BaseBall america®
2010 ALMANAC

BASEBALL AMERICA INC. · DURHAM, N.C.

BaseBall america
2010 ALMANAC

A COMPREHENSIVE REVIEW OF THE 2009 SEASON, FEATURING STATISTICS AND COMMENTARY

Editor
WILL LINGO

Assistant Editors
BEN BADLER, JIM CALLIS, J.J. COOPER, MATT EDDY, CONOR GLASSEY,
AARON FITT, JOSH LEVENTHAL, JOHN MANUEL, NATHAN RODE, JIM SHONERD

Database and Application Development
GREG LEVINE, BRENT LEWIS

Contributing Writer
JOHN PERROTTO

Photo Editor
NATHAN RODE

Editorial Assistants
DAN BUDREIKA, JESSE BURKHART,
MATT FORMAN, POWELL LATIMER

Design & Production
SARA HIATT MCDANIEL, TIFFANY SCHWARZ, LINWOOD WEBB

Jacket Photo
CHASE UTLEY BY DAVID SCHOFIELD

BaseBall america

PRESIDENT/PUBLISHER: LEE FOLGER
EDITORS IN CHIEF: WILL LINGO, JOHN MANUEL
EXECUTIVE EDITOR: JIM CALLIS
DESIGN & PRODUCTION DIRECTOR: SARA HIATT MCDANIEL
TECHNOLOGY MANAGER: GREG LEVINE

DISTRIBUTED BY SIMON & SCHUSTER
ISBN-13: 978-1-932391-28-2

STATISTICS PROVIDED BY MAJOR LEAGUE BASEBALL ADVANCED MEDIA
AND COMPILED BY BASEBALL AMERICA

EDITOR'S NOTE: Major league statistics are based on final, unofficial 2009 averages. >> The organization statistics, which begin on page 43, include all players who participated in at least one game during the 2009 season. >> Pitchers' batting statistics are not included, nor are the pitching statistics of field players who pitched in less than two games. >> For players who played with more than one team in the same league, the player's cumulative statistics appear on the line immediately after the player's statistics with each team. >> Innings pitched have been rounded off to the nearest full inning.

TABLE OF CONTENTS

Torii Hunter and his Angels teammates played their season in memory of Nick Adenhart

LARRY GOREN

MAJOR LEAGUES

Baseball can't shake specter of steroids

BY JOHN PERROTTO

The biggest story in baseball throughout the first decade of the new millennium was the use of performance-enhancing drugs.

Seemingly every superstar in the game was either found to have used steroids or was linked to their usage at some point in the 2000s. Pressure from Congress led Commissioner Bud Selig and Major League Baseball Players Association executive director Don Fehr to not only reach agreement on a steroids testing policy in 2005 but to stiffen the punishments on three different occasions.

Thus, by the time 2009 rolled around, Selig, Fehr and others associated with baseball thought the steroids cloud that had hung over the game for so long had lifted.

Boy, were they wrong.

The PED issue returned to the forefront on the eve of spring training when Sports Illustrated reported that Yankees third baseman Alex Rodriguez had tested positive for using steroids while he was a member of the Rangers. It continued on May 8 when Dodgers left fielder Manny Ramirez was suspended 50 games for failing a drug test, violating MLB's joint drug prevention and treatment program. Steroids speculation again made the headlines in August when the New York Times reported that Red Sox DH David Ortiz had tested positive, though the results were disputed by the MLBPA.

Rodriguez and Ramirez both have hit more than 500 home runs in their careers and were considered surefire Hall of Famers until being ensnared in steroid controversies. The always-smiling Ortiz's immense popularity also took a hit with the reports that he had used PEDs.

"These players know they're getting tested and they're still getting caught. I don't understand it," Giants manager Bruce Bochy said. "I'm not surprised. It's disappointing these major league players are getting caught. It's not good for the game. It's not good for the kids who look up to players."

Said Diamondbacks first baseman Tony Clark: "Any time you have the superstars in your game find themselves in difficult situations, it can't help but cast a general cloud over the group as a whole."

Ramirez was the most prominent major leaguer suspended for PED use in 2009. That brought the total number of suspensions to 29 since MLB insti-

Manny Ramirez sat out 50 games after testing positive for a female fertility drug

LARRY GOREN

tuted penalties in 2005.

Ramirez had long been noted for his quirky and erratic behavior along with his flowing dreadlocks. However, he had never been linked to steroids until his suspension.

Testing showed Ramirez had used the female fertility drug human chorionic gonadotropin, or hCG, which typically is used by steroid users to restart their bodies' natural testosterone production as they come off a steroid cycle.

A test taken in spring training revealed that Ramirez had elevated levels of testosterone in his body. MLB followed up with a more comprehensive test that confirmed the testosterone had come from hCG.

"It's a dark day for baseball and certainly for this organization," Dodgers general manager Ned Colletti said. "This organization will never condone anything that isn't clean."

Ramirez did not appeal the suspension but said a physician administered the drug in Miami, where he makes his offseason home.

Ramirez, who lost more than $7 million of his

$25 million salary, returned July 3 and was not especially repentant about his suspension. The Dodgers also were able to survive without their slugger, going 29-21 in his absence and winning their second straight National League West title.

"I don't want to be a distraction for this team," Ramirez said upon his return. "What happened, happened. I spoke to (owner) Frank McCourt, I apologized, I spoke to (manager) Joe (Torre), my teammates and I'm ready to move on. I didn't kill nobody, I didn't rape nobody, so that's it. I'm just going to come and play the game."

Ramirez's suspension came after Rodriguez's tearful spring-training admission that he used steroids from 2001-03 in his first three seasons with the Rangers after signing a 10-year, $252 million free

agent contract, then the largest deal in professional sports history.

"When I arrived in Texas in 2001, I felt an enormous amount of pressure," Rodriguez said. "I felt like I had all the weight of the world on top of me and I needed to perform, and perform at a high level every day. Back then, (baseball) was a different culture. It was very loose. I was young. I was stupid. I was naive. And I wanted to prove to everyone that I was worth being one of the greatest players of all time. I did take a banned substance. And for that, I am very sorry and deeply regretful."

Rodriguez's admission resulted from a Sports Illustrated report that his name appeared on a list of 104 players who tested positive for banned substances in 2003. That season, MLB conducted survey tests to see if mandatory, random drug testing was warranted. The tests were supposed to be confidential under terms of the agreement between MLB and the MLBPA. But federal investigators seized the samples and records of all 104 players from baseball's drug-testing companies in 2004 as part of the BALCO steroids lab investigation into Barry Bonds and others prominent athletes. The list of players said to have tested positive, attached to a grand jury subpoena, was part of a five-year legal fight, with the union trying to force the government to return what federal agents took during raids.

Rodriguez had long said he had never used steroids, including during a 2007 interview on the television show "60 Minutes." He also initially denied the SI report until admitting it was true two days later.

"I was stupid for three years. I was very, very stupid," Rodriguez said. "The more honest we can all be, the quicker we can get baseball (back) to where it needs to be. When you take this gorilla and this monkey off your back, you realize that honesty is the only way. I'm finally beginning to grow up. I'm pretty tired of being stupid and selfish, you know, about myself. The truth needed to come out a long time ago. I'm glad it's coming out."

Ortiz landed on the 2003 list of alleged drug users and said he believes then-legal supplements and vitamins caused him to test positive. MLB later stated that 96 urine samples, at most, classified as positive under the testing rules in place in 2003. The MLBPA said 13 of those were in dispute.

Another player on the list whose name leaked out was Sammy Sosa, who hit 609 home runs in his 18-year career that ended in 2007.

"I definitely was a little bit careless back in those days when I was buying supplements and vitamins over the counter. But I never bought steroids or used steroids," Ortiz said. "I never thought that buying supplements and vitamins was going to hurt

PED SUSPENSIONS

Major League Baseball announced performance-enhancing drug suspensions for 28 different players during the decade—from Alex Sanchez in April 2005 to Manny Ramirez last May. Note that Neifi Perez received two suspensions for failing three tests for amphetamines (the first resulted only in a warning).

Data compiled by the meticulous BizOfBaseball.com.

Date	Player, Pos., Team	Substance	Games
2005			
April 3	Alex Sanchez, of, Devil Rays	PEDs	10
April 11	Jorge Piedra, of, Rockies	PEDs	10
April 20	Agustin Montero, rhp, Rangers	PEDs	10
April 26	Jamal Strong, of, Mariners	PEDs	10
May 2	Juan Rincon, rhp, Twins	PEDs	10
July 8	Rafael Betancourt, rhp, Indians	PEDs	10
Aug. 1	Rafael Palmeiro, 1b, Orioles	PEDs	10
Aug. 2	Ryan Franklin, rhp, Mariners	PEDs	10
Sept. 7	Mike Morse, ss, Mariners	PEDs	10
Oct. 4	Carlos Almanzar, rhp, Rangers	PEDs	10
Oct. 18	Felix Heredia, lhp, Mets	PEDs	10
Nov. 2	Matt Lawton, of, (free agent)	PEDs	10
2006			
April 28	Yusaku Iriki, rhp, Mets	PEDs	50
June 12	Jason Grimsley, rhp, (free agent)	PEDs	50
Nov. 1	Guillermo Mota, rhp, Mets	PEDs	50
2007			
May 7	Juan Salas, rhp, Devil Rays	PEDs	50
July 6	Neifi Perez, ss, Tigers	Stimulant	25
Aug. 3	Neifi Perez, ss, Tigers	Stimulant	80
Sept. 7	Ryan Jorgensen, c, Reds	PEDs	50
Oct. 31	Mike Cameron, of, (free agent)	Stimulant	25
Nov. 27	Dan Serafini, lhp, (free agent)	PEDs	50
Dec. 6	Jay Gibbons, of, Orioles	PEDs	15
Dec. 6	Jose Guillen, of, Royals	PEDs	15
2008			
April 30	Eliezer Alfonzo, c, Giants	PEDs	50
May 28	Humberto Cota, c, Rockies	PEDs	50
2009			
Jan. 6	Sergio Mitre, rhp, Yankees	PEDs	50
Jan. 6	J.C. Romero, lhp, Phillies	PEDs	50
March 23	Kelvin Pichardo, rhp, Giants	PEDs	50
May 7	Manny Ramirez, of, Dodgers	PEDs	50

anybody's feelings."

Many current and retired players called for the MLBPA to make the list public, their rationale being that the public would suspect everyone who played in the major leagues in 2003 of being guilty of using PEDs without having evidence to the contrary. However, the union refused to bow to the pressure.

"To do that would, one, be illegal, and, two, be wrong," MLBPA general counsel Michael Weiner said. "It's illegal because it's covered by court order, and it would be wrong because a promise was made by the commissioner's office and the union to every player who was tested in 2003 that the results would be anonymous."

Astros shortstop Miguel Tejada became the first high-profile player convicted of a crime stemming from baseball's steroids era. He was sentenced to one year of probation for misleading Congress. Tejada, who had to leave Astros camp in the midst of spring training to appear in federal court in Washington, tearfully pled guilty.

Tejada faced up to a year imprisonment and a fine up to $100,000, but U.S. Magistrate Judge Alan Kay followed the recommendation of prosecutors who said he deserved a lighter punishment, issuing a sentence of probation, 100 hours of community service and a $5,000 fine.

Tejada's case has its roots in the March 17, 2005, congressional hearings on steroids in baseball at which Mark McGwire refused to "talk about the past" and Rafael Palmeiro—then Tejada's teammate with the Orioles—pointed a finger toward lawmakers and denied using drugs.

Palmeiro earned a suspension that August after failing a drug test. When a House panel looked into whether Palmeiro should be investigated for perjury, he told them that the positive test must have been caused by a tainted B-12 vitamin injection given to him by Tejada.

That led investigators to question Tejada. Though not under oath, court documents said he was advised "of the importance of providing truthful answers."

Selig, as always, was sensitive to the never-ending cycle of steroids news and took umbrage to the idea he should have taken stronger measures against PED users earlier.

"I don't want to hear the commissioner turned a blind eye to this or he didn't care about it," Selig said. "That annoys the you-know-what out of me. You bet I'm sensitive to the criticism. The reason I'm so frustrated is, if you look at our whole body of work, I think we've come farther than anyone ever dreamed possible. I honestly don't know how anyone could have done more than we've already done."

Braves third baseman Chipper Jones would not pass judgment on Selig but admitted that baseball in the 2000s would always be defined by PED use.

"You can't have arguably the greatest pitcher of our era, arguably the two greatest players of our era and now another very, very good player be under this cloud of suspicion and not feel like it has ruined it for everybody," Jones said, referring to Roger Clemens, Bonds, Rodriguez and Ramirez. "But what are you going to do? You can't be born in a different era. It is the Steroid Era."

Off To The Races

For the third straight year, the regular season stretched on an extra day because of the need for a tiebreaker game. Just as it had in 2008, the 163rd game involved the Twins in a one-game playoff for American League Central supremacy. Minnesota fell to the White Sox in 2008 and the Rockies eked past the Padres in 2007.

The Twins beat the Tigers 6-5 in a 12-inning thriller at Mall of America Field (better known as the Metrodome) in Minneapolis. Alexi Casilla singled home the winning run in a game that took numerous twists and turns. The Twins' victory also capped a wild comeback for the division title as they made up a seven-game deficit to the Tigers by going 17-4 down the stretch.

Both teams scored in the 10th inning and Casilla was thrown out at home plate by left fielder Ryan Raburn as he tried to score the winning run on a potential sacrifice fly. The Tigers thought they had taken the lead in the top of the 12th when Brandon Inge appeared to be hit by a pitch from Bobby Keppel with the bases loaded. However, home plate umpire Randy Marsh ruled that the ball did not strike Inge's billowing jersey.

"This is the most unbelievable game I've ever played in or seen," Twins shortstop Orlando Cabrera said.

It was a bitter defeat for the Tigers, who became the first team in history to blow a three-game lead with four games remaining.

"I guess it's fitting to say there was a loser in this game because we lost the game, but it's hard for me to believe there was a loser in this game," Tigers manager Jim Leyland said. "Both teams played their hearts out. You can't ask for anything more than that."

The Yankees won the AL East with a 103-59 record, best in the majors. They finished eight games ahead of the wild card-winning Red Sox. The Yankees, buoyed by a $423.5 million offseason spending spree in free agency that netted lefthander C.C. Sabathia, righthander A.J. Burnett and first

CONTINUED ON PAGE 11

Hometown Hero

LARRY GOREN

Twins all-star catcher Joe Mauer

BY JERRY CRASNICK

MINNEAPOLIS Flash back to spring training, and Joe Mauer didn't have the luxury of thinking about another trip to the All-Star Game or a run at a third batting title. The Twins catcher began the season on the disabled list, and his main objective was to get his aching back healthy and return by May.

Mauer, true to form, approached his extended stay at the Twins' spring training site in Fort Myers, Fla., with an upbeat mindset and maximum dedication. He worked with minor league rehab coordinator Lanny Tucker on core exercises that would benefit him over the long run. In the meantime, he hung out with his older brother Jake, manager of the Twins' Rookie-level Gulf Coast League club, and felt energized by the company of all those farmhands.

"I was able to stay with my brother and get back to enjoying the game," Mauer said. "Sometimes you get up here and it gets so serious and businesslike. Being around those younger guys and seeing how much enthusiasm they had was a really good thing for me."

Mauer went 7-for-10 in his return against the Royals in early May, and that was the harbinger for a big season. Before it was through:

■ Mauer hit .365 to outlast the Mariners' Ichiro Suzuki and win his third career batting title. National Leaguers Bubbles Hargrave (1926) and Ernie Lombardi (1938 and '42) are the only other catchers to win even one title.

■ Mauer led the AL with a .388 average at home and a .345 mark on the road. He was the first AL player to pull off that double since Rod Carew hit .401 at home and .374 on the road for the 1977 Twins.

Mauer's 28 homers more than doubled his previous career high of 13. He's so naturally gifted, his fellow Twins have to step back on occasion and remind themselves that they're watching something historic unfold.

"To tell you the truth, I do it all the time," says manager Ron Gardenhire. "I sit in the dugout, and say, 'Nothing he does can amaze me now.' It's a constant."

Mauer's offensive exploits alone were enough to earn him BA's Player of the Year, but that's only part of the equation. Mauer showed leadership in helping Minnesota overcome a seven-game deficit and the loss of Justin Morneau to an injury to overtake Detroit for the AL Central title.

Mauer already has achieved so much of what was predicted for him at Cretin-Derham Hall in St. Paul. He was sufficiently skilled on the football field that Florida State offered him a scholarship to play quarterback, but the Twins swayed him toward baseball by choosing him first in the 2001 draft and giving him a club-record $5.15 million bonus.

Mauer has been worth every dime. At 26, he has already bagged BA's High School, Minor League and Major League Player of the Year awards—a hat trick achieved by no other player. After Mauer hit .339 in two minor league stops at age 20, Twins scouting director Mike Radcliff made it clear he wasn't long for the farm. "He's not a normal prospect," Radcliff said in 2003.

PREVIOUS 10 WINNERS

1999: Pedro Martinez, rhp, Red Sox
2000: Alex Rodriguez, ss, Mariners
2001: Barry Bonds, of, Giants
2002: Alex Rodriguez, ss, Rangers
2003: Barry Bonds, of, Giants
2004: Barry Bonds, of, Giants
2005: Albert Pujols, 1b, Cardinals
2006: Johan Santana, lhp, Twins
2007: Alex Rodriguez, 3b, Yankees
2008: C.C. Sabathia, lhp, Indians/Brewers
Full list: BaseballAmerica.com/awards

CONTINUED FROM PAGE 9

baseman Mark Teixeira, returned to the postseason a year after their streak of 13 straight playoff appearances ended. They also won their first division crown since 2006.

The Angels captured their third AL West title in a row and fifth in sixth years, taking the division with a 10-game cushion on the Rangers.

The Dodgers posted the best record in the NL at 95-67, winning the West Division for a second straight season. However, they had to hold off a spirited charge by the Rockies, who finished three games back after trailing by as many as 15½ games on June 3. The Rockies wound up claiming the wild card.

The Phillies won their third straight NL East title, with six games separating them from the Marlins. The Cardinals broke the Cubs' two-year hold on the NL Central to win their first division title since 2006, finishing 7½ games in front of Chicago.

A Year For Milestones

When Tom Glavine notched his 300th career win in 2007, many experts suggested he would be the last pitcher to achieve that milestone. The reasoning was that the practice of using five-man rotations would rob pitchers of the opportunity to win so many games.

However, Giants 46-year-old lefthander Randy Johnson defied those predictions when he recorded victory No. 300 on June 4 against the Nationals at Nationals Park in Washington. The 6-foot-10 fire-baller got through six innings on a rainy night in the nation's capital and allowed one unearned run and two hits in the 5-1 triumph. He left the game with a bruised left shoulder suffered while he slipped while trying to field a comebacker.

"My senior moment," Johnson joked of the injury.

Johnson has often come across as surly during his career and hardly the sentimental type. However, he admitted that becoming the 24th pitcher to accumulate 300 wins was special.

"I think it kind of hit me when I walked on the field at the end of the game," Johnson said. "It's a long-range achievement. It's not a one-game or a one-year achievement. It's a career achievement. Who knows how many teammates I've had over my 21 years? But they had a great deal to do with my success. I'm going to think about this for a long time."

"He didn't want to make a big deal out of it," Bochy said. "But you could see after the game what it meant to him."

Mets outfielder Gary Sheffield became the 25th player to hit 500 home runs on April 17 when the 40-year-old connected for the milestone shot off Brewers lefty Mitch Stetter at Citi Field in New York.

"Now I can say I'm in the club and, you know, it's like getting your degree," Sheffield said. "Nobody can ever take that away from you."

The home run was Sheffield's first with the Mets after they signed him two weeks earlier after the Tigers released him during the last week of spring training. He hit just .178 during the exhibition season.

AMERICAN LEAGUE STANDINGS

EAST	W	L	PCT	GB	Manager	General Manager	Attendance	Average	Last Penn.
New York Yankees	103	59	.636	—	Joe Girardi	Brian Cashman	3,719,358	45,918	2009
*Boston Red Sox	95	67	.586	8	Terry Francona	Theo Epstein	3,062,699	37,811	2007
Tampa Bay Rays	84	78	.519	19	Joe Maddon	Andrew Friedman	1,874,962	23,148	2008
Toronto Blue Jays	75	87	.463	28	Cito Gaston	J.P. Ricciardi	1,876,129	23,162	1993
Baltimore Orioles	64	98	.395	39	Dave Trembley	Andy MacPhail	1,907,163	23,545	1983
CENTRAL	W	L	PCT	GB	Manager	General Manager	Attendance	Average	Last Penn.
Minnesota Twins	87	76	.534	—	Ron Gardenhire	Bill Smith	2,416,237	29,466	1991
Detroit Tigers	86	77	.528	1	Jim Leyland	Dave Dombrowski	2,567,165	31,693	2006
Chicago White Sox	79	83	.488	7½	Ozzie Guillen	Ken Williams	2,284,163	28,552	2005
Cleveland Indians	65	97	.401	21½	Eric Wedge	Mark Shapiro	1,766,242	22,357	1997
Kansas City Royals	65	97	.401	21½	Trey Hillman	Dayton Moore	1,797,891	22,474	1985
WEST	W	L	PCT	GB	Manager	General Manager	Attendance	Average	Last Penn.
Los Angeles Angels	97	65	.599	—	Mike Scioscia	Tony Reagins	3,240,386	40,005	2002
Texas Rangers	87	75	.537	10	Ron Washington	Jon Daniels	2,156,016	27,641	Never
Seattle Mariners	85	77	.525	12	Don Wakamatsu	Jack Zduriencik	2,195,533	27,105	Never
Oakland Athletics	75	87	.463	22	Bob Geren	Billy Beane	1,408,783	17,392	1990

*Wild card

PLAYOFFS—Division Series: Yankees defeated Twins 3-0 and Angels defeated Red Sox 3-0 in best-of-five series.
League Championship Series: Yankees defeated Angels 4-2 in best-of-seven series.

"Everything happens for a reason, you know," Sheffield said. "There was a reason why I hit 19 home runs instead of 20 last year. I could have done it then, but there was a reason why I got released and then came here and did it on the biggest stage of all in New York City. It makes it that much more special for me as well as my family."

Citi Field also was the setting for another milestone when Yankees closer Mariano Rivera became the second reliever to record 500 saves. He joined Trevor Hoffman in that exclusive club by getting the final four outs of a 4-2 victory against the Mets on June 28.

In typical fashion, Rivera downplayed his personal achievement.

"Don't get me wrong, it's definitely special. But I had one thing in mind when I got to the mound and that was to try to do something to win the game," the 39-year-old said.

"He's the definition of consistency," Yankees shortstop Derek Jeter said. "Nobody can compare."

Coincidentally, Rivera got the first RBI of his 14-year career in the game when he singled in a run in the top of the ninth inning in just his third career plate appearance.

White Sox lefthander Mark Buehrle didn't miss his second chance at a perfect game, throwing the 17th in history on July 23 when he shut down the Rays 5-0 at U.S. Cellular Field in Chicago. He nearly threw a perfect game on April 18, 2007, against the Rangers, facing the minimum 27 batters, but that day he settled for a no-hitter after walking

Sammy Sosa in the fifth inning and then picking him off two pitches later.

This time, an outstanding defensive play by center fielder Dewayne Wise with one out in the ninth inning allowed Buehrle to be perfect. Put into the game as a replacement at the start of the inning, Wise jumped and extended his hand above the top of the eight-foot wall in an attempt to catch Gabe Kapler's drive. The ball popped out of Wise's glove momentarily when he bounced off the wall, but he grabbed it with his bare hand as he fell to the ground.

"I was hoping it was staying in there (to) give him enough room to catch it," Buehrle said. "I know the guys were doing everything they could to save the no-hitter, the perfect game, whatever it might be."

"It was kind of crazy because when I jumped, the ball hit my glove at the same time I was hitting the wall," Wise said. "So I didn't realize I had caught it until I fell down and the ball was coming out of my glove, so I reached out and grabbed it."

When Buehrle set down the first 17 batters in his next start against the Twins on July 28, he set a major league record by retiring 45 straight batters. The streak ended when he walked Alexi Casilla with two outs in the sixth inning, three batters after he broke the record set by the Giants' Jim Barr in 1972. Buehrle's White Sox teammate Bobby Jenks matched that standard in 2007, pitching exclusively in relief.

Giants lefthander Jonathan Sanchez settled for a no-hitter on July 10, but he was perfect for seven innings in an 8-0 victory against the Padres at Pac Bell Park in San Francisco. The only runner to reach

NATIONAL LEAGUE STANDINGS

EAST	W	L	PCT	GB	Manager	General Manager	Attendance	Average	Last Penn.
Philadelphia Phillies	93	69	.574	—	Charlie Manuel	Ruben Amaro Jr.	3,600,693	44,453	2009
Florida Marlins	87	75	.537	6	Fredi Gonzalez	Larry Beinfest	1,464,109	18,771	2003
Atlanta Braves	86	76	.531	7	Bobby Cox	Frank Wren	2,373,631	29,304	1999
New York Mets	70	92	.432	23	Jerry Manuel	Omar Minaya	3,168,571	39,118	2000
Washington Nationals	59	103	.364	34	M. Acta/J. Riggleman	J. Bowden/M. Rizzo	1,817,226	22,715	Never
CENTRAL	W	L	PCT	GB	Manager	General Manager	Attendance	Average	Last Penn.
St. Louis Cardinals	91	71	.562	—	Tony La Russa	John Mozeliak	3,343,252	41,275	2005
Chicago Cubs	83	78	.516	7½	Lou Piniella	Jim Hendry	3,168,859	39,611	1945
Milwaukee Brewers	80	82	.494	11	Ken Macha	Doug Melvin	3,037,451	37,499	^1982
Cincinnati Reds	78	84	.481	13	Dusty Baker	Walt Jocketty	1,747,919	21,579	1990
Houston Astros	74	88	.457	17	C. Cooper/D. Clark	Ed Wade	2,521,076	31,124	2005
Pittsburgh Pirates	62	99	.385	28½	John Russell	Neal Huntington	1,577,853	19,480	1979
WEST	W	L	PCT	GB	Manager	General Manager	Attendance	Average	Last Penn.
Los Angeles Dodgers	95	67	.586	—	Joe Torre	Ned Colletti	3,761,655	46,440	1988
*Colorado Rockies	92	70	.568	3	C. Hurdle/J. Tracy	Dan O'Dowd	2,665,080	32,902	2007
San Francisco Giants	88	74	.543	7	Bruce Bochy	Brian Sabean	2,862,110	35,335	2002
San Diego Padres	75	87	.463	20	Bud Black	Kevin Towers	1,919,603	23,699	1998
Arizona Diamondbacks	70	92	.432	25	B. Melvin/A.J. Hinch	Josh Byrnes	2,128,765	26,281	2001

*Wild card ^American League

PLAYOFFS—Division Series: Phillies defeated Rockies 3-1 and Dodgers defeated Cardinals 3-0 in best-of-five series.
League Championship Series: Phillies defeated Dodgers 4-1 in best-of-seven series.

against Sanchez resulted from a fielding error by third baseman Juan Uribe in the eighth inning.

"It's the game. It can happen," Sanchez said of the error. "I could have given up a hit, too. It doesn't matter. I just want to win. I'm more than happy to pitch a no-hitter."

Like Buehrle, Sanchez got help from his center fielder with one out in the ninth inning. Aaron Rowand made a leaping catch at the wall to rob pinch-hitter Edgar Gonzalez of extra bases.

"I was going to go up and over and land on the other side of the fence if I had to, to try to make the catch," Rowand said.

Mariners right fielder Ichiro Suzuki continued his amazing show of consistency by collecting at least 200 hits for a record ninth consecutive season. Suzuki finished the year with 225 hits and has reached the milestone each season since coming to the United States following a stellar career in his native Japan.

Suzuki broke the record set by Wee Willie Keeler from 1894-1901 with an infield single off Rangers lefthander Derek Holland on Sept. 13 at Rangers Ballpark in Arlington.

"To see a 108-year-old record broken is pretty special," Mariners manager Don Wakamatsu said.

Two days earlier, Jeter broke a long-standing record when he moved past Lou Gehrig and into first place on the Yankees' all-time hit list with 2,722. He singled off Orioles righthander Chris Tillman at Yankee Stadium.

"For those who say today's game can't produce legendary players, I have two words: Derek Jeter," Yankees owner George Steinbrenner said in a prepared statement. "Game in and game out, he just produces.

"As historic and significant as becoming the Yankees' all-time hit leader is, the accomplishment is all the more impressive because Derek is one of the finest young men playing the game today. That combination of character and athletic ability is something he shares with the previous record holder, Lou Gehrig."

Mauer Wins Third Title

Twins catcher Joe Mauer continued rewriting the history books in becoming the first major league catcher to win three batting titles—when no other AL catcher had won even one. He hit a career-high .365 and also led the AL in on-base percentage (.444) and slugging (.587). Baseball America recognized the 26-year-old as its Major League Player of the Year.

Marlins shortstop Hanley Ramirez hit .342 to become the first shortstop to win the NL batting title since the Pirates' Dick Groat in 1960.

No pitcher won 20 games for only the second

AMERICAN LEAGUE: BEST TOOLS

A Baseball America survey of American League managers, conducted at midseason 2009, ranked players with the best tools.

BEST HITTER
1. Joe Mauer, Twins
2. Ichiro Suzuki, Mariners
3. Miguel Cabrera, Tigers

BEST CONTROL
1. Roy Halladay, Blue Jays
2. Mark Buehrle, White Sox
3. Zack Greinke, Royals

BEST POWER
1. Justin Morneau, Twins
2. Alex Rodriguez, Yankees
3. Mark Teixeira, Yankees

BEST PICKOFF MOVE
1. Andy Pettitte, Yankees
2. Mark Buehrle, White Sox
3. Dallas Braden, Athletics

BEST BUNTER
1. Ichiro Suzuki, Mariners
2. Chone Figgins, Angels
3. Erick Aybar, Angels

BEST RELIEVER
1. Mariano Rivera, Yankees
2. Joe Nathan, Twins
3. Jonathan Papelbon, Red Sox

BEST STRIKE-ZONE JUDGEMENT
1. Bobby Abreu, Angels
2. Joe Mauer, Twins
3. Jim Thome, White Sox

BEST DEFENSIVE CATCHER
1. Joe Mauer, Twins
2. Gerald Laird, Tigers
3. Kurt Suzuki, Athletics

BEST HIT-AND-RUN ARTIST
1. Placido Polanco, Tigers
2. Orlando Cabrera, Athletics
3. Derek Jeter, Yankees

BEST DEFENSIVE 1B
1. Mark Teixeira, Yankees
2. Carlos Pena, Rays
3. Kevin Youkilis, Red Sox

BEST BASERUNNER
1. Chone Figgins, Angels
2. Carl Crawford, Rays
3. Ichiro Suzuki, Mariners

BEST DEFENSIVE 2B
1. Dustin Pedroia, Red Sox
2. Placido Polanco, Tigers
3. Robinson Cano, Yankees

FASTEST BASERUNNER
1. Carl Crawford, Rays
2. Ichiro Suzuki, Mariners
3. Jacoby Ellsbury, Red Sox

BEST DEFENSIVE 3B
1. Evan Longoria, Rays
2. Adrian Beltre, Mariners
3. Scott Rolen, Blue Jays

MOST EXCITING PLAYER
1. Carl Crawford, Rays
2. Ichiro Suzuki, Mariners
3. Joe Mauer, Twins

BEST DEFENSIVE SS
1. Jason Bartlett, Rays
2. Elvis Andrus, Rangers
3. Erick Aybar, Angels

BEST PITCHER
1. Roy Halladay, Blue Jays
2. Zack Greinke, Royals
3. Felix Hernandez, Mariners

BEST INFIELD ARM
1. Brandon Inge, Tigers
2. Adrian Beltre, Mariners
3. Erick Aybar, Angels

BEST FASTBALL
1. Justin Verlander, Tigers
2 (tie). Joel Zumaya, Tigers
2 (tie). Zack Greinke, Royals

BEST DEFENSIVE OUTFIELDER
1. Torii Hunter, Angels
2. Ichiro Suzuki, Mariners
3. Curtis Granderson, Tigers

BEST CURVEBALL
1. Justin Verlander, Tigers
2. A.J. Burnett, Yankees
3. Josh Beckett, Red Sox

BEST OUTFIELD ARM
1. Ichiro Suzuki, Mariners
2. B.J. Upton, Rays
3. Josh Hamilton, Rangers

BEST SLIDER
1 (tie). Zack Greinke, Royals
1 (tie). Felix Hernandez, Mariners
2. Roy Halladay, Blue Jays

BEST MANAGER
1. Mike Scioscia, Angels
2. Jim Leyland, Tigers
3. Joe Maddon, Rays

BEST CHANGEUP
1. Mark Buehrle, White Sox
2. James Shields, Rays
3. Jered Weaver, Angels

time in a non-shortened season since 1900. It last happened in 2006.

With 19 wins, C.C. Sabathia tied Mariners

CONTINUED ON PAGE 15

Pirates Treasure

Center fielder Andrew McCutchen won over jaded Pirates fans with his talent

GEORGE GOJKOVICH

BY JOHN PERROTTO

PITTSBURGH Pirates top prospect Andrew McCutchen was called up from Triple-A Indianapolis on the morning of June 4, just hours after the club had traded veteran center fielder Nate McLouth to the Braves.

McLouth had assumed the role of face of the franchise in February when he signed a three-year, $15.75 million contract. He won a Gold Glove and made the all-star team last year in his first season as a regular.

Thus, McCutchen was not only being asked to become the Pirates' starting center fielder and leadoff hitter, but also take the spot of their most popular player. He handled it about as well as any 22-year-old could.

McCutchen came strolling into the clubhouse about two hours before a 12:35 p.m. game against the Mets. He stopped to hug several of his new teammates, settled in at his locker at PNC Park and calmly held court with several media members.

"I'm not the type of guy who gets upset very easily," McCutchen said. "I try to go with the flow."

He batted .286/.365/.471 in 433 big league at-bats, with 12 home runs and 22 stolen bases in 27 attempts. For his efforts, McCutchen was named BA Rookie of the Year.

McCutchen's rookie season fulfilled the great hopes harbored by the Pirates since they selected him in the first round of the 2005 draft, following his senior season at Fort Meade (Fla.) High.

"There has been so much talk about Andrew, so much hype the last few years," Pirates manager John Russell said. "He had a lot of expectations to live up to, and he did. He got to the major leagues and was comfortable. You don't see that in every player who comes up from the minor leagues. That's what separates the really good players."

He added excitement to the moribund Pirates, who finished 62-99 and set a major North American professional sports record with their 17th consecutive losing season.

McCutchen showed outstanding speed, good plate discipline (54 walks, 83 strikeouts), developing power and the ability to go from gap to gap to chase down fly balls.

"I was probably 5 years old when I first started playing T-ball and I knew then that playing in the big leagues is what I wanted to do," McCutchen said.

"I've always prided myself on being the best I could possibly be. I have high standards for myself, and I expect to reach them."

McCutchen already has replaced McLouth as the face of the franchise. Jerseys and T-shirts bearing his name and No. 22 were by far the biggest seller at PNC Park souvenir stands.

McCutchen has the personality to be both a fan favorite and a leader. He has a warm smile and a good sense of humor off the field. On the field, he plays with great joy but is also a fierce competitor who takes losing and personal failure to heart.

PREVIOUS 10 WINNERS

1999: Carlos Beltran, of, Royals
2000: Rafael Furcal, ss/2b, Braves
2001: Albert Pujols, of/3b/1b, Cardinals
2002: Eric Hinske, 3b, Blue Jays
2003: Brandon Webb, rhp, Diamondbacks
2004: Khalil Greene, ss, Padres
2005: Huston Street, rhp, Athletics
2006: Justin Verlander, rhp, Tigers
2007: Ryan Braun, 3b, Brewers
2008: Geovany Soto, c, Cubs

Full list: BaseballAmerica.com/awards

ALL-ROOKIE TEAM 2009

POS, PLAYER, TEAM	AGE	AB	AVG	OBP	SLG	2B	HR	RBI	SB	RUNDOWN
C Matt Wieters, Orioles	23	354	.288	.340	.412	15	9	43	0	Second-half improvement points to '10 breakout
1B Garrett Jones, Pirates	28	314	.293	.372	.567	21	21	44	10	Incredible value as minor league free agent sign
2B Casey McGehee, Brewers	26	355	.301	.360	.499	20	16	66	0	Waiver wire pickup helped cover for infield losses
3B Gordon Beckham, White Sox	23	378	.270	.347	.460	28	14	63	7	Hit for power, got on base while learning hot corner
SS Elvis Andrus, Rangers	21	480	.267	.329	.373	17	6	40	33	Strong glovework shored up Rangers' pitching staff
LF Chris Coghlan, Marlins	24	504	.321	.390	.460	31	9	47	8	Top hitting rookie helped keep Marlins in the hunt
CF Andrew McCutchen, Pirates	22	433	.286	.365	.471	26	12	54	22	New face of franchise seemed to improve daily
RF Dexter Fowler, Rockies	23	433	.266	.363	.406	29	4	34	27	Led off, patrolled center field for wild-card Rockies
DH Nolan Reimold, Orioles	25	358	.279	.365	.466	18	15	45	8	Slugging left fielder hit well from start to finish

POS, PLAYER, TEAM	AGE	W	L	ERA	IP	SO	BB	SV	RUNDOWN
SP Tommy Hanson, Braves	23	11	4	2.89	128	116	46	0	Lived up to potential, nearly pitched Braves to playoffs
SP J.A. Happ, Phillies	26	12	4	2.93	166	119	56	0	Seamless move to rotation pushed Phils to third East title
SP Jeff Niemann, Rays	26	13	6	3.94	181	125	59	0	Made 30 starts in AL East—2.93 ERA in 3 versus Yankees
SP Rick Porcello, Tigers	20	14	9	3.96	171	89	52	0	Rare effectiveness and efficiency for such a young hurler
RP Andrew Bailey, Athletics	25	6	3	1.84	83	91	24	26	Career took off after shift to bullpen; made all-star team

CONTINUED FROM PAGE 13

righthander Felix Hernandez and Tigers righthander Justin Verlander for the AL lead. Cardinals righthander Adam Wainwright also won 19 to top the NL. Sabathia and Wainwright both lost in their final starts of the season to fall just short.

Royals righthander Zack Grienke led the AL with a 2.16 ERA, the lowest in the league since Pedro Martinez rolled to a 1.74 mark in 2000. Cardinals righthander Chris Carpenter bounced back from two seasons of elbow and shoulder injuries to lead the NL with a 2.24 ERA. Verlander topped the AL with 269 strikeouts and Giants righthander Tim Lincecum led the NL for the second straight year with 261. Greinke and Lincecum topped off their seasons with Cy Young Awards.

Cardinals first baseman Albert Pujols won his first NL home run crown with 47 despite not hitting any in his final 79 at-bats of the season. He slugged .658, topping the league for the third time. Rays first baseman Carlos Pena, whose season ended Sept. 7 because of two broken fingers, tied Mark Teixeira for the AL title with 39 home runs.

Brewers first baseman Prince Fielder, who finished one home run behind Pujols, tied Phillies first baseman Ryan Howard for the NL RBI lead with 141. Teixeira topped the AL with 122.

Suzuki paced the AL with his 225 hits and Brewers left fielder Ryan Braun led the NL with 203.

Red Sox center fielder Jacoby Ellsbury won the AL stolen base title with 70 in 82 attempts (85 percent) and Astros center fielder Michael Bourn paced the NL with 61 in 73 tries (84 percent).

Diamondbacks third baseman Mark Reynolds broke his own infamous record by striking out 223 times, surpassing his total of 203 from 2008.

Teams combined to hit 2.07 home runs per game, compared with 2.01 in 2008. The uptick represented the highest mark since the 2.22 that teams averaged in 2006.

The AL dominated interleague play again, going 137-114 against the NL. It marked the sixth straight year that the AL won the season series.

The Pirates set a major North American professional sports record for futility with their 17th consecutive losing season. They went 63-99, breaking their tie with the 1933-48 Phillies. "Even though none of us have been here for the whole streak, it's still embarrassing to be a part of something like this," Pirates third baseman Andy LaRoche said. "You really feel bad for the fans. It's tough to support a team that hasn't won in this long."

Adenhart, Kalas Pass Away

Two tragic events marred the early stages of the season. Angels rookie righthander Nick Adenhart was killed in an automobile accident on April 9 in Fullerton, Calif., and longtime Phillies broadcaster Harry Kalas dropped dead four days later in the visiting television booth before a game against the Nationals in Washington.

Adenhart and two others were killed by a suspected drunk driver just hours after the 22-year-old made his first start of the season. He had pitched six shutout innings against the Athletics at Angel Stadium in Anaheim.

"It's a tragedy that will never be forgotten," Angels manager Mike Scioscia said.

Adenhart was a passenger in a silver Mitsubishi Eclipse that was broadsided in an intersection at 12:30 a.m. by a minivan that apparently ran a red light. The impact spun around both vehicles, and one then struck another car.

The minivan driver, Andrew Thomas Gallo, fled the crash on foot and was captured about 30 minutes later. Police said he had a suspended license because of a previous drunken-driving conviction.

Adenhart died in surgery at the University of California, Irvine Medical Center. Henry Nigel Pearson, a 25-year-old passenger in the car, and the driver, 20-year-old Courtney Frances Stewart, a cheerleader at Cal State Fullerton, were pronounced dead at the scene. Another passenger, 24-year-old Jon Wilhite, a former catcher at Cal State Fullerton, suffered severe injuries but survived.

Adenhart and the others had gone dancing at a club about a block away from the crash site. The Angels honored Adenhart by wearing a patch with his No. 34 on their jerseys and also kept his locker intact throughout the season.

"He was a very funny kid and he's going to be missed," Angels center fielder Torii Hunter said. "A lot of these guys in this clubhouse have never lost anybody in their family that's close to them. I hate that this happened, but this is part of life. This is the real deal. That's why you've got to kiss your kids, kiss your family every day when you get up in the morning and before you leave for work."

Kalas, 73, had missed a majority of spring training after having what the Phillies deemed "minor surgery." He returned by Opening Day and threw out the ceremonial first pitch before the Phillies received their World Series rings prior to the second game of the season.

Kalas was found dead in the booth, the victim of heart disease, by his co-workers about an hour before the April 13 game at Nationals Park. He had been with the Phillies since 1971 and had received the Ford C. Frick award for broadcasting excellence during the Hall of Fame induction ceremonies in 2002.

"We lost our voice," Phillies president David Montgomery said. "He has loved our game and made just a tremendous contribution to our sport and certainly to our organization."

When the Phillies won the second World Series title in their 125-year history in 2008, it was Kalas who called the final out on radio. He then joined the on-field celebration and sang Frank Sinatra's "High Hopes."

Kalas was an icon in Philadelphia and many Phillies' fans asked him to record outgoing messages on answering machines or cell phone voice mail using his "Outta here!" home run call.

"Players come and go but 'Outta here!' is forever," Phillies radio broadcaster Scott Franzke said.

Yankees Christen New Park

Two palatial stadiums opened in New York in

NATIONAL LEAGUE: BEST TOOLS

A Baseball America survey of National League managers, conducted at midseason 2009, ranked players with the best tools.

BEST HITTER
1. Albert Pujols, Cardinals
2. Hanley Ramirez, Marlins
3. Todd Helton, Rockies

BEST POWER
1. Albert Pujols, Cardinals
2. Prince Fielder, Brewers
3. Ryan Howard, Phillies

BEST BUNTER
1. Juan Pierre, Dodgers
2. Willy Taveras, Reds
3. Michael Bourn, Astros

BEST STRIKE-ZONE JUDGEMENT
1. Albert Pujols, Cardinals
2. Adrian Gonzalez, Padres
3. Nick Johnson, Nationals

BEST HIT-AND-RUN ARTIST
1. David Eckstein, Padres
2. Ryan Theriot, Cubs
3. Jack Wilson, Pirates

BEST BASERUNNER
1 (tie). Nyjer Morgan, Nationals
1 (tie). Juan Pierre, Dodgers
3. Jimmy Rollins, Phillies

FASTEST BASERUNNER
1. Michael Bourn, Astros
2. Willy Taveras, Reds
3. Nyjer Morgan, Nationals

MOST EXCITING PLAYER
1. Albert Pujols, Cardinals
2. Hanley Ramirez, Marlins
3. Pablo Sandoval, Giants

BEST PITCHER
1. Tim Lincecum, Giants
2. Johan Santana, Mets
3. Dan Haren, Diamondbacks

BEST FASTBALL
1. Jonathan Broxton, Dodgers
2. Brian Wilson, Giants
3. Tim Lincecum, Giants

BEST CURVEBALL
1. Tim Lincecum, Giants
2. Adam Wainwright, Cardinals
3. Yovani Gallardo, Brewers

BEST SLIDER
1. Carlos Marmol, Cubs
2. Jake Peavy, Padres
3. Brad Lidge, Phillies

BEST CHANGEUP
1. Johan Santana, Mets
2. Trevor Hoffman, Brewers
3. Cole Hamels, Phillies

BEST CONTROL
1. Dan Haren, Diamondbacks
2. Chris Carpenter, Cardinals
3. Cole Hamels, Phillies

BEST PICKOFF MOVE
1. Doug Davis, Diamondbacks
2. Jamie Moyer, Phillies
3. Cole Hamels, Phillies

BEST RELIEVER
1. Jonathan Broxton, Dodgers
2. Francisco Rodriguez, Mets
3. Huston Street, Rockies

BEST DEFENSIVE CATCHER
1. Yadier Molina, Cardinals
2. Russell Martin, Dodgers
3. Bengie Molina, Giants

BEST DEFENSIVE 1B
1. Albert Pujols, Cardinals
2 (tie). Todd Helton, Rockies
2 (tie). Adrian Gonzalez, Padres

BEST DEFENSIVE 2B
1. Orlando Hudson, Dodgers
2. Chase Utley, Phillies
3. Brandon Phillips, Reds

BEST DEFENSIVE 3B
1. Ryan Zimmerman, Nationals
2. Pedro Feliz, Phillies
3. David Wright, Mets

BEST DEFENSIVE SS
1. Jimmy Rollins, Phillies
2. Troy Tulowitzki, Rockies
3. Hanley Ramirez, Marlins

BEST INFIELD ARM
1. Rafael Furcal, Dodgers
2. Troy Tulowitzki, Rockies
3. Yunel Escobar, Braves

BEST DEFENSIVE OF
1. Shane Victorino, Phillies
2. Matt Kemp, Dodgers
3. Nyjer Morgan, Nationals

BEST OUTFIELD ARM
1. Jeff Francoeur, Mets
2 (tie). Jay Bruce, Reds
2 (tie). Brad Hawpe, Rockies

BEST MANAGER
1. Tony La Russa, Cardinals
2. Bobby Cox, Braves
2. Joe Torre, Dodgers

2009, including an updated version of one of the most famous venues in sports, Yankee Stadium.

The new Yankee Stadium, which cost a staggering $1.5 billion to build, replaced the 85-year-old edifice across the street in the Bronx that was home to 26 World Series champions. However, the first game turned out to be a flop for the throng of 48,271 home fans. The Indians rolled to a 10-2 victory, keyed by shortstop Jhonny Peralta's tie-breaking, two-run double in the seventh inning off righthander Jose Veras. Cleveland center fielder Grady Sizemore added a grand slam.

The pre-game ceremonies lasted an hour and included the West Point Marching Band, which played the "Washington Post March" and "Stars and Stripes Forever" by John Philip Sousa. He led the Seventh Regiment Band before the first game at the old stadium in 1923.

John Fogerty followed by playing "Centerfield," and former Yankees center fielder Bernie Williams strummed an acoustic guitar version of "Take Me Out to the Ball Game." A group of nearly 50 former Yankees, all wearing special jackets commemorating the new stadium, were introduced and lined the back of the infield dirt. Yankees legend Yogi Berra threw out the ceremonial first pitch.

Dozens of blue-vested waiters and waitresses from three restaurants and lounges in the stadium filled the aisles to attend to the first nine rows wrapping the infield, where the seats started at $500 and a season ticket cost as much as $202,500.

The Mets also lost their first game at $800 million Citi Field on April 13, falling 6-5 to the Padres.

Padres center fielder Jody Gerut gave the place a memorable beginning as he led off the game with a home run. It was the first time in major league history that the first batter homered in a new stadium.

Most of the 41,007 fans filed in through the stately Jackie Robinson Rotunda, many snapping photos and searching for souvenirs only steps from where Shea Stadium was razed to make room for Citi Field's parking lot. Pregame ceremonies included Hall of Fame righthander Tom Seaver throwing the ceremonial first pitch to former Mets all-star catcher Mike Piazza.

With its intricate brickwork and archways, Citi Field was modeled after Ebbets Field, home of the Brooklyn Dodgers from 1913-57. Mets owner Fred Wilpon grew up in Brooklyn.

Meanwhile, the Twins said goodbye to the Metrodome following 28 seasons when they lost to the Yankees in Game 3 of the AL Division Series. While it was far from the most aesthetic baseball venue, the Twins did win seven division titles and two World Series there, and opponents lost scores of pop flies in the cream-colored roof that required 250,000 cubic feet of air pressure to keep in place.

CONTINUED ON PAGE 19

ALL-TIME ACHIEVEMENTS

300 WINS

No. Pitcher	Wins		
1. Cy Young	511	14. Nolan Ryan	324
2. Walter Johnson	417	Don Sutton	324
3. Pete Alexander	373	16. Phil Niekro	318
Christy Mathewson	373	17. Gaylord Perry	314
5. Pud Galvin	364	18. Tom Seaver	311
6. Warren Spahn*	363	19. Charley Radbourn	309
7. Kid Nichols	361	20. Mickey Welch	307
8. Greg Maddux	355	21. Tom Glavine*	305
9. Roger Clemens	354	22. Randy Johnson*	303
12. John Clarkson	328	23. Lefty Grove*	300
13. Eddie Plank*	326	Early Wynn	300

* Lefthanded pitcher. Active player in bold.

Pitching for the Giants, a 45-year-old Randy Johnson notched win No. 300 on June 4, two seasons after Tom Glavine gained passage into the club. Roger Clemens and Greg Maddux got there earlier in the decade, while Mike Mussina opted to retire with 270 wins following the 2008 season. Four 200-game winners pitched in 2009—Jamie Moyer (258), Andy Pettitte (229), Pedro Martinez (219) and John Smoltz (213)—but none seemed particularly likely to stick around long enough to reach 300.

So who's next? Roy Halladay is nearly half the way there with 148 wins, and he's just 32 years old. Additionally, three lefthanders age 29 or 30 stand out from the pack: C.C. Sabathia (136 wins), Mark Buehrle (135) and Johan Santana (122).

500 HOME RUNS

No. Batter	HR		
1. Barry Bonds*	762	13. Reggie Jackson*	563
2. Hank Aaron	755	14. Mike Schmidt	548
3. Babe Ruth*	714	15. Manny Ramirez	546
4. Willie Mays	660	16. Mickey Mantle#	536
5. Ken Griffey Jr.*	630	17. Jimmie Foxx	534
6. Sammy Sosa	609	18. Willie McCovey*	521
7. Frank Robinson	586	Frank Thomas	521
8. Mark McGwire	583	Ted Williams*	521
Alex Rodriguez	583	21. Ernie Banks	512
10. Harmon Killebrew	573	Eddie Mathews*	512
11. Rafael Palmeiro*	569	23. Mel Ott*	511
12. Jim Thome*	564	24. Gary Sheffield	509
		25. Eddie Murray#	504

* Lefthanded batter. # Switch-hitter. Active players in bold.

Gary Sheffield smacked his 500th home runs on April 17, giving the club 25 members. Alex Rodriguez smashed an even 30 homers to finish with 583, tying him for eighth all time with Mark McGwire, who retired in 2001 in sole possession of the No. 5 spot. In the ensuing eight years, Barry Bonds, Ken Grifey Jr., Sammy Sosa and now Rodriguez all tied or passed him.

With 473 career clouts, first baseman Carlos Delgado would need to smack 27 home runs in 2010 to reach 500. He hit but four in an injury-plagued 2009 season, and he turns 38 in June. Beyond him, Chipper Jones (426), Jason Giambi (409) and Vladimir Guerrero (407) are the only active players with at least 400.

Phillies' success changes outlook

BY JAYSON STARK

PHILADELPHIA A long, long time ago, they set out on a journey that has led them to this place. For the Phillies of Jimmy Rollins and Chase Utley and Ryan Howard, the mission has never been just about winning. It's been about history erasing history.

They had to wipe away the ghosts of 10,000 losses, of the historic El Foldo of 1964. They had to heal the scars from the two decades of futility that preceded the arrival of this generation.

They even had to remind their city just what a beautiful game baseball can be, because it seems like only yesterday that millions of Philadelphians would rather have attended an arena-football game than a Phillies game. But they've healed those scars. They've lifted their sport to the top of their city's mountaintop.

And then, on a gorgeous Wednesday night in the third week of October, the 2009 Phillies arrived at a place where no Phillies team before them had ever been—in the World Series for consecutive years.

These Phillies accomplished the metamorphosis of an entire franchise. "You know, it's not only the franchise that's different now, but the city," Phillies right fielder Jayson Werth said. "It's the fans. Everything. It's all different now."

Before October 2008, this team had won only four postseason series in the history of the franchise. It wasn't so long ago that this franchise had played in two World Series in its first 97 seasons of existence.

Their closer Brad Lidge played on a World Series team in Houston in 2005—and watched

DAVID SCHOFIELD

Jimmy Rollins has helped the Phillies exorcise the ghosts of a painful past

that same team fade to just two games over .500 the next year. So he knows what can happen The Next Year.

"But there's just something different about these guys," he said. "It's really hard to explain, other than it's the talent. And the belief. When they keep coming back over and over, it's not luck. They really have the talent, and they really believe this is how it's supposed to be."

These Phillies know how many championship teams talked that talk The Next Year through all those no-repeat decades.

"Maybe some teams have success, and they forget how hard it is to get there," said Jimmy Rollins, the longest-tenured Phillie. "Maybe they feel like what happened last year is supposed to happen again. But to do that, you're going to be tested."

"It would have been really easy, after winning the World Series, to come in this spring and set the cruise control," injured pitcher Jamie Moyer said. "But this team never did that. You always go through ups and downs in any year. But with this team, the attitude was always, 'We're going to win. And whatever happens, we're going to find a way to win.'"

PREVIOUS 10 WINNERS
1999: Oakland Athletics
2000: Chicago White Sox
2001: Houston Astros
2002: Minnesota Twins
2003: Florida Marlins
2004: Minnesota Twins
2005: Atlanta Braves
2006: Los Angeles Dodgers
2007: Colorado Rockies
2008: Tampa Bay Rays
Full list: BaseballAmerica.com/awards

The Twins are scheduled to move into Target Field, an outdoor stadium in downtown Minneapolis, in time for Opening Day 2010.

"We're going to miss the Dome, but hey, we're going outside," Twins second baseman Nick Punto said. "It's going to be great for the fans and we're looking forward to it. But you can't really simulate 55,000 fans screaming and cheering and bringing the house down. It was like at times the Metrodome was just going to crumble."

Fehr Steps Aside

Don Fehr was the man the players loved and the owners loved to hate during his eventful 25-year tenure as the MLBPA's executive director. However, approaching retirement age as he turned 61 in July, Fehr announced in June that he would step down from his post.

Michael Weiner, the union's general counsel, was tabbed to succeed Fehr. The 47-year-old will lead negotiations for the next Collective Bargaining Agreement between the players and owners after the current one expires following the 2011 season.

Weiner, along with Steve Fehr, Don's brother, handled the primary negotiations for the labor contracts in 2002 and 2006. Those agreements were the first achieved without a work stoppage since 1970.

"I think I have some sense of what I'm getting into," said Weiner, who began working for the MLBPA in 1988.

Fehr became the top lawyer to MLBPA founder Marvin Miller in 1977 and took over as acting executive director in December 1983 after the players fired Kenneth Moffett, the former federal mediator who succeeded Miller, following a 50-day strike during the 1981 season. Fehr led negotiations for five labor agreements and felt that was enough.

"After a while, it wears you down," Fehr said. "I think it will be good for everybody."

Fehr led players through a two-day strike in 1985 then guided the MLBPA successfully through charges that management conspired to collude against free agents following the 1985, 1986 and 1987 seasons. The owners eventually paid the association $280 million to settle. During Fehr's tenure, the average player's salary rose from $289,000 in 1983 to $3.24 million in 2009.

The biggest criticism leveled at Fehr was that he was too zealous in trying to keep the players from being drug tested. He reasoned that his constituents' civil liberties would be violated.

"If we had known or understood what the circumstances were a little better, then perhaps we would have moved sooner," Fehr said.

In addition to the brief strike in 1985, Fehr presided over two other work stoppages—a 32-day lockout in spring training that delayed the start of the 1990 season and a 7½-month strike in 1994-95 that forced the cancellation of the playoffs. MLB was set to begin the 1995 season with replacement players until the National Labor Relations Board, at the MLBPA's request, obtained an 11th-hour injunction to restore previous working rules so that new terms could be negotiated. U.S. District Judge Sonia Sotomayor handed down that injunction, and, coincidentally, President Barack Obama appointed her to the Supreme Court in 2009.

"It was very satisfying at the end to say that the players got through it," Fehr said. "They got through it in one piece and regardless of what it took to get there, they got a very good agreement. It's my proudest achievement."

Cubs Bought For Record Sum

One of the longest sale proceedings of a franchise in major league history came to a close in September when the other 29 owners unanimously approved the sale of the Cubs from the bankrupt Tribune Co. to the family of online brokerage billionaire Joe Ricketts for a record $845 million.

The Tribune Co., which owns the Chicago Tribune and the Los Angeles Times among other newspaper and television properties, bought the Cubs in 1981 for $20.5 million from chewing gum manufacturer William Wrigley Jr. The Ricketts family, whose wealth comes primarily from its stake in Omaha-based TD Ameritrade Holding Corp., bought a 95 percent stake in the team and Wrigley Field along with a 25 percent share of the Comcast SportsNet Chicago regional cable network.

Tribune Co. announced on Opening Day 2007 that the franchise and ballpark would be sold by the end of that season. However, the process was slowed because chief executive officer Sam Zell held out for higher bids and then was forced to declare bankruptcy in 2008 amid a steep decline in the circulation and advertising revenues of newspapers throughout the nation.

The transaction was the largest in baseball history, surpassing the $660 million paid for the Red Sox, Fenway Park and New England Sports Network in 2002.

Former Diamondbacks chief executive officer Jeff Moorad began his acquisition of the Padres from John Moores in March, buying a 35 percent stake in the team and gaining control of the franchise.

CONTINUED ON PAGE 21

MAJOR LEAGUE *ALL-STARS*

LARRY GOREN

Zack Greinke's 2.16 ERA was the lowest since Pedro Martinez's 1.74 mark in 2000

MORRIS FOSTOFF

Hanley Ramirez turned in his third straight 20-20 season and won his first batting title

FIRST TEAM

POS	PLAYER, TEAM	AVG	OBP	SLG	AB	R	H	2B	3B	HR	RBI	SB	CS	BB	SO
C	Joe Mauer, Twins	.365	.444	.587	523	94	191	30	1	28	96	4	1	76	63
1B	Albert Pujols, Cardinals	.327	.443	.658	568	124	186	45	1	47	135	16	4	115	64
2B	Chase Utley, Phillies	.282	.397	.508	571	112	161	28	4	31	93	23	0	88	110
3B	Pablo Sandoval, Giants	.330	.387	.556	572	79	189	44	5	25	90	5	5	52	83
SS	Hanley Ramirez, Marlins	.342	.410	.543	576	101	197	42	1	24	106	27	8	61	101
LF	Ryan Braun, Brewers	.320	.386	.551	635	113	203	39	6	32	114	20	6	57	121
CF	Matt Kemp, Dodgers	.297	.352	.490	606	97	180	25	7	26	101	34	8	52	139
RF	Ichiro Suzuki, Mariners	.352	.386	.465	639	88	225	31	4	11	46	26	9	32	71
DH	Mark Teixeira, Yankees	.292	.383	.565	609	103	178	43	3	39	122	2	0	81	114

POS	PITCHER, TEAM	W	L	ERA	G	GS	CG	SV	IP	H	BB	SO	HR	G/F	AVG
SP	Zack Greinke, Royals	16	8	2.16	33	33	6	0	229	195	51	242	11	0.71	.230
SP	Roy Halladay, Blue Jays	17	10	2.79	32	32	9	0	239	234	35	208	22	1.05	.256
SP	Felix Hernandez, Mariners	19	5	2.49	34	34	2	0	239	200	71	217	15	1.17	.227
SP	Tim Lincecum, Giants	15	7	2.48	32	32	4	0	225	168	68	261	10	0.99	.206
RP	Mariano Rivera, Yankees	3	3	1.76	66	0	0	44	66	48	12	72	7	1.16	.197

SECOND TEAM

POS	PLAYER, TEAM	AVG	OBP	SLG	AB	R	H	2B	3B	HR	RBI	SB	CS	BB	SO
C	Victor Martinez, Indians/Red Sox	.303	.381	.480	588	88	178	33	1	23	108	1	0	75	74
1B	Prince Fielder, Brewers	.299	.412	.602	591	103	177	35	3	46	141	2	3	110	138
2B	Ben Zobrist, Rays	.297	.405	.543	501	91	149	28	7	27	91	17	6	91	104
3B	Ryan Zimmerman, Nationals	.292	.364	.525	610	110	178	37	3	33	106	2	0	72	119
SS	Derek Jeter, Yankees	.334	.406	.465	634	107	212	27	1	18	66	30	5	72	90
LF	Jason Bay, Red Sox	.267	.384	.537	531	103	142	29	3	36	119	13	3	94	162
CF	Denard Span, Twins	.311	.392	.415	578	97	180	16	10	8	68	23	10	70	89
RF	Andre Ethier, Dodgers	.272	.361	.508	596	92	162	42	3	31	106	6	4	72	116
DH	Ryan Howard, Phillies	.279	.360	.571	616	105	172	37	4	45	141	8	1	75	186

POS	PITCHER, TEAM	W	L	ERA	G	GS	CG	SV	IP	H	BB	SO	HR	G/F	AVG
SP	Chris Carpenter, Cardinals	17	4	2.24	28	28	3	0	193	156	38	144	7	1.91	.226
SP	Cliff Lee, Indians/Phillies	14	13	3.22	34	34	6	0	232	245	43	181	17	0.78	.272
SP	Jon Lester, Red Sox	15	8	3.41	32	32	2	0	203	186	64	225	20	0.96	.242
SP	Justin Verlander, Tigers	19	9	3.45	35	35	3	0	240	219	63	269	20	0.60	.243
RP	Joe Nathan, Twins	2	2	2.10	70	0	0	47	69	42	22	89	7	0.74	.171

EXECUTIVE OF THE YEAR

Dan O'Dowd

The Rockies won a franchise-record 92 games and captured their second NL wild card in three years, owing much of their success to astute trades and player development.

The Rockies cultivated several of their best players—including Brad Hawpe, Ubaldo Jimenez and Troy Tulowitzki—on the watch of general manager Dan O'Dowd, who signed on after the 1999 season. The continuity in Colorado's scouting (Bill Schmidt) and international (Rolando Fernandez) departments have allowed for a consistent philosophy. Oh, and the trades for Rafael Betancourt, Carlos Gonzalez, Jason Marquis and Huston Street didn't hurt.

PREVIOUS 10 WINNERS

1999: Jim Bowden, Reds
2000: Walt Jocketty, Cardinals
2001: Pat Gillick, Mariners
2002: Billy Beane, Athletics
2003: Brian Sabean, Giants
2004: Terry Ryan, Twins
2005: Mark Shapiro, Indians
2006: Dave Dombrowski, Tigers
2007: Jack Zduriencik, Brewers
2008: Theo Epstein, Red Sox

Full list: BaseballAmerica.com/awards

MANAGER OF THE YEAR

Mike Scioscia

The Angels cruised to a third consecutive AL West title—and their fifth in the past six years—while integrating rookies like Jason Bulger, Kevin Jepsen, Matt Palmer and Sean O'Sullivan into the pitching staff and dealing with the free agent departure of Mark Teixeira.

Manager Mike Scioscia, who just completed his 10th year at the helm (900-720, .556) kept the club together in between the unfortunate death of Nick Adenhart and the mid-May return of John Lackey.

First baseman Kendry Morales (34 homers) helped offset the loss of Teixeira, while Erick Aybar blossomed into a top AL shortstop.

PREVIOUS 10 WINNERS

1999: Jimy Williams, Red Sox
2000: Dusty Baker, Giants
2001: Lou Piniella, Mariners
2002: Mike Scioscia, Angels
2003: Jack McKeon, Marlins
2004: Bobby Cox, Braves
2005: Ozzie Guillen, White Sox
2006: Jim Leyland, Tigers
2007: Terry Francona, Red Sox
2008: Ron Gardenhire, Twins

Full list: BaseballAmerica.com/awards

CONTINUED FROM PAGE 19

Moorad and a group of investors intend to acquire full ownership during a period of up to five years at a reported price of $500 million.

Moores began entertaining offers for the Padres in 2008 while going through a contentious divorce with his wife Becky. Before joining the Diamondbacks, Moorad had been a high-profile agent whose crowning achievement was negotiating an eight-year, $160 million contract for free agent Manny Ramirez with the Red Sox in 2000.

Organization Shakeups

A new ownership group in San Diego marked the end of the line for Kevin Towers, the longest-tenured GM in the game, on the last weekend of the season following a 14-year run. The Padres won four division titles and one NL pennant under Towers.

Towers spent 26 years in the Padres organization, dating back to his first-round selection in 1982 as a pitcher from Brigham Young. He left only for a two-year stint as a scout with the Pirates.

The Padres finished 75-87 in 2009 but did go 37-25 in their final 62 games. However, Moorad believed it was time for a change and opted to fire Towers and hire Red Sox assistant GM Jed Hoyer as his replacement.

"We want to have a team that can consistently compete for the NL West," Moorad said. "Once you get into the postseason, anything can happen. But we want to have a chance to win each and every year. That's the goal."

Another longtime GM, the Blue Jays' J.P. Ricciardi, also got fired during the season's final weekend. Toronto also finished at 75-87, but did so following a 27-14 start. Ricciardi spent eight years on the job and the Blue Jays finished as high as second place in the AL East only once in that time.

Blue Jays assistant GM Alex Anthopoulos was promoted to replace Ricciardi.

"I'm certainly excited about the upside of this club because of the work J.P. has done," Anthopoulos said. "The arrow is pointing up in this organization. It may not seem that way right now, but there's a lot to look forward to."

The embattled Jim Bowden resigned as GM of the Nationals on March 1, while the organization was under federal investigation into the alleged skimming of signing bonuses given to Latin American prospects.

"I've become a distraction," Bowden said. "It saddens me, but I feel it's in the best interest of two of the things I love the most and those are the Washington Nationals and baseball."

Bowden met in 2008 with FBI investigators, who were reportedly looking at Bowden's actions as far back as 1994 when he was GM of the Reds. However, no charges had been filed against Bowden through the end of October and he maintained his innocence.

Bowden's resignation came three days after Washington fired Jose Rijo, a special assistant to the GM, in the aftermath of an MLB investigation that determined that a top Nationals prospect from the Dominican Republic had falsified his identity and age. Shortstop Esmailyn Gonzalez, who received a $1.4 million bonus in July 2006, was really Carlos Alvarez, and he was 19, rather than 16, when he signed. Alvarez did not secure a work visa to play in the U.S. in 2009, so he played in the Dominican Summer League after spending the previous two seasons in the Gulf Coast League.

Five managers were fired over the course of the season. The Diamondbacks' Bob Melvin and Rockies' Clint Hurdle lost their jobs less than two years after facing off in the 2007 NL Championship Series.

Melvin, the NL Manager of the Year in '07, was let go on May 8 and replaced by 34-year-old A.J. Hinch, the Diamondbacks' vice president for player development, who had never managed at any level. The Diamondbacks went 12-17 under Melvin and then went 58-75 afterward, finishing last in the NL West with a 70-92 record. Melvin went 337-440 (.434) in four-plus seasons.

The Rockies were 18-28 on May 29 when they bid goodbye to Hurdle, who guided them to the franchise's lone World Series appearance in 2007. Colorado promoted bench coach Jim Tracy to interim manager and the Rockies took flight, going 74-42 and winning the NL wild card. Hurdle compiled a 534-625 (.461) record in a little more than seven full seasons.

After the Nationals went 26-61 in the first half of the season, the organization fired Manny Acta on July 13, over the all-star break. Bench coach Jim Riggleman became interim manager and guided the Nationals to a 59-103 finish after they went 33-42 following the switch. Acta was 158-252 (.385) over 2½ seasons.

The Astros finished 74-88 and Cecil Cooper paid

DECADE LEADERS

Using the power of Baseball-Reference.com, we present the various major league department leaders for the years 2000 to 2009. Batters need 3,000 plate appearances and pitchers 1,000 innings to qualify for percentage titles.

BATTING			PITCHING		
AVG	Albert Pujols	.334	ERA	Pedro Martinez	3.01
OBP	Barry Bonds	.517	PCT	Pedro Martinez	.691
SLG	Barry Bonds	.724	AVG	Pedro Martinez	.216
OPS	Barry Bonds	1.241	SO/9	Randy Johnson	10.42
G	Miguel Tejada	1,581	BB/9	Brad Radke	1.36
PA	Bobby Abreu	6,932	HR/9	Brandon Webb	0.63
AB	Miguel Tejada	6,263	H/9	Kerry Wood	7.13
R	Alex Rodriguez	1,190	WHIP	Pedro Martinez	1.04
H	Ichiro Suzuki	2,030	K/BB	Curt Schilling	6.01
2B	Todd Helton	431	W	Andy Pettitte	148
3B	Jimmy Rollins	95	L	Livan Hernandez	124
HR	Alex Rodriguez	435	SV	Mariano Rivera	397
RBI	Alex Rodriguez	1,243	G	Dave Weathers	713
BB	Barry Bonds	1,128	GS	Livan Hernandez	332
SO	Adam Dunn	1,433	SHO	Roy Halladay	14
XBH	Albert Pujols	767	IP	Livan Hernandez	2,201⅓
TB	Alex Rodriguez	3,362	R	Livan Hernandez	1,165
SB	Juan Pierre	459	HR	Jamie Moyer	270
CS	Juan Pierre	155	PO	Mark Buehrle	66
HBP	Jason Kendall	159	HBP	Tim Wakefield	107
GIDP	Miguel Tejada	223	GIDP	Mark Buehrle	240

for it with his job on Sept. 21 with his team's record at 70-79. Third-base coach Dave Clark ran the club for the remainder of the season, but the Astros then turned to Red Sox bench coach Brad Mills as the permanent replacement. Cooper spent just over two full seasons and compiled a 171-170 (.501) mark.

The Indians' Eric Wedge, just two years removed from winning AL manager of the year honors, was the final skipper to take a fall. Cleveland fired him following a disastrous 65-97 season. Wedge, who was 561-573 (.495) in seven seasons, was replaced by Acta after the season.

Henderson, Rice Enshrined

Rickey Henderson and Jim Rice were the headliners among three players inducted into the Hall of Fame in Cooperstown.

Henderson, who played primarily left field, finished his 25-year career in 2003 as the all-time leader in stolen bases (1,406), runs scored (2,295) and walks (2,190)—though Barry Bonds eclipsed his walks total in 2004. The most dynamic leadoff hitter of all time, Henderson batted .279/.401/.419 with 297 home runs for his career, while being selected to 10 All-Star Games and winning the AL MVP award in 1990. His 81 home runs leading off a game are the most ever.

CONTINUED ON PAGE 24

AL extends streak to 13

CLIFF WELCH

A game-saving catch helped Rays left fielder Carl Crawford earn MVP honors

ST. LOUIS Perhaps the surest bet in baseball in recent years is that the American League will win the All-Star Game.

The AL continued its dominance in 2009, using a highlight-reel catch by Rays left fielder Carl Crawford, a clutch hit from Tigers center fielder Curtis Granderson and outstanding relief pitching to beat the National League 4-3 at Busch Stadium in St. Louis.

The AL ran its mark to 12-0-1 in the last 13 All-Star Games, including seven straight wins since Major League Baseball began awarding home-field advantage to the winning league in 2003.

Crawford earned Most Valuable Player honors primarily on the strength of a catch he made in the seventh inning to preserve a 3-3 tie. Rockies right fielder Brad Hawpe hit a long drive to left-center but Crawford leaped and got his glove above the eight-foot fence to make the play.

Granderson then tripled with one out in the eighth off losing pitcher Heath Bell of the Padres. He scored the winning run on a sacrifice fly by Orioles center fielder Adam Jones.

Crawford became the first non-pitcher to win the MVP without an RBI since Willie Mays in 1968.

"It's probably the best catch I've ever made," Crawford said. "I didn't think it was going to carry that far. I just tried to find the wall and I was able to jump up and make a play on it."

Rays correspondent Marc Topkin reported that Crawford owes an assist to Rays' Triple-A outfielder Jon Weber for his MVP trophy. Crawford didn't want to break in a new glove in spring training, so he gave it to Weber and took his to use for the season.

Three of the game's premier closers finished the game for the AL. Jonathan Paplebon of the Red Sox pitched a scoreless seventh for the win and the Twins' Joe Nathan worked a scoreless eighth for the hold.

Making his eighth All-Star Game appearance, the Yankees' Mariano Rivera finished with a 1-2-3 ninth for his record fourth ASG save.

—John Perrotto

ALL-STAR GAME

JULY 14 IN ST. LOUIS

American League 4, National League 3

AMERICAN	AB	R	H	BI	NATIONAL	AB	R	H	BI
Suzuki, I, rf	3	0	1	0	Ramirez, H, ss	3	0	0	0
Jackson, E, p	0	0	0	0	Hoffman, p	0	0	0	0
Morneau, 1b	2	0	0	0	Gonzalez, A, 1b	0	0	0	0
Jeter, ss	2	2	0	0	Utley, 2b	2	0	0	0
Bartlett, ss	1	0	0	0	Hudson, O, ph-2b	2	0	1	0
Mauer, c	3	1	1	1	Pujols, 1b	3	0	0	0
Granderson, cf	1	1	1	0	Cordero, p	0	0	0	0
Teixeira, 1b	3	0	0	0	Bell, p	0	0	0	0
Martinez, V, c	0	0	0	0	Howard, ph	1	0	0	0
Bay, lf	2	0	1	0	Rodriguez, F, p	0	0	0	0
Jones, A, rf	1	0	0	1	Braun, rf-lf	2	0	0	0
Hamilton, cf	3	0	1	1	Upton, J, ph-lf	2	0	0	0
Hernandez, F, p	0	0	0	0	Ibanez, lf	2	0	0	0
Papelbon, p	0	0	0	0	Hawpe, rf	2	0	0	0
Youkilis, ph	1	0	1	0	Wright, D, 3b	2	1	1	0
Nathan, p	0	0	0	0	Billingsley, p	0	0	0	0
Rivera, Ma, p	0	0	0	0	Tejada, ss	2	0	0	0
Young, M, 3b	3	0	1	0	Victorino, cf	2	1	1	0
Zobrist, ph-2b	1	0	0	0	Werth, cf	1	0	0	0
Hill, A, 2b	3	0	0	0	Molina, Y, c	2	1	1	0
Inge, 3b	1	0	0	0	McCann, ph-c	1	0	0	0
Halladay, p	1	0	0	0	Lincecum, p	0	0	0	0
Buehrle, p	0	0	0	0	Fielder, ph	1	0	1	1
Greinke, p	0	0	0	0	Franklin, p	0	0	0	0
Crawford, ph-lf	3	0	1	0	Haren, p	0	0	0	0
					Zimmerman, R, 3b	2	0	0	0
Totals	**34**	**4**	**8**	**3**	**Totals**	**32**	**3**	**5**	**2**

American	200 010 010	—4
National	030 000 000	—3

LOB—American 6, National 3. **2B**—Mauer, Fielder. **3B**—Granderson. **GIDP**—Young, M. **SF**—Jones, A. **SB**—Hudson, O. **E**—Hamilton, Pujols. **IBB**—Martinez, V. **HBP**—Jeter.

AMERICAN	IP	H	R	ER	BB	SO	NATIONAL	IP	H	R	ER	BB	SO
Halladay	2	4	3	2	0	0	Lincecum	2	2	2	1	0	1
Buehrle	1	0	0	0	0	0	Franklin	1	0	0	0	0	0
Greinke	1	0	0	0	0	2	Haren	1	1	0	0	0	0
Jackson, E	1	0	0	0	0	0	Billingsley (BS)	1	2	1	1	0	0
Hernandez, F	1	0	0	0	0	0	Hoffman	1	1	0	0	0	0
Papelbon (W)	1	0	0	0	0	1	Cordero	1	0	0	0	0	0
Nathan	1	1	0	0	1	1	Bell (L)	1	2	1	1	1	1
Rivera, Ma (S)	1	0	0	0	0	1	Rodriguez, F	1	0	0	0	0	1
Totals	**9**	**5**	**3**	**2**	**1**	**5**	**Totals**	**9**	**8**	**4**	**3**	**1**	**3**

Umpires: HP—Dana DeMuth. **1B**—Brian Gorman. **2B**—Jeff Kellogg. **3B**—Angel Hernandez. **LF**—Tim Timmons. **RF**—Paul Nauert.
T—2:31. **A**—46,760.

CONTINUED FROM PAGE 22

All in all, it was quite a career for Henderson, who as an amateur at Oakland Technical High was better noted for his skills as a running back on the football field than for what he did on the baseball diamond. He spent the majority of his career, 14 seasons, with the hometown A's.

"My dream was to play football for the Oakland Raiders, but my mother thought I would get hurt playing football, so she choose baseball for me," Henderson said. "I guess moms do know best."

Rice gained election from the Baseball Writers Association of America in his 15th and final year on the ballot. The left fielder spent his entire 16-year career with the Red Sox, retiring after the 1989 season with eight all-star nods and one AL MVP from 1978. He batted .298/.352/.502 with 382 homers and 1,423 RBIs.

"It doesn't matter that the call came 15 years later," Rice said. "What matters is that I got it. It's hard to comprehend. I am in awe of being in this elite company."

The veterans committee selected Joe Gordon for enshrinement. A second baseman for 11 seasons from 1938-50 with the Yankees and Indians, Gordon batted .268/.357/.466 with 253 home runs while appearing in nine All-Star Games and winning the 1942 AL MVP. Gordon died at age 63 in 1978 and his final request was to not have a funeral.

"We consider Cooperstown and the National Baseball Hall of Fame as his final resting place, somewhere where he will be remembered forever," said Gordon's daughter Judy.

Nick Peters, who covered the Giants for 47 seasons for various San Francisco-area newspapers, was honored with the J.G. Taylor Spink Award for meritorious service to baseball writing. Tony Kubek, most noted for his work on NBC TV's Game of the Week, received the Frick Award.

Active Trading Deadline

Fans who look forward to the July 31 trading deadline were not disappointed by either the quality or quantity of prominent players who switched sides in 2009.

The Cardinals started the flurry of moves by acquiring left fielder Matt Holliday from the Athletics for a package of three prospects, headlined by Brett Wallace, St. Louis' first-round pick in 2008. Holliday went on to hit .353/.419/.604 with 11 home runs and 55 RBIs in 63 games to help the Cardinals win the NL Central.

The Phillies made a difference-making trade of their own when they acquired lefthander Cliff Lee from the Indians in exchange for four prospects, three of who had reached the Triple-A level. The 2008 AL Cy Young Award winner, Lee went 7-4, 3.39 in 12 starts as he helped the Phillies win their third straight NL East title.

The Indians traded catcher/first baseman Victor Martinez to the Red Sox for three young pitchers, just two weeks after he had been their lone representative at the All-Star Game. Martinez played a major role in the Red Sox winning the AL wild card by batting .336/.405/.507 with eight homers and 41 RBIs in 56 games.

The Padres traded righthander Jake Peavy, who won the NL Cy Young Award in 2007, to the White Sox for four young pitchers. Peavy, who missed a large chunk of the season with a right ankle tendon injury, had invoked his no-trade clause to veto a trade to the White Sox in May but then changed his mind in the final moments before the deadline. Peavy made just three starts for the White Sox, going an impressive 3-0, 1.35 but was viewed more as a long-term acquisition.

Other notable players who were dealt included Blue Jays third baseman Scott Rolen to the Reds, A's shortstop Orlando Cabrera to the Twins and Mariners lefthander Jarrod Washburn to the Tigers. Pittsburgh dealt away its double-play combination, sending second baseman Freddy Sanchez to the Giants and shortstop Jack Wilson to the Mariners.

Revenues Stung By Economy

Major League attendance figures dropped by 6.9 percent from 2008, proving that the game was not entirely immune to the country's deep recession in 2009.

While many clubs ran specials on discounted tickets, concessions and souvenirs, 22 of the 30 franchises saw decreases in attendance and three others had increases of less than 1 percent. The average attendance of 30,276 per game was also the lowest mark since 2006.

"I think we did quite well considering the circumstances," Selig said. "Our clubs worked extremely hard to provide value to fans in extremely challenging times."

Opening Day team payrolls were down 1.7 percent from 2008 as clubs spent $47 million less on players.

"We're seeing the continuation of the trend of mid-market and small-market teams developing their own talent and keeping their own talent," MLB chief operating officer Bob DuPuy said. "Teams were also concerned about the impact the economy might have on their revenues and adjusted their spending accordingly."

MAJOR LEAGUE *DEBUTS*

ARIZONA DIAMONDBACKS

Allen, Brandon	Aug. 22
Augenstein, Bryan	May 13
Hester, John	Aug. 28
Mulvey, Kevin	Sept. 3
Oeltjen, Trent	Aug. 6
Parra, Gerardo	May 13
Ryal, Rusty	Aug. 10
Schlereth, Daniel	May 29
Vasquez, Esmerling	April 26
Zavada, Clay	May 21

ATLANTA BRAVES

Canizares, Barbaro	June 11
Gorecki, Reid	Aug. 17
Hanson, Tommy	June 7
Hernandez, Diory	May 21
Kawakami, Kenshin	April 11
Medlen, Kris	May 21
Schafer, Jordan	April 5
Valdez, Luis	July 12

BALTIMORE ORIOLES

Bergesen, Brad	May 24
Berken, Jason	June 24
Hernandez, David	May 28
Matusz, Brian	Aug. 4
Reimold, Nolan	May 14
Tillman, Chris	July 29
Turner, Justin	Sept. 8
Uehara, Koji	May 23
Wieters, Matt	May 29

BOSTON RED SOX

Bard, Daniel	June 12
Bates, Aaron	July 6
Brown, Dusty	June 23
Jones, Hunter	April 20
Reddick, Josh	July 31
Richardson, Dustin	Sept. 28
Tazawa, Junichi	Aug. 7

CHICAGO CUBS

Atkins, Mitch	July 29
Berg, Justin	Aug. 13
Caridad, Esmailin	Aug. 10
Colvin, Tyler	Sept. 21
Patton, David	April 8
Scales, Bobby	May 5
Stevens, Jeff	July 10
Waddell, Jason	May 31

CHICAGO WHITE SOX

Beckham, Gordon	June 4
Egbert, Jack	April 21
Flowers, Tyler	Sept. 3
Hudson, Dan	Sept. 4
Nunez, Jhonny	Aug. 2
Poreda, Aaron	June 12
Torres, Carlos	Sept. 3
Whisler, Wes	June 2

CINCINNATI REDS

Fisher, Carlos	May 24
Francisco, Juan	Sept. 14
Maloney, Matt	June 6
Manuel, Robert	July 9
Stubbs, Drew	Aug. 19
Sutton, Drew	July 2
Tatum, Craig	July 21
Viola, Pedro	Sept. 8

CLEVELAND INDIANS

Brantley, Michael	Sept. 1
Carrasco, Carlos	Sept. 1
Crowe, Trevor	April 9
Gimenez, Chris	June 3
Huff, David	May 23
LaPorta, Matt	May 3
Romero, Niuman	Sept. 8
Sipp, Tony	June 24
Toregas, Wyatt	Aug. 1

COLORADO ROCKIES

Chacin, Jhoulys	July 25
Daley, Matt	April 25
McCoy, Mike	Sept. 9
Rogers, Esmil	Sept. 12
Young, Eric Jr.	Aug. 25

DETROIT LIONS

Avila, Alex	Aug. 6
Dlugach, Brent	Sept. 13
Fien, Casey	July 26
Figaro, Alfredo	June 27
French, Luke	May 15
Ni, Fu-Te	June 29
Perry, Ryan	June 13
Porcello, Rick	June 12
Ramirez, Wilkin	May 20

FLORIDA MARLINS

Coghlan, Chris	May 8
Hayes, Brett	May 22
Leroux, Chris	May 26
Martinez, Cristhian	May 21
Taylor, Graham	April 26
West, Sean	May 23
Wood, Tim	June 25

HOUSTON ASTROS

Gervacio, Samuel	Aug. 14
Johnson, Chris	Sept. 9
Lopez, Wilton	Aug. 28
Manzella, Tommy	Sept. 8
Norris, Bud	July 29

KANSAS CITY ROYALS

Hughes, Dusty	Sept. 6
Marte, Victor	Sept. 6

LOS ANGELES ANGELS

Bell, Trevor	Aug. 12
Davidson, Daniel	April 19
Mosebach, Robert	July 25
Ortega, Anthony	April 25
O'Sullivan, Sean	June 16
Pettit, Chris	Sept. 11
Rodriguez, Fernando	May 2
Rodriguez, Rafael	April 15

LOS ANGELES DODGERS

Belisario, Ronald	April 7
Hoffmann, Jamie	May 22
Jones, Mitch	June 16
Leach, Brent	May 7
Paul, Xavier	May 7
Schlichting, Travis	June 7

MILWAUKEE BREWERS

Axford, John	Sept. 15
Butler, Josh	Sept. 21
Corporan, Carlos	May 6

MINNEOSTA TWINS

Duensing, Brian	April 10
Gabino, Armando	Aug. 25
Manship, Jeff	May 14
Swarzak, Anthony	June 13

NEW YORK METS

Martinez, Fernando	May 26
Stoner, Tobi	Sept. 10
Takahashi, Ken	May 2
Thole, Josh	Sept. 3

NEW YORK YANKEES

Dunn, Michael	Sept. 4
Melancon, Mark	July 10
Pena, Ramiro	April 6

OAKLAND ATHLETICS

Anderson, Brett	April 29
Bailey, Andrew	June 14
Cahill, Trevor	June 14
Carson, Matt	Sept. 18

Everidge, Tommy	July 28
Kilby, Brad	Sept. 2
Mazzaro, Vin	June 12
Powell, Landon	April 11
Rodriguez, Henry	Sept. 21

PHILADELPHIA PHILLIES

Bastardo, Antonio	June 2
Escalona, Sergio	May 17
Mayberry, John Jr.	May 23

PITTSBURGH PIRATES

Claggett, Anthony	Oct. 3
Hacker, Eric	Sept. 22
Jackson, Steven	June 1
Jaramillo, Jason	April 16
McCutchen, Andrew	June 4
McCutchen, Daniel	Aug. 31
Veal, Donald	April 7
Walker, Neil	Sept. 1

ST. LOUIS CARDINALS

Freese, David	April 6
Greene, Tyler	April 30
Hawksworth, Blake	June 6
Hoffpauir, Jarrett	July 3
Mortensen, Clay	June 29
Pagnozzi, Matt	Sept. 29
Rasmus, Colby	April 7
Robinson, Shane	May 7
Todd, Jess	June 5
Walters, P.J.	April 17

SAN DIEGO PADRES

Blanks, Kyle	June 19
Burke, Greg	May 16
Cabrera, Everth	April 8
Carrillo, Cesar	Aug. 13
Durango, Luis	Sept. 15
Frieri, Ernesto	Sept. 26
Gregerson, Luke	April 6
Latos, Mat	July 19
Lobaton, Jose	July 5
Lopez, Arturo	April 29
Moreno, Edwin	April 7
Perdomo, Luis	April 15
Ramos, Cesar	Sept. 16
Silva, Walter	April 8

Webb, Ryan	July 8

SAN FRANCISCO GIANTS

Bumgarner, Madison	Sept. 8
Downs, Matt	June 16
Guzman, Jesus	May 21
Joaquin, Waldis	Aug. 4
Martinez, Joe	April 7
Posey, Buster	Sept. 11
Runzler, Dan	Sept. 4
Sadowski, Ryan	June 28

SEATTLE MARINERS

Carp, Mike	June 17
Fister, Doug	Aug. 8
Jakubauskas, Chris	June 13
Kelley, Shawn	April 10
Moore, Adam	Sept. 17
Saunders, Michael	July 25

TAMPA BAY RAYS

Davis, Wade	Sept. 6
Thayer, Dale	May 22

TEXAS RANGERS

Andrus, Elvis	April 6
Borbon, Julio	June 29
Feliz, Neftali	Aug. 3
Gentry, Craig	Sept. 6
Holland, Derek	May 22
Moscoso, Guillermo	May 30
Richardson, Kevin	Aug. 17
Strop, Pedro	Aug. 28

TORONTO BLUE JAYS

Cecil, Brett	June 20
Mills, Brad	June 18
Phillips, Kyle	Sept. 14
Ray, Robert	May 2
Romero, Ricky	June 16
Rzepczynski, Marc	July 7

WASHINGTON NATIONALS

Desmond, Ian	Sept. 10
Garate, Victor	Sept. 5
Martin, J.D.	July 20
Padilla, Jorge	Aug. 5
Stammen, Craig	May 21
Zimmermann, Jordan	April 20

Orioles catcher Matt Wieters made his much-anticipated debut on May 29

DIAMOND IMAGES

CLUB BATTING

	AVG	G	AB	R	H	2B	3B	HR	RBI	BB	SO	SB	CS	OBP	SLG
Los Angeles	.285	162	5622	883	1604	293	33	173	841	547	1054	148	63	.350	.441
New York	.283	162	5660	915	1604	325	21	244	881	663	1014	111	28	.362	.478
Minnesota	.274	163	5608	817	1539	271	40	172	770	585	1021	85	32	.345	.429
Boston	.270	162	5543	872	1495	335	25	212	822	659	1120	126	39	.352	.454
Baltimore	.268	162	5618	741	1508	307	19	160	708	517	1013	76	37	.332	.415
Toronto	.266	162	5696	798	1516	339	13	209	766	548	1028	73	23	.333	.440
Cleveland	.264	162	5568	773	1468	314	28	161	730	582	1211	84	31	.339	.417
Tampa Bay	.263	162	5462	803	1434	297	36	199	765	642	1229	194	61	.343	.439
Oakland	.262	162	5584	759	1464	307	21	135	723	527	1046	133	48	.328	.397
Detroit	.260	163	5540	743	1443	245	35	183	718	540	1114	72	33	.331	.416
Texas	.260	162	5526	784	1436	296	27	224	748	472	1253	149	36	.320	.445
Kansas City	.259	162	5532	686	1432	276	51	144	657	457	1091	88	29	.318	.405
Chicago	.258	162	5463	724	1410	246	20	184	695	534	1022	113	49	.329	.411
Seattle	.258	162	5543	640	1430	280	19	160	613	421	1093	89	33	.314	.402

CLUB PITCHING

	ERA	G	CG	SHO	SV	IP	H	R	ER	HR	BB	SO	AVG
Seattle	3.87	162	4	10	49	1453	1359	692	625	172	534	1043	.247
Chicago	4.14	162	4	11	36	1440	1438	732	663	169	507	1119	.261
New York	4.26	162	3	8	51	1450	1386	753	687	181	574	1260	.251
Oakland	4.26	162	2	10	38	1447	1486	761	685	156	523	1124	.265
Detroit	4.29	163	4	9	42	1447	1449	745	690	182	594	1102	.263
Tampa Bay	4.33	162	3	5	41	1427	1421	754	686	183	515	1125	.257
Boston	4.35	162	8	11	41	1437	1494	736	695	167	530	1230	.267
Texas	4.38	162	8	11	45	1435	1432	740	698	171	531	1016	.260
Los Angeles	4.45	162	9	13	51	1445	1513	761	715	180	523	1062	.272
Toronto	4.47	162	10	10	25	1451	1509	771	720	181	551	1181	.270
Minnesota	4.50	163	4	7	48	1453	1542	765	726	185	466	1052	.272
Kansas City	4.83	162	10	9	34	1426	1486	842	765	166	600	1153	.269
Cleveland	5.06	162	5	6	25	1434	1570	865	806	183	598	986	.280
Baltimore	5.15	162	2	3	31	1429	1633	876	817	218	546	933	.288

CLUB FIELDING

	PCT	PO	A	E	DP		PCT	PO	A	E	DP
Toronto	.988	4353	1740	76	469	Cleveland	.984	4302	1651	97	466
Minnesota	.987	4359	1565	76	371	Oakland	.983	4342	1592	105	410
Boston	.986	4310	1452	82	330	Tampa Bay	.983	4282	1511	98	364
Los Angeles	.986	4335	1623	85	475	Seattle	.982	4358	1525	105	397
Baltimore	.985	4287	1663	90	413	Texas	.982	4304	1603	106	458
Detroit	.985	4341	1616	88	449	Chicago	.981	4319	1669	113	432
New York	.985	4350	1493	86	360	Kansas City	.981	4278	1569	116	423

INDIVIDUAL BATTING LEADERS *(MINIMUM 3.1 PA/TEAM GAME)*

	AVG	G	AB	R	H	2B	3B	HR	RBI	BB	SO	SB
Mauer, Joe, Minnesota	.365	138	523	94	191	30	1	28	96	76	63	4
Suzuki, Ichiro, Seattle	.352	146	639	88	225	31	4	11	46	32	71	26
Jeter, Derek, New York	.334	153	634	107	212	27	1	18	66	72	90	30
Cabrera, Miguel, Detroit	.324	160	611	96	198	34	0	34	103	68	107	6
Young, Michael, Texas	.322	135	541	76	174	36	2	22	68	47	90	8
Cano, Robinson, New York	.320	161	637	103	204	48	2	25	85	30	63	5
Bartlett, Jason, Tampa Bay	.320	137	500	90	160	29	7	14	66	54	89	30
Aybar, Erick, Los Angeles	.312	137	504	70	157	23	9	5	58	30	54	14
Span, Denard, Minnesota	.311	145	578	97	180	16	10	8	68	70	89	23
Ordonez, Magglio, Detroit	.310	131	465	54	144	24	2	9	50	51	65	3

INDIVIDUAL PITCHING LEADERS *(MINIMUM 1 IP/TEAM GAME)*

	W	L	ERA	G	GS	CG	SHO	SV	IP	H	R	ER	BB	SO
Greinke, Zack, Kansas City	16	8	2.16	33	33	6	3	0	229	195	64	55	51	242
Hernandez, Felix, Seattle	19	5	2.49	34	34	2	1	0	239	200	81	66	71	217
Halladay, Roy, Toronto	17	10	2.79	32	32	9	4	0	239	234	82	74	35	208
Sabathia, C.C., New York	19	8	3.37	34	34	2	1	0	230	197	96	86	67	197
Lester, Jon, Boston	15	8	3.41	32	32	2	0	0	203	186	80	77	20	225
Verlander, Justin, Detroit	19	9	3.45	35	35	3	1	0	240	219	99	92	63	269
Jackson, Edwin, Detroit	13	9	3.62	33	33	1	0	0	214	200	93	86	70	161
Millwood, Kevin, Texas	13	10	3.67	31	31	3	0	0	199	195	88	81	71	123
Weaver, Jered, Los Angeles	16	8	3.75	33	33	4	2	0	211	196	91	88	66	174
Danks, John, Chicago	13	11	3.77	32	32	1	0	0	200	184	89	84	73	149

AWARD WINNERS

Selected by Baseball Writers Association of America

MOST VALUABLE PLAYER

Player	1st	2nd	3rd	Total
Joe Mauer, Minn.	27	1	—	387
Mark Teixeira, N.Y.	—	15	6	225
Derek Jeter, N.Y.	—	9	5	193
Miguel Cabrera, Det.	1	1	5	171
Kendry Morales, L.A.	—	—	3	170
Kevin Youkilis, Bos.	—	2	7	150
Jason Bay, Bos.	—		1	78
Ben Zobrist, T.B.	—	—	—	34
Ichiro Suzuki, Sea.	—	—	—	33
Alex Rodriguez, N.Y.	—		1	31
Chone Figgins, L.A.	—	—	—	31
Aaron Hill, Tor.	—	—	—	23
Bobby Abreu, L.A.	—	—	—	23
Mariano Rivera, N.Y.	—	—	—	17
Adam Lind, Tor.	—	—	—	14
Michael Young, Tex.	—	—	—	13
Zack Greinke, K.C.	—	—	—	12
Robinson Cano, N.Y.	—	—	—	12
Evan Longoria, T.B.	—	—	—	9
Justin Verlander, Det.	—	—	—	7
C.C. Sabathia, N.Y.	—	—	—	4
Michael Cuddyer, Minn.	—	—	—	4
Victor Martinez, Cle./Bos.	—	—	—	4
Jason Kubel, Minn.	—	—	—	3
Placido Polanco, Det.	—	—	—	2
Felix Hernandez, Sea.	—	—	—	1
Ian Kinsler, Tex.	—	—	—	1

CY YOUNG AWARD

Pitchers	1st	2nd	3rd	Total
Zack Greinke, K.C.	25	3	—	134
Felix Hernandez, Sea.	2	23	1	80
Justin Verlander, Det.	1	—	9	14
C.C. Sabathia, N.Y.	—	2	7	13
Roy Halladay, Tor.	—	—	11	11

ROOKIE OF THE YEAR

Player	1st	2nd	3rd	Total
Andrew Bailey, Oak.	13	6	5	88
Elvis Andrus, Tex.	8	6	7	65
Rick Porcello, Det.	7	8	5	64
Jeff Niemann, T.B.	—	5	6	21
Gordon Beckham, Chi.	—	2	4	10
Brett Anderson, Oak.	—	1	1	4

MANAGER OF THE YEAR

Managers	1st	2nd	3rd	Total
Mike Scioscia, L.A.	15	10	1	106
Ron Gardenhire, Minn.	6	12	6	72
Joe Girardi, N.Y.	4	3	5	34
Don Wakamatsu, Sea.	2	2	3	19
Ron Washington, Tex.	1	1	11	19
Jim Leyland, Det.	—	—	2	2

GOLD GLOVE AWARDS

Selected by AL managers
C—Joe Mauer, Minn. 1B—Mark Teixeira, N.Y.
2B—Placido Polanco, Det. 3B—Evan Longoria, T.B.
SS—Derek Jeter, N.Y. OF—Torii Hunter, L.A.; Adam Jones, Balt.; Ichiro Suzuki, Sea. P—Mark Buehrle, Chi.

SILVER SLUGGER AWARDS

Selected by AL managers, coaches
C—Joe Mauer, Minn. 1B—Mark Teixeira, N.Y. 2B—Aaron Hill, Tor. 3B—Evan Longoria, T.B. SS—Derek Jeter, N.Y. OF—Jason Bay, Bos.; Torii Hunter, L.A.; Ichiro Suzuki, Sea. DH—Adam Lind, Tor.

BATTING

GAMES
Cano, Robinson, Yankees	161
Inge, Brandon, Tigers	161
Markakis, Nick, Orioles	161
Cabrera, Miguel, Tigers	160
Cabrera, Orlando, A's/Twins	160
Granderson, Curtis, Tigers	160

AT-BATS
Hill, Aaron, Blue Jays	682
Cabrera, Orlando, A's/Twins	656
Markakis, Nick, Orioles	642
Suzuki, Ichiro, Mariners	639
Cano, Robinson, Yankees	637

PLATE APPEARANCES
Hill, Aaron, Blue Jays	734
Figgins, Chone, Angels	729
Roberts, Brian, Orioles	717
Jeter, Derek, Yankees	716
Pedroia, Dustin, Red Sox	714

RUNS
Pedroia, Dustin, Red Sox	115
Figgins, Chone, Angels	114
Roberts, Brian, Orioles	110
Damon, Johnny, Yankees	107
Jeter, Derek, Yankees	107

HITS
Suzuki, Ichiro, Mariners	225
Jeter, Derek, Yankees	212
Cano, Robinson, Yankees	204
Cabrera, Miguel, Tigers	198
Hill, Aaron, Blue Jays	195

TOTAL BASES
Teixeira, Mark, Yankees	344
Hill, Aaron, Blue Jays	340
Cabrera, Miguel, Tigers	334
Cano, Robinson, Yankees	331
Lind, Adam, Blue Jays	330

DOUBLES
Roberts, Brian, Orioles	56
Butler, Billy, Royals	51
Cano, Robinson, Yankees	48
Pedroia, Dustin, Red Sox	48
Lind, Adam, Blue Jays	46

TRIPLES
Ellsbury, Jacoby, Red Sox	10
Span, Denard, Twins	10
Aybar, Erick, Angels	9
DeJesus, David, Royals	9
Five tied at	8

EXTRA-BASE HITS
Teixeira, Mark, Yankees	85
Lind, Adam, Blue Jays	81
Morales, Kendry, Angels	79
Longoria, Evan, Rays	77
Cano, Robinson, Yankees	75

HOME RUNS
Pena, Carlos, Rays	39
Teixeira, Mark, Yankees	39
Bay, Jason, Red Sox	36
Hill, Aaron, Blue Jays	36
Lind, Adam, Blue Jays	35

RUNS BATTED IN
Teixeira, Mark, Yankees	122
Bay, Jason, Red Sox	119
Lind, Adam, Blue Jays	114
Longoria, Evan, Rays	113
Hill, Aaron, Blue Jays	108

Mark Teixeira

DIAMOND IMAGES

Martinez, Victor, Ind./R. Sox	108
Morales, Kendry, Angels	108

SACRIFICES
Everett, Adam, Tigers	15
Gutierrez, Franklin, Mariners	13
Punto, Nick, Twins	13
Three tied at	12

SACRIFICE FLIES
Byrd, Marlon, Rangers	10
Cabrera, Orlando, A's/Twins	10
Markakis, Nick, Orioles	10
Abreu, Bobby, Angels	9
Murphy, David, Rangers	9

HIT BY PITCH
Shoppach, Kelly, Indians	18
Inge, Brandon, Tigers	17
Choo, Shin-Soo, Indians	17
Youkilis, Kevin, Red Sox	16

Quentin, Carlos, White Sox	15

WALKS
Figgins, Chone, Angels	101
Swisher, Nick, Yankees	97
Abreu, Bobby, Angels	94
Bay, Jason, Red Sox	94
Cust, Jack, Athletics	93

INTENTIONAL WALKS
Suzuki, Ichiro, Mariners	15
Cabrera, Miguel, Tigers	14
Mauer, Joe, Twins	14
Morneau, Justin, Twins	12
Longoria, Evan, Rays	11
Pena, Carlos, Rays	11

STOLEN BASES
Ellsbury, Jacoby, Red Sox	70
Crawford, Carl, Rays	60
Figgins, Chone, Angels	42

Upton, B.J., Rays	42
Davis, Rajai, Athletics	41

CAUGHT STEALING
Figgins, Chone, Angels	17
Crawford, Carl, Rays	16
Upton, B.J., Rays	14
Podsednik, Scott, White Sox	13
Two tied at	12

STOLEN BASE PERCENTAGE
Getz, Chris, White Sox	92.6%
Choo, Shin-Soo, Indians	91.3%
Kinsler, Ian, Rangers	86.1%
Jeter, Derek, Yankees	85.7%
Ellsbury, Jacoby, Red Sox	85.4%

STRIKEOUTS
Cust, Jack, Athletics	185
Inge, Brandon, Tigers	170
Pena, Carlos, Rays	163
Bay, Jason, Red Sox	162
Upton, B.J., Rays	152

TOUGHEST TO STRIKE OUT (AT-BATS PER STRIKEOUT)
Pedroia, Dustin, Red Sox	13.91
Polanco, Placido, Tigers	13.43
Callaspo, Alberto, Royals	11.29
Betancourt, Yuniesky, M's/Roy.	10.68
Cano, Robinson, Yankees	10.11

GROUNDED INTO DOUBLE PLAYS
Longoria, Evan, Rays	27
Lopez, Jose, Mariners	25
Lowell, Mike, Red Sox	24
Cabrera, Miguel, Tigers	22
Cabrera, Orlando, A's/Twins	22
Cano, Robinson, Yankees	22
Cuddyer, Michael, Twins	22

MULTI-HIT GAMES
Suzuki, Ichiro, Mariners	73
Cano, Robinson, Yankees	67
Jeter, Derek, Yankees	66
Ellsbury, Jacoby, Red Sox	59
Three tied at	57

ON-BASE PERCENTAGE
Mauer, Joe, Twins	.444
Youkilis, Kevin, Red Sox	.413
Jeter, Derek, Yankees	.406
Zobrist, Ben, Rays	.405
Rodriguez, Alex, Yankees	.402

SLUGGING PERCENTAGE
Mauer, Joe, Twins	.587
Morales, Kendry, Angels	.569
Teixeira, Mark, Yankees	.565
Lind, Adam, Blue Jays	.562
Youkilis, Kevin, Red Sox	.548

ON-BASE PLUS SLUGGING
Mauer, Joe, Twins	1.031
Youkilis, Kevin, Red Sox	.961
Teixeira, Mark, Yankees	.948
Zobrist, Ben, Rays	.948
Cabrera, Miguel, Tigers	.942

PITCHING

WINS
Hernandez, Felix, Mariners	19
Sabathia, C.C., Yankees	19
Verlander, Justin, Tigers	19
Beckett, Josh, Red Sox	17
Feldman, Scott, Rangers	17
Halladay, Roy, Blue Jays	17

Felix Hernandez

LARRY GOREN

DEPARTMENT LEADERS

Justin Verlander

JASON POHUSKI

LOSSES

Guthrie, Jeremy, Orioles	17
Cahill, Trevor, Athletics	13
Contreras, Jose, White Sox	13
Hochevar, Luke, Royals	13
Holland, Derek, Rangers	13
Liriano, Francisco, Twins	13

GAMES

Guerrier, Matt, Twins	79
Breslow, Craig, Twins/A's	77
Lowe, Mark, Mariners	75
Springer, Russ, A's/Rays	74
Wilson, C.J., Rangers	74
Wuertz, Michael, Athletics	74

GAMES STARTED

Verlander, Justin, Tigers	35
Hernandez, Felix, Mariners	34
Sabathia, C.C., Yankees	34
Nine tied at	33

GAMES FINISHED

Rodney, Fernando, Tigers	65
Nathan, Joe, Twins	62
Papelbon, Jonathan, Red Sox	59
Fuentes, Brian, Angels	57
Rivera, Mariano, Yankees	55

COMPLETE GAMES

Halladay, Roy, Blue Jays	9
Greinke, Zack, Royals	6
Beckett, Josh, Red Sox	4
Weaver, Jered, Angels	4
Four tied at	3

SHUTOUTS

Halladay, Roy, Blue Jays	4
Greinke, Zack, Royals	3
Four tied at	2

SAVES

Fuentes, Brian, Angels	48
Nathan, Joe, Twins	47
Rivera, Mariano, Yankees	44
Aardsma, David, Mariners	38
Papelbon, Jonathan, Red Sox	38

INNINGS

Verlander, Justin, Tigers	240
Halladay, Roy, Blue Jays	239
Hernandez, Felix, Mariners	238.2
Sabathia, C.C., Yankees	230
Greinke, Zack, Royals	229.1

HITS ALLOWED

Blackburn, Nick, Twins	240
Shields, James, Rays	239
Pavano, Carl, Indians/Twins	235
Halladay, Roy, Blue Jays	234
Guthrie, Jeremy, Orioles	224

RUNS ALLOWED

Guthrie, Jeremy, Orioles	120
Pavano, Carl, Indians/Twins	119
Shields, James, Rays	113
Hochevar, Luke, Royals	109
Blackburn, Nick, Twins	103

HOME RUNS ALLOWED

Guthrie, Jeremy, Orioles	35
Saunders, Joe, Angels	29
Shields, James, Rays	29
Baker, Scott, Twins	28
Danks, John, White Sox	28

WALKS

Burnett, A.J., Yankees	97
Garza, Matt, Rays	79
Romero, Ricky, Blue Jays	79
Chamberlain, Joba, Yankees	76
Pettitte, Andy, Yankees	76

WALKS PER NINE INNINGS

Halladay, Roy, Blue Jays	1.32
Pavano, Carl, Indians/Twins	1.76
Blackburn, Nick, Twins	1.79
Buehrle, Mark, White Sox	1.90
Greinke, Zack, Royals	2.00

HIT BATSMEN

Chamberlain, Joba, Yankees	12
Garza, Matt, Rays	11
Millwood, Kevin, Rangers	11
Four tied at	10

STRIKEOUTS

Verlander, Justin, Tigers	269
Greinke, Zack, Royals	242
Lester, Jon, Red Sox	225
Hernandez, Felix, Mariners	217
Halladay, Roy, Blue Jays	208

STRIKEOUTS PER NINE INNINGS

Verlander, Justin, Tigers	10.09
Lester, Jon, Red Sox	9.96
Greinke, Zack, Royals	9.50
Burnett, A.J., Yankees	8.48
Beckett, Josh, Red Sox	8.43

STRIKEOUTS PER NINE INNINGS (RELIEVERS)

Robertson, David, Yankees	12.98
Tejeda, Robinson, Royals	11.79
Soria, Joakim, Royals	11.72
Wuertz, Michael, Athletics	11.67
Nathan, Joe, Twins	11.67

DOUBLE PLAYS

Romero, Ricky, Blue Jays	30
Buehrle, Mark, White Sox	28
Saunders, Joe, Angels	27
Laffey, Aaron, Indians	26
Anderson, Brett, Athletics	24
Porcello, Rick, Tigers	24

PICKOFFS

Buehrle, Mark, White Sox	8
Lester, Jon, Red Sox	6
Pettitte, Andy, Yankees	6
Richard, Clayton, White Sox	6
Two tied at	5

WILD PITCHES

Burnett, A.J., Yankees	17
Hernandez, Felix, Mariners	17
Kazmir, Scott, Rays/Angels	13
Bannister, Brian, Royals	12
Davies, Kyle, Royals	10

BALKS

Verlander, Justin, Tigers	4
Holland, Derek, Rangers	3
Nine tied at	2

OPPONENT AVERAGE

Hernandez, Felix, Mariners	.227
Greinke, Zack, Royals	.230
Sabathia, C.C., Yankees	.232
Garza, Matt, Rays	.233
Lester, Jon, Red Sox	.242

WORST ERA

Pavano, Carl, Indians/Twins	5.10
Guthrie, Jeremy, Orioles	5.04
Cahill, Trevor, Athletics	4.63
Saunders, Joe, Angels	4.60
Baker, Scott, Twins	4.37

FIELDING

PITCHER

PCT	Anderson, Brett, Athletics	1.000
	Baker, Scott, Twins	1.000
	Millwood, Kevin, Rangers	1.000
	Niemann, Jeff, Rays	1.000
	Pavano, Carl, Indians/Twins	1.000
	Sabathia, C.C., Yankees	1.000
PO	Hernandez, Felix, Mariners	29
A	Buehrle, Mark, White Sox	41
E	Holland, Derek, Rangers	5
TC	Buehrle, Mark, White Sox	55
DP	Anderson, Brett, Athletics	5
	Buehrle, Mark, White Sox	5
	Shields, James, Rays	5

CATCHER

PCT	Laird, Gerald, Tigers	.997
PO	Suzuki, Kurt, Athletics	923
A	Laird, Gerald, Tigers	78
E	Barajas, Rod, Blue Jays	8
	Buck, John, Royals	8

	Napoli, Mike, Angels	8
	Olivo, Miguel, Royals	8
DP	Wieters, Matt, Orioles	12
PB	Olivo, Miguel, Royals	10
CS%	Larid, Gerald, Tigers	.416

FIRST BASE

PCT	Overbay, Lyle, Blue Jays	.998
PO	Morales, Kendry, Angels	1274
A	Cabrera, Miguel, Tigers	105
E	Branyan, Russell, Mariners	10
	Butler, Billy, Royals	10
	Pena, Carlos, Rays	10
DP	Morales, Kendry, Angels	145

SECOND BASE

PCT	Polanco, Placido, Tigers	.997
PO	Cano, Robinson, Yankees	308
A	Hill, Aaron, Blue Jays	484
E	Callaspo, Alberto, Royals	17
DP	Hill, Aaron, Blue Jays	129

THIRD BASE

PCT	Mora, Melvin, Orioles	.971
PO	Inge, Brandon, Tigers	143
A	Figgins, Chone, Angels	314
E	Inge, Brandon, Tigers	20
DP	Longoria, Evan, Rays	43

SHORTSTOP

PCT	Jeter, Derek, Yankees	.986
PO	Andrus, Elvis, Rangers	261
A	Cabrera, Orlando, A's/Twins	428
E	Cabrera, Orlando, A's/Twins	25
DP	Aybar, Erick, Angels	102

OUTFIELD

PCT	Bay, Jason, Red Sox	1.000
	DeJesus, David, Royals	1.000
	Maier, Mitch, Royals	1.000
PO	Gutierrez, Franklin, Mariners	445
A	Bay, Jason, Red Sox	15
E	Abreu, Bobby, Angels	8
DP	Maier, Mitch, Royals	5

CLUB BATTING

	AVG	G	AB	R	H	2B	3B	HR	RBI	BB	SO	SB	CS	OBP	SLG
Los Angeles	.270	162	5592	780	1511	278	39	145	739	607	1068	116	48	.346	.412
New York	.270	162	5453	671	1472	295	49	95	631	526	928	122	44	.335	.394
Florida	.268	162	5572	772	1493	296	25	159	727	568	1226	75	35	.340	.416
Atlanta	.263	162	5539	735	1459	300	20	149	700	602	1064	58	26	.339	.405
Milwaukee	.263	162	5510	785	1447	281	37	182	757	610	1231	68	37	.341	.426
St. Louis	.263	162	5465	730	1436	294	29	160	694	528	1041	75	31	.332	.415
Colorado	.261	162	5398	804	1408	300	50	190	760	660	1277	106	55	.343	.441
Houston	.260	162	5436	643	1415	270	32	142	616	448	990	113	44	.319	.400
Philadelphia	.258	162	5578	820	1439	312	35	224	788	589	1155	119	28	.334	.447
Washington	.258	162	5493	710	1416	271	38	156	685	617	1208	73	40	.337	.406
San Francisco	.257	162	5493	657	1411	275	43	122	612	392	1158	78	28	.309	.389
Chicago	.255	161	5486	707	1398	293	29	161	678	592	1185	56	34	.332	.407
Arizona	.253	162	5565	720	1408	307	45	173	686	571	1298	102	40	.324	.418
Pittsburgh	.252	161	5417	636	1364	289	34	125	612	499	1142	90	32	.318	.387
Cincinnati	.247	162	5462	673	1349	260	25	158	637	531	1129	96	40	.318	.394
San Diego	.242	162	5425	638	1315	265	31	141	605	586	1182	82	29	.321	.381

CLUB PITCHING

	ERA	G	CG	SHO	SV	IP	H	R	ER	HR	BB	SO	AVG
Los Angeles	3.41	162	1	9	44	1473	1265	611	558	127	584	1272	.233
San Francisco	3.55	162	11	18	41	1446	1268	611	571	140	584	1302	.236
Atlanta	3.57	162	3	10	38	1463	1399	641	581	119	530	1232	.254
St. Louis	3.66	162	8	11	43	1441	1407	640	586	123	460	1049	.258
Chicago	3.84	161	3	8	40	1445	1329	672	616	160	586	1272	.246
Philadelphia	4.16	162	8	9	44	1456	1479	709	673	189	489	1153	.265
Cincinnati	4.18	162	6	12	41	1458	1420	723	677	188	577	1069	.258
Colorado	4.22	162	5	7	45	1438	1427	715	675	141	528	1154	.261
Florida	4.29	162	5	5	45	1446	1425	766	690	160	601	1248	.257
San Diego	4.37	162	2	9	45	1451	1422	769	704	167	603	1187	.258
Arizona	4.42	162	4	12	36	1448	1470	782	711	168	525	1158	.263
New York	4.45	162	3	12	39	1426	1452	757	705	158	616	1031	.264
Houston	4.54	162	5	10	39	1430	1521	770	722	176	546	1144	.275
Pittsburgh	4.59	161	5	7	28	1418	1491	768	723	152	563	919	.276
Milwaukee	4.83	162	1	8	44	1435	1498	818	770	207	607	1104	.268
Washington	5.00	162	6	3	33	1424	1533	874	791	173	629	911	.276

CLUB FIELDING

	PCT	PO	A	E	DP		PCT	PO	A	E	DP
Pittsburgh	.988	4255	1766	73	460	St. Louis	.985	4322	1855	96	453
Houston	.987	4290	1719	78	447	Milwaukee	.984	4305	1590	98	410
Philadelphia	.987	4367	1557	76	356	New York	.984	4278	1557	97	360
Colorado	.986	4315	1765	87	399	San Diego	.984	4352	1566	94	386
Los Angeles	.986	4420	1594	83	356	Chicago	.983	4336	1573	105	404
Atlanta	.985	4388	1714	96	431	Florida	.982	4339	1469	106	355
Cincinnati	.985	4375	1596	89	427	Arizona	.980	4343	1606	124	370
San Francisco	.985	4338	1511	88	362	Washington	.977	4273	1742	143	417

INDIVIDUAL BATTING LEADERS (MINIMUM 3.1 PA/TEAM GAME)

	AVG	G	AB	R	H	2B	3B	HR	RBI	BB	SO	SB
Ramirez, Hanley, Florida	.342	151	576	101	197	42	1	24	106	61	101	27
Sandoval, Pablo, San Francisco	.330	153	572	79	189	44	5	25	90	52	83	5
Pujols, Albert, St. Louis	.327	160	568	124	186	45	1	47	135	115	64	16
Helton, Todd, Colorado	.325	151	544	79	177	38	3	15	86	89	73	0
Votto, Joey, Cincinnati	.322	131	469	82	151	38	1	25	84	70	106	4
Coghlan, Chris, Florida	.321	128	504	84	162	31	6	9	47	53	77	8
Braun, Ryan, Milwaukee	.320	158	635	113	203	39	6	32	114	57	121	20
Tejada, Miguel, Houston	.313	158	635	83	199	46	1	14	86	19	48	5
Lopez, Felipe, Ariz./Mil.	.310	151	604	88	187	38	3	9	57	71	100	6
Morgan, Nyjer, Pitt./Wash.	.307	120	469	74	144	15	7	3	39	40	74	42

INDIVIDUAL PITCHING LEADERS (MINIMUM 1 IP/TEAM GAME)

	W	L	ERA	G	GS	CG	SHO	SV	IP	H	R	ER	BB	SO
Carpenter, Chris, St. Louis	17	4	2.24	28	28	3	1	0	193	156	49	48	38	144
Lincecum, Tim, San Francisco	15	7	2.48	32	32	4	2	0	225	168	69	62	68	261
Jurrjens, Jair, Atlanta	14	10	2.60	34	34	0	0	0	215	186	71	62	75	152
Wainwright, Adam, St. Louis	19	8	2.63	34	34	1	0	0	233	216	75	68	66	212
Kershaw, Clayton, Los Angeles	8	8	2.79	31	30	0	0	0	171	119	55	53	91	185
Vazquez, Javier, Atlanta	15	10	2.87	32	32	3	0	0	219	181	75	70	44	238
Cain, Matt, San Francisco	14	8	2.89	33	33	4	0	0	218	184	73	70	73	171
Happ, J.A., Philadelphia	12	4	2.93	35	23	3	2	0	166	149	55	54	56	119
Rodriguez, Wandy, Houston	14	12	3.02	33	33	1	1	0	206	192	77	69	63	193
Wells, Randy, Chicago	12	10	3.05	27	27	0	0	0	165	165	67	56	46	104

AWARD WINNERS

Selected by Baseball Writers Association of America

MOST VALUABLE PLAYER

Player	1st	2nd	3rd	Total
Albert Pujols, St.L.	32	—	—	448
Hanley Ramirez, Fla.	—	15	5	233
Ryan Howard, Phil.	—	6	8	217
Prince Fielder, Mil.	—	5	9	203
Troy Tulowitzki, Colo.	—	3	6	172
Andre Ethier, L.A.	—	2	—	113
Pablo Sandoval, S.F.	—	—	1	89
Chase Utley, Phil.	—	—	2	84
Derrek Lee, Chi.	—	1	—	66
Matt Kemp, L.A.	—	—	—	49
Ryan Braun, Mil.	—	—	—	43
Adrian Gonzalez, S.D.	—	—	—	30
Todd Helton, Colo.	—	—	1	28
Chris Carpenter, St.L.	—	—	—	25
Adam Wainwright, St.L.	—	—	—	16
Matt Holliday, St.L.	—	—	—	15
Jayson Werth, Phil.	—	—	—	10
Shane Victorino, Phil.	—	—	—	8
Tim Lincecum, S.F.	—	—	—	8
Yunel Escobar, Atl.	—	—	—	6
Mark Reynolds, Ariz.	—	—	—	6
Joey Votto, Cin.	—	—	—	4
Yadier Molina, St.L.	—	—	—	3
Miguel Tejada, Hou.	—	—	—	3
Huston Street, Colo.	—	—	—	2
Justin Upton, Ariz.	—	—	—	2
Ryan Zimmerman, Wash.	—	—	—	2
Jeremy Affeldt, S.F.	—	—	—	1
Chris Coghlan, Fla.	—	—	—	1
Brad Hawpe, Colo.	—	—	—	1

CY YOUNG AWARD

Pitchers	1st	2nd	3rd	Total
Tim Lincecum, S.F.	11	12	9	100
Chris Carpenter, St.L.	9	14	7	94
Adam Wainwright, St.L.	12	5	15	90
Javier Vazquez, Atl.	—	1	—	3
Dan Haren, Ariz.	—	—	1	1

ROOKIE OF THE YEAR

Player	1st	2nd	3rd	Total
Chris Coghlan, Fla.	17	6	2	105
J.A. Happ, Phil.	10	11	11	94
Tommy Hanson, Atl.	2	6	9	37
Andrew McCutchen, Pitt.	2	5	—	25
Casey McGehee, Mil.	1	3	4	18
Randy Wells, Chi.	—	1	—	3
Garrett Jones, Pitt.	—	2	2
Everth Cabrera, S.D.	—	—	1	1
Dexter Fowler, Colo.	—	—	1	1
Gerardo Parra, Ariz.	—	—	1	1
Colby Rasmus, St.L.	—	—	1	1

MANAGER OF THE YEAR

Managers	1st	2nd	3rd	Total
Jim Tracy, Colo.	29	2	—	151
Tony La Russa, St.L.	2	13	6	55
Joe Torre, L.A.	1	7	7	33
Bruce Bochy, S.F.	—	5	3	18
Bobby Cox, Atl.	—	3	6	15
Charlie Manuel, Phil.	—	2	4	10
Fredi Gonzalez, Fla.	—	—	4	4
Bud Black, S.D.	—	—	2	2

GOLD GLOVE AWARDS

Selected by NL managers

C—Yadier Molina, St.L. **1B**—Adrian Gonzalez, S.D. **2B**—Orlando Hudson, L.A. **3B**—Ryan Zimmerman, Wash. **SS**—Jimmy Rollins, Phil. **OF**—Michael Bourn, Hou.; Matt Kemp, L.A.; Shane Victorino, Phil. **P**—Adam Wainwright, St.L.

SILVER SLUGGER AWARDS

Selected by NL managers, coaches

C—Brian McCann, Atl. **1B**—Albert Pujols, St.L. **2B**—Chase Utley, Phil. **3B**—Ryan Zimmerman, Wash. **SS**—Hanley Ramirez, Fla. **OF**—Ryan Braun, Mil.; Andre Ethier, L.A.; Matt Kemp, L.A. **P**—Carlos Zambrano, Chi.

GAMES

Fielder, Prince, Brewers	162
Ethier, Andre, Dodgers	160
Gonzalez, Adrian, Padres	160
Howard, Ryan, Phillies	160
Lee, Carlos, Astros	160
Pujols, Albert, Cardinals	160

AT-BATS

Rollins, Jimmy, Phillies	672
Braun, Ryan, Brewers	635
Tejada, Miguel, Astros	635
Victorino, Shane, Phillies	620
Howard, Ryan, Phillies	616

PLATE APPEARANCES

Rollins, Jimmy, Phillies	725
Fielder, Prince, Brewers	719
Braun, Ryan, Brewers	708
Howard, Ryan, Phillies	703
Pujols, Albert, Cardinals	700

RUNS

Pujols, Albert, Cardinals	124
Braun, Ryan, Brewers	113
Utley, Chase, Phillies	112
Zimmerman, Ryan, Nationals	110
Howard, Ryan, Phillies	105

HITS

Braun, Ryan, Brewers	203
Tejada, Miguel, Astros	199
Ramirez, Hanley, Marlins	197
Sandoval, Pablo, Giants	189
Lopez, Felipe, D'backs/Brew.	187

TOTAL BASES

Pujols, Albert, Cardinals	374
Fielder, Prince, Brewers	356
Howard, Ryan, Phillies	352
Braun, Ryan, Brewers	350
Zimmerman, Ryan, Nationals	320

DOUBLES

Tejada, Miguel, Astros	46
Pujols, Albert, Cardinals	45
Sandoval, Pablo, Giants	44
Rollins, Jimmy, Phillies	43
Cantu, Jorge, Marlins	42
Ethier, Andre, Dodgers	42
Hawpe, Brad, Rockies	42
Ramirez, Hanley, Marlins	42

TRIPLES

Victorino, Shane, Phillies	13
Bourn, Michael, Astros	12
Drew, Stephen, Diamondbacks	12
Pagan, Angel, Mets	11
Fowler, Dexter, Rockies	10

EXTRA-BASE HITS

Pujols, Albert, Cardinals	93
Howard, Ryan, Phillies	86
Fielder, Prince, Brewers	84
Braun, Ryan, Brewers	77
Ethier, Andre, Dodgers	76

HOME RUNS

Pujols, Albert, Cardinals	47
Fielder, Prince, Brewers	46
Howard, Ryan, Phillies	45
Reynolds, Mark, D'backs	44
Gonzalez, Adrian, Padres	40

RUNS BATTED IN

Fielder, Prince, Brewers	141
Howard, Ryan, Phillies	141
Pujols, Albert, Cardinals	135
Braun, Ryan, Brewers	114

Ryan Braun

Lee, Derrek, Cubs	111

SACRIFICES

Vazquez, Javier, Braves	20
Castillo, Luis, Mets	19
Matsui, Kazuo, Astros	16
Four tied at	14

SACRIFICE FLIES

Molina, Bengie, Giants	11
Blake, Casey, Dodgers	10
Helton, Todd, Rockies	10
Five tied at	9

HIT BY PITCH

Utley, Chase, Phillies	24
Kendall, Jason, Brewers	17
Rowand, Aaron, Giants	14
Braun, Ryan, Brewers	13
Diaz, Matt, Braves	13

Adam Wainwright

WALKS

Ethier, Andre, Dodgers	13
Gonzalez, Adrian, Padres	119
Dunn, Adam, Nationals	116
Pujols, Albert, Cardinals	115
Fielder, Prince, Brewers	110
Jones, Chipper, Braves	101

INTENTIONAL WALKS

Pujols, Albert, Cardinals	44
Gonzalez, Adrian, Padres	22
Fielder, Prince, Brewers	21
Ramirez, Manny, Dodgers	21
Jones, Chipper, Braves	18

STOLEN BASES

Bourn, Michael, Astros	61
Morgan, Nyjer, Pirates/Nats	42
Kemp, Matt, Dodgers	34
Rollins, Jimmy, Phillies	31
Pierre, Juan, Dodgers	30

CAUGHT STEALING

Morgan, Nyjer, Pirates/Nats	17
Bourn, Michael, Astros	12
Pierre, Juan, Dodgers	12
Pence, Hunter, Astros	11
Tulowitzki, Troy, Rockies	11

STOLEN BASE PERCENTAGE

Utley, Chase, Phillies	100%
Werth, Jayson, Phillies	87%
Matsui, Kazuo, Astros	86.4%
Bourn, Michael, Astros	83.6%
McCutchen, Andrew, Pirates	81.5%

STRIKEOUTS

Reynolds, Mark, D'backs	223
Howard, Ryan, Phillies	186
Dunn, Adam, Nationals	177
Cameron, Mike, Brewers	156
Werth, Jayson, Phillies	156

TOUGHEST TO STRIKE OUT
(AT-BATS PER STRIKEOUT)

Tejada, Miguel, Astros	13.23
Molina, Yadier, Cardinals	12.33
Lee, Carlos, Astros	11.96
Eckstein, David, Padres	10.93
Rollins, Jimmy, Phillies	9.60

GROUNDED INTO DOUBLE PLAYS

Tejada, Miguel, Astros	29
Molina, Yadier, Cardinals	27
Kouzmanoff, Kevin, Padres	25
Pence, Hunter, Astros	25
Gonzalez, Adrian, Padres	23
Pujols, Albert, Cardinals	23

MULTI-HIT GAMES

Braun, Ryan, Brewers	64
Sandoval, Pablo, Giants	57
Tejada, Miguel, Astros	57
Ramirez, Hanley, Marlins	56
Fielder, Prince, Brewers	54

ON-BASE PERCENTAGE

Pujols, Albert, Cardinals	.443
Johnson, Nick, Nats/Marlins	.426
Helton, Todd, Rockies	.416
Votto, Joey, Reds	.414
Fielder, Prince, Brewers	.412

SLUGGING PERCENTAGE

Pujols, Albert, Cardinals	.658
Fielder, Prince, Brewers	.602
Lee, Derrek, Cubs	.579
Howard, Ryan, Phillies	.571
Votto, Joey, Reds	.567

ON-BASE PLUS SLUGGING

Pujols, Albert, Cardinals	1.101
Fielder, Prince, Brewers	1.014
Votto, Joey, Reds	.981
Lee, Derrek, Cubs	.972
Gonzalez, Adrian, Padres	.958

PITCHING

WINS

Wainwright, Adam, Cardinals	19
Carpenter, Chris, Cardinals	17
De La Rosa, Jorge, Rockies	16
Eight tied at	15

LOSSES

Duke, Zach, Pirates	16
Davis, Doug, Diamondbacks	14

DENNIS WIERZBICKI

LARRY GOREN

Harang, Aaron, Reds	14
Six tied at	13

GAMES

Feliciano, Pedro, Mets	88
Moylan, Peter, Braves	87
Gonzalez, Mike, Braves	80
Green, Sean, Mets	79
Madson, Rayn, Phillies	79
Marmol, Carlos, Cubs	79

GAMES STARTED

Davis, Doug, Diamondbacks	34
Jurrjens, Jair, Braves	34
Looper, Braden, Brewers	34
Lowe, Derek, Braves	34
Wainwright, Adam, Cardinals	34
Wolf, Randy, Dodgers	34

GAMES FINISHED

Rodriguez, Francisco, Mets	66
Wilson, Brian, Giants	60
Bell, Heath, Padres	59
Cordero, Francisco, Reds	59
Broxton, Jonathan, Dodgers	58

COMPLETE GAMES

Cain, Matt, Giants	4
Lincecum, Tim, Giants	4
Nine tied at	3

SHUTOUTS

Arroyo, Bronson, Reds	2
Hamels, Cole, Phillies	2
Happ, J.A., Phillies	2
Lincecum, Tim, Giants	2
Pineiro, Joel, Cardinals	2

SAVES

Bell, Heath, Padres	42
Cordero, Francisco, Reds	39
Franklin, Ryan, Cardinals	38
Wilson, Brian, Giants	38
Hoffman, Trevor, Brewers	37

INNINGS

Wainwright, Adam, Cards	233
Haren, Dan, D'backs	229.1
Lincecum, Tim, Giants	225.1
Arroyo, Bronson, Reds	220.1
Vazquez, Javier, Braves	219.1

HITS ALLOWED

Lowe, Derek, Braves	232
Duke, Zach, Pirates	231
Looper, Braden, Brewers	226

Tim Lincecum

BILL NICHOLS

Garland, Jon, D'backs/Dod.	225
Maholm, Paul, Pirates	221

RUNS ALLOWED

Looper, Braden, Brewers	123
Hernandez, Livan, Mets/Nats	112
Pelfrey, Mike, Mets	112
Nolasco, Ricky, Marlins	111
Lowe, Derek, Braves	109

HOME RUNS ALLOWED

Looper, Braden, Brewers	39
Arroyo, Bronson, Reds	31
Blanton, Joe, Phillies	30
Volstad, Chris, Marlins	29
Geer, Josh, Padres	27
Haren, Dan, Diamondbacks	27
Jamie Moyer, Phillies	27

WALKS

Davis, Doug, Diamondbacks	103
Gallardo, Yovani, Brewers	94
Kershaw, Clayton, Dodgers	91

Sanchez, Jonathan, Giants	88
Billingsley, Chad, Dodgers	86

WALKS PER NINE INNINGS

Pineiro, Joel, Cardinals	1.14
Haren, Dan, Diamondbacks	1.49
Carpenter, Chris, Cardinals	1.78
Vazquez, Javier, Braves	1.81
Lilly, Ted, Cubs	1.83

HIT BATSMEN

Bush, Dave, Brewers	15
Cueto, Johnny, Reds	14
Marmol, Carlos, Cubs	12
Suppan, Jeff, Brewers	11
Three tied at	10

STRIKEOUTS

Lincecum, Tim, Giants	261
Vazquez, Javier, Braves	238
Haren, Dan, Diamondbacks	223
Wainwright, Adam, Cards	212
Gallardo, Yovani, Brewers	204

STRIKEOUTS PER NINE INNINGS

Lincecum, Tim, Giants	10.42
Gallardo, Yovani, Brewers	9.89
Vazquez, Javier, Braves	9.77
Sanchez, Jonathan, Giants	9.75
Kershaw, Clayton, Dodgers	9.74

STRIKEOUTS PER NINE INNINGS (RELIEVERS)

Broxton, Jonathan, Dodgers	13.50
Soriano, Rafael, Braves	12.13
Marmol, Carlos, Cubs	11.31
Gregerson, Luke, Padres	11.16
Thatcher, Joe, Padres	11.00

DOUBLE PLAYS

Pineiro, Joel, Cardinals	29
Lannan, John, Nationals	28
Lowe, Derek, Braves	28
Maholm, Paul, Pirates	28
Marquis, Jason, Rockies	28

PICKOFFS

Davis, Doug, Diamondbacks	7
Kershaw, Clayton, Dodgers	7
Ohlendorf, Ross, Pirates	6
Hamels, Cole, Phillies	5
Four tied at	4

WILD PITCHES

Billingsley, Chad, Dodgers	14
Haren, Dan, Diamondbacks	13
Davis, Doug, Diamondbacks	12
De La Rosa, Jorge, Rockies	12
Suppan, Jeff, Brewers	12

BALKS

Pelfrey, Mike, Mets	6
Jimenez, Ubaldo, Rockies	3
Lilly, Ted, Cubs	3
Six tied at	2

OPPONENT AVERAGE

Kershaw, Clayton, Dodgers	.200
Lincecum, Tim, Giants	.206
Gallardo, Yovani, Brewers	.219
Sanchez, Jonathan, Giants	.221
Vazquez, Javier, Braves	.223

WORST ERA

Hernandez, Livan, Mets/Nats	5.44
Looper, Braden, Brewers	5.22
Nolasco, Ricky, Marlins	5.06
Pelfrey, Mike, Mets	5.03
Moyer, Jamie, Phillies	4.94

FIELDING

PITCHER

PCT	18 tied at	1.000
PO	Pineiro, Joel, Cardinals	27
	Wainwright, Adam, Cardinals	27
A	Jimenez, Ubaldo, Rockies	47
E	Davis, Doug, Diamondbacks	5
	De La Rosa, Jorge, Rockies	5
	Lilly, Ted, Cubs	5
TC	Jimenez, Ubaldo, Colorado	61
DP	Dempster, Ryan, Cubs	5
	Duke, Zach, Pirates	5

CATCHER

PCT	Hanigan, Ryan, Reds	.998
PO	Martin, Russell, Dodgers	1039
A	Martin, Russell, Dodgers	87
E	McCann, Brian, Braves	12
DP	Iannetta, Chris, Rockies	10
PB	Diaz, Robinzon, Pirates	7

	Hundley, Nick, Padres	7
	McCann, Brian, Atlanta	7
CS%	Hanigan, Ryan, Reds	.429

FIRST BASE

PCT	LaRoche, Adam, Pirates/Braves	.999
PO	Pujols, Albert, Cardinals	1473
A	Pujols, Albert, Cardinals	185
E	Howard, Ryan, Phillies	14
DP	Pujols, Albert, Cardinals	150

SECOND BASE

PCT	Eckstein, David, Padres	.996
PO	Utley, Chase, Phillies	354
A	Uggla, Dan, Marlins	426
E	Lopez, Felipe, D'backs/Brewers	17
DP	Lopez, Felipe, D'backs/Brewers	102

THIRD BASE

PCT	Kouzmanoff, Kevin, Padres	.990

PO	Wright, David, Mets	119
A	Zimmerman, Ryan, Nationals	325
E	Jones, Chipper, Braves	22
DP	Feliz, Pedro, Phillies	35

SHORTSTOP

PCT	Rollins, Jimmy, Phillies	.990
PO	Ramirez, Hanley, Marlins	221
A	Tejada, Miguel, Astros	475
E	Cabrera, Everth, Padres	23
DP	Tejada, Miguel, Astros	105

OUTFIELD

PCT	Winn, Randy, Giants	1.000
PO	Cameron, Mike, Brewers	404
A	Pence, Hunter, Astros	16
E	Upton, Justin, Diamondbacks	12
DP	Church, Ryan, Mets/Braves	5

TOMASSO DeROSA

Jorge Posada, Derek Jeter and Mariano Rivera (from left) celebrate their fourth World Series title as Yankees teammates; Jeter, Rivera and Andy Pettitte have won five championships together

Yankees bring Series trophy back to Bronx

BY JOHN PERROTTO

For most franchises, a nine-year wait for a World Series championship is a drop in the bucket.

The Cubs completed their 101st season without one in 2009. The Red Sox ended an 86-year drought in 2004, and the White Sox won their first in 88 years in 2005.

However, the Yankees aren't just any franchise. Their 27 Series titles are nearly triple the next team on the list, the Cardinals, who have 10. Thus, nine years without a championship for the Yankees felt like a lifetime.

And that explained why the Yankees, always so businesslike in their pinstriped uniforms, really cut loose when they beat the Phillies in six games in the 2009 World Series to win their first crown since 2000. The players piled into a big on-field scrum after a 7-3 victory in the series finale, then took a victory lap around the brand new $1.5 billion dollar Yankee Stadium, high-fiving fans, before heading to the clubhouse for what many long-time Yankees'

observers felt was their most raucous celebration.

"This is what the Steinbrenners strive for year after year after year as they try to deliver a championship to the city of New York," Yankees manager Joe Girardi said of the family that has been longtime owners of the team. "George Steinbrenner and his family are champions. To be able to deliver this to the Boss, the stadium that he has created and the atmosphere he has created around here is very gratifying to all of us."

"It feels better than I remember it," said shortstop and team captain Derek Jeter, who won his fifth World Series as a member of the Yankees along with lefthander Andy Pettitte and closer Mariano Rivera. Catcher Jorge Posada has taken part in four title runs. "It's been a long time."

However, the feeling was just as special to the new Yankees as it was the veterans who were around when the franchise won four World Series titles in a five-year span from 1996-2000. New York spent plenty of money in free agency in the previous offseason to bolster the roster after their run of 13 consecutive postseason appearances ended. They paid out $423.5 million to lefthander C.C. Sabathia, righthander A.J. Burnett and first baseman Mark Teixeira.

"I can't think of a better place to be than playing baseball in New York," Teixeira said. "This is the top. We knew from the first day of spring training that we potentially had a great team, but the biggest thing is that everyone contributed. It wasn't just two or three guys. We got contributions from everyone."

Designated hitter Hideki Matsui drove in six runs in Game Six as the Yankees wrapped up the Series. Despite being limited to pinch-hitting duty in the middle three games of the series at Citizens Bank Park in Philadelphia, Matsui was chosen as the Most Valuable Player.

Matsui, who became the first Japanese player to win the award, went 8-for-13 (.615) with three home runs and eight RBIs. His six RBIs in the clincher tied the World Series record set by Bobby Richardson for the Yankees in 1960 against the Pirates.

Matsui won three Japan Series titles while starring for the Yomiuri Giants, but he waited seven years for his first title in the United States after his much-ballyhooed signing with the Yankees prior to the 2003 season.

"You could say that this is the best moment of my life," Matsui said. "It's been a long road and very difficult journey. When I was in Japan, winning the Japan Series was the ultimate goal. Being here, winning the World Series, becoming world champions, that's what you strive for."

Matsui's 13 at-bats tied for the fewest ever by a World Series MVP, matching the Orioles' Rick Dempsey in 1983. Matsui also became the first MVP to make all his starts exclusively as a DH. Paul Molitor started four games at DH and three in left field for the Blue Jays in 1993.

Chase Utley tied Reggie Jackson's record by swatting five World Series home runs

"He hit everything we threw up there," Phillies manager Charlie Manuel said.

The Yankees won in a season that began with controversy when third baseman Alex Rodriguez confirmed a Sports Illustrated report on the eve of spring training that said he used steroids from 2001-03 when he played for the Rangers. Rodriguez also had hip surgery in spring training that kept him sidelined until May.

Rodriguez eradicated the label of being a postseason choker by hitting a combined .365 with six home runs and 18 RBIs in three series as the Yankees cruised to the Series. They swept the Twins in three games in the AL Division Series, then beat the Angels in six games in the Championship Series.

Sabathia was named MVP of the ALCS, winning both starts against the Angels, who swept the Red Sox in the other ALDS. He allowed just two runs and nine hits in 16 innings. However, it was Rodriguez who was in the spotlight throughout the postseason after the highest-paid player in baseball history drew heavy criticism for not delivering a championship during his first five seasons with the Yankees.

"My teammates and coaches and organization stood right next to me and now we stand together as world champs," Rodriguez said.

Meanwhile, the Phillies failed in their bid to become the first NL team to win consecutive World Series since the 1975-76 Reds. Second baseman Chase Utley tied the World Series record

POSTSEASON PERFORMERS

The most successful clubs of the decade, 2000-09, as measured by postseason glory:

World Series Titles: Red Sox 2, Yankees 2.
AL Pennants: Yankees 4.
NL Pennants: (tie) Cardinals, Phillies 2.
Most AL Division Titles: East—Yankees 8. Central—Twins 5. West—Angels 5. Wild Card—Red Sox 5.
Most NL Division Titles: East—Braves 6. Central—Cardinals 6. West—(tie) Diamondbacks, Dodgers 3. Wild Card—(tie) Astros, Rockies 2.
AL Playoff Appearances: Yankees 9.
NL Playoff Appearances: Cardinals 7.
Most Postseason Series Won: Yankees 11.

with five home runs, matching Reggie Jackson's performance with the 1977 Yankees, but first baseman Ryan Howard also set a World Series mark by striking out 13 times.

The Phillies made it back to the World Series by defeating the Rockies in four games in the NL Division Series and the Dodgers in five games in a Championship Series rematch. The Dodgers swept the Cardinals in their NLDS matchup.

Howard hit .333 with two home runs and eight RBIs to win MVP honors in the NLCS but then had a rough World Series.

"I feel cool," Howard said. "The only thing I can do now is go home and relax and come back for spring training. We would have liked to have won again, but we can't be disappointed. We made it back to the World Series, and that's a great accomplishment in its own right."

However, in the Yankees' world, the only accomplishment is winning the World Series. The Yankees used Steinbrenner as a rallying point from the start of the postseason, saying they wanted to

AMERICAN LEAGUE CHAMPIONS, 1901–2009

	PENNANT	PCT		PENNANT	PCT		PENNANT	PCT		PENNANT	PCT
1901	Chicago	.610	1918	Boston	.595	1935	Detroit	.616	1952	New York	.617
1902	Philadelphia	.610	1919	Chicago	.629	1936	New York	.667	1953	New York	.656
1903	Boston	.659	1920	Cleveland	.636	1937	New York	.662	1954	Cleveland	.721
1904	Boston	.617	1921	New York	.641	1938	New York	.651	1955	New York	.623
1905	Philadelphia	.622	1922	New York	.610	1939	New York	.702	1956	New York	.630
1906	Chicago	.616	1923	New York	.645	1940	Detroit	.584	1957	New York	.636
1907	Detroit	.613	1924	Washington	.597	1941	New York	.656	1958	New York	.597
1908	Detroit	.588	1925	Washington	.636	1942	New York	.669	1959	Chicago	.610
1909	Detroit	.645	1926	New York	.591	1943	New York	.636	1960	New York	.630
1910	Philadelphia	.680	1927	New York	.714	1944	St. Louis	.578	1961	New York	.673
1911	Philadelphia	.669	1928	New York	.656	1945	Detroit	.575	1962	New York	.593
1912	Boston	.691	1929	Philadelphia	.693	1946	Boston	.675	1963	New York	.646
1913	Philadelphia	.627	1930	Philadelphia	.662	1947	New York	.630	1964	New York	.611
1914	Philadelphia	.651	1931	Philadelphia	.704	1948	Cleveland	.626	1965	Minnesota	.630
1915	Boston	.669	1932	New York	.695	1949	New York	.630	1966	Baltimore	.606
1916	Boston	.591	1933	Washington	.651	1950	New York	.636	1967	Boston	.568
1917	Chicago	.649	1934	Detroit	.656	1951	New York	.636	1968	Detroit	.636

DIVISION ERA (1969-1993)
*Won pennant. ^ Won first half; defeated Milwaukee 3-2 in playoff. ^^ Won first half, defeated Kansas City 3-0.

	EAST	PCT	WEST	PCT	LCS		EAST	PCT	WEST	PCT	LCS
1969	Baltimore*	.673	Minnesota	.599	3-0		Milwaukee	.585	Kansas City	.566	
1970	Baltimore*	.667	Minnesota	.605	3-0	1982	Milwaukee*	.586	California	.574	3-2
1971	Baltimore*	.639	Oakland	.627	3-0	1983	Baltimore*	.605	Chicago	.611	3-1
1972	Detroit	.551	Oakland*	.600	3-2	1984	Detroit*	.642	Kansas City	.519	3-0
1973	Baltimore	.599	Oakland*	.580	3-2	1985	Toronto	.615	Kansas City*	.562	4-3
1974	Baltimore	.562	Oakland*	.556	3-1	1986	Boston*	.590	California	.568	4-3
1975	Boston*	.594	Oakland	.605	3-0	1987	Detroit	.605	Minnesota*	.525	4-1
1976	New York*	.610	Kansas City	.556	3-2	1988	Boston	.549	Oakland*	.642	4-0
1977	New York*	.617	Kansas City	.630	3-2	1989	Toronto	.549	Oakland*	.611	4-1
1978	New York*	.613	Kansas City	.568	3-1	1990	Boston	.543	Oakland*	.636	4-0
1979	Baltimore*	.642	California	.543	3-1	1991	Toronto	.562	Minnesota*	.586	4-1
1980	New York	.636	Kansas City*	.599	3-0	1992	Toronto*	.593	Oakland	.593	4-2
1981	New York*^	.607	Oakland^^	.587	3-0	1993	Toronto*	.586	Chicago	.580	4-2

WILD CARD ERA (1994-PRESENT)
*Won pennant. † Lost ALCS.

	EAST	PCT	CENTRAL	PCT	WEST	PCT	WILD CARD	PCT	LCS
1994	New York	.619	Chicago	.593	Texas	.456	None		
1995	Boston	.597	Cleveland*	.694	Seattle†	.545	New York (E)	.549	4-2
1996	New York*	.568	Cleveland	.615	Texas	.556	Baltimore (E)†	.543	4-1
1997	Baltimore†	.605	Cleveland*	.534	Seattle	.556	New York (E)	.593	4-2
1998	New York*	.704	Cleveland†	.549	Texas	.543	Boston (E)	.568	4-2
1999	New York*	.605	Cleveland	.599	Texas	.586	Boston (E)†	.580	4-1
2000	New York*	.540	Chicago	.586	Oakland	.565	Seattle (W)†	.562	4-2
2001	New York*	.594	Cleveland	.562	Seattle†	.716	Oakland (W)	.630	4-1
2002	New York	.640	Minnesota†	.584	Oakland	.636	Anaheim (W)*	.611	4-1
2003	New York*	.623	Minnesota	.556	Oakland	.593	Boston (E)†	.586	4-3
2004	New York†	.623	Minnesota	.568	Anaheim	.568	Boston (E)*	.605	4-3
2005	New York	.586	Chicago*	.611	Los Angeles†	.586	Boston (E)	.586	4-1
2006	New York	.599	Minnesota	.593	Oakland†	.574	Detroit (C)*	.586	4-0
2007	Boston*	.593	Cleveland†	.593	Los Angeles	.580	New York (E)	.580	4-3
2008	Tampa Bay*	.599	Chicago	.546	Los Angeles	.617	Boston (E)†	.586	4-3
2009	New York*	.636	Minnesota	.534	Los Angeles†	.599	Boston (E)	.586	4-2

win for the 79-year-old, who had been in failing health and made only two trips from his Tampa home to New York during the season—one for the first game at the new Yankee Stadium in April and the other for Game One of the World Series.

It was the seventh time the Yankees won the World Series since Steinbrenner bought the club in 1973, and it came just a year after he turned over control of the franchise to his son, Hal.

"He's the reason we're here," Jeter said. "First of all, we wouldn't be in this stadium if it wasn't

for him. We wouldn't have this group together if it wasn't for him. This is a special moment. We all tried to win it for him. He deserves it."

The pressure had been mounting on the Yankees to win a World Series. They kept coming up empty despite consistently having the highest payroll in the game. Thus, there was a feeling of relief along with jubilation when they accepted the championship trophy from commissioner Bud Selig.

"The Yankees won," club president Randy Levine said. "The world is right again."

NATIONAL LEAGUE CHAMPIONS, 1901–2009

	PENNANT	PCT		PENNANT	PCT		PENNANT	PCT		PENNANT	PCT
1901	Pittsburgh	.647	1918	Chicago	.651	1935	Chicago	.649	1952	Brooklyn	.627
1902	Pittsburgh	.741	1919	Cincinnati	.686	1936	New York	.597	1953	Brooklyn	.682
1903	Pittsburgh	.650	1920	Brooklyn	.604	1937	New York	.625	1954	New York	.630
1904	New York	.693	1921	New York	.614	1938	Chicago	.586	1955	Brooklyn	.641
1905	New York	.686	1922	New York	.604	1939	Cincinnati	.630	1956	Brooklyn	.604
1906	Chicago	.763	1923	New York	.621	1940	Cincinnati	.654	1957	Milwaukee	.617
1907	Chicago	.704	1924	New York	.608	1941	Brooklyn	.649	1958	Milwaukee	.597
1908	Chicago	.643	1925	Pittsburgh	.621	1942	St. Louis	.688	1959	Los Angeles	.564
1909	Pittsburgh	.724	1926	St. Louis	.578	1943	St. Louis	.682	1960	Pittsburgh	.617
1910	Chicago	.675	1927	Pittsburgh	.610	1944	St. Louis	.682	1961	Cincinnati	.604
1911	New York	.647	1928	St. Louis	.617	1945	Chicago	.636	1962	San Francisco	.624
1912	New York	.682	1929	Chicago	.645	1946	St. Louis	.628	1963	Los Angeles	.611
1913	New York	.664	1930	St. Louis	.597	1947	Brooklyn	.610	1964	St. Louis	.574
1914	Boston	.614	1931	St. Louis	.656	1948	Boston	.595	1965	Los Angeles	.599
1915	Philadelphia	.592	1932	Chicago	.584	1949	Brooklyn	.630	1966	Los Angeles	.586
1916	Brooklyn	.610	1933	New York	.599	1950	Philadelphia	.591	1967	St. Louis	.627
1917	New York	.636	1934	St. Louis	.621	1951	New York	.624	1968	St. Louis	.599

DIVISION ERA (1969-1993)
*Won pennant. ∧ Won first half; defeated Milwaukee 3-2 in playoff. ∧∧ Won first half, defeated Kansas City 3-0.

	EAST	PCT	WEST	PCT	LCS		EAST	PCT	WEST	PCT	LCS
1969	New York*	.617	Atlanta	.574	3-0		Philadelphia	.618	Houston	.623	
1970	Pittsburgh	.549	Cincinnati	.630	3-0	1982	St. Louis*	.568	Atlanta	.549	3-0
1971	Pittsburgh*	.599	San Francisco	.556	3-1	1983	Philadelphia*	.556	Los Angeles	.562	3-1
1972	Pittsburgh	.619	Cincinnati*	.617	3-2	1984	Chicago	.596	San Diego*	.568	3-2
1973	New York*	.509	Cincinnati	.611	3-2	1985	St. Louis*	.623	Los Angeles	.586	4-2
1974	Pittsburgh	.543	Los Angeles*	.630	3-1	1986	New York*	.667	Houston	.593	4-2
1975	Pittsburgh	.571	Cincinnati*	.667	3-0	1987	St. Louis*	.586	San Francisco	.556	4-3
1976	Philadelphia	.623	Cincinnati*	.630	3-0	1988	New York	.625	Los Angeles*	.584	4-3
1977	Philadelphia	.623	Los Angeles*	.605	3-1	1989	Chicago	.571	San Francisco*	.568	4-1
1978	Philadelphia	.556	Los Angeles*	.586	3-1	1990	Pittsburgh	.586	Cincinnati*	.562	4-2
1979	Pittsburgh*	.605	Cincinnati	.559	3-0	1991	Pittsburgh	.605	Atlanta*	.580	4-3
1980	Philadelphia*	.562	Houston	.571	3-2	1992	Pittsburgh	.593	Atlanta*	.605	4-3
1981	Montreal∧	.566	Los Angeles*∧∧	.632	3-2	1993	Philadelphia*	.599	Atlanta	.642	4-2

WILD CARD ERA (1994-PRESENT)
*Won pennant. † Lost ALCS.

	EAST	PCT	CENTRAL	PCT	WEST	PCT	WILD CARD	PCT	LCS
1994	Montreal	.649	Cincinnati	.593	Los Angeles	.509	None		
1995	Atlanta*	.625	Cincinnati†	.590	Los Angeles	.542	Colorado (W)	.535	4-2
1996	Atlanta*	.593	St. Louis†	.543	San Diego	.562	Los Angeles (W)	.556	4-3
1997	Atlanta†	.623	Houston	.519	San Francisco	.556	Florida (E)*	.568	4-2
1998	Atlanta†	.654	Houston	.630	San Diego*	.605	Chicago (C)	.552	4-2
1999	Atlanta*	.636	Houston	.599	Arizona	.617	New York (E)†	.595	4-2
2000	Atlanta	.586	St. Louis†	.586	San Francisco	.599	New York (E)*	.580	4-1
2001	Atlanta†	.543	Houston	.574	Arizona*	.568	St. Louis (C)	.574	4-1
2002	Atlanta	.631	St. Louis†	.599	Arizona	.605	San Francisco (W)*	.590	4-1
2003	Atlanta	.623	Chicago†	.543	San Francisco	.621	Florida (E)*	.562	4-3
2004	Atlanta	.593	St. Louis*	.648	Los Angeles	.574	Houston (C)†	.568	4-3
2005	Atlanta	.556	St. Louis*	.617	San Diego	.506	Houston (C)*	.549	4-2
2006	New York†	.599	St. Louis*	.516	San Diego	.543	Los Angeles (W)	.543	4-3
2007	Philadelphia	.549	Chicago	.525	Arizona†	.556	Colorado (W)*	.552	4-0
2008	Philadelphia*	.568	Chicago	.602	Los Angeles†	.519	Milwaukee (C)	.556	4-1
2009	Philadelphia*	.574	St. Louis	.562	Los Angeles†	.586	Colorado (W)	.568	4-1

World Series MVP Hideki Matsui drove in six runs in the Yankees' Game Six clincher

Year	Winner	Loser	Result
1903	Boston (AL)	Pittsburgh (NL)	5-3
1904	NO SERIES		
1905	New York (NL)	Philadelphia (AL)	4-1
1906	Chicago (AL)	Chicago (NL)	4-2
1907	Chicago (NL)	Detroit (AL)	4-0
1908	Chicago (NL)	Detroit (AL)	4-1
1909	Pittsburgh (NL)	Detroit (AL)	4-3
1910	Philadelphia (AL)	Chicago (NL)	4-1
1911	Philadelphia (AL)	New York (NL)	4-2
1912	Boston (AL)	New York (NL)	4-3-1
1913	Philadelphia (AL)	New York (NL)	4-1
1914	Boston (NL)	Philadelphia (AL)	4-0
1915	Boston (AL)	Philadelphia (NL)	4-1
1916	Boston (AL)	Brooklyn (NL)	4-1
1917	Chicago (AL)	New York (NL)	4-2
1918	Boston (AL)	Chicago (NL)	4-2
1919	Cincinnati (NL)	Chicago (AL)	5-3
1920	Cleveland (AL)	Brooklyn (NL)	5-2
1921	New York (NL)	New York (AL)	5-3
1922	New York (NL)	New York (AL)	4-0
1923	New York (AL)	New York (NL)	4-2
1924	Washington (AL)	New York (NL)	4-3
1925	Pittsburgh (NL)	Washington (AL)	4-3
1926	St. Louis (NL)	New York (AL)	4-3
1927	New York (AL)	Pittsburgh (NL)	4-0
1928	New York (AL)	St. Louis (NL)	4-0
1929	Philadelphia (AL)	Chicago (NL)	4-1
1930	Philadelphia (AL)	St. Louis (NL)	4-2
1931	St. Louis (NL)	Philadelphia (AL)	4-3
1932	New York (AL)	Chicago (NL)	4-0
1933	New York (NL)	Washington (AL)	4-1
1934	St. Louis (NL)	Detroit (AL)	4-3
1935	Detroit (AL)	Chicago (NL)	4-2
1936	New York (AL)	New York (NL)	4-2
1937	New York (AL)	New York (NL)	4-1
1938	New York (AL)	Chicago (NL)	4-0
1939	New York (AL)	Cincinnati (NL)	4-0
1940	Cincinnati (NL)	Detroit (AL)	4-3
1941	New York (AL)	Brooklyn (NL)	4-1
1942	St. Louis (NL)	New York (AL)	4-1
1943	New York (AL)	St. Louis (NL)	4-1
1944	St. Louis (NL)	St. Louis (AL)	4-2
1945	Detroit (AL)	Chicago (NL)	4-3
1946	St. Louis (NL)	Boston (AL)	4-3
1947	New York (AL)	Brooklyn (NL)	4-3
1948	Cleveland (AL)	Boston (NL)	4-2
1949	New York (AL)	Brooklyn (NL)	4-1
1950	New York (AL)	Philadelphia (NL)	4-0
1951	New York (AL)	New York (NL)	4-2
1952	New York (AL)	Brooklyn (NL)	4-3
1953	New York (AL)	Brooklyn (NL)	4-2
1954	New York (NL)	Cleveland (AL)	4-0
1955	Brooklyn (NL)	New York (AL)	4-3
1956	New York (AL)	Brooklyn (NL)	4-3
1957	Milwaukee (NL)	New York (AL)	4-3
1958	New York (AL)	Milwaukee (NL)	4-3
1959	Los Angeles (NL)	Chicago (AL)	4-2
1960	Pittsburgh (NL)	New York (AL)	4-3
1961	New York (AL)	Cincinnati (NL)	4-1
1962	New York (AL)	San Francisco (NL)	4-3
1963	Los Angeles (NL)	New York (AL)	4-0
1964	St. Louis (NL)	New York (AL)	4-3
1965	Los Angeles (NL)	Minnesota (AL)	4-3
1966	Baltimore (AL)	Los Angeles (NL)	4-0
1967	St. Louis (NL)	Boston (AL)	4-3
1968	Detroit (AL)	St. Louis (NL)	4-3
1969	New York (NL)	Baltimore (AL)	4-1
1970	Baltimore (AL)	Cincinnati (NL)	4-1
1971	Pittsburgh (NL)	Baltimore (AL)	4-3
1972	Oakland (AL)	Cincinnati (NL)	4-3
1973	Oakland (AL)	New York (NL)	4-3
1974	Oakland (AL)	Los Angeles (NL)	4-1
1975	Cincinnati (NL)	Boston (AL)	4-3
1976	Cincinnati (NL)	New York (AL)	4-0
1977	New York (AL)	Los Angeles (NL)	4-2
1978	New York (AL)	Los Angeles (NL)	4-2
1979	Pittsburgh (NL)	Baltimore (AL)	4-3
1980	Philadelphia (NL)	Kansas City (AL)	4-2
1981	Los Angeles (NL)	New York (AL)	4-2
1982	St. Louis (NL)	Milwaukee (AL)	4-3
1983	Baltimore (AL)	Philadelphia (NL)	4-1
1984	Detroit (AL)	San Diego (NL)	4-1
1985	Kansas City (AL)	St. Louis (NL)	4-3
1986	New York (NL)	Boston (AL)	4-3
1987	Minnesota (AL)	St. Louis (NL)	4-3
1988	Los Angeles (NL)	Oakland (AL)	4-1
1989	Oakland (AL)	San Francisco (NL)	4-0
1990	Cincinnati (NL)	Oakland (AL)	4-0
1991	Minnesota (AL)	Atlanta (NL)	4-3
1992	Toronto (AL)	Atlanta (NL)	4-2
1993	Toronto (AL)	Philadelphia (NL)	4-2
1994	NO SERIES		
1995	Atlanta (NL)	Cleveland (AL)	4-2
1996	New York (AL)	Atlanta (NL)	4-2
1997	Florida (NL)	Cleveland (AL)	4-3
1998	New York (AL)	San Diego (NL)	4-0
1999	New York (AL)	Atlanta (NL)	4-0
2000	New York (AL)	New York (NL)	4-1
2001	Arizona (NL)	New York (AL)	4-3
2002	Anaheim (AL)	San Francisco (NL)	4-3
2003	Florida (NL)	New York (AL)	4-2
2004	Boston (AL)	St. Louis (NL)	4-0
2005	Chicago (AL)	Houston (NL)	4-0
2006	St. Louis (NL)	Detroit (AL)	4-1
2007	Boston (AL)	Colorado (NL)	4-0
2008	Philadelphia (NL)	Tampa Bay (AL)	4-1
2009	New York (AL)	Philadelphia (NL)	4-2

WORLD SERIES BOX SCORES

GAME ONE October 28, 2009
PHILADELPHIA PHILLIES 6, NEW YORK YANKEES 1

PHILADELPHIA	AB	R	H	BI	BB	SO	NEW YORK	AB	R	H	BI	BB	SO
Rollins, ss	4	2	1	0	1	0	Jeter, ss	4	1	3	0	0	1
Victorino, cf	4	1	1	1	1	0	Damon, lf	4	0	1	0	0	0
Utley, 2b	4	2	2	2	1	1	Teixeira, 1b	4	0	0	0	0	2
Howard, 1b	5	0	2	1	0	2	Rodriguez, 3b	4	0	0	0	0	3
Werth, rf	2	0	1	0	2	1	Posada, c	4	0	1	0	0	2
Ibanez, dh	4	0	1	2	0	2	Matsui, dh	3	0	1	0	0	1
Francisco, lf	3	0	0	0	1	0	Cano, 2b	3	0	0	0	0	0
Feliz, 3b	4	0	0	0	0	1	Swisher, rf	3	0	0	0	0	1
Ruiz, c	4	1	1	0	0	0	Cabrera, M, cf	3	0	0	0	0	0
TOTALS	34	6	9	6	6	7	TOTALS	32	1	6	0	0	10

Philadelphia 001 001 022—6
New York 000 000 001—1

LOB—Phillies 7, Yankees 4. 2B—Howard 2 (2), Ruiz (1), Jeter (1). HR—Utley 2 (2). SB—Rollins (1). E—Rollins (1). A—Swisher.

PHILADELPHIA	IP	H	R	ER	BB	SO	NEW YORK	IP	H	R	ER	BB	SO
Lee, Cl (W)	9	6	1	0	0	10	Sabathia (L)	7	4	2	2	3	6
							Hughes	0	0	2	2	2	0
							Marte, D	⅔	0	0	0	0	0
							Robertson, D	⅓	1	0	0	1	0
							Bruney	⅓	3	2	2	0	0
							Coke	⅔	1	0	0	0	0

Hughes pitched to 2 batters in the 8th.
T—3:27. A—50,207.

GAME TWO October 29, 2009
NEW YORK YANKEES 3, PHILADELPHIA PHILLIES 1

PHILADELPHIA	AB	R	H	BI	BB	SO	NEW YORK	AB	R	H	BI	BB	SO
Rollins, ss	2	0	0	0	2	1	Jeter, ss	4	0	1	0	0	3
Victorino, cf	4	0	1	0	0	1	Damon, lf	4	0	0	0	0	1
Utley, 2b	3	0	0	0	1	0	Teixeira, 1b	3	1	1	1	0	1
Howard, 1b	4	0	0	0	0	4	Rodriguez, 3b	4	0	0	0	0	0
Werth, rf	4	0	1	0	0	0	Matsui, dh	3	1	2	1	1	1
Ibanez, lf	4	1	2	0	0	2	Cano, 2b	4	0	1	0	0	0
Stairs, dh	4	0	1	1	0	2	Hairston, J, rf	3	0	1	0	0	1
Feliz, 3b	3	0	0	0	0	1	1-Gardner, pr-cf	1	1	0	0	0	1
Ruiz, c	3	0	1	0	0	0	Cabrera, M, cf-rf	3	0	1	0	0	1
							Molina, J, c	1	0	0	0	1	0
							a-Posada, ph-c	1	0	1	1	0	0
TOTALS	31	1	6	1	3	11	TOTALS	31	3	8	3	2	12

Philadelphia 010 000 000—1
New York 000 101 10x—3

a-Singled for Molina, J in the 7th. 1-Ran for Hairston, J in the 7th.
LOB—Phillies 6, Yankees 7. 2B—Ibanez 2 (2), Ruiz 2 (2), Jeter (2). HR—Teixeira (1), Matsui (1). PO—Werth.

PHILADELPHIA	IP	H	R	ER	BB	SO	NEW YORK	IP	H	R	ER	BB	SO
Martinez, P (L)	6	6	3	3	2	8	Burnett (W)	7	4	1	1	2	9
Park	⅓	1	0	0	0	1	Rivera (S)	2	2	0	0	1	2
Eyre, S	⅔	0	0	0	0	0							
Madson	1	1	0	0	0	3							

Martinez, P pitched to 2 batters in the 7th.
IBB—Utley (by Burnett). HBP—Teixeira (by Madson).
T—3:25. A—50,181.

GAME THREE October 31, 2009
NEW YORK YANKEES 8, PHILADELPHIA PHILLIES 5

NEW YORK	AB	R	H	BI	BB	SO	PHILADELPHIA	AB	R	H	BI	BB	SO
Jeter, ss	5	1	1	0	0	0	Rollins, ss	4	0	1	1	1	0
Damon, lf	4	1	1	2	1	0	Victorino, cf	3	0	0	0	1	0
Teixeira, 1b	3	1	0	0	2	2	Utley, 2b	4	0	0	0	0	2
Rodriguez, 3b	2	1	1	2	1	0	Howard, 1b	4	0	0	0	0	3
Posada, c	5	0	1	1	0	0	Werth, rf	4	2	2	2	0	1
Cano, 2b	4	0	0	0	0	2	Ibanez, lf	4	0	0	0	0	2
Swisher, rf	4	2	2	1	0	0	Feliz, 3b	4	1	1	0	0	1
Gardner, cf	0	0	0	0	0	0	Ruiz, c	2	2	1	2	0	0
Cabrera, M, cf-rf	4	0	0	0	0	2	Hamels, p	1	0	1	0	0	0
Pettitte, p	3	1	1	1	0	1	Happ, p	0	0	0	0	0	0
Chamberlain, p	0	0	0	0	0	0	1-Bruntlett, ph	1	0	0	0	0	0
a-Matsui, ph	1	1	1	0	0	0	Durbin, C, p	0	0	0	0	0	0
Marte, D, p	0	0	0	0	0	0	Myers, p	0	0	0	0	0	0
Hughes, p	0	0	0	0	0	0	Madson, p	0	0	0	0	0	0
Rivera, p	0	0	0	0	0	0	2-Stairs, ph	1	0	0	0	0	0
TOTALS	35	8	8	8	4	8	TOTALS	32	5	6	5	3	9

New York 000 231 110—8
Philadelphia 030 001 001—5

a-Homered for Chamberlain in the 8th. 1-Flied out for Happ in the 6th. 2-Grounded out for Madson in the 9th.

LOB—Yankees 6, Phillies 5. 2B—Swisher (1), Damon (1), Feliz (1). HR—Rodriguez (1), Swisher (1), Matsui (2), Werth 2 (2), Ruiz (1). SH—Hamels. SF—Victorino. SB—Damon (1), Rollins (2). E—Rodriguez (1).

NEW YORK	IP	H	R	ER	BB	SO	PHILADELPHIA	IP	H	R	ER	BB	SO
Pettitte (W)	6	5	4	4	3	7	Hamels (L)	4⅓	5	5	5	2	3
Chamberlain	1	0	0	0	0	0	Happ	1⅓	1	1	1	0	1
Marte, D	1	0	0	0	0	2	Durbin, C	1	1	1	1	1	1
Hughes	⅓	1	1	1	0	0	Myers	1	1	1	1	0	2
Rivera	⅔	0	0	0	0	0	Madson	1	0	0	0	1	0

HBP—Rodriguez (by Hamels), Rodriguez (by Durbin, C).
T—3:25 (1:20 delay). A—46,061.

GAME FOUR November 1, 2009
NEW YORK YANKEES 7, PHILADELPHIA PHILLIES 4

NEW YORK	AB	R	H	BI	BB	SO	PHILLY	AB	R	H	BI	BB	SO
Jeter, ss	4	1	2	1	1	1	Rollins, ss	5	0	1	0	0	0
Damon, lf	5	2	3	1	0	1	Victorino, cf	4	1	1	0	1	0
Teixeira, 1b	4	1	0	1	0	1	Utley, 2b	4	1	2	2	0	0
Rodriguez, 3b	4	1	1	1	0	1	Howard, 1b	4	1	1	0	0	1
Posada, c	3	0	1	3	1	2	Werth, rf	3	0	0	0	1	0
Cano, 2b	4	0	1	0	0	0	Ibanez, lf	4	0	0	0	0	3
Swisher, rf	2	1	0	0	2	2	Feliz, 3b	4	1	3	2	0	0
Cabrera, M, cf	3	1	0	0	0	0	Ruiz, c	3	0	0	0	1	1
Gardner, cf	1	0	0	0	0	0	Blanton, p	2	0	0	0	0	2
Sabathia, p	3	0	0	0	0	2	1-Francisco, ph	1	0	0	0	0	0
Marte, D, p	0	0	0	0	0	0	Park, p	0	0	0	0	0	0
Chamberlain, p	0	0	0	0	0	0	Madson, p	0	0	0	0	0	0
a-Matsui, ph	1	0	0	0	0	0	Lidge, p	0	0	0	0	0	0
Rivera, p	0	0	0	0	0	0	2-Stairs, ph	1	0	0	0	0	0
TOTALS	34	7	9	7	4	11	TOTALS	35	4	8	4	3	9

New York 200 020 003—7
Philadelphia 100 100 110—4

a-Popped out for Chamberlain in the 9th. 1-Flied out for Blanton in the 6th. 2-Grounded out for Lidge in the 9th.
LOB—Yankees 7, Phillies 7. 2B—Damon (2), Rodriguez (1), Victorino (1), Utley (1). HR—Utley (3), Feliz (1). SF—Posada. SB—Damon 2 (3), Howard (1). E—Posada (1), Ibanez (1). A—Ibanez.

NEW YORK	IP	H	R	ER	BB	SO	PHILADELPHIA	IP	H	R	ER	BB	SO
Sabathia	6⅔	7	3	3	3	6	Blanton	6	5	4	4	2	7
Marte, D	⅓	0	0	0	0	0	Park	1	0	0	0	1	1
Chamberlain (W)	1	1	1	1	0	3	Madson	1	1	0	0	1	2
Rivera (S)	1	0	0	0	0	0	Lidge (L)	1	3	3	3	0	1

IBB—Werth (by Sabathia), Ruiz (by Sabathia). HBP—Rodriguez (by Blanton), Teixeira (by Lidge).
T—3:25. A—46,145.

GAME FIVE November 2, 2009
PHILADELPHIA PHILLIES 8, NEW YORK YANKEES 6

NEW YORK	AB	R	H	BI	BB	SO	PHILLY	AB	R	H	BI	BB	SO
Jeter, ss	5	0	1	0	0	0	Rollins, ss	4	1	2	0	1	1
Damon, lf	4	2	3	1	1	0	Victorino, cf	3	1	0	0	0	0
Teixeira, 1b	5	1	1	0	0	0	Francisco, cf	0	0	0	0	0	0
Rodriguez, 3b	4	1	2	3	0	0	Utley, 2b	3	3	2	4	1	0
Swisher, rf	3	0	0	0	1	0	Howard, 1b	2	1	0	0	2	2
Cano, 2b	3	0	1	0	0	0	Werth, rf	4	1	1	1	0	1
Gardner, cf	4	0	0	0	1	0	Ibanez, lf	4	1	2	1	0	1
Molina, J, c	1	0	0	0	0	0	Feliz, 3b	4	0	0	0	0	1
a-Posada, ph-c	3	1	1	0	1	1	Ruiz, c	4	0	1	1	0	1
Burnett, p	1	0	0	0	0	1	Lee, Cl, p	3	0	1	0	0	1
Robertson, D, p	0	0	0	0	0	0	Park, p	0	0	0	0	0	0

b-Hinske, ph	0	1	0	0	1	0	1-Stairs, ph	1	0	0	0	0	0
Aceves, A, p	0	0	0	0	0	0	Madson, p	0	0	0	0	0	0
c-Hairston, J, ph	1	0	0	0	0	0							
Coke, p	0	0	0	0	0	0							
Hughes p	0	0	0	0	0	0							
d-Matsui, ph	1	0	1	0	0	0							
TOTALS	**35**	**6**	**10**	**5**	**3**	**4**	**TOTALS**	**32**	**8**	**9**	**8**	**4**	**7**

New York 100 010 031—6
Philadelphia 303 000 20x—8

a-Grounded out for Molina, J in the 5th. b-Walked for Robertson, D in the 5th. c-Flied out for Aceves, A in the 7th. d-Singled for Hughes in the 9th. 1-Grounded into a double play for Park in the 8th.

LOB—Yankees 6, Phillies 5. **2B**—Rodriguez 2 (3), Teixeira (1), Posada (1). **HR**—Utley 2 (5), Ibanez (1). **SF**—Cano. **SB**—Utley (1).

NEW YORK	IP	H	R	ER	BB	SO	PHILADELPHIA	IP	H	R	ER	BB	SO
Burnett (L)	2	4	6	6	4	2	Lee, Cl (W)	7	7	5	5	3	3
Robertson, D	2	1	0	0	0	2	Park	1	0	0	0	0	
Aceves, A	2	1	0	0	0	1	Madson (S)	1	3	1	1	0	1
Coke	⅔	2	2	2	0	1							
Hughes	1⅓	1	0	0	0	1							

Burnett pitched to 4 batters in the 3rd. Lee, Cl pitched to 3 batters in the 8th.

WP—Aceves, A. **HBP**—Victorino (by Burnett).
T—3:26. **A**—46,178.

GAME SIX *November 4, 2009*

NEW YORK YANKEES 7, PHILADELPHIA PHILLIES 3

PHILADELPHIA	AB	R	H	BI	BB	SO	NEW YORK	AB	R	H	BI	BB	SO
Rollins, ss	4	0	0	1	0	0	Jeter, ss	5	2	3	0	0	0
Victorino, cf	4	0	1	0	1	0	Damon, lf	1	1	0	0	1	1
Utley, 2b	3	1	0	1	2	1	Hairston, lf	2	0	0	0	0	0
Howard, 1b	4	1	1	2	0	1	Teixeira, 1b	3	1	1	1	0	1
Werth, rf	2	0	0	0	2	2	Rodriguez, 3b	2	2	1	0	2	1
Ibanez, dh	3	0	2	0	1	0	Matsui, dh	4	1	3	6	0	1
Feliz, 3b	4	0	0	0	0	0	Posada, c	3	0	0	1	2	
Francisco, lf	3	0	0	0	0	2	Cano, 2b	4	0	0	0	0	2
a-Stairs, ph	1	0	0	0	0	0	Swisher, rf	3	0	0	1	1	
Ruiz, c	2	1	2	0	2	0	Gardner, cf	4	0	0	0	0	2
TOTALS	**30**	**3**	**6**	**3**	**7**	**7**	**TOTALS**	**31**	**7**	**8**	**7**	**5**	**11**

Philadelphia 001 002 000—3
New York 022 030 00x—7

a-Lined out for Francisco, B in the 9th.

LOB—Phillies 8, Yankees 7. **2B**—Ibanez 2 (4), Jeter (3), Matsui (1). **3B**—Ruiz (1). **HR**—Howard (1), Matsui (3). **SH**—Hairston, J. **SF**—Rollins. **SB**—Rollins (3), Rodriguez (1). **PB**—Posada (1).

PHILADELPHIA	IP	H	R	ER	BB	SO	NEW YORK	IP	H	R	ER	BB	SO
Martinez, P (L)	4	3	4	4	2	5	Pettitte (W)	5⅔	4	3	3	5	3
Durbin, C	⅓	2	3	3	1	0	Chamberlain	1	1	0	0	1	1
Happ	1	1	0	0	1	3	Marte, D	⅔	0	0	0	0	2
Park	1	1	0	0	0	1	Rivera	1⅓	1	0	0	1	1
Eyre, S	1⅓	0	0	0	1	2							
Madson	⅓	1	0	0	0	0							

WP—Pettitte. **IBB**—Posada (by Eyre, S). **HBP**—Teixeira (by Martinez, P).
T—3:52. **A**—50,315.

2009 WORLD SERIES

PHILADELPHIA

PLAYER, POS	AVG	G	AB	R	H	2B	3B	HR	RBI	BB	SO	SB
Joe Blanton, p	.000	1	2	0	0	0	0	0	0	0	2	0
Eric Bruntlett, ph	.000	1	1	0	0	0	0	0	0	0	0	0
Chad Durbin, p	—	1	0	0	0	0	0	0	0	0	0	0
Pedro Feliz, 3b	.174	6	23	2	4	1	0	1	2	0	4	0
Ben Francisco, lf	.000	4	7	0	0	0	0	0	0	1	2	0
Cole Hamels, p	1.000	1	1	0	1	0	0	0	0	0	0	0
J.A. Happ, p	—	1	0	0	0	0	0	0	0	0	0	0
Ryan Howard, 1b	.174	6	23	3	4	2	0	1	3	2	13	1
Raul Ibanez, lf	.304	6	23	2	7	4	0	1	4	1	9	0
Cliff Lee, p	.333	1	3	0	1	0	0	0	0	0	1	0
Brad Lidge, p	—	1	0	0	0	0	0	0	0	0	0	0

Ryan Madson, p	—	3	0	0	0	0	0	0	0	0	0	0
Brett Myers, p	—	1	0	0	0	0	0	0	0	0	0	0
Chan Ho Park, p	—	2	0	0	0	0	0	0	0	0	0	0
Jimmy Rollins, ss	.217	6	23	3	5	0	0	0	2	5	2	3
Carlos Ruiz, c	.333	6	18	4	6	2	1	1	2	5	2	0
Matt Stairs, dh	.125	5	8	0	1	0	0	0	1	0	2	0
Chase Utley, 2b	.286	6	21	7	6	1	0	5	8	4	5	1
Shane Victorino, cf	.182	6	22	3	4	1	0	0	2	3	1	0
Jayson Werth, rf	.263	6	19	3	5	0	0	2	3	5	7	0
Totals	**.227**	**6**	**194**	**27**	**44**	**11**	**1**	**11**	**27**	**26**	**50**	**5**

PITCHER	W	L	ERA	G	GS	SV	IP	H	R	ER	BB	SO
Joe Blanton	0	0	6.00	1	1	0	6.0	5	4	4	2	7
Chad Durbin	0	0	27.00	2	0	0	1.3	3	4	4	2	2
Scott Eyre	0	0	0.00	2	0	0	2.0	0	0	0	1	2
Cole Hamels	0	1	10.38	1	1	0	4.3	5	5	5	2	3
J.A. Happ	0	0	3.38	2	0	0	2.7	2	1	1	1	4
Cliff Lee	2	0	2.81	2	2	0	16.0	13	6	5	3	13
Brad Lidge	0	1	27.00	1	0	0	1.0	3	3	3	0	1
Ryan Madson	0	0	2.08	5	0	1	4.3	6	1	1	2	6
Pedro Martinez	0	2	6.30	2	2	0	10.0	9	7	7	4	13
Brett Myers	0	0	9.00	1	0	0	1.0	1	1	1	0	2
Chan Ho Park	0	0	0.00	4	0	0	3.3	2	0	0	1	3
Totals	**2**	**4**	**5.37**	**6**	**6**	**1**	**52.0**	**49**	**32**	**31**	**18**	**56**

NEW YORK

PLAYER, POS	AVG	G	AB	R	H	2B	3B	HR	RBI	BB	SO	SB
Alfredo Aceves, p	—	1	0	0	0	0	0	0	0	0	0	0
A.J. Burnett, p	.000	1	1	0	0	0	0	0	0	0	1	0
Melky Cabrera, cf	.154	4	13	1	2	0	0	0	0	3	0	0
Robinson Cano, 2b	.136	6	22	0	3	0	0	0	1	0	5	0
Joba Chamberlain, p	—	2	0	0	0	0	0	0	0	0	0	0
Phil Coke, p	—	1	0	0	0	0	0	0	0	0	0	0
Johnny Damon, lf	.364	6	22	6	8	2	0	0	4	3	3	3
Brett Gardner, cf	.000	5	10	1	0	0	0	0	0	0	4	0
Jerry Hairston, lf	.167	3	6	0	1	0	0	0	0	0	1	0
Eric Hinske, ph	—	1	1	0	0	0	0	0	0	1	0	0
Phil Hughes, p	—	2	0	0	0	0	0	0	0	0	0	0
Derek Jeter, ss	.407	6	27	5	11	3	0	0	1	1	6	0
Damaso Marte, p	—	2	0	0	0	0	0	0	0	0	0	0
Hideki Matsui, dh	.615	6	13	3	8	1	0	3	8	1	3	0
Jose Molina, c	.000	2	2	0	0	0	0	0	0	1	0	0
Andy Pettitte, p	.333	3	3	1	1	0	0	0	1	0	1	0
Jorge Posada, d	.263	6	19	1	5	1	0	0	5	2	7	0
Mariano Rivera, p	—	2	0	0	0	0	0	0	0	0	0	0
David Robertson, p	—	1	0	0	0	0	0	0	0	0	0	0
Alex Rodriguez, 3b	.250	6	20	5	5	3	0	1	6	3	8	1
CC Sabathia, p	.000	1	3	0	0	0	0	0	0	0	2	0
Nick Swisher, rf	.133	5	15	3	2	1	0	1	1	4	4	0
Mark Teixeira, 1b	.136	6	22	5	3	1	0	1	3	2	8	0
Totals	**.247**	**6**	**198**	**32**	**49**	**12**	**0**	**6**	**30**	**18**	**56**	**4**

PITCHER	W	L	ERA	G	GS	SV	IP	H	R	ER	BB	SO
Alfredo Aceves	0	0	0.00	1	0	0	2.0	1	0	0	1	1
Brian Bruney	0	0	54.00	1	0	0	0.3	3	2	2	0	0
A.J. Burnett	1	1	7.00	2	2	0	9.0	8	7	7	6	11
Joba Chamberlain	1	0	3.00	3	0	0	3.0	2	1	1	1	4
Phil Coke	0	0	13.50	2	0	0	1.3	3	2	2	0	1
Phil Hughes	0	0	16.20	3	0	0	1.7	2	3	3	2	1
Damaso Marte	0	0	0.00	2	0	0	2.7	0	0	0	0	5
Andy Pettitte	2	0	5.40	2	2	0	11.7	9	7	7	8	10
Mariano Rivera	0	0	0.00	4	0	2	5.3	3	0	0	2	3
David Robertson	0	0	0.00	2	0	0	2.3	2	0	0	1	2
C.C. Sabathia	0	1	3.29	2	2	0	13.7	11	5	5	6	12
Totals	**4**	**2**	**4.58**	**6**	**6**	**2**	**53.0**	**44**	**27**	**27**	**26**	**50**

E—Ibanez, Rollins, Posada, Rodriguez. **DP**—Philadelphia 3, N.Y. Yankees 5. **LOB**—Philadelphia 38, N.Y. Yankees 37. **SB**—Howard, Rollins 3, Utley, Damon 3, Rodriguez. **SH**—Hamels, Hairston. **SF**—Cano, Posada. **HBP**—Victorino (by Burnett), Rodriguez 3 (by Hamels, Durbin, Blanton), Teixeira 3 (by Madson, Lidge, Martinez). **IBB**—Ruiz (by Sabathia), Utley (by Burnett), Werth (by Sabathia), Posada (by Eyre). **WP**—Aceves, Pettitte. **PB**—Posada.

SCORE BY INNINGS

Philadelphia	445	104	333—27
NY Yankees	322	392	245—32

AMERICAN LEAGUE DIVISION SERIES
MINNESOTA VS. NEW YORK
MINNESOTA

PLAYER, POS	AVG	G	AB	R	H	2B	3B	HR	RBI	BB	SO	SB
Orlando Cabrera, ss	.154	3	13	1	2	0	0	0	0	2	3	1
Michael Cuddyer, 1b	.429	3	14	0	6	0	0	0	1	0	2	0
Carlos Gomez, cf	.000	1	4	1	0	0	0	0	0	1	2	0
Brendan Harris, 3b	.250	3	12	1	3	0	1	0	1	0	3	0
Jason Kubel, rf	.071	3	14	0	1	0	0	0	0	0	9	0
Joe Mauer, c	.417	3	12	1	5	1	0	0	1	2	4	0
Jose Morales, dh	.000	1	3	0	0	0	0	0	0	0	0	0
Nick Punto, 2b	.444	3	9	0	4	1	0	0	1	3	1	0
Denard Span, cf	.400	3	15	1	6	1	0	0	1	0	2	1
Matt Tolbert, 3b	.200	2	5	0	1	0	0	0	0	0	1	0
Delmon Young, lf	.083	3	12	1	1	1	0	0	0	1	5	1
Totals	.257	3	113	6	29	4	1	0	5	9	34	3

PITCHER	W	L	ERA	G	GS	SV	IP	H	R	ER	BB	SO
Nick Blackburn	0	0	1.59	1	1	0	5.7	3	1	1	2	3
Brian Duensing	0	1	9.64	1	1	0	4.7	7	5	5	1	3
Matt Guerrier	0	0	0.00	2	0	0	2.0	0	0	0	0	2
Francisco Liriano	0	0	4.50	1	0	0	2.0	1	2	1	1	1
Ron Mahay	0	0	5.40	3	0	0	1.7	0	1	1	1	2
Jose Mijares	0	1	13.50	2	0	0	0.7	1	1	1	1	0
Joe Nathan	0	0	9.00	2	0	0	2.0	5	2	2	1	2
Carl Pavano	0	1	2.57	1	1	0	7.0	5	2	2	0	9
Jon Rauch	0	0	6.75	3	0	0	1.3	1	1	1	2	0
Totals	0	3	4.67	3	3	0	27.0	23	15	14	9	22

NEW YORK

PLAYER, POS	AVG	G	AB	R	H	2B	3B	HR	RBI	BB	SO	SB
Melky Cabrera, cf	.167	3	12	1	2	0	0	0	0	0	5	0
Robinson Cano, 2b	.167	3	12	1	2	0	0	0	1	0	1	0
Francisco Cervelli, c	—	1	0	0	0	0	0	0	0	0	0	0
Johnny Damon, lf	.083	3	12	0	1	0	0	0	0	1	4	0
Brett Gardner, cf	—	3	0	0	0	0	0	0	0	0	0	1
Jerry Hairston, pr	—	1	0	0	0	0	0	0	0	0	0	0
Derek Jeter, ss	.400	3	10	4	4	2	0	1	2	3	0	0
Hideki Matsui, dh	.222	3	9	1	2	0	0	1	2	3	3	0
Jose Molina, c	.000	1	1	0	0	0	0	0	0	0	0	0
Jorge Posada, c	.364	3	11	1	4	0	0	1	2	0	2	0
Alex Rodriguez, 3b	.455	3	11	4	5	0	0	2	6	1	2	0
Nick Swisher, rf	.083	3	12	0	1	1	0	0	1	0	4	0
Mark Teixeira, 1b	.167	3	12	3	2	0	0	1	1	1	1	0
Totals	.225	3	102	15	23	3	0	6	15	9	22	1

PITCHER	W	L	ERA	G	GS	SV	IP	H	R	ER	BB	SO
Alfredo Aceves	0	0	0.00	1	0	0	1.0	1	0	0	1	1
A.J. Burnett	0	0	1.50	1	1	0	6.0	3	1	1	5	6
Joba Chamberlain	0	0	0.00	3	0	0	1.7	2	0	0	0	1
Phil Coke	0	0	0.00	2	0	0	0.7	0	0	0	0	1
Phil Hughes	0	0	9.00	3	0	0	2.0	5	2	2	1	3
Damaso Marte	0	0	—	1	0	0	0.0	2	0	0	0	0
Andy Pettitte	1	0	1.42	1	1	0	6.3	3	1	1	1	7
Mariano Rivera	0	0	0.00	3	0	1	3.7	4	0	0	1	7
David Robertson	1	0	0.00	1	0	0	1.0	1	0	0	0	0
CC Sabathia	1	0	1.35	1	1	0	6.7	8	2	1	0	8
Totals	3	0	1.55	3	3	1	29.0	29	6	5	9	34

DP—Minnesota 3, New York 1. **LOB**—Minnesota 32, New York 15. **SB**—Cabrera, Span, Young, Gardner. **HBP**—Tolbert (by Sabathia), Young (by Burnett). **IBB**—Jeter (by Nathan). **WP**—Sabathia. **PB**—Posada 2.

SCORE BY INNINGS

Minnesota	002 002 020	00	—6
New York	002 131 304	01	—15

BOSTON VS. LOS ANGELES
BOSTON

PLAYER, POS	AVG	G	AB	R	H	2B	3B	HR	RBI	BB	SO	SB
Brian Anderson, pr	—	1	0	0	0	0	0	0	0	0	0	0
Jason Bay, lf	.125	3	8	0	1	0	0	0	0	3	3	0
J.D. Drew, rf	.222	3	9	1	2	0	0	1	2	1	1	0
Jacoby Ellsbury, cf	.250	3	12	2	3	0	1	0	0	0	2	0
Joey Gathright, pr	—	1	0	1	0	0	0	0	0	0	0	1
Alex Gonzalez, ss	.167	3	6	1	1	0	0	0	0	1	1	0

C.C. Sabathia made five postseason starts, going 3-1, 1.98 with 32 whiffs in 36 innings

	AVG	G	AB	R	H	2B	3B	HR	RBI	BB	SO	SB
Casey Kotchman, 1b	.000	3	1	0	0	0	0	0	0	0	0	0
Mike Lowell, 3b	.200	3	10	1	2	0	0	0	1	1	0	0
Jed Lowrie, ss	.000	3	2	0	0	0	0	0	0	0	1	0
Victor Martinez, c	.182	3	11	0	2	0	0	0	2	1	2	0
David Ortiz, dh	.083	3	12	0	1	0	0	0	0	0	4	0
Dustin Pedroia, 2b	.167	3	12	1	2	1	0	0	2	1	0	0
Kevin Youkilis, 1b	.083	3	12	0	1	1	0	0	0	0	2	0
Totals	.158	3	95	7	15	2	1	1	7	8	16	1

PITCHER	W	L	ERA	G	GS	SV	IP	H	R	ER	BB	SO
Daniel Bard	0	0	0.00	2	0	0	3.0	0	0	0	0	4
Josh Beckett	0	1	5.40	1	1	0	6.7	5	4	4	1	3
Clay Buchholz	0	0	3.60	1	1	0	5.0	6	2	2	1	3
Jon Lester	0	1	4.50	1	1	0	6.0	4	3	3	4	5
Hideki Okajima	0	0	0.00	1	0	0	0.3	0	0	0	0	0
Jonathan Papelbon	0	1	13.50	2	0	0	2.0	4	3	3	2	1
Ramon Ramirez	0	0	—	1	0	0	0.0	1	2	2	1	0
Takashi Saito	0	0	0.00	1	0	0	1.0	2	0	0	0	0
Billy Wagner	0	0	18.00	2	0	0	1.0	2	2	2	1	2
Totals	0	3	5.76	3	3	0	25.0	24	16	16	10	18

LOS ANGELES

PLAYER, POS	AVG	G	AB	R	H	2B	3B	HR	RBI	BB	SO	SB
Bobby Abreu, rf	.556	3	9	4	5	2	0	0	1	4	0	0
Erick Aybar, ss	.364	3	11	2	4	1	1	0	2	0	1	0
Chone Figgins, 3b	.000	3	12	1	0	0	0	0	0	1	6	0
Vladimir Guerrero, dh	.400	3	10	2	4	0	0	0	2	2	1	0
Torii Hunter, cf	.200	3	10	2	2	1	0	1	3	2	1	0
Maicer Izturis, 2b	.143	2	7	1	1	0	0	0	1	0	2	1
Howard Kendrick, 2b	.200	2	5	1	1	0	0	0	0	0	2	1
Jeff Mathis, c	.333	2	3	0	1	0	0	0	0	0	2	0
Gary Matthews, ph	.000	1	1	0	0	0	0	0	0	0	0	0
Kendry Morales, 1b	.200	3	10	1	2	0	0	1	3	1	0	0
Mike Napoli, c	.250	2	4	1	1	0	0	0	0	0	1	0
Juan Rivera, lf	.273	3	11	1	3	1	0	0	2	0	2	1
Reggie Willits, lf	—	1	0	0	0	0	0	0	0	0	0	0
Totals	.258	3	93	16	24	6	1	2	14	10	18	3

PITCHER	W	L	ERA	G	GS	SV	IP	H	R	ER	BB	SO
Jason Bulger	0	0	0.00	1	0	0	1.0	0	0	0	1	1
Brian Fuentes	0	0	0.00	2	0	2	1.7	0	0	0	1	0
Kevin Jepsen	0	0	6.75	2	0	0	1.3	3	1	1	0	1
Scott Kazmir	0	0	7.50	1	1	0	6.0	5	5	5	3	1
John Lackey	1	0	0.00	1	1	0	7.3	4	0	0	1	4
Darren Oliver	1	0	0.00	3	0	0	2.3	1	0	0	0	2
Jered Weaver	1	0	1.23	1	1	0	7.3	2	1	1	2	7
Totals	3	0	2.33	3	3	2	27.0	15	7	7	8	16

E—Bay, Gonzalez, Lowell, Youkilis, Mathis. **DP**—Boston 2, Los Angeles 1. **LOB**—Boston 16, Los Angeles 18. **SB**—Gathright, Izturis, Kendrick, Rivera. **CS**—Abreu. **SH**—Figgins, Mathis. **SF**—Morales. **HBP**—Hunter (by Ramirez), Napoli 2 (by Beckett, Buchholz). **IBB**—Hunter (by Papelbon). **WP**—Lackey. **BK**—Buchholz.

SCORE BY INNINGS

Boston	003	300	010—7
Los Angeles	000	231	523—16

NATIONAL LEAGUE DIVISION SERIES
ST. LOUIS VS. LOS ANGELES
ST. LOUIS

PLAYER, POS	AVG	G	AB	R	H	2B	3B	HR	RBI	BB	SO	SB
Rick Ankiel, ph	.000	2	2	0	0	0	0	0	0	0	2	0
Mitchell Boggs, p	—	1	0	0	0	0	0	0	0	0	0	0
Chris Carpenter, p	.000	1	2	0	0	0	0	0	0	0	2	0
Mark DeRosa, 3b	.385	3	13	1	5	1	0	0	1	0	2	0
Ryan Franklin, p	—	2	0	0	0	0	0	0	0	0	0	0
Troy Glaus, ph	.000	2	2	0	0	0	0	0	0	0	1	0
Blake Hawksworth, p	—	1	0	0	0	0	0	0	0	0	0	0
Matt Holliday, lf	.167	3	12	1	2	0	0	1	1	0	2	0
Jason LaRue, ph	.000	1	1	0	0	0	0	0	0	0	0	0
Ryan Ludwick, rf	.333	3	12	1	4	0	0	0	1	1	0	0
Julio Lugo, 2b	.400	3	5	1	2	1	0	0	0	1	1	2
Kyle McClellan, p	—	1	0	0	0	0	0	0	0	0	0	0
Trever Miller, p	—	2	0	0	0	0	0	0	0	0	0	0
Yadier Molina, c	.308	3	13	0	4	1	0	0	0	0	1	0
Jason Motte, p	—	1	0	0	0	0	0	0	0	0	0	0
Joel Pineiro, p	.000	1	1	0	0	0	0	0	0	0	1	0
Albert Pujols, 1b	.300	3	10	0	3	0	0	0	1	3	1	0
Colby Rasmus, cf	.444	3	9	1	4	3	0	0	1	2	1	0
Dennys Reyes, p	—	2	0	0	0	0	0	0	0	0	0	0
Brendan Ryan, ss	.083	3	12	0	1	1	0	0	0	0	2	0
Skip Schumaker, 2b	.333	2	6	1	2	1	0	0	1	1	0	0
John Smoltz, p	—	1	0	0	0	0	0	0	0	0	0	0
Joe Thurston, ph	.000	1	1	0	0	0	0	0	0	0	1	0
Adam Wainwright, p	.000	1	2	0	0	0	0	0	0	0	0	0
Totals	**.262**	**3**	**103**	**6**	**27**	**8**	**0**	**1**	**6**	**8**	**17**	**2**

PITCHER	W	L	ERA	G	GS	SV	IP	H	R	ER	BB	SO
Mitchell Boggs	0	0	0.00	1	0	0	1.0	0	0	0	2	1
Chris Carpenter	0	1	7.20	1	1	0	5.0	9	4	4	4	3
Ryan Franklin	0	1	0.00	2	0	0	1.3	3	2	0	2	1
Blake Hawksworth	0	0	0.00	1	0	0	1.0	1	0	0	1	1
Kyle McClellan	0	0	0.00	1	0	0	0.7	1	0	0	1	0
Trever Miller	0	0	0.00	2	0	0	0.7	0	0	0	0	1
Jason Motte	0	0	0.00	1	0	0	1.0	0	0	0	0	0
Joel Pineiro	0	1	9.00	1	1	0	4.0	7	4	4	0	3
Dennys Reyes	0	0	9.00	2	0	0	1.0	1	1	1	0	2
John Smoltz	0	0	4.50	1	0	0	2.0	4	1	1	0	5
Adam Wainwright	0	0	1.13	1	1	0	8.0	3	1	1	1	7
Totals	**0**	**3**	**3.86**	**3**	**3**	**0**	**25.7**	**29**	**13**	**11**	**11**	**24**

LOS ANGELES

PLAYER, POS	AVG	G	AB	R	H	2B	3B	HR	RBI	BB	SO	SB
Ronald Belisario, p	—	2	0	0	0	0	0	0	0	0	0	0
Ronnie Belliard, 2b	.273	3	11	2	3	0	0	0	1	2	5	0
Casey Blake, 3b	.273	3	11	1	3	0	0	0	1	2	1	0
Jonathan Broxton, p	.000	3	1	0	0	0	0	0	0	0	1	0
Andre Ethier, rf	.500	3	12	5	6	2	1	2	3	1	2	0
Rafael Furcal, ss	.500	3	12	2	6	0	1	0	2	1	1	0
Orlando Hudson, 2b	—	3	0	0	0	0	0	0	0	0	0	0
Matt Kemp, cf	.143	3	14	2	2	0	0	1	2	0	8	0
Clayton Kershaw, p	.000	2	0	0	0	0	0	0	0	0	0	0
Hong-Chih Kuo, p	—	1	0	0	0	0	0	0	0	0	0	0
James Loney, 1b	.250	3	12	0	3	0	0	0	0	1	1	0
Mark Loretta, ph	1.000	1	1	0	1	0	0	0	1	0	0	0
Russell Martin, c	.111	3	9	0	1	0	0	0	1	3	1	0
Vicente Padilla, p	.000	1	3	0	0	0	0	0	0	0	1	0
Juan Pierre, lf	—	3	0	1	0	0	0	0	0	0	0	0
Manny Ramirez, lf	.308	3	13	0	4	3	0	0	2	1	2	0
George Sherrill, p	—	3	0	0	0	0	0	0	0	0	0	0
Jim Thome, ph	.000	3	2	0	0	0	0	0	0	0	1	0
Jeff Weaver, p	—	1	0	0	0	0	0	0	0	0	0	0
Randy Wolf, p	.000	1	2	0	0	0	0	0	0	0	0	0

Andre Ethier hit three home runs and drove in six runs in eight playoff games

LARRY GOREN

	AVG	G	AB	R	H	2B	3B	HR	RBI	BB	SO	SB
Totals	**.276**	**3**	**105**	**13**	**29**	**5**	**2**	**3**	**13**	**11**	**24**	**0**

PITCHER	W	L	ERA	G	GS	SV	IP	H	R	ER	BB	SO
Ronald Belisario	0	0	0.00	2	0	0	1.3	0	0	0	0	0
Jonathan Broxton	0	0	2.45	3	0	1	3.7	4	1	1	0	4
Clayton Kershaw	0	0	2.70	1	1	0	6.7	9	2	2	1	4
Hong-Chih Kuo	0	0	0.00	1	0	0	1.0	2	0	0	0	2
Vicente Padilla	1	0	0.00	1	1	0	7.0	4	0	0	1	4
George Sherrill	1	0	3.86	3	0	0	2.3	1	1	1	1	0
Jeff Weaver	1	0	0.00	1	0	0	1.3	1	0	0	0	1
Randy Wolf	0	0	4.91	1	1	0	3.7	6	2	2	5	2
Totals	**3**	**0**	**2.00**	**3**	**3**	**1**	**27.0**	**27**	**6**	**6**	**8**	**17**

E—Holliday, Pineiro. **DP**—St. Louis 1, Los Angeles 2. **LOB**—St. Louis 28, Los Angeles 31. **SB**—Lugo 2. **SH**—Carpenter, Wainwright, Pierre. **SF**—Furcal. **HBP**—Holliday (by Wolf), Schumaker (by Sherrill), Ethier (by Carpenter), Martin (by McClellan), Thome (by Wainwright). **IBB**—Pujols 3 (by Wolf 2, Kershaw). **WP**—Kershaw. **PB**—Molina.

SCORE BY INNINGS

St. Louis	110	100	111—6
Los Angeles	303	211	102—13

COLORADO VS. PHILADELPHIA
COLORADO

PLAYER, POS	AVG	G	AB	R	H	2B	3B	HR	RBI	BB	SO	SB
Garrett Atkins, 3b	.231	4	13	0	3	2	0	0	2	0	3	0
Clint Barmes, 2b	.000	4	14	0	0	0	0	0	0	0	2	0
Joe Beimel, p	—	3	0	0	0	0	0	0	0	0	0	0
Matt Belisle, p	.000	1	0	0	0	0	0	0	0	0	0	0
Rafael Betancourt, p	—	3	0	0	0	0	0	0	0	0	0	0
Jose Contreras, p	—	2	0	0	0	0	0	0	0	0	0	0
Aaron Cook, p	.500	1	2	1	1	0	0	0	0	0	1	0
Matt Daley, p	—	1	0	0	0	0	0	0	0	0	0	0
Dexter Fowler, cf	.214	4	14	1	3	0	0	0	2	1	3	0
Jason Giambi, ph	.333	3	3	1	1	0	0	0	1	0	1	0
Carlos Gonzalez, lf	.588	4	17	5	10	2	0	1	2	1	2	2
Jason Hammel, p	—	1	0	0	0	0	0	0	0	1	0	0
Brad Hawpe, rf	.000	2	4	0	0	0	0	0	0	0	1	0
Todd Helton, 1b	.188	4	16	5	3	0	0	0	2	3	2	0
Ubaldo Jimenez, p	.250	2	4	0	1	0	0	0	0	0	2	0
Jason Marquis, p	—	1	0	0	0	0	0	0	0	0	0	0
Franklin Morales, p	—	4	0	0	0	0	0	0	0	0	0	0
Seth Smith, lf	.200	3	5	0	1	0	0	0	0	1	1	0
Ryan Spilborghs, rf	.222	4	9	1	2	1	0	0	0	1	2	0
Ian Stewart, 3b	.000	2	1	0	0	0	0	0	0	1	1	0
Huston Street, p	—	3	0	0	0	0	0	0	0	0	0	0
Yorvit Torrealba, c	.357	4	14	1	5	2	0	1	4	0	5	0
Troy Tulowitzki, ss	.250	4	16	0	4	2	0	0	3	0	2	0

PLAYER, POS	AVG	G	AB	R	H	2B	3B	HR	RBI	BB	SO	SB
Eric Young, ph	.000	2	1	0	0	0	0	0	0	0	0	0
Totals	.254	4	134	15	34	9	0	2	15	10	27	2

PITCHER	W	L	ERA	G	GS	SV	IP	H	R	ER	BB	SO
Joe Beimel	0	0	0.00	3	0	0	0.7	1	0	0	0	0
Matt Belisle	0	0	0.00	2	0	0	2.0	0	0	0	1	2
Rafael Betancourt	0	0	3.86	3	0	0	2.3	2	1	1	1	3
Jose Contreras	0	0	4.50	2	0	0	2.0	3	1	1	2	3
Aaron Cook	1	0	5.40	1	1	0	5.0	7	3	3	2	4
Matt Daley	0	0	0.00	1	0	0	1.0	1	0	0	1	0
Jason Hammel	0	0	9.82	1	1	0	3.7	4	4	4	3	5
Ubaldo Jimenez	0	1	5.25	2	2	0	12.0	15	7	7	3	11
Jason Marquis	0	0	0.00	1	0	0	1.0	1	0	0	0	0
Franklin Morales	0	0	0.00	4	0	0	2.7	0	0	0	3	1
Huston Street	0	2	13.50	3	0	1	2.7	6	4	4	3	1
Totals	1	3	5.14	4	4	1	35.0	40	20	20	19	30

PHILADELPHIA

PLAYER, POS	AVG	G	AB	R	H	2B	3B	HR	RBI	BB	SO	SB
Antonio Bastardo, p	—	1	0	0	0	0	0	0	0	0	0	0
Joe Blanton, p	.000	2	1	0	0	0	0	0	0	0	1	0
Miguel Cairo, 3b	.000	2	3	0	0	0	0	0	0	0	0	0
Greg Dobbs, ph	.000	3	3	0	0	0	0	0	0	0	1	0
Chad Durbin, p	—	1	0	0	0	0	0	0	0	0	0	0
Scott Eyre, p	—	3	0	0	0	0	0	0	0	0	0	0
Pedro Feliz, 3b	.214	4	14	0	3	1	0	0	0	1	3	0
Ben Francisco, lf	.000	3	1	0	0	0	0	0	0	1	0	0
Cole Hamels, p	—	1	0	0	0	0	0	0	0	1	0	0
J.A. Happ, p	.000	2	1	0	0	0	0	0	0	0	1	0
Ryan Howard, 1b	.375	4	16	3	6	3	0	0	6	1	4	0
Raul Ibanez, lf	.308	4	13	2	4	1	0	0	5	4	2	0
Cliff Lee, p	.200	3	5	0	1	0	0	0	0	0	2	1
Brad Lidge, p	—	2	0	0	0	0	0	0	0	0	0	0
Ryan Madson, p	—	3	0	0	0	0	0	0	0	0	0	0
Brett Myers, p	—	1	0	0	0	0	0	0	0	0	0	0
Jimmy Rollins, ss	.263	4	19	1	5	1	0	0	0	0	5	0
Carlos Ruiz, c	.308	4	13	0	4	0	0	0	3	2	2	0
Matt Stairs, ph	.000	2	1	0	0	0	0	0	0	1	1	0
Chase Utley, 2b	.429	4	14	5	6	0	0	1	4	3	2	0
Shane Victorino, cf	.353	4	17	4	6	1	0	1	1	1	1	0
Jayson Werth, rf	.357	4	14	5	5	0	1	2	4	4	4	0
Totals	.296	4	135	20	40	7	1	4	20	19	30	4

PITCHER	W	L	ERA	G	GS	SV	IP	H	R	ER	BB	SO
Antonio Bastardo	0	0	0.00	1	0	0	0.3	0	0	0	0	1
Joe Blanton	0	0	4.91	2	0	0	3.7	4	2	2	0	1
Chad Durbin	1	0	0.00	1	0	0	1.0	0	0	0	0	0
Scott Eyre	0	0	4.50	3	0	0	2.0	4	1	1	0	1
Cole Hamels	0	1	7.20	1	1	0	5.0	7	4	4	0	5
J.A. Happ	0	0	9.00	2	1	0	3.0	6	3	3	2	4
Cliff Lee	1	0	1.10	2	2	0	16.3	11	4	2	3	10
Brad Lidge	0	0	0.00	2	0	2	1.3	0	0	0	2	1
Ryan Madson	1	0	3.38	3	0	0	2.7	2	1	1	1	4
Brett Myers	0	0	0.00	1	0	0	0.7	0	0	0	2	0
Totals	3	1	3.25	4	4	2	36.0	34	15	13	10	27

E—Barmes, Hawpe, Ibanez, Rollins. **DP**—Colorado 6, Philadelphia 5. **LOB**—Colorado 28, Philadelphia 32. **SB**—Gonzalez 2, Lee, Utley 2, Victorino. **CS**—Gonzalez, Howard. **SH**—Barmes, Fowler, Torrealba, Lee, Victorino. **SF**—Fowler 2, Tulowitzki, Howard. **HBP**—Tulowitzki (by Myers). **IBB**—Smith (by Madson), Spilborghs (by Myers), Howard (by Jimenez), Werth (by Morales). **WP**—Daley, Lee 2, Madson.

SCORE BY INNINGS

Colorado	301	311	231—15
Philadelphia	200	328	014—20

AMERICAN LEAGUE CHAMPIONSHIP SERIES
LOS ANGELES VS. NEW YORK
LOS ANGELES

PLAYER, POS	AVG	G	AB	R	H	2B	3B	HR	RBI	BB	SO	SB
Bobby Abreu, rf	.160	6	25	2	4	2	0	0	2	4	8	0
Erick Aybar, ss	.250	6	20	2	5	1	0	0	1	1	1	3
Chone Figgins, 3b	.130	6	23	2	3	0	0	0	1	3	3	0
Vladimir Guerrero, dh	.370	6	27	3	10	3	0	1	5	1	5	0
Torii Hunter, cf	.304	6	23	2	7	1	0	0	2	5	4	1
Maicer Izturis, 2b	.100	4	10	1	1	1	0	0	1	1	1	0
Howard Kendrick, 2b	.286	4	14	3	4	0	1	1	1	1	1	0

Cliff Lee went 4-0, 1.56 in five postseason starts, winning both World Series turns

PLAYER, POS	AVG	G	AB	R	H	2B	3B	HR	RBI	BB	SO	SB
Jeff Mathis, c	.583	5	12	2	7	5	0	0	1	0	2	0
Gary Matthews, lf	.000	3	4	1	0	0	0	0	0	1	3	0
Kendry Morales, 1b	.167	6	24	1	4	0	0	1	4	1	6	0
Mike Napoli, c	.111	5	9	0	1	0	0	0	0	0	3	0
Juan Rivera, lf	.200	6	25	0	5	1	0	0	0	0	1	0
Reggie Willits, lf	—	3	0	0	0	0	0	0	0	0	0	0
Totals	.236	6	216	19	51	14	1	3	18	18	38	4

PITCHER	W	L	ERA	G	GS	SV	IP	H	R	ER	BB	SO
Jason Bulger	0	0	3.86	3	0	0	2.3	1	1	1	3	4
Brian Fuentes	0	0	3.00	3	0	1	3.0	1	1	1	3	3
Kevin Jepsen	1	0	2.45	3	0	0	3.7	5	1	1	2	2
Scott Kazmir	0	1	7.71	2	1	0	4.7	6	5	4	5	3
John Lackey	0	1	3.65	2	2	0	12.3	15	7	5	6	10
Darren Oliver	0	0	4.26	5	0	0	6.3	6	3	3	4	6
Matt Palmer	0	0	13.50	2	0	0	2.7	5	4	4	1	2
Ervin Santana	1	1	1.59	4	0	0	5.7	5	3	1	4	5
Joe Saunders	0	1	4.35	2	2	0	10.3	13	5	5	6	5
Jered Weaver	0	0	4.26	3	1	0	6.3	5	3	3	4	7
Totals	2	4	4.40	6	6	1	57.3	62	33	28	38	47

NEW YORK

PLAYER, POS	AVG	G	AB	R	H	2B	3B	HR	RBI	BB	SO	SB
Alfredo Aceves, p	—	1	0	0	0	0	0	0	0	0	0	0
Melky Cabrera, cf	.391	6	23	3	9	2	0	0	4	3	6	0
Robinson Cano, 2b	.261	6	23	4	6	1	2	0	4	4	3	0
Francisco Cervelli, ph	.000	1	1	0	0	0	0	0	0	0	1	0
Johnny Damon, lf	.300	6	30	4	9	1	0	2	5	1	2	0
Brett Gardner, cf	.667	6	3	2	2	0	0	0	0	0	0	0
Freddy Guzman, pr	.000	2	1	0	0	0	0	0	0	0	1	0
Jerry Hairston, lf	.500	2	2	1	1	0	0	0	0	0	1	0
Derek Jeter, ss	.259	6	27	5	7	0	0	2	3	6	5	0
Hideki Matsui, dh	.238	6	21	1	5	1	0	0	3	5	4	0
Jose Molina, c	.333	2	3	0	1	0	0	0	0	0	1	0
Jorge Posada, c	.200	6	20	3	4	1	0	1	1	5	5	1
Mariano Rivera, p	—	1	0	0	0	0	0	0	0	0	0	0
David Robertson, p	—	1	0	0	0	0	0	0	0	0	0	0
Alex Rodriguez, 3b	.429	6	21	6	9	2	0	3	6	8	3	1
Nick Swisher, rf	.150	6	20	2	3	0	0	0	0	3	7	0
Mark Teixeira, 1b	.222	6	27	2	6	1	0	0	4	3	8	0
Totals	.279	6	222	33	62	9	2	8	30	38	47	2

PITCHER	W	L	ERA	G	GS	SV	IP	H	R	ER	BB	SO
Alfredo Aceves	0	1	13.50	2	0	0	1.3	3	2	2	0	0
A.J. Burnett	0	0	5.84	2	2	0	12.3	11	8	8	5	7
Joba Chamberlain	0	0	5.40	4	0	0	1.7	5	1	1	0	2
Phil Coke	0	0	0.00	2	0	0	0.7	1	0	0	1	1

Chad Gaudin	0	0	0.00	1	0	0	1.0	0	0	0	0	0
Phil Hughes	0	1	3.38	3	0	0	2.7	4	1	1	1	3
Damaso Marte	0	0	0.00	3	0	0	1.3	0	0	0	0	0
Andy Pettitte	1	0	2.84	2	2	0	12.7	14	4	4	2	8
Mariano Rivera	0	0	1.29	5	0	2	7.0	3	1	1	2	4
David Robertson	1	0	0.00	2	0	0	2.0	1	0	0	2	1
CC Sabathia	2	0	1.13	2	2	0	16.0	9	2	2	3	12
Totals	**4**	**2**	**2.91**	**6**	**6**	**2**	**58.7**	**51**	**19**	**19**	**18**	**38**

E—Abreu, Figgins, Hunter, Izturis, Kazmir, Kendrick, Lackey, Rivera, Cano 2, Jeter. **DP**—Los Angeles 7, New York 8. **LOB**—Los Angeles 46, New York 64. **SB**—Aybar 3, Hunter, Posada, Rodriguez. **CS**—Hunter, Gardner, Jeter. **SH**—Aybar 2, Figgins 2, Cabrera 2, Gardner, Swisher. **SF**—Izturis, Rodriguez, Teixeira. **HBP**—Figgins (by Burnett), Morales (by Burnett), Cano 2 (by Bulger, Fuentes), Swisher (by Santana). **IBB**—Abreu 3 (by Aceves, Robertson, Rivera), Izturis (by Robertson), Cano (by Santana), Jeter (by Oliver), Rodriguez 3 (by Fuentes 2, Oliver). **WP**—Bulger, Kazmir, Burnett 2.

SCORE BY INNINGS

Los Angeles	401 142 410	020	0—19
New York	311 741 653	010	1—33

NATIONAL LEAGUE CHAMPIONSHIP SERIES
PHILADELPHIA VS. LOS ANGELES
PHILADELPHIA

PLAYER, POS	AVG	G	AB	R	H	2B	3B	HR	RBI	BB	SO	SB
Antonio Bastardo, p	—	1	0	0	0	0	0	0	0	0	0	0
Joe Blanton, p	.000	1	2	0	0	0	0	0	0	0	0	0
Eric Bruntlett, pr	—	1	0	1	0	0	0	0	0	0	0	0
Miguel Cairo, ph	.000	2	2	0	0	0	0	0	0	0	1	0
Greg Dobbs, ph	.000	2	1	0	0	0	0	0	0	0	0	0
Chad Durbin, p	—	4	0	0	0	0	0	0	0	0	0	0
Scott Eyre, p	—	2	0	0	0	0	0	0	0	0	0	0
Pedro Feliz, 3b	.118	5	17	3	2	0	1	1	2	1	4	0
Ben Francisco, lf	.000	4	3	0	0	0	0	0	0	0	0	0
Cole Hamels, p	.000	2	1	0	0	0	0	0	0	1	1	0
J.A. Happ, p	—	3	0	0	0	0	0	0	0	0	0	0
Ryan Howard, 1b	.333	5	15	5	5	1	1	2	8	6	4	0
Raul Ibanez, lf	.167	5	18	4	3	1	0	1	4	1	6	0
Cliff Lee, p	.333	1	3	1	1	0	0	0	0	0	1	0
Brad Lidge, p	—	3	0	0	0	0	0	0	0	0	0	0
Ryan Madson, p	—	4	0	0	0	0	0	0	0	0	0	0
Pedro Martinez, p	.000	1	2	0	0	0	0	0	0	0	0	0
Chan Ho Park, p	—	4	0	0	0	0	0	0	0	0	0	0
Jimmy Rollins, ss	.227	5	22	5	5	2	0	0	3	0	3	0
Carlos Ruiz, c	.385	5	13	4	5	1	0	1	4	5	0	1
Matt Stairs, ph	.000	2	1	0	0	0	0	0	0	1	0	0
Chase Utley, 2b	.211	5	19	3	4	0	0	1	4	4	0	0
Shane Victorino, cf	.368	5	19	4	7	1	1	2	6	2	2	1
Jayson Werth, rf	.222	5	18	5	4	0	0	3	6	2	7	0
Totals	**.231**	**5**	**156**	**35**	**36**	**6**	**3**	**10**	**34**	**23**	**33**	**2**

PITCHER	W	L	ERA	G	GS	SV	IP	H	R	ER	BB	SO
Antonio Bastardo	0	0	—	1	0	0	0.0	1	0	0	0	0
Joe Blanton	0	0	4.50	1	1	0	6.0	6	4	3	2	2
Chad Durbin	1	0	0.00	4	0	0	3.0	0	0	0	0	1
Scott Eyre	0	0	0.00	2	0	0	0.3	2	0	0	0	0
Cole Hamels	1	0	6.52	2	2	0	9.7	13	7	7	2	7
J.A. Happ	0	0	0.00	3	0	0	0.7	0	0	0	3	0
Cliff Lee	1	0	0.00	1	1	0	8.0	3	0	0	0	10
Brad Lidge	1	0	0.00	3	0	1	2.7	1	0	0	1	3
Ryan Madson	0	0	5.40	4	0	0	3.3	6	2	2	3	4
Pedro Martinez	0	0	0.00	1	1	0	7.0	2	0	0	0	3
Chan Ho Park	0	1	8.10	4	0	0	3.3	4	3	3	1	3
Totals	**4**	**1**	**3.07**	**5**	**5**	**1**	**44.0**	**38**	**16**	**15**	**12**	**33**

LOS ANGELES

PLAYER, POS	AVG	G	AB	R	H	2B	3B	HR	RBI	BB	SO	SB
Ronald Belisario, p	—	4	0	0	0	0	0	0	0	0	0	0
Ronnie Belliard, 2b	.316	5	19	2	6	0	0	0	0	0	2	1
Chad Billingsley, p	.000	1	1	0	0	0	0	0	0	0	1	0
Casey Blake, 3b	.105	5	19	0	2	0	0	0	1	0	5	1
Jonathan Broxton, p	—	3	0	0	0	0	0	0	0	0	0	0
Juan Castro, 3b	—	1	0	0	0	0	0	0	0	0	0	0
Scott Elbert, p	—	1	0	0	0	0	0	0	0	0	0	0
Andre Ethier, rf	.263	5	19	2	5	1	0	1	3	2	4	0
Rafael Furcal, ss	.143	5	21	0	3	1	0	0	1	1	3	1
Orlando Hudson, 2b	.250	5	4	1	1	0	0	1	1	0	1	0
Matt Kemp, cf	.250	5	20	2	5	0	0	1	2	1	8	0
Clayton Kershaw, p	—	2	0	0	0	0	0	0	0	0	1	0
Hong-Chih Kuo, p	—	4	0	0	0	0	0	0	0	0	0	0
Hiroki Kuroda, p	—	1	0	0	0	0	0	0	0	0	0	0
James Loney, 1b	.353	5	17	3	6	0	0	2	3	2	2	0
Mark Loretta, 3b	.000	2	2	0	0	0	0	0	0	0	1	0
Russell Martin, c	.250	5	16	2	4	1	0	0	2	1	3	0
Vicente Padilla, p	.000	2	1	0	0	0	0	0	0	0	0	0
Juan Pierre, lf	.000	4	2	1	0	0	0	0	0	0	0	0
Manny Ramirez, lf	.263	5	19	3	5	0	0	1	2	1	4	0
George Sherrill, p	—	3	0	0	0	0	0	0	0	0	0	0
Jim Thome, ph	1.000	2	1	0	1	0	0	0	0	0	1	0
Ramon Troncoso, p	—	3	0	0	0	0	0	0	0	0	0	0
Randy Wolf, p	.000	2	3	0	0	0	0	0	0	0	0	0
Totals	**.232**	**5**	**164**	**16**	**38**	**3**	**0**	**6**	**15**	**12**	**33**	**3**

PITCHER	W	L	ERA	G	GS	SV	IP	H	R	ER	BB	SO
Ronald Belisario	0	0	10.80	4	0	0	3.3	5	4	4	1	0
Chad Billingsley	0	0	5.40	1	0	0	3.3	2	2	2	2	3
Jonathan Broxton	0	1	6.00	3	0	1	3.0	2	2	2	1	1
Scott Elbert	0	0	0.00	1	0	0	0.3	0	0	0	0	0
Clayton Kershaw	0	1	9.45	2	1	0	6.7	5	7	7	6	6
Hong-Chih Kuo	1	0	2.25	4	0	0	4.0	2	1	1	0	6
Hiroki Kuroda	0	1	40.50	1	1	0	1.3	6	6	6	1	1
Vicente Padilla	0	1	6.10	2	2	0	10.3	8	7	7	3	9
George Sherrill	0	0	13.50	3	0	0	2.0	2	3	3	3	2
Ramon Troncoso	0	0	0.00	3	0	0	3.0	0	0	0	3	3
Randy Wolf	0	0	5.06	1	1	0	5.3	4	3	3	2	2
Totals	**1**	**4**	**7.38**	**5**	**5**	**1**	**42.7**	**36**	**35**	**35**	**23**	**33**

E—Feliz, Utley 2. **DP**—Philadelphia 2, Los Angeles 4. **LOB**—Philadelphia 24, Los Angeles 32. **SB**—Ruiz, Victorino, Belliard, Blake, Furcal. **CS**—Victorino, Ethier, Kemp. **SH**—Hamels 2, Lee, Padilla 2. **SF**—Furcal, Rollins, Victorino. **HBP**—Rollins 2 (by Troncoso, Kershaw), Ruiz (by Broxton), Victorino 2 (by Sherrill 2), Martin (by Martinez). **WP**—Lidge, Belisario, Elbert, Kershaw 3, Sherrill. **PB**—Martin.

SCORE BY INNINGS

Philadelphia	930	373	172—35
Los Angeles	120	251	050—16

Ryan Howard and Jayson Werth balanced playoff power (10 HR) with strikeouts (39)

LARRY GOREN

ORGANIZATION STATISTICS

Arizona Diamondbacks

SEASON IN A SENTENCE: Arizona hoped to return to contention in 2009, but a slow start led to farm director A.J. Hinch replacing Bob Melvin as manager and the rest of the season serving as an audition for 2010.

HIGH POINT: You could pick just about any Dan Haren start, but his July 10 shutout against the Marlins was probably his best. In an 8-0 win he registered 10 strikeouts and allowed just four hits and one walk. The offensive performances of outfielder Justin Upton and third baseman Mark Reynolds (and his amazing 44 home runs and 223 strikeouts) also should give Arizona something to build around.

LOW POINT: Things got off to a terrible start for the Diamondbacks, as they not only lost the opener 9-8 to the Rockies—kicking off the 12-18 start that cost Melvin his job—but also saw the only start ace righthander Brandon Webb would make all season. He tried to rehab a shoulder injury but finally had surgery in August. Arizona picked up his option and hopes he will be healthy for 2010.

NOTABLE ROOKIES: With Eric Byrnes missing time due to injuries again and Chris Young taking a huge step back, Gerardo Parra's emergence was a key development in the Arizona outfield. He opened the season at Double-A Mobile but jumped straight to the big leagues a month into the season. Lefthander Clay Zavada, an independent league discovery, emerged as a reliable set-up man and averaged better than a strikeout per inning.

KEY TRANSACTIONS: The Diamondbacks quickly realized they were sellers, and while they didn't make any major deals they did unload pitchers Jon Garland, Tony Pena and Jon Rauch to contenders in July and August. None of the players they got back will be stars, but Tony Abreu, Brandon Allen and Kevin Mulvey should be big league contributors.

DOWN ON THE FARM: The bad news continued in the minors, with top prospect Jarrod Parker getting shut down in July and having Tommy John surgery in October. The unconventional decision to promote Hinch from farm director to major league manager led to upheaval in the player-development department, with Mike Berger taking over as farm director. The organization finished 26th in minor league winning percentage and will rely on the 2009 draft to restock the system.

OPENING DAY PAYROLL: $73,516,666

ORGANIZATION LEADERS

BATTING
Minimum 250 at-bats

MAJORS

*AVG	Justin Upton	.300
*OPS	Justin Upton	.899
HR	Mark Reynolds	44
RBI	Mark Reynolds	102

MINORS

*AVG	Schmidt, Konrad, Visalia/Reno	.309
*OBP	Gotay, Ruben, Reno	.429
*SLG	Ryal, Rusty, Reno	.527
R	Linton, Ollie, Visalia	81
H	Harbin, Taylor, Visalia/Reno	145
	Linton, Ollie, Visalia	145
TB	Harbin, Taylor, Visalia/Reno	225
2B	Hankerd, Cyle, Mobile	33
	Ryal, Rusty, Reno	33
3B	Oeltjen, Trent, Reno	14
HR	Ryal, Rusty, Reno	17
RBI	Greene, Kyle, Reno/Visalia	80
BB	Gotay, Ruben, Reno	102
SO	Greene, Kyle, Reno/Visalia	149
SB	Ciriaco, Pedro, Mobile	38

PITCHING
†Minimum 75 innings

MAJORS

W	Dan Haren	14
†ERA	Dan Haren	3.14
SO	Dan Haren	223

MINORS

W	Barnette, Tony, Reno	14
L	Moorhouse, Brett, South Bend	14
†ERA	Cook, Ryan, South Bend	3.66
G	Urquidez, Jason, Mobile/Reno	50
GS	Barnette, Tony, Reno	29
SV	Korecky, Bobby, Reno	13
IP	Torra, Matt, Mobile	180
BB	Barnette, Tony, Reno	62
SO	Collmenter, Joshua, Visalia	152
†AVG	Collmenter, Joshua, Visalia	.238

2009 PERFORMANCE

General Manager: Josh Byrnes. **Farm Director:** A.J. Hinch/Mike Berger. **Scouting Director:** Tom Allison.

Class	Team	League	W	L	PCT	Finish*	Manager(s)
Majors	Arizona Diamondbacks	National	70	92	.432	t-13th (16)	Bob Melvin/A.J. Hinch
Triple-A	Reno Aces	Pacific Coast	79	64	.552	3rd (16)	Brett Butler
Double-A	Mobile BayBears	Southern	66	74	.471	5th (10)	Hector De La Cruz
High A	Visalia Rawhide	California	64	76	.457	6th (10)	Mike Bell
Low A	South Bend Silver Hawks	Midwest	59	78	.431	10th (14)	Mark Haley
Short-season	Yakima Bears	Northwest	28	48	.368	8th (8)	Bob Didier
Rookie	Missoula Osprey	Pioneer	40	36	.526	5th (8)	Audo Vicente
Overall 2009 Minor League Record			336	376	.472	26th (30)	

*Finish in overall standings (No. of teams in league). †League champion.

ORGANIZATION STATISTICS

ARIZONA DIAMONDBACKS

NATIONAL LEAGUE

Batting	B-T	HT	WT	DOB	AVG	vLH	vRH	G	AB	R	H	2B	3B	HR	RBI	BB	HBP	SH	SF	SO	SB	CS	SLG	OBP
Allen, Brandon	L-R	6-2	235	2-12-86	.202	.091	.232	32	104	13	21	7	0	4	14	12	0	0	0	40	0	0	.385	.284
Byrnes, Eric	R-R	6-2	215	2-16-76	.226	.228	.225	84	239	26	54	14	1	8	31	12	3	2	2	30	9	3	.393	.270
Carlin, Luke	B-R	5-11	185	12-20-80	.167	.100	.250	10	18	3	3	0	0	0	1	3	0	0	0	3	0	0	.167	.286
Clark, Tony	B-R	6-7	245	6-15-72	.182	.211	.170	36	66	7	12	4	0	4	11	11	0	0	1	24	0	0	.424	.295
Drew, Stephen	L-R	6-0	185	3-16-83	.261	.200	.282	135	533	71	139	29	12	12	65	49	1	5	7	87	5	1	.428	.320
Hester, John	R-R	6-3	220	9-14-83	.250	.167	.400	15	28	4	7	2	0	1	4	2	0	0	0	7	0	0	.429	.300
Jackson, Conor	R-R	6-2	215	5-7-82	.182	.172	.186	30	99	8	18	4	0	1	14	11	0	0	0	16	5	0	.253	.264
Lopez, Felipe	B-R	6-0	205	5-12-80	.301	.313	.298	85	345	44	104	18	1	6	25	34	1	1	2	59	6	3	.412	.364
2-team total (66 Milwaukee)					.310	—	—	151	604	88	187	38	3	9	57	71	2	1	2	100	6	6	.427	.383
Montero, Miguel	L-R	5-11	190	7-9-83	.294	.329	.286	128	425	61	125	30	0	16	59	38	3	2	2	78	1	2	.478	.355
Oeltjen, Trent	L-L	6-1	190	2-28-83	.243	.158	.275	24	70	11	17	4	1	3	4	1	0	1	1	13	3	1	.457	.250
Ojeda, Augie	B-R	5-9	175	12-20-74	.246	.203	.263	103	264	38	65	17	3	1	16	32	6	6	1	28	3	1	.345	.340
Parra, Gerardo	L-L	5-11	195	5-6-87	.290	.220	.310	120	455	59	132	21	8	5	60	25	1	4	6	89	5	7	.404	.324
Reynolds, Mark	R-R	6-2	220	8-3-83	.260	.235	.266	155	578	98	150	30	1	44	102	76	5	0	3	223	24	9	.543	.349
Roberts, Ryan	R-R	5-11	195	9-19-80	.279	.325	.250	110	305	41	85	17	2	7	25	40	3	2	1	55	7	3	.416	.367
Romero, Alex	L-R	6-0	200	9-9-83	.248	.192	.261	66	145	14	36	6	2	1	18	11	1	0	0	23	2	0	.338	.306
Ryal, Rusty	R-R	6-2	200	3-16-83	.271	.273	.267	30	59	11	16	6	2	3	9	6	2	0	1	21	0	0	.593	.353
Snyder, Chris	R-R	6-4	245	2-12-81	.200	.161	.220	61	165	20	33	7	0	6	22	32	2	1	2	47	0	0	.352	.333
Tracy, Chad	L-R	6-2	215	5-22-80	.237	.146	.258	98	257	29	61	15	0	8	39	26	1	0	4	38	1	0	.389	.306
Upton, Justin	R-R	6-2	205	8-25-87	.300	.377	.277	138	526	84	158	30	7	26	86	55	2	1	4	137	20	5	.532	.366
Whitesell, Josh	L-L	6-1	225	4-14-82	.194	.208	.190	46	108	7	21	7	0	1	14	24	1	0	0	29	0	0	.287	.346
Wilson, Josh	R-R	6-0	175	3-26-81	.231	.111	.294	11	26	1	6	1	0	0	2	3	1	0	0	3	0	0	.269	.333
2-team total (16 San Diego)					.156	—	—	27	64	3	10	3	0	0	3	6	2	1	0	12	0	0	.203	.250
Young, Chris	R-R	6-2	200	9-5-83	.212	.262	.196	134	433	54	92	28	4	15	42	59	4	3	2	133	11	4	.400	.311

Pitching	B-T	HT	WT	DOB	W	L	ERA	G	GS	CG	SV	IP	H	R	ER	HR	BB	SO	AVG	vLH	vRH	K/9	BB/9
Augenstein, Bryan	R-R	6-6	230	7-11-86	0	1	7.94	7	2	0	0	17	23	16	15	2	6	6	.333	.250	.378	3.18	3.18
Boyer, Blaine	R-R	6-3	215	7-11-81	0	1	2.68	30	0	0	0	37	39	20	11	0	12	18	.273	.263	.284	4.38	2.92
3-team total (3 Atlanta, 15 St. Louis)					0	2	4.12	48	0	0	0	55	56	36	25	1	20	29	—	—	—	4.77	3.29
Buckner, Billy	R-R	6-2	215	8-27-83	4	6	6.40	16	13	0	0	77	94	57	55	12	39	64	.306	.347	.270	7.45	5.38
Cabrera, Daniel	R-R	6-9	260	5-28-81	0	1	6.55	6	1	0	0	11	11	8	8	0	7	7	.262	.125	.346	5.73	5.73
2-team total (9 Washington)					0	6	6.00	15	9	0	0	51	59	47	34	4	42	23	—	—	—	4.06	7.41
Davis, Doug	R-L	6-4	215	9-21-75	9	14	4.12	34	34	0	0	203	203	101	93	25	103	146	.267	.264	.268	6.46	4.56
Garland, Jon	R-R	6-6	210	9-27-79	8	11	4.29	27	27	1	0	168	188	90	80	19	52	83	.286	.271	.302	4.46	2.79
2-team total (6 Los Angeles)					11	13	4.01	33	33	1	0	204	225	106	91	23	61	109	—	—	—	4.81	2.69
Gordon, Tom	R-R	5-10	200	11-18-67	0	1	21.60	3	0	0	0	2	3	4	4	0	3	0	.429	.000	.600	0.00	16.20
Gutierrez, Juan	R-R	6-3	210	7-14-83	4	3	4.06	65	0	0	9	71	67	33	32	2	30	66	.250	.297	.207	8.37	3.80
Haren, Dan	R-R	6-5	215	9-17-80	14	10	3.14	33	33	3	0	229	192	83	80	27	38	223	.224	.229	.219	8.75	1.49
Korecky, Bobby	R-R	5-11	185	9-16-79	0	0	13.50	5	0	0	0	6	11	9	9	0	4	3	.423	.455	.400	4.50	6.00
Mulvey, Kevin	R-R	6-2	195	5-26-85	0	3	7.04	6	4	0	0	23	23	18	18	5	12	18	.264	.189	.382	7.04	4.70
Pena, Tony	R-R	6-2	220	1-9-82	5	3	4.24	37	0	0	1	34	41	20	16	3	11	26	.295	.317	.276	6.88	2.91
Petit, Yusmeiro	R-R	6-1	255	11-22-84	3	10	5.82	23	17	0	0	90	102	62	58	19	34	74	.276	.282	.269	7.43	3.41
Qualls, Chad	R-R	6-5	220	8-17-78	2	2	3.63	51	0	0	24	52	53	23	21	5	7	45	.256	.298	.214	7.79	1.21
Rauch, Jon	R-R	6-11	290	9-27-78	2	2	4.14	58	0	0	2	54	57	27	25	5	17	35	.266	.255	.277	5.80	2.82
Rosales, Leo	R-R	6-1	205	5-28-81	2	1	4.76	33	0	0	0	45	40	24	24	5	12	31	.237	.235	.238	6.15	2.38
Scherzer, Max	R-R	6-3	215	7-27-84	9	11	4.12	30	30	0	0	170	166	94	78	20	63	174	.253	.265	.239	9.19	3.33
Schlereth, Daniel	L-L	6-0	210	5-9-86	1	4	5.89	21	0	0	0	18	15	13	12	1	15	22	.221	.222	.220	10.80	7.36
Schoeneweis, Scott	L-L	6-0	190	10-2-73	1	2	7.13	45	0	0	0	24	29	20	19	6	13	14	.287	.276	.302	5.35	4.88
Slaten, Doug	L-L	6-5	215	2-4-80	0	0	7.11	11	0	0	0	6	10	5	5	1	1	4	.345	.389	.273	5.68	1.42
Vasquez, Esmerling	R-R	6-1	175	11-7-83	3	3	4.42	53	0	0	0	53	52	27	26	4	29	45	.255	.196	.304	7.64	4.92
Webb, Brandon	R-R	6-2	230	5-9-79	0	0	13.50	1	1	0	0	4	6	6	6	2	2	2	.353	.222	.500	4.50	4.50
Zavada, Clay	L-L	6-1	195	6-28-84	3	3	3.35	49	0	0	0	51	45	22	19	5	24	52	.236	.284	.205	9.18	4.24

Fielding

Catcher	PCT	G	PO	A	E	DP	PB
Carlin	1.000	4	24	1	0	0	1
Hester	1.000	8	45	3	0	0	0
Montero	.989	111	733	60	9	4	4
Snyder	1.000	56	363	21	0	1	3

First Base	PCT	G	PO	A	E	DP
Allen	.993	32	260	11	2	23
Clark	.979	21	128	13	3	11
Jackson	.977	6	42	1	1	5
Reynolds	.975	28	186	11	5	28
Ryal	.978	10	39	5	1	2
Snyder	1.000	1	1	0	0	0
Tracy	.996	66	471	37	2	39

	PCT	G	PO	A	E	DP
Whitesell	.996	30	246	12	1	16

Second Base	PCT	G	PO	A	E	DP
Lopez	.977	82	138	243	9	56
Ojeda	1.000	35	44	93	0	19
Roberts	.991	57	99	117	2	18
Ryal	1.000	13	9	27	0	7

Third Base	PCT	G	PO	A	E	DP
Ojeda	.886	28	14	25	5	5
Reynolds	.945	130	88	240	19	30
Roberts	.927	19	14	24	3	3
Tracy	1.000	8	5	9	0	0

Shortstop	PCT	G	PO	A	E	DP
Drew	.980	132	173	362	11	70
Ojeda	.972	34	31	74	3	15
Wilson	.951	8	12	27	2	6

Outfield	PCT	G	PO	A	E	DP
Byrnes	.976	58	118	3	3	0
Jackson	.972	23	35	0	1	0
Oeltjen	.974	18	36	2	1	0
Parra	.975	113	229	8	6	0
Roberts	.957	16	22	0	1	0
Romero	.985	44	64	2	1	0
Upton	.961	136	294	4	12	1
Young	.993	124	287	3	2	1

RENO ACES   TRIPLE-A
PACIFIC COAST LEAGUE

Batting	B-T	HT	WT	DOB	AVG	vLH	vRH	G	AB	R	H	2B	3B	HR	RBI	BB	HBP	SH	SF	SO	SB	CS	SLG	OBP
Allen, Brandon	L-R	6-2	235	2-12-86	.324	.366	.308	38	145	33	47	8	1	12	32	20	2	0	0	25	6	0	.641	.413
Byrne, Bryan	L-R	6-3	200	4-30-84	.133	.143	.130	35	98	9	13	5	0	0	12	16	5	0	1	20	0	0	.184	.283
Byrnes, Eric	R-R	6-2	215	2-16-76	.279	.286	.277	16	68	14	19	7	1	2	9	5	1	0	1	4	1	0	.500	.333
Carlin, Luke	B-R	5-11	185	12-20-80	.321	.254	.347	72	237	45	76	17	0	7	35	45	1	1	1	55	4	4	.481	.430
Clark, Tony	B-R	6-7	245	6-15-72	.160	.273	.071	7	25	1	4	1	0	1	2	5	0	0	0	4	0	0	.320	.300
Drew, Stephen	L-R	6-0	185	3-16-83	.333	.200	.500	2	9	0	3	0	1	0	1	0	0	0	0	1	0	0	.556	.333
Gillespie, Cole	R-R	6-1	205	6-20-84	.304	.366	.278	42	138	33	42	6	4	5	27	27	2	0	3	31	8	0	.514	.418
2-team total (75 Nashville)					.265	—	—	117	374	62	99	18	9	12	54	58	5	3	7	87	14	5	.457	.365
Gotay, Ruben	B-R	5-11	190	12-25-82	.272	.176	.301	118	371	65	101	29	2	11	57	102	1	3	2	69	2	4	.450	.429
Greene, Kyle	L-R	6-2	200	5-26-86	.500	.333	.667	3	6	1	3	0	0	1	3	0	0	0	1	0	0	0	1.000	.429
Harbin, Taylor	R-R	5-9	175	2-13-86	.381	.333	.389	6	21	5	8	3	1	0	6	1	1	1	0	1	0	1	.619	.435
Hester, John	R-R	6-3	220	9-14-83	.328	.320	.332	92	329	61	108	31	5	9	66	22	3	0	1	65	13	3	.535	.375
Mercado, Orlando	R-R	5-9	210	3-13-85	.289	.400	.200	17	45	6	13	2	0	0	6	9	0	0	1	2	0	0	.333	.400
Murillo, Agustin	R-R	6-3	195	5-5-82	.275	.221	.297	76	233	37	64	16	1	2	32	31	0	2	4	33	4	1	.378	.354
Nunez, Abraham	B-R	5-11	200	3-16-76	.249	.269	.240	84	253	28	63	8	2	2	32	48	1	5	3	40	4	3	.320	.367
Oeltjen, Trent	L-L	6-1	190	2-28-83	.303	.302	.304	114	442	78	134	29	14	10	64	31	10	4	1	101	22	8	.500	.362
Reyes, Guillermo	B-R	5-9	177	12-29-81	.229	.263	.216	31	70	9	16	3	0	0	2	10	0	0	0	14	0	0	.271	.325
Roberson, Chris	B-R	6-2	180	8-23-79	.261	.309	.242	127	425	73	111	27	8	7	59	34	3	2	3	60	30	8	.412	.318
Roberts, Ryan	R-R	5-11	195	9-19-80	.310	.333	.292	10	42	10	13	1	1	1	10	6	0	0	0	6	7	0	.452	.396
Rogers, Ed	R-R	6-0	190	8-29-78	.280	.347	.253	69	254	44	71	18	0	4	42	14	2	6	8	42	10	3	.398	.313
Romero, Alex	L-R	6-0	200	9-9-83	.348	.270	.376	70	279	40	97	20	3	2	47	32	3	0	3	26	7	4	.462	.416
Ryal, Rusty	R-R	6-2	200	3-16-83	.290	.336	.273	103	404	65	117	33	6	17	70	33	4	2	3	94	5	3	.527	.347
Schmidt, Konrad	R-R	6-0	225	8-2-84	.438	.667	.300	5	16	1	7	2	0	0	4	0	0	0	0	1	0	0	.563	.438
Snyder, Chris	R-R	6-4	245	2-12-81	.308	.400	.250	3	13	2	4	1	0	1	4	0	0	0	0	3	0	0	.615	.308
Tracy, Chad	L-R	6-2	215	5-22-80	.286	.333	.276	10	35	4	10	1	1	0	4	3	1	0	1	8	0	1	.371	.350
Watson, Brandon	L-R	6-1	170	9-30-81	.279	.270	.282	128	463	72	129	16	5	5	49	29	2	15	4	29	18	10	.367	.321
Whitesell, Josh	L-L	6-1	225	4-14-82	.293	.290	.295	63	225	35	66	14	1	8	58	40	3	0	6	48	1	1	.471	.398
Wilson, Josh	R-R	6-0	175	3-26-81	.260	.000	.283	15	50	5	13	3	1	1	10	7	1	1	2	8	1	1	.420	.350
2-team total (16 Tacoma)					.252	—	—	31	103	15	26	5	1	2	13	9	2	4	3	14	2	1	.379	.316
Young, Chris	R-R	6-2	200	9-5-83	.370	.412	.351	13	54	17	20	5	1	3	9	9	0	0	0	13	2	2	.667	.460

Pitching	B-T	HT	WT	DOB	W	L	ERA	G	GS	CG	SV	IP	H	R	ER	HR	BB	SO	AVG	vLH	vRH	K/9	BB/9
Ambriz, Hector	L-R	6-2	235	5-24-84	9	9	5.57	23	22	0	0	128	164	88	79	12	40	103	.312	.313	.312	7.26	2.82
Augenstein, Bryan	R-R	6-6	230	7-11-86	2	5	5.50	8	7	0	0	36	43	23	22	2	7	29	.299	.300	.298	7.25	1.75
Barnette, Tony	R-R	6-1	190	11-9-83	14	8	5.79	29	29	0	0	165	185	107	106	24	62	121	.285	.281	.289	6.61	3.39
Blackley, Travis	L-L	6-3	200	11-4-82	4	7	4.85	38	12	0	3	111	133	65	60	11	38	101	.296	.264	.309	8.16	3.07
Buckner, Billy	R-R	6-2	215	8-27-83	9	3	3.32	18	16	1	0	103	91	41	38	5	45	96	.239	.251	.228	8.39	3.93
Cabrera, Daniel	R-R	6-9	260	5-28-81	0	1	6.14	4	4	0	0	15	15	10	10	1	10	11	.283	.368	.235	6.75	6.14
Coutlangus, Jon	L-L	6-1	185	10-21-80	1	0	6.52	21	0	0	1	29	41	23	21	2	15	18	.339	.385	.326	5.59	4.66
Dohmann, Scott	R-R	6-1	200	2-13-78	0	1	6.75	14	0	0	4	19	22	14	14	2	5	13	.289	.273	.302	6.27	2.41
Ellis, Josh	R-R	6-1	190	8-7-84	3	1	7.91	15	0	0	0	19	28	17	17	1	6	19	.329	.294	.353	8.84	2.79
Etherton, Seth	R-R	6-1	195	10-17-76	11	8	5.04	28	26	0	0	161	189	96	90	27	40	118	.300	.318	.286	6.61	2.24
Gordon, Tom	R-R	5-10	200	11-18-67	0	0	11.77	11	1	0	0	10	19	14	12	0	14	4	.452	.588	.360	3.72	13.03
Korecky, Bobby	R-R	5-11	185	9-16-79	2	1	2.10	27	0	0	13	30	26	9	7	1	3	25	.232	.167	.271	7.50	0.90
MacLane, Evan	L-L	6-2	185	11-4-82	0	2	6.75	3	2	0	0	15	23	11	11	0	4	3	.365	.375	.364	1.84	2.45
2-team total (24 Memphis)					8	11	4.02	27	26	0	0	166	194	84	74	23	24	95	—	—	—	5.16	1.30
Mahon, Reid	R-R	6-3	215	6-1-83	1	2	6.63	14	0	0	2	19	25	14	14	2	7	14	.313	.303	.319	6.63	3.32
Maine, Scott	L-L	6-3	195	2-2-85	1	2	3.68	12	0	0	2	15	13	7	6	0	7	15	.228	.250	.216	9.20	4.30
Marte, Jose	R-R	6-6	215	9-4-83	4	1	4.52	47	0	0	2	72	68	37	36	3	34	63	.253	.263	.245	7.91	4.27
Petit, Yusmeiro	R-R	6-1	255	11-22-84	1	0	6.89	5	5	0	0	16	21	13	12	4	5	13	.318	.355	.286	7.47	2.87
Rosales, Leo	R-R	6-1	205	5-28-81	2	1	1.40	17	0	0	3	19	12	3	3	1	8	12	.182	.185	.179	5.59	3.72
Schlereth, Daniel	L-L	6-0	210	5-9-86	0	0	0.00	1	0	0	0	1	1	0	0	0	1	1	.250	.500	.000	9.00	9.00
Slaten, Doug	L-L	6-5	215	2-4-80	3	2	3.09	39	0	0	9	44	41	17	15	3	15	40	.247	.197	.276	8.24	3.09
Spottiswood, Billy	R-R	6-3	208	4-24-85	1	0	4.28	17	0	0	0	27	22	15	13	4	11	16	.216	.225	.210	5.27	3.62
Urquidez, Jason	R-R	6-0	175	9-12-82	4	1	4.53	38	0	0	1	48	42	24	24	3	19	35	.244	.221	.263	6.61	3.59

Valdez, Cesar	R-R	6-2	200	3-17-85	7	6	4.78	19	18	0	0	96	103	58	51	16	30	60	.272	.294	.254	5.63	2.81
Vasquez, Esmerling	R-R	6-1	175	11-7-83	0	0	0.93	6	0	0	1	10	7	2	1	0	3	9	.200	.357	.095	8.38	2.79
Woody, Abe	R-R	5-11	200	11-9-82	1	2	7.67	38	1	0	0	59	78	52	50	9	33	21	.333	.284	.363	3.22	5.06

Fielding

Catcher	PCT	G	PO	A	E	DP	PB
Carlin	1.000	60	392	37	0	3	5
Hester	.989	79	475	59	6	7	5
Mercado	.982	8	50	4	1	1	1
Schmidt	1.000	4	35	1	0	0	0
Snyder	1.000	3	18	0	0	0	1

First Base	PCT	G	PO	A	E	DP
Allen	.991	35	321	22	3	30
Byrne	.990	29	182	22	2	20
Carlin	.974	11	67	8	2	7
Clark	1.000	3	23	2	0	3
Hester	1.000	1	4	0	0	0
Murillo	1.000	16	105	9	0	16
Tracy	1.000	3	17	3	0	2
Whitesell	.992	57	461	56	4	51

Second Base	PCT	G	PO	A	E	DP
Gotay	.961	41	84	88	7	22

	PCT	G	PO	A	E	DP
Harbin	.913	6	7	14	2	5
Nunez	.987	31	51	102	2	21
Reyes	1.000	12	9	11	0	4
Roberts	.980	9	19	29	1	9
Rogers	1.000	1	2	2	0	0
Ryal	.982	59	105	161	5	45

Third Base	PCT	G	PO	A	E	DP
Byrne	.800	3	3	1	1	0
Gotay	.913	67	26	120	14	13
Greene	—	1	0	0	0	0
Murillo	.966	49	32	81	4	8
Nunez	1.000	5	4	7	0	1
Ryal	.905	32	20	56	8	2
Tracy	1.000	3	1	4	0	0

Shortstop	PCT	G	PO	A	E	DP
Drew	.900	2	2	7	1	1
Harbin	1.000	1	3	2	0	2

Murillo	1.000	1	0	2	0	0
Nunez	.966	47	64	132	7	32
Reyes	.976	15	18	22	1	8
Roberts	.667	1	1	1	1	1
Rogers	.972	68	98	175	8	46
Ryal	.950	10	13	25	2	9
Wilson	.895	15	20	48	8	9

Outfield	PCT	G	PO	A	E	DP
Byrnes	.957	12	22	0	1	0
Gillespie	.987	39	76	1	1	0
Oeltjen	.986	102	196	9	3	1
Roberson	.982	112	269	9	5	3
Romero	.975	64	153	3	4	2
Ryal	1.000	3	6	0	0	0
Watson	.986	110	198	12	3	2
Young	1.000	12	23	1	0	1

MOBILE BAYBEARS

DOUBLE-A

SOUTHERN LEAGUE

Batting	B-T	HT	WT	DOB	AVG	vLH	vRH	G	AB	R	H	2B	3B	HR	RBI	BB	HBP	SH	SF	SO	SB	CS	SLG	OBP
Bordes, Greg	R-R	5-9	160	6-3-85	.171	.200	.150	18	35	7	6	0	0	0	1	11	2	0	0	8	0	0	.171	.396
Byrne, Bryan	L-R	6-3	200	4-30-84	.272	.295	.267	84	276	43	75	17	1	2	40	51	9	0	5	53	1	2	.362	.396
Ciriaco, Pedro	R-R	6-0	160	9-27-85	.296	.286	.300	121	469	56	139	15	3	4	54	16	2	5	5	71	38	10	.367	.319
Clifford, Pete	L-R	6-0	190	12-20-83	.236	.136	.262	105	280	26	66	12	0	4	32	22	2	2	3	49	5	2	.321	.293
Coughlin, Sean	L-R	6-1	215	5-14-85	.304	.333	.295	50	161	24	49	8	0	7	20	35	2	0	1	19	0	0	.484	.432
Davis, Chris	R-R	6-0	200	9-22-86	.200	.200	.200	3	10	0	2	0	0	0	1	0	0	0	0	3	0	1	.200	.200
Frey, Evan	L-L	6-0	170	6-7-86	.267	.262	.268	134	506	62	135	21	6	1	52	58	7	3	3	78	31	14	.338	.348
Hallberg, Mark	R-R	5-11	170	12-9-85	.257	.231	.266	132	455	51	117	22	1	2	42	39	8	5	3	43	14	4	.323	.325
Hankerd, Cyle	R-R	6-3	215	1-24-85	.266	.284	.259	132	440	57	117	33	1	7	67	41	17	1	11	80	1	5	.393	.344
Mercado, Orlando	R-R	5-9	210	3-13-85	.294	.377	.260	71	238	26	70	14	1	2	36	33	1	0	2	25	0	0	.387	.380
Parra, Gerardo	L-L	5-11	195	5-6-87	.361	.290	.390	29	108	23	39	3	1	3	12	22	0	0	0	13	7	4	.491	.469
Rahl, Chris	R-R	5-10	185	12-5-83	.280	.266	.286	124	435	72	122	22	9	5	48	36	3	0	5	104	20	7	.407	.333
Reyes, Guillermo	B-R	5-9	177	12-29-81	.091	.000	.111	7	11	2	1	0	0	0	2	1	0	0	1	3	1	1	.091	.154
Rumler, Eli	R-R	5-8	185	12-30-84	.132	.222	.103	15	38	5	5	2	0	0	5	1	0	1	1	7	1	0	.184	.150
Sanchez, Yunesky	B-R	6-2	212	5-3-84	.286	.196	.291	64	199	27	57	3	2	2	18	14	0	0	0	26	3	4	.352	.315
Skelton, James	L-R	5-11	165	10-28-85	.182	.151	.193	68	214	34	39	8	2	0	16	52	0	6	1	40	9	3	.238	.341
Sosa, Ricardo	R-R	6-1	200	5-24-84	.260	.298	.245	123	443	61	115	25	0	12	71	38	9	1	4	81	3	1	.397	.328
Tupman, Matt	L-R	5-11	185	11-25-79	.254	.200	.264	38	126	10	32	4	1	1	19	11	0	1	4	15	0	0	.325	.305

Pitching	B-T	HT	WT	DOB	W	L	ERA	G	GS	CG	SV	IP	H	R	ER	HR	BB	SO	AVG	vLH	vRH	K/9	BB/9
Ambriz, Hector	L-R	6-2	235	5-24-84	3	2	2.17	5	5	0	0	29	18	7	7	1	6	32	.180	.217	.148	9.93	1.86
Augenstein, Bryan	R-R	6-6	230	7-11-86	5	0	0.99	9	9	0	0	46	27	5	5	0	8	36	.172	.221	.135	7.09	1.58
Bongiovanni, Vince	R-R	6-5	215	1-11-83	2	0	6.00	5	0	0	0	9	9	6	6	1	3	6	.265	.250	.273	6.00	3.00
Christianson, Chase	R-R	6-5	220	12-11-84	1	0	3.00	4	0	0	0	9	6	3	3	2	8	4	.194	.300	.143	4.00	8.00
Dietz, Jeff	R-R	6-3	215	1-28-86	0	0	9.45	4	0	0	0	7	9	9	7	1	5	7	.333	.636	.125	9.45	6.75
Ellis, Josh	R-R	6-1	190	8-7-84	4	2	1.94	25	0	0	1	42	30	12	9	1	14	48	.197	.278	.153	10.37	3.02
Enright, Barry	R-R	6-3	220	3-30-86	10	9	3.98	27	27	0	0	156	171	73	69	16	37	103	.284	.293	.278	5.94	2.13
Evans, Cody	R-R	6-5	190	9-3-83	5	11	5.40	28	24	0	0	137	159	94	82	24	47	54	.293	.276	.305	3.56	3.10
Layne, Tom	L-L	6-3	185	11-2-84	0	3	4.94	6	6	0	0	31	27	21	17	0	19	24	.229	.143	.265	6.97	5.52
Mahon, Reid	R-R	6-3	215	6-1-83	5	2	3.41	23	0	0	3	32	35	16	12	0	10	21	.278	.288	.270	5.97	2.84
Maine, Scott	L-L	6-3	195	2-2-85	3	3	2.66	36	0	0	5	47	56	16	14	2	15	46	.298	.348	.270	8.75	2.85
Mercedes, Roque	R-R	6-3	185	9-28-86	1	0	3.32	15	0	0	1	19	14	7	7	2	10	25	.200	.250	.158	11.84	4.74
Newby, Kyler	R-R	6-4	225	2-22-85	2	3	3.99	42	2	0	4	65	67	34	29	10	24	48	.265	.235	.285	6.61	3.31
Norberto, Jordan	L-L	6-0	195	12-8-86	0	2	7.99	19	0	0	2	24	29	23	21	4	18	30	.302	.219	.344	11.41	6.85
Parker, Jarrod	R-R	6-1	180	11-24-88	4	4	3.68	16	16	0	0	78	82	35	32	2	34	74	.272	.278	.267	8.50	3.91
Roemer, Wes	R-R	6-0	205	10-7-86	9	9	4.28	22	22	1	0	135	132	71	64	13	43	98	.260	.257	.263	6.55	2.87
Sanchez, Ramon	R-R	6-2	212	6-6-84	0	1	3.48	17	0	0	0	21	19	11	8	2	25	17	.241	.167	.273	7.40	10.89
Schlereth, Daniel	L-L	6-0	210	5-9-86	0	0	1.01	21	0	0	4	27	14	3	3	1	16	39	.161	.222	.133	13.16	5.40
Septimo, Leyson	L-L	6-0	150	7-7-85	0	1	7.85	19	0	0	3	18	20	17	16	2	18	25	.278	.321	.250	12.27	8.84
Stange, Daniel	R-R	6-3	185	12-22-85	0	4	4.88	39	0	0	10	52	66	35	28	4	15	44	.316	.316	.316	7.66	2.61
Summers, Houston	R-R	5-10	180	8-20-87	0	1	7.20	1	1	0	0	5	5	4	4	1	4	3	.278	.375	.200	5.40	7.20
Torra, Matt	R-R	6-3	225	6-24-84	10	13	3.75	28	28	4	0	180	192	91	75	24	28	116	.276	.266	.284	5.80	1.40
Urquidez, Jason	R-R	6-0	175	9-12-82	1	0	3.15	12	0	0	1	20	13	7	7	0	6	20	.181	.167	.194	9.00	2.70
Woody, Abe	R-R	5-11	200	11-9-82	0	1	2.84	5	0	0	0	6	8	2	2	0	3	5	.308	.214	.417	7.11	4.26
Zavada, Clay	L-L	6-1	195	6-28-84	1	0	2.60	11	0	0	0	17	10	5	5	2	7	18	.169	.125	.186	9.35	3.63

Fielding

Catcher	PCT	G	PO	A	E	DP	PB
Coughlin	.988	14	81	4	1	0	2
Davis	1.000	3	17	0	0	0	0
Mercado	.981	50	335	34	7	5	5
Skelton	.964	47	304	19	12	2	4
Tupman	1.000	32	238	14	0	3	2

First Base	PCT	G	PO	A	E	DP
Byrne	.995	74	571	43	3	51
Clifford	.973	22	131	12	4	11
Coughlin	.985	31	247	20	4	24
Mercado	.985	14	113	15	2	12
Sanchez	.990	12	86	11	1	11

Second Base	PCT	G	PO	A	E	DP
Bordes	.985	14	30	35	1	8
Ciriaco	.989	23	35	53	1	9
Hallberg	.993	69	118	180	2	41
Reyes	1.000	2	2	6	0	0
Rumler	1.000	6	13	11	0	2
Sanchez	.966	18	35	49	3	10
Skelton	.965	19	28	54	3	11

Third Base	PCT	G	PO	A	E	DP
Byrne	.889	4	5	3	1	0
Hallberg	.936	18	12	32	3	1
Rumler	1.000	3	5	6	0	2

	PCT	G	PO	A	E	DP
Sanchez	1.000	18	5	30	0	1
Sosa	.922	108	66	169	20	15

Shortstop	PCT	G	PO	A	E	DP
Ciriaco	.960	93	145	242	16	54
Hallberg	.984	44	71	118	3	28
Sanchez	1.000	10	6	19	0	2

Outfield	PCT	G	PO	A	E	DP
Clifford	.988	54	79	3	1	0
Frey	.983	130	328	12	6	2
Hankerd	.972	117	197	15	6	5
Parra	.982	28	51	3	1	0
Rahl	.995	115	195	4	1	1

VISALIA RAWHIDE HIGH CLASS A
CALIFORNIA LEAGUE

Batting	B-T	HT	WT	DOB	AVG	vLH	vRH	G	AB	R	H	2B	3B	HR	RBI	BB	HBP	SH	SF	SO	SB	CS	SLG	OBP
Cooper, David	L-R	5-8	170	6-18-85	.226	.165	.265	76	248	34	56	2	1	0	26	39	3	6	0	54	16	6	.242	.338
Corniel, Jorge	R-R	5-8	180	1-4-88	.267	.200	.300	5	15	2	4	1	0	0	0	0	0	0	0	5	0	0	.333	.267
Coughlin, Sean	L-R	6-1	215	5-14-85	.260	.233	.279	27	104	18	27	7	0	4	20	12	0	0	1	20	0	0	.442	.333
Cowgill, Collin	R-L	5-9	195	5-22-86	.277	.280	.275	61	220	39	61	9	5	6	36	29	7	0	4	49	11	4	.445	.373
Duffy, Brendan	L-L	6-1	185	5-16-85	.279	.196	.313	53	179	28	50	5	2	0	13	22	8	0	0	37	6	3	.330	.383
Easley, Ed	R-R	6-0	200	12-21-85	.228	.222	.231	106	378	50	86	18	1	3	38	48	7	5	2	86	0	1	.304	.324
Ferrer, Manuel	R-R	5-9	201	2-15-85	.127	.103	.138	40	126	5	16	2	0	1	10	12	0	2	1	48	1	1	.167	.201
Fie, Andrew	R-R	6-3	205	10-25-87	.207	.195	.217	45	174	14	36	12	0	1	18	11	0	1	1	62	0	0	.293	.253
Gomez, Nelson	R-R	6-1	210	10-21-86	.192	.143	.211	8	26	1	5	1	0	0	3	4	1	0	0	8	0	0	.231	.323
Greene, Kyle	L-R	6-2	200	5-26-86	.237	.212	.253	125	460	53	109	25	3	11	77	44	10	0	6	149	0	2	.376	.313
Harbin, Taylor	R-R	5-9	175	2-13-86	.259	.278	.247	127	529	70	137	27	3	14	60	26	10	5	3	91	12	7	.401	.305
Jackson, Conor	R-R	6-2	215	5-7-82	.000	.000	.000	3	10	1	0	0	0	0	1	1	0	0	0	1	0	0	.000	.091
Linton, Ollie	L-L	5-8	160	4-7-86	.295	.245	.329	128	491	81	145	28	10	1	51	65	18	4	4	104	28	14	.399	.394
Pimentel, Jhoan	R-R	5-10	195	7-13-89	.444	.500	.400	3	9	1	4	1	0	0	2	0	0	0	0	2	0	0	.556	.444
Ramirez, Ramon	B-R	6-2	170	2-22-86	.342	.333	.345	9	38	4	13	5	0	0	4	0	0	1	0	7	0	0	.474	.342
Rodriguez, Daniel	R-R	6-2	195	1-20-87	.145	.050	.200	22	55	6	8	3	0	0	5	7	2	0	0	25	1	0	.200	.266
Rumler, Eli	R-R	5-8	185	12-30-84	.205	.242	.176	75	268	29	55	12	0	3	20	18	14	5	1	41	3	4	.284	.289
Schmidt, Konrad	R-R	6-0	225	8-2-84	.304	.282	.318	106	411	54	125	28	1	9	50	30	7	0	3	75	0	3	.443	.359
Skelton, James	L-R	5-11	165	10-28-85	.236	.171	.284	51	178	28	42	8	0	4	26	34	2	6	3	51	5	2	.348	.359
Snyder, Chris	R-R	6-4	245	2-12-81	.143	.000	.167	3	7	1	1	0	0	0	0	3	1	0	0	3	0	0	.143	.455
Thomson, Greg	L-L	6-1	205	6-13-84	.220	.237	.210	51	159	25	35	14	0	4	18	9	10	0	1	34	1	1	.384	.302
Upton, Justin	R-R	6-2	205	8-25-87	.250	—	.250	2	8	1	2	0	0	1	6	1	0	0	0	3	1	0	.625	.333
Walker, Derrick	R-R	6-4	215	10-10-85	.200	.198	.202	62	210	22	42	5	0	0	18	25	1	0	1	66	12	7	.224	.287
White, Ryne	L-L	5-11	205	10-17-86	.266	.212	.298	116	418	62	111	18	1	6	52	65	6	0	2	87	3	3	.356	.371

Pitching	B-T	HT	WT	DOB	W	L	ERA	G	GS	CG	SV	IP	H	R	ER	HR	BB	SO	AVG	vLH	vRH	K/9	BB/9
Beltre, Cristian	R-R	6-1	195	5-10-85	6	11	6.37	26	24	0	0	123	156	99	87	17	43	81	.310	.357	.276	5.93	3.15
Capellan, Victor	R-R	6-2	195	7-24-89	0	0	9.53	5	0	0	0	6	12	6	6	1	3	6	.429	.500	.409	9.53	4.76
Christianson, Chase	R-R	6-5	220	12-11-84	1	4	6.44	37	0	0	3	64	80	49	46	7	30	46	.319	.339	.303	6.44	4.20
Collmenter, Josh	R-R	6-4	235	2-7-86	8	10	4.15	27	27	1	0	145	127	76	67	8	55	152	.238	.227	.247	9.41	3.41
Dietz, Jeff	R-R	6-3	215	1-28-86	4	7	3.14	40	0	0	6	66	57	32	23	5	17	71	.224	.200	.239	9.68	2.32
Elliott, Matt	R-R	5-11	200	4-6-84	2	2	4.50	18	0	0	2	26	28	13	13	2	12	29	.275	.286	.267	10.04	4.15
Gordon, Tom	R-R	5-10	200	11-18-67	0	0	9.00	1	0	0	0	1	1	1	1	0	2	1	.250	.000	.500	9.00	18.00
Harden, Trevor	B-R	6-2	215	9-1-87	2	9	4.43	17	17	0	0	91	115	61	45	11	23	63	.304	.254	.344	6.21	2.27
Henry, Bryan	R-R	6-3	205	2-15-85	5	5	3.15	38	7	0	0	106	111	46	37	7	21	90	.266	.265	.271	7.67	1.79
Hose, T.J.	R-R	5-10	185	4-15-86	0	0	2.78	15	0	0	1	23	22	8	7	1	5	27	.262	.243	.277	10.72	1.99
Layne, Tom	L-L	6-3	185	11-2-84	4	2	2.86	29	4	0	0	66	63	27	21	1	25	43	.254	.130	.302	5.86	3.41
McAnaney, Pat	R-L	6-3	185	3-11-86	10	8	4.41	28	28	0	0	147	162	81	72	19	47	146	.285	.270	.290	8.94	2.88
Miley, Wade	L-L	6-2	190	11-13-86	1	1	4.80	3	0	0	0	15	18	10	8	0	4	11	.295	.190	.350	6.60	2.40
Norberto, Jordan	L-L	6-0	195	12-8-86	4	1	1.61	29	0	0	2	45	36	9	8	1	22	59	.226	.180	.248	11.89	4.43
Parker, Jarrod	R-R	6-1	180	11-24-88	1	0	0.95	4	4	0	0	19	12	2	2	0	4	21	.179	.172	.184	9.95	1.89
Perez, Jorge	R-R	5-11	167	1-16-86	3	2	4.14	44	0	0	5	67	65	31	31	10	18	84	.258	.230	.281	11.23	2.41
Rodriguez, Pira	R-R	6-0	190	6-20-89	0	1	14.40	5	0	0	0	5	7	8	8	1	4	2	.333	.333	.333	3.60	7.20
Roemer, Wes	R-R	6-0	205	10-7-86	3	1	2.05	6	6	0	0	31	33	14	7	0	13	18	.282	.269	.300	5.28	3.82
Sanchez, Ramon	R-R	6-2	212	6-6-84	0	0	6.97	9	0	0	0	10	13	11	8	1	10	15	.295	.286	.304	13.06	8.71
Scherzer, Max	R-R	6-3	215	7-27-84	0	0	1.93	1	1	0	0	5	1	2	1	0	4	5	.067	.143	.000	9.64	7.71
Septimo, Leyson	L-L	6-0	150	7-7-85	2	1	3.52	26	0	0	6	38	29	18	15	1	26	44	.212	.222	.207	10.33	6.10
Shaw, Bryan	B-R	6-1	210	11-8-87	3	7	4.70	30	19	0	0	107	96	65	56	7	40	95	.236	.265	.212	7.97	3.35
Spottiswood, Billy	R-R	6-3	208	4-24-85	5	4	4.54	27	0	0	8	40	46	22	20	3	9	29	.301	.354	.261	6.58	2.04

Fielding

Catcher	PCT	G	PO	A	E	DP	PB
Corniel	.973	5	35	1	1	0	2
Coughlin	1.000	5	32	6	0	0	0
Easley	.994	53	434	42	3	4	8
Pimentel	1.000	3	15	3	0	0	0

	PCT	G	PO	A	E	DP	PB
Schmidt	.979	67	512	54	12	6	11
Skelton	.974	13	106	5	3	1	0
Snyder	1.000	1	5	0	0	0	0

First Base	PCT	G	PO	A	E	DP
Coughlin	1.000	8	67	4	0	7

	PCT	G	PO	A	E	DP
Easley	.995	23	188	15	1	23
Fie	.982	7	51	3	1	5
Gomez	1.000	3	17	4	0	2
Greene	.993	17	125	12	1	14
Ramirez	.981	6	50	3	1	3

Rodriguez	—	1	0	0	0	0
Schmidt	.932	5	37	4	3	4
White	.992	78	596	58	5	72

Second Base	PCT	G	PO	A	E	DP
Cooper	.946	46	93	119	12	36
Ferrer	.991	24	42	65	1	19
Harbin	.983	25	48	65	2	19
Rumler	.959	34	58	106	7	26
Skelton	.975	19	31	47	2	9

Third Base	PCT	G	PO	A	E	DP
Easley	.889	11	8	16	3	3
Ferrer	1.000	13	6	28	0	2

Fie	.929	13	5	34	3	4
Greene	.916	95	65	154	20	18
Harbin	.833	4	2	8	2	1
Ramirez	.857	3	3	3	1	0
Rumler	.857	4	3	3	1	0

Shortstop	PCT	G	PO	A	E	DP
Cooper	.937	31	43	75	8	16
Harbin	.952	96	135	245	19	67
Rumler	.945	15	29	40	4	11

Outfield	PCT	G	PO	A	E	DP
Cowgill	.953	56	116	7	6	2
Duffy	.962	50	66	9	3	1

Fie	.969	19	28	3	1	0
Jackson	1.000	1	1	0	0	0
Linton	.996	125	264	11	1	1
Rodriguez	.917	14	21	1	2	0
Rumler	1.000	21	28	2	0	0
Skelton	.971	17	29	5	1	1
Thomson	.958	47	90	1	4	1
Upton	—	1	0	0	0	0
Walker	.968	57	118	4	4	0
White	.975	28	39	0	1	0

SOUTH BEND SILVER HAWKS

LOW CLASS A

MIDWEST LEAGUE

Batting	B-T	HT	WT	DOB	AVG	vLH	vRH	G	AB	R	H	2B	3B	HR	RBI	BB	HBP	SH	SF	SO	SB	CS	SLG	OBP
Asencio, Isaias	R-R	6-0	169	12-31-87	.211	.244	.201	99	332	31	70	22	3	5	32	17	9	4	3	101	6	3	.340	.266
Babineau, Ryan	R-R	6-2	205	12-13-86	.125	.000	.174	10	32	4	4	2	1	0	1	7	0	0	0	13	0	0	.250	.282
Conner, Clayton	R-R	6-3	210	10-8-86	.220	.143	.234	24	91	11	20	5	0	1	9	4	2	0	0	24	1	0	.308	.268
Davis, Chris	R-R	6-0	200	9-22-86	.173	.211	.153	52	168	23	29	10	0	4	17	12	7	0	3	40	2	0	.304	.253
Diaz, Alberto	R-R	6-1	180	9-3-88	.232	.284	.217	119	436	43	101	15	0	8	44	28	7	0	1	109	3	1	.321	.288
Duffy, Brendan	L-L	6-1	180	5-16-85	.308	.190	.340	54	201	37	62	7	5	0	15	25	12	2	1	42	17	8	.393	.414
Elmore, Jake	R-R	5-10	180	6-15-87	.258	.253	.260	117	387	62	100	21	3	3	38	61	5	2	2	55	13	7	.351	.365
Estevez, Victor	R-R	5-11	183	9-8-88	.261	.238	.269	100	329	47	86	15	1	2	23	21	13	4	1	88	5	6	.331	.330
Gomez, Nelson	R-R	6-1	210	10-21-86	.218	.198	.225	95	325	27	71	24	1	2	31	20	7	0	2	69	0	2	.317	.277
Krauss, Marc	L-R	6-3	235	10-5-87	.304	.294	.306	32	115	14	35	12	1	2	17	14	0	0	1	21	0	1	.478	.377
Marte, Alfredo	R-R	6-1	170	3-31-89	.251	.255	.249	120	475	49	119	27	3	7	71	25	4	2	0	78	5	2	.364	.294
Navarro, Reynaldo	B-R	5-10	175	12-22-89	.262	.286	.256	121	451	57	118	25	5	0	46	27	5	6	4	85	12	4	.339	.308
Parker, Justin	R-R	6-1	205	3-14-87	.252	.250	.252	91	322	46	81	23	2	4	45	49	2	0	5	77	0	2	.373	.349
Perez, Rossmel	B-R	5-10	180	8-26-89	.272	.224	.280	97	353	29	96	16	0	0	35	30	9	1	2	31	1	0	.337	.343
Pollock, A.J.	R-R	6-2	200	12-5-87	.271	.319	.260	63	255	36	69	12	3	3	22	16	3	1	2	36	10	4	.376	.319
Ramirez, Ramon	B-R	6-2	170	2-22-86	.225	.179	.236	56	187	14	42	6	3	1	23	7	1	1	2	38	0	0	.305	.254
Van Winkle, Tyson	R-R	6-1	190	2-2-88	.059	.000	.091	6	17	0	1	0	0	0	1	1	0	0	0	2	0	0	.059	.111
Wheeler, Ryan	L-R	6-4	220	7-10-88	.345	.333	.346	8	29	4	10	1	1	1	5	5	2	0	0	4	0	1	.552	.472

Pitching	B-T	HT	WT	DOB	W	L	ERA	G	GS	CG	SV	IP	H	R	ER	HR	BB	SO	AVG	vLH	vRH	K/9	BB/9
Capellan, Victor	R-R	6-2	195	7-24-89	0	2	1.01	21	0	0	2	36	17	7	4	1	10	37	.138	.114	.152	9.34	2.52
Cook, Ryan	R-R	6-3	200	6-30-87	11	11	3.66	25	25	0	0	143	140	71	58	5	44	103	.265	.302	.234	6.50	2.78
Harden, Trevor	B-R	6-2	215	9-1-87	5	1	2.39	6	6	1	0	38	28	10	10	3	7	31	.207	.231	.198	7.41	1.67
Hose, T.J.	R-R	5-10	185	4-15-86	3	2	1.70	27	0	0	11	37	24	15	7	1	12	43	.176	.164	.185	10.46	2.92
Mace, Justin	L-R	6-3	205	3-11-86	3	2	1.90	40	0	0	12	52	40	17	11	3	12	44	.212	.247	.188	7.62	2.08
Meaker, Jordan	R-R	6-6	220	9-22-86	4	1	5.67	29	3	0	0	60	69	44	38	4	37	40	.289	.245	.321	5.97	5.52
Miley, Wade	L-L	6-2	190	11-13-86	5	9	4.12	21	21	0	0	114	127	60	52	8	29	115	.283	.263	.294	7.21	2.30
Moorhouse, Brett	R-R	6-2	190	6-28-87	5	14	4.52	25	25	0	0	131	148	78	66	9	42	84	.288	.317	.268	5.76	2.88
Morgan, Sean	R-R	6-3	215	1-15-86	2	2	4.19	23	7	0	0	58	58	35	27	5	25	50	.261	.247	.271	7.76	3.88
Ortega, Yonata	R-R	6-1	200	11-11-86	0	2	6.87	30	0	0	1	38	49	31	29	2	24	38	.308	.360	.262	9.00	5.68
Quezada, Rafael	R-R	6-3	180	11-21-86	0	3	9.45	4	3	0	0	13	18	16	14	3	7	8	.310	.167	.412	5.40	4.72
Rodriguez, Randy	R-R	5-11	170	1-6-88	5	11	5.67	21	21	0	0	113	144	84	71	10	23	48	.314	.395	.251	3.83	1.84
Sinclair, Taylor	L-L	6-3	180	12-23-85	3	5	3.22	21	15	0	1	89	85	35	32	5	30	72	.257	.179	.293	7.25	3.02
Smith, Eric	R-R	6-3	215	10-15-88	0	0	2.76	3	3	0	0	16	16	7	5	2	6	10	.250	.278	.224	5.51	3.31
Sosa, Keny	L-L	6-0	167	3-26-87	2	3	2.19	7	7	0	0	37	27	12	9	4	12	30	.209	.175	.225	7.30	2.92
Summers, Houston	R-R	5-10	180	8-20-87	0	0	17.18	2	0	0	0	4	5	7	7	1	4	5	.333	.167	.444	12.27	9.82
Vasquez, Daniel	R-R	6-0	195	3-4-86	4	1	4.57	29	1	0	1	69	72	41	35	5	19	55	.258	.253	.271	7.17	2.48
Wilson, Brad	R-R	6-1	185	5-26-87	0	0	0.00	1	0	0	0	4	2	0	0	0	1	1	.143	.000	.167	2.08	2.08
Woodall, Bryan	R-R	6-1	200	10-24-86	4	5	3.24	36	0	0	2	67	73	32	24	2	17	73	.273	.306	.252	9.85	2.30
Zepeda, Bayron	L-L	5-10	185	8-29-87	3	4	4.58	37	0	0	1	53	64	30	27	0	12	43	.311	.299	.318	7.30	2.04

Fielding

Catcher	PCT	G	PO	A	E	DP	PB
Babineau	1.000	10	53	11	0	0	0
Davis	.987	50	335	38	5	5	9
Perez	.982	75	522	69	11	6	9
Van Winkle	1.000	6	25	6	0	0	1

First Base	PCT	G	PO	A	E	DP
Conner	.975	14	109	10	3	9
Gomez	.985	79	659	43	11	66
Ramirez	.982	42	357	21	7	37
Wheeler	1.000	8	67	2	0	2

Second Base	PCT	G	PO	A	E	DP
Elmore	.980	108	193	308	10	64
Estevez	.956	30	49	82	6	17

Third Base	PCT	G	PO	A	E	DP
Estevez	.953	46	20	102	6	8
Gomez	.833	12	9	16	5	1
Parker	.887	73	53	136	24	11
Ramirez	.913	8	3	18	2	2

Shortstop	PCT	G	PO	A	E	DP
Elmore	.929	4	5	8	1	5

	PCT	G	PO	A	E	DP
Estevez	.943	15	28	55	5	7
Navarro	.949	118	180	360	29	75

Outfield	PCT	G	PO	A	E	DP
Asencio	.977	92	160	7	4	1
Diaz	.978	111	211	8	5	2
Duffy	.987	43	73	4	1	0
Estevez	1.000	1	2	0	0	0
Gomez	—	1	0	0	0	0
Krauss	.974	23	34	3	1	1
Marte	.961	82	140	7	6	0
Pollock	.994	62	166	5	1	1

ARIZONA DIAMONDBACKS

Batting	B-T	HT	WT	DOB	AVG	vLH	vRH	G	AB	R	H	2B	3B	HR	RBI	BB	HBP	SH	SF	SO	SB	CS	SLG	OBP
Aguila, Roidany	R-R	5-10	175	10-22-90	.119	.100	.125	21	42	1	5	1	0	0	5	1	1	1	1	13	0	0	.143	.156
Button, Evan	R-L	6-0	195	9-5-86	.143	.000	.154	5	14	0	2	0	0	0	0	0	1	0	0	3	0	0	.143	.200
Canelo, Adonys	B-R	5-11	165	1-23-89	.208	.167	.222	11	24	0	5	1	1	0	3	2	0	0	0	8	2	0	.333	.269
Conner, Clayton	R-R	6-3	210	10-8-86	.259	.167	.283	45	174	22	45	10	0	9	39	14	5	0	1	45	8	3	.471	.330
Corniel, Jorge	R-R	5-8	180	1-4-88	.269	.346	.244	40	108	8	29	6	0	0	13	8	0	1	1	18	0	0	.324	.316
Davidson, Matt	R-R	6-3	210	3-26-91	.241	.277	.229	72	270	29	65	15	0	2	28	21	7	1	0	75	0	2	.319	.312
Fie, Andrew	R-R	6-3	205	10-25-87	.273	.333	.231	11	22	3	6	1	0	1	5	3	0	0	0	12	3	0	.455	.360
Greer, Brent	R-R	6-0	185	10-16-87	.300	.246	.316	69	273	38	82	12	2	7	31	14	10	8	0	66	5	4	.436	.357
Helm, Matt	R-R	6-2	190	9-1-90	.291	.231	.310	16	55	6	16	1	0	1	5	4	0	0	0	16	2	0	.364	.339
Inciarte, Astolfo	L-L	5-8	170	2-9-88	.222	.222	.222	57	153	16	34	5	1	1	8	20	0	1	1	23	3	2	.288	.310
Kaczrowski, Dan	R-R	5-9	170	6-17-87	.266	.250	.271	71	274	43	73	16	1	1	20	28	6	4	2	42	12	3	.343	.345
Montilla, Gerson	R-R	5-10	168	11-13-89	.220	.205	.224	66	227	27	50	7	2	5	24	17	2	2	2	42	5	8	.335	.278
Pimentel, Jhoan	R-R	5-10	195	7-13-89	.250	.500	.167	4	8	1	2	0	0	0	1	0	0	0	0	2	0	0	.250	.333
Rodriguez, Roberto	L-L	6-0	156	3-22-89	.162	.158	.163	58	142	14	23	5	1	0	11	12	2	1	0	48	13	1	.211	.236
Sherlock, Tim	L-L	5-11	175	11-30-86	.238	.150	.249	65	193	23	46	10	1	2	24	28	4	0	3	66	1	3	.332	.342
Van Winkle, Tyson	R-R	6-1	190	2-2-88	.244	.333	.217	51	156	14	38	10	0	0	14	25	6	0	1	35	4	2	.308	.367
Varnell, Zach	R-R	6-1	200	6-25-86	.108	.136	.067	29	37	7	4	1	0	0	4	8	0	0	0	20	1	0	.135	.267
Wheeler, Ryan	L-R	6-4	220	7-10-88	.363	.383	.358	64	234	44	85	20	3	5	36	37	7	0	2	28	7	4	.538	.461
Worthington, Tyrell	R-R	6-0	190	8-2-88	.204	.157	.222	65	186	26	38	10	0	1	16	13	2	2	0	62	8	4	.274	.264

Pitching	B-T	HT	WT	DOB	W	L	ERA	G	GS	CG	SV	IP	H	R	ER	HR	BB	SO	AVG	vLH	vRH	K/9	BB/9
Albert, Justin	L-L	6-3	235	5-27-87	0	1	7.00	18	0	0	0	18	21	15	14	1	6	20	.284	.279	.290	10.00	3.00
Brea, Ariel	L-L	5-10	155	5-14-89	0	2	8.84	15	0	0	0	18	25	20	18	0	14	12	.321	.282	.359	5.89	6.87
Budrow, Brian	R-R	6-3	215	11-12-86	3	3	2.38	22	0	0	6	34	30	9	9	0	12	28	.250	.245	.254	7.41	3.18
Dollar, Ben	R-R	6-4	225	9-19-86	0	3	5.94	17	3	0	0	33	51	22	22	2	8	18	.364	.338	.397	4.86	2.16
Gemberling, Brad	R-R	6-1	205	12-9-86	0	1	6.43	18	6	0	0	42	56	32	30	3	20	44	.326	.333	.318	9.43	4.29
Hale, Jake	R-R	6-7	200	12-11-85	2	1	5.29	12	0	0	0	17	19	10	10	2	6	14	.302	.280	.316	7.41	3.18
Hamrick, Randy	R-R	6-2	195	8-27-86	2	4	6.47	19	2	0	2	32	37	25	23	5	16	30	.291	.351	.243	8.44	4.50
Harvil, Will	R-R	6-5	220	6-17-87	2	2	3.34	21	0	0	1	32	27	12	12	3	19	25	.231	.261	.211	6.96	5.29
Odegaard, Chris	R-R	6-3	215	4-17-87	2	8	4.10	15	15	0	0	79	76	43	36	4	35	46	.261	.280	.247	5.24	3.99
Orosco Jr., Jesse	R-R	6-2	200	7-3-87	0	0	0.00	1	0	0	0	1	0	0	0	0	0	0	.333	.000	.500	0.00	0.00
Quezada, Rafael	R-R	6-3	180	11-21-86	0	7	6.13	17	13	0	0	62	79	57	42	4	42	40	.302	.294	.309	5.84	6.13
Rodriguez, Pira	R-R	6-0	190	6-20-89	2	3	5.61	20	0	0	0	26	41	24	16	2	9	17	.373	.341	.391	5.96	3.16
Summers, Houston	R-R	5-10	180	8-20-87	3	1	7.07	14	1	0	0	36	49	32	28	2	19	18	.343	.377	.303	4.54	4.79
Suss, Clayton	R-R	6-2	190	10-2-88	1	0	11.57	14	0	0	0	14	24	22	18	0	15	18	.375	.429	.333	11.57	9.64
Taveras, Ricardo	R-R	6-2	210	10-17-87	0	2	4.42	7	7	0	0	37	33	20	18	5	13	32	.248	.211	.263	7.85	3.19
Taylor, Dan	L-L	6-0	205	7-25-87	5	1	3.53	17	9	0	0	64	56	28	25	6	20	79	.231	.200	.243	11.17	2.83
Thieroff, Alex	R-R	6-2	210	10-6-86	1	0	3.04	21	0	0	2	27	24	12	9	1	10	22	.233	.152	.298	7.43	3.38
Wilson, Brad	R-R	6-1	185	5-26-87	2	3	5.65	18	5	0	1	37	28	27	23	2	27	39	.219	.203	.234	9.57	6.63
Wolcott, Andrew	R-R	6-5	245	9-8-87	3	5	4.87	14	14	0	0	65	77	39	35	6	14	29	.293	.252	.321	4.04	1.95

Fielding

Catcher	PCT	G	PO	A	E	DP	PB
Aguila	.986	17	63	7	1	1	3
Corniel	.976	32	176	28	5	4	3
Pimentel	1	5	0	0	0	0	0
Van Winkle	.993	39	238	44	2	1	6
Varnell	1.000	13	34	3	0	0	2

First Base	PCT	G	PO	A	E	DP
Conner	1.000	27	254	21	0	25
Helm	1.000	9	73	3	0	14
Inciarte	.857	3	6	0	1	1
Kaczrowski	1.000	2	4	0	0	1
Wheeler	.988	42	380	24	5	34

Second Base	PCT	G	PO	A	E	DP
Button	1.000	4	10	11	0	4
Canelo	1.000	1	1	5	0	2
Kaczrowski	.973	18	29	44	2	10
Montilla	.979	64	135	196	7	47

Third Base	PCT	G	PO	A	E	DP
Davidson	.934	67	37	148	13	14
Fie	1.000	1	3	0	1	0
Kaczrowski	.971	11	9	25	1	2

Shortstop	PCT	G	PO	A	E	DP
Canelo	.875	3	2	5	1	3
Greer	.941	68	90	182	17	37

Kaczrowski	1.000	11	19	39	0	11

Outfield	PCT	G	PO	A	E	DP
Button	—	1	0	0	0	0
Fie	1.000	7	6	1	0	0
Inciarte	1.000	45	48	0	0	0
Kaczrowski	.978	41	41	3	1	0
Rodriguez	.956	54	83	3	4	0
Sherlock	.950	62	73	3	4	0
Varnell	.875	9	7	0	1	0
Wheeler	1.000	3	2	1	0	0
Worthington	.960	61	141	3	6	2

MISSOULA OSPREY

ROOKIE

PIONEER LEAGUE

Batting	B-T	HT	WT	DOB	AVG	vLH	vRH	G	AB	R	H	2B	3B	HR	RBI	BB	HBP	SH	SF	SO	SB	CS	SLG	OBP
Aguila, Roidany	R-R	5-10	175	10-22-90	.000	.000	.000	6	13	0	0	0	0	0	0	0	0	0	0	6	0	0	.000	.000
Borchering, Bobby	B-R	6-4	195	10-25-90	.241	.211	.250	22	87	10	21	8	1	2	11	5	1	0	0	27	0	0	.425	.290
Broxton, Keon	R-R	6-3	187	5-7-90	.246	.277	.237	72	272	38	67	11	9	11	37	19	3	2	1	93	6	1	.474	.302
Canelo, Adonys	B-R	5-11	165	1-23-89	.235	.000	.267	20	34	8	8	1	1	1	3	1	0	1	0	10	2	1	.412	.257
Castillo, Ramon	R-R	5-11	190	9-6-88	.278	.316	.266	63	241	35	67	13	0	9	39	18	13	0	4	41	0	1	.444	.355
Goldschmidt, Paul	R-R	6-4	220	9-10-87	.334	.343	.332	74	287	51	96	27	3	18	62	36	3	0	5	74	4	3	.638	.408
Gomez, Raywilly	B-R	5-11	170	1-25-90	.302	.315	.297	59	202	32	61	7	3	0	21	26	0	7	1	13	1	0	.366	.380
Herrnberger, Alex	B-R	6-0	182	7-6-86	.000	—	.000	7	10	2	0	0	0	0	2	1	0	0	0	2	0	0	.000	.091
Hollinger, Errol	R-R	6-4	210	6-14-87	.202	.222	.194	43	129	15	26	5	0	2	17	6	2	4	1	24	0	0	.287	.261
Inciarte, Ender	L-L	5-11	155	10-29-90	.325	.308	.330	66	237	33	77	14	1	1	22	15	0	5	1	40	10	4	.405	.364
Kim, Jae Yun	R-R	6-1	185	9-16-90	.230	.192	.241	33	113	11	26	3	0	3	14	9	2	0	2	40	1	0	.336	.294
Narodowski, David	R-R	5-10	195	8-3-88	.233	.121	.277	66	206	40	48	5	1	7	22	53	4	1	2	47	7	5	.369	.396

Batting	B-T	HT	WT	DOB	AVG	vLH	vRH	G	AB	R	H	2B	3B	HR	RBI	BB	HBP	SH	SF	SO	SB	CS	SLG	OBP
Nick, David	R-R	6-2	175	2-3-90	.286	.323	.274	66	273	46	78	18	3	6	35	22	6	4	1	49	16	8	.440	.351
Noboa, Michael	R-R	5-8	160	6-21-87	.250	.286	.238	20	28	4	7	0	0	0	3	5	1	1	0	6	1	1	.250	.382
Owings, Chris	R-R	5-11	170	8-12-91	.306	.250	.321	24	108	20	33	5	1	2	10	3	0	0	0	25	3	0	.426	.324
Santiago, Alan	L-R	6-1	170	7-24-90	.288	.167	.304	21	52	13	15	5	0	1	8	10	1	1	0	18	1	0	.442	.413
Sepulveda, Antonio	B-R	5-9	150	12-31-91	.500	—	.500	1	2	0	1	0	0	0	2	0	0	0	0	0	0	0	.500	.500
Stone, Bobby	L-L	6-2	205	11-14-89	.240	.147	.271	74	296	46	71	15	3	16	68	29	4	0	7	95	1	1	.473	.310
Zabala, Henry	R-R	6-1	175	10-20-89	.254	.000	.333	31	59	15	15	3	1	1	5	13	0	1	0	15	0	0	.390	.389

Pitching	B-T	HT	WT	DOB	W	L	ERA	G	GS	CG	SV	IP	H	R	ER	HR	BB	SO	AVG	vLH	vRH	K/9	BB/9
Allen, Scottie	R-R	6-1	165	7-3-91	1	0	0.51	12	0	0	0	18	9	4	1	0	7	16	.145	.143	.146	8.15	3.57
Anderson, Chase	R-R	6-1	175	11-30-87	3	1	2.38	18	4	0	0	45	35	17	12	1	13	48	.206	.205	.207	9.53	2.58
Belfiore, Mike	R-L	6-3	200	10-3-88	2	2	2.17	14	11	0	0	58	59	29	14	2	13	55	.259	.235	.266	8.53	2.02
Brewer, Charles	R-R	6-4	205	4-7-88	7	2	2.47	17	7	0	0	55	43	24	15	4	15	61	.216	.232	.205	10.04	2.47
Burgos, Enrique	R-R	6-4	200	11-23-90	5	3	6.26	16	16	0	0	65	77	50	45	10	39	61	.292	.186	.343	8.49	5.43
Cantwell, Keith	R-R	6-5	215	9-9-87	4	0	4.11	18	0	0	0	35	36	19	16	1	5	44	.252	.286	.238	11.31	1.29
De La Rosa, Eury	L-L	5-9	150	2-24-90	0	2	5.35	14	4	0	0	37	47	28	22	5	16	32	.303	.231	.328	7.78	3.89
De Los Santos, Sammy	R-R	6-1	185	12-9-89	1	1	4.40	13	0	0	1	29	37	15	14	5	6	27	.308	.442	.234	8.48	1.88
Eichhorn, Kevin	R-R	6-0	170	2-6-90	0	2	3.38	10	0	0	0	16	13	7	6	1	9	25	.224	.200	.242	14.06	5.06
Hagens, Bradin	R-R	6-1	175	5-12-89	1	1	3.42	15	0	0	4	26	29	12	9	0	6	13	.312	.364	.283	4.94	2.28
Hale, Jake	R-R	6-7	200	12-11-85	1	1	6.00	6	0	0	0	9	13	9	6	1	2	10	.317	.385	.286	10.00	2.00
Hogben, Kable	R-R	6-2	176	7-6-90	1	1	5.57	13	0	0	0	21	25	13	13	3	19	18	.301	.192	.351	7.29	3.86
Pena, Miguel	R-R	6-0	160	9-18-90	3	5	5.32	15	15	0	0	71	81	49	42	1	29	48	.287	.313	.269	6.08	3.68
Reagan, Miles	R-R	6-2	200	11-16-90	0	1	11.91	10	0	0	0	11	7	17	15	2	15	11	.175	.167	.179	8.74	11.91
Robowski, Ryan	L-L	6-0	185	2-3-88	3	3	4.20	21	0	0	6	30	34	14	14	2	6	23	.283	.214	.321	6.90	1.80
Rosario, Diogenes	R-R	6-0	170	9-1-88	1	1	2.05	17	0	0	4	31	31	10	7	1	6	38	.252	.271	.234	11.15	1.76
Schuster, Patrick	R-L	6-2	165	10-30-90	0	0	3.60	5	0	0	0	5	4	2	2	0	4	6	.211	.500	.176	10.80	7.20
Smith, Anthony	L-L	6-1	205	3-28-85	0	1	9.41	7	4	0	0	22	36	25	23	1	14	11	.379	.520	.329	4.50	5.73
Smith, Eric	R-R	6-3	215	10-15-88	0	3	4.21	9	7	0	0	26	22	14	12	1	16	21	.232	.212	.242	7.36	5.61
Sosa, Keny	L-L	6-0	167	3-26-87	2	2	5.31	8	8	0	0	39	58	27	23	2	9	28	.358	.281	.377	6.46	2.08
Worthington, Adam	R-R	5-10	190	8-20-87	5	4	1.82	19	0	0	2	30	26	16	6	3	3	36	.222	.323	.186	10.92	0.91

Fielding

Catcher	PCT	G	PO	A	E	DP	PB
Aguila	.900	6	15	3	2	1	0
Gomez	1.000	7	31	1	0	0	4
Herrnberger	.955	6	20	1	1	0	5
Hollinger	.986	43	297	44	5	7	8
Kim	.979	32	249	25	6	2	6

First Base	PCT	G	PO	A	E	DP
Castillo	.967	6	55	4	2	5
Goldschmidt	.994	66	648	43	4	58
Gomez	1.000	1	4	1	0	0
Stone	.926	5	25	0	2	1

Second Base	PCT	G	PO	A	E	DP
Canelo	1.000	3	7	9	0	2
Gomez	1.000	2	4	14	0	3
Narodowski	.900	5	10	8	2	2
Nick	.971	64	99	171	8	37
Noboa	1.000	8	3	19	0	4

Third Base	PCT	G	PO	A	E	DP
Borchering	.881	20	4	33	5	1
Broxton	1.000	1	0	1	0	0
Canelo	.833	4	2	3	1	0
Gomez	.888	50	24	87	14	8
Narodowski	.933	7	3	11	1	1
Noboa	.500	3	0	3	3	0

Shortstop	PCT	G	PO	A	E	DP
Canelo	.810	6	5	12	4	3
Narodowski	.939	53	84	178	17	30
Owings	.915	22	39	69	10	23
Sepulveda	.871	1	1	3	1	1

Outfield	PCT	G	PO	A	E	DP
Broxton	.967	70	111	7	4	1
Goldschmidt	1.000	1	3	0	0	0
Inciarte	.952	65	113	5	6	1
Narodowski	1.000	2	2	0	0	0
Santiago	1.000	15	11	1	0	0
Stone	.916	70	95	3	9	2
Zabala	.920	26	19	4	2	1

DSL DIAMONDBACKS — ROOKIE

DOMINICAN SUMMER LEAGUE

Batting	B-T	HT	WT	DOB	AVG	vLH	vRH	G	AB	R	H	2B	3B	HR	RBI	BB	HBP	SH	SF	SO	SB	CS	SLG	OBP
Alegria, Jose	R-R	6-1	200	11-5-90	.245	.118	.273	54	184	21	45	9	0	1	22	29	8	0	2	44	0	1	.310	.368
Delgado, Elvin	R-R	5-11	177	8-17-90	.132	.059	.149	35	91	10	12	3	0	0	7	7	8	1	1	26	1	0	.165	.252
Dicent, Jose	R-R	6-2	176	10-1-90	.202	.185	.207	32	114	14	23	5	1	0	5	12	2	1	1	45	2	3	.263	.287
Felix, Ruben	R-R	—		8-28-88	.222	.333	.182	32	90	4	20	3	0	2	11	6	3	1	1	19	0	1	.322	.290
Gomez, Jeremia	R-R	6-3	185	2-10-91	.266	.333	.250	45	177	28	47	9	5	3	20	22	2	0	1	46	4	2	.424	.351
Javier, Kelvin	R-R	—		10-7-90	.206	.237	.197	56	175	19	36	7	0	0	24	28	5	1	5	61	4	0	.246	.324
Jimenez, Bernardino	R-R	6-1	160	8-7-90	.238	.222	.242	35	126	18	30	0	0	0	10	17	6	0	0	40	3	5	.238	.356
Jose, Juan	L-L	—		7-21-90	.160	.100	.173	51	169	20	27	5	1	3	14	26	3	0	0	78	1	1	.254	.283
Mejia, Yermis	B-R	6-0	165	1-5-90	.216	.111	.250	20	37	8	8	3	0	0	6	8	0	1	0	9	0	0	.297	.356
2-team total (9 Rays)					.224	—	—	29	67	12	15	3	1	1	12	11	0	1	1	19	1	0	.343	.329
Navarro, Raul	R-R	5-11	160	2-5-92	.280	.226	.294	67	271	43	76	12	1	1	11	35	4	1	0	42	12	8	.343	.371
Ortiz, Roberto	R-R	6-1	195	10-28-88	.262	.170	.288	66	237	28	62	5	2	0	31	25	19	4	2	51	18	3	.300	.375
Pacheco, Jose	B-R	5-11	160	6-3-91	.246	.222	.250	17	61	7	15	1	1	0	3	3	0	0	1	14	2	1	.295	.277
Pena, Fidel	R-R	5-11	165	7-19-91	.267	.306	.259	51	202	38	54	6	2	1	26	26	4	2	4	33	5	3	.332	.356
Perez, Jonathan	R-R	6-0	205	10-4-90	.196	.217	.191	39	112	22	22	7	2	2	21	30	6	2	0	40	4	0	.348	.392
Santana, Wilmer	L-L	6-0	170	2-19-92	.077	.200	.000	5	13	1	1	0	0	0	1	2	0	0	0	5	0	0	.077	.200
Soriano, Domingo	R-R	—		10-29-89	.279	.296	.275	65	258	43	72	15	3	5	38	17	7	2	2	53	10	9	.419	.338
Sosa, Miguel	R-R	6-5	210	2-10-91	.667	1.000	.500	1	3	1	2	1	0	0	0	0	0	0	0	1	0	0	1.000	.667

Pitching	B-T	HT	WT	DOB	W	L	ERA	G	GS	CG	SV	IP	H	R	ER	HR	BB	SO	AVG	vLH	vRH	K/9	BB/9
Acosta, Victor	R-R	5-11	175	3-10-91	1	2	4.91	9	0	0	0	37	17	10	8	0	6	14	.293	.385	.267	8.59	3.68
Collado, Juan	R-R	6-1	175	4-4-90	1	1	4.66	18	0	0	2	29	40	24	15	0	15	33	.323	.273	.341	10.24	4.66
Cruz, Berling	R-R	6-1	183	6-3-91	7	2	2.23	14	13	0	0	69	65	30	17	3	22	50	.245	.234	.250	6.55	2.88
De Jesus, Cesse	R-R	5-11	155	5-16-90	0	0	0.00	1	0	0	0	1	0	0	0	0	0	1	.000	—	.000	9.00	0.00
De La Rosa, Javi	L-L	6-3	185	9-9-91	0	2	8.72	12	5	0	0	22	20	30	21	0	27	24	.222	.250	.220	9.97	11.22

Escanio, Bryan	R-R	6-1	185	12-17-91	3	3	3.65	8	6	0	0	37	43	19	15	2	12	25	.291	.245	.313	6.08	2.92
Gil, Manuel	R-R	—	—	3-17-91	0	1	2.08	3	1	0	0	4	2	3	1	0	4	5	.143	.333	.000	10.38	8.31
Gonzalez, Gabriel	R-R	6-2	170	5-27-91	5	5	2.77	15	14	0	0	78	83	33	24	4	12	58	.268	.294	.255	6.69	1.38
Gutierrez, Teo	R-R	—	—	5-23-90	4	6	3.53	15	15	0	0	82	89	41	32	4	12	64	.271	.304	.256	7.05	1.32
Guzman, Francisco	L-L	6-5	190	7-2-89	0	0	2.57	6	0	0	0	7	5	3	2	0	9	12	.200	.000	.217	15.43	11.57
Jaime, Johan	L-L	5-11	185	12-7-89	0	1	2.18	13	2	0	0	33	20	12	8	1	29	39	.179	.000	.200	10.64	7.91
Jimenez, Carlos	R-R	6-3	195	11-18-91	0	0	3.06	9	0	0	3	18	15	9	6	1	12	21	.227	.235	.224	10.70	6.11
Leon, Danny	R-R	6-5	180	9-16-89	1	1	4.26	15	0	0	1	25	19	17	12	2	15	31	.202	.296	.164	11.01	5.33
Lujan, Mario	R-R	6-2	180	11-7-90	0	1	6.14	5	1	0	0	7	10	8	5	0	2	5	.303	.400	.286	6.14	2.45
Mariano, Ramon	B-L	6-1	187	11-1-87	0	0	1.50	2	0	0	0	6	3	2	1	0	2	7	.130	.333	.100	10.50	3.00
Martinez, Gustavo	R-R	6-2	162	3-13-90	1	0	4.02	15	0	0	3	31	18	15	14	0	31	29	.167	.208	.155	8.33	8.90
Ramirez, Jhoan	R-R	6-0	155	5-4-89	0	1	6.14	6	0	0	0	7	6	7	5	0	11	2	.207	.375	.143	2.45	13.50
Santana, Diony	L-L	6-0	150	1-15-91	3	3	3.00	14	12	0	0	63	58	37	21	2	31	50	.247	.310	.238	7.14	4.43
Santana, Frank	R-R	6-2	200	2-21-89	7	1	1.89	21	0	0	4	38	34	11	8	1	8	31	.234	.325	.200	7.34	1.89

Fielding

Catcher	PCT	G	PO	A	E	DP	PB
Alegria	.986	18	132	13	2	0	7
Delgado	.967	33	226	37	9	0	7
Felix	.971	22	120	16	4	0	6
Pena	.966	8	50	7	2	0	1

First Base	PCT	G	PO	A	E	DP
Alegria	.969	20	157	1	5	11
Dicent	.945	5	51	1	3	5
Javier	.979	28	204	29	5	10
Pena	1.000	10	92	4	0	6
Perez	.979	11	88	6	2	7
Santana	1.000	5	33	0	0	5

Second Base	PCT	G	PO	A	E	DP
Jimenez	.955	34	68	82	7	13
Mejia	.840	9	9	12	4	2
Pacheco	.899	16	25	37	7	5
Pena	.973	18	29	44	2	7
Perez	1.000	1	1	3	0	1

Third Base	PCT	G	PO	A	E	DP
Delgado	1.000	1	0	1	0	0
Dicent	.853	25	21	43	11	4
Javier	.667	1	1	1	1	1
Mejia	.778	4	3	4	2	0
Pena	.926	15	14	36	4	3
Perez	.878	28	29	57	12	3

Sosa	1.000	1	1	1	0	0

Shortstop	PCT	G	PO	A	E	DP
Jimenez	.667	3	1	11	6	2
Navarro	.907	67	103	189	30	27
Pacheco	.750	2	1	2	1	0
Pena	1.000	1	1	0	0	0

Outfield	PCT	G	PO	A	E	DP
Gomez	.918	40	82	8	8	2
Javier	.868	28	31	2	5	0
Jose	.962	35	45	5	2	0
Ortiz	.958	62	105	8	5	3
Pena	1.000	1	1	0	0	0
Soriano	1.000	49	91	4	0	1

Atlanta Braves

SEASON IN A SENTENCE: The Braves got off to a mediocre start, and were at 53-53 on Aug. 3, but they closed strong and finished 10 games over .500, even making a late run at a wild-card berth behind a rebuilt pitching staff led by Javier Vazquez, Jair Jurrjens, Kenshin Kawakami and Derek Lowe.

HIGH POINT: When Atlanta beat the Marlins 4-0 on Sept. 28, Braves fans started to believe a playoff miracle was possible. It capped a seven-game win streak and 15 of 17 run that put Atlanta just two games out of the wild card, with Chipper Jones hitting a home run and Jurrjens winning his fourth straight start. The air went out of the balloon when the Braves lost their next game, and they closed with six straight losses.

LOW POINT: The Braves spent most of the season right around .500, but a 1-0 loss to the Red Sox on June 27 put them at 34-40, capping a four-game losing streak and six-game stretch when they lost four of six to the Yankees and Red Sox. The only wins in those two series were starts by rookie righthander Tommy Hanson.

NOTABLE ROOKIES: Hanson had an argument for rookie of the year honors, with an 11-4, 2.89 mark, and would have been a slam-dunk choice if he had made more than 21 starts. Braves fans also had to wonder if they would have seen playoff baseball had Hanson not made 11 starts in Triple-A. Jordan Schafer's debut in the outfield didn't go well, but he'll get another chance in 2010.

KEY TRANSACTIONS: Credit the Braves for not standing pat with their season mired in mediocrity. In addition to calling up Hanson, they brought back first baseman Adam LaRoche by sending Casey Kotchman to the Red Sox, and sent prospects to the Pirates in order to get Nate McLouth to man center field. They also gave up on right fielder Jeff Francoeur, trading him to the Mets for Ryan Church.

DOWN ON THE FARM: Outfielder Jason Heyward looks like the next big thing for Atlanta, winning Baseball America's Minor League Player of the Year award while tearing through three levels of the farm system. Beyond him, though, the minor league talent is thinner after the trades for McLouth and Vazquez. Scouting director Roy Clark also left to become an assistant general manager with the Nationals, with former Orioles scouting director Tony DeMacio getting promoted to take his place.

OPENING DAY PAYROLL: $96,726,166

PLAYERS OF THE YEAR

MAJOR LEAGUE	MINOR LEAGUE
Javier Vazquez rhp	**Jason Heyward of**
15-10, 2.87	(High A/AA/AAA)
10th straight season	.323/.408/.555
with at least 198 IP	BA Minor League POY

ORGANIZATION LEADERS

BATTING   *Minimum 250 at-bats

MAJORS

*AVG	Martin Prado	.307
*OPS	Brian McCann	.834
HR	Brian McCann	21
RBI	Brian McCann	94

MINORS

*AVG	Heyward, Jason, M.B./Miss./Gwinnett	.323
R	Young, Matt, Mississippi/Gwinnett	87
H	Canizares, Barbaro, Gwinnett	149
TB	Rodriguez, Gerardo, Rome/Myrtle Beach	226
2B	Linares, Donell, Myrtle Beach	32
3B	Young, Matt, Mississippi/Gwinnett	10
HR	Johnson, Cody, Myrtle Beach/Mississippi	32
RBI	Johnson, Cody, Myrtle Beach/Mississippi	87
	Linares, Donell, Myrtle Beach	87
BB	Young, Matt, Mississippi/Gwinnett	97
SO	Johnson, Cody, Myrtle Beach/Mississippi	180
SB	Young, Matt, Mississippi/Gwinnett	43
*OBP	Timmons, Wes, Gwinnett	.416
*SLG	Heyward, Jason, M.B./Miss./Gwinnett	.555

PITCHING   †Minimum 75 innings

MAJORS

W	Derek Lowe	15
†ERA	Jair Jurrjens	2.60
SO	Javier Vazquez	238

MINORS

W	Cofield, Kyle, Mississippi	10
L	Sullivan, Richard, Rome/Miss./Myrtle Beach	14
†ERA	Spruill, Zeke, Rome	3.03
G	Valdez, Luis, Gwinnett	58
GS	Venters, Jonny, Mississippi/Gwinnett	29
SV	Valdez, Luis, Gwinnett	27
IP	Venters, Jonny, Mississippi/Gwinnett	157
BB	Cofield, Kyle, Mississippi	89
SO	Hoover, J.J., Myrtle Beach/Rome	150
†AVG	Ortegano, Jose, Myrtle Beach/Mississippi	.232

2009 PERFORMANCE

General Manager: Frank Wren. **Farm Director:** Kurt Kemp. **Scouting Director:** Roy Clark.

Class	Team	League	W	L	PCT	Finish*	Manager(s)
Majors	Atlanta Braves	National	86	76	.531	7th (16)	Bobby Cox
Triple-A	Gwinnett Braves	International	81	63	.563	4th (14)	Dave Brundage
Double-A	Mississippi Braves	Southern	65	73	.471	4th (10)	Phillip Wellman
High A	Myrtle Beach Pelicans	Carolina	53	84	.387	8th (8)	Rocket Wheeler
Low A	Rome Braves	South Atlantic	66	73	.475	11th (16)	Randy Ingle
Rookie	Danville Braves	Appalachian	47	21	.691	†1st (10)	Paul Runge
Rookie	GCL Braves	Gulf Coast	26	34	.433	13th (16)	Luis Ortiz
Overall 2009 Minor League Record			338	348	.493	18th (30)	

*Finish in overall standings (No. of teams in league). †League champion.

ORGANIZATION STATISTICS

ATLANTA BRAVES

NATIONAL LEAGUE

Batting	B-T	HT	WT	DOB	AVG	vLH	vRH	G	AB	R	H	2B	3B	HR	RBI	BB	HBP	SH	SF	SO	SB	CS	SLG	OBP
Anderson, Garret	L-L	6-3	225	6-30-72	.268	.283	.262	135	496	52	133	27	0	13	61	27	2	0	9	73	1	0	.401	.303
Barton, Brian	R-R	6-3	190	4-25-82	—	—	—	1	0	0	0	0	0	0	0	0	0	0	0	0	0	1	—	—
Blanco, Gregor	L-L	5-11	170	12-12-83	.186	.083	.226	24	43	5	8	0	1	0	1	4	0	1	0	9	2	0	.233	.255
Canizares, Barbaro	R-R	6-3	240	11-21-79	.190	.333	.133	5	21	1	4	1	0	0	0	0	0	0	0	6	0	0	.238	.190
Church, Ryan	L-L	6-2	220	10-14-78	.260	.281	.253	44	127	20	33	12	0	2	18	16	1	0	0	22	0	0	.402	.347
2-team total (67 New York)					.273	—	—	111	359	46	98	28	0	4	40	33	3	2	2	58	6	2	.384	.338
Conrad, Brooks	B-R	5-11	190	1-16-80	.204	.222	.200	30	54	7	11	1	2	2	8	3	1	0	0	14	0	0	.407	.259
Diaz, Matt	R-R	6-1	215	3-3-78	.313	.412	.255	125	371	56	116	18	4	13	58	35	13	5	1	90	12	5	.488	.390
Escobar, Yunel	R-R	6-2	200	11-2-82	.299	.232	.327	141	528	89	158	26	2	14	76	57	10	7	2	62	5	4	.436	.377
Francoeur, Jeff	R-R	6-4	220	1-8-84	.250	.303	.228	82	304	32	76	12	2	5	35	12	3	1	4	46	5	1	.352	.282
2-team total (75 New York)					.280	—	—	157	593	72	166	32	4	15	76	23	6	1	9	92	6	4	.423	.309
Gorecki, Reid	R-R	6-1	200	12-22-80	.200	.400	.150	31	25	6	5	0	0	0	3	1	0	0	1	12	1	0	.200	.222
Hernandez, Diory	R-R	6-0	185	4-8-84	.141	.087	.161	33	85	6	12	3	0	1	6	6	0	2	0	22	0	1	.212	.198
Infante, Omar	R-R	6-0	180	12-26-81	.305	.323	.298	70	203	24	62	9	1	2	27	19	1	2	4	28	2	0	.389	.361
Johnson, Kelly	L-R	6-1	205	2-22-82	.224	.325	.188	106	303	47	68	20	3	8	29	32	3	6	2	54	7	2	.389	.303
Jones, Brandon	L-R	6-1	210	12-10-83	.308	1.000	.250	5	13	2	4	0	0	0	1	4	0	0	0	3	0	0	.308	.471
Jones, Chipper	B-R	6-4	210	4-24-72	.264	.289	.252	143	488	80	129	23	2	18	71	101	1	0	6	89	4	1	.430	.388
Kotchman, Casey	L-L	6-3	215	2-22-83	.282	.267	.288	87	298	28	84	20	0	6	41	32	3	0	3	28	0	0	.409	.354
LaRoche, Adam	L-L	6-3	205	11-6-79	.325	.279	.344	57	212	30	69	11	1	12	40	28	0	0	2	59	0	0	.557	.401
2-team total (87 Pittsburgh)					.278	—	—	144	536	76	149	36	2	24	80	69	0	0	5	140	2	2	.487	.357
McCann, Brian	L-R	6-3	230	2-20-84	.281	.225	.308	138	488	63	137	35	1	21	94	49	5	3	6	83	4	1	.486	.349
McLouth, Nate	L-R	5-11	180	10-28-81	.257	.192	.285	84	339	59	87	20	1	11	36	47	5	3	2	70	12	6	.419	.354
2-team total (45 Pittsburgh)					.256	—	—	129	507	86	130	27	2	20	70	68	9	3	4	99	19	6	.436	.352
Norton, Greg	B-R	6-1	205	7-6-72	.145	.286	.113	95	76	3	11	2	0	0	7	20	1	0	0	20	0	0	.171	.330
Prado, Martin	R-R	6-1	190	10-27-83	.307	.301	.309	128	450	64	138	38	0	11	49	36	2	11	4	59	1	3	.464	.358
Ross, David	R-R	6-2	240	3-19-77	.273	.250	.284	54	128	18	35	9	0	7	20	21	1	1	0	39	0	0	.508	.380
Sammons, Clint	R-R	6-0	200	5-15-83	.182	.250	.143	6	11	1	2	0	0	0	1	0	0	0	0	3	0	0	.182	.250
Schafer, Jordan	L-R	6-1	200	9-4-86	.204	.212	.200	50	167	18	34	8	0	2	8	27	0	0	1	63	2	1	.287	.313

Pitching	B-T	HT	WT	DOB	W	L	ERA	G	GS	CG	SV	IP	H	R	ER	HR	BB	SO	AVG	vLH	vRH	K/9	BB/9
Acosta, Manny	B-R	6-4	170	5-1-81	1	1	4.34	36	0	0	0	37	45	19	18	4	19	32	.300	.297	.302	7.71	4.58
Bennett, Jeff	R-R	6-3	200	6-10-80	2	4	3.18	33	0	0	0	34	42	13	12	2	21	23	.316	.327	.308	6.09	5.56
Boyer, Blaine	R-R	6-3	215	7-11-81	0	1	40.50	3	0	0	0	1	3	6	6	0	3	2	.429	.500	.400	13.50	20.25
3-team total (30 Arizona, 15 St. Louis)					0	2	4.12	48	0	0	0	55	56	36	25	1	20	29	—	—	—	4.77	3.29
Campillo, Jorge	R-R	6-1	225	8-10-78	1	0	4.15	5	0	0	0	4	7	3	2	0	3	3	.389	.500	.300	6.23	6.23
Carlyle, Buddy	L-R	6-3	210	12-21-77	0	1	8.86	16	0	0	0	21	35	23	21	5	12	12	.380	.316	.426	5.06	5.06
Gonzalez, Mike	R-L	6-2	215	5-23-78	5	4	2.42	80	0	0	10	74	56	28	20	7	33	90	.209	.194	.218	10.90	4.00
Hanson, Tommy	R-R	6-6	220	8-28-86	11	4	2.89	21	21	0	0	128	105	42	41	10	46	116	.225	.256	.192	8.18	3.24
Hudson, Tim	R-R	6-1	170	7-14-75	2	1	3.61	7	7	0	0	42	49	17	17	4	13	30	.295	.329	.271	6.38	2.76
Jurrjens, Jair	R-R	6-1	200	1-29-86	14	10	2.60	34	34	0	0	215	186	71	62	15	75	152	.237	.264	.212	6.36	3.14
Kawakami, Kenshin	R-R	5-11	200	6-22-75	7	12	3.86	32	25	0	1	156	153	73	67	15	57	105	.260	.252	.268	6.04	3.28
Logan, Boone	R-L	6-5	215	8-13-84	1	1	5.19	20	0	0	0	17	21	12	10	1	9	10	.292	.231	.364	5.19	4.67
Lowe, Derek	R-R	6-6	230	6-1-73	15	10	4.67	34	34	0	0	195	232	109	101	16	63	111	.301	.300	.303	5.13	2.91
Medlen, Kris	B-R	5-10	190	10-7-85	3	5	4.26	37	4	0	0	68	65	34	32	5	30	72	.256	.183	.328	9.58	3.99
Moylan, Peter	R-R	6-2	200	12-2-78	6	2	2.84	87	0	0	0	73	65	29	23	0	35	61	.245	.309	.211	7.52	4.32
Nunez, Vladimir	R-R	6-4	240	3-15-75	0	0	36.00	1	0	0	0	1	2	4	4	2	2	1	.400	.333	.500	9.00	18.00
O'Flaherty, Eric	L-L	6-2	220	2-5-85	2	1	3.04	78	0	0	0	56	52	23	19	2	18	39	.248	.215	.282	6.23	2.88
Parr, James	R-R	6-1	185	2-27-86	0	0	5.79	8	0	0	0	14	17	9	9	1	5	12	.293	.367	.214	7.71	3.21
Reyes, Jo-Jo	L-L	6-2	230	11-20-84	0	2	7.00	6	5	0	0	27	27	25	21	4	13	21	.262	.156	.310	7.00	4.33
Soriano, Rafael	R-R	6-1	220	12-19-79	1	6	2.97	77	0	0	27	76	53	25	25	6	27	102	.194	.258	.138	12.13	3.21
Valdez, Luis	R-R	6-2	205	5-5-84	0	1	3.38	3	0	0	0	3	3	1	1	0	2	0	.273	.750	.000	0.00	6.75
Vazquez, Javier	R-R	6-2	210	7-25-76	15	10	2.87	32	32	3	0	219	181	75	70	20	44	238	.223	.235	.212	9.77	1.81

Fielding

Catcher	PCT	G	PO	A	E	DP	PB
McCann	.988	127	924	58	12	7	7
Ross	.997	52	314	37	1	6	5
Sammons	1.000	6	23	2	0	0	0

First Base	PCT	G	PO	A	E	DP
Canizares	1.000	5	33	2	0	3
Kotchman	1.000	85	674	61	0	51
LaRoche	.998	57	520	43	1	61
Norton	1.000	3	21	2	0	1
Prado	.994	28	160	14	1	25

Second Base	PCT	G	PO	A	E	DP
Conrad	1.000	11	22	31	0	10
Hernandez	1.000	4	4	5	0	1

	PCT	G	PO	A	E	DP
Infante	.981	30	42	62	2	12
Johnson	.973	84	135	222	10	56
Prado	.986	63	116	162	4	37

Third Base	PCT	G	PO	A	E	DP
Conrad	—	1	0	0	0	0
Hernandez	1.000	3	1	5	0	2
Infante	.938	10	1	14	1	0
Jones	.930	133	85	208	22	30
Prado	.975	41	14	65	2	8

Shortstop	PCT	G	PO	A	E	DP
Escobar	.979	139	191	409	13	83
Hernandez	.989	22	26	61	1	18
Infante	1.000	10	11	21	0	3

Outfield	PCT	G	PO	A	E	DP
Anderson	.980	124	193	4	4	0
Barton	1.000	1	1	0	0	0
Blanco	.957	14	21	1	1	0
Church	.986	41	67	3	1	2
Diaz	.981	109	157	2	3	0
Francoeur	1.000	80	157	6	0	0
Gorecki	.963	28	25	1	1	0
Infante	1.000	16	24	0	0	0
Jones	1.000	4	5	0	0	0
McLouth	.995	84	196	4	1	2
Prado	—	1	0	0	0	0
Schafer	1.000	50	127	4	0	1

GWINNETT BRAVES

INTERNATIONAL LEAGUE

TRIPLE-A

Batting	B-T	HT	WT	DOB	AVG	vLH	vRH	G	AB	R	H	2B	3B	HR	RBI	BB	HBP	SH	SF	SO	SB	CS	SLG	OBP
Barton, Brian	R-R	6-3	190	4-25-82	.266	.267	.265	114	369	47	98	17	4	7	46	45	7	2	3	101	17	7	.390	.354
Blanco, Gregor	L-L	5-11	170	12-12-83	.228	.203	.236	90	333	54	76	9	1	2	30	50	1	7	6	70	10	3	.279	.326
Borchard, Joe	B-R	6-4	230	11-25-78	.119	.000	.167	12	42	5	5	1	0	1	5	6	1	0	0	14	0	0	.214	.245
Boscan, J.C.	R-R	6-2	215	12-26-79	.250	.385	.194	13	44	5	11	4	0	0	2	2	1	1	0	9	0	0	.341	.298
Burke, Chris	R-R	5-11	195	3-11-80	.285	.323	.273	73	274	39	78	19	2	3	32	22	7	4	2	46	13	2	.401	.351
Canizares, Barbaro	R-R	6-3	240	11-21-79	.294	.322	.286	130	506	55	149	31	2	12	79	52	7	0	4	67	2	2	.435	.366
Colina, Alvin	R-R	6-3	210	12-26-81	.262	.341	.243	67	225	31	59	12	0	8	42	25	4	0	2	55	1	1	.422	.344
Conrad, Brooks	B-R	5-11	190	1-16-80	.269	.274	.267	110	398	66	107	25	0	12	64	53	7	2	9	108	13	1	.422	.358
Gorecki, Reid	R-R	6-1	200	12-22-80	.286	.299	.280	106	371	57	106	27	6	9	49	34	5	3	3	73	14	7	.464	.351
Hernandez, Diory	R-R	6-0	185	4-8-84	.319	.298	.417	54	204	18	65	16	1	1	32	21	7	1	1	34	8	6	.422	.399
Heyward, Jason	L-L	6-4	220	8-9-89	.364	—	.364	3	11	3	4	0	0	0	2	2	0	0	0	2	1	0	.364	.462
Holt, J.C.	L-R	5-9	175	12-8-82	.282	.222	.291	81	266	44	75	12	3	0	30	27	2	3	4	50	14	4	.350	.348
Infante, Omar	R-R	6-0	180	12-26-81	.333	—	.333	1	3	1	1	0	0	1	2	0	1	0	0	0	0	0	1.333	.500
Johnson, Kelly	L-R	6-1	205	2-22-82	.308	.300	.313	13	52	9	16	2	2	3	16	4	0	0	3	8	1	0	.596	.339
Johnson, Benji	R-R	6-1	195	7-17-86	.125	—	.125	3	8	0	1	0	0	0	0	1	1	0	0	3	0	0	.125	.300
Jones, Brandon	L-R	6-1	210	12-10-83	.281	.250	.291	107	384	50	108	28	2	7	57	50	1	1	7	76	6	3	.419	.360
Kirkland, Kody	R-R	6-4	200	6-9-83	.289	.417	.231	13	38	5	11	2	0	1	2	4	2	0	0	13	1	1	.342	.386
Kotchman, Casey	L-L	6-3	215	2-22-83	.000	—	.000	2	3	2	0	0	0	0	0	3	1	0	0	1	0	0	.000	.200
McCann, Brian	L-R	6-3	230	2-20-84	.333	—	.333	1	3	0	1	1	0	0	1	1	0	0	0	0	0	0	.667	.500
Norton, Greg	B-R	6-1	205	7-6-72	.324	.500	.240	12	37	3	12	0	1	1	10	3	0	0	1	7	1	0	.459	.366
Perez, Antonio	R-R	5-9	190	1-26-80	.190	.310	.131	49	126	18	24	5	2	1	8	13	1	5	2	23	4	2	.286	.288
Pope, Van	R-R	6-0	200	2-26-84	.202	.275	.173	106	322	39	65	15	0	4	28	33	3	6	4	62	2	1	.286	.279
Sammons, Clint	R-R	6-0	200	5-15-83	.214	.218	.213	80	299	34	64	12	0	9	37	20	3	1	5	61	7	0	.344	.266
Schafer, Jordan	L-L	6-0	200	9-4-86	.229	.250	.222	9	35	6	8	0	0	2	3	2	0	0	1	10	3	1	.400	.263
Timmons, Wes	R-R	6-0	190	7-12-79	.283	.338	.268	105	322	62	91	20	2	1	31	62	15	9	5	36	12	5	.366	.416
Young, Matt	L-R	5-8	180	10-3-82	.192	.500	.167	7	26	6	5	1	0	1	3	3	0	0	0	5	1	1	.346	.276

Pitching	B-T	HT	WT	DOB	W	L	ERA	G	GS	CG	SV	IP	H	R	ER	HR	BB	SO	AVG	vLH	vRH	K/9	BB/9
Acosta, Manny	B-R	6-4	170	5-1-81	1	3	2.63	18	0	0	2	27	21	8	8	4	13	25	.210	.164	.267	8.23	4.28
Armas Jr., Tony	R-R	6-3	225	4-29-78	1	2	4.37	13	11	0	0	60	67	40	29	8	22	38	.282	.307	.263	5.73	3.32
Bennett, Jeff	R-R	6-3	200	6-10-80	0	1	18.00	2	2	0	0	2	5	4	4	0	1	0	.500	.500	.500	0.00	4.50
2-team total (3 Durham)					1	1	6.75	5	5	0	0	13	19	10	10	1	6	8	—	—	—	5.40	4.05
Brownlie, Bobby	R-R	6-0	225	10-5-80	5	2	4.13	14	7	0	0	57	60	26	26	7	17	47	.276	.265	.287	7.46	2.70
Bueno, Francisley	L-L	5-11	200	3-5-81	4	1	3.13	33	5	0	1	55	47	21	19	1	21	33	.234	.266	.213	5.43	3.46
Campillo, Jorge	R-R	6-1	225	8-10-78	0	0	6.00	1	0	0	1	3	4	2	2	1	0	1	.308	.750	.111	3.00	0.00
Carlyle, Buddy	L-R	6-3	210	12-21-77	3	1	1.76	12	1	0	0	15	13	3	3	0	1	23	.228	.167	.273	13.50	0.59
Cruz, Rafael	R-R	6-2	225	5-19-77	1	1	0.00	8	0	0	1	9	6	1	0	0	2	5	.207	.125	.238	5.19	2.08
Gamble, Jerome	R-R	6-4	235	4-5-80	1	3	5.60	6	4	0	0	18	25	24	11	3	13	17	.329	.432	.231	8.66	6.62
Glavine, Tom	L-L	6-0	205	3-25-66	1	0	3.38	2	2	0	0	8	11	3	3	1	2	3	.333	.500	.280	3.38	2.25
Gomez, Mariano	L-L	6-6	240	9-12-82	8	4	1.99	47	0	0	8	72	51	18	16	3	29	36	.203	.218	.193	4.48	3.61
Gunderson, Kevin	R-L	5-10	165	9-16-84	0	0	13.50	4	0	0	0	3	3	4	4	0	3	2	.300	.250	.333	6.75	10.13
Halama, John	L-L	6-5	215	2-22-72	4	7	4.48	16	13	0	0	90	92	47	45	8	33	54	.267	.261	.269	5.38	3.29
Hanson, Tommy	R-R	6-6	220	8-28-86	3	3	1.49	11	11	0	0	66	40	16	11	5	17	90	.169	.179	.161	12.21	2.31
Heath, Deunte	R-R	6-4	215	8-8-85	0	1	9.64	7	2	0	0	19	27	21	20	2	12	18	.325	.417	.255	8.68	5.79
Huber, Jon	R-R	6-2	195	7-7-81	0	0	4.25	27	0	0	1	42	44	20	20	3	7	42	.262	.333	.228	8.93	1.49
Hudson, Tim	R-R	6-1	170	7-14-75	1	0	3.38	4	4	0	0	19	24	7	7	0	2	11	.320	.229	.400	5.30	0.96
Kimbrel, Craig	R-R	5-11	205	5-28-88	0	0	0.00	2	0	0	0	2	0	0	0	0	4	3	.000	.000	.000	13.50	18.00
Logan, Boone	R-L	6-5	215	8-13-84	4	2	3.28	29	0	0	2	36	26	15	13	2	17	39	.205	.245	.179	9.84	4.29
Lyman, Jeff	R-R	6-3	215	1-14-87	0	2	4.91	5	2	0	0	11	11	6	6	0	10	11	.244	.294	.214	9.00	8.18
Marek, Stephen	L-R	6-2	240	9-3-83	0	1	7.94	6	0	0	0	6	7	5	5	1	7	4	.350	.500	.286	6.35	11.12
Medlen, Kris	B-R	5-10	190	10-7-85	5	0	1.19	8	4	0	0	38	20	5	5	0	10	44	.157	.139	.188	10.51	2.39
Morton, Charlie	R-R	6-4	190	11-12-83	7	2	2.51	10	10	1	0	65	52	18	18	3	16	55	.222	.215	.230	7.65	2.23
2-team total (1 Indianapolis)					7	2	2.26	11	11	1	0	72	56	18	18	3	17	62	—	—	—	7.79	2.13
Nunez, Vladimir	R-R	6-4	240	3-15-75	3	2	2.16	45	2	0	5	83	69	23	20	7	37	79	.227	.277	.195	8.53	4.00
Parr, James	R-R	6-1	185	2-27-86	1	1	5.40	7	6	0	0	30	34	18	18	5	5	20	.286	.264	.303	6.00	1.50

	B-T	HT	WT	DOB	W	L	ERA	G	GS	CG	SV	IP	H	R	ER	HR	BB	SO	AVG	vLH	vRH	K/9	BB/9
Perez, Juan	R-L	6-0	180	9-3-78	2	4	3.47	47	0	0	1	57	40	28	22	7	36	59	.191	.171	.201	9.32	5.68
Redmond, Todd	R-R	6-3	215	5-17-85	9	6	4.41	27	24	0	0	145	152	85	71	21	47	106	.269	.244	.290	6.58	2.92
Reyes, Jo-Jo	L-L	6-2	230	11-20-84	4	2	2.86	15	14	0	0	66	68	23	21	6	24	32	.272	.311	.250	4.36	3.27
Reynoso, Ryne	L-R	6-2	215	3-15-85	0	1	10.80	1	1	0	0	5	7	6	6	1	2	0	.318	.429	.267	0.00	3.60
Valdez, Luis	R-R	6-2	205	5-5-84	5	4	3.28	58	0	0	27	71	66	37	26	4	19	75	.237	.219	.249	9.46	2.40
Venters, Jonny	L-L	6-3	185	3-20-85	4	7	5.62	17	17	0	0	91	103	64	57	7	42	58	.285	.283	.286	5.72	4.14

Fielding

Catcher	PCT	G	PO	A	E	DP	PB
Boscan	.992	12	111	7	1	0	1
Colina	.990	56	366	34	4	2	5
Johnson	1.000	1	1	1	0	0	0
McCann	1.000	1	7	3	0	0	0
Sammons	.995	76	541	36	3	3	9

First Base	PCT	G	PO	A	E	DP
Boscan	1.000	1	2	0	0	0
Canizares	.989	90	677	54	8	73
Conrad	.978	10	84	6	2	8
Kirkland	1.000	4	20	2	0	1
Kotchman	1.000	2	8	0	0	1
Norton	1.000	2	19	2	0	1
Perez	1.000	2	13	1	0	1
Timmons	.991	50	324	25	3	28

Second Base	PCT	G	PO	A	E	DP
Burke	1.000	16	26	51	0	8

Conrad	.960	67	127	161	12	45
Holt	.987	39	66	85	2	17
Johnson	1.000	11	14	30	0	7
Perez	.926	7	12	13	2	6
Timmons	1.000	14	15	26	0	7
Young	1.000	1	1	2	0	0

Third Base	PCT	G	PO	A	E	DP
Conrad	.950	8	10	9	1	1
Kirkland	1.000	1	1	1	0	0
Pope	.961	101	69	153	9	10
Timmons	.952	45	29	70	5	6

Shortstop	PCT	G	PO	A	E	DP
Burke	.975	41	66	130	5	30
Conrad	.935	20	23	49	5	11
Hernandez	.945	53	89	135	13	29
Infante	.889	1	4	4	1	1
Kirkland	.844	8	7	20	5	4

Perez	.955	30	30	75	5	13
Timmons	—	1	0	0	0	0

Outfield	PCT	G	PO	A	E	DP
Barton	.959	108	230	6	10	2
Blanco	.981	87	199	5	4	2
Borchard	1.000	7	8	2	0	1
Burke	.900	14	18	0	2	0
Conrad	1.000	1	4	0	0	0
Gorecki	.969	97	239	10	8	4
Heyward	1.000	3	11	0	0	0
Holt	1.000	33	61	1	0	0
Jones	.994	80	154	4	1	1
Norton	1.000	4	9	1	0	0
Perez	1.000	3	3	0	0	0
Schafer	1.000	9	26	0	0	0
Young	1.000	6	16	0	0	0

MISSISSIPPI BRAVES   DOUBLE-A

SOUTHERN LEAGUE

Batting	B-T	HT	WT	DOB	AVG	vLH	vRH	G	AB	R	H	2B	3B	HR	RBI	BB	HBP	SH	SF	SO	SB	CS	SLG	OBP
Anderson, Chris	R-R	6-0	210	10-27-85	.143	.200	.000	3	7	2	1	1	0	0	0	1	0	0	0	3	0	0	.286	.250
Boscan, J.C.	R-R	6-2	215	12-26-79	.260	.298	.251	73	250	20	65	12	0	0	30	33	2	2	2	50	2	1	.308	.348
Britton, Phillip	R-R	6-0	205	9-25-84	.222	.273	.212	39	126	9	28	10	0	0	12	6	0	4	1	24	1	3	.302	.256
Cabrera, Willie	R-R	5-11	185	8-3-86	.275	.310	.264	107	371	44	102	19	2	8	53	33	3	1	7	51	3	7	.402	.333
Camarena, Jose	B-R	5-10	170	5-29-84	.157	.227	.134	32	89	3	14	4	0	0	7	1	1	1	2	15	1	1	.202	.222
Campbell, Eric	R-R	6-0	205	8-6-85	.241	.238	.242	104	369	28	89	16	1	5	38	36	2	1	6	56	1	3	.331	.308
Creek, Greg	L-R	6-3	225	8-29-82	.234	.161	.242	104	320	26	75	14	1	5	42	25	3	1	4	65	2	3	.331	.293
Freeman, Freddie	L-R	6-5	220	9-12-89	.248	.268	.241	41	149	15	37	8	0	2	24	11	4	0	5	19	0	0	.342	.308
Guzman, Javier	B-R	6-0	170	5-4-82	.087	.000	.111	12	23	3	2	0	0	0	1	0	0	0	0	4	0	0	.087	.125
Hernandez, Gorkys	R-R	6-0	175	9-7-87	.316	.373	.294	52	212	33	67	11	2	0	19	15	0	1	0	54	10	8	.387	.361
Heyward, Jason	L-L	6-4	220	8-9-89	.352	.304	.371	47	162	32	57	13	4	7	30	28	2	0	3	19	5	1	.611	.446
Hicks, Brandon	R-R	6-2	200	9-14-85	.237	.288	.222	128	464	63	110	25	4	10	48	53	5	8	4	131	17	1	.373	.319
Johnson, Cody	L-R	6-4	195	8-18-88	.182	.083	.300	6	22	4	4	0	0	3	4	0	0	0	0	9	1	0	.182	.280
Johnson, Benji	R-R	6-1	195	7-17-86	.179	.000	.263	8	28	3	5	2	0	1	3	0	0	0	0	5	0	0	.357	.179
Jones, Travis	R-R	5-9	190	11-10-85	.249	.272	.242	121	366	41	91	22	1	5	40	50	9	6	3	93	23	8	.355	.350
Ka'aihue, Kala	R-R	6-2	230	3-29-85	.157	.167	.153	69	191	17	30	6	1	4	15	36	5	0	0	64	1	1	.262	.306
Kirkland, Kody	R-R	6-4	200	6-9-83	.201	.262	.181	92	264	33	53	13	3	3	20	20	4	2	2	63	4	4	.307	.266
Marcial, Robert	R-R	5-10	170	4-21-84	.077	—	.077	4	13	0	1	0	0	0	0	2	0	0	0	7	1	0	.077	.200
McLouth, Nate	L-R	5-11	180	10-28-81	.000	.000	.000	2	3	1	0	0	0	0	0	2	0	0	0	1	0	0	.000	.400
Mejia, Ernesto	R-R	6-6	190	12-2-85	.229	.300	.200	9	35	3	8	0	0	2	3	0	0	0	0	11	0	0	.229	.289
Owings, Jon	R-R	6-4	195	4-4-85	.500	.500	.500	3	6	1	3	1	0	1	2	0	0	0	1	3	1	.167	.500
Perez, Antonio	R-R	5-9	190	1-26-80	.333	.500	.250	3	12	3	4	0	0	1	1	0	0	0	3	0	0	.583	.333
Rodriguez, Concepcion	R-R	6-2	170	9-19-86	.263	.230	.273	116	395	43	104	19	1	3	32	29	1	5	6	69	9	9	.339	.312
Young, Matt	L-R	5-8	180	10-3-82	.289	.314	.283	130	460	81	133	22	10	4	33	94	12	3	2	59	42	16	.407	.421

Pitching	B-T	HT	WT	DOB	W	L	ERA	G	GS	CG	SV	IP	H	R	ER	HR	BB	SO	AVG	vLH	vRH	K/9	BB/9
Armas Jr., Tony	R-R	6-3	225	4-29-78	0	0	0.00	1	1	0	0	5	3	0	0	0	1	2	.176	.333	.091	3.86	1.93
Beachey, Brandon	R-R	6-2	210	9-3-86	0	0	0.00	1	0	0	0	1	1	0	0	0	0	0	.250	1.000	.000	0.00	0.00
Broadway, Mike	R-R	6-5	190	3-30-87	0	0	0.00	4	1	0	0	9	9	2	0	1	5	4	.250	.250	.250	4.00	4.42
Butts, Brett	R-R	6-1	190	4-24-86	7	3	2.58	53	0	0	5	73	63	23	21	5	36	68	.233	.218	.245	8.35	4.42
Campillo, Jorge	R-R	6-1	225	8-10-78	0	0	0.00	1	1	0	0	2	1	0	0	0	1	2	.143	.200	.000	9.00	4.50
Cofield, Kyle	R-R	6-5	190	1-23-87	10	5	3.90	26	24	1	0	141	122	74	61	9	89	87	.236	.199	.267	5.57	5.69
Cruz, Rafael	R-R	6-2	225	5-19-77	0	2	4.76	22	0	0	12	23	27	13	12	3	8	20	.290	.286	.294	7.94	3.18
Darrow, Rudy	R-R	5-10	180	2-11-84	1	0	9.31	9	0	0	0	10	11	11	10	0	10	9	.289	.250	.308	8.38	9.31
Diamond, Scott	L-L	6-3	190	7-30-86	5	10	3.50	23	23	0	0	131	152	68	51	9	53	111	.294	.192	.327	7.63	3.64
Dumesnil, Bryan	R-L	6-3	210	9-19-83	1	7	4.41	38	0	0	2	49	46	28	24	5	28	49	.172	.292	10.10	5.14
Gamble, Jerome	R-R	6-4	235	4-5-80	2	1	3.05	29	1	0	3	44	33	20	15	4	24	44	.206	.219	.198	8.93	4.87
Gearrin, Cory	R-R	6-3	200	4-14-86	1	2	2.84	20	0	0	2	25	19	9	8	2	8	20	.213	.167	.231	7.11	2.84
Glavine, Tom	L-L	6-0	205	3-25-66	0	0	4.50	1	1	0	0	2	3	1	1	1	1	0	.300	.400	.000	0.00	4.50
Gunderson, Kevin	R-L	5-10	190	9-16-84	1	3	2.55	42	0	0	2	49	45	14	14	3	20	38	.247	.322	.211	6.93	3.65
Gustafson, Tim	R-R	6-3	185	12-29-84	2	3	3.79	20	7	0	1	62	57	29	26	3	32	49	.249	.212	.284	7.15	4.67
Heath, Deunte	R-R	6-4	215	8-8-85	2	5	4.16	25	12	0	1	80	80	43	37	4	38	70	.260	.313	.220	7.88	4.28
Hyde, Lee	R-L	6-2	185	2-14-85	2	1	4.35	7	0	0	0	10	9	5	5	1	4	13	.231	.143	.280	11.32	3.48
Kimbrel, Craig	R-R	5-11	205	5-28-88	2	1	0.77	12	0	0	6	12	3	1	1	0	7	17	.083	.118	.053	13.11	5.40

	B-T	HT	WT	DOB	W	L	ERA	G	GS	CG	SV	IP	H	R	ER	HR	BB	SO	AVG	vLH	vRH	K/9	BB/9
Lyman, Jeff	R-R	6-3	215	1-14-87	5	7	3.12	33	8	0	0	87	70	36	30	3	43	76	.218	.206	.228	7.89	4.47
Marek, Stephen	L-R	6-2	240	9-3-83	3	3	5.72	38	0	0	2	39	40	31	25	2	29	31	.267	.211	.301	7.09	6.64
Ortegano, Jose	L-L	6-1	145	8-5-87	5	2	2.83	8	8	1	0	48	46	19	15	2	15	42	.247	.049	.303	7.93	2.83
Osuna, Edgar	L-L	6-1	165	11-25-87	4	4	3.72	13	12	0	0	77	74	38	32	7	21	49	.251	.254	.250	5.70	2.44
Palica, Tommy	L-L	6-3	215	7-21-87	1	0	2.79	8	0	0	0	10	8	3	3	0	4	9	.235	.267	.211	8.38	3.72
Reynoso, Ryne	L-R	6-2	215	3-15-85	7	9	3.47	25	24	0	0	148	127	66	57	12	59	89	.236	.298	.188	5.41	3.59
Sullivan, Richard	L-L	6-3	235	4-14-87	0	1	9.45	3	3	0	0	13	21	15	14	0	10	8	.389	.571	.325	5.40	6.75
Venters, Jonny	L-L	6-3	185	3-20-85	4	4	2.76	12	12	1	0	65	60	24	20	2	35	40	.251	.145	.283	5.51	4.82

Fielding

Catcher	PCT	G	PO	A	E	DP	PB
Anderson	1.000	3	16	2	0	0	0
Boscan	.993	71	497	53	4	5	6
Britton	.978	38	241	25	6	3	8
Camarena	.971	29	155	14	5	1	5
Johnson	.982	7	53	1	1	0	0

First Base	PCT	G	PO	A	E	DP
Camarena	1.000	1	1	0	0	0
Creek	.995	44	358	34	2	25
Freeman	.994	40	309	18	2	35
Jones	1.000	1	15	1	0	0
Ka'aihue	.987	45	363	29	5	33
Kirkland	1.000	4	15	2	0	0
Mejia	.955	9	63	1	3	3

Second Base	PCT	G	PO	A	E	DP
Campbell	—	1	0	0	0	0
Creek	1.000	1	1	2	0	0
Guzman	1.000	5	7	12	0	2
Jones	.961	104	187	256	18	57
Kirkland	.968	24	47	45	3	8
Marcial	1.000	2	1	5	0	0
Perez	1.000	3	3	8	0	1
Young	.947	6	8	10	1	4

Third Base	PCT	G	PO	A	E	DP
Campbell	.931	101	63	165	17	11
Creek	.920	10	9	14	2	3
Guzman	1.000	1	1	2	0	0
Kirkland	.917	30	22	44	6	1
Marcial	.833	1	0	5	1	0

Shortstop	PCT	G	PO	A	E	DP
Hicks	.952	128	204	351	28	71
Kirkland	.984	12	22	39	1	10
Marcial	1.000	1	0	2	0	1

Outfield	PCT	G	PO	A	E	DP
Cabrera	.995	95	187	7	1	2
Hernandez	.993	52	139	6	1	1
Heyward	.992	44	113	5	1	1
Johnson	1.000	5	9	1	0	1
Kirkland	1.000	3	4	1	0	0
McLouth	1.000	2	6	0	0	0
Owings	1.000	1	2	0	0	0
Rodriguez	.981	99	200	8	4	3
Young	1.000	125	275	10	0	3

MYRTLE BEACH PELICANS   HIGH CLASS A

CAROLINA LEAGUE

Batting	B-T	HT	WT	DOB	AVG	vLH	vRH	G	AB	R	H	2B	3B	HR	RBI	BB	HBP	SH	SF	SO	SB	CS	SLG	OBP
Anderson, Chris	R-R	6-0	210	10-27-85	.143	.167	.125	4	14	2	2	0	0	1	1	2	0	0	0	9	0	0	.357	.250
Davis, Quentin	L-R	5-10	170	3-7-83	.227	.211	.234	17	66	8	15	2	2	0	3	4	1	1	0	11	1	2	.318	.282
Fisher, Michael	B-R	6-2	188	3-22-85	.238	.234	.239	113	425	50	101	17	1	2	31	32	2	5	1	99	4	5	.296	.293
Freeman, Freddie	L-R	6-5	220	9-12-89	.302	.260	.327	70	255	43	77	19	0	6	34	26	14	0	2	41	1	4	.447	.394
Fuller, Chais	R-R	5-11	190	8-11-84	.306	.375	.250	10	36	2	11	1	1	0	0	1	0	0	0	9	0	1	.389	.324
Gress, Randy	R-R	6-3	180	12-6-84	.194	.180	.200	62	196	16	38	7	0	3	14	15	0	4	0	50	2	2	.276	.251
Heyward, Jason	L-L	6-4	220	8-9-89	.296	.364	.260	49	189	34	56	12	0	10	31	21	2	0	2	30	4	0	.519	.369
Johnson, Cody	L-R	6-4	195	8-18-88	.242	.239	.243	122	422	59	102	18	1	32	84	64	4	0	3	171	10	7	.517	.345
Johnson, Benji	R-R	6-1	195	7-17-86	.221	.226	.219	61	199	18	44	10	0	7	30	20	5	1	1	63	2	3	.377	.307
Kennelly, Matt	R-R	6-1	180	3-21-89	.195	.222	.181	47	159	13	31	4	0	1	6	14	0	1	0	44	0	3	.239	.260
Lee, C.J.	R-R	6-3	195	8-12-84	.239	.255	.230	89	289	40	69	15	3	4	19	21	6	2	1	85	8	9	.353	.303
Linares, Donell	R-R	6-0	190	10-28-83	.287	.269	.296	130	505	63	145	32	1	15	87	22	11	2	4	41	5	5	.444	.328
Lundahl, Chad	R-R	6-2	190	8-18-84	.157	.079	.191	60	204	15	32	8	0	2	12	6	2	0	0	34	1	1	.225	.189
Marcial, Robert	R-R	5-10	170	4-21-84	.195	.213	.185	67	215	23	42	3	0	3	17	10	2	12	0	51	6	2	.251	.238
McCann, Brian	L-R	6-3	230	2-20-84	.333	.400	.000	2	6	1	2	2	0	0	1	1	0	0	0	2	0	0	.667	.429
Mejia, Ernesto	R-R	6-6	190	12-2-85	.293	.385	.267	17	58	8	17	7	0	3	12	4	3	0	2	16	0	1	.569	.358
Miles, Cole	B-R	5-8	165	3-24-87	.266	.272	.263	119	421	64	112	6	7	4	27	43	4	12	4	70	16	7	.342	.337
Milligan, Adam	L-R	6-3	210	3-14-88	.167	.125	.188	6	24	2	4	1	0	1	6	1	0	0	0	8	0	0	.333	.200
Owings, Jon	R-R	6-4	195	4-4-85	.198	.208	.192	60	202	18	40	9	4	2	15	13	2	1	0	65	3	5	.312	.253
Rodriguez, Gerardo	R-R	6-1	195	10-25-87	.281	.299	.272	60	224	34	63	9	2	12	41	15	2	0	1	72	4	1	.500	.331
Shehan, Chris	R-R	6-0	205	5-5-87	.261	.244	.268	39	138	15	36	15	0	1	6	5	1	0	0	38	3	3	.391	.293
Shults, Stephen	R-R	6-2	190	12-27-86	.258	.231	.278	10	31	4	8	3	0	0	4	3	1	0	0	9	0	1	.355	.343
Sucre, Jesus	R-R	6-0	200	4-30-88	.259	.219	.278	53	197	17	51	8	1	5	20	8	0	0	1	33	3	1	.386	.286
Sumoza, Luis	R-R	6-0	170	7-15-88	.189	.273	.154	9	37	1	7	1	0	0	2	3	0	0	0	9	0	2	.216	.250
Whitmer, Jace	R-R	6-4	225	12-18-87	.000	—	.000	2	7	0	0	0	0	0	0	3	0	0	0	3	0	0	.000	.300

Pitching	B-T	HT	WT	DOB	W	L	ERA	G	GS	CG	SV	IP	H	R	ER	HR	BB	SO	AVG	vLH	vRH	K/9	BB/9
Barrett, Eric	L-L	6-3	180	12-19-86	1	2	6.08	20	0	0	0	24	24	16	16	1	23	24	.267	.273	.263	9.13	8.75
Beachey, Brandon	R-R	6-2	210	9-3-86	4	3	3.41	22	8	0	1	58	59	31	22	2	15	47	.267	.273	.261	7.29	2.33
Broadway, Mike	R-R	6-5	190	3-30-87	2	7	4.50	35	1	0	0	58	59	32	29	5	36	53	.266	.306	.228	8.22	5.59
Castro, Yeliar	R-R	6-3	180	12-3-87	0	0	3.00	1	0	0	0	3	0	1	1	0	1	5	.000	.000	.000	15.00	3.00
Chapman, Jaye	R-R	6-0	180	5-22-87	1	2	4.08	27	0	0	0	35	35	18	16	3	20	37	.257	.306	.216	9.42	5.09
Cordier, Erik	R-R	6-3	195	2-25-86	7	8	3.87	25	25	1	0	121	115	62	52	13	74	88	.257	.271	.243	6.55	5.50
Currin, Patrick	R-R	6-0	188	5-12-84	1	0	3.28	20	0	0	1	16	18	10	9	3	11	20	.272	.190	.328	7.30	4.01
Darrow, Rudy	R-R	5-10	180	2-11-84	3	6	6.07	24	0	0	0	30	37	22	20	1	19	26	.314	.355	.268	7.89	5.76
Francis, David	R-R	6-1	200	2-8-88	0	0	7.02	4	4	0	0	17	16	14	13	2	13	22	.258	.323	.194	11.88	7.02
Gearrin, Cory	R-R	6-3	200	4-14-86	0	1	1.84	27	0	0	17	29	22	6	6	3	3	32	.198	.208	.190	9.82	0.92
Gustafson, Tim	R-R	6-3	185	12-29-84	0	0	2.03	10	0	0	0	13	15	7	3	1	7	8	.278	.269	.286	5.40	4.72
Hernandez, Moises	R-R	6-1	168	3-18-84	0	2	21.60	5	0	0	0	5	13	13	12	2	4	4	.500	.588	.333	7.20	7.20
Hodges, Casey	R-R	6-2	195	3-29-85	0	0	11.20	7	0	0	0	14	20	18	17	2	6	10	.328	.200	.452	6.59	3.95
Hoover, J.J.	R-R	6-3	215	8-13-87	0	0	9.00	1	1	0	0	3	3	3	3	1	5	2	.250	.375	.000	6.00	15.00
Hudson, Tim	R-R	6-1	170	7-14-75	0	1	5.79	2	2	0	0	5	5	3	3	0	2	3	.263	.231	.333	5.79	3.86
Hyde, Lee	R-L	6-2	185	2-14-85	3	1	1.21	17	0	0	1	22	13	4	3	0	9	28	.163	.154	.171	11.28	3.63
Kimbrel, Craig	R-R	5-11	205	5-28-88	0	2	5.47	19	0	0	2	26	18	19	16	2	28	45	.200	.275	.103	15.38	9.57
Locke, Jeff	L-L	6-2	180	11-20-87	1	4	5.52	10	10	0	0	46	47	31	28	1	26	43	.272	.274	.270	8.47	5.12

2-team total (17 Lynchburg)			5	8	4.59	27	27	0	0	127	145	75	65	5	44	99	—	—	—	7.00	3.11
Mehlich, Mike	R-R	6-2 180	9-5-87	1	5	8.07	23	0	0	2	36	45	39	32	4	22	30	.302	.264	.338	7.57	5.55
Ortegano, Jose	L-L	6-1 145	8-5-87	4	5	3.49	21	12	0	0	70	56	30	27	4	19	59	.220	.165	.246	7.62	2.45
Osuna, Edgar	L-L	6-1 165	11-25-87	3	6	4.33	14	14	1	0	73	82	40	35	4	14	56	.275	.294	.265	6.94	1.73
Palica, Tommy	L-L	6-3 215	7-21-87	5	1	3.31	41	0	0	6	52	46	24	19	4	21	59	.238	.270	.218	10.28	3.66
Pruneda, Benino	R-R	5-9 170	8-8-88	2	3	5.47	36	0	0	3	51	54	35	31	3	32	64	.273	.287	.256	11.29	5.65
Rivas, Carlos	L-L	6-3 160	1-3-85	2	3	7.52	8	5	0	0	26	33	27	22	0	16	17	.297	.263	.315	5.81	5.47
2-team total (13 Wilmington)			5	3	4.98	21	5	0	1	47	45	32	26	0	25	36	—	—	—	6.89	4.79
Rodgers, Chad	L-R	6-3 185	11-23-87	0	1	6.75	4	0	0	0	4	5	4	3	0	2	4	.313	.273	.400	9.00	4.50
Rohrbough, Cole	L-L	6-3 205	5-23-87	6	8	5.77	23	22	0	0	117	129	80	75	12	48	100	.280	.327	.259	7.69	3.69
Sullivan, Richard	L-L	6-3 235	4-14-87	2	12	4.25	19	19	1	0	112	115	66	53	5	39	80	.266	.254	.271	6.41	3.12
Thompson, Jacob	R-R	6-6 215	11-19-86	5	4	3.57	16	14	0	0	91	88	40	36	8	42	78	.260	.247	.274	7.74	4.17
Wilson, Tyler	L-L	6-1 210	7-11-86	0	2	4.58	15	0	0	0	18	12	11	9	1	14	15	.190	.100	.233	7.64	7.13

Fielding

Catcher	PCT	G	PO	A	E	DP	PB
Anderson	.969	4	29	2	1	0	0
Johnson	.995	43	333	35	2	1	4
Kennelly	.980	44	318	31	7	3	6
Sucre	.976	46	356	53	10	5	10
Whitmer	.913	2	21	0	2	0	0

First Base	PCT	G	PO	A	E	DP
Freeman	.990	69	548	44	6	42
Fuller	1.000	1	6	0	0	0
Gress	1.000	4	36	4	0	2
Linares	1.000	10	87	4	0	7
Lundahl	.956	5	41	2	2	4
Mejia	.988	9	77	5	1	8
Rodriguez	.983	44	329	21	6	26
Shults	1.000	1	4	0	0	2

Second Base	PCT	G	PO	A	E	DP
Fisher	.967	107	220	306	18	65
Gress	1.000	2	0	4	0	1
Lee	—	1	0	0	0	0
Marcial	.946	13	18	35	3	4
Miles	.974	18	27	48	2	6

Third Base	PCT	G	PO	A	E	DP
Fisher	.800	2	2	2	1	1
Fuller	.833	1	2	3	1	1
Gress	.909	19	9	31	4	2
Linares	.918	109	68	179	22	12
Lundahl	.909	6	2	8	1	2
Marcial	.846	3	2	9	2	1

Shortstop	PCT	G	PO	A	E	DP
Fuller	.935	9	17	26	3	4
Gress	.940	35	52	89	9	19
Lundahl	.949	49	80	106	10	26

	PCT	G	PO	A	E	DP
Marcial	.941	49	67	141	13	21
Miles	1.000	1	1	0	0	0

Outfield	PCT	G	PO	A	E	DP
Davis	1.000	15	35	0	0	0
Heyward	.968	41	81	9	3	0
Johnson	.961	91	139	8	6	2
Johnson	—	1	0	0	0	0
Lee	.958	85	153	5	7	1
Marcial	1.000	1	3	0	0	0
Miles	.989	92	174	7	2	1
Milligan	1.000	6	11	0	0	0
Owings	.949	34	55	1	3	0
Rodriguez	1.000	5	7	0	0	0
Shehan	.900	36	60	3	7	0
Shults	1.000	5	4	0	0	0
Sumoza	.938	9	13	2	1	1

ROME BRAVES   LOW CLASS A

SOUTH ATLANTIC LEAGUE

Batting	B-T	HT	WT	DOB	AVG	vLH	vRH	G	AB	R	H	2B	3B	HR	RBI	BB	HBP	SH	SF	SO	SB	CS	SLG	OBP
Anderson, Chris	R-R	6-0	210	10-27-85	.063	.000	.077	7	16	2	1	0	0	0	3	0	0	0	0	12	0	0	.063	.211
Barba, Ryan	R-R	6-0	190	12-6-84	.201	.222	.194	120	378	41	76	20	0	2	30	26	5	13	2	74	4	0	.270	.260
Berres, David	L-R	6-1	185	12-16-86	.200	.000	.227	6	25	1	5	1	0	0	1	3	0	0	0	2	0	0	.240	.286
Campusano, Albaro	R-R	5-11	200	12-14-86	.288	.278	.291	103	382	55	110	15	4	5	35	28	6	1	4	52	15	5	.387	.343
Coe, Adam	R-R	6-0	190	6-7-88	.172	.167	.174	8	29	1	5	0	0	0	1	0	0	0	0	10	0	1	.172	.172
Culver, Calvin	R-R	6-2	220	10-7-88	.225	.203	.231	86	316	28	71	20	0	4	29	22	4	1	3	62	2	5	.326	.281
Fuller, Chais	R-R	5-11	190	8-11-84	.207	.185	.214	77	246	21	51	11	1	1	25	15	4	2	4	51	2	3	.272	.260
Gress, Randy	R-R	6-3	180	12-9-85	.333	.667	.250	6	15	2	5	0	0	0	1	3	0	0	1	3	0	0	.333	.421
Hiller, Layton	R-R	6-3	220	5-18-88	.111	.000	.182	7	18	0	2	0	0	0	0	3	0	2	1	0	1	0	.111	.200
Infante, Omar	R-R	6-0	180	12-26-81	.294	.333	.273	5	17	1	5	0	0	0	0	3	0	0	0	2	1	0	.294	.400
Kennelly, Matt	R-R	6-1	180	3-21-89	.255	.235	.260	46	157	11	40	7	0	1	16	13	2	0	1	36	1	2	.318	.318
Kramer, Matt	R-R	6-3	215	5-7-86	.385	.500	.286	4	13	5	5	1	0	2	3	1	0	0	0	2	0	0	.923	.429
Lee, C.J.	R-R	6-3	195	8-12-84	.239	.313	.200	14	46	4	11	2	0	0	5	3	0	2	1	11	1	1	.283	.280
Maddox, Craig	L-R	5-10	190	4-10-85	.231	.000	.237	11	39	2	9	0	0	0	1	1	1	0	0	15	1	0	.231	.268
McLouth, Nate	L-R	5-11	180	10-28-81	.000	.000	—	1	2	0	0	0	0	0	0	1	0	0	0	1	0	0	.000	.333
Miles, Kuyaunnis	L-R	5-11	175	5-15-87	.279	.167	.297	14	43	4	12	3	0	0	1	1	1	2	0	17	1	1	.349	.311
Milligan, Adam	L-R	6-3	210	3-14-88	.345	.270	.363	52	197	28	68	14	2	10	33	12	4	0	1	43	4	5	.589	.393
Moody, Shayne	R-R	6-0	200	10-24-84	.262	.246	.266	84	298	37	78	9	0	1	28	22	4	7	1	43	11	8	.302	.320
Rodriguez, Gerardo	R-R	6-1	195	10-25-87	.258	.313	.237	63	240	29	62	9	5	11	42	12	4	0	3	69	4	1	.475	.301
Ross, David	R-R	6-2	240	3-19-77	.500	—	.500	2	6	1	3	0	0	1	4	1	0	0	0	1	0	0	1.000	.571
Santamaria, Jahdiel	R-R	6-3	170	4-5-87	.274	.259	.279	62	212	26	58	8	2	0	14	12	3	1	1	37	5	7	.330	.320
Schlehuber, Braeden	R-R	6-3	190	1-7-88	.199	.153	.214	100	351	41	70	23	0	5	37	18	14	3	2	59	5	1	.308	.265
Shehan, Chris	R-R	6-0	205	5-5-87	.248	.327	.224	66	214	32	53	9	2	2	19	17	3	1	3	56	3	6	.336	.308
Shults, Stephen	R-R	6-2	190	12-27-86	.228	.241	.225	67	232	24	53	16	0	4	21	14	3	2	3	68	2	2	.349	.278
Sime, Samuel	R-R	6-2	180	4-20-87	.242	.211	.252	108	368	47	89	18	4	2	27	23	2	2	1	79	13	7	.329	.289
Sucre, Jesus	R-R	6-0	200	4-30-88	.325	.450	.287	45	169	14	55	15	0	1	18	6	1	0	0	17	1	4	.432	.352
Sumoza, Luis	R-R	6-0	170	7-15-88	.271	.286	.266	119	461	48	125	27	2	4	47	28	3	1	1	100	8	9	.364	.316
Ware, L.V.	R-R	5-10	185	3-18-87	.130	.200	.111	17	46	5	6	0	1	1	5	2	1	2	0	14	3	1	.239	.184
Wiley, Derek	R-R	6-4	217	4-9-87	.176	.000	.220	15	51	6	9	1	0	0	2	8	1	0	0	13	0	1	.196	.300

Pitching	B-T	HT	WT	DOB	W	L	ERA	G	GS	CG	SV	IP	H	R	ER	HR	BB	SO	AVG	vLH	vRH	K/9	BB/9
Beachey, Brandon	R-R	6-2	210	9-3-86	0	0	5.60	12	0	0	0	18	20	11	11	0	4	17	.290	.269	.302	8.66	2.04
Bullard, Adam	R-R	6-6	225	2-10-87	0	1	20.25	6	0	0	0	5	11	15	12	1	6	5	.407	.333	.467	8.44	10.13
Carlyle, Buddy	L-R	6-3	210	12-21-77	0	0	0.00	1	1	0	0	2	1	0	0	0	0	1	.200	.000	.250	4.50	0.00
Castro, Yeliar	R-R	6-3	180	12-3-87	4	4	4.50	31	3	0	1	64	59	36	32	3	32	73	.250	.269	.238	10.27	4.50
Chapman, Jaye	R-R	6-0	180	5-22-87	1	0	0.40	19	0	0	13	23	9	3	1	0	4	29	.113	.138	.098	11.51	1.59
Clemens, Paul	R-R	6-4	170	2-14-88	6	5	5.91	26	11	0	3	85	105	67	56	7	49	64	.296	.303	.291	6.75	5.17

Name	B-T	HT	WT	DOB	W	L	ERA	G	GS	CG	SV	IP	H	R	ER	HR	BB	SO	AVG	vLH	vRH	K/9	BB/9
Delgado, Dimasther	L-L	6-2	180	3-3-89	5	7	3.61	17	17	0	0	100	89	43	40	4	26	104	.237	.229	.240	9.39	2.35
Delgado, Randall	R-R	6-3	165	2-9-90	5	10	4.35	25	25	1	0	124	123	70	60	9	49	141	.256	.201	.299	10.23	3.56
DeVall, Brett	R-L	6-3	215	1-8-90	4	4	3.52	10	10	1	0	54	50	22	21	3	14	41	.245	.258	.239	6.88	2.35
Francis, David	R-R	6-1	200	2-8-88	5	7	3.67	30	6	0	3	88	101	43	36	5	30	73	.293	.325	.268	7.44	3.06
Glavine, Tom	L-L	6-0	205	3-25-66	1	0	0.00	1	1	0	0	6	3	0	0	0	0	2	.143	—	.143	3.00	0.00
Gustafson, Tim	R-R	6-3	185	12-29-84	0	1	7.36	4	1	0	0	7	11	7	6	0	3	4	.333	.333	.333	4.91	3.68
Harris, Ty'Relle	R-R	6-4	235	12-12-86	2	0	0.77	9	0	0	0	12	5	1	1	0	5	15	.132	.077	.160	11.57	3.86
Hernandez, Moises	R-R	6-1	168	3-18-84	1	0	3.52	7	0	0	0	15	14	7	6	0	5	5	.250	.308	.200	2.93	2.93
Hodges, Casey	R-R	6-2	195	3-29-85	0	0	12.00	2	0	0	0	3	5	4	4	0	2	2	.417	.400	.429	6.00	6.00
Hoover, J.J.	R-R	6-3	215	8-13-87	7	6	3.35	25	18	0	1	134	135	58	50	9	25	148	.259	.276	.248	9.92	1.67
Kimbrel, Craig	R-R	5-11	205	5-28-88	0	0	0.90	16	0	0	10	20	9	2	2	0	6	38	.132	.125	.139	17.10	2.70
McMillan, Clayton	L-L	6-3	180	9-19-86	2	3	3.32	35	0	0	1	38	46	22	14	0	13	32	.303	.431	.238	7.58	3.08
Mehlich, Mike	R-R	6-2	180	9-5-87	1	2	5.28	10	0	0	0	29	32	18	17	3	10	25	.276	.282	.273	7.76	3.10
Minor, Mike	R-L	6-3	200	12-26-87	0	1	0.64	4	4	0	0	14	10	1	1	0	0	17	.208	.091	.243	10.93	0.00
Paulino, Angelo	R-R	6-4	190	12-15-86	6	4	2.67	37	0	0	2	64	58	28	19	2	27	78	.233	.221	.241	10.97	3.80
Pruneda, Benino	R-R	5-9	170	8-8-88	0	0	0.00	8	0	0	6	8	2	0	0	0	1	13	.080	.167	.000	14.63	1.13
Railsback, Cody	R-R	6-4	175	6-3-87	0	0	3.86	8	0	0	1	12	12	5	5	0	5	7	.279	.333	.250	5.40	3.86
Small, Matt	R-R	6-3	185	12-29-87	1	3	3.41	25	0	0	6	34	25	13	13	2	13	36	.203	.173	.225	9.44	3.41
Spruill, Zeke	B-R	6-4	184	9-11-89	8	6	3.03	20	19	0	1	116	120	54	39	9	24	95	.261	.234	.277	7.37	1.86
Sullivan, Richard	L-L	6-3	235	4-14-87	4	1	3.72	5	5	1	0	29	37	18	12	2	5	27	.306	.310	.304	8.38	1.55
Teheran, Julio	R-R	6-2	150	1-27-91	1	3	4.78	7	7	0	0	38	42	20	20	2	11	28	.288	.250	.309	6.69	2.63
Thompson, Jacob	R-R	6-6	215	11-19-86	2	5	5.20	11	11	0	0	64	74	41	37	5	14	41	.298	.282	.310	5.77	1.97
Wilson, Andrew	R-R	6-2	180	7-30-87	0	0	0.00	2	0	0	0	3	1	0	0	0	0	3	.100	.000	.125	9.00	0.00

Fielding

Catcher	PCT	G	PO	A	E	DP	PB
Anderson	1.000	1	1	0	0	0	0
Kennelly	.997	38	301	24	1	2	4
Kramer	1.000	1	5	0	0	0	0
Ross	1.000	2	5	1	0	0	0
Schlehuber	.988	74	581	60	8	6	8
Sucre	.990	31	274	36	3	3	7

First Base	PCT	G	PO	A	E	DP
Anderson	1.000	1	7	1	0	1
Coe	1.000	3	17	0	0	1
Fuller	.993	36	269	13	2	22
Gress	1.000	2	12	2	0	4
Kramer	.889	1	8	0	1	0
Rodriguez	.989	58	492	28	6	44
Shults	.987	27	217	10	3	13
Wiley	1.000	15	117	7	0	9

Second Base	PCT	G	PO	A	E	DP
Campusano	.974	96	170	245	11	61

(Second Base cont.)	PCT	G	PO	A	E	DP
Fuller	.951	15	28	30	3	7
Gress	1.000	1	1	1	0	0
Infante	.750	1	2	1	1	0
Moody	.984	32	50	75	2	13
Sime	1.000	1	2	2	0	0

Third Base	PCT	G	PO	A	E	DP
Coe	1.000	3	0	5	0	0
Fuller	.894	20	19	40	7	5
Gress	.500	1	1	0	1	0
Infante	1.000	1	0	3	0	1
Moody	.948	46	30	79	6	6
Shults	.857	16	9	21	5	2
Sime	.901	65	44	128	19	13

Shortstop	PCT	G	PO	A	E	DP
Barba	.945	120	169	314	28	61
Fuller	.971	9	5	28	1	4
Gress	.800	3	1	3	1	0
Infante	.833	1	2	3	1	0

(Shortstop cont.)	PCT	G	PO	A	E	DP
Moody	1.000	2	3	4	0	2
Sime	.913	12	13	29	4	5

Outfield	PCT	G	PO	A	E	DP
Berres	1.000	6	14	0	0	0
Culver	.974	80	143	7	4	0
Hiller	1.000	6	9	0	0	0
Infante	1.000	1	1	0	0	0
Lee	1.000	14	23	0	0	0
McLouth	1.000	1	1	0	0	0
Miles	1.000	12	21	0	0	0
Milligan	.958	48	67	2	3	0
Santamaria	.990	59	98	6	1	0
Shehan	.944	65	112	5	7	5
Shults	1.000	15	15	3	0	0
Sime	.750	3	3	0	1	0
Sumoza	.951	108	184	11	10	3
Ware	.909	16	19	1	2	0

DANVILLE BRAVES   ROOKIE
APPALACHIAN LEAGUE

Batting	B-T	HT	WT	DOB	AVG	vLH	vRH	G	AB	R	H	2B	3B	HR	RBI	BB	HBP	SH	SF	SO	SB	CS	SLG	OBP
Adair, Travis	L-R	5-10	175	12-23-87	.206	.071	.227	36	102	12	21	3	1	0	13	11	1	2	0	14	3	2	.255	.289
Anderson, Chris	R-R	6-0	210	10-27-85	.000	—	.000	2	3	0	0	0	0	0	0	0	0	0	0	2	0	0	.000	.000
Barnett, Tyler	L-R	5-9	175	2-22-86	.125	.200	.000	6	8	2	1	0	0	0	1	2	1	1	0	1	1	0	.125	.364
Bethancourt, Christian	R-R	6-2	175	9-2-91	.260	.182	.282	14	50	10	13	5	0	2	8	6	0	0	0	16	1	1	.480	.339
Curley, Chris	R-R	6-0	185	8-25-87	.158	.333	.077	11	19	0	3	1	0	0	2	2	0	0	0	4	1	0	.211	.238
Elorriaga-Matra, Daniel	R-R	6-0	185	12-28-88	.127	.217	.103	38	110	9	14	7	0	0	8	7	4	0	2	34	0	1	.191	.203
Gress, Randy	R-R	6-3	180	12-6-84	.324	.200	.370	10	37	7	12	3	1	0	8	2	1	0	0	7	0	1	.459	.375
Harrilchak, Cory	L-L	5-10	175	10-27-87	.324	.235	.340	60	222	43	72	10	5	2	41	27	2	1	1	22	19	2	.441	.401
Hefflinger, Robby	R-R	6-5	225	1-3-90	.242	.293	.231	61	240	23	58	11	1	7	37	16	1	0	3	76	1	0	.383	.288
Jones, Mycal	R-R	5-10	165	5-30-87	.258	.160	.284	64	244	50	63	18	6	4	27	26	5	3	4	55	19	4	.430	.337
Kreke, Jordan	R-R	6-1	205	5-21-87	.271	.415	.237	63	218	35	59	10	1	2	15	23	8	1	1	32	2	2	.353	.360
Marval, Osman	B-R	6-1	185	11-26-86	.297	.400	.276	37	118	17	35	10	0	1	20	9	0	0	1	12	1	0	.407	.344
Miles, Kuyaunnis	L-R	5-11	175	5-15-87	.197	.200	.197	30	76	10	15	2	1	2	6	4	1	0	1	30	1	4	.329	.244
Milligan, Adam	R-R	6-3	210	3-14-88	.439	.500	.419	9	41	9	18	5	1	2	10	3	2	0	0	7	0	0	.756	.500
Odreman, Alberto	R-R	6-3	210	3-12-89	.333	—	.333	1	3	1	1	0	0	0	0	0	0	0	0	1	0	0	.333	.333
Rauh, Bobby	R-R	6-0	172	11-25-87	.229	.188	.239	29	83	15	19	6	1	0	8	8	2	3	0	31	9	1	.325	.312
Rose, Kyle	R-R	6-0	165	5-24-89	.600	1.000	.333	1	5	1	3	0	0	0	0	0	0	0	0	0	1	0	.600	.600
Shimabukuro, Ryohei	L-R	6-0	205	9-1-89	.333	—	.333	2	6	0	2	0	0	0	0	0	0	0	0	0	0	0	.333	.333
Spanjer-Furstenburg, Riaan	R-R	6-2	235	2-8-88	.359	.440	.337	62	234	36	84	19	0	8	53	16	8	0	5	37	0	3	.543	.411
Ware, L.V.	R-R	5-10	185	3-18-87	.293	.367	.270	62	249	40	73	16	5	0	24	12	8	3	3	39	24	4	.398	.342
Weaver, Matt	R-R	6-0	175	1-27-90	.291	.292	.291	35	110	11	32	5	0	1	16	4	2	3	2	27	4	6	.364	.322
Whitmer, Jace	R-R	6-4	225	12-18-87	.242	.148	.279	25	95	8	23	4	0	0	5	4	3	0	1	28	1	0	.284	.291
Wiley, Derek	R-R	6-4	217	4-9-87	.231	.333	.191	25	65	10	15	3	0	2	5	2	4	1	1	17	0	0	.369	.292

Pitching

Pitching	B-T	HT	WT	DOB	W	L	ERA	G	GS	CG	SV	IP	H	R	ER	HR	BB	SO	AVG	vLH	vRH	K/9	BB/9
Accomando, Dennis	L-L	6-1	181	7-16-87	0	0	6.75	9	1	0	0	15	16	12	11	1	8	6	.271	.000	.333	3.68	4.91
Avilan, Luis	L-L	6-2	165	7-19-89	0	2	3.05	14	3	0	2	38	25	14	13	1	17	34	.185	.158	.196	7.98	3.99
Barrett, Eric	L-L	6-3	180	12-19-86	1	0	7.36	6	0	0	0	7	10	9	6	0	8	5	.323	.200	.346	6.14	9.82
Berryhill, Thomas	R-R	5-10	185	12-9-87	1	1	2.55	16	0	0	6	18	15	5	5	1	9	12	.231	.227	.233	6.11	4.58
Bullard, Adam	R-R	6-6	225	2-10-87	0	1	6.92	6	0	0	0	13	13	16	10	1	10	12	.245	.250	.243	8.31	6.92
Crim, Matt	L-L	6-0	195	8-14-87	10	2	3.18	13	11	0	0	68	70	26	24	5	10	48	.265	.345	.243	6.35	1.32
Hale, David	R-R	6-2	200	9-27-87	2	1	1.13	7	1	0	1	16	7	4	2	0	5	12	.130	.217	.065	6.75	2.81
Harris, Ty'Relle	R-R	6-4	235	12-12-86	0	0	1.59	3	0	0	1	6	1	1	1	0	0	9	.227	.333	.154	14.29	0.00
Himpsl, Derick	L-L	6-4	240	6-4-86	3	0	5.48	14	0	0	1	21	17	17	13	1	22	35	.198	.111	.221	14.77	9.28
Hodges, Casey	R-R	6-2	195	3-29-85	2	0	2.75	14	0	0	6	20	20	10	6	0	11	17	.247	.174	.276	7.78	5.03
Lorick, Jeff	L-L	6-0	195	12-18-87	2	1	4.09	17	3	0	3	33	30	17	15	1	13	42	.236	.167	.252	11.45	3.55
Masters, Chris	L-L	6-0	230	10-1-87	8	4	1.42	13	11	1	0	70	53	17	11	1	9	85	.206	.200	.208	10.98	1.16
Mora, Edigson	R-R	6-1	195	10-20-87	0	1	3.55	5	1	0	1	13	17	6	5	1	3	12	.309	.235	.342	8.53	2.13
Oberholtzer, Brett	L-L	6-2	190	7-1-89	6	2	2.01	12	12	1	0	67	46	17	15	1	6	56	.191	.217	.180	7.52	0.81
Railsback, Cody	R-R	6-4	175	6-3-87	1	0	1.93	8	0	0	1	9	5	2	2	0	5	8	.147	.250	.115	7.71	4.82
Rasmus, Cory	R-R	6-1	220	11-6-87	4	2	3.48	13	6	1	1	52	34	21	20	1	26	57	.189	.179	.198	9.93	4.53
Stovall, Tyler	L-L	6-1	180	12-27-89	3	2	3.12	12	12	0	0	52	36	22	18	1	56	57	.202	.147	.215	9.87	9.69
Surinach, Julio	R-R	6-1	157	7-29-88	2	1	3.07	14	0	0	3	44	35	15	15	0	16	36	.224	.250	.205	7.36	3.27
Teheran, Julio	R-R	6-2	150	1-27-91	2	1	2.68	7	7	0	0	44	36	17	13	2	7	39	.229	.310	.182	8.04	1.44

Fielding

Catcher	PCT	G	PO	A	E	DP	PB
Anderson	1.000	2	9	1	0	0	0
Bethancourt	.974	11	103	8	3	1	5
Elorriaga-Matra	.993	37	258	43	2	3	5
Marval	.973	16	93	14	3	0	2
Whitmer	.983	16	110	8	2	0	1

First Base	PCT	G	PO	A	E	DP
Gress	1.000	2	1	0	1	0
Marval	1.000	4	40	1	0	1
Shimabukuro	1.000	1	8	0	0	0
Spanjer-Furstenburg	.989	54	506	30	6	40
Wiley	1.000	15	101	8	0	3

Second Base	PCT	G	PO	A	E	DP
Adair	.973	34	57	85	4	16
Barnett	1.000	5	2	9	0	1
Gress	1.000	6	14	13	0	2
Weaver	.952	33	54	86	7	16

Third Base	PCT	G	PO	A	E	DP
Curley	.895	7	5	12	2	0
Gress	.900	2	1	8	1	0
Kreke	.913	61	41	138	17	10
Weaver	1.000	1	0	1	0	0

Shortstop	PCT	G	PO	A	E	DP
Barnett	.500	1	1	0	1	0

	PCT	G	PO	A	E	DP
Curley	1.000	1	0	1	0	0
Gress	1.000	3	5	6	0	0
Jones	.936	64	73	190	18	26
Kreke	1.000	2	0	5	0	2
Weaver	.818	2	3	6	2	0

Outfield	PCT	G	PO	A	E	DP
Harrilchak	.980	58	92	4	2	1
Hefflinger	.949	51	55	1	3	0
Miles	1.000	11	10	1	0	0
Milligan	1.000	7	6	0	0	0
Rauh	.974	23	37	1	1	1
Rose	1.000	1	1	0	0	0
Ware	.990	62	94	5	1	1

GCL BRAVES

GULF COAST LEAGUE

ROOKIE

Batting	B-T	HT	WT	DOB	AVG	vLH	vRH	G	AB	R	H	2B	3B	HR	RBI	BB	HBP	SH	SF	SO	SB	CS	SLG	OBP
Bethancourt, Christian	R-R	6-2	175	9-2-91	.284	.200	.314	32	116	22	33	9	1	2	19	11	1	0	3	22	7	0	.431	.344
Blanco, Elys	B-R	5-11	160	4-8-89	.240	.182	.264	34	75	17	18	1	0	0	3	13	4	1	1	20	9	4	.253	.376
Coe, Adam	R-R	6-0	190	6-7-88	.176	.250	.154	5	17	1	3	0	0	0	0	1	0	0	0	5	0	0	.176	.222
Contreras, Luis	L-L	6-0	170	3-31-91	.182	.188	.180	44	77	9	14	2	0	0	8	13	1	2	0	19	3	1	.208	.308
Coury, Daniel	R-R	6-4	205	9-5-86	.125	.167	.111	9	24	0	3	2	0	0	2	3	0	0	0	6	0	0	.208	.222
Dalfonso, Jakob	L-R	6-3	200	1-25-90	.259	.206	.276	41	139	19	36	7	0	0	19	10	3	0	0	20	7	2	.309	.322
De Los Santos, Fernando	R-R	6-1	180	1-18-90	.229	.345	.184	36	105	15	24	4	2	1	12	7	1	5	2	25	1	1	.333	.278
Falcon, Daniel	R-R	6-1	220	12-27-88	.257	.182	.278	45	148	13	38	7	2	3	15	7	0	0	1	42	2	2	.392	.288
Feliz, Anthony	R-R	6-2	195	10-7-87	.261	.325	.235	46	142	20	37	9	2	2	10	8	2	2	0	26	4	2	.394	.309
Hanson, Jake	R-R	6-0	180	11-20-89	.279	.323	.265	44	129	26	36	9	2	3	14	19	5	0	0	39	4	2	.450	.392
Hiller, Layton	R-R	6-3	220	5-18-88	.274	.245	.284	53	197	25	54	17	0	8	45	5	7	0	0	62	2	1	.482	.316
Kramer, Matt	R-R	6-3	215	5-7-86	.254	.273	.244	29	63	11	16	3	0	4	10	1	4	1	1	14	0	0	.492	.304
Linger, Jim	R-R	5-11	195	9-6-90	.273	.316	.255	41	132	15	36	4	1	2	8	9	1	0	0	11	3	4	.364	.324
Lovett, Chris	R-R	6-0	180	12-21-88	.231	.250	.225	35	104	12	24	7	1	1	12	13	2	3	0	16	2	3	.346	.328
Mejia, Ernesto	R-R	6-6	190	12-2-85	.214	.111	.263	10	28	3	6	1	0	1	3	2	0	1	0	5	0	0	.357	.324
Odreman, Alberto	R-R	6-3	210	3-12-89	.251	.240	.255	55	195	24	49	3	1	9	29	12	3	0	0	47	1	0	.415	.305
Owings, Jon	R-R	6-4	195	4-4-85	.167	.333	.000	2	6	1	1	1	0	0	1	0	0	0	0	3	0	0	.333	.286
Payne, Mike	L-R	6-0	190	12-3-85	.282	.429	.250	17	39	4	11	1	0	0	3	1	0	0	1	8	0	0	.308	.293
Rose, Kyle	R-R	6-0	165	5-24-89	.282	.333	.264	47	142	26	40	4	1	1	10	20	6	0	1	26	14	4	.345	.391
Weaver, Matt	R-R	6-0	175	1-27-90	.136	.333	.063	11	22	4	3	0	1	0	2	1	1	0	0	6	1	0	.227	.208
Whitmer, Jace	R-R	6-4	225	12-18-87	.156	.000	.208	10	32	3	5	1	1	0	2	2	0	0	1	9	0	0	.250	.200

Pitching	B-T	HT	WT	DOB	W	L	ERA	G	GS	CG	SV	IP	H	R	ER	HR	BB	SO	AVG	vLH	vRH	K/9	BB/9
Acord, Joshua	R-R	6-3	200	3-10-90	1	1	2.92	9	0	0	1	12	6	4	4	1	8	18	.140	.136	.143	13.14	5.84
Alvarez, Danilo	R-R	6-0	210	1-14-90	1	1	3.79	13	0	0	1	19	16	9	8	2	4	18	.235	.300	.184	8.53	1.89
Brewer, Caleb	R-R	6-3	205	2-2-89	3	3	2.82	12	10	0	0	45	20	14	14	0	31	65	.132	.132	.133	13.10	6.25
Darrow, Rudy	R-R	5-10	180	2-11-84	1	1	3.00	2	0	0	0	3	4	4	1	0	0	3	.333	.667	.222	9.00	0.00
Escobar, Reidy	R-R	6-4	170	11-27-89	1	1	4.26	11	0	0	0	19	21	10	9	1	7	21	.276	.241	.298	9.95	3.32
Estevez, Wilton	R-R	6-1	175	5-30-87	0	2	4.03	13	0	0	2	22	15	10	10	1	14	30	.188	.259	.151	12.09	5.64
Farrell, Kyle	R-R	6-4	210	5-6-89	0	3	6.92	12	5	0	0	39	44	37	30	4	19	31	.284	.286	.282	7.15	4.38
Hayes, Jamie	R-R	6-0	195	10-21-87	0	1	0.61	12	0	0	4	15	12	4	1	0	2	11	.226	.273	.194	6.75	1.23
Hernandez, Moises	R-R	6-1	168	3-18-84	2	1	3.07	9	2	0	0	15	17	6	5	2	5	13	.293	.423	.188	7.98	3.07
Huang, Wei	R-R	6-0	180	3-6-90	2	1	3.18	12	0	0	0	17	17	6	6	0	6	11	.246	.200	.282	5.82	3.18
Hyde, Lee	R-L	6-2	185	2-14-85	0	0	3.00	2	0	0	0	3	0	1	1	0	2	4	.000	.000	.000	12.00	6.00
LaPoint, Lucas	R-R	6-3	215	3-30-91	1	4	4.15	11	3	0	0	26	29	17	12	2	18	22	.271	.326	.230	7.62	6.23

					W	L	ERA	G	GS	CG	SV	IP	H	R	ER	HR	BB	SO	AVG	vLH	vRH	K/9	BB/9
Lopez, Robinson	R-R	6-2	190	3-2-91	3	1	1.29	11	8	0	0	49	41	13	7	1	12	42	.229	.207	.253	7.77	2.22
Mora, Edigson	R-R	6-1	195	10-20-87	2	0	0.95	7	0	0	2	19	6	2	2	2	2	17	.098	.065	.133	8.05	0.95
Niekro, Lance	R-R	6-3	225	1-29-79	1	3	5.61	14	4	1	0	34	37	34	21	3	17	22	.280	.255	.296	5.88	4.54
Northcraft, Aaron	R-R	6-4	225	5-28-90	1	2	4.50	11	10	0	0	40	33	26	20	2	21	31	.229	.188	.263	6.98	4.72
Pacheco, Ronan	L-L	6-6	170	7-29-88	1	4	4.54	11	6	0	0	34	39	25	17	4	13	31	.289	.182	.324	8.29	3.48
Parr, James	R-R	6-1	185	2-27-86	0	0	0.00	3	3	0	0	6	0	1	0	0	1	9	.000	.000	.000	13.50	1.50
Perez, Carlos	L-L	6-2	195	11-20-91	1	2	5.28	10	5	0	0	31	35	23	18	2	13	23	.292	.190	.313	6.75	3.82
Rodgers, Chad	L-L	6-3	185	11-23-87	1	0	4.50	3	0	0	0	4	3	2	2	1	0	2	.214	.000	.231	4.50	0.00
Spruill, Zeke	B-R	6-4	184	9-11-89	1	0	4.58	4	4	0	0	20	24	15	10	2	5	23	.289	.371	.229	10.53	2.29
Weber, Ryan	R-R	6-0	170	8-12-90	0	0	1.74	7	0	0	2	10	8	2	2	0	0	13	.216	.182	.231	11.32	0.00
Wilson, Andrew	R-R	6-2	180	7-30-87	2	3	4.82	12	0	0	2	19	19	10	10	1	8	22	.253	.313	.209	10.61	3.86

Fielding

Catcher	PCT	G	PO	A	E	DP	PB
Bethancourt	.983	27	214	24	4	1	8
Coury	1.000	8	43	9	0	1	1
Kramer	.976	12	78	4	2	2	5
Payne	.966	15	77	8	3	2	3
Whitmer	1.000	8	66	9	0	0	1

First Base	PCT	G	PO	A	E	DP
Kramer	.963	13	75	2	3	13
Mejia	.983	8	54	4	1	5
Odreman	.986	49	335	23	5	22

Second Base	PCT	G	PO	A	E	DP
Blanco	.875	27	29	48	11	10
De Los Santos	1.000	7	7	10	0	1
Linger	.976	39	50	73	3	13
Weaver	1.000	2	1	1	0	0

Third Base	PCT	G	PO	A	E	DP
Coe	1.000	5	3	8	0	0
Dalfonso	.887	28	21	42	8	3
Hanson	.798	33	25	46	18	5

Shortstop	PCT	G	PO	A	E	DP
De Los Santos	.949	29	39	72	6	14
Linger	1.000	1	2	2	0	0
Lovett	.932	32	49	74	9	11
Weaver	.923	6	5	7	1	1

Outfield	PCT	G	PO	A	E	DP
Contreras	1.000	40	47	2	0	1
Falcon	.961	38	45	4	2	1
Feliz	.940	43	57	6	4	2
Hiller	1.000	46	64	0	0	0
Rose	.955	45	82	2	4	0

DSL BRAVES   ROOKIE

DOMINICAN SUMMER LEAGUE

Batting	B-T	HT	WT	DOB	AVG	vLH	vRH	G	AB	R	H	2B	3B	HR	RBI	BB	HBP	SH	SF	SO	SB	CS	SLG	OBP
Alcantara, Aris	R-R	6-2	170	5-5-90	.253	.289	.243	53	186	28	47	12	0	1	29	23	5	2	2	28	1	2	.333	.347
Cadette, Victor	R-R	6-0	180	12-6-90	.251	.214	.259	44	175	19	44	5	3	1	25	9	3	2	5	27	7	3	.331	.292
De Los Santos, Ramon	R-R	6-0	190	12-26-89	.248	.188	.259	34	101	8	25	5	1	0	18	4	7	1	0	19	0	0	.317	.321
Epifano, Erick	R-R	6-1	160	3-31-90	.305	.348	.297	42	141	24	43	9	2	0	19	16	2	6	0	10	2	2	.397	.384
Flores, Juan	R-R	6-0	189	10-2-86	.368	.217	.404	27	117	25	43	10	4	1	16	5	2	0	0	12	1	2	.547	.403
Franco, Carlos	R-R	6-2	170	12-20-91	.181	.154	.186	31	83	15	15	4	1	1	5	10	1	0	1	30	0	3	.289	.274
Gamboa, Freddy	L-L	6-3	187	7-27-92	.000	—	.000	2	6	0	0	0	0	0	0	1	0	0	0	6	0	0	.000	.143
Garcia, Hector	R-R	6-2	170	6-19-92	.165	.190	.156	30	85	11	14	2	1	0	4	5	3	1	1	25	1	2	.212	.234
Gimenez, Carlos	R-R	5-11	175	5-14-90	.319	.300	.322	19	69	12	22	4	0	0	4	6	2	2	1	9	2	3	.377	.385
Guzman, Luis	R-R	6-2	195	4-17-90	.258	.200	.269	11	31	7	8	1	0	0	2	5	1	0	0	6	1	0	.290	.378
Llapur, Omar	L-L	6-3	220	6-27-86	.211	.000	.286	6	19	0	4	0	0	0	2	0	1	0	0	9	0	0	.211	.250
Luna, Ronald	R-R	6-0	145	8-18-82	.204	.227	.198	30	108	15	22	4	0	0	6	7	2	2	0	21	2	0	.241	.265
Marte, Felix	R-R	6-1	180	11-14-90	.243	.308	.230	46	152	15	37	4	3	2	16	18	0	0	1	46	5	1	.349	.322
Nunez, Anthony	R-R	6-3	205	2-2-90	.187	.059	.216	29	91	9	17	3	0	0	7	8	1	1	0	11	4	2	.220	.260
Perez, Ricardo	R-R	5-11	171	2-19-92	.154	.250	.000	4	13	0	2	0	0	0	1	1	0	0	0	3	0	1	.154	.214
Puello, Ramon	R-R	6-3	195	8-31-88	.237	.154	.254	22	76	11	18	3	0	1	8	4	2	0	1	14	2	3	.316	.289
Ramos, Abdiel	R-R	6-3	195	8-6-91	.254	.391	.227	41	142	21	36	5	0	0	16	22	1	0	1	27	7	2	.289	.355
Reyes, Elmer	R-R	5-11	150	11-26-90	.275	.222	.286	37	109	18	30	5	2	0	17	12	5	1	2	16	3	1	.358	.367
Reyes, Gerardo	R-R	5-10	170	2-7-91	.208	.280	.184	30	101	15	21	1	0	0	9	5	2	2	0	12	6	2	.257	.259
Rivera, Wilson	R-R	6-1	195	10-30-89	.273	.400	.243	38	132	27	36	7	3	2	8	17	9	4	0	33	5	1	.417	.392
Sanchez, Edison	R-R	6-4	195	11-1-90	.283	.313	.276	49	159	36	45	7	4	4	39	34	14	0	1	45	9	2	.453	.447
Vizcaya, Johnder	R-R	6-0	175	2-18-89	.195	.500	.169	23	77	9	15	3	0	0	5	9	1	0	0	20	3	0	.234	.287

Pitching	B-T	HT	WT	DOB	W	L	ERA	G	GS	CG	SV	IP	H	R	ER	HR	BB	SO	AVG	vLH	vRH	K/9	BB/9
Briceno, Rafael	R-R	6-2	175	10-29-90	0	0	3.18	14	0	0	1	17	14	10	6	0	8	11	.222	.211	.227	5.82	4.24
Caicedo, Oriel	R-R	6-1	185	3-25-91	0	0	1.35	8	0	0	0	13	7	3	2	0	13	12	.163	.091	.188	8.10	8.78
Castillo, Eduardo	R-R	6-2	170	7-27-90	1	3	5.36	18	11	0	0	49	51	33	29	0	25	37	.267	.279	.264	6.84	4.62
de Luna, Luis	R-R	6-4	200	6-16-90	9	2	2.08	18	13	0	0	74	49	19	17	2	11	66	.188	.208	.181	8.06	1.34
Escobar, Reidy	R-R	6-4	170	11-27-89	0	1	1.42	5	0	0	0	13	10	7	2	0	4	11	.200	.333	.143	7.82	2.84
Gaxiola, Amilcar	L-L	6-2	170	10-27-90	4	0	0.71	6	0	0	0	13	9	1	1	0	0	10	.205	.200	.205	7.11	0.00
Geronimo, Ignacio	R-R	6-1	170	6-1-91	1	1	6.23	9	0	0	0	9	11	7	6	0	9	7	.355	.500	.304	7.27	9.35
Martinez, Luis	R-R	6-2	165	2-19-91	0	0	3.12	6	0	0	0	9	5	3	3	0	8	5	.161	.000	.185	5.19	8.31
Mejia, Henry	R-R	6-1	185	4-2-89	0	1	2.79	9	0	0	0	10	3	4	3	0	10	13	.088	.111	.080	12.10	9.31
Mendez, Henry	R-R	6-3	195	4-12-89	0	0	2.16	7	0	0	0	8	4	2	2	0	8	10	.138	.375	.048	10.80	8.64
Milander, Garlton	R-R	6-0	175	11-2-89	2	3	4.67	19	0	0	0	35	30	26	18	1	19	23	.238	.303	.215	5.97	4.93
Nin, Amable	R-R	6-2	190	6-2-90	1	2	4.50	18	0	0	1	22	18	18	11	0	12	17	.222	.056	.270	6.95	4.91
Otero, Andy	L-L	5-9	160	6-3-92	6	1	0.84	18	12	0	0	64	38	11	6	1	26	93	.175	.222	.168	13.08	3.66
Paulino, Jorge	R-R	6-2	200	7-8-89	2	2	1.20	28	0	0	8	30	7	7	4	0	28	49	.073	.038	.086	14.70	8.40
Perez, Williams	R-R	6-0	183	5-21-91	2	2	2.35	17	11	0	0	69	50	19	18	3	15	57	.206	.243	.191	7.43	1.96
Pinto, Alexis	L-L	6-0	170	1-21-90	5	1	1.47	19	2	0	1	43	21	10	7	0	19	50	.142	.053	.155	10.47	3.98
Reyes, Manolo	R-R	6-1	190	11-14-89	1	3	10.24	6	2	0	0	10	13	15	11	0	13	11	.342	.500	.313	10.24	12.10
Silva, Ernesto	R-R	6-4	180	2-5-92	4	1	4.15	12	12	0	0	52	56	32	24	0	10	32	.277	.286	.274	5.54	1.73
Torres, Carlos	R-R	6-2	205	5-13-90	0	0	2.81	18	0	0	0	26	20	9	8	0	10	25	.230	.300	.193	8.77	3.51
Vargas, Isaac	L-L	6-2	170	4-27-89	0	1	19.29	2	0	0	0	2	4	8	5	1	4	0	.364	—	.364	0.00	15.43

Fielding

Catcher	PCT	G	PO	A	E	DP	PB
De Los Santos	.978	33	229	32	6	1	2
Guzman	.989	11	83	5	1	0	4
Nunez	.987	29	211	18	3	4	4
Perez	1.000	4	26	4	0	0	1

First Base	PCT	G	PO	A	E	DP
Alcantara	.982	48	405	21	8	31
Epifano	1.000	1	2	0	0	0
Llapur	.980	5	47	2	1	3
Sanchez	1.000	1	2	0	0	0
Vizcaya	.982	14	103	9	2	7

Second Base	PCT	G	PO	A	E	DP
Epifano	.957	35	71	64	6	20
Gimenez	.973	16	29	42	2	7
Luna	1.000	7	8	10	0	3
Reyes	.965	16	43	40	3	6
Sanchez	1.000	1	1	1	0	0

Third Base	PCT	G	PO	A	E	DP
Epifano	1.000	9	5	6	0	0
Franco	.867	16	6	20	4	3
Luna	1.000	1	1	0	0	0
Sanchez	.905	47	43	81	13	9
Vizcaya	1.000	2	1	0	0	0

Shortstop	PCT	G	PO	A	E	DP
Cadette	.889	1	4	4	1	1
Luna	.918	25	25	65	8	8
Reyes	.942	37	56	89	9	15
Reyes	.947	11	12	24	2	3

Outfield	PCT	G	PO	A	E	DP
Alcantara	.857	4	6	0	1	0
Flores	.981	27	48	4	1	1
Gamboa	.833	2	4	1	1	0
Garcia	.969	25	29	2	1	1
Marte	.880	42	43	1	6	0
Puello	.889	19	16	0	2	0
Ramos	.948	41	50	5	3	0
Rivera	.955	38	60	3	3	1
Vizcaya	1.000	7	8	1	0	0

Baltimore Orioles

SEASON IN A SENTENCE: The Orioles showed promise on offense and continued to integrate talented youngsters such as Matt Wieters into the lineup, but abysmal pitching again held the team down as it actually finished worse than 2008 with a 64-98 record.

HIGH POINT: Baltimore couldn't have seriously harbored hopes of reaching the playoffs going into the 2009 season, but a 7-5, extra-inning win over the Rangers on April 14 meant they won each of their first three series. Aubrey Huff, Adam Jones and Luke Scott each hit home runs, though the Orioles had to use six pitchers after starter Alfredo Simon couldn't get out of the second inning.

LOW POINT: Baltimore treaded water through the first half of the season, but everything fell apart in the second half. It culminated in a 5-3 loss to the Rays on Sept. 30, which gave the Orioles a 13-game losing streak, third-longest in franchise history. Rookie righthander David Hernandez started the game and dropped his seventh straight decision.

NOTABLE ROOKIES: Four of the organization's top five prospects coming into the season made their major league debuts. Wieters didn't put up overwhelming numbers in his major league debut, but he held his own and the Orioles clearly view him as a franchise cornerstone. Outfielder Nolan Reimold's success was a pleasant surprise, and his 15 home runs led American League rookies. Righthander Chris Tillman and lefthander Brian Matusz had mixed results but will be expected to front future rotations, and righthander Brad Bergesen showed he might be able to join them. Hernandez and righthander Jason Berken didn't perform as well but could still contribute down the road.

KEY TRANSACTIONS: Most of Baltimore's key moves involved calling up rookies, but the team also shipped out closer George Sherrill to the Dodgers at the trade deadline and got third base prospect Josh Bell (as well as righthander Steve Johnson).

DOWN ON THE FARM: With so many prospects graduating to the major leagues, the farm system talent thinned out considerably and Orioles affiliates had the 25th-best record in baseball. Third baseman Brandon Waring, acquired from the Reds in a trade before the 2009 season, was the organization's best offensive performer, batting .273/.354/.520 with 26 home runs.

OPENING DAY PAYROLL: $67,101,666

PLAYERS OF THE YEAR

MAJOR LEAGUE	MINOR LEAGUE
Brian Roberts	**Brian Matusz**
2b	**lhp**
.283/.356/.451	(High A/AA)
16 HR, 30 SB,	11-2, 1.91
led AL with 56 2B	121 SO in 113 IP

ORGANIZATION LEADERS

BATTING		*Minimum 250 at-bats
MAJORS		
*AVG	Nick Markakis	.293
*OPS	Luke Scott	.828
HR	Luke Scott	25
RBI	Nick Markakis	101
MINORS		
*AVG	Turner, Justin, Norfolk	.300
R	Angle, Matt, Frederick/Bowie	84
H	Angle, Matt, Frederick/Bowie	148
TB	Waring, Brandon, Frederick/Bowie	259
2B	Waring, Brandon, Frederick/Bowie	38
3B	Avery, Xavier, Delmarva	8
HR	Waring, Brandon, Frederick/Bowie	27
RBI	Waring, Brandon, Frederick/Bowie	96
BB	Angle, Matt, Frederick/Bowie	63
SO	Henson, Tyler, Frederick/Bowie	130
	Waring, Brandon, Frederick/Bowie	130
SB	Angle, Matt, Frederick/Bowie	42
*OBP	Fiorentino, Jeff, Bowie/Norfolk	.375
*SLG	Waring, Brandon, Frederick/Bowie	.521

PITCHING		†Minimum 75 innings
MAJORS		
W	Jeremy Guthrie	10
†ERA	Jeremy Guthrie	5.04
SO	Jeremy Guthrie	110
MINORS		
W	Four tied at	11
L	Gleason, Sean, Bowie/Frederick	14
†ERA	Matusz, Brian, Frederick/Bowie	1.91
G	Perrault, Josh, Bowie/Norfolk	59
GS	Arrieta, Jake, Bowie/Norfolk	28
SV	Cooney, Brandon, Delmarva/Frederick	22
IP	Pauley, David, Norfolk	152
BB	Arrieta, Jake, Bowie/Norfolk	56
SO	Arrieta, Jake, Bowie/Norfolk	148
†AVG	Matusz, Brian, Frederick/Bowie	.211

2009 PERFORMANCE

General Manager: Andy MacPhail. **Farm Director:** David Stockstill. **Scouting Director:** Joe Jordan.

Class	Team	League	W	L	PCT	Finish*	Manager(s)
Majors	Baltimore Orioles	American	64	98	.395	14th (14)	Dave Trembley
Triple-A	Norfolk Tides	International	71	71	.500	7th (14)	Gary Allenson
Double-A	Bowie Baysox	Eastern	73	69	.514	4th (12)	Brad Komminsk
High A	Frederick Keys	Carolina	64	75	.460	6th (8)	Richie Hebner
Low A	Delmarva Shorebirds	South Atlantic	66	70	.485	10th (16)	Orlando Gomez
Short-season	Aberdeen IronBirds	New York-Penn	30	44	.405	12th (14)	Gary Kendall
Rookie	Bluefield Orioles	Appalachian	33	35	.485	5th (10)	Einar Diaz
Rookie	GCL Orioles	Gulf Coast	30	26	.536	5th (16)	Ramon Sambo

Overall 2009 Minor League Record 367 390 .485 25th (30)
*Finish in overall standings (No. of teams in league). †League champion.

ORGANIZATION STATISTICS

BALTIMORE ORIOLES
AMERICAN LEAGUE

Batting	B-T	HT	WT	DOB	AVG	vLH	vRH	G	AB	R	H	2B	3B	HR	RBI	BB	HBP	SH	SF	SO	SB	CS	SLG	OBP
Andino, Robert	R-R	6-0	195	4-25-84	.222	.226	.221	78	198	31	44	7	0	2	10	15	0	0	2	47	3	3	.288	.274
Aubrey, Michael	L-L	6-0	195	4-15-82	.289	.150	.329	31	90	12	26	7	0	4	14	5	0	0	0	10	0	0	.500	.326
Fiorentino, Jeff	L-R	6-1	185	4-14-83	.281	.364	.238	24	64	8	18	1	0	0	8	8	0	1	2	16	2	0	.297	.351
Freel, Ryan	R-R	5-9	180	3-8-76	.133	.000	.222	9	15	2	2	0	0	0	1	5	0	0	0	4	0	0	.133	.350
2-team total (18 Kansas City)					.217	—	—	27	60	10	13	2	0	0	4	9	0	0	0	16	0	0	.250	.319
Huff, Aubrey	L-R	6-4	235	12-20-76	.253	.237	.264	110	430	51	109	24	1	13	72	41	4	0	5	74	0	6	.405	.321
2-team total (40 Detroit)					.241	—	—	150	536	59	129	30	1	15	85	51	5	0	5	87	0	6	.384	.310
Izturis, Cesar	B-R	5-9	190	2-10-80	.256	.290	.238	114	387	34	99	14	4	2	30	18	3	4	0	38	12	4	.328	.294
Jones, Adam	R-R	6-2	210	8-1-85	.277	.246	.295	119	473	83	131	22	3	19	70	36	7	0	3	93	10	4	.457	.335
Markakis, Nick	L-L	6-2	195	11-17-83	.293	.262	.314	161	642	94	188	45	2	18	101	56	5	0	10	98	6	2	.453	.347
Moeller, Chad	R-R	6-3	210	2-18-75	.258	.160	.297	30	89	6	23	8	1	2	10	7	1	1	2	16	0	0	.438	.313
Montanez, Lou	R-R	6-1	200	12-15-81	.183	.114	.234	29	82	5	15	5	0	1	6	5	2	1	1	16	0	1	.280	.244
Mora, Melvin	R-R	5-11	200	2-7-72	.260	.242	.270	125	450	44	117	20	0	8	48	34	8	1	3	60	3	3	.358	.321
Pie, Felix	L-L	6-2	170	2-8-85	.266	.250	.269	101	252	38	67	10	3	9	29	24	0	2	3	58	1	3	.437	.326
Reimold, Nolan	R-R	6-4	205	10-12-83	.279	.271	.284	104	358	49	100	18	2	15	45	47	3	0	3	77	8	2	.466	.365
Roberts, Brian	B-R	5-9	175	10-9-77	.283	.294	.278	159	632	110	179	56	1	16	79	74	2	1	8	112	30	7	.451	.356
Rodriguez, Guillermo	R-R	5-11	230	5-15-78	.000	.000	.000	7	5	1	0	0	0	0	1	2	0	0	0	1	0	0	.000	.286
Salazar, Oscar	R-R	6-0	195	6-27-78	.419	.545	.350	17	31	4	13	0	0	2	6	2	0	0	0	4	0	0	.613	.455
Scott, Luke	L-R	6-0	210	6-25-78	.258	.260	.257	128	449	61	116	26	1	25	77	55	1	0	1	104	0	0	.488	.340
Turner, Justin	R-R	5-11	180	11-23-84	.167	.429	.000	12	18	2	3	0	0	0	3	4	0	0	0	3	0	0	.167	.318
Wieters, Matt	B-R	6-5	230	5-21-86	.288	.248	.313	96	354	35	102	15	1	9	43	28	1	0	2	86	0	0	.412	.340
Wigginton, Ty	R-R	6-0	190	10-11-77	.273	.252	.285	122	410	44	112	19	0	11	41	23	2	0	1	57	1	2	.400	.314
Zaun, Gregg	B-R	5-10	205	4-14-71	.244	.220	.252	56	168	21	41	10	0	4	13	27	2	0	0	30	0	0	.375	.335
2-team total (34 Tampa Bay)					.260	—	—	90	262	34	68	17	0	8	27	31	3	0	0	48	0	2	.416	.345

Pitching	B-T	HT	WT	DOB	W	L	ERA	G	GS	CG	SV	IP	H	R	ER	HR	BB	SO	AVG	vLH	vRH	K/9	BB/9
Albers, Matt	L-R	6-0	205	1-20-83	3	6	5.51	56	0	0	0	67	80	43	41	3	36	49	.303	.342	.273	6.58	4.84
Baez, Danys	R-R	6-1	235	9-10-77	4	6	4.02	59	0	0	0	72	59	36	32	8	22	40	.222	.248	.197	5.02	2.76
Bass, Brian	R-R	6-2	215	1-6-82	5	3	4.90	48	0	0	0	86	106	52	47	11	44	54	.306	.298	.314	5.63	4.59
Bergesen, Brad	L-R	6-2	215	9-25-85	7	5	3.43	19	19	1	0	123	126	52	47	11	32	65	.265	.263	.267	4.74	2.34
Berken, Jason	R-R	6-0	175	11-27-83	6	12	6.54	24	24	0	0	120	164	92	87	19	44	66	.327	.335	.318	4.96	3.31
Castillo, Alberto	L-L	6-3	220	7-5-75	0	0	2.25	20	0	0	0	12	12	4	3	0	4	8	.279	.269	.294	6.00	3.00
Eaton, Adam	R-R	6-2	215	11-23-77	2	5	8.56	8	8	0	0	41	56	39	39	9	19	28	.322	.358	.278	6.15	4.17
Guthrie, Jeremy	R-R	6-1	195	4-8-79	10	17	5.04	33	33	1	0	200	224	120	112	35	60	110	.281	.289	.274	4.95	2.70
Hendrickson, Mark	L-L	6-9	240	6-23-74	6	5	4.37	53	11	0	1	105	116	59	51	16	33	61	.280	.275	.282	5.23	2.83
Henn, Sean	R-L	6-4	225	4-23-81	0	0	9.00	6	0	0	0	3	6	3	3	0	4	6	.400	.273	.750	18.00	12.00
2-team total (14 Minnesota)					0	3	7.53	20	0	0	0	14	15	12	12	2	12	15	—	—	—	9.42	7.53
Hernandez, David	R-R	6-3	215	5-13-85	4	10	5.42	20	19	0	0	101	118	62	61	27	46	68	.288	.280	.297	6.04	4.09
Hill, Rich	L-L	6-5	205	3-11-80	3	3	7.80	14	13	0	0	58	68	53	50	7	40	46	.296	.267	.303	7.18	6.24
Johnson, Jim	R-R	6-5	225	6-27-83	4	6	4.11	64	0	0	10	70	73	32	32	8	23	49	.270	.262	.278	6.30	2.96
Lambert, Chris	R-R	6-1	205	3-8-83	0	0	4.76	4	0	0	0	6	8	3	3	2	1	7	.320	.462	.167	11.12	1.59
2-team total (2 Detroit)					0	1	10.22	6	0	0	0	12	20	14	14	5	7	11	—	—	—	8.03	5.11
Liz, Radhames	R-R	6-2	185	10-6-83	0	0	67.50	2	0	0	0	1	8	10	10	1	2	1	.667	.250	.875	6.75	13.50
Matusz, Brian	L-L	6-5	200	2-11-87	5	2	4.63	8	8	0	0	45	52	24	23	6	14	38	.292	.200	.315	7.66	2.82
McCrory, Bob	R-R	6-1	205	5-3-82	0	0	17.18	7	0	0	0	7	17	19	14	3	10	4	.447	.500	.375	4.91	12.27
Meredith, Cla	R-R	6-0	190	6-4-83	0	0	3.77	29	0	0	0	29	26	12	12	3	12	17	.252	.213	.286	5.34	3.77
Mickolio, Kam	R-R	6-9	255	5-10-84	0	2	2.63	11	0	0	0	14	11	4	4	0	7	14	.220	.043	.370	9.22	4.61
Ray, Chris	R-R	6-3	225	1-12-82	0	4	7.27	46	0	0	0	43	64	36	35	8	23	39	.352	.449	.279	8.10	4.78
Sarfate, Dennis	R-R	6-4	225	4-9-81	0	1	5.09	20	0	0	0	23	21	15	13	3	14	20	.250	.256	.244	7.83	5.48
Sherrill, George	L-L	6-0	230	4-19-77	0	1	2.40	42	0	0	20	41	34	11	11	3	13	39	.219	.133	.255	8.49	2.83
Simon, Alfredo	R-R	6-4	230	5-8-81	0	1	9.95	2	2	0	0	6	8	7	7	5	2	3	.308	.333	.273	4.26	2.84
Tillman, Chris	R-R	6-5	195	4-15-88	2	5	5.40	12	12	0	0	65	74	40	39	15	24	39	.297	.254	.341	5.40	3.32
Uehara, Koji	R-R	6-1	190	4-3-75	2	4	4.05	12	12	0	0	67	71	33	30	7	12	48	.270	.273	.266	6.48	1.62

	B-T	HT	WT	DOB	W	L	ERA	G	GS	CG	SV	IP	H	R	ER	HR	BB	SO	AVG	vLH	vRH	K/9	BB/9
Walker, Jamie	L-L	6-2	195	7-1-71	0	0	5.11	22	0	0	0	12	19	8	7	5	0	9	.373	.458	.296	6.57	0.00
Waters, Chris	L-L	6-0	170	8-17-80	1	0	5.40	5	1	0	0	12	9	7	7	3	5	5	.205	.214	.200	3.86	3.86

Fielding

Catcher	PCT	G	PO	A	E	DP	PB
Moeller	1.000	30	194	6	0	0	3
Rodriguez	1.000	6	10	0	0	0	0
Wieters	.991	86	489	35	5	12	3
Zaun	.984	54	294	17	5	1	2

First Base	PCT	G	PO	A	E	DP
Aubrey	1.000	25	189	17	0	23
Huff	.995	93	822	59	4	82
Salazar	1.000	2	20	1	0	0
Scott	.983	10	54	3	1	4
Wigginton	.989	40	315	30	4	30

Second Base	PCT	G	PO	A	E	DP
Andino	1.000	8	12	8	0	4
Freel	1.000	2	0	1	0	0

	PCT	G	PO	A	E	DP
Roberts	.984	158	249	432	11	106
Turner	1.000	3	3	3	0	1
Wigginton	1.000	8	8	11	0	2

Third Base	PCT	G	PO	A	E	DP
Andino	1.000	2	0	1	0	0
Freel	—	2	0	0	0	0
Mora	.971	124	113	254	11	20
Salazar	1.000	5	4	0	0	0
Turner	1.000	7	3	7	0	1
Wigginton	.951	39	24	54	4	4

Shortstop	PCT	G	PO	A	E	DP
Andino	.968	62	76	163	8	37
Izturis	.984	112	171	337	8	70
Salazar	.667	2	0	2	1	0

	PCT	G	PO	A	E	DP
Wigginton	1.000	9	3	8	0	1

Outfield	PCT	G	PO	A	E	DP
Andino	1.000	2	1	0	0	0
Fiorentino	1.000	22	36	2	0	0
Freel	1.000	6	8	0	0	0
Jones	.986	118	349	9	5	1
Markakis	.981	161	298	13	6	1
Montanez	1.000	22	37	0	0	0
Pie	.990	83	197	5	2	0
Reimold	.973	90	173	7	5	1
Salazar	—	1	0	0	0	0
Scott	1.000	26	53	0	0	0
Wigginton	1.000	2	1	0	0	0

NORFOLK TIDES   TRIPLE-A

INTERNATIONAL LEAGUE

Batting	B-T	HT	WT	DOB	AVG	vLH	vRH	G	AB	R	H	2B	3B	HR	RBI	BB	HBP	SH	SF	SO	SB	CS	SLG	OBP
Aubrey, Michael	L-L	6-0	195	4-15-82	.287	.318	.275	44	164	14	47	13	0	3	23	11	0	0	4	13	1	1	.421	.324
2-team total (57 Columbus)					.290	—	—	101	376	41	109	29	1	8	52	20	2	1	8	38	2	2	.436	.323
Booker, Zach	R-R	6-0	220	4-24-85	.000	.000	.000	2	4	0	0	0	0	0	0	2	0	0	0	2	0	0	.000	.333
Cabrera, Jolbert	R-R	6-1	215	12-8-72	.262	.298	.248	78	294	30	77	18	1	7	50	12	4	1	2	60	9	2	.401	.298
Christian, Justin	R-R	6-1	190	4-3-80	.270	.277	.267	88	356	54	96	18	5	3	25	20	2	5	3	51	26	3	.374	.310
Concepcion, Ambiorix	R-R	6-2	180	3-19-82	.241	.667	.130	8	29	3	7	0	1	1	6	0	0	0	0	8	1	1	.414	.241
Costanzo, Mike	L-R	6-3	215	9-9-83	.206	.125	.231	22	68	8	14	4	2	0	8	13	1	0	1	21	0	0	.324	.337
Davis, Blake	L-R	5-11	165	12-22-83	.211	.111	.236	55	180	21	38	4	2	1	14	14	1	1	1	40	3	2	.272	.270
Diaz, Victor	R-R	6-0	210	12-10-81	.229	.297	.194	31	109	12	25	5	0	1	9	8	2	0	0	36	1	0	.303	.294
Dorta, Melvin	R-R	5-11	160	1-15-82	.252	.333	.226	94	321	31	81	13	0	3	23	23	1	9	4	43	8	5	.321	.301
Fiorentino, Jeff	L-R	6-1	185	4-14-83	.312	.301	.316	102	365	70	114	26	5	12	67	48	0	3	6	62	13	6	.510	.387
Gathright, Joey	L-R	5-10	185	4-27-81	.329	.351	.322	80	322	49	106	11	2	0	20	27	3	10	0	41	24	7	.376	.386
2-team total (3 Pawtucket)					.325	—	—	83	332	50	108	11	2	0	20	27	3	11	0	42	24	8	.370	.381
Guzman, Freddy	B-R	5-10	165	1-20-81	.192	.059	.232	20	73	7	14	1	1	0	3	5	0	0	1	9	13	0	.233	.241
3-team total (62 Pawtucket, 6 Scranton/W-B)					.224	—	—	88	308	39	69	7	4	2	14	23	0	3	2	49	41	7	.292	.276
Hammock, Robby	R-R	5-10	185	5-13-77	.209	.129	.231	82	278	28	58	16	0	4	26	25	4	0	1	63	2	1	.309	.282
Hughes, Rhyne	L-L	6-2	175	9-9-83	.264	.389	.222	20	72	9	19	2	1	3	7	7	2	0	0	22	0	0	.444	.346
2-team total (56 Durham)					.301	—	—	76	286	40	86	24	3	10	33	19	6	0	0	91	0	0	.510	.357
Krynzel, Dave	L-L	6-1	185	11-7-81	.379	.200	.474	8	29	6	11	0	1	1	3	3	0	0	0	4	4	0	.552	.438
Moeller, Chad	R-R	6-3	210	2-18-75	.203	.379	.146	35	118	7	24	6	0	0	10	5	1	1	0	22	0	1	.254	.242
Montanez, Lou	R-R	6-1	200	12-15-81	.429	.125	.500	10	42	8	18	3	0	3	5	1	0	0	0	9	3	0	.500	.500
Moore, Scott	L-R	6-2	195	11-17-83	.252	.265	.247	32	123	19	31	7	0	7	21	8	4	0	1	22	1	0	.480	.316
Murphy, Donnie	R-R	5-10	185	3-10-83	.222	.000	.250	3	9	1	2	0	0	1	1	1	0	0	0	3	0	0	.556	.300
Pinckney, Brandon	R-R	5-10	165	4-12-82	.291	.262	.301	71	254	27	74	10	2	1	21	5	2	5	1	36	0	3	.358	.309
Reimold, Nolan	R-R	6-4	205	10-12-83	.394	.517	.350	31	109	21	43	11	0	9	27	18	2	0	1	25	6	1	.743	.485
Rodriguez, Guillermo	R-R	5-11	230	5-15-78	.222	.148	.267	18	72	4	16	6	0	0	9	1	0	1	0	11	0	0	.306	.233
Rojas, Carlos	R-R	6-1	186	1-11-84	.179	.273	.140	74	223	18	40	5	1	0	13	18	0	7	2	30	2	3	.211	.239
Salazar, Oscar	R-R	6-0	195	6-27-78	.372	.462	.340	50	199	31	74	17	1	10	43	13	0	0	1	27	0	3	.618	.408
Snyder, Brandon	R-R	6-2	215	11-23-86	.248	.269	.247	73	262	36	65	18	2	2	43	24	5	0	6	64	3	1	.355	.316
Torrealba, Steve	R-R	6-0	220	2-24-78	.247	.200	.266	33	89	6	22	7	0	2	11	10	1	1	0	19	0	0	.393	.330
Tucker, Jonathan	R-R	5-7	170	7-2-83	.348	.222	.429	7	23	4	8	1	1	0	4	6	0	0	0	4	3	0	.478	.483
Turner, Justin	R-R	5-11	180	11-23-84	.300	.359	.281	108	387	54	116	28	0	2	43	34	8	4	8	37	9	4	.388	.362
Wieters, Matt	B-R	6-5	230	5-21-86	.305	.324	.298	39	141	25	43	9	2	5	30	20	0	0	2	30	0	0	.504	.387

Pitching	B-T	HT	WT	DOB	W	L	ERA	G	GS	CG	SV	IP	H	R	ER	HR	BB	SO	AVG	vLH	vRH	K/9	BB/9
Albers, Matt	L-R	6-0	205	1-20-83	1	0	5.68	10	0	0	0	13	19	11	8	1	5	12	.328	.333	.321	8.53	3.55
Arrieta, Jake	R-R	6-4	225	3-6-86	5	8	3.93	17	17	0	0	92	97	46	40	9	33	78	.276	.271	.282	7.66	3.24
Bergesen, Brad	R-R	6-2	215	9-25-85	1	1	2.45	2	2	0	0	11	6	4	3	0	3	9	.154	.111	.250	7.36	2.45
Berken, Jason	R-R	6-0	175	11-27-83	2	0	1.05	5	5	0	0	26	19	3	3	1	6	16	.211	.196	.231	5.61	2.10
Castillo, Alberto	L-R	6-3	220	7-5-75	2	3	2.77	50	0	0	13	52	49	23	16	2	17	54	.250	.164	.301	9.35	2.94
Chiasson, Scott	R-R	6-3	210	8-14-77	0	0	0.00	3	0	0	0	3	0	0	0	0	0	3	.000	.000	.000	8.10	0.00
Clark, Zach	R-R	6-0	195	7-11-83	0	0	3.86	2	0	0	0	5	5	2	2	0	3	2	.278	.000	.500	5.79	5.79
Deza, Fredy	R-R	6-2	175	12-11-82	2	1	5.14	5	1	0	1	14	16	10	8	2	8	5	.291	.292	.290	3.21	5.14
George, Chris	L-L	6-2	185	9-16-79	1	1	1.86	5	5	0	0	29	27	6	6	2	3	19	.250	.214	.263	5.90	0.93
2-team total (12 Pawtucket)					2	1	3.08	17	5	0	0	50	48	20	17	4	9	29	—	—	—	5.26	1.63
Hernandez, David	R-R	6-3	215	5-13-85	3	2	3.30	11	11	0	0	57	42	26	21	5	18	79	.199	.222	.170	12.40	2.83
Hill, Rich	L-L	6-5	205	3-11-80	1	1	1.35	3	3	0	0	13	5	2	2	1	9	14	.116	.188	.074	9.45	6.07
Lambert, Chris	R-R	6-1	205	3-8-83	1	2	6.94	3	3	0	0	12	18	9	9	3	3	9	.360	.385	.333	6.94	2.31
2-team total (21 Toledo)					7	9	3.84	24	24	1	0	138	139	63	59	11	34	115	—	—	—	7.48	2.21
Livingston, Bobby	L-L	6-3	205	9-3-82	1	0	1.80	3	3	0	0	20	21	5	4	2	1	11	.269	.208	.296	4.95	0.45
3-team total (1 Columbus, 1 Indianapolis)					1	0	2.70	5	4	0	0	30	33	13	9	3	4	17	—	—	—	5.10	1.20

BALTIMORE ORIOLES

BALTIMORE ORIOLES

Name	B-T	HT	WT	DOB	W	L	ERA	G	GS	CG	SV	IP	H	R	ER	HR	BB	SO	AVG	vLH	vRH		
Liz, Radhames	R-R	6-2	185	10-6-83	0	3	5.68	17	6	0	0	44	56	31	28	2	12	37	.315	.299	.324	7.51	2.44
McCrory, Bob	R-R	6-1	205	5-3-82	0	3	3.88	50	0	0	5	63	66	28	27	6	24	43	.268	.345	.203	6.18	3.45
Mickolio, Kam	R-R	6-9	255	5-10-84	3	3	3.50	35	0	0	0	44	32	21	17	4	16	52	.203	.191	.211	10.72	3.30
Miller, Jim	R-R	6-1	200	4-28-82	4	4	2.64	54	0	0	17	65	64	20	19	3	19	59	.256	.324	.207	8.21	2.64
Mitchell, Andy	R-R	6-3	205	9-10-78	11	5	5.24	37	13	0	0	113	126	73	66	13	52	58	.288	.305	.274	4.61	4.13
Patton, Troy	B-L	6-1	185	9-3-85	1	3	6.45	9	9	0	0	45	62	35	32	12	14	26	.337	.439	.308	5.24	2.82
Pauley, David	R-R	6-2	210	6-13-83	9	12	4.37	27	26	1	0	152	171	87	74	15	45	108	.284	.278	.289	6.38	2.66
Perrault, Josh	R-R	6-3	205	6-11-82	1	2	2.53	24	0	0	2	32	27	11	9	4	9	33	.221	.268	.182	9.28	2.53
Ray, Chris	R-R	6-3	225	1-12-82	0	1	2.25	8	0	0	1	12	5	3	3	0	4	13	.125	.133	.120	9.75	3.00
Sarfate, Dennis	R-R	6-4	225	4-9-81	1	1	6.39	12	0	0	0	13	13	10	9	4	2	13	.260	.250	.269	9.24	1.42
Tillman, Chris	R-R	6-5	195	4-15-88	8	6	2.70	18	18	0	0	97	85	36	29	5	26	99	.232	.234	.231	9.22	2.42
Waters, Chris	L-L	6-0	170	8-17-80	9	7	4.49	29	20	0	0	114	114	66	57	12	47	71	.259	.205	.278	5.59	3.70
Wolf, Ross	R-R	6-0	180	10-18-82	4	2	3.95	47	0	0	1	82	70	38	36	5	33	73	.228	.216	.237	8.01	3.62

Fielding

Catcher	PCT	G	PO	A	E	DP	PB
Booker	1.000	1	2	0	0	0	0
Hammock	.995	53	404	23	2	4	6
Moeller	1.000	34	237	10	0	2	1
Rodriguez	1.000	16	103	8	0	1	2
Torrealba	1.000	12	69	5	0	0	2
Wieters	.996	27	214	13	1	0	2

First Base	PCT	G	PO	A	E	DP
Aubrey	1.000	12	76	7	0	12
Cabrera	.983	23	168	8	3	15
Costanzo	1.000	5	60	6	0	4
Hughes	.992	14	115	7	1	13
Moeller	1.000	1	1	0	0	1
Moore	1.000	5	48	3	0	4
Rodriguez	1.000	1	8	2	0	1
Salazar	.996	31	221	20	1	32
Snyder	.991	50	413	22	4	51
Torrealba	.957	8	22	0	1	1

Second Base	PCT	G	PO	A	E	DP
Dorta	.960	35	67	78	6	29
Murphy	1.000	1	3	7	0	1
Pinckney	.953	10	17	24	2	6
Rojas	.990	20	33	70	1	20
Tucker	1.000	2	6	4	0	2
Turner	.963	80	130	212	13	53

Third Base	PCT	G	PO	A	E	DP
Cabrera	.960	15	9	15	1	4
Costanzo	.964	10	9	18	1	4
Dorta	.882	33	20	55	10	6
Hammock	1.000	2	0	1	0	0
Moore	.898	23	16	37	6	4
Pinckney	.962	42	23	78	4	4
Rojas	1.000	5	0	3	0	0
Snyder	.913	9	2	19	2	2
Turner	.895	15	10	24	4	4

Shortstop	PCT	G	PO	A	E	DP
Cabrera	.988	23	37	43	1	13
Davis	.938	54	68	143	14	34
Dorta	.878	10	9	27	5	8
Murphy	1.000	2	4	3	0	1
Rojas	.965	49	72	146	8	30
Turner	.930	14	19	34	4	8

Outfield	PCT	G	PO	A	E	DP
Aubrey	1.000	4	6	0	0	0
Cabrera	.867	14	13	0	2	0
Christian	1.000	84	220	8	0	2
Concepcion	1.000	8	16	0	0	0
Diaz	.895	13	15	2	2	1
Dorta	1.000	19	30	3	0	0
Fiorentino	.991	102	201	12	2	3
Gathright	.991	79	216	8	2	3
Guzman	.978	20	44	1	1	0
Hammock	1.000	8	9	0	0	0
Krynzel	.923	8	11	1	1	0
Montanez	1.000	10	12	1	0	0
Pinckney	.971	24	33	1	1	1
Reimold	1.000	25	38	0	0	0
Salazar	.958	18	22	1	1	0
Tucker	.889	6	8	0	1	0

BOWIE BAYSOX

DOUBLE-A

EASTERN LEAGUE

Batting	B-T	HT	WT	DOB	AVG	vLH	vRH	G	AB	R	H	2B	3B	HR	RBI	BB	HBP	SH	SF	SO	SB	CS	SLG	OBP
Abreu, Miguel	R-R	6-0	190	11-14-84	.290	.322	.277	130	489	55	142	31	1	4	45	12	3	5	1	53	25	8	.382	.311
Angle, Matt	L-R	5-10	175	9-10-85	.357	.333	.368	8	28	6	10	1	0	0	1	4	0	0	0	5	2	0	.393	.438
Bell, Josh	B-R	6-3	235	11-13-86	.289	.129	.349	33	114	18	33	5	0	9	24	11	0	0	2	28	0	0	.570	.346
Binick, Kraig	R-L	5-10	180	2-10-85	.364	.250	.667	3	11	2	4	1	0	0	2	0	0	0	0	1	0	0	.455	.364
Britton, Buck	L-R	6-1	163	5-16-86	.000	—	.000	1	3	0	0	0	0	0	0	0	0	0	0	0	0	0	.000	.000
Cardona, Rodolfo	R-R	5-10	155	11-27-86	.000	.000	.000	6	14	2	0	0	0	0	1	1	0	0	1	2	0	0	.000	.063
Concepcion, Ambiorix	R-R	6-2	180	3-19-82	.251	.264	.246	121	430	46	108	27	2	8	54	35	2	0	3	82	15	6	.379	.309
Conley, Brian	L-R	6-2	195	5-7-86	.143	.500	.000	4	7	1	1	0	0	0	0	2	0	0	0	4	0	1	.143	.333
Costanzo, Mike	L-R	6-3	215	9-9-83	.201	.212	.196	60	204	25	41	12	1	3	29	27	0	0	2	58	0	2	.314	.292
Crozier, Eric	L-L	6-4	200	8-11-78	.217	.178	.236	64	217	32	47	7	4	10	34	36	0	2	4	68	1	2	.424	.323
Donahie, Adam	R-R	6-1	215	3-3-84	.215	.299	.169	88	275	25	59	19	0	5	33	45	0	0	6	79	0	3	.338	.319
Dorta, Melvin	R-R	5-11	160	1-15-82	.327	.250	.349	31	110	20	36	8	1	1	12	13	0	3	2	8	4	6	.445	.392
Figueroa, Danny	R-R	5-11	182	2-19-83	.319	.365	.299	78	238	43	76	10	3	2	24	39	16	8	2	52	11	4	.412	.444
Figueroa, Paco	R-R	5-11	180	2-19-83	.305	.367	.283	62	226	32	69	18	6	0	28	30	2	4	1	37	13	3	.438	.390
Fiorentino, Jeff	L-R	6-1	185	4-14-83	.087	.000	.091	7	23	1	2	1	0	0	3	0	0	0	4	2	0	0	.130	.192
Florimon, Pedro	B-R	6-2	165	12-10-86	.091	.125	.071	7	22	0	2	0	0	0	1	1	0	1	0	9	0	1	.091	.130
Freel, Ryan	R-R	5-9	180	3-8-76	.111	.000	.167	3	9	2	1	0	0	0	2	1	0	0	0	1	1	0	.111	.200
Henson, Tyler	R-R	6-1	190	5-21-87	.250	.250	.250	7	20	3	5	0	0	1	3	3	0	1	1	5	0	0	.400	.333
Izturis, Cesar	B-R	5-9	190	2-10-80	.333	.667	.000	2	6	2	2	0	0	0	0	1	0	0	0	1	0	0	.333	.429
Krynzel, Dave	L-L	6-1	185	11-7-81	.249	.281	.239	109	365	35	91	13	3	7	35	30	4	2	1	108	15	6	.359	.313
Montanez, Lou	R-R	6-1	200	12-15-81	.375	.000	.500	2	8	2	3	0	0	0	2	0	0	0	0	0	0	0	.375	.375
Nowicki, Joe	L-L	6-2	210	11-12-82	.217	.216	.218	58	184	20	40	8	0	5	25	13	1	1	1	53	2	2	.342	.271
Pinckney, Brandon	R-R	5-10	165	4-12-82	.293	.357	.259	10	41	3	12	3	0	1	5	1	0	1	1	5	0	0	.439	.302
Rodriguez, Guillermo	R-R	5-11	230	5-15-78	.251	.254	.250	71	227	24	57	14	1	5	21	13	2	5	4	43	6	0	.388	.293
Rojas, Carlos	R-R	6-1	186	1-11-84	.162	.160	.163	24	74	9	12	1	0	0	1	4	1	2	0	11	0	1	.176	.215
Snyder, Brandon	R-R	6-2	215	11-23-86	.343	.370	.335	58	201	24	69	19	1	10	45	27	2	0	3	45	0	1	.597	.421
Stephen, Jedidiah	R-R	6-2	195	4-30-84	.111	—	.111	4	9	0	1	0	0	0	0	1	0	0	0	5	1	0	.111	.200
Torrealba, Steve	R-R	6-0	220	2-24-78	.242	.208	.263	26	62	6	15	2	0	3	13	21	1	0	3	10	0	0	.419	.425
Tucker, Jonathan	R-R	5-7	170	7-2-83	.265	.260	.267	120	430	71	114	24	5	1	36	49	7	7	5	55	31	12	.351	.346
Valido, Robert	R-R	6-2	210	5-16-85	.219	.219	.218	100	334	36	73	10	6	3	23	15	3	5	5	44	7	3	.311	.255
Waring, Brandon	R-R	6-4	195	1-2-86	.292	.000	.412	8	24	4	7	3	0	1	6	3	2	0	0	9	0	0	.542	.414
White, Jason	L-R	6-1	175	6-7-84	.195	.143	.206	28	77	12	15	0	1	0	3	9	2	0	1	32	2	0	.221	.292

Pitching	B-T	HT	WT	DOB	W	L	ERA	G	GS	CG	SV	IP	H	R	ER	HR	BB	SO	AVG	vLH	vRH	K/9	BB/9
Arrieta, Jake	R-R	6-4	225	3-6-86	6	3	2.59	11	11	2	0	59	45	21	17	4	23	70	.208	.189	.236	10.68	3.51
Bascom, Tim	R-R	6-1	205	1-4-85	3	7	4.30	15	14	0	0	82	82	40	39	4	29	59	.267	.263	.272	6.50	3.20
Beato, Pedro	R-R	6-6	230	10-27-86	1	3	4.50	6	5	0	0	32	33	16	16	6	7	18	.268	.273	.265	5.06	1.97
Berken, Jason	R-R	6-0	175	11-27-83	1	1	5.63	2	2	0	0	8	4	5	5	1	6	8	.148	.118	.200	9.00	6.75
Clark, Zach	R-R	6-0	195	7-11-83	2	1	5.06	13	0	0	0	27	34	16	15	1	8	16	.315	.302	.323	5.40	2.70
Deza, Fredy	R-R	6-2	175	12-11-82	6	7	3.79	31	7	0	0	78	69	36	33	12	32	51	.240	.284	.193	5.86	3.68
Egan, Pat	R-R	6-8	225	10-25-84	1	0	2.08	3	2	0	0	13	14	5	3	1	2	11	.280	.333	.176	7.62	1.38
Erbe, Brandon	R-R	6-4	180	12-25-87	5	3	2.34	14	14	2	0	73	44	27	19	5	35	62	.170	.208	.134	7.64	4.32
Gamboa, Eddie	R-R	6-2	195	12-21-84	1	0	0.00	7	0	0	1	12	7	3	0	0	7	11	.167	.111	.208	8.25	5.25
Gleason, Sean	L-R	6-0	190	8-21-85	3	5	5.96	10	10	0	0	51	72	38	34	4	22	20	.338	.314	.370	3.51	3.86
Hernandez, David	R-R	6-3	215	5-13-85	0	0	2.25	1	1	0	0	4	2	1	1	0	1	4	.143	.200	.111	9.00	2.25
Hoey, Jim	R-R	6-6	210	12-30-82	2	6	4.50	36	0	0	0	48	48	27	24	4	32	47	.274	.275	.274	8.81	6.00
Johnson, Steve	R-R	6-1	200	8-31-87	3	2	2.84	7	7	0	0	38	24	13	12	3	17	37	.179	.169	.187	8.76	4.03
Keefer, Ryan	L-R	6-3	225	8-10-81	0	1	7.36	18	3	0	0	26	27	22	21	3	29	22	.276	.235	.319	7.71	10.17
Lebron, Luis	R-R	6-1	172	3-15-85	1	0	1.98	24	0	0	9	27	8	6	6	3	13	39	.093	.088	.096	12.84	4.28
Livingston, Bobby	L-L	6-3	205	9-3-82	6	2	3.62	13	12	0	0	70	85	33	28	2	21	34	.300	.310	.296	4.39	2.71
2-team total (9 Akron)					8	7	4.50	22	21	1	0	126	144	70	63	5	32	57	—	—	—	4.07	2.29
Liz, Radhames	R-R	6-2	185	10-6-83	4	1	2.63	8	8	0	0	48	46	18	14	1	14	39	.256	.269	.237	7.31	2.63
Mariotti, John	L-R	6-0	225	8-19-84	2	9	3.72	18	13	0	0	82	87	49	34	4	42	30	.282	.241	.327	3.28	4.59
Matusz, Brian	L-L	6-5	200	2-11-87	7	0	1.55	8	8	1	0	46	31	9	8	2	11	46	.189	.077	.224	8.94	2.14
Ouellette, Ryan	R-R	5-11	185	10-4-85	4	6	3.28	37	0	0	5	49	50	20	18	2	21	27	.275	.341	.220	4.93	3.83
Parker, Brian	R-R	6-4	195	6-4-85	0	0	3.60	2	0	0	1	5	5	4	2	1	3	6	.263	.111	.400	10.80	5.40
Patton, Troy	B-L	6-1	185	9-3-85	6	2	1.99	11	11	0	0	63	50	18	14	4	18	47	.211	.182	.222	6.68	2.56
Perez, Wilfrido	L-L	6-0	145	8-12-84	2	0	1.37	24	0	0	7	26	12	5	4	1	22	29	.136	.132	.140	9.91	7.52
Perrault, Josh	R-R	6-3	205	6-11-82	0	2	1.80	35	0	0	16	40	30	13	8	3	9	41	.199	.203	.194	9.23	2.03
Ray, Chris	R-R	6-3	225	1-12-82	0	0	0.00	3	0	0	0	3	0	0	0	0	2	2	.000	.000	.000	6.00	6.00
Rodriguez, Ryan	L-L	6-4	233	7-10-84	1	2	7.16	26	2	0	1	44	59	36	35	4	23	28	.326	.300	.339	5.73	4.70
Sarfate, Dennis	R-R	6-4	225	4-9-81	0	0	0.00	1	0	0	0	1	0	0	0	0	1	2	.000	.000	.000	18.00	9.00
Tanaka, Ryohei	R-R	6-0	169	11-18-82	4	4	3.00	21	12	0	3	75	74	31	25	6	25	53	.257	.281	.238	6.36	3.00
Thall, Chad	L-L	6-4	220	8-2-85	2	2	2.69	53	0	0	1	60	48	20	18	3	28	55	.214	.188	.236	8.20	4.18

Fielding

Catcher	PCT	G	PO	A	E	DP	PB
Donachie	.989	72	499	41	6	3	5
Rodriguez	.990	59	348	45	4	5	6
Torrealba	.979	13	86	9	2	2	1

First Base	PCT	G	PO	A	E	DP
Costanzo	1.000	9	64	9	0	10
Crozier	.994	61	511	28	3	53
Donachie	1.000	2	12	0	0	1
Dorta	1.000	3	24	1	0	2
Figueroa	1.000	1	12	0	0	1
Snyder	.989	56	441	30	5	42
Torrealba	1.000	8	41	3	0	3
Waring	1.000	7	41	2	0	6

Second Base	PCT	G	PO	A	E	DP
Abreu	.960	102	208	276	20	58
Britton	1.000	1	0	4	0	0
Cardona	.941	3	5	11	1	6
Dorta	—	1	0	0	0	0
Figueroa	1.000	23	42	59	0	15
Freel	1.000	1	1	1	0	0
Rojas	1.000	11	20	28	0	12

Stephen	1.000	3	5	5	0	3
Tucker	—	1	0	0	0	0
Valido	1.000	1	5	4	0	3
White	1.000	1	5	1	0	0

Third Base	PCT	G	PO	A	E	DP
Abreu	.774	14	11	13	7	3
Bell	.860	26	12	31	7	2
Costanzo	.950	51	28	86	6	7
Dorta	.976	17	13	27	1	2
Figueroa	1.000	7	4	14	0	2
Freel	.500	1	0	1	1	0
Pinckney	1.000	3	3	7	0	1
Rodriguez	1.000	1	0	2	0	1
Tucker	.889	13	16	24	5	2
Waring	.833	2	1	4	1	1
White	.886	13	6	25	4	3

Shortstop	PCT	G	PO	A	E	DP
Cardona	—	1	0	0	0	0
Costanzo	1.000	1	2	5	0	2
Dorta	.941	8	16	16	2	8
Florimon	.964	7	10	17	1	6

Izturis	1.000	2	2	5	0	2
Pinckney	.966	6	10	18	1	1
Rojas	.967	15	18	41	2	8
Tucker	1.000	1	2	1	0	0
Valido	.965	97	143	238	14	60
White	.978	13	18	27	1	4

Outfield	PCT	G	PO	A	E	DP
Abreu	1.000	9	16	1	0	0
Angle	1.000	8	23	1	0	1
Concepcion	.959	108	200	9	9	1
Conley	1.000	4	5	1	0	0
Crozier	1.000	4	3	0	0	0
Figueroa	.993	64	134	1	1	1
Fiorentino	1.000	1	2	1	0	0
Freel	—	1	0	0	0	0
Henson	1.000	7	16	2	0	0
Krynzel	.975	87	146	9	4	3
Montanez	1.000	2	6	0	0	0
Nowicki	.958	39	66	2	3	1
Tucker	.991	104	212	12	2	3

FREDERICK KEYS   HIGH CLASS A

CAROLINA LEAGUE

Batting	B-T	HT	WT	DOB	AVG	vLH	vRH	G	AB	R	H	2B	3B	HR	RBI	BB	HBP	SH	SF	SO	SB	CS	SLG	OBP
Adams, Ryan	R-R	6-0	195	4-21-87	.288	.253	.307	59	215	27	62	14	0	2	25	19	1	0	0	41	2	4	.381	.349
Angle, Matt	L-R	5-10	175	9-10-85	.289	.298	.284	123	478	78	138	17	4	1	32	59	4	10	2	72	40	12	.347	.370
Binick, Kraig	R-L	5-10	180	2-10-85	.225	.209	.237	55	204	32	46	7	0	5	25	12	6	1	2	21	9	0	.333	.286
Britton, Buck	L-R	6-1	163	5-16-86	.243	.125	.276	13	37	3	9	1	0	0	2	2	0	1	0	7	2	1	.270	.282
Cardona, Rodolfo	R-R	5-10	155	11-27-86	.238	.227	.250	14	42	2	10	1	1	0	1	1	0	1	1	16	1	1	.310	.250
Cash, David	B-R	6-3	180	11-22-85	.219	.214	.221	69	215	17	47	3	1	0	17	8	2	2	1	54	6	5	.242	.252
Crancer, Wally	L-R	6-0	215	7-7-84	.302	.243	.315	64	215	29	65	8	2	8	34	13	2	1	4	40	0	3	.470	.342
Florimon, Pedro	B-R	6-2	165	12-10-86	.267	.270	.266	115	430	76	115	32	5	9	68	42	5	4	5	107	26	9	.428	.336
Henson, Tyler	R-R	6-1	190	12-15-87	.267	.303	.252	125	460	68	123	31	2	8	71	38	6	1	4	125	18	6	.396	.329
Hudson, Kyle	L-L	5-11	175	1-7-87	.250	.250	.250	6	20	4	5	0	0	0	4	1	1	0	6	3	0	.250	.400
Joseph, Caleb	R-R	6-3	180	6-18-86	.284	.303	.272	104	380	50	108	23	2	12	60	26	5	0	1	64	2	1	.450	.337
Killian, Billy	L-R	6-0	210	6-12-86	.216	.267	.207	33	97	13	21	1	0	0	9	3	0	3	1	21	0	0	.227	.280
Mahoney, Joe	L-L	6-7	255	2-1-87	.267	.167	.333	7	30	2	8	4	0	1	5	0	0	0	1	10	0	1	.500	.258
Miclat, Greg	B-R	5-9	180	7-23-87	.208	.111	.267	6	24	4	5	1	0	0	1	3	0	0	0	4	1	0	.250	.296
Montanez, Lou	R-R	6-1	200	12-15-81	.333	.400	.250	2	9	0	3	0	0	0	0	0	0	1	0	0	0	0	.333	.300

Batting	B-T	HT	WT	DOB	AVG	vLH	vRH	G	AB	R	H	2B	3B	HR	RBI	BB	HBP	SH	SF	SO	SB	CS	SLG	OBP
Rowell, Bill	L-R	6-5	205	9-10-88	.225	.258	.210	120	423	51	95	20	0	9	39	35	1	2	2	122	3	2	.336	.284
Stephen, Jedidiah	R-R	6-2	195	4-30-84	.150	.167	.143	6	20	3	3	1	0	0	1	1	0	0	0	11	0	0	.200	.190
Stevens, Bobby	R-R	6-0	190	3-30-87	.272	.269	.275	81	246	39	67	9	1	7	25	23	13	8	3	79	10	6	.402	.361
Tucker, Matt	B-R	6-2	185	6-5-83	.317	.295	.326	41	139	19	44	8	2	4	20	15	2	0	2	32	1	5	.489	.386
Vinyard, Chris	R-R	6-4	230	12-15-85	.208	.238	.193	34	125	12	26	5	0	4	15	15	0	0	2	30	0	1	.344	.289
Waring, Brandon	R-R	6-4	195	1-2-86	.273	.245	.286	128	473	70	129	35	2	26	90	51	12	1	6	121	5	3	.520	.354
White, Jason	L-R	6-1	175	6-7-84	.195	.375	.152	13	41	6	8	0	0	0	4	6	2	0	0	15	1	1	.195	.327
Widlansky, Robbie	L-R	6-2	210	11-6-84	.340	.366	.330	86	326	49	111	31	1	7	59	29	3	1	4	48	5	1	.506	.395

Pitching	B-T	HT	WT	DOB	W	L	ERA	G	GS	CG	SV	IP	H	R	ER	HR	BB	SO	AVG	vLH	vRH	K/9	BB/9
Barb, Andy	R-R	6-3	190	10-6-84	0	0	3.93	10	0	0	1	18	15	10	8	2	13	18	.224	.065	.361	8.84	6.38
Bascom, Tim	R-R	6-1	205	1-4-85	4	5	3.40	12	11	0	0	53	59	35	20	6	13	32	.278	.301	.261	5.43	2.21
Beato, Pedro	R-R	6-6	230	10-27-86	5	7	4.53	20	20	1	0	105	125	60	53	12	40	70	.297	.315	.278	5.98	3.42
Bordes, Brett	L-L	5-10	175	11-30-83	3	4	8.23	27	0	0	1	27	36	29	25	2	15	15	.319	.238	.366	4.94	8.23
Britton, Zach	L-L	6-2	172	12-22-87	9	6	2.70	25	24	0	0	140	123	64	42	6	55	131	.232	.240	.228	8.42	3.54
Clark, Zach	R-R	6-0	195	7-11-83	0	0	1.13	4	0	0	0	8	4	2	1	1	2	7	.160	.250	.118	7.88	2.25
Cooney, Brandon	R-R	6-6	240	8-2-85	0	2	0.60	12	0	0	6	15	7	3	1	0	2	12	.140	.160	.120	7.20	1.20
Egan, Pat	R-R	6-8	225	10-25-84	2	3	1.33	20	2	0	2	47	27	8	7	1	9	33	.163	.210	.118	6.27	1.71
Esposito, Joe	L-R	5-11	220	5-15-85	1	2	4.46	20	0	0	3	40	37	21	20	1	22	41	.253	.187	.324	9.15	4.91
Flagello, Cliff	R-R	5-10	200	1-3-85	1	2	7.55	21	0	0	1	31	41	34	26	6	25	27	.323	.412	.263	7.84	7.26
Gamboa, Eddie	R-R	6-2	195	12-21-84	4	0	0.55	14	0	0	1	33	27	3	2	0	7	29	.227	.179	.270	7.91	1.91
Gleason, Sean	R-R	6-0	190	8-21-85	4	9	4.93	18	17	0	0	97	114	63	53	8	31	61	.295	.260	.346	5.68	2.89
Hill, Rich	L-L	6-5	205	3-11-80	0	1	3.00	1	1	0	0	3	1	1	1	0	0	3	.100	.000	.143	9.00	0.00
Jacobson, Brett	R-R	6-6	205	11-9-86	1	2	6.30	7	0	0	0	10	7	7	7	1	9	11	.206	.154	.238	9.90	8.10
Kantakevich, Pat	R-R	6-2	198	8-11-86	1	0	1.50	1	1	0	0	6	5	2	1	1	0	3	.227	.133	.429	4.50	0.00
Lebron, Luis	R-R	6-1	172	3-15-85	2	3	3.00	28	0	0	11	33	20	11	11	2	20	52	.168	.157	.176	14.18	5.45
Mariotti, John	L-R	6-0	225	8-19-84	1	2	4.37	7	2	0	0	23	19	12	11	2	9	21	.226	.278	.188	8.34	3.57
Mathews, Shane	R-R	6-3	210	3-28-85	0	0	27.00	2	0	0	0	2	8	6	6	0	1	1	.571	.500	.667	4.50	4.50
Matusz, Brian	L-L	6-5	200	2-11-87	4	2	2.16	11	11	0	0	67	56	22	16	5	21	75	.225	.213	.230	10.13	2.84
Moreland, Kenny	R-R	5-11	200	4-2-86	4	2	4.72	9	9	0	0	48	43	26	25	10	7	29	.230	.236	.222	5.48	1.32
Nery, Nate	R-L	6-4	210	8-25-85	4	5	5.00	19	19	1	0	99	117	62	55	8	33	73	.289	.227	.319	6.64	3.00
Ouellette, Ryan	R-R	5-11	185	10-4-85	0	1	3.38	11	0	0	1	18	9	7	7	1	2	14	.247	.250	.262	6.75	0.96
Parker, Brian	R-R	6-4	195	8-21-85	4	3	4.31	35	0	0	0	65	59	35	31	9	26	64	.247	.317	.193	8.91	3.62
Renshaw, Jake	R-R	6-3	215	4-29-86	1	0	2.08	5	0	0	0	9	8	3	2	0	5	7	.242	.385	.150	7.27	5.19
Rodriguez, Ryan	L-L	6-4	233	7-10-84	1	0	0.00	14	0	0	4	15	9	0	0	4	15	.176	.125	.200	9.00	2.40
Salberg, Chris	R-L	6-1	185	5-8-84	1	3	6.80	16	5	0	0	41	49	40	31	5	28	26	.290	.295	.287	5.71	6.15
Sarfate, Dennis	R-R	6-4	225	4-9-81	1	0	9.00	1	0	0	0	2	2	2	2	0	1	2	.250	.400	.000	9.00	4.50
Spoone, Chorye	R-R	6-1	215	9-16-85	0	2	9.42	4	4	0	0	14	17	16	15	3	14	12	.298	.226	.385	7.53	8.79
Stevens, Jake	L-L	6-2	215	3-15-85	5	6	4.42	34	0	0	0	59	65	37	29	6	31	49	.273	.242	.293	7.47	4.73
Zagone, Rick	L-L	6-4	215	9-30-86	1	3	5.10	13	13	0	0	67	70	41	38	7	22	59	.277	.164	.308	7.93	2.96

Fielding

Catcher	PCT	G	PO	A	E	DP	PB
Crancer	.986	18	123	14	2	0	9
Joseph	.986	98	685	84	11	6	11
Killian	1.000	29	178	22	0	4	2
Stephen	.857	2	2	4	1	0	
Stevens	.984	57	98	154	4	29	
Tucker	.910	14	33	38	7	13	
White	1.000	5	7	17	0	4	
Miclat	.893	6	8	17	3	2	
Stevens	1.000	9	9	22	0	0	
White	.963	7	8	18	1	2	

First Base	PCT	G	PO	A	E	DP
Crancer	1.000	3	12	1	0	0
Mahoney	1.000	6	58	4	0	2
Vinyard	.974	9	70	5	2	11
Waring	.991	69	613	48	6	47
Widlansky	.992	54	470	47	4	38

Second Base	PCT	G	PO	A	E	DP
Adams	.929	53	87	135	17	21
Britton	1.000	4	5	8	0	1
Cardona	.975	8	18	21	1	2
Cash	1.000	2	3	3	0	0
Henson	.800	3	5	3	2	1

Third Base	PCT	G	PO	A	E	DP
Britton	1.000	7	2	12	0	1
Henson	.905	68	46	144	20	13
Stephen	1.000	1	1	1	0	0
Stevens	.857	3	2	4	1	0
Tucker	.875	4	3	4	1	0
Waring	.925	60	48	99	12	5
White	—	1	0	0	0	0

Shortstop	PCT	G	PO	A	E	DP
Cardona	.880	6	8	14	3	1
Florimon	.935	115	167	339	35	65
Henson	.857	1	2	4	1	1

Outfield	PCT	G	PO	A	E	DP
Angle	.993	123	268	12	2	1
Binick	.967	53	83	4	3	2
Cash	.988	55	81	2	1	1
Crancer	1.000	2	2	0	0	0
Henson	.949	50	90	3	5	1
Hudson	1.000	6	10	0	0	0
Mahoney	1.000	1	2	0	0	0
Montanez	1.000	1	2	0	0	0
Rowell	.904	110	135	7	15	2
Tucker	1.000	10	23	2	0	0
Widlansky	.967	20	29	0	1	0

DELMARVA SHOREBIRDS   LOW CLASS A

SOUTH ATLANTIC LEAGUE

Batting	B-T	HT	WT	DOB	AVG	vLH	vRH	G	AB	R	H	2B	3B	HR	RBI	BB	HBP	SH	SF	SO	SB	CS	SLG	OBP
Avery, Xavier	L-L	5-11	180	1-1-90	.262	.308	.247	129	473	55	124	15	8	2	36	27	4	3	2	111	30	10	.340	.306
Bernardo, Luis	R-R	6-0	170	1-16-88	.213	.200	.218	82	253	21	54	11	1	1	25	12	3	10	1	51	2	0	.277	.257
Black, Dustin	R-R	6-0	205	12-8-86	.159	.231	.129	18	44	3	7	2	0	2	4	4	1	0	0	14	1	0	.341	.245
Britton, Buck	L-R	6-1	163	5-16-86	.455	—	.455	3	11	1	5	2	0	0	1	0	0	0	0	1	0	0	.636	.455
Cardona, Rodolfo	R-R	5-10	155	11-27-86	.235	.200	.253	46	132	19	31	8	3	1	22	11	2	5	1	35	3	3	.364	.301
Carolus, Levi	R-R	6-0	160	9-24-87	.250	.320	.200	17	60	5	15	3	1	1	7	3	1	2	0	15	3	2	.383	.297
Castillo, Victor	B-R	5-11	180	9-12-84	.188	.222	.174	27	64	6	12	2	0	1	7	6	0	0	0	16	1	0	.266	.257
Conley, Brian	L-R	6-2	195	5-7-86	.156	.118	.170	29	64	12	10	1	0	1	7	16	0	2	0	18	1	0	.219	.325
Flacco, Mike	R-R	6-5	220	1-17-87	.158	.000	.231	5	19	3	3	1	0	0	1	1	1	0	0	7	1	0	.211	.238
Helmick, Gary	R-R	5-11	185	8-29-87	.059	.000	.100	6	17	5	1	1	0	0	1	4	0	0	0	6	0	0	.118	.238
Hoes, L.J.	R-R	6-1	181	3-5-90	.260	.299	.243	119	431	42	112	19	0	2	47	23	3	4	4	80	20	5	.318	.299

Batting	B-T	HT	WT	DOB	AVG	vLH	vRH	G	AB	R	H	2B	3B	HR	RBI	BB	HBP	SH	SF	SO	SB	CS	SLG	OBP
Hudson, Kyle	L-L	5-11	175	1-7-87	.284	.291	.281	117	398	61	113	8	2	0	21	49	2	7	0	85	31	16	.314	.365
Julius, Jacob	L-L	6-5	185	3-13-86	.228	.200	.240	57	171	23	39	8	3	2	12	17	2	3	1	60	7	5	.345	.304
Kolodny, Tyler	R-R	6-2	210	3-9-88	.226	.202	.234	107	363	52	82	20	3	9	42	42	17	4	3	97	10	4	.372	.332
Mahoney, Joe	L-L	6-7	255	2-1-87	.278	.245	.290	108	395	61	110	16	7	7	53	30	3	0	4	93	29	1	.408	.331
Miclat, Greg	B-R	5-9	180	7-23-87	.228	.304	.201	111	400	49	91	14	2	0	22	42	0	9	3	79	25	6	.273	.299
Monaghan, Brendan	R-R	6-2	210	4-11-85	.222	.214	.225	39	99	13	22	5	1	1	16	11	1	1	1	28	1	0	.323	.304
Polanco, Elvin	B-L	6-3	190	3-3-87	.246	.205	.262	126	459	34	113	20	0	6	59	23	2	3	5	112	1	3	.329	.282
Ricardo, Dashenko	R-R	6-0	160	3-1-90	.133	.333	.000	6	15	2	2	1	0	0	2	1	0	0	0	3	0	0	.200	.188
Rosa, Garabez	R-R	6-2	166	10-12-89	.125	.100	.136	11	32	2	4	0	0	1	5	1	0	0	0	7	0	1	.219	.152
Santana, Javier	B-R	6-1	160	7-31-87	.000	.000	.000	1	4	0	0	0	0	0	0	0	0	0	0	3	0	0	.000	.000
Scott, Luke	L-R	6-0	210	6-25-78	.750	1.000	.500	2	4	1	3	0	0	1	1	2	0	0	0	0	0	0	1.500	.833
Stephen, Jedidiah	R-R	6-2	195	4-30-84	.232	.292	.200	20	69	7	16	2	0	1	10	4	1	0	1	25	2	0	.304	.280
Welty, Ronnie	R-R	6-2	180	1-19-88	.290	.341	.269	121	431	60	125	24	2	10	67	46	12	0	2	120	13	5	.425	.373

Pitching	B-T	HT	WT	DOB	W	L	ERA	G	GS	CG	SV	IP	H	R	ER	HR	BB	SO	AVG	vLH	vRH	K/9	BB/9
Allar, Brent	R-R	6-3	230	3-1-85	1	5	4.70	33	3	0	1	67	62	40	35	0	55	77	.243	.294	.218	10.34	7.39
Allen, Colin	R-R	6-1	175	10-14-86	0	3	7.04	12	2	0	0	23	31	21	18	4	16	22	.316	.276	.333	8.61	6.26
Bordes, Brett	L-L	5-10	175	11-30-83	3	2	2.08	17	0	0	4	22	11	8	5	0	16	16	.151	.207	.114	6.65	6.65
Cooney, Brandon	R-R	6-6	240	8-2-85	2	5	2.68	38	0	0	16	44	39	22	13	2	17	36	.234	.193	.255	7.42	3.50
Drake, Oliver	R-R	6-4	210	1-13-87	8	9	4.34	25	24	0	0	131	138	72	63	6	42	104	.277	.313	.250	7.16	2.89
Egan, Pat	R-R	6-8	225	10-25-84	0	0	2.78	13	2	0	2	32	28	12	10	0	5	31	.237	.200	.256	8.63	1.39
Esposito, Joe	L-R	5-11	220	5-15-85	3	0	1.08	18	0	0	2	33	26	9	4	1	14	52	.203	.280	.154	14.04	3.78
Flagello, Cliff	R-R	5-10	200	1-3-85	1	2	1.76	20	0	0	6	31	19	11	6	0	10	35	.181	.220	.156	10.27	2.93
Gamboa, Eddie	R-R	6-2	195	12-21-84	6	0	1.86	18	0	0	1	39	30	8	8	5	3	35	.219	.182	.237	8.15	0.70
Haughian, Nick	L-L	6-0	205	1-1-87	0	1	3.09	2	2	0	0	12	9	4	4	2	2	5	.225	.000	.273	3.86	1.54
Kantakevich, Pat	R-R	6-2	198	8-11-86	0	0	6.43	2	2	0	0	7	7	5	5	0	6	7	.259	.250	.267	9.00	7.71
Keating, Travis	R-R	6-6	205	9-16-85	5	5	3.74	27	0	0	2	46	34	22	19	2	11	43	.202	.161	.226	8.47	2.17
Mathews, Shane	R-R	6-3	210	3-28-85	1	4	4.15	27	1	0	0	52	57	28	24	0	19	44	.284	.343	.252	7.62	3.29
Mattaliano, Mick	R-R	6-3	200	1-17-85	0	2	12.00	11	0	0	0	9	15	13	12	1	5	2	.395	.400	.394	2.00	5.00
McCurry, Cole	L-L	6-2	180	9-25-85	6	9	2.71	26	25	0	0	140	118	51	42	8	46	145	.229	.195	.236	9.34	2.96
Mechaw, Blake	L-L	6-2	200	8-19-88	0	0	0.00	2	0	0	0	2	1	0	0	0	3	1	.143	.000	.250	3.86	11.57
Moreau, Nathan	L-L	6-4	222	9-15-86	5	3	3.61	20	20	0	0	87	78	39	35	9	43	95	.241	.231	.243	9.79	4.43
Mueller, Scott	R-R	6-3	175	6-9-86	2	0	7.04	14	0	0	0	23	32	20	18	1	10	20	.337	.300	.354	7.83	3.91
Nery, Nate	R-L	6-4	210	8-25-85	3	0	1.17	5	4	0	0	23	16	3	3	1	7	19	.190	.000	.239	7.43	2.74
O'Shea, Ryan	L-R	6-1	200	5-29-86	8	8	3.60	25	25	1	0	138	133	63	55	8	47	100	.254	.247	.258	6.54	3.07
Procner, Stephen	L-L	6-2	200	12-27-84	0	0	2.25	2	0	0	0	4	1	1	1	0	3	2	.077	.000	.091	4.50	6.75
Rivero, Raul	R-R	6-0	165	5-6-86	4	2	4.06	22	1	0	0	51	46	26	23	5	20	47	.235	.264	.218	8.29	3.53
Salberg, Chris	R-L	6-1	185	5-8-84	3	3	4.31	13	13	0	0	63	60	41	30	2	22	51	.253	.278	.249	7.32	3.16
Schindling, Andy	R-R	6-2	175	8-15-86	0	2	36.00	3	0	0	0	1	3	4	4	0	6	5	.400	.333	.429	22.50	27.00
Smith, Jacob	L-L	6-4	210	10-1-85	1	0	0.00	2	0	0	0	5	2	0	0	0	0	1	.125	.500	.071	1.80	0.00
Zagone, Rick	L-L	6-4	215	9-30-86	4	5	4.66	13	12	0	0	64	59	35	33	3	27	59	.249	.167	.264	8.34	3.82

Fielding

Catcher	PCT	G	PO	A	E	DP	PB
Bernardo	.984	81	560	109	11	7	15
Black	.987	10	70	6	1	0	4
Castillo	1.000	22	138	12	0	1	3
Monaghan	.991	32	198	23	2	0	6
Ricardo	.974	6	33	5	1	0	1

First Base	PCT	G	PO	A	E	DP
Flacco	1.000	3	30	4	0	3
Julius	.967	7	27	2	1	1
Kolodny	1.000	2	1	0	0	0
Mahoney	.992	68	576	45	5	42
Polanco	.992	66	555	47	5	42

Second Base	PCT	G	PO	A	E	DP
Britton	.909	3	6	4	1	1

	PCT	G	PO	A	E	DP
Cardona	.967	14	29	30	2	7
Hoes	.939	107	186	247	28	49
Rosa	1.000	5	6	16	0	4
Stephen	.977	9	20	22	1	8

Third Base	PCT	G	PO	A	E	DP
Bernardo	1.000	1	1	1	0	0
Cardona	.938	13	4	26	2	0
Carolus	.939	17	8	38	3	2
Kolodny	.916	102	73	189	24	10
Rosa	.500	1	0	1	1	0
Stephen	.833	5	3	7	2	0

Shortstop	PCT	G	PO	A	E	DP
Cardona	.968	14	20	40	2	8
Helmick	.923	6	11	25	3	4

	PCT	G	PO	A	E	DP
Kolodny	1.000	1	3	5	0	0
Miclat	.945	110	149	284	25	55
Rosa	.929	4	1	12	1	2
Santana	1.000	1	2	2	0	1
Stephen	.917	6	2	20	2	0

Outfield	PCT	G	PO	A	E	DP
Avery	.951	122	225	10	12	0
Conley	.953	23	40	1	2	0
Hudson	.988	113	151	7	2	2
Julius	.980	42	46	3	1	0
Mahoney	1.000	2	1	0	0	0
Monaghan	1.000	3	1	0	0	0
Scott	—	1	0	0	0	0
Welty	.991	119	207	11	2	2

ABERDEEN IRONBIRDS   SHORT-SEASON

NEW YORK-PENN LEAGUE

Batting	B-T	HT	WT	DOB	AVG	vLH	vRH	G	AB	R	H	2B	3B	HR	RBI	BB	HBP	SH	SF	SO	SB	CS	SLG	OBP
Baxter, T.J.	L-R	6-1	208	12-13-85	.280	.300	.270	62	232	32	65	10	5	1	17	21	3	3	2	50	16	5	.379	.345
Bonevacia, Arthur	B-R	5-9	160	5-16-88	.195	.167	.214	40	118	7	23	5	2	0	12	12	1	1	2	28	3	2	.271	.271
Booker, Zach	R-R	6-0	220	4-24-85	.000	.000	.000	2	6	0	0	0	0	0	1	0	1	0	0	2	0	0	.000	.143
Britton, Buck	L-R	6-1	163	5-16-86	.241	.286	.225	17	54	4	13	3	0	1	5	3	1	3	0	9	1	2	.352	.293
Bumbry, Steve	L-L	5-11	185	4-4-88	.234	.204	.253	45	128	15	30	8	3	2	10	20	1	3	0	55	5	3	.391	.342
Carolus, Levi	R-R	6-0	160	9-22-87	.320	.193	.384	44	169	20	54	13	1	1	25	8	0	3	2	38	9	3	.426	.346
Conley, Brian	L-R	6-2	195	7-16-86	.263	.257	.266	31	99	23	26	4	2	1	8	22	1	2	2	26	4	1	.374	.395
D'Oleo, Richard	L-L	6-2	165	5-5-86	.205	.159	.223	63	220	27	45	12	5	1	20	21	1	2	2	64	7	1	.318	.275
Dalles, Justin	R-R	6-2	205	12-30-88	.225	.183	.244	48	187	13	42	9	1	0	21	10	3	0	0	39	0	0	.283	.275
Davis, Blake	L-R	5-11	165	12-20-83	.320	.333	.310	13	50	6	16	2	0	1	5	4	0	0	2	7	0	0	.420	.357
Edwards, Tom	L-R	6-2	200	10-15-85	.240	.158	.275	39	129	7	31	2	1	0	8	15	2	3	0	28	0	0	.271	.329
Gioioso, Mike	R-R	6-0	190	2-14-85	.155	.150	.158	23	58	6	9	2	0	0	3	11	0	2	0	11	1	0	.190	.290

	B-T	HT	WT	DOB	AVG	vLH	vRH	G	AB	R	H	2B	3B	HR	RBI	BB	HBP	SH	SF	SO	SB	CS	SLG	OBP
Kelly, Ty	L-R	6-0	185	7-20-88	.265	.267	.264	61	226	31	60	5	1	1	18	33	2	5	5	29	3	3	.310	.357
Mooney, Mike	B-R	5-8	160	6-12-88	.230	.275	.211	46	174	21	40	5	2	1	15	20	4	2	2	37	1	3	.299	.320
Rook, Jason	L-R	6-1	200	8-28-87	.202	.125	.227	37	99	9	20	3	0	2	8	12	1	1	0	40	3	2	.293	.295
Rosa, Garabez	R-R	6-2	166	10-12-89	.218	.176	.240	64	220	28	48	8	6	6	25	8	6	3	2	72	1	2	.391	.263
Stifler, Jason	R-R	6-0	215	8-12-86	.030	.063	.000	13	33	0	1	0	0	0	1	2	0	0	0	16	0	0	.030	.086
Townsend, Tyler	L-R	6-3	215	5-14-88	.143	.107	.154	31	119	11	17	7	0	4	16	10	3	0	1	39	1	1	.303	.226
Ward, Brian	R-R	5-11	200	10-17-85	.252	.270	.243	36	107	10	27	2	1	1	13	20	5	2	3	16	1	0	.318	.385
West, Lance	R-R	6-2	215	11-8-87	.194	.071	.294	13	31	5	6	1	1	2	7	6	0	0	0	14	0	1	.484	.324

Pitching	B-T	HT	WT	DOB	W	L	ERA	G	GS	CG	SV	IP	H	R	ER	HR	BB	SO	AVG	vLH	vRH	K/9	BB/9
Allen, Colin	R-R	6-1	175	10-14-86	2	6	5.45	15	15	0	0	69	89	51	42	5	25	56	.310	.271	.344	7.27	3.25
Anderson, Justin	L-L	6-4	195	10-21-87	0	0	5.40	1	1	0	0	5	8	3	3	0	1	2	.364	.400	.333	3.60	1.80
Barajas, Jose	R-R	6-4	190	2-25-88	3	3	4.32	21	0	0	1	33	30	23	16	0	16	26	.234	.217	.250	7.02	4.32
Brandhorst, James	R-R	6-4	240	8-26-87	0	1	1.30	21	0	0	4	28	23	7	4	0	7	32	.240	.200	.258	10.41	2.28
Butler, Tony	L-L	6-7	220	11-18-87	0	0	67.50	1	0	0	0	1	5	5	5	0	2	0	.714	.667	.750	0.00	27.00
Cowan, Jacob	L-R	6-3	165	6-30-88	1	2	2.25	8	4	0	0	24	15	7	6	1	11	27	.179	.182	.175	10.13	4.13
Dowdy, Josh	R-R	5-11	165	1-18-87	1	3	4.20	13	0	0	7	15	15	8	7	0	9	13	.259	.160	.333	7.80	5.40
Eastham, Dan	R-R	6-2	200	12-30-84	0	0	—	1	0	0	0	0	0	3	3	0	1	0	—	—	—	—	—
Erbe, Brandon	R-R	6-4	180	12-25-87	0	1	4.61	4	4	0	0	14	13	9	7	3	2	11	.245	.333	.211	7.24	1.32
Frabizio, Vito	R-R	0-0	0	6-28-89	0	1	18.00	1	1	0	0	3	7	6	6	1	1	0	.467	.500	.429	0.00	3.00
Haughian, Nick	L-L	6-0	205	1-1-87	6	3	2.05	13	12	0	0	75	61	25	17	2	20	54	.221	.186	.237	6.51	2.41
Kantakevich, Pat	R-R	6-2	198	8-11-86	3	5	3.34	13	13	0	0	73	60	30	27	2	26	57	.228	.296	.176	7.06	3.22
Landry, Kevin	R-R	6-7	220	5-9-88	0	0	5.27	14	0	0	0	27	26	17	16	2	18	43	.255	.234	.273	14.16	5.93
Mattaliano, Mick	R-R	6-3	200	1-17-85	0	2	7.59	7	0	0	1	11	15	10	9	1	4	5	.319	.158	.429	4.22	3.38
Moreland, Kenny	R-R	5-11	200	4-2-86	6	1	0.88	8	1	0	0	51	32	7	5	2	3	39	.178	.175	.181	6.88	0.53
Mueller, Scott	R-R	6-3	175	6-9-86	1	0	0.95	9	0	0	2	19	10	2	2	1	5	17	.154	.167	.138	8.05	2.37
Phelps, Thomas	R-R	6-2	215	10-12-87	0	1	0.00	2	0	0	0	5	3	1	0	2	1	.167	.250	.100	1.80	3.60
Phillips, Chase	R-R	6-4	175	9-14-86	0	0	4.00	4	0	0	0	9	7	5	4	1	6	6	.212	.333	.143	6.00	6.00
Procner, Stephen	L-L	6-2	200	12-27-84	0	3	5.02	17	2	0	3	38	40	26	21	2	12	26	.280	.304	.268	6.21	2.87
Sexton, Tyler	L-L	6-4	205	7-24-85	3	7	3.39	15	13	0	0	80	71	38	30	4	32	62	.243	.256	.238	7.00	3.62
Sisk, Brian	L-L	5-10	200	8-21-87	0	2	4.20	17	0	0	0	30	32	17	14	2	12	21	.267	.162	.313	6.30	3.60
Smith, Jacob	L-L	6-4	210	10-1-85	3	3	2.15	19	0	0	0	38	32	12	9	0	18	33	.234	.233	.234	7.88	4.30
Spoone, Chorye	R-R	6-1	215	9-16-85	0	0	0.00	1	1	0	0	3	1	0	0	0	3	3	.100	.250	.000	9.00	9.00
Tolliver, Ashur	L-L	6-0	170	1-24-88	1	0	0.00	3	0	0	0	8	6	0	0	0	2	7	.231	.200	.250	7.88	2.25
Walters, David	R-R	6-3	190	8-13-87	0	0	2.70	2	0	0	0	3	2	1	0	0	4	.167	.000	.250	10.80	0.00

Fielding

Catcher	PCT	G	PO	A	E	DP	PB
Dalles	.978	35	235	27	6	3	9
Stifler	1.000	6	42	0	0	0	4
Ward	.983	35	268	25	5	1	5

First Base	PCT	G	PO	A	E	DP
Baxter	.997	31	274	27	1	20
Edwards	.981	21	188	18	4	14
Townsend	.991	24	209	21	2	24

Second Base	PCT	G	PO	A	E	DP
Britton	.929	13	19	33	4	8
Gioioso	.944	18	30	38	4	5

	PCT	G	PO	A	E	DP
Kelly	.985	14	22	42	1	9
Mooney	.988	36	58	105	2	27
Rosa	1.000	2	1	7	0	1

Third Base	PCT	G	PO	A	E	DP
Carolus	.900	17	6	39	5	6
Edwards	.906	13	7	22	3	5
Kelly	.910	41	22	79	10	5
Rosa	.882	7	3	12	2	1

Shortstop	PCT	G	PO	A	E	DP
Davis	1.000	10	14	27	0	7
Mooney	.923	14	20	28	4	5

	PCT	G	PO	A	E	DP
Rosa	.950	57	76	154	12	25

Outfield	PCT	G	PO	A	E	DP
Baxter	.974	22	34	3	1	0
Bonevacia	.983	38	55	3	1	0
Bumbry	.971	43	97	3	3	1
Conley	.962	30	49	2	2	0
D'Oleo	.986	62	131	8	2	4
Rook	.968	36	55	5	2	2
West	.900	12	9	0	1	0

BLUEFIELD ORIOLES   ROOKIE

APPALACHIAN LEAGUE

Batting	B-T	HT	WT	DOB	AVG	vLH	vRH	G	AB	R	H	2B	3B	HR	RBI	BB	HBP	SH	SF	SO	SB	CS	SLG	OBP
Casamayor, Omar	B-R	5-11	170	11-3-86	.279	.246	.291	57	215	37	60	7	1	1	21	14	5	6	1	39	13	8	.335	.336
Flacco, Mike	R-R	6-5	220	1-17-87	.272	.255	.277	60	228	25	62	14	5	3	34	15	4	0	2	37	7	2	.417	.325
Guerrero, Janensi	R-R	6-0	170	5-21-89	.186	.250	.154	20	59	6	11	2	0	0	4	4	1	1	0	15	1	0	.220	.250
Helmick, Gary	R-R	5-11	185	8-29-87	.275	.222	.298	45	149	31	41	10	4	4	13	17	1	1	4	22	5	3	.477	.345
Kianes, Jose	B-L	6-2	182	5-1-87	.218	.167	.225	38	101	18	22	5	1	4	12	5	0	2	0	25	4	1	.406	.255
Meyer, Edinho	R-R	6-2	170	2-7-88	.252	.303	.235	37	131	17	33	6	1	2	15	9	5	0	1	32	0	1	.359	.322
Planeta, Mike	R-R	6-3	195	10-17-89	.288	.305	.282	61	229	29	66	12	2	3	29	9	2	1	1	68	8	5	.397	.320
Polanco, Joel	R-R	6-2	190	9-27-85	.268	.200	.292	39	97	8	26	6	0	3	19	6	3	0	0	15	0	0	.423	.330
Ramirez, Luis	L-L	6-3	170	4-24-88	.220	.325	.194	56	205	19	45	7	4	3	32	9	8	1	1	46	4	7	.337	.278
Ricardo, Dashenko	R-R	6-0	160	3-1-90	.243	.300	.228	49	169	13	41	8	2	0	17	5	2	1	0	34	3	1	.314	.273
Rivera, Larry	B-R	6-1	170	5-26-88	.174	.182	.170	40	121	11	21	1	0	0	6	15	3	3	1	39	4	4	.182	.279
Santana, Javier	B-R	6-1	160	7-31-87	.242	.231	.246	51	165	18	40	4	1	1	14	13	4	2	1	51	5	2	.297	.311
Schutz, Kipp	L-L	6-4	170	3-21-88	.252	.250	.252	40	135	26	34	6	1	0	15	18	0	0	3	23	2	3	.319	.340
Thomas, Corey	R-R	6-2	201	9-23-88	.233	.184	.250	57	193	30	45	10	3	5	21	20	3	2	0	72	3	2	.394	.315
Tucker, Matt	B-R	6-2	185	6-5-83	.556	1.000	.333	3	9	4	5	1	0	0	0	2	0	0	0	2	0	0	.667	.636
West, Lance	R-R	6-2	215	11-8-87	.150	.273	.079	19	60	3	9	3	0	0	4	6	3	0	0	27	0	3	.267	.239

Pitching	B-T	HT	WT	DOB	W	L	ERA	G	GS	CG	SV	IP	H	R	ER	HR	BB	SO	AVG	vLH	vRH	K/9	BB/9
Almanzar, Jorge	R-R	6-2	160	7-25-86	1	3	4.32	9	6	0	0	33	37	20	16	2	20	30	.289	.310	.279	8.10	5.40
Anderson, Justin	L-L	6-4	195	10-21-87	2	1	2.50	14	3	0	0	40	42	18	11	1	15	34	.278	.340	.250	7.71	3.40
Beal, Jesse	B-R	6-6	210	7-12-90	5	5	4.26	13	13	0	0	74	77	44	35	3	8	41	.267	.183	.324	4.99	0.97
Bundy, Bobby	R-R	6-2	215	1-13-90	2	7	5.10	12	12	1	0	55	47	38	31	6	19	38	.229	.217	.235	6.26	3.13

	B-T	HT	WT	DOB	W	L	ERA	G	GS	CG	SV	IP	H	R	ER	HR	BB	SO	AVG	vLH	vRH	K/9	BB/9
Dowdy, Josh	R-R	5-11	165	1-18-87	2	0	1.13	9	0	0	3	16	14	3	2	0	3	20	.233	.250	.225	11.25	1.69
Frabizio, Vito	R-R	0-0	0	6-28-89	4	4	2.96	12	12	0	0	70	57	27	23	5	16	64	.223	.250	.208	8.23	2.06
Hobgood, Matt	R-R	6-4	245	8-3-90	1	2	4.72	8	8	0	0	27	32	17	14	0	8	16	.305	.289	.317	5.40	2.70
Holloway, Brandon	L-L	6-3	245	4-26-86	3	3	4.03	14	2	0	0	45	49	31	20	2	12	34	.269	.256	.273	6.85	2.42
Huebner, Andrew	R-R	6-2	200	11-5-86	0	1	4.50	8	0	0	1	12	14	7	6	0	4	12	.280	.118	.364	9.00	3.00
McCrory, Pat	R-R	5-9	175	12-9-86	1	1	9.00	7	0	0	1	8	11	10	8	2	8	10	.324	.267	.368	11.25	9.00
Mechaw, Blake	L-L	6-2	200	8-19-88	1	0	6.75	12	0	0	0	25	26	21	19	2	12	16	.263	.222	.278	5.68	4.26
Moore, Justin	R-R	6-3	190	7-26-89	4	3	3.11	13	12	0	0	64	67	27	22	1	15	37	.278	.300	.265	5.23	2.12
Palsha, Ryan	R-R	6-1	180	5-17-90	2	1	4.33	11	0	0	3	27	27	14	13	1	6	40	.255	.375	.182	13.33	2.00
Phelps, Thomas	R-R	6-2	215	10-12-87	2	2	3.43	16	0	0	1	39	38	16	15	3	12	33	.253	.261	.250	7.55	2.75
Phillips, Chase	R-R	6-4	175	9-14-86	1	0	0.56	9	0	0	0	16	11	1	1	1	8	20	.200	.208	.194	11.25	4.50
Taveras, Sam	R-R	6-3	180	1-4-88	2	1	2.66	20	0	0	5	24	24	11	7	0	7	20	.258	.343	.207	7.61	2.66
Walters, David	R-R	6-3	190	8-13-87	0	1	4.74	11	0	0	1	19	21	13	10	2	6	19	.259	.333	.208	9.00	2.84

Fielding

Catcher	PCT	G	PO	A	E	DP	PB
Guerrero	.987	20	138	11	2	2	7
Polanco	.917	5	20	2	2	0	1
Ricardo	.982	49	314	58	7	3	12

First Base	PCT	G	PO	A	E	DP
Flacco	.986	32	324	19	5	30
Meyer	.980	19	185	7	4	18
Thomas	.989	19	164	8	2	13

Second Base	PCT	G	PO	A	E	DP
Casamayor	.977	50	95	155	6	33

	PCT	PO	A	E	DP	
Helmick	.967	21	32	55	3	15
Tucker	1.000	1	0	1	0	0

Third Base	PCT	G	PO	A	E	DP
Casamayor	.882	7	3	12	2	0
Flacco	.921	26	18	64	7	4
Thomas	.895	36	22	89	13	10

Shortstop	PCT	G	PO	A	E	DP
Helmick	.948	21	28	63	5	10
Santana	.924	51	73	159	19	33
Tucker	1.000	1	1	1	0	0

Outfield	PCT	G	PO	A	E	DP
Kianes	.941	21	31	1	2	1
Planeta	.963	56	103	1	4	0
Ramirez	.972	53	98	8	3	3
Rivera	.941	40	44	4	3	1
Schutz	.933	33	39	3	3	1
West	1.000	12	19	1	0	0

GCL ORIOLES
ROOKIE

GULF COAST LEAGUE

Batting	B-T	HT	WT	DOB	AVG	vLH	vRH	G	AB	R	H	2B	3B	HR	RBI	BB	HBP	SH	SF	SO	SB	CS	SLG	OBP
Anderson, David	R-R	6-6	240	9-1-87	.271	.239	.281	50	181	28	49	11	3	4	35	36	2	0	2	32	0	1	.431	.394
Calderon, David	R-R	6-1	180	1-30-90	.205	.000	.281	15	44	7	9	2	0	0	6	6	1	0	1	6	0	0	.250	.308
Childers, Anderson	L-R	6-1	187	8-21-86	.213	.139	.237	40	150	19	32	6	2	0	16	18	1	1	3	39	5	0	.280	.297
Cintron, Edwin	B-R	5-11	175	6-29-90	.230	.189	.242	43	161	19	37	4	3	0	10	10	6	3	1	31	11	7	.292	.298
Ciriaco, Moises	R-R	5-11	185	8-31-88	.261	.200	.277	51	188	26	49	7	1	1	19	8	6	4	1	28	14	6	.324	.310
Figueroa, Paco	R-R	5-11	180	2-19-83	.286	.333	.267	6	21	5	6	1	1	0	5	4	0	0	0	1	2	0	.429	.400
Ford, Bo	R-R	6-0	180	10-6-84	.268	.182	.300	13	41	4	11	3	0	0	5	2	0	0	0	10	2	0	.341	.302
Gonzalez, Grolmann	R-R	6-1	180	10-12-88	.226	.294	.207	45	155	25	35	6	7	2	16	20	1	3	1	40	5	2	.394	.316
Hoppy, Kyle	L-L	6-0	195	5-8-91	.111	—	.111	3	9	0	1	0	0	0	2	0	0	0	0	4	0	1	.111	.111
Lopez, Xavier	B-R	6-1	175	1-18-90	.208	.111	.241	23	72	9	15	2	1	0	8	9	2	0	0	14	9	0	.264	.313
Melenciano, Jaynnertt	R-R	6-1	170	11-13-87	.253	.300	.237	46	158	19	40	8	3	1	24	18	7	3	1	38	3	4	.361	.353
Montanez, Lou	R-R	6-1	200	12-15-81	.333	.000	.400	2	6	0	2	0	0	0	1	0	1	0	0	0	0	0	.333	.429
Nivar, Jose	B-R	6-1	170	2-28-89	.102	.222	.075	16	49	4	5	2	0	0	3	3	0	1	0	12	1	1	.143	.154
Ohlman, Michael	R-R	6-4	205	12-14-90	.182	1.000	.000	4	11	1	2	1	0	0	1	0	0	0	0	3	1	0	.273	.250
Parra, Freuny	R-R	5-11	195	11-2-87	.324	.333	.320	12	37	4	12	2	0	0	2	5	0	0	0	9	0	0	.378	.405
Perez, Dennis	B-R	5-11	185	7-30-88	.236	.133	.263	24	72	9	17	3	0	0	6	13	0	1	0	6	2	0	.278	.353
Rivera, David	L-R	6-0	190	3-20-91	.197	.194	.198	40	142	12	28	3	2	1	10	11	0	3	2	34	1	1	.268	.252
Stampone, Tyler	R-R	6-2	215	5-21-87	.312	.303	.315	36	141	19	44	6	0	2	3	26	8	0	1	18	5	1	.475	.380
Tejeda, Anyi	R-R	6-3	173	1-19-89	.238	.265	.229	48	193	26	46	6	0	0	12	13	2	2	1	38	4	1	.269	.292
Webb, Brenden	L-L	6-3	190	2-24-90	.186	.077	.233	13	43	7	8	2	0	0	1	10	1	0	0	14	2	0	.233	.352

Pitching	B-T	HT	WT	DOB	W	L	ERA	G	GS	CG	SV	IP	H	R	ER	HR	BB	SO	AVG	vLH	vRH	K/9	BB/9
Alfonso, Orlando	R-R	6-5	230	8-15-89	1	2	2.20	9	0	0	0	16	11	5	4	0	10	11	.204	.296	.111	6.06	5.51
Baker, David	R-R	6-4	195	4-17-91	1	0	2.30	8	0	0	0	16	13	6	4	0	3	20	.224	.238	.216	11.49	1.72
Butler, Tony	L-L	6-7	220	11-18-87	0	1	2.92	10	0	0	1	12	11	4	4	0	7	6	.268	.400	.250	4.38	5.11
Carder, Dustin	R-R	6-5	220	2-2-87	2	2	2.40	14	0	0	2	30	31	13	8	0	11	22	.265	.281	.250	6.60	3.30
Centanni, Joey	R-L	6-0	175	1-15-87	0	1	4.38	10	0	0	0	12	13	6	6	0	3	19	.277	.063	.387	13.86	2.19
Cespedes, Angel	R-R	6-2	170	8-27-89	5	3	2.51	12	10	0	0	72	64	27	20	1	15	34	.241	.227	.254	4.27	1.88
Clark, Zach	R-R	6-0	195	7-11-83	0	0	0.00	4	4	0	0	9	5	1	0	0	9	5	.161	.125	.200	9.00	0.00
De La Cruz, Jairo	R-R	6-3	183	7-15-87	3	4	3.71	12	11	0	0	53	44	27	22	4	22	39	.224	.281	.178	6.58	3.71
Goodin, Joshua	R-R	6-1	200	8-17-86	1	1	0.47	11	0	0	3	19	8	2	1	0	4	23	.121	.120	.122	10.89	1.89
Gross, Billy	R-R	0-0	0	9-3-87	0	1	2.60	12	0	0	1	17	21	5	5	0	4	16	.313	.250	.340	8.31	2.08
Hallerman, Jason	R-R	6-3	190	1-12-88	0	1	8.71	11	0	0	0	10	9	12	10	0	19	4	.243	.300	.176	3.48	16.55
Hervey, Chris	R-R	6-2	190	12-10-86	1	1	9.69	13	0	0	1	13	15	14	14	0	7	8	.283	.389	.229	5.54	4.85
Huebner, Andrew	R-R	6-2	200	11-5-86	0	0	0.00	1	0	0	1	1	0	0	0	0	1	1	.000	.000	.000	9.00	9.00
McCrory, Pat	R-R	5-9	175	12-9-86	0	0	0.00	1	0	0	0	1	0	0	0	0	1	2	.000	.000	.000	18.00	9.00
Petersime, Zach	R-R	6-3	175	1-19-89	4	2	3.61	11	8	0	1	47	45	21	19	2	25	36	.257	.264	.252	6.85	4.75
Ramirez, Eiri	R-R	6-0	173	8-2-88	2	2	2.78	7	5	0	0	32	28	14	10	0	10	16	.230	.264	.203	4.45	2.78
Reyes, Jean Carlos	R-R	6-1	150	6-22-87	1	0	3.86	5	0	0	0	5	3	2	2	0	4	3	.200	.125	.286	5.79	7.71
Schmitt, Chris	R-R	6-0	190	12-31-86	3	0	2.97	15	0	0	2	30	21	12	10	0	8	21	.204	.102	.296	6.23	2.37
Spoone, Chorye	R-R	6-1	215	9-16-85	0	1	4.38	5	0	0	0	12	9	6	6	1	2	11	.220	.214	.222	8.03	1.46
Tavarez, Daurin	R-R	6-6	160	2-8-89	4	2	1.37	12	9	0	1	66	53	15	10	0	9	44	.220	.220	.220	6.03	1.23
Walters, David	R-R	6-3	190	8-13-87	0	1	4.50	5	0	0	1	10	9	5	5	0	0	9	.237	.125	.318	8.10	0.00
Wirsch, Aaron	R-L	6-6	200	11-15-90	1	0	2.16	7	4	0	0	17	12	4	4	0	10	18	.207	.083	.239	9.72	5.40

Fielding

Catcher	PCT	G	PO	A	E	DP	PB
Calderon	.987	12	68	9	1	0	6
Lopez	.987	17	135	12	2	2	2
Ohlman	.952	4	15	5	1	0	0
Parra	.985	10	55	10	1	1	3
Perez	1.000	17	100	10	0	2	2

First Base	PCT	G	PO	A	E	DP
Anderson	.995	48	505	46	3	51
Perez	1.000	2	23	3	0	5
Stampone	.983	6	49	9	1	5

Second Base	PCT	G	PO	A	E	DP
Childers	.987	28	57	95	2	14

	PCT	G	PO	A	E	DP	PB
Ciriaco	.932	17	31	51	6	15	
Figueroa	1.000	4	5	10	0	2	
Ford	.921	7	10	25	3	5	
Perez	.895	5	5	12	2	0	

Third Base	PCT	G	PO	A	E	DP
Anderson	1.000	1	2	0	0	0
Ciriaco	.911	11	12	29	4	3
Stampone	.925	28	25	49	6	5
Tejeda	.953	16	7	34	2	5

Shortstop	PCT	G	PO	A	E	DP
Calderon	—	1	0	0	0	0
Childers	.923	7	8	16	2	5

	PCT	G	PO	A	E	DP
Ciriaco	.937	17	36	53	6	13
Tejeda	.961	32	48	124	7	27

Outfield	PCT	G	PO	A	E	DP
Cintron	1.000	42	67	1	0	1
Ciriaco	1.000	3	8	0	0	0
Gonzalez	1.000	42	61	3	0	0
Hoppy	1.000	2	2	0	0	0
Melenciano	.969	42	57	6	2	1
Montanez	—	1	0	0	0	0
Nivar	1.000	4	7	1	0	0
Rivera	.978	31	43	2	1	0
Webb	.950	7	16	3	1	1

DSL ORIOLES   ROOKIE

DOMINICAN SUMMER LEAGUE

Batting	B-T	HT	WT	DOB	AVG	vLH	vRH	G	AB	R	H	2B	3B	HR	RBI	BB	HBP	SH	SF	SO	SB	CS	SLG	OBP
Arias, Moises	R-R	6-6	205	2-3-89	.091	.000	.100	10	11	1	1	0	0	0	1	1	0	0	0	4	0	0	.091	.167
2-team total (19 Orioles/Brewers)					.146	—	—	29	48	5	7	0	0	0	3	5	0	1	0	15	0	1	.146	.226
Cleofa, Rojean	R-R	5-11	176	9-11-90	.240	.225	.245	48	150	19	36	3	1	0	7	23	4	5	2	19	18	3	.273	.352
Familia, Elvis	R-R	6-1	190	5-2-91	.197	.125	.220	45	132	13	26	7	1	0	11	11	4	2	0	34	5	2	.265	.279
Feliz, Esteylin	L-R	6-1	190	9-24-88	.132	.083	.146	22	53	6	7	1	0	0	2	3	1	1	0	16	1	0	.151	.193
Gomez, Nelson	R-R	6-2	171	1-6-92	.258	.304	.243	31	97	15	25	2	1	0	5	3	3	3	1	21	4	3	.299	.311
Gonzalez, Henry	L-L	6-4	210	3-31-92	.193	.174	.199	67	212	21	41	8	1	3	22	35	2	0	0	60	3	1	.283	.313
Leonora, Dudley	R-R	6-1	154	12-15-91	.241	.241	.241	67	257	26	62	6	2	1	21	8	7	5	0	24	7	2	.292	.283
Moranci, Gino	L-L	6-4	188	1-27-90	.268	.128	.304	65	228	29	61	9	2	1	30	39	2	2	0	44	6	3	.338	.379
Nivar, Jose	B-R	6-1	170	2-28-89	.288	.125	.333	30	111	10	32	5	2	0	9	8	3	0	0	17	3	2	.369	.352
Paez, Carlos	R-R	6-0	180	6-18-91	.186	.167	.195	27	59	13	11	2	1	1	5	5	4	3	0	15	2	0	.305	.294
2-team total (5 Orioles/Brewers)					.186	—	—	32	70	13	13	3	1	1	6	5	4	3	0	21	3	0	.300	.278
Parra, Gustavo	R-R	5-11	172	8-4-90	.176	.235	.162	36	85	7	15	3	0	0	3	7	4	3	0	18	1	1	.212	.271
Perez, Pedro	R-R	5-11	170	5-8-91	.177	.313	.150	33	96	7	17	2	0	0	7	5	3	1	0	18	3	0	.198	.240
Ramirez, Freidderyx	R-R	6-3	175	4-28-92	.151	.150	.151	39	106	8	16	4	1	0	7	8	3	2	0	39	1	0	.208	.231
Santana, Yigui	R-R	6-2	180	3-2-92	.172	.200	.167	38	64	9	11	2	0		5	6	0	1	1	27	4	2	.250	.239
Schoop, Jonathan	R-R	6-1	187	10-6-91	.239	.122	.269	68	247	28	59	7	3	0	35	24	6	1		39	11	3	.291	.320
Serrata, Martin	B-R	6-1	170	11-3-88	.265	.271	.264	62	230	42	61	8	2	0	16	23	1	11	2	41	36	7	.317	.332
Zorrilla, Alexander	R-R	6-1	169	5-16-91	.237	.255	.232	65	215	33	51	7	4	1	28	29	7	5	1	57	9	4	.321	.345

Pitching	B-T	HT	WT	DOB	W	L	ERA	G	GS	CG	SV	IP	H	R	ER	HR	BB	SO	AVG	vLH	vRH	K/9	BB/9
Castillo, Yancarlos	R-R	6-2	175	1-7-91		3	4.50	13	5	0	0	34	24	27	17	2	18	12	.200	.265	.174	3.18	4.76
Florentino, Angel	R-R	6-2	160	9-29-89	1	0	3.00	7	0	0	1	15	19	9	5	1	4	4	.306	.118	.378	2.40	2.40
Garcia, Rafael	R-R	6-3	170	9-15-89	2	2	3.82	15	0	0	1	33	33	18	14	2	8	18	.260	.259	.260	4.91	2.18
Jimenez, Enrico	L-L	6-3	195	2-7-89	5	6	3.00	13	12	0	0	69	56	41	23	1	26	68	.220	.269	.215	8.87	3.39
Jimenez, Joan	R-R	6-2	179	6-27-90	1	0	0.00	1	1	0	0	5	5	2	0		3	6	.263	.333	.250	10.80	5.40
2-team total (14 Orioles/Brewers)					5	5	3.67	15	13	0	0	69	72	39	28	2	17	62	—	—		8.13	2.23
Mejias, Jesus	L-L	6-0	190	6-20-90	0	0	8.23	16	1	0	0	27	25	30	25	1	36	24	.243	.167	.247	7.90	11.85
Montas, Lorenzo	R-R	6-1	180	9-5-90	2	4	2.62	30	0	0	12	34	23	17	10	0	30	29	.190	.317	.125	7.60	7.86
Mota, Jose	R-R	5-11	180	12-18-89	0	0	6.75	1	0	0	0	1	3	1	1	0	1	2	.429	.667	.250	13.50	6.75
2-team total (12 Orioles/Brewers)					3	3	2.76	13	8	0	0	62	67	23	19	0	15	62	—	—		9.00	2.18
Noel, Luis	R-R	6-1	175	9-29-87	4	5	2.99	15	14	0	1	90	78	37	30	0	24	76	.235	.247	.230	7.57	2.39
Nunez, Julio	R-R	6-5	200	11-30-88	0	0	0.00	1	0	0	0	2	0	0	0	0	0	1	.000	.000	.000	5.40	0.00
Princivil, William	R-R	6-2	180	4-12-90	2	3	2.01	27	3	0	2	58	54	24	13	0	24	37	.255	.250	.257	5.71	3.70
Ramirez, Eiri	R-R	6-0	173	8-2-88	0	3	1.23	4	4	0	0	22	22	10	3	0	9	18	.275	.421	.230	7.36	3.68
Reyes, Julio	L-L	5-10	168	11-21-79	0	0	27.00	1	0	0	0	1	2	3	3	0	2	0	.400	.000	.500	0.00	18.00
Rivera, Jorge	L-L	6-0	200	10-30-90	0	2	8.59	4	0	0	0	7	10	8	7	0	9	7	.357	1.000	.333	8.59	11.05
Rojas, Yorky	R-R	6-4	185	5-4-91	0	6	6.99	14	9	0	0	37	44	43	29	1	42	24	.297	.410	.257	5.79	10.13
Salas, Domingo	R-R	6-2	170	5-11-91	0	3	2.35	8	0	0	0	15	10	7	4	0	13	6	.185	.294	.135	3.52	7.63
Sanchez, Bruno	R-R	6-6	170	11-8-86	4	4	2.47	16	14	0	0	91	91	35	25	3	14	65	.265	.318	.246	6.43	1.38
Sosa, Israel	L-L	6-2	180	6-6-89	3	3	4.38	16	8	0	0	51	57	30	25	2	28	45	.288	.333	.282	7.89	4.91
Soto, Luis	R-R	6-0	190	8-22-89	0	0	11.12	7	0	0	0	6	6	10	7	0	10	4	.273	.167	.313	6.35	15.88

Fielding

Catcher	PCT	G	PO	A	E	DP	PB
Paez	.979	27	123	17	3	1	9
Parra	.965	35	172	23	7	1	9
Perez	.977	33	180	37	5	2	5

First Base	PCT	G	PO	A	E	DP
Arias	1.000	10	34	3	0	1
Feliz	1.000	6	39	1	0	7
Gonzalez	.981	31	247	12	5	29
Moranci	.991	37	309	18	3	33
Ramirez	1.000	2	18	2	0	2
Ramirez	.943	5	33	0	2	1

Second Base	PCT	G	PO	A	E	DP
Feliz	1.000	5	9	6	0	1

	PCT	G	PO	A	E	DP
Leonora	1.000	3	7	8	0	3
Santana	.900	10	19	17	4	5
Zorrilla	.947	59	116	169	16	41

Third Base	PCT	G	PO	A	E	DP
Feliz	.789	5	6	9	4	2
Leonora	.908	43	41	88	13	10
Moranci	.667	1	1	3	2	0
Ramirez	.808	25	16	47	15	8
Santana	.844	10	4	23	5	1
Schoop	—	1	0	0	0	0

Shortstop	PCT	G	PO	A	E	DP
Feliz	.500	1	0	1	1	0
Ramirez	.758	10	10	15	8	6

	PCT	G	PO	A	E	DP
Santana	.800	2	1	3	1	1
Schoop	.944	67	113	223	20	38

Outfield	PCT	G	PO	A	E	DP
Cleofa	.981	46	93	12	2	3
Familia	.926	42	47	3	4	0
Gomez	.891	31	38	3	5	1
Leonora	.943	30	30	3	2	1
Moranci	.978	32	39	5	1	3
Ramirez	—	1	0	0	0	0
Serrata	.956	61	105	35	5	2

DOMINICAN SUMMER LEAGUE

Batting	B-T	HT	WT	DOB	AVG	vLH	vRH	G	AB	R	H	2B	3B	HR	RBI	BB	HBP	SH	SF	SO	SB	CS	SLG	OBP
Abreu, Joan	R-R	5-11	180	7-15-90	.196	.160	.208	37	102	6	20	2	1	0	6	16	2	1	0	28	1	6	.235	.317
Aguirre, Wilder	R-R	6-0	160	4-16-92	.240	.385	.189	26	50	2	12	0	0	0	4	2	3	0	0	16	2	1	.240	.309
Arias, Hitaniel	R-R	6-6	202	9-20-90	.246	.188	.264	20	69	9	17	4	0	1	3	5	2	0	0	23	1	2	.348	.316
Arias, Moises	R-R	6-6	205	2-3-89	.162	.286	.133	19	37	4	6	0	0	0	2	4	0	1	0	11	0	0	.162	.244
2-team total (10 Orioles)					.146	—	—	29	48	5	7	0	0	0	3	5	0	1	0	15	0	0	.146	.226
Avila, Eliecer	R-R	6-2	175	1-30-90	.205	.176	.212	33	83	9	17	2	0	0	11	8	1	3	1	16	3	2	.229	.280
Barrini, Juan	R-R	6-2	175	1-1-92	.188	.087	.209	50	133	23	25	4	0	1	10	7	6	2	2	42	7	2	.241	.257
Bido, Felix	R-R	6-2	170	8-7-91	.149	.182	.143	48	141	8	21	7	0	0	12	6	4	0	0	54	1	1	.199	.205
Chirinos, Luis	R-R	6-1	215	8-30-92	.243	.375	.203	33	103	5	25	4	0	0	18	12	2	1	2	38	2	6	.282	.328
Guanipa, Dick	R-R	6-0	180	6-20-90	.091	.143	.083	28	55	4	5	1	0	0	3	11	2	0	0	19	0	0	.109	.265
Jabalera, Jose	R-R	6-2	175	8-2-88	.256	.200	.267	39	125	17	32	4	1	0	11	4	1	5	1	18	5	2	.304	.282
Javier, Jhonatan	R-R	6-1	197	9-16-87	.344	.447	.322	64	221	48	76	17	5	6	45	17	17	1	5	30	12	4	.548	.423
Martinez, Andres	R-R	6-2	188	1-26-92	.158	.185	.153	54	158	27	25	4	2	3	15	19	1	6	0	68	6	1	.266	.253
Paez, Carlos	R-R	6-0	180	6-18-91	.182	—	.182	5	11	0	2	1	0	0	1	0	0	0	0	6	1	0	.273	.182
2-team total (27 Orioles)					.186	—	—	32	70	13	13	3	1	1	6	5	4	3	0	21	3	0	.300	.278
Portes, Wilmer	R-R	6-1	193	3-25-91	.269	.281	.266	51	160	27	43	9	0	3	13	26	1	0	0	39	7	13	.381	.374
Puello, Ronny	R-R	6-6	200	10-23-89	.343	.000	.400	12	35	2	12	2	1	1	7	0	2	1	0	9	0	0	.543	.378
Rodriguez, Pedro	B-R	5-11	145	4-20-90	.227	.240	.225	57	194	45	44	5	3	0	18	28	3	3	1	27	18	10	.284	.332
Roson, Deibisson	R-R	6-4	210	8-12-89	.185	.174	.188	43	124	20	23	6	1	2	16	27	5	0	0	32	7	4	.298	.353
Wilson, Edwin	R-R	6-1	170	11-10-89	.189	.243	.175	63	180	22	34	2	1	1	15	25	10	6	0	49	9	4	.228	.321
Wilson, Octavio	R-R	6-2	162	10-11-89	.184	.222	.174	48	136	13	25	5	1	1	13	18	4	3	0	44	4	3	.257	.297

Pitching	B-T	HT	WT	DOB	W	L	ERA	G	GS	CG	SV	IP	H	R	ER	HR	BB	SO	AVG	vLH	vRH	K/9	BB/9
Cespedes, Angel	R-R	6-2	170	8-27-89	1	1	2.75	5	3	0	1	20	23	9	6	1	5	14	.303	.276	.319	6.41	2.29
Espiritu, Alexander	R-R	6-0	190	3-30-91	0	2	13.50	7	1	0	0	9	12	16	14	0	14	13	.308	.250	.323	12.54	13.50
Hodge, Humberto	R-R	6-4	170	11-6-87	0	0	9.00	1	0	0	0	5	6	5	5	0	2	5	.300	.000	.333	9.00	3.60
Jean, Samuel	L-L	6-1	175	6-22-88	2	4	4.01	15	12	1	0	67	79	40	30	0	23	48	.299	.269	.303	6.42	3.07
Jimenez, Joan	R-R	6-2	179	6-27-90	4	5	3.96	14	12	0	0	64	67	37	28	2	14	56	.272	.281	.270	7.92	1.98
2-team total (1 Orioles)					5	5	3.67	15	13	0	0	69	72	39	28	2	17	62	—	—	—	8.13	2.23
King, Jaime	R-R	6-4	219	9-27-89	0	1	4.91	7	1	0	0	11	10	7	6	1	12	16	.233	.167	.258	13.09	9.82
Linares, Edwin	R-R	6-2	198	10-15-89	4	5	1.77	29	0	0	11	46	35	15	9	1	22	37	.210	.087	.256	7.29	4.34
Lorenzo, Leonard	R-R	6-0	190	7-16-91	0	0	13.50	2	0	0	0	3	3	4	4	0	5	3	.333	—	.333	10.13	16.88
Mambru, Dionicio	R-R	6-1	180	4-8-89	1	1	7.61	13	1	0	0	24	28	25	20	1	20	27	.292	.261	.301	10.27	7.61
Montano, Eliezer	L-L	6-7	160	10-21-91	0	2	2.84	18	3	0	1	38	30	22	12	0	30	35	.216	.211	.217	8.29	7.11
Mota, Jose	R-R	5-11	180	12-18-89	3	3	2.67	12	8	0	0	61	64	22	18	0	14	60	.269	.222	.283	8.90	2.08
2-team total (1 Orioles)					3	3	2.76	13	8	0	0	62	67	23	19	0	15	62	—	—	—	9.00	2.18
Pascual, Rolando	B-R	6-6	245	2-8-89	2	3	6.05	15	4	0	0	42	31	34	28	0	42	58	.211	.184	.220	12.53	9.07
Perez, Julio	R-R	6-2	175	1-16-92	2	5	6.38	14	11	0	1	48	40	38	34	1	38	36	.220	.186	.230	6.75	7.13
Ramos, Jose	L-L	6-5	228	6-14-89	3	4	6.52	23	0	0	2	39	55	42	28	1	25	29	.335	.391	.326	6.75	5.82
Rivero, Francisco	R-R	6-2	204	3-11-91	0	0	0.00	3	0	0	0	8	5	0	0	0	2	6	.185	.077	.286	6.48	2.16
Rodriguez, Mike	L-L	6-1	165	4-24-89	0	2	7.39	14	6	0	0	35	38	34	29	2	36	44	.270	.235	.274	11.21	9.17
Santana, Kelvin	R-R	6-4	190	4-15-90	1	1	7.54	18	0	0	0	37	49	38	31	0	33	27	.329	.313	.337	6.57	8.03

Fielding

Catcher	PCT	G	PO	A	E	DP	PB
Aguirre	.966	23	118	24	5	1	2
Avila	.943	33	201	45	15	0	12
Javier	.971	29	199	38	7	2	10
Paez	1.000	5	19	1	0	0	1

First Base	PCT	G	PO	A	E	DP
Arias	.972	17	133	7	4	9
Arias	.966	14	78	6	3	9
Bido	.952	8	37	3	2	5
Guanipa	.985	21	127	6	2	5
Jabalera	1.000	10	49	3	0	6
Wilson	.975	29	231	7	6	20

Second Base	PCT	G	PO	A	E	DP
Abreu	.943	26	53	62	7	15
Araujo	.920	11	22	24	4	6

	PCT	G	PO	A	E	DP
Rodriguez	.968	40	93	117	7	30
Wilson	.889	4	10	6	2	3

Third Base	PCT	G	PO	A	E	DP
Abreu	1.000	1	0	2	0	0
Araujo	.875	4	1	6	1	0
Bido	.869	39	30	56	13	2
Jabalera	.879	23	19	39	8	4
Martinez	.929	5	5	8	1	0
Rodriguez	—	1	0	0	0	0
Wilson	.845	25	16	33	9	1

Shortstop	PCT	G	PO	A	E	DP
Jabalera	1.000	2	2	4	0	0
Martinez	.906	45	55	119	18	22
Rodriguez	.972	14	26	43	2	10
Wilson	.898	21	32	47	9	7

Outfield	PCT	G	PO	A	E	DP
Araujo	—	2	0	0	0	0
Arias	1.000	1	2	0	0	0
Arias	—	1	0	0	0	0
Barrini	.892	47	60	6	8	0
Chirinos	.889	23	22	2	3	1
Guanipa	—	1	0	0	0	0
Jabalera	1.000	9	12	3	0	1
Lorenzo	1.000	23	24	1	0	0
Martinez	—	1	0	0	0	0
Portes	.978	47	81	8	2	2
Puello	1.000	12	15	1	0	0
Rodriguez	—	2	0	0	0	0
Roson	.974	36	34	4	1	1
Wilson	.953	39	39	2	2	0

Boston Red Sox

SEASON IN A SENTENCE: Boston led the American League East until July 20 but lost six straight in early August—including a four-game sweep in New York at the hands of the Yankees—to fall into wild-card land, then lost their first playoff series in four tries against the Angels, getting swept in three games.

HIGH POINT: The Red Sox won their first eight games against the Yankees, capped by a three-run eighth-inning rally to beat C.C. Sabathia 4-3 on June 11. The Red Sox took over first place in that series and held it for a month before an inconsistent offense and rotation doomed them, though twin aces Josh Beckett and Jon Lester kept them in the playoff picture.

LOW POINT: Boston had just swept the Blue Jays to pull within 6½ games of New York when it opened a series at Fenway Park against the Yankees. With Brad Penny starting, the Red Sox fell into a 10-1 hole before losing 20-11, starting a series loss and setting a season high in runs allowed.

NOTABLE ROOKIES: Reserve catcher George Kottaras was the lone rookie to get more than 100 at-bats for Boston, while righthander Daniel Bard broke into a prominent relief role and was one of the game's most exciting rookies. A first-round pick in 2006, Bard went 2-2, 3.65 with 63 strikeouts in 49 innings, flashing one of the game's best fastballs that regularly reached 100 mph.

KEY TRANSACTIONS: With 37-year-old catcher Jason Varitek slowing offensively, the Red Sox bolstered their lineup by acquiring Victor Martinez from the Indians. Martinez hit .336/.405/.507 for Boston with eight home runs, though he did cost Boston its top pitching prospect, lefthander Nick Hagadone, as well as righthander Justin Masterson. Offseason acquisitions Penny and John Smoltz flopped, combining to go 9-13, 6.24 in 32 starts.

DOWN ON THE FARM: Low Class A Greenville lost in the South Atlantic League finals, and was the lone Red Sox farm club to reach the playoffs. No. 1 prospect Lars Anderson struggled at Double-A Portland and ceded that title after batting just .233/.328/.345. Casey Kelly split his season between pitching in the first half and playing shortstop thereafter. Kelly's performance on the mound was exciting (7-5, 2.08 in 95 innings between two Class A stops), while his bat (.224/.305/.313) made scouts think he was a better fit as a pitcher.

OPENING DAY PAYROLL: $121,745,999

PLAYERS OF THE YEAR

MAJOR LEAGUE	MINOR LEAGUE
Jon Lester	**Casey Kelly**
lhp	**rhp/ss**
15-8, 3.41	(Low A/High A)
225 SO (3rd in AL) in	7-5, 2.08 in 95 IP
203 IP, 5th in AL ERA	.222/.302/.340

ORGANIZATION LEADERS

BATTING	*Minimum 250 at-bats	
MAJORS		
*AVG	Kevin Youkilis	.305
*OPS	Kevin Youkilis	.961
HR	Jason Bay	36
RBI	Jason Bay	119
MINORS		
*AVG	Federowicz, Tim, Greenville/Salem	.305
R	Kalish, Ryan, Salem/Portland	84
H	Jimenez, Jorge, Portland	144
TB	Kalish, Ryan, Salem/Portland	231
2B	Still, Jon, Portland	40
3B	Mailman, David, Greenville/Salem	7
HR	Lavarnway, Ryan, Greenville	21
RBI	Still, Jon, Portland	89
BB	Kalish, Ryan, Salem/Portland	68
SO	Still, Jon, Portland	148
SB	Lin, Che-Hsuan, Salem	26
*OBP	Rizzo, Anthony, Greenville/Salem	.368
*SLG	Lavarnway, Ryan, Greenville	.540

PITCHING	†Minimum 75 innings	
MAJORS		
W	Josh Beckett	17
†ERA	Jon Lester	3.41
SO	Jon Lester	225
MINORS		
W	Mills, Adam, Portland/Pawtucket	12
L	Johnson, Kris, Pawtucket/Portland	16
†ERA	Bowden, Michael, Pawtucket	3.13
G	Large, T.J., Portland/Pawtucket	56
	Rhoades, Chad, Portland	56
GS	Three tied at	26
SV	Cabrera, Fernando, Pawtucket	22
IP	Mills, Adam, Portland/Pawtucket	141
BB	Zink, Charlie, Pawtucket	93
SO	Portice, Eammon, Salem	141
†AVG	Bowden, Michael, Pawtucket	.228

General Manager: Theo Epstein. **Farm Director:** Mike Hazen. **Scouting Director:** Jason McLeod.

Class	Team	League	W	L	PCT	Finish*	Manager(s)
Majors	Boston Red Sox	American	95	67	.586	3rd (14)	Terry Francona
Triple-A	Pawtucket Red Sox	International	61	82	.427	12th (14)	Ron Johnson
Double-A	Portland Sea Dogs	Eastern	67	74	.475	9th (12)	Arnie Beyeler
High A	Salem Red Sox	Carolina	67	72	.482	5th (8)	Chad Epperson
Low A	Greenville Drive	South Atlantic	73	65	.529	5th (16)	Kevin Boles
Short-season	Lowell Spinners	New York-Penn	45	30	.600	t-3rd (14)	Gary DiSarcina
Rookie	GCL Red Sox	Gulf Coast	26	27	.491	10th (16)	Dave Tomlin

| **Overall 2009 Minor League Record** | | | 339 | 350 | .492 | 19th (30) | |

*Finish in overall standings (No. of teams in league). †League champion.

ORGANIZATION STATISTICS

BOSTON RED SOX

AMERICAN LEAGUE

Batting	B-T	HT	WT	DOB	AVG	vLH	vRH	G	AB	R	H	2B	3B	HR	RBI	BB	HBP	SH	SF	SO	SB	CS	SLG	OBP
Anderson, Brian	R-R	6-2	215	3-11-82	.294	.375	.222	21	17	7	5	0	0	2	5	3	0	0	1	5	0	0	.647	.381
2-team total (65 Chicago)					.243	—	—	86	202	32	49	9	0	4	18	23	3	2	1	54	3	6	.347	.328
Bailey, Jeff	R-R	6-2	200	11-19-78	.208	.400	.115	26	77	14	16	3	2	3	9	10	4	0	0	21	0	0	.416	.330
Baldelli, Rocco	R-R	6-4	200	9-25-81	.253	.290	.193	62	150	23	38	4	1	7	23	11	2	0	1	37	1	0	.433	.311
Bates, Aaron	R-R	6-4	230	3-10-84	.364	.333	.400	5	11	2	4	2	0	0	2	1	0	0	0	4	0	0	.545	.417
Bay, Jason	R-R	6-2	205	9-20-78	.267	.292	.257	151	531	103	142	29	3	36	119	94	9	0	4	162	13	3	.537	.384
Brown, Dusty	R-R	6-0	180	6-19-82	.333	.500	.000	6	3	1	1	0	0	1	1	1	0	0	0	0	0	0	1.333	.500
Carter, Chris	L-L	6-3	225	9-16-82	.000	.000	.000	4	5	0	0	0	0	0	0	0	0	0	1	4	0	0	.000	.000
Drew, J.D.	L-R	6-1	200	11-20-75	.279	.272	.281	137	452	84	126	30	4	24	68	82	3	1	1	109	2	6	.522	.392
Ellsbury, Jacoby	L-L	6-1	185	9-11-83	.301	.318	.294	153	624	94	188	27	10	8	60	49	6	6	6	74	70	12	.415	.355
Gathright, Joey	L-L	5-10	185	4-27-81	.313	.250	.333	17	16	7	5	0	0	0	1	0	0	2	1	0	3	1	.313	.353
Gonzalez, Alex	R-R	5-11	215	2-15-77	.284	.188	.330	44	148	26	42	10	0	5	15	5	2	4	0	29	2	0	.453	.316
Green, Nick	R-R	6-0	180	9-10-78	.236	.235	.236	103	276	35	65	18	0	6	35	20	8	2	3	69	1	4	.366	.303
Kotchman, Casey	L-L	6-3	215	2-22-83	.218	.182	.231	39	87	9	19	3	0	1	7	7	1	0	0	14	1	0	.287	.284
Kotsay, Mark	L-L	6-0	205	12-2-75	.257	.200	.266	27	74	4	19	2	0	1	5	4	0	0	1	12	2	1	.324	.291
2-team total (40 Chicago)					.278	—	—	67	187	16	52	9	0	4	23	15	0	1	3	21	3	2	.390	.327
Kottaras, George	L-R	6-0	185	5-10-83	.237	.111	.267	45	93	15	22	11	0	1	10	11	0	0	3	25	0	0	.387	.308
LaRoche, Adam	L-L	6-3	205	11-6-79	.263	.167	.308	6	19	2	5	2	0	1	3	0	0	0	0	2	0	0	.526	.263
Lowell, Mike	R-R	6-3	210	2-24-74	.290	.301	.285	119	445	54	129	29	1	17	75	33	1	0	5	61	2	1	.474	.337
Lowrie, Jed	B-R	6-0	180	4-17-84	.147	.211	.122	32	68	5	10	2	0	2	11	6	0	0	2	20	0	0	.265	.211
Lugo, Julio	R-R	6-1	175	11-16-75	.284	.333	.260	37	109	16	31	4	1	1	8	12	0	1	1	18	3	0	.367	.352
Martinez, Victor	B-R	6-2	210	12-23-78	.336	.323	.342	56	211	32	71	12	0	8	41	24	1	0	1	23	1	0	.507	.405
2-team total (99 Cleveland)					.303	—	—	155	588	88	178	33	1	23	108	75	3	0	6	74	1	0	.480	.381
Ortiz, David	L-L	6-4	230	11-18-75	.238	.212	.250	150	541	77	129	35	1	28	99	74	5	0	7	134	0	2	.462	.332
Pedroia, Dustin	R-R	5-9	180	8-17-83	.296	.277	.302	154	626	115	185	48	1	15	72	74	5	3	6	45	20	8	.447	.371
Reddick, Josh	L-R	6-2	180	2-19-87	.169	.200	.167	27	59	5	10	4	0	2	4	2	1	0	0	17	0	0	.339	.210
Van Every, Jon	L-L	6-1	190	11-27-79	.364	.000	.400	7	11	1	4	0	0	1	3	2	0	0	0	5	0	0	.636	.462
Varitek, Jason	B-R	6-2	230	4-11-72	.209	.231	.200	109	364	41	76	24	0	14	51	54	3	0	4	90	0	0	.390	.313
Velazquez, Gil	R-R	6-3	190	10-17-79	.000	—	.000	6	2	0	0	0	0	0	0	0	1	0	0	0	0	0	.000	.333
Woodward, Chris	R-R	6-0	190	6-27-76	.083	.000	.091	13	12	0	1	0	0	0	0	2	2	0	0	4	0	0	.083	.313
2-team total (20 Seattle)					.215	—	—	33	79	7	17	1	0	0	5	7	2	1	1	19	1	0	.228	.292
Youkilis, Kevin	R-R	6-1	220	3-15-79	.305	.309	.304	136	491	99	150	36	1	27	94	77	16	0	4	125	7	2	.548	.413

Pitching	B-T	HT	WT	DOB	W	L	ERA	G	GS	CG	SV	IP	H	R	ER	HR	BB	SO	AVG	vLH	vRH	K/9	BB/9
Bard, Daniel	R-R	6-4	200	6-25-85	2	2	3.65	49	0	0	1	49	41	24	20	5	22	63	.228	.263	.200	11.49	4.01
Beckett, Josh	R-R	6-5	220	5-15-80	17	6	3.86	32	32	4	0	212	198	99	91	25	55	199	.244	.258	.226	8.43	2.33
Bowden, Michael	R-R	6-3	210	9-9-86	1	1	9.56	8	1	0	0	16	23	17	17	3	6	12	.333	.395	.258	6.75	3.38
Buchholz, Clay	L-R	6-3	190	8-14-84	7	4	4.21	16	16	0	0	92	91	44	43	13	36	68	.256	.284	.228	6.65	3.52
Byrd, Paul	R-R	6-1	190	12-3-70	1	3	5.82	7	6	0	0	34	47	22	22	4	11	11	.331	.405	.250	2.91	2.91
Cabrera, Fernando	R-R	6-4	225	11-16-81	0	0	8.44	6	0	0	0	5	7	5	5	0	4	8	.304	.500	.235	13.50	6.75
Delcarmen, Manny	R-R	6-2	205	2-16-82	5	2	4.53	64	0	0	0	60	64	34	30	5	34	44	.270	.221	.322	6.64	5.13
Gonzalez, Enrique	R-R	5-10	225	7-14-82	0	0	4.91	2	0	0	0	4	5	2	2	1	2	1	.313	.091	.800	2.45	4.91
Jones, Hunter	L-L	6-4	235	1-10-84	0	0	9.24	11	0	0	0	13	16	13	13	3	7	9	.302	.200	.364	6.39	4.97
Lester, Jon	L-L	6-2	190	1-7-84	15	8	3.41	32	32	2	0	203	186	80	77	20	64	225	.242	.257	.237	9.96	2.83
Lopez, Javier	L-L	6-4	210	7-11-77	0	2	9.26	14	0	0	0	12	20	13	12	1	9	5	.392	.420	.367	3.86	6.94
Masterson, Justin	R-R	6-6	250	3-22-85	3	3	4.50	31	6	0	0	72	72	38	36	7	25	67	.271	.313	.230	8.38	3.13
2-team total (11 Cleveland)					4	10	4.52	42	16	1	0	129	128	73	65	12	60	119	—	—	—	8.28	4.18
Matsuzaka, Daisuke	R-R	6-0	185	9-13-80	4	6	5.76	12	12	0	0	59	81	38	38	10	30	54	.325	.340	.304	8.19	4.55
Okajima, Hideki	L-L	6-1	195	12-25-75	6	0	3.39	68	0	0	6	61	56	33	23	8	21	53	.242	.167	.309	7.82	3.10
Papelbon, Jonathan	R-R	6-4	225	11-23-80	1	1	1.85	66	0	0	38	68	54	15	14	5	24	76	.213	.187	.242	10.06	3.18
Penny, Brad	R-R	6-4	230	5-24-78	7	8	5.61	24	24	0	0	132	160	89	82	17	42	89	.299	.277	.321	6.08	2.87
Ramirez, Ramon	R-R	5-10	190	8-31-81	7	4	2.84	70	0	0	0	70	61	26	22	7	32	52	.233	.244	.220	6.72	4.13
Richardson, Dustin	L-L	6-6	220	1-9-84	0	0	0.00	3	0	0	0	4	1	0	0	0	1	2	.250	.200	.286	0.00	2.70
Saito, Takashi	L-R	6-2	215	2-14-70	3	3	2.43	56	0	0	2	56	50	16	15	6	25	52	.244	.195	.304	8.41	4.04

	B-T	HT	WT	DOB	W	L	ERA	G	GS	CG	SV	IP	H	R	ER	HR	BB	SO	AVG	vLH	vRH	K/9	BB/9
Smoltz, John	R-R	6-3	220	5-15-67	2	5	8.32	8	8	0	0	40	59	37	37	8	9	33	.343	.444	.232	7.43	2.03
Tazawa, Junichi	R-R	5-11	180	6-6-86	2	3	7.46	6	4	0	0	25	43	23	21	4	9	13	.374	.323	.440	4.62	3.20
Traber, Billy	L-L	6-5	205	9-18-79	0	0	12.27	1	0	0	0	4	9	5	5	2	1	1	.474	.429	.500	2.45	2.45
Wagner, Billy	L-L	5-11	205	7-25-71	1	1	1.98	15	0	0	0	14	8	5	3	1	7	22	.174	.125	.200	14.49	4.61
Wakefield, Tim	R-R	6-2	210	8-2-66	11	5	4.58	21	21	2	0	130	137	67	66	12	50	72	.270	.280	.263	5.00	3.47

Fielding

Catcher	PCT	G	PO	A	E	DP	PB
Brown	1.000	6	6	2	0	0	0
Kottaras	.995	39	196	8	1	1	8
Martinez	.982	33	215	8	4	1	1
Varitek	.997	108	856	37	3	4	1

First Base	PCT	G	PO	A	E	DP
Bailey	.988	23	158	11	2	13
Bates	.972	5	35	0	1	3
Kotchman	1.000	29	185	19	0	12
Kotsay	1.000	19	103	11	0	9
LaRoche	1.000	4	29	6	0	1
Martinez	1.000	23	160	3	0	14
Ortiz	.980	6	42	6	1	2
Youkilis	.998	78	565	52	1	56

Second Base	PCT	G	PO	A	E	DP
Green	1.000	7	12	17	0	2
Lowrie	—	2	0	0	0	0

Pedroia	.991	154	253	404	6	93
Woodward	1.000	6	5	6	0	0

Third Base	PCT	G	PO	A	E	DP
Baldelli	—	1	0	0	0	0
Green	.889	9	4	4	1	0
Kottaras	1.000	1	0	2	0	0
Lowell	.966	107	82	174	9	14
Lowrie	1.000	4	1	4	0	0
Velazquez	.750	2	0	3	1	0
Woodward	1.000	3	1	1	0	0
Youkilis	.974	63	52	99	4	5

Shortstop	PCT	G	PO	A	E	DP
Gonzalez	.994	44	51	107	1	17
Green	.956	81	104	198	14	41
Lowrie	.987	26	22	52	1	16
Lugo	.928	32	39	51	7	8
Velazquez	1.000	4	3	3	0	1

Woodward	.667	4	0	2	1	0

Outfield	PCT	G	PO	A	E	DP
Anderson	1.000	19	6	0	0	0
Bailey	1.000	3	4	0	0	0
Baldelli	.958	45	66	3	3	1
Bay	1.000	150	310	15	0	2
Carter	1.000	1	2	0	0	0
Drew	.992	131	242	5	2	2
Ellsbury	.994	153	357	4	2	1
Gathright	1.000	11	13	0	0	0
Green	.750	3	3	0	1	0
Kotsay	1.000	9	8	0	0	0
Lopez	—	1	0	0	0	0
Reddick	.968	23	30	0	1	0
Van Every	1.000	6	6	0	0	0
Youkilis	.800	2	3	1	1	0

PAWTUCKET RED SOX   TRIPLE-A
INTERNATIONAL LEAGUE

Batting	B-T	HT	WT	DOB	AVG	vLH	vRH	G	AB	R	H	2B	3B	HR	RBI	BB	HBP	SH	SF	SO	SB	CS	SLG	OBP
Ambres, Chip	R-R	6-0	200	12-19-79	.259	.333	.238	52	185	18	48	9	1	3	18	21	1	0	2	38	2	4	.368	.335
2-team total (80 Buffalo)					.261	—	—	132	464	54	121	27	1	12	58	45	2	0	5	83	3	6	.401	.326
Anderson, Brian	R-R	6-2	215	3-11-82	.200	.148	.226	24	80	9	16	4	0	4	8	7	2	1	0	22	0	2	.400	.281
2-team total (11 Charlotte)					.228	—	—	35	123	15	28	5	1	6	13	9	2	2	0	38	0	3	.431	.291
Bailey, Jeff	R-R	6-2	200	11-19-78	.262	.270	.259	63	229	34	60	7	0	10	27	35	3	0	4	51	2	0	.424	.362
Baldelli, Rocco	R-R	6-4	200	9-25-81	.077	.000	.125	4	13	1	1	0	0	0	1	0	1	0	1	5	0	0	.077	.133
Bates, Aaron	R-R	6-4	230	3-10-84	.213	.203	.217	76	272	28	58	10	0	5	18	22	6	0	2	59	0	0	.305	.285
Bell, Bubba	L-R	6-0	195	10-9-82	.208	.196	.212	71	240	24	50	8	2	1	18	31	0	0	1	53	2	1	.271	.298
Borowiak, Zach	R-R	6-1	185	5-18-81	.000	—	.000	2	3	0	0	0	0	0	0	0	1	2	0	2	0	0	.000	.250
Brown, Dusty	R-R	6-0	180	6-19-82	.264	.262	.265	86	295	22	78	13	0	2	23	37	0	0	1	74	0	0	.329	.345
Carter, Chris	L-L	6-0	230	9-16-82	.294	.287	.297	116	428	50	126	25	0	16	61	42	3	0	5	63	0	0	.465	.358
Chavez, Angel	R-R	6-0	185	7-22-81	.253	.255	.253	127	442	41	112	23	0	4	39	18	1	0	3	48	3	2	.333	.282
Corsaletti, Jeff	L-R	6-0	190	2-22-83	.128	.000	.161	13	39	3	5	0	0	0	1	3	0	0	0	8	1	1	.128	.190
Daeges, Zach	L-R	6-4	225	11-16-83	.172	.273	.111	9	29	1	5	2	0	0	1	3	0	0	0	6	0	0	.241	.250
Danielson, Sean	B-R	5-8	165	8-6-82	.240	.206	.250	52	154	18	37	6	1	1	19	21	0	5	3	33	9	3	.312	.326
Denker, Travis	R-R	5-9	205	8-5-85	.238	.235	.238	117	400	43	95	21	1	5	43	48	4	2	6	85	3	2	.343	.321
Duncan, Chris	L-R	6-5	230	5-5-81	.188	.125	.213	27	85	8	16	3	0	2	10	7	1	0	1	20	0	0	.294	.255
Gathright, Joey	L-R	5-10	185	4-27-81	.200	.000	.222	3	10	1	2	0	0	0	0	0	0	1	0	1	0	1	.200	.200
2-team total (80 Norfolk)					.325	—	—	83	332	50	108	11	2	0	20	27	3	11	0	42	24	8	.370	.381
Guzman, Freddy	B-R	5-10	165	1-20-81	.229	.200	.237	62	214	25	49	6	2	2	10	13	0	3	1	35	21	7	.304	.272
3-team total (20 Norfolk, 6 Scranton/W-B)					.224	—	—	88	308	39	69	7	4	2	14	23	0	3	2	49	41	7	.292	.276
Kotsay, Mark	L-L	6-0	205	12-2-75	.303	.222	.333	10	33	2	10	1	0	0	5	0	0	0	1	1	1	0	.333	.294
Kottaras, George	L-R	6-0	185	5-10-83	.292	.333	.278	10	24	1	7	3	0	0	6	0	0	0	0	6	0	0	.417	.433
Lowrie, Jed	B-R	6-0	180	4-17-84	.176	.125	.192	22	68	9	12	3	0	3	8	13	1	0	1	13	0	0	.353	.313
Lugo, Julio	R-R	6-1	175	11-16-75	.235	.000	.267	4	17	1	4	1	0	0	0	2	0	0	0	5	0	0	.294	.316
Madera, Sandy	R-R	6-2	176	8-11-80	.125	.000	.250	5	16	0	2	0	0	0	0	2	0	0	0	3	0	0	.125	.222
Maldonado, Carlos	R-R	6-2	250	1-3-79	.225	.067	.262	24	80	9	18	2	0	2	15	10	0	0	2	14	0	0	.325	.304
McAnulty, Paul	L-R	5-11	225	2-24-81	.233	.156	.257	90	326	36	76	20	1	11	48	45	4	0	3	83	0	1	.402	.331
Natale, Jeff	R-R	5-9	180	8-24-82	.282	.345	.270	58	170	23	48	9	1	3	19	31	2	1	1	26	0	1	.400	.397
Ochoa, Ivan	R-R	5-9	160	12-16-82	.227	.265	.213	45	128	25	29	3	2	2	8	20	2	5	0	22	9	0	.328	.340
Otness, John	R-R	5-11	200	9-15-81	.320	.571	.222	8	25	2	8	2	0	0	3	4	0	0	1	5	0	0	.400	.400
Reddick, Josh	L-R	6-2	180	2-19-87	.127	.077	.156	18	71	1	9	0	2	0	6	6	0	0	2	13	0	1	.183	.190
Suarez, Iggy	R-R	5-11	165	5-9-82	.167	.143	.170	20	60	5	10	2	0	1	8	8	1	1	0	16	1	0	.250	.275
Van Every, Jon	L-L	6-1	190	11-27-79	.215	.063	.265	20	65	7	14	4	0	4	10	16	1	0	0	25	0	0	.462	.378
Velazquez, Gil	R-R	6-3	190	10-17-79	.193	.247	.174	93	290	26	56	13	0	3	18	19	0	4	3	49	3	1	.269	.240
Wagner, Mark	R-R	6-1	205	6-11-84	.214	.200	.221	43	154	12	33	12	0	3	20	11	1	0	2	29	0	0	.351	.268
Wilkerson, Brad	L-L	6-0	190	6-1-77	.111	.000	.167	2	9	1	1	0	0	0	1	0	0	0	0	4	0	0	.111	.200
Woodward, Chris	R-R	6-0	190	6-27-76	.129	.167	.120	12	31	1	4	0	0	0	0	5	0	1	0	7	0	1	.129	.250
Youkilis, Kevin	R-R	6-1	220	3-15-79	.000	—	.000	2	6	0	0	0	0	0	0	1	0	0	0	2	0	0	.000	.143

Pitching	B-T	HT	WT	DOB	W	L	ERA	G	GS	CG	SV	IP	H	R	ER	HR	BB	SO	AVG	vLH	vRH	K/9	BB/9
Bard, Daniel	R-R	6-4	200	6-25-85	1	0	1.13	11	0	0	6	16	6	2	2	2	5	29	.115	.091	.133	16.31	2.81
Bierd, Randor	R-R	6-4	190	3-14-84	3	1	4.55	25	7	0	0	61	68	37	31	7	21	55	.275	.274	.277	8.07	3.08
Bowden, Michael	R-R	6-3	215	9-9-86	4	6	3.13	24	24	0	0	126	106	47	44	11	47	88	.228	.266	.202	6.27	3.35
Buchholz, Clay	L-R	6-3	190	8-14-84	7	2	2.36	17	16	1	0	99	67	30	26	7	30	89	.188	.241	.142	8.09	2.73

Name	B-T	HT	WT	DOB	W	L	ERA	G	GS	CG	SV	IP	H	R	ER	HR	BB	SO	AVG	vLH	vRH	K/9	BB/9
Byrd, Paul	R-R	6-1	190	12-3-70	0	1	3.27	2	2	0	0	11	9	4	4	1	1	7	.220	.188	.240	5.73	0.82
Cabrera, Fernando	R-R	6-4	225	11-16-81	0	3	1.71	43	0	0	22	53	40	11	10	3	22	51	.208	.233	.189	8.72	3.76
Cherry, Rocky	R-R	6-5	235	8-19-79	3	1	2.57	38	1	0	0	63	63	22	18	1	36	44	.267	.294	.252	6.29	5.14
Coello, Robert	R-R	6-5	250	11-23-84	0	0	0.00	1	0	0	0	1	1	0	0	0	0	1	.200	—	.200	6.75	0.00
George, Chris	L-L	6-2	185	9-16-79	1	0	4.79	12	0	0	0	21	21	14	11	2	6	10	.269	.118	.311	4.35	2.61
2-team total (5 Norfolk)					2	1	3.08	17	5	0	0	50	48	20	17	4	9	29	—	—		5.26	1.63
Gonzalez, Enrique	R-R	5-10	225	7-14-82	8	11	5.12	26	23	0	0	139	159	85	79	20	53	99	.285	.308	.269	6.41	3.43
Hansack, Devern	R-R	6-2	180	2-5-78	0	0	9.00	1	0	0	0	1	2	1	1	0	0	0	.400	.500	.000	0.00	0.00
Johnson, Kris	L-L	6-4	170	10-14-84	3	13	6.35	22	22	0	0	96	128	77	68	8	44	65	.320	.287	.331	6.07	4.11
Jones, Hunter	L-L	6-4	235	1-10-84	4	3	4.25	36	0	0	2	53	45	27	25	7	24	39	.232	.206	.244	6.62	4.08
Large, T.J.	R-R	6-4	185	5-28-83	3	4	7.04	22	0	0	1	31	38	26	24	1	22	10	.322	.231	.367	2.93	6.46
Lopez, Javier	L-L	6-4	220	7-11-77	1	1	3.18	38	0	0	0	40	35	15	14	2	13	23	.245	.196	.276	5.22	2.95
Matsuzaka, Daisuke	R-R	6-0	185	9-13-80	0	1	2.25	4	4	0	0	16	13	4	4	2	6	17	.217	.333	.139	9.56	3.38
McBeth, Marcus	R-R	6-2	185	8-23-80	2	3	2.69	44	1	0	3	67	43	20	20	5	30	66	.189	.200	.181	8.87	4.03
Mills, Adam	R-R	5-11	190	11-19-84	2	2	3.48	6	6	0	0	31	39	15	12	1	4	16	.315	.277	.338	4.65	1.16
Richardson, Dustin	L-L	6-6	220	1-9-84	0	0	1.69	7	0	0	0	11	8	2	2	1	2	16	.211	.250	.192	13.50	1.69
Smoltz, John	R-R	6-3	220	5-15-67	1	1	3.38	3	3	1	0	16	10	6	6	2	4	11	.179	.182	.174	6.19	2.25
Tazawa, Junichi	R-R	5-11	180	6-6-86	0	2	2.38	2	2	0	0	11	7	4	3	0	1	6	.184	.353	.048	4.76	0.79
Traber, Billy	L-L	6-5	205	9-18-79	7	8	3.52	38	7	0	0	84	88	36	33	8	25	33	.272	.293	.263	3.52	2.67
Vaquedano, Jose	R-R	6-4	167	7-9-81	4	2	3.76	43	0	0	3	65	52	33	27	6	41	34	.223	.178	.252	4.73	5.71
Wakefield, Tim	R-R	6-2	210	8-2-66	1	1	2.89	2	2	0	0	9	5	3	3	1	2	7	.152	.000	.200	6.75	1.93
Zink, Charlie	R-R	6-1	190	8-26-79	6	15	5.59	27	23	1	0	135	134	88	84	10	93	47	.270	.255	.281	3.13	6.18

Fielding

Catcher	PCT	G	PO	A	E	DP	PB
Brown	.991	81	521	45	5	5	10
Kottaras	1.000	4	23	1	0	0	0
Maldonado	.979	22	136	7	3	1	1
Otness	1.000	8	55	2	0	1	1
Wagner	1.000	35	164	20	0	1	3

First Base	PCT	G	PO	A	E	DP
Bailey	.985	17	122	13	2	12
Bates	.993	72	564	44	4	63
Carter	1.000	11	75	12	0	7
Chavez	1.000	1	3	1	0	0
Kotsay	.933	3	13	1	1	1
McAnulty	.979	32	265	14	6	26
Natale	1.000	13	97	9	0	13
Velazquez	1.000	4	24	2	0	4
Youkilis	1.000	1	3	0	0	0

Second Base	PCT	G	PO	A	E	DP
Denker	.981	102	193	216	8	62
Natale	.991	25	50	62	1	14

	PCT	G	PO	A	E	DP
Ochoa	.961	11	18	31	2	11
Suarez	1.000	1	1	0	0	0
Velazquez	.983	15	28	29	1	11
Woodward	1.000	5	8	12	0	3

Third Base	PCT	G	PO	A	E	DP
Chavez	.965	121	116	240	13	22
Denker	.865	21	15	30	7	5
Suarez	1.000	2	1	10	0	2
Velazquez	1.000	8	8	11	0	1
Woodward	.667	2	4	0	2	0

Shortstop	PCT	G	PO	A	E	DP
Borowiak	1.000	2	1	8	0	3
Chavez	1.000	8	13	18	0	2
Lowrie	.938	20	18	43	4	9
Lugo	.933	3	6	8	1	1
Ochoa	.984	36	47	79	2	22
Suarez	.971	17	25	42	2	12
Velazquez	.961	73	105	192	12	38
Woodward	1.000	5	7	18	0	4

Outfield	PCT	G	PO	A	E	DP
Ambres	1.000	49	110	4	0	2
Anderson	.986	24	66	3	1	1
Bailey	.945	31	50	2	3	0
Bates	1.000	3	3	1	0	1
Bell	.976	70	156	7	4	2
Carter	.975	59	112	4	3	2
Corsaletti	1.000	11	17	0	0	0
Daeges	1.000	8	11	0	0	0
Danielson	.978	50	86	1	2	0
Duncan	.970	17	30	2	1	1
Gathright	1.000	3	11	0	0	0
Guzman	.994	59	162	4	1	1
Kotsay	1.000	5	1	0	0	0
McAnulty	.981	32	49	3	1	2
Natale	1.000	3	2	0	0	0
Reddick	1.000	18	55	2	0	0
Van Every	.959	20	46	1	2	1
Velazquez	—	2	0	0	0	0
Wilkerson	1.000	1	3	0	0	0

PORTLAND SEA DOGS · DOUBLE-A

EASTERN LEAGUE

Batting	B-T	HT	WT	DOB	AVG	vLH	vRH	G	AB	R	H	2B	3B	HR	RBI	BB	HBP	SH	SF	SO	SB	CS	SLG	OBP
Anderson, Lars	L-L	6-4	215	9-25-87	.233	.221	.237	119	447	50	104	23	0	9	51	63	1	0	1	114	2	0	.345	.328
Apodaca, Juan	R-R	5-11	180	7-15-86	.245	.326	.224	61	216	26	53	12	0	5	29	20	1	0	1	55	1	0	.370	.317
Bates, Aaron	R-R	6-4	230	3-10-84	.340	.426	.309	52	206	41	70	13	0	7	39	17	7	0	2	49	1	0	.505	.405
Bell, Bubba	L-R	6-0	195	10-9-82	.275	.200	.305	53	211	37	58	13	1	5	20	27	0	0	2	37	8	2	.417	.354
Borowiak, Zach	R-R	6-1	185	5-18-81	.217	.273	.191	25	69	13	15	5	1	0	9	12	2	1	0	10	2	2	.319	.349
Diaz, Argenis	R-R	5-11	155	2-12-87	.253	.178	.279	76	277	21	70	14	1	0	24	21	2	6	1	60	7	4	.310	.309
Engel, Reid	L-R	6-3	190	5-7-87	.234	.204	.242	74	214	28	50	15	0	3	21	24	1	2	3	67	5	0	.346	.310
Exposito, Luis	R-R	6-3	210	1-20-87	.337	.462	.288	23	92	14	31	5	0	3	12	4	1	0	0	27	1	2	.489	.371
Jimenez, Jorge	L-R	6-1	210	9-12-84	.289	.234	.310	133	498	63	144	23	2	13	87	52	11	0	5	70	3	2	.422	.366
Kalish, Ryan	L-L	6-1	205	3-28-88	.271	.242	.285	103	391	63	106	19	4	13	56	42	1	0	3	87	14	3	.440	.341
Khoury, Ryan	R-R	5-10	180	3-19-84	.223	.220	.224	109	368	61	82	23	2	2	32	63	8	2	3	103	3	1	.313	.346
Lowrie, Jed	B-B	6-0	180	4-17-84	.600	.333	1.000	1	5	1	3	1	0	0	2	0	0	0	0	0	0	0	.800	.600
Nava, Daniel	B-L	5-10	200	2-22-83	.364	.371	.361	32	118	25	43	10	1	4	23	25	1	0	0	12	0	0	.568	.479
Navarro, Yamaico	R-R	5-11	170	10-31-87	.185	.214	.178	39	135	16	25	6	2	2	11	14	2	0	1	28	5	1	.304	.270
Otness, John	R-R	5-11	200	9-15-81	.226	.350	.192	27	93	9	21	7	0	1	13	10	3	0	0	13	0	0	.333	.321
Place, Jason	R-R	6-3	205	5-8-88	.262	.286	.255	42	141	21	37	6	0	4	16	17	2	0	1	52	1	2	.390	.348
Reddick, Josh	L-R	6-2	180	2-19-87	.277	.234	.292	63	256	47	71	17	3	13	29	30	0	0	1	62	5	5	.520	.352
Sheely, Matt	R-R	5-9	160	8-30-86	.181	.194	.173	41	83	9	15	2	0	0	4	18	5	4	1	34	3	4	.205	.355
Still, Jon	R-R	6-2	210	11-16-84	.233	.231	.233	134	507	53	118	40	1	17	89	44	8	0	5	148	2	0	.416	.301
Suarez, Iggy	R-R	5-11	165	5-3-81	.175	.191	.170	67	194	31	34	7	0	1	13	27	4	1	2	60	8	2	.227	.286
Wagner, Mark	R-R	6-1	205	6-11-84	.301	.262	.315	42	153	21	46	18	0	3	23	28	3	0	4	26	1	0	.477	.410

Pitching	B-T	HT	WT	DOB	W	L	ERA	G	GS	CG	SV	IP	H	R	ER	HR	BB	SO	AVG	vLH	vRH	K/9	BB/9
Beazley, Travis	R-R	6-0	175	6-17-83	0	1	12.46	1	1	0	0	4	7	6	6	2	2	3	.350	.400	.300	6.23	4.15
Cox, Bryce	R-R	6-4	205	8-10-84	1	5	2.88	45	0	0	12	56	64	24	18	2	28	37	.286	.333	.236	5.91	4.47
Dobies, Andrew	L-L	6-1	180	4-20-83	2	3	3.69	27	0	0	0	39	32	17	16	1	13	39	.227	.175	.262	9.00	3.00

Name	B-T	HT	WT	DOB	W	L	ERA	G	GS	CG	SV	IP	H	R	ER	HR	BB	SO	AVG	vLH	vRH	K/9	BB/9
Doubront, Felix	L-L	6-2	165	10-23-87	8	6	3.35	26	26	1	0	121	119	59	45	8	52	101	.255	.255	.256	7.51	3.87
Fernandes, Kyle	L-L	6-0	190	9-12-85	0	0	33.75	1	0	0	0	1	4	5	5	1	3	0	.500	.667	.400	0.00	20.25
Gabbard, Kason	L-L	6-3	200	4-8-82	0	4	20.77	5	5	0	0	13	26	30	30	2	28	12	.413	.556	.356	8.31	19.38
Hedrick, Justin	R-R	6-3	225	6-8-82	1	2	6.49	17	1	0	1	26	33	20	19	3	14	14	.317	.350	.273	4.78	4.78
Hottovy, Tommy	L-L	6-1	195	7-9-81	0	2	3.46	16	0	0	0	26	26	12	10	2	10	29	.263	.258	.265	10.04	3.46
Johnson, Kris	L-L	6-4	170	10-14-84	0	3	6.35	3	3	0	0	17	22	14	12	1	5	12	.310	.417	.255	6.35	2.65
Large, T.J.	R-R	6-4	185	5-28-83	3	0	1.08	34	0	0	8	42	31	7	5	1	14	34	.207	.193	.226	7.34	3.02
Latimer, Will	L-L	6-3	190	12-4-85	0	0	4.50	3	0	0	0	4	6	3	2	0	5	2	.353	.600	.250	4.50	11.25
Lawson, Ryne	L-R	6-2	180	6-21-85	3	12	5.93	23	23	1	0	115	124	83	76	10	57	57	.278	.267	.289	4.45	4.45
Lentz, Richie	R-R	6-2	210	8-6-84	1	0	6.75	29	0	0	0	36	33	32	27	2	33	48	.243	.200	.295	12.00	8.25
Loop, Derrick	L-L	6-3	220	12-11-83	1	0	6.23	4	0	0	0	4	5	3	3	0	2	4	.333	.400	.300	8.31	4.15
Matsuzaka, Daisuke	R-R	6-0	185	9-13-80	0	1	22.50	1	1	0	0	2	4	5	5	1	3	2	.444	.500	.400	9.00	13.50
Maxwell, Blake	R-R	6-5	255	8-1-84	7	8	5.32	32	18	0	0	112	131	73	66	9	33	59	.292	.309	.273	4.76	2.66
Miller, Ryne	R-R	6-4	230	9-25-85	2	2	2.75	14	3	0	1	39	28	18	12	2	13	38	.196	.226	.173	8.69	2.97
Mills, Adam	R-R	5-11	190	11-19-84	10	5	4.24	20	20	0	0	110	121	57	52	11	26	73	.278	.261	.298	5.95	2.12
Papelbon, Josh	R-R	6-1	210	6-24-83	1	0	3.60	2	0	0	0	5	4	4	2	0	3	4	.211	.222	.200	7.20	5.40
Plummer, Jarod	R-R	6-5	200	1-27-84	8	7	4.01	23	21	0	0	112	110	55	50	6	51	91	.257	.275	.236	7.29	4.09
Province, Chris	R-R	6-3	220	1-20-85	2	4	2.60	43	0	0	1	80	72	29	23	3	32	55	.240	.232	.250	6.21	3.62
Rhoades, Chad	R-R	5-10	175	3-10-83	6	2	3.94	56	0	0	2	82	71	39	36	4	36	82	.228	.222	.234	8.96	3.94
Richardson, Dustin	L-L	6-6	220	1-9-84	2	2	2.70	38	0	0	4	63	42	22	19	2	40	80	.186	.159	.201	11.37	5.68
Smoltz, John	R-R	6-3	220	5-15-67	0	0	2.70	1	1	0	0	3	3	1	1	0	0	2	.231	.167	.286	5.40	0.00
Tazawa, Junichi	R-R	5-11	180	6-6-86	9	5	2.57	18	18	0	0	98	80	31	28	8	26	88	.222	.218	.229	8.08	2.39

Fielding

Catcher	PCT	G	PO	A	E	DP	PB
Apodaca	.988	57	368	27	5	2	3
Exposito	.981	20	143	11	3	0	1
Otness	.989	27	164	14	2	1	1
Still	1.000	1	5	1	0	0	0
Wagner	.997	38	287	33	1	4	4

First Base	PCT	G	PO	A	E	DP
Anderson	.988	95	780	51	10	74
Jimenez	1.000	5	9	0	0	1
Still	.992	46	338	31	3	31

Second Base	PCT	G	PO	A	E	DP
Borowiak	.978	9	13	32	1	8

	PCT	G	PO	A	E	DP
Khoury	.969	106	188	287	15	56
Suarez	.975	30	66	90	4	23

Third Base	PCT	G	PO	A	E	DP
Borowiak	1.000	5	1	14	0	1
Jimenez	.932	126	112	203	23	24
Khoury	.833	3	2	3	1	1
Suarez	.917	17	7	15	2	0

Shortstop	PCT	G	PO	A	E	DP
Borowiak	.927	7	18	20	3	3
Diaz	.947	76	107	217	18	44
Lowrie	1.000	1	1	2	0	1
Navarro	.975	39	56	102	4	20

	PCT	G	PO	A	E	DP
Suarez	.949	21	48	45	5	13

Outfield	PCT	G	PO	A	E	DP
Bates	.939	47	90	2	6	0
Bell	.958	50	89	3	4	1
Engel	.991	65	107	2	1	1
Kalish	.983	101	232	6	4	1
Nava	.961	30	48	1	2	0
Place	.951	42	71	7	4	0
Reddick	.979	63	135	7	3	1
Sheely	.987	37	76	2	1	0
Suarez	1.000	2	3	1	0	0

SALEM RED SOX

HIGH CLASS A

CAROLINA LEAGUE

Batting	B-T	HT	WT	DOB	AVG	vLH	vRH	G	AB	R	H	2B	3B	HR	RBI	BB	HBP	SH	SF	SO	SB	CS	SLG	OBP
Borowiak, Zach	R-R	6-1	185	5-18-81	.223	.242	.213	75	264	29	59	13	0	2	22	24	3	4	1	55	3	3	.295	.295
Butler, Daniel	R-R	5-10	190	10-17-86	.000	.000	.000	2	3	0	0	0	0	0	0	0	0	0	0	1	0	0	.000	.000
Chiang, Chih-Hsien	L-R	6-2	170	2-21-88	.264	.237	.277	85	299	37	79	21	3	6	38	24	3	0	2	48	2	1	.415	.323
Correll, Brad	R-R	6-2	205	6-17-81	.274	.316	.262	24	84	14	23	5	0	2	13	10	0	0	1	18	3	1	.405	.347
Dent, Ryan	R-R	6-0	190	3-15-89	.268	.143	.294	13	41	6	11	4	0	0	3	0	1	1	1	10	1	0	.366	.279
Exposito, Luis	R-R	6-3	210	1-20-87	.271	.262	.278	76	288	28	78	24	1	6	45	23	4	0	4	49	3	1	.424	.329
Farkes, Zak	R-R	5-11	190	5-30-83	.229	.200	.255	34	105	12	24	9	1	2	13	7	1	1	2	24	1	0	.390	.278
Federowicz, Tim	R-R	5-10	213	8-5-87	.257	.300	.236	51	187	18	48	13	0	4	24	5	1	1	3	22	1	0	.390	.276
Hee, Jonathan	B-R	6-0	180	8-11-85	.236	.203	.255	87	322	38	76	15	0	3	35	28	3	3	5	40	3	3	.311	.299
Jones, Michael	L-R	6-3	220	6-14-85	.283	.302	.272	108	396	55	112	26	1	6	59	40	5	0	3	58	3	0	.399	.354
Kalish, Ryan	L-L	6-1	205	3-28-88	.304	.311	.296	32	115	21	35	5	2	5	21	26	1	0	1	20	7	3	.513	.434
Lin, Che-Hsuan	R-R	6-0	180	9-21-88	.265	.261	.268	131	479	75	127	23	2	7	54	66	5	4	8	75	26	11	.365	.355
Mailman, David	L-L	6-2	180	10-7-88	.186	.156	.200	61	199	15	37	4	0	1	12	19	2	2	4	49	1	3	.221	.264
Nava, Daniel	B-L	5-10	200	2-22-83	.339	.385	.298	29	109	18	37	12	1	1	13	18	1	1	1	21	0	2	.495	.434
Navarro, Yamaico	R-R	5-11	170	10-31-87	.319	.385	.273	23	94	10	30	9	0	4	17	6	2	0	0	12	2	2	.543	.373
Negron, Kris	R-R	6-0	180	2-1-86	.264	.262	.266	111	409	69	108	17	4	3	34	39	8	6	2	83	20	3	.347	.338
Place, Jason	R-R	6-3	205	5-8-88	.248	.260	.240	76	302	47	75	23	3	4	47	34	2	0	3	85	1	2	.384	.326
Reza, Aaron	R-R	5-7	180	6-25-85	.208	.250	.191	36	125	19	26	3	0	1	8	10	1	0	1	30	0	2	.256	.270
Rizzo, Anthony	L-L	6-3	220	8-8-89	.295	.264	.313	55	200	23	59	16	0	3	24	25	1	0	3	39	2	0	.420	.371
Segovia, Luis	B-R	5-10	150	7-19-86	.190	.173	.204	67	189	18	36	10	2	0	25	15	4	7	1	54	2	3	.265	.263
Sheely, Matt	R-R	5-9	160	8-8-86	.256	.256	.256	35	82	13	21	2	0	0	6	13	0	3	0	15	10	2	.280	.358
Stanley, Jered	R-R	6-3	220	9-18-84	.211	.236	.188	48	152	17	32	7	1	0	11	26	3	0	0	51	1	1	.270	.337
Vazquez, Will	R-R	6-2	190	2-22-85	.180	.239	.145	43	122	9	22	8	1	1	18	11	5	3	0	37	1	0	.287	.275
Weeden, Ty	R-R	6-2	220	9-26-87	.200	.240	.171	18	60	8	12	1	0	1	5	8	0	0	0	20	0	0	.267	.294

Pitching	B-T	HT	WT	DOB	W	L	ERA	G	GS	CG	SV	IP	H	R	ER	HR	BB	SO	AVG	vLH	vRH	K/9	BB/9
Alvarez, Jose	L-L	5-11	150	5-6-89	1	1	4.74	12	0	0	0	25	32	15	13	1	6	11	.308	.324	.299	4.01	2.19
Blackey, Jason	R-R	6-4	206	4-11-83	2	0	2.08	13	0	0	6	17	12	5	4	0	11	17	.197	.172	.219	8.83	5.71
Capellan, Jose	L-L	6-2	170	7-18-86	6	4	6.34	29	16	0	1	94	122	73	66	14	65	63	.314	.276	.332	6.05	6.25
Coello, Robert	R-R	6-5	250	11-23-84	5	3	2.05	33	0	0	2	66	38	22	15	4	34	82	.167	.196	.138	11.18	4.64
Dobies, Andrew	L-L	6-1	180	4-20-83	0	0	5.06	3	0	0	0	5	5	3	0	0	2	3	.227	.286	.200	5.06	3.38
Fernandes, Kyle	L-L	6-0	190	9-12-85	5	3	3.48	43	0	0	2	83	74	36	32	7	30	74	.242	.260	.233	8.06	3.27
Fife, Stephen	R-R	6-3	210	10-4-86	3	2	4.44	10	10	0	0	51	58	28	25	7	10	51	.283	.307	.253	9.06	1.78

Garrison, Seth	B-R	6-5	220	8-13-85	8	11	3.90	26	25	0	1	132	136	72	57	12	40	90	.271	.248	.297	6.15	2.73
Kelly, Casey	R-R	6-3	194	10-4-89	1	4	3.09	8	8	0	0	47	33	21	16	4	7	35	.196	.233	.138	6.75	1.35
Loop, Derrick	R-L	6-3	220	12-11-83	3	3	1.61	47	1	0	18	67	51	15	12	2	22	78	.217	.219	.216	10.48	2.96
McKae, Dave	R-R	6-2	190	11-24-81	2	6	4.32	20	16	0	0	85	95	49	41	6	18	64	.276	.263	.291	6.75	1.90
Miller, Ryne	R-R	6-4	230	9-25-85	8	2	2.77	27	0	0	0	55	50	18	17	3	18	59	.244	.204	.293	9.60	2.93
Papelbon, Josh	R-R	6-1	210	6-24-83	5	2	2.87	34	0	0	2	60	56	21	19	2	15	40	.249	.286	.208	6.03	2.26
Plummer, Jarod	R-R	6-5	200	1-27-84	0	1	3.60	1	1	0	0	5	4	3	2	0	1	5	.200	.111	.273	9.00	1.80
Portice, Eammon	R-R	6-2	185	6-18-85	8	8	4.35	25	25	0	0	128	128	67	62	12	36	141	.259	.295	.220	9.89	2.52
Povich, Chad	R-R	6-0	185	6-13-86	0	1	4.70	6	0	0	1	8	7	4	4	2	4	10	.226	.400	.063	11.74	4.70
Price, Bryan	R-R	6-4	210	11-13-86	1	6	6.54	11	11	0	0	52	62	43	38	4	19	57	.288	.294	.283	9.80	3.27
2-team total (7 Kinston)					3	10	5.89	18	18	0	0	89	100	65	58	13	29	87	—	—		8.83	2.94
Rice, Jason	R-R	6-0	190	5-13-86	1	3	2.44	41	0	0	0	70	38	20	19	2	41	94	.160	.125	.188	12.09	5.27
Weiland, Kyle	L-R	6-4	195	9-12-86	7	9	3.46	26	26	0	0	133	119	65	51	4	57	112	.240	.294	.192	7.60	3.87
Zerpa, Armando	L-L	5-11	175	2-13-87	1	3	4.85	16	0	0	0	30	26	17	16	2	21	27	.236	.139	.284	8.19	6.37

Fielding

Catcher	PCT	G	PO	A	E	DP	PB
Butler	1.000	2	10	0	0	0	1
Exposito	.988	67	513	69	7	5	9
Federowicz	.991	38	307	39	3	6	4
Vazquez	.995	26	171	21	1	0	2
Weeden	1.000	11	79	9	0	0	3

First Base	PCT	G	PO	A	E	DP
Borowiak	1.000	5	30	2	0	1
Farkes	.975	7	37	2	1	4
Jones	.992	66	564	43	5	51
Rizzo	.992	51	443	43	4	33
Stanley	.972	11	101	5	3	3
Vazquez	1.000	8	53	2	0	4

Second Base	PCT	G	PO	A	E	DP
Borowiak	.970	21	39	57	3	15

	PCT	G	PO	A	E	DP
Hee	.959	14	29	41	3	10
Negron	.982	31	64	96	3	21
Reza	.965	29	38	73	4	9
Segovia	.964	56	64	152	8	20

Third Base	PCT	G	PO	A	E	DP
Borowiak	.877	26	17	40	8	5
Farkes	.871	27	12	42	8	7
Hee	.966	75	42	159	7	11
Reza	1.000	7	3	11	0	1
Segovia	.909	3	2	8	1	2
Vazquez	.909	9	3	17	2	3

Shortstop	PCT	G	PO	A	E	DP
Borowiak	.920	26	41	62	9	8
Dent	.969	13	27	36	2	10
Navarro	.938	21	33	42	5	11

	PCT	G	PO	A	E	DP
Negron	.943	76	105	174	17	33
Segovia	.944	6	6	11	1	4

Outfield	PCT	G	PO	A	E	DP
Chiang	.926	43	47	3	4	0
Correll	1.000	24	26	2	0	0
Kalish	.983	24	56	3	1	1
Lin	.963	128	269	18	11	7
Mailman	.968	61	85	5	3	1
Nava	.959	29	45	2	2	0
Negron	1.000	6	10	1	0	0
Place	.964	75	126	6	5	1
Sheely	.974	32	37	1	1	1
Stanley	1.000	16	16	1	0	0

GREENVILLE DRIVE

LOW CLASS A

SOUTH ATLANTIC LEAGUE

Batting	B-T	HT	WT	DOB	AVG	vLH	vRH	G	AB	R	H	2B	3B	HR	RBI	BB	HBP	SH	SF	SO	SB	CS	SLG	OBP
Almanzar, Michael	R-R	6-3	190	12-2-90	.207	.118	.227	49	188	13	39	7	0	3	17	9	5	0	1	53	0	0	.293	.261
Dening, Mitch	L-R	6-1	165	8-17-88	.261	.253	.263	106	391	57	102	24	3	3	39	39	4	1	2	95	20	5	.361	.333
Dent, Ryan	R-R	6-0	190	3-15-89	.252	.167	.272	99	345	59	87	24	3	6	48	49	5	8	4	112	17	5	.391	.350
DiBenedetto, Tom	R-R	6-1	190	11-3-85	.308	.400	.250	4	13	2	4	2	0	0	1	1	0	0	1	3	0	0	.462	.333
Federowicz, Tim	R-R	5-10	213	8-5-87	.345	.283	.361	55	226	34	78	19	0	10	34	15	4	0	2	42	1	0	.562	.393
Gentile, Zach	L-R	5-8	165	11-1-86	.281	.254	.287	88	306	45	86	11	2	1	27	36	4	4	1	45	7	6	.340	.363
Hassan, Alex	R-R	6-3	195	4-1-88	.313	1.000	.267	8	32	6	10	3	1	1	7	2	0	0	0	7	0	0	.563	.353
Hazelbaker, Jeremy	L-R	6-3	190	8-4-86	.167	.133	.175	45	150	16	25	5	1	1	9	23	1	1	1	58	11	2	.233	.280
Hee, Jonathan	B-R	6-0	180	8-11-85	.200	.227	.190	26	80	11	16	3	1	0	11	7	3	0	0	20	0	1	.263	.289
Hissey, Pete	L-L	6-1	180	1-17-90	.279	.240	.289	106	369	50	103	13	6	0	37	39	7	6	4	88	22	9	.347	.356
Keowen, Kade	R-R	6-5	215	4-18-86	.241	.310	.221	85	315	40	76	15	0	10	32	17	7	1	0	91	3	1	.384	.295
Lavarnway, Ryan	R-R	6-4	225	8-7-87	.285	.268	.290	106	404	60	115	36	2	21	87	50	6	0	6	113	1	2	.540	.367
Mailman, David	L-L	6-2	180	10-7-88	.297	.270	.303	58	212	33	63	13	7	3	32	19	2	1	2	28	10	2	.467	.357
Marks, David	L-R	6-0	190	3-23-87	.198	.125	.213	29	91	12	18	5	0	4	12	7	0	0	3	34	1	2	.385	.248
McGuiness, Chris	L-L	6-1	210	4-11-88	.150	.000	.167	6	20	2	3	1	0	0	1	3	2	0	0	5	0	0	.200	.320
Middlebrooks, Will	R-R	6-4	200	9-9-88	.265	.241	.271	103	374	53	99	25	3	7	57	48	2	0	3	123	7	4	.404	.349
Rizzo, Anthony	L-L	6-3	220	8-8-89	.298	.283	.302	64	245	40	73	21	0	9	42	25	2	0	2	60	2	1	.494	.365
Sanchez, Maykol	R-R	5-11	176	5-30-88	.000	—	.000	1	4	0	0	0	0	0	0	0	0	0	0	3	0	0	.000	.000
Stanley, Jered	R-R	6-3	220	9-18-84	.228	.211	.232	30	101	14	23	6	1	1	13	22	2	0	5	28	2	2	.317	.362
Tejeda, Oscar	R-R	6-1	177	12-26-89	.257	.274	.252	99	370	50	95	13	3	3	50	30	3	0	9	89	3	5	.332	.311
Thomas, Michael	R-R	6-3	215	12-5-88	.183	.143	.189	17	60	8	11	1	0	4	8	2	1	0	0	23	0	0	.400	.222
Weeden, Ty	R-R	6-2	220	9-26-87	.248	.229	.254	43	157	22	39	12	1	1	15	22	3	0	0	58	0	0	.357	.352
Wilkerson, Shannon	R-R	6-0	198	7-20-88	.241	.207	.253	29	112	18	27	7	2	2	12	7	0	0	1	17	2	0	.393	.283

Pitching	B-T	HT	WT	DOB	W	L	ERA	G	GS	CG	SV	IP	H	R	ER	HR	BB	SO	AVG	vLH	vRH	K/9	BB/9
Blackey, Jason	R-R	6-4	206	4-11-83	1	1	7.15	8	0	0	3	11	15	12	9	3	6	13	.313	.357	.294	10.32	4.76
Castillo, Yeiper	R-R	6-3	158	9-6-88	0	4	7.04	9	4	0	1	31	36	27	24	2	15	28	.286	.319	.266	8.22	4.40
Clay, Caleb	R-R	6-2	180	2-15-88	6	7	4.01	25	16	0	3	110	102	53	49	11	38	67	.249	.264	.239	5.48	3.11
Fife, Stephen	R-R	6-3	210	10-4-86	0	3	2.70	8	8	0	0	37	32	13	11	1	4	35	.230	.283	.204	8.59	0.98
Hagadone, Nick	L-L	6-5	230	1-1-86	0	2	2.52	10	10	0	0	25	13	8	7	0	14	32	.149	.176	.143	11.52	5.04
2-team total (5 Lake County)					0	3	2.50	15	15	0	0	40	21	12	11	0	19	53	—	—		12.03	4.31
Herold, Mitch	L-L	6-0	200	6-18-86	5	1	1.92	33	0	0	4	66	58	19	14	1	24	71	.238	.275	.223	9.73	3.29
Huntzinger, Brock	R-R	6-3	200	7-2-88	10	9	4.09	25	25	0	0	125	127	64	57	7	32	102	.261	.247	.269	7.32	2.30
Kehrt, Jeremy	R-R	6-2	190	12-21-85	2	2	3.29	11	4	0	2	55	48	24	20	4	13	33	.231	.270	.209	5.43	2.14
Kelly, Casey	R-R	6-3	194	10-4-89	6	1	1.12	9	9	0	0	48	32	9	6	0	9	39	.184	.175	.189	7.26	1.68
Latimer, Will	L-L	6-3	190	12-4-85	1	1	2.92	7	0	0	0	12	11	6	4	2	5	11	.224	.167	.243	8.03	3.65
Lee, Michael	R-R	6-7	220	11-18-86	3	4	3.50	18	4	0	1	72	77	37	28	3	23	71	.275	.287	.268	8.88	2.88
Marin, Leandro	R-R	5-11	165	11-9-88	3	2	2.89	27	0	0	0	44	31	21	14	1	28	56	.200	.211	.194	11.54	5.77

Name	B-T	HT	WT	DOB	W	L	ERA	G	GS	CG	SV	IP	H	R	ER	HR	BB	SO	AVG	vLH	vRH	K/9	BB/9
McClain, Lance	R-L	6-1	175	3-26-87	2	2	3.51	36	0	0	6	67	63	35	26	7	25	84	.253	.267	.249	11.34	3.37
Neuman, Dennis	R-R	5-11	185	10-18-89	0	0	4.15	2	0	0	0	4	5	2	2	1	2	2	.294	.111	.500	4.15	4.15
Pimentel, Stolmy	R-R	6-3	186	2-1-90	10	7	3.82	24	23	1	0	118	135	62	50	12	29	103	.290	.301	.284	7.88	2.22
Povich, Chad	R-R	6-0	185	6-13-86	2	0	8.83	11	1	0	1	17	28	18	17	1	6	17	.368	.250	.438	8.83	3.12
Price, Bryan	R-R	6-4	210	11-13-86	3	2	2.45	8	8	0	0	44	37	16	12	2	12	40	.223	.154	.254	8.18	2.45
Rosario, Charle	R-R	5-10	158	7-23-88	0	0	1.42	2	0	0	0	6	6	4	1	1	2	6	.231	.167	.286	8.53	2.84
Rutter, Kyle	R-R	6-3	175	7-12-86	0	1	3.52	5	0	0	1	8	11	4	3	0	4	6	.379	.500	.294	7.04	4.70
Smoltz, John	R-R	6-3	220	5-15-67	0	0	1.13	2	2	0	0	8	5	1	1	0	0	8	.172	.077	.250	9.00	0.00
Strickland, Hunter	R-R	6-5	200	9-24-88	5	4	3.35	18	12	0	1	83	85	39	31	11	13	51	.264	.252	.271	5.51	1.40
2-team total (8 West Virginia)					9	6	3.49	26	20	0	1	126	127	62	49	14	19	74	—	—	—	5.27	1.35
Ventura, Felix	R-R	5-11	165	4-27-84	3	7	4.52	36	0	0	8	72	74	38	36	8	20	58	.269	.262	.274	7.28	2.51
Williamson, Fabian	R-L	6-2	175	10-20-88	10	5	2.42	28	12	0	5	108	71	34	29	3	53	104	.189	.196	.186	8.67	4.42
Zerpa, Armando	L-L	5-11	175	2-13-87	1	0	1.20	22	0	0	2	45	19	6	6	0	14	51	.125	.056	.147	10.20	2.80

Fielding

Catcher	PCT	G	PO	A	E	DP	PB
Federowicz	.986	46	373	39	6	3	0
Lavarnway	.989	66	505	51	6	4	26
Sanchez	.889	1	8	0	1	1	0
Thomas	.985	17	116	18	2	5	1
Weeden	.979	11	85	7	2	0	2

First Base	PCT	G	PO	A	E	DP
Almanzar	1.000	9	95	2	0	9
Hee	1.000	9	73	2	0	2
Keowen	.983	14	108	6	2	5
McGuiness	1.000	6	43	5	0	4
Rizzo	.997	59	527	43	2	43
Stanley	.955	14	98	7	5	7
Weeden	.982	31	259	15	5	13

Second Base	PCT	G	PO	A	E	DP
Dent	.975	65	115	157	7	30
DiBenedetto	1.000	4	5	12	0	1
Gentile	.993	67	104	173	2	34
Hee	.969	7	9	22	1	3

Third Base	PCT	G	PO	A	E	DP
Almanzar	.943	34	17	66	5	3
Gentile	.933	11	4	10	1	0
Hee	1.000	6	8	8	0	0
Middlebrooks	.934	91	53	144	14	11

Shortstop	PCT	G	PO	A	E	DP
Dent	.964	34	46	116	6	22
Gentile	1.000	1	2	2	0	0
Kelly	.902	20	28	55	9	5

Outfield	PCT	G	PO	A	E	DP
Tejeda	.933	84	112	224	24	37
Dening	.980	105	193	8	4	1
Gentile	1.000	3	1	0	0	0
Hassan	1.000	8	9	1	0	0
Hazelbaker	.989	42	84	3	1	2
Hee	1.000	1	3	0	0	0
Hissey	.991	105	203	8	2	4
Keowen	.967	54	88	1	3	0
Mailman	.936	54	81	7	6	1
Marks	.982	25	53	2	1	1
Stanley	1.000	10	17	0	0	0
Wilkerson	.950	27	57	0	3	0

LOWELL SPINNERS   SHORT-SEASON

NEW YORK-PENN LEAGUE

Batting	B-T	HT	WT	DOB	AVG	vLH	vRH	G	AB	R	H	2B	3B	HR	RBI	BB	HBP	SH	SF	SO	SB	CS	SLG	OBP
Almanzar, Michael	R-R	6-3	190	12-2-90	.230	.203	.242	59	222	29	51	7	3	1	29	16	3	0	2	52	1	2	.302	.288
Bermudez, Ronald	R-R	6-1	165	6-6-88	.258	.291	.243	70	252	31	65	11	1	1	27	9	5	2	3	54	12	4	.321	.294
Blair, Carson	R-R	6-1	190	10-18-89	.500	—	.500	1	2	0	1	0	0	0	1	0	0	0	1	0	0	1.000	.667
Butler, Daniel	R-R	5-10	190	10-17-86	.179	.125	.194	22	78	7	14	3	1	1	10	4	5	0	1	14	0	1	.282	.261
Chen, Chia-Chu	L-R	5-10	175	4-7-89	.188	.167	.192	23	64	9	12	3	1	1	11	5	0	1	2	8	0	0	.313	.239
DiBenedetto, Tom	R-R	6-1	190	11-3-85	.286	.313	.269	18	42	2	12	2	0	0	1	3	2	0	0	9	0	1	.333	.362
Dominguez, Drew	R-R	5-11	195	12-27-86	.184	.250	.167	14	38	4	7	1	0	0	4	1	3	0	0	14	1	0	.211	.262
Feliz, Roberto	R-R	6-1	180	12-30-87	.175	.231	.148	13	40	7	7	0	0	1	5	3	0	0	0	8	1	0	.250	.233
Garcia, Joantoni	R-R	5-11	165	9-9-90	.178	.116	.209	61	208	26	37	15	1	2	28	27	3	1	1	77	3	0	.288	.280
Gibson, Derrik	R-R	6-1	170	12-5-89	.290	.216	.329	67	255	54	74	15	4	0	25	39	6	2	1	42	28	5	.380	.395
Hassan, Alex	R-R	6-3	195	4-1-88	.333	.423	.299	26	93	14	31	5	1	1	11	8	0	1	1	11	1	1	.441	.382
Hazelbaker, Jeremy	L-R	6-3	190	8-14-87	.125	.000	.200	3	8	0	1	0	0	0	0	4	0	1	0	3	0	0	.125	.417
Hedman, Drew	L-L	6-2	200	7-20-86	.265	.217	.286	45	151	16	40	19	0	0	21	15	3	1	1	39	0	3	.391	.341
Holmes, Willie	R-R	5-11	215	8-20-87	.264	.233	.279	27	91	15	24	3	1	2	14	7	4	0	3	28	0	2	.385	.333
Killeen, Sean	R-R	6-0	205	3-2-87	.250	.267	.239	23	76	7	19	3	0	0	3	7	1	0	0	16	0	2	.289	.321
Lowrie, Jed	B-R	6-0	180	4-17-84	.182	.250	.143	3	11	2	2	2	0	0	1	2	0	0	0	1	0	0	.364	.308
McGuiness, Chris	L-L	6-1	210	4-11-88	.255	.266	.250	54	196	26	50	17	0	6	38	36	2	0	1	40	0	1	.434	.374
Navarro, Yamaico	R-R	5-11	170	10-31-87	.238	.000	.313	5	21	1	5	1	0	0	2	2	0	0	1	3	0	2	.286	.304
Pichardo, Wilfred	B-R	5-9	146	10-21-89	.302	.315	.297	62	245	39	74	14	1	2	21	18	1	2	1	76	32	9	.392	.351
Roque, Kenneth	L-R	5-11	162	9-20-88	.313	.273	.333	10	32	6	10	1	2	0	3	4	0	1	0	8	1	1	.469	.389
Thomas, Michael	R-R	6-3	215	12-5-88	.286	.333	.250	2	7	0	2	0	0	0	0	1	0	0	0	4	0	0	.286	.375
Vazquez, Christian	R-R	5-9	195	8-21-90	.123	.045	.163	21	65	4	8	2	0	2	9	11	0	0	0	16	0	0	.246	.250
Westmoreland, Ryan	L-R	6-2	195	4-27-90	.296	.257	.315	60	223	38	66	15	3	7	35	38	3	0	3	49	19	0	.484	.401
Wilkerson, Shannon	R-R	6-0	190	12-8-88	.264	.255	.269	31	125	15	33	10	5	0	11	5	3	1	0	2	5	1	.424	.308

Pitching	B-T	HT	WT	DOB	W	L	ERA	G	GS	CG	SV	IP	H	R	ER	HR	BB	SO	AVG	vLH	vRH	K/9	BB/9
Alvarez, Jose	L-L	5-11	150	5-6-89	8	3	1.52	14	12	2	0	83	60	17	14	4	10	63	.203	.221	.198	6.83	1.08
Angeloni, Chez	R-R	6-2	190	1-23-87	1	1	3.72	4	0	0	0	10	11	4	4	0	1	2	.275	.375	.125	1.86	0.93
Batista, Anatanaer	R-R	5-10	150	2-2-89	3	0	2.59	14	0	0	1	31	25	14	9	1	8	34	.208	.250	.172	9.77	2.30
Bayer, Jeremiah	R-R	6-2	200	12-26-85	0	0	4.15	14	0	0	2	26	26	16	12	1	7	27	.255	.264	.245	9.35	2.42
Britton, Drake	L-L	6-2	200	5-22-89	0	0	1.93	3	3	0	0	5	4	1	1	0	3	8	.235	.286	.200	15.43	5.79
Bugary, Michael	L-L	6-4	215	10-11-87	3	1	2.82	16	0	0	1	22	18	9	7	0	22	30	.222	.286	.189	12.09	8.87
Cabral, Cesar	L-L	6-3	175	2-11-89	1	6	4.03	15	9	0	4	60	66	35	27	2	17	47	.265	.203	.294	7.01	2.54
Castillo, Yeiper	R-R	6-3	158	9-6-88	6	1	2.92	15	15	0	0	77	65	31	25	3	26	64	.226	.252	.197	7.48	3.04
Ebert, Tom	R-R	6-6	245	10-31-87	4	0	6.00	11	0	0	0	24	28	19	16	2	11	22	.292	.286	.296	8.25	4.13
Flasher, Jordan	R-R	5-11	165	10-14-87	1	0	0.00	6	0	0	2	7	4	0	0	0	2	9	.167	.143	.200	11.57	2.57
Gabbard, Kason	L-L	6-3	200	4-8-82	2	1	2.53	5	5	0	0	21	19	6	6	0	15	15	.260	.263	.259	6.33	6.33
Hottovy, Tommy	L-L	6-1	195	7-9-81	1	0	2.25	5	0	0	0	8	4	2	2	1	3	12	.148	.167	.143	13.50	3.38
Kehrt, Jeremy	R-R	6-2	190	12-21-85	1	2	2.49	5	1	0	0	22	17	10	6	0	2	30	.198	.179	.213	12.46	0.83
Latimer, Will	L-L	6-3	190	12-4-85	1	0	2.78	13	0	0	1	23	19	11	7	0	12	26	.218	.273	.200	10.32	4.76
Lentz, Richie	R-R	6-2	210	8-6-84	2	0	3.95	9	0	0	0	14	8	6	6	0	6	26	.167	.167	.167	17.12	3.95

BOSTON RED SOX

	B-T	HT	WT	DOB	W	L	ERA	G	GS	CG	SV	IP	H	R	ER	HR	BB	SO	AVG	vLH	vRH	K/9	BB/9
Lin, Wang-Yi	R-R	6-2	192	6-28-88	0	2	17.18	3	0	0	1	4	7	9	7	2	3	4	.389	.250	.500	9.82	7.36
Neuman, Dennis	R-R	5-11	185	10-18-89	1	0	1.45	26	0	0	7	31	15	6	5	0	12	35	.147	.111	.175	10.16	3.48
Perez, Pedro	R-R	6-4	170	5-3-88	2	5	3.28	17	6	0	2	49	39	25	18	2	25	38	.219	.237	.198	6.93	4.56
Povich, Chad	R-R	6-0	185	6-13-86	0	1	9.45	5	0	0	0	7	10	7	7	0	6	6	.400	.467	.300	8.10	8.10
Pressly, Ryan	R-R	6-3	175	12-15-88	6	4	3.17	13	11	0	0	60	48	22	21	1	25	64	.220	.175	.276	9.65	3.77
Rosario, Charle	R-R	5-10	158	7-23-88	1	1	4.86	8	0	0	0	17	22	10	9	1	5	20	.324	.400	.242	10.80	2.70
Rutter, Kyle	R-R	6-3	175	7-12-86	1	1	1.50	15	0	0	1	18	14	3	3	1	13	21	.226	.276	.182	10.50	6.50
Wilson, Alex	R-R	6-1	205	11-3-86	0	1	0.50	13	13	0	0	36	10	3	2	0	7	33	.085	.113	.054	8.25	1.75
Wogee, Doug	B-R	6-3	190	9-9-88	0	0	6.00	2	0	0	0	3	2	2	2	1	0	2	.182	.333	.000	6.00	0.00

Fielding

Catcher	PCT	G	PO	A	E	DP	PB
Butler	.990	21	176	13	2	2	3
Chen	1.000	22	146	19	0	2	2
Killeen	.978	23	164	10	4	1	2
Thomas	1.000	2	20	2	0	0	1
Vazquez	.986	15	121	19	2	0	2

First Base	PCT	G	PO	A	E	DP
Almanzar	1.000	2	4	0	0	0
Hedman	.991	26	205	13	2	14
McGuiness	.992	52	441	30	4	35

Second Base	PCT	G	PO	A	E	DP
Bayer	1.000	1	0	1	0	0
DiBenedetto	1.000	5	1	12	0	0
Dominguez	.933	12	16	26	3	5

	PCT	G	PO	A	E	DP
Garcia	.950	25	42	71	6	14
Gibson	.951	30	53	83	7	18
Roque	.975	9	14	25	1	6

Third Base	PCT	G	PO	A	E	DP
Almanzar	.890	58	29	92	15	4
Blair	.500	1	0	1	1	0
DiBenedetto	.947	11	3	15	1	1
Garcia	1.000	5	0	8	0	0
Holmes	.857	2	1	5	1	0
Roque	—	1	0	0	0	0
Vazquez	.917	5	2	9	1	0

Shortstop	PCT	G	PO	A	E	DP
Garcia	.933	33	43	83	9	16
Gibson	.939	38	66	88	10	22

	PCT	G	PO	A	E	DP
Lowrie	.933	3	10	4	1	0
Navarro	1.000	4	4	12	0	3

Outfield	PCT	G	PO	A	E	DP
Bermudez	.986	69	133	3	2	0
DiBenedetto	1.000	2	3	0	0	0
Feliz	.909	11	9	1	1	0
Hassan	.977	26	39	3	1	0
Hazelbaker	1.000	3	3	0	0	0
Hedman	.933	13	14	0	1	0
Holmes	.889	15	8	0	1	0
Pichardo	.917	62	94	6	9	0
Westmoreland	1.000	8	12	0	0	0
Wilkerson	.985	31	64	2	1	1

GCL RED SOX — ROOKIE

GULF COAST LEAGUE

Batting	B-T	HT	WT	DOB	AVG	vLH	vRH	G	AB	R	H	2B	3B	HR	RBI	BB	HBP	SH	SF	SO	SB	CS	SLG	OBP
Blair, Carson	R-R	6-1	190	10-18-89	.210	.118	.224	39	124	15	26	8	0	2	20	16	0	0	7	46	0	1	.323	.286
Bonifacio, Juan	R-R	6-2	168	12-7-88	.208	.154	.219	30	77	9	16	5	1	1	5	2	1	0	19	2	1	.338	.274
Escobar, Leonel	R-R	5-10	175	9-4-90	.226	.125	.244	21	53	9	12	3	0	0	7	8	2	0	0	9	0	1	.283	.349
Fuentes, Reymond	L-L	6-0	160	2-12-91	.290	.190	.306	40	145	16	42	6	2	1	14	7	3	2	2	24	9	5	.379	.331
Garcia, Jose	R-R	5-11	165	4-23-91	.214	.292	.201	49	168	21	36	8	1	2	16	15	4	0	1	39	5	6	.310	.293
Head, Miles	R-R	6-0	215	5-2-91	.103	.000	.125	10	29	1	3	0	0	0	3	0	0	0	8	0	0	.103	.188
Jacobs, Brandon	R-R	5-11	240	12-8-90	.250	.000	.273	8	24	1	6	2	0	0	0	2	1	0	0	8	0	0	.333	.333
Lora, Eddie	B-L	6-2	215	3-21-89	.222	.091	.239	34	99	9	22	6	2	3	7	9	0	0	0	34	0	0	.414	.287
Moanaroa, Boss	L-R	6-1	200	7-12-91	.289	.200	.305	29	97	8	28	4	0	0	7	12	0	0	1	26	0	0	.330	.364
Moanaroa, Moko	L-L	6-0	215	12-22-89	.273	.100	.324	16	44	3	12	2	0	0	4	4	1	0	0	6	1	0	.318	.347
Ochoa, Ivan	R-R	5-9	160	12-16-82	.438	.167	.600	5	16	1	7	2	0	0	0	1	1	0	0	5	1	0	.563	.500
Peterson, Bryan	L-R	6-3	190	3-21-90	.214	.200	.215	20	70	6	15	3	1	1	9	10	0	0	0	8	3	1	.329	.313
Ramos, Roberto	B-R	5-10	160	9-4-88	.253	.091	.278	38	83	12	21	5	0	0	10	4	0	3	2	18	7	2	.313	.281
Reza, Aaron	R-R	5-7	180	6-25-85	.222	.000	.250	3	9	0	2	1	1	0	0	0	2	0	0	4	0	0	.556	.364
Roque, Kenneth	L-R	5-11	162	9-20-89	.317	.263	.327	40	123	17	39	9	5	2	23	17	0	0	0	23	5	4	.520	.400
Sallis, Jordan	B-R	5-8	165	7-2-88	.156	.333	.143	28	45	11	7	1	0	0	2	15	2	3	0	22	3	0	.178	.387
Sanchez, Felix	B-R	6-0	165	6-2-90	.246	.100	.271	40	138	17	34	7	3	1	11	9	0	2	1	39	10	4	.362	.291
Sanchez, Maykol	R-R	5-11	176	5-30-88	.300	.200	.314	17	40	3	12	0	0	0	3	5	1	0	0	10	0	0	.300	.391
Schwindenhammer, Seth	L-R	6-2	205	7-1-91	.194	.188	.194	36	124	11	24	6	2	0	10	8	2	0	1	41	0	1	.274	.252
Thompson, Jason	B-R	6-1	180	7-30-90	—	—	—	1	0	0	0	0	0	0	0	1	0	0	0	0	0	0	—	1.000
Vazquez, Christian	R-R	5-9	195	8-21-90	.278	.286	.276	10	36	5	10	5	0	0	7	4	1	0	0	7	0	0	.417	.366
Yockey, Tyler	L-L	6-1	196	10-16-89	.260	.231	.266	26	77	16	20	3	2	3	12	6	0	0	2	33	1	0	.455	.306

Pitching	B-T	HT	WT	DOB	W	L	ERA	G	GS	CG	SV	IP	H	R	ER	HR	BB	SO	AVG	vLH	vRH	K/9	BB/9
Angeloni, Chez	R-R	6-2	190	1-23-87	3	1	3.42	13	0	0	0	26	24	11	10	1	7	13	.226	.216	.232	4.44	2.39
Blackey, Jason	R-R	6-4	206	4-11-83	1	0	1.13	6	0	0	1	8	5	1	1	0	5	9	.200	.400	.067	10.13	5.63
Britton, Drake	L-L	6-2	200	5-22-89	0	0	0.00	4	4	0	0	7	2	0	0	0	4	11	.080	.000	.118	14.14	5.14
Byrd, Paul	R-R	6-1	190	12-3-70	0	1	5.14	2	2	0	0	7	10	8	4	1	0	3	.313	.286	.333	3.86	0.00
Cervenka, Hunter	L-L	6-0	225	1-3-90	2	2	4.84	11	5	0	1	22	16	14	12	0	26	18	.219	.000	.239	7.25	10.48
Consuegra, Randy	R-R	6-2	211	10-14-89	4	4	2.98	12	9	0	0	45	36	21	15	0	22	49	.216	.205	.223	9.73	4.37
Erasmus, Justin	R-R	5-10	175	1-22-90	2	2	2.05	15	0	0	5	26	20	8	6	0	11	25	.213	.275	.167	8.54	3.76
Flasher, Jordan	R-R	5-11	165	10-14-87	0	0	0.00	6	0	0	0	9	7	0	0	0	6	6	.219	.188	.250	5.79	5.79
Huijer, Swen	R-R	6-9	205	11-7-90	1	1	3.67	13	0	0	0	27	24	14	11	1	1	20	.235	.167	.273	6.67	0.33
Lennox, Michael	R-R	6-4	195	8-25-89	2	2	3.47	11	0	0	1	23	24	14	9	0	2	21	.247	.205	.286	8.10	0.77
Matsuzaka, Daisuke	R-R	6-0	185	9-13-80	0	0	0.00	1	1	0	0	3	1	0	0	0	0	4	.100	.000	.167	12.00	0.00
Mendez, Roman	R-R	6-2	180	7-25-90	2	3	1.99	12	10	0	0	50	33	11	11	1	8	47	.184	.219	.160	8.52	1.45
Mercadante, Dustin	R-R	6-7	230	10-24-88	0	1	5.40	14	0	0	3	15	17	12	9	0	8	8	.270	.120	.368	4.80	4.80
Rivera, Manuel	L-L	6-0	170	9-1-89	1	3	1.19	12	9	0	0	53	40	14	7	0	14	50	.206	.200	.208	8.49	2.38
Rosario, Charle	R-R	5-10	158	7-23-88	3	0	0.00	5	1	0	0	15	11	0	0	0	0	10	.200	.053	.278	6.00	0.00
Ruiz, Pete	R-R	6-3	205	8-21-87	3	2	3.83	11	6	0	0	47	51	23	20	2	15	33	.285	.267	.294	6.32	2.87
Stroup, Kyle	R-R	6-6	235	3-13-90	1	1	4.50	12	0	0	0	24	28	12	12	0	14	19	.301	.368	.255	7.13	5.25
Wasielewski, Richie	L-L	6-4	240	9-23-89	0	2	6.26	12	1	0	1	23	25	22	16	1	16	20	.278	.167	.295	7.83	6.26
Wilson, Tyler	L-R	6-5	192	12-24-89	0	2	5.63	6	5	0	0	8	7	5	5	1	4	11	.241	.231	.250	12.38	4.50
Wogee, Doug	B-R	6-3	190	9-9-88	1	0	0.00	3	0	0	0	3	2	0	0	0	0	1	.200	.200	.200	3.00	0.00

Fielding

Catcher	PCT	G	PO	A	E	DP	PB
Blair	.993	21	133	11	1	0	5
Escobar	.983	21	106	12	2	2	1
Sanchez	1.000	16	92	14	0	0	1
Vazquez	1.000	6	49	7	0	0	1

First Base	PCT	G	PO	A	E	DP
Lora	.988	29	238	9	3	26
Moanaroa	.988	29	242	12	3	19

Second Base	PCT	G	PO	A	E	DP
Ochoa	.947	5	6	12	1	1
Ramos	1.000	4	4	2	0	0
Roque	.977	30	41	84	3	18

	PCT	G	PO	A	E	DP
Sallis	.950	22	29	47	4	9
Third Base	**PCT**	**G**	**PO**	**A**	**E**	**DP**
Blair	.862	10	5	20	4	1
Head	.909	9	7	13	2	2
Ramos	.884	27	16	45	8	4
Roque	.810	9	5	12	4	0
Vazquez	.875	4	1	6	1	1
Shortstop	**PCT**	**G**	**PO**	**A**	**E**	**DP**
Garcia	.910	34	60	123	18	21
Kelly	.933	4	4	10	1	5
Ramos	.917	4	3	8	1	1
Reza	.917	2	1	10	1	1

	PCT	G	PO	A	E	DP
Sallis	1.000	1	0	3	0	2
Thompson	1.000	1	1	0	0	0
Outfield	**PCT**	**G**	**PO**	**A**	**E**	**DP**
Bonifacio	1.000	23	37	3	0	2
Fuentes	.981	30	51	2	1	0
Jacobs	1.000	2	1	0	0	0
Moanaroa	1.000	16	19	0	0	0
Peterson	.952	12	20	0	1	0
Sanchez	.971	34	65	1	2	0
Schwindenhammer	.938	34	42	3	3	0
Yockey	.973	22	31	5	1	1

DSL RED SOX   ROOKIE

DOMINICAN SUMMER LEAGUE

Batting	B-T	HT	WT	DOB	AVG	vLH	vRH	G	AB	R	H	2B	3B	HR	RBI	BB	HBP	SH	SF	SO	SB	CS	SLG	OBP
Chourio, Pedro	R-R	6-2	211	3-13-90	.258	.317	.246	61	236	28	61	12	1	5	38	27	12	0	1	51	4	4	.381	.362
De La Cruz, Keury	L-L	5-11	170	11-28-91	.259	.200	.270	67	251	31	65	16	4	3	50	42	4	0	5	43	13	8	.390	.368
Doran, Curtney	R-R	6-0	180	4-30-92	.214	.368	.178	60	201	46	43	10	2	2	28	47	5	0	3	60	21	7	.313	.371
Escobar, Leonel	R-R	5-10	175	9-4-90	.333	.000	.400	6	24	5	8	4	0	0	4	2	0	0	0	0	0	0	.500	.385
Gonzalez, Aly	R-R	6-1	185	2-9-91	.223	.292	.206	36	121	19	27	3	1	0	15	23	1	0	0	20	0	0	.264	.352
Gonzalez, Pedro	L-L	6-0	185	3-17-90	.178	.000	.195	14	45	7	8	4	1	0	8	5	0	0	1	16	0	1	.311	.255
Guerrero, Dreily	B-R	5-11	162	10-12-90	.253	.250	.253	51	174	28	44	1	5	0	19	32	1	1	1	38	12	5	.316	.370
Gutierrez, Javier	R-R	6-0	170	8-26-90	.195	.100	.209	30	77	14	15	3	1	2	9	14	5	1	2	22	3	0	.338	.347
Menses, Heiker	R-R	5-9	160	7-1-91	.199	.194	.200	65	216	48	43	2	6	1	17	34	13	4	1	68	25	5	.278	.341
Perez, Oscar	R-R	6-1	185	11-9-91	.210	.226	.207	52	195	26	41	11	1	1	23	17	5	0	1	41	4	0	.292	.289
Pinto, Derwin	R-R	5-10	196	2-20-90	.200	.467	.156	30	105	16	21	2	1	0	14	14	1	2	1	25	1	2	.238	.298
Ruiz, Derward	L-R	5-9	190	11-11-91	.286	.167	.302	26	49	12	14	1	0	0	5	10	0	0	0	9	5	2	.306	.407
Soto, Alfredo	R-R	6-0	190	10-23-91	.233	.212	.237	52	189	30	44	11	1	5	30	21	7	0	0	50	1	0	.381	.332
Ugas, Juan	R-R	6-0	160	3-21-80	.203	.048	.228	48	148	20	30	5	0	0	9	27	5	3	1	37	4	0	.236	.343
Urena, Lewis	R-R	5-8	145	5-6-91	.246	.289	.235	43	179	21	44	1	1	1	27	52	4	5	2	35	22	6	.353	.390

Pitching	B-T	HT	WT	DOB	W	L	ERA	G	GS	CG	SV	IP	H	R	ER	HR	BB	SO	AVG	vLH	vRH	K/9	BB/9
Alvarado, Antony	R-R	6-2	175	3-31-90	0	0	0.00	2	0	0	0	2	3	1	0	0	1	3	.375	.000	.429	13.50	4.50
Bastardo, Luis	R-R	6-1	165	5-14-90	4	2	4.17	19	0	0	5	37	38	26	17	2	22	27	.270	.226	.282	6.63	5.40
Cuevas, William	R-R	6-0	160	10-14-90	4	1	3.17	18	0	0	3	48	44	19	17	1	11	36	.246	.259	.240	6.70	2.05
Diaz, Luis	R-R	6-3	210	4-9-92	0	3	3.75	15	2	0	2	36	36	25	15	0	18	22	.255	.273	.250	5.50	4.50
Dilon, Danny	R-R	6-1	170	7-30-89	2	2	3.82	16	0	0	0	33	34	18	14	1	16	18	.270	.275	.267	4.91	4.36
Garcia, Samuel	R-R	5-10	150	11-6-90	0	0	8.59	13	0	0	1	15	21	14	14	0	11	10	.339	.500	.292	6.14	6.75
Jimenez, Javier	R-R	6-3	143	7-28-89	0	0	9.00	1	0	0	0	1	1	1	1	0	0	0	.250	—	.250	0.00	4.38
Juan, Ronaldo	R-R	6-1	170	1-15-90	5	2	5.11	15	0	0	1	37	44	27	21	1	18	19	.310	.333	.299	4.62	4.38
Lastreto, Nestor	L-L	6-0	160	9-28-89	7	2	3.00	15	15	1	0	66	65	27	22	0	19	55	.259	.263	.259	7.50	2.59
Mateo, Alexander	R-R	5-11	165	4-10-91	1	0	0.90	5	0	0	0	10	10	6	1	0	6	5	.238	.308	.207	4.50	5.40
Medina, Eduardo	R-R	6-0	170	2-24-92	2	0	7.71	7	0	0	0	9	13	9	8	0	9	4	.310	.182	.355	3.86	8.68
Ortega, Yunior	R-R	5-11	170	8-10-91	5	1	1.84	13	13	0	0	64	50	20	13	2	15	58	.206	.172	.216	8.20	2.12
Reyes, Ernesto	L-L	6-0	190	7-31-90	1	2	5.13	15	0	0	5	26	25	17	15	4	19	22	.260	.000	.272	7.52	6.49
Rodriguez, Josue	R-R	6-5	165	12-12-88	3	1	1.55	15	12	0	1	64	37	15	11	0	30	78	.172	.207	.159	11.03	4.24
Santana, Wilfi	R-R	6-0	185	11-8-88	4	5	3.54	19	1	0	5	48	52	25	19	1	11	32	.286	.377	.248	5.96	2.05
Taveras, Francisco	L-L	6-0	180	5-23-90	3	2	1.71	13	13	0	0	58	39	13	11	0	29	71	.190	.150	.195	11.02	4.50
Vellette, Raynel	R-R	6-2	165	6-10-91	3	2	2.47	14	13	0	0	58	40	20	16	3	28	48	.200	.204	.199	7.41	4.32

Fielding

Catcher	PCT	G	PO	A	E	DP	PB
Escobar	1.000	4	27	2	0	1	0
Gonzalez	1.000	5	30	3	0	0	2
Perez	.984	46	314	61	6	2	11
Pinto	.994	19	132	37	1	1	1

First Base	PCT	G	PO	A	E	DP
Chourio	.986	59	516	33	8	44
Gonzalez	1.000	7	48	1	0	2
Gonzalez	1.000	5	39	1	0	3

Second Base	PCT	G	PO	A	E	DP
Guerrero	1.000	3	5	6	0	1

	PCT	G	PO	A	E	DP
Ruiz	.897	11	15	20	4	7
Urena	.975	63	127	144	7	22
Third Base	**PCT**	**G**	**PO**	**A**	**E**	**DP**
Gonzalez	.893	13	15	35	6	1
Guerrero	.815	10	4	18	5	1
Ugas	.907	48	40	106	15	8
Urena	—	2	0	0	0	0
Shortstop	**PCT**	**G**	**PO**	**A**	**E**	**DP**
Guerrero	1.000	2	6	7	0	3
Menses	.920	63	130	192	28	36
Ruiz	.833	8	11	14	5	1

Outfield	PCT	G	PO	A	E	DP
Chourio	1.000	1	1	0	0	0
De La Cruz	.971	66	127	6	4	2
Doran	.941	59	105	7	7	0
Gonzalez	1.000	1	2	0	0	0
Gonzalez	1.000	6	5	0	0	0
Guerrero	.964	24	25	2	1	1
Gutierrez	.926	26	23	2	2	0
Pinto	1.000	1	3	1	0	0
Soto	.985	36	60	7	1	0
Urena	1.000	1	0	1	0	0

Chicago Cubs

SEASON IN A SENTENCE: In the whole scope of Cubs history, a third straight winning season could be considered an accomplishment, but finishing 7½ games out in a mediocre National League Central was a major disappointment for a team with the third-highest payroll in baseball and significant playoff aspirations.

HIGH POINT: After being acquired from the Pirates in a trade deadline deal, lefthander Tom Gorzelanny won his Cubs debut (and chipped in an RBI single as well) in Cincinnati on Aug. 4, beating the Reds 6-3, keeping the Cubs in first place in the NL Central before they dropped seven of eight and ceded the division to the Cardinals.

LOW POINT: Just a month after being in first place in their division, the Cubs dropped a 6-2 decision to the Mets on Sept. 4 to fall just one game above .500 and six games back in the wild card race. Chicago recovered slightly to finish five games above .500 but never seriously challenged for the postseason again.

NOTABLE ROOKIES: With an experienced veteran team, the Cubs weren't counting on rookies in any major roles, but they wound up getting a surprise contribution from 27-year-old righthander Randy Wells. Wells, who was selected by the Blue Jays in the 2007 major league Rule 5 draft but was later returned to the Cubs, led the team in ERA (and finished 10th in the NL) with a 12-10, 3.05 record. Jake Fox and Micah Hoffpauir proved to be useful bats off the bench.

KEY TRANSACTIONS: Chicago thought it was addressing a key weakness in its mostly right-handed lineup when it signed switch-hitting outfielder Milton Bradley as a free agent, but the deal proved disastrous as Bradley was unproductive on the field and destructive off it, upsetting the team's clubhouse chemistry and getting suspended in late September for the balance of the season. The team made a couple of minor deadline deals in July, getting second baseman Jeff Baker from the Rockies and lefthanders Gorzelanny and John Grabow from the Pirates.

DOWN ON THE FARM: After a period of decline marked by weak drafts and the departure of top prospects in trades for veterans, things were looking up with the performances of first-round picks Josh Vitters (2007) and Brett Jackson (2009) in the lower minors. Most of Chicago's best farmhands are at least a couple of years away from making an impact in the major leagues.

OPENING DAY PAYROLL: $134,809,000

PLAYERS OF THE YEAR

MAJOR LEAGUE
Derrek Lee
1b
.306/.393/.579
3rd in NL in slugging,
4th in OPS (.972)

MINOR LEAGUE
Starlin Castro
ss
(High A/AA)
.299/.342/.392
23 2B, 28 SB

ORGANIZATION LEADERS

BATTING		*Minimum 250 at-bats
MAJORS		
*AVG	Derrek Lee	.306
*OPS	Derrek Lee	.972
HR	Derrek Lee	35
RBI	Derrek Lee	111
MINORS		
*AVG	Harrison, Josh, Peoria/Daytona	.327
R	Burke, Kyler, Peoria	93
H	Ridling, Rebel, Peoria	166
TB	Ridling, Rebel, Peoria	250
2B	Burke, Kyler, Peoria	43
3B	Fuld, Sam, Iowa	10
HR	Flaherty, Ryan, Peoria	20
RBI	Ridling, Rebel, Peoria	97
BB	Burke, Kyler, Peoria	78
SO	Lake, Junior, Peoria	138
SB	Campana, Tony, Peoria/Daytona	66
*OBP	Burke, Kyler, Peoria	.405
*SLG	Burke, Kyler, Peoria	.505

PITCHING		†Minimum 75 innings
MAJORS		
W	Ted Lilly	12
ERA	Randy Wells	3.05
SO	Ryan Dempster	172
MINORS		
W	Coleman, Casey, Tennessee	14
L	Atkins, Mitch, Iowa	12
†ERA	Carpenter, Chris, Peoria/Daytona/Tenn.	2.82
G	Ruhlman, Jayson, Iowa/Tennessee	59
	Schlitter, Brian, Tennessee	59
GS	Four tied at	27
SV	Parker, Blake, Tennessee/Iowa	25
IP	Coleman, Casey, Tennessee	149
BB	Archer, Christopher, Peoria	66
SO	Atkins, Mitch, Iowa	127
	Jackson, Jay, Tennessee/Daytona/Iowa	127
†AVG	Carpenter, Chris, Peoria/Daytona/Tenn.	.210

General Manager: Jim Hendry. **Farm Director:** Oneri Fleita. **Scouting Director:** Tim Wilken.

Class	Team	League	W	L	PCT	Finish*	Manager(s)
Majors	Chicago Cubs	National	83	78	.516	8th (16)	Lou Piniella
Triple-A	Iowa Cubs	Pacific Coast	72	72	.500	9th (16)	Bobby Dickerson
Double-A	Tennessee Smokies	Southern	71	69	.507	3rd (10)	Ryne Sandberg
High A	Daytona Cubs	Florida State	64	71	.474	9th (12)	Buddy Bailey
Low A	Peoria Chiefs	Midwest	81	57	.587	2nd (14)	Marty Pevey
Short-season	Boise Hawks	Northwest	34	42	.447	t-6th (8)	Casey Kopitzke
Rookie	AZL Cubs	Arizona	29	27	.518	4th (11)	Juan Cabreja
Overall 2009 Minor League Record			351	338	.509	12th (30)	

*Finish in overall standings (No. of teams in league). †League champion.

ORGANIZATION STATISTICS

CHICAGO CUBS

NATIONAL LEAGUE

Batting	B-T	HT	WT	DOB	AVG	vLH	vRH	G	AB	R	H	2B	3B	HR	RBI	BB	HBP	SH	SF	SO	SB	CS	SLG	OBP
Baker, Jeff	R-R	6-2	210	6-21-81	.305	.308	.305	69	203	27	62	15	1	4	21	17	2	0	2	46	0	0	.448	.362
2-team total (12 Colorado)					.288	—	—	81	226	27	65	15	2	4	24	18	2	0	2	53	1	0	.425	.343
Blanco, Andres	B-R	5-10	190	4-11-84	.252	.250	.253	53	123	15	31	8	0	1	12	8	1	6	0	14	0	2	.341	.303
Bradley, Milton	B-R	6-0	225	4-15-78	.257	.333	.231	124	393	61	101	17	1	12	40	66	11	2	1	95	2	3	.397	.378
Colvin, Tyler	L-L	6-3	190	9-5-85	.176	.000	.214	6	17	1	3	0	0	0	2	2	0	0	1	5	0	0	.176	.250
Fontenot, Mike	L-R	5-8	170	6-9-80	.236	.212	.240	135	377	38	89	22	2	9	43	35	2	0	5	83	4	1	.377	.301
Fox, Jake	R-R	6-0	210	7-20-82	.259	.250	.263	82	216	23	56	12	0	11	44	14	5	0	6	47	0	0	.468	.311
Freel, Ryan	R-R	5-9	180	3-8-76	.143	.167	.125	14	28	1	4	0	0	0	1	2	1	1	0	7	1	0	.143	.226
Fukudome, Kosuke	L-R	6-0	185	4-26-77	.259	.164	.270	146	499	79	129	38	5	11	54	93	3	3	5	112	6	10	.421	.375
Fuld, Sam	L-L	5-10	185	11-20-81	.299	.308	.296	65	97	17	29	6	1	1	2	17	1	0	0	10	2	1	.412	.409
Gathright, Joey	L-R	5-10	185	4-27-81	.214	.000	.231	20	14	2	3	0	0	0	0	1	0	0	0	6	1	2	.214	.267
Hill, Koyie	B-R	6-0	190	3-9-79	.237	.256	.233	83	253	26	60	12	2	2	24	27	1	2	1	78	0	0	.324	.312
Hoffpauir, Micah	L-L	6-3	215	3-1-80	.239	.172	.249	105	234	28	56	12	1	10	35	20	1	0	2	46	1	0	.427	.300
Johnson, Reed	R-R	5-10	180	12-8-76	.255	.324	.206	65	165	23	42	10	2	4	22	13	6	1	1	27	2	1	.412	.330
Lee, Derrek	R-R	6-5	245	9-6-75	.306	.300	.308	141	532	91	163	36	2	35	111	76	3	0	4	109	1	0	.579	.393
Miles, Aaron	B-R	5-8	180	12-15-76	.185	.206	.179	74	157	17	29	7	1	0	5	8	0	5	0	21	3	0	.242	.224
Ramirez, Aramis	R-R	6-1	215	6-25-78	.317	.350	.312	82	306	46	97	14	1	15	65	28	8	0	0	43	2	1	.516	.389
Scales, Bobby	B-R	6-0	185	10-4-77	.242	.208	.250	51	124	15	30	8	2	3	15	11	2	0	1	32	0	0	.411	.312
Soriano, Alfonso	R-R	6-1	180	1-7-76	.241	.184	.256	117	477	64	115	25	1	20	55	40	3	0	2	118	9	2	.423	.303
Soto, Geovany	R-R	6-1	225	1-20-83	.218	.205	.221	102	331	27	72	19	1	11	47	50	3	0	5	77	1	0	.381	.321
Taguchi, So	R-R	5-10	170	7-2-69	.273	.222	.500	6	11	1	3	1	0	0	1	0	0	0	0	4	0	0	.364	.333
Theriot, Ryan	R-R	5-11	175	12-7-79	.284	.306	.279	154	602	81	171	20	5	7	54	51	6	13	5	93	21	10	.369	.343

Pitching	B-T	HT	WT	DOB	W	L	ERA	G	GS	CG	SV	IP	H	R	ER	HR	BB	SO	AVG	vLH	vRH	K/9	BB/9
Ascanio, Jose	R-R	6-0	170	5-2-85	0	1	3.52	14	0	0	0	15	18	6	6	1	9	18	.295	.476	.200	10.57	5.28
2-team total (2 Pittsburgh)					0	2	4.00	16	0	0	0	18	22	8	8	1	9	20	—	—	—	10.00	4.50
Atkins, Mitch	R-R	6-3	230	10-1-85	0	0	0.00	2	0	0	0	2	1	0	0	0	0	0	.143	.000	.250	0.00	0.00
Berg, Justin	R-R	6-3	230	6-7-84	0	0	0.75	11	0	0	0	12	10	1	1	0	1	7	.227	.263	.200	5.25	0.75
Caridad, Esmailin	R-R	5-10	195	10-28-83	1	0	1.40	14	0	0	0	19	15	4	3	0	3	17	.221	.194	.243	7.91	1.40
Cotts, Neal	L-L	6-1	200	3-25-80	0	2	7.36	19	0	0	0	11	14	9	9	3	9	9	.311	.318	.304	7.36	7.36
Dempster, Ryan	R-R	6-2	215	5-3-77	11	9	3.65	31	31	1	0	200	196	94	81	22	65	172	.260	.281	.241	7.74	2.93
Fox, Chad	R-R	6-3	215	9-3-70	0	0	135.00	2	0	0	0	0	2	5	5	0	3	0	.667	1.000	.500	0.00	81.00
Gorzelanny, Tom	L-L	6-2	200	7-12-82	4	2	5.63	13	7	0	0	38	39	25	24	6	13	40	.262	.226	.271	9.39	3.05
2-team total (9 Pittsburgh)					7	3	5.55	22	7	0	0	47	45	30	29	6	17	47	—	—	—	9.00	3.26
Grabow, John	L-L	6-2	205	11-4-78	0	0	3.24	30	0	0	0	25	19	9	9	1	12	16	.209	.133	.246	5.76	4.32
2-team total (45 Pittsburgh)					3	0	3.36	75	0	0	0	72	62	28	27	5	40	57	—	—	—	7.09	4.98
Gregg, Kevin	R-R	6-6	240	6-20-78	5	6	4.72	72	0	0	23	69	60	38	36	13	30	71	.229	.195	.257	9.31	3.93
Guzman, Angel	R-R	6-3	200	12-14-81	3	3	2.95	55	0	0	1	61	41	20	20	8	23	47	.192	.189	.194	6.93	3.39
Harden, Rich	L-R	6-1	195	11-30-81	9	9	4.09	26	26	0	0	141	122	74	64	23	67	171	.234	.251	.220	10.91	4.28
Hart, Kevin	R-R	6-4	220	12-29-82	3	1	2.60	8	4	0	0	28	23	8	8	3	18	13	.242	.333	.179	4.23	5.86
2-team total (10 Pittsburgh)					4	9	5.44	18	14	0	0	81	97	55	49	11	44	52	—	—	—	5.78	4.89
Heilman, Aaron	R-R	6-5	225	11-12-78	4	4	4.11	70	0	0	1	72	68	34	33	9	34	65	.257	.210	.288	8.09	4.23
Lilly, Ted	L-L	6-1	190	1-4-76	12	9	3.10	27	27	0	0	177	151	66	61	22	36	151	.230	.219	.233	7.68	1.83
Marmol, Carlos	R-R	6-2	180	10-14-82	2	4	3.41	79	0	0	15	74	43	29	28	2	65	93	.170	.136	.200	11.31	7.91
Marshall, Sean	L-L	6-7	220	8-30-82	3	7	4.32	55	9	1	0	85	91	43	41	10	32	68	.274	.243	.289	7.17	3.38
Patton, David	R-R	6-3	205	5-18-84	3	1	6.83	20	0	0	0	28	31	22	21	4	19	23	.279	.243	.297	7.48	6.18
Samardzija, Jeff	R-R	6-5	220	1-23-85	1	3	7.53	20	2	0	0	35	46	29	29	7	15	21	.329	.361	.304	5.45	3.89
Stevens, Jeff	R-R	6-2	205	9-5-83	1	0	7.11	11	0	0	0	13	14	10	10	2	8	9	.286	.318	.259	6.39	5.68
Vizcaino, Luis	R-R	5-11	210	8-6-74	0	0	0.00	4	0	0	0	4	2	0	0	0	3	3	.154	.000	.182	7.36	0.00
Waddell, Jason	R-L	6-2	200	6-11-81	0	0	5.40	3	0	0	0	2	3	1	1	0	0	2	.375	.333	.500	10.80	0.00
Wells, Randy	R-R	6-3	230	8-28-82	12	10	3.05	27	27	0	0	165	165	67	56	14	46	104	.261	.310	.221	5.66	2.50
Zambrano, Carlos	B-R	6-5	255	6-1-81	9	7	3.77	28	28	1	0	169	155	78	71	10	78	152	.246	.258	.235	8.08	4.15

Fielding

Catcher	PCT	G	PO	A	E	DP	PB
Fox	1.000	3	6	1	0	0	0
Hill	.995	79	573	46	3	8	2
Soto	.994	96	720	50	5	9	3

First Base	PCT	G	PO	A	E	DP
Baker	1.000	2	8	0	0	2
Fox	.953	7	40	1	2	3
Hoffpauir	.993	27	136	10	1	11
Lee	.995	139	1088	94	6	110

Second Base	PCT	G	PO	A	E	DP
Baker	.995	49	103	116	1	33
Blanco	1.000	40	52	71	0	20
Fontenot	.989	70	112	149	3	36
Miles	.986	35	71	69	2	21
Scales	.971	11	14	19	1	4

	PCT	G	PO	A	E	DP
Soriano	—	2	0	0	0	0
Third Base	PCT	G	PO	A	E	DP
Baker	.960	17	6	18	1	0
Fontenot	.963	50	26	77	4	7
Fox	.958	27	8	38	2	2
Freel	.923	7	2	10	1	1
Hill	—	1	0	0	0	0
Miles	1.000	4	1	1	0	0
Ramirez	.948	79	45	137	10	14
Scales	.944	8	6	11	1	1
Soriano	—	1	0	0	0	0

Shortstop	PCT	G	PO	A	E	DP
Blanco	.939	15	15	31	3	7
Miles	1.000	8	7	13	0	2
Theriot	.976	151	206	411	15	90

Outfield	PCT	G	PO	A	E	DP
Bradley	.985	109	197	5	3	4
Colvin	1.000	6	16	0	0	0
Fox	.925	26	36	1	3	0
Freel	1.000	3	1	0	0	0
Fukudome	.994	140	305	5	2	2
Fuld	.985	53	65	1	1	0
Gathright	1.000	11	6	0	0	0
Hoffpauir	.982	36	55	1	1	0
Johnson	.989	54	83	3	1	1
Marshall	1.000	1	0	0	0	0
Scales	1.000	20	35	0	0	0
Soriano	.950	116	201	7	11	2
Taguchi	1.000	3	2	1	0	0

IOWA CUBS — TRIPLE-A

PACIFIC COAST LEAGUE

Batting	B-T	HT	WT	DOB	AVG	vLH	vRH	G	AB	R	H	2B	3B	HR	RBI	BB	HBP	SH	SF	SO	SB	CS	SLG	OBP
Barney, Darwin	R-R	5-10	180	11-8-85	.264	.322	.242	63	212	25	56	12	1	0	17	13	0	2	2	32	4	1	.330	.304
Blanco, Andres	B-R	5-10	190	4-11-84	.304	.263	.318	64	230	30	70	17	2	6	29	17	3	3	5	28	6	1	.474	.353
Camp, Matt	L-R	6-0	175	5-29-84	.282	.279	.282	99	348	47	98	13	1	2	44	21	3	5	3	43	18	3	.342	.325
Clevenger, Steve	L-R	6-0	195	4-5-86	.265	.301	.248	68	230	21	61	12	1	0	26	15	1	2	3	31	4	3	.326	.309
Craig, Matt	B-R	6-3	215	4-16-81	.269	.298	.257	59	197	27	53	14	0	4	27	16	2	0	1	34	1	0	.401	.329
2-team total (31 New Orleans)					.264	—	—	90	292	39	77	20	0	7	35	28	2	0	2	53	1	0	.404	.330
Deeds, Doug	L-L	6-2	195	6-2-81	.257	.195	.276	52	175	25	45	10	2	4	19	10	2	1	1	41	5	2	.406	.303
Dubois, Jason	R-R	6-5	220	3-26-79	.302	.306	.299	91	275	38	83	20	1	11	50	32	9	0	2	77	2	1	.502	.390
Fox, Jake	R-R	6-0	210	7-20-82	.409	.356	.429	45	164	44	67	14	3	17	53	21	8	0	1	31	2	1	.841	.495
Freel, Ryan	R-R	5-9	180	3-8-76	.417	.333	.429	7	24	6	10	4	0	0	4	3	1	0	0	4	5	1	.583	.500
2-team total (2 Oklahoma City)					.400	—	—	9	30	6	12	4	0	0	5	3	2	0	0	6	5	1	.533	.486
Fuld, Sam	L-L	5-10	185	11-20-81	.284	.318	.267	84	328	62	93	17	10	2	33	38	1	1	2	24	23	5	.415	.358
2-team total (16 Albuquerque)					.268	—	—	105	340	39	91	29	3	5	40	36	5	0	5	87	5	2	.415	.342
Hoffpauir, Micah	L-L	6-3	215	3-1-80	.217	.333	.161	23	83	12	18	4	0	3	13	6	0	0	1	12	2	0	.373	.267
Johnson, Mark	L-R	6-0	200	9-12-75	.169	.231	.155	22	71	6	12	0	1	0	4	8	3	0	0	14	2	2	.197	.280
Machado, Anderson	B-R	6-0	185	1-25-81	.172	.132	.231	28	64	7	11	2	0	0	6	13	0	4	2	17	5	1	.203	.304
Macias, David	B-R	5-9	175	3-7-86	.226	.148	.286	22	62	7	14	1	0	0	3	4	0	2	0	6	1	0	.242	.273
Matulia, Matt	B-R	6-0	185	5-24-84	.150	.143	.152	26	40	6	6	3	1	1	2	3	0	0	0	10	0	0	.350	.209
Miles, Aaron	B-R	5-8	180	12-15-76	.253	.286	.231	21	87	8	22	4	0	0	8	2	0	1	1	14	1	2	.299	.267
Reynolds, Kyle	L-R	6-2	190	9-1-83	.220	.154	.243	19	50	7	11	3	0	1	3	2	0	1	0	14	3	0	.340	.250
Rivas, Luis	R-R	5-11	190	8-30-79	.236	.315	.167	63	191	23	45	14	2	1	16	20	1	2	2	18	3	0	.346	.308
Robinson, Chris	R-R	6-0	200	5-12-84	.326	.306	.337	91	310	37	101	22	3	2	48	13	0	1	7	44	9	3	.435	.345
Robnett, Richie	L-L	5-10	210	9-17-83	.143	.167	.133	8	21	3	3	0	2	0	1	2	0	0	0	6	0	1	.333	.217
Scales, Bobby	B-R	6-0	185	10-4-77	.278	.304	.265	91	306	41	85	15	1	5	39	46	5	1	2	61	8	8	.382	.379
Snyder, Brad	L-L	6-3	200	5-25-82	.278	.290	.274	69	237	39	66	16	3	14	44	20	1	0	2	68	10	4	.549	.335
Spears, Nate	L-R	5-11	165	5-3-85	.253	.241	.256	128	368	48	93	20	4	2	37	35	2	4	2	43	6	5	.345	.319
Taguchi, So	R-R	5-10	170	7-2-69	.248	.248	.248	85	258	37	64	8	1	4	29	32	9	1	4	32	4	4	.333	.347

Pitching	B-T	HT	WT	DOB	W	L	ERA	G	GS	CG	SV	IP	H	R	ER	HR	BB	SO	AVG	vLH	vRH	K/9	BB/9
Ascanio, Jose	R-R	6-0	170	5-2-85	2	4	3.16	12	12	0	0	51	47	23	18	1	18	47	.247	.316	.202	8.24	3.16
Astacio, Ezequiel	R-R	6-3	200	11-4-79	0	1	10.29	3	1	0	0	7	13	8	8	2	3	4	.394	.474	.286	5.14	3.86
Atkins, Mitch	R-R	6-3	230	10-1-85	8	12	6.58	27	27	1	0	146	164	113	107	26	52	127	.284	.282	.285	7.81	3.20
Berg, Justin	R-R	6-3	200	6-7-84	6	2	2.43	37	0	0	0	56	41	17	15	2	29	35	.205	.250	.180	5.66	4.69
Cales, David	R-R	5-11	200	7-27-87	0	0	5.40	1	0	0	0	2	4	5	1	2	2	2	.444	.333	.500	10.80	10.80
Caridad, Esmailin	R-R	5-10	195	10-28-83	5	10	4.17	25	25	0	0	132	139	71	61	17	46	114	.271	.336	.223	7.79	3.14
Cotts, Neal	L-L	6-1	200	3-25-80	1	1	2.84	12	0	0	1	13	7	4	4	1	6	11	.159	.071	.200	7.82	4.26
Estrada, Jesse	R-R	6-8	260	10-27-83	1	1	10.50	13	0	0	0	18	28	22	21	4	6	5	.354	.333	.364	2.50	3.00
Fossum, Casey	L-L	6-1	160	1-6-78	6	4	4.12	13	12	0	0	68	59	32	31	8	22	70	.231	.240	.228	9.31	2.93
Fox, Chad	R-R	6-3	215	9-3-70	1	0	1.59	11	0	0	2	11	8	3	2	0	3	10	.211	.100	.250	7.94	2.38
Gaub, John	R-L	6-2	200	4-28-85	1	1	1.72	26	0	0	1	31	17	6	6	1	16	40	.157	.211	.129	11.49	4.60
Guzman, Angel	R-R	6-3	200	12-14-81	0	0	0.00	1	1	0	0	1	1	0	0	0	0	1	.200	.333	.000	6.75	6.75
Harden, Rich	L-R	6-1	195	11-30-81	0	0	1.93	1	1	0	0	5	3	2	1	0	2	6	.176	.000	.250	11.57	3.86
Hart, Kevin	R-R	6-4	220	12-29-82	3	3	3.10	22	6	0	3	52	39	20	18	5	20	57	.206	.203	.209	9.80	3.44
Jackson, Jay	R-R	6-1	195	10-27-87	1	0	1.50	1	1	0	0	6	5	1	1	1	3	6	.227	.200	.250	6.00	4.50
Lambert, Casey	L-L	5-11	175	12-11-85	1	1	7.07	7	1	0	0	14	20	12	11	2	7	10	.339	.227	.405	6.43	4.50
Mathes, J.R.	L-L	6-3	210	11-9-81	12	8	3.62	26	21	0	0	129	150	59	52	11	14	51	.291	.271	.296	3.55	0.97
Papelbon, Jeremy	R-L	6-1	205	6-24-83	0	1	9.64	2	1	0	0	5	10	5	5	0	2	2	.417	.333	.444	3.86	3.86
Parker, Blake	R-R	6-3	225	6-19-85	2	3	3.00	45	0	0	22	51	36	20	17	3	27	58	.196	.238	.160	10.24	4.76
Patton, David	R-R	6-3	205	5-18-84	1	1	5.14	5	1	0	0	7	5	4	4	1	2	7	.227	.600	.118	5.14	9.00
Perkins, Vince	L-R	6-5	240	9-27-81	6	2	3.48	45	0	0	3	75	73	32	29	2	50	58	.258	.290	.239	6.96	6.00
Reinhard, Greg	L-R	6-2	215	8-11-83	2	4	5.30	42	5	0	0	73	75	43	43	8	34	89	.268	.235	.287	10.97	4.19
Ruhlman, Jayson	L-L	6-1	180	8-17-84	0	0	8.03	12	0	0	0	12	23	12	11	2	4	9	.404	.438	.390	6.57	2.92

Name	B-T	HT	WT	DOB	W	L	ERA	G	GS	CG	SV	IP	H	R	ER	HR	BB	SO	AVG	vLH	vRH	K/9	BB/9
Russell, James	L-L	6-4	205	1-8-86	3	3	3.43	26	7	0	0	66	71	25	25	6	19	46	.269	.231	.285	6.30	2.60
Ryan, B.J.	L-L	6-5	250	12-28-75	0	0	0.00	5	0	0	0	6	0	0	0	0	5	4	.000	.000	.000	6.35	7.94
Samardzija, Jeff	R-R	6-5	220	1-23-85	6	6	4.35	18	17	1	0	89	98	46	43	12	27	71	.283	.308	.270	7.18	2.73
Stevens, Jeff	R-R	6-2	205	9-5-83	1	3	2.03	42	0	0	2	58	35	15	13	1	25	61	.175	.176	.174	9.52	3.90
Waddell, Jason	R-L	6-2	200	6-11-81	0	1	3.25	26	0	0	0	28	26	12	10	1	8	20	.248	.325	.200	6.51	2.60
Wells, Randy	R-R	6-3	230	8-28-82	3	0	2.77	5	5	0	0	26	19	8	8	1	7	21	.204	.257	.172	7.27	2.42
Williamson, Hank	R-R	6-5	233	11-1-85	0	0	4.70	3	0	0	0	8	6	5	4	0	4	5	.222	.333	.133	5.87	4.70

Fielding

Catcher	PCT	G	PO	A	E	DP	PB
Clevenger	.984	51	362	18	6	2	5
Fox	1.000	2	17	2	0	1	2
Johnson	.986	20	131	12	2	1	3
Robinson	.998	75	551	39	1	5	5

First Base	PCT	G	PO	A	E	DP
Clevenger	1.000	12	78	3	0	7
Craig	.997	37	289	14	1	23
Deeds	1.000	24	165	10	0	14
Dubois	1.000	6	20	1	0	1
Fox	.989	33	251	22	3	23
Hoffpauir	.984	20	105	15	2	10
Matulia	1.000	2	8	2	0	1
Reynolds	1.000	3	6	0	0	1
Rivas	.889	2	8	0	1	0
Robinson	1.000	4	25	2	0	1
Scales	1.000	31	202	18	0	24
Spears	1.000	1	1	0	0	1

Second Base	PCT	G	PO	A	E	DP
Barney	.947	11	16	20	2	4
Blanco	1.000	1	0	6	0	3
Camp	.957	13	19	26	2	10

	PCT	G	PO	A	E	DP
Freel	1.000	1	0	3	0	0
Machado	1.000	1	2	0	0	0
Macias	1.000	20	51	42	0	9
Matulia	.727	5	3	5	3	1
Miles	.982	12	23	31	1	5
Rivas	.990	53	90	108	2	20
Scales	.982	15	21	34	1	7
Spears	.988	42	73	93	2	28

Third Base	PCT	G	PO	A	E	DP
Blanco	.950	8	3	16	1	1
Camp	.920	25	19	27	4	1
Clevenger	1.000	1	0	1	0	0
Craig	1.000	2	2	1	0	0
Fox	1.000	1	0	1	0	0
Freel	1.000	5	2	5	0	0
Matulia	1.000	2	0	1	0	1
Miles	.933	7	5	9	1	0
Reynolds	.927	13	6	32	3	2
Rivas	.917	4	2	9	1	1
Scales	.928	47	24	79	8	9
Spears	.939	62	37	87	8	10

Shortstop	PCT	G	PO	A	E	DP
Barney	.963	51	81	151	9	28
Blanco	.968	55	71	143	7	25
Camp	.963	8	10	16	1	3
Machado	.942	24	26	55	5	16
Matulia	1.000	1	0	1	0	1
Miles	.769	4	2	8	3	3
Rivas	.500	1	0	1	1	0
Spears	.952	15	9	31	2	6

Outfield	PCT	G	PO	A	E	DP
Camp	1.000	59	126	7	0	2
Deeds	1.000	31	34	1	0	0
Dubois	.938	57	87	3	6	0
Fox	1.000	10	8	0	0	0
Freel	1.000	2	1	0	0	0
Fuld	.981	81	195	11	4	2
Griffin	.982	78	108	3	2	0
Hoffpauir	1.000	8	14	2	0	0
Robnett	.909	6	10	0	1	0
Scales	1.000	13	17	0	0	0
Snyder	.985	68	129	2	2	0
Taguchi	1.000	78	123	7	0	1

TENNESSEE SMOKIES — DOUBLE-A
SOUTHERN LEAGUE

Batting	B-T	HT	WT	DOB	AVG	vLH	vRH	G	AB	R	H	2B	3B	HR	RBI	BB	HBP	SH	SF	SO	SB	CS	SLG	OBP
Adduci, Jim	L-L	6-2	185	5-15-85	.300	.295	.302	131	467	63	140	21	4	4	51	58	0	9	0	76	35	12	.388	.377
Barney, Darwin	R-R	5-10	180	11-8-85	.317	.415	.271	74	252	30	80	12	0	3	32	23	0	4	5	33	5	1	.401	.368
Camp, Matt	L-R	6-0	175	5-29-84	.298	.571	.250	14	47	5	14	3	0	0	5	5	0	0	1	4	1	1	.362	.358
Canzler, Russ	R-R	6-2	215	4-11-86	.258	.159	.299	90	233	27	60	15	0	6	35	31	1	1	1	41	2	5	.399	.346
Castillo, Welington	R-R	6-0	200	4-24-87	.232	.263	.219	95	319	27	74	16	0	11	39	15	4	1	0	71	1	0	.386	.275
Castro, Starlin	R-R	6-1	160	3-24-90	.288	.346	.271	31	111	11	32	6	3	0	14	10	0	1	0	12	6	0	.396	.347
Chirinos, Robinson	R-R	6-1	185	6-5-84	.257	.200	.267	12	35	4	9	3	0	0	5	7	0	0	1	4	0	1	.343	.372
Clevenger, Steve	L-R	6-0	195	4-5-86	.364	.368	.397	26	77	12	28	4	3	1	10	10	1	1	0	8	0	0	.532	.443
Colvin, Tyler	L-L	6-3	190	9-5-85	.300	.320	.290	84	307	51	92	13	7	14	50	16	1	4	2	57	5	1	.524	.334
Deeds, Doug	L-L	6-2	195	6-2-81	.305	.389	.283	61	174	32	53	20	1	6	19	12	2	0	2	37	0	1	.534	.353
Guyer, Brandon	R-R	6-1	210	1-28-86	.190	.148	.211	57	189	22	36	12	2	1	14	10	2	2	2	33	7	5	.291	.236
Lalli, Blake	L-R	6-1	210	5-12-83	.314	.367	.297	118	373	49	117	25	0	5	52	32	4	1	2	50	0	2	.421	.372
Mota, Jonathan	R-R	6-0	180	6-1-87	.238	.240	.237	107	320	32	76	16	2	2	22	35	7	6	2	59	2	6	.319	.324
Reed, Mark	L-R	5-11	175	4-13-86	.160	.250	.143	28	75	5	12	1	0	0	9	1	0	1	1	20	0	0	.173	.169
Reynolds, Kyle	L-R	6-2	190	9-1-83	.088	.158	.053	21	57	4	5	2	0	1	3	4	0	0	0	16	1	1	.175	.148
Robnett, Richie	L-L	5-10	210	9-17-83	.184	.095	.218	30	76	10	14	1	1	2	8	7	0	0	0	18	5	0	.303	.253
Samson, Nate	R-R	6-0	170	8-19-87	.292	.286	.295	20	65	8	19	1	0	0	4	3	0	0	0	5	2	0	.308	.324
Smith, Marquez	R-R	5-10	210	3-20-85	.280	.270	.285	113	410	56	115	34	1	10	49	33	4	1	2	82	4	0	.441	.339
Soto, Geovany	R-R	6-1	225	1-20-83	.333	.429	.000	3	9	2	3	0	0	2	4	2	0	0	0	1	0	0	1.000	.455
Thomas, Tony	R-R	5-10	180	7-10-86	.251	.336	.220	125	427	66	107	24	1	11	41	50	11	5	4	106	13	13	.389	.341
Wright, Ty	R-R	6-0	200	2-26-85	.290	.310	.279	128	442	66	128	23	2	9	58	35	8	7	5	60	5	3	.412	.349

Pitching	B-T	HT	WT	DOB	W	L	ERA	G	GS	CG	SV	IP	H	R	ER	HR	BB	SO	AVG	vLH	vRH	K/9	BB/9
Blackford, Todd	L-R	6-4	205	6-10-85	1	3	6.84	17	0	0	0	26	36	25	20	2	17	13	.330	.347	.317	4.44	5.81
Cales, David	R-R	5-11	200	7-27-87	3	0	5.40	16	0	0	2	25	29	16	15	1	21	21	.302	.385	.246	7.56	3.96
Carpenter, Chris	R-R	6-4	215	12-26-85	0	3	4.78	7	7	0	0	32	30	20	17	0	11	25	.246	.304	.197	7.03	3.09
Carrillo, Marco	R-R	5-11	215	2-1-87	4	1	4.21	31	0	0	0	51	51	27	24	6	29	46	.258	.272	.248	8.06	5.08
Cashner, Andrew	R-R	6-6	210	9-11-86	3	4	3.39	12	12	0	0	58	45	30	22	0	27	41	.210	.198	.220	6.33	4.17
Chen, Hung-Wen	R-R	5-11	210	2-3-86	8	11	4.48	27	27	0	0	143	166	81	71	13	32	98	.294	.355	.247	6.18	2.02
Coleman, Casey	L-R	6-1	180	7-3-87	14	6	3.68	27	27	1	0	149	142	63	61	8	58	84	.256	.284	.237	5.07	3.50
Estrada, Jesse	R-R	6-8	260	10-27-83	0	1	9.64	3	2	0	0	9	19	13	10	3	2	5	.442	.500	.407	4.82	1.93
Gaub, John	R-L	6-2	200	4-28-85	3	1	2.83	26	0	0	4	29	19	12	9	3	17	40	.188	.200	.183	12.56	5.34
Jackson, Jay	R-R	6-1	195	10-27-87	5	5	3.70	16	16	1	0	83	73	35	34	7	39	77	.236	.231	.240	8.38	4.25
Lambert, Casey	L-L	5-11	175	12-11-85	6	5	3.95	24	13	0	0	82	91	45	36	6	25	43	.289	.354	.267	4.72	2.74
Maestri, Alessandro	R-R	5-11	180	6-1-85	4	2	3.69	54	0	0	3	85	71	36	35	8	52	73	.234	.286	.204	7.70	5.48
Mateo, Marcos	R-R	6-1	160	4-18-84	3	6	4.07	34	14	0	0	97	97	47	44	9	43	70	.258	.253	.262	6.47	3.98
Muyco, Jake	R-R	6-0	190	9-16-84	3	3	4.19	34	0	0	1	43	56	20	20	8	17	25	.337	.400	.297	5.23	3.56
Papelbon, Jeremy	R-L	6-1	205	6-24-83	6	5	3.38	31	14	0	0	104	115	43	39	9	26	77	.280	.260	.289	6.66	2.25

Parker, Blake	R-R	6-3	225	6-19-85	0	0	1.46	10	0	0	3	12	8	2	2	0	8	19	.195	.143	.222	13.86	5.84
Patton, David	R-R	6-3	205	5-18-84	0	1	3.52	3	3	0	0	8	7	6	3	1	1	6	.219	.182	.238	7.04	1.17
Perkins, Vince	L-R	6-5	240	9-27-81	1	0	0.00	8	0	0	2	11	6	1	0	0	7	10	.162	.133	.182	7.94	5.56
Ruhlman, Jayson	L-L	6-1	180	8-17-84	2	1	3.83	47	0	0	4	49	42	22	21	4	24	37	.228	.214	.237	6.75	4.38
Russell, James	L-L	6-4	205	1-8-86	2	3	5.11	11	5	0	0	37	45	24	21	5	9	26	.302	.327	.289	6.32	2.19
Sasser, Dustin	L-L	6-0	200	9-13-85	2	0	1.65	12	0	0	0	16	13	3	3	0	10	10	.241	.261	.226	5.51	5.51
Schlitter, Brian	R-R	6-5	240	12-21-85	1	7	4.38	59	0	0	22	62	62	36	30	8	24	51	.261	.318	.211	7.44	3.50

Fielding

Catcher	PCT	G	PO	A	E	DP	PB
Castillo	.990	93	565	58	6	8	10
Chirinos	1.000	11	70	5	0	0	1
Clevenger	.988	21	146	13	2	2	0
Lalli	1.000	6	18	1	0	0	1
Reed	1.000	21	95	8	0	0	5
Soto	1.000	3	19	0	0	0	1

First Base	PCT	G	PO	A	E	DP
Canzler	.985	51	366	21	6	41
Chirinos	1.000	1	0	0	0	0
Clevenger	1.000	1	1	0	0	0
Deeds	.987	10	72	2	1	10
Lalli	.991	83	655	36	6	69
Mota	—	1	0	0	0	0
Reynolds	.990	13	90	10	1	12

Second Base	PCT	G	PO	A	E	DP
Barney	1.000	1	1	1	0	1
Mota	1.000	23	46	61	0	15
Samson	.909	6	13	17	3	6
Thomas	.971	118	257	303	17	85

Third Base	PCT	G	PO	A	E	DP
Barney	1.000	1	0	1	0	0
Camp	1.000	9	4	15	0	3
Canzler	1.000	3	1	2	0	0
Clevenger	—	1	0	0	0	0
Mota	.945	33	21	48	4	9
Reynolds	.750	2	3	3	2	1
Smith	.959	109	60	223	12	34

Shortstop	PCT	G	PO	A	E	DP
Barney	.949	69	101	198	16	37
Camp	1.000	3	1	8	0	4
Castro	.950	29	44	89	7	16
Mota	.940	35	49	91	9	25
Samson	.950	12	17	21	2	5
Smith	.500	1	1	0	1	0

Outfield	PCT	G	PO	A	E	DP
Adduci	.980	124	281	14	6	4
Camp	1.000	5	8	0	0	0
Canzler	.923	17	12	0	1	0
Colvin	.980	75	137	8	3	1
Deeds	.986	40	72	0	1	0
Guyer	.983	55	116	1	2	1
Mota	1.000	13	20	1	0	1
Reed	—	1	0	0	0	0
Robnett	1.000	12	21	1	0	0
Wright	.963	117	198	8	8	0

DAYTONA CUBS   HIGH CLASS A

FLORIDA STATE LEAGUE

Batting	B-T	HT	WT	DOB	AVG	vLH	vRH	G	AB	R	H	2B	3B	HR	RBI	BB	HBP	SH	SF	SO	SB	CS	SLG	OBP
Campana, Tony	L-L	5-8	160	5-30-86	.284	.306	.276	108	430	56	122	8	2	0	25	34	0	7	2	78	55	16	.312	.335
Canzler, Russ	R-R	6-2	215	4-11-86	.270	.273	.270	28	100	14	27	8	1	2	14	7	0	0	1	24	2	0	.430	.315
Castro, Starlin	R-R	6-1	160	3-24-90	.302	.298	.303	96	358	45	108	17	3	3	35	19	3	5	2	41	22	11	.391	.340
Chirinos, Robinson	R-R	6-1	185	6-5-84	.300	.322	.292	69	227	40	68	13	5	11	47	35	5	0	3	40	2	2	.546	.400
Colvin, Tyler	L-L	6-3	190	9-5-85	.250	.375	.229	32	112	18	28	5	2	1	10	13	1	0	3	27	3	1	.357	.326
Contreras, John	R-R	6-0	185	4-17-86	.094	.000	.150	11	32	0	3	0	0	0	2	1	0	0	0	7	0	0	.094	.121
Flores, Luis	R-R	5-10	195	11-2-86	.169	.345	.124	49	142	9	24	5	0	0	12	16	2	3	3	31	0	0	.204	.258
Gonzalez, Marwin	B-R	6-1	186	3-14-89	.241	.196	.255	120	424	43	102	15	4	2	34	26	2	8	1	77	9	8	.309	.287
Guyer, Brandon	R-R	6-1	210	1-28-86	.347	.292	.365	73	265	40	92	16	3	2	32	24	8	0	8	34	23	2	.453	.407
Guzman, Francisco	L-L	6-1	160	4-12-88	.263	.500	.200	6	19	4	5	0	0	0	1	3	0	0	0	4	1	0	.263	.364
Harrison, Josh	R-R	5-8	175	7-8-87	.286	.308	.281	18	70	10	20	3	1	1	9	6	1	1	0	7	10	1	.400	.351
Johnston, Dylan	L-R	6-0	180	3-25-87	.185	.114	.203	50	173	19	32	6	0	4	13	18	0	1	2	71	3	1	.289	.259
Jones, Jericho	R-R	6-5	215	7-21-87	.181	.214	.150	41	116	8	21	5	0	0	14	11	3	1	1	37	0	1	.224	.267
Keedy, Ryan	L-R	6-3	220	8-15-85	.236	.222	.239	27	89	9	21	0	0	0	14	9	1	0	3	24	0	0	.336	.304
Made, Jose	R-R	5-8	175	10-23-85	.156	.000	.179	17	45	3	7	0	0	0	3	0	0	1	0	12	0	1	.156	.156
Opitz, Jake	L-R	6-0	180	7-28-86	.272	.319	.261	104	356	45	97	21	5	2	36	39	4	2	4	56	6	4	.376	.347
Reed, Mark	L-R	5-11	175	4-13-86	.190	.231	.183	54	168	13	32	6	2	0	13	12	3	4	1	50	1	2	.250	.255
Rosa, Jovan	R-R	6-2	180	10-26-87	.220	.236	.216	69	245	16	54	19	2	2	33	11	1	0	3	65	2	1	.339	.254
Rundle, Drew	L-L	6-4	180	11-5-87	.190	.167	.194	15	42	3	8	3	0	0	4	5	0	2	0	19	0	0	.262	.277
Samson, Nate	R-R	6-0	170	8-19-87	.255	.294	.241	93	326	51	83	7	2	2	43	31	4	6	6	24	3	5	.307	.322
Smith, Marquez	R-R	5-10	210	3-20-85	.266	.167	.273	15	50	9	13	1	0	5	18	5	0	0	0	13	1	1	.580	.327
Soto, Kevin	R-R	6-1	170	10-12-88	.333	.222	.417	6	21	7	7	0	0	0	4	1	0	0	0	5	1	0	.333	.391
Vitters, Josh	R-R	6-3	200	8-27-89	.238	.167	.259	50	189	21	45	7	2	3	22	5	1	0	1	23	2	1	.344	.260
Wyatt, Jonathan	L-R	5-10	180	9-6-84	.232	.205	.240	116	396	44	92	10	1	2	33	35	0	4	0	67	9	5	.278	.295

Pitching	B-T	HT	WT	DOB	W	L	ERA	G	GS	CG	SV	IP	H	R	ER	HR	BB	SO	AVG	vLH	vRH	K/9	BB/9
Alburquerque, Al	R-R	6-0	150	6-10-86	1	0	2.08	24	0	0	2	35	26	11	8	4	14	44	.203	.262	.174	11.42	3.63
Blackford, Todd	L-R	6-4	205	6-10-85	2	0	3.60	8	0	0	0	10	11	6	4	1	3	4	.268	.278	.261	3.60	2.70
Cales, David	R-R	5-11	200	7-27-87	3	0	0.78	37	0	0	14	46	29	5	4	1	11	43	.187	.241	.155	8.41	2.15
Carpenter, Chris	R-R	6-4	215	12-26-85	2	1	1.44	5	5	0	0	25	15	7	4	1	8	33	.163	.105	.204	11.88	2.88
Carrillo, Marco	R-R	5-11	215	2-1-87	0	0	0.00	1	0	0	0	1	1	0	0	0	0	0	.333	.500	.000	0.00	0.00
Cashner, Andrew	R-R	6-6	210	9-11-86	0	0	1.50	12	12	0	0	42	31	8	7	1	15	34	.201	.157	.238	7.29	3.21
Dolis, Rafael	R-R	6-3	180	1-10-88	3	9	3.79	27	25	0	0	100	78	46	42	4	53	75	.221	.245	.202	6.77	4.79
Jackson, Jay	R-R	6-1	195	10-27-87	2	2	1.64	7	7	0	0	38	31	12	7	3	4	46	.218	.154	.273	10.80	0.94
Leverton, James	R-L	6-2	185	5-13-86	9	11	4.35	26	25	0	0	122	115	71	59	14	61	75	.253	.258	.251	5.53	4.50
Martinez, Oswaldo	R-R	6-0	180	9-25-88	0	0	0.59	6	3	0	0	15	5	1	1	0	5	9	.102	.133	.088	5.28	2.93
Mateo, Marcos	R-R	6-1	160	4-18-84	0	0	0.00	3	3	0	0	9	4	0	0	0	2	7	.143	.308	.000	7.00	2.00
McDaniel, Dan	R-R	6-3	220	4-18-86	6	9	4.78	29	15	0	1	92	101	56	49	3	49	79	.284	.282	.285	7.70	4.78
Muldowney, Billy	R-R	6-1	215	8-9-84	0	2	6.55	6	1	0	0	11	16	8	8	2	4	9	.364	.308	.387	7.36	3.27
Muschko, Craig	R-R	6-2	192	8-17-85	7	3	3.31	31	12	0	0	103	90	39	38	8	19	85	.231	.253	.215	7.40	1.65
Muyco, Jake	R-R	6-0	190	9-16-84	1	2	4.35	13	1	0	2	21	14	10	10	1	8	18	.266	.317	.211	7.84	3.48
Pena, Julio	R-R	6-3	185	3-1-89	0	0	4.50	2	0	0	0	2	3	1	1	0	1	3	.333	.000	.429	13.50	4.50
Perconte, Mike	R-R	6-4	170	3-18-86	1	1	3.64	17	0	0	1	30	25	14	12	2	10	32	.223	.186	.246	9.71	3.03
Pina, Jose	R-R	6-2	150	11-2-85	3	2	4.19	37	0	0	1	58	67	34	27	1	30	39	.290	.281	.296	6.05	4.66
Rosario, Jose	R-R	6-1	170	8-29-90	0	0	0.00	2	0	0	0	3	1	0	0	0	2	3	.100	.000	.125	9.00	6.00

Name	B-T	HT	WT	DOB	W	L	ERA	G	GS	CG	SV	IP	H	R	ER	BB	SO	AVG	vLH	vRH	K/9	BB/9
Sasser, Dustin	L-L	6-0	200	9-13-85	5	4	1.60	35	0	0	0	62	45	18	11	3	25	51	.200	.193	.204	7.40	3.63
Searle, Ryan	R-R	6-0	190	6-22-89	7	11	4.42	26	24	0	0	116	121	71	57	5	43	68	.264	.319	.225	5.28	3.34
Siegfried, Chris	L-L	6-5	195	12-12-85	3	2	3.38	12	0	0	1	16	18	7	6	0	5	16	.295	.273	.308	9.00	2.81
Simokaitis, Joe	R-R	6-1	200	12-27-82	0	0	4.91	3	0	0	0	4	5	3	2	0	1	1	.313	.500	.125	2.45	2.45
Sommer, Luke	L-L	6-3	190	6-22-85	2	4	2.13	51	0	0	3	72	76	20	17	5	11	67	.275	.218	.309	8.38	1.38
Vento, Steve	R-R	6-3	210	3-28-86	0	3	4.82	17	0	0	0	28	30	18	15	0	13	26	.273	.271	.274	8.36	4.18
Williamson, Hank	R-R	6-5	233	11-1-85	7	4	4.93	38	1	0	1	84	94	52	46	4	31	87	.283	.283	.284	9.32	3.32
Zambrano, Carlos	B-R	6-5	255	6-1-81	0	1	9.82	1	1	0	0	4	5	4	4	0	3	1	.313	.300	.333	2.45	7.36

Fielding

Catcher	PCT	G	PO	A	E	DP	PB
Chirinos	.986	54	374	39	6	3	6
Contreras	.500	1	1	0	1	0	0
Flores	.990	49	333	48	4	0	3
Reed	.985	37	235	22	4	2	5

First Base	PCT	G	PO	A	E	DP
Canzler	.992	24	226	26	2	25
Chirinos	1.000	8	70	8	0	3
Contreras	.986	7	68	4	1	5
Keedy	.987	18	150	6	2	14
Opitz	.983	34	269	15	5	32
Reed	.979	13	91	3	2	9
Rosa	.989	38	337	16	4	29

Second Base	PCT	G	PO	A	E	DP
Chirinos	1.000	1	0	2	0	1
Gonzalez	.969	27	44	83	4	13

	PCT	G	PO	A	E	DP
Harrison	1.000	5	5	15	0	5
Made	.965	11	20	35	2	8
Opitz	.957	20	35	55	4	13
Samson	.971	81	152	251	12	59
Smith	1.000	1	2	3	0	1

Third Base	PCT	G	PO	A	E	DP
Canzler	1.000	1	0	3	0	1
Gonzalez	.922	24	12	47	5	10
Harrison	1.000	5	4	12	0	0
Opitz	.888	31	19	60	10	6
Rosa	.966	29	13	44	2	3
Samson	—	0	0	0	0	0
Smith	.923	13	9	27	3	3
Vitters	.922	42	26	69	8	5

Shortstop	PCT	G	PO	A	E	DP
Castro	.933	90	146	299	32	63

	PCT	G	PO	A	E	DP
Gonzalez	.916	38	54	87	13	19
Samson	.906	11	21	27	5	10

Outfield	PCT	G	PO	A	E	DP
Campana	.978	107	212	11	5	1
Canzler	1.000	2	1	0	0	0
Colvin	.875	12	19	2	3	1
Gonzalez	.962	38	47	3	2	0
Guyer	.981	66	99	3	2	0
Guzman	1.000	6	17	0	0	0
Harrison	1.000	8	10	1	0	0
Johnston	.930	43	52	1	4	0
Jones	.500	3	1	0	1	0
Rundle	1.000	14	19	0	0	0
Soto	1.000	6	14	0	0	0
Wyatt	.984	110	179	6	3	1

PEORIA CHIEFS
LOW CLASS A
MIDWEST LEAGUE

Batting	B-T	HT	WT	DOB	AVG	vLH	vRH	G	AB	R	H	2B	3B	HR	RBI	BB	HBP	SH	SF	SO	SB	CS	SLG	OBP
Andersen, Cliff	L-L	6-2	185	7-24-87	.240	.217	.250	29	75	7	18	3	1	0	5	4	0	0	0	25	0	0	.307	.278
Bautista, Robert	B-R	6-1	165	8-20-88	.059	.333	.000	8	17	2	1	0	1	0	0	1	0	0	0	9	0	0	.176	.111
Brenly, Michael	R-R	6-3	210	10-14-86	.265	.264	.266	94	339	35	90	18	0	4	36	20	3	2	6	55	2	2	.354	.307
Burke, Kyler	L-L	6-3	205	4-20-88	.303	.291	.307	132	465	93	141	43	3	15	89	78	6	0	6	99	14	2	.505	.405
Campana, Tony	L-L	5-8	160	5-30-86	.283	.333	.273	18	53	14	15	1	1	0	5	5	0	0	0	6	11	2	.340	.345
Fitzgerald, D.J.	R-R	6-0	190	12-20-88	.231	.250	.226	19	65	6	15	1	0	1	3	4	1	0	0	22	1	1	.292	.286
Flaherty, Ryan	L-R	6-3	200	7-27-86	.276	.219	.294	131	485	81	134	24	5	20	81	50	2	2	4	98	7	6	.470	.344
Flores, Nelson	R-R	5-10	195	11-2-86	.208	.231	.200	18	48	7	10	6	0	2	4	12	2	2	0	11	0	1	.458	.387
Guzman, Francisco	L-L	6-1	160	4-12-88	.095	.000	.105	8	21	3	2	0	0	0	3	0	0	0	0	7	3	1	.095	.208
Harrison, Josh	R-R	5-8	175	7-8-87	.337	.310	.347	79	303	51	102	17	7	4	33	16	5	9	2	25	16	9	.479	.377
Jackson, Brett	L-R	6-2	210	8-2-88	.295	.370	.271	26	112	30	33	5	1	7	17	11	5	0	0	32	11	1	.545	.383
Johnson, Reed	R-R	5-10	180	12-8-76	.333	—	.333	3	6	2	2	0	0	0	1	1	0	0	0	0	0	0	.333	.500
Lake, Junior	R-R	6-2	200	3-27-90	.248	.279	.239	131	463	71	115	19	7	7	42	18	2	4	4	138	10	7	.365	.277
Lemahieu, D.J.	R-R	6-4	185	7-13-88	.316	.405	.287	38	152	19	48	4	2	0	30	12	2	1	1	22	2	2	.368	.371
Macias, David	B-R	5-9	175	3-7-86	.244	.259	.238	92	312	44	76	12	1	1	29	31	5	8	2	50	4	5	.298	.320
Made, Jose	R-R	5-8	175	10-23-85	.273	.286	.267	15	22	3	6	0	1	0	3	3	1	0	0	8	0	1	.364	.385
Mercedes, Mario	R-R	5-10	160	11-22-86	.271	.273	.270	50	155	15	42	11	0	1	14	5	1	0	2	11	1	1	.361	.294
Perez, Nelson	L-R	6-3	215	11-16-87	.251	.204	.263	120	427	48	107	19	4	11	65	21	4	0	6	130	2	0	.391	.288
Ramirez, Aramis	R-R	6-1	215	6-25-78	.500	.500	.500	3	6	2	3	1	0	0	1	3	0	0	0	0	0	0	.667	.667
Ridling, Rebel	R-R	6-4	230	5-22-86	.310	.325	.305	136	536	74	166	34	1	16	97	40	3	0	7	95	2	1	.466	.357
Rosa, Jovan	R-R	6-2	180	10-26-87	.301	.267	.309	40	153	17	46	13	0	4	32	9	2	0	5	27	2	1	.464	.337
Rundle, Drew	L-L	6-4	180	11-5-87	.219	.140	.242	81	192	26	42	10	2	3	19	32	3	4	0	63	3	3	.339	.339
Valdez, Jose	R-R	6-1	170	9-5-87	.375	.333	.391	8	32	9	12	2	1	0	5	1	1	0	1	4	8	1	.500	.400
Vitters, Josh	R-R	6-3	200	8-27-89	.316	.338	.308	70	269	42	85	12	1	15	46	7	9	0	3	42	4	0	.535	.351

Pitching	B-T	HT	WT	DOB	W	L	ERA	G	GS	CG	SV	IP	H	R	ER	BB	SO	AVG	vLH	vRH	K/9	BB/9
Antigua, Jeffry	R-L	6-1	170	6-23-90	4	0	3.62	7	7	0	0	37	30	16	15	4	9	33	.214	.118	.228	7.96	2.17
Archer, Chris	R-R	6-3	180	9-26-88	6	4	2.81	27	26	0	0	109	78	41	34	0	66	119	.202	.240	.172	9.83	5.45
Beliveau, Jeff	L-L	6-1	197	1-17-87	5	4	3.54	29	7	0	3	97	77	40	38	5	45	117	.216	.182	.230	10.89	4.19
Bibens-Dirkx, Austin	R-R	6-2	190	4-29-85	7	2	2.04	12	8	1	1	71	55	19	16	4	9	50	.215	.213	.216	6.37	1.15
Bristow, Justin	R-R	6-4	220	3-6-87	5	8	4.49	23	23	0	0	100	102	54	50	8	29	73	.266	.286	.250	6.55	2.60
Buchter, Ryan	L-L	6-3	185	2-13-87	3	0	1.33	38	0	0	5	61	36	18	9	1	34	79	.171	.230	.148	11.66	5.02
Cabrera, Alberto	R-R	6-4	170	10-25-88	8	2	4.48	27	8	0	1	96	94	53	48	6	54	73	.256	.248	.262	6.82	5.04
Carpenter, Chris	R-R	6-4	215	12-26-85	4	3	2.44	15	15	1	0	74	55	23	20	4	33	60	.210	.183	.232	7.33	4.03
de Leon, Manolin	R-R	6-0	175	11-23-86	5	3	2.84	31	0	0	2	51	37	19	16	3	17	47	.197	.225	.176	8.35	3.02
Guzman, Angel	R-R	6-3	200	12-14-81	0	0	0.00	1	1	0	0	1	0	0	0	0	0	2	.000	.000	.000	18.00	0.00
Hamren, Erik	R-R	6-1	195	8-21-86	3	4	5.98	38	0	0	7	59	64	43	39	3	32	42	.279	.351	.243	6.44	4.91
Hart, Kevin	R-R	6-4	220	12-29-82	0	0	4.50	1	1	0	0	4	3	2	2	1	1	3	.200	.333	.000	6.75	2.25
Hatley, Marcus	R-R	6-5	190	3-26-88	6	6	4.64	30	16	0	0	95	103	60	49	10	41	64	.278	.289	.269	6.06	3.88
Huseby, Chris	R-R	6-7	220	1-11-88	4	5	1.83	40	0	0	18	54	43	11	11	3	10	73	.213	.222	.207	12.17	1.67
Kreier, Kevin	R-R	6-1	195	8-31-87	5	4	3.77	37	0	0	4	74	73	32	31	4	20	47	.253	.327	.208	5.72	2.43
Lilly, Ted	L-L	6-1	190	1-4-76	1	0	0.00	1	1	0	0	5	2	0	0	0	1	2	.125	.333	.000	3.60	1.80
Perconte, Mike	R-R	6-4	170	3-18-86	3	1	3.69	18	0	0	2	32	33	15	13	3	14	24	.270	.250	.282	6.82	3.98

	B-T	HT	WT	DOB	W	L	ERA	G	GS	CG	SV	IP	H	R	ER	HR	BB	SO	AVG	vLH	vRH	K/9	BB/9
Pina, Jose	R-R	6-2	150	11-2-85	0	0	22.50	4	0	0	1	2	4	7	5	0	6	0	.364	.667	.250	0.00	27.00
Shafer, Aaron	L-R	6-5	185	12-2-86	11	8	4.49	25	24	0	0	116	122	67	58	14	31	81	.266	.325	.234	6.27	2.40
Siegfried, Chris	L-L	6-5	195	12-12-85	0	2	3.38	20	0	0	1	45	37	20	17	2	26	35	.227	.196	.241	6.95	5.16
Whitlock, Josh	R-R	6-1	195	3-12-86	1	1	5.24	12	0	0	1	22	23	15	13	2	1	18	.264	.303	.241	7.25	0.40
Zambrano, Carlos	B-R	6-5	255	6-1-81	0	0	0.00	1	1	0	0	5	4	0	0	0	0	5	.211	.182	.250	9.00	0.00

Fielding

Catcher	PCT	G	PO	A	E	DP	PB
Brenly	.997	87	665	73	2	3	5
Flores	.986	17	130	13	2	1	1
Mercedes	.993	39	270	32	2	1	1

First Base	PCT	G	PO	A	E	DP
Bautista	1.000	1	2	0	0	0
Brenly	.933	2	14	0	1	1
Burke	1.000	10	15	3	0	2
Macias	1.000	2	3	0	0	0
Ridling	.990	133	1081	103	12	92
Rosa	.968	4	27	3	1	2

Second Base	PCT	G	PO	A	E	DP
Bautista	1.000	2	1	4	0	0
Fitzgerald	.818	2	3	6	2	2
Flaherty	.992	55	93	161	2	25
Harrison	.949	16	23	33	3	8
Lake	.943	45	85	112	12	20

	PCT	G	PO	A	E	DP
Lemahieu	.974	9	17	21	1	8
Macias	.913	17	30	33	6	9

Third Base	PCT	G	PO	A	E	DP
Bautista	.000	1	0	0	1	0
Flaherty	.902	19	7	30	4	3
Harrison	.967	12	5	24	1	1
Lake	.818	3	1	8	2	0
Macias	.981	24	13	40	1	3
Made	.875	5	1	6	1	0
Ramirez	1.000	2	1	1	0	0
Ridling	1.000	1	1	0	0	0
Rosa	.930	24	22	44	5	2
Vitters	.914	62	40	99	13	8

Shortstop	PCT	G	PO	A	E	DP
Bautista	1.000	1	1	1	0	0
Flaherty	.951	40	59	116	9	25
Lake	.912	75	110	181	28	37

	PCT	G	PO	A	E	DP
Lemahieu	.982	24	37	71	2	7
Made	1.000	2	1	0	0	0

Outfield	PCT	G	PO	A	E	DP
Andersen	1.000	15	18	1	0	0
Bautista	—	1	0	0	0	0
Burke	.982	123	205	14	4	1
Campana	1.000	17	23	0	0	0
Fitzgerald	1.000	7	4	0	0	0
Guzman	1.000	8	18	0	0	0
Harrison	.980	29	40	8	1	1
Jackson	.985	26	64	1	1	0
Johnson	1.000	2	8	0	0	0
Macias	.990	54	96	3	1	1
Made	1.000	2	1	0	0	0
Perez	.937	98	168	11	12	2
Rundle	.971	74	99	2	3	0
Valdez	1.000	8	18	1	0	1

BOISE HAWKS   SHORT-SEASON
NORTHWEST LEAGUE

Batting	B-T	HT	WT	DOB	AVG	vLH	vRH	G	AB	R	H	2B	3B	HR	RBI	BB	HBP	SH	SF	SO	SB	CS	SLG	OBP
Andersen, Cliff	L-L	6-2	185	7-24-87	.228	.235	.225	16	57	2	13	4	0	0	6	3	0	0	0	20	0	0	.298	.267
Bour, Justin	L-R	6-4	250	5-28-88	.258	.154	.287	48	182	17	47	13	0	2	27	20	3	0	2	28	1	0	.363	.338
Cerda, Matt	L-R	5-9	165	6-20-90	.174	.111	.214	7	23	1	4	0	0	0	3	3	0	0	1	3	0	0	.174	.259
Contreras, John	R-R	6-0	185	4-17-86	.143	.500	.000	3	7	1	1	0	0	0	0	0	0	0	0	2	0	0	.143	.250
Davis, Runey	R-R	6-0	185	1-2-89	.245	.161	.265	47	163	20	40	6	4	0	18	13	4	0	2	58	8	1	.331	.313
Fitzgerald, D.J.	R-R	6-0	190	12-20-88	.267	.333	.253	27	105	13	28	4	1	2	5	4	0	1	0	22	3	0	.381	.294
Guevara, Jose	R-R	6-1	180	3-17-88	.257	.250	.258	9	35	4	9	6	0	0	4	1	1	0	0	12	0	0	.429	.297
Guzman, Francisco	L-L	6-1	160	4-12-88	.118	.500	.067	6	17	2	2	0	0	0	1	6	0	0	0	5	1	1	.118	.348
Ha, Jae-Hoon	R-R	6-1	185	10-29-90	.242	.226	.246	65	248	31	60	15	0	2	37	6	2	0	2	31	5	5	.327	.264
Hoorelbeke, Sean	R-R	6-0	220	5-26-85	.188	.000	.250	6	16	3	3	0	0	0	1	1	1	0	0	3	0	0	.188	.278
Jackson, Brett	L-R	6-2	210	8-2-88	.330	.280	.349	24	88	14	29	1	1	1	15	17	1	0	0	20	2	1	.398	.443
Jones, Richard	L-R	6-4	215	1-31-88	.244	.100	.273	33	119	10	29	5	1	2	15	6	2	1	1	41	0	1	.353	.289
Lee, Hak-Ju	L-R	6-2	170	11-4-90	.330	.328	.330	68	264	56	87	14	2	2	33	31	1	6	2	50	25	8	.420	.399
Matheus, George	R-R	6-0	170	7-20-88	.229	.295	.211	59	210	22	48	5	1	0	22	20	1	3	0	41	2	4	.262	.299
Petraitis, Jordan	R-R	6-2	210	8-30-86	.135	.091	.146	17	52	6	7	2	0	0	2	7	1	0	2	17	0	0	.173	.242
Rohan, Greg	R-R	6-0	205	5-11-86	.249	.216	.258	61	233	34	58	14	1	4	21	16	7	1	1	36	1	0	.369	.315
Sosa, Alvaro	L-R	6-0	181	6-7-86	.191	.091	.222	15	47	6	9	0	0	1	2	2	0	2	0	11	0	0	.255	.224
Soto, Kevin	R-R	6-1	170	10-12-88	.071	.125	.050	10	28	4	2	1	0	0	1	3	1	0	0	6	0	1	.107	.188
Valdez, Jose	B-R	6-0	170	9-5-87	.302	.366	.285	54	192	21	58	2	1	0	11	14	1	3	0	32	17	7	.323	.353
Wagner, Bobby	L-R	6-3	205	7-9-86	.265	.320	.250	31	113	15	30	11	2	5	25	11	0	1	1	32	0	2	.531	.328
Watkins, Logan	L-R	5-11	170	8-29-89	.326	.262	.346	72	279	48	91	14	2	0	29	27	3	7	2	31	14	7	.391	.389
Williams, Matt	R-R	5-11	220	2-23-87	.167	.167	.167	31	108	9	18	3	0	0	11	8	2	1	0	25	1	0	.194	.237

Pitching	B-T	HT	WT	DOB	W	L	ERA	G	GS	CG	SV	IP	H	R	ER	HR	BB	SO	AVG	vLH	vRH	K/9	BB/9
Antigua, Jeffry	R-L	6-1	170	6-23-90	2	1	2.30	7	5	0	0	31	19	8	8	3	10	35	.171	.238	.156	10.05	2.87
Figueroa, Eduardo	R-R	6-1	185	11-30-88	3	4	7.11	11	1	0	0	25	39	26	20	2	10	17	.364	.452	.308	6.04	3.55
Gonzalez, Yohan	R-R	6-4	210	4-15-90	3	3	4.21	23	0	0	0	47	44	28	22	3	7	31	.234	.250	.225	5.94	1.34
Grife, Steve	R-R	6-0	177	11-4-86	0	0	0.00	3	0	0	2	5	4	0	0	0	2	4	.235	.111	.375	7.71	3.86
Hernandez, Robert	R-R	6-2	165	10-7-88	4	3	3.36	15	15	0	0	72	62	30	27	6	22	67	.229	.244	.217	8.34	2.74
Jung, Su-Min	R-R	6-2	190	4-1-90	0	0	4.38	8	7	0	0	25	23	14	12	4	11	17	.253	.194	.291	6.20	4.01
Keefe, Danny	R-R	6-4	185	8-15-87	2	1	7.71	26	0	0	0	35	50	34	30	4	14	31	.338	.476	.283	7.97	3.60
Kirk, Austin	L-L	6-1	200	5-22-90	1	1	5.40	2	0	0	0	5	2	4	3	1	3	5	.100	.143	.077	9.00	5.40
Martin, Corey	R-R	6-3	195	5-1-87	2	2	5.21	21	0	0	0	38	43	27	22	3	9	21	.289	.286	.290	4.97	2.13
McNutt, Trey	R-R	6-4	205	8-2-89	3	0	1.33	7	2	0	0	20	9	7	3	1	12	21	.132	.292	.045	9.30	5.31
Mitchell, Tarlandas	R-R	5-8	190	3-9-90	0	1	7.58	8	5	0	0	19	17	16	16	0	21	22	.239	.167	.293	10.42	9.95
Nagel, Jon	R-R	6-4	230	1-18-87	0	2	4.58	14	14	0	0	35	43	28	18	1	14	30	.299	.283	.306	7.64	3.57
Nunez, Dionis	R-R	6-4	170	9-28-88	3	3	2.84	21	0	0	5	38	22	14	12	1	23	30	.169	.179	.165	7.11	5.45
Perconte, Mike	R-R	6-4	170	3-18-86	1	1	4.70	7	0	0	2	8	4	5	4	0	4	5	.160	.143	.167	5.87	4.70
Quezada, Andres	B-R	5-11	170	3-15-86	3	2	4.84	18	0	0	0	35	43	19	19	1	9	29	.303	.228	.353	7.39	2.29
Raley, Brooks	L-L	6-3	185	6-29-88	0	0	1.42	2	0	0	0	6	3	1	1	1	1	2	.150	.286	.077	2.84	1.42
Rhee, Dae-Eun	L-R	6-2	190	3-23-89	0	1	11.25	2	2	0	0	4	8	5	5	2	1	4	.421	.500	.286	9.00	2.25
Rusin, Chris	L-L	6-2	185	10-22-86	0	4	3.48	8	8	0	0	31	33	14	12	1	9	27	.270	.333	.260	7.84	2.61
Sierra, Miguel	R-R	6-5	170	7-28-88	0	1	13.06	5	1	0	0	10	23	16	15	0	4	7	.426	.370	.481	6.10	3.48
Simokaitis, Joe	R-R	6-1	200	12-27-82	0	3	8.68	8	0	0	0	9	14	9	9	2	3	5	.341	.250	.429	4.82	2.89
Sontag, Ryan	L-L	5-10	195	9-13-85	2	1	4.25	25	0	0	3	30	32	18	14	3	25	26	.276	.088	.354	7.89	7.58

	B-T	HT	WT	DOB	W	L	ERA	G	GS	CG	SV	IP	H	R	ER	HR	BB	SO	AVG	vLH	vRH	K/9	BB/9
Suarez, Larry	R-R	6-4	245	12-20-89	1	0	10.38	8	1	0	0	13	21	19	15	1	16	13	.368	.333	.394	9.00	11.08
Whitenack, Robert	R-R	6-5	185	11-20-88	0	4	4.80	15	12	0	0	54	66	36	29	1	20	33	.296	.299	.294	5.47	3.31
Whitlock, Josh	R-R	6-1	195	3-12-86	3	3	5.72	14	3	0	0	39	47	29	25	4	10	27	.292	.288	.294	6.18	2.29

Fielding

Catcher	PCT	G	PO	A	E	DP	PB
Cerda	.900	4	25	2	3	0	2
Guevara	.967	7	47	11	2	1	2
Jones	.995	24	172	16	1	2	5
Sosa	1.000	13	83	9	0	1	4
Williams	.983	30	201	24	4	1	9

First Base	PCT	G	PO	A	E	DP
Bour	.989	46	420	22	5	45
Contreras	1.000	1	11	0	0	0
Hoorelbeke	1.000	4	26	5	0	4
Jones	1.000	1	11	0	0	0
Petraitis	.985	6	59	5	1	4
Rohan	1.000	20	214	7	0	15

Sosa	1.000	1	6	0	0	0

Second Base	PCT	G	PO	A	E	DP
Cerda	1.000	2	3	2	0	2
Matheus	.948	12	27	28	3	7
Watkins	.956	63	96	185	13	38

Third Base	PCT	G	PO	A	E	DP
Matheus	.895	27	19	49	8	4
Petraitis	.933	9	9	19	2	1
Rohan	.915	31	27	59	8	3
Wagner	.850	10	1	16	3	3

Shortstop	PCT	G	PO	A	E	DP
Lee	.919	61	92	215	27	35
Matheus	.934	18	28	57	6	14

Outfield	PCT	G	PO	A	E	DP
Andersen	.933	11	14	0	1	0
Davis	.949	41	73	1	4	0
Fitzgerald	.909	14	19	1	2	0
Guzman	1.000	6	12	1	0	0
Ha	.980	61	92	8	2	1
Jackson	.941	20	31	1	2	0
Jones	1.000	1	1	0	0	0
Rohan	1.000	3	7	0	0	0
Soto	.923	10	12	0	1	0
Valdez	.946	50	98	8	6	2
Wagner	1.000	15	23	1	0	0
Watkins	1.000	2	3	0	0	0

AZL CUBS   ROOKIE

ARIZONA LEAGUE

Batting	B-T	HT	WT	DOB	AVG	vLH	vRH	G	AB	R	H	2B	3B	HR	RBI	BB	HBP	SH	SF	SO	SB	CS	SLG	OBP
Bautista, Robert	B-R	6-1	165	8-20-88	.223	.233	.221	49	166	26	37	5	5	1	18	10	1	5	1	61	15	3	.331	.270
Bour, Justin	L-R	6-4	250	5-28-88	.273	.000	.319	14	55	7	15	4	0	2	13	5	0	0	2	17	1	0	.455	.323
Burruel, Sergio	L-R	5-11	210	7-22-91	.264	.000	.292	15	53	7	14	3	0	0	10	5	0	0	2	9	0	1	.321	.317
Cook, Glenn	L-L	6-1	220	12-13-84	.167	.176	.164	34	84	11	14	4	1	0	8	11	7	0	1	32	1	4	.238	.311
Darvill, Wes	L-R	6-2	175	9-10-91	.223	.250	.218	34	130	18	29	1	0	0	15	13	1	2	2	31	7	1	.231	.295
Davis, Runey	R-R	6-0	185	1-2-89	.250	.250	.250	6	20	5	5	1	0	2	5	4	2	0	1	8	3	0	.600	.407
Fitzgerald, D.J.	R-R	6-0	190	12-20-88	.500	.625	.455	8	30	9	15	4	2	1	8	2	0	0	0	4	2	0	.867	.531
Guevara, Jose	R-R	6-1	180	3-17-88	.088	.000	.115	13	34	0	3	1	0	0	4	6	0	0	0	9	0	0	.118	.225
Guzman, Francisco	L-L	6-1	160	4-12-88	.264	.265	.264	53	182	49	48	3	2	0	18	41	1	4	1	36	32	8	.302	.400
Jackson, Brett	L-R	6-2	210	8-2-88	.455	.000	.500	3	11	6	5	0	1	0	4	3	0	0	1	4	0	0	.636	.533
Jones, Richard	L-R	6-0	215	1-31-88	.319	.500	.302	12	47	11	15	1	0	7	17	2	0	0	1	15	0	0	.787	.340
Kemp, Dwayne	B-R	5-8	160	2-24-88	.248	.208	.260	25	101	13	25	2	6	1	12	6	2	0	0	25	2	1	.416	.303
Lemahieu, D.J.	R-R	6-4	185	7-13-88	.417	.333	.444	3	12	2	5	0	1	0	4	1	0	0	1	3	1	0	.583	.429
May, Brandon	R-R	6-1	205	1-7-88	.296	.667	.250	7	27	1	8	1	0	0	3	7	0	0	0	12	1	1	.333	.441
Medina, Juan	R-R	6-1	185	6-13-86	.266	.217	.282	30	94	12	25	4	0	0	17	8	4	0	1	18	4	2	.309	.346
Morelli, Jesus	R-R	6-3	186	4-25-90	.279	.313	.275	38	136	26	38	2	3	0	14	15	4	1	1	24	8	4	.338	.365
Petraitis, Jordan	R-R	6-2	210	8-30-86	.231	.250	.228	32	117	16	27	7	0	3	16	8	5	0	1	36	4	2	.368	.305
Snyder, Brad	L-L	6-3	200	5-25-82	.278	.500	.250	5	18	1	5	1	1	1	3	1	0	0	0	7	0	0	.611	.316
Sosa, Alvaro	L-R	6-0	181	6-7-86	.226	.500	.181	24	84	7	19	6	0	1	10	4	1	0	0	13	3	2	.333	.270
Soto, Geovany	R-R	6-1	225	1-20-83	.333	—	.333	4	3	0	1	0	0	2	0	0	0	0	1	0	0	.667	.333
Soto, Kevin	R-R	6-1	170	10-12-88	.328	.158	.358	37	128	17	42	5	3	0	11	7	3	2	1	35	16	9	.414	.374
Springfield, Blair	R-R	5-11	190	2-18-91	.202	.231	.197	31	89	12	18	1	1	0	5	14	1	1	1	28	4	1	.236	.314
Thomas, Charles	R-R	6-4	225	7-2-88	.306	.333	.301	45	160	19	49	11	3	1	23	13	1	0	4	43	1	2	.431	.354
Wagner, Bobby	L-R	6-3	205	7-9-86	.339	.167	.360	15	56	12	19	4	3	3	11	7	2	0	1	13	1	1	.679	.424
Weimer, Chris	R-R	6-2	215	7-24-86	.239	.143	.256	16	46	10	11	3	0	0	6	5	4	0	1	11	2	1	.304	.357
Williams, Matt	R-R	5-11	220	2-23-87	.360	.429	.333	6	25	5	9	2	0	0	2	1	0	0	0	2	0	0	.440	.385
Williams, Sean	L-L	5-11	180	7-9-90	.364	.500	.286	3	11	2	4	1	0	0	1	0	0	0	0	0	0	0	.364	.364

Pitching	B-T	HT	WT	DOB	W	L	ERA	G	GS	CG	SV	IP	H	R	ER	HR	BB	SO	AVG	vLH	vRH	K/9	BB/9
Carmona, Rogelino	R-R	6-3	210	8-30-89	1	3	6.00	15	0	0	0	18	22	16	12	0	3	26	.275	.280	.273	13.00	1.50
Clubb, Tim	R-R	6-3	195	9-4-86	1	0	3.98	16	1	0	4	20	22	13	9	0	9	14	.268	.435	.203	6.20	3.98
Cox, Daley	L-L	5-9	170	10-4-88	0	0	13.03	7	0	0	0	10	16	15	14	0	3	7	.372	.400	.364	6.52	2.79
Encarnacion, Diego	R-R	6-2	190	3-4-90	1	2	4.15	15	3	0	0	30	33	21	14	2	16	31	.264	.229	.286	9.20	4.75
Figueroa, Eduardo	R-R	6-1	185	11-30-88	2	0	2.84	5	3	0	0	19	18	7	6	0	2	16	.247	.167	.273	7.58	0.95
Ginley, Jesse	R-R	6-5	180	1-7-90	0	0	5.14	14	1	0	1	21	29	14	12	2	8	21	.337	.364	.328	9.00	3.43
Grife, Steve	R-R	6-0	177	11-4-86	1	1	6.61	14	0	0	2	16	19	13	12	1	15	22	.284	.182	.304	12.12	8.27
Hams, Cody	L-L	6-5	210	11-23-89	1	3	6.75	14	3	0	0	28	35	28	21	0	30	22	.302	.333	.293	7.07	9.64
Jung, Su-Min	R-R	6-2	190	4-1-90	0	0	0.00	2	2	0	0	3	2	0	0	0	2	3	.182	.000	.222	9.00	6.00
Kirk, Austin	L-L	6-1	200	5-22-90	1	0	3.12	5	2	0	0	9	8	3	3	0	4	10	.267	.143	.304	10.38	4.15
Liria, Luis	B-R	6-2	170	1-15-90	2	1	5.33	10	5	0	0	25	30	17	15	1	12	23	.294	.348	.278	8.17	4.26
Martin, Corey	R-R	6-3	195	5-1-87	0	0	3.00	2	0	0	0	3	4	1	1	0	2	2	.308	.429	.167	6.00	6.00
Matchulat, Toby	R-R	6-5	195	2-7-89	2	2	3.13	11	7	0	0	32	26	17	11	1	17	27	.228	.243	.221	7.67	4.83
McNutt, Trey	R-R	6-4	205	8-2-89	0	1	0.00	6	4	0	0	7	5	5	0	0	3	7	.167	.000	.250	8.59	3.68
Mincone, John	L-L	6-1	215	7-23-89	2	0	3.12	3	1	0	0	9	8	3	3	0	1	7	.242	.000	.296	7.27	1.04
Muldowney, Billy	R-R	6-1	215	8-9-84	0	0	0.00	2	1	0	0	3	1	0	0	0	0	3	.100	.250	.000	9.00	0.00
Pena, Julio	R-R	6-3	185	3-1-89	4	1	3.07	14	5	0	0	44	46	15	15	1	5	40	.264	.255	.268	8.18	1.02
Perez, Marcos	L-R	6-1	175	1-1-90	2	1	3.51	15	0	0	0	26	27	11	10	1	9	22	.278	.222	.311	7.71	3.16
Pineda, George	R-R	6-3	175	7-19-88	3	1	3.31	14	0	0	0	16	13	6	6	0	5	18	.217	.286	.196	9.92	2.76
Raley, Brooks	L-L	6-3	185	6-29-88	0	1	4.15	3	3	0	0	4	2	4	2	1	2	3	.125	.000	.154	6.23	4.15
Rhee, Dae-Eun	L-R	6-2	190	3-23-89	0	0	7.71	3	2	0	0	5	4	4	4	0	5	3	.235	.250	.231	5.79	9.64
Rojas, Carlos	R-R	6-1	170	5-22-90	1	4	5.58	16	5	0	0	31	41	22	19	0	27	24	.323	.385	.295	7.92	3.52

Name	B-T	HT	WT	DOB	W	L	ERA	G	GS	CG	SV	IP	H	R	ER	HR	BB	SO	AVG	vLH	vRH	K/9	BB/9
Rosario, Jose	R-R	6-1	170	8-29-90	2	1	4.76	11	1	0	1	17	15	9	9	1	6	21	.234	.300	.205	11.12	3.18
Rusin, Chris	L-L	6-2	185	10-22-86	0	0	0.00	2	1	0	0	5	1	0	0	0	3	2	.067	.000	.077	3.60	5.40
Schmidt, Jake	R-R	6-3	200	3-29-87	0	0	0.00	2	0	0	0	2	2	0	0	0	1	3	.250	.333	.200	13.50	4.50
Sierra, Miguel	R-R	6-5	170	7-28-88	2	1	2.96	10	3	0	0	27	31	10	9	1	6	21	.290	.214	.316	6.91	1.98
Simokaitis, Joe	R-R	6-1	200	12-27-82	0	0	0.00	2	0	0	0	2	0	0	0	0	0	3	.000	.000	.000	13.50	0.00
Spencer, Adam	R-R	6-3	190	9-24-89	0	0	6.43	12	0	0	1	14	19	12	10	3	3	15	.328	.278	.350	9.64	1.93
Suarez, Larry	R-R	6-4	245	12-20-89	1	1	6.23	6	1	0	0	17	24	14	12	0	8	12	.333	.455	.280	6.23	4.15
Vasquez, Melvin	L-L	5-11	180	5-13-88	0	2	6.52	14	0	0	0	19	25	16	14	0	3	12	.325	.278	.339	5.59	1.40

Fielding

Catcher	PCT	G	PO	A	E	DP	PB
Burruel	1.000	8	74	5	0	2	4
Guevara	.976	10	66	15	2	0	4
Jones	1.000	6	37	8	0	0	3
Medina	.984	16	103	19	2	0	9
Sosa	.982	19	140	24	3	1	5
Williams	1.000	3	17	1	0	0	2

First Base	PCT	G	PO	A	E	DP
Bour	1.000	9	84	7	0	8
Burruel	.923	2	12	0	1	2
Jones	.960	3	24	0	1	0
May	1.000	3	30	2	0	3
Medina	1.000	3	13	0	0	0
Petraitis	.981	5	50	3	1	4
Sosa	.967	4	26	3	1	3
Thomas	.989	21	177	11	2	10
Wagner	1.000	6	53	4	0	7
Weimer	1.000	6	57	3	0	4

Second Base	PCT	G	PO	A	E	DP
Bautista	.971	10	15	19	1	6
Darvill	.974	13	28	46	2	4
Fitzgerald	.967	5	10	19	1	2
Kemp	.970	14	28	36	2	8
Lemahieu	1.000	1	1	1	0	0
May	.500	1	1	0	1	0
Medina	1.000	1	1	0	0	0
Morelli	1.000	2	2	1	0	0
Springfield	.920	20	34	35	6	4
Weimer	1.000	3	2	3	0	1

Third Base	PCT	G	PO	A	E	DP
Guevara	.000	1	0	0	1	0
Kemp	.963	12	7	19	1	1
May	1.000	1	1	0	0	0
Petraitis	.911	28	17	55	7	3
Thomas	.769	9	3	7	3	0
Wagner	.923	6	4	8	1	0
Weimer	.933	7	2	12	1	0

Shortstop	PCT	G	PO	A	E	DP
Bautista	.917	37	49	117	15	21
Darvill	.896	22	27	59	10	8
Lemahieu	.800	1	2	2	1	0
Weimer	.800	1	1	3	1	1

Outfield	PCT	G	PO	A	E	DP
Cook	.829	25	27	2	6	0
Davis	1.000	6	7	1	0	0
Fitzgerald	1.000	1	1	1	0	0
Guzman	.961	52	114	8	5	0
Jackson	1.000	1	2	0	0	0
May	.667	2	2	0	1	0
Morelli	.962	37	69	6	3	0
Petraitis	—	1	0	0	0	0
Snyder	.667	3	2	0	1	0
Soto	.925	34	43	6	4	0
Springfield	1.000	5	6	0	0	0
Wagner	1.000	4	4	0	0	0
Weimer	1.000	4	3	0	0	0
Williams	—	1	0	0	0	0
Williams	1.000	3	2	0	0	0

DSL CUBS #1 — ROOKIE

DOMINICAN SUMMER LEAGUE

Batting	B-T	HT	WT	DOB	AVG	vLH	vRH	G	AB	R	H	2B	3B	HR	RBI	BB	HBP	SH	SF	SO	SB	CS	SLG	OBP
Alcantara, Arismendy	B-R	5-10	160	10-29-91	.275	.261	.280	65	258	44	71	11	8	3	32	30	1	1	3	47	20	2	.415	.349
Astacio, Yohan	R-R	6-2	180	2-3-92	.284	.317	.274	55	176	25	50	5	3	0	21	24	1	2	2	41	9	3	.347	.369
Batista, Xavier	R-R	6-3	190	1-18-92	.241	.215	.250	68	257	42	62	15	2	8	38	33	4	1	3	85	4	2	.409	.333
Bieneme, Vismeldy	B-R	5-10	160	3-19-90	.245	.171	.275	41	143	25	35	5	2	1	11	27	3	3	1	38	25	10	.329	.374
2-team total (25 Cubs 2)					.260	—	—	66	242	40	63	6	3	1	20	41	4	4	2	62	42	16	.322	.374
Damian, Alejandro	R-R	6-2	190	6-17-90	.158	.143	.167	6	19	4	3	1	0	0	3	7	0	0	1	7	1	0	.211	.370
Fuenmayor, Yonan	R-R	5-9	170	4-15-92	.255	.400	.214	48	161	19	41	6	1	4	34	10	3	4	3	32	2	2	.379	.305
Gonzalez, Eduardo	L-L	5-10	170	2-9-92	.333	.333	.333	2	6	1	2	0	0	0	1	0	1	0	0	1	1	0	.333	.429
Gonzalez, Gregori	R-R	5-9	170	7-11-89	.175	.167	.176	23	63	6	11	3	0	0	3	3	0	0	0	17	8	3	.222	.212
2-team total (10 Cubs 2)					.190	—	—	33	100	8	19	3	0	0	8	6	0	0	1	22	9	6	.220	.234
Hernandez, Albert	R-R	6-1	170	2-25-89	.295	.238	.315	45	166	34	49	7	1	5	26	24	4	1	0	26	5	1	.440	.397
Liria, Yamel	R-R	5-11	190	11-5-89	.167	.333	.133	6	18	0	3	1	0	0	1	1	0	0	1	4	1	0	.222	.250
Montecino, Jose	B-R	5-11	175	7-31-90	.226	.182	.235	23	62	5	14	1	0	0	4	13	2	3	0	14	4	2	.242	.377
2-team total (36 Cubs 2)					.272	—	—	59	169	26	46	3	0	0	15	31	4	4	2	28	16	7	.290	.393
Pena, Juan	R-R	6-3	190	5-29-90	.258	.298	.246	65	244	48	63	18	5	5	40	32	6	0	5	53	2	2	.434	.352
Pestana, Manuel	R-R	6-0	150	3-9-90	.239	.192	.258	28	92	18	22	3	2	0	6	9	5	2	0	13	5	7	.315	.340
Ramirez, Alvaro	L-L	5-9	160	4-5-86	.372	.362	.375	58	199	40	74	7	4	2	30	21	12	4	2	17	24	7	.477	.457
Rodriguez, Jesus	B-R	6-0	170	9-5-91	.213	.205	.217	54	164	28	35	2	1	0	9	28	0	4	1	53	16	6	.238	.326
Romero, Carlos	R-R	6-1	180	5-28-90	.176	.200	.168	54	153	13	27	3	1	0	9	15	5	7	0	25	1	0	.209	.272
Valdez, Rander	R-R	6-2	180	3-28-91	.052	.000	.071	18	58	3	3	0	0	0	1	1	0	0	1	24	3	1	.052	.067
Vigay, Jose	R-R	5-10	185	12-10-88	.261	.000	.333	18	46	2	12	1	0	0	7	4	1	2	0	10	2	0	.283	.333

Pitching	B-T	HT	WT	DOB	W	L	ERA	G	GS	CG	SV	IP	H	R	ER	HR	BB	SO	AVG	vLH	vRH	K/9	BB/9
Batista, Frank	R-R	5-10	170	4-26-89	4	2	3.55	15	9	1	3	58	63	29	23	3	7	63	.263	.339	.236	9.72	1.08
Cruz, Willengton	R-L	6-2	170	8-8-90	1	0	3.63	8	4	0	0	22	16	10	9	0	24	21	.208	.000	.229	8.46	9.67
2-team total (7 Cubs 2)					1	2	6.10	15	10	0	0	38	37	30	26	1	43	31	—	—	—	7.28	10.10
Encarnacion, Diego	R-R	6-2	190	3-4-90	0	1	3.00	2	2	0	0	6	3	4	2	0	6	5	.150	.250	.083	7.50	9.00
Estrada, Denis	L-L	6-1	176	6-16-89	0	2	4.43	6	2	0	0	20	25	14	10	2	4	10	.287	.250	.291	4.43	1.77
Fransua, William	R-R	6-0	180	8-17-90	0	0	4.32	9	1	0	0	17	10	10	8	0	10	14	.167	.000	.196	7.56	5.40
Galvez, Carlos	L-L	6-1	170	4-26-90	0	1	3.07	4	2	0	0	15	12	8	5	1	8	14	.222	.167	.229	8.59	4.91
Garcia, Ramon	R-R	6-2	170	8-2-91	1	3	5.21	6	3	0	0	19	24	17	11	1	3	9	.300	.300	.300	4.26	1.42
Gonzalez, Enyel	R-R	6-2	195	9-4-91	0	1	4.35	6	1	0	2	10	12	7	5	0	3	7	.279	.308	.267	6.10	2.61
Jimenez, Alvido	R-R	6-1	160	11-22-91	0	0	2.20	7	4	0	0	29	31	14	7	1	7	28	.258	.216	.277	8.79	1.88
2-team total (8 Cubs 2)					1	1	3.00	15	7	0	0	54	59	31	18	1	16	52	—	—	—	8.67	2.67
Liria, Luis	B-R	6-2	170	1-15-90	1	0	3.00	7	5	0	0	27	14	12	9	2	12	32	.149	.189	.123	10.67	4.00
Mayora, Hector	R-R	6-1	178	6-22-89	3	2	2.06	12	7	0	0	39	37	15	9	0	13	32	.248	.129	.280	7.32	2.97
Mendez, Jadel	R-R	6-2	170	11-21-88	1	2	6.23	9	3	0	1	26	41	22	18	0	6	21	.360	.227	.391	7.27	2.08
2-team total (6 Cubs 2)					1	2	3.63	15	6	0	1	52	66	32	21	1	9	40	—	—	—	6.92	1.56
Pena, Enyelberth	R-R	6-2	175	9-8-90	2	0	5.68	9	3	0	0	25	27	22	16	0	17	14	.267	.261	.269	4.97	6.04

	B-T	HT	WT	DOB	W	L	ERA	G	GS	CG	SV	IP	H	R	ER	HR	BB	SO	AVG	vLH	vRH	K/9	BB/9
2-team total (4 Cubs 2)					2	2	5.94	13	5	0	0	36	42	34	24	0	23	23	—	—	—	5.70	5.70
Peralta, Starlin	R-R	6-4	180	11-11-90	1	3	4.10	7	3	0	0	26	32	13	12	2	4	22	.299	.421	.273	7.52	1.37
Pichardo, Roderick	R-R	5-10	180	9-24-90	1	1	2.77	4	1	0	0	13	11	5	4	0	8	9	.229	.353	.161	6.23	5.54
Pineda, Francory	R-R	6-1	180	5-25-89	2	2	2.60	9	1	0	1	28	25	15	8	1	10	11	.238	.310	.211	3.58	3.25
Reyes, Ramon	B-R	6-3	185	1-2-89	3	2	3.60	13	3	0	0	35	31	15	14	1	10	23	.237	.275	.220	5.91	2.57
Rivera, Ramon	R-R	6-0	174	7-22-88	0	1	9.00	1	0	0	0	1	3	1	1	0	0	1	.500	1.000	.400	9.00	0.00
Rodriguez, Jhon	R-R	6-0	185	7-18-90	2	0	3.38	4	1	0	1	16	11	6	6	1	2	17	.190	.261	.143	9.56	1.13
Rosa, Melvin	R-R	6-3	215	9-5-87	2	2	3.41	9	6	0	0	34	19	17	13	2	20	42	.157	.273	.114	11.01	5.24
Ruiz, Adner	L-L	6-1	180	4-1-89	5	4	2.37	24	0	0	5	38	22	14	10	1	31	30	.171	.091	.178	7.11	7.34
Sanchez, Julio	L-R	6-4	185	12-6-88	0	1	3.65	12	2	0	1	25	20	13	10	1	16	17	.217	.250	.211	6.20	5.84
Tineo, Jose	R-R	5-10	170	8-29-90	0	0	0.00	1	0	0	0	1	0	0	0	1	0	1	.500	—	.500	27.00	27.00
Turbi, Francisco	R-R	6-4	210	2-19-88	3	1	5.56	20	3	0	2	44	54	37	27	1	28	21	.314	.258	.326	4.33	5.77
Vargas, Roberto	R-R	6-1	170	11-8-91	4	2	3.94	9	3	0	0	30	25	19	13	0	11	21	.225	.208	.230	6.37	3.34

Fielding

Catcher	PCT	G	PO	A	E	DP	PB
Fuenmayor	.974	23	124	26	4	1	16
Liria	.500	2	1	0	1	0	0
Liria	1.000	2	22	3	0	0	1
Romero	.988	46	290	40	4	1	7
Vigay	.919	13	50	7	5	1	4

First Base	PCT	G	PO	A	E	DP
Astacio	.987	30	284	10	4	20
Fuenmayor	1.000	1	1	0	0	1
Hernandez	.987	25	217	11	3	21
Liria	1.000	1	2	1	0	0
Liria	1.000	1	9	0	0	1
Pena	.961	5	47	2	2	5
Rodriguez	1.000	6	38	2	0	5
Romero	1.000	7	63	4	0	4

Second Base	PCT	G	PO	A	E	DP
Vigay	—	1	0	0	0	0
Alcantara	.942	13	23	26	3	4
Astacio	1.000	2	5	5	0	0
Bieneme	.972	8	14	21	1	2
Gonzalez	.930	11	28	25	4	4
Montecino	1.000	12	28	42	0	11
Rodriguez	.940	26	72	85	10	22

Third Base	PCT	G	PO	A	E	DP
Astacio	.926	8	6	19	2	2
Bieneme	.938	7	6	24	2	1
Pena	.843	56	36	120	29	11
Rodriguez	—	1	0	0	0	0

Shortstop	PCT	G	PO	A	E	DP
Alcantara	.874	52	65	163	33	27

Bieneme	1.000	2	3	2	0	0
Rodriguez	.881	17	31	65	13	9

Outfield	PCT	G	PO	A	E	DP
Astacio	.857	8	6	0	1	0
Batista	.913	68	90	5	9	0
Bieneme	.933	21	25	3	2	0
Damian	1.000	5	2	0	0	0
Gonzalez	.900	2	9	0	1	0
Gonzalez	—	1	0	0	0	0
Hernandez	.867	19	26	0	4	0
Liria	—	1	0	0	0	0
Montecino	1.000	4	8	2	0	0
Pestana	.972	20	35	0	1	0
Ramirez	.965	56	104	6	4	1
Valdez	.905	18	18	1	2	0

DSL CUBS #2   *ROOKIE*

DOMINICAN SUMMER LEAGUE

Batting	B-T	HT	WT	DOB	AVG	vLH	vRH	G	AB	R	H	2B	3B	HR	RBI	BB	HBP	SH	SF	SO	SB	CS	SLG	OBP
Altagracia, Joel	R-R	6-2	180	9-1-91	.206	.125	.228	60	228	28	47	17	0	5	25	21	4	1	1	82	3	1	.346	.283
Bieneme, Vismeldy	B-R	5-10	160	3-19-90	.283	.160	.324	25	99	15	28	1	1	0	9	14	1	1	1	24	17	6	.313	.374
2-team total (41 Cubs 1)					.260	—	—	66	242	40	63	6	3	1	20	41	4	4	2	62	42	16	.322	.374
Camarena, Melvin	R-R	6-4	210	10-12-89	.271	.230	.288	57	221	38	60	9	1	4	29	12	4	1	1	68	8	2	.376	.319
Contreras, Willson	R-R	6-1	175	5-13-92	.205	.214	.202	29	112	13	23	5	2	1	6	10	6	2	0	26	2	2	.313	.305
Disla, Rafael	B-R	5-10	160	3-27-91	.248	.290	.236	41	141	25	35	6	2	0	15	36	2	3	0	34	19	4	.319	.408
Figueroa, Darlyn	R-R	6-3	190	12-21-89	.216	.206	.218	50	153	26	33	8	1	0	15	23	7	0	0	44	6	5	.281	.344
Gonzalez, Gregori	R-R	5-9	170	7-11-89	.216	.500	.182	10	37	2	8	0	0	0	5	3	0	0	1	5	1	3	.216	.268
2-team total (23 Cubs 1)					.190	—	—	33	100	8	19	3	0	0	8	6	0	0	1	22	9	6	.220	.234
Gonzalez, Jasly	R-R	6-3	190	1-28-91	.178	.109	.201	56	185	26	33	3	5	3	18	21	5	3	0	49	4	4	.297	.280
Gonzalez, Miguel	R-R	6-0	180	10-30-89	.285	.314	.273	43	123	10	35	7	1	0	15	6	7	1	2	16	2	3	.358	.348
Henry, Carlos	L-R	5-11	170	5-11-92	.162	.140	.169	58	198	22	32	5	4	1	16	21	4	4	1	45	8	6	.242	.254
Medina, Pedro	R-R	6-2	170	6-15-90	—	—	—	1	0	0	0	0	0	0	0	0	0	0	0	0	0	0	—	—
Montecino, Jose	B-R	5-11	175	7-31-90	.299	.355	.276	36	107	21	32	2	0	0	11	18	2	1	2	14	12	5	.318	.403
2-team total (23 Cubs 1)					.272	—	—	59	169	26	46	3	0	0	15	31	4	4	2	28	16	7	.290	.393
Parra, Ricardo	R-R	6-0	180	5-30-91	.230	.053	.291	28	74	5	17	2	0	0	3	3	3	0	1	26	0	0	.257	.284
Perez, Melido	L-R	5-10	160	10-22-90	.318	.333	.316	6	22	2	7	0	2	0	1	2	1	0	0	6	1	1	.500	.400
Robles, Gregorio	R-R	6-1	170	3-4-91	.222	.196	.232	56	189	27	42	4	2	0	12	18	2	3	0	45	10	9	.265	.297
Suarez, Hector	B-R	6-1	170	5-5-92	.221	.233	.218	41	131	14	29	6	1	0	19	16	6	1	1	31	2	0	.282	.331

Pitching	B-T	HT	WT	DOB	W	L	ERA	G	GS	CG	SV	IP	H	R	ER	HR	BB	SO	AVG	vLH	vRH	K/9	BB/9
Castro, Darlin	R-R	6-0	175	5-29-92	1	5	7.71	17	5	0	0	30	42	37	26	1	26	29	.313	.286	.326	8.60	7.71
Cruz, Willengton	R-L	6-2	170	8-8-90	0	2	9.56	7	4	0	0	16	21	20	17	1	19	10	.333	.200	.345	5.63	10.69
2-team total (8 Cubs 1)					1	2	6.10	15	10	0	0	38	37	30	26	1	43	31	—	—	—	7.28	10.10
Encarnacion, Antonio	R-R	6-1	170	11-6-91	0	4	4.47	14	7	0	0	46	51	37	23	2	19	33	.285	.302	.279	6.41	3.69
Jimenez, Alvido	R-R	6-1	160	11-22-91	1	1	3.91	8	3	0	0	25	28	17	11	0	10	24	.275	.214	.297	8.53	3.55
2-team total (7 Cubs 1)					1	1	3.00	15	7	0	0	54	59	31	18	1	16	52	—	—	—	8.67	2.67
Leyba, Richard	L-L	6-4	210	10-25-91	1	0	10.05	14	0	0	1	14	25	26	16	1	16	16	.347	.333	.348	10.05	10.05
Martinez, Eric	R-R	6-2	185	1-25-90	0	2	5.59	13	7	0	0	47	59	40	29	3	17	23	.299	.292	.302	4.44	3.28
Mejia, Roneidy	R-R	6-3	180	5-14-90	1	1	3.48	27	0	0	7	41	38	30	16	2	16	27	.235	.333	.200	5.88	3.48
Mendez, Jadel	R-R	6-2	170	11-21-88	0	0	1.04	6	3	0	0	26	25	10	3	1	3	19	.250	.222	.256	6.58	1.04
2-team total (9 Cubs 1)					1	2	3.63	15	6	0	1	52	66	32	21	1	9	40	—	—	—	6.92	1.56
Padron, Loiger	R-R	6-0	180	1-31-91	2	5	6.91	14	4	0	0	27	28	28	21	0	24	24	.248	.276	.238	7.90	7.90
Paulino, Amaury	R-R	6-1	175	8-31-91	0	4	4.22	15	7	0	0	32	33	29	15	0	26	22	.264	.222	.276	6.19	7.31
Pena, Enyelberth	R-R	6-2	175	9-8-90	0	2	6.55	4	2	0	0	11	15	12	8	0	6	9	.341	.286	.367	7.36	4.91
2-team total (9 Cubs 1)					2	2	5.94	13	5	0	0	36	42	34	24	0	23	23	—	—	—	5.70	5.70
Pena, Felix	R-R	6-2	186	2-25-90	1	4	3.58	14	6	0	0	50	53	30	20	2	15	38	.266	.356	.240	6.79	2.68
Pena, Genezaret	R-R	6-5	200	6-6-89	1	0	14.40	12	0	0	0	10	12	20	16	1	16	8	.279	.167	.323	7.20	14.40
Reyes, Roeldwin	R-R	6-1	160	5-14-89	3	4	5.00	22	1	0	0	45	52	36	25	1	18	38	.275	.378	.250	7.60	3.60

Robles, Albert	R-R	6-1	165	4-27-92	1	1	13.86	14	0	0	0	12	15	20	19	0	20	7	.300	.308	.297	5.11	14.59
Rodriguez, Santo	L-R	6-1	185	9-29-89	0	6	3.43	12	7	0	0	39	45	32	15	0	13	28	.281	.273	.283	6.41	2.97
Rosario, Braulio	R-R	6-3	175	9-21-89	0	2	1.80	4	0	0	0	5	5	6	1	1	2	4	.263	.200	.286	7.20	3.60
Rosario, Jose	R-R	6-1	170	8-29-90	2	2	2.49	7	3	0	0	22	12	11	6	0	13	28	.148	.130	.155	11.63	5.40
Sanchez, Yilver	R-R	6-2	198	7-31-90	1	5	3.45	15	7	1	0	60	63	36	23	3	13	46	.256	.292	.243	6.90	1.95
Severino, Deuris	R-R	6-1	170	8-26-90	0	2	9.00	19	0	0	1	27	30	33	27	2	23	25	.270	.214	.289	8.33	7.67

Fielding

Catcher	PCT	G	PO	A	E	DP	PB
Gonzalez	.940	32	149	38	12	3	16
Parra	.983	20	97	16	2	1	7
Suarez	.952	34	198	19	11	1	22

First Base	PCT	G	PO	A	E	DP
Altagracia	.974	17	141	10	4	10
Borges	.968	22	190	19	7	20
Camarena	.958	27	191	14	9	10
Gonzalez	.892	4	30	3	4	0
Parra	1.000	1	6	1	0	0
Suarez	.923	1	12	0	1	1

Second Base	PCT	G	PO	A	E	DP
Bieneme	.875	4	11	3	2	2
Gonzalez	.920	4	10	13	2	2
Henry	.880	39	90	78	23	13
Montecino	.920	19	38	43	7	11
Perez	.889	4	8	8	2	1
Suarez	1.000	2	2	0	0	0

Third Base	PCT	G	PO	A	E	DP
Altagracia	.824	38	30	78	23	7
Bieneme	.667	5	1	9	5	0
Contreras	.787	21	13	46	16	3
Disla	1.000	3	0	2	0	0
Henry	.900	4	8	10	2	3

Shortstop	PCT	G	PO	A	E	DP
Bieneme	.927	9	16	22	3	5
Disla	.876	36	62	100	23	16
Gonzalez	.870	4	5	15	3	3
Montecino	.816	9	15	16	7	2

Outfield	PCT	G	PO	A	E	DP
Bieneme	.900	5	8	1	1	0
Borges	.982	34	50	5	1	0
Camarena	.957	25	41	4	2	0
Figueroa	.890	41	59	6	8	0
Gonzalez	1.000	2	2	2	0	1
Gonzalez	.899	54	84	5	10	3
Robles	.949	55	123	6	7	2

Chicago White Sox

SEASON IN A SENTENCE: General manager Ken Williams never stopped trying to improve his roster and was able to pry Jake Peavy away from the Padres in his most significant deal, but the White Sox never got more than a half-game lead in the American League Central and fell out of playoff contention by going 11-17 in August.

HIGH POINT: Ace Mark Buehrle pitched the 17th perfect game in baseball history—which was preserved thanks to an amazing ninth-inning catch from center fielder DeWayne Wise—in a 5-0 win over the Rays on July 23, putting the White Sox in first place as they won for the fifth time in seven games. White Sox fan Barack Obama even called with congratulations after the game.

LOW POINT: The White Sox lost their fourth straight game (and ninth of 10) when the Twins scored in the bottom of the ninth for a 4-3 victory on Sept. 1. The Twins were in the midst of surging toward the AL Central title, while the White Sox were in the middle of their worst stretch of the season.

NOTABLE ROOKIES: Gordon Beckham, the club's first-round pick in 2008, reached the big leagues in less than a year and was a revelation at third base, proving to be one of the best rookies in the American League. He batted .270/.347/.460 after getting called up in June. The only other rookie to play a significant role was lefthander Aaron Poreda, who contributed in the bullpen before going to San Diego in the Peavy deal.

KEY TRANSACTIONS: After trying to get Peavy for most of the year, the White Sox finally succeeded at the trade deadline by sending lefthanders Poreda and Clayton Richard and two other pitchers to the Padres. The deal ended up not paying big dividends in 2009 because Peavy had a bad ankle, and by the time he returned to the mound the White Sox were effectively out of it. He is under contract through at least 2012, however. When the Sox fell out of the race, Williams traded away Jim Thome and Jose Contreras for a couple of minor prospects.

DOWN ON THE FARM: White Sox affiliates had the third-best winning percentage in baseball, and both Double-A Birmingham and low Class A Kannapolis had the best overall records in their leagues. The farm system is thinner after the graduation of Beckham and trades that shipped out four of their top nine prospects heading into the 2009 season.

OPENING DAY PAYROLL: $96,068,500

PLAYERS OF THE YEAR

RODGER WOOD

MAJOR LEAGUE	MINOR LEAGUE
Mark Buehrle lhp	**Daniel Hudson** rhp
13-10, 3.84	(Lo A/Hi A/AA/AAA)
4th All-Star Game,	14-5, 2.32
first Gold Glove	166 SO in 147 IP

ORGANIZATION LEADERS

BATTING *Minimum 250 at-bats

MAJORS

*AVG	Scott Podsednik	.304
*OPS	Paul Konerko	.842
HR	Paul Konerko	28
RBI	Paul Konerko	88

MINORS

*AVG	Marrero, Christian, Winston-Salem/Birm.	.308
R	Cook, David, Charlotte/Birmingham	89
H	Restovich, Michael, Charlotte	142
	Retherford, C.J., Birmingham	142
TB	Restovich, Michael, Charlotte	247
2B	Retherford, C.J., Birmingham	46
3B	Escobar, Eduardo, Kannapolis	7
HR	Cook, David, Charlotte/Birmingham	26
RBI	Gartrell, Stefan, Birmingham/Charlotte	89
BB	Flowers, Tyler, Birmingham/Charlotte	67
SO	Paiml, Greg, Winston-Salem	152
SB	Shelby III, John, Birmingham	30
*OBP	Flowers, Tyler, Birmingham/Charlotte	.423
*SLG	Loman, Seth, Kannapolis/Winston-Salem	.519

PITCHING †Minimum 75 innings

MAJORS

W	Mark Buehrle	13
†ERA	John Danks	3.77
SO	Gavin Floyd	163

MINORS

W	Three tied at	14
L	Maxwell, Levi, Winston-Salem	14
†ERA	Hudson, Dan, Kannapolis/W-S/Birm./Charlotte	2.32
G	Hernandez, Fernando, Birmingham/Charlotte	57
GS	Three tied at	27
SV	Remenowsky, Dan, Kannapolis	24
IP	Leesman, Charles, Kannapolis	158
BB	Harrell, Lucas, Birmingham/Charlotte	69
SO	Hudson, Dan, Kannapolis/W-S/Birm./Charlotte	166
†AVG	Hudson, Dan, Kannapolis/W-S/Birm./Charlotte	.200

2009 PERFORMANCE

General Manager: Ken Williams. **Farm Director:** Buddy Bell. **Scouting Director:** Doug Laumann.

Class	Team	League	W	L	PCT	Finish*	Manager(s)
Majors	Chicago White Sox	American	79	83	.488	9th (14)	Ozzie Guillen
Triple-A	Charlotte Knights	International	67	76	.469	11th (14)	Chris Chambliss
Double-A	Birmingham Barons	Southern	92	47	.662	1st (10)	Ever Magallanes
High A	Winston-Salem Dash	Carolina	73	65	.529	3rd (8)	Joe McEwing
Low A	Kannapolis Intimidators	South Atlantic	82	57	.590	1st (16)	Ernie Young
Rookie	Bristol White Sox	Appalachian	27	39	.409	8th (10)	Ryan Newman
Rookie	Great Falls Voyagers	Pioneer	42	34	.553	3rd (8)	Chris Cron
Overall 2009 Minor League Record			383	318	.546	3rd (30)	

*Finish in overall standings (No. of teams in league). †League champion.

ORGANIZATION STATISTICS

CHICAGO WHITE SOX
AMERICAN LEAGUE

Batting	B-T	HT	WT	DOB	AVG	vLH	vRH	G	AB	R	H	2B	3B	HR	RBI	BB	HBP	SH	SF	SO	SB	CS	SLG	OBP
Anderson, Brian	R-R	6-2	215	3-11-82	.238	.167	.267	65	185	25	44	9	0	2	13	20	3	2	0	49	3	6	.319	.322
2-team total (21 Boston)					.243	—	—	86	202	32	49	9	0	4	18	23	3	2	1	54	3	6	.347	.328
Beckham, Gordon	R-R	6-0	190	9-16-86	.270	.318	.250	103	378	58	102	28	1	14	63	41	6	1	4	65	7	4	.460	.347
Betemit, Wilson	B-R	6-3	230	11-2-81	.200	.200	.200	20	45	2	9	5	0	0	3	5	0	0	0	13	0	0	.311	.280
Castro, Ramon	R-R	6-3	245	3-1-76	.184	.257	.122	31	76	8	14	3	0	4	12	8	0	0	0	23	0	0	.382	.262
Dye, Jermaine	R-R	6-5	245	1-28-74	.250	.292	.236	141	503	78	126	19	1	27	81	64	5	0	2	108	0	2	.453	.340
Fields, Josh	R-R	6-2	225	12-14-82	.222	.243	.213	79	239	29	53	5	2	7	30	25	2	2	0	76	2	3	.347	.301
Flowers, Tyler	R-R	6-4	245	1-24-86	.188	.250	.125	10	16	3	3	1	0	0	3	1	0	0	0	8	0	0	.250	.350
Getz, Chris	L-R	6-0	185	8-30-83	.261	.246	.265	107	375	49	98	18	4	2	31	30	6	1	3	54	25	2	.347	.324
Konerko, Paul	R-R	6-2	215	3-5-76	.277	.338	.253	152	546	75	151	30	1	28	88	58	10	0	7	89	1	0	.489	.353
Kotsay, Mark	L-L	6-0	205	12-2-75	.292	.227	.308	40	113	12	33	7	0	3	18	11	0	1	2	9	1	1	.434	.349
2-team total (27 Boston)					.278	—	—	67	187	16	52	9	0	4	23	15	0	1	3	21	3	2	.390	.327
Lillibridge, Brent	R-R	5-11	190	9-18-83	.158	.214	.134	46	95	9	15	2	0	0	3	14	1	2	0	26	6	3	.179	.273
Miller, Corky	R-R	6-1	245	3-18-76	.205	.353	.091	14	39	5	8	3	0	0	5	3	0	0	0	9	0	0	.282	.262
Nix, Jayson	R-R	5-11	185	8-26-82	.224	.256	.194	94	255	36	57	11	0	12	32	28	4	1	2	64	10	2	.408	.308
Owens, Jerry	L-L	6-3	195	2-16-81	.083	.500	.000	12	12	0	1	0	0	0	0	3	0	0	0	3	1	0	.083	.267
Pierzynski, A.J.	L-R	6-3	230	12-30-76	.300	.277	.307	138	504	57	151	22	1	13	49	24	1	3	3	52	1	1	.425	.331
Podsednik, Scott	L-L	6-2	190	3-18-76	.304	.320	.297	132	537	75	163	25	6	7	48	39	3	6	2	74	30	13	.412	.353
Quentin, Carlos	R-R	6-1	230	8-28-82	.236	.213	.245	99	351	47	83	14	0	21	56	31	15	0	2	52	3	0	.456	.323
Ramirez, Alexei	R-R	6-2	170	9-22-81	.277	.370	.248	148	542	71	150	14	1	15	68	49	1	6	8	66	14	5	.389	.333
Rios, Alex	R-R	6-5	215	2-18-81	.199	.243	.183	41	146	11	29	6	0	3	9	6	0	1	1	29	5	2	.301	.229
2-team total (108 Toronto)					.247	—	—	149	582	63	144	31	2	17	71	37	6	1	7	107	24	5	.395	.296
Thome, Jim	L-R	6-3	250	8-27-70	.249	.216	.261	107	345	55	86	15	0	23	74	69	0	0	3	116	0	0	.493	.372
Wise, Dewayne	L-L	6-1	190	2-24-78	.225	.400	.205	84	142	17	32	8	3	2	11	3	4	4	0	27	4	5	.366	.262

Pitching	B-T	HT	WT	DOB	W	L	ERA	G	GS	CG	SV	IP	H	R	ER	HR	BB	SO	AVG	vLH	vRH	K/9	BB/9
Broadway, Lance	R-R	6-3	195	8-20-83	0	1	5.06	8	0	0	0	16	19	10	9	0	9	9	.288	.323	.257	5.06	5.06
Buehrle, Mark	L-L	6-2	230	3-23-79	13	10	3.84	33	33	1	0	213	222	97	91	20	45	105	.275	.298	.267	4.43	1.90
Carrasco, D.J.	R-R	6-3	220	4-12-77	5	1	3.76	49	1	0	0	93	103	42	39	5	29	62	.281	.317	.251	5.98	2.80
Colon, Bartolo	R-R	5-11	245	5-24-73	3	6	4.19	12	12	0	0	62	69	42	29	13	21	38	.280	.288	.273	5.49	3.03
Contreras, Jose	R-R	6-4	255	12-6-71	5	13	5.42	21	21	0	0	115	121	83	69	11	45	89	.267	.243	.291	6.99	3.53
Danks, John	L-L	6-1	205	4-15-85	13	11	3.77	32	32	1	0	200	184	89	84	28	73	149	.245	.244	.246	6.69	3.28
Dotel, Octavio	R-R	6-0	215	11-25-73	3	3	3.32	62	0	0	0	62	54	26	23	7	36	75	.239	.248	.226	10.83	5.20
Egbert, Jack	R-R	6-3	220	5-12-83	0	0	27.00	2	0	0	0	3	8	8	8	1	2	0	.533	.750	.455	0.00	6.75
Floyd, Gavin	R-R	6-5	230	1-27-83	11	11	4.06	30	30	1	0	193	178	93	87	21	59	163	.244	.232	.256	7.60	2.75
Garcia, Freddy	R-R	6-4	260	10-6-76	3	4	4.34	9	9	0	0	56	56	27	27	4	12	37	.259	.196	.316	5.95	1.93
Gobble, Jimmy	L-L	6-3	210	7-19-81	0	0	7.50	12	0	0	0	12	14	10	10	3	7	10	.280	.227	.321	7.50	5.25
Hudson, Dan	R-R	6-4	220	3-9-87	1	1	3.38	6	2	0	0	19	16	9	7	3	9	14	.225	.194	.257	6.75	4.34
Jenks, Bobby	R-R	6-3	275	3-14-81	3	4	3.71	52	0	0	29	53	52	24	22	9	16	49	.250	.309	.202	8.27	2.70
Linebrink, Scott	R-R	6-2	210	8-4-76	3	7	4.66	57	0	0	2	56	70	34	29	9	23	55	.304	.297	.310	8.84	3.70
MacDougal, Mike	B-R	6-4	190	3-5-77	0	0	12.46	5	0	0	0	4	7	6	6	0	7	2	.389	.571	.273	5.23	14.54
Nunez, Jhonny	L-R	6-3	185	11-26-85	0	0	9.53	7	0	0	0	6	10	6	6	1	2	3	.370	.667	.222	4.76	3.18
Peavy, Jake	R-R	6-1	195	5-31-81	3	0	1.35	3	3	0	0	20	11	3	3	1	6	18	.162	.132	.200	8.10	2.70
Pena, Tony	R-R	6-2	220	1-9-82	1	2	3.75	35	0	0	1	36	40	17	15	4	9	29	.272	.255	.283	7.25	2.25
Poreda, Aaron	L-L	6-6	240	10-1-86	1	0	2.45	10	0	0	0	11	9	3	3	0	8	12	.231	.357	.160	9.82	6.55
Richard, Clayton	L-L	6-5	240	9-12-83	4	3	4.65	26	14	1	0	89	94	50	46	10	37	66	.276	.213	.299	6.67	3.74
Thornton, Matt	L-L	6-6	235	9-15-76	6	3	2.74	70	0	0	4	72	58	22	22	5	20	87	.217	.208	.223	10.82	2.49
Torres, Carlos	R-R	6-2	195	10-22-82	1	2	6.04	8	5	0	0	28	30	20	19	5	17	22	.286	.264	.308	6.96	5.40
Whisler, Wes	L-L	6-5	240	4-7-83	0	0	13.50	3	0	0	0	1	0	2	2	0	3	2	.000	.000	.000	13.50	20.25
Williams, Randy	L-L	6-3	190	9-18-75	0	1	4.58	25	0	0	0	18	13	9	9	2	12	22	.206	.162	.269	11.21	6.11

CHICAGO WHITE SOX

Fielding

Catcher
Catcher	PCT	G	PO	A	E	DP	PB
Castro	.983	29	163	7	3	2	0
Flowers	1.000	6	20	0	0	0	0
Miller	1.000	11	68	3	0	1	1
Pierzynski	.995	131	879	50	5	8	7

First Base
First Base	PCT	G	PO	A	E	DP
Betemit	.980	7	41	7	1	6
Fields	1.000	17	100	4	0	9
Konerko	.997	134	1159	79	4	112
Kotsay	1.000	22	155	12	0	13

Second Base
Second Base	PCT	G	PO	A	E	DP
Getz	.986	106	196	298	7	75
Lillibridge	.973	23	29	43	2	6
Nix	.973	52	81	137	6	34

Third Base
Third Base	PCT	G	PO	A	E	DP
Beckham	.952	102	73	205	14	21
Betemit	.500	6	0	4	4	0
Fields	.941	49	27	101	8	9
Lillibridge	—	1	0	0	0	0
Nix	.957	12	2	20	1	2

Shortstop
Shortstop	PCT	G	PO	A	E	DP
Lillibridge	.938	7	8	7	1	2
Nix	.906	15	19	39	6	10
Ramirez	.969	148	220	410	20	94

Outfield
Outfield	PCT	G	PO	A	E	DP
Anderson	.984	64	118	3	2	1
Dye	.980	133	238	9	5	3
Kotsay	1.000	11	18	1	0	0
Lillibridge	.6941	12	15	1	1	1
Nix	1.000	7	11	0	0	0
Owens	1.000	7	11	0	0	0
Podsednik	.992	116	258	6	2	2
Quentin	.988	88	157	6	2	2
Rios	.979	41	93	0	2	0
Wise	.990	70	96	6	1	3

CHARLOTTE KNIGHTS   TRIPLE-A

INTERNATIONAL LEAGUE

Batting	B-T	HT	WT	DOB	AVG	vLH	vRH	G	AB	R	H	2B	3B	HR	RBI	BB	HBP	SH	SF	SO	SB	CS	SLG	OBP
Allen, Brandon	L-R	6-2	235	2-12-86	.262	.385	.229	15	61	6	16	4	0	1	8	0	0	0	0	13	0	0	.377	.262
Anderson, Brian	R-R	6-2	215	3-11-82	.279	.462	.200	11	43	6	12	1	1	2	5	2	0	1	0	16	0	1	.488	.311
2-team total (24 Pawtucket)					.228	—	—	35	123	15	28	5	1	6	13	9	2	2	0	38	0	3	.431	.291
Armstrong, Cole	R-R	6-3	210	8-24-83	.252	.242	.254	69	246	28	62	13	0	10	32	12	1	0	2	51	0	0	.427	.287
Beckham, Gordon	R-R	6-0	190	9-16-86	.464	.375	.500	7	28	6	13	6	0	0	3	0	0	1	1	2	1	0	.679	.448
Betemit, Wilson	B-R	6-3	230	11-2-81	.241	.257	.235	72	261	36	63	19	0	11	49	21	0	0	4	73	2	0	.441	.294
Broussard, Ben	L-L	6-2	230	9-24-76	.130	.333	.059	7	23	0	3	0	0	0	2	3	0	0	1	5	1	0	.130	.222
Cannizaro, Andy	R-R	5-10	170	12-19-78	.208	.200	.211	22	77	5	16	3	0	0	4	5	1	3	0	11	0	0	.247	.265
2-team total (50 Columbus)					.249	—	—	72	237	18	59	13	0	1	23	20	6	6	1	30	0	1	.316	.322
Castillo, Javier	R-R	6-3	210	8-29-83	.262	.348	.230	47	168	16	44	11	2	2	15	13	1	0	0	40	0	1	.387	.319
2-team total (78 Buffalo)					.249	—	—	125	442	40	110	25	3	7	39	28	3	0	1	87	1	2	.367	.297
Cook, David	R-R	5-11	205	7-21-81	.192	.313	.000	7	26	2	5	0	0	1	2	1	0	1	0	9	0	0	.308	.222
Dawkins, Gookie	R-R	6-1	180	5-12-79	.229	.174	.255	20	70	6	16	6	0	0	1	2	1	0	0	17	2	1	.314	.260
Fields, Josh	R-R	6-2	225	12-14-82	.265	.214	.286	27	98	15	26	5	0	5	13	13	1	2	0	22	1	2	.469	.357
Fischer, Lee	R-R	6-4	170	7-31-86	.500	—	.500	1	2	0	1	0	0	0	0	1	0	0	0	0	0	0	1.000	.667
Flowers, Tyler	R-R	6-4	245	1-24-86	.286	.371	.243	31	105	13	30	10	0	2	13	10	3	1	0	32	0	0	.438	.364
Fulgencio, Jose	R-R	6-1	162	12-16-86	.174	.429	.063	7	23	2	4	0	0	0	0	1	0	1	0	5	1	0	.174	.174
Fuller, Justin	L-R	6-1	190	7-10-83	.308	.333	.300	5	13	1	4	0	0	0	1	3	0	0	0	4	1	1	.308	.438
Gartrell, Stefan	R-R	6-3	230	1-14-84	.265	.333	.244	31	113	14	30	11	1	4	19	7	1	0	0	29	0	2	.487	.314
Gerst, Kent	L-R	5-10	170	2-6-88	.148	.429	.050	8	27	1	4	0	0	1	4	2	0	0	1	9	1	1	.259	.200
Getz, Chris	L-R	6-0	185	8-30-83	.267	.125	.429	5	15	4	4	0	0	0	0	3	1	0	0	1	2	0	.267	.421
Ginter, Keith	R-R	5-10	195	5-5-76	.262	.245	.269	107	363	35	95	22	1	6	33	39	5	6	1	71	2	2	.377	.341
Gonzalez, Miguel	R-R	6-0	200	12-3-90	.182	.000	.250	3	11	1	2	0	0	0	1	0	0	0	0	2	0	0	.182	.182
Hopper, Norris	R-R	5-11	205	5-29-79	.329	.314	.341	20	76	12	25	3	0	0	5	7	0	0	0	4	3	3	.368	.386
3-team total (52 Louisville, 34 Syracuse)					.281	—	—	106	409	49	115	14	3	0	35	35	1	5	3	25	23	8	.330	.337
Knoedler, Justin	R-R	6-2	215	7-17-80	.222	.364	.125	8	27	3	6	0	0	1	1	0	0	0	0	7	0	0	.333	.222
Kroeger, Josh	L-L	6-3	230	8-31-82	.267	.266	.268	128	501	59	134	27	0	17	56	36	2	0	1	86	23	7	.423	.319
Lillibridge, Brent	R-R	5-11	190	9-18-83	.252	.240	.257	67	246	34	62	9	4	3	24	29	4	3	1	57	17	1	.358	.339
Lucy, Donny	R-R	6-2	205	8-8-82	.216	.266	.180	45	153	14	33	8	0	2	10	10	0	2	3	38	2	2	.307	.259
Miller, Corky	R-R	6-1	245	3-18-76	.143	.000	.333	4	7	0	1	0	0	0	0	2	1	0	0	2	0	0	.143	.400
2-team total (23 Louisville)					.274	—	—	27	84	13	23	5	0	0	8	10	4	2	0	9	0	0	.333	.378
Myrow, Brian	L-R	5-11	210	9-4-76	.277	.200	.288	48	159	23	44	10	0	7	25	22	5	1	1	37	0	1	.472	.380
2-team total (62 Indianapolis)					.307	—	—	110	365	60	112	22	1	15	59	65	10	1	6	70	3	2	.496	.419
Negron, Miguel	L-L	6-1	190	8-22-82	.279	.270	.282	103	384	41	107	15	3	4	38	26	1	4	2	62	14	13	.365	.324
Nix, Jayson	R-R	5-11	185	8-26-82	.450	.333	.471	5	20	4	9	1	0	0	5	4	0	0	0	1	0	0	.500	.542
Owens, Jerry	L-L	6-3	195	2-16-81	.143	.500	.000	2	7	1	1	0	0	0	2	1	0	0	0	3	0	0	.143	.250
Phillips, Andy	R-R	6-0	215	4-6-77	.295	.354	.275	49	190	24	56	9	1	5	27	15	0	1	2	26	1	1	.432	.343
2-team total (7 Indianapolis)					.300	—	—	56	217	26	65	9	1	6	29	17	1	1	3	30	1	1	.433	.349
Podsednik, Scott	L-L	6-2	190	3-18-76	.262	.143	.321	10	42	6	11	4	0	0	2	5	2	0	0	5	1	0	.357	.367
Quentin, Carlos	R-R	6-1	230	8-28-82	.378	.278	.474	12	37	10	14	3	0	1	9	5	2	0	1	2	0	0	.541	.467
Restovich, Michael	R-R	6-6	240	1-3-79	.290	.269	.299	135	489	83	142	36	3	21	61	58	2	0	3	118	0	1	.505	.366
Shoemaker, Brady	R-R	6-0	205	5-10-87	.103	.000	.150	8	29	3	3	1	0	1	2	1	0	0	0	6	0	0	.241	.133
Torres, Eider	B-R	5-8	165	1-16-83	.240	.252	.234	92	359	36	86	12	1	1	29	24	3	2	1	63	13	7	.287	.292
Ward, Daryle	L-L	6-2	240	6-27-75	.255	.175	.283	69	247	31	63	11	0	8	36	31	2	0	3	49	2	1	.397	.339
2-team total (30 Syracuse)					.252	—	—	99	341	41	86	13	0	13	49	43	3	0	5	69	2	1	.405	.337
Wise, Dewayne	L-L	6-1	190	2-24-78	.333	.500	.235	7	27	2	9	3	1	0	3	1	0	0	0	4	0	0	.519	.357

Pitching	B-T	HT	WT	DOB	W	L	ERA	G	GS	CG	SV	IP	H	R	ER	HR	BB	SO	AVG	vLH	vRH	K/9	BB/9
Asselin, Kevin	L-R	6-1	180	2-16-85	0	0	12.00	2	0	0	0	3	3	4	4	1	2	4	.273	.250	.333	12.00	6.00
Broadway, Lance	R-R	6-3	195	8-20-83	0	2	5.63	3	3	0	0	16	18	11	10	2	4	15	.273	.368	.143	8.44	2.25
2-team total (16 Buffalo)					5	9	6.17	19	17	1	0	101	119	74	69	8	38	56	—	—		5.01	3.40
Cassel, Justin	R-R	6-2	215	9-25-84	3	9	5.06	18	12	0	0	75	86	47	42	10	27	53	.281	.246	.304	6.39	3.25
Colon, Bartolo	R-R	5-11	245	5-24-73	1	1	3.75	2	2	0	0	12	10	5	5	2	4	1	.233	.200	.250	0.75	3.00
Contreras, Jose	R-R	6-4	255	12-6-71	1	1	2.70	5	5	1	0	33	19	12	10	2	16	27	.164	.229	.118	7.29	4.32
DeFoor, Brent	R-R	6-2	175	1-9-86	0	0	6.75	2	0	0	0	3	2	2	2	0	2	4	.200	.250	.167	13.50	6.75
Egbert, Jack	L-R	6-3	220	5-12-83	6	11	5.05	30	18	0	1	109	132	73	61	13	33	78	.293	.270	.309	6.46	2.73
Garcia, Freddy	R-R	6-4	260	10-6-76	0	1	3.00	1	1	0	0	6	8	2	2	1	0	9	.320	.500	.263	13.50	0.00

	B-T	HT	WT	DOB	W	L	ERA	G	GS	CG	SV	IP	H	R	ER	HR	BB	SO	AVG	vLH	vRH		
2-team total (2 Buffalo)					0	3	6.35	3	3	0	0	17	20	12	12	3	5	15	—	—	—	7.94	2.65
Gobble, Jimmy	L-L	6-3	210	7-19-81	0	1	5.25	11	0	0	1	12	8	8	7	2	4	19	.174	.059	.241	14.25	3.00
Harrell, Lucas	B-R	6-2	205	6-3-85	4	1	3.29	11	11	0	0	66	58	26	24	3	37	42	.246	.225	.261	5.76	5.07
Hernandez, Fernando	R-R	5-11	190	7-31-84	1	1	1.59	13	0	0	0	17	11	4	3	0	8	17	.180	.217	.158	9.00	4.24
Hudson, Dan	R-R	6-4	220	3-9-87	2	0	3.00	5	5	0	0	24	22	10	8	1	9	24	.247	.171	.296	9.00	3.38
Hynick, Brandon	R-R	6-3	205	3-7-85	1	0	1.29	1	1	0	0	7	4	1	1	0	2	2	.167	.100	.214	2.57	2.57
Jimenez, Kelvin	R-R	6-2	195	10-27-80	6	3	4.02	40	4	0	1	78	97	40	35	11	20	55	.307	.308	.306	6.32	2.30
Johnston, Mike	L-L	6-3	220	3-30-79	0	0	0.00	5	0	0	0	5	5	0	0	0	2	1	.294	.250	.333	1.93	3.86
Link, Jon	R-R	6-1	190	3-23-84	1	2	3.99	48	0	0	13	56	55	26	25	5	27	66	.256	.314	.217	10.54	4.31
Long, Matt	R-R	6-5	220	2-23-84	0	0	5.40	1	1	0	0	5	7	3	3	0	1	6	.333	.364	.300	10.80	1.80
Marquez, Jeff	R-R	6-2	190	8-10-84	2	8	9.85	11	11	0	0	46	72	51	50	12	22	27	.362	.333	.388	5.32	4.34
Nunez, Jhonny	L-R	6-3	185	11-26-85	2	0	3.33	16	0	0	1	24	19	9	9	3	5	22	.221	.265	.192	8.14	1.85
Omogrosso, Brian	R-R	6-4	230	4-26-84	0	0	15.88	4	0	0	0	6	12	10	10	2	3	6	.429	.727	.235	9.53	4.76
Peavy, Jake	R-R	6-1	195	5-31-81	1	1	2.93	4	4	0	0	15	14	6	5	1	4	17	.237	.259	.219	9.98	2.35
Poreda, Aaron	L-L	6-6	240	10-1-86	0	0	3.60	2	2	0	0	10	8	4	4	0	3	9	.216	.000	.242	8.10	2.70
Rodriguez, Derek	R-R	6-1	190	5-17-83	0	3	3.49	36	1	0	2	57	56	24	22	3	23	44	.264	.280	.255	6.99	3.65
Rote, Ryan	R-R	6-4	225	8-8-82	0	0	1.93	3	0	0	0	5	3	2	1	0	5	4	.188	.000	.300	7.71	9.64
Russell, Adam	R-R	6-8	255	4-14-83	2	2	3.20	34	0	0	5	56	39	20	20	5	18	51	.200	.234	.178	8.15	2.88
Santos, Sergio	R-R	6-3	225	7-4-83	0	1	9.00	3	0	0	0	5	5	5	5	0	7	5	.263	.333	.231	12.60	12.60
Thompson, Taylor	R-R	6-5	225	6-18-87	0	0	0.00	2	0	0	0	4	2	0	0	0	4	1	.154	.333	.000	2.25	9.00
Torres, Carlos	R-R	6-2	195	10-22-82	10	4	2.39	23	20	2	1	128	96	38	34	4	56	130	.207	.226	.190	9.14	3.94
Van Benschoten, John	R-R	6-4	215	4-14-80	2	8	6.35	22	13	0	0	78	97	66	55	9	30	67	.298	.292	.301	7.73	3.46
Wassermann, Ehren	B-R	6-0	190	12-6-80	7	3	3.68	43	0	0	1	64	72	30	26	3	18	57	.290	.366	.253	8.06	2.54
Whisler, Wes	L-L	6-5	240	4-7-83	10	12	4.01	26	26	1	0	153	165	83	68	10	56	77	.276	.311	.265	4.54	3.30
Williams, Randy	L-L	6-3	190	9-18-75	3	0	3.44	33	0	0	1	37	31	17	14	3	11	40	.220	.246	.200	9.82	2.70
Wiltz, Danny	R-R	6-1	200	2-13-87	0	0	162.00	1	0	0	0	0	6	6	6	1	3	1	.857	.667	1.000	27.00	81.00
Zaleski, Matt	R-R	6-1	190	12-2-81	0	1	2.25	3	3	0	0	16	13	4	4	2	3	15	.213	.077	.250	8.44	1.69

Fielding

Catcher	PCT	G	PO	A	E	DP	PB
Armstrong	.990	63	464	34	5	4	2
Flowers	.984	28	178	10	3	1	3
Gonzalez	1.000	3	17	0	0	0	1
Knoedler	1.000	7	48	3	0	1	3
Lucy	.988	45	290	31	4	5	4
Miller	1.000	2	8	0	0	0	0

First Base	PCT	G	PO	A	E	DP
Allen	1.000	13	122	7	0	15
Betemit	1.000	17	140	16	0	17
Broussard	.973	4	36	0	1	2
Kroeger	.987	32	276	17	4	35
Myrow	.995	22	193	10	1	13
Phillips	.995	21	189	11	1	18
Ward	.990	35	285	23	3	24

Second Base	PCT	G	PO	A	E	DP
Cannizaro	1.000	1	0	1	0	1
Dawkins	1.000	5	11	18	0	2
Fischer	1.000	1	1	2	0	1
Fulgencio	.963	6	11	15	1	2
Fuller	1.000	1	1	1	0	0

	PCT	G	PO	A	E	DP
Getz	1.000	4	5	7	0	2
Ginter	.980	84	170	226	8	63
Lillibridge	1.000	1	1	2	0	0
Nix	1.000	1	5	1	0	1
Phillips	.978	12	18	26	1	4
Torres	.993	31	45	90	1	19

Third Base	PCT	G	PO	A	E	DP
Beckham	.923	6	2	22	2	1
Betemit	.942	37	16	98	7	4
Cannizaro	1.000	2	3	5	0	1
Castillo	.907	44	25	82	11	7
Dawkins	1.000	2	3	2	0	0
Fields	.907	25	17	51	7	5
Ginter	.935	22	19	53	5	2
Phillips	.800	7	1	7	2	0

Shortstop	PCT	G	PO	A	E	DP
Beckham	.857	1	2	4	1	3
Betemit	1.000	2	4	6	0	5
Cannizaro	.941	19	21	43	4	11
Dawkins	.966	5	6	22	1	2
Fulgencio	1.000	1	3	5	0	1

	PCT	G	PO	A	E	DP
Fuller	.944	4	6	11	1	3
Lillibridge	.967	49	72	159	8	46
Nix	1.000	4	5	9	0	4
Torres	.960	60	85	157	10	29

Outfield	PCT	G	PO	A	E	DP
Anderson	1.000	9	21	1	0	0
Cook	.917	4	10	1	1	0
Dawkins	1.000	8	23	0	0	0
Gartrell	1.000	28	44	0	0	0
Gerst	1.000	8	25	0	0	0
Hopper	1.000	19	43	3	0	2
Kroeger	.963	92	172	8	7	1
Lillibridge	1.000	18	46	0	0	0
Negron	.987	101	219	9	3	1
Owens	1.000	2	2	0	0	0
Phillips	1.000	7	7	1	0	0
Podsednik	.920	9	23	0	2	0
Quentin	1.000	8	11	1	0	0
Restovich	.993	108	145	4	1	0
Shoemaker	1.000	8	8	0	0	0
Ward	1.000	3	4	0	0	0
Wise	1.000	6	16	0	0	0

BIRMINGHAM BARONS   DOUBLE-A

SOUTHERN LEAGUE

Batting	B-T	HT	WT	DOB	AVG	vLH	vRH	G	AB	R	H	2B	3B	HR	RBI	BB	HBP	SH	SF	SO	SB	CS	SLG	OBP
Allen, Brandon	L-R	6-2	235	2-12-86	.290	.301	.286	62	241	39	70	12	3	7	35	30	2	0	1	47	1	2	.452	.372
Beckham, Gordon	R-R	6-0	190	9-16-86	.299	.325	.290	38	147	23	44	17	0	4	22	14	2	2	1	24	1	0	.497	.366
Colina, Javier	R-R	6-1	200	2-15-79	.260	.264	.259	91	315	41	82	15	2	6	41	21	3	2	2	57	2	3	.378	.311
Cook, David	R-R	5-11	205	7-21-81	.264	.304	.245	117	421	87	111	24	3	25	84	64	8	0	3	84	9	7	.513	.369
Cruz, Lee	R-R	6-2	205	6-13-83	.256	.333	.224	65	227	28	58	18	0	6	36	12	1	0	5	51	0	1	.414	.290
Danks, Jordan	L-R	6-4	210	8-7-86	.243	.254	.240	73	284	50	69	12	1	6	20	37	4	4	1	73	7	3	.356	.337
Flowers, Tyler	R-R	6-4	245	1-24-86	.302	.343	.287	77	248	54	75	18	2	13	43	57	9	0	3	76	3	0	.548	.445
Gallagher, Jimmy	L-L	6-1	195	9-3-85	.280	.077	.358	27	93	17	26	8	1	2	20	16	0	0	0	21	0	1	.452	.385
Gartrell, Stefan	R-R	6-3	205	1-14-84	.285	.333	.269	101	361	72	103	20	4	19	70	46	4	0	1	99	6	0	.521	.371
Hudson, Robert	R-R	6-0	170	8-31-83	.251	.270	.243	91	315	40	79	7	1	3	29	14	0	10	5	37	15	3	.308	.278
Lang, C.J.	R-R	5-8	170	4-24-84	.286	.300	.282	29	91	14	26	3	0	0	9	14	0	2	1	10	1	1	.319	.377
Lucy, Donny	R-R	6-2	205	8-8-82	.217	.235	.212	20	69	6	15	1	0	0	2	2	1	1	0	23	0	0	.232	.250
Marrero, Christian	L-L	6-1	185	7-30-86	.301	.268	.312	65	229	28	69	15	1	11	40	18	0	1	9	50	1	1	.520	.340
Nix, Jayson	R-R	5-11	185	8-26-82	.300	.333	.250	3	10	1	3	0	0	0	3	2	0	0	0	0	0	0	.300	.417
Price, Jared	R-R	6-1	230	3-18-82	.220	.250	.209	56	173	18	38	8	0	5	17	6	5	5	0	61	1	0	.353	.266
Retherford, C.J.	R-R	5-10	190	8-14-85	.297	.368	.270	128	478	70	142	46	4	10	76	30	5	5	8	70	3	3	.473	.340
Ricks, Adam	B-R	5-10	190	9-24-82	.231	.000	.316	9	26	1	6	1	0	0	4	2	0	0	0	6	0	0	.269	.286
Shelby III, John	R-R	5-10	185	8-6-85	.243	.326	.203	115	428	64	104	32	3	10	49	49	3	10	3	77	30	9	.402	.323
Viciedo, Dayan	R-R	5-11	240	3-10-89	.280	.273	.282	130	504	72	141	20	0	12	78	23	7	0	6	89	5	2	.391	.317

Pitching	B-T	HT	WT	DOB	W	L	ERA	G	GS	CG	SV	IP	H	R	ER	HR	BB	SO	AVG	vLH	vRH	K/9	BB/9
Aselton, Kyle	R-L	6-5	215	2-28-83	0	0	15.43	5	0	0	0	5	9	8	8	1	7	8	.391	.571	.313	15.43	13.50
2-team total (4 Carolina)					0	1	17.28	9	0	0	0	8	17	16	16	2	12	13	—	—	—	14.04	12.96
Brooks, Ricky	R-R	6-3	180	7-18-84	3	1	2.68	25	0	0	1	37	24	13	11	2	5	35	.178	.220	.145	8.51	1.22
Cassel, Justin	R-R	6-2	215	9-25-84	4	2	4.01	9	7	0	0	52	59	27	23	3	20	26	.309	.308	.310	4.53	3.48
Ely, John	R-R	6-1	200	5-17-86	14	2	2.82	27	27	1	0	156	140	63	49	9	50	125	.241	.271	.217	7.20	2.88
Harrell, Lucas	B-R	6-2	205	6-3-85	8	3	3.25	14	14	0	0	80	78	38	29	4	32	51	.264	.273	.255	5.71	3.59
Hernandez, Fernando	R-R	5-11	190	7-31-84	2	3	1.71	44	0	0	20	53	34	12	10	2	18	53	.181	.173	.187	9.06	3.08
Hudson, Dan	R-R	6-4	220	3-9-87	7	0	1.60	9	9	0	0	56	37	11	10	1	10	63	.188	.131	.230	10.07	1.60
Johnston, Mike	L-L	6-3	220	3-30-79	0	0	0.77	11	0	0	1	12	10	1	1	0	5	8	.238	.050	.409	6.17	3.86
Long, Matt	R-R	6-5	220	2-23-84	6	3	2.98	21	8	0	0	60	53	22	20	1	19	40	.236	.238	.233	5.97	2.83
Lowe, Johnnie	R-R	6-5	220	3-21-85	0	4	9.25	6	5	0	0	24	42	29	25	4	5	10	.382	.436	.352	3.70	1.85
Lujan, John	R-R	6-1	200	5-10-84	3	5	4.45	37	0	0	1	59	51	32	29	1	28	51	.234	.264	.205	7.82	4.30
Mabee, Henry	R-R	6-4	230	7-10-85	2	2	3.34	21	0	0	1	30	22	16	11	0	13	22	.208	.192	.222	6.67	3.94
Marceaux, Jacob	R-R	6-1	195	2-14-84	0	0	27.00	1	0	0	0	1	4	2	2	0	1	0	.667	.500	1.000	13.50	0.00
McCulloch, Kyle	R-R	6-3	190	3-20-85	9	9	4.58	28	24	0	1	149	185	86	76	8	32	64	.308	.339	.283	3.86	1.93
Nunez, Jhonny	L-R	6-3	185	11-26-85	3	0	2.14	26	0	0	3	46	38	12	11	3	21	57	.229	.293	.167	11.07	4.08
Omogrosso, Brian	R-R	6-4	230	4-26-84	7	2	4.19	13	13	0	0	73	67	40	34	4	40	64	.245	.325	.177	7.89	4.93
Poreda, Aaron	L-L	6-6	240	10-1-86	5	4	2.38	11	11	1	0	64	47	20	17	1	35	69	.206	.170	.217	9.65	4.90
Rodriguez, Derek	R-R	6-1	190	5-17-83	2	0	0.00	7	0	0	2	7	2	0	0	0	2	7	.091	.000	.154	8.59	2.45
Rote, Ryan	R-R	6-4	225	8-8-82	0	0	7.58	18	0	0	0	19	22	19	16	0	22	20	.282	.314	.256	9.47	10.42
Santeliz, Clevelan	R-R	6-0	180	9-1-86	4	0	0.96	40	0	0	10	56	43	10	6	2	35	52	.216	.238	.200	8.31	5.59
Santos, Sergio	R-R	6-3	225	7-4-83	0	1	10.38	7	0	0	0	9	15	10	10	0	7	6	.375	.471	.304	6.23	7.27
Shirek, Charlie	R-R	6-3	205	10-25-85	6	4	3.39	15	14	1	0	90	97	40	34	8	17	32	.279	.280	.278	3.19	1.69
Socolovich, Miguel	R-R	6-1	155	7-24-86	1	0	0.00	4	0	0	0	4	2	0	0	0	0	0	.125	.250	.000	0.00	0.00
Zaleski, Matt	R-R	6-1	190	12-2-81	6	2	2.05	20	8	0	1	75	75	23	17	4	21	44	.270	.290	.252	5.30	2.53

Fielding

Catcher	PCT	G	PO	A	E	DP	PB
Flowers	.994	67	452	33	3	6	7
Lucy	.982	19	103	9	2	1	2
Price	.989	56	338	29	4	7	7
Ricks	.983	8	50	7	1	1	0

First Base	PCT	G	PO	A	E	DP
Allen	.993	57	485	49	4	58
Colina	.993	29	244	24	2	30
Gallagher	.990	22	177	19	2	29
Marrero	.984	33	293	19	5	30
Viciedo	1.000	2	16	2	0	0

Second Base	PCT	G	PO	A	E	DP
Beckham	.947	4	7	11	1	5

Catcher (cont.)	PCT	G	PO	A	E	DP	PB
Colina	.975	8	13	26	1	5
Hudson	.950	5	7	12	1	2
Lang	1.000	4	4	11	0	0
Retherford	.981	123	218	396	12	102

Third Base	PCT	G	PO	A	E	DP
Beckham	1.000	2	0	6	0	2
Colina	.935	26	14	44	4	6
Hudson	—	2	0	0	0	0
Viciedo	.894	114	56	198	30	15

Shortstop	PCT	G	PO	A	E	DP
Beckham	.960	31	51	93	6	17
Colina	.977	9	18	24	1	11
Hudson	.971	78	132	238	11	70

	PCT	G	PO	A	E	DP
Lang	.957	25	35	76	5	16
Nix	.952	3	7	13	1	3

Outfield	PCT	G	PO	A	E	DP
Colina	—	1	0	0	0	0
Cook	.974	101	178	13	5	3
Cruz	1.000	17	27	0	0	0
Danks	1.000	71	164	7	0	3
Gallagher	1.000	4	6	0	0	0
Gartrell	.969	93	145	13	5	4
Hudson	1.000	3	7	0	0	0
Marrero	.971	29	61	5	2	2
Shelby III	.977	106	241	13	6	2

WINSTON-SALEM DASH   HIGH CLASS A
CAROLINA LEAGUE

Batting	B-T	HT	WT	DOB	AVG	vLH	vRH	G	AB	R	H	2B	3B	HR	RBI	BB	HBP	SH	SF	SO	SB	CS	SLG	OBP
Cruz, Lee	R-R	6-2	205	6-13-83	.263	.250	.275	26	95	14	25	8	0	3	14	4	2	0	1	16	0	0	.442	.304
Curtis, John	L-R	6-2	210	11-22-84	.212	.185	.222	30	99	9	21	4	0	1	9	12	0	4	0	24	0	1	.283	.297
Danks, Jordan	L-R	6-4	210	8-7-86	.322	.322	.322	30	118	25	38	11	2	3	21	18	0	1	1	32	5	1	.525	.409
Gallagher, Jimmy	L-L	6-1	195	9-3-85	.270	.259	.277	101	381	43	103	21	1	9	49	48	2	1	4	72	4	2	.402	.352
Gerst, Kent	L-R	5-10	170	2-6-88	.239	.216	.248	49	142	16	34	5	3	2	16	13	0	2	1	46	4	4	.359	.301
Grace, Mike	R-R	6-1	220	4-27-84	.231	.304	.172	16	52	6	12	4	0	2	3	2	0	0	9	2	0	.308	.298
Greene, Justin	R-R	6-0	185	10-10-85	.240	.250	.236	49	175	24	42	6	0	2	13	16	8	1	0	52	12	5	.309	.332
Johnson, Logan	L-T	5-9	175	11-22-83	.269	.277	.266	74	242	37	65	13	1	11	35	25	12	2	3	48	0	0	.467	.362
Kuhn, Tyler	L-R	5-10	185	9-9-86	.281	.368	.244	68	256	28	72	14	2	0	19	14	2	6	3	38	7	7	.352	.320
Lang, C.J.	R-R	5-8	170	4-12-84	.230	.233	.227	33	87	9	20	8	0	0	10	21	2	2	0	14	5	1	.322	.391
Loman, Seth	L-R	6-4	225	12-16-85	.262	.243	.269	81	286	42	75	18	0	15	53	17	15	1	1	85	0	1	.483	.335
Marrero, Christian	L-L	6-1	185	7-30-86	.314	.242	.366	62	226	35	71	15	1	7	34	11	4	0	0	44	2	3	.482	.357
Mollenhauer, Dale	L-R	5-10	170	6-26-86	.259	.291	.242	124	478	75	124	25	4	6	45	46	4	2	1	79	20	10	.366	.329
Morales, Sergio	R-R	6-1	190	12-17-87	.143	.286	.086	15	49	2	7	3	0	0	3	6	0	0	1	19	2	0	.204	.232
Morel, Brent	R-R	6-1	220	4-21-87	.281	.313	.266	128	481	82	135	33	1	16	79	38	3	1	3	66	25	9	.453	.335
Paiml, Greg	R-R	6-0	185	8-3-84	.238	.243	.235	132	508	59	121	29	1	4	46	34	9	8	5	152	10	9	.323	.295
Persichina, Joe	L-R	6-0	190	12-14-84	.230	.211	.239	58	191	19	44	9	0	1	25	12	0	7	0	30	5	2	.293	.276
Ricks, Adam	B-R	5-10	190	9-24-82	.265	.289	.246	34	102	21	27	5	1	1	14	21	0	0	1	17	0	0	.363	.387
Sanchez, Salvador	R-R	6-6	195	1-19-85	.256	.314	.224	114	437	63	112	24	0	16	63	23	5	2	1	80	20	6	.421	.300
Shelton, Kyle	R-R	6-0	184	5-15-86	.324	.383	.250	31	108	17	35	8	0	1	15	9	2	1	0	25	1	0	.426	.387
Sierra, Luis	L-R	5-11	150	7-23-87	.000	—	.000	2	4	0	0	0	0	0	0	1	0	0	0	0	0	0	.000	.200

Pitching	B-T	HT	WT	DOB	W	L	ERA	G	GS	CG	SV	IP	H	R	ER	HR	BB	SO	AVG	vLH	vRH	K/9	BB/9
Albritton, Dan	R-R	6-0	200	11-10-84	0	0	3.38	4	0	0	0	11	9	4	4	1	2	9	.231	.292	.133	7.59	1.69
Asselin, Kevin	L-R	6-1	180	2-16-85	0	0	10.38	3	0	0	1	4	6	5	5	0	2	3	.316	.400	.286	6.23	4.15
Axelrod, Dylan	R-R	6-0	195	7-30-85	2	1	1.91	5	5	0	0	28	29	7	6	2	4	17	.274	.125	.364	5.40	1.27
Brooks, Ricky	R-R	6-3	180	7-18-84	0	1	4.26	10	0	0	0	13	10	6	6	2	6	9	.222	.292	.143	6.39	4.26
Burdie, Charlis	R-R	6-1	185	9-8-85	4	1	2.89	11	0	0	0	19	15	6	6	0	10	22	.217	.080	.295	10.61	4.82
Carter, Anthony	L-R	6-3	180	4-4-86	11	7	4.36	27	27	1	0	155	149	80	75	21	43	119	.256	.258	.254	6.92	2.50

Name	B-T	HT	WT	DOB	W	L	ERA	G	GS	CG	SV	IP	H	R	ER	HR	BB	SO	AVG	vLH	vRH	K/9	BB/9
Corley, Tyson	R-R	6-6	200	1-26-86	0	1	2.61	17	0	0	6	21	18	7	6	2	5	14	.250	.407	.156	6.10	2.18
Dubee, Michael	R-R	6-3	185	1-12-86	0	1	6.00	2	0	0	0	3	5	2	2	0	0	1	.417	.333	.500	3.00	0.00
2-team total (23 Lynchburg)					2	1	1.45	25	0	0	6	37	27	7	6	1	3	53	—	—	—	12.78	0.72
Edwards, Justin	L-L	6-0	180	9-7-87	6	2	4.23	14	14	0	0	79	84	43	37	7	22	25	.284	.259	.289	2.86	2.52
Hudson, Dan	R-R	6-4	220	3-9-87	4	3	3.40	8	8	1	0	45	31	19	17	3	13	49	.195	.158	.229	9.80	2.60
Infante, Gregory	R-R	6-2	185	7-10-87	1	2	7.84	6	5	0	0	21	18	20	18	3	23	10	.243	.306	.184	4.35	10.02
Jones, Nathan	R-R	6-5	190	1-28-86	2	1	3.65	32	0	0	0	49	44	20	20	4	13	43	.244	.200	.273	7.84	2.37
Long, Matt	R-R	6-5	220	2-23-84	0	3	8.37	5	5	0	0	24	35	24	22	4	13	20	.350	.296	.413	7.61	4.94
Lowe, Johnnie	R-R	6-5	220	3-21-85	7	5	4.04	20	20	0	0	123	127	62	55	11	39	76	.271	.305	.241	5.58	2.86
Luis, Santo	R-R	6-4	200	1-27-84	5	4	4.34	47	0	0	14	56	50	34	27	11	23	79	.227	.293	.174	12.70	3.70
Mabee, Henry	R-R	6-4	230	7-10-85	4	1	3.06	20	0	0	8	32	32	13	11	1	15	23	.262	.186	.333	6.40	4.18
Maxwell, Levi	R-R	6-2	200	12-22-84	5	14	4.54	27	16	1	1	101	109	68	51	11	43	48	.278	.289	.268	4.28	3.83
Perez, Wander	L-L	6-3	160	1-5-85	2	1	4.88	33	2	0	1	59	63	35	32	4	28	47	.275	.256	.286	7.17	4.27
Rasner, Jacob	R-R	6-4	210	12-4-86	4	7	4.72	31	19	0	1	128	115	72	67	11	42	98	.241	.232	.248	6.91	2.96
Rote, Ryan	R-R	6-4	225	8-8-82	0	0	3.00	3	0	0	0	3	2	9	1	0	7	2	.154	.167	.143	6.00	21.00
Santiago, Hector	R-L	6-0	210	12-16-87	4	4	3.88	38	0	0	1	58	54	34	25	5	25	66	.252	.246	.255	10.24	3.88
Santos, Sergio	R-R	6-3	225	7-4-83	0	0	5.87	8	0	0	0	8	9	5	5	2	3	7	.290	.429	.176	8.22	3.52
Shirek, Charlie	R-R	6-3	205	10-25-85	8	1	3.88	11	11	0	0	65	63	30	28	0	16	44	.251	.263	.241	6.09	2.22
Socolovich, Miguel	R-R	6-1	155	7-24-86	3	4	4.80	29	5	0	7	54	65	30	29	6	20	41	.307	.311	.303	6.79	3.31
Zaleski, Matt	R-R	6-1	190	12-2-81	1	1	3.38	5	1	0	1	16	12	7	6	2	4	14	.214	.241	.185	7.88	2.25

Fielding

Catcher	PCT	G	PO	A	E	DP	PB
Curtis	.995	30	203	18	1	2	8
Grace	.960	8	44	4	2	0	1
Johnson	.983	67	410	47	8	5	25
Ricks	.993	34	257	31	2	6	5

First Base	PCT	G	PO	A	E	DP
Gallagher	.990	97	853	51	9	65
Grace	1.000	2	20	1	0	1
Loman	.996	26	244	8	1	23
Marrero	1.000	3	30	2	0	2
Persichina	.971	11	93	8	3	9

Second Base	PCT	G	PO	A	E	DP
Kuhn	.968	6	11	19	1	2

	PCT	G	PO	A	E	DP
Lang	.963	11	13	39	2	9
Mollenhauer	.989	118	218	337	6	77
Persichina	1.000	3	2	8	0	0
Sierra	—	1	0	0	0	0

Third Base	PCT	G	PO	A	E	DP
Lang	.833	6	3	12	3	2
Morel	.969	123	95	245	11	22
Persichina	1.000	7	3	16	0	1
Shelton	1.000	3	2	4	0	0

Shortstop	PCT	G	PO	A	E	DP
Lang	.962	7	8	17	1	2
Paiml	.964	131	197	393	22	76

Outfield	PCT	G	PO	A	E	DP
Cruz	.950	10	18	1	1	0
Danks	.982	30	54	2	1	1
Gallagher	1.000	3	5	1	0	0
Gerst	.977	42	83	1	2	0
Greene	1.000	49	100	3	0	0
Kuhn	.991	62	106	4	1	1
Marrero	.976	55	75	7	2	2
Morales	.963	15	25	1	1	0
Persichina	1.000	25	47	1	0	0
Sanchez	.955	111	222	10	11	2
Shelton	1.000	14	32	0	0	0
Sierra	1.000	1	1	0	0	0

KANNAPOLIS INTIMIDATORS   LOW CLASS A
SOUTH ATLANTIC LEAGUE

Batting	B-T	HT	WT	DOB	AVG	vLH	vRH	G	AB	R	H	2B	3B	HR	RBI	BB	HBP	SH	SF	SO	SB	CS	SLG	OBP
Black, Dan	L-R	6-5	240	7-2-87	.209	.121	.227	57	196	25	41	7	2	1	17	31	8	0	3	49	1	1	.281	.336
Castillo, Jorge	L-R	6-2	225	9-26-86	.242	.194	.252	53	194	19	47	9	0	4	27	10	0	0	5	20	0	0	.351	.273
Cheatham, Jordan	L-L	5-10	185	11-2-87	.202	.063	.235	30	84	7	17	3	2	1	6	9	1	0	0	21	5	1	.321	.287
Curtis, John	L-R	6-2	210	11-22-84	.265	.294	.261	52	170	22	45	8	0	0	13	27	5	0	1	35	1	1	.312	.379
Escobar, Eduardo	B-R	5-10	150	1-5-89	.256	.238	.262	128	464	64	119	10	7	3	41	29	1	17	3	91	20	6	.328	.300
Fischer, Lee	R-R	6-4	170	7-31-86	.216	.250	.200	20	51	10	11	3	0	0	4	6	3	2	0	15	1	0	.275	.333
Garcia, Drew	B-R	6-1	175	4-22-86	.269	.243	.276	112	458	58	123	23	3	6	62	21	7	7	6	78	5	5	.371	.307
Gerst, Kent	L-R	5-10	170	2-6-88	.115	.000	.125	9	26	2	3	1	0	2	4	0	1	0	10	0	0	.231	.233
Gilmore, Jon	R-R	6-3	195	8-23-88	.274	.261	.278	130	504	60	138	27	1	5	67	34	4	1	4	83	4	3	.361	.322
Greene, Justin	R-R	6-0	185	10-10-85	.303	.275	.312	81	284	56	86	13	3	7	24	30	14	8	2	66	16	7	.444	.394
Inouye, Matt	R-R	5-10	190	5-20-84	.125	.063	.188	13	32	5	4	2	0	1	4	4	3	1	2	9	2	0	.281	.268
Kuhn, Tyler	L-R	5-10	185	9-9-86	.299	.311	.295	58	221	27	66	10	3	0	27	18	1	1	1	30	19	4	.371	.353
Larson, Zack	R-R	6-4	230	10-15-86	.235	.433	.079	19	68	5	16	3	0	0	5	2	1	0	0	19	0	1	.279	.268
Lee, Ryan	R-R	6-0	185	2-11-86	.185	.211	.174	20	65	9	12	1	0	0	5	9	1	1	1	14	3	0	.200	.289
Loman, Seth	L-R	6-4	225	12-16-85	.303	.476	.256	27	99	19	30	4	2	8	29	6	8	0	1	29	0	0	.626	.386
Mitchell, Jared	L-L	6-0	195	10-13-88	.296	.250	.310	34	115	13	34	12	2	0	10	23	1	0	0	40	5	3	.435	.417
Morales, Sergio	R-R	6-1	190	12-17-87	.237	.217	.244	93	325	42	77	14	4	6	38	26	9	3	3	99	18	2	.360	.309
Persichina, Joe	L-R	6-0	190	12-14-84	.287	.313	.282	26	87	13	25	6	0	1	6	5	1	0	0	19	3	1	.391	.333
Phegley, Josh	R-R	5-10	215	2-12-88	.224	.271	.209	52	196	27	44	9	0	9	33	11	4	1	2	40	1	1	.408	.277
Quentin, Carlos	R-R	6-1	230	8-28-82	.333	—	.333	2	3	0	1	1	0	0	1	2	0	0	0	0	0	0	.667	.600
Shelton, Kyle	R-R	6-0	184	5-15-86	.263	.250	.273	23	76	10	20	5	0	4	17	6	0	4	2	25	0	0	.487	.310
Short, Brandon	R-R	6-1	175	9-9-88	.284	.301	.279	97	345	56	98	19	3	7	55	27	5	10	3	78	12	1	.417	.342
Sierra, Luis	L-R	5-11	150	7-23-87	.268	.333	.263	38	149	18	40	11	0	4	25	11	0	1	2	28	3	2	.423	.315
Vargas, Jose	R-R	6-3	225	12-15-87	.191	.242	.169	31	110	8	21	5	0	3	12	2	1	2	1	32	0	0	.318	.211
Vaughn, Rob	R-R	5-10	190	7-7-87	.250	—	.250	2	8	1	2	1	0	1	6	0	0	0	0	1	0	0	.750	.250
Wagner, Daniel	L-R	6-0	185	7-12-88	.293	1.000	.256	11	41	5	12	2	0	1	2	4	0	0	0	7	1	2	.415	.356
Williams Jr., Kenny	B-R	6-0	180	5-22-86	.255	.218	.268	81	302	41	77	17	3	4	27	21	4	1	0	87	7	3	.371	.312

Pitching	B-T	HT	WT	DOB	W	L	ERA	G	GS	CG	SV	IP	H	R	ER	HR	BB	SO	AVG	vLH	vRH	K/9	BB/9
Albritton, Dan	R-R	6-0	200	11-10-84	1	0	1.76	10	0	0	2	15	12	6	3	2	2	18	.207	.182	.222	10.57	1.17
Albury, James	L-R	6-3	185	4-1-86	5	2	4.79	9	9	0	0	47	59	30	25	6	17	34	.319	.370	.286	6.51	3.26
Asselin, Kevin	L-R	6-1	180	2-16-85	6	3	2.74	26	1	0	0	49	41	19	15	0	24	49	.224	.343	.150	8.94	4.38
Axelrod, Dylan	R-R	6-0	195	7-30-85	0	0	2.08	2	0	0	0	4	3	2	1	0	1	3	.158	.222	.100	6.23	2.08
Ballinger, J.R.	R-R	6-1	190	4-2-88	0	3	9.00	4	3	0	0	13	18	13	13	1	10	9	.340	.345	.333	6.23	6.92
Bellamy, Kyle	R-R	6-5	215	10-25-87	2	0	1.42	17	0	0	2	19	14	5	3	1	2	30	.189	.111	.214	14.21	0.95

CHICAGO WHITE SOX

Player	B-T	HT	WT	DOB	W	L	ERA	G	GS	CG	SV	IP	H	R	ER	HR	BB	SO	AVG	vLH	vRH	K/9	BB/9
Bowling, Adam	R-R	6-4	180	1-16-84	0	1	5.68	8	2	0	0	13	18	8	8	0	4	6	.353	.350	.355	4.26	2.84
Braun, Ryan	R-R	6-1	220	7-29-80	0	0	0.00	2	0	0	0	2	0	0	0	0	1	3	.000	—	.000	13.50	4.50
Burdie, Charlis	R-R	6-1	185	9-8-85	4	5	1.76	37	0	0	2	56	22	11	11	1	28	60	.122	.194	.079	9.59	4.47
Carter, Dexter	R-R	6-6	195	2-5-87	6	2	3.13	19	19	0	0	118	103	44	41	9	32	143	.236	.265	.217	10.91	2.44
Colon, Bartolo	R-R	5-11	245	5-24-73	0	1	2.57	1	1	0	0	7	7	2	2	0	1	8	.280	.300	.267	10.29	1.29
Corley, Tyson	R-R	6-6	200	1-26-86	3	1	0.95	30	0	0	4	38	33	6	4	0	9	38	.229	.296	.189	9.00	2.13
Edwards, Justin	L-L	6-0	180	9-7-87	4	3	3.80	8	8	0	0	45	48	21	19	2	7	30	.265	.200	.276	6.00	1.40
Garcia, Freddy	R-R	6-4	260	10-6-76	0	0	0.00	1	1	0	0	3	2	0	0	0	1	3	.222	—	.222	9.00	3.00
Gouvea, Murillo	R-R	6-2	190	9-15-88	0	0	3.00	1	1	0	0	3	6	6	1	0	0	3	.375	.333	.400	9.00	0.00
Griffith, Nevin	R-R	6-2	165	3-23-89	5	5	3.86	13	12	0	0	68	69	35	29	4	26	35	.274	.370	.201	4.66	3.46
Hudson, Dan	R-R	6-4	220	3-9-87	1	2	1.23	4	4	0	0	22	15	5	3	0	2	30	.190	.161	.208	12.27	0.82
Hunt, Leroy	R-R	6-6	240	11-28-87	3	3	4.48	46	0	0	1	62	65	43	31	3	34	43	.284	.393	.214	6.21	4.91
Infante, Gregory	R-R	6-2	185	7-10-87	3	5	3.26	15	15	0	0	88	76	37	32	4	37	75	.239	.252	.232	7.64	3.77
Johnson, Garrett	L-L	6-10	205	9-2-87	4	4	6.70	17	7	0	0	47	63	40	35	5	12	42	.321	.143	.370	8.04	2.30
Jones, Nathan	R-R	6-5	190	1-28-86	2	0	2.41	13	0	0	1	19	8	5	5	0	9	25	.129	.190	.098	12.05	4.34
Lechuga, Enrique	L-L	6-0	180	6-6-86	0	1	3.60	12	0	0	1	10	10	4	4	1	1	8	.270	.235	.300	7.20	0.90
Leesman, Charlie	L-L	6-4	210	3-10-87	13	5	3.08	27	27	1	0	158	165	66	54	4	58	117	.275	.207	.291	6.68	3.31
O'Neil, Drew	R-R	6-3	200	11-8-85	4	1	2.54	40	0	0	1	60	51	22	17	0	36	35	.236	.323	.199	5.22	5.37
Remenowsky, Dan	R-R	6-5	245	4-7-86	7	3	1.99	54	0	0	24	63	40	18	14	3	16	109	.176	.167	.181	15.49	2.27
Rodriguez, Santos	L-L	6-5	180	1-2-88	0	0	0.00	3	0	0	0	4	3	0	0	0	1	8	.200	.333	.167	18.00	2.25
Santos, Sergio	R-R	6-3	225	7-4-83	0	1	7.36	8	0	0	0	7	8	6	6	0	3	10	.286	.571	.190	12.27	3.68
Sauer, Stephen	R-R	6-2	185	8-13-86	6	5	3.36	28	22	0	0	142	163	62	53	4	19	123	.290	.321	.271	7.80	1.20
Serafin, Joe	L-L	5-10	185	2-27-86	3	1	2.98	7	7	0	0	42	40	14	14	2	9	38	.255	.313	.240	8.08	1.91

Fielding

Catcher	PCT	G	PO	A	E	DP	PB
Curtis	.992	50	438	50	4	7	6
Inouye	.990	12	87	11	1	1	1
Larson	.987	19	136	11	2	0	2
Phegley	.984	47	378	48	7	2	11
Sierra	.988	11	73	7	1	0	4
Vaughn	1.000	2	23	1	0	0	1
Garcia	.973	93	206	294	14	67	
Kuhn	.922	17	32	39	6	9	
Sierra	1.000	2	2	6	0	2	
Wagner	1.000	11	11	2	0	2	

First Base	PCT	G	PO	A	E	DP
Black	.986	54	469	30	7	41
Castillo	1.000	44	387	26	0	39
Persichina	.986	8	66	5	1	5
Shelton	.985	13	123	6	2	13
Sierra	1.000	1	12	0	0	1
Vargas	.975	22	179	14	5	17

Second Base	PCT	G	PO	A	E	DP
Escobar	.958	9	9	14	1	5
Fischer	.980	10	29	21	1	9

Third Base	PCT	G	PO	A	E	DP
Fischer	1.000	1	1	2	0	0
Gilmore	.894	126	81	255	40	23
Kuhn	1.000	1	0	2	0	0
Persichina	.800	3	2	2	1	0
Shelton	1.000	2	1	3	0	0
Sierra	.500	1	0	1	0	0
Vargas	.875	6	3	11	2	2

Shortstop	PCT	G	PO	A	E	DP
Escobar	.961	119	169	372	22	74
Fischer	1.000	1	0	3	0	0
Garcia	.948	19	25	66	5	17
Kuhn	1.000	1	3	3	0	2

Outfield	PCT	G	PO	A	E	DP
Cheatham	.903	30	28	0	3	0
Fischer	1.000	7	8	1	0	0
Gerst	.938	9	13	2	1	1
Greene	.978	78	125	6	3	4
Kuhn	1.000	27	30	3	0	1
Lee	1.000	20	35	2	0	0
Loman	1.000	4	8	0	0	0
Mitchell	.972	34	68	2	2	0
Morales	.966	92	131	9	5	3
Persichina	1.000	9	8	1	0	0
Quentin	1.000	1	1	1	0	0
Shelton	1.000	6	5	3	0	0
Short	.987	96	146	9	2	1
Sierra	1.000	21	37	3	0	0
Vargas	1.000	2	4	0	0	0
Williams Jr.	1.000	2	2	0	0	0

BRISTOL SOX   ROOKIE

APPALACHIAN LEAGUE

Batting	B-T	HT	WT	DOB	AVG	vLH	vRH	G	AB	R	H	2B	3B	HR	RBI	BB	HBP	SH	SF	SO	SB	CS	SLG	OBP
Baines Jr., Harold	L-L	5-10	165	12-18-87	.147	.067	.167	25	75	4	11	1	0	0	5	7	0	0	0	13	0	2	.160	.220
Black, Dan	L-R	6-5	240	7-2-87	.333	.000	.400	3	12	1	4	0	0	0	1	0	0	0	0	2	0	0	.333	.333
Buckridge, Shaydron	R-R	5-10	170	5-12-88	.163	.077	.204	25	80	8	13	3	0	1	5	8	4	1	0	21	1	0	.238	.272
Casarai, A.J.	L-R	6-1	175	2-21-88	.211	.278	.198	40	114	14	24	5	1	0	9	10	3	1	0	40	9	2	.272	.291
Davis, Kyle	R-R	5-11	160	1-8-87	.233	.210	.242	60	223	24	52	6	1	0	14	25	1	3	0	63	3	0	.269	.313
Ferreiras, Angel	R-R	6-1	184	8-12-88	.132	.100	.152	16	53	3	7	3	0	0	4	3	0	0	0	8	0	0	.189	.179
Fischer, Lee	R-R	6-4	170	7-31-86	.333	.000	1.000	1	3	1	1	1	0	0	0	0	0	0	0	0	0	0	.667	.333
Fulgencio, Jose	R-R	6-1	162	12-16-86	.184	.163	.200	34	98	6	18	6	1	0	3	1	0	3	1	27	2	1	.265	.190
Gonzalez, Miguel	R-R	6-0	200	12-3-90	.311	.313	.311	45	151	24	47	15	1	4	19	16	2	4	0	25	2	1	.503	.385
Lee, Ryan	R-R	6-0	185	2-11-86	.292	.351	.263	44	171	25	50	8	1	0	10	23	3	3	2	26	17	5	.351	.382
McDonald, Jared	L-R	6-1	180	3-1-88	.171	.250	.157	29	82	6	14	2	0	1	8	13	2	1	3	22	2	0	.232	.290
Pangilinan, Leighton	L-R	6-3	230	3-6-91	.299	.138	.339	44	144	11	43	10	0	4	22	6	1	1	2	34	0	1	.451	.327
Patino, Jeffer	R-R	5-10	163	10-8-88	.188	.378	.125	46	149	12	28	2	2	1	12	16	0	2	1	21	1	3	.248	.265
Shoemaker, Brady	R-R	6-0	200	5-10-87	.351	.309	.372	57	205	38	72	21	0	9	34	25	3	0	2	53	0	0	.585	.426
Tavarez, Misael	R-R	6-5	190	12-6-87	.207	.151	.233	45	169	20	35	13	0	3	14	8	6	0	2	57	5	2	.337	.265
Thompson, Trayce	R-R	6-3	195	3-15-91	.188	.136	.206	25	85	8	16	3	1	0	10	4	3	0	1	33	2	0	.247	.247
Vaughn, Rob	R-R	5-10	190	7-7-87	.226	.321	.185	27	93	10	21	1	0	4	7	3	2	1	0	24	0	0	.366	.265
Wagner, Daniel	L-R	6-0	185	7-12-88	.258	.254	.260	56	217	23	56	10	1	1	26	12	1	4	2	33	12	4	.327	.297
Williams, Dallas	R-R	6-1	160	11-13-84	.217	.333	.143	10	23	1	5	0	0	0	3	0	1	0	0	7	0	0	.217	.308

Pitching	B-T	HT	WT	DOB	W	L	ERA	G	GS	CG	SV	IP	H	R	ER	HR	BB	SO	AVG	vLH	vRH	K/9	BB/9
Ballinger, J.R.	R-R	6-1	190	4-2-88	0	0	7.71	1	0	0	0	2	5	2	2	0	1	2	.417	.500	.333	7.71	3.86
Bellamy, Kyle	R-R	6-5	215	10-25-87	0	0	0.00	3	0	0	1	3	0	0	0	0	0	2	.000	.000	.000	6.00	0.00
Braun, Ryan	R-R	6-1	220	7-29-80	0	1	0.90	7	0	0	0	10	5	1	1	0	1	12	.143	.214	.095	10.80	0.90
Cooney, Chase	R-R	6-8	245	12-18-87	0	0	7.36	3	0	0	0	4	5	3	3	1	1	8	.357	.500	.300	2.45	2.45
DeFoor, Brent	R-R	6-2	175	1-9-86	2	2	2.31	19	0	0	3	35	24	12	9	2	10	32	.198	.255	.162	8.23	2.57
Delk, Trey	R-R	6-0	190	12-17-85	3	7	6.22	13	12	0	0	55	67	43	38	4	21	48	.290	.268	.306	7.85	3.44
Farotto, Alex	L-L	5-11	195	3-28-87	0	1	1.10	13	0	0	4	16	10	2	2	1	4	22	.179	.091	.200	12.12	2.20

	B-T	HT	WT	DOB	W	L	ERA	G	GS	CG	SV	IP	H	R	ER	HR	BB	SO	AVG	vLH	vRH	K/9	BB/9
Garcia, Rene	R-R	6-2	200	6-15-86	2	1	2.35	6	2	0	0	15	12	8	4	1	7	18	.203	.250	.179	10.57	4.11
Garcia, Freddy	R-R	6-4	260	10-6-76	0	0	1.64	2	2	0	0	11	6	3	2	0	0	7	.158	.154	.160	5.73	0.00
Gouvea, Murillo	R-R	6-2	190	9-15-88	0	1	5.82	7	4	0	0	22	25	16	14	4	15	27	.301	.371	.250	11.22	6.23
2-team total (9 Greeneville)					1	3	4.65	16	4	0	0	50	48	30	26	7	23	57	—	—	—	10.19	4.11
Griffith, Nevin	R-R	6-2	165	3-23-89	0	1	5.00	2	2	0	0	9	10	7	5	0	7	7	.294	.091	.391	7.00	7.00
Heidenreich, Matt	L-R	6-5	185	1-17-91	0	1	4.50	16	0	0	0	22	22	14	11	1	12	12	.256	.375	.152	4.91	4.91
Holmberg, David	R-L	6-4	220	7-19-91	2	2	4.72	14	7	0	0	40	40	26	21	5	18	37	.256	.233	.265	8.32	4.05
Negus, Phil	R-R	6-2	210	11-10-87	2	0	2.38	15	4	0	1	34	26	14	9	3	11	34	.208	.273	.173	9.00	2.91
Rienzo, Andre	R-R	6-3	160	6-5-88	2	6	4.14	13	9	0	0	54	55	28	25	4	13	49	.263	.258	.267	8.12	2.15
Rodriguez, Santos	L-L	6-5	180	1-2-88	2	0	1.33	19	0	0	4	27	18	5	4	0	17	42	.189	.238	.176	14.00	5.67
Serafin, Joe	L-L	5-10	185	2-27-86	4	1	1.64	7	5	0	0	33	25	7	6	2	5	20	.216	.120	.242	5.45	1.36
Simmons, Goldy	R-R	6-4	210	10-29-88	0	3	5.56	12	3	0	1	23	26	16	14	3	4	19	.286	.200	.353	7.54	1.59
Thompson, Taylor	R-R	6-5	225	6-18-87	0	0	2.40	7	3	0	2	15	10	4	4	0	10	17	.189	.273	.129	10.20	6.00
Upchurch, Steven	R-R	6-4	180	9-14-89	3	10	6.95	13	13	1	0	66	94	53	51	8	17	42	.338	.348	.331	5.73	2.32
Wiltz, Danny	R-R	6-1	200	2-13-87	4	2	2.78	18	0	0	1	36	34	12	11	3	8	39	.248	.176	.291	9.84	2.02
Zagyi, Chris	R-R	6-5	215	8-5-89	0	1	8.10	15	0	0	0	23	31	22	21	2	13	20	.330	.436	.255	7.71	5.01

Fielding

Catcher	PCT	G	PO	A	E	DP	PB
Buckridge	1.000	8	64	12	0	1	3
Gonzalez	.971	38	289	46	10	4	8
Vaughn	.995	22	162	26	1	1	3

First Base	PCT	G	PO	A	E	DP
Black	1.000	2	23	0	0	3
Buckridge	.992	16	123	9	1	11
Ferreiras	1.000	8	86	5	0	5
McDonald	.986	9	68	4	1	6
Pangilinan	.990	32	292	8	3	22

Second Base	PCT	G	PO	A	E	DP
McDonald	1.000	4	9	14	0	4
Patino	.971	10	7	26	1	5
Wagner	.952	54	84	156	12	30

Third Base	PCT	G	PO	A	E	DP
Black	1.000	1	1	1	0	0
Fischer	1.000	1	0	3	0	1
Fulgencio	.903	23	7	49	6	3
McDonald	.821	11	10	13	5	0
Patino	.944	33	16	68	5	2

Shortstop	PCT	G	PO	A	E	DP
Davis	.926	60	93	145	19	37
Fulgencio	.900	7	10	17	3	3
McDonald	.714	1	1	4	2	0

Outfield	PCT	G	PO	A	E	DP
Baines Jr.	1.000	13	14	2	0	0
Casario	.959	31	45	2	2	0
Lee	.978	44	84	3	2	0
Shoemaker	.984	39	60	2	1	0
Tavarez	.941	43	78	2	5	1
Thompson	.976	23	38	2	1	2
Williams	1.000	9	7	1	0	1

GREAT FALLS VOYAGERS   ROOKIE
PIONEER LEAGUE

Batting	B-T	HT	WT	DOB	AVG	vLH	vRH	G	AB	R	H	2B	3B	HR	RBI	BB	HBP	SH	SF	SO	SB	CS	SLG	OBP
Avila, Jesus	R-L	6-0	165	11-26-88	.261	.205	.275	55	226	31	59	9	1	3	33	16	5	2	2	33	5	3	.350	.321
Blackwood, Chase	R-R	5-10	205	11-24-87	.198	.067	.268	24	86	13	17	5	0	3	7	2	1	0	1	33	4	1	.360	.222
Celis, Johny	L-R	6-0	165	3-26-86	.281	.250	.290	63	203	26	57	14	0	7	50	36	2	0	5	46	0	2	.453	.386
Cheatham, Jordan	L-L	5-10	185	11-2-87	.330	.255	.352	61	206	33	68	10	2	2	34	21	1	2	1	43	14	10	.427	.393
Ciolli, Nick	L-R	6-2	215	12-6-87	.317	.314	.318	63	240	45	76	17	1	7	36	26	3	0	1	49	23	4	.483	.389
Colligan, Kyle	R-R	6-2	210	4-23-87	.273	.314	.255	66	231	48	63	13	2	7	38	34	12	0	5	62	20	5	.437	.387
Cummings, Robby	R-R	6-2	195	8-14-87	.264	.316	.236	46	163	22	43	12	0	2	26	13	1	0	2	60	1	0	.374	.318
Dubler, Kevin	L-R	6-1	200	2-18-87	.223	.190	.230	42	121	19	27	7	1	0	11	18	3	1	1	35	4	1	.298	.336
Gilbert, Ken	L-L	6-2	185	2-6-89	.277	.333	.250	12	47	5	13	0	1	0	3	2	0	0	0	13	2	1	.319	.306
Gossage, Todd	L-R	6-2	190	6-8-84	.231	.150	.247	37	117	14	27	3	0	0	11	10	4	2	2	21	1	1	.256	.308
Hamme, Ryan	L-R	6-3	210	3-13-87	.278	.250	.287	61	198	31	55	9	1	0	24	8	4	1	0	30	13	2	.333	.319
Harughty, Matt	R-R	6-0	180	7-28-86	.238	.233	.240	42	105	19	25	5	2	0	9	22	4	2	0	29	6	2	.324	.389
Kayne, Zach	B-R	5-10	185	11-22-86	.266	.260	.268	54	177	28	47	10	2	0	15	21	1	0	1	44	9	3	.345	.345
Larson, Zack	R-R	6-4	230	10-15-86	.177	.227	.158	24	79	8	14	2	0	0	6	15	1	0	2	14	1	0	.203	.309
Santos, Orlando	R-R	6-0	187	12-10-86	.238	.333	.167	7	21	4	5	1	1	0	1	4	0	1	0	6	1	0	.381	.360
Tezak, Jeff	B-R	5-10	180	2-23-88	.280	.283	.279	56	200	37	56	3	1	0	23	27	6	5	2	32	10	5	.305	.379
Thennis, Doug	R-R	6-2	195	2-19-86	.094	.056	.143	11	32	4	3	0	0	1	2	5	0	0	0	16	2	0	.188	.216
Thompson, Trayce	R-R	6-3	195	3-15-91	.222	.333	.222	7	21	2	5	0	0	0	3	3	0	1	0	8	1	0	.238	.333
Vargas, Jose	R-R	6-3	225	12-15-87	.333	.324	.336	36	144	30	48	12	0	7	35	10	3	0	3	28	2	0	.563	.381

Pitching	B-T	HT	WT	DOB	W	L	ERA	G	GS	CG	SV	IP	H	R	ER	HR	BB	SO	AVG	vLH	vRH	K/9	BB/9
Albritton, Dan	R-R	6-0	200	11-10-84	2	0	3.60	8	0	0	3	15	14	6	6	0	1	17	.230	.222	.233	10.20	0.60
Ballinger, J.R.	R-R	6-1	190	4-2-88	3	0	3.83	10	10	0	0	42	35	22	18	5	15	30	.217	.179	.230	6.38	3.19
Bayne, Cameron	R-R	6-2	195	2-14-88	0	2	6.26	19	1	0	2	27	35	25	19	2	14	27	.318	.375	.295	8.89	4.61
Billeaud, Josh	R-R	6-3	210	3-22-87	1	0	5.00	4	4	0	0	18	22	12	10	1	5	15	.286	.318	.273	7.50	2.50
Buch, Ryan	R-R	6-3	205	11-8-87	1	2	3.38	16	0	0	0	21	13	10	8	0	21	29	.183	.222	.170	12.23	8.86
Burnside, Paul	R-R	6-4	225	11-20-86	2	0	4.50	9	0	0	0	10	5	8	5	0	6	20	.135	.091	.154	18.00	5.40
Coker, Jarrett	R-R	6-2	190	11-26-86	3	2	5.32	8	2	0	0	22	23	13	13	3	9	21	.280	.238	.295	8.59	3.68
Collop, Justin	R-R	6-1	185	5-30-88	3	2	2.72	15	7	0	0	40	38	20	12	1	23	33	.257	.306	.241	7.49	5.22
Curry, Nelson	R-R	6-0	190	1-14-87	6	3	3.05	18	4	0	1	41	41	20	14	3	13	39	.263	.111	.308	8.49	2.83
Doyle, Terry	R-R	6-4	225	11-2-85	5	1	2.98	12	10	0	0	57	51	20	19	1	15	75	.244	.314	.209	11.77	2.33
Graffy, Brett	R-R	6-2	185	3-12-87	1	3	10.22	8	0	0	1	12	24	15	14	0	8	11	.393	.435	.368	8.03	5.84
Hopps, Matt	R-R	6-5	235	10-8-85	1	4	3.38	18	0	0	4	24	24	14	9	2	10	29	.247	.227	.253	10.88	3.75
Johnson, Garrett	L-L	6-10	205	4-2-88	0	3	5.80	11	10	0	0	45	57	35	29	1	20	33	.329	.409	.318	6.60	4.00
Johnson, Greg	R-R	6-2	228	12-30-86	1	2	3.06	11	0	0	2	18	15	6	6	1	2	10	.234	.267	.224	5.09	1.02
Kloess, Brandon	R-R	6-2	195	12-9-84	2	0	2.45	18	2	0	4	59	49	22	16	4	17	72	.229	.308	.204	11.05	2.61
Kuehn, Justin	R-R	6-2	190	6-9-87	0	0	7.20	5	0	0	0	5	5	7	4	0	8	4	.227	.143	.267	7.20	14.40
Lechuga, Enrique	L-L	6-0	180	6-26-86	3	2	5.23	11	0	0	0	21	24	15	12	2	9	14	.296	.125	.338	6.10	3.92
Martinez, Joucer	R-R	6-2	160	2-3-86	3	4	4.44	16	15	0	0	79	85	48	39	7	24	52	.276	.308	.265	5.92	2.73
Puls, Dan	R-L	6-7	200	1-30-86	0	1	4.44	13	0	0	2	24	25	13	12	1	14	30	.272	.211	.288	11.10	5.18

Player	B-T	HT	WT	DOB	W	L	ERA	G	GS	CG	SV	IP	H	R	ER	HR	BB	SO	AVG	vLH	vRH	K/9	BB/9
Wickswat, Matt	L-L	6-2	210	8-4-86	2	2	3.84	15	15	0	0	77	92	36	33	7	14	91	.297	.289	.298	10.59	1.63
Wilson, Jake	R-R	6-0	195	8-12-87	3	1	4.50	14	0	0	0	20	15	10	10	1	9	30	.211	.286	.180	13.50	4.05

Fielding

Catcher	PCT	G	PO	A	E	DP	PB
Blackwood	.977	17	160	13	4	3	2
Dubler	.990	38	285	25	3	2	4
Larson	.981	20	187	20	4	1	7
Santos	.958	7	62	6	3	0	2

First Base	PCT	G	PO	A	E	DP
Cummings	1.000	1	8	0	0	0
Gossage	.981	34	250	11	5	17
Hamme	.977	13	78	7	2	9
Thennis	.978	11	86	2	2	5
Vargas	.996	26	222	15	1	31

Second Base	PCT	G	PO	A	E	DP
Avila	.952	32	43	76	6	15
Kayne	.951	9	20	19	2	5
Tezak	.962	38	75	101	7	28

Third Base	PCT	G	PO	A	E	DP
Avila	.893	22	11	56	8	7
Cummings	.903	45	25	87	12	4
Haughty	.842	6	0	16	3	0
Vargas	.889	9	5	11	2	1

Shortstop	PCT	G	PO	A	E	DP
Haughty	.921	32	39	66	9	18

	PCT	G	PO	A	E	DP
Kayne	.939	39	63	106	11	20
Tezak	.964	15	19	34	2	7

Outfield	PCT	G	PO	A	E	DP
Celis	1.000	5	7	0	0	0
Cheatham	.974	59	72	2	2	0
Ciolli	.967	61	78	9	3	2
Colligan	.957	64	130	4	6	1
Gilbert	.786	8	10	1	3	1
Hamme	.985	40	60	4	1	0
Thompson	.923	6	12	0	1	0

DSL WHITE SOX   ROOKIE

DOMINICAN SUMMER LEAGUE

Batting	B-T	HT	WT	DOB	AVG	vLH	vRH	G	AB	R	H	2B	3B	HR	RBI	BB	HBP	SH	SF	SO	SB	CS	SLG	OBP
Acuna, Hector	B-R	6-2	200	8-26-88	.308	.400	.276	26	78	20	24	6	2	1	19	31	8	0	1	19	0	1	.474	.534
Alcala, Julio	R-R	6-0	165	12-24-90	.295	.417	.258	61	207	39	61	19	7	0	30	25	10	0	3	29	6	6	.454	.392
Becerra, Ifran	L-R	5-10	155	6-13-91	.213	.286	.200	25	47	6	10	0	0	0	4	6	1	0	0	13	2	0	.213	.315
Buda, Maurizio	R-R	6-1	175	1-7-92	.254	.286	.246	26	71	12	18	5	0	1	11	10	4	1	0	21	1	3	.366	.376
Cabrera, Raldy	R-R	6-0	180	9-25-89	.154	.000	.167	6	13	0	2	0	0	0	1	1	0	0	0	2	0	0	.154	.214
Del Carmen, Jaime	B-R	6-1	170	1-3-90	.299	.222	.316	43	144	29	43	3	0	2	28	20	9	1	1	24	8	3	.361	.414
Ferreiras, Angel	R-R	6-1	184	8-12-88	.333	.429	.316	11	45	10	15	2	0	1	11	5	3	1	0	12	0	2	.444	.434
Garcia, Miguel	R-R	6-1	150	5-16-90	.286	.250	.294	15	42	2	12	0	0	0	6	1	1	1	0	6	0	2	.286	.318
Lora, Ronald	R-R	6-1	180	3-31-89	.200	.500	.161	16	35	7	7	0	0	1	5	5	0	1	1	13	1	0	.286	.293
Lugo, Antoni	R-R	6-1	187	6-16-88	.248	.206	.260	51	161	28	40	7	1	9	29	18	5	1	1	27	2	2	.472	.341
Mercedes, Daurys	R-R	6-1	165	2-26-90	.319	.189	.347	55	207	48	66	11	9	1	26	31	1	3	0	39	7	5	.473	.410
Pascual, Oliver	R-R	5-10	170	11-13-89	.271	.250	.274	43	133	19	36	10	1	1	17	7	1	1	2	29	3	8	.383	.308
Puentes, Jerry	R-R	6-1	170	7-18-91	.302	.250	.316	45	169	30	51	6	2	0	17	21	3	2	1	26	13	6	.361	.387
Ramirez, Juan	R-R	6-4	196	8-28-90	.292	.244	.306	55	216	47	63	11	5	1	30	19	7	1	1	58	4	0	.403	.366
Ramos, Luis	R-R	6-3	185	6-19-88	.167	.333	.095	9	30	2	5	1	0	1	1	2	0	0	0	9	1	0	.300	.219
Reyes, Rafi	R-R	6-2	195	7-31-91	.200	.250	.194	13	35	3	7	1	0	0	3	3	1	0	0	14	0	0	.229	.282
Sanchez, Carlos	R-R	5-11	175	6-29-92	.156	.222	.130	22	32	7	5	0	0	0	3	8	1	1	0	10	1	0	.156	.341
Sanchez, Leopoldo	R-R	6-1	180	6-5-91	.264	.333	.250	48	129	30	34	3	3	0	12	41	4	0	1	19	5	2	.333	.451
Silverio, Juan	R-R	6-1	175	4-18-91	.321	.250	.342	61	243	52	78	11	10	8	56	16	3	0	3	47	5	6	.547	.366
Trujillo, Rather	R-R	6-0	185	2-23-89	.286	.222	.304	61	206	36	59	9	1	2	21	29	8	4	5	24	9	8	.369	.387
Williams, Ariel	R-R	5-11	155	11-13-88	.220	.182	.225	28	82	9	18	4	3	1	9	6	0	0	1	22	2	3	.378	.270
Yepez, Daniel	R-R	6-1	190	5-6-91	.237	.316	.211	26	76	6	18	2	0	0	12	2	1	2	0	6	1	1	.263	.266

Pitching	B-T	HT	WT	DOB	W	L	ERA	G	GS	CG	SV	IP	H	R	ER	HR	BB	SO	AVG	vLH	vRH	K/9	BB/9
Bautista, Jose	L-L	6-1	175	3-31-92	0	0	7.36	9	3	0	0	11	8	10	9	1	14	15	.200	.333	.189	12.27	11.45
Calixto, Tiago	R-R	6-0	180	5-6-89	0	2	2.89	10	1	0	1	9	10	10	3	0	5	5	.263	.091	.333	4.82	4.82
Cueva, Jorge	R-R	6-3	205	3-24-89	4	0	3.72	30	0	0	4	39	42	29	16	0	36	28	.290	.273	.297	6.52	8.38
Duque, Jean	R-R	6-3	190	7-17-89	4	3	6.10	24	5	0	1	41	49	39	28	4	33	44	.292	.327	.277	9.58	7.19
Echezuria, Luis	R-R	6-0	179	5-10-91	2	5	6.75	23	0	0	2	33	34	29	25	1	27	33	.258	.222	.271	8.91	7.29
Hernandez, Abel	R-R	6-0	180	2-12-89	0	0	3.60	6	2	0	0	5	6	3	2	0	4	3	.353	.667	.286	5.40	7.20
Jean, Dominque	R-R	6-2	170	11-24-88	2	1	5.37	26	1	0	2	54	51	43	32	7	32	45	.245	.193	.265	7.55	5.37
Matos, Darwin	R-R	6-0	170	8-4-90	3	4	3.57	17	13	0	1	68	59	31	27	2	34	82	.233	.235	.232	10.85	4.50
Mercedes, Raffy	R-R	6-1	185	12-17-88	8	4	3.84	20	8	0	0	77	79	42	33	4	25	83	.253	.295	.235	9.66	2.91
Mota, Arismendy	R-R	6-2	165	2-16-87	7	2	1.81	16	15	1	0	97	67	26	18	0	19	80	.208	.231	.199	8.03	1.91
Ortega, Yorvix	R-R	5-11	175	8-1-89	4	2	3.68	14	11	0	0	64	58	28	26	2	38	59	.262	.418	.211	8.34	5.37
Payano, Luis	R-R	6-1	176	3-31-87	5	3	3.08	15	11	0	0	76	68	30	26	4	25	64	.248	.241	.251	7.58	2.96
Rosario, Carlos	L-L	5-10	160	3-13-88	2	0	2.21	19	0	0	2	20	14	7	5	0	15	18	.200	.000	.219	7.97	6.64
Tejada, Silvio	R-R	6-6	190	9-6-88	1	2	7.71	18	0	0	2	21	20	19	18	0	25	22	.250	.261	.246	9.43	10.71

Fielding

Catcher	PCT	G	PO	A	E	DP	PB
Del Valle	.967	26	181	25	7	1	4
Pascual	.977	39	253	51	7	2	15
Yepez	1.000	23	159	15	0	1	3

First Base	PCT	G	PO	A	E	DP
Acuna	.983	20	159	14	3	21
Del Valle	.983	17	157	12	3	8
Ferreiras	.953	5	38	3	2	1
Lugo	.992	30	247	16	2	27
Sanchez	—	1	0	0	0	0
Sanchez	1.000	1	4	0	0	0
Yepez	.714	1	4	1	2	0

Second Base	PCT	G	PO	A	E	DP
Becerra	.915	21	21	22	4	5

	PCT	G	PO	A	E	DP
Mercedes	.940	36	41	85	8	11
Puentes	.978	9	21	23	1	6
Sanchez	1.000	7	3	8	0	1
Silverio	.935	5	14	15	2	2
Williams	.984	15	27	34	1	5

Third Base	PCT	G	PO	A	E	DP
Garcia	.919	11	7	27	3	3
Lugo	.889	7	6	10	2	1
Mercedes	—	1	0	0	0	0
Puentes	.889	3	3	5	1	0
Sanchez	.929	43	35	96	10	12
Silverio	.857	21	11	31	7	0

Shortstop	PCT	G	PO	A	E	DP
Mercedes	.885	23	27	50	10	9

	PCT	G	PO	A	E	DP
Puentes	.948	25	64	64	7	8
Sanchez	1.000	11	11	13	0	6
Sanchez	1.000	1	2	5	0	0
Silverio	.920	26	51	64	10	11

Outfield	PCT	G	PO	A	E	DP
Alcala	.974	59	70	5	2	2
Buda	.958	24	22	1	1	0
Cabrera	1.000	5	2	1	0	0
Lora	.938	15	13	2	1	0
Ramirez	.883	51	49	4	7	1
Ramos	.923	6	11	1	1	0
Reyes	.786	13	10	1	3	0
Trujillo	.989	61	85	3	1	0
Williams	1.000	6	5	1	0	0

Cincinnati Reds

SEASON IN A SENTENCE: The Reds once again sat in the netherworld between playing for the future and competing for a playoff spot, finishing 13 games out in the National League Central and with a losing record (78-84) for the ninth straight season.

HIGH POINT: On the Fourth of July, Cincinnati found itself just two games out of first place, having won five of its last seven in a stretch that saw Homer Bailey pick up his first win of the season and Johnny Cueto combine with three relievers on a shutout of Arizona.

LOW POINT: Outfielder Jay Bruce broke his wrist in mid-July, righthander Edinson Volquez blew out his elbow and catcher Ramon Hernandez injured his right knee. Between the onslaught of injuries and a generally ineffective lineup, Cincinnati went 1-15 over a miserable stretch in late July and early August that ended any hopes of a playoff spot.

NOTABLE ROOKIES: Catcher Ryan Hannigan showed a solid glove and an ability to get on base when he was forced into the starting catching job after Hernandez's knee injury. Drew Stubbs' range and surprising power quickly earned him the starting center field job. Paul Janish earned the starting shortstop job whether he was ready or not because of Alex Gonzalez's injury. Adam Rosales filled a utility role, showing defensive versatility while he struggled at the plate. Unheralded lefthander Danny Ray Herrera's guile enabled him to post a 3.06 ERA despite a fastball that rarely broke 80 mph.

KEY TRANSACTIONS: Even after their playoff hopes faded away, the Reds traded pitching prospects Zach Stewart and Josh Roenicke along with third baseman Edwin Encarnacion to the Blue Jays for 34-year-old third baseman Scott Rolen. For a team with a limited budget, Rolen's $11 million salary further reduces the team's financial flexibility for 2010.

DOWN ON THE FARM: Most of the team's best prospects began the season at Double-A Carolina and ended up at Triple-A Louisville—which had the best record in the International League but was the only full-season affiliate with a winning record. Travis Wood regained his prospect status by posting a 1.21 ERA at Carolina, while teammate Chris Heisey hit .314/.379/.521 between Carolina and Louisville. Juan Francisco led the organization with 27 home runs before a callup to Cincinnati.

OPENING DAY PAYROLL: $73,558,500

PLAYERS OF THE YEAR

MAJOR LEAGUE

Joey Votto
1b
.322/.414/.567
38 2B, 25 HR, 3rd in
NL in OPS (.981)

MINOR LEAGUE

Travis Wood
lhp
(Double-A/Triple-A)
13-5, 1.77
135 SO in 168 IP

ORGANIZATION LEADERS

BATTING		*Minimum 250 at-bats
MAJORS		
*AVG	Joey Votto	.322
*OPS	Joey Votto	.981
HR	Joey Votto	25
RBI	Brandon Phillips	98
MINORS		
*AVG	Heisey, Chris, Carolina/Louisville	.314
R	Heisey, Chris, Carolina/Louisville	91
H	Heisey, Chris, Carolina/Louisville	162
TB	Francisco, Juan, Carolina/Louisville	274
2B	Frazier, Todd, Carolina/Louisville	45
3B	Sappelt, Dave, Dayton/Sarasota	10
HR	Francisco, Juan, Carolina/Louisville	27
RBI	Francisco, Juan, Carolina/Louisville	93
BB	Wiley, Byron, Dayton	76
SO	Puckett, Cody, Sarasota/Dayton	142
SB	Sappelt, Dave, Dayton/Sarasota	47
*OBP	Wiley, Byron, Dayton	.395
*SLG	Barker, Kevin, Louisville	.551

PITCHING		†Minimum 75 innings
MAJORS		
W	Bronson Arroyo	15
†ERA	Bronson Arroyo	3.84
SO	Aaron Harang	142
MINORS		
W	Wood, Travis, Carolina/Louisville	13
L	Horst, Jeremy, Sarasota/Carolina	17
†ERA	Wood, Travis, Carolina/Louisville	1.77
G	Ondrusek, Logan, Sara./Carolina/Louisville	56
GS	Horst, Jeremy, Sarasota/Carolina	28
SV	Ondrusek, Logan, Sara./Carolina/Louisville	19
IP	Wood, Travis, Carolina/Louisville	168
BB	Gil, Jerry, Sarasota/Carolina	77
SO	Fairel, Matt, Dayton/Sarasota	137
†AVG	Wood, Travis, Carolina/Louisville	.204

CINCINNATI REDS

2009 PERFORMANCE

General Manager: Walt Jocketty. **Farm Director:** Terry Reynolds. **Scouting Director:** Chris Buckley.

Class	Team	League	W	L	PCT	Finish*	Manager(s)
Majors	Cincinnati Reds	National	78	84	.481	10th (16)	Dusty Baker
Triple-A	Louisville Bats	International	84	58	.592	1st (14)	Rick Sweet
Double-A	Carolina Mudcats	Southern	65	74	.468	t-6th (10)	David Bell
High A	Sarasota Reds	Florida State	54	83	.394	12th (12)	Joe Ayrault
Low A	Dayton Dragons	Midwest	59	80	.424	11th (14)	Todd Benzinger
Rookie	Billings Mustangs	Pioneer	24	52	.316	8th (8)	Julio Garcia
Rookie	GCL Reds	Gulf Coast	28	27	.509	8th (16)	Pat Kelly
Overall 2009 Minor League Record			314	374	.456	27th (30)	

*Finish in overall standings (No. of teams in league). †League champion.

ORGANIZATION STATISTICS

CINCINNATI REDS

NATIONAL LEAGUE

Batting	B-T	HT	WT	DOB	AVG	vLH	vRH	G	AB	R	H	2B	3B	HR	RBI	BB	HBP	SH	SF	SO	SB	CS	SLG	OBP
Balentien, Wladimir	R-R	6-2	220	7-2-84	.264	.111	.293	40	110	12	29	7	1	3	11	15	0	0	0	27	1	1	.427	.352
Barker, Kevin	L-L	6-2	195	7-26-75	.281	.000	.310	29	32	2	9	3	0	0	3	3	0	0	1	9	0	0	.375	.333
Bruce, Jay	L-L	6-3	225	4-3-87	.223	.210	.229	101	345	47	77	15	2	22	58	38	2	1	1	75	3	3	.470	.303
Castillo, Wilkin	B-R	6-0	200	6-1-84	.667	1.000	.500	4	3	0	2	0	0	0	1	0	0	0	0	0	0	0	.667	.667
Dickerson, Chris	L-L	6-3	230	4-10-82	.275	.243	.280	97	255	31	70	13	3	2	15	39	1	2	2	66	11	3	.373	.370
Encarnacion, Edwin	R-R	6-2	230	1-7-83	.209	.281	.187	43	139	10	29	6	1	5	16	24	2	0	0	38	1	1	.374	.333
Francisco, Juan	L-R	6-2	180	6-24-87	.429	.333	.444	14	21	4	9	1	0	1	7	3	1	0	0	7	0	0	.619	.520
Gomes, Jonny	R-R	6-1	225	11-22-80	.267	.307	.244	98	281	39	75	17	0	20	51	26	5	0	2	85	3	1	.541	.338
Gonzalez, Alex	R-R	5-11	215	2-15-77	.210	.235	.203	68	243	16	51	12	0	3	26	15	2	6	4	36	0	1	.296	.258
Hairston Jr., Jerry	R-R	5-10	190	5-29-76	.254	.253	.255	86	307	47	78	18	1	8	27	21	3	6	3	46	7	3	.397	.305
Hanigan, Ryan	R-R	6-0	200	8-16-80	.263	.291	.255	90	251	22	66	6	1	3	11	37	2	2	1	31	0	0	.331	.361
Hernandez, Ramon	R-R	6-0	225	5-20-76	.258	.288	.246	81	287	25	74	13	1	5	37	33	3	4	4	34	1	0	.362	.336
Janish, Paul	R-R	6-2	195	10-12-82	.211	.230	.203	90	256	36	54	21	0	1	16	26	5	5	0	40	2	0	.305	.296
McDonald, Darnell	R-R	5-11	210	11-17-78	.267	.365	.216	170	47	105	12	28	6	1	2	10	5	1	0	0	31	1	0	.400	.306
Miller, Corky	R-R	6-1	245	3-18-76	.179	.071	.214	21	56	4	10	1	0	1	10	9	1	2	1	14	0	0	.250	.299
Nix, Laynce	L-L	6-1	220	10-30-80	.239	.156	.249	116	309	42	74	26	1	15	46	22	2	0	4	81	0	1	.476	.291
Phillips, Brandon	R-R	6-0	195	6-28-81	.276	.301	.267	153	584	78	161	30	5	20	98	44	6	2	8	75	25	9	.447	.329
Richar, Danny	L-R	6-1	195	6-9-83	.250	—	.250	7	8	1	2	0	0	0	1	0	0	0	1	0	0	.250	.333
Rolen, Scott	R-R	6-4	240	4-4-75	.270	.435	.237	40	137	24	37	7	1	3	24	19	3	0	3	20	1	2	.401	.364
Rosales, Adam	R-R	6-2	195	5-20-83	.213	.255	.200	87	230	23	49	10	1	4	19	26	5	2	3	46	1	2	.317	.303
Stubbs, Drew	R-R	6-4	205	10-4-84	.267	.286	.261	42	180	27	48	5	1	8	17	15	0	1	0	49	10	4	.439	.323
Sutton, Drew	B-R	6-3	185	6-30-83	.212	.167	.217	42	66	10	14	4	1	1	9	7	1	2	0	20	0	2	.348	.297
Tatum, Craig	R-R	6-1	225	3-18-83	.162	.000	.175	26	68	3	11	1	0	1	6	7	1	1	0	10	0	0	.221	.250
Taveras, Willy	R-R	6-0	160	12-25-81	.240	.219	.247	102	404	56	97	11	2	1	15	18	2	11	2	58	25	6	.285	.275
Votto, Joey	L-R	6-3	235	9-10-83	.322	.329	.319	131	469	82	151	38	1	25	84	70	4	0	1	106	4	1	.567	.414

Pitching	B-T	HT	WT	DOB	W	L	ERA	G	GS	CG	SV	IP	H	R	ER	HR	BB	SO	AVG	vLH	vRH	K/9	BB/9
Arroyo, Bronson	R-R	6-5	195	2-24-77	15	13	3.84	33	33	3	0	220	214	101	94	31	65	127	.256	.278	.236	5.19	2.66
Bailey, Homer	R-R	6-3	210	5-3-86	8	5	4.53	20	20	0	0	113	115	61	57	12	52	86	.266	.283	.248	6.83	4.13
Burton, Jared	R-R	6-5	230	6-2-81	1	0	4.40	53	0	0	0	59	61	30	29	5	23	45	.261	.222	.289	6.83	3.49
Cordero, Francisco	R-R	6-3	240	5-11-75	2	6	2.16	68	0	0	39	67	58	21	16	2	30	58	.243	.228	.256	7.83	4.05
Cueto, Johnny	R-R	5-10	200	2-15-86	11	11	4.41	30	30	0	0	171	172	90	84	24	61	132	.262	.250	.274	6.93	3.20
Fisher, Carlos	R-R	6-4	225	2-22-83	1	1	4.47	39	0	0	0	52	50	26	26	4	31	48	.262	.337	.204	8.25	5.33
Harang, Aaron	R-R	6-7	260	5-9-78	6	14	4.21	26	26	2	0	162	186	82	76	24	43	142	.287	.285	.289	7.87	2.38
Herrera, Daniel Ray	L-L	5-6	165	10-21-84	4	4	3.06	70	0	0	0	62	63	30	21	5	24	44	.276	.183	.361	6.42	3.50
Lehr, Justin	R-R	6-2	215	8-3-77	5	3	5.37	11	11	1	0	65	72	39	39	14	28	33	.286	.234	.324	4.55	3.86
Lincoln, Mike	R-R	6-2	220	4-10-75	1	1	8.22	19	0	0	0	23	29	21	21	7	19	9	.326	.405	.269	3.52	7.43
Maloney, Matt	L-L	6-4	220	1-16-84	2	4	4.87	7	7	0	0	41	43	22	22	9	8	28	.281	.286	.280	6.20	1.77
Manuel, Robert	R-R	6-3	205	7-9-83	0	0	0.00	3	0	0	0	4	5	0	0	0	1	2	.294	.125	.444	4.15	2.08
Masset, Nick	R-R	6-4	235	5-17-82	5	1	2.37	74	0	0	0	76	54	22	20	6	24	70	.203	.219	.194	8.29	2.84
Owings, Micah	R-R	6-5	220	9-28-82	7	12	5.34	26	19	0	1	120	126	75	71	18	64	68	.272	.272	.271	5.11	4.81
Ramirez, Ramon	R-R	6-0	190	9-16-82	0	0	3.65	11	0	0	0	12	8	5	5	2	4	8	.186	.273	.156	5.84	2.92
Rhodes, Arthur	L-L	6-2	210	10-24-69	1	1	2.53	66	0	0	0	53	37	16	15	3	20	48	.198	.141	.245	8.10	3.38
Roenicke, Josh	R-R	6-3	195	8-4-82	0	0	2.70	11	0	0	0	13	13	4	4	0	4	14	.260	.273	.250	9.45	2.70
Viola, Pedro	L-L	6-1	185	6-29-83	0	0	5.14	9	0	0	0	7	7	4	4	2	3	5	.269	.077	.462	6.43	3.86
Volquez, Edinson	R-R	6-0	210	7-3-83	4	2	4.35	9	9	0	0	50	34	25	24	6	32	47	.191	.202	.181	8.52	5.80
Weathers, David	R-R	6-3	240	9-25-69	3	3	3.32	43	0	0	1	38	27	14	14	7	17	27	.199	.192	.202	6.39	4.03
2-team total (25 Milwaukee)					4	6	3.92	68	0	0	1	62	53	29	27	10	28	37	—	—	—	5.37	4.06
Wells, Kip	R-R	6-3	205	4-21-77	2	3	4.66	10	7	0	0	46	37	24	24	5	22	25	.222	.233	.213	4.86	4.27
2-team total (23 Washington)					2	5	5.33	33	7	0	2	73	60	43	43	6	40	43	—	—	—	5.33	4.95

Fielding

Catcher	PCT	G	PO	A	E	DP	PB
Hanigan	.998	88	494	44	1	6	3
Hernandez	.997	55	353	26	1	2	0
Miller	1.000	21	125	12	0	3	1
Tatum	.993	26	137	10	1	0	0

First Base	PCT	G	PO	A	E	DP
Barker	1.000	6	32	1	0	5
Hernandez	.984	30	238	12	4	30
Rosales	1.000	11	68	11	0	5
Votto	.991	130	960	101	10	108

Second Base	PCT	G	PO	A	E	DP
Hairston Jr.	.974	9	16	22	1	5
Phillips	.988	151	307	409	9	100
Richar	—	1	0	0	0	0
Rosales	1.000	4	2	3	0	1

	PCT	G	PO	A	E	DP
Sutton	1.000	8	9	11	0	2

Third Base	PCT	G	PO	A	E	DP
Encarnacion	.959	43	25	69	4	8
Francisco	.900	4	1	8	1	2
Hairston Jr.	.913	33	33	40	7	7
Hernandez	1.000	1	1	0	0	0
Janish	1.000	2	1	3	0	1
Richar	.750	4	1	2	1	0
Rolen	1.000	39	29	64	0	3
Rosales	.944	57	37	81	7	8
Sutton	1.000	2	1	1	0	0

Shortstop	PCT	G	PO	A	E	DP
Gonzalez	.977	68	97	163	6	42
Hairston Jr.	.981	31	47	56	2	8
Janish	.991	82	110	212	3	54

	PCT	G	PO	A	E	DP
Rosales	1.000	6	4	12	0	2
Sutton	1.000	7	7	16	0	4

Outfield	PCT	G	PO	A	E	DP
Balentien	.986	36	67	1	1	0
Bruce	.991	98	200	11	2	2
Dickerson	.981	77	146	5	3	3
Gomes	.991	70	103	5	1	1
Hairston Jr.	1.000	17	35	0	0	0
McDonald	.969	36	61	2	2	1
Nix	.986	85	141	2	2	2
Stubbs	1.000	42	111	4	0	0
Sutton	1.000	6	11	0	0	0
Taveras	.986	98	266	7	4	2

LOUISVILLE BATS — TRIPLE-A
INTERNATIONAL LEAGUE

Batting	B-T	HT	WT	DOB	AVG	vLH	vRH	G	AB	R	H	2B	3B	HR	RBI	BB	HBP	SH	SF	SO	SB	CS	SLG	OBP
Bankston, Wes	R-R	6-4	215	11-27-83	.267	.320	.246	122	457	57	122	26	3	17	75	30	2	1	3	88	2	1	.449	.313
Barker, Kevin	L-L	6-2	195	7-26-75	.285	.319	.273	101	354	58	101	22	3	22	69	54	2	0	7	80	1	1	.551	.376
Bolivar, Luis	R-R	6-0	180	2-15-81	.232	.219	.237	107	353	60	82	16	5	5	32	16	4	4	3	70	28	5	.348	.271
Bruce, Jay	L-L	6-3	225	4-3-87	.278	.333	.267	5	18	3	5	0	0	0	0	2	0	0	0	3	0	1	.278	.350
Castillo, Wilkin	B-R	6-0	200	6-1-84	.221	.242	.213	37	122	12	27	5	1	2	7	1	1	3	0	20	3	1	.328	.234
Denove, Chris	R-R	6-1	215	12-9-82	.307	.294	.310	25	75	8	23	4	0	1	11	4	1	2	3	19	0	1	.400	.337
Dickerson, Chris	L-L	6-3	230	4-10-82	.250	—	.250	4	12	2	3	0	0	0	1	3	0	0	0	4	2	0	.250	.400
Dorn, Danny	L-L	6-2	190	7-20-84	.275	.189	.297	112	357	45	98	21	1	14	47	30	5	1	3	78	2	1	.457	.337
Encarnacion, Edwin	R-R	6-2	230	1-7-83	.270	.167	.290	11	37	5	10	1	0	2	8	8	0	0	0	6	0	0	.459	.400
Eymann, Eric	R-R	6-2	191	2-9-84	.178	.143	.184	33	90	11	16	4	2	1	7	6	1	0	1	19	0	1	.300	.235
Feiner, Korey	R-R	5-11	210	9-25-81	.375	.333	.400	2	8	1	3	1	0	0	0	0	0	0	0	1	0	0	.500	.375
Ford, Lew	R-R	6-0	200	8-12-76	.158	.067	.217	11	38	6	6	0	1	1	6	7	0	0	1	7	0	0	.289	.283
Francisco, Juan	L-R	6-2	180	6-24-87	.359	.308	.379	22	92	17	33	5	1	5	19	4	1	0	2	24	0	0	.598	.384
Frazier, Todd	R-R	6-3	220	2-12-86	.302	.400	.256	16	63	9	19	5	0	2	9	6	0	0	0	12	2	0	.476	.362
Gomes, Jonny	R-R	6-1	225	11-22-80	.282	.387	.250	37	131	18	37	10	1	9	27	12	4	0	0	36	4	1	.580	.361
Gonzalez, Alex	R-R	5-11	215	2-15-77	.077	.000	.083	4	13	1	1	0	0	0	1	2	0	0	0	1	0	0	.077	.200
Griffin, Michael	R-R	5-10	195	10-1-83	.205	.196	.209	64	171	15	35	5	2	2	16	6	1	4	4	33	2	2	.292	.231
Hanigan, Ryan	R-R	6-0	200	8-16-80	.389	.500	.357	5	18	4	7	2	0	0	2	0	0	0	0	0	0	0	.500	.421
Heisey, Chris	R-R	6-0	200	12-14-84	.278	.346	.259	63	245	37	68	17	1	9	37	14	5	2	5	43	8	2	.465	.323
Hopper, Norris	R-R	5-11	205	3-24-79	.280	.254	.293	52	214	22	60	9	3	0	20	14	0	1	3	9	13	2	.350	.320
3-team total (20 Charlotte, 34 Syracuse)					.281	—	—	106	409	49	115	14	3	0	35	35	1	5	3	25	23	8	.330	.337
McDonald, Darnell	R-R	5-11	210	11-17-78	.314	.380	.292	73	280	42	88	22	7	9	40	16	1	3	4	56	8	3	.539	.349
Miller, Corky	R-R	6-1	245	3-18-76	.286	.421	.241	23	77	13	22	5	0	0	8	8	3	2	0	9	0	0	.351	.375
2-team total (4 Charlotte)					.274	—	—	27	84	13	23	5	0	0	8	10	4	2	0	9	0	0	.333	.378
Peterson, Brian	R-R	6-2	225	10-22-78	.125	.000	.138	14	32	3	4	1	0	1	2	9	1	0	0	2	0	0	.250	.333
2-team total (6 Scranton/W-B)					.143	—	—	20	49	6	7	2	0	1	3	13	1	0	0	19	0	0	.245	.333
Richar, Danny	L-R	6-1	195	6-9-83	.290	.240	.299	47	169	20	49	11	1	4	16	10	0	2	0	17	2	3	.438	.330
Rolen, Scott	R-R	6-4	240	4-4-75	.333	—	.333	2	6	1	2	0	0	0	1	0	0	0	0	1	0	0	.333	.333
Rosales, Adam	R-R	6-2	195	5-20-83	.349	.370	.341	30	109	27	38	8	2	5	20	12	1	0	3	15	4	0	.596	.408
Stubbs, Drew	R-R	6-4	205	10-4-84	.268	.257	.272	107	411	57	110	25	2	3	39	51	4	4	2	104	46	8	.360	.353
Sutton, Drew	B-R	6-3	185	6-30-83	.261	.370	.204	44	157	32	41	14	2	5	22	26	5	1	1	39	1	2	.471	.381
Tatum, Craig	R-R	6-1	225	3-18-83	.239	.304	.217	64	213	22	51	12	0	3	21	17	2	0	1	55	0	0	.338	.300
Valaika, Chris	R-R	6-0	215	8-14-85	.235	.233	.236	95	366	32	86	20	1	6	36	16	4	1	5	76	1	0	.344	.271

Pitching	B-T	HT	WT	DOB	W	L	ERA	G	GS	CG	SV	IP	H	R	ER	HR	BB	SO	AVG	vLH	vRH	K/9	BB/9
Atencio, Greg	R-R	6-2	191	7-15-81	2	1	8.44	4	0	0	0	5	7	6	5	0	2	7	.292	.200	.357	11.81	3.38
Baez, Federico	R-R	6-2	190	8-4-81	3	1	4.17	30	0	0	0	37	48	18	17	4	11	30	.314	.259	.343	7.36	2.70
Bailey, Homer	R-R	6-3	210	5-3-86	8	5	2.71	14	14	2	0	90	87	33	27	10	27	82	.253	.295	.218	8.23	2.71
Bray, Bill	L-L	6-3	220	6-5-83	0	0	0.00	3	0	0	0	3	3	0	0	0	1	6	.118	.400	.000	10.80	1.80
Burton, Jared	R-R	6-5	230	6-2-81	3	0	0.82	10	0	0	0	11	8	1	1	0	3	10	.195	.273	.105	8.18	2.45
Cochran, Tom	L-L	6-2	195	10-16-82	1	0	3.07	3	0	0	0	15	18	7	5	0	9	12	.300	.143	.348	7.36	5.52
Del Rosario, Enerio	R-R	6-2	165	10-16-85	1	0	1.09	15	0	0	4	25	24	6	3	1	6	12	.258	.361	.193	4.38	2.19
Fisher, Carlos	R-R	6-4	225	2-22-83	2	0	2.00	13	0	0	2	18	11	4	4	0	4	21	.175	.280	.105	10.50	2.00
Jukich, Ben	L-L	6-5	205	10-17-82	9	6	4.10	29	17	0	0	123	125	64	56	16	40	106	.264	.244	.271	7.76	2.93
Kennard, Jeff	R-R	6-2	220	7-26-81	3	1	2.83	40	0	0	2	54	45	23	17	4	21	48	.225	.260	.203	8.00	3.50
Klinker, Matt	R-R	6-5	220	10-8-84	2	2	2.48	5	5	0	0	29	22	10	8	0	13	30	.204	.220	.194	9.31	4.03
Krebs, Joseph	L-L	6-0	200	9-14-84	0	0	0.00	2	0	0	0	3	1	0	0	0	1	2	.091	.000	.100	6.00	3.00
LeCure, Sam	R-R	6-1	205	5-4-84	10	8	4.46	25	25	0	0	143	143	76	71	17	44	125	.264	.331	.227	7.85	2.76
Lehr, Justin	R-R	6-2	215	8-3-77	8	1	2.51	12	11	1	0	75	57	22	21	3	10	40	.210	.211	.209	4.78	1.19
2-team total (8 Lehigh Valley)					13	3	3.31	20	18	2	0	117	100	45	43	8	26	60	—	—	—	4.62	2.00
Mallett, Justin	R-R	6-6	210	11-11-81	0	0	0.00	2	0	0	0	4	3	0	0	0	0	4	.214	.200	.222	9.00	0.00
Maloney, Matt	L-L	6-4	220	1-16-84	9	9	3.08	22	22	3	0	143	143	56	49	11	24	125	.262	.288	.254	7.87	1.51
Manuel, Robert	R-R	6-3	205	7-9-83	3	4	2.70	36	0	0	10	47	37	17	14	2	10	38	.215	.161	.245	7.33	1.93

Name	B-T	HT	WT	DOB	W	L	ERA	G	GS	CG	SV	IP	H	R	ER	HR	BB	SO	AVG	vLH	vRH	K/9	BB/9
Ondrusek, Logan	R-R	6-7	205	2-13-85	0	0	1.74	19	0	0	12	21	16	4	4	1	2	11	.219	.261	.200	4.79	0.87
Owings, Micah	R-R	6-5	220	9-28-82	1	0	0.87	2	2	0	0	10	8	1	1	1	7	5	.222	.154	.261	4.35	6.10
Pettyjohn, Adam	R-L	6-3	200	6-11-77	1	6	4.68	18	6	0	0	50	66	35	26	5	22	27	.316	.292	.326	4.86	3.96
2-team total (9 Buffalo)					4	11	4.09	27	14	0	0	106	129	59	48	10	31	57	—	—	—	4.85	2.64
Ramirez, Ramon	R-R	6-0	190	9-16-82	6	7	4.03	31	20	0	0	127	122	68	57	13	50	78	.256	.199	.304	5.51	3.53
Roenicke, Josh	R-R	6-3	195	8-4-82	1	0	2.57	27	0	0	12	28	30	9	8	0	6	32	.268	.353	.197	10.29	1.93
Stewart, Zach	R-R	6-2	205	9-28-86	0	0	0.73	9	0	0	2	12	11	2	1	0	8	16	.234	.250	.222	11.68	5.84
Tabor, Lee	L-L	6-2	175	12-17-84	2	0	3.10	9	0	0	0	20	21	7	7	1	6	14	.273	.333	.250	6.20	2.66
Thompson, Daryl	R-R	6-0	185	11-2-85	1	2	6.59	8	6	0	0	29	34	22	21	3	7	8	.288	.212	.348	2.51	2.20
Vazquez, Camilo	L-L	5-11	205	10-3-83	0	0	5.52	5	2	0	0	15	25	10	9	1	3	7	.391	.563	.333	4.30	1.84
Viola, Pedro	L-L	6-1	185	6-29-83	2	2	5.47	54	0	0	8	49	48	30	30	7	33	57	.251	.229	.269	10.40	6.02
Watson, Sean	R-R	6-2	215	7-24-85	0	1	1.93	4	0	0	0	5	4	2	1	1	4	3	.235	.250	.231	5.79	7.71
Wells, Kip	R-R	6-3	205	4-21-77	1	0	3.07	5	1	0	0	15	12	5	5	2	5	16	.226	.296	.154	9.82	3.07
2-team total (2 Syracuse)					2	0	2.81	7	3	0	0	26	21	8	8	3	7	27	—	—	—	9.47	2.45
Wood, Travis	R-L	5-11	166	2-6-87	4	2	3.14	8	8	0	0	49	43	17	17	4	16	32	.240	.250	.238	5.92	2.96

Fielding

Catcher	PCT	G	PO	A	E	DP	PB
Castillo	.973	21	131	15	4	0	2
Denove	.995	24	174	12	1	2	4
Feiner	.895	2	16	1	2	1	1
Hanigan	1.000	5	33	1	0	0	0
Miller	1.000	23	167	13	0	2	2
Peterson	.976	11	78	3	2	0	0
Tatum	.988	63	449	37	6	1	6

First Base	PCT	G	PO	A	E	DP
Bankston	.992	40	332	21	3	32
Barker	.990	72	556	40	6	49
Dorn	.979	26	172	16	4	17
Eymann	1.000	3	20	2	0	2
Rosales	1.000	3	24	0	0	0
Sutton	1.000	6	46	5	0	7

Second Base	PCT	G	PO	A	E	DP
Bolivar	.968	42	73	111	6	23
Castillo	1.000	1	1	1	0	1
Eymann	1.000	5	10	15	0	4
Frazier	.944	14	26	41	4	9

	PCT	G	PO	A	E	DP
Griffin	1.000	17	22	45	0	12
Richar	.968	41	71	81	5	19
Rosales	.933	4	7	7	1	2
Sutton	.967	12	25	33	2	7
Valaika	.985	18	20	47	1	8

Third Base	PCT	G	PO	A	E	DP
Bankston	.845	42	24	58	15	6
Bolivar	.864	14	7	12	3	3
Castillo	.931	13	9	18	2	1
Encarnacion	.952	9	10	10	1	2
Eymann	.975	19	7	32	1	2
Francisco	.938	21	14	46	4	6
Griffin	.932	25	12	29	3	2
Rolen	—	2	0	0	0	0
Rosales	.962	12	4	21	1	1
Sutton	.917	13	12	21	3	0

Shortstop	PCT	G	PO	A	E	DP
Bolivar	.938	31	49	73	8	13
Eymann	.957	4	9	13	1	6
Gonzalez	1.000	4	3	7	0	3

	PCT	G	PO	A	E	DP
Richar	1.000	7	12	17	0	4
Rosales	.980	11	15	35	1	5
Sutton	.979	14	18	29	1	1
Valaika	.977	77	89	214	7	47

Outfield	PCT	G	PO	A	E	DP
Bankston	1.000	17	33	0	0	0
Bolivar	1.000	14	26	1	0	0
Bruce	1.000	5	10	0	0	0
Castillo	1.000	2	3	0	0	0
Dickerson	1.000	4	7	0	0	0
Dorn	.982	62	104	3	2	0
Ford	1.000	11	20	2	0	1
Francisco	1.000	2	3	0	0	0
Frazier	1.000	1	1	0	0	0
Gomes	.951	31	56	2	3	0
Griffin	.857	16	23	1	4	0
Heisey	.985	61	127	4	2	0
Hopper	.991	48	108	3	1	0
McDonald	.987	62	144	6	2	0
Stubbs	.993	106	294	8	2	4

CAROLINA MUDCATS

DOUBLE-A

SOUTHERN LEAGUE

Batting	B-T	HT	WT	DOB	AVG	vLH	vRH	G	AB	R	H	2B	3B	HR	RBI	BB	HBP	SH	SF	SO	SB	CS	SLG	OBP
Alonso, Yonder	L-R	6-2	215	4-8-87	.295	.242	.319	29	105	12	31	11	0	2	14	14	0	0	2	15	1	0	.457	.372
Bour, Jason	R-R	6-3	215	7-2-86	.237	.160	.275	26	76	3	18	6	0	0	4	5	1	2	2	21	0	0	.316	.286
Castro, Jose	B-R	5-11	172	11-5-86	.270	.280	.267	104	333	30	90	13	2	1	29	11	3	8	3	30	2	4	.330	.297
Chapman, Stephen	L-L	6-0	205	10-12-85	.215	.167	.225	49	135	15	29	4	1	5	17	6	1	1	2	46	4	4	.370	.250
Cozart, Zack	R-R	6-1	185	8-12-85	.262	.303	.248	131	462	72	121	29	2	10	59	63	10	2	4	87	10	2	.398	.360
Cumberland, Shaun	L-R	6-2	185	8-1-84	.236	.243	.235	111	296	31	70	16	2	3	31	27	2	1	1	70	12	6	.334	.304
Denove, Chris	R-R	6-1	215	12-9-82	.264	.315	.233	48	144	14	38	13	0	3	18	15	5	2	1	18	0	1	.417	.352
Eymann, Eric	R-R	6-2	191	2-9-84	.234	.265	.221	74	222	21	52	12	0	1	21	19	6	0	3	38	1	2	.302	.308
Feiner, Korey	R-R	5-11	210	9-25-81	.153	.105	.167	29	85	5	13	0	0	0	4	7	4	1	0	14	0	0	.153	.250
Francisco, Juan	L-R	6-2	180	6-24-87	.281	.235	.299	109	437	64	123	26	2	22	74	20	4	0	3	91	6	2	.501	.317
Frazier, Todd	R-R	6-3	220	2-12-86	.290	.320	.279	119	451	59	131	40	2	14	68	42	2	0	5	67	7	8	.481	.350
Griffin, Michael	R-R	5-10	195	10-1-83	.248	.244	.250	36	133	12	33	9	0	1	5	7	0	1	0	13	2	2	.338	.286
Heisey, Chris	R-R	6-0	200	12-14-84	.347	.366	.340	71	271	54	94	18	2	13	40	34	5	2	2	34	13	1	.572	.426
Henry, Sean	R-R	5-10	180	8-18-85	.271	.308	.257	121	420	66	114	22	1	11	38	40	5	3	1	66	23	9	.407	.341
Kahaulelio, Jake	R-R	5-10	182	6-7-85	.297	.316	.289	19	64	11	19	7	1	0	3	7	0	0	0	11	1	0	.438	.366
Kainer, Carson	R-R	6-1	210	10-27-84	.243	.164	.290	57	148	11	36	6	0	1	13	8	1	0	1	33	1	1	.304	.285
Kroski, Chris	L-R	6-2	225	5-17-82	.202	.167	.209	33	104	16	21	6	1	2	13	16	0	1	1	28	0	1	.337	.306
Long, Jacob	R-R	6-1	180	4-17-86	.194	.286	.172	11	36	5	7	5	0	1	3	3	0	0	0	18	0	0	.417	.256
Louwsma, Jason	R-R	6-2	210	9-9-83	.333	.333	—	1	3	0	1	0	0	0	0	1	0	0	0	0	0	0	.333	.500
Negron, Kris	R-R	6-0	180	2-1-86	.241	.333	.194	15	54	11	13	2	0	2	5	8	4	1	0	7	4	1	.389	.379
Parker, Logan	L-L	6-3	215	7-18-84	.222	.179	.236	125	392	37	87	18	4	6	48	53	1	2	2	97	5	6	.334	.315
Peterson, Brian	R-R	6-2	225	10-22-78	.323	.000	.417	9	31	3	10	2	0	1	9	2	0	0	1	7	0	0	.484	.353
Phipps, Denis	R-R	6-2	177	7-22-85	.000	.000	.000	3	4	0	0	0	0	0	0	0	0	0	0	1	0	0	.000	.000
Tordi, Justin	R-R	6-1	208	4-9-84	.117	.238	.051	25	60	4	7	2	0	0	2	7	0	2	0	21	0	0	.150	.209

Pitching	B-T	HT	WT	DOB	W	L	ERA	G	GS	CG	SV	IP	H	R	ER	HR	BB	SO	AVG	vLH	vRH	K/9	BB/9
Aselton, Kyle	R-L	6-5	215	2-28-83	0	1	9.64	4	0	0	0	4	8	8	8	1	5	5	.400	.400	.400	12.27	12.27
2-team total (5 Birmingham)					0	1	17.28	9	0	0	0	8	17	16	16	2	12	13	—	—	—	14.04	12.96
Atencio, Greg	R-R	6-2	191	7-15-81	1	1	3.38	8	0	0	0	11	10	4	4	0	3	8	.244	.133	.308	6.75	2.53
Avery, James	R-R	6-1	210	6-10-84	2	3	2.89	10	10	0	0	56	53	26	18	3	19	32	.248	.269	.231	5.14	3.05
Baez, Federico	R-R	6-2	190	8-4-81	3	2	3.38	13	0	0	0	21	19	12	8	2	9	18	.241	.219	.255	7.59	3.80
Beal, Josh	R-R	6-2	220	10-21-87	0	0	2.45	2	0	0	0	4	1	1	1	1	0	3	.091	.000	.143	7.36	0.00

Pitching	B-T	HT	WT	DOB	W	L	ERA	G	GS	CG	SV	IP	H	R	ER	HR	BB	SO	AVG	vLH	vRH	K/9	BB/9
Buck, Dallas	R-R	6-2	195	11-11-84	2	3	4.82	8	8	0	0	37	49	23	20	1	18	25	.327	.380	.278	6.03	4.34
Carroll, Scott	R-R	6-5	210	9-24-84	0	0	9.00	2	2	0	0	5	9	6	5	0	3	3	.391	.333	.455	5.40	5.40
Cochran, Tom	L-L	6-2	195	10-16-82	4	6	3.18	17	15	1	1	88	79	42	31	8	34	70	.241	.269	.227	7.19	3.49
DeJesus, Misael	R-R	6-2	235	11-5-84	1	4	9.85	7	7	0	0	28	34	37	31	4	26	14	.327	.356	.305	4.45	8.26
Del Rosario, Enerio	R-R	6-2	165	10-16-85	0	0	1.59	4	0	0	1	6	2	1	1	0	0	9	.105	.222	.000	14.29	0.00
Geronimo, Ramon	R-R	6-0	185	10-8-83	4	3	4.87	50	0	0	5	65	65	39	35	6	41	46	.266	.292	.246	6.40	5.71
Gil, Jerry	R-R	6-3	200	10-14-82	3	4	8.21	24	4	0	0	49	51	50	45	9	48	30	.262	.250	.272	5.47	8.76
Horst, Jeremy	L-L	6-4	220	10-1-85	1	4	6.21	5	5	0	0	29	35	20	20	7	10	21	.310	.250	.342	6.52	3.10
Kelly, Chris	R-R	6-3	200	7-14-82	0	1	7.88	17	0	0	0	24	28	23	21	1	17	12	.301	.293	.308	4.50	6.38
Klinker, Matt	R-R	6-5	220	10-8-84	3	2	2.95	6	6	0	0	37	27	12	12	6	13	40	.206	.265	.143	9.82	3.19
Krebs, Joseph	L-L	6-0	200	9-14-84	0	1	0.40	11	1	0	2	22	11	4	1	0	11	17	.149	.182	.135	6.85	4.43
Lutz, Derrik	R-R	6-0	210	4-22-85	1	2	1.99	20	0	0	2	23	18	7	5	0	10	17	.212	.161	.241	6.75	3.97
Mallett, Justin	R-R	6-6	210	11-11-81	0	2	3.68	5	5	0	0	29	31	12	12	1	7	21	.274	.291	.259	6.44	2.15
Maloney, Matt	L-L	6-4	220	1-16-84	0	0	1.29	1	1	0	0	7	3	1	1	1	2	5	.136	.000	.167	6.43	2.57
Medina, Ruben	R-R	5-11	157	7-29-86	2	4	3.95	51	0	0	11	59	33	31	6	48	52	.241	.268	.213	6.62	6.11
Montano, Luis	R-R	6-0	180	3-20-85	0	6	6.86	7	7	0	0	39	54	32	30	5	17	18	.329	.329	.330	4.12	3.89
Ondrusek, Logan	R-R	6-7	205	2-13-85	2	1	1.65	24	0	0	7	33	21	7	6	0	12	24	.184	.218	.153	6.61	3.31
Otterness, Steven	L-L	6-4	210	10-30-84	1	0	0.00	1	0	0	0	2	0	0	0	0	1	1	.000	.000	.000	3.86	3.86
Partch, Curtis	R-R	6-5	200	12-13-87	1	0	1.80	1	1	0	0	5	5	1	1	0	2	2	.238	.231	.250	3.60	3.60
Smit, Alexander	L-L	6-3	215	10-2-85	4	3	3.04	21	10	0	0	71	54	27	24	9	42	73	.220	.234	.213	9.25	5.32
Smith, Jordan	R-R	6-4	220	2-4-86	5	3	3.44	13	13	0	0	73	77	37	28	4	21	39	.277	.287	.266	4.79	2.58
Stewart, Zach	R-R	6-2	205	9-28-86	3	0	1.46	7	7	0	0	37	29	7	6	1	10	31	.218	.278	.130	7.54	2.43
Tabor, Lee	L-L	6-2	175	12-17-84	1	2	3.13	9	5	0	0	32	28	15	11	3	8	15	.239	.194	.256	4.26	2.27
Valiquette, Philippe	L-L	6-0	175	2-14-87	1	1	2.76	27	0	0	3	33	25	13	10	2	20	27	.217	.222	.215	7.44	5.51
Vazquez, Camilo	L-L	5-11	205	10-3-83	5	4	5.29	34	11	0	0	78	85	52	46	6	42	77	.280	.231	.300	8.85	4.83
Ward, Zach	R-R	6-3	250	1-14-84	2	4	13.50	10	3	0	0	17	31	27	25	0	20	13	.431	.375	.458	7.02	10.80
Watson, Sean	R-R	6-2	215	7-24-85	4	4	4.48	46	0	0	8	66	54	33	33	6	42	63	.228	.222	.233	8.55	5.70
Wood, Travis	R-L	5-11	166	2-6-87	9	3	1.21	19	19	1	0	119	78	23	16	2	37	103	.189	.194	.187	7.79	2.80

Fielding

Catcher	PCT	G	PO	A	E	DP	PB
Bour	.955	23	134	14	7	2	4
Denove	.992	45	330	33	3	2	5
Feiner	1.000	26	185	14	0	4	3
Kroski	.990	30	188	19	2	1	8
Long	.989	11	84	6	1	1	0
Peterson	.962	9	65	11	3	0	1

First Base	PCT	G	PO	A	E	DP
Alonso	.987	27	212	24	3	24
Chapman	1.000	2	2	0	0	1
Denove	1.000	1	1	0	0	0
Eymann	1.000	9	44	7	0	6
Frazier	.992	15	111	7	1	12
Louwsma	1.000	1	8	2	0	2
Parker	.990	98	697	63	8	81
Tordi	1.000	8	48	8	0	5

Second Base	PCT	G	PO	A	E	DP
Castro	.991	58	98	111	2	28

(Second Base, cont.)	PCT	G	PO	A	E	DP
Eymann	.974	50	86	103	5	32
Frazier	.971	23	42	60	3	18
Griffin	.974	10	17	20	1	3
Henry	—	1	0	0	0	0
Kahaulelio	1.000	9	13	22	0	5
Negron	.965	10	26	29	2	7
Tordi	1.000	1	1	0	0	0

Third Base	PCT	G	PO	A	E	DP
Castro	.962	27	10	40	2	3
Eymann	1.000	6	6	18	0	4
Francisco	.871	104	59	178	35	22
Frazier	1.000	4	3	1	0	0
Griffin	1.000	1	1	2	0	0
Kahaulelio	1.000	2	5	3	0	2
Negron	.500	1	1	0	1	0
Tordi	1.000	2	2	3	0	0

Shortstop	PCT	G	PO	A	E	DP
Castro	.960	9	9	15	1	3

Shortstop (cont.)	PCT	G	PO	A	E	DP
Cozart	.959	118	209	335	23	83
Eymann	.955	5	5	16	1	4
Kahaulelio	1.000	4	7	9	0	3
Negron	1.000	1	2	2	0	0
Tordi	.976	8	14	26	1	10

Outfield	PCT	G	PO	A	E	DP
Chapman	.973	35	69	2	2	0
Cumberland	.975	79	149	9	4	2
Frazier	.979	78	126	16	3	4
Griffin	1.000	26	64	5	0	0
Heisey	.973	68	139	3	4	1
Henry	.948	108	206	12	12	2
Kahaulelio	—	2	0	0	0	0
Kainer	.974	41	71	4	2	0
Negron	1.000	3	8	1	0	0
Parker	.969	21	27	4	1	0
Phipps	—	1	0	0	0	0

SARASOTA REDS   HIGH CLASS A

FLORIDA STATE LEAGUE

Batting	B-T	HT	WT	DOB	AVG	vLH	vRH	G	AB	R	H	2B	3B	HR	RBI	BB	HBP	SH	SF	SO	SB	CS	SLG	OBP
Alonso, Yonder	L-R	6-2	215	4-8-87	.303	.231	.315	49	175	21	53	13	0	7	38	24	0	0	2	30	0	1	.497	.383
Bour, Jason	R-R	6-3	215	7-2-86	.263	.130	.286	44	156	13	41	8	0	2	13	8	2	1	1	45	1	0	.353	.305
Brown, Tony	L-L	6-0	200	1-26-88	.189	.000	.194	12	37	3	7	1	0	1	4	2	1	0	1	9	1	0	.297	.244
Buchholz, Alex	R-R	6-0	182	9-30-87	.237	.200	.247	90	334	38	79	18	2	2	34	23	7	1	3	59	3	4	.320	.297
Carlson, Shane	R-R	6-0	185	4-7-87	.210	.300	.167	41	124	9	26	5	0	0	8	4	3	3	0	33	3	1	.250	.252
Chapman, Stephen	L-L	6-0	205	10-12-85	.100	.200	.080	10	30	0	3	0	0	0	0	1	0	0	0	9	0	0	.100	.129
Day, Kyle	L-R	5-11	200	7-13-86	.234	.063	.264	33	107	8	25	4	1	1	9	16	1	0	2	40	1	0	.318	.333
Feiner, Kevyn	R-R	6-1	170	6-11-87	.195	.083	.241	21	41	4	8	2	0	0	3	1	1	3	0	6	1	2	.244	.233
Gregorius, Mariekson	L-R	6-1	160	2-18-90	.254	.429	.234	22	71	8	18	4	0	0	2	1	1	1	0	9	0	0	.310	.274
Gualdron, Jose	R-R	5-11	165	7-18-87	.231	.120	.265	36	108	7	25	4	1	2	10	2	0	0	2	16	0	1	.343	.241
Jones, Kel	L-L	5-9	170	9-21-85	.130	.000	.150	8	23	2	3	0	0	0	3	1	0	1	2	6	1	0	.130	.154
Kahaulelio, Jake	R-R	5-10	182	6-7-85	.241	.229	.244	58	216	11	52	16	0	1	10	15	7	0	0	46	10	2	.329	.311
Kainer, Carson	R-R	6-1	210	10-27-84	.266	.242	.270	57	218	28	58	8	1	2	9	9	1	0	1	34	1	1	.339	.297
Konstanty, Mike	R-R	6-4	225	4-17-86	.067	.250	.000	5	15	2	1	1	0	0	1	0	0	0	0	5	0	0	.133	.125
Kuo, Yen-Wen	L-R	5-10	175	10-25-88	.000	—	.000	1	3	0	0	0	0	0	0	0	0	0	0	2	0	0	.000	.000
Long, Jacob	R-R	6-1	180	4-17-86	.165	.083	.167	18	48	4	7	3	0	0	1	4	0	1	1	17	0	0	.208	.208
Louwsma, Jason	R-R	6-2	210	9-9-83	.193	.241	.178	100	347	26	67	18	1	4	27	18	0	2	4	68	1	1	.285	.230
McMurray, Chris	R-R	6-1	195	10-12-86	.080	.182	.000	9	25	0	2	0	0	0	0	1	0	0	0	9	0	0	.080	.115
Mesoraco, Devin	R-R	6-1	220	6-19-88	.228	.255	.222	92	312	32	71	22	1	8	37	35	4	3	3	76	0	1	.381	.311
Negron, Kris	R-R	6-0	180	2-1-86	.208	.333	.190	8	24	6	5	0	0	1	2	5	0	0	0	8	3	1	.333	.345
Perales, Daniel	L-L	6-0	195	3-18-85	.206	.143	.214	20	63	7	13	4	1	1	13	1	0	0	4	9	1	0	.349	.206

Name	B-T	HT	WT	DOB	AVG	vLH	vRH	G	AB	R	H	2B	3B	HR	RBI	BB	HBP	SH	SF	SO	SB	CS	SLG	OBP
Phipps, Denis	R-R	6-2	177	7-22-85	.239	.233	.241	134	493	51	118	32	5	10	55	31	5	5	6	108	18	8	.385	.288
Puckett, Cody	R-R	5-10	175	4-3-87	.056	.000	.059	5	18	1	1	0	0	0	1	2	0	0	1	4	1	0	.056	.143
Reed, Justin	L-R	5-11	179	11-29-87	.222	.267	.209	124	478	60	106	13	9	2	26	55	3	6	0	130	21	10	.299	.306
Sappelt, David	R-R	5-9	195	1-2-87	.295	.206	.324	62	251	27	74	10	3	4	21	13	2	4	1	29	21	11	.406	.333
Soto, Neftali	R-R	6-2	180	2-28-89	.248	.243	.249	131	505	53	125	21	2	11	57	23	3	2	4	95	1	3	.362	.282
Tordi, Justin	R-R	6-1	208	4-9-84	.167	.204	.156	67	209	12	35	4	1	1	15	4	2	2	2	66	1	0	.211	.189
Votto, Joey	L-R	6-3	235	9-10-83	.000	—	.000	1	2	0	0	0	0	0	0	0	0	0	0	1	0	0	.000	.333
Wideman, Jordan	R-R	5-11	200	3-14-89	.250	.400	.206	14	44	3	11	2	0	0	3	5	0	0	0	16	0	0	.295	.327

Pitching	B-T	HT	WT	DOB	W	L	ERA	G	GS	CG	SV	IP	H	R	ER	HR	BB	SO	AVG	vLH	vRH	K/9	BB/9
Beal, Josh	R-R	6-2	220	10-21-87	1	3	3.44	31	0	0	0	52	63	30	20	5	19	32	.301	.365	.258	5.50	3.27
Bohana, Michael	R-R	6-1	190	10-14-85	0	1	7.71	5	0	0	0	9	11	8	8	1	6	5	.289	.444	.150	4.82	5.79
Carnevale, Jesus	L-L	6-0	200	7-18-84	0	1	5.79	8	0	0	1	9	15	8	6	0	3	10	.357	.250	.400	9.64	2.89
Carroll, Scott	R-R	6-5	210	9-24-84	2	2	2.68	7	6	0	0	40	40	18	12	5	6	14	.260	.329	.198	3.12	1.34
Davis, Ben	B-R	6-4	240	3-10-77	0	1	3.09	9	0	0	4	12	10	4	4	1	2	14	.233	.263	.208	10.80	1.54
Del Rosario, Enerio	R-R	6-2	165	10-16-85	2	1	1.98	31	0	0	7	50	40	14	11	2	6	33	.215	.225	.208	5.94	1.08
Driessen, Nathan	L-L	6-2	190	6-28-91	0	0	6.00	1	0	0	0	3	3	2	2	0	1	0	.273	.000	.429	0.00	3.00
Fairel, Matt	L-L	6-3	203	7-8-87	3	3	3.24	8	8	0	0	50	46	21	18	0	19	30	.251	.327	.221	5.40	3.42
Fisher, Carlos	R-R	6-4	225	2-22-83	0	0	0.00	2	0	0	0	2	1	0	0	0	2	2	.143	.000	.333	9.00	9.00
Freeman, Justin	R-R	6-1	170	10-22-86	2	5	3.48	37	0	0	3	65	75	34	25	1	10	49	.292	.317	.275	6.82	1.39
Gil, Jerry	R-R	6-3	200	10-14-82	3	7	7.74	12	10	0	0	48	66	46	41	7	29	30	.338	.237	.439	5.66	5.48
Gonzalez, Aguido	L-L	5-10	185	9-19-86	1	0	3.77	10	0	0	1	14	19	7	6	1	8	5	.345	.316	.361	3.14	5.02
Gonzalez, Rafael	R-R	6-1	232	3-21-86	3	5	5.23	14	12	0	0	64	74	40	37	8	34	37	.291	.360	.236	5.23	4.81
Guerrero, Daniel	R-R	6-1	180	7-21-85	1	0	8.71	5	0	0	0	10	19	11	10	1	2	6	.388	.409	.370	5.23	1.74
Horst, Jeremy	L-L	6-4	220	10-1-85	6	13	3.25	23	23	1	0	133	136	61	48	15	41	101	.268	.278	.264	6.83	2.77
Janke, Lance	R-R	6-2	190	10-8-86	0	5	3.73	6	6	0	0	31	36	18	13	2	10	26	.298	.292	.306	7.47	2.87
Kelly, Chris	R-R	6-3	200	7-14-82	1	1	4.76	4	0	0	0	6	5	3	3	0	1	3	.263	.200	.286	4.76	1.59
Klinker, Matt	R-R	6-5	220	10-8-84	2	2	4.89	9	9	0	0	42	53	26	23	3	8	42	.306	.370	.260	8.93	1.70
Krebs, Joseph	L-L	6-0	200	9-14-84	3	1	2.45	32	0	0	1	55	53	18	15	2	19	39	.245	.174	.279	6.38	3.11
Molina, Marcos	R-R	6-1	185	4-4-88	0	0	0.00	1	0	0	0	1	0	0	0	0	0	2	.000	—	.000	18.00	0.00
Montano, Luis	R-R	6-0	180	3-20-85	8	9	4.43	23	15	1	1	85	93	47	42	10	30	54	.284	.260	.304	5.70	3.16
Ondrusek, Logan	R-R	6-7	205	2-13-85	2	0	0.96	13	0	0	0	19	7	4	2	0	7	12	.117	.111	.119	5.79	3.38
Otterness, Steven	L-L	6-4	210	10-30-84	2	2	3.93	20	0	0	1	34	25	15	15	6	20	25	.202	.216	.195	6.55	5.24
Partch, Curtis	R-R	6-5	200	2-13-87	3	2	4.35	7	7	0	0	39	38	22	19	0	18	25	.257	.222	.289	5.72	4.12
Pawelek, Mark	L-L	6-3	190	8-18-86	0	2	4.67	18	0	0	0	27	18	15	14	1	33	23	.189	.333	.149	7.67	11.00
Smit, Alexander	L-L	6-3	215	10-2-85	0	0	4.26	3	2	0	0	13	12	7	6	1	7	12	.267	.333	.242	8.53	4.97
Stewart, Zach	R-R	6-2	205	9-28-86	1	1	2.13	7	7	1	0	42	47	17	10	1	8	32	.283	.338	.242	6.80	1.70
Tabor, Lee	L-L	6-2	175	12-17-84	0	0	12.00	2	0	0	0	3	9	4	4	1	0	1	.529	.000	.563	3.00	0.00
Thurman, Mace	L-L	6-1	180	4-5-87	0	2	1.10	30	0	0	8	49	30	10	6	0	14	47	.172	.204	.158	8.63	2.57
Valiquette, Philippe	L-L	6-0	175	2-14-87	1	1	2.29	17	0	0	6	20	11	5	5	2	9	19	.175	.211	.159	8.69	4.12
Villarreal, Pedro	R-R	6-1	215	12-9-87	0	3	5.46	9	3	0	0	31	30	20	19	2	18	12	.252	.290	.211	3.45	5.17
Walker, Justin	L-L	6-5	200	11-3-86	0	0	0.00	1	0	0	0	1	2	0	0	0	0	0	.400	.333	.500	0.00	0.00
Ward, Zach	R-R	6-3	250	1-14-84	0	0	0.00	2	2	0	0	4	2	1	0	0	4	5	.125	.000	.222	10.38	8.31
Webb, Travis	L-L	6-4	205	8-2-84	7	10	3.99	27	27	0	0	129	127	62	57	10	64	105	.258	.259	.257	7.34	4.48

Fielding

Catcher	PCT	G	PO	A	E	DP	PB
Bour	.988	24	145	16	2	4	7
Day	1.000	2	19	0	0	0	2
Long	.989	17	84	6	1	1	3
McMurray	1.000	9	58	9	0	0	0
Mesoraco	.985	75	481	37	8	7	10
Wideman	.990	14	90	10	1	1	3

First Base	PCT	G	PO	A	E	DP
Alonso	.988	42	373	22	5	42
Chapman	.900	1	8	1	1	2
Konstanty	1.000	1	4	0	0	1
Louwsma	.990	86	744	53	8	75
Soto	.986	8	64	9	1	10
Tordi	1.000	2	3	0	0	0
Votto	1.000	1	10	0	0	1

Second Base	PCT	G	PO	A	E	DP
Buchholz	.978	51	127	140	6	42

	PCT	G	PO	A	E	DP
Feiner	.935	16	18	40	4	7
Gualdron	.963	5	12	14	1	6
Kahaulelio	.982	52	110	157	5	38
Kuo	1.000	1	6	2	0	1
Puckett	.938	5	9	6	1	2
Tordi	.976	15	33	49	2	10

Third Base	PCT	G	PO	A	E	DP
Carlson	.800	3	3	1	1	1
Gualdron	.952	29	15	64	4	7
Louwsma	1.000	6	3	14	0	4
Soto	.901	96	56	199	28	25
Tordi	.909	6	0	10	1	1

Shortstop	PCT	G	PO	A	E	DP
Buchholz	.937	34	31	88	8	19
Carlson	.943	36	57	93	9	18
Feiner	1.000	1	1	0	0	0
Gregorius	.937	22	38	66	7	14

	PCT	G	PO	A	E	DP
Kahaulelio	1.000	2	2	4	0	1
Negron	.964	6	8	19	1	4
Tordi	.946	45	55	121	10	33

Outfield	PCT	G	PO	A	E	DP
Brown	1.000	7	6	0	0	0
Chapman	1.000	7	14	0	0	0
Day	.909	8	9	1	1	0
Jones	1.000	8	10	1	0	0
Kahaulelio	1.000	3	4	0	0	0
Kainer	.972	44	65	5	2	1
Konstanty	1.000	2	3	0	0	0
Louwsma	1.000	3	4	0	0	0
Negron	1.000	3	4	0	0	0
Perales	1.000	18	28	4	0	0
Phipps	.975	130	294	19	8	6
Reed	.958	123	241	9	11	2
Sappelt	.989	62	175	5	2	2

DAYTON DRAGONS   LOW CLASS A

MIDWEST LEAGUE

Batting	B-T	HT	WT	DOB	AVG	vLH	vRH	G	AB	R	H	2B	3B	HR	RBI	BB	HBP	SH	SF	SO	SB	CS	SLG	OBP
Brown, Tony	L-L	6-0	200	1-26-88	.255	.250	.256	58	200	25	51	11	4	4	29	10	6	1	1	76	2	1	.410	.309
Chapman, Stephen	L-L	6-0	205	10-12-85	.219	.071	.260	37	128	21	28	6	1	3	12	15	2	1	0	43	14	3	.352	.310
Coddington, Kevin	R-R	6-4	205	7-21-87	.278	.244	.289	99	363	39	101	23	2	2	42	24	5	4	3	61	11	2	.369	.329
Day, Kyle	L-R	5-11	200	7-13-86	.258	.326	.241	67	233	26	60	7	3	4	26	30	4	1	3	52	1	1	.365	.348
Feiner, Kevyn	R-R	6-1	170	6-11-87	.275	.244	.286	52	178	20	49	10	1	2	24	5	3	4	2	33	9	5	.376	.303
Fellhauer, Josh	L-L	5-11	180	3-24-88	.280	.250	.287	57	236	31	66	16	2	7	23	19	7	2	0	34	7	4	.453	.351

	B-T	HT	WT	DOB	AVG	vLH	vRH	G	AB	R	H	2B	3B	HR	RBI	BB	HBP	SH	SF	SO	SB	CS	SLG	OBP
Gualdron, Jose	R-R	5-11	165	7-18-87	.205	.333	.183	25	83	10	17	8	0	1	9	8	0	0	1	18	0	0	.337	.272
Konstanty, Mike	R-R	6-4	225	4-17-86	.218	.114	.259	46	156	15	34	4	4	3	21	14	1	0	1	52	2	1	.353	.285
Kuo, Yen-Wen	L-R	5-10	175	10-25-88	.231	.286	.219	15	39	4	9	2	0	0	8	3	0	1	0	10	1	0	.282	.286
Long, Jacob	R-R	6-1	180	4-17-86	.152	.333	.111	9	33	3	5	0	0	1	3	1	0	0	0	5	0	0	.242	.176
Means, Andrew	R-R	6-1	215	9-11-86	.262	.353	.228	53	187	27	49	11	1	2	10	9	8	8	0	42	19	0	.364	.324
Menchaca, Brandon	R-R	5-11	195	4-15-85	.150	.167	.147	13	40	3	6	1	0	0	2	1	0	0	0	7	0	0	.175	.171
Mendez, Carlos	R-R	6-0	195	9-15-86	.308	.290	.313	115	455	64	140	18	6	5	67	29	2	1	9	50	4	1	.407	.345
Oliveras, Alex	L-R	6-0	180	3-29-89	.307	.083	.328	35	140	24	43	9	2	2	17	2	0	0	0	31	5	2	.443	.317
Pfister, Frank	R-R	6-1	205	8-25-86	.214	.242	.203	32	112	7	24	6	0	0	11	5	1	0	0	21	0	0	.268	.254
Puckett, Cody	R-R	5-10	175	4-3-87	.263	.308	.251	125	482	76	127	35	1	19	67	39	7	5	5	138	19	1	.459	.325
Rojas, Miguel	R-R	5-9	175	2-24-89	.273	.333	.257	130	469	50	128	16	3	3	49	35	4	15	4	44	14	8	.339	.326
Sappelt, David	R-R	5-9	195	1-2-87	.269	.311	.256	74	301	44	81	14	7	3	25	23	2	2	3	46	26	11	.392	.322
Sosa, Humberto	R-R	5-11	235	10-13-85	.260	.263	.260	80	292	34	76	21	0	4	37	29	1	1	0	50	1	1	.373	.329
Stovall, Tyler	R-R	6-1	215	10-19-85	.164	.211	.143	18	61	7	10	1	0	1	4	4	0	0	0	20	1	0	.230	.215
Votto, Joey	L-R	6-3	235	9-10-83	.429	1.000	.333	2	7	3	3	0	0	1	3	2	0	0	0	3	1	0	.857	.556
Weems, Chase	L-R	6-2	170	1-17-89	.179	.143	.183	18	67	5	12	5	0	0	5	4	0	0	0	26	0	1	.254	.225
Wideman, Jordan	R-R	5-11	200	3-14-89	.178	.211	.169	31	90	9	16	3	0	0	6	11	4	0	2	16	0	1	.211	.290
Wiley, Byron	L-L	6-1	200	12-12-86	.275	.241	.285	110	382	62	105	25	5	12	64	76	3	0	5	114	9	6	.461	.395

Pitching	B-T	HT	WT	DOB	W	L	ERA	G	GS	CG	SV	IP	H	R	ER	HR	BB	SO	AVG	vLH	vRH	K/9	BB/9
Astorga, Leonardo	R-R	6-2	175	3-25-86	1	3	15.43	4	0	0	0	19	38	33	32	3	14	9	.422	.513	.353	4.34	6.75
Bohana, Michael	R-R	6-1	190	10-14-85	1	2	4.91	18	0	0	2	26	32	19	14	4	10	28	.296	.250	.339	9.82	3.51
Bowman, Drew	R-L	6-4	190	11-8-85	2	7	4.82	39	1	0	1	71	63	52	38	4	51	79	.235	.167	.270	10.01	6.46
Burton, Jared	R-R	6-5	230	6-2-81	1	0	0.00	1	0	0	0	1	0	0	0	0	0	3	.250	.333	.000	27.00	0.00
Carnevale, Jesus	L-L	6-5	200	7-18-84	0	1	8.53	3	0	0	0	6	6	6	6	1	4	3	.240	.333	.211	4.26	5.68
Castro, Oscar	R-R	6-2	200	3-29-89	2	5	7.56	25	16	0	0	89	120	81	75	15	38	48	.336	.343	.330	4.84	3.83
Fairel, Matt	L-L	6-3	203	7-8-87	8	5	2.93	19	19	0	0	111	98	38	36	9	37	107	.238	.243	.237	8.70	3.01
Gaffney, Scott	R-R	6-3	190	3-13-86	4	4	3.88	41	0	0	6	49	56	26	21	1	20	46	.283	.241	.315	8.51	3.70
Gonzalez, Aguido	L-L	5-10	185	9-19-86	0	5	4.25	33	0	0	11	42	32	22	20	1	24	55	.212	.349	.157	11.69	5.10
Hotchkiss, Jordan	R-R	6-4	220	4-3-86	3	6	2.73	33	5	0	3	86	78	29	26	5	19	75	.250	.230	.268	7.88	2.00
Infante, Ezequiel	L-L	5-10	185	8-31-88	2	2	3.44	15	7	0	0	52	51	21	20	2	9	46	.262	.232	.273	7.91	1.55
James, Mark	R-R	6-1	185	7-24-87	1	7	5.10	34	1	0	2	65	87	45	37	2	17	45	.321	.454	.247	6.20	2.34
Janke, Lance	R-R	6-2	190	10-8-86	5	5	4.06	20	15	0	0	93	92	49	42	11	25	86	.256	.264	.250	8.32	2.42
Joseph, Donnie	L-L	6-3	180	11-1-87	2	2	4.35	16	0	0	4	21	13	10	10	0	10	31	.176	.095	.208	13.50	4.35
Martinez, Junior	R-R	6-0	240	4-30-86	1	2	9.15	17	0	0	0	21	18	21	21	2	26	13	.247	.192	.277	5.66	11.32
Otterness, Steven	L-L	6-4	210	10-30-84	0	0	2.45	13	0	0	1	22	13	7	6	2	13	17	.176	.192	.167	6.95	5.32
Partch, Curtis	R-R	6-5	200	2-13-87	8	7	4.67	19	19	0	0	104	107	62	54	11	39	77	.270	.344	.219	6.66	3.38
Ravin, Josh	R-R	6-4	220	1-21-88	3	8	3.67	15	15	0	0	81	65	42	33	4	40	66	.220	.232	.212	7.33	4.44
Santana, Hector	R-R	6-1	186	2-4-88	0	0	2.92	6	0	0	0	12	12	6	4	0	1	5	.255	.235	.267	3.65	0.73
Serrano, Mark	L-R	6-1	185	9-14-85	3	1	2.20	11	8	0	0	49	37	14	12	2	12	57	.204	.246	.183	10.47	2.20
Snowden, Shea	L-L	6-1	165	10-6-88	1	1	5.88	7	3	0	0	26	33	20	17	4	9	19	.306	.206	.351	6.58	3.12
Sulbaran, Juan Carlos	R-R	6-2	220	11-9-89	5	5	5.24	21	21	0	0	93	94	68	54	19	51	100	.265	.299	.242	9.71	4.95
Thurman, Mace	L-L	6-1	180	4-5-87	3	0	2.93	15	0	0	0	31	24	12	10	3	11	35	.209	.317	.149	10.27	3.23
Walker, Justin	L-L	6-5	200	11-3-86	1	2	2.39	6	3	0	1	26	22	9	7	2	7	27	.218	.222	.216	9.23	2.39
Ware, Chase	R-R	6-6	200	7-16-87	1	1	4.13	9	2	0	0	28	25	15	13	5	9	15	.240	.280	.204	4.76	2.86

Fielding

Catcher	PCT	G	PO	A	E	DP	PB
Coddington	.983	82	629	66	12	8	3
Day	.987	11	62	13	1	1	1
Long	.970	7	57	8	2	0	1
Sosa	1.000	2	14	0	0	0	1
Weems	.978	16	126	7	3	0	5
Wideman	.988	29	210	28	3	4	4

First Base	PCT	G	PO	A	E	DP
Chapman	.987	10	68	6	1	5
Day	1.000	7	36	4	0	3
Konstanty	.986	36	277	11	4	24
Mendez	1.000	24	181	8	0	15
Sosa	.984	68	498	49	9	45
Votto	1.000	2	16	3	0	2

Second Base	PCT	G	PO	A	E	DP
Feiner	.979	19	50	44	2	12
Gualdron	.977	10	21	21	1	3
Kuo	1.000	4	6	13	0	1
Mendez	—	2	0	0	0	0
Puckett	.980	108	208	231	9	46

Third Base	PCT	G	PO	A	E	DP
Feiner	.833	13	9	26	7	1
Gualdron	.826	10	3	16	4	1
Kuo	.833	4	2	3	1	0
Mendez	.925	85	49	147	16	12
Pfister	.956	32	30	56	4	5

Shortstop	PCT	G	PO	A	E	DP
Kuo	.889	3	4	4	1	0
Puckett	.912	10	9	22	3	5
Rojas	.977	130	220	340	13	72

Outfield	PCT	G	PO	A	E	DP
Brown	.948	35	55	0	3	0
Chapman	.979	25	45	1	1	0
Coddington	—	1	0	0	0	0
Day	.969	21	28	3	1	0
Feiner	1.000	17	28	1	0	0
Fellhauer	.975	53	112	4	3	1
Konstanty	.750	3	3	0	1	0
Means	.982	50	106	2	2	0
Menchaca	1.000	13	22	2	0	0
Oliveras	.974	33	70	4	2	2
Sappelt	.994	72	172	7	1	2
Stovall	1.000	15	20	1	0	0
Wiley	.961	92	169	5	7	2

GCL REDS   ROOKIE

GULF COAST LEAGUE

Batting	B-T	HT	WT	DOB	AVG	vLH	vRH	G	AB	R	H	2B	3B	HR	RBI	BB	HBP	SH	SF	SO	SB	CS	SLG	OBP
Alonso, Yonder	L-R	6-2	215	4-8-87	.133	.333	.083	6	15	0	2	0	0	0	0	3	0	0	0	1	0	0	.133	.278
Barnhart, Tucker	B-R	5-8	175	1-7-91	.208	.063	.281	14	48	5	10	2	0	0	6	6	0	0	1	9	0	0	.250	.291
Bowe, Theodis	L-R	5-9	160	8-5-90	.287	.375	.271	31	101	15	29	5	1	0	9	14	2	1	3	21	15	4	.356	.375
Buchholz, Alex	R-R	6-0	182	9-30-87	.250	—	.250	4	16	4	4	2	0	0	2	0	0	0	1	0	0	0	.375	.333
Cech, Petr	L-R	5-10	185	10-13-87	.154	.333	.139	17	39	0	6	0	0	0	4	3	0	0	1	5	0	0	.154	.209
Doran, Ryan	R-R	5-11	175	8-14-86	.135	.000	.161	16	37	4	5	0	0	0	2	0	0	0	0	14	4	1	.135	.179
Duran, Juan	R-R	6-5	190	9-2-91	.177	.267	.157	45	164	15	29	7	4	0	17	8	1	0	1	52	0	0	.268	.218

Name	B-T	HT	WT	DOB	AVG	vLH	vRH	G	AB	R	H	2B	3B	HR	RBI	BB	HBP	SH	SF	SO	SB	CS	SLG	OBP
Gonzalez, Yovan	R-R	5-10	186	11-11-89	.208	.000	.233	26	48	3	10	1	0	0	5	4	2	1	1	5	0	0	.229	.291
Guerrero, Sergio	R-R	6-0	179	11-13-87	.200	.167	.206	17	40	5	8	2	0	0	4	5	0	0	0	11	0	0	.250	.289
Hamilton, Billy	R-R	6-1	160	9-9-90	.205	.135	.225	43	166	19	34	6	3	0	11	11	0	2	1	47	14	3	.277	.253
Hernandez, Danny	R-R	6-0	200	10-9-88	.202	.105	.227	29	94	15	19	4	0	1	9	10	5	0	2	23	1	1	.277	.306
Lowery, Derrick	L-L	6-1	215	5-3-88	.260	.200	.275	15	50	6	13	1	0	0	3	6	0	0	0	13	0	0	.280	.339
Lutz, Donald	L-R	6-4	230	2-6-89	.169	.250	.157	16	59	9	10	1	2	1	10	5	1	0	0	14	2	1	.305	.246
Manz, Trey	L-R	6-1	185	9-1-87	.316	.200	.357	13	38	7	12	5	0	2	4	5	0	0	0	7	0	1	.605	.395
Morrison, Carter	L-L	6-4	195	6-23-90	.206	.074	.240	36	131	13	27	4	1	0	15	9	2	1	3	21	2	0	.252	.262
Pimentel, Mauricio	B-R	6-0	165	12-11-88	.308	.429	.263	9	26	3	8	0	0	0	2	4	0	0	0	4	2	0	.308	.400
Rodriguez, Cristobal	R-R	5-11	165	11-1-89	.310	.333	.306	25	87	10	27	2	1	0	10	2	0	0	1	16	1	3	.356	.322
Rodriguez, Henry	B-R	5-10	150	2-9-90	.322	.280	.331	42	152	24	49	10	1	1	19	7	1	0	1	18	9	0	.421	.354
Rodriguez, Yorman	R-R	6-3	180	8-15-92	.274	.250	.276	22	84	9	23	2	1	0	2	10	0	0	1	23	5	0	.321	.347
Santos, Oliver	R-R	6-0	190	2-5-87	.214	.333	.163	24	70	11	15	0	1	1	9	9	3	0	0	13	3	1	.286	.329
Sierra, Jefry	R-R	5-10	165	4-16-90	.336	.500	.289	34	107	9	36	3	2	0	12	7	1	1	4	25	8	5	.402	.370
Silva, Juan	L-L	6-0	190	1-8-91	.280	.200	.306	43	143	26	40	9	7	1	16	21	0	2	0	45	7	4	.462	.372
Stewart, Dave	R-R	6-6	230	11-23-88	.158	.286	.083	7	19	1	3	0	0	0	2	0	1	0	0	4	0	0	.158	.200
Vicioso, Danny	R-R	6-0	190	10-27-88	.288	.250	.300	23	52	5	15	4	0	2	8	2	1	0	0	6	0	0	.481	.327

Pitching	B-T	HT	WT	DOB	W	L	ERA	G	GS	CG	SV	IP	H	R	ER	HR	BB	SO	AVG	vLH	vRH	K/9	BB/9
Adames, Jesus	R-R	6-4	195	1-25-91	0	1	4.42	12	2	1	1	39	34	20	19	1	16	24	.243	.296	.209	5.59	3.72
Albino, Reinaldo	R-R	6-2	165	3-16-89	0	0	0.00	1	0	0	0	1	0	0	0	0	0	0	.000	.000	.000	0.00	0.00
Buck, Dallas	R-R	6-2	195	11-11-84	0	0	6.00	2	2	0	0	3	6	2	2	0	0	6	.400	.714	.125	18.00	0.00
Carson, Blair	R-R	6-2	200	10-3-87	1	2	3.94	4	4	0	0	16	21	10	7	1	2	11	.313	.406	.229	6.19	1.13
Chiu, Tzu-Kai	L-L	6-2	220	9-14-87	1	0	0.95	6	2	0	1	19	13	3	2	0	1	17	.200	.222	.191	8.05	0.47
Clarke, Mitchell	R-L	6-2	220	8-29-90	1	1	3.77	7	1	0	0	14	15	6	6	0	3	12	.273	.091	.318	7.53	1.88
Cline, Tyler	R-R	6-2	215	6-24-90	5	1	2.09	12	10	0	0	60	41	17	14	2	21	43	.187	.200	.179	6.41	3.13
Corcino, Daniel	R-R	5-11	165	8-26-90	0	1	0.00	2	0	0	0	3	5	2	0	0	1	2	.455	.500	.429	6.75	3.38
DeJesus, Misael	R-R	6-2	235	11-5-84	0	0	2.25	4	3	0	0	8	6	2	2	0	3	5	.222	.133	.333	5.63	3.38
Driessen, Nathan	L-L	6-2	190	6-28-91	2	1	3.41	13	0	0	0	29	24	12	11	1	3	21	.218	.250	.209	6.52	0.93
Henry, Mike	R-R	6-3	205	9-1-89	1	1	4.23	11	4	0	0	28	25	18	13	0	24	20	.248	.347	.154	6.51	7.81
Johnson, Jacob	R-R	6-4	215	9-12-90	2	3	2.83	11	0	0	0	48	38	19	15	1	16	37	.217	.235	.202	6.99	3.02
Machuca, Luis	R-R	6-1	190	3-16-88	2	1	2.40	3	1	0	0	15	16	4	4	3	3	12	.271	.286	.250	7.20	1.80
Martinez, Porfirio	R-R	5-10	175	11-29-89	0	0	20.25	3	0	0	1	3	5	6	6	0	5	1	.417	.600	.286	3.38	16.88
Molina, Marcos	R-R	6-1	185	4-4-88	4	1	2.18	16	0	0	4	33	25	8	8	1	15	27	.214	.132	.253	7.36	4.09
Pizziconi, Matteo	L-L	6-2	172	10-30-89	2	2	1.88	10	0	0	0	14	10	8	3	1	10	8	.192	.222	.186	5.02	6.28
Rodriguez, Ramon	R-R	6-2	180	2-14-88	1	0	4.11	11	0	0	1	15	12	10	7	1	5	13	.218	.278	.189	7.63	2.93
Rodriguez, Raul	R-R	6-3	190	10-16-90	2	3	2.73	18	0	0	4	26	23	8	8	1	18	26	.240	.214	.259	8.89	6.15
Smit, Alexander	L-L	6-3	215	10-2-85	0	0	0.00	2	2	0	0	4	0	0	0	0	0	2	.000	.000	.000	4.50	0.00
Smith, Ryan	R-R	6-3	205	11-4-89	0	2	10.80	2	2	0	0	5	10	6	6	1	2	2	.435	.429	.438	3.60	3.60
Thompson, Daryl	R-R	6-0	185	11-2-85	0	0	27.00	1	1	0	0	1	2	3	2	0	2	1	.500	1.000	.000	13.50	27.00
Tuttle, Daniel	R-R	6-1	175	8-21-90	1	2	1.67	9	7	0	0	32	32	14	6	1	10	30	.258	.240	.270	8.35	2.78
Villarreal, Pedro	R-R	6-1	215	12-9-87	1	2	1.47	5	5	0	0	18	15	6	3	1	6	9	.242	.219	.267	4.42	2.95
Ware, Chase	R-R	6-6	200	7-16-87	1	1	4.50	6	0	0	1	22	25	11	11	0	2	21	.278	.344	.241	8.59	0.82
Wiley, Jake	R-R	6-1	195	10-4-86	1	2	4.60	13	0	0	6	16	16	8	8	0	9	12	.262	.292	.243	6.89	5.17

Fielding

Catcher	PCT	G	PO	A	E	DP	PB
Barnhart	1.000	8	42	13	0	1	1
Cech	1.000	16	61	10	0	0	1
Gonzalez	.984	26	97	24	2	2	1
Manz	.987	11	69	5	1	1	7
Vicioso	.956	23	91	18	5	4	2

First Base	PCT	G	PO	A	E	DP
Alonso	1.000	4	20	2	0	1
Cech	1.000	1	6	1	0	2
Hernandez	.983	19	170	2	3	14
Lowery	.991	12	101	5	1	9
Lutz	.983	16	168	2	3	26
C. Rodriguez	1.000	2	17	0	0	2
Santos	1.000	6	34	6	0	4

Stewart	1.000	1	1	0	0	0

Second Base	PCT	G	PO	A	E	DP
Buchholz	1.000	1	0	3	0	2
Doran	.778	1	2	5	2	0
Pimentel	.918	8	24	21	4	3
C. Rodriguez	1.000	3	4	8	0	1
H. Rodriguez	1.000	15	35	50	0	13
Sierra	.927	29	65	75	11	23

Third Base	PCT	G	PO	A	E	DP
Hernandez	.952	11	3	17	1	4
C. Rodriguez	.949	14	9	28	2	5
H. Rodriguez	.907	15	13	26	4	2
Santos	.892	16	7	26	4	4
Sierra	1.000	3	1	3	0	0

Shortstop	PCT	G	PO	A	E	DP
Buchholz	1.000	1	1	7	0	2
Hamilton	.955	41	54	136	9	19
C. Rodriguez	.806	7	7	22	7	6
H. Rodriguez	.963	6	12	14	1	4

Outfield	PCT	G	PO	A	E	DP
Bowe	1.000	25	51	2	0	1
Doran	1.000	2	5	0	0	0
Duran	.912	32	50	2	5	1
Guerrero	.947	15	16	2	1	2
Morrison	.980	33	47	2	1	2
Y. Rodriguez	.957	22	40	5	2	1
Sierra	1.000	3	7	0	0	0
Silva	.986	42	67	3	1	1

BILLINGS MUSTANGS   ROOKIE
PIONEER LEAGUE

Batting	B-T	HT	WT	DOB	AVG	vLH	vRH	G	AB	R	H	2B	3B	HR	RBI	BB	HBP	SH	SF	SO	SB	CS	SLG	OBP
Brown, Tony	L-L	6-0	200	1-26-88	.667	—	.667	1	3	1	2	0	1	0	1	1	0	0	0	1	0	0	1.333	.750
Carlson, Shane	R-R	6-0	185	4-7-87	.222	.000	.250	8	27	2	6	2	0	0	3	5	0	0	0	4	0	0	.296	.344
Cech, Petr	L-R	5-10	185	10-13-87	.333	—	.333	9	3	1	3	0	0	0	1	0	0	0	0	3	0	0	.333	.400
Conner, Sean	L-R	6-2	198	7-28-87	.237	.143	.256	64	241	26	57	18	2	6	31	15	3	2	0	66	1	1	.402	.290
Contreras, Efrain	R-R	6-1	165	2-6-87	.301	.294	.303	46	153	30	46	7	2	2	14	20	4	1	0	39	6	1	.412	.395
Dao, John	R-R	5-11	175	12-15-85	.189	.294	.139	19	53	6	10	1	0	0	4	2	1	0	2	8	2	0	.208	.271
Fleury, Mark	L-R	6-0	189	5-4-88	.198	.148	.212	39	121	8	24	4	2	4	17	15	1	1	1	27	0	1	.382	.284
Garton, Josh	L-R	6-2	215	4-27-88	.205	.250	.194	37	127	17	26	12	0	2	7	9	3	0	1	45	1	1	.346	.271
Gregorius, Mariekson	L-R	6-1	160	2-18-90	.314	.304	.316	50	204	28	64	10	1	1	16	12	5	2	2	27	8	6	.387	.363

Batting	B-T	HT	WT	DOB	AVG	vLH	vRH	G	AB	R	H	2B	3B	HR	RBI	BB	HBP	SH	SF	SO	SB	CS	SLG	OBP
Kuo, Yen-Wen	L-R	5-10	175	10-25-88	.265	.214	.274	48	185	19	49	10	1	1	22	17	0	3	2	41	2	0	.346	.324
Lowery, Derrick	L-L	6-1	215	5-3-88	.333	1.000	.000	1	3	0	1	0	0	0	0	1	0	0	0	1	0	0	.333	.500
Manz, Trey	L-R	6-1	185	9-1-87	.306	.214	.343	15	49	6	15	1	0	3	7	3	0	0	2	17	0	1	.510	.333
McMurray, Chris	R-R	6-1	195	10-12-86	.235	.273	.222	26	85	8	20	5	2	3	11	7	3	0	0	23	0	0	.447	.316
Nurre, Tommy	R-R	6-3	235	2-11-87	.224	.235	.220	33	116	14	26	5	0	5	13	6	5	1	0	21	0	0	.397	.291
Oliveras, Alex	L-R	6-0	180	3-29-89	.270	.360	.247	28	122	17	33	5	1	1	16	10	0	0	0	27	7	1	.352	.326
Pfister, Firenns	R-R	6-1	205	8-25-86	.259	.327	.236	63	220	21	57	11	1	1	24	10	1	3	2	25	3	3	.332	.292
Pimentel, Mauricio	B-R	6-0	165	12-11-88	.196	.240	.179	33	92	10	18	2	0	0	7	10	2	2	1	22	4	2	.217	.286
Richburg, Chris	R-R	6-2	210	12-29-85	.274	.323	.262	46	157	17	43	10	0	3	20	22	5	1	0	42	2	1	.395	.380
Rodriguez, Cristobal	R-R	5-11	165	11-1-89	.190	.138	.207	33	116	12	22	6	0	2	15	5	0	0	1	33	1	1	.293	.221
Rodriguez, Yorman	R-R	6-3	180	8-15-92	.219	.255	.206	46	183	21	40	10	2	3	17	9	1	0	0	61	5	2	.344	.259
Sosa, Humberto	R-R	5-11	235	10-13-85	.359	.231	.385	21	78	11	28	9	1	2	13	10	0	0	1	12	2	0	.577	.427
Stovall, Tyler	R-R	6-1	215	10-19-85	.244	.267	.235	44	160	22	39	7	0	1	13	10	4	0	0	35	3	1	.306	.305
Stramp, Will	R-R	6-3	180	5-29-86	.220	.444	.094	17	50	6	11	2	0	0	1	5	0	0	0	23	3	0	.260	.291

Pitching	B-T	HT	WT	DOB	W	L	ERA	G	GS	CG	SV	IP	H	R	ER	HR	BB	SO	vLH	vRH	K/9	BB/9
Astorga, Leonardo	R-R	6-2	175	3-25-86	2	8	5.01	15	15	0	0	74	95	54	41	4	25	44	.321	.339	.310	5.38	3.05
Bohana, Michael	R-R	6-1	190	10-14-85	2	0	7.71	5	0	0	0	7	13	9	6	2	6	12	.371	.313	.421	15.43	7.71
Bowen, Ricky	R-R	6-3	178	8-6-87	0	2	6.28	8	4	0	0	14	15	20	10	0	16	16	.250	.417	.208	10.05	10.05
Braun, Jason	R-R	6-5	190	11-24-86	1	3	5.35	18	0	0	1	34	37	23	20	2	12	30	.282	.343	.260	8.02	3.21
Cannon, Forest	R-R	6-3	190	6-5-88	0	0	4.35	7	0	0	0	10	7	5	5	1	7	9	.194	.125	.214	7.84	6.10
Carson, Blair	R-R	6-2	200	10-3-87	1	5	4.67	11	9	0	0	52	56	30	27	3	11	28	.279	.333	.239	4.85	1.90
Castro, Oscar	R-R	6-2	200	3-29-89	1	1	5.32	5	5	0	0	24	18	16	14	4	8	18	.209	.333	.161	6.85	3.04
Chiu, Tzu-Kai	L-L	6-0	220	9-14-87	1	2	5.96	8	1	0	0	23	32	17	15	1	5	11	.360	.667	.312	4.37	1.99
Corcino, Daniel	R-R	5-11	165	8-26-90	1	4	4.91	20	0	0	3	26	23	16	14	2	15	30	.245	.310	.215	10.52	5.26
Crabbe, Tim	R-R	6-4	195	2-20-88	1	7	4.86	14	14	0	0	50	56	39	27	2	27	53	.275	.323	.254	9.54	4.86
Gardner, Bryan	L-L	5-11	190	10-8-86	1	0	8.02	19	0	0	0	34	34	33	30	3	32	32	.270	.103	.320	8.55	8.55
Henry, Mike	R-R	6-3	205	9-1-89	0	1	7.36	3	0	0	0	7	10	11	6	2	9	7	.323	.154	.444	8.59	11.05
Infante, Ezequiel	L-L	5-10	185	8-31-88	1	0	1.42	3	0	0	0	6	5	1	1	1	2	7	.200	.500	.143	9.95	2.84
Joseph, Donnie	L-L	6-3	180	11-1-87	2	1	0.77	8	0	0	0	12	6	6	1	0	4	11	.146	.000	.167	8.49	3.09
Kummet, Adian	R-R	6-4	200	4-15-87	1	2	4.31	19	1	0	3	31	36	19	15	0	10	25	.281	.273	.286	7.18	2.87
Panerati, Luca	L-L	6-2	167	12-2-89	3	7	5.96	14	14	2	0	71	89	57	47	8	14	43	.302	.378	.291	5.45	1.77
Pearl, Brian	L-R	6-1	190	5-17-88	1	0	3.77	20	0	0	8	29	31	13	12	2	10	43	.267	.308	.247	13.50	3.14
Santana, Hector	R-R	6-1	186	2-4-88	0	1	3.38	10	0	0	0	21	25	10	8	0	5	16	.294	.375	.245	6.75	2.11
Serrano, Mark	L-R	6-1	185	9-14-85	0	0	1.42	3	0	0	0	6	3	2	1	0	3	8	.143	.143	.143	11.37	4.26
Snowden, Shea	L-L	6-1	165	10-6-88	2	2	4.17	7	7	0	0	37	41	22	17	4	18	18	.295	.185	.321	4.42	4.42
Walczak, Jamie	R-R	6-2	195	5-4-87	2	2	3.94	18	0	0	0	30	33	17	13	0	17	33	.280	.216	.309	10.01	5.16
Walker, Justin	L-L	6-5	200	11-3-86	0	3	4.75	8	5	0	0	30	37	23	16	6	3	27	.287	.333	.278	8.01	0.89
Wiley, Jake	R-R	6-1	195	10-4-86	1	1	6.52	8	1	0	0	19	23	14	14	3	5	11	.311	.353	.298	5.12	2.33

Fielding

Catcher	PCT	G	PO	A	E	DP	PB
Cech	1.000	3	13	0	0	0	0
Fleury	.978	37	244	29	6	6	14
Manz	.981	9	51	2	1	1	1
McMurray	.985	26	168	24	3	2	0
Sosa	.986	9	66	4	1	0	3

First Base	PCT	G	PO	A	E	DP
Nurre	.980	31	235	14	5	23
Pfister	.667	1	2	0	1	0
Richburg	.990	35	279	25	3	25
Sosa	.981	13	100	5	2	10

Second Base	PCT	G	PO	A	E	DP
Carlson	1.000	1	1	1	0	0

	PCT	G	PO	A	E	DP
Dao	.923	12	21	27	4	6
Gregorius	1.000	1	3	1	0	1
Kuo	.947	23	40	50	5	10
Pimentel	.911	28	48	75	12	16
Rodriguez	.913	17	35	49	8	12

Third Base	PCT	G	PO	A	E	DP
Carlson	—	1	0	0	0	0
Kuo	.895	16	12	22	4	3
Pfister	.908	62	47	120	17	12
Stramp	1.000	1	1	1	0	0

Shortstop	PCT	G	PO	A	E	DP
Carlson	.867	7	13	26	6	5
Dao	.839	7	8	18	5	1

	PCT	G	PO	A	E	DP
Gregorius	.922	47	78	124	17	34
Kuo	1.000	1	2	3	0	1
Rodriguez	.887	15	18	45	8	6

Outfield	PCT	G	PO	A	E	DP
Brown	1.000	1	2	0	0	0
Conner	.960	63	130	15	6	5
Contreras	.975	42	71	6	2	0
Garton	.974	25	33	4	1	0
Oliveras	.957	27	66	1	3	0
Rodriguez	.941	46	91	5	6	0
Stovall	.958	19	22	1	1	1
Stramp	1.000	9	12	0	0	0

DSL REDS ROOKIE

DOMINICAN SUMMER LEAGUE

Batting	B-T	HT	WT	DOB	AVG	vLH	vRH	G	AB	R	H	2B	3B	HR	RBI	BB	HBP	SH	SF	SO	SB	CS	SLG	OBP
Arias, Brayan	R-R	6-2	180	11-27-91	.133	.182	.118	13	45	0	6	0	0	0	1	2	2	0	0	14	1	3	.133	.204
Arias, Junior	R-R	6-2	178	1-9-92	.231	.189	.240	55	208	33	48	11	2	6	27	19	3	0	0	66	10	6	.389	.304
Baez, Ariel	R-R	6-0	183	1-22-91	.227	.321	.206	52	154	20	35	10	0	4	16	23	5	0	2	34	1	1	.370	.342
Chacoa, Miguel	B-R	5-11	165	11-27-88	.301	.158	.341	51	176	23	53	10	0	1	30	21	1	3	3	22	12	5	.375	.373
Diaz, Samuel	B-R	5-11	170	2-28-91	.268	.175	.289	59	220	35	59	3	3	0	19	23	2	4	4	20	11	9	.309	.337
Estevez, Wilfrel	R-R	6-0	177	8-11-90	.272	.250	.277	53	184	22	50	8	1	2	22	14	3	1	2	27	1	0	.359	.330
Felipe, Ayeudi	R-R	6-1	175	3-12-90	.220	.167	.234	54	200	30	44	7	6	1	27	19	7	3	1	54	9	4	.330	.308
Flores, Ponceano	R-R	6-1	182	4-6-90	.250	.000	.313	8	20	1	5	0	0	0	1	1	0	0	0	3	0	0	.250	.286
Galindez, Ronald	R-R	6-0	170	7-29-90	.281	.150	.304	42	135	19	38	5	0	0	8	18	3	4	0	26	6	6	.319	.378
Lopez, Frederman	L-L	6-1	185	1-11-90	.218	.100	.244	22	55	7	12	4	0	0	6	10	3	0	2	18	2	0	.291	.357
Lopez, Yimmy	R-R	6-0	216	8-19-92	.232	.400	.187	34	95	9	22	6	1	0	9	11	7	1	1	24	0	0	.316	.351
Moreno, William	R-R	5-11	170	1-17-92	.258	.308	.247	29	90	15	23	3	2	1	9	14	6	0	0	15	0	1	.367	.391
Ortuno, Jose	R-R	6-1	185	12-23-90	.205	.138	.221	52	151	17	31	7	0	0	11	13	4	2	0	42	2	0	.252	.286
Pineda, Lorgi	R-R	6-1	173	10-31-91	.159	.136	.164	46	132	13	21	1	0	0	8	20	0	3	1	65	1	1	.167	.268
Quintero, Jose	L-R	6-1	175	12-6-90	.224	.133	.243	35	85	21	19	4	0	0	2	17	2	5	0	21	6	2	.271	.365

Sanchez, Carlos	L-L	5-10	175	4-4-91	.234	.209	.240	55	197	35	46	17	4	5	37	19	1	1	4	35	4 1	.437 .299
Santoni, Andres	R-R	5-11	170	6-6-91	.063	.500	.033	15	32	4	2	1	1	0	3	1	4	0	0	14	0 1	.156 .189
Victor, Jose	R-R	6-2	170	5-25-90	.156	.222	.141	32	96	8	15	1	1	0	10	8	5	0	1	25	0 4	.188 .255

Pitching	B-T	HT	WT	DOB	W	L	ERA	G	GS	CG	SV	IP	H	R	ER	HR	BB	SO	AVG	vLH	vRH	K/9	BB/9
Caceres, Cesar	R-R	6-3	180	8-28-88	0	2	6.58	16	0	0	0	26	30	23	19	0	27	28	.300	.182	.333	9.69	9.35
Chiquiin, Jose	R-R	6-1	164	4-24-90	2	0	6.53	13	0	0	0	21	24	20	15	1	13	21	.279	.364	.226	9.15	5.66
Contreras, Carlos	R-R	6-0	165	1-8-91	4	4	5.60	14	12	0	0	72	65	49	45	6	30	58	.242	.279	.224	7.22	3.73
Correa, Jonathan	R-R	6-1	168	9-13-90	0	1	0.68	6	6	0	0	13	8	4	1	0	8	14	.170	.182	.167	9.45	5.40
Gerson, Starlin	R-R	6-4	175	8-26-88	6	6	3.55	14	12	1	1	76	62	35	30	2	26	67	.223	.257	.211	7.93	3.08
Lora, Luis	R-R	6-4	193	12-28-89	1	1	4.24	14	4	0	0	34	23	19	16	0	21	29	.193	.176	.200	7.68	5.56
Machuca, Luis	R-R	6-1	190	3-16-88	6	3	2.34	10	10	0	0	62	51	20	16	3	13	40	.230	.196	.241	5.84	1.90
Marizan, Jose	L-L	6-1	170	2-7-88	3	1	2.25	22	0	0	3	40	30	16	10	1	22	50	.203	.231	.200	11.25	4.95
Marmolejo, Jose	R-R	6-0	185	9-9-89	0	0	7.78	13	0	0	0	20	28	19	17	1	19	9	.341	.381	.328	4.12	8.69
Martinez, Daniel	L-L	6-2	170	6-4-90	2	4	4.21	18	0	0	1	36	35	23	17	2	18	29	.261	.313	.254	7.18	4.46
Martinez, Porfirio	R-R	5-10	175	11-29-89	1	2	5.82	21	0	0	11	22	23	19	14	0	12	18	.284	.300	.279	7.48	4.98
Mercedes, Elvin	R-R	6-4	150	3-2-89	0	4	7.39	17	2	0	1	35	48	39	29	2	14	24	.312	.255	.336	6.11	3.57
Morillo, JR	L-L	5-11	167	10-30-91	2	7	3.90	12	12	0	0	55	66	44	24	0	22	48	.293	.257	.300	7.81	3.58
Quezada, Radhames	R-R	6-2	175	7-6-90	2	5	2.06	13	11	0	0	66	59	31	15	0	26	51	.234	.258	.226	6.99	3.56
Sierra, Waldy	R-R	6-2	190	8-23-86	0	0	19.50	7	1	0	0	6	12	15	13	0	7	4	.375	.333	.391	6.00	10.50
Tineo, Carlos	R-R	—	—	3-12-91	0	0	9.00	14	0	0	0	11	12	12	11	0	21	9	.286	.000	.343	7.36	17.18

Fielding

Catcher	PCT	G	PO	A	E	DP	PB
Chacoa	1.000	1	0	1	0	0	0
Flores	1.000	5	15	0	0	0	5
Lopez	.984	28	163	19	3	0	21
Ortuno	.982	52	332	41	7	2	12

First Base	PCT	G	PO	A	E	DP
Arias	1.000	1	13	0	0	2
Chacoa	1.000	4	36	2	0	5
Estevez	.975	12	75	3	2	5
Lopez	1.000	1	6	2	0	0
Lopez	.955	2	19	2	1	1
Sanchez	.992	54	449	25	4	46

Second Base	PCT	G	PO	A	E	DP
Chacoa	.949	10	22	15	2	4
Diaz	.980	51	117	130	5	29
Pineda	.933	7	18	24	3	7
Santoni	.952	5	12	8	1	3

Third Base	PCT	G	PO	A	E	DP
Baez	.858	38	21	88	18	10
Chacoa	.890	30	29	68	12	4
Pineda	.955	8	5	16	1	1
Santoni	1.000	2	1	2	0	1

Shortstop	PCT	G	PO	A	E	DP
Arias	.898	38	56	111	19	21

Chacoa	.941	8	10	22	2	6
Diaz	.667	1	1	3	2	0
Pineda	.862	30	35	77	18	9

Outfield	PCT	G	PO	A	E	DP
Arias	.846	7	11	0	2	0
Estevez	1.000	34	45	2	0	0
Felipe	.960	53	115	5	5	1
Galindez	.986	39	71	2	1	0
Lopez	.818	10	9	0	2	0
Moreno	.966	25	28	0	1	0
Quintero	1.000	26	33	2	0	1
Victor	.980	32	48	2	1	0

Cleveland Indians

SEASON IN A SENTENCE: A season that began with expectations turned ugly early, as Grady Sizemore got hurt, star veterans such as Victor Martinez and Cliff Lee were traded away, and manager Eric Wedge got fired after the season.

HIGH POINT: Cleveland's 5-3 mark against Tampa Bay was its best record against an American League team in 2009, and a four-game sweep of the Rays from May 25-28 pulled Cleveland to its best record at 21-28. The four-game sweep included two double-figure scoring games by the offense and two one-run efforts by the pitching staff.

LOW POINT: Pick one. The Indians opened with a five-game losing streak, never got closer than 10 games out of first place after getting swept by the Cubs in a mid-June interleague series and lost their last five to finish with their worst record since 1991. The end of July was the real punch in the gut as Cleveland traded away Lee on July 29 to the Phillies, followed by the Martinez trade to Boston two days later. Cleveland fans had to watch the last two American League Cy Young Award winners (Lee and C.C. Sabathia) square off in the World Series in other uniforms while their team's top winner, rookie David Huff, posted a 5.61 ERA.

NOTABLE ROOKIES: Plenty of rookies got opportunities, such as Huff, who had a 4.75 ERA over his last 12 starts. Relievers Tony Sipp and Chris Perez solidified the bullpen in the second half, while Luis Valbuena emerged as a power threat at second base, allowing Asdrubal Cabrera to move to shortstop. Matt LaPorta and Michael Brantley, acquired from Milwaukee in the Sabathia deal, also showed promising signs at the plate.

KEY TRANSACTIONS: Trading Lee (and Ben Francisco) to Philly and Martinez to Boston brought power arms into the organization, with Carlos Carrasco reaching Cleveland while Jason Knapp and Nick Hagadone were a bit further away. Other veterans traded away by the Indians included Mark DeRosa (Cardinals), righthander Rafael Betancourt (Rockies) and first baseman Ryan Garko (Giants). In return, Cleveland got prospects such as righthanders Perez and Connor Graham and lefty Scott Barnes.

DOWN ON THE FARM: Led by Eastern League MVP Carlos Santana, Akron won 89 games and the EL championship and was BA's Team of the Year. Lonnie Chisenhall, Cleveland's 2008 first-round pick, had a strong first full season, belting 22 home runs and shining in Akron's playoff run.

OPENING DAY PAYROLL: $81,579,166

PLAYERS OF THE YEAR

RODGER WOOD

MAJOR LEAGUE	MINOR LEAGUE
Cliff Lee	**Carlos Santana**
lhp	c
7-9, 3.14	(Double-A)
Led team with 152 IP,	.290/.413/.530
107 SO in 22 starts	30 2B, 23 HR, 97 RBI

ORGANIZATION LEADERS

BATTING		*Minimum 250 at-bats
MAJORS		
*AVG	Asdrubal Cabrera	.308
*OPS	Shin Soo Choo	.883
HR	Shin Soo Choo	20
RBI	Shin Soo Choo	86
MINORS		
*AVG	Brown, Jordan, Columbus	.336
R	Constanza, Jose, Akron	98
H	Webb, Donnie, Lake County/Columbus	147
TB	McBride, Matt, Kinston/Akron	238
2B	McBride, Matt, Kinston/Akron	44
3B	Webb, Donnie, Lake County/Columbus	12
HR	Santana, Carlos, Akron	23
RBI	McBride, Matt, Kinston/Akron	99
BB	Phelps, Cord, Kinston	93
SO	Sanchez, Karexon, Lake County	136
SB	Constanza, Jose, Akron	49
*OBP	Santana, Carlos, Akron	.413
*SLG	Brown, Jordan, Columbus	.532

PITCHING		†Minimum 75 innings
MAJORS		
W	David Huff	11
†ERA	Cliff Lee	3.14
SO	Cliff Lee	107
MINORS		
W	Tomlin, Josh, Akron	14
L	House, T.J., Lake County	11
	Lofgren, Chuck, Akron/Columbus	11
†ERA	Berger, Eric, Kinston/Akron	2.50
G	Landis, Kyle, Lake County/Kinston	52
GS	Berger, Eric, Kinston/Akron	27
SV	Smith, Steve, Lake County/Kinston	26
IP	Gomez, Jeanmar, Kinston/Akron	147
BB	Haley, Trey, Lake County	65
SO	Rondon, Hector, Akron/Columbus	137
†AVG	Espino, Paolo, Akron/Lake Co./Kinston	.220

General Manager: Mark Shapiro. **Farm Director:** Ross Atkins. **Scouting Director:** Brad Grant.

Class	Team	League	W	L	PCT	Finish*	Manager(s)
Majors	Cleveland Indians	American	65	97	.401	t-12th (14)	Eric Wedge
Triple-A	Columbus Clippers	International	57	85	.401	13th (14)	Torey Lovullo
Double-A	Akron Aeros	Eastern	89	53	.627	†1st (12)	Mike Sarbaugh
High A	Kinston Indians	Carolina	60	78	.435	7th (8)	Chris Tremie
Low A	Lake County Captains	South Atlantic	71	66	.518	6th (16)	Aaron Holbert
Short-season	Mahoning Valley Scrappers	New York-Penn	49	27	.645	1st (14)	Travis Fryman
Rookie	AZL Indians	Arizona	24	32	.429	t-8th (11)	Ted Kubiak
Overall 2009 Minor League Record			350	341	.507	t-13th (30)	

*Finish in overall standings (No. of teams in league). †League champion.

ORGANIZATION STATISTICS

CLEVELAND INDIANS

AMERICAN LEAGUE

Batting	B-T	HT	WT	DOB	AVG	vLH	vRH	G	AB	R	H	2B	3B	HR	RBI	BB	HBP	SH	SF	SO	SB	CS	SLG	OBP
Barfield, Josh	R-R	6-0	190	12-17-82	.400	.400	.400	17	20	5	8	1	0	0	2	0	0	0	0	7	0	1	.450	.400
Brantley, Michael	L-L	6-2	200	5-15-87	.313	.462	.267	28	112	10	35	4	0	0	11	8	0	1	0	19	4	4	.348	.358
Cabrera, Asdrubal	B-R	6-0	170	11-13-85	.308	.306	.309	131	523	81	161	42	4	6	68	44	1	10	3	89	17	4	.438	.361
Carroll, Jamey	R-R	5-9	170	2-18-74	.276	.271	.278	93	315	53	87	10	2	2	26	36	3	3	1	63	4	2	.340	.355
Choo, Shin-Soo	L-L	5-11	200	7-13-82	.300	.275	.312	156	583	87	175	38	6	20	86	78	17	0	7	151	21	2	.489	.394
Crowe, Trevor	B-R	6-0	190	11-17-83	.235	.255	.228	68	183	22	43	9	3	1	17	11	1	4	3	39	6	0	.333	.278
Dellucci, David	L-L	5-11	205	10-31-73	.275	.250	.278	14	40	3	11	3	0	1	2	2	0	1	12	0	0		.350	.333
2-team total (8 Toronto)					.185	—	—	22	65	5	12	4	0	0	3	5	3	0	1	19	0	0	.246	.270
DeRosa, Mark	R-R	6-1	205	2-26-75	.270	.339	.251	71	278	47	75	13	0	13	50	29	3	1	3	63	1	1	.457	.342
Francisco, Ben	R-R	6-1	190	10-23-81	.250	.269	.245	89	308	48	77	21	1	10	33	33	8	4	2	59	13	3	.422	.336
Garko, Ryan	R-R	6-2	225	1-2-81	.285	.333	.265	78	239	29	68	10	0	11	39	20	10	2	2	40	0	0	.464	.362
Gimenez, Chris	R-R	6-2	200	12-27-82	.144	.143	.144	45	111	12	16	2	0	3	7	17	0	1	1	36	1	1	.243	.256
Graffanino, Tony	R-R	6-1	190	6-6-72	.130	.000	.188	7	23	1	3	1	0	0	1	0	0	0	0	5	0	0	.174	.167
Hafner, Travis	L-R	6-3	240	6-3-77	.272	.210	.292	94	338	46	92	19	0	16	49	41	3	0	1	67	0	0	.470	.355
LaPorta, Matt	R-R	6-2	210	1-8-85	.254	.211	.266	52	181	29	46	13	0	7	21	12	3	0	2	37	2	0	.442	.308
Marson, Lou	R-R	6-1	200	6-26-86	.250	.111	.286	14	44	6	11	6	0	0	4	7	0	0	1	14	0	0	.386	.346
Marte, Andy	R-R	6-1	205	10-21-83	.232	.167	.244	47	155	20	36	6	1	6	25	14	1	1	4	30	0	0	.400	.293
Martinez, Victor	B-R	6-2	210	12-23-78	.284	.246	.300	99	377	56	107	21	1	15	67	51	2	0	5	51	0	0	.464	.368
2-team total (56 Boston)					.303	—	—	155	588	88	178	33	1	23	108	75	3	0	6	74	1	0	.480	.381
Peralta, Jhonny	R-R	6-1	210	5-28-82	.254	.235	.261	151	582	57	148	35	1	11	83	51	4	2	6	134	0	2	.375	.316
Romero, Niuman	B-R	6-0	160	1-24-85	.143	.000	.200	10	14	2	2	0	0	0	1	0	0	0	5	0	0		.143	.200
Shoppach, Kelly	R-R	6-0	220	4-29-80	.214	.304	.191	89	271	33	58	14	0	12	40	33	18	2	3	98	0	0	.399	.335
Sizemore, Grady	L-L	6-2	200	8-2-82	.248	.216	.262	106	436	73	108	20	6	18	64	60	4	2	1	92	13	8	.445	.343
Toregas, Wyatt	R-R	5-11	200	12-2-82	.176	.333	.128	19	51	1	9	1	0	0	6	6	1	0	2	12	0	0	.196	.267
Valbuena, Luis	L-R	5-10	195	11-30-85	.250	.205	.255	103	368	52	92	25	3	10	31	26	0	2	2	83	2	3	.416	.298

Pitching	B-T	HT	WT	DOB	W	L	ERA	G	GS	CG	SV	IP	H	R	ER	HR	BB	SO	AVG	vLH	vRH	K/9	BB/9
Abreu, Winston	R-R	6-2	170	4-5-77	0	0	23.14	3	0	0	0	2	7	7	6	2	2	3	.500	.400	.556	11.57	7.71
2-team total (2 Tampa Bay)					0	0	10.50	5	0	0	0	6	10	8	7	2	4	6	—	—	—	9.00	6.00
Aquino, Greg	R-R	6-1	190	1-11-78	1	2	4.50	10	0	0	0	16	13	8	8	1	15	11	.228	.182	.257	6.19	8.44
Betancourt, Rafael	R-R	6-2	200	4-29-75	1	2	3.52	29	0	0	1	31	25	15	12	3	15	32	.225	.295	.179	9.39	4.40
Carmona, Fausto	R-R	6-4	230	12-7-83	5	12	6.32	24	24	0	0	125	151	97	88	16	70	79	.295	.331	.245	5.67	5.03
Carrasco, Carlos	R-R	6-3	215	3-21-87	0	4	8.87	5	5	0	0	22	40	23	22	6	11	11	.400	.367	.431	4.43	4.43
Chulk, Vinnie	R-R	6-2	195	12-19-78	0	1	3.75	8	0	0	0	12	10	6	5	1	10	4	.233	.056	.360	3.00	7.50
Gosling, Mike	L-L	6-2	210	9-23-80	0	0	5.04	15	0	0	0	25	30	15	14	5	11	13	.291	.289	.292	4.68	3.96
Herges, Matt	L-R	6-0	210	4-1-70	2	1	3.55	21	0	0	0	25	24	10	10	6	18	10	.240	.250	.232	6.39	2.13
Huff, David	L-L	6-2	190	8-22-84	11	8	5.61	23	23	0	0	128	159	82	80	16	41	65	.301	.317	.292	4.56	2.88
Jackson, Zach	L-L	6-5	220	5-13-83	0	0	9.35	3	1	0	0	9	14	10	9	2	4	10	.350	.300	.367	10.38	4.15
Kobayashi, Masahide	R-R	6-0	195	5-24-74	0	0	8.38	10	0	0	0	10	12	9	9	2	4	4	.300	.294	.304	3.72	3.72
Laffey, Aaron	L-L	6-0	185	4-15-85	7	9	4.44	25	19	0	1	122	140	69	60	9	57	59	.294	.255	.310	4.36	4.22
Lee, Cliff	L-L	6-3	190	8-30-78	7	9	3.14	22	22	3	0	152	165	53	53	10	33	107	.278	.216	.303	6.34	1.95
Lewis, Jensen	R-R	6-3	210	5-16-84	2	4	4.61	47	0	0	1	66	62	37	34	13	29	62	.249	.299	.205	8.41	3.93
Lewis, Scott	B-L	6-0	185	9-26-83	0	0	8.31	1	1	0	0	4	7	4	4	2	1	3	.368	.500	.353	6.23	2.08
Masterson, Justin	R-R	6-6	250	3-22-85	1	7	4.55	11	10	1	0	57	56	35	29	5	35	52	.258	.333	.165	8.16	5.49
2-team total (31 Boston)					4	10	4.52	42	16	1	0	129	128	73	65	12	60	119	—	—	—	8.28	4.18
Ohka, Tomo	B-R	6-1	200	3-18-76	1	5	5.96	18	6	0	0	71	77	47	47	18	19	31	.278	.256	.299	3.93	2.41
Pavano, Carl	R-R	6-5	240	1-8-76	9	8	5.37	21	21	1	0	126	150	80	75	19	23	88	.299	.281	.318	6.30	1.65
2-team total (12 Minnesota)					14	12	5.10	33	33	1	0	199	235	119	113	26	39	147	—	—	—	6.64	1.76
Perez, Chris	R-R	6-4	230	7-1-85	0	1	4.32	32	0	0	1	33	24	16	16	5	12	38	.205	.163	.230	10.26	3.24
Perez, Rafael	L-L	6-3	195	5-15-82	4	3	7.31	54	0	0	0	48	66	41	39	5	25	32	.335	.412	.277	6.00	4.69
Reyes, Anthony	R-R	6-2	230	10-16-81	1	1	6.57	8	8	0	0	38	40	30	28	5	23	22	.274	.292	.257	5.17	5.40
Rundles, Rich	L-L	6-5	210	6-3-81	0	0	0.00	1	0	0	0	1	1	0	0	0	1	1	.250	.000	.333	9.00	9.00

Name	B-T	HT	WT	DOB	W	L	ERA	G	GS	CG	SV	IP	H	R	ER	HR	BB	SO	AVG	vLH	vRH	K/9	BB/9
Sipp, Tony	L-L	6-0	190	7-12-83	2	0	2.93	46	0	0	0	40	27	16	13	5	25	48	.194	.208	.179	10.80	5.63
Smith, Joe	R-R	6-2	205	3-22-84	0	0	3.44	37	0	0	0	34	30	16	13	4	13	30	.236	.355	.198	7.94	3.44
Sowers, Jeremy	L-L	6-1	180	5-17-83	6	11	5.25	23	22	0	0	123	134	73	72	11	52	51	.281	.291	.277	3.72	3.79
Todd, Jess	R-R	5-11	210	4-20-86	0	1	7.40	19	0	0	0	21	31	17	17	3	7	18	.356	.400	.310	7.84	3.05
Veras, Jose	R-R	6-5	235	10-20-80	1	2	4.38	22	0	0	0	25	19	16	12	3	14	22	.213	.212	.214	8.03	5.11
2-team total (25 New York)					4	3	5.19	47	0	0	0	50	42	33	29	8	28	40	—	—	—	7.15	5.01
Vizcaino, Luis	R-R	5-11	210	8-6-74	1	3	5.40	11	0	0	1	12	8	7	7	2	12	9	.190	.056	.292	6.94	9.26
Wood, Kerry	R-R	6-5	210	6-16-77	3	3	4.25	58	0	0	20	55	48	26	26	7	28	63	.233	.255	.208	10.31	4.58

Fielding

Catcher	PCT	G	PO	A	E	DP	PB
Gimenez	1.000	8	36	4	0	0	0
Marson	.990	14	95	8	1	1	0
Martinez	1.000	52	285	14	0	2	3
Shoppach	.992	81	476	31	4	3	6
Toregas	1.000	19	119	9	0	0	1

First Base	PCT	G	PO	A	E	DP
DeRosa	.977	7	41	1	1	3
Garko	.993	51	418	36	3	53
Gimenez	.993	18	133	4	1	6
LaPorta	.976	10	78	4	2	8
Marte	.988	45	380	23	5	47
Martinez	.992	47	348	17	3	41
Romero	1.000	1	7	0	0	0

Second Base	PCT	G	PO	A	E	DP
Barfield	1.000	8	12	12	0	4
Cabrera	.993	28	59	82	1	30
Carroll	.996	56	89	137	1	26
Graffanino	.952	4	10	10	1	3
Valbuena	.985	77	162	228	6	64

Third Base	PCT	G	PO	A	E	DP
Carroll	.960	23	11	37	2	8
DeRosa	.925	42	25	74	8	12
Graffanino	1.000	3	0	8	0	0
Peralta	.951	104	78	211	15	19
Romero	—	1	0	0	0	0
Valbuena	1.000	1	0	1	0	0

Shortstop	PCT	G	PO	A	E	DP
Cabrera	.980	100	143	288	9	75

	PCT	G	PO	A	E	DP
Peralta	.979	41	62	123	4	36
Romero	1.000	4	1	6	0	1
Valbuena	.957	28	37	73	5	6

Outfield	PCT	G	PO	A	E	DP
Barfield	—	1	0	0	0	0
Brantley	.983	28	59	0	1	0
Carroll	.944	10	17	0	1	0
Choo	.979	143	317	11	7	2
Crowe	.971	65	130	4	4	0
Dellucci	1.000	1	1	0	0	0
DeRosa	1.000	25	38	1	0	0
Francisco	.995	85	183	5	1	3
Garko	.944	12	16	1	1	0
Gimenez	1.000	20	28	0	0	0
LaPorta	.976	39	77	3	2	0
Sizemore	1.000	92	259	1	0	0

COLUMBUS CLIPPERS   TRIPLE-A

INTERNATIONAL LEAGUE

Batting	B-T	HT	WT	DOB	AVG	vLH	vRH	G	AB	R	H	2B	3B	HR	RBI	BB	HBP	SH	SF	SO	SB	CS	SLG	OBP
Arnal, Cristo	R-R	6-0	180	9-17-85	.500	—	.500	3	8	2	4	2	0	0	1	0	0	0	0	0	0	0	.750	.500
Aubrey, Michael	L-L	6-0	195	4-15-82	.292	.309	.287	57	212	27	62	16	1	5	29	9	1	4	25	1	1	.448	.322
2-team total (44 Norfolk)					.290	—	—	101	376	41	109	29	1	8	52	20	2	1	8	38	2	2	.436	.323
Barfield, Josh	R-R	6-0	190	12-17-82	.252	.273	.246	73	305	27	77	15	0	3	35	8	1	2	3	48	5	3	.331	.271
Blair, Ryan	L-R	6-2	185	4-6-86	.200	.250	.167	4	10	1	2	0	1	0	1	0	0	0	0	5	0	0	.400	.200
Brantley, Michael	L-L	6-2	200	5-15-87	.267	.264	.268	116	457	80	122	21	2	6	37	59	1	8	3	48	46	5	.361	.350
Brown, Jordan	L-L	6-0	205	12-18-83	.336	.301	.349	111	417	65	140	35	1	15	67	30	2	3	3	64	2	4	.532	.381
2-team total (22 Charlotte)					.249	—	—	72	237	18	59	13	0	1	23	20	6	6	1	30	0	1	.316	.322
Carroll, Jamey	R-R	5-9	170	2-18-74	.273	.333	.250	3	11	2	3	1	0	0	0	0	0	0	0	3	0	0	.364	.273
Childs, Dwight	R-R	6-2	175	7-23-88	—	—	—	1	0	0	0	0	0	0	0	0	0	0	0	0	0	0	—	—
Crowe, Trevor	B-R	6-0	190	11-17-83	.297	.351	.273	49	185	27	55	11	1	2	20	30	2	2	0	31	14	7	.400	.401
Dellucci, David	L-L	5-11	205	10-31-73	.414	.000	.522	7	29	7	12	1	1	0	2	3	0	0		4	2	0	.517	.469
Donald, Jason	R-R	6-1	195	9-4-84	.257	.222	.269	10	35	10	9	2	0	1	3	2	0	0		11	1	0	.400	.350
2-team total (51 Lehigh Valley)					.239	—	—	61	243	36	58	17	1	2	17	17	7	1	2	64	7	0	.342	.305
Espino, Damaso	R-R	6-1	210	5-8-83	.261	.311	.244	49	176	19	46	10	0	2	14	13	1	2	0	15	0	1	.352	.316
Gimenez, Chris	R-R	6-2	200	12-27-82	.235	.267	.226	39	136	20	32	8	0	6	15	15	3	2	1	40	0	0	.426	.323
Graffanino, Tony	R-R	6-1	190	6-6-72	.264	.333	.244	69	261	39	69	24	0	6	40	17	3	0	5	46	3	0	.425	.311
Hafner, Travis	L-R	6-3	240	6-3-77	.333	.500	.276	12	39	6	13	4	0	1	8	9	0	0	0	3	0	0	.513	.458
Hall, Mickey	L-L	6-2	195	5-20-85	.159	.086	.182	49	145	13	23	5	3	2	8	15	2	2	0	45	1	1	.276	.247
Head, Stephen	L-L	6-3	220	1-13-84	.246	.167	.281	74	280	28	69	16	0	6	31	17	2	2	3	34	1	2	.368	.291
Hodges, Wes	R-R	6-2	205	9-14-84	.265	.275	.261	86	332	33	88	24	0	5	38	19	3	1	4	64	8	5	.383	.307
LaPorta, Matt	R-R	6-2	210	1-8-85	.299	.226	.323	93	338	63	101	23	2	17	60	42	9	1	3	56	1	3	.530	.388
Lombard, George	L-R	6-0	210	9-14-75	.368	.500	.333	8	19	5	7	3	0	0	4	2	0	1	0	7	2	2	.526	.429
Mackowiak, Rob	L-R	5-11	210	6-20-76	.156	.250	.146	13	45	1	7	1	0	0	3	3	0	0	1	9	0	1	.178	.204
2-team total (2 Buffalo)					.137	—	—	15	51	2	7	1	0	0	4	3	0	0	2	11	0	1	.157	.179
Marson, Lou	R-R	6-1	200	6-26-86	.243	.292	.228	28	103	10	25	5	1	1	9	10	2	0	1	19	1	0	.340	.319
2-team total (63 Lehigh Valley)					.277	—	—	91	314	42	87	18	1	2	33	40	2	0	1	59	4	1	.360	.361
Marte, Andy	R-R	6-1	205	10-21-83	.327	.314	.330	82	300	48	98	24	1	18	66	22	0	1	3	50	3	0	.593	.369
Merchan, Jesus	R-R	6-0	185	3-26-81	.280	.276	.282	27	100	9	28	5	1	0	8	4	2	2	0	15	1	0	.350	.321
Romero, Niuman	B-R	6-0	160	1-24-85	.254	.294	.244	81	252	34	64	10	1	1	27	21	2	6	3	27	10	4	.313	.313
Toregas, Wyatt	R-R	5-11	200	12-2-82	.284	.326	.272	60	208	22	59	10	0	7	29	16	2	0	3	43	0	1	.433	.336
Valbuena, Luis	L-R	5-10	195	11-30-85	.321	.182	.375	22	78	15	25	4	2	3	13	16	0	1	0	13	3	3	.538	.436
Valdez, Wilson	R-R	5-11	170	5-20-78	.198	.156	.213	41	121	17	24	1	0	0	6	10	1	4	1	19	5	1	.207	.263
2-team total (36 Buffalo)					.247	—	—	77	235	30	58	5	0	0	12	17	2	7	2	29	6	2	.268	.301
Webb, Donnie	B-R	5-11	190	4-30-86	.367	.400	.350	7	30	3	11	4	0	0	6	2	0	0	1	7	1	0	.500	.394

Pitching	B-T	HT	WT	DOB	W	L	ERA	G	GS	CG	SV	IP	H	R	ER	HR	BB	SO	AVG	vLH	vRH	K/9	BB/9
Aquino, Greg	R-R	6-1	190	1-11-78	1	2	3.13	30	1	0	16	32	26	15	11	3	15	27	.220	.273	.175	7.67	4.26
Betancourt, Rafael	R-R	6-2	200	4-29-75	1	0	0.00	3	0	0	0	3	0	0	0	1	0	4	.000	.000	.000	10.80	2.70
Carmona, Fausto	R-R	6-4	230	12-7-83	1	3	3.55	5	5	0	0	33	32	13	13	5	6	27	.250	.214	.267	7.36	1.64
Carrasco, Carlos	R-R	6-3	215	3-21-87	5	1	3.19	6	6	0	0	42	31	18	15	3	7	36	.196	.170	.210	7.65	1.49
2-team total (20 Lehigh Valley)					11	10	4.64	26	26	0	0	157	149	91	81	17	45	148	—	—	—	8.48	2.58
Cassel, Jack	R-R	6-2	205	8-8-80	5	7	5.78	15	15	2	0	90	109	63	58	11	38	51	.298	.284	.308	5.08	3.79

Name	B-T	HT	WT	DOB	W	L	ERA	G	GS	CG	SV	IP	H	R	ER	HR	BB	SO	AVG	vLH	vRH	SO/9	BB/9
Chulk, Vinnie	R-R	6-2	195	12-19-78	1	0	2.08	18	0	0	4	22	22	7	5	0	7	16	.275	.280	.273	6.65	2.91
Edell, Ryan	L-L	6-1	215	7-6-83	0	6	6.36	15	6	0	0	47	68	35	33	7	15	37	.338	.404	.315	7.14	2.89
Gosling, Mike	L-L	6-2	210	9-23-80	0	3	5.29	8	4	0	0	32	45	21	19	5	7	30	.341	.250	.361	8.35	1.95
2-team total (21 Rochester)					7	4	4.81	29	4	0	1	67	78	38	36	7	24	73	—			9.76	3.21
Grening, Brian	R-R	5-11	200	6-10-85	0	0	0.00	1	1	0	0	2	1	0	0	0	2	5	.125	.000	.143	19.29	7.71
Herges, Matt	L-R	6-0	210	4-1-70	1	2	5.40	11	0	0	4	10	12	6	6	0	5	7	.316	.333	.308	6.30	4.50
Herrmann, Frank	L-R	6-4	220	5-30-84	2	3	2.96	44	0	0	2	76	83	33	25	3	13	50	.279	.278	.279	5.92	1.54
Huff, David	L-L	6-2	190	8-22-84	5	1	4.35	7	7	0	0	39	35	19	19	5	16	32	.241	.275	.229	7.32	3.66
Jackson, Zach	L-L	6-5	220	5-13-83	4	8	6.05	30	14	0	0	100	128	76	67	13	33	67	.313	.305	.315	6.05	2.98
Kobayashi, Masahide	R-R	6-0	195	5-24-74	2	2	4.66	18	0	0	1	19	28	10	10	4	7	11	.350	.333	.358	5.12	3.26
Laffey, Aaron	L-L	6-0	185	4-15-85	0	2	11.32	3	3	0	0	10	21	13	13	2	5	4	.457	.600	.439	3.48	4.35
Lewis, Jensen	R-R	6-3	210	5-16-84	1	0	0.00	12	0	0	0	19	13	0	0	0	7	28	.200	.320	.125	13.50	3.38
Lewis, Scott	B-L	6-0	185	9-26-83	0	1	18.00	1	1	0	0	2	5	4	4	1	1	2	.500	.750	.333	9.00	4.50
Livingston, Bobby	L-L	6-3	205	9-3-82	0	0	12.00	1	0	0	0	3	6	6	4	1	1	3	.400	.333	.417	9.00	3.00
3-team total (1 Indianapolis, 3 Norfolk)					1	0	2.70	5	4	0	0	30	33	13	9	3	4	17	—			5.10	1.20
Lofgren, Chuck	L-L	6-3	205	1-29-86	6	10	5.31	17	17	0	0	98	94	63	58	15	33	62	.247	.216	.255	5.67	3.02
Meloan, John	R-R	6-3	225	7-11-84	0	0	5.52	25	2	0	0	44	52	27	27	6	17	37	.289	.310	.275	7.57	3.48
3-team total (10 Durham, 6 Indianapolis)					0	0	4.57	41	2	0	0	65	68	33	33	9	28	60	—			8.31	3.88
Meyer, Matt	L-L	6-4	220	1-17-85	1	0	4.50	2	0	0	0	2	3	1	1	0	1	1	.375	.000	.429	4.50	4.50
Neal, Blaine	L-R	6-5	240	4-6-78	0	1	6.07	12	0	0	0	13	21	11	9	2	7	5	.350	.381	.333	3.38	4.72
Newsom, Randy	R-R	6-2	200	5-6-82	0	0	5.40	2	0	0	0	2	3	1	1	1	1	1	.429	.600	.000		5.40
Ohka, Tomo	B-R	6-1	200	3-18-76	3	3	3.42	9	9	0	0	53	53	20	20	6	9	26	.272	.270	.274	4.44	1.54
Perez, Rafael	L-L	6-3	195	5-15-82	1	0	0.83	16	0	0	3	22	23	3	2	0	5	23	.271	.346	.237	9.55	2.08
Pino, Yohan	R-R	6-0	190	12-26-83	2	0	1.29	2	2	0	0	14	12	2	2	0	2	14	.231	.133	.270	9.00	1.29
2-team total (8 Rochester)					4	2	2.49	10	10	0	0	65	49	20	18	5	13	58	—			8.03	1.80
Ray, Ken	R-R	6-2	200	11-27-74	2	10	6.90	20	15	0	0	90	127	85	69	12	33	68	.334	.284	.364	6.80	3.30
Roehl, Scott	R-R	6-1	195	8-19-81	0	0	3.38	3	0	0	1	5	5	2	2	0	3	6	.250	.000	.313	10.13	5.06
Rondon, Hector	R-R	6-3	180	2-26-88	4	5	4.00	12	12	0	0	74	83	38	33	8	13	64	.282	.289	.279	7.75	1.57
Rundles, Rich	L-L	6-5	210	6-3-81	2	2	4.75	45	0	0	1	42	54	29	22	3	17	36	.312	.269	.340	7.78	3.67
Saarloos, Kirk	R-R	6-0	180	5-23-79	3	10	5.61	15	15	2	0	87	112	67	54	14	35	53	.313	.324	.305	5.50	3.63
Salas, Juan	R-R	6-2	230	11-7-78	0	0	0.00	1	0	0	0	1	1	0	0	0	1	1	.250	—	.250	9.00	9.00
Sipp, Tony	L-L	6-0	190	7-12-83	1	0	3.71	12	0	0	1	17	17	8	7	1	6	22	.254	.105	.313	11.65	3.18
Smith, Joe	R-R	6-2	205	3-22-84	0	0	5.00	5	0	0	0	5	4	0	0	0	1	6	.211	.200	.214	10.80	1.80
Sowers, Jeremy	L-L	6-1	180	5-17-83	2	2	2.89	6	6	0	0	37	36	12	12	2	9	27	.247	.286	.237	6.51	2.17
Swindle, R.J.	L-L	6-3	190	7-12-83	1	0	4.05	6	0	0	0	7	9	4	3	2	3	5	.333	.455	.250	6.75	4.05
Tejera, Michael	L-L	5-10	195	10-18-76	0	0	7.79	8	0	0	0	17	24	15	15	2	6	10	.320	.250	.345	5.19	3.12
Todd, Jess	R-R	5-11	210	4-20-86	0	0	0.00	3	0	0	1	4	1	0	0	0	0	7	.077	.000	.167	15.75	0.00
Veras, Jose	R-R	6-5	235	10-20-80	0	1	1.29	7	0	0	0	7	3	1	1	1	2	9	.136	.125	.143	11.57	2.57
Wright, Steven	R-R	6-1	200	8-30-84	0	0	4.76	2	1	0	0	6	5	3	3	0	0	4	.217	.000	.385	6.35	0.00

Fielding

Catcher	PCT	G	PO	A	E	DP	PB
Childs	—	1	0	0	0	0	0
Espino	.989	36	245	15	3	1	5
Gimenez	.994	24	147	16	1	1	2
Marson	.991	27	211	14	2	1	3
Toregas	.997	58	342	23	1	3	5

First Base	PCT	G	PO	A	E	DP
Aubrey	.994	36	291	24	2	32
Brown	.988	22	157	6	2	21
Espino	.989	12	88	4	1	13
Gimenez	1.000	3	28	2	0	5
Head	.993	16	133	11	1	9
LaPorta	.982	46	378	13	7	33
Marte	1.000	6	36	1	0	5
Romero	1.000	7	35	5	0	4

Second Base	PCT	G	PO	A	E	DP
Arnal	1.000	2	3	3	0	1
Barfield	.973	52	110	139	7	31
Cannizaro	.938	17	30	30	4	15
Carroll	1.000	1	0	3	0	1
Graffanino	.984	39	83	102	3	30
Merchan	.932	17	36	32	5	10
Romero	1.000	8	8	9	0	1
Valbuena	.983	12	32	26	1	8
Valdez	—	1	0	0	0	0

Third Base	PCT	G	PO	A	E	DP
Cannizaro	.833	2	0	5	1	0
Carroll	1.000	1	0	6	0	0
Graffanino	1.000	5	2	10	0	1
Hodges	.858	50	27	64	15	1
Marte	.960	74	47	170	9	24
Romero	.870	8	3	17	3	0
Valbuena	1.000	5	2	10	0	0

Shortstop	PCT	G	PO	A	E	DP
Arnal	1.000	1	0	2	0	0
Cannizaro	.944	21	22	63	5	15
Donald	.946	9	10	25	2	3
Graffanino	.964	6	7	20	1	4
Merchan	.933	9	6	22	2	3
Romero	.954	58	76	153	11	29
Valbuena	1.000	6	6	16	0	2
Valdez	.976	37	59	101	4	30

Outfield	PCT	G	PO	A	E	DP
Barfield	.981	21	48	3	1	0
Blair	1.000	4	3	0	0	0
Brantley	.993	115	293	7	2	1
Brown	.978	68	133	3	3	0
Crowe	.992	49	118	6	1	1
Dellucci	1.000	2	3	0	0	0
Gimenez	1.000	11	14	3	0	1
Hall	.991	48	107	4	1	0
Head	.971	46	99	3	3	1
LaPorta	.977	46	82	3	2	0
Lombard	.929	6	11	2	1	0
Mackowiak	.848	13	28	0	5	0
Valdez	.900	4	9	0	1	0
Webb	1.000	7	22	0	0	0

AKRON AEROS   DOUBLE-A

EASTERN LEAGUE

Batting	B-T	HT	WT	DOB	AVG	vLH	vRH	G	AB	R	H	2B	3B	HR	RBI	BB	HBP	SH	SF	SO	SB	CS	SLG	OBP
Arnal, Cristo	R-R	6-0	180	9-17-85	.275	.273	.276	79	251	38	69	8	0	6	16	26	3	13	2	23	18	6	.307	.348
Cabrera, Asdrubal	B-R	6-0	170	11-13-85	.250	.000	.267	4	16	5	4	1	0	0	0	1	1	0	0	2	2	0	.313	.333
Camacaro, Armando	R-R	5-11	215	4-6-79	.222	.286	.200	44	135	15	30	5	0	1	11	7	4	4	2	18	1	1	.281	.277
Chisenhall, Lonnie	L-R	6-1	200	10-4-88	.183	.174	.186	24	93	13	17	5	1	4	13	7	0	0	1	16	1	0	.387	.238
Constanza, Jose	B-L	5-9	150	9-1-83	.282	.259	.291	130	486	98	137	15	7	0	46	75	1	11	2	65	49	14	.342	.378
Drennen, John	L-L	5-11	195	8-26-86	.274	.200	.298	93	325	45	89	23	5	8	40	21	2	4	2	59	0	2	.449	.320
Espino, Damaso	R-R	6-1	210	5-8-83	.197	.160	.217	21	71	6	14	4	1	0	9	3	0	0	1	2	0	0	.282	.227
Goedert, Jared	R-R	6-2	200	5-25-85	.224	.235	.219	92	313	34	70	22	1	5	37	34	6	3	3	47	1	0	.348	.309
Haines, Kyle	B-R	6-1	170	7-28-82	.233	.133	.267	19	60	7	14	0	0	0	5	2	0	1	0	8	1	1	.233	.292

Name	B-T	HT	WT	DOB	AVG	vLH	vRH	G	AB	R	H	2B	3B	HR	RBI	BB	HBP	SH	SF	SO	SB	CS	SLG	OBP
Hall, Mickey	L-L	6-1	195	5-20-85	.250	.219	.263	39	108	15	27	2	0	2	18	28	0	1	3	30	4	1	.324	.396
Head, Jerad	R-R	6-1	205	11-15-82	.282	.273	.288	98	326	49	92	23	4	6	47	23	12	5	2	72	6	2	.433	.350
McBride, Matt	R-R	6-2	215	5-23-85	.247	.262	.240	98	361	48	89	29	0	12	63	18	14	4	9	42	1	1	.427	.301
Merchan, Jesus	R-R	6-0	185	3-26-81	.366	.455	.333	10	41	9	15	1	0	0	3	6	0	1	1	5	0	0	.390	.438
Mills, Beau	L-R	6-3	220	8-15-86	.267	.237	.283	134	516	59	138	33	1	14	83	31	4	2	11	95	1	2	.417	.308
Rivero, Carlos	R-R	6-3	210	5-20-88	.242	.268	.231	132	480	50	116	24	2	7	58	50	1	5	10	73	1	0	.344	.309
Rodriguez, Josh	R-R	6-0	185	12-18-84	.295	.353	.268	33	105	18	31	4	0	0	12	23	1	2	0	30	2	3	.333	.426
Romero, Niuman	B-R	6-0	160	1-24-85	.209	.204	.212	38	115	13	24	4	0	0	8	12	2	4	1	19	3	1	.243	.292
Santana, Carlos	B-R	5-11	190	4-8-86	.290	.329	.270	130	428	91	124	30	2	23	97	90	7	0	10	83	2	2	.530	.413
Weglarz, Nick	L-L	6-3	245	12-16-87	.227	.261	.210	105	339	69	77	17	2	16	65	75	9	0	4	78	2	3	.431	.377

Pitching	B-T	HT	WT	DOB	W	L	ERA	G	GS	CG	SV	IP	H	R	ER	HR	BB	SO	AVG	vLH	vRH	K/9	BB/9
Barnes, Scott	L-L	6-4	185	9-5-87	2	2	5.68	6	6	0	0	32	35	22	20	7	14	29	.292	.241	.308	8.24	3.98
Berger, Eric	L-L	6-2	205	4-22-86	3	1	2.67	6	6	0	0	34	32	14	10	1	16	33	.250	.318	.214	8.82	4.28
Carmona, Fausto	R-R	6-4	230	12-7-83	1	0	1.29	1	1	1	0	7	4	1	1	1	0	5	.167	.182	.154	6.43	0.00
Edell, Ryan	L-L	6-1	215	7-6-83	4	1	2.32	17	16	0	0	89	82	27	23	8	19	91	.247	.234	.253	9.17	1.91
Espino, Paolo	R-R	5-10	190	1-10-87	0	1	3.00	1	0	0	0	3	2	2	1	1	0	2	.167	.000	.286	6.00	0.00
Finocchi, Mike	R-R	6-0	190	4-28-85	0	0	6.75	5	0	0	0	5	8	6	4	1	9	3	.364	.571	.267	5.06	15.19
Gomez, Jeanmar	R-R	6-4	190	2-10-88	10	4	3.43	22	22	1	0	123	117	56	47	11	40	109	.249	.280	.215	7.95	2.92
Graham, Connor	R-R	6-6	235	12-30-85	1	3	4.93	8	7	0	0	38	40	21	21	3	25	39	.268	.250	.288	9.16	5.87
Grening, Brian	R-R	5-11	200	6-10-85	1	0	0.82	6	0	0	0	11	5	1	1	1	7	9	.135	.200	.091	7.36	5.73
Herrmann, Frank	L-R	6-4	220	5-30-84	2	1	2.93	5	5	0	0	31	27	11	10	4	5	12	.243	.300	.222	3.52	1.47
Judy, Josh	R-R	6-4	200	2-9-86	4	3	3.10	36	1	0	11	49	35	19	17	2	18	63	.198	.173	.219	11.49	3.28
Laffey, Aaron	L-L	6-0	185	4-15-85	0	0	3.68	2	2	0	0	6	3	3	0	0	7	6	.231	.286	.211	7.36	8.59
Lewis, Scott	B-L	6-0	185	9-26-83	0	0	1.17	2	2	0	0	8	3	1	1	0	3	6	.111	.182	.063	7.04	3.52
Livingston, Bobby	L-L	6-3	205	9-3-82	2	5	5.59	9	9	1	0	56	59	37	35	3	11	23	.268	.314	.247	3.67	1.76
2-team total (13 Bowie)					8	7	4.50	22	21	1	0	126	144	70	63	5	32	57	—	—		4.07	2.29
Lofgren, Chuck	L-L	6-3	205	1-29-86	3	1	1.48	8	8	0	0	43	24	9	7	1	15	31	.160	.094	.178	6.54	3.16
Meyer, Matt	L-L	6-4	220	1-17-85	0	1	7.36	23	0	0	0	22	27	21	18	2	20	22	.310	.241	.424	9.00	8.18
Newsom, Randy	R-R	6-2	200	5-6-82	2	0	2.38	8	0	0	1	11	6	4	3	0	7	3	.154	.091	.179	2.38	5.56
2-team total (5 Altoona)					4	1	6.75	13	0	0	1	16	14	13	12	1	13	5	—	—		2.81	7.31
Pestano, Vinnie	R-R	6-0	205	2-20-85	2	3	2.86	34	0	0	24	35	30	11	11	2	13	31	.234	.255	.219	8.05	3.38
Putnam, Zach	R-R	6-2	225	7-3-87	4	2	4.13	33	0	0	2	57	59	29	26	2	18	57	.261	.255	.266	9.05	2.86
Roehl, Scott	R-R	6-1	195	8-19-81	0	0	3.63	10	0	0	0	17	16	7	7	3	6	9	.242	.150	.283	4.67	3.12
Rondon, Hector	R-R	6-3	180	2-26-88	7	5	2.75	15	13	1	0	72	60	23	22	3	16	73	.227	.171	.281	9.13	2.00
Smith, Carlton	L-R	6-2	205	1-23-86	6	2	2.72	37	2	0	3	79	68	36	24	5	23	40	.230	.288	.178	4.54	2.61
Stiller, Erik	R-R	6-5	210	7-10-84	8	3	3.23	41	5	0	0	70	56	30	25	2	30	68	.215	.195	.230	8.78	3.88
Tejera, Michael	L-L	5-10	195	10-18-76	2	2	5.56	4	4	0	0	23	29	15	14	1	12	13	.315	.310	.317	5.16	4.76
Tomlin, Josh	R-R	6-1	195	10-19-84	14	9	4.16	26	25	0	0	145	149	81	67	21	27	125	.266	.263	.269	7.76	1.68
Wagner, Neil	R-R	6-0	195	1-1-84	1	3	2.95	46	0	0	2	61	48	24	20	3	32	69	.214	.213	.215	10.18	4.72
Westbrook, Jake	R-R	6-3	215	9-29-77	0	1	2.00	3	3	0	0	9	8	2	2	1	1	6	.242	.214	.263	6.00	1.00
Wright, Steven	R-R	6-1	200	8-30-84	10	0	2.32	36	5	0	2	81	72	24	21	1	20	64	.235	.202	.260	7.08	2.21

Fielding

Catcher	PCT	G	PO	A	E	DP	PB
Camacaro	.993	38	282	17	2	1	6
Espino	.979	16	88	6	2	0	2
Santana	.988	94	682	52	9	5	1

First Base	PCT	G	PO	A	E	DP
Espino	1.000	1	1	0	0	1
Head	.955	4	21	0	1	2
McBride	1.000	16	120	4	0	10
Mills	.990	124	993	76	11	86

Second Base	PCT	G	PO	A	E	DP
Arnal	.975	69	104	168	7	38
Goedert	.929	4	7	6	1	0
Haines	.967	8	10	19	1	3

	PCT	G	PO	A	E	DP
Head	.984	18	22	40	1	6
Merchan	.972	7	10	25	1	5
Rodriguez	.966	29	51	93	5	21
Romero	.988	18	31	52	1	5

Third Base	PCT	G	PO	A	E	DP
Arnal	.923	4	6	6	1	0
Chisenhall	1.000	22	13	33	0	4
Goedert	.924	76	40	119	13	7
Haines	.813	6	2	11	3	0
Head	.907	24	13	26	4	1
Romero	.939	14	6	25	2	3

Shortstop	PCT	G	PO	A	E	DP
Arnal	1.000	1	3	0	0	0

	PCT	G	PO	A	E	DP
Cabrera	.933	3	2	12	1	2
Haines	1.000	4	4	9	0	4
Merchan	1.000	1	3	1	0	0
Rivero	.972	131	181	313	14	72
Romero	.917	3	6	5	1	2

Outfield	PCT	G	PO	A	E	DP
Arnal	1.000	5	5	0	0	0
Constanza	.983	122	288	5	5	1
Drennen	.989	89	180	5	2	1
Hall	.947	38	70	1	4	0
Head	.981	52	97	7	2	2
McBride	.982	54	105	2	2	0
Weglarz	.965	78	136	2	5	0

KINSTON INDIANS   HIGH CLASS A

CAROLINA LEAGUE

Batting	B-T	HT	WT	DOB	AVG	vLH	vRH	G	AB	R	H	2B	3B	HR	RBI	BB	HBP	SH	SF	SO	SB	CS	SLG	OBP
Allman, John	R-R	6-2	220	4-18-85	.257	.320	.222	20	70	2	18	4	0	0	7	2	2	1	2	17	0	0	.314	.289
Arnal, Cristo	R-R	6-0	180	9-17-85	.297	.462	.208	13	37	6	11	0	1	1	5	3	0	1	0	8	1	0	.432	.350
Blair, Ryan	L-R	6-2	185	4-6-86	.195	.172	.205	55	185	17	36	6	1	1	15	10	0	4	1	38	3	1	.254	.235
Brown, Matt	L-R	6-1	183	2-21-85	.268	.273	.265	48	183	22	49	9	1	1	25	27	0	1	2	34	2	1	.344	.358
Castillo, Alex	R-R	6-2	195	11-29-85	.236	.253	.228	74	242	27	57	11	1	2	28	24	1	3	2	70	6	1	.314	.305
Chisenhall, Lonnie	L-L	6-1	200	10-4-88	.276	.252	.289	99	388	59	107	26	2	18	79	37	5	1	1	92	1	2	.492	.346
Davis, Adam	B-R	5-9	190	10-15-84	.228	.222	.231	114	382	48	87	16	1	8	40	51	0	8	1	92	8	11	.338	.318
Drennen, John	L-L	5-11	195	8-26-86	.270	.136	.341	17	63	10	17	6	1	0	5	12	1	1	0	10	1	2	.397	.395
Fedroff, Tim	L-R	5-11	220	2-4-87	.278	.278	.278	99	378	70	105	23	2	4	39	64	3	0	4	95	13	3	.381	.383
Haines, Kyle	B-R	6-0	170	7-28-82	.222	.143	.250	11	27	3	6	2	0	0	1	6	0	0	0	7	2	0	.296	.364
Martinez, Richard	R-R	6-0	185	6-19-87	.227	.290	.193	52	176	19	40	5	0	3	18	4	2	3	1	57	1	0	.307	.251
McBride, Matt	R-R	6-2	215	5-23-85	.405	.293	.459	31	126	24	51	15	0	6	36	11	1	0	1	15	0	0	.667	.453

Batting	B-T	HT	WT	DOB	AVG	vLH	vRH	G	AB	R	H	2B	3B	HR	RBI	BB	HBP	SH	SF	SO	SB	CS	SLG	OBP
Montero, Lucas	B-R	5-11	180	10-18-84	.260	.247	.268	129	465	81	121	17	9	5	39	70	7	7	0	97	35	16	.368	.365
Pena, Roman	L-L	6-0	190	9-2-86	.204	.170	.224	92	313	38	64	14	2	5	37	46	4	4	4	85	7	10	.310	.311
Perlozzo, Eric	R-R	5-9	175	9-7-84	.080	.000	.143	10	25	4	2	1	0	0	1	4	0	1	0	5	0	0	.120	.207
Phelps, Cord	B-R	6-2	200	1-23-87	.261	.317	.231	130	479	72	125	27	5	4	53	93	6	2	2	97	17	14	.363	.386
Pickens, Doug	R-R	6-0	190	6-19-85	.288	.297	.282	52	191	19	55	7	1	4	26	14	0	0	1	33	1	1	.398	.335
Recknagel, Nate	R-R	6-2	220	4-29-86	.233	.393	.161	25	90	10	21	5	0	1	8	6	0	1	0	17	0	1	.322	.281
Rivas, Ronald	R-R	6-2	184	1-16-88	.253	.233	.263	115	431	40	109	18	2	0	37	30	4	8	1	97	5	1	.304	.307
Sheldon, Ole	R-R	6-4	225	11-25-82	.267	.277	.262	72	258	39	69	14	0	13	54	32	0	0	5	42	1	0	.473	.360
Thompson, Mark	R-R	5-9	165	11-26-84	.296	.182	.375	7	27	2	8	5	0	0	6	0	1	1	1	6	0	0	.481	.310
White, Adam	B-R	5-10	190	4-21-85	.250	.125	.500	8	12	4	3	1	0	0	0	3	0	0	0	3	4	0	.333	.400
Willard, Matt	R-R	5-11	177	12-31-85	.156	.100	.182	12	32	0	5	0	0	0	1	4	0	0	1	4	0	1	.156	.243

Pitching

Pitching	B-T	HT	WT	DOB	W	L	ERA	G	GS	CG	SV	IP	H	R	ER	HR	BB	SO	AVG	vLH	vRH	K/9	BB/9
Barnes, Scott	L-L	6-4	185	9-5-87	0	0	2.13	3	3	0	0	13	14	3	3	1	6	10	.280	.357	.250	7.11	4.26
Berger, Eric	L-L	6-2	205	4-22-86	7	8	2.45	21	21	0	0	110	93	38	30	4	45	100	.227	.221	.230	8.16	3.67
Campfield, Gary	R-R	6-1	200	5-29-84	1	2	6.02	38	0	0	0	49	44	38	33	7	47	60	.238	.256	.224	10.95	8.57
Cawiezell, Dallas	R-R	6-6	255	9-4-85	1	4	3.21	49	0	0	8	67	65	28	24	4	31	56	.258	.294	.233	7.49	4.14
De La Cruz, Kelvin	L-L	6-5	187	1-8-88	2	0	1.50	2	2	0	0	12	6	2	2	1	2	19	.146	.095	.200	14.25	1.50
Espino, Paolo	R-R	5-10	190	1-10-87	9	6	2.59	22	21	0	1	118	89	41	34	9	34	101	.206	.207	.206	7.68	2.59
Frias, Santo	R-R	6-3	189	12-8-87	0	2	5.14	17	0	0	1	28	30	16	16	2	19	27	.275	.311	.250	8.68	6.11
Gomez, Jeanmar	R-R	6-4	190	2-10-88	2	2	2.63	4	4	0	0	24	17	8	7	2	5	15	.202	.245	.143	5.63	1.88
Hagadone, Nick	L-L	6-5	230	1-1-86	0	0	5.06	2	2	0	0	5	5	3	3	0	5	6	.250	.000	.417	10.13	8.44
Holt, Jonathan	L-R	6-2	210	3-10-86	4	5	5.02	42	4	0	0	81	86	52	45	8	29	51	.274	.292	.260	5.69	3.24
Jones, Chris	L-L	6-2	165	9-19-84	1	1	7.50	4	4	0	0	18	22	17	15	5	8	21	.306	.250	.317	10.50	4.00
Judy, Josh	R-R	6-4	200	2-9-86	0	0	0.00	5	0	0	3	5	4	0	0	0	0	7	.235	.273	.167	13.50	0.00
Landis, Kyle	R-R	6-1	185	5-30-86	2	4	3.05	44	0	0	8	59	53	24	20	5	17	64	.238	.292	.197	9.76	2.59
Lee, Chen	R-R	5-11	175	10-21-86	4	6	3.35	45	0	0	2	83	67	33	31	5	28	97	.220	.246	.200	10.48	3.02
Lewis, Scott	B-L	6-0	185	9-26-83	0	0	2.45	1	1	0	0	4	1	1	1	0	1	0	.154	.250	.111	0.00	2.45
Mahalic, Joey	R-R	6-3	205	11-28-88	0	1	19.64	1	1	0	0	4	7	8	8	1	8	0	.412	.455	.333	0.00	19.64
McGuire, Mike	R-R	6-7	240	6-29-86	0	3	5.46	9	8	0	0	28	34	20	17	2	15	24	.309	.360	.267	7.71	4.82
Meyer, Matt	L-L	6-4	220	1-17-85	2	1	3.49	19	0	0	0	28	19	12	11	2	9	25	.192	.171	.207	7.94	2.86
Miller, Ryan	L-L	6-0	195	12-14-86	0	1	9.00	8	5	0	0	18	17	22	18	1	25	18	.250	.280	.233	9.00	12.50
Morris, Ryan	L-L	6-3	175	1-10-88	4	8	4.86	16	15	0	0	80	77	58	43	9	48	72	.252	.262	.248	8.13	5.42
Perez, Alexander	R-R	6-2	156	7-24-89	1	2	2.87	8	7	0	0	31	32	10	10	1	9	31	.264	.273	.250	8.90	2.59
Pontius, Mike	R-R	6-2	235	10-26-87	1	0	2.45	2	0	0	0	4	3	1	1	0	5	4	.231	.400	.125	9.82	12.27
Price, Bryan	R-R	6-4	210	11-13-86	2	4	4.95	7	7	0	0	36	38	22	20	9	10	30	.268	.288	.253	7.43	2.48
2-team total (11 Salem)					3	10	5.89	18	18	0	0	89	100	65	58	13	29	87	—	—	—	8.83	2.94
Putnam, Zach	R-R	6-2	225	7-3-87	2	0	4.13	5	5	0	0	24	22	12	11	1	5	23	.247	.267	.227	8.63	1.88
Roberts, David	L-R	6-3	215	10-29-86	2	5	4.12	24	0	0	4	39	36	24	18	1	15	29	.245	.221	.271	6.64	3.43
Smith, Steve	R-R	6-0	195	10-27-85	0	0	0.00	2	0	0	0	1	1	0	0	0	3	1	.333	1.000	.000	13.50	40.50
Stowell, Bryce	R-R	6-2	205	9-23-86	4	6	5.31	19	6	0	0	61	64	40	36	6	34	62	.270	.267	.273	9.15	5.02
Taylor, Heath	L-L	6-0	215	5-26-86	3	1	5.20	17	0	0	2	38	30	26	16	2	14	18	.270	.268	.271	10.73	4.55
Turek, Travis	R-R	6-1	170	9-2-87	0	0	2.93	12	0	0	1	15	13	8	5	2	9	11	.228	.208	.242	6.46	5.28
Young, Russell	L-L	6-4	205	11-27-85	6	6	3.28	22	22	0	0	129	126	51	47	7	22	78	.255	.285	.242	5.44	1.53

Fielding

Catcher	PCT	G	PO	A	E	DP	PB
Castillo	.989	72	544	61	7	3	13
Martinez	.993	51	364	39	3	3	5
Pickens	.988	22	153	11	2	0	1
Davis	1.000	3	5	6	0	0	
Haines	1.000	2	5	5	0	2	
Perlozzo	.968	7	12	18	1	6	
Phelps	.993	118	229	328	4	78	
Willard	1.000	6	14	15	0	4	
Perlozzo	—	1	0	0	0	0	
Rivas	.946	111	151	291	25	72	
Thompson	1.000	2	3	5	0	2	
Willard	.889	3	2	6	1	1	

First Base	PCT	G	PO	A	E	DP
Allman	.971	15	127	5	4	15
Arnal	1.000	4	19	3	0	1
Blair	.970	10	57	7	2	7
Haines	—	1	0	0	0	0
McBride	.984	22	170	13	3	21
Pickens	1.000	18	130	7	0	12
Recknagel	.995	25	207	14	1	15
Sheldon	.993	52	399	30	3	47

Second Base	PCT	G	PO	A	E	DP
Arnal	1.000	4	4	12	0	2

Third Base	PCT	G	PO	A	E	DP
Chisenhall	.897	78	53	139	22	11
Davis	.930	54	39	94	10	9
Haines	1.000	1	1	1	0	0
Thompson	.941	6	5	11	1	1
Willard	1.000	1	3	0	0	0

Shortstop	PCT	G	PO	A	E	DP
Arnal	.857	5	5	13	3	1
Davis	.973	16	28	44	2	10
Haines	.941	7	8	8	1	2

Outfield	PCT	G	PO	A	E	DP
Allman	1.000	3	7	0	0	0
Blair	.986	44	66	3	1	0
Brown	.965	38	79	4	3	2
Davis	.989	40	90	2	1	1
Drennen	1.000	13	17	0	0	0
Fedroff	.988	86	166	5	2	0
McBride	1.000	3	2	0	0	0
Montero	.984	108	175	7	3	1
Pena	.971	84	190	8	6	2
Perlozzo	1.000	1	1	0	0	0
White	1.000	5	8	0	0	0

LAKE COUNTY CAPTAINS
SOUTH ATLANTIC LEAGUE

LOW CLASS A

Batting	B-T	HT	WT	DOB	AVG	vLH	vRH	G	AB	R	H	2B	3B	HR	RBI	BB	HBP	SH	SF	SO	SB	CS	SLG	OBP
Abraham, Adam	R-R	6-0	210	3-27-87	.257	.297	.242	104	339	38	87	23	2	6	31	36	5	5	3	59	4	4	.389	.334
Abreu, Abner	R-R	6-3	170	10-24-89	.305	.342	.289	63	246	36	75	16	4	7	30	11	7	0	1	68	3	3	.488	.351
Allman, John	R-R	6-2	220	4-18-85	.295	.226	.318	66	210	40	62	17	1	6	32	23	12	2	1	48	6	4	.471	.394
Baker, Trent	R-L	6-0	175	6-14-90	.071	.000	.125	7	14	2	1	1	0	0	0	0	0	1	0	2	0	0	.143	.071
Blair, Ryan	L-R	6-2	185	4-6-86	.266	.143	.300	17	64	8	17	3	0	1	2	3	0	0	0	20	0	1	.359	.299
Camargo, Jose	R-R	6-0	175	9-6-89	.250	.200	.263	10	24	1	6	1	0	0	1	3	1	0	0	4	0	0	.292	.357
Cid, Delvi	R-R	6-2	170	7-19-89	.271	.283	.266	93	362	53	98	11	3	2	27	31	6	8	0	109	33	16	.334	.338
DeGeorge, Dan	R-R	5-10	180	2-19-87	.170	.171	.169	35	106	12	18	4	1	0	14	8	1	2	1	25	2	1	.226	.233

Name	B-T	HT	WT	DOB	AVG	vLH	vRH	G	AB	R	H	2B	3B	HR	RBI	BB	HBP	SH	SF	SO	SB	CS	SLG	OBP
Diaz, Walter	R-R	6-0	180	11-13-85	.218	.322	.162	58	170	24	37	3	1	0	10	30	2	7	1	28	6	3	.247	.340
Greenwell, Bo	L-L	6-0	185	10-15-88	.290	.280	.293	60	214	29	62	16	1	2	26	21	2	4	0	23	7	3	.402	.359
Hodges, Wes	R-R	6-2	205	9-14-84	.400	.333	.429	5	10	1	4	2	0	0	2	2	1	0	0	1	0	1	.600	.538
Nash, Chris	R-R	6-5	235	2-22-87	.250	.198	.269	115	412	50	103	23	1	5	62	29	13	0	8	99	5	3	.347	.314
Perez, Roberto	R-R	6-0	200	12-23-88	.240	.333	.200	17	50	10	12	1	0	0	5	8	4	0	1	10	0	1	.260	.381
Pickens, Doug	R-R	6-0	190	6-19-85	.120	.400	.050	8	25	0	3	0	0	0	2	1	0	2	0	7	0	0	.120	.154
Recknagel, Nate	R-R	6-2	220	4-29-86	.280	.315	.266	92	336	46	94	21	4	13	67	49	8	1	5	73	2	4	.482	.379
Sanchez, Karexon	B-R	5-11	175	8-22-87	.234	.197	.248	129	453	70	106	23	4	11	57	70	11	7	1	136	25	10	.375	.350
Thompson, Mark	R-R	5-9	165	11-26-84	.257	.151	.298	95	311	60	80	14	0	11	48	39	12	9	4	73	13	6	.408	.358
Tice, Jeremie	R-R	6-1	225	9-25-86	.268	.242	.277	65	239	31	64	16	1	3	30	30	2	1	1	65	2	2	.381	.353
Valadez, Michael	R-R	6-1	220	5-31-86	.207	.239	.195	52	169	15	35	4	0	4	24	5	3	1	1	28	4	3	.302	.242
Webb, Donnie	B-R	5-11	190	4-30-86	.289	.301	.284	122	471	69	136	17	12	7	57	40	6	6	2	110	35	9	.420	.351
White, Adam	B-R	5-10	190	4-21-85	.255	.225	.267	53	145	21	37	5	3	1	12	21	5	7	2	47	15	6	.352	.364
Willard, Matt	R-R	5-11	177	12-31-85	.246	.333	.219	40	138	12	34	3	0	0	10	11	0	1	1	45	3	1	.268	.300

Pitching	B-T	HT	WT	DOB	W	L	ERA	G	GS	CG	SV	IP	H	R	ER	HR	BB	SO	AVG	vLH	vRH	K/9	BB/9
Burns, Eddie	R-R	6-8	225	9-21-85	2	1	2.38	16	0	0	1	34	36	12	9	3	7	44	.261	.217	.283	11.65	1.85
Campfield, Gary	R-R	6-1	200	5-29-84	0	1	5.40	1	0	0	0	2	2	1	1	0	1	3	.286	.500	.200	16.20	5.40
Carmona, Fausto	R-R	6-4	230	12-7-83	1	0	0.00	1	1	0	0	6	1	0	0	0	1	7	.050	.250	.000	9.95	1.42
Espino, Paolo	R-R	5-10	190	1-10-87	2	1	6.75	5	2	0	0	13	19	10	10	1	2	14	.339	.241	.444	9.45	1.35
Frias, Santo	R-R	6-3	189	12-8-87	2	1	3.74	19	0	0	0	34	22	16	14	2	13	42	.182	.259	.119	11.23	3.48
Grening, Brian	R-R	5-11	200	6-10-85	0	0	1.78	16	1	0	1	25	21	5	5	2	8	31	.239	.250	.233	11.01	2.84
Hagadone, Nick	L-L	6-5	230	1-1-86	0	1	2.45	5	5	0	0	15	8	4	4	0	5	21	.163	.333	.140	12.89	3.07
2-team total (10 Greenville)					0	3	2.50	15	15	0	0	40	21	12	11	0	19	53	—	—	—	12.03	4.31
Haley, Trey	R-R	6-3	180	6-21-90	4	8	5.56	19	16	0	0	78	70	55	48	6	65	57	.241	.167	.292	6.61	7.53
House, T.J.	R-L	6-2	215	9-29-89	6	11	3.15	26	26	0	0	134	127	56	47	8	49	109	.250	.233	.254	7.30	3.28
Jimenez, Francisco	L-L	5-11	164	10-2-88	7	0	2.35	14	0	0	1	31	26	10	8	0	6	34	.226	.114	.275	9.98	1.76
Jones, Chris	L-L	6-2	165	9-19-88	5	3	4.07	12	7	0	0	55	60	32	25	1	19	50	.276	.262	.280	8.13	3.09
Knapp, Jason	R-R	6-5	235	8-31-90	0	0	5.40	4	4	0	0	12	10	10	7	0	8	12	.238	.235	.240	9.26	6.17
2-team total (17 Lakewood)					2	7	4.18	21	21	0	0	97	73	55	45	3	47	123	—	—	—	11.41	4.36
Landis, Kyle	R-R	6-1	185	5-30-86	2	0	1.64	8	0	0	1	11	9	2	2	0	4	12	.220	.231	.214	9.82	3.27
Langwell, Matt	R-R	6-3	220	5-6-86	1	4	1.97	45	0	0	4	69	54	21	15	4	22	68	.217	.232	.207	8.91	2.88
Lewis, Scott	B-L	6-0	185	9-26-83	0	0	0.00	1	1	0	0	3	0	0	0	0	0	3	.000	.000	.000	9.00	0.00
Mahalic, Joey	R-R	6-3	205	11-28-88	1	1	1.91	6	6	0	0	28	20	9	6	2	9	22	.208	.267	.157	6.99	2.86
Martinez, Anillins	L-L	6-2	176	4-6-87	2	3	3.65	36	0	0	0	62	63	36	25	1	30	53	.265	.273	.262	7.74	4.38
McFarland, T.J.	L-L	6-3	190	6-8-89	9	4	3.58	25	23	0	1	121	128	58	48	6	42	85	.275	.295	.269	6.34	3.13
McGuire, Mike	R-R	6-7	240	6-29-86	5	3	3.18	20	1	0	1	45	35	20	16	2	22	42	.206	.200	.210	8.34	4.37
Mead, Kaimi	L-L	5-11	195	8-19-85	5	3	3.62	15	3	0	1	32	32	17	13	3	13	24	.260	.200	.284	6.68	3.62
Miller, Ryan	L-L	6-0	195	12-14-86	0	2	11.57	10	1	0	0	16	18	22	21	5	17	23	.269	.143	.302	12.67	9.37
Morales, Alexander	R-R	6-0	161	7-26-89	1	0	1.50	3	2	0	0	12	6	3	2	0	5	7	.146	.174	.111	5.25	3.75
Perez, Alexander	R-R	6-2	156	7-24-89	5	4	3.04	15	15	1	0	83	69	36	28	9	24	76	.223	.200	.242	8.24	2.60
Roberts, David	L-R	6-3	215	10-29-86	2	1	2.44	18	0	0	0	44	36	12	12	2	14	38	.239	.185	.264	7.92	2.84
Salazar, Danny	R-R	6-0	180	1-11-90	5	7	4.44	21	20	0	0	107	114	60	53	10	40	65	.271	.253	.282	5.45	3.35
Sarianides, Nick	R-R	6-1	200	8-29-89	1	0	3.18	3	0	0	0	6	4	2	2	0	2	4	.200	.400	.133	6.35	3.18
Smith, Steve	R-R	6-0	195	10-27-85	2	3	2.36	47	0	0	26	53	42	17	14	4	12	62	.214	.237	.200	10.46	2.03
Stowell, Bryce	R-R	6-2	205	9-23-86	0	0	1.00	3	1	0	0	9	4	1	1	1	3	15	.133	.273	.053	15.00	3.00
Turek, Travis	R-R	6-1	170	9-2-87	2	3	2.73	21	0	0	1	53	41	17	16	4	15	41	.220	.265	.195	7.01	2.56
Urena, Jose	L-L	6-2	186	3-14-88	0	0	0.00	1	0	0	0	2	1	1	0	0	0	1	.125	1.000	.000	4.50	0.00
Young, Russell	L-L	6-4	205	11-27-85	0	1	5.14	4	2	0	0	14	17	12	8	0	3	12	.304	.313	.300	7.71	1.93

Fielding

Catcher	PCT	G	PO	A	E	DP	PB
Abraham	.987	75	489	55	7	0	24
Perez	.993	17	129	16	1	2	3
Pickens	.969	6	56	7	2	0	1
Valadez	.986	52	378	54	6	7	3

First Base	PCT	G	PO	A	E	DP
Abraham	1.000	3	19	1	0	2
Allman	.979	8	43	4	1	2
Nash	.991	98	878	45	8	75
Recknagel	.984	34	300	16	5	35

Second Base	PCT	G	PO	A	E	DP
Camargo	.929	3	4	9	1	2
DeGeorge	1.000	21	35	45	0	9
Diaz	1.000	5	9	13	0	4
Sanchez	.979	78	124	201	7	42

	PCT	G	PO	A	E	DP
Thompson	.984	27	46	77	2	20
Willard	.971	12	29	39	2	11

Third Base	PCT	G	PO	A	E	DP
Abraham	.833	19	7	23	6	2
DeGeorge	.906	14	3	26	3	3
Diaz	.897	35	19	51	8	1
Hodges	.778	4	3	4	2	0
Recknagel	.833	2	5	0	1	0
Tice	.911	57	26	97	12	5
Willard	.924	21	16	45	5	4

Shortstop	PCT	G	PO	A	E	DP
Blair	.833	1	1	4	1	1
Camargo	.909	7	7	13	2	2
DeGeorge	.667	1	0	2	1	0
Diaz	.972	20	24	46	2	9

	PCT	G	PO	A	E	DP
Sanchez	.931	45	57	145	15	31
Thompson	.941	67	95	191	18	46
Willard	.962	6	9	16	1	4

Outfield	PCT	G	PO	A	E	DP
Abreu	.968	48	88	4	3	3
Allman	.975	46	76	2	2	2
Baker	1.000	6	7	1	0	0
Blair	1.000	14	16	0	0	0
Cid	.973	91	175	2	5	0
Greenwell	.979	57	92	3	2	1
Pickens	—	1	0	0	0	0
Webb	.987	114	219	9	3	1
White	.978	48	84	3	2	1
Willard	1.000	2	2	0	0	0

MAHONING VALLEY SCRAPPERS — SHORT-SEASON

NEW YORK-PENN LEAGUE

Batting	B-T	HT	WT	DOB	AVG	vLH	vRH	G	AB	R	H	2B	3B	HR	RBI	BB	HBP	SH	SF	SO	SB	CS	SLG	OBP
Allman, John	R-R	6-2	220	4-18-85	.333	.417	.282	17	63	8	21	5	0	1	14	9	1	0	1	14	1	1	.460	.419
Aponte, Juan	R-R	6-0	185	3-2-88	.304	.188	.340	22	69	12	21	4	0	2	11	4	1	4	0	21	0	0	.449	.351
Basabe, Lurvin	B-R	5-8	179	9-23-89	.226	.200	.235	25	93	12	21	1	1	1	8	11	3	1	0	24	3	2	.290	.327
Bellows, Kyle	R-R	6-3	210	8-19-88	.240	.284	.214	54	200	29	48	4	4	7	32	20	1	1	1	30	8	2	.405	.311

	B-T	HT	WT	DOB	AVG	vLH	vRH	G	AB	R	H	2B	3B	HR	RBI	BB	HBP	SH	SF	SO	SB	CS	SLG	OBP
Brito, Jesus	R-R	6-1	160	12-25-87	.333	.360	.323	25	90	16	30	7	2	0	18	14	0	2	1	15	0	1	.456	.419
Carlson, Ben	L-L	6-3	230	10-8-87	.228	.150	.256	62	224	22	51	7	2	3	27	18	7	0	4	58	0	0	.317	.300
Chen, Chun-Hsiu	R-R	6-1	200	11-1-88	.215	.306	.173	59	195	24	42	15	0	1	19	31	2	2	1	42	9	2	.308	.328
Childs, Dwight	R-R	6-2	175	7-23-88	.093	.167	.065	15	43	3	4	0	0	1	5	3	3	1	0	11	0	1	.163	.204
Folgia, Greg	B-R	5-10	194	10-14-87	.272	.213	.299	65	232	34	63	17	3	3	36	33	10	2	2	49	3	5	.409	.383
Frawley, Casey	R-R	5-11	170	9-17-87	.300	.289	.305	39	150	20	45	6	1	2	20	10	2	0	1	28	1	0	.393	.350
Greenwell, Bo	L-L	6-0	185	10-15-88	.346	.125	.444	7	26	5	9	2	0	0	4	2	0	0	0	2	2	0	.423	.393
Head, Stephen	L-L	6-3	220	1-13-84	.286	—	.286	2	7	2	2	0	0	1	3	0	0	0	0	1	0	0	.714	.286
Henry, Jordan	L-R	6-3	175	6-13-88	.286	.291	.284	67	248	48	71	12	0	0	23	49	2	7	0	37	22	1	.335	.408
Kipnis, Jason	L-R	5-10	175	4-3-87	.306	.294	.312	29	111	19	34	8	3	1	19	15	1	0	2	18	3	3	.459	.388
Martinez, Argenis	B-R	5-11	160	4-8-90	.357	.333	.364	6	14	4	5	0	0	0	3	3	1	1	0	2	2	1	.357	.500
Montero, Moises	R-R	6-0	210	11-4-89	.000	.000	.000	4	6	1	0	0	0	0	1	1	1	0	0	1	0	0	.000	.250
Palincsar, Tim	L-L	6-3	190	4-4-87	.208	.115	.244	55	183	26	38	7	1	3	18	17	3	0	1	49	1	0	.306	.284
Perez, Roberto	R-R	6-0	200	12-23-88	.214	.000	.375	4	14	3	3	1	0	0	1	1	0	0	0	4	0	0	.286	.267
Smit, Jason	R-R	6-0	165	10-27-89	.279	.278	.279	43	165	29	46	8	4	1	23	15	7	0	2	30	7	0	.394	.360
Smith, Kyle	R-R	6-1	185	12-25-87	.242	.297	.207	51	190	26	46	3	2	0	12	21	6	3	0	40	8	0	.279	.336
Toole, Justin	R-R	6-0	180	9-10-86	.156	.000	.192	9	32	1	5	1	0	0	2	1	0	0	0	3	2	0	.188	.182
Vera, Rafael	R-R	6-1	180	11-21-87	.240	.218	.248	58	204	19	49	11	1	1	18	13	3	3	3	56	6	1	.319	.291

Pitching	B-T	HT	WT	DOB	W	L	ERA	G	GS	CG	SV	IP	H	R	ER	HR	BB	SO	AVG	vLH	vRH	K/9	BB/9
Adams, Austin	R-R	5-11	185	8-19-86	3	1	4.86	17	0	0	1	37	39	22	20	4	15	29	.269	.306	.250	7.05	3.65
Anthony, Ryan	L-L	6-4	218	4-2-86	0	2	13.50	2	2	0	0	4	8	6	6	0	4	2	.421	.400	.429	4.50	9.00
Brach, Brett	R-R	6-3	185	3-29-88	5	2	2.19	15	15	0	0	78	62	25	19	1	20	61	.215	.181	.237	7.04	2.31
Burns, Cory	R-R	6-1	180	10-9-87	3	2	1.93	22	0	0	11	33	18	8	7	2	6	37	.157	.163	.153	10.19	1.65
Cook, Clayton	R-R	6-3	175	7-23-90	5	3	2.79	14	14	0	0	68	55	24	21	2	26	64	.224	.191	.242	8.51	3.46
Fonseca, Guido	R-R	6-0	260	9-15-85	1	2	4.32	22	0	0	5	33	26	22	16	1	13	20	.217	.263	.195	5.40	3.51
Grening, Brian	R-R	5-11	200	6-10-85	3	0	2.79	5	0	0	2	10	8	3	3	1	3	13	.216	.211	.222	12.10	2.79
Guilmet, Preston	R-R	6-2	200	7-27-87	6	6	4.09	15	15	0	0	70	70	41	32	8	16	62	.255	.330	.200	7.93	2.05
Hubbard, Antwonie	R-R	6-3	250	7-30-88	2	0	2.05	13	0	0	1	26	16	6	6	0	10	26	.172	.189	.161	8.89	3.42
Johnson, Jeremy	R-R	5-10	165	1-7-87	2	2	1.95	19	0	0	0	37	37	11	8	2	8	29	.257	.255	.258	7.05	1.95
Kirk, Nick	L-L	6-0	195	12-16-86	3	1	4.15	21	0	0	1	35	33	22	16	3	14	41	.248	.255	.244	10.64	3.63
Mead, Kaimi	L-L	5-11	195	8-19-85	1	0	1.80	3	1	0	1	10	2	2	2	1	4	10	.065	.091	.050	9.00	3.60
Nuno, Vidal	L-L	5-11	195	7-26-87	5	0	2.05	13	8	0	0	57	43	16	13	3	14	48	.207	.276	.180	7.58	2.21
Packer, Matt	L-L	6-0	200	8-28-87	0	0	2.38	5	0	0	1	11	8	3	3	1	1	13	.186	.133	.214	10.32	0.79
Popham, Marty	R-R	6-6	235	8-4-87	6	1	2.76	14	14	0	0	75	75	29	23	7	10	83	.253	.311	.215	9.96	1.20
Smith, Kyle C.	R-R	6-6	220	9-5-87	0	2	3.00	6	5	0	0	18	19	10	6	1	11	12	.264	.324	.211	6.00	5.50
Sturdevant, Tyler	R-L	6-1	170	12-20-85	2	1	2.75	19	0	0	3	36	34	13	11	1	13	42	.245	.294	.216	10.50	3.25
Urena, Jose	L-L	6-2	186	3-14-88	2	2	3.98	14	2	0	0	32	34	17	14	0	17	26	.283	.179	.333	7.39	4.83

Fielding

Catcher	PCT	G	PO	A	E	DP	PB
Aponte	.990	14	95	4	1	0	7
Chen	.983	48	373	28	7	1	9
Childs	.972	13	98	8	3	3	2
Montero	1.000	4	25	3	0	0	0
Perez	1.000	4	32	5	0	0	0

First Base	PCT	G	PO	A	E	DP
Allman	1.000	2	17	0	0	1
Aponte	.976	6	40	1	1	3
Carlson	.981	46	391	19	8	37
Smit	.984	16	118	8	2	8
Vera	.973	11	73	0	2	7

Second Base	PCT	G	PO	A	E	DP
Basabe	.868	22	43	62	16	13

	PCT	G	PO	A	E	DP
Folgia	.833	3	4	6	2	1
Frawley	.966	35	53	91	5	22
Martinez	1.000	5	12	10	0	2
Toole	.933	7	13	15	2	8
Vera	.923	9	16	20	3	5

Third Base	PCT	G	PO	A	E	DP
Bellows	.957	46	36	97	6	8
Brito	.900	22	12	51	7	4
Smith	1.000	1	0	1	0	0
Vera	.795	9	9	22	8	2

Shortstop	PCT	G	PO	A	E	DP
Bellows	.933	5	4	10	1	1
Frawley	—	1	0	0	0	0
Martinez	.900	1	4	5	1	2

	PCT	G	PO	A	E	DP
Smith	.966	50	68	130	7	31
Toole	.909	2	3	7	1	0
Vera	.943	21	25	57	5	9

Outfield	PCT	G	PO	A	E	DP
Allman	1.000	8	17	1	0	1
Folgia	.972	58	95	8	3	0
Frawley	—	1	0	0	0	0
Greenwell	1.000	6	9	1	0	0
Head	1.000	2	2	0	0	0
Henry	.993	60	142	3	1	0
Kipnis	1.000	25	48	0	0	0
Palincsar	.957	49	64	3	3	0
Smit	.975	24	38	1	1	0
Vera	1.000	5	5	0	0	0

AZL INDIANS

ROOKIE

ARIZONA LEAGUE

Batting	B-T	HT	WT	DOB	AVG	vLH	vRH	G	AB	R	H	2B	3B	HR	RBI	BB	HBP	SH	SF	SO	SB	CS	SLG	OBP
Aponte, Juan	R-R	6-0	185	3-2-88	.462	.667	.400	3	13	4	6	1	0	1	5	1	0	0	0	4	0	0	.769	.500
Baker, Trent	R-L	6-0	175	6-14-90	.237	.216	.242	50	215	30	51	10	2	0	19	25	3	2	2	42	13	5	.302	.322
Basabe, Lurvin	B-R	5-8	179	9-23-89	.300	.385	.277	19	60	10	18	2	1	0	6	5	0	0	0	12	4	2	.367	.354
Brito, Jesus	R-R	6-1	160	12-25-87	.366	.407	.355	35	134	36	49	12	8	3	25	18	1	2	1	26	2	1	.642	.439
Brown, Matt	L-R	6-1	183	2-21-85	.364	1.000	.222	4	11	1	4	0	0	0	1	0	2	0	0	1	0	0	.364	.462
Camargo, Jose	R-R	6-0	175	9-6-89	.232	.324	.207	41	155	24	36	7	2	2	23	12	2	0	2	29	3	2	.342	.292
DeGeorge, Dan	R-R	5-10	180	2-19-87	.267	.000	.286	7	15	3	4	0	1	0	0	1	1	0	0	2	0	1	.400	.353
Fontanez, Kevin	R-R	5-11	170	6-21-90	.467	.600	.400	5	15	5	7	3	0	0	4	3	0	0	0	1	0	1	.667	.556
Frawley, Casey	R-R	5-11	170	9-17-87	.302	.222	.324	14	43	7	13	4	0	0	5	6	0	0	1	13	1	0	.442	.380
Kersten, Chris	R-R	6-4	225	12-28-85	.328	.441	.301	45	180	33	59	20	2	4	33	12	8	0	1	48	5	0	.528	.393
Martinez, Argenis	B-R	5-11	160	4-8-90	.289	.313	.284	51	201	34	58	7	4	0	17	14	1	5	2	48	13	7	.363	.335
Merchan, Jesus	R-R	6-0	185	3-26-81	.316	.375	.273	6	19	4	6	1	0	0	1	1	0	0	1	0	0	0	.368	.381
Montero, Moises	R-R	6-0	210	11-4-89	.235	.174	.250	31	119	12	28	4	0	1	14	6	1	0	3	26	2	0	.328	.271
Perez, Roberto	R-R	6-0	200	12-23-88	.351	.333	.356	34	131	24	46	12	0	3	31	16	5	1	1	28	4	1	.511	.438
Petit, Rolando	B-R	6-2	205	4-27-90	.220	.261	.211	30	118	16	26	4	0	2	19	12	3	0	1	38	4	2	.305	.306

	B-T	HT	WT	DOB	AVG	vLH	vRH	G	AB	R	H	2B	3B	HR	RBI	BB	HBP	SH	SF	SO	SB	CS	SLG	OBP
Read, Darling	R-R	6-1	190	5-29-88	.209	.129	.231	40	148	17	31	7	1	3	15	5	5	1	0	62	4	4	.331	.259
Rucker, Kevin	R-R	6-1	185	9-14-89	.293	.265	.301	44	157	19	46	6	2	1	21	16	2	0	0	46	9	5	.376	.366
Tice, Jeremie	R-R	6-1	225	9-25-86	.231	.000	.300	4	13	0	3	0	0	0	0	1	0	0	0	4	0	0	.231	.286
Toole, Justin	R-R	6-0	180	9-10-86	.340	.250	.359	14	47	9	16	2	0	0	7	2	3	0	0	3	1	0	.383	.404
Torres, Joel	R-R	6-0	185	7-4-89	.225	.182	.235	37	120	9	27	3	1	1	6	12	3	2	0	51	2	2	.292	.311
Urshela, Giovanny	R-R	6-0	185	10-11-91	.257	.368	.233	32	105	10	27	2	0	0	11	10	1	1	2	12	3	0	.276	.322

Pitching	B-T	HT	WT	DOB	W	L	ERA	G	GS	CG	SV	IP	H	R	ER	HR	BB	SO	AVG	vLH	vRH	K/9	BB/9
Bryson, Rob	R-R	6-1	200	12-11-87	0	0	12.00	3	3	0	0	3	4	5	4	2	2	5	.308	.000	.400	15.00	6.00
Campos, Jose	R-R	6-4	207	8-18-90	1	4	5.44	10	7	0	0	41	61	38	25	3	14	38	.332	.321	.336	8.27	3.05
Colon, Joseph	R-R	6-0	167	2-18-90	0	3	5.63	11	7	0	0	32	44	28	20	1	17	26	.324	.452	.286	7.31	4.78
De La Cruz, Kelvin	L-L	6-5	187	1-8-88	0	2	9.39	3	3	0	0	8	10	8	8	1	5	5	.323	.143	.375	5.87	5.87
Dickerson, Dale	R-R	6-2	210	9-11-86	0	0	3.91	21	0	0	3	25	19	14	11	1	16	24	.216	.240	.206	8.53	5.68
Flores, Jose	R-R	6-3	185	6-4-89	0	2	4.55	18	0	0	0	28	35	22	14	3	10	25	.297	.342	.275	8.13	3.25
Goryl, J.D.	R-R	6-0	205	5-29-86	3	2	4.60	15	0	0	1	29	32	17	15	3	5	24	.283	.361	.247	7.36	1.53
Hubbard, Antwonie	R-R	6-3	250	7-30-88	0	0	9.00	1	0	0	0	1	1	1	1	1	0	2	.250	.000	.333	18.00	0.00
Jimenez, Danny	L-L	6-2	205	9-23-89	4	1	3.68	11	1	0	0	37	33	16	15	3	14	25	.248	.214	.257	6.14	3.44
Jimenez, Francisco	L-L	5-11	164	10-2-88	1	0	2.16	5	1	0	0	17	14	4	4	1	1	25	.237	.000	.250	13.50	0.54
Lara, Juan	R-L	6-2	190	1-26-81	0	1	4.24	15	0	0	0	17	24	9	8	1	8	19	.333	.222	.370	10.06	4.24
Lewis, Scott	B-L	6-0	185	9-26-83	0	0	1.29	2	2	0	0	7	4	3	1	1	0	11	.154	.250	.136	14.14	0.00
Moncrief, Carlos	L-R	6-1	210	11-3-88	1	2	6.51	19	0	0	0	28	30	23	20	0	12	39	.275	.389	.219	12.69	3.90
Morales, Alexander	R-R	6-0	161	7-26-89	5	2	4.99	11	8	0	0	49	56	31	27	5	15	53	.290	.226	.314	9.80	2.77
Nuno, Vidal	L-L	5-11	195	7-26-87	0	0	5.14	4	0	0	1	7	10	4	4	0	1	11	.333	.333	.333	14.14	1.29
Pontius, Mike	R-R	6-2	235	10-26-87	0	0	6.00	3	0	0	0	3	3	2	2	1	3	4	.250	.333	.167	12.00	9.00
Rayl, Mike	L-L	6-5	180	11-1-88	1	2	3.74	10	8	0	0	34	36	18	14	3	10	41	.267	.364	.248	10.96	2.67
Rosario, Gregorio	R-R	6-4	180	8-26-88	0	1	3.38	8	7	0	0	11	4	4	4	0	4	7	.125	.176	.067	5.91	3.38
Salas, Juan	R-R	6-2	230	11-7-78	0	0	8.10	4	2	0	0	3	4	3	3	0	2	6	.267	.222	.333	16.20	5.40
Sarianides, Nick	R-R	6-1	200	8-29-89	2	3	2.33	14	0	0	1	27	21	12	7	2	10	28	.216	.143	.246	9.33	3.33
Soto, Franklin	L-L	6-2	170	9-18-89	0	1	6.57	9	0	0	1	12	11	11	9	0	10	18	.234	.211	.250	13.14	7.30
Tseng, Sung-Wei	R-R	5-10	195	12-28-84	1	1	17.55	7	0	0	0	7	10	13	13	0	11	9	.345	.500	.263	12.15	14.85
Valera, Francisco	R-R	6-1	170	10-19-89	4	2	4.81	17	0	0	0	39	32	27	21	6	24	35	.215	.250	.200	8.01	5.49
Wetmore, Kirk	L-L	6-2	205	3-17-89	1	3	4.19	11	7	0	0	43	43	23	20	4	11	45	.261	.231	.266	9.42	2.30

Fielding

Catcher	PCT	G	PO	A	E	DP	PB
Aponte	1.000	1	6	1	0	0	0
Montero	.974	19	159	30	5	2	5
Perez	.983	26	251	31	5	3	6
Petit	.978	12	113	19	3	4	12

First Base	PCT	G	PO	A	E	DP
Aponte	1.000	2	10	0	0	0
Camargo	.976	11	74	8	2	12
Kersten	.981	36	299	13	6	31
Petit	.989	11	87	1	1	7

Second Base	PCT	G	PO	A	E	DP
Basabe	.928	15	33	31	5	7
DeGeorge	.900	3	5	4	1	0

	PCT	G	PO	A	E	DP
Frawley	1.000	3	2	11	0	3
Martinez	.967	37	81	94	6	28
Merchan	1.000	1	2	1	0	0

Third Base	PCT	G	PO	A	E	DP
Brito	.846	25	15	51	12	5
Camargo	.727	3	2	6	3	0
Tice	.750	3	2	4	2	0
Urshela	.866	30	22	49	11	4

Shortstop	PCT	G	PO	A	E	DP
Brito	1.000	1	0	3	0	0
Camargo	.922	24	29	65	8	13
DeGeorge	1.000	3	8	6	0	2
Fontanez	.857	3	5	1	1	0

	PCT	G	PO	A	E	DP
Frawley	.906	9	8	21	3	6
Martinez	.857	10	4	26	5	2
Merchan	.700	3	3	4	3	1
Toole	.959	14	12	35	2	7

Outfield	PCT	G	PO	A	E	DP
Baker	.968	50	110	11	4	2
Brito	.818	6	8	1	2	0
Brown	1.000	3	2	0	0	0
Frawley	—	1	0	0	0	0
Kersten	.857	6	6	0	1	0
Read	.975	39	73	4	2	2
Rucker	.915	40	39	4	4	0
Torres	.870	35	38	2	6	0

DSL INDIANS   ROOKIE
DOMINICAN SUMMER LEAGUE

Batting	B-T	HT	WT	DOB	AVG	vLH	vRH	G	AB	R	H	2B	3B	HR	RBI	BB	HBP	SH	SF	SO	SB	CS	SLG	OBP
Aguilar, Jesus	R-R	6-3	241	6-30-90	.305	.359	.292	55	200	33	61	16	0	5	46	31	6	0	1	24	5	1	.460	.412
Avila, Agustin	B-R	5-10	167	6-3-90	.223	.268	.211	62	202	39	45	5	1	1	15	34	4	3	3	42	19	10	.272	.342
Avila, Jack	B-R	6-1	165	5-30-92	.154	.083	.175	17	52	3	8	1	1	0	1	5	5	1	0	17	0	1	.212	.290
Bonifacio, Joan	R-R	6-2	175	3-6-90	.174	.000	.235	13	23	5	4	0	0	0	1	7	0	0	0	9	2	0	.174	.367
Bryan, Wally	R-R	6-0	160	2-17-89	.262	.200	.280	65	248	38	65	9	1	0	24	23	5	2	1	47	7	7	.306	.336
Cabrera, Jose	R-R	6-3	185	2-17-91	.283	.417	.253	55	198	27	56	6	1	2	29	26	7	4	2	57	9	7	.354	.382
Fermin, Joly	R-R	5-11	162	2-18-91	.250	.261	.247	62	228	33	57	11	1	0	21	14	8	1	2	58	11	2	.307	.313
Fernandez, Yileiviu	R-R	6-0	189	1-5-91	.170	.214	.163	35	94	10	16	5	0	0	7	8	1	1	1	35	0	0	.223	.240
Gonzalez, Erik	R-R	6-1	165	8-31-91	.248	.271	.242	61	234	33	58	9	3	0	27	15	5	2	0	36	14	2	.312	.307
Izaguirre, Nelson	R-R	5-11	175	3-31-90	.237	.455	.148	17	38	6	9	1	0	0	6	10	0	0	0	5	1	0	.263	.396
Monsalve, Alex	R-R	6-2	185	4-22-92	.274	.234	.284	61	230	28	63	14	0	0	22	18	4	0	0	54	6	2	.335	.337
Moreno, Henry	R-R	6-0	219	12-17-90	.219	.207	.224	39	114	12	25	2	0	1	14	18	2	0	2	26	2	2	.254	.331
Robles, Dioris	R-R	5-11	180	5-21-92	.310	.255	.324	70	268	55	83	18	8	3	36	26	11	1	1	68	21	11	.470	.392
Tejeda, Aderlin	R-R	6-2	175	11-23-91	.148	.111	.159	48	162	15	24	7	1	0	10	13	9	0	0	53	3	2	.204	.250
Urshela, Giovanny	R-R	6-0	185	10-11-91	.269	.273	.267	27	108	10	29	8	1	1	24	7	1	0	1	14	2	2	.389	.316

Pitching	B-T	HT	WT	DOB	W	L	ERA	G	GS	CG	SV	IP	H	R	ER	HR	BB	SO	AVG	vLH	vRH	K/9	BB/9
Castillo, Luis	R-R	6-3	195	10-23-91	1	0	10.29	16	1	0	0	21	26	24	24	1	21	10	.339	.320	.319	4.29	9.00
Cespedes, Ramon	R-R	6-2	174	11-1-90	6	3	2.17	24	0	0	6	50	35	16	12	1	22	41	.200	.245	.180	7.43	3.99
Del Carmen, Carlos	R-R	6-0	170	5-12-90	4	0	2.55	19	2	0	1	49	36	19	14	0	16	39	.201	.208	.198	7.11	2.92
Encarnacion, Isaias	L-L	6-4	200	7-10-91	0	2	6.48	19	6	0	1	42	52	45	30	0	30	24	.306	.368	.298	5.18	6.48
Flores, Fernando	R-R	6-3	230	11-11-90	3	6	4.91	15	12	0	0	55	60	35	30	1	18	27	.287	.279	.291	4.42	2.95
Guerrero, Harold	L-L	6-3	215	5-21-90	1	5	2.60	13	12	0	0	52	41	30	15	1	17	48	.211	.261	.205	8.31	2.94

Montano, Francisco	R-R	6-1	175	6-4-89	0	3	6.27	15	0	0	1	19	28	20	13	2	7	9	.341	.346	.339	4.34	3.38
Munoz, Oswell	R-R	6-5	179	11-22-90	6	1	2.20	14	12	0	0	61	48	17	15	7	7	52	.211	.175	.226	7.63	1.03
Pacheco, Enriquez	R-R	6-3	165	12-10-89	2	1	3.98	16	11	0	0	63	64	31	28	11	16	51	.267	.203	.290	7.25	2.27
Pereira, Orlando	R-R	6-5	180	9-10-91	0	4	4.99	7	7	0	0	31	29	22	17	3	5	20	.252	.206	.272	5.87	1.47
Pinales, Wady	R-R	6-5	224	12-4-89	2	3	11.22	18	2	0	0	22	29	39	27	4	36	26	.312	.400	.270	10.80	14.95
Quintero, Jesus	R-R	6-2	165	5-16-89	0	2	6.82	13	1	0	0	32	44	28	24	4	11	31	.326	.372	.304	8.81	3.13
Ramirez, Moisses	R-R	5-11	170	3-8-90	3	1	1.88	15	0	0	3	29	17	11	6	0	10	20	.173	.167	.177	6.28	3.14
Ramirez, Wuilmer	L-L	6-6	190	12-5-91	0	1	15.88	5	0	0	0	6	12	18	10	3	8	3	.414	.000	.462	4.76	12.71
Robles, Jefry	R-R	6-4	205	7-7-90	0	2	8.00	4	4	0	0	9	10	9	8	1	8	9	.286	.154	.364	9.00	8.00
Rolando, Cariel	R-R	6-0	165	9-23-91	2	3	1.65	22	1	0	4	44	31	16	8	2	18	48	.195	.189	.198	9.89	3.71
Valdez, Phillip	R-R	6-2	160	11-16-91	2	2	3.66	13	0	0	0	20	11	10	8	2	19	12	.164	.050	.213	5.49	8.69
Villa, Alejandro	R-R	6-2	160	5-29-92	0	0	5.40	10	0	0	0	20	18	17	12	3	22	16	.254	.250	.254	7.20	9.90

Fielding

Catcher	PCT	G	PO	A	E	DP	PB
Avila	.971	7	31	3	1	0	3
Fernandez	.955	15	59	4	3	0	2
Izaguirre	.988	16	80	5	1	0	8
Monsalve	.966	45	291	47	12	4	13
Moreno	.968	9	30	0	1	0	1

First Base	PCT	G	PO	A	E	DP
Aguilar	.996	48	419	28	2	26
Avila	1.000	1	9	0	0	1
Fermin	.900	2	16	2	2	2
Fernandez	1.000	7	62	5	0	10
Monsalve	.983	7	59	0	1	4

	PCT	G	PO	A	E	DP
Moreno	1.000	13	102	1	0	9
Second Base	**PCT**	**G**	**PO**	**A**	**E**	**DP**
Avila	.887	12	23	24	6	5
Fermin	.926	11	19	31	4	8
Gonzalez	.947	53	118	133	14	28
Third Base	**PCT**	**G**	**PO**	**A**	**E**	**DP**
Avila	.333	2	0	1	2	0
Fermin	.894	45	48	113	19	7
Urshela	.910	26	33	68	10	5
Shortstop	**PCT**	**G**	**PO**	**A**	**E**	**DP**
Bryan	.921	65	100	179	24	33

	PCT	G	PO	A	E	DP
Gonzalez	.884	9	13	25	5	2
Outfield	**PCT**	**G**	**PO**	**A**	**E**	**DP**
Aguilar	.875	6	5	2	1	0
Avila	.948	50	88	4	5	1
Bonifacio	.857	11	11	1	2	0
Cabrera	.921	44	53	5	5	1
Fermin	1.000	4	7	2	0	0
Fernandez	1.000	2	3	0	0	0
Robles	.958	67	107	7	5	4
Robles	1.000	1	4	0	0	0
Tejeda	.887	42	51	4	7	0

CLEVELAND INDIANS

Colorado Rockies

SEASON IN A SENTENCE: After a slow start that led to manager Clint Hurdle getting fired and had them 12 games below .500 at the beginning of June, the Rockies surged in the second half and won the National League wild card to reach the playoffs for the second time in three years.

HIGH POINT: The Rockies responded to new manager Jim Tracy and played better than .600 ball in the second half. While it started with an 11-game win streak in June, an eight-game streak in September brought the Rockies within two games of the Dodgers and cemented them as a playoff contender. The streak was topped off by a dramatic Sept. 11 win when the Rockies scored four runs in the ninth to beat the Padres 4-1.

LOW POINT: A sweep by the Dodgers left the Rockies at 18-28 and fading fast, so on May 28 general manager Dan O'Dowd fired Hurdle and replaced him with Tracy. Hurdle was already on a short leash after the team had replaced much of his coaching staff in the offseason.

NOTABLE ROOKIES: The Rockies are a young and largely homegrown team—Todd Helton was the only significant contributor over the age of 30—but the only rookies to make a splash in 2009 were center fielder Dexter Fowler and righthanded reliever Matt Daley. Fowler, the organization's top prospect coming into the season, batted .266/.363/.406, while the unheralded Daley compiled a 4.24 ERA in 57 appearances—the second-most on the team behind Huston Street.

KEY TRANSACTIONS: O'Dowd made three offseason acquisitions that shored up the pitching staff, though his most important move came in May when he fired Hurdle. He traded for Jason Marquis (from the Cubs) and Jason Hammel (from the Rays), and that duo combined for 393 innings in a rotation that was amazingly stable. He also got closer Huston Street, outfielder Carlos Gonzalez and lefthander Greg Smith from the Athletics for outfielder Matt Holliday. Street returned to form with 35 saves, and Gonzalez showed he could be an important contributor in the future.

DOWN ON THE FARM: All but one of the Rockies' full-season affiliates had a winning record, and low Class A Asheville was just two games below .500. The team scored a coup in the draft by getting high school lefthander Tyler Matzek, whose price tag scared teams even though he was regarded as one of the best pitchers available. He went with the 11th overall pick and signed for $3.9 million.

OPENING DAY PAYROLL: $75,201,000

PLAYERS OF THE YEAR

MAJOR LEAGUE	MINOR LEAGUE
Troy Tulowitzki	**Christian Friedrich**
ss	rhp
.297/.377/.552	(Low A/High A)
25 2B, 32 HR, 20 SB,	6-5, 2.41
10th in NL in OPS	159 SO in 120 IP

ORGANIZATION LEADERS

BATTING		*Minimum 250 at-bats
MAJORS		
*AVG	Todd Helton	.325
*OPS	Troy Tulowitzki	.930
HR	Troy Tulowitzki	32
RBI	Troy Tulowitzki	92
MINORS		
*AVG	Roling, Kiel, Asheville	.331
R	Young, Eric, Colorado Springs	118
H	Blackmon, Charles, Modesto	169
TB	Miller, Matt, Colorado Springs	249
2B	Van Kooten, Jason, Modesto	45
3B	Young, Eric, Colorado Springs	10
HR	Harvey, Ryan, Tulsa	23
RBI	Miller, Matt, Colorado Springs	98
BB	McCoy, Mike, Colorado Springs	80
SO	Christensen, David, Asheville	166
SB	Young, Eric, Colorado Springs	58
*OBP	McCoy, Mike, Colorado Springs	.405
*SLG	Roling, Kiel, Asheville	.593

PITCHING		†Minimum 75 innings
MAJORS		
W	Jorge de la Rosa	16
†ERA	Ubaldo Jimenez	3.47
SO	Ubaldo Jimenez	198
MINORS		
W	Williamson, Joey, Tulsa/Modesto	13
L	Weiser, Keith, Tulsa	15
†ERA	Friedrich, Christian, Asheville/Modesto	2.41
	Nicasio, Juan, Asheville	2.41
G	Baker, Craig, Modesto	62
GS	Durden, Brandon, Modesto/Tulsa	28
	Durst, Kenneth, Modesto	28
SV	Baker, Craig, Modesto	33
IP	Riordan, Cory, Modesto	170
BB	Deduno, Samuel, Tulsa/Colorado Springs	76
SO	Friedrich, Christian, Asheville/Modesto	159
†AVG	Deduno, Samuel, Tulsa/Colorado Springs	.204

2009 PERFORMANCE

General Manager: Dan O'Dowd. **Farm Director:** Marc Gustafson. **Scouting Director:** Bill Schmidt.

Class	Team	League	W	L	PCT	Finish*	Manager(s)
Majors	Colorado Rockies	National	92	70	.568	3rd (16)	Clint Hurdle/Jim Tracy
Triple-A	Colorado Springs Sky Sox	Pacific Coast	73	69	.514	6th (16)	Tom Runnells/Stu Cole
Double-A	Tulsa Drillers	Texas	74	66	.529	2nd (8)	Stu Cole/Ron Gideon
High A	Modesto Nuts	California	75	65	.536	t-3rd (10)	Jerry Weinstein
Low A	Asheville Tourists	South Atlantic	68	70	.493	7th (16)	Joe Mikulik
Short-season	Tri-City Dust Devils	Northwest	47	29	.618	2nd (8)	Fred Ocasio
Rookie	Casper Ghosts	Pioneer	28	46	.378	7th (8)	Tony Diaz

| **Overall 2009 Minor League Record** | | | 365 | 345 | .514 | 9th (30) | |

*Finish in overall standings (No. of teams in league). †League champion.

ORGANIZATION STATISTICS

COLORADO ROCKIES

NATIONAL LEAGUE

Batting	B-T	HT	WT	DOB	AVG	vLH	vRH	G	AB	R	H	2B	3B	HR	RBI	BB	HBP	SH	SF	SO	SB	CS	SLG	OBP
Atkins, Garrett	R-R	6-3	215	12-12-79	.226	.268	.199	126	354	37	80	12	1	9	48	41	2	0	2	58	0	0	.342	.308
Baker, Jeff	R-R	6-2	210	6-21-81	.130	.111	.143	12	23	0	3	0	1	0	3	1	0	0	0	7	1	0	.217	.167
2-team total (69 Chicago)					.288	—	—	81	226	27	65	15	2	4	24	18	2	0	2	53	1	0	.425	.343
Barmes, Clint	R-R	6-1	210	3-6-79	.245	.245	.246	154	550	69	135	32	3	23	76	31	10	6	7	121	12	10	.440	.294
Bellorin, Edwin	R-R	5-9	225	2-21-82	.250	.000	.333	2	8	1	2	0	0	0	1	0	0	0	1	0	0	0	.250	.333
Fowler, Dexter	B-R	6-4	185	3-22-86	.266	.321	.240	135	433	73	115	29	10	4	34	67	1	14	3	116	27	10	.406	.363
Giambi, Jason	L-R	6-3	240	1-8-71	.292	.333	.286	19	24	4	7	1	0	2	11	7	0	0	0	8	0	0	.583	.452
Gonzalez, Carlos	L-L	6-1	215	10-17-85	.284	.276	.286	89	278	53	79	14	7	13	29	28	3	5	3	70	16	4	.525	.353
Hawpe, Brad	L-L	6-3	205	6-22-79	.285	.243	.303	145	501	82	143	42	3	23	86	79	4	0	4	145	1	3	.519	.384
Helton, Todd	L-L	6-2	210	8-20-73	.325	.311	.332	151	544	79	177	38	3	15	86	89	2	0	10	73	0	1	.489	.416
Iannetta, Chris	R-R	6-0	225	4-8-83	.228	.296	.202	93	289	41	66	15	2	16	52	43	11	1	6	75	0	1	.460	.344
McCoy, Mike	R-R	5-9	175	4-2-81	.000	.000	.000	12	5	1	0	0	0	0	0	0	0	1	0	2	0	0	.000	.000
Murton, Matt	R-R	6-1	220	10-3-81	.250	.233	.273	29	52	7	13	5	0	1	6	4	0	0	0	14	2	0	.404	.304
Phillips, Paul	R-R	5-11	205	4-15-77	.311	.125	.351	17	45	5	14	2	0	1	9	7	0	1	1	3	0	0	.422	.396
Quintanilla, Omar	L-R	5-9	190	10-24-81	.172	.083	.196	58	58	7	10	2	0	0	2	8	0	3	0	27	0	0	.207	.273
Smith, Seth	L-L	6-1	215	9-30-82	.293	.259	.300	133	335	61	98	20	4	15	55	46	2	1	3	67	4	1	.510	.378
Spilborghs, Ryan	R-R	6-1	195	9-5-79	.241	.230	.250	133	352	55	85	24	3	8	48	34	2	3	2	79	9	5	.395	.310
Stewart, Ian	L-R	6-3	215	4-5-85	.228	.178	.244	147	425	74	97	19	3	25	70	56	5	0	5	138	7	4	.464	.322
Torrealba, Yorvit	R-R	5-11	200	7-19-78	.291	.220	.318	64	213	27	62	11	1	2	31	21	1	3	4	42	1	1	.380	.351
Tulowitzki, Troy	R-R	6-3	205	10-10-84	.297	.269	.307	151	543	101	161	25	9	32	92	73	3	0	9	112	20	11	.552	.377
Young Jr., Eric	B-R	5-10	180	5-25-85	.246	.304	.206	30	57	7	14	1	0	1	1	4	0	0	0	12	4	4	.316	.295

Pitching	B-T	HT	WT	DOB	W	L	ERA	G	GS	CG	SV	IP	H	R	ER	HR	BB	SO	AVG	vLH	vRH	K/9	BB/9
Beimel, Joe	L-L	6-3	215	4-19-77	0	1	4.02	26	0	0	0	16	19	7	7	2	4	11	.317	.303	.333	6.32	2.30
2-team total (45 Washington)					1	6	3.58	71	0	0	1	55	57	24	22	5	19	35	—	—	—	5.69	3.09
Belisle, Matt	R-R	6-4	230	6-6-80	3	1	5.52	24	0	0	0	31	35	21	19	6	5	22	.280	.241	.313	6.39	1.45
Betancourt, Rafael	R-R	6-2	200	4-29-75	3	1	1.78	32	0	0	1	25	17	5	5	1	5	29	.189	.231	.157	10.30	1.78
Chacin, Jhoulys	R-R	6-3	200	1-7-88	0	1	4.91	9	1	0	0	11	6	6	6	1	11	13	.167	.263	.059	10.64	9.00
Contreras, Jose	R-R	6-4	255	12-6-71	1	0	1.59	7	2	0	0	17	20	3	3	2	8	17	.308	.321	.297	9.00	4.24
Cook, Aaron	R-R	6-3	215	2-8-79	11	6	4.16	27	27	1	0	158	175	76	73	19	47	78	.284	.282	.285	4.44	2.68
Corpas, Manny	R-R	6-3	170	12-3-82	1	3	5.88	35	0	0	1	34	44	22	22	3	7	24	.326	.400	.267	6.42	1.87
Daley, Matt	R-R	6-2	175	6-23-82	1	1	4.24	57	0	0	0	51	43	24	24	6	18	55	.231	.266	.206	9.71	3.18
De La Rosa, Jorge	L-L	6-1	210	4-5-81	16	9	4.38	33	32	0	0	185	172	95	90	20	83	193	.249	.204	.262	9.39	4.04
Eaton, Adam	R-R	6-2	215	11-23-77	1	0	5.63	4	0	0	0	8	9	5	5	1	8	7	.281	.250	.313	7.88	9.00
Embree, Alan	L-L	6-2	200	1-23-70	2	2	5.84	36	0	0	0	25	28	18	16	3	12	12	.292	.326	.264	4.38	4.38
Flores, Randy	L-L	6-0	190	7-31-75	0	1	5.25	27	0	0	0	12	14	7	7	2	2	14	.280	.265	.313	10.50	1.50
Fogg, Josh	R-R	6-0	205	12-13-76	0	2	3.74	24	1	0	0	46	32	20	19	7	20	27	.198	.221	.176	5.32	3.94
Grilli, Jason	R-R	6-5	225	11-11-76	0	1	6.05	22	0	0	1	19	29	13	13	2	13	22	.345	.375	.327	10.24	6.05
Hammel, Jason	R-R	6-6	220	9-2-82	10	8	4.33	34	30	1	0	177	203	94	85	17	42	133	.290	.289	.290	6.78	2.14
Herges, Matt	L-R	6-0	210	4-1-70	1	0	2.89	9	0	0	0	9	10	4	3	2	2	8	.263	.333	.176	7.71	1.93
Jimenez, Ubaldo	R-R	6-4	200	1-22-84	15	12	3.47	33	33	1	0	218	183	87	84	13	85	198	.229	.251	.206	8.17	3.51
Marquis, Jason	R-R	6-1	210	8-21-78	15	13	4.04	33	33	2	0	216	218	104	97	15	80	115	.267	.275	.258	4.79	3.33
Morales, Franklin	L-L	6-0	170	1-24-86	3	2	4.50	40	2	0	7	40	38	22	20	4	23	41	.250	.205	.265	9.23	5.18
Peralta, Joel	R-R	5-11	195	3-23-76	0	3	6.20	27	0	0	0	25	27	17	17	3	12	22	.278	.348	.216	8.03	4.38
Rincon, Juan	R-R	5-11	210	1-23-79	3	2	7.52	26	0	0	0	26	18	23	22	2	20	25	.191	.167	.212	8.54	6.84
Rogers, Esmil	R-R	6-1	150	8-14-85	0	0	4.50	1	1	0	0	4	3	2	2	0	2	3	.231	.250	.200	6.75	4.50
Rusch, Glendon	L-L	6-1	225	11-7-74	2	0	6.75	11	0	0	0	19	35	15	14	3	3	13	.398	.368	.406	6.27	1.45
Speier, Ryan	R-R	6-7	210	7-24-79	0	0	4.76	5	0	0	0	6	6	3	3	0	3	2	.316	.222	.400	3.18	4.76
Street, Huston	R-R	6-0	190	8-2-83	4	1	3.06	64	0	0	35	62	43	22	21	7	13	70	.194	.167	.217	10.22	1.90

Fielding

Catcher	PCT	G	PO	A	E	DP	PB
Bellorin	1.000	2	11	0	0	0	0
Iannetta	.992	89	542	59	5	10	2

	PCT	G	PO	A	E	DP	PB
Phillips	.990	15	95	8	1	0	2
Torrealba	1.000	64	505	27	0	2	2

First Base	PCT	G	PO	A	E	DP
Atkins	.992	28	124	5	1	8
Baker	1.000	1	3	0	0	2

	PCT	G	PO	A	E	DP
Giambi	1.000	5	29	2	0	3
Helton	.998	149	1349	96	3	115

Second Base	PCT	G	PO	A	E	DP
Baker	.900	3	4	5	1	1
Barmes	.982	139	241	413	12	91
McCoy	—	2	0	0	0	0
Quintanilla	.981	25	23	28	1	11
Stewart	.963	21	36	43	3	9
Young Jr.	1.000	6	8	10	0	1

Third Base	PCT	G	PO	A	E	DP
Atkins	.956	78	37	137	8	13
Baker	1.000	3	0	2	0	0
Quintanilla	1.000	10	1	6	0	0
Stewart	.969	121	43	176	7	11

Shortstop	PCT	G	PO	A	E	DP
Barmes	.984	16	13	49	1	8
Quintanilla	.966	13	13	15	1	5
Tulowitzki	.986	151	215	433	9	89

Outfield	PCT	G	PO	A	E	DP
Fowler	.984	127	247	5	4	2
Gonzalez	.988	80	152	6	2	0
Hawpe	.978	141	213	5	5	1
McCoy	1.000	1	1	0	0	0
Murton	1.000	16	13	0	0	0
Smith	.993	86	135	4	1	1
Spilborghs	.975	106	150	7	4	1
Stewart	1.000	9	5	1	0	0
Young Jr.	1.000	5	4	0	0	0

COLORADO SPRINGS SKY SOX

TRIPLE-A

PACIFIC COAST LEAGUE

Batting	B-T	HT	WT	DOB	AVG	vLH	vRH	G	AB	R	H	2B	3B	HR	RBI	BB	HBP	SH	SF	SO	SB	CS	SLG	OBP
Baker, Jeff	R-R	6-2	210	6-21-81	.217	.000	.250	7	23	3	5	2	0	1	1	4	0	0	0	3	0	0	.435	.333
Bellhorn, Mark	B-R	6-1	205	8-23-74	.270	.276	.268	74	196	30	53	13	2	10	34	32	0	0	1	50	0	0	.510	.371
Bellorin, Edwin	R-R	5-9	225	2-21-82	.277	.213	.305	57	202	15	56	10	1	1	28	9	1	2	2	18	0	2	.351	.308
Colonel, Christian	R-R	6-2	210	12-25-81	.279	.252	.289	122	391	55	109	17	2	7	69	39	5	0	5	58	2	3	.386	.348
Fasano, Sal	R-R	6-2	225	8-10-71	.236	.318	.214	61	212	23	50	12	0	4	21	10	5	0	4	63	3	0	.349	.281
Frey, Chris	L-L	6-1	180	8-11-83	.269	.259	.272	108	320	45	86	9	5	4	30	22	3	16	4	53	15	1	.366	.318
Giambi, Jason	L-R	6-3	240	1-8-71	.444	—	.444	6	18	4	8	1	0	2	4	6	0	0	0	3	0	1	.833	.583
Gomez, Leuris	R-R	6-0	170	10-20-86	.000	—	.000	1	1	0	0	0	0	0	0	0	0	0	0	0	0	0	.000	.000
Gonzalez, Carlos	L-L	6-1	215	10-17-85	.339	.360	.331	48	192	43	65	12	7	10	59	22	5	3	1	32	6	3	.630	.418
Herrera, Jonathan	B-R	5-9	150	11-3-84	.268	.286	.261	119	381	63	102	11	5	2	33	49	3	14	3	51	16	5	.339	.353
Iannetta, Chris	R-R	6-0	225	4-8-83	.333	.250	.364	4	15	3	5	2	0	1	3	2	0	0	0	6	0	0	.667	.412
McAnulty, Paul	L-R	5-11	225	2-24-81	.182	.143	.195	20	55	4	10	3	0	2	6	5	0	0	1	12	0	0	.345	.246
McCoy, Mike	R-R	5-9	175	4-2-81	.307	.298	.311	132	462	102	142	27	5	2	52	80	3	16	11	70	40	6	.400	.405
Miller, Matt	R-R	6-2	210	12-26-82	.319	.289	.332	133	523	83	167	39	8	9	98	51	6	0	9	78	4	1	.476	.380
Murton, Matt	R-R	6-1	220	10-3-81	.324	.337	.320	97	373	72	121	27	1	12	79	39	5	0	7	52	12	2	.499	.389
Ortmeier, Dan	B-L	6-4	230	5-11-81	.295	.292	.296	122	431	59	127	17	5	7	73	51	10	0	12	92	11	5	.406	.373
Perez, Kenny	B-R	6-2	190	9-28-81	.292	.326	.279	108	315	35	92	21	3	3	48	32	1	0	6	43	2	1	.406	.353
Phillips, Paul	R-R	5-11	205	4-15-77	.276	.297	.267	38	123	11	34	6	2	1	14	4	0	1	2	18	0	0	.382	.295
Rauch, Austin	R-R	6-3	210	3-30-88	.250	.000	.333	2	4	0	1	0	0	0	0	0	0	0	0	0	0	0	.250	.250
Torrealba, Yorvit	R-R	5-11	200	7-19-78	.267	.000	.364	4	15	1	4	0	0	0	1	1	0	0	0	0	0	0	.267	.313
Young Jr., Eric	B-R	5-10	180	5-25-85	.299	.266	.313	119	472	118	141	21	10	7	43	56	12	12	0	79	58	14	.430	.387

Pitching	B-T	HT	WT	DOB	W	L	ERA	G	GS	CG	SV	IP	H	R	ER	HR	BB	SO	AVG	vLH	vRH	K/9	BB/9
Belisle, Matt	R-R	6-4	230	6-6-80	1	1	3.09	33	4	0	9	58	58	20	20	2	15	47	.264	.172	.331	7.25	2.31
Birkins, Kurt	L-L	6-2	190	8-11-80	3	2	3.49	25	12	0	0	67	68	29	26	8	27	58	.267	.200	.297	7.79	3.63
Chacin, Jhoulys	R-R	6-3	200	1-7-88	1	2	3.77	4	4	0	0	14	11	7	6	2	13	11	.220	.167	.250	6.91	8.16
Corpas, Manny	R-R	6-3	170	12-3-82	0	0	0.00	3	0	0	0	3	2	0	0	1	3	.222	.000	.333	10.13	3.38
Daley, Matt	R-R	6-2	175	6-23-82	0	0	0.90	7	0	0	0	10	8	1	1	0	1	19	.216	.278	.158	17.10	0.90
Deduno, Samuel	R-R	6-3	190	7-2-83	0	1	6.35	1	1	0	0	6	5	4	4	0	4	8	.250	.250	12.71	6.35
Eaton, Adam	R-R	6-2	215	11-23-77	4	3	3.18	14	12	0	0	79	81	33	28	4	16	50	.265	.231	.286	5.67	1.82
Flores, Randy	L-L	6-0	190	7-31-75	0	2	4.26	38	0	0	0	32	37	20	15	2	11	33	.294	.297	.290	9.38	3.13
Fogg, Josh	R-R	6-0	205	12-13-76	3	1	5.80	8	8	0	0	40	44	26	26	8	17	16	.284	.257	.309	3.57	3.79
Grube, Jarrett	R-R	6-4	220	11-5-81	1	2	6.00	13	0	0	0	18	32	16	12	3	7	11	.410	.382	.432	5.50	3.50
Herges, Matt	L-R	6-0	210	4-1-70	3	2	1.96	13	0	0	0	18	13	4	4	1	4	14	.191	.148	.220	6.87	1.96
Hirsh, Jason	R-R	6-8	250	2-20-82	7	6	6.66	20	16	0	0	101	130	78	75	14	35	59	.310	.315	.305	5.24	3.11
Hynick, Brandon	R-R	6-3	205	3-7-85	10	9	3.83	26	26	2	0	155	153	77	66	17	48	92	.257	.255	.259	5.34	2.79
Johnson, Alan	R-R	6-1	180	8-24-83	10	6	5.66	26	24	0	0	143	169	105	90	22	53	76	.293	.287	.298	4.78	3.34
Julianel, Ben	B-L	6-2	200	9-4-79	3	1	5.46	25	0	0	1	28	35	21	17	2	12	29	.302	.286	.313	9.32	3.86
Mattheus, Ryan	R-R	6-3	215	11-10-83	1	1	4.32	13	0	0	0	17	19	8	8	3	8	20	.288	.273	.295	10.80	4.32
Morales, Franklin	L-L	6-0	170	1-24-86	2	2	3.48	8	8	0	0	41	39	17	16	4	19	37	.253	.243	.256	8.06	4.14
Moss, Damian	R-L	6-0	183	11-24-76	8	3	3.30	59	4	0	0	76	87	32	28	5	47	58	.299	.336	.277	6.84	5.54
Munter, Scott	R-R	6-6	260	3-7-80	4	6	4.88	46	0	0	1	55	56	40	30	3	28	36	.264	.222	.290	5.86	4.55
Nunez, Franklin	R-R	6-0	175	1-24-80	1	0	6.64	13	2	0	1	20	25	15	15	2	15	15	.321	.381	.250	6.64	6.64
Ortiz, Russ	R-R	6-1	215	6-5-74	0	1	7.07	3	2	0	0	14	18	12	11	2	10	9	.316	.190	.389	5.79	6.43
Peralta, Joel	R-R	5-11	195	3-23-76	6	0	2.45	31	0	0	4	37	31	11	10	3	11	32	.225	.190	.250	7.85	2.70
Register, Steven	R-R	6-1	180	5-16-83	0	2	4.50	16	0	0	6	16	22	11	8	3	9	13	.333	.387	.286	7.31	5.06
Reynolds, Greg	R-R	6-7	225	7-3-85	0	0	10.38	1	1	0	0	4	6	5	5	0	3	3	.316	.375	.273	6.23	6.23
Rincon, Juan	R-R	5-11	210	1-23-79	1	0	1.56	14	0	0	3	17	8	3	3	1	7	22	.138	.100	.158	11.42	3.63
Rogers, Esmil	R-R	6-1	150	8-14-85	3	5	7.42	12	11	0	0	61	77	50	50	9	35	46	.317	.367	.293	6.82	5.19
Smith, Greg	L-L	6-1	190	12-22-83	1	2	7.28	7	7	0	0	30	34	24	24	5	11	15	.309	.440	.271	4.55	3.34
Speier, Ryan	R-R	6-7	210	7-24-79	2	2	4.70	30	0	0	0	31	42	19	16	3	14	24	.323	.293	.337	7.04	4.11
Timlin, Mike	R-R	6-4	210	3-10-66	0	3	3.86	4	0	0	0	5	7	2	2	1	2	6	.350	.429	.308	11.57	3.86
Wilhite, Matt	R-R	5-11	185	7-3-81	0	4	6.87	32	0	0	10	38	41	30	29	7	11	26	.270	.313	.250	6.16	2.61
2-team total (6 Salt Lake)					0	4	7.21	38	0	0	10	49	59	41	39	8	13	32	—	—	—	5.92	2.40

Fielding

Catcher	PCT	G	PO	A	E	DP	PB
Bellorin	.997	56	306	26	1	6	4
Fasano	.998	60	391	33	1	2	0
Iannetta	.941	4	15	1	1	0	3
Phillips	.990	35	177	19	2	1	1

	PCT	G	PO	A	E	DP	
Rauch	1.000	2	5	1	0	0	
Torrealba	1.000	3	14	0	0	1	0

First Base	PCT	G	PO	A	E	DP
Bellhorn	.994	20	156	11	1	17
Bellorin	1.000	1	9	0	0	1
Colonel	.994	20	147	11	1	12
Giambi	1.000	1	8	0	0	1
McAnulty	.963	4	23	3	1	6
Ortmeier	.991	85	649	39	6	67
Perez	.996	34	211	13	1	22

Torrealba	1.000	1	8	2	0	1

Second Base	PCT	G	PO	A	E	DP
Baker	.909	2	8	2	1	0
Bellhorn	.967	15	27	31	2	12
Herrera	.991	21	50	55	1	19
McCoy	.970	6	14	18	1	6
Young Jr.	.973	109	235	336	16	64

Third Base	PCT	G	PO	A	E	DP
Baker	.857	2	3	3	1	0

Bellhorn	1.000	8	5	10	0	1
Colonel	.900	89	62	137	22	14
McAnulty	1.000	1	0	1	0	0
McCoy	.966	38	22	62	3	3
Perez	.917	27	13	31	4	6

Shortstop	PCT	G	PO	A	E	DP
Herrera	.977	98	156	266	10	60
McCoy	.973	60	101	187	8	36

Outfield	PCT	G	PO	A	E	DP
Colonel	1.000	3	6	0	0	0
Frey	1.000	102	199	8	0	4
Gonzalez	.983	48	116	3	2	1
McAnulty	1.000	3	7	0	0	0
McCoy	1.000	40	55	3	0	0
Miller	.986	128	210	9	3	1
Murton	.966	94	167	5	6	0
Ortmeier	.984	38	61	2	1	1
Young Jr.	.964	11	26	1	1	0

TULSA DRILLERS
TEXAS LEAGUE

DOUBLE-A

Batting	B-T	HT	WT	DOB	AVG	vLH	vRH	G	AB	R	H	2B	3B	HR	RBI	BB	HBP	SH	SF	SO	SB	CS	SLG	OBP
Bowden, Johnny	R-R	6-3	205	8-15-84	.083	.000	.091	3	12	1	1	0	0	1	3	1	0	0	0	6	0	0	.333	.154
Buller, Dayton	R-R	6-0	190	6-22-81	.261	.286	.256	26	92	8	24	3	1	1	7	8	3	0	2	30	0	0	.348	.333
Carte, Daniel	R-R	6-0	190	5-18-84	.214	.286	.179	77	252	23	54	9	1	5	28	17	7	4	2	68	3	1	.317	.281
Corley, Brad	R-R	6-2	198	12-28-83	.227	.263	.210	62	181	18	41	9	1	3	14	15	2	2	1	46	2	3	.337	.291
Fowler, Dexter	B-R	6-4	185	3-22-86	.400	.333	.429	3	10	3	4	2	0	0	3	3	0	0	0	3	1	0	.600	.538
Garner, Cole	R-R	6-2	210	12-15-84	.288	.330	.270	112	396	65	114	25	4	16	64	23	12	4	5	78	13	5	.492	.342
Gonzalez, Jose	R-R	6-1	165	6-23-87	.211	.200	.217	12	38	6	8	2	1	1	4	3	0	0	1	10	0	0	.395	.262
Harvey, Ryan	R-R	6-5	240	8-30-84	.246	.297	.222	103	345	44	85	21	2	23	82	30	3	0	4	100	3	0	.519	.309
Holcomb, Darin	R-R	5-11	205	12-7-85	.271	.296	.260	128	479	67	130	26	1	13	52	54	4	6	4	50	3	1	.411	.348
Jackson, Anthony	B-R	5-8	175	6-17-84	.220	.198	.229	116	422	61	93	11	4	4	34	44	7	12	5	58	27	5	.294	.301
Kindel, Jeff	L-L	6-3	205	9-1-83	.265	.239	.276	128	464	62	123	26	2	6	64	68	6	0	5	87	7	5	.369	.363
Mayora, Daniel	R-R	5-11	145	7-27-85	.286	.255	.299	122	441	60	126	23	1	7	49	40	3	9	3	80	20	8	.390	.347
McKenry, Michael	R-R	5-10	200	3-4-85	.279	.310	.263	102	358	52	100	25	1	12	50	54	2	2	1	69	2	2	.455	.376
Nelson, Chris	R-R	5-11	175	9-3-85	.280	.087	.333	29	107	21	30	5	2	4	17	12	1	1	1	21	5	2	.477	.355
Paulk, Mike	L-L	6-2	195	4-23-84	.288	.255	.300	124	413	63	119	19	2	8	60	63	1	2	4	69	7	6	.402	.380
Rundgren, Rex	R-R	6-1	170	11-20-80	.238	.248	.233	101	341	30	81	15	2	1	24	19	5	9	5	52	2	1	.302	.284
Sandoval, Danny	R-R	6-1	205	4-7-79	.264	.289	.256	58	201	22	53	5	0	1	15	12	2	6	1	17	4	2	.303	.310

Pitching	B-T	HT	WT	DOB	W	L	ERA	G	GS	CG	SV	IP	H	R	ER	HR	BB	SO	AVG	vLH	vRH	K/9	BB/9
Alburquerque, Al	R-R	6-0	150	6-10-86	1	3	3.76	23	0	0	0	26	23	13	11	0	13	31	.240	.216	.254	10.59	4.44
Baumgardner, Tommy	L-L	6-3	220	10-15-83	2	2	2.81	53	0	0	2	58	62	26	18	1	22	41	.272	.303	.252	6.40	3.43
Birkins, Kurt	L-L	6-2	190	8-11-80	0	1	6.00	2	2	0	0	9	11	8	6	1	2	4	.324	.500	.300	4.00	2.00
Bright, Adam	L-L	5-11	175	8-11-84	1	2	4.30	36	0	0	1	38	35	18	18	3	23	31	.250	.156	.329	7.41	5.50
Cedeno, Xavier	L-L	6-1	165	8-26-86	3	2	4.79	28	0	0	0	47	46	30	25	6	22	25	.253	.309	.219	4.79	4.21
Chacin, Jhoulys	R-R	6-3	200	1-7-88	8	6	3.14	18	18	1	0	103	87	45	36	10	35	86	.227	.236	.216	7.49	3.05
Chambliss, Austin	L-R	6-2	185	2-19-87	1	2	4.76	24	0	0	0	28	33	19	15	1	10	22	.300	.256	.324	6.99	3.18
Deduno, Samuel	R-R	6-3	190	7-2-83	12	4	2.57	24	24	1	0	133	94	48	38	3	72	123	.202	.172	.230	8.32	4.87
Durden, Brandon	R-L	6-3	215	7-20-84	7	4	3.46	17	17	0	0	101	95	44	39	8	24	38	.253	.196	.274	3.38	2.13
Escalona, Edgmer	R-R	6-4	175	10-6-86	1	2	2.45	31	0	0	4	37	33	12	10	5	11	32	.232	.327	.172	7.85	2.70
George, Jon	R-R	6-4	220	7-6-84	4	2	6.23	32	0	0	0	48	57	35	33	9	21	31	.311	.311	.312	5.85	3.97
Graham, Andy	R-R	6-4	210	6-29-84	4	4	4.38	33	10	0	0	84	69	43	41	8	31	73	.221	.255	.203	7.79	3.31
Grube, Jarrett	R-R	6-4	220	11-5-81	0	1	8.44	5	0	0	0	5	4	5	5	0	4	9	.200	.333	.176	15.19	6.75
Johnston, Andrew	R-R	6-5	205	4-20-84	2	4	3.69	56	0	0	31	54	63	28	22	3	20	38	.300	.398	.222	6.37	3.35
Lindsay, Shane	R-R	6-1	205	1-25-85	3	1	2.60	22	0	0	1	28	12	8	8	0	19	36	.129	.071	.176	11.71	6.18
Lo, Ching-Lung	R-R	6-6	190	8-20-85	0	1	6.39	3	3	0	0	13	17	10	9	0	5	8	.327	.308	.346	5.68	3.55
Mattheus, Ryan	R-R	6-3	215	11-10-83	0	1	3.60	3	0	0	0	5	3	2	2	0	1	5	.200	.333	.111	9.00	1.80
Nix, Michael	R-R	6-5	235	5-21-83	0	0	5.87	6	0	0	0	8	10	5	5	1	3	2	.313	.300	.318	2.35	3.52
Reynolds, Matt	L-L	6-5	240	10-2-84	1	2	4.21	21	0	0	1	26	23	12	12	3	9	29	.237	.125	.274	10.17	3.16
Roe, Chaz	R-R	6-5	180	10-9-86	7	3	3.15	20	20	1	0	117	105	47	41	7	43	77	.241	.257	.230	5.92	3.31
Rogers, Esmil	R-R	6-1	150	8-14-85	8	2	2.48	15	15	0	0	94	87	30	26	2	19	83	.243	.239	.247	7.92	1.81
Smith, Greg	L-L	6-1	190	12-22-83	0	1	7.88	2	2	0	0	8	12	7	7	3	1	5	.353	.333	.357	5.63	1.13
Speier, Ryan	R-R	6-7	210	7-24-79	0	0	3.00	3	0	0	0	3	3	1	1	0	2	2	.300	.667	.143	6.00	6.00
Weiser, Keith	R-L	6-2	190	9-21-84	9	15	5.23	27	27	0	0	157	195	115	91	23	29	97	.305	.295	.309	5.57	1.67
Williamson, Joey	R-R	6-2	210	1-28-86	0	0	0.00	2	2	0	0	7	3	0	0	0	4	4	.143	.333	.067	5.40	5.40

Fielding

Catcher	PCT	G	PO	A	E	DP	PB
Bowden	1.000	3	20	1	0	0	0
Buller	.986	26	197	17	3	1	2
Corley	1.000	1	0	1	0	0	0
Gonzalez	.968	12	86	6	3	1	1
McKenry	.987	102	630	77	9	4	1

First Base	PCT	G	PO	A	E	DP
Kindel	.990	110	1032	67	11	99
Paulk	.990	32	263	26	3	22

Second Base	PCT	G	PO	A	E	DP
Jackson	.904	8	14	33	5	10

Mayora	.966	73	148	218	13	51
Nelson	—	1	0	0	0	0
Rundgren	.969	59	102	177	9	37
Sandoval	.947	9	12	24	2	2

Third Base	PCT	G	PO	A	E	DP
Holcomb	.951	126	81	252	17	16
Mayora	.951	17	11	28	2	3

Shortstop	PCT	G	PO	A	E	DP
Mayora	.939	32	49	106	10	13
Nelson	.939	28	30	63	6	15
Rundgren	.983	39	68	103	3	30

Sandoval	.945	46	52	138	11	30

Outfield	PCT	G	PO	A	E	DP
Carte	.974	65	111	3	3	2
Corley	.964	45	77	4	3	2
Fowler	.750	2	3	0	1	0
Garner	.974	100	184	2	5	0
Harvey	.975	78	145	8	4	0
Jackson	.986	104	262	15	4	4
Paulk	.946	41	51	2	3	0

CALIFORNIA LEAGUE

Batting	B-T	HT	WT	DOB	AVG	vLH	vRH	G	AB	R	H	2B	3B	HR	RBI	BB	HBP	SH	SF	SO	SB	CS	SLG	OBP
Baker, Jeff	R-R	6-2	210	6-21-81	.400	—	.400	2	5	1	2	1	0	0	1	1	0	0	0	1	0	0	.600	.500
Beerer, Scott	R-R	6-1	200	7-4-82	.346	.311	.368	52	191	38	66	8	5	7	40	21	3	0	3	27	5	2	.550	.413
Blackmon, Charlie	L-L	6-2	185	7-1-86	.307	.305	.309	133	550	87	169	34	7	7	69	39	19	3	5	83	30	13	.433	.370
Clark, Kevin	L-L	6-0	195	12-10-85	.241	.143	.273	12	29	4	7	3	0	0	4	3	0	0	0	9	1	0	.345	.313
Cox, Jay	L-R	6-0	200	10-30-84	.294	.187	.335	111	388	58	114	22	6	12	51	44	4	3	3	102	8	3	.474	.369
Cunningham, Jeff	L-R	6-3	220	3-22-86	.249	.215	.258	102	317	54	79	21	7	9	52	30	6	1	7	101	1	2	.445	.319
Davis, Lars	L-R	6-3	205	11-7-85	.233	.211	.243	93	348	36	81	12	2	1	34	15	6	11	3	80	2	2	.287	.274
Goff, Andy	R-R	5-11	180	9-2-85	.000	.000	.000	5	3	0	0	0	0	0	0	2	0	0	0	2	0	0	.000	.400
Gomez, Hector	R-R	6-2	180	3-5-88	.275	.265	.282	83	338	39	93	21	4	7	46	15	5	4	6	68	10	4	.423	.310
Gonzalez, Maikol	R-R	5-10	175	3-25-86	.282	.314	.257	111	369	59	104	15	7	2	42	43	3	2	2	60	19	7	.377	.360
Mitchell, Mike	R-R	6-1	200	8-24-85	.226	.187	.258	118	340	48	77	10	1	1	34	31	7	8	1	75	24	7	.271	.303
Nazario, Radames	R-R	6-0	166	6-14-87	.252	.257	.249	99	353	51	89	27	1	4	27	24	15	11	2	63	3	10	.368	.325
Rauch, Austin	R-R	6-3	210	3-30-88	.120	.091	.143	11	25	0	3	1	0	0	0	3	0	0	0	10	1	0	.160	.214
Repec, Matt	R-R	6-1	190	8-30-83	.297	.285	.304	94	344	53	102	30	2	11	62	27	4	2	6	94	7	3	.491	.349
Rike, Brian	L-L	6-2	200	12-13-85	.196	.153	.221	104	368	44	72	18	5	11	59	34	7	9	8	147	4	3	.361	.271
Rosario, Wilin	R-R	5-11	190	2-23-89	.266	.333	.209	58	203	17	54	12	2	4	33	10	1	3	5	55	2	1	.404	.297
Schaeffer, Warren	R-R	6-0	180	1-28-85	.218	.165	.275	70	165	21	36	5	1	2	20	8	3	3	3	38	3	1	.297	.263
Van Kooten, Jason	R-R	6-0	170	9-1-84	.302	.345	.274	120	441	76	133	45	7	10	55	28	8	5	5	92	19	7	.503	.351

Pitching	B-T	HT	WT	DOB	W	L	ERA	G	GS	CG	SV	IP	H	R	ER	HR	BB	SO	AVG	vLH	vRH	K/9	BB/9
Baker, Craig	R-R	6-2	210	1-31-85	4	2	2.30	62	0	0	33	63	49	23	16	1	21	75	.212	.165	.250	10.77	3.02
Billings, Bruce	R-R	6-0	200	11-18-85	6	10	4.17	21	20	0	0	99	91	60	46	10	38	122	.238	.187	.276	11.05	3.44
Cedeno, Xavier	L-L	6-1	165	8-26-86	1	2	4.32	16	0	0	0	17	15	10	8	0	9	21	.221	.375	.136	11.34	4.86
Chambliss, Austin	L-R	6-2	185	2-19-87	2	1	3.60	35	0	0	0	55	41	25	22	4	29	41	.205	.269	.150	6.71	4.75
Durden, Brandon	R-L	6-3	215	7-20-84	3	4	4.05	11	11	1	0	67	77	35	30	7	12	33	.297	.306	.294	4.46	1.62
Durst, Kenny	B-L	6-0	195	10-1-85	4	13	5.25	28	28	0	0	153	163	98	89	13	59	95	.275	.272	.277	5.60	3.48
Escalona, Edgmer	R-R	6-4	175	10-6-86	2	0	2.48	28	0	0	0	33	25	10	9	3	7	34	.207	.250	.169	9.37	1.93
Friedrich, Christian	R-L	6-4	215	7-8-87	3	2	2.54	14	14	0	0	74	59	25	21	3	28	93	.215	.256	.197	11.26	3.39
Graham, Connor	R-R	6-6	235	12-30-85	7	4	3.14	16	16	0	0	80	68	35	28	2	41	87	.225	.213	.237	9.75	4.59
Hollingsworth, Ethan	R-R	6-2	200	5-4-87	3	3	4.83	11	10	0	0	60	77	39	32	3	16	56	.312	.298	.322	8.45	2.41
Jarrett, Sean	R-R	6-5	210	4-26-83	5	4	4.64	46	0	0	0	66	82	44	34	3	15	56	.305	.320	.293	7.64	2.05
Lo, Ching-Lung	R-R	6-6	190	8-20-85	1	1	3.86	16	2	0	0	30	30	15	13	1	11	25	.265	.271	.262	7.42	3.26
Luna, Carlos	R-R	5-11	175	10-5-86	1	1	5.52	22	0	0	0	29	35	20	18	3	12	24	.297	.224	.348	7.36	3.68
Malone, Chris	R-R	6-4	215	6-28-83	0	2	9.13	18	0	0	0	23	36	26	23	2	10	14	.367	.340	.396	5.56	3.97
Mattheus, Ryan	R-R	6-3	215	11-10-83	0	1	2.08	3	0	0	0	4	2	1	1	0	2	2	.133	.125	.143	4.15	4.15
Reynolds, Matt	L-L	6-5	240	10-2-84	5	3	1.29	39	0	0	3	49	32	8	7	2	8	58	.190	.206	.181	10.65	1.47
Riordan, Cory	R-R	6-4	200	5-25-86	12	7	3.93	28	27	2	0	170	185	87	74	11	48	134	.274	.288	.263	7.11	2.55
Smith, Greg	L-L	6-1	190	12-22-83	1	0	3.86	2	2	0	0	12	11	6	5	1	4	7	.250	.364	.212	5.40	3.09
Speier, Ryan	R-R	6-7	210	7-24-79	0	0	3.00	3	0	0	0	3	5	1	1	0	3	2	.455	1.000	.143	6.00	9.00
Taylor, Don	R-R	6-0	185	5-23-85	2	2	6.48	48	0	0	0	58	79	45	42	5	15	37	.324	.354	.303	5.71	2.31
Williamson, Joey	R-R	6-2	210	1-28-86	13	3	3.36	36	10	0	3	107	91	43	40	9	31	104	.230	.232	.229	8.75	2.61

Fielding

Catcher	PCT	G	PO	A	E	DP	PB
Davis	.982	87	713	54	14	10	22
Rauch	.979	6	43	4	1	0	3
Rosario	.983	49	351	43	7	0	7

First Base	PCT	G	PO	A	E	DP
Cox	1.000	2	4	0	0	0
Cunningham	.982	92	608	56	12	43
Repec	.990	61	378	27	4	30
Schaeffer	1.000	17	109	13	0	12

Second Base	PCT	G	PO	A	E	DP
Baker	1.000	1	2	0	0	0
Goff	1.000	3	3	1	0	0

Gonzalez	.968	58	101	140	8	29
Nazario	1.000	2	1	4	0	1
Schaeffer	1.000	2	3	9	0	3
Van Kooten	.949	88	165	209	20	34

Third Base	PCT	G	PO	A	E	DP
Baker	—	1	0	0	0	0
Goff	—	1	0	0	0	0
Gonzalez	.951	54	27	89	6	11
Nazario	.933	64	37	89	9	13
Repec	.896	47	30	56	10	4
Schaeffer	.875	6	3	4	1	0

Shortstop	PCT	G	PO	A	E	DP
Gomez	.949	66	129	168	16	32
Gonzalez	.857	2	1	5	1	0
Nazario	.963	51	64	120	7	16
Schaeffer	.969	45	51	74	4	14

Outfield	PCT	G	PO	A	E	DP
Beerer	1.000	32	55	2	0	0
Blackmon	.988	111	251	4	3	0
Clark	1.000	4	10	0	0	0
Cox	.979	82	136	6	3	1
Gonzalez	1.000	3	2	0	0	0
Mitchell	.970	111	216	10	7	4
Rike	.964	98	179	10	7	1

SOUTH ATLANTIC LEAGUE

Batting	B-T	HT	WT	DOB	AVG	vLH	vRH	G	AB	R	H	2B	3B	HR	RBI	BB	HBP	SH	SF	SO	SB	CS	SLG	OBP
Bowman, Bo	L-L	6-2	200	9-22-84	.048	.000	.083	6	21	0	1	1	0	0	0	0	0	0	0	7	0	0	.095	.048
Cesario, Jimmy	L-R	5-11	200	10-15-85	.285	.208	.310	126	488	74	139	28	2	11	68	31	7	3	6	76	18	11	.418	.333
Christensen, David	R-R	6-1	195	2-11-88	.234	.183	.251	118	431	62	101	26	7	18	63	26	11	2	3	166	27	9	.452	.293
Cleary, Delta	R-R	6-3	180	8-14-89	.256	.173	.282	105	399	53	102	19	4	7	45	31	5	8	3	87	32	11	.376	.315
Field, Thomas	R-R	5-9	175	2-22-87	.257	.254	.257	89	304	42	78	17	0	2	32	26	11	5	2	58	8	3	.332	.335
Goff, Andy	R-R	5-11	180	9-2-85	.150	.273	.103	14	40	5	6	1	0	0	2	5	1	2	0	3	0	1	.175	.261
Gonzalez, Maikol	R-R	5-10	175	3-25-86	.200	.333	.143	3	10	0	2	0	0	0	1	0	1	0	0	0	0	0	.300	.273
Martinez, Carlos	R-R	5-11	182	2-1-87	.197	.169	.205	91	295	33	58	12	1	0	19	14	9	5	2	92	12	6	.244	.253
Massey, Tyler	L-L	6-0	205	7-21-89	.220	.260	.211	110	404	31	89	12	5	2	38	23	1	3	5	100	8	9	.290	.261
Pacheco, Jordan	R-R	6-1	190	1-30-86	.322	.374	.305	117	451	67	145	30	4	13	79	38	8	3	7	44	12	2	.492	.379
Peisel, Ryan	R-R	6-3	200	6-14-86	.271	.224	.285	93	329	42	89	22	1	4	36	27	3	2	2	65	6	5	.380	.330

COLORADO ROCKIES

Name	B-T	HT	WT	DOB	AVG	vLH	vRH	G	AB	R	H	2B	3B	HR	RBI	BB	HBP	SH	SF	SO	SB	CS	SLG	OBP
Robinson, Scott	R-R	6-0	185	7-6-88	.309	.248	.328	124	501	94	155	34	5	3	37	20	12	5	3	111	46	13	.415	.349
Roling, Kiel	R-R	6-3	240	1-23-87	.331	.260	.352	94	344	54	114	26	2	20	66	39	2	1	2	92	0	2	.593	.401
Rose, Patrick	R-R	5-11	190	10-2-85	.243	.163	.269	52	173	28	42	8	0	1	14	16	2	6	0	52	5	3	.306	.314
Seabury, Beau	R-R	6-1	190	6-13-85	.238	.204	.249	71	227	15	54	11	0	1	20	23	6	9	3	64	4	4	.300	.320
Sims, James	R-R	6-0	200	4-11-86	.200	.375	.083	6	20	3	4	1	0	0	2	2	0	0	0	7	1	1	.250	.273
Wetzel, Erik	R-R	6-1	180	12-25-86	.300	.250	.313	13	40	7	12	0	0	0	2	8	0	4	0	6	6	0	.300	.417
Zuanich, Mike	R-L	6-4	225	7-10-86	.362	.436	.333	42	138	23	50	12	1	7	34	20	6	1	5	36	1	1	.616	.450

Pitching	B-T	HT	WT	DOB	W	L	ERA	G	GS	CG	SV	IP	H	R	ER	HR	BB	SO	AVG	vLH	vRH	K/9	BB/9
Aristil, Jonnathan	R-R	6-1	160	11-30-86	4	9	5.06	30	22	1	0	112	129	82	63	14	46	102	.285	.323	.258	8.20	3.70
Brothers, Rex	L-L	6-0	205	12-18-87	0	0	3.38	9	0	0	0	11	6	4	4	1	3	10	.171	.125	.185	8.44	2.53
Deratt, Alan	R-R	6-5	225	11-6-85	2	4	5.03	36	8	0	0	79	91	50	44	7	18	71	.285	.250	.311	8.12	2.06
Dodson, Stephen	R-R	6-5	200	8-29-85	7	1	2.45	25	0	0	0	40	36	12	11	2	14	43	.238	.200	.264	9.60	3.12
Fabian, Robinson	R-R	6-3	152	2-10-86	3	6	6.24	24	12	0	0	84	105	64	58	6	21	54	.310	.317	.305	5.81	2.26
2-team total (9 Hagerstown)					3	7	5.32	33	13	0	2	107	126	70	63	7	25	64	—	—	—	5.40	2.11
Frazier, Parker	R-R	6-5	159	11-11-88	10	7	4.48	23	23	1	0	131	158	70	65	7	33	98	.303	.296	.308	6.75	2.27
Friedrich, Christian	R-L	6-4	215	7-8-87	3	3	2.18	8	8	0	0	45	35	14	11	2	15	66	.215	.120	.232	13.10	2.98
Froneberger, Isaiah	L-L	5-8	200	6-23-89	3	3	4.58	43	1	0	0	59	61	32	30	7	29	71	.266	.200	.299	10.83	4.42
Hollingsworth, Ethan	R-R	6-2	200	5-4-87	5	6	4.05	16	15	2	0	87	87	43	39	9	18	76	.259	.231	.272	7.89	1.87
Houston, Dan	R-R	6-3	205	10-24-86	8	9	3.63	26	26	0	0	149	141	77	60	11	63	121	.250	.206	.281	7.33	3.81
Jorgenson, Adam	R-R	6-0	185	9-10-85	1	5	3.38	60	0	0	27	59	48	23	22	3	21	77	.242	.262	.200	11.81	3.22
Lindsay, Shane	R-R	6-1	205	1-25-85	1	1	1.59	5	0	0	0	6	4	1	1	0	4	7	.211	.250	.182	11.12	6.35
Luna, Carlos	R-R	5-11	175	10-5-86	0	1	5.89	4	4	0	0	18	22	12	12	1	7	15	.310	.304	.313	7.36	3.44
Marbry, Michael	R-R	6-3	185	9-3-84	5	3	3.46	46	0	0	2	65	67	27	25	1	15	54	.267	.247	.278	7.48	2.08
Nicasio, Juan	R-R	6-3	190	8-31-86	9	3	2.41	18	18	1	0	112	110	44	30	6	23	115	.252	.304	.214	9.24	1.85
Trice, Tyler	R-R	6-4	205	5-16-86	5	5	4.76	41	0	0	0	57	66	34	30	6	20	46	.289	.290	.289	7.31	3.18
Weatherford, Aaron	R-R	6-0	185	12-19-86	0	1	4.76	7	0	0	0	11	7	6	6	1	4	12	.175	.105	.238	9.53	3.18
Yacko, Kurt	R-R	5-11	180	8-22-87	2	2	3.52	50	1	0	4	69	73	31	27	5	15	86	.269	.313	.246	11.22	1.96

Fielding

Catcher	PCT	G	PO	A	E	DP	PB
Pacheco	.987	69	552	51	8	9	8
Seabury	.995	69	539	73	3	7	10

First Base	PCT	G	PO	A	E	DP
Bowman	1.000	2	23	1	0	3
Cesario	.988	37	315	23	4	18
Peisel	.986	9	65	3	1	5
Roling	.997	72	639	45	2	62
Zuanich	.990	23	184	13	2	14

Second Base	PCT	G	PO	A	E	DP
Cesario	.981	53	107	152	5	32

Field	PCT	G	PO	A	E	DP
Field	.984	31	40	83	2	12
Goff	1.000	12	19	29	0	3
Gonzalez	1.000	2	4	2	0	0
Martinez	.909	10	18	2	4	8
Rose	.979	25	34	61	2	14
Wetzel	.981	13	20	32	1	8

Third Base	PCT	G	PO	A	E	DP
Cesario	.897	38	22	74	11	12
Goff	1.000	1	2	2	0	0
Gonzalez	.667	1	0	2	1	1
Peisel	.904	75	47	151	21	9
Rose	.922	26	16	43	5	2

Shortstop	PCT	G	PO	A	E	DP
Field	.960	61	83	183	11	43
Goff	1.000	1	2	3	0	1
Martinez	.934	80	119	221	24	38

Outfield	PCT	G	PO	A	E	DP
Christensen	.952	89	154	6	8	1
Cleary	.968	103	168	13	6	5
Massey	.953	104	151	12	8	3
Robinson	.984	114	178	8	3	4
Sims	.857	6	6	0	1	0
Zuanich	1.000	6	3	0	0	0

TRI-CITY DUST DEVILS   SHORT-SEASON

NORTHWEST LEAGUE

Batting	B-T	HT	WT	DOB	AVG	vLH	vRH	G	AB	R	H	2B	3B	HR	RBI	BB	HBP	SH	SF	SO	SB	CS	SLG	OBP
Beerer, Scott	R-R	6-1	200	7-4-82	.558	.429	.583	11	43	13	24	5	1	1	14	2	1	0	0	2	1	1	.791	.587
Bowman, Bo	L-L	6-2	200	9-22-84	.328	.314	.331	55	192	31	63	9	4	7	46	24	0	1	2	41	2	1	.526	.399
Clark, Kevin	L-L	6-0	195	12-10-85	.260	.240	.263	59	181	32	47	11	1	5	28	35	5	1	1	39	19	4	.414	.392
Feinberg, Alex	R-R	6-0	185	4-29-86	.211	.242	.197	32	109	13	23	3	0	0	15	9	6	1	0	22	4	3	.239	.306
Gonzalez, Jose	R-R	6-1	165	6-23-87	.178	.259	.154	35	118	10	21	3	0	0	14	13	0	8	1	29	2	0	.203	.258
Lowe, Shane	B-R	6-3	190	8-14-87	.147	.115	.159	31	95	17	14	1	1	1	8	8	0	1	0	41	10	1	.211	.255
Matthes, Kent	R-R	6-2	215	1-8-87	.289	.318	.282	63	239	39	69	23	1	5	35	21	9	4	3	77	6	4	.456	.364
Paulsen, Ben	L-R	6-4	205	10-27-87	.280	.270	.283	44	175	28	49	10	2	1	25	12	1	0	3	32	2	1	.377	.325
Rauch, Austin	R-R	6-3	210	3-30-88	.164	.273	.136	16	55	6	9	3	1	0	8	4	3	0	0	26	1	0	.255	.258
Reyes, Leonardo	R-R	6-0	165	8-2-88	.194	.222	.184	41	139	16	27	6	0	1	17	11	2	1	1	30	3	3	.259	.261
Sammy, Jeremiah	L-R	6-2	190	7-13-87	.316	.364	.309	49	187	32	59	8	2	3	20	20	0	5	0	35	9	5	.428	.382
Sanders, Joseph	R-R	6-0	195	2-24-88	.251	.196	.264	62	243	27	61	17	1	3	33	8	2	5	4	51	6	1	.342	.276
Sanders, Matt	R-R	6-1	180	5-10-87	.244	.154	.281	18	45	5	11	1	0	0	3	6	1	1	1	7	2	0	.267	.340
Sandoval, Orlando	R-R	6-0	185	1-22-86	.279	.385	.250	39	122	23	34	6	3	1	14	12	7	0	1	37	10	1	.402	.373
Scott, Joe	R-R	6-0	185	8-22-86	.071	.250	.000	4	14	3	1	0	0	0	2	1	3	0	0	5	1	0	.071	.278
Tarleton, Dallas	L-R	5-11	200	8-5-87	.193	.231	.188	32	109	10	21	4	0	0	9	18	0	2	1	19	4	2	.229	.305
Valdez, Nick	R-R	5-11	212	5-26-86	.333	—	.333	1	3	1	1	0	0	0	1	1	0	0	0	0	0	0	.333	.600
Vasami, Chris	R-R	6-4	230	3-7-85	.333	—	.333	2	3	1	1	0	0	0	2	0	1	0	0	1	0	0	.333	.500
Wheeler, Tim	R-R	6-4	205	1-21-88	.256	.185	.274	68	273	44	70	13	3	5	35	29	3	2	2	60	10	4	.381	.332
Wong, Joey	L-R	5-10	175	4-12-88	.215	.200	.220	70	205	30	44	8	0	0	17	34	13	6	1	48	9	2	.254	.360
Zuanich, Mike	R-L	6-4	225	7-10-86	.340	.500	.308	15	47	17	16	1	0	7	16	8	6	0	2	10	0	0	.809	.476

Pitching	B-T	HT	WT	DOB	W	L	ERA	G	GS	CG	SV	IP	H	R	ER	HR	BB	SO	AVG	vLH	vRH	K/9	BB/9
Ballard, Rhett	R-R	6-5	235	11-13-85	4	1	2.08	26	0	0	1	43	27	12	10	1	19	40	.181	.167	.188	8.31	3.95
Bargas, Paul	L-L	6-1	205	10-13-88	3	1	1.59	13	0	0	0	23	12	5	4	1	7	24	.160	.056	.193	9.53	2.78
Baugh, Matt	L-L	6-1	190	1-25-86	0	3	9.35	7	7	0	0	26	43	28	27	2	8	29	.377	.448	.353	10.04	2.77
Bennigson, Craig	R-L	6-2	215	3-21-87	8	3	1.53	24	0	0	0	53	42	16	9	0	14	41	.219	.169	.241	6.96	2.38
Brothers, Rex	L-L	6-0	205	12-18-87	2	0	3.38	8	0	0	0	11	10	4	4	0	5	18	.256	.154	.308	15.19	4.22
Federico, Eric	R-R	5-11	175	9-4-87	4	3	4.30	25	0	0	0	46	47	25	22	4	12	35	.264	.227	.286	6.85	2.35

Name	B-T	HT	WT	DOB	W	L	ERA	G	GS	CG	SV	IP	H	R	ER	HR	BB	SO	AVG	vLH	vRH	K/9	BB/9
Harris, Will	R-R	6-4	225	8-28-84	0	0	0.00	1	0	0	0	1	1	0	0	0	0	2	.250	.500	.000	18.00	0.00
Hungerman, Josh	L-L	6-3	195	9-8-86	1	1	2.57	14	9	0	0	49	37	17	14	1	22	53	.208	.186	.215	9.73	4.04
Kuo, Sheng-An	R-R	6-2	190	1-1-86	4	3	5.12	15	13	0	0	65	81	47	37	4	23	50	.308	.283	.322	6.92	3.18
Luna, Carlos	R-R	5-11	175	10-5-86	1	0	5.16	9	4	0	0	23	22	15	13	1	19	15	.244	.265	.232	5.96	7.54
McAtee, Brad	R-R	6-5	215	3-15-87	2	4	7.42	15	7	0	0	44	48	36	36	1	38	24	.300	.459	.202	4.95	7.83
Musick, Wes	L-L	6-0	190	12-30-86	3	0	2.49	7	5	0	0	25	21	8	7	0	9	31	.226	.417	.198	11.01	3.20
Perkins, Dan	R-R	6-4	200	3-5-86	3	2	2.80	15	15	0	0	71	63	26	22	4	15	55	.241	.174	.289	7.00	1.91
Ruiz, Charlie	R-R	6-1	180	10-10-88	1	0	1.14	32	0	0	17	32	22	6	4	1	12	46	.186	.222	.171	13.07	3.41
Scahill, Rob	R-R	6-2	205	2-15-87	1	4	3.14	15	15	0	0	63	58	30	22	2	20	58	.245	.231	.253	8.29	2.86
Scurry, Rod	R-R	6-7	190	2-1-86	5	1	2.68	23	0	0	1	37	37	17	11	0	14	23	.259	.404	.163	5.59	3.41
Stavert, Erik	R-R	6-3	185	11-20-87	0	1	5.19	5	0	0	0	9	10	5	5	1	4	11	.303	.231	.350	11.42	4.15
Testa, Ricky	R-R	6-3	225	4-8-87	0	0	0.87	6	0	0	0	10	3	1	1	0	3	9	.097	.200	.048	7.84	2.61
Tilford, Clint	R-R	6-3	195	4-2-88	0	0	9.00	1	1	0	0	4	7	5	4	0	2	0	.412	.222	.625	0.00	4.50
Walker, Kyle	L-L	6-0	190	6-9-87	4	2	1.76	21	0	0	2	41	28	11	8	3	24	27	.194	.125	.221	5.93	5.27
Weatherford, Aaron	R-R	6-0	185	12-19-86	1	0	2.87	11	0	0	1	16	8	5	5	2	7	24	.148	.167	.139	13.79	4.02

Fielding

Catcher	PCT	G	PO	A	E	DP	PB
Gonzalez	.997	35	291	40	1	3	11
Rauch	1.000	9	76	7	0	0	3
Tarleton	.996	32	223	27	1	2	6
Valdez	1.000	1	9	0	0	0	0
Vasami	1.000	1	0	1	0	0	0

First Base	PCT	G	PO	A	E	DP
Bowman	.991	24	206	13	2	26
Paulsen	.991	40	322	24	3	33
Rauch	1.000	1	12	0	0	4
Vasami	1.000	1	8	0	0	0
Zuanich	.993	14	126	11	1	10

Second Base	PCT	G	PO	A	E	DP
Feinberg	1.000	25	50	68	0	13
Lowe	1.000	1	1	1	0	0
Sammy	.952	43	93	124	11	26
Sanders	.966	15	27	29	2	8
Scott	.889	2	4	4	1	0

Third Base	PCT	G	PO	A	E	DP
Beerer	1.000	3	4	6	0	2
Feinberg	.895	8	2	15	2	0
Rauch	.667	4	2	4	3	0
Sanders	.870	62	42	118	24	13
Sanders	1.000	1	1	1	0	0

Shortstop	PCT	G	PO	A	E	DP
Sammy	.926	8	6	19	2	4
Sanders	.750	2	0	3	1	0
Scott	.917	2	3	8	1	0
Wong	.985	70	118	219	5	51

Outfield	PCT	G	PO	A	E	DP
Beerer	1.000	1	1	0	0	0
Clark	.974	29	38	0	1	0
Lowe	1.000	28	34	1	0	0
Matthes	.979	59	86	6	2	0
Reyes	1.000	31	47	3	0	0
Sandoval	.985	35	61	3	1	1
Wheeler	.979	66	133	4	3	0

CASPER GHOSTS   ROOKIE
PIONEER LEAGUE

Batting	B-T	HT	WT	DOB	AVG	vLH	vRH	G	AB	R	H	2B	3B	HR	RBI	BB	HBP	SH	SF	SO	SB	CS	SLG	OBP
Altobelli, Dom	R-R	6-1	195	3-7-87	.233	.296	.216	39	129	13	30	5	1	0	16	13	0	0	3	31	6	3	.287	.297
Arenado, Nolan	R-R	6-1	205	4-16-91	.300	.216	.329	54	203	28	61	15	0	2	22	16	2	0	4	18	5	2	.404	.351
Barnes, Avery	R-L	6-1	170	9-17-86	.335	.311	.343	49	188	37	63	7	2	0	13	19	1	1	0	46	23	8	.394	.399
Clark, Jared	R-R	6-4	215	5-9-86	.348	.382	.336	58	198	33	69	13	1	11	44	29	0	1	4	34	5	5	.591	.424
Crousset, Juan	L-L	5-11	193	4-30-90	.288	.200	.306	15	59	4	17	1	1	0	4	3	0	1	0	11	1	2	.339	.323
DiNatale, David	R-R	6-1	202	2-9-87	.193	.143	.214	44	119	10	23	4	2	1	10	12	5	1	0	45	3	7	.286	.294
Garneau, Dustin	R-R	6-1	200	8-13-87	.250	.250	.250	23	72	11	18	4	1	1	13	13	4	0	0	14	1	0	.375	.393
Hernandez, David	R-R	6-2	165	2-1-88	.200	.167	.211	25	75	8	15	2	0	0	1	3	0	1	0	17	2	2	.227	.231
Hines, Nathan	L-R	5-10	180	12-9-85	.279	.414	.227	26	104	18	29	2	4	6	17	7	2	0	0	17	6	2	.548	.336
Jacobsen, Chad	R-R	6-1	210	4-3-86	.262	.382	.204	48	168	24	44	8	3	3	17	16	6	1	0	45	1	2	.399	.347
Kandilas, David	R-R	6-2	185	9-14-90	.205	.500	.152	29	78	10	16	1	2	0	10	8	0	0	1	13	5	1	.269	.276
Laurent, Chandler	R-R	5-10	180	10-17-87	.292	.280	.296	60	209	37	61	12	6	3	30	14	3	4	3	57	8	3	.450	.341
Mesa, Eliezer	R-R	5-11	180	11-24-88	.316	.400	.290	57	231	35	73	9	6	1	28	10	2	2	1	38	12	5	.420	.348
Nina, Angelys	R-R	5-11	165	11-16-88	.295	.459	.235	36	139	20	41	7	2	1	14	7	2	5	0	22	11	5	.396	.338
Rivera, Jose	R-R	5-10	170	4-18-90	.175	.000	.200	22	63	3	11	1	0	0	1	11	0	1	1	16	2	3	.190	.293
Scott, Joe	R-R	6-0	185	8-22-86	.205	.333	.152	35	112	16	23	7	1	1	13	8	4	2	1	31	5	6	.313	.280
Squier, Jeff	R-R	6-3	190	3-3-87	.154	.188	.143	42	123	10	19	7	1	1	16	10	2	3	4	50	9	2	.252	.223
Valdez, Nick	R-R	5-11	212	5-26-86	.231	.316	.208	31	91	15	21	3	0	1	13	13	3	1	2	15	1	0	.297	.339
Whitby, Brandon	R-R	6-2	205	1-9-87	.311	.194	.360	32	106	11	33	5	2	1	13	11	1	0	0	16	1	5	.425	.381

Pitching	B-T	HT	WT	DOB	W	L	ERA	G	GS	CG	SV	IP	H	R	ER	HR	BB	SO	AVG	vLH	vRH	K/9	BB/9
Balcom-Miller, Chris	R-R	6-2	190	3-3-89	4	0	1.58	11	11	1	0	57	37	13	10	3	10	60	.181	.224	.156	9.47	1.58
Bargas, Paul	L-L	6-1	205	10-13-88	0	0	3.52	6	1	0	2	8	5	3	3	0	1	10	.200	.200	.200	11.74	1.17
Barraza, Alejandro	R-R	6-1	205	10-25-90	4	0	3.94	17	1	0	0	32	31	18	14	2	10	21	.256	.200	.289	5.91	2.81
Born, David	L-L	6-3	195	6-7-86	1	3	4.96	16	0	0	0	16	21	17	9	3	11	15	.296	.350	.275	8.27	6.06
Cabrera, Edwar	L-L	6-0	160	10-20-87	0	0	3.38	9	1	0	0	21	19	10	8	2	12	28	.235	.167	.254	11.81	5.06
Ferrer, Ricardo	R-R	6-2	174	10-11-89	2	8	6.95	14	13	0	0	66	94	57	51	8	27	43	.344	.368	.329	5.86	3.68
Gagnon, Tyler	R-R	6-2	175	3-22-89	0	1	6.19	13	0	0	0	16	18	11	11	2	5	20	.281	.300	.273	11.25	2.81
Gibson, Trevor	R-R	6-3	225	9-6-86	1	1	3.76	18	0	0	0	26	23	14	11	1	5	28	.240	.342	.172	9.57	1.71
Gonzalez, Juan	R-R	6-2	206	4-5-90	1	6	7.13	14	13	1	0	66	89	58	52	7	35	39	.337	.310	.350	5.35	4.80
Hancock, Kyle	R-R	6-3	185	8-20-87	3	5	5.01	11	11	0	0	50	54	32	28	5	14	45	.281	.309	.266	8.05	2.50
Hungerman, Josh	L-L	6-3	195	9-8-86	0	0	0.00	1	0	0	0	1	1	0	0	0	0	1	.200	.250		9.00	0.00
Junker, Steve	L-L	6-5	180	9-18-86	0	2	6.23	14	0	0	0	17	24	17	12	0	17	14	.324	.286	.333	7.27	8.83
McKinney, Clint	L-L	6-1	200	11-17-86	0	3	6.00	18	0	0	1	21	30	14	14	2	8	14	.357	.481	.298	6.00	3.43
Rodriguez, Juan	B-R	6-2	186	9-15-88	0	0	12.79	7	0	0	0	6	5	11	9	0	17	4	.227	.286	.200	5.68	24.16
Rose, Chad	R-R	6-2	200	2-17-88	3	3	4.61	23	0	0	5	27	28	18	14	1	13	37	.252	.167	.284	12.18	4.28
Schnaitmann, Nick	R-R	6-6	190	11-16-89	1	2	3.91	5	4	0	0	23	28	14	10	2	5	15	.308	.250	.324	5.87	1.96
Testa, Ricky	R-R	6-3	225	4-8-87	0	0	4.50	7	0	0	0	13	15	6	5	1	3	6	.288	.350	.250	10.38	2.08
Tilford, Clint	R-R	6-3	195	4-2-88	2	4	6.94	11	5	0	1	35	45	32	27	3	19	27	.302	.295	.305	6.94	4.89
Timlin, Mike	R-R	6-4	210	3-10-66	0	0	0.00	2	1	0	0	2	1	0	0	0	0	4	.167	.250	.000	0.00	0.00
Vargas, Jonathan	L-L	6-2	150	5-29-89	4	5	4.61	13	13	0	0	57	58	36	29	5	32	31	.270	.400	.249	4.92	5.08

	B-T	HT	WT	DOB	W	L	ERA	G	GS	CG	SV	IP	H	R	ER	HR	BB	SO	AVG	vLH	vRH	K/9	BB/9
Vopinek, Billy	R-R	6-3	200	11-16-85	0	1	4.09	15	0	0	0	22	27	22	10	3	9	13	.297	.250	.317	5.32	3.68
Woods, Coty	R-R	6-2	190	3-14-88	2	1	4.43	17	0	0	2	22	21	12	11	1	10	19	.244	.333	.180	7.66	4.03

Fielding

Catcher	PCT	G	PO	A	E	DP	PB
Garneau	.994	22	156	24	1	4	7
Valdez	.980	30	176	18	4	3	4
Whitby	.969	28	201	17	7	4	8

First Base	PCT	G	PO	A	E	DP
Clark	.986	52	462	45	7	54
Jacobsen	.991	25	209	16	2	28

Second Base	PCT	G	PO	A	E	DP
Altobelli	.959	11	19	28	2	5
Hernandez	.900	3	3	6	1	1
Nina	.958	34	56	103	7	24

	PCT	G	PO	A	E	DP
Rivera	.977	17	38	48	2	19
Scott	1.000	1	2	2	0	0
Squier	.912	11	18	34	5	9

Third Base	PCT	G	PO	A	E	DP
Altobelli	.845	21	14	46	11	1
Arenado	.899	49	33	92	14	9
Rivera	.889	3	2	6	1	1
Squier	.917	4	5	6	1	3

Shortstop	PCT	G	PO	A	E	DP
Hernandez	.905	21	37	77	12	22
Rivera	.667	2	3	3	3	2

	PCT	G	PO	A	E	DP
Scott	.939	33	42	113	10	23
Squier	.864	20	26	50	12	15

Outfield	PCT	G	PO	A	E	DP
Barnes	1.000	48	59	4	0	1
Crousset	.818	5	9	0	2	0
DiNatale	.978	33	41	3	1	2
Hines	1.000	18	30	0	0	0
Kandilas	.929	25	33	6	3	2
Laurent	.927	54	71	5	6	1
Mesa	.951	56	97	1	5	0
Squier	1.000	2	1	0	0	0

DSL ROCKIES

ROOKIE

DOMINICAN SUMMER LEAGUE

Batting	B-T	HT	WT	DOB	AVG	vLH	vRH	G	AB	R	H	2B	3B	HR	RBI	BB	HBP	SH	SF	SO	SB	CS	SLG	OBP
Adames, Cristhian	B-R	6-0	160	7-26-91	.231	.263	.225	36	121	17	28	6	0	1	19	18	3	7	2	24	8	3	.306	.340
Castillo, Engels	R-R	6-3	194	7-25-90	.067	.000	.083	8	15	3	1	0	0	0	0	1	1	0	0	0	9	0	0	.067	.125
Ciriaco, Juan	R-R	5-9	155	7-6-90	.303	.200	.329	35	99	17	30	0	0	0	11	15	2	3	0	23	9	1	.303	.405
De Jesus, Kelvin	R-R	5-9	167	11-22-88	.267	.182	.278	27	90	16	24	3	0	0	17	14	3	3	3	9	3	3	.300	.373
De La Cruz, Robert	R-R	5-11	189	10-10-89	.190	.217	.183	44	116	5	22	3	1	0	5	9	2	5	0	31	1	2	.233	.260
De Leon, Miguel	R-R	6-2	195	8-5-91	.214	.207	.216	41	126	14	27	9	1	3	17	10	3	3	3	45	1	1	.373	.282
Mejia, Deyvi	R-R	6-2	195	11-3-89	.227	.211	.231	39	110	6	25	6	0	3	16	13	5	0	1	27	1	1	.364	.333
Ortega, Rafael	L-R	5-11	160	5-15-91	.324	.381	.313	70	256	45	83	7	8	0	39	32	2	6	6	23	39	12	.414	.395
Ramirez, Michael	R-R	5-10	165	4-27-90	.190	.111	.212	43	126	14	24	4	0	0	10	11	10	4	2	20	1	0	.222	.302
Reyes, Gabriel	R-R	6-0	166	4-28-91	.261	.267	.260	51	157	21	41	3	1	1	14	25	7	11	0	26	15	13	.312	.386
Rivera, Jose	R-R	5-10	170	4-18-90	.204	.286	.190	14	49	7	10	2	0	0	3	2	1	1	0	5	0	2	.245	.250
Rogers, John	R-R	6-2	189	12-13-89	.240	.125	.257	48	125	24	30	5	0	0	5	13	6	2	0	37	8	7	.280	.340
Roja, Yafistel	B-R	5-11	150	10-26-91	.255	.256	.255	63	247	32	63	3	1	0	12	25	0	6	1	45	15	9	.275	.322
Soriano, Wilson	R-R	5-9	140	12-31-91	.200	.261	.188	52	135	22	27	7	0	0	16	15	4	8	3	11	5	5	.252	.293
Sosa, Francisco	R-R	6-4	180	2-27-90	.291	.237	.304	57	199	23	58	8	1	2	29	22	8	1	2	54	16	6	.372	.381
Valera, Smit	R-R	6-1	168	7-14-90	.262	.250	.264	61	202	33	53	6	2	1	15	10	4	15	0	31	15	6	.327	.310
Yan, Julian	R-R	6-2	180	11-27-91	.197	.167	.205	47	152	17	30	7	1	2	14	22	2	5	0	45	1	7	.296	.307

Pitching	B-T	HT	WT	DOB	W	L	ERA	G	GS	CG	SV	IP	H	R	ER	HR	BB	SO	AVG	vLH	vRH	K/9	BB/9
Acosta, Amin	L-L	6-1	170	9-25-91	0	0	2.25	15	4	0	1	32	21	16	8	1	18	41	.174	.100	.180	11.53	5.06
Brazoban, Gustavo	R-R	6-3	159	8-13-91	2	2	2.09	9	8	0	0	39	31	13	9	0	18	34	.217	.278	.196	7.91	4.19
Cabrera, Edwar	L-L	6-0	160	10-20-87	1	0	1.16	7	3	0	0	31	16	5	4	0	10	50	.145	.111	.149	14.52	2.90
Campos, Albert	R-R	6-4	222	2-4-91	2	6	4.11	25	5	0	5	50	50	33	23	2	14	31	.259	.260	.259	5.54	2.50
Garcia, Carlos	L-L	6-0	175	3-25-91	1	0	4.38	11	0	0	0	12	9	7	6	0	8	6	.220	.500	.171	4.38	5.84
Garcia, Joan	L-L	6-2	158	3-26-91	0	0	3.86	10	0	0	0	12	13	6	5	0	8	7	.277	.333	.273	5.40	6.17
Gonzalez, Juan	R-R	6-2	206	4-5-90	2	2	1.25	4	4	0	0	22	11	8	3	0	6	19	.145	.100	.161	7.89	2.49
Gonzalez, Nelson	R-R	6-1	168	2-15-90	5	5	3.18	27	2	0	0	51	60	29	18	0	17	50	.294	.265	.303	8.82	3.00
Hernandez, Jefri	R-R	6-1	170	4-27-91	3	0	2.96	28	0	0	7	27	21	11	9	0	14	25	.214	.042	.270	8.23	4.61
Hurtado, Ramon	R-R	6-4	180	11-1-91	2	4	4.38	13	7	0	0	39	39	22	19	6	12	10	.265	.386	.214	2.31	2.77
Medrano, Carlos	R-R	6-0	190	1-28-91	0	1	9.82	8	2	0	0	7	15	11	8	0	6	4	.385	.625	.323	4.91	7.36
Mejias, Alving	R-R	6-1	185	12-26-91	5	1	1.24	13	11	0	0	72	51	16	10	0	6	70	.194	.184	.198	8.71	0.75
Montilla, Manuel	R-R		205	9-7-91	1	4	3.89	13	9	0	0	35	34	29	15	0	28	27	.248	.330	.221	7.01	7.27
Morillo, Scarly	R-R	6-1	175	6-17-89	0	0	10.80	6	0	0	0	5	9	6	6	0	8	6	.263	.375	.182	10.80	14.40
Ortiz, Elvin	L-L	6-3	180	11-8-91	1	0	9.82	7	0	0	0	7	7	11	8	1	10	6	.241	.333	.231	7.36	12.27
Pacheco, Anthony	R-R	6-1	160	10-6-89	2	2	5.19	11	0	0	0	17	20	12	10	2	6	16	.290	.238	.313	8.31	3.12
Pena, Raul	L-L	6-0	195	2-16-87	6	4	2.25	15	13	1	0	72	63	26	18	2	19	60	.232	.162	.243	7.50	2.88
Sanchez, Miguel	R-R	6-2	190	6-12-90	1	3	3.98	19	2	0	0	41	41	33	18	1	20	27	.261	.255	.264	5.98	4.43
Sanchez, Waler	R-R	6-1	180	3-23-92	0	0	5.40	6	0	0	0	3	4	3	2	0	3	3	.286	.300	.250	8.10	8.10
Santana, Argenis	R-R	6-1	190	11-14-90	0	0	10.00	9	0	0	0	9	10	11	10	0	9	7	.270	.100	.333	7.00	9.00
Suarez, Rafael	R-R	6-0	200	5-14-89	0	0	3.00	5	0	0	0	9	5	3	3	0	1	9	.152	.154	.150	9.00	1.00

Fielding

Catcher	PCT	G	PO	A	E	DP	PB
De Jesus	.991	25	186	24	2	0	8
Mejia	.978	14	76	14	2	0	2
Ramirez	.993	42	263	41	2	1	11

First Base	PCT	G	PO	A	E	DP
De Leon	.982	34	263	14	5	18
Reyes	.996	28	224	13	1	13
Rogers	.944	3	16	1	1	2
Valera	.987	19	142	5	2	11

Second Base	PCT	G	PO	A	E	DP
Adames	.875	2	4	3	1	1
Ciriaco	.875	5	15	6	3	0
Reyes	1.000	2	2	6	0	2

	PCT	G	PO	A	E	DP
Rivera	1.000	9	22	25	0	5
Roja	.932	39	92	99	14	24
Soriano	.945	22	33	53	5	7

Third Base	PCT	G	PO	A	E	DP
Adames	.923	9	7	29	3	2
De Leon	1.000	1	0	1	0	0
Reyes	.880	9	5	17	3	1
Rivera	1.000	2	0	4	0	0
Soriano	.885	18	14	32	6	2
Valera	.880	42	43	89	18	10

Shortstop	PCT	G	PO	A	E	DP
Adames	.923	23	39	57	8	7
Ciriaco	.933	23	34	64	7	6

	PCT	G	PO	A	E	DP
Roja	.895	22	39	63	12	12
Soriano	.942	9	13	36	3	2
Valera	.667	1	0	2	1	0

Outfield	PCT	G	PO	A	E	DP
Castillo	1.000	5	4	0	0	0
De La Cruz	.957	34	40	5	2	0
Ortega	.992	67	120	7	1	2
Reyes	1.000	12	23	1	0	0
Rogers	1.000	22	17	2	0	2
Sosa	.964	55	80	1	3	0
Yan	.929	47	61	4	5	1

Detroit Tigers

SEASON IN A SENTENCE: Detroit was in first place in the American League Central for most of the season, but faded badly down the stretch, allowing the Twins to catch them and force a one-game playoff, which the Tigers lost 6-5 in an epic 12 innings.

HIGH POINT: May 8 featured one of the best pitching duels of the season, when Tigers ace Justin Verlander outdueled Cleveland's Cliff Lee, tossing a two-hit shutout with 11 strikeouts as the Tigers won 1-0.

LOW POINT: In game 163, the Tigers got a run in the eighth inning to force extra innings. They took a one-run lead in the 10th, but the Twins tied it up in the bottom of the 10th against Tigers closer Fernando Rodney and won it in the 12th. The Metrodome was shaking with excitement and the wind was out of the Tigers' sails.

NOTABLE ROOKIES: Righthander Rick Porcello, the Tigers' first-round draft pick in 2007, was so impressive during big league spring training that he jumped from high Class A in 2008 to the Opening Day big league rotation. He more than held his own, going 14-9, 3.96. In the bullpen, righthander Ryan Perry, the team's No. 2 prospect behind Porcello heading into the year, compiled a 3.79 ERA in 53 appearances. Catcher Alex Avila was also a pleasant surprise in jumping from Double-A to the big league backup job; he remains rookie-eligible for 2010.

KEY TRANSACTIONS: The Tigers took a chance by trading outfielder Matt Joyce to the Rays for righthander Edwin Jackson before the season, and it paid off. Jackson went 13-9, 3.62 over 214 innings and made the American League all-star team. Detroit tried to bolster its rotation down the stretch by trading lefthanders Luke French and Mauricio Robles for lefthander Jarrod Washburn. Statistically, Washburn was in the middle of a career year, but he fizzled in Detroit, going 1-3, 7.33 and missing time with an injured knee.

DOWN ON THE FARM: The performance of graduated top prospects was a feather in the organization's cap, but many of their other top prospects stagnated or were plagued by injuries. Second baseman Scott Sizemore continued to impress with his steady bat. He broke his left ankle in the Arizona Fall League, but should be ready by spring training. First baseman Ryan Strieby and righthander Cody Satterwhite missed time this year with wrist and shoulder injuries, respectively.

OPENING DAY PAYROLL: $115,085,145

PLAYERS OF THE YEAR

MAJOR LEAGUE	MINOR LEAGUE
Justin Verlander rhp	**Alex Avila** c
19-9, 3.45	(Double-A)
Led AL in IP (245), SO	.264/.365/.450
(269), SO/9 (10.088)	23 2B, 12 HR

ORGANIZATION LEADERS

BATTING		*Minimum 250 at-bats
MAJORS		
*AVG	Miguel Cabrera	.324
*OPS	Miguel Cabrera	.942
HR	Miguel Cabrera	34
RBI	Miguel Cabrera	103
MINORS		
*AVG	Kelly, Don, Toledo	.331
R	Boesch, Brennan, Erie	89
H	Sizemore, Scott, Erie/Toledo	160
TB	Boesch, Brennan, Erie	269
2B	Sizemore, Scott, Erie/Toledo	39
3B	Nunez, Gustavo, West Michigan	10
HR	Boesch, Brennan, Erie	28
RBI	Boesch, Brennan, Erie	93
BB	Wyatt, Brent, West Michigan	67
SO	Hessman, Mike, Toledo	171
SB	Nunez, Gustavo, West Michigan	45
*OBP	Kelly, Don, Toledo	.404
*SLG	Boesch, Brennan, Erie	.510

PITCHING		†Minimum 75 innings
MAJORS		
W	Justin Verlander	19
†ERA	Justin Verlander	3.45
SO	Justin Verlander	269
MINORS		
W	Lugo, Ruddy, Toledo	13
L	Brown, Brooks, Erie/Toledo	13
†ERA	Putkonen, Luke, West Michigan	3.13
G	Stohr, Tyler, West Michigan	52
GS	Putkonen, Luke, West Michigan	28
SV	Stohr, Tyler, West Michigan	19
IP	Nickerson, Jonah, Erie	165
BB	Kibler, Jon, Erie	68
SO	Gagnier, L.J., Lakeland/Erie	134
†AVG	Gagnier, L.J., Lakeland/Erie	.246

General Manager: Dave Dombrowski. **Farm Director:** Dan Lunetta. **Scouting Director:** David Chadd.

Class	Team	League	W	L	PCT	Finish*	Manager(s)
Majors	Detroit Tigers	American	86	77	.528	6th (14)	Jim Leyland
Triple-A	Toledo Mud Hens	International	73	70	.510	6th (14)	Larry Parrish
Double-A	Erie SeaWolves	Eastern	71	70	.504	6th (12)	Tom Brookens
High A	Lakeland Flying Tigers	Florida State	55	75	.423	11th (12)	Andy Barkett
Low A	West Michigan Whitecaps	Midwest	81	59	.579	t-3rd (14)	Joe DePastino
Short-season	Oneonta Tigers	New York-Penn	35	39	.473	9th (14)	Howie Bushong
Rookie	GCL Tigers	Gulf Coast	29	30	.492	9th (16)	Basilio Cabrera

Overall 2009 Minor League Record 344 343 .501 16th (30)

*Finish in overall standings (No. of teams in league). †League champion.

ORGANIZATION STATISTICS

DETROIT TIGERS

AMERICAN LEAGUE

Batting	B-T	HT	WT	DOB	AVG	vLH	vRH	G	AB	R	H	2B	3B	HR	RBI	BB	HBP	SH	SF	SO	SB	CS	SLG	OBP
Anderson, Josh	L-R	6-2	195	8-10-82	.242	.211	.247	74	165	22	40	4	4	0	16	8	1	1	0	22	13	2	.315	.282
2-team total (44 Kansas City)					.240	—	—	118	283	42	68	7	4	1	24	13	1	1	0	43	25	5	.304	.276
Avila, Alex	L-R	5-11	210	1-29-87	.279	.400	.255	29	61	9	17	4	0	5	14	10	0	0	1	18	0	0	.590	.375
Cabrera, Miguel	R-R	6-4	240	4-18-83	.324	.315	.327	160	611	96	198	34	0	34	103	68	5	0	1	107	6	2	.547	.396
Dlugach, Brent	R-R	6-4	195	3-3-83	.000	.000	.000	5	3	1	0	0	0	0	0	0	0	0	0	2	0	0	.000	.000
Everett, Adam	R-R	6-0	180	2-5-77	.238	.273	.217	118	345	43	82	21	0	3	44	22	4	15	4	61	5	2	.325	.288
Granderson, Curtis	L-R	6-1	185	3-16-81	.249	.183	.275	160	631	91	157	23	8	30	71	72	2	3	2	141	20	6	.453	.327
Guillen, Carlos	B-R	6-1	215	9-30-75	.242	.244	.241	81	277	36	67	10	3	11	41	39	3	0	3	56	1	3	.419	.339
Huff, Aubrey	L-R	6-4	235	12-20-76	.189	.125	.194	40	106	8	20	6	2	2	13	10	1	0	0	13	0	0	.302	.265
2-team total (110 Baltimore)					.241	—	—	150	536	59	129	30	1	15	85	51	5	0	5	87	0	6	.384	.310
Inge, Brandon	R-R	5-11	190	5-19-77	.230	.243	.225	161	562	71	129	16	1	27	84	54	17	1	3	170	2	5	.406	.314
Kelly, Don	L-R	6-4	190	2-15-80	.250	.125	.271	31	56	8	14	3	1	0	3	4	1	1	0	10	1	0	.339	.311
Laird, Gerald	R-R	6-1	225	11-13-79	.225	.248	.218	135	413	49	93	23	2	4	33	40	10	10	4	68	5	0	.320	.306
Larish, Jeff	L-R	6-2	200	10-11-82	.216	.000	.235	32	74	13	16	3	1	4	7	15	0	0	1	25	0	1	.446	.344
Ordonez, Magglio	R-R	6-0	215	1-28-74	.310	.352	.291	131	465	54	144	24	2	9	50	51	0	0	2	65	3	1	.428	.376
Polanco, Placido	R-R	5-10	195	10-10-75	.285	.266	.292	153	618	82	176	31	4	10	72	36	9	7	5	46	7	2	.396	.331
Raburn, Ryan	R-R	6-0	185	4-17-81	.291	.278	.305	113	261	44	76	11	2	16	45	26	2	1	1	60	5	4	.533	.359
Ramirez, Wilkin	R-R	6-2	190	10-25-85	.364	.333	.500	15	11	6	4	0	1	1	3	1	0	0	1	3	0	0	.818	.385
Ryan, Dusty	R-R	6-4	220	9-2-84	.154	.083	.214	12	26	1	4	1	0	0	4	4	0	0	0	12	0	1	.192	.267
Santiago, Ramon	B-R	5-11	175	8-31-79	.267	.270	.267	93	262	29	70	6	2	7	35	17	4	10	3	57	1	2	.385	.318
Sardinha, Dane	R-R	6-0	215	4-8-79	.097	.077	.111	12	31	1	3	1	0	0	3	0	0	1	2	16	0	0	.129	.091
Thames, Marcus	R-R	6-2	220	3-6-77	.252	.257	.248	87	258	33	65	11	1	13	36	29	1	0	6	72	0	2	.453	.323
Thomas, Clete	L-R	5-11	195	11-14-83	.240	.245	.239	102	275	46	66	13	3	7	39	33	1	1	0	77	3	0	.385	.324
Treanor, Matt	R-R	6-0	210	3-3-76	.000	.000	.000	4	13	0	0	0	0	0	0	0	1	0	0	4	0	0	.000	.071

Pitching	B-T	HT	WT	DOB	W	L	ERA	G	GS	CG	SV	IP	H	R	ER	HR	BB	SO	AVG	vLH	vRH	K/9	BB/9
Bonderman, Jeremy	R-R	6-2	220	10-28-82	0	1	8.71	8	1	0	0	10	16	10	10	4	8	5	.364	.278	.423	4.35	6.97
Bonine, Eddie	R-R	6-5	220	6-6-81	1	1	4.46	10	4	0	0	34	40	19	17	7	12	19	.308	.299	.317	4.98	3.15
Dolsi, Freddy	R-R	6-0	160	1-9-83	1	0	1.69	6	0	0	0	11	13	6	2	0	4	3	.310	.368	.261	2.53	3.38
Fien, Casey	R-R	6-2	195	10-21-83	0	1	7.94	9	0	0	0	11	13	11	10	2	6	9	.289	.188	.345	7.15	4.76
Figaro, Alfredo	R-R	6-0	175	7-7-84	2	2	6.35	5	3	0	0	17	23	13	12	3	10	16	.324	.480	.239	8.47	5.29
French, Luke	L-L	6-4	220	9-13-85	1	2	3.38	7	5	0	0	29	33	13	11	2	11	19	.275	.277	.274	5.83	3.38
2-team total (8 Seattle)					4	5	5.21	15	12	0	0	67	87	45	39	11	28	42	—	—	—	5.61	3.74
Galarraga, Armando	R-R	6-4	180	1-15-82	6	10	5.64	29	25	0	0	144	158	93	90	24	67	95	.284	.309	.257	5.95	4.20
Jackson, Edwin	R-R	6-3	210	9-9-83	13	9	3.62	33	33	1	0	214	200	93	86	27	70	161	.247	.247	.248	6.77	2.94
Lambert, Chris	R-R	6-1	205	3-8-83	0	1	14.85	2	0	0	0	7	12	11	11	3	6	4	.400	.421	.364	5.40	8.10
2-team total (4 Baltimore)					0	1	10.22	6	0	0	0	12	20	14	14	5	7	11	—	—	—	8.03	5.11
Lyon, Brandon	R-R	6-1	195	8-10-79	6	5	2.86	65	0	0	3	79	56	25	25	7	31	57	.205	.205	.205	6.52	3.55
Miner, Zach	R-R	6-3	200	3-12-82	7	5	4.29	51	5	0	1	92	101	49	44	11	45	62	.281	.256	.302	6.04	4.39
Ni, Fu-Te	L-L	6-0	170	11-14-82	0	0	2.61	36	0	0	0	20	9	9	3	11	21	.187	.113	.289	6.10	3.19
Perry, Ryan	R-R	6-4	200	2-13-87	0	1	3.79	53	0	0	0	62	56	30	26	7	38	60	.246	.294	.206	8.76	5.55
Porcello, Rick	R-R	6-5	200	12-27-88	14	9	3.96	31	31	0	0	171	176	81	75	23	52	89	.267	.281	.248	4.69	2.74
Rapada, Clay	R-L	6-5	200	3-9-81	0	0	5.40	3	0	0	0	3	4	2	2	1	2	2	.286	.333	.250	5.40	5.40
Rincon, Juan	R-R	5-11	210	1-23-79	1	0	5.23	7	0	0	0	10	12	6	6	2	6	10	.293	.438	.200	8.71	5.23
Robertson, Nate	R-L	6-2	225	9-3-77	2	3	5.44	28	6	0	0	50	59	33	30	4	28	35	.295	.295	.295	6.34	5.07
Rodney, Fernando	R-R	5-11	220	3-18-77	2	5	4.40	73	0	0	37	76	70	38	37	8	41	61	.249	.269	.223	7.26	4.88
Seay, Bobby	L-L	6-2	235	6-20-78	6	3	4.25	67	0	0	0	49	46	23	23	3	17	37	.253	.261	.239	6.84	3.14
Verlander, Justin	R-R	6-5	225	2-20-83	19	9	3.45	35	35	3	0	240	219	99	92	20	63	269	.243	.248	.237	10.09	2.36
Washburn, Jarrod	L-L	6-1	195	8-13-74	1	3	7.33	8	8	0	0	43	51	35	35	12	16	21	.300	.204	.339	4.40	3.35
2-team total (20 Seattle)					9	9	3.78	28	28	1	0	176	160	77	74	23	49	100	—	—	—	5.11	2.51
Willis, Dontrelle	L-L	6-4	225	1-12-82	1	4	7.49	7	7	0	0	34	37	28	28	4	28	17	.294	.306	.289	4.54	7.49
Zumaya, Joel	R-R	6-3	210	11-9-84	3	3	4.94	29	0	0	1	31	34	18	17	5	22	30	.274	.344	.206	8.71	6.39

Fielding

Catcher	PCT	G	PO	A	E	DP	PB
Avila	1.000	25	101	7	0	0	4
Laird	.997	135	844	78	3	7	9
Ryan	1.000	12	60	6	0	0	1
Sardinha	1.000	12	90	7	0	2	1
Treanor	1.000	4	28	0	0	0	0

First Base	PCT	G	PO	A	E	DP
Cabrera	.995	153	1215	105	7	128
Guillen	1.000	2	19	0	0	2
Kelly	1.000	2	7	0	0	1
Laird	1.000	1	1	0	0	1
Larish	1.000	11	68	5	0	4
Raburn	1.000	10	35	2	0	6
Thames	1.000	2	3	0	0	1

Second Base	PCT	G	PO	A	E	DP
Kelly	—	1	0	0	0	0
Polanco	.997	151	290	439	2	112
Santiago	1.000	29	33	52	0	15

Third Base	PCT	G	PO	A	E	DP
Dlugach	1.000	2	1	3	0	0
Inge	.955	161	143	281	20	41
Kelly	1.000	4	2	5	0	1
Larish	1.000	1	1	1	0	0
Raburn	.600	6	2	4	4	0
Santiago	—	2	0	0	0	0

Shortstop	PCT	G	PO	A	E	DP
Dlugach	—	2	0	0	0	0

Everett	.969	116	161	282	14	70
Santiago	.975	69	78	159	6	35

Outfield	PCT	G	PO	A	E	DP
Anderson	.976	65	79	4	2	1
Granderson	.993	160	400	4	3	2
Guillen	.975	42	79	0	2	0
Kelly	1.000	20	29	1	0	0
Ordonez	.987	104	149	6	2	1
Raburn	.967	87	136	9	5	2
Ramirez	1.000	5	4	1	0	0
Thames	1.000	20	19	0	0	0
Thomas	.978	100	173	5	4	3

TOLEDO MUD HENS   TRIPLE-A

INTERNATIONAL LEAGUE

Batting	B-T	HT	WT	DOB	AVG	vLH	vRH	G	AB	R	H	2B	3B	HR	RBI	BB	HBP	SH	SF	SO	SB	CS	SLG	OBP
Ciriaco, Audy	R-R	6-3	195	6-16-87	.160	.222	.125	7	25	2	4	0	0	0	0	1	0	0	0	4	0	0	.160	.192
Clevlen, Brent	R-R	6-2	190	10-27-83	.265	.331	.235	128	479	61	127	26	5	16	64	42	3	6	1	139	10	1	.441	.328
Dlugach, Brent	R-R	6-4	195	3-3-83	.294	.317	.283	125	466	58	137	36	4	9	59	39	3	4	5	137	5	3	.446	.349
Flores, Angel	R-R	6-0	200	8-16-86	—	—	—	1	0	0	0	0	0	0	0	0	0	0	0	0	0	0	—	—
Frazier, Jeff	R-R	6-3	195	8-10-82	.308	.364	.281	105	399	52	123	24	1	11	54	20	1	0	9	49	1	2	.456	.336
Gosse, Mike	L-R	5-7	165	5-30-86	.313	.000	.500	4	16	1	5	0	0	1	3	0	0	0	0	2	0	0	.500	.313
Guillen, Carlos	R-L	6-1	215	9-30-75	.571	—	.571	2	7	2	4	0	0	0	1	2	0	0	0	1	0	0	.571	.667
Hernandez, Keith	R-R	5-11	212	8-13-84	.200	.333	.111	4	15	3	3	2	0	0	2	0	0	0	0	2	0	0	.333	.200
Hessman, Mike	R-R	6-5	215	3-5-78	.217	.254	.202	131	466	58	101	30	3	23	77	65	11	2	4	171	3	1	.442	.324
Kelly, Don	L-R	6-4	190	2-15-80	.331	.325	.333	105	372	57	123	20	6	6	40	43	3	2	0	51	27	4	.465	.404
Larish, Jeff	L-R	6-2	200	10-11-82	.265	.178	.312	61	211	38	56	13	0	6	26	42	4	0	0	56	2	2	.412	.397
Leon, Maxwell	B-R	5-11	190	6-27-84	.161	.333	.091	10	31	2	5	0	0	1	6	2	1	0	0	4	0	1	.258	.235
Raburn, Ryan	R-R	6-0	185	4-17-81	.255	.176	.300	12	47	11	12	3	0	5	9	7	1	0	1	13	2	1	.638	.357
Ramirez, Wilkin	R-R	6-2	190	10-25-85	.258	.304	.237	113	434	69	112	18	6	17	51	41	4	0	2	143	33	10	.445	.326
Rhymes, Will	L-R	5-9	155	4-1-83	.260	.291	.248	109	404	48	105	17	6	3	41	36	3	10	2	58	20	8	.354	.324
Roberson, Ryan	R-R	6-5	240	8-1-83	.227	.270	.205	84	295	27	67	19	0	7	36	24	5	0	2	89	1	3	.363	.294
Rockett, Michael	R-R	6-1	180	7-26-87	.167	.000	.200	2	6	1	1	1	0	0	0	0	0	0	0	1	0	0	.333	.167
Ryan, Dusty	R-R	6-2	220	9-2-84	.257	.311	.234	63	202	25	52	8	1	10	35	29	3	1	0	64	2	0	.455	.359
Sardinha, Dane	R-R	6-0	215	4-8-79	.178	.270	.136	38	118	10	21	7	0	3	16	11	1	3	2	34	0	0	.314	.250
Sizemore, Scott	R-R	6-0	185	1-4-85	.308	.298	.314	71	292	49	90	22	1	8	33	29	4	5	0	49	14	1	.473	.378
St. Pierre, Max	R-R	6-0	175	4-17-80	.248	.405	.187	45	149	16	37	8	0	6	18	10	1	2	0	15	0	0	.423	.300
Thames, Marcus	R-R	6-2	220	3-6-77	.245	.167	.270	12	49	6	12	0	0	2	6	5	0	0	0	14	0	0	.367	.315
Thomas, Clete	L-R	5-11	195	11-14-83	.291	.226	.320	45	175	27	51	17	1	1	17	26	3	0	1	49	18	3	.417	.390
Tyner, Jason	L-L	6-1	180	4-23-77	.172	.300	.148	20	64	6	11	0	1	0	2	4	2	2	0	11	1	1	.203	.243
Worth, Danny	R-R	6-1	185	9-30-85	.212	.245	.196	41	151	9	32	4	1	0	4	11	0	0	0	40	3	1	.252	.265

Pitching	B-T	HT	WT	DOB	W	L	ERA	G	GS	CG	SV	IP	H	R	ER	HR	BB	SO	AVG	vLH	vRH	K/9	BB/9
Bonderman, Jeremy	R-R	6-2	220	10-28-82	1	4	4.24	14	3	0	1	34	40	17	16	4	7	26	.290	.292	.289	6.88	1.85
Bonine, Eddie	R-R	6-5	220	6-6-81	4	5	4.41	17	17	1	0	102	112	54	50	9	16	51	.280	.302	.265	4.50	1.41
Brown, Brooks	L-R	6-3	210	6-20-85	3	13	4.71	20	18	0	0	113	120	63	59	9	55	48	.276	.296	.264	3.83	4.39
Bump, Nate	R-R	6-2	195	7-24-76	7	1	2.38	10	10	1	0	68	58	20	18	3	10	33	.235	.235	.235	4.37	1.32
Chiavacci, Ron	R-R	6-0	240	9-5-77	1	5	5.24	20	4	0	2	46	58	29	27	6	25	34	.309	.263	.339	6.60	4.86
Dolsi, Freddy	R-R	6-0	160	1-9-83	4	3	3.83	39	0	0	10	52	49	27	22	2	19	31	.249	.217	.263	5.40	3.31
Drucker, Scott	R-R	6-1	192	5-30-82	8	3	4.78	29	16	0	0	113	116	63	60	13	38	77	.267	.303	.247	6.13	3.03
Fien, Casey	R-R	6-2	195	10-21-83	2	1	3.41	42	0	0	14	58	51	23	22	5	15	66	.237	.268	.218	10.24	2.33
French, Luke	L-L	6-4	220	9-13-85	4	4	2.98	13	13	1	0	82	71	32	27	6	20	72	.237	.215	.245	7.93	2.20
Ketchner, Ryan	L-L	6-1	190	4-19-82	2	0	0.56	2	2	1	0	16	11	1	1	0	2	6	.196	.182	.200	3.38	1.13
Lambert, Chris	R-R	6-1	205	3-8-83	6	7	3.55	21	21	1	0	127	121	54	50	8	31	106	.250	.277	.235	7.53	2.20
2-team total (3 Norfolk)					7	9	3.84	24	24	1	0	138	139	63	59	11	34	115	—	—	—	7.48	2.21
Lugo, Ruddy	B-R	6-0	210	5-22-80	13	9	4.07	25	25	1	0	142	148	77	64	14	57	82	.273	.306	.254	5.21	3.62
Ni, Fu-Te	L-L	6-0	170	11-14-82	3	0	2.60	24	0	0	0	35	31	10	10	4	9	32	.240	.184	.275	8.31	2.34
Oliveros, Lester	R-R	5-11	178	5-28-88	0	0	0.00	1	0	0	0	2	2	0	0	0	1	3	.250	.500	.000	13.50	4.50
Perry, Ryan	R-R	6-4	200	2-13-87	1	0	2.63	8	0	0	3	14	13	4	4	1	4	12	.245	.261	.233	7.90	2.63
Rainwater, Josh	R-R	6-1	220	4-9-85	1	3	5.76	17	3	0	3	30	34	26	19	3	11	22	.288	.366	.247	6.67	3.34
Rapada, Clay	R-L	6-5	200	3-9-81	4	2	2.76	42	0	0	5	46	50	15	14	1	17	47	.282	.210	.322	9.26	3.35
Regas, Kris	L-L	6-4	205	11-15-79	0	1	5.63	7	0	0	0	8	9	5	5	4	1	8	.281	.200	.318	9.00	1.13
Regilio, Nick	R-R	6-2	205	9-4-78	0	1	3.60	8	0	0	0	15	16	8	6	1	13	11	.291	.150	.371	6.60	7.80
Robertson, Nate	R-L	6-2	225	9-3-77	1	1	1.89	5	5	0	0	19	19	7	4	1	4	21	.271	.250	.278	9.95	1.89
Rusch, Matt	R-R	5-11	180	5-20-83	2	4	4.86	38	1	0	1	74	90	45	40	9	24	48	.307	.320	.300	5.84	2.92
Sborz, Jay	R-R	6-4	210	1-24-85	1	0	2.25	2	0	0	0	4	1	1	1	1	1	5	.077	.200	.000	11.25	2.25
Simons, Zach	L-R	6-3	200	5-23-85	3	0	2.45	11	0	0	1	18	15	5	5	3	4	13	.231	.267	.220	6.38	1.96
Stanley, Patrick	R-R	6-7	200	5-6-84	0	0	0.00	1	0	0	0	3	2	0	0	0	2	5	.200	.250	.167	16.88	6.75
Williamson, Scott	R-R	6-0	195	2-17-76	0	0	11.81	5	0	0	2	5	10	8	7	0	3	4	.400	.545	.286	6.75	5.06
Willis, Dontrelle	L-L	6-4	225	1-12-82	1	2	4.81	5	5	0	0	24	22	13	13	1	17	15	.244	.261	.239	5.55	6.29
Zumaya, Joel	R-R	6-3	210	11-9-84	0	0	0.00	3	0	0	0	4	3	0	0	0	0	5	.200	.000	.273	11.25	0.00

Fielding

Catcher	PCT	G	PO	A	E	DP	PB
Flores	—	1	0	0	0	0	
Hernandez	.889	4	15	1	2	0	1
Hessman	1.000	1	0	0	0	0	
Ryan	.995	63	403	28	2	2	3
Sardinha	.988	38	231	17	3	4	2
St. Pierre	.980	45	268	24	6	4	1

First Base	PCT	G	PO	A	E	DP
Hernandez	—	1	0	0	0	0
Hessman	.963	14	96	8	4	14
Kelly	.993	14	121	14	1	11
Larish	.994	54	465	24	3	42
Leon	1.000	6	50	3	0	4
Roberson	.991	64	525	33	5	52

Second Base	PCT	G	PO	A	E	DP
Gosse	1.000	1	2	8	0	1
Hessman	—	1	0	0	0	0
Kelly	1.000	2	1	5	0	0

	PCT	G	PO	A	E	DP
Rhymes	.989	63	119	160	3	46
Sizemore	.971	62	131	173	9	48
Worth	.981	17	32	21	1	6

Third Base	PCT	G	PO	A	E	DP
Ciriaco	—	1	0	0	0	0
Dlugach	.857	3	4	8	2	2
Frazier	—	1	0	0	0	0
Gosse	1.000	1	1	0	0	0
Hessman	.968	110	66	239	10	21
Kelly	.917	6	6	16	2	2
Larish	.909	5	4	6	1	1
Leon	1.000	1	0	1	0	0
Rhymes	.966	11	3	25	1	3
Sizemore	—	1	0	0	0	0
Worth	1.000	14	12	32	0	2

Shortstop	PCT	G	PO	A	E	DP
Ciriaco	.926	7	7	18	2	1
Dlugach	.955	117	148	361	24	76

	PCT	G	PO	A	E	DP
Hessman	1.000	3	1	6	0	2
Kelly	1.000	1	0	4	0	0
Rhymes	.967	6	14	15	1	4
Sizemore	1.000	1	1	4	0	1
Worth	.980	11	20	28	1	6

Outfield	PCT	G	PO	A	E	DP
Clevlen	.976	118	271	12	7	4
Frazier	.981	69	145	7	3	3
Hessman	1.000	3	4	0	0	0
Kelly	.995	78	181	6	1	0
Leon	1.000	2	5	0	0	0
Raburn	.964	9	26	1	1	1
Ramirez	.945	98	183	5	11	1
Rhymes	1.000	2	10	0	0	0
Rockett	1.000	2	4	0	0	0
Thames	1.000	4	5	0	0	0
Thomas	.968	43	89	1	3	0
Tyner	.966	13	28	0	1	0

ERIE SEAWOLVES

DOUBLE-A

EASTERN LEAGUE

Batting	B-T	HT	WT	DOB	AVG	vLH	vRH	G	AB	R	H	2B	3B	HR	RBI	BB	HBP	SH	SF	SO	SB	CS	SLG	OBP
Avila, Alex	L-R	5-11	210	1-29-87	.264	.220	.284	93	329	52	87	23	1	12	55	52	1	3	2	77	2	1	.450	.365
Bertram, Michael	L-R	6-2	220	2-25-84	.285	.156	.330	33	123	21	35	7	3	8	30	13	0	0	0	31	0	0	.585	.353
Boesch, Brennan	L-L	6-6	210	4-12-85	.275	.258	.283	131	527	89	145	26	7	28	93	33	3	1	7	127	11	2	.510	.318
Bourquin, Ron	L-R	6-3	205	4-29-85	.228	.182	.253	37	127	14	29	5	2	5	19	16	0	0	1	42	0	2	.417	.313
Casanova, Adrian	R-R	6-1	210	5-6-83	.154	.250	.111	6	13	0	2	0	0	0	0	2	0	0	0	4	0	0	.154	.267
De Leon, Santo	R-R	6-2	175	11-1-83	.266	.290	.254	86	297	32	79	18	2	7	39	11	3	4	3	67	1	1	.411	.296
Dirks, Andy	L-L	6-0	195	1-24-86	.255	.265	.251	98	361	46	92	14	1	6	44	36	3	2	6	61	11	5	.349	.323
Frazier, Jeff	R-R	6-3	195	8-10-82	.322	.323	.321	23	87	11	28	10	0	1	13	7	1	0	1	13	0	1	.471	.375
Hollimon, Michael	B-R	6-1	185	6-14-82	.212	.240	.203	29	104	15	22	3	3	3	21	17	0	2	1	35	0	1	.385	.320
Iorg, Cale	R-R	6-2	180	9-6-85	.222	.222	.222	129	491	57	109	17	3	11	41	32	4	2	3	149	13	7	.336	.274
Kunkel, Jeffrey	B-R	5-11	200	3-11-83	.218	.211	.221	47	142	14	31	6	0	4	16	13	2	1	2	33	0	1	.345	.289
Leon, Maxwell	R-R	5-11	190	6-27-84	.256	.296	.239	62	234	37	60	11	4	7	31	24	3	8	0	47	6	2	.427	.333
Roof, Shawn	R-R	5-10	175	8-3-84	.261	.255	.264	56	184	21	48	2	3	1	16	12	5	3	1	39	4	2	.321	.322
Scram, Deik	L-R	6-0	180	2-1-84	.252	.263	.247	121	441	75	111	23	8	20	70	63	1	6	6	121	9	2	.476	.342
Sizemore, Scott	R-R	6-0	185	1-4-85	.307	.279	.317	59	228	39	70	17	4	9	33	35	2	3	1	46	7	3	.535	.402
St. Pierre, Max	R-R	6-0	175	4-17-80	.224	.143	.270	16	58	8	13	4	0	2	6	3	3	1	0	11	0	0	.397	.297
Strieby, Ryan	R-R	6-5	235	8-9-85	.303	.308	.301	86	294	64	89	18	1	19	58	57	8	1	2	80	2	0	.565	.427
Tucker, Joe	R-R	5-11	170	1-25-84	.239	.353	.204	26	71	15	17	3	0	2	7	4	0	1	0	15	0	1	.366	.337
Wells, Casper	R-R	6-2	210	11-23-84	.260	.277	.252	86	311	52	81	18	4	15	41	43	11	1	1	103	8	8	.489	.369
White, Christopher	B-R	5-11	170	11-12-87	.189	.143	.200	15	37	6	7	3	0	2	5	1	0	1	2	11	0	0	.432	.200
Worth, Danny	R-R	6-1	185	9-30-85	.239	.341	.193	75	285	33	68	17	3	0	24	26	3	3	1	74	4	5	.319	.308

Pitching	B-T	HT	WT	DOB	W	L	ERA	G	GS	CG	SV	IP	H	R	ER	HR	BB	SO	AVG	vLH	vRH	K/9	BB/9
Below, Duane	L-L	6-2	205	11-15-85	1	0	1.59	2	2	0	0	11	7	4	2	1	6	7	.175	.083	.214	5.56	4.76
Brown, Brooks	L-R	6-3	210	6-20-85	5	0	2.21	6	6	0	0	37	32	9	9	1	8	13	.246	.271	.232	3.19	1.96
Cain, Nolan	R-R	6-3	235	1-2-86	0	1	5.40	4	0	0	0	7	6	4	4	0	3	4	.261	.273	.250	5.40	4.05
Figaro, Alfredo	R-R	6-0	175	7-7-84	6	3	3.60	16	11	0	0	80	67	36	32	8	23	69	.225	.279	.177	7.76	2.59
Gagnier, L.J.	R-R	6-2	210	2-28-85	1	0	2.03	2	2	0	0	13	12	3	3	0	1	11	.231	.227	.233	7.43	2.03
Garcia, Ramon	L-L	6-2	165	10-30-84	4	4	6.14	35	12	0	2	92	132	71	63	12	22	44	.328	.347	.318	4.29	2.14
Gayhart, Jared	L-R	6-3	195	10-29-86	1	1	4.45	10	4	0	0	28	32	17	14	0	18	20	.294	.266	.333	6.35	5.72
Jensen, Brett	R-R	6-7	190	11-29-83	5	5	3.19	43	0	0	12	54	48	20	19	8	18	59	.240	.318	.183	9.89	3.02
Kibler, Jon	L-L	6-4	215	8-10-86	6	9	4.06	27	27	3	0	162	168	85	73	14	68	87	.277	.272	.278	4.84	3.79
Kite, Josh	L-L	6-2	190	3-2-82	2	4	4.04	23	0	0	0	36	39	20	16	5	18	28	.281	.234	.304	7.07	4.54
Marte, Luis	R-R	5-11	170	8-26-86	5	8	4.02	19	17	0	0	105	106	57	47	18	28	84	.259	.308	.220	7.18	2.39
Nickerson, Jonah	R-R	6-1	190	3-9-85	8	12	5.33	28	27	1	0	165	217	108	98	23	44	75	.321	.324	.319	4.08	2.40
Rainwater, Josh	R-R	6-1	220	4-9-85	2	1	2.59	22	2	0	2	42	33	15	12	1	14	32	.219	.298	.170	6.91	3.02
Regas, Kris	L-L	6-4	205	11-15-79	0	1	6.05	14	0	0	1	19	24	14	13	8	8	17	.296	.226	.340	7.91	3.72
Satterwhite, Cody	R-R	6-4	205	1-27-87	4	6	3.47	34	0	0	12	49	46	22	19	5	27	52	.246	.188	.290	9.49	4.93
Sborz, Jay	R-R	6-4	210	1-24-85	1	2	2.52	14	1	0	0	25	16	9	7	3	13	29	.184	.152	.204	10.44	4.68
Simons, Zach	L-R	6-3	200	5-23-85	1	2	2.82	31	0	0	3	51	39	21	16	1	21	50	.209	.192	.219	8.82	3.71
Stanley, Patrick	R-R	6-7	200	1-4-83	6	4	4.57	15	15	0	0	85	79	48	43	14	32	53	.244	.275	.209	5.63	3.40
Waddell, Jason	R-L	6-2	200	11-6-81	1	2	3.14	11	0	0	2	14	11	5	5	0	4	14	.212	.125	.286	8.79	2.51
Weber, Thad	R-R	6-2	200	9-28-84	7	3	4.06	13	13	1	0	75	78	38	34	7	18	44	.273	.226	.331	5.26	2.15
Weinhardt, Robbie	R-R	6-2	205	12-8-85	0	1	2.30	20	0	0	2	31	28	9	8	0	16	32	.233	.206	.263	9.19	4.60
Willis, Dontrelle	L-L	6-4	225	1-12-82	1	0	3.00	1	1	0	0	6	3	2	2	1	3	6	.150	.100	.200	9.00	4.50
Wise, Brendan	L-R	6-2	190	1-9-86	4	1	4.39	21	1	0	2	41	53	21	20	2	12	15	.325	.395	.264	3.29	2.63

Fielding

Catcher	PCT	G	PO	A	E	DP	PB
Avila	.993	82	512	58	4	3	11
Casanova	.968	6	29	1	1	0	0
Kunkel	.996	44	247	24	1	3	1
St. Pierre	.980	16	90	9	2	1	1

First Base	PCT	G	PO	A	E	DP
Avila	1.000	1	14	1	0	0
Bertram	.996	27	207	19	1	22
Bourquin	.991	27	211	13	2	21
Kunkel	.889	1	8	0	1	0
Leon	.982	22	154	11	3	19
Roof	1.000	4	29	2	0	0
Strieby	.993	72	543	44	4	62
Tucker	1.000	1	9	0	0	2

Second Base	PCT	G	PO	A	E	DP
De Leon	.500	1	1	0	1	0
Leon	1.000	1	1	0	0	0
Roof	.933	21	50	47	7	12
Scram	1.000	1	1	2	0	0

Sizemore	.961	56	135	157	12	52
Tucker	1.000	2	1	1	0	0
Worth	.972	65	132	180	9	39

Third Base	PCT	G	PO	A	E	DP
Bertram	.944	5	2	15	1	1
Bourquin	1.000	7	3	13	0	2
De Leon	.953	85	63	162	11	11
Hollimon	.896	27	22	47	8	8
Leon	.889	3	1	7	1	0
Roof	.907	19	14	25	4	3
Tucker	1.000	2	0	6	0	0

Shortstop	PCT	G	PO	A	E	DP
Iorg	.957	123	202	351	25	76

Roof	1.000	12	8	37	0	10
Worth	1.000	11	11	24	0	6

Outfield	PCT	G	PO	A	E	DP
Boesch	.974	122	244	15	7	3
Dirks	.979	61	135	3	3	1
Frazier	1.000	5	9	0	0	0
Leon	1.000	29	35	0	0	0
Roof	1.000	2	2	0	0	0
Scram	.983	92	216	9	4	1
Strieby	.909	20	28	2	3	0
Tucker	1.000	15	22	0	0	0
Wells	.982	83	211	10	4	4
White	.952	10	20	0	1	0

LAKELAND FLYING TIGERS

HIGH CLASS A

FLORIDA STATE LEAGUE

Batting	B-T	HT	WT	DOB	AVG	vLH	vRH	G	AB	R	H	2B	3B	HR	RBI	BB	HBP	SH	SF	SO	SB	CS	SLG	OBP
Alvino, Billy	R-R	5-11	200	9-2-87	.268	.222	.281	13	41	8	11	2	0	0	3	2	2	0	0	7	0	0	.317	.333
Bertram, Michael	L-R	6-2	220	2-25-84	.281	.333	.268	82	292	34	82	19	3	10	47	20	1	0	2	54	3	0	.469	.327
Carlson, Chris	R-R	6-4	230	1-7-84	.237	.254	.230	73	241	28	57	9	1	13	29	29	4	0	2	64	0	0	.444	.326
Casanova, Adrian	R-R	6-1	210	5-6-83	.158	.083	.181	51	152	18	24	5	1	1	15	13	5	2	1	45	0	1	.224	.246
Castillo, Luis	R-R	5-11	160	5-15-89	.200	—	.200	3	10	1	2	0	0	0	0	0	0	0	0	1	0	0	.200	.200
Ciriaco, Audy	R-R	6-3	195	6-16-87	.262	.320	.246	121	443	55	116	17	5	11	59	20	3	1	3	89	15	4	.397	.296
Cruz, Jordan	L-R	6-0	210	4-30-86	.162	.111	.179	11	37	3	6	0	1	0	2	1	0	0	0	11	0	0	.216	.184
De Leon, Santo	R-R	6-2	175	11-1-83	.262	.310	.236	26	84	12	22	5	0	0	5	4	0	0	1	17	0	0	.321	.292
Dirks, Andy	L-L	6-0	195	1-24-86	.330	.308	.338	27	103	11	34	5	0	0	18	13	1	0	0	11	10	2	.379	.410
Garcia, Avisail	R-R	6-3	190	6-12-91	.250	—	.250	3	8	1	2	0	0	0	0	0	0	0	0	2	0	0	.250	.250
Gosse, Mike	L-R	5-7	165	5-30-86	.243	.333	.231	24	74	9	18	3	1	1	12	5	0	0	0	9	2	2	.351	.291
Grullon, Luis	R-R	6-3	200	9-12-87	.184	.231	.167	18	49	5	9	2	0	0	3	4	2	0	0	18	0	0	.224	.273
Guillen, Carlos	B-R	6-1	215	9-30-75	.250	.000	.333	5	12	3	3	1	0	0	0	4	0	0	0	3	0	0	.333	.438
Henry, Justin	L-R	6-3	180	4-30-85	.257	.265	.255	116	424	56	109	14	4	0	43	45	2	6	1	40	22	7	.304	.331
Kaiser, Kody	B-R	5-9	185	4-6-85	.267	.216	.281	50	165	27	44	9	4	5	21	23	3	0	2	55	9	2	.461	.363
Kunkel, Jeffrey	B-R	5-11	200	3-11-83	.192	.000	.227	8	26	0	5	2	0	0	2	0	1	0	1	7	0	0	.269	.214
Laster, Jeramy	R-R	6-1	185	4-5-85	.231	.214	.236	86	295	37	68	13	2	12	35	19	2	1	4	109	4	4	.410	.278
Leon, Maxwell	B-R	5-11	190	6-27-84	.286	.667	.240	8	28	2	8	2	1	0	3	0	0	0	0	7	0	0	.429	.364
Loyola, Maiko	R-R	5-11	180	7-19-85	.209	.125	.226	42	139	11	29	8	1	0	10	8	0	1	2	34	1	4	.281	.248
Martinez, Francisco	R-R	6-1	180	9-1-90	.167	.375	.000	6	18	1	3	0	0	0	2	0	0	0	0	3	1	0	.167	.167
Newton, Jordan	R-R	5-10	195	8-29-85	.263	.293	.255	75	266	40	70	19	3	8	29	16	4	0	3	80	9	4	.447	.311
Perez, Hernan	R-R	6-0	160	3-26-91	.264	.278	.259	21	72	7	19	4	1	0	3	0	1	1	0	21	0	0	.347	.289
Peter, Kyle	L-R	6-2	185	2-4-86	.222	.357	.200	35	99	14	22	2	1	0	6	19	2	3	0	29	13	1	.263	.358
Rodriguez, Julio	R-R	6-2	200	8-3-89	.286	.200	.500	2	7	1	2	0	0	0	0	0	0	0	0	0	0	0	.286	.286
Roof, Shawn	R-R	5-10	175	8-3-84	.258	.600	.192	8	31	5	8	1	0	1	3	2	0	0	0	5	4	1	.355	.303
Thomas, Devin	B-R	5-11	195	2-22-85	.265	.274	.262	75	272	38	72	19	3	4	48	25	3	0	1	86	2	1	.401	.332
Tomas, Roger	B-R	5-8	185	4-17-86	.141	.174	.130	32	92	7	13	4	0	0	6	5	0	3	3	16	0	0	.185	.180
Tucker, Joe	R-R	5-11	170	1-25-84	.252	.262	.248	67	218	29	55	7	2	0	14	21	11	4	0	44	3	3	.303	.348
White, Christopher	B-R	5-11	170	11-12-87	.235	.237	.235	90	319	36	75	12	4	4	34	28	3	3	0	69	14	6	.335	.303
Workman, Josh	L-R	6-1	200	11-4-85	.297	.342	.283	55	158	21	47	8	1	1	12	20	1	3	1	38	3	3	.380	.378

Pitching	B-T	HT	WT	DOB	W	L	ERA	G	GS	CG	SV	IP	H	R	ER	HR	BB	SO	AVG	vLH	vRH	K/9	BB/9
Below, Duane	L-L	6-2	205	11-15-85	1	4	3.14	6	6	0	0	29	22	11	10	4	14	38	.208	.226	.200	11.93	4.40
Cain, Nolan	R-R	6-3	235	1-2-86	0	1	3.38	13	0	0	0	19	18	8	7	2	4	11	.254	.227	.265	5.30	1.93
Feeney, Trevor	R-R	6-1	185	6-4-86	2	6	4.44	32	10	0	3	79	117	47	39	4	20	49	.351	.355	.348	5.58	2.28
Furbush, Charlie	L-L	6-5	215	4-11-86	6	7	3.96	24	23	0	0	111	111	59	49	10	32	93	.257	.229	.266	7.52	2.59
Gagnier, L.J.	R-R	6-2	210	2-28-85	9	10	3.83	23	22	2	0	134	126	65	57	15	40	123	.247	.263	.234	8.26	2.69
Gayhart, Jared	L-R	6-3	195	10-29-86	0	0	0.77	7	0	0	0	12	5	1	1	0	0	10	.128	.176	.091	7.71	0.00
Graham, Drew	R-R	6-1	240	6-23-86	0	0	3.21	8	0	0	0	14	12	5	5	2	4	13	.245	.261	.231	8.36	2.57
Green, Scott	R-R	6-7	240	8-10-85	3	4	3.25	32	0	0	11	36	42	21	13	3	14	35	.296	.324	.268	8.75	3.50
Guichardo, Rayni	L-L	6-1	165	8-13-91	0	0	3.00	1	1	0	0	5	3	2	2	0	2	1	.200	.250	.231	1.80	3.60
Hess, Andrew	R-R	6-4	210	11-6-84	7	11	3.28	23	20	0	0	123	144	56	45	7	27	56	.295	.305	.286	4.09	1.97
Hoffman, Matt	L-L	6-2	195	11-18-88	3	7	6.79	16	10	1	0	62	79	52	47	9	21	32	.309	.286	.318	4.62	3.03
Jacobson, Brett	R-R	6-6	205	11-9-86	1	3	3.74	35	0	0	6	55	51	30	23	6	17	44	.243	.307	.197	7.16	2.77
Ketchner, Ryan	L-L	6-1	190	4-19-82	1	4	4.66	10	7	0	0	39	46	26	20	2	6	33	.289	.250	.303	7.68	1.40
Linder, Chad	R-L	6-2	210	1-30-85	4	3	5.40	32	1	0	2	50	51	34	30	3	20	35	.258	.267	.252	6.30	3.60
Mejia, Miguel	R-R	6-2	210	1-19-88	0	0	4.50	2	0	0	0	4	3	2	2	1	0	3	.214	.143	.286	6.75	0.00
Moody, Nolan	L-R	6-1	200	9-27-85	1	0	5.79	2	0	0	0	5	5	3	3	1	1	2	.278	.200	.375	1.93	5.79
Oliveros, Lester	R-R	5-11	178	5-28-88	4	2	4.17	34	0	0	2	54	53	27	25	5	16	58	.249	.277	.231	9.67	2.67
Perinar, Gary	R-R	6-0	200	2-10-86	0	0	27.00	1	0	0	0	1	2	3	3	0	4	1	.400	.667	.000	9.00	36.00
Robles, Mauricio	L-L	5-10	160	3-5-89	4	2	3.60	7	7	0	0	35	34	16	14	3	14	40	.256	.314	.235	10.29	3.60
Sborz, Jay	R-R	6-4	210	3-24-85	0	0	0.00	1	0	0	0	1	0	0	0	0	1	1	.125	.000	.250	3.38	3.38
Sorensen, Mark	R-R	6-3	205	2-21-86	1	2	6.88	7	7	0	0	34	57	29	26	7	7	17	.358	.321	.397	4.50	1.85
Stanley, Patrick	R-R	6-7	200	1-4-83	1	0	1.40	8	1	0	0	19	11	3	3	1	6	18	.162	.111	.195	8.38	2.79
Waite, Robb	R-R	6-3	210	1-9-87	1	0	3.86	10	0	0	0	16	13	7	7	1	6	3	.213	.200	.226	1.65	3.31
Weber, Thad	R-R	6-2	200	9-28-84	4	4	2.13	12	12	1	0	68	54	19	16	6	11	40	.217	.223	.212	5.32	1.46

	B-T	HT	WT	DOB	ERA	G				IP	H	R	ER	HR	BB	SO	AVG	vLH	vRH	K/9	BB/9

Name	B-T	HT	WT	DOB																					AVG	vLH	vRH	SLG	OBP
Weinhardt, Robbie	R-R	6-2	205	12-8-85	1	1	0.85	22	0	0	3	32	24	5	3	2	10	40	.200	.265	.155	11.37	2.84
Willis, Dontrelle	L-L	6-4	225	1-12-82	0	1	5.14	1	1	0	0	7	8	4	4	1	0	2	.308	.500	.250	2.57	0.00
Wise, Brendan	L-R	6-2	190	1-9-86	1	1	3.32	14	0	0	2	19	19	7	7	1	3	10	.271	.240	.289	4.74	1.42
Wood, Austin	L-L	6-2	195	11-2-86	0	0	0.00	3	0	0	0	5	4	0	0	0	4	.222	.167	.250	7.20	0.00
Zumaya, Joel	R-R	6-3	210	11-9-84	0	1	11.57	2	2	0	0	2	3	5	3	1	5	4	.300	.333	.286	15.43	19.29
Zumaya, Richard	R-R	6-0	180	11-10-89	0	1	7.11	4	0	0	0	6	6	5	5	0	6	3	.261	.333	.182	4.26	8.53

Fielding

Catcher	PCT	G	PO	A	E	DP	PB
Alvino	1.000	12	77	2	0	0	0
Casanova	.997	51	304	32	1	1	8
Kunkel	1.000	8	69	6	0	1	2
Newton	.993	62	361	36	3	2	8
Rodriguez	1.000	2	7	0	0	0	0

First Base	PCT	G	PO	A	E	DP
Bertram	.993	34	277	20	2	29
Carlson	.988	29	226	11	3	17
De Leon	1.000	1	2	1	0	0
Grullon	.966	8	52	5	2	3
Henry	1.000	2	3	0	0	0
Thomas	.988	63	532	26	7	42

Second Base	PCT	G	PO	A	E	DP
Gosse	.941	12	22	26	3	6
Henry	.979	86	148	222	8	50
Leon	.667	1	0	2	1	0

	PCT	G	PO	A	E	DP
Perez	.982	10	19	36	1	7
Roof	.857	2	2	4	1	0
Tomas	1.000	2	0	1	0	0
Tucker	.983	28	48	66	2	11

Third Base	PCT	G	PO	A	E	DP
Bertram	.900	33	22	50	8	3
De Leon	.895	26	19	49	8	3
Grullon	.667	3	0	2	1	0
Henry	1.000	7	6	13	0	3
Martinez	.889	5	3	5	1	0
Perez	.875	2	3	4	1	2
Roof	.900	6	3	15	2	1
Tomas	.954	27	16	46	3	3
Tucker	.875	33	16	47	9	4

Shortstop	PCT	G	PO	A	E	DP
Ciriaco	.944	120	161	342	30	66
Perez	.967	8	10	19	1	2

	PCT	G	PO	A	E	DP
Tomas	.833	2	2	3	1	0
Tucker	1.000	3	8	6	0	3

Outfield	PCT	G	PO	A	E	DP
Castillo	1.000	3	7	0	0	0
Cruz	.947	8	18	0	1	0
Dirks	1.000	26	46	1	0	0
Garcia	1.000	2	4	0	0	0
Guillen	1.000	1	2	0	0	0
Henry	1.000	28	66	4	0	1
Kaiser	.927	45	76	0	6	0
Laster	.963	78	124	5	5	0
Loyola	.988	41	82	3	1	0
Peter	.980	34	89	7	2	1
Tucker	1.000	2	3	0	0	0
White	.989	89	173	9	2	2
Workman	1.000	45	71	3	0	1

WEST MICHIGAN WHITECAPS
LOW CLASS A
MIDWEST LEAGUE

Batting	B-T	HT	WT	DOB	AVG	vLH	vRH	G	AB	R	H	2B	3B	HR	RBI	BB	HBP	SH	SF	SO	SB	CS	SLG	OBP
Bourquin, Ron	L-R	6-3	205	4-29-85	.283	.286	.282	81	297	40	84	25	1	3	58	48	4	1	9	77	8	3	.404	.380
Bowen, Joseph	B-R	6-1	190	9-25-87	.247	.237	.251	76	271	27	67	18	1	0	25	25	2	1	1	72	1	1	.321	.314
Carrithers, Alden	L-R	5-9	165	11-14-84	.307	.250	.325	45	150	29	46	3	3	0	19	24	0	4	3	22	9	5	.367	.395
Douglas, Brandon	R-R	6-0	185	8-27-85	.322	.319	.323	83	329	47	106	11	3	0	35	29	8	1	6	33	9	1	.374	.384
Flores, Angel	R-R	6-0	200	8-16-86	.203	.222	.200	52	182	14	37	4	0	1	12	13	3	0	0	27	1	2	.242	.268
Garcia, Avisail	R-R	6-3	190	6-12-91	.264	.312	.248	81	299	36	79	11	2	1	31	8	4	0	4	70	8	7	.324	.289
Gosse, Mike	L-R	5-7	165	5-30-86	.263	.279	.258	43	167	19	44	11	0	1	28	8	3	0	2	18	0	0	.347	.306
Guez, Ben	R-R	5-10	170	1-24-87	.275	.305	.265	104	404	64	111	34	7	12	64	18	10	3	3	95	11	4	.483	.320
Hernandez, Keith	R-R	5-11	212	8-13-84	.143	.167	.125	4	14	2	2	1	0	0	1	0	0	0	0	2	0	0	.214	.143
Lennerton, Jordan	L-L	6-2	230	2-16-86	.282	.194	.307	119	433	56	122	30	0	12	71	64	1	0	7	127	1	2	.434	.370
Newton, Jordan	R-R	5-10	195	8-29-85	.386	.357	.400	11	44	11	17	3	2	3	9	2	2	1	0	9	0	0	.750	.438
Nowlin, Billy	R-R	6-1	210	12-16-86	.311	.367	.294	112	418	69	130	29	2	13	77	37	20	0	5	67	2	0	.483	.390
Nunez, Gustavo	B-R	5-10	148	2-8-88	.315	.241	.339	112	464	82	146	16	10	5	40	25	11	9	5	62	45	25	.425	.360
Palacios, Luis	R-R	5-10	162	7-7-89	.193	.212	.186	40	135	16	26	7	0	2	11	1	3	0	3	39	1	0	.289	.211
Perez, Hernan	R-R	6-0	160	3-26-91	.227	.500	.200	12	44	0	10	0	1	0	5	0	0	1	0	8	2	1	.273	.227
Pounds, Bryan	R-R	6-0	195	10-4-85	.284	.266	.289	97	341	55	97	27	2	13	60	57	12	1	6	87	2	2	.402	.399
Salas, Luis	R-R	6-0	172	1-2-89	.240	.250	.238	74	254	33	61	11	4	4	27	11	4	0	2	96	6	3	.362	.280
Tang, Chao-Ting	L-R	5-11	176	10-12-87	.195	.300	.161	21	82	6	16	3	1	0	5	4	0	0	1	26	0	1	.256	.233
Wyatt, Brent	B-R	5-10	185	1-25-85	.242	.126	.274	126	475	87	115	23	6	3	53	67	23	7	5	71	23	9	.335	.360

Pitching	B-T	HT	WT	DOB	W	L	ERA	G	GS	CG	SV	IP	H	R	ER	HR	BB	SO	AVG	vLH	vRH	K/9	BB/9
Bonderman, Jeremy	R-R	6-2	220	10-28-82	1	0	2.57	1	1	0	0	7	6	2	2	0	1	4	.231	.222	.250	5.14	1.29
Cassavecchia, Nick	R-R	6-0	185	12-18-85	0	1	2.61	10	0	0	1	10	6	3	3	1	8	7	.171	.235	.111	6.10	6.97
Conn, Tyler	L-L	6-1	180	11-9-85	6	3	3.21	39	0	0	4	70	65	26	25	3	18	62	.249	.232	.257	7.97	2.31
Crichton, Erik	R-R	5-10	190	6-6-85	7	0	3.99	46	0	0	2	65	81	35	29	5	21	38	.306	.363	.270	5.23	2.89
Crosby, Casey	R-L	6-5	200	9-17-88	10	4	2.41	24	24	0	0	105	70	36	28	3	48	117	.195	.159	.207	10.06	4.13
Gayhart, Jared	L-R	6-3	195	10-29-86	5	3	1.97	24	0	0	3	46	24	11	10	2	15	49	.156	.107	.184	9.66	2.96
Hamilton, Brandon	R-R	6-3	220	12-25-88	5	5	7.09	30	20	0	0	99	112	79	78	11	61	71	.286	.310	.271	6.45	5.55
Hoffman, Matt	L-L	6-2	195	11-18-88	5	0	1.12	7	3	0	1	40	24	5	5	1	8	33	.169	.061	.202	7.36	1.79
Larez, Victor	R-R	6-3	160	5-28-87	5	10	4.33	37	3	0	3	108	107	59	52	8	24	81	.261	.286	.245	6.75	2.00
Mercedes, Melvin	R-R	6-3	190	11-2-90	0	1	11.57	3	0	0	0	2	1	4	3	0	3	1	.125	.000	.200	3.86	11.57
Putkonen, Luke	R-R	6-6	200	5-10-86	7	8	3.13	28	28	1	0	149	148	63	52	3	47	115	.260	.303	.232	6.93	2.83
Robles, Mauricio	L-L	5-10	160	3-5-89	4	4	4.63	11	11	0	0	56	45	29	29	6	27	71	.221	.264	.205	11.34	4.31
Sanz, Luis	R-R	6-1	173	11-19-87	0	1	8.64	8	1	0	0	17	21	16	16	1	8	10	.313	.250	.371	5.40	4.32
Shawler, Anthony	R-R	6-3	188	5-16-87	7	5	3.76	37	8	0	1	108	101	50	45	4	31	98	.253	.284	.231	8.19	2.59
Sorensen, Mark	R-R	6-3	205	2-21-86	8	2	2.44	14	14	1	0	92	83	31	25	3	20	52	.251	.246	.254	5.07	1.95
Stohr, Tyler	L-R	6-2	210	9-19-86	3	4	3.54	52	0	0	19	61	59	26	24	2	16	55	.254	.270	.245	8.11	2.36
Todd, Jade	R-L	6-2	190	3-22-90	0	1	4.41	6	1	0	0	16	10	8	8	0	7	1	.262	.217	.289	3.86	5.51
Villareal, Brayan	R-R	6-0	170	5-10-87	5	5	2.87	26	16	0	2	103	85	40	33	5	34	118	.231	.222	.239	10.28	2.96
Waite, Robb	R-R	6-3	210	1-9-87	1	1	4.56	24	3	0	2	53	50	28	27	1	16	39	.243	.317	.194	6.58	2.70
Wilk, Adam	L-L	6-2	175	12-9-87	2	1	1.49	7	7	0	0	36	30	7	6	2	2	33	.222	.316	.186	8.17	0.50

Fielding

Catcher	PCT	G	PO	A	E	DP	PB
Bowen	.992	76	570	69	5	4	10
Flores	.984	52	376	43	7	4	6
Hernandez	.957	3	22	0	1	1	0
Newton	.983	11	108	9	2	0	0

First Base	PCT	G	PO	A	E	DP
Bourquin	.997	39	361	18	1	32
Lennerton	.996	95	839	74	4	78
Nowlin	.981	5	51	2	1	5
Pounds	.952	3	19	1	1	0
Wyatt	1.000	1	1	0	0	0

Second Base	PCT	G	PO	A	E	DP
Carrithers	.991	26	41	70	1	8
Douglas	.983	81	131	222	6	49
Gosse	.982	23	40	68	2	20
Palacios	1.000	12	11	26	0	4

	PCT	G	PO	A	E	DP
Wyatt	.950	2	9	10	1	2

Third Base	PCT	G	PO	A	E	DP
Bourquin	.899	27	11	51	7	6
Gosse	.875	11	7	21	4	0
Palacios	1.000	13	5	32	0	1
Pounds	.926	86	44	156	16	12
Wyatt	1.000	6	2	18	0	4

Shortstop	PCT	G	PO	A	E	DP
Nunez	.958	112	184	340	23	69
Palacios	.894	12	13	29	5	5
Perez	.938	12	23	22	3	5

	PCT	G	PO	A	E	DP
Wyatt	1.000	6	9	20	0	6

Outfield	PCT	G	PO	A	E	DP
Carrithers	1.000	17	36	1	0	1
Garcia	.934	80	128	13	10	3
Guez	.992	102	252	11	2	4
Nowlin	.848	29	24	4	5	2
Salas	.955	71	101	6	5	0
Tang	1.000	21	28	2	0	0
Wyatt	.991	110	201	12	2	0

ONEONTA TIGERS

SHORT-SEASON

NEW YORK-PENN LEAGUE

Batting	B-T	HT	WT	DOB	AVG	vLH	vRH	G	AB	R	H	2B	3B	HR	RBI	BB	HBP	SH	SF	SO	SB	CS	SLG	OBP
Bishop, Rawley	R-R	6-3	205	11-19-85	.282	.284	.281	71	255	42	72	15	5	5	43	30	11	0	3	51	1	2	.439	.378
Carrithers, Alden	L-R	5-9	165	11-14-84	.182	.000	.200	5	11	1	2	0	0	0	0	3	0	0	0	2	1	0	.182	.357
Espinoza, Alexis	R-R	6-1	180	12-20-88	.256	.298	.230	65	223	24	57	15	6	2	24	14	10	0	1	64	9	6	.404	.327
Gaynor, Wade	R-R	6-4	225	4-19-88	.192	.228	.174	67	234	37	45	10	1	3	23	21	9	0	3	52	8	3	.282	.281
Gulliver, Jimmy	R-L	5-11	175	6-6-86	.196	.167	.205	52	148	20	29	2	1	0	18	19	1	2	4	38	3	1	.223	.285
Hernandez, Keith	R-R	5-11	212	8-13-84	.255	.255	.255	34	102	8	26	7	0	2	12	5	2	1	2	20	1	0	.382	.297
Jaime, Carmelo	B-R	5-9	170	7-16-85	.243	.222	.255	56	169	26	41	5	3	3	25	7	0	5	1	28	3	1	.361	.271
Johnson, Jamie	L-R	5-9	180	4-26-87	.241	.191	.267	73	270	38	65	11	7	3	20	41	2	1	0	50	7	4	.367	.345
Lamont, Wade	L-R	6-2	230	6-25-84	.000	—	.000	2	4	0	0	0	0	0	0	2	0	0	0	3	0	0	.000	.333
Mansilla, Matt	R-R	6-0	185	5-25-86	.175	.184	.169	42	120	11	21	5	0	2	10	15	3	5	1	34	4	1	.267	.281
Murrian, John	R-R	6-1	210	6-15-88	.296	.319	.282	54	186	16	55	16	2	4	35	16	2	3	1	33	2	1	.468	.356
Palacios, Luis	R-R	5-10	162	7-7-89	.248	.185	.309	35	109	14	27	5	1	1	7	6	3	2	0	26	1	1	.339	.305
Rockett, Michael	R-R	6-1	180	7-26-87	.274	.330	.247	70	266	36	73	7	6	3	27	10	3	6	2	41	6	2	.380	.306
Roof, Eric	R-L	6-5	185	11-15-86	.213	.226	.208	41	127	9	27	3	0	2	13	13	1	1	0	35	0	0	.283	.291
Sedon, Chris	R-R	5-10	175	11-6-87	.137	.125	.147	49	139	16	19	2	1	0	7	10	5	1	0	57	4	3	.165	.221

Pitching	B-T	HT	WT	DOB	W	L	ERA	G	GS	CG	SV	IP	H	R	ER	HR	BB	SO	AVG	vLH	vRH	K/9	BB/9
Cassavecchia, Nick	R-R	6-0	185	12-18-85	1	0	0.00	1	0	0	0	3	4	0	0	0	0	2	.333	.500	.167	6.00	0.00
Diaz, Jose	R-R	6-0	160	4-20-89	0	3	8.28	6	6	0	0	25	34	23	23	3	12	15	.333	.289	.368	5.40	4.32
Faulk, Kenny	L-L	6-0	210	5-27-87	2	2	2.83	25	0	0	9	29	22	13	9	3	15	28	.212	.303	.169	8.79	4.71
Gerbe, Jeff	R-R	6-3	200	7-4-84	1	0	6.00	5	5	0	0	15	16	10	10	0	12	14	.281	.375	.212	8.40	7.20
Hamilton, Cory	R-R	6-1	195	4-15-88	4	5	3.02	17	5	0	0	45	47	22	15	1	20	32	.269	.329	.229	6.45	4.03
Hess, Kevan	R-R	6-2	190	3-30-88	2	0	4.30	20	1	0	0	44	50	21	21	0	19	35	.278	.301	.258	7.16	3.89
Kapteyn, Wade	R-R	6-5	210	7-11-87	1	5	7.27	20	0	0	2	35	46	34	28	3	21	16	.311	.369	.265	4.15	5.45
LaLuna, Mike	R-R	6-2	205	2-11-86	3	5	4.96	22	4	0	2	53	46	31	29	3	29	53	.237	.280	.205	9.06	4.96
Mendoza, Clemente	R-R	6-0	170	7-24-90	5	5	3.19	16	11	1	0	73	69	27	26	3	19	50	.247	.246	.248	6.14	2.33
Morrison, Michael	R-R	6-1	210	12-17-88	1	1	3.26	12	0	0	0	19	16	7	7	0	10	26	.222	.167	.262	12.10	4.66
Newman, Nate	R-R	6-5	210	12-17-86	2	1	2.34	12	9	0	0	42	35	15	11	0	20	34	.219	.200	.243	7.23	4.25
Ortega, Jose	R-R	5-11	165	10-12-88	2	2	3.97	25	0	0	1	34	28	19	15	2	23	32	.220	.222	.219	8.47	6.09
Perinar, Gary	R-R	6-0	200	2-10-86	2	2	5.82	6	6	0	0	22	17	15	14	0	22	20	.224	.200	.244	8.31	9.14
Sanz, Luis	R-R	6-1	173	11-19-87	5	4	3.27	14	14	2	0	83	72	33	30	2	35	61	.243	.256	.234	6.64	3.81
Siso, Jose	L-L	5-11	155	3-22-89	0	3	6.84	6	0	0	0	26	40	23	20	0	15	16	.354	.412	.329	5.47	5.13
Torrealba, Michael	R-R	5-11	150	11-19-89	2	1	2.78	23	0	0	2	36	24	12	11	1	18	44	.197	.191	.200	11.10	4.54
Wilk, Adam	L-L	6-2	175	12-9-87	2	0	1.45	7	7	1	0	37	23	7	6	0	5	34	.173	.281	.139	8.20	1.21

Fielding

Catcher	PCT	G	PO	A	E	DP	PB
Hernandez	.993	21	135	9	1	2	4
Murrian	.996	38	247	31	1	6	3
Roof	.993	22	125	19	1	0	8

First Base	PCT	G	PO	A	E	DP
Bishop	.994	70	586	50	4	49
Lamont	1.000	1	3	1	0	0
Roof	1.000	4	24	4	0	1

Second Base	PCT	G	PO	A	E	DP
Carrithers	1.000	2	3	10	0	1
Jaime	.989	20	36	51	1	12
Palacios	.982	13	19	35	1	5
Sedon	.983	41	67	110	3	23

Third Base	PCT	G	PO	A	E	DP
Gaynor	.952	63	31	107	7	7
Jaime	.750	2	3	0	1	0
Palacios	.826	12	8	11	4	1

Shortstop	PCT	G	PO	A	E	DP
Gulliver	.886	47	60	103	21	19
Jaime	.968	30	44	77	4	15
Palacios	.917	3	3	8	1	1

Outfield	PCT	G	PO	A	E	DP
Espinoza	.959	46	70	1	3	0
Johnson	.994	73	159	7	1	2
Mansilla	.973	41	68	4	2	2
Rockett	.964	70	127	6	5	0

GCL TIGERS

ROOKIE

GULF COAST LEAGUE

Batting	B-T	HT	WT	DOB	AVG	vLH	vRH	G	AB	R	H	2B	3B	HR	RBI	BB	HBP	SH	SF	SO	SB	CS	SLG	OBP
Alvino, Billy	R-R	5-11	200	9-2-87	.176	.100	.208	12	34	4	6	0	0	0	2	3	3	1	1	3	0	0	.176	.293
Anderson, Brett	R-R	6-3	185	9-3-90	.216	.176	.235	30	102	9	22	1	0	1	7	5	2	0	2	25	1	2	.255	.261
Castillo, Luis	R-R	5-11	160	5-15-89	.219	.240	.211	52	178	17	39	6	0	1	14	13	1	3	1	25	7	1	.270	.275
Corcino, Edgar	B-R	6-2	190	6-7-92	.160	.333	.105	8	25	2	4	1	0	1	4	4	0	1	0	10	0	0	.320	.276
Cruz, Jordan	L-R	6-0	210	4-30-86	.265	.241	.277	48	166	28	44	15	3	6	29	24	4	1	0	37	7	2	.500	.371
Gomez, Edwin	B-R	6-3	175	8-26-91	.190	.122	.214	45	153	12	29	4	0	0	12	9	0	7	1	31	1	1	.216	.233
Grullon, Luis	R-R	6-3	200	9-12-87	.267	.333	.231	17	60	6	16	5	0	1	8	2	0	0	1	21	0	0	.400	.286
Hernandez, Keith	R-R	5-11	212	8-13-84	.200	.500	.000	2	5	0	1	1	0	0	0	0	0	0	0	2	0	0	.400	.200

Batting	B-T	HT	WT	DOB	AVG	vLH	vRH	G	AB	R	H	2B	3B	HR	RBI	BB	HBP	SH	SF	SO	SB	CS	SLG	OBP
Martinez, Francisco	R-R	6-1	180	9-1-90	.222	.283	.196	43	153	21	34	9	0	2	23	5	3	4	3	38	11	1	.320	.256
McKenna, Pat	R-R	5-10	170	6-24-87	.195	.105	.222	30	82	8	16	0	0	1	8	10	2	2	1	27	4	3	.232	.295
Nunez, Alexander	R-R	5-11	172	5-4-90	.308	.415	.265	41	143	18	44	7	5	5	17	7	3	2	0	31	4	3	.531	.353
Nunez, Gustavo	B-R	5-10	148	2-8-88	.190	.091	.300	6	21	5	4	0	0	1	4	1	1	1	0	5	3	0	.333	.261
Perez, Hernan	R-R	6-0	160	3-26-91	.222	.179	.245	21	81	9	18	9	1	1	9	3	1	1	0	14	2	0	.395	.259
Reina, Adolfo	R-R	6-1	190	1-22-90	.171	.250	.148	23	70	8	12	4	0	3	7	9	2	0	2	18	0	0	.357	.277
Robbins, James	L-L	6-0	225	9-26-90	.361	.286	.379	9	36	4	13	0	1	2	7	2	1	0	0	9	0	0	.583	.410
Rodriguez, Julio	R-R	6-2	200	8-3-89	.198	.211	.193	38	121	11	24	7	0	1	12	4	3	2	1	10	1	1	.281	.240
Rush, Eddie	R-R	5-11	174	1-4-87	.282	.308	.268	31	110	11	31	7	0	0	5	3	1	0	0	23	6	2	.345	.307
Soto, Elvin	L-R	6-2	190	5-6-89	.195	.286	.167	47	149	29	29	4	3	4	15	27	3	3	0	57	3	1	.342	.330
Tang, Chao-Ting	L-R	5-11	176	10-12-87	.307	.286	.315	22	75	13	23	5	0	1	11	8	0	0	0	8	2	0	.413	.373
Taylor, Londell	R-R	6-2	200	9-13-88	.139	.067	.169	41	101	10	14	2	0	2	6	11	2	2	0	47	5	1	.218	.237

Pitching	B-T	HT	WT	DOB	W	L	ERA	G	GS	CG	SV	IP	H	R	ER	HR	BB	SO	AVG	vLH	vRH	K/9	BB/9
Cain, Nolan	R-R	6-3	235	1-2-86	0	0	1.08	4	0	0	0	8	5	3	1	0	1	6	.167	.167	.167	6.48	1.08
Diaz, Jose	R-R	6-0	160	4-20-89	1	4	5.20	9	6	0	0	36	37	25	21	2	6	32	.270	.286	.261	7.93	1.49
Diaz, Robert	L-L	6-2	180	2-12-89	4	3	4.18	18	0	0	0	28	18	14	13	2	24	30	.194	.192	.194	9.64	7.71
Graham, Drew	R-R	6-1	240	6-23-86	0	0	0.00	5	0	0	0	7	2	0	0	0	1	6	.105	.143	.083	8.10	1.35
Guichardo, Rayni	L-L	6-1	165	8-13-91	4	4	1.73	11	11	1	0	68	43	14	13	6	31	48	.189	.185	.190	6.38	4.12
Lebron, Ramon	R-R	6-1	180	2-1-89	3	4	3.73	12	10	0	0	51	45	24	21	1	37	55	.249	.250	.248	9.77	6.57
Manus, Michael	L-L	6-3	240	8-25-86	1	1	6.00	17	0	0	0	24	28	19	16	2	11	21	.280	.250	.289	7.88	4.13
Mejia, Miguel	R-R	6-2	210	1-19-88	0	0	0.00	1	0	0	0	2	0	0	0	0	1	2	.000	—	.000	10.80	5.40
Mercedes, Melvin	R-R	6-0	190	11-2-90	1	1	1.82	26	0	0	16	25	19	9	5	0	14	20	.221	.293	.156	7.30	5.11
Moody, Nolan	L-R	6-1	200	9-23-85	2	1	2.76	10	0	0	1	16	10	5	5	1	5	18	.175	.133	.190	9.92	2.76
Nunez, Marcos	R-R	6-5	210	7-10-89	2	0	6.11	15	1	0	1	28	34	21	19	4	15	21	.304	.267	.328	6.75	4.82
Perinar, Gary	R-R	6-0	200	2-10-86	0	3	8.47	5	2	0	0	17	20	16	16	3	11	18	.303	.292	.310	9.53	5.82
Rondon, Bruce	R-R	6-2	190	12-9-90	0	1	4.76	3	3	0	0	11	12	6	6	0	8	15	.267	.333	.208	11.91	6.35
Samuels, Zach	L-R	6-2	180	10-8-86	2	2	2.56	10	10	0	0	56	53	19	16	3	17	44	.260	.263	.258	7.03	2.72
Siso, Jose	L-L	5-11	155	3-22-89	2	1	2.17	7	5	0	0	29	23	8	7	1	12	22	.213	.077	.232	6.83	3.72
Soto, Giovanni	L-L	6-4	150	5-18-91	4	0	1.18	13	6	0	1	46	33	7	6	0	20	37	.209	.304	.170	7.29	3.94
Todd, Jade	R-L	6-2	190	3-22-90	0	0	1.80	2	0	0	0	5	3	1	1		2	6	.176	.333	.143	10.80	3.60
Wesson, Jared	L-L	6-5	190	1-30-86	1	2	6.23	5	5	0	0	17	22	13	12	2	9	23	.324	.286	.328	14.02	4.67
Wood, Austin	L-L	6-2	195	11-2-86	1	0	9.00	1	0	0	0	1	2	1	1	0	0	1	.400	—	.400	9.00	0.00
Zumaya, Richard	R-R	6-0	180	11-10-89	1	3	5.26	17	0	0	0	26	32	15	15	2	9	31	.327	.250	.364	10.87	3.16

Fielding

Catcher	PCT	G	PO	A	E	DP	PB
Alvino	1.000	10	73	10	0	0	0
Hernandez	1.000	1	3	0	0	0	0
Reina	.974	16	100	12	3	2	5
Rodriguez	.985	38	280	41	5	2	9

First Base	PCT	G	PO	A	E	DP
Grullon	.987	10	75	3	1	7
Robbins	.980	5	48	1	1	11
Soto	.990	45	374	22	4	40

Second Base	PCT	G	PO	A	E	DP
McKenna	.982	26	45	63	2	15

	PCT	G	PO	A	E	DP
Nunez	.972	35	63	77	4	26
Nunez	1.000	1	2	1	0	1

Third Base	PCT	G	PO	A	E	DP
Anderson	.872	18	12	29	6	4
Corcino	1.000	4	2	6	0	0
Martinez	.945	39	38	99	8	9

Shortstop	PCT	G	PO	A	E	DP
Anderson	1.000	2	3	4	0	1
Gomez	.976	34	47	73	3	18
Martinez	—	1	0	0	0	0
McKenna	.875	2	5	1	1	

	PCT	G	PO	A	E	DP
Nunez	.917	4	9	13	2	5
Perez	.987	18	21	53	1	16

Outfield	PCT	G	PO	A	E	DP
Castillo	.991	52	112	4	1	1
Cruz	.969	48	60	2	2	0
Grullon	1.000	3	1	1	0	0
Rush	.967	30	29	0	1	0
Tang	1.000	21	33	1	0	0
Taylor	.981	37	51	1	1	0

DSL TIGERS   ROOKIE

DOMINICAN SUMMER LEAGUE

Batting	B-T	HT	WT	DOB	AVG	vLH	vRH	G	AB	R	H	2B	3B	HR	RBI	BB	HBP	SH	SF	SO	SB	CS	SLG	OBP
Aguasvivas, Juaner	R-R	6-3	225	9-15-89	.257	.327	.240	67	257	36	66	9	0	12	57	22	5	0	2	64	1	2	.432	.325
Azcona, Javier	R-R	6-1	185	9-28-91	.249	.163	.270	63	221	46	55	11	5	4	35	33	4	0	5	54	8	5	.398	.350
Espinoza, Ivan	R-R	6-0	165	1-16-89	.230	.292	.214	46	122	18	28	2	1	0	12	15	2	3	0	20	7	3	.262	.324
Figueroa, Robinson	R-R	6-0	160	3-11-90	.171	.176	.170	43	105	20	18	7	1	0	8	13	6	2	0	32	2	2	.257	.298
Gonzalez, Domingo	R-R	6-1	175	3-10-91	.214	.222	.213	34	98	17	21	2	0	1	12	14	6	0	1	28	3	1	.265	.345
Guzman, Raynolds	R-R	6-0	185	3-16-90	.249	.205	.260	60	225	24	56	6	0	1	20	8	9	0	1	20	3	3	.289	.300
Heredia, Santos	B-L	5-8	170	10-15-89	.235	.129	.259	55	166	33	39	2	1	1	14	40	7	2	0	44	24	9	.277	.404
Leiva, Raul	B-R	6-2	185	1-30-90	.228	.056	.252	47	145	21	33	5	0	0	11	18	2	4	2	20	2	0	.262	.317
Marte, Ernesto	R-R	6-2	190	9-11-89	1.000	—	1.000	1	1	1	1	0	0	0	0	0	0	0	0	0	0	0	1.000	1.000
Moya, Steven	L-R	6-6	220	9-8-91	.252	.324	.238	60	218	36	55	8	0	6	33	33	4	0	0	58	4	2	.372	.361
Ortiz, Samuel	R-R	5-11	155	6-12-91	.242	.208	.247	61	194	34	47	8	0	3	35	32	11	1	5	41	2	3	.330	.372
Pierre, Nelson	B-R	6-0	160	12-23-87	.253	.094	.288	51	178	44	45	5	2	0	15	26	1	3	0	35	32	2	.303	.351
Rijo, Samir	R-R	6-2	205	6-26-90	.279	.316	.272	66	222	39	62	14	6	5	36	34	6	1	1	35	2	2	.464	.388
Turiano, Franklin	B-R	5-11	175	1-16-89	.162	.200	.156	16	37	1	6	1	0	0	2	5	3	1	0	9	0	0	.189	.311

Pitching	B-T	HT	WT	DOB	W	L	ERA	G	GS	CG	SV	IP	H	R	ER	HR	BB	SO	AVG	vLH	vRH	K/9	BB/9
Acosta, Alvin	R-R	6-2	170	6-12-90	4	3	5.46	17	0	0	0	30	29	25	18	1	26	30	.246	.263	.242	9.10	7.89
Andujar, Billis	R-R	6-3	165	5-30-89	1	0	7.71	11	0	0	0	14	17	16	12	0	10	10	.283	.233	.298	6.43	6.43
Calderon, Yinio	R-R	6-4	170	11-16-90	1	0	6.04	14	0	0	0	22	26	18	15	0	24	20	.292	.417	.273	8.06	9.67
Cruz, Antonio	L-L	5-11	160	10-7-91	3	2	3.03	15	6	0	1	39	27	25	13	0	32	31	.182	.250	.176	7.22	7.45
De La Rosa, Edgar	R-R	6-6	215	11-20-90	3	3	5.70	17	11	0	1	54	64	40	34	1	28	40	.299	.333	.290	6.71	4.70
Del Orbe, Emmanuel	R-R	6-3	188	12-20-90	5	3	2.44	13	12	0	0	59	43	23	16	0	29	51	.204	.211	.202	7.78	4.42
Duran, Darlin	L-L	6-0	160	3-3-89	3	2	2.52	14	8	0	0	54	38	22	15	1	26	59	.193	.250	.186	9.89	4.36

	B-T	HT	WT	DOB	W	L	ERA	G	GS	CG	SV	IP	H	R	ER	HR	BB	SO	AVG	vLH	vRH	K/9	BB/9
Encarnacion, Jose	R-R	6-4	190	10-11-90	1	0	10.67	11	0	0	0	14	20	18	17	1	16	13	.333	.286	.340	8.16	10.05
Franco, Ramon	R-R	6-2	170	10-17-91	2	2	2.77	11	6	0	0	39	31	21	12	1	13	42	.209	.273	.191	9.69	3.00
Gonzalez, Eduardo	R-R	6-3	152	11-2-88	1	0	9.31	6	1	0	0	10	11	12	10	3	7	10	.289	.400	.273	9.31	6.52
Medina, Kelvin	L-L	6-4	147	7-30-90	4	3	2.15	14	13	1	0	63	51	28	15	2	27	55	.221	.148	.230	7.90	3.88
Morillo, Gregory	R-R	6-2	180	3-4-92	0	2	11.77	11	0	0	0	13	8	19	17	1	27	10	.178	.000	.195	6.92	18.69
Ortiz, Vladimir	R-R	6-2	186	3-24-89	2	3	3.95	30	0	0	12	43	34	25	19	0	22	39	.215	.313	.190	8.10	4.57
Palacios, Wilsen	R-R	6-3	180	12-15-89	0	1	3.48	7	0	0	1	10	11	4	4	0	0	14	.282	.417	.222	12.19	0.00
Polanco, Yadiel	L-L	6-2	185	3-21-91	1	2	3.18	14	12	0	0	65	60	31	23	2	21	37	.241	.281	.235	5.12	2.91
Stephenson, Zuriel	R-R	6-1	198	5-8-89	0	0	—	1	0	0	0	0	2	5	5	0	3	0	1.000	—	1.000	—
Valdez, Jose	R-R	6-1	167	3-1-90	4	5	5.23	26	0	0	4	31	25	24	18	2	23	30	.231	.250	.226	8.71	6.68

Fielding

Catcher	PCT	G	PO	A	E	DP	PB
Guzman	.988	52	378	44	5	1	12
Leiva	.980	15	84	14	2	0	9
Turiano	.974	7	31	6	1	0	2

First Base	PCT	G	PO	A	E	DP
Aguasvivas	.992	54	469	12	4	42
Leiva	.962	18	123	5	5	8

Second Base	PCT	G	PO	A	E	DP
Heredia	.921	16	31	27	5	10

Ortiz	.945	49	92	97	11	24
Pierre	.949	10	28	28	3	5

Third Base	PCT	G	PO	A	E	DP
Gonzalez	.816	32	16	86	23	4
Leiva	1.000	1	1	0	0	0
Pierre	.933	41	44	96	10	6

Shortstop	PCT	G	PO	A	E	DP
Azcona	.915	62	78	171	23	29
Ortiz	.875	13	14	21	5	4

Pierre	1.000	1	2	3	0	2

Outfield	PCT	G	PO	A	E	DP
Espinoza	.940	36	56	7	4	1
Figueroa	.935	29	41	2	3	0
Heredia	.962	33	50	1	2	1
Moya	.931	59	64	3	5	0
Rijo	.933	65	91	6	7	1

VSL TIGERS   ROOKIE

VENEZUELAN SUMMER LEAGUE

Batting	B-T	HT	WT	DOB	AVG	vLH	vRH	G	AB	R	H	2B	3B	HR	RBI	BB	HBP	SH	SF	SO	SB	CS	SLG	OBP
Alvarado, Jesus	R-R	6-1	160	11-25-91	.249	.227	.254	65	237	30	59	8	2	1	21	17	5	2	1	58	9	3	.312	.312
Cortez, Luis	R-R	6-0	155	1-8-92	.212	.244	.202	61	208	25	44	11	2	2	20	15	9	3	1	55	3	5	.313	.292
De Los Santos, Wondy	B-R	5-9	154	1-3-90	.202	.278	.185	35	99	13	20	5	2	0	9	8	3	1	2	23	3	1	.293	.277
Espinoza, Ivan	R-R	6-0	165	1-16-91	.231	.250	.226	12	39	5	9	1	0	2	2	2	0	0	0	12	1	0	.333	.302
Gomez, Gilbert	R-R	6-0	165	4-30-90	.253	.167	.270	49	146	23	37	11	0	11	27	13	7	0	1	46	1	3	.555	.341
Gomez, Oscar	R-R	5-11	155	3-25-91	.203	.240	.195	54	138	18	28	7	1	1	10	9	4	0	1	46	6	1	.290	.270
Hoyer, Wilfredo	R-R	6-1	180	5-14-91	.171	.083	.188	35	76	4	13	1	1	0	6	6	2	0	0	20	2	0	.211	.250
Machado, Dixon	R-R	6-0	140	2-22-92	.205	.255	.193	63	234	41	48	6	1	3	26	32	5	3	3	32	27	6	.278	.310
Moreno, Alexander	R-R	6-4	185	4-1-90	.275	.233	.284	65	240	37	66	10	4	4	42	24	1	0	3	74	2	2	.400	.340
Navia, Aldo	R-R	6-0	180	11-30-89	.206	.206	.206	47	160	19	33	5	1	1	11	9	4	0	0	27	6	3	.269	.266
Purroy, Gabriel	R-R	5-9	160	4-16-92	.267	.286	.261	65	240	28	64	11	2	7	39	13	5	2	6	40	3	2	.417	.315
Sanz, Luis	R-R	5-10	165	2-23-91	.328	.409	.308	65	229	36	75	11	1	2	30	34	3	0	6	12	4	3	.410	.412
Soledad, Jose	R-R	5-11	165	7-22-92	.194	.154	.204	49	129	9	25	2	0	1	9	19	2	0	2	24	2	0	.233	.206
Suarez, Eugenio	B-R	5-11	155	7-18-91	.262	.293	.255	57	206	29	54	9	3	1	15	17	15	1	1	32	8	4	.350	.360

Pitching	B-T	HT	WT	DOB	W	L	ERA	G	GS	CG	SV	IP	H	R	ER	HR	BB	SO	AVG	vLH	vRH	K/9	BB/9
Aguirre, Gino	R-R	6-2	155	9-12-90	3	3	3.86	13	10	0	2	51	61	34	22	6	9	34	.289	.250	.299	5.96	1.58
Alvarado, Carlos	R-R	6-4	175	10-22-89	0	2	6.47	15	1	0	1	32	48	33	23	3	11	17	.340	.250	.367	4.78	3.09
Alvarez, Carlos	R-R	6-1	175	1-15-91	0	1	13.50	9	0	0	0	9	10	16	14	1	10	7	.250	.385	.185	6.75	9.64
Briceno, Endrys	R-R	6-4	150	7-2-92	0	0	3.41	16	0	0	2	36	36	17	12	4	12	16	.265	.287	.243	4.55	3.41
Carreno, Josue	R-R	6-1	170	6-26-91	3	3	2.36	10	8	0	0	46	43	18	12	1	6	43	.242	.170	.267	8.47	1.18
Celis, Fernando	R-R	6-1	165	3-27-89	4	3	3.69	16	7	0	1	63	56	33	26	4	18	35	.245	.196	.260	4.97	2.56
Espinoza, Juan	L-L	5-11	155	10-20-91	0	5	5.70	11	7	0	0	36	43	31	23	8	14	24	.295	.200	.305	5.94	3.47
Guilarte, Julio	R-R	6-3	170	5-17-92	3	6	6.63	15	11	0	0	58	70	46	43	5	18	53	.298	.356	.278	8.18	2.78
Lopez, Yorfrank	R-R	6-3	170	12-1-90	2	3	2.23	6	6	0	0	32	29	15	8	3	5	22	.246	.313	.221	6.12	1.39
Lozano, Juan	L-L	6-0	175	9-14-89	0	1	6.27	12	0	0	1	19	25	18	13	3	11	14	.316	.300	.319	6.75	5.30
Morandi, Manuel	R-R	6-4	180	8-2-91	0	1	11.85	10	0	0	0	14	18	21	18	4	9	13	.300	.316	.293	8.56	5.93
Mosquera, Yonny	R-R	5-10	170	1-16-91	1	3	4.88	18	0	0	3	31	32	21	17	0	20	25	.278	.375	.253	7.18	5.74
Nesbitt, Angel	R-R	6-1	175	12-4-90	0	0	16.74	13	0	0	0	17	36	32	31	6	12	6	.444	.556	.389	3.24	6.48
Penalver, Frank	R-R	6-0	150	1-19-91	1	2	6.59	10	0	0	0	14	19	11	10	3	9	8	.339	.357	.333	5.27	5.93
Ramirez, Wilfredo	L-L	6-4	210	11-24-87	4	6	3.84	19	6	0	3	61	78	31	26	6	7	65	.313	.400	.306	9.59	1.03
Rondon, Bruce	R-R	6-2	190	12-9-90	0	0	13.50	3	0	0	0	4	5	6	6	0	7	4	.313	1.000	.267	9.00	15.75
Tablante, Jose	L-L	5-10	135	1-18-92	2	4	3.83	15	10	0	0	47	49	29	20	3	30	32	.277	.231	.280	6.13	5.74
Vasquez, Leonel	R-R	6-0	150	2-10-91	1	2	4.06	14	4	0	1	44	50	29	20	4	19	29	.281	.289	.278	5.89	3.86

Fielding

Catcher	PCT	G	PO	A	E	DP	PB
Gomez	1.000	1	1	1	0	0	0
Hoyer	.977	18	76	9	2	0	2
Purroy	.982	39	231	42	5	4	15
Sanz	.989	25	146	30	2	3	4

First Base	PCT	G	PO	A	E	DP
Gomez	.980	31	226	22	5	23
Gomez	.985	10	59	6	1	6
Hoyer	1.000	1	4	0	0	0
Sanz	.994	34	289	20	2	33
Soledad	.968	7	29	1	1	1

Second Base	PCT	G	PO	A	E	DP
Cortez	.940	47	75	114	12	31

De Los Santos	—	1	0	0	0	0
Gomez	.852	11	11	12	4	1
Machado	1.000	2	3	2	0	0
Soledad	.917	7	13	9	2	2
Suarez	.915	17	24	30	5	7

Third Base	PCT	G	PO	A	E	DP
Cortez	.917	5	4	7	1	0
Gomez	.917	22	16	28	4	3
Soledad	.717	25	8	35	17	1
Suarez	.928	40	31	72	8	6

Shortstop	PCT	G	PO	A	E	DP
Cortez	.933	11	11	17	2	2
Machado	.954	61	141	215	17	45

Suarez	.962	6	10	15	1	4

Outfield	PCT	G	PO	A	E	DP
Alvarado	.938	62	111	10	8	2
Alvarez	—	1	0	0	0	0
De Los Santos	.986	31	66	5	1	1
Espinoza	.950	10	18	1	1	1
Gomez	—	1	0	0	0	0
Gomez	.800	8	12	0	3	0
Moreno	.893	62	82	10	11	1
Navia	.962	46	97	3	4	0
Nesbitt	—	1	0	0	0	0

Florida Marlins

SEASON IN A SENTENCE: The Marlins again contended for a playoff spot despite having the game's lowest payroll, and their 87 wins was the third-highest total in franchise history, behind only the championship seasons of 1997 and 2003.

HIGH POINT: The Marlins raced out to an 11-1 start in April, though six of those wins came against the Nationals. The signature win came on April 12, when righthander Josh Johnson outdueled Mets ace Johan Santana in a 2-1 Florida win. Johnson threw a complete game and limited New York to a run on five hits while striking out seven.

LOW POINT: Memories of the Marlins' great start were erased over the next month as they endured an 8-24 stretch that left them 5½ games out of first in the National League East by the time they pulled out of their tailspin. One of the most difficult losses came May 20 in the second game of a doubleheader against Arizona. With the score tied in the late innings, the Marlins missed several chances to win the game and went on to lose 11-9 in 13 innings.

NOTABLE ROOKIES: Chris Coghlan was an infielder in the minors but moved to left field after being called up in May. All he did was hit .321/.390/.460 and win the National League rookie of the year award. Lefthander Sean West, the organization's top pitching prospect entering the season, was called up in May and held his own, though he fizzled in September en route to a 8-6, 4.79 mark. Outfielder Cameron Maybin struggled and was sent back to the minors in May, though he did hit better upon returning in September.

KEY TRANSACTIONS: Aside from calling up rookies like Coghlan and West, the Marlins mostly stood pat. They did try to bolster their playoff hopes at the trade deadline by sending lefthander Aaron Thompson, their first-round pick in 2005, to the Nationals for first baseman Nick Johnson.

DOWN ON THE FARM: Outfielder Mike Stanton cemented his reputation as one of the game's best young power hitters, slugging 28 home runs between high Class A Jupiter and Double-A Jacksonville. One of the organization's bigger disappointments was catcher Kyle Skipworth, a 2008 first-round pick who hit just .208 at low Class A Greensboro. Jacksonville captured the Southern League championship, and the Rookie-level Gulf Coast League affiliate had the best record in the league. Marlins affiliates finished with a 350-341 record, tying them for 13th-best in baseball.

OPENING DAY PAYROLL: $36,834,000

PLAYERS OF THE YEAR

MAJOR LEAGUE	MINOR LEAGUE
Hanley Ramirez ss	**Mike Stanton** of
.342/.410/.543	(High A/Double-A)
NL batting champion,	.255/.311/.455
24 HR, 42 2B, 27 SB	28 HR, 92 RBI

ORGANIZATION LEADERS

BATTING		*Minimum 250 at-bats
MAJORS		
*AVG	Hanley Ramirez	.342
*OPS	Hanley Ramirez	.954
HR	Dan Uggla	31
RBI	Hanley Ramirez	106
MINORS		
*AVG	Ryan, Michael, New Orleans	.300
R	Stanton, Mike, Jupiter/Jacksonville	76
H	Lasater, Ben, Greensboro	140
TB	Stanton, Mike, Jupiter/Jacksonville	240
2B	Lasater, Ben, Greensboro	34
3B	Cousins, Scott, Jacksonville	11
HR	Stanton, Mike, Jupiter/Jacksonville	28
RBI	Stanton, Mike, Jupiter/Jacksonville	92
BB	Mitchell, Lee, Jacksonville/New Orleans	70
SO	Burns, Greg, Jupiter	163
SB	Mattison, Kevin, Greensboro	41
*OBP	Ryan, Michael, New Orleans	.375
*SLG	Miller, Jai, New Orleans	.510

PITCHING		†Minimum 75 innings
MAJORS		
W	Josh Johnson	15
†ERA	Josh Johnson	3.23
SO	Ricky Nolasco	195
MINORS		
W	Dorn, Johnny, Greensboro	11
L	Hand, Brad, Greensboro	13
	Villanueva, Elih, Jupiter/Jacksonville	13
†ERA	Hensley, Clay, New Orleans	3.24
G	Speigner, Levale, New Orleans/Jacksonville	58
GS	Dorn, Johnny, Greensboro	27
	Villanueva, Elih, Jupiter/Jacksonville	27
SV	Peterson, Matt, Jacksonville	37
IP	Villanueva, Elih, Jupiter/Jacksonville	168
BB	Hand, Brad, Greensboro	66
SO	Hand, Brad, Greensboro	122
†AVG	Rosario, Jose, Greensboro/Jupiter	.231

2009 PERFORMANCE

General Manager: Larry Beinfest. **Farm Director:** Jim Fleming. **Scouting Director:** Stan Meek.

Class	Team	League	W	L	PCT	Finish*	Manager(s)
Majors	Florida Marlins	National	87	75	.537	6th (16)	Fredi Gonzalez
Triple-A	New Orleans Zephyrs	Pacific Coast	63	80	.441	14th (16)	Edwin Rodriguez
Double-A	Jacksonville Suns	Southern	82	58	.586	†2nd (10)	Brandon Hyde
High A	Jupiter Hammerheads	Florida State	67	70	.489	8th (12)	Tim Leiper
Low A	Greensboro Grasshoppers	South Atlantic	66	74	.471	13th (16)	Darin Everson
Short-season	Jamestown Jammers	New York-Penn	34	42	.447	11th (14)	Andy Haines
Rookie	GCL Marlins	Gulf Coast	38	17	.691	1st (16)	Jorge Hernandez
Overall 2009 Minor League Record			350	341	.507	t-13th (30)	

*Finish in overall standings (No. of teams in league). †League champion.

ORGANIZATION STATISTICS

FLORIDA MARLINS

NATIONAL LEAGUE

Batting	B-T	HT	WT	DOB	AVG	vLH	vRH	G	AB	R	H	2B	3B	HR	RBI	BB	HBP	SH	SF	SO	SB	CS	SLG	OBP
Amezaga, Alfredo	B-R	5-10	180	1-16-78	.217	.133	.241	27	69	6	15	3	0	0	5	5	0	0	1	16	1	1	.261	.267
Baker, John	L-R	6-1	230	1-20-81	.271	.171	.281	112	373	59	101	25	0	9	50	41	5	2	2	89	0	0	.410	.349
Bonifacio, Emilio	B-R	5-11	195	4-23-85	.252	.315	.223	127	461	72	116	11	6	1	27	34	2	8	4	95	21	9	.308	.303
Cantu, Jorge	R-R	6-3	205	1-30-82	.289	.322	.278	149	585	67	169	42	0	16	100	47	6	0	5	81	3	1	.443	.345
Carroll, Brett	R-R	6-0	210	10-3-82	.234	.258	.213	92	141	18	33	8	2	3	18	11	4	1	1	33	0	0	.383	.306
Coghlan, Chris	L-R	6-0	200	6-18-85	.321	.316	.323	128	504	84	162	31	6	9	47	53	4	3	1	77	8	5	.460	.390
De Aza, Alejandro	L-L	5-11	190	4-11-84	.250	.000	.294	22	20	6	5	1	0	0	3	5	0	1	1	5	0	0	.300	.385
Gload, Ross	L-L	6-1	190	4-5-76	.261	.194	.271	125	230	33	60	10	2	6	30	23	2	1	3	30	0	0	.400	.329
Gonzalez, Andy	R-R	6-3	205	12-15-81	.083	.143	.000	14	12	1	1	0	1	0	0	0	0	0	0	4	0	0	.250	.083
Hayes, Brett	R-R	6-1	200	2-13-84	.273	.333	.250	14	11	5	3	1	0	1	2	0	1	0	0	4	0	0	.636	.333
Helms, Wes	R-R	6-4	225	5-12-76	.271	.273	.270	113	214	18	58	11	0	3	33	13	3	1	3	54	1	1	.364	.318
Hermida, Jeremy	L-R	6-3	220	1-30-84	.259	.189	.282	129	429	48	111	14	2	13	47	56	4	0	2	101	5	2	.392	.348
Johnson, Nick	L-L	6-3	235	9-19-78	.279	.241	.293	35	104	24	29	8	0	2	18	36	6	1	3	18	0	2	.413	.477
2-team total (98 Washington)					.291	—	—	133	457	71	133	24	2	8	62	99	12	1	5	84	2	4	.405	.426
Maybin, Cameron	R-R	6-3	205	4-4-87	.250	.254	.248	54	176	30	44	12	2	4	13	17	1	4	1	51	1	3	.409	.318
Paulino, Ronny	R-R	6-3	245	4-21-81	.272	.290	.250	80	239	24	65	10	1	8	27	25	0	1	1	48	1	0	.423	.340
Ramirez, Hanley	R-R	6-3	225	12-23-83	.342	.316	.352	151	576	101	197	42	1	24	106	61	9	1	5	101	27	8	.543	.410
Ross, Cody	R-L	5-10	195	12-23-80	.270	.284	.266	151	559	73	151	37	1	24	90	34	9	0	2	122	5	2	.469	.321
Sanchez, Gaby	R-R	6-1	235	9-2-83	.238	.333	.200	21	21	2	5	0	0	2	3	2	0	0	0	3	0	0	.524	.304
Uggla, Dan	R-R	5-11	215	3-11-80	.243	.208	.253	158	564	84	137	27	1	31	90	92	7	1	4	150	2	1	.459	.354

Pitching	B-T	HT	WT	DOB	W	L	ERA	G	GS	CG	SV	IP	H	R	ER	HR	BB	SO	AVG	vLH	vRH	K/9	BB/9
Ayala, Luis	R-R	6-2	190	1-12-78	0	3	11.74	10	0	0	0	8	12	10	10	1	6	7	.364	.500	.304	8.22	7.04
Badenhop, Burke	R-R	6-5	220	2-8-83	7	4	3.75	35	2	0	0	72	71	32	30	5	24	57	.260	.250	.269	7.13	3.00
Calero, Kiko	R-R	6-1	210	1-9-75	2	2	1.95	67	0	0	0	60	36	13	13	1	30	69	.180	.187	.176	10.35	4.50
Davidson, Dave	L-L	6-1	200	4-23-84	0	0	45.00	1	0	0	0	1	4	5	5	0	4	3	.571	.500	.667	27.00	36.00
Donnelly, Brendan	R-R	6-3	240	7-4-71	3	0	1.78	30	0	0	2	25	22	8	5	1	9	25	.239	.262	.220	8.88	3.20
Johnson, Josh	L-R	6-7	250	1-31-84	15	5	3.23	33	33	2	0	209	184	77	75	14	58	191	.237	.242	.231	8.22	2.50
Kensing, Logan	R-R	6-1	190	7-3-82	0	1	9.82	6	0	0	0	7	14	8	8	1	5	7	.412	.444	.375	8.59	6.14
2-team total (26 Washington)					1	2	8.92	32	0	0	1	35	54	35	35	8	17	19	—	—	—	4.84	4.33
Koronka, John	L-L	6-0	200	7-3-80	0	2	11.05	2	2	0	0	7	11	11	9	4	7	4	.344	.400	.318	4.91	8.59
Leroux, Chris	L-R	6-6	210	4-14-84	0	0	10.80	5	0	0	0	7	11	8	8	0	4	2	.355	.412	.286	2.70	5.40
Lindstrom, Matt	R-R	6-3	220	2-11-80	2	1	5.89	54	0	0	15	47	54	35	31	5	24	39	.281	.278	.284	7.42	4.56
Martinez, Carlos	R-R	6-2	220	5-26-82	0	0	3.86	2	0	0	0	2	3	1	1	1	2	2	.300	.000	.375	7.71	7.71
Martinez, Cristhian	R-R	6-1	160	3-6-82	1	1	5.13	15	0	0	0	26	27	16	15	2	8	18	.262	.163	.352	6.15	2.73
Meyer, Dan	R-L	6-2	220	7-3-81	3	2	3.09	71	0	0	2	58	47	24	20	7	21	56	.219	.228	.211	8.64	3.24
Miller, Andrew	L-L	6-7	205	5-21-85	3	5	4.84	20	14	0	0	80	85	52	43	7	43	59	.273	.309	.261	6.64	4.84
Nolasco, Ricky	R-R	6-2	230	12-13-82	13	9	5.06	31	31	2	0	185	188	111	104	23	44	195	.259	.251	.268	9.49	2.14
Nunez, Leo	R-R	6-2	180	8-14-83	4	6	4.06	75	0	0	26	69	53	33	31	13	27	60	.230	.234	.225	7.86	3.54
Penn, Hayden	R-R	6-3	200	10-13-84	1	0	7.77	16	1	0	0	22	30	27	19	3	20	27	.319	.400	.245	11.05	8.18
Pinto, Renyel	L-L	6-4	265	7-8-82	4	1	3.23	73	0	0	0	61	53	25	22	4	45	58	.237	.277	.208	8.51	6.60
Sanches, Brian	R-R	6-0	190	8-8-78	4	2	2.56	47	0	0	0	56	50	18	16	5	26	51	.235	.245	.227	8.15	4.15
Sanchez, Anibal	R-R	6-0	220	2-27-84	4	8	3.87	16	16	0	0	86	84	39	37	10	46	71	.253	.231	.276	7.43	4.81
Taylor, Graham	L-L	6-3	225	5-25-84	0	2	8.18	3	3	0	0	11	16	14	10	0	12	5	.340	.455	.306	4.09	9.82
VandenHurk, Rick	R-R	6-5	220	5-22-85	3	2	4.30	11	11	0	0	59	57	29	28	11	21	49	.252	.273	.224	7.52	3.22
Volstad, Chris	R-R	6-8	225	9-23-86	9	13	5.21	29	29	1	0	159	169	100	92	29	59	107	.278	.255	.302	6.06	3.34
West, Sean	L-L	6-8	240	6-15-86	8	6	4.79	20	20	0	0	103	115	62	55	11	44	70	.280	.338	.267	6.10	3.83
Wood, Tim	R-R	6-1	185	11-16-82	1	0	2.82	18	0	0	0	22	22	8	7	2	10	16	.272	.219	.306	6.45	4.03

Fielding

Catcher	PCT	G	PO	A	E	DP	PB
Baker	.992	105	748	42	6	2	5
Paulino	.996	77	511	46	2	1	3

First Base	PCT	G	PO	A	E	DP
Cantu	.993	111	829	38	6	72
Gload	.997	41	266	20	1	23

	PCT	G	PO	A	E	DP
Hayes	1.000	1	2	0	0	1
Helms	.974	4	33	5	1	2
Johnson	.977	33	192	24	5	22

Sanchez	1.000	1	12	0	0	1

Second Base	PCT	G	PO	A	E	DP
Bonifacio	1.000	7	6	13	0	4
Coghlan	1.000	1	2	0	0	0
Uggla	.977	158	264	426	16	95

Third Base	PCT	G	PO	A	E	DP
Bonifacio	.934	86	48	151	14	13
Cantu	.910	45	26	45	7	9
Gonzalez	1.000	2	0	1	0	0

Helms	.935	70	31	70	7	11

Shortstop	PCT	G	PO	A	E	DP
Amezaga	1.000	5	5	15	0	1
Bonifacio	.935	20	11	32	3	5
Gonzalez	1.000	4	0	2	0	0
Ramirez	.983	146	221	349	10	77

Outfield	PCT	G	PO	A	E	DP
Amezaga	1.000	17	33	0	0	0
Bonifacio	1.000	17	23	0	0	0

Carroll	1.000	75	97	5	0	1
Coghlan	.977	123	209	3	5	1
De Aza	.950	11	19	0	1	0
Gload	.917	10	11	0	1	0
Hermida	.995	120	201	3	1	1
Maybin	.992	52	124	1	1	0
Ross	.991	151	337	6	3	3

NEW ORLEANS ZEPHYRS

TRIPLE-A

PACIFIC COAST LEAGUE

Batting	B-T	HT	WT	DOB	AVG	vLH	vRH	G	AB	R	H	2B	3B	HR	RBI	BB	HBP	SH	SF	SO	SB	CS	SLG	OBP
Carroll, Brett	R-R	6-0	210	10-3-82	.233	.214	.240	27	103	16	24	3	1	5	12	8	1	0	0	23	0	1	.427	.295
Coghlan, Chris	L-R	6-0	200	6-18-85	.344	.333	.347	25	96	21	33	9	1	3	22	12	1	0	1	10	9	1	.552	.418
Craig, Matt	B-R	6-3	215	4-16-81	.253	.250	.254	31	95	12	24	6	0	3	8	12	0	0	1	19	0	0	.411	.333
2-team total (59 Iowa)					.264	—	—	90	292	39	77	20	0	7	35	28	2	0	2	53	1	0	.404	.330
Davis, Brad	R-R	6-1	190	12-29-82	.114	.125	.105	10	35	1	4	2	0	0	4	2	0	0	1	10	1	0	.171	.158
Dawkins, Gookie	R-R	6-1	180	5-12-79	.244	.280	.227	90	311	35	76	13	1	5	26	27	6	6	0	78	7	4	.341	.317
De Aza, Alejandro	L-L	5-11	190	4-11-84	.300	.309	.296	87	267	45	80	21	5	8	34	27	4	7	2	53	11	5	.506	.370
Gonzalez, Andy	R-R	6-3	205	12-15-81	.259	.312	.235	102	352	45	91	11	0	8	43	48	3	0	1	79	8	2	.358	.351
Hayes, Brett	R-R	6-1	200	2-13-84	.240	.260	.231	90	321	27	77	15	0	4	37	20	1	4	7	66	2	0	.324	.281
Jenkins, Andy	R-R	6-0	205	7-23-83	.231	.250	.222	5	13	1	3	0	0	1	1	0	0	0	0	2	0	0	.462	.231
Klosterman, Ryan	R-R	5-11	190	5-28-82	.240	.222	.250	12	25	4	6	0	0	1	2	1	0	0	0	5	1	0	.360	.269
Knoedler, Justin	R-R	6-2	215	7-17-80	.182	.222	.167	9	33	3	6	3	0	1	4	1	0	0	1	8	0	0	.364	.200
Lindsey, John	R-R	6-1	245	1-30-77	.251	.228	.259	133	443	53	111	22	1	19	83	38	17	0	4	112	1	2	.433	.331
Matranga, Dave	R-R	6-0	185	1-8-77	.272	.299	.261	95	232	35	63	12	2	7	28	46	7	3	2	64	3	1	.431	.404
Maybin, Cameron	R-R	6-3	205	4-4-87	.319	.387	.288	82	298	44	95	18	8	3	39	38	3	2	2	58	8	2	.463	.399
Mayorson, Manny	R-R	5-9	195	3-10-83	.249	.253	.248	97	337	40	84	11	2	1	20	13	1	10	1	23	11	4	.303	.278
2-team total (5 Las Vegas)					.243	—	—	102	354	42	86	12	2	1	22	15	2	10	1	24	12	4	.297	.277
Miller, Jai	R-R	6-3	205	1-17-85	.289	.276	.295	102	343	55	99	24	2	16	52	38	3	1	5	106	6	3	.510	.360
Mitchell, Lee	R-R	6-1	200	4-21-82	.246	.208	.267	21	69	10	17	4	2	1	8	8	1	0	1	26	0	0	.406	.329
Ontiveros, Emilio	R-R	5-11	170	1-2-85	.188	.167	.200	4	16	1	3	1	0	0	1	0	0	0	0	3	0	0	.250	.188
Purdom, John	R-R	6-2	230	5-28-81	.203	.125	.229	20	64	3	13	2	0	1	11	3	0	2	0	12	0	0	.281	.239
Raynor, John	R-R	6-1	205	1-4-84	.257	.270	.251	123	447	63	115	24	2	6	36	42	6	5	3	121	19	8	.360	.327
Ryan, Michael	L-R	5-11	220	7-6-77	.300	.255	.318	109	367	61	110	25	0	14	66	47	1	0	6	64	2	1	.482	.375
Sanchez, Gaby	R-R	6-1	235	9-2-83	.289	.341	.269	55	190	30	55	18	1	5	33	22	5	1	5	44	5	0	.475	.374
Wilson, Neil	R-R	6-1	190	12-7-83	.250	.130	.298	24	80	6	20	4	0	0	5	5	0	1	0	13	0	0	.300	.294

Pitching	B-T	HT	WT	DOB	W	L	ERA	G	GS	CG	SV	IP	H	R	ER	HR	BB	SO	AVG	vLH	vRH	K/9	BB/9
Ayala, Luis	R-R	6-2	190	1-12-78	0	0	0.00	9	0	0	4	10	4	0	0	0	3	10	.114	.095	.143	9.00	2.70
Badenhop, Burke	R-R	6-5	220	2-8-83	0	1	6.75	2	2	0	0	9	14	7	7	0	4	6	.341	.357	.333	5.79	3.86
Barone, Daniel	R-R	6-2	185	4-24-83	2	6	5.51	13	10	0	0	51	64	31	31	10	11	25	.309	.329	.297	4.44	1.95
Battisto, A.J.	R-R	6-0	193	9-30-83	0	1	3.24	5	0	0	0	8	9	3	3	1	1	9	.281	.421	.077	9.72	1.08
Buente, Jay	R-R	6-2	185	9-28-83	5	1	3.39	35	0	0	1	61	59	24	23	6	32	56	.253	.263	.244	8.26	4.72
Collazo, Willie	L-L	5-8	180	11-7-79	9	5	3.70	34	16	0	0	126	125	57	52	14	35	74	.264	.212	.282	5.27	2.49
Davidson, Dave	L-L	6-1	200	4-23-84	0	0	2.53	10	0	0	0	11	7	5	3	0	4	14	.189	.000	.233	11.81	3.38
DeSalvo, Matt	R-R	6-0	180	9-11-80	1	2	2.70	9	2	0	4	17	16	5	5	1	7	11	.258	.343	.148	5.94	3.78
Field, Nate	R-R	6-2	210	12-11-75	5	4	3.25	49	0	0	9	55	43	25	20	7	22	62	.210	.275	.158	10.08	3.58
Glen, Willie	R-R	6-1	185	10-30-77	1	3	6.92	9	5	0	0	26	36	30	20	4	20	11	.327	.239	.465	3.81	6.92
Glover, Gary	R-R	6-4	225	12-3-76	1	0	0.00	1	1	0	0	5	4	0	0	2	1	7	.211	.250	.182	12.60	1.80
Gunderson, Kyle	R-R	6-3	215	1-31-85	0	0	0.00	1	0	0	0	1	0	0	0	0	0	0	.000	.000	.000	0.00	0.00
Harker, Brett	R-R	6-3	185	7-9-84	0	0	3.18	2	1	0	0	6	8	2	2	1	3	4	.348	.500	.267	6.35	4.76
Hensley, Clay	R-R	5-11	190	8-31-79	8	4	3.24	19	19	1	0	114	105	46	41	8	38	82	.246	.230	.265	6.47	3.00
2-team total (6 Round Rock)					9	4	3.56	25	20	1	0	124	117	55	49	9	45	87	—	—	—	6.31	3.27
Koronka, John	L-L	6-0	200	7-3-80	4	10	4.83	30	23	0	0	129	159	79	69	17	43	77	.303	.285	.308	5.39	3.01
Lawrence, Brian	R-R	6-0	195	5-14-76	3	0	3.00	5	5	0	0	30	25	10	10	5	5	23	.234	.322	.125	6.90	1.50
2-team total (9 Portland)					7	4	5.10	14	13	0	0	83	99	50	47	9	19	49	—	—	—	5.31	2.06
Martinez, Carlos	R-R	6-2	220	5-26-82	0	2	6.75	17	0	0	0	17	23	14	13	4	8	14	.329	.316	.333	7.27	4.15
Miller, Andrew	L-L	6-7	205	5-21-85	1	2	7.71	3	3	0	0	12	9	10	10	0	13	16	.209	.000	.220	12.34	10.03
Mobley, Chris	R-R	5-11	170	8-16-83	3	3	4.37	42	0	0	3	60	76	36	29	5	21	42	.315	.326	.309	6.34	3.17
Nolasco, Ricky	R-R	6-2	230	12-13-82	1	1	2.40	2	2	1	0	15	12	4	4	0	3	12	.222	.227	.219	7.20	1.80
Penn, Hayden	R-R	6-3	200	10-13-84	2	4	4.11	14	13	2	0	70	71	35	32	9	26	62	.258	.253	.264	7.97	3.34
Pinto, Renyel	L-L	6-4	265	7-8-82	0	0	0.00	2	0	0	0	2	1	0	0	0	0	1	.167	.000	.200	4.50	0.00
Sanches, Brian	R-R	6-0	190	8-8-78	1	1	2.04	16	0	0	4	18	13	6	4	1	4	22	.206	.100	.256	11.21	2.04
Santos, Jarrett	R-R	6-4	215	8-18-81	3	5	4.50	23	6	0	0	62	77	39	31	6	6	24	.296	.256	.329	3.48	0.87
Sinkbeil, Brett	R-R	6-2	205	12-26-84	2	8	6.07	47	8	0	0	83	106	65	56	9	44	52	.315	.310	.317	5.64	4.77
Speigner, Levale	R-R	5-11	170	9-24-80	5	3	2.93	35	0	0	1	55	54	24	18	3	15	29	.250	.322	.202	4.72	2.44
Standridge, Jason	R-R	6-4	235	11-9-78	0	0	7.82	6	0	0	0	13	15	11	11	0	11	9	.326	.538	.242	6.39	7.82
Stone, Brad	R-R	6-3	190	5-20-84	0	0	5.17	7	0	0	0	16	17	9	9	1	7	9	.323	.350	.311	5.12	4.02
Trahern, Dallas	R-R	6-3	235	11-29-85	1	3	6.28	6	0	0	0	29	40	20	20	2	13	19	.345	.455	.278	5.97	4.08
Tucker, Ryan	R-R	6-1	205	12-6-86	1	2	8.04	4	4	0	0	16	18	14	14	1	14	7	.295	.233	.355	4.02	8.04
VandenHurk, Rick	R-R	6-5	220	5-22-85	5	2	2.87	11	11	0	0	59	48	20	19	3	16	51	.195	.186	.206	7.69	2.41

	B-T	HT	WT	DOB	W	L	ERA	G	GS	CG	SV	IP	H	R	ER	HR	BB	SO	AVG	vLH	vRH	K/9	BB/9
Vasquez, Carlos	L-L	6-3	230	12-6-82	0	0	11.12	9	0	0	0	11	15	16	14	2	12	14	.300	.286	.306	11.12	9.53
Volstad, Chris	R-R	6-8	225	9-23-86	0	1	6.75	1	1	0	0	4	5	3	3	2	2	7	.333	.182	.750	15.75	4.50
Wood, Mike	R-R	6-2	220	4-26-80	0	2	9.53	8	5	0	1	23	35	24	24	3	14	10	.365	.333	.381	3.97	5.56
2-team total (2 Oklahoma City)					0	2	9.49	10	5	0	1	25	37	26	26	3	14	13	—	—	—	4.74	5.11
Wood, Tim	R-R	6-1	185	11-16-82	1	2	3.18	31	0	0	0	40	42	16	14	1	17	37	.269	.284	.258	8.39	3.86

Fielding

Catcher

	PCT	G	PO	A	E	DP	PB
Davis	.957	10	60	7	3	0	0
Hayes	.995	86	569	40	3	7	6
Jenkins	1.000	3	19	1	0	0	0
Knoedler	1.000	9	48	2	0	0	2
Purdom	.958	15	83	9	4	1	8
Wilson	.994	23	159	8	1	0	3

First Base

	PCT	G	PO	A	E	DP
Craig	1.000	2	10	0	0	0
Hayes	1.000	1	1	0	0	0
Lindsey	.992	95	746	71	7	71
Matranga	1.000	1	7	0	0	0
Mitchell	1.000	4	33	4	0	3
Purdom	1.000	4	15	0	0	0
Ryan	1.000	4	18	4	0	2
Sanchez	.995	45	359	20	2	39

Second Base

	PCT	G	PO	A	E	DP
Coghlan	1.000	14	33	30	0	4

Second Base

	PCT	G	PO	A	E	DP
Dawkins	.994	36	79	93	1	21
Gonzalez	.971	23	30	71	3	7
Hayes	1.000	1	1	2	0	0
Klosterman	.952	6	7	13	1	2
Matranga	.980	32	59	86	3	20
Mayorson	.981	46	100	102	4	27
Mitchell	1.000	3	6	10	0	3

Third Base

	PCT	G	PO	A	E	DP
Coghlan	.966	11	9	19	1	1
Craig	.951	26	14	44	3	3
Dawkins	.966	20	9	48	2	4
Gonzalez	1.000	4	3	3	0	1
Jenkins	1.000	1	1	1	0	0
Matranga	.952	37	17	62	4	7
Mayorson	.900	5	7	11	2	1
Mitchell	.929	15	8	18	2	3
Sanchez	.879	41	19	68	12	3

Shortstop

	PCT	G	PO	A	E	DP
Dawkins	.950	38	64	89	8	27
Gonzalez	.957	70	113	218	15	46
Klosterman	1.000	1	0	5	0	1
Matranga	1.000	3	2	7	0	0
Mayorson	.972	32	48	93	4	17
Ontiveros	1.000	4	10	14	0	4

Outfield

	PCT	G	PO	A	E	DP
Carroll	.952	25	57	3	3	2
Coghlan	—	1	0	0	0	0
De Aza	.933	64	123	3	9	0
Gonzalez	.833	4	4	1	1	0
Jenkins	1.000	1	2	0	0	0
Lindsey	1.000	8	6	0	0	0
Maybin	.978	76	220	6	5	0
Miller	.957	92	217	5	10	1
Raynor	.984	104	178	11	3	1
Ryan	.979	74	138	4	3	2

JACKSONVILLE SUNS   DOUBLE-A
SOUTHERN LEAGUE

Batting	B-T	HT	WT	DOB	AVG	vLH	vRH	G	AB	R	H	2B	3B	HR	RBI	BB	HBP	SH	SF	SO	SB	CS	SLG	OBP
Cousins, Scott	L-L	6-1	195	1-22-85	.263	.225	.278	130	482	60	127	31	11	12	74	42	3	1	5	107	27	9	.448	.323
Craig, Matt	B-R	6-3	215	4-16-81	.300	.278	.306	20	80	9	24	4	1	4	11	5	1	0	2	18	0	0	.525	.341
Davis, Brad	R-R	6-1	190	12-29-82	.236	.185	.251	88	280	36	66	23	0	10	43	28	3	2	1	62	0	0	.425	.311
De La Cruz, Chris	B-R	6-0	175	5-3-82	.273	.215	.298	112	308	46	84	15	3	2	23	37	2	3	2	50	4	1	.360	.352
Dominguez, Matt	R-R	6-1	210	8-28-89	.186	.222	.171	31	97	10	18	7	0	2	9	14	1	1	1	24	0	0	.320	.292
Hatcher, Chris	R-R	6-2	190	1-12-85	.218	.262	.202	51	156	29	34	9	3	8	27	14	4	2	3	43	1	0	.468	.294
Jenkins, Andy	R-R	6-0	205	7-23-83	.266	.253	.271	79	256	29	68	21	0	1	18	14	2	0	3	44	4	0	.359	.305
Klosterman, Ryan	R-R	5-11	190	5-28-82	.251	.223	.263	100	334	53	84	20	2	7	35	38	4	7	4	81	12	3	.386	.332
McDougall, Brandon	R-R	6-3	180	2-7-84	.158	.154	.167	13	19	7	3	1	0	0	3	10	1	0	2	5	2	1	.211	.438
Mitchell, Lee	R-R	6-1	200	4-21-82	.227	.223	.228	110	362	43	82	20	1	11	54	62	4	0	8	129	1	0	.378	.339
Morrison, Logan	L-L	6-3	245	8-25-87	.277	.232	.296	79	278	48	77	18	2	8	47	63	1	0	1	46	9	4	.442	.411
Perez, Smelin	B-R	5-10	150	5-28-84	.192	.125	.222	15	26	3	5	1	0	0	1	2	0	2	0	5	0	0	.231	.250
Petersen, Bryan	L-R	6-0	200	4-9-86	.297	.299	.297	121	431	64	128	15	7	7	49	49	0	0	9	66	13	12	.413	.368
Randel, Kevin	L-R	6-1	180	6-11-81	.253	.188	.263	123	352	55	89	21	2	12	49	62	6	3	3	92	4	1	.426	.371
Scott, Lorenzo	L-L	6-3	210	3-1-82	.265	.214	.283	123	400	65	106	14	9	4	46	61	0	1	6	124	20	13	.385	.358
Stanton, Mike	R-R	6-5	240	11-8-89	.231	.208	.239	79	299	49	69	15	2	16	53	31	6	0	5	99	1	1	.455	.311
Torres, Tim	B-R	6-2	180	11-12-83	.228	.271	.201	84	224	25	51	8	2	1	27	24	1	1	3	58	8	1	.295	.302
Wilson, Neil	R-R	6-1	190	12-7-83	.222	.000	.250	4	9	2	2	1	0	0	1	1	2	0	0	2	0	0	.333	.417

Pitching	B-T	HT	WT	DOB	W	L	ERA	G	GS	CG	SV	IP	H	R	ER	HR	BB	SO	AVG	vLH	vRH	K/9	BB/9
Allison, Jeff	R-R	6-2	195	11-7-84	1	0	3.60	1	1	0	0	5	6	2	2	0	1	3	.333	.222	.444	5.40	1.80
Battisto, A.J.	R-R	6-0	193	9-30-83	1	0	2.70	11	0	0	0	13	9	4	4	0	5	10	.265	.267	.172	6.75	3.38
Buente, Jay	R-R	6-2	185	9-28-83	0	1	2.45	16	0	0	1	22	17	6	6	1	11	23	.215	.219	.213	9.41	4.50
Doolittle, Todd	R-R	5-10	175	11-1-82	0	0	10.80	3	0	0	0	3	5	4	4	1	2	2	.333	.333	.333	5.40	5.40
Glen, Willie	R-R	6-1	185	10-30-77	2	7	3.69	15	14	0	0	78	79	42	32	7	30	59	.261	.258	.263	6.81	3.46
Gogal, Jeff	R-L	6-2	195	6-10-82	0	0	8.10	4	0	0	0	3	4	3	3	0	3	2	.286	.444	.000	5.40	8.10
Harker, Brett	R-R	6-3	185	7-9-84	1	0	9.00	5	1	0	0	10	13	12	10	0	7	7	.302	.211	.375	6.30	6.30
Hill, Ronald	R-R	6-3	225	11-29-82	0	0	4.11	11	0	0	0	15	16	7	7	1	6	10	.276	.360	.212	5.87	3.52
Jennings, Dan	L-L	6-3	190	4-17-87	0	0	0.00	3	0	0	0	2	2	0	0	0	1	2	.286	.500	.200	10.80	5.40
Leroux, Chris	L-R	6-6	210	4-14-84	5	3	2.70	46	0	0	2	60	59	19	18	0	17	55	.258	.266	.252	8.25	2.55
Lindstrom, Matt	R-R	6-3	220	2-11-80	0	1	9.00	2	2	0	0	2	2	2	1	0	0	3	.250	.000	.333	13.50	0.00
Martinez, Cristhian	R-R	6-1	160	3-6-82	9	3	2.94	17	16	0	0	104	96	39	34	7	22	62	.249	.273	.230	5.37	1.90
McCall, Derell	R-R	6-2	230	9-22-81	0	1	5.06	1	1	0	0	5	7	3	3	1	3	6	.333	.143	.429	10.13	5.06
Mendez, Adalberto	R-R	6-2	160	2-22-82	2	4	3.50	27	0	0	0	36	29	15	14	2	16	32	.220	.196	.237	8.00	4.00
Miller, Andrew	L-L	6-7	205	5-21-85	0	0	1.50	1	1	0	0	6	5	1	1	0	2	5	.238	—	.238	7.50	3.00
Mobley, Chris	R-R	5-11	170	8-16-83	0	0	4.50	2	0	0	0	2	3	1	0	1	1	3	.375	.667	.200	13.50	4.50
Olenberger, Kasey	R-R	6-4	235	3-18-78	7	1	1.10	52	1	0	3	66	48	9	8	1	19	64	.203	.177	.221	8.77	2.60
Owens, Henry	R-R	6-2	220	4-23-79	0	0	0.00	8	0	0	0	10	4	0	0	0	0	8	.133	.273	.053	7.45	9.31
Parcell, Garrett	R-R	6-5	220	7-12-84	0	0	0.25	23	0	0	1	37	16	5	1	0	15	42	.128	.160	.107	10.31	3.68
Peterson, Matt	R-R	6-5	220	2-11-82	4	4	3.86	56	0	0	37	58	50	26	25	3	27	53	.224	.204	.250	8.18	4.17
Sanchez, Anibal	R-R	6-0	220	2-27-84	1	0	2.61	2	2	0	0	10	5	3	3	1	3	8	.139	.231	.087	6.97	2.61
Santos, Jarrett	R-R	6-4	215	8-18-81	5	3	3.11	17	9	0	0	55	55	29	19	2	11	31	.261	.272	.252	5.07	1.80
Speigner, Levale	R-R	5-11	170	9-24-80	3	1	1.86	23	0	0	0	29	22	8	6	2	5	21	.222	.189	.242	6.52	1.55
Stone, Brad	R-R	6-3	190	5-20-84	6	3	2.23	27	11	0	0	81	65	25	20	3	16	44	.215	.183	.240	4.91	1.79

Name	B-T	HT	WT	DOB	W	L	ERA	G	GS	CG	SV	IP	H	R	ER	HR	BB	SO	AVG	vLH	vRH	K/9	BB/9
Taylor, Graham	L-L	6-3	225	5-25-84	8	7	3.69	23	23	0	0	127	115	62	52	9	54	71	.246	.256	.242	5.04	3.84
Thompson, Aaron	L-L	6-2	190	2-28-87	5	9	4.11	20	20	0	0	114	121	63	52	7	43	75	.268	.209	.289	5.92	3.39
Ungs, Nic	R-R	6-1	220	9-3-79	10	3	2.37	18	18	0	0	106	84	33	28	7	30	79	.218	.212	.223	6.69	2.54
Vasquez, Carlos	L-L	6-3	230	12-6-82	1	1	4.50	18	0	0	0	20	17	12	10	2	14	22	.221	.270	.175	9.90	6.30
Villanueva, Elih	R-R	6-2	235	7-26-86	0	1	4.50	2	2	0	0	10	12	5	5	0	3	5	.293	.364	.211	4.50	2.70
Voss, Jay	L-L	6-4	195	4-22-87	3	0	2.97	30	0	0	1	36	26	14	12	2	15	36	.200	.190	.205	8.92	3.72
West, Sean	L-L	6-8	240	6-15-86	7	3	4.78	12	11	0	0	64	68	37	34	12	28	65	.267	.214	.286	9.14	3.94
Winters, Kyle	R-R	6-4	190	4-22-87	1	2	5.40	7	7	0	0	35	44	21	21	1	13	25	.312	.267	.346	6.43	3.34

Fielding

Catcher	PCT	G	PO	A	E	DP	PB
Davis	.992	83	571	47	5	6	4
Hatcher	.990	46	285	26	3	1	6
Jenkins	.986	13	65	6	1	0	2
Wilson	1.000	4	26	0	0	0	0

First Base	PCT	G	PO	A	E	DP
Craig	.990	8	92	4	1	4
Jenkins	.992	41	331	21	3	30
Mitchell	1.000	14	106	11	0	11
Morrison	.996	74	632	54	3	54
Randel	.983	8	52	7	1	3
Torres	1.000	2	7	0	0	1

Second Base	PCT	G	PO	A	E	DP
De La Cruz	1.000	27	33	62	0	10
Klosterman	.958	35	54	83	6	18
Mitchell	.962	5	10	15	1	5
Perez	.941	8	14	18	2	5
Randel	.960	86	144	189	14	40
Torres	.926	7	10	15	2	6

Third Base	PCT	G	PO	A	E	DP
Craig	.913	9	2	19	2	3
De La Cruz	.944	7	4	13	1	2
Dominguez	.944	30	16	52	4	7
Klosterman	.938	6	3	12	1	0
Mitchell	.949	90	52	154	11	16
Randel	.875	4	3	4	1	0
Torres	.850	11	4	13	3	1

Shortstop	PCT	G	PO	A	E	DP
De La Cruz	.960	55	98	140	10	24
Klosterman	.942	62	87	158	15	26
Torres	.960	39	50	94	6	16

Outfield	PCT	G	PO	A	E	DP
Cousins	.988	121	242	10	3	3
Jenkins	.955	9	20	1	1	0
McDougall	1.000	9	15	2	0	0
Morrison	1.000	2	2	0	0	0
Petersen	1.000	108	167	6	0	0
Scott	.978	103	212	6	5	2
Stanton	.963	72	175	8	7	2
Torres	1.000	12	13	5	0	0

JUPITER HAMMERHEADS   HIGH CLASS A

FLORIDA STATE LEAGUE

Batting	B-T	HT	WT	DOB	AVG	vLH	vRH	G	AB	R	H	2B	3B	HR	RBI	BB	HBP	SH	SF	SO	SB	CS	SLG	OBP
Amezaga, Alfredo	B-R	5-10	180	1-16-78	.333	.000	.429	3	9	0	3	0	0	0	1	2	0	0	0	1	0	0	.333	.455
Blackwood, Jake	R-R	6-0	195	9-14-85	.174	.214	.156	27	92	7	16	1	0	2	10	4	0	0	0	21	1	0	.250	.208
Burns, Greg	L-L	6-2	185	11-7-86	.242	.148	.272	132	475	64	115	20	7	4	35	64	4	7	3	163	37	15	.339	.335
Curry, Ryan	R-R	5-10	185	4-18-85	.277	.372	.234	92	278	42	77	18	2	10	32	20	2	8	2	54	4	7	.464	.328
Dominguez, Matt	R-R	6-1	210	8-28-89	.262	.276	.259	103	381	49	100	25	1	11	53	38	5	0	5	68	1	0	.420	.333
Fermin, Miguel	R-R	5-11	175	2-11-85	.209	.224	.203	92	302	27	63	10	0	1	24	11	6	7	4	62	16	3	.252	.248
Garcia, Dan	R-R	6-0	165	12-27-87	.333	—	.333	3	6	2	2	0	1	0	3	0	0	0	1	1	0	0	.667	.286
Harrison, Ben	R-R	6-4	203	9-18-81	.203	.250	.184	68	227	32	46	7	0	10	32	34	2	0	3	83	1	2	.366	.308
Hatcher, Chris	R-R	6-2	190	1-12-85	.333	1.000	.200	6	18	4	6	1	0	0	2	1	1	0	0	8	0	1	.389	.400
Hickman, Tom	L-L	6-1	180	4-18-88	.129	.154	.123	23	70	5	9	4	0	1	4	14	0	0	0	33	0	0	.229	.274
Johnson, Nick	L-L	6-3	235	9-19-78	.333	1.000	.000	2	3	0	1	1	0	0	0	0	0	0	0	2	0	0	.667	.333
Martinez, Ozzie	R-R	5-10	170	5-7-88	.254	.248	.256	130	433	54	110	16	5	1	45	41	4	5	2	51	16	4	.321	.323
McDougall, Brandon	R-R	6-3	180	2-7-84	.224	.214	.229	66	196	31	44	12	2	3	20	21	1	4	1	64	10	3	.352	.301
Mense, Hunter	L-L	5-11	185	8-30-84	.236	.254	.232	105	364	33	86	16	2	4	30	31	6	2	3	54	2	2	.324	.304
Morrison, Logan	L-L	6-3	245	8-25-87	.273	.250	.286	3	11	0	3	1	0	0	2	1	0	0	0	2	0	1	.364	.333
Ontiveros, Emilio	R-R	5-11	170	1-2-85	.000	—	.000	2	4	0	0	0	0	0	0	0	0	0	0	0	0	0	.000	.000
Ott, Louis	B-R	6-0	185	2-22-85	.280	.194	.294	64	218	27	61	7	0	2	23	39	1	4	2	53	5	6	.339	.388
Perez, Smelin	B-R	5-10	150	8-26-85	.181	.107	.205	34	116	11	21	1	0	2	6	10	2	4	1	18	5	3	.241	.256
Schultz, Brian	L-L	6-0	200	10-15-84	.200	—	.200	3	5	0	1	0	0	0	1	1	0	0	0	3	0	0	.200	.333
Smith, Jameson	L-R	5-11	190	10-9-86	.243	.074	.281	49	148	18	36	8	0	1	13	20	0	3	0	32	1	0	.318	.333
Stanton, Mike	R-R	6-5	240	11-8-89	.294	.286	.297	50	180	27	53	9	3	12	39	28	1	0	1	45	2	2	.578	.390
Synan, Jeremy	L-R	6-0	193	7-14-86	.178	.219	.155	26	90	7	16	2	1	1	10	12	0	0	0	18	1	1	.278	.275
Torres, Tim	B-R	6-2	180	11-12-83	.276	.275	.276	85	304	37	84	14	3	9	42	36	2	1	1	24	6	1	.402	.359
Tripp, Brandon	L-R	6-2	200	4-2-85	.278	.210	.295	87	313	42	87	14	2	11	41	26	8	0	1	80	1	0	.441	.348
Valentin, Geraldo	R-R	6-0	184	9-8-82	.261	.253	.264	98	337	32	88	9	2	1	31	28	8	2	0	37	3	4	.309	.332

Pitching	B-T	HT	WT	DOB	W	L	ERA	G	GS	CG	SV	IP	H	R	ER	HR	BB	SO	AVG	vLH	vRH	K/9	BB/9
Allison, Jeff	R-R	6-2	195	11-7-84	7	9	3.68	25	25	3	0	139	151	66	57	13	30	71	.275	.296	.260	4.59	1.94
Andrelczyk, Pete	R-R	6-1	185	11-10-85	2	1	5.06	6	0	0	0	11	13	6	6	0	2	11	.295	.444	.192	9.28	1.69
Badenhop, Burke	R-R	6-5	220	2-8-83	0	0	0.00	2	2	0	0	8	2	1	0	0	1	8	.071	.071	.071	9.00	1.13
Battisto, A.J.	R-R	6-0	193	9-30-83	4	3	2.75	28	0	0	5	39	30	13	12	1	9	42	.211	.190	.226	9.61	2.06
Calero, Kiko	R-R	6-1	210	1-9-75	0	0	0.00	2	0	0	0	1	0	0	0	0	0	1	.000	.000	.000	4.50	0.00
Caminero, Arquimedes	R-R	6-4	185	6-16-87	0	0	30.86	2	0	0	0	2	7	8	8	3	2	2	.500	.571	.429	7.71	7.71
Cishek, Steven	R-R	6-6	200	6-18-86	3	4	2.84	37	0	0	2	57	36	23	18	2	16	45	.182	.237	.148	7.11	2.53
Crawford, Skyler	R-R	6-1	175	4-20-88	0	0	4.50	6	0	0	1	12	8	6	6	0	8	7	.200	.294	.130	5.25	6.00
Donnelly, Brendan	R-R	6-3	240	7-4-71	0	0	0.00	1	1	0	0	1	1	0	0	0	0	0	.250	.000	.500	0.00	0.00
Doolittle, Todd	R-R	5-10	175	11-1-82	2	2	9.64	8	0	0	0	9	12	13	10	0	7	11	.308	.313	.304	10.61	6.75
Evans, Bryan	R-R	6-3	205	2-25-87	0	0	12.00	1	1	0	0	3	5	4	4	0	1	5	.385	.333	.429	15.00	3.00
Fulton, Jonathan	R-R	6-4	200	12-1-83	0	2	2.42	17	0	0	0	22	22	6	6	1	13	33	.259	.286	.240	13.30	5.24
Gunderson, Kyle	R-R	6-3	215	1-31-85	1	3	3.12	38	0	0	14	40	39	14	14	1	11	36	.252	.333	.212	8.03	2.45
Harker, Brett	R-R	6-3	185	7-9-84	4	4	3.49	24	15	0	0	98	95	47	38	7	21	47	.256	.205	.300	4.32	1.93
Harvey, Kris	R-R	6-2	195	1-5-84	6	7	4.38	37	3	0	1	72	67	39	35	3	34	54	.248	.248	.248	6.75	4.25
Hernandez, Ricardo	L-L	5-10	152	1-3-88	0	0	0.00	1	0	0	0	2	0	0	0	0	0	0	.667	1.000	.500	0.00	0.00
Jennings, Dan	L-L	6-3	190	4-17-87	0	0	0.00	8	0	0	6	12	5	0	0	0	4	13	.132	.133	.130	10.03	3.09
Jones, Blake	R-R	6-5	220	4-15-81	0	1	8.53	7	0	0	2	6	13	6	6	0	3	3	.481	.455	.500	4.26	4.26

	B-T	HT	WT	DOB	W	L	ERA	G	GS	CG	SV	IP	H	R	ER	HR	BB	SO	AVG	vLH	vRH	K/9	BB/9
Koehler, Tom	R-R	6-3	235	6-29-86	4	1	3.38	6	6	0	0	35	35	15	13	0	9	25	.271	.341	.239	6.49	2.34
Korpi, Wade	R-L	6-0	185	3-10-86	2	0	3.52	18	4	0	0	31	21	13	12	3	15	30	.196	.175	.209	8.80	4.40
Lindstrom, Matt	R-R	6-3	220	2-11-80	0	0	0.00	2	0	0	0	2	1	0	0	0	0	1	.167	.000	.333	4.50	0.00
Loomis, Andy	L-L	5-10	175	11-25-85	0	0	0.00	1	0	0	0	1	1	0	0	0	2	0	.250	.000	.333	0.00	18.00
Madden, Corey	R-R	6-1	195	3-30-84	1	0	1.29	4	0	0	0	7	5	1	1	0	3	4	.227	.111	.308	5.14	3.86
Marinez, Jhan	R-R	6-1	165	8-12-88	1	1	3.14	29	0	0	1	43	28	17	15	4	20	42	.185	.167	.200	8.79	4.19
McCall, Derell	R-R	6-2	230	9-22-81	1	3	6.47	10	8	0	0	40	52	30	29	6	15	27	.317	.362	.292	6.02	3.35
Miller, Andrew	L-L	6-7	205	5-21-85	0	0	2.25	1	1	0	0	4	3	1	1	0	1	5	.200	.500	.154	11.25	2.25
Owens, Henry	R-R	6-2	220	4-23-79	0	0	2.25	3	0	0	1	4	2	1	1	0	2	3	.167	.286	.000	6.75	4.50
Parcell, Garrett	R-R	6-5	220	7-12-84	1	0	2.25	3	0	0	0	4	3	1	1	0	0	2	.200	.400	.100	4.50	0.00
Pinto, Renyel	L-L	6-4	265	7-8-82	0	0	0.00	2	0	0	0	2	0	0	0	0	1	1	.000	.000	.000	4.50	4.50
Ramirez, Andy	R-R	6-1	164	10-10-87	0	0	3.00	1	0	0	0	3	3	1	1	0	1	1	.273	.250	.286	3.00	0.00
Rosario, Jose	R-R	6-0	170	2-16-86	8	7	3.14	22	18	0	0	109	90	45	38	4	25	91	.221	.213	.226	7.51	2.06
Sanabia, Alejandro	R-R	6-1	165	9-8-88	9	5	3.45	19	18	0	0	104	89	45	40	6	36	68	.231	.220	.239	5.87	3.11
Sanchez, Anibal	R-R	6-0	220	2-27-84	1	0	0.68	3	3	0	0	13	7	2	1	0	3	12	.156	.167	.143	8.10	2.03
Stone, Brad	R-R	6-3	190	5-20-84	0	3	3.07	9	0	0	2	15	10	5	5	0	2	7	.196	.304	.107	4.50	1.23
Teague, Sean	R-R	6-0	190	3-16-86	0	0	0.00	1	0	0	0	2	1	1	0	0	1	2	.167	.000	.333	9.00	4.50
Ungs, Nic	R-R	6-1	220	9-3-79	0	1	2.25	1	1	0	0	4	2	1	1	0	0	4	.154	.167	.143	9.00	0.00
VandenHurk, Rick	R-R	6-5	220	5-22-85	0	0	3.00	1	1	0	0	3	3	1	1	0	2	3	.250	.143	.400	9.00	6.00
Vieira, Matt	L-L	6-1	185	8-9-85	0	0	4.50	1	0	0	0	2	3	1	1	0	1	0	.333	.333	.333	4.50	4.50
Villanueva, Elih	R-R	6-2	235	7-26-86	9	12	3.47	26	25	2	0	158	159	68	61	10	18	110	.259	.271	.249	6.27	1.03
Voss, Jay	L-L	6-4	195	4-22-87	0	1	2.03	10	0	0	0	13	14	5	3	0	3	10	.269	.267	.270	6.75	2.03
Winters, Kyle	R-R	6-4	190	4-22-87	1	0	0.87	5	5	0	0	31	27	4	3	0	4	15	.235	.231	.238	4.35	1.16

Fielding

Catcher	PCT	G	PO	A	E	DP	PB
Fermin	.991	91	578	52	6	6	5
Hatcher	1.000	6	41	8	0	3	0
Smith	.986	48	249	25	4	2	10

First Base	PCT	G	PO	A	E	DP
Blackwood	.981	23	197	14	4	19
Dominguez	1.000	1	7	0	0	0
Johnson	1.000	2	9	3	0	2
McDougall	.981	30	243	9	5	21
Mense	.989	87	710	42	8	52
Morrison	1.000	1	14	1	0	1
Ott	.952	3	17	3	1	3

Second Base	PCT	G	PO	A	E	DP
Amezaga	1.000	1	2	2	0	1
Blackwood	1.000	1	2	4	0	0
Curry	.982	81	137	189	6	36

Garcia	1.000	3	6	6	0	2
Ontiveros	1.000	1	1	1	0	0
Ott	.938	30	44	78	8	14
Perez	.966	23	37	75	4	15
Torres	1.000	7	8	10	0	2

Third Base	PCT	G	PO	A	E	DP
Blackwood	1.000	3	0	1	0	0
Curry	1.000	1	1	0	0	0
Dominguez	.949	101	73	190	14	17
McDougall	1.000	1	1	0	0	0
Ott	.941	10	5	11	1	1
Torres	.975	24	19	59	2	6

Shortstop	PCT	G	PO	A	E	DP
Amezaga	1.000	1	0	1	0	0
Martinez	.953	129	155	336	24	67
Ontiveros	1.000	1	2	3	0	0

Perez	1.000	8	11	12	0	1
Torres	1.000	1	1	3	0	1

Outfield	PCT	G	PO	A	E	DP
Amezaga	1.000	1	3	1	0	0
Burns	.989	132	354	7	4	1
Harrison	.985	27	63	2	1	2
Hickman	1.000	21	38	1	0	0
McDougall	.964	30	50	3	2	0
Mense	1.000	16	20	2	0	1
Schultz	1.000	1	3	0	0	0
Stanton	.960	40	70	2	3	0
Synan	.971	21	33	1	1	0
Torres	1.000	4	12	0	0	0
Tripp	.989	54	89	2	1	1
Valentin	.966	81	156	13	6	2

GREENSBORO GRASSHOPPERS

LOW CLASS A

SOUTH ATLANTIC LEAGUE

Batting	B-T	HT	WT	DOB	AVG	vLH	vRH	G	AB	R	H	2B	3B	HR	RBI	BB	HBP	SH	SF	SO	SB	CS	SLG	OBP
Bass, Justin	R-R	6-0	205	12-11-85	.258	.186	.277	99	337	45	87	17	2	14	57	17	7	1	1	89	8	4	.445	.307
Ceballos, Jose	R-R	6-0	190	12-27-89	.200	.000	.238	11	25	4	5	1	0	1	4	1	3	0	1	7	0	0	.360	.300
Dayleg, Terrence	R-R	6-0	170	9-19-87	.167	.250	.125	4	12	1	2	0	0	0	1	0	0	0	0	3	0	0	.167	.231
Galloway, Isaac	R-R	6-2	190	10-10-89	.268	.239	.275	83	340	44	91	24	3	3	30	12	2	1	4	89	15	9	.382	.293
Gran, Paul	R-R	5-11	182	4-7-86	.261	.284	.255	118	449	67	117	24	2	4	48	50	10	1	5	91	12	3	.350	.344
Hickman, Tom	L-L	6-1	180	4-18-88	.322	.350	.314	28	90	14	29	9	1	7	19	17	2	0	0	27	2	2	.678	.440
Jacobs, Justin	R-R	6-1	180	7-31-88	.236	.270	.226	87	271	46	64	19	0	9	35	41	3	4	4	86	13	6	.406	.339
Keedy, Ryan	L-R	6-3	220	8-15-85	.304	.286	.306	47	168	30	51	12	1	8	40	14	1	1	1	28	3	0	.530	.359
Langley, Torre	R-R	5-9	175	10-9-87	.223	.333	.189	67	229	16	51	6	0	4	25	11	2	2	3	38	2	1	.301	.261
Lasater, Ben	R-R	6-3	195	5-24-86	.290	.280	.292	126	483	73	140	34	2	16	76	39	10	0	5	119	4	1	.468	.352
Mattison, Kevin	L-L	6-0	180	9-20-85	.250	.203	.260	95	360	61	90	15	1	15	47	30	9	3	4	81	41	6	.422	.323
Ontiveros, Emilio	R-R	5-11	170	1-2-85	.213	.174	.224	73	216	26	46	11	0	1	20	16	10	3	1	40	0	0	.278	.296
Pasek, Mike	R-R	5-9	160	4-18-88	.143	—	.143	2	7	1	1	0	0	0	0	0	0	0	0	2	0	0	.143	.143
Perez, Smelin	B-R	5-10	150	8-26-85	.205	.083	.259	10	39	3	8	3	0	0	3	5	2	1	0	8	0	1	.282	.262
Pertusati, Danny	R-R	6-1	185	4-27-90	.251	.242	.254	123	446	59	112	22	3	4	38	34	8	4	0	77	9	6	.341	.316
Skipworth, Kyle	L-R	6-4	205	3-1-90	.208	.068	.236	70	264	28	55	14	1	7	37	18	2	1	1	91	1	2	.348	.263
Smolinski, Jake	R-R	5-11	185	2-9-89	.283	.340	.271	77	279	50	79	25	0	7	31	38	5	0	0	45	2	5	.448	.379
Staples, Joel	R-R	6-2	205	5-26-87	.198	.182	.203	33	91	12	18	0	1	0	10	17	6	0	2	18	4	2	.220	.353
Synan, Jeremy	L-R	6-0	193	7-14-86	.291	.365	.276	100	375	54	109	31	1	13	63	33	5	0	4	84	4	6	.483	.353
Taylor, Robert	R-R	6-2	210	10-10-85	.212	.091	.236	22	66	11	14	2	0	2	12	6	2	0	1	22	1	0	.333	.293
Turner, Brandon	L-R	6-1	185	2-15-87	.280	.240	.290	41	132	17	37	4	0	2	16	23	2	1	0	21	1	0	.356	.395

Pitching	B-T	HT	WT	DOB	W	L	ERA	G	GS	CG	SV	IP	H	R	ER	HR	BB	SO	AVG	vLH	vRH	K/9	BB/9
Alexander, Stu	R-R	6-5	210	10-25-84	1	1	9.24	5	1	0	0	13	23	13	13	0	4	6	.371	.381	.366	4.26	2.84
Andrelczyk, Pete	R-R	6-1	185	11-10-85	2	5	2.29	44	0	0	19	59	55	28	15	2	14	74	.242	.261	.230	11.29	2.14
Benjamin, Ramon	R-L	6-2	180	6-14-87	1	0	1.00	6	0	0	0	9	5	1	1	0	7	11	.147	.091	.174	11.00	7.00
Caminero, Arquimedes	R-R	6-4	185	6-16-87	0	0	5.65	10	0	0	0	14	16	14	9	1	8	17	.276	.250	.300	10.67	5.02
Chirinos, Luis	R-R	6-2	170	4-22-90	0	0	0.00	1	0	0	0	3	0	0	0	0	1	1	.000	.000	.000	3.00	3.00

Name	B-T	HT	WT	DOB	W	L	ERA	G	GS	CG	SV	IP	H	R	ER	HR	BB	SO	AVG	vLH	vRH	K/9	BB/9
Dilone, Natividad	R-R	6-0	160	9-8-82	2	0	0.00	2	2	0	0	11	4	0	0	0	6	11	.118	.083	.136	9.28	5.06
Dorn, Johnny	R-R	6-3	210	8-4-85	11	10	4.18	27	27	1	0	157	181	84	73	11	42	94	.292	.296	.290	5.38	2.40
Encarnacion, Rodolfo	R-R	5-11	180	5-8-86	1	0	1.04	19	0	0	2	35	20	7	4	1	15	51	.161	.145	.174	13.24	3.89
Evans, Bryan	R-R	6-3	205	2-25-87	3	7	3.97	39	5	0	0	100	115	56	44	7	27	75	.293	.290	.294	6.77	2.44
Hand, Brad	L-L	6-2	185	3-20-90	7	13	4.86	26	26	0	0	128	130	83	69	12	66	122	.264	.264	.264	8.60	4.65
Jennings, Dan	L-L	6-3	190	4-17-87	1	2	2.74	34	0	0	0	49	42	21	15	1	21	54	.237	.282	.225	9.85	3.83
Johnson, Graham	R-R	6-6	215	10-13-89	6	7	4.83	20	20	0	0	91	100	59	49	8	47	52	.277	.331	.237	5.12	4.63
Kaminska, Kyle	L-R	6-4	180	10-5-88	9	9	4.16	26	25	0	0	143	162	91	66	10	36	112	.284	.304	.269	7.07	2.27
Koehler, Tom	R-R	6-3	235	6-29-86	5	5	3.20	18	18	0	0	98	88	37	35	9	39	82	.238	.236	.239	7.51	3.57
Korpi, Wade	R-L	6-0	185	3-10-86	2	2	3.99	18	2	0	0	38	41	20	17	7	17	42	.273	.261	.279	9.86	3.99
Loomis, Andy	L-L	5-10	175	11-25-85	2	3	4.23	41	0	0	1	66	68	33	31	7	23	58	.265	.254	.268	7.91	3.14
Roberts, Josh	R-R	6-5	230	5-12-84	0	1	8.00	3	3	0	0	9	15	11	8	1	4	5	.375	.182	.448	5.00	4.00
Rosario, Jose	R-R	6-0	170	2-16-86	2	0	5.14	4	4	0	0	21	24	14	12	3	6	14	.282	.300	.273	6.00	2.57
Rosario, Sandy	R-R	6-1	170	8-22-85	3	2	5.13	7	7	0	0	40	57	28	23	4	6	36	.322	.306	.333	8.03	1.34
Teague, Sean	R-R	6-0	190	3-16-86	0	0	0.00	1	0	0	0	1	0	0	0	2	1		.000	.000	.000	9.00	18.00
Todd, Brandon	R-R	6-1	205	4-5-85	4	3	3.28	43	0	0	3	58	40	23	21	3	25	59	.194	.195	.194	9.21	3.90
Yecker, Jared	R-R	6-6	210	12-8-86	3	4	5.57	40	0	0	4	65	71	45	40	8	31	79	.284	.220	.327	10.99	4.31

Fielding

Catcher	PCT	G	PO	A	E	DP	PB
Ceballos	.986	11	66	4	1	1	1
Langley	.987	65	467	74	7	7	10
Skipworth	.983	64	472	50	9	1	13
Taylor	.933	6	37	5	3	0	1

	PCT	G	PO	A	E	DP
Ontiveros	.941	4	7	9	1	3
Perez	1.000	4	7	5	0	0
Pertusati	.954	116	198	317	25	58
Smolinski	.970	8	12	20	1	1
Turner	1.000	1	2	1	0	0

Shortstop	PCT	G	PO	A	E	DP
Dayleg	.963	4	9	17	1	6
Gran	.938	49	69	144	14	21
Ontiveros	.972	61	71	175	7	27
Perez	.929	2	2	11	1	2
Staples	.933	32	20	91	8	14

First Base	PCT	G	PO	A	E	DP
Keedy	.983	28	222	9	4	21
Lasater	.989	106	932	49	11	75
Ontiveros	1.000	4	16	1	0	0
Smolinski	1.000	1	5	2	0	0
Taylor	1.000	2	12	1	0	2
Turner	1.000	8	57	4	0	4

Third Base	PCT	G	PO	A	E	DP
Gran	.931	61	37	124	12	11
Lasater	.947	8	6	12	1	2
Ontiveros	1.000	4	0	8	0	0
Pasek	.800	2	2	2	1	0
Perez	.909	4	3	7	1	0
Smolinski	.879	55	29	94	17	10
Turner	.882	15	9	21	4	1

Outfield	PCT	G	PO	A	E	DP
Bass	.976	89	161	4	4	0
Galloway	.974	82	178	6	5	2
Hickman	.979	26	44	2	1	0
Jacobs	.946	68	100	5	6	1
Mattison	.974	90	212	9	6	1
Synan	.989	68	88	5	1	0
Taylor	1.000	10	4	1	0	0

Second Base	PCT	G	PO	A	E	DP
Gran	.868	10	15	18	5	4

JAMESTOWN JAMMERS   SHORT-SEASON

NEW YORK-PENN LEAGUE

Batting	B-T	HT	WT	DOB	AVG	vLH	vRH	G	AB	R	H	2B	3B	HR	RBI	BB	HBP	SH	SF	SO	SB	CS	SLG	OBP
Austin, Chase	R-R	6-2	185	12-4-87	.252	.330	.209	64	246	34	62	10	3	3	26	18	1	2	3	45	7	1	.354	.302
Brady, Mike	R-R	6-0	200	3-21-87	.333	.500	.000	4	6	0	2	0	0	0	0	2	1	0	0	2	1	0	.333	.556
Brantley, Harold	L-R	5-10	180	5-19-88	.000	.000	.000	3	4	1	0	0	0	0	0	0	0	0	0	1	0	0	.000	.000
Ceballos, Jose	R-R	6-0	190	12-27-89	.171	.061	.245	27	82	6	14	4	1	1	7	3	6	1	1	24	0	0	.280	.250
Cregar, Chad	L-R	6-4	221	10-30-86	.219	.091	.286	8	32	5	7	1	0	1	2	0	0	0	0	7	0	1	.344	.219
Dickerson, Dustin	L-R	6-4	205	9-30-87	.214	.245	.198	46	159	14	34	5	0	0	18	13	0	0	0	46	0	0	.245	.273
Hord, Dallas	R-R	6-0	175	11-25-87	.143	.000	.200	2	7	0	1	0	0	0	0	0	0	0	0	5	0	0	.143	.143
Jensen, Kyle	R-L	6-4	230	5-20-88	.280	.224	.313	55	182	24	51	10	5	4	24	18	5	0	4	46	3	0	.456	.354
Kanaby, Erik	L-R	6-1	185	7-26-85	.260	.282	.248	65	208	21	54	6	1	0	14	37	2	4	2	34	9	3	.298	.373
Krick, Taylor	R-R	6-1	200	3-31-88	.222	.429	.091	6	18	1	4	0	0	0	0	2	0	0	0	4	3	0	.222	.300
Manzanillo, Ernesto	R-R	5-11	165	12-24-88	.168	.179	.163	40	119	12	20	1	0	2	11	6	2	2	1	39	0	1	.227	.219
Markel, Austin	L-R	6-1	195	9-12-86	.295	.314	.286	29	105	21	31	6	2	4	17	11	0	2	2	43	0	2	.505	.356
Moore, Zach	L-R	6-4	205	8-6-88	.208	.136	.228	39	101	16	21	6	1	0	8	8	2	2	0	31	6	3	.287	.279
Orton, Ricky	L-R	6-4	225	9-7-86	.235	.311	.188	43	162	22	38	11	1	3	28	21	3	0	0	48	0	0	.370	.333
Pasek, Mike	R-R	5-9	160	9-8-89	.210	.270	.175	40	100	12	21	4	0	0	9	15	1	2	0	29	1	0	.250	.319
Paulino, Carlos	R-R	6-0	167	9-24-89	.291	.298	.287	42	141	13	41	11	1	1	14	11	0	0	1	27	2	1	.404	.340
Simon, Nate	L-R	6-1	185	11-19-86	.213	.267	.200	27	80	6	17	1	0	0	3	4	1	3	2	22	0	2	.225	.253
Smith, Rand	R-R	6-0	190	6-11-87	.305	.316	.299	30	105	11	32	2	0	0	9	8	1	1	1	27	5	3	.324	.357
Stonecipher, Sequoyah	R-R	6-0	195	11-6-87	.264	.298	.247	41	144	20	38	11	1	2	10	11	1	2	1	31	4	0	.396	.318
Taylor, Robert	R-R	6-2	210	10-10-85	.263	.321	.239	29	95	12	25	7	0	3	20	8	0	0	2	24	3	0	.432	.314
Thieme, Konrad	R-R	6-3	205	2-15-85	.333	.000	.500	1	3	0	1	0	0	0	1	0	0	0	0	2	0	0	.333	.333
Torres, Jose	R-R	6-0	170	10-22-90	.248	.231	.255	56	210	19	50	7	0	0	17	4	2	2	1	23	3	3	.282	.268
Wade, Chris	R-R	6-0	170	9-25-87	.277	.344	.238	47	166	24	46	6	3	0	18	14	7	8	1	29	5	4	.349	.356
Wyatt, Mark	R-R	5-11	210	9-29-86	.207	.444	.100	11	29	7	6	1	0	0	3	2	1	2	2	8	0	0	.241	.265

Pitching	B-T	HT	WT	DOB	W	L	ERA	G	GS	CG	SV	IP	H	R	ER	HR	BB	SO	AVG	vLH	vRH	K/9	BB/9
Armstrong, Austin	R-R	6-3	205	1-17-87	0	0	0.00	1	1	0	0	5	2	0	0	0	1	4	.125	.222	.000	7.20	1.80
2-team total (17 Auburn)					2	4	7.22	18	1	0	0	29	35	27	23	4	13	21	—	—	—	6.59	4.08
Barrow, Brandon	L-L	6-4	195	4-18-89	1	0	4.76	4	0	0	0	6	5	3	3	0	5	7	.227	.250	.214	11.12	7.94
Benjamin, Ramon	R-L	6-2	180	6-14-87	1	1	3.77	18	0	0	0	29	25	12	12	1	11	31	.243	.179	.267	9.73	3.45
Brewer, Blake	R-R	6-5	177	3-2-90	0	3	32.40	3	3	0	0	3	9	15	12	0	12	6	.450	.400	.467	16.20	32.40
Bukvich, Brett	R-R	6-4	237	8-26-85	0	0	0.00	1	0	0	0	1	0	1	0	0	3	1	.000	.000	.000	6.75	20.25
Caminero, Arquimedes	R-R	6-4	185	6-16-87	3	1	3.00	15	0	0	0	24	19	9	8	1	16	42	.218	.206	.226	15.75	6.00
Carrillo, Erick	R-R	6-1	185	1-3-87	4	2	2.05	14	11	0	1	61	49	17	14	1	18	50	.216	.215	.216	7.34	2.64
Crawford, Skyler	R-R	6-1	175	4-20-88	4	4	3.82	13	3	0	0	35	33	20	15	5	19	28	.256	.245	.263	7.13	4.84
Dilone, Natividad	R-R	6-0	160	9-8-82	1	0	2.13	4	0	0	0	13	12	3	3	0	4	15	.261	.190	.320	10.66	2.84

Name	B-T	HT	WT	DOB	W	L	ERA	G	GS	CG	SV	IP	H	R	ER	HR	BB	SO	AVG	vLH	vRH	K/9	BB/9
Encarnacion, Rodolfo	R-R	5-11	180	5-8-86	0	0	4.91	2	0	0	0	4	1	2	2	0	4	2	.077	.000	.111	4.91	9.82
Fernandez, Kenny	R-R	6-2	170	2-19-87	0	2	5.98	18	3	0	0	41	51	30	27	4	12	33	.298	.338	.272	7.30	2.66
Fry, Casey	R-L	6-0	175	11-9-89	0	0	1.04	2	2	0	0	9	4	2	1	0	4	8	.138	.000	.167	8.31	4.15
Hodges, Josh	R-R	6-7	235	6-21-91	1	0	4.50	1	0	0	0	4	5	2	2	1	0	6	.294	.500	.267	13.50	0.00
Mahoney, Dan	R-R	6-3	195	2-17-88	1	6	8.04	10	10	0	0	31	48	35	28	4	15	25	.348	.293	.371	7.18	4.31
Matos, Wilson	R-R	6-2	180	4-10-88	2	1	4.10	20	0	0	2	26	25	14	12	5	18	28	.238	.233	.242	9.57	6.15
Miller, David	L-R	6-10	210	9-29-84	0	0	2.45	1	1	0	0	4	5	3	1	0	2	1	.333	.286	.375	2.45	4.91
2-team total (15 Auburn)					0	3	6.16	16	1	0	0	31	36	25	21	2	18	24	—	—	—	7.04	5.28
Montgomery, Matt	R-R	6-4	210	7-21-87	1	0	0.00	2	2	0	0	9	4	0	0	0	0	9	.129	.286	.000	4.00	0.00
O'Gara, Joey	R-R	6-7	205	4-20-88	3	4	6.46	15	3	0	0	39	53	32	28	4	14	28	.338	.316	.358	6.46	3.23
Olmos, Edgar	L-L	6-5	180	4-12-90	0	0	2.25	1	1	0	0	4	3	1	1	0	2	4	.214	.000	.333	9.00	4.50
Petersen, Curtis	R-R	6-3	180	8-28-89	3	5	4.29	15	15	0	0	63	61	41	30	3	31	50	.250	.196	.295	7.14	4.43
Ramirez, Andy	R-R	6-1	164	10-10-87	2	3	4.03	20	1	0	0	45	44	25	20	2	17	49	.262	.297	.240	9.87	3.43
Ramos, A.J.	R-R	5-10	210	9-20-86	2	2	2.14	25	0	0	9	34	22	9	8	0	14	50	.182	.178	.184	13.37	3.74
Richards, Stephen	L-L	6-0	180	8-10-88	0	1	3.14	10	0	0	1	14	13	7	5	0	8	12	.232	.200	.250	7.53	5.02
Roberts, Josh	R-R	6-5	230	5-12-84	0	3	3.86	8	7	0	0	35	37	17	15	1	6	23	.261	.349	.222	5.91	1.54
Rosario, Sandy	R-R	6-1	170	8-22-85	4	2	1.70	9	9	0	0	42	48	12	8	1	8	41	.277	.192	.314	8.72	1.70
Shafer, Chris	R-R	6-2	245	5-16-89	1	0	1.43	20	1	0	1	38	35	13	6	0	14	37	.241	.259	.230	8.84	3.35
Sprague, Holden	R-R	6-2	210	7-24-87	0	2	4.30	3	3	1	0	15	19	9	7	2	2	11	.306	.385	.250	6.75	1.23
Vieira, Matt	L-L	6-1	185	8-9-85	0	0	2.29	7	0	0	0	20	20	5	5	1	4	13	.253	.250	.254	5.95	1.83

Fielding

Catcher	PCT	G	PO	A	E	DP	PB
Ceballos	.987	27	210	19	3	4	9
Hord	1.000	1	6	0	0	0	0
Krick	1.000	1	2	0	0	0	1
Paulino	.989	37	256	22	3	2	3
Taylor	.976	8	76	4	2	0	0
Thieme	1.000	1	7	0	0	0	0
Wyatt	.962	9	68	8	3	0	3

First Base	PCT	G	PO	A	E	DP
Dickerson	.966	24	162	7	6	14
Jensen	1.000	5	28	2	0	2
Orton	.980	35	267	28	6	22
Taylor	.960	14	111	8	5	11

Second Base	PCT	G	PO	A	E	DP
Brady	1.000	2	3	5	0	0

	PCT	G	PO	A	E	DP
Manzanillo	.932	26	42	40	6	12
Pasek	.925	20	33	41	6	9
Simon	.964	14	25	29	2	7
Torres	.968	23	42	49	3	13
Wade	.944	4	6	11	1	2

Third Base	PCT	G	PO	A	E	DP
Austin	.903	54	35	96	14	6
Krick	.833	2	1	4	1	0
Manzanillo	.842	10	3	13	3	2
Pasek	.900	14	5	31	4	1

Shortstop	PCT	G	PO	A	E	DP
Austin	.893	5	8	17	3	2
Pasek	1.000	2	2	4	0	0
Torres	.923	32	43	89	11	12
Wade	.937	39	51	97	10	21

Outfield	PCT	G	PO	A	E	DP
Brantley	1.000	2	2	1	0	0
Cregar	1.000	6	14	0	0	0
Dickerson	1.000	5	9	0	0	0
Jensen	.971	42	63	3	2	0
Kanaby	.986	62	136	4	2	2
Markel	.980	28	47	1	1	0
Moore	.930	30	39	1	3	0
Simon	.933	11	14	0	1	0
Smith	.985	29	64	3	1	0
Stonecipher	.958	30	38	8	2	0
Taylor	1.000	3	4	0	0	0

GCL MARLINS — ROOKIE

GULF COAST LEAGUE

Batting	B-T	HT	WT	DOB	AVG	vLH	vRH	G	AB	R	H	2B	3B	HR	RBI	BB	HBP	SH	SF	SO	SB	CS	SLG	OBP
Bautista, Samuel	L-R	6-1	148	12-12-88	.174	.000	.211	7	23	3	4	2	0	0	3	1	0	0	1	12	0	0	.261	.200
Brady, Mike	R-R	6-0	200	3-21-87	.034	.091	.000	11	29	6	1	0	0	0	2	8	1	0	1	7	0	0	.034	.256
Brantley, Harold	L-R	5-10	180	5-19-88	.154	.143	.160	24	39	8	6	1	0	0	2	5	1	2	1	9	8	0	.179	.261
Cooper, Marquise	R-R	5-9	175	10-16-91	.193	.277	.151	39	140	19	27	3	1	1	14	18	8	3	1	27	6	4	.250	.317
Dayleg, Terrence	R-R	6-0	170	9-19-87	.269	.294	.253	35	130	24	35	9	2	1	19	16	6	1	1	18	0	1	.392	.373
Diaz, Aury	R-R	6-1	155	5-29-90	.244	.244	.244	33	119	23	29	4	0	1	18	12	1	0	1	19	0	1	.303	.316
Dunn, Chris	R-R	5-10	180	3-8-84	.333	.000	.500	1	3	0	1	0	0	0	1	0	0	0	0	0	0	0	.333	.333
Garcia, Dan	R-R	6-0	165	12-27-87	.222	.067	.333	10	36	6	8	1	1	0	2	3	2	0	0	8	0	0	.306	.317
Gimenez, Wilfredo	R-R	6-0	180	12-18-90	.279	.316	.258	35	104	17	29	7	0	1	22	14	0	2	2	9	1	1	.375	.358
Hickman, Tom	L-L	6-1	180	4-18-88	.273	.222	.308	6	22	5	6	2	0	1	4	1	1	0	0	9	0	0	.500	.333
Hord, Dallas	R-R	6-0	175	11-25-87	.200	.000	.500	3	5	1	1	1	0	0	2	0	0	0	0	0	0	0	.400	.429
Kam, Adam	L-R	5-11	180	7-31-91	.000	—	.000	2	1	0	0	0	0	0	0	0	0	0	0	0	0	0	.000	.500
Keys, Brent	L-R	6-1	210	7-14-90	.288	.341	.269	50	163	23	47	5	0	0	19	28	2	3	2	20	13	4	.319	.395
Krick, Taylor	R-R	6-3	190	3-31-88	.174	.000	.222	8	23	6	4	1	1	0	1	5	1	1	0	0	0	0	.304	.345
Lokken, Matt	R-R	6-4	200	9-18-88	.237	.333	.219	16	38	5	9	1	0	0	3	8	2	0	0	9	0	0	.263	.396
Markel, Austin	L-R	6-1	195	9-12-86	.250	.200	.273	7	16	5	4	1	0	0	2	5	1	0	0	5	2	0	.313	.455
Morales, Jobduan	B-R	5-10	180	6-7-91	.227	.200	.238	34	110	14	25	5	0	0	6	18	1	1	3	24	0	0	.273	.333
Nunez, Jose	B-R	5-9	160	5-27-86	.194	.136	.225	22	62	12	12	3	1	1	5	16	2	1	1	17	2	2	.323	.378
Ozuna, Marcell	R-R	6-2	190	11-12-90	.313	.254	.340	55	214	32	67	22	0	5	39	22	3	0	5	52	4	2	.486	.377
Paulino, Carlos	R-R	6-0	167	9-24-89	.333	.000	.375	3	9	1	3	0	0	0	3	0	0	0	0	1	0	0	.333	.333
Peralta, Rony	L-R	6-0	160	8-19-90	.204	.234	.192	43	167	20	34	5	1	0	9	15	1	4	1	31	3	4	.246	.272
Perio, Noah	L-R	6-0	170	11-14-91	.429	.000	.462	4	14	2	6	1	1	0	2	6	0	0	1	0	1	0	.643	.429
Peters, David	R-R	6-0	195	1-26-91	.081	.077	.083	26	86	5	7	0	0	0	6	5	2	1	1	22	1	1	.081	.149
Rabelo, Mike	B-R	6-0	210	1-17-80	.143	.091	.176	9	28	3	4	2	0	0	2	6	2	0	0	6	0	0	.214	.333
Simon, Nate	L-R	6-1	185	11-19-86	.235	.200	.250	5	17	2	4	0	0	0	2	4	0	0	2	2	1	1	.235	.316
Wade, Chris	R-R	6-0	190	9-25-87	.200	—	.200	1	5	0	1	0	0	0	0	1	0	0	0	1	0	0	.400	.333
Weaver, Brent	R-R	6-1	175	3-2-85	.269	.339	.234	53	186	32	50	9	0	3	33	16	5	0	1	37	4	1	.366	.341
Wilson, Neil	R-R	6-0	190	12-7-83	.292	.600	.211	7	24	3	7	1	0	1	5	0	1	0	0	6	0	0	.458	.320

Pitching	B-T	HT	WT	DOB	W	L	ERA	G	GS	CG	SV	IP	H	R	ER	HR	BB	SO	AVG	vLH	vRH	K/9	BB/9
Badenhop, Burke	R-R	6-5	220	2-8-83	0	1	0.00	2	2	0	0	3	2	3	0	0	0	4	.167	.000	.182	12.00	0.00
Barrow, Brandon	L-L	6-4	195	4-18-89	0	0	6.43	5	0	0	0	7	8	6	5	1	5	6	.333	.250	.350	7.71	6.43

FLORIDA MARLINS

Name	B-T	HT	WT	DOB	W	L	ERA	G	GS	CG	SV	IP	H	R	ER	HR	BB	SO	AVG	vLH	vRH	K/9	BB/9
Brewer, Blake	R-R	6-5	177	3-2-90	1	0	3.95	11	0	0	0	14	7	9	6	0	22	16	.152	.111	.162	10.54	14.49
Bukvich, Brett	L-L	6-4	237	8-26-85	2	0	0.00	2	0	0	0	3	3	0	0	0	0	2	.273	.000	.300	6.00	0.00
Chirinos, Luis	R-R	6-2	170	4-22-90	3	2	1.35	18	0	0	4	27	20	7	4	0	9	23	.198	.176	.202	7.76	3.04
Conley, Jordan	R-R	6-1	180	7-19-86	0	2	0.90	9	0	0	4	10	6	4	1	0	4	13	.182	.429	.115	11.70	3.60
Doolittle, Todd	R-R	5-10	175	11-1-82	1	0	0.00	7	1	0	0	8	6	1	0	0	2	6	.194	.200	.192	6.75	2.25
Eskew, Jared	L-L	6-2	175	12-10-86	7	1	2.23	14	7	0	0	48	40	15	12	1	10	44	.217	.308	.203	8.19	1.86
Estevez, Alvaro	R-R	6-2	180	3-15-89	3	1	2.22	13	10	0	0	53	42	16	13	2	14	52	.216	.224	.214	8.89	2.39
Fry, Casey	R-L	6-0	175	11-9-89	1	1	3.34	11	7	0	0	30	22	16	11	0	22	33	.214	.083	.231	10.01	6.67
Gonzalez, Saul	R-R	6-1	182	9-19-88	7	0	3.67	16	5	0	0	42	37	20	17	0	11	33	.250	.351	.216	7.13	2.38
Hernandez, Ricardo	L-L	5-10	152	1-23-88	2	1	1.10	15	0	0	2	33	20	4	4	0	7	24	.179	.143	.184	6.61	1.93
Hodges, Josh	R-R	6-7	235	6-21-91	2	1	4.02	5	2	0	0	16	15	8	7	0	8	14	.238	.417	.196	8.04	4.60
Kainer, Andy	L-L	6-1	215	8-22-86	1	0	4.00	7	0	0	0	9	5	4	4	0	8	10	.167	.167	.167	10.00	8.00
Madden, Corey	R-R	6-1	195	3-30-84	0	0	0.00	4	0	0	0	4	2	0	0	0	1	4	.154	.250	.111	9.00	2.25
Miller, Andrew	L-L	6-7	205	5-21-85	0	0	2.57	2	2	0	0	7	8	2	2	0	4	10	.286	.000	.296	12.86	5.14
Montgomery, Matt	R-R	6-4	210	7-21-87	0	0	4.50	1	0	0	0	2	1	1	1	0	0	2	.167	.000	.250	9.00	0.00
Morales, Isaac	L-L	6-0	188	5-4-87	1	1	2.54	20	0	0	5	28	25	11	8	0	10	26	.238	.308	.228	8.26	3.18
Olmos, Edgar	L-L	6-5	180	4-12-90	0	0	0.00	2	2	0	0	5	1	0	0	0	2	5	.077	.000	.091	9.00	3.60
Peale, Tommy	R-R	6-3	225	11-11-86	0	0	3.00	3	1	0	0	6	6	2	2	0	3	3	.273	.333	.231	4.50	4.50
Roberts, Josh	R-R	6-5	230	5-12-84	0	0	2.57	2	2	0	0	7	8	2	2	0	3	6	.286	.333	.273	7.71	3.86
Sanchez, Anibal	R-R	6-0	220	2-27-84	0	0	3.38	1	1	0	0	3	3	1	1	0	2	0	.273	.250	.286	0.00	6.75
Sprague, Holden	R-R	6-2	210	7-24-87	1	1	3.79	12	9	0	0	38	38	21	16	2	7	24	.266	.351	.236	5.68	1.66
Teague, Sean	R-R	6-0	190	3-16-86	2	3	2.63	14	0	0	0	24	25	10	7	0	10	22	.260	.348	.233	8.25	3.75
Topp, Tyler	R-R	6-2	175	11-14-86	2	1	2.84	20	2	0	4	38	38	13	12	1	4	36	.270	.467	.216	8.53	0.95
Tucker, Ryan	R-R	6-1	205	12-6-86	1	0	2.25	2	2	0	0	8	5	2	2	0	2	7	.179	—	.179	7.88	2.25
Williamson, Scott	R-R	6-0	195	2-17-76	0	0	81.00	1	0	0	0	0	2	3	3	0	2	1	.667	1.000	.500	27.00	54.00

Fielding

Catcher	PCT	G	PO	A	E	DP	PB
Gimenez	.979	32	203	31	5	2	4
Hord	1.000	3	14	3	0	0	1
Krick	.889	2	8	0	1	0	1
Morales	.992	16	114	15	1	0	1
Paulino	.900	2	9	0	1	0	0
Peters	.981	7	42	9	1	1	2
Wilson	1.000	5	38	0	0	0	0

First Base	PCT	G	PO	A	E	DP
Kam	1.000	1	2	0	0	0
Krick	1.000	1	2	0	0	0
Lokken	.987	11	75	3	1	7
Morales	.991	12	109	6	1	5
Weaver	.991	38	330	14	3	27

Second Base	PCT	G	PO	A	E	DP
Brady	1.000	1	1	0	0	0
Diaz	.951	31	64	73	7	16
Garcia	1.000	8	15	28	0	8
Nunez	1.000	14	20	29	0	9
Peralta	.929	3	3	10	1	2
Simon	1.000	5	10	11	0	1

Third Base	PCT	G	PO	A	E	DP
Brady	.909	8	5	15	2	1
Dayleg	.919	22	12	56	6	1
Diaz	1.000	1	0	2	0	0
Garcia	.500	2	1	0	1	0
Krick	.917	3	1	10	1	1
Nunez	.950	6	5	14	1	5
Weaver	.972	15	9	26	1	2

Shortstop	PCT	G	PO	A	E	DP
Dayleg	.941	11	15	33	3	6
Peralta	.905	40	45	146	20	19
Perio	.857	4	6	6	2	2
Wade	1.000	1	1	2	0	0

Outfield	PCT	G	PO	A	E	DP
Bautista	1.000	7	9	0	0	0
Brantley	.952	20	18	2	1	0
Cooper	.986	39	71	2	1	1
Dunn	1.000	1	1	0	0	0
Hickman	.500	3	1	0	1	0
Keys	.988	49	76	3	1	1
Markel	1.000	6	12	0	0	0
Ozuna	.959	54	88	5	4	2
Peters	—	1	0	0	0	0

DSL MARLINS   ROOKIE

DOMINICAN SUMMER LEAGUE

Batting	B-T	HT	WT	DOB	AVG	vLH	vRH	G	AB	R	H	2B	3B	HR	RBI	BB	HBP	SH	SF	SO	SB	CS	SLG	OBP
Acosta, Pedro	R-R	6-2	213	0-0-00	.000	.000	.000	5	12	0	0	0	0	0	0	0	0	0	0	3	0	0	.000	.000
Bautista, Juan	B-R	5-10	170	1-25-90	.234	.206	.243	41	141	21	33	7	0	1	19	15	3	2	0	16	0	1	.305	.321
Bautista, Samuel	L-R	6-1	148	12-12-88	.143	.167	.138	22	70	6	10	4	1	0	3	13	2	0	0	34	3	2	.229	.294
Cuevas, Carlos	R-R	6-1	170	11-26-91	.444	.667	.333	3	9	3	4	1	0	1	5	1	0	0	0	0	0	0	.889	.500
Gomez, Raul	L-R	6-1	160	2-23-89	.208	.265	.179	29	101	11	21	3	1	0	11	11	1	1	1	20	1	2	.257	.289
Gonzalez, Jorge	L-L	6-3	183	12-22-90	.200	.368	.130	21	65	7	13	2	0	0	3	9	0	1	0	12	4	4	.231	.297
Hernandez, Yeison	B-R	5-10	150	6-29-92	.202	.130	.222	34	104	16	21	2	0	0	2	25	0	0	1	19	7	8	.221	.354
Jimenez, Joel	R-R	5-11	189	4-30-92	.122	.125	.121	14	41	3	5	0	0	0	0	8	1	0	0	14	0	1	.122	.280
Martinez, Juancito	R-R	6-1	170	6-10-89	.284	.333	.269	53	225	36	64	5	7	3	26	16	2	2	0	63	26	6	.409	.337
Martinez, Julio	R-R	6-1	145	3-5-91	.063	.167	.000	5	16	3	1	0	0	0	0	3	0	0	0	4	0	0	.063	.211
Mendoza, Pedro	R-R	6-0	148	5-11-91	.314	.195	.351	48	70	20	55	5	2	0	17	17	7	3	2	13	3	1	.366	.393
Morfe, Arsenio	R-R	5-10	173	12-15-88	.224	.100	.262	32	85	19	19	1	2	0	6	17	1	1	0	22	5	7	.282	.359
Munoz, Felix	L-L	6-1	193	4-7-92	.242	.270	.234	65	264	31	64	14	0	1	28	31	1	0	2	31	2	1	.307	.322
Ortiz, Luis	B-R	5-10	161	3-14-92	.264	.279	.260	53	174	28	46	8	1	0	16	28	4	1	3	24	16	9	.322	.373
Osuna, Hector	B-R	6-1	170	10-17-90	.246	.259	.242	39	122	14	30	3	2	2	20	16	3	1	2	23	3	1	.352	.343
Perez, Yefri	R-R	5-11	162	2-24-91	.236	.241	.235	59	220	37	52	9	4	0	29	30	3	4	2	28	21	2	.314	.333
Ramirez, Marc	R-R	6-2	185	7-17-91	.278	.292	.274	61	227	30	63	8	4	3	36	18	8	2	3	60	12	7	.388	.348
Solorzano, Jesus	R-R	6-0	190	8-8-90	.109	.000	.128	23	55	6	6	0	1	1	6	5	3	1	1	18	2	1	.200	.219
Soto, Mayobanex	R-R	6-3	185	5-5-91	.241	.347	.211	61	224	39	54	15	0	1	23	32	11	1	4	51	2	3	.321	.358
Urena, Maicol	R-R	6-0	165	11-11-90	.133	.000	.154	6	15	1	2	0	0	0	4	3	0	0	1	4	2	0	.133	.263

Pitching	B-T	HT	WT	DOB	W	L	ERA	G	GS	CG	SV	IP	H	R	ER	HR	BB	SO	AVG	vLH	vRH	K/9	BB/9
Arias, Gregory	R-R	6-2	187	7-21-92	1	0	4.50	3	0	0	0	4	5	2	2	0	3	4	.313	1.000	.267	9.00	6.75
Baez, Jaby	L-L	5-11	176	12-28-91	1	0	3.86	11	1	0	1	30	19	15	13	2	14	32	.176	.286	.168	9.49	4.15
Buret, Alfredo	R-R	6-1	160	8-22-87	1	0	1.53	5	0	0	1	18	17	6	3	0	5	10	.262	.273	.259	5.09	2.55
Caracas, Jhondervisth	R-R	6-1	165	1-10-92	0	1	5.40	6	0	0	0	7	5	7	4	0	10	6	.208	.375	.125	8.10	13.50
Cova, Kleyber	R-R	5-11	160	3-15-92	0	1	27.00	1	0	0	0	1	2	2	2	0	3	0	.333	.000	.500	0.00	40.50
Del Orbe, Ramon	R-R	5-11	177	2-17-92	3	2	2.97	19	0	0	8	33	36	14	11	0	22	22	.298	.458	.258	5.94	5.94

FLORIDA MARLINS

Delgadillo, Yonalis	R-R	6-2	170	1-26-91	0	1	8.44	5	0	0	0	5	4	6	5	1	8	4	.211	.200	.214	6.75	13.50
Estevez, Alvaro	R-R	6-2	180	3-15-89	3	0	2.20	4	3	0	0	16	10	6	4	0	6	18	.167	.000	.185	9.92	3.31
Fermin, Yeraldo	R-R	5-11	136	10-2-91	2	1	4.01	8	5	0	0	34	30	17	15	1	11	23	.240	.239	.241	6.15	2.94
Ferreira, Kelvin	L-L	6-0	156	10-31-90	4	2	1.08	15	0	0	2	33	35	14	4	0	10	29	.271	.214	.278	7.83	2.70
Gil, Daniel	R-R	6-5	184	3-28-90	4	3	1.76	8	8	0	0	51	39	20	10	1	7	54	.206	.274	.173	9.53	1.24
Jorge, Eduardo	R-R	6-0	194	12-19-91	0	2	2.91	5	4	0	0	22	20	9	7	1	6	23	.260	.320	.231	9.55	2.49
Joseph, Michael	R-R	6-4	170	5-28-92	0	1	2.63	14	0	0	1	27	30	17	8	1	6	24	.265	.321	.247	7.90	1.98
Lopez, Cesar	R-R	6-2	176	3-14-92	0	0	16.20	5	0	0	0	3	11	8	6	1	0	4	.524	.400	.563	10.80	0.00
Lopez, Jose	L-L	6-0	165	11-11-90	0	1	13.50	5	1	0	0	5	6	15	7	1	12	3	.300	.000	.316	5.79	23.14
Manzueta, Jheyson	R-R	6-2	162	12-5-89	0	3	2.36	11	11	0	0	53	38	22	14	1	34	57	.197	.147	.208	9.62	5.74
Oviedo, Grabiel	R-R	6-4	187	10-30-89	0	0	27.00	1	0	0	0	1	6	4	4	0	2	0	.545	—	.545	0.00	13.50
Reyes, Helpi	R-R	6-1	175	7-27-92	0	2	5.63	11	0	0	0	16	17	12	10	1	11	15	.274	.176	.311	8.44	6.19
Rodriguez, Jose	R-R	6-1	195	9-24-90	4	4	2.15	13	13	0	0	80	70	32	19	0	16	53	.234	.254	.229	5.99	1.81
Rojas, Wilfredo	R-R	6-2	150	8-31-89	2	5	4.62	14	8	0	0	60	65	45	31	2	21	30	.275	.341	.240	4.48	3.13
Solano, Aneurys	R-R	6-1	180	11-18-88	2	2	4.25	15	8	0	0	55	50	32	26	1	30	55	.245	.350	.220	9.00	4.91
Suero, Miguel	R-R	6-2	180	3-7-91	0	0	0.00	1	0	0	0	1	0	0	0	0	0	2	.000	—	.000	18.00	0.00
Tamares, Joel	R-R	—	—	8-13-90	1	3	3.29	10	4	0	0	27	22	22	10	2	18	21	.216	.269	.197	6.91	5.93
Urena, Jose	R-R	6-3	172	9-12-91	3	3	6.75	14	2	0	2	27	36	22	20	0	11	15	.313	.333	.308	5.06	3.71

Fielding

Catcher	PCT	G	PO	A	E	DP	PB
Acosta	1.000	5	19	1	0	0	1
Bautista	.969	40	259	51	10	2	11
Jimenez	.980	13	80	18	2	0	3
Osuna	.971	20	135	31	5	2	4

First Base	PCT	G	PO	A	E	DP
Gomez	1.000	1	3	0	0	0
Mendoza	1.000	1	1	0	0	1
Munoz	.986	46	398	24	6	29
Osuna	.979	5	42	4	1	2
Solorzano	1.000	1	1	0	0	0
Soto	.987	27	214	12	3	8

Second Base	PCT	G	PO	A	E	DP
Hernandez	.857	4	6	0	1	0

	PCT	G	PO	A	E	DP
Mendoza	.947	4	9	9	1	4
Morfe	.859	15	21	34	9	7
Ortiz	.964	44	95	117	8	19
Perez	.934	11	27	30	4	4

Third Base	PCT	G	PO	A	E	DP
Cuevas	1.000	1	0	2	0	0
Mendoza	.942	33	37	61	6	2
Morfe	1.000	5	0	5	0	0
Ortiz	.900	6	5	13	2	1
Soto	.810	32	12	73	20	1

Shortstop	PCT	G	PO	A	E	DP
Hernandez	.870	20	33	54	13	7
Mendoza	.956	8	9	34	2	3
Perez	.902	41	95	136	25	22

Outfield	PCT	G	PO	A	E	DP
Bautista	.941	13	15	1	1	0
Gomez	.900	25	24	3	3	2
Gonzalez	.923	19	23	1	2	0
Martinez	.954	53	98	5	5	1
Martinez	1.000	5	6	1	0	1
Morfe	.900	5	6	3	1	0
Munoz	.886	25	27	4	4	0
Ortiz	.000	1	0	0	1	0
Ramirez	.969	58	84	9	3	0
Solorzano	.957	19	22	0	1	0
Urena	1.000	2	2	0	0	0

Houston Astros

SEASON IN A SENTENCE: In spite of an aging, patchwork roster, the mediocrity of the National League Central kept the Astros in playoff contention through most of July until things finally fell apart and cost manager Cecil Cooper his job in September.

HIGH POINT: Houston never got more than four games over .500 and never had more than a four-game winning streak, and both high-water marks came for the last time on July 24, when Mike Hampton outdueled Johan Santana and hit a two-run home run as the Astros beat the Mets 5-4. You won't be surprised to learn that Hampton went on the disabled list shortly thereafter, later having shoulder surgery that will knock him out for 2010.

LOW POINT: The Astros staggered to the finish, going 10-17 in September (including a nine-game losing streak) to finish 74-88, 27th in baseball in scoring and 23rd in runs allowed. Ace Roy Oswalt, who won a career-low eight games, was shut down with a couple of weeks left in the season with back and hip pain.

NOTABLE ROOKIES: Years of focusing on the major league team at the expense of the farm system meant that Houston had little to offer in the way of rookie reinforcements. Righthander Felipe Paulino got 17 starts even though he compiled a 3-11, 6.27 mark in 98 innings. Righthander Bud Norris looked a bit more promising when he got called up in the second half, going 6-3, 4.53 in 56 innings.

KEY TRANSACTIONS: For a team that has been on a clear slide toward mediocrity (17 games below .500 since playing in the 2005 World Series), the Astros did little more than tweak their roster, signing Hampton and catcher Ivan Rodriguez as free agents before the season. They were neither buyers nor sellers at the trade deadline, though they did send Rodriguez to the Rangers in August for a few marginal prospects.

DOWN ON THE FARM: The lack of talent manifested itself in the minor leagues as well, where the Astros ranked dead last in organization winning percentage. Six of their seven affiliates had either the worst or second-worst records in their respective leagues. Hope for the future lies with the last two first-round picks, catcher Jason Castro (2008), who could reach Houston in 2010, and shortstop Jiovanni Mier (2009), the top position prospect in the Rookie-level Appalachian League.

OPENING DAY PAYROLL: $102,996,414

PLAYERS OF THE YEAR

MAJOR LEAGUE	MINOR LEAGUE
Wandy Rodriguez lhp	**Koby Clemens** c
14-12, 3.02	(High A/Double-A)
193 SO in 206 IP,	.341/.415/.620
9th in NL in ERA	45 2B, 22 HR

ORGANIZATION LEADERS

BATTING   *Minimum 250 at-bats

MAJORS

*AVG	Miguel Tejada	.313
*OPS	Lance Berkman	.907
HR	Carlos Lee	26
RBI	Carlos Lee	102

MINORS

*AVG	Clemens, Koby, Corpus Christi/Lancaster	.341
R	Gaston, Jonathan, Lancaster	119
H	Shuck, Jack, Lancaster	175
TB	Gaston, Jonathan, Lancaster	310
2B	Clemens, Koby, Corpus Christi/Lancaster	45
3B	Gaston, Jonathan, Lancaster	15
HR	Gaston, Jonathan, Lancaster	35
RBI	Clemens, Koby, Corpus Christi/Lancaster	123
BB	Pellegrini, Brian, Lancaster/Lexington	73
SO	Gaston, Jonathan, Lancaster	164
SB	Abercrombie, Reggie, Round Rock	26
*OBP	Clemens, Koby, Corpus Christi/Lancaster	.415
*SLG	Clemens, Koby, Corpus Christi/Lancaster	.620

PITCHING   †Minimum 75 innings

MAJORS

W	Wandy Rodriguez	14
†ERA	Wandy Rodriguez	3.02
SO	Wandy Rodriguez	193

MINORS

W	Trinidad, Polin, Corpus Christi/Round Rock	13
L	Duncan, David, Lancaster/Lexington	13
	Greenwalt, Kyle, Lexington	13
†ERA	Norris, Bud, Round Rock	2.63
G	Meszaros, Daniel, Lexington/Corpus Christi	51
GS	Perez, Sergio, Corpus Christi	27
SV	Paronto, Chad, Round Rock	24
IP	Trinidad, Polin, Corpus Christi/Round Rock	170
BB	Muecke, Josh, Round Rock	67
SO	Lyles, Jordan, Lexington	167
†AVG	Norris, Bud, Round Rock	.237

2009 PERFORMANCE

General Manager: Ed Wade. **Farm Director:** Ricky Bennett. **Scouting Director:** Bobby Heck.

Class	Team	League	W	L	PCT	Finish*	Manager(s)
Majors	Houston Astros	National	74	88	.457	12th (16)	Cecil Cooper/Dave Clark
Triple-A	Round Rock Express	Pacific Coast	63	81	.438	15th (16)	Marc Bombard
Double-A	Corpus Christi Hooks	Texas	61	79	.436	t-7th (8)	Luis Pujols
High A	Lancaster JetHawks	California	56	84	.400	10th (10)	Wes Clements
Low A	Lexington Legends	South Atlantic	68	72	.486	9th (16)	Tom Lawless
Short-season	Tri-City ValleyCats	New York-Penn	27	48	.360	13th (14)	Jim Pankovits
Rookie	Greeneville Astros	Appalachian	27	40	.403	9th (10)	Rodney Linares
Rookie	GCL Astros	Gulf Coast	18	38	.321	16th (16)	Omar Lopez
Overall 2009 Minor League Record			320	442	.420	30th (30)	

*Finish in overall standings (No. of teams in league). †League champion.

ORGANIZATION STATISTICS

HOUSTON ASTROS

NATIONAL LEAGUE

Batting	B-T	HT	WT	DOB	AVG	vLH	vRH	G	AB	R	H	2B	3B	HR	RBI	BB	HBP	SH	SF	SO	SB	CS	SLG	OBP
Berkman, Lance	B-L	6-1	220	2-10-76	.274	.231	.291	136	460	73	126	31	1	25	80	97	1	0	4	98	7	4	.509	.399
Blum, Geoff	B-R	6-3	205	4-26-73	.247	.345	.239	120	381	34	94	14	1	10	49	33	7	0	6	61	0	1	.367	.314
Boone, Aaron	R-R	6-3	205	3-9-73	.000	.000	.000	10	13	0	0	0	0	0	0	0	0	0	0	2	0	0	.000	.071
Bourn, Michael	L-R	5-11	180	12-27-82	.285	.287	.285	157	606	97	173	27	12	3	35	63	2	5	2	140	61	12	.384	.354
Coste, Chris	R-R	6-1	210	2-4-73	.204	.200	.205	43	103	3	21	5	0	0	10	8	0	0	1	28	0	0	.252	.259
2-team total (45 Philadelphia)					.224	—		88	205	15	46	13	0	2	18	22	1	1	1	55	0	0	.317	.301
Erstad, Darin	L-L	6-2	215	6-4-74	.194	.154	.198	107	134	13	26	8	2	2	11	14	0	1	1	31	0	2	.328	.268
Johnson, Chris	R-R	6-3	220	10-1-84	.091	.000	.133	11	22	1	2	0	0	0	1	1	0	0	0	6	0	0	.091	.130
Kata, Matt	B-R	6-1	185	3-14-78	.200	.143	.209	40	50	2	10	1	0	0	5	0	1	0	1	5	1	0	.220	.212
Keppinger, Jeff	R-R	6-0	185	4-21-80	.256	.314	.227	107	305	35	78	13	3	7	29	27	3	7	2	33	0	2	.387	.320
Lee, Carlos	R-R	6-2	265	6-20-76	.300	.325	.293	160	610	65	183	35	1	26	102	41	3	0	8	51	5	3	.489	.343
Manzella, Tommy	R-R	6-2	200	4-16-83	.200	.500	.000	7	5	0	1	0	0	0	0	0	0	0	0	4	0	0	.200	.200
Matsui, Kazuo	B-R	5-10	180	10-23-75	.250	.271	.244	132	476	56	119	20	2	9	46	34	3	16	4	85	19	3	.357	.302
Maysonet, Edwin	R-R	6-1	190	10-17-81	.290	.313	.283	39	69	9	20	2	0	1	7	5	0	4	1	19	0	0	.362	.333
Michaels, Jason	R-R	6-0	210	5-4-76	.237	.268	.215	102	135	17	32	12	1	4	16	16	1	0	0	38	1	2	.430	.322
Pence, Hunter	R-R	6-4	220	4-13-83	.282	.294	.279	159	585	76	165	26	5	25	72	58	1	0	3	109	14	11	.472	.346
Quintero, Humberto	R-R	5-9	205	8-2-79	.236	.273	.226	60	157	11	37	8	1	4	14	7	4	0	0	41	0	0	.376	.286
Rodriguez, Ivan	R-R	5-9	190	11-30-71	.251	.303	.238	93	327	41	82	15	2	8	34	13	1	1	2	74	0	2	.382	.280
Smith, Jason	L-R	6-3	195	7-24-77	.000	.000	.000	21	25	1	0	0	0	0	1	0	0	1	1	9	0	0	.000	.000
Tejada, Miguel	R-R	5-9	215	5-25-74	.313	.326	.310	158	635	83	199	46	1	14	86	19	11	0	8	48	5	2	.455	.340
Towles, J.R.	R-R	6-2	195	2-11-84	.188	.286	.147	16	48	7	9	2	0	2	3	3	1	1	0	16	0	0	.354	.250

Pitching	B-T	HT	WT	DOB	W	L	ERA	G	GS	CG	SV	IP	H	R	ER	HR	BB	SO	AVG	vLH	vRH	K/9	BB/9
Arias, Alberto	R-R	5-11	155	10-14-83	2	1	3.35	42	0	0	0	46	49	21	17	1	19	39	.272	.276	.269	7.69	3.74
Backe, Brandon	R-R	6-0	195	4-5-78	0	0	10.38	5	1	0	0	13	21	15	15	5	6	10	.362	.370	.355	6.92	4.15
Bazardo, Yorman	R-R	6-2	220	7-11-84	1	3	7.88	10	6	0	0	32	37	31	28	2	22	17	.296	.293	.299	4.78	6.19
Brocail, Doug	L-R	6-5	235	5-16-67	1	0	4.58	20	0	0	0	18	21	9	9	4	13	9	.309	.355	.270	4.58	6.62
Byrdak, Tim	L-L	5-11	195	10-31-73	1	2	3.23	76	0	0	0	61	39	23	22	10	36	58	.178	.184	.172	8.51	5.28
Fulchino, Jeff	R-R	6-5	275	11-26-79	6	4	3.40	61	0	0	0	82	70	33	31	7	27	71	.233	.261	.209	7.79	2.96
Geary, Geoff	R-R	6-0	180	8-26-76	1	3	8.10	16	0	0	0	20	30	19	18	4	10	12	.357	.355	.358	5.40	4.50
Gervacio, Samuel	R-R	6-0	175	1-10-85	1	1	2.14	29	0	0	0	21	16	5	5	1	8	25	.219	.250	.208	10.71	3.43
Hampton, Mike	R-L	5-10	195	9-9-72	7	10	5.30	21	21	0	0	112	128	71	66	13	46	74	.298	.238	.316	5.95	3.70
Hawkins, LaTroy	R-R	6-5	215	12-21-72	1	4	2.13	65	0	0	11	63	60	16	15	7	16	45	.253	.203	.303	6.39	2.27
Lopez, Wilton	R-R	6-0	200	7-19-83	0	2	8.38	8	2	0	0	19	32	21	18	4	8	9	.386	.377	.400	4.19	3.72
Moehler, Brian	R-R	6-3	225	12-31-71	8	12	5.47	29	29	1	0	155	187	101	94	21	51	91	.298	.280	.316	5.30	2.97
Norris, Bud	R-R	6-0	225	3-2-85	6	3	4.53	11	10	0	0	56	59	29	28	9	25	54	.272	.200	.323	8.73	4.04
Ortiz, Russ	R-R	6-1	215	6-5-74	3	6	5.57	23	13	0	0	86	95	56	53	8	48	65	.289	.272	.305	6.83	5.04
Oswalt, Roy	R-R	6-0	190	8-29-77	8	6	4.12	30	30	3	0	181	183	83	83	19	42	138	.265	.279	.252	6.85	2.08
Paronto, Chad	R-R	6-5	285	7-28-75	0	0	12.15	6	0	0	0	7	15	9	9	4	1	3	.455	.467	.444	4.05	1.35
Paulino, Felipe	R-R	6-2	260	10-5-83	3	11	6.27	23	17	0	0	98	126	73	68	20	37	93	.317	.354	.286	8.57	3.41
Rodriguez, Wandy	R-L	5-11	195	1-18-79	14	12	3.02	33	33	1	0	206	192	77	69	21	63	193	.250	.192	.264	8.45	2.76
Sadler, Billy	R-R	6-0	195	9-21-81	0	0	13.50	1	0	0	0	1	2	2	2	0	1	2	.333	.500	.000	13.50	6.75
Sampson, Chris	R-R	6-1	205	5-23-78	4	2	5.04	49	0	0	3	55	66	34	31	2	21	33	.293	.315	.272	5.37	3.42
Valverde, Jose	R-R	6-4	280	3-24-78	4	2	2.33	52	0	0	25	54	40	15	14	5	21	56	.207	.281	.144	9.33	3.50
Wright, Wesley	R-L	5-11	175	1-28-85	3	4	5.44	49	0	0	0	45	53	27	27	9	25	47	.299	.359	.265	9.47	5.04

Fielding

Catcher	PCT	G	PO	A	E	DP	PB
Coste	1.000	26	116	5	0	0	0
Quintero	.987	59	358	36	5	6	5
Rodriguez	.994	90	618	41	4	4	5
Towles	1.000	15	83	8	0	0	1

First Base	PCT	G	PO	A	E	DP
Berkman	.995	131	1107	116	6	122
Blum	1.000	10	58	3	0	2
Boone	1.000	2	9	1	0	1
Coste	.992	15	118	7	1	16
Erstad	1.000	15	94	7	0	13

Kata	1.000	1	5	0	0	1
Lee	1.000	1	2	0	0	0
Second Base	**PCT**	**G**	**PO**	**A**	**E**	**DP**
Kata	1.000	7	9	24	0	4
Keppinger	.988	22	33	48	1	12

	PCT	G	PO	A	E	DP
Matsui	.991	130	279	373	6	99
Maysonet	.971	15	22	46	2	9
Smith	1.000	5	4	8	0	5

Third Base	PCT	G	PO	A	E	DP
Blum	.986	102	45	164	3	15
Boone	1.000	1	0	2	0	0
Johnson	1.000	7	2	5	0	0
Keppinger	.955	67	38	110	7	16
Maysonet	1.000	7	1	8	0	0

	PCT	G	PO	A	E	DP
Smith	1.000	1	0	1	0	0

Shortstop	PCT	G	PO	A	E	DP
Blum	—	1	0	0	0	0
Keppinger	1.000	11	5	13	0	2
Manzella	1.000	2	1	3	0	1
Maysonet	1.000	3	1	1	0	0
Smith	—	1	0	0	0	0
Tejada	.970	158	214	475	21	105

Outfield	PCT	G	PO	A	E	DP
Bourn	.992	154	371	11	3	0
Erstad	1.000	28	15	0	0	0
Kata	—	4	0	0	0	0
Keppinger	1.000	2	0	1	0	0
Lee	.991	154	211	9	2	0
Michaels	1.000	45	52	0	0	0
Pence	.985	157	316	16	5	2

ROUND ROCK EXPRESS   TRIPLE-A
PACIFIC COAST LEAGUE

Batting	B-T	HT	WT	DOB	AVG	vLH	vRH	G	AB	R	H	2B	3B	HR	RBI	BB	HBP	SH	SF	SO	SB	CS	SLG	OBP
Abercrombie, Reggie	R-R	6-3	215	7-15-81	.271	.299	.259	134	517	64	140	28	6	11	52	29	5	2	4	159	26	10	.412	.314
Blum, Geoff	B-R	6-3	205	4-26-73	.143	.000	.200	2	7	0	1	1	0	0	1	0	0	0	0	1	0	0	.286	.143
Bogusevic, Brian	L-L	6-3	215	2-18-84	.271	.231	.283	138	520	68	141	25	3	6	53	53	3	5	0	118	22	3	.365	.342
Boone, Aaron	R-R	6-3	205	3-9-73	.091	.200	.000	4	11	1	1	0	0	0	0	0	0	0	0	1	0	0	.091	.091
Esposito, Brian	R-R	6-1	190	2-24-79	.318	.250	.333	31	88	7	28	4	0	2	16	4	2	0	1	14	0	0	.432	.358
Fixler, Jon	R-R	6-1	205	6-13-86	.000	.000	.000	2	7	0	0	0	0	0	0	1	0	0	0	4	0	0	.000	.000
Gall, John	R-R	6-0	200	4-2-78	.246	.262	.241	125	398	34	98	19	0	9	45	41	3	0	3	67	4	4	.362	.319
Iorg, Eli	R-R	6-4	215	3-14-83	.209	.364	.156	20	43	3	9	2	1	0	4	1	0	0	0	13	1	0	.302	.227
Johnson, Chris	R-R	6-3	220	10-1-84	.281	.324	.264	104	384	48	108	20	5	13	42	21	4	0	3	90	2	1	.461	.323
Kata, Matt	B-R	6-1	185	3-14-78	.269	.313	.252	66	227	22	61	10	1	2	22	12	3	1	1	25	8	0	.348	.313
Manzella, Tommy	R-R	6-2	200	4-16-83	.289	.240	.308	133	530	68	153	31	5	9	56	40	1	7	2	99	12	3	.417	.339
Maysonet, Edwin	R-R	6-1	190	10-17-81	.235	.264	.224	59	187	21	44	11	0	1	14	26	1	2	1	39	3	0	.310	.330
Quintero, Humberto	R-R	5-9	205	8-2-79	.100	.000	.143	4	10	0	1	1	0	0	1	0	2	0	0	4	0	0	.200	.250
Ramirez, Yordany	R-R	6-1	190	7-31-84	.256	.239	.263	133	457	41	117	22	1	11	47	11	2	4	3	64	14	8	.381	.275
Saccomanno, Mark	R-R	6-3	225	4-30-80	.278	.259	.283	137	493	67	137	23	5	15	67	34	6	1	5	87	5	0	.436	.329
Santangelo, Lou	R-R	6-1	205	3-16-83	.212	.288	.184	84	269	24	57	18	2	5	26	21	1	1	2	79	0	0	.349	.270
Smith, Jason	L-R	6-3	195	7-24-77	.198	.250	.191	83	262	32	52	6	2	6	28	13	3	4	3	83	11	2	.305	.242
Spann, Chad	R-R	6-1	195	10-25-83	.246	.191	.277	63	130	17	32	5	0	1	8	10	2	0	0	32	0	0	.308	.310
Sutton, Drew	B-B	6-3	185	6-30-83	.267	1.000	.214	5	15	1	4	0	0	0	0	2	1	0	0	2	0	0	.267	.389
Towles, J.R.	R-R	6-2	195	2-11-84	.276	.432	.208	56	145	23	40	12	1	4	22	22	6	2	3	27	3	0	.455	.386
Vallejo, Jose	R-R	6-0	175	9-11-86	.350	.333	.364	7	20	2	7	3	0	0	0	0	0	0	0	4	0	0	.500	.350
2-team total (84 Oklahoma City)					.240			91	329	34	79	10	5	2	28	22	0	1	2	77	3	2	.319	.286

Pitching	B-T	HT	WT	DOB	W	L	ERA	G	GS	CG	SV	IP	H	R	ER	BB	SO	AVG	vLH	vRH	K/9	BB/9
Abreu, Erick	R-R	6-1	170	8-9-83	2	2	7.90	6	5	0	0	27	36	24	24	7	14	14	.319	.263	.375	4.61	4.61
Arias, Alberto	R-R	5-11	155	10-14-83	2	2	3.86	4	3	0	0	16	14	9	7	1	10	15	.237	.211	.250	8.27	5.51
Backe, Brandon	R-R	6-0	195	4-5-78	0	1	4.50	2	2	0	0	10	13	5	5	0	3	4	.317	.294	.333	3.60	2.70
Bazardo, Yorman	R-R	6-2	220	7-11-84	9	6	3.20	23	20	3	0	135	121	51	48	15	32	80	.244	.255	.236	5.33	2.13
Benitez, Armando	R-R	6-4	260	11-3-72	2	0	3.86	7	0	0	1	9	7	5	4	4	3	9	.200	.158	.250	8.68	2.89
Brocail, Doug	L-R	6-5	235	5-16-67	0	1	5.14	7	0	0	0	7	8	5	4	0	2	3	.296	.267	.333	3.86	2.57
Burton, T.J.	L-R	6-3	185	7-30-83	0	1	6.06	9	0	0	0	16	20	11	11	3	7	7	.308	.290	.324	3.86	3.86
Capellan, Jose	R-R	6-4	245	1-13-81	2	10	7.07	30	14	0	0	98	133	80	77	12	49	74	.328	.322	.335	6.80	4.50
Corcoran, Roy	R-R	5-10	185	5-11-80	0	0	4.12	13	1	0	0	20	24	12	9	0	7	11	.312	.333	.286	5.03	3.20
2-team total (3 Tacoma)					1	0	3.57	16	1	0	0	27	13	9	0	7	13	—	—		5.16	2.78
Daigle, Casey	R-R	6-5	240	4-4-81	4	3	2.91	49	0	0	5	56	61	19	18	3	25	53	.285	.294	.279	8.57	4.04
Donnelly, Brendan	R-R	6-3	240	7-4-71	2	0	1.75	24	0	0	6	26	21	6	5	0	7	23	.233	.290	.203	8.06	2.45
Englebrook, Evan	R-R	6-8	225	4-28-82	1	1	6.97	9	0	0	0	10	14	8	8	1	3	8	.326	.444	.240	6.97	2.61
Fulchino, Jeff	R-R	6-5	275	11-26-79	0	0	6.75	2	1	0	0	4	3	3	3	0	2	3	.200	.143	.250	6.75	4.50
Geary, Geoff	R-R	6-0	180	8-26-76	1	3	4.95	26	0	0	2	40	53	23	22	4	11	26	.323	.284	.356	5.85	2.48
Gervacio, Samuel	R-R	6-0	175	1-10-85	2	2	4.82	39	0	0	0	52	43	30	28	5	21	58	.223	.250	.204	9.97	3.61
Hensley, Clay	R-R	5-11	190	8-31-79	1	0	7.20	6	1	0	0	10	12	9	8	1	7	5	.324	.364	.267	4.50	6.30
2-team total (19 New Orleans)					9	4	3.56	25	20	1	0	124	117	55	49	9	45	87	—	—		6.31	3.27
Johnson, Jeremy	R-R	6-3	170	7-19-82	5	8	3.51	21	13	0	2	95	96	45	37	4	27	57	.260	.261	.260	5.40	2.56
Lumsden, Tyler	L-L	6-4	215	5-9-83	0	0	4.42	14	0	0	0	18	23	9	9	2	12	10	.315	.148	.413	4.91	5.89
McKeller, Ryan	R-R	6-5	220	7-8-83	1	2	6.54	17	0	0	0	32	32	25	23	3	10	33	.264	.263	.266	9.38	2.84
McLemore, Mark	L-L	6-2	220	10-9-80	5	10	4.87	18	18	0	0	92	97	52	50	7	34	49	.279	.250	.290	4.78	3.31
Moehler, Brian	R-R	6-3	225	12-31-71	0	0	2.25	1	1	0	0	4	3	2	1	0	3	0	.188	.500	.000	0.00	6.75
Muecke, Josh	L-L	6-3	195	1-9-82	7	11	4.90	29	20	0	0	136	149	90	74	15	67	85	.284	.275	.288	5.63	4.43
Musser, Neal	L-L	6-1	235	8-25-80	0	0	5.14	4	0	0	0	7	4	4	4	0	4	7	.321	.200	.389	9.00	5.14
Norris, Bud	R-R	6-0	225	3-2-85	4	9	2.63	19	19	0	0	120	104	42	35	6	53	112	.237	.250	.228	8.40	3.98
Paronto, Chad	R-R	6-5	285	7-28-75	2	1	1.39	44	0	0	24	52	34	8	8	1	14	39	.194	.224	.172	6.79	2.44
Paulino, Felipe	R-R	6-2	260	10-5-83	2	1	3.12	7	7	0	0	35	30	13	12	1	23	29	.233	.273	.173	7.53	5.97
Sadler, Billy	R-R	6-0	195	9-21-81	0	0	3.52	3	3	0	0	8	9	4	3	0	2	6	.310	.188	.462	7.04	2.35
2-team total (13 Fresno)					5	3	5.12	16	16	0	0	63	73	38	36	4	31	57	—	—		8.10	4.41
Sampson, Chris	R-R	6-1	205	5-23-78	0	0	7.50	6	0	0	0	6	7	5	5	0	2	5	.292	.286	.300	7.50	3.00
Trinidad, Polin	L-L	6-3	195	11-19-84	6	5	4.53	13	12	0	0	87	90	46	44	18	25	59	.260	.310	.236	6.08	2.58
Van Hekken, Andy	R-L	6-3	185	7-31-79	1	1	3.86	6	3	0	0	26	32	12	11	1	6	16	.314	.300	.327	5.61	2.10
Wright, Wesley	R-L	5-11	175	1-28-85	2	1	3.32	13	1	0	0	19	13	7	7	0	10	18	.206	.194	.219	8.53	4.74

Fielding

Catcher	PCT	G	PO	A	E	DP	PB
Esposito	.979	28	131	8	3	1	5
Fixler	1.000	2	11	0	0	0	0
Quintero	1.000	4	21	1	0	0	0
Santangelo	.991	81	515	45	5	5	6
Towles	.990	45	268	25	3	1	3

First Base	PCT	G	PO	A	E	DP
Boone	1.000	2	10	0	0	0
Gall	.987	37	280	16	4	28
Saccomanno	.990	110	896	58	10	89
Santangelo	1.000	1	1	0	0	0
Smith	1.000	9	34	1	0	2

Second Base	PCT	G	PO	A	E	DP
Gall	—	1	0	0	0	0

	PCT	G	PO	A	E	DP
Kata	.952	31	52	86	7	16
Maysonet	.982	45	94	127	4	20
Smith	.993	54	116	151	2	35
Spann	.986	18	33	36	1	11
Sutton	1.000	5	9	15	0	6
Vallejo	1.000	7	10	10	0	3

Third Base	PCT	G	PO	A	E	DP
Blum	1.000	2	1	8	0	0
Boone	1.000	2	2	4	0	0
Johnson	.947	102	56	193	14	15
Kata	.962	13	10	15	1	3
Maysonet	.833	5	2	8	2	1
Saccomanno	.909	13	6	24	3	2
Smith	—	2	0	0	0	0
Spann	.921	19	9	26	3	4

Shortstop	PCT	G	PO	A	E	DP
Manzella	.977	130	182	369	13	80
Maysonet	.957	9	9	13	1	2
Smith	1.000	9	15	18	0	6

Outfield	PCT	G	PO	A	E	DP
Abercrombie	.972	127	278	2	8	0
Bogusevic	.983	134	283	7	5	2
Gall	1.000	33	37	4	0	1
Iorg	.933	9	14	0	1	0
Kata	1.000	20	28	2	0	1
Maysonet	—	1	0	0	0	0
Ramirez	.980	128	341	8	7	4
Smith	1.000	6	10	2	0	0
Spann	1.000	1	1	0	0	0

CORPUS CHRISTI HOOKS

DOUBLE-A

TEXAS LEAGUE

Batting	B-T	HT	WT	DOB	AVG	vLH	vRH	G	AB	R	H	2B	3B	HR	RBI	BB	HBP	SH	SF	SO	SB	CS	SLG	OBP
Barnes, Brandon	R-R	6-2	210	5-15-86	.095	.250	.000	7	21	2	2	0	0	1	3	0	0	0	7	0	0	.238	.208
Boone, Aaron	R-R	6-3	205	3-9-73	.200	.125	.286	7	15	2	3	1	0	0	1	3	0	0	0	3	0	0	.267	.333
Castro, Jason	L-R	6-3	210	6-18-87	.293	.302	.290	63	239	38	70	11	1	3	29	25	2	0	2	35	2	1	.385	.362
Clemens, Koby	R-R	5-11	193	12-4-86	.235	.000	.267	5	17	2	4	0	0	0	2	3	0	0	1	2	0	0	.235	.333
DeLome, Collin	L-R	6-2	195	12-18-85	.255	.225	.264	125	467	79	119	18	10	20	61	37	11	5	2	141	15	8	.465	.323
Diaz, Mike	L-R	5-10	160	4-11-87	.000	—	.000	1	1	0	0	0	0	0	0	0	0	0	0	1	0	0	.000	.000
Duran, German	R-R	5-10	185	8-3-84	.136	.273	.091	14	44	2	6	1	0	0	2	4	3	0	1	11	1	0	.159	.250
Einertson, Mitch	R-R	5-10	178	4-4-86	.260	.230	.271	88	288	36	75	13	0	8	33	23	3	1	1	50	3	1	.389	.321
Erstad, Darin	L-L	6-2	215	6-4-74	.333	.000	.500	2	9	1	3	2	0	0	1	0	0	0	0	2	0	0	.556	.333
Esposito, Brian	R-R	6-1	190	2-24-79	.209	.292	.177	49	172	16	36	5	1	3	22	5	4	3	0	27	0	0	.302	.249
Fixler, Jon	R-R	6-1	205	6-13-86	.194	.190	.195	34	108	15	21	5	1	9	23	10	2	0	2	24	0	0	.509	.270
Florentino, Jhon	R-R	6-0	155	8-22-83	.266	.283	.260	112	399	43	106	15	6	5	43	30	2	2	3	70	6	1	.371	.318
Flores, Josh	R-R	6-0	200	11-18-85	.239	.300	.220	45	163	25	39	10	2	1	10	14	2	0	0	34	9	2	.344	.307
Locke, Drew	R-R	6-1	205	2-28-83	.338	.366	.328	129	503	81	170	31	3	20	109	46	1	0	8	84	2	2	.531	.389
Lopez, Jose	R-R	5-11	195	3-8-85	.000	.000	.000	2	4	0	0	0	0	0	0	0	0	0	0	0	0	0	.000	.000
Matsui, Kazuo	B-R	5-10	180	10-23-75	.214	.000	.273	4	14	3	3	0	0	0	2	2	0	0	0	4	0	0	.214	.313
Meyer, Drew	L-R	5-10	200	8-29-81	.291	.330	.278	120	443	70	129	29	1	5	51	50	1	5	3	74	2	0	.395	.362
Molina, Felix	L-R	5-8	180	5-5-83	.239	.196	.252	70	209	28	50	8	2	5	25	11	1	1	3	22	2	2	.368	.310
Moresi, Nick	R-R	6-4	180	11-22-84	.208	.277	.184	56	183	21	38	10	1	7	22	8	2	0	1	52	1	0	.383	.247
Ori, Mark	L-R	6-4	225	12-16-83	.262	.294	.252	125	423	52	111	28	0	1	45	41	6	0	3	88	0	1	.336	.334
Sadler, Ray	R-R	6-1	190	8-23-83	.129	.154	.122	16	62	5	8	2	0	1	7	4	1	0	0	15	0	0	.210	.194
Spann, Chad	R-R	6-1	195	10-25-83	.129	.125	.130	21	62	2	8	2	0	0	2	4	0	0	0	14	0	0	.161	.182
Sutil, Wladimir	R-R	5-10	155	10-31-84	.273	.317	.258	125	472	77	129	21	0	1	37	44	12	5	3	42	19	13	.324	.348
Van Ostrand, Jimmy	R-R	6-4	210	8-7-84	.283	.265	.291	113	367	44	104	18	1	16	71	43	5	0	3	67	0	0	.469	.364

Pitching	B-T	HT	WT	DOB	W	L	ERA	G	GS	CG	SV	IP	H	R	ER	HR	BB	SO	AVG	vLH	vRH	K/9	BB/9
Abad, Fernando	L-L	6-2	170	12-17-85	0	1	3.21	3	3	0	0	14	12	7	5	1	3	13	.222	.179	.269	8.36	1.93
Abreu, Erick	R-R	6-1	170	8-9-83	0	2	2.06	27	1	0	0	48	44	12	11	4	11	47	.250	.216	.284	8.81	2.06
Arguello, Doug	L-L	6-3	190	11-21-84	3	4	3.36	14	14	1	0	75	70	30	28	4	26	55	.249	.172	.272	6.60	3.12
Backe, Brandon	R-R	6-0	195	4-5-78	3	0	1.38	4	4	0	0	26	18	4	4	0	7	17	.200	.250	.143	5.88	2.42
Baugh, Kenny	R-R	6-4	225	2-5-79	4	4	5.12	12	12	0	0	65	59	46	37	6	29	38	.244	.236	.255	5.26	4.02
Brocail, Doug	L-R	6-5	235	5-16-67	1	0	0.00	2	0	0	0	2	2	0	0	0	0	1	.250	.200	.333	4.50	0.00
Burton, T.J.	L-R	6-3	185	7-30-83	0	3	4.59	28	0	0	12	33	42	20	17	8	7	18	.307	.303	.311	4.86	1.89
Englebrook, Evan	R-R	6-8	225	4-28-82	2	0	3.16	21	0	0	9	26	19	12	9	2	9	16	.207	.130	.316	5.61	3.16
Estrada, Paul	R-R	6-1	220	9-10-82	0	1	10.80	7	0	0	1	7	11	8	8	1	5	4	.367	.100	.500	5.40	6.75
Hudspeth, Casey	R-R	6-0	165	10-1-84	4	6	6.23	14	14	1	0	74	93	58	51	12	34	29	.306	.345	.259	3.54	4.15
James, Brad	R-R	6-2	210	6-19-84	2	10	6.69	23	21	1	0	108	127	84	80	10	62	55	.303	.322	.284	4.60	5.18
Lo, Chia-Jen	R-R	5-11	181	4-7-86	0	2	2.31	30	0	0	2	39	30	12	10	1	20	39	.213	.236	.188	9.00	4.62
Lopez, Wilton	R-R	6-0	200	7-19-83	4	5	4.73	29	1	0	0	110	133	62	58	8	13	69	.297	.319	.272	5.63	1.06
Lumsden, Tyler	L-L	6-4	215	5-9-83	2	4	5.15	16	4	0	0	44	50	32	25	6	25	14	.294	.321	.281	2.89	5.15
McKeller, Ryan	R-R	6-5	220	7-8-83	2	4	3.81	28	0	0	0	50	57	26	21	4	15	45	.282	.303	.262	8.15	2.72
Meszaros, Danny	R-R	6-0	170	9-6-85	3	3	3.36	37	0	0	1	62	63	25	23	7	17	48	.268	.307	.222	7.01	2.48
Moehler, Brian	R-R	6-3	225	12-31-71	0	0	14.40	1	1	0	0	5	11	8	8	0	0	2	.423	.545	.333	3.60	0.00
Perez, Sergio	R-R	6-3	230	12-5-84	11	11	4.68	27	27	0	0	142	167	88	74	14	60	72	.291	.321	.261	4.55	3.79
Salamida, Chris	L-L	6-0	180	5-7-84	1	2	7.80	22	0	0	0	15	21	16	13	2	5	10	.336	.278	.368	5.70	3.00
Semerano, Rob	R-R	6-1	210	7-18-81	0	1	8.87	12	0	0	3	22	33	22	22	1	9	5	.340	.349	.333	2.01	3.63
Trinidad, Polin	L-L	6-3	195	11-19-84	7	5	2.94	13	12	2	1	83	87	36	27	7	10	53	.272	.263	.276	5.77	1.09
Valverde, Jose	R-R	6-4	280	3-24-78	0	0	0.00	2	0	0	0	2	0	0	0	0	0	2	.000	.000	.000	9.00	9.00
Van Hekken, Andy	R-L	6-3	185	7-31-79	7	5	4.05	27	10	0	0	98	105	48	44	7	20	59	.277	.310	.261	5.41	1.84
Wagler, Chad	R-R	6-1	185	9-11-83	1	3	4.44	11	1	0	1	24	27	12	12	3	4	16	.281	.211	.328	5.92	1.48
Weatherby, Charlie	R-R	6-0	208	12-23-78	1	5	4.66	19	1	0	0	37	39	21	19	4	15	23	.275	.278	.270	5.65	3.68

Fielding

Catcher	PCT	G	PO	A	E	DP	PB
Castro	.974	57	300	32	9	2	6
Clemens	.968	5	29	1	1	0	1
Esposito	.986	49	250	28	4	3	5
Fixler	.995	32	179	12	1	1	4
Lopez	1.000	2	10	1	0	0	0

First Base	PCT	G	PO	A	E	DP
Boone	1.000	2	13	0	0	1
Erstad	1.000	1	9	1	0	1
Ori	.987	97	884	73	13	93
Van Ostrand	.991	48	407	36	4	51

Second Base	PCT	G	PO	A	E	DP
Duran	.981	10	23	29	1	4
Florentino	1.000	4	5	11	0	1

Matsui	1.000	4	7	7	0	1
Meyer	.978	99	177	323	11	76
Molina	.988	32	55	109	2	25
Spann	.889	3	3	5	1	2

Third Base	PCT	G	PO	A	E	DP
Boone	1.000	5	3	8	0	1
Duran	.923	4	2	10	1	2
Florentino	.933	100	48	146	14	17
Meyer	1.000	2	3	4	0	1
Molina	.909	29	15	45	6	3
Spann	.857	13	9	27	6	2

Shortstop	PCT	G	PO	A	E	DP
Florentino	.867	3	2	11	2	2
Meyer	.965	14	19	36	2	10

Molina	1.000	1	1	4	0	0
Sutil	.957	124	216	365	26	98

Outfield	PCT	G	PO	A	E	DP
Barnes	1.000	7	16	2	0	0
DeLome	.985	120	262	2	4	0
Einertson	.977	81	166	3	4	1
Erstad	1.000	1	1	0	0	0
Flores	.991	42	103	2	1	1
Locke	.977	114	201	15	5	4
Moresi	.975	55	116	3	3	2
Sadler	1.000	15	38	0	0	0
Spann	—	1	0	0	0	0
Van Ostrand	1.000	2	4	0	0	0

LANCASTER JETHAWKS   HIGH CLASS A
CALIFORNIA LEAGUE

Batting	B-T	HT	WT	DOB	AVG	vLH	vRH	G	AB	R	H	2B	3B	HR	RBI	BB	HBP	SH	SF	SO	SB	CS	SLG	OBP
Barnes, Brandon	R-R	6-2	210	5-15-86	.293	.422	.235	68	266	51	78	19	3	12	52	15	5	3	2	74	1	2	.523	.340
Brown, Steve	R-R	6-0	180	9-3-86	.200	.200	.200	7	30	4	6	2	0	3	6	0	0	0	0	10	0	0	.567	.200
Cabral, Marcos	R-R	5-11	185	4-4-84	.298	.273	.308	124	477	74	142	33	6	11	71	44	2	1	2	77	2	3	.461	.358
Castro, Jason	L-R	6-3	210	6-18-87	.309	.311	.308	56	207	27	64	20	1	7	44	30	3	0	3	41	1	1	.517	.399
Clemens, Koby	R-R	5-11	193	12-4-86	.345	.368	.337	116	423	74	146	45	6	22	121	51	9	0	9	109	4	1	.636	.419
Comadena, Jordan	R-R	5-10	210	11-16-85	.219	.125	.232	28	64	7	14	2	0	0	2	6	2	0	0	14	1	0	.250	.306
Corrado, Craig	R-R	6-2	185	9-10-84	.247	.254	.244	112	417	35	103	17	5	2	36	15	2	7	3	79	14	10	.326	.275
Fixler, Jon	R-R	6-1	205	6-13-86	.239	.259	.225	21	67	5	16	2	1	1	10	7	1	0	3	12	1	0	.343	.308
Flores, David	R-R	6-2	220	10-13-84	.242	.243	.242	72	264	28	64	18	2	4	26	5	12	2	0	47	4	2	.371	.288
Gaston, Jon	L-R	6-0	210	10-13-86	.278	.235	.296	139	518	119	144	31	15	35	100	71	8	0	10	164	14	4	.598	.367
Jackson, Chris	R-R	5-11	185	12-30-86	.183	.100	.219	58	197	22	36	7	1	1	15	11	4	4	1	61	3	3	.244	.239
Johnson, Chris	R-R	6-3	220	10-1-84	.438	.250	.500	4	16	5	7	5	0	0	6	1	0	0	0	3	0	0	.750	.471
Minaker, Chris	R-R	6-0	195	3-24-84	.319	.500	.253	31	113	16	36	8	0	1	15	5	1	0	1	14	1	3	.416	.350
Moresi, Nick	R-R	6-4	180	11-22-84	.244	.289	.227	45	135	24	33	13	0	4	10	9	1	1	0	43	0	1	.430	.297
Pellegrini, Brian	R-R	6-1	240	10-3-84	.171	.097	.203	30	105	17	18	3	0	7	15	15	2	0	0	40	0	0	.400	.287
Ramirez, Ronald	R-R	5-11	165	1-30-86	.239	.216	.248	43	142	13	34	10	0	0	13	6	3	2	0	41	0	0	.310	.285
Rosario, Ebert	R-R	6-3	165	5-27-87	.250	.304	.230	42	172	25	43	5	0	3	29	13	3	1	1	24	0	2	.331	.312
Shuck, J.B.	L-L	5-11	185	6-18-87	.315	.256	.338	133	556	98	175	30	11	1	36	64	4	4	0	55	18	9	.414	.389
Simunic, Andy	R-R	6-0	170	8-7-85	.286	.143	.333	21	56	5	16	1	0	0	4	9	0	1	1	12	2	1	.304	.379
Steele, T.J.	R-R	6-3	185	9-21-86	.345	.294	.364	50	194	27	67	11	8	5	40	9	4	0	1	40	6	1	.562	.385
Suarez, Gabe	R-R	6-0	170	12-14-84	.323	.391	.287	37	133	26	43	6	4	0	12	11	2	3	0	40	1	1	.429	.384
Suttle, Eric	R-R	6-0	190	7-17-84	.375	.500	.300	12	32	4	12	2	0	0	7	5	0	0	0	6	1	0	.438	.459
Taylor, Tip	R-R	6-3	195	7-29-85	.185	.182	.188	9	27	5	5	1	0	0	4	4	2	0	0	7	1	0	.222	.333
Weston, Matt	L-L	6-3	215	5-20-84	.300	.370	.276	86	327	61	98	32	3	17	67	38	2	0	2	107	0	3	.572	.374

Pitching	B-T	HT	WT	DOB	W	L	ERA	G	GS	CG	SV	IP	H	R	ER	HR	BB	SO	AVG	vLH	vRH	K/9	BB/9
Abad, Fernando	L-L	6-2	170	12-17-85	4	6	4.14	41	0	0	6	83	78	42	38	8	8	79	.252	.255	.251	8.60	0.87
Abreu, Erick	R-R	6-1	170	8-9-83	1	1	2.77	8	0	0	3	13	16	4	4	0	5	13	.302	.320	.286	9.00	3.46
Cespedes, Leandro	R-R	5-11	160	4-19-87	9	10	5.06	24	22	0	0	132	152	88	74	13	52	116	.287	.298	.274	7.93	3.55
Dominguez, Jason	R-R	6-2	193	12-17-85	0	0	15.88	4	0	0	0	6	15	10	10	2	2	4	.500	.500	.500	6.35	3.18
Duncan, David	L-L	6-9	230	6-1-86	0	9	8.51	11	10	0	0	49	82	56	46	8	17	33	.383	.427	.356	6.10	3.14
Duran, Jose	R-R	6-1	205	5-1-85	2	5	8.06	27	7	0	0	64	89	62	57	10	29	43	.331	.342	.317	6.08	4.10
Fairchild, Tip	R-R	6-2	200	12-5-83	3	3	7.06	8	8	1	0	51	62	43	40	15	12	44	.292	.280	.304	7.76	2.12
Hallberg, Bryan	R-R	6-0	185	4-23-85	3	5	5.34	32	7	0	3	86	105	56	51	8	41	56	.307	.282	.331	5.86	4.29
Hicks, Chris	R-R	6-4	205	2-17-87	9	11	6.12	26	26	0	0	129	180	105	88	22	39	103	.328	.334	.321	7.17	2.71
Hudspeth, Casey	R-R	6-5	165	10-1-84	3	3	5.30	6	6	1	0	37	43	23	22	1	16	24	.297	.329	.254	5.79	3.86
Icenogle, Jeff	L-L	6-2	205	5-30-84	0	1	6.79	19	8	0	0	53	76	44	40	6	23	49	.341	.309	.359	8.32	3.91
Kelly, Reid	R-R	6-1	182	10-31-86	2	1	5.23	21	3	0	2	43	50	30	25	3	13	43	.286	.319	.247	9.00	2.72
Lo, Chia-Jen	R-R	5-11	181	4-7-86	1	0	1.78	12	0	0	1	25	10	6	5	1	13	36	.120	.047	.200	12.79	4.62
Mowdy, Ashton	R-R	6-0	185	6-21-86	1	1	9.30	15	0	0	0	20	32	26	21	5	11	21	.337	.279	.385	9.30	4.87
Pacella, J.J.	R-R	6-6	212	12-26-83	0	0	6.43	15	0	0	0	21	28	16	15	1	10	10	.308	.353	.250	4.29	4.29
Powell, Jordan	R-R	6-2	205	9-25-84	4	2	4.13	42	0	0	3	72	82	34	33	9	23	40	.292	.331	.244	5.00	2.88
Rummel, Philip	R-R	6-5	235	6-26-85	2	5	6.55	28	6	0	0	56	89	47	41	5	21	34	.363	.438	.269	5.43	3.36
Salamida, Chris	L-L	6-0	180	5-7-84	4	3	6.75	18	7	1	1	55	65	45	41	10	15	41	.294	.213	.325	6.75	2.47
Severino, Sergio	L-L	5-11	150	9-1-84	0	1	8.56	10	0	0	0	14	23	16	13	2	6	12	.371	.367	.375	7.90	3.95
Tilghman, Jack	R-R	6-2	205	5-19-87	0	4	6.91	25	6	0	3	42	56	40	32	5	23	35	.315	.293	.342	7.56	4.97
Urckfitz, Pat	L-L	6-2	190	7-21-88	0	1	4.15	7	0	0	1	9	9	4	4	0	5	7	.310	.357	.267	7.27	5.19
Wagler, Chad	R-R	6-1	185	9-11-83	3	2	6.80	8	7	0	0	45	65	35	34	8	12	13	.346	.350	.341	2.60	2.40
Wolf, Shane	L-L	6-3	225	9-10-86	5	7	5.34	28	17	1	0	121	142	75	72	9	30	101	.293	.253	.313	7.49	2.23

Fielding

Catcher	PCT	G	PO	A	E	DP	PB
Castro	.985	44	292	39	5	4	3
Clemens	.983	66	412	49	8	6	18

Comadena	.993	27	135	16	1	2	3
Fixler	.977	17	115	12	3	3	1

First Base	PCT	G	PO	A	E	DP
Cabral	.994	18	158	14	1	10
Flores	1.000	1	4	0	0	0

Minaker	.982	18	155	12	3	3
Pellegrini	.991	13	109	7	1	5
Suarez	1.000	1	3	0	0	2
Taylor	.988	9	71	11	1	6
Weston	.994	85	711	61	5	57

Second Base	PCT	G	PO	A	E	DP
Cabral	.964	12	18	36	2	4
Corrado	.972	85	124	227	10	29
Ramirez	.947	30	36	72	6	18
Simunic	.978	11	17	27	1	4
Suarez	1.000	13	24	33	0	7

Third Base	PCT	G	PO	A	E	DP
Cabral	.920	11	7	16	2	1

Corrado	—	1	0	0	0	0
Flores	.925	64	43	105	12	8
Johnson	.944	4	5	12	1	0
Minaker	1.000	4	3	8	0	1
Ramirez	1.000	3	1	3	0	1
Rosario	.899	42	28	70	11	5
Suarez	.949	17	11	26	2	3
Weston	1.000	1	3	1	0	1

Shortstop	PCT	G	PO	A	E	DP
Cabral	.958	71	113	164	12	33
Jackson	.931	57	102	167	20	24
Minaker	1.000	7	11	9	0	1
Ramirez	.929	12	19	20	3	5

Suarez	.909	5	4	6	1	1

Outfield	PCT	G	PO	A	E	DP
Barnes	.977	58	123	5	3	2
Brown	1.000	7	18	0	0	0
Clemens	1.000	16	17	1	0	0
Corrado	1.000	5	3	0	0	0
Gaston	.959	120	197	16	9	1
Moresi	.970	39	59	5	2	4
Pellegrini	.969	15	30	1	1	0
Shuck	.985	121	244	16	4	3
Simunic	.920	10	22	1	2	0
Steele	.992	44	119	2	1	0
Suttle	1.000	10	17	2	0	0

LEXINGTON LEGENDS

LOW CLASS A

SOUTH ATLANTIC LEAGUE

Batting	B-T	HT	WT	DOB	AVG	vLH	vRH	G	AB	R	H	2B	3B	HR	RBI	BB	HBP	SH	SF	SO	SB	CS	SLG	OBP
Austin, Jay	L-L	5-11	170	8-10-90	.267	.212	.285	101	397	49	106	22	6	1	33	31	0	7	0	78	23	13	.360	.320
Barnes, Brandon	R-R	6-2	210	5-15-86	.264	.386	.229	57	197	23	52	11	3	5	25	10	4	2	2	52	3	6	.426	.310
Bonfante, Ricardo	R-R	5-9	140	10-21-88	.145	.176	.135	24	69	8	10	1	1	0	6	9	0	3	1	10	5	2	.188	.241
Brown, Steve	R-R	6-0	180	9-3-86	.247	.213	.255	88	292	45	72	15	5	6	43	17	6	3	4	80	8	5	.394	.298
Cartwright, Albert	R-R	5-10	180	10-31-87	.236	.202	.248	100	348	65	82	17	4	7	34	36	14	4	2	92	23	8	.368	.330
Comadena, Jordan	R-R	5-10	210	11-16-85	.125	—	.125	3	8	1	1	0	0	0	0	0	0	0	0	2	1	0	.125	.125
De Leon, Jorge	R-R	6-0	168	8-15-87	.187	.148	.198	43	123	14	23	5	1	0	9	3	2	2	0	38	2	2	.244	.219
Diaz, Mike	L-R	5-10	160	4-11-87	.241	.160	.256	89	320	22	77	11	1	3	31	15	6	1	1	46	6	3	.309	.287
Disher, Phil	R-R	6-2	215	6-17-85	.156	.185	.149	39	128	12	20	2	0	4	17	18	1	0	1	51	0	0	.266	.264
Dixon, Russell	L-R	6-2	205	8-28-85	.167	.261	.151	50	162	18	27	8	0	1	13	13	3	2	1	29	1	1	.235	.240
Gonzalez, Pedro	L-R	5-11	180	10-29-86	.114	.167	.105	17	44	6	5	1	0	0	4	6	0	2	0	13	0	0	.136	.220
Hernandez, Federico	B-R	6-0	170	2-9-88	.231	.258	.221	103	347	39	80	14	1	6	35	17	2	3	3	65	1	0	.329	.268
Hinze, Kody	R-R	6-0	225	7-29-87	.175	.231	.164	27	80	14	14	3	0	4	14	9	1	0	0	28	0	0	.363	.267
Hulett, Jeff	R-R	6-0	185	11-16-87	.259	.310	.241	32	108	7	28	2	2	0	15	9	3	0	2	31	1	0	.315	.328
Jackson, Chris	R-R	5-11	185	12-30-86	.197	.167	.207	41	152	10	30	3	2	0	11	9	4	1	2	44	3	5	.243	.257
Metroka, Nathan	R-R	6-2	220	8-30-86	.150	.133	.160	12	40	3	6	1	0	0	2	4	0	0	0	13	1	0	.175	.227
Miller, Kyle	R-R	6-1	200	9-1-86	.213	.162	.246	32	94	6	20	6	0	2	10	5	1	0	0	38	0	1	.340	.260
Parra, Wilder	R-R	6-0	175	3-2-91	.000	—	.000	4	6	0	0	0	0	0	0	0	0	0	0	4	0	0	.000	.000
Pellegrini, Brian	R-R	6-1	240	10-3-84	.291	.277	.295	103	351	64	102	18	1	27	74	58	6	0	4	102	10	4	.578	.396
Pestana, Reinaldo	R-L	6-1	180	5-24-87	.141	.240	.108	34	99	4	14	1	0	1	7	7	1	4	0	24	0	0	.182	.206
Ramirez, Ronald	R-R	5-11	165	1-30-86	.248	.282	.237	52	153	14	38	7	1	3	13	8	1	3	1	39	0	3	.366	.288
Rosario, Ebert	R-R	6-3	165	5-27-87	.272	.267	.273	88	320	32	87	14	3	4	31	10	7	1	2	50	2	6	.372	.307
Simunic, Andy	R-R	6-0	170	8-7-85	.287	.217	.314	55	167	27	48	3	0	0	6	29	4	3	0	26	8	4	.305	.405
Suttle, Eric	R-R	6-0	190	7-17-84	.235	.242	.233	82	285	38	67	13	1	1	27	39	1	5	1	58	10	7	.298	.328
Wikoff, Brandon	L-R	5-9	170	4-5-88	.276	.235	.287	39	156	16	43	2	2	0	17	10	0	0	1	20	3	5	.314	.317
Williams, Marques	R-R	6-0	185	10-24-85	.258	.241	.266	33	93	10	24	6	0	0	8	8	1	3	0	19	3	2	.323	.324

Pitching	B-T	HT	WT	DOB	W	L	ERA	G	GS	CG	SV	IP	H	R	ER	HR	BB	SO	AVG	vLH	vRH	K/9	BB/9
Bono, Robert	R-R	6-2	175	12-12-88	10	8	3.20	25	25	3	0	143	158	65	51	5	19	66	.276	.255	.291	4.14	1.19
Duncan, David	L-L	6-9	230	6-1-86	4	4	4.29	10	10	0	0	57	67	31	27	6	9	52	.305	.237	.319	8.26	1.43
Dydalewicz, Brad	L-L	6-1	180	3-24-90	8	5	3.93	22	22	0	0	110	93	58	48	6	51	78	.221	.221	.222	6.38	4.17
Godfrey, Kyle	R-R	6-4	200	2-6-86	1	3	1.88	20	0	0	3	38	31	14	8	2	8	33	.218	.203	.229	7.75	1.88
Greenwalt, Kyle	R-R	6-0	200	9-29-88	8	13	4.20	25	25	0	0	139	154	72	65	7	28	90	.278	.331	.239	5.81	1.81
Hacker, Mike	L-L	5-9	175	11-6-85	1	1	9.16	16	0	0	0	19	27	25	19	0	17	21	.338	.333	.340	10.13	8.20
Leon, Arcenio	R-R	6-1	162	9-22-86	4	2	5.86	41	4	0	0	71	82	53	46	6	49	52	.287	.212	.330	6.62	6.24
Lyles, Jordan	R-R	6-4	185	10-19-90	7	11	3.24	26	26	0	0	145	134	56	52	5	38	167	.247	.216	.265	10.39	2.36
Meszaros, Danny	R-R	6-0	170	9-6-85	0	0	0.71	16	0	0	9	13	5	1	1	0	3	19	.116	.111	.120	13.50	2.13
Mowdy, Ashton	R-R	6-0	185	6-21-86	0	0	1.72	26	0	0	3	37	21	14	7	4	8	33	.157	.104	.186	8.10	1.96
Nevarez, Matt	R-R	6-5	220	2-26-87	1	0	0.00	8	0	0	4	8	3	0	0	0	0	13	.103	.222	.050	14.04	0.00
2-team total (34 Hickory)					2	4	2.28	42	0	0	13	43	25	14	11	1	15	63	—	—		13.08	3.12
Noguera, Antonio	L-L	6-3	194	2-26-88	0	0	4.15	6	0	0	0	9	9	7	4	3	5	4	.250	.400	.226	4.15	5.19
Rivers, Kirkland	L-L	6-1	195	1-6-86	1	1	6.75	20	0	0	0	19	22	18	14	2	19	15	.314	.300	.320	7.23	9.16
Seaton, Ross	L-R	6-4	213	9-18-89	8	10	3.29	24	24	1	0	137	137	69	50	11	39	88	.261	.235	.278	5.80	2.57
Tilghman, Jack	R-R	6-2	205	5-19-87	1	3	2.57	11	0	0	1	21	18	8	6	1	6	16	.228	.276	.200	6.86	2.57
Trinidad, Jose	R-R	5-11	150	7-13-87	0	3	4.71	13	0	0	1	21	23	14	11	0	12	17	.274	.382	.200	7.29	5.14
Urckfitz, Pat	L-L	6-3	190	7-21-88	4	1	2.57	42	0	0	13	49	44	17	14	5	13	42	.243	.176	.269	7.71	2.39
Villar, Henry	R-R	5-11	150	5-24-87	3	4	2.60	43	3	0	5	90	80	36	26	6	18	109	.235	.208	.251	10.90	1.80
Wabick, Brian	R-R	6-0	180	8-3-87	7	3	3.96	40	1	0	0	86	87	47	38	4	21	66	.266	.264	.267	6.88	2.19

Fielding

Catcher	PCT	G	PO	A	E	DP	PB
Comadena	1.000	3	22	1	0	0	1
Gonzalez	1.000	17	91	18	0	0	2
Hernandez	.989	95	623	78	8	6	14
Hulett	1.000	1	3	0	0	0	0
Parra	1.000	4	13	3	0	0	0
Pestana	.987	34	204	24	3	0	3

First Base	PCT	G	PO	A	E	DP
Diaz	.984	8	53	8	1	9
Disher	.984	31	293	7	5	20
Hernandez	1.000	2	9	1	0	0
Hinze	.975	9	74	3	2	5
Miller	1.000	9	78	2	0	7
Pellegrini	.995	87	783	39	4	58

Ramirez	1.000	2	6	0	0	0
Simunic	1.000	3	20	3	0	1

Second Base	PCT	G	PO	A	E	DP
Cartwright	.963	89	174	242	16	54
Diaz	.981	29	35	66	2	11
Ramirez	1.000	10	7	27	0	1
Simunic	.981	22	39	67	2	16

HOUSTON ASTROS

Third Base	PCT	G	PO	A	E	DP
Diaz	.875	2	3	4	1	1
Hulett	.863	27	17	52	11	6
Jackson	.829	18	6	28	7	1
Miller	.789	8	6	9	4	1
Ramirez	.923	7	1	11	1	1
Rosario	.902	85	62	178	26	16
Simunic	.875	2	2	12	2	1

Shortstop	PCT	G	PO	A	E	DP
Bonfante	.936	23	21	82	7	10

	PCT	G	PO	A	E	DP
De Leon	.901	42	62	101	18	15
Diaz	1.000	3	0	2	0	0
Jackson	.930	17	20	46	5	8
Ramirez	.908	31	37	72	11	14
Rosario	1.000	1	0	1	0	0
Wikoff	.976	38	45	118	4	19

Outfield	PCT	G	PO	A	E	DP
Austin	.980	99	191	10	4	3
Barnes	.983	57	106	7	2	4
Brown	.994	77	168	8	1	2

	PCT	G	PO	A	E	DP
Diaz	1.000	1	3	0	0	0
Dixon	.973	44	68	3	2	0
Hinze	1.000	1	1	0	0	0
Metroka	1.000	12	15	0	0	0
Pellegrini	1.000	10	7	0	0	0
Simunic	.956	30	39	4	2	0
Suttle	.957	78	123	11	6	2
Williams	.959	28	47	0	2	0

TRI-CITY VALLEYCATS

SHORT-SEASON

NEW YORK-PENN LEAGUE

Batting	B-T	HT	WT	DOB	AVG	vLH	vRH	G	AB	R	H	2B	3B	HR	RBI	BB	HBP	SH	SF	SO	SB	CS	SLG	OBP
Altuve, Jose	R-R	5-5	148	5-6-90	.250	.304	.226	21	76	13	19	5	0	0	7	8	2	1	0	10	7	2	.316	.337
Barksdale, Sean	R-R	6-0	210	10-18-86	.175	.151	.200	37	103	11	18	5	1	2	8	8	0	1	0	34	2	3	.301	.234
Butera, Barry	L-R	5-11	175	6-5-87	.267	.350	.232	61	202	24	54	11	0	0	11	23	3	6	0	52	16	3	.322	.351
Castro, Erik	L-R	6-4	200	11-13-87	.266	.296	.254	60	192	29	51	13	1	7	36	26	1	1	3	38	0	1	.453	.351
De Leon, Jorge	R-R	6-0	168	8-15-87	.242	.318	.205	23	66	7	16	4	2	0	7	4	1	0		13	1	0	.364	.296
Dixon, Russell	L-R	6-2	205	8-28-85	.302	.241	.320	38	126	11	38	4	1	1	11	10	0	0	1	22	2	1	.373	.350
Figueroa, Oscar	R-R	5-11	154	1-10-88	.143	.200	.000	2	7	0	1	0	0	0	0	0	0	0	0	2	0	1	.143	.143
Garcia, Rene	R-R	6-1	172	3-21-90	.202	.213	.196	52	173	9	35	6	1	1	9	12	3	2	0	24	2	0	.266	.266
Goebbert, Jake	L-L	6-0	200	9-24-87	.238	.191	.254	59	189	21	45	12	3	0	18	22	5	1	1	39	2	3	.333	.332
Gonzalez, Pedro	L-R	5-11	180	10-29-86	.195	.167	.207	28	82	4	16	0	1	0	10	5	0	2	0	12	0	0	.220	.241
Hulett, Jeff	R-R	6-0	185	11-16-87	.189	.192	.185	19	53	7	10	1	0	0	1	3	1	0	0	23	0	0	.208	.246
Iorg, Eli	R-R	6-4	215	3-14-83	.353	.500	.222	6	17	2	6	1	0	0	3	2	1	0	1	6	1	1	.412	.429
Kemp, Brian	R-R	5-9	180	9-2-88	.259	.265	.255	66	220	35	57	5	2	0	11	25	13	3	1	31	16	3	.300	.367
Martinez, J.D.	R-R	6-3	175	8-21-87	.326	.319	.331	53	187	25	61	15	2	7	33	15	3	0	3	30	1	0	.540	.380
Medrano, Jhonny	R-R	6-1	156	9-12-87	.213	.224	.206	47	169	13	36	9	0	1	23	10	2	0	2	37	5	0	.284	.262
Meier, Danny	R-R	6-3	205	10-28-85	.143	.500	.083	6	14	0	2	1	0	0	0	0	1	0	0	8	1	0	.214	.200
Orloff, Ben	R-R	5-11	170	4-26-87	.150	.087	.189	28	60	9	9	1	0	0	8	5	2	2	1	9	4	0	.167	.235
Stanley, Nick	L-R	6-2	195	5-12-87	.230	.180	.250	63	209	25	48	7	2	5	21	23	1	0	1	45	2	2	.354	.308
Tello, Renzo	R-R	6-1	155	6-30-87	.197	.148	.226	45	147	12	29	6	0	1	13	4	2	0	0	39	4	2	.259	.229
Wikoff, Brandon	L-R	5-9	170	4-5-88	.287	.295	.281	28	101	12	29	4	1	0	2	10	1	4	0	10	2	2	.347	.357

Pitching	B-T	HT	WT	DOB	W	L	ERA	G	GS	CG	SV	IP	H	R	ER	HR	BB	SO	AVG	vLH	vRH	K/9	BB/9
Alvino, Wander	R-R	5-11	159	2-10-87	4	7	5.17	13	13	0	0	71	72	41	41	8	29	49	.262	.317	.215	6.18	3.66
Arguello, Doug	L-L	6-3	190	11-21-84	1	1	5.63	3	3	0	0	8	9	5	5	0	2	7	.290	.125	.348	7.88	2.25
Berner, David	L-L	6-2	205	8-16-87	0	1	10.50	7	0	0	0	6	11	10	7	2	5	4	.367	.250	.409	6.00	7.50
Clark, Kirk	R-R	6-2	202	7-19-88	2	0	1.89	10	0	0	0	19	14	4	4	2	3	24	.215	.242	.188	11.37	1.42
Donovan, Robby	R-R	6-5	195	4-24-88	2	5	3.74	19	4	0	4	34	30	21	14	0	21	28	.233	.283	.197	7.49	5.61
Duncan, David	L-L	6-9	230	6-1-86	0	1	3.10	3	0	0	0	8	8	7	1	3	1	7	.233	.100	.283	7.52	1.33
Fearnow, Max	R-R	6-4	205	1-17-87	1	1	4.42	17	4	0	0	37	40	19	18	4	17	21	.288	.333	.256	5.15	4.17
Godfrey, Kyle	R-R	6-4	200	2-6-86	0	1	5.54	3	3	0	0	13	16	9	8	1	4	8	.296	.407	.185	5.54	2.77
Grimmett, Zach	R-R	6-3	185	2-5-90	0	7	7.34	12	12	0	0	42	63	41	34	5	16	28	.362	.369	.358	6.05	3.46
Harper, Justin	R-R	6-4	185	6-10-88	0	1	9.00	5	0	0	0	6	5	6	6	1	8	3	.263	.500	.091	4.50	12.00
Keuchel, Dallas	L-L	6-3	200	1-1-88	2	3	2.70	11	10	0	0	57	52	18	17	2	9	44	.240	.183	.261	6.99	1.43
MacDonald, J.B.	R-R	6-2	190	4-15-87	2	1	2.53	23	0	0	8	32	33	10	9	2	10	29	.264	.170	.321	8.16	2.81
Migl, Scott	R-R	6-4	190	9-1-87	0	0	14.54	8	0	0	0	9	16	15	14	0	13	7	.390	.417	.379	7.27	13.50
Modica, Mike	L-L	6-0	175	12-16-86	0	3	2.61	27	0	0	0	31	31	13	9	2	13	19	.279	.341	.243	5.52	3.77
Noguera, Antonio	L-L	6-3	194	2-26-88	2	0	3.62	14	0	0	0	27	25	11	11	2	8	21	.260	.192	.286	6.91	2.63
Pettus, Nate	R-R	6-1	200	10-9-88	2	1	1.71	10	0	0	2	21	18	8	4	1	9	17	.231	.286	.186	7.29	3.86
Pitkin, Colton	R-L	6-3	210	8-10-89	4	8	4.21	14	13	1	0	68	76	38	32	5	32	49	.285	.200	.315	6.45	4.21
Sarisky, Dan	R-R	6-1	175	5-25-88	0	0	3.27	12	0	0	0	22	24	9	8	0	9	24	.279	.349	.209	9.82	3.68
Schurz, Mike	R-R	6-2	205	9-12-86	1	0	0.66	8	0	0	0	14	9	1	1	0	7	15	.191	.143	.231	9.88	4.61
Stines, Brenden	R-R	6-2	190	1-12-87	3	0	4.93	24	0	0	0	38	44	25	21	2	17	23	.286	.250	.306	5.40	3.99
Walker, Brandt	R-R	6-1	165	11-9-87	1	7	7.92	16	10	0	1	50	59	45	44	10	36	39	.296	.326	.269	7.02	6.48

Fielding

Catcher	PCT	G	PO	A	E	DP	PB
Garcia	.991	51	293	39	3	2	9
Gonzalez	.971	27	179	21	6	0	0

First Base	PCT	G	PO	A	E	DP
Castro	1.000	13	100	9	0	14
Hulett	1.000	3	30	3	0	3
Martinez	1.000	1	9	1	0	0
Medrano	1.000	1	9	0	0	0
Stanley	.989	60	490	32	6	55

Second Base	PCT	G	PO	A	E	DP
Altuve	.978	20	27	63	2	15
Butera	.989	35	78	106	2	31

	PCT	G	PO	A	E	DP
Figueroa	1.000	1	1	2	0	0
Hulett	.952	7	21	19	2	4
Orloff	.970	19	30	35	2	15

Third Base	PCT	G	PO	A	E	DP
Butera	1.000	2	0	3	0	0
Castro	.877	36	21	72	13	12
Hulett	.667	1	0	2	1	0
Medrano	.884	40	29	85	15	12

Shortstop	PCT	G	PO	A	E	DP
Butera	.946	24	45	60	6	19
De Leon	.903	22	32	52	9	13
Figueroa	1.000	1	5	3	0	1

	PCT	G	PO	A	E	DP
Orloff	.941	4	6	10	1	1
Wikoff	.968	28	51	100	5	22

Outfield	PCT	G	PO	A	E	DP
Barksdale	1.000	34	47	2	0	0
Butera	—	1	0	0	0	0
Dixon	.978	26	44	1	1	0
Goebbert	.910	47	69	2	7	0
Iorg	1.000	5	13	0	0	0
Kemp	1.000	62	101	6	0	2
Martinez	.958	22	43	3	2	1
Meier	—	1	0	0	0	0
Tello	.987	43	67	7	1	0

GREENEVILLE ASTROS
APPALACHIAN LEAGUE

ROOKIE

Batting	B-T	HT	WT	DOB	AVG	vLH	vRH	G	AB	R	H	2B	3B	HR	RBI	BB	HBP	SH	SF	SO	SB	CS	SLG	OBP
Almonte, Frank	R-R	6-2	190	1-24-89	.246	.300	.231	38	138	19	34	8	1	5	23	11	3	0	1	40	1	2	.428	.314
Altuve, Jose	R-R	5-5	148	5-6-90	.324	.333	.322	45	179	45	58	20	2	3	18	26	0	2	1	16	21	4	.508	.408
Alvarez, Luis	R-R	5-11	198	2-28-90	.271	.125	.300	17	48	7	13	3	0	1	8	3	2	0	0	11	1	0	.396	.340
Arrendell, Miguel	L-R	6-0	165	3-26-88	.235	.074	.275	46	136	24	32	3	3	1	14	35	2	1	2	37	4	4	.368	.394
Bray, Aaron	R-L	6-0	180	7-4-87	.278	.176	.306	48	158	17	44	5	1	0	20	28	1	1	1	35	2	3	.323	.388
Figueroa, Oscar	R-R	5-11	154	1-10-88	.190	.118	.214	42	137	15	26	5	0	1	14	9	0	1	2	21	6	1	.248	.236
Hogue, Grant	R-R	6-1	190	6-26-86	.284	.226	.297	53	176	23	50	8	4	1	14	16	7	6	1	32	17	5	.392	.365
Humphrey, Ryan	R-R	6-0	190	9-19-88	.219	.207	.222	40	128	16	28	6	1	0	6	14	1	0	0	48	4	2	.281	.301
Infante, Wilton	R-R	6-1	175	8-11-87	.136	.125	.138	35	118	11	16	4	2	3	7	5	1	0	0	32	0	0	.280	.177
Martinez, J.D.	R-R	6-3	175	8-21-87	.403	.250	.431	19	77	17	31	9	1	5	23	5	1	0	0	14	0	0	.740	.446
Metroka, Nathan	R-R	6-2	220	8-30-86	.227	.147	.246	52	172	16	39	10	0	0	15	14	2	1	0	52	5	2	.285	.293
Meyer, Jonathan	R-R	6-1	195	11-1-90	.190	.106	.213	62	221	27	42	9	3	3	27	36	0	0	2	69	1	0	.299	.301
Mier, Jiovanni	R-R	6-2	175	8-26-90	.276	.314	.268	51	192	32	53	7	6	7	32	30	4	0	3	45	10	5	.484	.380
Miller, Kyle	R-R	6-1	200	9-1-86	.229	.217	.232	35	118	9	27	11	0	0	5	9	1	0	1	31	2	4	.322	.287
Mojica, Carlos	R-R	6-0	190	6-7-88	.273	.368	.241	27	77	10	21	4	0	1	8	3	3	0	1	22	0	0	.364	.321
Orloff, Ben	R-R	5-11	170	4-26-87	.189	.250	.172	11	37	7	7	2	0	0	5	3	2	1	2	2	0	0	.243	.273
Williams, Bubby	R-R	6-0	190	3-13-89	.202	.364	.168	39	129	17	26	4	1	4	16	4	3	0	2	42	0	0	.341	.239

Pitching	B-T	HT	WT	DOB	W	L	ERA	G	GS	CG	SV	IP	H	R	ER	HR	BB	SO	AVG	vLH	vRH	K/9	BB/9
Belliard, Joan	R-R	6-2	185	3-3-89	3	4	3.71	19	0	0	1	44	40	22	18	2	14	38	.240	.292	.206	7.83	2.89
Bullock, Garrett	L-L	6-3	195	6-9-86	0	0	4.26	5	0	0	0	6	5	3	0	4	4	.240	.600	.150	5.68	5.68
Castillo, Jeiler	R-R	6-0	155	10-26-87	1	1	5.61	19	0	0	3	34	44	26	21	5	14	34	.312	.351	.286	9.09	3.74
Cisnero, Jose	R-R	6-3	185	4-11-89	4	2	3.56	13	13	0	0	56	32	25	22	5	30	64	.165	.165	.165	10.35	4.85
Cruz, Luis	L-L	6-4	170	9-10-90	1	4	6.75	12	10	0	0	55	62	43	41	10	22	41	.290	.357	.266	6.75	3.62
Garcia, Gabriel	L-L	5-11	140	5-11-89	0	4	7.91	10	10	0	0	39	69	42	34	5	6	32	.401	.421	.396	7.45	1.40
Gonzalez, Abraham	R-R	5-11	185	12-13-86	1	1	1.23	8	0	0	1	15	9	2	2	0	3	18	.173	.136	.200	11.05	1.84
Gonzalez, Angel	R-R	6-0	160	8-12-88	5	4	7.38	13	10	0	0	54	68	51	44	9	16	42	.311	.352	.297	7.04	2.68
Gouvea, Murillo	R-R	6-2	190	9-15-88	1	2	3.77	9	0	0	0	29	23	14	12	3	8	30	.228	.333	.169	9.42	2.51
2-team total (7 Bristol)					1	3	4.65	16	4	0	0	50	48	30	26	7	23	57	—	—	—	10.19	4.11
Hyatt, B.J.	R-L	6-4	205	12-14-88	1	2	8.84	8	3	0	0	19	30	20	19	2	12	15	.349	.292	.371	6.98	5.59
Martinez, David	R-R	6-2	180	8-4-87	1	4	4.50	22	0	0	1	40	46	24	20	3	14	25	.282	.300	.272	5.63	3.15
McLean, Tio	R-R	6-4	190	4-6-86	0	1	13.50	8	0	0	0	11	17	17	16	4	6	9	.354	.385	.343	7.59	5.06
Migl, Scott	R-R	6-4	190	9-1-87	0	0	2.75	11	0	0	2	20	14	6	6	1	8	17	.200	.148	.233	7.78	3.66
Perez, Juri	R-R	5-11	148	8-8-90	3	1	2.79	15	8	0	0	52	43	22	16	7	19	60	.219	.188	.235	10.45	3.31
Pettus, Nate	R-R	6-1	200	10-9-88	1	1	2.60	15	0	0	6	17	14	7	5	2	5	18	.226	.036	.382	9.35	2.60
Quevedo, Carlos	R-R	6-1	222	9-30-89	2	7	5.60	13	13	0	0	55	67	40	34	9	9	55	.289	.267	.307	9.05	1.48
Sarisky, Dan	R-R	6-1	175	5-25-88	2	1	4.72	10	0	0	0	13	14	9	7	1	4	17	.259	.211	.286	11.48	2.70
Smink, Travis	L-L	6-2	200	4-10-87	1	1	6.14	21	0	0	5	29	41	24	20	5	7	14	.325	.243	.360	4.30	2.15

Fielding

Catcher	PCT	G	PO	A	E	DP	PB
Alvarez	.978	17	115	20	3	1	6
Mojica	.984	24	160	20	3	0	10
Williams	.975	38	246	26	7	0	8

First Base	PCT	G	PO	A	E	DP
Bray	.972	32	270	9	8	16
Figueroa	.971	19	158	7	5	18
Martinez	.917	1	10	1	1	1
Miller	.979	18	134	6	3	11

Second Base	PCT	G	PO	A	E	DP
Altuve	.963	43	81	127	8	31

Arrendell	.952	15	17	42	3	5
Bray	1.000	2	4	9	0	2
Figueroa	1.000	6	8	15	0	0
Orloff	.857	3	2	4	1	0

Third Base	PCT	G	PO	A	E	DP
Arrendell	1.000	2	2	5	0	2
Bray	1.000	1	1	2	0	1
Figueroa	.667	1	1	1	1	0
Meyer	.920	62	55	130	16	5
Miller	1.000	2	1	4	0	0

Shortstop	PCT	G	PO	A	E	DP
Arrendell	.857	8	8	16	4	2
Figueroa	.904	13	24	23	5	7
Mier	.922	51	87	125	18	20

Outfield	PCT	G	PO	A	E	DP
Almonte	.977	29	42	0	1	0
Hogue	.961	53	96	2	4	0
Humphrey	.946	40	69	1	4	0
Infante	.935	34	51	7	4	0
Martinez	1.000	8	12	1	0	0
Metroka	.958	52	86	6	4	1

GCL ASTROS
GULF COAST LEAGUE

ROOKIE

Batting	B-T	HT	WT	DOB	AVG	vLH	vRH	G	AB	R	H	2B	3B	HR	RBI	BB	HBP	SH	SF	SO	SB	CS	SLG	OBP
Baldee, Jan	R-R	6-2	170	12-8-90	.024	.000	.032	18	41	0	1	0	0	0	0	2	0	0	0	24	0	1	.024	.070
Bonfante, Ricardo	R-R	5-9	140	10-21-88	.667	.500	1.000	2	3	0	2	0	0	0	1	1	2	0	0	0	1	0	.667	.833
Bryan, Luis	R-R	6-2	165	11-26-90	.340	.289	.368	31	106	16	36	6	2	2	19	0	2	1	2	20	3	0	.491	.345
Duran, German	R-R	5-10	185	8-3-84	.385	.500	.333	4	13	2	5	1	0	0	1	2	0	0	0	3	0	0	.462	.467
Feliz, Pedro	B-R	6-0	150	12-7-90	.205	.136	.239	43	132	21	27	5	2	0	17	24	1	0	0	38	5	4	.273	.331
Garcia, Ricardo	R-R	5-9	142	1-20-89	.154	.143	.158	8	26	4	4	0	0	0	0	3	2	1	0	6	1	1	.154	.290
Genoves, Ernesto	R-R	5-11	203	6-4-91	.234	.263	.217	31	107	15	25	6	2	1	13	5	4	0	1	23	0	0	.355	.291
Hernandez, Enrique	R-R	5-11	170	8-24-91	.295	.290	.297	53	207	35	61	12	3	1	27	10	4	2	2	28	8	2	.396	.336
Hinze, Kody	R-R	6-0	225	7-29-87	.262	.258	.264	32	103	21	27	7	2	1	14	19	4	0	2	26	0	0	.398	.391
Infante, Wilton	R-R	6-1	175	8-11-87	.320	.333	.300	7	25	4	8	1	1	0	3	1	0	0	0	6	0	0	.440	.346
King, Emilio	R-R	6-1	180	8-17-89	.254	.283	.239	42	138	22	35	9	3	1	20	18	16	0	1	31	8	1	.384	.399
Lopez, Luis	R-R	5-11	195	3-8-85	.273	.000	.375	6	11	0	3	1	0	0	1	1	0	0	0	4	0	0	.364	.333
Nash, Telvin	R-R	6-1	230	2-20-91	.218	.217	.219	40	142	15	31	10	1	1	20	12	1	0	2	45	1	2	.324	.280
Parra, Wilder	R-R	6-0	175	3-2-91	.182	.125	.205	17	55	8	10	4	0	0	7	2	1	0	0	15	1	2	.255	.224

Name	B-T	HT	WT	DOB	AVG	vLH	vRH	G	AB	R	H	2B	3B	HR	RBI	BB	HBP	SH	SF	SO	SB	CS	SLG	OBP
Reyes, Carlos	R-R	6-0	180	12-5-87	.154	.188	.139	23	52	6	8	1	0	0	3	6	0	0	0	22	0	1	.173	.241
Sanchez, Ronald	L-R	5-10	180	8-9-91	.210	.111	.258	43	138	13	29	5	0	0	16	18	6	2	0	33	3	1	.246	.327
Santana, Nestor	R-R	6-0	190	5-30-90	.287	.474	.244	35	101	16	29	5	0	0	9	13	3	1	1	27	5	4	.337	.381
Suniaga, Gober	R-R	5-11	160	6-17-91	.193	.136	.218	38	145	18	28	2	2	1	20	11	1	0	1	47	4	1	.255	.253
Vargas, Jose	R-R	6-1	200	4-30-91	.232	.176	.250	25	69	8	16	3	0	2	14	7	3	0	1	22	0	0	.362	.325
Wilkerson, Brandon	R-R	6-2	170	4-18-88	.171	.194	.160	41	111	19	19	8	0	0	6	11	4	1	1	27	2	4	.243	.268
Wright, Garen	R-R	6-3	230	12-25-90	.185	.143	.200	34	108	10	20	2	1	0	7	15	1	2	0	35	4	1	.222	.290

Pitching	B-T	HT	WT	DOB	W	L	ERA	G	GS	CG	SV	IP	H	R	ER	HR	BB	SO	AVG	vLH	vRH	K/9	BB/9
Batista, Ricardo	L-L	6-1	170	8-19-91	0	4	5.97	9	0	0	0	35	46	30	23	1	18	22	.326	.292	.333	5.71	4.67
Bullock, Garrett	L-L	6-3	195	6-9-86	0	0	2.77	10	0	0	2	13	15	8	4	0	9	11	.294	.111	.333	7.62	6.23
Bushue, Tanner	R-R	6-4	180	6-20-91	1	0	2.42	5	5	0	0	22	18	8	6	2	5	19	.220	.160	.246	7.66	2.01
Cedano, Enmanuel	R-R	6-2	194	12-28-88	0	0	20.77	11	0	0	0	9	16	26	20	1	15	5	.364	.500	.300	5.19	15.58
Frawley, John	R-R	6-2	185	11-29-85	2	0	0.90	7	0	0	1	20	18	4	2	0	0	25	.243	.077	.279	11.25	0.00
Gil, Carlos	R-R	6-4	175	4-19-90	1	3	7.42	17	0	0	0	30	43	39	25	1	20	25	.321	.317	.323	7.42	5.93
Hylander, Spencer	L-L	6-1	195	6-12-86	4	3	3.23	15	1	0	0	39	36	20	14	1	9	26	.237	.194	.248	6.00	2.08
Jones, Mark	R-R	6-7	205	8-29-90	1	2	4.57	13	4	0	0	22	27	19	11	0	13	13	.314	.143	.369	5.40	5.40
Lucati, Andrea	R-R	6-3	247	1-17-90	1	2	4.86	13	5	0	0	33	41	27	18	3	23	31	.295	.321	.288	8.37	6.21
Luna, Rafael	L-L	6-6	175	1-20-90	0	3	5.87	17	0	0	0	31	41	29	20	2	21	24	.325	.318	.327	7.04	6.16
McLean, Tio	R-R	6-4	190	4-6-86	0	0	5.40	2	0	0	0	2	4	2	1	0	2	0	.667	1.000	.500	0.00	10.80
Minaya, Juan	R-R	6-4	185	9-18-90	3	3	4.27	12	12	0	0	53	45	30	25	1	18	30	.231	.268	.221	5.13	3.08
Perez, German	L-L	5-11	147	9-21-89	0	3	6.91	6	4	0	0	14	18	12	11	0	9	9	.333	.167	.381	5.65	5.65
Pio, Rafael	R-R	6-3	210	1-9-88	1	4	3.12	17	0	0	1	43	33	25	15	1	10	41	.205	.238	.193	8.52	2.08
Quezada, Euris	R-R	6-6	210	4-8-89	1	7	6.91	12	12	0	0	42	49	45	32	4	14	27	.272	.258	.280	5.83	3.02
Rivera, Raul	R-R	6-3	185	2-5-91	0	2	6.60	4	3	0	0	15	17	12	11	2	3	9	.298	.263	.316	5.40	1.80
Rorabaugh, Philip	R-R	6-0	185	10-5-86	1	1	3.89	15	0	0	1	35	49	26	15	1	7	26	.318	.333	.311	6.75	1.82
Sadler, Billy	R-R	6-0	195	9-21-81	0	1	3.38	3	1	0	0	5	2	2	2	0	1	12	.105	.000	.133	20.25	1.69
Schurz, Mike	R-R	6-2	205	9-12-86	2	0	2.25	15	0	0	6	16	10	4	4	1	6	22	.185	.000	.222	12.38	3.38

Fielding

Catcher	PCT	G	PO	A	E	DP	PB
Genoves	.973	31	204	15	6	2	16
Lopez	1.000	5	16	0	0	0	0
Parra	.957	17	101	10	5	1	8
Vargas	.961	13	66	8	3	1	7

First Base	PCT	G	PO	A	E	DP
Hinze	.990	20	189	10	2	28
Sanchez	.982	40	303	17	6	21

Second Base	PCT	G	PO	A	E	DP
Baldee	1.000	6	9	12	0	6
Duran	.750	3	1	2	1	0
Feliz	.922	27	37	57	8	14

	PCT	G	PO	A	E	DP
Hernandez	.951	31	56	81	7	21

Third Base	PCT	G	PO	A	E	DP
Baldee	—	1	0	0	0	0
Duran	1.000	2	0	4	0	0
Feliz	.908	20	19	50	7	7
Garcia	.900	8	4	14	2	0
Hernandez	—	1	0	0	0	0
Wilkerson	.885	37	32	68	13	7

Shortstop	PCT	G	PO	A	E	DP
Baldee	.759	8	6	16	7	0
Bryan	.893	30	35	74	13	14
Duran	—	1	0	0	0	0

	PCT	G	PO	A	E	DP
Feliz	.889	3	4	4	1	2
Hernandez	.893	25	20	55	9	11
Wilkerson	.818	3	3	6	2	0

Outfield	PCT	G	PO	A	E	DP
Infante	1.000	6	15	1	0	0
King	.973	40	100	9	3	3
Nash	.824	19	25	3	6	1
Reyes	1.000	14	18	2	0	0
Santana	.918	32	48	8	5	3
Suniaga	.908	38	66	3	7	0
Wright	.950	29	34	4	2	1

DSL ASTROS   ROOKIE

DOMINICAN SUMMER LEAGUE

Batting	B-T	HT	WT	DOB	AVG	vLH	vRH	G	AB	R	H	2B	3B	HR	RBI	BB	HBP	SH	SF	SO	SB	CS	SLG	OBP
Alcantara, Carlos	R-R	6-4	210	2-16-90	.158	.069	.197	36	95	12	15	5	0	4	14	22	3	0	0	40	4	0	.337	.333
Ayarza, Max	B-R	6-0	160	3-11-92	.149	.136	.152	33	101	10	15	3	1	0	7	9	0	0	0	21	2	4	.198	.218
Campusano, Fredwin	R-R	5-11	170	10-8-91	.222	.200	.230	45	135	17	30	2	1	0	8	16	3	2	1	34	8	2	.252	.316
De La Rosa, Luis	B-R	6-1	162	1-2-92	.202	.231	.194	38	119	7	24	4	2	1	9	2	1	1	1	28	3	2	.294	.226
Fulgencio, Lonny	R-R	5-11	175	2-14-90	.205	.167	.220	41	83	12	17	2	1	0	5	17	2	1	0	19	4	4	.253	.353
Gonzalez, Alfredo	R-R	6-1	190	7-13-92	.167	.350	.114	31	90	12	15	3	1	0	9	13	1	0	0	21	5	3	.222	.279
Gonzalez, Mario	L-R	6-1	195	12-25-91	.238	.167	.261	50	151	8	36	6	0	0	15	12	0	2	3	26	4	2	.278	.289
Heredia, Ricardo	R-R	6-2	170	3-1-89	.248	.304	.233	36	113	13	28	3	2	1	13	10	7	0	0	14	5	2	.336	.346
Hirland, Cristian	R-R	6-1	180	5-30-91	.100	.167	.063	26	50	5	5	2	0	1	1	13	0	0	0	16	0	0	.200	.286
Lopez, Jose	R-R	5-11	172	5-8-90	.209	.250	.192	49	148	18	31	10	0	0	14	23	6	1	1	36	5	2	.277	.337
Lopez, Raymer	R-R	5-10	145	3-31-91	.257	.227	.272	38	136	17	35	0	0	0	10	12	6	3	0	28	9	4	.331	.344
Monzon, Jose	R-R	6-0	170	12-30-91	.198	.133	.212	50	167	24	33	7	2	1	18	20	6	2	1	42	14	4	.281	.304
Moronta, Cristian	R-R	5-10	185	12-5-89	.246	.333	.219	52	138	20	34	10	4	1	29	13	8	1	1	16	5	3	.399	.344
Perez, Rainier	R-R	6-1	185	8-19-90	.218	.162	.238	48	142	22	31	6	2	1	8	21	1	5	0	48	10	3	.310	.323
Ramos, Eudy	L-L	6-2	210	1-5-91	.229	.261	.219	34	96	9	22	6	0	1	10	15	0	0	0	21	3	0	.323	.333
Rodriguez, Hector	R-R	5-11	150	8-8-89	.269	.273	.268	55	197	33	53	12	1	0	10	18	3	2	0	30	8	6	.340	.339
Rodriguez, Raul	R-R	6-1	176	7-28-90	.250	—	.250	1	4	0	1	0	0	0	1	1	0	0	0	0	1	0	.250	.400
Sierra, Andru	B-R	5-9	168	11-13-91	.042	.000	.056	15	24	7	1	0	0	0	0	5	0	0	0	11	6	1	.042	.207
Torres, Julio	R-R	5-11	166	7-28-90	.155	.107	.171	34	110	10	17	5	0	0	2	9	0	0	0	33	7	1	.200	.218

Pitching	B-T	HT	WT	DOB	W	L	ERA	G	GS	CG	SV	IP	H	R	ER	HR	BB	SO	AVG	vLH	vRH	K/9	BB/9
Alayon, Leonardo	R-R	6-2	187	4-29-92	7	2	2.32	17	1	0	2	50	44	16	13	0	22	34	.240	.256	.236	6.08	3.93
Baso, Xavier	R-R	6-0	182	12-1-91	7	3	2.34	19	0	0	5	62	50	24	16	4	15	61	.219	.204	.223	8.90	2.19
Carela, Freidy	R-R	6-3	160	11-28-88	2	2	6.42	15	4	0	1	34	45	33	24	1	10	25	.313	.515	.252	6.68	2.67
De La Cruz, Leonel	R-R	6-2	160	10-3-90	0	0	5.87	6	0	0	0	8	14	7	5	0	4	6	.400	.250	.419	7.04	4.70
De Leon, Elias	L-L	5-11	177	7-8-90	1	2	3.23	15	2	0	4	31	29	12	11	3	6	27	.246	.188	.255	7.92	1.76
Del Rio, Danilo	R-R	5-11	179	9-28-90	3	7	3.96	15	15	0	0	73	70	39	32	3	12	46	.248	.283	.240	5.70	1.49
Estrella, Joel	R-R	6-2	160	1-20-90	1	1	6.75	9	0	0	0	13	9	15	10	0	10	10	.191	.100	.216	6.75	6.75

	B-T	Ht	Wt	DOB	W	L	ERA	G	GS	CG	SV	IP	H	R	ER	HR	BB	SO	AVG	vLH	vRH	BB/9	SO/9
Farias, Rafael	R-R	6-3	160	9-27-89	5	2	3.30	20	1	0	0	46	48	32	17	2	27	36	.267	.243	.273	6.99	5.24
Feliz, Rafael	R-R	6-0	180	9-21-89	1	1	8.57	11	0	0	0	21	27	24	20	1	15	17	.310	.333	.303	7.29	6.43
Iturralde, Roliner	R-R	5-11	167	11-23-90	1	2	2.61	11	8	0	0	41	28	19	12	1	14	23	.181	.182	.180	5.01	3.05
Medrano, Amilcar	R-R	6-7	215	8-24-89	0	0	1.69	5	3	0	0	11	9	5	2	0	8	5	.220	.000	.237	4.22	6.75
Paul, Dieudone	L-L	6-2	187	9-28-87	2	0	1.65	16	6	0	2	55	37	19	10	0	24	66	.190	.238	.184	10.87	3.95
Perdomo, Jose	R-R	6-0	180	10-24-91	0	5	3.64	13	12	0	1	47	31	26	19	0	18	34	.178	.205	.170	6.51	3.45
Perdomo, Yeudy	L-L	6-1	155	12-19-91	0	1	3.38	3	0	0	0	5	5	4	2	0	4	2	.250	.000	.278	3.38	6.75
Ramirez, Felix	R-R	6-5	150	7-12-90	0	1	2.61	8	4	0	0	21	8	6	6	0	17	25	.111	.056	.130	10.89	7.40
Ramirez, Francis	R-R	6-5	205	1-12-92	2	2	4.03	10	5	0	0	29	27	15	13	0	14	15	.252	.278	.247	4.66	4.34
Tiburcio, Frederick	R-R	6-3	192	11-1-90	0	1	4.43	12	3	0	0	22	23	22	11	0	17	15	.271	.217	.290	6.04	6.85

Fielding

Catcher	PCT	G	PO	A	E	DP	PB
Gonzalez	.966	26	155	13	6	0	12
Hirland	.960	21	80	15	4	0	7
Moronta	.984	39	213	29	4	2	5

First Base	PCT	G	PO	A	E	DP
Alcantara	.953	17	135	6	7	11
Fulgencio	1.000	1	1	0	0	0
Gonzalez	.997	42	317	22	1	28
Hirland	1.000	4	7	1	0	1
Ramos	.982	21	162	6	3	12
Sierra	1.000	1	2	0	0	0

Second Base	PCT	G	PO	A	E	DP
Ayarza	1.000	1	2	2	0	0
Campusano	.903	25	46	56	11	9
De La Rosa	.955	28	43	63	5	14
Fulgencio	.909	10	15	25	4	7
Heredia	1.000	1	1	2	0	0
Lopez	.958	6	12	11	1	3
Sierra	.962	6	12	13	1	4

Third Base	PCT	G	PO	A	E	DP
Campusano	.886	15	11	28	5	6
De La Rosa	.818	4	5	4	2	0
Fulgencio	.826	10	4	15	4	1
Gonzalez	1.000	1	0	1	0	0
Lopez	.918	16	15	30	4	2
Rodriguez	.956	28	23	86	5	7
Rodriguez	1.000	1	0	2	0	0

Shortstop	PCT	G	PO	A	E	DP
Ayarza	.818	29	40	86	28	13
Fulgencio	.850	6	3	14	3	0
Lopez	.914	12	21	43	6	9
Rodriguez	.922	25	38	81	10	14

Outfield	PCT	G	PO	A	E	DP
Campusano	—	1	0	0	0	0
Fulgencio	.333	4	1	0	2	0
Heredia	1.000	32	37	4	0	0
Hirland	—	1	0	0	0	0
Lopez	.896	48	59	1	7	0
Monzon	.941	48	90	5	6	2
Perez	.967	46	56	2	2	0
Ramos	.714	5	5	0	2	0
Rodriguez	—	2	0	0	0	0
Rodriguez	1.000	1	3	0	0	0
Torres	.952	33	56	3	3	2

Kansas City Royals

SEASON IN A SENTENCE: Cy Young Award winner Zack Grienke led the American League with a 2.16 ERA and gave Royals fans something to cheer for every fifth day, but the other four days were filled with doom and gloom.

HIGH POINT: A month and a half into the season on May 15, Kansas City was in first place in the AL Central, such a remarkable event that the satirical newspaper The Onion was making jokes about the Royals' unexpected rise to first.

LOW POINT: There were many, but a season-worst 10-game losing streak in mid-July included three shutout losses. The streak began with a tough 1-0 loss to the Red Sox despite one of Brian Bannister's best starts of the season, but Kansas City allowed eight or more runs in five of the next nine games.

NOTABLE ROOKIES: For a team that was out of the pennant race in mid-June, the Royals played remarkably few rookies. Rookie catcher Brayan Pena hit .273/.318/.442 in 62 games, but he was the only rookie to see significant playing time. The only players to make their major league debuts were September callups Dusty Hughes and Victor Marte.

KEY TRANSACTIONS: General manager Dayton Moore's offseason moves struck out. Trade acquisition Mike Jacobs hit .228/.297/.401 to lose the DH job, while center fielder Coco Crisp played just 49 games before having season-ending shoulder surgery. Free-agent relievers Juan Cruz (3-4, 5.72) and Kyle Farnsworth (1-5, 4.78) failed to live up to their pricetags. After shortstop Mike Aviles was lost to Tommy John surgery, Kansas City had no viable options to take his place and traded for Mariners shortstop Yuniesky Betancourt. Betancourt failed to fill the team's offensive hole at shortstop, as he hit .240/.269/.370 for the Royals after the trade.

DOWN ON THE FARM: There was better news in the minors at the lower levels of the system. Mike Montgomery dominated two Class A levels in his first full pro season while fellow lefty Danny Duffy shut down Carolina League hitters to earn a spot in the Future's Game. Top hitting prospects Mike Moustakas and Eric Hosmer both struggled at the plate, but outfielder David Lough and shortstop Jeff Bianchi had breakout seasons that saw both of them earn midseason promotions to Double-A Northwest Arkansas. The system has lots of talent in Class A and below, but very little immediate help in Triple-A.

2009 OPENING DAY PAYROLL: $70,519,333

PLAYERS OF THE YEAR

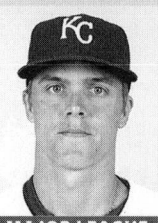
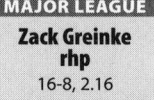

MAJOR LEAGUE	MINOR LEAGUE
Zack Greinke	**David Lough**
rhp	of
16-8, 2.16	(High A/Double-A)
AL Cy Young winner,	.325/.370/.496
242 SO in 229 IP	28 2B, 14 HR, 19 SB

ORGANIZATION LEADERS

BATTING		*Minimum 250 at-bats
MAJORS		
*AVG	Billy Butler	.301
*OPS	Billy Butler	.853
HR	Miguel Olivo	23
RBI	Billy Butler	93
MINORS		
*AVG	Lough, David, Wilmington/NW Arkansas	.325
R	Giavotella, Johnny, Wilmington	84
H	Bianchi, Jeff, Wilmington/NW Arkansas	151
TB	Smith, Corey, NW Arkansas	231
2B	Moustakas, Mike, Wilmington	32
3B	Giavotella, Johnny, Wilmington	8
	Mertins, Kurt, NW Arkansas	8
HR	Aldridge, Cory, Omaha	22
RBI	Smith, Corey, NW Arkansas	90
BB	Ka'aihue, Kila, Omaha	102
SO	Smith, Corey, NW Arkansas	132
SB	Robinson, Derrick, Wilmington	69
*OBP	Ka'aihue, Kila, Omaha	.392
*SLG	Aldridge, Cory, Omaha	.582

PITCHING		†Minimum 75 innings
MAJORS		
W	Zack Greinke	16
†ERA	Zack Greinke	2.16
SO	Zack Greinke	242
MINORS		
W	Four tied at	10
L	Santiago, Mario, Wilmington	13
†ERA	Duffy, Danny, Wilmington	2.98
G	Sisk, Brandon, Wilmington	45
GS	Runion, Sam, Burlington	28
SV	Sisk, Brandon, Wilmington	21
IP	Lerew, Anthony, NW Arkansas	152
BB	Kniginyzky, Matthew, NW Arkansas	57
SO	DiNardo, Lenny, Omaha	127
†AVG	Duffy, Danny, Wilmington	.230

2009 PERFORMANCE

General Manager: Dayton Moore. **Farm/Scouting Director:** J.J. Picollo.

Class	Team	League	W	L	PCT	Finish*	Manager(s)
Majors	Kansas City Royals	American	65	97	.401	t-12th (14)	Trey Hillman
Triple-A	Omaha Royals	Pacific Coast	64	80	.444	13th (16)	Mike Jirschele
Double-A	Northwest Arkansas Naturals	Texas	73	67	.521	3rd (8)	Brian Poldberg
High A	Wilmington Blue Rocks	Carolina	84	55	.604	1st (8)	Brian Rupp
Low A	Burlington Bees	Midwest	64	75	.460	8th (14)	Jim Gabella
Rookie	Burlington Royals	Appalachian	24	44	.353	10th (10)	Nelson Liriano
Rookie	AZL Royals	Arizona	20	35	.364	11th (11)	Julio Bruno
Rookie	Idaho Falls Chukars	Pioneer	43	31	.581	2nd (8)	Darryl Kennedy
Overall 2009 Minor League Record			372	387	.490	21st (30)	

*Finish in overall standings (No. of teams in league). †League champion.

ORGANIZATION STATISTICS

KANSAS CITY ROYALS

AMERICAN LEAGUE

Batting	B-T	HT	WT	DOB	AVG	vLH	vRH	G	AB	R	H	2B	3B	HR	RBI	BB	HBP	SH	SF	SO	SB	CS	SLG	OBP
Anderson, Josh	L-R	6-2	195	8-10-82	.237	.192	.250	44	118	20	28	3	0	1	8	5	0	0	0	21	12	3	.288	.268
2-team total (74 Detroit)					.240	—	—	118	283	42	68	7	4	1	24	13	1	1	0	43	25	5	.304	.276
Aviles, Mike	R-R	5-9	205	3-13-81	.183	.195	.177	36	120	10	22	3	1	1	8	4	0	2	1	26	1	0	.250	.208
Betancourt, Yuniesky	R-R	5-10	195	1-31-82	.240	.275	.226	71	246	25	59	10	5	4	27	11	0	3	3	26	0	2	.370	.269
2-team total (63 Seattle)					.245	—	—	134	470	40	115	20	6	6	49	21	0	11	6	44	3	3	.351	.274
Bloomquist, Willie	R-R	5-11	195	11-27-77	.265	.248	.275	125	434	52	115	11	8	4	29	27	1	4	2	73	25	6	.355	.308
Buck, John	R-R	6-3	230	7-7-80	.247	.213	.259	59	186	16	46	12	4	8	36	13	1	1	1	55	1	1	.484	.299
Butler, Billy	R-R	6-2	240	4-18-86	.301	.330	.289	159	608	78	183	51	1	21	93	58	2	0	4	103	1	0	.492	.362
Callaspo, Alberto	B-R	5-9	180	4-19-83	.300	.361	.273	155	576	79	173	41	8	11	73	52	1	0	5	51	2	1	.457	.356
Crisp, Coco	B-R	6-0	180	11-1-79	.228	.222	.231	49	180	30	41	8	5	3	14	29	1	4	1	23	13	2	.378	.336
DeJesus, David	L-L	6-0	190	12-20-79	.281	.290	.277	144	558	74	157	28	9	13	71	51	8	5	5	87	4	9	.434	.347
Freel, Ryan	R-R	5-9	180	3-8-76	.244	.176	.286	18	45	8	11	2	0	0	3	4	0	0	0	12	0	0	.289	.306
2-team total (9 Baltimore)					.217	—	—	27	60	10	13	2	0	0	4	9	0	0	0	16	0	0	.250	.319
Gordon, Alex	L-R	6-1	220	2-10-84	.232	.163	.261	49	164	28	38	6	0	6	22	21	2	1	1	43	5	0	.378	.324
Guillen, Jose	R-R	5-11	195	5-17-76	.242	.181	.273	81	281	30	68	8	0	9	40	22	8	0	1	50	1	0	.367	.314
Hernandez, Luis	B-R	5-10	180	6-26-84	.205	.250	.184	37	73	4	15	1	0	0	4	4	1	3	0	18	1	0	.219	.256
Hulett, Tug	L-R	5-10	185	2-28-83	.111	.500	.063	15	18	4	2	0	0	0	1	1	0	0	0	6	0	0	.111	.158
Jacobs, Mike	L-R	6-3	215	10-30-80	.228	.178	.243	128	434	46	99	16	1	19	61	41	2	0	1	132	0	0	.401	.297
Maier, Mitch	L-R	6-2	210	6-30-82	.243	.299	.224	127	341	42	83	15	3	3	31	43	4	7	2	76	9	2	.331	.333
Olivo, Miguel	R-R	6-0	230	7-15-78	.249	.265	.238	114	390	51	97	15	5	23	65	19	5	1	1	126	5	2	.490	.292
Pena, Brayan	B-R	5-11	245	1-7-82	.273	.258	.282	64	165	17	45	10	0	6	18	12	0	4	2	18	0	0	.442	.318
Teahen, Mark	L-R	6-3	210	9-6-81	.271	.287	.262	144	524	69	142	34	1	12	50	37	6	2	2	123	8	1	.408	.325

Pitching	B-T	HT	WT	DOB	W	L	ERA	G	GS	CG	SV	IP	H	R	ER	HR	BB	SO	AVG	vLH	vRH	K/9	BB/9
Bale, John	L-L	6-4	205	5-22-74	0	1	5.72	43	0	0	1	28	34	19	18	3	18	24	.296	.271	.321	7.62	5.72
Bannister, Brian	R-R	6-2	215	2-28-81	7	12	4.73	26	26	0	0	154	161	94	81	15	50	98	.268	.266	.270	5.73	2.92
Chen, Bruce	L-L	6-1	215	6-19-77	1	6	5.78	17	9	0	0	62	74	42	40	12	25	45	.301	.292	.305	6.50	3.61
Colon, Roman	R-R	6-6	235	8-13-79	2	3	4.83	43	0	0	0	50	50	27	27	7	22	29	.256	.265	.250	5.19	3.93
Cruz, Juan	R-R	6-2	165	10-15-78	3	4	5.72	46	0	0	2	50	46	34	32	6	29	38	.246	.244	.247	6.79	5.19
Davies, Kyle	R-R	6-2	220	9-9-83	8	9	5.27	22	22	1	0	123	122	76	72	18	66	86	.265	.239	.284	6.29	4.83
DiNardo, Lenny	L-L	6-2	220	9-19-79	0	3	10.13	5	5	0	0	21	41	28	24	2	15	8	.414	.450	.405	3.38	6.33
Farnsworth, Kyle	R-R	6-4	235	4-14-76	1	5	4.58	41	0	0	0	37	43	22	19	3	14	42	.287	.277	.294	10.13	3.38
Greinke, Zack	R-R	6-2	190	10-21-83	16	8	2.16	33	33	6	0	229	195	64	55	11	51	242	.230	.250	.211	9.50	2.00
Hochevar, Luke	R-R	6-5	210	9-15-83	7	13	6.55	25	25	2	0	143	167	109	104	23	46	106	.290	.292	.289	6.67	2.90
Hughes, Dusty	L-L	5-10	187	6-29-82	0	2	5.14	8	1	0	0	14	13	9	8	2	8	15	.245	.267	.237	9.64	5.14
Lerew, Anthony	L-R	6-3	220	10-28-82	0	1	4.05	3	2	0	0	13	14	8	6	4	8	7	.264	.294	.211	4.72	5.40
Mahay, Ron	L-L	6-2	195	6-28-71	1	1	4.79	41	0	0	0	41	55	26	22	9	19	34	.313	.278	.340	7.40	4.14
2-team total (16 Minnesota)					2	1	4.29	57	0	0	0	50	62	29	24	10	22	42	—	—	—	7.51	3.93
Marte, Victor	R-R	6-2	265	11-8-80	0	0	8.25	8	0	0	0	12	13	12	11	2	12	7	.283	.167	.357	5.25	9.00
Meche, Gil	R-R	6-3	215	9-8-78	6	10	5.09	23	23	1	0	129	144	81	73	17	58	95	.281	.268	.292	6.63	4.05
Ponson, Sidney	R-R	6-1	260	11-2-76	1	7	7.36	14	9	0	0	59	79	50	48	6	25	32	.332	.372	.284	4.91	3.84
Ramirez, Horacio	L-L	6-1	220	11-24-79	0	2	5.96	19	1	0	0	23	27	16	15	3	11	13	.293	.245	.349	5.16	4.37
Rosa, Carlos	R-R	6-1	210	9-21-84	0	0	3.38	7	0	0	1	10	4	4	4	1	3	6	.256	.158	.350	3.38	2.53
Soria, Joakim	R-R	6-3	204	5-18-84	3	2	2.21	47	0	0	30	53	44	14	13	5	16	69	.219	.224	.213	11.72	2.72
Tejeda, Robinson	R-R	6-3	250	3-24-82	4	2	3.54	35	6	0	0	74	43	30	29	4	50	87	.167	.209	.125	10.63	6.11
Waechter, Doug	R-R	6-4	225	1-28-81	0	0	8.44	5	0	0	0	5	9	5	5	2	3	3	.375	.214	.600	5.06	5.06
Wright, Jamey	R-R	6-5	225	12-24-74	3	5	4.33	65	0	0	0	79	73	51	38	8	44	60	.247	.200	.285	6.84	5.01
Yabuta, Yasuhiko	R-R	6-2	190	6-19-73	2	1	13.50	12	0	0	0	14	29	21	21	3	7	9	.420	.467	.385	5.79	4.50

Fielding

Catcher	PCT	G	PO	A	E	DP	PB
Buck	.976	46	309	14	8	4	2
Olivo	.990	103	718	47	8	5	10

Pena	1.000	30	168	7	0	2	2

First Base	PCT	G	PO	A	E	DP
Bloomquist	1.000	3	3	0	0	1

Butler	.992	145	1141	92	10	123
Jacobs	.982	15	94	14	2	13
Teahen	1.000	11	60	3	0	4

Second Base	PCT	G	PO	A	E	DP
Bloomquist	.967	14	24	35	2	10
Callaspo	.973	146	233	379	17	96
Freel	—	1	0	0	0	0
Hernandez	1.000	8	3	7	0	0
Hulett	1.000	5	2	7	0	1
Teahen	1.000	3	5	6	0	1

Third Base	PCT	G	PO	A	E	DP
Aviles	—	2	0	0	0	0
Bloomquist	1.000	3	2	5	0	0
Callaspo	1.000	14	11	13	0	2

Gordon	.920	49	21	94	10	8
Hernandez	1.000	5	4	2	0	0
Hulett	.000	1	0	0	1	0
Teahen	.956	107	66	171	11	14

Shortstop	PCT	G	PO	A	E	DP
Aviles	.973	34	51	92	4	29
Betancourt	.970	71	111	181	9	40
Bloomquist	.956	38	51	80	6	22
Callaspo	1.000	1	1	0	0	0
Hernandez	.986	23	20	52	1	13
Hulett	—	1	0	0	0	0

Pena Jr.	.936	40	29	44	5	9

Outfield	PCT	G	PO	A	E	DP
Anderson	.990	42	93	2	1	0
Bloomquist	.986	84	134	3	2	1
Crisp	.976	49	120	0	3	0
DeJesus	1.000	144	310	13	0	3
Freel	1.000	16	16	1	0	0
Guillen	.962	69	98	4	4	0
Hulett	1.000	3	2	0	0	0
Maier	1.000	123	250	11	0	5
Teahen	.975	32	39	0	1	0

OMAHA ROYALS

TRIPLE-A

PACIFIC COAST LEAGUE

Batting	B-T	HT	WT	DOB	AVG	vLH	vRH	G	AB	R	H	2B	3B	HR	RBI	BB	HBP	SH	SF	SO	SB	CS	SLG	OBP
Aldridge, Cory	L-R	6-1	225	6-13-79	.316	.341	.308	98	354	48	112	20	4	22	71	24	3	0	4	86	0	1	.582	.361
Buchanan, Brian	R-R	6-4	230	7-21-73	.238	.255	.227	34	122	10	29	7	0	7	26	7	0	0	0	19	1	0	.467	.279
Buck, John	R-R	6-3	230	7-7-80	.259	.200	.294	7	27	3	7	1	0	2	4	0	0	0	0	7	0	0	.519	.259
Clark, Cody	R-R	6-2	205	9-14-81	.500	1.000	.429	3	8	2	4	1	0	0	2	1	0	0	0	1	0	0	.625	.636
Costa, Shane	L-R	6-0	205	12-12-81	.500	—	.500	1	2	1	1	0	0	0	0	0	0	0	0	0	0	0	.500	.500
Duarte, Jose	R-R	5-10	165	3-7-85	.182	.154	.190	17	55	6	10	0	1	0	4	5	0	3	0	8	1	1	.218	.250
Falu, Irving	B-R	5-9	180	6-6-83	.269	.293	.257	122	465	64	125	19	5	2	40	52	2	8	5	35	12	5	.344	.342
Gordon, Alex	L-R	6-1	220	2-10-84	.313	.333	.302	18	67	17	21	4	1	2	10	13	3	0	2	16	0	0	.493	.435
Hernandez, Luis	B-R	5-10	180	6-26-84	.303	.362	.271	55	198	24	60	10	0	1	26	16	1	7	1	17	1	3	.369	.356
House, J.R.	R-R	6-0	215	11-11-79	.251	.291	.232	127	505	58	127	24	0	9	53	33	1	2	3	57	0	0	.352	.297
Hulett, Tug	L-R	5-10	185	2-28-83	.291	.283	.295	99	374	62	109	27	4	11	53	58	1	5	4	79	9	2	.473	.384
Ka'aihue, Kila	L-R	6-3	220	3-29-84	.252	.255	.250	131	441	83	111	27	1	17	57	102	4	1	7	85	0	1	.433	.392
Lisson, Mario	R-R	6-2	210	5-31-84	.236	.263	.225	95	339	34	80	23	0	12	43	19	3	4	1	89	7	4	.410	.282
Lubanski, Chris	L-L	6-3	210	3-24-85	.227	.265	.214	36	132	20	30	7	1	2	16	17	0	0	1	27	7	1	.341	.313
Lucas, Ed	R-R	6-3	205	5-21-82	.125	.000	.333	5	8	1	1	0	0	0	1	2	0	1	0	4	0	1	.125	.300
Maier, Mitch	L-R	6-2	210	6-30-82	.314	.316	.313	12	51	8	16	3	0	2	10	8	0	0	1	8	1	1	.490	.400
Metcalf, Travis	R-R	6-3	215	8-17-82	.219	.197	.229	110	388	45	85	18	2	9	47	33	5	4	6	80	2	1	.345	.285
2-team total (15 Oklahoma City)					.216			125	440	48	95	19	2	11	54	38	5	5	6	95	4	1	.343	.282
Murphy, Tommy	B-R	5-11	200	8-27-79	.228	.239	.224	79	272	35	62	13	1	3	14	31	2	6	1	63	16	6	.316	.310
Parraz, Jordan	R-R	6-2	210	10-8-84	.298	.333	.269	13	47	6	14	6	0	0	5	4	1	0	1	14	0	2	.426	.358
Pena, Brayan	B-R	5-11	245	1-7-82	.307	.412	.241	22	88	11	27	6	1	4	18	4	3	2	1	9	2	1	.534	.354
Raines Jr., Tim	B-R	5-10	190	8-31-79	.234	.242	.231	82	273	35	64	11	1	7	28	18	0	3	4	52	15	0	.359	.278
Shealy, Ryan	R-R	6-5	240	8-29-79	.345	.313	.352	25	87	15	30	7	0	0	12	18	1	0	2	25	0	0	.425	.454
Suomi, John	L-R	5-11	200	10-5-80	.145	.050	.179	23	76	4	11	3	0	1	6	2	1	2	0	14	0	1	.224	.177
Thorman, Scott	L-R	6-3	235	1-6-82	.297	.272	.308	97	367	45	109	12	2	19	63	21	9	3	5	66	5	3	.496	.346
2-team total (11 Oklahoma City)					.288	—		108	399	49	115	16	2	20	67	24	11	3	5	75	7	3	.489	.342
Tschepikow, Ben	L-R	5-11	200	9-22-85	.250	.250	.250	4	12	2	3	0	0	0	1	1	1	1	0	1	0	0	.250	.357
Tupman, Matt	L-R	5-11	185	11-25-79	.261	.182	.276	21	69	5	18	2	0	0	7	2	0	1	0	6	0	0	.290	.282

Pitching	B-T	HT	WT	DOB	W	L	ERA	G	GS	CG	SV	IP	H	R	ER	HR	BB	SO	AVG	vLH	vRH	K/9	BB/9
Atencio, Greg	R-R	6-2	191	7-15-81	2	7	7.04	27	0	0	2	38	46	31	30	3	16	44	.305	.278	.320	10.33	3.76
Bannister, Brian	R-R	6-2	215	2-28-81	0	1	3.46	3	3	0	0	13	12	5	5	1	8	24	.240	.200	.257	5.54	0.69
Chavez, Chris	L-R	6-3	195	9-11-84	1	2	3.00	5	1	0	0	18	15	6	6	1	4	15	.221	.154	.262	7.50	2.00
Chen, Bruce	L-L	6-1	215	6-19-77	4	2	3.40	14	13	3	0	82	57	33	31	8	23	69	.196	.145	.214	7.57	2.52
Colon, Roman	R-R	6-6	235	8-13-79	2	3	2.84	13	0	0	2	25	27	9	8	1	8	26	.278	.290	.273	9.24	2.84
Davies, Kyle	R-R	6-2	220	9-9-83	4	2	2.14	8	8	0	0	46	47	19	11	3	14	44	.264	.226	.298	8.55	2.72
De La Vara, Gilbert	L-L	5-10	190	10-4-84	0	0	1.29	3	0	0	0	7	6	2	1	0	7	3	.250	.250	.250	3.86	9.00
DiNardo, Lenny	L-L	6-2	220	9-19-79	10	5	3.32	29	23	0	2	152	139	61	56	5	38	127	.246	.273	.239	7.54	2.25
Duckworth, Brandon	R-R	6-1	210	1-23-76	3	6	5.31	20	19	0	0	105	105	63	62	12	37	67	.261	.281	.244	5.74	3.17
Farnsworth, Kyle	R-R	6-4	235	4-14-76	0	0	0.00	2	1	0	0	2	0	0	0	0	0	2	.000	.000	.000	9.00	0.00
Godin, Jason	R-R	6-5	170	9-23-84	1	0	4.26	3	0	0	0	6	10	4	3	0	3	10	.357	.364	.353	14.21	4.26
Hamulack, Tim	L-L	6-2	215	11-14-76	4	3	5.01	41	0	0	1	65	81	36	36	7	22	53	.320	.260	.347	7.38	3.06
Hartsock, Aaron	R-R	6-3	200	1-17-84	0	0	18.00	1	0	0	0	1	3	2	2	1	1	2	.500	.000	.600	18.00	9.00
Hayes, Chris	R-R	6-1	195	2-5-83	1	6	4.59	26	0	0	3	49	67	27	25	2	7	24	.328	.394	.297	4.41	1.29
Hochevar, Luke	R-R	6-3	210	9-15-83	5	1	1.50	8	8	1	0	48	41	11	8	2	12	36	.238	.310	.202	6.75	2.25
Holland, Greg	R-R	5-11	180	11-20-85	1	1	7.00	6	0	0	2	9	12	7	7	2	5	1	.343	.182	.615	1.00	5.00
Hughes, Dusty	L-L	5-10	187	6-29-82	3	3	3.50	34	11	0	1	87	79	35	34	6	41	76	.248	.208	.265	7.83	4.23
Liotta, Ray	L-L	6-3	220	4-3-83	0	1	7.56	2	2	0	0	8	11	7	7	1	6	5	.333	.667	.300	5.40	6.48
Marte, Victor	R-R	6-2	265	11-8-80	1	4	2.13	26	0	0	4	42	35	14	10	0	20	36	.224	.204	.235	7.65	4.25
Meche, Gil	R-R	6-3	215	9-8-78	1	1	3.12	2	2	0	0	9	3	3	3	0	7	4	.120	.167	.077	4.15	7.27
Newman, Josh	L-L	6-1	200	6-11-82	1	1	8.47	10	1	0	0	17	23	16	16	3	11	10	.338	.368	.327	5.29	5.82
Nicoll, Chris	R-R	6-3	190	10-30-83	2	2	6.67	6	5	0	0	27	30	20	20	4	9	18	.280	.304	.255	6.00	3.00
O'Connor, Mike	L-L	6-3	185	8-17-80	1	4	7.24	6	5	0	0	27	41	27	22	7	5	18	.347	.292	.362	5.93	1.65
2-team total (6 Portland)					1	4	6.81	12	6	0	0	40	58	36	30	7	9	24	—	—	—	5.45	2.04
Pena Jr., Tony	R-R	6-2	180	3-23-81	0	0	0.00	1	0	0	0	3	2	0	0	0	3	.200	.000	.250	9.00	0.00
Phillips, Heath	L-L	6-3	280	3-24-82	8	7	4.99	27	25	2	0	150	175	91	83	12	50	111	.301	.347	.288	6.67	3.01
Ponson, Sidney	R-R	6-1	260	11-2-76	2	1	2.18	6	6	0	0	33	34	8	8	2	5	19	.283	.323	.270	5.18	1.36
Randolph, Stephen	L-L	6-3	210	5-1-74	1	1	10.13	2	2	0	0	8	12	9	9	4	9	7	.364	.364	.364	7.88	10.13
2-team total (19 Albuquerque)					5	3	5.90	21	8	0	0	50	42	33	33	6	38	53	—	—	—	9.48	6.79

	B-T	HT	WT	DOB	W	L	ERA	G	GS	CG	SV	IP	H	R	ER	HR	BB	SO	AVG	vLH	vRH	K/9	BB/9
Rosa, Carlos	R-R	6-1	210	9-21-84	2	8	4.56	43	0	0	7	71	69	40	36	6	32	80	.258	.264	.256	10.14	4.06
Tejeda, Robinson	R-R	6-3	250	3-24-82	0	1	0.00	1	1	0	0	2	1	2	0	0	3	1	.143	.250	.000	4.50	13.50
Waechter, Doug	R-R	6-4	225	1-28-81	1	1	4.82	13	0	0	1	19	22	11	10	0	1	10	.301	.313	.293	4.82	0.48
Wright, Matt	R-R	6-4	270	3-13-82	1	5	6.75	9	8	0	0	40	47	30	30	3	15	29	.299	.250	.324	6.53	3.38
Yabuta, Yasuhiko	R-R	6-2	190	6-19-73	2	1	3.55	26	0	0	0	46	39	19	18	5	17	53	.228	.213	.236	10.45	3.35

Fielding

Catcher	PCT	G	PO	A	E	DP	PB
Buck	1.000	5	30	3	0	0	0
Clark	1.000	3	23	3	0	0	0
House	.993	101	728	36	5	5	3
Pena	.951	5	37	2	2	1	0
Suomi	.982	16	105	5	2	2	1
Tupman	.977	19	119	9	3	1	1

First Base	PCT	G	PO	A	E	DP
House	1.000	3	24	0	0	3
Ka'aihue	.997	118	1091	78	4	129
Metcalf	1.000	9	89	7	0	12
Shealy	1.000	8	70	5	0	3
Thorman	1.000	10	70	2	0	3

Second Base	PCT	G	PO	A	E	DP
Falu	.985	63	129	206	5	58
Hernandez	1.000	10	17	24	0	8
Hulett	.990	59	119	183	3	53

	PCT	G	PO	A	E	DP
Metcalf	1.000	6	8	20	0	5
Murphy	.962	5	12	13	1	2
Tschepikow	1.000	4	13	11	0	7

Third Base	PCT	G	PO	A	E	DP
Falu	1.000	2	0	7	0	2
Gordon	.886	9	4	27	4	3
Hulett	1.000	6	3	14	0	2
Lisson	.952	31	15	65	4	9
Metcalf	.951	95	53	217	14	24
Murphy	.667	2	0	2	1	0
Thorman	.933	5	1	13	1	3

Shortstop	PCT	G	PO	A	E	DP
Falu	.949	29	23	89	6	12
Hernandez	.980	46	62	139	4	37
Hulett	1.000	5	2	11	0	1
Lisson	.958	67	92	201	13	50

Outfield	PCT	G	PO	A	E	DP
Aldridge	.973	64	105	5	3	0
Buchanan	1.000	4	4	0	0	0
Costa	1.000	1	1	0	0	0
Duarte	.936	17	41	3	3	0
Falu	1.000	26	55	3	0	0
Hulett	1.000	21	37	0	0	0
Lubanski	1.000	36	57	5	0	0
Lucas	1.000	3	3	0	0	0
Maier	1.000	12	32	0	0	0
Murphy	.977	74	119	10	3	2
Parraz	.929	13	23	3	2	1
Pena	.923	9	12	0	1	0
Raines Jr.	.973	81	179	4	5	1
Suomi	.900	5	8	1	1	0
Thorman	.952	79	90	9	5	0

NORTHWEST ARKANSAS NATURALS   *DOUBLE-A*

TEXAS LEAGUE

Batting	B-T	HT	WT	DOB	AVG	vLH	vRH	G	AB	R	H	2B	3B	HR	RBI	BB	HBP	SH	SF	SO	SB	CS	SLG	OBP
Betancourt, Yuniesky	R-R	5-10	195	1-31-82	.154	.250	.111	3	13	2	2	0	0	1	1	0	0	0	0	1	0	0	.385	.154
Bianchi, Jeff	R-R	6-0	175	10-5-86	.315	.394	.289	68	270	42	85	17	1	5	42	19	1	2	5	58	10	4	.441	.356
Clark, Cody	R-R	6-2	205	9-14-81	.304	.283	.312	65	191	33	58	13	0	8	32	15	5	2	2	27	1	2	.497	.366
Dickerson, Joe	L-L	6-1	190	10-3-86	.230	.233	.229	34	126	15	29	7	2	0	13	18	3	2	1	19	5	1	.317	.338
Duarte, Jose	R-R	5-10	165	3-7-85	.248	.323	.217	93	326	50	81	14	3	4	39	47	0	6	1	67	18	10	.347	.342
Dyson, Jarrod	L-R	5-10	160	8-15-84	.258	.200	.281	63	248	38	64	7	4	0	14	27	0	8	0	54	37	6	.319	.331
Gordon, Alex	L-R	6-1	220	2-10-84	.367	.143	.435	8	30	4	11	3	0	2	10	5	0	0	0	5	0	0	.667	.457
Howell, Jeff	R-R	6-0	205	4-1-83	.262	.262	.262	62	195	22	51	10	1	4	24	16	1	1	3	36	0	2	.385	.316
Johnson, Josh	R-R	5-11	170	1-11-86	.189	.175	.196	51	132	26	25	3	0	0	9	29	1	2	0	24	2	2	.212	.340
Lisson, Mario	R-R	6-2	210	5-31-84	.206	.227	.196	36	136	20	28	4	0	2	17	14	3	1	4	29	4	3	.279	.287
Lough, David	L-L	6-0	180	1-20-86	.331	.186	.379	61	236	41	78	13	2	9	31	12	3	2	0	30	13	4	.517	.371
Lucas, Ed	R-R	6-3	205	5-21-82	.290	.354	.266	103	355	61	103	22	2	10	58	53	7	4	5	75	18	2	.448	.388
Maddox, Marc	R-R	5-11	185	9-16-83	.168	.075	.202	44	149	20	25	6	0	4	17	20	4	1	0	23	4	2	.289	.283
McConnell, Chris	R-R	5-11	175	12-18-85	.219	.283	.190	59	169	25	37	7	0	0	11	14	1	6	2	40	6	5	.272	.280
McFall, Brian	R-R	6-3	215	3-17-84	.250	.288	.232	59	204	29	51	13	0	7	37	19	8	0	2	57	3	1	.417	.335
Mertins, Kurt	R-R	6-0	175	4-22-86	.275	.295	.266	126	495	64	136	23	8	2	57	41	4	7	5	107	11	10	.366	.332
Parraz, Jordan	R-R	6-3	210	10-8-84	.358	.370	.353	64	226	35	81	17	3	7	42	29	11	1	2	25	4	8	.553	.451
Smith, Corey	R-R	6-1	200	4-15-82	.249	.282	.236	140	550	67	137	29	1	21	90	39	4	0	4	132	12	8	.420	.302
Strait, Cody	R-R	6-1	180	5-28-83	.278	.316	.261	87	320	59	89	22	1	4	38	31	0	5	2	65	14	4	.391	.340
Suomi, John	L-R	5-11	200	10-5-80	.311	.208	.337	37	119	23	37	6	2	0	19	13	1	1	2	17	0	2	.571	.378
Wilson, Vance	R-R	5-11	215	3-17-73	.270	.318	.256	59	204	27	55	9	0	10	32	16	7	1	1	46	0	1	.461	.342

Pitching	B-T	HT	WT	DOB	W	L	ERA	G	GS	CG	SV	IP	H	R	ER	HR	BB	SO	AVG	vLH	vRH	K/9	BB/9
Abreu, Juan	R-R	6-0	170	4-8-85	2	2	5.75	16	0	0	4	20	19	15	13	3	22	25	.247	.424	.114	11.07	9.74
Bale, John	L-L	6-4	205	5-22-74	0	0	1.35	6	0	0	0	7	4	2	1	0	1	5	.167	.286	.118	6.75	1.35
Bannister, John	R-R	6-4	200	1-20-84	1	0	5.02	8	0	0	0	14	12	8	8	1	6	9	.235	.125	.333	5.65	3.77
2-team total (24 Frisco)					4	3	5.89	32	0	0	1	44	41	29	29	5	20	31	—	—	—	6.29	4.06
Castaneda, Federico	R-R	6-3	187	1-26-84	0	3	4.28	12	2	0	1	27	20	13	13	2	11	27	.204	.143	.250	8.89	3.62
Cevette, Dan	L-L	6-3	195	10-19-83	0	0	5.32	14	2	0	0	22	25	13	13	1	11	13	.291	.344	.259	5.32	4.50
Chavez, Chris	L-R	6-3	195	9-11-84	0	1	3.86	3	0	0	0	5	3	2	2	0	5	3	.176	.111	.250	5.79	9.64
Cortes, Danny	R-R	6-6	215	3-4-87	6	6	3.92	16	15	0	0	80	77	43	35	3	50	57	.258	.259	.256	6.39	5.60
Crist, Kyle	R-R	6-3	194	6-27-83	0	0	8.38	8	0	0	0	10	14	12	9	0	10	4	.341	.316	.364	3.72	9.31
De La Vara, Gilbert	L-L	5-10	190	10-4-84	6	2	5.74	35	1	0	2	64	83	59	41	6	27	40	.304	.308	.302	5.60	3.78
Farnsworth, Kyle	R-R	6-4	235	4-14-76	0	0	0.00	3	0	0	0	4	1	0	0	1	0	3	.083	.000	.250	7.36	2.45
Godin, Jason	R-R	6-5	170	9-23-84	0	2	6.48	8	2	0	0	17	23	15	12	1	13	9	.324	.286	.349	4.86	7.02
Hardy, Rowdy	L-L	6-4	170	10-26-84	4	4	3.43	11	10	0	0	60	59	28	23	5	20	39	.258	.175	.289	5.82	2.98
Hartsock, Aaron	R-R	6-3	200	1-17-84	3	1	2.82	28	0	0	8	51	43	17	16	4	17	27	.223	.232	.216	4.76	3.00
Hayes, Chris	R-R	6-1	195	2-5-83	3	0	0.98	18	0	0	3	37	33	11	4	1	6	17	.237	.286	.188	4.17	1.47
Holland, Greg	R-R	5-11	180	11-20-85	3	2	3.18	29	0	0	8	45	46	16	16	2	19	49	.264	.312	.227	9.73	3.77
Johnson, Blake	R-R	6-5	200	10-4-85	8	8	4.57	24	24	0	0	122	148	70	62	11	41	61	.305	.305	.306	4.50	3.02
Kniginyzky, Matt	L-R	6-3	185	10-5-82	5	10	5.48	26	24	0	0	135	157	98	82	21	57	68	.297	.344	.256	4.54	3.81
Lerew, Anthony	L-R	6-3	220	10-28-82	10	6	4.09	27	27	1	0	152	164	79	69	14	55	101	.275	.290	.263	5.98	3.26
Marte, Victor	R-R	6-2	265	11-8-80	2	1	2.45	13	0	0	4	22	15	7	6	1	5	17	.190	.211	.171	6.95	2.05
Nicoll, Chris	R-R	6-3	190	10-30-83	7	0	3.50	33	0	0	1	62	60	32	24	4	26	58	.251	.248	.254	8.46	3.79
Orvella, Chad	R-R	5-11	195	10-1-80	1	1	1.64	8	1	0	0	11	7	2	2	1	0	6	.179	.286	.124	4.91	0.00

	B-T	HT	WT	DOB	W	L	ERA	G	GS	CG	SV	IP	H	R	ER	HR	BB	SO	AVG	vLH	vRH	K/9	BB/9
Sencion, Carlos	L-L	6-6	170	11-17-84	3	1	6.02	25	1	0	1	46	58	34	31	5	30	43	.307	.208	.368	8.35	5.83
Swaggerty, Ben	L-L	6-1	185	8-8-82	4	1	4.33	26	0	0	1	44	53	21	21	3	20	54	.298	.250	.322	11.13	4.12
Teaford, Everett	L-L	6-0	155	5-15-84	3	7	5.11	16	16	1	0	81	86	53	46	12	34	42	.269	.298	.257	4.67	3.78
Tejeda, Robinson	R-R	6-3	250	3-24-82	0	1	4.91	2	2	0	0	4	3	2	2	1	2	5	.250	.400	.143	12.27	4.91
Wood, Blake	R-R	6-4	225	8-8-85	2	8	5.83	17	13	1	0	79	92	52	51	8	28	49	.309	.329	.287	5.61	3.20

Fielding

Catcher	PCT	G	PO	A	E	DP	PB
Clark	.993	65	371	38	3	2	2
Howell	.979	49	248	36	6	3	4
Suomi	.988	24	137	26	2	3	2
Wilson	.989	18	81	7	1	1	0

First Base	PCT	G	PO	A	E	DP
Lucas	1.000	5	24	4	0	2
McFall	.981	35	291	22	6	32
Smith	.986	107	980	41	14	104

Second Base	PCT	G	PO	A	E	DP
Bianchi	1.000	2	7	4	0	2
Johnson	.949	7	14	23	2	9
Lucas	1.000	1	1	0	0	0

	PCT	G	PO	A	E	DP
Maddox	.994	29	61	104	1	32
McConnell	1.000	19	35	59	0	13
Mertins	.976	86	146	266	10	54

Third Base	PCT	G	PO	A	E	DP
Gordon	.846	5	6	5	2	0
Johnson	.920	23	9	37	4	5
Lucas	.947	53	30	96	7	9
Maddox	.933	14	2	26	2	1
Mertins	.910	26	18	43	6	5
Smith	.893	27	15	35	6	4

Shortstop	PCT	G	PO	A	E	DP
Betancourt	.900	3	2	7	1	1
Bianchi	.973	60	95	191	8	46

	PCT	G	PO	A	E	DP
Johnson	1.000	12	18	31	0	9
Lisson	.938	32	53	98	10	20
McConnell	.970	39	47	117	5	26

Outfield	PCT	G	PO	A	E	DP
Dickerson	.963	33	50	2	2	1
Duarte	.987	90	212	10	3	4
Dyson	.975	61	149	10	4	0
Lough	.967	58	115	4	4	0
Lucas	.924	47	91	6	8	2
McFall	1.000	1	3	0	0	0
Parraz	.971	63	124	9	4	2
Strait	.977	72	171	2	4	1

WILMINGTON BLUE ROCKS　　　　　　　　　　HIGH CLASS A

CAROLINA LEAGUE

Batting	B-T	HT	WT	DOB	AVG	vLH	vRH	G	AB	R	H	2B	3B	HR	RBI	BB	HBP	SH	SF	SO	SB	CS	SLG	OBP
Bianchi, Jeff	R-R	6-0	175	10-5-86	.300	.302	.299	60	220	32	66	12	2	4	28	20	1	3	1	47	12	2	.427	.360
Del Rosario, Luis	R-R	6-2	200	5-21-90	.125	.000	.143	3	8	0	1	1	0	0	0	2	0	0	0	1	0	0	.250	.300
Eigsti, Ryan	R-R	6-2	195	8-24-85	.201	.220	.191	104	324	41	65	14	1	3	35	42	8	6	2	95	4	2	.278	.306
Fontaine, Chase	L-R	6-1	200	10-22-85	.288	.222	.306	29	80	8	23	3	0	1	16	16	1	2	2	22	3	3	.363	.404
Giavotella, Johnny	R-R	5-8	185	7-10-87	.258	.290	.240	133	476	84	123	24	8	6	52	66	4	11	4	54	26	9	.380	.351
Hosmer, Eric	L-L	6-4	215	10-24-89	.206	.194	.213	27	97	9	20	2	2	1	10	9	1	0	0	22	0	0	.299	.280
Jimenez, Antonio	R-R	6-2	155	4-20-87	.087	.083	.091	8	23	0	2	0	0	0	0	1	1	0	0	6	0	0	.087	.160
Johnson, Josh	B-R	5-11	170	1-11-86	.333	.300	.346	12	36	4	12	3	1	0	4	3	0	0	1	6	3	1	.472	.375
Lough, David	L-L	6-0	180	1-20-86	.320	.295	.336	65	222	28	71	15	2	5	30	12	7	7	2	34	6	4	.473	.370
Morizio, Matt	L-R	6-3	215	12-14-83	.132	.125	.136	37	106	2	14	3	0	0	4	16	2	3	0	19	1	2	.160	.258
Moustakas, Mike	L-R	6-0	195	9-11-88	.250	.235	.259	129	492	66	123	32	2	16	86	32	2	1	3	90	10	6	.421	.297
Orlando, Paulo	R-R	6-3	185	11-1-85	.261	.218	.287	101	356	46	93	20	3	2	34	15	7	12	1	80	20	5	.351	.303
Ortiz, Adrian	R-R	6-0	172	1-14-87	.238	.263	.223	76	256	22	61	5	4	0	22	9	2	4	3	47	12	6	.289	.267
Robinson, Clint	L-L	6-4	225	2-16-85	.298	.305	.295	124	436	65	130	31	1	13	57	35	7	0	5	79	4	3	.463	.356
Robinson, Derrick	B-L	5-11	170	9-28-87	.239	.234	.243	128	522	72	125	19	5	5	47	35	3	9	2	90	69	23	.324	.290
Seratelli, Anthony	B-R	6-0	205	2-27-83	.268	.222	.292	103	317	41	85	12	3	3	31	33	4	8	2	82	21	8	.353	.343
Van Stratten, Nick	R-L	6-1	185	5-22-85	.288	.243	.304	42	139	18	40	7	0	3	14	12	1	2	1	19	5	2	.403	.371
Walton, Jamar	L-R	6-4	195	1-5-86	.255	.177	.289	93	314	31	80	10	1	4	39	26	4	0	3	76	7	8	.331	.317

Pitching	B-T	HT	WT	DOB	W	L	ERA	G	GS	CG	SV	IP	H	R	ER	HR	BB	SO	AVG	vLH	vRH	K/9	BB/9
Abreu, Juan	R-R	6-0	170	4-8-85	3	2	1.69	20	0	0	12	21	8	5	4	1	14	28	.114	.194	.051	11.81	5.91
Basurto, Eric	R-R	6-3	200	4-17-86	0	0	0.84	8	0	0	2	11	8	1	1	1	6	16	.216	.059	.350	13.50	5.06
Bowden, Barry	R-R	6-1	205	11-9-84	2	0	4.50	5	0	0	0	11	8	7	6	1	2	14	.222	.333	.143	12.60	1.80
Caldera, Alex	L-R	6-3	200	10-1-85	5	10	4.77	27	27	0	0	138	141	77	73	12	53	105	.268	.294	.241	6.86	3.46
Chavez, Chris	L-R	6-3	195	9-11-84	6	1	1.95	25	0	0	4	51	52	13	11	0	24	41	.272	.280	.267	7.28	4.26
Coleman, Louis	R-R	6-4	195	4-4-86	3	1	1.26	10	0	0	1	14	8	3	2	0	3	16	.157	.125	.185	10.05	1.88
Duffy, Danny	L-L	6-2	185	12-21-88	9	3	2.98	24	24	1	0	127	108	49	42	6	41	125	.230	.223	.232	8.88	2.91
Godin, Jason	R-R	6-5	170	9-23-84	3	0	1.63	15	3	0	0	39	34	15	7	1	13	32	.245	.298	.207	7.45	3.03
Gutierrez, Danny	R-R	6-1	180	3-8-87	1	0	1.65	8	4	0	0	27	17	5	5	0	7	25	.173	.128	.216	8.23	2.30
Hardy, Rowdy	L-L	6-4	170	10-26-82	3	1	1.88	12	6	0	0	48	52	14	10	2	9	29	.289	.228	.317	5.44	1.69
Hartsock, Aaron	R-R	6-3	200	1-17-84	1	0	0.48	15	0	0	11	19	13	4	1	1	3	17	.197	.176	.219	8.20	1.45
Keating, Patrick	R-R	6-2	215	6-9-87	1	0	0.00	2	0	0	1	3	1	0	0	0	0	1	.125	.200	.000	3.38	0.00
Kelley, Scott	R-R	6-0	190	10-2-86	0	1	67.50	1	0	0	0	1	3	6	5	0	1	0	.600	.600	—	0.00	13.50
Liotta, Ray	L-L	6-3	220	4-3-83	4	2	3.84	24	8	0	0	68	68	37	29	5	24	34	.265	.306	.244	4.50	3.18
Montgomery, Mike	L-L	6-5	180	7-1-89	4	1	2.25	9	9	0	0	52	38	15	13	0	12	46	.196	.191	.197	7.96	2.08
Paulino, Eduardo	R-R	5-11	176	9-29-85	10	6	3.63	26	22	1	0	139	129	61	56	15	39	84	.246	.247	.245	5.45	2.53
Peterson, Zach	R-R	6-1	165	11-6-84	2	0	2.15	23	0	0	3	38	31	11	9	2	9	15	.223	.229	.217	3.58	2.15
Rivas, Carlos	L-L	6-3	160	1-3-85	3	0	1.74	13	0	0	1	21	12	5	4	0	9	19	.164	.154	.170	8.27	3.92
2-team total (8 Myrtle Beach)					5	3	4.98	21	5	0	1	47	45	32	26	0	25	36	—	—	—	6.89	4.79
Rodriguez, Craig	L-L	6-4	210	6-27-85	0	1	6.75	6	0	0	0	7	6	7	5	1	4	8	.222	.400	.118	10.80	5.40
Santiago, Mario	R-R	6-2	210	12-16-84	6	13	4.30	25	24	1	0	136	159	79	65	8	34	97	.298	.347	.249	6.42	2.25
Sisk, Brandon	L-L	6-3	210	7-13-85	2	3	1.92	45	0	0	21	61	30	13	13	2	18	78	.151	.185	.138	11.51	2.66
Swaggerty, Ben	L-L	6-1	185	8-8-82	3	1	1.64	16	0	0	2	22	16	5	4	0	12	27	.211	.286	.182	11.05	4.91
Teaford, Everett	L-L	6-0	155	5-15-84	7	1	2.39	11	11	0	0	64	51	19	17	7	12	49	.219	.177	.234	6.89	1.69
Villa, Kelvin	L-L	5-10	170	12-14-85	6	8	3.38	35	1	0	2	77	91	37	29	3	22	67	.294	.284	.300	7.80	2.56

Fielding

Catcher	PCT	G	PO	A	E	DP	PB
Eigsti	.991	104	747	119	8	7	15
Morizio	.972	35	221	22	7	2	2

First Base	PCT	G	PO	A	E	DP
Fontaine	.880	3	20	2	3	3
Hosmer	.996	25	211	17	1	20

	PCT	G	PO	A	E	DP
Jimenez	1.000	6	46	5	0	5
Robinson	.990	94	769	43	8	72
Seratelli	.979	20	128	10	3	16

Second Base	PCT	G	PO	A	E	DP
Fontaine	1.000	1	2	2	0	0
Giavotella	.966	133	248	355	21	87
Jimenez	1.000	1	2	6	0	0
Johnson	1.000	1	0	4	0	0
Seratelli	.958	7	11	12	1	3

Third Base	PCT	G	PO	A	E	DP
Fontaine	.870	8	6	14	3	0
Jimenez	.750	1	0	3	1	0

Johnson	.600	3	0	3	2	0
Moustakas	.931	122	92	230	24	25
Seratelli	.905	8	3	16	2	1

Shortstop	PCT	G	PO	A	E	DP
Bianchi	.978	60	85	180	6	44
Fontaine	1.000	2	3	4	0	2
Johnson	1.000	9	6	14	0	1
Seratelli	.950	71	102	182	15	32

Outfield	PCT	G	PO	A	E	DP
Del Rosario	1.000	3	9	0	0	0
Lough	.988	46	78	3	1	0
Orlando	.994	92	170	9	1	0
Ortiz	.978	56	85	4	2	0
Robinson	.984	127	310	5	5	0
Van Stratten	.947	39	68	3	4	2
Walton	.951	58	97	0	5	0

BURLINGTON BEES

LOW CLASS A

MIDWEST LEAGUE

Batting	B-T	HT	WT	DOB	AVG	vLH	vRH	G	AB	R	H	2B	3B	HR	RBI	BB	HBP	SH	SF	SO	SB	CS	SLG	OBP
Alfaro, J.D.	R-R	5-9	170	4-28-88	.168	.300	.136	27	101	9	17	2	0	1	2	5	0	1	1	21	3	1	.218	.206
Bonilla, Jose	R-R	5-10	188	8-4-88	.217	.174	.230	100	351	43	76	12	3	5	36	29	3	2	2	92	6	4	.311	.281
Dyson, Jarrod	L-R	5-10	160	8-15-84	.343	.318	.356	17	67	14	23	2	1	0	5	5	1	2	0	14	9	4	.403	.397
Fontaine, Chase	L-R	6-1	200	10-22-85	.290	.281	.294	27	100	13	29	7	1	2	13	7	1	0	1	22	0	3	.440	.339
Francis, Nick	R-R	6-3	195	3-5-86	.275	.264	.279	113	415	59	114	24	4	16	66	28	1	0	3	122	13	6	.467	.320
Franco, Angel	B-R	5-10	152	5-23-90	.184	.182	.184	16	49	5	9	2	0	0	7	5	0	3	0	5	1	1	.224	.259
Garcia, Fernando	B-R	6-0	160	7-28-88	.260	.329	.234	96	296	50	77	12	5	1	22	61	4	10	1	56	29	15	.345	.392
Graterol, Juan	R-R	6-1	170	2-14-89	.310	.435	.266	29	87	10	27	4	0	0	10	6	1	2	2	12	2	0	.356	.354
Griffin, Shawn	B-R	6-3	200	8-9-86	.285	.136	.331	53	186	19	53	13	1	3	26	14	1	0	2	52	1	6	.414	.335
Hosmer, Eric	L-L	6-4	215	10-24-89	.254	.138	.300	79	280	31	71	17	2	5	49	44	0	0	3	68	3	2	.382	.352
Jimenez, Antonio	B-R	6-2	155	4-20-87	.218	.167	.238	58	197	20	43	9	4	1	22	2	2	0	3	49	5	3	.320	.230
Maddox, Marc	R-R	5-11	185	9-16-83	.137	.100	.146	15	51	8	7	1	0	0	1	10	2	1	1	8	2	1	.157	.297
Martin, Kyle	R-R	6-0	175	11-22-84	.187	.300	.154	37	134	18	25	6	1	1	13	11	4	0	4	28	3	0	.269	.261
McCauley, Sean	R-R	6-2	170	5-13-89	.222	.275	.205	51	167	16	37	8	1	1	14	14	1	2	1	29	2	0	.299	.284
Molina, Yeldrys	R-R	5-9	170	1-8-89	.189	.179	.194	34	95	8	18	4	2	0	12	10	1	2	2	22	2	0	.274	.269
Morales, Jason	R-R	6-0	205	12-9-85	.300	.389	.269	20	70	12	21	6	2	1	12	3	1	1	0	13	2	1	.486	.338
Norris, Patrick	B-R	6-2	190	3-17-86	.244	.160	.275	116	393	54	96	3	4	0	22	31	3	2	1	80	45	9	.272	.304
Ortiz, Adrian	L-R	6-0	172	1-14-87	.244	.194	.257	43	176	21	43	8	2	0	19	6	0	4	1	21	10	2	.313	.268
Perez, Alwin	L-R	6-0	150	4-4-87	.167	.200	.154	8	18	0	3	0	0	0	1	0	1	0	0	10	0	0	.167	.167
Perez, Salvador	R-R	6-3	175	5-10-90	.189	.194	.187	36	127	10	24	6	0	0	21	6	1	2	1	15	0	1	.236	.230
Richardson, Hilton	L-L	6-3	200	1-10-89	.154	.125	.167	8	26	2	4	2	0	0	2	1	0	1	0	10	2	0	.231	.185
Rivera, Juan	R-R	6-0	150	3-17-87	.229	.231	.228	35	118	11	27	2	2	1	9	5	0	0	1	26	7	4	.305	.258
Taylor, Jason	R-R	6-1	210	1-14-88	.272	.380	.237	57	202	29	55	14	2	2	27	26	1	0	1	31	17	10	.391	.357
Tucker, Will	R-R	6-1	205	1-14-85	.141	.071	.156	27	78	10	11	3	0	2	9	5	0	0	0	22	1	0	.256	.190
Van Stratten, Nick	R-R	6-1	185	5-22-85	.318	.257	.341	69	255	50	81	20	5	1	38	28	5	1	2	32	15	6	.447	.393
Wood, David	L-L	6-2	210	12-21-84	.270	.236	.282	111	411	55	111	26	3	8	62	29	1	1	3	70	7	4	.406	.318
Wood, Ryan	R-R	6-4	185	5-5-87	.237	.316	.218	33	97	19	23	5	1	2	13	13	1	1	2	20	1	0	.371	.327

Pitching	B-T	HT	WT	DOB	W	L	ERA	G	GS	CG	SV	IP	H	R	ER	HR	BB	SO	AVG	vLH	vRH	K/9	BB/9
Arias, Carlos	R-R	6-2	178	7-4-85	0	0	24.00	2	0	0	0	3	8	8	8	2	4	0	.500	.636	.200	0.00	12.00
Baez, Manauris	B-R	5-11	182	8-16-85	8	6	3.41	30	20	0	1	132	136	63	50	6	48	85	.269	.332	.231	5.80	3.27
Barrera, Henry	R-R	6-0	195	11-25-85	0	0	12.27	4	0	0	0	4	2	5	5	0	5	5	.154	.333	.100	12.27	12.27
Basurto, Eric	R-R	6-3	200	4-17-86	1	1	0.77	6	0	0	0	12	6	1	1	0	9	19	.154	.143	.160	14.66	6.94
Bowden, Barry	R-R	6-1	205	11-9-84	3	2	2.28	38	0	0	10	51	30	15	13	2	22	64	.168	.193	.156	11.22	3.86
Bryant, Carson	R-R	6-2	180	6-6-86	1	0	5.16	13	0	0	2	30	30	22	17	2	20	29	.273	.267	.277	8.80	6.07
Casey, Bryan	R-R	6-2	200	6-5-86	4	7	3.67	14	13	0	0	61	66	37	25	3	33	51	.281	.275	.286	7.48	4.84
Coleman, Louis	R-R	6-4	195	4-4-86	1	0	2.45	4	0	0	1	7	2	2	2	0	1	6	.091	.143	.067	7.36	1.23
Cota, Luis	R-R	6-2	200	8-19-85	0	2	4.26	4	4	0	0	19	22	12	9	2	5	15	.297	.433	.205	7.11	2.37
Fisher, Brent	L-L	6-2	190	8-6-87	0	2	6.19	4	4	0	0	16	24	16	11	1	8	11	.343	.273	.356	6.19	4.50
Garcia, Justin	R-R	6-0	185	10-19-84	4	6	3.86	31	0	0	0	70	80	36	30	7	15	59	.289	.283	.292	7.59	1.93
Hardy, Blaine	L-L	6-2	195	3-14-87	4	4	2.05	36	3	0	9	92	71	26	21	3	17	94	.215	.308	.173	9.16	1.66
Herrera, Kelvin	R-R	5-10	162	12-31-89	1	0	0.00	1	1	0	0	5	3	0	0	0	1	1	.176	.333	.143	1.80	0.00
Hodgson, Ivor	B-L	6-2	190	4-25-86	3	1	3.98	9	7	0	0	41	45	19	18	2	15	37	.285	.240	.306	8.19	3.32
Lehmann, Mike	R-R	6-2	185	5-3-89	5	7	5.85	22	18	1	0	95	108	70	62	9	56	51	.298	.250	.326	4.81	5.29
Melville, Tim	R-R	6-5	210	10-9-89	7	7	3.79	21	21	0	0	97	89	57	41	10	43	96	.245	.239	.249	8.88	3.98
Montgomery, Mike	L-L	6-5	180	7-1-89	2	3	2.17	12	12	0	0	58	42	19	14	1	24	52	.206	.286	.189	8.07	3.72
Odenbach, Dusty	R-R	6-3	225	9-3-87	2	1	3.97	11	0	0	0	23	23	12	10	1	12	23	.267	.184	.333	8.74	3.97
Pena, Riquy	R-R	6-2	160	6-17-85	2	2	4.35	25	0	0	0	41	27	29	20	1	33	32	.188	.127	.225	6.97	7.19
Pena Jr., Tony	R-R	6-2	180	3-23-81	1	2	3.14	7	1	0	0	14	8	6	5	1	5	14	.160	.267	.114	8.79	3.14
Peterson, Zach	B-R	6-1	165	11-6-84	3	2	3.63	10	6	0	0	40	37	21	16	6	10	21	.250	.189	.284	4.76	2.27
Rodriguez, Craig	L-L	6-4	210	6-27-85	0	0	3.00	4	1	0	0	6	7	2	2	0	4	7	.304	.273	.333	10.50	6.00
Runion, Sam	R-R	6-4	220	11-9-88	5	11	6.60	28	28	0	0	135	193	106	99	17	45	62	.337	.323	.349	4.13	3.00
Saito, Derrick	L-L	5-9	155	12-26-87	2	6	4.15	22	0	0	2	52	50	31	24	4	15	53	.249	.207	.266	9.17	2.60
2-team total (13 Clinton)					2	7	4.06	35	2	0	2	78	76	45	35	5	26	78	—	—	—	9.04	3.01
Thompson, James	R-R	6-3	195	8-15-87	5	3	2.71	44	0	0	8	66	52	25	20	5	51	79	.219	.315	.162	10.72	6.92
White, Cole	R-R	6-2	195	1-22-88	0	0	2.16	8	0	0	0	17	16	5	4	1	9	13	.258	.250	.262	7.02	4.86

Fielding

Catcher	PCT	G	PO	A	E	DP	PB
Bonilla	.986	77	547	78	9	11	15
Graterol	.983	15	103	12	2	2	2
McCauley	.981	29	180	31	4	4	3
Perez	.974	22	160	26	5	3	1

First Base	PCT	G	PO	A	E	DP
Graterol	.988	14	78	4	1	8
Hosmer	.992	60	445	41	4	46

Jimenez	1.000	4	31	2	0	2
Taylor	1.000	6	55	1	0	2
Wood	.993	66	541	31	4	61

Second Base	PCT	G	PO	A	E	DP
Alfaro	1.000	1	1	0	0	0
Fontaine	1.000	3	3	5	0	2
Franco	.923	3	4	8	1	0
Garcia	.958	94	157	232	17	59
Jimenez	.965	18	35	47	3	11
Maddox	.970	9	12	20	1	5
Martin	—	1	0	0	0	0
Molina	.983	15	23	34	1	5
Perez	.810	6	8	9	4	1

Third Base	PCT	G	PO	A	E	DP
Fontaine	.817	22	10	39	11	3
Franco	1.000	4	0	14	0	2
Jimenez	.946	23	15	55	4	5
Maddox	1.000	1	0	2	0	0
Martin	.973	28	29	43	2	5
Molina	.941	8	4	12	1	1
Morales	.925	18	9	40	4	5
Taylor	.875	43	22	62	12	7

Shortstop	PCT	G	PO	A	E	DP
Alfaro	.980	26	36	62	2	17
Franco	.886	9	11	28	5	6
Jimenez	.930	17	27	39	5	14
Maddox	.900	5	6	12	2	2
Martin	.952	9	17	23	2	7

Molina	.896	13	25	35	7	12
Rivera	.954	35	52	92	7	15
Wood	.924	32	34	76	9	18

Outfield	PCT	G	PO	A	E	DP
Dyson	.978	16	43	1	1	1
Fontaine	1.000	1	1	0	0	0
Francis	.968	112	227	13	8	6
Griffin	.952	29	40	0	2	0
Norris	.988	115	225	27	3	5
Ortiz	1.000	41	82	7	0	3
Perez	1.000	2	1	0	0	0
Richardson	1.000	8	11	0	0	0
Tucker	1.000	24	29	2	0	1
Van Stratten	.987	66	140	10	2	5
Wood	.957	30	42	2	2	2

BURLINGTON ROYALS   ROOKIE

APPALACHIAN LEAGUE

Batting	B-T	HT	WT	DOB	AVG	vLH	vRH	G	AB	R	H	2B	3B	HR	RBI	BB	HBP	SH	SF	SO	SB	CS	SLG	OBP
Beltre, Geulin	B-R	6-0	185	10-27-90	.217	.154	.250	61	226	29	49	14	2	6	27	12	3	5	2	64	8	6	.376	.263
Cruz, Diego	L-L	6-0	195	11-13-87	.212	.238	.203	27	85	4	18	3	1	1	7	3	1	0	1	17	0	0	.306	.244
Cruz, Fernando	B-R	6-2	205	3-28-90	.277	.264	.284	51	188	22	52	11	1	3	21	7	2	2	1	23	2	0	.394	.308
Culver, Malcolm	R-R	6-2	190	2-9-90	.217	.186	.232	61	184	18	40	4	3	3	19	25	2	2	1	37	8	4	.321	.316
Del Rosario, Luis	R-R	6-2	200	5-21-90	.268	.203	.295	57	213	19	57	8	3	3	17	19	1	1	0	60	19	7	.376	.330
Espinal, Yowill	R-R	6-0	185	4-1-91	.246	.257	.241	63	236	31	58	9	4	7	23	22	7	5	1	53	20	14	.407	.327
Hall, Gerard	B-R	5-9	170	7-9-88	.200	.000	.500	2	5	0	1	1	0	0	1	0	1	0	1	0	0	.400	.333
Jones, Travis	R-R	6-2	205	5-23-89	.144	.182	.127	43	146	10	21	7	0	2	10	13	2	0	1	42	0	0	.233	.222
Kuebler, Jake	R-R	6-5	200	9-3-89	.215	.190	.227	55	177	27	38	5	0	4	14	28	6	0	1	52	7	2	.311	.340
MacDougall, Gabe	R-R	6-1	190	4-13-87	.207	.167	.217	8	29	4	6	2	0	0	2	6	2	0	0	5	1	3	.276	.378
Moctezuma, Miguel	R-R	5-10	195	1-14-87	.208	.250	.196	23	72	6	15	6	2	0	7	5	1	2	1	19	0	0	.347	.266
Molina, Yeldrys	R-S	5-9	170	1-8-89	.074	.111	.056	9	27	2	2	1	0	0	0	3	0	1	0	8	2	0	.111	.167
Morales, Jason	R-R	6-0	205	12-9-85	.214	.500	.167	4	14	1	3	1	0	0	0	0	0	0	0	3	0	1	.286	.214
Myers, Wil	R-R	6-3	190	12-10-90	.125	.000	.154	4	16	1	2	0	1	1	4	0	0	0	0	3	0	0	.438	.125
Pickett, Jovan	·L-L	5-8	160	11-11-87	.259	.315	.231	46	162	15	42	2	2	0	9	10	4	5	0	32	23	7	.296	.318
Rodriguez, Derek	R-R	5-9	160	2-13-89	.227	.214	.233	31	88	11	20	1	1	0	3	6	2	2	0	26	9	3	.261	.292
Soto, Victor	R-R	5-11	175	10-16-88	.183	.158	.194	41	131	10	24	6	3	1	11	5	0	2	0	32	13	4	.298	.213
Tschepikow, Ben	L-R	5-11	200	9-22-85	.232	.241	.226	24	82	8	19	1	2	2	12	5	1	0	2	14	1	1	.366	.278
Wood, Ryan	R-R	6-4	185	5-5-87	.174	.200	.164	27	92	15	16	4	0	0	6	16	1	0	0	15	4	3	.217	.303

Pitching	B-T	HT	WT	DOB	W	L	ERA	G	GS	CG	SV	IP	H	R	ER	HR	BB	SO	AVG	vLH	vRH	K/9	BB/9
Baumann, Buddy	L-L	5-10	175	12-9-87	0	0	1.80	3	0	0	0	5	4	3	1	1	0	5	.211	.000	.333	9.00	0.00
Bavera, Claudio	L-L	5-10	200	6-30-87	0	0	9.00	1	0	0	0	2	3	2	2	0	1	1	.333	.000	.375	4.50	4.50
Billo, Greg	R-R	6-4	220	7-15-90	2	2	1.81	3	8	0	1	55	40	18	11	4	16	51	.205	.239	.185	8.40	2.63
Cuevas, Gary	R-R	6-2	200	5-23-88	0	5	6.63	13	1	0	1	38	44	30	28	3	16	33	.280	.218	.314	7.82	3.79
De La Cruz, Deivi	R-R	5-11	185	3-25-90	2	2	4.12	12	4	0	3	39	47	24	18	3	9	28	.285	.403	.214	6.41	2.06
Dennick, Ryan	L-L	6-0	185	1-10-87	1	2	2.43	14	1	0	1	33	27	12	9	2	11	34	.221	.212	.225	9.18	2.97
Fortuna, Carlos	R-R	6-2	205	3-31-90	3	6	4.09	13	8	0	1	51	50	34	23	7	25	43	.259	.258	.260	7.64	4.44
Hayenga, Keaton	R-R	6-4	190	7-10-88	4	7	3.66	13	13	0	0	66	68	40	27	2	16	34	.249	.230	.260	4.61	2.17
Hentges, Chase	R-R	6-5	195	5-15-90	0	3	5.31	12	6	0	1	42	49	27	25	2	20	20	.287	.306	.273	4.25	4.25
Hudnall, Jaeson	R-R	6-6	240	10-4-86	0	4	10.13	12	0	0	0	13	16	16	15	3	10	16	.281	.300	.270	10.80	6.75
Kelley, Scott	R-R	6-0	190	10-2-86	0	2	1.38	11	0	0	1	26	16	7	4	0	7	27	.176	.128	.212	9.35	2.42
Lamb, John	L-L	6-3	195	7-10-90	2	2	3.95	6	6	0	0	27	24	14	12	4	9	25	.238	.087	.282	8.23	2.96
Odenham, Dusty	R-R	6-3	225	9-3-87	1	0	0.55	6	0	0	2	16	12	3	1	0	5	13	.197	.143	.213	6.61	2.76
Perez, Leondy	R-R	6-1	190	8-19-89	2	5	3.84	13	12	0	0	63	56	28	27	7	21	62	.240	.297	.204	8.81	2.98
Richardson, Brett	R-R	6-3	205	3-2-88	0	0	3.96	17	0	0	4	25	28	11	11	1	5	15	.286	.333	.258	5.40	1.80
Roberts, Lee	R-R	6-0	185	1-24-86	2	1	4.50	4	0	0	0	12	13	7	6	1	2	12	.277	.222	.310	9.00	1.50
Sample, Tyler	L-R	6-7	245	6-27-89	4	2	2.84	12	9	0	1	51	34	22	16	2	20	44	.184	.191	.179	7.82	3.55
Sirrett, Onassis	R-R	5-11	190	12-15-88	1	1	3.98	14	0	0	4	20	28	12	9	2	6	22	.329	.242	.385	9.74	2.66

Fielding

Catcher	PCT	G	PO	A	E	DP	PB
Cruz	.995	25	171	18	1	1	10
Jones	.985	24	174	17	3	1	6
Moctezuma	.992	18	110	16	1	0	7
Myers	1.000	2	16	1	0	0	1

First Base	PCT	G	PO	A	E	DP
Cruz	.972	21	158	16	5	14
Cruz	.944	2	16	1	1	3
Kuebler	.976	43	393	22	10	27
Molina	.958	2	19	4	1	1
Morales	.969	4	29	2	1	4

Second Base	PCT	G	PO	A	E	DP
Espinal	.900	8	17	19	4	3
Molina	1.000	3	5	10	0	3
Soto	.920	18	30	50	7	12
Tschepikow	.981	24	38	68	2	15
Wood	.985	17	20	45	1	4

Third Base	PCT	G	PO	A	E	DP
Culver	.925	54	49	112	13	8
Hall	1.000	2	1	5	0	0
Kuebler	.848	13	12	16	5	3
Molina	—	1	0	0	0	0
Soto	1.000	1	0	4	0	0

Shortstop	PCT	G	PO	A	E	DP
Culver	.917	4	1	10	1	1
Espinal	.901	53	71	129	22	24
Soto	1.000	1	0	2	0	0
Wood	.913	10	9	33	4	5

Outfield	PCT	G	PO	A	E	DP
Beltre	.944	61	116	2	7	1
Del Rosario	.951	57	111	6	6	3
MacDougall	.800	8	12	0	3	0
Pickett	.958	44	67	1	3	0
Rodriguez	.918	29	54	2	5	0
Soto	.960	15	24	0	1	0

AZL ROYALS ROOKIE

ARIZONA LEAGUE

Batting	B-T	HT	WT	DOB	AVG	vLH	vRH	G	AB	R	H	2B	3B	HR	RBI	BB	HBP	SH	SF	SO	SB	CS	SLG	OBP
Adams, Lane	R-R	6-4	190	11-13-89	.233	.308	.222	29	103	18	24	2	2	0	10	16	1	1	1	32	14	1	.291	.339
Baldwin, Geoff	L-L	6-4	195	11-8-90	.251	.294	.241	48	171	25	43	7	5	3	21	21	4	1	0	59	3	1	.404	.347
Cabrera, Santos	R-R	5-10	170	1-28-90	.220	.200	.223	34	109	14	24	5	1	0	17	2	2	1	1	23	6	1	.284	.246
Cooper, Chanse	R-R	5-11	180	3-28-88	.214	.000	.240	10	28	8	6	0	0	0	2	7	2	1	0	12	9	1	.214	.405
Dickerson, Joe	L-L	6-1	190	10-3-86	.250	.000	.273	3	12	4	3	0	0	0	3	3	0	1	0	1	2	0	.250	.400
Escobar, Edul	R-R	5-11	185	9-2-90	.266	.308	.255	28	64	6	17	1	0	0	9	2	1	2	0	17	0	2	.281	.299
Figueroa, Yunior	B-R	6-0	170	8-8-90	.271	.237	.280	49	199	27	54	7	2	3	28	11	2	1	3	27	3	3	.372	.312
Gordon, Alex	L-R	6-1	220	2-10-84	.286	.000	.400	4	7	1	2	0	0	1	3	5	0	0	1	3	0	0	.714	.538
Henriquez, Edwin	B-R	6-2	168	11-7-88	.267	.167	.292	16	30	4	8	2	0	1	3	0	1	1	0	9	0	1	.433	.290
Howard, Anthony	L-L	6-1	180	11-9-90	.191	.190	.192	29	94	19	18	5	3	1	10	16	1	1	0	31	11	2	.340	.315
Howell, Jeff	R-R	6-0	205	4-1-83	.278	.500	.214	4	18	3	5	1	0	0	3	1	0	0	0	5	0	0	.333	.316
Llanos, Alex	R-R	6-1	160	9-21-90	.311	.500	.287	31	122	25	38	6	2	3	16	10	1	1	1	35	15	5	.467	.366
Lubanski, Chris	L-L	6-3	210	3-24-85	.467	.125	.591	7	30	8	14	5	0	3	13	4	0	0	0	8	0	0	.933	.529
Maddox, Marc	R-R	5-11	185	9-16-83	.231	.500	.182	4	13	3	3	2	0	0	1	2	0	0	0	2	1	0	.385	.333
Mariano, Miguel	L-R	6-0	170	10-11-88	.200	.143	.238	14	35	6	7	1	0	0	2	6	0	1	0	18	1	3	.229	.317
Martinez, Adrian	R-R	6-1	158	1-12-91	.220	.324	.189	45	164	26	36	4	2	0	20	15	0	2	0	42	12	3	.268	.285
Matos, Mauricio	R-R	6-0	185	9-10-90	.300	.375	.290	22	70	6	21	4	1	0	12	2	1	1	2	13	1	0	.386	.320
McConnell, Chris	R-R	5-11	175	12-18-85	.360	1.000	.333	7	25	8	9	4	0	1	4	5	1	0	0	3	0	0	.640	.484
Moreno, Henry	R-R	6-2	162	6-6-89	.222	.100	.239	30	81	8	18	5	0	0	8	5	3	0	1	21	0	1	.284	.289
Piterson, Luis	R-R	5-11	155	6-10-90	.311	.286	.315	47	177	28	55	8	1	0	16	13	2	1	2	34	11	3	.367	.361
Polonia, Juan	B-R	5-11	173	12-16-89	.225	.150	.242	40	111	18	25	2	2	2	18	16	5	3	2	46	18	7	.333	.343
Shortell, Eric	R-R	6-0	20	5-31-86	.214	.333	.182	6	14	0	3	0	0	0	1	1	2	0	0	3	1	1	.214	.353
Stovall, Ryan	R-R	5-11	190	12-16-86	.235	.316	.212	22	85	12	20	5	0	3	15	7	0	0	1	29	6	2	.400	.290
Trapp, Justin	R-R	6-1	175	10-7-90	.262	.267	.261	32	126	18	33	4	1	0	19	11	2	2	1	36	12	4	.310	.329
Tschepikow, Ben	L-R	5-11	200	9-22-85	.333	.500	.000	1	3	0	1	0	0	0	0	0	0	0	0	0	0	1	.333	.333

Pitching	B-T	HT	WT	DOB	W	L	ERA	G	GS	CG	SV	IP	H	R	ER	HR	BB	SO	AVG	vLH	vRH	K/9	BB/9
Adams, Jack	R-R	5-11	210	9-25-86	1	1	1.69	15	0	0	3	21	16	6	4	1	3	21	.205	.167	.222	8.86	1.27
Amador, Ezequiel	R-R	6-1	154	7-26-88	1	3	6.39	13	6	0	0	51	58	45	36	5	18	41	.289	.313	.277	7.28	3.20
Avinazar, Willian	R-R	6-4	195	2-27-89	4	5	6.43	14	9	0	0	56	69	52	40	6	22	59	.295	.303	.292	9.48	3.54
Batista, Geronimo	R-R	6-3	180	6-10-91	1	2	4.98	10	0	0	0	22	26	17	12	3	9	18	.292	.294	.292	7.48	3.74
Bavera, Claudio	L-L	5-10	200	6-30-87	4	0	0.44	15	0	0	2	21	14	4	1	0	11	21	.192	.182	.194	9.15	4.79
Castaneda, Federico	R-R	6-3	187	1-26-84	0	1	2.61	8	0	0	0	10	8	5	3	0	3	10	.200	.222	.182	8.71	2.61
De La Rosa, Starling	L-L	6-5	159	9-19-87	1	0	6.11	12	0	0	1	18	17	15	12	0	8	26	.254	.182	.268	13.25	4.08
Diaz, Eric	L-L	6-2	184	10-4-88	2	1	7.20	14	3	0	0	35	44	35	28	3	23	40	.312	.250	.325	10.29	5.91
Fisher, Brent	L-L	6-2	190	8-6-87	0	0	2.84	5	2	0	0	6	6	2	2	0	3	4	.286	.200	.313	5.68	4.26
Folmer, Richard	R-R	6-3	210	11-24-86	0	0	2.25	2	0	0	0	4	4	1	1	0	4	7	.250	.500	.167	15.75	9.00
Keck, Jonathon	L-L	6-6	215	6-18-87	1	1	9.00	12	0	0	0	24	35	27	24	1	14	24	.347	.077	.386	9.00	5.25
Mozingo, Harold	R-R	6-1	175	3-29-85	0	2	15.43	3	3	0	0	2	5	5	4	1	8	3	.385	.125	.800	11.57	3.86
Ortega, Luis	R-R	6-3	170	8-4-87	0	2	4.47	13	5	0	1	48	64	33	24	3	6	39	.312	.345	.300	7.26	1.12
Peacock, Brian	L-L	6-3	190	5-7-90	0	5	4.93	11	9	0	0	38	50	31	21	6	8	34	.318	.296	.323	7.98	1.88
Pena Jr., Tony	R-R	6-2	180	3-23-81	0	0	0.00	2	2	0	0	2	2	2	0	0	1	1	.250	.000	.286	4.50	4.50
Roberts, Lee	R-R	6-0	185	1-24-86	1	0	1.35	9	0	0	1	13	13	4	2	0	2	14	.271	.294	.258	9.45	1.35
Rodriguez, Craig	L-L	6-4	210	6-27-85	1	1	2.84	5	1	0	0	6	7	3	2	0	2	12	.269	.250	.273	17.05	2.84
Sample, Tyler	L-R	6-7	245	6-27-89	0	1	6.75	2	2	0	0	4	7	4	3	0	2	5	.412	.364	.500	11.25	4.50
Santiago, Leonel	R-R	6-0	178	12-23-89	1	3	5.40	13	10	0	0	58	81	45	35	3	16	66	.327	.409	.256	10.18	2.47
Shimek, Steve	R-R	6-4	220	1-21-87	0	0	0.00	2	0	0	0	2	1	0	0	0	0	0	.200	.000	.250	0.00	0.00
Wood, Blake	R-R	6-4	225	8-8-85	0	1	0.00	3	2	0	0	4	4	1	0	0	1	4	.250	.200	.273	9.00	2.25
Worrell, Josh	R-R	6-5	215	11-17-86	0	3	4.05	12	0	0	0	13	12	9	6	0	6	25	.245	.286	.229	16.88	4.05
Yambati, Robinson	R-R	6-3	155	11-15-91	2	3	8.89	12	1	0	1	27	41	35	27	3	14	18	.333	.295	.354	5.93	4.61

Fielding

Catcher	PCT	G	PO	A	E	DP	PB
Escobar	.989	28	164	24	2	4	10
Howell	.952	3	18	2	1	0	1
Matos	.984	22	163	23	3	0	5
Moreno	.993	23	129	17	1	0	12

First Base	PCT	G	PO	A	E	DP
Baldwin	.974	46	438	19	12	34
Henriquez	1.000	9	67	1	0	7
Moreno	.943	6	47	3	3	5

Second Base	PCT	G	PO	A	E	DP
Henriquez	.500	4	0	1	1	0
Maddox	.933	4	5	9	1	0
Martinez	.935	9	20	23	3	7

McConnell	1.000	3	4	16	0	3
Piterson	.981	31	57	96	3	28
Stovall	.833	6	8	17	5	3
Trapp	1.000	5	9	8	0	2
Tschepikow	1.000	1	0	1	0	0

Third Base	PCT	G	PO	A	E	DP
Figueroa	.911	42	14	98	11	9
Gordon	1.000	2	0	1	0	0
Piterson	.893	10	7	18	3	2
Stovall	.600	5	2	4	4	0

Shortstop	PCT	G	PO	A	E	DP
Martinez	.957	33	38	95	6	19
McConnell	.833	3	6	9	3	2

Piterson	1.000	2	0	4	0	0
Trapp	.870	21	27	80	16	13

Outfield	PCT	G	PO	A	E	DP
Adams	—	1	0	0	0	0
Adams	.943	22	32	1	2	0
Cabrera	.914	33	30	2	3	1
Cooper	1.000	10	12	1	0	0
Dickerson	1.000	3	5	1	0	0
Howard	.857	27	20	4	4	0
Llanos	.959	25	39	8	2	0
Lubanski	1.000	7	14	0	0	0
Mariano	.920	13	21	2	2	0
Polonia	.944	37	48	3	3	0
Shortell	—	2	0	0	0	0

IDAHO FALLS CHUKARS ROOKIE

PIONEER LEAGUE

Batting	B-T	HT	WT	DOB	AVG	vLH	vRH	G	AB	R	H	2B	3B	HR	RBI	BB	HBP	SH	SF	SO	SB	CS	SLG	OBP
Alfaro, J.D.	R-R	5-9	170	4-28-88	.254	.333	.230	59	209	27	53	14	3	3	26	19	2	4	2	63	6	6	.392	.319

	B-T	HT	WT	DOB	AVG	vLH	vRH	G	AB	R	H	2B	3B	HR	RBI	BB	HBP	SH	SF	SO	SB	CS	SLG	OBP
Aparicio, Julio	R-R	6-2	175	1-4-90	.209	.267	.193	60	211	31	44	14	2	5	22	22	5	4	2	66	8	4	.365	.296
Batista, Deivy	R-R	5-11	150	5-7-88	.262	.340	.241	61	248	50	65	8	6	13	56	19	1	1	7	68	9	5	.500	.309
Caldwell, Keven	L-L	5-11	170	3-29-88	.255	.241	.259	41	137	23	35	6	3	2	18	17	3	1	5	22	3	0	.387	.340
Cooper, Chanse	R-R	5-11	180	3-28-88	.148	.182	.140	20	54	11	8	0	1	0	4	6	2	0	0	23	4	2	.185	.258
Culver, Malcolm	R-R	6-2	190	2-9-90	.263	.500	.235	6	19	0	5	0	0	0	5	1	0	0	0	4	0	0	.263	.300
Espinosa, Alberto	R-R	5-11	210	9-15-86	.271	.282	.268	57	203	25	55	14	3	1	27	23	4	3	1	45	2	2	.384	.355
Franco, Angel	B-R	5-10	152	5-23-90	.301	.304	.300	67	266	42	80	7	5	2	28	28	3	8	1	42	17	8	.387	.372
Graterol, Juan	R-R	6-1	170	2-14-89	.286	.000	.400	3	7	2	2	0	0	0	1	2	1	2	1	1	0	0	.286	.455
Griffin, Shawn	B-R	6-3	200	8-9-86	.667	—	.667	1	3	3	2	1	0	0	0	1	0	0	0	0	0	0	1.000	.750
Lewis, Joey	R-R	6-4	220	10-13-87	.275	.400	.254	20	69	8	19	6	0	1	9	8	1	0	1	25	0	0	.406	.354
Llanos, Alex	R-R	6-1	160	9-21-90	.223	.211	.225	32	130	12	29	5	1	0	14	5	0	4	0	42	3	4	.277	.252
Morales, Jason	R-R	6-0	205	12-9-85	.262	.389	.227	27	84	9	22	5	2	1	14	8	0	0	0	21	1	1	.405	.326
Myers, Wil	R-R	6-3	190	12-10-90	.426	.533	.396	18	68	18	29	7	1	4	14	9	1	0	2	15	2	0	.735	.488
Parraz, Jordan	R-R	6-3	210	10-8-84	.353	.286	.400	4	17	4	6	3	0	1	5	0	0	0	0	4	0	0	.706	.353
Perez, Salvador	R-R	6-3	175	5-10-90	.309	.350	.295	59	233	35	72	14	3	2	38	19	1	1	5	25	0	1	.421	.357
Pickett, Jovan	L-L	5-8	160	11-11-87	.205	.077	.269	11	39	5	8	0	0	0	2	1	4	1	0	7	1	0	.205	.295
Richardson, Hilton	L-L	6-3	200	1-10-89	.313	.241	.328	48	166	34	52	12	2	1	17	19	3	1	1	44	20	1	.428	.392
Rodriguez, Derek	R-R	5-9	160	2-13-89	.316	.000	.353	6	19	3	6	0	0	0	1	1	0	0	0	4	1	1	.316	.316
Stovall, Ryan	R-R	5-11	190	12-16-86	.323	.391	.307	37	124	23	40	15	2	0	13	8	0	1	2	27	2	3	.476	.358
Taylor, Jason	R-R	6-1	210	1-14-88	.333	.375	.308	5	21	7	7	1	0	2	5	2	0	0	3	1	0	.667	.391
Testa, Carlo	L-L	6-3	218	12-16-86	.305	.355	.287	32	118	22	36	11	2	6	20	16	0	2	0	32	9	3	.585	.388
Theriot, Ben	L-R	6-1	190	12-8-87	.290	.583	.247	30	93	15	27	4	1	0	14	1	0	0	16	1	1	.333	.389

Pitching	B-T	HT	WT	DOB	W	L	ERA	G	GS	CG	SV	IP	H	R	ER	HR	BB	SO	AVG	vLH	vRH	K/9	BB/9
Arias, Carlos	R-R	6-2	178	7-4-85	3	4	5.80	16	2	0	1	40	44	30	26	6	21	41	.272	.327	.245	9.15	4.69
Basurto, Eric	R-R	6-3	200	4-17-86	0	0	0.00	1	0	0	0	1	0	0	0	0	0	3	.000	.000	.000	20.25	0.00
Dennick, Ryan	L-L	6-0	185	1-10-87	1	1	3.68	3	0	0	0	7	6	3	3	0	7	6	.273	.000	.286	7.36	8.59
Dwyer, Chris	R-L	6-3	210	4-8-88	0	0	4.15	4	4	0	0	9	12	5	4	1	8	15	.324	.500	.290	15.58	8.31
Folmer, Richard	R-R	6-3	210	11-24-86	1	2	4.36	23	0	0	8	33	35	18	16	4	15	42	.278	.351	.247	11.45	4.09
Garcia, Justin	R-R	6-0	185	10-19-84	0	0	0.90	5	1	0	0	10	11	2	1	0	0	6	.268	.438	.160	5.40	0.00
Garrido, Santiago	R-R	6-0	178	10-4-89	3	3	5.01	14	14	0	0	65	66	44	36	6	31	44	.264	.279	.256	6.12	4.31
Halliman, Pernell	R-R	6-7	240	12-20-86	5	1	5.59	15	3	0	1	47	55	29	29	2	28	39	.307	.375	.282	7.52	5.40
Hodge, Mitch	R-R	6-2	210	6-15-89	0	2	4.22	20	0	0	2	32	41	24	15	1	13	24	.313	.317	.311	6.75	3.66
Hodgson, Ivor	B-L	6-2	190	4-25-86	2	0	2.49	5	5	0	0	22	17	6	6	1	7	16	.213	.250	.206	6.65	2.91
Keating, Patrick	R-R	6-2	215	6-9-87	5	1	1.78	22	0	0	8	30	20	8	6	1	10	46	.187	.167	.195	13.65	2.97
Kelley, Scott	R-R	6-0	190	10-2-86	1	0	0.00	5	0	0	2	15	8	0	0	0	5	19	.163	.130	.192	11.40	3.00
Lafferty, Brendan	L-L	6-3	180	5-27-86	4	1	2.85	15	2	0	4	54	60	24	17	4	15	48	.284	.305	.276	8.05	2.52
Lamb, John	L-L	6-3	195	7-10-90	3	1	3.70	8	8	0	0	41	33	20	17	4	11	46	.217	.130	.233	10.02	2.40
Marimon, Sugar Ray	R-R	6-1	168	9-30-88	3	3	5.78	15	13	0	0	62	77	44	40	5	30	47	.313	.263	.335	6.79	4.33
Morgan, Ryan	R-R	6-1	190	1-29-87	2	2	5.01	17	1	0	0	23	31	18	13	2	14	22	.304	.435	.266	8.49	5.40
Paukovits, Bryan	R-R	6-7	240	6-29-87	4	3	4.34	13	12	0	0	56	67	28	27	6	18	57	.293	.329	.273	9.16	2.89
Shimek, Steve	R-R	6-4	220	1-21-87	0	3	8.84	12	0	0	0	18	30	19	18	2	8	13	.366	.393	.352	6.38	3.93
Toribio, Aneidy	L-L	6-1	172	5-21-88	0	0	4.24	11	0	0	0	17	21	10	8	1	5	12	.313	.200	.346	6.35	2.65
White, Cole	R-R	6-2	195	1-22-88	3	2	1.29	12	0	0	3	21	15	7	3	1	13	23	.205	.400	.155	9.86	5.57
Wooley, Nick	R-R	6-2	160	4-18-88	3	2	4.78	13	9	0	0	49	56	28	26	4	10	40	.279	.271	.282	7.35	1.84

Fielding

Catcher	PCT	G	PO	A	E	DP	PB
Graterol	1.000	1	13	4	0	0	0
Lewis	1.000	1	13	2	0	0	0
Myers	.989	9	78	13	1	1	5
Perez	.993	42	366	48	3	5	5
Theriot	.977	24	149	23	4	4	4

First Base	PCT	G	PO	A	E	DP
Espinosa	.983	57	489	27	9	50
Graterol	1.000	2	20	1	0	2
Lewis	.976	10	74	7	2	7
Morales	.971	7	63	3	2	6
Theriot	1.000	1	3	0	0	0

Second Base	PCT	G	PO	A	E	DP
Alfaro	.950	8	11	27	2	8

Batista	.952	8	17	23	2	6
Franco	.981	60	128	174	6	38
Stovall	.750	2	3	3	2	0

Third Base	PCT	G	PO	A	E	DP
Alfaro	.897	26	12	40	6	2
Batista	.889	4	2	6	1	1
Culver	.909	6	2	8	1	1
Morales	.930	19	7	33	3	3
Stovall	.900	21	13	32	5	4
Taylor	.923	5	2	10	1	2

Shortstop	PCT	G	PO	A	E	DP
Alfaro	.956	22	23	64	4	12
Batista	.925	49	56	141	16	31
Franco	.821	7	10	13	5	3

Outfield	PCT	G	PO	A	E	DP
Aparicio	.959	57	86	8	4	0
Caldwell	.959	37	68	3	3	2
Cooper	.897	14	25	1	3	0
Llanos	.939	30	43	3	3	0
Parraz	1.000	4	9	2	0	0
Pickett	.960	11	22	2	1	0
Richardson	.943	41	61	5	4	1
Rodriguez	1.000	6	7	1	0	0
Stovall	.933	9	11	3	1	1
Testa	.976	22	37	4	1	2

DSL ROYALS   ROOKIE

DOMINICAN SUMMER LEAGUE

Batting	B-T	HT	WT	DOB	AVG	vLH	vRH	G	AB	R	H	2B	3B	HR	RBI	BB	HBP	SH	SF	SO	SB	CS	SLG	OBP
Alcantara, Ysmelin	R-R	6-2	180	5-13-90	.256	.288	.245	61	199	31	51	11	1	5	33	25	3	4	2	44	7	2	.397	.345
Alvarez, Jhonson	R-R	5-11	160	1-2-90	.177	.188	.175	31	79	11	14	3	0	0	10	7	5	0	0	18	0	1	.215	.286
Bello, Rainier	B-R	5-10	165	6-11-92	.293	.342	.280	50	181	24	53	8	0	0	25	12	1	1	1	29	0	0	.337	.338
Blanco, Jerico	R-R	6-1	160	5-25-92	.240	.275	.228	47	167	31	40	5	4	2	28	12	14	1	1	30	8	3	.353	.340
Carmona, Samuel	R-R	6-1	183	2-8-91	.134	.105	.146	26	67	13	9	3	0	0	8	13	3	0	1	24	0	1	.179	.298
Cordova, Jesus	B-R	5-11	155	1-29-91	.236	.300	.212	34	72	19	17	3	2	0	4	17	4	0	0	24	7	5	.333	.409
Fortuna, Juan	R-R	5-11	185	1-12-89	.250	.261	.245	23	76	7	19	1	0	0	6	18	0	0	0	13	1	1	.263	.394
Garcia, Carlos	R-R	6-0	176	3-18-92	.150	.217	.133	43	113	18	17	0	1	0	6	27	4	6	0	25	5	6	.168	.333

Garcia, Jeifrich	R-R	6-1	181	11-26-90	.213	.241	.206	48	136	23	29	2	1	0	6	28	1	3	1	44	8	6	.243	.349
Gomez, Moises	R-R	5-11	190	1-20-92	.190	.273	.167	37	100	10	19	2	1	0	8	17	2	2	0	18	0	3	.230	.319
Lugo, Rafael	R-R	6-2	187	1-17-91	.238	.290	.223	47	143	17	34	4	2	4	19	23	6	1	0	43	2	2	.378	.366
Mariano, Miguel	L-R	6-0	170	10-11-88	.250	.250	.250	13	36	3	9	2	1	1	4	3	1	1	0	11	3	1	.444	.325
Mateo, Daniel	B-R	6-1	178	8-10-91	.254	.333	.228	61	213	29	54	13	5	2	27	23	5	3	1	37	12	6	.390	.339
Nivar, Pedro	R-R	5-10	170	1-13-92	.233	.348	.190	28	86	13	20	5	0	0	10	13	8	1	1	20	7	0	.291	.380
Pereira, Vicni	R-R	6-1	175	1-20-91	.171	.273	.125	12	35	4	6	1	0	0	2	4	1	1	0	13	0	0	.200	.275
Rosario, George	R-R	6-2	170	8-21-90	—	—	—	2	0	0	0	0	0	0	0	0	0	0	0	0	0	0	—	—
Santos, Ramon	R-R	6-3	193	11-5-91	.209	.161	.227	64	206	18	43	12	2	1	23	15	7	4	1	56	8	4	.301	.284
Vasquez, Jhorman	R-R	6-4	205	3-30-91	.116	.111	.120	21	43	3	5	1	0	1	1	5	2	1	0	15	0	0	.209	.240
Wilmore, Juan	B-R	6-1	175	5-27-89	.175	.129	.193	51	114	15	20	3	1	0	7	12	5	5	0	36	8	6	.219	.282

Pitching	B-T	HT	WT	DOB	W	L	ERA	G	GS	CG	SV	IP	H	R	ER	HR	BB	SO	AVG	vLH	vRH	K/9	BB/9
Baez, Angel	R-R	6-3	196	2-14-91	0	6	3.88	14	11	0	0	49	54	32	21	0	19	45	.280	.360	.252	8.32	3.51
De La Cruz, Giancarlos	R-R	6-0	166	10-21-86	1	2	3.41	9	6	0	1	34	32	14	13	0	11	38	.246	.241	.248	9.96	2.88
De La Rosa, Rafael	L-L	6-0	180	5-12-88	3	2	4.54	10	4	0	0	34	34	19	17	1	11	19	.276	.250	.278	5.08	2.94
Diaz, Frankelis	R-R	6-0	190	9-25-91	3	2	2.41	14	2	0	2	37	27	15	10	0	12	29	.205	.216	.200	6.99	2.89
Garcia, Dilson	R-R	6-2	184	9-9-91	2	3	3.21	14	7	1	1	53	47	26	19	0	12	41	.227	.253	.212	6.92	2.03
Garcia, Juan	R-R	6-1	196	3-27-89	0	1	9.00	3	0	0	0	5	5	6	5	0	4	3	.313	.000	.333	5.40	7.20
Guete, Elkin	R-R	6-1	170	12-24-91	3	0	1.74	9	0	0	0	21	23	10	4	0	13	15	.277	.235	.288	6.53	5.66
Guzman, Luis	R-R	6-3	222	7-21-91	0	1	8.10	8	0	0	0	7	12	8	6	0	14	7	.375	.500	.333	9.45	18.90
Melgar, Luis	R-R	6-3	153	2-5-92	0	0	4.50	1	0	0	0	2	2	1	1	0	0	1	.250	.400	.000	4.50	0.00
Nina, Aroni	R-R	6-4	160	4-9-90	0	1	7.04	5	0	0	0	8	6	8	6	0	11	6	.222	.286	.200	7.04	12.91
Penalo, Victor	R-R	5-10	154	7-12-91	1	2	6.23	15	0	0	3	22	31	29	15	2	11	17	.326	.350	.320	7.06	4.57
Rodriguez, Freddy	R-R	6-3	188	12-1-90	2	5	4.75	13	3	0	1	36	46	38	19	3	8	19	.303	.283	.311	4.75	2.00
Rodriguez, Jonathan	R-R	6-1	165	12-13-88	3	1	0.80	17	4	0	2	45	25	5	4	0	15	46	.159	.269	.137	9.20	3.00
Rosario, Sergio	R-R	5-11	184	8-20-90	3	4	3.23	14	6	0	0	39	39	20	14	1	21	45	.252	.227	.261	10.38	4.85
Soto, Jorge	R-R	6-3	180	11-1-91	1	5	5.28	12	9	0	0	46	50	30	27	1	17	40	.260	.125	.280	7.83	3.33
Velasquez, Angelo	R-R	6-0	160	9-19-91	0	3	2.29	14	3	0	2	35	31	12	9	1	12	34	.238	.286	.221	8.66	3.06
Ventura, Yordano	R-R	5-11	140	6-3-91	0	1	2.78	10	5	0	3	23	28	11	7	0	5	11	.304	.333	.301	4.37	1.99
Violi, Willer	R-R	6-1	165	5-29-90	2	2	3.24	14	2	0	0	33	28	20	12	0	20	22	.255	.235	.263	5.94	5.40
Yambati, Robinson	R-R	6-3	185	1-15-91	2	0	0.77	5	5	0	0	23	16	7	2	1	9	16	.198	.120	.232	6.17	3.47

Fielding

Catcher	PCT	G	PO	A	E	DP	PB
Alvarez	.981	27	133	23	3	1	6
Bello	.960	26	167	26	8	0	7
Fortuna	1.000	1	1	0	0	0	0
Gomez	.975	29	151	45	5	2	6
Vasquez	1.000	1	7	1	0	0	0

First Base	PCT	G	PO	A	E	DP
Bello	.977	6	41	2	1	1
Carmona	.991	26	201	12	2	10
Fortuna	.995	23	203	14	1	16
Lugo	.962	12	94	7	4	2
Wilmore	.966	11	80	6	3	5

Second Base	PCT	G	PO	A	E	DP
Cordova	1.000	14	20	19	0	3

	PCT	G	PO	A	E	DP
Garcia	.910	16	26	35	6	6
Garcia	.918	22	37	53	8	2
Nivar	.931	22	47	47	7	15
Wilmore	.967	9	14	15	1	3

Third Base	PCT	G	PO	A	E	DP
Cordova	.889	9	8	16	3	1
Garcia	.882	14	8	37	6	2
Lugo	.842	23	14	34	9	4
Vasquez	.861	17	15	16	5	0
Wilmore	.900	31	23	40	7	3

Shortstop	PCT	G	PO	A	E	DP
Cordova	1.000	1	1	2	0	0
Garcia	.903	26	31	53	9	6
Lugo	—	1	0	0	0	0

	PCT	G	PO	A	E	DP
Mateo	.915	50	67	149	20	20
Wilmore	1.000	1	1	0	0	0

Outfield	PCT	G	PO	A	E	DP
Alcantara	.975	60	74	3	2	0
Blanco	.988	47	72	7	1	2
Cordova	1.000	2	1	0	0	0
Garcia	1.000	3	2	2	0	0
Mariano	1.000	11	16	1	0	0
Pereira	1.000	8	12	0	0	0
Ramirez	.957	30	42	3	2	1
Rosario	1.000	2	2	0	0	0
Santos	.939	62	86	6	6	0
Wilmore	.667	4	2	0	1	0

Los Angeles Angels

SEASON IN A SENTENCE: Adversity dogged the Angels all season, from early-season injuries to the shocking death of young pitcher Nick Adenhart, but manager Mike Scioscia rallied the Angels around its homegrown core and imported veterans such as Torii Hunter, and the Angels won the division for the fifth time in six seasons, swept the Red Sox in the Division Series and lost a six-game League Championship Series to the Yankees.

HIGH POINT: The Angels had two cathartic moments, clinching the division at home and beating Boston in Fenway Park. Adenhart's jersey went to the dugout every day of the season, and the Angels celebrated winning the American League West by gathering in front of the outfield-wall memorial to their fallen teammate, then included the jersey in their clubhouse celebration. Beating the Red Sox was a major accomplishment for the Angels, who lost to Boston in the playoffs in 2008, 2007, 2004 and 1986.

LOW POINT: Adenhart died April 9 in a post-game car accident when the vehicle he was in was struck by a drunk driver. His death didn't just cast a pall over the start of the season; it took away a quality starter from a team already short of pitching, with John Lackey, Kelvim Escobar and Ervin Santana all on the shelf. The Angels wound up giving starts to 14 different pitchers, including the likes of Anthony Ortega, Trevor Bell and Shane Loux.

NOTABLE ROOKIES: All those injuries opened opportunities in the pitching staff. Minor league veteran Matt Palmer won 11 games as a spot starter and reliever, while Kevin Jepsen and Jason Bulger provided power arms to make up for Scot Shields' injury-plagued season. The Angels also got 10 starts and four victories from 21-year-old Sean O'Sullivan, a 2006 draft-and-follow signee.

KEY TRANSACTIONS: The Angels flexed some financial muscle in August by adding Scott Kazmir when the Rays decided he'd be too expensive. They traded infielder Sean Rodriguez and lefthander Alex Torres for Kazmir, who went 2-2, 1.73 in six starts but faltered in the LCS against the Yankees.

DOWN ON THE FARM: Four Angels clubs made the playoffs, with Orem winning the Rookie-level Pioneer League. The Angels had six of the first 80 picks in the 2009 draft, and prep outfielders Randal Grichuk and Mike Trout—the club's pair of first-round picks—helped the Rookie-level Arizona League club to a 38-18 mark.

OPENING DAY PAYROLL: $113,709,000

PLAYERS OF THE YEAR

MAJOR LEAGUE	MINOR LEAGUE
Kendry Morales 1b	**Chris Pettit** of
.306/.355/.569	(Triple-A/Rookie)
34 HR, 2nd in AL in	.322/.386/.481
SLG, 3rd in XBH (79)	31 2B, 19 SB

ORGANIZATION LEADERS

BATTING	*Minimum 250 at-bats	
MAJORS		
*AVG	Erick Aybar	.312
*OPS	Kendry Morales	.924
HR	Kendry Morales	34
RBI	Kendry Morales	108
MINORS		
*AVG	Pettit, Chris, Salt Lake	.321
R	Evans, Terry, Salt Lake	104
H	Evans, Terry, Salt Lake	156
TB	Evans, Terry, Salt Lake	279
2B	Amarista, Alexia, Cedar Rapids	39
3B	Bourjos, Peter, Arkansas	14
HR	Rodriguez, Sean, Salt Lake	29
RBI	Rodriguez, Sean, Salt Lake	93
BB	Fuller, Clay, Rancho Cucamonga	71
SO	Moore, Jeremy, Arkansas/Rancho Cuca.	151
SB	Auer, Tyson, Cedar Rapids	43
*OBP	Rodriguez, Sean, Salt Lake	.400
*SLG	Rodriguez, Sean, Salt Lake	.616

PITCHING	†Minimum 75 innings	
MAJORS		
W	Joe Saunders	16
†ERA	Jered Weaver	3.75
SO	Jered Weaver	174
MINORS		
W	Torres, Alexander, Rancho Cuca./Arkansas	13
L	MacDonald, Mike, Salt Lake	13
†ERA	Reckling, Trevor, Rancho Cuca./Arkansas	2.68
G	Cassevah, Bobby, Arkansas	57
	Hill, Jeremy, Arkansas/Salt Lake	57
GS	Four tied at	27
SV	Carmona, Ismael, Rancho Cucamonga	20
	Hill, Jeremy, Arkansas/Salt Lake	20
IP	Kiely, Tim, Rancho Cucamonga/Arkansas	168
BB	Torres, Alexander, Rancho Cuca./Arkansas	80
SO	Torres, Alexander, Rancho Cuca./Arkansas	149
†AVG	Chaffee, Ryan, Cedar Rapids	.206

2009 PERFORMANCE

General Manager: Tony Reagins. **Farm Director:** Abe Flores. **Scouting Director:** Eddie Bane.

Class	Team	League	W	L	PCT	Finish*	Manager(s)
Majors	Los Angeles Angels	American	97	65	.599	2nd (14)	Mike Scioscia
Triple-A	Salt Lake Bees	Pacific Coast	72	71	.503	8th (16)	Bobby Mitchell
Double-A	Arkansas Travelers	Texas	61	79	.436	t-7th (8)	Bobby Magallanes
High A	Rancho Cucamonga Quakes	California	61	79	.436	t-7th (10)	Keith Johnson
Low A	Cedar Rapids Kernels	Midwest	78	60	.565	5th (14)	Bill Mosiello
Rookie	AZL Angels	Arizona	38	18	.679	2nd (11)	Tyrone Boykin
Rookie	Orem Owlz	Pioneer	51	25	.671	†1st (8)	Tom Kotchman

| **Overall 2009 Minor League Record** | | | 361 | 332 | .521 | 6th (30) | |

*Finish in overall standings (No. of teams in league). †League champion.

ORGANIZATION STATISTICS

LOS ANGELES ANGELS

AMERICAN LEAGUE

Batting	B-T	HT	WT	DOB	AVG	vLH	vRH	G	AB	R	H	2B	3B	HR	RBI	BB	HBP	SH	SF	SO	SB	CS	SLG	OBP
Abreu, Bobby	L-R	6-0	210	3-11-74	.293	.267	.305	152	563	96	165	29	3	15	103	94	1	0	9	113	30	8	.435	.390
Aybar, Erick	B-R	5-10	170	1-14-84	.312	.325	.305	137	504	70	157	23	9	5	58	30	5	12	5	54	14	7	.423	.353
Budde, Ryan	R-R	5-11	210	8-15-79	.000	.000	.000	3	3	0	0	0	0	0	0	0	0	0	0	2	0	0	.000	.000
Evans, Terry	R-R	6-3	205	1-19-82	.286	1.000	.167	11	7	2	2	0	0	0	1	0	0	0	0	2	0	0	.286	.286
Figgins, Chone	B-R	5-8	180	1-22-78	.298	.246	.323	158	615	114	183	30	7	5	54	101	1	8	4	114	42	17	.393	.395
Guerrero, Vladimir	R-R	6-3	235	2-9-75	.295	.250	.311	100	383	59	113	16	1	15	50	19	4	0	1	56	2	1	.460	.334
Hunter, Torii	R-R	6-2	225	7-18-75	.299	.336	.287	119	451	74	135	26	1	22	90	47	3	0	5	92	18	4	.508	.366
Izturis, Maicer	B-R	5-8	170	9-12-80	.300	.380	.288	114	387	74	116	22	3	8	65	35	5	3	7	41	13	5	.434	.359
Kendrick, Howie	R-R	5-10	200	7-12-83	.291	.313	.278	105	374	61	109	21	3	10	61	20	4	2	0	71	11	4	.444	.334
Mathis, Jeff	R-R	6-0	200	3-31-83	.211	.228	.203	84	237	26	50	8	0	5	28	22	4	8	1	73	2	3	.308	.288
Matthews Jr., Gary	B-R	6-3	225	8-25-74	.250	.221	.261	103	316	44	79	19	2	4	50	40	2	0	2	74	4	1	.361	.336
Morales, Kendry	B-R	6-1	225	6-20-83	.306	.296	.309	152	566	86	173	43	2	34	108	46	2	0	8	117	3	7	.569	.355
Napoli, Mike	R-R	6-0	215	10-31-81	.272	.330	.253	114	382	60	104	22	1	20	56	40	7	0	3	103	3	3	.492	.350
Pettit, Chris	R-R	6-0	195	8-15-84	.286	.000	.400	10	7	2	2	0	0	0	0	0	0	0	0	1	0	0	.286	.286
Quinlan, Robb	R-R	6-1	215	3-17-77	.243	.257	.220	54	115	13	28	5	0	2	14	5	0	0	0	30	1	1	.339	.275
Rivera, Juan	R-R	6-2	230	7-3-78	.287	.333	.271	138	529	72	152	24	1	25	88	36	2	0	5	57	0	1	.478	.332
Rodriguez, Sean	R-R	6-1	215	4-26-85	.200	.091	.286	12	25	4	5	0	0	2	4	3	0	0	1	7	0	0	.440	.276
Sandoval, Freddy	B-R	6-1	200	8-16-82	.182	.333	.125	5	11	1	2	1	0	0	0	0	0	0	0	3	0	0	.273	.182
Willits, Reggie	B-R	5-11	185	5-30-81	.213	.222	.210	49	80	16	17	2	0	0	6	5	0	6	1	17	5	1	.238	.256
Wilson, Bobby	R-R	6-0	220	4-8-83	.200	—	.200	12	5	0	1	0	0	0	0	0	0	1	0	1	0	0	.400	.200
Wood, Brandon	R-R	6-3	210	3-2-85	.195	.217	.167	18	41	5	8	1	0	1	3	3	1	1	0	19	0	0	.293	.267

Pitching	B-T	HT	WT	DOB	W	L	ERA	G	GS	CG	SV	IP	H	R	ER	HR	BB	SO	AVG	vLH	vRH	K/9	BB/9
Adenhart, Nick	R-R	6-3	185	8-24-86	0	0	0.00	1	1	0	0	6	7	0	0	0	3	5	.292	.250	.333	7.50	4.50
Arredondo, Jose	R-R	6-0	175	3-30-84	2	3	6.00	43	0	0	0	45	47	30	30	6	23	47	.269	.238	.295	9.40	4.60
Bell, Trevor	L-R	6-2	186	10-12-86	1	2	9.74	8	4	0	0	20	40	25	22	3	11	14	.412	.469	.354	6.20	4.87
Bulger, Jason	R-R	6-4	210	12-6-78	6	1	3.56	64	0	0	1	66	46	26	26	7	30	68	.207	.196	.217	9.32	4.11
Davidson, Danny	L-L	6-4	210	1-8-81	0	0	5.40	4	0	0	0	2	3	1	1	0	3	0	.375	.429	.000	0.00	16.20
Escobar, Kelvim	R-R	6-1	230	4-11-76	0	1	3.60	1	1	0	0	5	4	2	2	0	4	5	.235	.000	.571	9.00	7.20
Fuentes, Brian	L-L	6-4	230	8-9-75	1	5	3.93	65	0	0	48	55	53	24	24	6	24	46	.254	.239	.261	7.53	3.93
Jepsen, Kevin	R-R	6-3	215	7-26-84	6	4	4.94	54	0	0	1	55	63	33	30	2	19	48	.292	.373	.208	7.90	3.13
Kazmir, Scott	L-L	6-0	190	1-24-84	2	2	1.73	6	6	0	0	36	28	8	7	1	10	26	.212	.207	.214	6.44	2.48
2-team total (20 Tampa Bay)					10	9	4.89	26	26	0	0	147	149	85	80	16	60	117	—	—	—	7.15	3.67
Lackey, John	R-R	6-6	245	10-23-78	11	8	3.83	27	27	1	0	176	177	84	75	17	47	139	.263	.276	.247	7.09	2.40
Loux, Shane	R-R	6-2	235	8-31-79	2	3	5.86	18	6	0	0	58	84	42	38	4	19	19	.343	.385	.291	2.93	2.93
Mosebach, Bobby	R-R	6-4	195	9-14-84	0	0	7.71	3	0	0	0	2	4	3	2	0	3	2	.364	.375	.333	7.71	11.57
Moseley, Dustin	R-R	6-4	215	12-26-81	1	0	4.30	3	3	0	0	15	20	8	7	3	3	8	.323	.281	.367	4.91	1.84
O'Sullivan, Sean	R-R	6-2	230	9-1-87	4	2	5.92	12	10	0	0	52	60	34	34	12	16	29	.296	.263	.324	5.05	2.79
Oliver, Darren	R-L	6-2	200	10-6-70	5	1	2.71	63	1	0	0	73	61	22	22	5	22	65	.237	.263	.217	8.01	2.71
Ortega, Anthony	R-R	6-0	210	8-24-85	0	2	9.24	3	3	0	0	13	19	15	13	4	6	7	.345	.273	.455	4.97	4.26
Palmer, Matt	R-R	6-2	225	3-21-79	11	2	3.93	40	13	1	0	121	105	55	53	12	55	69	.240	.279	.197	5.12	4.08
Rodriguez, Fernando	R-R	6-3	215	6-18-84	0	0	27.00	1	0	0	0	1	1	3	2	1	2	1	.250	.500	.000	13.50	27.00
Rodriguez, Rafael	R-R	6-1	175	9-24-84	0	1	5.58	18	0	0	0	31	47	22	19	4	9	10	.356	.371	.343	2.93	2.64
Santana, Ervin	R-R	6-2	185	12-12-82	8	8	5.03	24	23	2	0	140	159	83	78	24	47	107	.288	.323	.248	6.89	3.03
Saunders, Joe	L-L	6-3	210	6-16-81	16	7	4.60	31	31	1	0	186	202	102	95	29	64	101	.279	.257	.287	4.89	3.10
Shields, Scot	R-R	6-1	180	7-22-75	1	3	6.62	20	0	0	1	18	16	14	13	1	12	12	.239	.250	.229	6.11	7.64
Speier, Justin	R-R	6-3	205	11-6-73	4	2	5.18	41	0	0	0	40	44	23	23	7	15	39	.277	.328	.239	8.78	3.38
Thompson, Rich	R-R	6-1	180	7-1-84	0	0	5.12	13	0	0	0	19	27	11	11	6	7	21	.329	.351	.311	9.78	3.26
Weaver, Jered	R-R	6-7	205	10-4-82	16	8	3.75	33	33	4	0	211	196	91	88	26	66	174	.246	.276	.208	7.42	2.82

Fielding

Catcher	PCT	G	PO	A	E	DP	PB
Budde	1.000	2	7	1	0	0	0
Mathis	.988	79	507	58	7	5	6
Napoli	.986	96	526	48	8	7	5
Wilson	1.000	11	19	1	0	0	0

First Base	PCT	G	PO	A	E	DP
Morales	.994	152	1274	86	8	145
Quinlan	1.000	17	119	16	0	11
Wilson	1.000	1	5	0	0	0
Wood	1.000	4	35	5	0	4

Second Base	PCT	G	PO	A	E	DP
Figgins	1.000	2	2	2	0	0
Izturis	.993	68	114	180	2	49

	PCT	G	PO	A	E	DP
Kendrick	.991	95	156	271	4	70
Rodriguez	1.000	5	5	6	0	4
Sandoval	1.000	3	4	8	0	1

Third Base	PCT	G	PO	A	E	DP
Figgins	.968	154	109	314	14	38
Izturis	1.000	5	3	4	0	0
Quinlan	.857	9	2	4	1	0
Sandoval	1.000	2	0	3	0	0
Wood	1.000	9	6	1	0	0

Shortstop	PCT	G	PO	A	E	DP
Aybar	.983	136	240	378	11	102
Izturis	.977	28	33	52	2	15
Wood	.824	5	6	8	3	3

Outfield	PCT	G	PO	A	E	DP
Abreu	.972	136	269	10	8	4
Evans	1.000	8	6	0	0	0
Figgins	—	1	0	0	0	0
Guerrero	1.000	2	4	0	0	0
Hunter	.997	115	308	2	1	0
Izturis	—	1	0	0	0	0
Matthews Jr.	.985	91	193	2	3	0
Pettit	1.000	5	4	0	0	0
Quinlan	1.000	23	20	1	0	0
Rivera	.992	128	237	11	2	3
Rodriguez	1.000	7	3	0	0	0
Willits	1.000	39	36	0	0	0

SALT LAKE BEES   TRIPLE-A

PACIFIC COAST LEAGUE

Batting	B-T	HT	WT	DOB	AVG	vLH	vRH	G	AB	R	H	2B	3B	HR	RBI	BB	HBP	SH	SF	SO	SB	CS	SLG	OBP
Brown, Matt	R-R	6-0	200	8-8-82	.245	.330	.218	107	388	57	95	27	0	13	69	45	8	2	4	92	5	5	.415	.333
Budde, Ryan	R-R	5-11	210	8-15-79	.223	.167	.244	83	273	32	61	16	1	7	31	31	1	1	1	73	1	1	.366	.304
Colmenares, Carlos	B-R	6-0	175	2-11-86	.250	—	.250	1	4	0	1	0	0	0	0	0	0	0	0	0	0	0	.250	.250
Coon, Brad	L-L	6-0	175	12-11-82	.276	.240	.291	119	442	78	122	15	3	4	36	62	5	10	3	75	23	8	.351	.369
Evans, Terry	R-R	6-3	205	1-19-82	.291	.304	.286	135	537	104	156	33	6	26	90	40	5	2	8	146	28	5	.520	.341
Figueroa, Luis	B-R	5-9	165	2-16-74	.241	.211	.256	34	116	9	28	7	1	1	15	5	0	0	2	8	0	1	.345	.268
Gutierrez, Chris	R-R	5-9	185	3-12-84	.222	—	.222	3	9	1	2	1	0	0	0	1	1	1	0	4	0	0	.333	.364
Johnson, Ben	B-R	6-0	220	10-17-81	.252	.111	.281	35	107	15	27	9	2	1	6	8	3	1	0	24	0	2	.402	.322
Kendrick, Howie	R-R	5-10	200	7-12-83	.346	.333	.350	20	78	11	27	6	1	2	11	7	2	0	0	12	4	2	.526	.414
Nieves, Abel	R-R	5-11	175	8-14-85	.262	.273	.260	20	61	5	16	2	0	0	5	12	0	0	5	10	0	2	.295	.384
Patchett, Gary	R-R	6-2	180	9-25-78	.244	.231	.249	91	307	37	75	9	2	4	26	18	5	5	3	58	0	6	.326	.294
Pavkovich, Adam	R-R	6-2	205	12-31-81	.242	.271	.231	111	397	44	96	20	2	6	44	28	1	7	3	69	8	2	.348	.291
Pettit, Chris	R-R	6-0	195	8-15-84	.321	.442	.273	96	371	70	119	34	3	8	58	31	8	1	3	62	18	2	.482	.383
Rodriguez, Sean	R-R	6-1	215	4-26-85	.299	.345	.285	103	365	81	109	17	6	29	93	51	13	3	3	119	9	2	.616	.400
Sandoval, Freddy	B-R	6-1	200	8-16-82	.300	.329	.289	67	277	46	83	16	5	6	46	26	0	0	3	39	12	3	.458	.360
Segura, Jean	R-R	5-11	155	3-17-90	.421	.400	.429	7	19	2	8	2	0	0	2	0	0	0	0	4	0	0	.526	.421
Smith, Coby	R-R	6-0	200	9-21-80	.143	.000	.182	4	14	1	2	0	0	0	0	0	0	0	0	1	0	1	.143	.143
Statia, Hainley	B-R	5-10	160	1-19-86	.000	—	.000	4	6	2	0	0	0	0	0	2	0	0	0	0	0	0	.000	.250
Sumi, Ikko	R-R	5-9	200	10-20-87	.000	—	.000	1	1	0	0	0	0	0	0	0	0	0	0	0	0	0	.000	.000
Sutton, Nate	L-R	6-0	195	9-1-82	.250	.158	.277	24	84	12	21	4	3	0	10	9	1	1	2	13	3	0	.369	.323
Willits, Reggie	B-R	5-11	185	5-30-81	.261	.235	.275	62	234	40	61	10	1	1	27	34	2	4	6	44	11	4	.325	.351
Wilson, Bobby	R-R	6-0	220	4-8-83	.271	.278	.269	97	354	38	96	19	1	8	55	22	1	4	0	56	0	0	.398	.316
Wipke, Flint	R-R	6-0	215	1-22-83	.214	1.000	.154	5	14	2	3	0	0	1	3	2	0	0	0	3	0	0	.429	.313
Wood, Brandon	R-R	6-3	210	3-2-85	.293	.293	.293	99	386	65	113	28	4	22	72	36	2	4	0	80	1	1	.557	.353

Pitching	B-T	HT	WT	DOB	W	L	ERA	G	GS	CG	SV	IP	H	R	ER	HR	BB	SO	AVG	vLH	vRH	K/9	BB/9
Arredondo, Jose	R-R	6-0	175	3-30-84	1	1	2.18	19	0	0	1	21	13	7	5	1	14	24	.188	.212	.167	10.45	6.10
Austen, David	R-R	6-1	185	5-21-81	2	5	7.17	10	8	0	0	43	59	37	34	4	13	20	.330	.389	.262	4.22	2.74
Bell, Trevor	L-R	6-2	186	10-12-86	3	4	3.15	11	11	2	0	71	67	27	25	5	15	38	.250	.237	.263	4.79	1.89
Boshiers, Buddy	L-L	6-3	205	5-9-88	0	0	0.00	2	0	0	0	1	1	0	0	0	0	1	.200	.000	.333	6.75	0.00
Cabrera, Francis	R-R	6-1	184	5-27-87	0	0	4.50	2	0	0	0	2	2	1	1	0	1	1	.286	.000	.400	4.50	4.50
Davidson, Danny	L-L	6-4	210	1-8-81	2	3	7.33	45	0	0	0	50	66	44	41	12	24	46	.328	.309	.342	8.23	4.29
Denham, Dan	R-R	6-2	195	12-24-82	9	9	4.97	29	22	0	0	129	151	88	71	16	61	62	.297	.306	.288	4.34	4.27
Escobar, Kelvim	R-R	6-1	230	4-11-76	0	0	7.20	1	1	0	0	5	8	5	4	0	2	1	.400	.500	.000	1.80	3.60
Fish, Robert	L-L	6-3	225	1-19-88	0	0	0.00	1	0	0	0	1	0	0	0	0	1	0	.000	.000	.000	0.00	13.50
Hill, Jeremy	R-R	5-11	200	8-8-77	3	4	4.68	55	0	0	20	60	63	31	31	7	27	55	.274	.288	.259	8.30	4.07
Hurst, Kyle	R-R	6-4	230	8-23-85	0	0	9.00	1	0	0	0	1	2	1	1	0	1	1	.400	1.000		9.00	9.00
Jepsen, Kevin	R-R	6-3	215	7-26-84	1	0	9.00	14	0	0	2	18	30	24	18	4	16	20	.349	.408	.270	10.00	8.00
Knox, Brad	R-R	6-2	230	5-27-82	9	5	5.20	28	25	1	0	152	178	96	88	23	51	70	.299	.291	.306	4.14	3.01
Lackey, John	R-R	6-6	245	10-23-78	0	1	2.79	2	2	0	0	10	6	3	3	1	1	8	.176	.235	.118	7.45	0.93
Leon, Sammy	R-R	6-0	160	5-19-85	1	0	0.00	1	0	0	0	2	2	0	0	0	0	3	.250	.000	.400	13.50	0.00
Loux, Shane	R-R	6-2	235	8-31-79	1	2	3.96	8	5	0	0	25	24	12	11	2	14	13	.261	.265	.256	4.68	5.04
MacDonald, Michael	R-R	6-1	215	10-29-81	8	13	6.37	30	27	0	0	147	181	109	104	15	60	80	.305	.338	.269	4.90	3.67
McKiernan, John	R-R	5-11	160	3-21-89	0	1	6.75	6	0	0	0	11	9	8	8	2	3	2	.220	.176	.250	2.53	2.53
Mendoza, Tommy	R-R	6-2	195	8-18-87	2	1	2.91	4	4	0	0	22	18	8	7	3	11	10	.228	.097	.313	4.15	4.57
Mosebach, Bobby	R-R	6-4	195	9-14-84	2	2	2.23	33	0	0	7	40	33	11	10	1	18	31	.232	.233	.232	6.92	4.02
O'Sullivan, Sean	R-R	6-2	230	9-1-87	6	4	5.48	14	13	1	0	69	74	42	42	9	20	48	.270	.281	.259	6.26	2.61
Ortega, Anthony	R-R	6-0	210	8-24-85	2	1	9.64	4	4	0	0	19	30	21	20	5	6	5	.366	.236	.630	2.41	2.89
Palmer, Matt	R-R	6-2	225	3-21-79	1	1	11.74	2	2	0	0	8	13	10	10	2	3	5	.382	.318	.500	5.87	3.52
Peguero, Jailen	R-R	6-0	185	1-4-81	0	1	9.98	16	0	0	1	15	24	20	17	4	9	15	.343	.436	.226	8.80	5.28
2-team total (8 Oklahoma City)					0	2	7.33	24	0	0	2	27	32	25	22	6	17	29	—	—	—	9.67	5.67
Rodriguez, Fernando	R-R	6-3	215	6-18-84	1	1	7.54	23	0	0	0	37	44	33	31	5	23	25	.312	.280	.356	6.08	5.59
Rodriguez, Frank	R-R	6-3	215	2-26-83	5	4	3.96	44	1	0	0	77	67	35	34	8	40	60	.244	.219	.265	6.98	4.66
Rodriguez, Rafael	R-R	6-1	175	9-24-84	1	0	1.85	22	0	0	3	34	27	7	7	3	10	23	.225	.250	.200	6.09	2.65
Salmon, Brad	L-R	6-4	225	1-3-80	8	4	4.56	37	17	0	1	109	114	60	55	11	60	87	.270	.291	.251	7.21	4.97

Name	B-T	HT	WT	DOB	W	L	ERA	G	GS	CG	SV	IP	H	R	ER	HR	BB	SO	AVG	vLH	vRH	K/9	BB/9
Santana, Ervin	R-R	6-2	185	12-12-82	1	0	3.60	1	1	0	0	5	3	2	2	0	1	4	.158	.125	.182	7.20	1.80
Seanez, Rudy	R-R	6-1	225	10-20-68	0	0	4.00	9	0	0	0	9	8	4	4	2	4	7	.235	.227	.250	7.00	4.00
Thompson, Rich	R-R	6-1	180	7-1-84	3	1	3.12	29	0	0	0	43	41	19	15	7	11	51	.246	.293	.207	10.59	2.28
Wilhite, Matt	R-R	5-11	185	7-3-81	0	0	8.44	6	0	0	0	11	18	11	10	1	2	6	.375	.360	.391	5.06	1.69
2-team total (32 Colorado Springs)					0	4	7.21	38	0	0	10	49	59	41	39	8	13	32	—	—	—	5.92	2.40

Fielding

Catcher	PCT	G	PO	A	E	DP	PB
Budde	.982	69	397	51	8	10	1
Johnson	1.000	2	2	0	0	0	0
Wilson	.988	74	425	53	6	4	2
Wipke	1.000	4	20	2	0	1	0

First Base	PCT	G	PO	A	E	DP
Brown	.987	83	677	62	10	82
Budde	.972	12	92	13	3	10
Johnson	.992	12	112	5	1	12
Nieves	1.000	5	46	2	0	6
Pavkovich	1.000	2	15	0	0	0
Sandoval	.973	14	100	10	3	15
Wilson	1.000	12	120	12	0	13
Wood	1.000	6	63	2	0	9

Second Base	PCT	G	PO	A	E	DP
Figueroa	.978	24	60	74	3	22
Kendrick	.990	19	37	65	1	11

	PCT	G	PO	A	E	DP/PB
Nieves	1.000	2	4	5	0	2
Patchett	.955	15	31	33	3	10
Rodriguez	.979	75	154	261	9	68
Sandoval	1.000	3	3	0	2	
Segura	1.000	5	8	14	0	1
Statia	1.000	1	1	3	0	1
Sutton	1.000	5	8	19	0	7

Third Base	PCT	G	PO	A	E	DP
Brown	.885	12	12	11	3	0
Colmenares	1.000	1	3	2	0	0
Gutierrez	1.000	2	0	2	0	0
Nieves	1.000	4	2	3	0	1
Pavkovich	.925	36	27	59	7	9
Sandoval	.933	44	24	73	7	7
Wood	.956	46	33	75	5	12

Shortstop	PCT	G	PO	A	E	DP
Figueroa	.929	5	8	18	2	8

	PCT	G	PO	A	E	DP
Gutierrez	1.000	1	1	3	0	0
Patchett	.976	76	127	235	9	57
Rodriguez	.934	19	34	51	6	18
Statia	.875	2	0	7	1	2
Wood	.979	44	79	109	4	28

Outfield	PCT	G	PO	A	E	DP
Coon	.997	114	283	5	1	1
Evans	.979	119	226	11	5	1
Johnson	1.000	5	4	0	0	0
Pavkovich	.990	54	97	4	1	0
Pettit	.980	76	140	4	3	1
Rodriguez	1.000	6	12	0	0	0
Smith	1.000	4	10	0	0	0
Sutton	1.000	10	19	1	0	0
Willits	.993	50	132	1	1	0

ARKANSAS TRAVELERS

DOUBLE-A

TEXAS LEAGUE

Batting	B-T	HT	WT	DOB	AVG	vLH	vRH	G	AB	R	H	2B	3B	HR	RBI	BB	HBP	SH	SF	SO	SB	CS	SLG	OBP
Bourjos, Peter	R-R	6-1	180	3-31-87	.281	.358	.257	110	437	72	123	16	14	6	51	49	3	10	5	77	32	12	.423	.354
Brannon, Nolan	L-R	6-2	185	7-5-85	.000	.000	—	1	1	0	0	0	0	0	0	0	0	0	0	0	0	0	.000	.000
Breen, Pat	L-L	6-3	210	6-23-82	.198	.063	.225	34	96	16	19	2	0	2	6	23	5	0	0	34	3	2	.281	.379
Caligiuri, Jay	R-R	6-0	190	3-29-80	.195	.254	.159	56	174	16	34	5	0	4	20	24	4	1	2	30	1	0	.293	.304
Conger, Hank	B-R	6-1	220	1-29-88	.295	.316	.287	123	458	61	135	20	3	11	68	55	2	3	6	68	4	2	.424	.369
Contreras, Ivan	B-R	5-9	155	1-3-87	.261	.297	.248	54	142	16	37	4	1	0	9	10	1	4	1	30	4	3	.303	.312
Florence, Branden	R-R	6-0	200	4-3-78	.301	.208	.339	46	166	22	50	9	0	1	13	10	5	0	0	24	1	2	.373	.359
Fox, Chris	L-L	5-10	205	3-21-86	.000	.000	—	1	1	0	0	0	0	0	0	0	0	0	0	0	0	0	.000	.000
Gutierrez, Chris	R-R	5-9	185	3-12-84	.279	.178	.348	33	111	22	31	5	1	1	11	21	1	0	1	23	0	0	.369	.396
Johnson, Ben	B-R	6-0	220	10-17-81	.184	.139	.200	41	141	18	26	7	1	4	22	17	2	1	3	20	3	2	.333	.276
Kiniry, Rian	L-R	5-10	160	12-12-86	.500	—	.500	1	4	2	2	1	0	0	0	0	0	1	0	0	0	0	.750	.500
Majewski, Val	L-L	6-2	220	6-19-81	.235	.195	.253	36	132	18	31	4	1	4	18	15	3	0	1	21	4	1	.371	.325
Moore, Jerome	L-R	6-1	190	6-29-87	.333	.200	.375	7	21	5	7	0	1	0	2	10	3	1	0	1	7	1	1	.714	.423
Mount, Ryan	L-R	6-0	190	8-17-86	.252	.211	.266	84	305	36	77	16	0	4	31	20	2	1	2	64	5	7	.344	.301
Nieves, Abel	R-R	5-11	175	8-14-85	.269	.500	.200	8	26	3	7	1	0	0	2	3	0	1	0	9	0	0	.308	.345
Ortiz, Wilberto	R-R	5-10	180	1-30-85	.257	.298	.242	119	435	43	112	15	2	0	42	35	6	8	1	47	9	8	.301	.321
Patchett, Gary	R-R	6-2	180	9-25-78	.333	—	.333	2	6	2	2	0	0	0	0	2	0	0	0	3	0	1	.333	.500
Ramos, Kevin	R-R	5-11	170	6-6-86	.263	.333	.143	8	19	0	5	0	0	0	2	1	0	1	0	5	0	1	.263	.300
Smith, Coby	R-R	6-0	200	9-21-80	.262	.262	.262	116	450	68	118	18	3	8	47	37	6	13	2	55	41	12	.369	.325
Statia, Hainley	B-R	5-10	160	1-19-86	.243	.263	.236	111	375	46	91	21	2	1	43	34	2	13	2	34	13	3	.317	.308
Sumi, Ikko	R-R	5-9	200	10-20-87	.000	—	.000	1	4	0	0	0	0	0	0	1	0	0	0	0	0	0	.000	.000
Sutton, Nate	L-R	6-0	195	9-1-82	.305	.330	.295	104	371	54	113	20	3	2	40	48	4	5	3	55	21	8	.391	.387
Trumbo, Mark	R-R	6-4	220	1-16-86	.291	.289	.291	137	533	54	155	35	3	15	88	37	1	2	8	100	6	3	.452	.333
Walker, Brian	L-R	6-0	215	7-16-85	.267	.250	.268	19	60	4	16	2	0	0	7	6	2	0	1	21	0	0	.300	.348
Wipke, Flint	R-R	6-0	215	1-22-83	.228	.328	.168	53	171	24	39	9	0	4	19	22	0	3	4	58	3	2	.351	.310

Pitching	B-T	HT	WT	DOB	W	L	ERA	G	GS	CG	SV	IP	H	R	ER	HR	BB	SO	AVG	vLH	vRH	K/9	BB/9
Albano, Marco	R-R	5-11	215	8-26-83	6	6	3.77	30	10	0	0	88	74	43	37	10	37	87	.223	.240	.212	8.86	3.77
Aldridge, Ryan	R-R	6-2	210	9-10-83	0	1	4.50	15	0	0	0	18	23	10	9	1	10	11	.315	.455	.255	5.50	5.00
Anton, Mike	L-L	6-3	195	4-3-85	3	8	5.07	20	17	1	0	82	83	52	46	6	44	64	.263	.329	.240	7.05	4.85
Bell, Trevor	L-R	6-2	186	10-12-86	4	3	2.23	11	11	0	0	69	54	24	17	1	20	51	.212	.196	.223	6.68	2.62
Blackwell, Chad	R-R	5-11	145	1-7-83	1	0	9.26	8	0	0	0	12	21	17	12	2	3	9	.356	.545	.243	6.94	2.31
Brasier, Ryan	R-R	6-0	200	8-26-87	2	1	5.56	8	0	0	2	11	13	8	7	1	6	23	.283	.500	.188	4.76	5.56
Browning, Barrett	L-L	6-2	205	12-28-84	3	10	4.17	48	7	0	0	91	92	54	42	3	45	73	.266	.237	.281	7.25	4.47
Cabrera, Francis	R-R	6-1	184	5-27-87	0	1	—	1	0	0	0	0	1	3	3	0	3	0	1.000	—	1.000	—	—
Cassevah, Bobby	R-R	6-3	195	9-11-85	3	7	3.68	57	0	0	4	73	64	40	30	2	37	45	.236	.295	.199	5.52	4.54
Diaz, Amalio	R-R	6-2	170	9-10-86	3	7	3.65	36	14	0	0	113	114	55	46	10	33	83	.263	.259	.265	6.59	2.62
Herndon, David	R-R	6-5	230	9-4-85	5	6	3.03	50	0	0	11	65	70	25	22	9	14	35	.282	.323	.255	4.82	1.93
Hill, Jeremy	R-R	5-11	200	8-8-77	0	0	10.80	2	0	0	0	2	6	3	2	0	2	4	.500	.833	.167	21.60	10.80
Kiely, Tim	R-R	6-1	190	8-26-85	4	3	4.85	15	15	1	0	95	104	59	51	15	18	48	.277	.265	.284	4.56	1.71
Mendoza, Tommy	R-R	6-2	195	8-18-87	7	7	3.36	20	20	0	0	129	130	60	48	10	31	86	.260	.257	.262	6.02	2.17
Mosebach, Bobby	R-R	6-4	195	9-14-84	2	0	0.34	19	0	0	6	26	12	1	1	0	9	16	.140	.147	.135	5.47	3.08
O'Sullivan, Sean	R-R	6-2	230	9-1-87	1	1	5.30	3	3	0	0	19	21	11	11	1	0	16	.288	.217	.407	6.75	0.00
Reckling, Trevor	L-L	6-1	195	5-22-89	8	7	2.93	23	23	1	0	135	118	50	44	4	75	106	.244	.165	.271	7.05	4.99
Rembisz, Bryan	R-R	5-8	185	8-16-85	2	3	4.25	40	0	0	0	59	56	30	28	9	19	35	.255	.200	.289	5.31	2.88

								ERA	G	GS			IP	H	R	ER	HR	BB	SO	AVG	vLH	vRH	K/9	BB/9
Rodriguez, Fernando	R-R	6-3	215	6-18-84	3	1		1.28	26	0	0	4	42	20	7	6	0	22	52	.137	.109	.154	11.06	4.68
Thorne, Jeremy	R-R	6-4	260	10-4-85	0	0		2.45	2	2	0	0	11	8	3	3	1	1	5	.229	.125	.259	4.09	0.82
Torres, Alex	L-L	5-10	175	12-8-87	3	1		2.77	5	5	0	0	26	23	10	8	0	17	25	.245	.474	.187	8.65	5.88
Walden, Jordan	R-R	6-5	240	11-16-87	1	5		5.25	13	13	0	0	60	72	39	35	4	29	57	.301	.306	.298	8.55	4.35

Fielding

Catcher	PCT	G	PO	A	E	DP	PB
Conger	.978	87	573	58	14	3	3
Johnson	.958	6	41	5	2	0	3
Sumi	.889	1	8	0	1	0	0
Walker	.985	9	60	7	1	2	0
Wipke	.973	41	227	28	7	3	8

First Base	PCT	G	PO	A	E	DP
Caligiuri	1.000	24	175	13	0	21
Johnson	.968	3	29	1	1	0
Nieves	1.000	2	20	0	0	4
Sutton	1.000	2	22	0	0	1
Trumbo	.990	108	965	63	10	91
Wipke	1.000	2	24	1	0	1

Second Base	PCT	G	PO	A	E	DP
Contreras	.953	18	35	47	4	12
Gutierrez	.929	3	5	8	1	3

	PCT	G	PO	A	E	DP
Mount	.969	79	163	215	12	47
Ortiz	.969	12	29	34	2	11
Ramos	.955	7	13	8	1	2
Statia	1.000	1	5	4	0	4
Sutton	.976	26	49	73	3	15

Third Base	PCT	G	PO	A	E	DP
Caligiuri	.905	16	8	30	4	3
Gutierrez	.957	25	13	53	3	5
Nieves	.909	5	4	6	1	0
Ortiz	.898	75	35	141	20	10
Sutton	.939	23	17	45	4	4

Shortstop	PCT	G	PO	A	E	DP
Contreras	1.000	3	3	7	0	2
Gutierrez	1.000	5	8	8	0	1
Ortiz	.936	24	33	69	7	18
Patchett	1.000	2	2	4	0	2

	PCT	G	PO	A	E	DP
Statia	.964	109	188	354	20	70
Sutton	.778	2	1	6	2	1

Outfield	PCT	G	PO	A	E	DP
Bourjos	.997	109	294	7	1	5
Brannon	—	1	0	0	0	0
Breen	.906	19	28	1	3	0
Contreras	.925	30	46	3	4	0
Florence	.973	32	70	1	2	0
Fox	—	1	0	0	0	0
Johnson	.974	21	33	4	1	0
Kiniry	1.000	1	1	0	0	0
Majewski	.984	34	61	1	1	0
Moore	1.000	7	12	2	0	0
Ortiz	1.000	1	1	0	0	0
Smith	.979	115	225	7	5	0
Sutton	.978	51	80	8	2	3
Trumbo	1.000	10	23	1	0	1

RANCHO CUCAMONGA QUAKES   HIGH CLASS A

CALIFORNIA LEAGUE

Batting	B-T	HT	WT	DOB	AVG	vLH	vRH	G	AB	R	H	2B	3B	HR	RBI	BB	HBP	SH	SF	SO	SB	CS	SLG	OBP
Bressoud, C.J.	R-R	6-2	200	5-12-85	1.000	—	1.000	1	2	1	2	0	0	0	1	0	0	0	0	0	0	0	1.000	1.000
Brossman, Jay	R-R	6-1	210	1-17-85	.245	.239	.247	71	245	32	60	15	1	10	45	21	6	4	5	52	4	2	.437	.314
Colmenares, Carlos	B-R	6-0	175	2-11-86	.298	.313	.291	93	302	43	90	21	6	0	29	26	2	11	1	53	8	6	.407	.356
Estrella, Hector	R-R	5-11	175	12-22-84	.263	.247	.270	90	315	48	83	14	3	4	45	42	5	1	3	52	9	6	.365	.356
Fuller, Clay	B-R	6-2	190	6-17-87	.232	.214	.240	129	452	89	105	18	4	9	48	71	6	10	5	127	30	8	.350	.341
Guerrero, Vladimir	R-R	6-3	235	2-9-75	.500	—	.500	2	6	2	3	2	0	0	2	0	0	0	0	1	0	0	.833	.500
Hunter, Torii	R-R	6-2	225	7-18-75	.333	.333	.333	3	9	3	3	0	0	1	3	3	0	0	0	2	1	0	.667	.500
Kiniry, Rian	L-R	5-10	160	12-12-86	.236	.217	.242	31	89	9	21	4	1	0	7	10	0	2	0	22	5	1	.303	.313
Long, Matt	L-R	5-11	170	4-30-87	.250	.200	.273	5	16	1	4	1	0	1	2	1	0	0	0	3	0	0	.500	.294
Moore, Jerome	L-R	6-1	190	6-29-87	.279	.322	.259	124	470	61	131	20	12	11	58	34	4	4	4	144	17	13	.443	.330
Navarro, Efren	L-L	6-0	200	5-14-86	.287	.265	.296	130	481	64	138	32	3	5	61	53	3	1	2	72	3	2	.397	.360
Nieves, Abel	R-R	5-11	175	8-14-85	.266	.229	.286	42	139	23	37	5	3	0	17	26	1	0	0	38	0	3	.410	.386
Norman, Anthony	R-R	6-0	185	10-20-84	.238	.269	.222	27	80	13	19	4	1	0	12	7	4	1	1	15	0	0	.438	.326
Perez, Julio	R-R	6-2	160	9-28-85	.265	.270	.262	82	310	46	82	17	3	10	51	16	2	2	6	74	8	6	.435	.299
Phillips, P.J.	R-R	6-3	170	9-23-86	.233	.276	.217	126	455	51	106	23	5	10	56	25	3	5	6	113	23	12	.371	.274
Ramos, Kevin	R-R	5-11	170	6-6-86	—			1	0	0	0	0	0	0	0	0	0	0	0	0	0	0	—	—
Rife, Jake	L-L	5-11	206	6-7-87	.253	.250	.254	31	87	10	22	7	1	0	11	3	3	0	1	24	2	0	.356	.298
Romine, Andrew	B-R	6-1	190	12-24-85	.278	.310	.262	131	479	68	133	13	9	1	36	51	5	16	4	83	26	11	.349	.351
Rosario, Alberto	R-R	5-10	190	1-10-87	.232	.152	.260	104	314	38	73	15	4	0	35	13	8	6	2	43	9	4	.306	.279
Rosenbaum, Chris	R-R	6-1	205	4-2-84	.319	.111	.392	31	69	13	22	1	0	1	7	11	5	0	1	14	1	2	.377	.442
Sweeney, Matt	L-R	6-3	215	4-4-88	.299	.185	.338	58	211	39	63	17	1	9	44	26	2	1	1	37	2	0	.517	.379
Walker, Brian	L-R	6-0	215	7-16-85	.291	.295	.288	38	117	10	34	7	0	5	21	6	1	2	3	40	1	2	.479	.323

Pitching	B-T	HT	WT	DOB	W	L	ERA	G	GS	CG	SV	IP	H	R	ER	HR	BB	SO	AVG	vLH	vRH	K/9	BB/9
Anton, Mike	L-L	6-3	195	4-3-85	1	0	3.00	3	2	0	1	15	14	7	5	0	2	16	.241	.143	.297	9.60	1.20
Brasier, Ryan	R-R	6-0	200	8-26-87	5	4	5.23	27	14	0	0	98	103	63	57	17	32	93	.270	.279	.260	8.54	2.94
Carmona, Ysmael	R-R	6-1	190	2-12-85	0	8	5.74	42	0	0	20	42	45	28	27	5	26	55	.274	.293	.256	11.69	5.53
Escobar, Kelvim	R-R	6-1	230	4-11-76	0	0	0.00	2	2	0	0	11	2	1	0	0	1	12	.059	.000	.118	10.13	0.84
Fish, Robert	L-L	6-3	225	1-19-88	1	6	6.39	16	13	0	0	69	94	59	49	12	28	54	.331	.322	.335	7.04	3.65
Flores, Manuel	L-L	6-2	170	6-1-87	2	3	4.32	6	6	0	0	33	44	23	16	4	3	19	.310	.278	.321	5.13	0.81
Geltz, Steve	R-R	5-10	170	11-1-87	7	1	3.76	34	0	0	0	65	52	29	27	7	32	73	.225	.186	.263	10.16	4.45
Haynes, Jeremy	R-R	6-2	180	5-28-86	0	5	4.36	39	0	0	0	66	64	45	32	3	51	67	.255	.322	.199	9.14	6.95
Howard, Cephas	R-R	6-5	240	9-5-84	0	1	18.00	5	0	0	0	4	8	8	8	0	3	5	.421	.364	.500	6.75	11.25
Jimenez, Esmerlin	R-R	6-2	184	8-1-84	2	3	8.14	10	9	0	0	42	71	42	38	7	28	26	.413	.423	.400	5.57	6.00
Kenney, Mike	R-R	6-4	210	8-16-86	1	7	5.54	36	11	0	0	88	102	56	54	12	40	66	.293	.299	.287	6.78	4.11
Kiely, Tim	R-R	6-1	190	8-26-85	5	5	4.44	12	12	1	0	73	85	42	36	7	8	44	.286	.305	.263	5.42	0.99
Kohn, Michael	R-R	6-2	200	6-26-86	2	0	0.94	22	0	0	3	29	13	3	3	0	16	43	.141	.190	.100	13.50	4.40
Leon, Sammy	R-R	6-0	160	5-19-85	2	2	10.80	15	0	0	0	18	25	25	22	3	13	19	.313	.318	.306	9.33	6.38
Lopez, Baudilio	R-R	6-1	190	11-20-90	0	0	0.00	1	0	0	0	1	1	0	0	0	1	2	.333	.500	.000	18.00	9.00
Loux, Shane	R-R	6-2	235	8-31-79	0	0	0.00	1	1	0	0	1	1	0	0	0	0	2	.250	1.000	.000	0.00	18.00
McKiernan, Eddie	R-R	5-11	160	3-21-89	5	4	3.81	45	0	0	4	57	60	30	24	6	22	52	.269	.262	.276	8.26	3.49
Miller, Jayson	L-L	5-11	180	11-25-85	6	10	5.09	26	25	0	0	141	180	91	80	15	24	87	.314	.296	.321	5.54	1.53
Nabors, Kevin	R-R	6-3	210	8-12-85	0	1	6.98	16	0	0	0	19	23	16	15	2	10	21	.303	.333	.279	9.78	4.66
Pugliese, Nick	R-R	6-1	205	9-18-85	0	0	7.04	6	0	0	0	8	8	7	6	2	5	7	.250	.231	.263	8.22	5.87
Reckling, Trevor	L-L	6-1	195	5-22-89	1	2	0.95	3	3	0	0	19	9	3	2	2	3	16	.138	.059	.167	7.58	1.42
Santana, Ervin	R-R	6-2	185	12-12-82	0	0	5.79	1	1	0	0	5	4	3	3	2	0	3	.222	.250	.167	5.79	0.00
Schoeninger, Tim	R-R	6-3	220	9-7-84	1	1	4.15	5	5	0	0	22	28	10	10	4	7	15	.315	.308	.324	6.23	2.91

Name	B-T	HT	WT	DOB	W	L	ERA	G	GS	CG	SV	IP	H	R	ER	HR	BB	SO	AVG	vLH	vRH	K/9	BB/9
Shoemaker, Matt	R-R	6-2	225	9-27-86	1	0	3.12	3	3	0	0	17	14	7	6	2	1	13	.212	.211	.214	6.75	0.52
Taylor, Drew	R-L	6-2	190	8-18-86	1	0	9.53	5	0	0	0	6	8	8	6	2	8	8	.320	.286	.333	12.71	12.71
Thorne, Jeremy	R-R	6-4	260	10-4-85	4	8	4.83	14	14	0	0	82	101	50	44	11	29	49	.310	.322	.295	5.38	3.18
Tobin, Mason	R-R	6-4	220	7-8-87	0	0	0.00	3	0	0	1	3	2	4	0	0	2	2	.167	.250	.000	6.75	6.75
Torres, Alex	L-L	5-10	175	12-8-87	10	3	2.74	21	19	0	0	121	93	43	37	4	63	124	.217	.195	.225	9.20	4.67
Towns, Jordan	R-R	6-2	220	9-21-85	0	3	8.74	9	0	0	0	11	18	13	11	2	7	9	.346	.345	.348	7.15	5.56
Wilding, Taylor	R-R	6-1	190	10-22-84	4	2	3.43	39	0	0	3	58	52	25	22	5	16	55	.237	.300	.185	8.58	2.50

Fielding

Catcher	PCT	G	PO	A	E	DP	PB
Bressoud	1.000	1	1	0	0	0	1
Rosario	.986	103	723	103	12	4	16
Rosenbaum	.990	21	100	4	1	0	0
Walker	.989	36	236	23	3	1	2

First Base	PCT	G	PO	A	E	DP
Brossman	1.000	11	89	10	0	5
Colmenares	1.000	5	39	5	0	5
Navarro	.989	125	1077	85	13	102
Nieves	1.000	1	10	1	0	1

Second Base	PCT	G	PO	A	E	DP
Colmenares	.955	16	29	35	3	9
Estrella	.983	28	55	63	2	8

	PCT	G	PO	A	E	DP
Nieves	.975	26	44	73	3	16
Phillips	.955	73	146	214	17	43

Third Base	PCT	G	PO	A	E	DP
Brossman	.950	45	30	102	7	7
Colmenares	.940	40	17	61	5	8
Estrella	.917	21	13	31	4	2
Nieves	1.000	7	3	14	0	1
Sweeney	.908	33	8	51	6	6

Shortstop	PCT	G	PO	A	E	DP
Colmenares	.937	18	21	53	5	7
Nieves	1.000	2	3	8	0	1
Phillips	.750	1	0	3	1	0
Ramos	—	1	0	0	0	0

	PCT	G	PO	A	E	DP
Romine	.967	125	220	359	20	74

Outfield	PCT	G	PO	A	E	DP
Colmenares	1.000	7	11	0	0	0
Fuller	.975	123	219	11	6	1
Hunter	—	2	0	0	0	0
Kiniry	.980	28	50	0	1	0
Long	1.000	4	10	1	0	1
Moore	.961	115	184	12	8	0
Norman	.960	22	24	0	1	0
Perez	.950	77	128	5	7	2
Phillips	.946	37	79	8	5	1
Rife	.892	24	33	0	4	0

CEDAR RAPIDS KERNELS

LOW CLASS A

MIDWEST LEAGUE

Batting	B-T	HT	WT	DOB	AVG	vLH	vRH	G	AB	R	H	2B	3B	HR	RBI	BB	HBP	SH	SF	SO	SB	CS	SLG	OBP
Almanzar, Jean	B-R	5-7	150	2-7-89	.091	.000	.143	3	11	0	1	0	0	0	0	0	0	1	0	0	2	0	0	.091	.167
Amarista, Alexia	B-R	5-8	150	4-6-89	.319	.245	.341	125	477	84	152	39	10	4	49	50	8	18	4	61	38	20	.468	.390
Auer, Tyson	R-R	6-0	188	10-24-85	.277	.252	.285	122	491	84	136	18	5	2	39	45	7	5	3	117	43	18	.346	.344
Bailey, Dwayne	B-R	6-2	200	8-11-86	.219	.286	.174	59	155	18	34	6	1	0	12	25	2	4	1	48	9	0	.271	.333
Brannon, Nolan	L-R	6-0	185	7-5-85	.300	.286	.304	11	30	2	9	1	0	0	2	1	1	1	1	4	0	0	.333	.333
Bressoud, C.J.	R-R	6-2	200	5-12-85	.167	.500	.000	3	6	0	1	0	0	0	0	0	0	0	0	4	0	0	.167	.167
Brooks, Beau	L-R	6-1	200	8-3-87	.248	.224	.253	97	322	63	80	17	3	5	47	67	3	2	5	86	5	1	.366	.378
Castillo, Angel	R-R	6-3	190	6-7-89	.242	.290	.225	112	393	56	95	20	1	12	61	29	17	5	9	111	16	2	.389	.315
Colmenares, Carlos	B-R	6-0	175	2-11-86	.211	.300	.191	17	57	9	12	2	0	0	4	7	0	0	0	15	5	1	.246	.297
Crawford, Matt	B-R	6-0	165	5-9-86	.285	.281	.286	126	474	57	135	18	4	2	53	40	5	12	2	76	24	16	.352	.345
De Los Santos, Anel	R-R	6-3	216	6-19-88	.212	.195	.219	76	273	24	58	6	1	5	31	8	3	9	0	95	5	0	.297	.243
Estrella, Hector	R-R	5-11	175	12-22-84	.208	.077	.250	16	53	7	11	3	0	1	11	11	1	0	0	13	4	1	.321	.354
Fox, Chris	L-L	5-10	205	3-21-86	.250	.667	.176	9	20	5	5	1	0	0	1	1	0	0	0	4	0	0	.300	.286
Gomez, Rolando	L-R	5-7	145	6-18-89	.111	.000	.125	5	18	1	2	1	0	0	1	1	0	0	1	4	0	0	.167	.150
Groth, Ryan	L-L	6-2	200	7-23-86	.195	.063	.230	26	77	10	15	4	1	2	9	6	2	0	0	27	2	0	.351	.271
Jacobo, Gabe	R-R	6-2	190	4-14-87	.257	.227	.268	118	440	59	113	27	9	10	72	31	11	0	7	84	6	8	.427	.317
Jones, Jeff	R-R	6-4	189	1-22-87	.204	.190	.214	19	49	5	10	1	0	0	5	3	1	0	1	16	1	0	.224	.259
Lopez, Roberto	R-R	6-0	195	10-1-85	.271	.272	.271	94	354	61	96	18	0	11	67	40	17	1	8	52	5	7	.415	.365
Perez, Darwin	B-R	5-10	160	7-27-89	.261	.301	.247	106	352	55	92	14	4	2	42	49	0	16	0	84	11	7	.341	.352
Townsend, Jon	R-R	6-0	190	9-24-84	.229	.309	.195	69	227	32	52	9	0	5	32	15	6	5	3	59	8	3	.335	.291
Trout, Mike	R-R	6-1	200	8-7-91	.267	.250	.273	5	15	1	4	0	0	0	0	4	0	1	0	6	0	0	.267	.421
Wing, Michael	R-R	6-1	180	10-25-88	—	—	—	1	0	0	0	0	0	0	0	0	0	0	0	0	0	1	—	—
Younger, Adam	R-R	6-2	207	8-25-85	.228	.257	.218	84	281	30	64	13	3	4	39	27	15	5	5	100	5	5	.338	.323

Pitching	B-T	HT	WT	DOB	W	L	ERA	G	GS	CG	SV	IP	H	R	ER	HR	BB	SO	AVG	vLH	vRH	K/9	BB/9
Armstrong, Chris	L-L	5-10	195	2-10-88	3	2	4.73	38	1	0	0	59	62	36	31	4	39	47	.277	.212	.304	7.17	5.95
Boshiers, Buddy	L-L	6-3	205	5-9-88	3	1	5.97	6	6	1	0	32	31	21	21	5	7	27	.254	.257	.253	7.67	1.99
Cabrera, Francis	R-R	6-1	184	5-27-87	1	4	9.42	10	0	0	0	14	20	15	15	0	5	7	.333	.321	.344	4.40	3.14
Chaffee, Ryan	R-R	6-2	190	5-18-88	8	8	4.33	23	23	0	0	116	84	63	56	6	65	121	.206	.240	.183	9.36	5.03
Chatwood, Tyler	R-R	5-11	175	12-16-89	8	7	4.02	24	24	0	0	116	99	60	52	3	66	106	.237	.267	.215	8.20	5.11
Correa, Manuarys	R-R	6-3	170	1-9-86	8	10	4.47	27	27	2	0	163	176	92	81	16	43	69	.276	.253	.297	3.81	2.37
Davitt, Michael	R-R	6-6	230	9-8-86	1	0	4.32	3	0	0	0	17	18	8	8	0	7	17	.290	.357	.235	9.18	3.78
Dorado, Reyes	L-R	6-1	195	1-10-86	0	0	24.30	4	0	0	0	3	11	13	9	1	3	4	.458	.400	.500	10.80	8.10
Flores, Manuel	L-L	6-2	170	6-1-87	7	4	3.59	19	19	1	0	120	122	50	48	9	23	74	.263	.223	.277	5.53	1.72
Hellweg, John	R-R	6-7	200	10-29-88	0	0	1.35	5	0	0	2	7	4	3	1	0	7	7	.160	.100	.200	9.45	9.45
Hurst, Kyle	R-R	6-4	230	8-23-85	1	2	4.64	15	2	0	0	33	26	19	17	4	8	17	.213	.224	.205	4.64	2.18
Kohn, Michael	R-R	6-2	200	6-26-86	4	1	2.19	28	0	0	6	37	20	9	9	1	12	60	.161	.192	.139	14.59	2.92
Miller, Jayson	L-L	5-11	180	11-25-85	1	1	3.00	2	2	0	0	12	11	4	4	0	1	11	.234	.333	.200	8.25	0.75
Nabors, Kevin	R-R	6-3	210	8-12-85	3	3	3.00	33	0	0	1	51	47	20	17	1	22	40	.251	.253	.250	7.06	3.88
Pugliese, Nick	R-R	6-1	205	9-18-85	3	2	2.52	24	0	0	2	36	33	13	10	0	6	46	.243	.275	.224	11.61	1.51
Rocco, Michael	R-R	6-3	210	8-19-85	1	0	1.80	2	0	0	0	5	3	1	1	0	2	3	.158	.000	.231	10.80	3.60
Scholl, Chris	R-R	5-11	195	10-27-87	3	2	3.42	45	0	0	9	84	64	36	32	7	37	90	.213	.206	.218	9.60	3.95
Shoemaker, Matt	R-R	6-2	225	9-27-86	4	1	3.39	20	5	0	0	64	53	29	24	5	23	54	.227	.180	.257	7.63	3.25
Smith, Will	R-L	6-5	215	7-10-89	10	5	3.76	20	19	0	0	115	109	61	48	11	24	95	.249	.211	.258	7.43	1.88
Taylor, Drew	R-L	6-2	190	8-18-86	3	0	1.23	40	0	0	8	51	29	7	7	0	19	83	.166	.131	.184	14.55	3.33
Thorne, Jeremy	R-R	6-4	260	10-4-85	3	3	2.39	19	2	0	3	38	33	14	10	2	9	24	.226	.203	.244	5.73	2.15
Veras, Vladimir	R-R	6-0	150	1-10-86	3	4	3.00	38	0	0	11	54	43	20	18	0	18	59	.219	.224	.217	9.83	3.00

Fielding

Catcher	PCT	G	PO	A	E	DP	PB
Brannon	1.000	11	65	12	0	0	2
Bressoud	1.000	2	5	0	0	0	0
Brooks	.985	50	355	32	6	0	10
De Los Santos	.991	76	580	72	6	10	7
Lopez	.985	11	58	8	1	0	4

First Base	PCT	G	PO	A	E	DP
Bailey	1.000	19	104	5	0	5
Colmenares	.978	9	82	6	2	5
Jacobo	.995	108	973	64	5	61
Lopez	.987	15	141	11	2	14

Second Base	PCT	G	PO	A	E	DP
Almanzar	.600	2	1	2	2	1
Amarista	.975	120	199	346	14	63

	PCT	G	PO	A	E	DP	PB
Bailey	.920	10	10	13	2	1	
Estrella	1.000	2	2	2	0	0	
Perez	.982	11	18	38	1	4	

Third Base	PCT	G	PO	A	E	DP
Almanzar	1.000	1	0	3	0	0
Bailey	.944	25	15	36	3	7
Colmenares	1.000	2	0	4	0	0
Estrella	.943	12	8	25	2	2
Gomez	1.000	5	2	6	0	0
Townsend	.950	63	33	139	9	7
Wing	—	1	0	0	0	0
Younger	.947	36	17	73	5	6

Shortstop	PCT	G	PO	A	E	DP
Almanzar	1.000	1	0	1	0	0

	PCT	G	PO	A	E	DP
Gomez	1.000	1	0	2	0	0
Perez	.951	94	121	249	19	44
Younger	.953	44	43	119	8	13

Outfield	PCT	G	PO	A	E	DP
Auer	.993	120	278	9	2	3
Castillo	.964	104	181	7	7	4
Colmenares	1.000	5	12	1	0	0
Crawford	.986	114	194	13	3	1
Fox	1.000	6	9	0	0	0
Groth	.960	14	21	3	1	0
Jones	1.000	18	28	0	0	0
Lopez	.962	40	47	4	2	0
Trout	1.000	5	12	0	0	0

AZL ANGELS
ROOKIE
ARIZONA LEAGUE

Batting	B-T	HT	WT	DOB	AVG	vLH	vRH	G	AB	R	H	2B	3B	HR	RBI	BB	HBP	SH	SF	SO	SB	CS	SLG	OBP
Almanzar, Jean	B-R	5-7	150	2-7-89	.310	.333	.305	29	116	15	36	6	2	0	18	7	0	1	3	17	0	0	.397	.341
Alvarez, Ricky	R-R	5-11	217	2-7-89	.273	.333	.262	54	205	38	56	10	6	4	41	11	10	1	5	48	6	2	.439	.333
Bando, Phil	R-L	5-10	175	5-7-86	.238	.333	.222	8	21	4	5	0	0	0	3	1	0	0	0	6	0	1	.238	.273
Barkley, Alibay	R-L	6-3	255	11-16-89	.389	.400	.385	6	18	4	7	2	0	0	3	1	0	0	0	5	0	0	.500	.421
Brossman, Jay	R-R	6-1	210	1-17-85	.500	—	.500	4	10	2	5	3	0	0	1	2	1	0	1	0	0	0	.800	.571
Brown, Matt	R-R	6-0	200	8-8-82	.400	.333	.429	3	10	1	4	0	0	0	2	1	0	0	1	3	0	1	.400	.417
Cates, Rich	R-L	5-11	180	12-11-86	.600	.667	.571	3	10	5	6	2	1	0	4	2	1	0	0	1	0	0	1.000	.692
Demperio, Michael	R-R	5-10	170	2-17-88	.167	.400	.140	14	48	13	8	1	0	1	4	11	2	1	0	15	4	0	.250	.344
Drake, Jordan	R-R	5-9	180	2-18-91	.222	.333	.167	10	9	2	2	0	0	0	1	0	0	0	0	4	1	1	.222	.300
Farnsworth, Nick	L-L	6-2	210	6-17-89	.193	.182	.196	20	57	8	11	3	0	0	12	13	4	2	2	23	1	1	.246	.368
Figueroa, Luis	B-R	5-9	165	2-16-74	.467	—	.467	4	15	2	7	1	0	0	3	1	0	0	0	0	0	0	.533	.500
Gillan, Jeremy	R-R	6-2	195	10-20-86	.193	.000	.220	17	57	8	11	2	0	1	7	7	3	1	1	14	1	1	.281	.309
Gomez, Rolando	L-R	5-7	145	6-18-89	.304	.267	.311	45	181	48	55	13	5	2	19	32	0	4	0	43	12	4	.464	.408
Grichuk, Randal	R-R	6-1	195	8-13-91	.322	.351	.317	53	236	47	76	13	10	7	53	9	4	3	4	64	6	4	.551	.352
Hatton, Wes	R-R	5-10	165	12-28-90	.200	.167	.208	20	65	11	13	1	1	0	11	9	0	0	1	22	0	1	.246	.293
Jimenez, Jose	L-R	5-10	240	1-2-87	.214	.077	.235	32	98	19	21	6	0	3	17	26	0	2	1	22	0	0	.367	.376
Long, Matt	L-R	5-11	170	4-30-87	.283	.273	.285	50	184	37	52	7	9	1	29	26	2	4	3	23	3	3	.435	.372
Mallard, Jamie	R-R	6-0	265	8-23-90	.297	.111	.333	30	111	16	33	4	0	5	28	12	0	0	2	25	1	0	.468	.360
Mount, Ryan	L-R	6-0	190	8-17-86	.375	.250	.417	4	16	5	6	0	0	1	2	0	0	0	0	4	0	0	.375	.444
Nieves, Abel	R-R	5-11	175	8-14-85	.429	—	.429	2	7	1	3	1	0	0	4	2	0	0	2	0	0	.571	.556
Oliver, Eric	R-R	6-1	215	1-29-87	.274	.071	.314	49	168	36	46	7	1	4	35	28	6	4	2	25	2	0	.399	.392
Pettit, Chris	R-R	6-0	195	8-15-84	.357	.750	.200	4	14	2	5	1	0	0	1	3	0	0	0	6	1	0	.429	.471
Rickard, John	R-R	6-0	185	3-23-90	.286	.250	.300	19	42	8	12	1	0	1	12	7	1	2	2	16	0	1	.381	.385
Rife, Jake	L-L	5-11	206	6-7-87	.348	.400	.333	7	23	5	8	0	1	0	5	2	2	0	0	1	3	1	.435	.444
Sandoval, Freddy	B-R	6-1	200	8-16-82	.263	.167	.308	6	19	5	5	1	0	0	1	4	1	0	0	2	1	0	.316	.417
Soto, Eduardo	R-R	6-0	165	4-25-91	.213	.250	.205	18	47	7	10	2	3	0	6	2	2	1	0	12	1	1	.383	.275
Sweeney, Matt	L-R	6-3	215	4-4-88	.267	.000	.286	4	15	3	4	1	0	0	2	1	0	0	4	0	0	.333	.389
Trout, Mike	R-R	6-1	200	8-7-91	.360	.379	.356	39	164	29	59	7	7	1	25	18	0	3	2	28	13	2	.506	.418
Washington, Demetrius	R-R	6-0	185	7-13-89	.222	.000	.267	6	18	7	4	0	0	0	1	3	0	0	0	6	3	0	.222	.333
Witherspoon, Travis	R-R	6-2	190	4-16-89	.231	.500	.111	5	13	2	3	1	0	0	1	0	0	0	0	3	0	0	.308	.286

Pitching	B-T	HT	WT	DOB	W	L	ERA	G	GS	CG	SV	IP	H	R	ER	HR	BB	SO	AVG	vLH	vRH	K/9	BB/9
Aldridge, Ryan	R-R	6-2	210	9-10-83	0	0	2.70	6	0	0	0	7	7	4	2	0	2	13	.259	.250	.261	17.55	2.70
Bachanov, Jon	R-R	6-4	210	1-30-89	4	0	3.14	16	0	0	0	29	26	10	10	0	4	47	.239	.190	.269	14.76	1.26
Baez, Suammy	R-R	6-4	200	9-28-88	3	2	2.70	23	0	0	1	30	31	14	9	1	8	30	.256	.268	.250	9.00	2.40
Blanco, Josh	L-L	6-2	190	11-16-89	3	2	3.04	12	8	0	0	50	40	20	17	3	13	63	.217	.133	.234	11.26	2.32
Calderon, Leonardo	L-L	5-11	170	7-31-86	0	0	12.27	3	0	0	0	4	8	5	5	0	2	5	.421	1.000	.389	12.27	4.91
Cisterna, Ryan	R-R	6-1	200	6-25-86	0	0	4.50	6	0	0	0	6	2	3	3	0	3	4	.100	.000	.111	6.00	4.50
Dorado, Reyes	L-R	6-1	195	1-10-86	0	0	0.00	2	0	0	0	1	3	0	0	0	0	3	.429	.500	.400	20.25	0.00
Fish, Robert	L-L	6-3	225	1-19-88	0	0	3.00	5	0	0	0	6	1	2	2	0	1	9	.050	.000	.067	13.50	1.50
Hellweg, John	R-R	6-7	200	10-29-88	2	1	2.96	18	0	0	6	24	16	8	8	0	8	25	.186	.105	.209	9.25	2.96
Jang, Pil Joon	R-R	6-3	190	4-8-88	6	3	3.83	14	14	0	0	82	77	42	35	5	10	72	.244	.216	.254	7.87	1.09
Jung, Youngil	R-R	6-2	190	11-16-88	0	0	0.00	2	0	0	0	2	1	0	0	0	0	3	.143	.000	.200	13.50	0.00
Lopez, Baudilio	R-R	6-1	190	11-20-90	4	2	3.72	13	6	0	0	46	54	22	19	0	16	35	.298	.265	.319	6.85	3.13
Martinez, Fabio	R-R	6-3	190	10-29-89	3	2	3.26	14	13	0	0	61	45	33	22	1	36	92	.197	.182	.202	13.65	5.34
Nichols, Heath	R-R	6-2	180	11-23-88	1	0	2.19	18	0	0	0	25	23	13	6	2	11	23	.230	.267	.214	8.39	4.01
Oye, Matt	R-R	6-5	230	2-25-86	2	0	2.57	7	2	0	0	14	11	6	4	1	1	10	.095	.310	6.43	0.64
Pena, Ariel	R-R	6-3	186	5-20-89	5	4	3.83	14	6	0	0	49	46	26	21	2	15	47	.247	.203	.277	8.57	2.74
Perez, Jose	R-R	6-2	180	9-14-87	1	0	3.46	4	4	0	0	13	9	5	5	0	3	20	.191	.211	.179	13.85	2.08
Rocco, Michael	R-R	6-3	210	8-19-85	2	2	2.43	22	0	0	5	30	26	9	8	1	5	36	.236	.289	.200	10.92	1.52
Santana, Ervin	R-R	6-2	185	12-12-82	0	0	0.00	1	1	0	0	3	3	0	0	0	0	7	.231	—	.231	18.90	0.00
Skaggs, Tyler	L-L	6-4	180	7-13-91	0	0	0.00	3	2	0	0	6	4	0	0	0	1	7	.182	.333	.125	10.50	1.50

Fielding

Catcher	PCT	G	PO	A	E	DP	PB
Gillan	1.000	17	148	17	0	0	0
Jimenez	.997	31	285	28	1	1	3
Rickard	.987	19	144	12	2	1	7

First Base	PCT	G	PO	A	E	DP
Barkley	1.000	1	4	0	0	0
Brown	1.000	3	21	0	0	1
Farnsworth	.980	17	135	11	3	11
Oliver	.983	42	326	21	6	14

Second Base	PCT	G	PO	A	E	DP
Almanzar	.944	10	11	23	2	3
Bando	.889	6	9	15	3	3
Demperio	.813	8	12	14	6	4

	PCT	G	PO	A	E	DP
Figueroa	.923	4	3	9	1	1
Hatton	.930	19	26	40	5	5
Mount	.909	4	3	7	1	0
Sandoval	1.000	1	2	2	0	0
Soto	.947	12	15	21	2	4

Third Base	PCT	G	PO	A	E	DP
Almanzar	.857	6	5	7	2	2
Alvarez	.912	52	31	72	10	1
Brossman	1.000	2	0	3	0	0
Nieves	1.000	1	0	1	0	0
Sandoval	1.000	3	0	4	0	0

Shortstop	PCT	G	PO	A	E	DP
Almanzar	.939	15	18	44	4	5

	PCT	G	PO	A	E	DP
Figueroa	.000	1	0	0	1	0
Gomez	.913	43	60	130	18	14

Outfield	PCT	G	PO	A	E	DP
Cates	.833	3	4	1	1	0
Demperio	1.000	6	8	0	0	0
Drake	1.000	5	6	0	0	0
Gomez	1.000	2	2	1	0	0
Grichuk	.987	53	72	4	1	1
Long	1.000	48	74	3	0	1
Pettit	1.000	4	4	0	0	0
Rife	1.000	6	3	0	0	0
Trout	.986	38	67	1	1	0
Washington	1.000	6	7	1	0	0
Witherspoon	.875	5	7	0	1	0

OREM OWLZ
ROOKIE

PIONEER LEAGUE

Batting	B-T	HT	WT	DOB	AVG	vLH	vRH	G	AB	R	H	2B	3B	HR	RBI	BB	HBP	SH	SF	SO	SB	CS	SLG	OBP
Alliman, Terrell	R-R	6-3	185	10-15-88	.307	.326	.301	61	202	36	62	18	0	0	24	26	1	2	1	27	12	3	.396	.387
Baird, Dillon	L-R	6-3	190	1-13-88	.372	.304	.391	57	215	39	80	17	2	7	49	28	5	0	2	33	1	1	.567	.452
Bass, Justin	B-R	5-11	190	4-6-89	.282	.250	.291	64	234	35	66	16	3	4	34	26	4	4	3	38	6	4	.427	.360
Brannon, Nolan	L-R	6-0	185	7-5-85	.250	.400	.200	7	20	3	5	1	0	0	4	1	0	0	0	2	1	0	.300	.286
Cates, Rich	R-L	5-11	180	12-11-86	.300	.333	.294	63	237	50	71	8	3	1	43	31	6	7	0	38	3	3	.371	.394
Champagnie, Marcel	R-R	5-11	170	10-18-85	.095	.333	.056	7	21	3	2	0	0	0	1	5	0	0	0	5	0	0	.095	.269
Demperio, Michael	R-R	5-10	170	2-17-88	.138	—	.138	12	29	5	4	2	0	0	0	5	1	0	0	9	1	0	.207	.286
Eichelberger, Dan	R-R	6-0	175	12-30-87	.268	.261	.270	35	97	14	26	2	3	0	10	10	2	0	0	32	6	3	.351	.349
Haerther, Casey	R-R	6-2	210	10-5-87	.350	.300	.365	50	206	37	72	18	2	0	35	12	2	2	3	28	0	2	.456	.386
Karcich, Jon	R-R	6-2	195	9-10-87	.235	.220	.240	53	187	37	44	11	0	5	22	30	8	3	1	40	3	1	.374	.363
Mann, Tyler	L-R	6-2	195	7-21-89	.270	.217	.284	36	111	18	30	7	1	2	29	13	2	2	3	55	0	0	.405	.349
Pardo, Braulio	B-R	5-11	180	10-10-86	.230	.100	.258	36	113	12	26	5	0	0	5	9	1	3	0	30	1	0	.274	.293
Ramirez, Carlos	R-R	5-11	205	3-19-88	.376	.406	.368	42	149	34	56	18	0	7	36	35	4	0	2	26	0	0	.638	.500
Ramos, Kevin	R-R	5-11	170	6-6-86	.304	.405	.259	49	181	33	55	18	2	2	28	20	4	6	1	35	6	2	.459	.383
Rife, Jake	L-L	5-11	206	6-7-87	.423	.000	.478	9	26	9	11	3	0	1	5	2	1	0	0	5	2	0	.654	.483
Segura, Jean	R-R	5-11	155	3-17-90	.346	.326	.353	36	162	33	56	10	4	3	21	11	2	1	1	11	11	3	.512	.392
Sierra, Raddy	R-R	6-0	175	9-21-87	.154	.000	.200	5	13	2	2	0	0	1	2	1	1	2	0	5	0	0	.385	.267
Sumi, Ikko	R-R	5-9	200	10-20-87	.232	.385	.186	21	56	5	13	2	0	0	5	6	2	0	0	14	1	0	.268	.328
Wing, Michael	R-R	6-1	180	10-25-88	.315	.250	.333	64	238	42	75	22	4	4	40	31	2	1	2	57	4	1	.492	.396
Witherspoon, Travis	R-R	6-2	190	4-16-89	.227	.278	.215	58	194	37	44	3	6	6	26	10	5	9	1	61	10	1	.397	.281

Pitching	B-T	HT	WT	DOB	W	L	ERA	G	GS	CG	SV	IP	H	R	ER	HR	BB	SO	AVG	vLH	vRH	K/9	BB/9
Almeida, Yeison	R-R	5-11	150	3-30-90	5	0	1.83	27	0	0	6	34	31	15	7	2	10	40	.237	.295	.207	10.49	2.62
Andrew, Carson	R-R	6-2	205	10-7-87	1	0	2.68	19	5	0	2	50	55	18	15	3	14	40	.281	.294	.273	7.15	2.50
Arenas, Orangel	R-R	6-0	165	3-31-89	4	3	4.65	15	15	0	0	70	76	44	36	7	18	48	.281	.305	.267	6.20	2.33
Bachanov, Jon	R-R	6-4	210	1-30-89	0	0	2.70	2	0	0	0	3	5	1	1	0	1	5	.333	.333	.333	13.50	2.70
Berg, Jeremy	R-R	6-0	180	7-17-86	5	0	1.35	15	0	0	0	27	19	5	4	1	2	24	.204	.227	.197	8.10	0.68
Boshiers, Buddy	L-L	6-3	205	5-9-88	2	1	2.55	5	5	0	0	25	24	11	7	2	8	23	.247	.250	.246	8.39	2.92
Cabrera, Francis	R-R	6-1	184	5-27-87	2	1	2.78	11	0	0	0	23	16	7	7	1	13	20	.208	.267	.170	7.94	5.16
Carpenter, David	R-R	6-3	185	9-1-87	2	2	2.36	25	0	0	8	34	26	12	9	2	11	42	.202	.222	.194	11.01	2.88
Clerici, Adam	L-R	6-5	215	10-4-85	2	1	3.70	16	0	0	0	24	25	11	10	2	6	23	.253	.385	.205	8.51	2.22
Corbin, Pat	L-L	6-3	165	7-19-89	4	2	5.05	13	12	0	0	46	59	34	26	6	11	46	.291	.205	.311	8.94	2.14
Dorado, Reyes	L-R	6-1	195	1-10-86	1	1	9.19	9	0	0	0	16	22	20	16	2	5	18	.301	.353	.256	10.34	2.87
Garrett, Jonathan	R-R	6-3	200	3-31-86	5	1	4.06	22	0	0	2	38	46	22	17	1	9	28	.291	.340	.267	6.69	2.15
Gonzalez, Abraham	R-R	5-11	185	12-13-86	1	1	9.00	5	0	0	0	6	10	7	6	1	2	7	.370	.308	.429	10.50	3.00
Graham, Caleb	R-R	6-2	201	1-18-87	0	1	8.31	4	1	0	0	9	12	8	8	4	1	7	.324	.385	.292	7.27	1.04
Hurst, Kyle	R-R	6-4	230	8-23-85	0	0	9.00	1	0	0	0	2	2	2	2	1	1	3	.250	1.000	.143	13.50	4.50
Kehrer, Tyler	L-L	6-3	210	3-22-88	3	3	4.75	14	14	0	0	55	57	36	29	6	22	57	.266	.179	.286	9.33	3.60
Kelly, T.J.	R-R	6-2	240	9-27-87	0	1	4.50	6	0	0	0	12	12	7	6	1	4	8	.245	.292	.200	6.00	3.00
Kinzer, Taylor	R-R	6-3	213	1-7-88	0	0	6.04	17	0	0	1	28	41	24	19	2	13	26	.342	.340	.343	8.26	4.13
Locke, Stephen	L-L	6-1	188	5-6-86	6	4	4.02	15	14	0	0	69	70	40	31	9	11	46	.261	.219	.275	5.97	1.43
Martinez, Fabio	R-R	6-3	190	10-29-89	1	0	3.86	2	2	0	0	7	5	4	3	2	2	10	.192	.333	.118	12.86	2.57
Piazza, Mike	R-R	6-4	205	11-24-86	2	1	2.01	16	0	0	0	31	32	8	7	3	15	30	.271	.286	.263	8.62	4.31
Richards, Garrett	R-R	6-3	210	5-27-88	3	1	1.53	8	8	0	0	35	37	6	6	0	4	30	.278	.359	.245	7.64	1.02
Roberson, Kyle	R-R	6-2	205	3-21-87	1	1	4.61	19	0	0	1	27	24	14	14	2	13	23	.238	.250	.230	7.57	4.28
Skaggs, Tyler	L-L	6-4	180	7-13-91	0	0	4.50	2	0	0	0	4	5	4	2	0	1	6	.278	.250	.300	13.50	2.25

Fielding

Catcher	PCT	G	PO	A	E	DP	PB
Brannon	.960	6	21	3	1	0	0
Pardo	.979	36	237	40	6	1	4
Ramirez	.993	32	257	20	2	3	3
Sumi	.989	15	80	7	1	0	2

First Base	PCT	G	PO	A	E	DP
Baird	.993	56	525	34	4	40
Mann	.981	26	192	12	4	16

Second Base	PCT	G	PO	A	E	DP
Demperio	.976	11	20	20	1	4
Ramos	.956	35	60	91	7	22

	PCT	G	PO	A	E	DP
Segura	.963	36	63	117	7	20

Third Base	PCT	G	PO	A	E	DP
Haerther	.904	42	20	84	11	5
Ramos	.893	13	5	20	3	0
Wing	.909	27	19	51	7	2

Shortstop	PCT	G	PO	A	E	DP
Karcich	.942	53	92	170	16	30
Ramos	.857	1	4	2	1	1
Wing	.886	24	29	88	15	16

Outfield	PCT	G	PO	A	E	DP
Alliman	.951	60	89	8	5	1
Bass	.914	32	27	5	3	0
Cates	.948	62	85	6	5	1
Champagnie	1.000	6	11	1	0	0

Eichelberger	.912	28	30	1	3	0
Rife	1.000	7	11	0	0	0
Sierra	.917	4	11	0	1	0
Witherspoon	.983	56	109	5	2	1

DSL ANGELS   ROOKIE

DOMINICAN SUMMER LEAGUE

Batting	B-T	HT	WT	DOB	AVG	vLH	vRH	G	AB	R	H	2B	3B	HR	RBI	BB	HBP	SH	SF	SO	SB	CS	SLG	OBP
Adames, Waskal	R-R	5-11	195	2-28-89	.282	.222	.299	48	170	42	48	10	1	3	27	17	2	1	2	36	20	6	.406	.351
Batista, Hamsem	L-L	6-2	195	7-12-90	.161	.222	.136	13	31	2	5	1	0	0	4	3	0	0	0	13	2	3	.194	.235
Beltran, Glenn	R-R	6-2	220	12-23-91	.193	.125	.208	30	88	13	17	6	0	0	7	3	5	0	0	33	0	1	.261	.260
Diaz, Jairo	R-R	6-0	195	5-27-91	.118	.105	.122	24	68	5	8	2	0	0	5	15	4	1	0	26	0	2	.147	.310
Dionicio, Ismael	B-R	5-10	165	7-19-91	.206	.077	.247	36	107	19	22	5	1	0	5	16	2	1	0	30	8	4	.271	.320
Dubeau, Jose	R-R	6-1	200	4-22-91	.150	.111	.157	19	60	5	9	2	0	0	7	0	0	2	0	28	0	0	.183	.145
Garcia, Sergio	R-R	6-1	185	9-20-90	.246	.233	.248	50	179	25	44	12	1	3	36	17	3	1	3	42	23	7	.374	.317
Grance, Moises	R-R	5-11	160	12-1-91	.214	.192	.219	44	140	22	30	5	1	0	14	17	2	2	1	33	6	2	.264	.306
Hernandez, Jonattan	B-R	5-11	175	7-11-90	.000	.000	.000	4	9	1	0	0	0	0	0	1	0	0	0	3	0	0	.000	.100
Linares, Raul	B-R	5-11	160	10-4-90	.225	.219	.227	49	151	22	34	4	5	0	16	13	3	5	1	38	8	3	.318	.298
Lugo, Carlos	R-R	6-0	190	11-20-89	.168	.121	.181	48	149	18	25	4	1	0	12	13	3	5	0	47	5	1	.228	.248
Martinez, Joaquin	R-R	6-1	195	6-1-90	.279	.368	.259	32	104	11	29	5	0	0	13	11	0	4	1	23	0	3	.327	.345
Orozco, Jose	L-L	5-10	170	10-17-90	.168	.031	.205	44	149	15	25	6	5	2	20	15	1	3	2	29	3	2	.315	.246
Piron, Lorenzo	R-L	6-0	200	8-25-90	.186	.240	.169	34	102	9	19	7	0	1	10	12	6	0	1	23	1	3	.284	.306
Rodriguez, Angel	R-R	5-10	170	4-28-92	.248	.161	.273	43	141	18	35	5	2	0	7	11	2	4	0	23	2	2	.312	.312
Rodriguez, Domingo	R-R	6-2	190	10-28-91	.208	.000	.263	11	24	3	5	1	0	0	6	0	2	0	0	12	3	1	.250	.367
Rodriguez, Jose	R-R	6-4	190	3-10-90	.145	.071	.161	25	76	9	11	3	1	0	2	3	1	0	0	31	2	0	.211	.188
Suriel, Alexander	B-L	6-2	190	9-27-90	.188	.036	.227	44	138	13	26	9	1	0	16	33	2	2	2	43	4	5	.268	.349
Toribio, Pedro	R-R	5-10	158	7-21-90	.250	.136	.283	55	196	37	49	5	6	1	23	28	2	1	3	33	21	6	.352	.345

Pitching	B-T	HT	WT	DOB	W	L	ERA	G	GS	CG	SV	IP	H	R	ER	HR	BB	SO	AVG	vLH	vRH	K/9	BB/9
Araujo, Joan	R-L	6-3	170	4-22-91	1	1	3.38	13	1	0	0	16	16	16	6	0	17	17	.235	.200	.238	9.56	9.56
Cedano, Rikelvin	R-R	5-10	155	10-22-89	0	1	4.50	4	0	0	1	6	4	5	3	0	4	11	.174	.000		16.50	6.50
Cruz, Junior	R-R	6-1	180	4-5-90	5	8	3.24	15	15	1	0	89	81	48	32	1	42	42	.244	.264	.237	4.25	4.25
De La Cruz, Cesar	L-L	6-5	215	2-20-91	0	0	7.59	7	0	0	0	11	5	12	9	0	23	9	.156	.000	.179	7.59	19.41
Garcia, Franklin	R-R	6-3	195	3-23-90	0	3	3.38	13	4	0	1	35	29	19	13	0	17	24	.223	.222	.223	6.23	4.41
Gomez, Jordany	R-R	6-3	180	9-1-90	1	2	3.94	15	0	0	2	30	28	18	13	0	17	34	.239	.280	.228	10.31	5.16
Hurtado, Daniel	R-R	6-3	180	7-25-92	1	3	4.50	14	1	0	2	24	27	19	12	1	10	17	.278	.316	.269	6.38	3.75
Jimenez, Eswarlin	L-L	6-1	187	11-27-91	5	3	2.57	15	15	0	0	88	77	37	25	1	20	55	.233	.290	.227	5.65	2.05
Mesa, Renedin	R-R	6-3	185	10-10-91	2	3	4.36	8	8	0	0	43	43	26	21	2	27	24	.276	.318	.269	4.98	5.61
Perez, Gabriel	R-R	6-0	185	6-3-91	8	2	2.22	14	14	0	0	89	63	27	22	1	27	70	.199	.170	.211	7.05	2.72
Pichardo, Pedro	R-R	6-1	190	7-16-88	2	0	2.25	12	0	0	3	16	13	5	4	1	7	10	.224	.333	.204	5.63	3.94
Santiago, Yancarlos	L-L	6-0	180	1-23-91	2	1	1.91	16	6	0	1	47	37	13	10	0	19	43	.218	.125	.227	8.23	3.64
Santos, Edward	R-R	6-2	220	10-22-89	0	4	5.08	17	0	0	1	28	29	16	16	1	15	18	.279	.304	.272	5.72	4.76
Toribio, Roberto	R-R	6-0	180	11-2-89	0	3	3.91	14	0	0	1	25	24	15	11	0	20	18	.255	.176	.273	6.39	7.11

Fielding

Catcher	PCT	G	PO	A	E	DP	PB
Diaz	.970	22	148	11	5	0	13
Hernandez	1.000	1	1	0	0	0	0
Lugo	.961	47	276	42	13	2	7

First Base	PCT	G	PO	A	E	DP
Dubeau	.979	7	44	3	1	2
Rodriguez	1.000	19	165	5	0	14
Suriel	.985	44	386	18	6	32

Second Base	PCT	G	PO	A	E	DP
Dionicio	.971	20	55	47	3	12

Grance	.989	16	47	45	1	10
Linares	.951	27	88	68	8	14
Rodriguez	.875	4	8	6	2	0

Third Base	PCT	G	PO	A	E	DP
Grance	.923	6	2	10	1	1
Linares	.860	13	18	31	8	3
Piron	.800	15	11	29	10	1
Rodriguez	.888	38	29	90	15	4

Shortstop	PCT	G	PO	A	E	DP
Grance	.908	18	22	57	8	11

Rodriguez	1.000	1	1	1	0	0
Toribio	.936	51	78	172	17	25

Outfield	PCT	G	PO	A	E	DP
Adames	.982	39	52	3	1	0
Batista	.750	10	8	1	3	0
Beltran	1.000	28	28	2	0	0
Garcia	.910	50	83	8	9	0
Martinez	.969	31	56	6	2	1
Orozco	.973	42	67	6	2	2
Rodriguez	1.000	11	18	2	0	2

Los Angeles Dodgers

SEASON IN A SENTENCE: The Dodgers completed their second straight run to the National League Championship Series (and second straight 4-1 series loss to the Phillies) and made their fourth playoff appearance in the last six years, though the suspension of Manny Ramirez and domestic problems of the team's ownership took some of the shine off an otherwise sterling year.

HIGH POINT: Los Angeles led the NL West nearly wire-to-wire, running off an eight-game win streak after a 2-3 start and never looking back. A young, talented team got as high as 31 games above .500, and the final 95-67 record was the franchise's best since 1985.

LOW POINT: Falling short of the World Series again was a bummer, but couldn't compare to the disappointment of Ramirez's 50-game suspension in early May. The benefit was that it shined the spotlight on young players like outfielders Andre Ethier and Matt Kemp and righthanders Chad Billingsley and Clayton Kershaw, and the team didn't lose any ground during Manny's absence. The bitter, public divorce battle between Frank and Jamie McCourt after the season at best was embarrassing and at worst threatened the stability of the franchise.

NOTABLE ROOKIES: While the Dodgers are built around a homegrown core, they didn't get many contributions from rookies in 2009. The exceptions were righthanders Ronald Belisario and James McDonald. Belisario made 69 appearances compiled a 2.04 ERA. McDonald couldn't hold down a rotation spot (which the Dodgers struggled all year to fill) but ended up contributing as a middle reliever, with a 4.00 ERA in 63 innings.

KEY TRANSACTIONS: Signing free agents Orlando Hudson and Randy Wolf and re-signing Rafael Furcal and Ramirez before the season were important, and Los Angeles traded for veterans Jon Garland, George Sherrill and Jim Thome to bolster the roster, but the biggest find came when they grabbed Vicente Padilla off the scrap heap after the Rangers released him in August. Padilla went 4-0, 3.20 in seven regular season starts, then made three playoff starts, including seven shutout innings against the Cardinals in the Division Series.

DOWN ON THE FARM: Trades and graduation have thinned out the Dodgers farm system, but good news came when hard-throwing righthander Chris Withrow pitched 114 innings, after compiling just 13 in his first season and a half.

OPENING DAY PAYROLL: $100,414,592

PLAYERS OF THE YEAR

JON SOOHOO/LA DODGERS

MAJOR LEAGUE	**MINOR LEAGUE**
Andre Ethier of	**Trayvon Robinson** of
.272/.361/.508	(High A/Double-A)
31 HR, 106 RBI, won first Silver Slugger	.300/.373/.493 29 2B, 17 HR, 47 SB

ORGANIZATION LEADERS

BATTING		*Minimum 250 at-bats
MAJORS		
*AVG	Matt Kemp	.297
*OPS	Andre Ethier	.869
HR	Andre Ethier	31
RBI	Andre Ethier	106
MINORS		
*AVG	Tomlin, James, Chattanooga	.315
R	Pedroza, Jaime, Great Lakes	100
H	Gordon, Dee, Great Lakes	162
TB	Van Slyke, Scott, Inland Empire/Albuquerque	266
2B	Van Slyke, Scott, Inland Empire/Albuquerque	42
3B	Gordon, Dee, Great Lakes	12
HR	Jones, Mitch, Albuquerque	35
RBI	Jones, Mitch, Albuquerque	103
BB	Pedroza, Jaime, Great Lakes	78
SO	Russell, Kyle, Great Lakes	180
SB	Gordon, Dee, Great Lakes	73
*OBP	Tomlin, James, Chattanooga	.401
*SLG	Jones, Mitch, Albuquerque	.651

PITCHING		†Minimum 75 innings
MAJORS		
W	Chad Billingsley	12
†ERA	Clayton Kershaw	2.79
SO	Clayton Kershaw	185
MINORS		
W	Redding, Jon Michael, Great Lakes	16
L	Miller, Justin, Great Lakes/Inland Empire	14
	Sexton, Timothy, Inland Empire	14
†ERA	Alvarado, Giancarlo, Albuquerque	3.49
G	Guerra, Javy, Great Lakes/Chattanooga	51
GS	Miller, Justin, Great Lakes/Inland Empire	28
SV	Strickland, Scott, Albuquerque	32
IP	Sexton, Timothy, Inland Empire	157
BB	Adkins, James, Chattanooga	72
SO	Alvarado, Giancarlo, Albuquerque	139
†AVG	Alvarado, Giancarlo, Albuquerque	.240

General Manager: Ned Colletti. **Farm Director:** De Jon Watson. **Scouting Director:** Logan White.

Class	Team	League	W	L	PCT	Finish*	Manager(s)
Majors	Los Angeles Dodgers	National	95	67	.586	1st (16)	Joe Torre
Triple-A	Albuquerque Isotopes	Pacific Coast	80	64	.556	2nd (16)	Tim Wallach
Double-A	Chattanooga Lookouts	Southern	65	74	.468	t-6th (10)	John Valentin
High A	Inland Empire 66ers	California	59	81	.421	9th (10)	Carlos Subero
Low A	Great Lakes Loons	Midwest	81	59	.579	t-3rd (14)	Juan Bustabad
Rookie	AZL Dodgers	Arizona	24	32	.429	t-8th (11)	Jeff Carter
Rookie	Ogden Raptors	Pioneer	42	34	.553	4th (8)	Damon Berryhill
Overall 2009 Minor League Record			351	344	.505	15th (30)	

*Finish in overall standings (No. of teams in league). †League champion.

ORGANIZATION STATISTICS

LOS ANGELES DODGERS

NATIONAL LEAGUE

Batting	B-T	HT	WT	DOB	AVG	vLH	vRH	G	AB	R	H	2B	3B	HR	RBI	BB	HBP	SH	SF	SO	SB	CS	SLG	OBP
Abreu, Tony	B-R	5-9	200	11-13-84	.250	—	.250	6	8	0	2	0	0	0	1	3	0	0	0	2	0	1	.250	.455
Ausmus, Brad	R-R	5-11	190	4-14-69	.295	.286	.299	36	95	9	28	4	0	1	9	5	2	5	0	21	1	0	.368	.343
Belliard, Ronnie	R-R	5-10	210	4-7-75	.351	.467	.323	24	77	13	27	7	0	5	17	6	0	0	0	16	1	0	.636	.398
2-team total (86 Washington)					.277	—	—	110	264	39	73	14	1	10	39	20	0	1	2	56	3	0	.451	.325
Blake, Casey	R-R	6-2	205	8-23-73	.280	.320	.270	139	485	84	136	25	6	18	79	63	6	1	10	116	3	4	.468	.363
Castro, Juan	R-R	5-11	190	6-20-72	.277	.240	.287	57	112	18	31	4	0	1	9	6	0	2	1	25	0	0	.339	.311
DeWitt, Blake	L-R	5-11	205	8-20-85	.204	.200	.205	31	49	4	10	3	0	2	4	3	0	0	1	7	0	0	.388	.245
Ellis, A.J.	R-R	6-2	225	4-9-81	.100	.000	.125	8	10	0	1	0	0	0	1	0	0	0	0	1	0	0	.100	.100
Ethier, Andre	L-L	6-2	210	4-10-82	.272	.194	.302	160	596	92	162	42	3	31	106	72	13	0	4	116	6	4	.508	.361
Furcal, Rafael	B-R	5-8	185	10-24-77	.269	.296	.261	150	613	92	165	28	5	9	47	61	1	3	2	89	12	6	.375	.335
Hoffmann, Jamie	R-R	6-3	235	8-20-84	.182	.167	.188	14	22	2	4	2	0	1	7	0	0	0	2	5	0	0	.409	.167
Hu, Chin-Lung	R-R	5-11	195	2-2-84	.400	—	.400	5	5	2	2	1	0	0	2	0	0	0	1	2	0	0	.600	.333
Hudson, Orlando	B-R	6-0	190	12-12-77	.283	.293	.280	149	551	74	156	35	6	9	62	62	4	9	5	99	8	1	.417	.357
Jones, Mitch	R-R	6-5	215	10-15-77	.308	.286	.333	8	13	1	4	1	0	0	0	0	2	0	0	6	0	0	.385	.400
Kemp, Matt	R-R	6-2	225	9-23-84	.297	.362	.278	159	606	97	180	25	7	26	101	52	3	6	139	34	8		.490	.352
Loney, James	L-L	6-3	220	5-7-84	.281	.274	.283	158	576	73	162	25	2	13	90	70	0	1	4	68	7	3	.399	.357
Loretta, Mark	R-R	6-0	200	8-14-71	.232	.273	.214	107	181	19	42	8	0	0	25	20	1	0	2	21	1	1	.276	.309
Martin, Russell	R-R	5-10	210	2-15-83	.250	.275	.243	143	505	63	126	19	0	7	53	69	11	2	1	80	11	6	.329	.352
Mientkiewicz, Doug	L-R	6-0	210	6-19-74	.333	.333	.333	20	18	0	6	1	0	0	3	1	1	0	0	6	0	0	.389	.400
Paul, Xavier	L-R	5-9	205	2-25-85	.214	.200	.222	11	14	3	3	1	0	1	1	2	0	0	0	4	0	1	.500	.313
Pierre, Juan	L-L	5-10	185	8-14-77	.308	.320	.304	145	380	57	117	16	8	0	31	27	8	9	1	27	30	12	.392	.365
Ramirez, Manny	R-R	6-0	200	5-30-72	.290	.270	.295	104	352	62	102	24	2	19	63	71	7	0	1	81	0	1	.531	.418
Repko, Jason	R-R	5-10	190	12-27-80	.000	.000	.000	10	5	1	0	0	0	0	0	1	0	1	0	2	1	0	.000	.143
Thome, Jim	L-R	6-3	250	8-27-70	.235	.000	.286	17	17	0	4	0	0	0	3	0	0	0	0	7	0	0	.235	.235

Pitching	B-T	HT	WT	DOB	W	L	ERA	G	GS	CG	SV	IP	H	R	ER	HR	BB	SO	AVG	vLH	vRH	K/9	BB/9
Belisario, Ronald	R-R	6-3	235	12-31-82	4	3	2.04	69	0	0	0	71	52	21	16	4	29	64	.201	.270	.157	8.15	3.69
Billingsley, Chad	R-R	6-1	245	7-29-84	12	11	4.03	33	32	0	0	196	173	94	88	17	86	179	.244	.257	.229	8.21	3.94
Broxton, Jonathan	R-R	6-4	295	6-16-84	7	2	2.61	73	0	0	36	76	44	24	22	4	29	114	.165	.138	.190	13.50	3.43
Elbert, Scott	L-L	6-1	215	8-13-85	2	0	5.03	19	0	0	0	20	19	11	11	4	7	21	.253	.222	.282	9.61	3.20
Garland, Jon	R-R	6-6	210	9-27-79	3	2	2.72	6	6	0	0	36	37	16	11	4	9	26	.262	.269	.257	6.44	2.23
2-team total (27 Arizona)					11	13	4.01	33	33	1	0	204	225	106	91	23	61	109	—	—	—	4.81	2.69
Haeger, Charlie	R-R	6-1	210	9-19-83	1	1	3.32	6	3	0	0	19	13	7	7	4	7	15	.188	.125	.222	7.11	3.32
Kershaw, Clayton	L-L	6-3	225	3-19-88	8	8	2.79	31	30	0	0	171	119	55	53	7	91	185	.200	.173	.208	9.74	4.79
Kuo, Hong-Chih	L-L	6-1	240	7-23-81	2	0	3.00	35	0	0	0	30	21	10	10	2	13	32	.198	.152	.219	9.60	3.90
Kuroda, Hiroki	R-R	6-1	220	2-10-75	8	7	3.76	21	20	0	0	117	110	59	49	12	24	87	.243	.233	.253	6.67	1.84
Leach, Brent	L-L	6-4	220	11-18-82	2	0	5.75	38	0	0	0	20	16	13	13	3	12	19	.213	.256	.156	8.41	5.31
McDonald, James	L-R	6-5	195	10-19-84	5	5	4.00	45	4	0	0	63	60	34	28	6	34	54	.254	.213	.282	7.71	4.86
Milton, Eric	L-L	6-1	220	8-4-75	2	1	3.80	5	5	0	0	24	30	12	10	2	6	20	.303	.281	.313	7.61	2.28
Mota, Guillermo	R-R	6-5	235	7-25-73	3	4	3.44	61	0	0	0	65	53	25	25	6	24	39	.224	.202	.238	5.37	3.31
Ohman, Will	L-L	6-2	210	8-13-77	1	0	5.84	21	0	0	1	12	12	8	8	4	8	7	.261	.296	.211	5.11	5.84
Padilla, Vicente	R-R	6-2	220	9-27-77	4	0	3.20	8	7	0	0	39	36	15	14	4	12	38	.252	.256	.246	8.69	2.75
Schlichting, Travis	R-R	6-4	215	10-19-84	0	0	3.38	2	0	0	0	3	1	2	1	1	5	2	.111	.143	.000	6.75	16.88
Schmidt, Jason	R-R	6-5	220	1-29-73	2	2	5.60	4	4	0	0	18	16	12	11	1	12	8	.239	.226	.250	4.08	6.11
Sherrill, George	L-L	6-0	230	4-19-77	1	0	0.65	30	0	0	1	28	19	2	2	1	11	22	.192	.121	.227	7.16	3.58
Stults, Eric	L-L	6-1	220	12-9-79	4	3	4.86	10	10	1	0	50	51	27	27	3	26	33	.268	.262	.270	5.94	4.68
Troncoso, Ramon	R-R	6-1	220	2-16-83	5	4	2.72	73	0	0	6	83	83	30	25	3	34	55	.268	.289	.251	5.99	3.70
Vargas, Claudio	R-R	6-4	235	6-19-78	0	0	1.64	8	0	0	0	11	7	2	2	1	4	10	.184	.267	.130	8.18	3.27
2-team total (28 Milwaukee)					1	0	1.74	36	0	0	0	41	25	8	8	3	15	30	—	—	—	6.53	3.27
Wade, Cory	R-R	6-1	190	5-28-83	2	3	5.53	27	0	0	0	28	28	17	17	3	10	18	.257	.283	.238	5.86	3.25
Weaver, Jeff	R-R	6-5	200	8-22-76	6	4	3.65	28	7	0	0	79	87	34	32	7	33	64	.281	.286	.277	7.29	3.76
Wolf, Randy	L-L	5-10	200	8-22-76	11	7	3.23	34	34	0	0	214	178	81	77	24	58	160	.227	.159	.246	6.72	2.44

Fielding

Catcher	PCT	G	PO	A	E	DP	PB
Ausmus	1.000	30	203	11	0	1	2
Ellis	1.000	7	36	2	0	0	0
Martin	.994	137	1039	87	7	9	3

First Base	PCT	G	PO	A	E	DP
Blake	1.000	2	2	0	0	0
Loney	.995	155	1269	85	7	110
Loretta	1.000	17	122	9	0	12
Mientkiewicz	1.000	4	9	0	0	0

Second Base	PCT	G	PO	A	E	DP
Abreu	1.000	1	4	3	0	1
Belliard	.968	10	11	19	1	6
Castro	.964	20	29	24	2	7
DeWitt	1.000	2	2	1	0	0
Hudson	.988	145	325	359	8	77
Loretta	1.000	3	2	2	0	1

Third Base	PCT	G	PO	A	E	DP
Abreu	1.000	1	1	3	0	0
Belliard	1.000	10	8	13	0	1
Blake	.973	134	99	263	10	32
Castro	1.000	8	2	5	0	0
DeWitt	.947	14	5	13	1	1
Loretta	.955	23	11	31	2	3
Martin	—	1	0	0	0	0

Shortstop	PCT	G	PO	A	E	DP
Castro	.983	28	20	39	1	6
DeWitt	1.000	2	1	2	0	0
Furcal	.968	149	187	419	20	76
Hu	1.000	3	1	1	0	0

Outfield	PCT	G	PO	A	E	DP
Blake	—	2	0	0	0	0
Castro	—	2	0	0	0	0
Ethier	.976	158	279	6	7	0
Hoffmann	1.000	5	10	1	0	1
Jones	1.000	1	2	0	0	0
Kemp	.995	158	377	14	2	4
Paul	1.000	4	2	0	0	0
Pierre	.994	103	156	1	1	0
Ramirez	.973	101	139	3	4	0
Repko	1.000	7	3	0	0	0

ALBUQUERQUE ISOTOPES   TRIPLE-A
PACIFIC COAST LEAGUE

Batting	B-T	HT	WT	DOB	AVG	vLH	vRH	G	AB	R	H	2B	3B	HR	RBI	BB	HBP	SH	SF	SO	SB	CS	SLG	OBP
Abreu, Tony	B-R	5-9	200	11-13-84	.353	.357	.351	54	218	36	77	18	3	11	48	12	1	2	3	37	3	1	.615	.385
Ardoin, Danny	R-R	6-0	225	7-8-74	.269	.182	.293	30	104	11	28	7	1	0	10	5	1	0	0	19	0	1	.356	.309
Arp, Ryan	R-R	6-0	185	11-16-85	.000	—	.000	1	1	0	0	0	0	0	0	0	0	0	0	1	0	0	.000	.000
Brown, Dee	L-R	6-0	235	3-27-78	.290	.233	.311	121	396	79	115	35	0	19	80	57	3	2	2	63	9	3	.523	.382
Castro, Juan	R-R	5-11	190	6-20-72	.182	.167	.200	3	11	1	2	0	0	0	0	0	0	0	0	3	0	0	.182	.182
Closser, J.D.	B-R	5-10	200	1-15-80	.295	.250	.324	69	220	28	65	14	0	2	31	29	0	1	2	41	4	3	.386	.375
DeWitt, Blake	L-R	5-11	205	8-20-85	.256	.279	.246	92	352	64	90	21	9	7	47	48	4	0	3	44	2	2	.426	.349
Ellis, A.J.	R-R	6-2	225	4-9-81	.314	.253	.340	90	283	48	89	13	2	0	39	64	3	4	6	44	2	2	.375	.438
Garcia, Sergio	R-R	5-10	170	3-29-80	.232	.200	.247	85	211	32	49	12	0	1	14	23	5	11	3	34	1	1	.303	.318
Gonzalez, Juan	B-R	6-0	160	2-23-82	.256	.154	.304	29	82	11	21	4	0	0	9	11	0	2	1	16	3	0	.305	.340
Griffin, John-Ford	L-L	6-2	215	11-19-79	.122	.000	.147	16	41	1	5	2	0	0	3	0	1	0	0	13	1	0	.171	.143
2-team total (89 Iowa)					.268	—	—	105	340	39	91	29	3	5	40	36	5	0	5	87	5	2	.415	.342
Harper, Brett	L-R	6-2	245	7-31-81	.363	.409	.345	24	80	11	29	7	0	4	16	5	1	0	2	8	0	0	.500	.398
2-team total (79 Las Vegas)					.292	—	—	103	390	46	114	25	1	19	71	26	1	0	6	48	0	0	.508	.333
Hoffmann, Jamie	R-R	6-3	235	8-20-84	.284	.282	.285	68	257	44	73	14	3	8	48	32	0	1	3	37	10	8	.455	.360
Hu, Chin-Lung	R-R	5-11	195	2-2-84	.294	.277	.303	130	496	66	146	21	5	6	53	25	5	14	4	54	14	5	.393	.332
Jansen, Kenley	B-R	6-2	220	9-30-87	.185	.000	.294	8	27	1	5	0	0	2	1	0	0	0	7	0	0	.185	.214
Jones, Mitch	R-R	6-0	215	10-15-77	.297	.298	.297	108	387	72	115	26	3	35	103	40	0	3	4	102	9	3	.651	.364
Luna, Hector	R-R	6-0	225	2-1-80	.351	.430	.318	91	313	59	110	18	6	17	62	28	7	0	2	52	4	2	.610	.414
Maza, Luis	R-R	5-8	195	6-20-80	.300	.245	.327	100	327	55	98	19	4	5	44	17	5	2	4	40	0	1	.428	.340
Mientkiewicz, Doug	L-R	6-0	210	6-19-74	.306	.375	.273	11	49	9	15	6	1	1	10	1	0	0	2	6	0	0	.531	.308
Pascucci, Val	R-R	6-6	270	11-17-78	.211	.114	.240	61	194	31	41	8	1	8	29	34	2	0	1	55	2	0	.387	.333
2-team total (65 Portland)					.248	—	—	126	436	62	108	25	2	19	77	66	4	0	5	119	3	0	.445	.348
Paul, Xavier	L-R	5-9	205	2-25-85	.328	.241	.356	31	116	13	38	10	2	2	16	10	0	2	1	22	8	2	.500	.378
Ramirez, Manny	R-R	6-0	200	5-30-72	.000	.000	.000	2	3	0	0	0	0	0	0	1	0	0	0	1	0	0	.000	.250
Repko, Jason	R-R	5-10	190	12-27-80	.277	.298	.268	110	393	70	109	20	4	16	47	28	5	2	5	81	24	7	.471	.329
Rosario, Jovanny	B-R	5-9	160	4-12-85	.264	.219	.284	51	106	15	28	1	2	1	4	1	0	9	0	15	4	1	.340	.271
Rose, Mike	B-R	6-1	225	8-25-76	.000	—	.000	5	8	0	0	0	0	0	0	0	0	0	0	3	0	0	.000	.000
Van Slyke, Scott	R-R	6-5	195	7-24-86	.167	.000	.250	3	6	1	1	0	0	0	0	2	0	0	1	0	0	0	.167	.375
Young, Delwyn	B-R	5-10	190	6-30-82	.111	.000	.167	3	9	1	0	0	0	0	1	0	0	0	2	0	0	.111	.200

Pitching	B-T	HT	WT	DOB	W	L	ERA	G	GS	CG	SV	IP	H	R	ER	HR	BB	SO	AVG	vLH	vRH	K/9	BB/9
Alvarado, Carlo	R-R	6-0	210	1-24-78	13	10	3.49	27	25	1	0	152	139	65	59	17	51	139	.240	.269	.213	8.21	3.01
Arias, Marlon	L-L	6-3	150	9-1-84	0	0	11.37	5	0	0	0	6	8	8	8	3	5	7	.308	.200	.333	9.95	7.11
Bastardo, Alberto	L-L	6-0	160	4-6-84	0	0	0.00	1	0	0	0	1	2	0	0	0	0	1	.400	.333	.500	9.00	0.00
Bonilla, Henry	R-R	6-0	190	8-16-78	3	11	6.03	41	5	0	3	78	90	55	52	7	29	59	.295	.286	.302	6.84	3.36
Cali, Carmen	L-L	5-8	220	11-2-78	0	2	4.22	9	0	0	0	11	17	5	5	1	2	11	.354	.333	.361	11.81	1.69
Choi, Hyang-Nam	R-R	6-2	190	3-28-71	9	2	2.34	33	0	0	0	58	51	18	15	6	21	77	.236	.329	.182	12.02	3.28
Corcoran, Tim	R-R	6-2	205	4-15-78	2	0	4.71	6	5	0	0	29	25	16	15	2	12	26	.240	.184	.291	8.16	3.77
DeBarr, Nick	R-R	6-3	245	8-24-83	2	0	7.36	23	0	0	0	29	39	25	24	8	12	25	.317	.362	.277	7.67	3.68
Durbin, J.D.	R-R	6-0	210	2-24-82	0	6	6.43	10	9	0	0	49	55	41	35	6	30	35	.282	.333	.229	6.43	5.51
Elbert, Scott	L-L	6-1	215	8-13-85	2	1	3.74	8	7	1	0	34	34	16	14	2	14	38	.262	.250	.264	10.16	3.74
Estes, Shawn	R-L	6-0	205	2-18-73	3	4	3.07	13	13	2	0	73	73	27	25	3	27	40	.264	.206	.282	4.91	3.31
Felix, Francisco	R-R	5-11	191	7-28-81	1	0	3.38	14	0	0	1	21	23	8	8	1	7	24	.277	.176	.347	10.13	2.95
Garcia, Harvey	R-R	6-2	220	3-16-84	0	1	10.80	2	0	0	0	2	3	2	2	1	2	1	.500	.333	.667	5.40	10.80
Haeger, Charlie	R-R	6-1	200	9-19-83	11	6	3.55	22	22	4	0	145	134	63	57	16	58	103	.247	.318	.194	6.41	3.61
Kuo, Hong-Chih	L-L	6-1	240	7-23-81	0	0	4.50	2	0	0	0	2	1	1	1	0	1	1	.286	.333	.250	4.50	4.50
Leach, Brent	L-L	6-4	220	11-18-82	2	0	6.75	18	0	0	1	19	17	17	14	2	16	20	.254	.192	.293	9.64	7.71
Lindblom, Josh	R-R	6-5	240	6-15-87	3	0	2.54	20	3	0	1	39	34	11	11	3	12	36	.236	.185	.278	8.31	2.77
Mazone, Brian	L-L	6-2	220	7-26-76	0	1	8.44	13	0	0	0	16	24	15	15	1	8	13	.338	.353	.333	7.31	4.50
McDonald, James	L-R	6-5	195	10-19-84	1	0	3.26	6	6	0	0	30	21	11	11	2	14	40	.196	.158	.217	11.87	4.15
Milton, Eric	L-L	6-1	220	8-4-75	3	2	2.83	7	7	0	0	35	29	12	11	3	6	27	.225	.148	.245	6.94	1.54
Ohman, Will	L-L	6-2	210	8-13-77	0	0	1.17	8	1	0	0	8	3	1	1	1	3	9	.120	.250	.059	10.57	3.52
Padilla, Vicente	R-R	6-2	220	9-27-77	1	0	3.60	1	1	0	0	5	3	2	2	1	2	5	.167	.143	.182	9.00	5.40

Name	B-T	HT	WT	DOB	W	L	ERA	G	GS	CG	SV	IP	H	R	ER	HR	BB	SO	AVG	vLH	vRH	K/9	BB/9
Pinango, Miguel	R-R	6-1	190	1-20-83	2	5	7.55	11	11	0	0	54	73	49	45	8	18	30	.332	.307	.358	5.03	3.02
Pollok, Dwayne	R-R	6-3	195	11-12-80	3	4	6.01	36	6	0	0	76	91	61	51	13	23	53	.296	.293	.300	6.25	2.71
Randolph, Stephen	L-L	6-3	210	5-1-74	4	2	5.10	19	6	0	0	42	30	24	24	2	29	46	.203	.257	.186	9.78	6.17
2-team total (2 Omaha)					5	3	5.90	21	8	0	0	50	42	33	33	6	38	53	—	—		9.48	6.79
Schlichting, Travis	R-R	6-4	215	10-19-84	1	0	1.42	13	0	0	0	13	8	3	2	0	8	7	.186	.118	.231	4.97	5.68
Schmidt, Jason	R-R	6-5	220	1-29-73	2	0	4.18	6	5	0	0	32	35	16	15	3	7	25	.289	.234	.324	6.96	1.95
Strickland, Scott	R-R	5-10	220	4-26-76	2	1	2.98	50	0	0	32	48	40	18	16	5	23	57	.220	.244	.202	10.61	4.28
Stults, Eric	L-L	6-1	220	12-9-79	5	4	5.20	12	11	0	0	64	86	43	37	5	24	40	.330	.400	.304	5.63	3.38
Sturtze, Tanyon	R-R	6-5	230	10-12-70	0	1	6.14	8	0	0	4	7	9	6	5	1	5	7	.300	.308	.294	8.59	6.14
Threets, Erick	L-L	6-5	240	11-4-81	3	0	1.52	33	0	0	1	41	29	10	7	1	16	28	.203	.176	.217	6.10	3.48
Vargas, Claudio	R-R	6-4	235	6-19-78	0	0	3.46	7	0	0	1	13	15	5	5	3	1	12	.288	.346	.231	8.31	0.69
Wade, Cory	R-R	6-1	190	5-28-83	1	1	6.75	18	0	0	1	23	20	17	17	5	7	19	.235	.158	.298	7.54	2.78
Weaver, Jeff	R-R	6-5	200	8-22-76	1	0	3.55	5	1	0	1	13	11	6	5	1	2	12	.224	.192	.261	8.53	1.42

Fielding

Catcher	PCT	G	PO	A	E	DP	PB
Ardoin	.988	21	151	14	2	0	3
Closser	.982	31	247	20	5	2	2
Ellis	.991	86	633	51	6	2	11
Jansen	1.000	8	55	6	0	1	2
Rose	.944	2	15	2	1	0	0

First Base	PCT	G	PO	A	E	DP
Ardoin	1.000	7	61	3	0	8
Closser	.988	36	229	21	3	20
Garcia	1.000	18	128	13	0	13
Harper	.989	22	161	17	2	15
Jones	.974	13	69	7	2	4
Luna	.975	26	182	14	5	18
Pascucci	.986	47	388	30	6	38

Second Base	PCT	G	PO	A	E	DP
Abreu	.981	35	67	87	3	20
Castro	.900	2	4	5	1	1
DeWitt	.979	45	89	99	4	28

	PCT	G	PO	A	E	DP
Garcia	1.000	13	15	31	0	4
Gonzalez	.980	13	19	31	1	6
Hu	1.000	6	16	19	0	6
Luna	1.000	3	3	14	0	1
Maza	.988	41	64	97	2	21

Third Base	PCT	G	PO	A	E	DP
Abreu	.958	12	5	18	1	3
Ardoin	1.000	1	0	2	0	0
Closser	—	1	0	0	0	0
DeWitt	.976	39	25	58	2	3
Garcia	.974	23	10	27	1	3
Gonzalez	1.000	10	6	15	0	2
Jones	.800	3	1	3	1	0
Luna	.949	56	21	91	6	8
Maza	.938	15	11	19	2	1

Shortstop	PCT	G	PO	A	E	DP
Abreu	.900	7	7	11	2	3
Castro	1.000	1	4	4	0	3

	PCT	G	PO	A	E	DP
DeWitt	.935	7	11	18	2	5
Garcia	.959	14	20	27	2	6
Hu	.977	120	182	335	12	68

Outfield	PCT	G	PO	A	E	DP
Brown	.970	97	125	4	4	1
Closser	1.000	1	3	0	0	0
Garcia	1.000	6	6	0	0	0
Griffin	1.000	13	20	0	0	0
Hoffmann	.959	67	136	5	6	0
Jones	.993	91	149	3	1	0
Maza	1.000	28	41	1	0	0
Paul	.964	29	51	3	2	0
Ramirez	1.000	2	1	0	0	0
Repko	.996	106	217	5	1	1
Rosario	.932	31	53	2	4	0
Van Slyke	.750	3	3	0	1	0
Young	1.000	2	1	0	0	0

CHATTANOOGA LOOKOUTS DOUBLE-A

SOUTHERN LEAGUE

Batting	B-T	HT	WT	DOB	AVG	vLH	vRH	G	AB	R	H	2B	3B	HR	RBI	BB	HBP	SH	SF	SO	SB	CS	SLG	OBP
Abreu, Tony	B-R	5-9	200	11-13-84	.292	.267	.305	23	89	11	26	4	1	0	5	1	0	0	0	12	0	2	.360	.300
Becker, Joseph	R-R	5-11	175	11-8-85	.238	.188	.269	20	42	7	10	4	0	0	4	3	0	1	0	7	0	1	.333	.289
Bell, Josh	B-R	6-3	235	11-13-86	.296	.212	.335	94	334	47	99	30	2	11	52	50	2	0	5	70	3	5	.497	.386
Closser, J.D.	B-R	5-10	200	1-15-80	.228	.304	.205	30	101	9	23	7	0	1	12	13	0	0	1	21	1	0	.327	.313
Giles, Tommy	L-L	6-0	179	8-28-83	.251	.143	.272	82	179	30	45	11	0	11	31	32	1	1	2	58	0	1	.497	.364
Godwin, Adam	R-R	5-11	170	12-13-82	.254	.259	.252	95	248	30	63	12	2	1	22	17	3	7	0	50	13	7	.331	.310
Gonzalez, Juan	B-R	6-0	160	2-23-82	.215	.132	.243	58	149	13	32	8	0	0	13	35	1	5	2	42	0	0	.268	.364
Gutierrez, Gabriel	R-R	5-11	190	11-24-83	.267	.333	.238	35	90	9	24	8	1	0	14	8	3	1	0	12	0	0	.378	.347
Hoffmann, Jamie	R-R	6-3	235	8-20-84	.307	.321	.301	29	101	25	31	9	2	2	16	22	6	0	0	18	5	3	.495	.457
Lambo, Andrew	L-L	6-3	190	8-11-88	.256	.293	.241	130	492	70	126	39	1	11	61	39	3	0	7	95	4	3	.407	.311
Martinez, Gaby	L-R	6-2	180	5-17-83	.296	.175	.335	72	260	32	77	15	0	9	44	29	3	0	1	71	0	2	.458	.372
May, Lucas	R-R	5-11	195	10-24-84	.306	.391	.271	68	235	32	72	18	1	6	32	31	5	0	6	58	3	1	.468	.390
Mercedes, Victor	B-R	5-11	190	4-15-79	.148	.176	.138	36	128	6	19	4	2	0	8	8	1	1	4	24	4	3	.211	.199
Mier, Jessie	R-R	6-1	215	3-5-85	.000	—	.000	1	4	0	0	0	0	0	0	0	0	0	0	1	0	0	.000	.000
Mitchell, Russ	R-R	6-2	205	1-2-85	.241	.277	.226	131	456	63	110	30	3	13	63	36	2	4	3	84	4	1	.406	.298
Nivar, Ramon	R-R	5-10	185	2-22-80	.298	.241	.325	45	171	29	51	16	3	2	20	5	4	5	0	19	14	6	.480	.333
Perez, Eduardo	B-R	6-1	175	8-30-84	.281	.276	.282	90	292	46	82	22	1	11	47	30	7	0	0	73	0	2	.476	.362
Robinson, Trayvon	R-B	5-10	175	9-1-87	.246	.091	.283	19	57	8	14	1	2	2	10	10	0	3	0	18	4	2	.439	.358
Rosario, Jovanny	B-R	5-9	160	4-12-85	.278	.400	.258	12	36	1	10	0	0	0	5	0	0	3	1	6	1	0	.278	.270
Rose, Mike	B-R	6-1	225	8-25-76	.216	.222	.213	32	97	7	21	0	1	2	6	10	0	2	0	31	1	0	.299	.284
Rottino, Vinny	R-R	6-1	220	4-7-80	.315	.214	.339	31	73	18	23	5	0	0	7	15	0	0	1	8	5	1	.384	.427
2-team total (98 Huntsville)					.261	—		129	414	64	108	18	0	4	55	62	2	0	6	53	14	2	.333	.355
Sellers, Justin	R-R	5-10	160	2-1-86	.280	.300	.271	116	393	44	110	27	1	2	33	50	10	6	5	70	10	8	.369	.371
Tomlin, James	R-R	6-0	183	8-12-82	.315	.288	.328	108	387	55	122	23	4	2	34	54	3	4	2	73	12	10	.411	.401

Pitching	B-T	HT	WT	DOB	W	L	ERA	G	GS	CG	SV	IP	H	R	ER	HR	BB	SO	AVG	vLH	vRH	K/9	BB/9
Adkins, James	L-L	6-6	230	11-26-85	6	10	4.48	27	26	0	0	139	144	82	69	8	72	81	.270	.256	.274	5.26	4.67
Alvarez, Mario	R-R	6-0	205	3-26-84	0	1	9.00	1	1	0	0	3	6	3	3	2	1	3	.400	.500	.364	9.00	3.00
Bastardo, Alberto	L-L	6-0	160	4-6-84	6	3	4.23	13	13	1	0	72	72	42	34	6	30	58	.262	.329	.235	7.22	3.73
Batista, Kendy	R-R	6-2	165	7-5-81	5	1	2.17	24	5	0	1	58	41	16	14	2	24	56	.205	.282	.163	8.69	3.72
Cali, Carmen	L-L	5-8	220	11-2-78	0	1	3.55	7	0	0	0	13	11	6	5		5	12	.229	.231	.229	8.53	3.55
Castillo, Jesus	R-R	6-0	195	5-31-84	7	9	4.31	29	27	0	0	150	151	74	72	10	56	69	.262	.312	.233	5.33	3.35
Chick, Travis	R-R	6-2	220	6-10-84	8	7	4.22	23	21	0	0	113	110	58	53	12	46	98	.253	.277	.235	7.81	3.66
Corcoran, Tim	R-R	6-2	205	4-15-78	4	7	5.48	28	8	0	1	71	83	50	43	7	31	53	.286	.323	.258	6.75	3.95
Durbin, J.D.	R-R	6-0	210	2-24-82	2	3	2.05	20	5	0	3	53	39	12	12	1	21	34	.212	.278	.170	5.81	3.59
Elbert, Scott	L-L	6-1	215	8-13-85	2	3	3.90	12	11	0	0	62	59	32	27	5	30	87	.248	.145	.279	12.56	4.33

Pitching	B-T	HT	WT	DOB	W	L	ERA	G	GS	CG	SV	IP	H	R	ER	HR	BB	SO	AVG	vLH	vRH	K/9	BB/9
Felix, Francisco	R-R	5-11	191	7-28-83	3	2	2.93	29	2	0	2	55	48	22	18	3	20	54	.233	.238	.230	8.78	3.25
Garate, Victor	L-L	6-2	210	9-25-84	0	1	2.04	47	0	0	4	53	36	12	12	1	23	56	.191	.216	.175	9.51	3.91
Garcia, Harvey	R-R	6-2	220	3-16-84	0	1	2.70	12	0	0	5	13	8	4	4	1	4	15	.167	.182	.154	10.13	2.70
Guerra, Javy	R-R	6-1	195	10-31-85	3	1	4.13	23	0	0	0	28	32	15	13	2	16	29	.291	.347	.246	9.21	5.08
Johnson, Steve	R-R	6-1	200	8-31-87	1	1	1.69	2	2	0	0	11	8	5	2	1	3	15	.205	.105	.300	12.66	2.53
Koss, Paul	R-R	6-4	215	6-17-85	0	0	3.00	15	0	0	2	18	11	7	6	1	9	19	.169	.190	.159	9.50	4.50
Leach, Brent	L-L	6-4	220	11-18-82	0	1	0.69	9	0	0	1	13	12	3	1	1	8	17	.231	.188	.250	11.77	5.54
Lindblom, Josh	R-R	6-5	240	6-15-87	3	5	4.71	14	11	0	0	57	55	35	30	4	14	46	.250	.309	.206	7.22	2.20
Meque, Jacobo	L-L	6-0	230	10-1-83	1	4	11.81	10	0	0	0	11	17	15	14	1	11	13	.378	.200	.429	10.97	9.28
Rodriguez, Jesus	R-R	6-0	180	9-13-85	6	5	3.47	46	1	0	1	80	86	35	31	10	20	42	.273	.218	.318	4.71	2.24
Sartor, Matt	R-R	6-6	250	8-18-84	4	6	4.27	49	0	0	11	72	65	39	34	7	28	76	.236	.216	.249	9.54	3.52
Schlichting, Travis	R-R	6-4	215	10-19-84	1	0	0.66	9	0	0	1	14	7	5	1	1	7	12	.146	.050	.214	7.90	4.61
Schreiber, Zach	R-R	6-1	220	6-24-82	1	0	2.42	15	0	0	2	26	24	7	7	3	10	29	.245	.256	.236	10.04	3.46
Withrow, Chris	R-R	6-3	195	4-1-89	2	2	3.95	6	6	0	0	27	24	14	12	2	12	26	.240	.235	.245	8.56	3.95

Fielding

Catcher	PCT	G	PO	A	E	DP	PB
Closser	.984	28	234	16	4	2	3
Gutierrez	.991	28	191	25	2	2	2
May	.981	65	463	57	10	5	20
Mier	1.000	1	13	0	0	0	0
Rose	.986	18	130	13	2	1	3
Rottino	1.000	2	18	1	0	0	0

First Base	PCT	G	PO	A	E	DP
Martinez	.992	31	221	24	2	21
Mitchell	.990	50	377	31	4	25
Perez	.990	69	578	39	6	46
Rottino	1.000	2	2	0	0	0

Second Base	PCT	G	PO	A	E	DP
Abreu	.960	18	28	44	3	9
Becker	1.000	2	3	6	0	0
Gonzalez	.967	30	44	72	4	12

	PCT	G	PO	A	E	DP
Mercedes	.974	33	68	80	4	12
Mitchell	.973	30	38	72	3	13
Nivar	.963	35	78	104	7	25
Sellers	1.000	1	2	2	0	1

Third Base	PCT	G	PO	A	E	DP
Becker	—	1	0	0	0	0
Bell	.929	91	59	163	17	15
Gonzalez	1.000	5	2	1	0	0
Martinez	.889	14	10	22	4	4
Mitchell	.959	27	16	55	3	5
Rottino	.882	9	4	11	2	0

Shortstop	PCT	G	PO	A	E	DP
Abreu	1.000	4	2	8	0	2
Becker	.939	10	12	19	2	2
Gonzalez	1.000	16	16	35	0	6
Mercedes	1.000	2	1	3	0	0

	PCT	G	PO	A	E	DP
Nivar	.897	7	9	17	3	4
Sellers	.957	109	155	268	19	45

Outfield	PCT	G	PO	A	E	DP
Giles	.986	48	69	4	1	1
Godwin	.975	65	110	6	3	0
Hoffmann	1.000	28	81	4	0	0
Lambo	.977	127	211	4	5	1
Martinez	.960	14	24	0	1	0
Mitchell	1.000	18	22	2	0	0
Robinson	1.000	18	26	3	0	2
Rosario	1.000	9	18	0	0	0
Rose	1.000	3	4	0	0	0
Rottino	1.000	14	16	1	0	0
Tomlin	.996	100	220	6	1	2

INLAND EMPIRE 66ERS   HIGH CLASS A
CALIFORNIA LEAGUE

Batting	B-T	HT	WT	DOB	AVG	vLH	vRH	G	AB	R	H	2B	3B	HR	RBI	BB	HBP	SH	SF	SO	SB	CS	SLG	OBP
Baez, Pedro	R-R	6-2	195	3-11-88	.286	.247	.300	79	308	48	88	17	1	10	61	16	4	0	3	84	5	1	.445	.326
Becker, Joseph	R-R	5-11	175	11-8-85	.286	.286	.286	11	42	6	12	2	1	0	6	5	0	0	0	9	1	1	.381	.362
Caseres, Steven	L-R	6-4	220	3-26-87	.260	.155	.297	113	393	61	102	25	6	15	55	54	10	0	4	116	1	0	.468	.360
Cilladi, Steve	R-R	5-9	182	3-15-87	.000	.000	—	1	1	0	0	0	0	0	0	0	0	0	0	1	0	0	.000	.000
Fuller, Justin	L-R	6-1	190	7-10-83	.254	.167	.277	56	177	29	45	11	3	4	17	19	4	5	0	38	3	6	.418	.340
Garabedian, Alex	R-R	6-2	210	8-26-85	.236	.215	.246	84	280	34	66	12	1	6	35	38	2	2	1	62	1	1	.350	.330
Garcia, Johan	R-R	6-0	170	9-6-86	.162	.116	.191	40	111	8	18	1	0	0	4	10	1	2	0	23	7	3	.171	.238
Gibson, Chris	L-R	6-2	210	6-20-84	.067	.250	.000	5	15	0	1	0	0	0	1	0	0	0	0	6	0	0	.067	.067
Giles, Tommy	L-L	6-0	190	8-28-83	.344	.273	.381	16	64	8	22	4	0	4	17	6	0	0	2	14	1	1	.594	.389
Gonzalez, Adolfo	R-R	5-11	160	6-13-85	.271	.254	.277	59	236	35	64	9	2	4	24	11	4	2	2	54	2	5	.377	.312
Green, Garett	R-R	5-11	190	2-24-85	.219	.241	.204	49	151	18	33	3	0	4	25	17	1	3	3	46	0	2	.318	.297
Herrera, Elian	B-R	5-11	190	2-1-85	.290	.315	.278	99	389	64	113	18	5	4	35	35	3	2	2	95	42	5	.393	.352
Jansen, Kenley	B-R	6-2	220	9-30-87	.202	.130	.227	26	89	7	18	6	0	1	11	7	1	1	0	21	0	1	.303	.268
Lara, Christian	B-R	5-11	150	4-11-85	.256	.261	.253	115	391	48	100	15	5	6	46	25	1	5	3	102	11	11	.366	.300
Mattingly, Preston	R-R	6-3	205	8-28-87	.238	.254	.231	115	454	59	108	25	1	8	36	35	4	5	3	150	26	13	.350	.296
Mientkiewicz, Doug	R-R	6-2	210	6-19-74	.222	.250	.200	3	9	2	2	0	0	1	2	2	1	0	0	3	0	0	.444	.417
Mier, Jessie	R-R	6-1	215	3-5-85	.225	.233	.222	35	111	11	25	4	0	3	7	9	0	4	0	21	4	0	.342	.283
Ortiz, Jaime	L-L	6-1	220	7-14-88	.245	.250	.242	56	188	20	46	12	0	5	24	22	3	1	2	49	2	1	.388	.330
Perez, Andres	R-R	6-0	200	5-23-84	.340	.333	.343	26	103	13	35	7	1	5	20	7	2	0	0	23	2	3	.573	.393
Perez, Eduardo	B-R	6-1	175	8-30-84	.353	.500	.292	38	150	23	53	13	5	3	22	14	3	0	2	47	2	1	.567	.414
Ramirez, Manny	R-R	6-0	200	5-30-72	.429	.500	.333	3	7	2	3	0	0	1	1	2	0	0	0	4	0	0	.857	.556
Robinson, Trayvon	B-R	5-10	175	9-1-87	.306	.296	.311	117	470	82	144	28	9	15	54	50	4	1	4	125	43	18	.500	.375
Rosario, Jovanny	R-R	5-9	160	4-12-85	.240	.194	.273	18	75	5	18	2	2	0	2	3	0	0	0	15	9	0	.320	.269
Van Slyke, Scott	R-R	6-5	195	7-24-86	.294	.301	.291	132	496	75	146	42	4	23	100	61	3	0	3	128	10	7	.534	.373
Washington, Johnny	R-R	5-11	165	5-6-84	.286	.000	.500	2	7	1	2	0	0	0	0	0	0	0	0	0	0	0	.286	.286
Ynoa, Rafael	R-R	5-10	162	8-7-87	.054	.000	.087	14	37	3	2	0	0	0	1	6	0	4	0	13	0	0	.054	.186

Pitching	B-T	HT	WT	DOB	W	L	ERA	G	GS	CG	SV	IP	H	R	ER	HR	BB	SO	AVG	vLH	vRH	K/9	BB/9
Akin, Brian	R-R	6-3	185	10-13-81	0	0	12.86	5	0	0	0	7	10	10	10	2	8	10	.333	.214	.438	12.86	10.29
Alvarez, Mario	R-R	6-0	205	3-26-84	5	6	4.45	18	11	1	1	85	76	42	42	5	24	66	.242	.243	.241	6.99	2.54
Arias, Marlon	L-L	6-3	150	9-1-84	1	1	4.34	10	1	0	1	19	21	13	9	2	9	20	.288	.333	.261	9.64	4.34
Bastardo, Alberto	L-L	6-0	160	4-6-84	6	2	3.84	14	14	0	0	75	73	35	32	6	23	71	.259	.301	.238	8.52	2.76
Batista, Kendy	R-R	6-2	165	7-5-81	1	2	4.99	12	4	0	0	31	33	20	17	5	9	39	.266	.254	.279	11.45	2.64
Belisario, Ronald	R-R	6-3	235	12-31-82	0	0	0.00	2	2	0	0	2	2	0	0	0	1	3	.250	.400	.000	13.50	4.50
Brannon, Blake	R-R	6-2	225	3-5-85	0	3	4.54	19	1	0	0	36	37	18	18	3	16	30	.266	.254	.276	7.57	4.04
Johnson, Steve	R-R	6-1	200	8-31-87	8	4	3.82	18	16	0	1	97	94	50	41	14	42	102	.260	.271	.252	9.50	3.91
Jones, Joe	R-R	6-5	210	11-16-82	0	0	8.84	12	0	0	0	18	35	19	18	5	7	11	.427	.385	.465	5.40	3.44

Pitching	B-T	HT	WT	DOB	W	L	ERA	G	GS	CG	SV	IP	H	R	ER	HR	BB	SO	AVG	vLH	vRH	SO/9	BB/9
Krebs, Eric	R-R	6-3	210	5-16-85	0	2	3.24	22	0	0	0	25	16	10	9	1	25	31	.182	.194	.175	11.16	9.00
Kuo, Hong-Chih	L-L	6-1	240	7-23-81	0	0	0.00	4	0	0	0	4	3	0	0	0	0	6	.214	.250	.200	13.50	0.00
Kuroda, Hiroki	R-R	6-1	220	2-10-75	0	0	3.29	3	3	0	0	14	15	9	5	0	1	10	.273	.304	.250	6.59	0.66
McCarter, Jake	R-R	6-2	200	8-31-84	3	3	3.33	34	0	0	7	46	31	20	17	2	26	51	.193	.179	.208	9.98	5.09
Melgarejo, Thomas	L-L	6-1	216	1-10-87	2	2	5.70	20	2	0	0	36	36	24	23	7	16	31	.263	.231	.282	7.68	3.96
Meque, Jacobo	L-L	6-0	230	10-1-83	1	3	5.14	20	0	0	1	21	28	14	12	3	16	36	.304	.313	.300	15.43	6.86
Miller, Greg	L-L	6-6	215	11-3-84	0	1	9.26	25	0	0	1	12	7	12	12	0	11	10	.179	.160	.214	7.71	8.49
Miller, Justin	R-R	6-3	190	8-2-87	0	7	8.13	7	7	0	0	34	52	38	31	3	18	14	.371	.357	.386	3.67	4.72
Milton, Eric	L-L	6-1	220	8-4-75	1	0	0.00	1	1	0	0	5	4	0	0	0	1	3	.235	.125	.333	5.06	1.69
Ohman, Will	L-L	6-2	210	8-13-77	0	0	13.50	3	1	0	0	3	5	4	4	0	1	2	.417	.250	.500	6.75	3.38
Orenduff, Justin	R-R	6-3	215	5-27-83	1	0	3.98	15	0	0	3	20	24	9	9	2	14	21	.289	.250	.326	9.30	6.20
Pfeiffer, David	L-L	6-3	190	8-17-85	3	3	3.56	34	0	0	4	48	46	25	19	1	17	38	.253	.177	.292	7.13	3.19
Prado, Marcel	R-R	6-4	226	11-22-87	2	2	4.06	41	0	0	7	44	48	25	20	2	28	20	.277	.316	.245	4.06	5.68
Ramirez, Miguel	R-R	5-11	180	7-15-83	0	0	0.00	3	0	0	0	4	0	0	0	0	2	4	.000	.000	.000	8.31	4.15
Rondon, Daigoro	R-R	6-2	163	11-4-86	1	2	7.62	10	0	0	1	13	17	11	11	2	8	10	.315	.481	.148	6.92	5.54
Sanfler, Miguel	L-L	5-11	165	10-5-84	1	0	5.48	40	2	0	1	69	72	45	42	7	41	47	.276	.295	.265	6.13	5.35
Schmidt, Jason	R-R	6-5	220	1-29-73	1	1	2.25	2	2	0	0	12	8	4	3	0	7	12	.182	.154	.222	9.00	5.25
Schreiber, Zach	R-R	6-1	220	6-24-82	1	0	3.18	9	0	0	2	11	7	5	4	2	6	7	.189	.235	.150	5.56	4.76
Sexton, Tim	R-R	6-6	185	6-10-87	8	14	3.96	27	22	0	0	157	178	92	69	17	34	100	.284	.296	.268	5.73	1.95
Smit, Kyle	R-R	6-3	165	10-14-87	0	4	7.84	5	5	0	0	21	23	18	18	2	10	18	.288	.286	.289	7.84	4.35
Smith, Matt	R-R	6-6	195	11-2-86	0	1	12.86	6	1	0	0	7	20	10	10	3	5	3	.541	.533	.545	3.86	6.43
Stults, Eric	L-L	6-1	220	12-9-79	0	0	1.23	2	2	0	0	7	5	2	1	0	0	5	.185	.182	.188	6.14	0.00
Torres, Joe	L-L	6-2	195	9-3-82	0	0	0.98	13	0	0	1	18	19	3	2	1	9	17	.271	.300	.250	8.35	4.42
Vargas, Claudio	R-R	6-4	235	6-19-78	0	1	5.40	3	3	0	0	5	3	3	3	1	1	3	.158	.182	.125	5.40	1.80
Vasquez, Luis	R-R	6-4	155	4-3-86	0	2	9.95	7	1	0	0	13	16	16	14	3	10	11	.291	.323	.250	7.82	7.11
Wade, Cory	R-R	6-1	190	5-28-83	0	0	0.00	1	1	0	0	1	0	0	0	0	2	1	.000	.000	.000	9.00	18.00
Wall, Josh	R-R	6-6	190	1-21-87	5	8	5.98	23	22	0	0	111	135	85	74	9	51	77	.310	.317	.304	6.22	4.12
Withrow, Chris	R-R	6-3	195	4-1-89	6	6	4.69	19	16	0	0	86	80	50	45	3	45	105	.252	.283	.219	10.95	4.69

Fielding

Catcher	PCT	G	PO	A	E	DP	PB
Cilladi	1.000	1	1	0	0	0	0
Garabedian	.987	84	631	69	9	7	11
Jansen	.955	26	215	20	11	0	3
Mier	.989	35	232	37	3	3	6

First Base	PCT	G	PO	A	E	DP
Caseres	.989	77	653	39	8	62
Gibson	1.000	2	8	0	0	0
Gonzalez	1.000	7	38	1	0	3
Green	1.000	2	3	0	0	1
Ortiz	.991	40	298	26	3	32
Perez	1.000	2	19	3	0	0
Perez	.982	18	154	8	3	13

Second Base	PCT	G	PO	A	E	DP
Becker	.963	5	9	17	1	2
Fuller	.965	22	31	51	3	5
Garcia	1.000	2	1	7	0	1
Gonzalez	.988	37	70	101	2	28

Second Base (cont.)	PCT	G	PO	A	E	DP
Green	.994	33	58	100	1	25
Herrera	.980	32	54	95	3	18
Lara	.895	4	10	7	2	2
Perez	.947	3	7	11	1	1
Washington	1.000	2	3	10	0	0
Ynoa	.945	11	14	38	3	6

Third Base	PCT	G	PO	A	E	DP
Baez	.910	78	47	124	17	9
Becker	1.000	3	0	4	0	0
Fuller	1.000	2	1	0	0	0
Garcia	.930	34	17	63	6	3
Gonzalez	.935	10	7	22	2	1
Green	.893	14	6	19	3	1
Herrera	.963	7	10	16	1	1
Perez	1.000	1	2	0	0	0

Shortstop	PCT	G	PO	A	E	DP
Becker	.750	2	2	1	1	0
Fuller	.955	27	37	68	5	25

Shortstop (cont.)	PCT	G	PO	A	E	DP
Garcia	1.000	2	3	3	0	1
Gonzalez	1.000	5	3	17	0	4
Herrera	1.000	1	5	1	0	0
Lara	.955	110	193	290	23	64
Ynoa	1.000	3	3	7	0	1

Outfield	PCT	G	PO	A	E	DP
Fuller	1.000	8	9	0	0	0
Giles	1.000	15	19	2	0	0
Herrera	.961	38	64	10	3	0
Mattingly	.966	100	137	7	5	3
Mier	—	1	0	0	0	0
Perez	.926	10	24	1	2	0
Perez	1.000	1	1	0	0	0
Ramirez	1.000	1	1	0	0	0
Robinson	.974	113	251	11	7	4
Rosario	1.000	18	44	2	0	0
Van Slyke	.969	124	234	18	8	4

GREAT LAKES LOONS

LOW CLASS A

MIDWEST LEAGUE

Batting	B-T	HT	WT	DOB	AVG	vLH	vRH	G	AB	R	H	2B	3B	HR	RBI	BB	HBP	SH	SF	SO	SB	CS	SLG	OBP
Becker, Joseph	R-R	5-11	175	11-8-85	.339	.421	.300	17	59	10	20	4	1	1	11	7	0	0	1	12	0	0	.492	.403
Buss, Nick	L-R	6-0	180	12-15-86	.260	.165	.296	110	416	55	108	15	5	10	63	21	4	5	6	75	14	3	.392	.298
Calfee, Clay	L-R	6-6	220	6-2-86	.125	.000	.200	11	40	3	5	1	0	0	3	4	0	0	0	21	0	0	.150	.205
Dalton, Parker	R-R	6-1	185	7-7-83	.169	.190	.160	55	148	19	25	9	1	1	14	11	1	1	0	44	1	1	.264	.231
Delmonico, Tony	R-R	6-0	194	4-27-87	.285	.280	.287	100	365	53	104	22	2	9	43	46	13	2	2	86	5	0	.430	.383
Gallagher, Austin	L-R	6-5	210	11-16-88	.257	.241	.262	60	226	28	58	11	0	3	30	21	1	0	3	43	1	1	.345	.319
Gordon, Dee	L-R	5-11	150	4-22-88	.301	.281	.309	131	538	96	162	17	12	3	35	43	10	7	3	90	73	25	.394	.362
Hatch, Anthony	L-R	6-3	200	8-30-83	.294	.248	.311	130	479	80	141	36	6	11	73	51	2	0	2	70	6	2	.463	.363
Herrera, Elian	B-R	5-11	190	2-1-85	.250	.455	.172	13	40	6	10	0	0	0	2	1	0	0	1	9	1	2	.250	.262
Kanaby, Erik	L-R	6-1	185	7-26-85	.143	.286	.071	9	21	5	3	1	0	0	5	8	0	0	1	3	1	1	.190	.367
Lopez, Steven	R-R	6-1	210	6-20-84	.203	.180	.214	49	148	13	30	5	0	3	22	12	5	1	2	37	1	0	.297	.281
Mathews, Brian	R-R	6-0	230	8-26-87	.182	.375	.139	13	44	4	8	1	0	0	2	1	2	0	0	8	1	0	.205	.234
Pedroza, Jaime	B-R	5-8	167	9-12-86	.260	.216	.278	136	520	100	135	33	6	15	78	78	6	2	3	162	36	14	.433	.361
Russell, Kyle	L-L	6-5	195	6-27-86	.272	.235	.287	133	481	90	131	39	7	26	102	72	6	0	4	180	20	2	.545	.371
Sands, Jerry	R-R	6-4	210	9-28-87	.260	.250	.263	32	104	22	27	7	2	5	19	15	2	1	1	32	1	0	.510	.361
Silverio, Alfredo	R-R	6-1	185	5-6-87	.284	.271	.289	132	490	75	139	34	6	13	61	26	2	1	4	104	2	5	.457	.320
Songco, Angelo	L-R	6-0	190	9-9-88	.150	.179	.136	33	120	8	18	6	2	1	16	10	2	1	1	28	1	0	.258	.226
Vetters, Travis	R-R	6-2	190	9-11-83	.227	.225	.228	36	119	16	27	3	3	1	19	11	4	1	2	40	0	1	.328	.309
Wallach, Matt	L-R	6-1	205	2-17-86	.251	.183	.275	107	351	36	88	20	1	4	48	38	3	2	3	69	2	1	.348	.327

Pitching

Pitching	B-T	HT	WT	DOB	W	L	ERA	G	GS	CG	SV	IP	H	R	ER	HR	BB	SO	AVG	vLH	vRH	K/9	BB/9
Aguasviva, Geison	L-L	6-2	166	8-3-87	4	2	1.58	19	4	0	1	63	53	16	11	1	20	46	.236	.203	.248	6.61	2.87
Blevins, Bobby	R-R	6-0	200	1-16-85	11	10	4.16	27	27	2	0	154	159	82	71	11	32	97	.263	.300	.239	5.68	1.87
Boothe, Robert	R-R	6-2	190	1-30-86	2	3	4.95	37	0	0	2	56	55	35	31	2	29	78	.253	.247	.257	12.46	4.63
Brannon, Blake	R-R	6-2	225	3-5-85	1	0	2.81	12	0	0	0	26	19	9	8	1	11	25	.204	.139	.246	8.77	3.86
Dutton, Jon	L-L	6-1	155	9-30-87	0	3	3.60	17	1	0	0	20	19	10	8	1	10	23	.244	.242	.244	10.35	4.50
Eovaldi, Nathan	R-R	6-3	195	2-13-90	3	5	3.27	26	16	0	1	96	95	48	35	2	41	71	.265	.252	.271	6.63	3.83
Feliciano, Roberto	L-L	6-0	214	8-16-90	0	0	2.70	6	0	0	0	7	7	3	2	0	5	5	.259	.556	.111	6.75	6.75
Garcia, Luis	R-R	6-2	212	1-30-87	5	3	2.92	34	0	0	5	71	68	27	23	5	15	55	.245	.255	.240	6.97	1.90
Guerra, Javy	R-R	6-1	195	10-31-85	3	1	1.54	28	0	0	16	41	23	7	7	1	15	55	.161	.203	.131	12.07	3.29
Martin, Ethan	R-R	6-2	195	6-6-89	6	8	3.87	27	19	0	1	100	85	55	43	4	61	120	.232	.258	.218	10.80	5.49
Miller, Aaron	L-L	6-3	200	9-18-87	3	1	2.08	7	7	0	0	30	22	7	7	3	10	38	.208	.115	.238	11.27	2.97
Miller, Justin	R-R	6-3	190	8-2-87	5	7	4.70	21	21	0	0	115	125	73	60	7	46	66	.275	.260	.284	5.17	3.60
Pratt, Jordan	R-R	6-3	195	5-17-85	3	4	4.58	36	0	0	2	57	46	30	29	2	42	65	.222	.171	.248	10.26	6.63
Redding, Jon Michael	R-R	6-1	195	11-16-87	16	3	4.60	26	26	0	0	133	149	79	68	9	39	96	.281	.324	.249	6.50	2.64
Rondon, Daigoro	R-R	6-2	163	11-4-86	0	0	0.00	3	0	0	0	4	3	0	0	0	5	5	.214	.125	.333	11.25	0.00
Smit, Kyle	R-R	6-3	165	10-14-87	1	3	5.36	21	2	0	0	47	55	33	28	5	18	43	.284	.300	.274	8.23	3.45
Smith, Steve	R-R	6-2	215	5-15-86	4	1	2.67	28	0	0	3	67	63	23	20	1	28	54	.252	.309	.218	7.22	3.74
St. Clair, Cole	L-L	6-5	225	7-30-86	4	1	2.48	30	0	0	15	36	30	10	10	3	13	45	.226	.216	.229	11.15	3.22
Walter, Josh	R-R	6-4	250	4-5-85	10	4	3.27	32	17	0	0	110	92	41	40	10	49	113	.228	.266	.200	9.25	4.01

Fielding

Catcher	PCT	G	PO	A	E	DP	PB
Delmonico	.993	49	391	37	3	1	11
Lopez	.997	48	352	30	1	2	5
Wallach	.980	53	346	48	8	4	2

First Base	PCT	G	PO	A	E	DP
Calfee	.982	10	102	5	2	8
Delmonico	.966	17	167	5	6	14
Gallagher	.984	33	288	13	5	19
Hatch	1.000	2	5	1	0	0
Lopez	1.000	1	5	0	0	2
Mathews	1.000	7	68	4	0	11
Sands	.984	22	176	6	3	25
Vetters	1.000	1	3	0	0	1

Wallach	.978	51	407	28	10	33

Second Base	PCT	G	PO	A	E	DP
Becker	.974	8	12	25	1	8
Dalton	.966	14	22	34	2	7
Pedroza	.953	122	204	342	27	67

Third Base	PCT	G	PO	A	E	DP
Dalton	.981	21	11	40	1	4
Hatch	.948	123	81	210	16	12
Wallach	1.000	1	3	0	0	0

Shortstop	PCT	G	PO	A	E	DP
Becker	.750	1	2	1	1	0
Dalton	.971	16	20	46	2	6

Gordon	.941	127	197	343	34	78
Hatch	1.000	1	1	2	0	1
Pedroza	1.000	2	0	1	0	1

Outfield	PCT	G	PO	A	E	DP
Buss	.980	109	244	6	5	0
Herrera	1.000	11	18	1	0	1
Kanaby	1.000	8	15	0	0	0
Russell	.973	125	244	9	7	2
Sands	1.000	7	14	1	0	1
Silverio	.976	124	198	6	5	1
Songco	1.000	27	30	1	0	0
Vetters	.952	15	19	1	1	0

AZL DODGERS

ROOKIE

ARIZONA LEAGUE

Batting	B-T	HT	WT	DOB	AVG	vLH	vRH	G	AB	R	H	2B	3B	HR	RBI	BB	HBP	SH	SF	SO	SB	CS	SLG	OBP
Akins, Nick	R-R	6-1	180	12-25-87	.333	.400	.311	32	120	21	40	12	3	7	34	11	3	0	2	30	3	1	.658	.397
Arp, Ryan	R-R	6-0	185	11-16-85	.170	.222	.158	17	47	6	8	1	0	1	8	4	1	1	3	10	0	0	.255	.236
Aviles, Adrian	L-L	6-2	155	4-7-89	1.000	1.000	—	1	1	0	1	0	0	0	0	0	0	0	0	0	0	0	1.000	1.000
Banks, Stetson	R-R	6-1	185	1-14-88	.231	.306	.212	44	169	31	39	4	3	2	11	16	3	2	0	42	11	4	.325	.309
Becker, Joseph	R-R	5-11	175	11-8-85	.364	1.000	.300	3	11	3	4	1	0	0	2	0	0	1	0	0	0	0	.455	.462
Calfee, Clay	L-R	6-6	220	6-2-86	.270	.174	.308	16	63	10	17	4	1	2	12	4	1	0	1	18	1	0	.460	.319
Cilladi, Steve	R-R	5-9	182	3-15-87	.122	.000	.139	14	41	0	5	0	1	0	3	3	2	0	0	18	0	0	.171	.217
DeJesus Jr., Ivan	R-R	5-11	190	5-1-87	.200	.000	.333	4	10	1	2	1	0	0	3	1	1	0	1	6	0	0	.300	.308
Garcia, Johan	R-R	6-0	170	9-6-86	.250	.000	.353	12	48	9	12	0	1	0	6	2	1	0	0	10	6	0	.292	.280
Garcia, Jonathan	R-R	5-11	175	11-11-91	.304	.303	.305	41	138	22	42	16	1	3	21	10	3	2	1	37	4	0	.500	.362
Green, Garett	R-R	5-11	190	2-24-85	.274	.333	.260	17	62	6	17	4	2	0	7	6	0	2	0	17	1	0	.403	.338
Grider, Casio	R-R	6-1	165	8-17-87	.263	.244	.271	47	171	42	45	5	2	2	15	15	14	2	0	53	22	2	.351	.370
Henderson, Chris	R-L	5-11	190	6-23-88	.255	.250	.256	47	165	18	42	11	2	0	18	16	2	0	3	47	1	1	.345	.323
Hunt, Jeff	L-R	6-2	190	2-13-91	.172	.154	.176	18	64	4	11	1	1	0	2	6	0	0	0	19	2	0	.219	.243
Jean, Ramon	R-R	6-0	160	10-10-87	.280	.227	.298	44	175	28	49	9	2	0	23	10	1	0	0	23	14	3	.360	.323
King, Austin	R-R	6-2	200	12-1-88	.244	.150	.281	28	78	10	19	3	0	3	12	5	2	1	0	16	6	2	.397	.306
Luna, Hector	R-R	6-0	225	2-1-80	.250	.000	.286	3	8	4	2	1	0	0	1	2	1	0	0	0	0	0	.375	.455
Martinez, Gaby	L-R	6-2	180	5-17-83	.286	.333	.273	4	14	3	4	0	0	1	3	1	0	0	0	4	0	0	.500	.333
Nam, Tae-Hyeok	R-R	6-0	209	3-13-91	.000	—	.000	1	3	0	0	0	0	0	0	1	0	0	0	1	0	0	.000	.250
Pericht, Mike	R-R	6-5	225	5-23-88	.211	.222	.198	35	109	16	23	6	1	4	19	18	7	0	5	41	0	0	.394	.345
Perry, Taiwan	R-R	6-0	185	6-1-88	.050	.000	.061	18	40	3	2	1	0	0	2	5	0	0	0	17	0	0	.075	.156
Ray, Melvin	R-R	6-4	205	4-23-89	.130	.136	.130	29	92	13	12	2	0	2	6	5	0	0	1	55	4	0	.217	.173
Ruggiano, Brian	R-R	6-0	175	6-9-86	.120	.167	.111	7	25	1	3	0	0	0	1	2	1	0	1	11	0	0	.120	.207
Smith, Blake	L-R	6-2	220	12-9-87	.227	.000	.313	6	22	3	5	1	0	0	2	2	1	0	0	9	0	0	.273	.346
Tavarez, Pedro	R-R	6-0	198	6-28-87	.325	.300	.325	43	151	20	49	4	0	1	26	16	2	1	1	19	3	1	.371	.394
Vazquez, Jan	B-R	5-10	165	4-29-87	.216	.200	.222	25	74	8	16	3	0	0	3	7	2	0	0	20	0	0	.257	.301
Vetters, Travis	R-R	6-2	190	9-11-83	.333	.500	.250	4	12	5	4	1	0	0	1	6	1	0	0	1	0	0	.417	.579
Ynoa, Rafael	R-R	5-10	162	8-7-87	.500	—	.500	2	6	0	3	1	0	0	3	2	1	0	0	1	0	0	.667	.556

Pitching	B-T	HT	WT	DOB	W	L	ERA	G	GS	CG	SV	IP	H	R	ER	HR	BB	SO	AVG	vLH	vRH	K/9	BB/9
Akin, Brian	R-R	6-3	185	10-13-81	1	1	3.77	10	5	0	0	14	10	8	6	0	9	14	.196	.167	.222	8.79	5.65
Arias, Marlon	L-L	6-3	150	11-9-84	0	0	9.00	1	0	0	0	1	2	1	1	0	0	0	.400	.000	.500	0.00	0.00
Childs, K.J.	R-B	6-2	195	4-21-87	0	0	6.14	11	0	0	0	15	17	10	10	1	5	13	.298	.143	.349	7.98	3.07
Danielson, Danny	R-R	6-4	220	12-12-88	5	2	3.08	14	9	0	0	61	65	30	21	5	12	77	.257	.195	.284	11.30	1.76

	B-T	HT	WT	DOB	W	L	ERA	G	GS	CG	SV	IP	H	R	ER	HR	BB	SO	AVG	vLH	vRH	K/9	BB/9
De La Rosa, Rubby	R-R	6-1	170	3-4-89	0	1	6.06	5	2	0	0	16	17	12	11	0	11	22	.266	.259	.270	12.12	6.06
Dignelli, Justin	R-R	6-4	220	2-26-87	1	1	7.71	11	0	0	1	14	11	12	12	1	11	18	.216	.083	.256	11.57	7.07
Feliciano, Roberto	L-L	6-0	214	8-16-90	1	2	1.50	10	0	0	2	24	16	6	4	0	6	27	.195	.250	.186	10.13	2.25
Frias, Carlos	R-R	6-4	170	11-13-89	5	5	4.28	14	9	0	0	61	64	37	29	1	24	67	.267	.147	.321	9.89	3.54
Fructuoso, Beyker	R-R	6-3	195	4-8-90	1	5	6.28	13	1	0	1	29	36	25	20	8	8	29	.295	.387	.264	9.10	2.51
Gonzalez, Cristian	B-R	6-1	169	6-6-88	0	0	2.25	9	0	0	0	12	16	7	3	0	1	7	.333	.313	.344	5.25	0.75
Guzman, Amauri	R-R	6-3	200	10-12-86	0	0	3.38	10	0	0	0	13	15	6	5	0	4	13	.294	.188	.343	8.78	2.70
Handke, Chris	R-R	6-10	235	3-19-88	0	0	13.50	2	0	0	0	1	3	5	2	0	1	0	.429	1.000	.333	0.00	6.75
Hernandez, Bobby	R-R	6-0	190	6-21-87	2	1	1.88	12	0	0	0	14	17	10	3	2	7	12	.293	.278	.300	7.53	4.40
Kuo, Hong-Chih	L-L	6-1	240	7-23-81	0	0	0.00	3	1	0	0	3	2	0	0	0	1	5	.182	.000	.250	15.00	3.00
Lee, Ji-Mo	R-R	6-1	188	10-30-86	0	0	—	1	0	0	0	0	4	5	4	0	1	0	.800	1.000	.750	—	—
Marshall, Jimmy	R-R	6-6	195	4-13-87	0	1	4.09	10	0	0	3	11	8	5	5	1	6	12	.211	.182	.222	9.82	4.91
Martinez, Brandon	R-R	6-4	150	11-25-90	0	4	9.86	10	5	0	0	21	38	29	23	2	11	23	.388	.385	.390	9.86	4.71
Medina, Bolivar	L-L	6-2	175	8-11-88	3	2	2.89	13	4	0	2	47	43	27	15	1	13	42	.235	.182	.247	8.10	2.51
Melgarejo, Thomas	L-L	6-1	216	1-10-87	0	1	9.64	4	2	0	0	5	7	5	5	0	2	9	.333	.333	.333	17.36	3.86
Miller, Aaron	L-L	6-3	200	9-18-87	0	0	6.35	3	3	0	0	6	8	5	4	0	2	10	.320	.250	.333	15.88	3.18
Miller, Greg	L-L	6-6	215	11-3-84	0	0	0.00	5	1	0	0	5	3	0	0	0	2	5	.176	.000	.188	8.44	3.38
Perez, Tommy	R-R	6-4	167	8-10-86	0	0	9.00	2	0	0	0	2	4	2	2	0	0	4	.400	.000	.444	0.00	0.00
Pfeiffer, David	L-L	6-3	190	8-17-85	0	0	0.00	2	0	0	0	4	0	1	0	0	0	2	.000	.000	.000	4.50	0.00
Santiago, Andres	R-R	6-2	200	10-26-89	3	4	7.17	14	3	0	2	43	54	45	34	2	14	38	.298	.323	.284	8.02	2.95
Schlichting, Travis	R-R	6-4	215	10-19-84	0	0	0.00	3	3	0	0	3	2	0	0	0	0	4	.182	.400	.000	12.00	0.00
Tavarez, Gari	R-R	6-4	170	10-26-87	0	0	6.75	12	0	0	1	19	26	16	14	2	8	20	.321	.500	.246	9.64	3.86
Urriola, Marlon	R-R	6-2	165	7-1-88	0	1	13.50	2	0	0	0	2	5	5	3	0	3	3	.455	.500	.429	13.50	13.50
Webster, Allen	R-R	6-2	165	2-10-90	2	1	2.08	12	8	0	0	48	35	19	11	0	14	56	.197	.167	.210	10.57	2.64

Fielding

Catcher	PCT	G	PO	A	E	DP	PB
Cilladi	1.000	7	55	8	0	0	6
Pericht	.991	10	97	11	1	1	5
Tavarez	.984	26	216	32	4	2	10
Vazquez	.963	19	141	17	6	2	4

First Base	PCT	G	PO	A	E	DP
Arp	.966	7	55	8	2	4	14
Calfee	.978	15	122	11	3	11
Green	.957	2	22	0	1	3
Henderson	.981	18	145	11	3	3
Luna	.917	1	10	1	1	0
Martinez	1.000	3	15	0	0	1
Pericht	.978	7	45	0	1	7

Second Base	PCT	G	PO	A	E	DP
Banks	1.000	9	26	23	0	7
Garcia	1.000	3	2	7	0	1

Green	.950	5	10	9	1	2
Grider	.941	12	20	28	3	8
Jean	.907	26	38	60	10	11
Ruggiano	.909	3	4	6	1	1
Ynoa	1.000	2	3	12	0	1

Third Base	PCT	G	PO	A	E	DP
Garcia	.917	7	1	10	1	2
Green	.857	6	4	8	2	1
Henderson	.827	28	15	47	13	3
Hunt	.933	18	10	32	3	3
Luna	.000	1	0	0	1	0
Martinez	1.000	1	2	0	0	0
Nam	.714	1	2	3	2	1

Shortstop	PCT	G	PO	A	E	DP
Becker	1.000	3	2	13	0	1
DeJesus Jr.	1.000	3	0	2	0	1

Garcia	.933	3	4	10	1	1
Grider	.904	35	50	91	15	12
Jean	.872	17	19	56	11	12
Luna	1.000	1	3	1	0	0

Outfield	PCT	G	PO	A	E	DP
Akins	.935	28	40	3	3	2
Banks	.967	34	56	2	2	0
Garcia	.919	41	54	3	5	0
King	.955	23	40	2	2	0
Perry	1.000	15	13	1	0	1
Ray	.959	26	46	1	2	0
Ruggiano	1.000	3	3	0	0	0
Smith	1.000	6	10	0	0	0
Vetters	1.000	4	3	0	0	0

OGDEN RAPTORS   ROOKIE

PIONEER LEAGUE

Batting	B-T	HT	WT	DOB	AVG	vLH	vRH	G	AB	R	H	2B	3B	HR	RBI	BB	HBP	SH	SF	SO	SB	CS	SLG	OBP
Akins, Nick	R-R	6-1	180	12-25-87	.260	.222	.274	27	100	15	26	8	1	4	16	13	3	0	1	33	0	1	.480	.359
Calfee, Clay	L-R	6-6	220	6-2-86	.354	.250	.388	17	65	10	23	4	0	3	12	6	0	0	0	19	0	1	.554	.408
Cavazos-Galvez, Brian	R-R	6-0	215	5-17-87	.322	.293	.332	71	301	59	97	29	3	18	63	10	7	0	5	43	17	8	.618	.353
Collado, Keyter	R-R	5-11	178	6-8-86	.273	.000	.375	9	22	1	6	1	0	0	5	1	0	0	0	3	0	0	.318	.304
Erickson, Gorman	B-R	6-3	205	3-11-88	.305	.340	.292	55	197	40	60	18	1	5	36	24	1	0	3	36	0	0	.482	.378
Guerrero, Pedro	R-R	6-3	181	12-3-88	.259	.200	.279	62	232	36	60	13	1	4	29	9	4	1	1	65	3	1	.375	.297
Hernandez, Bryant	R-R	5-8	170	3-5-88	.276	.367	.237	44	163	20	45	6	2	2	16	21	4	1	0	48	8	4	.374	.370
Iden, David	R-R	5-9	160	3-4-87	.239	.226	.246	32	92	11	22	3	0	0	5	12	0	1	0	19	5	6	.272	.327
Jacobs, Chris	R-R	6-5	260	11-25-88	.277	.300	.265	42	148	22	41	10	1	4	17	21	1	1	0	49	0	0	.439	.371
McGee, Lenell	R-R	6-2	185	8-10-88	.268	.268	.268	45	168	23	45	11	1	2	22	8	6	2	2	35	3	4	.381	.321
Nam, Tae-Hyeok	R-R	6-0	209	3-13-91	.333	.400	.250	2	9	2	3	0	0	1	0	0	0	0	5	0	0	.333	.333
Orr, Kyle	L-R	6-5	205	9-29-88	.223	.188	.233	40	148	19	33	7	2	3	27	10	1	1	2	47	0	0	.358	.273
Ruggiano, Brian	R-R	6-0	175	6-9-86	.371	.449	.338	54	229	57	85	14	5	9	38	20	7	1	0	57	22	5	.594	.438
Sands, Jerry	R-R	6-4	210	9-28-87	.350	.469	.298	41	163	41	57	9	2	14	39	22	0	0	0	28	0	1	.687	.427
Smith, Blake	L-R	6-2	220	12-9-87	.212	.161	.233	30	104	14	22	7	0	1	12	13	2	1	0	38	0	0	.308	.311
Songco, Angelo	L-R	6-0	190	9-9-88	.306	.350	.288	36	144	27	44	11	1	9	29	10	3	0	1	41	0	1	.583	.361
Wise, J.T.	R-R	6-1	205	6-2-86	.338	.455	.287	39	145	26	49	9	0	8	23	16	0	2	1	31	0	0	.566	.401
Ynoa, Rafael	R-R	5-10	162	8-7-87	.183	.077	.218	35	104	16	19	6	1	0	5	17	1	3	1	20	4	2	.260	.301
Yount, Austin	L-R	6-0	185	10-9-86	.257	.261	.256	38	140	20	36	6	0	3	21	28	0	0	0	35	0	0	.364	.381

Pitching	B-T	HT	WT	DOB	W	L	ERA	G	GS	CG	SV	IP	H	R	ER	HR	BB	SO	AVG	vLH	vRH	K/9	BB/9
Ames, Steven	R-R	6-1	205	3-15-88	1	1	2.10	17	0	0	7	30	20	7	7	2	6	47	.192	.250	.167	14.10	1.80
Castillo, Antonio	L-L	5-11	180	3-5-88	4	3	6.04	13	3	0	0	48	58	35	32	4	34	39	.301	.302	.300	7.36	6.42
Contreras, Edwin	R-R	6-2	165	9-17-88	5	1	4.06	15	15	0	0	75	83	39	34	5	30	48	.280	.240	.300	5.73	3.58
Ferreras, Luis	R-R	6-0	150	12-28-89	2	1	2.50	15	0	0	0	18	14	5	5	0	12	11	.241	.333	.189	5.50	6.00
Frias, Carlos	R-R	6-4	170	11-13-89	0	1	3.52	2	0	0	0	8	10	6	3	0	4	6	.313	.214	.389	7.04	4.70
Gaudi, Nick	R-R	6-5	215	8-2-86	2	4	2.96	18	0	0	0	27	25	13	9	3	5	39	.234	.161	.263	12.84	1.65

	B-T	HT	WT	DOB	W	L	ERA	G	GS	CG	SV	IP	H	R	ER	HR	BB	SO	AVG	vLH	vRH	K/9	BB/9
Gould, Garrett	R-R	6-4	190	7-19-91	0	1	10.13	3	3	0	0	3	4	5	3	1	2	4	.333	.250	.375	13.50	6.75
Lee, Ji-Mo	R-R	6-1	188	10-30-86	0	0	6.00	3	0	0	0	3	6	2	2	0	2	1	.429	.000	.545	3.00	6.00
Magill, Matt	R-R	6-3	175	11-10-89	6	3	4.00	15	15	0	0	72	59	43	32	7	30	55	.224	.247	.212	6.88	3.75
Miller, Graham	L-L	6-2	205	10-18-86	1	0	4.30	9	0	0	0	15	10	8	7	0	11	14	.204	.077	.250	8.59	6.75
Paxson, J.B.	R-R	6-3	250	7-28-86	1	3	5.52	17	0	0	3	29	37	23	18	1	11	29	.301	.333	.289	8.90	3.38
Pimentel, Elisaul	R-R	6-2	170	7-10-88	4	4	4.73	13	12	0	0	59	71	39	31	4	15	48	.300	.309	.295	7.32	2.29
Quintero, Fredy	R-R	6-3	180	12-29-87	0	2	1.93	15	0	0	1	33	30	13	7	0	13	32	.246	.270	.235	8.82	3.58
Roberts, Jordan	L-L	6-1	180	1-5-86	1	0	2.70	13	0	0	1	27	21	11	8	1	8	12	.216	.235	.213	4.05	2.70
Rondon, Daigoro	R-R	6-2	163	11-4-86	3	4	3.98	19	0	0	7	20	24	11	9	1	7	24	.286	.297	.277	10.62	3.10
Solano, Javier	R-R	6-0	177	3-31-90	2	0	4.64	16	0	0	1	33	35	19	17	3	16	31	.278	.310	.262	8.45	4.36
Suiter, Andy	L-L	6-3	210	6-6-87	2	0	4.02	14	0	0	0	16	11	10	7	0	18	15	.200	.211	.194	8.62	10.34
Thompson, Eric	R-R	6-6	210	4-4-88	1	1	5.79	14	0	0	0	28	27	20	18	2	11	15	.241	.235	.244	4.82	3.54
Vasquez, Luis	R-R	6-4	155	4-3-86	3	3	5.09	13	13	0	0	58	56	40	33	8	35	40	.258	.325	.216	6.17	5.40
Wallach, Brett	R-R	6-2	180	12-2-88	0	1	5.23	12	12	0	0	31	34	20	18	4	15	38	.279	.333	.256	11.03	4.35
Webster, Allen	R-R	6-2	165	2-10-90	2	0	3.00	4	3	0	0	21	23	8	7	1	4	21	.277	.364	.246	9.00	1.71
Wilborn, Greg	L-L	6-2	175	6-3-87	2	1	7.45	12	0	0	0	19	25	20	16	3	16	23	.325	.200	.368	10.71	7.45

Fielding

Catcher	PCT	G	PO	A	E	DP	PB
Collado	.985	9	62	4	1	0	0
Erickson	.988	48	332	66	5	7	10
Wise	.982	24	187	31	4	3	10
Yount	1.000	1	2	0	0	0	0

First Base	PCT	G	PO	A	E	DP
Calfee	.973	7	69	4	2	5
Jacobs	.988	34	292	24	4	36
Orr	.986	37	319	33	5	25

Second Base	PCT	G	PO	A	E	DP
Guerrero	.931	13	21	33	4	3

	PCT	G	PO	A	E	DP
Hernandez	.938	11	15	45	4	10
Iden	.972	25	57	82	4	22
Ynoa	.958	28	76	85	7	25

Third Base	PCT	G	PO	A	E	DP
Guerrero	.850	7	6	11	3	1
Iden	.667	2	0	4	2	1
Ruggiano	.925	48	25	99	10	7
Yount	.891	21	11	31	5	6

Shortstop	PCT	G	PO	A	E	DP
Guerrero	.931	41	76	139	16	33
Hernandez	.912	32	42	92	13	15

	PCT	G	PO	A	E	DP
Ynoa	1.000	3	3	13	0	3

Outfield	PCT	G	PO	A	E	DP
Akins	.976	23	40	0	1	0
Calfee	1.000	4	5	0	0	0
Cavazos-Galvez	.974	66	102	9	3	3
McGee	.965	43	79	4	3	1
Ruggiano	1.000	3	4	0	0	0
Sands	.973	38	67	5	2	1
Smith	.955	26	39	3	2	0
Songco	1.000	30	39	1	0	0

DSL DODGERS — ROOKIE

DOMINICAN SUMMER LEAGUE

Batting	B-T	HT	WT	DOB	AVG	vLH	vRH	G	AB	R	H	2B	3B	HR	RBI	BB	HBP	SH	SF	SO	SB	CS	SLG	OBP
Aguilar, Alexis	R-R	5-11	162	6-17-91	.275	.250	.282	45	131	23	36	4	1	1	19	17	5	2	1	19	9	2	.344	.377
Bens, Edward	R-R	6-1	189	1-15-89	.266	.208	.282	41	109	13	29	6	0	1	14	10	4	0	0	12	1	1	.349	.350
Capellan, Jose	R-R	6-0	190	10-10-90	.248	.212	.258	50	161	19	40	8	0	1	11	13	5	3	0	28	2	2	.317	.324
Charles, Wilner	R-R	5-11	160	4-6-91	.268	.308	.256	51	164	29	44	3	1	1	18	22	7	2	0	35	10	6	.317	.378
Franco, Bladimir	R-R	6-1	172	2-4-91	.282	.326	.269	60	213	42	60	9	3	9	32	39	4	1	1	75	7	3	.479	.401
Infante, Jorky	B-R	6-0	155	2-24-91	.143	.000	.167	26	35	3	5	0	0	0	3	4	0	1	0	7	2	0	.143	.225
Lugo, Jose	R-R	6-1	200	6-19-90	.223	.188	.229	41	112	11	25	2	1	0	13	14	4	3	1	25	1	0	.259	.328
Lugo, Ronny	R-R	6-2	170	2-18-90	.246	.333	.218	63	228	30	56	8	5	0	26	20	4	2	4	44	5	5	.325	.313
Mercedes, Carlos	R-R	6-2	190	7-26-91	.133	.219	.102	42	120	15	16	3	1	2	12	18	3	0	1	46	0	2	.225	.261
Morales, Enlly	R-R	5-11	168	9-13-89	.317	.236	.340	64	243	35	77	19	1	3	29	31	7	1	2	23	4	5	.440	.406
Nieto, Abdul	R-R	6-3	180	12-9-91	.153	.111	.164	30	85	5	13	1	0	1	6	6	4	2	0	33	0	1	.200	.242
Oguisten, Faustino	R-R	6-2	165	1-17-91	.190	.176	.194	24	79	9	15	0	0	0	6	7	2	5	0	22	2	0	.190	.273
Perez, Freudys	R-R	5-10	160	8-13-91	.198	.190	.200	38	111	12	22	5	0	2	14	17	2	1	2	34	1	1	.297	.311
Ramirez, Jose	R-R	6-2	200	9-24-88	.213	.263	.200	51	188	28	40	10	1	2	21	21	5	2	3	37	10	6	.309	.304
Sanchez, Jose	R-R	6-2	175	5-11-90	.200	.000	.250	1	5	0	1	0	0	0	0	0	0	0	0	2	0	0	.200	.200
Sucre, Marlon	R-R	6-2	160	3-12-90	.255	.270	.250	47	149	25	38	5	1	3	22	7	17	1	0	31	5	2	.362	.358

Pitching	B-T	HT	WT	DOB	W	L	ERA	G	GS	CG	SV	IP	H	R	ER	HR	BB	SO	AVG	vLH	vRH	K/9	BB/9
Acevedo, Noel	L-L	5-11	160	4-12-90	0	0	4.50	3	0	0	0	4	4	2	2	0	4	1	.308	—	.308	2.25	9.00
Beras, Leonel	L-L	5-11	143	5-7-91	0	3	7.07	9	1	0	0	14	16	11	11	1	20	14	.200	.000	.227	9.00	12.86
Bustillos, Florencio	R-R	6-0	209	4-17-89	4	2	3.70	19	4	0	2	49	52	33	20	6	10	56	.260	.298	.248	10.36	1.85
Chavez, Giordanny	R-R	6-3	185	4-19-91	0	1	6.38	12	1	0	1	18	23	17	13	1	10	12	.303	.474	.246	5.89	4.91
De Aza, Carlos	R-R	6-3	178	5-4-90	4	2	1.30	18	0	0	1	28	14	8	4	0	20	24	.149	.105	.160	7.81	6.51
Dominguez, Jose	R-R	6-0	160	8-7-90	4	5	3.64	15	13	0	1	59	52	31	24	14	24	57	.233	.242	.230	8.65	3.64
Eugenia, Ivan	R-R	6-1	185	9-17-91	1	1	5.79	9	0	0	0	14	17	13	9	0	9	15	.288	.450	.205	9.64	5.79
Garcia, Jose	L-L	5-11	185	4-20-91	0	0	13.50	10	0	0	2	7	7	11	11	0	14	7	.259	.333	.250	8.59	17.18
Garcia, Yimi	R-R	6-1	175	8-18-90	3	2	1.67	16	5	0	0	54	37	13	10	0	15	51	.202	.197	.205	8.50	2.50
Gomez, Gustavo	R-R	6-1	150	5-24-91	2	3	2.70	14	13	0	0	60	55	28	18	2	19	63	.241	.271	.231	9.45	2.85
Lima, Joel	R-R	6-0	165	8-7-89	2	1	2.97	22	1	0	2	30	32	13	10	1	9	24	.276	.250	.289	7.12	2.67
Martinez, Geraldo	L-L	6-0	162	1-22-88	0	2	9.00	4	0	0	0	6	11	10	6	0	2	3	.355	.600	.308	4.50	3.00
Mateo, Jose	R-R	6-2	190	3-17-89	1	2	8.16	13	0	0	0	14	19	16	13	1	12	12	.322	.400	.295	7.53	7.53
Mendez, Irvit	R-R	6-6	225	4-11-90	0	0	27.00	3	1	0	0	1	4	4	4	0	7	2	.500	.750	.250	13.50	47.25
Mesa, Luis	R-R	6-4	170	7-13-90	0	3	6.37	12	6	0	0	30	36	27	21	2	12	17	.286	.286	.286	5.16	3.64
Nunez, Jonady	R-R	6-1	185	11-27-89	1	1	2.86	18	0	0	0	28	26	17	9	2	18	15	.248	.286	.238	4.76	5.72
Ozoria, Arismendy	R-R	6-0	195	8-7-90	3	2	2.53	15	8	0	1	57	44	23	16	3	23	54	.216	.196	.222	8.53	3.63
Rosano, Luis	R-R	6-2	190	4-25-91	3	5	4.98	12	11	0	0	43	46	26	24	3	16	26	.275	.184	.314	5.40	3.32
Tamares, Daniel	R-R	6-3	170	12-20-89	1	5	7.11	17	3	0	0	38	48	44	30	3	20	42	.314	.222	.342	9.95	4.74
Tamarez, Moises	R-R	6-3	195	3-6-93	1	0	4.31	13	3	0	0	31	31	16	15	1	13	10	.270	.154	.303	2.87	3.73

Fielding

Catcher	PCT	G	PO	A	E	DP	PB
Bens	.962	18	68	8	3	0	3
Capellan	.977	45	281	52	8	0	2
Lugo	.975	12	72	6	2	0	5
Perez	.962	19	88	14	4	0	4

First Base	PCT	G	PO	A	E	DP
Bens	.960	24	139	5	6	16
Lugo	.991	29	206	7	2	21
Mercedes	.981	31	242	14	5	19
Mirabal	1.000	1	5	0	0	1

Second Base	PCT	G	PO	A	E	DP
Aguilar	.957	17	33	33	3	10
Charles	.907	17	34	34	7	7
Infante	.935	13	24	19	3	4
Mirabal	.982	13	37	17	1	8
Morales	.931	29	71	64	10	21

Third Base	PCT	G	PO	A	E	DP
Franco	.892	55	60	139	24	15
Mirabal	.875	12	10	25	5	5
Morales	.917	4	5	6	1	0
Perez	.833	2	2	3	1	1

Shortstop	PCT	G	PO	A	E	DP
Aguilar	.887	12	17	30	6	3
Infante	.727	2	3	5	3	2
Mirabal	.947	38	63	117	10	19
Oguisten	.888	21	30	57	11	11

Outfield	PCT	G	PO	A	E	DP
Aguilar	1.000	5	7	0	0	0
Charles	.915	30	40	3	4	0
Lugo	1.000	1	1	0	0	0
Lugo	.967	61	80	9	3	2
Mercedes	.889	13	15	1	2	0
Nieto	.892	30	28	5	4	0
Ramirez	.987	51	67	8	1	4
Sanchez	1.000	1	1	0	0	0
Sucre	.939	39	59	3	4	1

Milwaukee Brewers

SEASON IN A SENTENCE: Without C.C. Sabathia (departed free agent) and Ben Sheets (injured free agent) at the top of the rotation, the Brewers could not muster a repeat of their 2008 playoff run, ranking next-to-last in ERA in the National League at 4.84, ahead of only 103-loss Washington.

HIGH POINT: Prince Fielder and Ryan Braun provided most of the highlights for the Brewers in 2009, combining for 78 home runs and 255 RBIs. Righthander Yovani Gallardo, however, was both the staff ace and a slugger, hitting a pair of home runs in April. His solo shot on April 29 backed up his eight shutout innings with 11 strikeouts in a 1-0 victory against Pittsburgh, and Gallardo beat the Reds 5-2 a month later, on May 31, to put the Brewers a season-high 10 games over .500.

LOW POINT: On July 5, Braun told reporters that the Brewers' pitching wasn't good enough and that a midseason trade would be needed to get the team to the playoffs. General manager Doug Melvin didn't agree and said so publicly in a strongly worded response, calling Braun's remarks "inappropriate" and "irresponsible," among other things. The Brewers were only a game out at the time but never got back into first place.

NOTABLE ROOKIES: An injury shelved Rickie Weeks after just 37 games. While the club missed Weeks, who was having a breakout season, his injury opened playing time for Casey McGehee, who was claimed in October 2008 off waivers from the Cubs. McGehee eventually shifted to third base from second and hit 16 home runs, while his 66 RBIs led all big league rookies.

KEY TRANSACTIONS: The Brewers traded for Felipe Lopez in July to replace Weeks, shifting McGehee to third. Bill Hall had fallen out of favor and was designated for assignment in August, so Milwaukee dealt him to Seattle for minor league righthander Ruben Flores. The Brewers still have to pay Hall $8.4 million in 2010 and have a $500,000 buyout for 2011.

DOWN ON THE FARM: High Class A Brevard County had many of the Brewers' better prospects and best stories in 2009, as the team went 79-48 and had a no-hitter from righthander Evan Anundsen. Top prospect Alcides Escobar graduated to the majors and performed well enough to prompt the team to trade J.J. Hardy after the season to the Twins, clearing the way for Escobar to become the team's shortstop in 2010.

OPENING DAY PAYROLL: $80,182,502

PLAYERS OF THE YEAR

MAJOR LEAGUE	MINOR LEAGUE
Prince Fielder	**Caleb Gindl**
1b	of
.284/.381/.550	(High A)
Led NL with 141 RBIs,	.277/.363/.459
2nd in HR (46)	15 2B, 17 HR

ORGANIZATION LEADERS

BATTING		*Minimum 250 at-bats
MAJORS		
*AVG	Ryan Braun	.320
*OPS	Prince Fielder	1.014
HR	Prince Fielder	46
RBI	Prince Fielder	141
MINORS		
*AVG	Bourgeois, Jason, Nashville	.316
R	Schafer, Logan, Huntsville/Brevard County	80
H	Schafer, Logan, Huntsville/Brevard County	148
TB	Katin, Brendan, Nashville	229
2B	Katin, Brendan, Nashville	33
3B	Duran, Jose, Wisconsin	8
	Gillespie, Cole, Brevard County/Reno	8
HR	Katin, Brendan, Nashville	24
	Koshansky, Joe, Nashville	24
RBI	Katin, Brendan, Nashville	92
BB	Lucroy, Jonathan, Huntsville	78
SO	Kjeldgaard, Brock, Wisconsin	172
SB	Farris, Eric, Brevard County	70
*OBP	Heether, Adam, Huntsville/Nashville	.396
*SLG	Heether, Adam, Huntsville/Nashville	.506

PITCHING		†Minimum 75 innings
MAJORS		
W	Braden Looper	14
†ERA	Yovani Gallardo	3.73
SO	Yovani Gallardo	204
MINORS		
W	Three tied at	13
L	Watten, Trey, Wisconsin	14
†ERA	Bowman, Michael, Wisconsin/Brevard Co.	2.60
G	Hinton, Robert, Huntsville/Nashville	53
	Wooten, Robert, Brevard County/Huntsville	53
GS	Cody, Chris, Huntsville/Nashville	26
	Holliman, Mark, Huntsville	26
SV	Wooten, Robert, Brevard County/Huntsville	29
IP	Cody, Chris, Huntsville/Nashville	152
BB	Frederickson, Evan, Wisconsin	82
SO	Rivas, Amaury, Brevard County	123
†AVG	Anundsen, Evan, Brevard County	.216

2009 PERFORMANCE

General Manager: Doug Melvin. **Farm Director:** Reid Nichols. **Scouting Director:** Bruce Seid.

Class	Team	League	W	L	PCT	Finish*	Manager(s)
Majors	Milwaukee Brewers	National	80	82	.494	9th (16)	Ken Macha
Triple-A	Nashville Sounds	Pacific Coast	75	69	.521	5th (16)	Don Money
Double-A	Huntsville Stars	Southern	63	75	.457	9th (10)	Robert Miscik
High A	Brevard County Manatees	Florida State	79	48	.622	1st (12)	Mike Guerrero
Low A	Wisconsin Timber Rattlers	Midwest	58	81	.417	12th (14)	Jeff Isom
Rookie	AZL Brewers	Arizona	25	31	.446	t-6th (11)	Tony Diggs
Rookie	Helena Brewers	Pioneer	32	44	.421	6th (8)	Rene Gonzales
Overall 2009 Minor League Record			332	348	.488	22nd (30)	

*Finish in overall standings (No. of teams in league). †League champion.

ORGANIZATION STATISTICS

MILWAUKEE BREWERS

NATIONAL LEAGUE

Batting	B-T	HT	WT	DOB	AVG	vLH	vRH	G	AB	R	H	2B	3B	HR	RBI	BB	HBP	SH	SF	SO	SB	CS	SLG	OBP
Bourgeois, Jason	R-R	5-9	190	1-4-82	.189	.240	.083	24	37	6	7	0	0	1	3	3	0	0	0	7	3	0	.270	.250
Braun, Ryan	R-R	6-1	200	11-17-83	.320	.395	.302	158	635	113	203	39	6	32	114	57	13	0	3	121	20	6	.551	.386
Cameron, Mike	R-R	6-2	205	1-8-73	.250	.271	.244	149	544	78	136	32	3	24	70	75	4	0	5	156	7	3	.452	.342
Catalanotto, Frank	L-R	6-0	205	4-27-74	.278	.091	.293	77	144	18	40	6	3	1	9	14	2	0	2	23	2	0	.382	.346
Corporan, Carlos	B-R	6-2	220	1-7-84	1.000	—	1.000	1	1	1	1	0	0	0	0	0	0	0	0	0	0	0	1.000	1.000
Counsell, Craig	L-R	6-0	180	8-21-70	.285	.237	.290	130	404	61	115	22	8	4	39	42	6	3	4	54	3	4	.408	.357
Duffy, Chris	L-L	5-9	185	4-20-80	.125	.000	.138	19	32	3	4	1	0	0	3	4	0	1	0	12	0	0	.156	.222
Escobar, Alcides	R-R	6-1	180	12-16-86	.304	.480	.260	38	125	20	38	3	1	1	11	4	2	2	1	18	4	2	.368	.333
Fielder, Prince	L-R	5-11	270	5-9-84	.299	.292	.303	162	591	103	177	35	3	46	141	110	9	0	9	138	2	3	.602	.412
Gamel, Mat	L-R	6-0	200	7-26-85	.242	.304	.229	61	128	11	31	6	1	5	20	18	1	0	1	54	1	0	.422	.338
Gerut, Jody	L-L	6-0	190	9-18-77	.236	.143	.245	85	161	23	38	7	0	5	21	14	1	0	1	21	4	2	.373	.299
2-team total (37 San Diego)					.230	—		122	274	40	63	13	0	9	35	19	1	0	4	43	6	2	.376	.279
Hall, Bill	R-R	6-0	210	12-28-79	.201	.244	.174	76	214	22	43	12	0	6	24	19	0	0	1	72	1	0	.341	.265
Hardy, J.J.	R-R	6-2	190	8-19-82	.229	.169	.245	115	414	53	95	16	2	11	47	43	2	1	5	85	0	1	.357	.302
Hart, Corey	R-R	6-6	230	3-24-82	.260	.248	.264	115	419	64	109	24	3	12	48	43	6	1	3	92	11	6	.418	.335
Iribarren, Hernan	L-R	6-1	195	6-29-84	.231	.000	.273	12	13	1	3	2	0	0	1	1	0	0	0	5	0	0	.385	.286
Kendall, Jason	R-R	6-0	190	6-26-74	.241	.218	.246	134	452	48	109	19	2	2	43	46	17	6	5	58	7	2	.305	.331
Lopez, Felipe	B-R	6-0	205	5-12-80	.320	.328	.318	66	259	44	83	20	2	3	32	37	1	0	0	41	0	3	.448	.407
2-team total (85 Arizona)					.310	—		151	604	88	187	38	3	9	57	71	2	1	2	100	6	6	.427	.383
McGehee, Casey	R-R	6-1	195	10-12-82	.301	.303	.301	116	355	58	107	20	1	16	66	34	1	0	4	67	0	2	.499	.360
Nelson, Brad	L-R	6-2	265	12-23-82	.000	.000	.000	19	21	0	0	0	0	0	0	2	0	0	0	9	0	0	.000	.087
Patterson, Corey	L-R	5-10	175	8-13-79	.071	—	.071	11	14	0	1	0	0	0	0	0	0	1	0	7	0	1	.071	.071
2-team total (5 Washington)					.103	—		16	29	0	3	0	0	0	0	1	0	1	0	13	2	1	.103	.103
Rivera, Mike	R-R	6-1	235	9-8-76	.228	.267	.214	41	114	10	26	7	0	2	14	15	2	0	1	32	1	0	.342	.326
Weeks, Rickie	R-R	5-10	215	9-13-82	.272	.276	.271	37	147	28	40	5	2	9	24	12	3	0	0	39	2	2	.517	.340

Pitching	B-T	HT	WT	DOB	W	L	ERA	G	GS	CG	SV	IP	H	R	ER	HR	BB	SO	AVG	vLH	vRH	K/9	BB/9
Axford, John	R-R	6-5	195	4-1-83	0	0	3.52	7	0	0	1	8	5	3	3	0	6	9	.179	.067	.308	10.57	7.04
Burns, Mike	R-R	6-1	210	7-14-78	3	5	5.75	15	8	0	0	52	60	36	33	10	17	39	.294	.295	.293	6.79	2.96
Bush, Dave	R-R	6-2	205	11-9-79	5	9	6.38	22	21	0	0	114	131	84	81	19	37	89	.294	.293	.295	7.01	2.91
Butler, Josh	R-R	6-5	200	12-11-84	0	0	9.00	3	0	0	0	4	7	4	4	0	6	3	.368	.417	.286	6.75	13.50
Coffey, Todd	R-R	6-4	240	9-9-80	4	4	2.90	78	0	0	2	84	76	28	27	8	21	65	.247	.282	.223	6.99	2.26
Colome, Jesus	R-R	6-2	240	12-23-77	0	0	5.68	5	0	0	0	6	11	4	4	1	0	3	.393	.385	.400	4.26	0.00
2-team total (16 Washington)					1	1	7.59	21	0	0	0	21	34	18	18	2	6	15	—	—	—	6.33	2.53
DiFelice, Mark	R-R	6-2	190	8-23-76	4	1	3.66	59	0	0	0	52	49	21	21	6	15	48	.245	.278	.233	8.36	2.61
Dillard, Tim	R-R	6-4	225	7-19-83	0	1	12.46	2	0	0	0	4	7	6	6	1	5	1	.412	.500	.364	2.08	10.38
Gallardo, Yovani	R-R	6-2	220	2-27-86	13	12	3.73	30	30	1	0	186	150	78	77	21	94	204	.219	.213	.225	9.89	4.56
Hoffman, Trevor	R-R	6-0	220	10-13-67	3	2	1.83	55	0	0	37	54	35	11	11	2	14	48	.183	.222	.149	8.00	2.33
Julio, Jorge	R-R	6-1	225	3-3-79	1	1	7.79	15	0	0	0	17	15	17	15	2	15	13	.217	.269	.186	6.75	7.79
Looper, Braden	R-R	6-3	235	10-28-74	14	7	5.22	34	34	0	0	195	226	123	113	39	64	100	.289	.302	.278	4.62	2.96
McClung, Seth	L-R	6-6	260	2-7-81	3	3	4.94	41	2	0	0	62	62	34	34	11	39	40	.267	.291	.243	5.81	5.66
Narveson, Chris	L-L	6-3	205	12-20-81	2	0	3.83	21	4	0	0	47	45	22	20	7	16	46	.247	.313	.224	8.81	3.06
Parra, Manny	L-L	6-3	215	10-30-82	11	11	6.36	27	27	0	0	140	179	108	99	19	77	116	.306	.287	.311	7.46	4.95
Riske, David	R-R	6-2	190	10-23-76	0	0	18.00	1	0	0	0	1	4	2	2	0	0	0	.800	1.000	.500	0.00	0.00
Smith, Chris	R-R	6-2	200	4-9-81	0	0	4.11	35	0	0	0	46	41	21	21	11	19	35	.232	.232	.232	6.85	3.72
Stetter, Mitch	L-L	6-4	210	1-16-81	4	1	3.60	71	0	0	1	45	37	19	18	4	27	44	.216	.178	.259	8.80	5.40
Suppan, Jeff	R-R	6-2	230	1-2-75	7	12	5.29	30	30	0	0	162	200	106	95	25	74	80	.309	.311	.306	4.45	4.12
Swindle, R.J.	L-L	6-3	190	7-7-83	0	0	16.20	6	0	0	0	7	12	12	12	3	4	8	.375	.385	.368	10.80	5.40
Vargas, Claudio	R-R	6-4	235	6-19-78	1	0	1.78	28	0	0	0	30	18	6	6	2	11	20	.175	.182	.169	5.93	3.26
2-team total (8 Los Angeles)					1	0	1.74	36	0	0	0	41	25	8	8	3	14	30	—	—	—	6.53	3.27
Villanueva, Carlos	R-R	6-2	230	11-28-83	4	10	5.34	64	6	0	3	96	102	58	57	13	35	83	.268	.257	.278	7.78	3.28
Weathers, David	R-R	6-3	240	9-25-69	1	3	4.88	25	0	0	0	24	26	15	13	3	11	10	.283	.257	.298	3.75	4.13
2-team total (43 Cincinnati)					4	6	3.92	68	0	0	1	62	53	29	27	10	28	37	—	—	—	5.37	4.06

Fielding

Catcher	PCT	G	PO	A	E	DP	PB
Corporan	1.000	1	2	1	0	0	0
Kendall	.992	133	882	61	8	2	4
Rivera	1.000	34	234	14	0	1	2

First Base	PCT	G	PO	A	E	DP
Fielder	.995	162	1387	66	7	142
McGehee	1.000	3	3	0	0	0

Second Base	PCT	G	PO	A	E	DP
Catalanotto	1.000	3	1	0	0	0
Counsell	1.000	50	92	131	0	37
Iribarren	1.000	2	3	4	0	2
Lopez	.972	62	105	176	8	46

	PCT	G	PO	A	E	DP
McGehee	.980	22	37	61	2	13
Weeks	.964	35	66	95	6	21

Third Base	PCT	G	PO	A	E	DP
Counsell	.955	43	27	58	4	5
Gamel	.885	27	19	35	7	5
Hall	.975	66	33	123	4	13
Iribarren	—	1	0	0	0	0
McGehee	.916	71	31	111	13	11

Shortstop	PCT	G	PO	A	E	DP
Counsell	.991	27	35	70	1	20
Escobar	.962	37	59	94	6	20
Hardy	.983	112	146	318	8	61

Outfield	PCT	G	PO	A	E	DP
Bourgeois	1.000	7	14	0	0	0
Braun	.994	158	304	8	2	2
Cameron	.990	147	404	4	4	1
Catalanotto	.985	37	64	2	1	0
Duffy	1.000	10	21	1	0	0
Gerut	.986	52	69	1	1	0
Hall	1.000	7	16	0	0	0
Hart	.974	112	187	3	5	0
Iribarren	—	1	0	0	0	0
McGehee	—	1	0	0	0	0
Nelson	1.000	2	4	0	0	0
Patterson	1.000	4	6	0	0	0

NASHVILLE SOUNDS TRIPLE-A

PACIFIC COAST LEAGUE

Batting	B-T	HT	WT	DOB	AVG	vLH	vRH	G	AB	R	H	2B	3B	HR	RBI	BB	HBP	SH	SF	SO	SB	CS	SLG	OBP
Almonte, Erick	R-R	6-2	180	2-1-78	.291	.284	.296	105	247	29	72	11	0	2	31	27	2	0	1	53	4	0	.360	.365
Anderson, Drew T.	L-R	6-2	200	6-9-81	.125	.000	.182	5	16	2	2	0	1	0	1	2	0	0	0	3	0	0	.250	.222
Arlis, Patrick	R-R	6-0	215	12-18-80	.300	.333	.282	22	60	8	18	4	0	0	5	9	0	1	1	12	0	0	.367	.386
Bourgeois, Jason	R-R	5-9	190	1-4-82	.316	.293	.325	105	424	61	134	18	6	2	41	22	4	2	2	40	36	7	.401	.354
Corporan, Carlos	B-R	6-2	220	1-7-84	.201	.233	.191	57	179	9	36	9	1	1	18	9	5	2	7	43	0	1	.279	.250
Duffy, Chris	L-L	5-9	185	4-20-80	.167	.250	.000	3	6	1	1	0	0	0	0	1	0	2	0	2	0	1	.167	.286
Escobar, Alcides	R-R	6-1	180	12-16-86	.298	.356	.272	109	430	76	128	24	6	4	34	32	5	19	1	65	42	10	.409	.353
Gamel, Mat	L-R	6-0	200	7-26-85	.278	.338	.256	75	273	42	76	18	1	11	48	38	3	1	5	89	1	0	.473	.367
Garciaparra, Michael	R-R	6-1	165	4-2-83	.271	.286	.250	22	48	4	13	2	0	1	2	4	0	3	0	7	0	0	.375	.327
Gillespie, Cole	R-R	6-1	205	6-20-84	.242	.216	.253	75	236	29	57	12	5	7	27	31	3	3	4	56	6	5	.424	.332
2-team total (42 Reno)					.265	—	—	117	374	62	99	18	9	12	54	58	5	3	7	87	14	5	.457	.365
Gwynn Jr., Tony	L-R	5-11	195	10-4-82	.309	.404	.260	38	152	34	47	8	1	1	9	20	0	2	1	21	15	1	.395	.387
Hall, Bill	R-R	6-0	210	12-28-79	.286	.375	.167	4	14	1	4	1	0	1	4	1	0	0	0	4	1	0	.571	.333
Hardy, J.J.	R-R	6-2	190	8-19-82	.254	.350	.216	18	71	7	18	2	0	4	12	3	0	0	0	9	0	0	.451	.284
Hart, Corey	R-R	6-6	230	3-24-82	.500	.500	.500	4	10	5	5	1	0	1	3	2	0	0	0	2	0	0	.900	.643
Heether, Adam	R-R	6-0	195	1-14-82	.293	.288	.295	112	379	62	111	29	1	16	59	59	11	0	3	84	5	1	.501	.400
Iribarren, Hernan	L-R	6-1	195	6-29-84	.311	.304	.314	105	379	46	118	19	5	3	54	28	4	7	3	63	13	7	.412	.362
Katin, Brendan	R-R	6-1	235	1-28-83	.244	.254	.240	127	459	67	112	33	6	24	92	35	7	1	4	164	2	0	.499	.305
Knott, Jon	R-R	6-3	225	8-4-78	.111	.000	.143	5	9	1	1	0	0	1	1	1	0	0	0	4	0	0	.444	.200
Koshansky, Joe	L-L	6-4	230	5-26-82	.218	.212	.219	135	455	72	99	21	3	24	80	64	5	0	7	166	7	4	.435	.316
Maldonado, Martin	R-R	6-1	210	8-16-86	.333	.286	.364	7	18	1	6	1	0	0	3	1	0	0	1	2	0	0	.389	.350
Parejo, Freddy	R-R	6-2	175	10-16-84	.262	.182	.290	16	42	3	11	1	0	0	3	1	0	1	0	7	0	1	.286	.279
Patterson, Corey	L-R	5-10	175	8-13-79	.331	.323	.333	29	124	24	41	12	3	5	22	8	0	1	2	25	7	3	.597	.366
Raburn, Johnny	B-R	6-0	165	2-16-79	.304	.286	.311	36	102	16	31	3	2	2	10	11	0	3	2	11	2	1	.431	.365
Redman, Tike	L-L	5-11	175	3-10-77	.255	.250	.257	15	55	6	14	1	0	0	6	8	0	1	1	8	0	0	.273	.344
Rivera, Mike	R-R	6-1	235	9-8-76	.231	.000	.333	3	13	1	3	1	0	0	3	0	0	0	0	5	0	0	.308	.231
Salome, Angel	R-R	5-7	200	6-8-86	.286	.317	.274	82	283	32	81	14	2	6	44	22	2	0	7	55	0	0	.413	.334
Stern, Adam	L-R	5-11	185	2-12-80	.310	.227	.339	18	84	12	26	4	0	1	8	4	1	0	0	12	3	1	.393	.348
Tyner, Jason	L-L	6-1	180	4-23-77	.095	.000	.125	9	21	2	2	0	0	0	2	2	0	0	1	2	0	0	.095	.167

Pitching	B-T	HT	WT	DOB	W	L	ERA	G	GS	CG	SV	IP	H	R	ER	HR	BB	SO	vLH	vRH	K/9	BB/9
Axford, John	R-R	6-5	195	4-1-83	5	0	3.55	22	0	0	0	33	23	13	13	2	19	37	.197	.227	.178	10.09	5.18
Burns, Mike	R-R	6-1	210	7-14-78	8	3	2.62	14	14	2	0	93	89	32	27	9	16	63	.249	.229	.270	6.12	1.55
Butler, Josh	R-R	6-5	200	12-11-84	1	1	3.60	3	3	0	0	15	15	6	6	2	1	15	.263	.314	.182	9.00	0.60
Cody, Chris	L-L	6-1	195	1-7-84	8	8	4.90	17	16	1	0	94	108	53	51	13	30	58	.289	.288	.289	5.57	2.88
Colome, Jesus	R-R	6-2	240	12-23-77	1	0	0.00	2	0	0	0	7	3	0	0	0	2	11	.120	.200	.067	14.14	2.57
Dillard, Tim	R-R	6-4	225	7-19-83	11	7	4.51	24	24	2	0	148	162	86	74	11	52	64	.287	.257	.314	3.90	3.17
Ginter, Matt	R-R	6-1	220	12-24-77	3	3	3.81	38	3	0	2	76	85	41	32	7	24	52	.282	.254	.301	6.19	2.85
Green, Nick	R-R	6-4	200	8-20-84	4	4	6.68	13	11	0	0	65	82	49	48	14	14	49	.305	.250	.355	6.82	1.95
Gulin, Lindsay	L-L	6-2	175	11-22-76	7	10	4.78	27	24	1	0	139	127	80	74	9	77	97	.244	.312	.218	6.27	4.97
Hinton, Robert	R-R	6-1	195	8-13-84	0	0	5.12	10	0	0	1	19	21	11	11	2	8	16	.284	.417	.220	7.45	3.72
Hoffman, Trevor	R-R	6-0	220	10-13-67	0	0	9.00	2	1	0	0	2	4	2	2	0	0	2	.500	.000	.571	9.00	0.00
Houston, Ryan	R-R	6-4	230	9-22-79	5	4	3.62	40	0	0	7	50	47	22	20	3	24	42	.258	.263	.255	7.61	4.35
Johnson, David	R-R	6-5	205	8-25-82	3	1	3.72	47	0	0	5	56	62	23	23	3	20	41	.290	.218	.331	6.63	3.23
Jones, Mike	R-R	6-4	220	4-23-83	1	2	6.53	4	4	0	0	21	32	18	15	4	13	14	.364	.483	.305	6.10	5.66
Littleton, Wes	R-R	6-3	200	9-2-82	4	1	7.14	23	0	0	0	29	36	27	23	4	26	24	.313	.261	.348	7.45	8.07
Narron, Sam	L-L	6-7	200	7-12-81	1	7	5.62	18	9	0	0	75	104	53	47	7	20	40	.327	.375	.317	4.78	2.39
Narveson, Chris	L-L	6-3	205	12-20-81	4	4	3.70	26	6	0	5	75	59	36	31	3	26	76	.209	.235	.199	9.08	3.11
Parra, Manny	L-L	6-3	215	10-30-82	1	2	2.92	4	4	0	0	25	16	10	8	0	13	19	.180	.200	.176	6.93	4.74
Sandoval, Juan	R-R	6-2	170	1-13-81	0	0	4.82	7	0	0	0	9	9	5	5	1	5	11	.257	.294	.222	10.61	4.82
Smith, Chris	R-R	6-2	200	4-9-81	2	0	1.27	28	0	0	17	43	31	7	6	3	6	49	.204	.176	.226	10.34	1.27
Suppan, Jeff	R-R	6-2	230	1-2-75	0	1	12.27	1	1	0	0	4	8	5	5	0	0	3	.444	.333	.556	7.36	0.00
Swindle, R.J.	L-L	6-3	190	7-7-83	3	1	1.03	31	0	0	2	44	30	6	5	1	13	41	.194	.148	.218	8.45	2.68
Wright, Chase	L-L	6-2	205	2-8-83	9	7	4.51	26	24	0	0	132	152	83	66	14	50	57	.291	.220	.313	3.90	3.42

Fielding

Catcher

	PCT	G	PO	A	E	DP	PB
Arlis	1.000	19	105	10	0	0	1
Corporan	.984	54	350	24	6	3	4
Maldonado	.972	6	32	3	1	0	0
Rivera	.950	3	19	0	1	0	0
Salome	.976	72	379	31	10	4	8

First Base

	PCT	G	PO	A	E	DP
Almonte	1.000	31	248	14	0	31
Heether	1.000	1	1	1	0	0
Koshansky	.997	114	1016	72	3	78

Second Base

	PCT	G	PO	A	E	DP
Escobar	.879	7	14	15	4	3
Garciaparra	.952	8	10	30	2	7
Heether	.947	16	30	41	4	8
Iribarren	.990	98	214	276	5	63
Raburn	.991	22	59	48	1	10

Third Base

	PCT	G	PO	A	E	DP
Almonte	.909	8	2	8	1	1
Gamel	.910	74	39	144	18	12
Garciaparra	—	1	0	0	0	0
Heether	.976	61	29	134	4	10
Iribarren	1.000	3	1	8	0	0

Shortstop

	PCT	G	PO	A	E	DP
Escobar	.975	102	156	316	12	59
Garciaparra	.889	5	3	13	2	2
Hall	.889	2	1	7	1	0
Hardy	.976	16	29	51	2	14
Heether	.925	15	12	37	4	4
Raburn	.960	9	8	16	1	3

Outfield

	PCT	G	PO	A	E	DP
Almonte	1.000	1	3	0	0	0
Anderson	1.000	5	11	0	0	0
Bourgeois	.967	103	233	4	8	0
Duffy	1.000	2	7	0	0	0
Garciaparra	1.000	2	3	0	0	0
Gillespie	.988	74	156	2	2	0
Gwynn Jr.	1.000	38	92	2	0	2
Hall	1.000	2	2	0	0	0
Hart	1.000	4	5	0	0	0
Heether	.970	17	30	2	1	1
Katin	.967	117	228	8	8	4
Knott	1.000	4	5	0	0	0
Parejo	1.000	13	20	1	0	0
Patterson	.987	28	73	3	1	1
Redman	1.000	15	30	1	0	0
Stern	1.000	18	31	3	0	0
Tyner	1.000	7	9	0	0	0

HUNTSVILLE STARS

SOUTHERN LEAGUE

DOUBLE-A

Batting	B-T	HT	WT	DOB	AVG	vLH	vRH	G	AB	R	H	2B	3B	HR	RBI	BB	HBP	SH	SF	SO	SB	CS	SLG	OBP
Anderson, Drew T.	L-R	6-2	200	6-9-81	.301	.307	.299	108	389	56	117	25	2	10	57	45	4	1	4	77	9	5	.452	.376
Brownstein, Mike	R-R	5-10	175	8-9-87	.375	.500	.333	5	8	0	3	2	0	0	1	0	0	0	2	0	0	.625	.444
Cain, Lorenzo	R-R	6-2	185	4-13-86	.214	.171	.231	42	145	17	31	6	0	4	15	10	3	1	1	35	3	3	.338	.277
Catalanotto, Frank	L-R	6-0	205	4-27-74	.250	—	.250	3	12	2	3	2	0	0	3	2	0	0	0	0	0	0	.417	.357
Caufield, Chuck	R-R	6-1	180	7-6-83	.255	.235	.262	103	302	34	77	13	1	4	36	20	10	2	6	56	2	2	.344	.317
Errecart, Chris	R-L	6-1	210	2-11-85	.149	.100	.170	18	67	8	10	2	1	0	6	4	2	0	0	21	1	0	.209	.219
Fermaint, Charlie	R-S	5-8	198	10-11-85	.000	.000	.000	5	10	0	0	0	0	0	0	0	0	0	0	3	0	0	.000	.000
Garciaparra, Michael	R-R	6-1	165	4-2-83	.206	.125	.229	50	141	4	29	4	0	0	11	18	3	2	1	36	0	2	.234	.307
Green, Taylor	L-R	5-10	195	11-2-86	.258	.288	.250	87	306	34	79	15	0	5	43	33	2	0	4	37	0	2	.356	.330
Heether, Adam	R-R	6-0	195	1-14-82	.325	.250	.344	9	40	5	13	3	0	2	12	1	2	0	2	10	0	0	.550	.356
Hopf, J.R.	L-R	6-1	205	11-4-82	.250	.222	.253	85	192	18	48	13	0	3	23	19	2	0	3	37	1	0	.365	.319
Justis, Shane	R-R	5-10	175	3-11-83	.277	.286	.274	127	473	71	131	28	4	5	50	34	18	8	4	65	10	5	.385	.346
Kemp, Corey	R-R	6-0	240	2-24-86	.000	.000	.000	6	16	0	0	0	0	0	0	1	0	0	0	4	0	0	.000	.059
Lawrie, Brett	R-R	5-11	200	1-18-90	.269	.400	.238	13	52	6	14	0	1	0	0	0	1	0	0	14	0	2	.308	.283
Lucroy, Jonathan	R-R	6-0	185	6-13-86	.267	.273	.266	125	419	61	112	32	2	9	66	78	2	1	6	66	1	1	.418	.380
Melillo, Kevin	L-R	5-11	185	5-14-82	.249	.176	.267	113	385	60	96	22	3	9	52	60	0	1	8	68	4	3	.392	.344
Parejo, Freddy	R-R	6-2	175	10-16-84	.229	.254	.221	92	258	28	59	13	1	2	23	16	1	2	2	49	3	2	.310	.274
Perez, Yohannis	R-R	6-0	190	10-11-82	.262	.254	.265	85	248	26	65	14	0	3	18	19	2	0	2	37	1	1	.355	.317
Raburn, Johnny	B-R	6-0	165	2-16-79	.233	.200	.239	54	133	19	31	3	0	1	9	30	0	3	1	19	4	3	.278	.372
Rottino, Vinny	R-R	6-1	220	4-7-80	.249	.309	.231	98	341	46	85	13	0	4	48	47	2	0	5	45	9	1	.323	.339
2-team total (31 Chattanooga)					.261	—	—	129	414	64	108	18	0	4	55	62	2	0	6	53	14	2	.333	.355
Schafer, Logan	L-L	6-1	180	9-8-86	.217	.250	.211	7	23	4	5	0	1	0	0	4	2	1	0	3	1	0	.304	.379
Stern, Adam	L-R	5-11	185	2-12-80	.280	.293	.277	104	404	64	113	17	6	3	32	41	4	5	3	51	28	10	.374	.350

Pitching	B-T	HT	WT	DOB	W	L	ERA	G	GS	CG	SV	IP	H	R	ER	HR	BB	SO	AVG	vLH	vRH	K/9	BB/9
Aguilar, Omar	R-R	5-11	220	3-31-85	1	0	7.71	23	0	0	6	26	36	32	22	3	18	33	.313	.233	.361	11.57	6.31
Axford, John	R-R	6-5	195	4-1-83	0	0	3.52	4	0	0	1	8	7	3	3	1	3	9	.250	.500	.150	10.57	3.52
Baron, Casey	L-L	6-2	185	11-29-84	4	6	2.44	37	0	0	1	48	46	15	13	4	15	46	.256	.226	.271	8.63	2.81
Braddock, Zach	L-L	6-4	230	8-23-87	2	1	2.87	12	0	0	0	16	16	9	5	2	3	22	.262	.273	.256	12.64	1.72
Bramhall, Bobby	L-L	5-10	170	7-13-85	6	7	5.29	31	16	0	0	97	105	62	57	8	48	91	.279	.308	.265	8.44	4.45
Bucci, Nick	R-R	6-2	180	7-16-90	1	0	6.75	3	0	0	0	4	3	3	3	2	2	3	.231	.500	.182	6.75	4.50
Bush, Dave	R-R	6-2	205	11-9-79	0	2	9.95	2	2	0	0	6	7	7	7	0	5	4	.318	.400	.250	5.68	7.11
Butler, Josh	R-R	6-5	200	12-11-84	2	1	2.85	8	8	0	0	41	37	17	13	2	13	33	.242	.294	.200	7.24	2.85
Cody, Chris	L-L	6-1	195	1-7-84	5	1	2.30	10	10	0	0	59	42	16	15	5	10	48	.195	.189	.198	7.36	1.53
Ellison, Derrick	L-L	6-2	195	9-6-78	2	2	4.45	19	0	0	2	28	21	18	14	3	15	26	.202	.222	.195	8.26	4.76
Green, Nick	R-R	6-4	200	8-20-84	1	6	4.30	7	7	0	0	44	49	22	21	1	6	23	.285	.260	.305	4.70	1.23
Hand, Donovan	R-R	6-4	190	4-20-86	8	5	3.56	27	12	0	1	99	102	44	39	12	21	51	.268	.274	.265	4.65	1.92
Henderson, Jim	L-R	6-5	190	10-21-82	1	0	2.57	5	0	0	0	7	8	3	2	0	4	5	.276	.286	.267	6.43	5.14
Hinton, Robert	R-R	6-1	195	8-13-84	0	6	4.20	43	0	0	11	56	50	29	26	4	30	58	.240	.274	.222	9.38	4.85
Holliman, Mark	R-R	6-0	195	9-19-83	7	10	4.64	26	26	0	0	138	150	77	71	19	57	89	.282	.312	.259	5.82	3.73
Jeffress, Jeremy	R-R	6-0	195	9-21-87	1	3	7.57	8	8	0	0	27	26	29	23	1	33	34	.255	.282	.238	11.20	10.87
Jones, Mike	R-R	6-2	180	4-23-83	1	5	4.59	13	13	0	0	69	74	38	35	6	19	47	.282	.343	.240	6.16	2.49
Kintzler, Brandon	R-R	6-1	180	8-1-84	1	2	4.54	9	6	0	0	36	41	21	18	5	9	32	.285	.333	.240	8.07	2.27
Littleton, Wes	R-R	6-3	200	9-2-82	0	1	5.40	12	0	0	0	17	19	11	10	0	13	14	.302	.250	.333	7.56	7.02
McClendon, Mike	R-R	6-5	215	4-3-85	4	3	3.30	41	2	0	3	85	86	40	31	4	20	57	.268	.291	.255	6.06	2.13
Narron, Sam	L-L	6-7	200	7-12-81	0	1	2.13	2	2	0	0	13	11	4	3	0	2	9	.224	.267	.206	6.39	1.42
Sandoval, Juan	R-R	6-2	170	1-13-81	4	3	4.93	42	0	0	2	49	52	36	27	1	24	38	.271	.277	.268	6.93	4.38
Scarpetta, Cody	R-R	6-3	240	8-25-88	0	0	5.40	1	1	0	0	5	5	3	3	1	1	3	.263	.250	.286	1.80	1.80
Wahpepah, Josh	R-R	6-0	195	7-17-84	1	2	5.18	33	4	0	0	66	70	43	38	2	44	52	.273	.217	.305	7.09	6.00
Welch, David	R-L	6-4	215	6-2-83	8	8	4.03	24	21	1	0	118	136	62	53	12	31	66	.291	.288	.292	5.02	2.36
Wooten, Rob	R-R	6-1	210	7-21-85	0	1	4.28	27	0	0	11	27	26	15	13	3	9	34	.245	.333	.154	11.20	2.96

Fielding

Catcher	PCT	G	PO	A	E	DP	PB
Hopf	.982	28	148	16	3	0	3
Lucroy	.991	108	727	70	7	4	12
Rottino	.973	11	68	4	2	0	0

First Base	PCT	G	PO	A	E	DP
Errecart	.994	17	148	11	1	13
Garciaparra	.955	3	20	1	1	4
Green	1.000	10	59	4	0	5
Hopf	.982	18	150	12	3	18
Kemp	1.000	3	14	0	0	1
Melillo	.990	49	342	48	4	43
Raburn	1.000	1	12	0	0	0
Rottino	.991	53	388	41	4	29

Second Base	PCT	G	PO	A	E	DP
Heether	1.000	1	2	5	0	0
Justis	.974	110	230	288	14	72

Lawrie	1.000	13	22	34	0	8
Melillo	.962	12	25	25	2	8
Raburn	.964	9	12	15	1	2

Third Base	PCT	G	PO	A	E	DP
Brownstein	1.000	2	0	5	0	1
Garciaparra	.909	5	3	7	1	0
Green	.931	76	40	135	13	13
Heether	1.000	2	1	6	0	0
Justis	.941	7	4	12	1	0
Melillo	.927	42	22	79	8	4
Raburn	1.000	3	0	2	0	0
Rottino	.857	9	2	16	3	1

Shortstop	PCT	G	PO	A	E	DP
Garciaparra	.947	39	47	97	8	21
Heether	.903	7	5	23	3	2
Perez	.967	76	103	186	10	43

Raburn	.938	35	48	89	9	21

Outfield	PCT	G	PO	A	E	DP
Anderson	.967	101	172	2	6	0
Cain	.989	39	84	2	1	0
Catalanotto	1.000	1	1	0	0	0
Caufield	.966	83	137	6	5	0
Fermaint	1.000	2	2	0	0	0
Hopf	—	1	0	0	0	0
Melillo	—	1	0	0	0	0
Parejo	.974	81	146	3	4	1
Raburn	—	1	0	0	0	0
Rottino	.970	34	61	3	2	0
Schafer	1.000	6	20	0	0	0
Stern	1.000	99	213	5	0	1

BREVARD COUNTY MANATEES HIGH CLASS A
FLORIDA STATE LEAGUE

Batting	B-T	HT	WT	DOB	AVG	vLH	vRH	G	AB	R	H	2B	3B	HR	RBI	BB	HBP	SH	SF	SO	SB	CS	SLG	OBP
Alfonso, Derrick	R-R	6-0	210	7-6-85	.222	.250	.200	10	27	5	6	0	1	0	1	0	0	1	0	7	0	0	.296	.222
Brewer, Brent	R-R	6-2	198	12-19-87	.222	.250	.213	104	356	42	79	18	1	1	29	33	1	7	2	109	19	7	.287	.288
Corporan, Carlos	B-R	6-2	220	1-7-84	.261	.429	.231	14	46	1	12	1	0	0	6	1	1	0	0	10	0	0	.283	.292
De La Rosa, Anderson	R-R	6-0	190	8-1-84	.207	.182	.218	36	111	13	23	4	0	0	5	0	2	1	0	32	1	4	.243	.221
Errecart, Chris	R-L	6-1	210	2-11-85	.245	.183	.265	90	335	40	82	20	2	8	43	26	10	0	4	86	4	5	.388	.315
Farris, Eric	R-R	5-10	170	3-3-86	.298	.297	.299	124	473	68	141	18	1	7	49	29	3	26	3	46	70	6	.385	.341
Gillespie, Cole	R-R	6-1	205	6-20-84	.349	.333	.351	12	43	10	15	2	3	1	9	7	0	0	1	11	4	0	.605	.431
Gindl, Caleb	L-L	5-9	185	8-31-88	.277	.206	.301	112	394	61	109	15	3	17	71	57	1	2	8	92	18	4	.459	.363
Haydel, Lee	L-L	5-11	175	7-15-87	.275	.186	.303	124	491	66	135	16	5	2	50	17	4	6	5	110	39	10	.340	.302
Maldonado, Martin	R-R	6-1	210	8-16-86	.199	.277	.172	81	251	25	50	9	0	2	28	33	0	7	9	2	51	2	1	.259	.300
Miranda, Sergio	B-R	5-9	180	3-5-87	.297	.268	.305	82	259	27	77	13	3	1	28	23	3	1	2	34	7	3	.382	.359
Roberts, Michael	R-R	6-2	185	8-28-87	.143	.500	.059	7	21	1	3	1	0	0	0	0	0	0	0	9	0	0	.190	.143
Sanchez, Juan	R-R	5-11	167	1-16-87	.229	.167	.241	15	35	2	8	2	0	0	1	3	0	1	0	9	0	0	.286	.289
Schafer, Logan	L-L	6-1	180	9-8-86	.313	.336	.305	113	457	76	143	31	6	6	58	38	5	1	4	53	16	8	.446	.369
Wheeler, Zelous	R-R	5-10	220	1-16-87	.268	.232	.280	125	410	50	110	23	3	7	64	60	12	2	10	78	13	3	.390	.370
Whiteside, Brett	R-R	6-2	210	3-29-88	.071	.000	.100	14	28	4	2	0	1	0	2	1	2	0	0	16	0	0	.143	.161
Wilson, Steffan	R-R	6-1	220	5-24-86	.272	.284	.268	122	445	63	121	15	4	13	60	58	2	0	6	110	14	7	.411	.354

Pitching	B-T	HT	WT	DOB	W	L	ERA	G	GS	CG	SV	IP	H	R	ER	HR	BB	SO	AVG	vLH	vRH	K/9	BB/9
Aguilar, Omar	R-R	5-11	220	3-31-85	2	1	2.12	18	0	0	8	30	16	8	7	1	9	37	.160	.108	.190	11.22	2.73
Almonte, Rigoberto	R-R	6-2	172	1-4-87	0	1	3.60	9	0	0	0	10	8	4	4	0	10	12	.229	.313	.158	10.80	9.00
Anundsen, Evan	R-R	6-3	200	5-17-88	10	8	2.69	24	23	2	0	130	101	51	39	2	41	118	.216	.232	.202	8.15	2.83
Axford, John	R-R	6-5	195	4-1-83	4	1	1.63	19	0	0	0	28	14	5	5	0	16	43	.151	.152	.150	13.99	5.20
Bowman, Michael	R-R	6-2	195	5-2-87	5	4	2.57	16	16	0	0	88	86	37	25	5	39	60	.258	.301	.228	6.16	4.00
Braddock, Zach	L-L	6-4	230	8-23-87	1	1	1.09	14	0	0	0	25	12	3	3	2	4	40	.143	.167	.133	14.59	1.46
Butler, Josh	R-R	6-5	200	12-11-84	6	2	2.47	9	9	0	0	51	44	16	14	0	23	32	.235	.242	.229	5.65	4.06
Fiers, Michael	R-R	6-3	205	6-15-85	1	0	1.98	6	0	0	2	14	10	3	3	2	2	16	.204	.227	.185	10.54	1.32
Flores, Ruben	R-R	6-4	170	5-19-84	0	0	1.29	5	0	0	1	7	2	1	1	1	2	6	.091	.000	.125	7.71	2.57
Henderson, Jim	R-R	6-5	190	10-21-82	3	0	2.76	15	0	0	4	29	16	11	9	2	14	20	.160	.150	.167	6.14	4.30
Jeffress, Jeremy	R-R	6-0	195	9-21-87	2	1	2.18	6	5	1	0	33	16	13	8	2	22	36	.145	.145	.145	9.82	6.00
Jones, Mike	R-R	6-4	220	4-23-83	4	0	4.06	7	7	0	0	38	36	21	17	4	13	26	.269	.288	.241	6.21	3.11
Krestalude, Damon	R-R	6-4	185	6-5-89	0	0	1.35	2	1	0	0	7	4	1	1	0	5	4	.200	.222	.182	5.40	6.75
Lluberes, Rafael	L-L	6-4	215	9-21-84	3	4	3.51	43	0	0	5	51	41	25	20	2	39	38	.228	.254	.214	6.66	6.84
Luetge, Lucas	L-L	6-3	180	3-24-87	6	7	4.48	27	7	0	2	92	93	55	46	6	38	75	.266	.291	.254	7.31	3.70
Mercedes, Roque	B-R	6-3	185	9-28-86	1	1	1.08	29	0	0	6	42	26	7	5	0	15	45	.179	.172	.185	9.72	3.24
Merklinger, Daniel	L-L	6-1	195	11-19-85	4	1	2.58	8	4	0	0	38	27	16	11	2	15	40	.201	.278	.173	9.39	3.52
Miller, Mitch	R-R	6-3	195	11-15-85	0	0	5.40	1	0	0	0	2	2	1	1	0	0	0	.333	.500	.250	0.00	0.00
Periard, Alex	L-R	6-1	205	6-15-87	3	2	5.23	9	9	0	0	31	37	20	18	1	13	22	.296	.300	.292	6.39	3.77
Ramlow, Mike	L-L	6-6	185	3-2-86	0	0	3.60	2	0	0	0	5	4	2	2	0	1	6	.211	.333	.154	10.80	1.80
Rapoza, Brandon	R-R	6-2	220	11-14-85	3	2	2.13	41	0	0	0	68	61	23	16	2	19	46	.237	.274	.212	6.12	2.53
Rivas, Amaury	R-R	6-2	189	12-20-85	13	7	2.98	26	23	0	0	133	109	55	44	11	43	123	.220	.257	.191	8.32	2.91
Rogers, Mark	R-R	6-2	225	1-30-86	1	3	1.67	23	22	0	0	65	46	16	12	2	29	67	.201	.213	.190	9.32	4.04
Willinsky, Mark	R-R	6-4	250	3-14-87	5	2	3.73	36	0	0	2	60	54	25	25	3	34	45	.250	.237	.260	6.71	5.07
Wooten, Rob	R-R	6-1	210	7-21-85	1	1	1.20	26	0	0	18	30	21	7	4	0	13	44	.191	.229	.161	13.20	3.90

Fielding

Catcher	PCT	G	PO	A	E	DP	PB
Alfonso	1.000	9	34	13	0	2	1
Corporan	.992	14	110	11	1	2	6
De La Rosa	.987	29	195	38	3	3	4
Maldonado	.995	81	630	95	4	3	17
Miranda	—	1	0	0	0	0	0

Roberts	1.000	2	6	1	0	0	0
Whiteside	1.000	2	2	0	0	0	1

First Base	PCT	G	PO	A	E	DP
Errecart	.988	60	528	44	7	59
Miranda	.991	10	96	10	1	8
Whiteside	1.000	2	12	0	0	5

Wilson	.994	58	475	36	3	39

Second Base	PCT	G	PO	A	E	DP
Brewer	.833	1	0	5	1	0
Farris	.985	118	230	362	9	79
Miranda	.963	7	8	18	1	8
Sanchez	1.000	1	1	1	0	0

	PCT	G	PO	A	E	DP			PCT	G	PO	A	E	DP			PCT	G	PO	A	E	DP
Wheeler	1.000	3	4	6	0	0		Farris	.900	2	5	4	1	0		Gindl	.965	103	154	11	6	3
Third Base	**PCT**	**G**	**PO**	**A**	**E**	**DP**		Miranda	.945	15	12	40	3	6		Haydel	.981	121	196	6	4	2
Brewer	.944	5	3	14	1	2		Sanchez	.909	3	4	6	1	1		Miranda	1.000	3	2	0	0	0
Miranda	.889	12	8	16	3	1		Wheeler	.954	18	21	41	3	8		Roberts	1.000	3	6	0	0	0
Sanchez	—	1	0	0	0	0		**Outfield**	**PCT**	**G**	**PO**	**A**	**E**	**DP**		Sanchez	1.000	10	9	0	0	0
Wheeler	.931	105	74	183	19	29		De La Rosa	1.000	6	7	0	0	0		Schafer	.996	108	210	14	1	4
Wilson	.850	10	8	9	3	2		Errecart	—	1	0	0	0	0		Whiteside	1.000	2	3	0	0	0
Shortstop	**PCT**	**G**	**PO**	**A**	**E**	**DP**		Farris	—	1	0	0	0	0		Wilson	.981	32	50	3	1	0
Brewer	.923	95	140	257	33	52		Gillespie	1.000	3	6	0	0	0								

WISCONSIN TIMBER RATTLERS

LOW CLASS A

MIDWEST LEAGUE

Batting	B-T	HT	WT	DOB	AVG	vLH	vRH	G	AB	R	H	2B	3B	HR	RBI	BB	HBP	SH	SF	SO	SB	CS	SLG	OBP
Alfonso, Derrick	R-R	6-0	210	7-6-85	.286	.750	.176	7	21	1	6	1	0	0	2	2	0	0	1	7	1	1	.333	.333
Braun, Steve	R-R	6-0	185	5-17-85	.265	.000	.310	12	34	5	9	3	0	0	4	5	1	1	0	6	0	2	.353	.375
Brownstein, Mike	R-R	5-10	175	8-9-87	.186	.571	.111	13	43	10	8	2	0	0	0	10	0	1	0	11	3	2	.233	.340
Cain, Lorenzo	R-R	6-2	185	4-13-86	.192	.167	.196	15	52	3	10	4	0	0	3	9	0	0	0	15	0	0	.269	.311
Delaney, John	R-R	5-9	180	12-30-85	.207	.176	.215	70	237	19	49	17	0	1	22	36	7	2	1	77	3	4	.291	.327
Dennis, Chris	L-R	6-1	205	9-15-88	.318	.333	.313	38	132	20	42	15	1	4	18	19	2	0	1	39	2	0	.538	.409
Dhanani, Kyle	R-R	6-2	195	9-6-87	.169	.133	.180	19	65	9	11	1	0	0	5	5	3	1	0	15	0	0	.215	.260
Duran, Jose	R-R	5-11	190	11-27-86	.221	.206	.226	90	298	31	66	7	8	0	27	28	4	1	2	88	16	7	.299	.295
Dykstra, Cutter	R-R	5-11	180	6-29-89	.212	.286	.192	29	99	16	21	4	1	1	7	12	2	0	0	27	4	2	.303	.310
Fatse, Peter	R-L	5-10	170	8-3-87	.236	.143	.259	59	212	22	50	9	5	1	14	28	6	3	1	65	5	5	.340	.340
Green, Taylor	L-R	5-10	195	11-2-86	.400	.250	.438	6	20	6	8	1	0	1	5	4	2	0	0	4	0	0	.600	.538
Kemp, Corey	R-R	6-0	240	2-24-86	.282	.287	.280	108	373	54	105	31	0	4	56	54	4	0	3	73	3	4	.397	.376
Kjeldgaard, Brock	R-R	6-5	215	1-22-86	.250	.271	.244	133	472	65	118	30	4	20	74	58	12	0	7	172	12	6	.458	.342
Komatsu, Erik	L-L	5-10	190	10-1-87	.242	.188	.260	21	66	6	16	2	0	1	5	8	3	1	2	14	0	2	.318	.342
Lawrie, Brett	R-R	5-11	200	1-18-90	.274	.321	.261	105	372	48	102	18	5	13	65	41	4	0	6	70	19	11	.454	.348
Maldonado, Martin	R-R	6-1	210	8-16-86	.105	.200	.071	7	19	1	2	0	0	0	2	2	0	0	1	7	1	0	.105	.182
Marseco, Michael	R-R	5-9	145	1-7-87	.189	.143	.204	93	322	30	61	9	5	0	26	22	0	12	1	54	9	5	.248	.241
McCraw, Sean	L-R	6-0	185	3-11-86	.211	.115	.241	76	218	24	46	15	0	1	21	37	3	3	2	54	1	1	.294	.331
McPhearson, Derrick	R-R	6-0	200	5-8-86	.160	.111	.173	45	125	11	20	3	1	0	10	12	3	0	0	48	8	2	.200	.250
Miller, Erik	R-R	6-3	200	8-23-87	.241	.222	.248	90	323	46	78	10	2	3	22	20	7	5	2	81	18	7	.313	.298
Prince, Josh	R-R	6-0	180	1-26-88	.221	.226	.220	31	122	18	27	5	0	1	10	15	1	0	2	21	12	5	.287	.307
Sanchez, Juan	R-R	5-11	167	1-16-87	.253	.200	.266	100	380	54	96	22	1	1	27	23	10	7	3	76	8	7	.324	.310
Sizemore, Brandon	R-R	6-0	205	12-10-86	.304	.222	.357	6	23	5	7	1	0	1	2	1	0	0	0	8	1	0	.478	.333
Trejo, Edgar	R-R	6-3	200	7-28-89	.198	.182	.205	30	106	11	21	5	0	2	10	3	0	0	1	32	1	2	.302	.218
Vass, Mike	R-R	6-1	210	4-19-85	.240	.257	.234	91	292	36	70	19	1	7	36	26	3	1	2	83	3	1	.384	.307
Zarraga, Shawn	R-R	6-2	215	1-21-89	.152	.100	.167	21	46	1	7	1	0	0	7	10	0	0	3	14	0	0	.174	.288

Pitching	B-T	HT	WT	DOB	W	L	ERA	G	GS	CG	SV	IP	H	R	ER	HR	BB	SO	AVG	vLH	vRH	K/9	BB/9
Adams, Cody	R-R	6-2	180	11-26-86	3	6	5.93	16	12	0	0	58	74	46	38	3	33	37	.322	.342	.302	5.77	5.15
Almonte, Rigoberto	R-R	6-2	172	1-4-87	0	4	7.36	32	0	0	0	44	54	38	36	3	26	49	.303	.260	.337	10.02	5.32
Bowman, Michael	R-R	6-2	195	5-2-87	3	1	2.66	8	8	0	0	44	45	19	13	1	14	41	.262	.291	.237	8.39	2.86
Bush, Dave	R-R	6-2	205	11-9-79	0	0	0.00	2	2	0	0	8	4	1	0	0	1	9	.148	.077	.214	10.57	1.17
Dabrowiecki, Kris	R-R	6-4	200	3-23-86	0	1	15.95	6	0	0	0	7	18	15	13	3	5	9	.439	.462	.429	11.05	6.14
Fiers, Michael	R-R	6-3	205	6-15-85	0	0	0.00	3	0	0	1	6	4	0	0	0	2	8	.190	.286	.143	12.00	3.00
Frederickson, Evan	L-L	6-6	240	9-23-86	3	9	5.27	29	16	0	2	97	99	67	57	5	82	93	.270	.221	.288	8.60	7.58
Frerichs, Corey	R-R	5-11	200	5-7-86	0	0	11.37	8	0	0	0	6	8	8	8	0	9	5	.333	.333	.333	7.11	12.79
Henderson, Jim	L-R	6-5	190	10-21-82	0	0	1.07	26	0	0	17	25	19	4	3	0	8	26	.207	.182	.229	9.24	2.84
Lambertus, Pedro	R-R	5-10	190	6-4-88	0	1	4.15	16	0	0	1	30	33	19	14	3	13	22	.275	.255	.292	6.53	3.86
Lasker, Maverick	R-R	6-2	190	2-17-90	1	1	5.00	2	2	0	0	9	9	7	5	0	5	4	.257	.313	.211	4.00	5.00
Meadows, Dan	L-L	6-5	235	11-3-87	13	6	4.01	33	11	1	2	117	122	57	52	8	32	108	.271	.309	.256	8.33	2.47
Merklinger, Daniel	L-L	6-1	195	11-19-85	3	2	2.55	11	8	0	1	53	45	18	15	3	17	53	.231	.171	.244	9.00	2.89
Nieves, Efrain	L-L	6-0	169	11-15-89	5	7	5.70	27	11	0	1	95	116	62	60	7	35	86	.311	.294	.317	8.18	3.33
Ohlmann, Liam	R-R	6-0	241	9-15-86	3	4	6.09	40	0	0	1	65	75	52	44	8	43	56	.288	.291	.287	7.75	5.95
Peralta, Wily	R-R	6-2	225	5-8-89	4	4	3.47	27	15	0	1	104	91	45	40	5	46	118	.235	.256	.216	10.24	3.99
Periard, Alex	L-R	6-1	205	6-15-87	0	0	3.18	3	3	0	0	11	14	5	4	0	2	5	.298	.238	.346	3.97	1.59
Ritchie, Brandon	L-L	6-4	230	12-10-86	5	1	1.54	48	0	0	4	70	47	20	12	2	28	58	.190	.167	.199	7.42	3.58
Scarpetta, Cody	R-R	6-3	240	8-25-88	4	11	3.43	26	18	0	0	105	83	53	40	5	55	116	.217	.197	.228	9.94	4.71
Seidel, R.J.	R-R	6-5	200	9-3-87	1	3	6.91	8	7	0	0	29	33	26	22	4	18	24	.287	.327	.258	7.53	5.65
Sherrill, Garrett	R-R	6-5	210	9-4-87	1	0	6.10	6	0	0	0	10	10	7	7	1	10	9	.263	.200	.286	7.84	8.71
Suppan, Jeff	R-R	6-2	230	1-2-75	0	1	10.80	1	1	0	0	3	5	4	4	0	0	1	.333	.300	.400	2.70	0.00
Tyson, Nick	R-R	6-3	185	1-13-88	4	5	3.29	38	1	0	6	63	59	28	23	2	17	43	.250	.250	.250	6.14	2.43
Watten, Trey	R-R	6-3	180	12-16-86	5	14	4.71	27	24	0	1	134	146	90	70	9	58	96	.282	.332	.248	6.46	3.91

Fielding

Catcher	PCT	G	PO	A	E	DP	PB		First Base	PCT	G	PO	A	E	DP		Trejo	.959	6	46	1	2	4
Alfonso	.962	7	44	7	2	0	0		Dhanani	.966	4	27	1	1	1		Zarraga	1.000	1	7	0	0	0
Kemp	.987	47	333	38	5	0	7		Duran	1.000	3	25	0	0	2		**Second Base**	**PCT**	**G**	**PO**	**A**	**E**	**DP**
Maldonado	1.000	6	45	3	0	0	0		Kemp	.990	45	366	15	4	36		Braun	.955	9	20	22	2	9
McCraw	.980	75	558	70	13	11	6		Kjeldgaard	.985	82	701	35	11	60		Brownstein	1.000	11	29	32	0	4
Zarraga	1.000	15	95	7	0	2	0		Sizemore	.972	5	28	7	1	3		Delaney	1.000	1	0	4	0	0

MILWAUKEE BREWERS

	PCT	G	PO	A	E	DP
Dhanani	1.000	2	4	3	0	0
Duran	.913	6	9	12	2	2
Fatse	.972	8	14	21	1	3
Lawrie	.964	100	176	248	16	58
Sanchez	1.000	7	13	22	0	7
Third Base	**PCT**	**G**	**PO**	**A**	**E**	**DP**
Brownstein	1.000	2	1	5	0	0
Delaney	.904	45	23	80	11	4
Dhanani	.632	7	0	12	7	1
Duran	.899	41	17	81	11	7
Fatse	1.000	9	9	12	0	2

	PCT	G	PO	A	E	DP
Green	.938	5	6	9	1	2
Sanchez	.969	26	24	38	2	7
Trejo	.975	17	10	29	1	1
Shortstop	**PCT**	**G**	**PO**	**A**	**E**	**DP**
Duran	.875	2	2	5	1	1
Marseco	.970	93	114	274	12	53
Prince	.945	31	49	71	7	19
Sanchez	.941	16	12	36	3	3
Outfield	**PCT**	**G**	**PO**	**A**	**E**	**DP**
Cain	1.000	15	33	0	0	0

	PCT	G	PO	A	E	DP
Delaney	1.000	5	5	0	0	0
Dennis	.947	37	51	3	3	0
Dykstra	.975	26	37	2	1	2
Fatse	.915	41	60	5	6	1
Kjeldgaard	.968	52	88	4	3	0
Komatsu	1.000	9	17	0	0	0
McPhearson	.942	37	61	4	4	1
Miller	.995	90	181	9	1	2
Sanchez	.956	54	98	10	5	2
Vass	.961	69	93	5	4	2

AZL BREWERS   ROOKIE
ARIZONA LEAGUE

Batting	B-T	HT	WT	DOB	AVG	vLH	vRH	G	AB	R	H	2B	3B	HR	RBI	BB	HBP	SH	SF	SO	SB	CS	SLG	OBP
Brownstein, Mike	R-R	5-10	175	8-9-87	.435	.667	.400	6	23	8	10	1	1	0	3	9	0	0	0	1	2	1	.565	.594
Cain, Lorenzo	R-R	6-2	185	4-13-86	.444	.250	.600	3	9	1	4	1	0	0	1	1	0	0	1	0	0	0	.556	.455
Cequea, Allixon	R-R	6-1	175	6-16-90	.245	.320	.230	43	147	12	36	5	2	0	14	7	5	3	1	34	1	4	.306	.300
Davis, Khris	R-R	6-0	195	12-21-87	.243	1.000	.222	10	37	7	9	0	2	2	8	6	1	0	1	11	4	0	.514	.356
Dedrick, Wayne	R-R	6-3	185	11-21-89	.227	.207	.231	46	176	25	40	9	4	0	22	14	5	0	3	43	7	5	.324	.298
Dennis, Chris	L-R	6-1	205	9-15-88	.167	—	.167	3	6	1	1	1	0	0	1	1	0	0	0	1	0	0	.333	.286
Garcia, Jose	R-R	6-3	195	3-5-91	.244	.235	.245	35	123	16	30	6	5	1	18	2	2	0	2	33	5	1	.398	.264
George, Carlos	R-R	6-2	165	2-6-89	.285	.273	.288	45	179	26	51	10	3	0	12	8	6	4	3	35	20	6	.374	.332
Halton, Sean	R-R	6-5	235	6-7-87	.330	.455	.292	25	94	13	31	7	1	3	17	8	3	0	1	18	3	0	.521	.396
Komatsu, Erik	L-L	5-10	190	10-1-87	.308	.200	.375	5	13	1	4	0	0	0	3	2	0	0	2	2	0	0	.308	.353
Lind, Connor	R-R	5-11	170	6-10-87	.205	.179	.211	47	161	14	33	4	1	0	11	8	3	1	1	26	3	4	.242	.254
McKelvie, Demetrius	R-L	6-3	210	10-27-90	.210	.120	.232	35	124	18	26	7	0	1	8	12	4	1	0	48	7	1	.290	.300
Pechek, Tony	B-R	6-2	195	10-12-86	.178	.333	.154	15	45	4	8	3	0	0	6	2	0	0	0	15	0	0	.244	.213
Requena, Jonathan	R-R	5-11	215	3-25-89	.238	.375	.191	22	63	4	15	5	0	0	9	1	1	0	1	16	0	1	.317	.258
Roberts, Tyler	R-R	6-0	226	10-25-90	.292	.333	.283	24	72	11	21	1	1	1	8	3	1	1	0	19	2	0	.375	.407
Rodriguez, Orton	R-R	6-2	187	9-15-89	.276	.333	.250	16	58	6	16	2	1	2	9	3	1	0	1	11	0	1	.448	.317
Sizemore, Brandon	R-R	6-0	205	12-10-86	.291	.357	.278	48	172	36	50	15	3	7	33	18	9	1	3	42	11	1	.535	.381
Stockfisch, Austin	B-R	6-2	205	4-26-86	.333	—	.333	2	3	1	1	0	0	0	0	0	0	0	0	0	0	0	.667	.333
Walla, Max	L-L	5-11	195	4-12-91	.199	.250	.188	48	186	18	37	5	2	2	19	15	8	0	3	82	4	2	.280	.283

Pitching	B-T	HT	WT	DOB	W	L	ERA	G	GS	CG	SV	IP	H	R	ER	HR	BB	SO	AVG	vLH	vRH	K/9	BB/9
Baron, Casey	L-L	6-2	185	11-29-84	0	0	2.25	3	0	0	0	4	1	1	1	1	0	4	.077	.000	.125	9.00	0.00
Billings, Blake	R-R	6-5	200	1-8-90	2	5	7.14	14	8	0	0	47	54	40	37	5	30	42	.290	.403	.227	8.10	5.79
Butler, Josh	R-R	6-5	200	12-11-84	0	1	4.76	4	3	0	0	11	15	6	6	0	6	16	.319	.261	.375	12.71	4.76
Capuano, Chris	L-L	6-2	225	8-19-78	0	0	6.00	3	3	0	0	3	5	2	2	0	2	4	.385	.000	.500	12.00	6.00
Costello, Matt	L-L	6-1	190	12-17-86	1	4	1.49	15	3	0	0	36	31	10	6	0	8	40	.233	.324	.202	9.91	1.98
Cravy, Tyler	R-R	6-3	180	7-13-89	2	1	4.45	12	4	0	0	32	28	16	16	1	12	34	.235	.184	.259	9.46	3.34
Dabrowiecki, Kris	R-R	6-4	200	3-23-86	0	0	2.93	12	1	0	3	15	10	7	5	0	8	12	.182	.167	.186	7.04	4.70
DeLaughter, Ryan	R-R	6-3	210	12-31-86	0	1	5.06	6	4	0	0	5	6	5	3	1	5	4	.261	.111	.357	6.75	8.44
Dunn, Andrew	R-R	6-5	205	9-3-86	0	0	1.29	8	0	0	0	14	8	2	2	0	3	9	.163	.154	.167	5.79	1.93
Frerichs, Corey	R-R	5-11	200	5-7-86	0	0	0.00	1	1	0	0	1	2	0	0	0	1		.400	.333	.500	9.00	0.00
Green, Nick	R-R	6-4	200	8-20-84	1	0	4.50	2	0	0	0	8	13	4	4	1	3	9	.361	.278	.444	10.13	3.38
Guerrero, Luis	R-R	6-0	170	6-20-90	1	4	8.45	15	2	0	0	38	50	45	36	1	27	45	.313	.315	.310	10.57	6.34
Howell, Del	L-L	6-3	185	9-6-87	1	0	0.00	2	0	0	0	3	3	0	0	0	1	2	.273	.000	.333	6.00	3.00
Lambertus, Pedro	R-R	5-10	190	6-4-88	0	0	5.68	4	0	0	0	6	4	5	4	1	3	5	.167	.000	.190	7.11	4.26
Lasker, Maverick	R-R	6-2	190	2-17-90	5	1	3.26	13	1	0	0	47	43	19	17	2	9	39	.246	.231	.255	7.47	1.72
Lintz, Seth	R-R	6-1	170	2-7-90	0	5	4.91	15	2	0	2	40	38	32	22	5	38	41	.241	.258	.236	9.15	8.48
Miller, Mitch	R-R	6-3	195	11-15-85	0	0	1.80	2	1	0	0	5	6	1	1	0	1	3	.316	.500	.182	5.40	1.80
Morales, Joel	R-R	6-3	206	3-12-89	0	0	0.00	1	0	0	0	2	2	1	0	0	1	2	.222	.500	.000	7.71	3.86
Nevakshonoff, Travis	R-R	6-0	180	7-22-89	0	0	0.00	2	1	0	0	2	0	0	0	0	0	0	.000		.000	0.00	0.00
Oviedo, Jose	R-R	6-2	165	11-30-88	2	1	3.13	13	2	0	1	32	25	19	11	0	17	29	.214	.308	.167	8.24	4.83
Platt, Ryan	L-R	6-1	195	8-25-85	0	1	9.64	2	1	0	0	5	6	5	5	1	3	9	.286	.143	.357	17.36	5.79
Romero, Jose	L-L	6-0	170	6-2-86	0	1	4.96	10	6	0	0	16	17	9	9	1	5	12	.274	.200	.288	6.61	2.76
Sanchez, Jose	R-R	6-1	180	10-4-88	0	1	5.17	11	0	0	1	16	14	9	9	0	7	14	.233	.261	.216	8.04	4.02
Sauter, Andrew	L-R	6-1	190	7-15-86	1	0	2.93	9	0	0	3	15	14	6	5	1	2	22	.237	.286	.211	11.91	1.17
Seidel, R.J.	R-R	6-5	200	9-3-87	0	3	6.67	6	6	0	0	28	43	24	21	0	8	23	.361	.436	.325	7.31	2.54
Thielbar, Caleb	L-L	6-0	200	1-31-87	6	1	1.59	14	2	0	0	45	44	16	8	1	7	46	.246	.136	.261	9.13	1.39
Wawrzasek, Stosh	R-R	6-0	225	8-30-90	3	1	3.74	11	3	0	1	22	19	15	9	1	9	23	.224	.188	.245	9.55	3.74

Fielding

Catcher	PCT	G	PO	A	E	DP	PB
Pechek	1.000	13	75	10	0	0	2
Requena	.994	20	147	20	1	0	12
Roberts	.982	21	147	20	3	1	9
Rodriguez	.973	13	91	17	3	0	7
Stockfisch	1.000	2	7	0	0	0	0

First Base	PCT	G	PO	A	E	DP
Cequea	.993	17	141	7	1	16
Halton	.995	20	191	12	1	18
Sizemore	.990	22	178	18	2	11

Second Base	PCT	G	PO	A	E	DP
Brownstein	.938	3	6	9	1	2
Cequea	1.000	1	1	5	0	1
Lind	.976	37	65	96	4	22
Sizemore	.988	17	21	60	1	15

Third Base	PCT	G	PO	A	E	DP
Cequea	.923	21	10	26	3	0
Dedrick	.915	36	21	87	10	8
Sizemore	.600	1	0	3	2	0

Shortstop	PCT	G	PO	A	E	DP
Brownstein	1.000	1	0	2	0	0
George	.887	45	56	140	25	27
Lind	1.000	10	19	38	0	12

Outfield	PCT	G	PO	A	E	DP
Cain	1.000	3	3	0	0	0
Cequea	1.000	1	4	0	0	0
Davis	1.000	8	10	1	0	0

	PCT					
Dedrick	1.000	8	9	0	0	0
Garcia	1.000	23	33	1	0	0
Komatsu	1.000	5	2	0	0	0
McKelvie	.870	26	40	0	6	0

	PCT					
Romero	.984	53	113	12	2	3
Walla	.951	47	74	4	4	0

HELENA BREWERS   ROOKIE

PIONEER LEAGUE

MILWAUKEE BREWERS

Batting	B-T	HT	WT	DOB	AVG	vLH	vRH	G	AB	R	H	2B	3B	HR	RBI	BB	HBP	SH	SF	SO	SB	CS	SLG	OBP
Alfonso, Derrick	R-R	6-0	210	7-6-85	.250	.000	.500	1	4	0	1	0	0	0	1	0	0	0	0	1	0	0	.250	.250
Arias, Hitaniel	R-R	6-6	202	9-20-90	.196	.333	.132	15	56	7	11	3	1	1	10	3	2	0	0	21	1	1	.339	.262
Brownstein, Mike	R-R	5-10	175	8-9-87	.305	.300	.307	44	167	35	51	9	2	0	22	27	2	1	5	19	17	6	.383	.398
Davis, Khris	R-R	6-0	195	12-21-87	.000	.000	—	1	1	0	0	0	0	0	0	0	0	0	0	0	0	0	.000	.000
Dhanani, Kyle	R-R	6-2	195	9-6-87	.267	.300	.258	27	86	14	23	7	1	0	15	8	5	0	0	26	6	1	.372	.364
Dykstra, Cutter	R-R	5-11	180	6-29-89	.244	.173	.268	61	209	35	51	5	1	5	26	27	1	1	1	50	14	4	.349	.332
Ellington, Chris	R-R	6-1	195	11-30-85	.285	.308	.277	70	284	40	81	17	2	10	45	14	3	0	5	58	6	4	.465	.320
Fatse, Peter	R-L	5-10	170	8-3-87	.250	.250	.250	4	16	4	4	0	1	0	2	3	0	0	0	6	0	0	.375	.368
Garfield, Cameron	R-R	6-1	195	5-23-91	.248	.173	.271	59	218	26	54	11	0	4	21	10	6	0	0	61	3	4	.353	.299
George, Carlos	R-R	6-2	165	2-6-89	.333	.333	.333	4	15	1	5	0	0	0	1	0	0	1	0	1	0	0	.333	.333
Halton, Sean	R-R	6-5	235	6-7-87	.354	.425	.331	44	161	27	57	14	0	3	28	9	4	0	2	38	4	4	.497	.398
Krieger, Scott	R-R	6-0	215	1-30-87	.253	.277	.245	68	277	41	70	16	3	13	53	21	0	0	4	103	9	2	.473	.301
Marseco, Michael	R-R	5-9	145	1-7-87	.240	.139	.280	33	129	18	31	4	2	0	14	5	2	4	2	21	5	0	.302	.275
McPhearson, Derrick	R-R	6-0	200	5-8-86	.357	.000	.500	4	14	5	5	1	1	0	1	2	0	0	0	2	4	0	.571	.438
Paciorek, Joey	R-R	6-2	225	9-20-88	.236	.159	.262	54	174	24	41	5	0	3	29	19	3	3	2	35	8	4	.316	.318
Prince, Josh	R-R	6-0	180	1-26-88	.298	.270	.308	36	141	32	42	5	1	0	8	33	0	0	2	25	26	7	.348	.426
Roberts, Michael	R-R	6-2	185	8-28-87	.193	.264	.155	49	150	20	29	6	3	4	22	19	4	2	1	42	5	2	.353	.299
Roberts, Tyler	R-R	6-0	226	10-25-90	.125	—	.125	3	8	0	1	0	0	0	1	0	0	0	0	3	0	0	.125	.125
Stang, Chad	R-R	6-2	190	3-26-89	.229	.340	.191	52	188	24	43	5	4	1	18	13	2	1	1	59	5	2	.314	.284
Trejo, Edgar	R-R	6-3	200	7-28-89	.255	.256	.255	45	149	22	38	11	1	2	10	11	1	0	1	35	4	2	.383	.309
Walla, Max	L-L	5-11	195	4-12-91	.250	—	.250	4	8	2	2	0	0	0	0	0	0	0	0	5	0	0	.250	.250
Zarraga, Shawn	R-R	6-2	215	1-21-89	.266	.263	.267	31	94	15	25	1	1	0	11	11	4	1	1	20	1	1	.298	.364

Pitching	B-T	HT	WT	DOB	W	L	ERA	G	GS	CG	SV	IP	H	R	ER	HR	BB	SO	AVG	vLH	vRH	K/9	BB/9
Arnett, Eric	R-R	6-5	230	1-25-88	0	4	4.41	14	9	0	0	35	33	30	17	1	21	35	.228	.222	.232	9.09	5.45
Brandt, Donald	L-L	6-3	210	12-29-85	2	1	5.96	8	2	0	0	26	31	19	17	3	6	33	.292	.286	.295	11.57	2.10
Bucci, Nick	R-R	6-2	180	7-16-90	6	3	4.41	13	12	0	0	69	59	39	34	7	21	66	.231	.204	.252	8.57	2.73
Bueno, Kristian	L-L	6-2	195	12-10-88	1	3	5.63	28	0	0	4	24	19	15	15	1	19	22	.224	.222	.224	8.25	7.13
Burgos, Hiram	R-R	6-1	210	8-4-87	3	2	5.62	14	7	0	0	58	75	45	36	7	14	53	.309	.253	.340	8.27	2.18
Capuano, Chris	L-L	6-2	225	8-19-78	0	0	1.50	3	3	0	0	6	3	2	1	1	0	4	.136	.000	.150	6.00	0.00
Costello, Matt	L-L	6-1	190	12-17-86	0	1	9.00	2	0	0	0	3	4	3	3	1	1	3	.333	.333	.333	9.00	3.00
Currie, Rob	R-R	6-6	230	4-29-87	4	2	3.57	24	0	0	3	35	34	18	14	3	11	35	.252	.184	.291	8.92	2.80
Fiers, Michael	R-R	6-3	205	6-15-85	1	0	1.29	13	0	0	8	21	10	3	3	2	1	35	.137	.154	.128	15.00	0.43
Heckathorn, Kyle	R-R	6-6	235	6-17-88	0	1	6.04	6	5	0	0	22	30	18	15	4	4	15	.326	.273	.356	6.04	1.61
Howell, Del	L-L	6-3	185	9-6-87	0	0	1.04	3	3	0	0	9	7	1	1	0	2	7	.219	.286	.200	7.27	2.08
Jeffers, Ben	R-R	6-1	200	8-30-87	0	3	7.30	22	0	0	1	25	33	21	20	3	15	28	.340	.371	.323	10.22	5.47
Krestalude, Damon	R-R	6-4	185	6-5-89	3	4	5.35	15	9	0	0	69	90	44	41	4	28	50	.314	.288	.330	6.52	3.65
Lamontagne, Andre	B-R	6-5	210	3-24-86	2	4	4.54	13	4	0	1	36	35	24	18	2	11	17	.250	.250	.250	4.29	2.78
Miller, Mitch	R-R	6-3	195	11-15-85	0	1	4.91	9	0	0	0	15	20	10	8	2	6	4	.323	.300	.333	2.45	3.68
Morales, Joel	R-R	6-3	206	3-12-89	1	2	7.67	18	0	0	0	27	40	31	23	5	14	16	.348	.340	.353	5.33	4.67
Odorizzi, Jake	R-R	6-2	175	3-27-90	1	4	4.40	12	10	0	0	47	55	27	23	3	9	43	.296	.306	.287	8.23	1.72
Oviedo, Jose	R-R	6-2	165	11-30-88	0	0	18.00	2	0	0	0	1	1	2	2	0	1	1	.250	.000	.333	9.00	9.00
Platt, Ryan	L-R	6-1	195	8-25-85	1	0	4.64	13	0	0	0	21	14	13	11	4	13	30	.182	.162	.200	12.66	5.48
Pokorny, Jon	R-L	6-2	225	4-4-88	3	2	3.38	16	2	0	1	40	43	24	15	4	14	43	.269	.244	.278	9.68	3.15
Robinson, Chad	R-R	6-5	210	11-13-87	1	0	3.60	8	2	0	1	10	9	5	4	1	2	8	.237	.222	.241	7.20	1.80
Rosario, Adrian	R-R	6-4	180	9-30-89	3	7	5.06	15	8	0	1	59	78	47	33	4	14	45	.322	.319	.324	6.90	2.15
Rusova, Ivan	R-R	6-1	180	11-5-86	0	0	27.00	2	0	0	0	1	3	4	4	0	4	4	.429	.000	.600	27.00	27.00
Salmon, Marcus	R-R	6-2	235	4-27-88	0	0	0.00	5	0	0	0	6	3	0	0	0	7	3	.158	.100	.222	4.50	10.50
Thielbar, Caleb	L-L	6-0	200	1-31-87	0	0	0.00	2	0	0	0	2	0	0	0	0	1	2	.000	.000	.000	10.80	5.40

Fielding

Catcher	PCT	G	PO	A	E	DP	PB
Garfield	.957	43	324	28	16	4	5
Roberts	.983	22	170	7	3	0	6
Roberts	1.000	3	17	3	0	0	
Zarraga	1.000	14	95	18	0	0	1

First Base	PCT	G	PO	A	E	DP
Arias	.961	14	109	14	5	12
Brownstein	1.000	1	9	0	0	0
Dhanani	.933	5	36	6	3	0
Halton	.990	41	361	43	4	27
Paciorek	.974	11	105	7	3	8
Trejo	.964	6	49	4	2	7
Zarraga	1.000	3	26	1	0	1

Second Base	PCT	G	PO	A	E	DP
Brownstein	.986	14	23	49	1	7

	PCT					
Dhanani	1.000	2	8	4	0	0
Dykstra	.923	55	76	165	20	28
Fatse	1.000	1	2	5	0	0
George	1.000	3	10	8	0	1
Paciorek	1.000	4	7	11	0	3

Third Base	PCT	G	PO	A	E	DP
Brownstein	.913	12	4	17	2	1
Dhanani	.848	20	15	24	7	3
George	.750	1	1	2	1	0
Paciorek	.853	35	13	80	16	9
Trejo	.868	14	7	26	5	1

Shortstop	PCT	G	PO	A	E	DP
Brownstein	1.000	8	11	24	0	6
George	.667	1	3	1	2	1
Marseco	.965	33	37	101	5	14

	PCT					
Prince	.943	36	52	114	10	18

Outfield	PCT	G	PO	A	E	DP
Brownstein	.944	11	17	0	1	0
Ellington	.965	69	102	8	4	1
Fatse	1.000	3	3	0	0	0
Halton	1.000	3	1	1	0	0
Krieger	.963	68	97	7	4	2
McPhearson	1.000	4	4	0	0	0
Roberts	1.000	17	28	0	0	0
Romero	1.000	5	6	1	0	0
Stang	.944	52	98	4	6	2
Walla	1.000	3	3	0	0	0

DOMINICAN SUMMER LEAGUE

Batting	B-T	HT	WT	DOB	AVG	vLH	vRH	G	AB	R	H	2B	3B	HR	RBI	BB	HBP	SH	SF	SO	SB	CS	SLG	OBP
Abreu, Joan	R-R	5-11	180	7-15-90	.196	.160	.208	37	102	6	20	2	1	0	6	16	2	1	0	28	1	6	.235	.317
Aguirre, Wilder	R-R	6-0	160	4-16-92	.240	.385	.189	26	50	2	12	0	0	0	4	2	3	0	0	16	2	1	.240	.309
Arias, Hitaniel	R-R	6-6	202	9-20-90	.246	.188	.264	20	69	9	17	4	0	1	3	5	2	0	0	23	1	2	.348	.316
Arias, Moises	R-R	6-6	205	2-3-89	.162	.286	.133	19	37	4	6	0	0	0	2	4	0	1	0	11	0	0	.162	.244
2-team total (10 Orioles)					.146	—	—	29	48	5	7	0	0	0	3	5	0	1	0	15	0	0	.146	.226
Avila, Eliecer	R-R	6-2	175	1-30-90	.205	.176	.212	33	83	9	17	2	0	0	11	8	1	3	1	16	3	2	.229	.280
Barrini, Juan	R-R	6-2	175	1-1-92	.188	.087	.209	50	133	23	25	4	0	1	10	7	6	2	2	42	7	2	.241	.251
Bido, Felix	R-R	6-2	170	8-7-91	.149	.182	.143	48	141	8	21	7	0	0	12	6	4	0	0	54	1	1	.199	.205
Chirinos, Luis	R-R	6-1	215	8-30-92	.243	.375	.203	33	103	5	25	4	0	0	18	12	2	1	2	38	2	6	.282	.328
Guanipa, Dick	R-R	6-0	180	6-20-90	.091	.143	.083	28	55	4	5	1	0	0	3	11	2	0	0	19	0	0	.109	.265
Jabalera, Jose	R-R	6-2	175	8-2-88	.256	.200	.267	39	125	17	32	4	1	0	11	4	1	5	1	18	5	2	.304	.282
Javier, Jhonatan	R-R	6-1	197	9-16-87	.344	.447	.322	64	221	48	76	17	5	6	45	17	1	5	0	30	12	4	.548	.423
Martinez, Andres	R-R	6-2	188	1-26-92	.158	.185	.153	54	158	27	25	4	2	3	15	19	1	6	0	68	6	1	.266	.253
Paez, Carlos	R-R	6-0	180	6-18-91	.182	—	.182	5	11	0	2	1	0	0	1	0	0	0	0	6	1	0	.273	.182
2-team total (27 Orioles)					.186	—	—	32	70	13	13	3	1	1	6	5	4	3	0	21	3	0	.300	.278
Portes, Wilmer	R-R	6-1	193	3-25-91	.269	.281	.266	51	160	27	43	9	0	3	13	26	1	0	0	39	7	13	.381	.374
Puello, Ronny	R-R	6-6	200	10-23-89	.343	.000	.400	12	35	2	12	2	1	1	7	0	2	1	0	9	0	0	.543	.378
Rodriguez, Pedro	B-R	5-11	145	4-20-90	.227	.240	.225	57	194	45	44	5	3	0	18	28	3	3	1	27	18	10	.284	.332
Roson, Deibisson	R-R	6-4	210	8-12-89	.185	.174	.188	43	124	20	23	6	1	2	16	27	5	0	0	32	7	4	.298	.353
Wilson, Edwin	R-R	6-1	170	11-10-89	.189	.243	.175	63	180	22	34	2	1	1	15	25	10	6	0	49	9	4	.228	.321
Wilson, Octavio	R-R	6-2	162	10-11-89	.184	.222	.174	48	136	13	25	5	1	1	13	18	4	3	0	44	4	3	.257	.297

Pitching	B-T	HT	WT	DOB	W	L	ERA	G	GS	CG	SV	IP	H	R	ER	HR	BB	SO	AVG	vLH	vRH	K/9	BB/9
Cespedes, Angel	R-R	6-2	170	8-27-89	1	1	2.75	5	3	0	1	20	23	9	6	1	5	14	.303	.276	.319	6.41	2.29
Espiritu, Alexander	R-R	6-0	190	3-30-91	0	2	13.50	7	1	0	0	9	12	16	14	0	14	13	.308	.250	.323	12.54	13.50
Hodge, Humberto	R-R	6-4	170	11-6-87	0	0	9.00	1	0	0	0	5	6	5	5	0	2	5	.300	.000	.333	9.00	3.60
Jean, Samuel	L-L	6-1	175	6-22-89	2	4	4.01	15	12	1	0	67	79	40	30	0	23	48	.299	.269	.303	6.42	3.07
Jimenez, Joan	R-R	6-2	179	6-27-90	4	5	3.96	14	12	0	0	64	67	37	28	2	14	56	.272	.281	.270	7.92	1.98
2-team total (1 Orioles)					5	5	3.67	15	13	0	0	69	72	39	28	2	17	62	—	—	—	8.13	2.23
King, Jaime	R-R	6-4	219	9-27-89	0	1	4.91	7	1	0	0	11	10	7	6	1	12	16	.233	.167	.258	13.09	9.82
Linares, Edwin	R-R	6-2	198	10-15-89	4	5	1.77	29	0	0	11	46	35	15	9	1	22	37	.210	.087	.256	7.29	4.34
Lorenzo, Leonard	R-R	6-0	190	7-16-91	0	0	13.50	2	0	0	0	3	3	4	4	0	5	3	.333	—	.333	10.13	16.88
Mambru, Dionicio	R-R	6-1	180	4-8-89	1	1	7.61	13	1	0	0	24	28	25	20	1	20	27	.292	.261	.301	10.27	7.61
Montano, Eliezer	L-L	6-2	170	10-21-91	0	2	2.84	18	3	0	1	38	30	22	12	0	30	35	.216	.211	.217	8.29	7.11
Mota, Jose	R-R	5-11	180	12-18-89	3	3	2.67	12	8	0	0	61	64	22	18	0	14	60	.269	.222	.283	8.90	2.08
2-team total (1 Orioles)					3	3	2.76	13	8	0	0	62	67	23	19	0	15	62	—	—	—	9.00	2.18
Pascual, Rolando	B-R	6-6	245	2-8-89	2	3	6.05	15	4	0	0	42	31	34	28	0	42	58	.211	.184	.220	12.53	9.07
Perez, Julio	R-R	6-2	175	1-16-92	2	5	6.38	14	11	0	1	48	40	38	34	1	38	36	.220	.186	.230	6.75	7.13
Ramos, Jose	L-L	6-5	228	6-14-89	3	4	6.52	23	0	0	2	39	55	42	28	1	25	29	.335	.391	.326	6.75	5.82
Rivero, Francisco	R-R	6-2	204	3-11-91	0	0	0.00	3	0	0	0	8	5	0	0	0	2	6	.185	.077	.286	6.48	2.16
Rodriguez, Mike	L-L	6-1	165	4-24-89	0	2	7.39	14	6	0	0	35	38	34	29	2	36	44	.270	.235	.274	11.21	9.17
Santana, Kelvin	R-R	6-4	190	4-15-90	1	1	7.54	18	0	0	0	37	49	38	31	0	33	27	.329	.313	.337	6.57	8.03

Fielding

Catcher	PCT	G	PO	A	E	DP	PB
Aguirre	.966	23	118	24	5	1	2
Avila	.943	33	201	45	15	0	12
Javier	.971	29	199	38	7	2	10
Paez	1.000	5	19	1	0	0	1

First Base	PCT	G	PO	A	E	DP
Arias	.972	17	133	7	4	9
Arias	.966	14	78	6	3	9
Bido	.952	8	37	3	2	5
Guanipa	.985	21	127	6	2	5
Jabalera	1.000	10	49	3	0	6
Wilson	.975	29	231	7	6	20

Second Base	PCT	G	PO	A	E	DP
Abreu	.943	26	53	62	7	15
Araujo	.920	11	22	24	4	6

	PCT	G	PO	A	E	DP
Rodriguez	.968	40	93	117	7	30
Wilson	.889	4	10	6	2	3

Third Base	PCT	G	PO	A	E	DP
Abreu	1.000	1	0	2	0	0
Araujo	.875	4	1	6	1	0
Bido	.869	39	30	56	13	2
Jabalera	.879	23	19	39	8	4
Martinez	.929	5	5	8	1	0
Rodriguez	—	1	0	0	0	0
Wilson	.845	25	16	33	9	1

Shortstop	PCT	G	PO	A	E	DP
Jabalera	1.000	2	2	4	0	0
Martinez	.906	45	55	119	18	22
Rodriguez	.972	14	26	43	2	10
Wilson	.898	21	32	47	9	7

Outfield	PCT	G	PO	A	E	DP
Araujo	—	2	0	0	0	0
Arias	1.000	1	2	0	0	0
Arias	—	1	0	0	0	0
Barrini	.892	47	60	6	8	0
Chirinos	.889	23	22	2	3	1
Guanipa	—	1	0	0	0	0
Jabalera	1.000	9	12	3	0	1
Lorenzo	1.000	23	24	1	0	0
Martinez	—	1	0	0	0	0
Portes	.978	47	81	8	2	2
Puello	1.000	12	15	1	0	0
Rodriguez	—	2	0	0	0	0
Roson	.974	36	34	4	1	1
Wilson	.953	39	39	2	2	0

Minnesota Twins

SEASON IN A SENTENCE: Minnesota was under .500 as late as Sept. 12, but the brilliance of Major League Player of the Year Joe Mauer—and the mediocrity of the American League Central—helped lift the Twins to a 17-4 finish, including a Game 163 victory to claim the division title over the Tigers.

HIGH POINT: In the last regular-season baseball game ever played at the Hubert H. Humphrey Metrodome, the Twins rallied from an early 3-0 deficit and won their tiebreaker game with the Tigers 6-5 in the bottom of the 12th on a walk-off single by Alexi Casilla, who hit just .202 on the season with 17 RBIs.

LOW POINT: The Twins crashed back to earth in the AL Division Series, losing three straight to the Yankees to fall to 0-10 against them on the season. Closer Joe Nathan, who saved 47 games in the regular season, coughed up a 3-1 lead in the ninth inning of Game Two on a home run to Alex Rodriguez, and the Twins couldn't recover.

NOTABLE ROOKIES: Catcher Jose Morales hit his way to the big leagues and onto the postseason roster, batting .311/.381/.361 once arriving. Lefthanders Jose Mijares (2-2, 2.34) and Brian Duensing (5-2, 3.64) combined for just 145 innings but were crucial pieces, Mijares as the team's top lefty reliever and set-up complement to Matt Guerrier, and Duensing as a starter down the stretch. Duensing wound up starting and losing Game One of the Division Series.

KEY TRANSACTIONS: The Twins shored up key holes on the roster with three August acquisitions, trading for reliever Jon Rauch (from the Diamondbacks), righty Carl Pavano (Indians) and shortstop Orlando Cabrera (Athletics). Cabrera wound up playing more innings at short than any Twin despite his Aug. 1 arrival and provided a solid bat to go with veteran savvy and playoff experience. Rauch posted a 1.72 ERA in 16 innings, while Pavano made 12 starts and was the Game Three Division Series starter.

DOWN ON THE FARM: Only low Class A Beloit had a truly awful season as high Class A Fort Myers posted the best record in the Florida State League, while Double-A New Britain, Rookie-level (advanced) Elizabethton and the Rookie-level Gulf Coast League teams all made the playoffs. Outfielder Aaron Hicks, the Twins' 2008 first-round pick, ranked as the No. 1 prospect in the Midwest League.

OPENING DAY PAYROLL: $65,299,266

PLAYERS OF THE YEAR

MAJOR LEAGUE	MINOR LEAGUE
Joe Mauer	**David Bromberg**
c	rhp
.365/.444/.587	(High A)
AL batting champion,	13-4, 2.70
BA Player of the Year	148 SO in 153 IP

ORGANIZATION LEADERS

BATTING   *Minimum 250 at-bats

MAJORS

*AVG	Joe Mauer	.365
*OPS	Joe Mauer	1.031
HR	Michael Cuddyer	32
RBI	Jason Kubel	103

MINORS

*AVG	Revere, Ben, Fort Myers	.311
R	Valencia, Danny, New Britain/Rochester	79
H	Revere, Ben, Fort Myers	145
TB	Valencia, Danny, New Britain/Rochester	227
2B	Dinkelman, Brian, New Britain	38
	Valencia, Danny, New Britain/Rochester	38
3B	Singleton, Steve, Fort Myers/New Britain	11
HR	Huber, Justin, Rochester	22
RBI	Huber, Justin, Rochester	76
BB	Parmelee, Chris, Fort Myers	65
SO	Parmelee, Chris, Fort Myers	109
SB	Revere, Ben, Fort Myers	45
*OBP	Dinkelman, Brian, New Britain	.383
	Santana, Ramon, Beloit/New Britain	.383
*SLG	Huber, Justin, Rochester	.482

PITCHING   †Minimum 75 innings

MAJORS

W	Scott Baker	15
†ERA	Nick Blackburn	4.03
SO	Scott Baker	162

MINORS

W	McCardell, Mike, Fort Myers/New Britain	14
L	DeVries, Cole, New Britain	14
†ERA	Hirschfeld, Steve, Fort Myers	2.23
G	Delaney, Rob, New Britain/Rochester	62
	Slama, Anthony, New Britain/Rochester	62
GS	Mullins, Ryan, New Britain	27
SV	Slama, Anthony, New Britain/Rochester	29
IP	Bromberg, David, Fort Myers	153
BB	Bromberg, David, Fort Myers	63
SO	Bromberg, David, Fort Myers	148
†AVG	Hirschfeld, Steve, Fort Myers	.215

2009 PERFORMANCE

General Manager: Bill Smith. **Farm Director:** Jim Rantz. **Scouting Director:** Deron Johnson.

Class	Team	League	W	L	PCT	Finish*	Manager(s)
Majors	Minnesota Twins	American	87	76	.534	5th (14)	Ron Gardenhire
Triple-A	Rochester Red Wings	International	70	74	.486	10th (14)	Stan Cliburn
Double-A	New Britain Rock Cats	Eastern	72	69	.511	5th (12)	Tom Nieto
High A	Fort Myers Miracle	Florida State	80	58	.580	2nd (12)	Jeff Smith
Low A	Beloit Snappers	Midwest	57	83	.407	13th (14)	Nelson Prada
Rookie	Elizabethton Twins	Appalachian	45	23	.662	2nd (10)	Ray Smith
Rookie	GCL Twins	Gulf Coast	34	21	.618	3rd (16)	Jake Mauer
Overall 2009 Minor League Record			358	328	.522	5th (30)	

*Finish in overall standings (No. of teams in league). †League champion.

ORGANIZATION STATISTICS

MINNESOTA TWINS

AMERICAN LEAGUE

Batting	B-T	HT	WT	DOB	AVG	vLH	vRH	G	AB	R	H	2B	3B	HR	RBI	BB	HBP	SH	SF	SO	SB	CS	SLG	OBP
Buscher, Brian	L-R	6-0	220	4-18-81	.235	.200	.240	61	136	14	32	3	1	2	12	24	3	0	1	35	0	0	.316	.360
Cabrera, Orlando	R-R	5-9	185	11-2-74	.289	.333	.265	59	242	42	70	13	3	5	36	11	0	1	6	32	2	0	.430	.313
2-team total (101 Oakland)					.284	—	—	160	656	83	186	36	3	9	77	36	0	6	10	71	13	4	.389	.316
Casilla, Alexi	B-R	5-9	180	7-20-84	.202	.182	.210	80	228	25	46	7	3	0	17	22	3	2	1	36	11	0	.259	.280
Crede, Joe	R-R	6-2	230	4-26-78	.225	.202	.235	90	333	42	75	16	1	15	48	29	2	0	3	56	0	0	.414	.289
Cuddyer, Michael	R-R	6-2	215	3-27-79	.276	.307	.263	153	588	93	162	34	7	32	94	54	6	0	2	118	6	1	.520	.342
Gomez, Carlos	R-R	6-4	215	12-4-85	.229	.204	.242	137	315	51	72	15	5	3	28	22	4	7	1	72	14	7	.337	.287
Harris, Brendan	R-R	6-1	210	8-26-80	.261	.302	.238	123	414	44	108	22	1	6	37	29	3	1	6	78	0	2	.362	.310
Huber, Justin	R-R	6-2	205	7-1-82	.500	1.000	.000	1	2	0	1	0	0	0	0	0	0	0	0	0	0	0	.500	.500
Kubel, Jason	L-R	6-0	220	5-25-82	.300	.243	.322	146	514	73	154	35	2	28	103	56	3	0	5	106	1	1	.539	.369
Mauer, Joe	L-R	6-5	225	4-19-83	.365	.345	.377	138	523	94	191	30	1	28	96	76	2	0	5	63	4	1	.587	.444
Morales, Jose	B-R	5-11	195	2-20-83	.311	.412	.294	54	119	14	37	6	0	0	7	14	0	0	1	22	0	0	.361	.381
Morneau, Justin	L-R	6-4	235	5-15-81	.274	.277	.272	135	508	85	139	31	1	30	100	72	3	0	7	86	0	0	.516	.363
Pridie, Jason	L-R	6-1	205	10-9-83	—	—	—	1	0	0	0	0	0	0	0	0	0	0	0	0	0	0	—	—
Punto, Nick	B-R	5-9	190	11-8-77	.228	.236	.225	125	359	56	82	15	1	1	38	61	1	13	6	70	16	3	.284	.337
Redmond, Mike	R-R	5-11	200	5-5-71	.237	.320	.188	45	135	9	32	5	1	0	7	11	1	0	0	19	0	0	.289	.299
Span, Denard	L-L	6-0	205	2-27-84	.311	.330	.303	145	578	97	180	16	10	8	68	70	10	12	6	89	23	10	.415	.392
Tolbert, Matt	B-R	6-0	185	5-4-82	.232	.321	.200	71	198	28	46	7	1	2	19	21	0	10	2	37	6	2	.308	.303
Young, Delmon	R-R	6-3	200	9-14-85	.284	.310	.271	108	395	50	112	16	2	12	60	12	4	0	5	92	2	5	.425	.308

Pitching	B-T	HT	WT	DOB	W	L	ERA	G	GS	CG	SV	IP	H	R	ER	HR	BB	SO	AVG	vLH	vRH	K/9	BB/9
Ayala, Luis	R-R	6-2	190	1-12-78	1	2	4.18	28	0	0	0	32	38	18	15	4	8	21	.306	.372	.272	5.85	2.23
Baker, Scott	R-R	6-4	220	9-19-81	15	9	4.37	33	33	1	0	200	190	99	97	28	48	162	.247	.217	.275	7.29	2.16
Blackburn, Nick	R-R	6-4	225	2-24-82	11	11	4.03	33	33	3	0	206	240	103	92	25	41	98	.290	.300	.277	4.29	1.79
Breslow, Craig	L-L	6-1	180	8-8-80	1	2	6.28	17	0	0	0	14	11	11	10	3	11	11	.220	.211	.226	6.91	6.91
2-team total (60 Oakland)					8	7	3.36	77	0	0	0	70	48	31	26	8	29	55	—	—	—	7.11	3.75
Crain, Jesse	R-R	6-1	215	7-5-81	7	4	4.70	56	0	0	0	52	48	28	27	3	27	43	.250	.297	.220	7.49	4.70
Dickey, R.A.	R-R	6-2	215	10-29-74	1	1	4.62	35	1	0	0	64	74	34	33	8	30	42	.290	.246	.326	5.88	4.20
Duensing, Brian	L-L	5-11	195	2-22-83	5	2	3.64	24	9	0	0	84	84	37	34	7	31	53	.263	.244	.269	5.68	3.32
Gabino, Armando	R-R	6-3	210	8-31-83	0	0	17.18	2	1	0	0	4	9	7	7	1	5	2	.450	.400	.600	4.91	12.27
Guerrier, Matt	R-R	6-3	195	8-2-78	5	1	2.36	79	0	0	1	76	58	23	20	10	16	47	.207	.194	.215	5.54	1.89
Henn, Sean	R-L	6-4	225	4-23-81	0	3	7.15	14	0	0	0	11	9	9	9	2	8	9	.225	.350	.100	7.15	6.35
2-team total (6 Baltimore)					0	3	7.53	20	0	0	0	14	15	12	12	2	12	15	—	—	—	9.42	7.53
Humber, Philip	R-R	6-4	220	12-21-82	0	0	8.00	8	0	0	0	9	17	8	8	1	9	9	.415	.385	.429	9.00	9.00
Keppel, Bob	R-R	6-5	215	6-11-82	1	1	4.83	37	0	0	0	54	63	30	29	4	21	32	.297	.317	.278	5.33	3.50
Liriano, Francisco	L-L	6-2	225	10-26-83	5	13	5.80	29	24	0	0	137	147	93	88	21	65	122	.279	.255	.287	8.03	4.28
Mahay, Ron	L-L	6-2	195	6-28-71	1	0	2.00	16	0	0	0	9	7	3	2	1	3	8	.206	.208	.200	8.00	3.00
2-team total (41 Kansas City)					2	1	4.29	57	0	0	0	50	62	29	24	10	22	42	—	—	—	7.51	3.93
Manship, Jeff	R-R	6-2	200	1-16-85	1	1	5.68	11	5	0	0	32	39	21	20	4	15	21	.310	.318	.300	5.97	4.26
Mijares, Jose	L-L	6-0	230	10-29-84	2	2	2.34	71	0	0	0	62	50	17	16	7	23	55	.224	.155	.283	8.03	3.36
Morillo, Juan	R-R	6-3	190	11-5-83	0	0	22.50	3	0	0	0	2	3	5	5	1	3	1	.333	.200	.500	4.50	13.50
Mulvey, Kevin	R-R	6-2	195	5-26-85	0	0	27.00	2	0	0	0	1	6	4	4	0	0	0	.600	.750	.500	0.00	0.00
Nathan, Joe	R-R	6-4	225	11-22-74	2	2	2.10	70	0	0	47	69	42	16	16	7	22	89	.171	.160	.181	11.67	2.88
Pavano, Carl	R-R	6-5	240	1-8-76	5	4	4.64	12	12	0	0	74	85	39	38	7	16	59	.284	.255	.315	7.21	1.95
2-team total (21 Cleveland)					14	12	5.10	33	33	1	0	199	235	119	113	26	39	147	—	—	—	6.64	1.76
Perkins, Glen	L-L	6-0	200	3-2-83	6	7	5.89	18	17	0	0	96	120	64	63	13	23	45	.304	.333	.295	4.20	2.15
Rauch, Jon	R-R	6-11	290	9-27-78	5	1	1.72	17	0	0	0	16	13	3	3	1	6	14	.245	.125	.297	8.04	3.45
Slowey, Kevin	R-R	6-3	195	5-4-84	10	3	4.86	16	16	0	0	91	113	50	49	15	15	75	.309	.354	.267	7.44	1.49
Swarzak, Anthony	R-R	6-4	225	9-10-85	3	7	6.25	12	12	0	0	59	76	43	41	12	20	34	.311	.331	.292	5.19	3.05

Fielding

Catcher	PCT	G	PO	A	E	DP	PB
Mauer	.996	109	724	31	3	3	9
Morales	.980	29	135	9	3	0	5
Redmond	1.000	44	228	8	0	2	2

First Base	PCT	G	PO	A	E	DP
Buscher	1.000	13	69	6	0	13
Cuddyer	.986	34	278	14	4	27
Harris	1.000	3	11	0	0	0
Huber	—	1	0	0	0	0
Morneau	.997	123	952	90	3	88
Tolbert	1.000	1	1	0	0	1

Second Base	PCT	G	PO	A	E	DP
Casilla	.984	72	141	170	5	35
Cuddyer	1.000	1	1	1	0	1
Harris	1.000	11	19	24	0	2
Punto	1.000	63	119	150	0	36
Tolbert	.989	36	74	110	2	29

Third Base	PCT	G	PO	A	E	DP
Buscher	.980	25	19	31	1	4
Crede	.983	84	60	171	4	18
Harris	.928	44	20	57	6	1
Punto	1.000	5	3	6	0	1
Tolbert	.964	27	11	43	2	5

Shortstop	PCT	G	PO	A	E	DP
Cabrera	.959	57	102	155	11	35
Casilla	1.000	2	0	1	0	1
Harris	.973	56	64	150	6	25
Punto	.973	58	100	153	7	29
Tolbert	1.000	3	2	4	0	2

Outfield	PCT	G	PO	A	E	DP
Cuddyer	.991	117	209	5	2	0
Gomez	.997	132	297	3	1	0
Kubel	1.000	58	103	1	0	0
Span	.986	145	350	6	5	2
Young	.973	98	175	4	5	1

ROCHESTER RED WINGS

TRIPLE-A

INTERNATIONAL LEAGUE

Batting	B-T	HT	WT	DOB	AVG	vLH	vRH	G	AB	R	H	2B	3B	HR	RBI	BB	HBP	SH	SF	SO	SB	CS	SLG	OBP
Buscher, Brian	L-R	6-0	220	4-18-81	.179	.276	.122	23	78	6	14	0	0	1	2	11	0	0	0	20	0	1	.218	.281
Butera, Drew	R-R	6-1	210	8-9-83	.211	.256	.193	99	298	23	63	16	1	2	25	22	2	8	3	49	0	1	.292	.268
Casilla, Alexi	B-R	5-9	180	7-20-84	.340	.261	.373	40	156	21	53	3	4	2	17	11	0	2	2	23	9	6	.449	.379
Christy, Jeff	R-R	6-1	210	4-13-84	.169	.250	.140	21	59	5	10	1	0	0	4	6	0	1	0	16	0	0	.186	.246
De San Miguel, Allan	R-R	5-9	200	2-1-88	1.000	—	1.000	2	1	0	1	0	0	0	0	0	0	0	0	0	0	0	1.000	1.000
Huber, Justin	R-R	6-2	205	7-1-82	.273	.257	.280	121	440	60	120	22	2	22	76	51	9	0	6	84	4	3	.482	.356
Hughes, Luke	R-R	5-11	205	8-24-84	.259	.370	.231	37	135	19	35	8	2	6	28	18	1	0	3	38	2	0	.481	.344
Machado, Alejandro	B-R	6-0	185	4-26-82	.222	.100	.250	18	54	2	12	1	0	0	5	8	1	0	1	6	6	1	.241	.328
Macri, Matt	R-R	6-2	215	5-29-82	.225	.216	.228	114	365	57	82	25	3	11	42	35	4	3	5	85	5	5	.400	.296
Martin, Dustin	L-L	6-2	215	4-4-84	.254	.238	.259	124	422	58	107	16	5	5	53	39	4	0	5	92	26	8	.351	.319
Morales, Jose	R-R	5-11	195	2-20-83	.336	.279	.360	58	211	30	71	13	1	2	26	28	1	0	2	27	1	3	.436	.413
Peterson, Brock	R-R	6-3	230	11-20-83	.304	.299	.306	99	316	47	96	18	2	10	43	34	4	0	2	77	0	0	.468	.376
Plouffe, Trevor	R-R	6-2	195	6-15-86	.260	.242	.268	118	430	53	112	23	5	10	60	34	2	4	7	68	3	6	.407	.313
Pridie, Jason	L-R	6-1	205	10-9-83	.265	.247	.273	121	513	69	136	23	5	9	53	19	5	3	6	85	25	7	.382	.295
Span, Denard	L-L	6-0	205	2-27-84	.333	.500	.250	2	6	1	2	1	0	0	0	1	0	0	0	1	1	1	.500	.500
Tolbert, Matt	B-R	6-0	185	5-4-82	.288	.321	.272	56	236	35	68	11	6	3	22	14	1	0	0	32	7	4	.424	.331
Tolleson, Steven	R-R	5-11	185	11-1-83	.270	.297	.254	92	352	57	95	17	1	6	27	36	2	1	3	52	7	6	.375	.338
Valencia, Danny	R-R	6-2	210	9-19-84	.286	.300	.278	71	269	35	77	24	0	7	41	8	1	0	4	37	0	2	.454	.305
Watkins, Tommy	R-R	5-10	225	6-18-80	.248	.190	.276	59	129	18	32	6	0	0	11	11	0	5	1	21	2	3	.295	.305
Winfree, David	R-R	6-3	230	8-5-85	.273	.250	.281	116	422	48	115	31	3	14	61	28	2	0	5	88	0	2	.460	.317

Pitching	B-T	HT	WT	DOB	W	L	ERA	G	GS	CG	SV	IP	H	R	ER	HR	BB	SO	AVG	vLH	vRH	K/9	BB/9
Crain, Jesse	R-R	6-1	215	7-5-81	1	0	2.55	12	0	0	1	18	13	5	5	0	8	22	.206	.227	.195	11.21	4.08
Delaney, Rob	L-R	6-3	235	9-8-84	7	3	4.53	36	0	0	7	48	43	25	24	5	15	38	.240	.250	.235	7.17	2.83
Dickey, R.A.	R-R	6-2	215	10-29-74	2	1	5.13	5	5	1	0	33	39	20	19	1	9	18	.289	.256	.304	4.86	2.43
Duensing, Brian	L-L	5-11	195	2-22-83	4	6	4.66	13	13	0	0	75	87	40	39	2	19	44	.298	.210	.332	5.26	2.27
Gabino, Armando	R-R	6-3	210	8-31-83	6	4	2.94	38	7	1	1	98	80	34	32	7	24	64	.227	.230	.225	5.88	2.20
Gosling, Mike	L-L	6-2	210	9-23-80	7	1	4.37	21	0	0	1	35	33	17	17	2	17	43	.246	.286	.224	11.06	4.37
2-team total (8 Columbus)					7	4	4.81	29	4	0	1	67	78	38	36	7	24	73	—	—	—	9.76	3.21
Hendrickson, Ben	R-R	6-4	205	2-4-81	0	0	7.84	6	0	0	0	10	18	9	9	0	9	9	.400	.333	.444	7.84	7.84
Henn, Sean	R-L	6-4	225	4-23-81	1	1	2.33	28	0	0	6	39	37	18	10	3	16	45	.240	.164	.290	10.47	3.72
Humber, Philip	R-R	6-4	220	12-21-82	7	9	5.34	23	22	1	0	120	135	79	71	15	45	87	.280	.286	.277	6.54	3.38
Jones, Jason	R-R	6-5	225	11-20-82	5	11	5.75	31	22	1	0	135	172	93	86	20	39	73	.312	.341	.292	4.88	2.61
Julianel, Ben	B-L	6-2	200	9-4-79	1	0	8.18	8	0	0	0	11	12	11	10	3	5	8	.273	.333	.250	6.55	4.09
Keppel, Bob	R-R	6-5	215	6-11-82	3	3	2.43	23	3	1	1	56	51	18	15	1	13	28	.245	.273	.220	4.53	2.10
Lahey, Tim	R-R	6-6	250	2-7-82	2	3	5.72	41	0	0	1	57	70	40	36	6	21	44	.298	.341	.273	6.99	3.34
Lugo, Jason	L-L	6-1	180	4-10-84	0	0	4.00	9	0	0	1	9	9	6	4	0	11		.265	.300		11.00	9.00
Manship, Jeff	R-R	6-2	200	1-16-85	4	2	3.22	8	8	0	0	50	53	23	18	1	17	30	.277	.286	.270	5.36	3.04
Mijares, Jose	L-L	6-0	230	10-29-84	1	0	0.00	5	0	0	1	6	2	0	0	1	4		.100	.200	.067	5.68	1.42
Morillo, Juan	R-R	6-3	190	11-5-83	6	6	3.90	46	0	0	5	67	56	30	29	1	51	87	.226	.240	.215	11.69	6.85
Mulvey, Kevin	R-R	6-2	195	5-26-85	5	8	3.93	24	24	2	0	149	153	84	65	12	54	113	.268	.308	.244	6.83	3.26
Pignatiello, Carmen	R-L	6-0	205	9-12-82	0	1	14.14	4	1	0	0	7	12	11	11	1	3	6	.400	.556	.333	7.71	3.86
Pino, Yohan	R-R	6-0	190	12-26-83	2	2	2.82	8	8	0	0	51	37	18	16	5	11	44	.199	.256	.154	7.76	1.94
2-team total (2 Columbus)					4	2	2.49	10	10	0	0	65	49	20	18	5	13	58	—	—	—	8.03	1.80
Santos, Reid	L-L	6-1	170	8-24-82	2	6	4.70	25	18	0	0	98	132	67	51	10	34	66	.320	.242	.345	6.08	3.13
Slama, Anthony	R-R	6-3	207	1-6-84	0	2	3.45	11	0	0	4	16	11	6	6	0	8	19	.212	.333	.162	10.91	4.60
Swarzak, Anthony	R-R	6-4	225	9-10-85	4	5	3.28	13	13	0	0	80	79	31	29	4	21	45	.261	.269	.253	5.08	2.37

Fielding

Catcher	PCT	G	PO	A	E	DP	PB
Butera	.989	96	585	68	7	3	14
Christy	1.000	17	103	7	0	1	3
De San Miguel	1.000	2	5	0	0	0	0
Morales	.990	41	273	11	2	0	4
Watkins	1.000	1	1	0	0	0	0

First Base	PCT	G	PO	A	E	DP
Buscher	1.000	9	62	3	0	3
Huber	.988	27	224	23	3	17
Macri	1.000	38	279	20	0	28
Peterson	.994	77	607	47	4	69

Second Base	PCT	G	PO	A	E	DP
Buscher	1.000	1	1	0	0	0

	PCT	G	PO	A	E	DP
Casilla	.970	40	82	109	6	22
Machado	.974	8	19	18	1	5
Macri	1.000	25	58	66	0	21
Tolbert	.980	23	43	53	2	12
Tolleson	.954	54	91	135	11	36
Watkins	.800	3	3	1	1	0

Third Base	PCT	G	PO	A	E	DP
Buscher	1.000	4	3	9	0	0
Hughes	.891	31	23	59	10	7
Machado	1.000	2	1	7	0	0
Macri	.883	28	18	35	7	6
Tolbert	1.000	6	3	11	0	2
Tolleson	1.000	1	0	1	0	0
Valencia	.927	68	40	113	12	7
Watkins	.885	14	4	19	3	0

Shortstop	PCT	G	PO	A	E	DP
Macri	.953	22	21	60	4	9
Plouffe	.952	111	186	330	26	84
Tolbert	.974	10	19	18	1	7
Tolleson	.963	7	11	15	1	1
Watkins	1.000	3	1	1	0	0

Outfield	PCT	G	PO	A	E	DP
Huber	1.000	26	42	0	0	0
Martin	.965	119	215	6	8	0
Pridie	.989	120	336	9	4	2
Span	1.000	2	5	0	0	0
Tolbert	1.000	20	38	1	0	1
Tolleson	.981	34	52	1	1	0
Watkins	.957	29	41	3	2	0
Winfree	.967	110	221	13	8	1

NEW BRITAIN ROCK CATS
DOUBLE-A
EASTERN LEAGUE

Batting	B-T	HT	WT	DOB	AVG	vLH	vRH	G	AB	R	H	2B	3B	HR	RBI	BB	HBP	SH	SF	SO	SB	CS	SLG	OBP
Berg, Daniel	R-R	6-0	200	11-21-84	.098	.158	.045	15	41	3	4	1	0	0	8	3	2	0	0	14	0	0	.122	.196
Christy, Jeff	R-R	6-1	210	4-13-84	.190	.045	.246	29	79	5	15	1	0	0	7	7	0	3	0	15	0	0	.203	.256
De San Miguel, Allan	R-R	5-9	200	2-1-88	.196	.217	.182	22	56	13	11	4	1	0	8	15	3	1	1	20	0	0	.304	.387
Dinkelman, Brian	L-R	5-11	195	11-10-83	.296	.282	.302	129	459	62	136	38	2	8	65	55	13	10	5	73	5	6	.440	.383
Gaetti, Joe	R-R	5-11	205	10-18-81	.139	.167	.111	9	36	1	5	3	1	0	2	1	1	0	1	14	0	0	.278	.179
Gardenhire, Toby	R-R	6-0	170	9-11-82	.265	.317	.212	71	200	21	53	8	0	0	19	14	4	6	0	36	2	1	.305	.326
Grudzielanek, Mark	R-R	6-1	200	6-30-70	.267	.250	.273	8	30	6	8	0	0	0	2	1	0	0	6	0	0	.267	.333
Hughes, Luke	R-R	5-11	205	8-2-84	.250	.259	.246	56	200	22	50	15	3	6	36	19	4	1	5	38	1	1	.445	.320
Lehmann, Danny	R-R	5-11	185	9-5-85	.190	.208	.183	56	168	11	32	8	0	0	10	12	1	7	1	18	0	1	.238	.247
Lis, Erik	L-L	6-1	220	3-8-84	.283	.286	.282	128	459	66	130	29	1	17	66	45	8	1	6	101	1	1	.462	.353
Machado, Alejandro	B-R	6-0	185	4-26-82	.200	.167	.214	12	40	7	8	3	0	1	6	4	1	0	0	8	0	1	.350	.289
Moses, Matt	L-R	6-0	210	2-20-85	.224	.082	.257	78	255	34	57	10	1	7	43	18	0	0	1	52	4	5	.353	.274
Ortiz, Yancarlos	B-R	5-9	150	9-15-84	.223	.260	.201	106	327	31	73	6	3	0	26	38	3	13	3	68	2	3	.260	.307
Portes, Juan	R-R	5-11	170	11-26-85	.297	.320	.281	100	327	45	97	21	3	6	40	34	3	4	2	45	7	3	.434	.366
Ramos, Wilson	R-R	6-0	220	8-10-87	.317	.348	.302	54	205	31	65	16	0	4	29	6	2	0	1	23	0	0	.454	.341
Robbins, Whit	R-R	6-0	205	9-25-84	.278	.276	.278	117	425	53	118	23	2	9	49	43	4	1	2	75	0	3	.405	.348
Roberts, Brandon	L-R	6-0	185	11-9-84	.287	.245	.302	103	397	65	114	18	2	3	37	29	12	7	2	60	21	7	.365	.352
Santana, Ramon	R-R	5-9	152	6-20-86	.267	.333	.250	4	15	4	4	1	0	0	1	1	0	0	3	0	0	.333	.353
Singleton, Steve	L-R	5-11	189	9-12-85	.291	.278	.295	46	158	15	46	11	3	1	18	7	0	0	1	23	1	1	.418	.319
Solarte, Yangervis	B-R	5-11	176	7-7-87	.143	.000	.167	3	7	0	1	0	0	0	0	0	0	0	0	1	0	0	.143	.143
Tolleson, Steven	R-R	5-11	185	11-1-83	.258	.268	.255	38	151	21	39	10	2	2	13	16	4	1	1	20	6	2	.391	.343
Tosoni, Rene	L-R	6-0	195	7-2-86	.271	.185	.308	122	425	64	115	25	4	15	71	45	16	1	3	98	8	8	.454	.360
Valencia, Danny	R-R	6-2	210	9-19-84	.284	.323	.269	57	218	44	62	14	4	7	29	31	1	0	2	40	0	2	.482	.373

Pitching	B-T	HT	WT	DOB	W	L	ERA	G	GS	CG	SV	IP	H	R	ER	HR	BB	SO	AVG	vLH	vRH	K/9	BB/9
Burnett, Alex	R-R	6-0	190	7-26-87	1	2	1.79	40	0	0	9	55	36	14	11	2	19	52	.187	.159	.207	8.46	3.09
Davis, Tony	B-L	5-11	185	1-16-88	0	0	0.00	2	0	0	0	3	1	0	0	0	0	1	.111	.250	.000	3.00	0.00
Delaney, Rob	L-R	6-3	235	9-8-84	1	1	2.00	26	0	0	0	36	32	11	8	1	6	40	.242	.254	.231	10.00	1.50
Devries, Cole	R-R	6-2	185	2-12-85	7	14	4.84	26	26	1	0	138	162	88	74	16	46	90	.291	.312	.268	5.88	3.01
Fox, Matt	R-R	6-3	192	12-4-82	9	9	3.58	28	26	1	0	151	143	67	60	12	56	120	.250	.249	.252	7.15	3.34
Guerra, Deolis	R-R	6-5	200	4-17-89	6	3	5.17	12	11	1	0	63	62	38	36	4	17	49	.258	.211	.302	7.04	2.44
Gutierrez, Carlos	R-R	6-3	205	9-22-86	1	3	6.19	22	6	0	0	52	62	36	36	6	24	32	.300	.279	.314	5.50	4.13
Lugo, Jose	L-L	6-1	180	4-10-84	4	2	4.19	50	0	0	3	58	54	36	27	2	28	56	.237	.241	.232	8.69	4.34
Manship, Jeff	R-R	6-2	200	1-16-85	6	4	4.28	13	13	0	0	76	72	37	36	2	20	45	.249	.269	.226	5.35	2.38
Mata, Frank	R-R	6-0	168	3-11-84	2	5	3.78	53	5	0	3	79	83	49	33	3	34	60	.268	.277	.259	6.86	3.89
McCardell, Mike	R-R	6-5	220	4-13-85	5	2	4.10	9	9	0	0	48	45	22	22	4	16	40	.247	.181	.318	7.45	2.98
Mullins, Ryan	L-L	6-0	180	11-13-83	11	11	4.03	28	27	1	0	145	175	78	65	13	36	133	.298	.324	.286	8.26	2.23
Pino, Yohan	R-R	6-0	190	12-26-83	5	1	3.19	32	4	0	0	62	61	24	22	4	16	64	.257	.303	.209	9.29	2.32
Rainville, Jay	R-R	6-3	230	10-16-85	3	3	5.56	19	13	0	0	70	90	51	43	6	24	40	.315	.272	.353	5.17	3.10
Slama, Anthony	R-R	6-3	207	1-6-84	4	2	2.48	51	0	0	25	65	46	18	18	5	32	93	.201	.286	.129	12.81	4.41
Steedley, Spencer	L-L	6-2	194	5-31-85	2	1	3.38	20	0	0	0	19	16	9	7	2	10	16	.239	.143	.400	7.71	4.82
Van Mil, Loek	R-R	7-1	232	9-15-84	1	1	2.45	8	0	0	1	7	7	2	2	0	6	5	.269	.214	.333	6.14	7.36
Waldrop, Kyle	R-R	6-5	215	10-27-85	2	3	1.46	31	0	0	0	56	51	14	9	2	18	30	.246	.287	.212	4.85	2.91
Ward, Zach	R-R	6-3	250	1-14-84	2	2	6.75	22	1	0	0	29	30	27	22	3	25	17	.250	.235	.261	5.22	7.67

Fielding

Catcher	PCT	G	PO	A	E	DP	PB
Christy	.982	29	149	11	3	0	1
De San Miguel	.988	22	147	16	2	3	2
Gardenhire	1.000	2	1	0	0	0	0
Lehmann	.998	56	389	23	1	5	4
Ramos	.989	45	313	36	4	7	4

First Base	PCT	G	PO	A	E	DP
Berg	—	1	0	0	0	0
Gardenhire	.967	4	24	5	1	5
Lis	.983	42	308	39	6	22
Machado	1.000	1	1	0	0	0
Robbins	.990	99	826	91	9	86

Second Base	PCT	G	PO	A	E	DP
Dinkelman	.983	80	131	207	6	46
Gardenhire	.952	22	32	48	4	13
Grudzielanek	.938	6	11	19	2	3
Hughes	1.000	7	7	15	0	1
Machado	.925	10	19	18	3	6
Singleton	1.000	22	26	38	0	7
Solarte	1.000	1	3	6	0	0
Tolleson	.963	7	10	16	1	5

Third Base	PCT	G	PO	A	E	DP
Gardenhire	.907	19	9	40	5	3
Hughes	.914	47	22	74	9	8
Machado	—	1	0	0	0	0
Ortiz	—	2	0	0	0	0
Portes	.931	18	7	20	2	0
Santana	1.000	3	3	6	0	1
Singleton	—	1	0	0	0	0
Valencia	.941	56	31	96	8	8

Shortstop	PCT	G	PO	A	E	DP
Gardenhire	1.000	4	2	8	0	0
Ortiz	.961	94	148	251	16	61
Singleton	.955	25	42	63	5	9
Tolleson	.927	24	35	54	7	11

Outfield	PCT	G	PO	A	E	DP
Berg	1.000	14	20	1	0	0
Dinkelman	.987	44	74	4	1	1
Gaetti	1.000	9	18	1	0	0
Gardenhire	1.000	4	7	0	0	0
Hughes	1.000	1	1	0	0	0
Moses	1.000	68	102	7	0	0

Ortiz	1.000	6	13	1	0	0
Portes	.979	75	131	12	3	1
Roberts	.991	97	213	8	2	3
Santana	—	1	0	0	0	0
Tolleson	1.000	8	12	0	0	0
Tosoni	.970	116	217	11	7	4

FORT MYERS MIRACLE   HIGH CLASS A

FLORIDA STATE LEAGUE

Batting	B-T	HT	WT	DOB	AVG	vLH	vRH	G	AB	R	H	2B	3B	HR	RBI	BB	HBP	SH	SF	SO	SB	CS	SLG	OBP
Benson, Joe	R-R	6-2	211	3-5-88	.285	.400	.239	80	263	46	75	10	3	5	29	46	13	3	2	74	14	7	.403	.414
Berg, Daniel	R-R	6-0	200	11-21-84	.239	.304	.212	45	159	23	38	9	2	1	18	16	5	1	1	53	1	1	.340	.326
Bigley, Evan	R-R	6-1	200	3-9-87	.280	.296	.274	95	328	39	92	22	2	5	46	22	6	5	1	71	1	5	.405	.336
Cates, Chris	R-R	5-3	145	4-15-85	.251	.239	.257	118	370	41	93	6	2	0	25	34	3	9	3	27	10	8	.278	.317
De Los Santos, Estarlin	B-R	5-10	165	1-20-87	.290	.294	.289	68	262	33	76	11	7	1	23	13	3	5	1	49	11	4	.397	.330
De San Miguel, Allan	R-R	5-9	200	2-1-88	.231	.444	.178	36	91	9	21	2	0	1	10	21	2	3	1	26	0	1	.286	.383
Dolenc, Mark	R-R	6-3	218	11-8-84	.288	.365	.255	110	386	44	111	19	5	4	42	24	3	6	3	84	27	6	.394	.332
Fernandez, Jair	R-R	6-1	170	12-10-86	.224	.250	.214	84	255	30	57	14	0	4	28	25	4	4	2	45	1	1	.325	.301
Lehmann, Danny	R-R	5-11	185	9-5-85	.294	.500	.220	25	68	9	20	3	0	1	5	9	0	1	2	7	2	0	.382	.367
Leveret, Rene	R-R	6-2	224	11-19-85	.286	.292	.283	92	301	25	86	17	1	5	38	30	7	0	1	65	1	2	.399	.363
Machado, Alejandro	B-R	6-0	185	4-26-82	.277	.091	.333	12	47	7	13	3	0	0	3	6	2	0	1	7	0	1	.340	.375
Mauer, Joe	L-R	6-5	225	4-19-83	.400	.000	.429	5	15	2	6	2	0	0	4	2	0	0	1	1	0	0	.533	.444
Parmelee, Chris	L-L	6-1	223	2-24-88	.258	.253	.260	123	422	61	109	27	1	16	73	65	6	0	8	109	2	2	.441	.359
Rams, Danny	R-R	6-2	205	12-19-88	.308	.400	.250	5	13	2	4	2	0	0	3	1	0	0	0	3	0	0	.462	.357
Revere, Ben	L-R	5-9	166	5-3-88	.311	.333	.303	121	466	75	145	13	4	2	48	40	7	1	3	34	45	17	.369	.372
Richardson, Juan	R-R	6-0	200	12-22-84	.210	.263	.186	22	62	4	13	1	0	0	6	2	0	0	1	8	0	1	.226	.231
Romero, Deibinson	R-R	6-1	200	9-24-86	.225	.210	.232	118	417	57	94	18	3	5	56	50	7	0	11	102	3	1	.319	.311
Romero, Nick	B-R	6-1	200	7-15-87	.240	.246	.237	76	242	28	58	11	3	4	29	38	5	0	2	46	4	0	.360	.352
Singleton, Steve	L-R	5-11	189	9-12-85	.269	.276	.267	80	297	41	80	15	8	5	39	23	4	6	1	26	6	3	.424	.329
Solarte, Yangervis	B-R	5-11	176	7-7-87	.188	.000	.200	4	16	2	3	1	0	0	1	0	0	0	0	1	0	0	.250	.188
Soto, Alexander	R-R	5-11	205	11-8-86	.212	.211	.212	26	85	7	18	2	0	1	7	6	0	0	0	25	0	0	.271	.264

Pitching	B-T	HT	WT	DOB	W	L	ERA	G	GS	CG	SV	IP	H	R	ER	HR	BB	SO	AVG	vLH	vRH	K/9	BB/9
Allen, Michael	R-R	6-3	220	5-27-87	1	0	3.38	10	0	0	0	13	11	7	5	0	7	12	.229	.313	.188	8.10	4.72
Arias, Henry	R-R	6-3	201	1-6-85	4	5	5.19	44	1	0	4	69	72	43	40	7	36	55	.269	.398	.200	7.14	4.67
Arias, Santos	R-R	5-11	162	3-17-87	6	3	2.15	38	9	0	3	101	90	26	24	1	27	72	.243	.250	.238	6.44	2.41
Baker, Scott	R-R	6-4	220	9-19-81	1	0	1.29	1	1	0	0	7	5	1	1	0	1	3	.227	.400	.176	3.86	1.29
Bonser, Boof	R-R	6-4	260	10-14-81	0	0	0.00	1	0	0	0	1	0	0	0	0	1	1	.000	.000	.000	9.00	9.00
Bromberg, David	L-R	6-5	241	9-14-87	13	4	2.70	27	26	1	0	153	125	52	46	6	63	148	.224	.197	.247	8.69	3.70
Burnett, Alex	R-R	6-0	190	7-26-87	2	1	1.99	18	0	0	4	23	14	6	5	0	7	26	.175	.129	.204	10.32	2.78
Erickson, Blair	R-R	6-1	212	10-28-84	1	5	4.39	44	0	0	15	53	50	30	26	2	32	63	.250	.358	.176	10.63	5.40
Guerra, Deolis	R-R	6-5	200	4-17-89	6	8	4.69	16	15	0	0	86	95	52	45	6	25	57	.278	.231	.308	5.94	2.61
Gutierrez, Carlos	R-R	6-3	205	9-22-86	2	3	1.32	11	10	0	0	55	37	20	8	1	22	33	.192	.200	.187	5.43	3.62
Hirschfeld, Steve	R-R	6-5	226	9-8-85	7	7	2.23	32	17	1	0	117	93	36	29	6	31	86	.215	.250	.194	6.62	2.38
Lanigan, Bobby	R-R	6-4	220	5-5-87	1	0	4.70	7	2	0	0	15	21	9	8	1	4	14	.318	.455	.250	8.22	2.35
McCardell, Mike	R-R	6-5	220	4-13-85	9	6	3.93	17	17	1	0	94	98	51	41	10	16	78	.272	.294	.253	7.47	1.53
Perkins, Glen	L-L	6-0	200	3-2-83	1	0	2.45	2	2	1	0	11	8	5	3	2	1	9	.195	.000	.216	7.36	0.82
Robertson, Tyler	L-L	6-5	220	12-23-87	8	8	3.33	26	26	0	0	143	139	64	53	7	51	103	.259	.197	.285	6.47	3.20
Steedley, Spencer	L-L	6-2	194	5-31-85	4	0	1.79	35	0	0	6	50	39	16	10	2	18	46	.214	.261	.186	8.23	3.22
Stuifbergen, Tom	R-R	6-3	200	9-26-88	0	1	10.13	1	1	0	0	3	5	4	3	0	1	3	.385	.000	.714	10.13	3.38
Tarsi, Mike	R-L	6-8	202	8-11-86	3	4	4.14	12	11	0	0	67	77	41	31	4	21	57	.281	.239	.296	7.62	2.81
Testa, Joe	L-L	5-10	175	12-18-85	5	0	1.22	22	0	0	1	37	29	13	5	2	18	53	.213	.191	.225	12.89	4.38
Van Mil, Loek	R-R	7-1	232	9-15-84	0	0	2.86	25	0	0	5	35	29	11	11	3	17	23	.236	.212	.254	5.97	4.41
Waldrop, Kyle	R-R	6-5	215	10-27-85	3	2	3.09	20	0	0	3	35	43	15	12	0	7	20	.312	.321	.305	5.14	1.80
Watts, Dakota	R-R	6-5	210	11-16-87	0	2	14.85	5	0	0	0	7	10	12	11	0	10	6	.370	.294	.500	8.10	13.50
Williams, Matt	R-R	6-1	180	2-28-87	3	0	2.88	16	0	0	1	25	22	9	8	3	5	30	.232	.222	.237	10.80	1.80

Fielding

Catcher	PCT	G	PO	A	E	DP	PB
De San Miguel	.986	28	191	16	3	2	3
Fernandez	.991	70	464	70	5	4	11
Lehmann	.994	24	143	18	1	0	2
Mauer	1.000	4	19	2	0	0	1
Rams	1.000	4	24	1	0	0	1
Richardson	.979	8	42	4	1	0	1
Soto	1.000	18	107	10	0	1	2

First Base	PCT	G	PO	A	E	DP
Berg	.990	21	187	7	2	16
De San Miguel	1.000	1	2	0	0	1
Leveret	.988	67	557	37	7	53
Machado	1.000	1	6	0	0	0
Parmelee	.988	62	465	31	6	45
Richardson	.909	4	8	2	1	0

Second Base	PCT	G	PO	A	E	DP
Berg	1.000	5	7	8	0	3
Cates	.950	27	40	74	6	18
De Los Santos	.974	11	14	23	1	4
Machado	1.000	7	11	18	0	3
Romero	.991	27	37	70	1	12
Singleton	.984	69	117	190	5	47

Third Base	PCT	G	PO	A	E	DP
Berg	.958	10	6	17	1	3
Cates	1.000	7	2	13	0	1
Machado	1.000	2	0	5	0	0
Richardson	.778	7	2	5	2	0
Romero	.919	98	55	193	22	16
Romero	.817	23	10	39	11	6

Shortstop	PCT	G	PO	A	E	DP
Cates	.971	84	119	251	11	57
De Los Santos	.905	54	66	144	22	21
Romero	1.000	4	8	8	0	4
Singleton	1.000	4	2	4	0	2

Outfield	PCT	G	PO	A	E	DP
Benson	.975	77	155	4	4	1
Berg	.800	3	3	1	1	0
Bigley	.985	82	129	6	2	0
De San Miguel	1.000	1	2	0	0	0
Dolenc	.979	105	176	8	4	0
Parmelee	.959	57	111	5	5	2
Revere	1.000	102	223	2	0	0
Richardson	1.000	1	1	0	0	0
Romero	1.000	10	16	0	0	0

MIDWEST LEAGUE

MINNESOTA TWINS

Batting	B-T	HT	WT	DOB	AVG	vLH	vRH	G	AB	R	H	2B	3B	HR	RBI	BB	HBP	SH	SF	SO	SB	CS	SLG	OBP
Beresford, James	L-R	6-1	155	1-19-89	.289	.323	.279	114	450	52	130	11	0	0	38	34	3	17	1	70	15	11	.313	.342
Bigley, Evan	R-R	6-1	200	3-9-87	.307	.318	.304	25	101	16	31	6	1	2	22	3	2	0	0	19	2	2	.446	.340
De La Osa, Dominic	R-R	5-11	205	1-13-86	.205	.176	.214	106	366	44	75	10	2	1	24	33	7	4	1	86	8	5	.251	.283
De San Miguel, Allan	R-R	5-9	200	2-1-88	.333	.286	.500	3	9	3	3	1	0	0	2	3	0	0	0	2	0	0	.444	.500
Hanson, Nate	R-R	6-0	195	2-8-87	.253	.203	.267	106	360	47	91	21	3	3	30	31	8	7	5	65	6	3	.353	.322
Harrington, Michael	L-R	6-0	200	10-6-85	.228	.167	.241	107	373	44	85	31	1	4	46	30	1	1	1	98	3	1	.349	.286
Hicks, Aaron	B-R	6-2	170	10-2-89	.251	.207	.264	67	251	43	63	15	3	4	29	40	1	2	3	55	10	8	.382	.353
Ladendorf, Tyler	R-R	6-0	210	3-7-88	.233	.083	.271	15	60	7	14	2	0	0	4	4	1	0	0	13	2	1	.267	.292
2-team total (35 Kane County)					.232	—	—	50	190	20	44	6	2	2	19	14	4	2	0	32	4	3	.316	.298
Lanning, Jeff	R-R	6-0	210	1-1-87	.250	.250	.250	52	164	18	41	9	1	2	17	15	0	2	3	39	2	0	.354	.308
Lewis, Ozzie	R-R	6-4	193	3-21-86	.272	.261	.275	108	401	43	109	22	1	7	53	24	5	1	6	91	7	4	.384	.317
Morales, Angel	R-R	6-1	180	11-24-89	.266	.276	.263	115	376	63	100	22	5	13	62	30	7	2	3	104	19	6	.455	.329
Munroe, Buddy	R-R	5-11	185	8-28-87	.263	.250	.267	5	19	3	5	1	0	0	0	1	0	0	0	5	0	0	.316	.300
Rams, Danny	R-R	6-2	205	12-19-88	.229	.237	.226	48	175	24	40	14	0	7	23	18	2	0	0	77	0	0	.429	.308
Richardson, Juan	R-R	6-0	200	12-27-86	.271	.294	.262	18	59	5	16	1	0	0	4	3	1	0	0	4	0	1	.288	.317
Romero, Nick	B-R	6-1	200	7-15-87	.222	.217	.224	31	108	18	24	2	1	2	14	16	2	2	3	29	4	1	.315	.326
Sanchez, Hank	R-R	6-3	235	11-29-86	.231	.250	.222	4	13	3	3	1	0	0	2	3	0	0	0	9	0	0	.308	.375
Santana, Ramon	R-R	5-9	152	6-20-86	.296	.315	.292	103	371	46	110	25	3	9	60	50	6	2	5	94	8	9	.453	.384
Severino, Adam	L-R	6-0	200	10-22-86	.171	.061	.218	45	111	19	19	5	1	0	4	13	0	7	0	33	4	6	.234	.258
Soto, Alexander	R-R	5-11	205	11-8-86	.240	.148	.260	50	154	15	37	6	0	5	26	19	1	1	1	38	0	1	.377	.326
Thompson, Drew	L-R	6-1	160	11-7-86	.242	.262	.237	91	302	37	73	15	8	2	31	38	0	3	2	70	6	5	.364	.325
Tintor, Eli	R-R	6-2	190	12-24-84	.184	.333	.138	12	38	6	7	1	0	0	3	7	0	0	0	14	0	2	.211	.311
Waltenbury, Jon	L-R	6-4	230	4-1-88	.236	.263	.230	109	402	48	95	17	2	5	38	41	0	0	1	91	3	1	.326	.306
Williams, Reggie	L-R	6-2	185	11-5-88	.600	.667	.571	3	10	2	6	2	0	0	2	2	0	0	0	2	0	1	.800	.667

Pitching	B-T	HT	WT	DOB	W	L	ERA	G	GS	CG	SV	IP	H	R	ER	HR	BB	SO	AVG	vLH	vRH	K/9	BB/9
Allen, Michael	R-R	6-3	220	5-27-87	2	8	4.89	27	11	1	0	77	95	55	42	4	32	67	.307	.286	.324	7.80	3.72
Berlind, Dan	R-R	6-7	215	12-3-87	5	13	4.76	31	21	2	2	129	131	83	68	8	56	97	.266	.276	.260	6.78	3.92
Blevins, Steve	R-R	6-2	215	11-17-86	3	5	3.52	50	0	0	3	77	79	38	30	2	26	67	.262	.266	.260	7.87	3.05
Bullock, Billy	R-R	6-6	225	2-27-88	3	0	2.73	26	0	0	8	26	25	11	8	0	12	35	.253	.270	.242	11.96	4.10
Carr, Kyle	R-L	6-5	200	11-11-86	0	2	3.42	16	0	0	0	24	26	14	9	2	9	27	.263	.240	.270	10.27	3.42
Hendriks, Liam	R-R	6-1	190	2-10-89	3	5	3.51	11	11	0	0	67	73	34	26	3	15	62	.278	.235	.297	8.37	2.03
Hernandez, Danny	R-R	6-2	180	11-19-85	0	0	9.00	3	0	0	0	5	6	6	5	0	4	7	.273	.375	.214	12.60	7.20
Hunt, Shooter	R-R	6-3	200	8-16-86	0	1	10.70	7	5	0	0	18	15	23	21	1	33	18	.246	.333	.209	9.17	16.81
Lanigan, Bobby	R-R	6-4	220	5-5-87	10	7	4.52	22	22	1	0	123	130	66	62	10	29	102	.265	.225	.294	7.44	2.12
Leavitt, Curtis	R-R	6-4	195	1-10-87	0	3	8.31	12	3	0	0	22	28	24	20	4	11	23	.311	.324	.302	9.55	4.57
Marquez, Winston	L-L	6-1	160	8-19-87	0	2	5.21	8	2	0	0	19	19	11	11	0	10	30	.260	.333	.224	14.21	4.74
Martin, Blake	L-L	6-2	182	6-19-86	3	1	4.06	22	0	0	1	31	29	17	14	3	22	41	.246	.239	.250	11.90	6.39
Osterbrock, Dan	R-L	6-3	190	1-27-87	7	10	5.19	28	26	1	0	137	173	95	79	15	35	140	.312	.379	.295	9.20	2.30
Pugh, Bruce	R-R	6-3	180	7-18-88	4	5	2.86	35	8	0	0	85	71	34	27	4	47	99	.228	.258	.209	10.48	4.98
Reyes, Henry	L-R	6-7	183	5-10-85	0	1	9.31	9	1	0	1	19	26	22	20	2	7	14	.329	.286	.345	6.52	3.26
Rondon, Danny	R-R	6-0	161	6-21-87	2	4	5.30	21	0	0	1	36	51	23	21	3	10	28	.342	.365	.330	7.07	2.52
Stillings, Brad	L-R	6-4	210	1-20-88	0	0	5.73	7	0	0	0	11	15	9	7	1	4	6	.306	.313	.303	4.91	3.27
Tarsi, Mike	R-L	6-8	202	8-11-86	4	1	1.84	11	5	0	0	44	41	10	9	1	15	41	.255	.196	.278	8.39	3.07
Testa, Joe	L-L	5-10	175	12-18-85	0	2	2.56	25	1	0	7	46	26	17	13	1	23	63	.161	.146	.168	12.42	4.53
Tippett, Brad	R-R	6-2	185	2-11-88	9	8	3.21	25	24	0	0	146	131	64	52	10	25	107	.239	.238	.239	6.60	1.54
Williams, Matt	R-R	6-1	180	2-28-87	1	2	2.70	32	0	0	8	43	40	20	13	5	14	40	.250	.295	.222	8.31	2.91
Wright, Tom	B-R	6-3	210	1-28-88	1	3	6.00	21	0	0	0	33	41	25	22	2	21	27	.301	.289	.308	7.36	5.73

Fielding

Catcher	PCT	G	PO	A	E	DP	PB
De San Miguel	.941	3	16	0	1	0	0
Lanning	.985	49	384	21	6	1	4
Munroe	.969	4	28	3	1	0	0
Rams	.983	33	269	28	5	3	13
Richardson	.977	7	40	2	1	0	2
Soto	.984	44	343	33	6	3	4
Tintor	.988	12	78	4	1	0	6

First Base	PCT	G	PO	A	E	DP
De La Osa	1.000	1	6	2	0	1
Hanson	.995	29	190	19	1	20
Harrington	1.000	1	3	3	0	2
Rams	.969	15	118	5	4	13
Sanchez	1.000	1	2	0	0	0
Soto	1.000	1	1	0	0	0
Waltenbury	.990	101	754	69	8	57

Second Base	PCT	G	PO	A	E	DP
Beresford	.932	8	20	21	3	7
De La Osa	.956	23	39	47	4	10
Hanson	—	1	0	0	0	0
Romero	.958	6	8	15	1	5
Santana	.968	27	55	65	4	17
Thompson	.955	85	128	192	15	31

Third Base	PCT	G	PO	A	E	DP
De La Osa	.880	30	11	33	6	1
Hanson	.950	71	43	128	9	10
Ladendorf	1.000	3	4	10	0	0
Lanning	—	1	0	0	0	0
Richardson	.933	7	5	9	1	0
Romero	.857	10	7	17	4	2
Santana	.882	30	18	57	10	9

Shortstop	PCT	G	PO	A	E	DP
Beresford	.952	102	157	275	22	51

	PCT	G	PO	A	E	DP
De La Osa	.818	2	4	5	2	0
Hanson	.667	3	0	2	1	0
Ladendorf	.958	10	17	29	2	9
Romero	.944	11	19	32	3	8
Santana	.921	11	12	23	3	7
Thompson	—	1	0	0	0	0
Williams	1.000	3	4	4	0	0

Outfield	PCT	G	PO	A	E	DP
Bigley	.977	23	41	2	1	0
De La Osa	.955	41	57	7	3	0
Harrington	.964	88	125	7	5	1
Hicks	.955	65	144	6	7	1
Lewis	.993	81	133	2	1	0
Morales	.966	106	220	8	8	0
Santana	1.000	8	6	0	0	0
Severino	.891	35	53	4	7	1

ELIZABETHTON TWINS   ROOKIE
APPALACHIAN LEAGUE

Batting	B-T	HT	WT	DOB	AVG	vLH	vRH	G	AB	R	H	2B	3B	HR	RBI	BB	HBP	SH	SF	SO	SB	CS	SLG	OBP
Dozier, Brian	R-R	6-0	185	5-15-87	.353	.406	.331	53	218	38	77	17	0	0	14	23	3	1	3	26	3	0	.431	.417
Goncalves, Jonathan	R-R	5-11	159	5-13-89	.256	.315	.229	49	172	27	44	7	0	4	20	11	1	2	1	55	7	4	.366	.303
Gonzales, Mike	L-R	6-6	245	6-16-88	.304	.288	.309	56	214	42	65	11	1	8	43	21	1	0	3	64	0	1	.477	.364
Herrmann, Chris	L-R	6-0	180	11-24-87	.297	.314	.289	59	236	45	70	14	1	7	30	33	5	1	2	40	2	2	.453	.391
Hidalgo, Anderson	R-R	5-9	172	9-5-88	.291	.241	.314	50	175	34	51	13	0	6	26	25	1	2	2	38	2	3	.469	.379
Klingsberg, Paul-Michael	L-R	6-4	215	3-24-88	.320	.188	.345	27	100	20	32	10	1	2	15	11	0	1	1	27	0	0	.500	.384
Ladendorf, Tyler	R-R	6-0	210	3-7-88	.410	.636	.360	17	61	18	25	7	0	4	17	11	1	0	1	7	1	0	.721	.500
Lara, Herbert	B-R	5-10	154	6-29-88	.218	.238	.214	44	147	18	32	2	2	4	17	12	3	0	1	17	2	0	.340	.288
Liddle, Steven	L-L	6-1	197	11-24-87	.360	.250	.381	13	50	14	18	2	0	2	5	8	0	0	1	11	0	0	.520	.441
McCallum, Derek	L-R	5-11	175	3-22-88	.241	.280	.230	57	228	38	55	11	3	5	38	23	2	2	5	55	1	1	.382	.310
Munroe, Buddy	R-R	5-11	185	8-28-87	.109	.063	.125	15	64	4	7	3	0	1	8	3	0	1	1	20	0	0	.203	.147
Pinto, Josmil	R-R	5-11	184	3-31-89	.332	.448	.286	53	205	34	68	14	2	13	55	19	2	0	4	39	0	1	.610	.387
Rams, Danny	R-R	6-2	205	12-19-88	.355	.500	.327	16	62	19	22	7	1	6	23	8	2	0	0	22	0	0	.790	.444
Rohlfing, Dan	R-R	6-0	185	2-12-89	.239	.295	.203	32	113	17	27	6	2	1	14	15	0	0	2	26	1	0	.354	.323
Streich, Tobias	R-R	6-0	190	4-5-88	.222	.173	.241	50	189	38	42	13	0	10	37	15	3	1	2	37	0	0	.450	.287
Williams, Reggie	L-R	6-2	185	11-5-88	.250	.258	.248	43	156	27	39	8	2	7	25	13	2	2	0	30	0	1	.462	.316

Pitching	B-T	HT	WT	DOB	W	L	ERA	G	GS	CG	SV	IP	H	R	ER	HR	BB	SO	AVG	vLH	vRH	K/9	BB/9
Acosta, Ramon	R-R	6-0	166	1-21-87	0	2	5.04	15	0	0	1	25	34	22	14	3	8	14	.318	.378	.286	5.04	2.88
Bashore, Matt	L-L	6-2	200	4-6-88	0	0	0.00	1	0	0	0	2	3	0	0	0	0	2	.375	.500	.333	9.00	0.00
Bullock, Billy	R-R	6-6	225	2-27-88	1	0	1.23	7	0	0	3	7	3	2	1	0	1	10	.125	.000	.200	12.27	1.23
Carr, Kyle	R-L	6-5	200	11-11-86	1	0	1.25	12	0	0	5	22	9	4	3	1	7	34	.120	.056	.140	14.12	2.91
Davis, Tony	B-L	5-11	185	1-16-88	2	3	5.35	21	0	0	6	35	43	23	21	2	21	47	.312	.480	.274	11.97	5.35
Garcia, Jhon	R-L	6-1	200	5-19-87	1	1	4.15	4	2	0	0	13	17	6	6	1	2	10	.321	.375	.297	6.92	1.38
Garcia, Martire	L-L	5-11	150	3-1-90	5	3	4.42	13	12	0	0	59	61	31	29	4	31	54	.274	.292	.269	8.24	4.73
Hendriks, Liam	R-R	6-1	190	2-10-89	2	0	3.71	3	3	0	0	17	19	8	7	0	1	13	.271	.150	.320	6.88	0.53
Holbrooks, Kane	R-R	6-3	220	6-8-87	2	2	5.04	17	1	0	0	25	33	18	14	0	12	29	.324	.324	10.44	4.32
Ibarra, Edgar	L-L	5-11	170	5-31-89	6	2	2.84	14	6	1	0	51	37	16	16	1	19	57	.213	.310	.182	10.13	3.38
Kennelly, Peter	R-R	6-3	205	11-15-87	3	1	2.01	12	0	0	1	22	17	6	5	1	17	27	.221	.167	.245	10.88	6.85
Marquez, Winston	L-L	6-1	160	8-19-87	1	0	3.27	7	0	0	0	11	10	5	4	0	7	15	.222	.182	.235	12.27	5.73
Mota, Kelvin	R-R	6-3	190	6-23-88	0	0	3.86	6	0	0	0	12	5	5	5	4	4	13	.125	.000	.192	10.03	3.09
Munoz, Miguel	R-R	6-2	182	8-4-88	5	4	4.96	13	13	0	0	69	82	44	38	6	14	62	.291	.365	.240	8.09	1.83
Sanchez, Angelo	R-R	6-2	215	6-7-89	5	1	5.52	12	12	0	0	60	64	38	37	15	20	64	.275	.291	.265	9.55	2.98
Stillings, Brad	L-R	6-4	210	1-20-88	0	1	4.19	10	6	0	0	39	45	24	18	5	13	26	.300	.292	.304	6.05	3.03
Stuifbergen, Tom	R-R	6-3	200	9-26-88	5	2	3.28	13	13	1	0	80	79	35	29	4	6	69	.257	.265	.253	7.79	0.68
Tone, Matt	L-L	6-1	210	2-17-88	4	1	1.31	16	0	0	1	34	13	5	5	1	23	45	.119	.280	.071	11.80	6.03
Tootle, Ben	R-R	6-1	180	1-9-88	0	0	0.00	6	0	0	2	6	4	0	0	0	2	1	.190	.143	.214	1.42	2.84
Watts, Dakota	R-R	6-5	210	11-16-87	2	0	2.70	11	0	0	1	13	9	4	4	0	12	12	.196	.250	.176	8.10	8.10

Fielding

Catcher	PCT	G	PO	A	E	DP	PB
Munroe	.968	14	129	21	5	1	1
Pinto	.985	22	177	19	3	2	4
Rams	.984	6	55	6	1	0	2
Streich	.992	26	225	27	2	6	3

First Base	PCT	G	PO	A	E	DP
Gonzales	.986	47	396	21	6	37
Klingsberg	.982	19	154	10	3	18
Rams	1.000	5	45	6	0	8

Second Base	PCT	G	PO	A	E	DP
McCallum	.973	56	136	153	8	44
Williams	.972	14	28	42	2	5

Third Base	PCT	G	PO	A	E	DP
Hidalgo	.919	49	26	87	10	8
Williams	.867	21	6	33	6	0

Shortstop	PCT	G	PO	A	E	DP
Dozier	.946	53	72	174	14	38
Ladendorf	.952	16	24	55	4	16

Outfield	PCT	G	PO	A	E	DP
Goncalves	.949	49	89	4	5	3
Gonzales	1.000	9	8	0	0	0
Herrmann	.972	59	65	5	2	1
Lara	.984	41	63	0	1	0
Liddle	1.000	13	24	1	0	0
Rohlfing	.980	32	44	4	1	0
Williams	.778	5	6	1	2	0

GCL TWINS   ROOKIE
GULF COAST LEAGUE

Batting	B-T	HT	WT	DOB	AVG	vLH	vRH	G	AB	R	H	2B	3B	HR	RBI	BB	HBP	SH	SF	SO	SB	CS	SLG	OBP
Arcia, Oswaldo	B-R	6-0	210	5-9-91	.275	.194	.294	44	167	20	46	11	2	5	24	15	2	0	3	18	8	0	.455	.337
Arias, Jhonatan	R-R	5-10	180	2-18-89	.244	.154	.261	27	82	12	20	6	0	0	7	10	2	3	0	12	2	0	.317	.340
Benson, Joe	R-R	6-2	211	3-5-88	.200	—	.200	2	5	1	1	0	0	0	0	2	0	0	0	1	1	0	.200	.429
Bistagne, Lee	R-R	5-11	175	10-13-87	.228	.190	.237	35	114	12	26	5	1	0	10	5	4	1	3	26	2	1	.289	.278
Choi, Hyeong-rok	R-R	5-11	189	8-23-89	.279	.100	.297	31	111	13	31	6	1	2	14	13	2	0	2	24	2	1	.405	.359
Choi, Hyun-wook	L-L	6-0	187	12-4-89	.215	.235	.211	31	107	14	23	4	1	1	10	10	0	1	2	15	2	1	.299	.277
De Los Santos, Estarlin	B-R	5-10	165	1-20-87	.250	—	.250	2	8	1	2	0	0	0	0	0	0	0	0	1	1	0	.250	.250
Dozier, Brian	R-R	6-0	185	5-15-87	.286	—	.286	5	14	1	4	0	0	0	2	0	0	0	0	1	0	0	.286	.375
Freitas, Nick	R-R	6-1	203	1-26-87	.246	.316	.232	32	118	13	29	8	0	1	10	13	3	0	0	38	6	0	.339	.336
Grudzielanek, Mark	R-R	6-1	200	6-30-70	.333	.000	.429	3	9	1	3	1	0	0	1	0	0	0	2	0	0	.444	.400
Hanvi, Frederic	R-R	6-2	180	5-2-89	.173	.167	.174	19	52	5	9	1	0	0	2	9	1	2	0	12	0	0	.192	.306
Hejma, Matej	R-R	6-6	215	5-4-90	.271	.529	.215	31	96	10	26	5	1	0	9	3	3	0	0	29	5	1	.344	.314
Hughes, Luke	R-R	5-11	205	8-2-84	.273	—	.273	4	11	0	3	0	0	0	4	0	0	0	1	0	0	0	.273	.467
Johnson, Trayvone	R-R	6-1	200	7-25-87	.182	.091	.205	19	55	5	10	3	0	1	2	5	0	0	0	20	0	1	.291	.250
Kang, In Kyun	L-R	6-1	200	4-21-89	.198	.333	.174	24	81	3	16	1	1	1	5	5	1	0	1	15	0	1	.272	.250
Lin, Wang-Wei	L-R	6-0	185	6-28-88	.364	.500	.355	10	33	6	12	3	0	1	7	4	0	0	0	3	2	0	.545	.432

Batting	B-T	HT	WT	DOB	AVG	vLH	vRH	G	AB	R	H	2B	3B	HR	RBI	BB	HBP	SH	SF	SO	SB	CS	SLG	OBP
Lockwood, Nick	R-R	6-1	175	1-7-91	.250	.167	.256	30	88	8	22	2	0	0	5	6	2	3	0	10	2	1	.273	.313
Machado, Alejandro	B-R	6-0	185	4-26-82	.556	.600	.500	3	9	1	5	1	0	0	0	1	0	0	0	3	2	0	.667	.600
Perez, Jairo	R-R	5-10	160	6-10-88	.217	.375	.177	37	120	14	26	7	1	1	8	17	3	0	2	12	4	1	.317	.324
Ramos, Wilson	R-R	6-0	220	8-10-87	.316	.500	.267	5	19	4	6	1	1	3	6	0	0	0	0	0	0	0	.947	.316
Rhodes, Rory	R-R	6-7	200	7-28-91	.198	.286	.179	35	116	11	23	6	1	0	7	9	2	0	2	28	0	0	.267	.264
Santana, Daniel	B-R	5-11	150	11-7-90	.265	.212	.277	44	170	30	45	7	5	3	25	8	2	3	2	27	12	1	.418	.302
Solarte, Yangervis	R-R	5-11	176	7-7-87	.179	.000	.200	9	28	4	5	0	0	0	4	5	1	1	2	1	0	0	.179	.306
Tindall, Nick	R-R	6-4	190	8-23-91	.185	.167	.188	17	54	8	10	4	0	0	8	2	5	1	0	20	0	0	.259	.279
Vargas, Kennys	B-R	6-5	215	8-1-90	.257	.316	.244	35	109	12	28	7	0	3	18	17	3	0	1	34	2	0	.404	.369

Pitching	B-T	HT	WT	DOB	W	L	ERA	G	GS	CG	SV	IP	H	R	ER	HR	BB	SO	AVG	vLH	vRH	K/9	BB/9
Alvarez, Edilson	L-R	6-3	163	8-4-88	3	0	4.24	12	0	0	1	17	19	11	8	0	6	6	.292	.375	.160	3.18	3.18
Calcano, Richard	R-R	6-1	183	1-15-91	0	0	6.75	3	0	0	0	3	0	2	2	0	2	3	.000	.000	.000	10.13	6.75
Cardenas, Eliecer	R-R	6-2	177	1-30-88	1	2	5.47	11	3	0	0	25	31	20	15	3	7	24	.298	.339	.244	8.76	2.55
Doran, Raynard	R-R	6-1	175	9-3-87	1	0	2.57	5	0	0	0	7	6	2	2	1	1	5	.222	.357	.077	6.43	1.29
Fuentes, Nelvin	L-L	6-0	196	4-7-89	1	1	1.29	12	0	0	2	21	16	7	3	0	4	24	.205	.053	.254	10.29	1.71
Garcia, Jhon	R-R	6-1	200	5-19-87	2	3	2.13	7	7	0	0	38	33	13	9	2	3	28	.228	.192	.264	6.63	0.71
Gonzalez, Jose	L-L	5-9	166	2-3-90	1	0	1.42	8	0	0	1	13	9	3	2	0	2	10	.196	.143	.219	7.11	1.42
Hermsen, B.J.	R-R	6-6	230	12-1-89	6	2	1.35	10	10	1	0	53	32	12	8	0	4	42	.171	.152	.182	7.09	0.68
Hunt, Shooter	R-R	6-3	200	8-16-86	0	4	9.60	7	5	0	0	15	10	16	16	0	25	8	.200	.240	.160	4.80	15.00
Lobanov, Andrei	L-L	6-3	171	1-25-90	2	1	0.82	15	0	0	7	22	14	5	2	1	1	35	.173	.000	.215	14.32	0.41
Mijares, Jean	L-L	5-11	149	1-10-88	1	0	2.81	12	0	0	0	16	5	6	5	1	14	17	.100	.250	.053	9.56	7.88
Mota, Kelvin	R-R	6-3	190	6-23-88	0	0	1.00	6	0	0	0	9	8	1	1	1	2	4	.267	.333	.222	4.00	2.00
Parra, Leonardo	R-R	6-2	160	7-18-86	1	0	7.71	9	0	0	0	14	18	13	12	2	5	11	.305	.286	.323	7.07	3.21
Perkins, Glen	L-L	6-0	200	3-2-83	0	0	0.00	1	1	0	0	1	0	0	0	0	0	0	.000	.000	.000	0.00	0.00
Rehacek, Jan	L-L	6-2	202	12-1-86	1	0	0.00	4	0	0	1	6	1	1	0	0	1	7	.053	.000	.063	10.50	1.50
Salcedo, Adrian	R-R	6-4	175	4-24-91	3	2	1.46	11	10	0	0	62	60	25	10	1	3	58	.241	.306	.188	8.46	0.44
See, Zach	R-R	6-2	185	11-23-88	2	0	0.69	13	0	0	2	26	16	3	2	0	10	34	.178	.195	.163	11.77	3.46
Sosa, Oswaldo	R-R	6-4	225	9-19-85	1	1	2.00	6	0	0	0	9	9	4	2	1	4	12	.257	.238	.286	12.00	4.00
Tonkin, Mike	R-R	6-7	215	11-19-89	3	4	3.62	11	9	0	0	55	55	30	22	2	9	60	.258	.314	.204	9.88	1.48
Watts, Dakota	R-R	6-5	210	11-16-87	0	0	0.00	6	0	0	4	9	1	1	0	0	3	10	.034	.100	.000	9.64	2.89
Weller, Blayne	R-R	6-5	220	1-30-90	5	1	1.58	11	10	0	0	57	46	12	10	1	8	49	.216	.221	.212	7.74	1.26

Fielding

Catcher	PCT	G	PO	A	E	DP	PB
Arias	.989	27	230	28	3	3	3
Hanvi	1.000	16	86	10	0	1	7
Johnson	.946	7	30	5	2	0	2
Ramos	1.000	3	14	2	0	0	0
Tindall	1.000	9	65	11	0	1	3

First Base	PCT	G	PO	A	E	DP
Kang	.991	20	194	15	2	11
Rhodes	.973	11	72	0	2	6
Vargas	.988	27	234	16	3	15

Second Base	PCT	G	PO	A	E	DP
Bistagne	.900	3	2	7	1	0
Choi	.966	26	49	64	4	13
Grudzielanek	1.000	2	2	4	0	1

	PCT	G	PO	A	E	DP
Lockwood	.924	21	30	55	7	10
Machado	1.000	1	1	1	0	0
Perez	.963	5	12	14	1	4
Solarte	1.000	1	2	3	0	0

Third Base	PCT	G	PO	A	E	DP
Choi	.900	4	3	6	1	0
Hughes	.625	3	2	3	3	0
Lockwood	.800	2	2	2	1	0
Perez	.878	25	12	67	11	3
Rhodes	.949	23	22	52	4	2

Shortstop	PCT	G	PO	A	E	DP
Bistagne	.857	4	5	7	2	0
De Los Santos	1.000	2	5	8	0	3
Dozier	1.000	3	5	4	0	1

	PCT	G	PO	A	E	DP
Lockwood	.870	7	8	12	3	1
Machado	1.000	2	1	3	0	0
Perez	.600	1	0	3	2	1
Santana	.918	37	57	100	14	15
Solarte	.950	5	7	12	1	3

Outfield	PCT	G	PO	A	E	DP
Arcia	1.000	37	51	6	0	1
Benson	1.000	2	3	0	0	0
Bistagne	1.000	24	26	3	0	1
Choi	1.000	31	37	1	0	0
Freitas	.986	31	64	5	1	1
Hejma	1.000	31	49	2	0	0
Lin	1.000	10	13	1	0	1
Perez	1.000	1	3	0	0	0
Santana	1.000	6	5	0	0	0

DSL TWINS   ROOKIE

DOMINICAN SUMMER LEAGUE

Batting	B-T	HT	WT	DOB	AVG	vLH	vRH	G	AB	R	H	2B	3B	HR	RBI	BB	HBP	SH	SF	SO	SB	CS	SLG	OBP
Arias, Victor	B-R	5-11	170	3-26-91	.250	.136	.284	34	96	11	24	4	2	0	10	11	5	3	1	25	5	5	.333	.354
Blanco, Juan	R-R	5-10	152	4-24-89	.285	.340	.266	47	186	34	53	10	0	1	24	5	5	4	0	9	14	8	.355	.321
Ciprian, Ernesto	R-R	6-2	175	2-9-91	.183	.130	.196	43	120	15	22	4	0	0	14	19	1	1	1	22	3	3	.217	.298
De Oliveira, Alexandre	L-R	6-1	185	7-15-92	.169	.125	.175	23	71	9	12	1	0	0	7	12	1	0	0	18	1	0	.183	.298
Estaba, Pedro	B-R	5-10	165	8-4-92	.278	.318	.265	28	90	15	25	4	1	0	20	12	3	0	0	15	4	1	.344	.381
Franco, Yancarlo	R-R	5-9	145	8-29-88	.252	.219	.261	46	151	25	38	6	1	3	21	15	2	3	2	33	8	5	.364	.324
Gallardo, Felix	R-R	5-10	178	6-25-91	.224	.250	.216	18	49	4	11	3	0	0	6	10	4	0	1	14	0	0	.286	.391
Galvan, Lesther	R-R	5-10	178	4-10-90	.190	.188	.190	29	100	11	19	2	0	0	7	8	1	1	1	31	3	1	.210	.255
Gonzalez, Erick	R-R	6-1	184	5-4-91	.095	.000	.125	8	21	1	2	0	0	0	1	2	2	0	0	7	1	2	.095	.240
Guillen, Wander	R-R	5-11	170	8-24-92	.336	.364	.330	31	110	15	37	3	1	1	19	19	2	0	0	23	2	3	.409	.443
Martinez, Felix	R-R	2-0	190	12-6-88	.224	.059	.313	16	49	7	11	1	0	0	4	11	2	0	1	18	1	1	.245	.381
Martinez, Yorby	B-R	6-0	170	1-12-89	.265	.132	.301	49	181	25	48	6	2	0	31	22	6	1	3	23	11	4	.320	.358
Murillo, Jose	R-R	6-1	175	7-15-92	.188	.238	.169	28	80	6	15	3	0	0	7	8	2	2	1	17	3	1	.225	.275
Ortiz, Kelvin	R-R	5-11	178	10-19-91	.181	.172	.183	48	149	28	27	6	1	1	11	25	6	1	0	57	8	4	.255	.322
Pimentel, Candido	B-R	5-11	160	7-19-90	.293	.286	.294	54	188	53	55	8	3	1	21	42	1	1	3	42	20	5	.383	.419
Pina, Randy	R-R	6-0	189	5-1-91	.125	.150	.118	30	88	10	11	3	0	1	7	15	7	1	2	27	2	0	.193	.295
Rodriguez, Jairo	R-R	5-11	180	8-24-88	.235	.289	.222	54	196	19	46	15	1	0	25	16	4	2	3	16	1	1	.321	.301
Sepulveda, Emilio	R-R	6-2	170	8-27-91	.180	.250	.157	42	111	16	20	2	0	0	7	13	1	2	0	28	9	3	.198	.272
Silvania, Kelvin	L-L	6-1	185	10-3-90	.283	.364	.265	16	60	11	17	4	1	2	12	5	4	0	1	8	1	0	.483	.371
Trinidad, Romy	R-R	6-2	170	5-14-91	.312	.200	.350	46	157	28	49	5	0	1	15	32	5	3	0	31	15	5	.363	.443

Pitching

Pitching	B-T	HT	WT	DOB	W	L	ERA	G	GS	CG	SV	IP	H	R	ER	HR	BB	SO	AVG	vLH	vRH	K/9	BB/9
Arevalo, Ricardo	R-R	6-3	210	2-28-91	0	1	2.48	17	0	0	1	33	22	12	9	2	11	19	.195	.258	.171	5.23	3.03
Carrillo, Carlos	R-R	6-4	180	11-25-89	1	2	1.71	13	0	0	2	21	11	7	4	1	10	12	.155	.136	.163	5.14	4.29
Ciurcina, Cesar	R-R	5-11	192	10-23-90	9	2	1.39	15	13	0	0	84	50	18	13	0	8	72	.172	.169	.173	7.71	0.86
Frias, Frank	R-R	6-3	170	8-15-89	1	1	3.38	17	0	0	0	24	16	11	9	0	18	19	.198	.308	.176	7.13	6.75
Guerra, Pedro	R-R	6-0	180	1-9-90	7	0	0.38	14	11	0	1	71	44	4	3	0	12	75	.181	.197	.175	9.51	1.52
Nunez, Francisco	R-R	6-3	180	12-28-91	3	2	3.35	24	1	0	8	46	46	22	17	1	7	52	.256	.283	.244	10.25	1.38
Nunez, Luis	L-L	5-11	160	9-26-91	1	3	3.11	23	1	0	4	46	42	23	16	3	14	53	.237	.273	.232	10.29	2.72
Reverol, Renzo	R-R	6-2	192	1-24-91	4	1	2.08	7	5	0	0	35	21	16	8	1	4	35	.164	.146	.172	9.09	1.04
Sanchez, Wilson	R-R	6-1	175	5-6-91	7	2	1.47	14	14	0	0	73	51	23	12	1	16	76	.188	.169	.196	9.33	1.96
Santana, Eddy	R-R	6-1	165	9-21-87	4	1	4.46	23	0	0	8	38	43	25	19	3	16	30	.285	.257	.293	7.04	3.76
Veras, Luis	R-R	6-3	185	12-9-90	0	0	27.00	2	0	0	0	1	2	5	4	0	5	2	.333	.000	.400	13.50	33.75
Villaroel, Orlando	R-R	6-1	190	3-8-90	3	4	4.39	16	10	0	2	55	66	31	27	1	17	40	.303	.333	.295	6.51	2.77

Fielding

Catcher	PCT	G	PO	A	E	DP	PB
Estaba	1.000	1	2	0	0	0	0
Gallardo	.994	17	140	13	1	1	5
Martinez	.968	8	49	12	2	0	1
Pina	.979	22	167	22	4	0	5
Rodriguez	1.000	30	186	27	0	0	7

First Base	PCT	G	PO	A	E	DP
De Oliveira	.986	10	71	2	1	6
Franco	.990	11	96	4	1	9
Gallardo	1.000	1	7	1	0	1
Martinez	1.000	2	15	0	0	2
Martinez	1.000	18	168	7	0	12
Murillo	.952	1	19	1	1	0
Pina	1.000	5	38	0	0	5
Rodriguez	1.000	10	97	3	0	7
Silvania	.957	15	130	5	6	10

Second Base	PCT	G	PO	A	E	DP
Arias	.933	16	25	31	4	7

	PCT	G	PO	A	E	DP
Blanco	.984	36	77	106	3	22
De Oliveira	1.000	1	0	3	0	0
Estaba	1.000	18	26	33	0	7
Franco	.950	4	9	10	1	3
Gonzalez	.750	1	2	1	1	0
Martinez	1.000	1	1	2	0	0

Third Base	PCT	G	PO	A	E	DP
Arias	1.000	2	1	4	0	1
Blanco	1.000	7	3	13	0	1
Estaba	.750	2	4	5	3	0
Franco	.818	3	1	8	2	0
Galvan	.882	19	8	52	8	6
Guillen	.925	23	26	48	6	4
Martinez	.921	19	13	45	5	2
Murillo	1.000	2	1	3	0	1

Shortstop	PCT	G	PO	A	E	DP
Arias	.804	10	14	23	9	8
Blanco	1.000	3	6	9	0	1

	PCT	G	PO	A	E	DP
Estaba	.800	5	6	10	4	1
Franco	.920	22	22	59	7	8
Gonzalez	1.000	4	4	9	0	1
Martinez	.926	12	15	35	4	6
Murillo	.897	15	18	34	6	5

Outfield	PCT	G	PO	A	E	DP
Blanco	1.000	3	1	0	0	0
Ciprian	.959	40	45	2	2	0
De Oliveira	.875	8	7	0	1	1
Franco	1.000	5	7	1	0	0
Murillo	—	1	0	0	0	0
Ortiz	.967	42	54	5	2	2
Pimentel	1.000	52	88	8	0	1
Sepulveda	.986	37	67	2	1	1
Trinidad	.952	38	79	1	4	0

New York Mets

SEASON IN A SENTENCE: The Mets weren't quite The Worst Team Money Could Buy (the 1993 club that won just 59 games), but the 2009 edition moved into new Citi Field and performed about as well as the bailed-out bank that gave its name to the park, as no Met hit more than 12 home runs and injuries (Carlos Beltran, Carlos Delgado, Jose Reyes) ravaged the team.

HIGH POINT: On June 25, the Mets beat St. Louis 3-2 behind seven strong innings from ace Johan Sanana and the 20th save for closer Francisco Rodriguez. But after taking three of four from the Cardinals to pull within a half-game of the Phillies, the Mets were swept at home by the Yankees. They lost 11 of 14 to fall out of contention and never threatened again.

LOW POINT: It actually came before the high-water mark. With K-Rod trying to nail down an 8-7 lead against the Yankees in the interleague opener, Luis Castillo dropped a pop fly to deep second base. Two Yankees raced around to score and the Mets lost 9-8 on a play that symbolized their futility. Another low came on Sept. 30, when the Mets were swept by the Nationals and fell to 67-92, a season-worst 25 games under .500.

NOTABLE ROOKIES: In a year with so many injuries, the Mets still had few rookies make an impact. Lefthander Jonathon Niese went down after five starts with a torn hamstring, and injuries limited Fernando Martinez to 100 at-bats. Hard-throwing righthander Bobby Parnell logged 88 innings, throwing well in relief (3-3, 3.46) and getting pounded as a starter (1-5, 7.93).

KEY TRANSACTIONS: After splurging in the offseason to sign K-Rod and keep free agent Oliver Perez, the Mets just tinkered during the season and came up with spare parts, such as 40-year-old Gary Sheffield, who hit career homer No. 500 in a Mets uniform, and minor league veteran Omir Santos, who wound up as the regular catcher. They did pick up some power by trading Ryan Church to the Braves for Jeff Francoeur, who hit 10 homers in 75 games as a Met while batting .311/338/.498.

DOWN ON THE FARM: Short-season Brooklyn was the lone farm club to have a big season, going 45-30 before losing in the New York-Penn League playoffs. The Mets made more news when vice president Tony Bernazard, who oversaw the farm system, was fired in July after a string of incidents, including challenging several Double-A Binghamton players to fight.

OPENING DAY PAYROLL: $149,373,987

PLAYERS OF THE YEAR

MAJOR LEAGUE	MINOR LEAGUE
David Wright	**Ike Davis**
3b	**1b**
.307/.390/.447	(High A/Double-A)
39 2B, 27 SB, 4th	.298/.381/.524
straight All-Star Game	31 2B, 20 HR

ORGANIZATION LEADERS

BATTING		*Minimum 250 at-bats
MAJORS		
*AVG	David Wright	.307
*OPS	David Wright	.837
HR	Daniel Murphy	12
RBI	David Wright	72
MINORS		
*AVG	Thole, Josh, Binghamton	.328
R	Nieuwenhuis, Kirk, St. Lucie/Binghamton	99
H	Feliciano, Jesus, Buffalo	154
TB	Nieuwenhuis, Kirk, St. Lucie/Binghamton	246
2B	Satin, Joshua, Savannah/St. Lucie	40
3B	Reyes, Raul, Savannah	9
HR	Davis, Ike, St. Lucie/Binghamton	20
RBI	Ratliff, Sean, Savannah/St. Lucie	74
BB	Satin, Joshua, Savannah/St. Lucie	78
SO	Ratliff, Sean, Savannah/St. Lucie	141
SB	Garcia, Emmanuel, Binghamton	19
	Tejada, Ruben, Binghamton	19
*OBP	Thole, Josh, Binghamton	.395
*SLG	Davis, Ike, St. Lucie/Binghamton	.524

PITCHING		†Minimum 75 innings
MAJORS		
W	Johan Santana	13
†ERA	Johan Santana	3.13
SO	Johan Santana	146
MINORS		
W	Familia, Jeurys, Savannah	10
	Schwinden, Chris, Savannah/St. Lucie	10
L	Brown, Eric, Binghamton	14
†ERA	Figueroa, Nelson, Buffalo	2.25
G	Merritt, Roy, Binghamton	56
GS	Niesen, Eric, St. Lucie/Binghamton	27
SV	Cruz, Rhiner, Savannah	22
IP	Shaw, Scott, St. Lucie	150
BB	Niesen, Eric, St. Lucie/Binghamton	57
	Shaw, Scott, St. Lucie	57
SO	Niesen, Eric, St. Lucie/Binghamton	134
†AVG	Familia, Jeurys, Savannah	.221

2009 PERFORMANCE

General Manager: Omar Minaya. **Farm Director:** Adam Wogan. **Scouting Director:** Rudy Terrasas.

Class	Team	League	W	L	PCT	Finish*	Manager(s)
Majors	New York Mets	National	70	92	.432	t-13th (16)	Jerry Manuel
Triple-A	Buffalo Bisons	International	56	87	.392	14th (14)	Ken Oberkfell
Double-A	Binghamton Mets	Eastern	54	86	.386	12th (12)	Mako Oliveras
High A	St. Lucie Mets	Florida State	66	68	.493	7th (12)	Tim Teufel
Low A	Savannah Sand Gnats	South Atlantic	65	72	.474	12th (16)	Edgar Alfonzo
Short-season	Brooklyn Cyclones	New York-Penn	45	30	.600	t-3rd (14)	Pedro Lopez
Rookie	Kingsport Mets	Appalachian	30	35	.462	6th (10)	Mike DiFelice
Rookie	GCL Mets	Gulf Coast	22	34	.393	14th (16)	Julio Franco
Overall 2009 Minor League Record			338	412	.451	29th (30)	

*Finish in overall standings (No. of teams in league). †League champion.

ORGANIZATION STATISTICS

NEW YORK METS

NATIONAL LEAGUE

Batting	B-T	HT	WT	DOB	AVG	vLH	vRH	G	AB	R	H	2B	3B	HR	RBI	BB	HBP	SH	SF	SO	SB	CS	SLG	OBP
Anderson, Marlon	L-R	5-11	200	1-6-74	.000	—	.000	4	4	0	0	0	0	0	0	0	0	0	0	1	0	0	.000	.000
Beltran, Carlos	B-R	6-1	200	4-24-77	.325	.326	.324	81	308	50	100	22	1	10	48	47	1	0	1	43	11	1	.500	.415
Berroa, Angel	R-R	6-0	195	1-27-78	.148	.200	.118	14	27	4	4	1	0	0	2	3	0	1	0	6	0	0	.185	.233
Brown, Emil	R-R	6-2	210	12-29-74	.200	.200	—	3	5	0	1	0	0	0	0	1	0	0	0	0	0	0	.200	.333
Cancel, Robinson	R-R	6-0	240	5-4-76	.000	.000	—	1	1	0	0	0	0	0	0	0	0	0	0	0	0	0	.000	.000
Castillo, Luis	B-R	5-11	195	9-12-75	.302	.264	.319	142	486	77	147	12	3	1	40	69	1	19	5	58	20	6	.346	.387
Castro, Ramon	R-R	6-3	245	3-1-76	.253	.158	.283	26	79	5	20	5	0	3	13	8	0	0	0	16	0	0	.430	.322
Church, Ryan	L-L	6-2	220	10-14-78	.280	.167	.310	67	232	26	65	16	0	2	22	17	2	2	2	36	6	2	.375	.332
2-team total (44 Atlanta)					.273	—	—	111	359	46	98	28	0	4	40	33	3	2	2	62	8	2	.384	.318
Cora, Alex	L-R	6-0	200	10-18-75	.251	.292	.238	82	271	31	68	11	1	1	18	25	3	8	1	28	8	3	.310	.320
Delgado, Carlos	L-R	6-3	245	6-25-72	.298	.333	.289	26	94	15	28	7	1	4	23	12	4	0	2	20	0	0	.521	.393
Evans, Nick	R-R	6-2	220	1-30-86	.231	.321	.162	30	65	5	15	5	1	1	7	4	0	0	0	20	0	0	.385	.275
Francoeur, Jeff	R-R	6-4	220	1-8-84	.311	.392	.284	75	289	40	90	20	1	10	41	11	3	0	5	46	1	3	.498	.338
2-team total (82 Atlanta)					.280	—	—	157	593	72	166	32	4	15	76	23	6	1	9	92	6	4	.423	.309
Green, Andy	R-R	5-10	180	7-7-77	.250	1.000	.000	4	4	0	1	0	0	0	1	0	0	0	0	1	0	0	.250	.400
Hernandez, Anderson	B-R	5-9	185	10-30-82	.252	.250	.253	46	135	14	34	6	2	2	14	13	0	0	1	22	2	2	.370	.315
2-team total (77 Washington)					.251	—	—	123	366	39	92	15	4	3	37	33	0	3	2	63	7	5	.339	.312
Martinez, Fernando	L-R	6-1	200	10-10-88	.176	.158	.181	29	91	11	16	6	0	1	8	5	3	1	0	14	2	0	.275	.242
Martinez, Ramon	R-R	6-0	190	10-10-72	.167	.300	.125	12	42	1	7	2	0	0	4	1	0	0	1	9	1	0	.214	.182
Murphy, Daniel	L-R	6-2	215	4-1-85	.266	.223	.275	155	508	60	135	38	4	12	63	38	0	4	6	69	4	2	.427	.313
Pagan, Angel	B-R	6-2	195	7-2-81	.306	.280	.316	88	343	54	105	22	11	6	32	25	0	5	3	56	14	7	.487	.350
Reed, Jeremy	L-L	6-0	210	6-15-81	.242	.400	.232	126	161	9	39	6	2	0	9	14	0	1	1	36	0	3	.304	.301
Reyes, Argenis	B-R	5-10	165	9-25-82	.118	.000	.143	9	17	0	2	0	0	0	1	0	0	0	0	4	1	0	.118	.167
Reyes, Jose	B-R	6-0	200	6-11-83	.279	.400	.248	36	147	18	41	7	2	2	15	18	0	0	1	19	11	2	.395	.355
Santos, Omir	R-R	6-0	215	4-29-81	.260	.218	.283	96	281	28	73	14	1	7	40	15	2	2	6	44	0	0	.391	.296
Schneider, Brian	L-R	6-1	210	11-26-76	.218	.000	.230	59	170	11	37	11	0	3	24	18	1	2	3	21	0	0	.335	.292
Sheffield, Gary	R-R	6-0	215	11-18-68	.276	.294	.268	100	268	44	74	13	2	10	43	40	2	0	2	46	2	1	.451	.372
Sullivan, Cory	L-L	6-0	200	8-20-79	.250	.167	.263	64	136	17	34	2	5	2	15	19	0	0	2	22	7	1	.382	.338
Tatis, Fernando	R-R	5-11	185	1-1-75	.282	.278	.285	125	340	42	96	21	4	8	48	22	9	4	4	54	4	1	.438	.339
Thole, Josh	L-R	6-1	205	10-28-86	.321	.200	.349	17	53	2	17	2	1	0	9	4	0	0	2	5	1	0	.396	.356
Valdez, Wilson	R-R	5-11	170	5-20-78	.256	.115	.317	41	86	11	22	3	2	0	7	8	1	0	0	10	0	1	.337	.326
Wright, David	R-R	6-0	210	12-20-82	.307	.416	.277	144	535	88	164	39	3	10	72	74	3	0	6	140	27	9	.447	.390

Pitching	B-T	HT	WT	DOB	W	L	ERA	G	GS	CG	SV	IP	H	R	ER	HR	BB	SO	AVG	vLH	vRH	K/9	BB/9
Broadway, Lance	R-R	6-3	195	8-20-83	0	0	6.75	8	0	0	0	15	19	11	11	0	6	9	.317	.379	.258	5.52	3.68
Dessens, Elmer	R-R	5-11	200	1-13-71	0	0	3.31	28	0	0	0	33	24	12	12	5	10	14	.211	.193	.228	3.86	2.76
Feliciano, Pedro	L-L	5-10	190	8-25-76	6	4	3.03	88	0	0	0	59	51	25	20	7	18	59	.231	.215	.264	8.95	2.73
Figueroa, Nelson	R-R	6-1	180	5-18-74	3	8	4.09	16	10	1	0	70	80	33	32	8	24	59	.286	.274	.294	7.55	3.07
Fossum, Casey	L-L	6-1	160	1-6-78	0	0	2.25	3	0	0	0	4	4	1	1	0	4	3	.267	.000	.333	6.75	9.00
Green, Sean	R-R	6-6	225	4-20-79	1	4	4.52	79	0	0	1	70	64	37	35	5	36	54	.240	.223	.250	6.98	4.65
Hernandez, Livan	R-R	6-2	245	2-20-75	7	8	5.47	23	23	1	0	135	164	83	82	16	51	75	.312	.294	.333	5.00	3.40
2-team total (8 Washington)					9	12	5.44	31	31	2	0	184	220	112	111	19	67	102	—	—	—	5.00	3.28
Maine, John	R-R	6-4	200	5-8-81	7	6	4.43	15	15	0	0	81	67	42	40	8	38	55	.224	.159	.304	6.09	4.20
Misch, Pat	R-L	6-2	195	8-18-81	3	4	4.12	22	7	1	0	59	62	27	27	9	19	23	.278	.316	.257	3.51	2.90
2-team total (4 San Francisco)					3	4	4.48	26	7	1	0	62	68	31	31	9	22	23	—	—	—	3.32	3.18
Niese, Jon	L-L	6-4	215	10-27-86	1	1	4.21	5	5	0	0	26	27	12	12	1	9	18	.276	.333	.242	6.31	3.16
Nieve, Fernando	R-R	6-0	220	7-15-82	3	3	2.95	8	7	0	0	37	36	13	12	4	19	23	.263	.200	.351	5.65	4.66
O'Day, Darren	R-R	6-4	220	10-22-82	0	0	0.00	4	0	0	0	3	5	2	0	0	1	2	.357	.333	.364	6.00	3.00
Parnell, Bobby	R-R	6-4	200	9-8-84	4	8	5.30	68	8	0	1	88	101	56	52	8	46	74	.281	.270	.290	7.54	4.69
Pelfrey, Mike	R-R	6-7	230	1-14-84	10	12	5.03	31	31	0	0	184	213	112	103	18	66	107	.289	.284	.294	5.22	3.22
Perez, Oliver	L-L	6-3	210	8-15-81	3	4	6.82	14	14	0	0	66	69	51	50	12	58	62	.273	.200	.306	8.45	7.91
Putz, J.J.	R-R	6-5	250	2-22-77	1	4	5.22	29	0	0	2	29	29	18	17	1	19	19	.257	.296	.220	5.83	5.83

Name	B-T	HT	WT	DOB	W	L	ERA	G	GS	CG	SHO	IP	H	R	ER	HR	BB	SO	AVG	vLH	vRH		
Redding, Tim	R-R	5-11	230	2-12-78	3	6	5.10	30	17	0	0	120	122	72	68	18	50	76	.263	.278	.247	5.70	3.75
Rodriguez, Francisco	R-R	6-0	195	1-7-82	3	6	3.71	70	0	0	35	68	51	34	28	7	38	73	.203	.185	.223	9.66	5.03
Santana, Johan	L-L	6-0	210	3-13-79	13	9	3.13	25	25	0	0	167	156	67	58	20	46	146	.244	.267	.235	7.88	2.48
Stokes, Brian	R-R	6-1	210	9-7-79	2	4	3.97	69	0	0	0	70	72	33	31	6	38	45	.267	.330	.219	5.76	4.86
Stoner, Tobi	B-R	6-2	215	12-3-84	0	0	4.00	4	0	0	0	9	9	4	4	2	3	5	.281	.176	.400	5.00	3.00
Switzer, Jon	L-L	6-3	210	8-13-79	0	0	8.10	4	0	0	0	3	4	3	3	1	2	3	.286	.333	.250	8.10	5.40
Takahashi, Ken	L-L	6-0	200	4-16-69	0	1	2.96	28	0	0	0	27	23	9	9	2	14	23	.235	.302	.156	7.57	4.61
Wagner, Billy	L-L	5-11	205	7-25-71	0	0	0.00	2	0	0	0	2	0	0	0	0	1	4	.000	.000	.000	18.00	4.50

Fielding

Catcher	PCT	G	PO	A	E	DP	PB
Castro	.988	23	159	9	2	3	0
Santos	.994	91	502	26	3	4	3
Schneider	.997	57	329	25	1	3	1
Thole	.987	16	72	3	1	0	3

First Base	PCT	G	PO	A	E	DP
Cora	—	1	0	0	0	0
Delgado	.990	25	192	9	2	16
Evans	.974	5	36	2	1	1
Murphy	.989	101	790	74	10	81
Reed	.964	4	26	1	1	4
Tatis	.997	41	274	28	1	20

Second Base	PCT	G	PO	A	E	DP
Castillo	.982	137	266	344	11	71
Cora	.975	19	38	40	2	7
Green	1.000	1	0	1	0	0

	PCT	G	PO	A	E	DP
Hernandez	1.000	8	11	14	0	4
Martinez	1.000	2	3	6	0	3
Reyes	1.000	3	4	3	0	0
Tatis	1.000	7	8	13	0	0
Valdez	—	1	0	0	0	0

Third Base	PCT	G	PO	A	E	DP
Green	.000	1	0	0	1	0
Tatis	.971	27	22	45	2	3
Valdez	—	1	0	0	0	0
Wright	.950	142	119	224	18	19

Shortstop	PCT	G	PO	A	E	DP
Berroa	.935	8	7	22	2	4
Cora	.976	56	106	140	6	36
Hernandez	.955	38	40	88	6	16
Martinez	.905	10	12	26	4	6
Reyes	1.000	1	2	3	0	2

	PCT	G	PO	A	E	DP
Reyes	.966	35	50	90	5	12
Tatis	1.000	2	4	2	0	1
Valdez	.991	32	41	69	1	16

Outfield	PCT	G	PO	A	E	DP
Beltran	.991	77	208	3	2	1
Brown	1.000	1	1	0	0	0
Church	.992	64	120	3	1	3
Evans	1.000	10	16	1	0	0
Francoeur	.993	74	137	5	1	0
Martinez	1.000	25	49	1	0	0
Murphy	.950	27	56	1	3	1
Pagan	.989	84	183	5	2	0
Reed	1.000	69	79	1	0	0
Sheffield	.980	63	96	4	2	0
Sullivan	1.000	44	68	3	0	0
Tatis	1.000	28	56	0	0	0
Valdez	1.000	2	2	0	0	0

BUFFALO BISONS   TRIPLE-A
INTERNATIONAL LEAGUE

Batting	B-T	HT	WT	DOB	AVG	vLH	vRH	G	AB	R	H	2B	3B	HR	RBI	BB	HBP	SH	SF	SO	SB	CS	SLG	OBP
Abreu, Michel	R-R	6-3	245	1-2-79	.228	.208	.237	56	171	17	39	8	0	4	19	14	0	0	0	39	0	0	.345	.286
Ambres, Chip	R-R	6-0	200	12-19-79	.262	.219	.277	80	279	36	73	18	0	9	40	24	1	0	3	45	1	2	.423	.319
2-team total (52 Pawtucket)					.261	—	—	132	464	54	121	27	1	12	58	45	2	0	5	83	3	6	.401	.326
Arroyo, Rafael	R-R	5-10	170	10-26-82	.000	.000	.000	3	8	1	0	0	0	0	0	2	0	0	0	7	2	0	.000	.200
Berroa, Angel	R-R	6-0	195	1-27-78	.250	—	.250	2	8	0	2	0	0	0	1	0	0	0	0	2	0	0	.250	.250
2-team total (14 Scranton/W-B)					.308	—	—	16	65	7	20	4	0	2	14	4	1	0	1	9	0	2	.462	.352
Brown, Emil	R-R	6-2	210	12-29-74	.256	.259	.255	34	125	14	32	7	0	2	13	6	1	0	0	30	0	3	.360	.295
Cancel, Robinson	R-R	6-0	240	5-4-76	.248	.294	.237	77	258	25	64	12	2	2	16	18	1	3	2	29	7	3	.333	.297
Castillo, Javier	R-R	6-3	210	8-29-83	.241	.283	.229	78	274	24	66	14	1	5	24	15	2	0	1	47	1	1	.354	.284
2-team total (47 Charlotte)					.249	—	—	125	442	40	110	25	3	7	39	28	3	0	1	87	1	2	.367	.297
Cooper, Jason	L-R	6-2	215	1-26-80	.169	.333	.132	26	65	6	11	4	1	0	4	4	2	0	0	18	1	0	.262	.239
Cora, Alex	L-R	6-0	200	10-18-75	.214	.286	.143	3	14	0	3	1	0	0	0	0	0	0	0	0	0	0	.286	.214
Coronado, Jose	B-R	6-1	190	4-13-86	.141	.105	.152	29	85	4	12	2	0	0	3	11	0	4	0	22	2	0	.165	.240
Del Campo, Rogelio	L-R	5-11	198	7-25-86	.000	—	.000	1	1	0	0	0	0	0	0	0	0	0	0	0	0	0	.000	.000
Diaz, Frank	R-R	6-0	211	10-6-83	.000	.000	.000	3	2	0	0	0	0	0	0	0	1	0	0	2	0	0	.000	.333
Dubois, Jason	R-R	6-5	220	3-26-79	.206	.192	.211	30	102	10	21	3	0	6	12	4	3	0	0	34	0	0	.412	.257
Evans, Nick	R-R	6-2	220	1-30-86	.211	.254	.197	66	237	27	50	12	3	10	30	23	0	0	1	55	0	0	.414	.280
Feliciano, Jesus	L-L	6-0	174	6-6-79	.311	.250	.330	130	495	57	154	30	1	1	42	25	5	4	4	44	13	5	.382	.348
Green, Andy	R-R	5-10	180	7-7-77	.259	.317	.241	50	174	24	45	7	1	4	20	18	1	5	1	32	3	0	.379	.330
Kielty, Bobby	B-R	6-1	225	8-5-76	.231	.286	.211	8	26	3	6	0	0	1	3	7	0	0	0	7	1	2	.346	.394
Kiger, Mark	R-R	5-10	195	5-30-80	.000	—	.000	2	4	0	0	0	0	0	0	0	0	0	0	1	0	0	.000	.000
Lamb, Mike	L-R	6-1	205	8-9-75	.261	.220	.274	119	440	44	115	29	2	5	53	21	3	1	5	34	0	0	.370	.299
Mackowiak, Rob	L-R	5-11	210	6-20-76	.000	—	.000	2	6	1	0	0	0	0	0	1	0	0	0	2	0	0	.000	.000
2-team total (13 Columbus)					.137	—	—	15	51	2	7	1	0	0	4	3	0	0	2	11	0	1	.157	.179
Malo, Jonathan	R-R	6-2	180	9-29-83	.186	.172	.190	36	129	10	24	3	1	0	3	12	0	2	0	28	2	0	.225	.255
Martinez, Fernando	L-R	6-1	200	10-10-88	.290	.317	.281	45	176	24	51	16	2	8	28	11	2	0	1	33	2	1	.540	.337
Martinez, Ramon	R-R	6-0	190	10-10-72	.290	.125	.348	9	31	5	9	1	0	0	1	4	0	0	0	5	0	1	.323	.371
Nickeas, Mike	R-R	6-0	210	2-13-83	.000	.000	.000	2	6	0	0	0	0	0	0	1	0	0	0	3	0	0	.000	.143
Pagan, Angel	B-R	6-2	195	7-2-81	.286	.200	.333	3	14	2	4	0	0	2	0	0	0	0	3	0	0	.571	.286
Pena, Wily Mo	R-R	6-3	270	1-23-82	.276	.316	.262	41	145	12	40	5	0	5	21	5	0	0	2	28	0	0	.414	.296
Petersen, Joshua	R-R	6-3	215	4-15-83	.248	.200	.268	31	101	10	25	4	0	1	5	5	0	1	0	17	1	0	.317	.283
Reyes, Argenis	B-R	5-10	165	9-25-82	.282	.244	.294	101	379	43	107	19	4	3	31	29	2	5	1	46	10	3	.377	.336
Rivera, Luis	R-R	6-1	187	1-25-84	.316	.250	.340	46	136	19	43	5	0	0	10	7	2	3	1	15	0	0	.353	.356
Rivera, Rene	R-R	5-10	230	7-31-83	.233	.254	.226	68	240	22	56	14	0	9	30	12	2	1	4	66	0	0	.404	.271
Santos, Omir	R-R	6-0	215	4-29-81	.231	—	.231	3	13	1	3	0	0	0	0	1	0	0	0	2	0	0	.231	.333
Sullivan, Cory	L-L	6-0	200	8-20-79	.290	.267	.296	85	286	37	83	16	0	2	24	29	0	2	3	30	2	2	.367	.352
Valdez, Wilson	R-R	5-11	170	5-20-78	.298	.316	.295	36	114	13	34	4	0	0	6	7	1	3	1	10	1	1	.333	.341
2-team total (41 Columbus)					.247	—	—	77	235	30	58	5	0	0	12	17	2	7	2	29	6	2	.268	.301
Valentin, Jose	B-R	5-10	210	9-19-75	.260	.368	.224	23	77	6	20	3	0	3	10	12	0	0	0	11	0	0	.416	.360
Watson, Matt	L-R	5-11	205	9-5-78	.188	.000	.214	5	16	2	3	0	0	0	0	3	0	0	0	3	0	0	.188	.316

Pitching

Pitching	B-T	HT	WT	DOB	W	L	ERA	G	GS	CG	SV	IP	H	R	ER	HR	BB	SO	AVG	vLH	vRH	K/9	BB/9
Antonini, Mike	R-L	6-2	200	8-6-85	0	1	12.27	2	2	0	0	7	16	10	10	1	3	6	.432	.333	.480	7.36	3.68
Bostick, Adam	L-L	6-1	225	3-17-83	0	3	3.26	28	1	0	3	39	33	16	14	5	18	43	.226	.211	.231	10.01	4.19
Broadway, Lance	R-R	6-3	195	8-20-83	5	7	6.27	16	14	1	0	85	101	63	59	6	34	41	.300	.262	.321	4.36	3.61
2-team total (3 Charlotte)					5	9	6.17	19	17	1	0	101	119	74	69	8	38	56	—	—	—	5.01	3.40
Dessens, Elmer	R-R	5-11	200	1-13-71	3	2	2.31	27	0	0	11	35	26	9	9	2	9	28	.205	.160	.234	7.20	2.31
Ellison, Derrick	L-L	6-2	195	9-6-78	0	0	2.70	6	1	0	0	10	11	3	3	2	1	12	.268	.333	.241	10.80	0.90
Figueroa, Nelson	R-R	6-1	180	5-18-74	7	5	2.25	17	17	1	0	112	91	29	28	5	24	94	.225	.253	.207	7.55	1.93
Fossum, Casey	L-L	6-1	160	1-6-78	0	0	0.82	2	2	0	0	11	5	1	1	0	5	12	.152	.000	.208	9.82	4.09
2-team total (10 Scranton/W-B)					3	3	2.92	12	12	0	0	62	55	25	20	7	21	55	—	—	—	8.03	3.06
Garcia, Freddy	R-R	6-4	260	10-6-76	0	2	8.18	2	2	0	0	11	12	10	10	3	3	5	.286	.211	.348	4.91	4.09
2-team total (1 Charlotte)					0	3	6.35	3	3	0	0	17	20	12	12	3	5	15	—	—	—	7.94	2.65
Gee, Dillon	R-R	6-1	200	4-28-86	1	3	4.10	9	9	1	0	48	47	22	22	5	16	42	.253	.259	.248	7.82	2.98
Knight, Brandon	L-R	6-0	200	10-1-75	4	9	5.06	20	14	1	3	89	101	51	50	10	29	80	.294	.283	.303	8.09	2.93
Kunz, Eddie	R-R	6-6	265	4-8-86	4	5	5.02	40	0	0	1	61	54	35	34	8	31	38	.241	.313	.199	5.61	4.57
Lopez, Arturo	L-L	5-10	165	2-22-83	0	2	3.86	15	1	0	0	30	36	17	13	1	13	19	.295	.242	.315	5.64	3.86
Mason, Chris	R-R	6-1	190	7-1-84	1	1	5.09	3	3	0	0	18	20	10	10	2	4	13	.286	.385	.227	6.62	2.04
2-team total (1 Durham)					1	1	5.82	4	4	0	0	22	28	14	14	3	5	16	—	—	—	6.65	2.08
McNab, Tim	R-R	6-0	175	6-4-80	5	4	4.03	36	2	0	4	58	71	34	26	5	18	27	.305	.281	.319	4.19	2.79
Misch, Pat	R-L	6-2	195	8-18-81	1	2	4.26	6	4	1	0	25	27	14	12	1	4	21	.267	.286	.263	7.46	1.42
Muniz, Carlos	R-R	6-1	190	3-12-81	0	3	5.95	12	0	0	0	20	22	18	13	4	14	14	.286	.240	.308	6.41	6.41
Niese, Jon	L-L	6-4	215	10-27-86	5	6	3.82	16	16	2	0	94	95	47	40	7	26	82	.258	.273	.254	7.82	2.48
Nieve, Fernando	R-R	6-0	220	7-15-82	3	0	3.70	4	4	0	0	24	18	10	10	2	10	23	.205	.278	.154	8.51	3.70
Perez, Oliver	L-L	6-3	210	8-15-81	0	2	3.86	2	2	0	0	9	8	4	4	1	9	9	.229	.286	.214	8.68	8.68
Pettyjohn, Adam	R-L	6-3	200	6-11-77	3	5	3.56	9	8	0	0	56	63	24	22	5	9	30	.289	.203	.321	4.85	1.46
2-team total (18 Louisville)					4	11	4.09	27	14	0	0	106	129	59	48	10	31	57	—	—	—	4.85	2.64
Ramirez, Edgar	R-R	6-4	250	11-30-83	0	0	4.50	1	0	0	0	2	3	1	1	1	1	0	.375	.500	.333	0.00	4.50
Redding, Tim	R-R	5-11	230	2-12-78	0	0	2.77	2	2	0	0	13	13	4	4	1	2	9	.265	.167	.323	6.23	1.38
Robertson, Connor	R-R	6-2	220	9-10-81	0	3	5.46	22	0	0	0	28	32	18	17	4	10	23	.286	.316	.270	7.39	3.21
Sanchez, Jose	R-R	6-0	170	5-12-84	0	1	4.91	3	2	0	0	11	12	6	6	1	5	9	.273	.357	.233	7.36	4.09
Snyder, Kyle	B-R	6-8	230	9-9-77	3	8	4.23	33	14	0	1	104	115	54	49	12	32	74	.279	.342	.241	6.38	2.76
Stoner, Tobi	B-R	6-2	215	12-3-84	7	7	3.96	16	16	1	0	98	92	45	43	9	34	64	.249	.229	.263	5.90	3.13
Switzer, Jon	L-L	6-3	210	8-13-79	1	3	3.29	41	0	0	4	52	46	23	19	4	23	49	.236	.230	.240	8.48	3.98
Takahashi, Ken	L-L	6-0	200	4-16-69	1	3	2.38	18	7	1	0	57	55	21	15	2	23	38	.253	.212	.267	6.04	3.65
Warden, Jim Ed	R-R	6-7	190	5-7-79	2	0	2.95	12	0	0	2	21	15	7	7	0	10	26	.190	.077	.245	10.97	4.22

Fielding

Catcher	PCT	G	PO	A	E	DP	PB
Arroyo	1.000	3	16	1	0	0	0
Cancel	.990	74	449	39	5	5	14
Nickeas	1.000	2	12	2	0	0	0
Rivera	.992	63	436	36	4	2	2
Santos	.970	3	31	1	1	1	2

First Base	PCT	G	PO	A	E	DP
Abreu	.992	42	327	26	3	31
Brown	1.000	1	8	0	0	1
Cooper	1.000	3	16	0	0	3
Evans	1.000	30	235	17	0	25
Lamb	.993	47	380	24	3	42
Pena	.984	16	118	6	2	14
Valentin	1.000	12	112	3	0	9

Second Base	PCT	G	PO	A	E	DP
Green	.987	16	27	48	1	12
Lamb	.909	5	8	12	4	4
Malo	.914	13	19	34	5	5
Martinez	1.000	4	4	5	0	0
Reyes	.991	68	149	190	3	52

	PCT	G	PO	A	E	DP
Rivera	.984	36	82	101	3	23
Valdez	1.000	6	18	18	0	2
Third Base	PCT	G	PO	A	E	DP
Castillo	.891	40	29	69	12	8
Cooper	.600	3	1	2	2	0
Evans	.667	1	1	1	1	0
Green	.925	27	22	40	5	4
Lamb	.932	63	40	97	10	5
Mackowiak	1.000	2	1	0	0	0
Malo	.960	8	6	18	1	4
Rivera	.769	3	2	8	3	2
Valentin	1.000	4	1	7	0	1
Shortstop	PCT	G	PO	A	E	DP
Berroa	1.000	2	0	6	0	1
Castillo	.959	23	30	64	4	14
Cora	1.000	2	4	6	0	1
Coronado	.948	28	37	73	6	14
Green	.889	5	5	11	2	4
Kiger	1.000	2	1	5	0	1
Malo	.941	15	23	41	4	9

	PCT	G	PO	A	E	DP
Martinez	.917	6	10	12	2	4
Reyes	.976	32	35	88	3	19
Rivera	.941	9	11	21	2	7
Valdez	.993	29	47	87	1	19
Outfield	PCT	G	PO	A	E	DP
Ambres	.988	72	155	7	2	2
Brown	.963	17	25	1	1	0
Cooper	1.000	8	21	0	0	0
Dubois	1.000	21	32	1	0	0
Evans	.986	37	66	3	1	0
Feliciano	.992	125	254	8	2	2
Green	1.000	1	1	0	0	0
Kielty	1.000	7	12	1	0	1
Martinez	.967	37	57	1	2	0
Pagan	1.000	3	4	2	0	0
Pena	1.000	10	19	0	0	0
Petersen	.972	19	35	0	1	0
Sullivan	1.000	73	180	5	0	1
Valdez	1.000	1	1	0	0	0
Watson	.900	5	9	0	1	0

BINGHAMTON METS

DOUBLE-A

EASTERN LEAGUE

Batting	B-T	HT	WT	DOB	AVG	vLH	vRH	G	AB	R	H	2B	3B	HR	RBI	BB	HBP	SH	SF	SO	SB	CS	SLG	OBP
Arroyo, Rafael	R-R	5-10	170	10-26-82	.000	.000	.000	7	20	0	0	0	0	0	0	4	0	0	0	8	0	0	.000	.167
Bouchard, Matt	R-R	6-0	185	12-12-86	.155	.000	.214	15	58	4	9	1	0	0	2	4	1	0	1	14	0	1	.172	.219
Bowman, Shawn	R-R	6-4	230	12-9-84	.294	.368	.261	91	347	42	102	24	3	9	44	25	4	3	1	101	0	0	.458	.346
Coronado, Jose	B-R	6-1	190	4-13-86	.271	.320	.252	99	361	37	98	16	1	1	40	27	2	11	5	66	11	4	.330	.322
Davis, Ike	L-L	6-5	195	3-22-87	.309	.268	.331	55	207	30	64	14	0	13	43	26	0	0	0	60	0	0	.565	.386
Duda, Lucas	L-R	6-5	240	2-3-86	.281	.192	.320	110	395	49	111	29	1	9	53	61	5	1	5	91	2	2	.428	.380
Eigsti, Jake	R-R	6-0	185	6-13-84	.192	.333	.118	13	26	1	5	0	0	1	2	1	0	0	0	5	0	0	.308	.222
Evans, Nick	R-R	6-2	220	1-30-86	.276	.381	.250	25	105	16	29	9	1	3	9	10	2	0	0	22	2	0	.467	.350
Garcia, Emmanuel	L-R	6-2	185	3-4-86	.246	.164	.275	130	491	66	121	16	4	4	40	39	4	11	4	113	19	10	.320	.305
Guzman, Carlos	R-R	6-1	185	5-24-86	.130	.000	.167	6	23	2	3	0	0	1	3	1	1	0	0	7	0	0	.261	.200
Kiger, Mark	R-R	5-10	195	5-30-80	.240	.267	.228	54	146	19	35	5	0	1	11	37	3	0	0	47	5	5	.295	.403
Loadenthal, Carl	L-L	5-10	190	12-27-81	.239	.163	.262	59	188	25	45	6	2	1	18	31	2	1	2	33	10	8	.309	.350

	B-T	HT	WT	DOB	AVG	vLH	vRH	G	AB	R	H	2B	3B	HR	RBI	BB	HBP	SH	SF	SO	SB	CS	SLG	OBP
Lutz, Zach	R-R	6-1	220	6-3-86	.207	.500	.185	8	29	0	6	1	0	0	2	5	0	0	0	7	0	0	.241	.324
Malo, Jonathan	R-R	6-2	180	9-29-83	.245	.270	.233	73	237	31	58	6	3	1	28	24	4	6	2	36	8	3	.308	.322
Nickeas, Mike	R-R	6-0	210	2-13-83	.182	.056	.243	18	55	3	10	1	0	0	7	9	0	2	1	9	0	0	.200	.292
Nieuwenhuis, Kirk	L-R	6-3	210	8-7-87	.406	.200	.444	8	32	8	13	3	1	1	2	4	0	0	0	9	1	1	.656	.472
Paniagua, Salvador	R-R	6-1	240	5-21-83	.217	.261	.196	51	143	8	31	7	0	3	15	14	0	0	1	54	0	0	.329	.285
Petersen, Joshua	R-R	6-3	215	4-15-83	.326	.392	.280	57	181	21	59	10	1	3	27	24	2	0	1	25	1	2	.442	.409
Stewart, Caleb	R-R	6-2	230	6-11-82	.225	.220	.230	66	204	32	46	14	0	3	16	32	9	0	0	62	2	2	.338	.355
Tejada, Ruben	R-R	5-11	165	9-1-89	.289	.289	.289	134	488	59	141	24	3	5	46	37	11	15	2	59	19	3	.381	.351
Thole, Josh	L-R	6-1	205	10-28-86	.328	.328	.328	103	384	48	126	29	2	1	46	42	6	1	9	34	8	4	.422	.395
Wabick, D.J.	R-R	6-2	185	5-30-84	.296	.247	.309	120	426	41	126	31	1	4	55	19	1	2	5	78	5	3	.401	.324
Watson, Matt	L-R	5-11	205	9-5-78	.200	—	.200	2	5	1	1	0	0	0	0	0	0	0	0	3	0	0	.200	.200

Pitching	B-T	HT	WT	DOB	W	L	ERA	G	GS	CG	SV	IP	H	R	ER	HR	BB	SO	AVG	vLH	vRH	K/9	BB/9
Abel, Nick	R-R	6-4	200	2-18-83	1	1	10.44	15	1	0	0	25	41	29	29	1	20	16	.387	.362	.417	5.76	7.20
Alfonzo, Edgar	L-L	5-10	170	12-14-84	4	5	3.97	49	1	0	0	70	78	38	31	3	30	42	.290	.276	.301	5.37	3.84
Antonini, Mark	R-L	6-2	200	8-6-85	7	5	5.32	25	20	0	0	115	137	70	68	9	34	86	.299	.278	.306	6.73	2.66
Bostick, Adam	L-L	6-1	225	3-17-83	3	0	2.60	11	0	0	0	17	16	5	5	1	4	20	.254	.258	.250	10.38	2.08
Brown, Eric	R-R	6-6	225	2-23-84	7	14	5.83	32	15	0	0	117	145	84	76	13	35	77	.305	.295	.315	5.91	2.68
Clyne, Stephen	B-R	6-2	215	9-22-84	1	0	7.31	17	0	0	0	28	45	23	23	1	20	17	.366	.339	.391	5.40	6.35
Coultas, Ryan	R-R	6-3	180	4-24-82	4	3	2.78	11	11	0	0	65	60	21	20	2	19	33	.249	.214	.287	4.59	2.64
De La Cruz, Julio	R-R	6-1	161	10-7-80	0	4	5.18	30	0	0	4	40	45	23	23	2	24	37	.294	.227	.359	8.32	5.40
De La Torre, Jose	R-R	5-9	175	10-17-85	3	2	2.67	18	0	0	2	30	23	14	9	1	17	37	.200	.191	.206	10.98	5.04
Ellison, Derrick	L-L	6-2	195	9-6-78	1	0	0.00	3	0	0	0	7	0	0	0	0	2	2	.000	.000	.000	2.70	2.70
Frederick, Emary	R-L	6-0	180	1-17-84	0	1	5.46	23	0	0	0	30	29	20	18	4	19	23	.250	.283	.222	6.98	5.76
Holt, Brad	R-R	6-4	194	10-13-86	3	6	6.21	11	11	0	0	58	58	42	40	9	23	45	.270	.264	.275	6.98	3.57
Madden, John	R-R	6-4	229	12-2-82	0	0	8.49	12	0	0	0	12	16	12	11	2	8	5	.340	.250	.407	3.86	6.17
Mason, Chris	R-R	6-1	190	7-1-84	1	1	2.87	4	3	0	0	16	15	6	5	0	7	9	.246	.233	.278	5.17	4.02
McNab, Tim	R-R	6-0	175	6-4-80	0	0	3.27	8	0	0	0	11	12	4	4	3	1	4	.267	.381	.167	3.27	0.82
Mejia, Jenrry	R-R	6-0	162	10-11-89	0	5	4.47	10	10	0	0	44	44	28	22	2	23	47	.263	.259	.268	9.54	4.67
Merritt, Roy	L-L	6-0	170	9-22-85	4	5	3.45	56	0	0	14	63	68	36	24	8	25	56	.285	.209	.355	8.04	3.59
Niesen, Eric	L-L	6-0	192	9-4-85	4	7	4.66	16	16	1	0	83	75	46	43	6	41	85	.246	.218	.256	9.22	4.45
Nieve, Fernando	R-R	6-0	220	7-15-82	0	1	4.91	5	4	0	0	18	16	10	10	1	6	19	.239	.235	.242	9.33	2.95
Owen, Dylan	R-R	5-11	185	7-12-86	4	10	5.93	23	23	0	0	123	152	88	81	13	53	84	.307	.258	.370	6.15	3.88
Ramirez, Edgar	R-R	6-4	250	11-30-83	0	2	6.66	14	3	0	0	26	40	20	19	1	13	15	.377	.364	.392	5.26	4.56
Robertson, Connor	R-R	6-2	220	9-10-81	2	1	3.19	25	0	0	11	31	24	12	11	2	9	31	.212	.245	.183	9.00	2.61
Ruckle, Jake	R-R	6-1	180	5-27-86	2	4	7.20	17	5	0	1	50	60	43	40	10	17	36	.305	.317	.292	6.48	3.06
Sanchez, Jose	R-R	6-0	170	5-12-84	1	6	6.88	10	10	0	0	52	72	42	40	6	22	33	.336	.357	.297	5.68	3.78
Stoner, Tobi	B-R	6-2	215	12-3-84	2	2	2.68	7	7	1	0	47	28	15	14	5	13	28	.170	.157	.184	5.36	2.49
Warden, Jim Ed	R-R	6-7	190	5-7-79	0	1	1.42	20	0	0	1	25	22	9	4	3	8	21	.237	.300	.189	7.46	2.84

Fielding

Catcher	PCT	G	PO	A	E	DP	PB
Arroyo	.948	7	50	5	3	1	0
Nickeas	.993	18	137	11	1	1	1
Paniagua	.985	30	185	17	3	4	1
Thole	.992	89	574	54	5	7	9

First Base	PCT	G	PO	A	E	DP
Davis	.990	51	361	38	4	46
Duda	.996	49	420	39	2	36
Eigsti	1.000	1	4	0	0	0
Evans	.992	15	117	11	1	14
Kiger	.984	17	115	9	2	10
Paniagua	.976	5	38	2	1	3
Petersen	1.000	2	2	1	0	2
Thole	1.000	1	1	0	0	0
Wabick	1.000	7	42	3	0	5

Second Base	PCT	G	PO	A	E	DP
Bouchard	.965	14	17	38	2	9
Coronado	.966	80	134	205	12	51
Eigsti	1.000	2	6	8	0	3
Garcia	1.000	1	0	1	0	0
Kiger	1.000	6	10	17	0	2
Malo	.967	28	48	71	4	16
Tejada	.955	14	34	30	3	3

Third Base	PCT	G	PO	A	E	DP
Bowman	.975	88	75	163	6	19
Eigsti	1.000	5	1	9	0	2
Kiger	.973	16	10	26	1	3
Lutz	.870	7	4	16	3	2
Malo	.972	24	22	48	2	7
Petersen	.929	4	3	10	1	1

Shortstop	PCT	G	PO	A	E	DP
Bouchard	.000	1	0	0	1	0
Coronado	.986	19	30	42	1	6
Malo	1.000	2	7	4	0	1
Tejada	.966	120	199	307	18	76

Outfield	PCT	G	PO	A	E	DP
Davis	.750	2	3	0	1	0
Duda	.975	42	74	3	2	0
Evans	1.000	10	19	0	0	0
Garcia	.986	126	349	10	5	1
Guzman	1.000	6	16	1	0	0
Kiger	1.000	3	2	0	0	0
Loadenthal	.989	53	82	6	1	0
Malo	.981	20	48	3	1	0
Nieuwenhuis	1.000	8	17	0	0	0
Petersen	1.000	44	65	5	0	0
Stewart	1.000	52	101	3	0	2
Wabick	.977	77	113	12	3	4
Watson	.750	2	3	0	1	0

ST. LUCIE METS   HIGH CLASS A

FLORIDA STATE LEAGUE

Batting	B-T	HT	WT	DOB	AVG	vLH	vRH	G	AB	R	H	2B	3B	HR	RBI	BB	HBP	SH	SF	SO	SB	CS	SLG	OBP
Abruzzo, Jordan	B-R	6-3	230	8-2-84	.100	.000	.111	5	10	1	1	0	0	0	0	2	0	0	0	0	0	0	.100	.250
Arroyo, Rafael	R-R	5-10	170	10-26-82	.094	.143	.080	22	64	4	6	3	0	0	3	10	2	1	1	24	2	1	.141	.234
Bouchard, Matt	R-R	6-0	185	12-12-86	.242	.375	.195	43	153	12	37	6	0	2	12	9	2	1	0	39	7	1	.320	.293
Campbell, Eric	R-R	6-3	220	4-9-87	.273	.250	.278	7	22	5	6	2	0	0	0	5	1	0	0	1	0	0	.364	.429
Davis, Ike	L-L	6-5	195	3-22-87	.288	.197	.323	59	222	28	64	17	3	7	28	31	1	0	1	52	0	2	.486	.376
Doyle, Dock	L-R	6-0	200	3-24-86	1.000	—	1.000	1	3	1	3	0	0	0	0	1	0	0	0	0	0	0	1.000	1.000
Eigsti, Jake	R-R	6-0	185	6-13-84	.227	.346	.196	42	128	15	29	5	0	0	11	9	2	4	1	24	0	2	.266	.286
Guzman, Carlos	L-R	6-3	195	5-24-86	.290	.202	.318	126	472	59	137	28	2	15	64	39	4	1	4	95	6	5	.453	.347
Havens, Reese	L-R	6-1	195	10-20-86	.247	.235	.252	97	360	53	89	19	1	14	52	55	11	1	3	73	3	2	.422	.361
Henriquez, Ralph	B-R	6-1	190	4-7-87	.444	.333	.467	6	18	1	8	2	0	0	5	1	0	0	0	3	0	0	.556	.474
Lutz, Zach	R-R	6-1	220	6-3-86	.284	.290	.281	99	356	46	101	19	2	11	62	50	7	0	2	72	1	1	.441	.381
Maccani, Tony	R-R	6-3	191	9-24-84	.185	.167	.190	8	27	3	5	0	0	0	1	2	0	0	0	8	0	0	.185	.241

	B-T	HT	WT	DOB	AVG	vLH	vRH	G	AB	R	H	2B	3B	HR	RBI	BB	HBP	SH	SF	SO	SB	CS	SLG	OBP
Maldonado, Brahiam	R-R	5-11	205	9-18-85	.273	.270	.274	122	410	62	112	19	3	18	73	43	7	2	6	126	13	4	.466	.348
Nieuwenhuis, Kirk	L-R	6-3	210	8-7-87	.274	.233	.289	123	482	91	132	35	5	16	71	53	10	1	1	118	16	4	.467	.357
Nieves, Luis	R-R	5-11	160	12-15-88	.250	—	.250	1	4	0	1	0	0	0	0	0	0	0	0	0	0	0	.250	.250
Pagan, Angel	B-R	6-2	195	7-2-81	.417	.000	.500	4	12	4	5	2	0	0	3	4	0	0	0	2	2	0	.583	.563
Pellot, Hector	R-R	5-11	184	2-8-87	.277	.330	.256	100	354	48	98	17	4	3	39	37	5	6	2	70	15	11	.373	.352
Pena, Francisco	R-R	6-2	230	10-12-89	.224	.211	.230	100	392	43	88	15	1	8	44	15	4	1	3	78	0	1	.329	.258
Pena, Richard	R-R	6-2	175	8-15-87	.222	.207	.230	34	90	16	20	4	0	1	7	14	1	1	0	22	2	2	.300	.333
Ratliff, Sean	L-L	6-3	185	2-24-87	.286	.000	.364	7	28	3	8	2	0	0	6	0	0	0	0	10	0	0	.357	.286
Rivera, Julio	R-R	5-11	200	7-20-87	.250	.000	.333	2	8	1	2	0	0	0	1	0	0	0	1	1	0	0	.250	.222
Rivera, Luis	R-R	6-1	187	1-25-84	.128	.125	.129	12	39	2	5	2	0	0	3	2	0	0	1	7	1	0	.179	.167
Satin, Josh	R-R	6-2	200	12-23-84	.364	.500	.333	7	22	6	8	2	0	1	5	5	0	0	1	7	0	0	.591	.464
Stegall, Daniel	L-R	6-3	180	9-24-87	.200	.000	.333	2	5	1	1	0	0	1	1	1	0	0	0	1	0	0	.800	.333
Veloz, Greg	B-R	6-1	175	6-3-88	.232	.238	.231	91	357	38	83	15	2	2	19	28	5	4	1	81	18	8	.303	.297
Watson, Matt	L-R	5-11	205	9-5-78	.444	.000	.571	3	9	1	4	1	1	0	2	2	0	0	1	1	0	0	.778	.500
Welch, Stefan	L-R	6-3	175	8-12-88	.278	.230	.297	56	216	38	60	10	2	5	37	20	5	0	2	37	0	0	.412	.350
Williams, Seth	R-R	6-2	205	11-21-85	.264	.295	.250	60	197	26	52	10	0	3	11	12	18	2	0	30	2	4	.360	.361

Pitching	B-T	HT	WT	DOB	W	L	ERA	G	GS	CG	SV	IP	H	R	ER	HR	BB	SO	AVG	vLH	vRH	K/9	BB/9
Aguilar, Sal	R-R	6-0	190	1-9-82	1	2	6.00	4	4	0	0	18	22	15	12	3	5	10	.301	.241	.341	5.00	2.50
Alvarez, Manuel	R-R	5-11	200	12-18-85	4	3	5.09	35	0	0	9	46	58	33	26	4	24	32	.305	.333	.288	6.20	4.70
Burns, Brad	R-R	6-4	182	5-28-86	0	0	3.00	1	0	0	0	3	1	1	1	0	4	.100	.000	.167	12.00	0.00
Calero, Angel	L-L	6-1	210	9-25-86	3	11	4.61	22	22	1	0	107	119	68	55	10	46	93	.283	.337	.268	7.80	3.86
Carr, Nick	R-R	6-1	195	4-19-87	2	3	3.59	14	2	0	3	43	36	21	17	1	28	42	.237	.292	.212	8.86	5.91
Carrillo, Matias	L-L	6-3	224	12-13-86	1	1	9.28	9	0	0	0	11	17	13	11	2	5	8	.347	.176	.438	6.75	4.22
Clyne, Stephen	B-R	6-2	215	9-22-84	3	1	1.27	26	0	0	2	35	21	6	5	0	17	29	.179	.146	.197	7.39	4.33
De La Torre, Jose	R-R	5-9	175	10-17-85	3	3	2.77	26	0	0	3	39	33	16	12	1	17	35	.229	.185	.256	8.08	3.92
Frederick, Emary	R-R	6-0	180	1-17-84	2	5	3.32	27	0	0	4	41	37	16	15	4	20	27	.240	.224	.250	5.98	4.43
Holt, Brad	R-R	6-4	194	10-13-86	4	1	3.12	9	9	0	0	43	34	16	15	5	13	54	.215	.190	.230	11.22	2.70
Johnson, Jimmy	L-L	6-0	195	11-24-85	1	1	4.26	12	0	0	1	19	22	9	9	0	4	14	.286	.160	.346	6.63	1.89
Kaplan, Jeff	R-R	6-0	190	7-9-85	3	5	3.39	10	9	0	0	58	56	28	22	3	19	47	.253	.292	.224	7.25	2.93
Maine, John	R-R	6-4	200	5-8-81	0	0	1.13	2	1	0	0	8	4	1	1	0	4	7	.154	.182	.133	7.88	4.50
Mason, Chris	R-R	6-1	190	7-1-84	0	0	4.50	3	2	0	0	10	11	5	5	0	3	6	.314	.333	.304	5.40	2.70
Mejia, Jenrry	R-R	6-0	162	10-11-89	4	1	1.97	9	9	0	0	50	41	18	11	0	16	44	.217	.200	.227	7.87	2.86
Morgan, Will	R-R	6-2	205	11-3-85	1	1	2.70	2	0	0	0	3	5	2	1	0	0	4	.333	.600	.200	10.80	0.00
Moviel, Scott	R-R	6-11	235	5-7-88	4	5	3.92	13	13	0	0	64	61	37	28	1	24	46	.250	.265	.236	6.44	3.36
Niesen, Eric	L-L	6-0	192	9-4-85	3	4	3.28	11	11	0	0	58	52	25	21	5	16	49	.237	.208	.247	7.65	2.50
Owen, Dylan	R-R	5-11	185	7-12-86	1	1	1.50	3	2	0	1	18	13	5	3	0	1	13	.194	.129	.250	6.50	0.50
Perez, Oliver	L-L	6-3	210	8-15-81	0	1	6.00	1	1	0	0	3	7	6	2	1	1	3	.438	.000	.467	9.00	3.00
Rackel, Trey	R-R	6-1	215	5-17-88	1	0	0.00	2	0	0	0	3	1	0	0	0	0	3	.111	.500	.000	0.00	0.00
Ramirez, Edgar	R-R	6-4	250	11-30-83	3	1	2.36	24	0	0	3	53	41	14	14	1	16	47	.209	.254	.186	7.93	2.70
Ruckle, Jake	R-R	6-1	180	5-27-86	1	0	5.40	2	0	0	0	5	6	3	3	0	3	2	.211	.100	.333	5.40	3.60
Rustich, Brant	R-R	6-6	230	1-23-85	1	1	2.45	19	3	0	2	48	44	20	13	0	17	46	.240	.290	.215	8.69	3.21
Sanchez, Jose	R-R	6-0	170	5-12-84	0	0	3.68	4	1	0	0	7	12	3	3	0	2	4	.375	.417	.350	4.91	2.45
Schwinden, Chris	R-R	6-3	215	9-22-86	1	0	3.97	2	2	0	0	11	9	6	5	0	3	4	.279	.400	.174	3.18	2.38
Shaw, Scott	R-R	6-5	230	8-3-86	8	8	3.73	26	26	1	0	150	140	69	62	13	57	118	.253	.253	.252	7.10	3.43
Stinson, Josh	R-R	6-4	210	3-14-88	3	1	1.98	25	0	0	6	36	22	12	8	0	19	35	.168	.146	.181	8.67	4.71
Stronach, Tim	L-R	6-5	185	12-20-85	3	4	4.06	15	8	0	0	58	64	35	26	2	24	42	.277	.320	.246	6.55	3.75
Waechter, Nick	R-R	6-3	200	11-30-84	4	4	5.52	31	9	0	3	93	95	58	57	9	33	80	.265	.261	.268	7.74	3.19
Wagner, Billy	L-L	5-11	205	7-25-71	0	0	0.00	5	0	0	0	5	3	0	0	0	0	8	.188	.000	.273	14.40	0.00

Fielding

Catcher	PCT	G	PO	A	E	DP	PB
Arroyo	.975	21	134	22	4	0	7
Doyle	1.000	1	5	2	0	0	0
Henriquez	.962	4	21	4	1	3	0
Maccani	.963	8	50	2	2	1	1
Pena	.991	100	707	89	7	8	9
Rivera	.952	2	20	0	1	0	0

First Base	PCT	G	PO	A	E	DP
Davis	.991	59	535	43	5	45
Eigsti	.967	7	53	6	2	9
Lutz	.990	14	94	6	1	6
Nieuwenhuis	1.000	1	1	0	0	0
Welch	.994	56	461	51	3	54

Second Base	PCT	G	PO	A	E	DP
Bouchard	.913	6	12	9	2	6
Eigsti	1.000	1	1	1	0	0
Pellot	.969	73	116	201	10	49
Rivera	1.000	6	10	11	0	4
Satin	.923	4	6	6	1	3
Veloz	.963	50	99	132	9	36

Third Base	PCT	G	PO	A	E	DP
Bouchard	.871	12	1	26	4	1
Campbell	.833	3	0	5	1	0
Eigsti	.789	10	4	11	4	0
Lutz	.944	80	31	136	10	10
Pellot	.822	20	12	25	8	4
Rivera	1.000	4	2	7	0	1
Veloz	.872	12	10	24	5	4

Shortstop	PCT	G	PO	A	E	DP
Bouchard	.968	19	21	39	2	8
Eigsti	.946	20	29	59	5	14
Havens	.952	97	150	270	21	55
Rivera	1.000	2	5	9	0	4

Outfield	PCT	G	PO	A	E	DP
Arroyo	1.000	1	1	0	0	0
Campbell	1.000	5	8	0	0	0
Guzman	.982	121	219	4	4	1
Maldonado	.973	91	172	6	5	1
Nieuwenhuis	.992	106	226	9	2	3
Pagan	1.000	3	5	1	0	1
Pellot	—	2	0	0	0	0
Pena	.978	25	43	2	1	1
Ratliff	1.000	7	22	0	0	0
Stegall	1.000	2	4	0	0	0
Watson	1.000	2	4	1	0	0
Williams	.959	49	67	3	3	1

SAVANNAH SAND GNATS — LOW CLASS A

SOUTH ATLANTIC LEAGUE

Batting	B-T	HT	WT	DOB	AVG	vLH	vRH	G	AB	R	H	2B	3B	HR	RBI	BB	HBP	SH	SF	SO	SB	CS	SLG	OBP
Abruzzo, Jordan	B-R	6-3	230	8-2-84	.220	.529	.149	23	91	12	20	4	0	3	8	4	0	0	1	20	0	0	.363	.250
Alen, Luis	R-R	6-1	175	4-16-85	.143	.250	.125	24	56	6	8	2	0	0	1	7	2	2	0	8	1	0	.179	.262
Alvarez, Imbewer	R-R	6-1	180	5-15-86	.190	.000	.250	25	58	4	11	2	0	0	4	2	2	2	1	24	1	1	.224	.238

Batting	B-T	HT	WT	DOB	AVG	vLH	vRH	G	AB	R	H	2B	3B	HR	RBI	BB	HBP	SH	SF	SO	SB	CS	SLG	OBP
August, Joey	L-L	6-1	190	9-23-86	.210	.294	.196	41	124	12	26	5	1	1	20	10	1	3	2	23	0	3	.290	.270
Blaquiere, Jean Luc	R-R	6-0	196	2-27-86	.238	.194	.253	70	240	25	57	11	1	5	21	26	6	0	1	57	4	2	.354	.326
Campbell, Eric	R-R	6-3	220	4-9-87	.248	.229	.254	95	339	42	84	23	0	5	47	48	5	0	3	57	6	4	.360	.347
Eigsti, Jake	R-R	6-0	185	6-13-84	.214	.400	.111	5	14	1	3	0	0	0	2	2	0	0	0	3	1	1	.214	.313
Fernandez, Rafael	L-L	6-1	171	8-3-88	.254	.194	.272	73	299	38	76	16	3	1	14	20	1	2	1	68	10	6	.338	.302
Flagg, Jeff	R-R	6-6	246	11-7-85	.174	.000	.200	7	23	1	4	2	0	0	3	4	0	0	0	12	1	0	.261	.296
Flores, Wilmer	R-R	6-3	175	8-6-91	.264	.255	.267	125	488	44	129	20	2	3	36	22	9	3	6	72	3	3	.332	.305
Gaski, Matt	L-R	5-10	185	5-12-86	.389	.500	.367	10	36	7	14	2	0	0	3	2	0	1	0	5	1	0	.444	.421
Giarraputo, Nick	R-R	6-3	200	5-29-88	.397	.250	.435	20	78	7	31	2	0	2	13	3	0	0	1	15	0	1	.500	.415
Gronauer, Kai	R-R	6-1	205	11-28-86	.243	.175	.258	67	230	27	56	7	0	6	23	13	5	0	4	45	0	1	.352	.294
Harris, Alonzo	R-R	5-11	165	11-16-89	.200	.250	.190	7	25	3	5	0	0	0	3	2	0	0	0	8	0	0	.200	.259
Henriquez, Ralph	B-R	6-1	190	4-7-87	.265	.200	.316	9	34	2	9	1	0	0	2	1	0	0	0	9	0	0	.294	.286
Jimenez, Jose	R-R	6-2	185	5-9-87	.149	.200	.123	28	87	7	13	4	0	0	2	8	3	0	0	37	0	0	.195	.245
Lagares, Juan	R-R	6-1	175	3-17-89	.274	.270	.275	47	168	23	46	6	2	0	13	6	2	0	1	42	9	4	.333	.305
LeBlanc, Evan	R-R	6-4	218	9-9-86	.198	.207	.196	43	131	16	26	5	0	1	14	12	3	1	1	30	4	0	.260	.279
Marte, Jefry	R-R	6-1	187	6-21-91	.233	.202	.243	123	485	58	113	21	6	6	41	25	8	2	6	117	5	5	.338	.279
Moras, Michael	R-R	6-1	200	9-11-85	.308	.429	.263	8	26	3	8	0	0	0	1	3	0	0	1	5	0	1	.308	.367
Ratliff, Sean	L-L	6-3	185	2-24-87	.265	.174	.295	122	468	64	124	28	7	15	68	31	4	0	6	131	11	6	.451	.312
Reyes, Raul	L-L	6-0	195	12-30-86	.253	.211	.263	111	371	44	94	15	9	9	51	42	3	7	2	97	3	4	.415	.333
Satin, Josh	R-R	6-2	200	12-23-84	.284	.260	.291	125	440	62	125	38	0	7	60	73	2	0	5	103	0	3	.418	.385
Stegall, Daniel	R-R	6-0	180	9-24-87	.146	.000	.158	11	41	2	6	0	0	1	3	1	1	0	0	13	0	1	.220	.186
Valdespin, Jordany	L-R	6-0	174	12-23-87	.322	.324	.322	39	152	30	49	9	3	3	18	11	0	0	1	32	7	2	.480	.366
Welch, Stefan	L-R	6-3	175	8-12-88	.239	.250	.236	26	92	7	22	3	1	2	10	4	0	0	0	19	0	0	.359	.271

Pitching	B-T	HT	WT	DOB	W	L	ERA	G	GS	CG	SV	IP	H	R	ER	HR	BB	SO	AVG	vLH	vRH	K/9	BB/9
Aldama, Eduardo	R-R	6-1	175	12-23-89	0	1	21.00	1	1	0	0	3	9	7	7	1	2	3	.500	.400	.625	9.00	6.00
Allen, Kyle	R-R	6-3	195	2-12-90	9	6	3.45	25	19	0	2	125	109	57	48	8	51	111	.234	.186	.261	7.97	3.66
Beaulac, Eric	R-R	6-5	190	11-13-86	7	7	2.95	26	19	0	2	116	110	53	38	6	41	133	.250	.250	.250	10.32	3.18
Burns, Brad	R-R	6-4	182	5-28-86	0	2	1.98	7	1	0	0	14	16	8	3	0	9	19	.276	.235	.293	12.51	5.93
Carson, Robert	L-L	6-3	220	1-23-89	8	10	3.21	25	25	2	0	132	139	68	47	4	45	90	.270	.281	.268	6.15	3.08
Church, John	R-R	6-3	235	11-4-86	1	4	5.28	21	0	0	0	29	34	18	17	3	14	34	.288	.277	.296	10.55	4.34
Cruz, Rhiner	R-R	6-2	205	11-1-86	3	3	1.92	50	0	0	22	61	42	14	13	2	31	55	.199	.222	.187	8.11	4.57
Familia, Jeurys	R-R	6-3	185	10-10-89	10	6	2.69	24	23	0	0	134	109	49	40	3	46	109	.221	.227	.218	7.32	3.09
Goldberg, Jake	R-R	6-3	185	11-28-85	1	2	2.89	25	0	0	1	37	32	13	12	2	10	27	.234	.237	.261	6.51	2.41
Hoge, Lance	L-L	5-10	185	5-6-87	0	2	4.50	5	3	0	0	16	21	10	8	1	0	13	.300	.235	.321	7.31	0.00
Johnson, Jimmy	L-L	6-0	195	11-24-85	1	1	1.09	25	0	0	4	33	23	4	4	1	8	33	.198	.158	.218	9.00	2.18
Kaplan, Jeff	R-R	6-0	190	7-9-85	4	2	1.46	10	9	0	0	56	51	13	9	1	17	47	.250	.225	.263	7.60	2.75
Lynn, Mike	R-R	5-10	170	10-11-84	0	1	0.00	7	0	0	1	5	8	5	0	0	0	12	.151	.143	.156	7.20	0.00
Martinez, Samuel	R-R	5-11	175	7-6-87	0	0	3.65	8	0	0	0	12	13	6	5	0	2	13	.271	.571	.147	9.49	1.46
Olivares, Manuel	R-R	6-0	170	5-22-86	2	4	3.77	35	0	0	1	62	65	29	26	2	18	49	.270	.263	.274	7.11	2.61
Orta, Phillips	R-R	6-2	175	5-9-86	1	3	4.93	25	0	0	1	38	32	23	21	1	27	38	.227	.212	.236	8.92	6.34
Powers, Michael	R-R	6-3	180	4-7-86	1	0	3.00	9	0	0	0	15	18	5	5	0	2	11	.305	.333	.293	6.60	1.20
Ramirez, Elvin	R-R	6-3	208	10-10-87	3	7	4.09	15	15	0	0	73	73	40	33	2	39	48	.261	.219	.283	5.94	4.83
Rodriguez, Armando	R-R	6-2	185	1-28-88	2	1	2.16	3	3	1	0	17	5	4	4	0	9	24	.094	.080	.107	12.96	4.86
Rosa, Wendy	R-R	6-0	170	8-26-86	0	1	9.69	8	0	0	0	17	16	14	14	0	12	12	.340	.385	.324	8.31	8.31
Schwinden, Chris	R-R	6-3	215	9-22-86	9	6	3.28	21	17	0	0	115	126	51	42	6	15	88	.279	.259	.291	6.87	1.17
Smith, Tim	R-R	5-11	195	6-25-86	0	0	5.87	9	0	0	0	15	23	17	10	1	5	6	.333	.429	.268	3.52	2.93
Stinson, Josh	R-R	6-4	210	3-14-88	2	2	3.61	25	1	0	2	42	45	17	17	1	10	49	.287	.275	.292	10.42	2.13
Tabata, Marcos	R-R	5-10	175	6-12-86	0	0	3.00	2	0	0	0	3	3	4	1	0	4	7	.231	.167	.286	21.00	12.00
Turgeon, Erik	R-R	6-0	170	3-25-87	1	1	3.18	10	0	0	3	11	7	4	4	1	11	12	.179	.400	.103	9.53	8.74
Von Tersch, Zach	R-R	6-4	195	4-22-88	0	0	4.50	1	1	0	0	6	3	3	3	1	2	7	.150	.182	.111	10.50	3.00

Fielding

Catcher	PCT	G	PO	A	E	DP	PB
Alen	.982	18	102	7	2	3	1
Blaquiere	.984	56	394	42	7	2	9
Gronauer	.984	59	448	59	8	3	11
Henriquez	.974	4	32	6	1	1	1
Moras	.986	7	66	4	1	0	1

First Base	PCT	G	PO	A	E	DP
Alen	1.000	3	7	0	0	1
Campbell	.994	69	600	26	4	48
Flagg	1.000	6	31	5	0	4
Giarraputo	.974	10	67	8	2	6
Jimenez	1.000	13	107	10	0	8
Satin	.990	25	177	15	2	19
Welch	1.000	20	189	16	0	20

Second Base	PCT	G	PO	A	E	DP
Alvarez	.935	19	31	27	4	5
Eigsti	.875	5	3	4	1	0
Gaski	.971	9	14	19	1	4
Harris	.944	7	8	9	1	2
Satin	.983	79	129	210	6	52
Valdespin	.979	28	65	76	3	22

Third Base	PCT	G	PO	A	E	DP
Campbell	.958	11	6	17	1	0
Giarraputo	1.000	6	2	4	0	0
Jimenez	1.000	1	0	1	0	0
Lagares	1.000	1	0	1	0	0
Marte	.856	119	69	222	49	18
Satin	1.000	3	0	6	0	0

Shortstop	PCT	G	PO	A	E	DP
Alvarez	.778	3	3	4	2	0
Flores	.974	125	160	330	13	73
Lagares	1.000	2	0	1	0	0
Marte	1.000	1	1	4	0	1
Valdespin	.902	10	18	28	5	5

Outfield	PCT	G	PO	A	E	DP
Alvarez	—	2	0	0	0	0
August	.987	37	71	3	1	2
Campbell	1.000	18	22	2	0	0
Fernandez	.968	73	149	2	5	0
Lagares	.988	42	77	7	1	2
LeBlanc	.955	39	64	3	0	0
Ratliff	.976	118	230	10	6	3
Reyes	.966	97	162	7	6	5
Stegall	1.000	6	5	1	0	0

BROOKLYN CYCLONES   SHORT-SEASON

NEW YORK-PENN LEAGUE

Batting	B-T	HT	WT	DOB	AVG	vLH	vRH	G	AB	R	H	2B	3B	HR	RBI	BB	HBP	SH	SF	SO	SB	CS	SLG	OBP
August, Joey	L-L	6-1	190	9-23-86	.167	.000	.200	3	6	1	1	0	0	0	0	1	0	0	0	2	0	0	.167	.286

NEW YORK METS

Batting	B-T	HT	WT	DOB	AVG	vLH	vRH	G	AB	R	H	2B	3B	HR	RBI	BB	HBP	SH	SF	SO	SB	CS	OBP	SLG
Beltran, Carlos	B-R	6-1	200	4-24-77	.167	.000	.188	5	18	1	3	0	0	0	2	2	0	0	0	5	0	0	.167	.250
Berroa, Angel	R-R	6-0	195	1-27-78	.250	.200	.333	2	8	2	2	0	0	0	1	1	0	0	0	1	1	0	.250	.333
Bonfe, Joe	R-R	6-4	220	12-28-87	.091	.250	.000	6	11	1	1	0	0	0	0	2	1	0	0	3	0	0	.091	.286
Bouchard, Matt	R-R	6-0	185	12-12-86	.408	.286	.457	14	49	16	20	4	1	1	8	2	1	0	2	8	3	2	.592	.426
Centeno, Juan	L-R	5-9	172	11-16-89	.164	.219	.141	32	110	8	18	2	1	0	9	5	2	2	1	18	1	1	.200	.212
Doyle, Dock	L-R	6-0	200	3-24-86	.257	.229	.268	49	171	13	44	8	2	1	18	18	1	4	0	27	2	2	.345	.332
Eigsti, Jake	R-R	6-0	185	6-13-84	.276	.308	.267	14	58	7	16	5	0	0	2	5	0	1	0	8	1	0	.362	.333
Ewing, James	R-R	6-0	190	10-27-86	.143	.250	.100	5	14	1	2	2	0	0	0	1	0	0	0	2	0	0	.286	.200
Garber, Justin	R-R	6-0	190	12-3-84	.264	.222	.282	33	121	24	32	6	0	0	7	15	5	2	2	26	5	1	.314	.364
Gaski, Matt	L-R	5-10	185	5-12-86	.291	.313	.286	24	79	7	23	0	1	0	4	10	0	1	0	10	2	0	.316	.371
Giarraputo, Nick	R-R	6-3	200	5-29-88	.203	.154	.216	34	123	16	25	6	1	1	13	4	5	2	3	20	1	0	.293	.252
Green, Andy	R-R	5-10	180	7-7-77	.304	.200	.385	7	23	4	7	0	0	1	2	5	0	0	0	2	1	1	.435	.429
Gregory, Alex	R-R	6-0	210	11-7-86	.278	.293	.272	42	144	23	40	10	2	2	17	16	2	0	4	29	1	0	.417	.349
Grimes, Scott	R-R	6-1	200	9-15-83	.226	.235	.222	15	53	5	12	1	0	2	7	6	0	1	0	13	0	0	.358	.305
Harris, R.J.	L-L	6-2	205	2-19-87	.273	—	.273	4	11	1	3	1	0	0	1	0	0	0	0	6	0	0	.364	.273
Henriquez, Ralph	B-R	6-1	190	4-7-87	.261	.189	.281	48	165	20	43	8	1	2	16	10	1	0	1	28	0	2	.358	.305
Honeck, Sam	L-L	6-2	210	6-19-87	.250	.169	.281	65	236	24	59	10	4	1	29	31	3	4	4	48	0	0	.305	.339
LeBlanc, Evan	R-R	6-4	218	9-9-86	.083	.000	.111	4	12	0	1	0	0	0	1	0	0	0	0	4	0	0	.083	.154
Lucas, Richard	R-R	6-1	205	11-2-88	.250	.286	.231	16	60	4	15	5	2	0	6	7	0	0	2	14	1	1	.400	.319
Nieves, Luis	R-R	5-11	160	12-15-88	.142	.257	.090	35	113	11	16	2	0	1	11	6	0	2	1	20	4	0	.186	.183
Rivera, Luis	R-R	6-1	190	10-12-86	.297	.324	.286	66	222	38	66	14	3	4	34	37	4	0	3	53	13	3	.441	.402
Santomauro, Nick	R-L	6-3	205	6-13-88	.241	.114	.282	45	145	18	35	5	3	6	21	28	1	1	0	38	1	4	.441	.368
Schroeder, James	R-R	6-0	210	12-13-86	—	—	—	1	0	0	0	0	0	0	0	0	0	1	0	0	0	0	—	1.000
Servidio, John	R-R	6-1	194	8-22-85	.181	.218	.160	49	155	23	28	6	0	6	19	20	11	4	1	53	3	1	.335	.316
Shields, Robbie	R-R	6-1	195	12-7-87	.178	.237	.157	44	146	14	26	4	3	1	9	16	3	2	0	32	2	0	.267	.273
Valdespin, Jordany	L-R	6-0	174	12-23-87	.279	.304	.267	18	68	10	19	3	1	1	5	5	1	2	0	16	4	3	.397	.338
Vaughn, Tyler	R-R	6-2	200	3-21-85	.250	.333	.212	25	96	11	24	3	0	1	9	4	3	0	0	19	5	3	.313	.301
Williams, Seth	R-R	6-2	205	11-21-85	.333	—	.333	2	6	2	2	0	0	0	0	0	0	0	0	1	1	0	.333	.429

Pitching	B-T	HT	WT	DOB	W	L	ERA	G	GS	CG	SV	IP	H	R	ER	HR	BB	SO	AVG	vLH	vRH	K/9	BB/9
Carrillo, Matias	L-L	6-3	224	12-13-86	1	2	3.14	21	0	0	1	29	22	10	10	2	3	32	.208	.171	.231	10.05	0.94
Chism, T.J.	L-L	5-10	190	8-9-88	2	0	0.00	2	0	0	0	4	1	0	0	0	2	5	.091	.000	.200	11.25	4.50
Church, John	R-R	6-3	235	11-4-86	0	0	9.00	1	0	0	0	1	1	1	1	0	1	0	.250	.500	.000	0.00	9.00
Cohoon, Mark	L-L	6-2	195	9-15-87	9	2	2.15	14	14	2	0	92	69	26	22	4	20	70	.210	.154	.231	6.85	1.96
Cuan, Angel	L-L	5-11	150	5-29-89	0	2	6.75	2	2	0	0	8	15	7	6	0	2	9	.429	.583	.348	10.13	2.25
Fuller, Jim	L-L	5-10	180	6-1-87	3	6	2.86	12	11	1	0	63	58	24	20	4	15	67	.250	.254	.248	9.57	2.14
Gagg, Bobby	R-R	5-11	215	12-29-86	2	0	2.25	8	0	0	1	12	10	3	3	1	4	11	.233	.150	.304	8.25	3.00
Goldberg, Jake	R-R	6-0	185	11-28-85	0	0	1.93	6	0	0	0	9	2	2	2	0	3	16	.067	.111	.048	10.61	2.89
Gorski, Darin	L-L	6-4	210	10-6-87	3	4	4.91	13	11	0	0	62	51	44	34	6	26	50	.220	.194	.230	7.22	3.75
Hilliard, Chris	L-L	6-0	175	10-26-87	1	1	0.75	3	2	0	0	12	13	5	1	0	2	7	.283	.364	.257	5.25	1.50
Hoge, Lance	L-L	5-10	185	5-6-87	1	0	2.52	10	0	0	0	25	24	7	7	0	6	20	.250	.211	.276	7.20	2.16
Johnson, Michael	R-R	5-10	180	9-14-87	0	0	6.48	6	0	0	0	8	11	6	6	2	6	7	.324	.278	.375	7.56	6.48
Lynn, Mike	R-R	5-10	170	10-11-84	1	1	3.98	12	0	0	0	20	19	11	9	0	12	21	.244	.233	.257	9.30	5.31
Martinez, Samuel	R-R	5-11	175	7-6-87	0	0	4.63	9	0	0	0	12	10	7	6	1	8	17	.217	.214	.222	13.11	6.17
McHugh, Collin	R-R	6-2	195	6-19-87	8	2	2.76	14	14	1	0	75	61	25	23	1	21	79	.219	.244	.183	9.48	2.52
Moore, Brandon	R-R	6-3	190	1-24-86	6	3	2.09	13	13	2	0	82	61	23	19	4	17	71	.206	.195	.218	7.79	1.87
Olivares, Manuel	R-R	6-0	170	5-22-86	0	0	3.52	5	0	0	0	8	12	9	3	2	5	5	.343	.313	.368	5.87	5.87
Perez, Oliver	L-L	6-3	210	8-15-81	1	0	0.00	1	1	0	0	5	2	0	0	0	1	6	.125	.250	.083	10.80	1.80
Powers, Michael	R-R	6-3	180	4-7-86	3	3	4.01	30	0	0	17	34	31	15	15	1	13	33	.237	.250	.227	8.82	3.48
Sage, Brandon	L-L	6-2	210	10-3-86	3	3	2.03	16	0	0	1	31	26	11	7	1	11	15	.224	.205	.234	4.35	3.19
Turgeon, Erik	R-R	6-0	170	3-25-87	1	0	3.60	14	0	0	1	15	17	9	6	0	7	11	.288	.304	.278	6.60	4.20
Wrenn, Wes	R-R	5-11	186	4-17-86	2	1	4.15	13	7	0	1	48	56	23	22	6	8	41	.287	.298	.277	7.74	1.51

Fielding

Catcher	PCT	G	PO	A	E	DP	PB
Centeno	.986	32	256	22	4	0	5
Doyle	1.000	32	263	17	0	3	2
Henriquez	.978	13	79	8	2	1	2

First Base	PCT	G	PO	A	E	DP
Giarraputo	1.000	3	21	2	0	0
Gregory	1.000	11	77	7	0	6
Henriquez	1.000	1	2	0	0	0
Honeck	.994	63	578	45	4	42

Second Base	PCT	G	PO	A	E	DP
Bouchard	.971	9	11	23	1	4
Centeno	1.000	1	0	2	0	0
Eigsti	.959	12	20	27	2	3
Ewing	.857	5	0	12	2	2
Gaski	.980	22	36	61	2	11
Green	.958	6	12	11	1	4
Nieves	.983	13	18	40	1	6
Valdespin	.971	14	24	43	2	9

Third Base	PCT	G	PO	A	E	DP
Bonfe	1.000	4	2	13	0	1
Bouchard	.750	2	1	5	2	0
Giarraputo	.944	30	19	66	5	6
Green	1.000	0	1	0	0	0
Lucas	.925	16	12	25	3	2
Schroeder	1.000	1	0	2	0	1
Vaughn	.862	23	11	39	8	2

Shortstop	PCT	G	PO	A	E	DP
Berroa	1.000	2	0	5	0	0
Bouchard	1.000	2	3	7	0	0
Eigsti	1.000	2	0	4	0	1
Nieves	.959	22	45	71	5	14
Shields	.966	44	76	122	7	19
Valdespin	.923	6	4	8	1	2

Outfield	PCT	G	PO	A	E	DP
August	1.000	3	2	0	0	0
Beltran	1.000	4	3	1	0	0
Bonfe	—	1	0	0	0	0
Garber	.987	33	76	1	1	0
Gregory	.974	28	37	0	1	0
Grimes	.913	11	20	1	2	0
Harris	1.000	4	8	0	0	0
LeBlanc	1.000	1	3	0	0	0
Rivera	.989	64	85	8	1	0
Santomauro	.978	36	40	5	1	0
Servidio	1.000	49	78	9	0	1
Williams	1.000	2	6	0	0	0

KINGSPORT METS   ROOKIE
APPALACHIAN LEAGUE

Batting	B-T	HT	WT	DOB	AVG	vLH	vRH	G	AB	R	H	2B	3B	HR	RBI	BB	HBP	SH	SF	SO	SB	CS	SLG	OBP
Bonfe, Joe	R-R	6-4	220	12-28-87	.327	.278	.342	40	156	29	51	12	0	3	19	19	8	0	0	32	3	2	.462	.426
Ceciliani, Darrell	L-L	6-1	185	6-22-90	.234	.296	.221	42	158	29	37	6	0	2	13	13	5	0	0	31	14	2	.310	.313
Flagg, Jeff	R-R	6-6	246	11-7-85	.301	.213	.324	57	226	47	68	9	3	10	59	23	1	0	2	71	3	3	.500	.365
Freeman, Taylor	L-R	6-0	190	8-24-87	.221	.100	.257	39	131	10	29	8	0	1	16	10	0	1	3	38	0	0	.305	.271
Garber, Justin	R-R	6-0	190	12-3-84	.400	.200	.600	3	10	2	4	0	0	0	3	0	0	0	0	2	0	0	.400	.400
Harris, Alonzo	R-R	5-11	165	11-16-89	.273	.358	.250	58	253	49	69	4	5	10	39	17	2	2	2	59	15	6	.447	.321
Harris, R.J.	L-L	6-2	205	2-19-87	.293	.359	.276	48	184	40	54	2	3	5	25	23	5	0	2	64	13	5	.418	.383
Howe, Tyler	L-R	6-1	200	2-7-86	.245	.250	.244	21	49	11	12	4	0	1	8	14	15	1	1	17	3	2	.388	.519
LeBlanc, Evan	R-R	6-4	218	9-9-86	.333	1.000	.250	2	9	0	3	1	1	0	1	0	0	0	0	0	0	1	.667	.333
Lucas, Richard	R-R	6-1	205	11-2-88	.357	.313	.366	26	98	28	35	12	1	4	21	20	2	0	1	20	1	2	.622	.471
Mochizuki, Gered	L-R	5-7	155	7-7-85	.270	.167	.307	39	137	20	37	7	1	1	19	16	1	1	0	34	10	3	.358	.351
Mollica, Ryan	R-L	6-0	185	2-25-86	.287	.344	.265	30	115	21	33	6	0	1	19	12	4	0	2	23	4	3	.365	.368
Moras, Michael	R-R	6-1	200	9-11-85	.261	.294	.250	17	69	7	18	4	0	0	14	3	1	0	1	11	1	0	.319	.297
Nieves, Luis	R-R	5-11	160	12-15-88	.265	.083	.304	18	68	7	18	2	0	0	8	0	0	0	2	7	2	1	.294	.257
Puello, Cesar	R-R	6-2	195	4-1-91	.296	.383	.268	49	196	37	58	10	0	5	23	10	14	1	0	51	15	5	.423	.373
Schroeder, James	R-R	6-0	210	12-13-86	.200	.500	.125	6	20	1	4	0	0	0	2	2	1	1	0	3	0	0	.200	.304
Semel, John	R-R	6-0	182	3-31-88	.215	.162	.238	34	121	15	26	1	0	0	15	20	0	1	1	18	10	2	.223	.324
Steinhauer, Kurt	R-R	6-1	205	3-29-86	.364	.480	.308	24	77	17	28	5	0	5	22	10	4	3	1	21	1	2	.623	.457
Torres, Juan	R-R	6-1	180	10-7-88	.328	.316	.333	20	58	6	19	5	1	0	10	1	1	0	0	12	0	1	.448	.350
Vaughn, Tyler	R-R	6-2	200	3-21-85	.412	.400	.417	5	17	2	7	1	0	1	3	0	1	0	0	5	0	1	.647	.444
Zapata, Pedro	R-R	6-4	185	10-3-87	.329	.348	.321	41	152	31	50	12	1	0	21	6	1	1	0	36	15	3	.421	.358

Pitching	B-T	HT	WT	DOB	W	L	ERA	G	GS	CG	SV	IP	H	R	ER	HR	BB	SO	AVG	vLH	vRH	K/9	BB/9
Aldama, Eduardo	R-R	6-1	175	12-23-89	5	1	3.79	12	12	0	0	62	59	31	26	4	23	57	.253	.234	.266	8.32	3.36
Almonte, Yohan	R-R	6-1	150	11-9-89	3	1	4.40	8	8	0	0	43	46	21	21	3	8	37	.275	.238	.310	7.74	1.67
Babin, Travis	R-R	6-1	205	12-2-86	1	1	3.63	20	0	0	5	22	24	14	9	1	9	19	.264	.333	.218	7.66	3.63
Bello, Julio	L-R	6-5	175	10-16-86	1	2	5.93	8	0	0	0	14	18	12	9	0	14	10	.310	.200	.368	6.59	9.22
Chism, T.J.	L-L	5-10	190	8-9-88	1	1	5.12	17	0	0	0	19	23	12	11	1	13	20	.307	.214	.362	9.31	6.05
Cuan, Angel	L-L	5-11	150	5-29-89	1	3	4.83	12	11	0	0	60	76	36	32	5	14	45	.313	.419	.290	6.79	2.11
Gagg, Bobby	R-R	5-11	215	12-29-86	0	1	1.80	5	0	0	1	5	6	3	1	0	1	7	.286	.429	.214	12.60	1.80
Hilliard, Chris	L-L	6-0	175	10-26-87	3	3	2.83	11	4	0	0	41	38	18	13	2	7	27	.252	.250	.252	5.88	1.52
Leduc, Guillaume	R-R	6-4	192	7-28-87	2	2	5.48	13	5	0	2	44	57	33	27	4	15	29	.311	.373	.276	5.89	3.05
Melendez, Oscar	R-R	6-0	170	9-15-86	0	0	7.30	12	0	0	0	12	17	15	10	1	11	12	.315	.444	.250	8.76	8.03
Needham, Brian	R-R	6-6	185	9-21-86	1	3	5.72	15	0	0	0	28	33	19	18	3	14	21	.287	.311	.271	6.67	4.45
Rodriguez, Armando	R-R	6-2	185	1-28-88	3	1	2.96	9	9	0	0	46	39	20	15	2	20	36	.227	.217	.233	7.09	3.94
Rojas, Luis	R-R	5-10	185	7-29-89	0	1	21.32	5	0	0	0	6	13	15	15	0	13	7	.419	.375	.467	9.95	18.47
Rosenbaum, Zach	R-R	6-4	190	4-25-87	1	3	4.30	14	0	0	0	23	25	14	11	1	8	18	.260	.243	.271	7.04	3.13
Smith, Tim	R-R	5-11	195	6-25-86	1	1	3.46	9	0	0	0	13	6	5	5	2	6	12	.136	.118	.148	8.31	4.15
Taveras, Samuel	R-R	6-2	190	4-14-89	1	3	6.53	18	0	0	2	21	23	16	15	1	8	17	.274	.379	.218	7.40	3.48
Torres, Jhonathan	L-L	5-11	170	3-20-90	2	4	4.87	9	9	0	0	41	51	35	22	7	17	33	.309	.231	.324	7.30	3.76
Von Tersch, Zach	R-R	6-4	195	4-22-88	3	0	3.92	13	6	0	1	39	37	24	17	4	25	30	.248	.308	.216	6.92	5.77
White, Johnathan	R-R	6-1	205	1-19-88	1	4	6.33	12	1	0	1	27	37	20	19	1	11	21	.339	.275	.377	7.00	3.67

Fielding

Catcher	PCT	G	PO	A	E	DP	PB
Freeman	.981	35	217	35	5	6	2
Howe	.948	10	47	8	3	0	2
Moras	.991	14	104	11	1	2	1
Steinhauer	1.000	1	10	0	0	0	0
Torres	.969	11	90	5	3	0	4

First Base	PCT	G	PO	A	E	DP
Bonfe	.983	7	56	2	1	4
Flagg	.998	55	450	26	1	52
Howe	.929	3	24	2	2	3
Semel	1.000	1	9	1	0	0
Torres	1.000	2	11	1	0	1

Second Base	PCT	G	PO	A	E	DP
Harris	.975	57	119	154	7	35
Mollica	.886	10	21	18	5	5

Third Base	PCT	G	PO	A	E	DP
Bonfe	.907	28	30	58	9	9
Lucas	.944	24	22	45	4	6
Mollica	1.000	3	1	9	0	3
Schroeder	.867	6	7	2	0	0
Vaughn	.667	4	1	5	3	0

Shortstop	PCT	G	PO	A	E	DP
Mochizuki	.897	39	55	93	17	19
Mollica	.881	10	14	23	5	9
Nieves	.947	18	28	62	5	12

Torres	—		1	0	0	0

Outfield	PCT	G	PO	A	E	DP
Ceciliani	.961	41	94	4	4	2
Freeman	1.000	1	1	0	0	0
Garber	1.000	2	3	0	0	0
Harris	1.000	2	4	0	0	0
Harris	.961	34	72	2	3	0
LeBlanc	1.000	2	3	1	0	0
Mollica	1.000	1	2	0	0	0
Puello	.960	49	91	4	4	3
Semel	.981	28	50	3	1	2
Steinhauer	1.000	15	22	1	0	0
Zapata	.921	27	33	2	3	0

GCL METS   ROOKIE
GULF COAST LEAGUE

Batting	B-T	HT	WT	DOB	AVG	vLH	vRH	G	AB	R	H	2B	3B	HR	RBI	BB	HBP	SH	SF	SO	SB	CS	SLG	OBP
Concepcion, Julio	R-R	6-4	194	9-5-89	.306	.267	.322	45	160	21	49	4	2	0	12	10	4	0	4	34	11	4	.356	.354
Davis, Marshal	R-R	6-0	180	8-1-85	.150	.143	.154	13	20	7	3	0	0	0	4	5	4	1	0	9	0	0	.150	.414
Dunn, Josh	R-R	6-3	198	12-9-90	.100	.167	.083	11	30	2	3	1	0	0	3	3	0	1	0	8	0	0	.133	.182
Green, Andy	R-R	5-10	180	7-7-77	.167	.000	.250	2	6	1	1	0	0	0	2	3	0	0	0	1	0	0	.167	.444
Greene, Chase	R-R	5-11	180	4-22-90	.286	.304	.275	22	63	8	18	7	0	0	5	7	1	0	1	10	2	0	.397	.361
Grimes, Scott	R-R	6-1	200	9-15-83	.244	.222	.250	12	41	7	10	2	1	1	6	6	1	0	1	5	3	1	.415	.347
Hall, ZeErika	R-R	6-0	175	6-29-88	.297	.324	.284	38	111	23	33	9	0	0	10	21	2	0	0	25	5	1	.378	.418
Hinojosa, Charlie	R-R	6-3	190	6-16-89	.323	.405	.289	38	127	10	41	12	0	1	15	9	5	1	1	30	1	4	.441	.387

Batting	B-T	HT	WT	DOB	AVG	vLH	vRH	G	AB	R	H	2B	3B	HR	RBI	BB	HBP	SH	SF	SO	SB	CS	SLG	OBP
Holliday, Cody	L-L	6-3	215	9-30-87	.175	.067	.240	15	40	7	7	4	0	0	0	9	0	0	0	15	1	0	.275	.327
Kiger, Mark	R-R	5-10	195	5-30-80	.063	.250	.000	6	16	3	1	0	0	0	0	4	0	0	0	5	0	0	.063	.250
Lagares, Juan	R-R	6-1	175	3-17-89	.208	.083	.333	6	24	1	5	1	0	0	1	1	0	0	0	4	1	0	.250	.240
Lucas, Richard	R-R	6-1	205	11-2-88	.333	.333	.333	5	18	1	6	3	0	0	3	2	0	0	0	5	1	0	.500	.400
Maron, Cam	L-R	6-1	175	1-20-91	.293	.357	.259	12	41	8	12	2	0	1	7	7	1	0	0	7	1	0	.415	.408
Martinez, Ruben	R-R	6-0	172	9-15-86	.087	.000	.125	12	23	2	2	0	1	0	4	5	1	0	1	11	1	1	.174	.267
Ortiz, Giovanni	R-R	6-5	233	5-11-88	.167	.182	.159	21	66	4	11	4	0	0	6	7	1	1	0	22	0	0	.227	.257
Ozga, Travis	B-R	6-2	210	12-7-86	.194	.176	.203	32	93	7	18	3	0	0	2	10	1	0	0	31	4	3	.226	.279
Rodriguez, Aderlin	R-R	6-3	210	11-18-91	.290	.333	.268	17	62	5	18	3	0	1	10	9	1	0	0	15	1	1	.387	.389
Rodriguez, Javier	R-R	6-2	165	4-4-90	.230	.262	.216	36	139	9	32	7	1	2	19	10	1	0	1	39	2	1	.338	.285
Rodriguez, Orlando	R-R	6-2	185	11-23-88	.298	.250	.323	16	47	11	14	5	0	0	8	7	2	0	0	9	1	1	.404	.411
Steinhauer, Kurt	R-R	6-1	205	3-29-86	.267	.357	.226	12	45	8	12	2	1	0	7	7	1	0	0	7	2	1	.356	.377
Tejada, Miguel	R-R	6-1	175	11-11-90	.141	.190	.120	26	71	6	10	2	1	0	7	6	3	0	1	33	2	1	.197	.235
Torres, Juan	R-R	6-1	180	10-7-88	.345	.350	.190	8	29	5	10	3	1	0	3	2	1	0	0	3	1	0	.517	.406
Tovar, Wilfredo	R-R	5-10	150	8-11-91	.243	.294	.216	38	148	21	36	5	3	0	14	8	3	1	1	19	16	8	.318	.294
Valdespin, Jordany	L-R	6-0	174	12-23-87	.174	.143	.188	6	23	0	4	0	0	0	0	1	0	0	0	3	1	0	.174	.208
Valdez, Amauris	R-R	5-11	194	8-24-88	.278	.250	.289	20	54	7	15	3	1	0	2	1	1	0	0	11	0	1	.370	.304
Van Gurp, Ray	R-R	5-11	165	1-2-89	.252	.128	.295	45	151	25	38	6	1	0	21	27	0	1	2	22	16	5	.305	.361
Vernouij, Marinus	R-R	6-3	215	1-30-89	.197	.333	.164	27	76	7	15	2	0	0	7	4	2	0	1	24	1	1	.224	.253
Zapata, Nelfi	R-R	6-0	203	12-13-90	.261	.250	.265	35	119	18	31	6	2	1	13	11	4	0	1	26	0	1	.370	.341

Pitching	B-T	HT	WT	DOB	W	L	ERA	G	GS	CG	SV	IP	H	R	ER	HR	BB	SO	AVG	vLH	vRH	K/9	BB/9
Aguilar, Sal	R-R	6-0	190	1-9-82	0	1	6.43	5	5	0	0	14	16	12	10	2	2	12	.271	.375	.200	7.71	1.29
Almonte, Yohan	R-R	6-1	150	11-9-89	1	0	1.37	5	5	0	0	20	17	5	3	0	2	20	.221	.435	.130	9.15	0.92
Bierd, Jose	R-R	6-2	155	5-8-85	0	0	4.50	2	0	0	0	2	1	1	1	1	0	2	.143	.000	.250	9.00	0.00
Burns, Brad	R-R	6-4	182	5-28-86	1	0	0.00	3	0	0	0	5	4	1	0	0	1	5	.211	.250	.200	9.00	1.80
Carela, Daniel	R-R	6-3	225	9-18-87	0	2	5.79	13	0	0	0	19	19	13	12	1	13	22	.271	.207	.317	10.61	6.27
Feliz, Tony	R-R	6-4	205	11-3-85	0	1	6.00	3	0	0	1	6	9	5	4	0	3	1	.346	.333	.353	1.50	4.50
Gagg, Bobby	R-R	5-11	215	12-29-86	0	0	0.00	3	0	0	0	7	4	0	0	0	1	6	.167	.000	.235	7.71	1.29
Germen, Gonzalez	R-R	6-1	175	9-23-87	0	1	6.00	2	1	0	0	6	5	4	1	0	0	7	.250	.143	.294	10.50	0.00
Hebert, Mike	R-R	6-3	180	8-11-90	1	3	3.73	8	5	0	1	31	28	15	13	1	14	23	.239	.167	.272	6.61	4.02
Hodge, Lachlan	L-L	6-2	185	2-3-89	4	2	3.35	13	11	0	0	54	43	26	20	3	28	56	.225	.194	.232	9.39	4.70
Houck, Mitch	L-L	6-1	200	5-26-87	0	1	3.00	2	0	0	0	3	3	2	1	0	1	0	.300	1.000	.222	0.00	3.00
Morgan, Will	R-R	6-1	205	11-3-85	0	0	0.00	3	0	0	0	4	1	0	0	0	0	7	.071	.333	.000	15.75	0.00
Moviel, Scott	R-R	6-11	235	5-7-88	0	1	0.00	2	2	0	0	9	10	2	1	0	0	10	.270	.250	.273	10.00	0.00
Mueses, Jimber	R-R	6-3	220	7-10-87	0	1	8.15	14	0	0	0	18	18	17	16	0	22	17	.286	.368	.250	8.66	11.21
O'Neill, Adam	R-R	6-1	180	5-22-90	1	2	6.38	11	0	0	0	18	18	13	13	0	14	11	.243	.296	.213	5.40	6.87
Peralta, Ramiro	R-R	6-3	180	9-8-89	2	1	2.60	9	2	0	0	17	16	7	5	0	13	14	.258	.438	.196	7.27	6.75
Rackel, Trey	R-R	6-1	215	5-17-88	2	2	3.38	15	0	0	3	27	22	12	10	1	11	26	.224	.267	.206	8.78	3.71
Rojas, Luis	R-R	5-10	185	7-29-89	3	1	3.09	13	0	0	0	23	17	14	8	0	16	20	.198	.238	.185	7.71	6.17
Sanchez, Jose	R-R	6-0	170	5-12-84	0	1	4.09	3	3	0	0	11	8	5	5	0	3	8	.200	.167	.214	6.55	2.45
Tabata, Marcos	R-R	5-10	175	6-12-86	0	1	2.63	13	0	0	2	24	21	10	7	1	8	23	.226	.179	.246	8.63	3.00
Torres, Jhonathan	L-L	5-11	170	3-20-90	4	0	0.82	4	3	0	0	22	6	2	2	0	5	22	.085	.053	.096	9.00	2.05
Tovar, Orlando	L-L	6-3	213	3-26-88	1	5	4.31	12	9	0	0	54	48	30	26	1	15	40	.238	.143	.257	6.63	2.48
Valdez, Santiago	R-R	6-2	210	7-29-87	0	1	4.02	12	0	0	0	16	9	7	1	1	11	17	.254	.222	.268	9.77	6.32
Valenzuela, Brian	L-L	5-10	155	10-21-89	0	5	6.33	7	4	0	0	27	32	24	19	1	20	28	.305	.188	.326	9.33	6.67
Wagner, Billy	L-L	5-11	205	7-25-71	0	0	0.00	2	0	0	0	2	0	0	0	0	0	2	.000	.000	.000	9.00	0.00
Whitenton, Taylor	R-R	6-3	190	2-20-88	0	0	0.00	4	0	0	1	5	1	0	0	0	5	7	.067	.000	.091	12.60	9.00

Fielding

Catcher	PCT	G	PO	A	E	DP	PB
Maron	.979	9	90	5	2	0	4
Rodriguez	1.000	7	31	1	0	1	3
Valdez	.975	18	106	9	3	1	4
Zapata	.988	31	214	30	3	3	12

First Base	PCT	G	PO	A	E	DP
Greene	1.000	1	2	0	0	0
Ortiz	.986	17	134	9	2	21
Ozga	.976	22	157	8	4	13
Torres	.987	8	72	4	1	4
Vernouij	.969	17	113	12	4	13

Second Base	PCT	G	PO	A	E	DP
Davis	.935	9	17	12	2	4
Green	1.000	1	0	1	0	0
Greene	1.000	1	0	2	0	0
Kiger	1.000	1	1	0	0	0
Tejada	1.000	1	3	1	0	0
Tovar	1.000	2	4	6	0	2
Valdespin	.951	5	11	10	0	5
Van Gurp	.951	45	99	96	10	34

Third Base	PCT	G	PO	A	E	DP
Dunn	.889	11	9	15	3	0
Hinojosa	.878	14	6	30	5	3
Kiger	1.000	4	1	6	0	1
Lucas	1.000	3	2	11	0	1
Ozga	.889	8	4	4	1	1
Rodriguez	.774	17	11	30	12	1
Vernouij	.952	10	4	16	1	2

Shortstop	PCT	G	PO	A	E	DP
Davis	1.000	2	3	10	0	3
Tejada	.892	24	29	45	9	14
Tovar	1.000	1	1	2	0	0
Tovar	.928	37	51	129	14	23

Outfield	PCT	G	PO	A	E	DP
Concepcion	.906	37	47	1	5	0
Greene	1.000	12	22	0	1	0
Grimes	.933	10	13	1	1	1
Hall	1.000	33	41	0	0	0
Hinojosa	.800	5	4	0	1	0
Holliday	.933	14	13	1	1	0
Lagares	1.000	5	5	0	0	0
Martinez	1.000	12	15	1	0	1
Ozga	1.000	3	2	0	0	0
Rodriguez	.987	36	73	1	1	0
Steinhauer	1.000	12	11	1	0	0
Tejada	—	1	0	0	0	0

DSL METS   ROOKIE

DOMINICAN SUMMER LEAGUE

Batting	B-T	HT	WT	DOB	AVG	vLH	vRH	G	AB	R	H	2B	3B	HR	RBI	BB	HBP	SH	SF	SO	SB	CS	SLG	OBP
Avila, Wandel	R-R	6-2	190	4-10-91	.229	.143	.250	38	105	23	24	2	0	0	17	21	4	2	1	36	2	4	.248	.374
Barrera, Edwin	L-L	6-2	200	9-15-90	.279	.200	.299	40	147	19	41	14	2	0	18	13	3	0	3	30	4	2	.401	.343
Caba, Arickson	R-R	6-3	190	2-23-89	.230	.185	.255	22	74	9	17	2	1	3	9	4	1	0	0	24	3	2	.405	.278

Batting	B-T	HT	WT	DOB	AVG	vLH	vRH	G	AB	R	H	2B	3B	HR	RBI	BB	HBP	SH	SF	SO	SB	CS	SLG	OBP
Castillo, Edwin	R-R	6-0	181	5-30-90	.177	.111	.205	19	62	9	11	1	1	1	7	6	3	0	0	21	2	2	.274	.282
Cessa, Luis	R-R	6-3	190	4-25-92	.191	.190	.191	34	89	17	17	1	1	1	9	19	8	1	0	33	8	5	.258	.379
Cordero, Albert	R-R	5-11	175	1-14-90	.211	.000	.250	7	19	2	4	1	0	0	3	5	1	0	0	2	0	0	.263	.400
De La Cruz, Yucarybert	R-R	6-0	160	10-23-90	.296	.299	.295	71	284	61	84	20	2	2	44	39	5	4	0	31	26	6	.401	.390
De Leon, Daniel	R-R	6-2	174	5-29-92	.242	.191	.259	62	194	35	47	4	0	0	18	42	7	1	0	37	7	5	.263	.395
De Leon, Jeyckol	R-R	6-2	185	7-25-90	.294	.229	.313	44	163	22	48	10	0	4	25	12	7	0	0	37	3	4	.429	.368
De Wolf, Thomas	L-R	6-3	198	12-22-89	.254	.257	.252	43	138	29	35	3	1	0	16	39	6	1	2	49	7	4	.290	.432
Decena, Joan	R-R	6-3	195	9-9-91	.186	.125	.200	14	43	4	8	2	1	0	5	1	0	0	0	11	0	0	.279	.205
Gomez, Gilbert	R-R	6-3	190	3-8-92	.268	.230	.281	68	239	54	64	15	2	3	41	50	5	2	1	59	35	7	.385	.403
Guillen, Marcus	B-R	5-11	175	5-29-90	.202	.294	.184	49	104	29	21	2	3	0	15	24	1	1	1	37	19	4	.279	.354
Mejia, Humberto	R-R	6-1	195	10-13-90	.191	.167	.198	35	115	11	22	2	1	2	14	5	5	1	1	15	1	2	.278	.254
Perez, Andres	R-R	6-1	189	7-5-89	.375	.571	.333	10	40	7	15	2	0	0	5	3	0	0	0	5	0	1	.425	.419
Pina, Eudy	R-R	6-3	188	4-12-91	.250	.193	.269	63	224	40	56	8	3	6	43	30	11	1	3	77	27	6	.393	.362
Sanchez, Alexander	R-R	6-3	200	11-28-90	.372	.300	.397	47	191	30	71	13	2	4	42	12	5	0	5	19	1	0	.524	.413
Santana, Randoll	R-R	6-0	165	11-12-90	.281	.257	.290	67	256	59	72	10	5	2	33	17	13	2	3	55	47	14	.383	.353
Valdespin, Jordany	L-R	6-0	174	12-23-87	.333	.286	.375	4	15	0	5	0	2	0	5	3	0	0	1	1	1	1	.600	.421

Pitching	B-T	HT	WT	DOB	W	L	ERA	G	GS	CG	SV	IP	H	R	ER	HR	BB	SO	AVG	vLH	vRH	K/9	BB/9
Acosta, Jose	R-R	6-2	205	1-20-90	3	3	4.91	11	0	0	1	22	16	13	12	2	15	15	.213	.286	.185	6.14	6.14
Arias, Martires	R-R	6-7	207	11-10-90	0	0	4.13	16	0	0	0	24	21	21	11	1	21	19	.239	.263	.232	7.13	7.88
Batista, Eudy	L-L	6-1	175	8-6-90	2	0	4.86	14	5	0	0	37	35	25	20	0	20	38	.241	.333	.231	9.24	4.86
Camarena, Marcos	R-R	6-3	202	9-8-90	7	2	1.74	14	12	0	0	67	52	23	13	2	10	57	.212	.247	.198	7.62	1.34
De Jesus, Willy	R-R	6-6	200	3-25-91	0	2	7.71	6	0	0	0	5	7	5	4	0	5	6	.350	.600	.267	11.57	9.64
De Los Santos, Pedro	L-L	5-11	188	6-10-89	0	1	2.35	6	0	0	0	8	3	2	2	0	8	8	.136	.000	.143	9.39	9.39
Febrillet, Lefty	R-R	6-3	175	11-16-89	0	0	2.03	9	0	0	0	13	8	7	3	0	8	10	.160	.167	.158	6.75	5.40
Frias, Darwin	R-R	6-0	192	2-18-92	3	0	4.75	17	3	0	2	42	35	26	22	1	23	57	.232	.286	.216	12.31	4.97
Germen, Gonzalez	R-R	6-1	175	9-23-87	5	0	1.80	8	8	0	0	45	31	11	9	1	3	54	.189	.222	.176	10.80	0.60
Guzman, Edward	R-R	6-4	184	9-13-89	0	0	4.50	1	0	0	0	2	3	1	1	0	0	0	.286	.000	.333	0.00	0.00
Hernandez, Luis	R-R	5-11	168	12-17-90	0	2	0.70	13	0	0	5	38	24	8	3	0	10	25	.182	.206	.173	5.87	2.35
Javier, Yancarlos	L-L	6-3	170	4-7-91	4	0	3.38	12	6	0	0	37	29	17	14	0	19	40	.216	.111	.224	9.64	4.58
Lopez, Adalberto	R-R	6-0	180	8-5-89	1	0	7.94	6	0	0	0	6	9	5	5	0	4	4	.346	.333	.348	6.35	6.35
Mendez, Ismael	L-L	6-1	184	5-23-90	0	1	7.07	4	4	0	0	14	21	14	11	0	6	12	.328	.000	.362	7.71	3.86
Morel, Estarlin	R-R	6-0	185	10-2-89	4	2	2.09	16	4	0	2	47	37	15	11	1	11	44	.214	.213	.214	8.37	2.09
Ortega, Flabio	R-R	6-1	170	8-19-90	5	1	3.50	14	0	0	3	18	15	7	7	1	13	21	.242	.059	.311	10.50	6.50
Robles, Hansel	R-R	5-11	185	8-13-90	5	4	2.91	15	9	0	0	59	47	30	19	0	16	60	.216	.250	.207	9.20	2.45
Rojas, Leonel	L-L	6-4	167	8-19-86	0	0	3.52	2	2	0	0	8	7	5	3	1	7	3	.241	.400	.208	3.52	8.22
Sanchez, Erigson	R-R	6-1	180	11-3-90	1	1	2.53	15	8	0	1	57	54	22	16	0	14	39	.243	.170	.266	6.16	2.21
Soriano, Derlin	R-R	6-2	184	12-6-89	1	1	1.93	8	0	0	1	14	11	11	3	0	9	9	.196	.143	.229	5.79	5.79
Valdez, Santiago	R-R	6-2	210	7-29-87	0	0	0.00	1	0	0	0	1	0	0	0	0	0	2	.000	—	.000	18.00	0.00
Vasquez, Carlos	L-L	5-11	180	9-3-91	5	0	1.85	17	4	0	7	49	31	12	10	1	15	52	.199	.400	.192	9.62	2.77
Villasmil, Edioglis	R-R	6-2	164	4-10-92	0	1	5.79	4	0	0	1	5	3	4	3	0	5	8	.176	.000	.214	15.43	9.64
Yanez, Ernesto	R-R	6-0	162	1-22-90	0	0	0.00	3	0	0	0	6	2	0	0	0	1	4	.111	.000	.133	6.35	1.59

Fielding

Catcher	PCT	G	PO	A	E	DP	PB
Avila	.982	22	137	23	3	1	6
Caba	.978	8	38	7	1	1	0
Cordero	1.000	4	21	1	0	0	0
De Leon	.857	1	6	0	1	0	1
De Leon	.988	16	153	13	2	0	5
Mejia	.979	34	242	39	6	1	5

First Base	PCT	G	PO	A	E	DP
Avila	1.000	11	61	3	0	5
Barrera	1.000	6	62	3	0	4
Caba	—	1	0	0	0	0
De Leon	.972	26	201	10	6	20
Sanchez	.977	37	329	16	8	27

Second Base	PCT	G	PO	A	E	DP
Castillo	1.000	1	0	1	0	0
Cessa	.933	8	18	10	2	5
De La Cruz	.972	67	148	162	9	40
Valdespin	.929	2	6	7	1	1

Third Base	PCT	G	PO	A	E	DP
Avila	—	1	0	0	0	0
Castillo	.971	12	8	26	1	3
Cessa	.910	22	15	46	6	2
De Leon	.912	41	37	77	11	11
Sanchez	1.000	1	0	2	0	0

Shortstop	PCT	G	PO	A	E	DP
Cessa	1.000	1	0	1	0	0

	PCT	G	PO	A	E	DP
De Leon	.936	19	29	59	6	13
Santana	.882	58	105	135	32	29
Valdespin	1.000	2	2	7	0	2

Outfield	PCT	G	PO	A	E	DP
Barrera	.909	17	20	0	2	0
Caba	.800	5	4	0	1	0
Castillo	1.000	2	3	0	0	0
De Wolf	1.000	39	41	3	0	0
Decena	1.000	9	7	0	0	0
Gomez	.950	66	106	7	6	2
Guillen	.962	42	50	0	2	0
Perez	1.000	10	15	0	0	0
Pina	.937	60	86	3	6	0

VSL METS — ROOKIE

VENEZUELAN SUMMER LEAGUE

Batting	B-T	HT	WT	DOB	AVG	vLH	vRH	G	AB	R	H	2B	3B	HR	RBI	BB	HBP	SH	SF	SO	SB	CS	SLG	OBP
Alvarez, Hector	R-R	5-11	170	2-14-91	.248	.182	.265	36	105	13	26	4	0	1	12	11	4	3	0	28	1	0	.314	.342
Batista, Sneider	R-R	5-11	182	9-13-90	.226	.231	.225	40	106	14	24	3	1	1	3	6	3	2	0	18	4	5	.302	.287
Bellorin, Jose	R-R	6-0	160	12-14-90	.287	.233	.303	33	129	21	37	8	2	3	23	8	3	1	0	25	9	2	.450	.343
Castillo, Edwin	R-R	6-0	181	5-30-90	.278	.238	.294	23	72	5	20	4	1	0	8	5	2	0	0	20	1	4	.361	.342
Castillo, Jairo	R-R	6-2	190	1-9-89	.201	.145	.223	65	219	25	44	11	1	9	36	18	1	1	1	101	1	0	.384	.264
Cordero, Albert	R-R	5-11	175	1-14-90	.284	.358	.258	59	208	35	59	5	4	3	34	11	7	0	3	16	2	1	.438	.336
Decuba, Quintin	R-R	6-3	180	9-9-87	.218	.143	.246	24	78	15	17	5	1	3	8	13	4	0	0	29	4	1	.423	.358
Duncan, Dani	R-R	6-0	192	10-30-89	.174	.077	.212	22	46	7	8	0	0	2	4	7	1	0	0	26	3	1	.304	.296
Lorduy, Alejandro	R-R	6-2	182	9-3-91	.202	.206	.200	41	109	10	22	2	0	3	12	8	3	2	1	42	1	1	.303	.273
Marquez, Cesar	R-R	6-0	170	7-16-91	.097	.059	.109	25	72	7	7	1	0	1	6	3	3	1	0	19	2	1	.167	.167
Moreno, Nestor	B-R	5-11	195	6-21-88	.320	.388	.294	68	244	33	78	15	0	1	29	21	4	0	1	48	0	3	.393	.381
Perez, Andres	R-R	6-1	189	7-5-89	.311	.333	.304	67	241	25	75	14	1	5	44	18	1	0	4	47	2	5	.440	.356

	B-T	HT	WT	DOB	AVG	vLH	vRH	G	AB	R	H	2B	3B	HR	RBI	BB	HBP	SH	SF	SO	SB	CS	OBP	SLG
Petit, Jesus	R-R	6-1	189	12-26-91	.228	.238	.224	28	79	8	18	3	0	0	9	3	1	2	0	20	1	0	.266	.265
Pirela, Adrian	R-R	6-0	205	12-23-88	.162	.200	.148	12	37	4	6	2	0	1	3	6	2	0	0	16	0	0	.297	.311
Ponce, Dimas	R-R	5-11	140	1-22-91	.198	.111	.219	33	91	10	18	3	1	0	3	8	1	2	0	21	3	1	.253	.270
Rivero, Nohisglin	R-R	6-0	180	1-26-90	.308	.125	.347	34	91	11	28	0	4	1	4	4	1	1	0	23	7	1	.429	.344
Soto, Breiner	R-R	6-2	147	2-23-90	.298	.286	.302	49	188	30	56	11	6	1	8	8	1	2	0	41	11	5	.436	.330
Tijerina, Ismael	R-R	6-0	165	8-19-89	.276	.310	.263	60	214	36	59	6	2	2	19	23	1	7	1	25	6	5	.350	.347
Tovar, Wilfredo	R-R	5-10	150	8-11-91	.289	.429	.258	12	38	3	11	3	1	0	2	5	0	0	1	3	1	1	.421	.364

Pitching	B-T	HT	WT	DOB	W	L	ERA	G	GS	CG	SV	IP	H	R	ER	HR	BB	SO	AVG	vLH	vRH	K/9	BB/9
Avellones, Carlos	R-R	6-1	193	12-23-90	1	3	3.09	9	8	0	1	35	37	18	12	2	18	14	.287	.303	.281	3.60	4.63
Barreto, Jesus	R-R	6-8	186	9-5-91	2	0	3.81	14	1	0	1	28	28	15	12	3	13	14	.259	.143	.287	4.45	4.13
Castro, Rafael	R-R	6-2	200	8-8-91	0	1	9.39	6	1	0	0	8	11	15	8	0	9	5	.344	.200	.370	5.87	10.57
De Leon, Gabriel	R-R	6-4	205	9-20-90	0	2	8.71	9	0	0	0	21	32	25	20	1	10	12	.360	.308	.381	5.23	4.35
Delgado, Ruben	R-R	6-4	182	8-18-89	1	1	3.52	12	0	0	4	23	31	18	9	0	10	12	.330	.222	.355	4.70	3.91
Diaz, Miller	R-R	6-1	209	6-22-92	2	2	5.02	11	2	0	0	29	28	19	16	1	20	23	.255	.263	.253	7.22	6.28
Gomez, Carlos	R-R	6-1	160	3-30-91	0	0	6.11	9	0	0	1	18	19	16	12	1	9	10	.271	.300	.260	5.09	4.58
Guzman, Edward	R-R	6-4	184	9-13-89	2	2	2.47	14	1	0	2	44	46	18	12	1	11	19	.280	.216	.299	3.92	2.27
Hernandez, Jose	R-R	6-1	210	1-22-89	2	1	2.08	5	5	0	0	26	17	9	6	0	9	29	.189	.263	.169	10.04	3.12
Monroe, Isaac	L-L	5-10	155	10-9-90	1	4	4.50	17	1	0	1	36	37	32	18	0	20	19	.272	.154	.285	4.75	5.00
Peralta, Victor	L-L	5-11	178	7-2-89	1	3	4.17	11	7	0	2	37	37	24	17	2	19	34	.266	.154	.278	8.35	4.66
Perez, Andres E.	R-R	6-2	184	2-8-91	2	6	3.95	14	13	0	0	57	63	38	25	4	17	39	.275	.295	.270	6.16	2.68
Ramirez, Rickys	L-L	5-11	173	4-6-90	3	5	4.76	16	8	0	0	57	59	36	30	2	19	40	.268	.240	.272	6.35	3.02
Rengel, Luis	R-R	6-2	165	3-19-90	0	0	5.14	5	0	0	0	7	11	8	4	0	6	8	.324	.400	.310	10.29	7.71
Romero, Johan	R-R	5-11	200	12-13-89	0	3	3.16	5	5	0	0	26	22	13	9	1	6	18	.220	.211	.222	6.31	2.10
Velasquez, Gustavo	R-R	6-2	191	10-3-91	3	1	4.97	13	1	0	1	29	28	18	16	2	10	12	.272	.359	.219	3.72	3.10
Villasmil, Edioglis	R-R	6-2	164	4-10-92	1	6	4.27	15	7	0	2	59	47	33	28	8	16	54	.218	.217	.218	8.24	2.44
Yanez, Ernesto	R-R	6-0	162	1-22-90	7	1	2.34	14	10	2	0	69	56	20	18	0	24	42	.227	.222	.228	5.45	3.12

Fielding

Catcher	PCT	G	PO	A	E	DP	PB
Alvarez	.972	26	137	35	5	3	3
Cordero	.985	28	155	44	3	3	4
Moreno	.968	15	72	18	3	2	5
Rivero	.948	11	47	8	3	0	3

First Base	PCT	G	PO	A	E	DP
Alvarez	.968	9	58	2	2	11
Castillo	1.000	6	8	0	0	0
Cordero	.984	9	56	6	1	8
Decuba	.990	22	184	9	2	17
Lorduy	1.000	1	1	1	0	0
Moreno	.994	35	306	18	2	19
Pirela	1.000	4	21	0	0	3
Rivero	1.000	1	1	0	0	0

Second Base	PCT	G	PO	A	E	DP
Alvarez	1.000	1	1	0	0	0
Batista	.951	34	62	54	6	12
Bellorin	.939	6	18	13	2	7
Castillo	.932	15	27	28	4	5
Marquez	1.000	1	0	1	0	0
Ponce	.922	18	25	34	5	6
Tijerina	.909	3	6	4	1	0
Tovar	.936	10	20	24	3	9

Third Base	PCT	G	PO	A	E	DP
Bellorin	.833	1	3	2	1	1
Castillo	.800	5	2	10	3	0
Castillo	.850	61	58	117	31	8
Moreno	1.000	1	0	3	0	0
Ponce	.958	9	8	15	1	2
Rivero	—	1	0	0	0	0
Tijerina	.667	2	2	0	1	0

Shortstop	PCT	G	PO	A	E	DP
Bellorin	.939	11	16	30	3	6
Castillo	.750	4	1	2	1	0
Ponce	.900	5	6	12	2	2
Tijerina	.950	55	91	194	15	37
Tovar	.818	2	6	3	2	0

Outfield	PCT	G	PO	A	E	DP
Batista	1.000	1	1	0	0	0
Bellorin	1.000	5	12	0	0	0
Castillo	—	1	0	0	0	0
Decuba	1.000	2	5	0	0	0
Duncan	.955	18	20	1	1	0
Guzman	1.000	1	1	0	0	0
Lorduy	.902	35	50	5	6	1
Marquez	.967	23	27	2	1	1
Perez	.980	66	139	8	3	2
Petit	.973	27	34	2	1	1
Pirela	1.000	8	4	0	0	0
Rivero	.833	3	4	1	1	0
Soto	.904	45	102	2	11	0

New York Yankees

SEASON IN A SENTENCE: New York committed nearly $300 million to free agents in the offseason and opened the new $1.5 billion Yankee Stadium, and the Bronx Bombers bludgeoned opponents with 244 home runs, got enough starting pitching—especially from new ace C.C. Sabathia (19-8, 3.37)—and still had Mariano Rivera to win its 27th World Series championship

HIGH POINT: Alex Rodriguez had never won a championship in 16 major league seasons, and he started the year talking about steroids and rehabilitating a hip injury. His return on May 8 sparked New York, which went 13-15 without him. Rodriguez then had a boffo postseason as the Yankees beat the Twins, Angels and Phillies and dropped just four games in the process, hitting .365 with six home runs. His biggest hit was a ninth-inning double to drive in the go-ahead run off Brad Lidge in Game Five of the World Series, breaking a 4-4 tie and staking the Yankees to a 3-1 series lead.

LOW POINT: A 4-0 loss at Atlanta to rookie Tommy Hanson dropped Chien-Ming Wang to 0-6 and dropped the Yankees a season-high five games back of the Red Sox on June 23. While Wang made just two more starts, depleting the rotation's depth, the Yankees responded, winning 13 of 15 to climb back into contention.

NOTABLE ROOKIES: Center fielder Brett Gardner ranked second on the team with 26 steals and shared time with Melky Cabrera; he batted .270/.345/.379. Lefthander Phil Coke (4-3, 4.50) led the team with 72 appearances out of the bullpen, while righthander Alfredo Aceves ranked fourth on the team in victories while going 10-1, 3.54 and pitching 84 innings.

KEY TRANSACTIONS: Free-agent signees Sabathia and A.J. Burnett made up two-thirds of New York's postseason rotation. Free-agent Mark Teixeira gave the Yankees a Gold Glove defender at first base to go with a team-best .948 OPS, with 39 homers and 122 RBIs also leading the way. Midseason trade acquisition Jerry Hairston provided a versatile reserve with offensive skills.

DOWN ON THE FARM: High Class A Tampa (Florida State) and short-season Staten Island (New York-Penn) joined the parent club with championships. Jesus Montero advanced to Double-A before hitting age 20, batting .337/.389/.562 overall with 17 home runs in 347 at-bats. However, 2007 first-round pick Andrew Brackman struggled (2-12, 5.91).

OPENING DAY PAYROLL: $201,449,189

PLAYERS OF THE YEAR

MAJOR LEAGUE	MINOR LEAGUE
Derek Jeter	**Jesus Montero**
SS	C
.334/.406/.465	(High A/Double-A)
10th All-Star Game,	.337/.389/.562
4th Gold Glove	25 2B, 17 HR

ORGANIZATION LEADERS

BATTING   *Minimum 250 at-bats

MAJORS

*AVG	Derek Jeter	.334
*OPS	Mark Teixeira	.948
HR	Mark Teixeira	39
RBI	Mark Teixeira	122

MINORS

*AVG	Montero, Jesus, Tampa, Trenton	.337
R	Duncan, Shelley, Scranton/Wilkes-Barre	85
H	Nunez, Eduardo, Trenton	160
TB	Duncan, Shelley, Scranton/Wilkes-Barre	247
2B	Adams, David, Charleston/Tampa	40
3B	Sublett, Damon, Tampa	11
HR	Duncan, Shelley, Scranton/Wilkes-Barre	30
RBI	Duncan, Shelley, Scranton/Wilkes-Barre	99
BB	Krum, Austin, Tampa/Trenton	71
SO	Mesa, Melky, Charleston	168
SB	Almonte, Abraham, Charleston	36
*OBP	Russo, Kevin, Scranton/Wilkes-Barre	.397
*SLG	Montero, Jesus, Tampa/Trenton	.562

PITCHING   †Minimum 75 innings

MAJORS

W	C.C. Sabathia	19
†ERA	C.C. Sabathia	3.37
SO	C.C. Sabathia	197

MINORS

W	Phelps, David, Charleston/Tampa	13
L	Three tied at	12
†ERA	McAllister, Zach, Trenton	2.23
G	Venditte, Pat, Charleston/Tampa	49
GS	Bleich, Jeremy, Tampa/Trenton	27
SV	Hovis, Jonathan, Trenton/Tampa	22
	Venditte, Pat, Charleston/Tampa	22
IP	Phelps, David, Charleston/Tampa	151
BB	Brackman, Andrew, Charleston	76
SO	Pendleton, Lance, Tampa/Trenton	130
†AVG	McAllister, Zach, Trenton	.220
	Noesi, Hector, Charleston/Tampa	.220

2009 PERFORMANCE

General Manager: Brian Cashman. **Farm Director:** Mark Newman. **Scouting Director:** Damon Oppenheimer.

Class	Team	League	W	L	PCT	Finish*	Manager(s)
Majors	New York Yankees	American	103	59	.636	1st (14)	Joe Girardi
Triple-A	Scranton/Wilkes-Barre Yankees	International	81	60	.574	3rd (14)	Dave Miley
Double-A	Trenton Thunder	Eastern	69	72	.489	8th (12)	Tony Franklin
High A	Tampa Yankees	Florida State	77	56	.579	†3rd (12)	Luis Sojo
Low A	Charleston RiverDogs	South Atlantic	74	65	.532	4th (16)	Torre Tyson
Short-season	Staten Island Yankees	New York-Penn	47	29	.618	†2nd (14)	Josh Paul
Rookie	GCL Yankees	Gulf Coast	33	27	.550	4th (16)	Jody Reed
Overall 2009 Minor League Record			381	309	.552	2nd (30)	

*Finish in overall standings (No. of teams in league). †League champion.

ORGANIZATION STATISTICS

NEW YORK YANKEES

AMERICAN LEAGUE

Batting	B-T	HT	WT	DOB	AVG	vLH	vRH	G	AB	R	H	2B	3B	HR	RBI	BB	HBP	SH	SF	SO	SB	CS	SLG	OBP
Berroa, Angel	R-R	6-0	195	1-27-78	.136	.111	.154	21	22	6	3	1	0	0	1	0	1	1	0	6	0	0	.182	.174
Cabrera, Melky	B-L	5-11	200	8-11-84	.274	.268	.277	154	485	66	133	28	1	13	68	43	4	4	4	59	10	2	.416	.336
Cano, Robinson	L-R	6-0	205	10-22-82	.320	.309	.326	161	637	103	204	48	2	25	85	30	3	0	4	63	5	7	.520	.352
Cash, Kevin	R-R	6-0	200	12-6-77	.231	.429	.158	10	26	1	6	2	0	0	3	0	1	0	1	5	0	0	.308	.250
Cervelli, Francisco	R-R	6-1	210	3-6-86	.298	.345	.277	42	94	13	28	4	0	1	11	2	0	4	1	11	0	3	.372	.309
Damon, Johnny	L-L	6-2	205	11-5-73	.282	.269	.288	143	550	107	155	36	3	24	82	71	2	2	1	98	12	0	.489	.365
Duncan, Shelley	R-R	6-5	225	9-29-79	.200	.250	.143	11	15	1	3	0	0	0	1	0	0	0	0	5	0	0	.200	.200
Gardner, Brett	L-L	5-10	185	8-24-83	.270	.291	.264	108	248	48	67	6	6	3	23	26	3	6	1	40	26	5	.379	.345
Guzman, Freddy	B-R	5-10	165	1-20-81	.167	1.000	.000	10	6	2	1	0	0	0	1	0	0	0	1	1	4	1	.167	.143
Hairston Jr., Jerry	R-R	5-10	190	5-29-76	.237	.216	.256	45	76	15	18	5	0	2	12	11	3	2	1	8	0	1	.382	.352
Hinske, Eric	L-R	6-1	235	8-5-77	.226	.211	.231	39	84	13	19	3	0	7	14	10	2	0	2	25	1	0	.512	.316
Jeter, Derek	R-R	6-3	195	6-26-74	.334	.395	.311	153	634	107	212	27	1	18	66	72	5	4	1	90	30	5	.465	.406
Matsui, Hideki	L-R	6-2	210	6-12-74	.274	.282	.271	142	456	62	125	21	1	28	90	64	4	0	2	75	0	1	.509	.367
Miranda, Juan	L-L	6-0	220	4-25-83	.333	.500	.286	8	9	2	3	0	0	1	3	0	0	0	0	4	0	0	.667	.333
Molina, Jose	R-R	6-2	235	6-3-75	.217	.220	.216	52	138	15	30	4	0	1	11	14	1	1	1	28	0	0	.268	.292
Nady, Xavier	R-R	6-1	185	11-14-78	.286	.333	.273	7	28	4	8	4	0	0	2	1	0	0	0	6	0	0	.429	.310
Pena, Ramiro	B-R	5-11	165	7-18-85	.287	.120	.333	69	115	17	33	6	1	1	10	5	0	1	0	20	4	1	.383	.317
Posada, Jorge	B-R	6-2	215	8-17-71	.285	.290	.282	111	383	55	109	25	0	22	81	48	2	0	5	101	1	0	.522	.363
Ransom, Cody	R-R	6-2	215	2-17-76	.190	.158	.200	31	79	11	15	9	1	0	10	7	0	0	0	25	2	0	.329	.256
Rodriguez, Alex	R-R	6-3	230	7-27-75	.286	.277	.289	124	444	78	127	17	1	30	100	80	8	0	3	97	14	2	.532	.402
Swisher, Nick	B-L	5-11	210	11-25-80	.249	.244	.251	150	498	84	124	35	1	29	82	97	3	3	6	126	0	0	.498	.371
Teixeira, Mark	B-R	6-3	220	4-11-80	.292	.305	.287	156	609	103	178	43	3	39	122	81	12	0	5	114	2	0	.565	.383

Pitching	B-T	HT	WT	DOB	W	L	ERA	G	GS	CG	SV	IP	H	R	ER	HR	BB	SO	AVG	vLH	vRH	K/9	BB/9
Aceves, Alfredo	R-R	6-3	220	12-8-82	10	1	3.54	43	1	0	1	84	69	36	33	10	16	69	.220	.212	.228	7.39	1.71
Albaladejo, Jonathan	R-R	6-5	260	10-30-82	5	1	5.24	32	0	0	0	34	41	23	20	6	16	21	.306	.258	.353	5.50	4.19
Bruney, Brian	R-R	6-3	235	2-17-82	5	0	3.92	44	0	0	0	39	36	17	17	6	23	36	.243	.214	.269	8.31	5.31
Burnett, A.J.	R-R	6-4	230	1-3-77	13	9	4.04	33	33	1	0	207	193	99	93	25	97	195	.247	.217	.282	8.48	4.22
Chamberlain, Joba	R-R	6-2	230	9-23-85	9	6	4.75	32	31	0	0	157	167	94	83	21	76	133	.274	.266	.282	7.61	4.35
Claggett, Anthony	B-R	6-3	195	7-15-84	0	0	33.75	2	0	0	0	1	11	10	10	2	4	3	.579	.667	.500	10.13	13.50
Coke, Phil	L-L	6-1	210	7-19-82	4	3	4.50	72	0	0	2	60	44	34	30	10	20	49	.209	.195	.227	7.35	3.00
Dunn, Mike	L-L	6-1	195	5-23-85	0	0	6.75	4	0	0	0	4	3	3	3	1	5	5	.200	.000	.273	11.25	11.25
Gaudin, Chad	R-R	5-10	190	3-24-83	2	0	3.43	11	6	0	0	42	41	16	16	7	20	34	.252	.301	.211	7.29	4.29
Hughes, Phil	R-R	6-5	240	6-24-86	8	3	3.03	51	7	0	3	86	68	31	29	8	28	96	.217	.257	.184	10.05	2.93
Kennedy, Ian	R-R	6-0	195	12-19-84	0	0	0.00	1	0	0	0	1	0	0	0	0	2	1	.000	.000	.000	9.00	18.00
Marte, Damaso	L-L	6-2	215	2-14-75	1	3	9.45	21	0	0	0	13	15	14	14	3	6	13	.278	.120	.414	8.78	4.05
Melancon, Mark	R-R	6-2	215	3-28-85	0	1	3.86	13	0	0	0	16	13	8	7	0	10	10	.217	.276	.161	5.51	5.51
Mitre, Sergio	R-R	6-3	225	2-16-81	3	3	6.79	12	9	0	0	52	71	45	39	10	13	32	.321	.421	.246	5.57	2.26
Pettitte, Andy	L-L	6-5	225	6-15-72	14	8	4.16	32	32	0	0	195	193	101	90	20	76	148	.259	.282	.249	6.84	3.51
Ramirez, Edwar	R-R	6-3	165	3-28-81	0	0	5.73	20	0	0	0	22	25	15	14	6	18	22	.281	.302	.250	9.00	7.36
Rivera, Mariano	R-R	6-2	185	11-29-69	3	3	1.76	66	0	0	44	66	48	14	13	7	12	72	.197	.182	.211	9.77	1.63
Robertson, David	R-R	5-11	190	4-9-85	2	1	3.30	45	0	0	1	44	36	19	16	4	23	63	.216	.189	.237	12.98	4.74
Sabathia, C.C.	L-R	6-7	290	7-21-80	19	8	3.37	34	34	2	0	230	197	96	86	18	67	197	.232	.198	.242	7.71	2.62
Tomko, Brett	R-R	6-4	220	4-7-73	1	2	5.23	15	0	0	0	21	19	12	12	5	7	11	.247	.152	.318	4.79	3.05
2-team total (6 Oakland)					5	3	3.77	21	6	1	0	57	50	24	24	12	13	33	—	—	—	5.18	2.04
Towers, Josh	R-R	6-1	185	2-26-77	0	0	3.38	2	0	0	0	5	6	3	2	0	1	2	.273	.091	.455	3.38	1.69
Veras, Jose	R-R	6-5	235	10-20-80	3	1	5.96	25	0	0	0	26	23	17	17	5	14	18	.235	.292	.180	6.31	4.91
2-team total (22 Cleveland)					4	3	5.19	47	0	0	0	50	42	33	29	8	28	40	—	—	—	7.15	5.01
Wang, Chien-Ming	R-R	6-3	230	3-31-80	1	6	9.64	12	9	0	0	42	66	46	45	7	19	29	.365	.394	.329	6.21	4.07

Fielding

Catcher	PCT	G	PO	A	E	DP	PB						First Base	PCT	G	PO	A	E	DP
Cash	1.000	10	57	10	0	1	0	Molina	.997	49	366	21	1	1	3	Miranda	1.000	8	19	1	0	2
Cervelli	.995	40	207	14	1	1	0	Posada	.990	100	648	48	7	6	8	Molina	1.000	3	4	2	0	1

Posada	1.000	2	3	2	0	0
Ransom	1.000	1	5	2	0	1
Swisher	.989	20	89	5	1	7
Teixeira	.997	152	1222	49	4	110

Second Base	PCT	G	PO	A	E	DP
Cano	.984	161	308	424	12	96
Hairston Jr.	1.000	3	3	2	0	0
Pena	1.000	8	7	10	0	2
Ransom	1.000	1	4	2	0	1

Third Base	PCT	G	PO	A	E	DP
Berroa	.880	16	6	16	3	3

Hairston Jr.	.920	16	3	20	2	2
Hinske	1.000	10	3	3	0	0
Molina	—	1	0	0	0	0
Pena	.952	27	10	30	2	5
Ransom	.911	23	10	31	4	2
Rodriguez	.967	116	66	200	9	17

Shortstop	PCT	G	PO	A	E	DP
Hairston Jr.	1.000	11	6	10	0	2
Jeter	.986	150	206	340	8	75
Pena	.953	34	21	40	3	9
Ransom	1.000	3	2	5	0	0

Outfield	PCT	G	PO	A	E	DP
Cabrera	.990	151	300	3	3	1
Damon	.978	132	220	6	5	2
Duncan	1.000	8	5	0	0	0
Gardner	.990	99	186	3	2	2
Guzman	1.000	7	4	0	0	0
Hairston Jr.	1.000	19	22	1	0	0
Hinske	1.000	24	32	0	0	0
Nady	1.000	6	10	0	0	0
Swisher	.980	134	249	2	5	1

SCRANTON/WILKES-BARRE YANKEES

TRIPLE-A

INTERNATIONAL LEAGUE

Batting	B-T	HT	WT	DOB	AVG	vLH	vRH	G	AB	R	H	2B	3B	HR	RBI	BB	HBP	SH	SF	SO	SB	CS	SLG	OBP
Bernier, Doug	R-R	5-11	175	6-24-80	.181	.160	.192	79	227	33	41	9	2	0	20	34	7	4	1	71	1	0	.238	.305
Berroa, Angel	R-R	6-0	195	1-27-78	.316	.471	.250	14	57	7	18	4	0	2	13	4	1	0	1	7	0	2	.491	.365
2-team total (2 Buffalo)					.308	—	—	16	65	7	20	4	0	2	14	4	1	0	1	9	0	2	.462	.352
Cash, Kevin	R-R	6-0	200	12-6-77	.221	.133	.245	23	68	7	15	1	0	2	9	9	0	0	0	23	0	0	.324	.312
Cervelli, Francisco	R-R	6-1	210	3-6-86	.275	.231	.302	21	69	7	19	5	0	1	7	3	1	1	1	13	0	2	.391	.311
Corona, Reegie	B-R	5-11	160	11-7-86	.200	.175	.208	44	160	13	32	7	0	3	14	9	1	3	4	20	4	0	.300	.241
Curtis, Colin	L-L	6-1	200	2-1-85	.235	.207	.250	70	251	29	59	10	0	6	29	24	1	1	2	46	1	2	.347	.302
De Caster, Yurendell	R-R	6-0	215	9-26-79	.301	.379	.258	53	186	23	56	12	0	5	21	13	7	0	0	28	3	0	.446	.369
Duncan, Shelley	R-R	6-5	225	9-29-79	.277	.296	.269	123	452	85	125	30	1	30	99	64	6	0	5	94	2	0	.546	.370
Duncan, Eric	L-R	6-3	195	12-7-84	.204	.226	.197	95	323	35	66	12	1	4	24	16	1	2	3	69	1	0	.285	.242
Gardner, Brett	L-L	5-10	185	8-24-83	.091	.000	.100	4	11	3	1	0	0	0	0	5	0	0	0	1	3	0	.091	.375
Guzman, Freddy	B-R	5-10	165	1-20-81	.286	.222	.333	6	21	7	6	0	1	0	1	5	0	0	0	5	7	0	.381	.423
3-team total (20 Norfolk, 62 Pawtucket)					.224	—	—	88	308	39	69	7	4	2	14	23	0	3	2	49	41	7	.292	.276
Jackson, Austin	R-R	6-1	185	2-1-87	.300	.300	.299	132	504	67	151	23	9	4	65	40	6	1	6	123	24	4	.405	.354
Leone, Justin	R-R	6-1	200	3-9-77	.178	.148	.191	55	185	17	33	11	0	4	28	21	1	0	5	59	2	0	.303	.259
Linden, Todd	B-R	6-3	220	6-30-80	.312	.270	.328	60	237	43	74	17	5	7	42	27	1	0	3	61	5	0	.515	.381
Malec, Chris	R-R	5-11	195	8-28-82	.226	.133	.255	19	62	8	14	1	0	1	13	6	1	0	1	10	1	0	.290	.300
Mendoza, Carlos	B-R	6-0	191	11-27-79	.222	.250	.200	3	9	1	2	1	0	0	1	0	0	0	3	0	0	.333	.300
Miranda, Juan	L-L	6-0	220	4-25-83	.290	.289	.290	122	438	74	127	30	2	19	82	55	3	0	6	101	1	0	.498	.369
Molina, Jose	R-R	6-2	235	6-3-75	.250	.500	.000	2	4	0	1	1	0	0	1	1	0	0	0	0	0	0	.500	.400
Nady, Xavier	R-R	6-1	185	11-14-78	.200	.333	.000	2	5	0	1	1	0	0	1	0	0	0	0	1	0	0	.400	.333
Nunez, Luis	R-R	5-11	160	11-21-86	.214	.190	.224	25	70	11	15	2	0	0	4	4	0	1	0	7	2	1	.243	.257
Pena, Ramiro	B-R	5-11	165	7-18-85	.231	.288	.202	43	156	18	36	9	0	2	9	18	0	6	0	28	5	1	.327	.310
Peterson, Brian	R-R	6-2	225	10-22-78	.176	.250	.111	6	17	3	3	1	0	0	1	4	0	0	0	7	0	0	.235	.333
2-team total (14 Louisville)					.143	—	—	20	49	6	7	2	0	1	3	13	1	0	0	19	0	0	.245	.333
Pilittere, P.J.	R-R	6-0	215	11-23-81	.244	.250	.242	28	86	8	21	6	0	1	9	3	1	1	2	9	0	0	.349	.272
Ransom, Cody	R-R	6-2	190	2-17-76	.240	.273	.230	31	96	24	23	7	1	3	16	19	2	0	3	22	0	0	.427	.367
Robnett, Richie	L-L	5-10	210	9-17-83	.000	—	.000	2	2	0	0	0	0	0	0	0	0	0	0	2	0	0	.000	.000
Rodriguez, John	L-L	6-0	205	1-20-78	.261	.265	.259	93	322	47	84	18	2	14	59	37	10	2	3	85	0	2	.460	.352
Russo, Kevin	R-R	5-11	190	7-8-84	.326	.283	.341	90	353	51	115	18	2	5	31	42	3	3	5	55	13	7	.431	.397
Stewart, Chris	R-R	6-4	210	2-19-82	.280	.397	.232	78	232	33	65	11	0	1	18	25	11	5	1	29	1	1	.341	.375

Pitching	B-T	HT	WT	DOB	W	L	ERA	G	GS	CG	SV	IP	H	R	ER	HR	BB	SO	AVG	vLH	vRH	K/9	BB/9
Aceves, Alfredo	R-R	6-3	220	12-8-82	2	0	3.80	4	4	0	0	24	18	11	10	3	5	18	.202	.147	.236	6.85	1.90
Albaladejo, Jonathan	R-R	6-5	260	10-30-82	3	0	1.75	27	0	0	11	36	25	8	7	4	3	26	.189	.216	.173	6.50	0.75
Arbiso, Cory	R-R	6-3	210	4-21-86	0	0	6.00	1	1	0	0	6	4	4	4	1	4	1	.182	.200	.176	1.50	6.00
Bruney, Brian	R-R	6-3	235	2-17-82	0	0	9.00	1	1	0	0	1	2	1	1	0	0	1	.400	.250	1.000	9.00	0.00
Bush, Paul	R-R	6-1	195	10-5-79	2	2	4.86	7	2	0	0	17	13	10	9	1	7	20	.217	.150	.250	10.80	3.78
Claggett, Anthony	B-R	6-3	195	7-15-84	7	7	3.07	39	5	0	4	82	78	32	28	6	32	43	.252	.264	.243	4.72	3.51
Cox, J.B.	L-R	6-3	205	5-13-84	0	1	7.08	12	1	0	1	20	29	18	16	2	9	11	.326	.314	.333	4.87	3.98
Dunn, Mike	L-L	6-1	195	5-23-85	1	0	2.22	12	0	0	0	20	17	5	5	1	14	23	.230	.154	.271	10.35	6.30
Fossum, Casey	L-L	6-1	160	1-6-78	3	3	3.38	10	10	0	0	51	50	24	19	7	16	43	.258	.288	.246	7.64	2.84
2-team total (2 Buffalo)					3	3	2.92	12	12	0	0	62	55	25	20	7	21	55	—	—	—	8.03	3.06
Hacker, Eric	B-R	6-1	210	3-26-83	0	1	7.88	3	3	0	0	16	19	14	14	3	4	12	.311	.333	.297	6.75	2.25
2-team total (21 Indianapolis)					5	6	4.49	24	24	0	0	132	154	71	66	9	50	94	—	—	—	6.39	3.40
Hirsh, Jason	R-R	6-8	250	2-20-82	4	0	1.35	6	6	0	0	27	24	4	4	2	6	21	.238	.237	.238	7.09	2.03
Hughes, Phil	R-R	6-5	240	6-24-86	3	0	1.86	3	3	0	0	19	17	4	4	2	3	19	.233	.292	.204	8.84	1.40
Igawa, Kei	L-L	6-1	170	7-13-79	10	8	4.15	26	26	1	0	145	165	75	67	21	40	105	.284	.189	.320	6.50	2.48
Jackson, Steven	R-R	6-5	215	3-15-82	0	0	1.88	7	1	0	1	14	16	3	3	1	3	8	.276	.238	.297	5.02	1.88
2-team total (12 Indianapolis)					1	0	4.45	19	1	0	1	32	39	17	16	2	8	25	—	—	—	6.96	2.23
Johnson, Jason	R-R	6-6	225	10-27-73	2	2	5.50	7	7	0	0	38	49	27	23	4	16	14	.308	.254	.348	3.35	3.82
Kennedy, Ian	R-R	6-0	195	12-19-84	1	0	1.59	4	4	0	0	23	18	5	4	0	7	25	.220	.289	.159	9.93	2.78
Kontos, George	R-R	6-3	215	6-12-85	3	4	3.35	9	9	1	0	51	44	24	19	6	21	39	.229	.250	.213	6.88	3.71
Kroenke, Zach	R-L	6-2	210	4-21-84	7	1	1.99	36	2	0	4	72	54	24	16	4	30	55	.213	.186	.226	6.84	3.73
Marte, Damaso	L-L	6-2	215	2-14-75	0	1	2.45	11	0	0	0	11	10	3	3	2	4	9	.244	.160	.304	7.36	3.27
Melancon, Mark	R-R	6-2	215	3-28-85	4	0	2.89	32	0	0	3	53	37	22	17	3	11	54	.196	.218	.180	9.17	1.87
Mitre, Sergio	R-R	6-3	225	2-16-81	3	1	2.40	7	7	0	0	45	40	13	12	3	5	35	.241	.324	.184	7.00	1.00
Nova, Ivan	R-R	6-4	210	1-12-87	1	4	5.10	12	12	1	0	67	72	39	38	4	28	43	.285	.292	.278	5.78	3.76

	B-T	HT	WT	DOB	W	L	ERA	G	GS	CG	SV	IP	H	R	ER	HR	BB	SO	AVG	vLH	vRH	K/9	BB/9
Ortiz, Russ	R-R	6-1	215	6-5-74	2	1	1.59	3	3	0	0	17	14	4	3	1	8	12	.212	.194	.229	6.35	4.24
Prihoda, Luke	R-R	6-5	230	8-10-84	1	0	1.69	2	0	0	0	5	5	1	1	0	1	4	.250	.500	.188	6.75	1.69
Ramirez, Edwar	R-R	6-3	165	3-28-81	1	5	3.18	29	0	0	4	51	39	19	18	3	16	62	.205	.194	.211	10.94	2.82
Robertson, David	R-R	5-11	190	4-9-85	0	3	1.84	8	0	0	0	2	15	10	7	3	0	6	25	.196	.100	.258	15.34	3.68
Sanchez, Humberto	R-R	6-6	270	5-28-83	2	0	0.00	3	0	0	0	5	2	0	0	0	4	6	.133	.000	.182	10.80	7.20
Sanchez, Romulo	R-R	6-5	260	4-28-84	5	5	4.04	19	13	0	0	65	66	31	29	3	34	64	.266	.282	.255	8.91	4.73
2-team total (10 Indianapolis)					6	5	4.09	29	13	0	0	77	77	37	35	4	39	79	—	—	—	9.23	4.56
Sanit, Amaury	R-R	5-11	187	7-4-79	0	3	4.13	19	0	0	0	24	27	12	11	2	7	13	.290	.182	.350	4.88	2.63
Stephens, Jay	R-R	6-5	200	10-10-84	1	1	5.40	3	1	0	0	7	7	9	4	2	5	8	.241	.250	.235	10.80	6.75
Tomko, Brett	R-R	6-4	220	4-7-73	1	0	0.64	10	0	0	4	14	8	1	1	1	4	17	.163	.238	.107	10.93	2.57
Towers, Josh	R-R	6-1	185	2-26-77	7	6	2.74	19	18	0	0	102	89	32	31	13	24	55	.239	.223	.254	4.87	2.12
2-team total (1 Syracuse)					7	6	3.05	20	18	0	0	103	95	36	35	13	24	55	—	—	—	4.79	2.09
Valdez, Jose	R-R	6-4	186	1-22-83	2	1	4.19	9	0	0	0	19	23	9	9	2	10	18	.307	.433	.222	8.38	4.66
Wang, Chien-Ming	R-R	6-3	230	3-31-80	1	0	0.00	2	2	1	0	13	7	0	0	0	3	7	.159	.182	.136	4.85	2.08
Whelan, Kevin	R-R	6-0	200	1-8-84	0	0	2.84	14	0	0	1	13	7	4	4	0	13	22	.159	.286	.100	15.63	9.24
Williams, Jeff	R-R	6-5	220	8-24-83	0	0	0.00	1	0	0	0	2	0	0	0	0	0	0	.000	.000	.000	0.00	0.00
Wordekemper, Eric	R-R	6-1	200	8-8-83	2	0	4.32	10	0	0	1	17	19	8	8	2	2	12	.284	.455	.200	6.48	1.08

Fielding

Catcher	PCT	G	PO	A	E	DP	PB
Cash	1.000	22	146	10	0	1	3
Cervelli	.981	21	140	19	3	2	2
Molina	1.000	2	8	0	0	0	0
Peterson	.968	6	27	3	1	1	0
Pilittere	.987	25	138	17	2	1	1
Stewart	.991	76	495	51	5	9	7

First Base	PCT	G	PO	A	E	DP
De Caster	1.000	4	31	2	0	2
Duncan	1.000	5	43	4	0	3
Duncan	.992	16	117	11	1	16
Malec	1.000	2	19	1	0	1
Mendoza	1.000	1	8	0	0	0
Miranda	.991	116	971	80	10	98
Ransom	1.000	2	10	1	0	1

Second Base	PCT	G	PO	A	E	DP
Bernier	1.000	17	25	37	0	9
Berroa	1.000	2	3	7	0	0
Corona	.988	19	35	49	1	14
De Caster	1.000	2	3	6	0	0
Leone	.929	3	7	6	1	0
Malec	1.000	4	2	5	0	2
Mendoza	.917	2	4	7	1	2
Nunez	.975	17	34	43	2	9
Pena	.979	11	19	27	1	4
Ransom	1.000	6	5	15	0	3
Russo	.970	67	117	171	9	42

Third Base	PCT	G	PO	A	E	DP
Bernier	1.000	3	0	3	0	0
Berroa	1.000	1	3	3	0	0
Cash	.500	1	0	1	1	0
De Caster	.976	38	30	51	2	4
Duncan	.910	37	17	74	9	6
Leone	.916	34	17	59	7	8
Malec	.944	7	3	14	1	2
Nunez	1.000	3	4	2	0	2
Pena	1.000	3	5	6	0	1
Ransom	.880	11	6	16	3	3
Russo	.940	18	13	34	3	3

Shortstop	PCT	G	PO	A	E	DP
Bernier	.979	60	74	156	5	33
Berroa	.944	10	15	19	2	4
Corona	.941	25	44	68	7	18
Leone	.950	18	23	34	3	9
Nunez	1.000	3	0	6	0	1
Pena	.990	22	31	72	1	13
Ransom	.921	10	11	24	3	7
Russo	1.000	6	1	15	0	2

Outfield	PCT	G	PO	A	E	DP
Curtis	.983	70	167	5	3	2
Duncan	.986	80	134	7	2	3
Duncan	.974	23	36	1	1	0
Gardner	1.000	3	9	0	0	0
Guzman	1.000	6	11	1	0	0
Jackson	.993	132	266	5	2	1
Leone	—	1	0	0	0	0
Linden	.982	53	106	3	2	1
Nady	—	2	0	0	0	0
Pena	1.000	7	15	0	0	0
Robnett	—	1	0	0	0	0
Rodriguez	.989	57	86	3	1	0

TRENTON THUNDER   DOUBLE-A

EASTERN LEAGUE

Batting	B-T	HT	WT	DOB	AVG	vLH	vRH	G	AB	R	H	2B	3B	HR	RBI	BB	HBP	SH	SF	SO	SB	CS	SLG	OBP
Anson, Kyle	B-R	6-0	200	4-21-83	.227	.185	.248	57	163	23	37	9	0	2	24	36	4	0	3	33	1	0	.319	.374
Baker, Ryan J.	R-R	5-9	205	11-9-84	.125	1.000	.067	8	16	0	2	0	0	0	2	0	0	0	0	3	0	0	.125	.222
Cervelli, Francisco	R-R	6-1	210	3-6-86	.190	.333	.140	16	58	8	11	1	0	2	7	6	0	0	0	13	0	0	.310	.266
Cooper, James	L-R	5-10	190	2-18-84	.240	.292	.220	81	258	42	62	12	3	1	31	22	11	1	0	27	2	2	.322	.326
Corona, Reegie	B-R	5-11	160	11-7-86	.287	.242	.308	85	307	56	88	21	2	3	26	56	1	3	1	50	12	4	.397	.397
Curtis, Colin	L-L	6-1	200	2-1-85	.268	.354	.230	56	213	28	57	14	4	1	19	20	5	1	1	37	7	0	.385	.343
Cusick, Matt	L-R	5-10	190	5-5-86	.240	.216	.254	28	96	9	23	4	0	0	9	10	2	5	0	16	0	1	.281	.324
Fortenberry, Seth	L-L	6-2	175	9-1-83	.160	.160	.160	38	125	12	20	6	3	0	8	15	2	1	1	40	5	1	.256	.259
Gil, Jose	R-R	6-0	170	9-4-86	.194	.313	.100	12	36	2	7	2	0	2	4	0	0	1	7	0	0	.417	.194
Gonzalez, Edwar	R-R	5-10	200	1-1-83	.232	.298	.205	115	413	46	96	26	1	4	37	30	9	0	4	93	7	3	.329	.296
Hall, Noah	R-R	5-11	205	6-9-77	.245	.300	.208	59	200	29	49	7	3	3	33	21	3	1	4	23	5	2	.355	.320
Krum, Austin	L-L	6-0	190	1-19-86	.234	.244	.231	77	290	43	68	14	5	2	24	36	4	5	6	68	11	2	.338	.321
Malec, Chris	B-R	5-11	195	8-28-82	.279	.193	.320	117	430	42	120	23	2	8	56	42	8	0	4	63	0	1	.398	.351
Mendoza, Carlos	R-R	6-0	191	11-27-79	.286	.200	.500	7	14	2	4	1	0	0	1	0	0	0	0	3	0	0	.357	.286
Molina, Jose	R-R	6-2	235	6-3-75	.000	.000	.000	3	7	0	0	0	0	0	0	2	1	0	0	4	0	0	.000	.300
Montero, Jesus	R-R	6-4	225	11-28-89	.317	.308	.322	44	167	19	53	10	0	9	33	14	0	0	0	21	0	0	.539	.370
Nunez, Eduardo	R-R	6-0	155	6-15-87	.322	.351	.309	123	497	70	160	26	1	9	55	22	1	4	4	63	19	7	.433	.349
Pilittere, P.J.	R-R	6-0	215	11-23-81	.198	.138	.224	27	96	5	19	3	0	0	8	7	1	0	0	8	0	0	.229	.260
Robnett, Richie	L-L	5-10	210	9-17-83	.269	.367	.246	46	156	15	42	11	2	2	12	12	0	0	0	36	2	2	.404	.321
Rye, Jack	L-R	6-1	200	3-8-86	.111	.250	.000	3	9	0	1	1	0	0	0	2	1	0	0	3	0	0	.222	.333
Santana, Francisco	L-L	5-10	170	6-18-88	.000	.000	.000	5	7	2	0	0	0	0	0	0	0	0	0	2	0	0	.000	.000
Smith, Kevin	L-R	6-1	215	1-15-84	.247	.235	.250	48	158	19	39	7	1	2	14	10	1	0	0	44	0	1	.342	.296
Snyder, Justin	L-R	5-9	190	4-8-86	.195	.152	.213	94	262	25	51	9	0	3	29	29	2	4	1	49	1	1	.263	.279
Vazquez, Jorge Alberto	R-R	6-2	230	3-15-82	.329	.270	.352	57	225	30	74	15	1	13	56	8	3	0	2	45	0	0	.578	.357
Vechionacci, Marcos	B-R	6-2	170	8-7-86	.213	.328	.168	122	422	44	90	18	1	10	43	35	4	0	3	113	0	0	.332	.278

Pitching	B-T	HT	WT	DOB	W	L	ERA	G	GS	CG	SV	IP	H	R	ER	HR	BB	SO	AVG	vLH	vRH	K/9	BB/9
Arias, Wilkins	L-L	6-1	150	11-4-80	5	4	3.65	48	2	0	0	62	53	26	25	4	22	66	.231	.183	.275	9.63	3.21
Bartleski, Philip	R-R	6-7	240	4-22-83	0	1	12.00	2	0	0	0	3	6	4	4	0	1	3	.429	.400	.444	9.00	3.00
Bleich, Jeremy	L-L	6-2	195	6-18-87	3	6	6.65	13	13	0	0	65	84	54	48	6	34	60	.318	.293	.331	8.31	4.71

Pitching	B-T	HT	WT	DOB	W	L	ERA	G	GS	CG	SV	IP	H	R	ER	HR	BB	SO	AVG	vLH	vRH	K/9	BB/9
Bruney, Brian	R-R	6-3	235	2-17-82	0	0	0.00	1	1	0	0	1	0	0	0	0	0	0	.000	.000	—	0.00	0.00
Bush, Paul	R-R	6-1	195	10-5-79	1	1	1.33	5	5	0	0	20	8	3	3	1	11	23	.119	.158	.069	10.18	4.87
Castillo, Noel	R-R	6-1	160	10-5-83	0	0	11.25	6	0	0	0	8	11	10	10	1	10	12	.314	.300	.333	13.50	11.25
Cox, J.B.	L-R	6-3	205	5-13-84	0	2	8.31	5	0	0	0	4	5	4	4	1	6	4	.278	.300	.250	8.31	12.46
De La Rosa, Wilkin	L-L	6-0	185	2-21-85	4	5	3.48	16	16	0	0	83	67	37	32	11	41	77	.221	.159	.255	8.38	4.46
Duff, Grant	R-R	6-6	210	12-19-82	4	2	3.22	21	0	0	1	36	30	15	13	1	16	37	.222	.246	.197	9.17	3.96
Dunn, Mike	L-L	6-1	195	5-23-85	3	3	3.71	26	0	0	2	53	41	23	22	3	32	76	.211	.232	.196	12.83	5.40
Garcia, Christian	R-R	6-5	215	8-24-85	2	0	0.71	5	5	0	0	25	15	3	2	1	17	24	.172	.159	.186	8.53	6.04
Hacker, Eric	B-R	6-1	210	3-26-83	1	1	4.11	3	3	0	0	15	16	10	7	0	7	8	.281	.250	.320	4.70	4.11
Horne, Alan	R-R	6-4	195	1-5-83	0	3	11.15	5	4	0	0	15	25	21	19	3	16	13	.352	.469	.256	7.63	9.39
Hovis, Jonathan	R-R	5-11	185	12-27-83	0	1	4.91	2	0	0	0	4	4	3	2	1	1	4	.250	.500	.100	9.82	2.45
Johnson, Jason	R-R	6-6	225	10-27-73	0	2	14.54	2	2	0	0	9	20	14	14	3	4	8	.465	.458	.474	8.31	4.15
Kontos, George	R-R	6-3	215	6-12-85	1	1	2.66	4	4	0	0	20	19	7	6	0	9	24	.235	.256	.211	10.62	3.98
McAllister, Zach	R-R	6-6	230	12-8-87	7	5	2.23	22	22	0	0	121	98	39	30	4	33	96	.220	.223	.216	7.14	2.45
Nova, Ivan	R-R	6-4	210	1-12-87	5	4	2.36	12	12	0	0	72	65	27	19	3	31	47	.244	.188	.301	5.85	3.86
Olbrychowski, Adam	R-R	6-3	205	9-7-86	0	0	0.00	1	0	0	0	1	2	0	0	0	0	0	.400	.250	1.000	0.00	0.00
Pendleton, Lance	L-R	6-3	205	9-10-83	1	3	4.47	8	8	0	0	44	40	25	22	4	15	43	.241	.273	.205	8.73	3.05
Pope, Ryan	R-R	6-3	200	5-21-86	5	12	4.78	26	25	0	0	141	155	91	75	7	34	106	.277	.242	.315	6.75	2.17
Sanchez, Humberto	R-R	6-6	270	5-28-83	2	0	3.72	12	0	0	1	19	13	11	8	3	8	19	.183	.152	.211	8.84	3.72
Sanit, Amaury	R-R	5-11	187	7-4-79	1	2	2.95	21	0	0	10	21	13	7	7	1	8	18	.186	.143	.229	7.59	3.38
Schmidt, Josh	R-R	6-4	175	11-14-82	8	4	1.61	46	5	0	0	84	57	16	15	2	38	96	.196	.240	.152	10.33	4.09
Stephens, Jay	R-R	6-5	200	10-10-84	1	1	2.98	13	8	0	0	45	40	17	15	3	14	21	.240	.240	.239	4.17	2.78
Texeira, Kanekoa	R-R	6-0	210	2-6-86	9	6	2.84	41	6	0	2	101	90	39	32	7	43	88	.236	.238	.234	7.82	3.82
Valdez, Jose	R-R	6-4	186	1-22-83	1	1	3.05	34	0	0	10	38	32	17	13	2	23	42	.232	.197	.269	9.86	5.40
Whelan, Kevin	R-R	6-0	200	1-8-84	4	0	2.63	30	0	0	2	55	38	17	16	1	28	63	.200	.250	.144	10.37	4.61
Wordekemper, Eric	R-R	6-1	200	8-8-83	1	2	3.00	28	0	0	1	42	31	15	14	3	13	32	.204	.243	.171	6.86	2.79

Fielding

Catcher	PCT	G	PO	A	E	DP	PB
Anson	.982	56	390	42	8	11	7
Baker	1.000	8	48	6	0	0	0
Cervelli	.967	16	133	14	5	1	1
Gil	.988	11	77	6	1	0	3
Molina	1.000	2	9	1	0	0	0
Montero	1.000	33	261	19	0	1	8
Pilittere	1.000	26	214	8	0	1	3

First Base	PCT	G	PO	A	E	DP
Malec	.995	68	507	58	3	61
Mendoza	1.000	4	9	0	0	1
Smith	.983	36	257	29	5	26
Snyder	1.000	3	7	1	0	0

	PCT	G	PO	A	E	DP
Vazquez	.977	38	313	21	8	25

Second Base	PCT	G	PO	A	E	DP
Corona	.982	69	133	188	6	47
Cusick	1.000	2	35	64	0	8
Malec	.966	14	21	35	2	7
Snyder	.976	44	82	118	5	35

Third Base	PCT	G	PO	A	E	DP
Malec	.968	13	7	23	1	2
Mendoza	1.000	1	2	0	0	1
Snyder	.880	14	7	15	3	2
Vechionacci	.922	117	61	174	20	23

Shortstop	PCT	G	PO	A	E	DP
Corona	.971	16	28	40	2	14

	PCT	G	PO	A	E	DP
Nunez	.932	120	162	289	33	69
Snyder	.967	11	11	18	1	1

Outfield	PCT	G	PO	A	E	DP
Cooper	.992	78	119	5	1	0
Curtis	.989	55	87	1	1	0
Fortenberry	.984	36	63	0	1	0
Gonzalez	.977	113	205	7	5	1
Hall	1.000	27	35	2	0	0
Krum	.977	75	164	5	4	1
Robnett	.983	30	55	2	1	1
Rye	1.000	3	6	0	0	0
Santana	1.000	3	4	0	0	0
Snyder	1.000	17	24	0	0	0

TAMPA YANKEES
FLORIDA STATE LEAGUE

HIGH CLASS A

Batting	B-T	HT	WT	DOB	AVG	vLH	vRH	G	AB	R	H	2B	3B	HR	RBI	BB	HBP	SH	SF	SO	SB	CS	SLG	OBP
Adams, David	R-R	6-2	190	5-15-87	.281	.279	.282	65	231	37	65	17	6	7	41	26	4	1	3	39	3	4	.498	.360
Baisley, Brian	R-R	6-3	223	12-19-82	.170	.200	.160	33	106	8	18	3	0	0	6	9	4	0	0	37	2	0	.198	.261
Baldridge, Tommy	L-L	6-1	195	8-18-86	.204	.417	.135	17	49	6	10	2	0	0	3	0	0	0	0	8	2	0	.245	.250
Brewer, Dan	R-R	6-0	185	7-19-87	.290	.241	.306	59	224	32	65	7	3	4	29	22	3	2	2	46	13	3	.402	.359
Cusick, Matt	L-R	5-10	190	5-5-86	.313	.347	.304	63	217	27	68	14	3	1	17	25	1	8	2	23	5	3	.419	.384
Fortenberry, Seth	L-L	6-2	175	9-1-83	.175	.150	.181	59	189	18	33	7	2	6	27	20	4	1	2	58	3	0	.328	.265
Fryer, Eric	R-R	6-2	215	8-26-85	.250	.208	.263	59	224	34	56	11	2	2	24	27	2	0	2	43	11	5	.344	.333
Gil, Jose	R-R	6-0	170	9-4-86	.208	.167	.222	29	96	10	20	4	0	0	8	5	0	3	0	24	0	0	.250	.248
Hilligoss, Mitch	L-R	6-1	195	5-5-86	.233	.268	.221	51	163	15	38	7	2	0	14	11	0	1	0	25	5	2	.301	.282
Ibarra, Walter	B-R	5-11	180	11-1-87	.265	.260	.267	74	234	38	62	10	1	0	16	10	1	2	3	23	11	5	.316	.294
Krum, Austin	L-L	6-0	190	1-19-86	.272	.327	.250	53	191	32	52	7	3	0	14	35	5	1	2	43	7	4	.340	.395
Laird, Brandon	R-R	6-1	215	9-11-87	.266	.262	.267	124	451	53	120	20	4	13	75	39	6	0	5	75	1	1	.415	.329
Landoni, Emerson	R-R	5-10	146	2-18-89	.185	.125	.211	10	27	0	5	0	0	0	3	5	1	1	0	4	0	1	.185	.333
Maruszak, Addison	R-R	6-1	195	12-21-86	.148	.143	.150	24	81	8	12	1	0	0	4	7	1	2	1	14	2	3	.160	.222
Montero, Jesus	R-R	6-4	225	11-28-89	.356	.306	.374	48	180	26	64	15	1	8	37	14	2	1	1	26	0	0	.583	.406
Nunez, Luis	R-R	5-11	160	11-21-84	.304	.390	.274	48	158	23	48	10	3	3	23	14	2	2	3	16	4	5	.462	.362
Romine, Austin	R-R	6-2	210	11-22-88	.276	.303	.266	118	442	61	122	28	3	13	72	29	4	0	6	78	11	5	.441	.322
Rufino, Wady	R-R	6-2	220	4-8-85	.235	.244	.231	40	136	16	32	8	0	1	9	8	4	0	1	39	2	2	.316	.295
Rye, Jack	L-L	6-1	200	3-8-86	.256	.222	.271	75	238	31	61	13	5	1	21	40	2	5	2	42	7	11	.366	.365
Smith, Kevin	R-R	6-1	190	1-15-83	.317	.348	.303	63	218	30	69	15	2	1	29	19	2	1	4	48	4	0	.417	.390
Strausbaugh, Steve	R-R	5-9	200	11-4-85	.500	—	.500	1	4	0	2	0	0	0	0	0	0	0	0	1	0	0	.500	.500
Sublett, Damon	L-R	6-1	190	9-22-85	.270	.212	.290	114	397	68	107	24	11	4	41	65	4	5	2	93	11	7	.416	.376

Pitching	B-T	HT	WT	DOB	W	L	ERA	G	GS	CG	SV	IP	H	R	ER	HR	BB	SO	AVG	vLH	vRH	K/9	BB/9
Banuelos, Manuel	L-L	5-10	155	3-13-91	0	0	0.00	1	0	0	0	1	0	0	0	0	0	2	.000	.000	.000	18.00	0.00
Bartleski, Philip	R-R	6-7	240	4-22-83	4	1	2.86	16	0	0	1	28	23	9	9	2	8	30	.213	.216	.211	9.53	2.54
Betances, Dellin	R-R	6-8	245	3-23-88	2	5	5.48	11	11	0	0	44	48	29	27	2	27	44	.277	.242	.317	8.93	5.48
Bleich, Jeremy	L-L	6-2	195	6-18-87	6	4	3.40	14	14	0	0	79	79	34	30	4	22	56	.257	.245	.263	6.35	2.50

Pitching	B-T	HT	WT	DOB	W	L	ERA	G	GS	CG	SV	IP	H	R	ER	HR	BB	SO	AVG	vLH	vRH	K/9	BB/9
Castillo, Noel	R-R	6-1	160	10-5-83	3	2	2.91	31	2	0	2	59	52	24	19	1	31	56	.235	.174	.274	8.59	4.76
De La Rosa, Wilkin	L-L	6-0	185	2-21-85	1	0	1.29	3	3	0	0	14	9	2	2	0	4	17	.184	.176	.188	10.93	2.57
Duff, Grant	R-R	6-6	210	12-19-82	0	1	3.82	24	1	0	1	35	35	17	15	2	11	26	.248	.242	.253	6.62	2.80
Heredia, Jairo	R-R	6-1	190	10-8-89	2	2	6.91	4	4	1	0	14	25	14	11	2	5	10	.373	.345	.395	6.28	3.14
Heyer, Craig	R-R	6-3	205	11-15-85	4	3	3.11	30	6	0	1	72	73	30	25	1	9	29	.264	.302	.231	3.61	1.12
Hovis, Jonathan	R-R	5-11	185	12-27-83	2	2	3.38	44	0	0	22	48	44	19	18	2	13	41	.242	.247	.238	7.69	2.44
Lare, Trenton	L-L	6-4	195	8-25-84	0	0	9.00	1	0	0	0	2	2	2	2	1	0	2	.250	.000	.400	9.00	0.00
Marte, Ronny	R-R	6-1	173	2-26-86	1	0	1.93	2	0	0	0	5	3	1	1	0	2	3	.188	.200	.167	5.79	3.86
Mitchell, D.J.	R-R	6-0	170	5-13-87	8	6	2.87	19	18	1	0	103	93	41	33	1	38	83	.245	.297	.201	7.23	3.31
Mitre, Sergio	R-R	6-3	225	2-16-81	1	0	1.93	2	2	0	0	9	6	2	2	0	2	8	.250	.417	.179	7.71	1.93
Noesi, Hector	R-R	6-2	174	1-26-87	3	0	3.92	9	9	0	0	41	34	18	18	3	4	40	.224	.227	.221	8.71	0.87
Nolte, Charles	R-R	6-3	200	3-19-86	1	1	5.34	15	0	0	0	32	43	23	19	2	11	14	.321	.345	.303	3.94	3.09
Norton, Tim	R-R	6-5	230	5-23-83	2	1	2.75	23	0	0	0	36	31	12	11	1	9	30	.230	.276	.195	7.50	2.25
Olbrychowski, Adam	R-R	6-3	205	9-7-86	3	2	2.73	32	2	0	0	63	55	23	19	3	43	52	.233	.239	.228	7.47	6.18
Ortiz, Jonathan	R-R	5-10	170	10-29-85	3	3	4.67	24	0	0	8	27	35	16	14	3	7	36	.310	.328	.291	12.00	2.33
Pendleton, Lance	L-R	6-3	205	9-10-83	11	5	2.58	20	18	0	0	105	101	43	30	1	31	87	.256	.258	.254	7.48	2.67
Phelps, David	R-R	6-3	190	10-9-86	3	1	1.17	7	7	0	0	38	34	9	5	1	6	32	.234	.239	.230	7.51	1.41
Ramirez, Jose	R-R	6-1	155	1-21-90	0	0	0.00	1	0	0	0	3	1	0	0	0	0	2	.100	.000	.167	6.00	0.00
Rulon, Brad	L-R	5-11	185	6-22-86	3	0	3.47	14	0	0	2	23	18	10	9	2	13	22	.209	.243	.184	8.49	5.01
Sanchez, Humberto	R-R	6-6	270	5-28-83	0	1	4.76	9	3	0	0	11	7	7	6	1	4	11	.175	.235	.130	8.74	3.18
Sanit, Amaury	R-R	5-11	187	7-4-79	0	0	0.00	4	0	0	0	6	5	0	0	0	0	5	.208	.364	.077	7.50	0.00
Stephens, Jay	R-R	6-5	200	10-10-84	3	4	4.50	11	8	0	0	50	55	27	25	3	13	39	.282	.299	.265	7.02	2.34
Venditte, Pat	R-B	6-1	180	6-30-85	2	0	2.21	21	0	0	2	37	37	11	9	1	9	47	.261	.254	.268	11.54	2.21
Zink, Ryan	R-R	6-5	230	4-1-85	9	12	5.07	26	25	0	0	135	157	87	76	10	44	95	.297	.285	.308	6.33	2.93

Fielding

Catcher	PCT	G	PO	A	E	DP	PB
Fryer	1.000	5	18	0	0	0	1
Gil	.986	26	188	21	3	1	0
Montero	.989	26	162	14	2	3	3
Romine	.984	80	550	67	10	4	11

First Base	PCT	G	PO	A	E	DP
Baisley	.986	32	274	13	4	20
Gil	1.000	2	17	0	0	0
Hilligoss	.994	20	143	11	1	11
Laird	.996	23	213	17	1	12
Nunez	1.000	1	5	1	0	0
Rufino	1.000	1	9	0	0	1
Rye	1.000	2	4	1	0	1
Smith	1.000	58	481	37	0	46

Second Base	PCT	G	PO	A	E	DP
Adams	.982	56	106	170	5	34
Cusick	.950	22	38	57	5	10
Landoni	1.000	3	3	6	0	1
Nunez	.962	5	7	18	1	7
Sublett	.958	47	68	137	9	20

Third Base	PCT	G	PO	A	E	DP
Cusick	.965	19	14	41	2	3
Hilligoss	1.000	10	7	14	0	0
Laird	.931	91	45	158	15	15
Landoni	1.000	1	1	3	0	0
Nunez	.905	16	10	28	4	6

Shortstop	PCT	G	PO	A	E	DP
Hilligoss	.958	16	29	40	3	4
Ibarra	.955	72	78	178	12	33

	PCT	G	PO	A	E	DP
Landoni	.941	5	4	12	1	2
Maruszak	.956	24	45	64	5	13
Nunez	.944	20	28	39	4	8

Outfield	PCT	G	PO	A	E	DP
Baldridge	.975	17	36	3	1	0
Brewer	1.000	58	107	0	0	0
Fortenberry	.990	53	98	1	1	0
Fryer	.955	56	81	4	4	1
Hilligoss	.500	2	1	0	1	0
Krum	.992	52	116	5	1	2
Nunez	1.000	2	2	1	0	0
Rufino	.932	37	67	2	5	0
Rye	.984	68	121	5	2	0
Sublett	.985	62	126	3	2	0

CHARLESTON RIVERDOGS   LOW CLASS A

SOUTH ATLANTIC LEAGUE

Batting	B-T	HT	WT	DOB	AVG	vLH	vRH	G	AB	R	H	2B	3B	HR	RBI	BB	HBP	SH	SF	SO	SB	CS	SLG	OBP
Abeita, Mitch	R-R	6-0	185	4-7-86	.225	.197	.234	74	249	28	56	12	1	4	32	31	5	2	1	58	1	0	.329	.322
Adams, David	R-R	6-2	190	5-15-87	.290	.246	.303	67	259	32	75	23	2	0	34	35	7	0	3	49	8	4	.394	.385
Almonte, Abraham	B-R	5-9	205	6-27-89	.280	.273	.282	115	440	63	123	14	10	5	56	35	2	4	3	81	36	5	.391	.333
Angelini, Carmen	R-R	6-2	185	9-22-88	.197	.310	.165	33	132	18	26	5	0	1	8	8	3	1	2	32	6	1	.258	.255
Baisley, Brian	R-R	6-3	223	12-19-82	.339	.190	.375	29	109	12	37	12	0	2	23	12	2	0	4	31	0	0	.505	.402
Baldridge, Tommy	L-L	6-1	195	8-18-86	.184	.071	.198	42	125	13	23	3	0	1	8	8	0	0	0	19	3	0	.232	.233
Brewer, Dan	R-R	6-0	185	7-19-87	.323	.296	.333	58	201	38	65	18	3	2	25	33	5	1	1	49	9	5	.473	.429
Farnham, Jeff	R-R	6-1	195	8-30-87	.323	.250	.348	20	62	13	20	6	0	1	10	5	3	0	2	13	0	1	.468	.389
French, Neall	R-R	6-3	220	8-5-83	.238	.266	.226	64	210	25	50	6	1	2	22	29	5	1	0	70	0	0	.305	.344
Grote, Taylor	L-R	6-2	195	12-5-88	.232	.192	.241	113	418	54	97	22	0	4	42	48	1	0	3	139	8	3	.313	.311
Ibarra, Walter	B-R	5-11	180	11-1-87	.241	.000	.333	12	29	2	7	0	0	0	3	2	0	1	0	10	1	0	.241	.290
Joseph, Corban	L-R	6-0	168	10-28-88	.300	.302	.299	100	380	39	114	17	8	4	57	49	3	0	4	61	8	5	.418	.381
Kruml, Ray	L-R	5-11	175	8-5-85	.246	.156	.269	100	382	53	94	15	4	2	35	26	3	1	3	100	23	5	.322	.297
Lassiter, Garrison	L-R	6-1	185	12-22-89	.260	.235	.266	74	265	25	69	12	1	2	29	12	6	3	1	74	3	0	.336	.330
Lyon, Mike	R-R	6-2	220	8-13-86	.236	.213	.246	54	165	15	39	6	1	2	10	17	3	0	0	55	3	1	.321	.319
Maruszak, Addison	R-R	6-1	195	12-21-86	.263	.233	.274	64	217	29	57	4	1	2	20	32	6	1	4	44	6	1	.318	.367
Mesa, Melky	R-R	6-1	165	1-31-87	.225	.224	.226	133	497	76	112	24	7	20	74	51	11	0	5	168	18	6	.423	.309
Pirela, Jose	B-R	5-10	191	11-21-89	.295	.252	.310	97	404	65	119	23	6	0	46	37	1	4	1	65	9	8	.381	.354
Weems, Chase	L-R	6-2	170	1-17-89	.260	.286	.254	55	173	19	45	10	1	1	14	15	0	5	1	55	0	0	.347	.317

Pitching	B-T	HT	WT	DOB	W	L	ERA	G	GS	CG	SV	IP	H	R	ER	HR	BB	SO	AVG	vLH	vRH	K/9	BB/9
Arbiso, Cory	R-R	6-3	210	4-21-86	4	7	4.85	30	10	0	1	91	109	58	49	8	14	62	.302	.319	.292	6.13	1.38
Banuelos, Manuel	L-L	5-10	155	3-13-91	9	5	2.67	25	19	0	0	108	88	40	32	4	28	104	.219	.164	.230	8.67	2.33
Barreda, Manuel	R-R	5-11	165	10-8-88	1	0	13.50	2	0	0	0	3	1	4	4	0	4	2	.111	—	.111	6.75	13.50
Braboy, Brandon	R-R	6-0	195	10-31-85	4	5	3.97	33	9	0	1	93	81	41	8	24	77	.232	.235	.230	7.45	2.32	
Brackman, Andrew	R-R	6-10	240	12-4-85	2	12	5.91	29	19	0	0	107	106	79	70	8	76	103	.266	.270	.263	8.69	6.41
Erickson, Casey	R-R	6-3	187	8-28-85	3	3	2.25	21	3	0	0	44	51	14	11	0	13	37	.291	.344	.261	7.57	2.66
2-team total (15 West Virginia)					8	4	1.75	36	6	0	5	82	87	22	16	1	19	69	—	—	—	7.54	2.08

Name	B-T	HT	WT	DOB	W	L	ERA	G	GS	CG	SV	IP	H	R	ER	HR	BB	SO	AVG	vLH	vRH	K/9	BB/9
Flannery, Ryan	R-R	6-4	245	1-6-86	0	0	10.13	6	0	0	0	5	12	7	6	0	1	10	.414	.462	.375	16.88	1.69
Heidler, Paul	R-R	6-2	195	11-12-86	0	0	4.50	2	0	0	0	4	5	3	2	1	3	4	.313	.500	.250	9.00	6.75
Heredia, Jairo	R-R	6-1	190	10-8-89	1	1	2.37	4	4	0	0	19	14	6	5	1	1	17	.203	.250	.162	8.05	0.47
Horne, Alan	R-R	6-4	195	1-5-83	0	1	5.50	3	3	0	0	18	17	12	11	1	11	13	.258	.167	.292	6.50	5.50
Kapala, Dan	R-R	6-5	220	9-6-85	6	2	2.64	38	4	0	2	95	84	36	28	2	26	50	.237	.257	.228	4.72	2.45
Lare, Trenton	L-L	6-4	195	8-25-84	2	3	2.76	7	7	0	0	42	36	16	13	0	7	35	.235	.231	.236	7.44	1.49
Marquez, Dickson	R-R	6-2	170	4-19-86	1	0	0.00	2	0	0	0	4	1	0	0	0	4		.077	.000	.091	9.00	0.00
Marshall, Brett	R-R	6-0	195	3-22-90	3	6	5.56	17	17	0	0	87	98	67	54	7	37	60	.290	.231	.323	6.18	3.81
Mitchell, D.J.	R-R	6-0	170	5-13-87	4	1	1.95	6	6	0	0	37	31	16	8	1	6	42	.228	.273	.214	10.22	1.46
Noesi, Hector	R-R	6-2	174	1-26-87	3	4	2.38	17	11	0	0	76	62	24	20	3	11	78	.218	.248	.201	9.28	1.31
Nolte, Charles	R-R	6-3	200	3-19-86	4	3	5.26	22	2	0	1	51	59	31	30	5	17	39	.285	.407	.206	6.84	2.98
Ortiz, Jonathan	R-R	5-10	170	10-29-85	0	1	1.26	24	0	0	9	29	21	6	4	1	3	40	.202	.239	.172	12.56	0.94
Patterson, Garrett	L-L	6-2	220	5-11-82	0	0	20.25	1	0	0	0	1	5	4	3	0	1	1	.556	.500	.571	6.75	6.75
Patterson, Paul	R-R	6-7	200	5-8-84	0	0	1.59	2	1	0	0	6	8	1	1	0	1	4	.320	.500	.304	6.35	1.59
Phelps, David	R-R	6-3	190	10-9-86	10	3	2.80	19	19	0	0	113	117	48	35	9	25	90	.272	.276	.270	7.19	2.00
Prihoda, Luke	R-R	6-5	230	8-10-84	3	0	3.10	12	0	0	2	20	21	7	7	1	0	23	.273	.192	.314	10.18	0.00
Rodriguez, Wilton	R-R	6-3	190	11-6-90	1	0	6.75	2	2	0	0	9	11	8	7	1	2	8	.275	.167	.294	7.71	1.93
Rulon, Brad	L-R	5-11	185	6-22-86	4	1	1.18	29	0	0	1	53	35	11	7	2	12	58	.186	.175	.191	9.79	2.03
Smith, Brett	R-R	6-5	220	8-12-83	0	1	3.00	3	3	0	0	15	11	8	5	0	9	3	.208	.286	.179	1.80	5.40
Tatis, Gabriel	R-R	6-0	180	5-18-85	3	2	5.68	15	0	0	0	25	25	16	16	2	16	20	.255	.270	.246	7.11	5.68
Venditte, Pat	R-B	6-1	180	6-30-85	2	2	1.47	28	0	0	20	31	24	8	5	1	2	40	.212	.108	.263	11.74	0.59
Walker, Edwin	R-L	6-3	205	10-26-83	2	0	0.78	14	0	0	1	23	14	2	2	0	4	20	.171	.350	.113	7.83	1.57
Williams, Jeff	R-R	6-5	220	8-24-83	2	2	3.66	13	0	0	3	20	21	8	8	2	4	18	.276	.267	.283	8.24	1.83

Fielding

Catcher	PCT	G	PO	A	E	DP	PB
Abeita	.987	73	553	62	8	5	7
Farnham	.986	19	121	16	2	0	2
Weems	.993	55	378	52	3	4	12

First Base	PCT	G	PO	A	E	DP
Baisley	.993	28	267	17	2	21
Baldridge	.993	32	246	23	2	15
Brewer	.950	2	15	4	1	1
French	.995	44	398	15	2	30
Ibarra	—	1	0	0	0	0
Lyon	.996	34	266	17	1	32
Maruszak	1.000	9	92	3	0	9

Second Base	PCT	G	PO	A	E	DP
Adams	.978	51	110	152	6	40
Almonte	1.000	2	3	2	0	2
Ibarra	.500	2	1	1	2	1
Joseph	.957	56	104	140	11	28
Pirela	.963	31	62	69	5	16

Third Base	PCT	G	PO	A	E	DP
Adams	.947	14	13	41	3	4
Ibarra	.875	3	0	7	1	2
Joseph	.949	37	38	93	7	9
Lassiter	.889	67	27	149	22	8
Lyon	.900	12	9	27	4	4
Maruszak	1.000	9	4	18	0	1

Shortstop	PCT	G	PO	A	E	DP
Angelini	.888	33	55	88	18	20
Ibarra	.842	4	3	13	3	4
Maruszak	.930	44	69	117	14	21
Pirela	.959	64	78	200	12	36

Outfield	PCT	G	PO	A	E	DP
Almonte	.968	102	168	11	6	1
Baldridge	1.000	5	4	0	0	0
Brewer	.932	26	36	5	3	0
Grote	.962	84	141	10	6	1
Kruml	.960	84	115	4	5	2
Lyon	—	1	0	0	0	0
Mesa	.974	121	242	19	7	4

STATEN ISLAND YANKEES — SHORT-SEASON

NEW YORK-PENN LEAGUE

Batting	B-T	HT	WT	DOB	AVG	vLH	vRH	G	AB	R	H	2B	3B	HR	RBI	BB	HBP	SH	SF	SO	SB	CS	SLG	OBP
Afenir, Buck	R-R	6-1	205	5-3-87	.167	.000	.250	5	12	0	2	2	0	0	2	1	0	0	1	0	0	.333	.333
Almonte, Zoilo	B-R	5-11	165	6-10-89	.274	.301	.263	69	259	43	71	20	1	7	39	31	2	1	1	58	15	7	.440	.355
Angelini, Carmen	R-R	6-2	185	9-22-88	.190	.137	.208	59	200	18	38	5	1	3	14	15	2	1	0	34	3	2	.270	.253
Baker, Ryan J.	R-R	5-9	205	11-9-84	.241	.308	.188	10	29	3	7	1	0	2	6	3	0	0	0	8	0	0	.483	.313
Castro, Kelvin	R-R	6-3	164	12-14-87	.212	.219	.209	65	217	24	46	11	5	2	27	13	3	2	1	62	6	4	.336	.265
Gross, Chad	R-R	6-5	220	5-3-88	.145	.174	.125	21	55	4	8	2	1	1	4	4	0	0	0	32	2	0	.273	.203
Higashioka, Kyle	R-R	6-1	190	4-20-90	.253	.254	.253	60	217	24	55	11	0	2	32	26	1	1	2	31	0	1	.332	.333
Landoni, Emerson	B-R	5-10	146	2-18-89	.237	.200	.250	27	76	8	18	1	1	0	9	8	1	2	0	14	4	1	.276	.318
Lyerly, Rob	R-L	6-2	200	7-23-87	.268	.308	.244	20	71	8	19	8	0	0	7	2	2	1	0	16	0	2	.380	.307
Lyon, Mike	R-R	6-2	220	8-13-86	.217	.333	.193	20	69	10	15	5	0	1	7	8	1	1	0	19	0	0	.333	.308
Mack, DeAngelo	R-R	5-10	190	11-19-86	.306	.377	.276	66	232	27	71	19	4	7	41	21	4	1	1	44	2	4	.513	.372
Medchill, Neil	L-R	6-4	220	6-25-87	.278	.215	.305	62	216	42	60	13	2	14	41	24	1	1	2	66	7	2	.551	.350
Milo, Justin	L-R	5-8	180	2-23-87	.253	.154	.274	25	75	13	19	5	0	1	12	22	1	1	0	23	4	0	.360	.429
Murton, Luke	R-R	6-4	222	5-21-86	.295	.377	.262	69	237	45	70	17	1	8	35	23	8	1	2	61	4	0	.477	.374
Paredes, Jimmy	B-R	6-1	178	11-25-88	.302	.300	.303	54	205	36	62	8	4	2	17	10	2	1	3	30	23	9	.410	.336
Rabago, Hector	R-R	5-10	185	8-24-88	.216	.300	.185	34	111	10	24	2	0	1	5	13	5	2	0	16	3	2	.261	.326
Santana, Francisco	L-L	5-10	170	6-18-88	.236	.162	.262	40	140	17	33	6	1	1	10	10	1	1	1	29	5	4	.314	.289

Pitching	B-T	HT	WT	DOB	W	L	ERA	G	GS	CG	SV	IP	H	R	ER	HR	BB	SO	AVG	vLH	vRH	K/9	BB/9
Arbiso, Cory	R-R	6-3	210	4-21-86	0	1	1.17	2	1	0	0	6	3	1	0	0	6		.214	.333	.083	7.04	0.00
Bailey, Griffin	R-R	6-5	220	9-19-84	3	2	1.49	32	0	0	2	48	35	13	8	1	14	28	.193	.230	.160	5.21	2.61
Bartleski, Philip	R-R	6-7	240	4-22-83	0	0	0.00	2	0	0	0	4	1	0	0	0	7		.077	.000	.125	15.75	0.00
Black, Sean	R-R	6-3	185	4-23-88	6	0	1.62	10	10	0	0	50	30	14	9	2	9	34	.169	.169	.168	6.12	1.62
Brooks, Gavin	L-L	6-3	220	10-27-87	5	1	0.62	30	0	0	3	43	27	8	3	1	24	48	.180	.216	.169	9.97	4.98
Cotham, Caleb	R-R	6-3	215	11-6-87	0	1	4.50	2	2	0	0	6	5	3	3	1	3	8	.217	.273	.167	12.00	4.50
Elam, Sam	L-L	6-4	220	6-16-87	0	0	23.63	3	0	0	0	3	1	7	7	0	11	2	.111	.250	.000	6.75	37.13
Flannery, Ryan	R-R	6-4	245	1-6-86	4	2	1.45	34	0	0	6	43	32	10	7	0	12	41	.204	.212	.198	8.52	2.49
Hall, Shaeffer	R-L	6-0	180	10-2-87	0	0	1.86	2	2	0	0	9	9	2	2	0	0	11	.243	.222	.263	10.24	0.00
Lare, Trenton	L-L	6-4	195	8-25-84	3	2	1.07	6	6	0	0	34	20	9	4	3	3	38	.164	.173	.157	10.16	0.80
Marte, Ronny	R-R	6-1	173	2-26-86	6	3	4.24	31	0	0	7	40	36	25	19	2	13	45	.231	.224	.238	10.04	2.90
Miller, Dan	R-R	6-3	220	7-7-86	0	0	4.15	6	0	0	0	9	9	4	4	0	2	9	.273	.278	.267	9.35	2.08
Patterson, Paul	R-R	6-7	200	5-8-84	1	1	5.64	6	0	0	0	22	28	17	14	1	6	16	.295	.289	.289	6.45	2.42

Name	B-T	HT	WT	DOB	W	L	ERA	G	GS	CG	SV	IP	H	R	ER	HR	BB	SO	AVG	vLH	vRH	K/9	BB/9
Perez, Kelvin	R-R	6-1	140	10-10-85	3	2	2.06	13	9	0	0	52	50	24	12	0	24	48	.251	.222	.268	8.25	4.13
Richardson, Matt	R-R	6-1	175	5-28-90	0	3	6.56	9	9	0	0	36	45	31	26	2	23	30	.317	.362	.286	7.57	5.80
Rondon, Francisco	L-L	6-1	160	4-19-88	3	2	2.32	11	11	0	0	54	38	22	14	2	33	48	.196	.170	.206	7.95	5.47
Solbach, Michael	R-R	6-3	185	7-31-85	2	3	3.92	24	2	0	1	39	40	27	17	2	22	34	.265	.259	.269	7.85	5.08
Stoneburner, Graham	R-R	6-1	190	9-29-87	0	0	0.00	1	0	0	0	1	1	0	0	0	0	2	.250	.000	1.000	18.00	0.00
Vizcaino, Arodys	R-R	6-0	189	11-13-90	2	4	2.13	10	10	0	0	42	34	18	10	2	15	52	.211	.256	.169	11.06	3.19
Warren, Adam	R-R	6-1	200	8-25-87	4	2	1.43	12	12	0	0	57	49	12	9	1	10	50	.236	.271	.211	7.94	1.59
Watkins, Ben	R-R	6-3	225	3-11-87	5	0	2.47	25	2	0	0	47	38	16	13	0	11	43	.210	.259	.167	8.18	2.09

Fielding

Catcher	PCT	G	PO	A	E	DP	PB
Afenir	1.000	5	29	0	0	0	0
Baker	.969	5	23	8	1	0	1
Higashioka	.990	57	451	41	5	2	7
Rabago	1.000	13	82	8	0	0	5

First Base	PCT	G	PO	A	E	DP
Gross	.935	4	29	0	2	1
Lyerly	1.000	2	20	1	0	1
Lyon	.917	3	21	1	2	0
Murton	.987	68	613	61	9	47

Second Base	PCT	G	PO	A	E	DP
Castro	.944	9	11	40	3	10
Landoni	.917	18	24	42	6	8
Paredes	.931	36	47	102	11	16
Rabago	.958	17	25	43	3	8

Third Base	PCT	G	PO	A	E	DP
Angelini	1.000	1	0	3	0	0
Castro	.913	40	32	73	10	8
Landoni	—	1	0	0	0	0
Lyerly	.857	18	8	34	7	3
Lyon	.960	15	5	19	1	2
Paredes	.900	3	2	7	1	0
Rabago	1.000	4	3	5	0	0

Shortstop	PCT	G	PO	A	E	DP
Angelini	.956	57	81	158	11	28
Castro	.900	12	16	38	6	7
Landoni	.880	7	10	12	3	3
Rabago	1.000	1	3	1	0	2

Outfield	PCT	G	PO	A	E	DP
Almonte	.966	57	79	5	3	0
Gross	.938	14	14	1	1	0
Mack	.975	55	76	3	2	0
Medchill	.989	57	93	1	1	0
Milo	.923	12	12	0	1	1
Santana	.987	39	76	1	1	0

GCL YANKEES   ROOKIE

GULF COAST LEAGUE

Batting	B-T	HT	WT	DOB	AVG	vLH	vRH	G	AB	R	H	2B	3B	HR	RBI	BB	HBP	SH	SF	SO	SB	CS	SLG	OBP
Afenir, Buck	R-R	6-1	205	5-3-87	.400	.333	.417	6	15	3	6	4	0	1	5	0	0	0	5	0	0	.867	.400
Arcia, Francisco	B-R	6-0	155	9-14-89	.247	.238	.255	31	97	10	24	7	0	2	13	11	2	0	2	16	0	0	.381	.330
Cervelli, Francisco	R-R	6-1	210	3-6-86	.167	.000	.333	2	6	1	1	0	0	0	0	1	0	0	0	0	0	0	.167	.286
De Leon, Kelvin	R-R	6-2	180	10-29-90	.269	.324	.238	56	201	28	54	13	0	7	31	16	3	0	1	61	5	1	.438	.330
Delaney, Mitch	L-R	6-2	215	4-14-89	.178	.242	.147	40	101	8	18	6	1	3	15	17	3	0	1	41	0	1	.347	.311
Farnham, Jeff	R-R	6-1	195	8-30-87	.167	.500	.100	5	12	0	2	1	0	0	2	1	0	0	0	3	1	0	.250	.231
Flores, Ramon	L-L	5-10	150	3-26-92	.196	.220	.182	51	158	34	31	5	1	0	14	22	3	2	2	35	7	5	.241	.303
Golsan, Judd	R-R	6-1	180	12-6-90	.224	.182	.237	39	98	16	22	3	0	0	5	13	3	0	1	34	4	2	.255	.330
Harrow, Isaac	R-R	5-11	185	1-25-87	.186	.053	.224	30	86	7	16	4	1	1	8	10	0	0	1	25	0	1	.291	.268
Heathcott, Slade	L-L	6-1	190	9-28-90	.100	.167	.000	3	10	0	1	0	0	0	1	0	0	0	0	2	0	0	.100	.182
Landoni, Emerson	B-R	5-10	146	2-18-89	.000	.000	.000	1	3	0	0	0	0	0	0	1	0	0	0	0	0	0	.000	.000
Lassiter, Garrison	L-R	6-1	185	12-22-89	.500	1.000	.000	1	2	1	1	0	0	0	1	1	0	0	1	0	0	0	.500	.500
Liccien, Jhorge	R-R	6-0	165	10-10-90	.100	.111	.097	29	80	6	8	0	0	0	1	7	1	2	0	18	0	0	.100	.182
Mahoney, Kevin	L-R	6-1	205	5-11-87	.226	.231	.224	57	190	28	43	17	1	6	30	24	7	5	3	70	3	2	.421	.330
Milo, Justin	L-R	5-8	180	2-23-87	.267	.333	.250	7	15	2	4	1	0	0	3	4	1	0	0	2	2	0	.533	.450
Mojica, Jose	R-R	6-0	145	12-26-88	.278	.317	.259	55	198	18	55	11	2	1	22	10	3	1	1	20	4	1	.369	.321
Murphy, J.R.	B-R	5-10	170	5-13-91	.333	.273	.364	9	33	4	11	2	0	1	7	3	1	0	0	8	0	0	.485	.405
Smith, Chris	L-L	6-0	190	1-11-90	.091	.111	.086	17	44	5	4	1	0	1	1	8	2	0	0	17	1	1	.182	.259
Sosa, Eduardo	L-L	5-11	155	3-14-91	.200	.123	.241	49	165	24	33	7	1	2	14	16	3	1	2	47	11	4	.291	.280
Tabares, Yunior	R-R	6-5	215	7-15-85	.230	.167	.254	30	87	9	20	3	1	0	6	7	1	0	1	21	0	0	.287	.292
Toussen, Jose	L-L	6-1	155	11-13-89	.223	.191	.239	58	202	27	45	12	1	2	15	27	3	0	5	36	8	3	.322	.316

Pitching	B-T	HT	WT	DOB	W	L	ERA	G	GS	CG	SV	IP	H	R	ER	HR	BB	SO	AVG	vLH	vRH	K/9	BB/9
Acosta, Ryan	R-R	6-2	170	11-4-88	0	0	0.00	1	0	0	0	1	1	0	0	0	0	2	.250	—	.250	9.00	0.00
Arballo, Julian	R-R	6-2	225	10-9-87	0	3	2.81	20	0	0	11	26	24	9	8	0	17	26	.255	.211	.286	9.12	5.96
Barreda, Manuel	R-R	5-11	165	10-8-88	0	1	1.93	14	0	0	2	23	10	7	5	0	7	25	.123	.143	.113	9.64	2.70
Bartleski, Philip	R-R	6-7	240	4-22-83	0	0	4.50	1	0	0	0	2	2	1	1	0	1	0	.286	1.000	.167	0.00	4.50
Checo, Mariel	R-R	6-3	190	10-16-89	1	1	8.40	10	0	0	0	15	14	15	14	1	14	14	.250	.357	.214	8.40	8.40
Cotham, Caleb	R-R	6-3	215	11-6-87	0	0	0.00	1	1	0	0	2	2	0	0	0	0	5	.250	.333	.200	22.50	0.00
Elam, Sam	L-L	6-4	220	6-16-87	0	2	6.75	7	0	0	0	5	5	7	4	0	10	8	.238	.500	.211	13.50	16.88
Gerritse, Brett	R-R	6-4	220	3-4-91	0	1	3.93	6	5	0	0	18	15	11	8	0	7	20	.217	.167	.244	9.82	3.44
Gil, Daniel	R-R	6-3	187	4-24-89	4	3	3.00	13	7	0	0	45	41	21	15	3	10	31	.237	.234	.239	6.20	2.00
Greene, Shane	R-R	6-4	210	11-17-88	1	2	5.87	13	0	0	0	23	30	19	15	2	6	20	.297	.351	.266	7.83	2.35
Heidler, Paul	R-R	6-2	195	11-12-86	3	1	2.16	13	0	0	0	17	15	4	4	1	8	13	.250	.143	.308	7.02	4.32
Heredia, Jairo	R-R	6-1	190	10-8-89	0	0	1.80	2	2	0	0	5	3	2	1	0	2	5	.167	.200	.154	9.00	3.60
Horne, Alan	R-R	6-4	195	1-5-83	4	0	2.86	6	5	0	0	28	23	9	9	2	10	22	.219	.222	.216	6.99	3.18
Marquez, Dickson	R-R	6-2	170	4-19-86	1	3	1.86	20	0	0	1	29	19	9	6	1	2	21	.186	.204	.170	6.52	0.62
Marte, Damaso	L-L	6-2	215	2-14-75	0	0	4.50	2	2	0	0	2	2	1	1	0	0	2	.250	.000	.286	9.00	0.00
Martinez, Alejandro	R-R	5-10	165	2-11-89	1	0	0.00	2	0	0	0	3	3	1	0	0	0	6	.214	.400	.111	16.20	0.00
Miller, Dan	R-R	6-3	220	7-7-86	2	0	2.25	15	0	0	1	20	13	5	5	0	9	12	.178	.333	.115	5.40	4.05
O'Brien, Mikey	R-R	5-11	185	3-3-90	2	4	5.09	11	8	0	0	46	51	33	26	1	9	44	.285	.250	.308	8.61	1.76
Patterson, Paul	R-R	6-7	200	5-8-84	0	0	0.00	2	0	0	0	1	0	0	0	0	0	1	.000	.125	.167	0.00	0.00
Perez, Kelvin	R-R	6-1	140	10-10-85	2	0	1.50	2	0	0	0	6	4	1	1	0	3	8	.200	.111	.273	12.00	4.50
Ramirez, Jose	R-R	6-1	155	1-21-90	6	0	1.48	11	10	0	0	61	33	12	10	5	16	53	.159	.167	.155	7.82	2.36
Richardson, Matt	R-R	6-1	175	5-28-90	3	0	0.64	5	4	0	0	28	20	2	2	0	1	21	.206	.190	.218	6.75	0.32
Rodriguez, Wilton	R-R	6-3	195	11-6-90	0	1	3.32	8	2	0	1	19	15	8	7	3	2	18	.217	.292	.178	8.53	0.95
Smith, Brett	R-R	6-5	220	8-12-83	0	2	6.75	4	4	0	0	12	15	9	9	2	6	10	.306	.455	.263	7.50	4.50

	B-T	HT	WT	DOB																				
Tatis, Gabriel	R-R	6-0	180	5-18-85	2	0	0.84	6	0	0	3	11	10	2	1	1	1	14	.244	.214	.259	11.81	0.84	
Turley, Nik	L-L	6-7	195	9-11-89	2	3	2.82	11	10	0	0	54	45	21	17	1	23	46	.228	.310	.214	7.62	3.81	

Fielding

Catcher	PCT	G	PO	A	E	DP	PB
Afenir	.952	5	17	3	1	0	0
Arcia	.995	27	178	25	1	4	4
Cervelli	.900	2	8	1	1	0	2
Farnham	1.000	4	20	3	0	0	0
Liccien	.977	27	195	18	5	0	2
Murphy	1.000	3	19	3	0	0	1

First Base	PCT	G	PO	A	E	DP
Delaney	.987	39	293	13	4	20
Tabares	.991	30	203	13	2	16

Second Base	PCT	G	PO	A	E	DP
Harrow	.966	25	33	53	3	8
Toussen	.960	38	71	97	7	19

Third Base	PCT	G	PO	A	E	DP
Lassiter	—	1	0	0	0	0
Mahoney	.954	55	42	123	8	6
Toussen	.913	6	3	18	2	2

Shortstop	PCT	G	PO	A	E	DP
Landoni	1.000	1	3	1	0	1
Mojica	.925	49	67	119	15	22

	PCT	G	PO	A	E	DP
Toussen	.898	12	19	25	5	2
Outfield						
Brown	.900	14	9	0	1	0
De Leon	.959	46	68	2	3	0
Flores	.956	46	85	2	4	2
Golsan	.979	26	46	1	1	0
Heathcott	1.000	2	4	1	0	0
Milo	.800	2	4	0	1	0
Smith	.818	12	9	0	2	0
Sosa	.964	45	104	2	4	0

DSL YANKEES #1   ROOKIE
DOMINICAN SUMMER LEAGUE

Batting	B-T	HT	WT	DOB	AVG	vLH	vRH	G	AB	R	H	2B	3B	HR	RBI	BB	HBP	SH	SF	SO	SB	CS	SLG	OBP
Beard, Edwin	R-R	6-3	188	8-31-89	.290	.146	.331	55	217	30	63	9	1	2	26	24	7	0	2	44	8	3	.369	.376
Beltre, Harlington	R-R	6-0	165	1-21-91	.360	.444	.313	7	25	7	9	1	0	0	6	4	0	1	1	2	1	0	.400	.433
Calderon, Ronny	L-R	5-9	155	12-6-87	.500	.000	.667	1	4	0	2	0	0	0	0	0	0	0	0	0	0	0	.500	.500
2-team total (10 Yankees 2)					.273	—		11	33	2	9	2	0	0	1	0	0	0	0	2	0	0	.333	.294
Calderon, Yeick	L-L	6-2	185	12-23-91	.321	.220	.349	55	193	38	62	5	2	3	27	38	6	0	4	45	9	1	.415	.440
Castillo, Ali	R-R	5-10	165	6-19-89	.319	.344	.314	51	185	40	59	13	9	1	27	24	1	0	2	14	10	1	.503	.396
Duran, Francisco	R-R	6-2	185	10-3-91	.250	.333	.230	40	156	22	39	5	2	1	23	6	1	1	1	45	3	1	.327	.280
Fulgencio, Edwin	R-R	6-2	190	7-22-91	.172	.079	.197	53	180	28	31	9	2	4	17	32	4	0	0	95	3	1	.311	.310
Guzman, Miguel	R-R	5-11	157	7-18-90	.250	.222	.259	15	36	6	9	2	0	0	5	8	0	0	0	15	4	1	.306	.386
Lapaix, Arielkis	R-R	5-11	186	10-14-88	.333	.400	.310	34	78	21	26	4	1	1	10	13	1	0	0	22	2	1	.449	.435
Leonora, Ericson	R-R	5-11	174	8-25-92	.286	.339	.271	61	259	40	74	12	9	4	39	18	1	0	4	66	15	8	.448	.330
Lopez, Jerison	R-R	5-11	177	8-24-91	.238	.180	.252	58	252	51	60	8	4	3	33	23	3	2	1	55	10	2	.337	.308
Morillo, Ronald	R-R	5-11	155	1-15-90	.257	.313	.247	39	105	22	27	3	1	1	9	26	2	1	0	33	5	1	.333	.414
Ramirez, John	L-R	6-1	180	9-27-89	.143	.000	.182	5	14	2	2	0	0	1	3	3	1	0	0	6	0	0	.357	.333
2-team total (18 Giants)					.185	—		23	81	12	15	2	0	1	8	8	4	0	0	33	1	2	.247	.290
Ramos, Abraham	R-R	5-10	150	8-3-92	.182	.100	.206	15	44	7	8	3	0	0	2	4	0	0	0	8	1	0	.250	.250
Rodriguez, Josue	R-R	6-0	165	10-2-90	.500	.250	.583	10	16	5	8	3	1	0	3	2	1	0	0	3	0	1	.813	.579
Rosario, Jose	R-R	5-11	160	11-29-91	.253	.333	.238	23	75	13	19	4	0	0	6	14	0	1	0	23	3	3	.307	.371
Rosario, Melvin	R-R	6-3	177	11-2-90	.297	.294	.298	51	212	33	63	16	0	3	36	17	4	1	2	32	10	5	.415	.357
Santana, Ravel	R-R	6-2	160	5-1-92	.207	.250	.200	7	29	4	6	2	1	0	3	4	1	0	0	8	1	0	.345	.324
2-team total (43 Yankees 2)					.234	—		50	167	31	39	8	1	5	28	26	7	0	3	43	8	3	.383	.355
Taveras, Damian	R-R	6-1	205	11-28-89	.396	.250	.439	30	106	17	42	13	0	2	22	12	6	1	2	16	1	3	.575	.476
Urena, Carlos	R-R	6-1	183	11-17-89	.159	.346	.103	30	113	15	18	4	0	3	12	15	4	0	2	37	0	0	.274	.276

Pitching	B-T	HT	WT	DOB	W	L	ERA	G	GS	CG	SV	IP	H	R	ER	HR	BB	SO	AVG	vLH	vRH	K/9	BB/9
Alvarez, Isaias	R-R	6-2	175	12-9-89	1	2	4.63	16	0	0	1	35	43	24	18	4	13	17	.305	.240	.319	4.37	3.34
Alves, Maicon	R-R	5-11	165	3-27-90	1	5	10.96	14	0	0	1	23	44	31	28	4	6	23	.393	.355	.407	9.00	2.35
Beriguete, Victor	R-R	6-1	185	11-6-88	2	3	3.56	11	11	0	0	43	36	27	17	2	10	31	.217	.229	.212	6.49	2.09
Bravo, Wilfi	R-R	6-2	180	2-26-89	1	3	5.13	13	0	0	5	26	26	17	15	1	12	18	.263	.233	.275	6.15	4.10
Canela, Erick	R-R	6-1	155	10-2-90	3	1	4.22	16	8	0	0	49	46	34	23	2	34	54	.246	.234	.250	9.92	6.24
Classe, Luis	L-L	5-11	140	6-23-88	2	1	3.73	13	0	0	0	31	30	18	13	4	15	24	.252	.200	.257	6.89	4.31
Garce, Harold	R-R	6-4	205	11-28-85	2	3	3.80	13	9	0	0	47	39	29	20	0	32	37	.231	.306	.200	7.04	6.08
Garcia, Charlyn	R-R	6-1	165	6-9-86	1	2	4.20	13	11	0	0	49	48	31	23	1	24	47	.254	.270	.250	8.57	4.38
Jimenez, Antonio	R-R	6-0	175	3-1-91	4	2	5.58	18	1	0	1	31	26	32	19	1	35	27	.232	.190	.242	7.92	10.27
Jimenez, Warlin	R-R	6-0	165	9-14-89	2	1	2.51	9	6	0	0	29	24	12	8	0	11	22	.224	.250	.217	6.91	3.45
Licien, Bienvenido	R-R	6-1	160	3-21-91	2	2	8.06	13	0	0	0	22	29	24	20	1	19	18	.322	.229	.382	7.25	7.66
Marcano, Juan	L-L	6-1	165	8-24-90	2	1	2.20	12	11	0	0	45	27	13	11	1	20	70	.166	.167	.166	14.00	4.00
Martinez, Rafael	L-L	6-3	175	3-24-91	1	0	2.53	8	0	0	3	11	14	9	3	1	2	11	.326	.333	.325	8.44	1.69
Rodriguez, Ramon	R-R	6-1	170	7-23-91	2	2	6.31	15	0	0	0	26	32	28	18	4	21	21	.311	.227	.333	7.36	7.36
Rojas, Gerald	R-R	6-1	145	2-19-91	0	3	5.08	16	0	0	1	34	46	26	19	6	4	27	.331	.265	.352	7.22	1.07
Sanchez, Anthony	R-R	6-4	185	7-3-91	2	3	11.12	11	0	0	0	11	13	16	14	2	15	6	.317	.417	.276	4.76	11.91
Santana, Gabriel	R-R	6-2	170	11-9-89	0	0	27.00	2	0	0	0	2	3	5	5	1	5	1	.500	.000	.750	5.40	27.00
Tolentino, Israel	R-R	6-4	190	1-11-88	1	2	4.76	13	11	0	0	45	35	35	24	0	36	37	.217	.160	.243	7.35	7.15
Vargas, Cesar	R-R	6-1	160	12-30-91	2	1	3.50	16	0	0	3	36	39	23	14	0	11	30	.273	.264	.278	7.50	2.75

Fielding

Catcher	PCT	G	PO	A	E	DP	PB
Calderon	.833	1	9	1	2	0	0
Duran	.987	38	270	42	4	3	20
Rodriguez	.939	9	27	4	2	0	2
Taveras	.960	27	196	42	10	1	14

First Base	PCT	G	PO	A	E	DP
Beard	.988	52	466	14	6	43
Beltre	1.000	1	8	0	0	0
Lapaix	.969	5	30	1	1	3

	PCT	G	PO	A	E	DP
Morillo	1.000	4	14	0	0	2
Ramirez	1.000	4	25	0	0	2
Urena	.957	9	88	2	4	7

Second Base	PCT	G	PO	A	E	DP
Beard	.857	1	5	1	1	0
Beltre	1.000	2	2	1	0	0
Guzman	.889	4	10	6	2	1
Lopez	.948	58	115	157	15	46
Morillo	1.000	1	1	0	0	0

	PCT	G	PO	A	E	DP
Ramos	.944	5	9	8	1	1
Third Base						
Alcantara	.892	12	13	20	4	2
Castillo	.955	49	57	132	9	12
Guzman	1.000	5	3	11	0	1
Morillo	1.000	1	0	4	0	2
Ramos	.750	1	3	0	1	1
Rosario	.667	5	2	6	4	2

Shortstop	PCT	G	PO	A	E	DP
Alcantara	.878	11	11	25	5	5
Beltre	.833	5	11	9	4	4
Guzman	.875	1	3	4	1	2
Morillo	.925	31	44	80	10	12
Ramos	.808	9	6	15	5	2

	PCT	G	PO	A	E	DP
Rosario	.922	18	25	46	6	10
Outfield	**PCT**	**G**	**PO**	**A**	**E**	**DP**
Calderon	.805	38	30	3	8	0
Fulgencio	.912	45	49	3	5	1
Guzman	1.000	1	2	1	0	1
Lapaix	.926	25	21	4	2	1

	PCT	G	PO	A	E	DP
Leonora	.942	48	106	8	7	3
Morillo	—	1	0	0	0	0
Rosario	.955	42	80	4	4	0
Santana	1.000	6	10	0	0	0
Urena	1.000	14	16	0	0	0

DSL YANKEES #2   *ROOKIE*

DOMINICAN SUMMER LEAGUE

Batting	B-T	HT	WT	DOB	AVG	vLH	vRH	G	AB	R	H	2B	3B	HR	RBI	BB	HBP	SH	SF	SO	SB	CS	SLG	OBP
Arias, Gian	B-R	5-11	179	10-6-91	.227	.125	.244	62	225	47	51	7	2	0	26	48	5	4	6	49	7	5	.276	.366
Baez, Luigi	L-L	6-0	160	6-11-89	.222	.000	.240	12	27	5	6	2	0	0	5	1	0	0	6	0	0	.296	.364
Calderon, Ronny	L-R	5-9	155	12-6-87	.241	.250	.240	10	29	2	7	2	0	0	1	1	0	0	0	2	0	0	.310	.267
2-team total (1 Yankees 1)					.273	—	—	11	33	2	9	2	0	0	1	1	0	0	0	2	0	0	.333	.294
De La Rosa, Elio	R-R	6-0	185	4-18-91	.226	.182	.235	53	195	26	44	9	1	4	21	9	6	1	1	53	3	3	.344	.280
Duran, Kelvin	L-L	5-11	165	11-10-90	.302	.262	.309	62	262	59	79	9	12	3	39	26	2	1	2	45	28	7	.462	.366
Felix, Anderson	B-R	6-0	155	5-11-92	.254	.160	.274	40	142	35	36	5	3	1	16	21	1	0	0	36	7	2	.352	.354
Flores, Ramon	L-L	5-10	150	3-26-92	.256	.444	.200	11	39	8	10	0	3	1	5	11	0	1	5	0	1	.487	.423
Lopez, Daniel	R-R	6-2	175	1-17-92	.259	.143	.277	18	54	16	14	2	2	0	7	4	8	1	0	19	2	1	.370	.394
Nunez, Reymond	R-R	6-4	210	9-25-90	.296	.225	.311	59	223	32	66	12	1	10	57	21	9	0	3	44	2	2	.493	.375
Palomo, Jesus	R-R	5-11	170	12-15-89	.263	.250	.264	23	80	11	21	1	2	1	7	6	3	1	0	26	2	0	.363	.337
Parache, Luis	L-R	5-8	175	11-25-88	.275	.500	.239	36	102	20	28	3	5	0	14	8	2	1	2	7	4	0	.402	.333
Pena, Henry	L-R	6-0	180	10-26-90	.315	.267	.323	57	197	44	62	15	4	4	36	42	2	1	2	57	5	2	.492	.436
Perez, Nixton	R-R	5-11	165	7-16-88	.325	.200	.351	38	117	13	38	6	0	1	20	7	3	1	1	10	3	4	.402	.375
Ramirez, Alcibiades	B-R	5-11	165	1-27-89	.150	.000	.176	11	20	4	3	1	0	0	3	4	0	0	0	7	0	0	.200	.292
Reynoso, Victor	R-R	6-3	190	10-31-91	.269	.306	.263	62	234	38	63	18	2	6	51	11	8	0	5	61	5	3	.440	.318
Rodriguez, Keny	R-R	6-1	170	2-25-90	.333	.300	.342	40	96	23	32	6	0	0	10	20	0	1	0	15	5	4	.396	.448
Santana, Ravel	R-R	6-2	160	5-1-92	.239	.190	.248	43	138	27	33	6	0	5	25	22	6	0	3	35	7	3	.391	.361
2-team total (7 Yankees 1)					.234	—	—	50	167	30	39	8	1	5	28	26	7	0	3	43	8	3	.383	.355
Valera, Jackson	R-R	6-1	175	4-8-92	.217	.250	.211	53	184	31	40	7	0	2	23	24	6	2	3	26	0	0	.288	.323

Pitching	B-T	HT	WT	DOB	W	L	ERA	G	GS	CG	SV	IP	H	R	ER	HR	BB	SO	AVG	vLH	vRH	K/9	BB/9
Arias, Justo	R-R	6-2	145	10-29-88	1	0	7.20	5	0	0	0	5	9	4	4	1	1	5	.409	.667	.313	9.00	1.80
Croussett, Melvin	L-L	6-1	168	12-28-88	1	1	1.61	22	0	0	13	28	17	5	5	0	14	45	.173	.000	.185	14.46	4.50
Cruz, Dawerd	R-R	6-1	170	12-7-88	6	2	3.48	16	1	0	1	31	25	14	12	2	15	29	.217	.308	.191	8.42	4.35
de Leon, Nestor	R-R	6-2	200	6-22-89	3	0	4.29	13	0	0	0	21	17	15	10	3	13	23	.210	.231	.206	9.86	5.57
Eusebio, Wilkinson	R-R	6-2	178	9-26-90	2	2	10.59	17	0	0	0	17	25	23	20	3	14	15	.338	.368	.327	7.94	7.41
Gonzalez, Felipe	R-R	6-2	165	8-15-91	0	1	0.00	2	0	0	0	1	3	6	0	0	1	0	.375	—	.375	0.00	9.00
Heredia, Juan	L-L	6-3	160	1-20-89	2	0	0.32	13	13	0	0	57	34	3	2	0	20	63	.179	.143	.182	9.95	3.16
Marte, Joel	R-R	5-11	195	1-18-88	4	2	3.89	20	0	0	2	39	44	36	17	3	13	43	.277	.367	.256	9.84	2.97
Mejia, Edison	R-R	6-1	185	7-2-90	3	0	4.50	12	8	0	0	38	45	24	19	2	14	24	.298	.282	.304	5.68	3.32
Mojica, Deivi	R-R	6-1	185	3-19-91	2	4	3.17	14	11	0	0	60	68	29	21	1	11	64	.291	.215	.320	9.65	1.66
Moreta, Francis	L-L	6-1	160	8-27-86	0	0	15.43	3	0	0	0	2	5	7	4	0	3	1	.417	.000	.455	3.86	11.57
Orozco, Elvin	R-R	6-1	195	10-24-88	4	0	2.08	19	0	0	1	39	36	11	9	0	14	42	.250	.333	.216	9.69	3.23
Pena, Jose	R-R	6-0	190	3-22-91	2	0	1.42	5	0	0	1	13	6	2	2	0	4	11	.143	.143	.143	7.82	2.84
Quintana, Jose	L-L	6-0	170	1-24-89	2	1	2.32	14	14	0	0	50	25	17	13	0	37	80	.149	.053	.161	14.30	6.62
Ramirez, Jose	R-R	6-1	160	10-29-88	1	0	2.84	19	0	0	3	25	17	12	8	1	10	25	.179	.250	.160	8.88	3.55
Regalado, Melvin	R-R	6-3	190	11-20-91	4	2	4.73	15	1	0	0	32	41	21	17	2	13	18	.306	.323	.301	5.01	3.62
Reyes, Yobanny	R-R	6-0	165	11-29-88	2	1	3.54	11	1	0	0	20	19	11	8	1	9	13	.250	.381	.200	5.75	3.98
Rodino, Manuel	R-R	6-3	190	3-7-90	6	1	3.94	18	0	0	2	32	34	21	14	5	8	32	.260	.250	.262	9.00	2.25
Sanchez, Omar	R-R	5-11	160	3-5-91	4	2	1.76	14	8	0	0	46	33	13	9	1	17	54	.198	.176	.207	10.57	3.33
Tapia, Eric	L-L	6-1	193	9-6-87	3	1	1.36	13	13	0	0	53	33	11	8	1	13	42	.177	.313	.165	7.13	2.21

Fielding

Catcher	PCT	G	PO	A	E	DP	PB
Calderon	.986	8	68	5	1	1	1
Palomo	.968	20	166	17	6	0	4
Perez	1.000	1	3	0	0	0	0
Ramirez	.972	11	64	5	2	0	1
Valera	.995	41	337	36	2	1	10

First Base	PCT	G	PO	A	E	DP
Baez	1.000	1	13	2	0	1
Nunez	.978	56	457	25	11	34
Palomo	1.000	3	28	0	0	1
Perez	.982	13	105	7	2	10
Rodriguez	1.000	2	1	0	0	0

Second Base	PCT	G	PO	A	E	DP
Felix	.923	36	59	73	11	11

	PCT	G	PO	A	E	DP
Parache	.984	15	24	36	1	9
Perez	1.000	1	0	1	0	0
Rodriguez	.975	25	26	53	2	8
Third Base	**PCT**	**G**	**PO**	**A**	**E**	**DP**
De La Rosa	.888	51	38	89	16	8
Parache	—	2	0	0	0	0
Perez	.827	17	8	35	9	3
Rodriguez	.833	9	1	9	2	1
Shortstop	**PCT**	**G**	**PO**	**A**	**E**	**DP**
Arias	.918	53	75	127	18	21
Arias	1.000	2	5	6	0	1
Felix	1.000	1	3	0	0	0
Flores	.750	1	2	4	2	2
Parache	.896	19	25	35	7	5

	PCT	G	PO	A	E	DP
Perez	1.000	1	1	1	0	0
Rodriguez	—	1	0	0	0	0
Valera	—	1	0	0	0	0
Outfield	**PCT**	**G**	**PO**	**A**	**E**	**DP**
Baez	.750	7	3	0	1	0
Duran	.941	54	89	7	6	2
Felix	1.000	1	1	0	0	0
Flores	1.000	9	9	0	0	0
Lopez	.824	15	14	0	3	0
Pena	.982	41	51	4	1	2
Perez	—	1	0	0	0	0
Reynoso	.934	56	80	5	6	2
Santana	.914	41	49	4	5	0

Oakland Athletics

SEASON IN A SENTENCE: The Athletics featured the majors' youngest rotation, with all of its regular members age 25 or younger, and one of the weaker offenses as the A's finished last in the American League in home runs with 135 en route to a third consecutive losing season at 75-87.

HIGH POINT: The A's might have singlehandedly knocked the Rangers out of the playoff race with a three-game sweep of Texas in Arlington Sept. 14-16. The series culminated with a 4-0 Oakland victory in which rookie righthander Trevor Cahill allowed only one hit over seven innings while striking out seven.

LOW POINT: After enjoying a strong September when it compiled a 17-10 record, Oakland ended the season on a seven-game losing streak, its longest of the season, after getting swept in back-to-back series by the Mariners and Angels. Oakland scored four runs or fewer in all seven games, the worst of which was a 7-0 loss in Seattle on Sept. 30 in which the A's mustered just two hits.

NOTABLE ROOKIES: Four of Oakland's top five pitching prospects graduated to the major leagues, led by Cahill and lefthander Brett Anderson. Those two were the only Athletics pitchers to post double-digit win totals, but another of their rookie pitchers made the biggest splash of all. Less heralded righthander Andrew Bailey won the AL rookie of the year award after posting 26 saves, a 1.84 ERA and allowing just 49 hits in 83 innings. Landon Powell also broke in as the backup to catcher Kurt Suzuki.

KEY TRANSACTIONS: Most expected outfielder Matt Holliday's tenure in Oakland to be brief, and sure enough, the A's dealt him to the Cardinals at the trade deadline. Oakland received three prospects in return, most notably third baseman Brett Wallace, the Cardinals' first-round pick in the 2008 draft. The A's also traded shortstop Orlando Cabrera to the Twins for a prospect, and sent three arms to the Padres for outfielder Scott Hairston.

DOWN ON THE FARM: Three of Oakland's four full-season affiliates made the playoffs, with Double-A Midland winning the Texas League title. A's affiliates finished 359-336, good for seventh-best in baseball. With most of the top pitchers moving on to the majors, the minor league focus shifted to the offensive side, where slugging first baseman Chris Carter was the top performer. Carter batted .329/.422/.570 with 28 home runs, spending most of the season at Midland.

OPENING DAY PAYROLL: $62,310,000

ORGANIZATION LEADERS

BATTING		*Minimum 250 at-bats
MAJORS		
*AVG	Ryan Sweeney	.293
*OPS	Jack Cust	.773
HR	Jack Cust	25
RBI	Kurt Suzuki	88
MINORS		
*AVG	Everidge, Tommy, Midland/Sacramento	.335
R	Carter, Chris, Midland/Sacramento	115
H	Carter, Chris, Midland/Sacramento	179
TB	Carter, Chris, Midland/Sacramento	310
2B	Carter, Chris, Midland/Sacramento	43
3B	Patterson, Eric, Sacramento	11
HR	Desme, Grant, Kane County, Stockton	31
RBI	Carter, Chris, Midland/Sacramento	115
BB	Carter, Chris, Midland/Sacramento	85
SO	Coleman, Dusty, Kane County/Stockton	154
SB	Patterson, Eric, Sacramento	43
*OBP	Carter, Chris, Midland/Sacramento	.422
*SLG	Carter, Chris, Midland/Sacramento	.570

PITCHING		†Minimum 75 innings
MAJORS		
W	Brett Anderson	11
†ERA	Brett Anderson	4.06
SO	Brett Anderson	150
MINORS		
W	Hernandez, Carlos, Sac./Stockton/Midland	15
L	Haviland, Shawn, Kane County	11
†ERA	Smalley, Kenny, Kane County	2.73
G	Benacka, Michael, Midland/Sacramento	55
	Demel, Sam, Midland/Sacramento	55
GS	Three tied at	28
SV	Storey, Mickey, Kane Co./Sac./Stock./Midland	18
IP	Godfrey, Graham, Midland	159
BB	Figueroa, Pedro, Kane County/Stockton	66
SO	Capra, Anthony, Kane County/Stockton	170
†AVG	Capra, Anthony, Kane County/Stockton	.206

OAKLAND ATHLETICS

2009 PERFORMANCE

General Manager: Billy Beane. **Farm Director:** Keith Lieppman. **Scouting Director:** Eric Kubota.

Class	Team	League	W	L	PCT	Finish*	Manager(s)
Majors	Oakland Athletics	American	75	87	.463	t-10th (14)	Bob Geren
Triple-A	Sacramento River Cats	Pacific Coast	86	57	.601	1st (16)	Tony DeFrancesco
Double-A	Midland RockHounds	Texas	78	62	.557	†1st (8)	Darren Bush
High A	Stockton Ports	California	61	79	.436	t-7th (10)	Aaron Nieckula
Low A	Kane County Cougars	Midwest	76	64	.543	6th (14)	Steve Scarsone
Short-season	Vancouver Canadians	Northwest	36	40	.474	5th (8)	Rick Magnante
Rookie	AZL Athletics	Arizona	22	34	.393	10th (11)	Marcus Jensen
Overall 2009 Minor League Record			359	336	.517	7th (30)	

*Finish in overall standings (No. of teams in league). †League champion.

ORGANIZATION STATISTICS

OAKLAND ATHLETICS

AMERICAN LEAGUE

Batting	B-T	HT	WT	DOB	AVG	vLH	vRH	G	AB	R	H	2B	3B	HR	RBI	BB	HBP	SH	SF	SO	SB	CS	SLG	OBP
Barton, Daric	L-R	6-0	220	8-16-85	.269	.333	.257	54	160	31	43	12	1	3	24	26	2	1	3	25	0	2	.413	.372
Buck, Travis	L-R	6-2	230	11-18-83	.219	.143	.231	36	105	11	23	3	0	3	10	10	0	0	0	20	1	1	.333	.287
Cabrera, Orlando	R-R	5-9	185	11-2-74	.280	.223	.301	101	414	41	116	23	0	4	41	25	0	5	4	39	11	4	.365	.318
2-team total (59 Minnesota)					.284	—	—	160	656	83	186	36	3	9	77	36	0	6	10	71	13	4	.389	.316
Carson, Matt	R-R	6-2	200	7-1-81	.286	.308	.250	10	21	1	6	0	0	1	5	0	0	0	1	7	0	0	.429	.273
Chavez, Eric	L-R	6-1	220	12-7-77	.100	.111	.083	8	30	0	3	1	0	0	1	1	0	0	0	7	0	0	.133	.129
Crosby, Bobby	R-R	6-3	205	1-12-80	.223	.265	.184	97	238	35	53	10	2	6	29	24	2	4	4	44	2	1	.357	.295
Cunningham, Aaron	R-R	5-11	205	4-24-86	.151	.176	.139	23	53	6	8	2	0	1	6	3	1	0	0	16	0	0	.245	.211
Cust, Jack	L-R	6-1	240	1-7-79	.240	.221	.247	149	513	88	123	16	0	25	70	93	2	0	4	185	4	1	.417	.356
Davis, Rajai	R-R	5-11	195	10-19-80	.305	.316	.299	125	390	65	119	27	5	3	48	29	7	2	4	70	41	12	.423	.360
Denorfia, Chris	R-R	6-0	205	7-15-80	.000	—	.000	4	2	1	0	0	0	0	1	0	0	0	0	0	0	0	.000	.000
Ellis, Mark	R-R	5-11	195	6-6-77	.263	.260	.264	105	377	52	99	23	0	10	61	23	2	3	5	54	10	3	.403	.305
Everidge, Tommy	R-R	6-0	240	4-20-83	.224	.333	.180	24	85	13	19	6	0	2	7	8	2	1	1	17	0	0	.365	.302
Garciaparra, Nomar	R-R	6-0	190	7-23-73	.281	.297	.267	65	160	17	45	8	0	3	16	8	0	0	1	28	2	0	.388	.314
Giambi, Jason	L-R	6-3	240	1-8-71	.193	.209	.186	83	269	39	52	13	0	11	40	50	7	0	2	72	0	0	.364	.332
Hairston, Scott	R-R	6-0	195	5-25-80	.236	.259	.229	60	233	24	55	13	1	7	35	8	2	0	5	38	3	2	.391	.262
Hannahan, Jack	L-R	6-2	210	3-4-80	.193	.200	.191	52	119	12	23	6	2	1	8	13	1	1	0	36	0	0	.303	.278
2-team total (51 Seattle)					.213	—	—	103	267	27	57	14	2	4	19	30	2	1	1	71	1	1	.326	.297
Holliday, Matt	R-R	6-4	235	1-15-80	.286	.280	.289	93	346	52	99	23	1	11	54	46	6	0	2	58	12	3	.454	.378
Kennedy, Adam	L-R	6-1	195	1-10-76	.289	.241	.307	129	529	65	153	29	1	11	63	45	4	5	3	86	20	6	.410	.348
Munson, Eric	L-R	6-3	220	10-3-77	.000	.000	—	1	1	0	0	0	0	0	0	0	0	0	0	0	0	0	.000	.000
Patterson, Eric	L-R	5-11	170	4-8-83	.287	.375	.269	39	94	15	27	5	1	1	11	14	0	0	2	25	6	1	.394	.373
Pennington, Cliff	S-R	5-11	190	6-15-84	.279	.200	.307	60	208	27	58	11	3	4	21	19	1	1	0	46	7	5	.418	.342
Petit, Gregorio	R-R	5-10	200	12-10-84	.226	.308	.167	11	31	2	7	1	0	0	1	0	0	0	0	6	0	0	.258	.226
Powell, Landon	B-R	6-3	260	3-19-82	.229	.128	.267	46	140	19	32	7	0	7	30	14	0	0	1	36	0	0	.429	.297
Suzuki, Kurt	R-R	5-11	200	10-4-83	.274	.250	.283	147	570	74	156	37	1	15	88	28	8	1	7	59	8	2	.421	.313
Sweeney, Ryan	L-L	6-4	220	2-20-85	.293	.268	.301	134	484	68	142	31	3	6	53	40	3	2	5	67	6	5	.407	.348

Pitching	B-T	HT	WT	DOB	W	L	ERA	G	GS	CG	SV	IP	H	R	ER	HR	BB	SO	AVG	vLH	vRH	K/9	BB/9
Anderson, Brett	L-L	6-4	215	2-1-88	11	11	4.06	30	30	1	0	175	180	94	79	20	45	150	.265	.313	.247	7.70	2.31
Bailey, Andrew	R-R	6-3	235	5-31-84	6	3	1.84	68	0	0	26	83	49	17	17	5	24	91	.167	.146	.185	9.83	2.59
Blevins, Jerry	L-L	6-6	180	9-6-83	0	0	4.84	20	0	0	0	22	19	12	12	2	6	23	.229	.250	.218	9.27	2.42
Braden, Dallas	L-L	6-1	200	8-13-83	8	9	3.89	22	22	0	0	137	144	63	59	9	42	81	.268	.203	.290	5.33	2.77
Breslow, Craig	L-L	6-1	180	8-8-80	7	5	2.60	60	0	0	0	55	37	20	16	5	18	44	.191	.202	.181	7.16	2.93
2-team total (17 Minnesota)					8	7	3.36	77	0	0	0	70	48	31	26	8	29	55	—	—	—	7.11	3.75
Cahill, Trevor	R-R	6-3	210	3-1-88	10	13	4.63	32	32	0	0	179	185	99	92	27	72	90	.270	.286	.252	4.53	3.63
Cameron, Kevin	R-R	6-1	190	12-15-79	0	0	3.44	11	0	0	1	18	15	7	7	1	6	15	.221	.240	.209	7.36	2.95
Casilla, Santiago	R-R	6-0	200	7-25-80	1	2	5.96	46	0	0	0	48	61	36	32	6	25	35	.303	.354	.257	6.52	4.66
Eveland, Dana	L-L	6-1	225	10-29-83	2	4	7.16	13	9	0	0	44	70	39	35	4	26	22	.365	.373	.362	4.50	5.32
Gallagher, Sean	R-R	6-2	235	12-30-85	1	2	8.16	6	2	0	0	14	21	16	13	1	7	10	.350	.409	.316	6.28	4.40
Giese, Dan	R-R	6-2	200	5-19-77	0	3	5.32	7	1	0	0	22	22	13	13	5	9	11	.262	.243	.277	4.50	3.68
Gonzalez, Edgar	R-R	6-2	210	2-23-83	0	4	5.51	26	6	0	0	65	76	41	40	4	28	39	.292	.351	.230	5.37	3.86
Gonzalez, Gio	R-L	5-11	195	9-19-85	6	7	5.75	20	17	0	0	99	113	68	63	14	56	109	.288	.340	.271	9.94	5.11
Gray, Jeff	R-R	6-3	195	11-19-81	0	1	3.76	24	0	0	0	26	30	12	11	3	4	19	.278	.300	.259	6.49	1.37
Kilby, Brad	L-L	6-1	235	2-19-83	1	0	0.53	11	0	0	0	17	10	2	1	1	4	20	.164	.217	.132	10.59	2.12
Marshall, Jay	L-L	6-5	205	2-25-83	0	2	14.73	10	0	0	0	7	13	12	12	1	0	1	.406	.333	.450	1.23	0.00
Mazzaro, Vin	R-R	6-1	215	9-27-86	4	9	5.32	17	17	0	0	91	120	61	54	12	39	59	.319	.321	.316	5.81	3.84
Meloan, John	R-R	6-3	225	7-11-84	0	0	0.00	6	0	0	0	8	3	1	0	0	2	11	.111	.231	.000	11.88	2.16
Mortensen, Clay	R-R	6-4	180	4-10-85	2	4	7.81	6	6	0	0	28	37	28	24	5	12	11	.319	.358	.286	3.58	3.90
Outman, Josh	L-L	6-1	185	9-14-84	4	1	3.48	14	12	0	0	67	53	30	26	9	25	53	.212	.123	.238	7.08	3.34
Reineke, Chad	R-R	6-6	230	4-9-82	0	0	7.20	1	1	0	0	5	7	4	4	2	0	1	.333	.400	.273	1.80	0.00
Rodriguez, Henry	R-R	6-0	210	2-25-87	0	0	2.25	3	0	0	0	4	4	2	1	0	2	4	.235	.429	.100	9.00	4.50

Player	B-T	HT	WT	DOB	ERA	G	GS	CG	SV	IP	H	R	ER	HR	BB	SO	AVG	vLH	vRH	K/9	BB/9
Springer, Russ	R-R	6-4	225	11-7-68	0	1	4.10	48	0	0	0	42	52	20	19	5	14	47	.299	.357	.260	10.15	3.02
2-team total (26 Tampa Bay)					1	4	4.11	74	0	0	1	57	68	27	26	9	17	58	—	—	9.16	2.68
Tomko, Brett	R-R	6-4	220	4-7-73	4	1	2.95	6	1	0	1	37	31	12	12	7	6	22	.230	.250	.209	5.40	1.47
2-team total (15 New York)					5	3	3.77	21	6	1	0	57	50	24	24	12	13	33	—	—	5.18	2.04
Wuertz, Michael	R-R	6-3	205	12-15-78	6	1	2.63	74	0	0	4	79	52	25	23	6	23	102	.188	.183	.193	11.67	2.63
Ziegler, Brad	R-R	6-4	205	10-10-79	2	4	3.07	69	0	0	7	73	82	27	25	2	28	54	.293	.336	.265	6.63	3.44

Fielding

Catcher	PCT	G	PO	A	E	DP	PB
Powell	.987	36	214	13	3	4	2
Suzuki	.995	135	923	68	5	7	3

First Base	PCT	G	PO	A	E	DP
Barton	.998	51	418	25	1	39
Crosby	1.000	54	235	13	0	26
Everidge	.993	21	138	11	1	11
Garciaparra	1.000	16	95	5	0	13
Giambi	.993	58	441	17	3	45
Hannahan	1.000	1	1	0	0	0
Kennedy	1.000	1	1	0	0	0
Powell	.977	6	39	4	1	5

Second Base	PCT	G	PO	A	E	DP
Crosby	.952	5	12	8	1	3

	PCT	G	PO	A	E	DP	PB
Ellis	.990	105	197	285	5	68	
Hannahan	—	1	0	0	0	0	
Kennedy	.967	50	87	121	7	30	
Patterson	.900	5	9	9	2	1	
Petit	.967	8	14	15	1	5	

Third Base	PCT	G	PO	A	E	DP
Chavez	1.000	8	5	15	0	2
Crosby	.931	42	23	72	7	6
Garciaparra	1.000	6	1	8	0	0
Hannahan	.969	51	35	89	4	10
Kennedy	.941	82	50	156	13	8
Petit	1.000	3	1	4	0	0

Shortstop	PCT	G	PO	A	E	DP
Cabrera	.968	101	156	273	14	63

	PCT	G	PO	A	E	DP
Crosby	1.000	6	1	8	0	2
Pennington	.971	60	90	181	8	41

Outfield	PCT	G	PO	A	E	DP
Buck	1.000	32	61	0	0	0
Carson	1.000	9	12	0	0	0
Crosby	—	1	0	0	0	0
Cunningham	.917	23	22	0	2	0
Cust	.972	51	69	1	2	1
Davis	.986	116	265	8	4	1
Denorfia	—	3	0	0	0	0
Hairston	.992	56	120	1	1	1
Holliday	.980	93	189	6	4	1
Kennedy	1.000	1	1	0	0	0
Patterson	1.000	31	41	1	0	0
Sweeney	.991	132	319	11	3	2

SACRAMENTO RIVER CATS
TRIPLE-A
PACIFIC COAST LEAGUE

Batting	B-T	HT	WT	DOB	AVG	vLH	vRH	G	AB	R	H	2B	3B	HR	RBI	BB	HBP	SH	SF	SO	SB	CS	SLG	OBP
Baisley, Jeff	R-R	6-3	220	12-19-82	.248	.355	.210	98	355	44	88	21	1	9	38	26	5	2	3	82	2	0	.389	.306
Barton, Daric	L-R	6-0	220	8-16-85	.261	.239	.273	70	253	48	66	21	1	9	48	45	9	2	4	43	1	0	.458	.386
Buck, Travis	L-R	6-2	230	11-18-83	.272	.222	.283	62	232	37	63	13	3	5	29	23	5	2	4	44	3	1	.418	.345
Cardenas, Adrian	L-R	6-0	185	10-10-87	.251	.277	.243	51	183	23	46	15	2	1	24	17	2	2	3	29	3	2	.372	.317
Carson, Matt	R-R	6-2	200	7-1-81	.264	.258	.266	118	440	68	116	29	3	25	77	38	6	4	5	94	15	4	.514	.327
Carter, Chris	R-R	6-4	225	12-18-86	.259	.250	.261	13	54	7	14	2	0	4	14	3	0	0	1	14	0	1	.519	.293
Chen, Yung Chi	R-R	5-11	170	7-13-83	.283	.217	.304	27	92	13	26	2	0	1	8	10	0	1	0	18	4	0	.337	.353
Cobb, Larry	R-R	5-9	179	7-10-85	.240	.286	.222	10	25	2	6	3	0	0	2	1	0	0	0	7	0	0	.360	.269
Copeland, Ben	L-L	6-1	190	12-17-83	.500	—	.500	1	4	0	2	0	0	0	1	0	0	0	0	0	0	0	.500	.500
2-team total (97 Fresno)					.281	—		98	342	46	96	18	3	8	35	24	3	1	3	60	15	6	.421	.331
Cunningham, Aaron	R-R	5-11	205	4-24-86	.302	.286	.307	83	334	62	101	24	1	11	48	33	5	1	2	74	11	4	.479	.372
Denorfia, Chris	R-R	6-0	205	7-15-80	.271	.242	.283	107	432	62	117	18	5	9	49	31	1	4	6	52	15	6	.398	.317
Doolittle, Sean	L-L	6-3	190	9-26-86	.267	.333	.232	28	105	17	28	5	1	4	14	15	1	0	0	23	0	1	.448	.364
Ellis, Mark	R-R	5-11	195	6-6-77	.182	.333	.167	8	33	2	6	1	0	0	3	0	0	0	0	2	0	0	.212	.182
Everidge, Tommy	R-R	6-0	240	4-20-83	.368	.378	.365	52	201	39	74	15	1	12	41	23	1	0	4	34	0	0	.632	.428
Galarraga, Joel	R-R	6-0	155	3-20-82	.357	.438	.308	13	42	9	15	3	1	0	6	6	1	1	0	10	0	1	.476	.449
Hannahan, Jack	L-R	6-2	210	3-4-80	.222	.150	.246	21	81	8	18	7	0	2	11	7	0	0	0	27	0	1	.383	.284
Munson, Eric	L-R	6-3	220	10-3-77	.265	.267	.264	99	351	50	93	22	2	13	68	54	3	1	6	71	0	1	.450	.362
Padron, Raul	L-R	6-0	195	9-17-84	.214	.125	.333	5	14	2	3	0	0	0	2	2	0	0	0	7	0	0	.214	.313
Patterson, Eric	L-R	5-11	170	4-8-83	.307	.241	.336	110	466	91	143	29	11	12	56	52	2	6	4	81	43	6	.494	.376
Pennington, Cliff	B-R	5-11	190	6-15-84	.264	.323	.242	99	360	48	95	22	3	3	40	45	2	6	4	54	27	4	.367	.345
Petit, Gregorio	R-R	5-10	200	12-10-84	.244	.235	.247	98	357	45	87	18	0	5	32	26	1	7	7	83	0	2	.336	.292
Putnam, Danny	L-L	5-10	200	9-17-82	.245	.179	.269	39	143	14	35	3	1	4	21	10	0	1	1	31	1	1	.364	.292
2-team total (54 Portland)					.247			93	312	33	77	18	1	10	55	32	4	2	1	69	4	3	.407	.324
Recker, Anthony	R-R	6-2	240	8-29-83	.261	.259	.262	78	272	30	71	11	2	12	45	28	2	3	1	80	2	0	.449	.333
Valdez, Alex	B-R	6-1	160	9-2-84	—	—	—	1	0	0	0	0	0	0	0	0	0	0	0	0	0	0	—	—
Wallace, Brett	L-R	6-2	205	8-26-86	.302	.286	.307	44	182	32	55	10	0	9	28	14	5	0	2	40	1	1	.505	.365
2-team total (62 Memphis)					.297			106	404	54	120	21	0	15	47	29	9	0	4	82	1	2	.460	.354

Pitching	B-T	HT	WT	DOB	W	L	ERA	G	GS	CG	SV	IP	H	R	ER	HR	BB	SO	AVG	vLH	vRH	K/9	BB/9
Banwart, Travis	R-R	6-4	205	2-14-86	0	1	10.50	1	1	0	0	6	11	7	7	0	1	5	.440	.417	.462	7.50	1.50
Benacka, Mike	R-R	6-2	210	8-2-82	0	1	1.98	10	0	0	0	14	6	3	3	0	6	18	.133	.143	.125	11.85	3.95
Blevins, Jerry	L-L	6-6	180	9-6-83	5	3	3.84	45	0	0	2	63	65	28	27	5	18	62	.271	.286	.263	8.81	2.56
Cameron, Kevin	R-R	6-1	190	12-15-79	2	1	2.77	10	0	0	1	13	7	5	4	0	11	14	.159	.136	.182	9.69	7.62
Casilla, Santiago	R-R	6-0	200	7-25-80	0	0	0.00	1	1	0	0	1	0	0	0	0	0	0	.000	.000	.000	0.00	0.00
Chacon, Shawn	R-R	6-3	220	12-23-77	8	4	6.29	14	12	0	0	73	77	55	51	13	42	53	.271	.316	.241	6.53	5.18
Cramer, Bob	L-L	6-1	190	10-28-79	1	1	6.43	6	1	0	0	14	14	11	10	0	8	14	.387	.238	.463	9.00	5.14
Demel, Sam	R-R	6-0	200	10-23-85	2	3	3.62	28	0	0	3	32	27	14	13	1	21	33	.225	.231	.222	9.19	5.85
Duchscherer, Justin	R-R	6-3	200	11-19-77	0	0	0.00	1	1	0	0	4	2	0	0	0	1	3	.143	—	.143	6.75	2.25
Eveland, Dana	L-L	6-1	225	10-29-83	8	6	4.94	21	21	0	0	124	133	79	68	12	51	92	.273	.270	.274	6.68	3.70
Friend, Justin	R-R	6-1	200	6-21-86	0	0	13.50	1	0	0	1	2	2	2	2	0	1	3	.333	.000	.400	20.25	6.75
Gallagher, Sean	R-R	6-2	235	12-30-85	1	0	1.74	5	5	0	0	21	12	5	4	0	6	15	.167	.184	.147	6.53	2.61
2-team total (1 Portland)					1	1	2.91	6	6	0	0	22	15	8	7	1	6	16	—	—		6.65	2.49
Giese, Dan	R-R	6-2	200	5-19-77	1	0	2.25	1	0	0	0	4	3	1	1	0	0	2	.231	.250	.222	4.50	0.00
Gissell, Chris	R-R	6-5	210	1-4-78	0	1	3.52	2	2	0	0	8	10	4	3	0	2	5	.323	.333	.316	5.87	2.35
Gonzalez, Edgar	R-R	6-2	210	2-23-83	3	2	5.22	7	7	0	0	40	48	23	23	4	16	27	.300	.323	.284	6.13	3.63

Gonzalez, Gio	R-L 5-11 195 9-19-85	4	1	2.51	12	12	0	0	61	42	21	17	5	34	71	.194	.209	.188	10.48	5.02
Gordon, Derrick	L-L 5-9 185 10-16-83	0	0	5.40	1	0	0	0	2	1	1	1	0	2	2	.167	—	.167	10.80	10.80
Gray, Jeff	R-R 6-3 195 11-19-81	2	2	1.54	37	0	0	16	41	30	8	7	2	6	22	.200	.218	.189	4.83	1.32
Haigwood, Daniel	R-L 6-2 215 11-19-83	0	0	3.38	1	0	0	0	5	6	3	2	0	2	3	.261	.125	.333	5.06	3.38
Hampson, Justin	L-L 6-0 205 5-24-80	0	0	5.40	4	0	0	0	7	6	4	4	2	0	5	.222	.000	.316	6.75	0.00
Hernandez, Carlos	L-L 5-11 155 3-4-87	0	0	0.00	1	0	0	0	3	2	0	0	0	1	5	.182	.125	.333	13.50	2.70
Hodsdon, Scott	R-R 6-1 185 5-31-85	0	0	4.32	2	1	0	0	8	9	4	4	1	4	2	.273	.053	.571	2.16	4.32
Kilby, Brad	L-L 6-1 235 2-19-83	4	2	2.13	45	0	0	2	63	40	15	15	5	24	77	.179	.234	.150	10.94	3.41
Lansford, Jared	R-R 6-0 190 10-22-86	0	1	9.00	8	0	0	0	11	13	12	11	2	12	1	.289	.353	.250	0.82	9.82
Marshall, Jay	L-L 6-5 205 2-25-83	5	3	3.20	50	0	0	7	51	53	23	18	2	15	30	.280	.179	.362	5.33	2.66
Mazzaro, Vin	R-R 6-1 215 9-27-86	2	2	2.38	10	9	0	0	57	42	17	15	2	17	44	.205	.218	.189	6.99	2.70
Meloan, John	R-R 6-3 225 7-11-84	0	0	0.00	3	0	0	0	3	0	0	0	2	2	1	.000	.000	.000	3.00	6.00
Mortensen, Clay	R-R 6-4 180 4-10-85	2	2	4.45	6	6	0	0	32	40	20	16	2	14	18	.310	.311	.309	5.01	3.90
2-team total (17 Memphis)		9	8	4.39	23	23	1	0	137	143	78	67	13	48	100	—	—	—	6.55	3.15
Patterson, Scott	R-R 6-7 235 6-20-79	0	1	2.08	7	0	0	0	9	9	5	2	2	4	8	.273	.500	.143	8.31	4.15
2-team total (51 Portland)		3	4	3.96	58	0	0	1	64	61	34	28	4	44	72	—	—	—	10.18	6.22
Reineke, Chad	R-R 6-6 230 4-9-82	9	4	4.75	30	22	0	2	125	134	73	66	17	52	91	.272	.308	.244	6.55	3.74
Rodriguez, Henry	R-R 6-0 210 2-25-87	2	1	5.77	37	0	0	4	44	38	28	28	4	38	71	.228	.266	.204	14.63	7.83
Schroder, Chris	R-R 6-1 210 8-20-78	3	1	2.22	45	1	0	3	57	36	20	14	4	37	46	.180	.176	.183	7.31	5.88
Sharpe, Steve	R-R 6-1 195 7-20-81	3	0	6.00	11	1	0	0	18	19	12	12	3	10	10	.268	.375	.179	5.00	5.00
Simmons, James	R-R 6-3 220 9-29-86	7	7	5.72	23	22	1	0	120	139	81	76	8	47	81	.292	.299	.286	6.09	3.53
Storey, Mickey	R-R 6-2 185 3-16-86	0	0	0.00	2	0	0	0	3	0	0	0	0	4	4	.000	.000	.000	12.00	0.00
Tomko, Brett	R-R 6-4 220 4-7-73	0	0	7.94	3	2	0	0	6	9	6	5	0	2	8	.346	.000	.500	12.71	3.18
Webb, Ryan	R-R 6-6 215 2-5-86	7	1	4.34	31	2	0	2	46	57	22	22	3	15	39	.313	.243	.361	7.69	2.96
2-team total (3 Portland)		7	1	4.25	34	2	0	2	49	60	23	23	3	16	39	—	—	—	7.21	2.96
Williams, Jerome	R-R 6-3 240 12-4-81	5	6	5.58	27	14	0	0	102	116	66	63	15	41	52	.297	.330	.269	4.60	3.63

Fielding

Catcher	PCT	G	PO	A	E	DP	PB
Galarraga	.970	6	29	3	1	1	0
Munson	.996	73	490	33	2	4	9
Padron	1.000	4	26	1	0	0	0
Recker	.988	69	519	38	7	6	5

First Base	PCT	G	PO	A	E	DP
Baisley	1.000	30	214	17	0	26
Barton	.994	67	576	40	4	61
Carter	.984	7	59	4	1	5
Doolittle	1.000	3	19	3	0	2
Everidge	.993	34	279	16	2	29
Munson	.974	5	35	3	1	6
Patterson	1.000	1	2	0	0	1
Wallace	1.000	5	46	5	0	3

Second Base	PCT	G	PO	A	E	DP
Cardenas	.966	35	80	88	6	21
Chen	1.000	18	37	38	0	11
Cobb	1.000	2	2	7	0	0

	PCT	G	PO	A	E	DP	PB
Ellis	1.000	8	14	26	0	6	
Hannahan	.962	5	11	14	1	4	
Patterson	.988	48	108	134	3	41	
Pennington	.951	16	35	43	4	11	
Petit	.989	19	38	51	1	13	

Third Base	PCT	G	PO	A	E	DP
Baisley	.947	50	33	92	7	9
Cardenas	1.000	6	2	10	0	0
Chen	1.000	2	0	3	0	0
Cobb	1.000	1	1	0	0	0
Everidge	1.000	3	0	4	0	1
Hannahan	.951	16	9	30	2	4
Patterson	.789	10	2	13	4	0
Pennington	1.000	3	0	5	0	1
Petit	.953	22	13	48	3	4
Wallace	.922	35	29	54	7	7

Shortstop	PCT	G	PO	A	E	DP
Baisley	.833	3	0	5	1	1

	PCT	G	PO	A	E	DP
Cardenas	.926	5	6	19	2	3
Chen	.950	5	7	12	1	5
Pennington	.959	77	114	236	15	57
Petit	.963	55	97	160	10	34

Outfield	PCT	G	PO	A	E	DP
Buck	1.000	53	96	3	0	0
Carson	1.000	106	260	7	0	3
Carter	1.000	6	11	0	0	0
Chen	1.000	1	3	0	0	0
Cobb	.667	4	2	0	1	0
Copeland	1.000	1	2	0	0	0
Cunningham	.983	70	114	5	2	0
Denorfia	.987	98	223	6	3	2
Doolittle	1.000	24	33	3	0	0
Galarraga	—	1	0	0	0	0
Patterson	.978	47	87	2	2	1
Pennington	1.000	1	4	0	0	0
Putnam	1.000	36	64	3	0	1

MIDLAND ROCKHOUNDS   DOUBLE-A
TEXAS LEAGUE

Batting	B-T	HT	WT	DOB	AVG	vLH	vRH	G	AB	R	H	2B	3B	HR	RBI	BB	HBP	SH	SF	SO	SB	CS	SLG	OBP
Affronti, Mike	R-R 6-2 195			2-13-84	.243	.220	.254	52	189	20	46	6	0	3	21	12	5	2	3	26	1	2	.323	.301
Brown, Corey	L-L 6-2 210			11-26-85	.268	.323	.250	66	250	46	67	20	4	9	43	27	4	0	0	69	5	2	.488	.349
Cardenas, Adrian	L-R 6-0 185			10-10-87	.326	.264	.350	79	325	56	106	26	2	3	55	38	1	3	6	44	5	4	.446	.392
Carter, Chris	R-R 6-4 225			12-18-86	.337	.360	.330	125	490	108	165	41	2	24	101	82	11	0	10	119	13	5	.576	.435
Chen, Yung Chi	R-R 5-11 170			7-13-83	.324	.429	.296	17	68	12	22	6	0	0	10	7	0	0	0	9	2	0	.412	.387
Donaldson, Josh	R-R 6-1 215			12-8-85	.270	.288	.263	124	455	67	123	37	1	9	91	80	1	3	2	92	7	2	.415	.379
Everidge, Tommy	R-R 6-0 240			4-20-83	.306	.263	.320	55	229	41	70	18	0	8	53	28	0	0	1	34	0	1	.489	.380
Gilbert, Archie	R-R 5-8 184			7-8-83	.283	.230	.303	119	449	81	127	16	5	3	39	61	13	1	1	52	29	15	.361	.384
Herrera, Javier	R-R 5-11 225			4-9-85	.000	—	.000	1	2	0	0	0	0	0	0	0	0	0	0	0	0	0	.000	.000
Horton, Josh	L-R 6-1 195			2-19-86	.263	.231	.274	125	510	80	134	21	6	5	62	65	1	2	7	65	9	3	.357	.343
Ortiz, Gabriel	R-R 6-1 215			11-7-85	.280	.143	.333	8	25	4	7	2	0	1	8	0	0	0	2	5	2	0	.480	.259
Padron, Raul	L-R 6-0 195			9-10-84	.275	.333	.250	39	138	13	38	9	0	2	17	11	2	1	2	25	0	0	.384	.333
Peterson, Shane	L-L 6-0 195			2-11-88	.273	.263	.278	39	154	16	42	10	0	3	17	13	2	1	2	32	4	0	.396	.333
2-team total (18 Springfield, MO)					.276	—	—	57	228	26	63	14	1	4	24	18	3	1	2	42	6	0	.399	.335
Putnam, Danny	L-L 5-10 200			9-17-82	.301	.212	.333	30	123	28	37	7	0	7	22	16	0	0	0	26	4	1	.528	.381
Recker, Anthony	R-R 6-2 240			8-29-83	.298	.438	.244	16	57	11	17	4	0	3	9	6	0	0	0	11	0	0	.526	.385
Spencer, Matt	L-L 6-4 225			1-27-86	.294	.272	.304	93	371	59	109	29	3	9	62	26	7	0	5	75	2	3	.461	.347
Sulentic, Matt	L-R 5-10 170			10-6-87	.288	.226	.315	113	413	60	119	21	5	7	52	35	4	1	6	103	21	9	.414	.345
Valdez, Alex	B-R 6-1 160			9-2-84	.280	.247	.293	77	275	43	77	15	5	5	46	33	1	1	3	42	4	3	.425	.356
Weeks, Jemile	B-R 5-10 175			1-26-87	.238	.333	.182	30	105	10	25	5	0	2	13	10	1	4	3	16	4	0	.343	.303
Wimberly, Corey	B-R 5-8 180			10-26-83	.296	.319	.286	70	297	56	88	10	3	0	28	24	9	3	3	31	21	8	.350	.363

Pitching

Pitching	B-T	HT	WT	DOB	W	L	ERA	G	GS	CG	SV	IP	H	R	ER	HR	BB	SO	AVG	vLH	vRH	K/9	BB/9
Banwart, Travis	R-R	6-4	205	2-14-86	10	5	4.89	27	27	0	0	140	165	87	76	13	44	77	.290	.270	.308	4.95	2.83
Barone, Daniel	R-R	6-2	185	4-24-83	0	2	9.50	4	4	0	0	18	31	21	19	2	5	9	.392	.412	.378	4.50	2.50
Bell, Kristian	R-R	6-0	185	1-11-84	1	2	8.67	9	7	0	0	27	50	29	26	2	18	12	.403	.408	.396	4.00	6.00
Benacka, Mike	R-R	6-2	210	8-2-82	3	0	2.74	45	0	0	4	66	52	21	20	0	32	72	.218	.114	.328	9.87	4.39
Cramer, Bob	L-L	6-1	190	10-28-79	3	4	3.35	12	8	0	0	43	48	29	16	1	13	39	.274	.233	.288	8.16	2.72
Day, Dewon	R-R	6-2	220	9-29-80	0	0	9.15	16	0	0	0	21	31	25	21	1	16	22	.348	.385	.320	9.58	6.97
Demel, Sam	R-R	6-0	200	10-23-85	0	2	0.61	27	0	0	11	29	23	5	2	1	9	26	.209	.212	.207	7.98	2.76
Dowdy, Justin	L-L	6-1	175	8-13-83	3	0	5.21	14	0	0	0	19	19	12	11	2	11	12	.253	.276	.239	5.68	5.21
Farley, Chris	R-R	6-2	220	2-24-83	1	3	9.22	11	5	0	0	27	42	34	28	6	25	13	.368	.311	.434	4.28	8.23
Fernandez, Jason	R-R	6-2	175	1-8-85	8	8	4.97	30	18	1	0	125	150	76	69	13	55	74	.308	.353	.271	5.33	3.96
Friend, Justin	R-R	6-1	200	6-21-86	1	0	7.71	9	0	0	1	9	12	8	8	1	7	11	.316	.278	.350	10.61	6.75
Garcia, Angel	R-R	6-7	230	10-28-83	2	0	3.99	21	0	0	1	38	38	18	17	1	25	31	.259	.227	.284	7.28	5.87
Glushon, Jason	R-R	6-2	195	5-26-85	1	0	10.43	5	0	0	0	15	22	17	17	2	5	9	.386	.417	.364	5.52	3.07
Godfrey, Graham	R-R	6-3	205	8-9-84	11	8	3.50	28	28	1	0	159	153	70	62	8	51	110	.248	.268	.229	6.21	2.88
Haigwood, Daniel	R-L	6-2	215	11-19-83	1	2	7.03	7	5	0	0	24	36	23	19	2	11	11	.346	.303	.366	4.07	4.07
Hernandez, Carlos	L-L	5-11	155	3-4-87	6	1	4.62	9	6	0	0	39	55	22	20	2	16	21	.348	.257	.374	4.85	3.69
Heuser, James	L-L	6-5	215	3-30-84	0	2	6.03	32	0	0	1	37	40	28	25	3	33	37	.286	.193	.349	8.92	7.96
Hornbeck, Ben	R-L	6-5	180	7-22-87	0	1	16.20	1	1	0	0	3	5	7	6	0	4	1	.385	.333	.429	2.70	10.80
Hunton, Jon	R-R	6-9	250	11-30-82	4	4	3.33	40	0	0	4	54	45	23	20	2	13	46	.225	.253	.208	7.67	2.17
Lansford, Jared	R-R	6-0	190	10-22-86	1	2	2.36	36	0	0	12	46	43	12	12	2	20	29	.253	.297	.219	5.72	3.94
Leon, Arnold	R-R	6-1	205	9-6-88	2	3	3.51	33	7	0	1	74	71	35	29	3	28	63	.247	.252	.243	7.63	3.39
Madsen, Michael	R-R	6-0	160	11-29-82	0	1	7.50	3	1	0	0	6	9	5	5	2	6	1	.360	.300	.400	1.50	9.00
Middleton, Kyle	R-R	6-4	225	6-13-80	5	2	2.69	9	9	1	0	60	47	20	18	3	13	38	.209	.227	.191	5.67	1.94
Roquet, Rocky	R-R	6-2	215	11-6-82	1	3	5.37	43	0	0	1	59	79	39	35	4	26	46	.324	.318	.328	7.06	3.99
Ross, Tyson	R-R	6-5	215	4-22-87	5	4	3.96	9	9	1	0	50	40	22	22	3	20	31	.225	.224	.225	5.58	3.60
Sharpe, Steve	R-R	6-1	195	7-20-81	8	1	4.50	25	0	0	1	36	33	18	18	0	15	25	.256	.302	.212	6.25	3.75
Souza, Justin	R-R	6-1	185	10-22-85	0	2	10.35	5	5	0	0	20	32	28	23	1	10	13	.368	.348	.390	5.85	4.50
Storey, Mickey	R-R	6-2	185	3-16-86	1	0	0.00	4	0	0	0	8	3	0	0	0	1	9	.120	.118	.125	10.57	1.17

Fielding

Catcher	PCT	G	PO	A	E	DP	PB
Donaldson	.978	102	645	80	16	5	17
Ortiz	.945	8	49	3	3	0	1
Padron	.988	27	154	14	2	1	4
Recker	.944	8	47	4	3	0	1

First Base	PCT	G	PO	A	E	DP
Carter	.993	105	925	48	7	107
Donaldson	.943	4	27	6	2	4
Everidge	1.000	8	74	7	0	9
Padron	.982	5	51	4	1	6
Peterson	.981	22	190	13	4	20
Spencer	1.000	1	1	0	0	1

Second Base	PCT	G	PO	A	E	DP
Affronti	.966	25	62	82	5	27
Cardenas	.986	38	91	127	3	30

	PCT	G	PO	A	E	DP
Chen	1.000	6	8	16	0	3
Horton	.944	3	6	11	1	3
Valdez	.972	33	61	110	5	28
Weeks	.977	27	53	77	3	15
Wimberly	1.000	10	20	39	0	10

Third Base	PCT	G	PO	A	E	DP
Affronti	.909	5	1	9	1	0
Cardenas	.938	32	24	51	5	9
Carter	1.000	1	1	0	0	1
Chen	.914	12	9	23	3	3
Donaldson	.951	15	7	32	2	4
Everidge	.902	27	13	42	6	6
Valdez	.911	34	16	76	9	6
Wimberly	.922	17	14	33	4	2

Shortstop	PCT	G	PO	A	E	DP
Affronti	.895	14	17	34	6	6
Cardenas	.927	9	11	27	3	8
Horton	.953	91	164	279	22	77
Wimberly	.940	28	53	87	9	21

Outfield	PCT	G	PO	A	E	DP
Affronti	.833	5	5	0	1	0
Brown	.988	63	168	1	2	0
Carter	1.000	8	11	0	0	0
Gilbert	.982	116	260	6	5	1
Herrera	.000	1	0	0	1	0
Peterson	.977	18	40	2	1	0
Putnam	.986	30	66	2	1	1
Spencer	.957	73	128	5	6	1
Sulentic	.971	102	192	6	6	2
Wimberly	1.000	15	29	3	0	0

STOCKTON PORTS

HIGH CLASS A

CALIFORNIA LEAGUE

Batting	B-T	HT	WT	DOB	AVG	vLH	vRH	G	AB	R	H	2B	3B	HR	RBI	BB	HBP	SH	SF	SO	SB	CS	SLG	OBP
Affronti, Mike	R-R	6-2	195	2-13-84	.220	.190	.241	14	50	4	11	2	0	1	4	1	3	1	0	7	0	2	.320	.278
Barton, Daric	L-R	6-2	220	8-16-85	.000	.000	.000	1	4	0	0	0	0	0	0	0	0	0	0	0	0	0	.000	.000
Carter, Yusuf	R-R	6-2	205	2-6-85	.318	.320	.317	91	352	61	112	12	4	14	52	31	2	0	4	89	4	2	.494	.373
Cobb, Larry	R-R	5-9	179	7-10-85	.221	.227	.217	21	68	9	15	1	0	3	5	5	4	1	0	20	1	2	.368	.312
Coleman, Dusty	R-R	6-2	185	4-20-87	.220	.250	.203	26	100	14	22	4	2	1	8	10	2	0	0	39	2	2	.350	.304
Copeland, Ben	L-L	6-1	190	12-17-83	.444	.400	.500	2	9	1	4	1	0	0	0	0	0	0	0	2	0	0	.556	.444
2-team total (6 San Jose)					.294	—	—	8	34	2	10	4	0	0	1	2	0	0	0	5	0	0	.412	.333
Desme, Grant	R-R	6-2	205	4-4-86	.304	.345	.280	62	227	49	69	12	4	20	51	33	3	0	1	67	16	5	.656	.398
Dowling, Greg	L-L	6-3	231	11-15-83	.111	.105	.113	14	45	3	5	1	0	0	1	7	1	0	0	11	0	0	.133	.245
Ellis, Mark	R-R	5-11	195	6-6-77	.000	—	.000	2	4	0	0	0	0	0	0	1	0	0	0	1	0	0	.000	.200
Green, Grant	R-R	6-3	170	9-27-87	.316	.333	.308	5	19	2	6	1	0	0	3	1	0	0	0	5	1	0	.368	.350
Johnson, Toddric	L-L	6-1	202	12-17-84	.264	.198	.292	110	416	45	110	29	2	5	54	37	4	1	5	91	2	7	.380	.327
Ka'aihue, Kala	R-R	6-2	230	3-29-85	.131	.087	.158	18	61	12	8	1	1	2	6	10	0	0	0	26	0	0	.377	.254
Keough, Shane	B-R	6-3	196	9-11-86	.235	.206	.254	122	446	42	105	15	3	3	39	41	3	2	3	141	8	8	.303	.302
Kleen, Steve	R-R	6-4	200	5-21-83	.342	.380	.318	70	257	45	88	16	0	7	39	32	10	0	3	38	0	2	.486	.430
Love, Dante	R-R	5-11	195	4-8-87	.205	.000	.276	12	39	1	8	1	0	0	7	2	0	0	0	5	0	0	.231	.244
Martinez, Frank	B-R	6-0	164	7-19-85	.260	.253	.265	118	430	48	112	21	6	5	46	41	2	6	2	75	7	4	.372	.326
Mitchell, Jermaine	L-L	6-0	205	11-2-84	.247	.250	.245	124	450	63	111	15	6	3	34	73	1	8	5	128	17	10	.327	.350
Ortiz, Gabriel	R-R	6-1	215	11-7-85	.262	.400	.185	12	42	6	11	2	0	0	3	4	0	0	0	14	4	1	.310	.326
Padron, Raul	L-R	6-0	195	9-17-84	.263	.333	.235	61	167	23	44	2	0	5	26	10	1	0	2	51	2	0	.365	.306
Putnam, Danny	L-L	5-10	200	9-17-82	.091	.200	.000	3	11	1	1	1	0	0	1	1	0	0	0	2	0	0	.182	.167
Richard, Michael	R-R	5-11	180	8-20-84	.267	.264	.268	95	345	60	92	15	0	1	20	51	9	8	0	59	24	11	.319	.375

Name	B-T	HT	WT	DOB	AVG	vLH	vRH	G	AB	R	H	2B	3B	HR	RBI	BB	HBP	SH	SF	SO	SB	CS	SLG	OBP
Smith, Matt	R-R	5-11	215	1-30-86	.218	.296	.160	90	316	29	69	13	1	5	38	30	3	0	3	64	1	1	.313	.290
Spencer, Matt	L-L	6-4	225	1-27-86	.274	.237	.291	30	117	20	32	5	0	10	29	12	0	0	1	15	3	1	.573	.338
Thomas, David	B-R	5-11	180	7-29-86	.218	.211	.222	46	165	22	36	6	2	2	19	16	6	6	2	42	3	1	.315	.307
Valdez, Alex	B-R	6-1	160	9-2-84	.258	.250	.262	33	124	16	32	6	2	2	19	4	0	2	1	30	2	1	.387	.279
Vitters, Christian	L-R	6-3	201	6-26-85	.216	.148	.244	82	305	33	66	12	5	8	39	25	3	6	3	80	4	2	.367	.280
Weeks, Jemile	B-R	5-10	175	1-26-87	.299	.203	.348	50	201	29	60	9	2	7	31	26	3	1	1	40	5	1	.468	.385

Pitching	B-T	HT	WT	DOB	W	L	ERA	G	GS	CG	SV	IP	H	R	ER	HR	BB	SO	AVG	vLH	vRH	K/9	BB/9
Adames, Joselito	R-R	6-3	175	10-26-88	0	0	4.50	1	0	0	0	4	2	2	2	0	2	3	.167	.200	.000	6.75	4.50
Bell, Kristian	R-R	6-0	185	1-11-84	0	0	3.52	5	0	0	0	8	5	3	3	1	5	7	.185	.167	.200	8.22	5.87
Capra, Anthony	L-L	6-1	200	4-3-87	2	2	3.12	9	9	0	0	52	42	24	18	6	21	67	.223	.222	.224	11.60	3.63
Carignan, Andrew	R-R	5-11	205	7-23-86	0	0	4.50	2	0	0	0	2	1	1	1	0	3	2	.167	.500	.000	9.00	13.50
Casilla, Santiago	R-R	6-0	200	7-25-80	0	0	0.00	1	1	0	0	1	0	0	0	0	0	0	.000	.000	—	0.00	0.00
Cramer, Bob	L-L	6-1	190	10-28-79	1	0	1.59	2	0	0	0	6	4	1	1	1	2	6	.190	.286	.143	9.53	3.18
Currin, Patrick	R-R	6-0	188	5-12-84	2	3	4.93	21	0	0	0	38	42	26	21	3	11	30	.276	.355	.222	7.04	2.58
Duchscherer, Justin	R-R	6-3	200	11-19-77	0	0	0.00	1	1	0	0	2	0	0	0	0	0	2	.000	.000	.000	9.00	0.00
Espinal, Leonardo	R-R	6-3	226	2-6-84	0	3	5.34	28	0	0	7	29	29	27	17	1	17	35	.257	.348	.194	10.99	5.34
Figueroa, Pedro	L-L	6-1	164	11-23-85	3	4	3.56	11	11	0	0	66	62	27	26	3	35	67	.251	.250	.251	9.18	4.80
Friend, Justin	R-R	6-1	200	6-21-86	1	4	2.87	43	0	0	5	60	47	27	19	5	29	64	.213	.264	.188	9.65	4.37
Garcia, Hector	R-R	6-3	160	10-22-85	0	1	1.50	2	1	0	0	6	3	1	1	1	0	2	.150	.000	.188	3.00	0.00
Gordon, Derrick	L-L	5-9	185	10-16-83	5	6	3.78	39	1	0	1	86	70	48	36	6	33	90	.222	.179	.246	9.46	3.47
Haigwood, Daniel	R-L	6-2	215	11-19-83	3	1	3.16	8	7	0	0	43	29	22	15	2	18	44	.191	.213	.181	9.28	3.80
Hernandez, Carlos	L-L	5-11	155	3-4-87	9	7	3.99	19	19	0	0	108	107	59	48	9	36	90	.257	.269	.251	7.48	2.99
Hodsdon, Scott	R-R	6-1	185	5-31-85	6	10	5.22	27	21	0	0	128	153	94	74	14	37	103	.297	.314	.284	7.26	2.61
Hornbeck, Ben	R-L	6-5	180	7-22-87	5	4	3.52	21	11	0	0	77	64	36	30	3	32	111	.225	.233	.221	13.03	3.76
Hunton, Jon	R-R	6-9	250	11-30-82	2	0	1.80	13	0	0	6	20	14	4	4	1	6	27	.189	.176	.200	12.15	2.70
Italiano, Craig	R-R	6-4	210	7-22-86	5	6	5.63	16	16	0	0	77	83	55	48	6	40	75	.280	.292	.271	8.80	4.70
2-team total (19 Lake Elsinore)					5	7	4.42	35	16	0	0	108	107	65	53	6	50	119	—	—		9.92	4.17
Kerfoot, Chad	R-R	6-0	185	4-1-85	2	1	6.52	13	0	0	0	19	30	17	14	3	7	12	.357	.375	.341	5.59	3.26
LeBlanc Poirier, Mathieu	L-R	6-1	175	3-10-87	0	3	5.44	10	9	0	0	46	42	31	28	7	24	28	.247	.321	.174	5.44	4.66
Madsen, Michael	R-R	6-0	160	11-29-82	0	0	0.00	1	1	0	0	3	0	0	0	0	2	3	.000	.000	.000	9.00	6.00
Mitchinson, Scott	R-R	6-3	185	12-28-84	0	4	5.60	9	8	0	0	35	42	26	22	4	13	36	.288	.297	.280	9.17	3.31
Murray, Justin	R-R	6-4	200	5-11-87	1	4	6.04	7	3	0	0	25	31	28	17	3	11	19	.301	.273	.322	6.75	3.91
Pena, Jorge	R-R	6-6	226	12-31-88	0	1	6.00	1	1	0	0	3	4	3	2	0	4	3	.308	1.000	.250	9.00	12.00
Ramos, Julio	L-L	6-1	158	2-13-88	0	1	3.75	2	2	0	0	12	12	5	5	0	3	11	.267	.176	.321	8.25	2.25
Ray, Jason	R-R	5-11	195	7-14-84	2	2	2.22	24	0	0	4	28	15	8	7	1	12	32	.158	.093	.212	10.16	3.81
Richmond, Jamie	R-R	6-3	190	3-23-86	2	0	5.40	14	0	0	0	27	31	18	16	7	3	27	.277	.205	.315	9.11	1.01
Rodriguez, Henry	R-R	6-0	210	2-25-87	0	0	0.00	3	0	0	0	5	3	0	0	0	1	11	.167	.400	.077	19.80	1.80
Ross, Tyson	R-R	6-5	215	4-22-87	5	6	4.17	18	18	0	0	86	78	49	40	10	33	82	.237	.257	.223	8.55	3.44
Sattler, Dan	R-R	6-3	190	11-11-83	1	1	9.00	4	0	0	0	4	6	5	4	1	5	6	.333	.333	.333	13.50	11.25
Sewell, Lance	L-L	6-1	195	6-17-86	1	1	4.36	32	0	0	0	43	40	21	21	8	27	56	.244	.266	.230	11.63	5.61
Sharpe, Steve	R-R	6-1	195	7-20-81	1	0	0.53	10	0	0	0	17	8	2	1	1	5	20	.148	.105	.171	10.59	2.65
Storey, Mickey	R-R	6-2	185	3-16-86	1	1	2.28	22	0	0	9	24	19	10	6	2	6	35	.213	.097	.276	13.31	2.28
Thomas, Dan	R-R	6-2	200	2-10-86	0	1	13.50	5	0	0	1	3	7	7	5	2	3	6	.389	.545	.143	16.20	8.10
Walters, Nick	L-L	6-2	175	9-30-85	1	2	4.56	54	0	0	1	53	45	30	27	2	40	56	.228	.220	.236	9.45	6.75

Fielding

Catcher	PCT	G	PO	A	E	DP	PB
Carter	.994	63	583	59	4	3	37
Love	1.000	10	76	4	0	1	1
Ortiz	.977	8	84	2	2	0	5
Padron	.986	18	125	16	2	2	2
Smith	.989	46	401	29	5	5	10

First Base	PCT	G	PO	A	E	DP
Barton	1.000	1	6	1	0	0
Carter	.965	13	125	12	5	10
Dowling	.988	9	73	7	1	7
Ka'aihue	.978	6	41	3	1	5
Kleen	.991	59	414	31	4	30
Padron	.988	22	155	15	2	14
Spencer	.989	22	167	20	2	20
Thomas	1.000	3	9	0	0	0
Vitters	.978	13	85	5	2	6

Second Base	PCT	G	PO	A	E	DP
Affronti	1.000	2	9	3	0	2
Cobb	.956	10	21	22	2	3
Ellis	1.000	2	0	4	0	1
Martinez	.962	47	94	111	8	25
Richard	.931	26	38	83	9	21
Valdez	.912	9	7	24	3	4
Vitters	1.000	2	6	1	0	0
Weeks	.986	47	93	116	3	16

Third Base	PCT	G	PO	A	E	DP
Affronti	.950	7	6	13	1	1
Cobb	1.000	3	6	6	0	0
Kleen	.875	6	1	6	1	1
Martinez	.839	26	16	36	10	1
Smith	.914	17	5	27	3	1
Valdez	.866	23	12	46	9	7
Vitters	.894	62	38	89	15	8

Shortstop	PCT	G	PO	A	E	DP
Affronti	.895	5	3	14	2	4
Coleman	.961	26	32	66	4	11
Martinez	.912	42	69	96	16	22
Richard	.938	68	103	171	18	29

Outfield	PCT	G	PO	A	E	DP
Cobb	1.000	4	10	0	0	0
Copeland	1.000	2	6	0	0	0
Desme	.972	58	103	1	3	0
Johnson	.962	83	125	2	5	0
Keough	.949	110	174	12	10	0
Kleen	1.000	3	2	0	0	0
Mitchell	.986	116	204	7	3	1
Putnam	1.000	2	5	0	0	0
Spencer	1.000	7	9	2	0	1
Thomas	.992	43	115	5	1	2

KANE COUNTY COUGARS
LOW CLASS A

MIDWEST LEAGUE

Batting	B-T	HT	WT	DOB	AVG	vLH	vRH	G	AB	R	H	2B	3B	HR	RBI	BB	HBP	SH	SF	SO	SB	CS	SLG	OBP
Arrieche, Carlos	R-R	5-10	190	3-30-85	.180	.154	.190	73	239	14	43	3	0	1	16	13	4	3	3	48	0	4	.205	.232
Barfield, Jeremy	R-L	6-5	240	7-12-88	.262	.228	.272	116	404	48	106	23	2	8	52	48	4	0	4	98	1	5	.389	.343
Berroa, Chris	R-R	6-0	175	2-3-89	.219	.114	.252	64	187	27	41	6	2	1	12	21	1	0	0	60	8	4	.289	.301
Christian, Jason	L-R	6-3	170	6-16-87	.261	.173	.289	86	330	51	86	12	4	7	46	41	1	3	3	69	28	3	.385	.341
Coleman, Dusty	R-R	6-2	185	4-20-87	.254	.222	.266	93	346	56	88	22	4	8	42	40	8	0	0	115	18	8	.410	.345
Crumbliss, Conner	R-L	5-8	175	4-19-87	.280	.333	.273	14	50	11	14	4	1	0	3	11	3	1	0	9	2	1	.400	.438

Batting	B-T	HT	WT	DOB	AVG	vLH	vRH	G	AB	R	H	2B	3B	HR	RBI	BB	HBP	SH	SF	SO	SB	CS	SLG	OBP
Desme, Grant	R-R	6-2	205	4-4-86	.274	.290	.269	69	259	49	71	19	2	11	38	21	4	1	3	81	24	0	.490	.334
Gil, Leonardo	R-R	6-1	160	8-18-87	.263	.315	.245	53	217	27	57	8	1	1	15	16	3	2	0	46	9	8	.323	.322
Hernandez, Franklin	R-R	6-3	165	4-19-87	.225	.183	.239	121	454	50	102	24	6	6	53	23	5	1	2	115	4	2	.344	.269
Kleen, Steve	R-R	6-4	200	5-21-83	.282	.214	.300	70	259	42	73	14	1	8	46	28	5	0	4	45	3	3	.436	.358
Ladendorf, Tyler	R-R	6-0	210	3-7-88	.231	.240	.229	35	130	13	30	4	2	2	15	10	3	2	0	19	2	2	.338	.301
2-team total (15 Beloit)					.232	—	—	50	190	20	44	6	2	2	19	14	4	2	0	32	4	3	.316	.298
LeVier, Mitch	L-L	5-11	185	1-12-88	.246	.179	.266	35	122	18	30	7	0	2	18	7	3	1	3	25	3	0	.352	.296
Leyja, Nino	R-R	5-10	170	10-2-90	.231	.238	.230	33	121	18	28	4	2	2	5	13	0	1	0	33	7	2	.347	.306
Napoleon, Dusty	L-R	6-2	208	5-21-86	.218	.200	.223	78	229	25	50	12	0	0	16	51	4	5	2	49	0	3	.271	.367
Nunez, Juan	R-R	6-2	191	8-27-87	.224	.158	.244	51	161	18	36	7	0	1	10	7	1	5	1	44	1	0	.286	.259
Paramore, Petey	B-R	6-2	195	10-30-86	.230	.229	.230	101	326	33	75	9	0	4	36	55	3	1	3	55	1	2	.294	.344
Parker, Steve	L-R	6-2	200	9-3-87	.244	.217	.253	70	254	27	62	11	2	5	39	25	2	1	4	55	1	4	.362	.312
Ray, Matt	B-R	5-9	179	1-28-84	.222	.259	.208	54	203	24	45	7	1	2	20	25	1	4	0	49	7	6	.296	.310
Spina, Mike	R-R	6-1	220	12-17-86	.255	.273	.250	52	184	21	47	10	0	7	28	25	5	0	5	48	1	0	.424	.352
Thomas, David	B-R	5-11	180	7-29-86	.273	.257	.279	36	139	26	38	5	1	4	13	13	2	1	1	21	7	4	.410	.342

Pitching	B-T	HT	WT	DOB	W	L	ERA	G	GS	CG	SV	IP	H	R	ER	HR	BB	SO	AVG	vLH	vRH	K/9	BB/9
Barham, Trey	L-L	6-0	215	11-7-85	4	1	1.24	28	1	0	2	44	26	7	6	1	11	41	.177	.045	.233	8.45	2.27
Capra, Anthony	L-L	6-1	200	4-3-87	4	7	3.24	18	18	0	0	100	70	39	36	9	40	103	.197	.202	.195	9.27	3.60
Deal, Scott	R-R	6-3	195	12-11-86	1	3	3.56	41	1	0	3	73	68	34	29	3	20	53	.245	.252	.241	6.50	2.45
Espinal, Leonardo	R-R	6-3	226	2-6-84	1	0	0.93	9	0	0	1	10	5	2	1	0	2	13	.147	.200	.125	12.10	1.86
Figueroa, Pedro	L-L	6-1	164	11-23-85	10	2	3.23	16	16	0	0	86	89	37	31	6	31	78	.267	.289	.260	8.13	3.23
Fitts, Matt	R-R	6-1	205	9-14-85	3	7	5.73	32	9	0	2	88	98	72	56	5	41	59	.293	.341	.261	6.03	4.19
Guzman, Jose	R-R	5-11	185	11-5-87	2	1	5.01	25	0	0	4	32	34	19	18	2	11	34	.260	.175	.297	9.46	3.06
Hart, Michael	R-R	6-1	210	2-9-87	0	2	2.96	17	0	0	0	24	22	12	8	1	13	23	.239	.323	.197	8.51	4.81
Haviland, Shawn	R-R	6-2	200	11-10-85	6	11	4.71	28	28	0	0	153	170	90	80	9	53	121	.283	.272	.289	7.12	3.12
Hornbeck, Ben	R-L	6-5	180	7-22-87	4	0	1.27	7	4	0	0	36	19	6	5	2	10	47	.158	.179	.152	11.64	2.48
Hunter, Brett	R-R	6-4	215	6-27-87	0	1	6.85	21	8	0	0	47	38	42	36	2	59	55	.225	.259	.209	10.46	11.22
Huttenlocker, A.J.	L-L	6-3	190	8-5-86	1	2	2.74	13	0	0	0	23	13	9	7	1	3	28	.155	.120	.169	10.96	1.17
LeBlanc Poirier, Mathieu	L-R	6-1	175	3-10-87	5	7	4.13	14	13	0	0	70	71	40	32	3	29	49	.262	.343	.211	6.33	3.75
Lee, Chad	R-R	6-4	210	12-20-85	1	1	6.30	2	2	0	0	10	10	8	7	1	4	4	.244	.261	.222	3.60	3.60
Murray, Justin	R-R	6-4	200	5-11-87	5	1	2.84	37	0	0	12	44	43	16	14	5	14	45	.256	.222	.276	9.14	2.84
Ramirez, Anvioris	L-L	6-1	165	3-10-88	5	2	3.29	9	9	0	0	52	57	23	19	2	11	33	.278	.241	.291	5.71	1.90
Ray, Jason	R-R	5-11	195	7-14-84	2	0	2.30	11	1	0	0	16	14	4	4	0	5	11	.241	.364	.167	6.32	2.87
Richmond, Jamie	R-R	6-3	190	3-23-86	4	3	2.70	26	0	0	4	50	48	17	15	3	5	40	.245	.247	.244	7.20	0.90
Selenes, Josue	R-R	6-0	180	10-8-85	6	1	3.34	33	0	0	1	57	51	26	21	2	23	48	.239	.274	.217	7.62	3.65
Smalley, Ken	R-R	6-2	195	7-25-87	9	8	2.73	29	21	0	0	132	109	49	40	6	60	119	.226	.226	.225	8.13	4.10
Smith, Murphy	R-R	6-3	210	8-25-87	2	2	4.75	9	9	0	0	36	40	19	19	2	17	31	.292	.281	.301	7.75	4.25
Smyth, Paul	R-R	5-11	210	4-1-87	1	0	0.00	5	0	0	2	7	2	0	0	0	0	7	.083	.000	.105	9.00	0.00
Storey, Mickey	R-R	6-2	185	3-16-86	0	0	0.52	13	0	0	9	17	5	1	1	0	1	23	.088	.160	.031	11.94	0.52
Thomas, Dan	R-R	6-2	200	2-10-86	0	1	5.23	15	0	0	4	21	22	12	12	0	12	23	.275	.267	.280	10.02	5.23

Fielding

Catcher	PCT	G	PO	A	E	DP	PB
Napoleon	.989	26	171	8	2	2	3
Nunez	.978	50	392	43	10	2	12
Paramore	.993	72	538	70	4	5	8

First Base	PCT	G	PO	A	E	DP
Hernandez	1.000	1	7	0	0	0
Kleen	.990	66	573	36	6	48
Napoleon	.993	19	122	16	1	11
Parker	.996	57	485	35	2	42
Spina	.875	2	7	0	1	0

Second Base	PCT	G	PO	A	E	DP
Arrieche	.955	23	35	49	4	18
Christian	.912	15	24	28	5	5

	PCT	G	PO	A	E	DP
Crumbliss	.800	1	3	1	1	1
Gil	.984	27	51	70	2	13
Leyja	.920	26	64	62	11	12
Ray	.970	53	84	144	7	24

Third Base	PCT	G	PO	A	E	DP
Arrieche	.936	21	13	31	3	6
Christian	.948	64	32	115	8	6
Gil	.941	10	1	15	1	0
Napoleon	1.000	2	0	4	0	1
Parker	.957	11	4	18	1	2
Spina	.913	42	18	77	9	9

Shortstop	PCT	G	PO	A	E	DP
Arrieche	.870	7	9	11	3	1

	PCT	G	PO	A	E	DP
Coleman	.941	91	142	244	24	48
Gil	.953	13	18	43	3	6
Ladendorf	.941	32	48	111	10	13

Outfield	PCT	G	PO	A	E	DP
Arrieche	.970	26	32	0	1	0
Barfield	.966	106	234	19	9	3
Berroa	.977	55	83	3	2	1
Crumbliss	.974	14	38	0	1	0
Desme	.958	56	112	3	5	0
Hernandez	.976	114	159	7	4	1
LeVier	.967	30	54	4	2	1
Napoleon	—	1	0	0	0	0
Thomas	.987	36	75	2	1	1

VANCOUVER CANADIANS
SHORT-SEASON

NORTHWEST LEAGUE

Batting	B-T	HT	WT	DOB	AVG	vLH	vRH	G	AB	R	H	2B	3B	HR	RBI	BB	HBP	SH	SF	SO	SB	CS	SLG	OBP
Aliotti, Anthony	L-L	6-0	204	2-16-87	.239	.147	.255	60	218	19	52	8	0	0	25	36	3	2	2	63	6	1	.275	.351
Crisotomo, Jose	L-R	6-1	181	4-20-89	.297	.357	.285	47	158	23	47	5	0	0	16	15	1	2	1	25	4	4	.329	.360
Crumbliss, Conner	R-L	5-8	175	4-19-87	.293	.196	.321	57	205	40	60	9	4	2	25	49	1	2	4	28	11	2	.445	.425
Dixon, Rashun	R-R	6-2	210	8-27-90	.214	.293	.194	57	196	25	42	7	0	2	16	23	2	0	2	73	6	4	.281	.300
Gil, Leonardo	R-R	6-1	160	8-18-87	.250	.000	.333	9	32	8	8	1	2	0	8	4	1	0	1	8	0	0	.406	.342
Gilmartin, Michael	R-R	6-0	180	7-14-87	.232	.204	.241	60	228	34	53	10	1	3	22	25	5	6	1	51	5	2	.325	.320
House, Tyreace	R-R	5-10	175	3-1-88	.291	.333	.277	56	196	31	57	3	0	0	16	17	6	3	0	38	19	10	.306	.365
Jernigan, Ryne	R-R	5-10	175	6-27-85	.268	.208	.285	62	220	37	59	12	1	4	30	18	4	5	3	40	7	1	.386	.331
Leyja, Nino	R-R	5-10	170	10-2-90	.269	.438	.216	16	67	5	18	3	0	1	7	3	0	3	0	19	3	0	.358	.300
Luis, Marcos	R-R	5-11	180	11-21-85	.260	.250	.288	30	93	6	24	7	0	0	10	10	0	2	1	15	0	0	.355	.346
Ortiz, Gabriel	R-R	6-1	215	11-7-85	.255	.316	.241	26	98	12	25	4	1	1	13	3	0	1	1	30	2	1	.347	.275
Ortiz, Ryan	B-R	6-3	205	9-29-87	.258	.306	.243	48	151	25	39	12	1	4	24	26	6	0	0	29	3	0	.430	.388
Richard, Myrio	R-R	6-1	190	8-27-88	.255	.159	.284	53	192	26	49	4	2	1	22	26	4	2	5	41	4	2	.313	.348

	B-T	HT	WT	DOB	AVG	vLH	vRH	G	AB	R	H	2B	3B	HR	RBI	BB	HBP	SH	SF	SO	SB	CS	SLG	OBP
Rutherford, Rodney	R-R	5-10	185	6-7-85	.209	.200	.213	23	67	4	14	5	0	0	5	7	1	1	1	20	2	0	.284	.289
Sosa, Wilfredo	R-R	6-2	175	10-24-88	.213	.184	.223	41	141	23	30	10	0	2	19	12	4	5	2	49	3	1	.326	.289
Stassi, Max	R-R	5-10	205	3-15-91	.286	.250	.297	13	49	3	14	4	0	0	8	2	2	0	0	15	0	0	.367	.340
Walton, Kent	R-R	6-1	185	12-11-86	.296	.218	.316	67	270	28	80	20	1	2	36	19	2	1	3	45	5	2	.400	.344

Pitching	B-T	HT	WT	DOB	W	L	ERA	G	GS	CG	SV	IP	H	R	ER	HR	BB	SO	AVG	vLH	vRH	K/9	BB/9
Adames, Joselito	R-R	6-3	175	10-26-88	5	6	6.47	16	16	0	0	72	92	57	52	3	32	40	.315	.300	.327	4.98	3.98
Arrioja, Jorge	R-R	6-1	155	1-25-89	2	1	4.45	21	0	0	0	28	28	15	14	1	22	19	.262	.227	.286	6.04	6.99
Christensen, Kyle	R-R	6-3	225	9-18-88	5	0	4.94	12	0	0	0	24	27	13	13	3	12	21	.287	.325	.259	7.99	4.56
Garcia, Hector	R-R	6-3	160	10-22-85	0	0	10.13	6	4	0	0	16	24	20	18	0	13	9	.358	.200	.426	5.06	7.31
Gilliam, Rob	R-R	6-1	195	11-29-87	2	0	5.19	6	0	0	0	9	9	5	5	1	5	11	.290	.333	.263	11.42	5.19
Guzman, Jose	R-R	5-11	185	11-5-87	0	1	2.61	9	0	0	6	10	7	3	3	1	2	11	.200	.333	.172	9.58	1.74
Hoehn, Connor	R-R	6-1	205	7-5-89	0	1	1.00	15	0	0	7	18	9	3	2	0	7	25	.143	.132	.152	12.50	3.50
Hunter, Brett	R-R	6-4	215	6-27-87	0	0	7.20	4	0	0	0	5	5	5	4	0	3	4	.435	.500	.364	7.20	5.40
Joseph, Jonathan	R-R	6-1	180	5-17-88	0	2	4.94	16	8	0	0	55	65	40	30	4	25	35	.300	.292	.306	5.76	4.12
Krol, Ian	L-L	6-1	180	5-9-91	0	1	8.10	3	1	0	0	3	6	5	3	0	1	4	.375	.400	.364	10.80	2.70
Lee, Chad	R-R	6-4	210	12-20-85	2	0	0.00	3	3	0	0	15	1	0	0	0	6	17	.023	.050	.000	10.20	3.60
Long, Nathan	R-R	6-2	210	2-9-86	1	2	6.69	22	0	0	0	36	45	31	27	5	14	25	.298	.284	.310	6.19	3.47
Morla, Ronny	R-R	6-4	180	5-19-88	1	7	4.86	17	12	0	0	63	70	42	34	4	24	73	.285	.291	.279	10.43	3.43
Penalba, Ricardo	R-R	5-11	170	1-6-89	2	5	4.80	21	6	0	1	45	52	28	24	2	27	47	.286	.237	.321	9.40	5.40
Peterson, Max	L-L	6-2	210	6-27-88	2	1	4.71	17	1	0	0	21	30	20	11	2	16	25	.326	.263	.370	10.71	6.86
Ramos, Julio	L-L	6-1	158	2-13-88	6	5	2.38	13	13	0	0	72	67	30	19	4	18	64	.248	.313	.228	8.00	2.25
Schultz, Patrick	R-R	6-3	215	9-25-85	2	3	2.66	26	0	0	0	44	29	19	13	0	19	48	.185	.246	.136	9.82	3.89
Smith, Murphy	R-R	6-3	210	8-25-87	0	0	0.00	1	1	0	0	4	2	1	0	0	1	5	.143	.200	.111	11.25	2.25
Smyth, Paul	R-R	5-11	210	4-1-87	1	0	0.00	20	0	0	9	29	12	0	0	0	4	37	.122	.088	.141	11.35	1.23
Straily, Dan	R-R	6-2	220	12-1-88	5	3	4.12	16	11	0	0	59	66	27	27	5	18	66	.286	.303	.270	10.07	2.75
Street, Juston	R-R	6-2	200	8-27-85	0	1	5.57	21	0	0	0	32	39	27	20	3	17	30	.289	.258	.315	8.35	4.73
Vidal, Pedro	R-R	6-3	194	7-31-87	0	1	10.24	6	0	0	0	10	13	11	11	2	4	8	.325	.417	.286	7.45	3.72

Fielding

Catcher	PCT	G	PO	A	E	DP	PB
Ortiz	.987	26	218	18	3	2	9
Ortiz	.986	44	337	25	5	4	13
Rutherford	.889	2	8	0	1	0	1
Stassi	1.000	8	70	3	0	0	2

First Base	PCT	G	PO	A	E	DP
Aliotti	.991	60	491	51	5	56
Rutherford	.977	12	79	6	2	7
Sosa	1.000	7	53	5	0	7

Second Base	PCT	G	PO	A	E	DP
Crumbliss	.959	28	53	87	6	24

Jernigan	.952	24	38	62	5	13
Leyja	.951	16	34	44	4	12
Luis	.962	13	17	33	2	7

Third Base	PCT	G	PO	A	E	DP
Gil	.909	4	4	6	1	1
Jernigan	.846	37	20	57	14	7
Luis	.857	17	11	19	5	1
Sosa	.877	22	13	37	7	5

Shortstop	PCT	G	PO	A	E	DP
Gil	.897	6	7	19	3	4
Gilmartin	.952	60	92	164	13	41

Sosa	.893	12	20	30	6	6

Outfield	PCT	G	PO	A	E	DP
Crisotomo	.931	45	51	3	4	0
Crumbliss	.981	31	50	3	1	1
Dixon	.989	54	83	3	1	0
House	.977	55	119	6	3	1
Jernigan	1.000	1	0	1	0	0
Richard	.990	52	94	8	1	4

AZL ATHLETICS   ROOKIE

ARIZONA LEAGUE

Batting	B-T	HT	WT	DOB	AVG	vLH	vRH	G	AB	R	H	2B	3B	HR	RBI	BB	HBP	SH	SF	SO	SB	CS	SLG	OBP
Affinito, Chris	R-R	6-3	230	2-10-87	.300	.297	.301	48	180	21	54	11	1	5	36	18	3	0	3	56	0	1	.456	.368
Barton, Daric	L-R	6-0	220	8-16-85	.278	.000	.313	6	18	3	5	1	0	1	3	6	0	0	0	4	0	0	.500	.458
Brazoban, Yeudy	R-R	6-1	185	9-9-88	.220	.375	.194	30	109	11	24	5	1	0	5	2	0	1	0	29	3	1	.284	.234
Castillo, Gernaldo	R-R	5-11	145	7-17-89	.265	.188	.280	55	189	29	50	7	0	0	20	43	4	3	2	34	3	3	.302	.408
Chen, Yung Chi	R-R	5-11	170	7-13-83	.346	.250	.364	8	26	3	9	5	0	1	8	4	0	0	1	6	0	0	.654	.419
Clime, Neudy	R-R	5-11	185	2-1-89	.244	.192	.257	41	127	18	31	1	1	0	8	13	2	3	0	40	11	2	.268	.324
Consigli, Royce	L-R	6-2	205	7-7-91	.202	.188	.205	26	94	14	19	3	1	0	13	16	2	1	0	20	3	0	.255	.330
Crosby, Blake	R-R	6-1	185	9-11-84	.217	.143	.236	20	69	6	15	0	0	0	6	5	3	2	1	16	0	1	.217	.295
De Leon, Abraham	R-R	6-0	194	2-20-89	.140	.133	.143	24	50	6	7	0	0	1	4	5	1	1	2	22	0	0	.200	.224
Eusebio, Joel	R-R	5-8	175	2-1-85	.189	.375	.152	33	95	15	18	6	0	1	7	22	2	0	0	32	2	0	.284	.353
Garcia, Elvis	R-R	6-2	178	11-8-89	.225	.294	.212	32	102	10	23	4	0	0	7	5	0	3	1	26	1	0	.265	.259
Landaeta, Douglas	R-R	6-1	170	11-25-88	.248	.233	.252	39	141	18	35	6	5	0	18	13	1	0	1	27	3	1	.362	.314
Leyland, Josh	L-R	6-1	220	7-6-91	.150	.000	.158	7	20	3	3	0	0	0	1	4	3	0	0	11	0	1	.150	.370
Lopez, Diomes	R-R	6-2	195	1-30-89	.212	.000	.229	16	52	6	11	2	1	0	4	5	1	0	0	24	0	0	.288	.293
Made, Alcibiades	R-R	6-0	169	4-5-89	.242	.250	.240	43	128	18	31	2	4	1	13	18	4	2	1	41	4	1	.344	.351
Parker, Steve	L-R	6-2	200	9-3-87	.214	—	.214	9	14	2	3	2	0	0	2	1	0	0	0	6	0	0	.357	.267
Richard, Myrio	R-R	6-1	190	8-27-88	.308	.000	.333	4	13	1	4	2	0	0	0	1	0	0	0	3	2	0	.462	.357
Rosario, Robin	R-R	6-2	170	11-28-90	.163	.154	.165	29	98	15	16	4	2	2	8	10	0	0	1	37	1	0	.306	.239
Shaw, Anthione	R-R	6-1	187	8-22-87	.199	.179	.204	43	141	16	28	6	2	0	6	13	3	3	0	45	4	2	.270	.280
Soto, Ramon	R-R	6-2	190	11-3-87	.246	.267	.241	21	69	8	17	4	3	0	5	7	0	0	1	15	1	0	.391	.312
Spina, Mike	R-R	6-1	220	12-17-86	.500	—	.500	2	6	1	3	1	0	0	0	0	0	0	0	0	0	0	.667	.500
Stassi, Max	R-R	5-10	205	3-15-91	.000	—	.000	1	1	0	0	0	0	0	0	0	0	0	0	1	0	0	.000	.000
Wells, Jeremy	R-R	5-11	175	8-9-86	.291	.433	.254	45	148	27	43	7	3	0	17	21	6	1	1	21	15	3	.345	.398
Wimberly, Corey	B-R	5-8	180	10-26-83	.000	.000	.000	4	11	1	0	0	0	0	1	0	0	0	1	0	0	.000	.083

Pitching	B-T	HT	WT	DOB	W	L	ERA	G	GS	CG	SV	IP	H	R	ER	HR	BB	SO	AVG	vLH	vRH	K/9	BB/9
Acevedo, Rony	R-R	6-2	165	9-18-88	1	1	7.67	19	1	0	0	32	47	31	27	3	14	22	.353	.357	.351	6.25	3.98
Cameron, Kevin	R-R	6-1	190	12-15-79	0	0	0.00	1	1	0	0	1	0	0	0	0	0	2	.000	.000	.000	18.00	0.00
De Los Santos, Fautino	R-R	6-0	205	2-15-86	0	1	3.86	7	7	0	0	12	12	6	5	0	4	16	.279	.438	.185	12.34	3.09

Name	B-T	HT	WT	DOB	W	L	ERA	G	GS	CG	SV	IP	H	R	ER	HR	BB	SO	AVG	vLH	vRH	K/9	BB/9
Diaz, Victor	R-R	6-1	220	10-26-89	0	0	11.12	11	0	0	0	11	13	20	14	0	19	6	.295	.286	.304	4.76	15.09
Duchscherer, Justin	R-R	6-3	200	11-19-77	0	0	0.00	1	1	0	0	5	4	0	0	0	0	3	.235	.250	.231	5.40	0.00
Duran, Omar	L-L	6-3	209	2-26-90	1	1	5.40	12	1	0	0	15	14	17	9	0	11	21	.237	.294	.214	12.60	6.60
Ferreras, Ronald	R-R	6-1	180	2-8-87	3	0	6.62	18	0	0	0	35	36	28	26	4	23	20	.261	.283	.247	5.09	5.86
Garcia, Hector	R-R	6-3	160	10-22-85	0	1	7.45	7	5	0	0	19	15	22	16	0	18	18	.214	.217	.213	8.38	8.38
Gilliam, Rob	R-R	6-1	195	11-29-87	0	1	0.00	2	0	0	0	3	4	3	0	0	0	2	.286	.000	.333	6.00	0.00
Hoehn, Connor	R-R	6-1	205	7-5-89	0	1	4.50	2	1	0	0	2	1	1	1	0	2	3	.143	.000	.200	13.50	9.00
Hunter, Brett	R-R	6-4	215	6-27-87	0	1	1.93	4	3	0	0	5	0	2	1	0	1	5	.000	.000	.000	9.64	1.93
Huttenlocker, A.J.	L-L	6-3	190	8-5-86	1	1	2.70	10	0	0	3	13	14	6	4	0	1	17	.264	.182	.286	11.48	0.68
Jimenez, Deivi	R-R	6-3	205	12-30-89	2	5	6.49	14	9	0	0	51	68	47	37	7	15	46	.306	.281	.323	8.06	2.63
Krol, Ian	L-L	6-1	180	5-9-91	0	0	0.00	1	0	0	0	1	0	0	0	0	0	0	.000	.000	.000	0.00	0.00
Marks, Justin	L-L	6-3	170	1-12-88	0	1	—	1	1	0	0	0	3	6	6	1	4	0	1.000	1.000	—	—	0.00
Mederos, Chris	R-R	6-3	175	5-17-87	3	1	2.14	11	2	0	0	21	14	5	5	1	2	26	.194	.167	.208	11.14	0.86
Mitchell, Mike	R-R	6-2	200	10-27-81	0	0	0.00	1	0	0	0	1	0	0	0	0	0	0	.000	.000	.000	0.00	0.00
Mota, David	R-R	6-3	218	2-18-87	1	0	6.14	6	0	0	0	7	4	5	5	0	7	11	.160	.125	.176	13.50	8.59
Oliveros, Jose	R-R	6-0	170	9-29-89	3	2	2.89	10	0	0	0	19	24	12	6	1	9	16	.308	.375	.261	7.71	4.34
Paez, Argenis	R-R	6-3	180	10-20-90	0	5	3.68	15	9	0	0	51	44	26	21	1	21	46	.235	.207	.248	8.06	3.68
Pena, Jorge	R-R	6-6	226	12-31-88	1	1	2.87	4	3	0	0	16	12	5	5	1	4	17	.211	.167	.216	9.77	2.30
Peterson, Max	L-L	6-2	210	6-27-88	0	0	0.00	3	0	0	1	4	3	0	0	0		6	.200	.333	.111	13.50	0.00
Quigley, Ryan	L-L	6-4	220	9-11-87	3	2	4.62	17	0	0	0	25	25	18	13	0	16	31	.253	.174	.276	11.01	5.68
Ramirez, Anvioris	L-L	6-1	165	3-10-88	1	1	4.56	6	3	0	0	24	27	14	12	1	7	22	.284	.160	.329	8.37	2.66
Reyes, Luis	R-R	6-2	160	2-4-88	0	4	6.38	16	5	0	1	42	49	35	30	2	25	35	.299	.370	.264	7.44	5.31
Sanchez, Jose	R-R	6-2	170	10-24-89	2	0	3.41	15	0	0	0	29	27	11	11	1	17	24	.250	.282	.232	7.45	5.28
Smith, Murphy	R-R	6-3	210	8-25-87	0	1	6.00	3	2	0	0	6	4	4	1	0		4	.261	.273	.250	6.00	0.00
Tenholder, Daniel	R-R	6-2	198	7-6-88	0	2	5.26	19	0	0	1	26	31	17	15	1	10	26	.292	.276	.299	9.12	3.51
Thomas, Dan	R-R	6-2	200	2-10-86	0	0	4.50	2	1	0	0	2	1	1	1	0	1	2	.143	.333	.000	9.00	4.50
Vidal, Pedro	R-R	6-3	194	7-31-87	0	1	3.71	13	0	0	3	17	22	11	7	1	3	23	.301	.346	.277	12.18	1.59

Fielding

Catcher	PCT	G	PO	A	E	DP	PB
Affinito	.974	19	135	15	4	1	2
De Leon	.982	17	95	15	2	2	6
Leyland	1.000	1	2	1	0	0	0
Lopez	.987	11	65	13	1	1	5
Soto	.978	21	152	23	4	2	5
Stassi	1.000	1	4	0	0	0	0

First Base	PCT	G	PO	A	E	DP
Affinito	1.000	12	89	6	0	5
Barton	1.000	4	22	1	0	3
Clime	1.000	1	1	1	0	0
Crosby	1.000	7	61	2	0	2
Lopez	1.000	3	27	1	0	3
Made	.985	37	297	23	5	26
Parker	1.000	1	1	1	0	0

Spina	.846	1	11	0	2	1

Second Base	PCT	G	PO	A	E	DP
Clime	.838	9	10	21	6	3
Eusebio	.941	18	15	33	3	9
Wells	.949	40	75	113	10	19
Wimberly	1.000	2	2	6	0	0

Third Base	PCT	G	PO	A	E	DP
Chen	1.000	5	2	11	0	1
Clime	.855	29	9	56	11	0
Crosby	.947	12	10	26	2	3
Eusebio	.818	8	10	17	6	2
Made	.900	6	6	12	2	2
Parker	1.000	3	2	5	0	0
Spina	—	1	0	0	0	0
Wells	—	1	0	0	0	0

Shortstop	PCT	G	PO	A	E	DP
Castillo	.925	55	88	145	19	36
Chen	1.000	1	0	4	0	1
Clime	—	1	0	0	0	0
Wimberly	.875	1	3	4	1	1

Outfield	PCT	G	PO	A	E	DP
Brazoban	.914	28	30	2	3	0
Consigli	.889	23	39	1	5	1
Garcia	.981	32	50	1	1	1
Landaeta	.914	36	48	5	5	1
Richard	1.000	3	5	1	0	0
Rosario	.860	26	34	3	6	0
Shaw	.952	37	56	3	3	0

DSL ATHLETICS   ROOKIE
DOMINICAN SUMMER LEAGUE

Batting	B-T	HT	WT	DOB	AVG	vLH	vRH	G	AB	R	H	2B	3B	HR	RBI	BB	HBP	SH	SF	SO	SB	CS	SLG	OBP
Almonte, Edward	R-R	6-2	176	1-12-90	.200	.000	.231	9	30	5	6	0	0	0	2	2	0	0	0	8	2	0	.200	.250
Baez, Luis	R-R	6-3	165	5-24-91	.214	.280	.186	29	84	8	18	4	1	1	7	2	0	2	0	26	2	1	.321	.233
Blanco, Charli	R-R	6-0	155	2-23-91	.244	.276	.235	48	127	12	31	3	1	0	7	11	7	2	1	34	4	4	.283	.336
Brazoban, Yeudy	R-R	6-1	185	9-9-88	.107	.200	.087	9	28	3	3	0	0	1	5	1	0	0	2	4	0	0	.214	.129
Castillo, Gernaldo	R-R	5-11	145	7-17-89	.208	.667	.143	8	24	5	5	0	0	0	2	6	0	0	1	4	3	0	.208	.355
Contreras, Franklin	R-R	6-1	165	6-10-90	.157	.500	.073	15	51	8	8	1	1	0	1	5	0	0	0	15	4	1	.216	.232
Cruzado, Fernando	R-R	6-2	210	10-25-89	.212	.000	.226	10	33	5	7	0	0	1	5	2	2	0	0	8	1	1	.303	.297
De La Cruz, Jonatan	R-R	6-0	160	5-28-88	.265	.333	.243	43	151	25	40	4	3	2	24	11	2	2	0	12	7	6	.371	.323
De La Rosa, Anderson	R-R	6-1	180	8-12-91	.153	.147	.155	46	131	19	20	3	0	0	11	17	5	3	1	35	5	4	.176	.273
De Leon, Abraham	R-R	6-0	194	2-20-89	.222	—	.222	5	9	1	2	0	0	1	1	0	0	0	1	0	0	0	.222	.300
Garabito, Yeis	R-R	6-2	170	1-28-90	.189	.120	.215	27	90	9	17	7	0	0	3	8	0	1	0	34	5	2	.267	.255
Garcia, Elvis	R-R	6-2	178	11-8-89	.367	.222	.429	11	30	9	11	3	1	1	5	4	2	0	1	10	3	1	.633	.459
Ledezma, Diego	R-R	6-5	170	8-14-90	.229	.273	.208	23	70	1	16	3	0	0	9	4	0	0	2	18	1	2	.271	.263
Marte, Miguel	R-R	6-3	230	8-29-89	.304	.211	.325	39	102	10	31	9	0	0	17	18	1	0	2	28	2	1	.392	.407
Mateo, Reynaldo	R-R	5-9	209	7-16-89	.364	.536	.304	41	107	17	39	12	0	3	21	18	6	1	0	21	3	1	.561	.481
Osorio, Luis	B-R	6-1	155	4-5-91	.179	.206	.164	28	95	6	17	2	0	0	3	15	1	1	0	25	3	2	.200	.297
Peralta, Jensi	R-R	6-2	180	7-2-91	.246	.324	.225	52	179	20	44	6	2	1	14	10	6	0	0	48	6	7	.318	.308
Rojas, Kelvin	R-R	6-2	188	8-7-89	.265	.303	.256	49	162	29	43	12	2	5	20	14	7	0	3	39	8	5	.457	.344
Rosario, Jose	R-R	6-5	219	9-2-90	.169	.400	.122	31	89	7	15	6	0	0	6	14	1	3	0	26	2	2	.236	.288
Santana, Gabriel	R-R	6-0	165	8-24-90	.234	.200	.241	40	141	17	33	4	0	0	12	7	4	1	0	20	8	3	.262	.289
Sayegh, Jose	R-R	6-2	180	12-7-91	.143	.130	.147	31	91	4	13	0	0	0	2	3	3	0	0	49	2	2	.143	.196
Sena, Alan	R-R	6-0	180	9-24-90	.229	.179	.255	34	83	6	19	1	1	0	3	6	5	3	0	29	6	2	.265	.319
Soto, Michael	R-R	6-3	195	11-17-91	.224	.182	.240	49	165	17	37	8	0	2	19	22	1	1	0	40	4	1	.309	.319
Trinidad, Victor	R-R	6-0	173	12-23-90	.227	.222	.229	17	44	11	10	2	0	0	5	12	2	1	1	14	7	3	.273	.407
Zarraga, Jonesy	R-R	6-1	170	6-3-92	.191	.226	.181	53	136	22	26	5	4	3	13	15	16	5	0	55	5	6	.353	.341

Pitching

Pitching	B-T	HT	WT	DOB	W	L	ERA	G	GS	CG	SV	IP	H	R	ER	HR	BB	SO	AVG	vLH	vRH	K/9	BB/9
Acevedo, Rony	R-R	6-2	165	9-18-88	0	0	4.26	2	1	0	0	6	7	4	3	0	0	8	.304	.200	.333	11.37	0.00
Astacio, Andres	R-R	6-3	180	8-20-90	1	4	3.65	13	11	0	0	57	68	32	23	3	13	42	.296	.346	.281	6.67	2.06
Azor, Jose	R-R	6-2	185	10-12-88	2	3	3.83	14	8	0	0	49	31	25	21	0	33	28	.186	.281	.163	5.11	6.02
Bautista, William	L-L	6-4	173	8-20-91	3	2	3.79	15	2	0	0	36	46	23	15	2	15	17	.301	.167	.312	4.29	3.79
Benzant, Leonel	R-R	6-6	213	12-20-91	0	9	9.50	15	8	0	0	42	45	50	44	2	33	26	.283	.225	.303	5.62	7.13
Castillo, Jose	R-R	6-2	185	2-22-91	3	4	6.27	15	6	0	1	37	41	35	26	1	37	20	.299	.225	.330	4.82	8.92
Diaz, Victor	R-R	6-1	220	10-26-89	0	1	8.10	8	0	0	0	10	6	10	9	0	11	9	.182	.200	.174	8.10	9.90
Duran, Omar	L-L	6-3	209	2-26-90	0	0	1.00	3	1	0	0	9	2	2	1	0	3	14	.065	.000	.077	14.00	3.00
Ferreras, Ronald	R-R	6-1	180	2-8-87	0	0	47.25	2	1	0	0	1	1	8	7	0	5	1	.167	—	.167	6.75	33.75
Fortuna, Anderson	R-R	6-4	200	10-20-89	2	2	5.13	11	2	0	2	26	24	16	15	0	15	22	.245	.364	.211	7.52	5.13
Jose, Luis	R-R	6-4	195	9-26-87	3	4	1.93	21	0	0	2	42	28	15	9	2	20	25	.189	.205	.183	5.36	4.29
Juma, Alexis	R-R	6-1	180	5-23-88	1	0	1.72	10	3	0	1	31	25	10	6	1	10	20	.216	.150	.229	5.74	2.87
Merestil, Rene	L-L	6-3	185	12-30-86	1	6	2.10	14	9	0	0	60	42	23	14	2	29	58	.203	.118	.211	8.70	4.35
Nolasco, Alex	L-L	6-4	190	9-11-90	0	3	13.00	6	3	0	0	9	11	15	13	1	15	7	.324	.500	.313	7.00	15.00
Oliveros, Jose	R-R	6-0	170	9-29-89	0	0	2.25	3	3	0	0	12	8	3	3	0	0	14	.182	.111	.200	10.50	0.00
Paez, Argenis	R-R	6-3	180	10-20-90	1	1	6.75	3	1	0	0	7	9	5	5	0	4	6	.333	.250	.368	8.10	5.40
Ramirez, Benito	R-R	6-5	180	9-23-88	0	1	18.00	9	0	0	0	8	5	18	16	0	16	9	.185	.000	.208	10.13	18.00
Reyes, Luis	R-R	6-2	160	2-4-88	0	0	10.13	4	2	0	0	8	12	9	9	0	5	6	.343	.571	.286	6.75	5.63
Rodriguez, Kevin	L-L	6-4	190	6-26-91	0	2	4.00	9	6	0	0	27	20	15	12	2	15	22	.208	.333	.200	7.33	5.00
Suniaga, Elihoref	R-R	6-1	170	5-5-92	1	2	2.77	4	3	0	0	13	15	6	4	0	2	2	.306	.100	.359	1.38	1.38
Zapata, Roberto	R-R	6-4	171	6-28-89	1	2	4.41	17	0	0	0	33	28	20	16	0	16	20	.237	.269	.228	5.51	4.41

Fielding

Catcher	PCT	G	PO	A	E	DP	PB
Cruzado	.966	10	44	12	2	0	3
De Leon	.967	5	28	1	1	0	0
Ledezma	.946	23	119	20	8	1	8
Marte	.955	15	58	6	3	0	9
Mateo	.972	39	195	45	7	1	10

First Base	PCT	G	PO	A	E	DP
Baez	1.000	1	3	0	0	0
De La Cruz	1.000	2	12	0	0	2
Marte	.992	15	116	5	1	12
Osorio	1.000	4	39	1	0	4
Peralta	1.000	3	31	3	0	0
Rosario	.988	28	227	10	3	24
Soto	.991	23	209	7	2	9

Second Base	PCT	G	PO	A	E	DP
Baez	.925	9	18	19	3	5
Castillo	1.000	7	12	8	0	1

	PCT	G	PO	A	E	DP
Contreras	.826	5	7	12	4	2
De La Cruz	.977	12	18	25	1	10
Osorio	.951	16	25	33	3	5
Santana	.984	22	57	64	2	17
Trinidad	.955	10	20	22	2	3

Third Base	PCT	G	PO	A	E	DP
Baez	.667	1	1	1	1	0
Castillo	1.000	2	2	0	0	0
De La Cruz	.922	27	25	58	7	1
Garabito	.875	12	8	20	4	0
Osorio	.917	2	3	8	1	1
Peralta	.912	16	12	40	5	7
Soto	.878	15	9	27	5	3
Trinidad	—	1	0	0	0	0

Shortstop	PCT	G	PO	A	E	DP
Baez	.941	18	25	39	4	8
Contreras	.906	9	10	19	3	0

	PCT	G	PO	A	E	DP
Osorio	.917	7	9	24	3	3
Peralta	.967	29	33	86	4	10
Santana	.984	19	22	40	1	7

Outfield	PCT	G	PO	A	E	DP
Almonte	.900	7	8	1	1	0
Blanco	.981	41	46	5	1	2
Brazoban	1.000	5	3	1	0	0
De La Rosa	.983	42	57	2	1	2
Garabito	.833	5	10	0	2	0
Garcia	.923	10	11	1	1	1
Rojas	.985	35	66	1	1	0
Rosario	—	1	0	0	0	0
Sayegh	.969	25	31	0	1	0
Sena	.970	29	30	2	1	0
Zarraga	.968	46	83	8	3	0

Philadelphia Phillies

SEASON IN A SENTENCE: Buoyed by the July acquisition of Cliff Lee from the Indians in a prospects-for-ace deal, the Phillies ran away from the National League East and lost just twice in the NL playoffs to the Rockies and Dodgers before they lost the World Series to the Yankees in six games.

HIGH POINT: Defending a championship proved more difficult than winning one, but the Phillies had about as successful an encore as they could have short of winning another World Series. Philadelphia slogged through June with an 11-15 record, but got hot in July with a 10-game winning streak. Rookie lefthander J.A. Happ won twice during the streak, which sandwiched the all-star break, as did veteran lefty Jamie Moyer.

LOW POINT: Longtime broadcaster Harry Kalas died April 13, collapsing in the Nationals Park press box several hours before a scheduled game against Washington. The Phillies honored him by wearing an "HK" patch on their jerseys and by hanging one of his sportcoats and a pair of his distinctive white shoes in their dugout all season.

NOTABLE ROOKIES: When last year's ace Cole Hamels struggled, the Phillies needed starting pitching, and Happ delivered. After opening the season with 12 relief appearances, he became a rotation stalwart, throwing a shutout at Toronto on June 27 and winning his first seven decisions. He led NL rookies in innings, strikeouts and complete games. Lefthander Antonio Bastardo made five starts and made the Division Series roster.

KEY TRANSACTIONS: The Phillies sent four of last year's top 10 prospects to the Indians for Lee, but righties Carlos Carrasco and Jason Knapp, catcher Lou Marson and infielder Jason Donald were a small price to pay for an ace like Lee and solid fourth outfielder in Ben Francisco. Lee beat the Yankees twice, but the Phillies didn't have enough pitching to hold off the Yanks in the World Series. The Phillies pulled Pedro Martinez, 37, off the scrapheap in July, and he went 5-1, 3.63 and made two World Series starts.

DOWN ON THE FARM: The Phillies held onto top prospects Domonic Brown and Michael Taylor, both outfielders, and righthander Kyle Drabek. All three at some point played for Reading, which reached the Eastern League playoffs. Low Class A Lakewood won the South Atlantic League title behind two scoreless starts by righty Trevor May and the hot bats of prospects Travis d'Arnaud (.391) and Anthony Gose (.407).

OPENING DAY PAYROLL: $113,004,046

PLAYERS OF THE YEAR

DAVID SCHOFIELD

MAJOR LEAGUE	MINOR LEAGUE
Chase Utley	**Michael Taylor**
2b	of
.282/.397/.508	(Double-A/Triple-A)
4th Silver Slugger,	.320/.395/.549
1.072 playoff OPS	28 2B, 20 HR, 21 SB

ORGANIZATION LEADERS

BATTING	*Minimum 250 at-bats	
MAJORS		
*AVG	Shane Victorino	.292
*OPS	Ryan Howard	.931
HR	Ryan Howard	45
RBI	Ryan Howard	141
MINORS		
*AVG	Taylor, Michael, Reading/Lehigh Valley	.320
R	Berry, Quintin, Reading	89
H	Sellers, Neil, Reading	164
TB	Sellers, Neil, Reading	252
2B	d'Arnaud, Travis, Lakewood	38
3B	Gose, Anthony, Lakewood	9
HR	Tracy, Andy, Lehigh Valley	26
RBI	Tracy, Andy, Lehigh Valley	96
BB	Tracy, Andy, Lehigh Valley	74
SO	Durant, Michael, Clearwater	142
SB	Gose, Anthony, Lakewood	76
*OBP	Taylor, Michael, Reading/Lehigh Valley	.395
*SLG	Taylor, Michael, Reading/Lehigh Valley	.549

PITCHING	†Minimum 75 innings	
MAJORS		
W	Jamie Moyer	12
†ERA	J.A. Happ	2.93
SO	Cole Hamels	168
MINORS		
W	Savery, Joe, Reading/Lehigh Valley	16
L	Worley, Vance, Reading	12
†ERA	Drabek, Kyle, Clearwater/Reading	3.19
G	Schwimer, Michael, Clearwater/Reading	53
GS	Three tied at	27
SV	Rosenberg, B.J., Lakewood/Reading	22
IP	Cloyd, Tyler, Lakewood/Clearwater	165
BB	Savery, Joe, Reading/Lehigh Valley	77
SO	Drabek, Kyle, Clearwater/Reading	150
†AVG	Drabek, Kyle, Clearwater/Reading	.239

General Manager: Ruben Amaro Jr. **Farm Director:** Steve Noworyta. **Scouting Director:** Marti Wolever.

Class	Team	League	W	L	PCT	Finish*	Manager(s)
Majors	Philadelphia Phillies	National	93	69	.574	†2nd (16)	Charlie Manuel
Triple-A	Lehigh Valley IronPigs	International	71	73	.493	8th (14)	Dave Huppert
Double-A	Reading Phillies	Eastern	75	67	.528	3rd (12)	Steve Roadcap
High A	Clearwater Threshers	Florida State	67	69	.493	6th (12)	Ernie Whitt
Low A	Lakewood BlueClaws	South Atlantic	78	58	.574	†2nd (16)	Dusty Wathan
Short-season	Williamsport Crosscutters	New York-Penn	42	34	.553	5th (14)	Chris Truby
Rookie	GCL Phillies	Gulf Coast	31	28	.525	6th (16)	Rolando de Armas
Overall 2009 Minor League Record			364	329	.525	4th (30)	

*Finish in overall standings (No. of teams in league). †League champion.

ORGANIZATION STATISTICS

PHILADELPHIA PHILLIES
NATIONAL LEAGUE

Batting	B-T	HT	WT	DOB	AVG	vLH	vRH	G	AB	R	H	2B	3B	HR	RBI	BB	HBP	SH	SF	SO	SB	CS	SLG	OBP
Bako, Paul	L-R	6-3	210	6-20-72	.224	.000	.245	44	116	12	26	4	0	3	9	13	1	0	0	32	0	1	.336	.308
Bruntlett, Eric	R-R	6-0	200	3-29-78	.171	.229	.123	72	105	15	18	7	0	0	7	5	3	2	3	26	2	0	.238	.224
Cairo, Miguel	R-R	6-1	210	5-4-74	.267	.000	.286	27	45	6	12	2	1	1	2	0	1	1	0	4	0	0	.422	.283
Coste, Chris	R-R	6-1	210	2-4-73	.245	.235	.250	45	102	12	25	8	0	2	8	14	1	1	0	27	0	0	.382	.342
2-team total (43 Houston)					.224	—	—	88	205	15	46	13	0	2	18	22	1	1	1	55	0	0	.317	.301
Dobbs, Greg	L-R	6-1	210	7-2-78	.247	.429	.238	97	154	15	38	6	0	5	20	11	1	0	3	29	1	0	.383	.296
Feliz, Pedro	R-R	6-1	210	4-27-75	.266	.208	.282	158	580	62	154	30	2	12	82	35	3	2	5	68	0	1	.386	.308
Francisco, Ben	R-R	6-1	190	10-23-81	.278	.200	.313	37	97	10	27	9	0	5	13	5	1	0	1	24	1	4	.526	.317
Hoover, Paul	R-R	6-1	210	4-14-76	.750	.750	—	3	4	0	3	0	0	0	1	0	0	0	0	1	0	0	.750	.750
Howard, Ryan	L-L	6-4	260	11-19-79	.279	.207	.320	160	616	105	172	37	4	45	141	75	6	0	6	186	8	1	.571	.360
Ibanez, Raul	L-R	6-2	225	6-2-72	.272	.285	.267	134	500	93	136	32	3	34	93	56	4	0	5	119	4	0	.552	.347
Marson, Lou	R-R	6-1	200	6-26-86	.235	—	.235	7	17	3	4	1	0	0	3	0	0	0	0	7	0	0	.294	.350
Mayberry Jr., John	R-R	6-6	230	12-21-83	.211	.243	.150	39	57	8	12	3	0	4	8	2	1	0	0	23	0	0	.474	.250
Rollins, Jimmy	B-R	5-8	170	11-27-78	.250	.230	.257	155	672	100	168	43	5	21	77	44	2	2	5	70	31	8	.423	.296
Ruiz, Carlos	R-R	5-10	205	1-22-79	.255	.293	.242	107	322	32	82	26	1	9	43	47	4	4	2	39	3	2	.425	.355
Stairs, Matt	L-R	5-9	215	2-27-68	.194	.000	.200	99	103	15	20	4	0	5	17	23	3	0	0	30	0	0	.379	.357
Tracy, Andy	L-R	6-3	240	12-11-73	.417	.000	.455	9	12	1	5	0	1	0	1	0	0	0	0	3	0	0	.583	.417
Utley, Chase	L-R	6-1	190	12-17-78	.282	.288	.279	156	571	112	161	28	4	31	93	88	24	0	4	110	23	0	.508	.397
Victorino, Shane	B-R	5-9	185	11-30-80	.292	.314	.283	156	620	102	181	39	13	10	62	60	6	4	4	71	25	8	.445	.358
Werth, Jayson	R-R	6-5	215	5-20-79	.268	.302	.256	159	571	98	153	26	1	36	99	91	8	0	6	156	20	3	.506	.373

Pitching	B-T	HT	WT	DOB	W	L	ERA	G	GS	CG	SV	IP	H	R	ER	HR	BB	SO	AVG	vLH	vRH	K/9	BB/9
Bastardo, Antonio	L-L	5-11	195	9-21-85	2	3	6.46	6	5	0	0	24	26	18	17	4	9	19	.274	.303	.258	7.23	3.42
Blanton, Joe	R-R	6-3	250	12-11-80	12	8	4.05	31	31	0	0	195	198	89	88	30	59	163	.262	.252	.271	7.51	2.72
Carpenter, Drew	R-R	6-3	225	5-18-85	1	0	11.12	3	1	0	0	6	11	7	7	1	4	5	.423	.400	.455	7.94	6.35
Condrey, Clay	R-R	6-3	225	11-19-75	6	2	3.00	45	0	0	1	42	37	17	14	4	14	25	.233	.172	.267	5.36	3.00
Durbin, Chad	R-R	6-2	220	12-3-77	2	2	4.39	59	0	0	2	70	56	38	34	8	47	62	.220	.223	.218	8.01	6.07
Escalona, Sergio	L-L	6-0	170	8-3-84	1	0	4.61	14	0	0	0	14	12	7	7	0	5	10	.240	.200	.257	6.59	3.29
Eyre, Scott	L-L	6-1	225	5-30-72	2	1	1.50	42	0	0	0	30	22	6	5	3	16	22	.206	.210	.200	6.60	4.80
Hamels, Cole	L-L	6-3	190	12-27-83	10	11	4.32	32	32	2	0	194	206	95	93	24	43	168	.273	.242	.282	7.81	2.00
Happ, J.A.	L-L	6-6	200	10-19-82	12	4	2.93	35	23	3	0	166	149	55	54	24	56	119	.244	.216	.253	6.45	3.04
Kendrick, Kyle	R-R	6-3	205	8-26-84	3	1	3.42	9	2	0	0	26	27	11	10	1	9	15	.273	.267	.278	5.13	3.08
Lee, Cliff	L-L	6-3	190	8-30-78	7	4	3.39	12	12	3	0	80	80	35	30	7	10	74	.261	.316	.249	8.36	1.13
Lidge, Brad	R-R	6-5	215	12-23-76	0	8	7.21	67	0	0	31	59	72	51	47	11	34	61	.301	.319	.285	9.36	5.22
Lopez, Rodrigo	R-R	6-1	185	12-14-75	3	1	5.70	7	5	0	0	30	42	24	19	3	11	19	.339	.327	.348	5.70	3.30
Madson, Ryan	L-R	6-6	200	8-28-80	5	5	3.26	79	0	0	10	77	73	29	28	7	22	78	.251	.257	.245	9.08	2.56
Martinez, Pedro	R-R	5-11	195	10-25-71	5	1	3.63	9	9	0	0	45	48	18	18	7	8	37	.276	.268	.286	7.46	1.61
Moyer, Jamie	L-L	6-0	185	11-18-62	12	10	4.94	30	25	0	0	162	177	91	89	27	43	94	.279	.243	.290	5.22	2.39
Myers, Brett	R-R	6-4	240	8-17-80	4	3	4.84	18	10	0	0	71	74	38	38	18	23	50	.272	.233	.320	6.37	2.93
Park, Chan Ho	R-R	6-2	210	6-30-73	3	3	4.43	45	7	0	0	83	84	43	41	5	33	73	.264	.280	.248	7.88	3.56
Register, Steven	R-R	6-1	180	5-16-83	0	0	4.50	1	0	0	0	2	3	1	1	0	1	1	.333	.500	.200	4.50	4.50
Romero, J.C.	B-L	5-11	205	6-4-76	0	0	2.70	21	0	0	0	17	13	6	5	2	13	12	.224	.308	.156	6.48	7.02
Taschner, Jack	L-L	6-3	205	4-21-78	1	1	4.91	24	0	0	0	29	38	18	16	3	20	19	.317	.324	.313	5.83	6.14
Walker, Tyler	R-R	6-3	262	5-15-76	2	1	3.06	32	0	0	0	35	31	12	12	4	9	27	.230	.229	.230	6.88	2.29

Fielding

Catcher	PCT	G	PO	A	E	DP	PB
Bako	.981	42	254	9	5	1	6
Coste	1.000	29	164	6	0	1	3
Hoover	1.000	3	9	1	0	0	0
Marson	1.000	7	48	6	0	0	0
Ruiz	.996	107	707	49	3	7	1

First Base	PCT	G	PO	A	E	DP
Bruntlett	1.000	2	6	0	0	0
Coste	1.000	1	9	0	0	1
Dobbs	.962	6	24	1	1	3
Howard	.990	156	1300	95	14	109
Tracy	1.000	1	8	1	0	2

Second Base	PCT	G	PO	A	E	DP
Bruntlett	.952	13	20	20	2	6
Cairo	1.000	5	10	9	0	3
Utley	.984	155	354	408	12	97
Third Base	**PCT**	**G**	**PO**	**A**	**E**	**DP**
Bruntlett	1.000	7	0	1	0	0
Cairo	1.000	1	1	1	0	0

	PCT	G	PO	A	E	DP
Dobbs	1.000	16	3	25	0	1
Feliz	.966	155	110	312	15	35
Shortstop	**PCT**	**G**	**PO**	**A**	**E**	**DP**
Bruntlett	.969	9	13	18	1	2
Cairo	1.000	3	1	4	0	0

	PCT	G	PO	A	E	DP
Feliz	—	2	0	0	0	0
Rollins	.990	155	212	389	6	72
Outfield	**PCT**	**G**	**PO**	**A**	**E**	**DP**
Bruntlett	.909	10	9	1	1	0
Dobbs	1.000	15	23	0	0	0

	PCT	G	PO	A	E	DP
Francisco	1.000	22	51	2	0	0
Ibanez	.991	129	213	9	2	0
Mayberry Jr.	1.000	30	31	1	0	1
Stairs	1.000	15	23	2	0	2
Victorino	.997	149	336	8	1	1
Werth	.984	157	353	11	6	4

LEHIGH VALLEY IRONPIGS   TRIPLE-A
INTERNATIONAL LEAGUE

Batting	B-T	HT	WT	DOB	AVG	vLH	vRH	G	AB	R	H	2B	3B	HR	RBI	BB	HBP	SH	SF	SO	SB	CS	SLG	OBP
Cairo, Miguel	R-R	6-1	210	5-4-74	.287	.292	.286	78	296	44	85	12	2	5	33	15	2	1	1	40	8	1	.392	.325
Cervenak, Mike	R-R	5-11	200	8-17-76	.305	.393	.277	119	462	67	141	36	2	9	77	28	6	2	8	46	1	1	.450	.347
Donald, Jason	R-R	6-1	195	9-4-84	.236	.300	.225	51	208	26	49	15	1	1	16	14	5	1	2	53	6	0	.332	.297
2-team total (10 Columbus)					.239	—	—	61	243	36	58	17	1	2	17	17	7	1	2	64	7	0	.342	.305
Ellison, Jason	R-R	5-10	180	4-4-78	.261	.311	.242	125	449	54	117	20	0	5	37	43	7	2	4	84	15	4	.339	.332
Furmaniak, J.J.	R-R	6-0	190	7-31-79	.230	.186	.246	118	378	36	87	20	2	5	48	23	3	4	6	72	4	3	.333	.276
Gosewisch, Tuffy	R-R	5-11	190	8-17-83	.200	.308	.167	16	55	6	11	3	0	0	1	2	0	0	0	13	0	0	.255	.228
Guevara, Orlando	B-R	6-1	175	9-13-83	.333	—	.333	1	3	0	1	0	0	0	0	0	0	0	0	1	0	0	.333	.333
Hoover, Paul	R-R	6-1	210	4-14-76	.253	.344	.223	73	245	26	62	16	1	1	28	29	1	1	5	66	1	1	.339	.329
Ibanez, Raul	L-R	6-2	225	6-2-72	.400	—	.400	2	5	1	2	1	0	0	2	3	0	0	0	2	0	0	.600	.625
Leon, Carlos	B-R	5-10	181	8-31-79	.250	.800	.130	12	28	5	7	0	0	1	3	3	1	2	0	4	0	0	.357	.344
Marson, Lou	R-R	6-1	200	6-26-86	.294	.283	.297	63	211	32	62	13	0	1	24	30	0	0	0	40	3	1	.370	.382
2-team total (28 Columbus)					.277	—	—	91	314	42	87	18	1	2	33	40	2	0	1	59	4	1	.360	.361
Mayberry Jr., John	R-R	6-6	230	12-21-83	.256	.296	.243	89	316	44	81	20	2	13	43	34	4	0	4	94	6	2	.456	.332
Milner, Gus	R-R	6-5	240	4-21-84	.375	.600	.000	2	8	1	3	2	0	0	4	0	1	0	0	2	0	0	.625	.444
Nelson, Kevin	R-R	6-3	215	4-8-81	.250	.000	.333	4	12	2	3	2	0	0	0	2	0	0	0	1	0	0	.417	.357
Newhan, David	L-R	5-10	185	9-7-73	.275	.333	.257	108	356	42	98	21	3	6	48	33	3	1	8	73	4	2	.402	.335
Ozuna, Pablo	R-R	5-11	200	8-25-74	.294	.250	.306	51	187	25	55	15	2	0	15	9	5	1	1	24	8	2	.396	.342
Ruiz, Carlos	R-R	5-10	205	1-22-79	.231	.000	.333	4	13	1	3	1	0	0	2	3	0	0	0	2	0	0	.308	.375
Slayden, Jeremy	L-R	6-0	185	7-28-82	.229	.185	.242	38	118	11	27	8	0	4	12	10	1	1	0	29	0	0	.398	.295
Spidale, Mike	R-R	6-1	190	3-12-82	.289	.351	.245	31	90	17	26	4	0	0	7	5	2	3	0	13	5	2	.333	.340
Taylor, Michael	R-R	6-6	250	12-19-85	.282	.250	.295	30	110	15	31	6	1	5	19	13	2	0	3	19	3	1	.491	.359
Thompson, Rich	L-R	6-3	185	4-23-79	.265	.257	.267	119	445	69	118	22	7	3	36	38	8	2	0	73	26	4	.366	.334
Tiffee, Terry	B-R	6-3	215	4-21-79	.268	.324	.247	64	246	18	66	12	0	5	34	10	0	0	2	24	0	1	.378	.295
Tracy, Andy	L-R	6-3	240	12-11-73	.254	.273	.248	129	453	76	115	23	1	26	96	74	6	0	7	110	7	1	.481	.361
Velandia, Jorge	R-R	5-9	190	1-12-75	.182	.250	.167	10	22	2	4	0	0	0	1	1	0	0	0	7	0	0	.318	.280

Pitching	B-T	HT	WT	DOB	W	L	ERA	G	GS	CG	SV	IP	H	R	ER	HR	BB	SO	AVG	vLH	vRH	K/9	BB/9
Anderson, Jason	L-R	6-0	188	6-9-79	2	2	3.55	37	0	0	4	51	41	23	20	5	20	34	.232	.254	.219	6.04	3.55
Bastardo, Antonio	L-L	5-11	195	9-21-85	1	0	2.08	2	2	0	0	13	11	3	3	1	3	12	.234	.263	.214	8.31	2.08
Bisenius, Joe	R-R	6-4	205	9-18-82	0	1	8.38	7	1	0	0	10	14	9	9	1	4	12	.350	.400	.320	11.17	3.72
Borkowski, Dave	R-R	6-1	230	2-7-77	0	4	3.74	10	0	0	0	22	22	10	9	2	4	15	.275	.464	.173	4.15	3.32
Bowers, Cedrick	B-L	6-2	220	2-10-78	4	3	1.93	48	0	0	5	61	38	15	13	1	45	67	.182	.233	.154	9.94	6.68
Brummett, Tyson	R-R	6-0	150	8-15-84	0	1	11.25	1	1	0	0	4	7	6	5	1	1	3	.412	.571	.300	6.75	2.25
Butto, Francisco	R-R	6-1	200	5-11-80	1	0	4.80	8	0	0	0	15	23	9	8	0	7	12	.365	.417	.353	7.20	4.20
Carpenter, Drew	R-R	6-3	225	5-18-85	11	6	3.35	25	24	0	0	156	162	67	58	18	47	120	.271	.312	.241	6.92	2.71
Carrasco, Carlos	R-R	6-3	215	3-21-87	6	9	5.18	20	20	0	0	115	118	73	66	14	38	112	.262	.245	.276	8.79	2.98
2-team total (6 Columbus)					11	10	4.64	26	26	0	0	157	149	91	81	17	45	148	—	—	—	8.48	2.58
Chacin, Gustavo	L-L	5-11	205	11-4-80	8	4	3.21	18	18	1	0	107	105	44	38	9	41	62	.264	.277	.259	5.23	3.46
Concepcion, Alexander	R-R	6-1	180	9-27-84	0	0	3.86	6	0	0	1	14	15	6	6	1	1	8	.278	.250	.289	5.14	0.64
Durbin, Chad	R-R	6-2	220	12-3-77	0	0	0.00	1	1	0	0	1	1	0	0	0	0	1	.333	.000	.500	9.00	0.00
Ennis, John	R-R	6-5	220	10-17-79	0	0	135.00	1	0	0	0	0	4	5	5	0	0	1	.800	.000	1.000	27.00	0.00
Escalona, Sergio	L-L	6-0	170	8-3-84	0	2	5.95	15	1	0	2	20	21	15	13	4	8	15	.266	.200	.306	6.86	3.66
Green, Steve	R-R	6-2	200	1-26-78	0	1	9.64	6	1	0	0	9	14	10	10	1	13	7	.333	.294	.360	6.75	12.54
Kendrick, Kyle	R-R	6-3	205	8-26-84	9	7	3.34	24	24	1	0	143	133	59	53	9	35	62	.250	.280	.228	3.90	2.20
Koplove, Mike	R-R	6-0	160	8-30-76	1	3	1.14	21	0	0	6	24	15	8	3	2	11	20	.179	.233	.148	11.41	4.18
2-team total (22 Indianapolis)					4	4	1.82	43	0	0	8	54	42	16	11	2	21	50	—	—	—	8.28	3.48
Lehr, Justin	R-R	6-2	215	8-3-77	5	4	4.75	8	7	1	0	42	43	23	22	5	16	20	.272	.333	.232	4.32	3.46
2-team total (12 Louisville)					13	3	3.31	20	18	2	0	117	100	45	43	8	26	60	—	—	—	4.62	2.00
Lopez, Rodrigo	R-R	6-1	185	12-14-75	7	5	4.31	18	18	1	0	100	122	57	48	9	14	71	.303	.306	.300	6.37	1.26
Majewski, Gary	R-R	6-2	215	2-26-80	0	5	4.02	51	0	0	5	63	73	36	28	4	24	43	.298	.282	.306	6.18	3.45
Martinez, Pedro	R-R	5-11	195	10-25-71	0	1	7.20	1	1	0	0	5	3	5	4	1	3	4	.176	.375	.000	7.20	5.40
Mazone, Brian	L-L	6-2	220	7-26-76	2	6	3.50	11	11	0	0	54	63	23	21	4	9	33	.299	.325	.292	5.50	1.50
Myers, Brett	R-R	6-4	240	8-17-80	0	0	0.00	2	0	0	1	2	0	0	0	0	0	2	.000	.000	.000	13.50	0.00
Nestor, Scott	R-R	6-4	225	8-20-84	0	0	45.00	2	0	0	0	1	1	5	5	0	9	2	.250	.000	.333	18.00	81.00
Overholt, Pat	R-R	6-0	190	2-8-84	1	0	2.81	10	0	0	0	16	12	5	5	1	13	10	.235	.412	.147	5.63	7.31
Register, Steven	R-R	6-1	180	5-16-83	2	3	3.70	34	0	0	7	41	44	18	17	4	12	28	.272	.356	.239	6.10	2.61
Romero, J.C.	B-L	5-11	205	6-4-76	0	1	3.86	5	1	0	0	5	5	2	2	0	2	5	.278	.000	.357	9.64	3.86
Savery, Joe	L-L	6-3	215	11-4-85	4	2	4.38	7	7	1	0	39	42	23	19	0	24	19	.286	.250	.297	4.38	5.54
Taschner, Jack	L-L	6-3	205	4-21-78	0	2	2.08	20	0	0	2	22	16	6	5	1	10	15	.213	.206	.220	6.23	4.15
Walker, Tyler	R-R	6-3	262	5-15-76	2	1	1.40	15	0	0	3	19	8	4	3	1	3	20	.125	.138	.114	9.31	1.40
Woods, Jake	L-L	6-0	200	9-3-81	5	2	3.46	42	6	0	2	81	82	31	31	7	29	53	.263	.223	.282	5.91	3.24

Fielding

Catcher	PCT	G	PO	A	E	DP	PB
Gosewisch	.982	16	97	12	2	0	1
Guevara	1.000	1	5	0	0	1	0
Hoover	.991	60	402	38	4	3	5
Marson	.986	62	379	29	6	3	2
Nelson	1.000	4	16	3	0	0	0
Ruiz	1.000	3	21	1	0	0	0

First Base	PCT	G	PO	A	E	DP
Cairo	1.000	1	9	0	0	1
Cervenak	.996	28	231	13	1	36
Hoover	.990	10	96	6	1	10
Newhan	1.000	1	8	1	0	1
Tracy	.992	104	869	71	8	93

Second Base	PCT	G	PO	A	E	DP
Cairo	1.000	7	15	16	0	6
Donald	1.000	3	5	7	0	1

Furmaniak	.982	50	90	125	4	32
Leon	1.000	8	22	21	0	8
Newhan	.974	39	63	87	4	21
Ozuna	.977	47	81	129	5	41
Tiffee	1.000	1	2	0	0	
Velandia	.900	2	5	4	1	1

Third Base	PCT	G	PO	A	E	DP
Cairo	.846	6	2	9	2	1
Cervenak	.951	36	17	61	4	5
Donald	.800	3	1	3	1	0
Furmaniak	.957	30	24	64	4	14
Newhan	.946	15	4	31	2	6
Tiffee	.973	56	38	104	4	17
Velandia	.000	1	0	0	1	0

Shortstop	PCT	G	PO	A	E	DP
Cairo	.974	65	98	167	7	43

Donald	.982	45	67	147	4	28
Furmaniak	.968	31	34	87	4	16
Newhan	.800	2	2	6	2	2
Ozuna	1.000	2	4	3	0	0
Velandia	1.000	4	5	14	0	2

Outfield	PCT	G	PO	A	E	DP
Cervenak	.972	22	34	1	1	0
Ellison	.997	123	311	12	1	3
Ibanez	1.000	2	2	0	0	0
Mayberry Jr.	1.000	89	183	4	0	0
Milner	1.000	2	2	1	0	0
Newhan	1.000	22	38	0	0	0
Slayden	.920	29	45	1	4	1
Spidale	1.000	24	34	1	0	0
Taylor	.975	30	74	5	2	0
Thompson	.993	108	255	13	2	3

READING PHILLIES
EASTERN LEAGUE

DOUBLE-A

Batting	B-T	HT	WT	DOB	AVG	vLH	vRH	G	AB	R	H	2B	3B	HR	RBI	BB	HBP	SH	SF	SO	SB	CS	SLG	OBP
Bako, Paul	L-R	6-3	210	6-20-72	.357	.273	.387	10	42	5	15	1	0	0	10	1	0	0	0	8	0	0	.381	.372
Berry, Quintin	L-L	6-1	165	11-21-84	.266	.305	.249	135	516	89	137	17	2	5	28	63	9	10	0	118	48	14	.335	.355
Brown, Domonic	L-L	6-5	204	9-3-87	.279	.322	.250	37	147	20	41	9	4	3	20	14	1	0	0	37	8	1	.456	.346
Chavez, Ozzie	B-R	6-1	160	7-13-83	.259	.245	.264	112	363	37	94	17	0	1	34	30	1	10	0	58	7	1	.314	.317
Galvis, Freddy	B-R	5-10	154	11-14-89	.197	.167	.209	16	61	6	12	0	0	1	5	2	0	0	0	7	0	1	.246	.222
Gosewisch, Tuffy	R-R	5-11	190	8-17-83	.244	.365	.190	60	205	16	50	17	0	1	20	14	7	3	0	34	0	1	.341	.314
Gradoville, Tim	R-R	6-3	195	1-30-80	—	—	—	2	0	0	0	0	0	0	0	0	0	0	0	0	0	0	—	—
Guerra, Jorge	R-R	6-1	170	9-12-87	.000	—	.000	1	4	0	0	0	0	0	0	0	0	0	0	1	0	0	.000	.000
Guevara, Orlando	B-R	6-1	175	9-13-83	.154	.000	.222	4	13	0	2	0	0	0	1	0	0	1	0	6	0	0	.154	.154
Harman, Brad	R-R	6-1	205	11-19-85	.201	.205	.200	117	422	46	85	23	4	5	41	39	3	3	4	119	0	2	.310	.271
Ibanez, Raul	L-R	6-2	225	6-2-72	.000	—	.000	1	2	1	0	0	0	0	0	0	1	0	0	0	0	0	.000	.333
Kennelly, Timothy	R-R	6-0	180	12-5-86	.256	.207	.273	37	117	13	30	6	2	2	17	12	3	0	1	16	1	1	.393	.338
Leon, Carlos	B-R	5-10	181	8-31-79	.214	.231	.205	70	187	22	40	7	1	1	12	25	5	10	1	30	4	2	.278	.321
Mahar, Kevin	R-R	6-5	220	6-8-81	.314	.245	.351	117	407	59	128	18	2	12	54	25	3	1	1	81	7	3	.457	.358
Milner, Gus	R-R	6-5	240	4-21-84	.226	.221	.228	85	257	26	58	10	2	3	23	24	1	2	2	75	3	8	.315	.292
Nelson, Kevin	R-R	6-3	215	4-8-81	.253	.209	.270	53	158	19	40	7	1	9	27	21	1	4	5	34	0	1	.481	.335
Sellers, Neil	R-R	6-0	195	4-3-82	.317	.366	.298	139	518	71	164	33	2	17	86	48	12	1	7	71	5	5	.486	.383
Slayden, Jeremy	L-R	6-0	185	7-28-82	.281	.314	.269	46	139	23	39	7	0	3	16	9	30	20	2	0	33	0	1	.525	.372
Spidale, Mike	R-R	6-1	190	3-12-82	.297	.350	.264	81	263	38	78	10	4	3	27	11	5	3	1	28	12	5	.399	.336
Stavisky, Brian	L-R	6-3	230	7-6-80	.279	.235	.294	118	394	54	110	32	2	11	66	62	4	0	7	84	3	2	.454	.377
Susdorf, Steve	L-L	6-1	195	3-28-86	.221	.063	.262	24	77	12	17	4	0	2	7	7	4	0	0	26	0	0	.351	.318
Taylor, Michael	R-R	6-6	250	12-19-85	.333	.289	.353	86	318	59	106	22	4	15	65	35	7	0	3	51	18	4	.569	.408

Pitching	B-T	HT	WT	DOB	W	L	ERA	G	GS	CG	SV	IP	H	R	ER	HR	BB	SO	AVG	vLH	vRH	K/9	BB/9
Anderson, Jason	L-R	6-0	188	6-9-79	1	1	3.15	14	0	0	4	20	15	7	7	2	3	13	.200	.281	.140	5.85	1.35
Bastardo, Antonio	L-L	5-11	195	9-21-85	2	2	1.75	11	5	0	3	36	22	7	7	1	7	41	.179	.163	.188	10.25	1.75
Bisenius, Joe	R-R	6-4	205	9-18-82	0	1	2	11.25	1	0	0	0	12	15	15	15	3	9	17	.294	.400	.226	12.75	6.75
Brummett, Tyson	R-R	6-0	150	8-15-84	3	9	5.22	26	15	0	2	98	119	63	57	12	27	70	.303	.312	.294	6.41	2.47
Butto, Francisco	R-R	6-1	200	5-11-80	1	1	1.96	16	0	0	2	18	18	7	4	2	14	19	.240	.226	.250	9.33	6.87
Castro, Angel	R-R	5-11	200	11-14-82	2	1	7.00	14	0	0	1	18	26	21	14	2	12	10	.342	.306	.375	5.00	6.00
Chacin, Gustavo	L-L	5-11	205	11-4-80	1	0	3.12	2	1	0	0	9	9	3	3	1	3	4	.257	.100	.320	4.15	3.12
Chapman, Chance	R-R	6-4	210	2-27-84	7	1	2.73	38	1	0	1	53	43	16	16	3	18	49	.225	.227	.223	8.37	3.08
Cisco, Mike	R-R	5-11	190	5-23-87	2	4	4.58	7	7	0	0	39	44	21	20	4	9	20	.282	.228	.359	4.58	2.06
Concepcion, Alexander	R-R	6-1	180	9-27-84	2	3	3.10	32	7	0	2	81	69	30	28	9	11	47	.232	.196	.268	5.20	1.22
Crawford, Tristan	R-R	6-3	213	7-22-82	0	0	5.79	7	0	0	0	9	9	6	6	2	4	7	.257	.125	.368	6.75	3.86
Drabek, Kyle	R-R	6-0	185	12-8-87	8	2	3.64	15	14	0	0	96	92	40	39	9	31	76	.252	.322	.166	7.10	2.90
Escalona, Sergio	L-L	6-0	170	8-3-84	2	1	1.77	32	0	0	12	41	31	12	8	1	14	38	.208	.255	.181	8.41	3.10
Eyre, Scott	L-L	6-1	225	5-30-72	0	0	5.40	2	1	0	0	2	4	1	1	1	2	3	.444	.500	.429	16.20	10.80
Flande, Yohan	L-L	6-2	170	1-27-86	4	4	4.58	13	13	1	0	71	81	38	36	5	21	50	.296	.275	.304	6.37	2.67
German, Matt	L-L	6-0	190	6-27-84	0	1	1.17	11	0	0	0	15	10	2	2	1	8	19	.182	.136	.212	11.15	4.70
Lidge, Brad	R-R	6-5	215	12-23-76	0	0	0.00	1	1	0	0	1	1	0	0	0	2	2	.250	—	.250	18.00	0.00
Mackintosh, Jason	R-L	6-0	205	7-2-80	1	0	4.63	20	0	0	1	23	22	12	12	1	12	19	.239	.111	.362	7.33	4.63
Martinez, Pedro	R-R	5-11	195	10-25-71	0	1	4.50	1	1	0	0	6	5	4	3	1	0	11	.217	.200	.250	16.50	0.00
Mathieson, Scott	R-R	6-3	190	2-27-84	2	1	1.40	13	0	0	1	19	10	6	3	1	7	17	.149	.194	.097	7.91	3.26
Monasterios, Carlos	R-R	6-2	175	3-21-86	0	0	3.68	2	1	0	0	7	8	3	3	0	2	4	.308	.357	.250	4.91	2.45
Myers, Brett	R-R	6-4	240	8-17-80	0	1	2.25	2	1	0	0	4	2	1	1	1	1	7	.154	.143	.167	15.75	2.25
Nestor, Scott	R-R	6-4	225	8-20-84	0	0	11.25	3	0	0	0	4	3	5	5	1	6	4	.214	.143	.286	9.00	13.50
2-team total (33 Altoona)					2	3	5.83	36	0	0	10	46	38	31	30	8	35	51	—	—	—	9.91	6.80
Overholt, Pat	R-R	6-0	190	2-8-84	0	1	4.83	39	0	0	0	50	53	30	27	9	30	39	.273	.294	.257	6.97	5.36
Romero, J.C.	B-L	5-11	205	6-4-76	0	0	0.00	1	0	0	1	0	0	0	0	0	0	0	.000	—	.000	0.00	0.00
Rosenberg, B.J.	R-R	6-2	200	9-17-85	0	1	2.53	10	0	0	3	11	10	3	3	0	4	8	.263	.222	.300	6.75	3.38
Savery, Joe	L-L	6-3	215	11-4-85	12	4	4.41	21	20	1	0	112	111	55	55	13	53	77	.262	.246	.270	6.17	4.25

Name	B-T	HT	WT	DOB	W	L	ERA	G	GS	CG	SV	IP	H	R	ER	HR	BB	SO	AVG	vLH	vRH	K/9	BB/9
Schwimer, Michael	R-R	6-8	246	2-19-86	2	1	7.71	5	0	0	0	5	7	4	4	0	2	7	.350	.111	.545	13.50	3.86
Shortslef, Josh	R-L	6-4	250	2-1-82	4	2	3.86	16	0	0	0	16	11	7	7	0	13	8	.200	.091	.273	4.41	7.16
Sikaras, Pete	R-R	6-2	220	5-5-79	0	0	4.50	4	0	0	0	4	4	2	2	1	4	6	.267	.500	.231	13.50	9.00
Stutes, Mike	R-R	6-1	185	9-4-86	8	8	4.26	27	27	0	0	146	147	78	69	15	58	109	.265	.307	.220	6.73	3.58
Walls, Sam	R-R	5-11	195	10-31-83	0	1	9.00	4	0	0	0	5	6	5	5	1	1	2	.300	.200	.400	3.60	1.80
Worley, Vance	R-R	6-2	220	9-25-87	7	12	5.34	27	27	0	0	153	163	102	91	17	49	100	.275	.288	.261	5.87	2.88
Zagurski, Mike	L-L	6-0	225	1-27-83	3	4	3.57	45	0	0	8	53	42	24	21	7	27	63	.219	.260	.193	10.70	4.58

Fielding

Catcher	PCT	G	PO	A	E	DP	PB
Bako	1.000	7	52	4	0	1	1
Gosewisch	.987	60	407	43	6	5	3
Gradoville	1.000	2	1	0	0	0	0
Guerra	.909	1	10	0	1	0	0
Guevara	1.000	4	35	8	0	1	1
Kennelly	.970	25	180	15	6	2	2
Nelson	.991	50	298	34	3	2	4

First Base	PCT	G	PO	A	E	DP
Mahar	.987	52	416	40	6	36
Sellers	1.000	11	13	1	0	3
Stavisky	.986	99	797	50	12	64

Second Base	PCT	G	PO	A	E	DP
Chavez	.985	15	24	40	1	11
Harman	.981	116	226	300	10	66
Leon	.986	16	27	41	1	8
Sellers	1.000	3	4	6	0	2

Third Base	PCT	G	PO	A	E	DP
Kennelly	1.000	3	2	4	0	0
Leon	.875	17	4	10	2	0
Nelson	—	1	0	0	0	0
Sellers	.961	138	107	237	14	15

Shortstop	PCT	G	PO	A	E	DP
Chavez	.966	96	112	259	13	48
Galvis	.935	16	20	38	4	9

	PCT	G	PO	A	E	DP
Leon	.966	40	62	82	5	22

Outfield	PCT	G	PO	A	E	DP
Berry	.993	135	284	3	2	0
Brown	.929	36	51	1	4	0
Ibanez	—	1	0	0	0	0
Kennelly	1.000	5	7	1	0	0
Leon	1.000	1	1	0	0	0
Mahar	1.000	54	99	1	0	0
Milner	.983	80	166	4	3	1
Slayden	1.000	15	17	0	0	0
Spidale	.992	64	118	2	1	1
Susdorf	1.000	8	9	0	0	0
Taylor	.991	65	100	6	1	2

CLEARWATER THRESHERS

HIGH CLASS A

FLORIDA STATE LEAGUE

Batting	B-T	HT	WT	DOB	AVG	vLH	vRH	G	AB	R	H	2B	3B	HR	RBI	BB	HBP	SH	SF	SO	SB	CS	SLG	OBP
Arzeno, Luis Ramon	R-R	5-11	190	8-9-84	.206	.250	.192	44	131	9	27	7	2	1	11	4	2	2	0	41	1	1	.313	.241
Brown, Domonic	L-L	6-5	204	9-3-87	.303	.283	.309	66	238	41	72	12	3	11	44	34	2	0	6	48	15	8	.517	.386
Diaz, Francisco	B-R	5-10	158	3-21-90	.167	.500	.000	2	6	2	1	0	0	0	0	3	0	0	0	0	0	0	.167	.444
Diaz, Javis	L-L	5-10	165	6-25-84	.253	.091	.269	97	368	50	93	9	5	2	23	39	2	4	2	61	34	9	.321	.326
Durant, Mike	R-R	6-5	230	1-2-87	.211	.270	.192	113	375	43	79	20	1	12	37	51	5	1	2	142	0	3	.365	.312
Galvis, Freddy	B-R	5-10	154	11-14-89	.247	.186	.271	63	251	29	62	8	2	1	15	10	2	8	1	43	6	3	.307	.280
Guerra, Jorge	R-R	6-1	170	9-9-82	.083	.000	.125	6	12	0	1	0	0	0	1	0	0	0	0	4	0	0	.083	.154
Guevara, Orlando	B-R	6-1	175	9-13-83	.143	.000	.200	4	7	0	1	0	0	0	0	0	1	2	0	4	0	0	.143	.250
Hernandez, Fidel	R-R	5-11	160	1-18-86	.265	.330	.245	121	472	53	125	13	2	2	35	20	3	3	6	40	19	11	.314	.295
Kennelly, Timothy	R-R	6-0	180	12-5-86	.303	.321	.298	76	271	42	82	27	2	3	46	33	5	1	5	49	6	3	.450	.382
Milner, Gus	R-R	6-5	240	4-21-84	.239	.231	.241	29	109	12	26	2	0	3	11	2	5	1	2	29	2	2	.339	.280
Mitchell, Derrick	R-R	6-2	170	1-5-87	.208	.202	.211	101	331	34	69	25	0	11	31	19	2	0	3	94	7	1	.384	.254
Naughton, Joel	L-R	6-1	180	8-27-86	.240	.235	.241	82	279	34	67	11	1	7	37	26	0	2	4	50	1	0	.362	.301
Overbeck, Cody	R-R	6-1	200	6-5-86	.230	.314	.204	96	361	37	83	23	1	12	51	23	3	0	0	105	0	0	.399	.282
Quiroz, Arlon	R-R	6-0	170	11-13-86	.229	.282	.199	96	284	31	65	12	1	0	19	35	1	1	2	80	20	8	.278	.314
Rizzotti, Matt	L-L	6-5	235	12-24-85	.263	.121	.278	101	350	44	92	26	1	13	58	48	2	0	4	91	0	0	.454	.351
Rodriguez, Yonderman	R-R	5-11	160	2-17-87	.248	.243	.250	87	282	28	70	6	1	2	24	30	4	8	0	66	8	9	.298	.329
Susdorf, Steve	L-L	6-1	195	3-28-86	.371	.333	.381	40	151	20	56	12	0	3	22	11	2	0	0	23	3	0	.510	.421
Villegas Andino, Jesus	R-R	5-10	175	9-21-86	.236	.273	.224	66	225	27	53	8	1	4	23	12	5	3	2	41	9	2	.333	.287

Pitching	B-T	HT	WT	DOB	W	L	ERA	G	GS	CG	SV	IP	H	R	ER	HR	BB	SO	AVG	vLH	vRH	K/9	BB/9
Ayala, Manny	R-R	6-3	237	11-6-84	0	0	3.72	10	0	0	0	19	20	8	8	4	8	10	.260	.367	.191	4.66	3.72
Bastardo, Antonio	L-L	5-11	195	9-21-85	0	0	27.00	1	0	0	0	1	4	3	3	0	0	0	.800	1.000	.667	0.00	0.00
Bisenius, Joe	R-R	6-4	205	9-18-82	0	0	0.00	3	0	0	0	4	2	0	0	0	2	5	.154	.000	.250	11.25	4.50
Brauer, Dan	L-L	6-0	210	10-14-83	2	1	6.51	39	0	0	2	55	50	43	40	3	47	56	.238	.250	.232	9.11	7.64
Brummett, Tyson	R-R	6-0	150	8-15-84	0	0	9.00	4	0	0	0	5	5	7	5	0	4	3	.263	.444	.100	5.40	7.20
Byrd, Darren	R-R	6-3	170	10-04-86	5	7	3.99	24	14	0	1	88	94	45	39	4	37	61	.273	.293	.261	6.24	3.78
Chapman, Chance	R-R	6-4	210	2-27-84	1	0	0.77	11	1	0	1	23	14	2	2	0	7	18	.184	.217	.133	6.94	2.70
Cisco, Mike	R-R	5-11	190	5-23-87	7	3	3.31	15	14	0	0	73	69	32	27	9	15	51	.246	.225	.266	6.26	1.84
Cloyd, Tyler	R-R	6-3	190	5-16-87	5	6	4.11	13	12	0	0	77	83	43	35	4	23	39	.274	.246	.295	4.58	2.70
Condrey, Clay	R-R	6-3	225	11-19-75	0	0	0.00	2	0	0	0	3	1	0	0	0	0	2	.111	.000	.167	6.00	0.00
Crawford, Tristan	R-R	6-3	213	7-22-82	2	0	0.00	3	0	0	0	4	4	0	0	0	1	6	.267	.250	.273	13.50	2.25
Drabek, Kyle	R-R	6-0	185	12-8-87	4	1	2.48	10	9	1	0	62	49	19	17	0	19	74	.218	.235	.198	10.80	2.77
Durbin, Chad	R-R	6-2	220	12-3-77	0	0	0.00	2	1	0	0	3	3	0	0	0	1	4	.250	.273	.000	12.00	3.00
Ellis, Jordan	R-R	6-2	198	9-11-85	0	1	27.00	1	0	0	0	1	1	3	3	0	4	1	.250	.500	.000	9.00	36.00
Flande, Yohan	L-L	6-2	170	1-27-86	7	1	2.52	13	13	1	0	82	72	27	23	2	24	67	.238	.208	.254	7.35	2.63
Garcia, Edgar	R-R	6-2	190	9-20-87	1	4	4.32	8	8	0	0	42	38	24	20	3	9	27	.239	.225	.250	5.83	1.94
Hernandez, Santos	R-R	6-1	160	11-9-84	1	0	4.57	16	0	0	2	22	17	11	11	2	13	28	.207	.194	.216	11.63	5.40
Jimenez, Esmelvin	L-L	5-10	180	2-5-87	1	0	6.60	7	0	0	0	15	19	15	11	3	5	7	.311	.286	.325	4.20	3.00
Kissock, Chris	R-R	6-4	195	5-2-85	3	5	3.98	47	0	0	0	72	82	38	32	7	15	59	.288	.307	.272	7.34	1.87
Lidge, Brad	R-R	6-5	215	12-23-76	0	0	0.00	1	0	0	1	1	0	0	0	0	0	0	.000	.000	.000	0.00	9.00
Mackintosh, Jason	R-L	6-0	205	7-2-80	1	0	0.00	3	0	0	0	5	1	0	0	0	0	3	.063	.000	.111	5.40	0.00
Martinez, Pedro	R-R	5-11	195	10-25-71	0	0	0.00	1	1	0	0	1	1	0	0	0	0	1	.200	.250	.000	6.75	0.00
Mathieson, Scott	R-R	6-3	190	2-27-84	0	0	0.00	5	0	0	1	7	4	0	0	0	3	9	.167	.250	.125	11.57	3.86
Monasterios, Carlos	R-R	6-2	175	3-21-86	5	6	3.73	35	7	1	2	82	71	39	34	4	27	71	.237	.253	.222	7.79	2.96
Myers, Brett	R-R	6-4	240	8-17-80	0	0	0.00	1	0	0	1	2	0	0	0	0	0	0	.400	.250	1.000	0.00	0.00
Naylor, Drew	R-R	6-4	210	5-31-86	8	11	4.22	26	25	4	0	158	162	85	74	12	37	115	.265	.268	.262	6.55	2.11

Player	B-T	HT	WT	DOB	W	L	ERA	G	GS	CG	SV	IP	H	R	ER	HR	BB	SO	AVG	vLH	vRH	K/9	BB/9
Rocchio, Joe	R-R	6-4	200	10-15-84	0	0	8.59	5	0	0	0	7	11	8	7	2	5	4	.344	.412	.267	4.91	6.14
Romero, J.C.	B-L	5-11	205	6-4-76	0	0	0.00	1	0	0	0	0	0	0	0	0	0	1	.000	—	.000	27.00	27.00
Roth, Robert	R-R	6-1	195	8-5-88	0	0	10.80	3	0	0	1	3	5	4	4	1	1	4	.357	.571	.143	10.80	2.70
Sampson, Julian	R-R	6-5	210	1-21-89	3	9	7.36	17	15	0	0	70	93	59	57	10	27	37	.323	.318	.327	4.78	3.49
Schwimer, Michael	R-R	6-8	246	2-19-86	2	1	2.85	48	0	0	20	60	44	21	19	2	19	82	.204	.273	.145	12.30	2.85
Simon, Jared	R-R	6-1	185	8-15-84	1	1	10.13	11	0	0	6	11	17	12	12	3	5	12	.354	.261	.440	10.13	4.22
Sterner, Zack	R-R	6-2	170	11-7-85	2	1	2.65	12	0	0	0	17	19	9	5	1	4	7	.275	.179	.341	3.71	2.12
Tejeda, Walter	L-L	6-3	187	9-28-85	2	3	2.89	32	1	0	1	44	45	21	14	4	22	30	.266	.233	.284	6.18	4.53
Velasquez, Jon	R-R	6-0	169	10-15-85	2	6	3.33	13	13	0	0	70	67	34	26	6	27	52	.247	.255	.242	6.65	3.45
Walls, Sam	R-R	5-11	195	10-31-83	0	1	1.69	4	0	0	1	5	4	1	1	0	5	5	.235	.250	.222	8.44	8.44
Zagurski, Mike	L-L	6-0	225	1-27-83	0	0	0.00	3	2	0	0	3	2	0	0	0	0	1	.167	.000	.250	3.00	0.00

Fielding

Catcher	PCT	G	PO	A	E	DP	PB
Arzeno	.975	43	281	34	8	3	4
Diaz	1.000	1	7	1	0	0	0
Guerra	.935	6	28	1	2	0	0
Guevara	1.000	4	27	5	0	0	1
Kennelly	.970	11	87	11	3	2	1
Naughton	.986	81	512	39	8	2	3

First Base	PCT	G	PO	A	E	DP
Durant	.984	108	865	58	15	76
Kennelly	.978	5	40	5	1	8
Rizzotti	.976	28	223	16	6	18
Rodriguez	.857	1	6	0	1	0

Second Base	PCT	G	PO	A	E	DP
Hernandez	.984	117	215	325	9	61
Rodriguez	.968	20	36	56	3	11

Third Base	PCT	G	PO	A	E	DP
Galvis	1.000	1	0	1	0	0
Kennelly	.808	10	3	18	5	3
Mitchell	.750	2	2	1	1	0
Overbeck	.915	73	46	138	17	13
Rodriguez	.942	55	41	106	9	7
Villegas Andino	1.000	1	2	0	0	0

Shortstop	PCT	G	PO	A	E	DP
Galvis	.969	62	92	159	8	30

	PCT	G	PO	A	E	DP
Hernandez	.889	4	4	12	2	2
Rodriguez	.957	10	10	35	2	7
Villegas Andino	.928	64	104	168	21	36

Outfield	PCT	G	PO	A	E	DP
Brown	.961	66	115	9	5	2
Diaz	1.000	1	1	0	0	0
Diaz	.979	91	228	7	5	4
Kennelly	.989	37	83	5	1	2
Milner	.972	26	67	3	2	2
Mitchell	.989	86	171	8	2	4
Quiroz	.978	88	169	11	4	1
Rodriguez	—	1	0	0	0	0
Susdorf	.980	30	50	0	1	0

LAKEWOOD BLUECLAWS — LOW CLASS A

SOUTH ATLANTIC LEAGUE

Batting	B-T	HT	WT	DOB	AVG	vLH	vRH	G	AB	R	H	2B	3B	HR	RBI	BB	HBP	SH	SF	SO	SB	CS	SLG	OBP
Akashian, Brendan	L-R	6-1	215	5-18-85	.204	.182	.209	24	54	10	11	2	0	1	7	18	5	0	0	14	0	1	.296	.442
Arzeno, Luis Ramon	R-R	5-11	190	8-9-84	.000	.000	.000	1	4	1	0	0	0	0	0	1	0	0	0	1	0	0	.000	.200
Castro, Leandro	R-R	5-11	175	6-15-89	.152	.167	.143	22	66	9	10	4	0	0	6	5	2	0	1	15	2	1	.212	.230
Collier, Zach	L-L	6-2	185	9-8-90	.218	.163	.241	82	298	40	65	16	7	0	32	23	1	2	2	80	13	7	.319	.275
D'Arnaud, Travis	R-R	6-2	195	2-10-89	.255	.239	.262	126	482	71	123	38	1	13	71	41	8	0	9	75	8	4	.419	.319
De Los Santos, Vladimir	R-R	6-1	176	9-6-86	.221	.143	.254	48	163	10	36	8	0	3	20	10	0	0	2	50	1	0	.325	.263
Garcia, Harold	B-R	5-11	164	10-25-86	.291	.211	.321	118	444	64	129	21	5	8	55	29	16	5	8	100	42	12	.414	.350
Gose, Anthony	L-L	6-1	190	8-10-90	.259	.288	.248	131	510	72	132	24	9	2	52	35	15	9	3	110	76	20	.353	.323
Gugel, Ryan	L-R	6-0	200	7-24-87	.000	.000	.000	3	3	1	0	0	0	0	0	1	0	0	0	2	0	0	.000	.250
Gump, Brian	L-L	6-2	195	6-16-87	.000	.000	.240	10	25	6	7	0	0	0	2	5	1	0	0	9	1	0	.280	.317
Hamilton, Jeremy	L-L	6-1	180	11-11-86	.255	.200	.268	88	294	26	75	12	3	4	32	38	3	3	2	73	2	0	.357	.344
Hanzawa, Troy	R-R	5-9	155	9-12-85	.267	.284	.261	126	423	50	113	23	3	2	47	24	15	5	5	100	9	11	.350	.325
Lafrenz, Bronco	R-R	6-1	190	2-6-87	.208	.222	.200	15	48	1	10	3	0	0	5	2	0	0	1	22	0	0	.271	.235
Mattair, Travis	R-R	6-5	210	12-21-88	.236	.219	.241	126	450	55	106	27	4	3	39	54	9	2	6	131	12	2	.333	.326
Mintken, Korby	L-R	6-0	180	3-12-86	.217	.178	.233	60	161	30	35	4	1	0	11	28	1	1	1	47	17	6	.255	.335
Murphy, Jim	R-R	6-4	240	9-16-85	.279	.258	.288	114	398	55	111	27	3	14	67	59	19	0	5	131	0	3	.467	.393
Myers, D'Arby	R-R	6-3	175	12-9-88	.270	.262	.273	83	270	41	73	14	5	2	23	12	3	4	0	62	16	4	.381	.309
Sanchez, Jesus	R-R	5-11	160	9-24-87	—	—	—	1	0	0	0	0	0	0	0	0	0	0	0	0	0	0	—	—
Schoenberger, Alan	B-R	5-10	160	1-19-89	.143	.167	.133	9	21	1	3	2	0	0	2	2	0	0	0	8	1	0	.238	.217
Susdorf, Steve	L-L	6-1	195	3-28-86	.333	.429	.298	21	78	9	26	5	1	2	15	7	2	0	0	15	2	0	.500	.402
Valle, Sebastian	R-R	6-1	170	7-24-90	.223	.190	.245	45	157	16	35	12	1	1	15	16	5	0	1	37	1	2	.331	.313
Villegas Andino, Jesus	R-R	5-10	175	9-21-86	.358	.333	.370	19	67	9	24	2	0	1	14	9	0	1	0	13	0	2	.433	.434
Warren, T.J.	R-R	6-4	190	8-17-88	.183	.154	.191	23	60	11	11	3	2	0	3	9	1	1	0	20	7	0	.300	.300

Pitching	B-T	HT	WT	DOB	W	L	ERA	G	GS	CG	SV	IP	H	R	ER	HR	BB	SO	AVG	vLH	vRH	K/9	BB/9
Ariail, Ryan	L-L	6-4	215	10-16-84	0	0	6.11	12	0	0	0	18	21	12	12	0	5	8	.292	.368	.264	4.08	2.55
Ballestas, Freddy	R-R	6-3	170	10-4-86	1	3	4.98	18	4	0	0	47	53	32	26	2	16	46	.280	.300	.269	8.81	3.06
Bergh, Ryan	R-R	6-4	220	4-25-85	3	6	5.05	45	0	0	13	71	83	49	40	4	21	51	.286	.316	.267	6.43	2.65
Cloyd, Tyler	R-R	6-3	190	5-16-87	7	3	3.05	14	14	1	0	89	90	32	30	3	19	77	.268	.227	.297	7.82	1.93
Correa, Heitor	R-R	6-3	200	8-25-89	7	8	4.13	22	21	2	0	124	128	64	57	6	50	89	.266	.265	.264	6.44	3.62
De Fratus, Justin	B-R	6-4	215	10-21-87	5	6	3.19	36	12	0	3	110	108	44	39	3	16	101	.258	.291	.236	8.26	1.31
Diekman, Jacob	L-L	6-4	190	1-21-87	2	0	4.04	32	2	0	2	56	59	32	25	3	28	52	.266	.255	.269	8.41	4.53
Ellis, Jordan	R-R	6-2	198	9-11-85	4	4	6.42	17	0	0	1	34	36	24	24	2	14	44	.286	.341	.256	11.76	3.74
Hernandez, Santos	R-R	6-1	160	1-19-84	5	2	1.71	29	0	0	4	53	36	14	10	1	26	63	.190	.184	.195	10.77	4.44
Hyatt, Austin	R-R	6-2	180	5-23-86	0	0	7.71	1	1	0	0	5	5	4	4	0	2	8	.278	.286	.273	15.43	3.86
Jimenez, Esmelvin	L-L	5-10	180	2-5-87	0	1	7.11	11	0	0	0	13	16	11	10	0	5	15	.302	.250	.324	10.66	3.55
Knapp, Jason	R-R	6-5	235	8-31-90	2	7	4.01	17	17	0	0	85	63	45	38	3	39	111	.208	.210	.206	11.71	4.11
2-team total (4 Lake County)					2	7	4.18	21	21	0	0	97	73	55	45	3	47	123	—			11.41	4.36
May, Trevor	R-R	6-5	215	9-23-89	4	1	2.56	15	15	0	0	77	58	24	22	3	43	95	.211	.182	.234	11.06	5.00
McConnell, Eryk	R-R	6-1	185	7-29-85	1	4	4.07	12	0	0	1	24	28	11	11	1	4	17	.295	.306	.288	6.29	1.48
Myers, Brett	R-R	6-4	240	8-17-80	0	0	0.00	1	1	0	0	1	0	0	0	0	0	1	.000	.000	.000	9.00	0.00
Noles, Korey	L-L	5-11	185	7-18-85	1	0	1.17	2	1	0	0	8	4	1	1	0	2	9	.160	.143	.167	10.57	2.35
Romero, J.C.	B-L	5-11	205	6-4-76	0	0	0.00	1	0	0	0	2	0	0	0	0	0	2	.000	.000	.000	9.00	0.00

PHILADELPHIA PHILLIES

Pitching	B-T	HT	WT	DOB	W	L	ERA	G	GS	CG	SV	IP	H	R	ER	HR	BB	SO	AVG	vLH	vRH	K/9	BB/9
Rosenberg, B.J.	R-R	6-2	200	9-17-85	7	2	0.89	37	0	0	19	50	37	7	5	0	10	65	.200	.233	.179	11.62	1.79
Roth, Robert	R-R	6-1	195	8-5-88	4	4	6.54	28	5	0	0	52	60	45	38	1	29	30	.291	.216	.347	5.16	4.99
Simon, Jared	R-R	6-1	185	8-15-84	1	1	5.40	9	0	0	0	12	12	8	7	0	3	10	.267	.368	.192	7.71	2.31
Tejeda, Walter	L-L	6-3	187	9-28-85	0	0	4.05	4	0	0	0	7	7	3	3	0	4	8	.269	.250	.273	10.80	5.40
Velasquez, Jon	R-R	6-0	169	10-15-85	9	2	4.26	15	11	0	0	70	66	35	33	3	17	48	.248	.241	.253	6.20	2.20
Way, Matt	L-L	6-1	195	1-25-87	4	1	3.11	6	6	1	0	38	32	15	13	0	4	42	.221	.217	.221	10.04	0.96
Wertz, Luke	R-R	6-1	175	9-20-85	0	0	0.00	2	0	0	0	3	2	0	0	0	2	5	.167	.167	.167	13.50	5.40

Fielding

Catcher	PCT	G	PO	A	E	DP	PB
Akashian	.985	10	60	6	1	0	4
D'Arnaud	.993	99	817	68	6	7	9
Gugel	—	1	0	0	0	0	0
Lafrenz	.990	12	88	13	1	2	1
Valle	.995	20	173	15	1	1	4

First Base	PCT	G	PO	A	E	DP
De Los Santos	1.000	1	1	0	0	0
Hamilton	.987	61	502	36	7	31
Mintken	.875	1	6	1	1	1
Murphy	.997	78	658	49	2	37

Second Base	PCT	G	PO	A	E	DP
Garcia	.973	116	196	303	14	42

Catcher (cont.)	PCT	G	PO	A	E	DP
Mintken	.960	18	34	38	3	6
Schoenberger	.875	1	3	4	1	1
Villegas Andino	1.000	10	11	19	0	5

Third Base	PCT	G	PO	A	E	DP
Mattair	.948	126	83	262	19	17
Mintken	1.000	6	4	6	0	0
Murphy	—	1	0	0	0	0
Schoenberger	1.000	2	2	3	0	0
Villegas Andino	1.000	5	1	8	0	1

Shortstop	PCT	G	PO	A	E	DP
Hanzawa	.964	126	139	311	17	47
Mintken	.947	8	4	14	1	3
Schoenberger	.882	5	7	8	2	1

Outfield	PCT	G	PO	A	E	DP
Villegas Andino	.895	5	2	15	2	1
Castro	.940	19	45	2	3	1
Collier	.969	81	153	4	5	1
De Los Santos	.981	40	49	4	1	0
Gose	.971	130	224	13	7	2
Gump	1.000	10	11	0	0	0
Hamilton	—	1	0	0	0	0
Mintken	1.000	24	32	2	0	0
Myers	.968	77	118	4	4	1
Schoenberger	1.000	1	3	0	0	0
Susdorf	1.000	18	15	2	0	0
Warren	1.000	22	34	2	0	0

WILLIAMSPORT CROSSCUTTERS   SHORT-SEASON

NEW YORK-PENN LEAGUE

Batting	B-T	HT	WT	DOB	AVG	vLH	vRH	G	AB	R	H	2B	3B	HR	RBI	BB	HBP	SH	SF	SO	SB	CS	SLG	OBP
Barnes, Jeremy	R-R	5-10	190	4-13-87	.287	.158	.316	55	209	31	60	15	5	4	27	20	4	0	1	52	3	4	.464	.359
Batts, Stephen	R-R	6-0	200	2-14-86	.195	.200	.193	45	149	17	29	5	1	2	11	11	2	1	0	46	1	0	.282	.259
Buschini, Adam	R-R	6-2	205	5-6-87	.228	.156	.243	52	180	20	41	4	4	2	15	23	5	0	2	44	15	1	.328	.329
Castro, Leandro	R-R	5-11	175	6-15-89	.316	.379	.298	66	256	48	81	19	5	7	43	13	3	1	4	49	18	9	.512	.351
Collier, Zach	L-L	6-2	185	9-8-90	.226	.174	.237	34	137	21	31	10	1	1	13	9	2	1	2	42	7	0	.336	.280
Dabbs, Mike	L-R	6-0	185	3-29-87	.211	.313	.187	49	171	18	36	6	4	3	17	10	3	2	2	48	4	2	.345	.263
Doss, David	R-R	6-0	190	4-28-87	.228	.273	.222	29	92	12	21	3	0	2	12	5	1	3	1	11	2	1	.326	.273
Gugel, Ryan	L-R	6-0	200	7-24-87	.103	.143	.091	10	29	2	3	1	0	0	0	2	0	0	0	16	1	0	.138	.161
Hewitt, Anthony	R-R	6-1	190	4-27-89	.223	.146	.243	61	233	25	52	7	6	7	30	9	2	0	3	77	9	5	.395	.255
Lafrenz, Bronco	R-R	6-1	190	2-6-87	.111	.000	.143	5	18	0	2	1	0	0	1	0	1	0	0	5	0	0	.167	.158
Murillo, Francisco	R-R	6-0	196	10-18-86	.253	.216	.266	41	146	20	37	8	3	5	16	12	1	1	0	50	0	0	.452	.314
Porter, Evan	R-R	6-5	205	3-13-87	.183	.278	.163	31	104	6	19	5	1	0	5	6	2	1	0	23	0	0	.250	.241
Rodriguez, Jean Carlos	R-R	5-10	204	3-27-89	.250	.250	.250	3	12	1	3	0	0	0	2	0	0	0	0	3	0	0	.250	.250
Ruf, Darin	R-R	6-3	220	7-28-86	.301	.333	.295	37	133	17	40	17	0	3	24	14	3	0	1	22	0	1	.496	.377
Schoenberger, Alan	R-R	5-10	160	1-19-89	.228	.192	.240	31	101	15	23	7	0	1	9	15	0	0	1	28	4	1	.327	.325
Uhl, Carl	B-L	5-8	175	4-2-87	.237	.276	.228	44	152	23	36	5	5	1	9	12	3	4	1	18	10	2	.355	.304
Valle, Sebastian	R-R	6-1	170	7-24-90	.307	.286	.313	50	192	25	59	15	5	6	40	10	0	0	4	41	0	0	.531	.335
Villar, Jonathan	B-R	6-1	180	5-2-91	.231	.222	.233	11	39	6	9	1	1	0	5	4	0	1	0	14	6	0	.308	.302
Warren, T.J.	R-R	6-4	190	8-17-88	.286	.400	.246	22	77	12	22	4	1	0	12	8	0	0	0	18	9	2	.364	.337

Pitching	B-T	HT	WT	DOB	W	L	ERA	G	GS	CG	SV	IP	H	R	ER	HR	BB	SO	AVG	vLH	vRH	K/9	BB/9
Arroyo, Spencer	L-L	6-2	166	8-9-88	2	2	3.67	16	1	0	0	34	38	18	14	0	20	25	.281	.316	.268	6.55	5.24
Ballestas, Freddy	R-R	6-3	170	10-4-86	0	0	0.00	1	1	0	0	4	2	0	0	0	1	5	.133	.333	.000	12.27	2.45
Beal, Justin	R-R	6-2	205	5-21-86	0	1	5.19	6	0	0	0	9	13	8	5	0	6	9	.317	.333	.304	9.35	6.23
Bolsenbroek, Mike	R-R	6-8	210	3-11-87	0	0	1.93	2	0	0	1	5	3	1	1	0	1	6	.176	.111	.250	11.57	1.93
Ellis, Jordan	R-R	6-2	198	9-11-85	0	1	10.13	2	0	0	0	3	6	3	3	0	1	4	.462	.500	.444	13.50	3.38
Grieve, Sean	L-L	6-1	195	12-13-84	0	0	6.33	16	0	0	1	21	20	16	15	2	18	20	.250	.375	.196	8.44	7.59
Hernandez, Nick	L-L	6-4	205	7-30-88	8	1	2.70	15	15	0	0	80	72	27	24	2	20	67	.242	.216	.252	7.54	2.25
Hyatt, Austin	R-R	6-2	180	5-23-86	3	0	0.66	17	5	0	6	54	26	6	4	1	12	81	.141	.130	.150	13.42	1.99
Jimenez, Esmelvin	L-L	5-10	180	2-5-87	1	2	4.15	7	0	0	0	9	7	4	4	2	2	6	.226	.286	.208	6.23	2.08
Lebron, Siulman	R-R	6-1	170	6-11-87	5	6	4.48	16	16	0	0	88	98	51	44	4	18	67	.283	.341	.227	6.83	1.83
Long, Justin	R-R	6-2	220	12-12-85	1	3	5.34	21	0	0	0	32	32	24	19	2	26	29	.252	.260	.247	8.16	7.31
Lugo, Ebelin	R-R	6-2	—	4-23-90	3	1	3.21	17	0	0	0	34	35	12	12	1	11	41	.265	.345	.203	10.96	2.94
Massingham, Eric	R-R	6-2	205	11-19-86	2	1	0.76	13	0	0	4	24	15	5	2	0	8	32	.181	.192	.175	12.17	3.04
Noles, Korey	L-L	5-11	185	7-18-85	3	2	2.34	9	7	0	0	42	31	13	11	0	11	39	.203	.333	.137	8.29	2.34
Pettibone, Jon	L-R	6-5	200	7-19-90	2	4	5.35	9	8	0	0	35	37	28	21	0	16	36	.261	.170	.305	9.17	4.08
Poe, Chad	R-R	6-2	185	11-14-87	0	0	4.50	8	0	0	1	14	11	8	7	1	2	11	.220	.222	.217	7.07	1.29
Simon, Reginal	R-R	6-3	177	12-28-89	0	1	8.34	18	0	0	0	23	35	24	21	0	17	20	.343	.366	.328	7.94	6.75
Way, Matt	L-L	6-1	195	1-25-87	2	3	1.67	8	0	0	0	38	28	11	7	2	8	43	.197	.300	.170	10.27	1.91
Wertz, Luke	R-R	6-1	175	9-20-85	2	1	2.18	17	0	0	1	33	26	16	8	2	13	23	.213	.250	.192	6.27	3.55
Zeid, Josh	R-R	6-5	210	3-24-87	8	5	2.94	15	15	0	0	80	64	27	26	1	20	72	.217	.245	.200	8.13	2.26

Fielding

Catcher	PCT	G	PO	A	E	DP	PB
Doss	1.000	23	190	11	0	0	4
Gugel	1.000	5	35	2	0	0	2
Lafrenz	1.000	2	14	1	0	0	0

Catcher (cont.)	PCT	G	PO	A	E	DP	PB
Rodriguez	1.000	3	28	0	0	0	4
Valle	.992	47	371	23	3	0	7

First Base	PCT	G	PO	A	E	DP
Batts	1.000	26	205	13	0	19

Outfield	PCT	G	PO	A	E	DP
Murillo	.993	15	131	9	1	12
Ruf	.994	37	300	30	2	29

Second Base	PCT	G	PO	A	E	DP
Batts	.909	2	3	7	1	1

Buschini	.974	52	92	133	6	35
Porter	.970	15	19	45	2	6
Schoenberger	.958	9	9	14	1	4

Third Base	PCT	G	PO	A	E	DP
Hewitt	.827	56	19	105	26	6
Schoenberger	.880	21	8	36	6	2

Shortstop	PCT	G	PO	A	E	DP
Barnes	.930	50	61	138	15	31
Porter	.935	17	19	39	4	10
Villar	.892	11	8	25	4	3

Outfield	PCT	G	PO	A	E	DP
Batts	.900	11	27	0	3	0

Castro	.964	63	100	6	4	2
Collier	.981	33	50	1	1	0
Dabbs	.981	45	98	3	2	1
James	.979	30	45	2	1	0
Uhl	.985	36	65	0	1	0
Warren	.941	16	32	0	2	0

GCL PHILLIES   ROOKIE
GULF COAST LEAGUE

Batting	B-T	HT	WT	DOB	AVG	vLH	vRH	G	AB	R	H	2B	3B	HR	RBI	BB	HBP	SH	SF	SO	SB	CS	SLG	OBP
Altherr, Aaron	R-R	6-5	190	1-14-91	.214	.185	.228	28	84	10	18	3	0	1	11	8	0	0	0	15	6	1	.286	.283
Alvarez, Miguel	R-R	6-1	172	8-27-89	.260	.389	.218	24	73	5	19	6	1	0	7	5	0	0	0	16	5	2	.370	.308
Aviola, Phil	R-R	6-1	225	9-2-86	.171	.231	.136	25	35	4	6	2	0	1	3	2	4	0	0	6	2	0	.314	.293
Bollinger, Ryan	L-L	6-6	185	2-4-91	.174	.000	.308	7	23	2	4	1	0	0	2	0	0	0	0	7	0	0	.217	.240
Brown, Domonic	L-L	6-5	204	9-3-87	.500	.500	.500	3	10	4	5	0	2	0	6	1	1	0	0	1	0	1	.900	.583
Castillo, Lendy	R-R	6-1	170	4-8-89	.179	.045	.232	27	78	3	14	3	0	0	7	6	0	1	1	15	4	6	.218	.235
Diaz, Francisco	B-R	5-10	158	3-21-90	.222	.263	.200	29	54	6	12	0	0	0	4	8	0	0	0	11	0	0	.222	.323
Donald, Jason	R-R	6-1	195	9-4-84	.231	.400	.125	9	26	4	6	1	1	0	1	2	0	0	0	5	1	0	.346	.286
Dugan, Kelly	B-R	6-3	195	9-18-90	.233	.148	.281	45	150	18	35	8	1	0	8	12	2	2	1	30	9	5	.300	.297
Duran, Edgar	R-R	5-11	154	2-10-91	.221	.148	.254	32	86	10	19	5	0	0	7	6	1	0	2	15	5	2	.279	.274
Galvis, Freddy	R-R	5-10	154	11-14-89	.276	.286	.267	7	29	6	8	1	0	0	0	1	0	0	0	4	1	1	.310	.300
Guerra, Jorge	R-R	6-1	170	9-12-87	.156	.091	.176	19	45	5	7	1	1	0	2	2	1	0	0	8	0	0	.222	.208
Gump, Brian	L-L	6-2	195	6-16-87	.317	.325	.314	37	126	21	40	7	1	4	19	14	0	0	0	25	6	5	.484	.386
Hernandez, Cesar	B-R	5-10	166	5-23-90	.267	.277	.259	41	150	21	40	5	1	0	18	17	4	1	3	20	13	5	.313	.351
Hissey, David	R-R	5-11	175	11-9-85	.226	.125	.270	22	53	5	12	0	0	0	2	6	4	0	1	11	2	0	.226	.344
Hudson, Kyrell	R-R	6-1	185	12-6-90	.162	.333	.107	10	37	3	6	2	0	0	6	3	0	0	0	9	2	0	.216	.225
McConnell, Matt	L-R	5-10	185	9-6-86	.245	.235	.250	30	102	8	25	4	0	0	8	9	4	1	4	15	3	2	.284	.319
Mitchell, Marlon	L-R	6-1	180	9-30-90	.212	.400	.135	28	52	6	11	1	0	1	5	5	3	1	1	13	0	0	.288	.311
Paulino, Luis	R-R	6-2	185	6-16-89	.201	.204	.200	41	149	13	30	11	2	2	15	7	3	0	2	43	0	1	.342	.248
Ruf, Darin	R-R	6-3	220	7-28-86	.326	.333	.321	20	43	5	14	3	0	0	6	3	3	0	1	8	0	0	.395	.400
Santana, Domingo	R-R	6-5	200	8-5-92	.288	.262	.303	37	118	17	34	6	1	6	28	15	5	0	1	44	3	1	.508	.388
Singleton, Jonathan	L-L	6-2	215	9-18-91	.290	.355	.261	31	100	12	29	9	0	2	12	18	0	0	1	13	1	0	.440	.395
Sladek, Jakub	L-R	6-6	220	2-17-90	.188	.000	.250	9	16	3	3	2	0	0	0	3	0	0	0	8	0	0	.313	.316
Torres, Winder	R-R	5-11	160	8-2-90	.109	.059	.132	20	55	5	6	1	0	0	2	2	3	0	0	16	3	0	.127	.183
Villar, Jonathan	B-R	6-1	180	5-2-91	.277	.206	.317	31	94	14	26	7	1	0	14	13	1	1	2	24	11	2	.372	.364
Wine, Cory	L-L	6-5	210	10-15-86	.189	.154	.208	34	74	5	14	2	0	0	7	13	3	0	2	11	1	0	.216	.326

Pitching	B-T	HT	WT	DOB	W	L	ERA	G	GS	CG	SV	IP	H	R	ER	HR	BB	SO	AVG	vLH	vRH	K/9	BB/9
Angelle, Kevin	L-L	6-2	195	2-27-88	3	3	1.89	12	12	0	0	57	41	15	12	0	19	42	.204	.194	.206	6.63	3.00
Bastardo, Antonio	L-L	5-11	195	9-21-85	0	0	0.00	3	2	0	0	4	2	1	0	0	2	3	.133	.000	.167	6.23	4.15
Beal, Justin	R-R	6-2	205	5-21-86	3	0	1.37	14	0	0	4	26	18	5	4	0	4	18	.202	.250	.175	6.15	1.37
Bisenius, Joe	R-R	6-4	205	9-18-82	0	0	0.00	1	0	0	0	1	1	0	0	0	0	3	.250	.000	.333	27.00	0.00
Bolsenbroek, Mike	R-R	6-8	210	3-11-87	2	2	2.03	16	0	0	3	31	19	8	7	0	14	30	.171	.184	.164	8.71	4.06
Colvin, Brody	R-R	6-3	195	8-14-90	0	0	0.00	1	0	0	0	2	0	1	0	0	1	2	.000	.000	.000	9.00	4.50
Condrey, Clay	R-R	6-3	225	11-19-75	0	0	0.00	3	1	0	0	3	3	0	0	0	0	3	.273	.250	.286	9.00	0.00
Cosart, Jarred	R-R	6-3	180	5-25-90	2	2	2.22	7	5	0	0	24	12	8	6	0	7	25	.143	.171	.122	9.25	2.59
Doll, Mark	R-R	6-1	190	9-25-85	0	2	1.42	12	0	0	2	19	20	6	3	1	5	16	.267	.229	.300	7.58	2.37
Garcia, Edgar	R-R	6-2	190	9-20-87	1	0	0.00	1	0	0	0	4	1	0	0	0	0	4	.083	.000	.100	9.00	0.00
Inch, Steven	R-R	6-4	190	2-1-91	0	1	27.00	2	1	0	0	2	7	6	6	1	1	0	.500	.667	.375	0.00	4.50
Izurriaga, Ely	L-L	5-11	188	6-29-90	2	2	5.74	9	0	0	0	16	13	14	10	2	11	16	.217	.417	.167	9.19	6.32
Jimenez, Esmelvin	L-L	5-10	180	2-5-87	1	1	0.96	5	0	0	2	9	4	1	1	0	1	5	.133	.000	.160	4.82	0.00
Johnson, Chase	R-R	6-5	245	4-29-88	0	1	3.94	15	0	0	0	30	28	16	13	2	12	35	.257	.209	.288	10.62	3.64
Mathieson, Scott	R-R	6-3	190	2-27-84	2	0	0.00	4	0	0	0	6	3	1	0	0	2	8	.130	.200	.111	12.00	3.00
Matos, Miguel	R-R	6-1	178	10-26-87	4	4	3.54	15	1	0	1	28	22	13	11	1	11	29	.220	.247	.200	9.32	3.54
McConnell, Eryk	R-R	6-1	185	7-29-85	0	1	1.50	6	0	0	0	4	4	1	1	0	0	3	.211	.000	.308	4.50	0.00
Noles, Korey	L-L	5-11	185	7-18-85	0	0	0.50	5	3	0	0	18	12	1	1	0	7	20	.190	.182	.192	10.00	3.50
Poe, Chad	R-R	6-2	185	11-14-87	3	0	1.40	8	2	0	0	26	15	5	4	1	8	27	.174	.200	.157	9.47	2.81
Rodriguez, Julio	R-R	6-4	195	8-29-90	1	2	3.08	11	8	0	0	50	36	22	17	6	14	56	.197	.167	.206	10.15	2.54
Sampson, Julian	R-R	6-5	210	1-21-89	0	1	5.31	6	4	0	0	20	26	12	12	3	5	12	.321	.355	.300	5.31	2.21
Sasaki, Ryan	R-L	6-5	215	10-30-90	3	2	3.78	11	11	1	0	52	46	24	22	1	14	38	.240	.235	.242	6.54	2.41
Sosa, Juan	R-R	6-2	165	10-11-89	1	3	6.55	8	4	0	0	22	25	19	16	1	16	24	.287	.314	.269	9.82	6.55
Tolentino, Harol	R-L	6-4	165	11-8-88	0	0	3.00	7	0	0	0	9	6	3	3	1	4	7	.194	.000	.250	7.00	4.00
Van Steensel, Todd	R-R	6-1	190	1-14-91	2	1	5.83	12	5	0	0	29	38	21	19	3	8	29	.314	.255	.357	8.90	2.45
Zuber, Jessie	R-R	6-4	215	8-24-86	1	0	1.00	5	0	0	0	9	3	1	1	0	2	3	.111	.167	.095	3.00	2.00

Fielding

Catcher	PCT	G	PO	A	E	DP	PB
Aviola	.973	25	96	11	3	1	2
Diaz	.993	29	127	12	1	0	0
Guerra	.974	19	104	8	3	0	2
Mitchell	.979	28	121	22	3	1	4

First Base	PCT	G	PO	A	E	DP
Bollinger	1.000	4	29	5	0	2

Ruf	1.000	18	76	7	0	4
Singleton	.991	25	214	17	2	17
Sladek	1.000	8	25	1	0	1
Wine	.993	28	135	12	1	12

Second Base	PCT	G	PO	A	E	DP
Castillo	.952	7	6	14	1	2
Hernandez	.940	38	69	88	10	19

McConnell	.926	16	16	34	4	4

Third Base	PCT	G	PO	A	E	DP
Castillo	.970	12	6	26	1	1
McConnell	.906	11	7	22	3	5
Paulino	.860	39	22	70	15	4

Shortstop	PCT	G	PO	A	E	DP
Castillo	1.000	7	1	9	0	0

PHILADELPHIA PHILLIES

Donald	1.000	6	10	6	0	3
Duran	.968	31	36	55	3	7
Galvis	.950	5	8	11	1	1
Villar	.948	28	40	51	5	9

Outfield	PCT	G	PO	A	E	DP
Altherr	.926	27	49	1	4	1
Alvarez	1.000	19	22	1	0	0
Brown	1.000	3	3	0	0	0
Dugan	.977	42	86	0	2	0

Gump	.983	30	57	2	1	1
Hissey	1.000	16	21	2	0	0
Hudson	1.000	8	20	1	0	1
Santana	.984	33	59	2	1	0
Torres	.905	19	19	0	2	0

DSL PHILLIES   ROOKIE
DOMINICAN SUMMER LEAGUE

Batting	B-T	HT	WT	DOB	AVG	vLH	vRH	G	AB	R	H	2B	3B	HR	RBI	BB	HBP	SH	SF	SO	SB	CS	SLG	OBP
Beltre, Luis	R-R	6-1	190	2-1-92	.257	.362	.221	55	187	14	48	8	4	1	25	12	4	0	0	59	3	7	.358	.315
Berroa, Eladio	B-R	5-8	155	2-2-91	.246	.220	.255	62	211	35	52	8	2	0	27	25	8	4	1	22	9	8	.303	.347
Castillo, Jorge	B-R	5-10	170	10-19-90	.253	.244	.256	52	162	30	41	5	3	2	15	11	3	1	2	27	3	9	.358	.309
Checo, Emmanuel	R-R	6-0	190	12-18-87	.220	.182	.231	29	50	5	11	2	0	0	5	11	2	1	0	15	1	3	.260	.381
De La Cruz, Rafael	R-R	6-2	200	7-29-91	.162	.242	.136	45	136	21	22	8	0	0	10	12	8	1	0	33	2	2	.221	.269
Dicen, Francisco	R-R	6-3	180	9-9-90	.187	.125	.198	39	107	11	20	4	1	0	15	22	3	1	2	24	3	2	.243	.336
Esquea, Edwin	R-R	6-0	200	9-11-91	.242	.217	.248	37	124	4	30	6	0	0	12	13	2	0	4	26	1	0	.290	.315
Jimenez, Nevri	B-R	6-0	175	3-23-91	.347	.440	.323	31	121	33	42	11	2	2	15	14	3	1	0	20	12	8	.521	.428
Marine, Felix	R-R	6-0	180	5-25-90	.238	.176	.257	52	147	22	35	10	0	2	25	24	10	0	1	38	2	3	.347	.379
Mejia, Lissander	R-R	6-1	185	10-9-91	.196	.167	.202	42	107	19	21	6	0	0	7	12	2	0	0	26	6	4	.252	.289
Mendez, Geancarlo	R-R	6-2	170	11-17-89	.328	.391	.311	70	229	39	75	14	2	1	37	52	12	0	6	29	20	7	.419	.465
Morales, Yeisson	R-R	6-3	195	4-28-92	.200	.200	.200	33	90	13	18	4	0	0	4	20	5	0	0	25	4	3	.244	.374
Moscat, Anderson	R-R	6-2	188	5-31-89	.158	.136	.165	37	101	10	16	1	1	1	6	9	3	2	1	23	2	3	.218	.246
Trinidad, Jose	R-R	6-2	175	6-13-91	.333	.250	.355	14	39	8	13	2	0	0	6	4	2	1	0	13	1	1	.385	.422
Valenzuela, Carlos	R-R	5-11	170	9-18-90	.235	.149	.257	67	238	29	56	11	4	1	22	21	6	4	3	55	20	12	.328	.310
Ventura, Nelson	R-R	5-11	174	5-14-90	.231	.333	.200	6	13	2	3	0	0	0	1	0	0	0	0	4	0	0	.231	.231

Pitching	B-T	HT	WT	DOB	W	L	ERA	G	GS	CG	SV	IP	H	R	ER	HR	BB	SO	AVG	vLH	vRH	K/9	BB/9
Alvarez, Dario	L-L	6-1	170	1-17-89	3	4	2.59	14	13	2	0	83	80	34	24	0	20	79	.252	.250	.253	8.53	2.16
Arias, Gabirel	R-R	6-2	185	12-6-89	5	2	2.29	17	9	0	3	71	68	25	18	1	9	70	.245	.296	.232	8.92	1.15
Basil, Alvaro	R-R	6-3	170	10-28-90	0	1	15.00	3	1	0	0	3	4	7	5	0	5	3	.308	.800	.000	9.00	15.00
Bonilla, Lisalverto	R-R	6-1	164	6-6-90	6	2	1.41	11	11	2	0	70	48	20	11	2	16	76	.189	.148	.200	9.77	2.06
Brazoban, Domingo	R-R	6-2	175	8-8-89	0	2	12.79	8	0	0	0	6	16	11	9	1	6	3	.471	.500	.464	4.26	8.53
Cespedes, Felix	R-R	6-3	180	4-30-91	1	6	3.12	14	14	1	0	84	69	35	29	0	20	103	.228	.311	.213	11.08	2.15
Charles, Francique	R-R	6-0	178	2-28-89	1	1	4.40	16	0	0	0	29	21	17	14	2	18	37	.206	.105	.229	11.62	5.65
Coca, Marcos	R-R	6-3	156	1-19-90	2	2	1.80	7	1	0	1	10	6	8	2	0	6	6	.162	.500	.121	5.40	5.40
De La Cruz, Daniel	R-R	6-3	175	8-10-90	3	4	1.03	15	9	1	2	61	39	13	7	0	18	55	.181	.231	.169	8.11	2.66
Herrera, Saskuel	R-R	6-1	185	11-15-89	0	0	6.75	3	0	0	0	7	4	7	5	0	7	7	.167	.000	.333	9.45	9.45
Lora, Pedro	L-L	6-1	190	8-11-88	1	3	2.12	12	0	0	1	30	29	17	7	1	14	31	.254	.154	.267	9.40	4.25
Lorenzo, Jorge	R-R	6-2	175	9-29-90	0	1	12.60	5	1	0	0	5	5	7	7	0	7	3	.278	.000	.357	5.40	12.60
Pascual, Joan	L-L	6-0	180	3-6-90	0	2	7.90	7	1	0	1	14	17	14	12	0	11	13	.309	.000	.354	8.56	7.24
Ramirez, George	R-R	6-1	170	12-3-89	2	3	4.18	9	4	0	1	32	29	20	15	4	12	35	.232	.231	.232	9.74	3.34
Santana, Camilo	R-R	6-3	190	12-26-87	0	1	18.00	3	0	0	0	2	3	4	4	0	6	1	.429	1.000	.333	4.50	27.00
Sierra, Adrian	L-L	5-11	155	1-10-91	1	1	3.90	12	2	0	1	28	29	18	12	1	15	22	.264	.300	.260	7.16	4.88
Sosa, Yari	R-R	6-0	180	9-30-90	3	2	8.54	18	0	0	2	33	54	37	31	2	17	28	.362	.409	.354	7.71	4.68
Vasquez, Jose	L-L	5-11	200	12-11-89	0	0	9.00	1	0	0	0	1	1	1	1	0	0	2	.333	—	.333	18.00	0.00

Fielding

Catcher	PCT	G	PO	A	E	DP	PB
Checo	.962	16	66	10	3	0	2
De La Cruz	.937	15	78	26	7	0	4
Esquea	.987	16	132	21	2	0	7
Marine	.958	37	251	45	13	1	5
Ventura	.940	6	45	2	3	0	5
Moscat	.991	28	211	13	2	5	

First Base	PCT	G	PO	A	E	DP
Checo	.982	9	55	0	1	5
De La Cruz	.984	16	121	3	2	6
Dicen	1.000	2	12	0	0	0
Esquea	1.000	5	28	4	0	1
Marine	.990	13	98	6	1	8
Mejia	1.000	1	2	0	0	0
Mendez	1.000	12	86	2	0	10
Morales	1.000	2	13	0	0	3

Second Base	PCT	G	PO	A	E	DP
Berroa	.933	3	3	11	1	3
Castillo	.933	12	23	19	3	4
Jimenez	.947	4	8	10	1	4
Mendez	.973	22	32	40	2	7
Valenzuela	.936	40	48	69	8	11

Third Base	PCT	G	PO	A	E	DP
De La Cruz	1.000	12	14	27	0	0
Jimenez	.941	11	4	28	2	1
Morales	.825	29	18	62	17	2
Moscat	.684	4	3	10	6	1
Valenzuela	.896	20	11	49	7	2

Shortstop	PCT	G	PO	A	E	DP
Berroa	.936	60	119	157	19	21
De La Cruz	1.000	2	1	2	0	0
Jimenez	.769	6	4	6	3	1
Valenzuela	.838	8	10	21	6	9

Outfield	PCT	G	PO	A	E	DP
Beltre	.930	54	61	5	5	0
Castillo	.944	33	30	4	2	0
Dicen	1.000	34	48	2	0	1
Jimenez	.895	11	17	0	2	0
Marine	—	1	0	0	0	0
Mejia	.956	38	43	0	2	0
Mendez	1.000	1	2	0	0	0
Moscat	1.000	4	8	0	0	0
Olmo	.969	50	89	4	3	0
Trinidad	.917	12	9	2	1	0

VSL PHILLIES   ROOKIE
VENEZUELAN SUMMER LEAGUE

Batting	B-T	HT	WT	DOB	AVG	vLH	vRH	G	AB	R	H	2B	3B	HR	RBI	BB	HBP	SH	SF	SO	SB	CS	SLG	OBP
Astudillo, Willians	R-R	5-9	182	10-14-91	.250	.225	.257	58	188	20	47	5	2	1	21	8	9	0	4	10	7	2	.314	.306
Balentien, Rudney	R-R	6-0	160	11-3-89	.352	.321	.365	27	91	21	32	6	0	8	23	8	3	0	0	24	5	1	.681	.422
Barrios, Hector	R-R	5-10	187	6-16-91	.170	.200	.158	27	53	2	9	0	0	0	3	1	1	0	1	4	0	0	.170	.196
Bogle, Vernal	R-R	6-0	167	11-21-89	.245	.306	.224	54	143	20	35	7	1	0	10	18	6	5	0	31	6	9	.308	.353
Davalillo, Marco	R-R	6-1	210	11-5-90	.336	.308	.345	64	220	30	74	18	0	6	26	18	5	0	2	25	2	4	.500	.396
Fajardo, Rosmel	R-R	6-2	177	7-19-92	.169	.143	.176	31	65	4	11	0	0	0	5	6	2	1	0	22	5	2	.169	.260

Machado, Gregorio	B-R	6-1	184	10-28-91	.149	.083	.160	38	87	6	13	1	1	0	10	5	3	3	1	30	1	5	.184	.219
Martinez, Luis	R-R	6-5	183	12-22-89	.265	.233	.274	37	136	16	36	7	3	2	16	3	2	2	0	27	5	0	.404	.291
Nunez, Rosmer	R-R	5-10	165	6-12-92	.127	.182	.114	26	55	7	7	1	0	0	1	4	3	0	0	12	1	0	.145	.226
Perdomo, Carlos	R-R	5-10	168	4-25-90	.309	.250	.326	64	249	27	77	12	3	2	32	12	0	0	2	8	5	10	.406	.338
Rios, Nerio	B-R	6-0	150	10-5-91	.207	.229	.202	54	164	21	34	4	2	0	9	23	1	7	3	49	5	7	.256	.304
Salazar, Alexis	R-R	5-11	184	1-26-91	.247	.357	.227	39	89	9	22	4	0	0	8	7	4	1	0	12	1	3	.292	.330
Solarte, Bernardo	R-R	6-0	161	1-23-92	.260	.222	.268	16	50	7	13	3	1	0	10	6	2	1	1	11	2	0	.360	.356
Sosa, Nelson	R-R	5-11	148	9-30-89	.202	.250	.194	45	109	12	22	3	1	0	5	9	2	4	0	16	4	2	.248	.275
Tolo, Eduards	R-R	5-9	140	10-7-90	.284	.370	.257	57	194	28	55	12	1	0	12	26	3	5	2	14	7	11	.356	.373
Unda, Luis	L-L	6-1	155	1-28-90	.301	.278	.307	67	246	35	74	16	2	5	34	25	1	2	3	28	4	2	.443	.364
Villegas, Enderson	R-R	5-10	168	1-31-92	.245	.303	.226	55	139	18	34	10	1	1	19	12	6	1	0	31	2	5	.353	.331

Pitching	B-T	HT	WT	DOB	W	L	ERA	G	GS	CG	SV	IP	H	R	ER	HR	BB	SO	AVG	vLH	vRH	K/9	BB/9
Bastidas, Leonel	R-R	6-3	184	6-26-89	2	6	4.71	16	12	0	1	63	63	41	33	6	18	45	.253	.227	.259	6.43	2.57
Campo, Kirlian	B-L	6-0	180	5-17-90	3	0	1.78	16	0	0	0	30	22	8	6	1	13	32	.198	.000	.208	9.49	3.86
Diaz, Victor	R-R	6-6	229	5-19-89	0	0	4.50	2	0	0	0	2	2	1	1	0	3	4	.250	.500	.167	18.00	13.50
Escaray, Atilio	R-R	6-2	153	12-29-89	0	0	18.56	5	0	0	0	5	11	12	11	1	4	4	.423	.375	.444	6.75	6.75
Garces, Orlando	L-L	5-11	181	8-24-90	0	0	6.89	7	1	0	0	16	15	13	12	1	16	15	.250	.200	.255	8.62	9.19
Gomez, Juary	R-R	6-2	200	5-23-90	2	3	3.09	17	3	0	0	44	55	27	15	3	12	39	.304	.277	.313	8.04	2.47
Guevara, Rafael	R-R	5-11	166	11-19-90	1	0	4.41	12	0	0	0	16	13	8	8	0	4	8	.213	.333	.184	4.41	2.20
Guzman, Jorge	R-R	6-1	201	8-14-91	0	3	7.09	14	1	0	0	27	35	22	21	1	15	27	.333	.467	.311	9.11	5.06
Hernandez, Jose	R-R	6-2	170	1-21-88	2	2	3.71	6	3	0	0	17	11	8	7	0	10	18	.186	.238	.158	9.53	5.29
Honora, Zael	R-R	6-2	199	3-15-90	0	7	6.97	14	6	0	0	41	50	38	32	4	24	25	.311	.243	.331	5.44	5.23
Izurriaga, Ely	L-L	5-11	188	6-29-90	2	2	2.08	8	8	0	0	39	32	15	9	1	10	47	.222	.000	.234	10.85	2.31
Leon, Luis	R-R	6-2	166	11-24-89	2	2	3.31	24	0	0	8	33	30	15	12	0	11	35	.246	.357	.231	9.64	3.03
Lopez, Jean	R-R	6-2	175	3-31-88	0	2	4.45	14	0	0	0	30	34	27	15	1	19	23	.288	.261	.295	6.82	5.64
Manzanillo, Ervis	L-L	6-2	160	8-25-89	0	4	5.03	13	6	0	0	34	31	22	19	0	27	32	.258	.500	.241	8.47	7.15
Martinez, Jose	R-R	6-2	209	2-14-89	5	0	1.80	11	0	0	0	25	17	5	5	1	10	25	.189	.111	.208	9.00	3.60
Monzon, Yosber	R-R	6-0	176	11-4-89	5	3	3.68	14	14	0	0	66	49	32	27	4	30	43	.203	.232	.195	5.86	4.09
Pirela, Jesus	R-R	6-0	152	3-13-89	3	6	4.59	15	13	0	0	69	70	40	35	3	28	60	.266	.222	.280	7.86	3.67
Silva, Yovan	R-R	6-0	209	2-6-90	0	0	4.39	15	1	0	1	27	26	18	13	2	15	26	.265	.250	.269	8.78	5.06
Suarez, Jesus	R-R	6-3	200	12-5-88	0	2	5.82	9	1	0	1	17	21	13	11	2	9	9	.296	.400	.268	4.76	4.76

Fielding

Catcher	PCT	G	PO	A	E	DP	PB
Astudillo	.975	14	102	15	3	3	4
Barrios	.982	22	93	17	2	0	7
Davalillo	.966	31	200	30	8	1	4
Villegas	.966	20	123	18	5	0	8

First Base	PCT	G	PO	A	E	DP
Astudillo	1.000	5	35	2	0	1
Davalillo	.996	25	210	16	1	12
Perdomo	.833	2	5	0	1	0
Tolo	1.000	1	1	0	0	0
Unda	.994	33	299	16	2	27
Villegas	.992	17	115	9	1	10

Second Base	PCT	G	PO	A	E	DP
Astudillo	1.000	7	21	18	0	7

	PCT	G	PO	A	E	DP
Nunez	.889	12	23	17	5	5
Perdomo	.956	31	43	66	5	11
Sosa	.890	28	44	45	11	11
Tolo	1.000	5	6	4	0	0

Third Base	PCT	G	PO	A	E	DP
Astudillo	.857	1	2	4	1	0
Davalillo	.895	6	5	12	2	1
Nunez	1.000	2	1	3	0	0
Perdomo	.875	14	9	26	5	2
Sosa	.688	10	2	9	5	1
Tolo	.943	47	31	117	9	8

Shortstop	PCT	G	PO	A	E	DP
Nunez	.867	5	4	9	2	0
Perdomo	.970	22	27	69	3	8

	PCT	G	PO	A	E	DP
Rios	.917	53	67	154	20	22
Sosa	1.000	1	2	2	0	1

Outfield	PCT	G	PO	A	E	DP
Astudillo	1.000	3	5	0	0	0
Balentien	.975	23	36	3	1	0
Bogle	.948	48	69	4	4	1
Fajardo	.900	27	33	3	4	0
Machado	.857	30	29	1	5	0
Martinez	.936	36	41	3	3	2
Nunez	—	2	0	0	0	0
Perdomo	—	1	0	0	0	0
Salazar	.882	37	28	2	4	0
Solarte	1.000	16	28	3	0	2
Unda	.941	30	29	3	2	0

Pittsburgh Pirates

SEASON IN A SENTENCE: While the Steelers were winning another Super Bowl and the Penguins were winning another Stanley Cup, Pittsburgh's baseball team endured its 17th straight losing season, compiling the second-worst record in baseball at 62-99.

HIGH POINT: Outfielder Andrew McCutchen made his major league debut on June 4 and was Baseball America's Rookie of the Year, a legitimate cornerstone for a franchise that has turned over nearly its entire roster in the last two years.

LOW POINT: It's an embarrassment of riches for anyone looking for low moments. The Pirates were 16th in the National League in runs with 636, and 14th in ERA at 4.59. Perhaps most discouraging was their 9-22 mark to close the season, part of a 24-49 second half. It's a season so bad it included losing streaks of one, two, three, four, five (three times), six, eight (twice) and nine games. Only a seven-game losing streak was missing.

NOTABLE ROOKIES: McCutchen's shoulders had better be strong, because a lot of the Pirates' hopes rest on them. He looked dynamic enough in his rookie year that he could be a star. Pittsburgh broke in several other rookies, but they fall more under the heading of complementary players. Garrett Jones performed well above expectations after signing as a minor league free agent, batting .293/.372/.567 with 21 home runs, though he'll have to prove he can repeat those numbers.

KEY TRANSACTIONS: General manager Neal Huntington recognized the team's talent deficiency when he took over late in the 2007 season, so he has worked hard to change that. He made seven trades in June and July alone, sending away eight players—including the longtime middle-infield combo of Freddy Sanchez and Jack Wilson—and getting 15 in return. By the end of the season, just five players remained on the major league roster who were there when Huntington took over.

DOWN ON THE FARM: The Pirates have plowed more than $18 million into draft bonuses the last two years, with third baseman Pedro Alvarez the most notable product. While high Class A Lynchburg won the Carolina League title, Pirates affiliates were 339-358 overall, the 23rd-best minor league record in baseball. The Pirates will move their high Class A affiliation to the Florida State League in 2010 after purchasing the Sarasota franchise and moving it to their Bradenton, Fla., spring training base.

OPENING DAY PAYROLL: $48,693,000

PLAYERS OF THE YEAR

MAJOR LEAGUE	MINOR LEAGUE
Andrew McCutchen	**Pedro Alvarez**
of	3b
.286/.365/.471	(High A/Double-A)
26 2B, 12 HR, 22 SB,	.288/.378/.535
BA Rookie of the Year	32 2B, 27 HR, 95 RBI

ORGANIZATION LEADERS

BATTING		*Minimum 250 at-bats
MAJORS		
*AVG	Freddy Sanchez	.296
*OPS	Garrett Jones	.938
HR	Garrett Jones	21
RBI	Adam LaRoche	64
MINORS		
*AVG	Huber, Erik, Lynchburg/West Virginia	.301
R	Grossman, Robbie, West Virginia	83
H	Durham, Miles, Lynchburg/Altoona	139
TB	Alvarez, Pedro, Lynchburg/Altoona	249
2B	Durham, Miles, Lynchburg/Altoona	36
2B	Mercer, Jordy, Lynchburg	36
3B	Presley, Alex, Lynchburg	11
HR	Alvarez, Pedro, Lynchburg/Altoona	27
RBI	Alvarez, Pedro, Lynchburg/Altoona	95
BB	Grossman, Robbie, West Virginia	75
SO	Grossman, Robbie, West Virginia	164
SB	De Los Santos, Jose, Lynchburg	53
*OBP	Watts, Kris, Lynchburg	.405
*SLG	Alvarez, Pedro, Lynchburg/Altoona	.535

PITCHING		†Minimum 75 innings
MAJORS		
W	Zach Duke	11
†ERA	Ross Ohlendorf	3.92
SO	Paul Maholm	119
MINORS		
W	McCutchen, Daniel, Indianapolis	13
L	Welker, Duke, West Virginia	11
†ERA	Owens, Rudy, West Virginia/Lynchburg	2.10
G	Hamman, Corey, Altoona/Indianapolis	55
GS	Crotta, Michael, Altoona	27
SV	Rodriguez, R.J., Lynchburg	27
IP	Moskos, Danny, Altoona	149
BB	Welker, Duke, West Virginia	67
SO	Owens, Rudy, West Virginia/Lynchburg	113
†AVG	Owens, Rudy, West Virginia/Lynchburg	.219

General Manager: Neal Huntington. **Farm Director:** Kyle Stark. **Scouting Director:** Greg Smith.

Class	Team	League	W	L	PCT	Finish*	Manager(s)
Majors	Pittsburgh Pirates	National	62	99	.385	15th (16)	John Russell
Triple-A	Indianapolis Indians	International	70	73	.490	9th (14)	Frank Kremblas
Double-A	Altoona Curve	Eastern	62	80	.437	11th (12)	Matt Walbeck
High A	Lynchburg Hillcats	Carolina	73	66	.525	†4th (8)	P.J. Forbes
Low A	West Virginia Power	South Atlantic	67	70	.489	8th (16)	Gary Green
Short-season	State College Spikes	New York-Penn	38	38	.500	7th (14)	Gary Robinson
Rookie	GCL Pirates	Gulf Coast	29	31	.483	11th (16)	Tom Prince
Overall 2009 Minor League Record			339	358	.486	23rd (30)	

*Finish in overall standings (No. of teams in league). †League champion.

ORGANIZATION STATISTICS

PITTSBURGH PIRATES
NATIONAL LEAGUE

Batting	B-T	HT	WT	DOB	AVG	vLH	vRH	G	AB	R	H	2B	3B	HR	RBI	BB	HBP	SH	SF	SO	SB	CS	SLG	OBP
Bixler, Brian	R-R	6-1	195	10-22-82	.227	.500	.147	18	44	5	10	5	0	0	3	2	0	0	0	26	1	0	.341	.261
Cedeno, Ronny	R-R	6-0	180	2-2-83	.258	.259	.258	46	155	17	40	4	1	5	21	9	2	4	0	29	2	0	.394	.307
Cruz, Luis	R-R	6-1	215	2-10-84	.214	.172	.244	27	70	5	15	1	0	0	2	6	1	0	1	7	0	0	.229	.282
Diaz, Robinzon	R-R	5-11	220	9-19-83	.279	.237	.314	41	129	9	36	7	0	1	19	3	3	1	2	9	0	1	.357	.307
Doumit, Ryan	R-R	6-1	215	4-3-81	.250	.266	.244	75	280	31	70	16	0	10	38	20	1	0	3	49	4	0	.414	.299
Hinske, Eric	L-R	6-1	235	8-5-77	.255	.273	.250	54	106	18	27	9	0	1	11	17	3	0	0	27	0	0	.368	.373
Jaramillo, Jason	B-R	6-0	200	10-9-82	.252	.161	.269	63	206	20	52	14	0	3	26	17	0	1	0	33	1	0	.364	.309
Jones, Garrett	L-L	6-4	245	6-21-81	.293	.208	.333	82	314	45	92	21	1	21	44	40	1	0	3	76	10	2	.567	.372
LaRoche, Andy	R-R	6-1	210	9-13-83	.258	.285	.249	150	524	64	135	29	5	12	64	50	8	6	2	84	3	1	.401	.330
LaRoche, Adam	L-L	6-3	205	11-6-79	.247	.226	.257	87	324	46	80	25	1	12	40	41	0	0	3	81	2	2	.441	.329
2-team total (57 Atlanta)					.278	—	—	144	536	76	149	36	2	24	80	69	0	0	5	140	2	2	.487	.357
McCutchen, Andrew	R-R	5-11	175	10-10-86	.286	.310	.279	108	433	74	124	26	9	12	54	54	2	0	4	83	22	5	.471	.365
McLouth, Nate	L-R	5-11	180	10-28-81	.256	.298	.234	45	168	27	43	7	1	9	34	21	4	0	2	29	7	0	.470	.349
2-team total (84 Atlanta)					.256	—	—	129	507	86	130	27	2	20	70	68	9	3	4	99	19	6	.436	.352
Milledge, Lastings	R-R	6-0	205	4-5-85	.291	.327	.281	58	220	20	64	11	0	4	20	12	3	2	2	47	4	4	.395	.333
2-team total (7 Washington)					.279	—	—	65	244	21	68	11	0	4	21	13	4	2	2	47	7	4	.373	.323
Monroe, Craig	R-R	6-1	215	2-27-77	.215	.256	.167	34	79	8	17	2	0	3	16	7	1	0	0	21	0	0	.354	.287
Morgan, Nyjer	L-L	6-0	175	7-2-80	.277	.151	.322	71	278	39	77	6	5	2	29	25	5	5	4	49	18	10	.356	.351
2-team total (49 Washington)					.307	—	—	120	469	74	144	15	7	3	39	40	9	10	5	74	42	17	.388	.369
Moss, Brandon	L-R	6-0	205	9-16-83	.236	.232	.237	133	385	47	91	20	4	7	41	34	4	0	1	84	1	5	.364	.304
Pearce, Steve	R-R	5-11	215	4-13-83	.206	.268	.174	60	126	19	34	13	1	4	16	21	0	0	0	43	1	0	.370	.296
Salazar, Jeff	L-L	6-0	195	11-24-80	.043	.000	.053	21	23	1	1	0	0	0	1	3	0	0	0	7	1	0	.043	.154
Sanchez, Freddy	R-R	5-10	190	12-21-77	.296	.323	.285	86	355	45	105	28	3	6	34	20	2	2	3	60	5	1	.442	.334
2-team total (25 San Francisco)					.293	—	—	111	457	56	134	29	3	7	41	22	2	4	4	76	5	1	.416	.326
Vazquez, Ramon	L-R	5-11	170	8-21-76	.230	.290	.220	101	204	17	47	7	0	1	16	31	2	0	2	47	1	0	.279	.335
Walker, Neil	B-R	6-3	215	9-10-85	.194	.143	.207	17	36	5	7	1	0	0	4	0	0	0	0	11	1	0	.222	.275
Wilson, Jack	R-R	6-0	200	12-29-77	.267	.261	.269	75	266	26	71	18	1	4	31	15	0	3	2	31	2	1	.387	.304
Young, Delwyn	B-R	5-10	190	6-30-82	.266	.233	.282	124	354	40	94	16	2	7	43	29	3	1	1	90	2	0	.381	.326

Pitching	B-T	HT	WT	DOB	W	L	ERA	G	GS	CG	SV	IP	H	R	ER	HR	BB	SO	AVG	vLH	vRH	K/9	BB/9
Ascanio, Jose	R-R	6-0	170	5-2-85	0	1	6.75	2	0	0	0	3	4	2	2	0	0	2	.444	1.000	.286	6.75	0.00
2-team total (14 Chicago)					0	2	4.00	16	0	0	0	18	22	8	8	1	9	20	—	—	—	10.00	4.50
Bautista, Denny	R-R	6-5	195	8-23-80	1	1	5.27	14	0	0	0	14	15	8	8	1	7	15	.306	.318	.296	9.88	4.61
Bootcheck, Chris	R-R	6-5	210	10-24-78	0	0	11.05	13	0	0	0	15	16	18	18	1	9	13	.286	.250	.300	7.98	5.52
Burnett, Sean	L-L	6-1	200	9-17-82	1	2	3.06	38	0	0	1	32	22	12	11	3	15	23	.200	.189	.211	6.40	4.18
2-team total (33 Washington)					2	3	3.12	71	0	0	1	58	36	21	20	6	28	43	—	—	—	6.71	4.37
Capps, Matt	R-R	6-2	245	9-3-83	4	8	5.80	57	0	0	27	54	73	36	35	10	17	46	.324	.342	.306	7.62	2.82
Chavez, Jesse	R-R	6-2	170	8-21-83	1	4	4.01	73	0	0	0	67	69	33	30	11	22	47	.264	.228	.299	6.28	2.94
Claggett, Anthony	B-R	6-3	195	7-15-84	0	0	9.00	1	0	0	0	1	2	1	1	1	0	0	.400	1.000	.250	0.00	0.00
Duke, Zach	L-L	6-2	205	4-19-83	11	16	4.06	32	32	3	0	213	231	101	96	23	49	106	.285	.284	.285	4.48	2.07
Dumatrait, Phil	R-L	6-2	200	7-12-81	0	2	6.92	15	0	0	0	13	13	11	10	4	11	7	.250	.280	.222	4.85	7.62
Gorzelanny, Tom	L-L	6-2	200	7-12-82	3	1	5.19	9	0	0	0	9	6	5	5	0	4	7	.194	.300	.143	7.27	4.15
2-team total (13 Chicago)					7	3	5.55	22	7	0	0	47	45	30	29	6	17	47	—	—	—	9.00	3.26
Grabow, John	L-L	6-2	205	11-4-78	3	0	3.42	45	0	0	4	47	43	19	18	4	28	41	.246	.275	.234	7.80	5.32
2-team total (30 Chicago)					3	0	3.36	75	0	0	0	72	62	28	27	5	40	57	—	—	—	7.09	4.98
Hacker, Eric	B-R	6-1	210	3-26-83	0	0	6.00	3	0	0	0	3	4	2	2	0	2	1	.333	.375	.250	3.00	6.00
Hanrahan, Joel	R-R	6-4	250	10-6-81	0	1	1.72	33	0	0	0	31	23	12	6	0	20	37	.204	.208	.200	10.63	5.74
2-team total (34 Washington)					1	4	4.78	67	0	0	5	64	73	40	34	3	34	72	—	—	—	10.13	4.78
Hansen, Craig	R-R	6-6	225	11-15-83	0	0	5.68	5	0	0	0	6	6	4	4	1	4	5	.240	.000	.353	7.11	5.68
Hart, Kevin	R-R	6-4	220	12-29-82	1	8	6.92	10	10	0	0	53	74	47	41	8	26	39	.333	.336	.330	6.58	4.39
2-team total (8 Chicago)					4	9	5.44	18	14	0	0	97	55	49	11	44	52	—	—	—	5.78	4.89
Jackson, Steven	R-R	6-5	215	3-15-82	2	3	3.14	40	0	0	0	43	38	20	15	2	22	21	.236	.216	.253	4.40	4.60
Karstens, Jeff	R-R	6-3	185	9-24-82	4	6	5.42	39	13	0	0	108	115	66	65	12	45	52	.279	.263	.294	4.33	3.75

PITTSBURGH PIRATES

	B-T	HT	WT	DOB	W	L	ERA	G	GS	CG	SV	IP	H	R	ER	HR	BB	SO	AVG	vLH	vRH	K/9	BB/9
Maholm, Paul	L-L	6-2	225	6-25-82	8	9	4.44	31	31	0	0	195	221	102	96	14	60	119	.290	.182	.316	5.50	2.77
McCutchen, Daniel	R-R	6-2	215	9-26-82	1	2	4.21	6	6	0	0	36	38	17	17	6	11	19	.271	.262	.280	4.71	2.72
Meek, Evan	R-R	6-0	220	5-12-83	1	1	3.45	41	0	0	0	47	34	18	18	2	29	42	.209	.250	.176	8.04	5.55
Morton, Charlie	R-R	6-4	190	11-12-83	5	9	4.55	18	18	1	0	97	102	49	49	7	40	62	.276	.316	.236	5.75	3.71
Ohlendorf, Ross	R-R	6-4	235	8-8-82	11	10	3.92	29	29	0	0	177	165	80	77	25	53	109	.255	.286	.221	5.55	2.70
Snell, Ian	R-R	5-11	200	10-30-81	2	8	5.36	15	15	1	0	81	87	50	48	7	44	52	.282	.280	.283	5.80	4.91
Vasquez, Virgil	R-R	6-3	205	6-7-82	2	5	5.84	14	7	0	0	45	58	30	29	6	18	29	.320	.342	.305	5.84	3.63
Veal, Donald	L-L	6-4	230	9-18-84	1	0	7.16	19	0	0	0	16	18	13	13	2	20	16	.281	.200	.318	8.82	11.02
Yates, Tyler	R-R	6-4	250	8-7-77	0	2	7.50	15	0	0	0	12	14	12	10	2	7	9	.311	.600	.167	6.75	5.25

Fielding

Catcher	PCT	G	PO	A	E	DP	PB
Diaz	.991	33	188	23	2	1	7
Doumit	.987	71	418	53	6	9	2
Jaramillo	.989	62	322	28	4	5	4

First Base	PCT	G	PO	A	E	DP
Hinske	1.000	6	39	3	0	4
Jones	.996	30	246	37	1	26
LaRoche	.999	87	776	59	1	86
Pearce	.995	42	360	30	2	31

Second Base	PCT	G	PO	A	E	DP
Bixler	.941	5	4	12	1	1
Cruz	1.000	5	6	11	0	1
Sanchez	.995	85	184	224	2	63

Vazquez	1.000	22	33	50	0	13
Young	.983	53	102	131	4	37

Third Base	PCT	G	PO	A	E	DP
Hinske	1.000	3	0	3	0	0
LaRoche	.968	146	97	321	14	34
Vazquez	.964	14	7	20	1	3
Walker	.955	9	6	15	1	1

Shortstop	PCT	G	PO	A	E	DP
Bixler	.951	10	15	24	2	3
Cedeno	.980	42	66	133	4	27
Cruz	.977	17	37	48	2	9
Vazquez	.989	28	37	54	1	13
Wilson	.980	74	105	242	7	64

Outfield	PCT	G	PO	A	E	DP
Bixler	—	1	0	0	0	0
Doumit	1.000	1	2	0	0	0
Hinske	1.000	13	30	3	0	0
Jones	1.000	53	100	4	0	0
McCutchen	.993	108	263	10	2	1
McLouth	1.000	45	117	5	0	2
Milledge	1.000	56	111	6	0	0
Monroe	1.000	17	31	0	0	0
Morgan	.994	70	163	6	1	1
Moss	.991	99	217	9	2	4
Pearce	1.000	1	1	0	0	0
Salazar	1.000	4	7	1	0	0
Young	.971	30	66	1	2	0

INDIANAPOLIS INDIANS

TRIPLE-A

INTERNATIONAL LEAGUE

Batting	B-T	HT	WT	DOB	AVG	vLH	vRH	G	AB	R	H	2B	3B	HR	RBI	BB	HBP	SH	SF	SO	SB	CS	SLG	OBP
Barnwell, Chris	R-R	5-10	180	3-1-79	.193	.193	.192	87	270	24	52	13	0	2	15	17	7	7	0	61	3	4	.263	.259
Bixler, Brian	R-R	6-1	195	10-22-82	.275	.355	.241	108	403	71	111	23	8	9	43	35	7	5	1	128	13	3	.439	.343
Bozied, Tagg	R-R	6-3	215	7-24-79	.288	.253	.307	56	215	32	62	17	1	5	18	21	3	1	0	60	4	2	.447	.360
Broadway, Larry	L-L	6-4	230	12-17-80	.233	.130	.270	69	206	21	48	10	0	8	27	17	2	0	1	64	0	4	.398	.296
Clement, Jeff	L-R	6-1	215	8-21-83	.224	.286	.190	27	98	16	22	2	0	7	22	12	2	0	3	27	1	1	.459	.313
Cruz, Luis	R-R	6-1	215	2-10-84	.253	.323	.226	66	229	28	58	15	0	3	23	6	1	0	1	26	3	3	.358	.274
Delaney, Jason	R-R	6-3	215	11-9-82	.000	.000	.000	2	3	0	0	0	0	0	0	1	0	0	0	2	0	0	.000	.250
Diaz, Argenis	R-R	5-11	155	2-12-87	.233	.188	.255	43	146	14	34	1	0	0	8	8	0	4	0	27	1	1	.240	.273
Diaz, Robinzon	R-R	5-11	220	9-19-83	.262	.296	.242	44	149	18	39	4	0	3	15	9	1	3	0	12	0	1	.349	.308
Doumit, Ryan	B-R	6-1	215	4-3-81	.118	.200	.083	5	17	1	2	0	0	0	1	0	0	0	0	3	0	0	.118	.167
Ford, Shelby	R-R	6-3	185	12-15-84	.188	.157	.197	86	298	34	56	11	2	4	27	14	7	0	2	58	8	1	.279	.240
Gimenez, Hector	B-R	5-10	210	9-28-82	.268	.283	.259	48	168	16	45	12	0	2	20	13	0	1	1	35	0	1	.375	.319
Jones, Garrett	L-L	6-4	245	6-21-81	.307	.295	.312	72	277	44	85	18	0	12	50	18	1	0	3	47	14	4	.502	.348
Kratz, Erik	R-R	6-4	250	6-15-80	.273	.340	.243	93	319	45	87	30	0	11	43	31	1	0	2	72	7	0	.470	.337
Lopez, Pedro	R-R	6-1	190	4-28-84	.275	.327	.241	42	142	16	39	5	0	0	13	9	0	7	1	20	0	2	.310	.316
Machado, Anderson	B-R	6-0	185	1-25-81	.125	.200	.000	4	8	1	1	0	1	0	0	1	0	0	0	6	0	0	.375	.222
McCutchen, Andrew	R-R	5-11	175	10-10-86	.303	.361	.279	49	201	41	61	10	8	4	20	17	1	0	0	24	10	2	.493	.361
Melhuse, Adam	R-R	6-2	210	3-27-72	.176	.083	.205	17	51	6	9	2	0	0	2	9	0	0	1	13	0	0	.216	.295
Milledge, Lastings	R-R	6-0	205	4-5-85	.333	.278	.357	17	60	7	20	6	0	0	7	8	3	1	2	10	3	2	.433	.425
2-team total (22 Syracuse)					.288	—	—	39	139	18	40	11	0	0	11	11	3	1	3	26	9	3	.367	.346
Myrow, Brian	R-R	5-11	210	9-4-76	.330	.214	.373	62	206	37	68	12	1	8	34	43	5	0	5	33	3	1	.515	.448
2-team total (48 Charlotte)					.307	—	—	110	365	60	112	22	1	15	59	65	10	1	6	70	3	2	.496	.419
Pacheco, Jonel	R-R	5-9	170	10-3-82	.400	.500	.364	7	15	2	6	3	0	0	4	2	0	0	1	6	0	0	.600	.444
Pearce, Steve	R-R	5-11	215	4-13-83	.286	.309	.276	77	273	37	78	18	1	13	54	34	6	1	3	46	3	7	.502	.373
Perez, Miguel	R-R	6-3	235	9-25-83	.182	.200	.167	7	22	2	4	0	0	0	1	1	0	0	0	9	0	1	.182	.217
Phillips, Andy	R-R	6-0	215	4-6-77	.333	.364	.313	7	27	2	9	0	0	1	2	2	1	0	1	4	0	0	.444	.387
2-team total (49 Charlotte)					.300	—	—	56	217	26	65	9	1	6	29	17	1	1	3	30	1	1	.433	.349
Salazar, Jeff	L-L	6-0	195	11-24-80	.270	.260	.274	84	315	43	85	7	3	10	39	30	2	1	3	57	16	0	.406	.334
Snelling, Chris	L-L	5-10	205	12-3-81	.123	.091	.130	19	57	5	7	0	0	0	4	8	2	0	1	14	0	1	.123	.250
Tabata, Jose	R-R	5-11	215	8-12-88	.276	.347	.235	32	134	21	37	7	1	3	10	10	2	1	1	18	4	2	.410	.333
Walker, Neil	B-R	6-3	215	9-10-85	.264	.235	.278	95	356	38	94	31	2	14	69	26	1	1	6	60	5	2	.480	.311
Wilson, Jack	R-R	6-0	200	12-29-77	.333	.500	.250	2	6	0	2	0	0	0	3	0	0	0	1	2	0	0	.667	.286

Pitching	B-T	HT	WT	DOB	W	L	ERA	G	GS	CG	SV	IP	H	R	ER	HR	BB	SO	AVG	vLH	vRH	K/9	BB/9
Ascanio, Jose	R-R	6-0	170	5-2-85	0	1	2.70	1	1	0	0	7	6	2	2	1	1	9	.240	.263	.167	12.15	1.35
Barthmaier, Jimmy	R-R	6-5	215	1-6-84	0	0	—	1	1	0	0	0	0	0	0	0	0	2	0	—	—	—	—
Bautista, Denny	R-R	6-5	195	8-23-80	2	3	4.88	36	0	0	1	48	54	29	26	2	34	58	.284	.303	.272	10.88	6.38
Bootcheck, Chris	R-R	6-5	210	10-24-78	3	2	3.38	40	0	0	20	43	40	16	16	1	7	55	.248	.177	.293	11.60	1.48
Davidson, Dave	L-L	6-1	200	4-23-84	0	1	4.15	3	0	0	0	4	3	2	2	0	1	4	.200	.000	.231	8.31	2.08
Davis, Jason	R-R	6-6	230	5-8-80	0	8	6.06	35	7	0	0	62	72	51	42	2	36	25	.293	.306	.283	3.61	5.20
Dumatrait, Phil	L-L	6-2	200	7-12-81	0	2	4.20	4	2	0	0	15	16	11	7	2	4	5	.267	.235	.279	3.00	2.40
Gorzelanny, Tom	L-L	6-2	200	7-12-82	4	3	2.48	15	15	2	0	87	73	31	24	3	30	85	.228	.195	.239	8.79	3.10
Hacker, Eric	B-R	6-1	210	3-26-83	5	5	4.02	21	21	0	0	116	135	57	52	6	46	82	.299	.374	.248	6.34	3.56
2-team total (3 Scranton/W-B)					5	6	4.49	24	24	0	0	132	154	71	66	9	50	94	—	—	—	6.39	3.40
Hamman, Corey	L-L	6-2	200	4-12-80	1	2	8.01	26	0	0	0	30	38	30	27	2	15	32	.299	.214	.341	9.49	4.45

Name	B-T	HT	WT	DOB	W	L	ERA	G	GS	CG	SV	IP	H	R	ER	HR	BB	SO	AVG	vLH	vRH		
Herrera, Yoslan	R-R	6-2	200	4-28-81	1	1	2.30	4	2	0	0	16	12	4	4	1	7	7	.218	.176	.237	4.02	4.02
Jackson, Steven	R-R	6-5	215	3-15-82	1	0	6.50	12	0	0	0	18	23	14	13	1	5	17	.319	.231	.424	8.50	2.50
2-team total (7 Scranton/W-B)					1	0	4.45	19	1	0	1	32	39	17	16	2	8	25	—	—	—	6.96	2.23
Julio, Jorge	R-R	6-1	225	3-3-79	0	2	6.75	4	0	0	0	5	8	7	4	0	2	7	.333	.667	.222	11.81	3.38
2-team total (19 Durham)					0	3	6.11	23	0	0	0	28	30	23	19	2	17	31	—	—	—	9.96	5.46
Karstens, Jeff	R-R	6-3	185	9-24-82	0	0	0.00	3	0	0	0	6	4	0	0	0	0	7	.182	.333	.158	10.50	0.00
Koplove, Mike	R-R	6-0	160	8-30-76	3	1	2.35	22	0	0	2	31	27	8	8	0	10	20	.231	.208	.250	5.87	2.93
2-team total (21 Lehigh Valley)					4	4	1.82	43	0	0	8	54	42	16	11	2	21	50	—	—	—	8.28	3.48
Lincoln, Brad	L-R	6-0	215	5-25-85	6	2	4.70	12	12	0	0	61	72	37	32	7	10	42	.300	.352	.259	6.16	1.47
Livingston, Bobby	L-L	6-3	205	9-3-82	0	0	1.29	1	1	0	0	7	6	2	1	0	2	3	.231	.125	.278	3.86	2.57
3-team total (1 Columbus, 3 Norfolk)					1	0	2.70	5	4	0	0	30	33	13	9	3	4	17	—	—	—	5.10	1.20
Machi, Jean	R-R	5-11	245	2-1-82	1	1	2.12	13	0	0	6	17	8	4	4	1	6	12	.148	.143	.150	6.35	3.18
Mateo, Juan	R-R	6-2	235	12-17-82	7	7	3.79	48	0	0	4	71	69	33	30	4	16	45	.261	.287	.245	5.68	2.02
McCutchen, Daniel	R-R	6-2	215	9-26-82	13	6	3.47	24	24	0	0	143	145	63	55	10	29	110	.264	.242	.279	6.94	1.83
Meek, Evan	R-R	6-0	220	5-12-83	0	0	1.04	6	0	0	0	9	3	1	1	0	7	7	.107	.250	.033	7.27	7.27
Meloan, John	R-R	6-3	225	7-11-84	0	0	1.17	6	0	0	0	8	3	1	1	1	1	8	.120	.400	.050	9.39	1.17
3-team total (25 Columbus, 10 Durham)					0	0	4.57	41	2	0	0	65	68	33	33	9	28	60	—	—	—	8.31	3.88
Morton, Charlie	R-R	6-4	190	11-12-83	0	0	0.00	1	1	0	0	7	4	0	0	0	1	7	.174	.125	.200	9.00	1.29
2-team total (10 Gwinnett)					7	2	2.26	11	11	1	0	72	56	18	18	3	17	62	—	—	—	7.79	2.13
Powell, Jeremy	R-R	6-5	230	6-18-76	4	7	3.74	34	10	0	2	99	114	48	41	9	26	61	.286	.281	.290	5.56	2.37
Sanchez, Romulo	R-R	6-5	260	4-28-84	1	0	4.38	10	0	0	0	12	11	6	6	1	5	15	.239	.200	.269	10.95	3.65
2-team total (19 Scranton/W-B)					6	5	4.09	29	13	0	0	77	77	37	35	4	39	79	—	—	—	9.23	4.56
Slocum, Brian	R-R	6-2	215	3-27-81	1	3	3.94	19	0	0	2	32	30	14	14	1	19	28	.254	.235	.269	7.88	5.34
Smith, Sean	R-R	6-4	195	10-13-83	1	0	0.93	3	1	0	0	10	8	1	1	0	3	9	.242	.182	.273	8.38	2.79
Snell, Ian	R-R	5-11	200	10-30-81	2	2	0.96	6	6	1	0	37	28	7	4	0	13	47	.209	.190	.225	11.33	3.13
Sues, Jeff	R-R	6-4	230	6-8-83	0	0	6.00	8	0	0	0	12	13	10	8	1	8	12	.289	.167	.333	9.00	6.00
Taubenheim, Ty	R-R	6-5	255	11-17-82	7	9	3.65	26	19	0	0	106	108	53	43	8	37	63	.265	.316	.228	5.35	3.14
Vasquez, Virgil	R-R	6-3	205	6-7-82	7	4	3.93	19	19	1	0	108	116	50	47	14	16	72	.276	.286	.272	6.02	1.34
Veal, Donald	L-L	6-4	230	9-18-84	0	1	6.43	9	1	0	0	14	6	10	10	0	16	13	.136	.154	.129	8.36	10.29

Fielding

Catcher	PCT	G	PO	A	E	DP	PB
Diaz	.979	27	168	23	4	3	3
Doumit	1.000	4	17	2	0	0	0
Gimenez	1.000	6	39	1	0	1	1
Kratz	.991	91	628	55	6	5	8
Melhuse	1.000	16	92	6	0	0	1
Perez	1.000	6	41	3	0	0	3

First Base	PCT	G	PO	A	E	DP
Barnwell	1.000	1	5	0	0	0
Bozied	.989	11	87	5	1	11
Broadway	1.000	17	140	6	0	8
Clement	.995	22	181	7	1	15
Cruz	.952	3	19	1	1	1
Diaz	.941	4	31	1	2	1
Gimenez	.985	10	63	3	1	9
Jones	1.000	1	7	0	0	2
Kratz	1.000	2	5	0	0	0
Myrow	.991	13	94	13	1	11
Pearce	.993	64	528	38	4	62
Perez	1.000	1	5	0	0	1
Snelling	1.000	2	14	2	0	0

Second Base	PCT	G	PO	A	E	DP
Barnwell	.973	10	13	23	1	4
Bixler	.962	27	43	59	4	18
Cruz	1.000	5	12	19	0	5
Ford	.968	77	126	180	10	45
Lopez	.992	27	52	70	1	26
Machado	1.000	2	3	2	0	1
Phillips	1.000	4	9	5	0	3

Third Base	PCT	G	PO	A	E	DP
Barnwell	.930	16	9	31	3	2
Bixler	1.000	2	2	5	0	1
Bozied	.833	4	5	4	2	1
Cruz	.875	13	6	22	4	4
Diaz	.875	4	1	6	1	0
Gimenez	.885	12	5	18	3	0
Lopez	.857	8	4	8	2	2
Machado	1.000	1	0	1	0	0
Walker	.932	89	71	147	16	16

Shortstop	PCT	G	PO	A	E	DP
Barnwell	.943	16	17	33	3	6
Bixler	.976	61	88	155	6	37
Cruz	.993	30	49	86	1	23
Diaz	.969	43	55	131	6	24
Wilson	1.000	2	0	5	0	1

Outfield	PCT	G	PO	A	E	DP
Barnwell	.955	39	80	5	4	0
Bixler	.982	15	54	2	1	1
Bozied	.939	37	76	1	5	0
Broadway	1.000	19	30	2	0	0
Cruz	1.000	12	23	4	0	0
Delaney	1.000	1	3	0	0	0
Diaz	—	1	0	0	0	0
Gimenez	1.000	3	4	0	0	0
Jones	.987	69	147	0	2	0
Lopez	.833	4	5	0	1	0
McCutchen	1.000	48	118	5	0	2
Milledge	.951	17	37	2	2	1
Myrow	1.000	38	75	3	0	2
Pacheco	1.000	5	11	0	0	0
Pearce	.800	2	4	0	1	0
Salazar	.978	83	174	7	4	1
Snelling	1.000	15	18	1	0	0
Tabata	.987	32	72	2	1	1

ALTOONA CURVE

DOUBLE-A

EASTERN LEAGUE

Batting	B-T	HT	WT	DOB	AVG	vLH	vRH	G	AB	R	H	2B	3B	HR	RBI	BB	HBP	SH	SF	SO	SB	CS	SLG	OBP
Alvarez, Pedro	L-R	6-3	235	2-6-87	.333	.324	.338	60	222	42	74	18	0	13	40	34	0	0	2	59	1	0	.590	.419
Boone, James	B-R	6-2	195	3-16-83	.179	.071	.211	43	123	11	22	5	0	1	10	7	2	1	0	29	0	0	.244	.235
Chang, Ray	R-R	5-11	205	8-24-83	.291	.136	.373	41	127	22	37	14	0	2	19	15	5	3	2	16	1	2	.449	.383
Corley, Brad	R-R	6-2	198	12-28-83	.221	.222	.221	31	104	14	23	6	1	4	14	4	1	0	1	25	0	1	.413	.255
Corsaletti, Jeff	L-R	6-0	190	2-22-83	.230	.276	.218	89	278	31	64	14	3	2	23	50	1	1	1	33	6	3	.324	.348
Delaney, Jason	R-R	6-3	215	11-9-82	.271	.231	.287	125	435	49	118	25	5	7	65	57	2	1	2	90	1	3	.400	.357
Durham, Miles	R-R	6-4	205	3-21-83	.275	.253	.286	65	240	31	66	17	2	5	34	20	2	0	4	57	8	2	.425	.331
Ford, Shelby	B-R	6-3	185	12-15-84	.233	.194	.250	29	103	12	24	6	0	2	17	12	2	0	0	8	2	0	.350	.325
Friday, Brian	R-R	5-11	180	12-16-85	.265	.289	.255	110	407	48	108	22	3	7	46	51	11	5	2	69	7	5	.386	.361
Gimenez, Hector	B-R	5-10	210	9-28-82	.286	.368	.253	41	133	16	38	6	1	6	18	6	0	1	1	22	2	1	.481	.314
Gonzalez, Angel	L-R	5-11	165	12-28-85	.192	.208	.189	66	172	17	33	6	1	1	14	14	1	5	1	37	2	1	.256	.255
Hernandez, Gorkys	R-R	6-0	175	9-7-87	.262	.240	.270	86	344	45	90	14	2	3	31	24	2	2	2	76	9	8	.340	.312
Lerud, Steve	L-R	6-1	210	10-13-84	.240	.202	.256	95	304	31	73	17	0	4	26	38	10	6	5	53	2	1	.336	.339
Lopez, Pedro	R-R	6-1	190	4-28-84	.263	.396	.218	53	190	24	50	3	1	3	16	13	1	6	2	20	1	3	.337	.311
Machado, Anderson	B-R	6-0	185	1-25-81	.185	.192	.182	28	81	9	15	4	1	0	2	14	1	1	0	21	4	1	.259	.313
Negrych, Jim	L-R	5-10	180	3-2-85	.272	.268	.274	93	323	51	88	18	1	3	30	45	3	6	1	37	8	1	.362	.366

Name	B-T	HT	WT	DOB	AVG	vLH	vRH	G	AB	R	H	2B	3B	HR	RBI	BB	HBP	SH	SF	SO	SB	CS	SLG	OBP
Pacheco, Jonel	R-R	5-9	170	10-3-82	.275	.288	.270	122	432	58	119	24	2	14	58	27	5	1	4	89	15	12	.438	.323
Perez, Miguel	R-R	6-3	235	9-25-83	.262	.226	.283	30	84	14	22	5	0	2	12	8	4	0	1	21	0	0	.393	.351
Prasch, Eddie	L-R	6-1	191	1-25-86	.294	.000	.313	8	17	4	5	0	0	0	0	0	2	1	0	4	0	0	.294	.368
Reyes, Milver	R-R	5-11	200	9-3-82	.282	.500	.226	14	39	4	11	5	0	0	3	4	0	2	0	9	0	0	.410	.349
Romak, Jamie	R-R	6-2	220	9-30-85	.175	.259	.146	64	211	12	37	12	0	5	24	18	2	1	4	66	1	0	.303	.243
Tabata, Jose	R-R	5-11	215	8-12-88	.303	.317	.298	61	228	31	69	15	1	2	25	20	5	0	1	25	7	6	.404	.370

Pitching	B-T	HT	WT	DOB	W	L	ERA	G	GS	CG	SV	IP	H	R	ER	HR	BB	SO	AVG	vLH	vRH	K/9	BB/9
Alderson, Tim	R-R	6-6	217	11-3-88	3	1	4.66	7	7	0	0	39	39	23	20	4	13	18	.257	.253	.262	4.19	3.03
2-team total (13 Connecticut)					9	2	3.88	20	20	0	0	111	115	54	48	9	27	64	—	—	—	5.17	2.18
Bloom, Kyle	R-L	6-4	185	2-21-83	6	9	4.05	22	21	0	0	104	92	60	47	3	57	71	.238	.185	.261	6.12	4.92
Castorri, Christian	R-R	6-3	215	12-17-83	1	1	17.36	5	0	0	0	5	12	10	9	1	3	3	.500	.364	.615	5.79	5.79
Crotta, Mike	R-R	6-6	210	9-24-84	7	8	4.76	27	27	0	0	144	181	90	76	7	33	97	.304	.319	.286	6.08	2.07
Dubee, Michael	R-R	6-3	185	1-12-86	3	0	2.91	26	0	0	1	34	39	21	11	5	10	28	.277	.232	.306	7.41	2.65
Dumatrait, Phil	R-L	6-2	200	7-12-81	0	1	11.25	1	1	0	0	4	9	5	5	0	0	4	.450	.200	.533	9.00	0.00
Hamman, Corey	L-L	6-2	200	4-12-80	0	3	3.68	29	0	0	1	29	28	15	12	1	8	21	.259	.156	.333	6.44	2.45
Hankins, Derek	R-R	6-4	192	7-1-83	3	4	4.42	19	9	0	1	71	70	40	35	6	26	66	.252	.252	.252	8.33	3.28
Herrera, Yoslan	R-R	6-2	200	4-28-81	11	1	3.23	23	15	0	0	98	98	39	35	5	33	65	.268	.280	.257	5.99	3.04
Herron, Tyler	R-R	6-3	190	8-5-86	0	2	4.50	8	4	0	0	26	30	13	13	1	15	18	.294	.239	.339	6.23	5.19
Hill, Josh	R-R	6-3	225	3-27-83	0	1	5.45	22	0	0	0	35	41	24	21	4	11	21	.293	.284	.301	5.45	2.86
Holdzkom, Lincoln	R-R	6-5	245	3-23-82	0	1	0.00	14	0	0	0	17	15	7	0	1	10	10	.250	.192	.294	5.29	5.29
Hughes, Jared	R-R	6-7	220	7-4-85	1	6	3.88	17	7	0	3	46	55	31	20	1	16	36	.296	.304	.287	6.99	3.11
Krebs, Eric	R-R	6-3	210	5-16-85	2	4	4.86	10	0	0	0	17	11	12	9	1	17	15	.204	.211	.200	8.10	9.18
Lincoln, Brad	L-R	6-0	215	5-25-85	1	5	2.28	13	13	1	0	75	63	22	19	4	18	65	.228	.231	.225	7.80	2.16
Machi, Jean	R-R	5-11	245	2-1-82	2	3	2.08	28	0	0	6	35	28	12	8	2	13	25	.226	.294	.178	6.49	3.38
Mateo, Juan	R-R	6-2	235	12-17-82	0	0	0.00	1	0	0	0	1	1	0	0	0	0	1	.250	.000	.333	9.00	0.00
Molleken, Dustin	L-R	6-4	228	8-21-84	1	1	4.62	18	0	0	1	37	37	21	19	5	16	26	.257	.304	.213	6.32	3.89
Moskos, Danny	R-L	6-1	210	4-28-86	11	10	3.74	27	25	1	0	149	159	75	62	11	58	77	.279	.281	.279	4.65	3.50
Nestor, Scott	R-R	6-4	225	8-20-84	2	3	5.31	33	0	0	10	42	35	26	25	7	29	47	.229	.253	.205	9.99	6.17
2-team total (3 Reading)					2	3	5.83	36	0	0	10	46	38	31	30	8	35	51	—	—	—	9.91	6.80
Newsom, Randy	R-R	6-2	200	5-6-82	2	1	17.36	5	0	0	0	5	8	9	9	1	6	2	.421	.286	.500	3.86	11.57
2-team total (8 Akron)					4	1	6.75	13	0	0	1	16	14	13	12	1	13	5	—	—	—	2.81	7.31
Nottingham, Shawn	L-L	6-1	190	1-22-85	0	1	8.37	26	0	0	0	24	34	22	22	1	19	22	.333	.303	.348	8.37	7.23
Robles, Moises	R-R	6-2	170	4-17-84	1	0	6.48	6	0	0	0	8	12	6	6	3	2	7	.333	.400	.250	7.56	2.16
Smith, Sean	R-R	6-4	195	10-13-83	3	3	2.95	22	3	1	7	61	48	23	20	4	23	53	.219	.176	.261	7.82	3.39
2-team total (7 New Hampshire)					3	3	2.82	29	9	1	7	89	72	31	28	5	36	84	—	—	—	8.46	3.63
Sues, Jeff	R-R	6-4	230	6-8-83	2	6	4.46	40	0	0	2	79	66	43	39	7	37	74	.225	.205	.241	8.47	4.23
Vasquez, Samuel	R-R	6-4	175	12-21-84	0	2	2.84	8	0	0	4	13	8	4	4	0	6	13	.182	.111	.231	9.24	4.26
Veal, Donald	L-L	6-4	230	9-18-84	0	0	1.35	7	5	0	0	13	5	2	2	0	10	18	.116	.067	.143	12.15	6.75
Watson, Tony	L-L	6-4	223	5-30-85	0	3	8.22	5	5	0	0	15	22	18	14	2	11	14	.344	.353	.340	8.22	6.46

Fielding

Catcher	PCT	G	PO	A	E	DP	PB
Gimenez	.991	17	96	12	1	3	0
Lerud	.991	93	569	72	6	7	15
Perez	.983	29	170	6	3	1	4
Reyes	.988	14	80	4	1	0	2

First Base	PCT	G	PO	A	E	DP
Delaney	.988	43	369	35	5	39
Durham	.989	40	333	17	4	33
Gimenez	.958	2	23	0	1	2
Machado	.975	5	38	1	1	4
Romak	.986	57	460	42	7	62

Second Base	PCT	G	PO	A	E	DP
Chang	1.000	11	25	29	0	6
Ford	.978	29	47	85	3	20
Gonzalez	.955	11	28	35	3	14
Lopez	.935	6	11	18	2	5
Machado	.900	7	13	14	3	7
Negrych	.961	85	166	231	16	58
Prasch	1.000	2	2	2	0	1

Third Base	PCT	G	PO	A	E	DP
Alvarez	.917	51	40	93	12	11
Chang	.972	9	6	29	1	2
Gimenez	.958	17	10	36	2	2
Gonzalez	.891	43	28	62	11	10
Lopez	.915	16	12	31	4	1
Machado	.972	16	7	28	1	2
Prasch	.750	2	2	1	1	0

Shortstop	PCT	G	PO	A	E	DP
Chang	1.000	10	18	27	0	8
Friday	.948	102	159	300	25	69
Gonzalez	.853	8	12	17	5	4
Lopez	.951	25	48	88	7	30
Machado	.833	2	1	4	1	1

Outfield	PCT	G	PO	A	E	DP
Boone	.969	38	62	1	2	0
Chang	1.000	1	1	0	0	0
Corley	1.000	24	43	0	0	0
Corsaletti	.963	78	130	1	5	0
Delaney	.983	38	54	3	1	1
Durham	.939	21	30	1	2	1
Hernandez	.981	83	200	8	4	1
Lopez	1.000	3	5	0	0	0
Machado	1.000	3	4	0	0	0
Pacheco	.990	109	189	6	2	2
Tabata	.991	55	109	4	1	1

LYNCHBURG HILLCATS — HIGH CLASS A

CAROLINA LEAGUE

Batting	B-T	HT	WT	DOB	AVG	vLH	vRH	G	AB	R	H	2B	3B	HR	RBI	BB	HBP	SH	SF	SO	SB	CS	SLG	OBP
Alvarez, Pedro	L-R	6-3	235	2-6-87	.247	.218	.268	66	243	38	60	14	1	14	55	37	0	0	4	70	1	1	.486	.342
Chang, Ray	R-R	5-11	205	8-24-83	.303	.367	.242	36	122	22	37	9	0	0	28	14	4	2	2	14	1	1	.377	.387
Collins, Joel	R-R	6-1	200	4-24-86	.179	.143	.200	19	56	9	10	2	0	0	1	5	8	1	0	12	0	0	.214	.333
D'Arnaud, Chase	R-R	6-1	175	1-21-87	.295	.413	.245	54	210	45	62	19	4	4	26	30	9	2	2	41	14	5	.481	.402
Davis, Marcus	R-R	6-3	200	10-11-84	.180	.143	.200	17	61	9	11	2	1	2	4	5	2	1	0	24	4	1	.344	.265
De Los Santos, Jose L.	R-R	5-11	160	2-17-85	.247	.242	.250	114	453	70	112	5	6	0	31	29	3	9	3	96	53	8	.285	.295
Durham, Miles	R-R	6-4	205	3-21-83	.296	.295	.296	65	247	39	73	19	4	7	39	17	3	0	0	55	8	2	.490	.348
Fryer, Eric	R-R	6-2	215	8-26-85	.242	.238	.243	47	157	22	38	11	0	3	14	22	7	1	0	25	0	0	.369	.360
Gonzalez, Angel	L-R	5-11	165	12-28-85	.138	.000	.167	8	29	1	4	0	0	0	2	2	0	0	0	9	0	0	.138	.194
Hague, Matt	R-R	6-3	225	8-20-85	.293	.282	.299	122	454	52	133	30	0	8	50	40	8	0	6	67	3	2	.412	.356
Harrison, Josh	R-R	5-8	175	7-8-87	.270	.326	.242	34	141	15	38	8	1	1	13	1	4	6	3	19	4	1	.362	.289
Huber, Erik	R-R	6-6	230	3-6-85	.262	.308	.241	33	122	9	32	9	0	0	11	3	2	2	1	17	1	0	.336	.289

PITTSBURGH PIRATES

PITTSBURGH PIRATES

	B-T	HT	WT	DOB	AVG	vLH	vRH	G	AB	R	H	2B	3B	HR	RBI	BB	HBP	SH	SF	SO	SB	CS	SLG	OBP
Keel, Jared	R-R	6-1	190	8-3-84	.229	.284	.201	98	301	49	69	21	0	11	44	68	6	5	3	72	1	3	.409	.378
Loyola, Maiko	R-R	5-11	180	7-19-85	.198	.179	.207	43	131	20	26	7	1	5	22	12	0	3	3	34	4	3	.382	.260
Marte, Starling	R-R	6-1	170	10-9-88	1.000	—	1.000	1	2	0	2	0	0	0	1	0	0	0	0	0	0	0	1.000	1.000
Mercer, Jordy	R-R	6-3	191	8-27-86	.255	.253	.257	131	513	64	131	36	4	10	83	41	9	3	14	93	10	6	.400	.314
Milledge, Lastings	R-R	6-0	205	4-5-85	.250	.000	.273	3	12	3	3	1	0	2	4	1	0	0	0	3	0	0	.833	.308
Prasch, Eddie	L-R	6-1	191	1-25-86	.179	.159	.187	47	151	20	27	10	2	0	19	22	6	1	4	40	1	2	.272	.301
Presley, Alex	L-L	5-9	180	7-25-85	.257	.190	.284	115	417	51	107	17	11	4	37	30	0	7	2	87	9	5	.379	.305
Romak, Jamie	R-R	6-2	220	9-30-85	.213	.179	.223	42	160	15	34	9	0	3	14	14	5	0	1	44	0	2	.325	.294
Rosero, Ciro	R-R	6-1	160	7-25-86	.294	.300	.286	10	17	0	5	2	0	0	3	3	0	0	0	8	0	2	.412	.400
Sakamoto, Kent	R-R	6-0	229	11-3-83	.189	.231	.164	72	243	34	46	11	1	7	29	28	7	1	1	60	1	3	.329	.290
Sanchez, Tony	R-R	6-0	220	5-20-88	.200	.000	.250	3	10	2	2	2	0	0	1	1	0	0	0	4	0	0	.400	.385
Watts, Kris	L-R	6-1	209	7-15-84	.291	.260	.304	103	340	54	99	21	3	7	49	55	12	2	3	51	2	0	.432	.405

Pitching	B-T	HT	WT	DOB	W	L	ERA	G	GS	CG	SV	IP	H	R	ER	HR	BB	SO	AVG	vLH	vRH	K/9	BB/9
Adcock, Nathan	R-R	6-5	190	2-25-88	3	2	5.25	7	4	0	0	24	29	17	14	5	7	15	.296	.267	.321	5.63	2.63
Bishop, Harrison	R-R	6-3	210	8-17-84	2	4	5.02	35	0	0	2	81	74	51	45	5	24	73	.240	.258	.221	8.14	2.68
Boleska, Mike	R-R	6-0	190	7-30-86	1	1	1.60	16	0	0	0	39	39	10	7	2	4	22	.258	.291	.222	5.03	0.92
Castorri, Christian	R-R	6-3	215	12-17-83	2	1	7.20	13	0	0	0	20	32	16	16	2	7	19	.352	.356	.348	8.55	3.15
Cheng, Chi-Hung	L-L	6-1	210	6-20-85	7	3	4.16	20	16	0	0	84	98	43	39	9	23	39	.289	.288	.290	4.16	2.45
Colla, Mike	R-R	6-2	220	12-23-86	6	3	4.31	37	0	0	0	65	70	31	31	7	19	52	.269	.273	.265	7.24	2.64
Cullen, Chris	R-R	6-1	190	10-16-86	4	4	5.01	39	0	0	2	65	64	39	36	6	18	36	.264	.292	.238	5.01	2.51
Dubee, Michael	R-R	6-3	185	1-12-86	2	0	1.05	23	0	0	6	34	22	5	4	1	3	52	.182	.175	.188	13.63	0.79
2-team total (2 Winston-Salem)					2	1	1.45	25	0	0	6	37	27	7	6	1	3	53	—			12.78	0.72
Felix, Mike	L-L	5-11	206	8-13-85	0	0	7.71	7	0	0	0	9	8	9	8	0	9	5	.235	.375	.111	4.82	8.68
Garcia, Harvey	R-R	6-2	220	3-16-84	1	0	2.77	10	0	0	1	13	7	4	4	2	2	16	.152	.154	.150	11.08	1.38
Krol, Noah	B-R	6-2	185	6-6-84	1	1	1.80	3	0	0	0	5	4	1	1	0	1	4	.222	.333	.167	7.20	1.80
Locke, Jeff	L-L	6-2	180	11-20-87	4	4	4.08	17	17	0	0	82	98	44	37	4	18	56	.305	.310	.303	6.17	1.98
2-team total (10 Myrtle Beach)					5	8	4.59	27	27	0	0	127	145	75	65	5	44	99	—			7.00	3.11
McSwain, Matt	R-R	6-2	185	8-15-85	11	8	3.43	28	25	1	1	144	162	60	55	3	23	64	.285	.306	.261	3.99	1.43
Mildren, Paul	R-L	6-1	195	5-3-84	3	6	5.77	27	11	0	0	73	98	49	47	10	14	44	.328	.371	.307	5.40	1.72
Molleken, Dustin	L-R	6-4	228	8-21-84	3	1	3.48	18	1	0	1	41	36	17	16	2	8	42	.240	.240	.243	9.15	1.74
Morris, Bryan	L-R	6-3	200	3-28-87	4	9	5.57	15	15	0	0	73	87	58	45	2	34	32	.295	.308	.279	3.96	4.21
Owens, Rudy	L-L	6-3	215	12-18-87	1	1	3.86	6	6	0	0	23	29	10	10	3	2	22	.305	.333	.292	8.49	0.77
Robles, Moises	R-R	6-2	170	4-17-84	0	2	4.43	28	0	0	0	43	48	22	21	4	7	26	.287	.321	.256	5.48	1.48
Rodriguez, R.J.	R-R	6-0	175	7-5-84	6	3	3.08	48	0	0	27	50	37	19	17	2	27	41	.214	.182	.247	7.43	4.89
Uviedo, Ronald	R-R	6-1	160	10-7-86	5	5	3.36	23	18	0	3	102	98	42	38	12	28	79	.254	.257	.250	6.99	2.48
Vasquez, Samuel	R-R	6-4	175	12-21-84	1	0	2.49	11	0	0	0	22	20	10	6	1	9	22	.241	.174	.324	9.14	3.74
Wilson, Justin	L-L	6-2	233	8-18-87	6	8	4.50	26	26	0	0	116	118	64	58	14	55	94	.262	.245	.269	7.29	4.27

Fielding

Catcher	PCT	G	PO	A	E	DP	PB
Collins	.992	19	106	15	1	2	2
Fryer	.989	37	227	34	3	4	3
Sanchez	.909	2	8	2	1	0	0
Watts	.997	82	532	47	2	3	9

First Base	PCT	G	PO	A	E	DP
Chang	1.000	1	10	1	0	1
Durham	1.000	3	34	3	0	5
Hague	.995	117	1086	59	6	104
Sakamoto	.990	19	188	10	2	15

Second Base	PCT	G	PO	A	E	DP
Chang	1.000	12	14	38	0	7
D'Arnaud	.920	25	50	76	11	16
De Los Santos	.978	75	145	256	9	66
Gonzalez	.929	3	11	15	2	4
Harrison	.985	15	28	39	1	9
Prasch	1.000	10	18	23	0	4

Third Base	PCT	G	PO	A	E	DP
Alvarez	.923	58	41	115	13	5
Chang	1.000	8	5	14	0	2
De Los Santos	.895	10	2	15	2	1
Gonzalez	1.000	3	1	2	0	1
Hague	1.000	1	2	5	0	1
Harrison	.963	18	13	39	2	2
Mercer	.967	21	13	45	2	7
Prasch	.918	21	13	43	5	4

Shortstop	PCT	G	PO	A	E	DP
Chang	1.000	5	8	14	0	2
D'Arnaud	.975	26	50	68	3	19
Gonzalez	.800	2	3	1	1	0
Mercer	.964	107	166	344	19	86

Outfield	PCT	G	PO	A	E	DP
Davis	.973	17	35	1	1	0
De Los Santos	.931	29	65	2	5	0
Durham	.964	62	106	0	4	0
Harrison	1.000	1	1	0	0	0
Huber	1.000	33	65	1	0	1
Keel	.962	91	145	5	6	1
Loyola	1.000	38	78	1	0	0
Marte	1.000	1	1	0	0	0
Milledge	.833	3	5	0	1	0
Prasch	1.000	3	4	0	0	0
Presley	.966	109	223	4	8	1
Romak	.959	33	45	2	2	1
Rosero	1.000	5	7	0	0	0

WEST VIRGINIA POWER   LOW CLASS A

SOUTH ATLANTIC LEAGUE

Batting	B-T	HT	WT	DOB	AVG	vLH	vRH	G	AB	R	H	2B	3B	HR	RBI	BB	HBP	SH	SF	SO	SB	CS	SLG	OBP
Anderson, Calvin	R-R	6-7	240	5-8-87	.274	.230	.288	101	372	50	102	18	5	12	64	33	11	2	5	110	1	1	.446	.347
Biela, Butch	R-R	5-11	189	12-26-88	.000	.000	.000	4	12	0	0	0	0	0	1	1	0	0	1	3	0	0	.000	.071
Bomback, Daniel	B-R	5-11	185	9-5-84	.231	.212	.238	69	234	38	54	13	3	2	27	22	12	2	1	29	2	2	.338	.327
Chourio, Adenson	B-R	5-9	160	7-22-86	.243	.200	.255	98	301	40	73	7	1	0	21	31	7	7	1	71	27	9	.272	.326
D'Arnaud, Chase	R-R	6-1	175	1-21-87	.291	.302	.288	62	213	32	62	14	3	3	31	30	8	1	3	31	17	3	.427	.394
Davis, Marcus	R-R	6-3	200	11-11-84	.204	.250	.192	28	98	12	20	2	1	1	9	11	3	2	0	28	5	1	.276	.304
Farrell, Jeremy	R-R	6-3	200	11-11-86	.248	.246	.249	73	270	42	67	13	1	5	39	30	8	0	4	71	1	2	.359	.337
Garcia, Edward	R-R	6-1	152	8-17-88	.164	.158	.167	22	73	8	12	1	0	0	3	5	1	0	0	23	7	2	.178	.228
Gonzalez, Benji	R-R	5-11	160	1-16-90	.250	.333	.222	3	12	2	3	1	0	0	1	1	0	1	0	1	0	1	.333	.308
Grossman, Robbie	B-L	6-1	190	9-16-89	.266	.330	.248	116	451	83	120	21	2	5	42	75	2	7	0	164	35	12	.355	.373
Huber, Erik	R-R	6-6	230	3-6-85	.318	.300	.321	72	217	47	88	19	2	5	40	15	7	0	2	35	4	0	.455	.365
Latimore, Quincy	R-R	5-10	175	2-3-89	.251	.242	.253	118	479	63	120	24	10	11	70	23	8	1	2	116	3	3	.411	.295
Marte, Starling	R-R	6-1	170	10-9-88	.312	.320	.310	54	221	41	69	9	5	3	34	12	12	0	2	55	24	7	.439	.377
McClune, Austin	R-R	6-2	175	11-15-87	.256	.286	.247	87	308	41	79	16	1	1	28	28	4	8	4	59	12	4	.325	.323

	B-T	HT	WT	DOB	AVG	vLH	vRH	G	AB	R	H	2B	3B	HR	RBI	BB	HBP	SH	SF	SO	SB	CS	SLG	OBP
Morgan, Kyle	L-L	6-1	215	8-8-86	.296	.324	.288	43	159	34	47	12	0	9	32	20	4	1	3	38	1	0	.541	.382
Peley, Jose	R-R	6-0	177	12-24-87	.188	.205	.183	67	224	18	42	8	1	0	24	16	2	1	2	41	2	1	.232	.246
Picart, Greg	B-R	5-11	175	9-25-85	.308	.296	.311	67	237	29	73	10	4	2	25	31	6	3	2	27	6	7	.409	.399
Sanchez, Tony	R-R	6-0	220	5-20-88	.316	.500	.282	41	155	29	49	15	1	7	46	21	8	0	4	34	1	0	.561	.415
Spain, Bobby	L-R	6-4	215	5-2-85	.275	.306	.266	94	335	46	92	15	1	4	47	28	4	0	2	59	0	2	.361	.336
Walker, Andrew	R-R	6-0	210	1-22-86	.211	.265	.188	35	114	14	24	8	1	1	13	20	2	1	2	28	0	1	.325	.333
Willemburg, Brett	B-R	6-1	190	7-2-84	.103	.333	.077	11	29	4	3	0	0	0	3	5	0	0	0	10	1	0	.103	.235

Pitching	B-T	HT	WT	DOB	W	L	ERA	G	GS	CG	SV	IP	H	R	ER	HR	BB	SO	AVG	vLH	vRH	K/9	BB/9
Alvarado, Gabriel	R-R	6-2	175	5-19-87	6	10	5.05	25	21	1	2	114	135	82	64	11	33	96	.290	.284	.294	7.58	2.61
Amato, Gary	R-R	6-0	210	2-5-86	0	1	2.89	6	0	0	0	9	11	6	3	1	1	7	.306	.417	.250	6.75	0.96
Bankston, Maurice	R-R	6-4	205	6-17-87	1	4	4.98	9	9	0	0	43	48	26	24	3	16	25	.284	.293	.277	5.19	3.32
Brolsma, Owen	R-R	6-2	210	10-6-84	0	2	2.92	27	0	0	2	37	38	19	12	0	15	21	.262	.358	.207	5.11	3.65
Cox, Tyler	R-L	6-3	200	4-19-86	0	4	10.25	8	6	0	0	26	40	31	30	2	12	17	.360	.400	.349	5.81	4.10
De Los Santos, Rafael	R-R	6-4	191	12-10-86	0	3	6.68	14	8	0	1	32	29	32	24	1	35	23	.254	.225	.270	6.40	9.74
Erickson, Casey	R-R	6-3	187	8-28-85	5	1	1.17	15	3	0	5	38	36	8	5	1	6	32	.245	.258	.235	7.51	1.41
2-team total (21 Charleston, SC)					8	4	1.75	36	6	0	5	82	87	22	16	1	19	69	—	—	—	7.54	2.08
Hinkle, Brad	R-R	6-10	220	10-13-84	1	0	7.11	3	0	0	0	6	11	5	5	1	2	3	.393	.143	.476	4.26	2.84
Kelly, William	R-R	6-2	170	10-30-87	3	2	4.30	30	0	0	6	69	83	46	33	8	9	67	.293	.270	.310	8.74	1.17
Knotts, Alan	R-R	6-4	230	2-28-85	0	0	0.00	4	0	0	1	6	1	0	0	0	0	6	.053	.000	.091	9.00	0.00
Krol, Noah	B-R	6-2	185	6-6-84	5	0	2.92	21	0	0	2	37	39	21	12	3	11	32	.269	.255	.278	7.78	2.68
Laureano, Melkin	R-R	6-3	205	8-26-85	0	0	0.00	3	0	0	0	2	0	0	0	0	1	6	.000	.000	.000	27.00	4.50
Leach, Brian	R-R	6-3	195	4-14-86	7	4	2.96	32	12	0	0	109	91	49	36	8	39	88	.221	.215	.227	7.24	3.21
Lorin, Brett	L-R	6-7	245	3-31-87	3	1	1.57	7	7	0	0	34	33	10	6	2	10	29	.264	.265	.263	7.60	2.62
Martinez, Yoffri	R-R	6-4	210	12-17-85	4	5	6.57	29	0	0	0	37	33	30	27	5	27	29	.241	.160	.287	7.05	6.57
McPherson, Kyle	B-R	6-3	205	11-11-87	5	2	4.94	13	8	0	0	51	53	32	28	3	6	32	.269	.244	.288	5.65	1.06
Miller, Quinton	R-R	6-1	185	11-28-89	2	3	4.47	12	12	0	0	56	50	35	28	5	25	40	.245	.257	.239	6.39	3.99
Moreno, Diego	R-R	6-1	177	7-21-86	1	3	2.60	18	0	0	5	45	29	16	13	3	14	57	.182	.250	.146	11.40	2.80
Ortiz, Wilson	R-R	5-11	181	11-6-85	4	3	6.87	36	0	0	1	58	73	48	44	7	24	36	.313	.343	.291	5.62	3.75
Owens, Rudy	L-L	6-3	215	12-18-87	10	1	1.70	19	19	0	0	101	71	22	19	8	15	91	.197	.193	.197	8.14	1.34
Pena, Eddie	R-R	6-4	205	6-18-83	1	4	5.45	29	0	0	8	33	38	23	20	1	13	14	.286	.295	.278	3.82	3.55
Pribanic, Aaron	R-R	6-4	200	9-1-86	4	2	2.15	7	6	0	0	38	32	9	9	5	5	18	.230	.291	.190	4.30	1.19
Strickland, Hunter	R-R	6-5	200	9-24-88	4	2	3.77	8	8	0	0	43	42	23	18	3	6	23	.250	.203	.283	4.81	1.26
2-team total (18 Greenville)					9	6	3.49	26	20	0	1	126	127	62	49	14	19	74	—	—	—	5.27	1.35
Vasquez, Samuel	R-R	6-4	175	12-21-84	1	2	4.71	20	3	0	0	50	58	31	26	5	16	40	.294	.296	.293	7.25	2.90
Welker, Duke	L-R	6-7	220	2-10-86	0	11	5.79	31	15	0	2	101	96	80	65	7	67	69	.253	.247	.257	6.15	5.97

Fielding

Catcher	PCT	G	PO	A	E	DP	PB
Bomback	1.000	6	40	2	0	0	3
Peley	.994	66	414	75	3	6	16
Sanchez	.969	36	256	22	9	4	6
Walker	.981	32	192	20	4	1	8

First Base	PCT	G	PO	A	E	DP
Anderson	.980	58	462	39	10	40
Huber	1.000	38	278	35	0	20
Morgan	.992	41	344	22	3	26
Spain	.500	1	1	0	1	1
Willemburg	1.000	2	9	1	0	0

Second Base	PCT	G	PO	A	E	DP
Bomback	.953	49	82	121	10	20

	PCT	G	PO	A	E	DP
Chourio	.960	53	105	136	10	28
Peley	1.000	1	1	2	0	0
Picart	.969	34	70	86	5	16
Willemburg	.853	6	12	17	5	2

Third Base	PCT	G	PO	A	E	DP
Bomback	.800	3	2	6	2	0
Farrell	.870	70	45	123	25	12
Picart	.900	3	4	5	1	1
Spain	.904	63	41	119	17	7
Willemburg	.750	2	1	2	1	0

Shortstop	PCT	G	PO	A	E	DP
Chourio	.948	44	63	118	10	21
D'Arnaud	.976	61	108	175	7	32

	PCT	G	PO	A	E	DP
Gonzalez	.875	3	4	10	2	0
Picart	.965	30	52	87	5	13
Willemburg	.000	1	0	0	1	0

Outfield	PCT	G	PO	A	E	DP
Biela	1.000	3	4	0	0	0
Davis	.962	21	48	3	2	1
Garcia	.974	22	37	1	1	1
Grossman	.977	113	208	8	5	1
Huber	1.000	4	4	0	0	0
Latimore	.938	114	201	12	14	3
Marte	.950	54	128	5	7	0
McClune	.988	85	222	16	3	5

STATE COLLEGE SPIKES

SHORT-SEASON

NEW YORK-PENN LEAGUE

Batting	B-T	HT	WT	DOB	AVG	vLH	vRH	G	AB	R	H	2B	3B	HR	RBI	BB	HBP	SH	SF	SO	SB	CS	SLG	OBP
Benitez, Deybis	R-R	6-2	170	4-23-87	.133	.333	.000	8	15	1	2	0	0	0	2	3	0	2	0	3	0	2	.133	.278
Biela, Butch	R-R	5-11	189	12-26-88	.196	.189	.200	37	112	13	22	5	0	1	6	14	0	0	0	22	3	1	.268	.286
Byler, Justin	R-R	6-1	233	8-12-85	.256	.258	.255	63	215	34	55	19	2	6	41	24	9	0	2	51	1	0	.447	.352
Chambers, Evan	R-R	5-11	210	3-24-89	.245	.333	.215	58	200	45	49	15	0	4	22	50	0	1	2	78	6	0	.380	.393
Garcia, Edward	B-R	6-1	152	8-1-87	.189	.086	.228	38	127	9	24	2	2	0	17	5	0	1	2	42	6	3	.236	.216
Gonzalez, Elevys	B-R	5-11	175	10-23-89	.216	.294	.176	13	51	5	11	2	2	0	3	1	0	1	0	14	2	1	.333	.231
Hernandez, Jose	L-R	5-11	195	3-19-86	.263	.167	.308	8	19	1	5	1	0	0	1	2	2	0	0	4	1	0	.316	.391
Holt, Brock	L-L	5-10	165	6-11-88	.299	.253	.318	66	254	45	76	14	3	6	33	26	1	0	4	31	9	0	.449	.361
Irvine, Pat	R-L	6-0	197	1-27-86	.245	.283	.233	66	216	22	53	10	6	3	41	28	7	1	3	49	5	2	.389	.346
Mendez, Miguel	R-L	6-1	170	1-8-88	.161	.179	.151	36	112	8	18	2	0	0	6	12	1	2	1	22	0	0	.179	.246
Morgan, Kyle	L-L	6-1	215	8-8-86	.224	.000	.263	20	67	13	15	4	1	3	17	1	2	0	0	14	3	0	.448	.257
Parry, Craig	R-R	6-1	202	5-16-86	.198	.292	.175	44	121	22	24	4	1	1	18	21	3	1	3	32	5	1	.273	.324
Payne, Matt	R-R	6-1	200	3-18-86	.129	.273	.050	10	31	2	4	1	0	0	3	2	0	0	1	4	0	0	.161	.176
Pedron, Freicer	L-R	5-11	160	9-9-86	.167	.000	.200	2	6	0	1	0	0	0	0	0	0	0	0	3	0	0	.167	.167
Rosero, Ciro	R-R	6-1	160	7-25-86	.200	.000	.286	3	10	0	2	0	0	0	2	1	0	0	2	0	0	0	.200	.273
Rubinstein, David	R-R	6-2	190	5-18-87	.267	.319	.247	65	243	32	65	13	3	3	36	13	4	2	5	73	5	3	.383	.309
Sanchez, Tony	R-R	6-0	220	5-20-88	.308	.500	.222	4	13	2	4	1	0	0	1	1	0	0	0	2	0	0	.385	.357
Saukko, Kyle	L-R	5-11	175	12-21-88	.172	.000	.200	28	87	11	15	1	1	0	6	6	0	2	2	25	3	0	.207	.221

	B-T	HT	WT	DOB	AVG	vLH	vRH	G	AB	R	H	2B	3B	HR	RBI	BB	HBP	SH	SF	SO	SB	CS	SLG	OBP
Silva, Carlos	R-R	6-2	165	5-31-87	.357	.167	.409	9	28	2	10	4	0	0	3	1	1	0	0	6	1	1	.500	.400
Summerlin, Ty	R-L	5-11	175	10-6-86	.224	.213	.228	53	174	15	39	5	1	0	11	15	1	3	2	41	0	4	.264	.286
Vasquez, Andy	R-R	6-1	168	10-8-87	.190	.200	.188	42	147	18	28	5	3	0	5	10	1	3	1	37	6	4	.265	.245
Willemburg, Brett	R-R	6-1	190	7-2-84	.125	.000	.143	3	8	1	1	0	0	0	0	0	0	0	0	3	0	0	.125	.125

Pitching	B-T	HT	WT	DOB	W	L	ERA	G	GS	CG	SV	IP	H	R	ER	HR	BB	SO	AVG	vLH	vRH	K/9	BB/9
Baca, Marc	R-R	5-11	175	10-11-86	1	3	3.00	18	0	0	6	18	19	8	6	0	6	10	.271	.333	.250	5.00	3.00
Baker, Nate	L-L	6-3	190	12-27-87	0	0	1.69	6	1	0	0	16	11	4	3	0	2	9	.193	.261	.147	5.06	1.13
Bankston, Maurice	R-R	6-4	205	6-17-87	2	4	2.34	9	9	0	0	50	54	17	13	2	5	25	.271	.318	.248	4.50	0.90
Black, Victor	R-R	6-3	185	5-23-88	1	2	3.45	13	7	0	1	31	26	17	12	0	15	33	.213	.283	.159	9.48	4.31
Brolsma, Owen	R-R	6-2	210	10-6-84	0	0	5.68	5	0	0	1	6	9	4	4	1	3	3	.333	.167	.467	4.26	4.26
Cox, Tyler	R-L	6-3	200	4-19-86	8	3	3.93	15	10	0	0	73	81	42	32	3	15	57	.279	.232	.291	7.00	1.84
Dumatrait, Phil	L-L	6-2	200	7-12-81	0	1	3.60	1	1	0	0	5	5	4	2	1	0	4	.250	—	.250	7.20	0.00
Erickson, Jason	R-R	6-1	175	2-3-87	4	2	2.70	16	8	0	0	57	59	23	17	2	7	49	.263	.256	.269	7.78	1.11
Fagan, Albert	R-R	6-7	205	11-14-86	0	0	45.00	1	0	0	0	1	5	5	5	1	1	0	.714	.500	.800	0.00	9.00
Fallon, Teddy	R-R	6-2	190	10-29-86	1	2	5.51	17	0	0	1	16	17	14	10	0	16	14	.270	.278	.267	7.71	8.82
Felix, Mike	L-L	5-11	206	8-13-85	1	2	3.60	12	4	0	1	35	31	20	14	1	18	13	.235	.120	.262	3.34	4.63
Foster, Zach	R-R	6-6	220	5-24-87	2	0	1.24	20	0	0	1	29	13	5	4	1	16	26	.134	.079	.169	8.07	4.97
Garcia, Diomedes	R-R	—	—	8-13-85	0	0	0.00	2	0	0	0	2	2	0	0	0	0	1	.286	.250	.333	4.50	0.00
Holden, Brandon	R-R	6-4	185	1-1-88	1	0	4.50	19	0	0	0	18	17	9	9	2	7	3	.274	.273	.275	1.50	3.50
Inman, Jeff	R-R	6-3	180	11-24-87	0	0	0.00	2	2	0	0	4	4	0	0	0	2	2	.250	.000	.364	4.50	4.50
Irwin, Phillip	R-R	6-2	220	2-25-87	1	2	2.12	10	7	0	0	30	27	8	7	1	6	32	.243	.241	.246	9.71	1.82
Klinger, Brent	R-R	6-4	185	7-21-88	0	0	0.00	1	1	0	0	3	0	0	0	0	2	0	.000	.000	.000	0.00	6.00
Knotts, Alan	R-R	6-4	230	2-28-85	3	3	4.70	19	0	0	2	31	35	18	16	1	11	25	.289	.333	.260	7.34	3.23
McPherson, Kyle	B-R	6-3	205	11-11-87	4	3	2.99	13	13	0	0	75	70	27	25	5	11	57	.248	.254	.244	6.81	1.31
Miller, Quinton	R-R	6-1	185	11-28-89	0	1	3.86	2	2	0	0	7	10	5	3	0	3	4	.345	.455	.278	5.14	3.86
Moreno, Diego	R-R	6-1	177	7-21-86	0	0	1.80	2	0	0	0	5	4	1	1	1	4	2	.222	.250	.200	7.20	1.80
Paulino, Ricardo	R-R	6-1	182	8-8-86	2	3	2.59	15	6	0	1	59	52	24	17	4	10	44	.233	.250	.222	6.71	1.53
Pereira, Nelson	L-L	5-11	180	2-12-89	4	5	4.35	15	5	0	0	50	41	30	24	4	28	56	.223	.250	.210	10.15	5.07
Williams, Mike	L-L	6-5	235	8-11-86	3	2	3.71	19	0	0	0	34	35	22	14	2	15	29	.265	.310	.252	7.68	3.97

Fielding

Catcher	PCT	G	PO	A	E	DP	PB
Mendez	.979	36	263	21	6	0	4
Parry	.979	42	221	16	5	0	10
Sanchez	.962	4	22	3	1	0	2

First Base	PCT	G	PO	A	E	DP
Baker	.997	39	311	28	1	39
Benitez	1.000	1	3	0	0	0
Byler	.986	31	256	20	4	25
Morgan	1.000	1	7	0	3	0

Second Base	PCT	G	PO	A	E	DP
Benitez	.850	5	5	12	3	2
Gonzalez	.975	11	15	24	1	6
Holt	.989	18	41	49	1	16
Pedron	.667	1	1	1	1	1

		G	PO	A	E	DP
Silva	.800	3	1	3	1	0
Summerlin	.956	44	79	116	9	29
Vasquez	1.000	3	5	7	0	2
Willemburg	1.000	1	1	0	0	0

Third Base	PCT	G	PO	A	E	DP
Irvine	.882	47	24	88	15	5
Payne	.800	10	10	14	6	1
Pedron	.333	1	0	1	2	0
Silva	.929	7	1	12	1	1
Summerlin	.750	4	1	5	2	0
Vasquez	.912	14	8	23	3	4

Shortstop	PCT	G	PO	A	E	DP
Gonzalez	.857	3	1	5	1	1
Holt	.961	45	78	119	8	24

		G	PO	A	E	DP
Summerlin	.857	5	6	6	2	1
Vasquez	.940	27	52	88	9	22
Willemburg	1.000	2	1	3	0	2

Outfield	PCT	G	PO	A	E	DP
Biela	.983	36	58	1	1	0
Chambers	.980	58	143	4	3	1
Garcia	1.000	37	51	3	0	0
Hernandez	.800	6	4	0	1	0
Irvine	.960	16	24	0	1	0
Morgan	1.000	3	3	0	0	0
Rosero	1.000	2	1	0	0	0
Rubinstein	.976	58	113	7	3	0
Saukko	.966	28	54	2	2	0

GCL PIRATES

GULF COAST LEAGUE

ROOKIE

Batting	B-T	HT	WT	DOB	AVG	vLH	vRH	G	AB	R	H	2B	3B	HR	RBI	BB	HBP	SH	SF	SO	SB	CS	SLG	OBP
Acevedo, Andury	R-R	6-4	200	8-23-90	.174	.250	.158	8	23	3	4	3	0	0	2	0	0	0	0	9	0	0	.304	.174
Aguilera, Jesus	R-R	6-1	190	8-9-87	.143	.000	.174	15	28	0	4	1	0	0	4	3	2	0	1	9	0	1	.179	.265
Cabrera, Ramon	B-R	5-7	202	11-5-89	.291	.355	.271	37	127	15	37	11	1	1	16	16	1	2	1	16	2	1	.417	.372
De La Cruz, Melvin	R-R	5-11	180	3-5-90	.205	.259	.188	36	112	8	23	3	0	0	3	7	2	0	0	43	11	8	.232	.264
Doumit, Ryan	B-R	6-1	215	4-3-81	.000	.000	.000	2	7	0	0	0	0	0	0	1	0	0	0	2	0	0	.000	.125
Freeman, Wes	R-R	6-4	215	1-29-90	.210	.182	.218	50	157	18	33	9	0	4	12	14	0	1	0	59	6	4	.344	.275
Gonzalez, Benji	R-R	5-11	160	1-16-90	.289	.406	.260	49	159	23	46	5	1	0	13	17	2	5	1	33	7	5	.333	.363
Gonzalez, Elevys	B-R	5-11	175	10-23-89	.271	.217	.286	35	107	17	29	1	2	1	9	5	0	6	0	21	6	3	.346	.304
Gonzalez, Gemmy	R-R	6-0	189	6-22-88	.160	.214	.148	26	75	7	12	2	0	1	11	4	1	1	1	32	2	1	.227	.210
Gourley, Walker	R-R	6-0	185	6-28-91	.220	.250	.200	18	50	6	11	2	0	0	2	6	1	2	1	11	3	1	.260	.310
Henry, Henry	R-R	5-9	164	5-29-87	.220	.304	.191	29	91	13	20	0	1	1	3	7	1	2	0	8	7	2	.275	.283
Marquez, Jairo	R-R	6-0	170	4-7-88	.281	.263	.286	29	96	8	27	6	1	1	14	6	1	0	0	11	3	2	.396	.330
Marte, Starling	R-R	6-1	170	10-9-88	.000	.000	.000	2	7	1	0	0	0	0	0	0	0	0	0	1	0	0	.000	.000
Milledge, Lastings	R-R	6-0	205	4-5-85	.333	.250	.375	4	12	1	4	2	0	0	2	0	0	0	0	2	1	0	.500	.429
2-team total (3 Nationals)					.294	—	—	7	17	2	5	2	0	1	3	5	0	0	0	2	2	0	.588	.455
Ngoepe, Gift	B-R	6-0	165	1-18-90	.238	.256	.231	47	160	24	38	4	0	1	9	21	4	8	0	52	13	9	.281	.341
Noris, Rogelios	R-R	6-2	192	3-12-89	.250	.333	.235	41	136	16	34	10	2	6	24	11	5	2	2	51	2	1	.485	.325
Pena, Ronald	R-R	5-9	191	2-28-87	.182	.250	.000	4	11	0	2	0	0	0	1	2	0	0	0	4	0	0	.182	.308
Picart, Greg	B-R	5-11	175	9-25-85	.300	.375	.250	5	20	0	6	1	0	0	1	0	0	0	0	3	0	1	.350	.300
Rodriguez, Gerlis	B-R	6-2	185	5-9-88	.266	.208	.285	54	199	22	53	12	0	3	28	9	0	2	4	32	1	3	.372	.292
Roman, Edwin	R-R	5-10	160	4-8-90	.191	.296	.157	41	110	9	21	3	0	0	8	17	3	1	1	38	4	5	.218	.313
Schoenfeld, Joey	R-R	6-2	187	6-11-91	.000	.000	.000	5	14	0	0	0	0	0	0	4	1	0	0	5	1	1	.000	.263
Walker, Andrew	R-R	6-0	210	1-22-86	.253	.333	.230	25	79	13	20	10	1	3	17	11	7	1	0	20	0	2	.519	.392
Walker, Neil	B-R	6-3	215	9-10-85	.167	.100	.200	8	30	2	5	2	0	1	1	1	0	0	0	5	0	1	.333	.219

PITTSBURGH PIRATES

Pitching

Pitching	B-T	HT	WT	DOB	W	L	ERA	G	GS	CG	SV	IP	H	R	ER	HR	BB	SO	AVG	vLH	vRH	K/9	BB/9
Aure, Chris	L-L	6-0	180	10-13-89	0	0	1.69	3	0	0	0	5	3	1	1	1	2	5	.158	.200	.143	8.44	3.38
Beckman, Ryan	R-R	6-4	185	1-2-90	2	2	5.49	11	3	0	0	39	45	26	24	5	8	19	.281	.279	.282	4.35	1.83
Boleska, Tom	R-R	6-0	190	7-30-86	0	0	1.50	3	0	0	0	6	5	3	1	0	1	3	.208	.250	.188	4.50	1.50
Clapp, Brad	R-R	6-4	215	5-19-86	1	1	2.66	7	5	0	0	20	17	6	6	1	7	10	.230	.257	.205	4.43	3.10
Dodson, Zack	L-L	6-2	190	7-23-90	0	0	0.00	1	0	0	0	1	0	0	0	0	0	1	.000	.000	.000	9.00	0.00
Dumatrait, Phil	R-L	6-2	200	7-12-81	0	0	0.00	1	1	0	0	4	3	0	0	0	2	2	.214	.500	.167	4.50	4.50
Esparza, Gerardo	R-R	6-1	180	11-11-87	2	3	4.44	8	2	0	0	26	24	16	13	2	9	19	.253	.296	.235	6.49	3.08
Fagan, Albert	R-R	6-7	205	11-14-86	0	1	0.00	2	0	0	1	4	4	2	0	1	0	2	.235	.000	.444	4.50	0.00
Fienemann, Mitchell	R-R	6-4	186	5-28-90	1	6	3.79	12	6	0	0	40	38	22	17	5	3	26	.238	.200	.252	5.80	0.67
Fuesser, Zac	L-L	6-2	190	7-19-90	1	1	1.26	5	1	0	0	14	6	4	2	0	10	12	.133	.154	.125	7.53	6.28
Garcia, Diomedes	R-R	—	—	8-13-85	1	0	1.93	15	0	0	7	19	10	5	4	1	4	10	.149	.148	.150	4.82	1.93
Garcia, Harvey	R-R	6-2	220	3-16-84	0	0	9.00	2	0	0	0	2	1	2	2	0	2	3	.167	.000	.200	13.50	9.00
Gutierrez, Edgar	R-R	6-0	170	4-16-88	1	2	2.65	11	3	0	0	34	34	14	10	0	7	24	.254	.203	.293	6.35	1.85
Hughes, Jared	R-R	6-7	220	7-4-85	0	0	1.50	3	3	0	0	6	3	1	1	0	1	5	.158	.167	.154	7.50	1.50
Juan, Papiro	R-R	5-10	190	5-13-88	1	0	2.84	11	0	0	1	13	8	5	4	1	6	14	.170	.188	.161	9.95	4.26
Klinger, Brent	R-R	6-4	185	7-21-88	0	1	3.28	11	8	0	0	36	31	14	13	2	12	36	.235	.242	.227	9.08	3.03
Krol, Noah	B-R	6-2	185	6-6-84	0	0	0.00	1	0	0	0	1	0	0	0	0	0	0	.000	.000	.000	0.00	0.00
Laureano, Melkin	R-R	6-3	205	8-26-85	2	4	4.13	11	1	0	1	28	32	15	13	1	7	28	.283	.358	.217	8.89	2.22
Navarro, Eliecer	L-L	5-9	177	10-26-87	4	2	3.77	10	3	0	1	31	32	13	13	3	6	23	.267	.421	.195	6.68	1.74
Patel, Dinesh	R-R	5-11	185	5-8-89	1	0	1.42	6	0	0	0	6	5	2	1	0	0	4	.192	.200	.188	5.68	0.00
Pounders, Brooks	R-R	6-4	225	9-26-90	2	2	3.04	9	4	0	0	24	19	11	8	1	11	20	.218	.300	.175	7.61	4.18
Quintero, Rafael	R-R	6-1	145	9-3-87	2	1	9.50	9	1	0	0	18	29	19	19	3	5	10	.387	.452	.341	5.00	2.50
Ramos, Jhonatan	L-L	5-8	156	8-7-89	5	0	1.82	8	4	0	0	35	23	9	7	2	3	33	.192	.114	.224	8.57	0.78
Santos, Andres	L-L	6-2	189	11-8-86	0	0	7.50	7	0	0	0	6	10	5	5	0	0	4	.345	.500	.304	6.00	0.00
Septimo, Sandobal	R-R	6-0	175	11-24-89	2	1	4.38	11	4	0	1	37	46	18	18	3	3	23	.297	.304	.293	5.59	0.73
Singh, Rinku	L-L	6-2	190	8-8-88	1	2	5.84	11	0	0	0	12	14	9	8	0	4	8	.292	.385	.257	5.84	2.92
Stevenson, Trent	L-L	6-6	175	6-1-90	0	1	1.20	5	4	0	0	15	13	2	2	1	0	8	.245	.304	.200	4.80	0.00
Uviedo, Ronald	R-R	6-1	160	10-7-86	0	1	3.24	3	3	0	0	8	4	3	3	0	2	10	.229	.214	.238	10.80	2.16
Von Rosenberg, Zack	R-R	6-5	205	9-24-90	0	0	0.00	1	1	0	0	1	0	0	0	0	0	1	.000	—	.000	9.00	0.00

Fielding

Catcher	PCT	G	PO	A	E	DP	PB
Aguilera	1.000	11	51	3	0	0	1
Cabrera	.989	28	162	14	2	3	6
Doumit	1.000	1	6	0	0	0	0
Marquez	1.000	10	60	2	0	0	2
Pena	1.000	3	22	0	0	1	0
Walker	.989	13	80	12	1	0	0

First Base	PCT	G	PO	A	E	DP
Aguilera	1.000	4	27	0	0	0
Marquez	1.000	5	30	4	0	4
Rodriguez	.989	52	409	23	5	40

Second Base	PCT	G	PO	A	E	DP
Gonzalez	1.000	11	11	20	0	1

Gonzalez	1.000	8	17	18	0	2
Henry	.944	6	8	9	1	1
Ngoepe	.978	35	74	108	4	26
Picart	1.000	3	5	7	0	0

Third Base	PCT	G	PO	A	E	DP
Acevedo	.769	7	3	7	3	2
Gonzalez	.837	20	11	25	7	0
Gonzalez	.833	2	2	3	1	0
Gourley	.778	8	3	11	4	1
Henry	.838	23	20	42	12	8
Walker	.909	5	3	7	1	0

Shortstop	PCT	G	PO	A	E	DP
Gonzalez	.936	38	51	110	11	22

Gonzalez	1.000	5	8	16	0	2
Gourley	.933	4	7	7	1	2
Ngoepe	.961	12	20	29	2	1
Picart	.933	2	7	7	1	1

Outfield	PCT	G	PO	A	E	DP
De La Cruz	.973	34	69	3	2	1
Freeman	.981	50	96	5	2	2
Gonzalez	1.000	20	28	1	0	1
Marte	1.000	2	8	1	0	0
Milledge	1.000	4	10	0	0	0
Noris	.942	35	61	4	4	0
Rodriguez	1.000	3	5	0	0	0
Roman	1.000	40	81	3	0	1

DSL PIRATES   ROOKIE

DOMINICAN SUMMER LEAGUE

Batting	B-T	HT	WT	DOB	AVG	vLH	vRH	G	AB	R	H	2B	3B	HR	RBI	BB	HBP	SH	SF	SO	SB	CS	SLG	OBP
Acevedo, Andury	R-R	6-4	200	8-23-90	.381	.300	.406	12	42	10	16	4	0	0	5	4	1	2	0	11	3	0	.476	.447
Arias, Julio	R-R	6-5	230	11-16-89	.214	.188	.221	27	84	10	18	6	1	0	5	7	0	0	0	36	1	0	.310	.275
Avila, Eric	R-R	6-1	165	6-9-90	.315	.267	.329	67	267	50	84	21	0	9	50	17	4	1	5	20	8	6	.494	.358
Carvajal, Jodaneli	R-R	5-9	145	4-20-92	.259	.231	.267	33	116	24	30	1	5	1	11	12	1	4	1	22	17	0	.379	.331
Charles, Melvin	B-R	6-2	160	12-9-90	.262	.400	.236	34	65	12	17	4	0	0	9	3	1	0	17	7	4	.323	.317
Fortunato, Raul	R-R	6-2	190	9-5-90	.161	.053	.191	29	87	6	14	2	0	1	9	7	4	0	0	14	4	2	.218	.255
Gonzalez, Samuel	R-R	6-0	180	2-24-89	.261	.176	.280	32	92	13	24	5	1	0	12	7	3	1	0	7	3	3	.337	.333
Goris, Diego	R-R	6-2	165	12-8-90	.277	.302	.271	58	231	37	64	8	5	1	31	10	3	7	2	22	11	7	.368	.313
Guillermo, Luis	R-R	6-3	180	8-3-92	.000	—	.000	1	2	0	0	0	0	0	1	0	0	0	0	0	0	0	.000	.333
Guzman, Dagoberto	R-R	6-0	165	5-15-88	.262	.205	.286	46	149	16	39	13	1	0	13	9	7	2	2	40	5	3	.362	.329
Heredia, Angel	R-R	6-0	160	7-22-92	.224	.211	.229	19	67	14	15	5	1	0	2	7	1	1	0	4	4	2	.328	.307
Jimenez, Jhoanel	B-R	5-11	185	6-7-90	.278	.231	.304	24	36	5	10	4	0	0	1	11	1	0	0	7	2	1	.389	.458
Lopez, Juan	R-R	5-11	180	4-20-90	.286	.500	.250	15	14	2	4	0	0	0	1	0	0	0	4	0	1	.286	.333
Mejia, Leandro	R-R	6-0	195	6-4-90	.207	.147	.222	47	169	14	35	5	1	0	21	6	3	1	2	48	0	1	.249	.244
Nivar, Gavi	R-R	6-4	185	9-16-88	.224	.206	.230	62	254	29	57	9	5	1	28	4	3	5	2	42	11	9	.311	.243
Polanco, Gregory	L-L	6-4	170	9-14-91	.267	.240	.275	63	221	34	59	8	6	0	24	40	3	4	0	50	12	4	.357	.370
Rodriguez, Chris	R-R	5-11	185	1-22-90	.214	.200	.218	55	131	13	28	6	1	1	13	13	2	6	1	18	2	1	.298	.293
Valdemora, Alberto	R-R	6-4	190	12-7-89	.196	.111	.215	32	97	17	19	4	0	1	6	10	10	1	0	40	13	4	.268	.333
Vasquez, Jesus	R-R	6-2	180	12-10-91	.268	.256	.271	51	183	30	49	10	5	2	16	9	3	0	3	40	6	7	.459	.340

Pitching	B-T	HT	WT	DOB	W	L	ERA	G	GS	CG	SV	IP	H	R	ER	HR	BB	SO	AVG	vLH	vRH	K/9	BB/9
Cadet, Martires	L-L	6-2	170	5-9-91	6	1	3.13	18	0	0	0	63	51	29	22	4	16	61	.220	.148	.229	8.67	2.27
Campos, Fraylin	R-R	5-11	170	1-3-90	3	6	2.27	15	13	0	1	71	56	30	18	3	24	92	.204	.169	.217	11.61	3.03
De La Cruz, Dionicio	L-L	6-1	170	4-1-92	0	4	11.76	14	0	0	0	21	27	35	27	1	34	14	.307	.222	.316	6.10	14.81

Player	B-T	HT	WT	DOB	W	L	ERA	G	GS	CG	SV	IP	H	R	ER	HR	BB	SO	AVG	vLH	vRH	K/9	BB/9
De Leon, Emmanuel	B-R	6-1	175	12-25-90	2	4	4.25	14	14	0	0	49	35	32	23	2	33	52	.199	.163	.211	9.62	6.10
Garcia, Wilbin	R-R	6-4	175	3-15-89	0	0	9.68	9	3	0	0	18	24	24	19	1	7	12	.308	.290	.319	6.11	3.57
Gonzalez, Yoan	L-L	6-0	165	12-14-89	0	0	9.00	2	0	0	1	4	3	4	4	0	2	4	.200	—	.200	9.00	4.50
Guzman, Oliberto	R-R	5-10	170	8-5-90	1	1	2.25	7	0	0	5	20	14	9	5	2	2	15	.175	.063	.203	6.75	0.90
Hernandez, Jimy	R-R	0-0	0	5-22-92	1	0	10.64	6	0	0	0	11	18	17	13	1	13	8	.375	.389	.367	6.55	10.64
Igsema, Victor	R-R	6-2	172	11-16-85	1	0	3.00	2	0	0	1	3	2	2	1	0	0	2	.200	.333	.143	6.00	0.00
Jean-Luis, Wilner	R-R	6-3	185	7-13-91	1	2	14.90	5	0	0	1	10	12	17	16	1	10	7	.308	.250	.323	6.52	9.31
Lopez, Porfirio	L-L	5-10	160	3-24-90	2	1	1.23	11	9	0	1	44	18	8	6	2	11	61	.125	.125	.125	12.48	2.25
Mata, Jonathan	L-L	6-2	192	7-12-90	0	0	1.80	4	0	0	0	5	3	1	1	0	5	6	.167	.000	.200	10.80	9.00
Montero, Joan	R-R	6-0	186	10-26-88	0	1	6.75	2	0	0	0	1	1	1	1	0	3	1	.200	.000	.333	6.75	20.25
Ozoria, Jean	R-R	6-5	175	3-16-92	1	0	4.70	4	0	0	0	8	7	5	4	0	8	5	.259	.000	.318	5.87	9.39
Perez, Clario	R-R	6-1	185	8-30-92	3	3	3.69	15	4	0	0	46	42	29	19	3	10	35	.231	.298	.207	6.80	1.94
Perez, Ricky	R-R	6-3	205	5-31-90	1	1	3.60	12	0	0	1	30	30	17	12	1	13	22	.256	.158	.276	6.60	3.90
Pontier, Sadid	R-R	6-3	185	10-12-90	0	0	17.08	11	0	0	0	16	19	37	31	1	29	7	.302	.286	.310	3.86	15.98
Reyes, Angel	R-R	5-10	175	12-13-87	0	0	21.00	9	0	0	0	9	9	27	21	0	28	8	.257	.222	.269	8.00	28.00
Rodriguez, Joely	L-L	6-1	175	11-14-91	2	5	4.60	12	12	0	0	47	53	29	24	1	24	24	.291	.238	.298	4.60	4.60
Sierra, Yoldi	L-L	6-2	165	4-26-92	0	1	0.00	3	0	0	0	8	4	2	0	0	3	10	.154	—	.154	11.25	3.38
Taveras, Yerfi	R-R	6-2	160	11-7-88	1	3	5.89	12	12	0	0	47	57	42	31	3	17	30	.295	.195	.322	5.70	3.23
Vargas, Plasido	R-R	6-4	185	10-5-88	3	5	3.64	21	0	0	0	54	59	37	22	2	30	37	.284	.260	.257	6.13	4.97

Fielding

Catcher	PCT	G	PO	A	E	DP	PB
Gonzalez	.959	16	101	17	5	0	1
Jimenez	.988	19	72	12	1	0	3
Lopez	1.000	13	40	3	0	0	3
Rodriguez	.969	54	298	43	11	0	22

First Base	PCT	G	PO	A	E	DP
Acevedo	1.000	7	44	0	0	2
Arias	.964	19	156	7	6	8
Gonzalez	1.000	3	23	3	0	0
Guzman	1.000	7	58	2	0	4
Jimenez	1.000	1	2	0	0	0
Mejia	.983	39	337	14	6	22
Rodriguez	1.000	1	7	1	0	1

Second Base	PCT	G	PO	A	E	DP
Avila	.917	10	10	23	3	2
Carvajal	.971	7	16	18	1	5
Charles	.951	20	29	29	3	4
Goris	.961	28	56	68	5	13
Guzman	.907	11	16	23	4	1
Heredia	1.000	2	5	4	0	2

Third Base	PCT	G	PO	A	E	DP
Acevedo	.857	7	11	13	4	0
Avila	.896	56	50	140	22	6
Charles	.600	2	1	2	2	0
Guzman	.667	3	2	4	3	0
Mejia	.857	5	3	9	2	2

Shortstop	PCT	G	PO	A	E	DP
Charles	.769	4	3	7	3	1
Goris	.896	33	44	94	16	9
Guzman	.930	24	34	72	8	9
Heredia	.914	16	26	48	7	8

Outfield	PCT	G	PO	A	E	DP
Carvajal	—	1	0	0	0	0
Fortunato	.975	27	32	7	1	0
Guillermo	1.000	1	2	0	0	0
Guzman	1.000	5	8	0	0	0
Nivar	.970	62	123	7	4	0
Polanco	.940	61	76	3	5	0
Valdemora	.810	9	17	0	4	0
Vasquez	.951	47	56	2	3	1

VSL PIRATES

ROOKIE

VENEZUELAN SUMMER LEAGUE

Batting	B-T	HT	WT	DOB	AVG	vLH	vRH	G	AB	R	H	2B	3B	HR	RBI	BB	HBP	SH	SF	SO	SB	CS	SLG	OBP
Apomte, Carlos	B-R	5-11	135	2-9-91	.410	.421	.405	24	61	15	25	3	1	0	8	7	4	0	0	10	4	6	.492	.500
Aponte, Kelly	L-R	6-5	220	6-4-91	.277	.500	.256	17	47	7	13	5	0	2	12	8	0	0	0	11	1	0	.511	.382
Barrios, Jonathan	B-R	5-11	179	12-1-91	.241	.125	.279	54	162	33	39	11	0	2	13	12	5	1	2	41	2	3	.346	.309
Bishop, Jorge	R-R	5-10	152	3-12-91	.308	.291	.313	63	253	64	78	8	3	9	41	23	1	2	1	36	24	7	.470	.367
Cabrera, Eduardo	R-R	5-11	170	4-24-88	.371	.214	.396	38	105	17	39	5	1	0	15	9	0	1	1	22	0	3	.438	.417
Cabrera, Ramon	B-R	5-7	202	11-5-89	.312	.375	.295	20	77	10	24	6	0	2	19	12	0	0	1	11	1	2	.468	.400
Cardona, Luis	B-R	5-10	152	7-29-88	.279	.190	.300	35	111	29	31	12	1	1	13	19	4	3	3	17	10	3	.432	.394
Cayonez, Exicardo	L-L	6-0	183	10-9-91	.302	.351	.292	65	205	38	62	18	2	1	34	23	10	2	2	30	4	6	.424	.396
Elenes, Norman	L-R	5-11	172	10-7-92	.149	.143	.150	22	47	4	7	1	0	0	5	6	1	0	1	20	0	1	.170	.255
Gimenez, Jefferson	B-R	5-10	160	4-5-92	.083	.000	.125	18	12	2	1	0	0	0	1	0	1	0	1	5	1	0	.083	.154
Leal, Carlos	R-R	5-10	170	2-10-90	.236	.182	.246	52	144	30	34	10	0	3	29	23	2	0	0	44	7	4	.368	.349
Pino, David	R-R	5-11	150	4-28-91	.278	.268	.280	65	216	50	60	16	8	4	48	27	10	0	2	36	4	4	.481	.380
Ponce, Dimas	R-R	5-11	140	1-22-91	.268	.404	.229	59	213	41	57	13	0	1	24	23	6	10	1	30	14	7	.343	.354
Sosa, Junior	L-L	5-10	139	10-3-90	.303	.396	.279	64	238	42	72	7	6	0	32	34	6	4	2	34	25	15	.382	.400
Trinidad, Michaelangel	L-L	5-11	232	8-23-88	.318	.294	.323	58	192	36	61	13	0	14	56	27	6	0	3	39	0	1	.604	.412

Pitching	B-T	HT	WT	DOB	W	L	ERA	G	GS	CG	SV	IP	H	R	ER	HR	BB	SO	AVG	vLH	vRH	K/9	BB/9
Barraza, Jesus	R-R	5-10	150	11-3-90	2	0	3.68	12	0	0	2	22	23	10	9	2	4	17	.267	.333	.246	6.95	1.64
Denis, Julio	L-L	6-3	185	5-8-86	1	3	4.40	18	0	0	2	29	27	14	14	5	7	31	.245	.500	.241	9.73	2.20
Espinosa, Octavio	L-L	5-10	175	9-22-90	1	2	5.02	12	9	0	0	38	51	28	21	2	19	24	.317	.182	.327	5.73	4.54
Espinoza, Roberto	R-R	6-1	189	5-7-92	4	1	2.74	14	14	0	0	62	41	21	19	3	22	48	.188	.262	.170	6.93	3.18
Figuera, Luis	R-R	6-1	178	11-11-90	2	0	1.35	9	0	0	0	20	11	3	3	1	8	12	.162	.167	.161	5.40	3.60
Goatache, Deivis	L-L	6-0	160	6-23-88	5	3	3.88	20	0	0	1	46	42	23	20	5	10	36	.241	.167	.244	6.99	1.94
Iriarte, Humberto	R-R	6-0	165	3-26-88	2	1	1.45	13	0	0	3	19	15	4	3	1	6	17	.231	.000	.263	3.38	2.89
Joves, Julio	R-R	6-2	190	4-7-91	0	1	7.80	5	5	0	0	15	18	13	13	3	4	5	.290	.333	.286	3.00	2.40
Lopez, Jovany	L-L	5-10	155	3-11-91	2	1	5.64	11	0	0	0	22	25	18	14	3	3	15	.272	.333	.267	6.04	1.21
Marquez, Erick	L-L	5-11	151	2-9-91	2	2	3.24	11	0	0	0	25	24	10	9	3	3	15	.253	.000	.264	5.40	1.08
Pacheco, Alexis	R-R	6-0	194	10-21-87	0	2	1.93	7	4	0	0	19	15	5	4	0	8	13	.217	.200	.220	6.27	3.38
Pacheco, Yomar	R-R	6-3	200	10-4-89	2	1	1.97	15	8	0	1	46	40	19	10	2	11	27	.231	.320	.216	5.32	2.17
Rodriguez, Rafael	L-L	5-9	165	7-13-90	4	1	3.58	9	7	0	0	33	32	14	13	0	11	28	.264	.240	.269	7.71	3.03
Romo, Remberto	R-R	5-9	168	10-10-91	3	2	5.70	16	0	0	0	36	54	31	23	6	8	26	.348	.333	.351	6.44	1.98
Ruiz, Raul	L-L	5-10	158	12-4-90	7	0	0.53	20	0	0	6	34	23	4	2	0	3	29	.192	.200	.191	7.75	0.80
Sanchez, Yeyber	R-R	6-4	198	6-18-90	0	1	6.00	4	0	0	0	6	5	5	4	1	6	7	.250	.000	.278	10.50	9.00
Verdugo, Oscar	R-R	6-1	172	1-21-90	4	0	2.95	14	14	0	0	58	50	26	19	5	14	53	.236	.270	.229	8.22	2.17

Vilchez, Francisco	R-R	6-0	183	12-28-90	4	1	3.74	15	9	0	0	55	57	25	23	5	12	47	.259	.257	.259	7.64	1.95
Zapari, Mario	R-R	5-8	154	12-22-91	2	1	5.50	15	0	0	1	34	49	28	21	6	5	28	.327	.321	.328	7.34	1.31

Fielding

Catcher	PCT	G	PO	A	E	DP	PB
Cabrera	.978	29	161	13	4	3	4
Cabrera	1.000	10	57	10	0	1	2
Diaz	.978	41	222	51	6	2	4
Elenes	1.000	8	18	5	0	0	0

First Base	PCT	G	PO	A	E	DP
Aponte	1.000	3	13	1	0	0
Cabrera	1.000	4	21	0	0	2
Cabrera	1.000	1	8	1	0	0
Diaz	.992	18	123	3	1	7
Elenes	1.000	1	8	0	0	0
Gimenez	1.000	3	6	0	0	1
Leal	.989	10	86	1	1	2
Pino	1.000	1	3	0	0	0
Trinidad	.987	50	424	16	6	17

Second Base	PCT	G	PO	A	E	DP
Apomte	.926	19	41	46	7	7

	PCT	G	PO	A	E	DP
Barrios	1.000	6	6	7	0	2
Bishop	.957	25	37	52	4	3
Gimenez	1.000	3	0	2	0	0
Leal	1.000	2	5	6	0	0
Pino	.800	2	2	2	1	0
Ponce	.947	30	49	59	6	14

Third Base	PCT	G	PO	A	E	DP
Apomte	1.000	1	0	2	0	0
Barrios	1.000	3	3	6	0	0
Bishop	1.000	1	0	2	0	0
Leal	.861	31	16	52	11	3
Pino	.915	17	11	32	4	3
Ponce	.943	32	28	87	7	3

Shortstop	PCT	G	PO	A	E	DP
Apomte	—	1	0	0	0	0
Barrios	.945	35	40	98	8	7
Bishop	.897	40	48	100	17	13

	PCT	G	PO	A	E	DP
Leal	.938	8	5	10	1	1
Ponce	1.000	1	0	6	0	0

Outfield	PCT	G	PO	A	E	DP
Apomte	1.000	1	2	0	0	0
Cardona	.984	35	59	2	1	0
Cayonez	.921	57	68	2	6	1
Elenes	—	1	0	0	0	0
Gimenez	—	1	0	0	0	0
Leal	.667	2	2	0	1	0
Mendoza	.961	22	46	3	2	1
Pino	.953	51	76	6	4	1
Ponce	—	1	0	0	0	0
Sosa	.985	63	127	6	2	0
Trinidad	.889	8	14	2	2	1

St. Louis Cardinals

SEASON IN A SENTENCE: With yet another transcendent year from Albert Pujols, the resurrection of Chris Carpenter, the continuing growth of Adam Wainwright and the addition of Matt Holliday, St. Louis spent most of the season in first place in the National League Central before getting swept out of the playoffs by the Dodgers.

HIGH POINT: The Cardinals were in a virtual tie with the Cubs in the National League Central heading into August, but after acquiring Holliday they went on a 20-6 run through the month and left the rest of the Central in their rearview mirror. St. Louis topped it off with a four-game winning streak that ended with a 10-3 win over the Brewers on Sept. 2, as Chris Carpenter won his 10th straight decision.

LOW POINT: St. Louis returned to the playoffs for the first time since winning the 2006 World Series, but a three-game sweep in the Division Series at the hands of the Dodgers put a damper on things after the Cardinals had spent most of the season in first place.

NOTABLE ROOKIES: Ten players made their major league debuts for the Cardinals in 2009, with center fielder Colby Rasmus by far the most significant. He batted .251/.307/.407 but showed enough promise that the Cardinals still think they can build around him. Jason Motte flopped in his audition as closer, but he did end up making 69 relief appearances and compiled a 4.76 ERA in 57 innings.

KEY TRANSACTIONS: Getting Holliday from the Athletics was clearly the most important deal for the Cardinals, but they also brought in Mark DeRosa from the Indians to play third base. The deals cost the Cardinals five prospects, four of whom were expected to be major league contributors as soon as 2010. The most notable was third baseman Brett Wallace, their 2008 first-round pick who went to Oakland.

DOWN ON THE FARM: St. Louis is using the same formula that former general manager Walt Jocketty used to build seven playoff teams and one World Series winner, with GM John Mozeliak showing the same willingness to use his minor league talent to pull off big trades for veterans. The most notable success on the farm came when Triple-A Memphis won the Pacific Coast League championship, spurred by the return of lefthander Jaime Garcia and third baseman David Freese from surgeries.

OPENING DAY PAYROLL: $77,605,109

PLAYERS OF THE YEAR

MAJOR LEAGUE	MINOR LEAGUE
Albert Pujols	**Allen Craig**
1b	3b/of
.327/.443/.658	(Triple-A)
Led NL in R (124), HR	.322/.374/.547
(47), OPS (1.101)	26 2B, 26 HR

ORGANIZATION LEADERS

BATTING		*Minimum 250 at-bats
MAJORS		
*AVG	Albert Pujols	.327
*OPS	Albert Pujols	1.101
HR	Albert Pujols	47
RBI	Albert Pujols	135
MINORS		
*AVG	Craig, Allen, Memphis	.322
	Cutler, Charles, Quad Cities/Palm Beach	.322
R	Craig, Allen, Memphis	78
H	Craig, Allen, Memphis	152
TB	Craig, Allen, Memphis	258
2B	Henley, Tyler, Springfield	31
3B	Chambers, Adron, Palm Beach	16
HR	Craig, Allen, Memphis	26
RBI	Craig, Allen, Memphis	83
BB	Rapoport, James, Springfield	71
SO	Morales, Osvaldo, Quad Cities/Palm Beach	149
SB	Greene, Tyler, Memphis	31
*OBP	Cutler, Charles, Quad Cities/Palm Beach	.408
*SLG	Craig, Allen, Memphis	.547

PITCHING		†Minimum 75 innings
MAJORS		
W	Adam Wainwright	19
†ERA	Chris Carpenter	2.24
SO	Adam Wainwright	212
MINORS		
W	Hearne, Trey, Memphis/Springfield	14
L	Castillo, Richard, Palm Beach	13
†ERA	Lynn, Lance, P.B./Springfield/Memphis	2.85
G	Sanchez, Eduardo, Palm Beach/Springfield	60
GS	Ottavino, Adam, Memphis	27
SV	Todd, Jess, Memphis	24
IP	Hearne, Trey, Memphis/Springfield	154
BB	Ottavino, Adam, Memphis	82
SO	Lynn, Lance, P.B./Springfield/Memphis	124
†AVG	Gorgen, Scott, Palm Beach/Springfield	.221

2009 PERFORMANCE

General Manager: John Mozeliak. **Farm/Scouting Director:** Jeff Luhnow.

Class	Team	League	W	L	PCT	Finish*	Manager(s)
Majors	St. Louis Cardinals	National	91	71	.562	4th (16)	Tony La Russa
Triple-A	Memphis Redbirds	Pacific Coast	77	67	.535	†4th (16)	Chris Maloney
Double-A	Springfield Cardinals	Texas	71	69	.507	5th (8)	Ron Warner
High A	Palm Beach Cardinals	Florida State	61	77	.442	10th (12)	Tom Spencer
Low A	Quad Cities River Bandits	Midwest	61	78	.439	9th (14)	Steve Dillard
Short-season	Batavia Muckdogs	New York-Penn	37	39	.487	8th (14)	Mark Dejohn
Rookie	Johnson City Cardinals	Appalachian	37	30	.552	3rd (10)	Mike Shildt
Rookie	GCL Cardinals	Gulf Coast	25	31	.446	12th (16)	Steve Turco
Overall 2009 Minor League Record			369	391	.486	24th (30)	

*Finish in overall standings (No. of teams in league). †League champion.

ORGANIZATION STATISTICS

ST. LOUIS CARDINALS

NATIONAL LEAGUE

Batting	B-T	HT	WT	DOB	AVG	vLH	vRH	G	AB	R	H	2B	3B	HR	RBI	BB	HBP	SH	SF	SO	SB	CS	SLG	OBP
Ankiel, Rick	L-L	6-1	210	7-19-79	.231	.234	.230	122	372	50	86	21	2	11	38	26	3	0	3	99	4	3	.387	.285
Barden, Brian	R-R	5-11	200	4-2-81	.233	.191	.268	52	103	13	24	3	0	4	10	6	2	2	1	21	0	0	.379	.286
DeRosa, Mark	R-R	6-1	205	2-26-75	.228	.224	.229	68	237	31	54	10	1	10	28	18	4	1	2	58	2	1	.405	.291
Duncan, Chris	L-R	6-5	230	5-5-81	.227	.231	.226	87	260	25	59	15	2	5	32	41	0	0	3	67	0	1	.358	.329
Freese, David	R-R	6-2	220	4-28-83	.323	.176	.500	17	31	3	10	2	0	1	7	2	0	0	1	7	0	0	.484	.353
Glaus, Troy	R-R	6-5	240	8-3-76	.172	.000	.192	14	29	2	5	2	0	0	2	3	0	0	0	8	0	0	.241	.250
Greene, Tyler	R-R	6-2	190	8-17-83	.222	.188	.237	48	108	9	24	5	0	2	7	4	3	1	0	32	3	0	.324	.270
Greene, Khalil	R-R	5-11	185	10-21-79	.200	.180	.211	77	170	21	34	7	0	6	24	15	3	2	3	35	2	1	.347	.272
Hoffpauir, Jarrett	R-R	5-9	190	6-18-83	.250	.143	.400	8	12	1	3	2	0	0	2	4	0	0	0	2	0	0	.417	.438
Holliday, Matt	R-R	6-4	235	1-15-80	.353	.308	.366	63	235	42	83	16	2	13	55	26	4	0	5	43	2	4	.604	.419
LaRue, Jason	R-R	5-11	205	3-19-74	.240	.259	.234	51	104	10	25	3	0	2	6	3	2	4	1	0	22	1	0	.327	.288
Ludwick, Ryan	R-L	6-3	220	7-13-78	.265	.269	.264	139	486	63	129	20	1	22	97	41	7	1	4	106	4	2	.447	.329
Lugo, Julio	R-R	6-1	175	11-16-75	.277	.246	.299	51	148	24	41	9	4	2	13	17	1	2	2	27	6	0	.432	.351
Molina, Yadier	R-R	5-11	230	7-13-82	.293	.248	.307	140	481	45	141	23	1	6	54	50	6	6	1	39	9	3	.383	.366
Pagnozzi, Matt	R-R	6-2	205	11-10-82	.000	.000	.000	6	3	1	0	0	0	0	0	1	0	1	0	0	0	0	.000	.250
Pujols, Albert	R-R	6-3	230	1-16-80	.327	.338	.324	160	568	124	186	45	1	47	135	115	9	0	8	64	16	4	.658	.443
Rasmus, Colby	L-L	6-2	200	8-11-86	.251	.160	.277	147	474	72	119	22	2	16	52	36	3	5	2	95	3	1	.407	.307
Robinson, Shane	R-R	5-9	160	10-30-84	.240	.143	.278	11	25	1	6	1	0	0	1	0	0	0	1	2	1	0	.280	.231
Ryan, Brendan	R-R	6-2	195	3-26-82	.292	.265	.306	129	390	55	114	19	7	3	37	24	6	6	3	56	14	7	.400	.340
Schumaker, Skip	L-R	5-10	195	2-3-80	.303	.220	.322	153	532	85	161	34	1	4	35	52	0	1	1	69	2	2	.393	.364
Stavinoha, Nick	R-R	6-2	240	5-3-82	.230	.262	.200	39	87	6	20	7	0	2	17	2	0	0	2	15	1	0	.379	.242
Thurston, Joe	L-R	5-11	210	9-29-79	.225	.196	.231	124	267	27	60	17	4	1	25	33	3	3	1	56	4	2	.330	.316

Pitching	B-T	HT	WT	DOB	W	L	ERA	G	GS	CG	SV	IP	H	R	ER	HR	BB	SO	AVG	vLH	vRH	K/9	BB/9
Boggs, Mitchell	R-R	6-4	215	2-15-84	2	3	4.19	16	9	0	0	58	71	28	27	3	33	46	.311	.410	.234	7.14	5.12
Boyer, Blaine	R-R	6-3	215	7-11-81	0	0	4.41	15	0	0	0	16	14	10	8	1	5	9	.230	.154	.286	4.96	2.76
3-team total (30 Arizona, 3 Atlanta)					0	2	4.12	48	0	0	0	55	56	36	25	1	20	29	—	—	—	4.77	3.29
Carpenter, Chris	R-R	6-6	230	4-27-75	17	4	2.24	28	28	3	0	193	156	49	48	7	38	144	.226	.239	.214	6.73	1.78
Franklin, Ryan	R-R	6-3	190	3-5-73	4	3	1.92	62	0	0	38	61	49	13	13	2	24	44	.220	.196	.238	6.49	3.54
Hawksworth, Blake	R-R	6-3	195	3-1-83	4	0	2.03	30	0	0	0	40	29	10	9	2	15	20	.209	.246	.176	4.50	3.38
Kinney, Josh	R-R	6-1	215	3-31-79	1	0	8.80	17	0	0	0	15	23	15	15	2	11	8	.343	.235	.455	4.70	6.46
Lohse, Kyle	R-R	6-2	210	10-4-78	6	10	4.74	23	22	1	0	118	125	69	62	16	36	77	.269	.251	.285	5.89	2.75
McClellan, Kyle	R-R	6-2	215	6-12-84	4	4	3.37	66	0	0	3	67	56	27	25	4	34	51	.229	.198	.252	6.89	4.59
Miller, Trever	R-L	6-3	200	5-29-73	4	1	2.06	70	0	0	0	44	31	11	10	5	11	46	.197	.135	.295	9.48	2.27
Mortensen, Clay	R-R	6-4	180	4-10-85	0	0	6.00	1	0	0	0	3	5	6	2	1	1	2	.417	.000	1.000	6.00	3.00
Motte, Jason	R-R	6-0	195	6-22-82	4	4	4.76	69	0	0	0	57	57	32	30	10	23	54	.264	.341	.214	8.58	3.65
Perez, Chris	R-R	6-4	230	7-1-85	1	1	4.18	29	0	0	1	24	17	12	11	3	15	30	.195	.231	.180	11.41	5.70
Pineiro, Joel	R-R	6-1	200	9-25-78	15	12	3.49	32	32	3	0	214	218	94	83	11	27	105	.268	.272	.266	4.42	1.14
Reyes, Dennys	R-L	6-3	250	4-19-77	0	2	3.29	75	0	0	1	41	35	17	15	2	21	33	.233	.207	.276	7.24	4.61
Smoltz, John	R-R	6-3	220	5-15-67	1	3	4.26	7	7	0	0	38	36	18	18	3	9	40	.248	.211	.284	9.47	2.13
Thompson, Brad	R-R	6-1	190	1-31-82	2	6	4.84	32	8	0	0	80	85	45	43	8	23	34	.273	.255	.289	3.83	2.59
Todd, Jess	R-R	5-11	210	4-20-86	0	0	10.80	1	0	0	0	2	3	2	2	1	2	2	.375	.500	.250	10.80	10.80
Wainwright, Adam	R-R	6-7	230	8-30-81	19	8	2.63	34	34	1	0	233	216	75	68	17	66	212	.244	.275	.217	8.19	2.55
Walters, P.J.	R-R	6-4	200	3-12-85	0	0	9.56	8	1	0	0	16	21	19	17	6	9	14	.304	.355	.263	7.88	5.06
Wellemeyer, Todd	R-R	6-3	225	8-30-78	7	10	5.89	28	21	0	0	122	160	88	80	19	57	78	.328	.351	.305	5.74	4.19

Fielding

Catcher	PCT	G	PO	A	E	DP	PB
Freese	1.000	1	1	0	0	0	0
LaRue	.995	43	174	13	1	0	1
Molina	.995	138	884	82	5	6	4
Pagnozzi	1.000	5	9	1	0	1	0

First Base	PCT	G	PO	A	E	DP
DeRosa	1.000	3	6	0	0	2
Duncan	.935	6	26	3	2	1
Freese	1.000	3	7	0	0	1
Glaus	1.000	2	15	0	0	0
Greene	1.000	1	1	0	0	1

	PCT	G	PO	A	E	DP
LaRue	1.000	2	7	0	0	0
Molina	1.000	6	10	1	0	2
Pagnozzi	1.000	1	1	0	0	0
Pujols	.992	159	1473	185	13	150
Second Base	**PCT**	**G**	**PO**	**A**	**E**	**DP**
Barden	1.000	1	4	0	0	0

	PCT	G	PO	A	E	DP
DeRosa	—	2	0	0	0	0
Greene	1.000	7	4	6	0	2
Hoffpauir	1.000	5	1	10	0	2
Lugo	.979	30	33	59	2	12
Ryan	.981	19	21	31	1	9
Schumaker	.983	133	188	347	9	80
Thurston	.976	47	32	48	2	13

Third Base	PCT	G	PO	A	E	DP
Barden	.937	46	9	50	4	4
DeRosa	1.000	63	41	99	0	9
Freese	1.000	7	6	5	0	1

Glaus	.875	8	1	6	1	0
Greene	.917	11	3	8	1	1
Greene	.970	16	5	27	1	5
Hoffpauir	1.000	1	0	1	0	0
Thurston	.936	68	38	109	10	11

Shortstop	PCT	G	PO	A	E	DP
Barden	1.000	4	4	11	0	2
Greene	.969	30	28	65	3	12
Greene	.946	30	43	80	7	17
Lugo	.978	24	35	55	2	16
Ryan	.984	105	145	354	8	71

Outfield	PCT	G	PO	A	E	DP
Ankiel	.977	101	203	5	5	2
DeRosa	1.000	3	3	0	0	0
Duncan	.965	68	79	3	3	1
Greene	1.000	1	1	0	0	0
Holliday	.989	62	86	1	1	0
Ludwick	.996	134	213	9	1	4
Rasmus	.979	135	276	3	6	1
Robinson	1.000	7	6	0	0	0
Schumaker	.967	54	29	0	1	0
Stavinoha	1.000	23	12	0	0	0
Thurston	1.000	5	3	0	0	0

MEMPHIS REDBIRDS — TRIPLE-A

PACIFIC COAST LEAGUE

Batting	B-T	HT	WT	DOB	AVG	vLH	vRH	G	AB	R	H	2B	3B	HR	RBI	BB	HBP	SH	SF	SO	SB	CS	SLG	OBP
Anderson, Bryan	L-R	6-1	200	12-16-86	.245	.091	.285	53	163	22	40	7	3	4	11	10	1	0	0	42	1	0	.399	.293
Barden, Brian	R-R	5-11	200	4-2-81	.267	.270	.266	61	187	26	50	11	0	4	28	10	4	4	1	44	1	1	.390	.317
Barton, Brian	R-R	6-3	190	4-25-82	.107	.500	.042	10	28	2	3	0	0	0	1	4	0	0	0	9	3	0	.107	.219
Brito, Javier	R-R	6-1	245	3-25-83	.283	.000	.333	13	46	5	13	1	0	0	4	6	0	0	1	11	0	0	.304	.358
Craig, Allen	R-R	6-2	210	7-18-84	.322	.348	.311	126	472	78	152	26	1	26	83	37	6	0	6	95	3	0	.547	.374
Descalso, Daniel	L-R	5-10	190	10-19-86	.253	.276	.248	46	150	23	38	4	0	2	17	16	1	4	1	21	3	0	.320	.327
Folli, Mike	B-R	5-10	175	7-17-85	.042	.000	.063	8	24	0	1	1	0	0	0	0	1	1	0	6	0	0	.083	.080
Freese, David	R-R	6-2	220	4-28-83	.300	.383	.264	56	200	34	60	15	0	10	37	22	1	0	2	51	1	0	.525	.369
Glaus, Troy	R-R	6-5	240	8-3-76	.216	.250	.194	15	51	10	11	0	0	3	8	12	1	0	1	17	1	0	.392	.369
Greene, Tyler	R-R	6-2	190	8-17-83	.291	.211	.320	89	340	70	99	10	5	15	42	38	5	3	2	86	31	3	.482	.369
Greene, Khalil	R-R	5-11	185	10-21-79	.345	.320	.367	15	55	9	19	3	0	4	10	2	0	0	0	4	0	0	.618	.368
Hamilton, Mark	L-L	6-3	220	7-29-84	.308	.276	.317	46	130	22	40	11	0	6	19	13	1	0	0	34	0	0	.531	.375
Hoffpauir, Jarrett	R-R	5-9	190	6-18-83	.291	.351	.262	108	358	53	104	22	3	14	53	35	3	4	2	28	4	1	.486	.357
Jay, Jon	L-L	5-11	200	3-15-85	.281	.281	.281	136	505	72	142	23	2	10	54	34	12	8	5	64	20	8	.394	.338
Mather, Joe	R-R	6-4	215	7-23-82	.176	.171	.178	39	136	12	24	6	2	1	14	9	2	0	3	27	7	1	.272	.233
Pagnozzi, Matt	R-R	6-2	205	11-10-82	.221	.264	.190	86	253	21	56	7	0	5	32	26	3	7	2	78	0	1	.308	.299
Robinson, Shane	R-R	5-9	160	10-30-84	.238	.232	.240	100	345	46	82	18	3	5	40	28	8	4	4	42	16	3	.351	.306
Rowlett, Casey	R-R	5-8	175	2-8-83	.216	.216	.216	71	148	16	32	4	0	1	13	13	0	4	1	24	3	1	.264	.278
Ryan, Brendan	R-R	6-2	195	3-26-82	.000	.000	.000	3	11	0	0	0	0	0	0	0	0	0	0	5	0	0	.000	.000
Shorey, Mark	L-L	6-0	230	8-13-84	.291	.333	.283	94	258	20	75	13	0	5	27	16	1	0	0	50	3	2	.399	.335
Solano, Donovan	R-R	5-10	165	12-17-87	.317	.146	.388	52	164	22	52	7	0	0	14	10	2	2	0	27	3	0	.360	.364
Stavinoha, Nick	R-R	6-2	240	5-3-82	.282	.310	.271	72	259	39	73	17	2	11	56	25	6	0	5	48	2	0	.490	.353
Wallace, Brett	L-R	6-2	205	8-26-86	.293	.400	.253	62	222	22	65	11	0	6	19	15	4	0	2	42	0	1	.423	.346
2-team total (44 Sacramento)					.297	—	—	106	404	54	120	21	0	15	47	29	9	0	4	82	1	2	.460	.354
Yarbrough, Brandon	L-R	6-2	180	11-9-84	.286	.333	.277	53	119	14	34	7	1	1	12	21	0	1	0	42	0	1	.387	.393

Pitching	B-T	HT	WT	DOB	W	L	ERA	G	GS	CG	SV	IP	H	R	ER	HR	BB	SO	AVG	vLH	vRH	K/9	BB/9
Boggs, Mitchell	R-R	6-4	215	2-15-84	6	4	4.83	14	14	0	0	76	90	45	41	8	32	58	.293	.352	.251	6.84	3.77
Garcia, Jaime	L-L	6-2	230	7-8-86	2	0	3.86	4	4	0	0	21	17	14	9	5	9	22	.230	.267	.220	9.43	3.86
Gonzalez, Marco	R-R	6-2	205	5-28-84	0	0	5.59	5	0	0	0	10	12	6	6	0	7	4	.308	.333	.296	3.72	6.52
Hawksworth, Blake	R-R	6-3	195	3-1-83	5	4	3.58	12	12	1	0	73	61	31	29	3	20	57	.222	.235	.210	7.03	2.47
Hearne, Trey	R-R	6-1	195	8-19-83	2	1	3.38	4	4	0	0	27	23	12	10	4	6	16	.219	.282	.182	5.40	2.03
Kinney, Josh	R-R	6-1	215	3-31-79	3	3	3.86	38	0	0	1	44	43	21	19	6	20	52	.254	.254	.255	10.56	4.06
Lohse, Kyle	R-R	6-2	210	10-4-78	1	0	0.00	1	1	0	0	6	2	0	0	0	2	6	.100	.000	.133	9.00	3.00
Lynn, Lance	R-R	6-5	250	5-12-87	0	0	2.70	1	1	0	0	7	5	2	2	0	3	9	.200	.200	.200	12.15	4.05
MacLane, Evan	L-L	6-2	185	11-4-82	8	9	3.75	24	24	0	0	151	171	73	63	23	20	92	.283	.242	.298	5.48	1.19
2-team total (3 Reno)					8	11	4.02	27	26	0	0	166	194	84	74	23	24	95	—	—	—	5.16	1.30
Maekawa, Kat	L-L	6-0	215	9-25-78	1	2	5.08	18	4	0	0	39	46	26	22	4	32	33	.291	.292	.291	7.62	7.38
Manning, Charlie	L-L	6-2	185	3-31-79	1	2	3.94	44	0	0	1	48	47	22	21	2	21	43	.255	.300	.234	8.06	3.94
Mortensen, Clay	R-R	6-4	180	4-10-85	7	6	4.37	17	17	1	0	105	103	58	51	11	34	82	.259	.257	.261	7.03	2.91
2-team total (6 Sacramento)					9	8	4.39	23	23	1	0	137	143	78	67	13	48	100	—	—	—	6.55	3.15
Norrick, Tyler	L-L	6-3	190	9-27-83	0	0	6.75	6	0	0	0	7	8	5	5	2	5	7	.296	.167	.333	9.45	6.75
Ostlund, Ian	R-L	6-1	200	10-17-78	2	0	5.85	23	1	0	0	52	62	35	34	7	18	43	.298	.338	.280	7.39	3.10
Ottavino, Adam	R-R	6-5	230	11-22-85	7	12	4.75	27	27	0	0	144	141	80	76	12	82	119	.261	.267	.255	7.44	5.13
Parise, Pete	R-R	6-1	185	12-5-84	2	1	4.17	32	0	0	8	37	34	20	17	4	13	31	.252	.302	.220	7.61	3.19
Perez, Chris	R-R	6-4	230	7-1-85	1	0	0.00	3	0	0	2	4	0	0	0	0	3	4	.000	.000	.000	9.00	6.75
Perez, Oneli	R-R	6-2	200	5-26-83	4	3	2.82	18	10	0	0	67	66	27	21	7	22	61	.261	.337	.213	8.19	2.96
Ring, Royce	L-L	6-0	220	12-21-80	5	2	3.04	51	0	0	4	47	44	18	16	4	15	38	.250	.208	.279	7.23	2.85
Salas, Fernando	R-R	6-2	200	5-30-85	3	2	3.67	24	0	0	0	27	22	12	11	4	10	24	.220	.227	.214	8.00	3.33
Scherer, Matt	R-R	6-5	260	1-20-83	3	4	3.54	52	0	0	1	74	79	37	29	8	18	61	.271	.282	.266	7.41	2.20
Thompson, Brad	R-R	6-1	190	1-31-82	2	0	3.45	3	3	0	0	16	13	6	6	1	1	9	.228	.273	.200	5.17	0.57
Todd, Jess	R-R	5-11	210	4-20-86	4	2	2.20	41	0	0	24	49	39	13	12	3	13	59	.214	.246	.195	10.84	2.39
Walters, P.J.	R-R	6-4	200	3-12-85	8	10	4.54	21	20	2	0	121	128	73	61	6	44	113	.271	.303	.241	8.40	3.27
Wellemeyer, Todd	R-R	6-3	225	8-30-78	0	0	18.00	2	2	0	0	2	4	4	4	1	3	4	.400	.375	.500	18.00	13.50

ST. LOUIS CARDINALS

Fielding

Catcher

Catcher	PCT	G	PO	A	E	DP	PB
Anderson	.987	44	283	22	4	4	6
Pagnozzi	.997	83	540	46	2	3	5
Stavinoha	1.000	1	11	0	0	0	0
Yarbrough	.968	34	199	13	7	1	6

First Base

First Base	PCT	G	PO	A	E	DP
Anderson	1.000	1	1	0	0	0
Barden	.984	21	118	6	2	17
Brito	1.000	8	73	3	0	11
Craig	.997	42	339	25	1	32
Descalso	.980	9	47	1	1	6
Freese	1.000	9	80	0	0	9
Hamilton	1.000	26	194	11	0	18
Jay	1.000	1	1	0	0	0
Mather	1.000	4	13	1	0	2
Stavinoha	.990	34	262	26	3	27
Wallace	1.000	9	54	6	0	3

Second Base

Second Base	PCT	G	PO	A	E	DP
Barden	1.000	3	3	3	0	0
Descalso	.973	28	64	82	4	18
Folli	1.000	4	6	16	0	3
Hoffpauir	.979	96	174	255	9	73
Rowlett	.979	25	39	55	2	13
Solano	1.000	4	5	21	0	3

Third Base

Third Base	PCT	G	PO	A	E	DP
Barden	.944	13	3	14	1	0
Craig	.900	13	6	21	3	2
Freese	.941	45	26	69	6	6
Glaus	.909	14	11	19	3	7
Greene	1.000	6	5	15	0	1
Greene	1.000	7	5	14	0	0
Hoffpauir	.250	2	0	1	3	0
Rowlett	.895	15	4	13	2	3
Solano	1.000	1	2	1	0	0
Wallace	.929	52	38	93	10	11

Shortstop

Shortstop	PCT	G	PO	A	E	DP
Barden	.960	17	8	40	2	8
Folli	1.000	4	4	5	0	1
Greene	.947	81	102	235	19	44
Greene	.893	8	4	21	3	0
Hoffpauir	.882	5	3	12	2	3
Ryan	1.000	3	4	10	0	3
Solano	.961	43	72	100	7	26

Outfield

Outfield	PCT	G	PO	A	E	DP
Barden	1.000	13	22	1	0	0
Barton	1.000	3	7	0	0	0
Craig	.991	73	112	3	1	1
Folli	1.000	1	2	0	0	0
Glaus	1.000	1	3	0	0	0
Hamilton	1.000	1	1	0	0	0
Jay	.996	131	258	3	1	2
Mather	1.000	35	68	6	0	0
Pagnozzi	—	1	0	0	0	0
Robinson	.992	96	250	6	2	2
Rowlett	1.000	17	17	0	0	0
Shorey	1.000	63	97	4	0	0
Stavinoha	.964	32	53	1	2	1
Yarbrough	1.000	4	5	0	0	0

SPRINGFIELD CARDINALS   DOUBLE-A
TEXAS LEAGUE

Batting	B-T	HT	WT	DOB	AVG	vLH	vRH	G	AB	R	H	2B	3B	HR	RBI	BB	HBP	SH	SF	SO	SB	CS	SLG	OBP
Arburr, Matt	R-R	6-4	260	3-21-81	.195	.211	.190	28	77	8	15	2	0	6	15	7	0	0	1	38	1	0	.455	.259
Brown, Andrew	R-R	6-0	185	9-10-84	.285	.351	.249	74	263	40	75	11	2	13	42	31	6	0	2	49	1	0	.490	.371
Buckman, Brandon	L-L	6-6	205	2-14-84	.133	.667	.000	4	15	0	2	1	0	0	1	2	0	0	0	5	0	0	.200	.235
Cruz, Arnoldi	R-R	5-11	205	8-18-86	.220	.254	.206	110	404	44	89	25	2	10	48	34	1	2	3	85	1	0	.366	.281
DeJesus, Antonio	L-L	5-11	185	1-25-86	.229	.279	.213	75	179	27	41	6	2	1	19	26	10	6	1	39	4	2	.302	.356
Derba, Nick	R-R	5-10	190	9-9-85	.130	.108	.141	40	108	9	14	5	0	2	7	21	1	1	0	34	0	1	.231	.277
Descalso, Daniel	L-R	5-10	190	10-19-86	.323	.321	.324	73	288	46	93	26	5	8	51	31	4	1	0	41	0	1	.531	.396
Folli, Mike	B-R	5-10	175	7-17-85	.237	.143	.265	71	211	24	50	11	4	4	23	18	2	2	2	31	6	1	.384	.300
Freese, David	R-R	6-2	220	4-28-83	.375	.625	.125	4	16	3	6	1	0	1	5	2	0	0	0	2	0	0	.625	.444
Glaus, Troy	R-R	6-5	240	8-3-76	.222	.400	.000	3	9	1	2	0	0	0	2	3	0	0	0	1	0	0	.222	.417
Greene, Khalil	R-R	5-11	185	10-21-79	.143	.200	.111	3	14	1	2	0	0	1	1	0	0	0	0	4	0	0	.357	.143
Hamilton, Mark	L-L	6-3	220	7-29-84	.307	.286	.314	48	163	26	50	11	0	8	28	28	4	0	0	46	0	1	.521	.421
Henley, Tyler	L-L	5-10	200	6-10-85	.303	.295	.306	123	423	62	128	31	3	13	63	40	5	1	4	64	9	4	.482	.367
Hill, Steven	R-R	5-11	200	3-14-85	.282	.303	.273	120	464	62	131	26	2	19	64	36	2	0	6	106	1	2	.470	.333
Jones, Daryl	L-L	5-11	180	6-25-87	.279	.284	.278	80	294	50	82	14	3	3	29	33	6	0	3	65	7	4	.378	.360
Kozma, Pete	R-R	6-0	170	4-11-88	.216	.269	.194	113	407	52	88	15	3	6	37	42	1	4	5	88	4	2	.312	.288
Luna, Aaron	R-R	5-11	200	3-28-87	.232	.227	.234	29	69	9	16	4	0	3	8	6	1	0	0	18	2	1	.420	.361
Mather, Joe	R-R	6-4	215	7-23-82	.207	.174	.229	17	58	8	12	3	0	3	11	5	1	0	1	11	0	2	.414	.277
Peterson, Shane	L-L	6-0	195	2-11-88	.284	.435	.216	18	74	10	21	4	1	1	7	5	1	0	0	10	2	0	.405	.338
2-team total (39 Midland)					.276	—	—	57	228	26	63	14	1	4	24	18	3	1	2	42	6	0	.399	.335
Rapoport, Jim	L-L	5-11	160	6-25-85	.255	.282	.243	124	458	69	117	16	6	4	58	71	4	6	4	73	12	7	.343	.358
Sedbrook, Colt	R-R	5-11	180	7-28-85	.236	.288	.209	55	174	22	41	5	0	3	16	23	8	2	2	30	8	2	.316	.348
Smith, Curt	R-R	5-10	210	9-9-86	.308	.375	.298	24	65	13	20	2	1	2	9	3	2	0	0	9	0	0	.462	.357
Solano, Donovan	R-R	5-10	165	12-17-87	.207	.227	.196	64	251	27	52	7	1	1	16	21	1	3	0	39	1	0	.255	.271
Wallace, Brett	L-R	6-2	205	8-26-86	.281	.280	.282	32	128	22	36	5	0	5	16	18	8	0	0	34	0	0	.438	.403

Pitching	B-T	HT	WT	DOB	W	L	ERA	G	GS	CG	SV	IP	H	R	ER	HR	BB	SO	AVG	vLH	vRH	K/9	BB/9
Additon, Nick	L-L	6-3	170	12-16-87	2	3	3.19	8	8	0	0	48	36	21	17	5	21	26	.207	.212	.206	4.88	3.94
Broderick, Brian	R-R	6-6	205	9-1-86	0	5	5.90	7	5	0	0	29	43	27	19	4	8	12	.350	.280	.397	3.72	2.48
Daley, Gary	R-R	6-3	200	11-1-85	0	2	4.76	9	0	0	0	11	9	6	6	1	7	7	.225	.333	.105	5.56	5.56
Degerman, Eddie	R-R	6-4	205	9-14-83	2	2	7.42	26	0	0	0	30	29	26	25	2	40	23	.269	.235	.284	6.82	11.87
Dickson, Brandon	R-R	6-5	190	11-3-84	8	10	3.78	28	20	1	0	148	160	75	62	12	50	112	.280	.306	.264	6.83	3.05
Fick, Chuck	R-R	6-5	187	11-20-85	1	2	1.50	10	3	0	1	24	19	5	4	1	10	12	.221	.257	.196	4.50	3.75
Fiske, Justin	L-L	5-11	185	9-3-84	1	1	5.06	12	3	0	0	27	30	18	15	2	14	23	.275	.314	.257	7.76	4.72
Freeman, Sam	R-L	5-11	170	6-24-87	0	1	3.52	15	0	0	1	23	19	9	9	6	14	17	.241	.154	.283	6.65	5.48
Furnish, Brad	B-L	6-1	185	1-19-85	2	2	9.14	19	8	0	0	42	57	44	43	5	40	29	.328	.366	.316	6.17	8.50
Gonzalez, Marco	R-R	6-2	205	5-28-84	0	5	4.84	44	0	0	0	58	66	34	31	5	25	20	.301	.313	.294	3.12	3.90
Gorgen, Scott	R-R	5-10	190	1-27-87	4	5	5.20	11	11	0	0	55	52	38	32	8	36	46	.259	.272	.250	7.48	5.86
Hearne, Trey	R-R	6-1	195	8-19-83	12	3	2.82	24	18	1	0	128	113	44	40	7	43	81	.240	.229	.249	5.71	3.03
Hernandez, Elvis	R-R	6-3	180	4-27-85	3	2	4.91	11	0	0	0	15	13	9	8	1	14	8	.255	.353	.206	4.91	8.59
Herron, Tyler	R-R	6-3	190	8-5-86	2	4	4.34	9	9	0	0	46	48	27	22	2	22	37	.268	.362	.209	7.29	4.34
King, Blake	R-R	6-1	195	4-11-87	0	0	10.80	3	0	0	0	3	7	4	4	0	5	6	.438	.000	.538	16.20	13.50
Kopp, David	R-R	6-3	205	10-22-85	1	1	6.43	5	5	0	0	21	29	18	15	3	11	6	.337	.422	.244	2.57	4.71
Kulik, Ryan	L-L	5-11	205	12-3-85	6	10	5.40	24	23	0	0	125	156	83	75	17	43	54	.310	.271	.321	3.89	3.10
Linares, Kristhiam	L-L	6-1	175	5-17-86	0	0	3.27	10	0	0	0	11	13	4	4	0	11	5	.295	.533	.172	4.09	9.00
Lohse, Kyle	R-R	6-2	210	10-4-78	0	0	3.86	1	1	0	0	5	3	2	2	1	4	3	.176	.100	.286	5.79	7.71
Lynn, Lance	R-R	6-5	250	5-12-87	11	4	2.92	22	22	0	0	126	117	51	41	5	51	98	.251	.266	.240	6.98	3.63
Maiques, Kenny	R-R	6-1	185	6-25-85	0	1	14.73	5	0	0	0	4	3	7	6	0	13	4	.250	.286	.200	9.82	31.91

Player	B-T	HT	WT	DOB	W	L	ERA	G	GS	CG	SV	IP	H	R	ER	HR	BB	SO	AVG	vLH	vRH	K/9	BB/9
Mulligan, Casey	R-R	6-2	190	10-5-87	3	0	2.21	15	0	0	2	20	15	5	5	1	12	27	.214	.280	.178	11.95	5.31
Mura, Kyle	R-R	6-4	215	11-24-84	1	0	7.88	7	4	0	0	16	28	15	14	2	5	9	.389	.517	.302	5.06	2.81
Norrick, Tyler	L-L	6-3	190	9-27-83	3	1	4.12	52	0	0	5	59	48	34	27	4	44	78	.219	.177	.236	11.90	6.71
Parise, Pete	R-R	6-1	185	12-5-84	3	1	2.88	25	0	0	0	41	31	13	13	3	12	29	.221	.250	.205	6.42	2.66
Salas, Fernando	R-R	6-2	200	5-30-85	1	0	3.18	10	0	0	0	11	10	5	4	0	2	7	.244	.250	.242	5.56	1.59
Samuel, Francisco	R-R	6-2	185	12-20-86	3	4	5.66	52	0	0	22	48	36	33	30	2	46	59	.208	.214	.205	11.14	8.69
Sanchez, Eduardo	R-R	5-11	155	2-16-89	2	0	2.70	41	0	0	10	50	32	16	15	4	20	56	.187	.218	.172	10.08	3.60
Williams, Joe	L-L	6-2	220	4-8-81	0	0	7.50	4	0	0	0	6	9	5	5	2	3	3	.360	.500	.316	4.50	4.50

Fielding

Catcher	PCT	G	PO	A	E	DP	PB
Cruz	.996	72	459	75	2	8	5
Derba	.996	38	246	18	1	2	2
Hill	.988	40	214	24	3	3	8

First Base	PCT	G	PO	A	E	DP
Arburr	.978	19	169	12	4	22
Brown	.984	54	419	23	7	60
Buckman	1.000	4	28	3	0	5
Cruz	.929	2	13	0	1	2
Glaus	.960	2	24	0	1	1
Hamilton	.996	33	269	15	1	39
Hill	1.000	25	207	14	0	19
Mather	1.000	2	4	0	0	0
Peterson	1.000	2	13	0	0	1
Rapoport	1.000	1	3	0	0	0
Smith	.968	9	54	7	2	9

Second Base	PCT	G	PO	A	E	DP
Descalso	.978	73	169	227	9	72
Folli	1.000	9	20	31	0	9
Luna	.938	3	8	7	1	2
Sedbrook	.959	38	67	98	7	30
Solano	.980	20	40	57	2	16

Third Base	PCT	G	PO	A	E	DP
Cruz	.947	32	20	52	4	8
Folli	.980	38	22	75	2	6
Freese	.750	4	3	6	3	2
Greene	1.000	3	1	5	0	1
Mather	.818	5	2	7	2	3
Sedbrook	.903	11	8	20	3	0
Smith	.000	1	0	0	1	0
Solano	.986	23	22	46	1	4
Wallace	.975	30	29	50	2	3

Shortstop	PCT	G	PO	A	E	DP
Folli	.945	10	23	29	3	12
Greene	1.000	1	2	4	0	0
Kozma	.957	113	181	375	25	97
Sedbrook	.938	3	4	11	1	4
Solano	.937	19	31	43	5	10

Outfield	PCT	G	PO	A	E	DP
Brown	.900	5	9	0	1	0
DeJesus	.986	65	135	6	2	2
Folli	1.000	4	9	0	0	0
Henley	.971	102	188	12	6	2
Hill	.864	30	35	3	6	0
Jones	.947	73	100	8	6	0
Luna	.941	16	30	2	2	0
Mather	1.000	12	12	2	0	0
Peterson	.842	16	16	0	3	0
Rapoport	.982	121	312	8	6	5
Smith	1.000	4	2	0	0	0

PALM BEACH CARDINALS   HIGH CLASS A

FLORIDA STATE LEAGUE

Batting	B-T	HT	WT	DOB	AVG	vLH	vRH	G	AB	R	H	2B	3B	HR	RBI	BB	HBP	SH	SF	SO	SB	CS	SLG	OBP
Arburr, Matt	R-R	6-4	260	3-21-86	.157	.121	.179	29	89	10	14	2	0	5	9	8	1	0	0	44	0	0	.348	.235
Bolivar, Domnit	R-R	5-11	165	5-12-89	.227	.206	.234	73	256	19	58	12	1	1	19	13	1	4	0	76	4	2	.293	.267
Brown, Andrew	R-R	6-0	185	9-10-84	.182	.000	.286	4	11	1	2	1	1	0	2	2	1	0	0	4	0	0	.455	.357
Carpenter, Matt	L-R	6-3	200	11-26-85	.219	.091	.272	32	114	13	25	6	1	1	9	10	1	2	1	24	1	0	.342	.286
Castellanos, Alex	R-R	5-11	180	8-4-86	.189	.227	.161	21	53	5	10	1	1	1	2	2	1	0	0	19	0	2	.302	.232
Chambers, Adron	L-L	5-10	185	10-8-86	.283	.235	.301	122	448	66	127	17	16	1	46	47	16	4	2	96	21	12	.400	.370
Curtis, Jermaine	R-R	5-11	190	7-10-87	.197	.171	.205	90	314	36	62	7	0	1	24	34	14	4	3	52	7	4	.229	.301
Cutler, Charlie	L-R	6-0	200	7-29-86	.274	.268	.276	44	146	25	40	10	2	1	15	25	8	1	1	22	2	0	.390	.406
De La Cruz, Luis	R-R	5-10	165	5-6-89	.154	.200	.125	4	13	0	2	1	0	0	0	0	0	0	0	4	0	0	.231	.154
Derba, Nick	R-R	5-10	190	9-9-85	.198	.174	.206	30	91	13	18	4	0	1	2	20	2	1	0	31	1	1	.275	.354
Garcia, Jose	R-R	5-11	170	2-11-88	.258	.231	.271	74	244	36	63	10	1	1	17	15	1	7	3	30	14	6	.320	.300
Glaus, Troy	R-R	6-5	240	8-3-76	.200	.000	.208	6	25	2	5	1	0	0	4	1	0	0	0	6	0	0	.240	.231
Kingrey, Charlie	L-L	6-2	210	1-19-85	.128	.000	.136	14	47	5	6	2	0	0	1	2	1	0	0	18	0	0	.170	.180
Kozma, Pete	R-R	6-0	170	4-11-88	.315	.353	.304	18	73	8	23	5	0	0	8	8	1	0	2	16	1	0	.384	.381
Luna, Aaron	R-R	5-11	200	3-28-87	.253	.340	.223	54	186	29	47	11	4	8	34	22	16	1	3	41	3	2	.484	.374
Marmol, Oliver	R-R	5-10	165	7-2-86	.204	.226	.194	74	186	22	38	10	1	2	13	18	15	2	2	55	5	3	.301	.321
Morales, Osvaldo	R-R	6-2	217	7-4-87	.213	.207	.217	24	75	5	16	5	0	0	8	5	0	0	2	30	0	0	.280	.256
Moscatel, Kevin	R-R	6-1	175	5-16-91	.111	.000	.125	4	9	0	1	0	0	0	1	0	0	0	0	1	0	0	.111	.111
Murphy, Blake	R-R	6-2	215	5-19-85	.162	.176	.153	45	136	12	22	7	1	2	9	16	1	3	0	41	1	0	.272	.255
Peterson, Shane	L-L	6-0	195	2-11-88	.298	.250	.312	76	285	32	85	11	4	6	39	21	11	0	2	52	10	1	.428	.367
Pham, Tommy	R-R	6-1	175	3-8-88	.232	.264	.220	114	336	47	78	15	5	8	44	36	4	3	1	102	18	6	.378	.313
Rivera, Francisco	L-L	5-11	170	12-3-88	.251	.140	.274	99	338	27	85	18	3	3	38	20	3	0	3	52	2	1	.349	.297
Sedbrook, Colt	R-R	5-11	180	7-28-85	.223	.212	.227	67	224	29	50	7	2	1	19	29	16	5	1	48	10	3	.299	.352
Smith, Curt	R-R	5-10	210	9-9-86	.286	.287	.285	94	371	44	106	15	3	10	56	15	6	1	6	67	1	3	.423	.319
Swauger, Chris	L-L	6-0	195	8-11-86	.273	.301	.264	87	289	35	79	19	4	7	41	14	6	1	2	45	4	2	.439	.318
Vasquez, Paul	R-R	5-10	160	3-7-85	.253	.233	.258	44	150	11	38	6	1	3	17	3	2	1	0	29	1	2	.367	.277

Pitching	B-T	HT	WT	DOB	W	L	ERA	G	GS	CG	SV	IP	H	R	ER	HR	BB	SO	AVG	vLH	vRH	K/9	BB/9
Additon, Nick	L-L	6-3	170	12-16-87	4	3	3.06	19	15	0	0	79	69	40	27	1	37	66	.233	.286	.215	7.49	4.20
Bradford, Jared	R-R	6-1	177	4-3-86	0	0	1.17	10	0	0	1	15	11	6	2	1	1	9	.183	.280	.114	5.28	0.59
Broderick, Brian	R-R	6-6	205	9-1-86	9	7	4.61	21	19	0	0	109	136	62	56	4	17	64	.305	.348	.262	5.27	1.40
Brown, George	L-L	6-1	195	6-18-86	4	5	4.26	14	13	0	0	63	63	32	30	2	19	47	.258	.246	.263	6.68	2.70
Buursma, Jason	R-R	6-3	200	9-9-85	3	1	4.62	27	0	0	0	37	52	22	19	1	15	20	.327	.387	.289	4.86	3.65
Castillos, Richard	R-R	5-11	165	10-11-89	6	13	3.87	29	26	1	0	149	155	77	64	4	66	105	.270	.278	.262	6.36	4.00
Diapoules, Mark	R-R	6-2	200	5-31-88	1	4	5.72	15	6	0	0	39	41	33	25	3	28	30	.259	.247	.271	6.86	6.41
Eager, Thomas	R-R	6-2	200	8-12-85	4	6	5.25	52	0	0	0	70	66	51	41	2	46	75	.260	.267	.254	9.60	5.89
Fick, Chuck	R-R	6-5	187	11-20-85	3	3	4.92	20	7	0	0	57	67	33	31	6	8	26	.296	.327	.272	4.13	1.27
Freeman, Sam	R-L	5-11	170	6-24-87	2	1	1.64	26	0	0	1	33	18	7	6	0	13	30	.157	.147	.160	8.18	3.55
Furnish, Brad	B-L	6-1	185	1-19-85	1	1	3.55	13	4	0	0	33	34	13	13	2	16	22	.270	.289	.261	6.00	4.36
Garceau, Shaun	B-R	6-1	185	8-28-87	0	2	6.23	11	4	0	0	30	30	22	21	2	19	16	.259	.208	.294	4.75	5.64
Garcia, Jaime	L-L	6-2	230	7-8-86	0	1	0.71	3	2	0	0	13	4	1	1	0	4	16	.105	.143	.097	11.37	2.84

Gonzalez, Yonathan	R-R	6-1	170	10-13-87	0	1	3.79	11	0	0	0	19	26	19	8	3	6	10	.310	.395	.220	4.74	2.84
Gorgen, Scott	R-R	5-10	190	1-27-87	3	5	2.92	14	13	0	0	74	50	28	24	7	32	73	.192	.182	.200	8.88	3.89
Hernandez, Elvis	R-R	6-3	180	4-27-85	0	0	5.65	12	0	0	0	14	13	10	9	2	16	13	.250	.286	.226	8.16	10.05
King, Blake	R-R	6-1	195	4-11-87	9	3	2.84	41	2	0	0	76	41	29	24	0	58	96	.160	.197	.126	11.37	6.87
Kopp, David	R-R	6-3	205	10-22-85	5	3	3.12	15	13	0	0	69	67	25	24	3	26	58	.262	.284	.243	7.53	3.38
Kulik, Ryan	L-L	5-11	205	12-3-85	1	1	5.25	4	2	0	1	12	15	7	7	1	3	17	.300	.214	.333	12.75	2.25
Linares, Kristhiam	L-L	6-1	175	5-7-86	0	2	4.62	23	0	0	0	25	21	14	13	1	15	26	.221	.136	.294	9.24	5.33
Lynn, Lance	R-R	6-5	250	5-12-87	0	0	2.30	5	2	0	0	16	16	4	4	0	3	17	.276	.304	.257	9.77	1.72
Mulligan, Casey	R-R	6-2	190	10-5-87	1	2	1.61	26	0	0	5	28	20	9	5	1	12	34	.198	.250	.143	10.93	3.86
Nieto, Arquimedes	R-R	6-0	175	4-28-89	1	3	4.28	6	0	0	0	34	32	20	16	1	9	27	.239	.266	.214	7.22	2.41
Parisi, Mike	R-R	6-3	215	4-18-83	0	1	8.22	2	2	0	0	8	15	7	7	0	3	4	.441	.500	.400	4.70	3.52
Reifer, Adam	R-R	6-2	195	6-3-86	4	7	4.47	54	0	0	21	48	51	28	24	2	24	50	.270	.232	.299	9.31	4.47
Rondon, Jorge	R-R	6-1	175	9-16-88	0	1	7.71	8	2	0	0	16	24	17	14	1	10	11	.338	.361	.314	6.06	5.51
Sanchez, Eduardo	R-R	5-11	155	2-16-89	0	1	1.44	19	0	0	3	25	12	4	4	2	5	26	.146	.167	.135	9.36	1.80

Fielding

Catcher	PCT	G	PO	A	E	DP	PB
Cutler	.995	30	198	15	1	1	3
De La Cruz	1.000	4	27	6	0	1	1
Derba	.996	30	226	19	1	3	0
Moscatel	1.000	3	21	4	0	0	1
Murphy	.977	39	275	21	7	1	5
Vasquez	.979	40	248	31	6	4	6

First Base	PCT	G	PO	A	E	DP
Arburr	1.000	18	126	5	0	19
Brown	1.000	2	9	2	0	0
Glaus	1.000	3	11	4	0	1
Morales	.981	23	191	17	4	20
Peterson	.976	5	37	3	1	5
Rivera	.992	57	451	43	4	49
Smith	.986	48	319	22	5	27
Swauger	1.000	5	13	1	0	0

Second Base	PCT	G	PO	A	E	DP
Castellanos	1.000	7	14	14	0	3

	PCT	G	PO	A	E	DP
Curtis	.984	18	18	44	1	6
Garcia	.977	18	30	55	2	16
Luna	.957	19	32	58	4	20
Marmol	.950	56	77	133	11	29
Sedbrook	.973	36	58	87	4	19

Third Base	PCT	G	PO	A	E	DP
Bolivar	.903	15	8	20	3	5
Carpenter	.976	32	12	70	2	8
Castellanos	.889	2	2	6	1	1
Curtis	.922	69	54	123	15	13
Garcia	.800	4	2	6	2	0
Marmol	.923	4	2	10	1	1
Rivera	1.000	1	0	1	0	0
Sedbrook	.943	16	11	22	2	3

Shortstop	PCT	G	PO	A	E	DP
Bolivar	.903	54	78	136	23	27
Garcia	.936	41	75	100	12	20
Kozma	.903	18	40	44	9	14

	PCT	G	PO	A	E	DP
Marmol	.939	10	17	29	3	9
Sedbrook	.988	19	29	52	1	18

Outfield	PCT	G	PO	A	E	DP
Bolivar	—	1	0	0	0	0
Brown	1.000	2	3	0	0	0
Castellanos	.944	12	15	2	1	2
Chambers	.975	118	223	11	6	3
Cutler	1.000	10	19	0	0	0
Glaus	1.000	1	1	0	0	0
Kingrey	1.000	8	14	0	0	0
Luna	.982	25	53	1	1	1
Marmol	1.000	1	2	0	0	0
Peterson	.985	62	123	8	2	4
Pham	.981	107	196	6	4	2
Rivera	—	1	0	0	0	0
Smith	.953	40	58	3	3	0
Swauger	.967	62	84	3	3	2

QUAD CITIES RIVER BANDITS

LOW CLASS A

MIDWEST LEAGUE

Batting	B-T	HT	WT	DOB	AVG	vLH	vRH	G	AB	R	H	2B	3B	HR	RBI	BB	HBP	SH	SF	SO	SB	CS	SLG	OBP
Bogany, Jarred	R-R	6-3	200	1-4-87	.245	.319	.217	75	253	31	62	7	5	2	26	28	1	4	2	78	16	7	.336	.320
Bolivar, Domnit	R-R	5-11	165	5-12-89	.218	.214	.220	45	165	25	36	10	0	5	14	13	4	2	1	56	4	1	.370	.290
Buck, Brian	R-R	6-1	190	2-3-86	.100	.000	.132	19	50	5	5	0	0	0	3	7	2	1	0	19	0	2	.100	.237
Carpenter, Matt	L-R	6-3	200	11-26-85	.295	.238	.310	29	105	11	31	6	2	0	10	17	3	0	1	13	2	0	.390	.405
Castellanos, Alex	R-R	5-11	180	8-4-86	.270	.250	.276	82	311	51	84	21	4	5	34	20	12	1	2	89	21	4	.412	.336
Cawley, Jack	R-R	6-2	205	3-2-86	.222	.227	.221	30	99	11	22	5	0	2	13	14	2	1	3	24	0	0	.333	.322
Conley, Kyle	R-R	6-4	209	5-7-87	.200	.231	.188	15	45	5	9	3	0	0	1	3	2	0	1	17	0	0	.267	.275
Cruz, Paul	L-L	6-0	190	9-20-85	.260	.295	.250	54	196	20	51	8	1	3	20	19	3	3	1	24	4	3	.357	.333
Curtis, Jermaine	R-R	5-11	190	7-10-87	.304	.261	.315	30	112	20	34	12	0	1	10	19	5	0	0	12	2	2	.438	.424
Cutler, Charlie	L-R	6-0	200	7-29-86	.351	.410	.331	66	242	36	85	11	1	4	44	24	5	0	7	25	1	1	.455	.410
Edwards, Jon	R-R	6-5	230	1-8-88	.191	.205	.188	67	225	22	43	9	0	11	32	21	5	0	3	85	0	1	.378	.272
Espinoza, Roberto	R-R	5-10	165	3-24-87	.220	.226	.218	68	223	18	49	7	0	1	17	28	4	1	3	49	2	1	.265	.314
Garcia, Jose	R-R	5-11	170	2-11-88	.265	.182	.289	42	147	24	39	6	4	1	16	15	1	7	1	24	13	6	.381	.335
Ingram, D'Marcus	R-R	5-9	170	3-30-88	.246	.094	.302	30	118	17	29	8	0	0	11	17	1	3	2	18	7	5	.314	.341
Lilley, Brett	L-R	5-8	170	7-30-85	.229	.193	.243	60	205	35	47	9	1	1	17	32	13	3	1	44	1	1	.298	.367
Luna, Aaron	R-R	5-11	200	3-8-87	.125	.000	.182	6	16	5	2	1	0	0	1	5	2	0	0	5	2	0	.188	.391
Martinez, Jairo	R-R	6-1	180	5-27-87	.174	.045	.292	13	46	3	8	2	0	0	3	1	1	0	0	11	0	0	.217	.208
Mitchell, Travis	R-R	6-3	185	9-27-87	.254	.189	.276	58	205	28	52	8	2	0	7	3	2	3	0	55	9	0	.312	.271
Morales, Osvaldo	R-R	6-2	217	7-4-87	.216	.190	.223	100	361	42	78	16	0	15	74	35	4	0	5	119	1	0	.385	.289
Murphy, Blake	R-R	6-2	215	5-19-85	.286	.667	.000	3	7	0	2	0	0	0	2	1	0	0	0	0	0	0	.286	.375
Parejo, Frederick	R-R	6-0	165	7-5-90	.221	.217	.223	94	339	37	75	17	3	2	36	35	1	1	3	55	2	5	.307	.294
Racobaldo, Rich	R-R	6-1	220	7-10-85	.234	.258	.226	31	124	16	29	6	1	3	16	12	1	0	1	23	4	1	.371	.304
Rodriguez, Ryde	R-R	6-3	232	2-4-88	.222	.333	.184	54	198	16	44	9	1	2	19	7	3	0	1	51	3	0	.308	.258
Scruggs, Xavier	R-R	6-1	210	9-23-87	.295	.273	.302	34	129	17	38	7	1	7	33	23	2	0	0	43	2	1	.527	.409
Stidham, Jason	L-R	5-11	180	2-26-88	.261	.139	.286	56	211	23	55	17	2	1	22	18	3	4	1	48	2	3	.374	.326
Stock, Robert	R-R	6-0	175	11-21-89	.095	.200	.063	5	21	1	2	0	0	0	2	1	0	0	0	5	0	0	.095	.208
Swauger, Chris	L-L	6-0	195	8-11-86	.296	.148	.341	31	115	28	34	10	2	4	22	9	2	0	0	23	2	1	.522	.357
Toribio, Guillermo	B-R	6-0	160	3-3-87	.146	.136	.148	39	103	8	15	2	1	0	7	10	2	3	1	25	2	0	.184	.233
Vasquez, Niko	R-R	5-11	175	2-26-89	.197	.175	.205	61	208	27	41	6	1	1	14	28	2	3	3	58	2	2	.250	.295

Pitching	B-T	HT	WT	DOB	W	L	ERA	G	GS	CG	SV	IP	H	R	ER	HR	BB	SO	AVG	vLH	vRH	K/9	BB/9
Bravo, Jonny	L-L	5-7	175	8-23-86	0	1	21.94	3	1	0	0	5	12	14	13	1	9	6	.429	.000	.480	10.13	15.19
Brown, George	L-L	6-1	195	6-18-86	0	2	6.16	8	3	0	0	19	21	16	13	1	10	14	.273	.100	.333	6.63	4.74
Buursma, Jason	R-R	6-3	200	9-9-85	0	0	0.77	9	0	0	0	12	6	1	1	0	1	11	.150	.188	.125	8.49	0.77
Cardenas, Hector	L-L	6-3	180	12-14-86	6	4	3.61	18	14	0	1	77	74	43	31	3	22	49	.249	.232	.254	5.70	2.56

Name	B-T	HT	WT	DOB	W	L	ERA	G	GS	CG	SV	IP	H	R	ER	HR	BB	SO	AVG	vLH	vRH	K/9	BB/9
Carpenter, David	R-R	6-2	200	7-15-85	5	3	4.28	52	0	0	12	67	61	34	32	2	36	77	.244	.189	.288	10.29	4.81
Daley, Gary	R-R	6-3	200	11-1-85	4	3	6.93	32	10	0	0	77	89	65	59	7	51	72	.296	.263	.321	8.45	5.99
Delgado, Ramon	R-R	6-3	195	9-3-86	7	3	2.41	53	0	0	3	82	70	28	22	5	17	68	.229	.206	.247	7.46	1.87
Diapoules, Mark	R-R	6-2	200	5-31-88	1	0	3.00	3	0	0	0	6	5	2	2	0	1	8	.227	.308	.111	12.00	1.50
Fick, Chuck	R-R	6-5	187	11-20-85	0	2	4.24	4	3	0	0	17	21	9	8	1	4	13	.300	.357	.286	6.88	2.12
Fornataro, Eric	R-R	6-1	195	1-2-88	0	5	5.24	7	6	0	0	34	42	25	20	2	11	11	.302	.353	.254	2.88	2.88
Frevert, Matt	R-R	6-1	190	11-16-86	2	1	1.78	28	0	0	4	35	25	8	7	2	10	44	.195	.268	.139	11.21	2.55
Gonzalez, Yonathan	R-R	6-1	170	10-13-87	1	2	7.63	10	0	0	0	15	17	14	13	1	7	13	.270	.296	.250	7.63	4.11
McCully, Nick	R-R	5-11	195	9-5-88	1	0	7.20	16	0	0	0	20	24	17	16	3	14	19	.304	.375	.255	8.55	6.30
McGregor, Scott	R-R	6-2	193	12-19-86	7	11	5.56	34	17	0	1	115	141	92	71	5	26	78	.290	.272	.302	6.10	2.03
Miller, Shelby	R-R	6-3	195	10-10-90	0	0	6.00	2	2	0	0	3	5	3	2	0	2	2	.357	.000	.714	6.00	6.00
Mulligan, Casey	R-R	6-2	190	10-5-87	2	0	0.45	17	0	0	9	20	8	2	1	0	5	36	.114	.115	.114	16.20	2.25
Nieto, Arquimedes	R-R	6-0	175	4-28-89	3	9	4.01	23	16	0	0	101	94	49	45	6	26	89	.250	.243	.256	7.93	2.32
Pichardo, Joel	R-R	5-11	160	2-20-88	3	1	2.95	28	0	0	0	40	37	18	13	3	9	35	.237	.229	.244	7.94	2.04
Rondon, Jorge	R-R	6-1	175	9-16-88	1	5	4.27	10	10	0	0	53	59	29	25	7	13	37	.278	.281	.276	6.32	2.22
Rosales, Andres	R-R	6-0	140	6-13-88	2	4	5.53	18	3	0	0	41	36	28	22	5	24	43	.240	.224	.250	9.52	5.31
Schneider, Scott	R-R	6-0	175	6-7-88	1	3	3.45	5	5	1	0	31	26	17	12	3	5	29	.218	.262	.172	8.33	1.44
Tapia, Angel	R-R	6-1	198	2-6-88	3	4	4.90	33	8	0	0	83	89	52	45	4	41	63	.277	.308	.253	6.86	4.46
Thomas, Kevin	R-R	6-3	215	7-8-86	7	7	4.07	28	21	0	1	119	116	63	54	6	42	55	.254	.269	.242	4.15	3.17
Veres, Adam	R-R	6-4	230	3-19-88	3	5	4.00	33	10	0	0	81	89	50	36	6	33	75	.277	.268	.284	8.33	3.67
Wilson, Josh	R-R	6-0	180	9-6-86	1	0	6.61	4	2	0	0	16	19	14	12	5	4	11	.279	.233	.316	6.06	2.20
Zawacki, Brett	R-R	6-1	190	5-2-89	1	3	5.63	8	8	0	0	32	34	22	20	1	10	22	.270	.293	.250	6.19	2.81

Fielding

Catcher	PCT	G	PO	A	E	DP	PB
Cawley	.987	28	193	31	3	3	9
Cutler	.994	42	301	38	2	3	7
Espinoza	.988	67	438	51	6	4	14
Murphy	1.000	1	7	0	0	0	0
Stock	.978	5	41	3	1	1	3

First Base	PCT	G	PO	A	E	DP
Castellanos	.966	7	81	3	3	6
Cutler	1.000	2	10	0	0	1
Martinez	1.000	1	1	0	0	1
Morales	.989	93	770	58	9	56
Scruggs	.976	34	352	20	9	28
Swauger	1.000	7	47	2	0	5

Second Base	PCT	G	PO	A	E	DP
Castellanos	.964	36	52	108	6	16
Lilley	.973	32	62	84	4	16

	PCT	G	PO	A	E	DP
Luna	1.000	5	4	6	0	1
Stidham	.967	52	91	174	9	36
Toribio	.970	21	21	44	2	8

Third Base	PCT	G	PO	A	E	DP
Bolivar	.868	14	5	28	5	2
Carpenter	.955	28	21	63	4	7
Castellanos	.845	29	16	55	13	5
Curtis	.875	18	7	42	7	2
Lilley	.934	27	17	54	5	3
Racobaldo	.971	16	7	27	1	7
Toribio	1.000	10	5	11	0	0

Shortstop	PCT	G	PO	A	E	DP
Bolivar	.907	29	48	98	15	21
Garcia	.931	42	69	120	14	24
Stidham	.786	3	1	10	3	1
Toribio	.941	9	13	19	2	1

	PCT	G	PO	A	E	DP
Vasquez	.909	58	77	164	24	25

Outfield	PCT	G	PO	A	E	DP
Bogany	.942	57	94	4	6	0
Buck	.947	18	34	2	2	1
Castellanos	1.000	9	19	0	0	0
Conley	.938	7	15	0	1	0
Cruz	1.000	45	74	4	0	1
Edwards	.964	50	78	2	3	0
Ingram	.985	30	64	2	1	1
Martinez	1.000	5	4	1	0	0
Mitchell	.956	56	125	4	6	1
Parejo	.963	92	173	10	7	3
Rodriguez	.972	47	67	3	2	0
Swauger	.963	13	24	2	1	0

BATAVIA MUCKDOGS   SHORT-SEASON
NEW YORK-PENN LEAGUE

Batting	B-T	HT	WT	DOB	AVG	vLH	vRH	G	AB	R	H	2B	3B	HR	RBI	BB	HBP	SH	SF	SO	SB	CS	SLG	OBP
Adams, Matt	L-R	6-3	230	8-31-88	.346	.275	.378	31	130	16	45	11	0	4	27	11	0	0	1	21	0	0	.523	.394
Ahmady, Alan	R-R	5-11	200	12-14-87	.292	.234	.313	67	243	46	71	13	1	3	32	47	2	1	3	52	2	3	.391	.407
Alvarez, Hector	B-R	6-0	175	1-25-87	.250	—	.250	2	4	0	1	0	0	0	0	1	0	0	0	2	0	0	.250	.400
Carpenter, Matt	L-R	6-3	200	11-26-85	.469	.400	.481	9	32	9	15	3	0	0	3	4	1	0	0	2	0	1	.563	.541
Castro, Ivan	R-R	6-0	185	11-17-87	.207	.214	.204	39	145	20	30	3	2	2	11	8	0	0	0	36	1	0	.297	.248
Cawley, Jack	R-R	6-2	205	3-2-86	.300	.286	.304	9	30	5	9	1	0	0	1	6	0	0	0	5	1	0	.333	.417
Conley, Kyle	R-R	6-4	209	5-7-87	.385	.424	.368	29	109	21	42	16	0	8	23	13	1	0	1	20	2	3	.752	.452
De La Cruz, Luis	R-R	5-10	165	5-6-89	.220	.351	.180	46	159	20	35	6	2	0	17	10	2	0	0	28	4	2	.283	.275
Edwards, Jon	R-R	6-5	230	1-8-88	.232	.250	.224	29	112	11	26	4	1	2	13	5	1	0	1	46	1	0	.339	.269
Gomez, Edwin	R-R	5-11	170	5-4-88	.222	.000	.250	3	9	0	2	1	0	0	0	0	0	0	0	3	0	0	.333	.222
Goodwin, Devin	R-R	5-11	185	10-2-86	.239	.222	.245	55	209	31	50	19	1	3	22	25	0	2	3	36	2	2	.383	.316
Ingram, D'Marcus	R-R	5-9	170	3-30-88	.290	.484	.234	37	138	19	40	5	4	0	12	17	1	2	0	20	18	2	.384	.372
Jackson, Ryan	R-R	6-3	180	5-10-88	.216	.212	.218	67	245	29	53	4	1	0	14	29	0	7	2	37	4	3	.241	.297
Martinez, Jairo	R-R	6-1	180	5-27-87	.177	.227	.162	29	96	11	17	3	0	1	7	6	1	0	2	31	0	0	.240	.229
Mitchell, Travis	R-R	6-3	185	9-27-87	.155	.200	.132	19	58	4	9	1	0	0	4	4	0	0	1	21	3	2	.172	.206
Riportella, Beau	R-R	6-3	200	8-20-88	.191	.227	.183	42	115	16	22	1	0	2	12	12	1	4	2	28	6	1	.252	.269
Rodriguez, Ryde	B-R	6-3	232	2-2-88	.311	.258	.324	42	145	25	45	12	0	4	30	6	1	0	0	34	1	1	.473	.339
Scruggs, Xavier	R-R	6-1	210	9-23-87	.234	.321	.214	41	145	21	34	7	0	7	26	21	4	0	1	48	1	1	.428	.345
Swinson, Michael	L-R	6-2	185	9-24-89	.196	.115	.227	23	92	13	18	5	1	0	9	11	0	4	1	24	4	1	.272	.279
Toribio, Guillermo	B-R	6-0	160	3-3-87	.159	.154	.161	17	44	4	7	1	0	0	4	2	0	0	0	12	0	2	.182	.196
Vasquez, Niko	R-R	5-11	175	2-26-89	.209	.177	.219	70	249	19	52	11	2	2	21	26	1	0	3	56	1	1	.293	.283

Pitching	B-T	HT	WT	DOB	W	L	ERA	G	GS	CG	SV	IP	H	R	ER	HR	BB	SO	AVG	vLH	vRH	K/9	BB/9
Blazek, Michael	R-R	6-0	180	3-16-89	4	9	4.50	15	12	0	0	64	73	45	32	3	24	62	.284	.306	.265	8.72	3.38
Bravo, Jonny	L-L	5-7	175	8-23-86	3	1	4.58	13	0	0	0	18	21	9	9	1	8	22	.288	.231	.319	11.21	4.08
Calhoun, Daniel	L-L	6-3	220	9-6-88	2	0	1.86	12	0	0	0	48	40	14	10	1	6	42	.217	.179	.239	7.82	1.12
Corrigan, Chris	R-R	6-2	155	12-24-87	2	2	3.80	16	7	0	0	47	45	21	20	2	22	28	.256	.250	.259	5.32	4.18
Edwards, Justin	L-L	6-2	188	12-3-87	3	2	3.25	15	8	0	0	53	50	21	19	1	16	54	.254	.145	.296	9.23	2.73
Fornataro, Eric	R-R	6-1	195	1-2-88	4	0	2.15	8	5	0	0	38	23	9	9	0	6	14	.177	.193	.164	3.35	1.43

Name	B-T	HT	WT	DOB	W	L	ERA	G	GS	CG	SV	IP	H	R	ER	HR	BB	SO	AVG	vLH	vRH	K/9	BB/9
Hooker, Deryk	R-R	6-4	185	6-21-89	1	6	3.98	15	10	0	0	61	56	30	27	4	23	53	.243	.257	.233	7.82	3.39
Kelly, Joe	R-R	6-1	165	6-9-88	2	3	4.75	16	2	0	1	30	33	23	16	0	11	30	.273	.220	.323	8.90	3.26
Lavigne, Tyler	R-R	6-0	190	7-30-88	2	2	4.71	16	4	0	0	29	25	15	15	1	8	34	.236	.205	.254	10.67	2.51
Leach, Tyler	R-R	6-3	200	9-8-86	1	2	6.44	15	5	0	0	36	50	33	26	4	13	16	.321	.300	.333	3.96	3.22
Maertz, Santo	R-R	6-2	220	5-9-86	3	1	1.45	26	0	0	3	31	15	6	5	0	11	36	.142	.128	.149	10.45	3.19
Mayes, LaCurtis	R-R	5-11	185	8-2-88	1	2	3.20	26	0	0	6	25	18	13	9	1	13	33	.194	.135	.232	11.72	4.62
Moss, Andy	R-R	6-1	210	10-8-86	0	1	13.50	1	1	0	0	5	8	7	7	0	1	5	.421	.500	.400	9.64	1.93
Richardson, Dan	R-R	6-2	195	3-21-85	0	1	6.28	11	0	0	0	14	13	13	10	0	17	11	.271	.333	.242	6.91	10.67
Rosales, Andres	R-R	6-0	140	6-13-88	2	2	8.00	17	1	0	0	18	24	17	16	6	11	23	.308	.375	.261	11.50	5.50
Schneider, Scott	R-R	6-0	175	6-7-88	2	0	0.92	12	5	0	1	39	25	8	4	0	8	47	.175	.143	.195	10.75	1.83
Siegrist, Kevin	L-L	6-5	190	7-20-89	1	0	3.86	10	4	0	2	28	30	14	12	4	11	23	.273	.265	.276	7.39	3.54
Simpson, Jesse	R-R	6-0	180	1-29-87	0	1	2.78	7	3	0	0	23	17	7	7	0	10	30	.213	.167	.250	11.91	3.97
Smith, Justin	R-R	6-0	190	3-23-88	0	3	4.50	7	3	0	0	20	17	12	10	1	8	27	.236	.235	.237	12.15	3.60
Squatrito, Josh	R-R	6-1	210	3-12-87	4	1	1.37	20	0	0	1	26	21	5	4	0	6	35	.219	.167	.259	11.96	2.05
Terry, Aaron	R-R	5-11	185	12-28-86	0	0	18.00	2	0	0	0	2	6	5	4	1	0	1	.500	.667	.444	4.50	0.00

Fielding

Catcher	PCT	G	PO	A	E	DP	PB
Ahmady	1.000	3	2	0	0	0	1
Castro	.989	35	303	51	4	2	12
Cawley	.971	4	30	3	1	0	1
De La Cruz	.976	37	258	30	7	3	10

First Base	PCT	G	PO	A	E	DP
Adams	.979	19	173	11	4	9
Ahmady	.979	16	129	11	3	12
Carpenter	1.000	1	10	0	0	1
Martinez	1.000	1	2	0	0	0
Scruggs	.987	40	369	20	5	27

Second Base	PCT	G	PO	A	E	DP
Ahmady	1.000	1	2	5	0	0
Goodwin	.966	52	85	143	8	31
Toribio	.971	11	10	23	1	4
Vasquez	.984	13	23	39	1	6

Third Base	PCT	G	PO	A	E	DP
Ahmady	.956	32	18	68	4	5
Alvarez	1.000	1	3	3	0	1
Carpenter	1.000	7	1	11	0	1
Toribio	1.000	5	2	1	0	0
Vasquez	.900	37	23	49	8	5

Shortstop	PCT	G	PO	A	E	DP
Jackson	.958	67	93	184	12	33

Vasquez	.976	9	17	24	1	5

Outfield	PCT	G	PO	A	E	DP
Ahmady	1.000	2	5	0	0	0
Conley	.929	28	36	3	3	1
Edwards	.935	26	40	3	3	0
Gomez	—	2	0	0	0	0
Ingram	.984	35	60	2	1	0
Martinez	1.000	25	42	1	0	1
Mitchell	1.000	18	25	2	0	1
Riportella	1.000	37	65	0	0	0
Rodriguez	.984	41	59	2	1	1
Swinson	.977	22	41	1	1	1

JOHNSON CITY CARDINALS   ROOKIE

APPALACHIAN LEAGUE

Batting	B-T	HT	WT	DOB	AVG	vLH	vRH	G	AB	R	H	2B	3B	HR	RBI	BB	HBP	SH	SF	SO	SB	CS	SLG	OBP
Adams, Matt	L-R	6-3	230	8-31-88	.365	.400	.353	32	115	15	42	6	0	6	25	9	1	0	3	20	0	0	.574	.406
Alvarez, Hector	B-R	6-0	175	1-25-87	.228	.263	.206	40	101	16	23	4	1	1	5	13	2	4	0	35	5	2	.317	.328
Beatty, C.J.	B-R	5-10	190	9-28-88	.175	.222	.167	19	57	13	10	1	0	2	8	6	0	0	1	14	3	0	.298	.250
Castillo, Yunior	B-R	6-0	160	5-15-89	.259	.132	.316	50	170	19	44	8	2	2	10	0	1	2	0	39	2	4	.365	.263
Hage, Joey	R-R	6-0	180	2-17-89	.176	.214	.162	20	51	6	9	5	0	0	2	5	1	1	1	10	0	0	.275	.259
Lara, Edgar	R-R	6-3	210	3-2-89	.237	.221	.244	64	224	22	53	16	0	9	36	26	3	0	1	74	0	2	.429	.323
Mateo, Luis	R-R	6-0	160	5-23-90	.344	.375	.333	26	93	16	32	7	1	3	12	4	1	1	1	25	5	4	.538	.374
Obregon, Ted	B-R	5-11	170	5-4-90	.268	.217	.293	58	183	30	49	4	2	4	17	17	1	2	1	46	14	3	.377	.332
Perez, Audris	R-R	5-9	180	12-23-88	.258	.318	.226	40	128	22	33	7	1	9	23	8	0	0	0	28	1	0	.539	.301
Racobaldo, Rich	R-R	6-1	220	7-10-85	.408	.471	.385	35	125	28	51	11	0	4	26	15	3	0	4	21	5	2	.592	.469
Rigoli, Matt	R-R	5-11	210	11-19-85	.179	.261	.121	26	56	8	10	1	0	0	2	9	4	0	0	19	0	0	.196	.333
Rodriguez, Jonathan	R-R	6-2	205	8-21-89	.250	.273	.239	24	68	9	17	5	0	2	7	11	1	0	0	18	1	1	.412	.363
Rosario, Rainel	R-R	6-0	188	3-29-89	.272	.167	.315	36	125	20	34	12	1	1	14	12	3	0	0	35	3	5	.440	.350
Ruiz, Romulo	R-R	6-0	170	11-30-89	.134	.179	.103	32	97	8	13	2	0	5	17	9	0	0	2	34	0	0	.309	.204
Smith, Ross	R-R	6-2	175	10-6-87	.190	.207	.183	61	184	28	35	11	1	6	16	17	10	0	0	70	9	1	.359	.294
Stock, Robert	L-R	6-0	175	11-21-89	.322	.270	.339	41	149	25	48	9	2	7	24	11	5	0	1	28	0	1	.550	.386
Swinson, Michael	L-R	6-2	185	9-24-89	.338	.143	.383	21	74	18	25	4	1	3	14	11	1	0	1	17	6	1	.541	.425
Tartamella, Travis	R-R	5-11	200	12-17-87	.183	.219	.160	26	82	10	15	2	0	1	8	7	1	0	0	18	0	1	.244	.256
Teran, Kleininger	L-R	6-1	175	7-23-89	.245	.188	.273	32	98	12	24	7	0	0	14	15	1	0	1	11	0	1	.316	.348

Pitching	B-T	HT	WT	DOB	W	L	ERA	G	GS	CG	SV	IP	H	R	ER	HR	BB	SO	AVG	vLH	vRH	K/9	BB/9
Butler, Keith	R-R	6-0	180	1-30-89	0	0	0.00	2	0	0	0	2	0	0	0	0	1	4	.000	.000	.000	18.00	4.50
Daugherty, Pat	L-L	6-5	215	8-30-88	0	2	11.57	4	0	0	0	7	7	12	9	1	11	6	.269	.364	.200	7.71	14.14
De Jesus, Angel	R-R	6-6	188	2-3-89	0	2	6.46	5	2	0	0	15	23	12	11	1	1	11	.354	.353	.354	6.46	0.59
Durham, John	L-L	6-1	170	8-19-87	1	1	9.55	11	3	0	0	27	47	31	29	3	9	19	.373	.294	.402	6.26	2.96
Ferrara, Anthony	R-L	6-1	175	9-2-89	4	1	3.24	13	9	0	0	50	49	21	18	1	17	40	.263	.368	.236	7.20	3.06
Gonzalez, Reynier	R-R	6-3	180	11-5-88	2	5	6.08	13	8	0	0	40	49	40	27	3	15	37	.293	.324	.273	8.32	3.38
Heim, Kyle	L-L	6-4	220	9-30-87	0	1	7.71	16	0	0	0	19	23	17	16	3	11	21	.303	.375	.283	10.13	5.30
Johnson, Cale	R-R	6-2	200	8-26-87	2	1	4.01	8	4	0	0	25	36	15	11	3	3	12	.333	.325	.338	4.38	1.09
Kington, David	R-R	6-2	200	12-1-87	2	1	3.31	19	0	0	8	16	10	7	6	0	7	15	.169	.368	.075	8.27	3.86
Lawler, Travis	R-R	6-3	180	6-13-88	2	1	4.05	17	0	0	0	20	22	11	9	1	10	29	.272	.290	.260	13.05	4.50
Moss, Andy	R-R	6-1	210	10-8-86	1	2	1.32	13	6	0	1	55	38	14	8	2	17	48	.196	.216	.183	7.90	2.80
Notti, Chris	R-R	6-5	210	9-3-88	4	1	3.83	12	8	0	0	42	49	30	18	2	6	32	.277	.291	.270	6.80	1.28
Novak, Jason	R-R	6-1	205	10-19-87	0	1	6.00	19	0	0	1	21	24	15	14	2	7	24	.279	.357	.241	10.29	3.00
Ortiz, Pablo	R-R	6-4	175	6-11-88	2	0	6.75	5	3	0	0	13	13	12	10	0	7	17	.241	.217	.258	11.48	4.72
Rada, Jose	R-R	6-1	180	4-13-88	5	0	1.76	23	0	0	1	31	22	8	6	1	8	30	.202	.184	.211	8.80	2.35
Russell, Ronald	R-R	6-2	185	7-27-89	0	0	1.89	6	2	0	0	19	8	5	4	1	11	22	.125	.174	.098	10.42	5.21
Santos, Randy	R-R	6-2	190	8-21-88	1	7	5.40	12	9	0	0	48	50	41	29	4	20	40	.263	.317	.238	7.45	3.72
Simpson, Jesse	R-R	6-0	180	1-29-87	3	0	1.24	8	4	0	0	29	18	5	4	1	7	28	.176	.132	.203	8.69	2.17

	B-T	HT	WT	DOB	W	L	ERA	G	GS	CG	SV	IP	H	R	ER	HR	BB	SO	AVG	vLH	vRH	K/9	BB/9
Smith, Justin	R-R	6-0	190	3-23-88	1	1	3.70	7	3	0	0	24	18	12	10	5	7	37	.198	.207	.194	13.68	2.59
Terry, Aaron	R-R	5-11	185	12-28-86	6	0	2.08	21	0	0	6	26	16	7	6	2	9	36	.170	.303	.098	12.46	3.12
Thompson, Michael	L-R	6-0	200	8-28-86	1	3	7.25	14	6	0	0	36	58	30	29	6	10	44	.360	.296	.393	11.00	2.50

Fielding

Catcher	PCT	G	PO	A	E	DP	PB
Perez	1.000	13	112	6	0	0	0
Stock	.985	30	236	32	4	1	6
Tartamella	.991	24	194	19	2	0	4

First Base	PCT	G	PO	A	E	DP
Adams	.992	29	226	14	2	11
Rigoli	1.000	16	105	8	0	5
Rodriguez	.979	18	134	8	3	13
Ruiz	.984	12	116	5	2	10
Teran	1.000	1	12	0	0	0

Second Base	PCT	G	PO	A	E	DP
Alvarez	.500	5	1	1	2	0
Mateo	.908	20	23	36	6	5

Obregon	.955	50	73	117	9	25

Third Base	PCT	G	PO	A	E	DP
Alvarez	.897	12	6	20	3	0
Mateo	1.000	7	1	12	0	1
Obregon	.846	7	3	8	2	1
Racobaldo	.944	23	12	39	3	3
Rigoli	1.000	2	2	3	0	1
Ruiz	.833	3	4	1	1	0
Teran	.913	28	15	48	6	2

Shortstop	PCT	G	PO	A	E	DP
Alvarez	.915	23	23	63	8	9
Beatty	—	1	0	0	0	0
Castillo	.909	50	62	128	19	23

Obregon	.750	1	1	2	1	1

Outfield	PCT	G	PO	A	E	DP
Alvarez	—	1	0	0	0	0
Beatty	1.000	2	1	1	0	0
Hage	1.000	20	15	0	0	0
Lara	.968	62	87	5	3	2
Obregon	—	1	0	0	0	0
Perez	—	2	0	0	0	0
Racobaldo	.920	12	21	2	2	0
Rosario	.898	36	50	3	6	0
Smith	.972	61	99	6	3	0
Swinson	1.000	20	32	4	0	2

GCL CARDINALS   ROOKIE
GULF COAST LEAGUE

Batting	B-T	HT	WT	DOB	AVG	vLH	vRH	G	AB	R	H	2B	3B	HR	RBI	BB	HBP	SH	SF	SO	SB	CS	SLG	OBP
Anderson, Bryan	L-R	6-1	200	12-16-86	.313	.000	.357	5	16	3	5	0	0	1	2	4	0	0	0	4	1	0	.500	.450
Babrick, Joe	R-R	6-6	215	12-7-89	.204	.184	.212	46	137	18	28	5	4	4	18	18	4	0	0	68	4	2	.387	.314
Bighames, Tyler	R-R	6-2	190	4-12-91	.216	.056	.257	33	88	15	19	5	1	1	8	10	1	0	1	23	1	2	.330	.300
Brown, Andrew	R-R	6-0	185	9-10-84	.667	.000	1.000	1	3	1	2	0	0	0	0	0	0	0	0	0	0	0	.667	.667
Cabrera, Juan B	R-R	6-1	151	6-22-88	.167	.000	.176	7	18	0	3	1	0	0	0	2	0	0	0	3	0	0	.222	.250
De La Cruz, Roberto	R-R	6-2	180	11-10-91	.224	.302	.197	49	165	17	37	9	0	0	17	10	1	0	4	59	0	3	.279	.267
Freese, David	R-R	6-2	220	4-28-83	.455	.667	.375	4	11	2	5	2	0	1	6	1	0	0	0	3	0	0	.909	.500
Garcia, Anthony	R-R	6-0	180	1-4-92	.235	.200	.244	23	51	12	12	3	1	0	3	4	2	0	0	10	2	1	.333	.316
Gomez, Edwin	R-R	5-11	170	3-10-88	.286	.000	.333	3	7	2	2	1	0	0	1	2	1	0	0	4	0	0	.429	.500
Hage, Joey	R-R	6-0	180	2-17-89	.311	.100	.371	16	45	7	14	5	0	0	7	3	1	0	1	7	0	0	.422	.360
Hill, Virgil	R-R	5-11	186	9-9-89	.216	.125	.246	51	162	28	35	6	4	1	22	20	6	0	0	58	11	7	.321	.324
Mannbel, Gerardo	R-R	5-11	165	5-16-90	.222	.195	.233	45	144	19	32	4	0	0	10	15	12	1	1	15	2	2	.250	.343
Mather, Joe	R-R	6-4	215	7-23-82	.250	.000	.333	3	8	1	2	1	0	0	3	3	0	0	0	1	0	0	.375	.455
Medina, David	L-L	6-3	162	1-1-89	.271	.243	.280	43	144	22	39	6	1	3	18	18	1	1	0	40	0	2	.389	.356
Moscatel, Kevin	R-R	6-1	175	5-16-91	.212	.300	.174	28	66	4	14	3	0	0	13	8	0	1	1	13	0	0	.258	.293
Mosquera, Juan	B-R	5-10	154	1-23-88	.232	.273	.217	43	125	15	29	3	1	0	7	17	1	5	0	17	5	1	.272	.329
Polanco, Jeudis	R-R	6-1	190	6-16-90	.193	.235	.175	22	57	4	11	2	2	0	1	6	0	1	0	15	0	0	.298	.270
Rivero, Alberto	L-L	5-10	155	4-30-89	.224	.071	.298	36	85	8	19	3	1	0	8	9	1	2	2	12	2	1	.282	.299
Rodriguez, Jonathan	R-R	6-2	205	8-21-89	.351	.409	.333	30	97	12	34	8	1	0	15	18	2	0	0	14	3	0	.454	.462
Teran, Kleininger	L-R	6-1	175	7-23-89	.384	.217	.444	25	86	16	33	8	0	0	11	6	1	0	0	8	2	2	.477	.430
Valera, Cesar	R-R	6-1	180	3-8-92	.242	.264	.233	54	186	32	45	10	2	1	21	10	8	1	3	55	8	3	.333	.304
Vasquez, Paul	R-R	5-10	160	3-7-85	.242	.429	.192	9	33	4	8	2	0	0	3	2	0	0	0	8	0	0	.303	.286
Washington, David	L-L	6-5	200	11-20-90	.165	.208	.148	28	85	3	14	0	0	0	5	6	1	0	0	29	1	0	.165	.228

Pitching	B-T	HT	WT	DOB	W	L	ERA	G	GS	CG	SV	IP	H	R	ER	HR	BB	SO	AVG	vLH	vRH	K/9	BB/9
Arredondo, Jose	R-R	6-1	166	9-3-87	0	0	0.00	2	0	0	0	2	2	0	0	0	0	1	.250	.000	.286	4.50	0.00
Avendano, Javier	R-R	6-3	180	9-6-90	1	0	2.08	5	1	0	0	13	10	4	3	2	6	14	.208	.143	.220	9.69	4.15
Bradford, Jared	R-R	6-1	177	4-3-86	0	0	5.06	3	3	0	0	5	9	5	3	0	1	5	.391	.375	.400	8.44	1.69
Bravo, Jonny	L-L	5-7	175	8-23-86	2	0	7.50	4	0	0	0	6	8	5	5	0	3	6	.348	.750	.263	9.00	4.50
Butler, Keith	R-R	6-0	180	1-30-89	1	1	2.22	21	0	0	6	28	18	9	7	0	12	34	.182	.143	.197	10.80	3.81
Calero, Jose	R-R	6-3	185	3-7-90	0	4	9.95	15	0	0	0	19	32	28	21	1	7	7	.364	.375	.357	3.32	3.32
Cardenas, Hector	L-L	6-3	180	12-14-86	0	0	3.00	2	2	0	0	3	1	2	1	0	1	1	.091	.000	.100	3.00	3.00
Castellano, Julio	L-L	6-2	170	6-11-87	1	0	5.79	16	0	0	0	14	15	13	9	0	8	13	.268	.417	.227	8.36	5.14
Castillo, Amaury	R-R	6-5	210	11-9-90	2	2	6.97	14	4	0	0	31	28	28	24	4	27	19	.255	.378	.169	5.52	7.84
Cruz, Angel	R-R	6-4	200	4-25-88	1	2	6.86	10	3	0	0	20	18	16	15	0	10	21	.237	.444	.209	9.61	4.58
Daugherty, Pat	L-L	6-5	215	8-30-88	1	1	2.89	9	2	0	1	28	16	10	9	0	14	31	.163	.056	.188	9.96	4.50
De Jesus, Angel	R-R	6-6	188	2-3-89	0	1	2.51	7	4	0	0	32	25	16	9	0	10	23	.210	.143	.231	6.40	2.78
De La Cruz, Manuel	R-R	6-2	225	5-8-90	1	3	3.95	13	0	0	0	14	12	6	6	0	10	10	.240	.000	.273	6.59	6.59
Diapoules, Mark	R-R	6-2	200	5-31-88	0	0	3.27	5	0	0	0	11	11	4	4	0	2	14	.250	.222	.257	11.45	1.64
Diaz, Omar	R-R	6-0	170	1-7-88	2	0	2.08	11	0	0	0	13	9	4	3	0	10	13	.205	.000	.257	9.00	6.92
Fiske, Justin	L-L	5-11	185	9-3-84	0	0	0.00	1	1	0	0	1	1	0	0	0	0	1	.250	—	.250	9.00	0.00
Garcia, Jaime	L-L	6-2	230	7-8-86	0	1	4.50	2	2	0	0	4	4	2	2	0	1	3	.250	.500	.214	6.75	2.25
Hernandez, Hector	B-L	6-1	198	2-20-91	2	1	2.21	13	8	0	0	41	37	16	10	0	9	33	.234	.222	.236	7.30	1.99
Javier, Omar	R-R	6-3	165	10-4-87	0	3	7.40	7	5	0	0	24	40	23	20	0	4	16	.381	.400	.378	5.92	1.48
Johnson, Cale	R-R	6-2	200	8-26-87	0	0	2.25	4	1	0	0	12	8	3	3	0	2	14	.182	.200	.176	10.50	1.50
Linares, Kristhiam	L-L	5-11	175	5-17-86	0	0	0.00	1	1	0	0	1	1	0	0	0	0	2	.250	—	.250	18.00	0.00
Maiques, Kenny	R-R	6-1	185	6-25-85	1	0	4.50	2	0	0	0	2	1	1	1	0	3	0	.143	.333	.000	0.00	13.50
Munoz, Orlando	R-R	6-1	165	2-22-90	2	3	3.77	12	4	0	0	31	41	22	13	1	5	23	.311	.389	.281	6.68	1.45
Orozco, Luis	R-R	5-11	160	10-22-90	1	3	5.32	20	0	0	4	22	22	17	13	3	13	21	.256	.118	.290	8.59	5.32
Ortiz, Pablo	R-R	6-4	175	6-11-88	0	0	9.00	1	0	0	0	1	2	1	1	0	1	0	.500	.500	.500	0.00	9.00
Parisi, Mike	R-R	6-3	215	4-18-83	0	1	1.17	3	3	0	0	8	2	1	1	0	4	9	.083	.000	.100	10.57	4.70

Pasen, Jose	R-R	6-1	180	5-19-90	1	2	2.77	8	4	0	0	26	19	9	8	0	16	11	.204	.258	.177	3.81	5.54
Rios, Geney	R-R	5-11	175	2-12-88	2	1	2.70	15	0	0	2	20	15	8	6	0	8	11	.214	.056	.269	4.95	3.60
Rosenthal, Trevor	R-R	6-2	190	5-29-90	4	1	4.88	14	0	0	0	24	25	17	13	0	16	26	.269	.222	.280	9.75	3.75
Russell, Ronald	R-R	6-2	185	7-27-89	0	3	4.98	7	5	0	0	22	20	15	12	0	17	27	.260	.423	.176	11.22	7.06
Salas, Fernando	R-R	6-2	200	5-30-85	0	0	0.00	1	0	0	0	1	0	0	0	0	0	1	.000	—	.000	9.00	0.00

Fielding

Catcher	PCT	G	PO	A	E	DP	PB
Anderson	.955	3	21	0	1	0	1
Bighames	1.000	1	2	0	0	0	0
Garcia	.968	16	105	16	4	1	6
Moscatel	.961	22	112	11	5	0	2
Polanco	.962	22	158	19	7	2	0
Vasquez	.964	4	23	4	1	0	1

First Base	PCT	G	PO	A	E	DP
Brown	1.000	1	5	0	0	1
Medina	.983	36	256	27	5	24
Rodriguez	1.000	9	61	1	0	8
Teran	.987	8	69	7	1	4
Washington	.984	8	60	3	1	8

Second Base	PCT	G	PO	A	E	DP
Cabrera	.864	6	8	11	3	3
Mannbel	.968	35	71	82	5	20
Mosquera	.928	25	41	49	7	14

Third Base	PCT	G	PO	A	E	DP
Bighames	1.000	1	0	3	0	1
De La Cruz	.875	39	37	68	15	6
Freese	.833	4	0	5	1	2
Mannbel	1.000	16	8	12	0	1
Medina	1.000	1	0	1	0	0
Mosquera	1.000	1	1	0	0	0
Teran	.824	10	4	10	3	0

Shortstop	PCT	G	PO	A	E	DP
Mosquera	.792	8	6	13	5	1

Valera	.927	53	73	156	18	39

Outfield	PCT	G	PO	A	E	DP
Babrick	.953	43	59	2	3	0
Bighames	.914	23	29	3	3	1
Garcia	1.000	1	1	0	0	0
Gomez	1.000	3	3	1	0	0
Hage	.941	13	16	0	1	0
Hill	.968	48	91	1	3	0
Mather	1.000	3	3	0	0	0
Medina	1.000	4	3	1	0	0
Mosquera	1.000	14	20	0	0	0
Rivero	.977	34	40	2	1	2
Teran	1.000	4	3	0	0	0
Washington	.947	10	17	1	1	0

DSL CARDINALS
ROOKIE
DOMINICAN SUMMER LEAGUE

Batting	B-T	HT	WT	DOB	AVG	vLH	vRH	G	AB	R	H	2B	3B	HR	RBI	BB	HBP	SH	SF	SO	SB	CS	SLG	OBP
Alcala, Yorbel	B-R	6-0	160	1-17-90	.255	.194	.272	47	145	16	37	7	0	0	15	10	2	1	1	22	1	3	.303	.310
Avila, Michael	R-R	6-0	160	9-7-89	.188	.333	.125	28	69	12	13	2	0	0	6	10	3	1	0	25	5	4	.217	.317
Beras, Andres	R-R	6-2	175	11-30-90	.246	.158	.280	22	69	10	17	6	1	1	8	5	2	0	0	24	4	0	.406	.316
Cabrera, Juan B	R-R	6-1	151	6-22-88	.230	.235	.228	47	148	24	34	4	4	1	19	14	4	1	2	29	12	4	.331	.310
Castillo, Juan	R-R	5-11	160	12-13-89	.277	.296	.271	33	112	17	31	8	0	2	20	13	3	0	0	14	3	1	.402	.367
Encanacion, Victor	R-R	6-2	165	3-8-90	.217	.263	.200	57	143	28	31	10	1	0	16	25	5	1	2	42	15	3	.301	.349
Ferreira, Victor	R-R	5-11	180	2-1-91	.100	.167	.083	8	30	0	3	1	0	0	0	0	1	0	0	15	0	0	.133	.129
Hernandez, Grabiel	B-R	5-10	150	10-16-91	.308	.269	.322	67	250	58	77	9	10	2	32	29	7	3	2	42	26	4	.448	.392
Lopez, Jorge	R-R	5-11	175	10-28-91	.268	.263	.270	53	164	21	44	5	1	0	8	6	1	2	1	30	5	7	.311	.297
Martinez, Marcos	R-R	6-5	195	3-3-89	.000	—	.000	1	4	0	0	0	0	0	0	0	0	0	0	3	0	0	.000	.000
Montero, Jesus	R-R	5-11	185	6-21-91	.287	.308	.280	31	101	13	29	6	1	0	20	15	3	0	1	18	2	0	.366	.392
Pena, Jose	R-R	6-2	190	5-26-92	.150	.162	.144	46	127	11	19	6	1	2	16	22	3	0	1	68	1	1	.260	.288
Perez, Luis	R-R	5-10	160	7-24-91	.308	.267	.320	30	65	18	20	8	0	0	7	22	2	1	0	8	2	2	.431	.494
Perez, Wader	B-R	5-10	170	6-12-90	.275	.229	.286	51	182	33	50	8	2	0	19	30	4	2	0	24	13	7	.341	.389
Pimentel, Luis	R-R	6-1	180	12-30-88	.280	.378	.257	54	189	35	53	12	1	5	27	24	4	2	4	16	8	5	.434	.367
Reyes, Roberto	L-L	6-0	185	5-10-89	.261	.267	.260	71	218	40	57	8	5	5	33	37	5	1	1	72	22	4	.413	.379
Sandoval, Santo	R-R	6-1	180	4-20-89	.154	.294	.132	49	123	21	19	5	1	2	19	10	7	1	3	50	15	4	.260	.252
Taveras, Oscar	L-L	6-2	180	6-19-92	.257	.148	.290	65	237	35	61	13	8	1	42	28	3	0	4	36	9	4	.392	.338

Pitching	B-T	HT	WT	DOB	W	L	ERA	G	GS	CG	SV	IP	H	R	ER	HR	BB	SO	AVG	vLH	vRH	K/9	BB/9
Estalis, Eduard	R-R	6-1	172	12-19-88	2	5	4.60	20	0	0	9	31	38	20	16	3	11	26	.297	.438	.277	7.47	3.16
Herrera, Keury	L-L	6-0	180	5-22-91	2	2	3.34	16	8	0	3	57	52	23	21	3	32	61	.252	.400	.249	9.69	5.08
Jimenez, Charllan	R-R	6-1	180	11-29-89	6	0	2.14	15	7	0	1	63	45	18	15	4	23	75	.204	.211	.203	10.71	3.29
Lopez, Stalyn	L-L	5-9	160	12-18-91	4	1	3.70	16	5	0	0	41	40	19	17	2	18	29	.267	.500	.264	6.31	3.92
Martinez, Bryan	R-R	6-3	172	3-1-91	6	0	3.02	13	3	0	1	42	42	18	14	0	18	38	.273	.250	.275	8.21	3.89
Mata, Luis	R-R	6-2	190	4-27-91	0	0	5.63	4	1	0	0	8	3	8	5	1	12	9	.111	.000	.125	10.13	13.50
Mercedes, Juan	L-L	6-5	205	6-1-89	0	0	21.60	6	1	0	0	3	5	9	8	0	7	4	.313	.000	.333	10.80	18.90
Pasen, Jose	R-R	6-1	180	5-19-90	1	3	1.73	9	6	0	0	36	25	19	7	1	21	40	.208	.353	.184	9.91	5.20
Pena, Pedro	L-L	6-1	189	2-22-91	1	2	2.11	12	7	0	0	38	30	14	9	2	24	43	.211	—	.211	10.10	5.63
Pinales, Alejandro	R-R	6-4	228	9-21-88	6	3	3.65	15	7	3	1	57	56	30	23	4	9	45	.258	.467	.243	7.15	1.43
Rodriguez, Delvi	L-L	6-2	170	9-14-90	1	0	4.50	9	0	0	0	10	5	5	5	0	11	4	.139	.000	.147	3.60	9.90
Rudecindo, Rosalin	R-R	6-4	185	10-7-90	0	1	3.20	11	2	0	0	25	26	17	9	1	15	25	.250	.222	.253	8.88	5.33
Santana, Michael	R-R	6-0	155	7-1-90	2	2	3.10	15	6	0	0	49	44	22	17	2	16	40	.240	.318	.230	7.30	2.92
Segundo, Jefferson	R-R	6-3	165	9-30-89	2	0	8.04	12	1	0	1	16	7	15	14	0	25	17	.143	.000	.152	9.77	14.36
Tapia, Angel	R-R	5-11	180	5-21-90	4	2	3.65	14	6	0	1	49	41	29	20	1	24	32	.218	.238	.216	5.84	4.38
Urena, Ramon	R-R	6-0	170	2-25-90	4	3	3.89	12	4	0	1	37	38	23	16	1	16	29	.275	.333	.270	7.05	3.89
Uribe, Adriano	L-L	6-4	200	5-17-89	2	3	5.89	7	4	0	0	18	23	15	12	0	14	20	.303	—	.303	9.82	6.87

Fielding

Catcher	PCT	G	PO	A	E	DP	PB
Alcala	.993	36	245	56	2	2	16
Castillo	.975	13	100	15	3	1	0
Montero	.983	13	101	15	2	0	1
Perez	.965	23	152	13	6	1	4

First Base	PCT	G	PO	A	E	DP
Alcala	1.000	1	8	1	0	4
Cabrera	1.000	2	7	2	0	0
Castillo	.979	18	129	12	3	10

Ferreira	.962	3	23	2	1	1
Lopez	1.000	2	2	0	0	1
Martinez	1.000	1	9	0	0	1
Montero	.990	14	95	4	1	11
Pimentel	.988	24	159	8	2	12
Reyes	.965	21	132	6	5	15

Second Base	PCT	G	PO	A	E	DP
Avila	.857	12	19	23	7	3
Cabrera	.969	7	16	15	1	7

Hernandez	1.000	3	4	6	0	0
Lopez	.955	43	86	63	7	20
Perez	.971	30	35	2	8	

Third Base	PCT	G	PO	A	E	DP
Cabrera	.807	35	21	50	17	6
Perez	1.000	26	19	41	0	3
Pimentel	.864	19	13	44	9	3

Shortstop	PCT	G	PO	A	E	DP
Avila	.947	5	6	12	1	1

	PCT	G	PO	A	E	DP			PCT	G	PO	A	E	DP
Cabrera	1.000	1	0	3	0	1	**Outfield**	**PCT**	**G**	**PO**	**A**	**E**	**DP**	
Hernandez	.901	62	121	171	32	28	Beras	1.000	18	22	0	0	0	
Perez	.940	7	15	32	3	6	Encanacion	.989	56	84	7	1	2	
							Pena	.881	30	35	2	5	0	

	PCT	G	PO	A	E	DP
Perez	.000	1	0	0	1	0
Reyes	.976	53	75	7	2	2
Sandoval	.889	42	38	2	5	1
Taveras	.964	63	100	8	4	0

VSL CARDINALS   ROOKIE

VENEZUELAN SUMMER LEAGUE

Batting	B-T	HT	WT	DOB	AVG	vLH	vRH	G	AB	R	H	2B	3B	HR	RBI	BB	HBP	SH	SF	SO	SB	CS	SLG	OBP
Argenal, Jem	L-L	5-11	180	9-19-91	.276	.296	.272	59	185	20	51	4	1	2	19	13	2	0	3	44	1	2	.341	.325
Castellano, Alexander	B-R	6-1	160	11-19-88	.231	.192	.242	43	117	16	27	7	2	2	8	9	7	0	0	40	0	4	.376	.323
Cortez, Jose	R-R	6-0	165	1-29-90	.273	.286	.269	53	176	23	48	10	1	1	21	14	4	0	0	26	0	4	.358	.340
Fonseca, Anthony	R-R	6-1	175	2-8-89	.288	.263	.295	57	184	33	53	4	0	4	22	12	14	3	3	35	8	5	.375	.371
Garcia, Hector	R-R	6-1	185	5-16-90	.314	.381	.299	63	229	27	72	16	0	5	36	17	7	1	1	32	2	1	.450	.378
Inojoza, Kaizer	R-R	6-0	175	10-7-90	.233	.226	.235	51	150	30	35	8	3	5	25	22	8	0	1	49	4	3	.427	.359
Marquez, Moises	R-R	5-9	165	7-16-90	.244	.294	.230	42	78	12	19	5	0	1	8	13	3	2	0	25	0	5	.346	.372
Martina, Hayrich	R-R	6-0	170	8-3-90	.241	.250	.238	29	83	9	20	4	0	0	3	0	0	1	0	23	0	1	.289	.241
Martinez, Teharick	R-R	6-2	175	11-19-90	.190	.313	.159	33	79	9	15	1	1	0	6	3	2	1	1	28	2	1	.228	.235
Medina, Osmir	R-R	6-2	170	11-27-90	.207	.139	.228	45	150	19	31	5	2	0	9	17	4	2	1	39	9	2	.267	.302
Montero, Jesus	R-R	5-11	185	6-21-91	.089	.091	.088	15	45	1	4	1	0	0	2	9	2	0	0	14	0	0	.111	.268
Perez, Roberto	R-R	6-0	185	8-31-88	.262	.360	.231	63	210	28	55	13	0	8	30	35	6	0	3	42	1	1	.438	.378
Rivas, Limbert	R-R	6-1	185	2-21-90	.319	.321	.337	40	116	13	37	6	1	2	13	20	4	1	1	24	4	3	.440	.433
Vargas, Ildemaro	R-R	6-0	170	7-16-91	.264	.244	.270	52	163	22	43	7	4	1	13	20	7	0	0	29	9	8	.374	.368
Velasco, Gerwins	R-R	6-1	190	10-7-90	.192	.200	.190	24	73	8	14	7	0	0	10	11	0	0	0	22	0	1	.288	.298
Viloria, Omar	R-R	6-2	176	2-12-91	.206	.125	.231	27	68	7	14	1	0	2	5	6	8	0	0	17	2	0	.309	.341
Vivas, Wilfred	R-R	5-11	160	11-8-89	.302	.308	.300	17	63	12	19	2	1	0	5	7	0	1	0	7	3	3	.365	.371
Yeques, Carlos	R-R	5-11	175	10-20-90	.240	.273	.232	33	104	9	25	2	1	3	13	4	2	0	0	31	1	1	.365	.282

Pitching	B-T	HT	WT	DOB	W	L	ERA	G	GS	CG	SV	IP	H	R	ER	HR	BB	SO	AVG	vLH	vRH	K/9	BB/9
Alvarado, Ruben	L-L	6-1	170	7-19-91	1	0	6.30	14	0	0	0	20	30	17	14	2	9	18	.349	.111	.377	8.10	4.05
Avendano, Javier	R-R	6-3	180	9-6-90	6	3	1.79	13	13	0	0	65	59	24	13	0	21	60	.238	.276	.226	8.27	2.89
Bier, Deimer	R-R	6-2	174	1-6-91	5	3	2.29	13	13	0	0	63	50	20	16	3	19	72	.216	.271	.198	10.29	2.71
Cedeno, Fernando	R-R	6-1	186	11-15-89	3	5	8.31	21	0	0	1	30	50	33	28	2	9	27	.360	.444	.339	8.01	2.67
Colorado, Moises	L-L	6-3	170	12-8-89	3	3	4.33	18	6	0	0	44	45	25	21	2	27	45	.265	.421	.245	9.27	5.56
Corpas, Hector	R-R	6-3	170	1-5-90	3	2	1.56	16	0	0	9	35	23	7	6	0	7	30	.193	.216	.183	7.79	1.82
De Aguas, John	L-L	5-10	160	12-4-91	0	2	1.42	15	2	0	2	32	22	11	5	0	14	24	.195	.143	.198	6.82	3.98
Echeverria, Angelo	L-L	6-2	170	1-2-92	1	0	0.00	2	0	0	0	5	0	0	0	0	1	4	.000	—	.000	7.71	1.93
Marquez, Fabian	R-R	6-1	178	8-18-91	2	0	5.29	13	0	0	0	17	20	10	10	3	3	9	.294	.154	.327	4.76	1.59
Montanez, Fermin	R-R	6-4	200	1-1-91	0	0	3.48	6	0	0	1	10	11	4	4	0	3	3	.275	.000	.324	2.61	2.61
Nieves, Sergio	R-R	6-0	180	10-18-91	1	5	4.22	14	14	0	0	64	77	43	30	4	17	40	.301	.217	.327	5.63	2.39
Oraa, Carlos	R-R	6-3	170	10-5-89	5	2	3.04	14	14	0	0	68	65	25	23	1	13	48	.260	.321	.244	6.35	1.72
Polanco, Jhonny	R-R	6-3	191	4-28-92	0	0	10.61	9	0	0	0	9	12	11	11	0	10	2	.308	.400	.276	1.93	9.64
Ramos, Gregorio	R-R	5-11	170	9-27-89	1	0	6.00	15	0	0	0	24	31	17	16	0	12	12	.320	.296	.329	4.50	4.50
Solarte, Jackson	R-R	6-0	171	6-14-90	1	2	4.44	16	0	0	2	26	29	17	13	0	17	15	.287	.304	.282	5.13	5.81
Ulacio, Ramon	R-R	6-1	190	3-17-91	1	2	6.48	14	1	0	0	25	31	21	18	3	11	18	.295	.313	.292	6.84	3.96
Villanueva, Dail	L-L	6-1	180	1-23-90	0	1	3.86	7	3	0	0	16	15	9	7	0	10	4	.250	.500	.232	2.20	5.51
Weffer, Jose	L-L	6-1	180	5-12-92	0	3	13.91	10	3	0	0	11	16	22	17	4	20	6	.333	.500	.318	4.91	16.36

Fielding

Catcher	PCT	G	PO	A	E	DP	PB
Montero	.970	15	79	17	3	2	2
Rivas	.990	18	83	12	1	3	7
Velasco	.962	23	152	23	7	1	5
Viloria	.968	27	149	30	6	3	6

First Base	PCT	G	PO	A	E	DP
Argenal	.976	16	76	5	2	2
Garcia	1.000	3	7	0	0	2
Perez	.992	56	459	29	4	38
Rivas	1.000	9	67	2	0	9

Second Base	PCT	G	PO	A	E	DP
Marquez	.915	21	22	32	5	5

	PCT	G	PO	A	E	DP
Martina	.889	13	18	22	5	4
Vargas	.978	42	80	94	4	19
Vivas	.913	5	10	11	2	3
Yeques	.977	9	20	22	1	6

Third Base	PCT	G	PO	A	E	DP
Garcia	.933	59	40	126	12	6
Marquez	1.000	4	0	5	0	0
Martina	.700	7	1	6	3	0
Yeques	.750	12	3	15	6	2

Shortstop	PCT	G	PO	A	E	DP
Marquez	.979	9	16	30	1	5
Martina	1.000	1	0	3	0	0

	PCT	G	PO	A	E	DP
Medina	.908	44	87	130	22	29
Vargas	.911	10	18	33	5	7
Vivas	.884	9	11	27	5	4

Outfield	PCT	G	PO	A	E	DP
Argenal	.956	23	42	1	2	0
Castellano	.857	29	26	4	5	1
Cortez	.943	52	82	1	5	0
Fonseca	.961	55	93	6	4	1
Inojoza	.924	48	80	5	7	2
Marquez	.800	3	4	0	1	0
Martinez	.978	32	43	2	1	1

San Diego Padres

SEASON IN A SENTENCE: It's time for the Padres to look toward the future, with the team never really in playoff contention and making its biggest news off the field as Jeff Moorad took over ownership of the franchise and Kevin Towers was replaced by Jed Hoyer as general manager after another losing season.

HIGH POINT: Turning to rookies like right-hander Mat Latos, infielder Everth Cabrera, and outfielders Kyle Blanks and Will Venable as the new foundations of the team, the Padres went 37-25 to end the season. The highlight came on Aug. 11, when first baseman Adrian Gonzalez had six hits and San Diego had its best offensive output of the year in a 13-6 win over Milwaukee. Lefthander Clayton Richard, another rookie who was acquired from the White Sox in the Jake Peavy trade, was the winning pitcher in his third start for the team.

LOW POINT: San Diego dropped a 6-4 decision to the Reds on July 27, the end of a stretch when it lost 20 of 24 to fall to 38-62 overall. Rookie Josh Geer gave up three home runs in four innings of work to fall to 1-7 on the season. He was sent down in August and outrighted off the 40-man roster following the season.

NOTABLE ROOKIES: The Padres had an amazing 15 players make their major league debuts in San Diego in 2009, and that doesn't include Geer, Venable or Clayton, who debuted in 2008, or lefthander Aaron Poreda, who debuted in Chicago before the White Sox included him in the Peavy deal. Latos, who played all season at 21, stood out for leaping from Double-A into the major league rotation in just his second full professional season and holding his own.

KEY TRANSACTIONS: Trading Jake Peavy to the White Sox at midseason not only brought in four talented arms, including Richard and Poreda, but also clearly pointed the organization in a new direction. The Padres preceded that deal earlier in July by sending Scott Hairston to the Athletics for righthanders Shawn Gallagher, Craig Italiano and Ryan Webb.

DOWN ON THE FARM: San Diego still lacks impact prospects at the upper levels of the minors, but more talent at the lower levels led to a playoff appearance for high Class A Lake Elsinore and a Midwest League title for low Class A Fort Wayne, which finished with the best overall record in the minor leagues at 94-46 (.671).

OPENING DAY PAYROLL: $43,734,200

General Manager: Kevin Towers. **Farm Director:** Grady Fuson. **Scouting Director:** Bill Gayton.

Class	Team	League	W	L	PCT	Finish*	Manager(s)
Majors	San Diego Padres	National	75	87	.463	11th (16)	Bud Black
Triple-A	Portland Beavers	Pacific Coast	60	84	.417	16th (16)	Randy Ready/Gary Jones
Double-A	San Antonio Missions	Texas	70	70	.500	6th (8)	Terry Kennedy
High A	Lake Elsinore Storm	California	73	67	.521	5th (10)	Carlos Lezcano
Low A	Fort Wayne TinCaps	Midwest	94	46	.671	†1st (14)	Doug Dascenzo
Short-season	Eugene Emeralds	Northwest	34	42	.447	t-6th (8)	Greg Riddoch
Rookie	AZL Padres	Arizona	28	28	.500	5th (11)	Jose Flores
Overall 2009 Minor League Record			359	337	.516	8th (30)	

*Finish in overall standings (No. of teams in league). †League champion.

ORGANIZATION STATISTICS

SAN DIEGO PADRES
NATIONAL LEAGUE

Batting	B-T	HT	WT	DOB	AVG	vLH	vRH	G	AB	R	H	2B	3B	HR	RBI	BB	HBP	SH	SF	SO	SB	CS	SLG	OBP
Alfonzo, Eliezer	R-R	5-11	220	2-7-79	.175	.208	.167	37	114	6	20	3	0	2	8	3	0	0	0	34	0	0	.254	.197
Blanco, Henry	R-R	5-11	220	8-29-71	.235	.322	.200	67	204	21	48	12	0	6	16	26	0	1	1	50	0	0	.382	.320
Blanks, Kyle	R-R	6-6	285	9-11-86	.250	.220	.262	54	148	24	37	9	0	10	22	18	6	0	0	55	1	1	.514	.355
Burke, Chris	R-R	5-11	195	3-11-80	.207	.091	.250	32	82	8	17	5	0	1	5	6	1	0	0	16	4	1	.305	.270
Cabrera, Everth	B-R	5-10	175	11-17-86	.255	.239	.261	103	377	59	96	18	8	2	31	46	5	8	2	88	25	8	.361	.342
Durango, Luis	B-R	5-9	160	4-23-86	.545	.571	.500	9	11	3	6	0	0	0	2	0	1	0	2	2	1	.545	.615
Eckstein, David	R-R	5-7	175	1-20-75	.260	.244	.268	136	503	64	131	27	2	2	51	39	9	13	4	46	3	1	.334	.323
Floyd, Cliff	L-R	6-4	230	12-5-72	.125	.000	.133	10	16	0	2	0	0	0	1	0	0	0	7	0	0	.125	.176
Gerut, Jody	L-L	6-0	190	9-18-77	.221	.235	.219	37	113	17	25	6	0	4	14	5	0	0	3	22	2	0	.381	.248
2-team total (85 Milwaukee)					.230	—	—	122	274	40	63	13	0	9	35	19	1	0	4	43	6	2	.376	.279
Giles, Brian	L-L	5-10	205	1-20-71	.191	.136	.222	61	225	18	43	10	1	2	23	26	1	0	1	31	1	0	.271	.277
Gonzalez, Adrian	L-L	6-2	225	5-8-82	.277	.234	.305	160	552	90	153	27	2	40	99	119	5	1	4	109	1	1	.551	.407
Gonzalez, Edgar	R-R	6-0	180	6-14-78	.216	.204	.222	82	153	16	33	8	2	4	18	11	3	0	2	36	1	2	.373	.278
Gwynn Jr., Tony	L-R	5-11	195	10-4-82	.270	.215	.290	119	393	59	106	11	6	2	21	48	2	5	3	65	11	7	.344	.350
Hairston, Scott	R-R	6-0	195	5-25-80	.299	.360	.262	56	197	26	59	14	1	10	29	17	1	1	0	45	8	1	.533	.358
Headley, Chase	B-R	6-2	210	5-9-84	.262	.244	.270	156	543	62	142	31	2	12	64	62	5	0	2	133	10	2	.392	.342
Hundley, Nick	R-R	6-1	205	9-8-83	.238	.159	.267	78	256	23	61	15	2	8	30	28	1	1	3	76	5	1	.406	.313
Kouzmanoff, Kevin	R-R	6-1	210	7-25-81	.255	.291	.241	141	529	50	135	31	1	18	88	27	11	0	6	106	1	0	.420	.302
Lobaton, Jose	B-R	6-0	195	10-21-84	.176	—	.176	7	17	0	3	0	0	0	0	0	0	0	0	5	0	0	.176	.176
Macias, Drew	L-L	6-3	200	3-7-83	.197	.222	.190	51	76	8	15	6	0	1	7	13	1	0	0	15	0	1	.316	.322
Rodriguez, Luis	B-R	5-9	190	6-27-80	.202	.294	.172	93	208	18	42	6	0	2	16	37	0	3	3	23	1	0	.260	.319
Salazar, Oscar	R-R	6-0	195	6-27-78	.269	.311	.238	55	108	12	29	8	2	3	19	12	0	0	1	16	0	0	.463	.339
Stansberry, Craig	R-R	6-0	185	3-8-82	.000	.000	—	1	1	0	0	0	0	0	0	0	0	0	0	0	0	0	.000	.000
Venable, Will	L-L	6-2	210	10-29-82	.256	.225	.266	95	293	38	75	14	2	12	38	25	4	2	0	89	6	1	.440	.323
Wilson, Josh	R-R	6-0	175	3-26-81	.105	.083	.115	16	38	2	4	2	0	0	1	3	1	1	0	9	0	0	.158	.190
2-team total (11 Arizona)					.156	—	—	27	64	3	10	3	0	0	3	6	2	1	0	20	0	0	.203	.250

Pitching	B-T	HT	WT	DOB	W	L	ERA	G	GS	CG	SV	IP	H	R	ER	HR	BB	SO	AVG	vLH	vRH	K/9	BB/9
Adams, Mike	R-R	6-5	205	7-29-78	0	0	0.73	37	0	0	0	37	14	9	3	1	8	45	.111	.130	.088	10.95	1.95
Banks, Josh	R-R	6-3	210	7-18-82	1	1	7.15	6	3	0	0	23	30	18	18	6	4	9	.330	.357	.306	3.57	1.59
Bell, Heath	R-R	6-3	250	9-29-77	6	4	2.71	68	0	0	42	70	54	21	21	3	24	79	.213	.275	.138	10.21	3.10
Burke, Greg	R-R	6-4	215	9-21-82	3	3	4.14	48	0	0	0	46	48	23	21	4	23	33	.271	.346	.208	6.50	4.53
Carrillo, Cesar	R-R	6-3	175	4-29-84	1	2	13.06	3	3	0	0	10	16	15	15	4	12	4	.348	.250	.400	3.48	10.45
Correia, Kevin	R-R	6-3	200	8-24-80	12	11	3.91	33	33	1	0	198	194	92	86	17	64	142	.259	.247	.269	6.45	2.91
De La Cruz, Eulogio	R-R	5-10	215	3-12-84	0	0	5.40	3	0	0	0	3	2	2	2	0	6	2	.200	.250	.167	5.40	16.20
Ekstrom, Mike	R-R	5-11	190	8-30-83	0	0	6.38	12	0	0	0	18	21	14	13	3	8	19	.292	.286	.297	9.33	3.93
Frieri, Ernesto	R-R	6-2	200	7-19-85	0	0	0.00	2	0	0	0	2	0	0	0	0	1	2	.000	.000	.000	9.00	4.50
Gallagher, Sean	R-R	6-2	235	12-30-85	0	0	0.00	8	0	0	0	5	5	0	0	0	5	4	.250	.111	.364	6.75	8.44
Gaudin, Chad	R-R	5-10	190	3-24-83	4	10	5.13	20	19	0	0	105	105	69	60	7	56	105	.261	.346	.229	8.97	4.78
Geer, Josh	R-R	6-3	195	6-2-83	1	7	5.96	19	17	0	0	103	116	73	68	27	23	54	.288	.290	.286	4.73	2.02
Gregerson, Luke	L-R	6-3	200	5-14-84	2	4	3.24	72	0	0	1	75	62	29	27	3	31	93	.221	.285	.161	11.16	3.72
Hill, Shawn	R-R	6-2	225	4-28-81	1	1	5.25	3	3	0	0	12	15	7	7	1	3	7	.306	.286	.333	5.25	2.25
Latos, Mat	R-R	6-6	225	12-9-87	4	5	4.62	10	10	0	0	51	43	29	26	7	23	39	.232	.271	.200	6.93	4.09
LeBlanc, Wade	L-L	6-3	200	8-7-84	3	1	3.69	9	9	0	0	46	35	19	19	6	19	30	.210	.235	.203	5.83	3.69
Lopez, Arturo	L-L	5-10	165	2-22-83	0	0	19.29	4	0	0	0	2	7	5	5	2	3	0	.538	.400	.625	0.00	11.57
Meredith, Cla	R-R	6-0	190	6-4-83	4	2	4.17	35	0	0	0	37	47	19	17	1	13	20	.324	.333	.318	4.91	3.19
Moreno, Edwin	R-R	6-1	220	7-30-80	1	3	4.84	19	0	0	0	22	28	13	12	3	15	15	.311	.352	.250	6.04	6.04
Mujica, Edward	R-R	6-2	215	5-10-84	3	5	3.94	67	4	0	2	94	101	47	41	14	19	76	.273	.300	.247	7.30	1.83
Peavy, Jake	R-R	6-1	195	5-31-81	6	6	3.97	13	13	1	0	82	69	38	36	7	28	92	.228	.276	.173	10.14	3.09
Perdomo, Luis	R-R	6-0	170	4-27-84	1	0	4.80	35	0	0	0	60	57	36	32	11	34	55	.246	.293	.198	8.25	5.10
Poreda, Aaron	L-L	6-6	240	10-1-86	0	0	3.86	4	0	0	0	2	1	1	1	0	5	0	.143	.250	.000	0.00	19.29
Ramos, Cesar	L-L	6-2	205	6-22-84	0	1	3.07	5	2	0	0	15	19	5	5	0	4	10	.328	.118	.415	6.14	2.45

Name	B-T	HT	WT	DOB	W	L	ERA	G	GS	CG	SV	IP	H	R	ER	HR	BB	SO	AVG	vLH	vRH	K/9	BB/9
Richard, Clayton	L-L	6-5	240	9-12-83	5	2	4.08	12	12	0	0	64	60	31	29	7	34	48	.254	.262	.253	6.75	4.78
Russell, Adam	R-R	6-8	255	4-14-83	3	1	3.65	15	0	0	0	12	13	6	5	0	11	14	.260	.286	.241	10.22	8.03
Sanchez, Duaner	R-R	6-2	210	10-14-79	1	1	9.00	12	0	0	0	11	18	11	11	3	8	2	.383	.355	.438	1.64	6.55
Silva, Walter	R-R	6-1	190	1-4-77	0	2	8.76	6	6	0	0	25	34	28	24	4	15	11	.330	.323	.341	4.01	5.47
Stauffer, Tim	R-R	6-1	205	6-2-82	4	7	3.58	14	14	0	0	73	71	31	29	8	34	53	.259	.239	.279	6.53	4.19
Thatcher, Joe	L-L	6-2	230	10-4-81	1	0	2.80	52	0	0	0	45	37	14	14	2	18	55	.227	.182	.267	11.00	3.60
Webb, Ryan	R-R	6-6	215	2-5-86	2	1	3.86	28	0	0	0	26	27	14	11	3	11	19	.265	.250	.278	6.66	3.86
Young, Chris	R-R	6-10	280	5-25-79	4	6	5.21	14	14	0	0	76	70	47	44	12	40	50	.246	.210	.297	5.92	4.74

Fielding

Catcher	PCT	G	PO	A	E	DP	PB
Alfonzo	.996	30	203	23	1	5	3
Blanco	1.000	60	444	28	0	4	2
Hundley	.989	74	515	35	6	5	7
Lobaton	.982	6	52	2	1	0	0

First Base	PCT	G	PO	A	E	DP
Blanks	1.000	8	36	3	0	8
Gonzalez	.995	156	1224	136	7	116
Gonzalez	1.000	2	6	0	0	2
Headley	1.000	1	1	0	0	0
Salazar	1.000	6	30	4	0	2

Second Base	PCT	G	PO	A	E	DP
Burke	—	1	0	0	0	0
Eckstein	.996	131	228	326	2	79
Gonzalez	.930	15	20	20	3	4

Lobaton	—	1	0	0	0	0
Rodriguez	.976	30	51	69	3	15
Salazar	.833	3	4	6	2	1

Third Base	PCT	G	PO	A	E	DP
Blanco	—	1	0	0	0	0
Burke	1.000	2	1	0	0	0
Gonzalez	.889	5	2	6	1	0
Headley	.907	28	10	39	5	2
Kouzmanoff	.990	139	94	214	3	24
Rodriguez	—	1	0	0	0	0
Wilson	—	1	0	0	0	0

Shortstop	PCT	G	PO	A	E	DP
Burke	.929	25	27	52	6	9
Cabrera	.951	102	140	304	23	66
Rodriguez	.975	34	45	74	3	23

Wilson	.943	15	13	20	2	3

Outfield	PCT	G	PO	A	E	DP
Blanks	1.000	38	55	1	0	0
Durango	1.000	2	3	1	0	0
Gerut	1.000	27	63	2	0	0
Giles	1.000	58	113	6	0	3
Gonzalez	1.000	14	24	0	0	0
Gwynn Jr.	.974	110	297	5	8	1
Hairston	.991	51	106	2	1	0
Headley	.987	114	215	5	3	2
Hundley	1.000	1	1	0	0	0
Macias	.960	30	24	0	1	0
Salazar	1.000	19	25	0	0	0
Venable	.988	81	158	3	2	0

PORTLAND BEAVERS

TRIPLE-A

PACIFIC COAST LEAGUE

Batting	B-T	HT	WT	DOB	AVG	vLH	vRH	G	AB	R	H	2B	3B	HR	RBI	BB	HBP	SH	SF	SO	SB	CS	SLG	OBP
Adams, Russ	L-R	6-0	200	8-30-80	.267	.222	.283	36	135	16	36	7	1	1	12	14	0	1	1	16	2	2	.356	.333
2-team total (24 Las Vegas)					.285	—	—	60	207	31	59	14	3	2	21	19	1	1	3	33	2	2	.411	.343
Alfonzo, Eliezer	R-R	5-11	220	2-7-79	.309	.353	.294	55	204	27	63	11	0	14	36	7	4	1	3	51	1	0	.569	.339
Alley, Josh	L-L	5-8	180	9-6-83	.192	.000	.213	32	52	5	10	1	0	0	7	11	0	2	1	13	1	1	.212	.328
Antonelli, Matt	R-R	6-0	205	4-8-85	.196	.222	.185	59	189	25	37	11	2	4	22	26	2	2	0	30	1	1	.339	.300
Baxter, Mike	L-R	6-0	190	12-7-84	.277	.270	.280	82	303	38	84	17	4	5	34	38	3	0	1	53	9	5	.409	.362
Benedict, Griffin	L-R	6-0	185	7-4-87	.000	—	.000	1	3	0	0	0	0	0	0	0	0	0	0	1	0	0	.000	.000
Blanks, Kyle	R-R	6-6	285	9-11-86	.283	.345	.264	66	233	35	66	9	1	12	38	39	5	0	3	63	0	0	.485	.393
Brown, Emil	R-R	6-2	210	12-29-74	.260	.391	.236	41	146	22	38	13	0	4	22	19	1	0	2	27	2	2	.432	.345
Cabrera, Everth	B-R	5-10	175	11-17-86	.333	.222	.389	7	27	5	9	2	0	0	0	1	1	0	0	6	1	0	.407	.379
Ciofrone, Peter	L-R	5-10	200	9-28-83	.180	.086	.210	90	284	29	51	6	2	5	25	31	3	2	4	59	0	1	.268	.264
Codiroli, Jason	L-L	5-10	175	1-20-87	.211	.333	.154	6	19	2	4	1	1	0	3	2	0	0	0	5	0	0	.368	.286
Collins, Michael	R-R	6-3	213	7-18-84	.091	.143	.000	5	11	1	1	0	0	0	4	0	0	0	1	0	0	0	.091	.333
Dowdy, Brett	R-R	6-0	190	2-22-82	.237	.257	.227	90	329	30	78	16	0	3	20	18	3	3	2	49	6	3	.313	.281
Gonzalez, Edgar	R-R	6-0	180	6-14-78	.278	.286	.273	6	18	3	5	0	0	1	1	5	1	0	0	3	0	0	.444	.458
Haad, Yamid	R-R	6-2	220	9-2-77	.273	.242	.284	33	121	10	33	5	0	1	8	3	0	1	0	29	0	0	.339	.290
Hagerty, Jason	B-R	6-3	220	9-13-87	.133	.000	.286	5	15	3	2	1	0	0	1	2	0	0	0	4	0	0	.200	.235
Hartman, Chadd	L-R	6-0	195	11-9-86	.167	—	.167	2	6	0	1	0	0	0	0	0	0	0	0	3	0	0	.167	.167
Howard, Kevin	L-R	6-2	190	6-25-81	.247	.222	.250	26	89	10	22	3	0	0	6	10	0	1	0	9	1	1	.281	.323
2-team total (91 Las Vegas)					.310	—	—	117	429	68	133	29	1	13	59	48	1	4	1	51	5	3	.473	.380
Huffman, Chad	R-R	6-1	215	4-29-85	.269	.185	.301	135	469	65	126	30	2	20	68	57	12	0	2	115	8	5	.469	.361
Hundley, Nick	R-R	6-1	205	9-8-83	.250	.333	.231	5	16	2	4	1	0	1	2	2	0	0	0	4	0	0	.500	.333
Johnston, Seth	R-R	6-3	204	3-12-83	.375	.250	.450	9	32	6	12	3	0	4	6	2	0	0	0	8	0	0	.844	.412
Kazmar, Sean	R-R	5-9	160	8-5-84	.235	.240	.233	114	366	40	86	14	0	5	46	37	2	3	3	59	8	2	.314	.306
Lobaton, Jose	B-R	6-0	195	10-21-84	.241	.167	.262	39	133	14	32	6	0	3	8	10	0	4	1	35	0	0	.353	.292
Macias, Drew	L-L	6-3	200	3-7-83	.232	.306	.203	86	297	43	69	18	0	5	27	39	5	1	2	56	5	3	.343	.329
Martinez, Luis	R-R	6-0	210	4-3-85	.171	.154	.182	11	35	3	6	0	0	0	4	0	0	0	0	7	0	0	.171	.256
Pascucci, Val	R-R	6-6	220	11-17-78	.277	.227	.299	65	242	31	67	17	1	11	48	32	2	0	4	64	1	0	.492	.361
2-team total (61 Albuquerque)					.248	—	—	126	436	62	108	25	2	19	77	66	4	0	5	119	3	0	.445	.348
Putnam, Danny	L-L	5-10	200	9-17-82	.249	.218	.263	54	169	19	42	15	0	6	34	22	4	1	0	38	3	2	.444	.349
2-team total (39 Sacramento)					.247	—	—	93	312	33	77	18	1	10	55	32	4	2	1	69	4	3	.407	.324
Sinisi, Vince	L-L	6-0	195	11-7-81	.253	.276	.243	33	99	10	25	5	1	1	12	6	1	0	0	21	1	0	.313	.302
Stansberry, Craig	R-R	6-0	185	3-8-82	.269	.344	.239	118	427	52	115	25	4	7	41	45	3	3	2	72	9	4	.396	.342
Venable, Will	L-L	6-2	210	10-29-82	.260	.263	.259	53	200	33	52	10	3	12	30	20	2	1	3	46	1	0	.520	.329
Weems, Beamer	B-R	5-10	175	7-28-87	1.000	—	1.000	1	1	0	1	0	0	0	0	0	0	0	0	0	0	0	1.000	1.000

Pitching	B-T	HT	WT	DOB	W	L	ERA	G	GS	CG	SV	IP	H	R	ER	HR	BB	SO	AVG	vLH	vRH	K/9	BB/9
Adams, Mike	R-R	6-5	205	7-29-78	0	0	5.40	4	0	0	0	5	4	3	3	1	1	0	.222	.100	.375	0.00	1.80
Baek, Cha Seung	R-R	6-4	225	5-29-80	0	2	11.12	3	3	0	0	6	9	7	7	2	0	7	.375	.444	.333	11.12	0.00
Banks, Josh	R-R	6-3	210	7-18-82	7	7	3.46	26	17	0	0	125	120	52	48	6	36	95	.255	.265	.247	6.84	2.59
Britton, Chris	R-R	6-3	275	12-16-82	1	1	9.53	5	0	0	1	6	11	7	6	1	4	5	.423	.400	.438	7.94	6.35
Burke, Greg	R-R	6-4	215	9-21-82	3	0	2.25	13	0	0	7	16	8	4	4	1	4	14	.148	.050	.206	7.88	2.25
Buschmann, Matt	R-R	6-3	210	2-13-84	3	10	6.18	19	18	1	0	99	121	74	68	13	33	53	.309	.346	.277	4.82	3.00
Carrillo, Cesar	R-R	6-3	175	4-29-84	0	3	5.52	5	5	0	0	29	37	19	18	2	9	26	.308	.277	.329	7.98	2.76

SAN DIEGO PADRES

Pitching	B-T	HT	WT	DOB	W	L	ERA	G	GS	CG	SV	IP	H	R	ER	HR	BB	SO	AVG	vLH	vRH	K/9	BB/9
Cherry, Rocky	R-R	6-5	235	8-19-79	0	1	12.27	6	0	0	0	7	16	12	10	2	6	5	.444	.462	.435	6.14	7.36
De La Cruz, Eulogio	R-R	5-10	215	3-12-84	2	6	3.12	48	4	0	9	69	52	26	24	2	44	59	.208	.190	.221	7.66	5.71
DeHoyos, Gabe	R-R	5-11	260	4-14-80	1	1	0.56	9	0	0	0	16	10	1	1	0	9	12	.179	.222	.158	6.75	5.06
DeMark, Mike	R-R	6-0	198	5-20-83	0	0	0.00	3	0	0	4	3	0	0	0	0	3	3	.200	.500	.154	6.75	6.75
Ekstrom, Mike	R-R	5-11	190	8-30-83	4	2	1.73	42	1	0	0	62	44	12	12	2	16	43	.202	.230	.183	6.21	2.31
Ellis, Jonathan	R-R	6-0	190	10-3-82	7	3	4.13	51	0	0	1	72	73	36	33	9	33	55	.269	.276	.265	6.88	4.13
Gallagher, Sean	R-R	6-2	235	12-30-85	0	1	27.00	1	1	0	0	1	3	3	3	1	0	1	.500	.000	.750	9.00	0.00
2-team total (5 Sacramento)					1	1	2.91	6	6	0	0	22	15	8	7	1	6	16	—	—	—	6.65	2.49
Gaudin, Chad	R-R	5-10	190	3-24-83	0	0	0.00	2	2	0	0	9	4	0	0	0	2	10	.138	.167	.118	10.38	2.08
Geer, Josh	R-R	6-3	195	6-2-83	2	5	4.44	9	9	1	0	53	60	29	26	5	14	21	.294	.301	.287	3.59	2.39
Guevara, Carlos	R-R	5-11	190	3-18-82	0	0	0.00	1	0	0	0	1	0	0	0	0	1	1	.000	—	.000	9.00	9.00
Hefner, Jeremy	R-R	6-4	215	3-11-86	0	0	3.38	1	1	0	0	5	7	2	2	0	2	5	.318	.357	.250	8.44	3.38
Hudgins, John	R-R	6-2	195	8-31-81	0	0	6.53	12	1	0	1	21	22	15	15	4	14	17	.275	.297	.256	7.40	6.10
Inman, Will	R-R	6-0	215	2-6-87	1	4	6.71	12	12	0	0	63	83	49	47	15	25	41	.329	.259	.386	5.86	3.57
Lawrence, Brian	R-R	6-0	195	5-14-76	4	4	6.28	9	8	0	0	53	74	40	37	6	14	26	.330	.310	.343	4.42	2.38
2-team total (5 New Orleans)					7	4	5.10	14	13	0	0	83	99	50	47	9	19	49	—	—	—	5.31	2.06
LeBlanc, Wade	L-L	6-3	200	8-7-84	4	9	3.87	24	20	0	0	121	109	54	52	15	31	95	.240	.242	.239	7.07	2.31
Lopez, Arturo	L-L	5-10	165	2-22-83	0	0	3.77	20	0	0	0	31	27	14	13	0	13	23	.231	.235	.229	6.68	3.77
Moreno, Edwin	R-R	6-1	220	7-30-80	3	3	4.17	39	0	0	10	45	46	24	21	7	20	40	.271	.258	.279	7.94	3.97
O'Connor, Mike	L-L	6-3	185	8-17-80	0	0	5.84	6	1	0	0	12	17	9	8	0	4	6	.347	.185	.545	4.38	2.92
2-team total (6 Omaha)					1	4	6.81	12	6	0	0	40	58	36	30	7	9	24	—	—	—	5.45	2.04
Patterson, Scott	R-R	6-7	235	6-20-79	3	4	3.25	51	0	0	1	55	52	29	26	2	40	64	.242	.284	.208	10.47	6.55
2-team total (7 Sacramento)					3	4	3.96	58	0	0	1	64	61	34	28	4	44	72	—	—	—	10.18	6.22
Perdomo, Luis	R-R	6-0	170	4-27-84	0	0	18.00	1	0	0	0	1	3	2	2	0	1	1	.500	.000	.750	9.00	9.00
Poreda, Aaron	L-L	6-6	240	10-1-86	0	3	7.16	7	6	0	0	33	28	27	26	3	37	30	.239	.171	.268	8.27	10.19
Ramos, Cesar	L-L	6-2	205	6-22-84	5	6	3.99	15	15	1	0	77	84	42	34	7	31	45	.274	.238	.283	5.28	3.64
Russell, Adam	R-R	6-8	255	4-14-83	0	0	5.25	9	0	0	4	12	12	7	7	1	6	7	.261	.211	.296	5.25	4.50
Silva, Walter	R-R	6-1	190	1-4-77	7	5	6.09	23	13	0	0	81	98	57	55	10	27	56	.304	.325	.291	6.20	2.99
Startup, Will	L-L	6-0	195	8-4-84	0	0	2.45	3	0	0	0	4	4	1	1	1	2	1	.286	.286	.286	2.45	4.91
Stauffer, Tim	R-R	6-1	205	6-2-82	2	1	2.35	4	4	0	0	23	16	7	6	1	4	16	.198	.224	.156	6.26	1.57
Teague, Matt	R-L	6-3	210	12-14-84	0	1	9.39	3	1	0	0	8	12	8	8	2	2	0	.400	.375	.409	0.00	2.35
Thatcher, Joe	L-L	6-2	230	10-4-81	1	2	1.89	19	0	0	1	19	18	7	4	1	5	22	.240	.259	.229	10.42	2.37
Valdez, Rolando	R-R	6-1	191	1-8-86	0	1	18.00	1	1	0	0	1	2	2	2	0	3	1	.400	.333	.500	9.00	27.00
Watt, Michael	L-L	6-1	185	2-24-89	0	0	12.00	1	1	0	0	3	6	4	4	1	2	0	.462	.500	.455	0.00	6.00
Webb, Ryan	R-R	6-6	215	2-5-86	0	0	3.00	3	0	0	0	3	3	1	1	0	1	0	.300	.333	.286	0.00	3.00
2-team total (31 Sacramento)					7	1	4.25	34	2	0	2	49	60	23	23	3	16	39	—	—	—	7.21	2.96

Fielding

Catcher	PCT	G	PO	A	E	DP	PB
Alfonzo	.985	53	381	26	6	7	2
Benedict	1.000	1	1	1	0	0	0
Collins	.955	4	21	0	1	0	0
Haad	.984	32	182	8	3	2	2
Hagerty	1.000	5	31	0	0	0	0
Hundley	1.000	5	30	4	0	1	2
Lobaton	.977	39	231	23	6	6	2
Martinez	.971	11	61	5	2	1	1

First Base	PCT	G	PO	A	E	DP
Baxter	.995	21	176	16	1	17
Blanks	.994	59	440	29	3	45
Huffman	.986	17	134	12	2	16
Pascucci	.992	55	438	30	4	46
Sinisi	.971	5	30	4	1	1

Second Base	PCT	G	PO	A	E	DP
Adams	.963	20	45	60	4	14
Antonelli	.989	54	104	154	3	45
Dowdy	1.000	31	54	71	0	16
Gonzalez	1.000	2	1	3	0	1
Howard	1.000	22	50	52	0	11
Stansberry	.992	24	45	83	1	14

Third Base	PCT	G	PO	A	E	DP
Adams	1.000	4	2	6	0	1
Ciofrone	.932	54	42	81	9	4
Dowdy	.968	24	15	45	2	6
Gonzalez	—	1	0	0	0	0
Howard	1.000	1	1	2	0	0
Johnston	1.000	7	1	13	0	1
Stansberry	.924	62	41	93	11	7

Shortstop	PCT	G	PO	A	E	DP
Adams	.962	8	7	18	1	2
Cabrera	.967	6	12	17	1	0
Dowdy	1.000	5	5	7	0	1

	PCT	G	PO	A	E	DP
Kazmar	.973	109	155	309	13	70
Stansberry	.951	28	42	75	6	18

Outfield	PCT	G	PO	A	E	DP
Alley	1.000	11	18	2	0	0
Baxter	.992	62	129	3	1	2
Blanks	.947	15	17	1	1	0
Brown	.980	30	44	6	1	1
Ciofrone	.938	11	15	0	1	0
Codiroli	1.000	5	10	0	0	0
Dowdy	1.000	25	58	6	0	1
Gonzalez	—	1	0	0	0	0
Huffman	.989	103	171	8	2	2
Macias	.986	82	203	10	3	2
Putnam	.989	43	92	1	1	0
Sinisi	.961	23	47	2	2	2
Venable	.954	49	103	1	5	1

SAN ANTONIO MISSIONS   DOUBLE-A

TEXAS LEAGUE

Batting	B-T	HT	WT	DOB	AVG	vLH	vRH	G	AB	R	H	2B	3B	HR	RBI	BB	HBP	SH	SF	SO	SB	CS	SLG	OBP
Baxter, Mike	L-R	6-0	190	12-7-84	.376	.479	.344	51	202	38	76	23	1	4	45	23	2	0	2	42	5	2	.559	.441
Canham, Mitch	L-R	6-2	215	9-25-84	.263	.245	.268	111	407	48	107	20	3	6	53	46	3	1	4	68	5	4	.371	.339
Carroll, Sawyer	L-R	6-4	215	5-9-86	.317	.316	.317	28	82	17	26	5	3	1	14	18	0	0	0	16	1	1	.488	.440
Carter, Sam	R-R	6-4	205	6-5-83	.161	.111	.170	21	56	4	9	0	0	2	6	10	0	0	0	20	0	0	.268	.288
Collins, Michael	R-R	6-3	213	7-18-84	.240	.224	.248	53	150	13	36	9	0	3	20	24	9	0	1	32	0	0	.360	.375
Contreras, Anthony	L-R	5-11	185	9-26-83	.248	.100	.271	79	222	19	55	10	3	2	27	12	0	2	3	29	2	2	.347	.283
Cooper, Craig	R-L	6-1	220	10-27-84	.312	.322	.308	131	503	69	157	35	1	11	94	73	7	1	2	85	9	5	.451	.405
Denker, Travis	R-R	5-9	205	8-5-85	.250	.500	.000	1	4	1	1	0	0	1	2	0	0	0	0	2	0	0	1.000	.250
Durango, Luis	B-R	5-9	160	4-23-86	.281	.281	.281	129	456	78	128	9	2	0	25	81	2	19	2	70	44	17	.309	.390
Forsythe, Logan	R-R	6-1	195	1-14-87	.279	.316	.262	66	244	37	68	9	3	3	31	41	2	1	2	63	5	0	.377	.384
Howard, Kevin	L-R	6-2	190	6-25-81	.500	1.000	.333	1	4	1	2	0	0	0	0	0	0	0	0	0	0	0	.500	.500
Hunter, Cedric	L-L	6-0	185	3-10-88	.261	.231	.272	131	541	71	141	20	6	2	54	25	3	2	6	43	13	3	.331	.294
Johnston, Seth	R-R	6-3	204	3-12-83	.233	.261	.221	108	373	37	87	12	2	9	54	32	3	1	6	89	5	4	.349	.295
Joynt, Brian	R-R	6-4	205	3-14-85	.236	.278	.217	65	233	28	55	7	1	6	31	16	3	1	4	67	4	0	.352	.289

	B-T	HT	WT	DOB	AVG	vLH	vRH	G	AB	R	H	2B	3B	HR	RBI	BB	HBP	SH	SF	SO	SB	CS	SLG	OBP
Kulbacki, Kellen	L-L	5-11	185	11-21-85	.201	.229	.186	36	134	11	27	5	1	0	11	9	1	0	0	23	2	1	.254	.257
Lopez, Jesus	R-R	5-11	165	9-12-87	.232	.193	.250	90	259	28	60	14	1	1	23	23	0	5	1	34	3	0	.305	.293
Ruth, Keoni	R-R	5-11	200	3-21-85	.309	.300	.311	17	55	7	17	1	0	0	7	5	1	0	0	6	2	0	.327	.377
Sogard, Eric	L-R	5-10	180	5-22-86	.293	.214	.325	117	457	79	134	25	3	6	51	58	2	6	7	47	10	6	.400	.370
Solis, Ali	R-R	5-10	225	9-29-87	.148	.273	.063	10	27	4	4	0	0	0	3	1	0	0	0	10	0	0	.148	.179
Zawadzki, Lance	B-R	5-11	185	5-26-85	.289	.333	.266	92	346	59	100	19	5	5	43	44	2	0	0	74	14	1	.416	.372

Pitching	B-T	HT	WT	DOB	W	L	ERA	G	GS	CG	SV	IP	H	R	ER	HR	BB	SO	AVG	vLH	vRH	K/9	BB/9
Adams, Mike	R-R	6-5	205	7-29-78	1	0	2.25	4	1	0	0	4	3	1	1	1	2	6	.214	.000	.429	13.50	4.50
Baek, Cha Seung	R-R	6-4	225	5-29-80	0	1	10.29	2	2	0	0	7	15	12	8	2	2	3	.417	.450	.375	3.86	2.57
Barzilla, Philip	L-L	6-0	180	1-25-79	0	1	9.82	4	0	0	0	4	5	5	4	0	7	3	.333	.429	.250	7.36	17.18
Britton, Chris	R-R	6-3	275	12-16-82	1	1	10.80	10	0	0	0	15	28	18	18	3	4	5	.400	.560	.311	3.00	2.40
Buschmann, Matt	R-R	6-3	210	2-13-84	2	1	4.39	16	3	0	0	41	42	23	20	4	10	28	.271	.284	.257	6.15	2.20
Carrillo, Cesar	R-R	6-3	175	4-29-84	8	4	4.24	20	20	0	0	121	115	61	57	10	37	57	.257	.240	.270	4.24	2.75
Culp, Nate	L-L	6-2	180	10-9-84	8	9	4.21	28	28	0	0	158	172	83	74	14	29	68	.277	.270	.280	3.87	1.65
DeHoyos, Gabe	R-R	5-11	260	4-14-80	0	3	2.45	19	0	0	0	26	27	9	7	1	9	23	.270	.313	.231	8.06	3.16
DeMark, Mike	R-R	6-0	198	5-20-83	2	3	3.15	57	0	0	1	60	53	29	21	2	33	55	.233	.214	.248	8.25	4.95
Faris, Stephen	R-R	6-1	190	6-30-84	4	11	4.54	38	16	1	0	115	134	74	58	9	38	63	.296	.276	.310	4.93	2.97
Frieri, Ernesto	R-R	6-2	200	7-19-85	10	9	3.59	27	26	0	0	140	125	61	56	13	62	118	.237	.272	.206	7.57	3.98
Garrison, Steve	B-L	6-1	185	9-12-86	1	0	9.00	2	2	0	0	6	9	6	6	2	1	3	.391	.222	.500	4.50	1.50
Gomes, Brandon	R-R	5-11	175	7-15-84	4	1	2.63	65	0	0	3	72	54	27	21	4	28	100	.206	.226	.190	12.50	3.50
Guevara, Carlos	R-R	5-11	190	3-18-82	0	0	2.27	31	0	0	0	40	33	13	10	2	16	33	.231	.225	.236	7.49	3.63
Herr, Zach	L-L	5-9	185	12-1-86	0	1	16.20	3	0	0	0	3	8	6	6	1	3	3	.444	.500	.375	8.10	8.10
Hudgins, John	R-R	6-2	195	8-31-81	1	3	2.97	27	0	0	1	33	19	14	11	0	20	29	.164	.188	.147	7.83	5.40
Inman, Will	R-R	6-0	215	2-6-87	6	5	3.40	15	15	0	0	87	71	36	33	5	20	59	.218	.235	.206	6.08	2.06
Jamison, Neil	R-R	6-3	185	8-4-83	0	0	9.00	7	0	0	0	6	11	6	6	0	0	1	.393	.571	.333	1.50	0.00
Kluber, Corey	R-R	6-4	215	4-10-86	2	4	4.60	9	9	0	0	45	45	25	23	5	34	35	.266	.245	.293	7.00	6.80
Latos, Mat	R-R	6-6	225	12-9-87	5	1	1.91	9	9	0	0	47	32	11	10	0	9	46	.192	.253	.131	8.81	1.72
Luebke, Cory	R-L	6-4	200	3-4-85	3	2	3.70	9	9	0	0	41	38	21	17	3	15	32	.241	.205	.254	6.97	3.27
McDaid, Derek	R-R	6-3	220	9-27-83	0	2	7.45	16	0	0	0	19	33	19	16	4	8	17	.370	.452	.339	7.91	3.72
Rice, Scott	L-L	6-6	217	9-21-81	1	4	7.36	25	0	0	0	29	33	26	24	1	22	21	.284	.300	.268	6.44	6.75
Scribner, Evan	R-R	6-3	190	7-19-85	8	4	3.07	58	0	0	21	70	60	27	24	4	20	77	.224	.260	.191	9.85	2.56
Stauffer, Tim	R-R	6-1	205	6-2-82	1	0	1.89	12	0	0	1	19	13	5	4	1	4	12	.183	.265	.108	5.68	1.89
Valdez, Rolando	R-R	6-1	191	1-8-86	1	0	5.01	17	0	0	0	32	39	18	18	5	12	28	.300	.250	.338	7.79	3.34

Fielding

Catcher	PCT	G	PO	A	E	DP	PB
Canham	.988	102	671	50	9	6	8
Collins	1.000	37	225	24	0	1	6
Solis	.968	8	58	3	2	0	0

First Base	PCT	G	PO	A	E	DP
Baxter	1.000	3	7	0	0	0
Collins	1.000	14	88	5	0	10
Cooper	.987	124	1045	48	14	91
Johnston	.974	4	35	2	1	6
Joynt	1.000	2	19	2	0	0

Second Base	PCT	G	PO	A	E	DP
Contreras	.975	27	53	62	3	13
Howard	1.000	1	1	3	0	1
Johnston	1.000	1	0	2	0	1

	PCT	G	PO	A	E	DP
Lopez	1.000	8	17	20	0	5
Ruth	.960	7	11	13	1	4
Sogard	.971	107	223	278	15	69

Third Base	PCT	G	PO	A	E	DP
Contreras	.950	11	7	12	1	2
Denker	.500	1	0	2	2	0
Forsythe	.931	65	52	111	12	13
Johnston	.913	48	29	86	11	5
Joynt	.875	7	9	12	3	0
Ruth	.947	6	4	14	1	1
Zawadzki	.950	11	5	14	1	1

Shortstop	PCT	G	PO	A	E	DP
Contreras	.907	15	19	30	5	7
Lopez	.961	71	92	176	11	31

Zawadzki	.950	72	101	219	17	47

Outfield	PCT	G	PO	A	E	DP
Baxter	.979	43	89	3	2	0
Canham	1.000	3	4	1	0	0
Carroll	.967	28	56	2	2	2
Carter	1.000	12	22	0	0	0
Contreras	1.000	3	4	0	0	0
Cooper	1.000	6	4	0	0	0
Durango	.976	118	231	8	6	2
Hunter	.988	127	313	8	4	2
Johnston	1.000	28	50	3	0	3
Joynt	.991	51	101	5	1	1
Kulbacki	1.000	25	48	1	0	0

LAKE ELSINORE STORM   HIGH CLASS A

CALIFORNIA LEAGUE

Batting	B-T	HT	WT	DOB	AVG	vLH	vRH	G	AB	R	H	2B	3B	HR	RBI	BB	HBP	SH	SF	SO	SB	CS	SLG	OBP
Alvarez, Julian	R-R	6-2	195	5-9-86	.091	.000	.111	3	11	1	1	0	0	0	0	1	0	0	0	1	0	0	.091	.167
Baum, Justin	R-R	6-1	195	10-6-85	.213	.305	.143	42	136	18	29	10	0	2	15	14	1	2	3	27	0	0	.331	.286
Cabrera, Everth	B-R	5-10	175	11-17-86	.391	.400	.385	7	23	7	9	1	1	0	4	5	0	0	0	2	4	3	.522	.500
Carrasco, Felix	B-R	6-1	220	2-14-87	.252	.250	.254	115	416	49	105	24	4	9	69	54	6	1	3	132	6	6	.394	.344
Carroll, Sawyer	L-R	6-4	215	5-9-86	.320	.333	.314	37	147	28	47	15	5	2	42	22	1	0	4	33	4	2	.531	.402
Carvajal, Yefri	R-R	5-11	190	1-22-89	.262	.270	.258	61	229	24	60	13	1	4	29	11	0	2	1	35	6	5	.380	.295
Chalk, Brad	L-L	6-1	180	1-20-86	.301	.309	.298	130	525	95	158	21	12	2	63	41	6	11	2	72	33	8	.398	.357
Clark, Matt	L-R	6-5	215	12-10-86	.292	.194	.324	67	250	44	73	13	3	13	46	28	4	0	4	62	2	0	.524	.367
Darnell, James	R-R	6-2	195	1-19-87	.294	.357	.267	60	235	40	69	18	2	13	43	30	2	1	1	38	3	1	.553	.377
Figueroa, Cole	L-R	5-10	180	6-30-87	.187	.158	.196	21	75	5	14	3	0	0	9	6	1	1	0	14	5	0	.227	.256
Floyd, Cliff	L-R	6-4	230	12-5-72	.190	.200	.188	7	21	0	4	1	0	0	0	1	0	0	0	2	0	0	.238	.227
Forsythe, Logan	R-R	6-1	195	1-14-87	.322	.372	.297	66	236	46	76	13	3	8	30	61	7	0	1	48	6	2	.504	.472
Gelbrich, Logan	R-R	6-3	205	12-1-85	.152	.222	.135	16	46	2	7	2	0	0	3	0	1	0	0	11	0	0	.196	.204
Gonzalez, Edgar	R-R	6-0	180	6-14-78	.286	.333	.273	5	14	2	4	1	0	1	3	1	0	0	0	6	0	1	.571	.333
Hairston, Scott	R-R	6-0	195	5-25-80	.100	1.000	.000	3	10	1	1	0	0	0	0	1	2	0	0	3	0	0	.100	.308
Joynt, Brian	R-R	6-2	205	3-14-85	.259	.148	.294	28	112	17	29	6	2	6	19	4	1	0	1	36	1	0	.509	.288
Martinez, Luis	R-R	6-0	210	4-3-85	.300	.237	.324	83	280	39	84	20	0	4	41	34	7	0	0	58	2	1	.414	.389
Mercado, Angel	R-R	6-0	205	8-19-85	.246	.357	.186	63	199	24	49	14	0	3	21	23	5	0	2	48	7	2	.362	.336
Morton, Colt	R-R	6-5	228	4-10-82	.222	.333	.200	11	36	7	8	4	1	1	5	4	1	0	0	10	0	0	.472	.317

Batting	B-T	HT	WT	DOB	AVG	vLH	vRH	G	AB	R	H	2B	3B	HR	RBI	BB	HBP	SH	SF	SO	SB	CS	SLG	OBP
Parrino, Andy	B-R	6-0	185	10-31-85	.235	.164	.256	94	311	52	73	16	1	2	29	51	4	1	4	85	8	2	.312	.346
Payne, Danny	L-L	5-10	185	9-8-85	.245	.174	.268	114	364	69	89	22	3	8	41	79	3	2	3	106	18	9	.387	.381
Perry, Robert	L-L	5-10	185	10-3-84	.171	.214	.161	26	70	14	12	3	2	2	8	6	7	0	1	20	1	0	.357	.298
Railey, Joey	L-R	5-7	180	12-9-85	.000	.000	.000	1	4	0	0	0	0	0	0	0	0	0	0	1	0	0	.000	.000
Rodriguez, Luis	B-R	5-9	190	6-27-80	.286	.000	.364	4	14	1	4	0	0	1	1	0	0	0	0	2	0	0	.500	.286
Ruth, Keoni	R-R	5-11	200	3-21-85	.280	.277	.281	90	343	36	96	18	2	0	30	18	3	5	1	36	5	2	.344	.321
Solis, Ali	R-R	5-10	225	9-29-87	.203	.250	.178	45	138	16	28	4	3	2	19	7	2	3	2	37	1	0	.319	.248
Tremblay, Chris	R-R	5-10	180	11-13-86	.167	.167	.167	15	36	5	6	2	0	0	4	4	0	0	0	10	0	0	.222	.250
Weems, Beamer	B-R	5-10	175	7-28-87	.253	.243	.258	108	359	61	91	21	3	3	44	76	13	5	1	76	10	5	.354	.401
Winn, Kevin	R-L	5-11	185	6-5-87	.238	.500	.176	13	21	1	5	2	0	0	1	0	0	0	0	5	0	0	.333	.238
Zawadzki, Lance	B-R	5-11	185	5-26-85	.276	.326	.255	36	145	19	40	6	2	10	34	18	1	0	0	29	3	1	.552	.360

Pitching	B-T	HT	WT	DOB	W	L	ERA	G	GS	CG	SV	IP	H	R	ER	HR	BB	SO	AVG	vLH	vRH	K/9	BB/9
Axelrod, Dylan	R-R	6-0	195	7-30-85	0	0	4.50	11	0	0	0	12	12	6	6	0	5	6	.245	.240	.250	4.50	3.75
Baek, Cha Seung	R-R	6-4	225	5-29-80	0	1	7.27	2	2	0	0	9	6	7	7	1	4	7	.194	.294	.071	7.27	4.15
Bass, Anthony	R-R	6-2	190	11-1-87	3	0	3.51	10	8	0	0	33	33	17	13	3	14	20	.266	.313	.217	5.40	3.78
Berger, Jon	R-R	6-2	215	1-18-87	0	2	17.10	3	3	0	0	10	23	19	19	3	7	5	.451	.560	.346	4.50	6.30
Breit, Aaron	R-R	6-4	205	4-19-86	2	6	3.51	40	13	0	0	108	103	59	42	7	45	110	.252	.218	.292	9.20	3.76
Garrison, Steve	B-L	6-1	185	9-12-86	0	0	1.17	2	1	0	1	8	5	2	1	0	2	7	.185	.273	.125	8.22	2.35
Gonzalez, Eric	R-R	6-5	190	9-5-86	2	1	4.47	24	0	0	0	46	46	24	23	5	14	38	.260	.292	.227	7.38	2.72
Harrington, Allen	L-L	5-11	185	7-3-86	1	6	7.13	42	1	0	0	53	84	46	42	7	29	36	.365	.432	.333	6.11	4.92
Hefner, Jeremy	R-R	6-4	215	3-11-86	14	9	4.12	27	27	0	0	151	165	81	69	13	38	142	.284	.260	.307	8.48	2.27
Hinson, Ryan	L-L	6-3	220	5-12-87	0	1	4.97	8	0	0	0	13	13	8	7	1	7	15	.271	.250	.281	10.66	4.97
Hynes, Colt	L-L	5-11	200	6-28-85	3	3	2.90	49	0	0	2	59	60	25	19	0	17	44	.264	.256	.269	6.71	2.59
Italiano, Craig	R-R	6-4	210	7-22-86	0	1	1.44	19	0	0	0	31	24	10	5	0	10	44	.209	.231	.180	12.64	2.87
2-team total (16 Stockton)					5	7	4.42	35	16	0	0	108	107	65	53	6	50	119	—	—		9.92	4.17
Jamison, Neil	R-R	6-3	185	8-4-83	0	0	4.08	12	0	0	0	18	20	9	8	3	6	11	.286	.324	.242	5.60	3.06
Kluber, Corey	R-R	6-4	215	4-10-86	7	9	4.54	19	19	0	0	109	110	65	55	9	36	124	.261	.292	.231	10.24	2.97
Luebke, Cory	R-L	6-4	200	3-4-85	8	2	2.34	14	14	1	0	88	73	24	23	3	17	80	.227	.242	.221	8.15	1.73
Lynch, Colin	R-R	6-0	185	8-30-85	0	0	5.06	3	0	0	0	5	7	3	3	0	3	2	.304	.300	.308	3.38	5.06
McBryde, Jeremy	R-R	6-2	195	5-1-87	6	3	4.54	13	12	0	0	75	72	39	38	12	19	82	.250	.287	.202	9.80	2.27
Oland, Bryan	R-R	6-3	230	6-5-85	7	2	3.10	53	0	0	28	58	53	20	20	3	13	68	.244	.245	.243	10.55	2.02
Pelzer, Wynn	R-R	6-1	200	6-23-86	11	8	3.94	27	27	0	0	151	134	76	66	6	59	147	.244	.274	.210	8.78	3.52
Ramos, Cesar	L-L	6-2	205	6-22-84	1	0	1.00	2	1	0	0	9	9	1	1	0	5	6	.250	.182	.280	6.00	5.00
Schmidt, Nick	L-L	6-5	245	10-10-85	2	8	7.88	11	11	0	0	48	68	43	42	7	27	27	.349	.273	.371	5.06	5.06
Teague, Matt	R-L	6-3	210	12-14-84	2	2	5.75	45	0	0	1	72	99	49	46	7	23	51	.327	.312	.335	6.38	2.88
Vincent, Nick	R-R	6-0	175	7-12-86	4	2	3.08	59	0	0	2	64	66	27	22	3	18	74	.266	.322	.218	10.35	2.52
Wilkes, Chris	R-R	6-4	235	9-26-89	0	1	10.13	3	1	0	0	5	9	6	6	1	4	2	.391	.385	.400	3.38	6.75
Woodard, Robert	R-R	6-1	205	1-10-85	0	0	4.15	4	0	0	0	4	7	2	2	0	0	2	.412	.429	.400	4.15	0.00

Fielding

Catcher	PCT	G	PO	A	E	DP	PB
Gelbrich	1.000	14	85	6	0	0	1
Martinez	.986	83	686	76	11	8	2
Morton	1.000	9	70	4	0	0	0
Solis	.995	44	318	62	2	7	5

First Base	PCT	G	PO	A	E	DP
Baum	1.000	25	199	12	0	13
Carrasco	.976	73	678	39	18	52
Clark	.977	45	366	16	9	28
Parrino	1.000	4	14	1	0	4
Ruth	.958	4	18	5	1	1

Second Base	PCT	G	PO	A	E	DP
Baum	.833	3	3	7	2	2
Cabrera	1.000	3	5	5	0	3
Figueroa	.984	14	23	37	1	5
Gonzalez	1.000	3	6	13	0	2
Parrino	.972	50	72	133	6	23

	PCT	G	PO	A	E	DP
Railey	1.000	1	1	3	0	0
Ruth	.976	56	86	163	6	27
Weems	.938	10	10	20	2	3
Winn	.909	6	4	6	1	1
Zawadzki	.973	7	11	25	1	6

Third Base	PCT	G	PO	A	E	DP
Baum	.870	9	8	12	3	0
Darnell	.924	51	34	99	11	7
Forsythe	.920	61	37	113	13	13
Parrino	.891	20	13	36	6	3
Ruth	1.000	2	3	2	0	0

Shortstop	PCT	G	PO	A	E	DP
Cabrera	.846	6	3	8	2	0
Figueroa	1.000	7	13	17	0	5
Parrino	1.000	9	7	27	0	3
Rodriguez	.941	4	8	8	1	3
Tremblay	.900	12	10	26	4	8

	PCT	G	PO	A	E	DP
Weems	.976	99	129	275	10	43
Winn	1.000	1	0	2	0	0
Zawadzki	.958	14	10	36	2	3

Outfield	PCT	G	PO	A	E	DP
Alvarez	1.000	3	5	0	0	0
Carroll	.969	36	58	4	2	1
Carvajal	.898	57	94	3	11	0
Chalk	.988	129	223	18	3	4
Gonzalez	1.000	1	1	0	0	0
Hairston	1.000	2	2	0	0	0
Joynt	.917	27	50	5	5	1
Mercado	.986	51	67	3	1	1
Parrino	1.000	3	1	0	0	0
Payne	.981	114	193	19	4	5
Perry	.962	22	22	3	1	0

FORT WAYNE TINCAPS — LOW CLASS A

MIDWEST LEAGUE

Batting	B-T	HT	WT	DOB	AVG	vLH	vRH	G	AB	R	H	2B	3B	HR	RBI	BB	HBP	SH	SF	SO	SB	CS	SLG	OBP
Anna, Dean	L-R	5-11	180	11-24-86	.200	.167	.216	17	55	4	11	2	0	0	5	7	0	0	2	13	0	0	.236	.281
Baum, Justin	R-R	6-1	195	10-6-85	.200	.267	.175	47	165	22	33	4	0	4	22	24	3	0	6	40	2	2	.297	.303
Belnome, Vince	R-L	5-11	205	3-11-88	.500	.375	.542	10	32	4	16	3	1	0	10	4	0	1	0	5	1	0	.656	.556
Benedict, Griffin	L-R	6-0	185	7-4-87	.286	.333	.278	6	21	4	6	0	0	0	2	2	1	0	0	2	0	1	.286	.375
Carroll, Sawyer	L-R	6-4	215	5-9-86	.316	.339	.309	66	250	43	79	20	1	5	40	40	1	0	2	57	14	5	.464	.410
Carvajal, Yefri	R-R	5-11	190	1-22-89	.253	.323	.230	66	249	29	63	10	4	1	29	18	2	0	1	43	2	2	.337	.307
Clark, Matt	L-R	6-5	215	12-10-86	.266	.209	.286	64	252	41	67	22	0	11	55	33	1	0	1	72	0	0	.484	.352
Cumberland, Drew	L-R	5-10	175	1-13-89	.293	.276	.297	77	290	57	85	18	5	2	40	40	6	0	3	36	19	3	.410	.386
Darnell, James	R-R	6-2	195	1-19-87	.329	.288	.341	66	222	40	73	17	2	7	38	57	2	1	1	51	5	5	.518	.468
Decker, Cody	R-R	5-11	220	1-17-87	.111	.000	.167	7	18	2	2	1	0	0	1	6	0	0	0	5	0	0	.167	.333
Decker, Jaff	L-L	5-10	190	2-23-90	.299	.219	.319	104	358	78	107	25	2	16	64	85	10	0	3	92	10	6	.514	.442

	B-T	HT	WT	DOB	AVG	vLH	vRH	G	AB	R	H	2B	3B	HR	RBI	BB	HBP	SH	SF	SO	SB	CS	SLG	OBP
Drake, Brayden	R-R	5-11	190	4-17-87	.233	.350	.189	25	73	7	17	3	0	5	12	6	1	0	0	13	0	0	.479	.300
Dykstra, Allan	L-R	6-5	215	5-21-87	.226	.241	.221	125	411	71	93	22	3	11	60	104	16	0	6	103	1	2	.375	.397
Figueroa, Cole	L-R	5-10	180	6-30-87	.319	.254	.343	70	238	32	76	15	1	1	34	37	3	1	6	38	10	7	.403	.408
Hansen, Kevin	R-R	5-10	170	11-5-85	.254	.228	.263	97	339	44	86	13	0	0	32	21	5	2	1	48	2	3	.292	.306
Hartman, Chadd	L-R	6-0	195	11-9-86	.250	1.000	.000	2	4	0	1	0	0	0	0	0	2	0	0	2	0	0	.250	.500
Lara, Robert	R-R	6-2	190	11-25-86	.219	.304	.194	58	201	22	44	11	1	2	28	20	2	0	4	52	1	2	.313	.291
Mercado, Angel	R-R	6-0	205	8-19-85	.294	.200	.429	4	17	2	5	0	0	1	4	0	0	0	0	1	0	0	.471	.294
Parrino, Andy	B-R	6-0	185	10-31-85	.500	—	.500	5	18	3	9	2	0	0	3	3	0	0	0	3	0	0	.611	.571
Railey, Joey	L-R	5-7	180	12-9-85	.000	.000	.000	3	6	1	0	0	0	0	0	1	1	0	0	3	1	1	.000	.143
Robertson, Dan	R-R	5-8	175	9-30-85	.296	.356	.274	121	432	78	128	23	3	5	65	50	12	3	6	51	20	10	.398	.380
Solis, Ali	R-R	5-10	205	9-29-87	.208	.300	.184	13	48	10	10	2	0	4	10	4	1	0	1	14	0	0	.500	.278
Tekotte, Blake	L-R	5-11	175	5-24-87	.258	.234	.266	134	530	83	137	24	5	13	56	68	4	4	4	97	30	12	.396	.345
Valdez, Jeudy	R-R	5-11	155	5-5-89	.212	.220	.211	49	193	25	41	11	2	1	14	17	2	3	0	51	11	3	.306	.283
Zornes, Adam	R-R	6-0	215	4-2-86	.200	.267	.177	69	235	34	47	20	2	8	35	32	2	2	1	86	1	1	.404	.300

Pitching	B-T	HT	WT	DOB	W	L	ERA	G	GS	CG	SV	IP	H	R	ER	HR	BB	SO	AVG	vLH	vRH	K/9	BB/9
Bass, Anthony	R-R	6-2	190	11-1-87	9	3	2.19	18	18	0	0	90	79	31	22	5	25	69	.235	.243	.229	6.87	2.49
Brach, Brad	R-R	6-6	210	4-12-86	3	3	1.27	60	0	0	33	64	36	10	9	1	11	82	.164	.153	.170	11.59	1.55
Carter, Dexter	R-R	6-6	195	2-5-87	1	4	12.86	6	6	0	0	21	34	30	30	3	15	23	.370	.333	.396	9.86	6.43
Castro, Simon	R-R	6-5	203	4-9-88	10	6	3.33	28	27	1	0	140	118	61	52	9	37	157	.226	.232	.221	10.07	2.37
Davis, Erik	R-R	6-4	200	10-8-86	16	6	3.64	32	19	0	0	124	111	56	50	5	44	106	.240	.257	.228	7.71	3.20
Davis, Tom	R-R	6-2	215	6-3-86	1	0	1.42	11	0	0	0	19	19	4	3	0	4	14	.264	.316	.245	6.63	1.89
Fetter, Chris	R-R	6-8	230	12-23-85	2	1	2.22	5	4	0	1	24	26	6	6	0	6	21	.286	.161	.350	7.77	2.22
Gonzalez, Eric	R-R	6-0	195	9-5-86	2	1	4.19	27	1	0	0	39	41	19	18	3	7	38	.275	.345	.231	8.84	1.63
Greenwood, Nick	R-L	6-1	180	9-28-87	0	0	0.00	3	0	0	0	3	2	0	0	1	3	.222	.333	.167	9.00	3.00
Harrington, Allen	L-L	5-11	185	7-3-86	1	0	0.00	10	0	0	0	10	5	1	0	0	6	12	.147	.167	.136	11.17	5.59
Herr, Zach	L-L	5-9	185	12-1-86	5	2	4.13	54	0	0	2	57	50	30	26	4	20	80	.229	.197	.242	12.71	3.18
Hynes, Colt	L-L	5-11	200	6-28-85	2	0	1.62	13	0	0	0	17	13	4	3	0	7	17	.217	.167	.238	9.18	3.78
Lara, Alexis	R-R	6-0	150	3-23-87	4	0	3.03	52	0	0	2	65	39	23	22	4	28	80	.175	.155	.187	11.02	3.86
Latos, Mat	R-R	6-6	225	12-9-87	3	0	0.36	6	6	0	0	25	10	1	1	1	3	27	.120	.077	.159	9.59	1.07
Lynch, Colin	R-R	6-0	185	8-30-85	1	1	3.75	20	0	0	0	36	34	17	15	3	14	36	.248	.213	.267	9.00	3.50
Musgrave, Rob	L-L	6-1	205	9-26-85	2	4	4.92	33	9	0	0	79	79	52	43	13	27	90	.259	.250	.262	10.30	3.09
Osuna, Stiven	R-R	6-3	170	5-5-87	10	9	4.54	30	24	0	1	123	123	75	62	6	54	105	.259	.274	.249	7.68	3.95
Perez, Eduardo	R-R	6-2	185	2-3-88	5	2	4.52	30	1	0	2	66	72	37	33	4	15	58	.275	.260	.285	7.95	2.06
Schmidt, Nick	L-L	6-5	245	10-10-85	4	7	2.79	13	11	0	0	52	38	21	16	0	23	59	.195	.293	.169	10.28	4.01
Schumacher, Nick	R-R	6-4	210	7-24-85	6	0	1.11	37	0	0	0	57	47	9	7	1	14	55	.226	.269	.200	8.74	2.22
Watt, Michael	L-L	6-1	185	2-24-89	7	4	4.17	31	18	0	0	121	119	65	56	6	44	87	.259	.288	.249	6.47	3.27

Fielding

Catcher	PCT	G	PO	A	E	DP	PB
Benedict	.967	6	52	6	2	0	1
Lara	.986	56	439	42	7	6	3
Solis	.985	13	115	14	2	1	1
Zornes	.997	67	602	50	2	1	11

First Base	PCT	G	PO	A	E	DP
Baum	1.000	10	95	5	0	5
Clark	.994	37	310	28	2	18
Decker	.952	4	16	4	1	3
Dykstra	.988	91	689	52	9	52

Second Base	PCT	G	PO	A	E	DP
Anna	.967	8	13	16	1	3
Belnome	1.000	3	3	6	0	0
Cumberland	.917	7	4	18	2	3
Drake	.952	6	10	10	1	2

	PCT	G	PO	A	E	DP
Figueroa	.974	28	50	62	3	14
Hansen	.970	49	89	108	6	20
Parrino	1.000	1	2	2	0	0
Railey	1.000	2	4	6	0	3
Valdez	.952	49	81	119	10	18

Third Base	PCT	G	PO	A	E	DP
Anna	1.000	6	6	14	0	0
Baum	1.000	34	31	60	0	4
Belnome	.923	6	2	10	1	0
Darnell	.875	66	35	98	19	9
Drake	.975	18	15	24	1	2
Hansen	1.000	18	11	30	0	4

Shortstop	PCT	G	PO	A	E	DP
Anna	1.000	3	2	5	0	0
Cumberland	.949	69	104	156	14	25

	PCT	G	PO	A	E	DP
Figueroa	.986	43	52	92	2	17
Hansen	.962	30	31	69	4	7
Parrino	1.000	5	9	14	0	4

Outfield	PCT	G	PO	A	E	DP
Carroll	.982	61	100	8	2	2
Carvajal	.924	51	69	4	6	1
Decker	1.000	1	1	0	0	0
Decker	.963	90	119	11	5	1
Hartman	—	1	0	0	0	0
Mercado	1.000	4	4	0	0	0
Robertson	.983	98	163	12	3	2
Tekotte	.981	127	289	13	6	4

EUGENE EMERALDS

SHORT-SEASON

NORTHWEST LEAGUE

Batting	B-T	HT	WT	DOB	AVG	vLH	vRH	G	AB	R	H	2B	3B	HR	RBI	BB	HBP	SH	SF	SO	SB	CS	SLG	OBP
Anna, Dean	L-R	5-11	180	11-24-86	.310	.219	.336	39	145	27	45	13	1	5	26	23	4	2	1	28	7	6	.517	.416
Belnome, Vince	R-L	5-11	205	3-11-88	.297	.255	.308	65	236	53	70	16	1	10	44	52	5	0	2	55	0	0	.500	.431
Benedict, Griffin	L-R	6-0	185	7-4-87	.259	.048	.305	30	116	12	30	7	0	1	12	11	5	0	0	30	4	1	.345	.348
Codiroli, Jason	L-L	5-10	175	1-20-87	.290	.404	.260	59	224	42	65	5	2	4	29	39	5	1	2	37	15	8	.384	.404
Davis, Bo	R-R	6-0	185	8-28-85	.329	.417	.311	20	73	19	24	7	2	0	6	16	4	1	1	16	11	1	.479	.468
Drake, Brayden	R-R	5-11	190	4-17-87	.194	.143	.208	17	67	8	13	5	0	1	7	0	0	0	0	12	0	1	.284	.270
Freiman, Nate	R-R	6-7	225	12-31-86	.294	.219	.316	72	289	36	85	22	0	11	68	30	3	0	2	55	2	0	.484	.364
Hagerty, Jason	B-R	6-3	220	9-13-87	.225	.256	.216	47	173	34	39	12	0	6	26	26	3	0	1	47	0	0	.399	.335
Hartman, Chadd	R-R	6-0	195	11-9-86	.196	.136	.213	30	102	14	20	1	0	2	12	14	1	1	2	32	1	0	.265	.294
Loretelli, Kyle	R-L	5-11	185	6-30-86	.218	.154	.240	30	101	13	22	5	0	1	7	12	5	0	0	40	1	2	.297	.331
Quiles, Emmanuel	R-R	5-11	186	10-26-89	.262	.235	.270	37	145	19	38	7	0	4	15	7	2	1	0	38	1	1	.393	.305
Railey, Joey	L-R	5-7	180	12-9-85	.283	.474	.233	26	92	12	26	3	0	0	13	14	0	1	2	16	3	0	.315	.370
Rincon, Edinson	R-R	6-1	185	8-11-90	.300	.267	.309	70	267	47	80	18	3	7	47	46	9	0	3	60	5	0	.468	.415
Tremblay, Chris	R-R	5-10	180	11-13-86	.227	.207	.233	34	119	17	27	0	0	0	7	15	5	0	0	31	4	2	.227	.348
Vern, Matt	R-R	6-3	225	11-8-86	.237	.200	.247	54	207	27	49	6	5	4	24	15	6	0	1	71	7	1	.372	.306

Batting	B-T	HT	WT	DOB	AVG	vLH	vRH	G	AB	R	H	2B	3B	HR	RBI	BB	HBP	SH	SF	SO	SB	CS	SLG	OBP
Wideman, Kurt	R-R	5-11	220	5-21-86	.000	.000	.000	3	11	0	0	0	0	0	0	0	1	1	0	0	3	0	.000	.154
Williams, Everett	L-R	5-10	200	10-1-90	.200	.000	.263	6	25	1	5	2	0	1	3	4	0	0	0	11	0	0	.400	.310
Winn, Kevin	R-L	5-11	185	6-5-87	.242	.333	.216	25	95	15	23	3	0	0	9	7	1	1	2	11	2	2	.274	.295
Wright, Ty	R-R	6-1	235	8-10-87	.231	.409	.186	28	108	13	25	4	2	1	12	3	2	0	1	23	1	0	.333	.263

Pitching	B-T	HT	WT	DOB	W	L	ERA	G	GS	CG	SV	IP	H	R	ER	HR	BB	SO	AVG	vLH	vRH	K/9	BB/9
Angelucci, Alessio	R-R	6-2	190	7-28-88	1	2	7.08	22	0	0	0	34	42	33	27	6	32	16	.304	.278	.321	4.19	8.39
Bagley, Tyson	R-R	6-8	250	10-20-85	1	1	5.80	19	1	0	0	40	49	28	26	4	18	39	.297	.352	.270	8.70	4.02
Berger, Jon	R-R	6-2	215	1-18-87	3	0	2.93	7	7	0	0	43	41	14	14	3	4	30	.248	.260	.239	6.28	0.84
Bovich, Andrew	L-L	6-1	195	8-7-85	2	1	4.30	12	0	0	0	23	27	11	11	3	3	16	.297	.222	.328	6.26	1.17
De Paula, Jose	L-L	6-2	165	3-4-90	1	0	2.79	2	2	0	0	10	9	4	3	0	2	10	.243	.000	.265	9.31	1.86
Erickson, David	R-R	5-10	171	2-9-86	3	4	2.58	30	0	0	8	38	33	17	11	0	12	31	.232	.163	.269	7.28	2.82
Fetter, Chris	R-R	6-8	230	12-23-85	2	0	1.33	14	6	0	6	41	24	6	6	0	8	54	.164	.241	.120	11.95	1.77
Greenwood, Nick	R-L	6-1	180	9-28-87	4	1	1.71	17	9	0	5	63	52	18	12	1	16	50	.224	.151	.258	7.11	2.27
Hernandez, Pedro	L-L	5-10	200	4-12-89	0	2	9.92	6	4	0	0	16	31	21	18	4	4	15	.408	.308	.429	8.27	2.20
Hinson, Ryan	L-L	6-3	220	5-12-87	1	1	8.04	14	2	0	1	31	39	34	28	2	19	33	.312	.262	.337	9.48	5.46
Holland, Brett	R-R	6-2	185	6-30-87	0	0	12.00	2	0	0	0	3	6	5	4	1	1	2	.400	.750	.273	6.00	3.00
Ibarra, Jeff	L-L	6-6	180	8-18-87	1	3	3.80	26	0	0	0	43	47	24	18	3	10	42	.278	.214	.310	8.86	2.11
Jackson, Matt	R-R	6-4	175	12-18-87	3	7	4.97	18	11	0	0	58	64	39	32	2	12	44	.276	.250	.293	6.83	1.86
Mead, Tyler	L-R	6-1	180	8-15-87	0	0	15.00	4	0	0	0	3	6	8	5	0	6	1	.400	.500	.286	3.00	18.00
Mikolas, Miles	R-R	6-5	220	8-23-88	1	8	5.94	15	11	0	0	53	77	47	35	1	9	39	.332	.402	.277	6.62	1.53
Poynter, Gary	R-R	6-2	190	6-12-87	2	2	4.58	14	0	0	1	18	22	11	9	0	7	16	.306	.458	.229	8.15	3.57
Reyes, Jorge	R-R	6-3	195	12-7-87	1	1	1.38	3	3	0	0	13	9	3	2	1	2	12	.214	.278	.167	8.31	1.38
Sampson, Keyvius	R-R	6-0	185	1-6-91	0	0	3.60	2	1	0	0	5	3	2	2	0	3	5	.176	.125	.222	9.00	5.40
Sullivan, Jerry	R-R	6-4	220	1-18-88	5	3	4.02	16	9	0	0	54	44	26	24	5	27	58	.219	.205	.228	9.73	4.53
Tabachnik, Mauricio	R-R	6-2	198	11-8-89	2	4	5.94	24	4	0	1	50	67	38	33	1	17	40	.313	.364	.278	7.20	3.06
Wilkes, Chris	R-R	6-4	235	9-26-89	1	2	2.84	6	6	0	0	25	28	14	8	0	4	17	.272	.302	.250	6.04	1.42

Fielding

Catcher	PCT	G	PO	A	E	DP	PB
Benedict	1.000	11	89	4	0	0	2
Hagerty	.984	31	243	11	4	4	6
Quiles	.979	33	251	27	6	1	6
Wideman	1.000	1	6	1	0	0	0

First Base	PCT	G	PO	A	E	DP
Freiman	.994	67	589	53	4	66
Hagerty	1.000	8	75	6	0	5
Wideman	1.000	1	9	3	0	2

Second Base	PCT	G	PO	A	E	DP
Anna	.967	5	10	19	1	3
Belnome	.969	33	63	93	5	16

	PCT	G	PO	A	E	DP
Drake	.895	4	6	11	2	3
Railey	.968	21	31	60	3	13
Winn	.953	14	23	58	4	19

Third Base	PCT	G	PO	A	E	DP
Anna	1.000	1	0	1	0	0
Belnome	.926	20	13	37	4	5
Drake	.880	11	4	18	3	4
Rincon	.818	44	31	68	22	6

Shortstop	PCT	G	PO	A	E	DP
Anna	.948	31	52	94	8	26
Drake	.833	1	3	2	1	0
Tremblay	.935	34	51	106	11	21

	PCT	G	PO	A	E	DP
Winn	.925	11	17	32	4	6

Outfield	PCT	G	PO	A	E	DP
Benedict	.895	18	17	0	2	0
Codiroli	.973	59	108	0	3	0
Davis	.944	18	33	1	2	0
Hartman	.961	27	49	0	2	0
Loretelli	.939	26	44	2	3	0
Vern	.938	54	71	4	5	0
Williams	1.000	6	8	0	0	0
Wright	.979	26	45	1	1	0

AZL PADRES   ROOKIE

ARIZONA LEAGUE

Batting	B-T	HT	WT	DOB	AVG	vLH	vRH	G	AB	R	H	2B	3B	HR	RBI	BB	HBP	SH	SF	SO	SB	CS	SLG	OBP
Adamson, Corey	L-R	6-2	185	2-23-92	.143	.091	.158	15	49	4	7	1	0	0	4	4	1	1	0	17	0	0	.163	.222
Ahearn, Chris	R-R	5-11	180	5-8-86	.098	.333	.083	19	51	4	5	1	0	0	3	2	0	0	14	3	1	.118	.179	
Alia, Jon	R-R	6-3	230	12-6-85	.304	.300	.305	53	204	37	62	13	3	6	41	23	2	0	2	54	1	2	.485	.377
Alvarez, Julian	R-R	6-2	195	5-9-86	.203	.200	.203	30	74	10	15	3	2	1	7	11	5	0	1	25	2	0	.338	.341
Basham, Brett	R-R	6-2	205	9-8-86	.444	.000	.500	3	9	1	4	1	0	0	1	0	0	0	1	0	0		.556	.444
Decker, Cody	R-R	5-11	220	1-17-87	.354	.389	.346	52	198	46	70	21	3	15	63	19	7	0	4	42	0	0	.717	.421
Galvez, Jonathan	R-R	6-2	175	1-18-91	.295	.375	.275	52	193	45	57	16	3	6	27	30	4	0	1	44	14	6	.503	.399
Garce, Daniel	R-R	6-1	166	6-6-89	.222	.214	.224	29	72	9	16	5	0	0	11	4	4	0	5	22	1	0	.292	.282
Liriano, Rymer	R-R	6-0	211	6-20-91	.350	.256	.373	50	197	44	69	8	1	8	44	15	2	0	2	52	14	5	.523	.398
Minyeti, Jorge	B-R	5-10	180	11-7-90	.240	.241	.240	45	154	38	37	3	3	0	16	31	1	3	0	32	11	2	.299	.371
Monger, Cameron	R-R	6-2	210	8-5-88	.295	.318	.289	52	217	42	64	11	6	2	32	12	10	3	2	52	29	5	.429	.357
Olabisi, Wande	R-R	6-0	210	3-18-88	.255	.345	.233	43	149	21	38	3	1	6	28	10	6	0	1	52	11	3	.409	.325
Pozo, Jhonaldo	R-R	6-3	183	3-28-89	.196	.364	.173	33	92	14	18	4	1	2	14	9	1	0	2	29	0	0	.326	.269
Skube, Ryan	R-R	5-11	175	3-26-91	.243	.200	.253	32	103	17	25	6	1	1	11	6	4	1	3	26	4	3	.350	.302
Tonneson, Dylan	R-R	6-2	200	9-5-87	.203	.222	.196	24	69	7	14	3	0	0	6	8	5	0	0	16	1	0	.246	.329
Valdez, Jeudy	R-R	5-11	155	5-5-89	.318	.300	.324	12	44	8	14	3	2	0	6	6	0	0	0	10	3	2	.477	.400
Wideman, Kurt	R-R	5-11	220	5-21-86	.268	.364	.250	22	71	9	19	3	0	1	11	4	3	0	0	14	0	1	.352	.333
Williams, Everett	L-R	5-10	200	10-1-90	.389	.333	.400	4	18	1	7	2	1	0	6	1	0	0	0	7	2	1	.611	.421
Wright, Ty	R-R	6-1	235	8-10-87	.500	.300	.611	3	8	2	4	1	1	0	5	1	0	0	1	1	0	0	.607	.588

Pitching	B-T	HT	WT	DOB	W	L	ERA	G	GS	CG	SV	IP	H	R	ER	HR	BB	SO	AVG	vLH	vRH	K/9	BB/9
Arias, Rafeal	R-R	6-0	165	1-3-89	3	0	2.22	22	0	0	5	28	25	10	7	1	7	37	.231	.256	.217	11.75	2.22
Berger, Jon	R-R	6-2	215	1-18-87	2	1	3.00	5	5	0	0	27	20	10	9	2	2	33	.196	.280	.169	11.00	0.67
Berroa, Simon	R-R	6-4	165	10-28-87	1	4	5.54	9	6	0	0	26	31	21	16	0	12	13	.282	.260	.300	4.50	4.15
Bovich, Andrew	L-L	6-1	195	8-7-85	0	0	2.89	7	0	0	0	9	10	4	3	0	3	8	.278	.333	.259	7.71	0.00
Chavez, Juan	R-R	6-0	200	12-25-89	4	2	3.86	19	0	0	0	30	38	16	13	1	11	29	.314	.353	.299	8.60	3.26
De La Cruz, Luis	R-R	6-6	195	6-15-89	3	0	4.71	19	0	0	0	29	24	17	15	1	15	20	.231	.231	.231	6.28	4.71
DeHoyos, Gabe	R-R	5-11	260	4-14-80	0	0	3.12	7	1	0	0	9	11	7	3	0	3	10	.297	.231	.333	10.38	3.12
Garrison, Steve	B-L	6-1	185	9-12-86	0	0	6.20	9	0	0	0	22	14	14	1	5	22		.262	.077	.296	9.74	2.21

Name	B-T	HT	WT	DOB	W	L	ERA	G	GS	CG	SV	IP	H	R	ER	HR	BB	SO	AVG	vLH	vRH	K/9	BB/9
Hernandez, Pedro	L-L	5-10	200	4-12-89	4	0	3.78	7	5	0	0	33	33	15	14	2	4	31	.260	.091	.295	8.37	1.08
Holland, Brett	R-R	6-2	185	6-30-87	1	0	1.64	8	0	0	0	11	7	3	2	1	4	9	.179	.333	.133	7.36	3.27
Hussey, John	R-R	6-3	170	11-22-86	2	2	10.20	12	5	0	0	30	44	37	34	5	28	24	.355	.316	.372	7.20	8.40
Lollis, Matt	R-R	6-7	230	9-11-90	0	0	5.19	6	0	0	0	9	11	8	5	1	2	7	.297	.417	.240	7.27	2.08
Morton, Andrew	L-L	6-1	215	4-16-86	1	0	2.55	16	0	0	0	25	32	9	7	0	3	19	.311	.438	.287	6.93	1.09
Needy, James	R-R	6-6	205	3-30-91	1	1	2.65	5	3	0	0	17	14	6	5	1	5	13	.226	.250	.211	6.88	2.65
Orosco Jr., Jesse	R-R	6-2	200	7-3-87	0	0	2.79	8	0	0	0	10	7	4	3	0	4	8	.206	.214	.200	7.45	3.72
Porter, Tom	R-R	6-1	185	11-11-86	1	1	6.00	9	2	0	0	21	26	16	14	0	9	21	.295	.333	.265	9.00	3.86
Portillo, Adys	R-R	6-2	185	12-21-91	1	9	5.13	13	12	0	0	53	67	41	30	2	28	44	.321	.338	.312	7.52	4.78
Poutier, Robert	R-R	6-4	190	10-21-85	0	0	4.70	5	0	0	0	8	6	5	4	0	3	8	.214	.077	.333	9.39	3.52
Poynter, Gary	R-R	6-2	190	6-12-87	0	0	6.75	4	0	0	0	4	4	3	3	1	3	1	.333	.400	.308	2.25	6.75
Ramos, Cesar	L-L	6-2	205	6-22-84	0	1	2.25	4	2	0	0	8	8	3	2	0	0	8	.250	.143	.280	9.00	0.00
Sampson, Keyvius	R-R	6-0	185	1-6-91	0	0	3.00	2	1	0	0	3	1	1	1	0	0	3	.111	.333	.000	9.00	0.00
Sanchez, Deiber	R-R	5-10	170	3-29-89	4	2	3.00	14	5	0	0	51	43	26	17	5	15	45	.226	.203	.240	7.94	2.65
Startup, Will	L-L	6-0	195	8-4-84	0	0	5.87	8	0	0	0	8	13	6	5	1	0	7	.371	.286	.393	8.22	0.00
Valdez, Stalyn	R-R	6-3	185	11-14-89	0	3	5.02	17	0	0	0	29	37	20	16	2	7	17	.314	.375	.282	5.34	2.20

Fielding

Catcher	PCT	G	PO	A	E	DP	PB
Basham	1.000	3	17	3	0	1	0
Pozo	.961	26	178	19	8	0	8
Tonneson	.951	19	114	22	7	3	3
Wideman	.986	20	121	17	2	1	2

First Base	PCT	G	PO	A	E	DP
Alia	1.000	1	102	9	0	6
Decker	.995	44	374	28	2	39
Pozo	.923	5	21	3	2	2

Second Base	PCT	G	PO	A	E	DP
Galvez	.964	20	30	50	3	11
Garce	1.000	3	5	0	0	0
Minyeti	.982	12	18	37	1	10

	PCT	G	PO	A	E	DP
Pozo	—	1	0	0	0	0
Skube	.930	24	39	41	6	11
Valdez	.931	9	12	15	2	2

Third Base	PCT	G	PO	A	E	DP
Ahearn	.500	1	1	0	1	0
Alia	.938	35	31	75	7	7
Alvarez	—	1	0	0	0	0
Decker	.857	1	3	1	0	0
Garce	.690	12	6	14	9	1
Minyeti	.938	13	5	25	2	4

Shortstop	PCT	G	PO	A	E	DP
Ahearn	.940	16	19	28	3	3
Galvez	.870	29	45	69	17	19

	PCT	G	PO	A	E	DP
Garce	1.000	1	0	2	0	0
Minyeti	.895	22	22	55	9	11

Outfield	PCT	G	PO	A	E	DP
Adamson	.909	11	10	0	1	0
Alvarez	1.000	23	38	3	0	1
Liriano	.924	47	89	8	8	0
Monger	.957	49	87	1	4	1
Olabisi	.962	36	51	0	2	0
Skube	1.000	2	2	0	0	0
Williams	1.000	4	7	0	0	0
Wright	1.000	6	12	0	0	0

DSL PADRES   ROOKIE
DOMINICAN SUMMER LEAGUE

Batting	B-T	HT	WT	DOB	AVG	vLH	vRH	G	AB	R	H	2B	3B	HR	RBI	BB	HBP	SH	SF	SO	SB	CS	SLG	OBP
Aristy, Alvaro	R-R	6-1	170	12-9-91	.183	.136	.195	30	104	12	19	2	1	2	18	22	1	1	2	35	1	3	.279	.326
Cabrera, Felix	R-R	6-0	170	7-14-89	.184	.143	.200	57	179	37	33	6	1	0	18	44	12	0	3	53	10	4	.229	.374
Carrillo, Rosario	R-R	6-4	183	9-8-88	.163	.125	.179	47	135	18	22	2	1	0	16	13	3	2	1	43	6	2	.193	.250
Contreras, Rayner	R-R	6-0	150	9-21-86	.077	.000	.091	8	26	8	2	0	0	1	2	7	2	0	0	23	0		.192	.314
Del Castillo, Miguel	R-R	5-10	170	10-14-91	.198	.184	.205	41	126	21	25	2	0	0	10	22	3	0	0	28	2	3	.214	.331
Domoromo, Luis	L-L	6-1	185	2-4-92	.239	.123	.277	68	230	46	55	2	7	1	26	45	7	2	2	49	8	3	.322	.377
Escarra, Fernando	R-R	6-2	195	1-7-92	.212	.364	.171	22	52	3	11	2	0	0	7	5	2	0	0	15	0	0	.250	.305
Familia, Ariel	R-R	6-3	185	9-29-92	.258	.286	.250	33	89	20	23	7	1	1	15	14	3	2	1	22	2	5	.393	.374
Garcia, Carlos	R-R	6-3	165	3-29-89	.241	.164	.266	62	224	33	54	8	0	6	43	25	6	0	0	57	17	5	.357	.333
Gomez, Jairo	R-R	6-0	170	1-16-92	.200	.205	.199	55	195	17	39	10	1	1	19	19	7	1	1	41	5	3	.277	.293
Lopez, Yair	R-R	6-3	150	9-9-91	.293	.256	.303	49	181	41	53	10	2	3	18	38	2	0	1	46	14	7	.420	.419
Nuno, Manuel	R-R	6-0	264	1-11-89	.195	.167	.202	63	205	39	40	6	0	6	43	48	10	0	5	78	4	1	.351	.366
Sillis, Aaron	R-R	5-10	180	6-3-91	.221	.267	.205	41	113	23	25	5	1	0	7	20	6	0	0	19	0	1	.283	.367
Tiburcio, Miguel	R-R	6-3	200	1-29-91	.170	.121	.186	44	135	10	23	4	1	0	12	12	1	2	1	54	1	1	.215	.242
Velazquez, Adan	R-R	5-10	180	9-29-91	.289	.214	.309	57	204	36	59	12	6	5	45	22	8	2	3	40	12	3	.480	.376
Wilson, Hans	B-R	5-11	185	9-8-90	.221	.333	.189	32	95	20	21	5	0	0	8	15	4	1	1	15	1	0	.274	.348

Pitching	B-T	HT	WT	DOB	W	L	ERA	G	GS	CG	SV	IP	H	R	ER	HR	BB	SO	AVG	vLH	vRH	K/9	BB/9
Andujar, Rudi	R-R	6-2	190	5-14-91	0	0	13.17	13	0	0	0	14	20	21	20	1	22	9	.333	.200	.400	5.93	14.49
Castillo, Jeury	R-R	6-5	210	1-20-89	2	1	3.15	14	6	0	0	46	39	20	16	1	21	30	.234	.268	.216	5.91	4.14
Ceren, Amaury	R-R	6-6	165	1-10-89	2	3	2.92	13	2	0	1	25	29	17	8	0	10	22	.287	.194	.329	8.03	3.65
Claveria, Marlon	R-R	6-3	210	8-30-90	1	2	6.86	12	5	0	0	39	51	36	30	3	25	21	.325	.319	.327	4.81	5.72
Corpas, Jean	R-R	6-2	170	3-9-91	4	2	4.25	12	6	0	0	42	48	25	20	4	11	40	.271	.241	.285	8.50	2.34
Flores, Francisco	R-R	6-0	165	9-23-91	1	4	6.00	14	2	0	2	21	22	20	14	0	7	13	.256	.214	.276	5.57	3.00
Gutierrez, Ulises	L-L	6-3	190	5-3-91	3	0	1.15	13	0	0	0	16	10	5	2	0	6	9	.189	.333	.170	5.17	3.45
Henrique, Freddys	R-R	6-3	218	5-28-90	1	4	4.61	14	8	0	0	57	64	39	29	4	13	42	.282	.306	.268	6.67	2.06
Herrera, Juan	R-R	6-0	179	8-21-91	0	3	4.78	11	6	0	0	38	37	28	20	1	27	27	.261	.270	.253	6.45	6.45
Javier, Esteban	R-R	6-1	155	4-23-91	1	2	3.25	19	2	0	1	36	26	17	13	2	13	36	.200	.200	.200	9.00	3.25
Martinez, Pedro	L-L	6-3	251	9-6-90	2	3	4.95	15	5	0	1	40	33	31	22	2	20	47	.216	.278	.207	10.58	4.50
Mejia, Ruben	R-R	6-1	175	2-23-92	0	1	3.62	10	4	0	1	32	30	18	13	1	12	27	.244	.227	.248	7.52	3.34
Mozo, Harlen	R-R	6-2	210	8-12-89	1	0	6.59	17	0	0	0	14	20	13	10	1	8	9	.328	.421	.286	5.93	5.27
Ojeda, Erick	R-R	6-5	260	9-18-89	3	3	4.62	13	5	0	0	39	49	29	20	2	17	24	.320	.325	.319	5.54	3.92
Paz, Uber	R-R	6-4	194	5-4-91	1	5	5.06	14	6	0	0	37	30	25	21	2	21	30	.214	.153	.259	7.23	5.06
Perez, Severino	R-R	6-0	185	11-8-89	0	1	4.26	5	2	0	0	13	10	7	6	0	7	15	.217	.222	.214	10.66	4.97
Pimentel, Carlos	B-R	6-2	175	10-8-89	1	5	7.92	14	5	0	0	31	31	34	27	2	29	11	.261	.318	.227	3.23	8.51
Reyes, Eugenio	R-R	6-3	215	7-13-90	1	3	6.47	10	7	0	0	32	38	24	23	1	22	24	.299	.362	.263	6.75	6.19
Tavarez, Elvin	R-R	6-1	170	9-7-91	0	1	6.60	10	0	0	0	15	7	13	11	1	19	14	.137	.188	.114	8.40	11.40

Fielding

Catcher	PCT	G	PO	A	E	DP	PB
Del Castillo	.977	39	210	47	6	4	8
Escarra	.991	22	95	12	1	0	10
Wilson	.983	27	145	25	3	0	11

First Base	PCT	G	PO	A	E	DP
Carrillo	.958	12	87	5	4	7
Nuno	.976	62	548	27	14	43

Second Base	PCT	G	PO	A	E	DP
Cabrera	.915	9	16	27	4	4
Contreras	1.000	2	4	7	0	0
Del Castillo	1.000	1	3	2	0	1
Garcia	1.000	1	1	0	0	0

Gomez	.917	23	48	52	9	10
Sillis	1.000	1	4	1	0	0
Velazquez	.968	40	87	92	6	25

Third Base	PCT	G	PO	A	E	DP
Cabrera	.813	27	28	46	17	3
Contreras	.909	4	5	5	1	0
Gomez	.750	2	1	5	2	0
Sillis	.915	29	27	48	7	5
Velazquez	.926	15	17	33	4	4
Wilson	.800	1	1	3	1	0

Shortstop	PCT	G	PO	A	E	DP
Aristy	.912	30	52	82	13	13

Cabrera	.928	17	25	39	5	2
Gomez	.894	28	39	62	12	13
Velazquez	1.000	1	1	5	0	0

Outfield	PCT	G	PO	A	E	DP
Carrillo	1.000	27	28	0	0	0
Domoromo	.981	66	96	6	2	3
Familia	.941	26	30	2	2	0
Garcia	.983	42	53	5	1	2
Lopez	1.000	44	66	3	0	2
Tiburcio	.980	31	46	3	1	2
Wilson	1.000	1	1	0	0	0

San Francisco Giants

SEASON IN A SENTENCE: The Giants pitched their way back into contention and found a new offensive leader for the post-Barry Bonds era in Pablo Sandoval (also known as Kung Fu Panda), but he didn't have enough help as the Giants finished 88-74, seven games back of the Dodgers and four games out of the National League wild card.

HIGH POINT: Lefthander Jonathan Sanchez lacks consistency, but at his best he's a terrific complement to staff aces Tim Lincecum and Matt Cain. He proved it with a no-hitter against the Padres on July 10, striking out 11 in the process. Only a throwing error by Juan Uribe prevented it from being a perfect game.

LOW POINT: A 9-1 blowout loss to the Dodgers on Sept. 12 was the Giants' fourth straight and dropped San Francisco 8½ back in the West and 5½ back in the wild card. Veteran shortstop Edgar Renteria missed all but one game the rest of the way, closing a subpar season with bone chips and spurs in his elbow that required surgery.

NOTABLE ROOKIES: Righthander Joe Martinez made the Opening Day roster but was knocked out in his second start by a comebacker to the mound off the bat of Milwaukee's Mike Cameron. Martinez sustained a concussion and had three small skull fractures but returned to the rotation in August. Lefthanders Madison Bumgarner, a 2007 first-round pick, and Dan Runzler started the year at high Class A San Jose and finished in San Francisco.

KEY TRANSACTIONS: General manager Brian Sabean tried hard to improve his team's poor offense, but trades for Ryan Garko (.235, two home runs) and Freddy Sanchez (.284/.295/.324) didn't work out and cost pitching prospects Tim Alderson (Pirates) and Scott Barnes (Indians). Sabean and manager Bruce Bochy won contract extensions, though, for turning the team around.

DOWN ON THE FARM: Bumgarner helped Double-A Connecticut reach the Eastern League playoffs by going 12-2, 1.85 overall in 131 innings. San Jose won the Cal League title despite most of its top players—including catcher Buster Posey, the club's 2008 first-round pick—moving on as the season progressed. In October, first-base prospect Angel Villalona was charged with murder in his native Dominican Republic, and while he was released in November and the charges could be dropped, the status of his U.S. visa and his future were very much in doubt.

OPENING DAY PAYROLL: $82,616,450

PLAYERS OF THE YEAR

MAJOR LEAGUE	MINOR LEAGUE
Tim Lincecum rhp	**Madison Bumgarner** lhp
15-7, 2.48	(High A/Double-A)
Led NL in CG (4), SHO (2) and SO (261)	12-2, 1.85 92 SO in 131 IP

ORGANIZATION LEADERS

BATTING		*Minimum 250 at-bats
MAJORS		
*AVG	Pablo Sandoval	.330
*OPS	Pablo Sandoval	.943
HR	Pablo Sandoval	25
RBI	Pablo Sandoval	90
MINORS		
*AVG	Bowker, John, Fresno	.342
R	Neal, Thomas, San Jose	102
H	Neal, Thomas, San Jose	160
TB	Kieschnick, Roger, San Jose	275
	Neal, Thomas, San Jose	275
2B	Neal, Thomas, San Jose	41
3B	Boyer, Brad, Connecticut	10
HR	Kieschnick, Roger, San Jose	23
RBI	Kieschnick, Roger, San Jose	110
BB	Bowker, John, Fresno	74
SO	Crawford, Brandon, San Jose/Connecticut	132
SB	Ford, Darren, San Jose	35
	Graham, Tyler, Conn./Fresno/San Jose	35
*OBP	Bowker, John, Fresno	.451
*SLG	Bowker, John, Fresno	.596

PITCHING		†Minimum 75 innings
MAJORS		
W	Tim Lincecum	15
†ERA	Tim Lincecum	2.48
SO	Tim Lincecum	261
MINORS		
W	Clark, Craig, San Jose	16
L	Kinney, Matt, Fresno	14
†ERA	Bumgarner, Madison, San Jose/Connecticut	1.85
G	Paterson, Joe, Connecticut	55
GS	Kinney, Matt, Fresno	29
SV	Espineli, Geno, Fresno	19
	Otero, Dan, Connecticut	19
IP	Nicholson, Kyle, Augusta/San Jose	162
BB	Hammond, Steve, Fresno	71
SO	Surkamp, Eric, Augusta	169
†AVG	Bumgarner, Madison, San Jose/Connecticut	.211

2009 PERFORMANCE

General Manager: Brian Sabean. **Farm Director:** Fred Stanley. **Scouting Director:** John Barr.

Class	Team	League	W	L	PCT	Finish*	Manager(s)
Majors	San Francisco Giants	National	88	74	.543	5th (16)	Bruce Bochy
Triple-A	Fresno Grizzlies	Pacific Coast	71	73	.493	t-10th (16)	Dan Rohn
Double-A	Connecticut Defenders	Eastern	83	59	.585	2nd (12)	Steve Decker
High A	San Jose Giants	California	93	47	.664	†1st (10)	Andy Skeels
Low A	Augusta GreenJackets	South Atlantic	76	63	.547	3rd (16)	Dave Machemer
Short-season	Salem-Keizer Volcanoes	Northwest	49	27	.645	†1st (8)	Tom Trebelhorn
Rookie	AZL Giants	Arizona	39	17	.696	1st (11)	Mike Goff
Overall 2009 Minor League Record			411	286	.590	1st (30)	

*Finish in overall standings (No. of teams in league). †League champion.

ORGANIZATION STATISTICS

SAN FRANCISCO GIANTS
NATIONAL LEAGUE

Batting	B-T	HT	WT	DOB	AVG	vLH	vRH	G	AB	R	H	2B	3B	HR	RBI	BB	HBP	SH	SF	SO	SB	CS	SLG	OBP
Aurilia, Rich	R-R	6-1	200	9-2-71	.213	.250	.186	60	122	10	26	2	0	2	16	8	0	0	3	24	0	0	.279	.256
Bowker, John	L-L	6-2	200	7-8-83	.194	.000	.210	31	67	7	13	2	2	2	7	4	1	0	1	18	1	0	.373	.247
Burriss, Emmanuel	B-R	6-0	190	1-17-85	.238	.333	.208	61	202	18	48	6	0	0	13	14	2	1	1	34	11	4	.267	.292
Downs, Matt	R-R	6-0	190	3-19-84	.170	.100	.186	17	53	6	9	2	0	1	2	6	0	0	1	13	1	0	.264	.250
Frandsen, Kevin	R-R	6-0	185	5-24-82	.140	.154	.135	23	50	3	7	2	0	0	1	3	1	0	0	4	0	0	.180	.204
Garko, Ryan	R-R	6-2	225	1-2-81	.235	.271	.209	40	115	10	27	3	1	2	12	9	3	0	0	10	0	0	.330	.307
Guzman, Jesus	R-R	6-1	215	6-14-84	.250	.231	.286	12	20	0	5	0	0	0	0	0	0	0	0	3	0	0	.250	.250
Holm, Steve	R-R	6-0	210	10-21-79	.286	—	.286	4	7	1	2	0	0	0	2	0	0	0	0	0	0	0	.286	.444
Ishikawa, Travis	L-L	6-3	225	9-24-83	.261	.278	.259	120	326	49	85	10	2	9	39	30	4	1	2	89	2	2	.387	.329
Lewis, Fred	L-R	6-2	200	12-9-80	.258	.164	.279	122	295	49	76	21	3	4	20	36	5	0	0	84	8	4	.390	.348
Molina, Bengie	R-R	5-11	225	7-20-74	.265	.277	.261	132	491	52	130	25	1	20	80	13	5	0	11	66	4	1	.442	.285
Posey, Buster	R-R	6-1	205	3-27-87	.118	.000	.167	7	17	1	2	0	0	0	0	0	0	0	0	4	0	0	.118	.118
Renteria, Edgar	R-R	6-1	200	8-7-75	.250	.231	.257	124	460	50	115	19	1	5	48	39	1	5	5	69	7	2	.328	.307
Rohlinger, Ryan	R-R	6-1	195	10-7-83	.158	.000	.273	12	19	0	3	1	0	0	4	1	0	0	0	6	0	0	.211	.200
Rowand, Aaron	R-R	6-0	220	8-29-77	.261	.213	.276	144	499	61	130	30	2	15	64	30	14	0	3	125	4	1	.419	.319
Sanchez, Freddy	R-R	5-10	190	12-21-77	.284	.321	.270	25	102	11	29	1	0	1	7	2	0	2	1	16	0	0	.324	.295
2-team total (86 Pittsburgh)					.293	—	—	111	457	56	134	29	3	7	41	22	2	4	4	76	5	1	.416	.326
Sandoval, Pablo	B-R	5-11	245	8-11-86	.330	.379	.314	153	572	79	189	44	5	25	90	52	4	0	5	83	5	5	.556	.387
Schierholtz, Nate	L-R	6-2	215	2-15-84	.267	.370	.242	116	285	33	76	19	2	5	29	16	1	0	6	58	3	1	.400	.302
Torres, Andres	B-R	5-10	190	1-26-78	.270	.338	.210	75	152	30	41	6	8	6	23	16	1	1	0	45	6	1	.533	.343
Uribe, Juan	R-R	6-0	230	3-22-79	.289	.255	.299	122	398	50	115	26	4	16	55	25	1	3	5	82	3	1	.495	.329
Velez, Eugenio	B-R	6-1	160	5-16-82	.267	.200	.286	84	285	40	76	13	5	5	31	16	2	2	2	55	11	5	.400	.308
Whiteside, Eli	R-R	6-2	215	10-22-79	.228	.083	.262	49	127	15	29	6	1	2	13	4	3	0	0	30	0	0	.339	.269
Winn, Randy	B-R	6-2	195	6-9-74	.262	.158	.292	149	538	65	141	33	5	2	51	47	1	3	8	93	16	2	.353	.318

Pitching	B-T	HT	WT	DOB	W	L	ERA	G	GS	CG	SV	IP	H	R	ER	HR	BB	SO	AVG	vLH	vRH	K/9	BB/9
Affeldt, Jeremy	L-L	6-5	225	6-6-79	2	2	1.73	74	0	0	0	62	42	14	12	3	31	55	.197	.211	.187	7.94	4.48
Bumgarner, Madison	R-L	6-4	215	8-1-89	0	0	1.80	4	1	0	0	10	8	2	2	2	3	10	.229	.083	.304	9.00	2.70
Cain, Matt	R-R	6-3	245	10-1-84	14	8	2.89	33	33	4	0	218	184	73	70	22	73	171	.232	.233	.231	7.07	3.02
Hinshaw, Alex	L-L	6-4	190	10-31-82	0	0	12.00	9	0	0	0	6	10	8	8	2	7	2	.385	.400	.364	3.00	10.50
Howry, Bob	L-R	6-5	220	8-4-73	2	6	3.39	63	0	0	0	64	50	26	24	5	23	46	.214	.225	.207	6.50	3.25
Joaquin, Waldis	R-R	6-2	235	12-25-86	0	0	4.22	10	0	0	0	11	10	5	5	1	7	12	.238	.188	.269	10.13	5.91
Johnson, Randy	R-L	6-10	225	9-10-63	8	6	4.88	22	17	0	0	96	97	55	52	19	31	86	.262	.268	.260	8.06	2.91
Lincecum, Tim	L-R	5-11	170	6-15-84	15	7	2.48	32	32	4	0	225	168	69	62	10	68	261	.206	.209	.203	10.42	2.72
Martinez, Joe	L-R	6-2	195	2-26-83	3	2	7.50	9	5	0	0	30	46	27	25	4	12	19	.351	.429	.279	5.70	3.60
Matos, Osiris	R-R	6-1	200	8-6-84	0	0	9.00	5	0	0	0	6	11	7	6	2	1	5	.367	.313	.429	7.50	1.50
Medders, Brandon	R-R	6-1	195	1-26-80	5	1	3.01	61	0	0	1	69	63	26	23	6	32	58	.248	.258	.242	7.60	4.19
Miller, Justin	R-R	6-2	200	8-27-77	3	3	3.18	44	0	0	0	57	47	20	20	7	27	36	.236	.241	.233	5.72	4.29
Misch, Pat	R-L	6-2	195	8-18-81	0	0	10.80	4	0	0	0	3	6	4	4	0	3	0	.375	.500	.333	0.00	8.10
2-team total (22 New York)					3	4	4.48	26	7	1	0	62	68	31	31	9	22	23	—	—	—	3.32	3.18
Penny, Brad	R-R	6-4	230	5-24-78	4	1	2.59	6	6	1	0	42	31	13	12	5	9	20	.205	.205	.206	4.32	1.94
Romo, Sergio	R-R	5-11	190	3-4-83	5	2	3.97	45	0	0	2	34	30	15	15	1	11	41	.233	.188	.259	10.85	2.91
Runzler, Dan	L-L	6-4	230	3-30-85	0	0	1.04	11	0	0	0	9	6	1	1	1	5	11	.188	.059	.333	11.42	5.19
Sadowski, Ryan	R-R	6-4	195	10-4-82	2	4	4.45	6	6	0	0	28	28	15	14	2	17	17	.264	.291	.235	5.40	5.40
Sanchez, Jonathan	L-L	6-2	190	11-19-82	8	12	4.24	32	29	1	0	163	135	82	77	19	88	177	.221	.223	.220	9.75	4.85
Valdez, Merkin	R-R	6-5	230	11-10-81	2	1	5.66	48	0	0	0	49	57	33	31	5	28	38	.292	.250	.324	6.93	5.11
Wilson, Brian	R-R	6-1	195	3-16-82	5	6	2.74	68	0	0	38	72	60	27	22	3	27	83	.223	.189	.255	10.33	3.36
Zito, Barry	L-L	6-4	215	5-13-78	10	13	4.03	33	33	1	0	192	179	89	86	21	81	154	.250	.230	.256	7.22	3.80

Fielding

Catcher	PCT	G	PO	A	E	DP	PB			PCT	G	PO	A	E	DP	PB		First Base	PCT	G	PO	A	E	DP
Holm	1.000	4	14	1	0	0	0		Posey	1.000	7	32	4	0	0	0		Aurilia	1.000	22	125	14	0	13
Molina	.995	123	942	77	5	8	4		Sandoval	1.000	3	21	2	0	0	0		Bowker	1.000	4	15	0	0	0
									Whiteside	.984	47	286	25	5	2	5								

	PCT	G	PO	A	E	DP
Garko	.996	33	219	14	1	17
Guzman	1.000	3	10	0	0	1
Ishikawa	.996	113	745	55	3	83
Sandoval	.985	26	181	10	3	10
Second Base	**PCT**	**G**	**PO**	**A**	**E**	**DP**
Burriss	.972	61	115	131	7	33
Downs	1.000	17	31	42	0	13
Frandsen	.977	14	21	22	1	9
Rohlinger	1.000	1	5	3	0	1
Sanchez	.973	25	44	65	3	12

	PCT	G	PO	A	E	DP
Uribe	.993	38	59	82	1	20
Velez	.953	31	55	68	6	8
Third Base	**PCT**	**G**	**PO**	**A**	**E**	**DP**
Aurilia	1.000	13	3	11	0	2
Rohlinger	1.000	8	2	7	0	0
Sandoval	.960	120	70	195	11	13
Uribe	.960	44	28	67	4	8
Shortstop	**PCT**	**G**	**PO**	**A**	**E**	**DP**
Frandsen	.941	7	4	12	1	2
Renteria	.970	123	161	299	14	63

	PCT	G	PO	A	E	DP
Rohlinger	1.000	3	4	5	0	2
Uribe	.975	41	61	94	4	20
Outfield	**PCT**	**G**	**PO**	**A**	**E**	**DP**
Bowker	1.000	17	26	1	0	0
Lewis	.977	83	127	3	3	1
Rowand	.990	137	299	5	3	2
Schierholtz	.986	86	135	10	2	2
Torres	1.000	69	93	2	0	2
Velez	.957	51	65	2	3	0
Winn	1.000	146	282	5	0	2

FRESNO GRIZZLIES

PACIFIC COAST LEAGUE

TRIPLE-A

Batting	B-T	HT	WT	DOB	AVG	vLH	vRH	G	AB	R	H	2B	3B	HR	RBI	BB	HBP	SH	SF	SO	SB	CS	SLG	OBP
Aurilia, Rich	R-R	6-1	200	9-2-71	.143	.000	.200	2	7	1	1	0	0	1	2	1	0	0	0	0	0	0	.571	.250
Borchard, Joe	B-R	6-4	230	11-25-78	.250	.231	.257	84	304	48	76	20	3	14	50	18	2	0	2	79	0	1	.474	.294
Bowker, John	L-L	6-2	200	7-8-83	.342	.314	.355	104	366	82	125	22	4	21	83	74	4	0	6	64	10	6	.596	.451
Burriss, Emmanuel	B-R	6-0	190	1-17-85	.268	.316	.250	17	71	9	19	2	1	1	7	3	2	0	1	4	6	2	.366	.312
Ciriaco, Juan	R-R	6-0	160	8-15-83	.274	.208	.300	34	84	14	23	6	1	0	12	6	0	0	3	8	2	2	.369	.312
Copeland, Ben	L-L	6-1	190	12-17-83	.278	.309	.270	97	338	46	94	18	3	8	34	24	3	1	3	60	15	5	.420	.329
2-team total (1 Sacramento)					.281	—	—	98	342	46	96	18	3	8	35	24	3	1	3	60	15	6	.421	.331
Downs, Matt	R-R	6-2	190	3-19-84	.300	.267	.313	109	424	68	127	33	3	14	74	25	7	4	7	58	8	2	.491	.343
Frandsen, Kevin	R-R	6-0	185	5-24-82	.295	.271	.304	110	427	67	126	18	2	13	55	23	16	5	3	34	3	4	.438	.352
Frias, Vladimir	B-R	6-2	170	9-6-86	—	—	—	1	0	1	0	0	0	0	0	0	0	0	0	0	0	0	—	—
Graham, Tyler	R-R	6-0	180	1-25-84	.204	.208	.200	17	54	9	11	1	0	1	4	2	1	1	0	12	4	0	.278	.246
Guzman, Jesus	R-R	6-1	215	6-14-84	.321	.318	.322	115	452	75	145	26	5	16	71	37	7	1	3	82	0	1	.507	.379
Holm, Steve	R-R	6-0	210	10-21-79	.242	.125	.272	63	198	23	48	12	0	6	16	15	2	3	4	40	0	0	.394	.297
Horwitz, Brian	R-R	6-1	185	11-7-82	.290	.321	.271	76	210	27	61	10	2	4	26	24	2	0	1	36	0	1	.414	.367
Lowenstein, Aaron	R-R	6-1	195	6-9-85	—	—	—	1	0	0	0	0	0	0	0	0	0	0	0	0	0	0	—	—
Mantle, Ryan	R-R	6-2	210	7-12-86	.250	.000	.333	2	4	0	1	0	0	0	0	0	0	1	0	0	1	0	0	.250	.400
Maroul, David	R-R	6-2	215	2-15-83	.130	.167	.118	7	23	2	3	1	0	1	4	1	0	0	0	8	0	0	.304	.167
McBryde, Mike	R-R	6-2	215	3-22-85	.224	.200	.242	15	58	7	13	1	0	1	1	1	1	1	0	10	6	2	.276	.250
McClain, Scott	R-R	6-4	230	5-19-72	.275	.385	.222	13	40	8	11	3	0	1	6	11	0	0	1	9	0	1	.425	.423
Posey, Buster	R-R	6-1	205	3-27-87	.321	.333	.317	35	131	21	42	8	1	5	22	17	0	0	3	23	0	1	.511	.391
Rohlinger, Ryan	R-R	6-1	195	10-7-83	.281	.328	.265	126	474	74	133	37	2	16	78	42	12	2	5	90	4	2	.468	.351
Rojas, Nestor	R-R	6-0	200	11-18-83	.188	.179	.192	24	80	9	15	2	0	0	5	4	0	1	0	26	0	0	.213	.226
Sanchez, Freddy	R-5-10	190	12-21-77		.333	.000	.375	3	9	1	3	1	0	0	0	0	0	0	0	1	0	0	.444	.400
Schierholtz, Nate	L-R	6-2	215	2-15-84	.222	.375	.100	5	18	2	4	1	0	0	1	1	0	0	0	1	1	0	.278	.263
Shriner, Jesse	R-R	6-1	195	2-24-85	.500	.000	1.000	2	2	0	1	0	0	0	0	0	0	0	0	0	0	0	.500	.500
Stromsmoe, Skyler	R-R	5-10	175	3-30-84	.000	—	.000	3	3	0	0	0	0	0	0	0	0	0	0	2	0	0	.000	.000
Timpner, Clay	L-L	6-2	195	5-13-83	.250	.239	.253	119	392	46	98	20	4	7	42	32	3	4	3	50	6	6	.355	.309
Torres, Andres	B-R	5-10	190	1-26-78	.302	.231	.333	11	43	7	13	1	1	1	2	1	0	1	0	18	1	0	.442	.318
Velez, Eugenio	B-R	6-1	160	5-16-82	.297	.340	.280	45	182	30	54	13	3	3	26	13	0	2	2	26	16	9	.451	.340
Wald, Jake	R-R	6-2	195	2-8-81	.234	.267	.224	83	252	36	59	8	3	5	37	30	3	7	1	70	4	2	.349	.322
Whiteside, Eli	R-R	6-2	215	10-22-79	.241	.257	.235	34	116	16	28	7	1	6	24	8	0	2	0	40	0	0	.474	.290
Witter, Adam	L-R	6-1	175	2-17-83	.224	.200	.232	44	107	14	24	2	0	6	21	11	1	0	1	27	0	0	.411	.300

Pitching	B-T	HT	WT	DOB	W	L	ERA	G	GS	CG	SV	IP	H	R	ER	HR	BB	SO	AVG	vLH	vRH	K/9	BB/9
Brewer, T.J.	R-R	6-2	200	8-30-84	0	1	45.00	1	1	0	0	1	4	5	5	0	3	0	.667	.333	1.000	0.00	27.00
Broshuis, Garrett	R-R	6-2	185	12-18-81	0	1	9.00	1	1	0	0	4	6	4	4	2	3	2	.333	.200	.500	4.50	6.75
Edlefsen, Steve	B-R	6-2	180	6-27-85	5	0	2.40	22	0	0	2	30	23	9	8	2	16	24	.200	.245	.180	7.20	4.80
Espineli, Geno	L-L	6-4	195	9-8-82	3	4	3.64	52	0	0	19	59	70	28	24	2	13	31	.288	.265	.297	4.70	1.97
Hammond, Steve	R-L	6-2	205	4-30-82	11	12	5.73	29	28	0	0	157	175	102	100	27	71	92	.281	.284	.280	5.27	4.07
Hinshaw, Alex	L-L	6-4	190	10-31-82	1	2	3.96	46	0	0	1	52	42	25	23	3	32	72	.212	.278	.188	12.38	5.50
Joaquin, Waldis	R-R	6-2	235	12-25-86	1	0	0.00	8	0	0	1	10	5	0	0	0	2	16	.143	.200	.100	14.40	1.80
Kinney, Matt	R-R	6-5	230	12-16-76	8	14	5.43	30	29	1	0	157	180	104	95	33	45	134	.283	.360	.219	7.67	2.57
Martinez, Joe	L-R	6-2	195	2-26-82	0	2	4.89	7	5	0	0	35	39	21	19	1	8	22	.281	.254	.303	5.66	2.06
Matos, Osiris	R-R	6-1	200	8-6-84	3	3	3.48	45	0	0	2	54	56	23	21	7	13	48	.269	.247	.285	7.95	2.15
Misch, Pat	R-L	6-2	195	8-18-81	3	0	2.00	12	0	0	1	27	24	7	6	1	4	12	.245	.190	.286	4.00	1.33
Mixon, David	R-R	6-3	190	9-10-84	0	1	10.13	1	1	0	0	3	4	3	3	0	2	2	.500	.250	.750	6.75	6.75
Musgrave, Mike	R-R	6-2	199	4-10-84	0	0	6.00	3	0	0	0	3	2	1	1	0	2	2	.182	.200	.167	6.00	6.00
Ortiz, Ramon	R-R	6-0	175	5-23-73	5	6	3.05	35	16	2	0	130	124	53	44	11	34	114	.248	.283	.219	7.91	2.36
Palazzolo, Steve	R-R	6-10	260	3-31-82	3	3	4.90	44	1	0	1	68	74	45	37	7	26	50	.278	.239	.307	6.62	3.44
Pucetas, Kevin	R-R	6-2	225	11-27-84	10	6	5.04	28	28	1	0	159	173	95	89	15	50	96	.282	.234	.321	5.43	2.83
Ray, Ronnie	R-R	6-3	215	5-11-84	1	5	5.79	43	3	0	0	65	88	48	42	8	20	46	.320	.291	.342	6.34	2.76
Romero, Felix	R-R	6-2	200	6-18-80	5	5	4.28	50	0	0	4	74	75	37	35	4	16	69	.267	.248	.282	8.43	1.95
Romo, Sergio	R-R	5-11	190	3-4-83	0	0	0.00	3	0	0	0	3	2	1	0	0	0	3	.167	.333	.000	9.00	0.00
Runzler, Dan	L-L	6-4	230	3-30-85	0	2	0.00	2	0	0	0	2	2	0	0	0	2	6	.286	.000	.333	4.50	0.00
Sadler, Billy	R-R	6-0	195	9-21-81	5	3	5.34	13	13	0	0	56	64	34	33	4	29	51	.294	.288	.300	8.25	4.69
2-team total (3 Round Rock)					5	3	5.12	16	16	0	0	63	73	38	36	4	31	57	—			8.10	4.41
Sadowski, Ryan	R-R	6-1	195	10-4-82	6	3	5.04	18	17	0	0	89	84	54	50	14	43	73	.250	.258	.243	7.35	4.33
Takatsu, Shingo	R-R	6-0	180	11-25-68	0	1	6.87	14	0	0	1	18	25	14	14	6	4	16	.325	.342	.308	7.85	1.96
Turpen, Daniel	R-R	6-4	215	8-17-86	0	0	0.00	1	0	0	0	2	1	0	0	0	2	1	.143	.000	.250	3.86	7.71
Yabu, Keiichi	R-R	6-1	220	9-28-68	1	1	6.55	18	0	0	1	22	26	20	16	4	15	17	.292	.316	.275	6.95	6.14

Fielding

Catcher	PCT	G	PO	A	E	DP	PB
Holm	.997	58	356	23	1	2	0
Lowenstein	—	1	0	0	0	0	0
Posey	.985	33	255	16	4	2	4
Rojas	.993	21	127	8	1	2	0
Shriner	1.000	1	2	0	0	0	0
Whiteside	.983	33	202	24	4	2	6
Witter	.952	9	55	4	3	0	3

First Base	PCT	G	PO	A	E	DP
Aurilia	1.000	1	7	1	0	1
Bowker	.986	16	129	15	2	9
Frandsen	.992	17	118	9	1	11
Guzman	.991	107	864	60	8	92
McClain	1.000	3	27	0	0	1
Witter	.930	7	37	3	3	6

Second Base	PCT	G	PO	A	E	DP
Burriss	.966	17	36	49	3	15
Ciriaco	.923	2	9	3	1	3

	PCT	G	PO	A	E	DP
Downs	.970	90	195	221	13	54
Frandsen	.986	30	54	82	2	16
Rohlinger	1.000	5	7	14	0	2
Sanchez	1.000	3	6	5	0	1
Velez	.962	8	9	16	1	4

Third Base	PCT	G	PO	A	E	DP
Aurilia	—	1	0	0	0	0
Ciriaco	.938	8	2	13	1	2
Downs	.783	11	5	13	5	0
Frandsen	.952	5	6	14	1	0
Guzman	.500	1	0	1	1	0
Maroul	.889	6	4	4	1	0
McClain	.857	2	1	5	1	1
Rohlinger	.961	109	62	208	11	27
Wald	.944	5	3	14	1	1

Shortstop	PCT	G	PO	A	E	DP
Ciriaco	.927	11	15	23	3	3
Downs	—	1	0	0	0	0

	PCT	G	PO	A	E	DP
Frandsen	.943	60	81	166	15	33
Rohlinger	.978	11	16	28	1	3
Velez	1.000	1	1	4	0	1
Wald	.969	73	96	182	9	36

Outfield	PCT	G	PO	A	E	DP
Borchard	.988	40	80	3	1	0
Bowker	.979	86	182	9	4	3
Copeland	.980	90	192	4	4	0
Downs	.941	9	14	2	1	1
Graham	1.000	15	31	0	0	0
Horwitz	.979	55	90	3	2	0
Mantle	1.000	2	3	0	0	0
McBryde	.944	14	34	0	2	0
McClain	1.000	3	2	0	0	0
Schierholtz	1.000	5	12	2	0	0
Timpner	.975	101	232	2	6	1
Torres	.968	11	30	0	1	0
Velez	.967	34	86	1	3	0

CONNECTICUT DEFENDERS · DOUBLE-A

EASTERN LEAGUE

Batting	B-T	HT	WT	DOB	AVG	vLH	vRH	G	AB	R	H	2B	3B	HR	RBI	BB	HBP	SH	SF	SO	SB	CS	SLG	OBP
Bocock, Brian	R-R	5-11	185	3-9-85	.171	.125	.185	25	70	9	12	1	0	0	3	12	1	4	1	20	2	3	.186	.298
Bond, Brock	B-R	5-10	195	9-11-85	.333	.302	.343	122	450	93	150	21	5	1	33	67	9	4	1	69	13	15	.409	.429
Boyer, Brad	L-R	6-0	185	10-4-83	.294	.260	.300	106	367	49	108	22	10	3	41	29	5	8	4	69	10	5	.433	.351
Castro, Ramon A.	R-R	6-0	195	10-23-79	.277	.339	.221	48	130	19	36	8	0	3	13	11	2	2	0	24	0	1	.408	.343
Crawford, Brandon	L-R	6-2	200	1-21-87	.258	.207	.273	108	392	38	101	26	2	4	31	20	1	8	2	100	11	7	.365	.294
D'Alessio, Andy	L-R	6-4	227	9-23-84	.194	.100	.211	22	67	3	13	2	0	1	6	7	0	0	1	13	0	0	.269	.267
Felmy, Bobby	L-L	5-10	194	4-29-84	.253	.211	.262	126	388	48	98	18	4	7	50	28	6	5	2	62	9	7	.374	.311
Graham, Tyler	R-R	6-0	180	1-25-84	.217	.200	.222	11	23	3	5	0	0	0	1	1	0	0	0	3	3	2	.217	.250
La Torre, Tyler	L-R	6-0	219	4-22-83	.265	.241	.270	69	181	27	48	10	1	1	24	29	1	1	1	35	1	2	.348	.368
Maroul, David	R-R	6-2	215	2-15-83	.218	.200	.229	21	55	4	12	0	1	1	6	3	1	0	0	18	0	2	.309	.271
Martinez-Esteve, Eddy	R-R	6-2	215	7-14-83	.291	.281	.295	127	436	58	127	31	3	8	65	47	3	1	4	62	2	3	.431	.361
McBryde, Mike	R-R	6-1	215	3-22-85	.308	.417	.269	90	318	62	98	21	2	5	41	17	4	12	4	53	16	10	.434	.347
Mooney, Mike	R-R	6-1	205	6-8-83	.253	.296	.233	117	340	41	86	16	6	6	47	21	4	3	3	77	11	6	.388	.302
Phelps, Josh	R-R	6-3	225	5-12-78	.188	.125	.208	11	32	2	6	0	0	2	4	2	0	0	0	8	0	0	.375	.235
Pill, Brett	R-R	6-4	211	9-9-84	.298	.303	.296	139	527	71	157	37	1	19	109	37	8	0	9	72	6	3	.480	.348
Richardson, Antoan	B-R	5-8	165	10-8-83	.207	.240	.194	50	87	13	18	3	0	0	6	11	4	3	1	31	6	5	.287	.320
Schoop, Sharlon	R-R	6-2	190	4-15-87	.241	.236	.243	105	320	36	77	15	0	3	36	20	5	5	2	63	6	5	.316	.294
Williams, Jackson	R-R	5-11	200	5-14-86	.223	.216	.226	105	300	33	67	20	0	2	24	35	6	6	1	60	1	5	.310	.316
Witter, Adam	L-R	6-2	175	2-17-83	.176	.214	.172	47	136	9	24	5	2	2	12	11	0	0	2	30	0	0	.279	.235

Pitching	B-T	HT	WT	DOB	W	L	ERA	G	GS	CG	SV	IP	H	R	ER	HR	BB	SO	AVG	vLH	vRH	K/9	BB/9
Alderson, Tim	R-R	6-6	217	11-3-88	4	3	3.47	13	13	0	0	73	76	31	28	5	14	46	.265	.265	.265	5.70	1.73
2-team total (7 Altoona)					9	2	3.88	20	20	0	0	111	115	54	48	9	27	64	—	—		5.17	2.18
Broshuis, Garrett	R-R	6-2	185	12-18-81	6	4	3.84	12	12	0	0	61	80	36	26	4	18	34	.319	.304	.336	5.02	2.66
Bumgarner, Madison	R-L	6-4	215	8-1-89	9	1	1.93	20	19	1	0	107	80	23	23	6	30	69	.209	.118	.254	5.80	2.52
Calicutt, Steven	L-L	6-2	190	2-7-84	0	1	11.12	4	1	0	0	6	6	7	7	0	5	3	.300	.000	.429	4.76	7.94
Edlefsen, Steve	B-R	6-2	180	6-27-85	2	0	3.18	6	0	0	0	11	10	4	4	1	8	8	.250	.286	.231	6.35	6.35
English, Jesse	L-L	6-2	220	9-13-84	7	7	4.20	26	19	1	0	101	98	54	47	9	57	71	.261	.151	.330	6.35	5.10
Foppert, Jesse	R-R	6-6	220	7-10-80	0	3	6.27	10	8	0	0	33	39	25	23	4	27	22	.295	.259	.353	6.00	7.36
Garcia, Geivy	R-R	6-2	175	7-8-82	2	3	4.73	34	7	0	1	70	60	41	37	4	48	58	.232	.246	.217	7.42	6.14
Griffin, Daniel	R-R	6-7	245	9-29-84	8	7	5.42	46	1	0	0	73	85	51	44	6	23	86	.287	.267	.304	10.60	2.84
Joaquin, Waldis	R-R	6-2	235	12-25-86	4	5	2.67	36	0	0	1	54	36	17	16	0	28	40	.190	.125	.239	6.67	4.67
Kaufman, Shane	R-R	6-0	182	12-11-85	2	1	5.91	18	0	0	2	21	27	14	14	1	6	20	.300	.429	.242	8.44	2.53
Lively, Mitch	R-R	6-5	230	9-7-85	3	0	0.70	14	0	0	1	26	17	3	2	0	9	18	.193	.333	.131	6.31	3.16
Maday, Daryl	R-R	6-2	225	8-14-85	6	6	4.25	25	25	1	0	136	149	67	64	10	44	67	.284	.293	.274	4.44	2.92
McNiven, Brooks	R-R	6-5	190	6-19-81	1	4	4.84	16	13	0	0	58	74	41	31	4	14	20	.329	.364	.290	3.12	2.18
Millikan, Bryan	R-R	6-5	202	8-13-83	0	0	7.71	1	0	0	0	2	1	2	2	1	3	0	.125	.000	.500	0.00	11.57
Musgrave, Mike	R-R	6-2	199	4-10-84	3	0	5.76	23	1	0	0	30	34	20	19	1	23	23	.298	.347	.262	6.98	6.98
Otero, Danny	R-R	6-3	205	2-19-85	0	3	1.15	39	0	0	19	39	40	6	5	0	10	31	.270	.342	.200	7.15	2.31
Paterson, Joe	R-L	6-1	210	5-19-86	5	6	1.96	55	0	0	10	69	47	18	15	3	24	69	.197	.112	.276	9.00	3.13
Pereira, Nick	R-R	6-0	190	9-22-82	0	1	4.91	3	3	0	0	11	10	6	6	2	10	7	.256	.238	.278	5.73	8.18
Runzler, Dan	L-L	6-4	230	3-30-85	3	0	0.96	7	0	0	1	9	5	1	1	1	7	11	.172	.133	.214	10.61	6.75
Snyder, Ben	L-L	6-2	224	7-20-85	4	4	2.88	34	5	1	1	97	82	35	31	4	38	86	.230	.146	.296	7.98	3.53
Sosa, Henry	R-R	6-2	195	7-28-85	6	0	2.36	14	14	0	0	72	61	22	19	4	25	44	.231	.234	.227	5.47	3.11
Whitaker, Craig	R-R	6-4	210	11-19-84	0	0	2.30	10	1	0	0	16	10	4	4	1	12	15	.185	.318	.094	8.62	6.89
Yourkin, Matt	R-L	6-3	225	7-4-81	6	2	2.42	50	0	0	8	63	52	19	17	5	26	72	.222	.203	.241	10.23	3.69

Fielding

Catcher	PCT	G	PO	A	E	DP	PB
La Torre	.990	44	271	25	3	4	4
Williams	.989	105	640	52	8	6	10
Witter	1.000	6	42	3	0	0	2

First Base	PCT	G	PO	A	E	DP
Castro	1.000	4	35	6	0	4

	PCT	G	PO	A	E	DP					
D'Alessio	.972	5	34	1	1	7					
La Torre	1.000	2	11	1	0	1					
Maroul	1.000	1	5	0	0	0					
Phelps	.750	1	6	0	2	1					
Pill	.997	133	1082	97	4	108					
Witter	1.000	5	20	2	0	1					

Second Base	PCT	G	PO	A	E	DP
Bond	.973	115	186	314	14	79
Boyer	.889	4	10	6	2	3
Schoop	.983	32	48	70	2	18

Third Base	PCT	G	PO	A	E	DP
Boyer	.965	69	39	98	5	11
Castro	.983	30	19	38	1	5
La Torre	—	1	0	0	0	0
Maroul	.972	18	13	22	1	0
Schoop	.967	53	34	85	4	7

Shortstop	PCT	G	PO	A	E	DP
Bocock	.964	25	37	70	4	17
Crawford	.972	106	178	300	14	67
Schoop	.987	20	42	33	1	9

Outfield	PCT	G	PO	A	E	DP
Boyer	1.000	24	43	1	0	0
Castro	1.000	4	3	1	0	1
Felmy	.985	119	181	10	3	3
Graham	1.000	9	8	1	0	0
Martinez-Esteve	.984	103	177	9	3	1
McBryde	.983	89	214	14	4	4
Mooney	.991	113	207	10	2	2
Phelps	1.000	6	12	0	0	0
Richardson	1.000	32	56	1	0	0

SAN JOSE GIANTS

HIGH CLASS A

CALIFORNIA LEAGUE

Batting	B-T	HT	WT	DOB	AVG	vLH	vRH	G	AB	R	H	2B	3B	HR	RBI	BB	HBP	SH	SF	SO	SB	CS	SLG	OBP
Ambort, Michael	B-R	6-1	215	4-23-85	.302	.233	.329	29	106	13	32	7	0	1	11	3	2	0	0	17	0	0	.396	.333
Aurilia, Rich	R-R	6-1	200	9-2-71	.100	.000	.143	3	10	1	1	0	0	0	2	1	0	0	1	0	0	.400	.308
Bocock, Brian	R-R	5-11	185	3-9-85	.241	.223	.249	97	386	56	93	25	2	3	48	36	1	1	6	96	6	7	.339	.303
Copeland, Ben	L-L	6-1	190	12-17-83	.240	.125	.294	6	25	1	6	3	0	0	1	2	0	0	0	3	0	0	.360	.296
2-team total (2 Stockton)					.294	—		8	34	2	10	4	0	0	1	2	0	0	0	5	0	0	.412	.333
Crawford, Brandon	L-R	6-2	200	1-21-87	.371	.387	.365	25	105	21	39	2	2	6	17	10	4	0	0	32	2	4	.600	.445
Ford, Darren	R-R	5-11	195	10-1-85	.300	.347	.278	101	380	81	114	17	9	9	50	49	6	3	3	97	35	12	.463	.386
Frias, Vladimir	B-R	6-2	170	9-6-86	.196	.105	.243	16	56	8	11	1	0	0	5	6	1	1	0	13	2	2	.214	.286
Gillaspie, Conor	L-R	6-1	200	7-18-87	.286	.283	.287	126	469	62	134	31	2	4	67	55	3	2	1	68	2	3	.386	.364
Graham, Tyler	R-R	6-0	180	1-25-84	.272	.358	.221	73	287	53	78	6	1	9	40	24	4	3	2	62	28	8	.394	.334
Jordan, Shane	L-L	5-7	170	11-26-84	.237	.222	.240	64	156	20	37	5	2	0	11	14	1	4	0	25	5	4	.295	.304
Kieschnick, Roger	L-R	6-3	200	1-21-87	.296	.320	.283	131	517	86	153	37	8	23	110	36	5	0	5	130	9	1	.532	.345
Kline, Trent	B-R	5-10	170	7-22-84	.200	.276	.173	38	110	4	22	5	0	0	10	11	2	1	2	21	0	1	.245	.280
Lormand, Ryan	R-R	6-0	165	10-30-85	.233	.230	.235	50	159	25	37	10	3	1	15	12	3	1	0	34	6	1	.352	.299
Lowenstein, Aaron	R-R	6-1	195	6-9-85	.243	.129	.326	26	74	14	18	1	1	0	8	7	0	4	0	16	0	0	.284	.309
Maroul, David	R-R	6-2	215	2-15-83	.241	.286	.203	35	108	15	26	8	0	5	19	9	1	2	0	42	1	1	.454	.305
Neal, Thomas	R-R	6-1	205	8-17-87	.337	.347	.332	129	475	102	160	41	4	22	90	65	16	0	3	98	3	0	.579	.431
Noonan, Nick	L-R	6-0	180	5-4-89	.259	.198	.282	124	459	82	119	26	8	7	64	48	5	9	9	97	9	5	.397	.330
Posey, Buster	R-R	6-1	205	3-27-87	.326	.440	.280	80	291	63	95	23	0	13	58	45	8	2	4	45	6	0	.540	.428
Rojas, Nestor	R-R	6-0	200	11-18-83	.293	.263	.315	27	92	11	27	8	0	3	11	1	1	0	0	22	0	0	.478	.375
Stromsmoe, Skyler	B-R	5-10	175	3-30-84	.267	.262	.271	44	101	17	27	7	1	2	15	10	3	3	2	19	1	0	.416	.345
Torres, Andres	B-R	5-10	190	1-26-78	.100	.167	.000	3	10	1	1	0	0	0	0	0	0	0	0	5	0	0	.200	.100
Villalona, Angel	R-R	6-3	200	8-13-90	.267	.224	.285	74	292	47	78	11	0	9	42	9	8	0	1	73	0	1	.397	.306
Zambrano, Eliezer	B-R	5-11	175	9-16-86	.000	.000	.000	2	2	0	0	0	0	0	0	0	0	0	0	0	0	0	.000	.000
Ziegler, C.J.	R-R	6-4	225	11-27-85	.263	.259	.264	45	160	21	42	9	0	5	28	16	0	0	3	35	0	0	.413	.324

Pitching	B-T	HT	WT	DOB	W	L	ERA	G	GS	CG	SV	IP	H	R	ER	HR	BB	SO	AVG	vLH	vRH	K/9	BB/9
Alderson, Tim	R-R	6-6	217	11-3-88	1	1	4.15	5	5	0	0	26	31	12	12	4	3	20	.292	.327	.255	6.92	1.04
Barnes, Scott	L-L	6-4	185	9-5-87	12	3	2.85	18	18	0	0	98	82	36	31	7	29	99	.227	.203	.240	9.09	2.66
Brewer, T.J.	R-R	6-2	200	8-30-84	4	2	4.02	32	6	0	1	72	85	35	32	7	24	82	.304	.304	.303	10.30	3.01
Broshuis, Garrett	R-R	6-2	185	12-18-81	6	1	2.15	13	7	0	0	59	45	15	14	2	8	33	.220	.209	.228	5.06	1.23
Bumgarner, Madison	R-L	6-4	215	8-1-89	3	1	1.48	5	5	0	0	24	20	10	4	0	4	23	.217	.235	.207	8.51	1.48
Clark, Craig	L-L	6-2	200	7-9-84	16	2	2.86	26	25	0	0	148	131	53	47	19	36	135	.237	.185	.261	8.23	2.19
Cova, Rafael	R-R	6-2	175	3-5-82	0	0	0.00	12	0	0	8	11	5	2	0	0	12	19	.128	.154	.115	15.55	9.82
Cowart, Adam	R-R	6-2	190	8-18-83	2	2	7.56	9	0	0	0	17	31	17	14	3	5	8	.397	.323	.447	4.32	2.70
Edlefsen, Steve	B-R	6-2	180	6-27-85	1	1	0.96	21	0	0	7	28	15	4	3	1	13	40	.140	.156	.143	12.86	4.18
Lively, Mitch	R-R	6-5	230	9-7-85	0	0	5.23	16	0	0	0	21	25	13	12	6	15	20	.305	.275	.333	8.71	6.53
Martinez, Joe	L-R	6-2	195	2-26-83	0	0	2.45	2	2	0	0	7	3	2	2	1	2	7	.125	.273	.000	8.59	2.45
Mixon, David	R-R	6-3	190	9-10-84	3	1	3.29	39	2	0	2	63	52	24	23	3	22	52	.237	.239	.217	7.57	3.14
Musgrave, Mike	R-R	6-2	199	4-10-84	0	0	15.68	13	0	0	0	10	20	18	18	0	13	13	.417	.333	.455	11.32	11.32
Nicholson, Kyle	R-R	6-0	205	7-31-85	4	0	2.93	7	7	0	0	40	46	17	13	3	11	30	.291	.333	.256	6.75	2.48
Odle, Oliver	R-R	6-0	229	7-11-85	8	12	5.37	23	21	0	0	117	159	82	70	19	24	79	.329	.317	.344	6.06	1.84
Oseguera, Paul	L-L	6-0	180	1-6-84	7	7	3.77	17	17	1	0	105	91	46	44	9	21	97	.234	.250	.227	8.31	1.80
Quirarte, Edwin	R-R	6-2	185	12-20-86	0	3	4.57	16	0	0	4	22	27	13	11	1	5	18	.310	.275	.340	7.48	2.08
Rodriguez, Wilmin	L-L	6-2	211	5-13-85	4	1	2.72	48	0	0	3	60	44	20	18	1	25	50	.209	.181	.223	7.54	3.77
Romo, Sergio	R-R	5-11	190	3-4-83	0	0	0.00	3	1	0	0	5	2	0	0	0	2	6	.133	.143	.125	11.57	3.86
Runzler, Dan	L-L	6-4	230	3-30-85	1	0	0.84	19	0	0	5	21	8	3	2	1	4	26	.104	.069	.125	10.97	1.69
Sadowski, Ryan	R-R	6-4	195	10-4-82	1	0	0.00	1	1	0	0	6	5	1	0	0	1	8	.217	.308	.100	12.00	1.50
Shaver, Ryan	R-R	6-5	197	12-17-84	2	0	0.00	11	0	0	0	17	9	0	0	0	9	16	.167	.231	.107	8.64	4.86
Tanner, Clayton	R-L	6-1	202	12-7-87	12	6	3.17	26	23	0	0	139	132	62	49	18	42	121	.254	.224	.265	7.82	2.71
Turpen, Daniel	R-R	6-4	215	8-17-86	4	2	1.24	46	0	0	7	65	56	15	9	1	22	55	.234	.235	.234	7.58	3.03
Webb, Trey	R-R	6-0	170	2-11-82	1	1	2.66	19	0	0	2	24	13	7	7	2	19	18	.171	.042	.231	6.85	7.23
Whitaker, Craig	R-R	6-4	210	11-19-84	1	1	3.89	26	0	0	0	42	25	19	18	0	30	33	.179	.262	.114	7.13	6.48

Fielding

Catcher	PCT	G	PO	A	E	DP	PB
Kline	.985	38	236	25	4	1	3
Lowenstein	.991	26	191	25	2	1	5
Posey	.996	64	501	55	2	4	10
Rojas	.989	26	171	17	2	2	5
Zambrano	1.000	2	3	2	0	0	0

First Base	PCT	G	PO	A	E	DP
Ambort	.983	5	52	5	1	2
Maroul	.987	28	221	11	3	25
Villalona	.987	72	618	44	9	60
Ziegler	.989	42	339	24	4	37

Second Base	PCT	G	PO	A	E	DP
Aurilia	.857	1	1	5	1	0
Frias	.800	2	2	2	1	0
Lormand	.943	9	24	26	3	6
Noonan	.972	120	236	325	16	95
Stromsmoe	.980	14	17	33	1	9

Third Base	PCT	G	PO	A	E	DP
Aurilia	1.000	1	1	3	0	0
Frias	1.000	7	3	13	0	1
Gillaspie	.908	116	65	201	27	23

	PCT	G	PO	A	E	DP
Lormand	.750	7	1	2	1	0
Maroul	1.000	3	2	6	0	0
Stromsmoe	.941	14	7	25	2	1

Shortstop	PCT	G	PO	A	E	DP
Bocock	.956	95	145	308	21	70
Crawford	.976	25	51	71	3	16
Frias	.917	3	5	6	1	2
Lormand	.954	17	18	44	3	9
Stromsmoe	.889	4	8	8	2	3

Outfield	PCT	G	PO	A	E	DP
Copeland	.833	5	5	0	1	0
Ford	.978	97	218	7	5	1
Graham	1.000	44	61	3	0	0
Jordan	.989	55	88	4	1	0
Kieschnick	.990	116	192	11	2	1
Neal	.990	116	174	15	2	1
Stromsmoe	1.000	4	2	1	0	0
Torres	1.000	3	8	0	0	0

AUGUSTA GREENJACKETS

LOW CLASS A

SOUTH ATLANTIC LEAGUE

Batting	B-T	HT	WT	DOB	AVG	vLH	vRH	G	AB	R	H	2B	3B	HR	RBI	BB	HBP	SH	SF	SO	SB	CS	SLG	OBP
Adrianza, Ehire	B-R	6-1	155	8-21-89	.258	.274	.253	117	388	54	100	15	3	2	46	42	5	6	7	66	7	1	.327	.333
Collins, Joel	R-R	6-1	200	4-24-86	.333	—	.333	1	3	0	1	0	0	0	0	0	0	0	0	0	0	0	.333	.333
Culberson, Charlie	R-R	6-1	185	4-10-89	.246	.220	.254	132	509	71	125	19	3	2	36	33	10	4	2	110	15	4	.306	.303
D'Alessio, Andy	L-R	6-4	227	9-23-84	.300	.284	.305	94	343	44	103	26	1	7	44	34	1	0	4	86	3	3	.443	.361
Duggan, Dom	R-R	5-9	185	2-8-85	.220	.171	.235	92	296	51	65	8	5	3	33	31	7	7	2	59	23	11	.311	.307
Fairley, Wendell	L-R	6-2	190	3-17-88	.243	.182	.252	106	345	47	84	20	1	3	42	36	5	3	1	103	2	4	.333	.323
Flores, Jose	B-R	5-11	175	8-17-87	.122	.000	.146	18	49	5	6	1	0	0	1	6	0	0	0	10	1	0	.143	.218
Frias, Vladimir	B-R	6-2	170	9-6-86	.246	.237	.249	72	252	36	62	6	6	0	20	15	7	3	1	39	15	3	.317	.305
Klimas, Matt	R-R	5-11	185	7-3-87	.284	.171	.325	53	155	20	44	5	1	0	15	14	9	2	2	32	6	3	.329	.372
Loberg, Mike	L-R	6-4	225	3-24-85	.222	.188	.225	70	194	33	43	7	1	4	35	24	2	3	2	50	3	1	.330	.311
Lormand, Ryan	R-R	6-0	165	10-30-85	.288	.167	.325	17	52	7	15	2	0	0	5	3	0	1	1	12	7	0	.327	.321
Mazzola, Josh	R-R	6-2	195	4-10-86	.284	.277	.286	130	490	72	139	30	3	16	96	37	14	0	7	124	5	1	.455	.347
Monell, Johnny	L-R	5-11	205	3-27-86	.273	.278	.272	91	293	46	80	21	0	8	44	33	5	1	1	45	4	1	.427	.355
Peguero, Francisco	R-R	6-0	175	6-1-88	.340	.404	.320	58	238	28	81	12	4	1	34	5	4	1	4	39	15	5	.437	.359
Perez, Juan Carlos	R-R	5-11	185	11-13-86	.244	.279	.232	123	447	56	109	29	3	9	54	23	4	3	7	101	18	4	.383	.283
Simmons, James	R-R	6-3	190	9-3-85	.252	.289	.236	99	286	44	72	17	2	4	35	31	8	4	2	85	15	1	.367	.339
Weeks, Joel	L-R	5-9	180	11-30-84	.040	.000	.042	14	25	1	1	0	0	0	3	4	0	0	0	8	0	0	.040	.172
Woodbury, Ben	R-R	5-10	175	2-21-86	.336	.333	.337	41	131	19	44	10	2	0	16	6	0	2	3	10	5	2	.443	.357
Zambrano, Eliezer	B-R	5-11	175	9-16-86	.227	.333	.188	9	22	3	5	0	0	2	3	1	5	0	4	0	0		.227	.346
Ziegler, C.J.	R-R	6-4	225	11-27-85	.231	.400	.185	31	117	11	27	8	0	0	10	8	0	0	2	23	0	1	.299	.276

Pitching	B-T	HT	WT	DOB	W	L	ERA	G	GS	CG	SV	IP	H	R	ER	HR	BB	SO	AVG	vLH	vRH	K/9	BB/9
Calicutt, Steven	L-L	6-2	190	2-7-84	0	0	5.40	6	0	0	0	7	8	5	4	1	6	7	.320	.500	.286	9.45	8.10
Corgan, Chance	R-R	6-2	175	4-25-86	3	3	4.19	11	4	0	0	34	36	17	16	4	8	26	.277	.208	.325	6.82	2.10
Fitzgerald, Justin	R-R	6-5	225	3-3-86	2	2	3.70	39	0	0	0	56	59	32	23	4	27	63	.262	.265		10.13	4.34
Kaufman, Shane	R-R	6-0	185	12-11-85	2	1	4.89	26	0	0	1	35	33	26	19	4	16	35	.243	.156	.286	9.00	4.11
King, Aaron	L-L	6-4	205	4-27-89	7	6	3.70	22	22	0	0	105	90	54	43	9	52	88	.234	.171	.249	7.57	4.47
Lively, Mitch	R-R	6-5	230	9-7-85	0	0	4.58	13	0	0	0	18	17	9	9	1	6	5	.258	.333	.229	2.55	3.06
Loree, Mike	R-R	6-6	226	9-14-86	8	9	4.67	22	21	0	0	123	139	72	64	9	26	70	.279	.254	.291	5.11	1.90
Marte, Kelvin	R-R	6-0	180	11-24-87	1	1	3.00	5	5	0	0	21	24	10	7	0	8	11	.279	.346	.250	4.71	3.43
Millikan, Bryan	R-R	6-5	202	8-13-83	0	1	8.00	8	0	0	0	9	14	8	8	0	4	7	.368	.412	.333	7.00	4.00
Nicholson, Kyle	R-R	6-0	205	7-31-85	7	8	2.80	18	18	4	0	122	110	49	38	7	22	83	.240	.245	.237	6.11	1.62
Oseguera, Paul	L-L	6-0	180	1-6-84	1	1	1.89	3	3	0	0	19	13	6	4	1	5	25	.194	.083	.218	11.84	2.37
Quirarte, Edwin	R-R	6-2	185	12-20-86	6	4	4.42	30	0	0	8	37	49	24	18	2	11	18	.316	.218	.370	4.42	2.70
Reichard, Andy	R-R	6-4	235	12-4-86	4	4	2.30	17	8	0	1	67	55	20	17	3	7	40	.229	.205	.240	5.40	0.95
Ronick, Ari	L-L	6-4	205	3-25-86	7	6	2.65	24	23	2	0	136	111	62	40	10	34	114	.215	.187	.222	7.54	2.25
Runzler, Dan	L-L	6-4	230	3-30-85	1	1	0.68	19	0	0	11	26	8	2	2	0	13	45	.093	.147	.058	15.38	4.44
Stolp, Eric	R-R	6-3	182	8-18-84	3	2	4.17	32	6	0	0	78	91	44	36	4	29	24	.300	.273	.316	2.78	3.36
Surkamp, Eric	L-L	6-4	190	7-16-87	11	5	3.30	23	23	2	0	131	129	57	48	6	39	169	.257	.333	.242	11.61	2.68
Verdugo, Ryan	L-L	6-0	195	4-10-87	4	0	1.39	21	0	0	0	32	19	6	5	0	19	45	.170	.176	.167	12.53	5.29
Webb, Trey	R-R	6-0	170	2-11-82	1	0	1.26	24	0	0	0	29	26	12	4	0	16	37	.241	.172	.266	11.62	5.02
Wilson, Chris	R-R	6-2	205	11-17-86	5	5	3.83	40	0	0	9	52	50	27	22	5	8	67	.249	.218	.260	11.67	1.39
Woodruff, Kyle	R-R	6-6	225	5-2-86	3	2	4.46	22	0	0	1	42	48	25	21	1	13	29	.287	.327	.268	6.17	2.76
Yntema, Orlando	R-R	6-3	180	2-21-86	0	2	6.41	6	6	0	0	27	39	23	19	1	9	17	.336	.462	.273	5.74	3.04

Fielding

Catcher	PCT	G	PO	A	E	DP	PB
Collins	1.000	1	10	1	0	0	0
Klimas	.983	53	325	16	6	2	9
Monell	.990	84	600	75	7	5	18
Weeks	.833	2	10	0	2	0	1
Zambrano	1.000	9	77	0	0	0	1

First Base	PCT	G	PO	A	E	DP
D'Alessio	1.000	10	93	6	0	5
Loberg	.978	41	295	16	7	26
Mazzola	.995	88	701	42	4	63
Ziegler	.991	13	103	10	1	8

Second Base	PCT	G	PO	A	E	DP
Flores	.980	10	25	25	1	12

	PCT	G	PO	A	E	DP
Frias	.976	55	122	123	6	32
Lormand	.970	8	14	18	1	6
Perez	.952	72	150	190	17	36

Third Base	PCT	G	PO	A	E	DP
Culberson	.900	132	82	279	40	21
Flores	1.000	4	1	6	0	0
Lormand	.833	2	2	3	1	1
Mazzola	1.000	3	0	5	0	0
Weeks	1.000	2	1	4	0	0

Shortstop	PCT	G	PO	A	E	DP
Adrianza	.942	117	150	333	30	60
Flores	1.000	1	1	1	0	0
Frias	.959	17	26	45	3	10

	PCT	G	PO	A	E	DP
Lormand	1.000	6	7	14	0	3
Weeks	1.000	7	6	9	0	1

Outfield	PCT	G	PO	A	E	DP
Duggan	.987	78	153	4	2	2
Fairley	.952	102	133	6	7	2
Frias	—	1	0	0	0	0
Loberg	1.000	4	6	0	0	0
Mazzola	.961	37	67	7	3	1
Peguero	.971	57	127	7	4	2
Perez	.970	40	60	4	2	0
Simmons	.983	95	163	7	3	5
Woodbury	.962	34	46	5	2	0

NORTHWEST LEAGUE

SAN FRANCISCO GIANTS

Batting	B-T	HT	WT	DOB	AVG	vLH	vRH	G	AB	R	H	2B	3B	HR	RBI	BB	HBP	SH	SF	SO	SB	CS	SLG	OBP
Anders, Luke	L-L	6-6	225	10-2-86	.284	.217	.302	58	208	35	59	10	1	5	41	30	1	0	4	48	2	2	.413	.370
Biery, Drew	R-R	6-2	215	5-14-86	.326	.289	.335	59	215	43	70	14	1	6	48	27	4	0	3	39	4	1	.484	.406
Cavan, Ryan	B-R	5-10	180	6-28-87	.277	.280	.277	58	191	42	53	9	5	9	33	35	5	0	2	34	3	2	.518	.399
Cook, Dan	B-R	6-3	185	6-15-86	.294	.281	.298	61	235	39	69	11	4	2	37	18	5	4	2	36	7	3	.400	.354
Crawford, Evan	R-R	6-2	167	8-5-88	.316	.318	.315	31	114	23	36	8	2	1	23	9	3	1	2	30	5	2	.447	.375
Curry, Caleb	R-R	6-0	175	4-23-86	.204	.261	.177	43	142	23	29	7	1	0	13	11	12	4	3	24	10	3	.268	.310
Dominguez, Chris	R-R	6-3	215	11-22-86	.254	.263	.252	47	181	31	46	5	1	9	32	9	4	0	4	57	11	2	.442	.298
Eshleman, John	R-R	6-1	185	4-8-89	.304	.333	.300	8	23	3	7	2	0	0	2	7	0	0	0	5	1	0	.391	.467
Henson, Kyle	R-R	5-11	185	12-7-86	.223	.208	.229	30	94	14	21	7	0	1	8	3	3	0	1	26	1	1	.330	.267
Lindsley, Brooks	R-R	6-0	185	10-25-86	.173	.158	.177	38	98	15	17	2	0	3	17	4	3	0	2	20	5	4	.286	.224
Lollis, Ryan	L-L	6-1	185	12-16-86	.312	.381	.303	52	199	31	62	9	3	2	25	20	0	0	1	24	1	5	.417	.373
Lowenstein, Aaron	R-R	6-1	195	6-9-85	.125	.000	.143	11	32	4	4	0	0	0	6	3	2	2	0	10	0	0	.125	.243
Mantle, Ryan	R-R	6-3	210	7-12-86	.218	.293	.167	33	101	18	22	3	1	2	9	13	2	1	0	39	3	1	.327	.319
Martinez, Juan	R-R	5-10	190	12-26-86	.285	.276	.288	67	249	44	71	9	9	4	37	12	3	2	1	43	4	3	.442	.325
McArthur, Evan	R-R	6-2	200	6-29-84	.147	.167	.143	10	34	5	5	1	0	0	6	2	0	0	2	12	0	0	.176	.310
Medina, Jose	R-R	6-0	180	11-29-86	.178	.125	.189	34	90	15	16	3	1	0	7	6	2	4	0	28	0	1	.233	.245
Peguero, Francisco	R-R	6-0	175	6-1-88	.394	.222	.453	17	71	14	28	3	1	0	12	3	1	0	1	9	7	0	.465	.421
Price, Ryne	L-R	5-11	190	5-27-86	.089	.000	.109	20	56	4	5	0	0	0	1	6	1	0	0	11	1	0	.089	.190
Stromsmoe, Skyler	B-R	5-10	175	3-30-84	.222	—	.222	2	9	2	2	0	0	0	1	0	0	0	0	0	0	0	.222	.222
Villegas, Ydwin	B-R	5-10	165	9-1-90	.375	.750	.000	3	8	1	3	0	0	0	2	1	0	0	0	2	0	0	.375	.444
Weeks, Joel	L-R	5-9	180	11-30-84	.294	.211	.313	31	102	16	30	4	0	4	15	11	1	3	1	13	1	2	.451	.365
Zambrano, Eliezer	B-R	5-11	190	9-16-86	.200	.120	.233	32	85	11	17	2	2	1	16	5	1	2	3	9	1	2	.306	.245
Ziegler, C.J.	R-R	6-4	225	11-27-85	.404	.643	.303	14	47	10	19	7	0	2	13	12	2	0	1	7	0	0	.681	.532

Pitching	B-T	HT	WT	DOB	W	L	ERA	G	GS	CG	SV	IP	H	R	ER	HR	BB	SO	AVG	vLH	vRH	K/9	BB/9
Bowlin, Drew	R-R	6-1	190	12-28-86	1	1	2.60	22	0	0	6	28	20	9	8	2	10	33	.194	.265	.159	10.73	3.25
Bucardo, Jorge	R-R	6-1	155	10-18-89	6	3	2.64	15	15	0	0	82	65	28	24	3	21	64	.229	.283	.193	7.05	2.31
Bucardo, Wilber	R-R	6-2	175	11-20-87	4	1	3.02	13	9	0	1	57	49	22	19	3	15	32	.231	.221	.239	5.08	2.38
Calicutt, Steven	L-L	6-2	190	2-7-84	0	0	0.00	2	0	0	0	2	2	1	0	0	2	0	.286	.000	.333	0.00	10.80
Casilla, Jose	R-R	6-1	190	5-21-89	1	1	1.67	25	0	0	12	27	22	8	5	0	9	31	.210	.200	.215	10.33	3.00
Gloor, Chris	L-L	6-6	255	3-21-86	7	1	2.61	17	7	0	0	48	38	14	14	2	19	48	.221	.216	.223	8.94	3.54
Grabham, Brandon	R-R	6-5	230	1-30-86	0	0	7.71	4	0	0	0	7	12	6	6	0	7	8	.387	.500	.316	10.29	9.00
Graves, Brandon	L-L	6-1	190	8-7-86	2	2	3.69	21	0	0	0	32	41	24	13	4	12	28	.301	.291	.309	7.96	3.41
Hernandez, Javier	R-R	6-4	180	9-27-87	4	4	5.43	15	10	0	0	58	71	42	35	7	26	33	.303	.296	.310	5.12	4.03
Irving, Brian	R-R	6-2	205	4-24-86	0	0	16.20	2	0	0	0	2	5	3	3	0	4	2	.556	.667	.500	10.80	0.00
Moran, Gary	R-R	6-8	265	5-21-85	4	0	3.04	23	0	0	0	24	28	9	8	2	5	16	.289	.294	.286	6.08	1.90
Quinowski, David	L-L	5-10	170	4-23-86	2	1	1.77	22	0	0	0	41	30	9	8	2	18	53	.208	.179	.227	11.73	3.98
Rodriguez, Mario	L-L	6-2	190	8-21-88	1	1	5.14	23	0	0	0	28	31	18	16	2	12	25	.292	.357	.250	8.04	3.86
Rogers, Taylor	R-R	6-4	200	6-5-87	2	4	7.54	21	2	0	0	37	47	39	31	10	21	34	.297	.339	.275	8.27	5.11
Romo, Andrew	R-R	6-1	230	6-20-87	0	0	0.00	1	0	0	0	1	0	0	0	0	0	0	.000	.000	.000	0.00	0.00
Stoffel, Jason	R-R	6-2	220	9-15-88	1	0	0.00	8	0	0	2	10	6	1	0	0	1	13	.158	.167	.150	11.32	0.87
Toole, Jeremy	R-R	6-4	185	6-17-88	1	4	2.74	13	10	0	0	46	42	17	14	1	20	41	.240	.203	.264	8.02	3.91
Valdez, Jose	R-R	6-7	250	8-1-88	3	3	4.33	16	5	0	0	35	24	20	17	2	18	36	.188	.218	.164	9.17	4.58
Vazquez, Kyle	R-R	6-3	175	6-29-88	3	1	3.66	17	3	0	0	39	26	19	16	4	15	38	.184	.214	.165	8.69	3.43
Westcott, Craig	L-R	6-4	225	3-1-86	3	0	3.26	7	7	0	0	30	28	11	11	1	9	42	.241	.289	.211	12.46	2.67
Yntema, Orlando	R-R	6-3	180	2-21-86	8	1	2.80	8	8	1	0	45	44	17	14	4	11	26	.254	.222	.277	5.20	2.20

Fielding

Catcher	PCT	G	PO	A	E	DP	PB
Henson	.984	30	219	24	4	2	4
Lowenstein	.989	11	83	6	1	0	2
Price	.963	18	99	6	4	0	0
Weeks	1.000	2	4	1	0	0	0
Zambrano	.969	32	207	14	7	0	4

First Base	PCT	G	PO	A	E	DP
Anders	.996	50	431	35	2	47
Biery	1.000	5	43	2	0	3
Dominguez	.979	11	90	5	2	5
Lindsley	—	1	0	0	0	0
McArthur	1.000	1	9	1	0	0
Weeks	—	1	0	0	0	0
Ziegler	.971	11	94	6	3	11

Second Base	PCT	G	PO	A	E	DP
Martinez	.962	67	125	180	12	43
Stromsmoe	1.000	2	3	7	0	2
Weeks	.938	9	14	31	3	6

Third Base	PCT	G	PO	A	E	DP
Biery	.933	44	34	64	7	3
Cavan	.833	2	2	3	1	0
Cook	—	1	0	0	0	0
Dominguez	.898	27	13	40	6	9
Martinez	1.000	1	2	0	0	0
McArthur	.750	1	0	3	1	0
Villegas	1.000	1	0	1	0	0
Weeks	1.000	8	3	10	0	1

Shortstop	PCT	G	PO	A	E	DP
Cavan	.936	57	79	168	17	38

	PCT	G	PO	A	E	DP
Eshleman	1.000	8	8	28	0	4
Lindsley	.917	4	3	19	2	2
Villegas	.875	3	5	2	1	1
Weeks	.968	13	18	43	2	6

Outfield	PCT	G	PO	A	E	DP
Cook	.957	53	84	6	4	1
Crawford	.957	30	43	1	2	0
Curry	.988	40	75	5	1	1
Lindsley	1.000	16	10	3	0	0
Lollis	.986	49	68	2	1	0
Mantle	.976	27	38	2	1	0
Medina	.900	27	36	0	4	0
Peguero	1.000	14	37	0	0	0
Weeks	—	1	0	0	0	0

ARIZONA LEAGUE

Batting	B-T	HT	WT	DOB	AVG	vLH	vRH	G	AB	R	H	2B	3B	HR	RBI	BB	HBP	SH	SF	SO	SB	CS	SLG	OBP
Ambort, Michael	B-R	6-1	215	4-23-85	.222	.333	.167	3	9	2	2	1	0	0	0	0	0	0	0	3	0	0	.333	.222
Benusa, Gus	L-L	5-11	190	1-30-91	.230	.333	.203	21	74	16	17	2	1	0	12	7	1	0	0	17	1	0	.284	.305

	B-T	HT	WT	DOB	AVG	vLH	vRH	G	AB	R	H	2B	3B	HR	RBI	BB	SO	SB	CS						OBP	SLG
Crawford, Evan	R-R	6-2	167	8-5-88	.273	.222	.281	16	66	14	18	1	1	0	7	5	0	2	0	15	9	0	.318	.324		
Dibbens, Derek	L-R	6-0	200	8-7-87	.000	.000	.000	2	2	0	0	0	0	0	0	0	0	0	0	0	0	0	.000	.000		
Dominguez, Chris	R-R	6-3	215	11-22-86	.306	.167	.333	9	36	8	11	2	0	2	8	3	1	0	0	9	1	0	.528	.375		
Dunning, Jake	R-R	6-4	188	8-12-88	.227	.294	.211	22	88	11	20	3	2	0	11	1	1	1	0	19	3	2	.307	.244		
Izturis, Julio	B-R	5-11	165	8-29-89	.313	.438	.289	25	99	22	31	5	0	1	11	12	4	1	1	20	10	1	.394	.405		
Liles, Nick	R-R	6-0	165	7-23-87	.300	.290	.303	34	140	20	42	8	1	0	19	4	3	1	2	15	14	1	.371	.329		
Lopez, Josh	R-R	5-9	170	1-31-89	.284	.222	.291	29	88	12	25	3	2	0	8	8	1	1	0	31	4	0	.364	.351		
Mach, Kyle	R-R	5-10	190	11-8-86	.216	.125	.235	31	97	13	21	7	0	1	12	7	3	0	4	25	1	0	.320	.279		
McArthur, Evan	R-R	6-2	200	6-29-84	.213	.429	.167	20	80	11	17	5	0	0	7	5	1	2	1	18	3	1	.275	.264		
Munoz, Luis	R-R	6-0	165	10-10-91	.179	.167	.182	18	28	5	5	0	0	0	1	5	0	1	0	14	0	0	.179	.303		
Navarro, Jesus	R-R	6-0	180	1-3-88	.191	.167	.195	18	47	5	9	1	1	0	9	4	3	0	1	20	0	0	.255	.291		
Ochoa, Leo	L-R	6-0	180	10-20-89	.288	.263	.293	29	111	16	32	4	3	1	15	15	3	0	0	25	3	5	.405	.388		
Phelps, Josh	R-R	6-3	225	5-12-78	.333	.250	.385	6	21	8	7	3	0	0	2	5	0	0	0	4	1	0	.476	.462		
Price, Ryne	L-R	5-11	190	5-27-86	.200	—	.200	2	5	0	1	0	1	0	1	0	0	1	0	0	0	0	.600	.333		
Quintana, Carlos	R-R	6-3	180	6-14-87	.300	.368	.287	34	120	21	36	6	0	0	11	7	2	0	1	27	8	3	.350	.346		
Rodriguez, Rafael	R-R	6-5	198	7-13-92	.299	.300	.299	35	127	25	38	8	0	0	19	16	4	0	1	23	5	4	.362	.392		
Sanchez, Hector	B-R	6-0	185	11-17-89	.299	.217	.319	33	117	13	35	8	1	1	22	16	5	0	1	21	0	0	.410	.403		
Santana, Victor	R-R	6-1	192	11-21-88	.000	—	.000	1	4	1	0	0	0	0	0	0	0	0	0	0	1	0	.000	.000		
Scoma, Ryan	R-L	6-2	180	9-12-87	.270	.083	.295	25	100	10	27	6	1	0	14	8	1	0	1	19	2	0	.350	.327		
Shriner, Jesse	R-R	6-1	195	2-24-85	.297	.171	.331	41	165	21	49	17	1	2	24	10	2	1	1	31	5	2	.448	.343		
Torres, Andres	B-R	5-10	190	1-26-78	.333	.000	.400	3	6	1	2	1	0	0	1	4	0	0	0	3	1	1	.500	.600		
Villegas, Ydwin	B-R	5-10	165	9-1-90	.302	.324	.296	40	159	28	48	6	1	0	21	9	2	3	1	21	12	3	.352	.345		
White, Jonathan	L-L	6-2	198	6-16-86	.287	.364	.277	25	94	14	27	3	1	2	13	6	1	0	1	21	4	1	.404	.333		
Windster, Sundrendy	R-R	6-3	185	2-23-89	.223	.200	.229	39	148	24	33	8	3	3	20	14	3	0	0	54	2	1	.378	.303		
Woodbury, Ben	R-R	5-10	175	2-21-86	.250	—	.250	2	4	1	0	0	0	0	0	0	0	0	0	0	0	0	.250	.250		

Pitching

	B-T	HT	WT	DOB	W	L	ERA	G	GS	CG	SV	IP	H	R	ER	HR	BB	SO	AVG	vLH	vRH	K/9	BB/9
Acosta, Kelyn	R-R	6-1	205	4-24-85	0	0	7.36	4	0	0	0	4	5	3	3	0	1	5	.333	.200	.400	12.27	2.45
Burgos, Raul	B-R	6-1	210	8-18-87	2	0	5.82	15	0	0	0	17	16	11	11	1	13	15	.254	.160	.316	7.94	6.88
Calicutt, Steven	L-L	6-2	190	2-7-84	0	0	2.84	7	0	0	0	6	5	2	2	0	2	8	.217	.364	.083	11.37	2.84
Castro, Ricardo	L-L	6-5	178	2-9-89	0	0	108.00	1	0	0	0	0	3	4	4	1	1	0	.750	—	.750	0.00	27.00
Concepcion, Edward	R-R	6-3	190	10-3-88	4	3	4.61	13	12	0	0	55	55	33	28	3	26	70	.258	.190	.284	11.52	4.28
Cova, Rafael	R-R	6-2	175	3-5-82	0	0	0.00	4	0	0	1	4	2	1	0	0	1	8	.133	.167	.111	18.00	2.25
Davidson, Aaron	R-L	5-11	205	9-27-88	1	0	4.05	13	6	0	0	33	30	17	15	2	14	28	.244	.152	.278	7.56	3.78
Downing, Kaohi	R-R	5-11	180	5-7-86	0	0	3.07	14	0	0	0	15	16	6	5	0	5	13	.291	.200	.325	7.98	3.07
Flick, Brennan	R-R	6-1	180	9-12-89	3	2	2.50	15	0	0	0	18	12	5	5	1	10	16	.197	.118	.227	8.00	5.00
Heston, Chris	R-R	6-4	185	4-10-88	1	5	4.11	11	6	0	0	35	30	19	16	0	10	34	.233	.143	.276	8.74	2.57
Irving, Brian	R-R	6-2	205	4-24-86	4	1	1.19	19	0	0	1	23	14	6	3	0	4	37	.169	.156	.176	14.69	1.59
Jarvis, Jason	R-R	6-2	195	10-1-87	2	1	4.09	11	2	0	0	22	19	10	10	0	7	22	.232	.156	.280	9.00	2.86
Kline, Devan	R-R	6-1	195	10-15-87	0	0	6.14	9	0	0	0	7	7	5	5	0	7	11	.259	.286	.250	13.50	8.59
Lamb, Cameron	R-R	6-3	195	5-29-89	4	1	2.04	13	13	0	0	57	40	15	13	1	28	55	.205	.127	.242	8.63	4.40
Martinez, Joe	L-R	6-2	195	2-26-83	0	0	10.13	1	1	0	0	3	3	3	3	0	1	3	.364	1.000	.300	3.38	0.00
Millikan, Bryan	R-R	6-5	202	8-13-83	2	0	1.35	8	0	0	0	13	11	3	2	0	2	17	.229	.250	.222	11.48	1.35
Pichardo, Kelvin	R-R	6-0	215	10-13-85	0	0	4.50	2	0	0	0	2	2	1	1	0	1	3	.286	.000	.333	13.50	4.50
Proszek, A.J.	R-R	6-5	260	4-17-87	2	2	4.24	13	4	0	0	23	27	15	11	1	8	26	.287	.321	.273	10.03	3.09
Romo, Andrew	R-R	6-1	230	6-20-87	1	0	5.09	12	1	0	0	18	15	10	10	1	11	23	.238	.375	.154	11.72	5.60
Salsbury, B.J.	R-R	6-2	185	10-22-89	5	2	3.04	13	11	0	0	53	38	23	18	4	10	41	.196	.191	.198	6.92	1.69
Sanford, Shawn	R-R	6-0	200	8-28-88	0	1	5.31	21	0	0	8	20	26	13	12	0	8	31	.292	.344	.263	13.72	3.54
Santana, Audy	R-R	6-3	160	11-10-86	2	1	1.40	17	0	0	0	26	16	4	4	0	3	37	.172	.258	.129	12.97	1.05
Shaver, Ryan	R-R	6-5	197	12-17-84	0	0	3.24	7	0	0	1	8	5	4	3	0	4	9	.167	.000	.238	9.72	4.32
Stoffel, Jason	R-R	6-2	220	9-15-88	0	0	1.86	9	0	0	2	10	8	2	2	0	0	6	.211	.000	.267	5.59	0.00
Verdugo, Ryan	L-L	6-2	195	4-10-87	0	0	0.00	2	0	0	0	3	0	0	0	0	0	6	.000	.000	.000	18.00	0.00
Westcott, Craig	L-R	6-4	225	3-1-86	4	0	0.69	7	0	0	0	13	4	2	1	0	3	21	.098	.111	.087	14.54	2.08
Wilshire, Ben	R-R	6-4	200	3-25-85	2	0	2.13	20	0	0	2	25	15	6	6	1	9	25	.174	.200	.164	8.88	3.20

Fielding

Catcher	PCT	G	PO	A	E	DP	PB
Dibbens	1.000	2	6	1	0	0	0
Navarro	.994	18	137	20	1	1	4
Price	.950	2	19	0	1	0	1
Sanchez	.985	33	285	40	5	2	5
Shriner	.991	13	104	10	1	0	0

First Base	PCT	G	PO	A	E	DP
Dominguez	1.000	2	12	1	0	0
Mach	.986	8	67	5	1	7
McArthur	1.000	7	63	0	0	4
Ochoa	1.000	1	1	0	0	0
Quintana	.988	32	236	18	3	19
Santana	1.000	1	8	1	0	2
Shriner	.972	13	101	5	3	7

Second Base	PCT	G	PO	A	E	DP
Izturis	.983	24	55	60	2	16
Liles	.959	28	60	79	6	18
Lopez	1.000	6	3	17	0	2
Mach	1.000	3	1	5	0	0

Third Base	PCT	G	PO	A	E	DP
Dominguez	1.000	4	2	9	0	1
Dunning	.857	7	2	16	3	2
Lopez	.897	13	4	22	3	0
Mach	.950	17	11	27	2	0
McArthur	1.000	13	6	25	0	0
Ochoa	.941	7	2	14	1	1

Shortstop	PCT	G	PO	A	E	DP
Dunning	.957	12	13	32	2	4
Liles	1.000	1	0	1	0	0
Lopez	.806	7	6	19	6	3
Villegas	.938	40	60	121	12	30

Outfield	PCT	G	PO	A	E	DP
Benusa	.950	21	38	0	2	0
Crawford	.964	16	26	1	1	0
Munoz	.917	13	11	0	1	0
Ochoa	1.000	14	12	1	0	0
Phelps	1.000	4	6	0	0	0
Rodriguez	.865	30	31	1	5	0
Scoma	.974	24	36	1	1	0
Shriner	1.000	1	2	0	0	0
Torres	1.000	3	8	0	0	0
White	.938	23	15	0	1	0
Windster	.905	32	54	3	6	1
Woodbury	1.000	2	2	0	0	0

DSL GIANTS

ROOKIE

DOMINICAN SUMMER LEAGUE

Batting	B-T	HT	WT	DOB	AVG	vLH	vRH	G	AB	R	H	2B	3B	HR	RBI	BB	HBP	SH	SF	SO	SB	CS	SLG	OBP
Almonte, Gilberto	R-R	6-3	188	7-15-88	.244	.351	.220	59	205	31	50	7	2	1	25	26	0	3	4	30	2	5	.312	.323
Cedeno, Jose	R-R	6-0	185	5-30-90	.159	.067	.179	33	82	13	13	3	0	0	5	17	9	0	0	24	2	1	.195	.361
Cornier, Gabriel	B-R	6-0	190	6-10-92	.191	.206	.186	56	152	32	29	1	1	1	16	42	5	1	4	40	1	3	.230	.374
De La Cruz, Jose	R-R	0-0	0	4-28-91	.301	.302	.301	40	156	26	47	12	2	0	18	8	5	0	1	23	2	2	.404	.353
Duran, Rey	R-R	6-0	200	7-31-89	.278	.240	.288	63	234	32	65	11	1	11	50	22	6	0	2	43	2	2	.474	.352
Fuentes, Robedluis	R-R	6-4	180	9-13-88	.317	.304	.321	63	246	32	78	11	2	1	39	27	11	3	4	30	6	4	.390	.403
Galindo, Jesus	B-R	5-11	175	8-23-90	.244	.206	.254	58	168	49	41	5	2	0	16	37	8	9	0	49	22	4	.298	.404
Lopez, Eduardo	L-L	6-0	185	2-23-91	.156	.143	.159	45	141	17	22	2	0	1	13	17	8	1	1	51	3	2	.191	.281
Lopez, Jorge	R-R	6-2	180	9-9-91	.200	.211	.197	54	190	25	38	7	1	0	30	25	7	0	3	52	6	4	.247	.311
Osuna, Cesar	R-R	5-11	175	1-29-90	.250	.250	.250	52	204	20	51	7	1	0	37	18	3	2	3	19	2	2	.294	.316
Ramirez, John	L-R	6-1	180	9-27-89	.194	.083	.218	18	67	10	13	2	0	0	5	5	3	0	0	27	1	2	.224	.280
2-team total (5 Yankees 1)					.185	—	—	23	81	12	15	2	0	1	8	8	4	0	0	33	1	2	.247	.290
Soto, Cesar	B-R	5-11	170	4-17-91	.190	.140	.206	60	179	32	34	4	0	0	8	37	10	5	0	45	6	5	.212	.358
Vasquez, Luis	L-R	5-10	170	3-20-91	.216	.214	.217	27	74	11	16	1	0	0	4	11	0	1	0	14	2	0	.230	.318
Willoughby, Carlos	B-R	5-10	170	11-12-88	.327	.262	.349	68	251	74	82	5	10	1	43	55	14	5	4	33	46	12	.438	.466

Pitching	B-T	HT	WT	DOB	W	L	ERA	G	GS	CG	SV	IP	H	R	ER	HR	BB	SO	AVG	vLH	vRH	K/9	BB/9
Azocar, Luis	L-L	5-11	180	9-6-86	2	1	2.95	15	0	0	3	40	29	18	13	0	22	41	.210	.214	.210	9.30	4.99
De La Cruz, Diego	L-L	6-1	182	2-12-89	2	2	1.88	13	7	0	0	53	35	19	11	1	17	42	.185	.133	.190	7.18	2.91
Feliz, Keurin	R-L	6-0	180	8-17-90	6	4	4.32	15	13	0	0	67	66	43	32	4	20	40	.259	.148	.272	5.40	2.70
Fernandez, Ebert	L-L	6-3	192	10-28-90	1	1	4.55	7	6	0	0	28	30	17	14	0	9	13	.268	.316	.258	4.23	2.93
Ferrer, Miguel	R-R	6-3	168	8-7-90	3	0	1.21	11	6	0	1	45	30	10	6	0	5	36	.186	.162	.194	7.25	1.01
Flores, Kendry	R-R	6-2	175	11-24-91	7	2	2.18	13	13	0	0	66	45	19	16	1	24	57	.200	.213	.193	7.77	3.27
Garcia, Alexis	R-R	6-4	170	1-17-92	1	0	9.24	10	0	0	0	13	24	22	13	2	15	5	.393	.500	.362	3.55	10.66
Garcia, Bertoni	R-R	5-11	173	7-8-91	5	1	1.36	14	1	0	1	46	28	17	7	3	24	40	.179	.161	.184	7.77	4.66
Hernandez, Ariel	R-R	6-3	180	3-2-92	6	1	3.64	13	8	0	0	54	45	26	22	3	18	47	.226	.220	.228	7.79	2.98
Martinez, Rafael	R-R	6-3	185	7-9-88	2	1	1.29	26	0	0	15	28	21	10	4	1	8	27	.200	.240	.188	8.68	2.57
Mendoza, Lorenzo	R-R	5-10	190	8-6-91	8	0	2.51	12	10	1	0	61	58	19	17	1	9	36	.240	.191	.251	5.31	1.33
Montero, Raymundo	R-R	6-2	185	9-20-89	2	3	1.14	19	0	0	4	47	30	15	6	1	12	42	.178	.140	.190	7.99	2.28
Noel, Franklin	L-L	6-1	175	12-20-88	4	0	0.00	9	0	0	1	27	12	0	0	0	6	29	.130	.176	.120	9.67	2.00
Paniagua, Armando	R-R	5-11	155	1-11-90	1	2	3.73	10	6	0	0	31	25	19	13	3	11	34	.219	.226	.217	9.77	3.16
Perez, Luiyin	R-R	0-0	0	4-16-89	2	1	4.05	12	1	0	0	27	26	18	12	3	11	21	.250	.208	.263	7.09	3.71
Prada, Marcos	R-R	6-0	180	8-31-90	0	0	13.50	1	0	0	0	2	0	3	3	0	5	3	.000	.000	.000	13.50	22.50
Reyes, Henris	R-R	6-3	205	3-13-90	0	0	0.00	1	0	0	0	2	0	0	0	0	3	1	.000	.000	.000	4.50	13.50

Fielding

Catcher	PCT	G	PO	A	E	DP	PB
Cedeno	1.000	1	1	0	0	0	0
Cornier	.988	54	346	49	5	3	13
Duran	.963	5	24	2	1	0	3
Vasquez	.981	25	130	21	3	1	9

First Base	PCT	G	PO	A	E	DP
Almonte	.995	20	194	8	1	18
Cedeno	.969	6	61	1	2	4
Cornier	1.000	2	15	0	0	0
Duran	.984	38	360	17	6	26
Ramirez	.965	12	104	6	4	10

Second Base	PCT	G	PO	A	E	DP
Almonte	—	1	0	0	0	0
Osuna	.917	15	25	30	5	9
Willoughby	.970	59	120	172	9	38

Third Base	PCT	G	PO	A	E	DP
Almonte	.893	37	16	101	14	8
Cedeno	.750	4	2	7	3	1
Osuna	.957	38	30	102	6	8

Shortstop	PCT	G	PO	A	E	DP
Almonte	.941	6	8	8	1	0
Soto	.933	60	76	173	18	31
Willoughby	.966	10	18	39	2	6

Outfield	PCT	G	PO	A	E	DP
Cedeno	.500	2	1	0	1	0
De La Cruz	.915	39	53	1	5	0
Fuentes	.972	60	98	6	3	2
Galindo	.946	54	101	4	6	0
Lopez	.927	30	38	0	3	0
Lopez	.984	43	54	6	1	1

SAN FRANCISCO GIANTS

Seattle Mariners

SEASON IN A SENTENCE: After becoming the first team ever to lose more than 100 games with a $100 million payroll in 2008, the Mariners hired former Brewers scouting director, Jack Zduriencik, as general manager and he quickly improved the team to 85-77 record in 2009.

HIGH POINT: While the Mariners had, for all practical purposes, been eliminated from playoff contention, Ichiro's walkoff home run against Yankees closer Mariano Rivera on Sept. 18 was special, part of a 4-for-5 day that helped him finish the season with more than 200 hits for the ninth consecutive year.

LOW POINT: Righthander Brandon Morrow came in to save the May 14 game against the Rangers, and gave up a game-tying home run to Hank Blalock and then the game-winning home run to Chris Davis. The Mariners lost 3-2 and it gave the Rangers the sweep as part of a 1-9 stretch.

NOTABLE ROOKIES: Rob Johnson became the team's primary catcher, but didn't live up to his defensive reputation and was anemic at the plate. Righthander Doug Fister went 3-4, 4.39 over his first 61 innings. Shawn Kelley and local product Sean White both pitched well out of the bullpen. Outfielder Michael Saunders, catcher Adam Moore and infielders Matt Tuiasosopo and Mike Carp saw time in the big leagues but will still be rookie-eligible in 2010.

KEY TRANSACTIONS: Zduriencik pulled off a huge three-way trade with the Mets and Indians before the season, getting center fielder Franklin Gutierrez as part of a 12-player deal. Then he made several trades during the season with an eye to the future, dumping shortstop Yuniesky Betancourt (Royals) and lefthander Jarrod Washburn (Tigers) for pitching prospects, and acquiring righthander Ian Snell and shortstop Jack Wilson from the Pirates for catcher Jeff Clement and three pitching prospects.

DOWN ON THE FARM: While the Rookie-level Arizona League team won its league title, in general, it was a down year for Mariners prospects. Heading into the season, outfielder Greg Halman was the team's top prospect, but he struggled in Double-A, hitting .210/.278/.420 and striking out 191 times over 124 games. Righthander Phillippe Aumont was moved to the bullpen and shortstop Carlos Triunfel broke his leg on April 10 and missed most of the season.

OPENING DAY PAYROLL: $98,904,166

ORGANIZATION LEADERS

BATTING		*Minimum 250 at-bats
MAJORS		
*AVG	Ichiro Suzuki	.352
*OPS	Russell Branyan	.867
HR	Russell Branyan	31
RBI	Jose Lopez	96
MINORS		
*AVG	Liddi, Alex, High Desert	.345
R	Gillies, Tyson, High Desert	104
H	Gillies, Tyson, High Desert	170
	Liddi, Alex, High Desert	170
TB	Liddi, Alex, High Desert	293
2B	Liddi, Alex, High Desert	44
3B	Gillies, Tyson, High Desert	14
	Peguero, Carlos, High Desert	14
HR	Peguero, Carlos, High Desert	31
RBI	Dunigan, Joseph, High Desert	104
	Liddi, Alex, High Desert	104
BB	Hubbard, Thomas, West Tenn	72
SO	Halman, Greg, West Tenn	183
SB	Gillies, Tyson, High Desert	44
*OBP	Carrera, Ezequiel, West Tenn	.441
*SLG	Liddi, Alex, High Desert	.594

PITCHING		†Minimum 75 innings
MAJORS		
W	Felix Hernandez	19
†ERA	Felix Hernandez	2.49
SO	Felix Hernandez	217
MINORS		
W	Hume, Donald, High Desert	17
L	Baldwin, Andrew, Tacoma	11
†ERA	Kasparek, Kenn, Clinton	2.41
G	Richard, Steven, High Desert	56
GS	Hume, Donald, High Desert	27
	Ramirez, Juan, High Desert	27
SV	Messenger, Randy, Tacoma	25
IP	Baldwin, Andrew, Tacoma	152
	Hume, Donald, High Desert	152
BB	Munoz, Luis, Tacoma/West Tenn	58
SO	Hensley, Steven, Clinton/W. Tenn/High Desert	135
†AVG	Kasparek, Kenn, Clinton	.236

2009 PERFORMANCE

General Manager: Jack Zduriencik. **Farm Director:** Pedro Grifol. **Scouting Director:** Tom McNamara.

Class	Team	League	W	L	PCT	Finish*	Manager(s)
Majors	Seattle Mariners	American	85	77	.525	7th (14)	Don Wakamatsu
Triple-A	Tacoma Rainiers	Pacific Coast	74	70	.514	7th (16)	Daren Brown
Double-A	West Tenn Diamond Jaxx	Southern	62	78	.443	10th (10)	Phil Plantier
High A	High Desert Mavericks	California	83	57	.593	2nd (10)	Jim Horner
Low A	Clinton LumberKings	Midwest	69	68	.504	7th (14)	Scott Steinmann
Short-season	Everett AquaSox	Northwest	39	37	.513	3rd (8)	John Tamargo
Rookie	Pulaski Mariners	Appalachian	28	36	.438	7th (10)	Jose Moreno
Rookie	AZL Mariners	Arizona	33	22	.600	†3rd (11)	Andy Bottin
Overall 2009 Minor League Record			388	368	.513	10th (30)	

*Finish in overall standings (No. of teams in league). †League champion.

ORGANIZATION STATISTICS

SEATTLE MARINERS

AMERICAN LEAGUE

Batting	B-T	HT	WT	DOB	AVG	vLH	vRH	G	AB	R	H	2B	3B	HR	RBI	BB	HBP	SH	SF	SO	SB	CS	SLG	OBP
Balentien, Wladimir	R-R	6-2	220	7-2-84	.213	.180	.234	56	155	18	33	10	0	4	13	13	0	0	2	43	1	0	.355	.271
Beltre, Adrian	R-R	5-11	220	4-7-79	.265	.298	.253	111	449	54	119	27	0	8	44	19	7	0	2	74	13	2	.379	.304
Betancourt, Yuniesky	R-R	5-10	195	1-31-82	.250	.294	.237	63	224	15	56	10	1	2	22	10	0	8	3	18	3	1	.330	.278
2-team total (71 Kansas City)					.245	—	—	134	470	40	115	20	6	6	49	21	0	11	6	44	3	3	.351	.274
Branyan, Russell	L-R	6-3	230	12-19-75	.251	.222	.267	116	431	64	108	21	1	31	76	58	9	1	6	149	2	0	.520	.347
Burke, Jamie	R-R	6-0	225	9-24-71	.122	.250	.108	13	41	1	5	0	0	1	2	2	0	0	0	13	0	0	.195	.163
Carp, Mike	L-R	6-2	215	6-30-86	.315	.286	.319	21	54	7	17	3	1	1	5	8	2	0	1	10	0	0	.463	.415
Cedeno, Ronny	R-R	6-0	180	2-2-83	.167	.164	.168	59	186	15	31	4	2	5	17	10	1	9	0	50	3	2	.290	.213
Chavez, Endy	L-L	6-0	170	2-7-78	.273	.258	.277	54	161	17	44	3	1	2	13	14	0	5	2	22	9	1	.342	.328
Griffey Jr., Ken	L-L	6-3	230	11-21-69	.214	.213	.215	117	387	44	83	19	0	19	57	63	1	0	3	80	0	0	.411	.324
Gutierrez, Franklin	R-R	6-2	190	2-21-83	.283	.335	.262	153	565	85	160	24	1	18	70	46	3	13	2	122	16	5	.425	.339
Hall, Bill	R-R	6-0	210	12-28-79	.200	.188	.208	34	120	10	24	8	1	2	12	8	0	0	3	48	1	2	.333	.244
Hannahan, Jack	L-R	6-2	210	3-4-80	.230	.186	.258	51	148	15	34	8	0	3	11	17	1	0	1	35	1	1	.345	.311
2-team total (52 Oakland)					.213	—	—	103	267	27	57	14	2	4	19	30	2	1	1	71	1	1	.326	.297
Johjima, Kenji	R-R	6-0	205	6-8-76	.247	.244	.248	71	239	24	59	11	0	9	22	12	5	1	1	28	2	2	.406	.296
Johnson, Rob	R-R	6-1	215	7-22-82	.213	.171	.233	80	258	21	55	19	2	2	26	21	2	3	1	60	1	1	.326	.289
Langerhans, Ryan	L-L	6-3	220	2-20-80	.218	.212	.221	38	101	12	22	6	1	3	10	14	1	3	3	28	0	1	.386	.311
Lopez, Jose	R-R	6-0	205	11-24-83	.272	.286	.266	153	613	69	167	42	0	25	96	24	6	3	7	69	3	3	.463	.303
Moore, Adam	R-R	6-3	220	5-8-84	.217	.300	.154	6	23	4	5	1	0	1	2	0	1	0	0	7	1	0	.391	.250
Quiroz, Guillermo	R-R	6-1	215	11-29-81	.286	1.000	.231	4	14	0	4	0	0	0	2	0	0	1	0	3	0	0	.286	.286
Saunders, Michael	L-R	6-4	210	11-19-86	.221	.200	.239	46	122	13	27	1	3	0	4	6	0	1	0	40	4	1	.279	.258
Shelton, Chris	R-R	6-0	215	6-26-80	.231	.313	.100	9	26	1	6	2	0	0	4	2	0	0	0	11	0	0	.308	.286
Suzuki, Ichiro	L-R	5-11	170	10-22-73	.352	.339	.359	146	639	88	225	31	4	11	46	32	4	2	1	71	26	9	.465	.386
Sweeney, Mike	R-R	6-3	225	7-22-73	.281	.235	.340	74	242	25	68	15	0	8	34	17	4	0	3	31	0	0	.442	.335
Tuiasosopo, Matt	R-R	6-2	225	5-10-86	.227	.278	.000	7	22	2	5	1	0	1	2	2	0	0	1	5	0	0	.409	.280
Wilson, Jack	R-R	6-0	200	12-29-77	.224	.200	.236	31	107	11	24	5	1	1	6	6	0	2	1	17	1	0	.299	.263
Wilson, Josh	R-R	6-0	175	3-26-81	.250	.233	.259	45	128	16	32	8	1	3	10	6	2	2	0	32	1	2	.398	.294
Woodward, Chris	R-R	6-0	190	6-27-76	.239	.111	.325	20	67	7	16	1	0	5	5	0	1	1	15	1	0	.254	.288
2-team total (13 Boston)					.215	—	—	33	79	7	17	1	0	0	5	7	2	1	1	19	1	0	.228	.292

Pitching	B-T	HT	WT	DOB	W	L	ERA	G	GS	CG	SV	IP	H	R	ER	HR	BB	SO	AVG	vLH	vRH	K/9	BB/9
Aardsma, David	R-R	6-4	205	12-27-81	3	6	2.52	73	0	0	38	71	49	23	20	4	34	80	.197	.197	.183	10.09	4.29
Batista, Miguel	R-R	6-1	210	2-19-71	7	4	4.04	56	0	0	1	71	79	37	32	7	39	52	.282	.331	.242	6.56	4.92
Bedard, Erik	L-L	6-1	200	3-5-79	5	3	2.82	15	15	0	0	83	65	29	26	8	34	90	.212	.214	.211	9.76	3.69
Corcoran, Roy	R-R	5-10	185	5-11-80	2	0	6.16	16	0	0	0	19	25	13	13	2	17	6	.357	.345	.366	2.84	8.05
Fister, Doug	L-R	6-8	200	2-4-84	3	4	4.13	11	10	0	0	61	63	29	28	11	15	36	.264	.237	.298	5.31	2.21
French, Luke	L-L	6-4	220	9-13-85	3	3	6.63	8	7	0	0	38	54	32	28	9	17	23	.344	.372	.333	5.45	4.03
2-team total (7 Detroit)					4	5	5.21	15	12	0	0	67	87	45	39	11	28	42	—	—	—	5.61	3.74
Hernandez, Felix	R-R	6-3	225	4-8-86	19	5	2.49	34	34	2	0	239	200	81	66	15	71	217	.227	.228	.226	8.18	2.68
Jakubauskas, Chris	R-R	6-2	215	12-22-78	6	7	5.32	35	8	1	0	93	91	60	55	15	27	47	.254	.275	.235	4.55	2.61
Kelley, Shawn	R-R	6-2	215	4-26-84	5	4	4.50	41	0	0	0	46	45	23	23	9	9	41	.257	.209	.303	8.02	1.76
Lowe, Mark	L-R	6-3	210	6-7-83	2	7	3.26	75	0	0	3	80	71	39	29	7	29	69	.232	.253	.213	7.76	3.26
Messenger, Randy	R-R	6-6	265	8-13-81	0	1	4.35	12	0	0	0	10	13	5	5	3	0	5	.302	.320	.278	4.35	0.00
Morrow, Brandon	R-R	6-3	195	7-26-84	2	4	4.39	26	10	0	6	70	66	38	34	10	44	63	.248	.277	.212	8.14	5.68
Olson, Garrett	R-L	6-1	205	10-18-83	3	5	5.60	31	11	0	0	80	79	52	50	19	34	47	.258	.275	.251	5.27	3.81
Rowland-Smith, Ryan	L-L	6-3	240	1-26-83	5	4	3.74	15	15	0	0	96	87	43	40	9	27	52	.239	.195	.253	4.86	2.52
Silva, Carlos	R-R	6-4	250	4-23-79	1	3	8.60	8	6	0	0	30	41	29	29	5	11	10	.323	.380	.250	2.97	3.26
Snell, Ian	R-R	5-11	200	10-30-81	5	2	4.20	12	12	0	0	64	61	32	30	7	39	37	.247	.250	.243	5.18	5.46
Stark, Denny	R-R	6-2	210	10-27-74	0	1	6.55	9	0	0	0	11	13	9	8	2	10	7	.302	.333	.273	5.73	8.18
Vargas, Jason	L-L	6-0	215	2-2-83	3	6	4.91	23	14	0	0	92	98	53	50	16	24	54	.281	.290	.277	5.30	2.36
Washburn, Jarrod	L-L	6-1	195	8-13-74	8	6	2.64	20	20	1	0	133	109	42	39	11	33	79	.223	.168	.244	5.35	2.23
2-team total (8 Detroit)					9	9	3.78	28	28	1	0	176	160	77	74	23	49	100	—	—	—	5.11	2.51
White, Sean	R-R	6-4	210	4-25-81	3	2	2.80	52	0	0	1	64	50	23	20	3	20	28	.216	.191	.238	3.92	2.80

Fielding

Catcher

	PCT	G	PO	A	E	DP	PB
Burke	.974	12	68	6	2	1	1
Johjima	.998	70	413	35	1	2	4
Johnson	.993	80	511	42	4	5	9
Moore	1.000	6	40	2	0	0	1
Quiroz	1.000	4	25	2	0	0	1

First Base

	PCT	G	PO	A	E	DP
Branyan	.990	116	947	74	10	94
Burke	.889	1	7	1	1	2
Carp	1.000	16	115	15	0	13
Hannahan	1.000	17	92	8	0	8
Lopez	.992	16	115	8	1	12
Shelton	1.000	4	31	2	0	3
Sweeney	.935	5	29	0	2	3

Second Base

	PCT	G	PO	A	E	DP
Cedeno	.977	13	22	21	1	9
Hall	1.000	3	3	3	0	0
Lopez	.975	141	235	351	15	89
Tuiasosopo	1.000	6	12	20	0	4
Wilson	1.000	4	6	13	0	4
Woodward	1.000	5	8	3	0	1

Third Base

	PCT	G	PO	A	E	DP
Beltre	.959	111	103	224	14	19
Cedeno	1.000	2	0	3	0	0
Hall	1.000	3	1	4	0	1
Hannahan	.963	33	18	60	3	11
Wilson	1.000	5	2	6	0	0
Woodward	.922	15	9	38	4	6

Shortstop

	PCT	G	PO	A	E	DP
Betancourt	.967	62	101	159	9	38
Cedeno	.969	40	44	114	5	18
Hannahan	1.000	2	0	4	0	0
Wilson	.961	31	47	75	5	17
Wilson	.983	32	42	74	2	16
Woodward	1.000	1	2	0	0	0

Outfield

	PCT	G	PO	A	E	DP
Balentien	.989	47	88	5	1	0
Cedeno	1.000	7	11	0	0	0
Chavez	.991	48	104	2	1	1
Griffey Jr.	1.000	11	13	0	0	0
Gutierrez	.985	153	445	6	7	2
Hall	.986	30	65	3	1	0
Langerhans	1.000	36	85	1	0	0
Saunders	.989	39	89	0	1	0
Suzuki	.988	145	317	5	4	2

TACOMA RAINIERS   TRIPLE-A
PACIFIC COAST LEAGUE

Batting	B-T	HT	WT	DOB	AVG	vLH	vRH	G	AB	R	H	2B	3B	HR	RBI	BB	HBP	SH	SF	SO	SB	CS	SLG	OBP
Baez, Fleming	R-R	6-0	170	6-10-81	.500	.333	1.000	1	4	1	2	1	0	0	0	0	0	0	0	1	0	0	.750	.500
Betancourt, Yuniesky	R-R	5-10	195	1-31-82	.500	—	.500	1	2	0	1	1	0	0	1	0	0	0	0	0	0	0	1.000	.500
Billingsley, Ben	L-R	5-11	185	10-27-86	1.000	—	1.000	1	1	1	1	0	0	0	0	0	0	0	0	0	0	0	1.000	1.000
Burke, Chris	R-R	5-11	195	3-11-80	.237	.250	.233	10	38	7	9	2	0	1	3	7	0	0	0	11	2	1	.368	.356
Burke, Jamie	R-R	6-0	225	9-24-71	.284	.235	.297	22	81	7	23	7	0	0	11	5	0	0	1	12	0	0	.370	.322
Carp, Mike	L-R	6-2	215	6-30-86	.271	.269	.272	110	413	66	112	25	1	15	64	58	12	1	6	99	0	1	.446	.372
Cintron, Alex	B-R	6-2	210	12-17-78	.248	.250	.247	30	113	8	28	4	1	2	9	2	0	3	0	18	2	0	.354	.261
Clement, Jeff	L-R	6-1	215	8-21-83	.288	.222	.318	92	372	65	107	33	3	14	68	43	4	0	2	81	1	0	.505	.366
Crabbe, Callix	B-R	5-7	185	2-14-83	.210	.260	.197	75	238	25	50	10	4	3	27	29	4	8	3	34	3	5	.324	.303
Guzman, Freddy	B-R	5-10	165	1-20-81	.214	.000	.243	13	42	5	9	2	1	0	3	2	0	0	1	5	4	2	.310	.244
Johjima, Kenji	R-R	6-0	205	6-8-76	.286	.286	.286	4	14	2	4	0	0	0	0	0	0	0	0	3	0	0	.286	.286
LaHair, Bryan	L-R	6-5	220	11-5-82	.289	.231	.313	121	457	72	132	28	2	26	85	45	3	1	4	116	0	5	.530	.354
Monzon, Erick	R-R	6-0	190	11-30-81	.250	.500	.186	31	88	5	22	3	0	0	8	8	0	2	2	28	3	3	.284	.306
Moore, Adam	R-R	6-2	220	5-8-84	.294	.313	.287	91	340	41	100	19	0	9	43	26	1	1	0	51	1	1	.429	.346
Morse, Mike	R-R	6-5	230	3-22-82	.312	.338	.303	66	260	38	81	14	0	10	52	20	6	0	3	50	0	0	.481	.370
Moss, Steve	R-R	6-2	200	1-12-84	.000	.000	.000	4	3	2	0	0	0	0	0	0	1	0	0	2	0	0	.000	.250
Navarro, Oswaldo	R-R	6-0	155	10-2-84	.252	.273	.243	48	159	13	40	7	0	0	12	8	3	4	1	34	4	1	.296	.298
Nelson, Brad	L-R	6-2	265	12-23-82	.247	.231	.252	78	275	35	68	9	1	15	45	30	1	0	1	56	0	0	.451	.322
Nunez, Israel	R-R	6-1	200	9-1-85	.333	1.000	.000	1	3	0	1	0	0	0	0	0	0	0	0	1	0	0	.333	.333
Owens, Jerry	L-L	6-3	195	2-16-81	.323	.350	.316	100	390	74	126	10	9	3	37	44	1	6	4	48	23	8	.418	.390
Quiroz, Guillermo	R-R	6-1	215	11-29-81	.250	.250	.250	13	48	2	12	2	0	1	6	0	0	2	0	9	0	0	.354	.250
Redman, Prentice	R-R	6-3	185	8-23-79	.297	.294	.299	108	414	84	123	35	3	21	66	33	3	4	2	77	7	2	.548	.352
Saunders, Michael	L-R	6-4	210	11-19-86	.310	.247	.344	64	248	58	77	15	2	13	32	25	3	4	2	48	6	3	.544	.378
Shelton, Chris	R-R	6-0	215	6-26-80	.314	.354	.301	105	405	71	127	30	2	15	85	58	2	0	7	86	0	2	.509	.394
Tuiasosopo, Matt	R-R	6-2	225	5-10-86	.261	.257	.263	59	226	43	59	15	0	11	35	36	3	3	1	83	3	1	.473	.368
Wilson, Josh	R-R	6-0	175	3-26-81	.245	.375	.222	16	53	10	13	2	0	1	3	2	1	3	1	6	1	0	.340	.281
2-team total (15 Reno)					.252	—		31	103	15	26	5	1	2	13	9	2	4	3	14	2	1	.379	.316
Wilson, Mike	R-R	6-2	245	6-29-83	.164	.167	.164	40	146	19	24	4	0	5	18	15	5	0	3	50	1	0	.295	.260
Woodward, Chris	R-R	6-0	190	6-27-76	.299	.356	.279	51	174	24	52	12	1	1	15	19	1	2	1	30	4	0	.397	.369

Pitching	B-T	HT	WT	DOB	W	L	ERA	G	GS	CG	SV	IP	H	R	ER	HR	BB	SO	AVG	vLH	vRH	K/9	BB/9
Baldwin, Andy	R-R	6-5	215	10-20-82	6	11	4.57	31	21	1	0	152	161	90	77	21	38	103	.270	.296	.245	6.11	2.25
Corcoran, Roy	R-R	5-10	185	5-11-80	1	0	0.00	3	0	0	0	3	3	1	0	0	0	2	.231	.500	.000	6.00	0.00
2-team total (13 Round Rock)					1	0	3.57	16	1	0	0	23	27	13	9	0	7	13				5.16	2.78
Delgado, Jesus	R-R	6-0	225	4-19-84	3	3	6.59	33	1	0	0	56	71	44	41	5	29	39	.309	.337	.291	6.27	4.66
Downs, Brodie	R-R	6-4	235	7-19-79	4	1	6.58	23	0	0	0	40	46	33	29	4	29	24	.293	.278	.306	5.45	6.58
Esquibel, Andres	R-R	6-1	215	7-13-86	0	1	8.44	2	1	0	0	5	5	5	5	2	5	5	.250	.125	.333	8.44	5.06
Fister, Doug	L-R	6-8	200	2-4-84	6	4	3.81	22	17	0	0	106	132	51	45	10	11	79	.305	.301	.308	6.69	0.93
Hall, Josh	R-R	6-2	190	12-16-80	2	1	6.91	8	4	0	0	27	45	26	21	1	16	12	.366	.359	.373	3.95	5.27
Hernandez, Gaby	R-R	6-3	215	5-21-86	10	9	5.23	26	26	1	0	146	158	90	85	16	48	98	.276	.310	.248	6.03	2.95
Hull, Eric	R-R	5-11	185	12-3-79	7	3	6.13	39	3	0	1	69	75	54	47	9	33	61	.272	.233	.301	7.96	4.30
Jakubauskas, Chris	R-R	6-2	215	12-22-78	0	0	0.00	1	0	0	0	1	0	0	0	0	1	1	.000	.000	.000	9.00	9.00
Jimenez, Cesar	L-L	5-11	220	11-12-84	0	1	4.70	8	0	0	0	8	10	5	4	0	5	5	.313	.167	.346	5.87	5.87
Johnson, Tyler	B-L	6-2	200	6-7-81	0	1	27.00	4	0	0	0	3	8	9	8	2	2	1	.500	.500	.500	3.38	6.75
Kelley, Shawn	R-R	6-2	215	4-26-84	0	0	0.00	1	0	0	0	1	0	0	0	0	0	0	.000	.000	.000	0.00	0.00
Koplove, Mike	R-R	6-0	160	8-30-76	1	0	2.00	12	0	0	3	18	14	9	4	2	7	19	.200	.103	.268	9.50	3.50
Manuel, Robert	R-R	6-3	205	7-9-83	1	1	3.32	15	0	0	4	19	13	8	7	4	6	11	.188	.229	.147	5.21	2.84
Messenger, Randy	R-R	6-6	245	8-13-81	0	2	2.86	52	0	0	25	57	65	24	18	4	36	48	.286	.215	.336	6.35	2.22
Morrow, Brandon	R-R	6-3	195	7-26-84	5	3	3.60	10	10	1	0	55	50	24	22	2	23	40	.242	.194	.288	6.55	3.76
Munoz, Luis	R-R	6-2	195	1-10-82	0	3	6.75	4	3	0	0	19	25	14	14	6	9	16	.329	.304	.340	7.71	4.34
Newby, Joey	R-R	6-2	205	3-8-82	0	0	1.42	3	0	0	0	6	4	1	1	0	5	4	.190	.167	.222	5.68	7.11
Olson, Garrett	R-L	6-1	205	10-18-83	2	3	4.94	9	9	0	0	47	38	26	26	2	23	38	.222	.273	.205	7.23	4.37

Player	B-T	HT	WT	DOB	W	L	ERA	G	GS	CG	SV	IP	H	R	ER	HR	BB	SO	AVG	vLH	vRH	K/9	BB/9
Rowland-Smith, Ryan	L-L	6-3	240	1-26-83	5	3	4.31	10	10	0	0	56	61	28	27	5	10	38	.277	.295	.268	6.07	1.60
Seddon, Chris	L-L	6-3	220	10-13-83	9	8	4.51	25	24	0	0	132	140	74	66	17	54	80	.274	.291	.268	5.47	3.69
Shell, Steven	R-R	6-4	225	3-10-83	3	3	6.98	17	5	0	1	40	56	35	31	10	15	27	.322	.296	.344	6.08	3.38
Silva, Carlos	R-R	6-4	250	4-23-79	0	0	3.00	2	1	0	0	3	3	1	1	0	0	2	.250	.400	.143	6.00	0.00
Stark, Denny	R-R	6-2	210	10-27-74	2	2	5.79	38	0	0	1	51	55	33	33	6	35	43	.281	.241	.312	7.54	6.14
Thomas, Justin	L-L	6-3	215	1-18-84	2	4	4.48	53	0	0	6	60	67	33	30	5	40	53	.276	.228	.305	7.91	5.97
Vargas, Jason	L-L	6-0	215	2-2-83	4	3	3.14	9	9	0	0	52	48	19	18	3	15	46	.255	.288	.240	8.01	2.61
Wells, Jared	R-R	6-4	200	10-31-81	1	0	5.09	28	0	0	1	35	35	23	20	5	24	27	.252	.224	.272	6.88	6.11
White, Sean	R-R	6-4	210	4-25-81	0	0	4.15	2	0	0	0	4	4	2	2	0	0	1	.250	.200	.273	2.08	0.00

Fielding

Catcher

Catcher	PCT	G	PO	A	E	DP	PB
Baez	1.000	1	3	1	0	0	0
Burke	.981	22	145	8	3	1	0
Clement	.984	16	122	5	2	1	2
Johjima	1.000	3	13	0	0	0	0
Moore	.990	91	553	43	6	7	8
Nunez	1.000	1	7	0	0	0	0
Quiroz	.958	13	88	3	4	0	2

First Base	PCT	G	PO	A	E	DP
Carp	.990	82	617	63	7	64
Clement	.977	6	40	2	1	5
LaHair	1.000	38	255	15	0	26
Nelson	.988	20	155	14	2	17
Shelton	1.000	8	88	3	0	3

Second Base	PCT	G	PO	A	E	DP
Betancourt	1.000	1	1	3	0	0
Billingsley	1.000	1	0	2	0	0
Burke	.944	5	8	9	1	3
Cintron	.987	20	30	46	1	10

Catcher	PCT	G	PO	A	E	DP
Crabbe	.969	65	122	163	9	36
Monzon	.957	9	17	28	2	8
Morse	.966	19	41	44	3	16
Navarro	1.000	7	9	10	0	3
Tuiasosopo	.978	21	39	48	2	13
Wilson	1.000	1	1	3	0	0
Woodward	1.000	4	9	11	0	2

Third Base	PCT	G	PO	A	E	DP
Crabbe	1.000	1	2	0	0	0
Monzon	.882	8	4	11	2	2
Morse	.923	17	10	26	3	1
Navarro	.875	3	3	4	1	1
Nelson	1.000	2	0	1	0	0
Shelton	.908	8	39	139	18	15
Tuiasosopo	.963	31	26	53	3	6
Woodward	1.000	2	0	3	0	1

Shortstop	PCT	G	PO	A	E	DP
Cintron	.980	10	14	34	1	11
Crabbe	.963	7	7	19	1	3

	PCT	G	PO	A	E	DP
Monzon	.915	11	15	28	4	6
Morse	.959	25	39	54	4	11
Navarro	.968	38	56	94	5	16
Wilson	.985	15	25	42	1	7
Woodward	.960	45	71	145	9	33

Outfield	PCT	G	PO	A	E	DP
Burke	.947	5	18	0	1	0
Carp	.958	12	23	0	1	0
Crabbe	1.000	2	4	0	0	0
Guzman	.966	13	27	1	1	0
LaHair	1.000	86	181	7	0	2
Morse	1.000	4	4	0	0	0
Moss	1.000	4	1	0	0	0
Nelson	1.000	21	49	1	0	0
Owens	.993	98	288	1	2	0
Redman	.985	104	191	3	3	1
Saunders	.983	63	168	4	3	0
Wilson	.965	40	106	5	4	3

WEST TENN DIAMOND JAXX

DOUBLE-A

SOUTHERN LEAGUE

Batting	B-T	HT	WT	DOB	AVG	vLH	vRH	G	AB	R	H	2B	3B	HR	RBI	BB	HBP	SH	SF	SO	SB	CS	SLG	OBP
Baez, Fleming	R-R	6-0	170	6-10-81	.091	.000	.107	13	33	3	3	0	0	0	2	1	0	5	0	11	0	0	.091	.118
Bonilla, Leury	R-R	6-3	170	2-8-85	.153	.150	.154	26	85	9	13	3	0	1	6	7	1	1	0	21	2	1	.224	.226
Brito, Javier	R-R	6-1	245	3-25-83	.245	.217	.269	17	49	7	12	2	0	0	6	13	0	0	0	13	0	1	.286	.403
Carrera, Ezequiel	L-L	5-11	175	6-11-87	.337	.277	.362	91	329	68	111	12	4	2	38	59	4	10	3	62	27	13	.416	.441
Crabbe, Callix	B-R	5-7	185	2-14-83	.212	.244	.195	36	118	21	25	4	0	0	6	23	0	2	0	13	4	2	.246	.340
Diaz, Ogui	R-R	6-2	170	12-1-85	.185	.400	.059	9	27	0	5	0	0	0	3	1	0	1	3	4	1	1	.185	.194
Dickey, Gavin	R-R	5-11	200	9-29-83	.417	.500	.400	4	12	1	5	0	0	0	2	0	0	1	0	3	0	0	.417	.417
Dominguez, Jeff	B-R	6-2	160	7-31-86	.214	.185	.233	27	70	9	15	0	0	0	4	11	0	0	0	16	1	3	.214	.321
Espinosa, David	B-R	6-2	190	12-16-81	.212	.133	.248	60	193	28	41	7	2	2	28	26	0	0	0	39	9	3	.301	.306
Garcia, Travis	R-R	6-2	205	4-18-82	.258	.305	.228	44	151	19	39	9	1	4	22	8	0	3	2	39	1	1	.411	.292
Haad, Yamid	R-R	6-2	220	9-2-77	.231	.277	.207	42	134	15	31	9	0	5	18	12	0	3	2	29	1	2	.410	.291
Halman, Greg	R-R	6-4	190	8-26-87	.210	.190	.219	121	457	64	96	17	2	25	72	29	15	2	3	183	9	7	.420	.278
Hubbard, Marshall	L-R	6-2	215	4-16-82	.271	.246	.280	129	447	73	121	29	1	14	70	72	12	0	8	110	2	3	.434	.380
Johnson, Brent	R-R	6-2	190	5-21-82	.216	.247	.199	78	227	30	49	13	0	3	17	34	4	4	1	30	12	7	.313	.327
Limonta, Johan	L-L	6-0	205	8-4-83	.297	.221	.329	126	438	57	130	30	8	6	53	54	3	0	3	74	7	6	.443	.376
Mangini, Matt	L-R	6-4	220	12-1-85	.273	.218	.294	124	422	48	115	18	5	12	67	38	6	0	3	92	10	2	.424	.339
Mojica, Jimmy	R-R	5-11	170	11-3-83	.187	.273	.151	25	75	6	14	3	1	1	10	6	1	3	1	12	4	2	.293	.253
Monzon, Erick	R-R	6-0	190	11-30-81	.197	.200	.196	24	76	9	15	1	0	5	7	5	0	2	0	19	2	0	.408	.247
Moore, Adam	R-R	6-3	220	5-8-84	.263	.344	.222	27	95	14	25	5	0	3	13	16	2	0	3	21	0	0	.411	.371
Morton, Colt	R-R	6-5	228	4-10-82	.207	.231	.200	16	58	8	12	1	0	4	9	4	0	0	1	14	0	0	.431	.254
Navarro, Oswaldo	R-R	6-0	155	10-2-84	.258	.207	.280	63	190	23	49	6	1	1	13	33	3	4	0	44	4	2	.316	.376
Poythress, Rich	R-R	6-4	235	8-11-87	.230	.320	.194	26	87	11	20	2	0	1	9	15	0	0	2	24	1	0	.287	.337
Prettyman, Ronnie	L-R	6-2	190	4-8-84	.239	.167	.255	27	67	7	16	3	0	1	3	10	4	0	1	22	0	0	.418	.282
Quiroz, Guillermo	R-R	6-1	215	11-29-81	.242	.250	.238	47	157	18	38	9	1	5	25	11	1	0	2	25	0	0	.408	.292
Stocker, Mel	B-R	5-10	160	8-15-80	.233	.213	.240	98	305	42	71	16	4	2	22	35	9	11	1	48	35	6	.331	.329
Triunfel, Carlos	R-R	5-11	175	2-27-90	.231	.167	.250	7	26	2	6	1	0	0	4	1	1	0	0	2	0	0	.269	.286
Wilson, Mike	R-R	6-2	245	6-24-83	.247	.179	.279	26	89	15	22	2	5	1	12	14	5	0	3	31	5	0	.461	.380
Yepez, Jose	R-R	6-0	205	6-19-81	.239	.231	.242	19	46	5	11	4	0	1	7	7	4	0	1	4	0	0	.391	.379

Pitching	B-T	HT	WT	DOB	W	L	ERA	G	GS	CG	SV	IP	H	R	ER	HR	BB	SO	AVG	vLH	vRH	K/9	BB/9
Aumont, Phillippe	L-R	6-7	220	1-7-89	1	4	5.09	15	0	0	4	18	21	15	10	1	11	24	.292	.276	.302	12.23	5.60
Bray, Steve	R-R	6-1	195	12-22-80	7	8	3.11	26	22	2	0	145	131	55	50	12	34	89	.243	.284	.214	5.54	2.12
Christensen, Daniel	L-L	6-1	210	8-10-83	1	6	4.16	24	10	0	0	76	84	42	35	5	32	46	.284	.215	.309	5.47	3.81
Cortes, Danny	R-R	6-6	215	3-4-87	1	5	4.94	10	10	0	0	55	51	33	30	4	35	55	.248	.250	.246	9.05	5.76
Cotter, Aaron	R-R	6-4	250	1-2-84	0	1	7.08	17	1	0	1	34	45	27	27	6	10	13	.315	.345	.294	3.41	2.62
Downs, Brodie	R-R	6-4	235	7-19-79	1	1	10.13	8	3	0	0	16	27	21	18	1	10	14	.375	.481	.311	7.88	5.63
Fields, Joshua	R-R	6-0	185	8-19-85	2	2	6.48	31	0	0	1	33	33	33	24	2	22	36	.254	.236	.267	9.72	5.94
Fister, Doug	L-R	6-8	200	2-4-84	1	0	0.00	2	0	0	0	6	2	0	0	1	5	.111	.000	.250	7.94	1.59
Hensley, Steven	R-R	6-3	180	12-27-86	0	1	7.20	3	3	0	0	15	19	12	12	1	10	11	.322	.250	.340	6.60	6.00
Hill, Nick	L-L	6-0	190	1-30-85	5	6	3.10	36	9	3	2	96	84	44	33	5	24	100	.232	.268	.213	9.41	2.26

	B-T	HT	WT	DOB	W	L	ERA	G	GS	CG	SV	IP	H	R	ER	HR	BB	SO	AVG	vLH	vRH	K/9	BB/9
Hull, Eric	R-R	5-11	185	12-3-79	0	1	10.29	6	0	0	0	7	9	10	8	0	7	8	.333	.250	.348	10.29	9.00
Munoz, Luis	R-R	6-2	195	1-10-82	8	7	4.08	23	23	0	0	121	117	59	55	11	49	89	.254	.275	.237	6.60	3.63
Newby, Joey	R-R	6-2	205	3-8-82	1	1	2.72	28	0	0	0	43	41	17	13	1	29	33	.263	.298	.242	6.91	6.07
Orta, Ricky	R-R	6-2	195	11-6-84	3	2	1.94	24	3	0	3	42	29	14	9	1	18	41	.196	.188	.203	8.86	3.89
Paredes, Edward	L-L	6-0	175	9-30-86	0	0	12.00	3	0	0	0	3	3	4	4	1	7	2	.250	.250	.250	6.00	21.00
Parker, Kyle	R-R	6-3	205	4-8-85	5	5	3.55	25	19	1	0	117	109	52	46	9	52	73	.252	.230	.267	5.63	4.01
Pena, Luis	R-R	6-5	200	1-10-83	1	1	4.50	3	3	0	0	10	11	5	5	1	7	3	.289	.444	.150	2.70	6.30
Renfree, Matt	R-R	6-8	220	1-16-85	0	0	3.52	5	0	0	0	8	9	3	3	0	1	5	.281	.353	.200	5.87	1.17
Rivera, Mumba	R-R	6-5	205	12-10-80	6	6	4.50	42	0	0	1	64	59	37	32	5	43	62	.249	.239	.255	8.72	6.05
Rohrbaugh, Robert	R-L	6-2	195	12-28-83	3	3	3.40	9	9	0	0	48	47	19	18	5	12	42	.261	.304	.242	7.93	2.27
Ryan, Patrick	R-R	6-0	200	5-31-83	2	5	6.62	16	8	0	0	50	64	43	37	7	21	35	.306	.247	.353	6.26	3.75
Shell, Steven	R-R	6-4	225	3-10-83	3	0	0.43	5	3	0	0	21	9	2	1	0	6	16	.123	.091	.150	6.86	2.57
Souza, Justin	R-R	6-1	185	10-22-85	6	6	3.35	20	14	0	0	78	73	34	29	4	18	62	.247	.224	.263	7.15	2.08
Varvaro, Anthony	R-R	6-0	180	10-31-84	4	3	2.82	36	0	0	8	54	30	23	17	1	44	63	.163	.203	.144	10.44	7.29
Vega, Marwin	R-R	6-0	175	10-27-86	0	3	5.27	19	0	0	1	27	29	23	16	3	18	22	.279	.340	.228	7.24	5.93
Villarreal, Luis	L-L	6-1	215	12-20-79	0	1	10.13	5	0	0	0	5	7	6	6	2	2	4	.304	.222	.357	6.75	3.38
Wells, Jared	R-R	6-4	200	10-31-81	1	0	0.00	2	0	0	0	3	2	0	0	2	5		.182	.333	.000	15.00	6.00

Fielding

Catcher	PCT	G	PO	A	E	DP	PB
Baez	.967	13	73	14	3	1	2
Bonilla	1.000	1	1	1	0	1	1
Haad	.985	38	249	19	4	1	6
Moore	.989	22	171	15	2	1	6
Morton	.988	13	71	8	1	0	0
Quiroz	.988	47	307	30	4	3	11
Yepez	1.000	17	97	10	0	2	2

First Base	PCT	G	PO	A	E	DP
Bonilla	1.000	2	10	0	0	0
Brito	1.000	4	15	0	0	0
Haad	1.000	2	11	1	0	1
Hubbard	.996	72	523	39	2	47
Johnson	1.000	6	37	1	0	1
Limonta	.993	40	253	23	2	16
Mangini	1.000	2	16	0	0	1
Poythress	.988	19	150	15	2	8
Prettyman	1.000	2	22	1	0	2

Second Base	PCT	G	PO	A	E	DP
Bonilla	1.000	1	0	2	0	0
Crabbe	.974	35	44	68	3	12
Diaz	.917	9	15	18	3	2
Dominguez	.934	22	35	36	5	7

	PCT	G	PO	A	E	DP
Espinosa	.951	36	42	74	6	21
Garcia	1.000	1	4	3	0	0
Johnson	—	1	0	0	0	0
Mojica	1.000	4	12	6	0	2
Monzon	.983	15	23	35	1	4
Navarro	.923	4	3	9	1	1
Prettyman	.909	17	15	35	5	2
Stocker	.920	11	11	12	2	3
Triunfel	.727	2	3	5	3	0

Third Base	PCT	G	PO	A	E	DP
Bonilla	.900	7	7	11	2	1
Crabbe	1.000	1	0	1	0	0
Dominguez	1.000	1	0	1	0	0
Espinosa	1.000	2	0	1	0	0
Garcia	.957	9	9	13	1	0
Johnson	.938	8	4	11	1	0
Mangini	.925	116	83	187	22	14
Monzon	.875	4	2	5	1	1
Navarro	1.000	1	0	4	0	0
Triunfel	—	1	0	0	0	0

Shortstop	PCT	G	PO	A	E	DP
Bonilla	.967	10	9	20	1	2
Crabbe	.750	2	1	2	1	0

	PCT	G	PO	A	E	DP
Dominguez	.857	7	5	7	2	1
Espinosa	1.000	10	13	17	0	1
Garcia	.951	32	42	74	6	14
Mojica	.988	21	30	53	1	10
Monzon	1.000	6	6	12	0	2
Navarro	.964	59	78	139	8	23
Prettyman	.800	2	2	2	1	1
Triunfel	.875	4	5	9	2	2

Outfield	PCT	G	PO	A	E	DP
Bonilla	1.000	7	16	0	0	0
Carrera	.981	89	204	5	4	1
Dickey	1.000	4	4	1	0	1
Espinosa	1.000	5	5	0	0	0
Garcia	—	1	0	0	0	0
Halman	.973	118	320	5	9	1
Johnson	.966	58	103	11	4	2
Limonta	.981	55	95	6	2	0
Prettyman	—	2	0	0	0	0
Stocker	.983	87	217	10	4	1
Wilson	.958	22	42	4	2	1

HIGH DESERT MAVERICKS

HIGH CLASS A

CALIFORNIA LEAGUE

Batting	B-T	HT	WT	DOB	AVG	vLH	vRH	G	AB	R	H	2B	3B	HR	RBI	BB	HBP	SH	SF	SO	SB	CS	SLG	OBP
Baez, Fleming	R-R	6-0	170	6-10-81	.000	.000	.000	2	8	0	0	0	0	0	0	0	1	0	1	2	0	0	.000	.111
Benitez, Deybis	R-R	6-2	170	4-23-87	.400	.333	.500	8	10	3	4	0	0	0	0	2	0	0	0	1	0	0	.400	.500
Bladergroen, Ian	L-L	6-5	210	2-23-83	.264	.186	.301	79	269	42	71	17	4	11	46	27	6	1	5	56	0	0	.480	.339
Bonilla, Leury	R-R	6-3	170	2-8-85	.287	.465	.198	35	129	23	37	11	4	2	12	6	1	1	2	33	4	1	.481	.319
Colina, Edilio	R-R	6-2	175	10-10-88	.270	.322	.243	110	444	67	120	26	0	2	51	37	10	10	5	52	9	7	.342	.337
Diaz, Juan	B-R	6-3	180	12-12-88	.311	.327	.303	84	325	55	101	22	5	4	29	23	0	3	0	65	5	2	.446	.356
Dickey, Gavin	R-R	5-11	200	9-29-83	.296	.333	.267	12	27	7	8	3	0	0	4	1	1	0	0	4	0	0	.407	.345
Dominguez, Jeff	B-R	6-2	160	7-31-86	.261	.214	.280	80	284	48	74	17	4	4	37	19	6	1	1	57	10	3	.391	.319
Dunigan, Joe	L-L	6-1	215	3-29-86	.294	.258	.313	118	456	83	134	28	4	30	104	43	2	2	3	129	20	8	.570	.355
Fonseca, Alexis	R-R	6-1	215	1-4-84	.000	—	.000	2	1	0	0	0	0	0	0	0	1	0	0	0	0	0	.000	.500
Fuentes, Juan	R-R	6-0	170	1-28-86	.333	.200	.400	4	15	0	5	0	0	0	1	1	0	0	0	1	0	0	.333	.375
Garth, Ron	R-R	5-11	165	11-5-84	.173	.167	.179	15	52	10	9	4	0	2	6	5	2	0	1	11	0	0	.365	.267
Gillies, Tyson	L-R	6-2	190	10-31-88	.341	.331	.347	124	498	104	170	17	14	9	42	60	18	16	1	81	44	19	.486	.430
Johnson, Brent	R-R	6-2	190	5-21-82	.292	.296	.289	21	65	12	19	3	1	1	11	9	5	0	1	9	3	1	.415	.413
Liddi, Alex	R-R	6-2	176	8-14-88	.345	.404	.315	129	493	97	170	44	5	23	104	53	8	3	8	122	10	6	.594	.411
Lo, Kuo Hui	R-R	6-2	188	9-26-85	.277	.267	.282	99	376	61	104	13	12	14	70	26	5	2	7	78	13	9	.487	.326
McOwen, Jamie	L-R	6-0	200	9-26-85	.340	.387	.316	115	447	79	152	23	8	10	82	40	4	3	8	70	13	10	.494	.393
Peguero, Carlos	L-L	6-5	210	2-22-87	.271	.216	.298	126	491	92	133	21	14	31	98	42	7	1	3	172	3	4	.560	.335
Scott, Travis	L-R	6-3	220	4-24-85	.285	.309	.274	102	351	48	100	28	5	15	71	41	1	0	6	78	2	1	.521	.356
Seager, Kyle	L-R	5-10	175	11-3-87	.000	—	.000	2	5	1	0	0	0	0	0	0	0	0	0	0	0	0	.000	.000
Welsh, Guy	R-R	6-3	226	5-15-85	.250	—	.250	1	4	1	1	0	0	0	2	0	0	0	0	0	0	0	1.000	.250
Yepez, Jose	R-R	6-0	205	6-19-81	.338	.339	.337	44	145	27	49	10	0	5	21	15	4	1	3	17	0	1	.510	.407

Pitching	B-T	HT	WT	DOB	W	L	ERA	G	GS	CG	SV	IP	H	R	ER	HR	BB	SO	AVG	vLH	vRH	K/9	BB/9
Adcock, Nathan	R-R	6-5	190	2-25-88	5	7	5.29	21	19	1	0	102	103	72	60	10	54	71	.265	.273	.257	6.26	4.76
Aumont, Phillippe	L-R	6-7	220	1-7-89	5	7	3.24	29	0	0	12	33	24	14	12	3	12	35	.195	.194	.197	9.45	3.24
Dilone, Natividad	R-R	6-0	160	9-8-82	2	1	5.09	40	0	0	0	53	56	40	30	2	34	44	.276	.293	.261	7.47	5.77

Esquibel, Andres	R-R	6-1	215	7-13-86	0	1	14.54	1	1	0	0	4	12	10	7	1	1	4	.480	.455	.500	8.31	2.08
Flores, Ruben	R-R	6-4	170	5-19-84	1	0	13.06	8	0	0	0	10	20	17	15	5	7	8	.400	.444	.375	6.97	6.10
Harben, Adam	R-R	6-5	210	8-19-83	0	0	9.35	3	3	0	0	9	12	14	9	11	6	.316	.150	.500	6.23	11.42
Hensley, Steven	R-R	6-3	180	12-27-86	9	3	4.21	20	19	1	0	113	104	57	53	16	30	108	.246	.242	.249	8.58	2.38
Hume, Donnie	R-L	6-0	185	8-29-85	17	5	4.81	28	27	0	0	152	165	88	81	15	53	117	.274	.276	.273	6.94	3.15
Jensen, Aaron	R-R	6-2	180	6-11-84	3	2	3.20	40	0	0	1	59	60	23	21	5	20	36	.278	.305	.252	5.49	3.05
Mortimore, Travis	L-L	6-5	225	8-1-84	2	5	7.07	49	2	0	1	64	94	57	50	6	29	55	.341	.312	.355	7.77	4.10
Newby, Joey	R-R	6-2	205	3-8-82	0	0	0.00	3	0	0	0	4	0	0	0	2	3	.000	.000	.000	7.36	4.91
Paredes, Edward	L-L	6-0	175	9-30-86	8	4	4.69	42	3	0	3	71	74	45	37	6	22	64	.269	.256	.276	8.11	2.79
Penney, Stephen	R-R	6-7	240	8-14-86	2	2	4.85	21	1	0	0	39	52	24	21	2	6	32	.327	.286	.366	7.38	1.38
Pineda, Michael	R-R	6-5	180	1-18-89	4	2	2.84	10	8	0	0	44	29	16	14	3	6	48	.190	.203	.176	9.74	1.22
Pullen, Brandon	L-L	6-4	200	12-7-85	0	0	27.00	1	0	0	0	1	2	2	2	1	2	1	.500	.000	.667	13.50	27.00
Ramirez, J.C.	R-R	6-3	175	8-16-88	8	10	5.12	28	27	1	0	142	153	93	81	18	53	111	.276	.286	.267	7.02	3.35
Richard, Steve	R-R	6-3	240	3-5-85	8	1	5.03	56	0	0	13	59	72	40	33	2	27	64	.296	.319	.276	9.76	4.12
Robles, Mauricio	L-L	5-10	160	3-5-89	3	2	2.78	7	6	0	0	32	23	14	10	1	19	34	.202	.130	.220	9.46	5.29
Staehely, Christian	R-R	6-4	205	9-28-85	0	0	4.50	1	0	0	0	2	1	1	1	0	1	2	.143	.000	.167	9.00	4.50
Varvaro, Anthony	R-R	6-0	180	10-31-84	0	0	7.04	8	0	0	4	8	9	6	6	0	6	10	.273	.267	.278	11.74	7.04
Vega, Marwin	R-R	6-0	175	10-27-86	0	0	15.12	7	0	0	0	8	18	14	14	2	6	9	.439	.235	.583	9.72	6.48
Venegas, Alfredo	R-R	6-1	180	5-11-86	1	2	5.46	11	4	0	0	28	28	21	17	5	10	23	.257	.237	.280	7.39	3.21
Wild, Jake	R-R	6-5	195	8-18-84	6	8	4.09	34	20	2	0	132	146	75	60	10	37	116	.289	.268	.310	7.91	2.52
Zapata, Juan	R-R	6-3	180	8-6-84	3	0	6.85	47	0	0	0	67	83	57	51	10	31	63	.294	.307	.283	8.46	4.16

Fielding

Catcher	PCT	G	PO	A	E	DP	PB
Baez	1.000	2	17	1	0	1	0
Fonseca	1.000	1	2	1	0	0	0
Fuentes	.967	4	26	3	1	1	0
Scott	.980	97	692	79	16	5	8
Welsh	1.000	1	5	0	0	0	0
Yepez	.994	41	330	27	2	3	3

First Base	PCT	G	PO	A	E	DP
Bladergroen	.990	69	517	60	6	52
Bonilla	.980	12	90	10	2	10
Dominguez	1.000	7	50	3	0	2
Dunigan	.975	53	410	25	11	52
Johnson	1.000	6	39	2	0	3
Liddi	.987	7	64	10	1	4
Scott	1.000	1	9	1	0	2

Second Base	PCT	G	PO	A	E	DP
Benitez	1.000	4	4	5	0	1
Bonilla	.893	13	18	32	6	4
Colina	.976	84	167	236	10	52
Dominguez	.992	34	49	78	1	20
Garth	.930	9	9	31	3	4
Johnson	1.000	1	3	3	0	2
Seager	—	2	0	0	0	0

Third Base	PCT	G	PO	A	E	DP
Bonilla	.935	10	4	25	2	0
Colina	1.000	6	2	18	0	0
Dominguez	.000	1	0	0	2	0
Garth	1.000	2	0	4	0	0
Johnson	.800	1	1	3	1	0
Liddi	.945	121	96	211	18	20
Yepez	1.000	1	1	1	0	0

Shortstop	PCT	G	PO	A	E	DP
Benitez	—	1	0	0	0	0
Colina	.947	21	32	58	5	8
Diaz	.960	83	137	245	16	54
Dominguez	.939	37	53	117	11	23
Liddi	1.000	1	1	0	0	0

Outfield	PCT	G	PO	A	E	DP
Bonilla	.833	2	5	0	1	0
Dickey	1.000	7	7	0	0	0
Dominguez	1.000	1	1	0	0	0
Dunigan	1.000	20	28	3	0	1
Gillies	.993	123	273	18	2	1
Johnson	1.000	9	10	2	0	0
Lo	.946	81	135	5	8	2
McOwen	.978	106	168	9	4	2
Peguero	.928	79	165	15	14	2

CLINTON LUMBERKINGS — LOW CLASS A

MIDWEST LEAGUE

Batting	B-T	HT	WT	DOB	AVG	vLH	vRH	G	AB	R	H	2B	3B	HR	RBI	BB	HBP	SH	SF	SO	SB	CS	SLG	OBP
Almonte, Denny	B-R	6-2	187	9-24-88	.232	.200	.247	108	409	58	95	23	5	13	58	25	1	8	2	148	14	6	.408	.277
Baez, Fleming	R-R	6-0	170	6-10-81	.273	.125	.667	6	11	0	3	0	0	0	1	3	0	0	0	3	0	0	.273	.429
Billingsley, Ben	L-R	5-11	185	10-27-86	.143	.000	.182	5	14	1	2	1	0	0	1	1	0	0	0	2	0	0	.214	.200
Bladergroen, Ian	L-L	6-5	210	2-23-83	.230	.176	.241	25	100	8	23	6	1	0	14	5	0	0	1	18	1	0	.310	.264
Britton, Dwight	B-R	6-0	170	7-17-87	.192	.167	.200	11	26	3	5	0	0	0	1	4	0	1	0	8	3	0	.192	.300
Carroll, Dan	R-R	6-1	175	1-6-89	.220	.203	.227	75	254	37	56	8	2	2	22	21	12	3	0	76	22	9	.291	.310
Contreras, Henry	R-R	5-11	208	5-5-86	.167	.000	.222	4	12	0	2	2	0	0	2	2	1	0	0	1	0	0	.333	.333
Diaz, Ogui	R-R	6-2	170	12-1-85	.207	.241	.187	44	145	14	30	6	1	1	11	3	0	3	1	27	7	4	.283	.221
Dickey, Gavin	R-R	5-11	200	9-29-83	.188	.143	.222	5	16	2	3	1	1	0	0	2	1	0	0	8	1	0	.375	.316
Dotel, Welington	R-R	6-1	180	10-2-85	.286	.500	.200	19	49	9	14	5	0	1	11	5	1	0	3	11	5	2	.449	.345
Extrano, Jetsy	B-R	6-1	175	8-13-88	.045	.000	.067	6	22	2	1	0	0	0	1	2	0	0	0	10	1	0	.045	.160
Fuentes, Juan	R-R	6-1	170	1-28-86	.200	.250	.190	8	25	0	5	0	1	0	3	2	0	0	0	5	0	0	.280	.259
Hansen, Shaver	B-R	6-0	185	12-19-87	.205	.212	.202	36	122	17	25	7	2	0	7	15	4	1	0	38	6	0	.295	.312
Howell, Travis	R-R	6-2	205	1-19-85	.205	.148	.224	66	210	29	43	10	0	8	29	27	4	5	3	61	2	0	.367	.303
Johnson, Tommy	R-R	5-11	215	3-14-86	.167	.286	.091	5	18	2	3	0	0	0	2	0	0	0	0	8	0	0	.167	.250
Martinez, Mario	R-R	6-1	208	11-13-89	.214	.219	.212	61	229	20	49	13	2	2	24	11	5	6	1	51	1	0	.314	.264
Mendez, Maximo	L-L	6-2	150	11-24-86	.213	.213	.213	64	211	38	45	3	8	2	21	31	5	4	1	79	20	7	.332	.327
Moss, Steve	R-R	6-2	200	1-12-84	.238	.250	.228	43	143	14	34	9	0	4	26	15	3	3	4	34	2	1	.385	.315
Nunez, Israel	R-R	6-1	200	9-1-85	.195	.083	.241	11	41	1	8	0	0	0	3	0	3	0	0	8	0	0	.195	.250
Nunez, Luis	R-R	6-0	170	12-31-86	.284	.322	.271	115	429	57	122	14	0	1	33	20	2	11	3	70	20	15	.324	.317
Ochoa, Blake	R-R	6-0	180	9-5-85	.318	.311	.321	54	173	25	55	9	2	5	31	14	6	4	5	35	0	1	.480	.369
Royster, Ryan	L-L	6-1	170	10-13-85	.333	.200	.364	8	27	5	9	3	0	2	7	3	0	0	0	8	2	2	.667	.400
Sams, Kalian	R-R	6-3	220	8-25-86	.161	.316	.081	16	56	4	9	3	2	1	6	5	0	1	0	25	0	0	.339	.230
Sanchez, Kris	L-L	6-3	220	1-9-84	.291	.247	.309	72	254	34	74	20	1	10	41	40	4	0	4	69	0	0	.496	.391
Savastano, Scott	R-R	6-4	190	6-12-86	.300	.298	.301	112	413	67	124	15	5	6	53	56	7	2	3	74	12	1	.404	.390
Seager, Kyle	L-R	5-10	175	11-3-87	.275	.250	.279	41	153	17	42	8	0	1	22	22	0	0	3	20	4	2	.346	.360
Serrano, Terry	B-R	6-1	165	2-6-87	.236	.209	.248	75	216	40	51	6	4	1	22	53	2	11	1	69	18	5	.315	.390
Shaffer, Jake	L-L	6-1	190	8-16-87	.285	.265	.290	97	355	46	101	23	2	7	45	17	1	7	1	63	7	6	.420	.318
Tenbrink, Nate	L-R	6-2	202	12-21-86	.282	.275	.285	126	457	76	129	24	7	10	59	47	10	6	7	104	14	4	.431	.357

Pitching

Pitching	B-T	HT	WT	DOB	W	L	ERA	G	GS	CG	SV	IP	H	R	ER	HR	BB	SO	AVG	vLH	vRH	K/9	BB/9
Carraway, Andrew	R-R	6-2	200	9-4-86	4	0	2.50	7	7	0	0	40	36	11	11	0	5	39	.240	.230	.250	8.85	1.13
Cleto, Maikel	R-R	6-3	220	5-1-89	0	3	5.33	8	8	0	0	25	35	20	15	4	11	24	.321	.333	.313	8.53	3.91
Cooper, Daniel	R-R	6-3	205	11-6-86	0	1	9.28	8	0	0	0	11	18	12	11	1	5	11	.375	.412	.355	9.28	4.22
Esquibel, Andres	R-R	6-1	215	7-13-86	1	1	4.91	8	1	0	0	11	14	7	6	0	5	5	.318	.389	.269	4.09	4.09
Flores, Ruben	R-R	6-4	170	5-19-84	2	2	2.30	36	0	0	18	43	25	15	11	1	28	53	.166	.155	.172	11.09	5.86
Hann, Cheyne	R-R	6-6	235	9-17-84	2	2	1.32	51	0	0	12	68	48	12	10	2	8	74	.196	.211	.187	9.75	1.05
Harben, Adam	R-R	6-5	210	8-19-83	1	1	3.86	8	6	0	0	33	34	19	14	1	13	23	.264	.277	.256	6.34	3.58
Hensley, Steven	R-R	6-3	180	12-27-86	4	0	0.00	4	3	0	0	20	18	4	0	0	0	16	.250	.240	.255	7.32	0.00
Hesketh, John	L-L	6-0	175	6-3-86	1	1	12.60	3	1	0	0	5	10	7	7	1	1	6	.385	.375	.389	10.80	1.80
Jimenez, Jose	L-L	6-0	180	3-23-87	4	2	3.38	45	0	0	1	61	72	35	23	4	32	57	.289	.214	.327	8.36	4.70
Josselyn, Brandon	L-R	6-0	200	8-22-86	0	1	0.75	14	0	0	3	24	14	3	2	0	6	18	.177	.130	.196	6.75	2.25
Kasparek, Kenn	R-R	6-8	200	9-23-85	10	6	2.41	26	26	1	0	142	126	50	38	5	32	134	.236	.216	.248	8.51	2.03
Kirkland, Chris	R-R	6-4	220	10-6-85	0	1	5.00	4	0	0	0	9	5	5	1	5	1	5	.156	.077	.211	9.00	5.00
LaFromboise, Bobby	L-L	6-4	190	6-25-86	8	9	4.03	33	19	0	0	138	146	66	62	11	31	119	.275	.279	.273	7.74	2.02
Lorin, Brett	L-R	6-7	245	3-31-87	5	4	2.44	16	16	0	0	89	61	29	24	9	25	87	.192	.185	.196	8.83	2.54
Meyer, Keith	L-R	6-4	180	2-10-86	0	1	7.20	5	0	0	1	5	7	4	4	1	2	4	.318	.667	.188	7.20	3.60
2-team total (3 Lansing)					0	1	7.36	8	0	0	1	11	15	9	9	2	3	9	—	—	—	7.36	2.45
Moorer, Ryan	R-R	6-2	205	3-2-86	3	1	3.05	32	0	0	1	44	53	21	15	2	22	21	.310	.300	.315	4.26	4.47
Moran, Brian	L-L	6-3	185	9-30-88	0	3	2.89	12	0	0	0	19	14	7	6	0	7	17	.212	.200	.217	8.20	3.38
Moviel, Greg	L-L	6-6	220	12-19-84	2	3	4.58	30	0	0	0	35	25	22	18	0	34	29	.198	.216	.187	7.39	8.66
Nation, Blake	R-R	6-8	218	5-16-87	3	5	3.16	40	4	0	0	83	79	40	29	6	23	55	.251	.267	.241	5.99	2.50
Penney, Stephen	R-R	6-7	240	8-14-86	2	1	3.38	18	0	0	0	27	31	12	10	1	2	17	.284	.313	.273	5.74	0.68
Pribanic, Aaron	R-R	6-4	200	9-1-86	7	6	3.21	17	17	0	0	87	76	41	31	1	26	54	.231	.245	.220	5.59	2.69
Renfree, Matt	R-R	6-8	220	1-16-85	3	2	2.60	27	0	0	0	35	34	19	10	2	11	44	.239	.216	.253	11.42	2.86
Saito, Derrick	L-L	5-9	155	12-26-87	0	1	3.86	13	2	0	0	26	26	14	11	1	11	25	.255	.176	.294	8.77	3.86
2-team total (22 Burlington)					2	7	4.06	35	2	0	2	78	76	45	35	5	26	78	—	—	—	9.04	3.01
Suriel, Walter	R-R	6-2	190	7-21-86	0	4	6.61	9	6	0	0	33	34	28	24	6	15	32	.262	.304	.230	8.82	4.13
Vasquez, Anthony	L-L	6-0	175	9-19-86	3	3	5.66	7	7	0	0	35	47	25	22	2	8	24	.333	.283	.364	6.17	2.06
Venegas, Alfredo	R-R	6-1	180	5-11-86	4	4	4.33	14	14	0	0	69	88	49	33	8	24	46	.311	.320	.306	6.03	3.15

Fielding

Catcher	PCT	G	PO	A	E	DP	PB
Baez	.960	5	24	0	1	0	0
Contreras	.967	4	24	5	1	0	2
Fuentes	.949	8	51	5	3	0	3
Howell	.985	65	478	58	8	9	12
Johnson	.968	5	27	3	1	0	1
Nunez	.980	11	89	7	2	1	1
Ochoa	.990	52	362	33	4	5	5
Savastano	1.000	2	1	0	0	0	0

First Base	PCT	G	PO	A	E	DP
Bladergroen	.985	14	128	4	2	16
Howell	1.000	1	5	0	0	1
Martinez	.981	11	100	4	2	6
Ochoa	.833	3	5	0	1	2
Sanchez	1.000	19	165	12	0	11
Savastano	.990	45	382	29	4	28
Tenbrink	.988	56	379	27	5	33

Second Base	PCT	G	PO	A	E	DP
Billingsley	.857	2	2	4	1	1
Diaz	.940	15	27	36	4	10

	PCT	G	PO	A	E	DP
Hansen	.889	2	6	2	1	1
Nunez	.956	103	198	283	22	56
Savastano	1.000	2	0	1	0	1
Seager	.971	16	32	35	2	14
Serrano	1.000	1	2	3	0	0
Tenbrink	1.000	1	1	5	0	0

Third Base	PCT	G	PO	A	E	DP
Diaz	1.000	3	0	3	0	0
Hansen	.857	18	12	24	6	2
Martinez	.895	42	37	74	13	6
Nunez	.778	2	3	4	2	0
Savastano	.857	11	6	12	3	2
Seager	.947	14	12	24	2	2
Tenbrink	.895	56	51	119	20	9

Shortstop	PCT	G	PO	A	E	DP
Billingsley	1.000	4	3	6	0	0
Diaz	.947	23	28	62	5	4
Extrano	.969	6	10	21	1	5
Hansen	.903	15	22	34	6	6
Martinez	1.000	1	0	1	0	1

	PCT	G	PO	A	E	DP
Nunez	.963	5	11	15	1	4
Savastano	.961	20	21	52	3	9
Seager	.929	10	15	24	3	8
Serrano	.935	65	80	166	17	35
Tenbrink	.833	2	2	8	2	2

Outfield	PCT	G	PO	A	E	DP
Almonte	.987	106	224	11	3	4
Britton	1.000	9	12	0	0	0
Carroll	.965	75	131	6	5	1
Dickey	1.000	3	3	0	0	0
Dotel	.917	15	21	1	2	0
Mendez	.969	61	119	8	4	2
Moss	.966	33	56	1	2	0
Ochoa	—		1	0	0	0
Royster	1.000	8	18	0	0	0
Sams	1.000	11	18	0	0	0
Savastano	1.000	17	25	1	0	1
Serrano	1.000	11	17	1	0	0
Shaffer	.992	75	125	1	1	0
Tenbrink	.882	14	15	0	2	0

EVERETT AQUASOX

SHORT-SEASON

NORTHWEST LEAGUE

Batting	B-T	HT	WT	DOB	AVG	vLH	vRH	G	AB	R	H	2B	3B	HR	RBI	BB	HBP	SH	SF	SO	SB	CS	SLG	OBP
Avila, Gerardo	L-L	6-2	185	7-15-86	.333	.289	.343	54	213	32	71	10	2	13	54	12	2	0	4	49	0	0	.582	.368
Bantz, Brandon	R-R	6-1	211	1-7-87	.290	.500	.229	19	62	16	18	8	1	3	15	5	6	0	0	8	0	0	.597	.397
Bello, Fred	R-R	5-10	165	10-6-87	.200	—	.200	3	10	3	2	2	0	0	0	3	0	0	0	5	0	0	.400	.385
Benitez, Deybis	R-R	6-2	170	4-23-87	.231	.000	.300	4	13	2	3	0	0	0	2	2	0	0	0	1	0	0	.231	.333
Billingsley, Ben	L-R	5-11	185	10-27-86	.280	.250	.285	60	211	37	59	10	2	6	25	25	0	2	0	50	11	4	.431	.356
Cerione, Matt	L-L	6-2	192	1-4-88	.266	.147	.295	43	173	28	46	10	2	7	14	20	2	0	0	46	2	2	.468	.349
Coleman, Trevor	B-R	6-1	205	1-19-88	.184	.200	.180	32	114	11	21	4	1	2	13	17	3	0	0	24	0	0	.289	.306
Dotel, Welington	R-R	6-1	180	10-2-85	.341	.389	.328	46	170	31	58	10	2	6	24	6	7	4	1	40	7	5	.529	.386
Franklin, Nick	B-R	6-1	170	3-2-91	.400	.500	.389	6	20	4	8	2	1	0	1	0	0	0	2	1	0	.600	.429
Fuentes, Juan	R-R	6-1	170	1-28-86	.267	.281	.264	49	176	26	47	9	1	4	24	20	1	3	1	29	2	1	.398	.343
Gebbers, Hawkins	R-R	6-2	205	7-29-86	.301	.286	.305	54	209	30	63	13	0	2	21	16	3	2	0	34	0	4	.392	.360
Jones, James	R-R	6-4	195	9-24-88	.311	.333	.305	45	164	28	51	12	2	3	24	19	3	0	0	40	0	3	.463	.392
Mailloux, Kevin	R-R	6-0	200	3-5-86	.286	1.000	.231	4	14	3	4	2	0	0	2	1	0	0	0	1	1	0	.429	.333
Martinez, Mario	R-R	6-1	208	11-13-89	.308	.333	.302	71	302	45	93	20	5	3	33	11	4	0	1	59	4	0	.437	.340
Nunez, Israel	R-R	6-2	200	9-1-85	.250	—	.250	3	4	0	1	0	0	0	1	0	0	0	0	0	0	0	.250	.400
Phillips, Anthony	R-R	5-9	160	4-11-90	.247	.291	.234	68	239	29	59	8	3	7	28	14	3	3	2	65	3	8	.393	.295
Rivero, Jose	R-R	6-2	180	1-8-90	.251	.196	.269	62	207	35	52	10	3	4	32	23	4	2	2	66	8	8	.386	.335

Player	B-T	HT	WT	DOB	AVG	vLH	vRH	G	AB	R	H	2B	3B	HR	RBI	BB	HBP	SH	SF	SO	SB	CS	SLG	OBP
Royster, Ryan	L-L	6-1	170	10-13-85	.325	.318	.326	41	151	38	49	11	2	7	27	22	2	3	1	39	8	3	.563	.415
Sams, Kalian	R-R	6-3	220	8-25-86	.375	—	.375	4	16	5	6	1	0	3	6	1	0	0	0	7	2	0	1.000	.412
Trinkler, Blake	R-R	6-0	200	4-19-88	.229	.200	.241	41	118	12	27	9	2	2	18	13	2	0	1	43	0	1	.390	.313
Welsh, Guy	R-R	6-3	226	5-15-85	.271	.364	.243	16	48	5	13	6	0	1	8	9	1	0	1	10	0	0	.458	.390
Yepez, Mario	B-R	6-2	160	6-15-88	.000	—	.000	2	4	0	0	0	0	0	0	0	0	0	0	2	0	0	.000	.000

Pitching	B-T	HT	WT	DOB	W	L	ERA	G	GS	CG	SV	IP	H	R	ER	HR	BB	SO	AVG	vLH	vRH	K/9	BB/9
Brown, Kyle	R-L	6-2	210	1-2-86	1	0	14.73	6	0	0	0	7	10	13	12	0	13	5	.333	.333	.333	6.14	15.95
Burnett, Luke	R-R	6-8	260	12-10-86	2	4	4.66	14	0	0	0	66	69	45	34	8	42	52	.275	.313	.243	7.13	5.76
Carraway, Andrew	R-R	6-2	200	9-4-86	4	0	1.44	10	3	0	1	25	15	7	4	4	4	31	.174	.216	.143	11.16	1.44
Cooper, Daniel	R-R	6-3	205	11-6-86	0	1	4.41	17	0	0	8	16	21	8	8	2	7	17	.318	.364	.295	9.37	3.86
Cordero, Chad	R-R	6-0	225	3-18-82	0	2	11.74	8	0	0	1	8	13	10	10	2	2	7	.406	.563	.250	8.22	2.35
Czyz, Nick	L-L	6-2	215	4-10-87	2	2	3.34	5	5	0	0	30	25	12	11	1	11	31	.229	.381	.193	9.40	3.34
Esquibel, Andres	R-R	6-1	215	7-13-86	2	4	5.00	10	9	1	0	54	58	37	30	6	15	36	.278	.315	.248	6.00	2.50
Hernandez, Eddy	L-L	6-3	170	8-4-84	0	1	6.14	14	0	0	0	15	18	18	10	3	20	16	.295	.500	.222	9.82	12.27
Hesketh, John	L-L	6-0	175	6-5-86	1	0	1.67	7	4	0	0	27	18	6	5	1	4	39	.188	.304	.151	13.00	1.33
Kirkland, Chris	R-R	6-4	220	10-6-85	4	5	4.83	15	15	0	0	86	79	48	46	7	32	85	.242	.241	.243	8.93	3.36
Lewis, Taylor	R-R	6-4	190	6-2-88	3	1	7.82	5	5	0	0	25	29	22	22	7	10	17	.284	.393	.243	6.04	3.55
Martinez, Fray	R-R	6-3	170	5-20-89	0	0	4.98	15	0	0	1	22	24	13	12	2	11	18	.286	.320	.271	7.48	4.57
Moorer, Ryan	R-R	6-2	205	3-2-86	1	2	5.51	4	4	0	0	16	22	11	10	1	4	6	.355	.345	.364	3.31	2.20
Pullen, Brandon	L-L	6-4	200	12-7-85	3	3	4.73	25	0	0	1	32	42	19	17	5	8	30	.304	.268	.320	8.35	2.23
Reid, Brad	R-R	6-1	185	1-18-88	4	3	3.86	28	0	0	1	40	55	23	17	5	11	32	.335	.276	.368	7.26	2.50
Rios, Jose	L-L	5-10	178	3-2-90	1	2	3.35	23	1	0	1	38	34	22	14	1	17	37	.228	.146	.267	8.84	4.06
Roy, Philip	R-R	6-4	195	7-29-87	2	2	5.72	19	0	0	0	28	29	19	18	2	12	32	.259	.286	.243	10.16	5.40
Silva, Carlos	R-R	6-4	250	4-23-79	0	0	9.00	1	1	0	0	1	3	2	1	0	0	3	.429	.000	.600	27.00	0.00
Staehely, Christian	R-R	6-4	205	9-28-85	4	2	3.16	21	0	0	1	31	26	11	11	0	9	40	.228	.273	.200	11.49	2.59
Stanton, Taylor	R-R	6-2	230	1-15-88	5	3	3.50	15	15	0	0	87	82	48	34	9	25	81	.248	.241	.252	8.35	2.58
Valdez, Eric	R-R	6-1	195	5-4-87	0	0	3.38	9	0	0	0	13	13	6	5	2	7	13	.250	.259	.240	8.78	4.72

Fielding

Catcher	PCT	G	PO	A	E	DP	PB
Bantz	1.000	16	109	8	0	3	2
Coleman	.988	28	221	25	3	0	6
Fuentes	.995	21	181	23	1	5	2
Nunez	1.000	3	15	1	0	0	0
Welsh	1.000	14	104	9	0	1	4

First Base	PCT	G	PO	A	E	DP
Avila	.984	52	397	25	7	39
Fuentes	1.000	3	17	2	0	1
Jones	.984	7	60	2	1	7
Trinkler	1.000	20	165	8	0	15

Second Base	PCT	G	PO	A	E	DP
Bello	1.000	3	4	3	0	1

	PCT	G	PO	A	E	DP
Benitez	1.000	2	3	1	0	0
Billingsley	.953	27	35	67	5	16
Gebbers	.973	46	79	100	5	25
Mailloux	.905	4	8	11	2	3
Trinkler	1.000	1	1	3	0	1

Third Base	PCT	G	PO	A	E	DP
Billingsley	.933	5	2	12	1	0
Gebbers	.813	6	5	8	3	0
Martinez	.916	63	44	120	15	14
Trinkler	.864	7	5	14	3	0

Shortstop	PCT	G	PO	A	E	DP
Billingsley	.968	8	13	17	1	3
Franklin	.842	6	5	11	3	3

	PCT	G	PO	A	E	DP
Phillips	.964	67	113	206	12	45

Outfield	PCT	G	PO	A	E	DP
Billingsley	.944	12	14	3	1	1
Cerione	.951	43	74	4	4	0
Dotel	.954	45	79	4	4	1
Jones	.946	34	64	6	4	0
Rivero	.977	56	83	2	2	0
Royster	.984	40	53	7	1	1
Sams	1.000	4	9	0	0	0
Trinkler	.875	7	6	1	1	0
Yepez	—	1	0	0	0	0

PULASKI MARINERS
APPALACHIAN LEAGUE

ROOKIE

Batting	B-T	HT	WT	DOB	AVG	vLH	vRH	G	AB	R	H	2B	3B	HR	RBI	BB	HBP	SH	SF	SO	SB	CS	SLG	OBP
Bantz, Brandon	R-R	6-1	211	1-7-87	.231	.125	.278	10	26	6	6	2	0	0	1	6	3	0	0	5	0	0	.308	.429
Baron, Steve	R-R	6-0	195	12-7-90	.179	.143	.192	30	106	12	19	6	0	2	13	7	2	0	1	38	0	0	.292	.241
Bello, Fred	R-R	5-10	165	10-6-87	.250	.277	.235	42	132	22	33	5	5	2	12	14	0	3	1	38	8	7	.409	.320
Britton, Dwight	B-R	6-0	170	7-17-87	.288	.254	.308	44	163	33	47	8	0	7	23	11	6	3	2	45	13	5	.466	.352
Burgess, Jarrett	R-R	6-2	180	8-10-90	.187	.241	.165	60	193	31	36	3	1	5	22	20	6	0	1	76	12	7	.290	.282
Catricala, Vinnie	R-R	6-2	210	10-31-88	.301	.310	.297	59	219	33	66	14	2	8	40	18	5	1	3	34	6	1	.493	.363
DeJesus, Jharmidy	R-R	6-3	185	8-30-89	.249	.263	.241	48	169	19	42	7	2	4	24	14	10	0	1	43	0	2	.385	.340
Familia, Emmanuel	R-R	6-2	190	2-5-87	.235	.294	.216	24	68	7	16	4	0	2	9	3	0	1	1	30	0	0	.382	.264
Fonseca, Alexis	R-R	6-1	215	1-4-84	.000	—	.000	1	4	0	0	0	0	0	0	0	0	0	0	2	0	0	.000	.000
Fuentes, Cesar	R-R	6-0	180	4-12-87	.261	.245	.268	48	161	16	42	8	0	4	20	15	0	4	0	44	2	2	.385	.324
Haveman, Brandon	L-R	5-9	165	6-21-86	.339	.431	.298	49	165	33	56	9	4	5	18	18	1	3	1	26	4	3	.533	.405
Johnson, Tommy	R-R	5-11	215	3-14-86	.361	.250	.415	21	61	8	22	5	0	0	8	8	0	1	0	9	0	0	.443	.435
McGonigle, Mark	R-R	6-3	205	8-6-85	.283	.205	.315	41	152	15	43	8	1	2	14	10	1	0	0	39	6	3	.388	.331
Morban, Julio	L-L	6-1	190	2-13-92	.333	.000	.375	4	9	3	3	1	0	0	0	1	0	0	0	3	0	0	.444	.400
Morris, Tim	L-L	6-3	220	12-11-87	.214	.179	.226	50	154	18	33	4	0	4	24	17	9	0	2	39	0	0	.318	.324
Noriega, Gabriel	R-R	6-2	190	10-31-90	.311	.386	.282	61	206	27	64	14	2	4	26	16	1	4	2	60	8	6	.456	.360
van Heydoorn, Rudy	R-R	6-3	180	4-17-89	.071	.000	.083	4	14	1	1	0	0	0	1	0	0	0	0	6	0	0	.071	.133
Waddell, Greg	L-R	6-1	210	5-5-87	.195	.050	.246	27	77	10	15	2	1	2	6	10	0	0	0	34	1	2	.325	.287

Pitching	B-T	HT	WT	DOB	W	L	ERA	G	GS	CG	SV	IP	H	R	ER	HR	BB	SO	AVG	vLH	vRH	K/9	BB/9
Buckborough, Colin	R-R	6-5	185	4-6-89	2	0	8.38	13	0	0	1	19	29	20	18	1	17	16	.358	.424	.313	7.45	7.91
Chang, Yao Wen	R-R	6-2	202	10-31-90	0	6	5.89	13	9	0	0	44	62	45	29	7	17	30	.330	.329	.330	6.09	3.45
Cloud, Brian	R-R	6-4	200	12-2-85	1	1	5.40	16	0	0	1	30	28	20	18	6	13	27	.246	.368	.184	8.10	3.90
de Haas, Jeroen	R-R	6-5	175	1-1-91	0	0	8.10	3	0	0	0	7	11	6	6	2	2	3	.355	.429	.294	4.05	2.70
Diaz, Nolan	R-R	6-1	175	3-28-91	1	2	4.85	5	5	0	0	26	31	18	14	3	4	22	.282	.297	.274	7.62	1.38
Gillheeney, Jimmy	L-L	6-1	200	11-8-87	0	3	4.84	6	4	0	0	22	23	13	12	3	7	21	.264	.222	.275	8.46	2.82
Haas, Kyle	R-R	6-5	215	8-20-87	1	0	4.05	2	2	0	0	7	7	3	3	0	3	5	.292	.500	.250	6.75	4.05

Name	B-T	HT	WT	DOB	W	L	ERA	G	GS	CG	SV	IP	H	R	ER	HR	BB	SO	AVG	vLH	vRH	K/9	BB/9
Housey, John	L-R	6-4	180	6-4-88	3	2	2.62	8	8	0	0	45	32	15	13	3	17	47	.194	.225	.170	9.47	3.43
Josselyn, Brandon	L-R	6-3	200	8-22-86	0	1	3.18	8	0	0	1	17	15	9	6	0	6	18	.227	.280	.195	9.53	3.18
Lewis, Taylor	R-R	6-4	190	6-2-88	0	1	7.71	1	1	0	0	2	3	2	2	0	2	3	.273	.667	.125	11.57	7.71
Maurer, Brandon	R-R	6-5	200	7-3-90	3	4	3.61	13	12	1	0	67	67	36	27	4	18	51	.266	.260	.270	6.82	2.41
Merry, Jorden	R-R	6-1	190	6-30-87	2	1	3.06	16	0	0	5	35	30	14	12	1	14	45	.231	.245	.221	11.46	3.57
Moran, Brian	L-L	6-3	185	9-30-88	1	0	3.72	6	0	0	2	10	6	5	4	0	2	14	.167	.000	.240	13.03	1.86
Ortiz, Richard	L-L	6-2	185	11-26-87	1	2	5.67	16	1	0	0	27	36	23	17	2	14	38	.321	.270	.347	12.67	4.67
Rodriguez, Leonardo	R-R	6-2	185	4-15-88	0	2	8.68	6	5	0	0	19	26	20	18	2	19	17	.351	.371	.333	8.20	9.16
Sorce, Chris	R-R	6-0	190	10-28-87	2	1	3.45	7	0	0	1	16	17	6	6	0	7	22	.293	.231	.344	12.64	4.02
Suda, Kenta	R-R	6-0	172	7-22-89	3	2	4.76	11	5	0	0	34	42	24	18	6	10	31	.294	.259	.315	8.21	2.65
Thomas, Eric	R-R	5-11	170	10-8-86	0	1	6.75	3	0	0	0	4	3	4	3	1	1	3	.214	.000	.333	6.75	2.25
Tome, Jean	R-R	6-2	200	9-5-89	3	4	5.18	11	10	0	0	49	48	32	28	5	17	54	.262	.250	.270	9.99	3.14
Valdez, Eric	R-R	6-1	195	5-4-87	1	0	4.09	13	0	0	4	22	25	10	10	4	7	32	.284	.333	.255	13.09	2.86
Vasquez, Anthony	L-L	6-0	175	9-19-86	2	1	3.80	8	2	0	2	24	20	13	10	2	8	27	.225	.280	.203	10.27	3.04
Witten, Kyle	R-R	6-4	175	9-14-88	1	2	13.50	7	0	0	0	9	18	14	14	1	7	17	.409	.455	.333	16.39	6.75

Fielding

Catcher	PCT	G	PO	A	E	DP	PB
Bantz	1.000	9	68	9	0	2	0
Baron	.979	25	214	22	5	3	4
Familia	.994	21	152	19	1	0	6
Fonseca	1.000	1	11	3	0	0	1
Johnson	.982	14	102	7	2	0	6

First Base	PCT	G	PO	A	E	DP
Bantz	1.000	1	8	0	0	1
DeJesus	.961	30	220	24	10	15
Fuentes	1.000	2	1	1	0	0
Morris	.984	37	232	16	4	15

Second Base	PCT	G	PO	A	E	DP
Bello	.948	31	50	59	6	8
Fuentes	.947	37	64	79	8	18
Noriega	—	1	0	0	0	0

Third Base	PCT	G	PO	A	E	DP
Catricala	.904	53	34	79	12	4
DeJesus	1.000	2	2	2	0	0
Fuentes	.727	6	3	5	3	0
van Heydoorn	.600	4	0	3	2	0

Shortstop	PCT	G	PO	A	E	DP
Bello	.750	6	3	12	5	0

	PCT	G	PO	A	E	DP
Fuentes	1.000	2	0	1	0	0
Noriega	.960	60	87	180	11	30

Outfield	PCT	G	PO	A	E	DP
Bello	1.000	2	5	0	0	0
Britton	.940	41	59	4	4	1
Burgess	.933	59	122	4	9	1
Haveman	.908	38	66	3	7	2
McGonigle	.942	37	43	6	3	1
Morban	1.000	1	3	0	0	0
Waddell	.892	18	31	2	4	0

AZL MARINERS   ROOKIE

ARIZONA LEAGUE

Batting	B-T	HT	WT	DOB	AVG	vLH	vRH	G	AB	R	H	2B	3B	HR	RBI	BB	HBP	SH	SF	SO	SB	CS	SLG	OBP
Angelo, Mark	R-L	6-2	195	7-15-86	.272	.250	.276	39	125	16	34	2	1	1	14	19	4	0	0	25	2	1	.328	.385
Carroll, Dan	R-R	6-1	175	1-6-89	.211	.000	.286	4	19	2	4	1	0	0	4	2	0	0	0	9	1	0	.263	.286
Cintron, Alex	B-R	6-2	210	12-17-78	.333	—	.333	3	6	1	2	1	0	0	0	2	0	0	0	1	1	0	.500	.500
Contreras, Henry	R-R	5-11	208	5-5-86	.423	.429	.421	21	52	6	22	6	1	2	13	7	4	0	0	9	1	1	.692	.524
Diaz, Juan	B-R	6-3	180	12-12-88	1.000	—	1.000	1	3	3	3	0	0	1	1	1	0	0	0	0	0	0	2.000	1.000
Extrano, Jetsy	B-R	6-1	175	8-13-88	.272	.235	.282	40	151	29	41	9	2	5	30	12	6	0	2	39	6	2	.457	.345
Fonseca, Alexis	R-R	6-1	215	1-4-84	.367	.333	.370	14	30	4	11	0	1	0	3	1	0	0	0	5	1	2	.433	.387
Franklin, Nick	B-R	6-1	170	3-2-91	.302	.375	.259	10	43	6	13	2	0	1	4	1	0	0	0	6	0	0	.419	.318
Halman, Greg	R-R	6-4	190	8-26-87	.182	.500	.111	3	11	1	2	0	1	0	2	2	0	0	0	8	0	0	.364	.308
Jacobo, Hector	R-R	6-5	190	9-15-89	.224	.333	.200	19	49	10	11	1	0	0	5	8	0	0	1	8	1	1	.245	.328
Jimenez, Hassiel	R-R	6-0	195	5-8-91	.277	.250	.280	28	83	12	23	8	0	0	11	8	3	1	0	24	2	3	.373	.362
Mailloux, Kevin	R-R	6-0	200	3-5-86	.311	.429	.285	46	151	29	47	14	5	5	37	16	6	1	1	33	8	2	.570	.397
McGonigle, Mark	R-R	6-3	205	8-6-85	.500	1.000	.400	3	6	1	3	2	0	0	1	2	0	0	0	0	0	0	.833	.625
Mendez, Joel	R-R	6-3	175	5-7-88	.207	.182	.210	30	92	11	19	1	1	2	9	4	0	1	0	32	5	1	.304	.240
Morban, Julio	L-L	6-1	190	2-13-92	.266	.233	.274	42	154	28	41	9	7	5	23	7	2	0	2	49	8	3	.513	.303
Morla, Ramon	B-R	6-1	175	11-20-89	.294	.286	.296	28	102	20	30	2	1	2	12	6	2	0	0	29	4	2	.392	.345
Nunez, Efrain	B-R	6-3	190	2-17-91	.195	.143	.206	39	128	19	25	5	3	1	12	10	1	0	0	55	3	1	.305	.259
Nunez, Israel	R-R	6-1	200	9-1-85	.222	.000	.250	3	9	1	2	1	0	0	2	1	0	0	0	3	0	0	.333	.300
Poythress, Rich	R-R	6-4	235	8-11-87	.300	.000	.316	6	20	4	6	0	0	1	6	5	1	0	0	6	0	0	.450	.462
Rivero, Jose	R-R	6-2	180	1-8-90	.143	.000	.200	2	7	1	1	0	1	0	0	1	0	0	0	2	0	0	.429	.250
Rivers, Kevin	L-R	6-2	210	8-24-88	.231	.000	.300	16	52	10	12	5	0	2	4	8	2	0	0	18	2	1	.442	.355
Seager, Kyle	L-R	5-10	175	11-3-87	.000	—	.000	1	3	0	0	0	0	0	0	0	0	0	0	1	0	0	.000	.000
Sharpley, Evan	L-R	6-2	205	11-4-86	.333	.095	.378	37	132	31	44	12	2	7	29	21	2	0	1	46	5	2	.614	.429
Tanabe, Carlton	R-R	6-0	190	10-28-91	.220	.364	.167	20	41	2	9	2	0	0	4	4	0	0	1	7	1	0	.268	.283
Trinkler, Blake	R-R	6-0	200	4-19-88	.250	.000	.333	1	4	0	1	0	0	0	0	0	0	0	0	2	0	0	.250	.250
Triunfel, Carlos	R-R	5-11	175	2-27-90	.250	.286	.222	4	16	0	4	1	0	0	4	0	0	0	0	2	1	0	.313	.250
Tuiasosopo, Matt	R-R	6-2	225	5-10-86	.407	.333	.417	9	27	9	11	0	0	1	3	4	1	0	0	6	0	0	.519	.500
van Heydoorn, Rudy	B-R	6-3	180	4-17-89	.129	.056	.143	37	116	14	15	5	0	2	8	9	2	1	0	41	1	3	.224	.205
Yepez, Mario	B-R	6-2	160	6-15-88	.290	.293	.290	52	217	37	63	10	4	1	16	14	2	5	0	36	9	2	.387	.339
Zapata, Angel	R-R	6-2	185	11-25-87	.206	.300	.190	22	68	5	14	1	0	1	7	3	0	1	0	20	3	0	.250	.239

Pitching	B-T	HT	WT	DOB	W	L	ERA	G	GS	CG	SV	IP	H	R	ER	HR	BB	SO	AVG	vLH	vRH	K/9	BB/9
Breedlove, Jeff	R-R	6-0	200	5-17-87	2	1	1.52	20	0	0	10	30	23	9	5	0	3	29	.205	.222	.197	8.80	0.91
Brundridge, Tyler	R-R	0-0	0	10-28-86	1	1	7.80	12	0	0	0	15	22	15	13	0	9	10	.324	.500	.250	6.00	5.40
Celestino, Miguel	R-R	6-5	170	10-10-89	5	3	4.72	13	12	0	0	67	76	36	35	5	23	48	.293	.264	.308	6.48	3.11
Chang, Yao Wen	R-R	6-2	202	10-31-90	0	0	20.77	1	0	0	0	4	10	10	10	2	2	6	.435	.750	.368	12.46	4.15
Cleto, Maikel	R-R	6-3	220	5-1-89	0	1	13.50	1	0	0	0		3	6	1	0	1	1	.500	.000	.600	13.50	13.50
Cloud, Brian	R-R	6-4	200	12-2-85	0	0	0.00	1	0	0	0	1	0	0	0	0	0	4	.000	.000	.000	27.00	0.00
Cordero, Chad	R-R	6-0	225	3-18-82	0	1	6.75	6	6	0	0	7	10	5	5	0	3	8	.333	.438	.214	10.80	4.05
Cruz, Danny	R-R	6-0	180	4-20-89	0	0	0.00	3	0	0	0	3	1	0	0	0	2	6	.100	.000	.143	18.00	6.00
de Haas, Jeroen	R-R	6-5	175	1-1-91	1	0	12.08	11	0	0	0	13	20	18	17	2	4	8	.370	.250	.405	5.68	2.84

Name	B-T	HT	WT	DOB	W	L	ERA	G	GS	CG	SV	IP	H	R	ER	HR	BB	SO	AVG	vLH	vRH	K/9	BB/9
Esquibel, Andres	R-R	6-1	215	7-13-86	0	0	2.25	1	1	0	0	4	2	1	1	0	3	3	.154	—	.154	6.75	6.75
Fernandez, Anthony	L-L	6-4	180	6-8-90	5	3	3.40	13	2	0	0	53	56	30	20	0	13	53	.268	.326	.253	9.00	2.21
Franzblau, Jason	R-R	5-10	195	8-26-87	1	0	4.05	10	0	0	1	13	14	7	6	1	5	14	.280	.217	.333	9.45	3.38
Haas, Kyle	R-R	6-5	215	8-20-87	0	1	1.23	7	3	0	0	15	12	6	2	1	5	11	.218	.231	.214	6.75	3.07
Hall, Josh	R-R	6-2	190	12-16-80	0	1	0.00	3	3	0	0	5	6	4	0	1	0	4	.286	.222	.333	7.20	0.00
Hesketh, John	L-L	6-0	175	6-3-86	2	0	1.64	5	0	0	0	11	6	2	2	0	3	19	.158	.000	.167	15.55	2.45
Housey, John	L-R	6-4	180	6-4-88	3	1	2.96	6	5	0	0	27	20	10	9	1	8	32	.204	.160	.219	10.54	2.63
Hudson, Austin	R-R	6-4	185	1-6-88	1	1	5.25	8	0	0	0	12	15	10	7	0	1	5	.294	.176	.353	3.75	0.75
Jimenez, Cesar	L-L	5-11	220	11-12-84	0	1	3.00	5	4	0	0	6	8	3	2	0	2	8	.308	.250	.318	12.00	3.00
Kahn, Stephen	L-R	6-3	220	12-14-83	0	0	27.00	1	0	0	0	1	2	3	3	1	1	1	.400	.000	.667	9.00	9.00
Kelley, Shawn	R-R	6-2	215	4-26-84	0	0	0.00	2	2	0	0	2	0	0	0	0	0	3	.000	.000	.000	13.50	0.00
Kessinger, Chris	R-R	6-0	195	6-5-86	5	3	2.45	13	7	0	0	66	58	24	18	3	8	66	.241	.216	.247	9.00	1.09
Kitchen, Billy	R-R	6-4	190	9-4-87	1	0	0.00	5	0	0	0	6	3	3	0	0	0	6	.143	.000	.250	8.53	0.00
Martinez, Fray	R-R	6-3	170	5-20-89	0	0	1.80	3	0	0	0	5	3	1	1	0	2	8	.188	.500	.143	14.40	3.60
Merry, Jorden	R-R	6-1	190	6-30-87	0	0	3.38	1	0	0	0	3	0	1	1	0	2	4	.000	.000	.000	13.50	6.75
Mohr, Brooks	R-R	6-3	195	1-14-89	0	0	0.00	1	0	0	0	1	1	1	0	0	1	1	.250	.000	.333	9.00	9.00
Ortiz, Richard	L-L	6-2	185	11-26-87	0	1	10.13	2	0	0	0	3	4	3	3	0	5	4	.333	.500	.300	13.50	16.88
Otteman, Matt	R-R	6-1	210	11-2-86	0	1	1.88	16	0	0	1	24	22	7	5	0	5	28	.250	.344	.196	10.50	1.88
Pena, Luis	R-R	6-5	200	1-10-83	2	0	1.50	3	1	0	0	12	3	2	2	1	3	11	.081	.091	.077	8.25	2.25
Pineda, Michael	R-R	6-5	180	1-18-89	0	0	0.00	2	2	0	0	3	2	0	0	0	0	4	.200	.000	.222	12.00	0.00
Rodriguez, Leonardo	R-R	6-2	185	4-15-88	0	0	0.00	1	0	0	0	2	2	0	0	0	2	0	.286	.200	.500	9.00	0.00
Rohrbaugh, Robert	R-L	6-2	195	12-28-83	1	0	2.70	6	3	0	0	20	20	8	6	0	4	22	.263	.235	.271	9.90	1.80
Suda, Kenta	R-R	6-0	172	7-22-89	0	0	8.10	3	0	0	0	3	4	3	3	1	2	5	.286	.000	.308	13.50	5.40
Valdivia, Jose	R-R	6-4	195	3-19-92	0	1	9.95	7	0	0	0	6	9	7	7	1	2	1	.346	.167	.400	1.42	2.84
Witten, Kyle	R-R	6-4	175	9-14-88	0	0	1.50	4	0	0	1	6	2	1	1	0	1	6	.100	.167	.071	9.00	1.50
Zimmerman, Jeff	R-R	6-1	200	8-9-72	0	0	4.50	1	1	0	0	2	2	1	1	0	1	2	.222	.200	.250	9.00	4.50

Fielding

Catcher	PCT	G	PO	A	E	DP	PB
Contreras	.993	19	115	23	1	1	2
Fonseca	1.000	11	60	8	0	0	1
Jimenez	.953	28	189	16	10	1	10
Nunez	1.000	1	10	0	0	0	0
Tanabe	.982	18	98	9	2	1	4

First Base	PCT	G	PO	A	E	DP
Angelo	.993	17	142	10	1	9
Morla	1.000	4	36	1	0	2
Poythress	1.000	5	48	6	0	5
Sharpley	.989	29	256	16	3	26
van Heydoorn	.921	4	34	1	3	4

Second Base	PCT	G	PO	A	E	DP
Cintron	1.000	2	1	3	0	0
Extrano	1.000	3	5	10	0	0
Franklin	.875	3	5	9	2	0
Jacobo	1.000	9	9	16	0	4

	PCT	G	PO	A	E	DP
Mailloux	.971	41	78	90	5	25
Seager	1.000	1	1	0	0	0
Triunfel	—	1	0	0	0	0
Zapata	.897	6	12	14	3	5

Third Base	PCT	G	PO	A	E	DP
Angelo	—	1	0	0	0	0
Extrano	.909	4	1	9	1	1
Jacobo	.900	6	4	5	1	0
Morla	.875	12	6	22	4	1
Sharpley	.857	4	1	5	1	1
Trinkler	1.000	1	2	0	0	1
Tuiasosopo	.875	5	1	6	1	1
van Heydoorn	.914	32	17	68	8	4

Shortstop	PCT	G	PO	A	E	DP
Cintron	1.000	1	1	2	0	0
Diaz	1.000	1	2	3	0	0
Extrano	.977	32	48	125	4	23

	PCT	G	PO	A	E	DP
Franklin	.969	8	10	21	1	2
Mailloux	1.000	1	1	4	0	1
Morla	.931	11	17	37	4	8
Triunfel	1.000	3	3	3	0	0
Zapata	.500	1	0	1	1	0

Outfield	PCT	G	PO	A	E	DP
Angelo	.885	22	23	0	3	0
Carroll	1.000	4	5	0	0	0
McGonigle	1.000	1	2	0	0	0
Mendez	.941	28	31	1	2	0
Morban	.889	6	8	0	1	0
Nunez	.944	39	48	3	3	0
Rivero	1.000	2	2	0	0	0
Rivers	1.000	14	12	1	0	0
Yepez	.987	52	73	2	1	0
Zapata	.909	15	19	1	2	0

DSL MARINERS   ROOKIE

DOMINICAN SUMMER LEAGUE

Batting	B-T	HT	WT	DOB	AVG	vLH	vRH	G	AB	R	H	2B	3B	HR	RBI	BB	HBP	SH	SF	SO	SB	CS	SLG	OBP
Beltre, Marbin	B-R	6-3	180	3-30-90	.270	.333	.255	23	63	9	17	2	1	0	4	18	0	1	0	15	12	6	.333	.432
Brea, Ivan	R-R	6-2	190	7-5-88	.175	.231	.159	31	57	5	10	1	0	0	3	6	1	1	0	6	0	1	.193	.266
Brito, Bryan	R-R	6-2	170	2-16-92	.254	.308	.239	47	118	18	30	1	2	1	14	13	1	4	1	36	13	3	.322	.331
Carvajal, Ameilis	R-R	6-2	170	3-6-89	.218	.200	.225	41	110	18	24	5	1	0	8	14	1	3	3	39	4	3	.282	.305
Drullard, George	R-R	6-3	180	9-27-91	.277	.361	.248	53	137	25	38	7	0	0	16	24	1	3	0	27	14	12	.328	.389
Flores, Mario	R-R	6-3	195	10-9-87	.276	.357	.250	57	174	24	48	14	1	5	27	28	2	1	0	51	3	7	.454	.382
Garcia, Oliver	R-R	6-1	188	12-7-90	.136	.000	.214	6	22	1	3	1	0	0	0	1	0	0	0	8	0	0	.182	.174
Lara, Jordy	R-R	6-3	180	5-21-91	.202	.261	.187	50	114	21	23	6	2	2	18	32	3	5	0	31	6	3	.342	.389
Marcelino, Westlonder	R-R	6-4	200	3-2-91	.231	.167	.250	12	26	5	6	1	0	0	1	2	1	0	0	6	2	0	.385	.310
Marte, Augusto	R-R	6-2	190	8-17-89	.118	.154	.095	16	34	4	4	2	0	0	4	5	5	1	0	12	0	1	.176	.318
Martinez, Jose	R-R	6-1	180	7-22-92	.241	.260	.236	62	224	33	54	10	1	2	24	10	6	0	1	65	8	1	.321	.290
Matias, Luis	R-R	6-2	180	8-27-90	.135	.150	.130	34	74	8	10	2	0	0	2	14	2	0	0	15	9	3	.162	.289
Mercedes, Hector	R-R	6-1	200	11-10-87	.286	.227	.304	67	182	26	52	13	1	5	27	32	4	0	3	52	10	3	.451	.398
Ozuna, Victor	R-R	6-2	180	12-2-86	.221	.256	.210	61	163	36	36	6	1	4	13	24	4	2	1	51	13	4	.344	.333
Perez, Randy	R-R	6-3	180	2-23-89	.273	.333	.255	53	128	27	35	6	1	1	13	12	8	2	0	43	17	11	.359	.372
Rodriguez, Robert	R-R	6-4	180	7-22-90	.176	.094	.202	52	131	14	23	6	2	0	22	12	1	4	0	29	4	4	.252	.250
Sanchez, Miguel	R-R	6-2	180	9-27-91	.222	.400	.171	22	45	7	10	0	0	2	9	6	0	1	1	16	1	2	.356	.308
Sanon, Bertin	R-R	6-3	180	7-14-89	.195	.375	.152	22	41	4	8	2	0	0	7	0	0	1	1	13	4	1	.244	.306
Soto, George	R-R	6-2	190	11-19-89	.202	.240	.192	36	129	9	26	3	0	0	9	7	6	3	1	19	7	4	.225	.273
Wel, Axel	L-L	6-3	180	4-10-91	.179	.200	.174	50	117	13	21	1	2	0	12	14	1	1	1	17	3	2	.222	.276
Zorrilla, Janelfry	R-R	6-2	180	9-2-90	.257	.293	.246	58	175	30	45	6	2	4	18	12	4	2	2	35	13	4	.383	.316

SEATTLE MARINERS

Pitching	B-T	HT	WT	DOB	W	L	ERA	G	GS	CG	SV	IP	H	R	ER	HR	BB	SO	AVG	vLH	vRH	K/9	BB/9
Alcantara, Ariel	R-R	6-3	190	5-13-89	3	0	3.41	15	0	0	1	32	30	17	12	0	8	28	.242	.182	.264	7.96	2.27
Aquino, Gregorio	R-R	6-5	175	3-5-90	1	1	5.12	7	2	0	1	19	20	19	11	0	3	15	.256	.286	.254	6.98	1.40
Bravo, Oscar	L-L	6-0	210	4-19-92	0	0	15.43	6	0	0	0	9	17	16	16	5	6	6	.386	1.000	.341	5.79	5.79
Duarte, Victor	R-R	6-2	155	10-21-86	3	0	2.10	6	5	0	0	26	20	11	6	1	3	24	.206	.267	.195	8.42	1.05
Germocen, Nelson	R-R	6-5	200	9-16-88	3	1	0.41	17	0	0	12	22	8	5	1	0	14	32	.107	.150	.091	13.09	5.73
Hidalgo, Ambioris	R-R	6-2	196	2-4-91	4	2	2.51	15	14	0	0	68	56	23	19	1	26	75	.229	.219	.233	9.93	3.44
Martinez, Fray	R-R	6-3	170	5-20-89	0	0	1.74	9	0	0	0	21	15	5	4	0	4	33	.203	.167	.210	14.37	1.74
Mercedes, Bruno	R-R	6-3	170	10-6-88	6	1	1.65	25	0	0	2	55	38	14	10	1	13	53	.197	.286	.154	8.73	2.14
Mieses, George	R-R	6-2	180	5-3-91	5	4	2.19	16	15	1	0	70	59	26	17	1	22	79	.228	.333	.189	10.16	2.83
Nunez, Junior	R-R	6-3	210	3-1-92	3	5	3.18	15	11	0	0	62	47	31	22	3	21	44	.213	.232	.206	6.35	3.03
Perez, Henry	L-L	6-3	170	10-18-89	6	5	3.16	15	14	2	0	77	72	33	27	3	15	65	.241	.111	.249	7.60	1.75
Rosario, Enrique	R-R	6-1	180	6-23-91	6	1	2.82	20	0	0	2	51	47	23	16	1	17	48	.240	.368	.209	8.47	3.00
Vargas, Richard	R-R	6-3	170	4-19-91	7	3	1.69	17	6	0	0	64	50	20	12	1	23	49	.223	.243	.214	6.89	3.23
Vizcaino, Joan	R-R	6-6	195	4-25-89	0	0	7.59	7	0	0	0	11	9	10	9	0	7	9	.225	.333	.160	7.59	5.91
Yan, Fello	R-R	6-2	180	9-8-90	0	0	4.50	4	2	0	0	8	11	4	4	0	4	5	.344	.444	.304	5.63	4.50

Fielding

Catcher	PCT	G	PO	A	E	DP	PB
Brea	.973	31	153	28	5	1	6
Brito	1.000	1	0	1	0	0	0
Flores	.964	34	188	24	8	2	5
Mercedes	.984	25	164	18	3	2	3
Sanchez	.958	19	84	7	4	0	5

First Base	PCT	G	PO	A	E	DP
Flores	.978	27	172	8	4	8
Lara	.986	15	69	2	1	4
Marcelino	1.000	4	22	1	0	2
Mercedes	.985	33	191	8	3	13
Ozuna	.933	6	14	0	1	0
Wel	.981	27	144	12	3	12

Second Base	PCT	G	PO	A	E	DP
Carvajal	.976	8	21	19	1	5
Garcia	1.000	4	4	4	0	1

Martinez	1.000	2	3	2	0	0
Matias	.945	17	21	31	3	4
Ozuna	.924	22	37	36	6	7
Sanon	.636	5	3	4	4	0
Soto	.931	30	55	67	9	13

Third Base	PCT	G	PO	A	E	DP
Drullard	—	1	0	0	0	0
Garcia	.600	2	1	2	2	0
Lara	.878	22	19	53	10	2
Martinez	.896	42	32	80	13	9
Matias	.889	14	11	21	4	3
Ozuna	.667	3	0	6	3	0
Sanon	1.000	2	0	2	0	0
Soto	1.000	1	1	1	0	0

Shortstop	PCT	G	PO	A	E	DP
Brito	.921	46	48	104	13	10

Carvajal	.857	27	37	59	16	7
Drullard	—	1	0	0	0	0
Matias	1.000	3	0	1	0	0
Ozuna	1.000	1	1	1	0	0
Sanon	.860	12	12	25	6	4
Soto	1.000	2	2	1	0	0

Outfield	PCT	G	PO	A	E	DP
Beltre	1.000	21	28	0	0	0
Drullard	.987	46	71	4	1	1
Marte	.833	16	14	1	3	0
Ozuna	.941	15	15	1	1	0
Perez	.955	39	63	1	3	0
Rodriguez	.975	48	73	6	2	2
Wel	.875	14	18	3	3	1
Zorrilla	1.000	57	68	10	0	0

VSL MARINERS   ROOKIE
VENEZUELAN SUMMER LEAGUE

Batting	B-T	HT	WT	DOB	AVG	vLH	vRH	G	AB	R	H	2B	3B	HR	RBI	BB	HBP	SH	SF	SO	SB	CS	SLG	OBP
Acevedo, Michael	R-R	6-0	185	12-5-90	.263	.328	.238	67	236	38	62	17	3	3	34	25	7	1	6	33	4	2	.398	.343
Agudelo, Jorge	R-R	6-0	175	5-30-89	.272	.200	.296	64	217	39	59	14	3	1	30	23	10	3	0	32	11	5	.378	.368
Batista, Yidid	R-R	6-0	150	10-13-89	.238	.259	.226	36	80	22	19	2	0	1	12	14	2	2	0	8	4	2	.300	.365
Burin, Felipe	B-R	5-10	160	2-10-92	.203	.077	.227	39	79	11	16	3	0	0	9	8	0	3	0	9	0	2	.241	.276
Coronel, Ramon	R-R	5-11	155	2-2-92	.258	.222	.273	31	93	9	24	4	1	0	13	4	4	4	0	10	0	1	.323	.317
Diaz, Franklin	R-R	6-1	170	7-20-90	.245	.188	.270	22	53	8	13	1	0	0	7	11	0	2	0	10	0	1	.264	.375
Garcia, Eduardo	R-R	6-2	190	9-16-89	.157	.176	.151	29	70	8	11	1	0	0	4	4	1	0	2	22	1	0	.171	.208
Gonzalez, Larry	R-R	5-11	170	2-1-88	.324	.390	.296	42	139	16	45	10	0	4	30	10	1	4	0	18	0	1	.482	.373
Hart, Kenny	R-R	6-3	180	3-21-90	.276	.262	.280	56	174	32	48	8	3	3	16	30	9	4	1	47	4	1	.408	.407
Hernandez, Jose	R-R	6-1	165	1-12-88	.295	.250	.310	45	132	20	39	4	0	1	15	8	2	1	3	23	3	1	.348	.338
Lampe, Reginald	R-R	6-3	170	3-1-90	.244	.250	.242	37	90	8	22	5	2	0	9	9	2	1	1	21	2	4	.344	.324
Morillo, Junior	R-R	6-2	185	9-4-90	.208	.286	.176	14	24	3	5	1	0	1	3	0	5	0	0	10	0	0	.375	.345
Ramirez, Carlos	B-R	5-11	145	12-2-88	.336	.230	.376	65	226	43	76	17	1	2	36	35	7	4	1	29	4	1	.447	.439
Ramirez, Ivan	R-R	6-1	190	7-25-92	.315	.250	.338	57	200	32	63	13	1	2	37	15	11	1	1	28	2	0	.420	.392
Rangel, Rigoberto	R-R	6-1	167	6-21-89	.229	.220	.233	40	131	18	30	10	1	3	23	18	7	1	4	32	1	2	.389	.344
Torrealba, Rafael	R-R	6-2	175	9-5-89	.217	.196	.226	52	166	29	36	4	4	2	18	18	7	3	0	32	4	6	.325	.319
Ugueto, Jesus	R-R	6-0	170	5-30-91	.182	.300	.130	18	33	2	6	1	0	0	1	5	0	0	0	8	0	1	.212	.289
Velasquez, Roberto	B-R	5-11	160	2-14-90	.267	.286	.260	42	135	31	36	3	2	0	11	20	1	5	2	9	5	2	.319	.361

Pitching	B-T	HT	WT	DOB	W	L	ERA	G	GS	CG	SV	IP	H	R	ER	HR	BB	SO	AVG	vLH	vRH	K/9	BB/9
Campos, Jose	R-R	6-2	195	7-27-92	1	3	5.73	13	4	0	1	33	38	23	21	3	16	23	.297	.233	.316	6.27	4.36
Campos, Manuel	R-R	6-2	175	1-12-90	1	1	3.91	17	0	0	10	25	33	18	11	0	8	22	.308	.400	.287	7.82	2.84
Gonzalez, Isliexel	R-R	6-3	185	5-10-91	1	1	8.10	12	1	0	0	20	29	21	18	3	16	9	.341	.370	.328	4.05	7.20
Guaipe, Mayckol	R-R	6-3	175	8-11-90	2	2	5.46	14	2	0	2	31	36	24	19	0	16	22	.293	.333	.276	6.32	4.60
Guanire, Oberth	R-R	6-6	190	6-21-90	1	1	6.00	10	0	0	0	15	17	15	10	0	7	13	.283	.429	.239	7.80	4.20
Julio, Ivan	R-R	6-3	175	8-19-91	1	0	6.48	9	0	0	0	17	20	13	12	3	12	16	.303	.429	.288	8.64	6.48
Medina, Yoervis	R-R	6-3	210	7-27-88	3	4	2.65	15	13	0	1	68	46	22	20	1	23	62	.192	.186	.194	8.21	3.04
Olivero, Yovanny	R-R	6-2	176	3-5-88	6	2	2.97	14	14	0	0	73	76	33	24	3	18	54	.279	.360	.261	6.69	2.23
Pereira, Cruz	L-L	5-10	175	12-18-90	0	1	6.14	10	1	0	0	15	22	11	10	0	8	13	.355	.000	.361	7.98	4.91
Pereira, Ricardo	B-R	6-3	150	4-18-91	0	1	5.40	12	0	0	0	17	17	10	10	0	12	10	.266	.167	.304	5.40	6.48
Pirela, Jesus	R-R	6-3	190	9-17-91	0	3	6.23	11	2	0	0	28	17	15	15	0	12	15	.341	.200	.373	4.98	6.23
Raga, Angel	R-R	6-1	168	7-25-89	4	4	2.16	14	8	0	1	58	50	19	14	0	19	35	.231	.222	.240	5.40	2.93
Ramirez, Erasmo	R-R	5-11	180	5-2-90	11	1	0.51	14	13	0	0	88	54	10	5	1	5	80	.174	.182	.172	8.18	0.51
Sabala, Reynaldo	R-R	6-3	187	8-16-90	4	3	3.30	12	9	0	0	46	41	21	17	3	23	38	.234	.225	.237	7.38	4.47
Seco, Edlando	L-L	6-2	178	7-23-88	1	0	2.78	15	0	0	2	32	26	12	10	0	22	36	.218	.429	.205	10.02	6.12
Ynfantes, Maykel	R-R	6-0	190	12-6-90	3	1	2.58	15	2	0	1	38	32	15	11	1	10	31	.246	.258	.242	7.28	2.35

Fielding

Catcher	PCT	G	PO	A	E	DP	PB
Diaz	1.000	19	98	17	0	2	3
Gonzalez	.963	25	143	13	6	0	4
Hernandez	.981	34	176	32	4	1	6
Ramirez	.968	9	54	6	2	0	2

First Base	PCT	G	PO	A	E	DP
Acevedo	—	1	0	0	0	0
Agudelo	1.000	2	5	0	0	0
Diaz	.938	2	15	0	1	2
Garcia	.994	24	164	9	1	17
Hernandez	1.000	11	101	4	0	11
Morillo	1.000	8	34	3	0	3
Ramirez	1.000	10	53	2	0	4

	PCT	G	PO	A	E	DP
Ramirez	.994	35	296	16	2	24
Second Base	PCT	G	PO	A	E	DP
Agudelo	.923	7	14	10	2	3
Batista	.974	27	49	62	3	15
Burin	.966	6	12	16	1	3
Coronel	1.000	6	7	9	0	1
Ramirez	.986	42	97	108	3	25
Third Base	PCT	G	PO	A	E	DP
Agudelo	.909	59	41	109	15	13
Burin	1.000	5	1	3	0	1
Ramirez	.949	21	14	42	3	1
Shortstop	PCT	G	PO	A	E	DP
Burin	.909	15	18	32	5	7

	PCT	G	PO	A	E	DP
Coronel	.912	26	25	68	9	15
Ramirez	1.000	1	1	0	0	0
Velasquez	.938	41	55	143	13	24
Outfield	PCT	G	PO	A	E	DP
Acevedo	.899	66	74	6	9	2
Agudelo	—	1	0	0	0	0
Garcia	—	1	0	0	0	0
Hart	.953	48	78	3	4	1
Lampe	.944	19	17	0	1	0
Ramirez	1.000	3	2	1	0	0
Rangel	1.000	27	38	0	0	0
Torrealba	.984	50	58	4	1	0
Ugueto	.833	16	17	3	4	1

SEATTLE MARINERS

Tampa Bay Rays

SEASON IN A SENTENCE: While overcoming a 9-14 start to notch the second-best record in franchise history, the Rays couldn't come up with an encore for their 2008 American League pennant, as their offense never quite clicked and their bullpen failed to live up to the 2008 standard.

HIGH POINT: Akinori Iwamura went down with a knee injury in late May. Ben Zobrist, who had played mostly in right field, shifted to second to replace Iwamura and kept right on hitting. Zobrist had a career year, leading the team in OPS while clubbing 27 home runs and stealing 17 bases. Zobrist was one of five Rays who were on the AL all-star team, joining Jason Bartlett, Carl Crawford, Evan Longoria and Carlos Pena.

LOW POINT: A September swoon took the Rays out of the running for a wild-card spot. Tampa opened the month by losing two of three at home to the Red Sox, then was swept at home by the Tigers before a 2-9 road trip that included a four-game sweep at Yankee Stadium and three-game sweep at Fenway Park in which the Rays scored just eight runs total.

NOTABLE ROOKIES: Rookies Jeff Niemann and David Price combined for 23 wins in the Rays rotation. Niemann, a 2004 first-round pick, led the club in wins at 13-6, 3.94, and his ERA was the best among the team's starters. Price, the ballyhooed 2007 No. 1 overall pick and 2008 playoff hero, went 10-7, 4.42 in a slightly disappointing first season, but he pitched better in the final two months.

KEY TRANSACTIONS: The Rays traded Scott Kazmir in late August to the Angels, getting three prospects—infielders Sean Rodriguez and Matt Sweeney and lefthander Alex Torees—in return. Tampa also dealt righthander Edwin Jackson to Detroit before the season for outfielder Matt Joyce, who spent all but 11 games at Triple-A Durham; and got minor league righty Aneury Rodriguez in April from the Rockies for Jason Hammel, who lost the final rotation spot to Niemann.

DOWN ON THE FARM: Durham, led by Minor League Manager of the Year Charlie Montoyo and righthanders Wade Davis and Jeremy Hellickson, won the International League championship for the third time since 2002, then beat Memphis in the Triple-A National Championship game. The Rays remain stocked with pitching prospects, though several of their top arms were at their new at low Class A Bowling Green affiliate.

OPENING DAY PAYROLL: $63,313,034

PLAYERS OF THE YEAR

MAJOR LEAGUE	MINOR LEAGUE
Ben Zobrist	**Desmond Jennings**
2b/of	**of**
.260/.346/.459	(Double-A/Triple-A)
Appeared at every	.318/.401/.487
position but catcher	31 2B, 10 3B, 52 SB

ORGANIZATION LEADERS

BATTING   *Minimum 250 at-bats

MAJORS

*AVG	Jason Bartlett	.320
*OPS	Ben Zobrist	.948
HR	Carlos Pena	39
RBI	Evan Longoria	113

MINORS

*AVG	Jennings, Desmond, Montgomery/Durham	.318
R	Jennings, Desmond, Montgomery/Durham	92
H	Jennings, Desmond, Montgomery/Durham	158
TB	Jennings, Desmond, Montgomery/Durham	242
2B	Weber, Jon, Durham	46
3B	Jennings, Desmond, Montgomery/Durham	10
HR	Richard, Chris, Durham	24
RBI	Fields, Matt, Charlotte/Montgomery	77
BB	Jennings, Desmond, Montgomery/Durham	67
	Joyce, Matt, Durham	67
SO	Hughes, Rhyne, Montgomery/Norfolk	149
SB	Jennings, Desmond, Montgomery/Durham	52
*OBP	Jennings, Desmond, Montgomery/Durham	.401
*SLG	Richard, Chris, Durham	.521

PITCHING   †Minimum 75 innings

MAJORS

W	Jeff Niemann	13
†ERA	Jeff Niemann	3.94
SO	Matt Garza	189

MINORS

W	Hall, Jeremy, Charlotte	14
L	Rodriguez, Aneury, Montgomery	11
	Rollins, Heath, Montgomery/Durham	11
†ERA	Downs, Darin, Charlotte/Montgomery	2.23
G	Childers, Jason, Durham	55
GS	Davis, Wade, Durham	28
SV	Satow, Josh, Bowling Green/Charlotte	20
IP	Davis, Wade, Durham	159
BB	Moore, Matthew, Bowling Green	70
SO	Moore, Matthew, Bowling Green	176
†AVG	Hellickson, Jeremy, Montgomery/Durham	.178

General Manager: Andrew Friedman. **Farm Director:** Mitch Lukevics. **Scouting Director:** R.J. Harrison.

Class	Team	League	W	L	PCT	Finish*	Manager(s)
Majors	Tampa Bay Rays	American	84	78	.519	8th (14)	Joe Maddon
Triple-A	Durham Bulls	International	83	61	.576	†2nd (14)	Charlie Montoyo
Double-A	Montgomery Biscuits	Southern	65	74	.468	t-6th (10)	Billy Gardner
High A	Charlotte Stone Crabs	Florida State	71	66	.518	4th (12)	Jim Morrison
Low A	Bowling Green Hot Rods	South Atlantic	64	74	.464	14th (16)	Matt Quatraro
Short-season	Hudson Valley Renegades	New York-Penn	38	37	.507	6th (14)	Brady Williams
Rookie	Princeton Rays	Appalachian	36	31	.537	4th (10)	Jared Sandberg
Rookie	GCL Rays	Gulf Coast	19	36	.345	15th (16)	Joe Alvarez
Overall 2009 Minor League Record			376	379	.498	17th (30)	

*Finish in overall standings (No. of teams in league). †League champion.

TAMPA BAY RAYS

AMERICAN LEAGUE

Batting	B-T	HT	WT	DOB	AVG	vLH	vRH	G	AB	R	H	2B	3B	HR	RBI	BB	HBP	SH	SF	SO	SB	CS	SLG	OBP
Aybar, Willy	B-R	5-11	205	3-9-83	.253	.265	.247	105	296	38	75	12	0	12	41	34	2	1	3	54	1	0	.416	.331
Bartlett, Jason	R-R	6-0	190	10-30-79	.320	.338	.312	137	500	90	160	29	7	14	66	54	4	4	4	89	30	7	.490	.389
Brignac, Reid	L-R	6-3	195	1-16-86	.278	.050	.343	31	90	10	25	8	2	1	6	3	0	0	0	20	2	2	.444	.301
Burrell, Pat	R-R	6-4	235	10-10-76	.221	.202	.229	122	412	45	91	16	1	14	64	57	2	0	5	119	2	0	.367	.315
Crawford, Carl	L-L	6-2	215	8-5-81	.305	.269	.322	156	606	96	185	28	8	15	68	51	2	5	99	60	16	.452	.364
Dillon, Joe	R-R	6-2	215	8-2-75	.300	.158	.545	15	30	4	9	0	0	1	2	3	2	0	0	4	0	0	.400	.400
Gross, Gabe	L-R	6-3	220	10-21-79	.227	.172	.233	115	282	31	64	16	1	6	36	42	0	1	1	79	6	3	.355	.326
Hernandez, Michel	R-R	6-0	215	8-12-78	.242	.200	.261	35	99	12	24	3	1	1	12	7	0	1	0	12	2	1	.323	.292
Iwamura, Akinori	L-R	5-9	200	2-9-79	.290	.386	.248	69	231	28	67	16	2	1	22	24	1	1	3	44	9	1	.390	.355
Joyce, Matt	L-R	6-2	185	8-3-84	.188	.250	.179	11	32	3	6	1	0	3	7	3	1	0	1	7	1	0	.500	.270
Kapler, Gabe	R-R	6-2	205	7-31-75	.239	.276	.150	99	205	26	49	15	1	8	32	29	0	1	3	39	5	2	.439	.329
Longoria, Evan	R-R	6-2	210	10-7-85	.281	.289	.277	157	584	100	164	44	0	33	113	72	8	0	7	140	9	0	.526	.364
Navarro, Dioner	B-R	5-9	205	2-9-84	.218	.279	.182	115	376	38	82	15	0	8	32	18	5	8	3	51	5	2	.322	.261
Pena, Carlos	L-L	6-2	225	5-17-78	.227	.211	.236	135	471	91	107	25	2	39	100	87	9	0	3	163	3	3	.537	.356
Perez, Fernando	B-R	6-1	195	4-23-83	.206	.154	.238	18	34	4	7	0	0	0	2	0	0	1	0	11	0	2	.206	.206
Richard, Chris	L-L	6-2	210	6-7-74	.105	.000	.133	13	19	1	2	0	0	0	4	0	0	0	0	7	0	0	.105	.261
Riggans, Shawn	R-R	6-2	200	7-25-80	.143	.000	.182	7	14	2	2	0	0	1	1	0	0	0	0	3	0	0	.357	.143
Upton, B.J.	R-R	6-3	185	8-21-84	.241	.190	.262	144	560	79	135	33	4	11	55	57	3	3	3	152	42	14	.373	.313
Zaun, Gregg	B-R	5-10	205	4-14-71	.287	.200	.292	34	94	11	27	7	0	4	14	4	1	0	0	18	0	2	.489	.323
2-team total (56 Baltimore)					.260	—	—	90	262	34	68	17	0	8	27	31	3	0	0	48	0	2	.416	.345
Zobrist, Ben	B-R	6-3	200	5-26-81	.297	.319	.287	152	501	91	149	28	7	27	91	91	2	1	4	104	17	6	.543	.405

Pitching	B-T	HT	WT	DOB	W	L	ERA	G	GS	CG	SV	IP	H	R	ER	HR	BB	SO	AVG	vLH	vRH	K/9	BB/9
Abreu, Winston	R-R	6-2	170	4-5-77	0	0	2.45	2	0	0	0	4	3	1	1	0	2	3	.231	.200	.250	7.36	4.91
2-team total (3 Cleveland)					0	0	10.50	5	0	0	0	6	10	8	7	2	4	6	—	—	—	9.00	6.00
Balfour, Grant	R-R	6-2	195	12-30-77	5	4	4.81	73	0	0	4	67	59	38	36	6	33	69	.235	.240	.232	9.22	4.41
Bennett, Jeff	R-R	6-3	200	6-10-80	0	0	9.95	11	0	0	0	13	24	14	14	2	11	4	.414	.500	.292	2.84	7.82
Bradford, Chad	R-R	6-5	215	9-14-74	1	0	4.35	20	0	0	0	10	22	5	5	1	2	6	.431	.800	.391	5.23	1.74
Choate, Randy	L-L	6-1	200	9-5-75	1	0	3.47	61	0	0	5	36	28	15	14	4	11	28	.214	.141	.321	6.94	2.72
Cormier, Lance	R-R	6-1	200	8-19-80	3	3	3.26	53	0	0	2	77	75	31	28	6	25	36	.249	.239	.261	4.19	2.91
Davis, Wade	R-R	6-5	220	9-7-85	2	2	3.72	6	6	1	0	36	33	19	15	2	13	36	.243	.238	.250	8.92	3.22
Garza, Matt	R-R	6-4	215	11-26-83	8	12	3.95	32	32	0	0	203	177	93	89	25	79	189	.233	.196	.271	8.38	3.50
Howell, J.P.	L-L	6-0	180	4-25-83	7	5	2.84	69	0	0	17	67	47	22	21	7	33	79	.197	.280	.159	10.67	4.46
Isringhausen, Jason	R-R	6-3	230	9-7-72	0	1	2.25	9	0	0	0	8	6	2	2	0	5	6	.200	.167	.222	6.75	5.63
Kazmir, Scott	L-L	6-0	190	1-24-84	8	7	5.92	20	20	0	0	111	121	77	73	15	50	91	.273	.276	.271	7.38	4.05
2-team total (6 Los Angeles)					10	9	4.89	26	26	0	0	147	149	85	80	16	60	117	—	—	—	7.15	3.67
Nelson, Joe	R-R	6-1	205	10-25-74	3	0	4.02	42	0	0	3	40	32	22	18	7	27	36	.213	.212	.216	8.03	6.02
Niemann, Jeff	R-R	6-9	260	2-28-83	13	6	3.94	31	30	2	0	181	185	84	79	17	59	125	.266	.274	.258	6.23	2.94
Percival, Troy	R-R	6-3	255	8-9-69	0	1	6.35	14	0	0	6	11	14	8	8	3	5	7	.304	.478	.130	5.56	3.97
Price, David	L-L	6-6	225	8-26-85	10	7	4.42	23	23	0	0	128	119	72	63	17	54	102	.241	.236	.242	7.15	3.79
Shields, James	R-R	6-4	220	12-20-81	11	12	4.14	33	33	0	0	220	239	113	101	29	52	167	.275	.272	.279	6.84	2.13
Shouse, Brian	L-L	5-10	190	9-26-68	1	1	4.50	45	0	0	0	28	31	15	14	5	7	17	.277	.224	.356	5.46	2.25
Sonnanstine, Andy	R-R	6-3	190	3-18-83	6	9	6.77	22	18	0	0	100	131	85	75	19	34	60	.311	.275	.367	5.42	3.07
Springer, Russ	R-R	6-4	225	11-7-68	1	3	4.11	26	0	0	1	15	16	7	7	4	3	11	.276	.300	.271	6.46	1.76
2-team total (48 Oakland)					1	4	4.11	74	0	0	1	57	68	27	26	9	17	58	—	—	—	9.16	2.68
Thayer, Dale	R-R	6-0	195	12-17-80	0	0	4.61	11	0	0	1	14	18	9	7	3	1	8	.310	.208	.382	5.27	0.66
Wheeler, Dan	R-R	6-2	220	12-10-77	4	5	3.28	69	0	0	2	58	41	22	21	11	9	45	.199	.305	.156	7.02	1.40

Fielding

Catcher	PCT	G	PO	A	E	DP	PB							First Base	PCT	G	PO	A	E	DP
Hernandez	.991	35	217	11	2	2	1	Riggans	.968	7	29	1	1	0	0	Aybar	.995	31	168	18	1	16
Navarro	.994	113	732	47	5	7	6	Zaun	.994	29	168	6	1	1	0	Pena	.991	133	1055	71	10	102

	PCT	G	PO	A	E	DP
Richard	.984	13	59	2	1	2
Zobrist	.875	3	6	1	1	2

Second Base	PCT	G	PO	A	E	DP
Aybar	.942	28	35	46	5	13
Brignac	1.000	3	0	4	0	0
Dillon	1.000	2	1	1	0	0
Iwamura	.979	67	114	163	6	37
Zobrist	.989	91	143	225	4	44

Third Base	PCT	G	PO	A	E	DP
Aybar	.944	18	8	26	2	2
Dillon	1.000	3	0	1	0	0
Iwamura	1.000	1	1	0	0	0
Longoria	.970	151	112	302	13	43
Zobrist	—	1	0	0	0	0

Shortstop	PCT	G	PO	A	E	DP
Bartlett	.962	134	170	339	20	57
Brignac	.978	28	26	62	2	9
Zobrist	.926	13	9	16	2	5

Outfield	PCT	G	PO	A	E	DP
Burrell	1.000	2	2	0	0	0
Crawford	.988	154	327	6	4	1
Gross	.981	100	149	6	3	1
Joyce	1.000	9	15	0	0	0
Kapler	.987	88	143	5	2	0
Perez	1.000	14	29	0	0	0
Upton	.990	144	375	6	4	1
Zobrist	1.000	70	112	5	0	4

DURHAM BULLS · TRIPLE-A

INTERNATIONAL LEAGUE

Batting	B-T	HT	WT	DOB	AVG	vLH	vRH	G	AB	R	H	2B	3B	HR	RBI	BB	HBP	SH	SF	SO	SB	CS	SLG	OBP
Albernaz, Craig	R-R	5-8	195	10-30-82	.183	.194	.180	48	120	15	22	4	2	0	10	12	0	3	0	29	1	0	.250	.258
Brignac, Reid	L-R	6-3	195	1-16-86	.282	.265	.287	96	415	51	117	28	2	8	44	27	3	3	5	69	5	5	.417	.327
Chaves, Brandon	B-R	6-3	181	8-5-79	.271	.357	.244	18	59	7	16	2	0	0	7	11	1	1	0	9	0	3	.305	.394
Dillon, Joe	R-R	6-2	215	8-2-75	.244	.212	.256	35	123	18	30	5	0	2	13	14	6	0	4	17	4	0	.333	.340
Eldridge, Rashad	B-R	6-1	185	10-16-81	.305	.333	.293	26	105	13	32	5	0	1	7	12	0	0	0	14	5	3	.381	.376
Hall, Matt	R-R	6-2	180	3-10-87	.190	.000	.250	8	21	2	4	1	0	0	3	1	0	0	0	5	0	0	.238	.227
Hernandez, Michel	R-R	6-0	215	8-12-78	.196	.158	.222	13	46	2	9	0	0	0	6	6	0	0	3	7	0	0	.196	.273
Hughes, Rhyne	L-L	6-2	175	9-9-83	.313	.259	.331	56	214	31	67	22	2	7	26	12	4	0	0	69	0	0	.533	.361
2-team total (20 Norfolk)					.301	—	—	76	286	40	86	24	3	10	33	19	6	0	0	91	0	0	.510	.357
Iwamura, Akinori	L-R	5-9	200	2-9-79	.303	.308	.300	11	33	9	10	3	0	0	2	9	0	0	0	7	0	0	.394	.452
Jamieson, Alex	R-R	5-11	205	4-7-83	.107	.000	.120	10	28	1	3	0	0	0	1	3	0	0	0	9	0	0	.107	.194
Jaso, John	L-R	6-2	205	9-19-83	.266	.270	.265	104	331	42	88	14	2	5	30	46	6	0	4	49	1	0	.366	.362
Jennings, Desmond	R-R	6-2	180	10-30-86	.325	.231	.373	32	114	23	37	6	2	3	17	19	1	1	2	15	15	2	.491	.419
Johnson, Elliot	B-R	6-0	190	3-9-84	.262	.222	.274	63	233	31	61	9	1	11	35	17	3	6	1	56	7	2	.451	.319
Joyce, Matt	L-R	6-2	185	8-3-84	.273	.250	.282	111	417	73	114	35	2	16	66	67	3	0	6	98	14	5	.482	.373
Kennedy, Adam	L-R	6-1	195	1-10-76	.280	.333	.266	23	82	11	23	4	0	3	9	10	1	0	0	12	1	1	.439	.366
Mateo, Henry	B-R	6-0	175	10-14-76	.277	.250	.286	82	307	41	85	17	4	3	23	37	1	6	3	63	13	5	.388	.353
Nowak, Chris	R-R	6-5	225	2-21-83	.228	.286	.209	64	228	22	52	13	1	4	23	18	4	0	2	54	2	1	.346	.294
Olmedo, Ray	B-R	5-11	175	5-31-81	.250	.248	.251	115	412	40	103	13	2	6	47	20	4	12	2	73	8	7	.335	.290
Perez, Fernando	B-R	6-1	195	4-23-83	.278	.333	.267	13	36	10	10	3	0	0	2	7	0	0	0	17	8	1	.361	.395
Richard, Chris	L-L	6-2	210	6-7-74	.263	.220	.277	100	365	56	96	22	0	24	75	52	6	0	0	83	2	1	.521	.364
Riggans, Shawn	R-R	6-2	200	7-25-80	.200	.333	.143	11	40	4	8	2	0	1	5	1	1	0	0	7	0	0	.325	.238
Rodriguez, Sean	R-R	6-1	215	4-26-85	.200	.250	.167	5	20	4	4	2	0	1	5	4	0	0	0	3	0	0	.450	.333
Ruggiano, Justin	R-R	6-2	205	4-12-82	.253	.219	.262	123	471	71	119	28	1	15	72	51	5	1	4	147	23	4	.412	.330
Sadler, Ray	R-R	6-1	200	9-19-80	.216	.048	.258	86	319	39	69	11	1	13	47	27	6	1	3	56	5	5	.379	.287
Weber, Jon	L-L	5-10	190	1-20-78	.302	.293	.304	117	451	63	136	46	0	14	69	56	6	0	5	98	3	7	.497	.382

Pitching	B-T	HT	WT	DOB	W	L	ERA	G	GS	CG	SV	IP	H	R	ER	HR	BB	SO	AVG	vLH	vRH	K/9	BB/9
Abreu, Winston	R-R	6-2	170	4-5-77	3	1	1.94	37	0	0	15	51	23	11	11	4	16	77	.133	.179	.104	13.59	2.82
Bateman, Joe	R-R	6-1	185	5-6-80	6	2	3.02	44	2	0	4	63	43	21	21	0	35	64	.193	.194	.192	9.19	5.03
Bennett, Jeff	R-R	6-3	200	6-10-80	1	0	4.76	3	3	0	0	11	14	6	6	1	5	8	.311	.421	.231	6.35	3.97
2-team total (2 Gwinnett)					1	1	6.75	5	5	0	0	13	19	10	10	1	6	8	—			5.40	4.05
Bradford, Chad	R-R	6-5	215	9-14-74	1	0	5.79	4	0	0	0	5	7	3	3	0	1	2	.350	.333	.357	3.86	1.93
Childers, Jason	R-R	6-2	190	1-13-75	9	6	4.44	55	1	0	5	79	83	41	39	10	24	63	.264	.250	.273	7.18	2.73
Choate, Randy	L-L	6-1	200	9-5-75	3	0	3.72	21	0	0	0	19	16	8	8	0	9	15	.216	.242	.195	6.98	4.19
Cromer, Jason	R-L	6-4	225	12-11-80	7	3	2.25	20	19	0	0	112	106	32	28	5	36	67	.252	.276	.244	5.38	2.89
Davis, Wade	R-R	6-5	220	9-7-85	10	8	3.40	28	28	0	0	159	139	71	60	14	60	140	.231	.243	.223	7.94	3.40
Day, Dewon	R-R	6-2	220	9-29-80	3	1	4.76	22	0	0	1	28	35	19	15	3	15	21	.304	.364	.268	6.67	4.76
DePaula, Julio	R-R	6-0	180	12-31-82	2	3	3.87	48	2	0	1	79	82	40	34	6	40	57	.273	.340	.239	6.49	4.56
DeSalvo, Matt	R-R	6-0	180	9-11-80	0	4	6.44	13	11	0	0	57	56	45	41	5	39	36	.255	.313	.219	5.65	6.12
Hellickson, Jeremy	R-R	6-1	185	4-8-87	6	1	2.51	9	9	0	0	57	31	19	16	4	15	70	.157	.174	.148	10.99	2.35
Hernandez, Carlos	B-L	5-11	205	4-22-80	7	6	3.29	21	21	0	0	112	100	45	41	8	42	81	.242	.248	.239	6.51	3.38
Houser, James	L-L	6-4	205	12-15-84	4	5	5.16	18	15	0	0	82	83	52	47	10	50	44	.264	.312	.244	4.83	5.49
Isringhausen, Jason	R-R	6-3	230	9-7-72	0	0	5.14	6	0	0	0	7	7	4	4	0	2	0	.259	.375	.211	0.00	2.57
Julio, Jorge	R-R	6-1	225	3-3-79	0	1	5.96	19	0	0	0	23	22	16	15	2	15	24	.256	.412	.154	9.53	5.96
2-team total (4 Indianapolis)					0	3	6.11	23	0	0	0	28	30	23	19	2	17	31	—			9.96	5.46
Kazmir, Scott	L-L	6-0	190	1-24-84	1	0	1.50	1	1	0	0	6	5	1	1	0	0	5	.238	.200	.250	7.50	0.00
Mason, Chris	R-R	6-1	190	7-1-84	0	0	9.00	1	1	0	0	4	8	4	4	1	1	3	.421	.364	.500	6.75	2.25
2-team total (3 Buffalo)					1	1	5.82	4	4	0	0	22	28	14	14	3	5	16	—			6.65	2.08
Medlock, Calvin	R-R	5-10	195	11-8-82	4	1	2.98	24	2	0	0	51	46	19	17	6	12	43	.245	.247	.243	7.54	2.10
Meloan, John	R-R	6-3	225	7-11-84	0	0	3.38	10	0	0	0	13	13	5	5	2	10	15	.250	.190	.290	10.13	6.75
3-team total (25 Columbus, 6 Indianapolis)					0	0	4.57	41	2	0	0	65	68	33	33	9	28	60	—			8.31	3.88
Nelson, Joe	R-R	6-1	205	10-25-74	2	2	6.23	13	0	0	0	17	22	14	12	4	11	14	.314	.348	.298	7.27	5.71
Oliveros, Rayner	R-R	6-2	180	9-23-85	1	0	3.48	2	1	0	0	10	10	5	4	0	3	13	.250	.286	.231	11.32	2.61
Orvella, Chad	R-R	5-11	195	10-31-80	1	0	6.12	19	0	0	0	32	36	22	22	5	11	24	.277	.235	.304	6.68	3.06
Phillips, Paul	R-R	6-1	211	1-26-84	0	0	0.00	2	1	0	0	3	1	0	0	0	0	3	.148	.182	.125	3.52	3.52
Price, David	L-L	6-6	225	8-26-85	1	4	3.93	8	8	0	0	34	28	20	15	5	18	35	.231	.214	.237	9.17	4.72
Rollins, Heath	R-R	6-1	190	5-25-85	0	0	6.00	3	0	0	0	6	7	7	4	1	4	4	.259	.256	.263	6.00	6.00
Sonnanstine, Andy	L-R	6-3	190	3-18-83	5	3	4.40	9	9	0	0	57	68	29	28	4	9	36	.300	.270	.323	5.65	1.41
Talbot, Mitch	R-R	6-2	200	10-17-83	4	4	4.47	10	10	0	0	54	67	29	27	3	18	40	.307	.314	.302	6.63	2.98

TAMPA BAY RAYS

	B-T	HT	WT	DOB	W	L	ERA	G	GS	CG	SV	IP	H	R	ER	HR	BB	SO	AVG	vLH	vRH	K/9	BB/9
Thayer, Dale	R-R	6-0	195	12-17-80	2	5	2.27	51	0	0	17	63	59	24	16	3	15	44	.245	.226	.257	6.25	2.13
Wlodarczyk, Mike	L-L	6-5	230	12-2-82	0	0	0.00	1	0	0	0	2	0	0	0	0	0	2	.000	.000	.000	9.00	0.00

Fielding

Catcher	PCT	G	PO	A	E	DP	PB
Albernaz	.992	44	232	20	2	3	5
Hernandez	.990	11	97	5	1	1	0
Jamieson	1.000	5	30	3	0	0	0
Jaso	.987	98	660	36	9	6	11
Riggans	1.000	7	66	2	0	1	0

First Base	PCT	G	PO	A	E	DP
Dillon	.992	17	118	6	1	14
Hall	1.000	1	2	0	0	0
Hughes	.989	41	344	22	4	35
Jamieson	1.000	4	19	2	0	0
Kennedy	1.000	2	9	1	0	2
Mateo	1.000	2	18	0	0	3
Nowak	.992	15	113	6	1	9
Richard	.983	71	591	37	11	46
Riggans	1.000	1	5	0	0	0

Second Base	PCT	G	PO	A	E	DP
Albernaz	1.000	1	2	1	0	0
Brignac	1.000	8	17	13	0	3
Dillon	1.000	4	10	9	0	2
Iwamura	1.000	6	5	6	0	2
Johnson	.981	22	49	52	2	13
Kennedy	.985	17	33	32	1	5
Mateo	.961	72	130	162	12	36
Olmedo	.989	22	38	49	1	15
Rodriguez	1.000	3	6	6	0	3

Third Base	PCT	G	PO	A	E	DP
Dillon	.962	13	2	23	1	1
Hall	.895	6	6	11	2	0
Johnson	.895	21	13	38	6	4
Kennedy	.750	2	0	3	1	2
Mateo	.857	5	1	11	2	0
Nowak	.979	41	42	99	3	11
Olmedo	.950	64	41	110	8	11
Rodriguez	1.000	2	1	0	0	0

Shortstop	PCT	G	PO	A	E	DP
Brignac	.962	88	139	242	15	47
Chaves	1.000	18	23	46	0	10
Dillon	1.000	1	0	2	0	0
Johnson	.963	13	20	32	2	8
Mateo	1.000	2	3	2	0	0
Olmedo	.918	25	32	58	8	11

Outfield	PCT	G	PO	A	E	DP
Eldridge	.983	26	55	2	1	1
Jennings	.968	30	61	0	2	0
Johnson	.964	11	26	1	1	0
Joyce	.980	105	235	4	5	1
Mateo	1.000	1	1	0	0	0
Nowak	1.000	2	1	0	0	0
Olmedo	1.000	3	8	0	0	0
Perez	.950	11	18	1	1	0
Ruggiano	.996	114	274	10	1	1
Sadler	.994	77	158	2	1	0
Weber	.968	69	114	8	4	1

MONTGOMERY BISCUITS

DOUBLE-A

SOUTHERN LEAGUE

Batting	B-T	HT	WT	DOB	AVG	vLH	vRH	G	AB	R	H	2B	3B	HR	RBI	BB	HBP	SH	SF	SO	SB	CS	SLG	OBP
Albernaz, Craig	R-R	5-8	195	10-30-82	.077	.000	.083	4	13	1	1	0	0	0	0	2	1	0	0	2	0	0	.077	.250
Anderson, Drew M.	B-R	5-9	170	2-2-83	.220	.224	.218	74	255	28	56	16	5	1	15	21	1	4	1	41	2	0	.333	.281
Ashley, Nevin	R-R	6-1	215	8-14-84	.212	.278	.200	35	118	10	25	7	1	1	15	18	3	0	0	31	0	0	.314	.331
Bowers, Jason	R-R	5-10	183	1-27-78	.233	.171	.250	98	330	40	77	10	7	3	27	33	4	4	2	61	7	2	.333	.309
Burrell, Pat	R-R	6-4	235	10-10-76	.111	—	.111	2	9	1	1	0	0	0	0	1	0	0	0	4	0	0	.111	.200
Cannon, Chip	L-R	6-5	215	11-30-81	.103	.100	.105	8	29	4	3	0	0	3	4	5	0	0	1	21	0	0	.414	.229
Chaves, Brandon	B-R	6-3	181	8-5-79	.198	.293	.166	88	298	35	59	10	1	2	26	44	4	10	1	56	8	6	.258	.308
Cipriano, Cody	R-R	6-0	200	1-7-85	.204	.192	.207	44	147	18	30	6	1	2	13	16	1	0	2	35	0	0	.299	.283
Cortez, Fernando	L-R	6-1	175	8-10-81	.244	.265	.238	115	442	41	108	11	6	5	46	34	2	1	1	55	3	5	.330	.301
Eldridge, Rashad	B-R	6-1	185	10-16-81	.283	.253	.293	98	364	51	103	20	2	2	45	47	3	3	2	66	20	7	.365	.368
Fields, Matt	R-R	6-5	235	7-8-85	.246	.173	.263	77	284	38	70	14	1	5	32	18	8	0	2	85	1	0	.356	.308
Gaetti, Joe	R-R	5-11	205	10-18-81	.188	.111	.205	32	101	9	19	2	0	4	13	17	1	1	2	36	0	1	.327	.306
Hall, J.T	L-R	6-3	210	5-19-84	.221	.241	.216	92	299	43	66	14	3	7	32	44	2	3	2	86	4	3	.358	.323
Hall, Matt	R-R	6-2	180	3-10-87	.000	—	.000	1	1	0	0	0	0	0	0	0	0	0	0	1	0	0	.000	.000
Hughes, Rhyne	L-L	6-2	175	9-9-83	.252	.234	.259	58	226	31	57	11	0	15	46	25	6	0	2	80	4	0	.500	.340
Jennings, Desmond	R-R	6-2	180	10-30-86	.316	.380	.299	100	383	69	121	25	8	8	45	48	5	0	4	52	37	5	.486	.395
Lobaton, Jose	B-R	6-0	195	10-21-84	.262	.231	.268	26	84	13	22	7	0	3	11	15	1	1	1	19	0	0	.452	.376
Matulia, John	L-L	6-0	175	8-19-86	.081	.125	.069	11	37	3	3	1	0	1	2	5	0	0	0	12	0	0	.189	.190
Nowak, Chris	R-R	6-5	225	2-21-83	.311	.295	.315	55	209	27	65	11	1	2	36	21	2	0	4	38	6	1	.402	.373
Paxton, Ian	R-R	6-1	210	9-4-83	.122	.000	.156	12	41	3	5	0	0	0	1	1	0	0	0	13	0	0	.122	.143
Perry, Jason	L-R	6-0	200	8-18-80	.204	.192	.208	32	103	16	21	5	0	5	15	21	3	0	1	31	1	0	.398	.352
Powell, Pedro	B-R	5-7	145	5-20-84	.229	.222	.231	56	179	15	41	3	2	0	12	9	1	9	0	41	16	6	.268	.270
Riggans, Shawn	R-R	6-2	200	7-25-80	.286	—	.286	3	7	2	2	0	0	0	0	0	0	0	0	2	0	0	.286	.286
Spring, Matt	R-R	6-2	215	11-7-84	.196	.269	.174	68	224	23	44	13	0	8	33	22	2	1	2	74	0	0	.362	.272
Strait, Cody	R-R	6-1	180	5-28-83	.234	.240	.233	33	111	15	26	6	1	1	21	8	1	0	4	29	5	1	.333	.282
Suarez, Cesar	R-R	5-11	170	8-17-83	.224	.254	.211	67	246	29	55	17	1	4	23	15	4	0	2	28	6	4	.350	.277

Pitching	B-T	HT	WT	DOB	W	L	ERA	G	GS	CG	SV	IP	H	R	ER	HR	BB	SO	AVG	vLH	vRH	K/9	BB/9
Baker, Brian	R-R	6-5	190	1-10-83	5	6	4.54	31	18	0	0	121	127	65	61	10	40	102	.271	.246	.289	7.59	2.98
Bradford, Chad	R-R	6-5	215	9-14-74	0	0	4.50	2	0	0	0	2	3	1	1	0	1	2	.375	.500	.000	9.00	4.50
Castro, Angel	R-R	5-11	200	11-14-82	0	0	6.75	2	0	0	0	3	4	2	2	0	3	1	.364	.333	.375	3.38	10.13
Cromer, Jason	R-L	6-4	225	12-11-81	4	3	5.01	8	8	0	0	41	53	28	23	3	9	21	.315	.289	.323	4.57	1.96
Downs, Darin	R-L	6-3	190	12-26-84	0	2	4.76	2	2	0	0	11	13	6	6	1	4	9	.295	.412	.222	7.15	3.18
Frontz, Neal	R-R	6-3	190	4-6-84	2	0	5.29	43	0	0	1	65	65	38	38	6	28	45	.256	.261	.253	6.26	3.90
Gorgen, Matt	R-R	6-0	210	1-27-87	3	1	2.38	16	0	0	4	23	18	7	6	2	13	18	.214	.258	.189	7.15	5.16
Hellickson, Jeremy	R-R	6-1	185	4-8-87	3	1	2.38	11	11	0	0	57	41	16	15	4	14	62	.198	.194	.202	9.85	2.22
Isringhausen, Jason	R-R	6-3	230	9-7-72	0	0	2.25	4	0	0	0	4	2	1	1	0	4	3	.167	.200	.143	6.75	9.00
Mann, Brandon	L-L	6-2	165	5-16-84	7	9	4.44	27	21	0	1	126	134	68	62	6	48	72	.279	.228	.299	5.16	3.44
Mason, Chris	R-R	6-2	180	12-8-84	3	5	6.24	24	3	0	0	53	72	44	37	4	22	34	.326	.307	.338	5.74	3.71
Medlock, Calvin	R-R	5-10	195	11-8-82	0	1	3.52	23	0	0	13	34	23	13	12	6	4	37	.209	.208	.211	10.86	1.17
Mejias, Jose	R-R	6-0	150	8-18-85	0	0	0.00	3	0	0	0	4	1	0	0	0	1		.071	.000	.111	0.00	2.08
Morlan, Eduardo	R-R	6-2	220	3-1-86	7	5	3.99	48	0	0	4	70	67	34	31	8	30	62	.248	.243	.251	7.97	3.86
Morse, Ryan	L-L	6-3	190	5-21-83	4	6	4.84	20	14	0	0	74	80	43	40	7	38	40	.280	.348	.258	4.84	4.60
Oliveros, Rayner	R-R	6-2	180	9-23-85	5	3	3.25	20	8	1	1	69	57	27	25	6	18	51	.228	.283	.188	6.62	2.34
Phillips, Paul	R-R	6-1	211	1-26-84	3	3	2.43	29	0	0	7	37	23	10	10	1	14	38	.177	.157	.190	9.24	3.41
Reid, Ryan	L-R	5-11	215	4-24-85	0	1	4.17	42	0	0	1	58	65	32	27	3	28	50	.291	.333	.270	7.71	4.32
Rodriguez, Aneury	R-R	6-3	180	12-13-87	9	11	4.50	27	27	1	0	142	122	78	71	17	59	111	.231	.208	.248	7.04	3.74

Rollins, Heath	R-R	6-1	190	5-25-85	9	11	3.83	28	22	0	0	134	147	64	57	9	33	83	.281	.290	.272	5.57	2.22
Torres, Alex	L-L	5-10	175	12-8-87	0	2	3.12	2	2	0	0	9	7	6	3	1	5	7	.219	.091	.286	7.27	5.19
Wlodarczyk, Mike	L-L	6-5	230	12-2-82	1	4	5.40	47	3	0	5	65	72	44	39	2	26	46	.286	.253	.304	6.37	3.60

Fielding

Catcher	PCT	G	PO	A	E	DP	PB
Albernaz	.973	4	30	6	1	2	2
Ashley	.993	35	254	23	2	0	3
Lobaton	.982	25	148	15	3	2	0
Paxton	1.000	12	71	6	0	1	0
Riggans	1.000	2	8	1	0	0	0
Spring	.987	65	407	39	6	1	10

First Base	PCT	G	PO	A	E	DP
Cortez	.958	6	43	3	2	6
Fields	.980	75	564	33	12	58
Hughes	.992	56	460	21	4	43
Nowak	—	1	0	0	0	0
Spring	1.000	3	25	5	0	3

Second Base	PCT	G	PO	A	E	DP
Anderson	.973	68	107	177	8	43
Bowers	.989	23	35	59	1	14
Chaves	1.000	5	3	18	0	3
Cipriano	.972	41	79	93	5	24
Cortez	1.000	1	2	6	0	1
Suarez	1.000	7	14	19	0	4

Third Base	PCT	G	PO	A	E	DP
Bowers	.963	18	15	37	2	3
Cortez	.932	33	34	48	6	4
Nowak	.947	53	41	103	8	10
Suarez	.943	37	31	69	6	4

Shortstop	PCT	G	PO	A	E	DP
Bowers	.969	58	110	142	8	35

Chaves	.962	82	100	203	12	49
Cortez	.938	3	7	8	1	3
Hall	—	1	0	0	0	0

Outfield	PCT	G	PO	A	E	DP
Cortez	1.000	14	24	2	0	0
Eldridge	.992	96	243	4	2	1
Gaetti	.964	25	49	5	2	1
Hall	.974	80	145	6	4	1
Jennings	.996	92	258	4	1	0
Matulia	1.000	11	20	1	0	1
Perry	1.000	25	44	1	0	0
Powell	1.000	53	94	1	0	0
Strait	.974	31	74	2	2	1
Suarez	—	1	0	0	0	0

CHARLOTTE STONE CRABS   HIGH CLASS A
FLORIDA STATE LEAGUE

Batting	B-T	HT	WT	DOB	AVG	vLH	vRH	G	AB	R	H	2B	3B	HR	RBI	BB	HBP	SH	SF	SO	SB	CS	SLG	OBP
Anderson, Drew M.	B-R	5-9	170	2-2-83	.275	.194	.300	36	131	14	36	6	4	2	19	11	1	2	4	27	1	1	.427	.327
Ashley, Nevin	R-R	6-1	215	8-14-84	.240	.239	.240	62	200	22	48	7	3	2	21	22	11	0	3	47	1	4	.335	.343
Bartlett, Jason	R-R	6-0	190	10-30-79	.455	.000	.500	3	11	2	5	0	1	0	0	2	0	0	0	2	0	1	.636	.538
Burrell, Pat	R-R	6-4	235	10-10-76	.000	—	.000	1	4	0	0	0	0	0	0	0	0	0	0	2	0	0	.000	.000
Cipriano, Cody	R-R	6-0	200	1-7-85	.297	.255	.307	72	239	41	71	17	3	5	35	39	5	1	3	60	8	6	.456	.402
Fields, Matt	R-R	6-5	235	7-8-85	.259	.265	.257	51	201	24	52	9	1	11	45	5	6	0	3	62	2	2	.478	.293
Fronk, Reid	L-R	6-1	200	7-21-86	.201	.196	.202	112	343	43	69	17	0	4	32	47	16	7	5	88	9	6	.286	.321
Hall, Matt	R-R	6-2	180	3-10-87	.218	.153	.237	86	266	26	58	6	1	3	20	25	0	8	1	73	4	4	.282	.284
Lopez, Christian	R-R	6-1	185	10-10-84	.174	.235	.163	39	115	7	20	5	0	1	10	6	4	3	2	22	0	2	.243	.236
Luis, Diogenes	B-R	5-10	169	5-7-87	.000	.000	.000	6	9	1	0	0	0	0	0	1	0	0	0	3	1	0	.000	.100
Luna, Omar	R-R	5-11	165	12-13-86	.185	.167	.191	76	259	26	48	6	1	0	19	11	0	5	0	32	5	3	.216	.219
Matulia, John	L-L	6-0	175	8-19-86	.278	.179	.299	87	317	31	88	22	5	2	30	14	3	4	1	55	10	3	.397	.313
McCormick, Mike	R-R	6-2	200	9-6-86	.170	.280	.136	32	106	6	18	7	0	3	8	11	2	1	0	35	2	2	.321	.261
O'Malley, Shawn	R-R	5-11	160	12-28-87	.268	.341	.246	103	366	73	98	9	2	1	27	58	15	6	2	80	40	14	.311	.388
Paxton, Ian	R-R	6-1	210	9-4-83	.288	.316	.279	28	80	8	23	4	0	2	11	2	1	0	1	19	0	1	.413	.310
Perez, Fernando	B-R	6-1	195	4-23-83	.200	—	.200	3	10	1	2	0	0	0	1	0	0	0	0	1	2	0	.200	.273
Powell, Pedro	B-R	5-7	145	5-20-84	.304	.316	.300	26	79	11	24	4	0	0	10	9	0	3	0	14	12	1	.354	.375
Riggans, Shawn	R-R	6-2	200	7-25-80	.256	.143	.281	12	39	5	10	2	0	0	2	4	2	0	0	6	1	0	.308	.356
Royster, Ryan	R-R	6-2	210	7-25-86	.229	.213	.234	104	371	32	85	19	1	5	38	26	2	2	3	106	3	1	.326	.281
Salem, Emeel	L-L	6-0	180	2-11-85	.255	.241	.259	99	357	54	91	12	7	0	22	36	3	6	2	36	24	9	.328	.327
Sexton, Greg	R-R	6-2	205	2-8-85	.244	.260	.239	67	238	37	58	7	2	3	37	25	2	4	7	30	4	2	.328	.313
Sweeney, Matt	L-R	6-3	215	4-4-88	.158	.333	.125	6	19	1	3	1	0	0	3	0	0	0	0	8	0	0	.211	.273
Thomas, Mark	R-R	6-1	180	5-5-88	.375	.000	.500	2	8	2	3	2	0	0	1	0	0	0	0	2	0	0	.625	.375
Upton, B.J.	R-R	6-3	185	8-21-84	.444	.000	.500	3	9	1	4	0	0	0	2	4	1	0	0	2	4	3	.444	.643
Vogt, Stephen	L-R	6-3	215	11-1-84	.171	.125	.185	10	35	0	6	2	0	0	3	2	0	0	0	4	0	1	.229	.216
Williams, Shawn	B-R	6-2	190	9-18-83	.246	.155	.266	96	317	32	78	18	2	3	30	30	11	5	3	84	2	1	.344	.330
Wrigley, Henry	R-R	6-3	180	8-9-86	.246	.279	.236	70	260	26	64	15	2	6	43	9	0	0	4	44	5	1	.388	.267

Pitching	B-T	HT	WT	DOB	W	L	ERA	G	GS	CG	SV	IP	H	R	ER	HR	BB	SO	AVG	vLH	vRH	K/9	BB/9
Boggan, Kevin	R-R	6-2	195	5-2-85	2	6	4.28	34	0	0	1	55	64	35	26	5	16	36	.294	.362	.242	5.93	2.63
Bradford, Chad	R-R	6-5	215	9-14-74	1	0	0.00	6	0	0	0	6	4	0	0	0	0	5	.190	.111	.250	7.50	0.00
Castro, Angel	R-R	5-11	200	11-14-82	0	2	22.50	4	0	0	0	6	11	15	15	3	7	6	.379	.455	.333	9.00	10.50
Cobb, Alex	R-R	6-1	180	10-7-87	8	5	3.03	24	23	0	0	125	116	49	42	6	31	107	.249	.291	.210	7.72	2.24
Darcy, Jesse	R-R	6-4	205	6-13-85	3	9	5.24	22	16	1	0	103	128	66	60	14	21	45	.311	.344	.291	3.93	1.83
de los Santos, Richard	R-R	6-1	175	6-14-86	2	0	0.79	13	0	0	10	23	11	4	2	0	4	21	.145	.162	.128	8.34	1.59
Downs, Darin	R-L	6-3	190	12-26-84	12	4	2.00	20	19	1	0	122	117	35	27	11	23	111	.253	.231	.263	8.21	1.70
Fleming, Marquis	R-R	6-1	181	9-11-86	0	0	9.00	2	0	0	0	2	3	2	2	0	1	5	.300	.000	.333	22.50	4.50
Flores, Brian	L-L	5-10	190	1-1-85	1	7	5.06	31	8	0	1	84	89	51	47	7	43	52	.279	.309	.263	5.59	4.63
Garcia, Justin	R-R	6-1	195	12-14-86	7	5	4.66	32	0	0	2	58	59	32	30	3	12	62	.260	.209	.294	9.62	1.86
Gorgen, Matt	R-R	6-0	210	1-27-87	4	0	0.57	28	0	0	15	48	24	4	3	1	16	59	.151	.123	.170	11.14	3.02
Hall, Jeremy	R-R	6-3	200	9-16-83	14	7	3.62	25	25	1	0	139	129	63	56	9	35	115	.244	.207	.274	7.43	2.26
Hinkle, Austin	R-R	6-1	200	9-3-86	2	6	3.53	36	3	0	7	74	61	34	29	7	36	65	.228	.223	.230	7.91	4.38
James, Craig	R-R	6-1	175	3-10-83	0	1	9.82	2	0	0	0	4	7	7	4	1	2	4	.389	.375	.400	9.82	4.91
Kazmir, Scott	L-L	6-0	190	1-24-84	0	0	0.00	1	1	0	0	5	3	0	0	0	1	5	.167	.000	.231	9.64	1.93
Mavares, Deivis	R-R	5-11	156	9-19-86	0	0	0.00	1	0	0	0	1	0	0	0	0	2	0	.000	.000	.000	0.00	18.00
McGee, Jake	L-L	6-3	190	8-6-86	0	2	6.45	11	11	0	0	22	26	16	16	2	9	26	.299	.323	.286	10.48	3.63
Mejias, Jose	R-R	6-0	150	8-18-85	1	2	6.41	19	3	0	1	46	58	37	33	11	11	30	.301	.349	.262	5.83	2.14
Morse, Ryan	L-L	6-3	200	5-21-83	0	1	4.82	3	2	0	0	9	9	7	5	0	1	10	.225	.267	.200	9.64	0.96
Newmann, David	R-L	6-2	200	6-24-85	9	6	3.44	24	24	2	0	131	108	59	50	6	46	128	.223	.195	.233	8.79	3.16
Oliveros, Rayner	R-R	6-2	180	9-23-85	1	0	1.24	11	1	0	0	29	17	4	4	1	5	30	.165	.367	.082	9.31	1.55
Phillips, Paul	R-R	6-1	211	1-26-84	2	1	3.33	18	0	0	2	27	27	12	10	2	10	27	.257	.310	.222	9.00	3.33

Rafferty, Tommy	R-R	6-1	165	2-5-85	1	2	3.38	26	0	0	1	43	32	18	16	2	20	41	.211	.219	.205	8.65	4.22
Satow, Josh	L-L	5-10	155	12-18-85	0	0	0.00	2	0	0	0	2	3	0	0	1	2	.300	.000	.375	9.00	4.50
Shouse, Brian	L-L	5-10	190	9-26-68	0	0	2.25	4	0	0	1	4	5	1	1	0	0	2	.313	.400	.273	4.50	0.00
Talbot, Mitch	R-R	6-2	200	10-17-83	0	0	0.00	1	1	0	0	3	1	0	0	0	0	6	.111	.000	.143	18.00	0.00

Fielding

Catcher	PCT	G	PO	A	E	DP	PB
Ashley	.993	54	373	57	3	5	5
Lopez	.978	37	240	27	6	0	2
McCormick	.990	24	173	31	2	1	2
Paxton	.994	19	139	15	1	2	1
Riggans	1.000	5	22	0	0	0	0
Thomas	1.000	2	14	2	0	0	1
Vogt	1.000	5	32	6	0	0	1

First Base	PCT	G	PO	A	E	DP
Cipriano	.986	18	131	10	2	10
Fields	.990	44	383	21	4	31
Paxton	1.000	3	7	1	0	0
Sexton	.917	1	10	1	1	1
Vogt	1.000	1	10	0	0	0
Williams	.995	21	179	11	1	11
Wrigley	.994	56	423	39	3	45

Second Base	PCT	G	PO	A	E	DP
Anderson	.978	36	52	81	3	19
Cipriano	.970	38	67	93	5	18
Hall	1.000	16	30	40	0	10
Luis	1.000	2	1	3	0	0
Luna	.969	46	96	123	7	28
Williams	1.000	5	11	9	0	2

Third Base	PCT	G	PO	A	E	DP
Cipriano	1.000	1	1	5	0	1
Hall	.926	37	19	69	7	6
Luna	.833	4	0	5	1	0
Sexton	.899	57	31	102	15	10
Williams	.885	37	16	61	10	5
Wrigley	.875	6	2	12	2	1

Shortstop	PCT	G	PO	A	E	DP
Bartlett	.000	1	0	0	1	0
Hall	.979	36	55	85	3	22

Luis	.889	2	2	6	1	0
Luna	.900	9	9	27	4	2
O'Malley	.960	94	147	234	16	42

Outfield	PCT	G	PO	A	E	DP
Fronk	.985	109	194	6	3	0
Lopez	1.000	1	1	0	0	0
Luis	1.000	1	1	0	0	0
Luna	.962	15	20	5	1	1
Matulia	.994	85	153	4	1	0
Perez	1.000	3	8	1	0	1
Powell	.978	24	44	0	1	0
Royster	.955	78	144	3	7	0
Salem	.990	96	194	2	2	1
Upton	1.000	2	4	0	0	0
Vogt	1.000	3	3	1	0	1
Wrigley	.952	7	20	0	1	0

BOWLING GREEN HOT RODS   LOW CLASS A
SOUTH ATLANTIC LEAGUE

Batting	B-T	HT	WT	DOB	AVG	vLH	vRH	G	AB	R	H	2B	3B	HR	RBI	BB	HBP	SH	SF	SO	SB	CS	SLG	OBP
Beckham, Jeremy	R-R	5-10	175	6-1-86	.226	.277	.209	70	186	23	42	6	2	1	9	23	12	3	0	43	9	5	.296	.348
Beckham, Tim	R-R	6-0	190	1-27-90	.275	.212	.291	125	491	58	135	33	4	5	63	34	7	0	5	116	13	10	.389	.328
Corder, Jason	R-R	6-2	195	9-6-85	.229	.216	.233	56	201	18	46	19	1	3	30	14	5	1	0	30	1	1	.378	.295
Estrada, Robi	R-R	5-10	170	10-8-88	.225	.250	.219	89	289	31	65	8	3	1	27	13	0	5	6	51	5	4	.284	.253
Hauschild, Tyler	R-R	6-0	210	11-24-85	.203	.357	.169	23	79	7	16	3	0	1	3	3	3	1	0	33	0	0	.278	.259
Jefferies, Jake	L-R	6-2	200	10-30-87	.261	.243	.267	116	440	54	115	17	1	8	50	37	7	3	3	35	7	2	.359	.326
Kang, K.D.	L-L	6-2	200	2-6-88	.307	.305	.307	89	316	42	97	29	7	5	42	40	4	0	2	74	10	5	.491	.390
McCormick, Mike	R-R	6-2	200	9-6-86	.165	.132	.172	64	218	27	36	7	0	4	13	29	3	1	0	76	1	0	.252	.272
Mollicone, John	R-R	6-1	220	9-9-85	.223	.143	.256	53	166	18	37	7	0	5	25	14	6	2	1	47	0	1	.355	.305
Reynolds, Justin	R-R	6-3	195	11-13-86	.228	.205	.236	87	272	38	62	11	1	4	35	26	3	2	3	80	13	6	.320	.299
Scelfo, Anthony	L-R	5-10	195	9-19-86	.244	.170	.262	125	484	61	118	18	5	8	52	41	3	6	3	106	12	11	.351	.307
Sheridan, Mike	L-L	6-2	205	8-8-87	.238	.182	.251	122	442	51	105	16	5	14	57	26	2	8	8	38	4	2	.391	.278
Tweedy, Jason	L-R	6-0	170	9-29-86	.194	.193	.195	88	288	32	56	14	4	0	16	31	0	3	4	61	7	3	.271	.269
Velasquez, Isaias	R-R	5-11	155	5-7-88	.278	.256	.284	122	428	58	119	30	6	2	40	36	7	5	2	74	14	4	.390	.342
Wrigley, Henry	R-R	6-3	180	8-9-86	.220	.175	.234	45	177	20	39	5	1	4	17	5	1	0	1	30	3	4	.390	.245

Pitching	B-T	HT	WT	DOB	W	L	ERA	G	GS	CG	SV	IP	H	R	ER	HR	BB	SO	AVG	vLH	vRH	K/9	BB/9
Andujar, Chris	R-R	6-2	180	8-24-87	10	4	2.70	31	17	0	0	120	99	44	36	7	42	79	.220	.230	.214	5.93	3.15
Bagley, Jamie	R-R	6-3	215	7-16-87	2	5	6.67	36	0	0	9	57	65	45	42	6	20	47	.288	.321	.269	7.46	3.18
Barnese, Nick	R-R	6-2	170	1-11-89	6	5	2.53	15	15	0	0	75	56	30	21	3	25	62	.202	.183	.214	7.47	3.01
Cruz, Joe	R-R	6-4	190	7-20-88	5	8	4.04	21	21	0	0	98	110	54	44	5	26	99	.284	.287	.282	9.09	2.39
De Los Santos, Frank	L-L	6-0	165	11-17-87	4	10	3.65	27	27	1	0	136	136	69	55	7	45	81	.258	.165	.280	5.37	2.99
Dyer, Shane	R-R	6-3	185	3-9-88	1	10	5.06	25	16	0	0	101	121	65	57	3	32	76	.297	.315	.286	6.75	2.84
Echeverria, Diego	R-R	5-11	190	1-1-85	3	2	8.01	34	0	0	0	61	72	62	54	5	38	39	.290	.311	.278	5.79	5.64
Fleming, Marquis	R-R	6-1	181	9-11-86	2	7	2.86	42	0	0	5	63	53	29	20	2	30	68	.227	.235	.223	9.71	4.29
Hayes, Tyree	R-R	6-0	175	8-8-88	7	5	5.23	34	2	0	0	74	87	46	43	6	30	70	.297	.311	.289	8.51	3.65
Jarman, Michael	L-L	6-1	195	6-6-85	4	6	3.82	21	10	0	0	73	72	43	31	7	25	52	.254	.227	.261	6.41	3.08
Mavares, Deivis	R-R	5-11	156	9-19-86	0	0	4.50	2	0	0	0	6	4	3	3	2	1	5	.190	.250	.176	7.50	1.50
Moore, Matt	L-L	6-2	205	6-18-89	8	5	3.15	26	26	0	0	123	86	51	43	6	70	176	.195	.181	.198	12.88	5.12
Rafferty, Tommy	R-R	6-1	165	2-5-85	2	0	3.90	15	0	0	1	28	29	14	12	1	8	22	.266	.294	.253	7.16	2.60
Santana, Juan	R-R	6-0	180	3-5-86	0	1	3.55	10	2	0	1	25	18	10	10	3	14	12	.202	.161	.224	4.26	4.97
Satow, Josh	L-L	5-10	155	12-18-85	4	0	2.29	44	0	0	20	63	48	17	16	2	15	65	.206	.216	.203	9.29	2.14
Schenk, Neil	L-L	6-3	220	6-17-86	6	4	4.46	39	2	0	0	75	88	46	37	6	22	72	.288	.257	.297	8.68	2.65

Fielding

Catcher	PCT	G	PO	A	E	DP	PB
Hauschild	.977	23	195	19	5	2	3
Jefferies	.982	54	398	36	8	4	9
McCormick	.988	43	296	39	4	2	9
Mollicone	.982	21	150	16	3	1	2

First Base	PCT	G	PO	A	E	DP
Mollicone	.958	13	102	12	5	6
Scelfo	1.000	2	14	0	0	0
Sheridan	.995	121	1124	54	6	80
Wrigley	.962	6	47	3	2	5

Second Base	PCT	G	PO	A	E	DP
Beckham	.959	26	41	52	4	11
Estrada	.982	54	82	137	4	30
Tweedy	.923	11	14	22	3	7
Velasquez	.959	53	62	147	9	28

Third Base	PCT	G	PO	A	E	DP
Beckham	.885	33	23	69	12	4
Estrada	.882	17	8	37	6	3
Tweedy	.836	20	12	34	9	0
Velasquez	.898	64	30	146	20	9
Wrigley	.864	6	5	14	3	1

Shortstop	PCT	G	PO	A	E	DP
Beckham	.919	117	160	328	43	64
Estrada	.956	21	30	57	4	7
Velasquez	1.000	2	6	12	0	1

Outfield	PCT	G	PO	A	E	DP
Beckham	1.000	6	7	0	0	0
Corder	.973	53	102	7	3	1
Kang	.965	69	104	6	4	1
Reynolds	.984	84	123	2	2	1
Scelfo	.976	123	230	12	6	3
Tweedy	.952	56	74	6	4	1
Wrigley	.938	31	44	1	3	1

HUDSON VALLEY RENEGADES
SHORT-SEASON
NEW YORK-PENN LEAGUE

Batting	B-T	HT	WT	DOB	AVG	vLH	vRH	G	AB	R	H	2B	3B	HR	RBI	BB	HBP	SH	SF	SO	SB	CS	SLG	OBP
Acosta, Mayobanex	R-R	6-1	205	11-20-87	.255	.333	.213	55	188	16	48	9	1	2	20	18	0	0	3	34	8	5	.346	.316
Biell, Dustin	L-R	6-0	175	3-19-87	.277	.321	.261	59	191	34	53	5	3	2	17	18	8	6	1	41	12	3	.366	.362
Bortnick, Tyler	R-R	5-11	185	7-3-87	.300	.310	.295	65	217	37	65	17	4	4	26	27	4	6	1	38	24	8	.470	.386
Cohen, Gabe	R-R	6-2	205	11-7-87	.206	.220	.198	41	131	12	27	6	0	3	12	9	2	2	1	35	5	3	.321	.266
Davis, Bennett	R-R	5-10	180	2-9-86	.213	.250	.202	46	136	17	29	6	2	0	17	11	5	0	3	25	4	2	.287	.290
Genao, David	R-R	5-11	210	12-15-86	.211	.150	.239	41	128	7	27	4	0	0	13	13	6	0	1	29	5	5	.242	.311
Jones, D.J.	L-L	6-1	185	12-15-87	.215	.108	.255	47	135	14	29	6	2	1	9	4	0	2	0	31	7	3	.311	.237
Luis, Diogenes	B-R	5-10	169	5-7-87	.239	.257	.233	50	138	17	33	3	2	0	9	9	3	7	0	41	6	3	.290	.300
Murrill, Chris	L-L	6-2	190	6-5-88	.306	.322	.299	49	193	31	59	7	2	0	18	13	4	4	1	46	29	7	.363	.360
Nommensen, Brett	L-L	5-11	190	10-6-86	.258	.219	.279	57	186	21	48	4	4	1	26	20	7	4	3	37	15	5	.339	.347
Otero, Elias	B-R	6-2	166	12-19-87	.196	.211	.189	59	219	18	43	5	2	0	13	12	1	4	2	47	4	5	.237	.239
Reynolds, Burt	R-R	6-1	190	9-13-88	.230	.177	.267	38	148	15	34	7	4	1	9	2	0	0	1	42	9	3	.351	.238
Sonoqui, Eli	L-L	6-2	195	1-20-88	.269	.174	.313	57	216	26	58	11	0	4	30	9	2	1	1	61	3	1	.375	.303
Thomas, Mark	R-R	6-2	180	5-5-88	.268	.239	.284	60	205	18	55	10	1	4	29	24	4	0	1	44	3	3	.385	.355

Pitching	B-T	HT	WT	DOB	W	L	ERA	G	GS	CG	SV	IP	H	R	ER	HR	BB	SO	AVG	vLH	vRH	K/9	BB/9
Amargos, Jordi	R-R	5-11	165	2-5-86	0	4	7.52	16	0	0	0	26	34	27	22	1	14	18	.309	.386	.258	6.15	4.78
April, Dan	L-L	6-1	190	11-8-86	0	0	0.00	1	0	0	0	1	1	0	0	0	0	1	.200	.500	.000	6.75	0.00
Ayers, Kyle	R-R	6-4	220	9-6-89	3	1	2.45	7	5	0	0	26	18	11	7	2	7	13	.196	.186	.204	4.56	2.45
Chapa, Angel	R-R	6-2	170	5-14-87	3	4	4.15	18	0	0	0	39	41	20	18	2	15	28	.279	.291	.272	6.46	3.46
Chavez, Kevin	R-R	6-3	206	6-24-89	1	2	4.68	16	8	0	0	58	61	32	30	3	21	31	.277	.283	.271	4.84	3.28
Cinadr, Jeff	R-R	6-6	200	8-8-87	0	0	4.91	2	0	0	0	4	1	2	2	1	1	1	.083	.000	.167	2.45	2.45
Colome, Alexander	R-R	6-2	184	12-31-88	7	4	1.66	15	15	2	0	76	46	22	14	0	32	94	.174	.169	.178	11.13	3.79
de los Santos, Richard	R-R	6-1	175	6-1-84	2	0	2.81	8	0	0	4	16	12	5	5	0	6	13	.214	.174	.242	7.31	3.38
Dott, Aaron	R-L	6-4	215	5-17-88	1	4	4.12	13	9	0	0	44	52	28	20	0	16	29	.291	.200	.326	5.98	3.30
Florentino, Bladimir	R-R	6-2	187	9-20-84	2	3	4.11	21	0	0	4	35	38	17	16	2	13	37	.286	.320	.241	9.51	3.34
Fuller, Devin	R-R	6-2	225	12-15-88	4	2	2.92	13	0	0	0	49	44	22	16	6	13	31	.239	.235	.242	5.66	4.74
Gibson, Glenn	L-L	6-4	195	9-21-87	3	4	6.89	14	3	0	1	33	40	29	25	4	20	19	.292	.290	.292	5.23	5.51
Hill, Hunter	R-R	5-11	185	11-30-88	0	1	6.27	12	0	0	0	19	20	15	13	0	12	12	.278	.313	.250	5.79	5.79
Lobstein, Kyle	L-L	6-2	190	8-12-89	3	5	2.58	14	14	0	0	73	55	23	21	4	23	74	.204	.205	.203	9.08	2.82
McEachern, Jason	R-R	6-2	160	10-12-90	2	3	2.75	11	11	1	0	56	56	23	17	3	12	47	.260	.223	.295	7.60	1.94
Quate, Zach	R-R	6-1	200	9-12-87	1	0	0.35	18	0	0	13	26	15	2	1	0	4	34	.170	.200	.140	11.77	1.38
Salinas, Doug	R-R	6-4	195	12-5-88	5	0	2.61	22	0	0	0	41	30	13	12	2	8	36	.201	.232	.175	7.84	1.74
Santana, Juan	R-R	6-0	180	3-5-86	0	0	5.14	8	0	0	0	14	20	11	8	2	4	12	.333	.192	.441	7.71	2.57
Suarez, Albert	R-R	6-2	186	10-8-89	1	0	2.79	2	2	0	0	10	8	3	3	1	2	4	.222	.381	.000	3.72	1.86

Fielding

Catcher	PCT	G	PO	A	E	DP	PB
Acosta	.997	37	257	33	1	6	11
Genao	1.000	8	39	5	0	0	2
Thomas	.982	35	245	29	5	1	6

First Base	PCT	G	PO	A	E	DP
Genao	.968	21	173	9	6	8
Sonoqui	.986	56	457	37	7	32

Second Base	PCT	G	PO	A	E	DP
Bortnick	.952	5	8	12	1	3

	PCT	G	PO	A	E	DP	PB
Davis	.965	14	17	38	2	2
Otero	.964	58	110	128	9	19

Third Base	PCT	G	PO	A	E	DP
Bortnick	.933	13	5	23	2	1
Davis	.836	26	12	39	10	1
Luis	.895	7	4	13	2	0
Reynolds	.924	35	18	79	8	1

Shortstop	PCT	G	PO	A	E	DP
Bortnick	.952	43	75	102	9	22

	PCT	G	PO	A	E	DP
Luis	.924	37	37	85	10	10

Outfield	PCT	G	PO	A	E	DP
Biell	.985	57	126	4	2	3
Cohen	.952	37	59	0	3	0
Jones	.974	45	72	3	2	0
Luis	1.000	2	1	0	0	0
Murrill	.957	47	88	2	4	0
Nommensen	.980	51	88	9	2	2

PRINCETON DEVIL RAYS
ROOKIE
APPALACHIAN LEAGUE

Batting	B-T	HT	WT	DOB	AVG	vLH	vRH	G	AB	R	H	2B	3B	HR	RBI	BB	HBP	SH	SF	SO	SB	CS	SLG	OBP
Bryles, Brian	R-R	6-1	170	11-4-89	.181	.180	.182	58	226	37	41	8	4	1	12	22	2	4	3	57	6	8	.265	.257
Cedeno, Julio	R-R	6-2	185	8-25-89	.272	.234	.290	54	202	26	55	11	0	5	34	17	5	1	3	52	4	2	.401	.339
Francisco, Tomas	R-R	6-0	210	4-4-88	.224	.263	.207	37	125	10	28	6	1	0	20	5	2	0	1	31	1	3	.288	.263
Glynn, Geno	R-R	6-1	190	10-27-86	.253	.211	.268	25	75	13	19	6	1	1	11	10	0	1	1	14	2	0	.400	.337
Henry, Seth	R-R	5-9	178	3-23-87	.205	.171	.220	39	117	23	24	8	1	1	12	27	5	2	1	30	6	1	.316	.373
Morrison, Ty	L-R	6-2	170	7-22-90	.271	.269	.272	59	225	34	61	9	2	3	18	27	7	5	1	61	20	5	.369	.365
Novas, Ramon	R-R	6-2	170	10-14-87	.208	.244	.188	34	125	8	26	7	2	0	4	5	2	0	0	22	2	2	.296	.250
Patton, Jason	L-R	6-3	180	12-27-86	.278	.286	.275	45	169	19	47	8	4	3	24	13	1	1	1	36	7	2	.426	.332
Rhault, Dan	L-R	6-2	205	9-18-86	.196	.250	.178	50	158	18	31	5	0	0	9	22	0	1	0	36	2	0	.228	.294
Rogers, John	L-R	6-2	175	9-13-88	.303	.344	.284	52	198	33	60	7	6	6	37	20	0	0	2	54	14	1	.490	.364
Spraker, Kyle	R-R	5-11	170	1-10-86	.244	.235	.248	49	172	29	42	9	1	1	24	12	8	0	2	37	4	3	.326	.323
Torres, Alejandro	R-R	6-1	178	9-30-88	.222	.333	.194	34	117	16	26	5	0	1	5	2	0	0	0	24	1	2	.291	.235
Wendt, David	R-R	6-5	205	1-2-87	.298	.333	.282	19	57	2	17	6	0	0	12	4	1	1	0	9	0	0	.404	.355
Wiegand, Ryan	L-R	6-4	225	12-30-86	.324	.260	.356	59	222	37	72	19	0	5	35	23	1	0	1	29	2	0	.477	.389

Pitching	B-T	HT	WT	DOB	W	L	ERA	G	GS	CG	SV	IP	H	R	ER	HR	BB	SO	AVG	vLH	vRH	K/9	BB/9
Bencomo, Omar	R-R	6-1	168	2-10-89	2	1	3.47	9	9	0	0	36	37	20	14	5	5	29	.253	.283	.237	7.18	1.24
Cinadr, Jeff	R-R	6-6	200	8-8-87	2	0	4.94	10	0	0	0	27	34	18	15	3	5	25	.306	.282	.319	8.23	1.65
Dettrich, Julius	L-L	6-4	175	9-23-88	5	5	2.92	12	12	0	0	62	49	23	20	4	15	36	.213	.135	.228	5.25	2.19
Hill, Hunter	R-R	5-11	185	11-30-88	1	0	0.00	6	0	0	1	9	8	0	0	0	2	11	.242	.444	.167	10.61	1.93

	B-T	HT	WT	DOB	W	L	ERA	G	GS	CG	SV	IP	H	R	ER	HR	BB	SO	AVG	vLH	vRH	K/9	BB/9
Koronis, Alex	R-R	6-2	187	1-4-88	1	3	1.95	15	0	0	3	28	19	7	6	2	8	34	.198	.222	.188	11.06	2.60
Mavares, Deivis	R-R	5-11	156	9-19-86	5	1	2.81	14	4	0	1	51	40	19	16	4	20	49	.216	.195	.231	8.59	3.51
McEachern, Jason	R-R	6-2	160	10-12-90	0	0	1.06	3	3	0	0	17	11	2	2	1	0	15	.190	.077	.222	7.94	0.00
Oakes, Tyler	R-R	6-3	221	11-8-86	2	0	3.82	14	1	0	0	33	24	14	14	4	16	28	.205	.265	.162	7.64	4.36
Rodriguez, Wilking	R-R	6-1	160	3-2-90	1	6	3.21	13	13	0	0	56	44	24	20	5	12	52	.213	.149	.248	8.36	1.93
Rosscup, Zach	R-L	6-2	205	6-9-88	3	4	2.68	10	9	0	0	40	41	20	12	0	6	27	.263	.300	.254	6.02	1.34
Shull, Trevor	R-R	6-4	180	8-7-90	4	4	4.62	13	12	1	0	60	68	35	31	6	16	50	.275	.217	.305	7.46	2.39
Shuman, Scott	R-R	6-3	205	3-28-88	0	0	0.82	10	0	0	3	22	18	4	2	0	9	29	.222	.226	.220	11.86	3.68
Stabelfeld, Matt	L-L	5-10	185	8-21-86	1	0	3.10	16	0	0	0	20	19	15	7	0	12	18	.232	.200	.239	7.97	5.31
Sullivan, Jake	L-L	6-5	210	11-15-86	0	1	81.00	1	0	0	0	0	3	4	3	0	2	0	.750	—	.750	0.00	54.00
Yates, Kirby	R-R	5-10	170	3-25-87	0	1	2.39	14	0	0	4	26	22	7	7	0	8	49	.227	.297	.183	16.75	2.73

Fielding

Catcher	PCT	G	PO	A	E	DP	PB
Francisco	.984	31	225	27	4	3	2
Torres	.987	27	203	21	3	3	6
Wendt	1.000	15	80	10	0	0	1

First Base	PCT	G	PO	A	E	DP
Francisco	.982	7	48	6	1	5
Glynn	.970	8	61	3	2	5
Henry	—	1	0	0	0	0
Wiegand	.988	54	483	28	6	38

Second Base	PCT	G	PO	A	E	DP
Henry	.977	37	68	105	4	21
Spraker	.952	31	66	94	8	15

Third Base	PCT	G	PO	A	E	DP
Cedeno	.892	53	34	106	17	7
Glynn	.875	15	7	21	4	1

Shortstop	PCT	G	PO	A	E	DP
Henry	1.000	1	2	2	0	1

	PCT	G	PO	A	E	DP
Rhault	.943	50	53	128	11	22
Spraker	.908	18	20	49	7	11

Outfield	PCT	G	PO	A	E	DP
Bryles	.940	52	74	4	5	0
Morrison	.980	54	95	3	2	1
Novas	.907	28	48	1	5	1
Patton	.967	25	28	1	1	0
Rogers	.928	42	62	2	5	1

GCL RAYS   ROOKIE
GULF COAST LEAGUE

Batting	B-T	HT	WT	DOB	AVG	vLH	vRH	G	AB	R	H	2B	3B	HR	RBI	BB	HBP	SH	SF	SO	SB	CS	SLG	OBP
Cipriota, Jacinto	R-R	5-11	180	3-23-90	.000	—	.000	3	4	0	0	0	0	0	0	0	1	0	0	1	0	0	.000	.200
Contreras, Ruben	B-R	6-2	190	8-18-87	.226	.192	.233	50	159	21	36	6	3	3	15	13	0	1	1	38	11	5	.358	.283
Cuello, Juan	R-R	5-11	170	5-9-89	.239	.231	.241	44	138	17	33	6	0	1	12	8	3	0	1	21	4	2	.304	.293
Diaz, Alex	R-R	6-1	180	11-15-91	.179	.214	.171	42	145	9	26	5	0	0	8	3	0	0	1	40	2	1	.214	.195
Fukunaga, Claudio	B-R	5-10	165	11-5-87	.161	.000	.189	20	62	5	10	0	0	0	5	3	0	1	0	11	1	1	.161	.200
Glaesmann, Todd	R-R	6-4	220	10-24-90	.278	.000	.313	5	18	1	5	1	0	0	2	0	0	0	0	3	1	0	.333	.278
Gomez, Hector	L-L	6-2	187	2-13-88	.204	.077	.233	43	142	13	29	10	3	1	16	9	1	0	0	35	1	2	.338	.257
Gonzalez, Felix	B-R	5-10	165	4-4-90	.226	.318	.212	46	168	17	38	7	3	0	15	7	0	4	0	44	8	2	.304	.257
Jacobo, Astin	R-R	6-0	167	12-15-88	.133	.200	.111	31	60	5	8	2	1	0	3	3	0	1	1	30	1	3	.200	.172
Johnson, Elliot	B-R	6-0	190	3-9-84	.313	.000	.357	5	16	2	5	2	0	0	2	2	0	0	0	1	0	0	.438	.389
Malm, Jeff	L-L	6-3	225	10-31-90	.240	.000	.250	7	25	2	6	0	0	0	1	1	0	0	0	4	1	0	.240	.296
Marchena, Luis	R-R	5-10	155	11-21-89	.265	.125	.283	26	68	7	18	1	0	0	5	11	0	0	0	11	1	1	.279	.367
Nakandakare, Lucas	R-R	6-2	215	9-18-89	.172	.100	.185	27	64	3	11	0	0	0	7	7	2	1	0	13	0	1	.172	.274
Olivares, Gerardo	R-R	6-0	187	8-14-88	.257	.313	.245	51	179	16	46	12	1	0	21	11	4	0	2	24	0	0	.335	.311
Pace, Hunter	R-R	5-10	170	12-5-86	.215	.321	.193	47	163	16	35	3	1	0	12	15	4	0	1	27	11	4	.245	.295
Perez, Fernando	B-R	6-1	195	4-23-83	.000	—	.000	1	3	0	0	0	0	0	0	0	0	0	0	3	0	0	.000	.000
Perry, Jason	L-R	6-0	200	8-18-80	.333	—	.333	3	6	2	2	0	0	0	1	2	0	0	1	1	0	0	.333	.444
Segovia, Alejandro	R-R	6-0	181	4-27-90	.188	.462	.125	23	69	3	13	5	0	0	9	6	5	0	2	6	0	1	.261	.293
Simas, Travis	R-R	6-5	205	8-12-87	.191	.182	.192	32	89	11	17	5	0	0	3	13	4	0	1	26	0	0	.247	.318
Vasquez, Cristian	R-R	6-1	155	3-9-90	.171	.129	.183	46	146	15	25	4	0	0	12	10	0	2	0	53	10	2	.219	.248

Pitching	B-T	HT	WT	DOB	W	L	ERA	G	GS	CG	SV	IP	H	R	ER	HR	BB	SO	AVG	vLH	vRH	K/9	BB/9
Almonte, Wilmer	R-R	5-11	164	8-19-89	3	2	3.32	12	7	0	0	62	62	24	23	4	8	37	.262	.260	.263	5.34	1.16
Bellatti, Andrew	R-R	6-1	170	8-5-91	1	0	3.38	12	3	0	0	29	30	12	11	1	7	29	.265	.283	.250	8.90	2.15
De La Cruz, Jose	L-L	5-11	173	8-16-87	0	0	30.86	3	0	0	0	2	5	8	8	2	3	0	.417	.333	.444	0.00	11.57
Furdal, Brad	R-R	6-2	185	10-21-90	1	5	3.86	12	8	0	1	51	55	27	22	0	18	49	.271	.206	.330	8.59	3.16
James, Kevin	L-L	6-4	190	10-1-90	0	0	0.00	1	0	0	0	1	1	0	0	0	1	0	.250	.000	.333	9.00	0.00
Mateo, Victor	R-R	6-5	180	7-27-89	3	4	1.98	10	9	0	0	50	42	23	11	1	9	38	.226	.244	.208	6.84	1.62
McGee, Jake	L-L	6-3	190	8-6-86	0	2	3.52	5	5	0	0	8	5	4	3	0	3	14	.172	.273	.111	16.43	3.52
Mercedes, Aneuris	R-R	6-0	180	5-1-87	0	0	2.75	16	0	0	4	20	15	9	6	1	12	20	.208	.240	.191	9.15	5.49
Molina, Jose	L-L	5-11	160	6-26-91	2	3	6.00	15	0	0	0	24	32	19	16	1	9	16	.327	.429	.299	6.00	3.38
Monegro, Jose	R-R	6-2	180	3-22-90	2	5	5.40	11	0	0	0	20	25	15	12	2	6	12	.301	.342	.267	5.40	2.70
Partridge, Jacob	L-L	6-3	200	12-21-90	0	2	1.75	11	7	1	0	36	26	8	7	0	13	39	.202	.276	.180	9.75	3.25
Perez, Elvin	R-R	6-0	165	3-3-86	0	0	9.53	6	0	0	3	6	8	6	6	0	7	2	.348	.333	.375	4.76	11.12
Proctor, Marcus	R-R	6-0	170	8-21-91	0	1	1.80	3	0	0	0	5	4	1	1	0	0	6	.211	.143	.250	10.80	0.00
Romero, Enny	L-L	6-3	165	1-24-91	2	4	4.81	11	4	0	0	39	38	25	21	2	21	33	.255	.179	.282	7.55	4.81
Smith, Shawn	R-L	6-3	180	9-9-90	1	1	3.00	10	0	0	0	21	22	10	7	2	10	13	.278	.286	.276	5.57	4.29
Suero, Eliazer	R-R	6-4	170	6-7-89	2	3	3.38	12	5	0	1	51	48	23	19	1	12	39	.250	.259	.243	6.93	2.13
Swilley, Matt	R-R	6-2	175	12-19-90	1	1	5.91	9	0	0	1	11	12	8	7	0	11	10	.293	.316	.273	8.44	9.28
Talbot, Mitch	R-R	6-2	200	10-17-83	0	0	0.82	4	4	0	0	11	5	1	1	0	0	21	.132	.167	.071	17.18	0.00
Townsend, Wade	R-R	6-4	230	2-22-83	0	1	13.50	3	3	0	0	3	3	4	4	1	7	3	.273	.250	.286	10.13	23.63
Yendis, Luis	R-R	6-3	178	7-19-89	1	1	9.64	11	0	0	0	14	16	19	15	0	17	7	.296	.474	.200	4.50	10.93

Fielding

Catcher	PCT	G	PO	A	E	DP	PB
Nakandakare	1.000	2	1	0	0	0	0
Olivares	.977	29	187	27	5	3	2
Segovia	.991	15	98	18	1	1	2

Simas	.974	19	103	10	3	2	1

First Base	PCT	G	PO	A	E	DP
Contreras	1.000	2	3	0	0	0

	PCT	G	PO	A	E	DP
Gomez	.972	33	253	27	8	23
Malm	1.000	6	43	2	0	1
Nakandakare	1.000	21	162	4	0	15

Second Base	PCT	G	PO	A	E	DP
Cipriota	1.000	1	2	1	0	1
Cuello	1.000	10	15	30	0	7
Fukunaga	1.000	7	19	24	0	4
Gonzalez	.987	19	37	38	1	10
Johnson	1.000	4	7	9	0	4
Marchena	1.000	20	30	40	0	8

Third Base	PCT	G	PO	A	E	DP
Cuello	.909	33	22	58	8	8

Fukunaga	.947	8	2	16	1	2
Gonzalez	.933	8	8	20	2	3
Marchena	.842	6	3	13	3	2
Vasquez	.778	5	4	10	4	3

Shortstop	PCT	G	PO	A	E	DP
Gonzalez	.964	17	24	30	2	6
Vasquez	.909	41	48	111	16	18

Outfield	PCT	G	PO	A	E	DP
Contreras	.990	47	98	3	1	1

Diaz	.964	41	52	2	2	1
Fukunaga	1.000	2	4	0	0	0
Glaesmann	1.000	4	6	2	0	1
Gomez	1.000	11	12	0	0	0
Jacobo	1.000	25	37	2	0	0
Nakandakare	—	1	0	0	0	0
Pace	.976	46	79	4	2	0
Perez	—	1	0	0	0	0
Perry	1.000	2	2	0	0	0

DSL RAYS ROOKIE

DOMINICAN SUMMER LEAGUE

Batting	B-T	HT	WT	DOB	AVG	vLH	vRH	G	AB	R	H	2B	3B	HR	RBI	BB	HBP	SH	SF	SO	SB	CS	SLG	OBP
Caminero, Leandro	R-R	6-1	185	10-24-89	.260	.300	.252	50	177	31	46	10	2	0	18	13	3	3	6	30	12	1	.339	.312
De Castro, Raynill	R-R	6-3	175	12-11-89	.167	.000	.200	3	6	2	1	0	0	0	3	0	0	0	1	1	0	0	.167	.444
Dorville, Edward	R-R	6-1	185	11-5-88	.304	.194	.327	56	204	44	62	11	6	9	37	19	5	2	3	70	11	4	.549	.372
Eder, Federico	L-R	5-9	165	9-5-90	.284	.273	.286	21	74	16	21	3	0	0	16	7	3	2	2	18	7	4	.324	.360
Elie, Alexis	R-R	6-3	206	8-21-90	.248	.273	.241	37	105	19	26	5	0	1	14	11	11	0	1	27	1	0	.324	.375
Gomez, Jhonatan	R-R	6-1	180	11-13-88	.199	.250	.186	42	146	29	29	6	3	0	18	29	2	1	4	24	6	2	.281	.331
Guillen, Cesar	R-R	6-1	185	3-15-89	.375	.304	.389	34	136	31	51	12	0	0	26	19	2	1	1	7	15	3	.463	.456
Guzman, Braly	R-R	6-2	188	9-29-88	.188	.125	.208	33	101	15	19	2	0	0	11	13	5	1	1	22	3	2	.208	.308
Inirio, Jorge	B-R	5-11	170	6-21-87	.186	.182	.188	35	102	17	19	2	3	0	14	24	5	0	1	19	3	1	.265	.364
Isenia, Ludson	B-R	6-1	206	11-24-89	.216	.167	.226	29	74	22	16	3	1	0	8	18	0	0	1	23	5	3	.284	.366
Lafontaines, Jose	B-R	5-9	185	10-6-88	.322	.231	.338	24	90	13	29	5	3	1	17	11	5	0	2	16	11	5	.478	.417
Marte, Luis	R-R	6-3	180	2-23-91	.200	.250	.189	34	90	11	18	2	0	0	6	7	2	3	0	35	7	3	.222	.273
Martin, Juan	R-R	6-1	200	5-12-90	.288	.346	.261	37	118	19	33	6	0	0	15	6	6	4	2	28	2	1	.331	.341
Mejia, Yermis	B-R	6-0	165	1-5-90	.233	.250	.231	9	30	4	7	0	1	0	6	3	0	0	1	10	1	0	.400	.294
2-team total (20 Diamondbacks)					.224	—	—	29	67	12	15	3	1	1	12	11	0	1	1	19	1	0	.343	.329
Morillo, Julian	B-R	5-11	167	12-10-91	.291	.194	.314	52	189	38	55	6	2	0	27	30	10	0	1	21	11	9	.344	.413
Quinonez, Jonathan	R-R	6-1	187	11-27-90	.800	1.000	.750	3	5	5	4	0	0	1	1	3	0	0	0	1	0	0	1.400	.875
Rodriguez, Hector	R-R	6-2	210	11-5-89	.276	.216	.289	61	217	35	60	14	0	2	38	29	9	0	4	32	1	3	.369	.378
Rodriguez, Starlin	B-R	5-9	160	12-13-89	.227	.200	.235	8	22	7	5	0	0	0	2	5	3	0	0	7	3	1	.227	.433
Rosa, Adderly	B-R	6-0	167	7-4-91	.243	.105	.272	37	111	25	27	3	1	0	10	31	6	3	0	20	16	6	.288	.432
Rosario, Waldo	R-R	6-2	185	10-13-89	.258	.286	.252	47	155	24	40	6	0	0	17	18	3	1	1	50	16	9	.297	.345
Santana, Arturo	R-R	6-2	200	2-1-90	.260	.364	.242	30	73	14	19	3	0	4	12	8	4	0	1	21	0	1	.466	.360
Soriano, Ariel	R-R	5-11	160	11-24-90	1.000	—	1.000	1	1	1	1	0	0	0	0	0	0	1	0	0	0	0	1.000	1.000

Pitching	B-T	HT	WT	DOB	W	L	ERA	G	GS	CG	SV	IP	H	R	ER	HR	BB	SO	AVG	vLH	vRH	K/9	BB/9
Cedeno, Carlos	R-R	6-2	180	7-19-90	0	1	12.60	5	0	0	0	5	3	7	7	0	9	7	.167	.500	.125	12.60	16.20
De Leon, Noel	R-R	6-5	176	7-6-88	0	4	2.95	19	0	0	1	40	41	20	13	2	11	27	.256	.133	.285	6.13	2.50
Dominguez, Ney	L-L	6-2	160	7-17-91	1	2	6.27	17	5	0	0	37	43	30	26	2	32	25	.299	.267	.302	6.03	7.71
Fermin, Jose	R-R	6-1	180	9-16-90	4	3	6.10	14	7	0	0	38	36	28	26	1	34	34	.259	.326	.229	7.98	7.98
Galan, Genaro	L-L	6-2	196	1-20-88	0	1	4.55	10	5	0	0	28	20	15	0	27	20	.255	.667	.243	6.07	8.19
Guerrero, Joan	L-L	6-2	170	1-22-91	1	3	5.86	15	10	0	0	51	67	43	33	3	30	35	.319	.222	.333	6.22	5.33
Jasco, Joselo	R-R	6-0	170	10-12-88	1	3	8.10	10	0	0	0	13	14	20	12	0	15	10	.275	.278	.273	6.75	10.13
Lara, Braulio	L-L	6-1	180	12-20-88	5	3	3.58	13	8	1	0	55	52	29	22	2	21	58	.242	.333	.234	9.43	3.42
Linares, Joice	L-L	5-10	182	4-21-90	0	0	0.00	2	1	0	0	2	0	0	0	2	6	.091	.000	.105	9.00	3.00
Ozoria, Ronny	R-R	6-3	185	6-5-89	2	1	6.68	14	2	0	0	32	33	31	24	1	19	25	.264	.258	.266	6.96	5.29
Pie, Juan	R-R	6-3	164	7-17-90	2	0	3.00	9	0	0	0	15	12	5	5	0	11	12	.231	.333	.224	7.20	6.60
Reyes, Robinson	L-L	6-4	200	11-15-88	0	1	6.75	12	10	0	0	17	16	17	13	0	16	15	.246	.111	.268	7.79	8.31
Rodriguez, Junior	R-R	6-0	189	2-8-89	3	3	2.67	24	0	0	8	30	15	13	9	1	28	34	.147	.120	.156	10.09	8.31
Santamaria, Joaquin	R-R	6-4	175	9-21-89	1	2	6.48	13	0	0	0	17	18	18	12	0	19	20	.254	.286	.240	10.80	10.26
Silvestre, Pedro	R-R	6-2	185	10-23-89	3	2	4.99	23	0	0	2	49	60	35	27	2	31	30	.319	.368	.307	5.55	5.73
Suero, Bruedlin	L-L	6-4	170	2-28-90	2	1	3.83	19	0	0	2	42	39	23	18	2	30	34	.244	.276	.237	7.23	6.38
Thomas, Yamal	R-R	6-7	225	11-4-89	1	0	6.75	8	2	0	0	13	10	13	10	0	18	8	.222	.375	.189	5.40	12.15
Torres, Jose	R-R	6-2	180	4-18-91	3	3	5.80	11	6	0	0	36	32	27	23	1	18	17	.244	.273	.235	4.29	4.54
Wilsino, Juan	R-R	6-3	190	3-22-89	1	4	3.60	11	11	0	0	55	54	26	22	2	7	40	.257	.182	.284	6.55	1.15

Fielding

Catcher	PCT	G	PO	A	E	DP	PB
Gomez	.963	30	193	44	9	1	13
Martin	.954	23	125	21	7	1	7
Rodriguez	.941	13	85	11	6	1	5
Santana	.955	10	52	12	3	0	6

First Base	PCT	G	PO	A	E	DP
Gomez	1.000	6	40	4	0	3
Guillen	.990	11	101	3	1	4
Guzman	1.000	3	26	1	0	1
Isenia	.944	6	32	2	2	3
Martin	.923	3	22	2	2	2
Rodriguez	.982	37	308	14	6	37
Santana	.930	7	52	1	4	4

Second Base	PCT	G	PO	A	E	DP
Eder	.987	18	31	46	1	11
Gomez	.800	2	2	2	1	1
Inirio	.950	10	18	20	2	2
Lafontaines	.990	21	58	46	1	15
Mejia	.917	5	9	13	2	5
Morillo	.950	6	10	9	1	3
Rodriguez	.971	7	16	18	1	3
Rosa	.920	7	15	8	2	2

Third Base	PCT	G	PO	A	E	DP
Gomez	.727	4	3	5	3	0
Guzman	.896	28	23	63	10	5
Inirio	.921	24	23	59	7	5
Lafontaines	1.000	3	1	6	0	0

Mejia	.500	3	1	2	3	0
Morillo	1.000	2	1	0	0	0
Quinonez	.667	2	0	2	1	0
Rosa	.975	13	15	24	1	1
Santana	—	1	0	0	0	0
Soriano	1.000	1	0	1	0	0

Shortstop	PCT	G	PO	A	E	DP
Inirio	.846	3	3	8	2	0
Lafontaines	1.000	1	0	1	0	0
Mejia	1.000	1	0	2	0	0
Morillo	.929	45	85	136	17	23
Rosa	.931	20	42	66	8	16

Outfield	PCT	G	PO	A	E	DP
Caminero	.920	49	112	3	10	0

Dorville	.956	55	80	6	4	2		Guillen	.960	22	24	0	1	0		Marte	.944	31	34	0	2	0
Elie	.667	14	4	0	2	0		Isenia	1.000	16	20	2	0	0		Rosario	.926	38	59	4	5	1

VSL RAYS   ROOKIE

VENEZUELAN SUMMER LEAGUE

Batting

Batting	B-T	HT	WT	DOB	AVG	vLH	vRH	G	AB	R	H	2B	3B	HR	RBI	BB	HBP	SH	SF	SO	SB	CS	SLG	OBP
Acosta, Ronald	R-R	5-11	170	3-16-91	.264	.387	.224	45	129	19	34	9	0	1	13	11	6	1	0	17	4	2	.357	.349
Alcala, Franklin	L-L	6-2	200	3-9-91	.086	.000	.097	12	35	3	3	0	0	2	6	3	0	0	0	19	0	0	.257	.158
Antunez, Ismel	L-R	5-7	166	6-17-91	.237	.176	.250	41	93	18	22	3	0	0	2	22	3	3	0	36	8	6	.269	.398
Colmenares, Jose	R-R	5-11	158	3-8-90	.298	.319	.292	62	225	49	67	13	0	8	42	31	7	4	2	22	4	4	.462	.396
Correa, Leopoldo	L-R	6-0	186	12-3-91	.161	.000	.231	27	56	10	9	2	1	2	6	16	0	1	0	17	0	0	.339	.347
Dominguez, Wilmer	R-R	5-10	182	6-19-90	.252	.200	.269	37	103	13	26	5	2	1	10	8	1	0	0	26	0	1	.369	.313
Eder, Federico	L-R	5-9	165	9-5-90	.203	.125	.229	26	64	15	13	5	0	0	3	12	4	1	1	14	2	1	.281	.358
Guevara, Hector	R-R	5-11	170	10-7-91	.330	.194	.359	54	206	29	68	14	2	8	36	16	1	2	4	21	6	5	.534	.374
Hernandez, Nahum	R-R	6-0	180	9-20-89	.258	.455	.206	52	159	30	41	8	0	4	21	16	7	3	0	44	4	1	.384	.352
Maldonado, Darwin	R-R	6-0	160	7-10-89	.297	.258	.308	48	148	28	44	7	1	7	29	15	4	0	1	34	4	2	.500	.375
Nagahashi, Mauricio	R-R	6-1	165	4-12-90	.245	.077	.268	37	110	18	27	4	1	2	12	9	1	1	0	19	4	5	.355	.308
Narvaez, Omar	B-R	5-10	172	2-10-92	.315	.414	.294	47	165	23	52	7	3	0	27	19	2	2	1	13	4	4	.394	.390
Paz, Franklin	R-R	6-1	166	5-7-91	.185	.077	.220	23	54	12	10	4	0	1	6	9	0	0	0	19	0	0	.315	.302
Quinonez, Jonathan	R-R	6-1	187	11-27-90	.232	.125	.253	25	99	19	23	7	2	2	13	9	5	0	0	18	6	3	.404	.327
Reginatto, Leonardo	R-R	6-2	180	4-10-90	.328	.436	.299	54	186	31	61	7	2	1	29	9	6	4	5	14	2	5	.403	.369
Reyes, Keiverson	R-R	5-9	152	2-7-91	.241	.296	.225	43	116	25	28	7	0	4	16	15	5	1	1	33	4	2	.405	.350
Salas, Roan	R-R	5-11	175	6-9-90	.338	.410	.322	61	222	49	75	19	3	15	59	25	4	0	3	31	1	0	.653	.409
Segovia, Alejandro	R-R	6-0	181	4-27-90	.349	.278	.366	50	189	35	66	16	0	7	40	15	7	2	0	18	1	1	.545	.417
Silva, Wester	R-L	6-0	170	1-10-92	.429	.333	.455	7	14	5	6	0	0	0	1	3	0	0	0	3	0	0	.429	.529

Pitching

Pitching	B-T	HT	WT	DOB	W	L	ERA	G	GS	CG	SV	IP	H	R	ER	HR	BB	SO	AVG	vLH	vRH	K/9	BB/9
Aguilera, Hector	R-R	6-3	185	3-26-90	6	0	3.20	18	0	0	2	51	49	22	18	1	17	38	.250	.340	.221	6.75	3.02
Cabrera, Orlando	R-R	5-11	165	10-25-89	4	2	3.92	15	10	0	0	60	55	34	26	5	17	33	.235	.326	.213	4.98	2.56
Crespo, Ali	R-R	6-4	209	2-1-90	1	1	2.91	14	4	0	1	43	46	20	14	5	9	17	.272	.342	.252	3.53	1.87
Duarte, Hugo	R-R	6-1	169	1-7-90	1	2	5.56	18	1	0	4	23	26	19	14	3	20	22	.295	.238	.313	8.74	7.94
Echarry, Eli	R-R	6-1	150	7-1-92	1	2	6.25	14	7	0	1	32	40	24	22	5	17	27	.305	.303	.306	7.67	4.83
Gonzalez, Joynerd	R-R	6-1	150	7-22-92	0	0	4.39	13	3	0	1	27	23	21	13	4	11	20	.221	.259	.208	6.75	3.71
Linares, Joice	L-L	5-10	182	4-01-90	2	1	4.82	9	7	0	0	28	32	16	15	4	5	20	.283	.182	.294	6.43	1.61
Lopez, Kevin	R-R	6-2	173	10-22-88	1	0	2.81	7	0	0	0	16	17	7	5	2	15	7	.274	.143	.291	3.94	8.44
Lopez, Reinaldo	R-R	6-2	221	4-27-91	1	1	4.87	13	9	0	0	44	52	30	24	2	23	25	.302	.211	.328	5.08	4.67
Mayora, Raul	L-L	6-1	190	1-13-87	1	1	4.50	7	0	0	0	16	15	12	8	0	11	21	.242	.500	.224	11.81	6.19
Montilla, Ricardo	R-R	6-2	155	4-23-88	2	0	0.00	4	0	0	0	6	6	0	0	0	8	.250	.400	.211	12.00	0.00
Moya, Dennis	R-R	6-3	180	8-16-91	2	2	4.22	16	3	0	1	32	27	18	15	2	13	20	.229	.280	.215	5.63	3.66
Orasmo, Carlos	L-L	5-9	154	12-13-91	2	0	3.86	6	0	0	0	16	15	8	7	2	3	19	.246	1.000	.233	10.47	1.65
Quinonez, Eduar	R-R	6-3	182	8-9-89	2	6	6.10	14	12	0	0	49	56	43	33	4	20	24	.283	.348	.263	4.44	3.70
Rivero, Felipe	L-L	6-0	151	7-5-91	6	4	3.74	16	0	0	1	34	38	24	14	0	12	25	.286	.429	.269	6.68	3.21
Sabala, Wilmer	R-R	6-2	184	12-22-91	2	1	3.11	16	1	0	1	38	47	19	13	3	9	33	.307	.313	.306	7.88	2.15
Salazar, Danmar	L-L	6-1	172	7-23-92	0	1	15.43	3	2	0	0	2	4	5	4	0	6	3	.400	1.000	.333	11.57	23.14
Salinas, Guillermo	R-R	6-1	180	10-28-88	3	1	1.82	7	1	0	1	25	16	5	5	1	6	22	.180	.130	.197	8.03	2.19
Sanchez, Daniel	R-R	6-2	180	5-29-89	1	2	6.87	15	5	0	3	38	51	36	29	2	23	32	.333	.500	.296	7.58	5.45
Wilches, Luis	L-L	6-1	200	10-1-91	3	1	3.10	14	4	0	0	29	35	14	10	1	5	13	.297	.357	.288	4.03	1.55

Fielding

Catcher	PCT	G	PO	A	E	DP	PB
Colmenares	—	1	0	0	0	0	0
Dominguez	.979	27	122	19	3	3	4
Narvaez	.994	25	134	25	1	0	5
Segovia	.986	29	169	38	3	3	5

First Base	PCT	G	PO	A	E	DP
Acosta	.947	3	18	0	1	1
Alcala	1.000	1	17	0	0	1
Colmenares	1.000	10	49	1	0	6
Correa	1.000	4	4	1	0	1
Dominguez	1.000	4	33	1	0	1
Narvaez	.975	20	189	8	5	17
Salas	.995	21	207	7	1	17
Segovia	.982	18	152	9	3	18

Second Base	PCT	G	PO	A	E	DP
Acosta	.750	5	5	7	4	1
Colmenares	.947	37	105	109	12	31
Eder	1.000	4	0	2	0	0
Guevara	.957	16	38	50	4	10
Reginatto	.889	4	2	6	1	1
Reyes	.947	17	25	29	3	6

Third Base	PCT	G	PO	A	E	DP
Acosta	.828	10	4	20	5	0
Colmenares	1.000	1	2	4	0	0
Correa	.744	14	9	20	10	1
Quinonez	.905	20	15	52	7	4
Reginatto	.918	13	8	37	4	6
Salas	.872	27	20	62	12	5

Shortstop	PCT	G	PO	A	E	DP
Acosta	—	1	0	0	0	0
Guevara	.949	33	46	102	8	20
Reginatto	.890	28	51	95	18	11
Reyes	.831	20	20	39	12	9

Outfield	PCT	G	PO	A	E	DP
Acosta	1.000	24	36	1	0	0
Alcala	.786	8	11	0	3	0
Antunez	.915	36	52	2	5	1
Colmenares	1.000	19	21	2	0	0
Eder	.960	20	22	2	1	0
Hernandez	.959	51	88	5	4	1
Maldonado	.936	46	72	1	5	0
Nagahashi	.923	29	32	4	3	0
Quinonez	1.000	6	12	0	0	0
Reginatto	1.000	1	1	0	0	0
Silva	1.000	7	5	0	0	0

Texas Rangers

SEASON IN A SENTENCE: The Rangers' young core made them contenders sooner than expected, as Texas was just two games out of the wild card and 4½ back in the American League West as late as Sept. 9, before fading down the stretch.

HIGH POINT: Righthander Scott Feldman, who spent the first two years of his big league career in middle relief, was one of the biggest surprises in the AL. He emerged as a workhorse and a big-game pitcher atop the rotation, winning a franchise-record 12 games on the road and going 7-0, 2.29 over an eight-start stretch in August and September as the Rangers surged toward a postseason berth. He finished 17-8, 4.08.

LOW POINT: The Rangers' bats failed them during their mid-September swoon, producing only one run total during a five-game losing streak that torpedoed their hopes of making the playoffs for the first time since 1999. The centerpiece of the lineup, outfielder Josh Hamilton, was hampered by a bruised rib cage and a slight abdominal tear, limiting him to just 89 games and sapping his productivity when he was on the field. He finished with a .741 OPS, down from .901 in 2008.

NOTABLE ROOKIES: Texas began reaping the fruits of its top-ranked farm system in 2009. Elvis Andrus stepped into the everyday shortstop job as a 20-year-old and finished second in the AL rookie of the year voting. Center fielder Julio Borbon provided a spark in the second half, hitting .312 and stealing 19 bases. Top prospect Neftali Feliz was electric out of the bullpen after a midseason callup, posting a team-best 1.74 ERA and a 39-8 strikeout-walk ratio in 31 innings. And lefthander Derek Holland and righty Tommy Hunter each settled into roles in the rotation.

KEY TRANSACTIONS: The Rangers were careful to keep their core intact and avoid major trades. They did welcome back former franchise icon Ivan Rodriguez, acquiring him for low Class A righty Matt Nevarez on Aug. 19. The struggles of young catchers Jarrod Saltalamacchia and Taylor Teagarden—and a season-ending injury to the former—forced the Rangers to make the move.

DOWN ON THE FARM: The Rangers still have one of the best farm systems in baseball. Slugging first baseman Justin Smoak tore up Double-A in his first full pro season before scuffling in Triple-A. And lefthander Martin Perez, 18, established himself as one of the top pitching prospects in the minors.

OPENING DAY PAYROLL: $68,178,798

PLAYERS OF THE YEAR

JOHN SPEAR

MAJOR LEAGUE	MINOR LEAGUE
Michael Young	**Martin Perez**
3b	**lhp**
.322/.374/.518	(Low A/Double-A)
5th in AL in batting,	6-8, 2.90
sixth All-Star Game	119 SO in 115 IP

ORGANIZATION LEADERS

BATTING		*Minimum 250 at-bats
MAJORS		
*AVG	Michael Young	.322
*OPS	Michael Young	.892
HR	Nelson Cruz	33
RBI	Marlon Byrd	89
MINORS		
*AVG	Moreland, Mitch, Bakersfield/Frisco	.331
R	Gentry, Craig, Frisco	100
H	Moreland, Mitch, Bakersfield/Frisco	156
TB	Gomez, Mauro, Bakersfield	268
2B	Moreland, Mitch, Bakersfield/Frisco	38
3B	Golson, Greg, Oklahoma City	8
HR	Bianucci, Michael, Hickory/Bakersfield	30
RBI	Tracy, Chad, Frisco	107
BB	Whittleman, John, Frisco	80
SO	Butler, Joey, Bakersfield	146
	Greene, Jonathan, Bakersfield/Frisco	146
SB	Gentry, Craig, Frisco	49
*OBP	German, Esteban, Oklahoma City	.419
*SLG	Bianucci, Michael, Hickory/Bakersfield	.561

PITCHING		†Minimum 75 innings
MAJORS		
W	Scott Feldman	17
†ERA	Kevin Millwood	3.67
SO	Kevin Millwood	123
MINORS		
W	Poveda, Omar, Oklahoma City/Frisco	11
	Roark, Tanner, Frisco/Bakersfield	11
L	Bleier, Richard, Hickory/Bakersfield	12
†ERA	Perez, Martin, Hickory/Frisco	2.90
G	Strop, Pedro, Frisco/Oklahoma City	47
GS	Beavan, Blake, Bakersfield/Frisco	27
SV	Reed, Evan, Bakersfield	25
IP	Bleier, Richard, Hickory/Bakersfield	167
BB	Gomez, Kennil, Bakersfield	67
SO	Gomez, Kennil, Bakersfield	126
†AVG	Moscoso, Guillermo, Frisco/Okla. City	.229

General Manager: Jon Daniels. **Farm Director:** Scott Servais. **Scouting Director:** Ron Hopkins.

Class	Team	League	W	L	PCT	Finish*	Manager(s)
Majors	Texas Rangers	American	87	75	.537	4th (14)	Ron Washington
Triple-A	Oklahoma City RedHawks	Pacific Coast	69	75	.479	12th (16)	Bobby Jones
Double-A	Frisco RoughRiders	Texas	72	68	.514	4th (8)	Mike Micucci
High A	Bakersfield Blaze	California	75	65	.536	t-3rd (10)	Steve Buechele
Low A	Hickory Crawdads	South Atlantic	63	76	.453	15th (16)	Hector Ortiz
Short-season	Spokane Indians	Northwest	37	39	.487	4th (8)	Tim Hulett
Rookie	AZL Rangers	Arizona	25	31	.446	t-6th (11)	Bill Richardson
Overall 2009 Minor League Record			341	354	.491	20th (30)	

*Finish in overall standings (No. of teams in league). †League champion.

ORGANIZATION STATISTICS

TEXAS RANGERS

AMERICAN LEAGUE

Batting	B-T	HT	WT	DOB	AVG	vLH	vRH	G	AB	R	H	2B	3B	HR	RBI	BB	HBP	SH	SF	SO	SB	CS	SLG	OBP
Andrus, Elvis	R-R	6-0	185	8-26-88	.267	.279	.262	145	480	72	128	17	8	6	40	40	6	12	3	77	33	6	.373	.329
Arias, Joaquin	R-R	6-1	165	9-21-84	.000	.000	.000	3	8	0	0	0	0	0	0	0	0	1	0	3	0	0	.000	.000
Blalock, Hank	L-R	6-1	200	11-21-80	.234	.221	.239	123	462	62	108	21	4	25	66	26	3	0	4	108	2	0	.459	.277
Boggs, Brandon	B-R	5-11	205	1-9-83	.059	.100	.000	9	17	0	1	1	0	0	0	1	0	0	0	8	0	0	.118	.111
Borbon, Julio	L-L	6-1	180	2-20-86	.312	.125	.333	46	157	30	49	4	0	4	20	15	1	6	0	28	19	4	.414	.376
Byrd, Marlon	R-R	6-0	245	8-30-77	.283	.244	.300	146	547	66	155	43	2	20	89	32	10	0	10	98	8	4	.479	.329
Cruz, Nelson	R-R	6-3	230	7-1-80	.260	.235	.270	128	462	75	120	21	1	33	76	49	2	0	2	118	20	4	.524	.332
Davis, Chris	L-R	6-4	235	3-17-86	.238	.189	.260	113	391	48	93	15	1	21	59	24	2	0	2	150	0	0	.442	.284
Gentry, Craig	R-R	6-2	190	11-29-83	.118	.250	.077	11	17	4	2	1	0	0	1	2	0	0	0	5	0	0	.176	.211
German, Esteban	R-R	5-9	195	1-26-78	.304	.389	.250	19	46	9	14	4	0	4	4	0	0	0	7	1	0	.391	.360
Golson, Greg	R-R	6-0	190	9-17-85	.000	—	.000	1	1	0	0	0	0	0	0	0	0	0	0	1	0	0	.000	.000
Hamilton, Josh	L-L	6-4	235	5-21-81	.268	.327	.239	89	336	43	90	19	2	10	54	24	1	0	4	79	8	3	.426	.315
Jones, Andruw	R-R	6-1	240	4-23-77	.214	.218	.210	82	281	43	60	18	0	17	43	45	2	0	3	72	5	1	.459	.323
Kinsler, Ian	R-R	6-0	200	6-22-82	.253	.310	.230	144	566	101	143	32	4	31	86	59	6	3	6	77	31	5	.488	.327
Murphy, David	L-L	6-4	205	10-18-81	.269	.235	.279	128	432	61	116	24	1	17	57	49	1	2	9	106	9	4	.447	.338
Richardson, Kevin	R-R	6-3	230	9-12-80	.500	.000	.750	4	6	3	3	0	0	0	0	0	0	0	0	2	0	0	.500	.500
Rodriguez, Ivan	R-R	5-9	190	11-30-71	.245	.231	.250	28	98	14	24	8	0	2	13	5	0	0	1	18	1	0	.388	.279
Saltalamacchia, Jarrod	B-R	6-4	235	5-2-85	.233	.229	.235	84	283	34	66	12	0	9	34	22	1	3	1	97	0	2	.371	.290
Teagarden, Taylor	R-R	6-1	200	12-21-83	.217	.288	.192	60	198	26	43	13	0	6	24	14	1	3	2	76	0	0	.374	.270
Vizquel, Omar	B-R	5-9	175	4-24-67	.266	.485	.215	62	177	17	47	7	1	1	14	13	0	5	0	27	4	0	.345	.316
Young, Michael	R-R	6-1	200	10-19-76	.322	.297	.331	135	541	76	174	36	2	22	68	47	1	0	4	90	8	3	.518	.374

Pitching	B-T	HT	WT	DOB	W	L	ERA	G	GS	CG	SV	IP	H	R	ER	HR	BB	SO	AVG	vLH	vRH	K/9	BB/9
Benson, Kris	R-R	6-4	205	11-7-74	1	1	8.46	8	2	0	0	22	33	23	21	6	12	11	.340	.255	.452	4.43	4.84
Eyre, Willie	R-R	6-2	205	7-21-78	0	0	4.50	17	0	0	0	18	18	9	9	0	6	8	.281	.286	.278	4.00	3.00
Feldman, Scott	L-R	6-5	210	2-7-83	17	8	4.08	34	31	0	0	190	178	87	86	18	65	113	.250	.226	.277	5.36	3.08
Feliz, Neftali	R-R	6-3	190	5-2-88	1	0	1.74	20	0	0	2	31	13	6	6	2	8	39	.124	.155	.085	11.32	2.32
Francisco, Frank	R-R	6-3	230	9-11-79	2	3	3.83	51	0	0	25	49	40	21	21	6	15	57	.214	.238	.186	10.40	2.74
Grilli, Jason	R-R	6-5	225	11-11-76	2	2	4.78	30	0	0	0	26	21	14	14	2	14	27	.216	.192	.244	9.23	4.78
Guardado, Eddie	R-L	6-0	225	10-2-70	1	2	4.46	48	0	0	0	38	39	21	19	8	15	20	.267	.333	.228	4.70	3.52
Harrison, Matt	L-L	6-4	225	9-16-85	4	5	6.11	11	11	2	0	63	81	43	43	9	23	34	.316	.210	.351	4.83	3.27
Holland, Derek	B-L	6-2	185	10-9-86	8	13	6.12	33	21	1	0	138	160	98	94	26	47	107	.288	.287	.289	6.96	3.06
Hunter, Tommy	R-R	6-3	255	7-3-86	9	6	4.10	19	19	1	0	112	113	55	51	13	33	64	.259	.288	.228	5.14	2.65
Jennings, Jason	L-R	6-2	235	7-17-78	2	4	4.13	44	0	0	1	61	67	31	28	7	28	44	.286	.327	.257	6.49	4.13
Madrigal, Warner	R-R	6-0	200	3-21-84	0	0	9.95	13	0	0	0	13	18	14	14	2	12	5	.333	.481	.185	3.55	8.53
Mathis, Doug	R-R	6-3	220	6-8-83	0	1	3.16	24	2	0	1	43	39	17	15	4	10	25	.244	.250	.239	5.27	2.11
McCarthy, Brandon	R-R	6-7	200	7-7-83	7	4	4.62	17	17	1	0	97	96	55	50	13	36	65	.255	.264	.246	6.01	3.33
Mendoza, Luis	R-R	6-3	210	10-31-83	0	0	36.00	1	0	0	0	1	2	4	4	1	1	0	.400	1.000	.000	0.00	9.00
Millwood, Kevin	R-R	6-4	230	12-24-74	13	10	3.67	31	31	3	0	199	195	88	81	26	71	123	.257	.240	.272	5.57	3.22
Moscoso, Guillermo	R-R	6-1	165	11-14-83	0	0	3.21	10	0	0	0	14	15	7	5	1	6	12	.268	.412	.205	7.71	3.86
Nippert, Dustin	R-R	6-8	225	5-6-81	5	3	3.88	20	10	0	0	70	64	31	30	7	29	54	.245	.257	.231	6.98	3.75
O'Day, Darren	R-R	6-4	220	10-22-82	2	1	1.94	64	0	0	2	56	36	12	12	3	17	54	.188	.234	.164	8.73	2.75
Padilla, Vicente	R-R	6-2	220	9-27-77	8	6	4.92	18	18	0	0	108	120	61	59	12	42	59	.286	.319	.246	4.92	3.50
Rupe, Josh	R-R	6-2	210	8-18-82	0	0	15.43	4	0	0	0	5	12	8	8	2	5	2	.462	.200	.625	3.86	9.64
Strop, Pedro	R-R	6-0	160	6-13-85	0	0	7.71	7	0	0	0	7	6	6	6	0	4	9	.231	.154	.308	11.57	5.14
Wilson, C.J.	L-L	6-1	215	11-18-80	5	6	2.81	74	0	0	14	74	66	29	23	3	32	84	.234	.206	.249	10.26	3.91

Fielding

Catcher	PCT	G	PO	A	E	DP	PB
Richardson	1.000	4	13	0	0	0	0
Rodriguez	.984	25	168	11	3	1	2
Saltalamacchia	.987	83	502	28	7	4	2
Teagarden	.985	60	360	31	6	4	5

First Base	PCT	G	PO	A	E	DP
Blalock	.989	66	535	26	6	64
Davis	.997	100	845	47	3	82
German	—	1	0	0	0	0
Jones	1.000	8	32	1	0	6

Second Base	PCT	G	PO	A	E	DP
Arias	1.000	2	4	4	0	2
German	.944	6	4	13	1	3
Kinsler	.985	144	249	451	11	100
Vizquel	1.000	16	23	49	0	12

Third Base	PCT	G	PO	A	E	DP
Arias	—	1	0	0	0	0
Blalock	1.000	1	0	3	0	0
Davis	.895	11	9	8	2	1
German	.810	10	5	12	4	1
Vizquel	1.000	20	5	22	0	2
Young	.969	134	72	208	9	29

Shortstop	PCT	G	PO	A	E	DP
Andrus	.968	145	261	407	22	98
Vizquel	1.000	27	32	76	0	22

Outfield	PCT	G	PO	A	E	DP
Boggs	.900	6	9	0	1	0
Borbon	.927	20	38	0	3	0
Byrd	.991	143	332	6	3	4

	PCT	G	PO	A	E	DP
Cruz	.987	122	301	11	4	2
Gentry	1.000	9	11	1	0	1
German	—	1	0	0	0	0
Golson	1.000	1	1	0	0	0
Hamilton	.995	79	185	4	1	1
Jones	1.000	17	30	0	0	0
Murphy	.991	112	214	7	2	2

OKLAHOMA CITY REDHAWKS   TRIPLE-A

PACIFIC COAST LEAGUE

Batting	B-T	HT	WT	DOB	AVG	vLH	vRH	G	AB	R	H	2B	3B	HR	RBI	BB	HBP	SH	SF	SO	SB	CS	SLG	OBP
Arias, Joaquin	R-R	6-1	165	9-21-84	.266	.273	.262	118	504	63	134	14	3	5	52	20	3	5	5	47	24	3	.335	.295
Benjamin, Casey	L-R	6-2	190	8-1-80	.231	.236	.229	93	299	46	69	12	3	5	32	54	3	5	5	69	3	0	.341	.349
Boggs, Brandon	B-R	5-11	205	1-9-83	.268	.287	.259	93	332	45	89	15	2	8	47	59	3	1	3	98	9	2	.398	.380
Bolden, Jared	L-L	6-2	180	3-17-87	.350	.400	.333	6	20	3	7	0	0	1	2	2	0	0	0	5	1	0	.500	.409
Borbon, Julio	L-L	6-1	180	2-20-86	.307	.276	.325	96	407	71	125	12	7	2	34	33	7	8	2	40	25	7	.386	.367
Cruz, Nelson	R-R	6-3	230	7-1-80	.000	.000	.000	3	10	0	0	0	0	0	0	1	0	0	0	5	1	0	.000	.091
Davis, Chris	L-R	6-4	235	3-17-86	.327	.260	.357	44	165	27	54	12	1	6	30	25	2	0	2	39	0	1	.521	.418
Duran, German	R-R	5-10	185	8-3-84	.149	.148	.150	25	87	6	13	0	1	1	7	4	0	1	1	17	0	1	.207	.185
Fox, Adam	R-R	5-11	200	11-23-81	.186	.217	.170	22	70	4	13	3	0	1	5	3	1	2	0	18	1	0	.271	.230
Freel, Ryan	R-R	5-9	180	3-8-76	.333	.000	.400	2	6	0	2	0	0	0	1	0	1	0	0	2	0	0	.333	.429
2-team total (7 Iowa)					.400	—	—	9	30	6	12	4	0	0	5	3	2	0	0	6	5	1	.533	.486
Frostad, Emerson	L-R	6-1	210	1-13-83	.226	.196	.236	63	208	19	47	12	1	1	20	32	1	2	1	39	0	1	.308	.331
German, Esteban	R-R	5-9	195	1-26-78	.319	.284	.337	105	389	63	124	15	5	4	59	65	8	2	8	63	35	9	.414	.419
Gold, Nate	R-R	6-3	230	6-12-80	.256	.103	.340	25	82	12	21	8	0	2	15	13	2	1	3	14	0	1	.427	.360
Golson, Greg	R-R	6-0	190	9-17-85	.258	.262	.256	123	457	46	118	17	8	2	40	29	0	8	6	114	20	4	.344	.299
Hamilton, Josh	L-L	6-4	235	5-21-81	.179	.091	.235	7	28	3	5	2	1	0	0	4	0	0	0	7	1	0	.321	.281
Harrison, Ben	R-R	6-4	203	9-18-81	.218	.167	.243	16	55	7	12	4	0	1	8	5	3	0	0	16	1	0	.345	.317
Huffman, Royce	R-R	6-0	205	1-11-77	.293	.321	.277	122	440	51	129	29	0	7	54	56	6	2	3	83	5	0	.407	.378
Leone, Justin	R-R	6-1	200	3-9-77	.160	.000	.235	8	25	2	4	2	0	1	3	5	0	0	0	16	1	0	.360	.300
Majewski, Dustin	L-L	5-11	205	8-16-81	.167	.000	.188	5	18	2	3	0	0	1	3	3	0	0	1	4	0	0	.333	.273
Metcalf, Travis	R-R	6-3	215	8-17-82	.192	.200	.188	15	52	3	10	1	1	1	7	5	0	1	0	15	2	0	.327	.263
2-team total (110 Omaha)					.216	—	—	125	440	48	95	19	2	11	54	38	5	5	6	95	4	1	.343	.282
Murphy, Steve	L-R	6-2	210	4-22-84	.231	.182	.244	33	104	15	24	3	2	2	10	9	3	1	2	26	1	0	.356	.305
Ramirez, Max	R-R	5-11	175	10-11-84	.234	.319	.191	76	274	29	64	13	0	5	43	35	4	1	6	85	1	0	.336	.323
Richardson, Kevin	R-R	6-3	220	9-12-80	.216	.296	.166	74	255	33	55	10	1	13	36	19	4	3	0	105	0	0	.416	.281
Smoak, Justin	B-L	6-4	220	12-5-86	.244	.231	.250	54	197	25	48	11	0	4	23	35	3	0	2	45	0	0	.360	.363
Thompson, Kevin	R-R	5-10	195	9-18-79	.000	.000	.000	5	16	2	0	0	0	0	0	1	1	1	0	4	1	0	.000	.111
Thorman, Scott	L-R	6-3	235	1-6-82	.188	.167	.192	11	32	4	6	4	0	1	4	3	2	0	0	9	2	0	.406	.297
2-team total (97 Omaha)					.288	—	—	108	399	49	115	16	2	20	67	24	11	3	5	75	7	3	.489	.342
Vallejo, Jose	B-R	6-0	175	9-11-86	.233	.253	.224	84	309	32	72	7	5	2	28	22	0	1	2	73	3	2	.307	.282
2-team total (7 Round Rock)					.240	—	—	91	329	34	79	10	5	2	28	22	0	1	2	77	3	2	.319	.286
Zaneski, Zach	R-R	6-2	215	6-27-86	.300	.400	.200	4	10	0	3	0	0	0	2	3	0	0	1	2	0	0	.300	.429

Pitching	B-T	HT	WT	DOB	W	L	ERA	G	GS	CG	SV	IP	H	R	ER	HR	BB	SO	AVG	vLH	vRH	K/9	BB/9
Ballard, Mike	R-L	6-2	180	2-6-84	1	2	5.14	8	4	0	0	28	29	18	16	5	4	16	.259	.286	.253	5.14	1.29
Bannister, John	R-R	6-4	200	1-20-84	0	0	5.40	14	0	0	0	18	24	14	11	2	14	10	.329	.281	.366	4.91	6.87
Benson, Kris	R-R	6-4	205	11-7-74	4	5	5.24	11	10	1	0	69	78	45	40	5	23	49	.285	.281	.288	6.42	3.01
Cooper, Chris	L-L	5-11	195	10-31-78	0	1	5.06	2	1	0	0	5	8	4	3	1	0	4	.333	.429	.294	6.75	0.00
Corey, Bryan	R-R	6-0	175	10-21-73	7	9	5.34	31	15	0	0	116	148	70	69	11	23	77	.309	.269	.338	5.96	1.78
Diamond, Thomas	R-R	6-3	230	4-6-83	0	0	6.55	6	1	0	0	11	12	8	8	1	7	8	.273	.350	.208	6.55	5.73
Eyre, Willie	R-R	6-2	205	7-21-78	0	0	2.10	19	2	0	2	34	24	8	8	1	12	25	.205	.237	.172	6.55	3.15
Feliz, Neftali	R-R	6-3	190	5-2-88	4	6	3.49	25	13	0	0	77	69	36	30	2	30	75	.240	.256	.227	8.73	3.49
Gabbard, Kason	L-L	6-3	200	4-8-82	0	1	10.50	5	0	0	0	6	10	8	7	0	11	3	.357	.273	.412	4.50	16.50
Gordon, Brian	L-R	6-0	190	8-16-78	7	3	3.49	43	2	0	2	77	72	32	30	5	20	51	.247	.283	.223	5.94	2.33
Hamilton, Clay	R-R	6-5	205	6-15-82	0	0	4.44	15	1	0	2	24	27	13	12	1	6	18	.297	.303	.293	6.66	2.22
Hernandez, Orlando	R-R	6-2	220	10-11-69	2	0	2.45	8	0	0	0	11	4	4	3	1	4	12	.121	.071	.158	9.82	3.27
Hinckley, Mike	R-L	6-3	205	10-5-82	1	1	3.26	33	0	0	0	50	53	20	18	4	23	32	.276	.250	.289	5.80	4.17
Holland, Derek	B-L	6-2	185	10-9-86	0	1	9.00	1	1	0	0	4	5	4	4	1	3	5	.357	.500	.300	11.25	6.75
Hunter, Tommy	R-R	6-3	255	7-3-86	3	2	3.83	8	8	0	0	49	53	25	21	5	16	35	.280	.254	.295	6.39	2.92
Hyatt, Jared	R-R	6-5	205	5-15-84	0	2	10.24	2	2	0	0	10	13	11	11	2	7	4	.325	.167	.455	3.72	6.52
Madrigal, Warner	R-R	6-0	200	3-21-84	2	2	2.57	42	0	0	17	49	42	15	14	5	11	48	.231	.232	.230	8.82	2.02
Mathis, Doug	R-R	6-3	220	6-7-83	4	2	2.84	11	10	2	0	57	64	23	18	3	15	38	.286	.318	.266	6.00	2.37
McCarthy, Brandon	R-R	6-7	200	7-7-83	0	1	4.15	5	5	0	0	22	20	10	10	1	9	22	.247	.261	.229	9.14	3.74
Mendoza, Luis	R-R	6-3	210	10-31-83	7	4	4.53	25	18	2	0	111	130	62	56	4	50	78	.294	.295	.294	6.31	4.04
Moscoso, Guillermo	R-R	6-1	165	11-14-83	5	4	2.31	12	11	0	0	70	56	20	18	2	15	60	.218	.149	.263	7.71	1.93
Murray, A.J.	B-L	6-3	220	3-17-82	2	2	3.28	35	0	0	1	49	56	27	18	1	20	32	.292	.279	.298	5.84	3.65
Nippert, Dustin	R-R	6-8	225	5-6-81	1	0	1.80	1	1	0	0	5	2	1	1	1	2	6	.118	.000	.143	10.80	3.60
Peguero, Jailen	R-R	6-0	185	1-4-81	0	1	3.86	8	0	0	1	12	8	5	5	2	8	14	.205	.316	.100	10.80	6.17
2-team total (16 Salt Lake)					0	2	7.33	24	0	0	2	27	32	25	22	6	17	29	—	—	—	9.67	5.67
Poveda, Omar	R-R	6-4	215	9-28-87	0	1	5.14	1	1	0	0	7	5	4	4	0	4	3	.208	.125	.250	3.86	5.14
Ramirez, Elizardo	B-R	6-0	180	1-28-83	9	11	4.63	28	24	1	0	142	164	80	73	16	36	74	.287	.257	.307	4.69	2.28
Rupe, Josh	R-R	6-2	210	8-18-82	5	7	6.67	24	14	0	1	89	115	75	66	5	41	62	.322	.307	.333	6.27	4.15

Strop, Pedro	R-R	6-0	160	6-13-85	1	1	7.82	11	0	0	1	13	13	11	11	2	4	13	.271	.125	.417	9.24	2.84
Turnbow, Derrick	R-R	6-3	210	1-25-78	0	1	8.53	8	0	0	0	6	11	7	6	0	9	1	.407	.500	.333	1.42	12.79
Vaughan, Beau	B-R	6-4	230	6-4-81	4	2	4.62	28	0	0	0	39	42	22	20	2	19	37	.273	.228	.299	8.54	4.38
Wood, Mike	R-R	6-2	220	4-26-80	0	0	9.00	2	0	0	0	2	2	2	2	0	0	3	.222	.000	.333	13.50	0.00
2-team total (8 New Orleans)					0	2	9.49	10	5	0	1	25	37	26	26	3	14	13	—	—	—	4.74	5.11

Fielding

Catcher	PCT	G	PO	A	E	DP	PB
Frostad	.967	32	186	16	7	2	5
Ramirez	.991	42	290	28	3	5	4
Richardson	.988	69	445	32	6	3	12
Zaneski	1.000	4	22	0	0	0	0

First Base	PCT	G	PO	A	E	DP
Benjamin	1.000	1	1	0	0	1
Davis	.989	9	83	8	1	4
Frostad	.994	18	152	14	1	12
Gold	1.000	21	172	17	0	17
Huffman	.995	46	385	27	2	50
Smoak	.997	45	376	20	1	41
Thorman	.982	6	49	7	1	7

Second Base	PCT	G	PO	A	E	DP
Benjamin	.971	21	42	59	3	19
Duran	.966	18	46	40	3	11
Fox	.967	19	37	52	3	16

	PCT	G	PO	A	E	DP
German	.972	8	21	14	1	6
Vallejo	.978	83	161	233	9	46
Third Base	PCT	G	PO	A	E	DP
Benjamin	1.000	2	1	4	0	0
Davis	.930	23	16	24	3	4
Duran	.900	3	1	8	1	0
Fox	1.000	1	1	6	0	0
Frostad	.938	7	5	10	1	2
German	.940	84	39	163	13	14
Huffman	1.000	11	9	20	0	2
Metcalf	1.000	15	10	30	0	4
Richardson	1.000	1	0	1	0	0
Shortstop	PCT	G	PO	A	E	DP
Arias	.977	111	153	305	11	71
Benjamin	.951	27	50	66	6	22
Duran	1.000	3	4	10	0	0
German	.909	6	10	10	2	1

Outfield	PCT	G	PO	A	E	DP
Benjamin	1.000	39	76	1	0	0
Boggs	.994	86	154	3	1	1
Bolden	1.000	6	8	0	0	0
Borbon	.974	96	263	2	7	0
Cruz	1.000	3	6	2	0	0
Freel	—	1	0	0	0	0
German	.857	8	6	0	1	0
Golson	.986	122	284	8	4	2
Hamilton	.875	4	7	0	1	0
Harrison	.941	7	16	0	1	0
Huffman	1.000	30	62	3	0	0
Leone	1.000	2	4	0	0	0
Majewski	1.000	5	13	0	0	0
Murphy	.967	30	57	2	2	1
Thompson	1.000	4	2	0	0	0
Thorman	1.000	3	5	1	0	0

FRISCO ROUGHRIDERS
DOUBLE-A
TEXAS LEAGUE

Batting	B-T	HT	WT	DOB	AVG	vLH	vRH	G	AB	R	H	2B	3B	HR	RBI	BB	HBP	SH	SF	SO	SB	CS	SLG	OBP
Beltre, Engel	L-L	6-1	169	11-1-89	.071	.000	.091	4	14	1	1	0	0	0	0	0	0	1	0	.143	0	0	.143	.133
Fox, Adam	R-R	5-11	200	11-23-81	.286	.400	.235	81	294	45	84	10	2	18	47	22	5	1	2	66	6	3	.517	.344
Frostad, Emerson	L-R	6-1	210	1-13-83	.295	.250	.313	13	44	13	13	2	1	3	8	13	0	0	0	9	0	0	.591	.456
Gaetti, Joe	R-R	5-11	205	10-18-81	.158	.000	.167	8	19	4	3	0	0	0	1	6	0	0	1	6	0	0	.158	.346
Gentry, Craig	R-R	6-2	190	11-29-83	.303	.288	.307	127	512	100	155	21	7	8	53	49	16	6	5	64	49	6	.418	.378
Gradoville, Chris	R-R	6-1	220	7-10-84	.227	.258	.220	54	181	13	41	5	0	1	15	4	3	2	2	30	0	0	.271	.253
Greene, Jonathan	R-R	6-0	200	9-16-85	.172	.273	.149	17	58	4	10	1	0	4	11	6	1	0	1	22	2	1	.397	.258
Hamilton, Josh	L-L	6-4	235	5-21-81	.250	—	.250	1	4	1	1	0	0	0	1	1	0	0	0	1	1	0	.250	.400
Harrison, Ben	R-R	6-4	203	9-18-81	.154	.083	.185	11	39	3	6	2	0	0	1	2	1	0	0	13	1	0	.205	.214
Jones, Andruw	R-R	6-1	240	4-23-77	.222	.000	.333	3	9	0	2	0	0	0	0	3	0	0	0	1	1	0	.222	.417
Kinsler, Ian	R-R	6-0	200	6-22-82	.000	.000	.000	2	7	1	0	0	0	0	0	1	0	0	0	1	0	0	.000	.222
Lemon, Marcus	L-R	5-11	173	6-3-88	.262	.303	.251	126	451	56	118	19	5	1	41	42	2	13	2	70	7	4	.333	.326
Majewski, Dustin	L-L	5-11	205	8-16-81	.270	.259	.274	84	322	45	87	21	2	1	30	46	1	1	3	41	3	3	.357	.360
Moreland, Mitch	L-L	6-2	230	9-6-85	.326	.385	.305	73	301	51	98	19	3	8	59	23	1	0	2	42	1	1	.488	.373
Morrison, Erik	R-R	6-0	190	10-23-81	.000	.000	.000	2	5	0	0	0	0	0	0	0	0	0	1	0	0	0	.000	.000
Murphy, Steve	L-R	6-2	210	4-22-84	.200	.161	.212	73	255	40	51	15	1	10	41	19	5	1	4	66	3	2	.384	.265
Osuna, Renny	R-R	6-0	172	4-24-85	.246	.294	.228	72	252	36	62	7	1	0	18	22	1	2	2	33	0	4	.282	.307
Pina, Manny	R-R	5-11	185	6-5-87	.259	.259	.258	86	321	36	83	17	1	8	42	19	8	3	4	58	1	0	.393	.313
Rodriguez, Guilder	B-R	6-1	160	7-24-83	.267	.211	.286	80	277	34	74	4	4	1	21	26	1	4	1	40	9	6	.321	.331
Saltalamacchia, Jarrod	B-R	6-4	235	5-2-85	.000	—	.000	2	4	1	0	0	0	0	0	1	1	0	0	1	0	0	.000	.333
Sarmiento, Elio	R-R	5-11	202	6-20-86	.077	.091	.067	8	26	1	2	1	0	0	3	0	0	0	0	6	0	0	.115	.172
Smith, Tim	L-L	6-3	225	6-14-86	.309	.231	.340	36	139	22	43	9	0	3	32	14	3	2	2	21	8	1	.439	.380
Smoak, Justin	B-L	6-4	220	12-5-86	.328	.196	.379	50	183	30	60	10	0	6	29	39	3	0	2	35	0	0	.481	.449
Tracy, Chad	R-R	6-3	205	7-4-85	.279	.264	.283	136	535	70	149	32	1	26	107	46	3	0	10	103	5	2	.488	.333
Vallejo, Jose	B-R	6-0	175	9-11-86	.283	.353	.273	20	83	13	24	3	1	0	10	4	0	1	1	14	7	1	.349	.318
Whittleman, Johnny	L-R	6-2	195	2-11-87	.224	.169	.238	127	438	60	98	28	1	10	57	80	4	0	5	110	4	2	.361	.345

Pitching	B-T	HT	WT	DOB	W	L	ERA	G	GS	CG	SV	IP	H	R	ER	HR	BB	SO	AVG	vLH	vRH	K/9	BB/9
Ballard, Mike	R-L	6-2	180	2-6-84	7	6	3.71	20	18	2	0	124	134	60	51	12	26	80	.273	.290	.265	5.82	1.89
Bannister, John	R-R	6-4	200	1-20-84	3	3	6.30	24	0	0	1	30	29	21	21	4	14	22	.254	.192	.306	6.60	4.20
2-team total (8 NW Arkansas)					4	3	5.89	32	0	0	1	44	41	29	29	5	20	31	—	—	—	6.29	4.06
Beavan, Blake	R-R	6-7	250	1-17-89	4	4	4.01	15	15	0	0	90	113	47	40	4	13	34	.309	.328	.287	3.41	1.30
Benson, Kris	R-R	6-4	205	11-7-74	0	1	5.40	1	1	0	0	5	5	3	3	1	1	4	.263	.333	.200	7.20	1.80
Diamond, Thomas	R-R	6-3	230	4-6-83	1	3	3.63	32	0	0	1	45	43	26	18	3	37	50	.254	.307	.213	10.07	7.46
Diaz, Jose	R-R	6-4	300	2-27-84	3	1	3.63	36	0	0	10	40	30	16	16	2	23	37	.205	.281	.146	8.39	5.22
Francisco, Frank	R-R	6-3	230	9-11-79	0	0	0.00	2	1	0	0	2	1	0	0	0	1	.143	.000	.333	4.50	0.00	
Garr, Brennan	R-R	6-2	190	2-22-84	3	3	4.26	32	0	0	2	51	48	32	24	3	25	42	.251	.244	.257	7.46	4.44
Grilli, Jason	R-R	6-5	225	11-11-76	0	0	0.00	1	1	0	0	1	0	0	0	0	1	1	.000	.000	.000	9.00	9.00
Gutierrez, Danny	R-R	6-1	180	3-8-87	0	0	3.60	1	1	0	0	5	3	2	2	1	0	3	.158	.133	.250	5.40	0.00
Hamilton, Clay	R-R	6-5	205	6-15-82	1	4	4.47	25	4	0	3	46	51	24	23	4	14	27	.280	.277	.284	5.24	2.72
Harrison, Matt	L-L	6-4	225	9-16-85	0	1	3.00	3	3	0	0	9	9	3	3	0	4	7	.281	.167	.308	7.00	4.00
Hunter, Tommy	R-R	6-3	255	7-3-86	1	0	4.98	5	3	0	0	22	30	15	12	5	4	16	.313	.300	.333	6.65	1.66
Hyatt, Jared	R-R	6-5	205	5-15-84	2	4	6.27	10	6	0	0	37	47	26	26	6	11	19	.309	.313	.306	4.58	2.65
Jones, Beau	L-L	6-1	195	8-25-86	3	4	4.47	36	0	0	2	54	59	31	27	2	31	57	.272	.330	.233	9.44	5.13
Kiker, Kasey	L-L	5-10	170	11-19-87	7	7	3.86	25	23	0	0	126	108	63	54	9	66	120	.231	.178	.252	8.57	4.71

Name	B-T	HT	WT	DOB	W	L	ERA	G	GS	CG	SV	IP	H	R	ER	HR	BB	SO	AVG	vLH	vRH	K/9	BB/9
Kirkman, Michael	L-L	6-4	195	9-18-86	5	7	4.19	18	18	0	0	97	93	54	45	9	43	64	.254	.261	.251	5.96	4.00
Kometani, Paul	R-R	6-4	205	12-24-82	1	0	5.40	11	0	0	0	18	28	15	11	5	5	15	.341	.471	.250	7.36	2.45
Laughter, Andrew	R-R	6-4	227	2-24-85	3	2	4.83	28	1	0	0	41	52	24	22	2	18	17	.308	.299	.314	3.73	3.95
Moscoso, Guillermo	R-R	6-1	165	11-14-83	3	1	4.46	9	7	0	0	42	41	23	21	1	14	36	.246	.198	.303	7.65	2.98
Murray, A.J.	B-L	6-3	220	3-17-82	2	0	0.87	6	0	0	0	10	5	1	1	0	2	7	.147	.188	.111	6.10	1.74
Nippert, Dustin	R-R	6-8	225	5-6-81	0	1	2.84	4	3	0	0	13	8	4	4	1	6	8	.186	.200	.154	5.68	4.26
Perez, Martin	L-L	6-0	178	4-4-91	1	3	5.57	5	5	0	0	21	29	16	13	2	5	14	.326	.267	.356	6.00	2.14
Phillips, Zach	L-L	6-1	200	9-21-86	0	0	1.60	20	0	0	2	34	27	11	6	1	19	29	.211	.240	.192	7.75	5.08
Poveda, Omar	R-R	6-4	215	9-28-87	11	5	4.14	22	22	2	0	130	133	73	60	11	48	73	.263	.304	.225	5.04	3.31
Roark, Tanner	R-R	6-2	220	10-5-86	1	1	4.58	5	4	0	0	18	17	9	9	1	7	9	.262	.344	.182	4.58	3.57
Schlact, Michael	R-R	6-7	205	12-9-85	0	1	9.69	4	4	0	0	13	25	14	14	2	5	6	.424	.467	.379	4.15	3.46
Strop, Pedro	R-R	6-0	160	6-13-85	5	5	4.38	36	0	0	4	51	48	28	25	1	29	48	.245	.202	.280	8.42	5.08
Torres, Joe	L-L	6-2	195	9-3-82	1	1	3.68	17	0	0	0	22	19	13	9	0	22	28	.235	.216	.250	11.45	9.00
Vaughan, Beau	B-R	6-4	230	6-4-81	3	0	2.35	18	0	0	8	23	16	6	6	1	3	20	.198	.192	.200	7.83	1.17
Young, Corey	L-L	6-2	175	12-30-86	1	0	7.71	18	0	0	1	21	26	19	18	0	13	23	.313	.300	.321	9.86	5.57

Fielding

Catcher	PCT	G	PO	A	E	DP	PB
Frostad	1.000	1	6	0	0	0	0
Gradoville	.992	53	327	37	3	3	4
Pina	.990	84	511	72	6	8	4
Saltalamacchia	1.000	2	14	1	0	1	0
Sarmiento	1.000	8	45	8	0	2	1

First Base	PCT	G	PO	A	E	DP
Frostad	1.000	5	44	2	0	2
Gradoville	1.000	1	1	0	0	0
Jones	1.000	1	10	3	0	2
Moreland	1.000	9	73	6	0	5
Smoak	.988	44	379	27	5	31
Tracy	.980	81	685	51	15	68

Second Base	PCT	G	PO	A	E	DP
Fox	.957	19	38	51	4	10

	PCT	G	PO	A	E	DP
Kinsler	1.000	2	4	5	0	1
Lemon	.968	77	142	194	11	47
Osuna	.912	8	18	13	3	3
Rodriguez	.989	21	43	46	1	8
Vallejo	.968	18	37	53	3	6

Third Base	PCT	G	PO	A	E	DP
Fox	.951	30	21	56	4	7
Frostad	1.000	1	1	0	0	0
Greene	.946	11	7	28	2	3
Osuna	.895	5	3	14	2	2
Whittleman	.909	96	73	187	26	22

Shortstop	PCT	G	PO	A	E	DP
Lemon	.928	38	73	94	13	15
Osuna	.963	54	93	165	10	33
Rodriguez	.955	49	89	145	11	27

Outfield	PCT	G	PO	A	E	DP
Beltre	1.000	4	10	0	0	0
Fox	.981	21	51	0	1	0
Gaetti	.867	8	13	0	2	0
Gentry	.981	120	296	8	6	5
Greene	1.000	2	1	0	0	0
Harrison	1.000	8	15	0	0	0
Majewski	1.000	80	170	4	0	0
Moreland	.982	56	102	9	2	2
Morrison	1.000	1	3	0	0	0
Murphy	.980	69	141	6	3	2
Rodriguez	1.000	10	14	0	0	0
Smith	1.000	31	61	0	0	0
Tracy	1.000	24	32	1	0	0

BAKERSFIELD BLAZE

HIGH CLASS A

CALIFORNIA LEAGUE

Batting	B-T	HT	WT	DOB	AVG	vLH	vRH	G	AB	R	H	2B	3B	HR	RBI	BB	HBP	SH	SF	SO	SB	CS	SLG	OBP
Barto, Aja	R-R	6-5	225	9-26-86	.200	.235	.125	8	25	2	5	1	0	1	2	3	1	0	0	8	0	0	.360	.310
Beltre, Engel	L-L	6-1	169	11-1-89	.227	.213	.235	84	357	44	81	13	5	3	23	17	10	5	0	77	17	7	.317	.281
Bianucci, Mike	R-R	6-2	225	6-26-86	.232	.215	.244	50	198	35	46	8	1	15	41	14	3	0	3	69	1	0	.510	.289
Butler, Joey	R-R	6-2	210	3-12-86	.280	.216	.315	134	522	82	146	33	1	12	76	46	5	0	1	146	6	4	.416	.343
Dominguez, Carlos	R-R	6-1	177	6-8-86	.000	.000	—	1	1	0	0	0	0	0	0	0	0	0	0	0	0	0	.000	.000
Felix, Jose	R-R	5-10	198	6-28-88	.241	.229	.248	90	320	35	77	15	1	0	34	16	3	7	2	45	0	2	.294	.282
Fry, Eric	L-R	5-10	190	8-9-87	.150	.333	.135	11	40	2	6	3	1	0	0	1	4	1	0	15	0	0	.275	.244
Gac, Ian	R-R	6-3	240	8-10-85	.238	.258	.225	104	391	54	93	24	0	22	55	31	3	0	5	128	1	0	.468	.295
Garcia, Edwin	B-R	6-0	150	3-1-91	.105	.100	.111	6	19	0	2	0	0	0	1	1	0	0	0	4	0	0	.105	.150
Gomez, Mauro	R-R	6-2	190	9-7-84	.285	.284	.286	124	501	75	143	35	3	28	94	31	7	0	4	141	0	0	.535	.333
Greene, Jonathan	R-R	6-0	200	9-16-85	.273	.287	.265	109	411	60	112	27	1	20	77	28	21	1	6	124	3	0	.489	.345
Hogan, Doug	R-R	6-3	210	9-29-84	.156	.231	.105	9	32	4	5	4	0	0	1	3	1	0	0	14	1	0	.281	.250
Kaase, Jake	L-R	6-1	185	4-14-86	.266	.333	.246	47	177	23	47	12	0	2	20	5	1	5	3	23	2	0	.367	.285
Lawson, Matt	R-R	6-0	195	11-18-85	.293	.272	.305	131	478	69	140	26	2	10	57	32	14	3	8	127	8	5	.418	.350
Mendonca, Tommy	L-R	6-1	200	4-12-88	.209	.294	.154	11	43	5	9	3	0	0	2	1	2	0	0	12	1	0	.279	.261
Moreland, Mitch	L-L	6-2	230	9-6-85	.341	.289	.360	43	170	34	58	19	0	8	26	21	4	0	2	26	1	0	.594	.421
Morrison, Erik	R-R	6-0	190	10-23-85	.323	.222	.364	9	31	7	10	3	0	1	2	4	0	1	0	11	1	0	.516	.400
Osuna, Renny	R-R	6-0	172	4-24-85	.255	.250	.256	42	165	20	42	6	1	1	12	15	1	4	3	21	4	1	.321	.315
Paisano, David	R-R	6-1	165	11-26-87	.253	.255	.252	38	158	31	40	11	0	3	12	17	4	0	0	44	1	0	.380	.341
Podraza, Cody	R-R	5-8	185	11-6-87	.292	.250	.313	11	24	6	7	1	0	1	3	1	0	1	1	5	1	1	.458	.308
Rodriguez, Tim	R-R	6-2	210	1-24-87	.260	.321	.196	34	104	17	27	7	1	5	17	3	3	0	1	37	0	5	.490	.297
Sarmiento, Elio	R-R	5-11	202	6-20-86	.344	.255	.375	58	183	33	63	12	3	2	25	19	4	1	1	35	3	2	.475	.415
Smith, Tim	L-L	6-3	225	6-14-86	.333	.357	.326	35	120	18	40	5	0	4	19	10	7	0	1	20	7	1	.475	.413
Stoneburner, Davis	R-R	6-0	175	1-14-85	.273	.268	.276	106	418	56	114	33	2	6	54	29	10	4	2	79	9	2	.404	.333

Pitching	B-T	HT	WT	DOB	W	L	ERA	G	GS	CG	SV	IP	H	R	ER	HR	BB	SO	AVG	vLH	vRH	K/9	BB/9
Beavan, Blake	R-R	6-7	250	1-17-89	12	12	4.30	12	12	1	0	73	75	44	35	6	16	51	.264	.237	.297	6.26	1.96
Bleier, Richard	L-L	6-3	195	4-16-87	7	11	4.51	23	22	1	0	144	165	88	72	9	20	108	.283	.259	.293	6.77	1.25
Brader, Dustin	R-R	6-4	220	11-13-85	4	0	5.49	19	0	0	0	39	44	25	24	5	15	33	.289	.310	.272	7.55	3.43
Falcon, Ryan	R-L	6-0	195	8-27-84	2	2	2.44	35	1	0	1	66	56	20	18	5	13	70	.230	.242	.223	9.48	1.76
Flores, Adalberto	R-R	6-7	227	11-4-86	6	2	3.40	39	0	0	2	56	51	27	21	6	21	73	.236	.209	.267	11.80	3.40
Garr, Brennan	R-R	6-2	190	2-22-84	0	0	1.69	8	0	0	2	11	7	2	2	1	4	12	.189	.286	.063	10.13	3.38
Gomez, Kennil	R-R	6-3	170	4-8-88	8	10	5.27	26	26	0	0	135	147	93	79	11	67	126	.279	.308	.240	8.40	4.47
Hyatt, Jared	R-R	6-5	205	5-15-84	1	2	8.89	6	0	0	0	27	42	28	27	5	5	26	.356	.394	.308	8.56	1.65
Jones, Beau	L-L	6-1	195	8-25-86	1	0	0.55	9	0	0	0	16	8	2	1	1	2	26	.145	.077	.207	14.33	1.10
Kirkman, Michael	L-L	6-4	195	9-18-86	4	1	2.06	8	7	0	0	48	43	16	11	1	18	54	.244	.294	.213	10.13	3.38
Lueke, Josh	R-R	6-5	220	12-5-84	0	1	1.17	4	0	0	1	8	5	2	1	0	1	11	.179	.214	.143	12.91	1.17

Name	B-T	HT	WT	DOB			ERA	G				IP	H	R	ER	HR	BB	SO				AVG	vLH	vRH	K/9	BB/9
Main, Michael	R-R	6-1	170	12-14-88	4	6	6.83	14	12	0	0	58	72	48	44	9	37	49				.313	.298	.330	7.60	5.74
Miller, Justin	R-R	6-3	190	6-13-87	1	1	2.35	11	0	0	2	15	10	5	4	1	9	16				.192	.250	.143	9.39	5.28
Murphy, Tim	L-L	6-2	190	5-7-87	10	10	6.80	27	26	0	0	135	184	114	102	12	59	86				.326	.279	.349	5.73	3.93
Nelo, Hector	R-R	6-1	200	11-5-86	0	0	5.16	19	0	0	0	30	33	18	17	1	23	27				.275	.328	.226	8.19	6.98
Phillips, Zach	L-L	6-1	200	9-21-86	2	3	1.23	16	3	0	2	44	19	7	6	1	11	46				.123	.061	.169	9.41	2.25
Quintero, Jorge	R-R	6-1	175	4-17-87	0	0	6.00	2	0	0	0	3	2	2	2	0	0	2				.182	.200	.167	6.00	0.00
Reed, Evan	R-R	6-4	225	12-31-85	2	2	2.96	46	0	0	25	49	44	17	16	1	28	65				.244	.230	.263	12.02	5.18
Roark, Tanner	R-R	6-2	220	10-5-86	10	0	2.70	29	9	0	0	87	68	27	26	5	27	91				.217	.188	.247	9.45	2.80
Slusarz, John	R-R	6-3	185	7-19-84	0	0	33.75	1	0	0	0	1	4	5	5	1	4	1				.571	.500	.667	6.75	27.00
Swanson, Glenn	L-L	6-1	175	5-15-83	1	1	3.92	20	0	0	0	41	42	19	18	4	20	42				.266	.234	.287	9.15	4.35
Tatusko, Ryan	R-R	6-5	200	3-27-85	7	6	4.64	29	16	1	0	120	123	69	62	9	38	86				.265	.293	.237	6.43	2.84
Tufts, Tyler	R-R	6-3	195	12-5-86	0	0	3.86	6	0	0	1	7	5	3	3	0	3	8				.217	.111	.286	10.29	3.86
Young, Corey	L-L	6-2	175	12-30-86	0	3	2.29	25	0	0	1	39	27	13	10	3	18	46				.189	.130	.225	10.53	4.12

Fielding

Catcher	PCT	G	PO	A	E	DP	PB
Dominguez	1.000	1	5	0	0	0	0
Felix	.991	90	729	63	7	5	16
Hogan	.988	8	75	7	1	0	0
Sarmiento	.985	46	349	34	6	1	15

First Base	PCT	G	PO	A	E	DP
Gac	.991	69	610	38	6	54
Gomez	.993	43	376	25	3	34
Moreland	.996	30	255	24	1	22

Second Base	PCT	G	PO	A	E	DP
Garcia	.600	1	2	1	2	0
Kaase	.941	9	16	16	2	4
Lawson	.980	126	232	410	13	81
Morrison	1.000	1	2	2	0	1

Osuna	.967	6	12	17	1	4

Third Base	PCT	G	PO	A	E	DP
Gac	1.000	1	0	3	0	0
Gomez	.813	8	4	9	3	1
Greene	.915	80	50	144	18	13
Kaase	.867	25	15	37	8	5
Mendonca	.941	11	7	25	2	1
Stoneburner	.881	21	18	41	8	2

Shortstop	PCT	G	PO	A	E	DP
Garcia	.810	5	2	15	4	2
Kaase	.971	13	19	49	2	8
Osuna	.960	37	53	117	7	17
Stoneburner	.913	86	137	230	35	56

Outfield	PCT	G	PO	A	E	DP
Barto	1.000	8	11	1	0	0
Beltre	.958	83	171	10	8	2
Bianucci	.930	30	49	4	4	0
Butler	.967	133	199	6	7	0
Fry	1.000	7	7	2	0	0
Greene	.962	32	48	2	2	0
Lawson	1.000	3	4	0	0	0
Moreland	.929	12	12	1	1	0
Morrison	1.000	8	8	2	0	0
Paisano	1.000	38	83	2	0	1
Podraza	1.000	8	9	1	0	0
Rodriguez	.932	30	54	1	4	0
Sarmiento	.917	9	10	1	1	0
Smith	.978	31	43	2	1	0

HICKORY CRAWDADS

SOUTH ATLANTIC LEAGUE

LOW CLASS A

Batting	B-T	HT	WT	DOB	AVG	vLH	vRH	G	AB	R	H	2B	3B	HR	RBI	BB	HBP	SH	SF	SO	SB	CS	SLG	OBP
Alfonzo, Miguel	R-R	6-3	190	4-21-88	.262	.333	.240	20	65	8	17	3	0	1	11	5	4	1	0	17	3	1	.354	.351
Barto, Aja	R-R	6-5	225	9-26-86	.190	.111	.204	15	58	6	11	1	0	1	4	2	1	0	0	23	2	0	.259	.230
Bianucci, Mike	R-R	6-1	225	6-26-86	.331	.319	.335	72	260	50	86	21	2	15	49	24	9	0	4	50	8	5	.600	.401
Bolden, Jared	L-L	6-2	180	3-17-87	.238	.302	.219	107	369	62	88	11	3	1	34	38	1	4	4	89	14	4	.293	.308
De Los Santos, Leonel	R-R	5-10	170	10-2-89	.272	.269	.273	65	217	26	59	6	0	4	35	7	4	8	6	42	5	1	.355	.299
DiFazio, Vin	R-R	6-0	215	5-15-86	.290	.000	.327	18	62	12	18	5	1	5	17	12	3	0	1	11	0	0	.645	.423
Dominguez, Carlos	R-R	6-1	177	6-8-86	.111	.000	.130	8	27	4	3	1	0	0	3	5	2	0	0	5	0	0	.148	.294
Fry, Eric	L-R	5-10	190	8-9-87	.258	.238	.262	74	252	41	65	17	2	7	38	28	4	3	3	69	5	4	.425	.338
Garcia, Leury	B-R	5-7	153	3-18-91	.232	.230	.233	83	276	28	64	6	3	1	18	18	4	9	1	64	19	6	.286	.288
Hogan, Doug	R-R	6-3	210	9-29-84	.249	.297	.232	68	241	31	60	15	3	16	43	26	1	1	0	74	0	1	.535	.325
Hollander, Michael	R-R	5-9	180	10-30-85	.242	.247	.241	94	355	44	86	15	1	3	35	29	7	13	6	68	6	5	.315	.307
James, Andres	B-R	5-9	150	11-25-87	.269	.294	.262	43	156	14	42	8	1	1	6	3	0	4	0	30	4	5	.353	.283
Kaase, Jake	L-R	6-1	185	4-14-86	.259	.167	.283	52	201	25	52	11	4	4	22	12	1	4	1	33	5	3	.413	.302
Koncel, Ed	R-R	6-3	195	7-29-88	.138	.200	.127	20	65	5	9	5	0	1	4	3	1	1	1	26	1	0	.262	.186
Martinez, Edward	R-R	5-9	160	3-28-88	.196	.176	.206	29	102	13	20	1	1	0	7	2	0	1	0	23	5	2	.225	.212
Morrison, Erik	R-R	6-0	190	10-23-85	.297	.323	.288	94	353	55	105	32	3	18	66	31	10	1	3	80	10	5	.558	.368
Murphy, Clark	L-L	6-2	190	12-18-89	.218	.143	.244	33	110	11	24	6	0	0	12	11	0	1	3	23	0	0	.273	.282
Ogata, Jason	R-R	6-1	189	10-21-86	.191	.226	.175	29	94	11	18	6	1	0	7	7	4	1	2	16	2	0	.277	.274
Paisano, David	R-R	6-1	165	11-26-87	.268	.279	.263	72	291	45	78	22	2	1	30	16	13	6	1	61	10	7	.368	.333
Podraza, Cody	R-R	5-8	185	11-6-87	.278	.235	.291	38	151	24	42	7	1	1	8	12	4	2	0	22	13	2	.358	.347
Rodriguez, Tim	R-R	6-2	210	1-24-87	.217	.220	.215	35	106	9	23	3	0	2	11	3	1	2	1	25	2	4	.302	.243
Santana, Cristian	R-R	6-0	175	6-28-89	.224	.219	.226	83	312	39	70	19	0	18	56	19	4	2	3	113	2	2	.458	.275
West, Matt	R-R	6-1	215	11-21-88	.234	.261	.224	135	471	61	110	29	2	5	55	54	22	0	7	136	12	4	.335	.336
Zaneski, Zach	R-R	6-2	215	6-27-86	.250	.333	.214	6	20	2	5	1	0	0	1	1	0	1	0	7	1	0	.300	.286

Pitching	B-T	HT	WT	DOB	W	L	ERA	G	GS	CG	SV	IP	H	R	ER	HR	BB	SO	AVG	vLH	vRH	K/9	BB/9
Bleier, Richard	L-L	6-3	195	4-16-87	2	1	1.14	5	4	1	0	24	19	8	3	0	4	17	.216	.071	.283	6.46	1.52
Boscan, Wilfredo	R-R	6-2	187	10-26-89	6	8	3.59	23	21	0	0	105	105	57	42	7	19	59	.254	.225	.275	5.04	1.62
Brigham, Jake	R-R	6-3	210	2-10-88	2	11	5.52	25	17	0	1	90	104	70	55	10	38	81	.292	.338	.260	8.13	3.81
Castillo, Fabio	R-R	6-1	235	2-19-89	3	6	4.05	40	2	0	2	80	87	45	36	5	25	67	.269	.295	.251	7.54	2.81
Doyle, Andrew	R-R	6-3	200	11-12-87	1	1	9.45	5	0	0	0	7	11	10	7	0	2	9	.367	.444	.333	12.15	2.70
Eppley, Cody	R-R	6-5	205	10-8-85	1	3	2.93	37	0	0	6	68	65	31	22	4	6	76	.244	.337	.193	10.11	0.80
Font, Wilmer	R-R	6-4	210	5-24-90	8	3	3.49	29	24	0	0	108	93	51	42	4	59	105	.231	.234	.228	8.72	4.90
Hamburger, Mark	R-R	6-4	195	2-5-87	2	9	4.75	41	0	0	1	66	79	49	35	8	25	55	.282	.327	.256	7.46	3.39
Hurley, Trevor	R-R	6-3	215	7-28-87	1	0	3.00	5	0	0	9	9	3	3	0	3	9	.250	.467	.095	9.00	3.00
Nam, Yoon-Hee	L-L	6-2	190	8-4-87	9	1	3.77	37	4	0	0	88	76	45	37	8	34	102	.226	.218	.229	10.39	3.46
Nevarez, Matt	R-R	6-5	220	2-26-87	1	4	2.83	34	0	0	9	35	22	14	11	1	15	50	.177	.143	.195	12.86	3.86
2-team total (8 Lexington)					2	4	2.28	42	0	0	13	43	25	14	11	1	15	63	—	—	—	13.08	3.12
Ortiz, Joseph	L-L	5-7	175	8-13-90	0	1	6.00	4	0	0	0	6	11	5	4	1	4	6	.344	.455	.286	9.00	6.00
Perez, Martin	L-L	6-0	178	4-4-91	5	5	2.31	22	14	0	1	94	82	35	24	3	33	105	.236	.293	.220	10.09	3.17

TEXAS RANGERS

Player	B-T	HT	WT	DOB	W	L	ERA	G	GS	CG	SV	IP	H	R	ER	BB	SO	AVG	vLH	vRH	K/9	BB/9
Pimentel, Carlos	R-R	6-3	180	12-1-89	5	4	2.93	28	14	1	1	123	120	49	40	15	35	101	.256	.202	.290	7.39	2.56
Quintero, Jorge	R-R	6-1	175	4-17-87	3	0	1.38	5	0	0	0	13	9	2	2	0	4	6	.200	.190	.208	4.15	2.77
Ragsdale, Corey	R-R	6-4	175	11-10-82	1	1	2.43	15	0	0	2	30	18	8	8	17	14	24	.178	.209	.155	7.28	5.16
Ramirez, Neil	R-R	6-3	185	5-25-89	3	6	4.75	18	14	0	0	66	58	40	35	8	41	56	.235	.253	.225	7.60	5.56
Schlecht, Ryan	R-R	6-4	240	7-30-85	0	0	27.00	3	0	0	0	3	4	10	10	0	6	0	.333	.500	.000	0.00	16.20
Springston, Cliff	L-L	6-3	195	11-13-86	2	4	6.55	7	7	0	0	34	43	37	25	5	9	19	.305	.185	.333	4.98	2.36
Swanson, Glenn	L-L	6-1	175	5-15-83	1	0	1.84	6	0	0	0	15	8	4	3	1	4	13	.154	.182	.146	7.98	2.45
Tufts, Tyler	R-R	6-3	195	12-5-86	3	2	2.73	34	0	0	4	66	71	32	20	1	9	58	.272	.320	.241	7.91	1.23
Wieland, Joe	R-R	6-3	175	1-21-90	4	6	5.31	19	18	0	0	83	102	67	49	7	24	73	.299	.282	.313	7.92	2.60

Fielding

Catcher	PCT	G	PO	A	E	DP	PB
De Los Santos	.978	57	426	63	11	2	19
DiFazio	.980	10	92	6	2	0	3
Dominguez	1.000	8	66	7	0	0	3
Hogan	.984	60	433	46	8	1	8
Zaneski	1.000	6	55	5	0	1	1

First Base	PCT	G	PO	A	E	DP
Alfonzo	1.000	1	1	2	0	0
Bolden	.993	32	255	15	2	14
Koncel	.959	15	106	10	5	4
Morrison	.993	60	545	22	4	39
Murphy	.986	33	280	12	4	18
Ogata	1.000	4	28	0	0	1
Ragsdale	1.000	1	2	0	0	0
West	1.000	1	7	1	0	0

Second Base	PCT	G	PO	A	E	DP
De Los Santos	1.000	2	3	4	0	0
Hollander	.960	51	81	134	9	21
James	.950	26	41	55	5	6
Kaase	.960	27	49	72	5	13
Martinez	1.000	2	3	7	0	1
Morrison	.980	22	38	58	2	8
Ogata	.887	17	22	33	7	4
Ragsdale	—	1	0	0	0	0

Third Base	PCT	G	PO	A	E	DP
Hollander	.903	11	5	23	3	1
Kaase	1.000	2	0	3	0	0
Morrison	.933	11	6	22	2	1
West	.902	120	80	224	33	15

Shortstop	PCT	G	PO	A	E	DP
Garcia	.888	83	109	224	42	32

	PCT	G	PO	A	E	DP
James	.869	19	17	36	8	7
Kaase	.943	15	30	36	4	6
Martinez	.930	27	32	87	9	13

Outfield	PCT	G	PO	A	E	DP
Alfonzo	.943	20	32	1	2	1
Barto	.943	15	32	1	2	0
Bianucci	.952	68	110	8	6	2
Bolden	.967	63	140	5	5	2
De Los Santos	—	1	0	0	0	0
Fry	.956	50	82	5	4	2
Hollander	.909	7	9	1	1	0
Koncel	.833	4	5	0	1	0
Morrison	1.000	3	1	0	0	0
Paisano	.957	66	131	4	6	2
Podraza	.976	38	83	0	2	0
Rodriguez	.946	30	35	0	2	0
Santana	.932	75	116	8	9	1

SPOKANE INDIANS — SHORT-SEASON

NORTHWEST LEAGUE

Batting	B-T	HT	WT	DOB	AVG	vLH	vRH	G	AB	R	H	2B	3B	HR	RBI	BB	HBP	SH	SF	SO	SB	CS	SLG	OBP
Alfonzo, Miguel	R-R	6-3	190	4-21-88	.214	.000	.257	11	42	7	9	3	1	1	8	6	2	0	1	12	0	1	.405	.333
Barto, Aja	R-R	6-5	225	9-26-86	.263	.371	.239	52	190	27	50	6	3	7	27	14	4	0	1	71	8	0	.437	.325
Bonadonna, Joe	R-R	5-8	170	9-6-85	.217	.250	.205	48	175	27	38	9	1	0	19	29	2	2	2	33	15	1	.280	.332
De Jesus, Santo	R-R	6-1	195	10-15-85	.111	.000	.167	4	9	0	1	0	0	0	1	1	0	0	0	5	0	0	.111	.200
DiFazio, Vin	R-R	6-0	215	5-15-86	.274	.333	.259	47	168	36	46	14	0	7	29	29	12	0	1	38	3	0	.482	.414
Dove, Chris	R-R	6-2	185	4-8-86	.125	.000	.143	3	8	1	1	0	0	0	0	0	0	0	0	2	0	0	.125	.125
Duron, Denny	R-R	5-11	180	1-10-86	.279	.318	.266	53	172	21	48	12	1	1	17	10	1	3	1	28	2	2	.378	.321
Garcia, Edwin	B-R	6-0	150	3-1-91	.100	.000	.125	3	10	1	1	1	0	0	0	0	0	0	0	4	0	0	.200	.100
Landry, Shon	R-R	5-9	175	2-14-86	.056	.000	.067	5	18	1	1	0	0	0	1	2	1	1	0	8	1	0	.056	.190
Lima, Daniel	R-R	6-1	175	2-21-87	.291	.314	.285	43	172	21	50	7	1	0	15	5	3	3	0	38	4	2	.343	.322
Martinez, Edward	R-R	5-9	160	3-28-88	.231	.160	.253	36	108	6	25	3	0	0	11	7	2	3	0	19	10	4	.259	.291
Mendonca, Tommy	L-R	6-1	200	4-12-88	.309	.333	.301	49	188	33	58	12	2	9	26	9	7	0	1	66	0	0	.537	.361
Murphy, Clark	L-L	6-2	190	12-18-89	.228	.146	.248	56	206	21	47	9	1	3	20	17	2	1	3	77	0	0	.325	.289
O'Connor, William	R-R	5-11	180	1-2-87	.167	—	.167	3	6	1	1	0	0	0	0	0	0	0	0	1	0	0	.167	.167
Ogata, Jason	R-R	6-1	189	10-21-86	.366	.256	.395	51	191	23	70	15	1	5	42	15	10	0	5	29	3	1	.534	.430
Ortiz, Mike	L-L	6-2	200	5-2-89	.267	.000	.364	5	15	2	4	0	0	0	1	2	1	0	0	2	0	0	.267	.389
Podraza, Cody	R-R	5-8	185	11-6-87	.274	.235	.281	27	113	15	31	6	0	3	13	7	2	0	2	20	4	3	.407	.323
Prince, Jared	R-R	6-2	180	5-25-86	.283	.349	.265	55	198	36	56	9	6	6	29	28	6	0	0	29	3	2	.419	.388
Puello, Alberto	R-R	6-2	180	10-20-87	.210	.286	.188	21	62	3	13	4	0	0	8	6	1	0	0	17	0	0	.274	.290
Rhoad, Kyle	R-R	5-10	190	11-10-85	.232	.216	.238	53	177	40	41	3	1	0	14	25	5	3	3	52	18	3	.260	.338
Solis, Emmanuel	R-R	6-3	220	6-29-89	.170	.250	.154	12	47	4	8	3	0	2	5	4	1	0	0	20	0	0	.362	.250
Telis, Tomas	B-R	5-8	175	6-18-91	.400	.333	.429	7	20	4	8	1	0	2	2	0	0	0	0	4	0	0	.750	.400
Velazquez, Miguel	R-R	6-2	205	5-15-88	.297	.319	.290	54	209	33	62	12	2	10	40	19	2	0	1	43	9	2	.517	.359
Zaneski, Zach	R-R	6-2	215	6-27-86	.252	.240	.256	35	111	15	28	5	0	2	16	12	3	0	0	22	0	1	.351	.341

Pitching	B-T	HT	WT	DOB	W	L	ERA	G	GS	CG	SV	IP	H	R	ER	BB	SO	AVG	vLH	vRH	K/9	BB/9
Bermudez, Rainier	R-R	5-11	175	6-8-85	1	2	1.67	19	0	0	3	32	20	7	6	1	18	44	.179	.182	.176	12.25	5.01
Brown, Sam	R-R	6-5	215	6-10-87	2	1	3.45	17	0	0	0	31	38	15	12	1	8	30	.297	.308	.289	8.62	2.30
Campbell, Keith	L-R	6-2	190	10-12-87	0	0	4.22	13	4	0	0	21	16	12	10	1	16	19	.216	.212	.220	8.02	6.75
Castner, Kevin	R-R	6-4	230	8-3-87	0	1	59.40	4	0	0	0	2	8	12	11	1	4	2	.667	.600	.714	10.80	21.60
Doyle, Andrew	R-R	6-3	200	11-12-87	2	0	1.89	14	0	0	1	19	22	5	4	1	4	24	.282	.293	.270	11.37	1.89
Grullon, Geuris	L-L	6-5	185	12-20-89	0	1	7.57	16	0	0	2	27	39	25	23	1	17	32	.328	.455	.253	10.54	5.60
Gunter, Johnny	R-R	6-4	230	3-10-88	1	4	4.94	17	0	0	1	27	21	17	15	1	15	24	.212	.231	.200	7.90	4.94
Henry, Ben	R-R	6-4	190	4-9-89	2	5	6.04	15	11	0	0	51	62	41	34	6	33	48	.290	.372	.234	7.64	2.31
Hurley, Trevor	R-R	6-3	215	7-28-87	7	2	3.36	15	15	0	0	80	71	35	30	3	33	77	.235	.217	.250	8.63	3.70
King, Justin	R-R	6-5	185	10-6-86	3	2	3.00	21	0	0	3	30	22	12	10	1	21	29	.212	.188	.232	8.70	6.30
Matlock, Chris	R-R	6-2	180	7-4-86	1	7	4.46	19	0	0	3	34	25	17	17	3	10	30	.208	.250	.176	7.86	2.62
Miller, Justin	R-R	6-3	190	6-13-87	0	1	9.00	5	0	0	0	6	6	7	6	0	7	11	.273	.364	.182	16.50	10.50
O'Campo, Kyle	R-R	6-3	195	9-9-88	2	2	5.02	17	2	0	3	38	33	23	21	2	15	33	.237	.298	.195	7.88	3.58
Ortiz, Joseph	L-L	5-7	175	8-13-90	2	0	2.95	18	0	0	0	37	32	12	12	4	5	38	.237	.273	.220	9.33	1.23
Ross, Robbie	L-L	5-11	185	6-24-89	4	4	2.66	15	15	0	0	74	68	28	22	5	17	76	.240	.228	.245	9.20	2.06
Slusarz, John	R-R	6-3	185	7-19-84	0	0	0.00	1	0	0	0	1	0	0	0	0	0	1	.000	—	.000	9.00	0.00

Name	B-T	HT	WT	DOB	W	L	ERA	G	GS	CG	SV	IP	H	R	ER	HR	BB	SO	AVG	vLH	vRH	K/9	BB/9
Thompson, Matt	R-R	6-3	210	2-10-90	4	4	4.38	15	15	0	0	72	87	37	35	7	10	53	.301	.308	.295	6.63	1.25
Tullis, Braden	R-R	6-2	200	1-23-90	4	3	3.04	16	13	0	0	68	68	33	23	1	20	64	.252	.296	.207	8.47	2.65
Wilkins, Bobby	R-R	6-4	225	8-20-89	0	0	0.00	4	1	0	0	8	4	0	0	0	3	7	.160	.167	.154	7.88	3.38
Zegarac, Shane	L-L	6-3	225	8-15-85	2	0	3.60	9	0	0	0	10	12	4	0	10	10		.308	.385	.269	9.00	9.00

Fielding

Catcher	PCT	G	PO	A	E	DP	PB
DiFazio	.986	31	247	27	4	1	6
O'Connor	1.000	1	9	1	0	1	0
Puello	.973	15	93	14	3	0	5
Telis	1.000	1	12	1	0	0	0
Zaneski	.976	34	261	22	7	4	7

First Base	PCT	G	PO	A	E	DP
Murphy	.990	53	476	26	5	38
Ogata	.967	7	57	2	2	8
Ortiz	1.000	4	40	3	0	1
Prince	1.000	15	104	6	0	13
Puello	1.000	4	11	1	0	2

Second Base	PCT	G	PO	A	E	DP
Bonadonna	.950	35	59	93	8	23

	PCT	G	PO	A	E	DP
Duron	.778	2	2	5	2	2
Landry	1.000	5	3	15	0	3
Lima	.944	31	39	78	7	15
Martinez	.967	7	9	20	1	1
O'Connor	.800	2	1	3	1	0
Ogata	1.000	2	0	4	0	0

Third Base	PCT	G	PO	A	E	DP
Lima	.875	9	2	12	2	0
Martinez	1.000	5	4	9	0	2
Mendonca	.941	49	35	77	7	8
Ogata	.846	5	3	8	2	0
Solis	.964	11	10	17	1	0

Shortstop	PCT	G	PO	A	E	DP
Bonadonna	.971	10	12	21	1	3

	PCT	G	PO	A	E	DP
Duron	.923	47	65	150	18	21
Garcia	1.000	3	4	8	0	3
Martinez	.916	21	37	61	9	19

Outfield	PCT	G	PO	A	E	DP
Alfonzo	1.000	9	10	0	0	0
Barto	.973	46	68	3	2	1
Bonadonna	1.000	4	5	1	0	0
De Jesus	1.000	4	1	1	0	0
Dove	1.000	2	3	1	0	0
Lima	1.000	2	2	0	0	0
Ogata	.867	9	13	0	2	0
Podraza	1.000	27	41	0	0	0
Prince	.984	34	57	3	1	0
Rhoad	.989	48	86	1	1	0
Velazquez	.946	54	80	7	5	2

AZL RANGERS   ROOKIE

ARIZONA LEAGUE

Batting	B-T	HT	WT	DOB	AVG	vLH	vRH	G	AB	R	H	2B	3B	HR	RBI	BB	HBP	SH	SF	SO	SB	CS	SLG	OBP
Alfonzo, Edward	R-R	6-1	185	10-29-89	.197	.103	.223	43	132	17	26	3	1	0	13	19	1	3	0	56	10	3	.235	.303
Beltre, Engel	L-L	6-1	169	11-1-89	.300	.500	.250	3	10	4	3	1	1	0	0	0	1	0	0	3	2	0	.600	.364
Bonadonna, Joe	R-R	5-8	170	9-6-85	.379	.500	.333	8	29	8	11	2	0	0	1	3	2	0	0	3	2	0	.448	.471
Cafaro, Vicente	R-R	5-9	170	6-15-84	.280	.250	.294	10	25	2	7	2	0	0	2	5	2	0	0	4	1	1	.360	.438
De Jesus, Santo	R-R	6-1	195	10-15-85	.240	.185	.261	34	96	13	23	6	2	3	11	8	0	1	0	27	2	2	.438	.298
Dominguez, Carlos	R-R	6-1	177	6-8-86	.400	.667	.000	3	10	2	4	2	0	0	2	1	0	0	0	1	0	0	.600	.455
Garcia, Edwin	B-R	6-0	150	3-1-91	.265	.341	.244	53	204	27	54	11	4	0	23	14	1	4	3	37	4	1	.358	.311
Gonzalez, Alex	R-R	5-11	165	7-7-91	.243	.303	.225	42	144	29	35	4	1	0	7	13	4	3	0	39	16	2	.285	.323
Hogan, Doug	R-R	6-3	210	9-29-84	.294	.500	.267	5	17	4	5	1	1	0	1	0	1	0	0	7	0	0	.471	.333
Koncel, Ed	R-R	6-3	195	7-29-88	.220	.314	.185	37	127	22	28	9	1	6	23	16	0	0	3	44	4	1	.449	.301
Lane, Braxton	B-R	5-10	190	12-30-90	.185	.238	.159	22	65	6	12	0	1	0	5	3	0	0	0	33	1	1	.215	.221
O'Connor, William	R-R	5-11	180	1-2-87	.304	.188	.326	35	102	19	31	4	0	0	10	17	4	1	1	13	2	3	.343	.419
Ortiz, Mike	L-L	6-2	200	5-2-89	.304	.267	.317	49	184	22	56	10	2	2	28	24	2	0	0	38	5	3	.413	.390
Pimentel, Guillermo	R-R	6-1	190	11-12-89	.245	.171	.268	42	147	19	36	2	2	2	16	24	1	0	0	51	12	5	.327	.355
Ramirez, Max	R-R	5-11	175	10-11-84	.154	.500	.000	4	13	1	2	2	0	0	2	1	0	0	0	8	0	0	.308	.214
Rodriguez, Guilder	B-R	6-1	160	7-24-83	.500	—	.500	2	8	2	4	0	0	0	1	0	0	0	0	0	2	0	.500	.500
Sierra Jr., Ruben	L-L	6-2	172	3-10-91	.202	.130	.221	34	109	14	22	3	0	0	10	8	0	0	1	47	7	4	.229	.254
Smith, Tim	L-L	6-3	225	6-14-86	.333	.333	.333	3	12	2	4	1	0	1	2	0	0	0	1	4	2	0	.667	.308
Smoak, Justin	B-L	6-4	220	12-5-86	.667	—	.667	2	6	3	4	0	1	2	5	1	0	0	0	1	0	0	2.000	.714
Solis, Emmanuel	R-R	6-3	220	6-29-89	.183	.107	.211	29	104	9	19	3	0	2	11	7	2	0	2	37	5	0	.269	.243
Telis, Tomas	B-R	5-8	175	6-18-91	.322	.313	.325	46	183	30	59	11	5	2	28	4	1	0	4	15	8	1	.470	.333
Torres, Kevin	R-L	6-3	195	2-24-90	.254	.300	.233	25	63	5	16	3	0	0	4	3	0	0	0	13	0	0	.302	.288
Vail, Taylor	R-L	6-2	200	9-5-86	.269	.381	.241	32	108	16	29	8	3	0	16	11	1	0	1	30	4	3	.398	.339
Velazquez, Miguel	R-R	6-2	205	5-15-88	.294	.429	.259	9	34	7	10	0	2	1	6	4	1	0	0	11	1	0	.500	.385

Pitching	B-T	HT	WT	DOB	W	L	ERA	G	GS	CG	SV	IP	H	R	ER	HR	BB	SO	AVG	vLH	vRH	K/9	BB/9
Ahn, Tae Kyung	R-R	6-3	185	5-25-90	0	0	8.10	5	0	0	0	3	1	3	3	0	10	4	.091	.000	.111	10.80	27.00
Alvarez, Richard	R-R	6-2	180	8-14-92	2	3	5.49	11	9	0	0	41	42	29	25	1	19	35	.268	.214	.287	7.68	4.17
Arrendell, Kelvin	R-R	6-0	200	10-4-86	0	3	3.80	18	0	0	10	21	22	17	9	1	9	18	.262	.333	.233	7.59	3.80
De Los Santos, Ovispo	R-R	6-1	180	11-19-87	3	2	3.45	18	0	0	0	29	24	16	11	1	7	22	.224	.125	.253	6.91	2.20
Erlin, Robbie	L-L	6-0	175	10-8-90	0	0	2.25	3	0	0	0	4	5	1	1	0	1	9	.294	.000	.333	20.25	2.25
Escobar, Edwin	L-L	6-1	185	4-22-92	2	5	5.00	13	12	0	0	45	53	34	25	1	16	48	.279	.217	.287	9.60	3.20
Geglein, Jacob	R-R	6-4	180	5-19-86	1	0	0.00	3	0	0	0	3	2	2	0	0	2	2	.154	.333	.100	5.40	5.40
Grullon, Juan	L-L	6-0	185	3-4-90	1	1	3.51	8	5	0	0	26	23	13	10	2	10	25	.237	.429	.205	8.73	3.51
Jamison, Justin	R-R	6-3	225	1-10-91	0	2	8.78	15	0	0	0	13	9	16	13	0	23	15	.191	.222	.184	10.13	15.52
Laughter, Andrew	R-R	6-4	227	2-24-85	0	0	0.00	2	2	0	0	3	4	2	0	0	0	1	.286	1.000	.231	3.00	0.00
Main, Michael	R-R	6-1	170	12-14-88	0	0	2.00	2	0	0	0	3	3	1	1	0	0	3	.231	.143	.333	15.00	0.00
Melo, Carlos	R-R	6-3	180	2-27-91	1	4	7.09	12	12	0	0	47	60	44	37	5	24	45	.317	.333	.311	8.62	4.60
Miller, Justin	R-R	6-3	190	6-13-87	0	0	1.08	8	0	0	2	8	2	1	1	0	1	10	.074	.222	.000	10.80	1.08
Monegro, Jose	R-R	6-3	200	9-19-89	0	0	2.51	18	0	0	0	32	31	10	9	2	7	47	.242	.229	.247	13.08	1.95
Piper, Brock	R-R	6-3	250	9-25-87	0	0	4.91	9	0	0	0	11	7	7	6	1	4	13	.189	.333	.143	10.64	3.27
Poveda, Omar	R-R	6-4	215	9-28-87	0	0	0.00	1	1	0	0	3	2	0	0	0	0	2	.182	.000	.222	6.00	0.00
Quintero, Jorge	R-R	6-1	175	4-17-87	0	0	4.82	7	0	0	0	9	13	6	5	0	6	8	.342	.333	.345	7.71	5.79
Ragsdale, Corey	R-R	6-4	175	11-30-82	0	0	5.14	6	0	0	0	7	5	4	4	0	8	9	.269	.161	.300	9.29	5.14
Rijo, Ezequiel	R-R	6-4	190	9-12-90	4	6	4.86	13	11	0	0	54	56	37	29	7	22	27	.271	.212	.298	4.53	3.69
Rodriguez, Danniel	R-R	6-0	195	1-11-90	2	1	8.78	15	0	0	0	28	42	28	27	4	11	34	.350	.333	.357	11.06	3.58
Schrom, Jared	R-R	6-4	230	2-23-87	2	0	3.71	17	0	0	1	27	31	18	11	3	9	34	.287	.175	.353	11.48	3.04
Wilkins, Bobby	R-R	6-4	225	8-20-89	3	1	2.14	13	2	0	0	34	28	10	8	1	6	27	.226	.184	.244	7.22	1.60
Zegarac, Shane	L-L	6-3	225	8-15-85	1	1	3.57	9	0	0	0	18	17	11	7	0	8	21	.243	.143	.286	10.70	4.08

Fielding

Catcher	PCT	G	PO	A	E	DP	PB
Dominguez	.727	1	8	0	3	0	1
Hogan	1.000	2	9	1	0	0	0
O'Connor	.990	14	83	14	1	0	0
Ramirez	1.000	4	21	7	0	0	0
Telis	.979	33	250	29	6	0	6
Torres	.981	19	96	6	2	0	5

First Base	PCT	G	PO	A	E	DP
Koncel	1.000	1	3	1	0	2
Ortiz	.981	47	396	23	8	35
Smoak	.900	2	9	0	1	2
Solis	.976	5	39	1	1	1
Vail	.971	4	30	4	1	4

Second Base	PCT	G	PO	A	E	DP
Bonadonna	1.000	2	0	2	0	0

Cafaro	.976	9	16	25	1	8
Garcia	1.000	5	2	13	0	0
Gonzalez	.957	38	71	84	7	23
Koncel	1.000	3	2	2	0	0
O'Connor	.960	8	10	14	1	3

Third Base	PCT	G	PO	A	E	DP
Bonadonna	1.000	2	4	3	0	1
Koncel	.908	23	16	53	7	6
O'Connor	.909	13	9	21	3	2
Solis	.812	23	13	43	13	0
Vail	.500	1	0	2	2	0

Shortstop	PCT	G	PO	A	E	DP
Bonadonna	.929	2	5	8	1	2
Garcia	.944	49	57	129	11	27
Gonzalez	.750	2	3	3	2	1

Koncel	.846	5	4	7	2	0
Rodriguez	1.000	2	1	10	0	0

Outfield	PCT	G	PO	A	E	DP
Alfonzo	.966	42	77	9	3	2
Beltre	1.000	3	6	0	0	0
Bonadonna	—	1	0	0	0	0
De Jesus	.907	34	39	0	4	0
Koncel	1.000	8	15	0	0	0
Lane	.981	18	48	3	1	0
Pimentel	.948	41	52	3	3	1
Sierra Jr.	.953	32	39	2	2	1
Smith	1.000	2	4	0	0	0
Torres	—	1	0	0	0	0
Velazquez	1.000	9	16	0	0	0

DSL RANGERS #1

ROOKIE

DOMINICAN SUMMER LEAGUE

Batting	B-T	HT	WT	DOB	AVG	vLH	vRH	G	AB	R	H	2B	3B	HR	RBI	BB	HBP	SH	SF	SO	SB	CS	SLG	OBP
Arias, Jose	R-R	6-0	165	6-6-90	.230	.200	.235	38	100	14	23	3	0	2	8	24	0	3	0	27	3	2	.320	.379
2-team total (12 Rangers 2)					.192	—	—	50	125	16	24	3	0	2	9	32	0	3	1	34	5	2	.264	.354
Cabrera, Luis	R-R	6-2	185	8-14-90	.114	.227	.093	48	140	13	16	2	1	0	9	20	1	1	0	49	4	2	.143	.230
Castillo, Yefry	R-R	5-11	175	4-22-90	.324	.000	.375	12	37	5	12	4	0	0	7	3	0	0	1	2	3	0	.432	.366
2-team total (42 Rangers 2)					.272	—	—	54	191	28	52	8	1	2	26	12	3	2	1	11	7	4	.356	.324
Ceballo, Edward	L-R	5-11	180	10-8-90	.231	.300	.216	61	225	24	52	8	3	3	27	13	3	0	2	49	6	1	.333	.280
Frias, Andres	R-R	6-2	185	2-18-90	.202	.174	.209	30	109	13	22	0	1	0	12	8	6	1	0	24	5	2	.220	.293
Guarucano, Gilberto	B-R	5-11	165	6-9-91	.167	.217	.153	34	108	6	18	3	1	0	9	7	3	1	1	28	1	1	.213	.235
2-team total (6 Rangers 2)					.174	—	—	40	121	8	21	4	1	0	10	9	4	2	2	31	1	1	.223	.250
Mateo, Jose	L-L	6-0	190	6-18-90	.270	.143	.304	29	100	14	27	10	0	1	9	15	5	0	1	30	2	2	.400	.388
2-team total (14 Rangers 2)					.279	—	—	43	147	25	41	15	3	1	19	25	5	0	1	42	2	2	.442	.399
Montes De Oca, Miguel	R-R	6-0	170	8-6-90	.195	.150	.206	58	210	33	41	5	1	0	18	28	9	2	2	55	20	16	.229	.313
Moreno, Miguel	R-R	6-2	185	1-9-90	.246	.217	.252	41	130	16	32	2	1	0	16	24	3	1	0	28	2	1	.277	.376
2-team total (7 Rangers 2)					.233	—	—	48	146	18	34	2	1	1	11	27	3	1	0	34	2	1	.281	.364
Morillo, Robert	R-R	6-1	188	6-2-91	.139	.167	.134	23	79	3	11	2	0	1	4	4	2	1	0	16	0	0	.203	.200
2-team total (28 Rangers 2)					.241	—	—	51	174	15	42	5	4	3	14	18	2	2	0	32	1	1	.368	.320
Mota, Ramon	R-R	5-11	190	7-20-90	.280	.500	.261	8	25	8	7	0	0	3	4	2	0	0	5	6	0	.280	.419
2-team total (28 Rangers 2)					.216	—	—	36	111	20	24	5	3	1	17	11	6	2	1	34	8	0	.342	.318
Oropeza, Carlos	B-R	6-0	180	7-7-92	.302	.222	.312	34	86	9	26	3	1	0	8	17	1	0	0	24	0	1	.360	.423
Payano, Junior	B-R	6-1	175	2-20-90	.263	.184	.279	58	217	36	57	6	1	2	15	32	3	0	1	56	15	4	.327	.364
Pirela, Oswaldo	R-R	5-10	165	10-13-91	.091	—	.091	4	11	0	1	0	0	0	1	0	0	0	0	3	0	0	.091	.091
2-team total (25 Rangers 2)					.184	—	—	29	76	6	14	1	0	0	8	6	2	0	0	16	1	0	.197	.262
Santa, Johan	R-R	5-11	178	3-27-92	.197	.100	.216	37	122	11	24	6	0	0	4	8	3	0	0	36	2	4	.246	.263
2-team total (11 Rangers 2)					.194	—	—	48	155	14	30	7	0	0	6	13	3	0	1	44	2	4	.239	.267
Torres, Carlos	R-R	5-10	175	2-5-92	.206	.000	.259	13	34	4	7	2	0	0	3	5	3	0	0	12	1	2	.265	.357
Valdez, Jairo	R-R	6-2	190	11-6-88	.208	.103	.235	40	144	8	30	5	0	0	13	13	5	0	0	25	3	2	.243	.296
Villegas, Luis	R-R	5-10	175	5-24-92	.195	.138	.207	51	174	22	34	5	0	0	13	16	4	1	0	40	4	2	.224	.278

Pitching	B-T	HT	WT	DOB	W	L	ERA	G	GS	CG	SV	IP	H	R	ER	HR	BB	SO	AVG	vLH	vRH	K/9	BB/9
Aguasvivas, Domingo	R-R	6-2	180	10-18-89	0	1	6.00	3	1	0	0	6	7	5	4	0	2	1	.292	.500	.273	1.50	3.00
2-team total (2 Rangers 2)					0	1	5.00	5	1	0	0	9	9	6	5	0	3	5	—	—	—	5.00	3.00
Alvarez, Reynaldo	R-R	6-2	185	2-27-88	4	3	2.66	19	0	0	1	41	32	17	12	0	30	38	.225	.242	.220	8.41	6.64
Arrendell, Kelvin	R-R	6-0	200	10-4-86	0	1	3.68	7	0	0	0	7	7	6	3	0	4	5	.241	.200	.250	6.14	4.91
Bryan, Melvin	R-R	6-5	205	9-30-86	0	1	3.24	18	0	0	1	33	21	18	12	0	26	27	.176	.226	.159	7.29	7.02
Caraballo, Orlando	R-R	6-3	195	8-13-89	0	0	6.75	2	0	0	0	1	1	1	1	0	2	1	.200	.000	.500	6.75	13.50
2-team total (6 Rangers 2)					2	1	1.56	8	0	0	0	17	8	4	3	0	12	10	—	—	—	5.19	6.23
Cuevas, Gerson	R-R	6-3	183	11-8-89	0	1	2.66	13	0	0	0	24	21	13	7	0	12	14	.236	.294	.222	5.32	4.56
2-team total (3 Rangers 2)					1	1	2.36	16	0	0	0	27	21	13	7	0	13	15	—	—	—	5.06	4.39
De Jesus, Jorge	R-R	6-0	205	1-17-92	0	6	16.80	16	4	0	0	15	23	34	28	2	25	11	.343	.182	.375	6.60	15.00
Garces, Frank	L-L	5-11	155	1-17-90	0	2	4.96	8	1	0	0	16	24	16	9	0	9	12	.343	.286	.349	6.61	4.96
Gil, Leonel	L-L	6-0	160	2-5-91	2	1	1.67	14	2	0	1	54	43	19	10	1	11	45	.215	.188	.217	7.50	1.83
2-team total (4 Rangers 2)					2	1	1.83	18	2	0	1	59	50	23	12	1	12	46	—	—	—	7.02	1.83
Herrera, Hector	R-R	6-4	195	10-28-90	0	5	3.94	10	9	0	0	32	35	23	14	0	22	19	.276	.419	.229	5.34	6.19
2-team total (4 Rangers 2)					1	5	4.28	14	9	0	0	40	39	29	19	0	26	27	—	—	—	6.08	5.85
Mavare, Jose	R-R	6-0	175	2-19-90	3	2	1.93	12	5	0	0	42	33	14	9	1	12	41	.214	.196	.222	8.79	2.57
2-team total (8 Rangers 2)					4	2	1.36	20	5	0	2	60	43	15	9	1	19	58	—	—	—	8.75	2.87
Mendoza, Francisco	R-R	6-0	175	12-7-87	0	1	2.45	3	0	0	1	7	9	4	2	1	1	6	.300	.600	.240	7.36	1.23
2-team total (20 Rangers 2)					2	1	1.45	23	0	0	8	37	30	12	6	1	6	38	—	—	—	9.16	1.45
Monegro, Jose	R-R	6-3	200	9-19-89	0	0	0.00	4	0	0	0	8	5	2	0	0	1	14	.156	.000	.185	15.12	1.08
Ogando, Alexi	R-R	6-4	185	10-5-83	0	2	2.45	10	0	0	2	18	16	8	5	0	1	31	.229	.211	.235	15.22	0.49
Peralta, Denny	R-R	6-4	170	12-11-89	1	2	3.32	4	3	0	0	19	20	9	7	0	2	22	.256	.130	.309	10.42	0.95
2-team total (9 Rangers 2)					6	3	3.30	13	11	0	0	60	54	27	22	0	7	65	—	—	—	9.75	1.05
Ramirez, Carlos	R-R	6-2	180	4-9-91	2	4	3.83	14	6	0	1	52	47	26	22	1	14	39	.242	.208	.253	6.79	2.44

Name	B-T	HT	WT	DOB	W	L	ERA	G	GS	CG	SV	IP	H	R	ER	HR	BB	SO	AVG	vLH	vRH	K/9	BB/9
2-team total (5 Rangers 2)					3	4	4.14	19	6	0	1	59	55	32	27	2	15	46	—	—	—	7.06	2.30
Rodriguez, Danniel	R-R	6-0	195	1-11-90	1	1	4.85	3	3	0	0	13	12	10	7	1	3	11	.240	.000	.286	7.62	2.08
Rojas, Jonathan	R-R	6-2	205	3-22-88	3	4	3.86	12	5	1	0	44	34	21	19	4	13	54	.207	.225	.202	10.96	2.64
2-team total (5 Rangers 2)					6	6	3.52	17	10	1	0	69	66	38	27	4	17	76	—	—	—	9.91	2.22
Rosendo, Ender	R-R	6-3	220	9-15-89	0	2	5.11	4	3	0	0	12	12	13	7	0	6	12	.250	.300	.214	8.76	4.38
Taveras, Ramon	L-L	6-2	191	5-6-91	0	0	10.29	8	0	0	0	7	10	8	8	1	9	1	.333	.000	.370	1.29	11.57
Thompson, Aaron	R-R	6-0	205	1-11-91	1	4	4.50	11	11	1	0	40	36	29	20	2	26	28	.250	.071	.293	6.30	5.85
2-team total (3 Rangers 2)					2	5	4.50	14	14	1	0	50	50	35	25	2	32	33	—	—	—	5.94	5.76
Tirado, Pedro	L-L	6-2	180	12-18-90	1	3	3.92	12	11	0	0	41	38	26	18	1	21	18	.238	.235	.238	3.92	4.57
Urbina, Jose	R-R	6-3	190	9-8-88	0	1	6.75	2	0	0	0	3	3	4	2	1	3	4	.250	.500	.125	13.50	10.13

Fielding

Catcher	PCT	G	PO	A	E	DP	PB
Castillo	.969	10	82	12	3	1	2
Guarucano	.985	25	174	21	3	0	8
Moreno	.960	5	21	3	1	0	1
Oropeza	.959	21	128	11	6	0	10
Pirela	.947	2	17	1	1	0	1
Torres	.988	13	68	11	1	1	5

First Base	PCT	G	PO	A	E	DP
Ceballo	1.000	1	7	1	0	1
Guarucano	.979	5	45	2	1	4
Mateo	1.000	1	2	1	0	0
Moreno	.969	19	144	12	5	8
Oropeza	.980	7	48	2	1	5
Valdez	.978	35	277	30	7	18

Second Base	PCT	G	PO	A	E	DP
Arias	1.000	4	5	1	0	0
Cabrera	—	1	0	0	0	0
Payano	.500	1	1	0	1	0
Rojas	1.000	1	3	4	0	1
Santa	.920	20	42	38	7	7
Villegas	.939	41	81	73	10	14

Third Base	PCT	G	PO	A	E	DP
Arias	.750	4	1	8	3	0
Moreno	.935	15	12	31	3	1
Morillo	.898	23	24	55	9	4
Oropeza	1.000	1	1	0	0	0
Santa	.804	17	14	31	11	3
Villegas	.833	9	5	25	6	2

Shortstop	PCT	G	PO	A	E	DP
Arias	.891	31	36	78	14	8
Payano	.860	36	51	84	22	10
Villegas	1.000	1	0	2	0	0

Outfield	PCT	G	PO	A	E	DP
Cabrera	.932	46	78	4	6	1
Castillo	.500	1	1	0	1	0
Ceballo	1.000	56	83	6	0	1
Frias	.957	24	43	2	2	1
Guarucano	1.000	3	2	1	0	1
Mateo	.828	10	21	3	5	1
Montes De Oca	.953	57	78	3	4	0
Mota	1.000	5	11	1	0	1

DSL RANGERS #2　　　　　　　　　　　　　ROOKIE

DOMINICAN SUMMER LEAGUE

Batting	B-T	HT	WT	DOB	AVG	vLH	vRH	G	AB	R	H	2B	3B	HR	RBI	BB	HBP	SH	SF	SO	SB	CS	SLG	OBP
Abreu, Esdras	R-R	6-3	185	3-21-92	.203	.357	.169	56	158	29	32	11	0	3	17	32	9	1	0	65	5	0	.329	.367
Arias, Jose	R-R	6-0	165	6-6-90	.040	.000	.048	12	25	2	1	0	0	0	1	8	0	0	1	7	2	0	.040	.265
2-team total (38 Rangers 1)					.192	—	—	50	125	16	24	3	0	2	9	32	0	3	1	34	5	2	.264	.354
Castillo, Yefry	R-R	5-11	175	4-22-90	.260	.238	.268	42	154	23	40	4	1	2	19	9	3	2	0	9	4	4	.338	.313
2-team total (12 Rangers 1)					.272	—	—	54	191	28	52	8	1	2	26	12	3	2	1	11	7	4	.356	.324
Cedeno, Luis	R-R	6-1	190	7-2-92	.263	.250	.267	30	80	13	21	4	0	0	7	13	2	2	3	17	2	0	.313	.367
Chalas, Alfredo	R-R	6-0	160	6-24-91	.312	.379	.296	46	154	27	48	9	3	1	25	14	4	1	0	34	10	5	.429	.384
Chirino, Santiago	R-R	5-10	154	2-11-91	.270	.261	.273	56	211	37	57	9	1	0	28	19	10	2	5	14	18	11	.322	.351
Gomez, Jhonny	R-R	5-11	190	12-21-89	.280	.233	.296	51	168	29	47	9	1	1	25	30	10	2	2	27	4	4	.363	.414
Guarucano, Gilberto	B-R	5-11	165	6-9-91	.231	.000	.250	6	13	2	3	1	0	0	1	2	1	1	1	3	0	0	.308	.353
2-team total (34 Rangers 1)					.174	—	—	40	121	8	21	4	1	0	10	9	4	2	2	31	1	1	.223	.250
Herrera, David	L-R	5-11	165	12-29-91	.280	.208	.302	58	207	47	58	9	1	0	24	39	6	2	6	39	21	10	.333	.399
Lugo, Francisco	R-R	6-0	180	10-22-91	.246	.267	.241	48	142	23	35	4	0	0	16	21	5	5	2	8	2	3	.275	.359
Martinez, Hector	L-L	6-1	185	9-17-91	.262	.111	.294	33	103	17	27	6	0	1	14	11	3	1	3	30	4	1	.350	.342
Martinez, Teodoro	R-R	5-11	155	3-16-92	.276	.358	.248	53	210	37	58	8	1	0	16	19	6	2	0	19	34	8	.324	.353
Mateo, Jose	L-L	6-0	190	6-18-90	.298	.235	.333	14	47	11	14	5	3	0	10	10	0	0	0	10	0	0	.532	.421
2-team total (29 Rangers 1)					.279	—	—	43	147	25	41	15	3	1	19	25	5	0	1	40	2	2	.442	.399
Moreno, Miguel	R-R	6-2	185	1-9-90	.125	—	.125	7	16	2	2	0	0	1	1	3	0	0	0	6	0	0	.313	.263
2-team total (41 Rangers 1)					.233	—	—	48	146	18	34	2	1	1	11	27	3	1	0	34	2	1	.281	.364
Morillo, Robert	R-R	6-1	188	6-2-91	.326	.370	.309	28	95	12	31	3	4	2	10	14	0	1	0	16	1	1	.505	.413
2-team total (23 Rangers 1)					.241	—	—	51	174	15	42	5	4	3	14	18	2	2	0	32	1	1	.368	.320
Mota, Ramon	B-R	5-11	190	7-20-90	.198	.167	.214	28	86	12	17	5	3	1	14	7	4	2	1	29	2	0	.360	.286
2-team total (8 Rangers 1)					.216	—	—	36	111	20	24	5	3	1	17	11	6	2	1	34	8	2	.342	.318
Perez, Alison	R-R	5-11	190	9-3-89	.333	.500	.302	12	51	7	17	5	0	4	14	3	1	0	0	8	0	0	.667	.382
Pirela, Oswaldo	R-R	5-10	165	10-13-91	.200	.125	.224	25	65	6	13	1	0	0	7	6	2	0	0	13	1	0	.215	.288
2-team total (4 Rangers 1)					.184	—	—	29	76	6	14	1	0	0	8	6	2	0	0	16	1	0	.197	.262
Santa, Johan	R-R	5-11	178	3-27-92	.182	.333	.148	11	33	3	6	1	0	0	2	5	0	0	1	8	0	0	.212	.282
2-team total (37 Rangers 1)					.194	—	—	48	155	14	30	7	0	0	6	13	3	0	1	44	2	4	.239	.267
Villanueva, Christian	R-R	5-11	160	6-19-91	.208	.000	.227	8	24	2	5	1	0	0	3	6	1	1	1	5	1	0	.250	.375

Pitching	B-T	HT	WT	DOB	W	L	ERA	G	GS	CG	SV	IP	H	R	ER	HR	BB	SO	AVG	vLH	vRH	K/9	BB/9
Aguasvivas, Domingo	R-R	6-2	180	10-18-89	0	0	3.00	2	0	0	0	3	2	1	1	0	1	4	.182	.000	.200	12.00	3.00
2-team total (3 Rangers 1)					0	1	5.00	5	1	0	0	9	9	6	5	0	3	5	—	—	—	5.00	3.00
Beltre, Omar	R-R	6-3	190	8-24-81	0	0	0.00	6	0	0	0	7	5	3	0	0	3	10	.185	.286	.150	12.27	3.68
Caraballo, Orlando	R-R	6-3	195	8-13-89	2	1	1.13	6	0	0	0	16	7	3	2	0	10	9	.152	.167	.147	5.06	5.63
2-team total (2 Rangers 1)					2	1	1.56	8	0	0	0	17	8	4	3	0	12	10	—	—	—	5.19	6.23
Cuevas, Gerson	R-R	6-3	183	11-8-89	1	0	0.00	3	0	0	0	3	0	0	0	0	1	1	.000	.000	.000	3.00	3.00
2-team total (13 Rangers 1)					1	1	2.36	16	0	0	0	27	21	13	7	0	13	15	—	—	—	5.06	4.39
De Los Santos, Miguel	L-L	6-1	170	7-10-88	1	1	1.41	22	0	0	12	32	8	7	5	0	22	70	.074	.000	.081	19.69	6.19
Gil, Leonel	L-L	6-0	160	2-5-91	0	0	3.60	4	0	0	0	5	4	2	2	0	1	1	.318	.333	.316	1.80	1.80
2-team total (14 Rangers 1)					2	1	1.83	18	2	0	1	59	50	23	12	1	12	46	—	—	—	7.02	1.83
Herrera, Hector	R-R	6-4	195	10-28-90	1	0	5.63	4	0	0	0	8	4	6	5	0	4	8	.143	.286	.095	9.00	4.50
2-team total (10 Rangers 1)					1	5	4.28	14	9	0	0	40	39	29	19	0	26	27	—	—	—	6.08	5.85

Name	B-T	Ht	Wt	DOB	W	L	ERA	G	GS	CG	SV	IP	H	R	ER	HR	BB	SO	AVG	vLH	vRH		
Jimenez, Jose	R-R	6-3	200	9-22-86	2	0	3.12	12	0	0	1	17	17	8	6	0	5	15	.258	.200	.275	7.79	2.60
Mavare, Jose	R-R	6-0	175	2-19-90	1	0	0.00	8	0	0	2	18	10	1	0	0	7	17	.172	.273	.149	8.66	3.57
2-team total (12 Rangers 1)					4	2	1.36	20	5	0	2	60	43	15	9	1	19	58	—	—	—	8.75	2.87
Medina, Emiliano	R-R	6-3	175	7-18-90	0	0	0.00	3	0	0	0	3	1	1	0	0	0	2	.091	.000	.111	6.00	0.00
Mendoza, Francisco	R-R	6-0	175	12-7-87	2	0	1.20	20	0	0	7	30	21	8	4	0	5	32	.189	.161	.200	9.60	1.50
2-team total (3 Rangers 1)					2	1	1.45	23	0	0	8	37	30	12	6	1	6	38	—	—	—	9.16	1.45
Munoz, Miguel	R-R	6-4	180	6-29-88	3	2	3.62	8	4	0	1	32	33	16	13	0	7	17	.270	.125	.306	4.73	1.95
Parra, Luis	L-L	6-2	160	11-21-91	3	1	2.63	14	12	0	0	51	32	20	15	0	33	36	.178	.115	.188	6.31	5.79
Peralta, Denny	R-R	6-4	170	12-11-89	5	1	3.29	9	8	0	0	41	34	18	15	0	5	43	.218	.188	.226	9.44	1.10
2-team total (4 Rangers 1)					6	3	3.30	13	11	0	0	60	54	27	22	0	7	65	—	—	—	9.75	1.05
Perez, Roberto	R-R	6-4	150	1-8-92	0	1	1.20	6	4	0	0	15	8	3	2	1	5	9	.143	.000	.154	5.40	3.00
Polanco, Luis	R-R	6-1	170	6-11-85	7	2	2.48	14	13	0	0	69	51	23	19	4	14	71	.206	.243	.199	9.26	1.83
Ramirez, Carlos	R-R	6-2	180	4-9-91	1	0	6.43	5	0	0	0	7	8	6	5	1	1	7	.258	.200	.286	9.00	1.29
2-team total (14 Rangers 1)					3	4	4.14	19	6	0	1	59	55	32	27	2	15	46	—	—	—	7.06	2.30
Rojas, Jonathan	R-R	6-2	205	3-22-88	3	2	2.92	5	5	0	0	25	32	17	8	0	4	22	.308	.344	.292	8.03	1.46
2-team total (12 Rangers 1)					6	6	3.52	17	10	1	0	69	66	38	27	4	17	76	—	—	—	9.91	2.22
Rojas, Randol	R-R	6-0	160	9-28-90	8	0	0.80	13	12	0	0	67	42	11	6	1	6	48	.170	.079	.201	6.42	0.80
Sibid, Pepe	R-R	6-0	200	2-2-88	2	0	2.35	18	0	0	2	23	15	9	6	0	8	21	.174	.095	.200	8.22	3.13
Simeoli, Luis	R-R	6-3	194	6-28-88	1	1	2.77	21	0	0	2	26	14	15	8	0	19	28	.154	.150	.155	9.69	6.58
Stanford, Tim	R-R	6-0	191	5-7-89	3	1	3.69	23	1	0	0	39	46	22	16	1	9	36	.282	.296	.279	8.31	2.08
Thompson, Aaron	R-R	6-0	205	1-11-91	1	1	4.50	3	3	0	0	10	14	6	5	0	6	5	.333	.529	.200	4.50	5.40
2-team total (11 Rangers 1)					2	5	4.50	14	14	1	0	50	50	35	25	2	32	33	—	—	—	5.94	5.76

Fielding

Catcher	PCT	G	PO	A	E	DP	PB
Castillo	.995	22	162	22	1	1	2
Cedeno	.980	25	172	20	4	1	5
Chalas	1.000	1	6	0	0	0	0
Guaracano	1.000	6	19	5	0	0	0
Moreno	1.000	1	1	0	0	0	0
Perez	1.000	9	68	9	0	0	2
Pirela	.987	11	62	13	1	0	4

First Base	PCT	G	PO	A	E	DP
Chalas	.968	9	60	1	2	5
Gomez	.982	50	423	26	8	25
Gomez	1.000	1	9	0	0	1
Lugo	1.000	3	13	0	0	3
Mateo	.974	4	38	0	1	1
Moreno	1.000	1	3	0	0	0

	PCT	G	PO	A	E	DP
Pirela	.963	4	25	1	1	1

Second Base	PCT	G	PO	A	E	DP
Arias	1.000	3	5	8	0	1
Castillo	.943	10	16	17	2	2
Chalas	.909	6	6	14	2	2
Chirino	.989	43	72	103	2	14
Herrera	1.000	2	4	3	0	1
Santa	.895	3	11	6	2	1

Third Base	PCT	G	PO	A	E	DP
Arias	.857	4	1	5	1	0
Chalas	.920	31	18	63	7	5
Morillo	.884	25	18	58	10	5
Santa	.818	4	2	7	2	0
Villanueva	.861	8	8	23	5	1

Shortstop	PCT	G	PO	A	E	DP
Chirino	.933	13	28	42	5	6
Herrera	.863	51	78	137	34	18

Outfield	PCT	G	PO	A	E	DP
Abreu	.899	52	66	5	8	1
Arias	1.000	4	3	0	0	0
Castillo	—	1	0	0	0	0
Cedeno	.000	1	0	0	1	0
Chirino	—	1	0	0	0	0
Lugo	.986	44	69	3	1	0
Martinez	.897	30	49	3	6	1
Martinez	.949	50	73	2	4	0
Mateo	1.000	3	5	1	0	0
Mota	1.000	19	34	3	0	2
Pirela	1.000	2	2	0	0	0

Toronto Blue Jays

SEASON IN A SENTENCE: While it seemed in July that Blue Jays fans had seen the last of longtime ace Roy Halladay, general manager J.P. Ricciardi never consummated a trade and Halladay again shined for a fourth-place team, while Ricciardi was the one who left Toronto when he was fired at season's end.

HIGH POINT: The Blue Jays got off to a scorching start. A four-game sweep of the White Sox, topped with a 3-2 victory on May 18, gave the Jays a 27-14 record and 3½-game lead in the division. The Jays then lost nine straight, all on the road, and never got back to the top of the division.

LOW POINT: The Halladay trade talks became something of a circus as Toronto fell 10 games out by mid-July. On July 29, Halladay took a 3-2 loss at Seattle as trade winds swirled, and Halladay—clearly tired of the maelstrom of rumors—told reporters after the game, "I'm going to lock myself in a room and hide." Earlier in the day, the Phillies had jilted the Jays by trading for Cliff Lee instead.

NOTABLE ROOKIES: Outfielder Travis Snider, 21, was expected to be Toronto's top rookie, and the 2006 first-round pick had his moments, with nine home runs. But '05 first-rounder Ricky Romero overcame a minor league track record of wildness to emerge as the Jays' second-best starter, going 13-9, 4.30. Injuries prompted a parade of rookies in the Jays rotation, as lefties Brett Cecil (a 2007 first-round pick), Marc Rzcepczynski ('07 fifth round) and Brad Mills ('07 fourth round) all were rushed to the majors.

KEY TRANSACTIONS: The end of the Ricciardi era came after the season in Toronto, and the Jays promoted assistant GM Alex Anthopoulos to replace him. In his final year, Ricciardi did make moves that didn't involve Halladay, including losing Alexis Rios and his nearly $70 million contract (that runs through 2014) on waivers to the White Sox. The Jays trimmed more payroll by trading Scott Rolen to the Reds for Edwin Encarnacion and hard-throwing righthanders Josh Roenicke and Zach Stewart, and releasing closer B.J. Ryan, while still owing him $10 million in 2010.

DOWN ON THE FARM: The Rookie-level Gulf Coast League team was the only affiliate to finish above .500, and the farm system took a hit when it had to move its Triple-A affiliate from longtime home Syracuse to Las Vegas. The top performer on the farm was Cubs castoff Brian Dopirak, 25, who led the organization with 27 homers.

OPENING DAY PAYROLL: $80,538,300

PLAYERS OF THE YEAR

MAJOR LEAGUE	MINOR LEAGUE
Roy Halladay rhp	**Marc Rzepczynski** lhp
17-10, 2.79	(Double-A/Triple-A)
Led AL with 9 CG,	9-5, 2.66
4 SO, 3rd in ERA	104 SO in 88 IP

ORGANIZATION LEADERS

BATTING		*Minimum 250 at-bats
MAJORS		
*AVG	Adam Lind	.305
*OPS	Adam Lind	.932
HR	Aaron Hill	36
RBI	Adam Lind	114
MINORS		
*AVG	Howard, Kevin, Las Vegas	.326
R	Mastroianni, Darin, Dunedin/New Hampshire	94
H	Dopirak, Brian, New Hampshire/Las Vegas	173
TB	Dopirak, Brian, New Hampshire/Las Vegas	300
2B	Ruiz, Randy, Las Vegas	43
3B	Pastornicky, Tyler, Lansing/Dunedin	9
HR	Dopirak, Brian, New Hampshire/Las Vegas	27
RBI	Ruiz, Randy, Las Vegas	106
BB	Mastroianni, Darin, Dunedin/New Hampshire	76
SO	Chavez, Johermyn, Lansing	137
SB	Mastroianni, Darin, Dunedin/New Hampshire	70
*OBP	Mastroianni, Darin, Dunedin/New Hampshire	.398
*SLG	Ruiz, Randy, Las Vegas	.584

PITCHING		†Minimum 75 innings
MAJORS		
W	Roy Halladay	17
†ERA	Roy Halladay	2.79
SO	Roy Halladay	208
MINORS		
W	Page, Ryan, Dunedin	11
L	Liebel, Andrew, Dunedin/New Hampshire	13
	Page, Ryan, Dunedin	13
†ERA	Huggins, Charles, Lansing/Dunedin	2.82
G	Stidfole, Sean, New Hampshire/Las Vegas	55
GS	Castro, Fabio, New Hampshire/Las Vegas	29
	Liebel, Andrew, Dunedin/New Hampshire	29
SV	Farquhar, Daniel, Dunedin/New Hampshire	22
IP	Liebel, Andrew, Dunedin/New Hampshire	169
BB	Purcey, David, Las Vegas	78
SO	Liebel, Andrew, Dunedin/New Hampshire	130
†AVG	Huggins, Charles, Lansing/Dunedin	.233

General Manager: J.P. Ricciardi. **Farm Director:** Dick Scott. **Scouting Director:** John Lalonde.

Class	Team	League	W	L	PCT	Finish*	Manager(s)
Majors	Toronto Blue Jays	American	75	87	.463	t-10th (14)	Cito Gaston
Triple-A	Las Vegas 51s	Pacific Coast	71	73	.493	t-10th (16)	Michael Basso
Double-A	New Hampshire Fisher Cats	Eastern	64	78	.451	10th (12)	Gary Cathcart
High A	Dunedin Blue Jays	Florida State	67	67	.500	5th (12)	Omar Malave
Low A	Lansing Lugnuts	Midwest	54	84	.391	14th (14)	Clayton McCullough
Short-season	Auburn Doubledays	New York-Penn	26	49	.347	14th (14)	Dennis Holmberg
Rookie	GCL Blue Jays	Gulf Coast	30	28	.517	7th (16)	John Schneider
Overall 2009 Minor League Record			312	379	.452	28th (30)	

*Finish in overall standings (No. of teams in league). †League champion.

ORGANIZATION STATISTICS

TORONTO BLUE JAYS

AMERICAN LEAGUE

Batting	B-T	HT	WT	DOB	AVG	vLH	vRH	G	AB	R	H	2B	3B	HR	RBI	BB	HBP	SH	SF	SO	SB	CS	SLG	OBP
Adams, Russ	L-R	6-0	200	8-30-80	.200	.000	.211	8	20	2	4	0	0	0	0	1	0	0	0	1	0	0	.200	.238
Barajas, Rod	R-R	6-1	245	9-5-75	.226	.267	.213	125	429	43	97	19	0	19	71	20	1	3	7	76	1	0	.403	.258
Barrett, Michael	R-R	6-0	225	10-22-76	.167	.000	.231	7	18	3	3	0	0	1	2	1	0	0	0	5	0	0	.333	.211
Bautista, Jose	R-R	6-0	200	10-19-80	.235	.293	.202	113	336	54	79	13	3	13	40	56	4	6	2	85	4	0	.408	.349
Chavez, Raul	R-R	5-11	240	3-17-73	.258	.244	.263	51	159	10	41	8	0	2	15	6	0	3	0	23	1	1	.346	.285
Dellucci, David	L-L	5-11	205	10-31-73	.040	.000	.042	8	25	2	1	1	0	0	2	3	1	0	0	7	0	0	.080	.172
2-team total (14 Cleveland)					.185	—	—	22	65	5	12	4	0	0	3	5	3	0	1	19	0	0	.246	.270
Encarnacion, Edwin	R-R	6-2	230	1-7-83	.240	.214	.246	42	154	25	37	5	1	8	23	13	3	0	3	29	1	0	.442	.306
Hill, Aaron	R-R	5-11	205	3-21-82	.286	.298	.282	158	682	103	195	37	0	36	108	42	5	1	4	98	6	2	.499	.330
Inglett, Joe	L-R	5-9	185	6-29-78	.281	.000	.291	36	89	11	25	4	1	0	6	8	1	1	0	21	3	1	.348	.347
Lind, Adam	L-L	6-2	220	7-17-83	.305	.275	.317	151	587	93	179	46	0	35	114	58	5	0	4	110	1	1	.562	.370
McDonald, John	R-R	5-9	180	9-24-74	.258	.260	.257	73	151	18	39	7	0	4	13	1	2	1	1	18	0	2	.384	.271
Millar, Kevin	R-R	6-0	215	9-24-71	.223	.250	.191	78	251	29	56	14	0	7	29	31	1	0	0	49	0	0	.363	.311
Overbay, Lyle	L-L	6-2	230	1-28-77	.265	.190	.282	132	423	57	112	35	1	16	64	74	0	0	3	95	0	0	.466	.372
Phillips, Kyle	L-R	6-1	225	4-3-84	.278	.000	.333	5	18	1	5	3	0	0	2	0	0	0	0	4	0	0	.444	.278
Rios, Alex	R-R	6-5	215	2-18-81	.264	.266	.263	108	436	52	115	25	2	14	62	31	6	0	6	78	19	3	.427	.317
2-team total (41 Chicago)					.247	—	—	149	582	63	144	31	2	17	71	37	6	1	7	107	24	5	.395	.296
Rolen, Scott	R-R	6-4	240	4-4-75	.320	.359	.305	88	338	52	108	29	0	8	43	26	4	0	5	42	4	2	.476	.370
Ruiz, Randy	R-R	6-1	240	10-19-77	.313	.286	.322	33	115	25	36	7	0	10	17	10	4	0	1	35	1	1	.635	.385
Scutaro, Marco	R-R	5-9	175	10-30-75	.282	.269	.287	144	574	100	162	35	1	12	60	90	4	5	7	75	14	5	.409	.379
Snider, Travis	L-L	6-0	235	2-2-88	.241	.225	.244	77	241	34	58	14	1	9	29	29	3	2	1	78	1	1	.419	.328
Wells, Vernon	R-R	6-1	230	12-8-78	.260	.206	.278	158	630	84	164	37	3	15	66	48	1	0	5	86	17	4	.400	.311

Pitching	B-T	HT	WT	DOB	W	L	ERA	G	GS	CG	SV	IP	H	R	ER	HR	BB	SO	AVG	vLH	vRH	K/9	BB/9
Accardo, Jeremy	R-R	6-1	190	12-8-81	0	0	2.55	26	0	0	1	25	23	8	7	2	17	18	.267	.143	.386	6.57	6.20
Bullington, Bryan	R-R	6-4	210	9-30-80	0	0	3.00	4	0	0	0	6	7	2	2	0	6	5	.304	.000	.412	7.50	9.00
Burres, Brian	L-L	6-2	175	4-8-81	0	2	14.21	2	2	0	0	6	12	12	10	0	5	4	.375	.200	.407	5.68	7.11
Camp, Shawn	R-R	6-0	205	11-18-75	2	6	3.50	59	0	0	1	80	73	36	31	7	29	58	.245	.260	.230	6.55	3.28
Carlson, Jesse	L-L	6-0	160	12-31-80	1	6	4.66	73	0	0	0	68	67	37	35	7	21	51	.258	.272	.247	6.78	2.79
Cecil, Brett	R-L	6-2	225	7-2-86	7	4	5.30	18	17	0	0	93	116	59	55	17	38	69	.308	.295	.314	6.65	3.66
Downs, Scott	L-L	6-2	215	3-17-76	1	3	3.09	48	0	0	9	47	46	18	16	4	13	43	.251	.263	.246	8.29	2.51
Frasor, Jason	R-R	5-9	175	8-9-77	7	3	2.50	61	0	0	11	58	43	17	16	4	16	56	.209	.274	.140	8.74	2.50
Halladay, Roy	R-R	6-5	225	5-14-77	17	10	2.79	32	32	9	0	239	234	82	74	22	35	208	.256	.240	.278	7.83	1.32
Hayhurst, Dirk	L-R	6-2	195	3-24-81	0	0	2.78	15	0	0	0	23	23	7	7	2	9	13	.274	.326	.220	5.16	3.57
Janssen, Casey	R-R	6-3	225	9-17-81	2	4	5.85	21	5	0	1	40	59	29	26	5	14	24	.341	.313	.367	5.40	3.15
League, Brandon	R-R	6-2	200	3-16-83	3	6	4.58	67	0	0	0	75	72	40	38	8	21	76	.257	.270	.245	9.16	2.53
Litsch, Jesse	R-R	6-1	215	3-9-85	0	1	9.00	2	2	0	0	9	14	9	9	4	1	8	.350	.261	.471	8.00	1.00
Mills, Brad	L-L	5-11	185	3-5-85	0	1	14.09	2	2	0	0	8	14	12	12	4	6	9	.400	.375	.407	10.57	7.04
Murphy, Bill	L-L	5-11	195	5-9-81	0	0	3.18	8	0	0	0	11	4	4	4	1	8	6	.111	.125	.100	4.76	6.35
Purcey, David	L-L	6-4	240	4-22-82	1	3	6.19	9	9	0	0	48	54	35	33	6	30	39	.287	.156	.329	7.31	5.63
Ray, Robert	R-R	6-5	195	1-21-84	1	2	4.44	4	4	0	0	24	23	15	12	4	6	13	.253	.239	.267	4.81	2.22
Richmond, Scott	R-R	6-5	215	8-30-79	8	11	5.52	27	24	1	0	139	147	90	85	27	59	117	.268	.292	.233	7.59	3.83
Roenicke, Josh	R-R	6-3	195	8-4-82	0	0	7.13	13	0	0	0	18	19	15	14	2	12	19	.271	.400	.143	9.68	6.11
Romero, Ricky	R-L	6-0	215	11-6-84	13	9	4.30	29	29	0	0	178	192	88	85	18	79	141	.284	.297	.278	7.13	3.99
Ryan, B.J.	L-L	6-5	250	12-28-75	1	1	6.53	25	0	0	2	21	22	15	15	5	17	13	.293	.250	.333	5.66	7.40
Rzepczynski, Marc	L-L	6-1	205	8-29-85	2	4	3.67	11	11	0	0	61	51	27	25	7	30	60	.225	.220	.226	8.80	4.40
Tallet, Brian	L-L	6-6	215	9-21-77	7	9	5.32	37	25	0	0	161	169	99	95	20	72	120	.268	.290	.259	6.72	4.03
Wolfe, Brian	R-R	6-2	230	11-29-80	2	2	8.22	14	0	0	0	15	25	15	14	5	7	11	.379	.444	.333	6.46	4.11

Fielding

Catcher	PCT	G	PO	A	E	DP	PB
Barajas	.991	120	806	55	8	7	6
Barrett	1.000	7	34	1	0	0	1
Chavez	.995	51	327	40	2	2	5
Phillips	.968	5	28	2	1	0	1

First Base	PCT	G	PO	A	E	DP
Millar	.990	46	376	27	4	40
Overbay	.998	130	1028	102	2	113
Ruiz	1.000	3	7	1	0	1

Second Base	PCT	G	PO	A	E	DP
Hill	.991	156	307	484	7	129

Inglett	1.000	3	5	6	0	1
McDonald	1.000	8	8	30	0	7
Scutaro	1.000	2	0	2	0	0

Third Base	PCT	G	PO	A	E	DP
Bautista	.957	26	18	48	3	4
Encarnacion	.937	42	27	77	7	6
McDonald	.909	10	3	17	2	2
Millar	1.000	4	4	4	0	2
Rolen	.979	88	62	168	5	16

Shortstop	PCT	G	PO	A	E	DP
McDonald	.990	31	38	66	1	22

Scutaro	.984	143	190	421	10	99

Outfield	PCT	G	PO	A	E	DP
Adams	1.000	5	1	0	0	0
Bautista	.993	79	132	11	1	2
Dellucci	1.000	6	8	0	0	0
Inglett	.949	26	35	2	2	0
Lind	.988	55	80	1	1	0
McDonald	1.000	4	3	0	0	0
Rios	.988	108	236	4	3	0
Snider	.969	75	123	3	4	0
Wells	.997	155	352	6	1	1

LAS VEGAS 51S   TRIPLE-A
PACIFIC COAST LEAGUE

Batting	B-T	HT	WT	DOB	AVG	vLH	vRH	G	AB	R	H	2B	3B	HR	RBI	BB	HBP	SH	SF	SO	SB	CS	SLG	OBP
Adams, Russ	L-R	6-0	200	8-30-80	.319	.526	.245	24	72	15	23	7	2	1	9	5	1	0	2	17	0	0	.514	.363
2-team total (36 Portland)					.285	—	—	60	207	31	59	14	3	2	21	19	1	1	3	33	2	2	.411	.343
Arencibia, J.P.	R-R	6-0	215	1-5-86	.236	.263	.227	116	466	67	110	32	1	21	75	26	6	0	2	114	0	1	.444	.284
Barrett, Michael	R-R	6-0	225	10-22-76	.231	.500	.182	7	26	2	6	2	0	0	5	1	0	1	0	5	0	0	.308	.259
Calderone, Adam	L-R	6-2	205	3-17-84	.212	.125	.240	10	33	2	7	1	0	0	3	2	0	0	2	8	1	0	.242	.243
Campbell, Scott	L-R	6-0	190	9-25-84	.229	.286	.213	27	96	17	22	3	1	0	6	14	0	3	0	9	0	0	.281	.327
Chavez, Raul	R-R	5-11	240	3-18-73	.143	.000	.200	2	7	0	1	0	0	0	0	0	0	0	0	0	0	0	.143	.143
Clark, Howie	L-R	5-10	190	2-13-74	.313	.316	.311	96	387	66	121	24	1	6	50	34	2	10	1	27	3	2	.426	.370
Coats, Buck	L-R	6-3	200	6-9-82	.302	.264	.314	117	500	82	151	33	3	6	56	47	1	2	3	64	25	7	.416	.361
Dellucci, David	L-L	5-11	205	10-31-73	.317	.167	.353	16	63	10	20	6	0	3	6	6	1	0	1	18	1	0	.556	.380
Diaz, Jonathan	R-R	5-8	155	4-9-85	.150	.278	.113	29	80	15	12	0	0	0	4	14	3	7	0	13	0	0	.150	.299
Dopirak, Brian	R-R	6-4	230	12-20-83	.330	.264	.352	52	218	33	72	13	1	8	34	13	0	0	1	44	0	0	.509	.366
Ebarb, C.J.	L-R	6-0	205	6-11-83	.000	.000	.000	1	3	0	0	0	0	0	0	0	0	0	0	2	0	0	.000	.000
Harper, Brett	R-R	6-2	245	7-31-81	.274	.138	.310	79	310	35	85	18	1	15	55	21	0	0	4	40	0	0	.484	.316
2-team total (24 Albuquerque)					.292	—	—	103	390	46	114	25	1	19	71	26	1	0	6	48	0	0	.508	.333
Howard, Kevin	L-R	6-2	190	6-25-81	.326	.288	.337	91	340	58	111	26	1	13	53	38	1	3	1	42	4	2	.524	.395
2-team total (26 Portland)					.310	—	—	117	429	68	133	29	1	13	59	48	1	4	1	51	5	3	.473	.380
Inglett, Joe	L-R	5-9	185	6-29-78	.360	.353	.362	40	161	29	58	14	1	3	25	16	2	6	1	18	4	2	.516	.422
Lane, Jason	R-L	6-2	225	12-22-76	.253	.265	.249	113	411	65	104	41	3	13	47	58	4	1	5	70	4	2	.462	.347
Liuzza, Matt	R-R	5-11	225	2-3-84	.000	—	.000	1	2	0	0	0	0	0	0	0	2	0	0	0	0	0	.000	.500
Mathews, Aaron	R-R	5-10	215	5-10-82	.274	.243	.283	132	518	67	142	21	5	8	77	37	2	4	6	49	4	2	.380	.321
Mayorson, Manny	R-R	5-9	195	3-10-83	.118	.000	.167	5	17	2	2	1	0	0	2	2	1	0	0	1	1	0	.176	.250
2-team total (97 New Orleans)					.243	—	—	102	354	42	86	12	2	1	22	15	2	10	1	24	12	4	.297	.277
Phillips, Kyle	L-R	6-1	225	4-3-84	.300	.161	.340	76	277	37	83	13	0	8	29	29	4	4	2	53	0	0	.433	.372
Quintana, Al	R-R	5-11	205	11-9-82	.000	—	.000	1	1	0	0	0	0	0	0	0	0	0	0	0	0	0	.000	.000
Ruiz, Randy	R-R	6-1	240	10-19-77	.320	.260	.337	114	462	81	148	43	2	25	106	47	9	0	3	99	0	0	.584	.392
Sanchez, Angel	R-R	6-2	205	9-20-83	.305	.229	.326	126	449	67	137	29	4	6	60	39	4	10	4	67	1	2	.428	.363
Snider, Travis	L-L	6-0	235	2-2-88	.337	.396	.315	48	175	32	59	13	1	14	40	28	1	0	0	47	2	3	.663	.431

Pitching	B-T	HT	WT	DOB	W	L	ERA	G	GS	CG	SV	IP	H	R	ER	HR	BB	SO	AVG	vLH	vRH	K/9	BB/9
Accardo, Jeremy	R-R	6-1	190	12-8-81	2	1	3.00	27	0	0	13	30	32	11	10	1	8	27	.269	.268	.270	8.10	2.40
Bayliss, Jonah	R-R	6-0	205	8-13-80	7	2	3.96	38	0	0	5	50	39	24	22	5	24	48	.214	.246	.197	8.64	4.32
Beam, T.J.	R-R	6-6	200	8-28-80	8	4	5.42	39	13	0	0	120	137	77	72	11	30	88	.285	.251	.316	6.62	2.26
Boone, Randy	R-R	6-0	200	8-6-84	0	2	15.75	2	2	0	0	8	15	15	14	3	4	7	.395	.444	.350	7.88	4.50
Bullington, Bryan	R-R	6-4	210	9-30-80	1	3	3.52	28	0	0	3	38	42	21	15	2	7	43	.278	.242	.303	10.10	1.64
Burres, Brian	L-L	6-2	175	4-8-81	6	7	4.76	19	17	1	0	108	121	68	57	11	30	84	.281	.242	.296	7.02	2.51
Buzachero, Bubbie	R-R	5-11	180	6-13-81	4	2	3.05	34	0	0	8	41	29	18	14	4	10	34	.196	.217	.182	7.40	2.18
Castro, Fabio	L-L	5-7	180	1-20-85	7	6	4.49	25	25	0	0	142	148	78	71	7	64	81	.268	.240	.278	5.12	4.05
Cecil, Brett	R-L	6-2	225	7-2-86	1	5	5.69	9	9	1	0	49	53	37	31	2	19	32	.273	.296	.264	5.88	3.49
Garcia, Dumas	R-R	6-2	165	7-7-83	0	0	4.15	2	0	0	0	4	4	2	2	0	2	3	.267	.333	.167	6.23	4.15
Hayhurst, Dirk	R-R	6-2	195	3-24-81	4	6	3.75	25	6	0	0	58	69	33	24	6	12	48	.300	.258	.328	7.49	1.87
Janssen, Casey	R-R	6-3	225	9-17-81	0	0	5.40	7	0	0	0	7	4	4	4	0	1	7	.167	.091	.231	9.45	1.35
Lewis, Rommie	L-L	6-5	230	9-2-82	2	3	3.38	19	0	0	0	24	23	10	9	1	9	20	.253	.300	.230	7.50	3.38
Marcum, Shaun	R-R	5-10	195	12-14-81	0	0	4.50	1	0	0	0	2	2	1	1	0	1	0	.250	.400	.000	0.00	4.50
Martin, Adrian	R-R	6-0	165	9-2-84	1	0	4.85	5	2	0	0	13	18	8	7	0	3	11	.321	.320	.323	7.62	2.08
McLeary, Marty	R-R	6-4	225	10-26-74	4	1	3.38	6	6	0	0	37	34	15	14	4	9	25	.238	.219	.257	6.03	2.17
Michalak, Chris	L-L	6-2	195	1-4-71	0	0	94.50	2	0	0	0	1	6	7	7	1	1	1	.750	.667	1.000	13.50	13.50
Miller, Wade	R-R	6-2	195	9-13-76	1	2	3.77	6	6	0	0	29	26	21	12	3	17	24	.236	.236	.236	7.53	5.34
Mills, Brad	L-L	5-11	185	3-5-85	2	8	4.06	14	14	1	0	84	83	43	38	6	35	72	.263	.246	.267	7.68	3.74
Murphy, Bill	L-L	5-11	195	5-9-81	0	6	7.59	45	0	0	0	53	70	48	45	5	35	51	.314	.359	.290	8.61	5.91
Purcey, David	L-L	6-4	240	4-22-82	9	6	4.46	24	24	1	0	139	132	83	69	7	78	109	.254	.268	.248	7.04	5.04
Ray, Robert	R-R	6-5	195	1-21-84	0	0	0.00	1	1	0	0	4	2	0	0	0	3	3	.133	.400	.000	6.23	6.23
Richmond, Scott	R-R	6-5	215	8-30-79	0	1	1.69	1	1	0	0	5	3	2	1	1	1	5	.167	.200	.125	8.44	1.69
Romero, Davis	L-L	5-10	170	3-30-83	3	6	5.98	27	14	0	0	93	124	71	62	16	36	68	.325	.304	.335	6.56	3.47
Romero, Ricky	R-L	6-0	215	11-6-84	0	0	7.20	1	1	0	0	5	8	4	4	0	2	3	.333	.333	.400	5.40	3.60
Rzepczynski, Marc	L-L	6-1	205	8-29-85	2	0	0.79	2	2	0	0	11	7	1	1	0	4	16	.171	.125	.200	12.71	3.18
Stewart, Zach	R-R	6-2	205	9-28-86	0	0	3.38	11	0	0	0	13	18	8	5	1	6	14	.327	.087	.500	9.45	4.05

	B-T	HT	WT	DOB			ERA	G	GS	CG	SV	IP	H	R	ER	HR	BB	SO	AVG	vLH	vRH	K/9	BB/9
Stidfole, Sean	R-R	6-2	195	3-12-84	3	1	3.70	46	0	0	0	56	57	25	23	5	20	42	.265	.309	.229	6.75	3.21
Wolfe, Brian	R-R	6-2	230	11-29-80	2	3	5.05	34	0	0	3	46	59	29	26	3	12	27	.311	.318	.306	5.24	2.33

Fielding

Catcher	PCT	G	PO	A	E	DP	PB
Arencibia	.983	104	709	59	13	4	14
Barrett	.984	7	58	2	1	0	2
Chavez	.947	2	16	2	1	0	0
Phillips	.987	34	212	15	3	0	7
Quintana	1.000	1	2	0	0	0	0

First Base	PCT	G	PO	A	E	DP
Clark	.955	2	17	4	1	2
Dopirak	.981	41	348	23	7	27
Harper	.990	35	296	16	3	30
Lane	1.000	1	2	0	0	0
Phillips	.983	6	57	2	1	3
Ruiz	.993	60	519	28	4	49

Second Base	PCT	G	PO	A	E	DP
Adams	1.000	2	9	3	0	0

	PCT					
Campbell	.875	4	4	10	2	2
Clark	.973	86	141	223	10	42
Coats	—	1	0	0	0	0
Diaz	.989	17	41	53	1	11
Inglett	.950	26	58	74	7	12
Sanchez	1.000	10	20	38	0	12

Third Base	PCT	G	PO	A	E	DP
Campbell	.897	23	16	36	6	3
Clark	1.000	1	0	4	0	0
Diaz	1.000	2	1	9	0	1
Howard	.908	91	63	185	25	7
Phillips	.915	28	22	53	7	6

Shortstop	PCT	G	PO	A	E	DP
Adams	.938	10	13	32	3	7
Diaz	1.000	8	14	23	0	8

Inglett	.920	6	12	11	2	2
Mayorson	1.000	5	6	5	0	0
Sanchez	.970	116	184	368	17	69

Outfield	PCT	G	PO	A	E	DP
Adams	.857	7	6	0	1	0
Calderone	.889	10	16	0	2	0
Clark	1.000	4	13	0	0	0
Coats	.977	115	296	7	7	1
Dellucci	1.000	13	21	0	0	0
Harper	1.000	2	1	0	0	0
Inglett	.900	6	9	0	1	0
Lane	.992	110	233	4	2	1
Mathews	.985	129	253	17	4	2
Ruiz	1.000	2	3	0	0	0
Snider	.926	43	59	4	5	0

NEW HAMPSHIRE FISHER CATS — DOUBLE-A

EASTERN LEAGUE

Batting	B-T	HT	WT	DOB	AVG	vLH	vRH	G	AB	R	H	2B	3B	HR	RBI	BB	HBP	SH	SF	SO	SB	CS	SLG	OBP
Calderone, Adam	L-R	6-2	205	3-17-84	.242	.250	.240	97	368	55	89	22	5	12	49	26	6	2	2	73	7	4	.427	.301
Campbell, Scott	L-R	6-0	190	9-25-84	.269	.242	.275	52	182	31	49	8	1	3	19	28	2	1	0	26	4	0	.374	.373
Cooper, David	L-L	6-0	200	2-12-87	.258	.240	.265	128	473	62	122	32	0	10	66	59	2	0	4	92	0	0	.389	.340
Diaz, Jonathan	R-R	5-8	155	4-10-85	.214	.182	.225	65	182	22	39	9	0	1	14	34	3	4	0	32	3	4	.280	.347
Donovan, Todd	R-R	6-0	175	8-12-78	.249	.302	.232	99	353	57	88	15	4	3	24	74	3	2	4	75	37	9	.340	.380
Dopirak, Brian	R-R	6-4	230	12-20-83	.308	.338	.299	87	328	44	101	29	1	19	68	35	1	0	2	75	1	3	.576	.374
Emaus, Brad	R-R	5-11	210	3-28-86	.253	.232	.261	137	505	67	128	28	2	10	67	59	8	0	9	69	10	3	.376	.336
Gorneault, Nick	R-R	6-3	220	4-19-79	.210	.218	.207	118	415	51	87	24	2	10	56	35	3	1	3	114	10	5	.349	.274
Gutierrez, Chris	R-R	5-9	185	3-12-84	.242	.263	.233	21	62	5	15	3	0	0	2	7	1	0	0	20	0	1	.290	.329
Haerther, Cody	L-R	5-11	215	7-14-83	.220	.222	.219	43	132	13	29	6	1	1	13	14	1	2	1	21	0	1	.303	.297
Jeroloman, Brian	L-R	5-11	200	5-10-85	.217	.198	.223	108	364	32	79	16	1	6	32	62	1	2	3	120	1	0	.316	.330
Kervin, Bryan	L-R	5-10	185	3-23-85	.161	.091	.174	54	143	10	23	2	1	1	11	6	1	1	1	38	0	3	.210	.199
Mastroianni, Darin	R-R	5-11	190	8-26-85	.271	.276	.270	70	247	39	67	10	2	1	25	39	1	4	1	45	38	8	.340	.372
Mayorson, Manny	R-R	5-9	195	3-10-83	.244	.286	.226	12	45	4	11	2	0	0	4	3	1	1	0	4	2	0	.289	.306
Phillips, Kyle	L-R	6-1	225	4-3-84	.175	.091	.207	12	40	1	7	0	0	1	1	3	0	0	0	8	0	0	.250	.233
Quintana, Al	R-R	5-11	205	11-9-82	.227	.267	.208	93	317	34	72	17	1	4	35	19	2	2	2	69	0	0	.325	.274
Sanchez, Luis	B-R	5-11	200	5-27-87	.191	.200	.187	83	262	23	50	12	1	1	24	28	1	8	4	68	1	0	.256	.268
Shoffit, Sean	L-R	6-2	185	6-9-85	.180	.130	.195	34	100	11	18	3	3	0	10	17	1	1	1	40	4	5	.290	.303
Sierra, Moises	R-R	6-0	225	9-24-88	.353	.273	.391	8	34	1	12	1	0	1	6	1	0	0	1	8	0	1	.471	.361
Van Kirk, Brian	R-R	5-11	210	8-10-85	.111	.125	.100	10	36	3	4	2	0	0	1	1	0	0	0	17	0	0	.167	.135

Pitching	B-T	HT	WT	DOB	W	L	ERA	G	GS	CG	SV	IP	H	R	ER	HR	BB	SO	AVG	vLH	vRH	K/9	BB/9
Boone, Randy	R-R	6-0	200	8-6-84	9	8	3.70	25	23	0	0	129	127	63	53	4	42	90	.261	.258	.264	6.28	2.93
Boyd, Leon	R-R	6-5	209	8-30-83	1	5	5.47	36	0	0	6	53	53	36	32	2	43	38	.264	.307	.230	6.49	7.35
Buzachero, Bubbie	R-R	5-11	180	6-13-81	1	2	1.74	15	0	0	2	31	18	7	6	3	4	22	.168	.250	.091	6.39	1.16
Castro, Fabio	L-L	5-7	180	1-20-85	2	0	0.83	4	4	0	0	22	15	2	2	0	3	24	.197	.250	.183	9.97	1.25
Cate, Troy	L-L	6-1	220	10-21-80	1	0	3.38	1	1	0	0	5	4	2	2	0	1	3	.200	.000	.222	5.06	1.69
Collins, Tim	L-L	5-7	155	8-29-89	2	3	5.68	9	0	0	0	13	12	9	8	1	7	17	.255	.217	.292	12.08	4.97
Dials, Zach	R-R	6-0	200	7-22-85	1	5	3.14	24	0	0	1	29	24	13	10	1	20	18	.220	.256	.200	5.65	6.28
Dumesnil, Bryan	R-L	6-3	210	9-19-83	0	0	0.00	3	0	0	0	4	1	0	0	0	4	5	.077	.000	.143	4.91	7.36
Estanga, Edgar	L-L	5-9	240	10-18-85	3	4	4.41	44	0	0	2	63	62	35	31	4	31	64	.256	.248	.264	9.09	4.41
Farquhar, Danny	R-R	5-10	170	2-17-87	1	4	2.36	37	0	0	15	46	31	15	12	1	30	51	.193	.225	.167	10.05	5.91
Gonzalez, Rei	R-R	5-9	215	11-1-85	4	6	2.90	17	17	0	0	93	82	36	30	4	25	67	.236	.289	.172	6.48	2.42
Hensley, Matt	R-R	6-2	180	8-18-78	1	0	10.32	8	0	0	0	11	20	14	13	1	2	9	.400	.462	.333	7.15	1.59
Janssen, Casey	R-R	6-3	225	9-17-81	1	0	2.40	6	1	0	0	15	12	4	4	0	5	12	.218	.206	.238	7.20	3.00
Ledezma, Wilfredo	L-L	6-4	225	1-21-81	1	1	3.31	8	0	0	0	16	19	7	6	1	6	21	.297	.207	.371	11.57	3.31
Lewis, Rommie	L-L	6-5	230	9-2-82	2	4	2.57	26	0	0	1	42	35	12	12	2	22	45	.229	.188	.188	9.64	4.71
Liebel, Andrew	R-R	6-0	195	3-22-86	1	0	2.08	2	2	0	0	13	10	3	3	2	2	12	.213	.095	.308	8.31	1.38
Magee, Brandon	R-R	6-4	210	7-26-83	4	5	5.16	12	10	0	0	52	55	33	30	3	21	22	.271	.267	.276	3.78	3.61
Magnuson, Trystan	L-R	6-8	210	6-6-85	1	0	0.00	5	0	0	0	10	4	0	0	0	1	7	.118	.067	.158	6.30	0.90
Marcum, Shaun	R-R	5-10	195	12-14-81	0	1	1.17	2	2	0	0	8	8	5	1	1	2	8	.242	.250	.235	9.39	2.35
Martin, Adrian	R-R	6-0	165	9-2-84	3	2	4.03	29	9	0	2	80	82	37	36	12	24	63	.265	.286	.245	7.06	2.69
McLeary, Marty	R-R	6-4	225	10-26-74	3	3	2.98	8	8	1	0	42	39	14	14	3	21	30	.245	.253	.233	6.38	4.46
Perez, Luis	L-L	6-0	205	1-20-85	9	11	3.55	28	27	2	0	162	145	78	64	11	67	112	.239	.180	.261	6.21	3.71
Polanco, Celson	R-L	6-4	250	8-28-84	1	2	4.13	19	0	0	0	33	31	17	15	3	16	34	.252	.232	.269	9.37	4.41
Rodriguez, Kenny	R-R	6-2	190	3-17-85	4	5	4.50	13	13	0	0	68	65	36	34	6	33	52	.251	.221	.277	6.88	4.37
Romero, Davis	L-L	5-10	170	3-30-83	0	0	0.00	1	0	0	0	2	1	0	0	0	0	3	.143	.333	.000	13.50	0.00
Romero, Ricky	R-L	6-0	175	11-6-84	0	0	1.69	1	1	0	0	5	3	2	1	0	5	4	.188	.167	.200	6.75	8.44
Rzepczynski, Marc	L-L	6-1	205	8-29-85	7	5	2.93	14	14	0	0	77	80	38	25	1	36	88	.266	.207	.290	10.33	4.23
Shinskie, David	R-R	6-3	215	5-4-84	1	0	3.44	12	0	0	1	18	17	8	7	1	6	13	.246	.310	.200	6.38	2.95

TORONTO BLUE JAYS

Smith, Sean	R-R	6-4	195	10-13-83	0	0	2.54	7	6	0	0	28	24	8	8	1	13	31	.229	.216	.241	9.85	4.13
2-team total (22 Altoona)					3	3	2.82	29	9	1	7	89	72	31	28	5	36	84	—	—	—	8.46	3.63
Starner, Nathan	L-L	6-3	205	5-29-84	1	2	4.23	33	4	0	2	62	66	36	29	5	40	38	.278	.302	.265	5.55	5.84
Stidfole, Sean	R-R	6-2	195	3-12-84	0	0	4.00	9	0	0	0	9	15	8	4	2	3	6	.366	.381	.350	6.00	3.00

Fielding

Catcher	PCT	G	PO	A	E	DP	PB
Jeroloman	.993	107	808	54	6	14	5
Phillips	1.000	2	11	2	0	0	0
Quintana	.992	35	218	17	2	3	5

First Base	PCT	G	PO	A	E	DP
Cooper	.989	92	793	76	10	96
Dopirak	.986	50	400	24	6	50
Quintana	—	1	0	0	0	0

Second Base	PCT	G	PO	A	E	DP
Campbell	.909	4	4	6	1	1
Diaz	1.000	11	11	20	0	3
Emaus	.977	132	262	417	16	117
Kervin	.750	2	5	1	2	0

Mayorson	1.000	1	2	2	0	0

Third Base	PCT	G	PO	A	E	DP
Campbell	.895	27	17	51	8	4
Diaz	.935	14	6	23	2	2
Gutierrez	.879	15	4	25	4	2
Kervin	.905	32	24	43	7	6
Mayorson	1.000	5	3	13	0	1
Phillips	.919	10	8	26	3	0
Quintana	.896	55	37	75	13	9

Shortstop	PCT	G	PO	A	E	DP
Diaz	.982	39	60	106	3	27
Gutierrez	.900	5	4	14	2	5
Kervin	.984	19	21	42	1	10

Mayorson	.933	5	12	16	2	7
Sanchez	.948	81	117	266	21	65

Outfield	PCT	G	PO	A	E	DP
Calderone	.984	88	171	13	3	2
Campbell	1.000	1	1	0	0	0
Diaz	1.000	3	6	1	0	1
Donovan	.970	92	153	6	5	0
Gorneault	.980	105	185	9	4	3
Haerther	.983	32	55	2	1	0
Mastroianni	1.000	70	157	10	0	1
Quintana	.500	3	1	0	1	0
Shoffit	.959	34	66	5	3	1
Sierra	1.000	6	7	2	0	1
Van Kirk	1.000	3	4	0	0	0

DUNEDIN BLUE JAYS

HIGH CLASS A

FLORIDA STATE LEAGUE

Batting	B-T	HT	WT	DOB	AVG	vLH	vRH	G	AB	R	H	2B	3B	HR	RBI	BB	HBP	SH	SF	SO	SB	CS	SLG	OBP
Ahrens, Kevin	B-R	6-1	195	4-26-89	.215	.229	.211	105	377	35	81	17	2	4	36	37	1	1	7	76	1	1	.302	.282
Baksh, Jon	L-R	6-1	210	3-1-85	.125	.000	.250	2	8	0	1	0	0	0	1	1	0	0	0	4	0	0	.125	.222
Barrett, Michael	R-R	6-0	225	10-22-76	.125	.333	.000	3	8	1	1	0	0	0	0	1	0	0	0	1	0	0	.125	.222
Barron, Raul	B-R	5-10	180	4-4-86	.264	.300	.253	65	212	24	56	12	3	2	24	17	2	4	1	43	6	6	.377	.323
Campbell, Scott	L-R	6-0	190	9-25-84	.500	.333	.571	5	20	3	10	1	0	0	3	2	0	0	1	3	0	0	.550	.522
Ebarb, C.J.	L-R	6-0	205	6-11-83	.203	.111	.214	25	79	7	16	4	0	2	9	8	0	0	0	18	0	0	.329	.276
Emanuele, Chris	R-R	5-11	185	2-17-84	.197	.250	.179	21	76	12	15	4	1	4	12	7	1	0	0	15	2	0	.434	.274
Fernandez, Luis	R-R	5-11	170	11-16-87	.125	.000	.200	3	8	0	1	0	0	0	0	0	0	0	0	1	0	0	.125	.125
Gonzalez, Jesus	R-R	6-4	220	7-7-84	.234	.289	.218	98	381	45	89	26	1	14	62	10	5	1	2	99	7	2	.417	.261
Hurtado, Luis	R-R	5-11	175	11-4-88	.200	—	.200	2	5	0	1	0	0	0	0	0	0	0	0	1	0	0	.200	.200
Jackson, Justin	R-R	6-1	186	12-11-88	.213	.265	.200	78	249	44	53	12	1	0	17	39	2	1	3	87	17	4	.269	.321
Jaspe, Jonathan	B-R	5-9	205	4-11-85	.271	.300	.262	75	262	30	71	5	0	9	41	17	3	1	3	45	0	0	.416	.319
Liuzza, Matt	R-R	5-11	225	2-3-84	.254	.326	.231	59	193	40	49	13	0	9	28	40	2	0	0	56	1	0	.461	.387
Loewen, Adam	L-L	6-6	235	4-9-84	.236	.277	.222	103	335	47	79	22	3	4	31	50	4	0	2	114	5	2	.355	.340
Mastroianni, Darin	R-R	5-11	190	8-26-85	.235	.242	.338	61	231	55	75	11	2	0	26	37	4	2	0	38	32	7	.390	.426
McElroy, Brad	L-R	5-11	192	4-24-86	.269	.333	.255	49	175	33	47	10	2	3	21	31	5	3	2	39	15	2	.400	.390
Pastornicky, Tyler	R-R	5-11	170	12-13-89	.270	.333	.259	15	63	9	17	3	0	0	3	3	0	0	0	7	6	3	.317	.303
Quintana, Al	R-R	5-11	205	11-9-82	.167	.000	.333	2	6	0	1	1	0	0	1	2	0	0	0	2	0	0	.333	.375
Rodriguez, Manny	L-L	6-2	225	1-6-85	.263	.271	.261	105	396	39	104	23	2	9	66	24	0	0	10	101	0	0	.399	.298
Sanchez, Luis	B-R	5-11	180	5-27-87	.179	.211	.167	24	67	2	12	1	0	0	5	5	1	3	1	14	0	0	.194	.243
Shoffit, Sean	L-R	6-2	185	6-9-85	.219	.216	.220	69	210	37	46	10	2	4	20	34	3	0	0	66	7	3	.343	.336
Sierra, Moises	R-R	6-0	225	9-24-88	.286	.337	.270	110	405	56	116	24	2	5	56	34	15	1	4	66	10	2	.393	.360
Thames, Eric	L-R	6-0	205	11-10-86	.313	.298	.318	52	195	33	61	15	5	3	38	21	3	0	1	40	1	1	.487	.386
Tolisano, John	B-R	5-11	190	10-7-88	.232	.165	.250	106	401	53	93	19	2	12	58	44	1	1	6	78	5	4	.379	.305
Van Kirk, Brian	R-R	5-11	210	8-10-85	.300	.000	.333	6	20	5	6	0	0	2	8	6	0	0	1	8	0	0	.600	.444

Pitching	B-T	HT	WT	DOB	W	L	ERA	G	GS	CG	SV	IP	H	R	ER	HR	BB	SO	AVG	vLH	vRH	K/9	BB/9
Anderson, John	L-L	6-2	200	11-9-88	0	0	0.00	1	0	0	0	3	0	0	0	0	0	5	.000	.000	.000	15.00	0.00
Beck, Chad	R-R	6-4	245	1-17-85	0	0	4.35	9	0	0	0	10	12	9	5	1	6	14	.279	.190	.364	12.19	5.23
Bell, Bobby	B-R	6-3	190	8-26-85	4	1	2.43	42	10	0	0	96	66	29	26	5	22	112	.191	.186	.194	10.46	2.06
Bongiovanni, Vince	R-R	6-5	215	1-11-83	8	9	4.44	24	18	0	0	103	101	55	51	6	38	86	.264	.258	.269	7.49	3.31
Boyd, Leon	R-R	6-5	209	8-3-80	0	1	1.54	8	0	0	0	12	13	3	2	0	6	13	.302	.467	.214	10.03	4.63
Buckwalter, Ross	L-R	6-0	195	1-27-85	0	0	3.38	6	0	0	0	8	10	3	3	0	2	2	.313	.357	.278	2.25	0.00
Collins, Tim	L-L	5-7	155	8-29-89	7	4	2.37	40	0	0	3	65	47	21	17	2	28	99	.199	.088	.256	13.78	3.90
Crowell, Cody	L-L	6-3	205	8-28-85	3	0	6.11	13	0	0	0	18	26	12	12	2	7	16	.338	.517	.229	8.15	3.57
Daly, Matt	R-R	5-9	180	8-14-86	0	0	0.00	8	0	0	1	9	4	0	0	0	4	11	.129	.167	.120	10.61	3.86
DeLucia, Dan	L-L	6-4	220	6-1-85	1	3	2.36	20	0	0	1	27	26	8	7	0	11	16	.263	.314	.234	5.40	3.71
Dials, Zach	R-R	6-0	200	7-22-85	0	1	2.21	19	0	0	10	20	19	5	5	0	1	14	.241	.259	.231	6.20	0.44
Downs, Scott	L-L	6-2	215	3-17-76	0	0	3.86	3	2	0	0	2	3	1	1	0	1	2	.300	.333	.286	7.71	3.86
Estanga, Edgar	L-L	5-9	240	10-18-85	0	0	0.00	2	0	0	0	3	2	0	0	0	0	3	.200	.400	.000	10.13	0.00
Farina, Alan	R-R	5-11	190	8-9-86	1	3	6.51	27	2	0	5	37	47	32	27	4	24	34	.307	.358	.267	8.20	5.79
Farquhar, Danny	R-R	5-10	170	2-17-87	1	0	0.53	17	0	0	7	17	10	4	1	0	11	23	.164	.194	.133	12.18	5.82
Garcia, Dumas	R-R	6-2	165	7-7-83	6	2	2.20	38	1	0	2	45	39	21	11	1	18	36	.234	.203	.255	7.20	3.60
Ginley, Kyle	R-R	6-2	210	9-1-86	0	1	3.68	5	0	0	0	7	12	3	3	0	2	5	.364	.538	.250	6.14	2.45
Gracey, Scott	R-R	6-2	190	10-15-86	0	0	6.75	2	1	0	0	7	11	5	5	0	3	1	.393	.385	.400	1.35	4.05
Huggins, Chuck	L-L	6-0	185	5-6-86	5	3	3.25	18	17	0	0	100	90	38	36	12	30	83	.243	.227	.249	7.49	2.71
Janssen, Casey	R-R	6-3	225	9-17-81	0	0	0.69	4	3	0	0	13	6	1	1	0	2	10	.136	.111	.154	6.92	1.38
Ledezma, Wilfredo	L-L	6-4	225	1-21-81	0	0	0.00	3	0	0	0	3	1	0	0	0	2	.100	.000	.143	6.00	0.00
Liebel, Andrew	R-R	6-0	195	3-22-86	5	13	3.63	27	27	2	0	156	155	74	63	13	42	118	.262	.264	.259	6.81	2.42

TORONTO BLUE JAYS

Name	B-T	HT	WT	DOB	W	L	ERA	G	GS	CG	SV	IP	H	R	ER	HR	BB	SO	AVG	vLH	vRH	K/9	BB/9
Loftin, Lance	R-R	0-0	0	3-3-86	0	0	2.84	6	0	0	0	6	9	3	2	0	5	0	.375	.286	.412	0.00	7.11
Magee, Brandon	R-R	6-4	210	7-26-83	2	2	4.26	4	3	0	0	19	20	12	9	1	7	10	.263	.216	.308	4.74	3.32
Magnuson, Trystan	L-R	6-8	210	6-6-85	4	1	2.77	38	0	0	1	62	56	23	19	2	27	45	.248	.256	.243	6.57	3.94
Marcum, Shaun	R-R	5-10	195	12-14-81	0	1	3.00	2	2	0	0	6	7	2	2	0	0	5	.292	.286	.300	7.50	0.00
Michalak, Chris	L-L	6-2	195	1-4-71	1	0	13.50	3	0	0	0	3	4	4	4	0	2	3	.333	.167	.500	10.13	6.75
Moreno, Felix	R-R	6-4	174	8-18-88	0	0	0.00	1	0	0	0	0	0	0	0	0	1	0	.000	—	.000	0.00	27.00
Page, Ryan	L-L	6-1	205	9-16-85	11	13	3.88	28	28	1	0	155	188	90	67	9	32	83	.298	.294	.300	4.81	1.85
Polanco, Celson	R-R	6-4	250	8-28-84	0	1	4.50	9	0	0	0	12	16	7	6	0	1	10	.327	.350	.310	7.50	0.75
Potts, Jared	L-L	6-3	210	7-4-85	0	0	4.58	14	0	0	1	20	24	10	10	1	7	16	.316	.231	.360	7.32	3.20
Ray, Robert	R-R	6-5	195	1-21-84	0	1	2.70	2	2	0	0	7	8	3	2	0	4	4	.286	.417	.188	5.40	0.00
Rodriguez, Kenny	R-R	6-2	190	3-17-85	6	3	2.43	13	12	0	0	67	56	24	18	5	23	63	.227	.210	.242	8.50	3.11
Romero, Ricky	R-L	6-0	215	11-6-84	0	1	13.50	1	1	0	0	4	6	6	6	2	1	5	.333	.500	.250	11.25	2.25
Ryan, B.J.	L-L	6-5	250	12-28-75	0	1	3.00	3	0	0	0	3	1	1	1	0	1	2	.111	.000	.167	6.00	3.00
Starner, Nathan	L-L	6-3	205	5-29-84	0	1	4.76	2	1	0	0	6	5	5	3	0	2	3	.238	.333	.167	4.76	3.18
Walden, Marcus	R-R	5-10	185	9-13-88	2	1	8.64	4	4	0	0	17	30	20	16	1	10	8	.385	.441	.341	4.32	5.40

Fielding

Catcher	PCT	G	PO	A	E	DP	PB
Barrett	1.000	2	11	0	0	0	0
Ebarb	.982	22	155	13	3	1	5
Hurtado	.909	1	9	1	1	0	0
Jaspe	.986	62	417	64	7	4	6
Liuzza	.995	52	371	26	2	2	5

First Base	PCT	G	PO	A	E	DP
Gonzalez	.989	39	332	13	4	28
Loewen	.974	5	36	2	1	2
Rodriguez	.991	93	809	56	8	96

Second Base	PCT	G	PO	A	E	DP
Barron	.974	32	60	87	4	29
Campbell	1.000	3	7	9	0	2
Fernandez	1.000	1	0	1	0	0

	PCT	G	PO	A	E	DP
Tolisano	.959	101	198	293	21	79

Third Base	PCT	G	PO	A	E	DP
Ahrens	.926	90	49	175	18	23
Barron	.950	11	6	13	1	0
Campbell	—	2	0	0	0	0
Gonzalez	.926	30	19	69	7	11
Jaspe	.667	1	1	1	1	0
Quintana	.750	1	1	2	1	2
Sanchez	1.000	4	3	9	0	0

Shortstop	PCT	G	PO	A	E	DP
Barron	.972	23	25	78	3	12
Fernandez	.900	2	5	4	1	0
Gonzalez	1.000	6	8	13	0	5
Jackson	.946	76	89	224	18	47

	PCT	G	PO	A	E	DP
Pastornicky	.973	15	19	53	2	11
Sanchez	.972	20	22	47	2	13

Outfield	PCT	G	PO	A	E	DP
Baksh	1.000	2	8	0	0	0
Barron	1.000	2	1	0	0	0
Emanuele	.947	17	35	1	2	0
Gonzalez	1.000	1	2	0	0	0
Loewen	.977	78	123	2	3	1
Mastroianni	.960	51	110	9	5	2
McElroy	.988	46	81	3	1	0
Shoffit	.986	63	136	2	2	0
Sierra	.951	108	160	13	9	3
Thames	.980	37	48	2	1	0
Van Kirk	1.000	6	11	0	0	0

LANSING LUGNUTS   LOW CLASS A
MIDWEST LEAGUE

Batting	B-T	HT	WT	DOB	AVG	vLH	vRH	G	AB	R	H	2B	3B	HR	RBI	BB	HBP	SH	SF	SO	SB	CS	SLG	OBP
Brisker, Markus	R-R	6-3	210	8-21-90	.114	.071	.130	40	105	7	12	1	0	0	2	10	0	0	1	35	12	4	.124	.190
Chavez, Johermyn	R-R	6-3	220	1-26-89	.283	.299	.278	134	508	87	144	22	6	21	89	40	13	0	8	137	10	6	.474	.346
Del Campo, Jon	B-R	5-11	195	5-18-88	.212	.200	.217	31	118	12	25	4	2	0	8	4	0	0	0	16	0	0	.280	.238
Emanuele, Chris	R-R	5-11	185	2-17-84	.275	.342	.253	81	305	43	84	16	1	5	25	24	10	1	0	80	20	7	.384	.348
Fernandez, Luis	R-R	5-11	170	11-16-87	.233	.233	.234	54	180	21	42	12	0	2	14	7	5	2	0	30	3	3	.333	.281
Fuenmayor, Balbino	R-R	6-3	235	11-26-89	.263	.262	.263	113	419	43	110	21	3	8	54	9	2	1	4	119	1	3	.384	.279
Goins, Ryan	L-R	5-10	170	2-13-88	.198	.259	.167	19	81	6	16	4	0	0	9	7	0	0	1	23	1	2	.247	.258
House, Chris	L-R	5-10	185	2-3-89	.218	.148	.250	29	87	7	19	4	1	0	14	5	0	5	1	32	0	0	.287	.258
Jimenez, A.J.	R-R	5-11	200	5-1-90	.263	.323	.245	80	278	30	73	15	1	3	31	7	1	5	3	72	5	2	.356	.280
Kervin, Bryan	L-R	5-10	185	3-23-85	.130	.333	.059	8	23	2	3	0	0	0	2	3	1	0	0	6	1	0	.130	.259
McClanahan, Justin	R-R	5-11	210	8-22-85	.261	.250	.265	109	383	61	100	20	1	13	55	25	16	1	6	113	11	7	.420	.328
McDade, Mike	B-R	6-4	255	5-8-89	.277	.234	.293	108	408	50	113	27	1	16	57	32	5	0	2	109	0	0	.466	.336
Pastornicky, Tyler	R-R	5-11	170	12-13-89	.269	.311	.255	109	413	63	111	11	9	1	31	39	3	1	5	50	51	15	.346	.336
Ramirez, Welinton	R-R	6-0	205	4-13-87	.313	.368	.292	17	67	9	21	7	0	1	6	2	1	0	1	19	4	1	.463	.338
Sobolewski, Mark	R-R	6-0	190	12-24-86	.249	.255	.247	93	341	47	85	22	1	4	43	30	1	1	1	77	6	0	.355	.311
Talley, Jon	L-R	6-3	220	2-18-89	.228	.231	.227	76	241	23	55	10	1	3	25	28	5	2	1	71	0	0	.311	.320
Van Kirk, Brian	R-R	5-11	210	8-10-85	.278	.253	.287	105	370	54	103	21	2	13	63	60	8	0	2	95	5	0	.451	.389
Wilson, Kenny	R-R	5-10	185	1-30-90	.212	.202	.216	87	321	51	68	12	3	4	27	35	11	1	5	99	37	12	.305	.306

Pitching	B-T	HT	WT	DOB	W	L	ERA	G	GS	CG	SV	IP	H	R	ER	HR	BB	SO	AVG	vLH	vRH	K/9	BB/9
Alvarez, Henderson	R-R	6-0	190	4-18-90	9	6	3.47	23	23	1	0	124	121	54	48	1	19	92	.251	.256	.246	6.66	1.38
Anderson, John	L-L	6-2	200	11-9-88	3	6	4.52	21	21	0	0	100	130	64	50	6	30	76	.316	.262	.329	6.86	2.71
Antolin, Dustin	R-R	6-2	195	8-9-89	2	5	4.47	28	0	0	1	48	48	28	24	1	20	40	.261	.260	.261	7.45	3.72
Barbara, Michael	R-R	6-3	175	4-27-85	0	4	10.20	12	0	0	1	15	33	18	17	3	9	14	.452	.321	.533	8.40	5.40
Beck, Chad	R-R	6-4	245	1-17-85	6	8	5.94	20	20	1	0	111	135	78	73	10	29	85	.297	.326	.276	6.91	2.36
Carreno, Joel	R-R	6-0	190	3-7-87	2	4	3.62	14	14	0	0	80	76	36	32	5	29	62	.255	.317	.211	7.00	3.28
Cuotto, Jonas	R-R	6-0	215	9-21-86	3	7	5.82	36	6	0	1	87	124	67	56	8	36	68	.333	.352	.319	7.06	3.74
Daly, Matt	R-R	5-9	180	8-14-86	1	5	1.95	44	0	0	19	51	35	13	11	0	20	54	.188	.203	.179	9.53	3.55
Gailey, Frank	L-L	5-9	190	11-18-85	3	2	1.93	44	0	0	1	65	48	17	14	2	23	60	.202	.155	.227	8.27	3.17
Holguin, Chris	R-R	5-11	185	4-25-86	1	5	6.34	10	10	0	0	50	58	38	35	2	25	41	.290	.323	.257	7.43	4.53
Huggins, Chuck	L-L	6-0	185	5-6-86	1	1	1.57	7	7	0	0	34	24	6	6	1	11	40	.200	.233	.189	10.49	2.88
Koch, Ryan	R-R	6-4	200	10-16-85	2	8	7.96	34	6	0	0	84	135	89	74	8	24	39	.369	.434	.330	4.20	2.58
Lirette, Chase	R-R	6-4	220	6-9-85	4	3	5.70	20	14	1	0	85	105	57	54	12	19	53	.299	.323	.281	5.59	2.00
Mayora, Yorman	R-R	5-11	195	4-20-87	7	3	4.03	47	0	0	4	76	66	36	34	6	33	76	.235	.257	.222	9.00	3.91
Meyer, Keith	R-R	6-4	180	2-10-86	0	0	7.50	3	0	0	0	6	8	5	5	1	5	2	.320	.375	.222	7.50	1.50
2-team total (5 Clinton)					0	1	7.36	8	0	0	1	11	15	9	9	2	3	9	—	—	—	7.36	2.45
Moody, Hunter	L-L	6-1	205	1-31-86	1	2	3.16	31	0	0	1	31	24	14	11	2	18	40	.212	.068	.304	11.49	5.17
Potts, Jared	L-L	6-3	210	7-4-85	4	1	3.47	31	0	0	0	47	49	19	18	0	16	45	.277	.250	.289	8.68	3.09

	B-T	HT	WT	DOB	W	L	ERA	G	GS	CG	SV	IP	H	R	ER	HR	BB	SO	AVG	vLH	vRH	K/9	BB/9
Roenicke, Jason	R-R	5-11	200	10-25-85	2	5	4.13	17	0	0	1	33	35	17	15	2	8	24	.282	.255	.304	6.61	2.20
Shopshire, Ryan	R-R	6-5	200	11-8-85	0	0	2.37	4	4	0	0	19	17	5	5	0	6	6	.239	.222	.257	2.84	2.84
Wells, Josh	R-R	6-7	240	6-6-87	3	9	8.22	13	13	0	0	58	87	55	53	6	24	43	.345	.383	.314	6.67	3.72

Fielding

Catcher	PCT	G	PO	A	E	DP	PB
House	.979	24	180	11	4	0	2
Jimenez	.985	72	530	48	9	6	11
Talley	.991	47	302	26	3	4	3

	PCT	G	PO	A	E	DP
Fernandez	.914	20	39	46	8	9
Kervin	.955	6	7	14	1	3
McClanahan	.980	76	135	207	7	45
Sobolewski	.889	12	12	20	4	5

	PCT	G	PO	A	E	DP
Fernandez	.909	17	21	39	6	9
Goins	.980	19	35	62	2	14
Kervin	1.000	2	2	3	0	0
Pastornicky	.948	106	173	303	26	64

First Base	PCT	G	PO	A	E	DP
Fernandez	1.000	1	3	0	0	0
Fuenmayor	1.000	26	222	14	0	19
McClanahan	.978	13	85	4	2	7
McDade	.984	100	813	67	14	90
Talley	1.000	3	9	1	0	1

Third Base	PCT	G	PO	A	E	DP
Fernandez	.878	17	12	24	5	2
Fuenmayor	.915	55	30	100	12	5
Jimenez	1.000	2	3	6	0	1
McClanahan	.818	3	1	8	2	2
Sobolewski	.934	69	55	128	13	14

Outfield	PCT	G	PO	A	E	DP
Brisker	.988	39	76	6	1	2
Chavez	.971	129	223	11	7	5
Emanuele	.988	78	162	6	2	2
McClanahan	1.000	5	6	0	0	0
Ramirez	.972	16	34	1	1	1
Van Kirk	.976	79	121	3	3	0
Wilson	.972	83	202	5	6	2

Second Base	PCT	G	PO	A	E	DP
Del Campo	.940	30	51	75	8	21

Shortstop	PCT	G	PO	A	E	DP
Del Campo	1.000	1	0	1	0	0

AUBURN DOUBLEDAYS   SHORT-SEASON

NEW YORK-PENN LEAGUE

Batting	B-T	HT	WT	DOB	AVG	vLH	vRH	G	AB	R	H	2B	3B	HR	RBI	BB	HBP	SH	SF	SO	SB	CS	SLG	OBP
Brisker, Markus	R-R	6-3	210	8-21-90	.200	.193	.203	59	200	27	40	4	0	1	23	19	2	2	1	59	11	4	.235	.275
Del Campo, Jon	B-R	5-11	195	5-18-88	.105	.333	.063	7	19	1	2	0	1	0	1	1	0	0	0	6	0	1	.211	.150
Durham, Lance	L-R	5-11	210	2-20-88	.221	.173	.236	63	217	21	48	8	1	4	23	21	4	1	2	67	2	0	.323	.299
Eiland, Eric	L-L	6-2	220	9-16-88	.194	.140	.210	66	217	19	42	7	2	1	15	26	3	1	0	95	13	5	.258	.289
Fernandez, Jonathan	B-R	6-0	175	9-7-88	.217	.250	.204	26	69	12	15	1	0	0	2	17	1	1	1	21	3	0	.232	.375
Gilligan, Kyle	R-R	6-1	195	3-7-88	.232	.314	.204	44	138	9	32	8	0	0	6	3	10	0	1	33	5	7	.290	.296
Glenn, Brad	R-R	6-2	220	4-2-87	.221	.240	.215	64	213	27	47	14	0	8	38	18	4	0	2	68	4	2	.399	.291
Goins, Ryan	L-R	5-10	170	2-13-88	.297	.333	.286	24	101	15	30	5	1	0	8	8	0	1	0	23	2	2	.366	.349
Gomes, Yan	R-R	6-2	215	7-19-87	.296	.373	.273	60	223	22	66	23	2	2	44	22	2	0	1	37	0	2	.444	.363
Gonzalez, Arvin	R-L	6-1	190	2-25-88	.178	.188	.172	36	90	7	16	2	1	0	7	6	0	1	1	30	3	3	.222	.227
Hopkins, Chris	R-R	5-11	175	9-10-87	.217	.178	.232	55	157	35	34	10	1	0	12	24	1	4	0	45	10	1	.293	.324
Hurtado, Luis	R-R	5-11	175	11-4-88	.200	.250	.167	3	10	0	2	0	0	0	2	0	0	0	0	2	0	0	.200	.200
Murphy, Jack	B-R	6-4	235	4-6-88	.279	.067	.348	19	61	7	17	3	0	2	8	11	0	0	0	8	0	0	.426	.389
Nolan, Kevin	R-R	6-2	200	12-13-87	.191	.158	.202	48	157	10	30	4	0	0	10	7	2	4	1	29	2	2	.217	.234
Ochinko, Sean	R-R	5-11	205	10-21-87	.324	.391	.303	52	188	40	61	20	0	6	32	16	2	0	1	26	1	0	.527	.382
Ramirez, Welinton	R-R	6-0	205	4-13-87	.318	.271	.335	56	220	29	70	22	2	3	33	11	2	0	2	55	13	3	.477	.353
Schimpf, Ryan	L-R	5-9	181	3-11-88	.287	.152	.333	34	129	25	37	7	1	3	14	15	3	4	2	24	4	1	.426	.369
Schwartz, Randy	R-R	6-4	235	1-25-86	.265	.286	.259	10	34	7	9	0	1	4	8	3	0	0	0	5	0	0	.676	.324
Turkamani, Karim	R-R	5-9	215	1-20-87	.275	.231	.289	25	51	2	14	3	0	0	3	4	0	0	0	16	0	0	.333	.327

Pitching	B-T	HT	WT	DOB	W	L	ERA	G	GS	CG	SV	IP	H	R	ER	HR	BB	SO	AVG	vLH	vRH	K/9	BB/9
Anderson, Zach	R-R	6-0	195	10-20-86	0	1	5.30	16	0	0	0	19	24	13	11	1	9	14	.296	.118	.426	6.75	4.34
Armstrong, Austin	R-R	6-3	205	1-17-87	2	4	8.75	17	0	0	0	24	33	27	23	4	12	17	.314	.366	.281	6.46	4.56
2-team total (1 Jamestown)					2	4	7.22	18	1	0	0	29	35	27	23	4	13	21	—	—	—	6.59	4.08
Beck, Casey	R-R	6-1	215	3-28-87	1	3	2.84	29	0	0	0	32	22	12	10	0	17	43	.190	.111	.225	12.22	4.83
Carreno, Joel	R-R	6-0	190	3-7-87	1	0	0.82	2	0	0	0	11	6	2	1	0	3	12	.158	.071	.208	9.82	2.45
Crawford, Evan	R-L	6-1	175	9-2-86	1	5	4.06	14	14	1	0	58	60	35	26	1	31	38	.269	.286	.263	5.93	4.84
Gracey, Scott	R-R	6-2	190	10-15-86	2	8	5.30	15	15	0	0	73	85	53	43	8	22	58	.283	.295	.277	7.15	2.71
Griffith, Shawn	R-R	5-10	180	5-24-87	0	0	0.00	3	0	0	0	6	4	9	1	0	4	9	.182	.200	.176	12.79	5.68
Justice, Brian	R-R	6-3	195	10-20-85	1	5	4.05	21	2	0	1	40	37	24	18	4	17	45	.245	.288	.217	10.13	3.83
Lehman, James	R-R	6-2	185	3-14-85	1	2	6.67	19	1	0	0	28	37	25	21	1	17	22	.308	.333	.283	6.99	5.40
Mendez, Willi	L-L	6-2	190	8-11-86	1	0	5.91	18	0	0	0	21	24	15	14	1	19	20	.304	.238	.332	8.44	8.02
Miller, David	L-R	6-10	210	9-29-84	0	3	6.67	15	0	0	0	27	31	22	20	2	16	23	.282	.222	.323	7.67	5.33
2-team total (1 Jamestown)					0	3	6.16	16	1	0	0	31	36	25	21	2	18	24	—	—	—	7.04	5.28
Molina, Nestor	R-R	6-1	179	1-9-89	0	1	1.59	2	0	0	0	6	9	3	1	1	1	6	.346	.357	.333	9.53	1.59
Morgal, Matt	R-R	6-5	220	9-18-86	3	4	6.07	12	2	0	0	27	29	20	18	1	12	15	.282	.267	.293	5.06	4.05
Outman, Zach	R-R	6-2	180	12-29-87	1	1	5.87	17	0	0	0	23	30	24	15	2	20	19	.300	.344	.279	7.43	7.83
Sever, Dave	R-R	6-4	195	8-29-86	4	5	3.34	14	12	0	0	67	54	27	25	3	15	57	.212	.252	.184	7.62	2.00
Slovak, David	R-R	6-0	170	5-20-86	0	0	4.22	7	0	0	1	11	14	5	5	0	7	4	.326	.353	.308	3.38	5.91
Smith, Egan	L-L	6-4	195	3-16-89	2	1	2.56	9	9	0	0	39	37	14	11	2	11	36	.239	.333	.224	8.38	2.56
Teague, Evan	L-L	6-2	212	2-4-87	1	0	2.35	6	0	0	0	8	7	2	2	0	2	7	.233	.000	.368	8.22	2.35
Turnbull, Steve	R-R	6-3	215	11-25-86	2	2	2.45	19	6	0	0	44	45	24	12	1	13	37	.265	.214	.300	7.57	2.66
Wells, Josh	R-R	6-7	240	6-6-87	1	2	4.50	13	0	0	2	30	36	21	15	3	17	25	.303	.389	.265	7.50	5.10
Wright, Matt	L-L	5-9	170	5-7-87	2	2	3.77	16	12	0	0	60	55	34	25	2	23	73	.240	.218	.247	11.01	3.47

Fielding

Catcher	PCT	G	PO	A	E	DP	PB
Gomes	.993	30	238	27	2	2	3
Hurtado	.962	3	24	1	1	0	1
Murphy	.991	14	97	8	1	1	3
Ochinko	1.000	20	109	9	0	1	5
Turkamani	1.000	25	103	9	0	0	2

First Base	PCT	G	PO	A	E	DP
Durham	.982	55	443	39	9	30
Glenn	1.000	5	45	4	0	4
Ochinko	.992	15	111	10	1	11

Second Base	PCT	G	PO	A	E	DP
Del Campo	1.000	1	0	5	0	1

	PCT	G	PO	A	E	DP
Fernandez	.923	22	33	51	7	9
Gilligan	.976	13	17	23	1	6
Gonzalez	.973	9	18	18	1	5
Nolan	.950	4	5	14	1	2
Schimpf	.951	33	68	87	8	20

Third Base	PCT	G	PO	A	E	DP
Del Campo	.875	3	2	5	1	0
Gilligan	.907	22	15	34	5	0
Glenn	.898	35	29	59	10	6
Gonzalez	.929	12	3	10	1	1
Nolan	1.000	2	0	2	0	0

Schwartz	.875	10	6	22	4	1
Shortstop	**PCT**	**G**	**PO**	**A**	**E**	**DP**
Fernandez	1.000	2	1	3	0	0
Goins	.909	22	23	57	8	12
Gonzalez	.844	13	12	26	7	4
Nolan	.913	42	57	101	15	15

Outfield	PCT	G	PO	A	E	DP
Brisker	.957	56	131	1	6	0
Eiland	.965	62	134	3	5	1
Glenn	1.000	15	23	2	0	0
Hopkins	.988	49	77	3	1	0
Ramirez	.958	54	85	6	4	3

GCL BLUE JAYS — ROOKIE

GULF COAST LEAGUE

TORONTO BLUE JAYS

Batting	B-T	HT	WT	DOB	AVG	vLH	vRH	G	AB	R	H	2B	3B	HR	RBI	BB	HBP	SH	SF	SO	SB	CS	SLG	OBP
Aponte, Yeico	L-L	6-2	190	12-17-88	.202	.083	.220	38	94	11	19	0	2	1	2	9	2	0	0	34	5	2	.277	.286
Bidois, Nicholas	R-R	6-0	180	6-9-92	.000	.000	.000	7	0	0	0	0	0	0	0	2	0	0	0	3	0	0	.000	.222
Crouse, Michael	R-R	6-4	215	11-22-90	.218	.152	.239	55	188	28	41	9	4	2	17	23	2	0	1	53	25	5	.340	.308
Del Campo, Jon	B-R	5-11	195	5-18-88	.067	.000	.083	5	15	1	1	0	1	0	2	1	0	0	0	4	0	1	.200	.125
Denis-Fortier, Kevin	R-R	6-3	215	9-22-87	.187	.118	.207	30	75	4	14	2	1	0	4	4	5	1	1	21	0	0	.240	.271
Dominguez, Oliver	B-R	5-9	156	4-23-89	.225	.208	.229	49	142	17	32	6	0	3	16	15	0	2	1	32	13	0	.331	.297
Fernandez, Jonathan	B-R	6-0	175	9-17-87	.192	.100	.250	11	26	4	5	2	0	0	4	7	1	0	1	8	2	0	.269	.371
Goins, Ryan	L-R	5-10	170	2-13-88	.111	.000	.200	3	9	1	1	0	0	0	0	0	0	0	0	2	0	0	.111	.111
Gomes, Yan	R-R	6-2	215	7-19-87	.357	.000	.385	4	14	1	5	0	0	0	2	3	0	0	0	2	0	0	.357	.471
Hernandez, Yudelmis	R-R	6-4	205	5-18-87	.101	.105	.100	26	69	2	7	2	0	0	2	8	0	1	2	35	0	0	.130	.190
Hurtado, Luis	R-R	5-11	175	11-4-88	.333	.333	.333	8	12	4	4	0	0	0	1	0	1	1	0	1	0	0	.333	.385
McElroy, Brad	L-R	5-11	192	4-24-86	.167	.000	.188	6	18	0	3	1	0	0	0	0	0	0	0	5	0	1	.222	.167
Murphy, Jack	B-R	6-4	235	4-6-88	.261	.158	.290	28	88	12	23	8	0	1	14	11	0	0	0	17	1	1	.386	.343
Namba, Bryson	R-R	6-2	210	1-31-91	.169	.125	.180	27	77	9	13	2	0	4	8	6	2	0	1	28	1	1	.351	.244
Nuzzo, Matt	R-R	6-0	205	3-18-87	.239	.222	.243	34	92	8	22	4	2	1	7	9	2	2	2	30	1	0	.359	.314
Pena, Gari	R-R	5-11	178	3-10-92	.192	.300	.165	33	99	7	19	4	1	2	9	2	0	0	0	28	1	0	.313	.245
Perez, Carlos	R-R	6-0	193	10-27-90	.291	.290	.291	43	141	17	41	11	3	1	21	16	2	1	3	23	2	5	.433	.364
Pierre, Gustavo	R-R	6-2	183	12-28-91	.259	.195	.278	48	174	22	45	10	4	4	22	3	1	2	2	45	8	5	.431	.272
Roberts, John	L-L	6-1	215	7-24-86	.241	.172	.259	45	137	21	33	6	2	5	21	23	1	0	1	34	2	0	.423	.352
Rodriguez, Henry	R-L	5-11	182	10-19-87	.225	.125	.250	19	40	1	9	2	0	1	5	3	3	2	0	10	0	0	.350	.326
Schimpf, Ryan	L-R	5-9	181	3-11-88	.500	.500	.500	2	4	1	2	0	1	0	2	0	0	0	0	1	0	0	1.000	.667
Thames, Eric	L-R	6-0	205	11-10-86	.286	.286	.286	7	21	4	6	3	0	0	1	3	0	0	1	5	0	0	.429	.360
Valdez, Jonnathan	L-R	6-3	230	9-5-90	.143	.214	.122	24	63	6	9	3	0	0	4	9	1	1	0	26	0	0	.190	.260
Wilson, Kenny	R-R	5-10	185	1-30-90	.200	.167	.211	8	25	6	5	2	1	0	0	3	1	0	0	8	3	1	.360	.310
Zaleski, Nick	R-R	6-3	195	12-26-86	.279	.313	.270	48	147	19	41	13	0	1	21	17	1	0	2	31	1	0	.388	.353

Pitching	B-T	HT	WT	DOB	W	L	ERA	G	GS	CG	SV	IP	H	R	ER	HR	BB	SO	AVG	vLH	vRH	K/9	BB/9
Buckwalter, Ross	L-R	6-0	195	1-27-85	0	1	3.00	3	0	0	0	3	4	1	1	0	0	4	.308	.000	.364	12.00	0.00
DeLucia, Dan	L-L	6-4	220	6-1-85	0	0	0.00	3	0	0	0	3	3	0	0	0	1	3	.273	.000	.333	9.00	3.00
Fields, Matt	R-R	6-3	190	7-10-86	0	0	1.22	14	9	0	0	52	35	9	7	1	6	54	.192	.154	.214	9.41	1.05
Griffith, Shawn	R-R	5-10	180	5-24-87	2	2	0.66	22	0	0	9	27	9	3	2	0	6	43	.102	.088	.111	14.16	1.98
Hernandez, Juan	L-L	6-0	180	10-25-87	0	0	2.95	6	4	0	0	21	16	10	7	2	6	22	.200	.232	.194	9.28	2.53
Holguin, Chris	R-R	5-11	185	4-25-86	1	1	0.00	2	2	0	0	11	6	1	0	0	2	8	.162	.300	.111	6.55	1.64
Janssen, Casey	R-R	6-3	225	9-17-81	0	0	9.00	1	0	0	0	1	2	1	1	0	0	0	.400	.333	.500	0.00	0.00
Loftin, Lance	R-R	0-0	0	3-3-86	0	0	0.47	12	0	0	1	19	14	1	1	0	5	24	.200	.231	.182	11.17	2.33
Loup, Aaron	L-L	5-11	180	12-19-87	2	1	3.86	13	0	0	3	16	17	9	7	0	3	19	.274	.125	.296	10.47	1.65
Mella, Leandro	L-L	6-4	190	5-5-90	0	1	3.50	14	1	0	0	18	18	8	7	2	17	21	.261	.111	.314	10.50	8.50
Miller, Wade	R-R	6-2	210	9-13-76	0	0	6.75	2	2	0	0	5	10	4	4	1	1	9	.400	.385	.417	15.19	1.69
Molina, Nestor	R-R	6-1	179	1-9-89	3	0	1.69	15	2	0	1	37	31	8	7	0	4	32	.226	.214	.235	7.71	0.96
Moreno, Felix	R-R	6-4	174	8-18-88	2	3	4.19	15	0	0	0	19	22	18	9	3	11	18	.278	.355	.229	8.38	5.12
Pepe, Alex	L-L	6-2	190	4-14-87	1	3	2.55	13	1	0	0	18	12	6	5	0	10	22	.203	.154	.217	11.21	5.09
Pina, Carlos	L-L	5-11	169	3-5-90	3	2	1.57	12	10	0	0	52	46	23	9	2	16	35	.231	.270	.222	6.10	2.79
Ray, Robert	R-R	6-5	195	1-21-84	0	1	4.50	2	2	0	0	2	4	1	1	0	0	2	.400	.800	.000	9.00	0.00
Richmond, Scott	R-R	6-5	215	8-30-79	0	0	8.10	1	1	0	0	3	9	3	3	1	1	5	.500	.667	.467	13.50	2.70
Shopshire, Ryan	R-R	6-5	200	11-8-85	2	2	2.56	8	8	1	0	39	37	12	11	2	9	38	.253	.276	.239	8.84	2.09
Slovak, David	R-R	6-0	170	5-20-86	2	0	1.59	5	0	0	0	6	4	5	1	0	3	5	.182	.125	.214	7.94	4.76
Slover, Brian	R-R	6-3	230	6-10-88	2	0	0.77	11	0	0	0	12	8	4	1	0	4	12	.182	.100	.206	9.28	3.09
Strickland, Sam	L-L	6-5	210	6-9-87	1	5	4.32	11	11	0	0	42	43	30	20	2	23	29	.269	.267	.269	6.26	4.97
Teague, Evan	L-L	6-2	212	2-4-87	1	1	5.23	16	0	0	1	21	19	14	12	3	13	23	.232	.217	.237	10.02	5.66
Tepera, Ryan	R-R	6-1	180	11-3-87	3	1	1.72	11	5	1	0	37	19	11	7	4	4	42	.150	.140	.155	10.31	0.98
Ybarra, Tyler	L-L	6-2	170	12-11-89	2	4	6.64	16	0	0	0	20	29	20	15	1	10	11	.333	.083	.373	4.87	4.43

Fielding

Catcher	PCT	G	PO	A	E	DP	PB
Gomes	1.000	2	17	3	0	1	1
Hurtado	1.000	7	36	3	0	0	0
Murphy	1.000	14	108	9	0	0	2
Perez	.983	33	268	27	5	3	0
Rodriguez	1.000	10	50	6	0	0	1
Valdez	.962	15	123	5	5	15	

First Base	PCT	G	PO	A	E	DP
Denis-Fortier	1.000	28	188	11	0	13
Hernandez	.982	25	155	7	3	11

Second Base	PCT	G	PO	A	E	DP
Bidois	.929	5	4	9	1	1
Del Campo	1.000	3	1	7	0	1
Dominguez	.946	42	58	81	8	16
Fernandez	.967	6	16	13	1	8
Pena	.917	13	22	22	4	4
Schimpf	1.000	2	2	5	0	0

Third Base	PCT	G	PO	A	E	DP
Dominguez	.885	9	4	19	3	0
Fernandez	.889	3	2	6	1	0
Namba	.842	22	10	38	9	6
Nuzzo	.875	33	17	46	9	4

Shortstop	PCT	G	PO	A	E	DP
Goins	1.000	3	1	5	0	0
Pena	.905	21	25	42	7	10
Pierre	.920	40	60	101	14	17

Outfield	PCT	G	PO	A	E	DP
Aponte	.980	36	49	0	1	0
Crouse	.973	54	105	5	3	0

	PCT	G	PO	A	E	DP
McElroy	1.000	6	4	0	0	0
Roberts	1.000	41	40	1	0	0
Thames	1.000	5	6	1	0	0

	PCT	G	PO	A	E	DP
Wilson	1.000	6	4	1	0	0
Zaleski	.985	46	63	4	1	2

DSL BLUE JAYS   ROOKIE

DOMINICAN SUMMER LEAGUE

Batting	B-T	HT	WT	DOB	AVG	vLH	vRH	G	AB	R	H	2B	3B	HR	RBI	BB	HBP	SH	SF	SO	SB	CS	SLG	OBP
Arcila, Daniel	R-L	6-1	170	7-4-90	.209	.163	.222	50	187	29	39	11	2	1	19	19	4	6	0	61	16	3	.305	.295
Bejas, Emilio	L-L	5-11	170	8-30-89	.266	.100	.322	34	79	17	21	0	1	0	11	12	4	1	2	22	4	4	.291	.381
Betegon, Adair	R-R	6-1	185	10-22-88	.171	.200	.160	18	35	7	6	2	1	0	2	13	1	0	0	15	1	1	.286	.408
Blanco, Alvaro	R-R	5-11	175	4-29-92	.177	.214	.169	29	79	10	14	4	0	0	9	13	0	2	0	16	5	3	.228	.293
Delgado, John	L-R	6-3	210	9-10-90	.235	.333	.205	52	166	21	39	5	2	1	25	19	0	5	0	25	0	1	.307	.305
Falcon, Manuel	R-R	5-11	165	1-31-90	.314	.381	.295	54	191	31	60	9	0	0	24	30	7	5	6	32	9	6	.361	.415
Ferrini, Leonardo	R-R	6-0	147	4-17-89	.247	.341	.223	56	198	37	49	9	4	0	30	40	4	1	1	40	18	11	.333	.383
Gonzalez, Gonzalo	R-R	5-10	162	7-10-89	.255	.250	.258	32	98	21	25	8	3	0	12	15	5	3	0	22	3	3	.398	.381
Hernandez, Leonardo	R-R	5-11	182	2-22-90	.292	.370	.269	38	120	16	35	9	0	1	15	13	8	1	1	13	2	2	.392	.394
Javier, Sony	R-R	6-0	180	6-15-91	.243	.275	.234	50	177	23	43	7	2	1	23	16	4	0	2	42	2	2	.322	.317
Monge, Manuel	R-R	6-1	184	2-10-90	.184	.182	.185	36	103	14	19	2	1	0	5	9	2	3	1	41	9	3	.223	.261
Moreta, Ruddy	R-R	5-11	190	7-28-87	.297	.333	.284	26	91	12	27	6	0	1	10	11	3	1	1	12	2	4	.396	.387
Natera, Fausto	B-R	6-1	168	8-15-88	.300	.345	.286	61	240	43	72	8	7	0	27	31	4	4	2	33	22	5	.392	.386
Ortega, Carlos	R-R	6-1	155	3-20-89	.254	.353	.217	23	63	12	16	1	0	1	9	10	5	1	1	22	4	1	.317	.392
Ramirez, Carlos	R-R	6-3	172	4-24-91	.229	.188	.244	52	179	29	41	5	1	3	14	15	5	1	0	56	4	3	.318	.307
Rodriguez, Alexys	R-R	5-10	175	11-23-88	.263	.280	.257	28	95	14	25	6	2	1	14	12	3	0	0	14	3	0	.400	.364
Sabino, Luis	R-R	6-0	175	7-4-88	.250	.167	.261	17	52	6	13	7	0	0	10	4	2	0	0	13	2	0	.385	.328
Vasquez, Simon	R-R	5-11	201	6-18-88	.326	.432	.298	56	178	32	58	13	3	1	32	17	4	7	4	23	7	3	.449	.389

Pitching	B-T	HT	WT	DOB	W	L	ERA	G	GS	CG	SV	IP	H	R	ER	HR	BB	SO	AVG	vLH	vRH	K/9	BB/9
Avila, Jose	L-L	6-3	190	9-14-90	2	1	3.77	14	1	0	0	29	29	27	12	0	28	20	.257	.100	.272	6.28	8.79
Bello, Fernando	R-R	6-1	180	4-27-89	3	2	2.81	12	4	0	0	51	44	18	16	2	9	53	.229	.250	.226	9.29	1.58
Diaz, Grabiel	R-R	6-2	190	2-11-88	0	0	0.00	1	0	0	0	3	3	0	0	0	4	0	.231	.250	.222	10.80	0.00
Diaz, Misual	R-R	6-2	180	12-20-89	5	3	2.11	14	0	0	1	43	35	16	10	1	12	50	.217	.229	.214	10.55	2.53
Estrada, Deivy	R-R	5-11	178	8-22-92	1	0	2.66	13	10	0	0	44	40	13	13	1	13	48	.244	.175	.266	9.82	2.66
German, Victor	R-R	6-0	210	5-26-89	4	1	3.06	19	1	1	2	47	42	23	16	2	8	36	.235	.227	.239	6.89	1.53
Gil, Juan	R-R	6-0	185	6-24-92	0	1	5.14	4	3	0	0	7	10	7	4	0	1	8	.323	.600	.190	10.29	1.29
Mendez, Luis	R-R	6-5	225	10-14-89	2	0	6.52	17	2	0	0	29	35	29	21	1	19	25	.297	.265	.310	7.76	5.90
Ramirez, Alex	R-R	6-2	188	2-11-90	2	2	3.69	11	4	0	0	32	26	18	13	3	17	17	.234	.286	.211	4.83	4.83
Rodriguez, Richard	R-R	6-1	197	8-31-88	0	0	0.00	3	1	0	0	3	5	1	0	0	0	4	.417	.250	.500	0.00	0.00
Romero, Steven	R-R	6-2	180	8-2-90	1	0	3.38	13	0	0	0	32	25	13	12	1	15	24	.223	.281	.200	6.75	4.22
Santana, Kenllie	L-L	6-0	192	7-13-89	3	3	3.79	18	2	0	0	36	33	21	15	2	28	43	.254	.083	.271	10.85	7.07
Santana, Milciades	R-R	—	—	1-20-89	4	3	2.96	16	14	0	0	67	57	27	22	3	16	61	.236	.161	.261	8.19	2.15
Serra, Jorge	R-R	6-4	190	4-26-92	0	2	11.57	5	1	0	0	7	11	10	9	0	5	6	.379	.556	.300	7.71	6.43
Valdez, Denny	R-R	6-3	188	5-8-90	1	0	2.20	10	9	0	0	33	24	9	8	2	12	23	.214	.280	.195	6.34	3.31
Vargas, Adrian	R-L	6-4	165	5-7-88	2	1	6.00	10	0	0	5	12	11	8	8	0	10	8	.256	.000	.275	6.00	7.50
Vargas, Jose	L-L	6-0	166	7-19-90	6	3	1.34	18	6	1	1	67	52	17	10	0	17	51	.211	.125	.217	6.85	2.28
Velazquez, Hector	R-R	6-3	180	3-30-89	2	1	3.00	11	3	0	1	18	20	13	6	0	5	11	.267	.467	.217	5.50	2.50

Fielding

Catcher	PCT	G	PO	A	E	DP	PB
Betegon	.943	6	29	4	2	0	1
Hernandez	.982	35	234	44	5	1	8
Rodriguez	.981	27	172	34	4	1	8
Vasquez	.982	14	103	8	2	2	2

First Base	PCT	G	PO	A	E	DP
Betegon	.833	3	10	0	2	1
Delgado	.978	51	384	23	9	37
Gonzalez	1.000	1	10	0	0	0
Vasquez	1.000	31	203	13	0	19

Second Base	PCT	G	PO	A	E	DP
Blanco	—	1	0	0	0	0
Falcon	.979	20	49	43	2	9
Ferrini	.957	48	118	126	11	29
Natera	1.000	3	8	7	0	2

Third Base	PCT	G	PO	A	E	DP
Falcon	.903	31	33	79	12	7
Gonzalez	1.000	7	1	9	0	1
Natera	.919	37	40	84	11	9

Shortstop	PCT	G	PO	A	E	DP
Arcila	.906	48	96	146	25	22

	PCT	G	PO	A	E	DP
Blanco	.917	26	41	59	9	14
Natera	1.000	1	1	6	0	0

Outfield	PCT	G	PO	A	E	DP
Bejas	.927	28	34	4	3	1
Gonzalez	.900	17	17	1	2	0
Javier	.925	49	57	5	5	1
Monge	.941	31	43	5	3	0
Moreta	1.000	25	33	6	0	1
Ortega	.971	22	33	1	1	0
Ramirez	.917	51	72	5	7	0
Sabino	1.000	10	8	0	0	0

Washington Nationals

SEASON IN A SENTENCE: The Nationals lost their first seven games of the season and never recovered, finishing with the worst record in baseball (59-103) for the second straight year.

HIGH POINT: Washington did close the season with seven straight wins, but the biggest baseball story in the nation's capital was No. 1 overall draft pick Stephen Strasburg. The San Diego State right-hander was the most hyped and perhaps the best prospect in draft history. Agent Scott Boras made it clear Strasburg sought a precedent-setting contract, and the Nationals inked him to a $15.1 million deal—including a $7.5 million bonus—just before the Aug. 17 deadline.

LOW POINT: As disastrous as the major league season was, things were even gloomier in February, when shortstop Esmailyn Gonzalez, who signed for a $1.4 million bonus out of the Dominican Republic in 2006, turned out to be 23-year-old Carlos Alvarez. Gonzalez had been listed as 19. GM Jim Bowden resigned and assistant GM Jose Rijo was fired in the aftermath, amid a federal probe into Latin American bonus skimming.

NOTABLE ROOKIES: Top prospect Jordan Zimmermann showed a glimpse of his impressive talent in the first half, and he led Washington with 92 strikeouts despite pitching just 91 innings before having season-ending Tommy John surgery. Fellow righthander Tyler Clippard led the Nationals with a 2.69 ERA in 41 relief appearances. Lefty Ross Detwiler and righties J.D. Martin, Craig Stammen and Shairon Martis all made 14 or more starts, but none of them won more than five games.

KEY TRANSACTIONS: The Nats promoted Mike Rizzo from assistant GM to interim GM when Bowden resigned, and to full-time GM after handling the Strasburg negotiations. On July 1, he dealt outfielder Lastings Milledge and righty Joel Hanrahan to the Pirates for center fielder Nyjer Morgan and righty Sean Burnett. Morgan proved to be a stellar defender and a sparkplug atop the lineup, batting .351 with 24 steals after the trade.

DOWN ON THE FARM: A handful of Nats prospects took steps forward in 2009, led by catcher Derek Norris, who posted a .926 OPS in the low Class A South Atlantic League, but many others stalled or went backward, and farm director Bobby Williams was replaced by Doug Harris after the season. Washington also promoted Kris Kline from assistant scouting director to scouting director after Dana Brown left for a job with the Blue Jays.

OPENING DAY PAYROLL: $60,328,000

PLAYERS OF THE YEAR

MAJOR LEAGUE	MINOR LEAGUE
Ryan Zimmerman	**Derek Norris**
3b	c
.292/.364/.525	(Low A)
33 HR, 106 RBI, 110 R,	.286/.413/.513
won first Gold Glove	30 2B, 23 HR

ORGANIZATION LEADERS

BATTING		*Minimum 250 at-bats
MAJORS		
*AVG	Ryan Zimmerman	.292
*OPS	Adam Dunn	.928
HR	Adam Dunn	38
RBI	Ryan Zimmerman	106
MINORS		
*AVG	Desmond, Ian, Harrisburg/Syracuse	.330
R	Espinosa, Danny, Potomac	90
	Lombardozzi, Stephen, Hagerstown	90
H	Lombardozzi, Stephen, Hagerstown	147
TB	Norris, Derek, Hagerstown	224
2B	Espinosa, Danny, Potomac	31
3B	Three tied at	7
HR	Norris, Derek, Hagerstown	23
RBI	Moore, Tyler, Hagerstown	87
BB	Norris, Derek, Hagerstown	90
SO	Bynum, Seth, Harrisburg/Syracuse	139
SB	Whiting, Boomer, Potomac	54
*OBP	Norris, Derek, Hagerstown	.413
*SLG	Norris, Derek, Hagerstown	.513

PITCHING		†Minimum 75 innings
MAJORS		
W	John Lannan	9
†ERA	John Lannan	3.88
SO	Jordan Zimmermann	92
MINORS		
W	Three tied at	12
L	Jones, Justin, Harrisburg	13
†ERA	Meyers, Bradley, Potomac/Harrisburg	1.72
G	Segovia, Zack, Harrisburg/Syracuse	51
	Wilkie, Josh, Harrisburg/Syracuse	51
GS	Arnesen, Erik, Potomac/Harrisburg	27
SV	Kensing, Logan, Syracuse	17
IP	Arnesen, Erik, Potomac/Harrisburg	156
BB	Jones, Justin, Harrisburg	48
SO	Atwood, William, Potomac	118
†AVG	Meyers, Bradley, Potomac/Harrisburg	.223

2009 PERFORMANCE

General Manager: Jim Bowden/Mike Rizzo. **Farm Director:** Bobby Williams. **Scouting Director:** Dana Brown.

Class	Team	League	W	L	PCT	Finish*	Manager(s)
Majors	Washington Nationals	National	59	103	.364	16th (16)	Manny Acta/Jim Riggleman
Triple-A	Syracuse Chiefs	International	76	68	.528	5th (14)	Tim Foli
Double-A	Harrisburg Senators	Eastern	70	72	.493	7th (12)	John Stearns
High A	Potomac Nationals	Carolina	79	58	.577	2nd (8)	Trent Jewett
Low A	Hagerstown Suns	South Atlantic	56	78	.418	16th (16)	Matthew LeCroy
Short-season	Vermont Lake Monsters	New York-Penn	34	41	.453	10th (14)	Jeff Garber
Rookie	GCL Nationals	Gulf Coast	36	19	.655	†2nd (16)	Bob Henley
Overall 2009 Minor League Record			351	336	.511	11th (30)	

*Finish in overall standings (No. of teams in league). †League champion.

ORGANIZATION STATISTICS

WASHINGTON NATIONALS

NATIONAL LEAGUE

Batting	B-T	HT	WT	DOB	AVG	vLH	vRH	G	AB	R	H	2B	3B	HR	RBI	BB	HBP	SH	SF	SO	SB	CS	SLG	OBP
Bard, Josh	B-R	6-3	225	3-30-78	.230	.240	.228	90	274	20	63	18	0	6	31	24	1	1	1	50	0	1	.361	.293
Belliard, Ronnie	R-R	5-10	210	4-7-75	.246	.232	.252	86	187	26	46	7	1	5	22	14	0	1	2	40	2	0	.374	.296
2-team total (24 Los Angeles)					.277	—	—	110	264	39	73	14	1	10	39	20	0	1	2	56	3	0	.451	.325
Bernadina, Roger	L-L	6-2	200	6-12-84	.250	—	.250	3	4	1	1	1	0	0	0	1	0	0	0	1	1	0	.500	.400
Burke, Jamie	R-R	6-0	225	9-24-71	.100	.000	.111	6	10	0	1	0	0	0	1	1	0	1	1	5	0	0	.100	.167
Cintron, Alex	B-R	6-2	210	12-17-78	.077	.000	.083	21	26	1	2	0	0	0	2	0	0	0	0	7	0	0	.077	.143
Desmond, Ian	R-R	6-2	210	9-20-85	.280	.300	.278	21	82	9	23	7	2	4	12	5	0	1	1	14	1	0	.561	.318
Dukes, Elijah	R-R	6-1	250	6-26-84	.250	.243	.252	107	364	38	91	20	4	8	58	46	3	0	3	74	3	10	.393	.337
Dunn, Adam	L-R	6-6	285	11-9-79	.267	.268	.267	159	546	81	146	29	0	38	105	116	4	0	2	177	0	1	.529	.398
Flores, Jesus	R-R	6-1	230	10-26-84	.301	.276	.313	29	93	13	28	3	2	4	15	11	0	1	1	26	0	0	.505	.371
Gonzalez, Alberto	R-R	5-10	195	4-18-83	.265	.397	.228	105	291	31	77	16	3	1	33	14	3	2	6	27	1	1	.351	.299
Guzman, Cristian	B-R	6-0	210	3-21-78	.284	.307	.277	135	531	74	151	24	7	6	52	16	1	6	1	75	4	5	.390	.306
Harris, Willie	L-R	5-9	190	6-22-78	.235	.121	.248	137	323	47	76	18	6	7	27	57	9	3	1	62	11	4	.393	.364
Hernandez, Anderson	B-R	5-9	185	10-30-82	.251	.292	.240	77	231	25	58	9	2	1	23	20	0	3	1	41	5	3	.320	.310
2-team total (46 New York)					.251	—	—	123	366	39	92	15	4	3	37	33	0	3	2	63	7	5	.339	.312
Johnson, Nick	L-L	6-3	235	9-19-78	.295	.337	.277	98	353	47	104	16	2	6	44	63	6	0	2	66	2	2	.402	.408
2-team total (35 Florida)					.291	—	—	133	457	71	133	24	2	8	62	99	12	1	5	84	2	4	.405	.426
Kearns, Austin	R-R	6-3	245	5-20-80	.195	.122	.224	80	174	20	34	6	2	3	17	32	5	0	0	51	1	1	.305	.336
Maxwell, Justin	R-R	6-5	235	11-6-83	.247	.242	.250	40	89	13	22	4	1	4	9	12	1	0	0	32	6	1	.449	.343
Milledge, Lastings	R-R	6-0	205	4-5-85	.167	.333	.111	7	24	1	4	0	0	0	1	1	1	0	0	10	1	0	.167	.231
2-team total (58 Pittsburgh)					.279	—	—	65	244	21	68	11	0	4	21	13	4	2	2	47	7	4	.373	.323
Morgan, Nyjer	L-L	6-0	175	7-2-80	.351	.233	.373	49	191	35	67	9	2	1	12	11	4	5	1	25	24	7	.435	.396
2-team total (71 Pittsburgh)					.307	—	—	120	469	74	144	15	7	3	39	40	9	10	5	74	42	17	.388	.369
Morse, Mike	R-R	6-5	230	3-22-82	.250	.250	.250	32	52	4	13	3	0	3	10	3	0	0	0	16	0	0	.481	.291
Nieves, Wil	R-R	5-10	180	9-25-77	.259	.186	.276	72	224	20	58	6	0	1	26	17	3	0	5	45	1	0	.299	.313
Orr, Pete	L-R	6-1	195	6-8-79	.253	.143	.265	27	75	5	19	2	1	1	10	3	0	0	3	15	2	1	.347	.272
Padilla, Jorge	R-R	6-1	215	8-11-79	.120	.400	.050	29	25	3	3	0	0	0	1	0	0	0	0	8	0	0	.120	.154
Patterson, Corey	L-R	5-10	175	8-13-79	.133	.000	.154	5	15	0	2	0	0	0	0	0	0	0	0	6	2	0	.133	.133
2-team total (11 Milwaukee)					.103	—	—	16	29	0	3	0	0	0	0	1	0	1	3	2	1	.103	.103
Willingham, Josh	R-R	6-2	215	2-17-79	.260	.300	.251	133	427	70	111	29	0	24	61	61	12	0	2	104	4	3	.496	.367
Zimmerman, Ryan	R-R	6-3	230	9-28-84	.292	.270	.298	157	610	110	178	37	3	33	106	72	2	0	9	119	2	0	.525	.364

Pitching	B-T	HT	WT	DOB	W	L	ERA	G	GS	CG	SV	IP	H	R	ER	HR	BB	SO	AVG	vLH	vRH	K/9	BB/9
Balester, Collin	R-R	6-5	200	6-6-86	1	4	6.82	7	7	0	0	30	34	24	23	10	14	20	.281	.315	.254	5.93	4.15
Beimel, Joe	L-L	6-3	215	4-19-77	1	5	3.40	45	0	0	1	40	38	17	15	3	15	24	.253	.233	.267	5.45	3.40
2-team total (26 Colorado)					1	6	3.58	71	0	0	1	55	57	24	22	5	19	35	—	—	—	5.69	3.09
Bergmann, Jason	R-R	6-3	220	9-25-81	2	4	4.50	56	0	0	0	48	50	28	24	7	25	40	.278	.339	.246	7.50	4.69
Burnett, Sean	L-L	6-1	200	9-17-82	1	1	3.20	33	0	0	0	25	14	9	9	3	13	20	.157	.182	.133	7.11	4.62
2-team total (38 Pittsburgh)					2	3	3.12	71	0	0	1	58	36	21	20	6	28	43	—	—	—	6.71	4.37
Cabrera, Daniel	R-R	6-9	260	5-28-81	0	5	5.85	9	8	0	0	40	48	39	26	4	35	16	.291	.347	.203	3.60	7.88
2-team total (6 Arizona)					0	6	6.00	15	9	0	0	51	59	47	34	4	42	23	—	—	—	4.06	7.41
Clippard, Tyler	R-R	6-3	200	2-14-85	4	2	2.69	41	0	0	0	60	36	20	18	9	32	67	.172	.122	.234	9.99	4.77
Colome, Jesus	R-R	6-2	240	12-23-77	1	1	8.40	16	0	0	0	15	23	14	14	1	6	12	.348	.367	.333	7.20	3.60
2-team total (5 Milwaukee)					1	1	7.59	21	0	0	0	21	34	18	18	2	6	15	—	—	—	6.33	2.53
Detwiler, Ross	R-L	6-5	185	3-6-86	1	6	5.00	15	14	1	0	76	87	43	42	3	33	43	.289	.288	.289	5.11	3.93
Estrada, Marco	R-R	6-0	195	7-5-83	0	1	6.14	4	1	0	0	7	6	5	5	1	4	9	.214	.300	.167	11.05	4.91
Garate, Victor	L-L	6-2	210	9-25-84	0	0	22.50	4	0	0	0	2	5	5	5	1	3	0	.500	.000	.625	0.00	13.50
Hanrahan, Joel	R-R	6-4	250	10-6-81	1	3	7.71	34	0	0	5	33	50	28	28	3	14	35	.342	.310	.373	9.64	3.86
2-team total (33 Pittsburgh)					1	4	4.78	67	0	0	5	64	73	40	34	3	34	72	—	—	—	10.13	4.78
Hernandez, Livan	R-R	6-2	245	2-20-75	2	4	5.36	8	8	1	0	49	56	29	29	3	16	27	.295	.266	.323	4.99	2.96
2-team total (23 New York)					9	12	5.44	31	31	2	0	184	220	112	111	19	67	102	—	—	—	5.00	3.28
Hinckley, Mike	R-L	6-3	205	10-5-82	0	0	4.66	14	0	0	0	10	8	5	5	1	11	3	.258	.077	.389	2.79	10.24

Player	B-T	HT	WT	DOB	W	L	ERA	G	GS	CG	SV	IP	H	R	ER	BB	SO	HR	AVG	vLH	vRH	BB9	SO9
Kensing, Logan	R-R	6-1	190	7-3-82	1	1	8.68	26	0	0	1	28	40	27	27	7	12	12	.342	.234	.414	3.86	3.86
2-team total (6 Florida)					1	2	8.92	32	0	0	1	35	54	35	35	8	17	19	—	—	4.84	4.33
Lannan, John	L-L	6-4	215	9-27-84	9	13	3.88	33	33	2	0	206	210	100	89	22	68	89	.266	.290	.259	3.88	2.97
Ledezma, Wilfredo	L-L	6-4	225	1-21-81	0	0	9.53	5	0	0	0	6	8	7	6	1	4	8	.333	.273	.385	12.71	6.35
MacDougal, Mike	B-R	6-4	190	3-5-77	1	1	3.60	52	0	0	20	50	45	25	20	3	31	31	.247	.265	.226	5.58	5.58
Martin, J.D.	R-R	6-4	200	1-2-83	5	4	4.44	15	15	0	0	77	85	40	38	14	24	37	.279	.307	.252	4.32	2.81
Martis, Shairon	R-R	6-1	225	3-30-87	5	3	5.25	15	15	1	0	86	83	52	50	15	39	34	.255	.315	.182	3.57	4.10
Mock, Garrett	R-R	6-3	230	4-25-83	3	10	5.62	28	15	0	0	91	114	65	57	9	44	72	.308	.344	.271	7.09	4.34
Olsen, Scott	L-L	6-4	210	1-12-84	2	4	6.03	11	11	0	0	63	83	45	42	11	25	42	.320	.309	.324	6.03	3.59
Rivera, Saul	B-R	5-10	175	12-7-77	1	3	6.10	30	0	0	0	38	48	28	26	7	14	21	.310	.296	.321	4.93	3.29
Segovia, Zack	R-R	6-2	245	4-11-83	1	0	7.84	8	0	0	0	10	11	10	9	1	6	4	.282	.318	.235	3.48	5.23
Shell, Steven	R-R	6-4	225	3-10-83	0	0	5.40	4	0	0	0	5	5	3	3	1	2	5	.250	.000	.385	9.00	3.60
Sosa, Jorge	R-R	6-2	220	4-28-77	2	1	6.45	18	0	0	2	22	28	16	16	5	12	17	.311	.344	.293	6.85	4.84
Stammen, Craig	R-R	6-3	210	3-9-84	4	7	5.11	19	19	1	0	106	112	67	60	14	24	48	.271	.290	.247	4.09	2.04
Tavarez, Julian	L-R	6-2	195	5-22-73	3	7	4.89	42	0	0	1	35	34	27	19	1	27	32	.250	.315	.207	8.23	6.94
Villone, Ron	L-L	6-3	245	1-16-70	5	6	4.25	63	0	0	1	49	54	25	23	6	29	33	.283	.293	.272	6.10	5.36
Wells, Kip	R-R	6-3	205	4-21-77	0	2	6.49	23	0	0	2	26	23	19	19	1	18	18	.237	.275	.211	6.15	6.15
2-team total (10 Cincinnati)					2	5	5.33	33	7	0	2	73	60	43	43	6	40	43	—	—	5.33	4.95
Zimmermann, Jordan	R-R	6-2	220	5-23-86	3	5	4.63	16	16	0	0	91	95	51	47	10	29	92	.271	.279	.263	9.07	2.86

Fielding

Catcher	PCT	G	PO	A	E	DP	PB
Bard	.988	79	397	27	5	3	3
Burke	1.000	6	27	1	0	0	0
Flores	.993	24	139	10	1	0	2
Nieves	.986	71	380	41	6	4	4

First Base	PCT	G	PO	A	E	DP
Belliard	.971	15	31	3	1	3
Dunn	.986	67	531	37	8	63
Johnson	.992	96	833	67	7	73
Morse	1.000	11	46	6	0	6
Willingham	—	1	0	0	0	0

Second Base	PCT	G	PO	A	E	DP
Belliard	.984	50	73	116	3	28
Cintron	1.000	2	1	0	0	0
Desmond	.923	5	12	12	2	2
Gonzalez	.995	55	86	121	1	34

	PCT	G	PO	A	E	DP
Harris	.959	19	21	26	2	7
Hernandez	.981	66	132	174	6	33
Orr	.976	18	31	51	2	15

Third Base	PCT	G	PO	A	E	DP
Belliard	.833	2	0	5	1	1
Gonzalez	—	3	0	0	0	0
Harris	.923	4	3	4	8	1
Morse	1.000	1	1	2	0	0
Orr	.800	4	2	6	2	0
Zimmerman	.963	154	117	325	17	28

Shortstop	PCT	G	PO	A	E	DP
Cintron	.857	2	4	2	1	0
Desmond	.952	17	37	43	4	14
Gonzalez	.932	41	39	84	9	13
Guzman	.962	117	154	353	20	74

Outfield	PCT	G	PO	A	E	DP
Bernadina	1.000	3	4	0	0	0
Desmond	1.000	1	3	0	0	0
Dukes	.965	100	209	12	8	1
Dunn	.947	84	142	2	8	0
Harris	.994	98	177	1	1	0
Hernandez	—	1	0	0	0	0
Kearns	1.000	57	84	5	0	0
Maxwell	1.000	36	60	1	0	1
Milledge	1.000	5	11	0	0	0
Morgan	.979	47	135	7	3	1
Morse	1.000	5	11	0	0	0
Orr	—	1	0	0	0	0
Padilla	1.000	13	10	1	0	0
Patterson	1.000	4	6	0	0	0
Willingham	.971	118	233	2	7	2

SYRACUSE CHIEFS   TRIPLE-A

INTERNATIONAL LEAGUE

Batting	B-T	HT	WT	DOB	AVG	vLH	vRH	G	AB	R	H	2B	3B	HR	RBI	BB	HBP	SH	SF	SO	SB	CS	SLG	OBP
Bard, Josh	B-R	6-3	225	3-30-78	.175	.000	.212	13	40	2	7	1	0	0	1	4	0	0	0	5	0	0	.200	.250
Bernadina, Roger	L-L	6-2	200	6-12-84	.167	.333	.083	5	18	1	3	0	0	0	0	4	0	1	0	5	1	0	.167	.318
Bynum, Freddie	L-R	6-1	185	3-15-80	.375	.000	.429	3	8	1	3	0	0	1	3	1	0	0	0	1	0	.750	.444
Bynum, Seth	R-R	6-0	185	12-19-80	.262	.274	.258	134	465	58	122	24	3	19	67	31	1	4	7	138	6	3	.449	.306
Casto, Kory	L-R	6-0	215	12-8-81	.271	.195	.296	126	447	57	121	22	1	8	58	44	3	1	9	85	4	4	.378	.334
Cintron, Alex	B-R	6-2	210	12-17-78	.500	.200	.615	5	18	2	9	1	0	0	3	0	0	0	1	1	0	0	.556	.474
Daniel, Mike	L-R	6-3	180	8-17-84	.279	.316	.250	11	43	5	12	2	1	0	2	4	1	1	0	12	2	1	.372	.354
Davis, Leonard	L-R	5-10	215	12-24-83	.208	.158	.241	14	48	4	10	1	1	2	4	4	0	1	0	13	0	0	.396	.269
Desmond, Ian	R-R	6-2	210	9-20-85	.354	.296	.379	55	178	25	63	12	2	1	14	20	3	4	0	31	8	1	.461	.428
Dukes, Elijah	R-R	6-1	250	6-26-84	.279	.316	.265	20	68	8	19	8	0	3	0	0	0	9	5	1	.529	.388
Eldred, Brad	R-R	6-5	290	7-12-80	.269	.264	.271	105	353	53	95	26	0	17	59	30	11	0	1	96	6	4	.487	.344
Gonzalez, Alberto	R-R	5-10	195	4-18-83	.311	.368	.296	23	90	5	28	3	1	0	8	1	0	1	0	8	1	0	.367	.319
Guzman, Joel	R-R	6-5	245	11-24-84	.121	.000	.250	12	33	3	4	0	0	0	2	2	0	0	0	9	0	1	.121	.171
Harris, Willie	L-R	5-9	190	6-22-78	.222	.333	.200	5	18	2	4	1	0	0	1	2	1	0	0	3	0	1	.278	.333
Hernandez, Anderson	B-R	5-9	185	10-30-82	.000	.000	—	1	4	0	0	0	0	0	0	0	0	0	0	0	0	0	.000	.000
Herrera, Javi	R-R	6-0	205	1-8-81	.167	.000	.190	8	24	1	4	1	0	0	0	0	0	0	0	4	0	0	.208	.167
Hopper, Norris	R-R	5-11	205	3-24-79	.252	.273	.244	34	119	15	30	2	0	0	10	14	1	4	0	12	7	3	.269	.336
3-team total (20 Charlotte, 52 Louisville)					.281	—		106	409	49	115	14	3	0	35	35	1	5	3	25	23	8	.330	.337
Langerhans, Ryan	L-L	6-3	220	2-20-80	.278	.262	.282	64	205	34	57	16	0	9	40	30	2	2	3	50	7	6	.488	.371
Maxwell, Justin	R-R	6-5	235	11-6-83	.242	.232	.246	111	384	68	93	10	5	13	42	54	6	3	1	136	35	8	.396	.344
Milledge, Lastings	R-R	6-0	205	4-5-85	.253	.182	.281	22	79	11	20	5	0	4	3	0	0	1	0	16	6	1	.316	.277
2-team total (17 Indianapolis)					.288	—		39	139	18	40	11	0	0	11	11	3	1	3	26	9	3	.367	.346
Molina, Gustavo	R-R	6-1	245	2-24-82	.209	.345	.160	72	211	19	44	15	0	2	24	6	1	8	1	25	0	1	.308	.233
Montz, Luke	R-R	6-1	200	7-7-83	.172	.200	.158	12	29	1	5	1	0	0	1	6	0	0	0	7	0	1	.207	.314
Morse, Mike	R-R	6-5	230	3-22-82	.339	.297	.352	44	165	21	56	12	3	6	34	15	2	0	2	27	2	1	.558	.404
Orr, Pete	L-R	6-1	195	6-8-79	.245	.217	.253	120	412	50	101	13	5	9	50	27	11	8	6	77	18	8	.367	.305
Padilla, Jorge	R-R	6-1	215	8-11-79	.367	.378	.362	95	311	58	114	18	3	4	21	24	8	6	1	32	14	11	.482	.424
Patterson, Corey	L-R	5-10	175	8-13-79	.274	.250	.280	84	263	30	72	16	1	7	40	13	4	3	0	65	14	5	.422	.318
Poppert, John	R-R	6-0	185	4-14-82	.000	—	.000	2	1	0	0	0	0	0	0	0	0	0	0	0	0	0	.000	.000
Solano, Jhonatan	R-R	6-0	180	8-12-85	.202	.245	.187	63	183	17	37	11	0	1	17	9	1	2	4	24	2	1	.279	.239
Vento, Mike	R-R	6-0	195	5-25-78	.252	.184	.282	50	159	23	40	11	1	5	18	3	0	2	2	29	2	2	.428	.262
Ward, Daryle	L-L	6-2	240	6-27-75	.245	.241	.246	30	94	10	23	2	0	5	13	12	1	0	2	20	0	0	.426	.330

	AVG	vLH	vRH	G	AB	R	H	2B	3B	HR	RBI	BB	HBP	SH	SF	SO	SB	CS	SLG	OBP
2-team total (69 Charlotte)	.252	—	—	99	341	41	86	13	0	13	49	43	3	0	5	69	2	1	.405	.337
Whitney, Matt R-R 6-3 215 2-13-84	.263	.333	.200	6	19	4	5	0	0	1	1	3	1	0	0	3	0	0	.421	.391
Yepez, Marcos B-R 5-10 160 12-29-81	.255	.286	.243	47	102	9	26	5	0	0	11	10	2	3	1	23	3	2	.304	.330

Pitching	B-T	HT	WT	DOB	W	L	ERA	G	GS	CG	SV	IP	H	R	ER	HR	BB	SO	AVG	vLH	vRH	K/9	BB/9
Atilano, Luis	R-R	6-2	220	5-10-85	2	0	2.45	2	2	0	0	11	11	3	3	2	1	5	.262	.389	.167	4.09	0.82
Balester, Collin	R-R	6-5	200	6-6-86	7	10	4.44	20	20	0	0	107	129	58	53	5	37	71	.305	.299	.309	5.95	3.10
Bergmann, Jason	R-R	6-3	220	9-25-81	1	1	1.16	19	0	0	2	23	18	3	3	1	8	15	.212	.294	.157	5.79	3.09
Clippard, Tyler	R-R	6-2	200	2-14-85	4	1	0.92	24	0	0	1	39	20	8	4	2	15	42	.150	.091	.192	9.69	3.46
Colome, Jesus	R-R	6-2	240	12-23-77	0	2	6.10	9	0	0	3	10	10	10	7	4	2	9	.244	.238	.250	7.84	1.74
Detwiler, Ross	R-L	6-5	185	3-6-86	4	2	3.10	10	10	0	0	49	56	23	17	2	20	42	.281	.364	.258	7.66	3.65
Doyne, Cory	R-R	6-2	240	8-13-81	2	0	6.75	10	0	0	0	11	10	8	8	2	6	4	.270	.222	.316	3.38	5.06
Estrada, Marco	R-R	6-0	195	7-5-83	9	5	3.63	27	25	0	0	136	133	61	55	10	33	98	.256	.276	.237	6.47	2.18
Everts, Clint	B-R	6-2	170	8-10-84	2	0	3.38	11	0	0	0	11	14	4	4	1	10	11	.341	.429	.296	9.28	8.44
Glover, Gary	R-R	6-4	225	12-3-76	2	3	6.32	10	0	0	1	16	19	11	11	5	3	9	.311	.214	.394	5.17	1.72
Kensing, Logan	R-R	6-1	190	7-3-82	2	1	2.97	31	0	0	17	33	28	11	11	2	6	35	.224	.231	.219	9.45	1.62
Kown, Andrew	L-R	6-7	210	10-7-82	5	3	4.45	14	9	0	0	55	58	27	27	4	15	28	.267	.269	.266	4.61	2.47
Larrison, Preston	R-R	6-3	255	11-19-80	0	1	4.60	26	0	0	0	31	44	16	16	1	20	15	.349	.370	.333	4.31	5.74
Ledezma, Wilfredo	L-L	6-4	225	1-21-81	0	2	4.19	18	0	0	1	19	29	12	9	0	12	17	.358	.308	.382	7.91	5.59
MacDougal, Mike	R-R	6-4	190	3-5-77	0	0	3.24	8	0	0	2	8	7	3	3	1	5	6	.226	.313	.133	6.48	5.40
Martin, J.D.	R-R	6-4	200	1-2-83	8	3	2.66	16	15	0	0	88	75	33	26	4	10	63	.237	.264	.215	6.44	1.02
Martis, Shairon	R-R	6-1	225	3-30-87	4	4	4.96	13	13	0	0	74	90	42	41	9	18	40	.304	.287	.317	4.84	2.18
Mock, Garrett	R-R	6-3	230	4-25-83	5	1	2.65	13	8	1	2	51	36	15	15	2	13	48	.199	.241	.167	8.47	2.29
Novoa, Yunior	L-L	6-4	180	9-11-84	1	0	3.66	19	0	0	0	20	20	11	8	1	10	16	.270	.318	.250	7.32	4.58
O'Connor, Mike	L-L	6-3	185	8-17-80	2	5	5.45	11	7	0	0	36	46	27	22	3	12	27	.309	.138	.350	6.69	2.97
Olsen, Scott	L-L	6-4	210	1-12-84	1	0	5.68	3	3	0	0	13	19	9	8	2	6	9	.345	.250	.385	6.39	4.26
Ramirez, Horacio	L-L	6-1	220	11-24-79	3	7	5.40	16	16	1	0	85	111	53	51	10	24	35	.324	.286	.336	3.71	2.54
Rivera, Saul	B-R	5-10	175	12-7-77	2	5	3.55	30	0	0	2	46	57	26	18	1	25	32	.315	.310	.317	6.31	4.93
Segovia, Zack	R-R	6-2	245	4-11-83	2	2	2.54	27	0	0	5	28	18	8	8	1	8	27	.184	.227	.148	8.58	2.54
Sosa, Jorge	R-R	6-2	220	4-28-77	1	2	2.79	20	4	0	3	48	40	15	15	3	13	53	.226	.242	.217	9.87	2.42
Spradlin, Jack	R-L	6-2	170	9-23-84	0	1	6.53	12	2	0	0	21	28	15	15	0	9	13	.329	.333	.328	5.66	3.92
Stammen, Craig	R-R	6-3	210	3-9-84	4	2	1.80	7	7	0	0	40	33	10	8	4	8	14	.223	.188	.253	3.15	1.80
Towers, Josh	R-R	6-1	185	2-26-77	0	0	21.60	1	0	0	0	2	6	4	4	0	0	0	.545	.667	.500	0.00	0.00
2-team total (19 Scranton/W-B)					7	6	3.05	20	18	0	0	103	95	36	35	13	24	55	—	—		4.79	2.09
Villone, Ron	L-L	6-3	245	1-16-70	0	0	2.35	8	0	0	0	8	4	2	1	2	5		.160	.222	.125	5.87	2.35
Wagner, Ryan	R-R	6-3	205	7-15-82	0	0	6.11	13	0	0	2	18	17	13	12	1	12	11	.258	.258	.257	5.60	6.11
Wells, Kip	R-R	6-3	205	4-21-77	1	0	2.45	2	2	0	0	11	9	3	3	1	2	11	.225	.182	.241	9.00	1.64
2-team total (5 Louisville)					2	0	2.81	7	3	0	0	26	21	8	8	3	7	27	—	—		9.47	2.45
Wilkie, Josh	R-R	6-2	190	7-22-84	2	3	3.22	17	0	0	2	22	19	8	8	0	4	25	.235	.276	.212	10.07	1.61
Williams, Dave	L-L	6-3	215	3-12-79	0	1	7.89	19	0	0	0	22	37	23	19	6	10	19	.370	.226	.435	7.89	4.15
Zimmermann, Jordan	R-R	6-2	220	5-23-86	0	0	5.06	1	1	0	0	5	4	3	3	2	1	4	.200	.222	.182	6.75	1.69
Zinicola, Zech	R-R	6-1	220	3-2-85	0	1	7.56	26	0	0	0	33	47	30	28	2	10	31	.348	.323	.370	8.37	2.70

Fielding

Catcher	PCT	G	PO	A	E	DP	PB
Bard	1.000	12	77	6	0	0	0
Herrera	1.000	8	46	3	0	0	2
Molina	.986	68	378	31	6	2	4
Montz	1.000	10	59	7	0	0	0
Poppert	—	1	0	0	0	0	0
Solano	.990	62	378	35	4	8	4

First Base	PCT	G	PO	A	E	DP
Bynum	1.000	1	2	0	0	0
Casto	.994	21	144	9	1	23
Eldred	.991	63	507	31	5	50
Guzman	1.000	2	6	0	0	0
Langerhans	.989	23	168	11	2	20
Molina	1.000	1	6	1	0	2
Morse	.996	27	205	17	1	30
Padilla	.900	2	9	0	1	1
Vento	—	2	0	0	0	0
Ward	1.000	16	136	12	0	17
Whitney	1.000	4	31	1	0	5

Second Base	PCT	G	PO	A	E	DP
Bynum	.973	123	210	335	15	98
Harris	1.000	1	3	3	0	0
Hernandez	1.000	1	3	0	0	0
Orr	1.000	20	28	50	0	10
Padilla	1.000	1	2	1	0	0
Solano	1.000	1	1	1	0	1
Yepez	1.000	8	8	13	0	5

Third Base	PCT	G	PO	A	E	DP
Casto	.938	59	26	126	10	14
Guzman	.952	8	6	14	1	0
Morse	1.000	15	10	15	0	3
Orr	.956	58	42	110	7	14
Whitney	1.000	2	2	6	0	0
Yepez	.889	20	11	21	4	3

Shortstop	PCT	G	PO	A	E	DP
Bynum	.818	2	3	6	2	2
Bynum	.875	10	13	22	5	6
Cintron	.950	5	7	12	1	1
Desmond	.935	55	85	161	17	41
Gonzalez	.978	23	32	59	2	12

	PCT	G	PO	A	E	DP
Morse	1.000	1	0	1	0	0
Orr	.980	45	65	136	4	30
Yepez	.964	9	27	27	2	13

Outfield	PCT	G	PO	A	E	DP
Bernadina	1.000	5	9	0	0	0
Casto	.973	48	69	4	2	1
Daniel	.967	11	29	0	1	0
Davis	.966	14	27	1	1	0
Desmond	—	1	0	0	0	0
Dukes	.973	18	31	5	1	1
Harris	1.000	4	12	0	0	0
Hopper	.987	33	77	1	1	1
Langerhans	1.000	36	55	2	0	1
Maxwell	.992	109	254	5	2	1
Milledge	.977	20	42	1	1	0
Morse	1.000	4	3	0	0	0
Orr	—	2	0	0	0	0
Padilla	.967	82	137	8	5	1
Patterson	.986	66	130	8	2	0
Vento	.956	28	42	1	2	0

HARRISBURG SENATORS

DOUBLE-A

EASTERN LEAGUE

Batting	B-T	HT	WT	DOB	AVG	vLH	vRH	G	AB	R	H	2B	3B	HR	RBI	BB	HBP	SH	SF	SO	SB	CS	SLG	OBP
Arata, Nick	R-R	5-10	175	10-13-86	.167	.000	.250	5	12	0	2	0	0	0	1	0	1	3	0	4	0	0	.167	.231
Baez, Edgardo	R-R	6-2	190	7-12-85	.254	.250	.256	101	323	42	82	14	4	9	28	28	1	3	1	78	5	10	.406	.314
Bynum, Freddie	L-R	6-1	185	3-15-80	.241	.171	.273	66	224	29	54	10	1	2	13	9	3	6	1	50	9	4	.321	.278
Bynum, Seth	R-R	6-0	185	12-19-80	.400	.571	.250	4	15	1	6	0	0	1	2	1	0	0	0	1	1	0	.600	.438

WASHINGTON NATIONALS

Name	B-T	HT	WT	DOB	AVG	vLH	vRH	G	AB	R	H	2B	3B	HR	RBI	BB	HBP	SH	SF	SO	SB	CS	SLG	OBP
Castro, Ofilio	R-R	6-0	160	8-18-83	.296	.340	.274	96	301	31	89	16	1	4	36	37	1	2	2	50	0	4	.395	.372
Daniel, Mike	L-R	6-3	180	8-17-84	.250	.188	.271	107	380	47	95	15	6	7	42	31	3	8	0	75	11	4	.376	.312
Davis, Leonard	L-R	5-10	215	12-24-83	.281	.214	.307	112	392	47	110	19	5	14	51	32	4	5	1	95	14	2	.462	.340
Desmond, Ian	R-R	6-2	210	9-20-85	.306	.229	.336	42	170	29	52	12	1	6	18	16	2	1	0	40	13	4	.494	.372
Dukes, Elijah	R-R	6-1	250	6-26-84	.250	.250	.250	2	8	0	2	0	0	0	0	1	0	0	0	1	0	0	.250	.333
Fermaint, Charlie	R-R	5-8	198	10-11-85	.200	.167	.214	11	20	3	4	0	0	0	0	1	0	0	0	6	1	0	.200	.238
Flores, Jesus	R-R	6-1	230	10-26-84	.364	.500	.286	3	11	1	4	0	0	0	1	0	0	0	0	1	0	0	.364	.364
Guzman, Joel	R-R	6-5	245	11-24-84	.281	.365	.244	108	385	53	108	26	1	12	57	34	9	0	1	72	1	0	.447	.352
Herrera, Javi	R-R	6-0	205	1-8-81	.145	.063	.174	24	62	7	9	3	0	1	11	16	2	0	1	17	0	0	.242	.333
Lowrance, Marvin	L-L	6-0	215	7-16-84	.241	.149	.270	122	361	47	87	22	2	15	45	41	3	2	1	89	1	2	.438	.323
Marrero, Chris	R-R	6-3	210	7-2-88	.267	.333	.241	23	75	9	20	6	0	1	11	8	1	0	0	18	0	1	.387	.345
Martinez, Michael	B-R	5-9	145	9-16-82	.223	.205	.235	65	188	22	42	7	2	1	8	20	5	5	1	34	0	3	.298	.313
Montz, Luke	R-R	6-1	220	7-7-83	.182	.217	.162	91	291	32	53	14	0	9	35	41	1	1	0	62	1	3	.323	.285
Nanita, Ricardo	L-L	6-0	205	6-12-81	.294	.226	.316	41	126	17	37	10	1	5	19	9	0	3	1	18	1	2	.508	.338
Plasencia, Francisco	L-L	6-1	192	6-19-84	.230	.087	.294	29	74	8	17	3	2	1	5	8	2	2	0	19	1	1	.365	.321
Rhinehart, Bill	L-L	6-0	202	11-22-84	.239	.160	.264	129	414	42	99	24	1	12	56	31	1	2	3	105	7	1	.389	.292
Rooney, Sean	B-R	5-10	205	4-12-86	.227	.207	.235	34	110	12	25	5	1	0	6	5	0	1	3	25	0	0	.291	.254
Solano, Jhonatan	R-R	6-0	180	8-12-85	.280	.359	.222	26	93	7	26	7	0	1	11	2	0	0	0	16	0	0	.387	.295
Spearman, Jemel	R-R	6-0	190	12-27-80	.267	.262	.270	62	161	18	43	8	1	3	22	13	2	2	2	30	5	3	.385	.326
Veloz, Greg	B-R	6-1	175	6-3-88	.000	.000	.000	4	10	0	0	0	0	0	0	0	2	0	2	4	0	0	.000	.167
Whitney, Matt	R-R	6-3	215	2-13-84	.268	.270	.267	101	261	43	70	18	1	7	36	40	3	2	2	61	2	1	.425	.369
Young, Dmitri	B-R	6-2	295	10-11-73	.241	.000	.269	10	29	4	7	2	0	0	2	3	1	0	1	4	0	0	.310	.324

Pitching	B-T	HT	WT	DOB	W	L	ERA	G	GS	CG	SV	IP	H	R	ER	HR	BB	SO	AVG	vLH	vRH	K/9	BB/9
Alaniz, Adrian	R-R	6-2	200	3-12-84	3	4	4.76	24	10	0	1	64	69	35	34	9	33	53	.276	.330	.238	7.41	4.62
Arnesen, Erik	R-R	6-3	260	3-19-84	8	6	3.87	22	21	1	0	123	133	59	53	11	26	91	.279	.314	.246	6.64	1.90
Atilano, Luis	R-R	6-2	220	5-10-85	7	8	4.16	21	20	0	0	115	143	58	53	12	27	61	.308	.338	.279	4.79	2.12
Avery, Matt	R-R	6-6	230	9-7-83	1	1	4.53	28	0	0	1	48	54	27	24	6	26	35	.300	.254	.322	6.61	4.91
Carr, Adam	R-R	6-2	220	4-1-84	0	1	8.71	8	0	0	0	10	16	13	10	2	9	7	.372	.353	.385	6.10	7.84
Chico, Matt	L-L	5-11	220	6-10-83	2	4	4.29	12	12	0	0	50	54	27	24	2	28	36	.283	.250	.294	6.44	5.01
Detwiler, Ross	R-L	6-5	185	3-6-86	0	3	2.96	6	4	0	0	27	28	14	9	2	10	28	.257	.375	.224	9.22	3.29
Estrada, Jesse	R-R	6-8	260	10-27-83	0	0	2.57	5	1	0	1	14	9	4	4	3	3	10	.188	.190	.185	6.43	1.93
Everts, Clint	B-R	6-2	170	8-10-84	3	1	1.53	20	0	0	4	29	21	7	5	0	11	31	.206	.152	.250	9.51	3.38
Jones, Justin	L-L	6-3	215	9-25-84	4	13	4.75	36	17	1	1	116	123	72	61	11	48	94	.273	.254	.282	7.31	3.73
Kown, Andrew	L-R	6-7	210	10-7-82	3	0	2.28	13	0	0	1	28	21	8	7	0	6	15	.208	.265	.154	4.88	1.95
Leatherman, Dan	R-R	6-2	210	7-12-85	0	0	3.86	1	0	0	0	2	2	1	1	0	0	4	.200	.200	.200	15.43	0.00
Mandel, Jeff	B-R	6-3	190	4-30-85	4	2	2.94	8	8	0	0	52	47	18	17	5	12	35	.253	.247	.258	6.06	2.08
Martinez, Carlos	R-R	6-4	180	3-30-84	7	6	3.95	28	9	0	2	80	80	43	35	6	25	43	.260	.267	.253	4.86	2.82
Meyers, Brad	R-R	6-6	195	9-13-85	5	1	2.25	9	9	1	0	48	40	14	12	2	11	43	.225	.242	.203	8.06	2.06
Novoa, Yunior	L-L	6-4	180	9-11-84	1	2	3.99	19	1	0	2	29	32	14	13	3	12	24	.274	.308	.256	7.36	3.68
O'Connor, Mike	L-L	6-3	185	8-17-80	0	1	2.45	3	3	0	0	15	12	4	4	0	4	13	.222	.222	.222	7.98	2.45
Segovia, Zack	R-R	6-2	245	4-11-83	1	3	3.68	24	3	0	1	44	57	19	18	2	19	39	.328	.324	.330	7.98	3.89
Severino, Atahualpa	L-L	5-9	170	11-6-84	6	0	2.78	15	0	0	2	23	19	8	7	1	14	27	.235	.265	.213	10.72	5.56
Spradlin, Jack	R-L	6-2	170	9-23-84	4	2	2.87	35	0	0	4	53	43	20	17	3	18	45	.226	.192	.248	7.59	3.04
Storen, Drew	B-R	6-2	180	8-11-87	1	0	0.00	10	0	0	9	12	3	0	0	0	6	12	.077	.105	.050	8.76	4.38
Thompson, Aaron	L-L	6-2	190	2-28-87	0	3	3.31	6	6	0	0	33	32	18	12	3	11	27	.254	.194	.278	7.44	3.03
VanAllen, Cory	L-L	6-3	180	12-24-84	3	5	5.07	31	16	0	0	94	116	56	53	13	31	69	.309	.368	.282	6.61	2.97
Wilkie, Josh	R-R	6-2	190	7-22-84	5	2	2.37	34	0	0	3	49	48	14	13	2	13	40	.257	.232	.271	7.30	2.37
Williams, Dave	L-L	6-3	215	3-12-79	1	3	3.56	21	0	0	3	30	33	13	12	1	9	28	.287	.260	.308	8.31	2.67
Zinicola, Zech	R-R	6-1	220	3-2-85	1	1	1.74	17	0	0	5	21	20	5	4	0	9	16	.263	.222	.300	6.97	3.92

Fielding

Catcher	PCT	G	PO	A	E	DP	PB
Flores	1.000	2	4	2	0	0	0
Herrera	.980	23	130	15	3	2	2
Montz	.994	68	427	46	3	4	6
Rooney	1.000	30	192	16	0	1	6
Solano	.990	25	185	15	2	1	3

First Base	PCT	G	PO	A	E	DP
Castro	1.000	1	1	0	0	1
Guzman	1.000	3	13	2	0	1
Marrero	.976	23	158	7	4	3
Montz	1.000	6	54	1	0	10
Rhinehart	.987	85	628	63	9	70
Whitney	.991	39	289	25	3	33
Young	.986	9	71	2	1	8

Second Base	PCT	G	PO	A	E	DP
Arata	1.000	5	10	11	0	4
Bynum	1.000	3	7	9	0	4
Castro	.986	75	131	225	5	53
Davis	.990	25	38	57	1	13
Martinez	.969	31	62	65	4	21
Spearman	.966	27	51	62	4	14
Veloz	.950	4	9	10	1	4

Third Base	PCT	G	PO	A	E	DP
Bynum	—	2	0	0	0	0
Castro	.929	25	10	29	3	1
Davis	.905	12	5	14	2	2
Guzman	.951	93	46	148	10	19
Montz	.800	2	0	4	1	0
Spearman	1.000	3	0	1	0	0
Whitney	.908	31	14	55	7	13

Shortstop	PCT	G	PO	A	E	DP
Bynum	.934	61	89	166	18	39
Desmond	.953	42	86	135	11	39
Martinez	.937	30	49	85	9	17
Spearman	.892	15	14	19	4	8

Outfield	PCT	G	PO	A	E	DP
Baez	.971	99	155	13	5	1
Daniel	.990	106	188	2	2	0
Davis	.991	80	103	8	1	3
Dukes	.750	2	3	0	1	0
Fermaint	1.000	10	8	0	0	0
Guzman	1.000	20	16	2	0	0
Lowrance	.993	80	127	6	1	1
Nanita	.986	34	69	0	1	0
Plasencia	1.000	27	45	0	0	0
Rhinehart	.946	34	48	5	3	0
Spearman	1.000	13	16	0	0	0

POTOMAC NATIONALS   HIGH CLASS A
CAROLINA LEAGUE

Batting	B-T	HT	WT	DOB	AVG	vLH	vRH	G	AB	R	H	2B	3B	HR	RBI	BB	HBP	SH	SF	SO	SB	CS	SLG	OBP
Burgess, Michael	L-L	5-11	195	10-20-88	.235	.227	.240	131	480	63	113	23	2	19	71	54	10	0	1	135	12	8	.410	.325

	B-T	HT	WT	DOB	AVG	vLH	vRH	G	AB	R	H	2B	3B	HR	RBI	BB	HBP	SH	SF	SO	SB	CS	SLG	OBP
Espinosa, Danny	B-R	6-0	190	4-25-87	.264	.250	.273	133	474	90	125	31	4	18	72	74	13	10	5	129	29	11	.460	.375
Ivany, Devin	R-R	6-2	185	7-27-82	.269	.311	.245	52	171	27	46	14	0	7	31	25	1	0	3	30	2	4	.474	.360
King, Stephen	R-R	6-2	195	10-2-87	.222	.226	.220	91	315	40	70	12	2	7	35	34	5	2	4	98	14	8	.340	.304
Lyons, Dan	R-R	5-10	185	8-21-84	.183	.148	.205	46	142	18	26	6	1	2	17	29	2	5	2	30	11	3	.282	.326
Marrero, Chris	R-R	6-3	210	7-2-88	.287	.346	.252	112	414	58	119	21	2	16	65	42	8	0	5	97	2	3	.464	.360
Martinez, Michael	B-R	5-9	145	9-16-82	.293	.356	.256	49	198	40	58	14	5	4	29	16	1	2	1	31	10	6	.475	.347
Nelson, Dan	B-R	5-11	180	6-22-82	.262	.243	.272	92	317	48	83	22	3	6	39	49	2	2	2	57	16	7	.407	.362
Pahuta, Tim	L-R	6-4	225	5-3-83	.251	.220	.265	90	295	34	74	16	1	8	42	24	1	1	1	80	4	4	.393	.308
Peacock, Brian	R-R	6-1	185	8-26-84	.255	.284	.239	80	247	37	63	16	4	8	32	24	2	0	3	66	13	7	.449	.322
Plasencia, Francisco	L-L	6-1	192	6-19-84	.274	.226	.295	91	340	52	93	19	1	10	48	35	4	1	3	81	6	8	.424	.346
Reagan, Travis	R-R	6-1	205	8-31-84	.000	—	.000	3	3	1	0	0	0	0	0	0	0	0	0	1	0	0	.000	.000
Rooney, Sean	B-R	5-10	205	4-12-86	.300	.273	.318	60	217	26	65	18	0	6	40	24	0	2	2	33	3	2	.465	.366
Seuss, Aaron	R-R	6-1	195	3-5-85	.187	.200	.179	32	91	6	17	7	0	2	9	4	3	0	0	19	1	1	.330	.245
Valdez, Jesus	R-R	6-2	170	11-24-84	.297	.331	.277	89	343	51	102	20	2	9	55	18	5	0	1	53	6	3	.446	.341
Veloz, Greg	B-R	6-1	175	6-3-88	.137	.200	.097	19	51	14	7	1	1	1	3	6	0	0	0	12	3	1	.255	.228
Whiting, Boomer	R-R	5-10	170	11-5-83	.245	.331	.190	114	355	68	87	16	3	3	22	52	7	12	3	90	54	12	.332	.350
Young, Dmitri	B-R	6-2	295	10-11-73	.333	.500	.000	1	3	1	1	0	0	1	1	1	0	0	0	1	0	0	1.333	.500

Pitching	B-T	HT	WT	DOB	W	L	ERA	G	GS	CG	SV	IP	H	R	ER	HR	BB	SO	AVG	vLH	vRH	K/9	BB/9
Arnesen, Erik	R-R	6-3	260	3-19-84	4	1	2.23	6	6	0	0	32	37	16	8	1	7	25	.285	.345	.236	6.96	1.95
Atwood, Will	L-L	6-2	180	1-13-87	8	8	4.61	26	26	0	0	137	142	76	70	10	40	118	.269	.255	.276	7.77	2.63
Beimel, Joe	L-L	6-3	215	4-19-77	0	0	45.00	1	1	0	0	1	7	5	5	0	0	0	.778	.500	.857	0.00	0.00
Beno, Marty	R-R	6-0	180	8-24-86	1	4	4.54	27	0	0	0	36	31	20	18	1	29	26	.242	.286	.208	6.56	7.32
Carr, Adam	R-R	6-2	220	4-1-84	2	6	5.82	24	11	1	1	73	84	52	47	7	34	32	.296	.264	.331	3.96	4.21
Engles, Terry	R-R	6-4	170	11-12-85	4	3	3.12	9	8	0	0	49	43	19	17	2	17	48	.239	.174	.298	8.82	3.12
Estrada, Jesse	R-R	6-8	260	10-27-83	0	3	3.19	22	0	0	1	37	36	16	13	1	11	19	.263	.368	.159	4.66	2.70
Everts, Clint	B-R	6-2	170	8-10-84	3	0	0.90	13	0	0	2	20	14	4	2	2	5	26	.194	.300	.119	11.70	2.25
Garcia, Luis	R-R	6-2	212	1-30-87	1	0	0.00	2	0	0	0	4	0	0	0	0	1	7	.000	.000	.000	15.75	2.25
Gunderson, Kyle	R-R	6-3	215	1-31-85	2	0	2.84	5	0	0	0	6	3	3	2	0	4	4	.125	.200	.071	5.68	5.68
Holder, Trevor	R-R	6-2	185	1-8-87	2	3	9.26	6	6	0	0	23	33	27	24	4	9	18	.337	.319	.353	6.94	3.47
Kimball, Cole	R-R	6-3	225	8-1-85	4	5	6.36	39	0	0	9	47	49	37	33	4	28	52	.269	.256	.280	10.03	5.40
Kown, Andrew	L-R	6-7	210	10-7-82	1	1	4.50	11	0	0	3	18	18	9	9	4	4	15	.254	.273	.237	7.50	2.00
Leatherman, Dan	R-R	6-2	210	7-12-85	6	1	3.23	41	0	0	5	70	64	27	25	5	23	67	.242	.261	.227	8.66	2.97
Lehman, James	R-R	6-2	185	3-14-85	0	0	12.15	5	0	0	1	7	9	9	1	5	2	3	.310	.200	.368	2.70	6.75
Mandel, Jeff	B-R	6-3	190	4-30-85	8	4	3.61	17	17	1	0	100	94	52	40	7	31	54	.249	.245	.253	4.88	2.80
Martinez, Carlos	R-R	6-4	180	3-30-84	1	1	4.21	11	2	0	0	26	29	19	12	0	10	13	.284	.310	.267	4.56	3.51
McCoy, Patrick	L-L	6-4	200	8-3-88	0	2	5.14	15	1	0	0	21	30	16	12	2	4	9	.337	.303	.357	3.86	1.71
Meyers, Brad	R-R	6-6	195	9-13-85	6	2	1.43	15	14	0	0	88	71	17	14	1	21	65	.222	.247	.198	6.62	2.14
Milone, Tom	L-L	6-1	205	2-16-87	12	5	2.91	27	25	0	0	151	144	57	49	9	36	106	.257	.244	.262	6.30	2.14
Olsen, Scott	L-L	6-4	210	1-12-84	0	0	0.00	1	1	0	0	3	3	0	0	0	0	4	.273	.200	.333	12.00	0.00
Peacock, Brad	R-R	6-1	175	2-2-88	3	3	4.34	8	7	0	0	48	46	26	23	4	10	27	.253	.264	.242	5.10	1.89
Pecina, Ricardo	L-L	5-11	180	7-1-87	1	0	2.16	7	0	0	0	8	7	3	2	0	8	9	.226	.000	.280	9.72	8.64
Pena, Hassan	R-R	6-2	210	3-25-85	2	1	2.39	12	2	0	0	26	16	7	7	1	12	21	.174	.171	.175	7.18	4.10
Phillabaum, Justin	R-R	6-2	180	4-6-86	0	0	3.63	10	0	0	0	18	9	7	7	2	12	11	.261	.250	.267	5.71	6.23
Rivera, Chris	R-R	6-4	200	3-4-84	1	1	3.94	16	0	0	0	16	14	9	7	0	9	11	.233	.333	.200	6.19	5.06
Rodriguez, Osvaldo	R-R	5-11	180	6-10-84	1	0	2.25	16	2	0	0	24	20	7	6	2	16	23	.227	.219	.232	8.63	6.00
Severino, Atahualpa	L-L	5-9	170	11-6-84	4	0	2.54	29	0	0	13	46	35	14	13	4	14	39	.211	.172	.235	7.63	2.74
Storen, Drew	B-R	6-2	180	8-11-87	1	0	1.80	7	0	0	2	10	7	2	2	0	2	11	.206	.235	.176	9.90	1.80
Wells, Kip	R-R	6-3	205	4-21-77	0	0	1.80	4	1	0	0	5	3	1	1	0	1	1	.188	.111	.286	1.80	1.80
Willems, Colton	R-R	6-3	175	7-30-88	1	4	7.40	6	6	1	0	21	27	21	17	3	7	12	.325	.293	.357	5.23	3.05
Zimmermann, Jordan	R-R	6-2	220	5-23-86	0	0	2.70	1	1	0	0	3	2	2	1	1	1	6	.167	.286	.000	16.20	2.70

Fielding

Catcher	PCT	G	PO	A	E	DP	PB
Ivany	.997	39	265	25	1	4	2
Peacock	.984	53	327	47	6	3	4
Reagan	1.000	2	7	1	0	0	0
Rooney	.985	46	292	37	5	0	6

First Base	PCT	G	PO	A	E	DP
Ivany	1.000	1	6	0	0	0
Marrero	.984	105	896	73	16	80
Pahuta	.993	38	256	17	2	25

Second Base	PCT	G	PO	A	E	DP
King	1.000	1	2	1	0	0

	PCT	G	PO	A	E	DP
Lyons	.981	46	77	127	4	22
Martinez	.944	45	72	112	11	27
Nelson	.953	48	73	130	10	25
Veloz	1.000	6	10	14	0	2

Third Base	PCT	G	PO	A	E	DP
King	.899	78	47	113	18	7
Nelson	.767	20	10	13	7	1
Pahuta	.901	37	17	56	8	3
Veloz	.935	13	7	22	2	2

Shortstop	PCT	G	PO	A	E	DP
Espinosa	.965	128	219	383	22	84

	PCT	G	PO	A	E	DP
King	.878	10	19	24	6	5
Martinez	1.000	5	2	11	0	0
Nelson	—	1	0	0	0	0

Outfield	PCT	G	PO	A	E	DP
Burgess	.979	121	229	9	5	2
Nelson	.979	25	46	1	1	0
Peacock	—	1	0	0	0	0
Plasencia	.991	82	203	9	2	1
Seuss	.979	28	44	2	1	1
Valdez	.957	63	105	5	5	1
Whiting	.972	107	236	3	7	0

HAGERSTOWN SUNS

LOW CLASS A

SOUTH ATLANTIC LEAGUE

Batting	B-T	HT	WT	DOB	AVG	vLH	vRH	G	AB	R	H	2B	3B	HR	RBI	BB	HBP	SH	SF	SO	SB	CS	SLG	OBP
Arata, Nick	R-R	5-10	175	10-13-86	.236	.182	.256	87	288	42	68	9	2	0	22	25	14	0	1	66	9	2	.281	.326
Curran, Chris	L-R	5-9	170	12-21-87	.213	.160	.228	122	423	49	90	11	5	2	32	25	8	7	1	104	19	8	.277	.269
Fermaint, Charlie	R-R	5-8	198	10-11-85	.254	.266	.251	78	291	23	74	10	4	4	29	20	2	1	4	54	13	6	.333	.303
Guerrero, Michael	R-R	6-0	175	10-16-86	.203	.211	.200	89	296	28	60	9	2	5	33	27	7	2	3	73	2	0	.297	.282
Heredia, Valerio	B-R	5-10	150	3-14-86	.227	.217	.228	47	172	20	39	0	2	0	5	16	1	3	1	38	17	3	.250	.295

Batting	B-T	HT	WT	DOB	AVG	vLH	vRH	G	AB	R	H	2B	3B	HR	RBI	BB	HBP	SH	SF	SO	SB	CS	SLG	OBP
Higley, J.R.	R-R	6-3	210	6-21-88	.300	.182	.345	11	40	7	12	3	1	2	6	4	2	0	0	12	0	0	.575	.391
Jacobsen, Robby	R-R	6-1	205	8-30-84	.285	.346	.262	109	383	43	109	27	3	2	25	24	4	4	2	96	8	5	.386	.332
Jones, Marcus	R-R	6-2	190	9-9-86	.176	.111	.200	9	34	3	6	0	0	0	1	3	0	0	1	8	0	0	.176	.237
Keithley, James	R-R	6-2	185	2-18-87	.228	.219	.232	38	127	17	29	4	0	0	10	22	1	2	0	41	1	2	.260	.347
Labrie, Ronnie	R-R	6-3	205	10-22-86	.208	.353	.167	21	77	7	16	5	2	0	6	7	2	0	0	29	0	2	.325	.291
Leon, Sandy	B-R	5-11	175	3-13-89	.218	.318	.179	23	78	7	17	3	0	0	6	5	0	0	0	21	0	0	.256	.265
Lombardozzi, Steve	B-R	6-0	170	9-20-88	.296	.292	.298	128	496	90	147	26	7	3	58	62	5	6	7	80	16	7	.395	.375
Lozada, Jose	B-R	6-0	180	12-29-85	.247	.245	.248	49	186	26	46	8	1	0	5	14	2	2	1	34	4	1	.301	.305
Moore, Tyler	R-R	6-2	185	1-30-87	.297	.299	.296	111	421	38	125	30	3	9	87	40	8	0	8	111	2	2	.447	.363
Newsome, Brett	L-L	6-2	210	8-24-86	.400	.667	.222	4	15	3	6	2	0	0	4	2	0	0	0	3	0	0	.533	.471
Norris, Derek	R-R	6-0	210	2-14-89	.286	.282	.287	126	437	78	125	30	0	23	84	90	8	0	5	116	6	3	.513	.413
Reagan, Travis	R-R	6-1	205	8-31-84	.233	.273	.223	36	116	13	27	4	3	0	12	15	2	0	1	31	1	1	.319	.328
Seuss, Aaron	R-R	6-1	195	3-5-85	.222	.278	.204	20	72	3	16	1	0	1	6	6	3	0	3	16	1	0	.278	.298
Souza, Steven	R-R	6-3	205	4-24-89	.237	.198	.249	126	447	52	106	18	3	4	47	54	7	0	6	116	25	10	.318	.325

Pitching	B-T	HT	WT	DOB	W	L	ERA	G	GS	CG	SV	IP	H	R	ER	HR	BB	SO	AVG	vLH	vRH	K/9	BB/9
Arnold, Patrick	R-R	6-1	190	10-31-88	3	5	4.67	36	6	0	3	81	99	46	42	9	23	71	.307	.320	.297	7.89	2.56
Chico, Matt	L-L	5-11	220	6-10-83	0	0	2.45	3	3	0	0	11	11	3	3	2	0	8	.262	.364	.226	6.55	.00
Demny, Paul	R-R	6-2	200	8-3-89	3	11	5.14	23	23	0	0	105	101	69	60	8	42	110	.250	.213	.275	9.43	3.60
Dill, Clayton	R-L	5-11	190	1-3-86	2	0	9.00	3	0	0	0	4	4	4	4	1	1	4	.250	.250	.250	9.00	2.25
Engles, Terry	R-R	6-4	170	11-12-85	4	2	3.53	10	10	0	0	51	50	22	20	5	12	60	.259	.220	.294	10.59	2.12
Fabian, Robinson	R-R	6-3	152	2-10-86	0	1	1.96	9	1	0	2	23	21	6	5	1	4	10	.247	.324	.196	3.91	1.57
2-team total (24 Asheville)					3	7	5.32	33	13	0	2	107	126	70	63	7	25	64	—	—		5.40	2.11
Frias, Marcos	R-R	6-2	190	12-19-88	9	5	2.91	25	23	0	0	127	124	56	41	6	30	112	.254	.256	.253	7.96	2.13
Garrett, Austin	L-L	6-0	190	3-26-87	4	5	4.67	39	0	0	0	62	64	36	32	5	37	51	.274	.308	.260	7.44	5.40
Hicks, Graham	L-L	6-5	170	2-9-90	0	0	5.40	1	1	0	0	5	6	3	3	2	3	6	.300	.286	.308	10.80	5.40
Holder, Trevor	R-R	6-2	185	1-8-87	2	0	3.55	3	3	0	0	13	17	6	5	1	3	12	.333	.381	.300	8.53	2.13
Jaime, Juan	R-R	6-1	180	8-2-87	3	1	2.27	8	7	0	0	32	22	15	8	2	16	40	.193	.220	.177	11.37	4.55
Lehman, Pat	R-R	6-6	215	10-18-86	1	1	2.25	6	6	0	0	32	22	9	8	2	1	28	.190	.179	.200	7.88	0.28
Light, Kevin	L-L	6-0	190	8-27-87	3	2	5.00	40	0	0	1	63	70	37	35	4	28	56	.292	.339	.277	8.00	4.00
Lugo, Chris	R-R	6-1	185	11-10-86	5	2	4.21	35	0	0	2	62	72	36	29	5	13	54	.295	.274	.309	7.84	1.89
Matias, Randy	R-R	6-0	160	9-19-86	0	0	2.25	3	0	0	0	4	2	5	1	0	3	4	.133	.250	.091	9.00	6.75
McCoy, Patrick	L-L	6-4	200	8-3-88	2	3	5.82	11	4	0	0	43	55	29	28	6	10	39	.311	.351	.300	8.10	2.08
McGeary, Jack	L-L	6-3	195	3-19-89	0	6	6.79	13	13	0	0	56	58	48	42	4	45	44	.280	.333	.269	7.11	7.28
Morris, A.J.	R-R	6-2	185	12-1-86	0	4	3.82	8	8	0	0	38	44	23	16	2	8	36	.297	.295	.299	8.60	1.91
Peacock, Brad	R-R	6-1	175	2-2-88	5	8	4.05	19	17	0	0	100	104	49	45	10	32	77	.272	.238	.300	6.93	2.88
Pecina, Ricardo	L-L	5-11	180	7-1-87	1	3	2.53	18	6	0	1	57	53	23	16	4	26	48	.242	.205	.251	7.58	4.11
Pena, Hassan	R-R	6-2	210	3-25-85	1	0	1.13	3	3	0	0	16	8	2	2	0	4	11	.151	.231	.125	6.19	2.25
Peralta, Carlos	R-R	6-1	185	7-29-85	4	7	3.91	48	0	0	8	53	47	31	23	6	27	48	.239	.197	.262	8.15	4.58
Phillabaum, Justin	R-R	6-2	180	4-18-86	1	4	2.21	24	0	0	2	53	43	18	13	4	16	44	.224	.206	.234	7.47	2.72
Rivera, Chris	R-R	6-2	180	3-4-84	0	2	3.79	17	0	0	1	19	17	9	8	0	1	21	.227	.273	.208	9.95	0.47
Rodriguez, Osvaldo	R-R	5-11	180	6-10-84	2	3	3.06	30	0	0	10	35	33	12	12	4	13	47	.241	.192	.271	11.97	3.31
Slovak, David	R-R	6-0	170	5-20-86	1	1	4.32	7	0	0	1	8	9	4	4	1	3	2	.281	.462	.158	2.16	3.24
Storen, Drew	B-R	6-2	180	8-11-87	0	1	3.68	11	0	0	0	15	11	6	6	2	0	26	.193	.368	.105	15.95	0.00

Fielding

Catcher	PCT	G	PO	A	E	DP	PB
Leon	.979	18	108	31	3	1	2
Norris	.979	100	760	88	18	9	28
Reagan	.995	23	175	26	1	2	4

First Base	PCT	G	PO	A	E	DP
Jacobsen	.978	14	87	4	2	7
Labrie	.995	20	178	14	1	23
Moore	.990	102	798	70	9	67
Newsome	1.000	3	28	1	0	2
Reagan	1.000	1	1	0	0	0

Second Base	PCT	G	PO	A	E	DP
Arata	1.000	5	3	4	0	0

	PCT	G	PO	A	E	DP
Heredia	.833	3	2	3	1	0
Lombardozzi	.987	127	259	354	8	75
Lozada	1.000	4	8	11	0	1

Third Base	PCT	G	PO	A	E	DP
Arata	.936	40	21	67	6	4
Jacobsen	.800	3	3	1	1	1
Keithley	.894	38	26	67	11	2
Lozada	—	1	0	0	0	0
Souza	.880	65	40	92	18	3

Shortstop	PCT	G	PO	A	E	DP
Arata	.920	43	51	110	14	31
Lombardozzi	1.000	1	1	2	0	0
Lozada	.961	41	64	110	7	35
Souza	.941	56	94	145	15	27

Outfield	PCT	G	PO	A	E	DP
Arata	—	1	0	0	0	0
Curran	.978	119	256	9	6	1
Englund	1.000	18	29	3	0	0
Fermaint	.992	71	120	3	1	0
Guerrero	.955	72	99	7	5	0
Heredia	.936	39	65	8	5	2
Higley	1.000	11	25	0	0	0
Jacobsen	.949	67	89	4	5	1
Jones	.950	9	19	0	1	0
Seuss	.931	13	25	2	2	0

VERMONT LAKE MONSTERS — SHORT-SEASON

NEW YORK-PENN LEAGUE

Batting	B-T	HT	WT	DOB	AVG	vLH	vRH	G	AB	R	H	2B	3B	HR	RBI	BB	HBP	SH	SF	SO	SB	CS	SLG	OBP
Amar, Adam	R-R	6-4	240	11-30-85	.145	.121	.155	35	117	7	17	4	0	2	9	15	1	0	3	19	0	0	.231	.243
Arias, Dani	B-R	5-11	175	8-24-87	.244	.200	.261	43	127	16	31	2	0	0	10	14	1	1	1	26	4	0	.260	.322
Bloxom, Justin	R-B	6-1	205	4-29-88	.228	.213	.234	67	228	31	52	6	1	3	24	37	5	1	2	68	4	3	.303	.346
Higley, J.R.	R-R	6-3	210	6-21-88	.271	.269	.271	53	192	22	52	6	3	3	20	12	6	2	4	52	6	6	.380	.327
Hood, Destin	R-R	6-1	225	4-3-90	.246	.200	.262	38	138	12	34	4	1	2	24	11	3	0	7	45	2	1	.333	.302
Killian, Dan	L-R	6-4	195	1-14-89	.187	.263	.170	35	107	9	20	4	0	0	4	8	1	2	0	36	1	1	.224	.250
Kobernus, Jeff	R-R	6-2	210	6-30-88	.220	.100	.258	10	41	8	9	1	0	0	2	2	1	0	0	5	4	0	.244	.273
Labrie, Ronnie	R-R	6-3	205	10-22-86	.204	.233	.192	45	142	18	29	4	6	1	14	17	3	0	0	54	0	1	.338	.302
Leon, Sandy	B-R	5-11	175	3-13-89	.247	.235	.252	50	166	16	41	10	1	2	18	24	2	1	2	29	1	1	.355	.345
Lopez, Yhonson	L-L	6-1	160	10-27-88	.148	.125	.158	10	27	2	4	0	1	0	4	2	0	0	0	10	0	0	.222	.207

Batting	B-T	HT	WT	DOB	AVG	vLH	vRH	G	AB	R	H	2B	3B	HR	RBI	BB	HBP	SH	SF	SO	SB	CS	SLG	OBP
Nicol, Sean	R-R	5-10	175	9-25-86	.269	.250	.276	63	223	36	60	9	0	1	21	35	5	7	4	28	9	1	.323	.375
Nolan, Rick	R-R	6-0	180	4-23-86	.250	.364	.190	12	32	4	8	2	0	1	7	4	0	1	1	14	0	0	.406	.324
Pruitt, Brian	R-R	6-1	175	12-8-86	.208	.158	.241	17	48	6	10	2	1	0	5	9	1	1	0	11	1	2	.292	.345
Ramirez, J.P.	L-L	5-10	185	9-29-89	.264	.200	.288	72	295	35	78	18	6	4	39	14	4	0	1	45	6	9	.407	.306
Sferra, J.J.	L-L	5-10	160	12-16-85	.238	.258	.233	50	160	16	38	2	0	0	9	9	1	1	0	25	5	1	.250	.282
Soriano, Francisco	B-R	5-11	169	6-16-87	.291	.298	.289	60	199	39	58	10	3	1	27	36	0	2	1	40	16	9	.387	.398
Tejeda, Yeurys	R-R	6-1	150	2-24-88	.143	.400	.000	4	14	1	2	1	0	1	2	0	1	0	0	6	0	0	.429	.200
Walker, Jack	R-R	6-3	220	2-12-87	.214	.162	.231	51	145	21	31	7	0	1	18	42	2	1	2	49	1	2	.283	.393

Pitching	B-T	HT	WT	DOB	W	L	ERA	G	GS	CG	SV	IP	H	R	ER	HR	BB	SO	AVG	vLH	vRH	K/9	BB/9
Alaniz, Adrian	R-R	6-2	200	3-12-84	1	0	0.00	2	2	0	0	9	3	0	0	0	0	8	.100	.000	.200	8.00	0.00
Amato, Gary	R-R	6-0	210	2-5-86	1	1	1.64	18	0	0	0	38	27	18	7	0	9	42	.180	.127	.218	9.86	2.11
Applebee, Paul	L-L	6-3	195	5-17-88	0	1	3.06	4	4	0	0	18	16	8	6	2	2	13	.235	.182	.286	6.62	1.02
Bronson, Evan	L-L	6-3	195	2-13-87	3	0	0.55	20	0	0	4	49	28	7	3	0	3	38	.161	.172	.155	6.93	0.55
Clegg, Mitchell	R-L	6-5	225	12-22-86	2	4	2.20	13	10	1	0	57	56	19	14	1	13	30	.262	.257	.264	4.71	2.04
Crane, Dustin	R-R	6-2	195	8-13-86	1	0	2.29	10	0	0	0	20	14	8	5	1	9	13	.203	.190	.208	5.95	4.12
Dill, Clayton	R-L	5-11	190	1-3-86	4	5	3.07	19	0	0	8	29	20	15	10	3	11	42	.185	.194	.181	12.89	3.38
Erb, Shane	R-R	6-5	180	5-3-87	1	1	7.15	17	1	0	0	34	46	28	27	6	15	18	.338	.439	.266	4.76	3.97
Figuereo, Johan	R-R	6-2	195	3-2-86	0	1	2.92	17	0	0	1	25	21	9	8	0	9	23	.247	.297	.208	8.39	3.28
Hicks, Graham	L-L	6-5	170	2-9-90	2	5	7.12	9	9	0	0	37	53	37	29	2	21	18	.338	.222	.372	4.42	5.15
Holder, Trevor	R-R	6-2	185	1-8-87	0	0	5.06	2	2	0	0	5	10	4	3	0	2	3	.476	.444	.500	5.06	3.38
Jaime, Juan	R-R	6-1	180	8-2-87	2	1	1.88	6	5	0	0	24	15	6	5	0	15	36	.183	.222	.164	13.50	5.63
Jenkins, Chad	L-L	6-4	195	3-12-88	0	2	8.28	9	8	0	0	29	33	31	27	2	24	26	.287	.316	.273	7.98	7.36
Lehman, Pat	R-R	6-6	215	10-18-86	3	1	1.65	7	3	0	0	27	21	6	5	1	1	24	.216	.265	.190	4.61	0.33
McGeary, Jack	L-L	6-3	195	3-19-89	2	6	4.31	13	13	0	0	56	61	43	27	5	41	45	.274	.246	.284	7.19	6.55
Morrison, Kyle	R-R	6-1	190	12-22-87	3	4	3.44	14	9	0	0	55	56	25	21	6	21	44	.267	.274	.261	7.20	3.44
Novoa, Yunior	L-L	6-4	180	9-11-84	0	1	5.79	3	0	0	2	5	7	4	3	0	1	3	.333	.400	.313	5.79	1.93
Pinales, Jose	R-R	6-2	175	9-1-85	3	1	4.72	16	1	0	0	27	25	21	14	3	25	25	.248	.122	.333	8.44	8.44
Stewart, Steven	R-R	6-3	215	5-18-86	3	3	4.03	20	0	0	1	29	28	16	13	2	8	25	.255	.289	.236	7.76	2.48
Swynenberg, Matt	R-R	6-5	185	2-16-89	2	2	5.17	8	8	0	0	31	37	19	18	1	17	25	.285	.266	.303	7.18	4.88
Tanco, Federico	R-R	5-11	180	4-15-86	1	1	2.39	19	0	0	0	26	29	13	7	0	8	21	.279	.179	.338	7.18	2.73
Weaver, Dean	R-R	6-4	207	5-17-88	0	1	3.18	5	0	0	2	6	6	3	2	0	1	4	.316	.167	.385	6.35	1.59

Fielding

Catcher	PCT	G	PO	A	E	DP	PB
Killian	.993	21	128	12	1	1	5
Leon	.988	48	359	39	5	2	10
Nolan	1.000	9	43	2	0	0	0

First Base	PCT	G	PO	A	E	DP
Amar	.969	27	205	14	7	15
Bloxom	1.000	7	55	5	0	4
Labrie	.985	44	316	18	5	33

Second Base	PCT	G	PO	A	E	DP
Arias	.943	12	22	28	3	3

	PCT	G	PO	A	E	DP
Kobernus	1.000	7	16	13	0	2
Nicol	.889	2	5	3	1	1
Soriano	.946	56	123	157	16	37

Third Base	PCT	G	PO	A	E	DP
Arias	.818	9	1	17	4	2
Bloxom	.826	15	10	28	8	3
Tejeda	1.000	4	4	7	0	0
Walker	.914	51	47	101	14	16

Shortstop	PCT	G	PO	A	E	DP
Arias	.950	16	24	33	3	9

	PCT	G	PO	A	E	DP
Nicol	.943	60	88	128	13	22

Outfield	PCT	G	PO	A	E	DP
Bloxom	.975	22	37	2	1	0
Higley	.983	53	111	3	2	0
Hood	.928	33	63	1	5	0
Lopez	.500	4	1	0	1	0
Pruitt	1.000	16	27	0	0	0
Ramirez	.949	62	109	2	6	1
Sferra	.980	46	93	3	2	0

GCL NATIONALS   ROOKIE
GULF COAST LEAGUE

Batting	B-T	HT	WT	DOB	AVG	vLH	vRH	G	AB	R	H	2B	3B	HR	RBI	BB	HBP	SH	SF	SO	SB	CS	SLG	OBP
Bernadina, Roger	L-L	6-2	200	6-12-84	.250	—	.250	2	4	0	1	0	0	0	0	0	0	0	0	1	0	0	.250	.250
Breault, Kyle	R-R	6-1	160	10-5-90	.000	.000	.000	2	7	1	0	0	0	0	0	0	0	0	0	4	0	0	.000	.000
Bynum, Freddie	L-R	6-1	185	3-15-80	.385	.167	.571	4	13	2	5	0	0	0	1	1	0	0	0	2	1	0	.385	.429
Cuevas, Justino	R-R	5-10	160	11-30-88	.230	.323	.178	54	183	28	42	10	0	2	26	11	5	5	2	30	7	5	.317	.289
Hood, Destin	R-R	6-1	225	4-3-90	.330	.241	.373	25	88	18	29	10	3	3	24	8	1	0	1	30	0	3	.614	.388
Jimenez, Hendry	B-R	5-10	160	12-30-89	.333	.356	.320	50	162	39	54	10	2	1	25	28	4	7	2	24	12	3	.438	.439
King, Stephen	R-R	6-2	195	10-2-87	.500	.667	.000	3	4	3	2	1	0	0	0	2	1	0	0	1	0	0	.750	.714
Martinez, Ricardo	R-R	6-0	175	11-27-88	.300	.238	.345	15	50	9	15	5	1	0	10	2	4	0	0	7	2	0	.440	.375
Milledge, Lastings	R-R	6-0	205	4-5-85	.200	—	.200	3	5	1	1	0	0	1	3	3	0	0	0	1	0	0	.800	.500
2-team total (4 Pirates)					.294	—	—	7	17	2	5	2	0	1	3	5	0	0	0	2	2	0	.588	.455
Montilla, Angelberth	R-R	6-1	180	4-11-89	.205	.222	.198	47	127	23	26	3	0	1	18	12	3	3	1	32	3	4	.252	.287
Nanita, Ricardo	R-R	6-0	205	6-12-81	.286	.200	.333	9	28	7	8	1	0	1	7	4	0	0	2	6	1	0	.429	.353
Newsome, Brett	L-L	6-2	210	8-24-86	.327	.262	.364	51	168	36	55	17	4	6	35	31	2	1	2	42	3	2	.583	.433
Nieto, Adrian	B-R	6-0	200	11-12-89	.228	.273	.198	42	136	22	31	6	1	0	17	20	4	0	3	30	1	2	.287	.337
Pena, Wilfri	R-R	6-0	180	5-2-87	.246	.111	.302	25	61	14	15	5	0	1	12	9	1	1	0	11	1	0	.377	.352
Perez, Eury	R-R	6-0	180	5-30-90	.381	.338	.407	47	181	38	69	3	5	3	24	15	5	4	0	20	16	8	.503	.443
Perez, Roberto	R-R	6-1	180	4-4-91	.167	.400	.077	11	36	3	6	0	0	0	4	2	0	1	0	13	0	1	.167	.211
Phillips, Derrick	R-R	6-3	220	9-21-90	.242	.265	.228	32	91	11	22	2	1	1	13	8	2	0	0	37	5	3	.319	.317
Romero, Alexander	R-R	6-1	180	1-3-90	.250	.222	.267	26	48	5	12	2	1	0	4	3	1	0	0	18	2	2	.313	.308
Sanchez, Adrian	B-R	6-0	160	8-16-90	.246	.167	.277	24	65	13	16	7	0	0	5	3	0	4	2	6	3	0	.354	.271
Solis, Chris	R-R	6-2	215	1-22-86	.226	.375	.162	23	53	11	12	6	0	1	11	9	5	0	1	13	0	0	.396	.382
Tejeda, Yeurys	R-R	6-1	150	2-24-88	.246	.186	.280	35	118	22	29	5	1	3	23	7	1	0	2	25	2	1	.381	.289
Valdez, Jesus	R-R	6-2	170	11-24-85	.286	.000	.306	5	14	5	4	0	0	0	3	5	1	1	2	0	1	0	.929	.375
Washiya, Naoya	L-R	6-1	160	10-3-88	.246	.162	.284	40	118	21	29	6	1	0	14	13	2	3	0	23	12	0	.314	.331
Young, Dmitri	B-R	6-2	295	10-11-73	.167	.000	.250	3	6	2	1	0	0	0	0	1	1	0	0	0	0	0	.167	.375

Pitching	B-T	HT	WT	DOB	W	L	ERA	G	GS	CG	SV	IP	H	R	ER	HR	BB	SO	AVG	vLH	vRH	K/9	BB/9
Applebee, Paul	L-L	6-3	195	5-17-88	0	1	3.45	4	3	0	0	16	15	6	6	0	2	13	.268	.083	.318	7.47	1.15
Crane, Dustin	R-R	6-2	195	8-13-86	0	1	5.27	10	0	0	4	14	13	8	8	0	3	16	.265	.167	.297	10.54	1.98
De La Rosa, Ruben	R-R	5-9	165	4-2-87	4	1	0.96	15	0	0	3	28	22	6	3	1	10	44	.208	.250	.192	14.14	3.21
Englund, Stephen	R-R	6-3	200	6-6-88	0	0	0.00	3	1	0	0	3	0	0	0	0	0	4	.000	.000	.000	13.50	0.00
Eusebio, Wilson	R-R	6-0	170	8-20-88	2	0	3.22	13	2	0	1	22	25	16	8	0	12	18	.275	.316	.264	7.25	4.84
Hansen, Bobby	L-L	6-5	220	12-17-89	1	2	4.93	10	5	0	0	35	38	28	19	1	13	30	.273	.158	.292	7.79	3.38
Hicks, Graham	L-L	6-5	170	2-9-90	3	0	3.60	3	3	0	0	15	15	13	6	6	1	3	14	.245	.000	.289	8.40	1.80
Jenkins, Chad	L-L	6-4	195	3-12-88	0	1	4.22	4	2	0	0	11	8	6	5	0	7	14	.200	.111	.226	11.81	5.91
Jordan, Taylor	R-R	6-3	190	1-17-89	2	0	3.63	10	6	0	0	35	25	18	14	4	9	33	.194	.219	.186	8.57	2.34
King, Brandon	R-R	6-4	235	11-14-90	3	0	4.15	8	6	0	0	30	28	18	14	1	10	29	.235	.222	.238	8.60	2.97
Lopez, Kelvin	R-R	6-1	150	1-22-90	0	2	8.04	10	0	0	0	16	25	17	14	3	4	9	.373	.067	.462	5.17	2.30
McCatty, Shane	R-R	6-3	205	5-18-87	1	1	3.95	14	1	0	2	27	30	15	12	0	5	18	.270	.211	.301	5.93	1.65
Morris, A.J.	R-R	6-2	185	12-1-86	0	0	0.00	2	2	0	0	5	0	0	0	0	4	.000	.000	.000	7.20	0.00
Paez, Ironel	R-R	6-1	165	7-28-90	1	0	5.40	9	2	0	1	12	11	9	7	1	14	15	.256	.375	.229	11.57	10.80
Pena, Hassan	R-R	6-2	210	3-25-85	0	1	2.70	2	2	0	0	7	6	3	2	0	3	3	.261	.222	.286	4.05	4.05
Perez, Julio	R-R	5-11	165	10-26-87	0	0	3.60	8	1	0	0	10	11	8	4	0	7	11	.297	.200	.333	9.90	6.30
Rosenbaum, Danny	R-L	6-1	210	10-10-87	4	1	1.95	11	8	0	0	37	29	14	8	1	9	38	.215	.231	.213	9.24	2.19
Santiago, John	R-R	6-0	185	10-10-88	3	0	3.43	13	0	0	5	21	23	10	8	1	7	17	.277	.350	.254	7.29	3.00
Smoker, Josh	L-L	6-2	195	11-26-88	4	2	3.38	10	9	0	0	43	46	17	16	2	10	31	.275	.364	.262	6.54	2.11
Swynenberg, Matt	R-R	6-5	185	2-16-89	1	0	1.80	3	1	0	0	10	9	2	2	0	5	10	.257	.250	.258	9.00	4.50
Taveras, Jose	L-L	6-5	190	11-10-87	1	0	1.74	9	0	0	0	10	9	3	2	0	4	8	.237	.400	.212	6.97	3.48
Vasquez, Wanel	R-R	6-3	190	1-15-87	4	2	2.73	15	0	0	0	26	17	18	8	0	16	31	.181	.368	.133	10.59	5.47
Weaver, Dean	R-R	6-4	207	5-17-88	0	0	3.86	5	0	0	0	7	8	3	3	0	3	6	.296	.200	.318	7.71	3.86
Willems, Colton	R-R	6-3	175	7-30-88	0	0	13.50	3	1	0	0	3	6	5	5	0	1	4	.400	.200	.500	10.80	2.70
Wort, Rob	R-R	6-2	170	2-7-89	3	3	3.91	18	0	0	1	23	22	12	10	1	11	16	.247	.308	.222	6.26	4.30

Fielding

Catcher	PCT	G	PO	A	E	DP	PB
Martinez	.971	9	61	7	2	0	1
Nieto	.996	29	205	22	1	2	10
Pena	1.000	17	92	14	0	2	1
Solis	.987	11	68	10	1	1	3

First Base	PCT	G	PO	A	E	DP
Newsome	.986	51	408	22	6	42
Pena	—	1	1	0	0	0
Romero	1.000	1	1	0	0	0
Sanchez	1.000	1	0	1	0	0
Solis	1.000	4	19	2	0	2
Tejeda	1.000	3	18	1	0	0
Young	1.000	3	12	0	0	3

Second Base	PCT	G	PO	A	E	DP
Breault	1.000	2	1	3	0	0
Cuevas	1.000	3	9	2	0	1
Jimenez	.965	48	104	117	8	38
Romero	.944	8	11	6	1	2
Sanchez	1.000	1	3	2	0	1

Third Base	PCT	G	PO	A	E	DP
Cuevas	—	2	0	0	0	0
King	.800	2	2	2	1	2
Romero	.931	14	5	22	2	3
Sanchez	.843	17	8	35	8	5
Tejeda	.884	31	20	79	13	6

Shortstop	PCT	G	PO	A	E	DP
Bynum	1.000	3	1	6	0	0

	PCT	G	PO	A	E	DP
Cuevas	.930	49	61	126	14	30
Perez	.970	8	5	27	1	0
Romero	1.000	1	1	1	0	0
Sanchez	1.000	2	2	4	0	0

Outfield	PCT	G	PO	A	E	DP
Bernadina	1.000	2	1	0	0	0
Hood	.964	23	26	1	1	0
Milledge	1.000	3	1	0	0	0
Montilla	.987	44	72	5	1	2
Nanita	1.000	6	8	1	0	0
Perez	1.000	47	82	7	0	1
Phillips	.893	22	22	3	3	1
Valdez	1.000	5	5	0	0	0
Washiya	1.000	34	35	0	0	0

DSL NATIONALS   ROOKIE

DOMINICAN SUMMER LEAGUE

Batting	B-T	HT	WT	DOB	AVG	vLH	vRH	G	AB	R	H	2B	3B	HR	RBI	BB	HBP	SH	SF	SO	SB	CS	SLG	OBP
Altuve, Jose	R-R	6-1	185	2-20-88	.143	.077	.163	18	56	4	8	1	0	0	2	5	0	2	0	6	1	1	.161	.213
Alvarez, Carlos	B-R	5-11	175	11-25-85	.280	.275	.282	63	232	36	65	15	5	3	25	49	9	0	1	30	5	5	.427	.423
Ariza, Jesus	R-R	5-11	180	7-6-90	.194	.333	.167	16	36	2	7	0	0	0	2	7	1	0	1	12	0	1	.194	.333
Bernabel, Jairo	R-R	6-2	185	9-26-90	.149	.115	.157	43	134	20	20	3	0	1	8	26	3	2	1	59	1	3	.194	.299
Bocio, Anderson	R-R	5-11	180	11-13-88	.250	.226	.258	37	120	12	30	7	3	2	24	11	4	0	0	32	0	1	.408	.333
Cabreja, Joseph	R-R	6-3	190	1-22-90	.207	.190	.211	59	208	26	43	9	0	4	27	34	5	1	0	57	1	3	.308	.332
Chacin, Paul	R-R	6-0	180	2-27-91	.172	.136	.183	30	93	5	16	3	0	0	7	11	1	1	1	34	0	0	.204	.264
Hiraldo, Wily	B-R	5-11	153	8-9-88	.265	.200	.283	23	68	4	18	1	0	0	3	10	2	1	0	16	5	3	.279	.375
Hodge, Alejandro	R-R	6-0	160	11-15-89	.226	.282	.212	58	195	32	44	6	3	2	9	31	7	1	0	50	23	7	.318	.352
Martinez, Estarlin	R-R	6-1	185	3-8-92	.240	.172	.263	60	233	42	56	6	3	3	34	32	3	0	4	28	11	6	.330	.335
Morales, Jesus	R-R	6-1	165	12-4-89	.218	.167	.236	62	225	40	49	13	1	2	24	35	8	3	2	66	8	3	.311	.341
Norberto, Jose	L-R	6-0	0	8-23-90	.143	.500	.083	4	14	2	2	0	0	0	1	0	0	0	10	0	0	.143	.200
Pena, Bill	R-R	6-0	180	4-14-92	.185	.000	.222	19	65	9	12	1	0	2	10	4	3	0	0	11	5	1	.292	.264
Ramirez, Andruth	R-R	5-11	180	3-10-89	.234	.235	.234	31	94	15	22	6	2	1	13	12	1	0	0	21	2	2	.372	.327
Ramos, Wander	R-R	6-3	192	4-26-90	.198	.150	.211	26	91	13	18	6	0	1	8	21	6	1	0	31	12	3	.297	.381
Rodriguez, Aridio	L-L	6-1	175	11-24-88	.251	.250	.252	59	215	35	54	8	6	1	25	33	6	0	0	68	18	4	.358	.366
Rodriguez, Elvin	R-R	6-0	186	4-17-89	.293	.250	.304	31	99	13	29	9	0	1	13	10	2	0	1	16	4	1	.414	.366
Urdaneta, Juan	L-L	6-4	185	5-20-89	.170	.133	.178	47	165	14	28	3	0	1	19	21	3	0	2	51	1	0	.206	.272

Pitching	B-T	HT	WT	DOB	W	L	ERA	G	GS	CG	SV	IP	H	R	ER	HR	BB	SO	AVG	vLH	vRH	K/9	BB/9
Almonte, Raudy	L-L	6-6	190	2-27-89	2	4	5.74	25	0	0	2	47	44	36	30	1	34	25	.259	.263	.258	4.79	6.51
Baez, Gregory	L-L	6-3	185	5-5-92	1	3	2.57	10	6	0	0	35	21	13	10	0	19	30	.174	.000	.191	7.71	4.89
Berroa, Javier	R-R	5-11	180	8-5-87	0	1	4.34	22	0	0	2	29	27	21	14	3	17	22	.248	.130	.279	6.83	5.28
De La Cruz, Joel	B-R	6-1	190	6-9-90	0	4	7.27	13	0	0	0	26	37	29	21	0	17	14	.336	.400	.307	4.85	5.88
De La Rosa, Yunior	B-R	5-10	182	6-7-89	4	5	3.05	25	0	0	1	41	36	27	14	2	19	32	.234	.300	.211	6.97	4.14
Encarnacion, Pedro	R-R	6-4	175	6-26-91	3	5	3.50	13	13	0	0	46	50	33	18	0	25	23	.279	.311	.269	4.47	4.86
Gonzalez, Danubio	R-R	6-4	190	9-5-91	2	4	2.57	14	13	0	0	67	61	34	19	3	27	45	.244	.247	.243	6.07	3.64

Guerrero, Rafael	R-R	5-11	183	3-23-89	5	2	3.02	22	0	0	2	54	40	22	18	0	31	50	.209	.317	.180	8.39	5.20
Guzman, Antonio	R-R	6-1	145	12-15-87	8	2	1.44	15	14	1	0	88	59	20	14	3	20	64	.192	.224	.182	6.57	2.05
Guzman, Wandy	R-R	6-5	205	4-29-89	0	3	15.63	13	0	0	0	13	14	27	22	1	21	11	.264	.182	.286	7.82	14.92
Rivera, Manuel	R-R	6-2	170	7-2-87	0	5	3.68	15	15	0	0	66	63	36	27	2	24	49	.253	.300	.238	6.68	3.27
Rosa, George	—	0-0	0	7-25-90	0	0	0.00	1	0	0	0	1	0	0	0	0	1	0	.000	—	.000	0.00	9.00
Torres, Carlos	R-R	6-2	170	8-28-89	1	0	11.00	9	0	0	0	9	7	12	11	0	18	6	.206	.400	.172	6.00	18.00
Vasquez, Wanel	R-R	6-3	190	1-15-87	0	1	8.31	11	0	0	3	9	9	10	8	0	7	18	.243	.300	.222	18.69	7.27
Vizcaino, Francisco	L-L	6-0	160	7-26-88	2	2	5.61	18	10	0	0	59	67	51	37	3	29	52	.276	.370	.264	7.89	4.40

Fielding

Catcher	PCT	G	PO	A	E	DP	PB
Ariza	.953	16	88	13	5	1	4
Bocio	.962	23	130	22	6	3	1
Chacin	.947	5	16	2	1	0	3
Pena	.931	17	92	16	8	1	8
Ramirez	.960	26	152	17	7	1	7

First Base	PCT	G	PO	A	E	DP
Altuve	.978	18	128	5	3	17
Cabreja	.940	9	75	3	5	6
Rivera	1.000	1	9	1	0	1
Urdaneta	.992	47	446	22	4	37

Second Base	PCT	G	PO	A	E	DP
Bernabel	1.000	6	9	11	0	4

	PCT	G	PO	A	E	DP
Bocio	.857	1	1	5	1	0
Hiraldo	.972	21	50	55	3	22
Hodge	.970	6	17	15	1	4
Martinez	.942	42	114	144	16	23

Third Base	PCT	G	PO	A	E	DP
Bernabel	.855	36	25	81	18	7
Chacin	.845	26	17	43	11	5
Martinez	.860	14	10	39	8	3
Ramirez	1.000	1	0	2	0	0

Shortstop	PCT	G	PO	A	E	DP
Alvarez	.949	62	107	226	18	42
Bernabel	1.000	2	4	2	0	0
Hiraldo	.857	2	4	2	1	1

	PCT	G	PO	A	E	DP
Martinez	.818	5	11	7	4	2
Morales	—	1	0	0	0	0

Outfield	PCT	G	PO	A	E	DP
Cabreja	.977	26	40	3	1	0
Hodge	.949	39	54	2	3	0
Morales	.976	61	114	9	3	1
Norberto	1.000	4	2	1	0	1
Ramirez	—	1	0	0	0	0
Ramos	.950	26	35	3	2	3
Rodriguez	.950	55	71	5	4	1
Rodriguez	.957	15	21	1	1	0

WASHINGTON NATIONALS

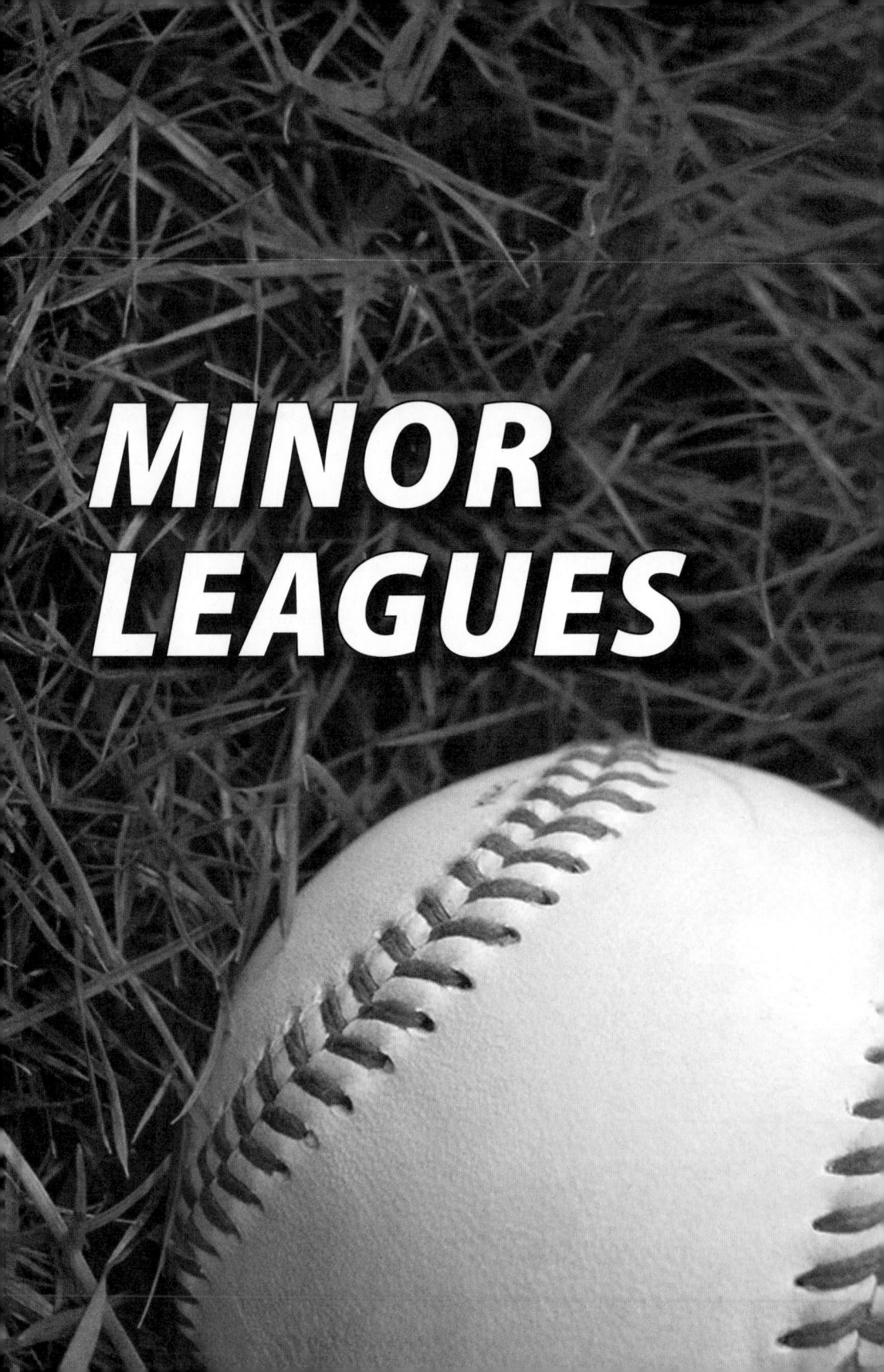

MINOR LEAGUES

Tough times hit Memphis in 2009 as the Redbirds defaulted on a loan for AutoZone Park

Minors fall short of record amid recession

BY JOSH LEVENTHAL

The minors are not immune.

That was the lesson taken from the 2009 season, as the sport buckled but did not break under the weight of a sour economy.

The high times that have been felt around the sport the last five years were replaced with apprehension, as attendance dipped and sponsorships sagged. The recession impacted the biggest markets—including Sacramento, the sport's top draw the past 10 years, and Memphis, one of its flagship franchises—as well as the smaller circuits—as 20 of 30 low Class A teams saw a dip in attendance.

The sport also proved that its affordable, family-friendly business model can survive tough times. The 2.9 percent decrease in average attendance was not nearly as bad as the 6.9 percent drop experienced by big league clubs in 2009.

And there was plenty of action on the field, from a record-setting hitting streak to an array of young talent ascending through the minors.

Statistics seemed to tell much of the story of the 2009 season, so we've decided to present our season in review in a by-the-numbers format.

41,644,518

Overall attendance in 2009, which was down for the first time in five years.

A big number indeed, but minor league baseball's overall attendance in 2009 was not enough to lift the sport to a sixth consecutive record.

The minors were down 1.6 million from the mark set in 2008, as baseball's first full season in the worst recession since the Great Depression left a cloud over the sport. In fact, many operators would take that argument quite literally, claiming bad weather was as much a factor in the decline as the recession. However, attendance figures would have been even worse if not for the debut of six new ballparks, accounting for a 920,000 increase in those markets from the previous year.

"This is a unique set of circumstances we're dealing with and our clubs fared very, very well. I'm proud of them," Minor League Baseball president Pat O'Conner said. "The phrase going around is that flat is the new up, and there are a lot of teams that were treading water. Given the circumstances, (if you held steady) then you've probably had a good year."

Not all teams accomplished that benchmark. In 2008, 78 of the sport's 160 teams saw an increase at the gate. In 2009, that figure dropped to 58 teams.

"We faced a lot of the same things that a lot of the industry did and our clubs had to bear down a do what they do a little bit better," said South Atlantic League president Eric Krupa, echoing the sentiment of many around the sport. "What we offered fans was a still an affordable night out. A family of four could go to the ballpark for just

MOST IMPROVED ATTENDANCE*

Team, League (Classification)	2009	2008	Increase	Avg.	Dates Lost
Visalia Rawhide, California (High A)	105,405	67,045	57.2%	1,528	1
Harrisburg Senators, Eastern (AA)	228,741	164,182	39.3%	3,574	7
Wisconsin Timber Rattlers, Midwest (low A)	253,240	190,263	33.0%	3,724	2
Bluefield Orioles, Appalachian (R)	34,510	26,897	28.3%	1,046	1
Lancaster Jethawks, California (High A)	150,970	124,934	20.8%	2,157	0
Vancouver Canadians, Northwest (SS)	149,297	129,073	15.6%	3,929	0
San Jose Giants, California (High A)	211,054	183,788	14.8%	3,015	0
Quad Cities River Bandits, Midwest (Low A)	236,401	207,048	14.1%	3,694	6
Casper Ghosts, Pioneer (R)	56,680	50,580	12.0%	1,718	5
Kannapolis Intimidators, South Atlantic (Low A)	132,342	119,668	10.5%	2,005	4

* Not including teams that opened new ballparks in 2009

BIGGEST ATTENDANCE DROPS

Team, League (Classification)	2009	2008	Decrease	Avg.	Dates Lost
Winston-Salem Dash, Carolina (High A)	57,665	169,963	-66.0%	901	6
Huntsville Stars, Southern (AA)	93,845	160,080	-41.3%	1,514	8
Oneonta Tigers, New York-Penn (SS)	23,521	39,609	-40.6%	692	4
Scranton/Wilkes-Barre Yankees, International (AAA)	358,888	496,658	-27.7%	6,188	14
Sarasota Reds, Florida State (High A)	33,788	43,088	-21.5%	528	6
Altoona Curve, Eastern (AA)	275,945	346,973	-20.4%	4,312	7
Peoria Chiefs, Midwest (Low A)	219,168	275,673	-20.4%	3,372	5
Batavia Muckdogs, New York-Penn (SS)	35,620	43,167	-17.4%	963	1
Rome Braves, South Atlantic (Low A)	183,750	222,168	-17.2%	2,827	5
Asheville Tourists, South Atlantic (Low A)	146,353	175,892	-16.7%	2,361	8

MINOR LEAGUES

over $52."

Even amid such gloom and doom, several teams saw a significant resurgence at the gate. Among those setting club records were the Tacoma Rainiers, New Britain Rock Cats, San Jose Giants, Visalia Rawhide, Wisconsin Timber Rattlers and Hudson Valley Renegades.

The secrets to teams' success (see chart above) varied from improved ownership (Lancaster) to ballpark renovations (Harrisburg, Visalia) to improved weather (Iowa, Quad Cities) to first-place teams (San Jose, Tacoma).

Visalia (California) and Harrisburg (Eastern) led all teams in increased attendance (not including the six that debuted new ballparks) and both had renovated facilities to thank. Visalia saw attendance jump 57 percent, from 67,045 in 2008 to 105,405 last season. Harrisburg enjoyed a 39 percent increase.

Renovations to Harrisburg's Commerce Bank Park transformed what was once a deteriorating island ballpark in the center of the Susquehanna River. Visalia increased its seating capacity to 2,600 by expanding right-field seating, added a canopy above the grandstand for relief from the summer heat and modernized concessions by building the first kitchen in 64-year-old Recreation Park's history.

The Wisconsin Timber Rattlers' record-breaking season had little to do with how they played the game, but rather who played it. It also proved once again, just like in Peoria and West Michigan, that affiliating with the hometown team pays off—quite literally.

In their first season since inking a player-development contract with the Brewers, the Timber Rattlers saw a 33 percent increase at the gate while drawing a club record 253,240 fans—all while fielding a team that finished third from the bottom in the Midwest League standings.

Losing had never been so much fun.

"This blew away our expectations," Wisconsin general manager Rob Zerjav said.

$1.625 million

The bond payment Triple-A Memphis failed to make on March 1, which led to the team's board of trustees dismissing its management group.

The plight of a team once considered a minor league success story was the most extreme example of the sinking economy's impact on the sport. Memphis drew just 474,764 fans in 2009—a decline of nearly 100,000 from last season and the fewest in the team's 10-year history. The Redbirds entered the season as one of the minors' highest-grossing teams (thanks largely to long-term contracts for their 44 luxury suites) but have still struggled to turn a profit due to annual $5.5 million ballpark payments.

The dismissal of Blues City Baseball also signaled the end of an era in Memphis and highlighted the complexities of operating the team, which is owned by a nonprofit charitable foundation and plays in the most expensive ballpark in minor league baseball history.

The team has been for sale for over a year, but the $50 million still owed on the ballpark makes it a difficult purchase.

"No one is going to write a check for $50 million to make the bondholders whole," said longtime Redbirds president of baseball operations Dave Chase, who was relieved of his duties.

9

Number of consecutive seasons Triple-A Sacramento led the minors in attendance before finishing second this season to Triple-A Columbus, which opened a new ballpark in 2009.

The River Cats had been the minors' best draw since the club debuted in 2000, and Sacramento still topped the Pacific Coast League with 657,095 fans this year. However, attendance was down from last year's mark of 700,168 and could not match Columbus' 666,797 fans.

The Clippers' brand-new Huntington Park was certainly the difference. The Clippers averaged 9,526 fans in 70 openings, up from 7,795 last year. Meanwhile, Sacramento averaged 9,126 in 72 openings, down from 9,725 last year.

6 out of 7

Number of new minor league ballparks that opened as scheduled in 2009.

The facilities that opened on time included Columbus (International), Triple-A Gwinnett (International), Triple-A Reno (Pacific Coast), high Class A Charlotte (Florida State), low Class A Bowling Green (South Atlantic) and low Class A Fort Wayne (Midwest).

However, minor league baseball's building boom hit a bump in the road in Winston-Salem, where the Carolina League affiliate was expected to debut a new $22 million ballpark on Opening Day. However the offseason breakup of team owners Billy Prim and Andrew Flipowski proved complicated and took longer than expected. Construction, meanwhile, ground to a halt as financing for the project dried up.

Winston-Salem was forced to play at its former home (the old Ernie Shore Field) and the city bailed out the team by contributing an additional $15.7 million to bring the new

ORGANIZATION STANDINGS

Cumulative farm club records for the 30 major league organizations, with winning percentages going back five years. Most organizations have six affiliates.

	2009						
	W	L	PCT	2008	2007	2006	2005
1. San Francisco	463	305	.603	.553	.562	.557	.555
2. N.Y. Yankees	459	369	.554	.586	.597	.551	.541
3. Chi. White Sox	425	346	.551	.503	.475	.496	.500
4. Minnesota	404	351	.535	.532	.534	.537	.525
5. Seattle	474	423	.528	.472	.443	.474	.482
6. L.A. Angels	389	368	.514	.542	.490	.534	.535
7. Colorado	401	380	.513	.499	.496	.487	.501
8. Philadelphia	422	410	.507	.462	.488	.426	.504
9. Boston	383	375	.505	.518	.501	.490	.489
10. Atlanta	377	372	.503	.506	.486	.506	.512
11. Tampa Bay	447	444	.502	.475	.527	.526	.429
12. Florida	381	378	.502	.530	.465	.537	.555
13. Cleveland	382	380	.501	.506	.535	.524	.492
14. San Diego	384	383	.501	.517	.465	.519	.454
15. Washington	380	378	.501	.481	.443	.481	.498
16. Pittsburgh	416	418	.499	.430	.480	.456	.517
17. L.A. Dodgers	381	384	.498	.484	.506	.530	.545
18. St. Louis	449	453	.498	.525	.478	.483	.464
19. Texas	406	415	.495	.556	.489	.495	.473
20. Oakland	378	387	.494	.520	.492	.499	.523
21. Detroit	405	419	.492	.448	.531	.513	.472
22. Milwaukee	332	348	.488	.469	.565	.491	.519
23. Chi. Cubs	402	424	.487	.488	.499	.525	.496
24. Kansas City	398	428	.482	.442	.497	.477	.509
25. Arizona	372	409	.476	.426	.494	.440	.438
26. Baltimore	393	435	.475	.468	.490	.499	.492
27. Toronto	355	405	.467	.511	.523	.504	.490
28. N.Y. Mets	415	476	.466	.453	.461	.465	.501
29. Cincinnati	343	415	.453	.476	.519	.423	.491
30. Houston	352	474	.426	.376	.441	.557	.494

POSTSEASON ROUNDUP

League	Champion	Runner-up
International	Durham	Scranton/Wilkes-Barre
Pacific Coast	Memphis	Sacramento
Eastern	Akron	Connecticut
Southern	Jacksonville	Tennessee
Texas	Midland	Northwest Arkansas
California	San Jose	High Desert
Carolina	Lynchburg	Salem
Florida State	Tampa	Charlotte
Midwest	Fort Wayne	Burlington
South Atlantic	Lakewood	Greenville
New York-Penn	Staten Island	Mahoning Valley
Northwest	Salem-Keizer	Tri-City
Appalachian	Danville	Elizabethton
Pioneer	Orem	Missoula
Arizona	Mariners	Giants
Gulf Coast	Nationals	Marlins

MINOR LEAGUES

ballpark's overall price tag to $40.1 million—the most expensive for a high Class A facility. Even a first-place team couldn't bring the fans out to the ballpark, as the newly named Dash averaged just 901 fans this season and saw attendance dip 66 percent.

The Dash weren't the only team to have a tough going. Double-A Huntsville never recovered from a disastrous start marred by rainy weather and Swine Flu fears. Triple-A Scranton/Wilkes-Barre lost 14 openings in 2009, including seven due to drainage problems with the field.

7-for-7

Triple-A Durham outfielder Desmond Jennings' club record performance in early September.

Jennings also became the first player in 10 years to collect seven hits in an International League game. The 22-year-old had six singles and a double, and boosted his overall average from .298 to .347.

"When he got to third base after his sixth hit, he looked up at me and said, 'Wow, I've never had six hits (in a game) before,'" said Durham manager Charlie Montoyo, who was coaching third base. "I looked down at my score book and told him he might get a shot at a seventh hit."

Sure enough, Jennings doubled home a run in his final at-bat.

$4.25 million/0 Innings

Latin American bonus record the Athletics gave Michael Ynoa last summer compared to his performance on the mound this season.

The Athletics' record investment in Dominican righthander Michael Ynoa has created plenty of buzz, but no results. Ynoa, whose signing bonus last year broke the Latin American record by nearly $2 million, debuted at Athletics camp last spring. But the 17-year-old did not throw a single pitch during a game this season and was shut down with elbow soreness in June.

68

The number of players suspended in 2009 (through October) under minor league baseball's drug prevention and treatment program.

The majority of the suspensions have come out of the Rookie-level Dominican Summer League, including Padres shortstop Alvaro Aristy. The 17-year-old who received a $1 million bonus last year was suspended 50 games after testing positive for a metabolite of Nandrolone.

Notable domestic suspensions included Brewers righthander Cody Adams, Astros outfielder Mitch Einerston, and a quartett of Burlington Royals—outfielders Nick Francis and Jarrod Dyson, third baseman Jason Taylor and shortstop Juan Rivera.

However, the suspension in the minors that gathered the most headlines was . . .

100/1

. . . Brewers top pitching prospect Jeremy Jeffress, who was suspended 100 games after his third failed drug test (for marijuana, reportedly) and has only one chance left before he faces a lifetime ban.

Jeffress was suspended for a "drug of abuse" in

June. He had previously been slapped with a 50-game suspension late in the 2007 season and then failed a club-administered test the next fall.

"Given he is a two- or three-time positive tester, it gives you a lot of concern," Brewers assistant general manager Gord Ash said. "Our job is to supply as much support as we can. It's tough to be shocked anymore about anything, but it's certainly surprising."

45

Consecutive games with a hit for high Class A High Desert outfielder Jamie McOwen.

The 23-year-old McOwen, a Mariners farmhand, set a standard that had not been matched in over a half century and along the way broke the California League record of 35 games. He surpassed the most recent streak of 43 games by Brandon Watson in 2007.

McOwen's streak was the longest since Roman Mejias hit in 55 straight games in 1954. Wichita's Joe Wilhoit hit in 69 straight Western League contests in 1919 for the recognized record.

14

High Class A California League players who ranked among the overall minor league leaders in batting average, home runs and RBIs.

Many hitter-friendly parks in the Cal League have long produced skewered offensive statistics, and this year was no exception. There was particularly something in the air at High Desert and Lancaster, where strong winds, thin air and warm temperatures keep baseballs soaring over the fence.

High Desert's Alex Liddi led the minors in average, while teammates Tyson Gillies and James McOwen finished in the top 5 (as did Lancaster's Koby Clemens). Meanwhile, Lancaster's Jonathan Gaston led the minor leagues in home runs (35) and Clemens was tops in RBIs (123).

51

Total runs scored in Lake Elsinore's 33-18 victory over High Desert

Speaking of the California League, High Desert's Mavericks Stadium earned its reputation as one of the most hitter-friendly ballparks in all of minor league baseball in this midseason contest. The game included 57 hits, 10 home runs 18 doubles and six errors. There were no stolen bases, but then again, why bother when the ball is sailing out with such regularity.

Unlike the California League's other extreme hitters park in Lancaster, the ball flies out in

CONTINUED ON PAGE 348

Braves' Heyward stands alone

BY MATT WINKELJOHN

The parallels between players are impossible to miss, yet it doesn't take long for Braves officials to try to distance Jason Heyward from former Braves phenom Jeff Francoeur.

Braves general manager Frank Wren and farm director Kurt Kemp are comfortable with the suggestion that Heyward, 20, is on track to one day be the face of the franchise, or at least join catcher Brian McCann in sharing the role as Chipper Jones' career winds down.

They just don't want to say that Heyward is following in Francoeur's footsteps—even if Francoeur blazed this very path four short years ago—lest there be some insinuation that he might follow that trail all the way off an ugly ledge like the one that resulted in Francoeur's trade to the Mets.

So they speak in a respectful yet hesitant way, mindful that there is only so much they can do to manage perceptions. It's natural for people to wonder if Francoeur left behind a cautionary tale, which the Braves used to create a new template that they're applying to Heyward.

"The answer to that, I would say, is no," Kemp said. "I can't give you an example of something we would do differently."

Heyward did not receive a September callup when rosters expanded, even though he may appear as ready as Francoeur was when he moved up in the middle of 2005. All Francoeur did was finish runner-up in voting for National

Jason Heyward

League rookie of the year in half a season. That was Francoeur's third full professional season, however, while this is Heyward's second.

And unlike Francoeur, who struggled in his first exposure to Double-A in 2004, Heyward has thrived. In fact, he improved after moving up from high Class A Myrtle Beach to Double-A Mississippi, batting .336/.434/.605 with seven home runs there after batting .296/.369/.519 with 10 homers for the Pelicans. He finished with overall .314/.399/.557 averages.

Heyward has lightning-quick bat speed, his defense and arm strength are above-average, he runs well, and at 6-foot-4, 225 pounds he could still grow more. He's been compared to Dave Parker, Willie McCovey, Fred McGriff and . . . you get the drift.

Yet many more players have the skills to make it to the majors than have the gray matter to excel over time once there, to hold the pieces together through the inevitable swoons. On these topics, Wren, Kemp and Mississippi manager Phillip Wellman are happy to opine about Heyward.

"We all know he has outstanding physical ability, but all of the other things along with it—his mental makeup, his approach, his work ethic, those peripheral things that go into his makeup are Jason's and Jason's alone," Kemp said.

PREVIOUS WINNERS

1981: Mike Marshall, 1b, Albuquerque (Dodgers)
1982: Ron Kittle, of, Edmonton (White Sox)
1983: Dwight Gooden, rhp, Lynchburg (Mets)
1984: Mike Bielecki, rhp, Hawaii (Pirates)
1985: Jose Canseco, of, Huntsville/Tacoma (Athletics)
1986: Gregg Jefferies, ss, Columbia/Lynchburg/Jackson (Mets)
1987: Gregg Jefferies, ss, Jackson/Tidewater (Mets)
1988: Tom Gordon, rhp, Appleton/Memphis/Omaha (Royals)
1989: Sandy Alomar, c, Las Vegas (Padres)
1990: Frank Thomas, 1b, Birmingham (White Sox)
1991: Derek Bell, of, Syracuse (Blue Jays)
1992: Tim Salmon, of, Edmonton (Angels)
1993: Manny Ramirez, of, Canton/Charlotte (Indians)
1994: Derek Jeter, ss, Tampa/Albany/Columbus (Yankees)

1995: Andruw Jones, of, Macon (Braves)
1996: Andruw Jones, of, Durham/Greenville/Richmond (Braves)
1997: Paul Konerko, 1b, Albuquerque (Dodgers)
1998: Eric Chavez, 3b, Huntsville/Edmonton (Athletics)
1999: Rick Ankiel, lhp, Arkansas/Memphis (Cardinals)
2000: Jon Rauch, rhp, Winston-Salem/Birmingham (White Sox)
2001: Josh Beckett, rhp, Brevard County/Portland (Marlins)
2002: Rocco Baldelli, of, Bakersfield/Orlando/Durham (Devil Rays)
2003: Joe Mauer, c, Fort Myers/New Britain (Twins)
2004: Jeff Francis, lhp, Tulsa/Colorado Springs (Rockies)
2005: Delmon Young, of, Montgomery/Durham (Devil Rays)
2006: Alex Gordon, 3b, Wichita (Royals)
2007: Jay Bruce, of, Sarasota/Chattanooga/Louisville (Reds)
2008: Matt Wieters, c, Frederick/Bowie (Orioles)

Diversified Young keeps busy

International League president Randy Mobley likes to joke that he never knows where Norfolk Tides president Ken Young is going to call in from on the road.

Young, a man of many hats with a unique perspective and background as a team owner, is the veritable "Where's Waldo" of minor league baseball.

There is Young in the International League, where he led an ownership group that purchased the Tides from the New York Mets in 1992 and has kept the team among the league's annual attendance leaders. Young can be spotted in the Pacific Coast League, too, where he guided the return of baseball to Albuquerque in 2003 and the renovation of a deteriorating ballpark into one of the minors' finest facilities.

Young pops up in the Eastern and Carolina leagues, where he holds ownership stakes and serves as team president for a pair of Orioles affiliates: Double-A Bowie and high Class A Frederick.

Remarkably, Young is equally active behind the scenes, serving as the Joint Triple-A Board of Trustees representative since the circuit folded from three into two leagues after the 1997 season. He is also chairman of the MILB marketing committee and serves on the sport's finance committee as well.

Young's background as founder of Ovations Food Services provides his fellow team owners and league officials a valued perspective into the hospitality aspect of the sport that few, if anyone, can match.

CONTINUED FROM PAGE 346

High Desert more because of temperature than wind. It was a balmy 100 degrees when the game began on a Sunday afternoon, which meant the ball was jumping even if the wind was only blowing at 7 mph. Every member of the Lake Elsinore lineup had at least two hits, and six different Storm batters had four hits or more. It wasn't much different for High Desert batters, as every member of the starting lineup except for Joe Dunigan had two or more hits—Dunigan went 0-for-5, which on this day had to feel like an 0-for-100 streak.

The biggest victim of the game was High Desert's Nathan Adcock. The righthander ranked in the top 10 in the league in ERA heading into the game, but after giving up eight runs in only two-thirds of an inning, Adcock saw his ERA jump by nearly a run to 4.54.

High Desert catcher Jose Yepez took a turn on the mound, faced six hitters and gave up four home runs.

11

First-round picks in 2009 who signed with a team but did not play this season.

The list includes: No. 1 overall pick Stephen Strasburg (Nationals), No. 2 Dustin Ackley (Mariners), No. 3 Donavan Tate (Padres), No. 6 Zack Wheeler (Giants), No. 8 Mike Leake (Reds), No. 9 Jacob Turner (Tigers), No. 11 Tyler Matzek (Rockies), No. 15 Alex White (Indians), No. 18 Chad James (Marlins), No. 20 Chad Jenkins (Blue Jays) and No. 22 Kyle Gibson (Twins).

Each player waited until the Aug. 17 deadline to sign.

90

Games won by each Birmingham, San Jose and Fort Wayne in 2009. No team won that many games last season.

Birmingham, which lost in the first round of the Southern League playoffs, were guided by six of the White Sox's top 10 prospects entering the season, including: Gordon Beckham (who reached the big leagues in June), lefthander Aaron Poreda (who was dealt to the Padres in the Jake Peavy deal), catcher Tyler Flowers, first baseman Brandon Allen and outfielders Jordan Danks and John Shelby III.

San Jose swept High Desert in the California League championship series after rolling through the season that they began with seven of the Giants'

Montoyo has winning touch

No shortage of talented prospects have traveled through the Rays system over the years. Yet one of the organization's brightest rising stars may very well be the man who managed all of those players: Charlie Montoyo.

After all, Montoyo's track record is as tough to beat as the teams he has managed. Montoyo, 45, completed his third season with the Bulls and guided the team to its third straight International League final. After a pair of runner-up finishes, the Bulls swept Scranton/Wilkes-Barre in three games before advancing to the Triple-A Championship, where they knocked off Pacific Coast League winners Memphis.

Montoyo's history of success did not begin with the Bulls. He led Double-A Montgomery to a Southern League title in 2006, and has also skippered winning teams at nearly every level of the organization's farm system since taking over Rookie-level Princeton in 1997.

Montoyo's disarming personality has helped him navigate clubhouses mixed with rising prospects and veterans to championship seasons.

MANAGER OF THE YEAR

PREVIOUS WINNERS

1989: Buck Showalter, Albany (Yankees)
1990: Kevin Kennedy, Albuquerque (Dodgers)
1991: Butch Hobson, Pawtucket (Red Sox)
1992: Grady Little, Greenville (Braves)
1993: Terry Francona, Birmingham (White Sox)
1994: Tim Ireland, El Paso (Brewers)
1995: Marc Bombard, Indianapolis (Reds)
1996: Carlos Tosca, Portland (Marlins)
1997: Gary Jones, Edmonton (Athletics)
1998: Terry Kennedy, Iowa (Cubs)
1999: John Mizerock, Wichita (Royals)
2000: Joel Skinner, Buffalo (Indians)
2001: Jackie Moore, Round Rock (Astros)
2002: John Russell, Edmonton (Twins)
2003: Dave Brundage, San Antonio (Mariners)
2004: Marty Brown, Buffalo (Indians)
2005: Ken Oberkfell, Norfolk (Mets)
2006: Todd Claus, Portland (Red Sox)
2007: Matt Wallbeck, Erie (Tigers)
2008: Rocket Wheeler, Myrtle Beach (Braves)

top 10 prospects. San Jose's Opening Day roster included lefthanders Madison Bumgarner and Scott Barnes, catcher Buster Posey, first baseman Angel Villalona, second baseman Nick Noonan and third baseman Conor Gillaspie.

The TinCaps, playing in a new ballpark, won a minors-best 94 games and swept the Midwest League championship series against Burlington. Outfielder Jaff Decker paced Fort Wayne in his first full season, topping the league with a .442 on-base percentage and finishing among the league leaders with a .299 average. Righthander Simon Castro led the league with 157 strikeouts while reliever Brad Brach topped the circuit with 33 saves.

45

Number of games White Sox third baseman Gordon Beckham spent in the minors before reaching the big leagues in his first full professional season.

Not even a year had passed since Gordon Beckham was busy leading the Georgia Bulldogs on a run to the College World Series finals before he made his debut for the White Sox. Three members of the 2008 draft class beat Beckham to the majors, but none had the same impact as Beckham, the eighth overall pick who helped keep

the White Sox in the AL Central race before a late-season collapse.

University of Arizona teammates Daniel Schlereth and Ryan Perry each reached the big leagues before Beckham in 2008, and Giants third baseman Conor Gillaspie had a cup of coffee in San Francisco at the end of '08 as part of his big league deal. Beckham, however, emerged as an AL rookie of the year candidate with the White Sox, this after batting .330/.381/.528 with four home runs and a minor league-leading 23 doubles in 176 at-bats, mostly with Double-A Birmingham. He went on to bat .270/.347/.460 with 14 home runs and 63 RBIs for the White Sox.

0

Mets full-season affiliates with a winning record during the 2009 season.

But the organization's dismal showing on the field may have been trumped by an embarrassing performance off of it.

New York dismissed vice president of player development Tony Bernazard after a series of his off-field confrontations was revealed by New York Daily News beat writer (and Baseball America correspondent) Adam Rubin. Rubin was later accused at a press conference by Mets GM Omar Minaya

TRIPLE-A

Pos	Player, Team (Organization), League	AVG	OBP	SLG	AB	R	H	2B	3B	HR	RBI	BB	SO	SB	CS
C	Adam Moore, Tacoma (Mariners), PCL	.294	.346	.429	340	41	100	19	0	9	43	26	51	1	1
1B	Jesus Guzman, Fresno (Giants), PCL	.321	.379	.507	452	75	145	26	5	16	71	37	82	0	2
2B	#Eric Young Jr., Colorado Springs (Rockies), PCL	.299	.387	.430	472	118	141	21	10	7	43	56	79	58	14
3B	Andy Marte, Columbus (Indians), IL	.327	.369	.593	300	48	98	24	1	18	66	22	50	3	0
SS	Alcides Escobar, Nashville (Brewers), PCL	.298	.353	.409	430	76	128	24	6	4	34	32	65	42	10
CF	Austin Jackson, Scranton/W-B (Yankees), IL	.300	.354	.405	504	67	151	23	9	4	65	40	123	24	4
OF	*Matt Joyce, Durham (Rays), IL	.273	.373	.482	417	73	114	35	2	16	66	67	98	14	5
OF	Matt LaPorta, Columbus (Indians), IL	.299	.388	.530	338	63	101	23	2	17	60	42	56	1	3
DH	*John Bowker, Fresno (Giants), PCL	.342	.451	.596	366	82	125	22	4	21	83	74	64	10	6

Pos	Pitcher, Team (Organization), League	W	L	ERA	G	GS	SV	IP	H	HR	BB	SO	G/F	WHIP	AVG
SP	Clay Buchholz, Pawtucket (Red Sox), IL	7	2	2.36	17	16	0	99	67	7	30	89	1.40	0.98	.188
SP	Bud Norris, Round Rock (Astros), PCL	4	9	2.63	19	19	0	120	104	6	53	112	1.22	1.31	.237
SP	Chris Tillman, Norfolk (Orioles), IL	8	6	2.70	18	18	0	97	85	5	26	99	0.98	1.15	.232
SP	Carlos Torres, Charlotte (White Sox), IL	10	4	2.39	23	20	1	128	96	4	56	130	1.23	1.19	.207
RP	Luis Valdez, Gwinnett (Braves), IL	5	4	3.28	58	0	27	71	66	4	19	75	1.05	1.19	.237

Player of the Year: Chris Tillman, rhp, Norfolk (Orioles). **Manager of the Year:** Tim Wallach, Albuquerque (Dodgers). **Team of the Year:** Durham (Rays).

DOUBLE-A

Pos	Player, Team (Organization), League	AVG	OBP	SLG	AB	R	H	2B	3B	HR	RBI	BB	SO	SB	CS
C	#Carlos Santana, Akron (Indians), EL	.290	.413	.530	428	91	124	30	2	23	97	90	83	2	2
1B	Chris Carter, Midland (Athletics), TL	.337	.435	.576	490	108	165	41	2	24	101	82	119	13	5
2B	C.J. Retherford, Birmingham (White Sox), SL	.297	.340	.473	478	70	142	46	4	10	76	30	70	3	3
3B	#Josh Bell, Chattanooga/Bowie (LAD/BAL), SL/EL	.295	.376	.516	448	65	132	35	2	20	76	61	98	3	5
SS	Eduardo Nunez, Trenton (Yankees), EL	.322	.349	.433	497	70	160	26	1	9	55	22	63	19	7
CF	Desmond Jennings, Montgomery (Rays), SL	.316	.395	.486	383	69	121	25	8	8	45	48	52	37	5
OF	Todd Frazier, Carolina (Reds), SL	.290	.350	.481	451	59	131	40	2	14	68	42	67	7	8
OF	Michael Taylor, Reading (Phillies), EL	.333	.408	.569	318	59	106	22	4	15	65	35	51	18	4
DH	Tyler Flowers, Birmingham (White Sox), SL	.302	.445	.548	248	54	75	18	2	13	43	57	76	3	0

Pos	Pitcher, Team (Organization), League	W	L	ERA	G	GS	SV	IP	H	HR	BB	SO	G/F	WHIP	AVG
SP	*Madison Bumgarner, Connecticut (Giants), EL	9	1	1.93	20	19	0	107	80	6	30	69	0.85	1.03	.209
SP	Samuel Deduno, Tulsa (Rockies), TL	12	4	2.57	24	24	0	133	94	3	72	123	2.10	1.25	.202
SP	Zach McAllister, Trenton (Yankees), EL	7	5	2.23	22	22	0	121	98	4	33	96	1.07	1.08	.220
SP	*Travis Wood, Carolina (Reds), SL	9	3	1.21	19	19	0	119	78	2	37	103	0.91	0.97	.189
RP	Anthony Slama, New Britain (Twins), EL	4	2	2.48	51	0	25	65	46	5	32	93	0.74	1.19	.201

Player of the Year: Chris Carter, 1b, Midland (Athletics). **Manager of the Year:** Ever Magallanes, Birmingham (White Sox). **Team of the Year:** Akron (Indians).

HIGH CLASS A

Pos	Player, Team (Organization), League	AVG	OBP	SLG	AB	R	H	2B	3B	HR	RBI	BB	SO	SB	CS
C	Buster Posey, San Jose (Giants), CAL	.326	.428	.540	291	63	95	23	0	13	58	45	45	6	0
1B	Brandon Waring, Frederick (Orioles), CAR	.273	.354	.520	473	70	129	35	2	26	90	51	121	5	3
2B	Eric Farris, Brevard County (Brewers), FSL	.298	.341	.385	473	68	141	18	1	7	49	29	46	70	6
3B	Alex Liddi, High Desert (Mariners), CAL	.345	.411	.594	493	97	170	44	5	23	104	53	122	10	6
SS	#Danny Espinosa, Potomac (Nationals), CAR	.264	.375	.460	474	90	125	31	4	18	72	74	129	29	11
CF	*Kirk Nieuwenhuis, St. Lucie (Mets), FSL	.274	.357	.467	482	91	132	35	5	16	71	53	118	16	4
OF	*Jon Gaston, Lancaster (Astros), CAL	.278	.367	.598	518	119	144	31	15	35	100	71	164	14	4
OF	Thomas Neal, San Jose (Giants), CAL	.337	.431	.579	475	102	160	41	4	22	90	65	98	3	0
DH	Koby Clemens, Lancaster (Astros), CAL	.345	.419	.636	423	74	146	45	6	22	121	51	109	4	1

Pos	Pitcher, Team (Organization), League	W	L	ERA	G	GS	SV	IP	H	HR	BB	SO	G/F	WHIP	AVG
SP	Evan Anundsen, Brevard County (Brewers), FSL	10	8	2.69	24	23	0	130	101	2	41	118	1.49	1.09	.216
SP	*Alex Torres, Rancho Cucamonga (Angels), CAL	10	3	2.74	21	19	0	121	93	4	63	124	2.66	1.29	.217
SP	David Bromberg, Fort Myers (Twins), FSL	13	4	2.70	27	26	0	153	125	6	63	148	0.78	1.23	.224
SP	*Craig Clark, San Jose (Giants), CAL	16	2	2.86	26	25	0	148	131	19	36	135	0.89	1.13	.237
RP	Scott Gorgen, Palm Beach (Cardinals), FSL	3	5	2.92	14	13	0	74	50	7	32	73	1.22	1.11	.192

Player of the Year: Thomas Neal, of, San Jose (Giants). **Manager of the Year:** Mike Guerrero, Brevard County (Brewers). **Team of the Year:** San Jose (Giants).

to be out for Bernazard's job—a claim Minaya later retracted.

Among Bernazard's transgressions was a recent clubhouse tirade at Double-A Binghamton in which he took off his shirt and challenged players to a fight.

"If you're developing people by saying, 'Look, I can fire you,' is that really development or is that intimidating people?" former Binghamton pitcher Nick Abel told the Daily News.

The Astros didn't fare much better on the field. For the second consecutive season, the Astros

LOW CLASS A

Pos	Player, Team (Organization), League	AVG	OBP	SLG	AB	R	H	2B	3B	HR	RBI	BB	SO	SB	CS
C	Derek Norris, Hagerstown (Nationals), SAL	.286	.413	.513	437	78	125	30	0	23	84	90	116	6	3
1B	Rebel Ridling, Peoria (Cubs), MWL	.310	.357	.466	536	74	166	34	1	16	97	40	95	2	1
2B	Brett Lawrie, Wisconsin (Brewers), MWL	.274	.348	.454	372	48	102	18	5	13	65	41	70	19	11
3B	James Darnell, Fort Wayne (Padres), MWL	.329	.468	.518	222	40	73	17	2	7	38	57	51	5	5
SS	*Dee Gordon, Great Lakes (Dodgers), MWL	.301	.362	.394	538	96	162	17	12	3	35	43	90	73	25
CF	*Anthony Gose, Lakewood (Phillies), SAL	.259	.323	.353	510	72	132	24	9	2	52	35	110	76	20
OF	*Kyler Burke, Peoria (Cubs), MWL	.303	.405	.505	465	93	141	43	3	15	89	78	99	14	2
OF	*Jaff Decker, Fort Wayne (Padres), MWL	.299	.442	.514	358	78	107	25	2	16	64	85	92	10	6
DH	*Kyle Russell, Great Lakes (Dodgers), MWL	.272	.371	.545	481	90	131	39	7	26	102	72	180	20	2

Pos	Pitcher, Team (Organization), League	W	L	ERA	G	GS	SV	IP	H	HR	BB	SO	G/F	WHIP	AVG
SP	Simon Castro, Fort Wayne (Padres), MWL	10	6	3.33	28	27	0	140	118	9	37	157	0.81	1.10	.226
SP	*Casey Crosby, West Michigan (Tigers), MWL	10	4	2.41	24	24	0	105	70	3	48	117	1.39	1.13	.195
SP	*Rudy Owens, West Virginia (Pirates), SAL	10	1	1.70	19	19	0	101	71	8	15	91	0.71	0.85	.197
SP	*Martin Perez, Hickory (Rangers), SAL	5	5	2.31	22	14	1	94	82	3	33	105	1.58	1.23	.236
RP	Brad Brach, Fort Wayne (Padres), MWL	3	3	1.27	60	0	33	64	36	1	11	82	0.71	0.74	164

Player of the Year: Jaff Decker, of, Fort Wayne (Padres). **Manager of the Year:** Dusty Wathan, Lakewood (Phillies). **Team of the Year:** Fort Wayne (Padres).

SHORT-SEASON

Pos	Player, Team (Organization), League	AVG	OBP	SLG	AB	R	H	2B	3B	HR	RBI	BB	SO	SB	CS
C	Sebastian Valle, Williamsport (Phillies), NYP	.307	.335	.531	192	25	59	15	5	6	40	10	41	0	0
1B	*Ryan Wheeler, Yakima (D'backs), NWL	.363	.461	.538	234	44	85	20	3	5	36	37	28	7	4
2B	*Logan Watkins, Boise (Cubs), NWL	.326	.389	.391	279	48	91	14	2	0	29	27	31	14	7
3B	Edinson Rincon, Eugene (Padres), NWL	.300	.415	.468	267	47	80	18	3	7	47	46	60	5	0
SS	*Hak-Ju Lee, Boise (Cubs), NWL	.330	.399	.420	264	56	87	14	2	2	33	31	50	25	8
CF	Miguel Velazquez, Spokane (Rangers), NWL	.297	.359	.517	209	33	62	12	2	10	40	19	43	9	2
OF	Leandro Castro, Williamsport (Phillies), NYP	.316	.351	.512	256	48	81	19	5	7	43	13	49	18	9
OF	*Neil Medchill, Staten Island (Yankees), NYP	.278	.360	.551	216	42	60	13	2	14	41	24	66	7	2
DH	*Ryan Westmoreland, Lowell (Red Sox), NYP	.296	.401	.484	223	38	66	15	3	7	35	38	49	19	0

Pos	Pitcher, Team (Organization), League	W	L	ERA	G	GS	SV	IP	H	HR	BB	SO	G/F	WHIP	AVG
SP	*Jose Alvarez, Lowell (Red Sox), NYP	8	3	1.52	14	12	0	83	60	4	10	63	0.97	0.84	.203
SP	Alex Colome, Hudson Valley (Rays), NYP	7	4	1.66	15	15	0	76	46	0	32	94	1.57	1.03	.174
SP	*Julio Ramos, Vancouver (Athletics), NWL	6	5	2.38	13	13	0	72	67	4	18	64	1.39	1.18	.248
SP	*Robbie Ross, Spokane (Rangers), NWL	4	4	2.66	15	15	0	74	68	5	17	76	3.21	1.14	.240
RP	Austin Hyatt, Williamsport (Phillies), NYP	3	0	0.66	17	5	6	54	26	1	12	81	0.52	0.70	.141

Player of the Year: Ryan Westmoreland, of, Lowell (Red Sox). **Manager of the Year:** Travis Fryman, Mahoning Valley (Indians). **Team of the Year:** Salem-Keizer (Giants).

ROOKIE

Pos	Player, Team (Organization), League	AVG	OBP	SLG	AB	R	H	2B	3B	HR	RBI	BB	SO	SB	CS
C	Christian Bethancourt, GCL/Danville (Braves), GCL/APP	.277	.342	.446	166	32	46	14	1	4	27	17	38	6	1
1B	Riaan Spanjer-Furstenburg, Danville (Braves), APP	.359	.411	.543	234	36	84	19	0	8	53	16	37	0	3
2B	Jean Segura, Orem (Angels), PIO	.346	.392	.512	162	33	56	10	4	3	21	11	11	11	3
3B	Vinnie Catricala, Pulaski (Mariners), APP	.301	.363	.493	219	33	66	14	2	8	40	18	34	6	1
SS	Jiovanni Mier, Greeneville (Astros), APP	.276	.380	.484	192	32	53	7	6	7	32	30	45	10	5
CF	Mike Trout, AZL Angels (Angels), AZL	.360	.418	.506	164	29	59	7	1	1	25	18	28	13	2
OF	Randal Grichuk, AZL Angels (Angels), AZL	.322	.352	.551	236	47	76	13	10	7	53	9	64	6	4
OF	Rymer Liriano, AZL Padres (Padres), AZL	.350	.398	.523	197	44	69	8	1	8	44	15	52	14	5
DH	Brian Cavazos-Galvez, Ogden (Dodgers), PIO	.322	.353	.618	301	59	97	29	3	18	60	10	43	17	8

Pos	Pitcher, Team (Organization), League	W	L	ERA	G	GS	SV	IP	H	HR	BB	SO	G/F	WHIP	AVG
SP	Chris Balcom-Miller, Casper (Rockies), PIO	4	0	1.58	11	11	0	57	37	3	10	60	2.86	0.82	.181
SP	*Mike Belfiore, Missoula (D'backs), PIO	2	2	2.17	14	11	0	58	59	2	13	55	1.85	1.24	.259
SP	B.J. Hermsen, GCL Twins (Twins), GCL	6	2	1.35	10	10	0	53	32	0	4	42	1.90	0.68	.171
SP	*Chris Masters, Danville (Braves), APP	8	4	1.42	13	11	0	70	53	1	9	85	1.01	0.89	.206
RP	*Santos Rodriguez, Bristol (White Sox), APP	2	0	1.33	19	0	4	27	18	0	17	42	1.06	1.30	.189

Player of the Year: Jiovanni Mier, ss, Greeneville (Astros). **Manager of the Year:** Tom Kotchman, Orem (Angels). **Team of the Year:** Orem (Angels).

MINOR LEAGUES

failed to field a club with a winning record.

No. 1

Our quote of the year, by low Class A Lansing pitching coach Antonio Caceres, on the emergence of righthander Henderson Alavarez.

"Even the other teams are like, 'Who's pitching tonight? Alvarez? We're (screwed),'" Caceres said. "'Henderson Alvarez? We're (screwed) today.' That's how good he is. All of a sudden he throws his changeup 3-2 and they're like 'Where'd that come from?' The hitter ain't got no chance."

CARL KLINE

Desmond Jennings racked up both 50 extra-base hits and 50 stolen bases

KEVIN PATAKY

Giants lefthander Madison Bumgarner posted a 1.85 ERA in 131 innings

FIRST TEAM

Pos	Player, Level (Organization), Age	AVG	OBP	SLG	G	AB	R	H	2B	3B	HR	RBI	BB	SO	SB
C	Buster Posey, HiA/AAA (Giants), 22	.325	.416	.531	115	422	84	137	31	1	18	80	62	68	6
1B	Chris Carter, AA/AAA (Athletics), 22	.329	.422	.570	138	544	115	179	43	2	28	115	85	133	13
2B	Scott Sizemore, AAA/AA (Tigers), 23	.308	.389	.500	130	520	88	160	39	5	17	66	64	95	21
3B	Pedro Alvarez, HiA/AA (Pirates), 22	.288	.378	.535	126	465	80	134	32	1	27	95	71	129	2
SS	Alcides Escobar, AAA (Brewers), 22	.298	.353	.409	109	430	76	128	24	6	4	34	32	65	42
CF	Desmond Jennings, AA/AAA (Rays), 22	.318	.401	.487	132	497	92	158	31	10	11	62	67	67	52
OF	Jaff Decker, LoA (Padres), 19	.299	.442	.514	104	358	78	107	25	2	16	64	85	92	10
OF	Jason Heyward, HiA/AA/AAA (Braves), 20	.323	.408	.555	99	362	69	117	25	4	17	63	51	51	10
DH	Carlos Santana, AA (Indians), 23	.290	.413	.530	130	428	91	124	30	2	23	97	90	83	2

Pos	Pitcher, Level (Organization), Age	W	L	ERA	G	GS	SV	IP	H	HR	BB	SO	G/F	AVG	WHIP
SP	Madison Bumgarner, AA/HiA (Giants), 20	12	2	1.85	25	24	0	131	100	6	34	92	0.82	.211	1.02
SP	Christian Friedrich, HiA/LoA (Rockies), 22	6	5	2.41	22	22	0	120	94	5	43	159	1.01	.215	1.15
SP	Jeremy Hellickson, AAA/AA (Rays), 22	9	2	2.45	20	20	0	114	72	8	29	132	0.77	.178	0.89
SP	Brian Matusz, HiA/AA (Orioles), 22	11	2	1.91	19	19	0	113	87	7	32	121	1.32	.211	1.05
RP	Dan Runzler, LoA/HiA/AA/AAA (Giants), 24	5	1	0.76	47	0	17	59	23	2	24	83	2.32	.116	0.80

SECOND TEAM

Pos	Player, Level (Organization), Age	AVG	OBP	SLG	G	AB	R	H	2B	3B	HR	RBI	BB	SO	SB
C	Derek Norris, LoA (Nationals), 20	.286	.413	.513	126	437	78	125	30	0	23	84	90	116	6
1B	Ike Davis, HiA/AA (Mets), 22	.298	.381	.524	114	429	58	128	31	3	20	71	57	112	0
2B	Brett Lawrie, LoA/AA (Brewers), 19	.274	.340	.436	118	424	54	116	18	6	13	65	41	84	19
3B	James Darnell, LoA/HiA (Padres), 22	.311	.424	.536	126	457	80	142	35	4	20	81	87	89	8
SS	Dee Gordon, LoA (Dodgers), 21	.301	.362	.394	131	538	96	162	17	12	3	35	43	90	73
CF	Chris Heisey, AA/AAA (Reds), 24	.314	.379	.521	134	516	91	162	35	3	22	77	48	77	21
OF	Thomas Neal, HiA (Giants), 22	.337	.431	.579	129	475	102	160	41	4	22	90	65	98	3
OF	Michael Taylor, AA/AAA (Phillies), 23	.320	.395	.549	116	428	74	137	28	5	20	84	48	70	21
DH	Jesus Montero, HiA/AA (Yankees), 19	.337	.389	.562	92	347	45	117	25	1	17	70	28	47	0

Pos	Pitcher, Level (Organization), Age	W	L	ERA	G	GS	SV	IP	H	HR	BB	SO	G/F	AVG	WHIP
SP	Kyle Drabek, AA/HiA (Phillies), 21	12	3	3.19	25	23	0	158	141	9	50	150	1.00	.239	1.21
SP	Dan Hudson, AA/HiA/AAA/LoA (White Sox), 22	14	5	2.32	26	26	0	147	105	5	34	166	0.86	.200	0.94
SP	Martin Perez, LoA/AA (Rangers), 18	6	8	2.90	27	19	1	115	111	5	38	119	1.51	.254	1.30
SP	Travis Wood, AA/AAA (Reds), 22	13	5	1.77	27	27	0	168	121	6	53	135	0.98	.204	1.04
RP	Pat Venditte, HiA/LoA (Yankees), 24	4	2	1.87	49	0	22	67	61	2	11	87	0.90	.239	1.07

Aeros soar to the top in 2009

BY STEPHANIE STORM

Before the 2009 season, there was little reason to predict the Indians' Double-A team was destined for a record-setting run.

Sure, the team had a group of good young arms, some expected up-and-coming bats and even a handful of notable prospects. But boasting a plethora of the Indians' top minor leaguers was nothing new, as many of the Aeros' teams this decade have been solid on paper from the start.

By the time the 2009 Aeros had cruised into the postseason and quickly wrapped up the Eastern League championship—the franchise's third since 2003—it was clear that talent plus chemistry and a strong yet approachable leader in manager Mike Sarbaugh proved to be a recipe for success.

"I know it sounds cliché, but this was a great group of guys to manage," said Sarbaugh, who was named the league's manager of the year. "They cared about each other, they cared about winning and yet they had fun each day along the way."

The Aeros got off to a 28-8 start and never looked back, leading the circuit from start to finish, culminating with a dominating 95-54 record between the regular season and playoffs. Along the way, the team set myriad franchise marks while winning a handful of individual honors.

In the playoffs, Akron needed just three games to dispatch the Reading Phillies in the Southern Division series, then rolled over the Connecticut Defenders three-games-to-one for the league title. Now, the Aeros add one more feather to their cap as Baseball America's Minor League Team of the Year.

"What's interesting about winning here is they have the (Eastern League's) manager of

the year, the pitcher of the year and the top hitter," Indians farm director Ross Atkins said as the team celebrated their title run with champagne in the nearby clubhouse. "They're not just solid professional baseball players, we're talking all major league core prospects who are very young and have a lot of upside."

Depth from the lower levels of the Indians system helped give Akron a needed push in the second of the season. Thus, there's no underestimating the importance that a handful of young players—including three 2008 draftees—made upon being promoted to Akron. This includes 2008 first-round pick Lonnie Chisenhall, who struggled initially in his debut with Akron after a promotion from high Class A Kinston. But the 20-year-old third baseman was a force in the playoffs. Chisenhall led all EL postseason players with a .467 average and .500 on-base percentage in seven games.

RODGER WOOD

Carlos Santana

Among the many accomplishments of the regular season was a perfect game in May thrown by righthander Jeanmar Gomez against Trenton en route to Gomez earning the league's pitcher of the year honors.

Righthander Hector Rondon was equally impressive in his stay with Akron, going 7-5, 2.75 with 73 strikeouts and 16 walks in 72 innings pitched.

There was no more dominant hitter in the Eastern League than league MVP Carlos Santana. The 23-year old switch-hitting catcher batted .290/.413/.530 during the regular season—proving mature beyond his age by drawing 90 walks and striking out just 83 times.

PREVIOUS WINNERS

1994: Wilmington/Carolina (Royals)
1995: Norfolk/International (Mets)
1996: Edmonton/Pacific Coast (Athletics)
1997: West Michigan/Midwest (Tigers)
1998: Mobile/Southern (Padres)

1999: Trenton/Eastern (Red Sox)
2000: Round Rock/Texas (Astros)
2001: Lake Elsinore/California (Padres)
2002: Akron/Eastern (Indians)
2003: Sacramento/Pacific Coast (Athletics)

2004: Lancaster/California (Diamondbacks)
2005: Jacksonville/Southern (Dodgers)
2006: Tucson/Pacific Coast (Diamondbacks)
2007: San Antonio/Texas (Padres)
2008: Frisco/Texas (Rangers)

MINOR LEAGUES

ST. LOUIS

The 11th annual Futures Game weathered its first-ever rain delay, but made up for it with impressive displays of speed on the bases and on radar guns, not to mention a final-inning comeback.

The World team built a four-run rally in the top of the seventh around three doubles and two misplays by U.S. defenders, rallying for a 7-5 victory after squandering an early 3-0 lead. Outfielder Rene Tosoni (Twins) earned the game's MVP award with a go-ahead pinch-hit double against Brad Lincoln (Pirates).

Originally scheduled for nine innings, the game was trimmed to seven after a four-hour, nine-minute rain delay, which immediately followed the World's two-run outburst in the top of the first. The shortened affair meant that Tosoni almost didn't get a chance to play.

"I didn't even think I was getting into the game until we got a couple more (runners) on," Tosoni said. "I got ready, I was standing in the dugout with my bat and my batting gloves on, ready to hit. It's awesome. I don't even have words to explain it."

The World's comeback started against lefty Trevor Reckling (Angels), who surrendered a leadoff double to Brett Lawrie (Brewers). Starlin Castro (Cubs) followed with an infield hit, with Lawrie scoring and Castro taking second on a wild pitch. Pedro Baez (Dodgers) then grounded out and Alcides Escobar (Brewers) followed with a chopper up the middle.

U.S. second baseman Jemile Weeks (Athletics) gloved the ball, but made an errant flip to shortstop Danny Espinosa (Nationals) in an attempt to keep Castro, the tying run, at third base. As the ball rolled away, Castro scored and Escobar took second.

Reckling struck out Tyson Gillies (Mariners) looking on a curveball to preserve the tie, then gave way to Lincoln. Tosoni ripped Lincoln's second pitch, a 94 mph fastball, off the glove of first baseman Chris Carter (Athletics) for the go-ahead run. Dayan Viciedo (White Sox) followed with an RBI double, and Carlos Santana (Indians) walked before Lincoln caught a soft pop-up from K.D. Kang (Rays) to end the inning.

Tosoni was the MVP, but the breakout player of the game was Gillies, like Tosoni, a Canadian who signed out of a U.S. junior college. Gillies beat out a bunt single and stole two bases (including one on an attempted pick-off) before

MINOR LEAGUES

FUTURES GAME BOX SCORE

JULY 13 IN ST. LOUIS
WORLD 7, U.S. 5

WORLD	AB	R	H	BI	U.S.	AB	R	H	BI
Escobar, ss	4	2	2	0	Young, 2b	2	1	1	1
Gillies, rf-cf	3	1	1	0	Weeks, 2b	2	0	0	0
Liddi, 3b-1b	1	1	0	0	Jennings, cf	3	1	0	0
Tosoni, ph-rf	1	1	1	1	Wallace, 3b	0	0	0	0
Canizares, 1b	2	0	1	1	Vitters, 3b	1	0	0	0
Viciedo, 3b	2	0	1	1	Carter, 1b	3	0	0	0
Montero, c	2	0	0	1	Alvarez, dh	2	0	1	1
Santana, c	1	0	0	0	Sizemore, dh	2	1	1	0
Weglarz, lf	2	0	0	0	Heisey, lf	2	0	0	0
Kang, ph-lf	1	0	0	0	Jones, lf	2	1	1	0
Lawrie, dh	3	1	1	0	Flowers, c	2	0	1	0
Flores, 2b	2	0	0	0	Castro, J, c	2	1	1	3
Castro, S, 2b	1	1	1	0	Heyward, rf	2	0	1	0
Durango, cf	2	0	1	0	Stanton, rf	1	0	0	0
Baez, ph-1b	1	0	0	0	Espinosa, ss	3	0	0	0
Totals	**28**	**7**	**9**	**4**	**Totals**	**29**	**5**	**7**	**5**

WORLD	201	000 4—7
U.S.	002	030 0—5

E: Flowers, Weeks. **LOB:** World 5, U.S. 11. **2B:** Lawrie, Tosoni, Viciedo. **HR:** Castro, J.; Young. **GIDP:** Canizares. **SB:** Durango, Gillies 2, Jennings 3. **CS:** Durango (by Duffy/Castro, J.)

NATIONAL	IP	H	R	ER	BB	SO	AMERICAN	IP	H	R	ER	BB	SO
Tazawa	0	0	0	0	0	0	Tillman	1	2	2	2	1	0
Feliz	1	0	0	0	0	0	Drabek	1	0	0	0	0	1
Flande	1	2	0	0	0	2	Matusz	1	1	1	1	1	0
Samuel	⅓	1	2	2	0	1	Latos	1	0	0	0	0	0
Septimo	⅔	1	0	0	0	2	Duffy	⅔	1	0	0	1	0
Chacin	1	0	0	1	2	Parker	⅓	0	0	0	0	0
Perez	1	3	3	3	0	1	Kelly	1	0	0	0	0	2
Lo (W)	1	0	0	0	2	1	Reckling (L)	⅓	3	3	3	0	1
Sulbaran (S)	1	0	0	2	0	0	Lincoln	½	2	1	1	1	0

Umpires: HP: Matt Schaufert. **1B:** Mike Jarboe. **2B:** Chris Ward. **3B:** Shaun Francis.

scoring a run. He also ended the game by snaring Weeks' hard line drive in deep center. e showed his top-of-the-line speed by racing to first base in 3.4 seconds on the bunt.

"He was almost like Jacoby Ellsbury for me, a lefthanded leadoff hitter with the speed to make things happen," a scout with a National League club said. "He's a high-energy guy who just seems like he does everything right. Looking at what he did in High Desert, the way that park is friendly to hitters, I was skeptical. But seeing him here had me pretty excited. I can't think of any major leaguers who could run that time from home to first on a drag bunt."

Besides Gillies, some of the minor leagues' other top burners showed their speed on the bases. Desmond Jennings (Rays) stole three bases while Luis Durango (Padres) swiped one and was nearly thrown out at third base by Jason Castro (Astros) on another attempt.

"Everyone wants to showcase what they can do, and for their team, they had a lot of guys who can run, so they were really running," Castro said.

TRIPLE-A: Indianapolis catcher Eric Kratz (Pirates) hit a go-ahead, two-run home run in the sixth inning and the International League held off a Pacific Coast League ninth-inning rally for a 6-5 win before the third-largest crowd in the event's history at Portland.

Louisville's Drew Stubbs (Reds) added a two-run home run and Bats' teammate Justin Lehr started the game with a perfect first inning. Lehigh Valley righthander Drew Carpenter (Phillies) earned the win after striking out the side in the second inning.

The PCL nearly pulled off a comeback in the ninth after Oklahoma City outfielder Esteban German's (Rangers) home run over the right-field fence cut the IL's lead to one. Fernando Cabrera struck out Eric Young Jr. (Rockies) to end the game.

Drew Stubbs

TEXAS LEAGUE: With the North leading 1-0 in the top of the eighth inning, Northwest Arkansas' Kurt Mertins (Royals) ripped a line drive single to center field to score Nate Sutton (Angels) with the winning run in the 2-1 victory. Northwest Arkansas infielder Corey Smith (Angels), who went 2-for-3 with a double, garnered player of the game honors. San Antonio righthander Mat Latos (Padres) pitched two scoreless innings and struck out three in the contest.

SOUTHERN LEAGUE: Carolina lefthander Travis Wood (Reds), the league's leader in both wins and ERA, pitched a perfect first inning, and nine other pitchers combined to allow just four hits for the North in its 7-0 win. Chattanooga left fielder Andrew Lambo (Dodgers) went 3-for-5, but Lookouts teammate Josh Bell went 2-for-5 with two RBIs to capture the MVP.

EASTERN LEAGUE: Bowie second baseman Miguel Abreu (Orioles) went 2-for-4 and Akron left fielder Nick Weglarz (Indians) scored the game's winning run to lead the South to a 5-3 victory in Trenton. Abreu was named MVP for both his offensive prowess and a diving catch that saved a run. Hometown catcher Jesus Montero (Yankees) went 2-for-2 just two days after playing in the Futures Game.

CALIFORNIA-CAROLINA LEAGUE: Lancaster outfielder Jon Gaston (Astros) led off the 10th inning with a home run to key the California League's 2-1, 10-inning victory over the Carolina League at Lake Elsinore. Gaston, who had struck out in his three previous plate appearances, sent the pitch by Salem lefthander Derrick Loop (Red Sox) to break up what had been a pitchers' duel. A total of 16 pitchers from the two teams combined for 25 strikeouts. Salem righthander Ryne Miller (Red Sox) struck out five over two innings, including three batters in the fifth inning who each watched a called third strike. Visalia lefthander Pat McAnaney (Diamondbacks) earned the victory with a scoreless bottom of the 10th inning.

FLORIDA STATE LEAGUE: Behind a perfect 4-for-4 performance at the plate from Daytona shortstop Starlin Castro (Cubs), the North squad defeated the South 6-4 in Fort Myers. Castro, 19, crushed an inside-the-park home run over the head of center fielder Ben Revere (Twins) and scored the first run in a six-run fourth inning to earn MVP honors. Jupiter righthander Kris Harvey (Marlins) surrendered five runs on three hits to earn the loss. Brevard County's Evan Anundsen (Brevard) started for the North, and allowed one hit in a 17-pitch scoreless inning.

SOUTH ATLANTIC LEAGUE: Just a few hours after blasting 13 home runs to win the home run derby, West Virginia first baseman Calvin Anderson (Pirates) connected on a single to center field that scored the game-winning run, leading the Northern Division to an 8-7 win. Anderson, who went 1-for-3 with two walks, impressed the hometown Charleston, W.Va., fans at Appalachian Power Park all night. But Lake County's Karexon Sanchez (Indians) was named MVP after going 2-for-2 with two RBIs, two walks and a stolen base. Bowling Green's Tim Beckham (Rays), the first overall pick in 2008, also went 3-for-5 with a triple.

MIDWEST LEAGUE: Helped by a three-run home run by West Michigan first baseman Ron Bourquin (Tigers), the East scored four in the fourth inning and went on to win 6-3. Fort Wayne outfielder Sawyer Carroll (Padres) took home the MVP award after going 4-for-4 and scoring a run. Fort Wayne righthander Anthony Bass (Padres) got the win by striking out two batters in the second inning.

(*Full-season teams only)

TEAM

WINS
Fort Wayne (Midwest)	94
San Jose (California)	93
Birmingham (Southern)	92
Akron (Eastern)	89
Sacramento (Pacific Coast)	86

LONGEST WINNING STREAK*
Cedar Rapids (Midwest)	13
Kannapolis (South Atlantic)	12
Wilmington (Carolina)	12
Scranton/WB (International)	11
Birmingham (Southern)	10
Fort Wayne (Midwest)	10
Great Lakes (Midwest)	10
Peoria (Midwest)	10
Visalia (California)	10
West Virginia (South Atlantic)	10

LOSSES
Buffalo (International)	87
Binghamton (Eastern)	86
Columbus (International)	85
Portland (Pacific Coast)	84
Lancaster (California)	84
Lansing (Midwest)	84
Myrtle Beach (Carolina)	84

LONGEST LOSING STREAK*
New Orleans (Pacific Coast)	13
Harrisburg (Eastern)	12
Tennessee (Southern)	12
Dayton (Midwest)	11
Lexington (South Atlantic)	11

BATTING AVERAGE*
High Desert (California)	.298
Las Vegas (Pacific Coast)	.290
Colorado Springs (Pacific Coast)	.289
Midland (Texas)	.288
Reno (Pacific Coast)	.286

RUNS
High Desert (California)	860
Midland (Texas)	811
Reno (Pacific Coast)	807
San Jose (California)	803
Lancaster (California)	782
Las Vegas (Pacific Coast)	782

HOME RUNS
Tacoma (Pacific Coast)	166
High Desert (California)	164
Erie (Eastern)	162
Las Vegas (Pacific Coast)	150
Fresno (Pacific Coast)	150
Sacramento (Pacific Coast)	150

STOLEN BASES
Lakewood (South Atlantic)	210
Brevard County (Florida State)	207
Wilmington (Carolina)	203
DSL Mets (Dominican)	193
Burlington (Midwest)	188

EARNED RUN AVERAGE*
Brevard County (Florida State)	2.75
Wilmington (Carolina)	3.10
Fort Myers (Florida State)	3.18
Jacksonville (Southern)	3.20
Savannah (South Atlantic)	3.23

STRIKEOUTS
Stockton (California)	1268
Fort Wayne (Midwest)	1224
Rome (South Atlantic)	1164
Bakersfield (California)	1155
Lake Elsinore (California)	1151

INDIVIDUAL BATTING

BATTING AVERAGE*
Alex Liddi (High Desert)	.345
John Bowker (Fresno)	.342
Tyson Gillies (High Desert)	.341
Koby Clemens (Corpus Christi, Lancaster)	.341
Jamie McOwen (High Desert)	.340

RUNS
Jon Gaston (Lancaster)	119
Eric Young Jr. (Colorado Springs)	118
Chris Carter (Midland, Sacramento)	115
Terry Evans (Salt Lake)	104
Tyson Gillies (High Desert)	104

HITS
Chris Carter (Midland, Sacramento)	179
Jack Shuck (Lancaster)	175
Brian Dopirak (New Hampshire, Las Vegas)	173
Tyson Gillies (High Desert)	170
Alex Liddi (High Desert)	170
Drew Locke (Corpus Christi)	170

TOP HITTING STREAKS
Jamie McOwen (High Desert)	45
Matt Murton (Colorado Springs)	29
Brady Shoemaker (Bristol)	28
Jesus Guzman (Fresno)	27
Eury Perez (GCL Nationals)	27

MOST HITS (ONE GAME)
Desmond Jennings (Durham)	7
Mike Bianucci (Hickory)	6
Randal Grichuk (AZL Angels)	6
Erik Huber (Lynchburg)	6
Jerry Owens (Tacoma)	6
Lance Zawadzki (San Antonio)	6

TOTAL BASES
Chris Carter (Midland, Sacramento)	310
Jon Gaston (Lancaster)	310
Brian Dopirak (New Hampshire, Las Vegas)	300
Alex Liddi (High Desert)	293
Terry Evans (Salt Lake)	279

EXTRA-BASE HITS
Jon Gaston (Lancaster)	81
Chris Carter (Midland, Sacramento)	73
Koby Clemens (Corpus Christi, Lancaster)	73
Alex Liddi (High Desert)	72
Kyle Russell (Great Lakes)	72

DOUBLES
C.J. Retherford (Birmingham)	46
Jon Weber (Durham)	46
Koby Clemens (Corpus Christi, Lancaster)	45
Todd Frazier (Carolina, Louisville)	45
Jason Van Kooten (Modesto)	45

TRIPLES
Adron Chambers (Palm Beach)	16
Jon Gaston (Lancaster)	15
Peter Bourjos (Arkansas)	14
Tyson Gillies (High Desert)	14
Trent Oeltjen (Reno)	14
Carlos Peguero (High Desert)	14

HOME RUNS
Jon Gaston (Lancaster)	35
Mitch Jones (Albuquerque)	35
Brian Pellegrini (Lancaster, Lexington)	34
Cody Johnson (Myrtle Beach, Mississippi)	32
Grant Desme (Kane County, Stockton)	31
Carlos Peguero (High Desert)	31

RUNS BATTED IN
Koby Clemens (Corpus Christi, Lancaster)	123
Chris Carter (Midland, Sacramento)	115
Roger Kieschnick (San Jose)	110
Drew Locke (Corpus Christi)	109
Brett Pill (Connecticut)	109

MOST RBIS, ONE GAME
Robinson Chirinos (Daytona)	8
Evan Crawford (Salem-Keizer)	8
Brian Dopirak (New Hampshire)	8
Layton Hiller (GCL Braves)	8
Matt McBride (Akron)	8
Chris Richard (Durham)	8

WALKS
Allan Dykstra (Fort Wayne)	104
Logan Forsythe (Lake Elsinore, San Antonio)	102
Ruben Gotay (Reno)	102
Kila Ka'aihue (Omaha)	102
Matt Young (Mississippi, Gwinnett)	97

STRIKEOUTS
Greg Halman (AZL Mariners, West Tenn)	191
Cody Johnson (Myrtle Beach, Mississippi)	180
Kyle Russell (Great Lakes)	180
Brock Kjeldgaard (Wisconsin)	172
Carlos Peguero (High Desert)	172

STOLEN BASES
Anthony Gose (Lakewood)	76
Dee Gordon (Great Lakes)	73
Eric Farris (Brevard County)	70
Darin Mastroianni (Dunedin, New Hampshire)	70
Derrick Robinson (Wilmington)	69

CAUGHT STEALING
Dee Gordon (Great Lakes)	25
Gustavo Nunez (GCL Tigers, West Michigan)	25
Derrick Robinson (Wilmington)	23
Dave Sappelt (Dayton, Sarasota)	22
Alexia Amarista (Cedar Rapids)	20
Anthony Gose (Lakewood)	20
Trayvon Robinson (Inland Empire, Chattanooga)	20

ON BASE PERCENTAGE*
John Bowker (Fresno)	.451
Jaff Decker (Fort Wayne)	.442
Ezequiel Carrera (West Tenn)	.441
Thomas Neal (San Jose)	.431
Tyson Gillies (High Desert)	.430

SLUGGING PERCENTAGE*
Mitch Jones (Albuquerque)	.651
Koby Clemens (Corpus Christi, Lancaster)	.620
Sean Rodriguez (Salt Lake, Durham)	.608
Jon Gaston (Lancaster)	.598
John Bowker (Fresno)	.596

ON BASE PLUS SLUGGING (OPS)*
John Bowker (Fresno)	1.047
Koby Clemens (Corpus Christi, Lancaster)	1.036
Mitch Jones (Albuquerque)	1.015
Thomas Neal (San Jose)	1.010
Alex Liddi (High Desert)	1.005
Sean Rodriguez (Salt Lake, Durham)	1.005

HIT BY PITCH
Aaron Luna (Quad Cities, Palm Beach, Springfield)	24
Colt Sedbrook (Palm Beach, Springfield)	24
Seth Loman (Kannapolis, Winston-Salem)	23
Brent Wyatt (West Michigan)	23
Jonathan Greene (Bakersfield, Frisco)	22
Justin Greene (Kannapolis, Winston-Salem)	22
Matt West (Hickory)	22

SACRIFICE FLIES
Jordy Mercer (Lynchburg)	14
Daniel Ortmeier (Colorado Springs)	12
Chris Carter (Midland, Sacramento)	11
Cyle Hankerd (Mobile)	11
Mike McCoy (Colorado Springs)	11
Beau Mills (Akron)	11
Deibinson Romero (Fort Myers)	11

SACRIFICE BUNTS
Eric Farris (Brevard County)	26
Luis Durango (San Antonio)	19
Alcides Escobar (Nashville)	19
Alexia Amarista (Cedar Rapids)	18
James Beresford (Beloit)	17
Eduardo Escobar (Kannapolis)	17

BATTING AVERAGE*
BY POSITION

CATCHERS
Koby Clemens (Corpus Christi, Lancaster)	.341
Jesus Montero (Tampa, Trenton)	.337
Josh Thole (Binghamton)	.328
Buster Posey (San Jose, Fresno)	.325
Charles Cutler (Quad Cities, Palm Beach)	.322

FIRST BASEMEN
Tommy Everidge (Midland, Sacramento)	.335
Kiel Roling (Asheville)	.331
Mitch Moreland (Bakersfield, Frisco)	.331
Chris Carter (Midland, Sacramento)	.329
Mike Morse (Tacoma, Syracuse)	.322

SECOND BASEMEN
Brock Bond (Connecticut)	.333
Kevin Russo (Scranton/WB)	.326
Alexia Amarista (Cedar Rapids)	.319
Howie Clark (Las Vegas)	.313
Kevin Howard (Portland, San Antonio, Las Vegas)	.312

THIRD BASEMEN
Alex Liddi (High Desert)	.345
Esteban German (Okla. City)	.319
Neil Sellers (Reading)	.317
Chris Shelton (Tacoma)	.314
James Darnell (Fort Wayne, Lake Elsinore)	.311

SHORTSTOPS
Ian Desmond (Harrisburg, Syracuse)	.330
Eduardo Nunez (Trenton)	.322
Gustavo Nunez (West Michigan)	.315
Jeff Bianchi (Wilmington, NW Arkansas)	.308
Mike McCoy (Colorado Springs)	.307

OUTFIELDERS
John Bowker (Fresno)	.342
Tyson Gillies (High Desert)	.341
Jamie McOwen (High Desert)	.340
Drew Locke (Corpus Christi)	.338
Ezequiel Carrera (West Tenn)	.337

DESIGNATED HITTERS
Billy Nowlin (West Michigan)	.311
Michael Aubrey (Columbus, Norfolk)	.290
Mauro Gomez (Bakersfield)	.285
Erik Lis (New Britain)	.283
Andy D'Alessio (Connecticut, Augusta)	.283

INDIVIDUAL PITCHING

EARNED RUN AVERAGE*
Brad Meyers (Potomac, Harrisburg)	1.72
Travis Wood (Carolina, Louisville)	1.77
Madison Bumgarner (San Jose, Connecticut)	1.85
Brian Matusz (Frederick, Bowie)	1.91
Rudy Owens (West Virginia, Lynchburg)	2.10
Brett Lorin (Clinton, West Virginia)	2.20
Steve Hirschfeld (Fort Myers)	2.23
Zach McAllister (Trenton)	2.23
Darin Downs (Charlotte, Montgomery)	2.23
Nelson Figueroa (Buffalo)	2.25

WORST ERA*
Tim Murphy (Bakersfield)	6.80
Sam Runion (Burlington)	6.60
Mitch Atkins (Iowa)	6.58
Mike MacDonald (Salt Lake)	6.37
Cristian Beltre (Visalia)	6.37

WINS
Donnie Hume (High Desert)	17
Craig Clark (San Jose)	16
Erik Davis (Fort Wayne)	16
Jon Michael Redding (Great Lakes)	16
Joe Savery (Reading, Lehigh Valley)	16

LOSSES
Jeremy Horst (Sarasota, Carolina)	17
Kris Johnson (Pawtucket, Portland)	16
Luis Montano (Sarasota, Carolina)	15
Keith Weiser (Tulsa)	15
Charlie Zink (Pawtucket)	15

GAMES
Brandon Gomes (San Antonio)	65

Craig Baker (Modesto)	62
Rob Delaney (New Britain, Rochester)	62
Colt Hynes (Fort Wayne, Lake Elsinore)	62
Anthony Slama (New Britain, Rochester)	62

GAMES STARTED
Tony Barnette (Reno)	29
Fabio Castro (New Hampshire, Las Vegas)	29
Matt Kinney (Fresno)	29
Andrew Liebel (Dunedin, New Hampshire)	29
Jonny Venters (Mississippi, Gwinnett)	29

COMPLETE GAMES
Charlie Haeger (Albuquerque)	4
Drew Naylor (Clearwater)	4
Kyle Nicholson (Augusta, San Jose)	4
Matt Torra (Mobile)	4
Jeff Allison (Jacksonville, Jupiter)	3
Yorman Bazardo (Round Rock)	3
Robert Bono (Lexington)	3
Bruce Chen (Omaha)	3
Nick Hill (West Tenn)	3
Jon Kibler (Erie)	3
Matt Maloney (Louisville, Carolina)	3
Alejandro Pinard (DSL Cardinals)	3

SHUTOUTS
Bruce Chen (Omaha)	3
Jose Alvarez (Salem, Lowell)	2
Jake Arrieta (Bowie, Norfolk)	2
Trevor Bell (Arkansas, Salt Lake)	2
Lisalverto Bonilla (DSL Phillies)	2
Steve Bray (West Tenn)	2
Brandon Hynick (Colorado Springs, Charlotte)	2
Brandon Moore (Brooklyn)	2
Jon Niese (Buffalo)	2
Matt Torra (Mobile)	2
Elih Villanueva (Jupiter, Jacksonville)	2

SAVES
Matt Peterson (Jacksonville)	37
Craig Baker (Modesto)	33
Brad Brach (Fort Wayne)	33
Scott Strickland (Albuquerque)	32
Andrew Johnston (Tulsa)	31

INNINGS PITCHED
Matt Torra (Mobile)	180.0
Polin Trinidad (Corpus Christi, Round Rock)	170.0
Cory Riordan (Modesto)	169.7
Andrew Liebel (Dunedin, New Hampshire)	169.0
Brandon Durden (Modesto, Tulsa)	168.0
Elih Villanueva (Jupiter, Jacksonville)	168.0

WALKS
Charlie Zink (Pawtucket)	93
Kyle Cofield (Mississippi)	89
Jack McGeary (Hagerstown, Vermont)	86
Danny Cortes (NW Arkansas, West Tenn)	85
Alex Torres (Mont., Arkansas, R. Cuca.)	85

STRIKEOUTS
Matt Moore (Bowling Green)	176
Anthony Capra (Kane County, Stockton)	170
Eric Surkamp (Augusta)	169
Jordan Lyles (Lexington)	167
Dexter Carter (Kannapolis, Fort Wayne)	166
Dan Hudson (Charlotte/Birm./W-S/Kann.)	166

HITS ALLOWED
Jonah Nickerson (Erie)	217
Keith Weiser (Tulsa)	195
Evan MacLane (Reno, Memphis)	194
Sam Runion (Burlington)	193
Matt Torra (Mobile)	192

HOME RUNS ALLOWED
Matt Kinney (Fresno)	33
Seth Etherton (Reno)	27
Steve Hammond (Fresno)	27
Mitch Atkins (Iowa)	26
Polin Trinidad (Corpus Christi, Round Rock)	25

STRIKEOUTS PER NINE INNINGS
(STARTERS)*
Matt Moore (Bowling Green)	12.88
Christian Friedrich (Asheville, Modesto)	11.96

Eric Surkamp (Augusta)	11.61
Dexter Carter (Kannapolis, Fort Wayne)	10.75
Mauricio Robles (W. Mich./Lakeland/High Desert)	10.57

STRIKEOUTS PER NINE INNINGS
(RELIEVERS)*
Dan Remenowsky (Kannapolis)	15.49
Craig Kimbrel (Rome/M.B./Miss./Gwinnett)	15.45
Henry Rodriguez (Stockton, Sacramento)	15.16
Drew Taylor (R. Cuca., Cedar Rapids)	14.37
Michael Kohn (Cedar Rapids, R. Cucamonga)	14.12

BATTING AVERAGE AGAINST
(STARTERS)*
Jeremy Hellickson (Montgomery, Durham)	.178
Matt Moore (Bowling Green)	.195
Dan Hudson (Charlotte/Birm./W-S/Kann.)	.200
Carlos Torres (Charlotte)	.200
Samuel Deduno (Tulsa, Colorado Springs)	.204

BATTING AVERAGE AGAINST
(RELIEVERS)*
Dan Runzler (Augusta, San Jose, Connecticut, Fresno)	.116
Winston Abreu (Durham)	.133
Garrett Parcell (Jupiter, Jacksonville)	.136
Luis Lebron (Frederick, Bowie)	.137
Charlis Burdie (Kannapolis, Winston-Salem)	.148

MOST STRIKEOUTS, ONE GAME
Ian Snell (Indianapolis)	17
Homer Bailey (Louisville)	15
Paul Oseguera (San Jose)	15
Mike Tonkin (GCL Twins)	15
Dexter Carter (Kannapolis)	14
Felix Cespedes (DSL Phillies)	14
Terry Doyle (Great Falls)	14
David Hernandez (Norfolk)	14
Corey Kluber (Lake Elsinore)	14
Jason Knapp (Lakewood)	14
P.J. Walters (Memphis)	14

WILD PITCHES
Leandro Cespedes (Lancaster)	28
Andrew Brackman (Charleston)	26
Victor Diaz (AZL Athletics, DSL Athletics)	23
Brad Hand (Greensboro)	22
Mathieu Leblanc Poirier (Stockton, Kane County)	22
Duke Welker (West Virginia)	22

BALKS
Luis Vasquez (Inland Empire, Ogden)	7
Oscar Castro (Dayton, Billings)	6
Manuel Banuelos (Charleston, Tampa)	5
Edwin Escobar (AZL Rangers)	5
Jeurys Familia (Savannah)	5
Juan Gonzalez (DSL Rockies, Casper)	5
Tyree Hayes (Bowling Green)	5
Lachlan Hodge (GCL Mets)	5
Jason Knapp (Lakewood, Lake County)	5
Eduardo Paulino (Wilmington)	5
Hassan Pena (Potomac, Hagerstown, GCL Nationals)	5
Martin Perez (Hickory, Frisco)	5
Luis Sanz (West Michigan, Oneonta)	5

HIT BATTERS
Charlie Zink (Pawtucket)	30
Heitor Correa (Lakewood)	21
Kennil Gomez (Bakersfield)	21
Mathieu Leblanc Poirier (Stockton, K. County)	20
Wynn Pelzer (Lake Elsinore)	18

INDIVIDUAL FIELDING

MOST ERRORS
Jefry Marte (Savannah)	49
Domnit Bolivar (Palm Beach, Quad Cities)	46
Davis Stoneburner (Bakersfield)	43
Tim Beckham (Bowling Green)	43
Junior Lake (Peoria)	42
Leury Garcia (Hickory)	42
Carlos Henry (DSL Cubs2)	42

MINOR LEAGUES

	INTERNATIONAL LEAGUE	PACIFIC COAST LEAGUE	EASTERN LEAGUE	SOUTHERN LEAGUE	TEXAS LEAGUE	CALIFORNIA LEAGUE	CAROLINA LEAGUE	FLORIDA STATE LEAGUE	MIDWEST LEAGUE	SOUTH ATLANTIC LEAGUE
Best Batting Prospect	Austin Jackson, Scranton/Wilkes-Barre	Brett Wallace, Memphis	Michael Taylor, Reading	Jason Heyward, Mississippi	Chris Carter, Midland	Thomas Neal, San Jose	Lonnie Chisenhall, Kinston	Ben Revere, Fort Myers	Josh Vitters, Peoria	Derek Norris, Hagerstown
Best Power Prospect	Nolan Reimold, Norfolk	Kyle Blanks, Portland	Brennan Boesch, Erie	Mike Stanton, Jacksonville	Chris Carter, Midland	Roger Kieschnick, San Jose	Cody Johnson, Myrtle Beach	Mike Stanton, Brevard County	Josh Vitters, Peoria	Derek Norris, Hagerstown
Best Strike-Zone Judgment	Michael Brantley, Columbus	Tommy Everidge, Sacramento	Carlos Santana, Akron	Tyler Flowers, Birmingham	Logan Forsythe, San Antonio	Logan Forsythe, Lake Elsinore	Cord Phelps, Kinston	Darin Mastroianni, Dunedin	Jaff Decker, Fort Wayne	Jordan Pacheco, Asheville
Best Baserunner	Drew Stubbs, Louisville	Eric Young Jr., Colorado Springs	Quintin Berry, Reading	Desmond Jennings, Montgomery	Craig Gentry, Frisco	Traynor Robinson, Inland Empire	Derrick Robinson, Wilmington	Eric Farris, Brevard County	Dee Gordon, Great Lakes	Anthony Gose, Lakewood
Fastest Baserunner	Andrew McCutchen, Indianapolis	Eric Young Jr., Colorado Springs	Jose Constanza, Akron	Desmond Jennings, Montgomery	Luis Durango, San Antonio	Darren Ford, San Jose	Derrick Robinson, Wilmington	Ben Revere, Fort Myers	Dee Gordon, Great Lakes	Anthony Gose, Lakewood
Best Pitching Prospect	Tommy Hanson, Gwinnett	Bud Norris, Round Rock	Brian Matusz, Bowie	Jarrod Parker, Mobile	Jhoulys Chacin, Tulsa	Cory Luebke, Lake Elsinore	Brian Matusz, Frederick	David Bromberg, Fort Myers	Casey Crosby, West Michigan	Jason Knapp, Lakewood
Best Fastball	Daniel Bard, Pawtucket	Neftali Feliz, Oklahoma City	Cody Satterwhite, Erie	Jarrod Parker, Mobile	Mat Latos, San Antonio	Ismael Carmona, Rancho Cucamonga	Craig Kimbrel, Myrtle Beach	Kyle Drabek, Clearwater	Casey Crosby, West Michigan	Jason Knapp, Lakewood
Best Breaking Pitch	Chris Tillman, Norfolk	Bud Norris, Round Rock	Brad Lincoln, Altoona	Jarrod Parker, Mobile	Trevor Reckling, Arkansas	Craig Baker, Modesto	Brian Matusz, Frederick	Chris Carpenter, Daytona	Cody Scarpetta, Wisconsin	Dexter Carter, Kannapolis
Best Changeup	Kris Medlen, Gwinnett	Wade LeBlanc, Portland	Brian Matusz, Bowie	Travis Wood, Carolina	Jhoulys Chacin, Tulsa	Josh Collmenter, Visalia	Danny Duffy, Wilmington	Kyle Drabek, Clearwater	Henderson Alvarez, Lansing	Rudy Owens, West Virginia
Best Control	J.D. Martin, Syracuse	Kevin Pucetas, Fresno	Zach McAllister, Trenton	Travis Wood, Carolina	Esmil Rogers, Tulsa	Cory Luebke, Lake Elsinore	Brad Meyers, Potomac	Kyle Drabek, Clearwater	Brad Tippett, Beloit	Rudy Owens, West Virginia
Best Reliever	Kam Mickolio, Norfolk	Jess Todd, Memphis	Vinnie Pestano, Akron	Matt Peterson, Jacksonville	Bobby Cassevah, Arkansas	Craig Baker, Modesto	Luis Lebron, Frederick	Matt Gorgen, Charlotte	Brad Brach, Fort Wayne	Pat Venditte, Charleston
Best Defensive Catcher	Drew Butera, Rochester	Bobby Wilson, Salt Lake	Jackson Williams, Connecticut	Tyler Flowers, Birmingham	Michael McKendry, Tulsa	Buster Posey, San Jose	Luis Exposito, Salem	Martin Maldonado, Brevard County	Anel de los Santos, Cedar Rapids	Tim Federowicz, Greenville
Best Defensive First Baseman	Michael Aubrey, Norfolk	Justin Smoak, Oklahoma City	Brett Pill, Connecticut	Freddie Freeman, Mississippi	Jeff Kindel, Tulsa	Efren Navarro, Rancho Cucamonga	Freddie Freeman, Myrtle Beach	Ike Davis, St. Lucie	Rebel Ridling, Peoria	Anthony Rizzo, Greenville
Best Defensive Second Baseman	Seth Bynum, Syracuse	Hernan Iribarren, Nashville	Reegie Corona, Trenton	C.J. Retherford, Birmingham	Colt Sedbrook, Springfield	Matt Lawson, Bakersfield	Cord Phelps, Kinston	Eric Farris, Brevard County	Alexia Amarista, Cedar Rapids	Karexon Sanchez, Lake County
Best Defensive Third Baseman	Van Pope, Gwinnett	Ryan Rohlinger, Fresno	Shawn Bowman, Binghamton	Josh Bell, Jacksonville	Jhon Florentino, Corpus Christi	Alex Liddi, High Desert	Brent Morel, Winston-Salem	Matt Dominguez, Jupiter	Jose Duran, Wisconsin	Travis Mattair, Lakewood
Best Defensive Shortstop	Reid Brignac, Durham	Alcides Escobar, Nashville	Cale Iorg, Erie	Pedro Ciriaco, Mobile	Pete Kozma, Springfield	Brian Bocock, San Jose	Danny Espinosa, Potomac	Starlin Castro, Daytona	Miguel Rojas, Dayton	Chase D'Arnaud, West Virginia
Best Infield Arm	Ian Desmond, Syracuse	Alcides Escobar, Nashville	Ian Desmond, Harrisburg	Pedro Ciriaco, Mobile	Lance Zawadzki, San Antonio	Hector Gomez, Modesto	Danny Espinosa, Potomac	Audy Ciriaco, Lakeland	Gustavo Nunez, West Michigan	Leury Garcia, Hickory
Best Defensive Outfielder	Drew Stubbs, Louisville	Yordany Ramirez, Round Rock	Jonathon Tucker, Bowie	Desmond Jennings, Montgomery	Peter Bourjos, Arkansas	Ollie Linton, Visalia	Che-Hsuan Lin, Salem	Dominic Brown, Clearwater	Tyson Auer, Cedar Rapids	Anthony Gose, Lakewood
Best Outfield Arm	Drew Stubbs, Louisville	Yordany Ramirez, Round Rock	Mike McBryde, Connecticut	Gerardo Parra, Mobile	Jarrod Dyson, Northwest Arkansas	Thomas Neal, San Jose	Che-Hsuan Lin, Salem	Moises Sierra, Dunedin	Johermyn Chavez, Lansing	Melky Mesa, Charleston
Most Exciting Player	Andrew McCutchen, Indianapolis	Alcides Escobar, Nashville	Michael Taylor, Reading	Desmond Jennings, Montgomery	Peter Bourjos, Arkansas	Tyson Gillies, High Desert	Jason Heyward, Myrtle Beach	Ben Revere, Fort Myers	Dee Gordon, Great Lakes	Anthony Gose, Lakewood
Best Manager Prospect	Torey Lovullo, Columbus	Tim Wallach, Albuquerque	Mike Sarbaugh, Akron	Brandon Hyde, Jacksonville	Mike Micucci, Frisco	Andy Skeels, San Jose	Joe McEwing, Winston-Salem	Jim Morrison, Charlotte	Doug Dascenzo, Fort Wayne	Dusty Wathan, Lakewood

Honoring excellence

TRIPLE-A: IOWA CUBS

One year after having its season almost washed away—literally—the Iowa Cubs returned to their rightful spot near the top of the Pacific Coast League attendance leaderboard.

The I-Cubs lost eight home dates in 2008 after a rainy and cold spring was replaced with historic flooding in June that left parts of the ballpark underwater and a fanbase in tatters. The Cubs wound up drawing 487,348 fans for the 2008 season, well down from a total of 576,310 in 2007.

"The city was limping along," Iowa general manager Sam Bernabe said. "There was a lot of damage and a lot of people who lost their businesses. They were hurting. That's always problematic for those of us in the business who are trying to sell tickets to the very same people."

Heading into 2009, the Cubs stayed with what they knew worked, and they were rewarded with attendance returning to the levels the team had become accustomed to, as the Cubs finished fourth in the PCL with 536,872 fans attending games in 2009. They were one of the few PCL teams to see its attendance rise in spite of the down economy, and the Cubs had easily the biggest jump of the teams in the league not opening new ballparks.

DOUBLE-A: NEW HAMPSHIRE FISHER CATS

The Fisher Cats have thrived despite being located just 40 miles outside of Boston by somehow penetrating the legion of fans who make up Red Sox Nation. The Fisher Cats entertained a franchise-record 386,991 fans in 2009 and their 5,500 per-game average was good for third in the Eastern League.

Not only does the team put on great shows—they had 20 fireworks nights—but its community involvement rivals some of the best in minors. Since 2006, the Fisher Cats have helped raise over $1.5 million for various charities and they awarded 10 scholarships of $2,500 to college-bound students from New Hampshire, and two more to Massachusetts students.

CLASS A: SAN JOSE GIANTS

The San Jose Giants' run of four consecutive seasons with an attendance record has hardly followed a traditional recipe for success.

Consider this: San Jose does not play in a new ballpark. The Giants affiliate is surrounded by a pair of major league teams competing for sports fans' attention. And they have had to endure annual rumors of being bounced out of town for a new Oakland Athletics ballpark.

Yet the Giants have kept the turnstiles spinning at Municipal Stadium through creative ticket packaging, goodwill in the community, and raising money for ballpark improvements. Among San Jose's 2009 highlights was a 14.8 percent increase in attendance from 2008.

SHORT-SEASON: TRI-CITY VALLEYCATS

If there is no better judge than your peers, then Tri-City has plenty of reasons to be proud.

Tri-City won three of the New York-Penn League's awards voted on by each club in 2009. They were recipients of the Leo Pickney award for promotional excellence in the NYPL. Meanwhile, ticket and merchandise manager Heather LaVine and assistant general manager Vic Christopher were honored by the league.

In fact, the ValleyCats have won an NYPL award in each of the past four years, including two in 2008: vice president/general manager Rick Murphy was named the league's executive of the year while team was named the outstanding club of the year.

The success has shown on at the ballpark, where the team has increased attendance every year for the past six seasons.

PREVIOUS WINNERS

TRIPLE-A	DOUBLE-A	CLASS A	SHORT-SEASON
2000: Edmonton (Pacific Coast)	**2000:** Reading (Eastern)	**2000:** Charleston, S.C. (South Atlantic)	**2000:** Lowell (New York-Penn)
2001: Buffalo (International)	**2001:** Mobile (Southern)	**2001:** Delmarva (South Atlantic)	**2001:** Salem-Keizer (Northwest)
2002: Memphis (Pacific Coast)	**2002:** Chattanooga (Southern)	**2002:** Fort Myers (Florida State)	**2002:** Ogden (Pioneer)
2003: Pawtucket (International)	**2003:** New Britain (Eastern)	**2003:** Modesto (California)	**2003:** Spokane (Northwest)
2004: Sacramento (Pacific Coast)	**2004:** Round Rock (Texas)	**2004:** Dayton (Midwest)	**2004:** Burlington (Appalachian)
2005: Toledo (International)	**2005:** Tulsa (Texas)	**2005:** Lakewood (South Atlantic)	**2005:** Brooklyn (New York-Penn)
2006: Durham (International)	**2006:** Altoona (Eastern)	**2006:** Daytona (Florida State)	**2006:** Aberdeen (New York-Penn)
2007: Albuquerque (Pacific Coast)	**2007:** Frisco (Texas)	**2007:** Lake Elsinore (California)	**2007:** Missoula (Pioneer)
2008: Columbus (International)	**2008:** Birmingham (Southern)	**2008:** Greensboro (South Atlantic)	**2008:** Greenville (Appalachian)

MINOR LEAGUES

MINOR LEAGUES

BY JOSH LEVENTHAL

The industry consensus at the start of the season was that the two best prospects in baseball were Orioles catcher Matt Wieters and Rays lefthander David Price. Both began the year in the International League, with Wieters staying in Norfolk just long enough to lock down the No. 1 spot on our IL Top 20 Prospects list. Price departed Durham too soon to qualify.

Both Gwinnett righthander Tommy Hanson (Braves) and Indianapolis center fielder Andrew McCutchen (Pirates) foreshadowed strong big league debuts by tearing up the IL for the first two months of the season. McCutchen closed out his Indianapolis career with a seven-game hitting streak before earning a promotion to Pittsburgh and ultimately winning BA Rookie of the Year honors. He edged Hanson as the top rookie after the Braves' future ace breezed through Gwinnett, going 3-3, 1.49. He helped keep the big league club in contention until the final weeks of the season.

Durham (Rays) cemented its legacy as the IL team of the decade by winning its third title of the 2000s while making a third straight appearance in the title game. The Bulls went on to knock off Memphis to win the Triple-A Championship in Oklahoma City.

The Bulls were boosted by a steady stream of prospects and a core of talent. Price and righthander Wade Davis proved to be a formidable combination to start the season, while the latter anchored the rotation throughout the year by going 10-8 while ranking seventh in the league in ERA (3.40) and second in strikeouts (140).

Righthander Jeremy Hellickson provided a midseason spark after earning a promotion from Double-A Montgomery, and carried the team through the playoffs after Davis was called

up to Tampa. Hellickson went 6-1, 2.51 with 70 strikeouts and 15 walks in 57 innings with Durham. Center fielder Desmond Jennings had a similar impact at the plate following a late-season promotion from Montgomery. Jennings hit .325/.419/.491 as a Bull, including a team-record 7-for-7 game against Charlotte (White Sox).

Durham's talent was recognized at the end of the season when Davis, Hellickson and shortstop Reid Brignac were ranked among the league's Top 10 Prospects. Jennings and Price did not play long enough with the club to qualify. Norfolk, which posted a 71-71 record and finished 11 games behind Durham in the Southern Division, also boasted three players in the Top 20.

The league had a new look as Columbus debuted a new ballpark, and promptly led the minor leagues in attendance, while the Braves began their tenure in Gwinnett after severing a 42-year relationship in Richmond after the 2008 season.

TOP 20 PROSPECTS

1. Matt Wieters, c, Norfolk (Orioles)
2. Tommy Hanson, rhp, Gwinnett (Braves)
3. Andrew McCutchen, of, Indianapolis (Pirates)
4. Chris Tillman, rhp, Norfolk (Orioles)
5. Wade Davis, rhp, Durham (Rays)
6. Jeremy Hellickson, rhp, Durham (Rays)
7. Austin Jackson, of, Scranton/Wilkes-Barre (Yankees)
8. Matt LaPorta, of/1b, Columbus (Indians)
9. Hector Rondon, rhp, Columbus (Indians)
10. Reid Brignac, ss, Durham (Rays)
11. Jake Arrieta, rhp, Norfolk (Orioles)
12. Fernando Martinez, of, Buffalo (Mets)
13. Jose Tabata, of, Indianapolis (Pirates)
14. Drew Stubbs, of, Louisville (Reds)
15. Michael Brantley, of, Columbus (Indians)
16. Jon Niese, lhp, Buffalo (Mets)
17. Carlos Carrasco, rhp, Lehigh Valley (Phillies)/Columbus (Indians)
18. Ross Detwiler, lhp, Syracuse (Nationals)
19. Ian Desmond, ss, Syracuse (Nationals)
20. Chris Heisey, of, Louisville (Reds)

STANDINGS

North	W	L	PCT	GB	Manager	Attendance	Average	Last Penn.
Scranton/Wilkes-Barre Yankees (Yankees)	81	60	.574	—	Dave Miley	358,888	6,188	2008
Syracuse Chiefs (Nationals)	76	68	.528	6½	Tim Foli	392,518	6,039	1976
Lehigh Valley IronPigs (Phillies)	71	73	.493	11½	Dave Huppert	641,335	9,162	1995
Rochester Red Wings (Twins)	70	74	.486	12½	Stan Cliburn	461,946	6,599	1997
Pawtucket Red Sox (Red Sox)	61	82	.427	21	Ron Johnson	625,561	8,937	1984
Buffalo Bisons (Mets)	56	87	.392	26	Ken Oberkfell	529,789	8,027	2004
South	**W**	**L**	**PCT**	**GB**	**Manager**	**Attendance**	**Average**	**Last Penn.**
Durham Bulls (Rays)	83	61	.576	—	Charlie Montoyo	488,385	6,783	2009
Gwinnett Braves (Braves)	81	63	.563	2	Dave Brundage	423,556	5,966	2007
Norfolk Tides (Orioles)	71	71	.500	11	Gary Allenson	387,153	5,956	1985
Charlotte Knights (White Sox)	67	76	.469	15½	Chris Chambliss	320,427	4,513	1999
West	**W**	**L**	**PCT**	**GB**	**Manager**	**Attendance**	**Average**	**Last Penn.**
Louisville Bats (Reds)	84	58	.592	—	Rick Sweet	612,525	8,750	2001
Toledo Mud Hens (Tigers)	73	70	.510	11½	Larry Parrish	559,037	7,986	2006
Indianapolis Indians (Pirates)	70	73	.490	14½	Frank Kremblas	549,552	8,202	2000
Columbus Clippers (Indians)	57	85	.401	27	Torey Lovullo	666,797	9,526	1996

PLAYOFFS—Semifinals: Scranton/Wilkes-Barre defeated Gwinnett 3-1 and Durham defeated Louisville 3-2 in best-of-five series. **Finals:** Durham defeated Scranton/Wilkes-Barre 3-0 in best-of-five series.

CLUB BATTING

	AVG	G	AB	R	H	2B	3B	HR	RBI	BB	SO	SB	CS	OBP	SLG
Columbus	.275	142	4792	646	1318	295	18	108	597	410	770	111	45	.335	.412
Norfolk	.272	142	4715	603	1283	259	30	78	563	386	814	132	44	.330	.389
Rochester	.266	144	4892	644	1301	259	40	110	596	414	901	98	59	.325	.403
Toledo	.265	143	4874	638	1291	275	36	135	600	489	1197	142	42	.337	.419
Durham	.264	144	4990	683	1315	295	22	137	644	539	1096	118	52	.340	.414
Charlotte	.263	143	4773	583	1256	264	18	116	540	414	983	91	48	.325	.399
Louisville	.263	142	4810	649	1267	271	39	129	607	390	976	132	34	.322	.416
Syracuse	.263	144	4693	601	1236	240	27	113	566	390	1019	144	66	.326	.398
Gwinnett	.262	144	4779	664	1251	260	28	86	615	539	965	131	47	.342	.382
Lehigh Valley	.262	144	4826	623	1265	274	24	91	590	430	942	97	26	.327	.385
Scranton/WB	.261	141	4603	654	1203	247	26	114	616	490	977	76	22	.337	.401
Indianapolis	.260	143	4776	627	1240	261	28	119	580	411	991	98	45	.323	.401
Buffalo	.255	143	4734	502	1207	239	20	80	454	335	785	49	24	.307	.365
Pawtucket	.234	143	4691	486	1099	216	13	87	465	508	926	57	28	.311	.342

CLUB PITCHING

	ERA	G	CG	SHO	SV	IP	H	R	ER	HR	BB	SO	AVG
Scranton/WB	3.32	141	4	16	36	1205	1124	507	445	109	405	950	.247
Louisville	3.46	142	6	15	52	1259	1223	555	484	107	396	1009	.255
Gwinnett	3.66	144	1	7	49	1270	1195	598	516	110	471	1030	.248
Durham	3.75	144	0	8	43	1310	1226	616	545	107	522	1050	.248
Lehigh Valley	3.80	144	5	10	38	1252	1258	600	529	106	450	894	.265
Indianapolis	3.81	143	4	8	37	1246	1263	605	528	79	419	970	.265
Norfolk	3.87	142	1	9	40	1225	1221	607	527	113	412	998	.260
Toledo	3.93	143	6	7	42	1256	1278	613	549	109	409	883	.266
Pawtucket	3.95	143	3	10	37	1257	1188	611	552	109	533	863	.252
Syracuse	4.02	144	2	12	43	1243	1320	620	555	98	398	894	.275
Buffalo	4.04	143	9	10	29	1229	1240	606	551	108	422	932	.263
Charlotte	4.19	143	4	13	27	1229	1255	649	573	111	469	998	.264
Rochester	4.27	144	7	7	29	1266	1334	685	601	99	449	948	.271
Columbus	4.70	142	4	2	34	1229	1407	731	642	138	390	923	.287

CLUB FIELDING

	PCT	PO	A	E	DP		PCT	PO	A	E	DP
Lehigh Valley	.983	3757	1480	92	415	Indianapolis	.977	3739	1390	120	374
Pawtucket	.980	3770	1409	108	378	Toledo	.977	3768	1458	121	371
Scranton/WB	.980	3616	1399	102	353	Columbus	.976	3686	1345	123	350
Buffalo	.978	3686	1417	115	363	Louisville	.976	3777	1388	127	318
Durham	.978	3929	1359	121	321	Gwinnett	.975	3810	1392	132	337
Syracuse	.978	3728	1519	117	434	Rochester	.975	3799	1433	135	364
Charlotte	.977	3688	1499	122	373	Norfolk	.974	3674	1366	134	396

INDIVIDUAL BATTING LEADERS (Minimum 3.1 PA/team game)

	AVG	G	AB	R	H	2B	3B	HR	RBI	BB	SO	SB
Brown, Jordan, Columbus	.336	111	417	65	140	35	1	5	67	30	64	2
Kelly, Don, Toledo	.331	105	372	57	123	20	6	6	40	43	51	27
Russo, Kevin, Scranton/WB	.326	90	353	51	115	18	2	5	31	42	55	13
Fiorentino, Jeff, Norfolk	.312	102	365	70	114	26	5	12	67	48	62	13
Feliciano, Jesus, Buffalo	.311	130	495	57	154	30	1	1	42	25	44	13
Frazier, Jeff, Toledo	.308	105	399	52	123	24	1	11	54	20	49	1
Myrow, Brian, Charlotte/Indianapolis	.307	110	365	60	112	22	1	15	59	65	70	3
Cervenak, Mike, Lehigh Valley	.305	119	462	67	141	36	2	9	77	28	46	1
Weber, Jon, Durham	.302	117	451	63	136	46	0	14	69	56	98	3
Turner, Justin, Norfolk	.300	108	387	54	116	28	0	2	43	34	37	9

INDIVIDUAL PITCHING LEADERS (Minimum 1 IP/team game)

	W	L	ERA	G	GS	CG	SV	IP	H	R	BB	SO
Torres, Carlos, Charlotte	10	4	2.39	23	20	2	1	128	96	38	56	130
Maloney, Matt, Louisville	9	9	3.08	22	22	3	0	143	143	56	24	125
Bowden, Michael, Pawtucket	4	6	3.13	24	24	0	0	126	106	47	47	88
Kendrick, Kyle, Lehigh Valley	9	7	3.34	24	24	1	0	143	133	59	35	62
Carpenter, Drew, Lehigh Valley	11	6	3.35	25	24	0	0	156	162	67	47	120
Davis, Wade, Durham	10	8	3.40	28	28	0	0	159	139	71	60	140
McCutchen, Daniel, Indianapolis	13	6	3.47	24	24	0	0	143	145	63	29	110
Lambert, Chris, Toledo/Norfolk	6	7	3.55	21	21	1	0	127	121	54	31	106
Estrada, Marco, Syracuse	9	5	3.63	27	25	0	0	136	133	61	33	98
Mulvey, Kevin, Rochester	5	8	3.93	24	24	2	0	149	153	84	54	113

ALL-STAR TEAM

C— Erik Kratz, Indianapolis. **1B**— Andy Tracy, Lehigh Valley. **2B**— Kevin Russo, Scranton/Wilkes-Barre. **3B**— Andy Marte, Columbus. **SS**— Brent Dlugach, Toledo. **OF**— Jordan Brown, Columbus; Shelley Duncan, Scranton/Wilkes-Barre; Jon Weber, Durham. **DH**— Barbaro Canizares, Gwinnett. **UTIL**— Don Kelly, Toledo. **SP**— Carlos Torres, Charlotte. **RP**— Luis Valdez, Gwinnett. **Most Valuable Player:** Shelley Duncan, Scranton/Wilkes-Barre. **Most Valuable Pitcher:** Justin Lehr, Louisville. **Rookie of the Year:** Austin Jackson, Scranton/Wilkes-Barre. **Manager of the Year:** Rick Sweet, Louisville.

DEPARTMENT LEADERS

BATTING

OBP	Myrow, Brian, Charlotte, Indianapolis	.419
SLG	Barker, Kevin, Louisville	.551
OPS	Barker, Kevin, Louisville	.927
R	Duncan, Shelley, Scranton/WB	85
H	Feliciano, Jesus, Buffalo	154
TB	Duncan, Shelley, Scranton/WB	247
	Restovich, Michael, Charlotte	247
XBH	Duncan, Shelley, Scranton/WB	61
2B	Weber, Jon, Durham	46
3B	Jackson, Austin, Scranton/WB	9
HR	Duncan, Shelley, Scranton/WB	30
RBI	Duncan, Shelley, Scranton/WB	99
SAC	Olmedo, Ray, Durham	12
BB	Tracy, Andy, Lehigh Valley	74
HBP	Timmons, Wes, Gwinnett	15
SO	Hessman, Mike, Toledo	171
SB	Brantley, Michael, Columbus	46
	Stubbs, Drew, Louisville	46
CS	Negron, Miguel, Charlotte	13
AB/SO	Hopper, Norris, Louisville, Charlotte, Syracuse	16.36

PITCHING

G	Valdez, Luis, Gwinnett	58
GS	Davis, Wade, Durham	28
GF	Valdez, Luis, Gwinnett	51
SV	Valdez, Luis, Gwinnett	27
W	Three tied at	13
L	Zink, Charlie, Pawtucket	15
IP	Davis, Wade, Durham	159
H	Jones, Jason, Rochester	172
R	Jones, Jason, Rochester	93
ER	Jones, Jason, Rochester	86
HB	Zink, Charlie, Pawtucket	30
BB	Zink, Charlie, Pawtucket	93
SO	Carrasco, Carlos, Lehigh Valley, Columbus	148
SO/9 (SP)	Torres, Carlos, Charlotte	9.16
SO/9 (RP)	Abreu, Winston, Durham	13.59
BB/9	Maloney, Matt, Louisville	1.51
WP	Broadway, Lance, Charlotte, Buffalo	11
BK	Ramirez, Ramon, Louisville	3
HR	Igawa, Kei, Scranton/WB	21
	Redmond, Todd, Gwinnett	21
AVG	Torres, Carlos, Charlotte	.207

FIELDING

C	FPCT	Sammons, Clint, Gwinnett	.995
	PO	Jaso, John, Durham	660
	A	Butera, Drew, Rochester	68
	E	Jaso, John, Durham	9
	DP	Stewart, Chris, Scranton/WB	9
	PB	Butera, Drew, Rochester	14
		Cancel, Robinson, Buffalo	14
1B	FPCT	Tracy, Andy, Lehigh Valley	.992
	PO	Miranda, Juan, Scranton/WB	971
	A	Miranda, Juan, Scranton/WB	80
	E	Richard, Chris, Durham	11
	DP	Miranda, Juan, Scranton/WB	98
2B	FPCT	Denker, Travis, Pawtucket	.981
	PO	Bynum, Seth, Syracuse	210
	A	Bynum, Seth, Syracuse	335
	E	Bynum, Seth, Syracuse	15
	DP	Bynum, Seth, Syracuse	98
3B	FPCT	Hessman, Mike, Toledo	.968
	PO	Chavez, Angel, Pawtucket	116
	A	Chavez, Angel, Pawtucket	240
	E	Castillo, Javier, Charlotte, Buffalo	23
	DP	Marte, Andy, Columbus	24
SS	FPCT	Dlugach, Brent, Toledo	.955
	PO	Plouffe, Trevor, Rochester	186
	A	Dlugach, Brent, Toledo	361
	E	Plouffe, Trevor, Rochester	26
	DP	Plouffe, Trevor, Rochester	84
OF	FPCT	Ellison, Jason, Lehigh Valley	.997
	PO	Pridie, Jason, Rochester	336
	A	Thompson, Rich, Lehigh Valley	13
		Winfree, David, Rochester	13
	E	Ramirez, Wilkin, Toledo	11
	DP	Four tied at	4

MINOR LEAGUES

BY JIM SHONERD

The Sacramento River Cats might have been the closest thing minor league baseball had to a dynasty, having won the last two Pacific Coast League titles, and four of the last six. But every dynasty's run ends eventually, as the River Cats' did at the hands of the Memphis Redbirds.

It might have taken a perfect team to deny Sacramento its third straight league title, and that's what the Redbirds were in the 2009 playoffs. Memphis went 6-0 in the postseason to win its first championship since 2000. A dominating pitching staff propelled the Redbirds' streak, which should have come as no surprise considering Memphis' hurlers had the PCL's best team ERA (4.05) during the regular season. The team won a division title despite an offense that ranked just 11th in both average and runs. In the playoffs, the Redbirds staff was led by veteran lefthander Evan MacLane, who won the clinching games in both of Memphis' playoff series, pitching 15 scoreless innings in the process. The Redbirds' rotation was also bolstered by the return of lefthander Jaime Garcia from Tommy John surgery. Garcia joined Memphis in August and allowed only one run over 12 innings in two playoff starts.

The Redbirds met Sacramento in the PCL finals and limited the River Cats, who had scored 34 runs over three games in their semifinal series against Tacoma, to just two runs in three games.

It was fitting that these two teams met in the final as they were connected by one of the season's biggest trades, with third baseman Brett Wallace and righthander Clay Mortensen going

TOP 20 PROSPECTS

1. Buster Posey, c, Fresno (Giants)
2. Neftali Feliz, rhp, Oklahoma City (Rangers)
3. Travis Snider, of, Las Vegas (Blue Jays)
4. Michael Saunders, of, Tacoma (Mariners)
5. Cameron Maybin, of, New Orleans (Marlins)
6. Alcides Escobar, ss, Nashville (Brewers)
7. Brett Wallace, 3b/1b, Memphis (Cardinals)/Sacramento (Athletics)
8. Kyle Blanks, 1b/of, Portland (Padres)
9. Justin Smoak, 1b, Oklahoma City (Rangers)
10. Vin Mazzaro, rhp, Sacramento (Athletics)
11. Bud Norris, rhp, Round Rock (Astros)
12. Esmil Rogers, rhp, Colorado Springs (Rockies)
13. Mat Gamel, 3b, Nashville (Brewers)
14. Brandon Allen, 1b, Reno (Diamondbacks)
15. Gio Gonzalez, lhp, Sacramento (Athletics)
16. Jeff Samardzija, rhp, Iowa (Cubs)
17. Adam Moore, c, Tacoma (Mariners)
18. Angel Salome, c, Nashville (Brewers)
19. Adrian Cardenas, 2b, Sacramento (Athletics)
20. Gaby Sanchez, 1b/3b, New Orleans (Marlins)

from Memphis to Sacramento when the Athletics shipped Matt Holliday to St. Louis.

Memphis outfielder Allen Craig enjoyed the hottest second half of the season of any PCL hitter, slugging 18 home runs after the all-star break in July to finish with a season total of 26. But he was a distant third to league home run champ Mitch Jones from Albuquerque, the minor league veteran who finished the year with 35 long balls.

Righthander Bud Norris captured the league's ERA title and its pitcher of the year award despite winning only four of his 19 starts while toiling for last place Round Rock. Fresno outfielder John Bowker won the league batting title with a .342 average, while Las Vegas first baseman Randy Ruiz captured MVP honors after batting .320 and leading the league in RBIs (106) and doubles (43).

STANDINGS

AMERICAN CONFERENCE

North	W	L	PCT	GB	Manager	Attendance	Average	Last Penn.
Memphis Redbirds (Cardinals)	77	67	.535	—	Chris Maloney	474,764	6,982	2009
Nashville Sounds (Brewers)	75	69	.521	2	Don Money	305,434	4,492	2005
Iowa Cubs (Cubs)	72	72	.500	5	Bobby Dickerson	536,872	7,895	Never
Omaha Royals (Royals)	64	80	.444	13	Mike Jirschele	371,046	5,457	Never

South	W	L	PCT	GB	Manager	Attendance	Average	Last Penn.
Albuquerque Isotopes (Dodgers)	80	64	.556	—	Tim Wallach	602,129	8,363	1994
Oklahoma City RedHawks (Rangers)	69	75	.479	11	Bobby Jones	397,219	5,675	1965
New Orleans Zephyrs (Marlins)	63	80	.441	16 ½	Edwin Rodriguez	362,771	5,258	2001
Round Rock Express (Astros)	63	81	.438	17	Marc Bombard	626,899	8,707	Never

PACIFIC CONFERENCE

North	W	L	PCT	GB	Manager	Attendance	Average	Last Penn.
Tacoma Rainiers (Mariners)	74	70	.514	—	Daren Brown	352,450	4,964	2001
Colorado Springs Sky Sox (Rockies)	73	69	.514	—	Stu Cole	300,185	4,351	1995
Salt Lake Bees (Angels)	72	71	.503	1 ½	Bobby Mitchell	492,321	7,240	1979
Portland Beavers (Padres)	60	84	.417	14	Randy Ready/Gary Jones	369,580	5,280	1983

South	W	L	PCT	GB	Manager	Attendance	Average	Last Penn.
Sacramento River Cats (Athletics)	86	57	.601	—	Tony DeFrancesco	657,095	9,126	2008
Reno Aces (Diamondbacks)	79	64	.552	7	Brett Butler	466,606	6,481	2006
Fresno Grizzlies (Giants)	71	73	.493	15 ½	Dan Rohn	480,627	6,675	Never
Las Vegas 51s (Blue Jays)	71	73	.493	15 ½	Mike Basso	337,388	4,752	1988

PLAYOFFS—Semifinals: Memphis defeated Albuquerque 3-0 and Sacramento defeated Tacoma 3-1 in best-of-five series; **Finals:** Memphis defeated Sacramento 3-0 in best-of-five series.

CLUB BATTING

	AVG	G	AB	R	H	2B	3B	HR	RBI	BB	SO	SB	CS	OBP	SLG
Las Vegas	.290	144	5075	782	1474	340	27	150	745	479	807	50	23	.354	.457
Colorado Springs	.289	142	4872	778	1407	257	56	87	710	520	824	169	45	.360	.418
Reno	.286	143	4891	807	1400	311	59	111	768	590	845	145	58	.365	.442
Albuquerque	.283	144	4894	774	1387	283	47	143	735	483	868	100	42	.350	.448
Tacoma	.280	144	5007	778	1403	290	30	146	728	516	1039	65	35	.351	.450
Fresno	.275	144	5025	755	1383	280	40	150	716	427	939	88	48	.337	.436
Sacramento	.273	143	5013	753	1368	294	38	150	705	509	1002	128	37	.342	.436
Salt Lake	.273	143	4844	752	1321	271	41	139	700	470	998	123	47	.342	.432
Iowa	.271	144	4812	658	1305	279	44	86	603	446	834	125	50	.337	.401
Nashville	.271	144	4786	671	1295	252	43	117	628	457	1097	144	43	.338	.415
Memphis	.268	144	4809	649	1288	226	23	134	601	415	981	103	23	.332	.408
Omaha	.262	144	4828	645	1267	252	24	132	615	492	868	79	34	.333	.407
New Orleans	.261	143	4857	648	1267	244	27	124	607	487	1081	94	34	.333	.399
Okla. City	.258	144	4851	613	1251	206	40	77	564	545	1054	137	31	.337	.364
Round Rock	.255	144	4910	559	1254	246	32	97	515	357	1086	111	31	.310	.378
Portland	.251	144	4801	590	1203	251	22	124	560	516	990	60	32	.328	.390

CLUB PITCHING

	ERA	G	CG	SHO	SV	IP	H	R	ER	HR	BB	SO	AVG
Memphis	4.05	144	4	6	41	1256	1264	641	565	125	453	1036	.261
Iowa	4.14	144	2	10	34	1250	1232	631	575	123	469	1043	.258
Nashville	4.25	144	6	6	41	1252	1305	669	592	112	462	882	.270
Round Rock	4.27	144	3	10	40	1274	1313	664	604	114	496	918	.270
Omaha	4.29	144	6	17	25	1260	1296	652	601	104	430	1013	.270
Sacramento	4.30	143	1	5	42	1297	1280	686	620	116	567	1038	.259
New Orleans	4.34	143	4	7	27	1262	1354	690	609	124	475	908	.275
Okla. City	4.35	144	6	8	27	1265	1360	684	611	91	446	915	.276
Albuquerque	4.36	144	8	8	46	1268	1274	677	614	133	497	1076	.263
Portland	4.58	144	3	5	35	1256	1304	691	639	125	503	907	.270
Las Vegas	4.65	144	4	11	33	1274	1365	764	658	105	483	994	.274
Fresno	4.67	144	4	6	32	1283	1370	735	666	150	454	994	.273
Colorado Springs	4.73	142	2	9	35	1244	1375	729	654	137	495	890	.283
Tacoma	4.82	144	3	6	42	1272	1392	762	681	141	495	915	.278
Reno	5.07	143	1	10	41	1264	1412	760	712	133	462	960	.285
Salt Lake	5.12	143	4	8	35	1248	1377	777	710	154	522	824	.283

CLUB FIELDING

	PCT	PO	A	E	DP		PCT	PO	A	E	DP
Omaha	.981	3779	1628	107	445	Memphis	.978	3768	1430	115	372
Okla. City	.980	3793	1432	108	376	Nashville	.978	3757	1527	118	332
Sacramento	.980	3890	1447	109	393	Reno	.978	3791	1517	117	394
Albuquerque	.979	3805	1424	110	328	Round Rock	.978	3823	1443	119	351
Iowa	.979	3749	1400	109	322	Tacoma	.977	3816	1357	124	346
Portland	.979	3768	1438	114	376	New Orleans	.976	3787	1491	130	343
Salt Lake	.979	3743	1535	112	443	Fresno	.975	3849	1412	133	341
Colorado Springs	.978	3732	1490	118	375	Las Vegas	.973	3821	1468	147	314

INDIVIDUAL BATTING LEADERS (MINIMUM 3.1 PA/TEAM GAME)

	AVG	G	AB	R	H	2B	3B	HR	RBI	BB	SO	SB
Bowker, John, Fresno	.342	104	366	82	125	22	4	21	83	74	64	10
Murton, Matt, Colorado Springs	.324	97	373	72	121	27	1	12	79	39	52	12
Owens, Jerry, Tacoma	.323	100	390	74	126	10	9	3	37	44	48	23
Craig, Allen, Memphis	.322	126	472	78	152	26	1	26	83	37	95	3
Guzman, Jesus, Fresno	.321	115	452	75	145	26	5	16	71	37	82	0
Pettit, Chris, Salt Lake	.321	96	371	70	119	30	3	8	58	31	62	18
Ruiz, Randy, Las Vegas	.320	114	462	81	148	43	2	25	106	47	99	0
Miller, Matt, Colorado Springs	.319	133	523	83	167	39	8	9	98	51	78	4
German, Esteban, Okla. City	.319	105	389	63	124	15	5	4	59	65	63	35
Bourgeois, Jason, Nashville	.316	105	424	61	134	18	6	2	41	22	40	36

INDIVIDUAL PITCHING LEADERS (MINIMUM 1 IP/TEAM GAME)

	W	L	ERA	G	GS	CG	SV	IP	H	R	BB	SO
Norris, Bud, Round Rock	4	9	2.63	19	19	0	0	120	104	42	53	112
Ortiz, Ramon, Fresno	5	6	3.05	35	16	2	0	130	124	53	34	114
Bazardo, Yorman, Round Rock	9	6	3.20	23	20	3	0	135	121	51	32	80
DiNardo, Lenny, Omaha	10	5	3.32	29	23	0	2	152	139	61	38	127
Banks, Josh, Portland	7	7	3.46	26	17	0	0	125	120	52	36	95
Alvarado, Carlos, Albuquerque	13	10	3.49	27	25	1	0	152	139	65	51	139
Haeger, Charlie, Albuquerque	11	6	3.55	22	22	4	0	145	134	63	58	103
Mathes, J.R., Iowa	12	8	3.62	26	21	0	0	129	150	59	14	51
Collazo, Willie, New Orleans	9	5	3.70	34	16	0	0	126	125	57	35	74
MacLane, Evan, Memphis, Reno	8	9	3.75	24	24	0	0	151	171	73	20	92

ALL-STAR TEAM

C: John Hester, Reno. **1B:** Randy Ruiz, Las Vegas. **2B:** Eric Young Jr., Colorado Springs. **3B:** Esteban German, Oklahoma City. **SS:** Alcides Escobar, Nashville. **OF:** John Bowker, Fresno; Terry Evans, Salt Lake; Matt Miller, Colorado Springs. **DH:** Mitch Jones, Albuquerque. **RHP:** Bud Norris, Round Rock. **LHP:** Lenny DiNardo, Omaha. **RP:** Scott Strickland, Albuquerque.
Most Valuable Player: Randy Ruiz, Las Vegas. **Pitcher of the Year:** Bud Norris, Round Rock. **Rookie of the Year:** Eric Young Jr., Colorado Springs. **Manager of the Year:** Tim Wallach, Albuquerque.

DEPARTMENT LEADERS

BATTING

OBP	Bowker, John, Fresno	.451
SLG	Jones, Mitch, Albuquerque	.651
OPS	Bowker, John, Fresno	.104
R	Young, Eric, Colorado Springs	118
H	Miller, Matt, Colorado Springs	167
TB	Evans, Terry, Salt Lake	279
XBH	Ruiz, Randy, Las Vegas	70
2B	Ruiz, Randy, Las Vegas	43
3B	Oeltjen, Trent, Reno	14
HR	Jones, Mitch, Albuquerque	35
RBI	Ruiz, Randy, Las Vegas	106
SAC	Escobar, Alcides, Nashville	19
BB	Gotay, Ruben, Reno	102
	Ka'aihue, Kila, Omaha	102
HBP	Lindsey, John, New Orleans	17
SO	Koshansky, Joe, Nashville	166
SB	Young, Eric, Colorado Springs	58
CS	Young, Eric, Colorado Springs	14
AB/SO	Watson, Brandon, Reno	15.97

PITCHING

G	Moss, Damian, Colorado Springs	59
GS	Barnette, Tony, Reno	29
	Kinney, Matt, Fresno	29
GF	Messenger, Randy, Tacoma	48
SV	Strickland, Scott, Albuquerque	32
W	Barnette, Tony, Reno	14
L	Kinney, Matt, Fresno	14
IP	MacLane, Evan, Reno, Memphis	166
H	MacLane, Evan, Reno, Memphis	194
R	Atkins, Mitch, Iowa	113
ER	Atkins, Mitch, Iowa	107
HB	Haeger, Charlie, Albuquerque	12
BB	Ottavino, Adam, Memphis	82
SO	Alvarado, Giancarlo, Albuquerque	139
SO/9 (SP)	Norris, Bud, Round Rock	8.40
SO/9 (RP)	Rodriguez, Henry, Sacramento	14.63
BB/9	Mathes, J.R., Iowa	0.97
WP	Sinkbeil, Brett, New Orleans	14
BK	Seddon, Chris, Tacoma	4
HR	Kinney, Matt, Fresno	33
AVG	Norris, Bud, Round Rock	.237

FIELDING

C	FPCT	Robinson, Chris, Iowa	.998
	PO	House, J.R., Omaha	728
	A	Arencibia, J.P., Las Vegas	59
		Hester, John, Reno	59
	E	Arencibia, J.P., Las Vegas	13
	DP	Budde, Ryan, Salt Lake	10
	PB	Arencibia, J.P., Las Vegas	14
1B	FPCT	Koshansky, Joe, Nashville	.997
	PO	Ka'aihue, Kila, Omaha	1091
	A	Ka'aihue, Kila, Omaha	78
	E	Three tied at	10
	DP	Ka'aihue, Kila, Omaha	129
2B	FPCT	Iribarren, Hernan, Nashville	.990
	PO	Young, Eric, Colorado Springs	235
	A	Young, Eric, Colorado Springs	336
	E	Young, Eric, Colorado Springs	16
	DP	Hoffpauir, Jarrett, Memphis	73
3B	FPCT	Rohlinger, Ryan, Fresno	.961
	PO	Wallace, Brett, Memphis, Sacramento	67
	A	Metcalf, Travis, Omaha, Oklahoma City	247
	E	Howard, Kevin, Portland, Las Vegas	25
	DP	Metcalf, Travis, Omaha, Oklahoma City	28
SS	FPCT	Hu, Chin-lung, Albuquerque	.977
	PO	Sanchez, Angel, Las Vegas	184
	A	Manzella, Tommy, Round Rock	369
	E	Greene, Tyler, Memphis	19
	DP	Manzella, Tommy, Round Rock	80
OF	FPCT	Carson, Matt, Sacramento	1.000
		Frey, Chris, Colorado Springs	1.000
	PO	Ramirez, Yordany, Round Rock	341
	A	Mathews, Aaron, Las Vegas	17
	E	Miller, Jai, New Orleans	10
	DP	Three tied at	4

MINOR LEAGUES

BY JOHN MANUEL

The Akron Aeros lost the league championship series to Trenton in 2008, and the Thunder entered 2009 as the two-time defending Eastern League champions. However, Akron would not be denied in 2009.

The Aeros had the league's best record at 89-53, getting off to a tremendous 28-8 start, shrugging off a five-game losing streak before the all-star break, then winning their final eight regular season games to enter the playoffs on a high. Akron brushed aside the talent-laden Reading in the playoffs, sweeping in three games and scoring 24 runs in the process. Then the Aeros beat Connecticut in four games to claim the league championship, their first since 2005 and third in the franchise's 21-year history.

Akron had several stalwarts who were with the team all season, starting with catcher Carlos Santana, who was named the EL's MVP. He batted .290/.413/.530 and finished second in the league in home runs (23), RBIs (97), on-base and slugging percentage. Lefthanded sluggers Beau Mills (.267/.308/.417, 14 homers, 33 doubles) and Nick Weglarz (.227/.377/.431) complemented him in the lineup while veteran center fielder Jose Constanza (.282/.378/.342, league-best 49 stolen bases and 98 runs) set the table.

When Weglarz left in September to play for Canada in the World Cup, 2008 first-round pick Lonnie Chisenhall stepped in and stepped up, batting .467 in seven playoff games.However, manager Mike Sarbaugh pointed to pitching as Akron's biggest reason for its championship. The Aeros overcame the promotion of ace righthander Hector Rondon, relying instead on solid starters Josh Tomlin (14-9, 4.16) and Jeamar Gomez (10-4, 3.43) down the stretch. Gomez, who was named the EL pitcher of the year, also had one of the league's highlights on May 21, throwing a perfect

TOP 20 PROSPECTS

1. Pedro Alvarez, 3b, Altoona (Pirates)
2. Madison Bumgarner, lhp, Connecticut (Giants)
3. Kyle Drabek, rhp, Reading (Phillies)
4. Carlos Santana, c, Akron (Indians)
5. Jesus Montero, c, Trenton (Yankees)
6. Domonic Brown, of, Reading (Phillies)
7. Junichi Tazawa, rhp, Portland (Red Sox)
8. Wilson Ramos, c, New Britain (Twins)
9. Michael Taylor, of, Reading (Phillies)
10. Brad Lincoln, rhp, Altoona (Pirates)
11. Hector Rondon, rhp, Akron (Indians)
12. Josh Reddick, of, Portland (Red Sox)
13. Ike Davis, 1b, Binghamton (Mets)
14. Marc Rzepczynski, lhp, New Hampshire (Blue Jays)
15. Jose Tabata, of, Altoona (Pirates)
16. Scott Sizemore, 2b, Erie (Tigers)
17. Jake Arrieta, rhp, Bowie (Orioles)
18. Nick Weglarz, of, Akron (Indians)
19. Zach McAllister, rhp, Trenton (Yankees)
20. Brandon Snyder, 1b, Bowie (Orioles)

game in a 3-0 victory against Trenton. (Erie's Thad Weber threw the league's other no-hitter, a 16-0 whitewashing of Akron on Aug. 22).

"Our pitching was solid all year long," Sarbaugh said. "Gomez and Tomlin were so solid for us all year. The other key for us was that we ended up with a really nice mix in the clubhouse."

Connecticut's loss in the championship series to Akron turned out to be the Defenders' EL swan song. The troubled Norwich, Conn.-based franchised announced its move to Richmond for 2010. The Richmond market should be a boon to the EL, especially if the team—renamed the Flying Squirrels—gets a new ballpark to replace the Diamond, whose poor condition was the reason the International League franchise left Richmond in the first place following the 2008 season.

Trenton had one of the league's most intriguing prospects in 19-year-old Jesus Montero, a man-child catcher/designated hitter who batted .317/.370/.539 in the EL. However, the Thunder's four-year playoff streak came to an end, as the team went just 69-72.

STANDINGS

North	W	L	PCT	GB	Manager	Attendance	Average	Last Penn.
Connecticut Defenders (Giants)	83	59	.585	—	Steve Decker	203,005	3,076	2002
New Britain Rock Cats (Twins)	72	69	.511	10 ½	Tom Nieto	366,682	5,556	2001
Trenton Thunder (Yankees)	69	72	.489	13 ½	Tony Franklin	371,602	5,546	2008
Portland Sea Dogs (Red Sox)	67	74	.475	15 ½	Arnie Beyeler	404,709	6,132	2006
New Hampshire Fisher Cats (Blue Jays)	64	78	.451	19	Gary Cathcart	386,991	5,609	2004
Binghamton Mets (Mets)	54	86	.386	28	Mako Oliveras	210,526	3,142	1994

South	W	L	PCT	GB	Manager	Attendance	Average	Last Penn.
Akron Aeros (Indians)	89	53	.627	—	Mike Sarbaugh	316,836	4,659	2009
Reading Phillies (Phillies)	75	67	.528	14	Steve Roadcap	460,791	6,678	2001
Bowie Baysox (Orioles)	73	69	.514	16	Brad Komminsk	247,660	3,810	Never
Erie SeaWolves (Tigers)	71	70	.504	17 ½	Tom Brookens	220,909	3,156	Never
Harrisburg Senators (Nationals)	70	72	.493	19	John Stearns	228,741	3,574	1999
Altoona Curve (Pirates)	62	80	.437	27	Matt Walbeck	275,945	4,312	Never

PLAYOFFS—Semifinals: Akron defeated Reading 3-0 and Connecticut defeated New Britain 3-1 in best-of-five series. **Finals:** Akron defeated Connecticut 3-1 in best-of-five series.

CLUB BATTING

	AVG	G	AB	R	H	2B	3B	HR	RBI	BB	SO	SB	CS	OBP	SLG
Binghamton	.268	140	4657	550	1250	248	23	64	513	485	992	93	48	.342	.373
Connecticut	.267	142	4696	622	1255	259	38	70	558	410	900	97	81	.331	.383
New Britain	.266	141	4678	624	1243	265	32	86	586	445	851	58	45	.338	.391
Reading	.266	142	4755	626	1263	244	30	101	580	457	966	116	53	.336	.393
Akron	.258	142	4569	682	1177	250	26	98	628	535	767	95	39	.340	.388
Erie	.258	141	4744	701	1223	245	49	162	662	503	1186	78	44	.334	.433
Altoona	.256	142	4676	580	1195	257	24	87	530	485	916	79	50	.331	.377
Bowie	.256	142	4482	561	1147	237	35	79	508	449	916	139	60	.327	.377
Portland	.256	141	4674	650	1196	279	18	105	603	558	1114	72	30	.341	.391
Trenton	.254	141	4625	571	1173	240	29	76	529	437	864	72	28	.324	.367
Harrisburg	.251	142	4586	555	1152	242	30	111	519	435	1019	73	45	.321	.390
New Hampshire	.238	142	4588	565	1090	241	25	84	526	550	1014	118	47	.322	.356

CLUB PITCHING

	ERA	G	CG	SHO	SV	IP	H	R	ER	HR	BB	SO	AVG
Akron	3.40	142	4	14	45	1219	1107	537	461	90	414	1041	.241
Bowie	3.44	142	5	15	44	1197	1096	538	457	85	506	916	.245
Connecticut	3.53	142	4	13	45	1245	1185	555	488	76	513	920	.254
Trenton	3.54	141	0	15	29	1211	1078	555	476	76	515	1110	.238
New Hampshire	3.57	142	3	11	32	1241	1160	580	492	75	534	1006	.248
Harrisburg	3.73	142	3	11	40	1210	1255	571	502	100	421	926	.271
New Britain	3.94	141	4	11	41	1212	1228	621	530	87	433	983	.263
Erie	4.08	141	5	7	38	1230	1278	638	558	132	428	845	.269
Altoona	4.11	142	3	10	36	1227	1246	673	560	87	501	918	.265
Reading	4.15	142	2	10	40	1240	1212	630	572	126	462	966	.258
Portland	4.21	141	2	6	29	1213	1198	649	567	81	529	966	.258
Binghamton	4.99	140	2	6	33	1204	1321	740	667	108	493	908	.283

CLUB FIELDING

	PCT	PO	A	E	DP		PCT	PO	A	E	DP
Connecticut	.981	3735	1437	99	368	Bowie	.975	3590	1376	128	361
Reading	.981	3720	1418	99	313	Erie	.975	3691	1425	132	372
Binghamton	.979	3611	1377	105	353	Harrisburg	.975	3630	1494	130	420
Akron	.978	3656	1305	114	288	Portland	.975	3639	1399	136	321
New Britain	.976	3635	1428	125	335	New Hampshire	.973	3724	1568	145	453
Trenton	.976	3634	1365	125	356	Altoona	.970	3681	1518	161	418

INDIVIDUAL BATTING LEADERS (MINIMUM 3.1 PA/TEAM GAME)

	AVG	G	AB	R	H	2B	3B	HR	RBI	BB	SO	SB
Bond, Brock, Connecticut	.333	122	450	93	150	21	5	1	33	67	69	13
Thole, Josh, Binghamton	.328	103	384	48	126	29	2	1	46	42	34	8
Nunez, Eduardo, Trenton	.322	123	497	70	160	26	1	9	55	22	63	19
Sellers, Neil, Reading	.317	139	518	71	164	33	2	17	86	48	71	5
Mahar, Kevin, Reading	.314	117	407	59	128	18	2	12	54	25	81	7
Pill, Brett, Connecticut	.298	139	527	71	157	37	1	19	109	37	72	6
Dinkelman, Brian, New Britain	.296	129	459	62	136	38	2	8	65	55	73	5
Wabick, D.J., Binghamton	.296	120	426	41	126	31	1	4	55	19	78	5
Boyer, Brad, Connecticut	.294	106	367	49	108	22	10	3	41	29	69	10
Martinez-Esteve, Eddy, Connecticut	.291	127	436	58	127	31	3	8	65	47	62	2

INDIVIDUAL PITCHING LEADERS (MINIMUM 1 IP/TEAM GAME)

	W	L	ERA	G	GS	CG	SV	IP	H	R	BB	SO
McAllister, Zach, Trenton	7	5	2.23	22	22	0	0	121	98	39	33	96
Doubront, Felix, Portland	8	6	3.35	26	26	1	0	121	119	59	52	101
Gomez, Jeanmar, Akron	10	4	3.43	22	22	1	0	123	117	56	40	109
Perez, Luis, New Hampshire	9	11	3.55	28	27	2	0	162	145	78	67	112
Fox, Matt, New Britain	9	9	3.58	28	26	1	0	151	143	67	56	120
Boone, Randy, New Hampshire	9	8	3.70	25	23	0	0	129	127	63	42	90
Moskos, Danny, Altoona	11	10	3.74	27	25	1	0	149	159	75	58	77
Arnesen, Erik, Harrisburg	8	6	3.87	22	21	1	0	123	133	59	26	91
Mullins, Ryan, New Britain	11	14	4.03	28	27	1	0	145	175	78	36	133
Kibler, Jon, Erie	6	9	4.06	27	27	3	0	162	168	85	68	87

ALL-STAR TEAM

C: Carlos Santana, Akron. **1B:** Brett Pill, Connecticut. **2B:** Brock Bond, Connecticut. **3B:** Neil Sellers, Reading. **SS:** Eduardo Nunez, Trenton. **OF:** Quintin Berry, Reading; Brennan Boesch, Erie; Michael Taylor, Reading. **DH:** Brian Dopirak, New Hampshire. **UTIL:** Brian Dinkleman, New Britain. **RHSP:** Jeanmar Gomez, Akron. **LHSP:** Joe Savery, Reading **RP:** Anthony Slama, New Britain.
Most Valuable Player: Carlos Santana, Akron. **Pitcher of the Year:** Jeanmar Gomez, Akron.
Manager of the Year: Mike Sarbaugh, Akron.

DEPARTMENT LEADERS

BATTING

OBP	Bond, Brock, Connecticut	.429
SLG	Dopirak, Brian, New Hampshire	.576
OPS	Santana, Carlos, Akron	.943
R	Constanza, Jose, Akron	98
H	Sellers, Neil, Reading	164
TB	Boesch, Brennan, Erie	269
XBH	Boesch, Brennan, Erie	61
2B	Still, Jon, Portland	40
3B	Boyer, Brad, Connecticut	10
HR	Boesch, Brennan, Erie	28
RBI	Pill, Brett, Connecticut	109
SAC	Tejada, Ruben, Binghamton	15
BB	Santana, Carlos, Akron	90
HBP	Figueroa, Daniel, Bowie	16
	Tosoni, Rene, New Britain	16
SO	Iorg, Cale, Erie	149
SB	Constanza, Jose, Akron	49
CS	Bond, Brock, Connecticut	15
AB/SO	Thole, Josh, Binghamton	11.29

PITCHING

G	Merritt, Roy, Binghamton	56
	Rhoades, Chad, Portland	56
GS	Seven tied at	27
GF	Slama, Anthony, New Britain	43
SV	Slama, Anthony, New Britain	25
W	Tomlin, Josh, Akron	14
L	Brown, Eric, Binghamton	14
	DeVries, Cole, New Britain	14
IP	Nickerson, Jonah, Erie	165
H	Nickerson, Jonah, Erie	217
R	Nickerson, Jonah, Erie	108
ER	Nickerson, Jonah, Erie	98
HB	Nickerson, Jonah, Erie	15
BB	Kibler, Jon, Erie	68
SO	Mullins, Ryan, New Britain	133
SO/9 (SP)	Mullins, Ryan, New Britain	8.27
SO/9 (RP)	Dunn, Michael, Trenton	12.83
BB/9	Tomlin, Josh, Akron	1.68
WP	Fox, Matt, New Britain	13
	Valdez, Jose, Trenton	13
BK	Four tied at	3
HR	Nickerson, Jonah, Erie	23
AVG	McAllister, Zach, Trenton	.220

FIELDING

C	FPCT	Jeroloman, Brian, New Hampshire	.993
	PO	Jeroloman, Brian, New Hampshire	808
	A	Lerud, Steven, Altoona	72
	E	Santana, Carlos, Akron	9
	DP	Jeroloman, Brian, New Hampshire	14
	PB	Lerud, Steven, Altoona	15
1B	FPCT	Pill, Brett, Connecticut	.997
	PO	Pill, Brett, Connecticut	1082
	A	Pill, Brett, Connecticut	97
	E	Stavisky, Brian, Reading	12
	DP	Pill, Brett, Connecticut	108
2B	FPCT	Harman, Brad, Reading	.981
	PO	Emaus, Brad, New Hampshire	262
	A	Emaus, Brad, New Hampshire	417
	E	Abreu, Miguel, Bowie	20
	DP	Emaus, Brad, New Hampshire	117
3B	FPCT	Sellers, Neil, Reading	.961
	PO	Jimenez, Jorge, Portland	112
	A	Sellers, Neil, Reading	237
	E	Jimenez, Jorge, Portland	23
	DP	Jimenez, Jorge, Portland	24
SS	FPCT	Rivero, Carlos, Akron	.972
	PO	Iorg, Cale, Erie	202
	A	Iorg, Cale, Erie	351
	E	Nunez, Eduardo, Trenton	33
	DP	Iorg, Cale, Erie	76
		Tejada, Ruben, Binghamton	76
OF	FPCT	Berry, Quintin, Reading	.993
	PO	Garcia, Emmanuel, Binghamton	349
	A	Boesch, Brennan, Erie	15
	E	Concepcion, Ambiorix, Bowie	9
	DP	Four tied at	4

MINOR LEAGUES

BY BEN BADLER

While Birmingham rolled to a 48-21 record in the first half of the season, Jacksonville was just a .500 team at the all-star break. Yet while Birmingham finished as the Southern League's only 90-win club, the Suns won the South Division's second-half crown with a 47-23 record, then swept the Barons 3-0 in the first round of the postseason before winning the championship series 3-1 against Tennessee.

Jacksonville got a boost in June when first baseman Logan Morrison returned after missing the first two months of the season with a broken bone in his right thumb. Morrison led the team at the plate, hitting .277/.411/.442 in 79 games to lead the team in on-base percentage. The second-half addition of 19-year-old right fielder Mike Stanton also helped, as Stanton hit 16 home runs in 79 games while batting .231/.311/.455.

Jacksonville's roster remained largely intact for most of the season, getting solid help from outfielders Bryan Peterson and Scott Cousins.

Birmingham led the league in runs scored and ranked second behind Jacksonville in runs allowed, but the loss of several of the White Sox's top prospects during the season hurt the Barons. Gordon Beckham was with the team through May before getting the callup to Chicago in early June. Tyler Flowers was a power-hitting, on-base machine for the Barons behind the dish, hitting .302/.445/.548 in 77 games before moving up to Triple-A Charlotte in July, while first baseman Brandon Allen and lefthander Aaron Poreda were among the prospects who began the year with the Barons and ended the season on another roster. Second baseman C.J. Retherford led the league in total bases, while outfielder David Cook tied West Tenn center fielder Greg Halman for the home run crown with 25.

While a a pair of hard-throwing lefties (Clayton Kershaw and David Price) reigned in the Southern League in 2008, the circuit's top prospects this year were a quartet of high-ceiling hitting prospects. Mississippi right fielder Jason Heyward looks

like a future superstar. Beckham established himself as a candidate for the American League rookie of the year after joining the White Sox and moving to third base. Montgomery center fielder Desmond Jennings moved on to propel Durham to the Triple-A championship, while Stanton has as much raw power as any minor league hitter.

On the mound, Carolina lefty Travis Wood's 1.21 ERA in 119 innings led the league and was less than half of the second-place finisher, Birmingham righthander John Ely, who finished with a 2.82 mark in 156 innings.

TOP 20 PROSPECTS

1. Jason Heyward, of, Mississippi (Braves)
2. Gordon Beckham, ss, Birmingham (White Sox)
3. Desmond Jennings, of, Montgomery (Rays)
4. Mike Stanton, of, Jacksonville (Marlins)
5. Jarrod Parker, rhp, Mobile (Diamondbacks)
6. Tyler Flowers, c, Birmingham (White Sox)
7. Logan Morrison, 1b, Jacksonville (Marlins)
8. Freddie Freeman, 1b, Misssissippi (Braves)
9. Jeremy Hellickson, rhp, Montgomery (Rays)
10. Josh Bell, 3b, Chattanooga (Dodgers)
11. Jay Jackson, rhp, Tennessee (Cubs)
12. Todd Frazier, of/2b/1b, Carolina (Reds)
13. Jonathan Lucroy, c, Huntsville (Brewers)
14. Chris Heisey, of, Carolina (Reds)
15. Dan Hudson, rhp, Birmingham (White Sox)
16. Jordan Danks, of, Birmingham (White Sox)
17. Sean West, lhp, Jacksonville (Marlins)
18. Andrew Lambo, of, Chattanooga (Dodgers)
19. Daniel Schlereth, lhp, Mobile (Diamondbacks)
20. Travis Wood, lhp, Carolina (Reds)

STANDINGS: SPLIT SEASON

FIRST HALF

North	W	L	PCT	GB
Huntsville	38	31	.551	—
Carolina	37	32	.536	1
Tennessee	32	38	.457	—
Chattanooga	30	39	.435	8
West Tenn	27	43	.386	11½

South	W	L	PCT	GB
Birmingham	48	21	.696	—
Mobile	37	33	.529	11½
Jacksonville	35	35	.500	—
Montgomery	33	37	.471	15½
Mississippi	31	39	.443	17½

SECOND HALF

North	W	L	PCT	GB
Tennessee	39	31	.557	—
Chattanooga	35	35	.500	4
West Tenn	35	35	.500	4
Carolina	28	42	.400	11
Huntsville	25	44	.362	13½

South	W	L	PCT	GB
Jacksonville	47	23	.671	—
Birmingham	44	26	.629	3
Mississippi	34	34	.500	12
Montgomery	32	37	.464	14½
Mobile	29	41	.414	18

PLAYOFFS—Semifinals: Jacksonville defeated Birmingham 3-0, Tennessee defeated Huntsville 3-1 in best-of-five series. **Finals:** Jacksonville defeated Tennessee 3-1 in best-of-five series.

OVERALL STANDINGS

Team	W	L	PCT	GB	Manager	Attendance	Average	Last Penn.
Birmingham Barons (White Sox)	92	47	.662	—	Ever Magallanes	287,185	4,418	2002
Jacksonville Suns (Marlins)	82	58	.586	10½	Brandon Hyde	354,553	5,138	2009
Tennessee Smokies (Cubs)	71	69	.507	21½	Ryne Sandberg	260,153	3,826	2004
Mississippi Braves (Braves)	65	73	.471	26½	Phillip Wellman	194,795	2,997	2008
Mobile BayBears (Diamondbacks)	66	74	.471	26½	Hector De La Cruz	209,742	3,084	2004
Carolina Mudcats (Reds)	65	74	.468	26½	David Bell	263,175	3,928	2003
Chattanooga Lookouts (Dodgers)	65	74	.468	26½	John Valentin	224,157	3,346	1988
Montgomery Biscuits (Rays)	65	74	.468	26½	Billy Gardner	266,818	4,043	2007
Huntsville Stars (Brewers)	63	75	.457	28½	Robert Miscik	93,845	1,514	2001
West Tenn Diamond Jaxx (Mariners)	62	78	.443	30½	Phil Plantier	129,778	2,060	2000

CLUB BATTING

	AVG	G	AB	R	H	2B	3B	HR	RBI	BB	SO	SB	CS	OBP	SLG
Birmingham	.271	139	4660	725	1261	277	25	139	678	457	955	85	36	.339	.430
Tennessee	.268	140	4654	591	1246	257	27	89	536	410	871	94	52	.331	.392
Chattanooga	.264	139	4594	599	1212	297	27	88	553	515	993	84	58	.342	.398
Mobile	.262	140	4618	595	1212	215	28	53	541	494	783	134	58	.339	.356
Huntsville	.254	138	4512	573	1144	229	23	65	520	493	786	77	40	.332	.358
Carolina	.253	139	4684	566	1184	274	20	99	524	421	907	92	51	.320	.383
Jacksonville	.249	140	4571	643	1138	246	41	110	583	570	1129	106	46	.334	.393
West Tenn	.249	140	4464	612	1110	206	31	105	555	539	1006	137	62	.336	.379
Mississippi	.247	138	4488	517	1107	222	30	60	466	501	943	123	69	.327	.350
Montgomery	.238	139	4540	565	1080	209	40	82	513	490	999	130	41	.317	.356

CLUB PITCHING

	ERA	G	CG	SHO	SV	IP	H	R	ER	HR	BB	SO	AVG
Jacksonville	3.20	140	0	15	45	1225	1104	512	436	73	433	933	.240
Birmingham	3.32	140	3	14	41	1218	1156	534	449	58	444	908	.253
Mississippi	3.57	138	3	8	36	1216	1131	573	482	71	577	953	.248
Chattanooga	3.83	139	1	10	34	1213	1149	593	516	91	501	1021	.250
Mobile	3.96	140	5	10	34	1215	1222	610	535	115	423	944	.263
Tennessee	3.99	140	2	9	41	1216	1228	610	539	102	491	900	.265
Carolina	4.01	140	2	11	29	1224	1137	635	545	95	599	936	.251
West Tenn	4.04	140	6	8	21	1194	1145	633	536	88	525	958	.253
Huntsville	4.25	138	1	7	38	1188	1226	659	561	101	455	925	.268
Montgomery	4.25	139	2	5	37	1199	1196	627	566	96	442	894	.261

CLUB FIELDING

	PCT	PO	A	E	DP		PCT	PO	A	E	DP
Montgomery	.979	3597	1286	107	329	Chattanooga	.975	3640	1379	131	275
Jacksonville	.976	3676	1403	124	305	Huntsville	.975	3564	1414	128	324
Mobile	.976	3644	1391	122	324	Mississippi	.974	3648	1350	132	297
Tennessee	.976	3647	1437	123	398	Carolina	.972	3670	1403	145	395
Birmingham	.975	3654	1537	132	443	West Tenn	.972	3582	1226	139	228

INDIVIDUAL BATTING LEADERS (MINIMUM 3.1 PA/TEAM GAME)

	AVG	G	AB	R	H	2B	3B	HR	RBI	BB	SO	SB
Carrera, Ezequiel, West Tenn	.337	91	329	68	111	12	4	2	38	59	62	27
Jennings, Desmond, Montgomery	.316	100	383	69	121	25	8	8	45	48	52	37
Tomlin, James, Chattanooga	.315	108	387	51	122	23	4	2	52	35	34	89
Lalli, Blake, Tennessee	.314	118	373	49	117	25	0	5	52	32	50	0
Anderson, Drew T., Huntsville	.301	108	389	56	117	25	2	10	57	45	77	9
Adduci, James, Tennessee	.300	131	467	63	140	21	4	4	51	58	76	35
Retherford, C.J., Birmingham	.297	128	478	70	142	46	4	10	76	30	70	3
Petersen, Bryan, Jacksonville	.297	121	431	64	128	15	7	7	49	50	66	13
Limonta, Johan, West Tenn	.297	126	438	57	130	30	8	6	53	54	74	7
Bell, Josh, Chattanooga	.296	94	334	47	99	30	2	11	52	50	70	3

INDIVIDUAL PITCHING LEADERS (MINIMUM 1 IP/TEAM GAME)

	W	L	ERA	G	GS	CG	SV	IP	H	R	BB	SO
Wood, Travis, Carolina	9	3	1.21	19	19	1	0	119	78	23	37	103
Ely, John, Birmingham	14	2	2.82	27	27	1	0	156	140	63	50	125
Bray, Steve, West Tenn	7	8	3.11	26	22	2	0	145	131	55	34	89
Reynoso, Ryne, Mississippi	7	9	3.47	25	24	0	0	148	127	66	59	89
Diamond, Scott, Mississippi	5	10	3.50	23	23	0	0	131	152	68	53	111
Parker, Kyle, West Tenn	5	5	3.55	25	19	1	0	117	109	52	52	73
Coleman, Casey, Tennessee	14	6	3.68	27	27	1	0	149	142	63	58	84
Taylor, Graham, Jacksonville	8	7	3.69	23	23	0	0	127	115	62	54	71
Torra, Matt, Mobile	10	13	3.75	28	28	4	0	180	192	91	28	116
Rollins, Heath, Montgomery	9	11	3.83	28	22	0	0	134	147	64	33	83

ALL-STAR TEAM

C: Tyler Flowers, Birmingham. **1B:** Blake Lalli, Tennessee. **2B:** C.J. Retherford, Birmingham. **3B:** Juan Francisco, Carolina. **SS:** Pedro Ciriaco, Mobile. **OF:** Ezequiel Carrera, West Tenn; David Cook, Birmingham; Stefan Gartrell, Birmingham; Desmond Jennings, Montgomery. **DH:** Greg Halman, West Tenn. **UTIL:** Todd Frazier, Carolina. **Best Hustler:** Matt Young, Mississippi. **RHP:** John Ely, Birmingham. **LHP:** Travis Wood, Carolina. **RP:** Matt Peterson, Jacksonville.
Most Valuable Player: Desmond Jennings, Montgomery. **Most Outstanding Pitcher:** Travis Wood, Carolina. **Manager of the Year:** Ever Magallanes, Birmingham.

DEPARTMENT LEADERS

BATTING

OBP	Carrera, Ezequiel, West Tenn	.441
SLG	Gartrell, Stefan, Birmingham	.521
OPS	Gartrell, Stefan, Birmingham	.892
R	Cook, David, Birmingham	87
H	Retherford, C.J., Birmingham	142
TB	Retherford, C.J., Birmingham	226
XBH	Retherford, C.J., Birmingham	60
2B	Retherford, C.J., Birmingham	46
3B	Cousins, Scott, Jacksonville	11
HR	Cook, David, Birmingham	25
	Halman, Greg, West Tenn	25
RBI	Cook, David, Birmingham	84
SAC	Stocker, Mel, West Tenn	11
BB	Young, Matt, Mississippi	94
HBP	Justis, Shane, Huntsville	18
SO	Halman, Greg, West Tenn	183
SB	Young, Matt, Mississippi	42
CS	Young, Matt, Mississippi	16
AB/SO	Hallberg, Mark, Mobile	10.58

PITCHING

G	Schlitter, Brian, Tennessee	59
GS	Torra, Matt, Mobile	28
GF	Peterson, Matt, Jacksonville	54
SV	Peterson, Matt, Jacksonville	37
W	Coleman, Casey, Tennessee	14
	Ely, John, Birmingham	14
L	Torra, Matt, Mobile	13
IP	Torra, Matt, Mobile	180
H	Torra, Matt, Mobile	192
R	Evans, Cody, Mobile	94
ER	Evans, Cody, Mobile	82
HB	Rodriguez, Aneury, Montgomery	12
BB	Cofield, Kyle, Mississippi	89
SO	Ely, John, Birmingham	125
SO/9 (SP)	Wood, Travis, Carolina	7.79
SO/9 (RP)	Nunez, Jhonny, Birmingham	11.07
BB/9	Torra, Matt, Mobile	1.40
WP	Maestri, Alex, Tennessee	15
BK	Heath, Deunte, Mississippi	4
HR	Evans, Cody, Mobile	24
	Torra, Matt, Mobile	24
AVG	Wood, Travis, Carolina	.189

FIELDING

C	FPCT	Boscan, J.C., Mississippi	.993
	PO	Lucroy, Jonathan, Huntsville	727
	A	Lucroy, Jonathan, Huntsville	70
	E	Skelton, James, Mobile	12
	DP	Castillo, Welington, Tennessee	8
	PB	May, Lucas, Chattanooga	20
1B	FPCT	Parker, Logan, Carolina	.990
	PO	Parker, Logan, Carolina	697
	A	Parker, Logan, Carolina	63
	E	Fields, Matt, Montgomery	12
	DP	Parker, Logan, Carolina	81
2B	FPCT	Retherford, C.J., Birmingham	.981
	PO	Thomas, Tony, Tennessee	257
	A	Retherford, C.J., Birmingham	396
	E	Jones, Travis, Mississippi	18
	DP	Retherford, C.J., Birmingham	102
3B	FPCT	Smith, Marquez, Tennessee	.959
	PO	Mangini, Matt, West Tenn	83
	A	Smith, Marquez, Tennessee	223
	E	Francisco, Juan, Carolina	35
	DP	Smith, Marquez, Tennessee	34
SS	FPCT	Ciriaco, Pedro, Mobile	.960
	PO	Cozart, Zack, Carolina	209
	A	Hicks, Brandon, Mississippi	351
	E	Hicks, Brandon, Mississippi	28
	DP	Cozart, Zack, Carolina	83
OF	FPCT	Three tied at	1.000
	PO	Frey, Evan, Mobile	328
	A	Frazier, Todd, Carolina	16
	E	Henry, Sean, Carolina	12
	DP	Hankerd, Cyle, Mobile	5

MINOR LEAGUES

BY WILL LINGO

While history will record that the Midland RockHounds won the Double-A Texas League playoff title, finished with the best overall record in the league and had several of the league's top prospects, it wasn't ever easy for the RockHounds.

Even the clinching playoff victory was a come-from-behind, extra-inning win on the road against the Northwest Arkansas Naturals (Royals), a 4-2 win in 12 innings that came courtesy of a two-run home run from Raul Padron, the team's backup catcher.

"It was very fitting," Midland manager Darren Bush told the Midland Reporter-Telegram after winning the championship. "The great thing about it is that it's somebody different every time. It's somebody different every day getting a big hit and that makes it even more enjoyable."

The RockHounds got off to a fast start, led by first baseman Tommy Everidge, but he was promoted to Triple-A Sacramento after batting .306/.380/.489 in 55 games and the team slipped to second place in its division at the end of the first half, losing five straight games and getting passed by San Antonio.

Midland also went through an eight-game losing streak in the second half, but the offensive production of Chris Carter got the team back in gear. Carter was the dominant offensive player in the league and batted .337/.435/.576 in 490 at-bats before being promoted to Sacramento at the end of August. The RockHounds held on to the second-half title, and Carter won the league MVP award.

The league's pitcher of the year was Tulsa right-hander Samuel Deduno, who went 12-4 and led the league with a 2.57 ERA. Playing their final season in Drillers Stadium before moving to a new downtown ballpark in 2010, Tulsa had the second-best overall record in the league but finished second in its division in both halves and missed the playoffs.

The league lacked a slam dunk top prospect this year, and most of those players who did rise to the top of the talent pool left before they even completed a circuit around the league. Five of the top seven players on the league prospect list were gone by the Fourth of July, with top prospect Mat Latos jumping straight to the big leagues and providing a glimpse of a brighter future in San Diego.

Carter departed for Triple-A Sacramento before the year was over, as did Adrian Cardenas—who made the league all-star team as a utilityman—leaving a supporting cast that included outfielders Corey Brown and Matt Sulentic to take Midland to the championship.

The RockHounds roster was representative of the league as a whole, with a few standouts and a depth of players who are interesting but are probably marginal major leaguers at best.

TOP 20 PROSPECTS

1. Mat Latos, rhp, San Antonio (Padres)
2. Justin Smoak, 1b, Frisco (Rangers)
3. Chris Carter, 1b, Midland (Athletics)
4. Jhoulys Chacin, rhp, Tulsa (Rockies)
5. Brett Wallace, 3b, Springfield (Cardinals)
6. Jason Castro, c, Corpus Christi (Astros)
7. Esmil Rogers, rhp, Tulsa (Rockies)
8. Trevor Reckling, lhp, Arkansas (Angels)
9. Peter Bourjos, of, Arkansas (Angels)
10. Hank Conger, c, Arkansas (Angels)
11. Kasey Kiker, lhp, Frisco (Rangers)
12. Lance Lynn, rhp, Springfield (Cardinals)
13. Daniel Descalso, 2b, Springfield (Cardinals)
14. Michael McKenry, c, Tulsa (Midland)
15. Adrian Cardenas, 2b/3b, Midland (Athletics)
16. Jeff Bianchi, 2b/ss, Northwest Arkansas (Royals)
17. Logan Forsythe, 3b, San Antonio (Padres)
18. Dan Cortes, rhp, Northwest Arkansas (Royals)
19. Corey Brown, of, Midland (Athletics)
20. Samuel Deduno, rhp, Tulsa (Rockies)

STANDINGS: SPLIT SEASON

FIRST HALF				
North	W	L	PCT	GB
Springfield	38	32	.543	—
Tulsa	38	32	.543	—
NW Arkansas	36	34	.514	2
Arkansas	28	42	.400	10
South	W	L	PCT	GB
San Antonio	39	31	.557	—
Midland	37	33	.529	2
Frisco	33	37	.471	6
Corpus Christi	31	39	.443	8

SECOND HALF				
North	W	L	PCT	GB
NW Arkansas	37	33	.529	—
Tulsa	36	34	.514	1
Arkansas	33	37	.471	4
Springfield	33	37	.471	4
South	W	L	PCT	GB
Midland	41	29	.586	—
Frisco	39	31	.557	2
San Antonio	31	39	.443	10
Corpus Christi	30	40	.429	11

PLAYOFFS—Semifinals: Northwest Arkansas defeated Springfield 3-0, Midland defeated San Antonio 3-1 in best-of-five series. **Finals:** Midland defeated Northwest Arkansas 3-1 in best-of-five series.

OVERALL STANDINGS

Team	W	L	PCT	GB	Manager	Attendance	Average	Last Penn.
Midland RockHounds (Athletics)	78	62	.557	—	Darren Bush	282,283	4,091	2009
Tulsa Drillers (Rockies)	74	66	.529	4	Stu Cole/Ron Gideon	316,365	4,652	1998
NW Arkansas Naturals (Royals)	73	67	.521	5	Brian Poldberg	318,056	4,819	1999
Frisco RoughRiders (Rangers)	72	68	.514	6	Mike Micucci	553,916	8,028	2004
Springfield Cardinals (Cardinals)	71	69	.507	7	Ron Warner	402,618	5,835	1994
San Antonio Missions (Padres)	70	70	.500	8	Terry Kennedy	300,669	4,358	2007
Arkansas Travelers (Angels)	61	79	.436	17	Bobby Magallanes	346,635	5,416	2008
Corpus Christi Hooks (Astros)	61	79	.436	17	Luis Pujols	443,628	6,429	2006

CLUB BATTING

	AVG	G	AB	R	H	2B	3B	HR	RBI	BB	SO	SB	CS	OBP	SLG
Midland	.288	140	4925	811	1419	303	36	103	749	576	887	133	58	.366	.427
NW Arkansas	.269	140	4694	703	1263	245	31	107	633	477	937	162	77	.342	.403
San Antonio	.269	140	4848	657	1306	225	35	62	598	549	857	125	47	.346	.369
Arkansas	.265	140	4639	602	1230	210	35	69	550	472	785	151	70	.337	.370
Frisco	.265	140	4773	680	1265	227	30	108	625	491	856	109	36	.338	.393
Corpus Christi	.261	140	4775	650	1244	233	29	106	603	429	909	62	33	.327	.388
Tulsa	.259	140	4660	616	1207	227	25	107	576	477	877	100	42	.333	.387
Springfield	.253	140	4719	642	1194	235	35	119	588	509	958	59	30	.333	.393

CLUB PITCHING

	ERA	G	CG	SHO	SV	IP	H	R	ER	HR	BB	SO	AVG
Arkansas	3.75	140	3	7	27	1227	1182	608	512	89	478	912	.254
Tulsa	3.78	140	3	17	40	1238	1186	612	520	97	447	932	.254
San Antonio	4.02	140	1	10	27	1248	1225	642	558	96	450	928	.257
Frisco	4.22	140	4	9	34	1240	1277	679	582	89	509	917	.265
Springfield	4.30	140	2	6	41	1231	1231	678	588	105	630	897	.265
NW Arkansas	4.42	140	3	4	33	1222	1306	704	600	110	520	833	.275
Corpus Christi	4.53	140	6	10	30	1224	1342	701	616	115	413	759	.280
Midland	4.63	140	4	12	37	1255	1379	737	646	80	533	888	.281

CLUB FIELDING

	PCT	PO	A	E	DP		PCT	PO	A	E	DP
San Antonio	.974	3744	1366	139	333	NW Arkansas	.972	3667	1521	149	404
Corpus Christi	.973	3673	1513	143	416	Tulsa	.972	3713	1564	152	365
Frisco	.973	3721	1431	145	322	Arkansas	.971	3682	1496	156	357
Springfield	.973	3693	1523	143	480	Midland	.971	3764	1521	159	425

INDIVIDUAL BATTING LEADERS *(MINIMUM 3.1 PA/TEAM GAME)*

	AVG	G	AB	R	H	2B	3B	HR	RBI	BB	SO	SB
Locke, Andrew, Corpus Christi	.338	129	503	81	170	31	3	20	109	46	84	2
Carter, Chris, Midland	.337	125	490	108	165	41	2	24	101	82	119	13
Cooper, Craig, San Antonio	.312	132	503	69	157	35	1	11	94	73	85	9
Sutton, Nate, Arkansas	.305	104	371	54	113	20	3	2	40	48	55	21
Gentry, Craig, Frisco	.303	127	512	100	155	21	7	8	53	49	64	49
Henley, Tyler, Springfield	.303	123	423	62	128	31	3	13	63	40	64	9
Conger, Hank, Arkansas	.295	123	458	61	135	20	3	11	68	55	68	4
Spencer, Matthew, Midland	.294	93	371	59	109	29	3	9	62	26	75	2
Sogard, Eric, San Antonio	.293	117	457	79	134	25	3	6	51	58	47	10
Meyer, Drew, Corpus Christi	.291	120	443	70	129	29	1	5	51	50	74	2

INDIVIDUAL PITCHING LEADERS *(MINIMUM 1 IP/TEAM GAME)*

	W	L	ERA	G	GS	CG	SV	IP	H	R	BB	SO
Deduno, Samuel, Tulsa	12	4	2.57	24	24	1	0	133	94	48	72	123
Hearne, Trey, Springfield	12	3	2.82	24	18	1	0	128	113	44	43	81
Lynn, Lance, Springfield	11	4	2.92	22	22	0	0	126	117	51	51	98
Reckling, Trevor, Arkansas	8	7	2.93	23	23	1	0	135	118	50	75	106
Roe, Chaz, Tulsa	7	3	3.15	20	20	1	0	117	105	47	43	77
Mendoza, Tommy, Arkansas	7	7	3.36	20	20	0	0	129	130	60	31	86
Godfrey, Graham, Midland	11	8	3.50	28	28	1	0	159	153	70	51	110
Frieri, Ernesto, San Antonio	10	9	3.59	27	26	0	0	140	125	61	62	118
Diaz, Amalio, Arkansas	3	7	3.65	36	14	0	0	113	114	55	33	83
Ballard, Michael, Frisco	7	6	3.71	20	18	2	0	124	134	60	26	80

ALL-STAR TEAM

C: Hank Conger, Arkansas. **1B:** Chris Carter, Midland. **2B:** Daniel Descalso, Springfield. **3B:** Darin Holcomb, Tulsa. **SS:** Wladimir Sutil, Corpus Christi. **OF:** Craig Gentry, Frisco; Tyler Henley, Springfield; Drew Locke, Corpus Christi. **DH:** Chad Tracy, Frisco. **UTIL:** Adrian Cardenas, Midland. **P:** Jhoulys Chacin, Tulsa; Samuel Deduno, Tulsa; Graham Godfrey, Midland; Trey Hearne, Springfield; Andrew Johnston, Tulsa; Lance Lynn, Springfield; Trevor Reckling, Arkansas.
Most Valuable Player: Chris Carter, Midland. **Pitcher of the Year:** Samuel Deduno, Tulsa. **Manager of the Year:** Darren Bush, Midland. Mike Coolbaugh **Coach of the Year:** Ken Patterson, Arkansas.

DEPARTMENT LEADERS

BATTING

OBP	Carter, Chris, Midland		.435
SLG	Carter, Chris, Midland		.576
OPS	Carter, Chris, Midland		.101
R	Carter, Chris, Midland		108
H	Locke, Andrew, Corpus Christi		170
TB	Carter, Chris, Midland		282
XBH	Carter, Chris, Midland		67
2B	Carter, Chris, Midland		41
3B	Bourjos, Peter, Arkansas		14
HR	Tracy, Chad, Frisco		26
RBI	Locke, Andrew, Corpus Christi		109
SAC	Durango, Luis, San Antonio		19
BB	Carter, Chris, Midland		82
HBP	Gentry, Craig, Frisco		16
SO	DeLome, Collin, Corpus Christi		141
SB	Gentry, Craig, Frisco		49
CS	Durango, Luis, San Antonio		17
AB/SO	Hunter, Cedric, San Antonio		12.58

PITCHING

G	Gomes, Brandon, San Antonio		65
GS	Culp, Nathan, San Antonio		28
	Godfrey, Graham, Midland		28
GF	Johnston, Andrew, Tulsa		51
	Scribner, Evan, San Antonio		51
SV	Johnston, Andrew, Tulsa		31
W	Deduno, Samuel, Tulsa		12
	Hearne, Trey, Springfield		12
L	Weiser, Keith, Tulsa		15
IP	Godfrey, Graham, Midland		159
H	Weiser, Keith, Tulsa		195
R	Weiser, Keith, Tulsa		115
ER	Weiser, Keith, Tulsa		91
HB	Kiker, Kasey, Frisco		17
BB	Reckling, Trevor, Arkansas		75
SO	Deduno, Samuel, Tulsa		123
SO/9 (SP)	Kiker, Kasey, Frisco		8.46
SO/9 (RP)	Gomes, Brandon, San Antonio		12.50
BB/9	Culp, Nathan, San Antonio		1.65
WP	Reckling, Trevor, Arkansas		14
BK	Eight tied at		2
HR	Weiser, Keith, Tulsa		23
AVG	Deduno, Samuel, Tulsa		.202

FIELDING

C	FPCT	Cruz, Tony, Springfield	.996
	PO	Canham, Mitch, San Antonio	671
	A	Donaldson, Josh, Midland	80
	E	Donaldson, Josh, Midland	16
	DP	Cruz, Tony, Springfield	8
		Pina, Manuel, Frisco	8
	PB	Donaldson, Josh, Midland	17
1B	FPCT	Carter, Chris, Midland	.993
	PO	Cooper, Craig, San Antonio	1045
	A	Ori, Mark, Corpus Christi	73
	E	Tracy, Chad, Frisco	15
	DP	Carter, Chris, Midland	107
2B	FPCT	Meyer, Drew, Corpus Christi	.978
	PO	Sogard, Eric, San Antonio	223
	A	Meyer, Drew, Corpus Christi	323
	E	Sogard, Eric, San Antonio	15
	DP	Meyer, Drew, Corpus Christi	76
3B	FPCT	Holcomb, Darin, Tulsa	.951
	PO	Holcomb, Darin, Tulsa	81
	A	Holcomb, Darin, Tulsa	252
	E	Whittleman, John, Frisco	26
	DP	Whittleman, John, Frisco	22
SS	FPCT	Statia, Hainley, Arkansas	.964
	PO	Sutil, Wladimir, Corpus Christi	216
	A	Kozma, Peter, Springfield	375
	E	Sutil, Wladimir, Corpus Christi	26
	DP	Sutil, Wladimir, Corpus Christi	98
OF	FPCT	Bourjos, Peter, Arkansas	.997
	PO	Hunter, Cedric, San Antonio	313
	A	Jackson, Anthony, Tulsa	15
		Locke, Andrew, Corpus Christi	15
	E	Lucas, Ed, NW Arkansas	8
	DP	Three tied at	5

MINOR LEAGUES

BY DAVE PERKIN

The San Jose Giants dominated the California League in 2009, posting a sensational 93-47 record and knocking off High Desert to win the league championship.

San Jose's prospect-laden roster was one of the most impressive in recent minor league history. The Giants'—and the league's—top prospect was Buster Posey, a superlative all-around catcher with plus offensive and defensive tools. Posey was joined in the lineup by hard-hitting left fielder Thomas Neal, powerful right fielder Roger Kieschnick and speedy center fielder Darren Ford—all players who could reach the big leagues by 2011 or 2012.

To no one's surprise, offense was the Cal League trademark in 2009. If speed is your preference, the league offered High Desert outfielder Tyson Gillies (44 steals) and Inland Empire outfielders Trayvon Robinson (43) and Ford (33). Fans of power hitters had Lancaster outfielder Jon Gaston (35 home runs), High Desert outfielders Carlos Peguero (31) and Joe Dunigan (30).

All-around hitting ability was displayed by Neal, Koby Clemens (Lancaster) and Alex Liddi (High Desert). Jamie McOwen (High Desert) compiled a league-record 45-game hitting streak.

In most seasons, the term "Cal League pitching" is an oxymoron. In 2009, however, several hurlers enjoyed outstanding seasons. Elite prospects Madison Bumgarner (Giants), Jarrod Parker (Diamondbacks) and Phillipe Aumont (Mariners) made cameo appearances in the Cal League.

Prior to being traded to the Rays for Scott Kazmir, Rancho Cucamonga lefthander Alexander Torres posted a 10-3, 2.74 mark. Modesto lefty Christian Friederich was another lefty who flourished and could be part of a future Rockies rotation with 2009 first-round pick Tyler Matzek.

Other notable pitchers in the Cal League included lefthander Cory Luebke and righty Wynn Pelzer of Lake Elsinore; San Jose's bookend starting tandem of Craig Clark and Clayton Tanner; hard throwing Chris Withrow of Inland Empire; Cory Riordan and Craig Baker of Modesto, and Tanner

Roark of Bakersfield.

The one pitcher who perhaps created the most conversation in the circuit was Stockton lefthander Pedro Figueroa. Scouts raved about Figueroa's mid-90s sinking fatsball and mid-80s slider.

Years from now, this 2009 Cal League season will be noted for the lavish individual talent present in the circuit, and for the accomplishments of the 2009 San Jose Giants, who will be remembered as one of the best ballclubs in Cal League history.

TOP 20 PROSPECTS

1. Buster Posey, c, San Jose (Giants)
2. Christian Friedrich, lhp, Modesto (Rockies)
3. Jason Castro, c, Lancaster (Astros)
4. Chris Withrow, rhp, Inland Empire (Dodgers)
5. Phillipe Aumont, rhp, High Desert (Mariners)
6. Alex Liddi, 3b, High Desert (Mariners)
7. Pedro Figueroa, lhp, Stockton (Athletics)
8. Wynn Pelzer, rhp, Lake Elsinore (Padres)
9. Thomas Neal, of, San Jose (Giants)
10. James Darnell, 3b, Lake Elsinore (Padres)
11. Roger Kieschnick, of, San Jose (Giants)
12. Cory Luebke, lhp, Lake Elsinore (Padres)
13. Tyson Gillies, of, High Desert (Mariners)
14. Alexander Torres, lhp, Rancho Cucamonga (Angels)
15. Trayvon Robinson, of, Inland Empire (Dodgers)
16. Grant Desme, of, Stockton (Athletics)
17. Logan Forsythe, 3b, Lake Elsinore (Padres)
18. Jemile Weeks, 2b, Stockton (Athletics)
19. Craig Italiano, rhp, Stockton/Lake Elsinore (Padres/Athletics)
20. Darren Ford, of, San Jose (Giants)

STANDINGS: SPLIT SEASON

FIRST HALF					SECOND HALF				
North	**W**	**L**	**PCT**	**GB**	**North**	**W**	**L**	**PCT**	**GB**
San Jose	42	28	.600	—	San Jose	51	19	.729	—
Modesto	40	30	.571	2	Bakersfield	41	29	.586	10
Visalia	39	31	.557	3	Stockton	36	34	.514	15
Bakersfield	34	36	.486	8	Modesto	35	35	.500	16
Stockton	25	45	.357	17	Visalia	25	45	.357	26
South	**W**	**L**	**PCT**	**GB**	**South**	**W**	**L**	**PCT**	**GB**
High Desert	43	27	.614	—	High Desert	40	30	.571	—
Lake Elsinore	39	31	.557	4	Lake Elsinore	34	36	.486	6
Inland Empire	32	38	.457	11	R. Cucamonga	31	39	.443	9
R. Cucamonga	30	40	.429	13	Lancaster	30	40	.429	10
Lancaster	26	44	.371	17	Inland Empire	27	43	.386	13

PLAYOFFS—Division Series: Rancho Cucamonga defeated Lake Elsinore 2-0 and Bakersfield defeated Modesto 2-1 in best-of-three series. **Semifinals:** High Desert defeated Rancho Cucamonga 3-2 and San Jose defeated Bakersfield 3-2 in best-of-five series. **Finals:** San Jose defeated High Desert 3-0 in a best-of-five series.

OVERALL STANDINGS

Team	W	L	PCT	GB	Manager	Attendance	Average	Last Penn.
San Jose Giants (Giants)	93	47	.664	—	Andy Skeels	211,054	3,015	2009
High Desert Mavericks (Mariners)	83	57	.593	10	Jim Horner	112,470	1,630	1997
Bakersfield Blaze (Rangers)	75	65	.536	18	Steve Buechele	65,656	952	1989
Modesto Nuts (Rockies)	75	65	.536	18	Jerry Weinstein	167,722	2,431	2004
Lake Elsinore Storm (Padres)	73	67	.521	20	Carlos Lezcano	235,174	3,458	2001
Visalia Rawhide (Diamondbacks)	64	76	.457	29	Mike Bell	105,405	1,528	1978
Rancho Cucamonga Quakes (Angels)	61	79	.436	32	Keith Johnson	266,773	3,811	1994
Stockton Ports (Athletics)	61	79	.436	32	Aaron Nieckula	203,327	2,905	2008
Inland Empire 66ers (Dodgers)	59	81	.421	34	Carlos Subero	202,728	2,896	2006
Lancaster JetHawks (Astros)	56	84	.400	37	Wes Clements	150,970	2,157	Never

CLUB BATTING

	AVG	G	AB	R	H	2B	3B	HR	RBI	BB	SO	SB	CS	OBP	SLG
High Desert	.298	140	4895	860	1461	287	80	164	791	452	1038	136	72	.364	.490
Lancaster	.283	140	4939	782	1400	323	66	136	741	444	1120	77	52	.349	.458
San Jose	.280	140	4830	803	1350	284	43	123	729	480	1051	115	50	.351	.433
Bakersfield	.269	140	4888	712	1313	301	22	144	653	348	1211	68	30	.328	.428
Modesto	.268	140	4777	686	1281	285	57	88	629	378	1107	139	65	.330	.407
Inland Empire	.266	140	4754	662	1266	256	46	122	606	454	1249	171	80	.335	.416
R. Cucamonga	.265	140	4648	664	1231	236	59	82	591	445	1009	149	78	.334	.394
Lake Elsinore	.264	140	4806	723	1271	273	50	96	658	603	1044	126	50	.353	.402
Stockton	.258	140	4772	638	1230	204	40	106	581	504	1143	106	63	.334	.384
Visalia	.248	140	4722	629	1170	231	27	68	554	505	1109	103	61	.332	.351

CLUB PITCHING

	ERA	G	CG	SHO	SV	IP	H	R	ER	HR	BB	SO	AVG
San Jose	3.27	140	1	13	39	1246	1162	526	452	108	401	1109	.249
Modesto	4.02	140	3	6	39	1252	1253	656	559	83	419	1121	.259
Stockton	4.15	140	0	4	36	1246	1170	717	575	113	526	1268	.247
Visalia	4.25	140	1	10	33	1246	1290	691	589	103	437	1138	.269
Lake Elsinore	4.26	140	1	8	34	1241	1306	672	588	94	424	1151	.273
Bakersfield	4.35	140	3	6	37	1253	1276	694	606	97	459	1155	.264
Rancho Cucamonga	4.69	140	1	6	32	1224	1324	741	638	136	485	1053	.278
Inland Empire	4.72	140	1	6	31	1231	1294	749	646	115	556	1064	.273
High Desert	5.02	140	5	5	34	1240	1349	806	691	129	480	1065	.278
Lancaster	5.92	140	4	2	23	1225	1549	907	806	151	426	957	.309

CLUB FIELDING

	PCT	PO	A	E	DP		PCT	PO	A	E	DP
San Jose	.976	3737	1519	128	382	Inland Empire	.971	3692	1490	155	342
Lake Elsinore	.972	3722	1529	150	294	Bakersfield	.969	3759	1527	171	327
Lancaster	.972	3676	1437	147	264	High Desert	.969	3718	1488	164	322
R. Cucamonga	.972	3673	1466	150	318	Modesto	.969	3757	1353	161	270
Visalia	.972	3738	1427	148	391	Stockton	.969	3737	1348	178	273

INDIVIDUAL BATTING LEADERS *(MINIMUM 3.1 PA/TEAM GAME)*

	AVG	G	AB	R	H	2B	3B	HR	RBI	BB	SO	SB
Clemens, Koby, Lancaster	.345	116	423	74	146	45	6	22	121	51	109	4
Liddi, Alex, High Desert	.345	129	493	97	170	44	5	23	104	53	122	10
Gillies, Tyson, High Desert	.341	124	498	104	170	17	14	9	42	60	81	44
McOwen, James, High Desert	.340	115	447	79	152	23	8	10	82	40	70	13
Neal, Thomas, San Jose	.337	129	475	102	160	41	4	22	90	65	98	3
Carter, Yusuf, Stockton	.318	91	352	61	112	12	4	14	52	31	89	4
Shuck, Jack, Lancaster	.315	133	556	98	175	30	11	1	36	64	55	18
Blackmon, Charles, Modesto	.307	133	550	87	169	34	7	7	69	39	83	30
Robinson, Trayvon, Inland Empire	.306	117	470	82	144	28	9	15	54	50	125	43
Schmidt, Konrad, Visalia	.304	106	411	54	125	28	1	9	50	30	75	0

INDIVIDUAL PITCHING LEADERS *(MINIMUM 1 IP/TEAM GAME)*

	W	L	ERA	G	GS	CG	SV	IP	H	R	BB	SO
Torres, Alexander, Rancho Cucamonga	10	3	2.74	21	19	0	0	121	93	43	63	124
Clark, Craig, San Jose	16	2	2.86	26	25	0	0	148	131	53	36	135
Tanner, Clayton, San Jose	12	6	3.17	26	23	0	0	139	132	62	42	121
Riordan, Cory, Modesto	12	7	3.93	28	27	2	0	170	185	87	48	134
Pelzer, Wynn, Lake Elsinore	11	8	3.94	27	27	0	0	151	134	76	59	147
Sexton, Timothy, Inland Empire	8	14	3.96	27	22	0	0	157	178	92	34	100
Wild, Jacob, High Desert	6	8	4.09	34	20	2	0	132	146	75	37	116
Hefner, Jeremy, Lake Elsinore	14	9	4.12	27	27	0	0	151	165	81	38	142
Collmenter, Joshua, Visalia	8	10	4.15	27	27	1	0	145	127	76	55	152
Hensley, Steven, High Desert	9	3	4.21	20	19	1	0	113	104	57	30	108

ALL-STAR TEAM

C: Koby Clemens, Lancaster. **1B:** Joe Dunigan, High Desert. **2B:** Jason Van Kooten, Modesto. **3B:** Alex Liddi, High Desert. **SS:** Beamer Weems, Lake Elsinore. **OF:** Thomas Neal, San Jose; Jon Gaston, Lancaster; Roger Kieschnick, San Jose. **DH:** Scott Van Slyke, Inland Empire. **SP:** Craig Clark, San Jose; Alex Torres, Rancho Cucamonga; Donnie Hume, High Desert. **RP:** Craig Baker, Modesto.
Most Valuable Player: Alex Liddi, High Desert. **Most Valuable Pitcher:** Craig Clark, San Jose.
Manager of the Year: Jim Horner, High Desert.

DEPARTMENT LEADERS

BATTING

OBP	Neal, Thomas, San Jose	.431
SLG	Clemens, Koby, Lancaster	.636
OPS	Clemens, Koby, Lancaster	.105
R	Gaston, Jonathan, Lancaster	119
H	Shuck, Jack, Lancaster	175
TB	Gaston, Jonathan, Lancaster	310
XBH	Gaston, Jonathan, Lancaster	81
2B	Clemens, Koby, Lancaster	45
	Van Kooten, Jason, Modesto	45
3B	Gaston, Jonathan, Lancaster	15
HR	Gaston, Jonathan, Lancaster	35
RBI	Clemens, Koby, Lancaster	121
SAC	Gillies, Tyson, High Desert	16
	Romine, Andrew, Rancho Cucamonga	16
BB	Payne, Danny, Lake Elsinore	79
HBP	Greene, Jonathan, Bakersfield	21
SO	Peguero, Carlos, High Desert	172
SB	Gillies, Tyson, High Desert	44
CS	Gillies, Tyson, High Desert	19
AB/SO	Shuck, Jack, Lancaster	10.11

PITCHING

G	Baker, Craig, Modesto	62
GS	Durst, Kenneth, Modesto	28
	McAnaney, Patrick, Visalia	28
GF	Baker, Craig, Modesto	52
	Oland, Bryan, Lake Elsinore	52
SV	Baker, Craig, Modesto	33
W	Hume, Donald, High Desert	17
L	Sexton, Timothy, Inland Empire	14
IP	Riordan, Cory, Modesto	170
H	Riordan, Cory, Modesto	185
R	Murphy, Tim, Bakersfield	114
ER	Murphy, Tim, Bakersfield	102
HB	Gomez, Kennil, Bakersfield	21
BB	Gomez, Kennil, Bakersfield	67
SO	Collmenter, Joshua, Visalia	152
SO/9 (SP)	Collmenter, Joshua, Visalia	9.41
SO/9 (RP)	Brewer, T.J., San Jose	12.06
BB/9	Bleier, Richard, Bakersfield	1.25
WP	Cespedes, Leandro, Lancaster	28
BK	Beltre, Christian, Visalia	3
HR	Hicks, Christopher, Lancaster	22
AVG	Torres, Alexander, Rancho Cucamonga	.217

FIELDING

C	FPCT	Felix, Jose, Bakersfield	.991
	PO	Felix, Jose, Bakersfield	729
	A	Rosario, Alberto, R.Cucamonga	103
	E	Scott, Travis, High Desert	16
	DP	Davis, Lars, Modesto	10
	PB	Carter, Yusuf, Stockton	37
1B	FPCT	Navarro, Efren, R. Cucamonga	.989
	PO	Navarro, Efren, R. Cucamonga	1077
	A	Navarro, Efren, Rancho Cucamonga	85
	E	Carrasco, Felix, Lake Elsinore	18
	DP	Navarro, Efren, R. Cucamonga	102
2B	FPCT	Lawson, Matthew, Bakersfield	.980
	PO	Noonan, Nick, San Jose	236
	A	Lawson, Matthew, Bakersfield	410
	E	Van Kooten, Jason, Modesto	20
	DP	Noonan, Nick, San Jose	95
3B	FPCT	Liddi, Alex, High Desert	.945
	PO	Liddi, Alex, High Desert	96
	A	Liddi, Alex, High Desert	211
	E	Gillaspie, Conor, San Jose	27
	DP	Gillaspie, Conor, San Jose	23
SS	FPCT	Weems, Beamer, Lake Elsinore	.976
	PO	Romine, Andrew, R. Cucamonga	220
	A	Romine, Andrew, R. Cucamonga	359
	E	Stoneburner, Davis, Bakersfield	35
	DP	Romine, Andrew, R. Cucamonga	74
OF	FPCT	Linton, Ollie, Visalia	.996
OF	PO	Gillies, Tyson, High Desert	273
OF	A	Payne, Danny, Lake Elsinore	19
OF	E	Peguero, Carlos, High Desert	14
OF	DP	Payne, Danny, Lake Elsinore	5

MINOR LEAGUES

BY BEN BADLER

L ynchburg's chances heading into the Carolina League playoffs seemed dim.

They qualified with a league-best 45-24 mark in the first half, but then the Hillcats tied Myrtle Beach for the league's worst second-half record at 28-42, thanks in part to the promotion of third baseman Pedro Alvarez to Double-A Altoona.

However, the Hillcats pulled off the improbable by sweeping Salem in a best-of-five series to win the Mills Cup championship.

Middle infielder Chase d'Arnaud, who was still in low Class A West Virginia when Lynchburg secured its first-half title, ignited the Hillcats in the postseason. He hit a game-tying two-run single in the finale and drove in eight runs in the series to earn the Mills Cup MVP award. First baseman Matt Hague, shortstop Jordy Mercer and outfielder Jamie Romak combined to drive in 11 runs in eight postseason games for Lynchburg.

For an eight-team league, the Carolina League featured more than its share of potential superstar talent and depth this season.

In Myrtle Beach outfielder Jason Heyward and Frederick lefthander Brian Matusz, the league featured arguably the best hitting and pitching prospects who appeared in the minors in 2009. Matusz, who moved so quickly that he finished the year in Baltimore, was the best of a strong CL group of lefthanders that also included Wilmington's Mike Montgomery and Danny Duffy and Frederick teammate Zach Britton.

Matusz ranked among the league leaders in ERA and topped the circuit in strikeouts at the time of his promotion to Double-A Bowie in late May, posting a 4-2, 2.16 mark with 75 strikeouts and 21 walks in 67 innings with the Keys. Heyward's stay in Myrtle Beach was interrupted in June by oblique and leg injuries, hit .296/.369/.519 in 189 at-bats before moving on to Double-A Mississippi.

Several 2008 first-round picks bolstered the CL with strong performances in their first full pro seasons. Alvarez struggled early in the season but went on to a power-hitting tear before his promotion,

and Kinston third baseman Lonnie Chisenhall and Salem righthander Casey Kelly also stood out.

Royals 2007 first-round pick Mike Moustakas put up underwhelming numbers in his second full pro season but still impressed Carolina League observers with a well-rounded set of offensive tools. Potomac shortstop Danny Espinosa (Nationals) emerged as the top shortstop prospect in the league with surprising power and above-average defensive tools.

The league will have a new look next year, as the Pirates ended their 15-year relationship with Lynchburg by swapping high Class A affiliates with the Reds (Sarasota/Florida State League).

TOP 20 PROSPECTS

1. Jason Heyward, of, Myrtle Beach (Braves)
2. Brian Matusz, lhp, Frederick (Orioles)
3. Pedro Alvarez, 3b, Lynchburg (Pirates)
4. Freddie Freeman, 1b, Myrtle Beach (Braves)
5. Lonnie Chisenhall, 3b, Kinston (Indians)
6. Casey Kelly, rhp, Salem (Red Sox)
7. Mike Montgomery, lhp, Wilmington (Royals)
8. Mike Moustakas, 3b, Wilmington (Royals)
9. Ryan Kalish, of, Salem (Red Sox)
10. Danny Espinosa, ss, Potomac (Nationals)
11. Danny Duffy, lhp, Wilmington (Royals)
12. Anthony Rizzo, 1b, Salem (Red Sox)
13. Chase D'Arnaud, ss/2b, Lynchburg (Pirates)
14. Jordan Danks, of, Winston-Salem (White Sox)
15. Zach Britton, lhp, Frederick (Orioles)
16. David Lough, of, Wilmington (Royals)
17. Luis Exposito, c, Salem (Red Sox)
18. Che-Hsuan Lin, of, Salem (Red Sox)
19. Jeff Bianchi, ss, Wilmington (Royals)
20. Brent Morel, 3b, Winston-Salem (White Sox)

STANDINGS: SPLIT SEASON

FIRST HALF					SECOND HALF				
North	**W**	**L**	**PCT**	**GB**	**North**	**W**	**L**	**PCT**	**GB**
Lynchburg	45	24	.652	—	Wilmington	46	24	.657	—
Potomac	37	30	.552	7	Potomac	42	28	.600	4
Wilmington	38	31	.551	7	Frederick	33	37	.471	13
Frederick	31	38	.449	14	Lynchburg	28	42	.400	18
South	**W**	**L**	**PCT**	**GB**	**South**	**W**	**L**	**PCT**	**GB**
Winston-Salem	38	30	.559	—	Winston-Salem	35	35	.500	—
Salem	32	37	.464	6½	Salem	35	35	.500	—
Kinston	27	41	.397	11	Kinston	33	37	.471	2
Myrtle Beach	25	42	.373	12½	Myrtle Beach	28	42	.400	7

PLAYOFFS—Semifinals: Salem defeated Winston-Salem 3-0 and Lynchburg defeated Wilmington 3-2 in best-of-five series.
Finals: Lynchburg defeated Salem 3-0 in best-of-five series.

OVERALL STANDINGS

Team	W	L	PCT	GB	Manager	Attendance	Average	Last Penn.
Wilmington Blue Rocks (Royals)	84	55	.604	—	Brian Rupp	288,094	4,723	1999
Potomac Nationals (Nationals)	79	58	.577	4	Trent Jewett	180,541	3,009	2008
Winston-Salem Dash (White Sox)	73	65	.529	10½	Joe McEwing	57,665	901	2003
Lynchburg Hillcats (Pirates)	73	66	.525	11	P.J. Forbes	164,328	2,490	2009
Salem Red Sox (Red Sox)	67	72	.482	17	Chad Epperson	231,186	3,451	2001
Frederick Keys (Orioles)	64	75	.460	20	Richie Hebner	293,438	4,585	2007
Kinston Indians (Indians)	60	78	.435	23½	Chris Tremie	133,049	1,901	2006
Myrtle Beach Pelicans (Braves)	53	84	.387	30	Rocket Wheeler	238,287	3,610	2000

CLUB BATTING

	AVG	G	AB	R	H	2B	3B	HR	RBI	BB	SO	SB	CS	OBP	SLG
Frederick	.268	139	4649	654	1248	252	23	103	605	411	1046	135	62	.334	.399
Winston-Salem	.262	138	4517	626	1183	263	17	98	565	392	948	124	61	.329	.393
Potomac	.258	137	4456	674	1149	256	31	127	611	514	1043	186	88	.341	.415
Wilmington	.256	139	4424	569	1134	213	35	66	509	385	869	203	84	.322	.365
Kinston	.255	138	4580	616	1166	232	29	76	560	553	1016	110	63	.339	.368
Lynchburg	.253	139	4592	643	1161	265	39	88	580	480	945	117	47	.333	.385
Salem	.252	139	4626	599	1167	270	22	62	548	477	916	93	43	.327	.360
Myrtle Beach	.245	137	4519	550	1105	209	23	114	503	353	1063	73	65	.307	.377

CLUB PITCHING

	ERA	G	CG	SHO	SV	IP	H	R	ER	HR	BB	SO	AVG
Wilmington	3.10	139	3	16	60	1191	1084	486	410	68	371	973	.244
Potomac	3.78	137	3	14	37	1180	1148	591	496	80	415	890	.256
Salem	3.80	139	0	10	33	1212	1146	599	511	88	457	1113	.249
Kinston	3.90	138	0	9	30	1203	1116	618	521	98	508	1075	.246
Frederick	4.11	139	2	5	31	1196	1188	664	546	105	477	992	.258
Lynchburg	4.11	139	1	9	43	1208	1278	621	552	96	342	855	.272
Winston-Salem	4.30	138	3	7	41	1173	1154	642	561	113	421	886	.260
Myrtle Beach	4.68	137	3	7	33	1186	1199	711	616	86	574	1062	.263

CLUB FIELDING

	PCT	PO	A	E	DP		PCT	PO	A	E	DP
Winston-Salem	.978	3519	1431	110	318	Salem	.972	3635	1455	149	296
Kinston	.976	3608	1360	124	340	Potomac	.969	3540	1404	158	307
Lynchburg	.976	3623	1494	127	387	Myrtle Beach	.967	3557	1370	166	280
Wilmington	.973	3574	1417	137	336	Frederick	.966	3587	1485	179	293

INDIVIDUAL BATTING LEADERS (MINIMUM 3.1 PA/TEAM GAME)

	AVG	G	AB	R	H	2B	3B	HR	RBI	BB	SO	SB
Widlansky, Robert, Frederick	.340	86	326	49	111	31	1	7	59	29	48	5
Robinson, Clint, Wilmington	.298	124	436	65	130	31	1	13	57	35	79	4
Hague, Matt, Lynchburg	.293	122	454	52	133	30	0	8	50	40	67	3
Watts, Kris, Lynchburg	.291	103	340	54	99	21	3	7	49	55	51	2
Angle, Matt, Frederick	.289	123	478	78	138	17	4	1	32	59	72	40
Marrero, Chris, Potomac	.287	112	414	58	119	21	2	16	65	42	97	2
Linares, Donell, Myrtle Beach	.287	130	505	63	145	32	1	15	87	22	41	5
Joseph, Caleb, Frederick	.284	104	380	50	108	23	2	12	60	26	64	2
Jones, Michael, Salem	.283	108	396	55	112	26	1	6	59	40	58	3
Morel, Brent, Winston-Salem	.281	128	481	82	135	33	1	16	79	38	66	25

INDIVIDUAL PITCHING LEADERS (MINIMUM 1 IP/TEAM GAME)

	W	L	ERA	G	GS	CG	SV	IP	H	R	BB	SO
Espino, Paolo, Kinston	9	6	2.59	22	21	0	1	118	89	41	34	101
Britton, Zach, Frederick	9	6	2.70	25	24	0	0	140	123	64	55	131
Milone, Tom, Potomac	12	5	2.91	27	25	0	0	151	144	57	36	106
Duffy, Danny, Wilmington	9	3	2.98	24	24	1	0	127	108	49	41	125
Young, Russell, Kinston	6	6	3.28	22	22	0	0	129	126	51	22	78
McSwain, Matt, Lynchburg	11	8	3.43	28	25	1	1	144	162	60	23	64
Weiland, Kyle, Salem	7	9	3.46	26	26	0	0	133	119	65	57	112
Paulino, Eduardo, Wilmington	10	6	3.63	26	22	1	0	139	129	61	39	84
Cordier, Erik, Myrtle Beach	7	8	3.87	25	25	1	0	121	115	62	74	88
Garrison, Seth, Salem	8	11	3.90	26	25	0	1	132	136	72	40	90

ALL-STAR TEAM

C: Caleb Joseph, Frederick. **1B:** Brandon Waring, Frederick; Chris Marrero, Potomac. **2B:** Cord Phelps, Kinston. **3B:** Brent Morel, Winston-Salem. **SS:** Danny Espinosa, Potomac. **OF:** Matt Angle, Frederick; Che-Hsuan Lin, Salem; Derrick Robinson, Wilmington. **DH:** Cody Johnson, Myrtle Beach. **UTIL IF:** Lonnie Chisenhall, Kinston. **UTIL OF:** Tim Fedroff, Kinston. **SP:** Zach Britton, Frederick. **RP:** R.J. Rodriguez, Lynchburg.
Most Valuable Player: Brandon Waring, Frederick. **Pitcher of the Year:** Zach Britton, Frederick.
Manager of the Year: Joe McEwing, Winston-Salem.

DEPARTMENT LEADERS

BATTING

OBP	Watts, Kris, Lynchburg	.405
SLG	Waring, Brandon, Frederick	.520
OPS	Waring, Brandon, Frederick	.874
R	Espinosa, Danny, Potomac	90
H	Linares, Donell, Myrtle Beach	145
TB	Waring, Brandon, Frederick	246
XBH	Waring, Brandon, Frederick	63
2B	Mercer, Jordy, Lynchburg	36
3B	Presley, Alex, Lynchburg	11
HR	Johnson, Cody, Myrtle Beach	32
RBI	Waring, Brandon, Frederick	90
SAC	Four tied at	12
BB	Phelps, Cord, Kinston	93
HBP	Loman, Seth, Winston, Salem	15
SO	Johnson, Cody, Myrtle Beach	171
SB	Robinson, Derrick, Wilmington	69
CS	Robinson, Derrick, Wilmington	23
AB/SO	Linares, Donell, Myrtle Beach	12.32

PITCHING

G	Cawiezell, Dallas, Kinston	49
GS	Three tied at	27
GF	Rodriguez, R.J., Lynchburg	43
SV	Rodriguez, R.J., Lynchburg	27
W	Milone, Tom, Potomac	12
L	Maxwell, Levi, Winston, Salem	14
IP	Carter, Anthony, Winston, Salem	155
H	McSwain, Matt, Lynchburg	162
R	Carter, Anthony, Winston, Salem	80
	Rohrbough, Cole, Myrtle Beach	80
ER	Carter, Anthony, Winston, Salem	75
	Rohrbough, Cole, Myrtle Beach	75
HB	Weiland, Kyle, Salem	16
BB	Cordier, Erik, Myrtle Beach	74
SO	Portice, Eammon, Salem	141
SO/9 (SP)	Portice, Eammon, Salem	9.89
SO/9 (RP)	Luis, Santo, Winston-Salem	12.70
BB/9	McSwain, Matt, Lynchburg	1.43
WP	Britton, Zach, Frederick	21
BK	Paulino, Eduardo, Wilmington	5
HR	Carter, Anthony, Winston, Salem	21
AVG	Espino, Paolo, Kinston	.206

FIELDING

C	FPCT	Watts, Kris, Lynchburg	.997
	PO	Eigsti, Ryan, Wilmington	747
	A	Eigsti, Ryan, Wilmington	119
	E	Joseph, Caleb, Frederick	11
	DP	Eigsti, Ryan, Wilmington	7
		Joseph, Caleb, Frederick	7
	PB	Johnson, Logan, Winston, Salem	25
1B	FPCT	Hague, Matt, Lynchburg	.995
	PO	Hague, Matt, Lynchburg	1086
	A	Marrero, Chris, Potomac	73
	E	Marrero, Chris, Potomac	16
	DP	Hague, Matt, Lynchburg	104
2B	FPCT	Phelps, Cord, Kinston	.993
	PO	Giavotella, Johnny, Wilmington	248
	A	Giavotella, Johnny, Wilmington	355
	E	Giavotella, Johnny, Wilmington	21
	DP	Giavotella, Johnny, Wilmington	87
3B	FPCT	Morel, Brent, Winston, Salem	.969
	PO	Morel, Brent, Winston, Salem	95
	A	Morel, Brent, Winston, Salem	245
	E	Moustakas, Mike, Wilmington	24
	DP	Moustakas, Mike, Wilmington	25
SS	FPCT	Espinosa, Danny, Potomac	.965
	PO	Espinosa, Danny, Potomac	219
	A	Paiml, Greg, Winston, Salem	393
	E	Florimon Jr., Pedro, Frederick	35
	DP	Mercer, Jordy, Lynchburg	86
OF	FPCT	Angle, Matt, Frederick	.993
	PO	Robinson, Derrick, Wilmington	310
	A	Lin, Che-Hsuan, Salem	18
	E	Rowell, Billy, Frederick	15
	DP	Lin, Che-Hsuan, Salem	7

MINOR LEAGUES

BY J.J. COOPER

T he Yankees' 2009 dominance extended beyond a World Series title and into their minor league system.

New York's Tampa farm club won the Florida State League championship, topping the Charlotte Stone Crabs (Rays) three games to two in the championship series.

Like the big league Yankees, Tampa was able to rely on some star power to earn their ring. Lefthander Ian Kennedy, down from Triple-A Scranton/Wilkes-Barre for a rehab start, made a surprise start in the opener of the championship series. Righthander D.J. Mitchell and Lefthander Trent Lare pitched the Yankees the rest of the way to the title with Lare, a former independent leaguer, winning the deciding Game Five by tossing five shutout innings while yielding just one hit and striking out six.

Brevard County had entered the playoffs as the favorite. Led by outfielders Logan Schafer, Caleb Gindl and righthander Logan Ondrusek, the Manatees led the league with a 79-48 record (five games better than Tampa), but Tampa swept them 2-0 in the first round of the playoffs.

Tampa had struggled through the first half of the season even as catcher Jesus Montero put together one of the best first halves offensively in the minors. But as July arrived, the Yankees turned into the best team in the Florida State League, going 47-19 after the all-star break.

Montero was one of a large number of top prospects who made a stopover in the Florida State League. Montero, Phillies top prospect Domonic Brown, Marlins top prospect Mike Stanton and Cubs top prospect Starlin Castro all began the season in the FSL before being promoted to Double-A. Montero's teammate, catcher Austin Romine, was named the league's player of the year.

While the league was filled with intriguing hitting prospects, speedsters dominated on the field. Four of the minors top eight basestealers spent all or most of the season in the Florida State League.

Most of the league's top pitchers, including Kyle Drabek, Zach Stewart, Andrew Cashner and Brad Holt, were promoted to Double-A before the midpoint of the season. Fort Myers' David Bromberg stuck around to win pitcher of the year honors.

The league will have a different look next year, as the Pirates will take over the Reds' affiliate in Sarasota and relocate the team to Bradenton—home the Pirates' spring training facility.

TOP 20 PROSPECTS

1. Mike Stanton, of, Jupiter (Marlins)
2. Jesus Montero, c, Tampa (Yankees)
3. Domonic Brown, of, Clearwater (Phillies)
4. Yonder Alonso, 1b, Sarasota (Reds)
5. Kyle Drabek, rhp, Clearwater (Phillies)
6. Starlin Castro, ss, Daytona (Cubs)
7. Jenrry Mejia, rhp, St. Lucie (Mets)
8. Ben Revere, of, Fort Myers (Twins)
9. Ike Davis, 1b, St. Lucie (Mets)
10. Austin Romine, c, Tampa (Yankees)
11. Carlos Gutierrez, rhp, Fort Myers (Twins)
12. Matt Dominguez, 3b, Jupiter (Marlins)
13. Kirk Nieuwenhuis, of, St. Lucie (Mets)
14. Josh Vitters, 3b, Daytona (Cubs)
15. David Bromberg, rhp, Fort Myers (Twins)
16. Caleb Gindl, of, Brevard County (Brewers)
17. Chris Parmelee, 1b, Fort Myers (Twins)
18. Shane Peterson, of, Palm Beach (Cardinals)
19. Freddy Galvis, ss, Clearwater (Phillies)
20. Mark Rogers, rhp, Brevard County (Brewers)

STANDINGS: SPLIT SEASON

FIRST HALF

North	W	L	PCT	GB
Brevard County	40	24	.625	—
Daytona	34	33	.507	7½
Dunedin	33	34	.493	8½
Clearwater	32	34	.485	9
Tampa	30	37	.448	11½
Lakeland	29	36	.446	11½

South	W	L	PCT	GB
Fort Myers	43	26	.623	—
Charlotte	37	31	.544	5½
Jupiter	34	33	.507	8
St. Lucie	34	34	.500	8½
Palm Beach	29	41	.414	14½
Sarasota	28	40	.412	14½

SECOND HALF

North	W	L	PCT	GB
Tampa	47	19	.712	—
Brevard County	39	24	.619	6½
Dunedin	34	33	.507	13½
Clearwater	35	35	.500	14
Daytona	30	38	.441	18
Lakeland	26	39	.400	20½

South	W	L	PCT	GB
Fort Myers	37	32	.536	—
Charlotte	34	35	.493	3
St. Lucie	32	34	.485	3½
Jupiter	33	37	.471	4½
Palm Beach	32	36	.471	4½
Sarasota	26	43	.377	11

PLAYOFFS—Semifinals: Tampa defeated Brevard County 2-0 and Charlotte defeated Fort Myers 2-1 in best-of-three series.
Finals: Tampa defeated Charlotte 3-2 in best-of-five series.

OVERALL STANDINGS

Team	W	L	PCT	GB	Manager	Attendance	Average	Last Penn.
Brevard County Manatees (Brewers)	79	48	.622	—	Mike Guerrero	68,596	1,183	2001
Fort Myers Miracle (Twins)	80	58	.580	4½	Jeff Smith	115,361	1,748	1985
Tampa Yankees (Yankees)	77	56	.579	5	Luis Sojo	92,671	1,519	2009
Charlotte Stone Crabs (Rays)	71	66	.518	13	Jim Morrison	171,314	2,855	1990
Dunedin Blue Jays (Blue Jays)	67	67	.500	15½	Omar Malave	35,683	585	Never
Clearwater Threshers (Phillies)	67	69	.493	16½	Ernie Whitt	169,559	2,494	2007
St. Lucie Mets (Mets)	66	68	.493	16½	Tim Teufel	95,598	1,471	2006
Jupiter Hammerheads (Marlins)	67	70	.489	17	Tim Leiper	68,741	1,074	1991
Daytona Cubs (Cubs)	64	71	.474	19	Buddy Bailey	147,921	2,425	2008
Palm Beach Cardinals (Cardinals)	61	77	.442	23½	Tom Spencer	68,562	1,008	2005
Lakeland Flying Tigers (Tigers)	55	75	.423	25½	Andy Barkett	49,569	885	1992
Sarasota Reds (Reds)	54	83	.394	30	Joe Ayrault	33,788	528	1963

CLUB BATTING

	AVG	G	AB	R	H	2B	3B	HR	RBI	BB	SO	SB	CS	OBP	SLG
Brevard County	.267	127	4182	554	1116	188	33	65	497	383	863	207	58	.333	.374
Fort Myers	.265	138	4566	585	1212	208	41	60	533	473	864	128	60	.341	.368
Tampa	.265	133	4257	573	1129	223	51	64	510	433	806	104	61	.337	.387
St. Lucie	.261	134	4460	609	1165	235	26	107	560	450	982	88	48	.338	.398
Daytona	.253	135	4395	527	1111	175	35	42	471	366	836	155	63	.313	.337
Dunedin	.251	134	4382	610	1101	239	28	86	566	470	1022	115	38	.328	.377
Clearwater	.250	136	4503	536	1124	221	23	87	487	401	1011	131	60	.315	.367
Lakeland	.248	130	4175	520	1035	192	40	70	471	353	974	115	45	.312	.363
Jupiter	.245	137	4403	528	1079	191	31	78	472	461	977	112	55	.322	.356
Palm Beach	.244	138	4509	532	1100	203	51	65	477	386	1005	106	50	.319	.355
Charlotte	.242	137	4389	526	1062	197	35	53	465	403	944	146	68	.315	.339
Sarasota	.231	137	4477	446	1034	213	28	60	401	305	985	90	47	.284	.331

CLUB PITCHING

	ERA	G	CG	SHO	SV	IP	H	R	ER	HR	BB	SO	AVG
Brevard County	2.75	127	3	18	46	1113	891	427	340	50	463	1005	.221
Fort Myers	3.18	138	5	11	42	1201	1112	523	424	63	421	998	.247
Daytona	3.44	135	0	13	26	1149	1066	527	439	63	433	955	.246
Dunedin	3.46	134	3	6	31	1147	1130	534	441	67	375	962	.258
Tampa	3.46	133	2	10	39	1125	1109	514	433	49	369	919	.257
Jupiter	3.48	137	5	12	35	1178	1082	519	456	65	333	858	.244
St. Lucie	3.61	134	2	7	37	1148	1089	560	460	66	436	955	.250
Charlotte	3.65	137	5	9	41	1173	1116	552	476	91	353	1004	.251
Sarasota	3.77	137	3	9	33	1194	1216	598	500	88	458	852	.266
Palm Beach	3.91	138	1	9	32	1195	1152	622	519	52	512	988	.253
Lakeland	3.94	130	4	9	29	1079	1130	556	472	97	313	818	.268
Clearwater	3.95	136	7	11	38	1197	1175	614	526	86	418	955	.256

CLUB FIELDING

	PCT	PO	A	E	DP		PCT	PO	A	E	DP
Jupiter	.977	3533	1325	114	289	Dunedin	.971	3441	1437	145	384
Brevard County	.975	3338	1363	119	331	Sarasota	.970	3581	1463	154	399
Tampa	.975	3375	1326	123	262	St. Lucie	.970	3445	1368	151	345
Charlotte	.974	3519	1355	132	279	Clearwater	.969	3592	1366	157	303
Fort Myers	.972	3603	1459	145	330	Palm Beach	.969	3584	1411	160	368
Lakeland	.972	3237	1277	130	271	Daytona	.966	3447	1468	171	356

INDIVIDUAL BATTING LEADERS *(MINIMUM 3.1 PA/TEAM GAME)*

	AVG	G	AB	R	H	2B	3B	HR	RBI	BB	SO	SB
Schafer, Logan, Brevard County	.313	113	457	76	143	31	6	6	58	38	53	16
Revere, Ben, Fort Myers	.311	121	466	75	145	13	4	2	48	40	34	45
Castro, Starlin, Daytona	.302	96	358	45	108	17	3	3	35	19	41	22
Farris, Eric, Brevard County	.298	124	473	68	141	18	1	7	49	29	46	70
Guzman, Carlos, St. Lucie	.290	126	472	59	137	28	2	15	64	39	95	6
Dolenc, Mark, Fort Myers	.288	110	386	44	111	19	5	4	42	24	84	27
Sierra, Moises, Dunedin	.286	110	405	56	116	24	2	5	56	34	66	10
Smith, Curt, Palm Beach	.286	94	371	44	106	15	3	10	56	15	67	1
Campana, Tony, Daytona	.284	108	430	56	122	8	2	0	25	34	78	55
Lutz, Zach, St. Lucie	.284	99	356	46	101	19	2	11	62	50	72	1

INDIVIDUAL PITCHING LEADERS *(MINIMUM 1 IP/TEAM GAME)*

	W	L	ERA	G	GS	CG	SV	IP	H	R	BB	SO
Downs, Darin, Charlotte	12	4	2.00	20	19	1	0	122	117	35	23	111
Hirschfeld, Steve, Fort Myers	7	7	2.23	32	17	2	0	117	93	36	31	86
Anundsen, Evan, Brevard County	10	8	2.69	24	23	2	0	130	101	51	41	118
Bromberg, David, Fort Myers	13	4	2.70	27	26	1	0	153	125	52	63	148
Rivas, Amaury, Brevard County	13	7	2.98	26	23	0	0	133	109	55	43	123
Cobb, Alex, Charlotte	8	5	3.03	24	23	0	0	125	116	49	31	107
Horst, Jeremy, Sarasota	6	13	3.25	23	23	1	0	133	136	61	41	101
Hess, Andrew, Lakeland	7	11	3.28	23	20	0	0	123	144	56	27	56
Robertson, Tyler, Fort Myers	8	8	3.33	26	26	0	0	143	139	64	51	103
Newmann, David, Charlotte	9	6	3.44	24	24	2	0	131	108	59	46	128

ALL-STAR TEAM

C: Austin Romine, Tampa; Robinson Chirinos, Daytona. **1B:** Chris Parmelee, Fort Myers. **2B:** Eric Farris, Brevard County. **3B:** Brandon Laird, Tampa. **SS:** Starlin Castro, Daytona. **LF:** Ben Revere, Fort Myers. **CF:** Logan Schafer, Brevard County. **RF:** Caleb Gindl, Brevard County. **DH:** Tim Kennelly, Clearwater. **UTIL IF:** Shawn O'Malley, Charlotte. **UTIL OF:** Kirk Nieuwenhuis, St. Lucie. **RHSP:** Lance Pendleton, Tampa; David Bromberg, Fort Myers; Amaury Rivas, Brevard County. **LHSP:** Darin Downs, Charlotte. **RHRP:** Matt Gorgen, Charlotte; Jonathan Hovis, Tampa.
Player of the Year: Austin Romine, Tampa. **Pitcher of the Year:** David Bromberg, Fort Myers.
Manager of the Year: Jeff Smith, Fort Myers.

DEPARTMENT LEADERS

BATTING

OBP	O'Malley, Shawn, Charlotte	.388
SLG	Nieuwenhuis, Kirk, St. Lucie	.467
OPS	Nieuwenhuis, Kirk, St. Lucie	.824
R	Nieuwenhuis, Kirk, St. Lucie	91
H	Revere, Ben, Fort Myers	145
TB	Nieuwenhuis, Kirk, St. Lucie	225
XBH	Nieuwenhuis, Kirk, St. Lucie	56
2B	Nieuwenhuis, Kirk, St. Lucie	35
3B	Chambers, Adron, Palm Beach	16
HR	Maldonado, Brahiam, St. Lucie	18
RBI	Laird, Brandon, Tampa	75
SAC	Farris, Eric, Brevard County	26
BB	Parmelee, Chris, Fort Myers	65
	Sublett, Damon, Tampa	65
HBP	Williams, Seth, St. Lucie	18
SO	Burns, Greg, Jupiter	163
SB	Farris, Eric, Brevard County	70
CS	Revere, Ben, Fort Myers	17
AB/SO	Revere, Ben, Fort Myers	13.71

PITCHING

G	Reifer, Adam, Palm Beach	54
GS	Page, Ryan, Dunedin	28
GF	Reifer, Adam, Palm Beach	45
SV	Hovis, Jonathan, Tampa	22
W	Hall, Jeremy, Charlotte	14
L	Four tied at	13
IP	Naylor, Drew, Clearwater	158
	Villanueva, Elih, Jupiter	158
H	Page, Ryan, Dunedin	188
R	Page, Ryan, Dunedin	90
ER	Zink, Ryan, Tampa	76
HB	Moviel, Scott, St. Lucie	16
BB	Castillo, Richard, Palm Beach	66
SO	Bromberg, David, Fort Myers	148
SO/9 (SP)	Newmann, David, Charlotte	8.79
SO/9 (RP)	Collins, Tim, Dunedin	13.78
BB/9	Villanueva, Elih, Jupiter	1.03
WP	Williamson, Henry, Daytona	17
BK	Eight tied at	2
HR	Gagnier, L.J., Lakeland	15
	Horst, Jeremy, Sarasota	15
AVG	Hirschfeld, Steve, Fort Myers	.215

FIELDING

C	FPCT	Maldonado, Martin, Brevard County	.995
	PO	Pena, Francisco, St. Lucie	707
	A	Maldonado, Martin, Brevard County	95
	E	Romine, Austin, Tampa	10
	DP	Pena, Francisco, St. Lucie	8
	PB	Maldonado, Martin, Brevard County	17
1B	FPCT	Rodriguez, Manuel, Dunedin	.991
	PO	Durant, Michael, Clearwater	865
	A	Durant, Michael, Clearwater	58
	E	Durant, Michael, Clearwater	15
	DP	Rodriguez, Manuel, Dunedin	96
2B	FPCT	Farris, Eric, Brevard County	.985
	PO	Farris, Eric, Brevard County	230
	A	Farris, Eric, Brevard County	362
	E	Tolisano, John, Dunedin	21
	DP	Farris, Eric, Brevard County	79
		Tolisano, John, Dunedin	79
3B	FPCT	Dominguez, Matt, Jupiter	.949
	PO	Wheeler, Zelous, Brevard County	74
	A	Soto, Neftali, Sarasota	199
	E	Soto, Neftali, Sarasota	28
	DP	Wheeler, Zelous, Brevard County	29
SS	FPCT	O'Malley, Shawn, Charlotte	.960
	PO	Ciriaco, Audy, Lakeland	161
	A	Ciriaco, Audy, Lakeland	342
	E	Brewer, Brent, Brevard County	33
	DP	Martinez, Osvaldo, Jupiter	67
OF	FPCT	Revere, Ben, Fort Myers	.100
	PO	Burns, Greg, Jupiter	354
	A	Phipps, Denis, Sarasota	19
	E	Reed, Justin, Sarasota	11
	DP	Phipps, Denis, Sarasota	6

MINOR LEAGUES

MINOR LEAGUES

BY JIM SHONERD

The newly re-branded Fort Wayne TinCaps dominated the Midwest League's regular season from wire to wire, but their playoff run to the title was anything but smooth.

Fort Wayne won 94 games during the regular season, the highest win total in minor league baseball, and captured Eastern Division titles for both halves of the season. They boasted a deep, prospect-laden lineup led by outfielder Jaff Decker, third baseman James Darnell (who was promoted at midseason) and Padres 2008 first round pick Allan Dykstra (who struggled for most of the season but came on late). The TinCaps were the league's highest scoring offense and had the second stingiest pitching staff, headlined by league strike-out leader Simon Castro.

After cruising through the regular season, the TinCaps needed late dramatics to survive their first two playoff series, both of which went to a decisive third game. In Game Three of their first-round series against South Bend, the TinCaps trailed by two runs in the bottom of the eighth before rallying for three runs in the frame, all of which scored with two outs, to escape with a 5-4 victory. Great Lakes was waiting for the TinCaps in the second round and won Game One, 11-10, in 11 innings. The TinCaps took Game Two, but trailed by a run late in Game Three before scoring the tying run in the bottom of the eighth. They won the game and the series in the bottom of the 10th on catcher Robert Lara's walk-off home run.

No such dramatics were needed in the championship series, where Fort Wayne swept Burlington, allowing just five runs over the three-game series.

Great Lakes teammates Dee Gordon and Kyle Russell were named the league's co-MVPs, as Gordon led the league in steals and triples while Russell won its home run and RBI crowns. Gordon and Russell were two members of a talented crop of hitters from the 2008 draft to pass through the MWL in 2009, including, Beloit outfielder Aaron Hicks, Burlington first baseman Eric Hosmer and Wisconsin second baseman Brett Lawrie.

TOP 20 PROSPECTS

1. Aaron Hicks, of, Beloit (Twins)
2. Dee Gordon, ss, Great Lakes (Dodgers)
3. Josh Vitters, 3b, Peoria (Cubs)
4. Brett Lawrie, 2b, Wisconsin (Brewers)
5. Mike Montgomery, lhp, Burlington (Royals)
6. Casey Crosby, lhp, West Michigan (Tigers)
7. Simon Castro, rhp, Fort Wayne (Padres)
8. Jaff Decker, of, Fort Wayne (Padres)
9. Cody Scarpetta, rhp, Wisconsin (Brewers)
10. Ethan Martin, rhp, Great Lakes (Dodgers)
11. Tim Melville, rhp, Burlington (Royals)
12. Eric Hosmer, 1b, Burlington (Royals)
13. A.J. Pollock, of, South Bend (Diamondbacks)
14. Wily Peralta, rhp, Wisconsin (Brewers)
15. James Darnell, 3b, Fort Wayne (Padres)
16. Chris Archer, rhp, Peoria (Cubs)
17. Kyle Russell, of, Great Lakes (Dodgers)
18. Grant Desme, of, Kane County (Athletics)
19. Pedro Figueroa, lhp, Kane County (Athletics)
20. Chris Carpenter, rhp, Peoria (Cubs)

STANDINGS: SPLIT SEASON

FIRST HALF

East	W	L	PCT	GB
Fort Wayne	45	25	.643	—
West Michigan	43	27	.614	2
Great Lakes	40	30	.571	5
Dayton	28	42	.400	17
South Bend	27	41	.397	17
Lansing	26	43	.377	18½

West	W	L	PCT	GB
Kane County	41	29	.586	—
Cedar Rapids	40	30	.571	1
Clinton	40	30	.571	1
Peoria	38	31	.551	2½
Wisconsin	34	36	.486	7
Quad Cities	30	40	.429	11
Burlington	29	41	.414	12
Beloit	27	43	.386	14

SECOND HALF

East	W	L	PCT	GB
Fort Wayne	49	21	.700	—
Great Lakes	41	29	.586	8
West Michigan	38	32	.543	11
South Bend	32	38	.457	17
Dayton	31	38	.449	17½
Lansing	28	41	.406	20½

West	W	L	PCT	GB
Peoria	43	26	.623	—
Cedar Rapids	38	30	.559	4½
Burlington	35	34	.507	8
Kane County	35	35	.500	8½
Quad Cities	31	38	.449	12
Clinton	29	38	.433	13
Beloit	30	40	.429	13½
Wisconsin	24	45	.348	19

PLAYOFFS—Division Series: Cedar Rapids defeated Peoria 2-0, Burlington defeated Kane County 2-0, Fort Wayne defeated South Bend 2-1 and Great Lakes defeated West Michigan 2-1 in best-of-three series. **Semifinals:** Burlington defeated Cedar Rapids 2-1, Fort Wayne defeated Great Lakes 2-1 in best-of-three series. **Finals:** Fort Wayne defeated Burlington 3-0 in best-of-five series.

OVERALL STANDINGS

Team	W	L	PCT	GB	Manager	Attendance	Average	Last Penn.
Fort Wayne TinCaps (Padres)	94	46	.671	—	Doug Dascenzo	378,529	5,408	2009
Peoria Chiefs (Cubs)	81	57	.587	12	Marty Pevey	219,168	3,372	2002
Great Lakes Loons (Dodgers)	81	59	.579	13	Juan Bustabad	271,146	4,047	2000
West Michigan Whitecaps (Tigers)	81	59	.579	13	Joe DePastino	356,642	5,245	2007
Cedar Rapids Kernels (Angels)	78	60	.565	15	Bill Mosiello	169,697	2,496	1994
Kane County Cougars (Athletics)	76	64	.543	18	Steve Scarsone	400,040	6,154	2001
Clinton LumberKings (Mariners)	69	68	.504	23½	Scott Steinmann	107,665	1,656	1991
Burlington Bees (Royals)	64	75	.460	29½	Jim Gabella	64,499	949	2008
Quad Cities River Bandits (Cardinals)	61	78	.439	32½	Steve Dillard	236,401	3,694	1990
South Bend Silver Hawks (Diamondbacks)	59	78	.431	33½	Mark Haley	155,403	2,428	2005
Dayton Dragons (Reds)	59	80	.424	34½	Todd Benzinger	586,193	8,496	Never
Wisconsin Timber Rattlers (Brewers)	58	81	.417	35½	Jeff Isom	253,240	3,724	1984
Beloit Snappers (Twins)	57	83	.407	37	Nelson Prada	83,480	1,265	1995
Lansing Lugnuts (Blue Jays)	54	84	.391	39	Clayton McCullough	346,935	5,257	2003

CLUB BATTING

	AVG	G	AB	R	H	2B	3B	HR	RBI	BB	SO	SB	CS	OBP	SLG
Peoria	.278	138	4708	701	1311	255	39	111	656	387	979	103	47	.338	.420
West Michigan	.274	140	4804	693	1316	267	45	63	631	441	1001	129	66	.345	.388
Fort Wayne	.266	140	4659	736	1237	268	32	97	661	681	978	130	65	.365	.399
Great Lakes	.263	140	4709	719	1239	264	54	106	646	476	1113	166	58	.336	.410
Dayton	.262	139	4734	612	1240	252	42	79	564	398	992	146	49	.325	.383
Cedar Rapids	.257	138	4575	663	1177	218	42	65	578	461	1068	187	90	.335	.366
Lansing	.255	138	4648	616	1184	229	32	94	555	367	1183	167	62	.318	.378
Clinton	.253	137	4590	627	1162	219	46	77	553	452	1133	162	65	.327	.371
Beloit	.252	140	4673	606	1177	240	32	66	534	458	1108	99	68	.323	.359
Burlington	.247	139	4547	596	1125	218	46	53	518	404	950	188	83	.311	.351
South Bend	.247	137	4505	534	1114	243	32	43	475	369	913	75	41	.315	.344
Kane County	.243	140	4615	598	1122	211	31	80	523	493	1085	127	61	.322	.354
Quad Cities	.240	139	4579	582	1101	223	32	71	524	466	1110	114	47	.320	.350
Wisconsin	.236	139	4472	546	1056	235	35	62	480	490	1160	130	76	.319	.346

CLUB PITCHING

	ERA	G	CG	SHO	SV	IP	H	R	ER	HR	BB	SO	AVG
Clinton	3.35	137	1	10	36	1216	1176	577	452	70	392	1043	.253
Fort Wayne	3.46	140	1	18	41	1232	1095	552	474	68	407	1224	.237
Peoria	3.59	138	2	10	46	1210	1075	555	482	77	479	1047	.237
West Michigan	3.61	140	2	15	38	1245	1134	560	500	61	418	1061	.245
Kane County	3.63	140	0	7	44	1231	1127	585	497	65	478	1090	.244
Great Lakes	3.66	140	2	13	46	1233	1168	588	501	64	484	1100	.249
Cedar Rapids	3.81	138	4	8	34	1228	1099	595	520	76	446	1064	.241
Burlington	3.99	139	1	7	33	1196	1188	648	530	87	510	980	.262
South Bend	4.06	137	1	5	31	1173	1208	635	529	74	374	907	.268
Beloit	4.28	140	5	5	31	1218	1273	701	579	81	460	1141	.269
Wisconsin	4.34	139	1	6	38	1195	1213	691	576	72	559	1076	.265
Dayton	4.48	139	0	1	31	1227	1221	710	611	113	501	1096	.260
Quad Cities	4.48	139	1	3	31	1202	1220	713	598	78	433	980	.261
Lansing	4.76	138	3	4	29	1205	1364	719	637	77	402	964	.285

CLUB FIELDING

	PCT	PO	A	E	DP		PCT	PO	A	E	DP
West Michigan	.978	3736	1526	120	334	South Bend	.969	3518	1459	160	332
Cedar Rapids	.975	3684	1478	132	263	Kane County	.968	3693	1458	171	294
Fort Wayne	.975	3697	1328	130	238	Lansing	.968	3615	1396	167	347
Dayton	.973	3682	1318	141	283	Beloit	.967	3654	1349	171	277
Great Lakes	.970	3700	1428	157	321	Wisconsin	.967	3583	1436	169	321
Peoria	.970	3630	1423	157	275	Clinton	.963	3647	1425	195	303
Burlington	.969	3588	1447	162	374	Quad Cities	.962	3606	1490	203	297

INDIVIDUAL BATTING LEADERS (MINIMUM 3.1 PA/TEAM GAME)

	AVG	G	AB	R	H	2B	3B	HR	RBI	BB	SO	SB
Amarista, Alexia, Cedar Rapids	.319	125	477	84	152	39	10	4	49	50	61	38
Nunez, Gustavo, West Michigan	.315	112	464	82	146	16	10	5	40	25	62	45
Nowlin, Billy, West Michigan	.311	112	418	69	130	29	2	13	77	37	67	2
Ridling, Rebel, Peoria	.310	136	536	74	166	34	1	16	97	40	95	2
Mendez, Carlos, Dayton	.308	115	455	64	140	18	6	5	67	29	50	4
Burke, Kyler, Peoria	.303	132	465	93	141	43	3	15	89	78	99	14
Gordon, Dee, Great Lakes	.301	131	538	96	162	17	12	3	35	43	90	73
Savastano, Scott, Clinton	.300	112	413	67	124	15	5	6	53	56	74	12
Decker, Jaff, Fort Wayne	.299	104	358	78	107	25	2	16	64	85	92	10
Santana, Ramon, Beloit	.296	103	371	46	110	25	3	9	60	50	94	8

INDIVIDUAL PITCHING LEADERS (MINIMUM 1 IP/TEAM GAME)

	W	L	ERA	G	GS	CG	SV	IP	H	R	BB	SO
Kasparek, Kenn, Clinton	10	6	2.41	26	26	1	0	142	126	50	32	134
Smalley, Kenny, Kane County	9	8	2.73	29	21	0	0	132	109	49	60	119
Putkonen, Luke, West Michigan	7	8	3.13	28	28	1	0	149	148	63	47	115
Tippett, Brad, Beloit	9	8	3.21	25	24	0	0	146	131	64	25	107
Castro, Simon, Fort Wayne	10	6	3.33	28	27	1	0	140	118	61	37	157
Baez, Manauris, Burlington	8	6	3.41	30	20	0	1	132	136	63	48	85
Alvarez, Henderson, Lansing	9	6	3.47	23	23	1	0	124	121	54	19	92
Flores, Manuel, Cedar Rapids	7	4	3.59	19	19	1	0	120	122	50	23	74
Davis, Erik, Fort Wayne	16	6	3.64	32	19	0	0	124	111	56	44	106
Cook, Ryan, South Bend	11	11	3.66	25	25	0	0	143	140	71	44	103

ALL-STAR TEAM

C: Tony Delmonico, Great Lakes. **1B:** Rebel Ridling, Peoria. **2B:** Alexi Amarista, Cedar Rapids. **3B:** Josh Vitters, Peoria. **SS:** Dee Gordon, Great Lakes. **OF:** Kyler Burke, Peoria; Josh Harrison, Peoria; Kyle Russell, Great Lakes. **DH:** Billy Nowlin, West Michigan. **RHSP:** Kenny Smalley, Kane County. **LHSP:** Casey Crosby, West Michigan. **RHRP:** Brad Brach, Fort Wayne. **LHRP:** Drew Taylor, Cedar Rapids.
Most Valuable Players: Dee Gordon, Great Lakes; Kyle Russell, Great Lakes. **Prospect of the Year:** Dee Gordon, Great Lakes. **Managers of the Year:** Doug Dascenzo, Fort Wayne; Marty Pevey, Peoria.

DEPARTMENT LEADERS

BATTING

OBP	Decker, Jaff, Fort Wayne	.442
SLG	Russell, Kyle, Great Lakes	.545
OPS	Decker, Jaff, Fort Wayne	.956
R	Pedroza, Jaime, Great Lakes	100
H	Ridling, Rebel, Peoria	166
TB	Russell, Kyle, Great Lakes	262
XBH	Russell, Kyle, Great Lakes	72
2B	Burke, Kyler, Peoria	43
3B	Gordon, Dee, Great Lakes	12
HR	Russell, Kyle, Great Lakes	26
RBI	Russell, Kyle, Great Lakes	102
SAC	Amarista, Alexia, Cedar Rapids	18
BB	Dykstra, Allan, Fort Wayne	104
HBP	Wyatt, Brent, West Michigan	23
SO	Russell, Kyle, Great Lakes	180
SB	Gordon, Dee, Great Lakes	73
CS	Gordon, Dee, Great Lakes	25
CS	Nunez, Gustavo, West Michigan	25
AB/SO	Perez, Rossmel, South Bend	11.39

PITCHING

G	Brach, Brad, Fort Wayne	60
GS	Three tied at	28
GF	Brach, Brad, Fort Wayne	57
SV	Brach, Brad, Fort Wayne	33
W	Davis, Erik, Fort Wayne	16
	Redding, Jon Michael, Great Lakes	16
L	Moorhouse, Brett, South Bend	14
	Watten, Trey, Wisconsin	14
IP	Correa, Manaurys, Cedar Rapids	163
H	Runion, Sam, Burlington	193
R	Runion, Sam, Burlington	106
ER	Runion, Sam, Burlington	99
HB	Three tied at	16
BB	Frederickson, Evan, Wisconsin	82
SO	Castro, Simon, Fort Wayne	157
SO/9 (SP)	Castro, Simon, Fort Wayne	10.17
SO/9 (RP)	Taylor, Andrew, Cedar Rapids	14.55
BB/9	Alvarez, Henderson, Lansing	1.38
WP	Frederickson, Evan, Wisconsin	20
BK	Three tied at	4
HR	Sulbaran, J.C., Dayton	19
AVG	Chaffee, Ryan, Cedar Rapids	.206

FIELDING

C	FPCT	Brenly, Michael, Peoria	.997
	PO	Brenly, Michael, Peoria	665
	A	Bonilla, Jose, Burlington	78
	E	McCraw, Sean, Wisconsin	13
	DP	Bonilla, Jose, Burlington	11
		McCraw, Sean, Wisconsin	11
	PB	Bonilla, Jose, Burlington	15
1B	FPCT	Lennerton, Jordan, West Michigan	.996
	PO	Ridling, Rebel, Peoria	1081
	A	Ridling, Rebel, Peoria	103
	E	McDade, Michael, Lansing	14
	DP	Ridling, Rebel, Peoria	92
2B	FPCT	Elmore, Jacob, South Bend	.980
	PO	Puckett, Cody, Dayton	208
	A	Amarista, Alexia, Cedar Rapids	346
	E	Pedroza, Jaime, Great Lakes	27
	DP	Pedroza, Jaime, Great Lakes	67
3B	FPCT	Hatch, Anthony, Great Lakes	.948
	PO	Hatch, Anthony, Great Lakes	81
	A	Hatch, Anthony, Great Lakes	210
	E	Parker, Justin, South Bend	24
	DP	Sobolewski, Mark, Lansing	14
SS	FPCT	Rojas, Miguel, Dayton	.977
	PO	Rojas, Miguel, Dayton	220
	A	Navarro, Reynaldo, South Bend	360
	E	Gordon, Dee, Great Lakes	34
	DP	Gordon, Dee, Great Lakes	78
OF	FPCT	Auer, Tyson, Cedar Rapids	.993
	PO	Tekotte, Blake, Fort Wayne	289
	A	Norris, Patrick, Burlington	27
	E	Perez, Nelson, Peoria	12
	DP	Francis, Nicholas, Burlington	6

MINOR LEAGUES

SOUTH ATLANTIC LEAGUE LOW CLASS A

BY MATT FORMAN

Lakewood BlueClaws catcher Travis d'Arnaud (Phillies) opened the 2009 campaign by hitting .192/.250/.345 with six home runs and nine doubles in April and May and was only one of several struggling young players who earned aggressive promotions to start the season.

D'Arnaud heated up with the summer weather, then stayed hot in the playoffs. In the final four months of the season, d'Arnaud hit .292/.359/.462 with 29 doubles and seven home runs. Then, he went 9-for-23 in six playoff at-bats. The 20-year-old catcher helped the BlueClaws go 5-1 in the postseason and led the team to the league championship. Lakewood swept Kannapolis (White Sox) in the opening round and beat Greenville (Red Sox) 3-1 in the finals to take its second SAL championship and first since 2006.

D'Arnaud was one of several catchers among the league's top prospects. Hagerstown backstop Derek Norris (Nationals) hit .286/.413/.513 line with 30 doubles and 23 home runs, earning praise as the league's best position player, best batting prospect and best power prospect. West Virginia catcher Tony Sanchez (Pirates), the fourth overall pick in June's draft, impressed with a .316/.415/.561 mark, including 23 extra-base hits. The league's best defensive catcher, Greenville's Tim Federovicz, did it with his bat too by knocking 19 doubles and 10 long balls in 55 games in the circuit. And that doesn't even account for the league's MVP, Asheville's Jordan Pacheco (Rockies). The 6-foot-1, 190-pounder hit .322/.379/.492 with 30 doubles, 13 home runs, 79 RBIs and 12 stolen bases.

As good as those players were at strapping on the tools of ignorance, pitching dominated the league. Seven of the league's top 11 prospects toed the rubber. Hickory turned in one of the league's best pitching staffs, led by lefthander Martin Perez, the league's top prospect. Rome's (Braves) impressive rotation, included Panamanian starters Dimasther Delgado and Randall Delgado, first-round picks Brett DeVall (2008) and Mike Minor (2009), and righthanders Zeke Spruill and Julio Teheran.

TOP 20 PROSPECTS

1. Martin Perez, lhp, Hickory (Rangers)
2. Casey Kelly, rhp/ss, Greenville (Red Sox)
3. Matt Moore, lhp, Bowling Green (Rays)
4. Derek Norris, c, Hagerstown (Nationals)
5. Tim Beckham, ss, Bowling Green (Rays)
6. Jordan Lyles, rhp, Lexington (Astros)
7. Jason Knapp, rhp, Lakewood (Phillies)/ Lake County (Indians)
8. Jared Mitchell, of, Kannapolis (White Sox)
9. Manny Banuelos, lhp, Charleston (Yankees)
10. Wilmer Flores, ss, Savannah (Mets)
11. Rudy Owens, lhp, West Virginia (Pirates)
12. Tony Sanchez, c, West Virginia (Pirates)
13. Anthony Gose, of, Lakewood (Phillies)
14. Tim Federowicz, c, Greenville (Red Sox)
15. Dexter Carter, rhp, Kannapolis (White Sox)
16. Nick Barnese, rhp, Bowling Green (Rays)
17. Travis D'Arnaud, c, Lakewood (Phillies)
18. Alex Perez, rhp, Lake County (Indians)
19. Trevor May, rhp, Lakewood (Phillies)
20. Melky Mesa, of, Charleston (Yankees)

STANDINGS: SPLIT SEASON

FIRST HALF

NORTH	W	L	PCT	GB
Lakewood	42	26	.618	—
Greensboro	37	33	.529	6
Kannapolis	37	33	.529	6
Delmarva	36	33	.522	6½
Hickory	33	36	.478	9½
Hagerstown	31	36	.463	10½
Lake County	31	36	.463	10½
West Virginia	27	43	.386	16

SOUTH	W	L	PCT	GB
Greenville	39	29	.574	—
Charleston	39	31	.557	1
Lexington	36	34	.514	4
Augusta	35	34	.507	4½
Rome	35	35	.500	5
Savannah	35	35	.500	5
Bowling Green	34	36	.486	6
Asheville	26	43	.377	13½

SECOND HALF

NORTH	W	L	PCT	GB
Kannapolis	45	24	.652	—
West Virginia	40	27	.597	4
Lake County	40	30	.571	5½
Lakewood	36	32	.529	8½
Delmarva	30	37	.448	14
Hickory	30	40	.429	15½
Greensboro	29	41	.414	16½
Hagerstown	25	42	.373	19

SOUTH	W	L	PCT	GB
Asheville	42	27	.609	—
Augusta	41	29	.586	1½
Charleston	35	34	.507	7
Greenville	34	36	.486	8½
Lexington	32	38	.457	10½
Rome	31	38	.449	11
Savannah	30	37	.448	11
Bowling Green	30	38	.441	11½

PLAYOFFS—Semifinals: Lakewood defeated Kannapolis 2-0, Greenville defeated Asheville 2-0 in best-of-three series. **Finals:** Lakewood defeated Asheville 3-1 in best-of-five series.

OVERALL STANDINGS

Team	W	L	PCT	GB	Manager	Attendance	Average	Last Penn.
Kannapolis Intimidators (White Sox)	82	57	.590	—	Ernie Young	132,342	2,005	2005
Lakewood BlueClaws (Phillies)	78	58	.574	2½	Dusty Wathan	429,221	6,312	2009
Augusta GreenJackets (Giants)	76	63	.547	6	Dave Machemer	194,437	2,902	2008
Charleston RiverDogs (Yankees)	74	65	.532	8	Torre Tyson	268,985	4,015	Never
Greenville Drive (Red Sox)	73	65	.529	8½	Kevin Boles	335,159	4,857	1998
Lake County Captains (Indians)	71	66	.518	10	Aaron Holbert	267,895	3,998	Never
Asheville Tourists (Rockies)	68	70	.493	13½	Joe Mikulik	146,353	2,361	1984
West Virginia Power (Pirates)	67	70	.489	14	Gary Green	177,691	2,820	1990
Lexington Legends (Astros)	68	72	.486	14½	Tom Lawless	332,588	4,964	2001
Delmarva Shorebirds (Orioles)	66	70	.485	14½	Orlando Gomez	214,575	3,576	2000
Rome Braves (Braves)	66	73	.475	16	Randy Ingle	183,750	2,827	2003
Savannah Sand Gnats (Mets)	65	72	.474	16	Edgar Alfonzo	110,846	1,732	1996
Greensboro Grasshoppers (Marlins)	66	74	.471	16½	Darin Everson	406,549	5,979	1982
Bowling Green Hot Rods (Rays)	64	74	.464	17½	Matt Quatraro	232,987	3,530	2007
Hickory Crawdads (Rangers)	63	76	.453	19	Hector Ortiz	131,414	1,905	2004
Hagerstown Suns (Nationals)	56	78	.418	23½	Matthew LeCroy	126,166	2,138	Never

CLUB BATTING

	AVG	G	AB	R	H	2B	3B	HR	RBI	BB	SO	SB	CS	OBP	SLG
Asheville	.269	138	4615	633	1241	261	32	89	558	349	1068	186	81	.329	.397
West Virginia	.262	137	4574	673	1199	226	42	71	600	458	1033	149	58	.341	.376
Augusta	.260	139	4635	648	1206	236	35	59	572	388	1006	144	45	.325	.364
Charleston	.260	139	4717	619	1228	232	46	55	548	495	1173	142	45	.337	.364
Greenville	.260	138	4699	663	1222	273	36	91	601	488	1234	109	48	.335	.392
Lake County	.260	137	4512	629	1172	224	38	79	549	471	1090	166	81	.341	.379
Kannapolis	.259	139	4673	622	1209	226	36	76	559	378	1025	127	44	.323	.371
Greensboro	.258	140	4679	662	1206	273	18	117	613	420	1067	121	55	.329	.399
Lakewood	.253	136	4486	588	1135	247	45	56	518	428	1115	210	75	.329	.366
Savannah	.252	137	4596	547	1159	226	35	70	481	382	1046	67	48	.315	.362
Hagerstown	.251	134	4500	561	1129	204	34	55	483	470	1097	125	53	.329	.348
Hickory	.250	139	4616	626	1155	251	30	105	572	368	1117	129	61	.316	.386
Delmarva	.248	136	4408	537	1094	183	43	49	468	375	1066	181	61	.313	.338
Rome	.248	139	4588	517	1137	229	23	57	445	297	957	88	67	.301	.345
Bowling Green	.243	138	4477	538	1088	234	40	65	479	372	894	99	58	.308	.357
Lexington	.237	140	4539	547	1076	186	34	75	485	380	1052	114	77	.304	.343

CLUB PITCHING

	ERA	G	CG	SHO	SV	IP	H	R	ER	HR	BB	SO	AVG
Savannah	3.23	137	3	9	39	1194	1133	538	429	47	430	1050	.251
Kannapolis	3.24	139	1	15	38	1226	1162	530	442	52	402	1135	.253
Greenville	3.38	138	1	12	38	1216	1121	552	457	81	391	1088	.244
Lake County	3.42	137	1	9	38	1209	1095	557	459	76	461	1078	.242
Augusta	3.45	139	8	8	31	1206	1171	593	462	72	379	1026	.253
Charleston	3.54	139	0	12	41	1230	1170	591	484	68	358	1062	.251
Lexington	3.59	140	4	7	39	1211	1195	605	483	73	363	981	.256
Delmarva	3.69	136	1	6	34	1153	1058	563	473	60	459	1056	.244
Hickory	3.78	139	2	10	27	1213	1196	672	510	89	416	1091	.254
Lakewood	3.79	136	4	9	43	1185	1141	572	499	39	402	1117	.253
Rome	3.83	139	3	10	48	1209	1209	609	515	66	383	1164	.259
Hagerstown	3.93	134	0	6	31	1169	1168	608	511	96	404	1069	.261
Bowling Green	4.05	138	1	4	36	1187	1160	639	534	73	446	1039	.253
Greensboro	4.06	140	1	4	29	1210	1259	670	546	95	447	1059	.267
Asheville	4.07	138	5	13	33	1192	1248	627	539	89	370	1124	.269
West Virginia	4.18	137	1	7	35	1177	1170	684	546	93	408	901	.253

CLUB FIELDING

	PCT	PO	A	E	DP		PCT	PO	A	E	DP
Lakewood	.978	3554	1388	111	218	Charleston	.968	3690	1553	175	330
Greenville	.974	3647	1371	135	261	Savannah	.968	3582	1375	164	314
Asheville	.972	3577	1450	147	324	Greensboro	.967	3629	1468	175	286
Kannapolis	.971	3679	1580	156	363	Lexington	.967	3633	1549	178	302
Delmarva	.970	3460	1460	153	261	Rome	.967	3627	1371	168	302
Hagerstown	.970	3508	1415	153	308	West Virginia	.964	3530	1406	185	270
Lake County	.970	3628	1451	156	341	Bowling Green	.963	3561	1483	192	282
Augusta	.968	3618	1451	168	309	Hickory	.955	3639	1420	236	225

INDIVIDUAL BATTING LEADERS (MINIMUM 3.1 PA/TEAM GAME)

	AVG	G	AB	R	H	2B	3B	HR	RBI	BB	SO	SB
Roling, Kiel, Asheville	.331	94	344	54	114	26	2	20	66	39	92	0
Pacheco, Jordan, Asheville	.322	117	451	67	145	30	4	13	79	38	44	12
Robinson, Scott, Asheville	.309	124	501	94	155	34	5	3	37	20	111	4
D'Alessio, Andy, Augusta	.300	94	343	44	103	26	1	7	44	34	86	3
Joseph, Corban, Charleston	.300	100	380	39	114	17	8	4	57	49	61	8
Morrison, Erik, Hickory	.297	94	353	55	105	32	3	18	66	31	80	10
Moore, Tyler, Hagerstown	.297	111	421	38	125	30	3	9	87	40	111	2
Lombardozzi, Stephen, Hagerstown	.296	128	496	90	147	26	7	3	58	62	80	16
Pirela, Jose, Charleston	.295	97	404	65	119	23	6	0	46	37	65	9
Synan, Jeremy, Greensboro	.291	100	375	54	109	31	1	13	63	33	84	4

INDIVIDUAL PITCHING LEADERS (MINIMUM 1 IP/TEAM GAME)

	W	L	ERA	G	GS	CG	SV	IP	H	R	BB	SO
Nicasio, Juan, Asheville	9	3	2.41	18	18	1	0	112	110	44	23	115
Ronick, Ari, Augusta	7	6	2.65	24	23	2	0	136	111	62	34	114
Familia, Jeurys, Savannah	10	6	2.69	24	23	0	0	134	109	49	46	109
Andujar, Chris, Bowling Green	10	4	2.70	31	17	0	0	120	99	44	42	79
McCurry, Cole, Delmarva	6	9	2.71	26	25	0	0	140	118	51	46	145
Nicholson, Kyle, Augusta	7	8	2.80	18	18	4	0	122	110	49	22	83
Phelps, David, Charleston	10	3	2.80	19	19	0	0	113	117	48	25	90
Frias, Marcos, Hagerstown	9	5	2.91	25	23	0	0	127	124	56	30	112
Pimentel, Carlos, Hickory	5	4	2.93	28	14	1	1	123	120	49	35	101
Beaulac, Eric, Savannah	7	7	2.95	26	19	0	2	116	110	53	41	133

ALL-STAR TEAM

C: Jordan Pacheco, Asheville. **1B:** Josh Mazzola, Augusta. **2B:** Steve Lombardozzi, Hagerstown. **3B:** Corban Joseph, Hagerstown. **SS:** Tim Beckham, Bowling Green. **OF:** Anthony Gose, Lakewood; Scott Robinson, Asheville; Ronnie Welty, Delmarva. **UTIL IF:** Erik Morrison, Hickory. **UTIL OF:** Melky Mesa, Charleston. **DH:** Derek Norris, Hagerstown. **RHP:** David Phelps, Charleston. **LHP:** Rudy Owens, West Virginia. **Most Valuable Player:** Jordan Pacheco, Asheville. **Most Outstanding Pitcher:** Rudy Owens, West Virginia. **Most Outstanding Prospect:** Derek Norris, Hagerstown. **Manager of the Year:** Dusty Wathan, Lakewood. **Coach of the Year:** Bob Kipper, Greenville.

DEPARTMENT LEADERS

BATTING

OBP	Norris, Derek, Hagerstown	.413
SLG	Roling, Kiel, Asheville	.593
OPS	Roling, Kiel, Asheville	.994
R	Robinson, Scott, Asheville	94
H	Robinson, Scott, Asheville	155
TB	Lasater, Ben, Greensboro	226
XBH	Lavarnway, Ryan, Greenville	59
2B	d'Arnaud, Travis, Lakewood	38
	Satin, Joshua, Savannah	38
3B	Webb, Donnie, Lake County	12
HR	Pellegrini, Brian, Lexington	27
RBI	Mazzola, Josh, Augusta	96
SAC	Escobar, Eduardo, Kannapolis	17
BB	Norris, Derek, Hagerstown	90
HBP	West, Matthew, Hickory	22
SO	Mesa, Melky, Charleston	168
SB	Gose, Anthony, Lakewood	76
CS	Gose, Anthony, Lakewood	20
AB/SO	Jefferies, Jake, Bowling Green	12.57

PITCHING

G	Jorgenson, Adam, Asheville	60
GS	Three tied at	27
GF	Jorgenson, Adam, Asheville	54
SV	Jorgenson, Adam, Asheville	27
W	Leesman, Charles, Kannapolis	13
L	Greenwalt, Kyle, Lexington	13
	Hand, Brad, Greensboro	13
IP	Leesman, Charles, Kannapolis	158
H	Dorn, Johnny, Greensboro	181
R	Kaminska, Kyle, Greensboro	91
ER	Dorn, Johnny, Greensboro	73
HB	Correa, Heitor, Lakewood	21
BB	Brackman, Andrew, Charleston	76
SO	Moore, Matthew, Bowling Green	176
SO/9 (SP)	Moore, Matthew, Bowling Green	12.88
SO/9 (RP)	Remenowsky, Dan, Kannapolis	15.49
BB/9	Schwinden, Chris, Savannah	1.17
WP	Brackman, Andrew, Charleston	26
BK	Five tied at	5
HR	Pimentel, Carlos, Hickory	15
AVG	Moore, Matthew, Bowling Green	.195

FIELDING

C	FPCT	d'Arnaud, Travis, Lakewood	.993
	PO	d'Arnaud, Travis, Lakewood	817
	A	Bernardo, Luis, Delmarva	109
	E	Norris, Derek, Hagerstown	18
	DP	Norris, Derek, Hagerstown	9
		Pacheco, Jordan, Savannah	9
	PB	Norris, Derek, Hagerstown	28
1B	FPCT	Sheridan, Michael, Bowling Green	.995
	PO	Sheridan, Michael, Bowling Green	1124
	A	Moore, Tyler, Hagerstown	70
	E	Lasater, Ben, Greensboro	11
	DP	Sheridan, Michael, Bowling Green	80
2B	FPCT	Lombardozzi, Stephen, Hagerstown	.987
	PO	Lombardozzi, Stephen, Hagerstown	259
	A	Lombardozzi, Stephen, Hagerstown	354
	E	Hoes, Jerome, Delmarva	28
	DP	Lombardozzi, Stephen, Hagerstown	75
3B	FPCT	Mattair, Travis, Lakewood	.948
	PO	Mattair, Travis, Lakewood	83
	A	Culberson, Charlie, Augusta	279
	E	Marte, Jefry, Savannah	49
	DP	Gilmore, Jon, Kannapolis	23
SS	FPCT	Flores, Wilmer, Savannah	.974
	PO	Barba, Ryan, Rome	169
		Escobar, Eduardo, Kannapolis	169
	A	Escobar, Eduardo, Kannapolis	372
	E	Beckham, Tim, Bowling Green	43
	DP	Escobar, Eduardo, Kannapolis	74
OF	FPCT	Welty, Ronnie, Delmarva	.991
	PO	Curran, Chris, Hagerstown	256
	A	Mesa, Melky, Charleston	19
	E	Latimore, Quincy, West Virginia	14
	DP	Five tied at	5

MINOR LEAGUES

BY AARON FITT

Staten Island and Mahoning Valley were the two best teams in the New York-Penn League during the 2009 regular season, so it was only fitting that the Yankees and Scrappers faced off for the best-of-three NY-P finals.

Staten Island won the opener and Mahoning Valley won Game Two before the Yankees broke a 2-2 tie with three runs in the eighth inning of Game Three to capture their fifth Penn League title, and their third in the last five years. Staten Island outfielder Neil Medchill, who hit a league-leading 14 home runs during the regular season despite playing the final month with a torn wrist ligament, had an infield hit to drive in the go-ahead run.

Staten Island caught fire down the stretch, winning 14 of its last 16, which included a club-record 13-game winning streak, to overtake Brooklyn for the McNamara Division title. The balanced Yankees led the NY-P in ERA (2.53) and ranked second with a .255 average. Staten Island and Lowell, the Stedler Division champ, were two of the Penn League's most prospect-laden teams, accounting for eight of the league's Top 20. Mahoning Valley, the Pinckney Division winner, placed just one player on the Top 20.

The league's fourth playoff team, McNamara runner-up Brooklyn, had a banner moment in August when 23-year-old righthander Brandon Moore threw the first no-hitter in franchise history. He gave up three walks and hit a batter while striking out six in a 5-0 win against Aberdeen on Aug. 23.

While 2008 was a strong year for the New York-Penn League, with catchers (led by Jason Castro and Derek Norris) and power arms (topped by Adam Reifer and Brad Holt) in abundance, most evalu-

ators were disappointed by the league's talent level in 2009. Lowell outfielder Ryan Westmoreland is a legitimate blue-chip prospect and Williamsport's Sebastian Valle established himself as one of the top young catchers in the lower minors, but the position-player crop dropped off quickly after that. The players who performed best lacked elite tools, while the players with the biggest tools struggled.

Dominican righthanders Alex Colome and Arodys Vizcaino led a decent supply of power arms Those two have a chance to be high-end starters, but most of the other electric arms in the league belong to older prospects who profile as relievers.

No 2009 first-round pick logged any meaningful time in the Penn League, and the league was dominated by several players with four years of college experience—including seniors such as Staten Island righthander Adam Warren and Batavia outfielder Kyle Conley, plus redshirt juniors such as Medchill, Mahoning Valley outfielder Jason Kipnis and Lowell righty Alex Wilson.

TOP 20 PROSPECTS

1. Ryan Westmoreland, of, Lowell (Red Sox)
2. Alex Colome, rhp, Hudson Valley (Rays)
3. Arodys Vizcaino, rhp, Staten Island (Yankees)
4. Sebastian Valle, c, Williamsport (Phillies)
5. Jason Kipnis, of, Mahoning Valley (Indians)
6. Victor Black, rhp, State College (Pirates)
7. Ramon Benjamin, lhp, Jamestown (Marlins)
8. Arquimedes Caminero, rhp, Jamestown (Marlins)
9. Alex Wilson, rhp, Lowell (Red Sox)
10. Kyle Lobstein, lhp, Hudson Valley (Rays)
11. Anthony Hewitt, 3b, Williamsport (Phillies)
12. Adam Warren, rhp, Staten Island (Yankees)
13. Destin Hood, of, Vermont (Nationals)
14. Jimmy Paredes, 2b, Staten Island (Yankees)
15. Derrik Gibson, 2b/ss, Lowell (Red Sox)
16. Leandro Castro, of, Williamsport (Phillies)
17. Kyle Conley, of, Batavia (Cardinals)
18. Neil Medchill, of, Staten Island (Yankees)
19. Michael Almanzar, 3b, Lowell (Red Sox)
20. Jim Fuller, lhp, Brooklyn (Mets)

STANDINGS

McNamara	W	L	PCT	GB	Manager	Attendance	Average	Last Penn.
Staten Island Yankees (Yankees)	47	29	.618	—	Josh Paul	206,635	5,904	2009
Brooklyn Cyclones (Mets)	45	30	.600	1½	Pedro Lopez	264,102	7,138	2001
Hudson Valley Renegades (Rays)	38	37	.507	8½	Brady Williams	161,332	4,609	1999
Aberdeen IronBirds (Orioles)	30	44	.405	16	Gary Kendall	247,061	6,502	1983

Pinckney	W	L	PCT	GB	Manager	Attendance	Average	Last Penn.
Mahoning Valley Scrappers (Indians)	49	27	.645	—	Travis Fryman	120,755	3,178	2004
Williamsport Crosscutters (Phillies)	42	34	.553	7	Chris Truby	68,130	1,893	2003
State College Spikes (Pirates)	38	38	.500	11	Gary Robinson	142,068	3,946	1994
Batavia Muckdogs (Cardinals)	37	39	.487	12	Mark Dejohn	35,620	963	2008
Jamestown Jammers (Marlins)	34	42	.447	15	Andy Haines	45,095	1,409	1991
Auburn Doubledays (Blue Jays)	26	49	.347	22½	Dennis Holmberg	55,804	1,594	2007

Stedler	W	L	PCT	GB	Manager	Attendance	Average	Last Penn.
Lowell Spinners (Red Sox)	45	30	.600	—	Gary DiSarcina	186,522	5,041	Never
Oneonta Tigers (Tigers)	35	39	.473	9½	Howie Bushong	23,521	692	1998
Vermont Lake Monsters (Nationals)	34	41	.453	11	Jeff Garber	84,114	2,549	1996
Tri-City ValleyCats (Astros)	27	48	.360	18	Jim Pankovits	145,976	4,293	1997

PLAYOFFS—Semifinals: Mahoning Valley defeated Brooklyn 2-0 and Staten Island defeated Lowell 2-1 in best-of-three series; **Finals:** Staten Island defeated Mahoning 2-1 in best-of-three series.

CLUB BATTING

	AVG	G	AB	R	H	2B	3B	HR	RBI	BB	SO	SB	CS	OBP	SLG
Mahoning Valley	.256	76	2559	363	654	119	24	28	317	291	534	78	20	.342	.354
Staten Island	.255	76	2421	332	618	136	21	52	308	235	544	78	38	.328	.393
Lowell	.253	75	2545	352	645	150	24	27	309	266	595	103	36	.332	.363
Hudson Valley	.250	75	2431	283	608	100	27	22	248	189	551	134	56	.314	.341
Batavia	.249	76	2531	333	630	125	19	37	290	264	564	52	24	.321	.357
Williamsport	.249	76	2551	334	636	137	45	45	304	192	629	96	32	.308	.391
Jamestown	.247	76	2496	292	616	110	19	24	261	216	597	52	24	.313	.335
Auburn	.245	75	2494	315	612	141	13	34	289	232	649	73	33	.317	.353
Tri-City	.242	75	2395	269	580	110	17	25	232	215	486	68	24	.314	.334
Brooklyn	.241	75	2423	305	583	105	21	31	250	258	506	52	24	.322	.340
Vermont	.239	75	2401	299	574	92	23	22	257	291	562	60	37	.327	.324
Oneonta	.237	74	2363	298	559	103	33	30	264	212	534	50	25	.311	.346
Aberdeen	.233	74	2459	275	573	101	31	25	238	258	620	56	29	.312	.330
State College	.233	76	2483	339	579	123	32	30	306	268	617	58	20	.313	.345

CLUB PITCHING

	ERA	G	CG	SHO	SV	IP	H	R	ER	HR	BB	SO	AVG
Staten Island	2.53	76	0	12	19	649	534	265	182	20	235	600	.220
Lowell	2.96	75	2	7	22	658	541	268	216	22	241	638	.222
Mahoning Valley	3.03	76	0	12	26	671	588	281	226	38	206	619	.232
Brooklyn	3.05	75	6	7	23	655	572	268	222	35	193	588	.234
State College	3.27	76	0	5	14	655	627	307	238	32	198	500	.251
Williamsport	3.35	76	0	4	24	661	599	302	246	20	231	636	.239
Aberdeen	3.46	74	1	9	18	660	603	313	254	29	238	545	.244
Hudson Valley	3.49	75	3	6	22	645	592	305	250	27	236	534	.244
Vermont	3.56	75	1	8	18	639	615	341	253	35	257	519	.253
Batavia	3.65	76	0	6	14	656	610	327	266	30	233	626	.245
Jamestown	3.76	76	1	9	14	657	654	341	274	36	265	615	.257
Oneonta	3.99	74	4	9	16	620	589	312	275	21	295	512	.251
Auburn	4.36	75	1	0	14	652	679	402	316	37	288	580	.263
Tri-City	4.52	75	1	2	15	625	664	357	314	50	271	476	.276

CLUB FIELDING

	PCT	PO	A	E	DP		PCT	PO	A	E	DP
Brooklyn	.977	1964	816	66	146	Hudson Valley	.966	1935	731	93	116
Batavia	.973	1967	769	76	154	State College	.965	1966	769	100	190
Oneonta	.973	1861	723	71	151	Mahoning Valley	.964	2012	750	104	173
Aberdeen	.969	1982	820	91	176	Staten Island	.964	1946	800	104	152
Lowell	.967	1973	756	94	147	Vermont	.962	1917	692	104	156
Tri-City	.967	1874	842	92	231	Jamestown	.961	1970	708	110	146
Williamsport	.967	1982	737	93	168	Auburn	.959	1957	738	116	137

INDIVIDUAL BATTING LEADERS (MINIMUM 3.1 PA/TEAM GAME)

	AVG	G	AB	R	H	2B	3B	HR	RBI	BB	SO	SB
Martinez, J.D., Tri-City	.326	53	187	25	61	15	2	7	33	15	30	1
Ochinko, Sean, Auburn	.324	52	188	40	61	20	0	6	32	16	26	1
Ramirez, Welinton, Auburn	.318	56	220	29	70	22	2	3	33	11	55	13
Castro, Leandro, Williamsport	.316	66	256	48	81	19	5	7	43	13	49	18
Valle, Sebastian, Williamsport	.307	50	192	25	59	15	5	6	40	10	41	0
Mack, Deangelo, Staten Island	.306	66	232	27	71	19	4	7	41	21	44	2
Murrill, Chris, Hudson Valley	.306	49	193	31	59	7	2	0	18	13	46	29
Paredes, Jimmy, Staten Island	.302	54	205	36	62	8	4	2	17	10	30	23
Pichardo, Wilfred, Lowell	.302	62	245	39	74	14	1	2	21	18	76	32
Bortnick, Tyler, Hudson Valley	.300	65	217	37	65	17	4	4	26	27	38	24

INDIVIDUAL PITCHING LEADERS (MINIMUM 1 IP/TEAM GAME)

	W	L	ERA	G	GS	CG	SV	IP	H	R	BB	SO
Alvarez, Jose, Lowell	8	3	1.52	14	12	2	0	83	60	17	10	63
Colome, Alex, Hudson Valley	7	4	1.66	15	15	2	0	76	46	22	32	94
Haughian, Nick, Aberdeen	6	3	2.05	13	12	0	0	75	61	25	20	54
Carrillo, Erick, Jamestown	4	2	2.05	14	11	0	1	61	49	17	18	50
Moore, Brandon, Brooklyn	6	3	2.09	13	13	2	0	82	61	23	17	71
Cohoon, Mark, Brooklyn	9	2	2.15	14	14	2	0	92	69	26	20	70
Brach, Brett, Mahoning Valley	5	2	2.19	15	15	0	0	78	62	25	20	61
Lobstein, Kyle, Hudson Valley	3	5	2.58	14	14	0	0	73	55	23	23	74
Hernandez, Nicholas, Williamsport	8	1	2.70	15	15	0	0	80	72	27	20	67
McHugh, Collin, Brooklyn	8	2	2.76	14	14	1	0	75	61	25	21	79
Popham, Marty, Mahoning Valley	6	1	2.76	14	14	0	0	75	75	29	10	83

DEPARTMENT LEADERS

BATTING

OBP	Henry, Jordan, Mahoning Valley	.408
SLG	Medchill, Neil, Staten Island	.551
OPS	Martinez, J.D., Tri, City	.920
R	Gibson, Derrik, Lowell	54
H	Castro, Leandro, Williamsport	81
TB	Castro, Leandro, Williamsport	131
XBH	Castro, Leandro, Williamsport	31
2B	Gomes, Yan, Auburn	23
3B	Baker, Aaron, State College	7
	Johnson, Jamie, Oneonta	7
HR	Medchill, Neil, Staten Island	14
RBI	Gomes, Yan, Auburn	44
SAC	Wade, Chris, Jamestown	8
BB	Chambers, Evan, State College	50
HBP	Kemp, Brian, Tri, City	13
SO	Eiland, Eric, Auburn	95
SB	Pichardo, Wilfred, Lowell	32
CS	Five tied at	9
AB/SO	Torres, Jose, Jamestown	8.78

PITCHING

G	Flannery, Ryan, Staten Island	34
GS	Lebron, Siulnan, Williamsport	16
GF	Powers, Michael, Brooklyn	27
SV	Powers, Michael, Brooklyn	17
W	Cohoon, Mark, Brooklyn	9
L	Blazek, Michael, Batavia	9
IP	Cohoon, Mark, Brooklyn	92
H	Lebron, Siulnan, Williamsport	98
R	Gracey, Scott, Auburn	53
ER	Lebron, Siulnan, Williamsport	44
	Walker, Brandt, Tri, City	44
HB	Grimmett, Zachary, Tri, City	11
BB	McGeary, Jack, Vermont	41
SO	Colome, Alexander, Hudson Valley	94
SO/9 (SP)	Colome, Alexander, Hudson Valley	11.13
SO/9 (RP)	Caminero, Arquimedes, Jamestown	15.75
BB/9	Alvarez, Jose, Lowell	1.08
WP	Blazek, Michael, Batavia	13
	Walker, Brandt, Tri, City	13
BK	Nuno, Vidal, Mahoning Valley	3
HR	Walker, Brandt, Tri, City	10
AVG	Colome, Alexander, Hudson Valley	.174

FIELDING

C	FPCT	Murrian, John, Oneonta	.996
	PO	Higashioka, Kyle, Staten Island	451
	A	Castro, Ivan, Batavia	51
	E	Chen, Chun-Hsiu, Mahoning Valley	7
		De La Cruz, Luis, Batavia	7
	DP	Acosta, Mayobanex, Hudson Valley	6
		Murrian, John, Oneonta	6
	PB	Castro, Ivan, Batavia	12
1B	FPCT	Bishop, Rawley, Oneonta	.994
	PO	Murton, Luke, Staten Island	613
	A	Murton, Luke, Staten Island	61
	E	Durham, Lance, Auburn	9
		Murton, Luke, Staten Island	9
	DP	Stanley, Nick, Tri, City	55
2B	FPCT	Buschina, Adam, Williamsport	.974
	PO	Soriano, Francisco, Vermont	123
	A	Soriano, Francisco, Vermont	157
	E	Basabe, Lurvin, Mahoning Valley	16
		Soriano, Francisco, Vermont	16
	DP	Soriano, Francisco, Vermont	37
3B	FPCT	Gaynor, Wade, Oneonta	.952
	PO	Walker, Jack, Vermont	47
	A	Gaynor, Wade, Oneonta	107
	E	Hewitt, Anthony, Williamsport	26
	DP	Walker, Jack, Vermont	16
SS	FPCT	Jackson, Ryan, Batavia	.958
	PO	Jackson, Ryan, Batavia	93
	A	Jackson, Ryan, Batavia	184
	E	Gulliver, Jimmy, Oneonta	21
	DP	Jackson, Ryan, Batavia	33
OF	FPCT	Kemp, Brian, Tri, City	.100
	PO	Johnson, Jamie, Oneonta	159
	A	Nommensen, Brett, Hudson Valley	9
		Servidio, John, Brooklyn	9
	E	Pichardo, Wilfred, Lowell	9
	DP	D Oleo, Richard, Aberdeen	4

BY CONOR GLASSEY

With one of the older teams in the eight-team circuit, the Salem-Keizer Volcanoes sported the league's best record at 49-27, two games better than the Tri-City Dust Devils.

Salem-Keizer and Tri-City met in the playoffs and the Volcanoes won the series 3-1 after a 13-inning marathon in what became the final game. The win gave the Volcanoes their second title in the past three years.

The Volcanoes had the league MVP in third baseman Drew Biery. A 22nd-round pick out of Kansas State, he certainly had a summer to remember, batting .326/.406/.484 and prompting his teammates to call him "Biery Bonds." On top of the standout performance, Biery also took five days off during the season to get married.

Nearly every Northwest League manager said it was a down year for pitching, as position players dominated the prospect scene in 2009. The first seven prospects on our Top 20 list are everyday players, beginning with a pair of international teenagers: Boise shortstop Hak-Ju Lee and Eugene third baseman Edinson Rincon. Prominent 2009 draftees also made their mark, with first-round outfielders Brett Jackson (Boise) and Tim Wheeler (Tri-City) standing out the most.

Lee, who signed out of Korea, hit .330/.399/.420 during his professional debut. He played excellent defense and also stole 25 bases. Rincon was one of the league's youngest players, not turning 19 until mid-August, and really stood out with what he did at the plate. Over 267 at-bats, he hit .300/.415/.468 with 18 doubles and seven home runs. Though he was rough defensively at third base, the bat showed a lot of promise.

Several other high-profile draftees, such as Everett shortstop Nick Franklin (first round, Mariners) and Vancouver catcher Max Stassi (fourth round, Athletics), performed well but signed too late to make much of an impact.

Last year's NWL crop featured a better balance between hitters and pitchers, with talented arms

TOP 20 PROSPECTS

1. Hak-Ju Lee, ss, Boise (Cubs)
2. Edinson Rincon, 3b, Eugene (Padres)
3. Brett Jackson, of, Boise (Cubs)
4. Mario Martinez, 3b, Everett (Mariners)
5. Tim Wheeler, of, Tri-City (Rockies)
6. Ryan Wheeler, 3b, Yakima (Diamondbacks)
7. Robbie Ross, lhp, Spokane (Rangers)
8. Francisco Peguero, of, Salem-Keizer (Giants)
9. Matt Davidson, 3b, Yakima (Diamondbacks)
10. Miguel Velazquez, of, Spokane (Rangers)
11. Tommy Mendonca, 3b, Spokane (Rangers)
12. James Jones, of, Everett (Mariners)
13. Chris Dominguez, 3b, Salem-Keizer (Giants)
14. Julio Ramos, lhp, Vancouver (Athletics)
15. Rob Scahill, rhp, Tri-City (Rockies)
16. Ben Paulsen, 1b, Tri-City (Rockies)
17. Jerry Sullivan, rhp, Eugene (Padres)
18. Connor Hoehn, rhp, Vancouver (Athletics)
19. Logan Watkins, 2b, Boise (Cubs)
20. Braden Tullis, rhp, Spokane (Rangers)

(Martin Perez, Christian Friedrich) who went on to bigger and better things in 2009. For the second straight summer, the league's best pitching prospect was a Spokane lefthander, as Robbie Ross followed in Perez's footsteps. The 20-year-old Ross went 4-4, 2.66 with 76 strikeouts and 17 walks in 74 innings. Tri-City lefty Rex Brothers, a supplemental first-round pick, went 2-0, 3.38 over eight relief appearances before earning a promotion to low Class A Asheville.

Another fun storyline from the league was the dominance of righthander Paul Smyth, a 35th-round pick by the Athletics out of Kansas. The 5-foot-11, 210-pound righthander comes at hitters from a sidearm delivery that creates a lot of deception. With a fastball he locates to both sides of the plate, along with a slider and a changeup, Smyth pitched very well for Vancouver, going 1-0, 0.00 with 12 hits, 37 strikeouts and four walks over 29 innings before a late-season promotion to low Class A Kane County.

"He's probably the most polished, most advanced relief pitcher I've had in four years," Vancouver manager Rick Magnante said. "He put up Nintendo-like numbers for us and was a very pleasant surprise for somebody that went that deep in the draft."

STANDINGS

EAST	W	L	PCT	GB	Manager	Attendance	Average	Last Penn.
Tri-City Dust Devils (Rockies)	47	29	.618	—	Fred Ocasio	84,198	2,216	Never
Spokane Indians (Rangers)	37	39	.487	10	Tim Hulett	174,941	4,604	2008
Boise Hawks (Cubs)	34	42	.447	13	Casey Kopitzke	103,783	2,731	2004
Yakima Bears (Diamondbacks)	28	48	.368	19	Bob Didier	72,881	1,918	2000

WEST	W	L	PCT	GB	Manager	Attendance	Average	Last Penn.
Salem-Keizer Volcanoes (Giants)	49	27	.645	—	Tom Trebelhorn	106,590	2,805	2009
Everett AquaSox (Mariners)	39	37	.513	10	John Tamargo	89,929	2,367	1985
Vancouver Canadians (Athletics)	36	40	.474	13	Rick Magnante	149,297	3,929	Never
Eugene Emeralds (Padres)	34	42	.447	15	Greg Riddoch	125,475	3,391	1980

PLAYOFFS: Salem-Keizer defeated Tri-City 3-1 in best-of-five series.

CLUB BATTING

	AVG	G	AB	R	H	2B	3B	HR	RBI	BB	SO	SB	CS	OBP	SLG
Everett	.285	76	2638	421	751	157	29	73	373	240	620	49	31	.353	.449
Salem-Keizer	.267	76	2584	443	691	116	32	51	398	251	526	67	34	.342	.396
Spokane	.267	76	2615	378	697	134	14	58	344	247	639	81	22	.343	.395
Eugene	.264	76	2595	409	686	134	16	58	367	344	616	64	25	.361	.395
Vancouver	.261	76	2581	349	673	134	13	22	302	295	585	80	30	.343	.344
Boise	.260	76	2586	339	673	120	16	21	289	220	526	80	38	.324	.343
Tri-City	.256	76	2597	398	665	132	20	38	362	276	612	101	33	.341	.366
Yakima	.250	76	2593	322	648	131	12	35	286	256	625	74	36	.328	.350

CLUB PITCHING

	ERA	G	CG	SHO	SV	IP	H	R	ER	HR	BB	SO	AVG
Tri-City	3.43	76	0	3	22	690	627	319	263	28	277	615	.244
Salem-Keizer	3.54	76	1	7	21	678	637	342	267	49	251	603	.247
Spokane	3.94	76	0	5	16	669	654	342	293	39	246	647	.255
Vancouver	4.41	76	0	5	23	671	703	402	329	40	290	624	.270
Eugene	4.44	76	0	5	22	665	720	403	328	37	216	570	.274
Everett	4.46	76	1	3	15	667	685	400	331	68	269	628	.266
Boise	4.76	76	0	4	16	670	704	422	354	47	275	531	.268
Yakima	5.18	76	0	3	12	672	754	449	387	48	305	531	.286

CLUB FIELDING

	PCT	PO	A	E	DP		PCT	PO	A	E	DP
Tri-City	.974	2071	864	78	207	Spokane	.964	2008	787	105	174
Yakima	.972	2017	911	83	227	Eugene	.963	1994	818	108	208
Everett	.970	2002	770	87	192	Vancouver	.962	2012	769	109	207
Salem-Keizer	.967	2035	820	96	195	Boise	.959	2009	847	122	190

INDIVIDUAL BATTING LEADERS (MINIMUM 3.1 PA/TEAM GAME)

	AVG	G	AB	R	H	2B	3B	HR	RBI	BB	SO	SB
Ogata, Jason, Spokane	.366	51	191	23	70	15	1	5	42	15	29	3
Wheeler, Ryan, Yakima	.363	64	234	44	85	20	3	5	36	37	28	7
Avila, Gerardo, Everett	.333	54	213	32	71	10	2	13	54	12	49	0
Lee, Hak-Ju, Boise	.330	68	264	56	87	14	2	2	33	31	50	25
Bowman, Bo, Tri-City	.328	55	192	31	63	9	4	7	46	24	41	2
Watkins, Logan, Boise	.326	72	279	48	91	14	2	0	29	27	31	14
Biery, Drew, Salem-Keizer	.326	59	215	43	70	14	1	6	48	27	39	4
Sammy, Jeremiah, Tri-City	.316	49	187	32	59	8	2	3	20	20	35	9
Lollis, Ryan, Salem-Keizer	.312	52	199	31	62	9	3	2	25	20	24	1
Mendonca, Tommy, Spokane	.309	49	188	33	58	12	2	9	26	9	66	0

INDIVIDUAL PITCHING LEADERS (MINIMUM 1 IP/TEAM GAME)

	W	L	ERA	G	GS	CG	SV	IP	H	R	BB	SO
Greenwood, Nick, Eugene	4	1	1.71	17	9	0	5	63	52	18	16	50
Ramos, Julio, Vancouver	6	5	2.38	13	13	0	0	72	67	30	18	64
Bucardo, Jorge, Salem-Keizer	6	3	2.64	15	15	0	0	82	65	28	21	64
Ross, Robert, Spokane	4	4	2.66	15	15	0	0	74	68	28	17	76
Perkins, Daniel, Tri-City	3	2	2.80	15	15	0	0	71	63	26	15	50
Tullis, Braden, Spokane	4	3	3.04	16	13	0	0	68	68	33	20	64
Scahill, Rob, Tri-City	1	4	3.14	15	15	0	0	63	58	30	20	58
Hernandez, Robert, Boise	4	3	3.36	15	15	0	0	72	62	30	22	67
Hurley, Trevor, Spokane	7	2	3.36	15	15	0	0	80	71	35	33	77
Stanton, Taylor, Everett	5	3	3.50	15	15	0	0	87	82	48	25	81

ALL-STAR TEAM

C: Vin DiFazio, Spokane. **1B:** Ryan Wheeler, Yakima. **2B:** Vince Belnome, Eugene. **3B:** Drew Biery, Salem-Keizer. **SS:** Hak-Ju Lee, Boise. **OF:** Ryan Royster, Everett; Joses Valdez, Boise; Miguel Velazquez, Spokane. **DH:** Drew Biery, Salem-Keizer. **LHP:** Nick Greenwood, Eugene. **LHSP:** Robbie Ross, Spokane. **RHSP:** Jorge Bucardo, Salem-Keizer. **LHRP:** Craig Benningson, Tri-City. **RHRP:** Charles Ruiz, Tri-City. **Most Valuable Player:** Drew Biery, Salem-Keizer. **Manager of the Year:** Freddie Ocasio, Tri-City.

DEPARTMENT LEADERS

BATTING

OBP	Wheeler, Ryan, Yakima	.461
SLG	Avila, Gerardo, Everett	.582
OPS	Wheeler, Ryan, Yakima	.999
R	Lee, Hak-Ju, Boise	56
H	Martinez, Mario, Everett	93
TB	Freiman, Nathan, Eugene	140
XBH	Freiman, Nathan, Eugene	33
2B	Matthes, Kent, Tri, City	23
3B	Martinez, Juan, Salem, Keizer	9
HR	Avila, Gerardo, Everett	13
RBI	Freiman, Nathan, Eugene	68
SAC	Gonzalez, Jose, Tri, City	8
	Greer, Brent, Yakima	8
BB	Belnome, Vincent, Eugene	52
HBP	Wong, Joey, Tri, City	13
SO	Matthes, Kent, Tri, City	77
	Murphy, Clark, Spokane	77
SB	Lee, Hak-Ju, Boise	25
CS	House, Tyreace, Vancouver	10
AB/SO	Watkins, Logan, Boise	9.00

PITCHING

G	Ruiz, Charles, Tri, City	32
GS	Adames, Joselito, Vancouver	16
GF	Ruiz, Charles, Tri, City	29
SV	Ruiz, Charles, Tri, City	17
W	Bennigson, Craig, Tri, City	8
L	Mikolas, Miles, Eugene	8
	Odegaard, Christopher, Yakima	8
IP	Stanton, Taylor, Everett	87
H	Adames, Joselito, Vancouver	92
R	Adames, Joselito, Vancouver	57
	Quezada, Rafael, Yakima	57
ER	Adames, Joselito, Vancouver	52
HB	Burnett, Luke, Everett	15
BB	Burnett, Luke, Everett	42
	Quezada, Rafael, Yakima	42
SO	Kirkland, Chris, Everett	85
SO/9 (SP)	Ross, Robert, Spokane	9.20
SO/9 (RP)	Ruiz, Charles, Tri-City	13.07
BB/9	Thompson, Matt, Spokane	1.25
WP	Kirkland, Chris, Everett	14
BK	Three tied at	3
HR	Rogers, Taylor, Salem, Keizer	10
AVG	Greenwood, Nick, Eugene	.224

FIELDING

C	FPCT	Van Winkle, Tyson, Yakima	.993
	PO	Ortiz, Ryan, Vancouver	337
	A	Van Winkle, Tyson, Yakima	44
	E	Zambrano, Eliezer, Salem, Keizer	7
		Zaneski, Zach, Spokane	7
	DP	Fuentes, Juan, Everett	5
	PB	Ortiz, Ryan, Vancouver	13
1B	FPCT	Freiman, Nathan, Eugene	.994
	PO	Freiman, Nathan, Eugene	589
	A	Freiman, Nathan, Eugene	53
	E	Avila, Gerardo, Everett	7
	DP	Freiman, Nathan, Eugene	66
2B	FPCT	Montilla, Gerson, Yakima	.979
	PO	Montilla, Gerson, Yakima	135
	A	Montilla, Gerson, Yakima	196
	E	Watkins, Logan, Boise	13
	DP	Montilla, Gerson, Yakima	47
3B	FPCT	Davidson, Matthew, Yakima	.934
	PO	Martinez, Mario, Everett	44
	A	Davidson, Matthew, Yakima	148
	E	Sanders, Joseph, Tri, City	24
	DP	Davidson, Matthew, Yakima	14
		Martinez, Mario, Everett	14
SS	FPCT	Wong, Joey, Tri, City	.985
	PO	Wong, Joey, Tri, City	118
	A	Wong, Joey, Tri, City	219
	E	Lee, Hak-Ju, Boise	27
	DP	Wong, Joey, Tri, City	51
OF	FPCT	Richard, Myrio, Vancouver	.990
	PO	Worthington, Tyrell, Yakima	141
	A	Three tied at	8
	E	Valdez, Jose, Boise	6
		Worthington, Tyrell, Yakima	6
	DP	Richard, Myrio, Vancouver	4

MINOR LEAGUES

BY MATT EDDY

Order was restored in the Appalachian League when Danville dispatched Elizabethton with a two-game sweep to win the title. Those two teams have tussled for supremacy in four of the past five seasons. Only Pulaski's surprise overtaking of the Braves in last year's Eastern Division broke the streak.

Danville squad brimmed with talent in 2009, though league No. 1 prospect Julio Teheran had matriculated to low Class A by the time the playoffs rolled around. Signed for $850,000 out of Colombia in 2007, he debuted with Danville last year but shoulder tendinitis capped his workload at 15 innings. In seven starts, Teheran went 2-1, 2.68 with 39 strikeouts and seven walks in 44 innings.

Braves catcher Christian Bethancourt, an 18-year-old Panamanian, arrived in mid-August to help pick up the slack. He batted .260/.339/.480 in 14 games for Danville, and then contributed a double and an RBI in the finals.

Danville benefited from five first-year pros, all four-year or junior college players, selected in the 2009 draft:

■ First baseman and league MVP Riaan Spanjer-Furstenburg, a 16th-round pick from Nova Southeastern (Fla.), hit .359/.411/.543 to win the batting title.

■ Lefthander Chris Masters, an 11th-round pick from Western Carolina, led the league with 85 strikeouts in 70 innings and narrowly missed winning the ERA title at 1.42. He expertly spots an 87-92 mph fastball.

■ Lefty Matt Crim, a 21st-round pick from The Citadel, won league pitcher of the year honors for his sterling 10-2, 3.18 record. He pounded the lower half of the strike zone on his way to a 3-to-1 groundout-to-flyout ratio.

■ Fourth-round shortstop Mycal Jones batted .258/.337/.430, stole 19 bases and led the league with 50 runs and six triples. Despite being a Miami Dade CC product, he debuted at age 22

TOP 20 PROSPECTS

1. Julio Teheran, rhp, Danville (Braves)
2. Jiovanni Mier, ss, Greeneville (Astros)
3. Wilking Rodriguez, rhp, Princeton (Rays)
4. Matt Hobgood, rhp, Bluefield (Orioles)
5. Gabriel Noriega, ss, Pulaski (Mariners)
6. David Holmberg, lhp, Bristol (White Sox)
7. John Lamb, lhp, Burlington (Royals)
8. Robert Stock, c, Johnson City (Cardinals)
9. Cesar Puello, of, Kingsport (Mets)
10. Juri Perez, rhp, Greeneville (Astros)
11. Trayce Thompson, of, Bristol (White Sox)
12. Tyler Ladendorf, ss, Elizabethton (Twins)
13. Steve Baron, c, Pulaski (Mariners)
14. Ty Morrison, of, Princeton (Rays)
15. Santos Rodriguez, lhp, Bristol (White Sox)
16. Tyler Stovall, lhp, Danville (Braves)
17. Mycal Jones, ss, Danville (Braves)
18. Jonathan Meyer, 3b, Greeneville (Astros)
19. Cody Rogers, of, Princeton (Rays)
20. Brett Oberholtzer, lhp, Danville (Braves)

because he spent two years North Florida.

■ Center fielder Cory Harrilchak, taken from Elon in the 14th round, batted .324/.401/.444 with 10 doubles and 19 stolen bases in 60 games.

Danville led the league in ERA (3.05) and fewest home runs allowed (18 in 68 games), and their pitching dominance was on full display in the finals when they limited Elizabethton to one run in two games. The Braves scored 12 times, batting .304 but without a homer.

While Danville had four players on the Top 20 Prospects list, Elizabethton featured just one. But shortstop Tyler Ladendorf didn't stick around for the playoffs. He went to the Athletics for Orlando Cabrera at the July 31 trading deadline.

A pair of first-round picks made their pro debuts in the league. Fourth overall pick Matt Hobgood, a righthander taken by the Orioles, showed diminished velocity with Bluefield, and he finished 1-2, 4.72 in eight starts with a 16-to-8 strikeout-to-walk ratio in 27 innings.

Greeneville shortstop Jiovanni Mier, the 21st overall pick by the Astros from a LaVerne, Calif., high school batted .276/.380/.484 with seven homers while showing impressive defensive range.

STANDINGS

Eastern Division	W	L	PCT	GB	Manager	Attendance	Average	Last Penn.
Danville Braves	47	21	.691	—	Paul Runge	35,743	1,083	2009
Princeton Rays	36	31	.537	10 ½	Jared Sandberg	25,944	927	1994
Bluefield Orioles	33	35	.485	14	Einar Diaz	34,510	1,046	2001
Pulaski Mariners	28	36	.438	17	Jose Moreno	30,526	954	Never
Burlington Royals	24	44	.353	23	Nelson Liriano	29,621	956	1993
Western Division	**W**	**L**	**PCT**	**GB**	**Manager**	**Attendance**	**Average**	**Last Penn.**
Elizabethton Twins	45	23	.662	—	Ray Smith	27,767	868	2008
Johnson City Cardinals	37	30	.552	7 ½	Mike Shildt	23,639	739	1976
Kingsport Mets	30	35	.462	13 ½	Mike DiFelice	33,691	1,087	1995
Bristol White Sox	27	39	.409	17	Ryan Newman	19,390	718	2002
Greeneville Astros	27	40	.403	17 ½	Rodney Linares	49,293	1,450	2004

PLAYOFFS: Danville defeated Elizabethton 2-0 in best-of-three series.

CLUB BATTING

	AVG	G	AB	R	H	2B	3B	HR	RBI	BB	SO	SB	CS	OBP	SLG
Kingsport	.286	65	2304	409	660	111	16	49	360	219	555	110	44	.362	.412
Elizabethton	.282	68	2390	433	674	145	15	80	387	251	514	19	13	.353	.456
Danville	.272	68	2338	349	636	138	23	33	307	184	492	88	31	.336	.393
Pulaski	.262	64	2079	294	544	100	18	51	260	188	571	60	38	.334	.401
Johnson City	.260	67	2180	325	567	122	12	65	280	205	562	54	28	.332	.417
Princeton	.251	67	2188	305	549	114	22	27	257	209	483	74	30	.324	.360
Bluefield	.248	68	2266	295	561	103	24	31	258	166	537	59	42	.310	.355
Greeneville	.244	67	2242	312	547	118	25	37	255	251	550	76	32	.327	.368
Bristol	.241	66	2147	241	517	110	9	28	209	183	509	56	21	.308	.340
Burlington	.222	68	2173	233	483	86	25	33	193	186	504	117	55	.293	.330

CLUB PITCHING

	ERA	G	CG	SHO	SV	IP	H	R	ER	HR	BB	SO	AVG
Danville	3.05	68	3	5	26	605	490	248	205	18	241	582	.219
Princeton	3.17	67	2	5	14	567	516	259	200	38	156	505	.240
Burlington	3.76	68	0	4	20	586	559	310	245	44	199	484	.247
Elizabethton	3.82	68	2	2	20	603	587	296	256	48	220	604	.257
Bluefield	3.84	68	1	2	15	593	594	318	253	31	179	484	.260
Bristol	4.11	66	1	6	17	565	556	302	258	44	200	521	.257
Johnson City	4.34	67	0	6	17	566	580	345	273	42	194	552	.261
Kingsport	4.62	65	0	2	12	571	629	363	293	42	238	464	.279
Pulaski	4.84	64	1	2	17	541	588	356	291	54	214	548	.276
Greeneville	5.18	67	0	1	19	586	639	399	337	73	201	533	.275

CLUB FIELDING

	PCT	PO	A	E	DP		PCT	PO	A	E	DP
Elizabethton	.972	1704	564	65	154	Bristol	.955	977	419	66	85
Danville	.970	1657	638	71	108	Princeton	.955	766	239	47	26
Kingsport	.965	1419	547	72	146	Burlington	.954	1677	676	114	136
Johnson City	.961	1651	601	92	116	Greeneville	.952	1166	632	90	105
Bluefield	.959	1270	571	78	122	Pulaski	.948	1263	565	100	87

INDIVIDUAL BATTING LEADERS (MINIMUM 3.1 PA/TEAM GAME)

	AVG	G	AB	R	H	2B	3B	HR	RBI	BB	SO	SB
Spanjer-Furstenburg, Riaan, Danville	.359	62	234	36	84	19	0	8	53	16	37	0
Dozier, Brian, Elizabethton	.353	53	218	38	77	17	0	0	14	23	26	3
Shoemaker, Brady, Bristol	.351	57	205	38	72	21	0	9	34	25	53	0
Haveman, Brandon, Pulaski	.339	49	165	33	56	9	4	5	18	18	26	4
Pinto, Josmil, Elizabethton	.332	53	205	34	68	14	2	13	55	19	39	0
Bonfe, Joe, Kingsport	.327	40	156	29	51	12	0	3	19	19	32	3
Harrilchak, Cory, Danville	.324	60	222	43	72	10	5	2	41	27	22	19
Wiegand, Ryan, Princeton	.324	59	222	37	72	19	0	5	35	23	29	2
Altuve, Jose, Greeneville	.324	45	179	45	58	20	2	3	18	26	16	14
Noriega, Gabriel, Pulaski	.311	61	206	27	64	14	2	4	26	16	60	8

INDIVIDUAL PITCHING LEADERS (MINIMUM 1 IP/TEAM GAME)

	W	L	ERA	G	GS	CG	SV	IP	H	R	BB	SO
Moss, Andy, Johnson City	1	2	1.32	13	6	0	1	55	38	14	17	48
Masters, Chris, Danville	8	4	1.42	13	11	0	0	70	53	17	9	85
Billo, Greg, Burlington	2	2	1.81	13	8	0	1	55	40	18	16	51
Oberholtzer, Brett, Danville	6	2	2.01	12	12	1	0	67	46	17	6	56
Dettrich, Julius, Princeton	5	5	2.92	12	12	0	0	62	49	23	15	36
Frabizio, Vito, Bluefield	4	4	2.96	12	12	0	0	70	57	27	16	64
Moore, Justin, Bluefield	4	3	3.11	13	12	0	0	64	67	27	15	37
Crim, Matt, Danville	10	2	3.18	13	11	0	0	68	70	26	10	48
Rodriguez, Wilking, Princeton	1	6	3.21	13	13	0	0	56	44	24	12	52
Stuifbergen, Tom, Elizabethton	5	2	3.28	13	13	1	0	80	79	35	6	69

ALL-STAR TEAM

C: Robert Stock, Johnson City. **1B:** Riaan Spanjer-Furstenburg, Danville. **2B:** Jose Altuve, Greeneville. **3B:** Vinnie Catricala, Pulaski; Rich Racobaldo, Johnson City. **SS:** Brian Dozier, Elizabethton. **UTIL INF:** Gabriel Noriega, Pulaski. **OF:** Cory Harrilchak, Danville; Cody Rogers, Princeton; Brady Shoemaker, Bristol. **UTIL OF:** Brandon Haveman, Pulaski. **DH:** Josmil Pinto, Elizabethton. **RHP:** Vito Frabizio, Bluefield. **LHP:** Matt Crim, Danville. **RP:** David Kington, Johnson City.
Player of the Year: Riaan Spanjer-Furstenburg, Danville. **Pitcher of the Year:** Matt Crim, Danville. **Manager of the Year:** Paul Runge, Danville.

DEPARTMENT LEADERS

BATTING

OBP	Bonfe, Joe, Kingsport	.426
SLG	Pinto, Josmil, Elizabethton	.610
OPS	Shoemaker, Brady, Bristol	.101
R	Jones, Mycal, Danville	50
H	Spanjer-Furstenburg, Riaan, Danville	84
TB	Spanjer-Furstenburg, Riaan, Danville	127
XBH	Shoemaker, Brady, Bristol	30
2B	Shoemaker, Brady, Bristol	21
3B	Three tied at	6
HR	Pinto, Josmil, Elizabethton	13
RBI	Flagg, Jeff, Kingsport	59
SAC	Casamayor, Omar, Bluefield	6
	Hogue, Grant, Greeneville	6
BB	Meyer, Jonathan, Greeneville	36
HBP	Howe, Tyler, Kingsport	15
SO	Burgess, Jarrett, Pulaski	76
	Hefflinger, Bobby, Danville	76
SB	Ware, L.V., Danville	24
CS	Espinal, Yowill, Burlington	14
AB/SO	Altuve, Jose, Greeneville	11.19

PITCHING

G	Rada, Jose, Johnson City	23
GS	Eight tied at	13
GF	Kington, David, Johnson City	17
	Taveras, Sam, Bluefield	17
SV	Kington, David, Johnson City	8
W	Crim, Matt, Danville	10
L	Upchurch, Steven, Bristol	10
IP	Stuifbergen, Tom, Elizabethton	80
H	Upchurch, Steven, Bristol	94
R	Upchurch, Steven, Bristol	53
ER	Upchurch, Steven, Bristol	51
HB	Three tied at	9
BB	Stovall, Tyler, Danville	56
SO	Masters, Chris, Danville	85
SO/9 (SP)	Cisnero, Jose, Greeneville	10.35
SO/9 (RP)	Yates, Kirby, Princeton	16.75
BB/9	Stuifbergen, Tom, Elizabethton	0.68
WP	Santos, Randy, Johnson City	15
BK	Seven tied at	2
HR	Sanchez, Angelo, Elizabethton	15
AVG	Cisnero, Jose, Greeneville	.165

FIELDING

C	FPCT	Elorriaga-Matra, Daniel, Danville	.993
	PO	Ricardo, Dashenko, Bluefield	314
	A	Ricardo, Dashenko, Bluefield	58
	E	Gonzalez, Miguel, Bristol	10
	DP	Freeman, John, Kingsport	6
		Streich, Tobias, Elizabethton	6
	PB	Ricardo, Dashenko, Bluefield	12
	CS%	Elorriaga-Matra, Daniel, Danville	.400
1B	FPCT	Flagg, Jeff, Kingsport	.998
	PO	Spanjer-Furstenburg, Riaan, Danville	506
	A	Spanjer-Furstenburg, Riaan, Danville	30
	E	De Jesus, Jharmidy, Pulaski	10
		Kuebler, Jacob, Burlington	10
	DP	Flagg, Jeff, Kingsport	52
2B	FPCT	Casamayor, Omar, Bluefield	.977
	PO	McCallum, Derek, Elizabethton	136
	A	Wagner, Daniel, Bristol	156
	E	Wagner, Daniel, Bristol	12
	DP	McCallum, Derek, Elizabethton	44
3B	FPCT	Culver, Malcom, Burlington	.925
	PO	Meyer, Jonathan, Greeneville	55
	A	Kreke, Jordan, Danville	138
	E	Cedeno, Julio, Princeton	17
		Kreke, Jordan, Danville	17
	DP	Kreke, Jordan, Danville	10
		Thomas, Corey, Bluefield	10
SS	FPCT	Noriega, Gabriel, Pulaski	.960
	PO	Davis, Kyle, Bristol	93
	A	Jones, Mycal, Danville	190
	E	Espinal, Yowill, Burlington	22
	DP	Dozier, Brian, Elizabethton	38
OF	FPCT	Ware, L.V., Danville	.990
	PO	Burgess, Jarrett, Pulaski	122
	A	Ramirez, Luis, Bluefield	8
	E	Burgess, Jarrett, Pulaski	9
	DP	Four tied at	3

MINOR LEAGUES

BY MATT EDDY

The Pioneer League season stretched to Sept. 11, making it anywhere from 10 days to two weeks longer than any other Rookie-level circuit. The quirky schedule gave several premium 2009 draft picks who signed near the Aug. 17 deadline enough time to qualify for the postseason prospect list, including Idaho Falls catcher Wil Myers and Missoula's duo of third baseman Bobby Borchering and shortstop Chris Owings.

The league benefited from the Angels' and Diamondbacks' surfeit of draft picks in June. The two clubs combined to send 10 players selected in the top five rounds directly to Orem and Missoula.

Righthander Garrett Richards (3-1, 1.53 in eight starts) and lefties Pat Corbin (4-2, 5.05 in 12 starts) and Tyler Kehrer (3-3, 4.75 in 14 starts) anchored an Owlz rotation that posted a composite 3.83 ERA, lowest in the league. They were the only club below 4.00, in fact. Richards and Kehrer were supplemental first-round picks, while Corbin went in the second. Ninth-round righthander David Carpenter posted a 2.36 ERA and led the team with eight saves

Orem manager Tom Kotchman credited Carlos Ramirez, former Arizona State catcher and eighth-round pick in June, as a key reason for the Owlz finishing with the league's best regular-season record. He signed in mid-July and batted .376/.500/.638 with seven homers, leading the league in on-base percentage.

The Osprey nearly put their entire infield on our postseason prospects list, with second baseman David Nick (fourth round) joining Borchering (first) and Owings (supplemental first). First baseman Paul Goldschmidt, an eighth-rounder, missed the cut but tied for the league lead with 18 homers.

Orem and Missoula met in the league finals, with the more experienced Owlz winning the series two games to one. The Osprey won the opener 7-6, but then dropped 10-0 and 13-10 decisions.

The Dodgers netted league player of the year Brian Cavazos-Galvez, a 22-year-old senior corner outfielder from New Mexico, in the 12th round. He batted .322/.353/.618 with 18 home runs and 63 RBIs for Ogden, leading the league in homers, runs (59), hits (97), doubles (29) and extra-base hits (50).

The league's pitcher of the year, Chris Balcom-Miller, a Rockies' sixth-round pick from West Valley (Calif.) JC, drew a comparison with Jason Marquis for his athleticism, repertoire and bulldog mentality. He throws a plus two-seam fastball that ranges form 89-93 mph and features plus sink and armside run. The Casper righthander went 4-0, 1.58 in 11 starts, notching 60 strikeouts and just 10 walks over 57 innings.

TOP 20 PROSPECTS

1. Wil Myers, c, Idaho Falls (Royals)
2. Jake Odorizzi, rhp, Helena (Brewers)
3. Bobby Borchering, 3b, Missoula (Diamondbacks)
4. Garrett Richards, rhp, Orem (Angels)
5. Pat Corbin, lhp, Orem (Angels)
6. Jean Segura, 2b, Orem (Angels)
7. Chris Owings, ss, Missoula (Diamondbacks)
8. Nolan Arenado, 3b, Casper (Rockies)
9. Chris Balcom-Miller, rhp, Casper (Rockies)
10. Eric Arnett, rhp, Helena (Brewers)
11. Yorman Rodriguez, of, Billings (Reds)
12. Mike Belfiore, lhp, Missoula (Diamondbacks)
13. Tyler Kehrer, lhp, Orem (Angels)
14. Carlos Ramirez, c, Orem (Angels)
15. John Lamb, lhp, Idaho Falls (Royals)
16. Brett Wallach, rhp, Ogden (Dodgers)
17. Nick Bucci, rhp, Helena (Brewers)
18. Mariekson Gregorius, ss, Billings (Reds)
19. David Nick, 2b, Missoula (Diamondbacks)
20. Salvador Perez, c, Idaho Falls (Royals)

STANDINGS: SPLIT SEASON

FIRST HALF

NORTH	W	L	PCT	GB
Great Falls	21	17	.553	—
Missoula	21	17	.553	—
Helena	20	18	.526	1
Billings	12	26	.316	9

SOUTH	W	L	PCT	GB
Ogden	24	14	.632	—
Idaho Falls	20	16	.556	3
Orem	20	18	.526	4
Casper	12	24	.333	11

SECOND HALF

NORTH	W	L	PCT	GB
Great Falls	21	17	.553	—
Missoula	19	19	.500	2
Billings	12	26	.316	9
Helena	12	26	.316	9

SOUTH	W	L	PCT	GB
Orem	31	7	.816	—
Idaho Falls	23	15	.605	8
Ogden	18	20	.474	13
Casper	16	22	.421	15

PLAYOFFS—Semifinals: Orem defeated Ogden 2-0 and Missoula defeated Great Falls 2-1 in best-of-three series; **Finals:** Orem defeated Missoula 2-1 in best-of-three series.

OVERALL STANDINGS

Team	W	L	PCT	GB	Manager	Attendance	Average	Last Penn.
Orem Owlz (Angels)	51	25	.671	—	Tom Kotchman	96,926	2,551	2009
Idaho Falls Chukars (Royals)	43	31	.581	7	Darryl Kennedy	94,674	2,630	2000
Great Falls Voyagers (White Sox)	42	34	.553	9	Chris Cron	103,909	2,734	2008
Ogden Raptors (Dodgers)	42	34	.553	9	Damon Berryhill	146,068	3,844	Never
Missoula Osprey (Diamondbacks)	40	36	.526	11	Audo Vicente	85,034	2,238	2006
Helena Brewers (Brewers)	32	44	.421	19	Rene Gonzales	33,478	905	1984
Casper Ghosts (Rockies)	28	46	.378	22	Tony Diaz	56,680	1,718	Never
Billings Mustangs (Reds)	24	52	.316	27	Julio Garcia	105,173	2,843	2001

CLUB BATTING

	AVG	G	AB	R	H	2B	3B	HR	RBI	BB	SO	SB	CS	OBP	SLG
Orem	.297	76	2691	484	800	181	30	43	419	312	531	68	24	.379	.435
Ogden	.289	76	2674	459	773	172	21	89	416	261	652	62	34	.359	.469
Idaho Falls	.277	74	2538	409	702	147	37	44	354	248	599	90	42	.345	.416
Great Falls	.271	76	2617	419	708	132	15	39	364	293	600	119	40	.352	.377
Missoula	.271	76	2649	419	717	140	27	80	376	272	625	53	25	.345	.435
Casper	.270	74	2467	345	667	113	35	33	295	223	536	107	63	.337	.385
Helena	.260	76	2565	392	667	120	24	46	339	235	637	119	44	.329	.379
Billings	.250	76	2564	315	642	141	16	40	269	207	604	50	22	.315	.365

CLUB PITCHING

	ERA	G	CG	SHO	SV	IP	H	R	ER	HR	BB	SO	AVG
Orem	3.83	76	0	5	20	680	713	362	289	60	199	611	.267
Great Falls	4.09	76	0	3	19	678	692	377	308	42	257	682	.266
Missoula	4.17	76	0	1	17	675	722	401	313	46	242	631	.271
Idaho Falls	4.29	74	0	3	29	653	705	367	311	51	269	609	.276
Ogden	4.32	76	0	1	20	673	683	397	323	50	305	592	.264
Helena	4.79	76	0	4	20	667	730	445	355	62	239	604	.276
Billings	5.01	76	2	1	15	647	726	457	360	50	264	533	.283
Casper	5.01	74	2	2	11	631	705	436	351	53	276	522	.284

CLUB FIELDING

	PCT	PO	A	E	DP		PCT	PO	A	E	DP
Great Falls	.968	1565	322	62	89	Orem	.961	1826	837	108	166
Ogden	.968	1902	669	85	163	Helena	.959	1502	611	90	122
Idaho Falls	.964	1879	755	98	192	Missoula	.955	1345	590	91	160
Casper	.961	1297	538	74	174	Billings	.948	1337	651	109	142

INDIVIDUAL BATTING LEADERS *(MINIMUM 3.1 PA/TEAM GAME)*

	AVG	G	AB	R	H	2B	3B	HR	RBI	BB	SO	SB
Baird, Dillon, Orem	.372	57	215	39	80	17	2	7	49	28	33	1
Ruggiano, Brian, Ogden	.371	54	229	57	85	14	5	9	38	20	57	22
Haerther, Casey, Orem	.350	50	206	37	72	18	2	9	33	20	34	0
Clark, Jared, Casper	.348	58	198	33	69	13	1	11	44	29	34	5
Barnes, Avery, Casper	.335	49	188	37	63	7	2	0	13	19	46	23
Goldschmidt, Paul, Missoula	.334	74	287	51	96	27	3	18	62	36	74	4
Cheatham, Jordan, Great Falls	.330	61	206	33	68	10	2	2	34	21	43	14
Inciarte, Ender, Missoula	.325	66	237	33	77	14	1	1	22	15	40	15
Cavazos-Galvez, Brian, Ogden	.322	71	301	59	97	29	3	18	63	10	43	17
Ciolli, Nick, Great Falls	.317	63	240	45	76	17	1	7	36	26	49	23

INDIVIDUAL PITCHING LEADERS *(MINIMUM 1 IP/TEAM GAME)*

	W	L	ERA	G	GS	CG	SV	IP	H	R	BB	SO
Wickswat, Matt, Great Falls	2	2	3.84	15	15	0	0	77	92	36	14	91
Magill, Matt, Ogden	6	3	4.00	15	15	0	0	72	59	43	30	55
Locke, Stephen, Orem	6	4	4.02	15	14	0	0	69	70	40	11	46
Contreras, Edwin, Ogden	5	1	4.06	15	15	0	0	75	83	39	30	48
Bucci, Nick, Helena	6	3	4.41	13	12	0	0	69	59	39	21	66
Martinez, Joucer, Great Falls	3	4	4.44	16	15	0	0	79	85	48	24	52
Arenas, Orangel, Orem	4	3	4.65	15	15	0	0	70	76	44	18	48
Astorga, Leonardo, Billings	2	8	5.01	15	15	0	0	74	95	54	25	44
Garrido, Santiago, Idaho Falls	3	3	5.01	14	14	0	0	65	66	44	31	44
Pena, Miguel, Missoula	3	5	5.32	15	15	0	0	71	81	49	29	48

ALL-STAR TEAM

C: Gorman Erickson, Ogden. **1B:** Dillon Baird, Orem. **2B:** David Nick, Missoula. **3B:** Brian Ruggiano, Ogden. **SS:** Mariekson Gregorius, Billings. **OF:** Brian Cavazos-Galvez, Ogden; Hilton Richardson, Idaho Falls; Jerry Sands, Ogden. **DH:** Jarred Clark, Casper. **P:** Chris Balcom-Miller, Casper; Nick Bucci, Helena; Terry Doyle, Great Falls; Brandon Kloess, Great Falls; Matt Wickswat, Great Falls.
Most Valuable Player: Brian Cavazos-Galvez, Ogden. **Pitcher of the Year:** Chris Balcom-Miller, Casper. **Manager of the Year:** Tom Kotchman, Orem.

DEPARTMENT LEADERS

BATTING

OBP	Ramirez, Carlos, Orem	.500
SLG	Goldschmidt, Paul, Missoula	.638
OPS	Goldschmidt, Paul, Missoula	.104
R	Cavazos-Galvez, Brian, Ogden	59
H	Cavazos-Galvez, Brian, Ogden	97
TB	Cavazos-Galvez, Brian, Ogden	186
XBH	Cavazos-Galvez, Brian, Ogden	50
2B	Cavazos-Galvez, Brian, Ogden	29
3B	Broxton, Keon, Missoula	9
HR	Cavazos-Galvez, Brian, Ogden	18
	Goldschmidt, Paul, Missoula	18
RBI	Stone, Bobby, Missoula	68
SAC	Witherspoon, Travis, Orem	9
BB	Narodowski, Dave, Missoula	53
HBP	Castillo, Ramon, Missoula	13
SO	Krieger, Scott, Helena	103
SB	Prince, Josh, Helena	26
CS	Cheatham, Jordan, Great Falls	10
AB/SO	Gomez, Raywilly, Missoula	15.54

PITCHING

G	Bueno, Kristian, Helena	28
GS	Burgos, Enrique, Missoula	16
GF	Almeida, Yeison, Orem	18
	Rondon, Daigoro, Ogden	18
SV	Five tied at	8
W	Brewer, Charles, Missoula	7
L	Astorga, Leonardo, Billings	8
	Ferrer, Ricardo, Casper	8
IP	Martinez, Joucer, Great Falls	79
H	Astorga, Leonardo, Billings	95
R	Gonzalez, Juan, Casper	58
ER	Gonzalez, Juan, Casper	52
HB	Martinez, Joucer, Great Falls	9
BB	Burgos, Enrique, Missoula	39
SO	Wickswat, Matt, Great Falls	91
SO/9 (SP)	Wickswat, Matt, Great Falls	10.59
SO/9 (RP)	Fiers, Michael, Helena	15.00
BB/9	Locke, Stephen, Orem	1.43
WP	Marimon, Sugar Ray, Idaho Falls	13
	Pena, Miguel, Missoula	13
BK	Gonzalez, Juan, Casper	5
	Vasquez, Luis, Ogden	5
HR	Burgos, Enrique, Missoula	10
AVG	Magill, Matt, Ogden	.224

FIELDING

C	FPCT	Perez, Salvador, Idaho Falls	.993
	PO	Perez, Salvador, Idaho Falls	366
	A	Erickson, Gorman, Ogden	66
	E	Garfield, Cameron, Helena	16
	DP	Erickson, Gorman, Ogden	7
		Hollinger, Errol, Missoula	7
	PB	Fleury, Mark, Billings	14
	CS%	Hollinger, Errol, Missoula	.350
1B	FPCT	Goldschmidt, Paul, Missoula	.994
	PO	Goldschmidt, Paul, Missoula	648
	A	Clark, Jared, Casper	45
	E	Espinosa, Alberto, Idaho Falls	9
	DP	Goldschmidt, Paul, Missoula	58
2B	FPCT	Franco, Angel, Idaho Falls	.981
	PO	Franco, Angel, Idaho Falls	128
	A	Franco, Angel, Idaho Falls	174
	E	Dykstra, Cutter, Helena	20
	DP	Franco, Angel, Idaho Falls	38
3B	FPCT	Pfister, Frank, Billings	.908
	PO	Pfister, Frank, Billings	47
	A	Pfister, Frank, Billings	120
	E	Pfister, Frank, Billings	17
	DP	Pfister, Frank, Billings	12
SS	FPCT	Karcich, Jon, Orem	.942
	PO	Karcich, Jon, Orem	92
	A	Narodowski, Dave, Missoula	178
	E	Gregorius, Mariekson, Billings	17
		Narodowski, Dave, Missoula	17
	DP	Gregorius, Mariekson, Billings	34
OF	FPCT	Witherspoon, Travis, Orem	.983
	PO	Colligan, Kyle, Great Falls	130
		Conner, Sean, Billings	130
	A	Conner, Sean, Billings	15
	E	Stone, Bobby, Missoula	9
	DP	Conner, Sean, Billings	5

MINOR LEAGUES

BY BILL MITCHELL

The Mariners and Giants had won four of the last five Arizona League championships, thus it was only appropriate that these same teams squared off in the 2009 final. This time, the Mariners prevailed in a thriller, winning 3-2 behind the pitching of 23-year-old righthander Chris Kessinger and closer Jeff Breedlove.

The Giants, who compiled the AZL's best overall record, edged the Angels 4-3 the previous evening to capture the East Division crown. The Mariners qualified for the title game by winning the West Division in both halves of the season.

In addition to having the most prospects in the AZL, the Angels compiled the best team batting average (.287) and ERA (3.16).

The league was split into two divisions in 2009, made necessary by the addition of the Dodgers and Indians, whose parent organizations migrated their training facilities from Florida to Arizona in late 2008. The league is expected to expand again in 2010 with the arrival of the Reds from Florida.

Baseball's three Southern California franchises dominated the league Top 20 Prospects list. The Angels, Dodgers and Padres combined to produce the five best players and top 11 overall, starting with 18-year-old outfielder Mike Trout (Angels). The first-round pick hit .360/.418/.506 in his debut season and impressed AZL observers with his plus speed, defense and bulldog approach.

For the second year in a row, a Padres prospect with the surname Decker won league MVP honors. But unlike outfielder Jaff, who was No. 2 on our 2008 Top 20, first baseman Cody (no relation) failed to crack our prospects list. Cody, a 22-year-old UCLA alum, made a run at the triple crown with a .354 average and league highs in homers (15) and RBIs (63).

Indians third-base prospect Jesus Brito, 21, led the league in hitting at .366 after three seasons in the Dominican Summer League. Cubs outfielder Francisco Guzman topped all AZL basestealers with 32.

TOP 20 PROSPECTS

1. Mike Trout, of, Angels
2. Fabio Martinez, rhp, Angels
3. Allen Webster, rhp, Dodgers
4. Rymer Liriano, of, Padres
5. Randal Grichuk, of, Angels
6. Julio Morban, of/dh, Mariners
7. Adys Portillo, rhp, Padres
8. Rafael Rodriguez, of, Giants
9. Jonathan Garcia, of, Dodgers
10. Jon Bachanov, rhp, Angels
11. Maverick Lasker, rhp, Brewers
12. Richard Alvarez, rhp, Rangers
13. Edward Concepcion, rhp, Giants
14. Jesus Brito, 3b, Indians
15. Hector Sanchez, c, Giants
16. Tomas Telis, c, Rangers
17. Rolando Gomez, ss, Angels
18. Jonathan Galvez, ss/2b, Padres
19. Danny Danielson, rhp, Dodgers
20. Max Walla, of, Brewers

STANDINGS: SPLIT SEASON

FIRST HALF

East	W	L	PCT	GB
Giants	19	9	.679	—
Angels	18	10	.643	1
Cubs	16	12	.571	3
Brewers	12	16	.429	7
Athletics	10	18	.357	9

West	W	L	PCT	GB
Mariners	17	11	.607	—
Dodgers	13	15	.464	4
Indians	13	15	.464	4
Padres	13	15	.464	4
Rangers	13	15	.464	4
Royals	10	18	.357	7

SECOND HALF

East	W	L	PCT	GB
Angels	20	8	.714	—
Giants	20	8	.714	—
Brewers	13	15	.464	7
Cubs	13	15	.464	7
Athletics	12	16	.429	8

West	W	L	PCT	GB
Mariners	16	11	.593	—
Padres	15	13	.536	1½
Rangers	12	16	.429	4½
Dodgers	11	17	.393	5½
Indians	11	17	.393	5½
Royals	10	17	.370	6

Semifinals: Giants defeated Angels in a one-game playoff.
Finals: Mariners defeated Giants in a one-game playoff.

Brewers lefthander Caleb Thielbar led all pitchers in ERA at 1.59, and also tied with Pil Joon Jang (Angels) for most wins at six. Righthander Fabio Martinez (Angels) ranked as the No. 2 prospect in the league and led in strikeouts with 92.

The most notable absentee from the AZL in 2009 was Athletics righthander Michael Ynoa, who signed last year for an international amateur-record $4.25 million. Ynoa was supposed to make his pro debut in the AZL but didn't take the mound at all in 2009 due to elbow tenderness.

OVERALL STANDINGS

Team	Complex	W	L	PCT	GB	Manager	Last Penn.
Angels	Tempe	38	18	.679	1	Tyrone Boykin	Never
Athletics	Phoenix	22	34	.393	17	Marcus Jensen	2001
Brewers	Phoenix	25	31	.446	14	Tony Diggs	1990
Cubs	Mesa	29	27	.518	10	Juan Cabreja	2002
Dodgers	Glendale	24	32	.429	9½	Jeff Carter	Never
Giants	Scottsdale	39	17	.696	—	Mike Goff	2008
Indians	Goodyear	24	32	.429	9½	Ted Kubiak	Never
Mariners	Peoria	33	22	.600	—	Andy Bottin	2009
Padres	Peoria	28	28	.500	5½	Jose Flores	2006
Rangers	Surprise	25	31	.446	8½	Bill Richardson	Never
Royals	Surprise	20	35	.364	13	Julio Bruno	2003

CLUB BATTING

	AVG	G	AB	R	H	2B	3B	HR	RBI	BB	SO	SB	CS	OBP	SLG
Angels	.287	56	1997	391	573	96	46	30	346	246	444	59	24	.371	.426
Padres	.279	56	1992	364	555	108	28	48	333	201	515	97	32	.358	.433
Indians	.278	56	2019	307	561	111	25	21	263	178	497	70	33	.346	.389
Giants	.272	56	2035	321	554	108	20	13	267	172	459	89	25	.339	.364
Mariners	.268	55	1917	312	513	100	31	39	264	177	522	65	27	.340	.413
Cubs	.263	56	1919	304	505	77	32	23	260	199	500	109	43	.341	.373
Rangers	.259	56	1932	283	500	88	27	21	227	186	522	90	30	.329	.365
Royals	.257	55	1894	295	487	80	22	21	254	183	509	127	42	.330	.356
Brewers	.248	56	1895	252	470	95	31	20	218	136	503	76	35	.313	.363
Dodgers	.248	56	1919	287	476	93	20	28	242	175	525	79	14	.325	.361
Athletics	.236	56	1901	252	449	74	24	12	192	234	517	54	16	.329	.319

CLUB PITCHING

	ERA	G	CG	SHO	SV	IP	H	R	ER	HR	BB	SO	AVG
Angels	3.16	56	0	3	12	513	456	231	180	17	154	587	.234
Giants	3.39	56	0	6	15	515	427	224	194	16	189	570	.225
Mariners	3.74	55	0	3	14	488	481	258	203	21	147	479	.257
Brewers	4.30	56	0	2	13	501	501	299	239	23	215	490	.258
Padres	4.39	56	0	0	5	497	536	303	242	26	170	437	.274
Dodgers	4.48	56	0	1	12	494	528	333	246	26	176	524	.268
Cubs	4.54	56	0	2	9	504	554	312	254	15	204	454	.278
Indians	4.79	56	0	3	7	507	541	336	270	42	205	525	.272
Rangers	4.85	56	0	2	14	494	515	338	266	30	216	481	.266
Athletics	5.10	56	0	0	9	496	520	353	281	26	234	470	.269
Royals	5.30	55	0	1	9	487	584	381	287	34	177	492	.296

CLUB FIELDING

	PCT	PO	A	E	DP		PCT	PO	A	E	DP
Giants	.966	1348	519	66	110	Cubs	.954	1163	557	83	88
Brewers	.965	1352	474	67	102	Athletics	.949	997	434	77	87
Angels	.963	1181	515	65	58	Dodgers	.948	1096	374	80	84
Royals	.962	1345	517	74	121	Indians	.945	1041	540	92	102
Mariners	.960	1036	493	63	91	Padres	.936	724	380	75	68
Rangers	.955	1391	541	91	113						

INDIVIDUAL BATTING LEADERS (MINIMUM 3.1 PA/TEAM GAME)

	AVG	G	AB	R	H	2B	3B	HR	RBI	BB	SO	SB
Brito, Jesus, Indians	.366	35	134	36	49	12	8	3	25	18	26	2
Trout, Mike, Angels	.360	39	164	29	59	7	7	1	25	18	28	13
Decker, Cody, Padres	.354	52	198	46	70	21	3	15	63	19	42	0
Perez, Roberto, Indians	.351	34	131	24	46	12	0	3	31	16	28	4
Liriano, Rymer, Padres	.350	50	197	44	69	8	1	8	44	15	52	14
Sharpley, Evan, Mariners	.333	37	132	31	44	12	2	7	29	21	46	5
Kersten, Chris, Indians	.328	45	180	33	59	20	2	4	33	12	48	5
Tavarez, Pedro, Dodgers	.325	43	151	20	49	4	0	1	26	16	19	3
Telis, Tomas, Rangers	.322	46	183	30	59	11	5	2	28	4	15	8
Grichuk, Randal, Angels	.322	53	236	47	76	13	10	7	53	9	64	6

INDIVIDUAL PITCHING LEADERS (MINIMUM 1 IP/TEAM GAME)

	W	L	ERA	G	GS	CG	SV	IP	H	R	BB	SO
Thielbar, Caleb, Brewers	6	1	1.59	14	2	0	0	45	44	16	7	46
Lamb, Cameron, Giants	4	1	2.04	13	13	0	0	57	40	15	28	55
Webster, Allen, Dodgers	2	1	2.08	12	8	0	0	48	35	19	14	56
Kessinger, Chris, Mariners	5	3	2.45	13	7	0	0	66	58	24	8	66
Medina, Bolivar, Dodgers	3	2	2.89	13	4	0	2	47	43	27	13	42
Sanchez, Deiber, Padres	4	2	3.00	14	5	0	0	51	43	26	15	45
Salsbury, Bryan, Giants	5	2	3.04	13	11	0	0	53	38	23	10	41
Blanco, Joshua, Angels	3	2	3.04	12	8	0	0	50	40	20	13	63
Pena, Julio, Cubs	4	1	3.07	14	5	0	0	44	46	15	5	40
Danielson, Danny, Dodgers	5	2	3.08	14	9	0	0	61	65	30	12	77

ALL-STAR TEAM

C: Pedro Tavarez, Dodgers. **1B:** Cody Decker, Padres. **2B:** Kevin Mailloux, Mariners. **3B:** Jesus Brito, Indians. **SS:** Rolando Gomez, Angels. **OF:** Nick Akins, Dodgers; Rymer Liriano, Padres; Mike Trout, Angels. **DH:** Eric Oliver, Angels. **LHSP:** Anthony Fernandez, Mariners. **RHSP:** Cameron Lamb, Giants. **LHRP:** Roberto Feliciano, Dodgers. **RHRP:** Jeff Breedlove, Mariners; Maverick Lasker, Brewers. **Most Valuable Player:** Cody Decker, Padres. **Manager of the Year:** Andy Bottin, Mariners.

DEPARTMENT LEADERS

BATTING

OBP	Brito, Jesus, Indians	.439
SLG	Decker, Cody, Padres	.717
OPS	Decker, Cody, Padres	.113
R	Guzman, Francisco, Cubs	49
H	Grichuk, Randal, Angels	76
TB	Decker, Cody, Padres	142
XBH	Decker, Cody, Padres	39
2B	Decker, Cody, Padres	21
3B	Grichuk, Randal, Angels	10
HR	Decker, Cody, Padres	15
RBI	Decker, Cody, Padres	63
SAC	Three tied at	5
BB	Castillo, Gernaldo, Athletics	43
HBP	Grider, Casio, Dodgers	14
SO	Walla, Maxwell, Brewers	82
SB	Guzman, Francisco, Cubs	32
CS	Soto, Kevin, Cubs	9
AB/SO	Telis, Tomas, Rangers	12.20

PITCHING

G	Baez, Suammy, Angels	23
GS	Jang, Pil Joon, Angels	14
GF	Breedlove, Jeff, Mariners	20
SV	Arrendell, Kelvin, Rangers	10
	Breedlove, Jeff, Mariners	10
W	Jang, Pil Joon, Angels	6
	Thielbar, Caleb, Brewers	6
L	Portillo, Adys, Padres	9
IP	Jang, Pil Joon, Angels	82
H	Santiago, Leonel, Royals	81
R	Avinazar, Willian, Royals	52
ER	Avinazar, Willian, Royals	40
HB	Amador, Ezequiel, Royals	12
BB	Lintz, Seth, Brewers	38
SO	Martinez Mesa, Fabio, Angels	92
SO/9 (SP)	Martinez Mesa, Fabio, Angels	13.66
SO/9 (RP)	Bachanov, Jon, Angels	14.76
BB/9	Kessinger, Chris, Mariners	1.09
WP	Billings, Blakeney, Brewers	16
	Frias, Carlos, Dodgers	16
BK	Escobar, Edwin, Rangers	5
HR	Fructuoso , Beyker, Dodgers	8
AVG	Salsbury, Bryan, Giants	.196

FIELDING

C	FPCT	Jimenez, Jose, Angels	.997
	PO	Jimenez, Jose, Angels	285
		Sanchez, Hector, Giants	285
	A	Sanchez, Hector, Giants	40
	E	Jimenez, Hassiel, Mariners	10
	DP	Escobar, Edul, Royals	4
		Petit, Rolando, Indians	4
	PB	Three tied at	12
1B	FPCT	Decker, Cody, Padres	.995
	PO	Baldwin, Geoffrey, Royals	438
	A	Decker, Cody, Padres	28
	E	Baldwin, Geoffrey, Royals	12
	DP	Decker, Cody, Padres	39
2B	FPCT	Lind, Connor, Brewers	.976
	PO	Martinez, Argenis, Indians	81
	A	Wells, Jeremy, Athletics	113
	E	Jean, Ramon, Dodgers	10
		Wells, Jeremy, Athletics	10
	DP	Martinez, Argenis, Indians	28
		Piterson, Luis, Royals	28
3B	FPCT	Alvarez, Ricky, Angels	.912
	PO	Alia, Jonathan, Padres	31
		Alvarez, Ricky, Angels	31
	A	Figueroa, Yunior, Royals	98
	E	Henderson, Chris, Dodgers	13
		Solis, Emmanuel, Rangers	13
	DP	Figueroa, Yunior, Royals	9
SS	FPCT	Garcia, Edwin, Rangers	.944
	PO	Castillo, Gernaldo, Athletics	88
	A	Castillo, Gernaldo, Athletics	145
	E	George, Carlos, Brewers	25
	DP	Castillo, Gernaldo, Athletics	36
OF	FPCT	Long, Matt, Angels	.100
	PO	Guzman, Francisco, Cubs	114
	A	Romero, Franklin, Brewers	12
	E	Liriano, Rymer, Padres	8
	DP	Romero, Franklin, Brewers	3

BY NATHAN RODE

The Gulf Coast League doesn't garner the same attention as others with playoff chases, hit streaks or attendance records. Still, a champion is crowned and players vie to lead the league in the important categories.

The Nationals took the 2009 title. They beat the Twins 1-0 in a first-round, single-elimination game, and then took down the Marlins 3-1 and 5-4 in a best-of-three championship series.

Nationals outfielder Eury Perez batted .381 over 181 at-bats to lead the league. His average was nearly 50 points higher than the closest contender. Braves first baseman Alberto Oderman was the top home run hitter with nine in 195 at-bats, edging teammate Layton Hiller, who had eight.

Tigers lefthander Giovanny Soto, who started as well as relieved, posted a league-best 1.18 ERA in 46 innings. Twins righthander B.J. Hermsen had the top ERA among full-time starters at 1.35 in 53 innings. Braves righthander Caleb Brewer led the league in strikeouts, sending 65 batters back to the bench in 45 innings.

As usual, the GCL was filled with young, raw prospects who flashed impressive tools but still needed plenty of seasoning. International position players dominated our GCL Top 20 list, starting with Braves catcher Christian Bethancourt, Yankees outfielder Kelvin De Leon and Red Sox outfielder Reymond Fuentes.

Bethancourt, a Panamanian, was the top catcher on the international market in 2008, and he hit .284/.344/.431 in 116 at-bats before moving on to Danville in the Appalachian League. De Leon, who signed for $1.1 million out of the Dominican Republic in 2007, hit .269/.330/.438 with seven home runs and 31 RBIs. Fuentes, a Puerto Rican,

TOP 20 PROSPECTS

1. Christian Bethancourt, c, Braves
2. Kelvin De Leon, of, Yankees
3. Reymond Fuentes, of, Red Sox
4. Jarred Cosart, rhp, Phillies
5. Carlos Perez, c, Blue Jays
6. Adrian Salcedo, rhp, Twins
7. Jonathan Singleton, 1b, Phillies
8. Destin Hood, of, Nationals
9. Tanner Bushue, rhp, Astros
10. Domingo Santana, of, Phillies
11. B.J. Hermsen, rhp, Twins
12. Roman Mendez, rhp, Red Sox
13. Billy Hamilton, ss, Reds
14. Eury Perez, of, Nationals
15. Brooks Pounders, rhp, Pirates
16. Yorman Rodriguez, of, Reds
17. Caleb Brewer, rhp, Braves
18. Jonathan Villar, ss, Phillies
19. Melvin Mercedes, rhp, Tigers
20. Daniel Tuttle, rhp, Reds

was subject to the draft, and Boston selected him 28th overall in June. He hit .290/.331/.379 in 145 at-bats.

The Phillies have an affinity for signing raw athletes who offer projection but require plenty of polish, so it was no surprise that they led all organizations with four players on the GCL list: righthander Jarred Cosart, first baseman Jonathan Singleton, outfielder Domingo Santana and shortstop Jonathan Villar.

Philadelphia's top pick (second round) in the 2009 draft, outfielder Kelly Dugan, didn't make the Top 20 but showed some potential as a switch-hitter with a solid frame and average speed.

Several 2009 draftees played well in the GCL but didn't log enough playing time to qualify for our ranking. Yankees catcher J.R. Murphy (second round), Pirates righthander Trent Stevenson (seventh) and Orioles lefty Aaron Wirsch (seventh) fell into that group.

STANDINGS

East	Complex	W	L	PCT	GB	Manager	Last Penn.
Marlins	Jupiter	38	17	.691	—	Jorge Hernandez	Never
Nationals	Melbourne	36	19	.655	2	Bob Henley	2009
Cardinals	Jupiter	25	31	.446	13 ½	Steve Turco	Never
Mets	Port St. Lucie	22	34	.393	16 ½	Julio Franco	Never
Astros	Kissimmee	18	38	.321	20 ½	Omar Lopez	Never

North	Complex	W	L	PCT	GB	Manager	Last Penn.
Yankees	Tampa	33	27	.550	—	Jody Reed	2007
Phillies	Clearwater	31	28	.525	1 ½	Rolando de Armas	2008
Blue Jays	Dunedin	30	28	.517	2	John Schneider	Never
Tigers	Lakeland	29	30	.492	3 ½	Basilio Cabrera	Never
Pirates	Bradenton	29	31	.483	4	Tom Prince	Never
Braves	Lake Buena Vista	26	34	.433	7	Luis Ortiz	2003

South	Complex	W	L	PCT	GB	Manager	Last Penn.
Twins	Fort Myers	34	21	.618	—	Jake Mauer	Never
Orioles	Sarasota	30	26	.536	4 ½	Ramon Sambo	Never
Reds	Sarasota	28	27	.509	6	Pat Kelly	Never
Red Sox	Fort Myers	26	27	.491	7	Dave Tomlin	2006
Rays	Port Charlotte	19	36	.345	15	Joe Alvarez	Never

PLAYOFFS—Semifinals: Marlins defeated Yankees 1-0 and Nationals defeated Twins 1-0 in one-game playoffs. **Finals:** Nationals defeated Marlins 2-0 in best-of-three series.

CLUB BATTING

	AVG	G	AB	R	H	2B	3B	HR	RBI	BB	SO	SB	CS	OBP	SLG
Nationals	.274	55	1766	334	484	100	19	27	281	193	365	75	31	.356	.398
Braves	.252	60	1932	270	487	92	15	37	226	160	426	72	26	.321	.373
Mets	.247	56	1847	235	456	96	15	7	193	202	433	73	36	.332	.326
Cardinals	.243	56	1819	245	442	87	18	12	199	192	466	42	26	.328	.330
Red Sox	.243	53	1649	195	400	87	21	17	169	164	439	48	26	.316	.352
Reds	.243	55	1786	218	434	70	24	9	177	155	398	73	24	.307	.324
Twins	.243	55	1776	209	431	89	15	22	182	166	346	53	10	.317	.347
Orioles	.239	56	1874	243	448	79	25	12	208	195	377	67	25	.321	.327
Marlins	.238	55	1813	277	431	87	8	15	226	229	350	46	22	.334	.319
Phillies	.238	59	1862	215	443	91	12	17	192	183	393	78	34	.317	.327
Pirates	.237	60	1810	206	429	87	9	23	178	164	467	69	51	.310	.333
Astros	.231	56	1833	253	424	88	19	10	218	181	482	46	25	.317	.316
Tigers	.227	59	1868	225	424	87	13	33	200	150	443	56	18	.294	.340
Blue Jays	.225	58	1777	206	400	90	22	26	183	179	485	66	22	.304	.344
Yankees	.220	60	1839	216	405	98	9	29	197	207	475	48	21	.309	.331
Rays	.211	55	1724	165	363	69	12	6	142	124	392	52	25	.274	.275

CLUB PITCHING

	ERA	G	CG	SHO	SV	IP	H	R	ER	HR	BB	SO	AVG
Twins	2.47	55	1	6	18	477	389	188	131	16	114	447	.218
Blue Jays	2.57	58	2	5	15	484	417	202	138	24	155	481	.230
Marlins	2.61	55	0	7	20	485	407	189	141	7	177	442	.228
Orioles	2.95	56	0	7	14	503	428	202	165	8	175	374	.233
Phillies	2.98	59	1	4	17	504	405	204	167	24	167	458	.221
Yankees	3.00	60	0	5	19	504	416	209	168	23	164	445	.223
Red Sox	3.01	53	0	4	12	443	383	190	148	8	163	378	.231
Reds	3.10	55	1	6	19	473	419	203	163	16	178	363	.238
Tigers	3.49	59	1	9	19	501	441	220	194	30	234	460	.243
Pirates	3.51	60	0	5	12	493	463	228	192	33	115	363	.246
Nationals	3.53	55	0	1	17	465	439	248	182	17	168	436	.248
Mets	3.76	56	0	5	8	484	411	254	202	15	235	431	.228
Braves	3.79	60	1	4	15	499	446	275	210	31	208	482	.237
Rays	3.90	55	1	6	10	464	457	247	201	18	174	390	.251
Cardinals	4.14	56	0	2	13	479	452	285	220	11	214	410	.249
Astros	4.84	56	0	0	11	478	528	368	257	21	203	377	.277

CLUB FIELDING

	PCT	PO	A	E	DP		PCT	PO	A	E	DP
Tigers	.975	1314	502	47	148	Red Sox	.962	1055	461	60	93
Orioles	.971	868	588	43	110	Marlins	.961	1046	532	64	110
Pirates	.970	1464	531	61	125	Reds	.961	997	522	61	133
Blue Jays	.969	1310	390	54	89	Twins	.961	874	475	55	61
Yankees	.969	1361	396	57	89	Braves	.958	1210	275	65	72
Nationals	.966	1382	567	69	149	Mets	.953	1044	462	74	146
Rays	.966	1289	538	64	127	Cardinals	.950	1400	554	102	140
Phillies	.964	1131	461	60	73	Astros	.943	1321	572	115	143

INDIVIDUAL BATTING LEADERS (Minimum 3.1 PA/team game)

	AVG	G	AB	R	H	2B	3B	HR	RBI	BB	SO	SB
Perez, Eury, Nationals	.381	47	181	38	69	3	5	3	24	15	20	16
Jimenez, Hendry, Nationals	.333	50	162	39	54	10	2	1	25	28	24	12
Newsome, Brett, Nationals	.327	51	168	36	55	17	4	5	35	31	42	3
Rodriguez, Henry, Reds	.322	42	152	24	49	10	1	1	19	7	18	9
Ozuna, Marcell, Marlins	.313	55	214	32	67	22	0	5	39	22	52	4
Stampone, Tyler, Orioles	.312	36	141	19	44	10	2	3	26	8	18	5
Nunez, Alexander, Tigers	.308	41	143	18	44	7	5	5	17	7	31	4
Concepcion, Julio, Mets	.306	45	160	21	49	4	2	0	12	10	34	11
Hernandez, Enrique, Astros	.295	53	207	35	61	12	3	1	27	10	28	8
Perez, Carlos, Blue Jays	.291	43	141	17	41	11	3	1	21	16	23	2

INDIVIDUAL PITCHING LEADERS (Minimum 1 IP/team game)

	W	L	ERA	G	GS	CG	SV	IP	H	R	BB	SO
Soto, Giovany, Tigers	4	0	1.18	13	6	0	1	46	33	7	20	37
Rivera, Manuel, Red Sox	1	3	1.19	12	9	0	0	53	40	14	14	50
Fields, Matt, Blue Jays	0	0	1.22	14	9	0	0	52	35	9	6	54
Lopez, Robinson, Braves	3	1	1.29	11	8	0	0	49	41	13	12	42
Hermsen, B.J., Twins	6	2	1.35	10	10	1	0	53	32	12	4	42
Tavarez, Daurin, Orioles	4	2	1.37	12	9	0	1	66	53	15	9	44
Salcedo, Adrian, Twins	3	2	1.46	11	10	0	0	62	60	25	3	58
Ramirez, Jose A., Yankees	6	0	1.48	11	10	0	0	61	33	12	16	53
Pina, Carlos, Blue Jays	3	2	1.57	12	10	0	0	52	46	23	16	35
Weller, Blayne, Twins	5	1	1.58	11	10	0	0	57	46	12	8	49

ALL-STAR TEAM

C: Carlos Perez, Blue Jays. **1B:** Brett Newsome, Nationals. **2B:** Hendry Jimenez, Nationals. **3B:** Tyler Stampone, Orioles. **SS:** Jose Mojica, Yankees. **OF:** Julio Concepcion, Mets; Marcell Ozuna, Marlins; Eury Perez, Nationals. **DH:** Layton Hiller, Braveys. **SP:** Jose Ramirez, Yankees. **RP:** Andrei Lobanov, Twins. **Most Valuable Player:** Eury Perez, Nationals. **Manager of the Year:** Jake Mauer, Twins.

DEPARTMENT LEADERS

BATTING

OBP	Perez, Eury, Nationals	.443
SLG	Newsome, Brett, Nationals	.583
OPS	Newsome, Brett, Nationals	.101
R	Jimenez, Hendry, Nationals	39
H	Perez, Eury, Nationals	69
TB	Ozuna, Marcell, Marlins	104
XBH	Newsome, Brett, Nationals	27
	Ozuna, Marcell, Marlins	27
2B	Ozuna, Marcell, Marlins	22
3B	Gonzalez, Grolmann, Orioles	7
	Silva, Juan, Reds	7
HR	Odreman, Alberto, Braves	9
RBI	Hiller, Layton, Braves	45
SAC	Ngoepe, Gift, Pirates	8
BB	Anderson, David, Orioles	36
HBP	King, Emilio, Astros	16
SO	Mahoney, Kevin, Yankees	70
SB	Rose, Kyle, Braves	26
CS	Ngoepe, Gift, Pirates	9
AB/SO	Mojica, Jose, Yankees	9.90

PITCHING

G	Mercedes, Melvin, Tigers	26
GS	Three tied at	12
GF	Mercedes, Melvin, Tigers	25
SV	Mercedes, Melvin, Tigers	16
W	Eskew, Jared, Marlins	7
	Gonzalez, Saul, Marlins	7
L	Quezada, Euris, Astros	7
IP	Cespedes, Angel, Orioles	72
H	Cespedes, Angel, Orioles	64
R	Quezada, Euris, Astros	45
ER	Quezada, Euris, Astros	32
HB	Northcraft, Aaron, Braves	9
	Quezada, Euris, Astros	9
BB	Lebron, Ramon, Tigers	37
SO	Brewer, Caleb, Braves	65
SO/9 (SP)	Lebron, Ramon, Tigers	10.64
SO/9 (RP)	Lobanov, Andrei, Twins	14.32
BB/9	Salcedo, Adrian, Twins	0.44
WP	Cedano, Enmanuel, Astros	11
	Henry, Michael, Reds	11
BK	Hodge, Lachlan, Mets	5
HR	Guichardo, Rayni, Tigers	6
	Rodriguez, Julio, Phillies	6
AVG	Brewer, Caleb, Braves	.132

FIELDING

C	FPCT	Nieto, Adrian, Nationals	.996
	PO	Rodriguez, Julio, Tigers	280
	A	Rodriguez, Julio, Tigers	41
	E	Polanco, Jeudis, Cardinals	7
	DP	Arcia, Francisco, Yankees	4
		Vicioso, Danny, Reds	4
	PB	Genoves, Ernesto, Astros	16
1B	FPCT	Anderson, David, Orioles	.995
	PO	Anderson, David, Orioles	505
	A	Anderson, David, Orioles	46
	E	Gomez, Hector, Rays	8
	DP	Anderson, David, Orioles	51
2B	FPCT	Linger, Jim, Marlins	.976
	PO	Jimenez, Hendry, Nationals	104
	A	Jimenez, Hendry, Nationals	117
	E	Blanco, Elys, Braves	11
		Sierra, Jefry, Reds	11
	DP	Jimenez, Hendry, Nationals	38
3B	FPCT	Mahoney, Kevin, Yankees	.954
	PO	Mahoney, Kevin, Yankees	42
	A	Mahoney, Kevin, Yankees	123
	E	Hanson, Jake, Braves	18
	DP	Martinez, Francisco, Tigers	9
SS	FPCT	Hamilton, Billy, Reds	.955
	PO	Valera, Cesar, Cardinals	73
	A	Valera, Cesar, Cardinals	156
	E	Peralta, Rony, Marlins	20
	DP	Valera, Cesar, Cardinals	39
OF	FPCT	Eight tied at	1.000
	PO	Castillo, Luis, Tigers	112
	A	King, Emilio, Astros	9
	E	Suniaga, Geber, Astros	7
	DP	King, Emilio, Astros	3
	DP	Santana, Nestor, Astros	3

MINOR LEAGUES

BY BEN BADLER
DOMINICAN SUMMER LEAGUE

After finishing with the Dominican Summer League's best record (52-19), the Giants stampeded through the postseason, defeating the Mariners, two games to none, in the semifinals before sweeping the Twins 3-0 in the championship series.

Second baseman Carlos Willoughby, 20, helped pace the Giants by hitting .327/.466/.438 in 68 games. Willoughby led the league in on-base percentage, walks (55) and runs scored (74), ranked second in stolen bases (46) and tied for second in triples (10). First baseman Rey Duran, 20, hit .278/.352/.474 for the Giants and finished second in the league with 11 home runs.

The Giants also were stingy allowing runs, finishing third in the league with a 2.66 ERA. Twins righthander Pedro Guerra's 0.38 ERA in 71 innings ranked first in the league.

STANDINGS

BOCA CHICA

NORTH	W	L	PCT	GB
Giants	52	19	.732	—
Mets	49	23	.681	3½
Red Sox	44	25	.638	7
Blue Jays	43	26	.623	8
Marlins	31	37	.456	19½
Yankees 1	31	37	.456	19½
Rays	30	37	.448	20
Pirates	29	38	.433	21
Dodgers	30	40	.429	21½

BASEBALL CITY	W	L	PCT	GB
Yankees 2	47	23	.671	—
Twins	46	23	.667	½
White Sox	42	28	.6	5
Tigers	37	32	.536	9½
Diamondbacks	36	33	.522	10½
Cubs 1	36	34	.514	11
Rockies	36	35	.507	11½
Indians	32	39	.451	15½
Reds	29	41	.414	18

	W	L	PCT	GB
Royals	26	41	.388	24
Orioles/Brewers	27	43	.386	24½
Cubs 2	15	52	.224	35

SANTO DOMINGO

NORTH	W	L	PCT	GB
Mariners	47	26	.644	—
Cardinals	46	27	.63	1
Phillies	31	39	.443	14½
Athletics	19	51	.271	26½

	W	L	PCT	GB
Nationals	29	42	.408	18½
Orioles	26	45	.366	21½
Padres	25	46	.352	22½

SAN PEDRO DE MACORIS	W	L	PCT	GB
Rangers 2	47	15	.758	—
Braves	39	24	.619	8½
Astros	32	32	.5	16
Angels	28	36	.438	20
Rangers 1	18	46	.281	30

INDIVIDUAL BATTING LEADERS
(MINIMUM 3.1 PA/TEAM GAME)

	AVG	G	AB	R	H	2B	3B	HR	RBI	BB	SO	SB
Ramirez, Alvaro, Cubs 1	.372	58	199	40	74	7	4	2	30	21	17	24
Sanchez, Alexander, Mets	.372	47	191	30	71	13	2	4	42	12	19	1
Javier, Jhonatan, O's/Brewers	.344	64	221	48	76	17	5	6	45	17	30	12
Mendez, Geancarlo, Phillies	.328	70	229	39	75	14	2	1	37	52	29	20
Willoughby, Carlos, Giants	.327	68	251	74	82	5	10	1	43	55	33	46
Vasquez, Simon, Blue Jays	.326	56	178	32	58	13	3	1	32	17	23	7
Ortega, Rafael, Rockies	.324	70	256	45	83	7	8	0	39	32	23	39
Calderon, Yeicok, Yankees 1	.321	55	193	38	62	5	2	3	27	38	45	9
Silverio, Juan, White Sox	.321	61	243	52	78	11	0	8	56	16	47	5
Castillo, Ali, Yankees 1	.319	51	185	40	59	13	9	1	27	24	14	10

INDIVIDUAL PITCHING LEADERS
(MINIMUM 1 IP/TEAM GAME)

	W	L	ERA	G	GS	CG	SV	IP	H	R	BB	SO
Heredia, Juan, Yankees 2	2	0	0.32	13	13	0	0	57	34	3	20	63
Guerra, Pedro, Twins	7	0	0.38	14	11	0	1	71	44	4	12	75
Rojas, Randol, Rangers 2	8	0	0.80	13	12	0	0	67	42	11	6	48
Otero, Andy, Braves	6	1	0.84	18	12	0	0	64	38	11	26	93
De La Cruz, Daniel, Phillies	3	4	1.03	15	9	1	2	61	39	13	18	55
Mejias, Alving, Rockies	5	1	1.24	13	11	1	0	72	51	16	6	70
Vargas, Jose, Blue Jays	6	3	1.34	18	6	1	1	67	52	17	17	51
Ciurcina, Cesar, Twins	9	2	1.39	15	13	0	0	84	50	18	8	72
Bonilla, Lisalverto, Phillies	6	2	1.41	11	11	2	0	70	48	20	16	76
Guzman, Antonio, Nationals	8	2	1.44	15	14	1	0	88	59	20	20	64

VENEZUELAN SUMMER LEAGUE

On the verge of elimination, the Rays rallied with an 8-7 victory and then an 8-2 victory against the Pirates in the championship series to win the Venezuelan Summer League title.

Rays third baseman/first baseman Roan Salas led the league in home runs (15), doubles (19), extra-base hits (37), total bases (145) and slugging (.653). Rays catcher Alejandro Segovia ranked second in on-base percentage (.417), while shortstop Hector Guevara, 17, hit .330/.374/.534 in 54 games, ranking fourth in the league in slugging.

The Pirates finished with the best regular season record, leading the league in runs scored (461) and ranking second to the Mariners in runs allowed (301). The Pirates received key contributions from 18-year-old middle infielder Jorge Bishop, who batted .308/.367/.470 with 24 steals in 63 games, and 17-year-old left fielder Exicardo Cayonez, who hit .302/.396/.424 in 65 games.

STANDINGS

	W	L	PCT	GB
Pirates	48	22	.686	—
Rays	41	28	.594	6½
Mariners	39	29	.574	8

	W	L	PCT	GB
Cardinals	34	35	.493	13½
Mets	28	41	.406	19½
Phillies	27	42	.391	20½
Tigers	24	44	.353	23

INDIVIDUAL BATTING LEADERS
(MINIMUM 3.1 PA/TEAM GAME)

	AVG	G	AB	R	H	2B	3B	HR	RBI	BB	SO	SB
Segovia, Alejandro, Rays	.349	50	189	35	66	16	0	7	40	15	18	1
Salas, Roan, Rays	.338	61	222	49	75	19	3	15	59	25	31	1
Davalillo, Marco, Phillies	.336	64	220	30	74	18	0	6	26	18	25	2
Ramirez, Carlos, Mariners	.336	65	226	43	76	17	1	2	36	35	29	4
Guevara, Hector, Rays	.330	54	206	29	68	14	2	8	36	16	21	6
Reginatto, Leonardo, Rays	.328	54	186	31	61	7	2	1	29	9	14	2
Sanz, Luis, Tigers	.328	65	229	36	75	11	1	2	30	34	12	4
Moreno, Nestor, Mets	.320	68	244	33	78	15	0	1	29	21	48	0
Trinidad, Michaelangel, Pirates	.31858		192	36	61	13	0	14	56	27	39	0
Narvaez, Omar, Rays	.315	47	165	23	52	7	3	0	27	19	13	4

INDIVIDUAL PITCHING LEADERS
(MINIMUM 1 IP/TEAM GAME)

	W	L	ERA	G	GS	CG	SV	IP	H	R	BB	SO
Ramirez, Erasmo, Mariners	11	1	0.51	14	13	0	0	88	54	10	5	80
Avendano, Javier, Cardinals	6	3	1.79	13	13	0	0	65	59	24	21	60
Raga, Angel, Mariners	4	4	2.16	14	8	0	1	58	50	19	19	35
Bier, Deimer, Cardinals	5	3	2.29	13	13	0	0	63	50	20	19	72
Yanez, Ernesto, Mets	7	1	2.34	14	10	2	0	69	56	20	24	42
Medina, Yoervis, Mariners	3	4	2.65	15	13	0	1	68	46	22	23	62
Espinoza, Roberto, Pirates	4	1	2.74	14	14	0	0	62	41	21	22	48
Verdugo, Oscar, Pirates	4	0	2.95	14	14	0	0	58	50	26	14	53
Olivero, Yovanny, Mariners	6	2	2.97	14	14	0	0	73	76	33	18	54
Oraa, Carlos, Cardinals	5	2	3.04	14	14	0	0	68	65	25	13	48

BY BILL MITCHELL

The 2009 Arizona Fall League championship game was supposed to be the occasion for No. 1 overall draft pick Stephen Strasburg to lead the Phoenix Desert Dogs to their sixth straight league championship in front of a national television audience.

Instead, local product C.J. Retherford (White Sox), who went undrafted in 2007 after his career at Arizona State, turned himself into the unlikely hero of the game. Retherford's two-run homer off Desert Dog reliever Josh Perrault (Orioles) in the bottom of the eighth inning gave the Peoria Javelinas a dramatic 5-4 victory for the AFL title.

Retherford hit a middle-in fastball on a 1-0 count for his winning blast. The home run capped a great day for Retherford, which saw the Peoria second baseman involved in four of the five Javelina runs.

"My family is here," said Retherford in a postgame interview just before getting doused by his teammates with a cooler of water. "It's awesome to be able to do it in Arizona and play at a high level."

Robbie Weinhardt (Tigers), in his second inning of relief, retired the Desert Dogs 1-2-3 in the ninth for the win. The righthanded reliever, who led the AFL in strikeouts with 29 in 18 innings, fanned four batters in his two-inning stint. He was relying primarily on his fastball, as he said after the game that his breaking ball wasn't working as well as usual.

Strasburg, who was the league's most hyped player since Michael Jordan, was originally scheduled to get the start for the Desert Dogs, but the Nationals prospect twisted his knee during pregame practice prior to the regular season finale. He returned to Arizona after a medical examination just in time to watch the championship game from the Phoenix dugout.

The Desert Dogs got on the scoreboard early when Matt Angle (Orioles) led off the game with a triple off Javelina starter Anthony Varvaro (Mariners), scoring one batter late on a Danny Espinosa (Nationals) ground ball out.

The Javelinas took a 2-1 lead in the bottom of the secondnd off Desert Dog starter Mitch Talbot (Rays) on Retherford's force out grounder, followed three batters later by a bases-loaded infield single by Dustin Ackley (Mariners), who was drafted one pick after Strasburg back in June.

Phoenix regained the lead in the top of the fourth on solo homers off Peoria reliever Scot

TOP 10 PROSPECTS

1. Stephen Strasburg, rhp, Nationals
2. Buster Posey, c, Giants
3. Domonic Brown, rf, Phillies
4. Dustin Ackley, of, Mariners
5. Josh Bell, 3b, Orioles
6. Jenrry Mejia, rhp, Mets
7. Freddie Freeman, 1b, Braves
8. Yonder Alonso, 1b, Reds
9. Starlin Castro, ss, Cubs
10. Ike Davis, 1b, Mets

Drucker (Tigers) by Grant Desme (Athletics) and Nevin Ashley (Rays).

Retherford was again in on the scoring as the Javelinas tied the game at three each in the bottom of the fourth inning, scoring from third base on a force out grounder by Jordan Danks (White Sox).

The game remained tied until the top of the seventh when Ashley scored from third on Shawn O'Malley's (Rays) single up the middle. After Weinhardt struck out the side in the top of the eighth, the stage was set for Retherford's heroics.

Perrault came on for the Desert Dogs, striking out Casper Wells (Tigers) for the first out. Jonathan Lucroy (Brewers) followed with a line-drive single to left field, bringing Retherford to the plate. After taking ball one, Retherford pounded Perrault's fastball deep into the left-field corner to give the Javelinas their 5-4 lead.

Javelinas infielder Russ Mitchell (Dodgers) won the Dernell Stenson Sportsmanship Award, named in memory of the former AFL player who was murdered in 2003 while a member of the Scottsdale Scorpions and given to the league's player who best exemplifies unselfishness, hard work and leadership. Mitchell hit .319/.396/.606, with five home runs for the Javelinas. He hit the first professional home run yielded by Strasburg on Oct. 22.

Desme won the league's Joe Black MVP Award. The righthanded-hitting outfielder hit .315/.413/.667 with a league-leading 11 home runs. He ranked second in the league in RBIs with 27. Corey Brown (A's) surpassed his Phoenix teammate Desme with a late-season rush to lead the league with 28 RBIs. Third baseman Brent Morel (White Sox), who replaced the injured Dayan Viciedo two weeks into the season, led the league with a .435 batting average. Shortstop Chase D'Arnaud (Pirates) was the leading base stealer with 13. Strasburg led all pitchers in wins with four; teammate Drew Storen (Nationals) was the league's top reliever with four saves.

MINOR LEAGUES

MINOR LEAGUES

STANDINGS

EAST	W	L	PCT	GB	WEST	W	L	PCT	GB
Phoenix Desert Dogs	19	13	.594	—	Peoria Javelinas	18	14	.563	—
Scottsdale Scorpions	15	16	.484	3½	Surprise Rafters	16	16	.500	2
Mesa Solar Sox	13	18	.419	5½	Peoria Saguaros	14	18	.438	4

INDIVIDUAL BATTING LEADERS
(MINIMUM 2 PLATE APPEARANCES/LEAGUE GAME)

PLAYER, TEAM	AVG	G	AB	R	H	HR	RBI
Morel, Brent, Javelinas	.435	16	62	14	27	2	11
Curtis, Colin, Surprise	.397	20	78	19	31	5	18
Tabata, Jose, Scottsdale	.392	28	120	21	47	1	21
Petersen, Byan, Mesa	.379	21	95	20	36	3	12
McBride, Matt, Saguaros	.378	22	74	15	28	4	18
Castro, Starlin, Mesa	.376	26	101	18	38	1	10
Ashley, Nevin, Phoenix	.366	18	71	13	26	2	14
Snyder, Brandon, Phoenix	.354	17	65	17	23	3	18
Vitters, Josh, Mesa	.353	16	68	6	24	1	8
Wells, Casper, Javelinas	.351	21	77	18	27	4	25

INDIVIDUAL PITCHING LEADERS
(MINIMUM .4 INNINGS/LEAGUE GAME)

PITCHER, TEAM	W	L	ERA	IP	H	BB	SO
Storen, Drew, Phoenix	2	0	0.66	14	16	3	13
Yanuki, Toshiyuki, Phoenix	0	0	0.66	14	10	8	14
Russell, James, Mesa	0	1	1.26	14	12	2	14
Reynolds, Matt, Scottsdale	0	0	1.29	14	9	4	15
Leake, Mike, Saguaros	1	2	1.37	20	20	3	15
Judy, Josh, Saguaros	2	2	1.59	17	13	8	20
Mandel, Jeff, Phoenix	0	0	1.88	14	14	0	10
Edlefsen, Steve, Scottsdale	3	0	2.08	13	8	9	11
Watson, Tony, Scottsdale	0	0	2.13	13	7	6	12
Veal, Donnie, Scottsdale	3	1	2.14	21	17	7	22

MESA SOLAR SOX

BATTERS	AVG	AB	R	H	2B	3B	HR	RBI	BB	SO	SB
Brenly, Michael, c	.240	25	4	6	1	0	1	3	0	3	0
* Burns, Greg, of	.297	37	5	11	1	1	0	2	16	15	3
Castillo, Welington, c	.357	14	1	5	0	0	1	2	2	5	0
Castro, Starlin, ss	.376	101	18	38	5	1	1	10	3	14	9
# Conger, Hank, c	.211	57	10	12	3	0	2	9	9	11	0
* Cooper, David, 1b	.231	78	6	18	5	0	1	5	6	18	0
Dominguez, Matt, 3b	.188	48	7	9	4	0	2	7	2	9	1
Exposito, Luis, c	.314	51	7	16	3	0	1	4	4	7	0
Iglesias, Jose, ss	.275	69	9	19	4	0	2	12	4	11	3
* Kalish, Ryan, of	.301	73	14	22	3	0	1	15	10	22	6
Kelly, Casey, 3b	.171	41	5	7	1	1	0	6	5	17	1
* Mount, Ryan, 2b	.208	53	1	11	1	1	0	5	3	13	2
* Parmelee, Chris, 1b	.250	80	10	20	8	2	4	21	11	24	1
Petersen, Bryan, of	.379	95	20	36	6	3	3	12	6	14	4
Phillips, P.J., of	.281	64	11	18	6	0	1	7	6	13	1
* Singleton, Steve, 2b	.289	76	18	22	5	1	3	15	1	12	0
Stanton, Mike, of	.478	23	2	11	0	0	1	2	3	8	4
* Tosoni, Rene, of	.218	87	13	19	1	3	1	10	12	24	0
Vitters, Josh, 3b	.353	68	6	24	4	1	1	8	2	11	0

PITCHERS	W	L	ERA	G	GS	SV	IP	H	BB	SO	AVG
Albano, Marco	0	0	8.16	11	0	0	14	16	8	8	.276
Bierd, Randor	3	2	6.04	7	7	0	25	25	12	17	.266
Buente, Jay	0	0	5.11	10	0	0	12	15	2	15	.294
* Burnett, Alex	0	0	3.38	10	0	3	11	6	10	11	.162
Cashner, Andrew	2	3	4.58	6	6	0	20	22	5	19	.278
* Gaub, John	1	1	9.31	10	0	0	10	13	6	15	.333
Haynes, Jeremy	0	1	9.69	10	0	0	13	18	9	10	.360
Hirschfeld, Steve	1	3	11.15	9	4	0	15	22	8	17	.328
Kiely, Tim	0	0	8.31	10	2	0	13	19	6	7	.333
Lentz, Richard	1	0	4.11	10	0	0	15	13	3	16	.224
McCardell, Mike	0	0	7.27	3	3	0	9	9	5	11	.257
Mendoza, Tommy	2	1	5.21	6	5	0	19	23	4	12	.299
* Miller, Andrew	0	1	5.28	5	5	0	15	13	11	13	.245
Parcell, Garrett	0	0	5.68	11	0	0	13	18	5	14	.321
Parker, Blake	2	1	4.50	11	0	2	12	12	6	11	.261
Province, Chris	0	2	3.46	10	0	2	13	9	5	9	.200
* Richardson, Dustin	0	1	5.40	11	0	0	12	13	10	18	.277
* Russell, James	0	1	1.26	11	0	0	14	12	2	14	.211
* Steedley, Spencer	0	1	4.50	11	0	0	14	16	14	8	.291
* Voss, Jay	1	0	4.91	11	0	0	15	18	7	12	.316

PEORIA JAVELINAS

BATTERS	AVG	AB	R	H	2B	3B	HR	RBI	BB	SO	SB
* Ackley, Dustin, of	.315	73	13	23	5	0	1	12	12	19	1
Cain, Lorenzo, of	.242	66	14	16	4	0	0	6	13	21	8
* Danks, Jordan, of	.343	99	31	34	7	0	3	23	20	26	5
# Diaz, Juan, ss	.067	15	3	1	1	0	0	1	7	5	1
* Dunigan, Joe, 1b	.280	75	12	21	5	0	3	14	8	18	1
* Green, Taylor, 3b	.212	52	9	11	1	0	1	6	9	9	1
Iorg, Cale, ss	.217	60	10	13	2	0	2	5	4	22	5
* Lambo, Andrew, of	.330	91	13	30	6	1	2	18	4	15	2
Lucroy, Jon, c	.310	58	8	18	4	0	2	10	5	11	0
May, Lucas, c	.325	40	7	13	6	0	2	12	5	9	0
Mier, Jessie, c	.167	36	6	6	1	0	0	1	5	10	0
Mitchell, Russ, 1b	.319	94	20	30	10	1	5	25	11	14	1
Morel, Brent, 3b	.435	62	14	27	2	0	2	11	4	7	2
Retherford, C.J., 2b	.246	69	11	17	0	2	1	12	7	9	0
Sellers, Justin, ss	.237	38	7	9	3	0	0	3	5	10	1
Sizemore, Scott, 2b	.368	19	7	7	2	0	3	9	5	3	0
Triunfel, Carlos, 2b	.204	49	6	10	2	0	0	6	2	10	0
Viciedo, Dayan, 3b	.333	18	6	6	1	0	1	6	1	6	0
Wells, Casper, of	.351	77	18	27	6	3	4	25	11	26	2

PITCHERS	W	L	ERA	G	GS	SV	IP	H	BB	SO	AVG
Aguilar, Omar	0	0	7.11	9	0	0	13	16	10	11	.314
Aumont, Phillipe	1	1	12.00	10	0	0	12	19	8	18	.339
Bellamy, Kyle	0	0	1.59	5	0	0	6	4	4	7	.200
* Braddock, Zach	0	0	5.25	11	0	3	12	12	8	8	.267
Butler, Josh	3	2	11.93	6	6	0	14	30	13	16	.429
Cassel, Justin	2	2	7.85	7	7	0	18	25	10	13	.333
Drucker, Scot	1	1	7.00	7	6	0	18	20	9	13	.282
Fields, Josh	0	0	1.64	11	0	0	11	6	6	10	.154
Guerra, Javy	0	0	0.84	10	0	0	11	7	9	8	.179
* Hill, Nick	0	2	10.50	7	7	0	18	38	10	17	.427
Jansen, Kenley	0	0	9.64	5	0	0	5	5	3	9	.263
Krebs, Eric	2	0	2.63	12	0	1	14	13	11	19	.250
Long, Matt	2	1	3.48	5	0	0	10	9	7	7	.231
* Miller, Aaron	0	0	2.08	3	0	0	4	3	3	5	.188
* Oliver, Andrew	1	1	2.81	11	0	0	16	13	9	16	.217
Rasner, Jacob	1	0	9.45	6	0	0	7	13	6	4	.433
Rogers, Mark	0	0	15.19	8	1	0	11	20	9	7	.392
Santos, Sergio	1	2	6.14	11	0	0	15	15	10	20	.254
Schlichting, Travis	2	1	4.20	6	5	0	15	16	11	14	.281
Varvaro, Anthony	1	0	4.05	10	0	2	13	12	3	11	.240
Weber, Thad	0	0	4.50	8	0	1	12	18	2	13	.360
* Weinhardt, Robbie	0	0	3.93	11	0	0	18	17	7	29	.243
Wooten, Robert	1	1	5.00	8	0	0	9	10	1	12	.286

PEORIA SAGUAROS

BATTERS	AVG	AB	R	H	2B	3B	HR	RBI	BB	SO	SB
* Alonso, Yonder, 1b	.267	86	15	23	3	1	2	23	12	15	0
* Canham, Mitch, c	.152	33	3	5	0	1	0	3	5	9	1
* Castro, Jason, c	.143	42	4	6	0	0	1	4	6	11	0
Cozart, Zack, ss	.340	50	9	17	5	0	2	10	5	9	3
* Fedroff, Tim, of	.111	36	3	4	0	0	0	2	3	8	0
* Freeman, Freddie, 1b	.267	45	5	12	3	0	1	5	4	15	0
* Gaston, Jon, of	.239	92	15	22	1	5	3	19	16	38	3
Heisey, Chris, of	.297	91	18	27	6	3	5	14	10	27	5
* Heyward, Jason, of	.286	14	3	4	3	0	0	1	2	1	2
Hicks, Brandon, 3b	.310	87	15	27	5	1	1	11	14	17	7
* Hunter, Cedric, of	.247	97	11	24	4	0	0	9	5	7	3
McBride, Matt, c	.378	74	15	28	4	2	4	18	19	9	2
Rivero, Carlos, 3b	.318	88	13	28	6	1	2	13	8	19	2
Rodriguez, Josh, 2b	.222	54	7	12	3	1	1	4	5	23	1
# Rooney, Sean, c	.111	18	0	2	0	0	0	0	2	4	0
# Vallejo, Jose, 2b	.275	80	14	22	0	1	1	8	7	18	8
* Weglarz, Nick, of	.240	25	3	6	1	0	0	1	7	7	0
# Zawadzki, Lance, ss	.324	105	20	34	8	1	2	18	9	25	9

PITCHERS	W	L	ERA	G	GS	SV	IP	H	BB	SO	AVG
Boxberger, Brad	1	1	11.37	8	2	0	13	17	7	13	.333
DeMark, Mike	0	1	7.43	11	0	0	13	19	7	15	.333
Englebrook, Evan	0	0	7.11	11	0	0	13	17	4	12	.309
* Garrison, Steve	2	2	3.86	6	6	0	19	17	6	11	.243
Gomes, Brandon	0	0	3.00	11	0	0	15	14	3	16	.241
Graham, Connor	1	1	6.08	11	0	1	13	14	18	16	.280
* Hyde, Lee	0	0	3.00	13	0	0	12	7	7	13	.167

PITCHERS	W	L	ERA	G	GS	SV	IP	H	BB	SO	AVG
Judy, Josh	2	2	1.59	11	0	0	17	13	8	20	.210
Kimbrel, Craig	0	1	10.45	11	0	0	10	7	16	18	.189
Leake, Mike	1	2	1.37	6	5	0	20	20	3	15	.256
Lo, Chia-Jen	1	0	3.48	6	0	0	10	7	2	12	.189
Lopez, Wilton	3	1	3.72	6	5	0	19	19	3	13	.264
Lyman, Jeff	0	1	7.07	11	2	0	14	18	6	11	.310
Meszaros, Daniel	0	0	4.63	12	0	1	12	8	3	15	.190
* Minor, Mike	1	0	4.86	7	7	0	17	23	6	12	.343
Ondrusek, Logan	2	1	13.50	10	0	1	10	22	2	8	.415
Pestano, Vinnie	0	1	7.36	4	0	0	4	5	4	5	.333
Putnam, Zach	0	1	8.76	5	5	0	12	18	3	18	.333
Scribner, Evan	0	1	1.59	12	0	2	11	6	8	14	.146
Smith, Carlton	0	1	5.14	12	0	0	14	22	4	6	.333
Watson, Sean	0	1	7.11	10	0	0	13	23	6	12	.371

PHOENIX DESERT DOGS

BATTERS	AVG	AB	R	H	2B	3B	HR	RBI	BB	SO	SB
* Angle, Matt, of	.237	76	18	18	3	0	1	10	11	18	7
Ashley, Nevin, c	.366	71	13	26	6	4	2	14	2	16	2
# Bell, Josh, 3b	.319	91	16	29	10	1	2	19	10	18	0
* Brown, Corey, of	.333	105	18	35	6	3	6	28	11	29	1
Cipriano, Cody, of	.250	4	1	1	1	0	0	1	0	2	0
Desme, Grant, of	.315	108	30	34	5	0	11	27	16	34	2
Emaus, Brad, 3b	.317	60	9	19	3	0	1	10	7	3	2
# Espinosa, Danny, ss	.345	87	24	30	5	1	1	14	15	20	3
Jimenez, A.J., c	.157	51	5	8	1	1	1	8	3	15	1
* Loewen, Adam, of	.200	70	10	14	1	0	2	9	9	32	2
* Marrero, Chris, 1b	.349	83	11	29	7	0	3	21	8	16	0
Mastroianni, Darin, of	.250	44	10	11	1	0	0	4	8	5	2
# O'Malley, Shawn, ss	.313	64	15	20	2	0	0	5	17	14	2
Snyder, Brandon, 1b	.354	65	17	23	5	1	3	18	13	11	1
Waring, Brandon, 3b	.257	35	7	9	2	1	2	10	3	13	1
# Weeks, Jemile, 2b	.241	87	19	21	6	4	1	11	10	16	5

PITCHERS	W	L	ERA	G	GS	SV	IP	H	BB	SO	AVG
Demel, Sam	0	0	5.73	11	0	1	11	16	4	10	.320
Erbe, Brandon	0	0	2.00	3	3	0	9	8	2	9	.242
Friend, Justin	3	1	3.97	9	0	0	11	6	5	9	.150
Gamboa, Eddie	0	0	2.70	8	0	1	10	12	2	5	.316
Gonzalez, Reidier	2	0	3.38	7	1	0	16	19	6	11	.288
Gorgen, Matt	0	1	10.38	10	0	1	9	18	6	12	.450
* Katayama, Hiroshi	0	0	1.71	12	0	0	12	9	7	11	.220
Mandel, Jeff	0	0	1.88	10	0	0	14	14	0	10	.259
Perrault, Josh	1	1	3.38	11	0	1	11	11	5	6	.289
Phillips, Paul	0	1	4.82	9	0	0	9	9	5	4	.250
Ray, Robert	2	1	4.81	7	7	0	24	34	7	25	.315
Rollins, Heath	0	0	8.03	10	0	0	12	21	5	9	.404
Simmons, James	1	4	4.50	6	6	0	24	29	8	11	.296
Storen, Drew	2	0	0.66	12	0	4	14	16	3	13	.286
Storey, Mickey	0	0	3.97	9	0	0	11	11	3	13	.250
Strasburg, Stephen	4	1	4.26	5	5	0	19	15	7	23	.217
Talbot, Mitch	3	0	4.37	6	6	0	23	27	6	15	.303
Tanaka, Ryohei	1	1	6.86	7	4	0	20	32	4	16	.360
Wilkie, Josh	0	1	4.26	10	0	0	13	17	4	12	.315
Yanuki, Toshiyuki	0	0	0.66	10	0	0	14	10	8	14	.213

SCOTTSDALE SCORPIONS

BATTERS	AVG	AB	R	H	2B	3B	HR	RBI	BB	SO	SB
* Allen, Brandon, 1b	.177	113	13	20	6	1	1	12	22	33	3
* Brown, Domonic, of	.229	118	10	27	9	2	2	18	10	27	0
Ciriaco, Pedro, ss	.258	66	10	17	4	0	0	4	3	13	5
* Crawford, Brandon, 3b	.312	77	18	24	3	1	2	10	12	22	4
D'Arnaud, Chase, 2b	.296	81	12	24	5	1	0	6	11	19	13
Friday, Brian, 2b	.245	49	7	12	1	1	0	7	4	13	0
Gillespie, Cole, of	.333	72	9	24	7	0	1	7	17	6	2
Gomez, Hector, ss	.299	67	10	20	8	1	1	14	0	12	1
Gosewisch, Tuffy, c	.318	44	1	14	2	0	0	5	1	6	0
Hanzawa, Troy, ss	.080	25	5	2	1	0	0	3	3	8	2
Holcomb, Darin, 3b	.250	44	9	11	1	0	1	5	7	9	0
Neal, Thomas, of	.284	74	15	21	3	1	1	10	11	14	12
Posey, Buster, c	.225	71	13	16	2	0	2	12	13	18	0
Rosario, Wilin, c	.304	56	11	17	3	0	4	12	3	18	1
* Susdorf, Steve, of	.200	55	6	11	3	0	2	6	8	11	1
Tabata, Jose, of	.392	120	21	47	6	3	1	21	10	13	4

PITCHERS	W	L	ERA	G	GS	SV	IP	H	BB	SO	AVG
Abe, Kenta	0	0	20.25	3	0	0	1	4	3	0	.571
Augenstein, Bryan	1	4	4.15	6	6	0	17	22	4	15	.301
Baker, Craig	1	1	4.63	11	0	1	12	9	5	9	.205
Cisco, Michael	1	2	3.38	6	6	0	19	14	8	13	.203
Edlefsen, Steve	3	0	2.08	13	0	0	13	8	9	11	.174
Garcia, Edgar	2	2	5.29	10	1	0	17	23	4	10	.324
Johnston, Andrew	0	0	7.59	10	0	2	11	18	5	7	.375
* Layne, Tom	0	0	4.97	12	0	0	13	13	7	11	.265
* Maine, Scott	0	0	16.20	2	0	0	2	3	4	2	.500
Martinez, Joe	1	0	6.08	7	7	0	24	31	8	26	.316
Mathieson, Scott	0	0	2.84	11	0	0	13	10	8	15	.227
* Moskos, Danny	1	1	5.28	11	0	0	15	22	8	13	.349
Murata, Tooru	1	2	5.73	9	0	1	11	10	3	8	.233
Nishimura, Ken	0	0	5.68	4	0	0	6	5	4	4	.227
* Reynolds, Matt	0	0	1.29	10	0	2	14	9	4	15	.173
Roe, Chaz	0	2	4.50	5	5	0	12	19	4	10	.365
Schwimer, Michael	0	0	4.26	10	0	0	13	12	8	8	.250
* Tsujiuchi, Takanobu	0	0	9.83	8	0	0	10	15	9	2	.349
Turpen, Daniel	1	0	3.94	11	0	0	16	14	8	13	.237
Valdez, Cesar	0	1	10.50	9	0	0	12	19	6	12	.339
* Veal, Donnie	3	1	2.14	7	7	0	21	17	7	22	.221
* Watson, Tony	0	0	2.13	11	0	0	13	7	6	12	.152

SURPRISE RAFTERS

BATTERS	AVG	AB	R	H	2B	3B	HR	RBI	BB	SO	SB
* Anderson, Bryan, c	.255	47	7	12	0	1	0	6	8	12	0
Bianchi, Jeff, ss	.265	68	10	18	2	1	2	13	7	10	1
* Curtis, Colin, of	.397	78	19	31	7	2	5	18	11	14	3
* Davis, Ike, 1b	.341	85	13	29	7	0	4	16	8	23	0
Descalso, Daniel, 2b	.220	82	11	18	4	0	0	3	11	10	1
* Duda, Lucas, of	.400	5	1	2	1	0	0	2	1	0	0
* Dyson, Jarrod, of	.310	71	10	22	3	2	0	7	6	15	2
Evans, Nick, of	.171	35	4	6	1	0	2	4	2	11	0
* Havens, Reese, 2b	.368	38	9	14	3	1	2	5	8	9	0
* Henley, Tyler, of	.300	60	11	18	4	1	2	7	6	9	0
Hogan, Doug, c	.212	52	8	11	2	0	4	10	4	22	0
* Jones, Daryl, of	.205	88	17	18	5	1	2	6	13	26	6
Laird, Brandon, 3b	.333	90	18	30	9	0	6	24	10	20	0
* Lemon, Marcus, of	.343	67	11	23	3	2	4	13	5	11	2
* Moreland, Mitch, of	.300	70	12	21	2	0	3	12	11	14	0
* Moustakas, Mike, 3b	.267	75	13	20	5	1	5	19	2	11	1
Romine, Austin, c	.400	15	2	6	0	0	0	2	1	4	0
* Teagarden, Taylor, c	.212	52	7	11	2	0	3	8	4	18	0
Tejada, Ruben, ss	.254	59	9	15	4	0	1	9	6	9	4

PITCHERS	W	L	ERA	G	GS	SV	IP	H	BB	SO	AVG
Crow, Aaron	0	2	5.87	4	4	0	15	17	7	12	.288
Daley, Gary	0	0	8.03	10	0	1	12	17	6	9	.315
Duff, Grant	0	0	2.89	10	0	2	9	7	5	4	.212
* Dunn, Michael	1	2	4.35	10	0	1	10	11	10	20	.268
Garr, Brennan	1	1	4.38	10	0	0	12	11	6	8	.244
Gorgen, Scott	0	1	7.15	11	0	1	11	17	9	11	.354
Gutierrez, Danny	2	0	4.08	6	2	0	18	14	7	16	.212
Harrison, Matt	1	2	5.00	5	4	0	9	5	6	6	.156
Hartsock, Aaron	1	0	4.11	11	0	0	15	15	4	10	.254
Kennedy, Ian	2	1	4.25	7	7	0	30	30	5	28	.250
* Kroenke, Zach	1	0	5.28	11	0	2	15	15	4	14	.250
Mejia, Jenrry	1	3	12.56	6	6	0	14	25	13	16	.362
Moviel, Scott	1	0	2.45	8	0	0	15	14	8	9	.250
* Niesen, Eric	0	0	24.55	4	0	0	4	8	3	2	.444
Parisi, Mike	3	2	4.44	7	6	0	26	26	6	15	.257
Reed, Evan	1	1	12.00	6	0	0	6	11	4	7	.393
Reifer, Adam	0	0	7.59	11	0	0	11	11	6	7	.268
Scheppers, Tanner	0	0	5.73	7	0	0	11	9	4	9	.237
* Sisk, Brandon	0	0	2.25	6	0	0	8	6	4	7	.231
Stinson, Josh	0	0	3.65	9	0	0	12	13	11	9	.302
* Swaggerty, Ben	0	0	9.45	6	0	0	7	7	7	4	.318
Wood, Blake	1	1	6.75	8	3	0	15	20	5	12	.345

INDEPENDENT LEAGUES

Rough economy leads to rocky year for indy ball

BY J.J. COOPER

Back in the mid-1990s, when independent leagues were popping up on every street corner, survival was an accomplishment in itself. While the Northern and Frontier leagues were gaining solid footing, leagues like the Atlantic Coast, Golden State, Mid-America and North Central were shutting down seemingly weeks after they got started.

Independent baseball thought it had left the bad old days behind, but a recession brought things back to the roots in 2009. Once again, survival was an accomplishment. Well before the 2009 season began, team owners and general managers around independent baseball knew that it was going to be a tough year. In boom years, GMs aimed to set attendance records; in 2009 everyone hunkered down to survive and sell tickets for another season.

Not everyone made it. The Can-Am League shed two teams before the season and lost another one as the season ended. The United League went into bankruptcy before the season, although it did reorganize in time to return for the 2009 season. It is a sign to the stability of independent baseball that every team that started the 2009 season finished it, even if some just barely made it to collapse across the finish line. It's not a sure bet that everyone will be back to the 2010 season, but when the 2009 season began, experienced independent league officials weren't sure that everyone would even make it through the season.

If anyone needed a sign that 2009 wasn't going to be a normal year, it came when the Golden League announced that it was dropping its Tijuana affiliate because of the swine flu epidemic.

That wasn't the Golden League's last noteworthy decision. As the season began, the league announced that it had sold the Yuma Scorpions to big leaguer Edgar Renteria and his brother Edinson. As part of the sale, the Scorpions became an affiliate for Colombian League players. The all-Colombian Scorpions finished with the worst record in the league (29-47), but they did produce league rookie of the year Reynaldo Rodriguez, who signed with the Red Sox after the season.

Of all the leagues, the Can-Am League suffered the most from the economic downturn. The league was forced to scramble before the season ever began to revise its eight-team schedule to a more compact six. The Atlantic City Surf announced they were

Tanner Scheppers starred in St. Paul before being drafted by the Texas Rangers

folding because they couldn't find a buyer. The league had already been planning to subsidize the Ottawa club, but the loss of the Surf forced it to drop from eight to six teams. The league suffered another blow at the end of the season when the American Defenders of New Hampshire were locked out of their ballpark for money owed to the city government. The team finished the season by playing a home series on the road, but its troubles meant the league was entering the offseason needing to find a solid sixth team instead of trying to expand back to eight.

The Northern League also had to delay its plans to grow to eight teams for at least a year due to the economy. The league had been working to line up two expansion clubs for 2009, but when the stock market crashed new ownership groups disappeared when they found their net worth plummeting with the Dow. The league stuck to its six-team format for 2009 but did announce during the season that it will expand to eight teams in 2010. The Rockford Riverhawks are moving from the Frontier League to join the Northern League, while the Lake County Fielders of Zion, Ill., will begin play in 2010.

By the time the Fielders open their doors, everyone in independent baseball hopes they'll find a much improved economic climate.

INDEPENDENT LEAGUES

Porter finds new life with Wingnuts

Greg Porter knows that baseball is a never-ending roller coaster. Just when you think you're reaching the top, you find yourself at the bottom.

Just two years ago, Porter was coming off of an excellent season in Triple-A and figuring he was one break away from a big league job. A year ago, he was unable to land a job in affiliated baseball.

He admits that he thought about giving up on baseball. But in the end, he decided that he didn't want his career to end on a down note. So he signed on with the Wichita Wingnuts to give baseball one more chance.

Whatever happens now, Porter put his troubles behind him. Porter hit .372/.453/.617 and led the American Association in average, on-base percentage, slugging percentage and home runs as he helped Wichita to the best record in the league. On the strength of that season, Porter was Baseball America's 2009 Independent League Player of the Year.

It was an interesting trip from Texas A&M to Wichita. Porter was a 45th-round pick of the Angels in 2001, but he was only a part-time baseball player until 2004 because he also played tight end for the Aggies. He signed a pro football contract with Houston and went to minicamp with the team, but decided to focus on baseball full-time after talking to Texans general manager Charley Casserly.

His baseball career picked up after the decision as he finally could focus on hitting. He spent a couple of years in Double-A and made it to Triple-A for the first time in 2007, hitting

Greg Porter

.345/.403/.510 in 200 at-bats with Salt Lake.

Porter headed into minor league free agency with the expectation that he would land a solid Triple-A job with the potential for a midseason callup. The Yankees were one of the first teams to call, and while Porter knew he wouldn't be making the team out of spring training, the offer of a spot in big league camp was a healthy inducement to sign. A strong spring training—he hit .318 with four extra-base hits in 22 at-bats—just added to the expectations.

When Opening Day arrived, however, Porter was stuck on the Triple-A Scranton/Wilkes-Barre bench. It was something he would grow accustomed to, playing in just five of the team's first 11 games. With sporadic playing time, Porter's swing got out of whack and his stats suffered. He was released midway through the season and found himself as an out-of-work free agent after a poor stint with Triple-A Columbus late in the season.

He thought about giving up, but his agent Steve Canter persuaded him to give independent baseball a chance.

Porter hopes that one day he'll get to the point where his swing doesn't need daily maintenance, but he admits that he's not there yet. Given a chance to play every day with Wichita, Porter quickly became the cornerstone of the lineup. After hitting .246 with one home run in May, he hit .481 with six home runs in June. His batting average never dipped below .365 again.

"He was getting two hits every single night it seemed," Wichita manager Kevin Hooper said. "He can flat-out hit. He hits the ball the other way with some authority. He just handles the bat. There's no streakiness to him."

PREVIOUS WINNERS

1996: Darryl Motley, of, Fargo-Moorhead (Nothern)
1997: Mike Meggers, of, Winnipeg/Duluth (Northern)
1998: Morgan Burkhart, 1b, Richmond (Frontier)
1999: Carmine Cappucio, of, New Jersey (Frontier)
2000: Anthony Lewis, 1b, Duluth-Superior (Northern)
2001: Mike Warner, of, Somerset (Atlantic)
2002: Bobby Madritsch, lhp, Winnipeg (Northern)

2003: Jason Shelley, rhp, Rockford (Frontier)
2004: Victor Rodriguez, ss, Somerset (Atlantic)
2005: Eddie Lantigua, 3b, Quebec (Can-Am)
2006: Ian Church, of, Kalamazoo (Frontier)
2007: Darryl Brinkley, of, Calgary (Northern)
2008: Patrick Breen, of, Orange County (Golden)

1, 2, 3 Indicates played for multiple teams
* Lefthander # Switch hitter

AMERICAN ASSOCIATION

Marty Scott has one of the most varied careers of anyone in minor league baseball. He's been a minor league manager, scout and front office executive in affiliated baseball. He's been a manager and front office executive in independent baseball and he's worked as an agent as well. And wherever he has gone, there's a pretty good chance titles will follow.

Scott's Lincoln Saltdogs knocked off Pensacola in the American Association championship series, led by Jim Paduch's pitching (3-0 in the playoffs) and Rafael Alvarez (.424-2-7 in the playoffs).

Along their way to the title, Lincoln knocked off Wichita in the semifinals. Wichita had run off to the best record in the league behind the hitting of league MVP Greg Porter and the pitching of all-stars Brad Davis and Derek Blacksher.

FIRST HALF

NORTH	W	L	PCT	GB
Wichita	32	16	.553	—
St. Paul	23	25	.479	9
Lincoln	22	26	.458	10
Sioux City	22	26	.458	10
Sioux Falls	21	27	.438	11
SOUTH	W	L	PCT	GB
Fort Worth	30	18	.625	—
Pensacola	24	24	.500	6
Grand Prairie	23	25	.479	7
Shreveport-Bossier	22	26	.458	8
El Paso	21	27	.438	9

SECOND HALF

NORTH	W	L	PCT	GB
Lincoln	27	21	.563	—
Wichita	26	22	.542	1
St. Paul	26	22	.542	1
Sioux Falls	19	29	.396	8
Sioux City	18	30	.375	9
SOUTH	W	L	PCT	GB
Pensacola	29	19	.604	—
Shreveport-Bossier	26	22	.542	3
Grand Prairie	25	23	.521	4
Fort Worth	23	25	.479	6
El Paso	21	27	.438	8

PLAYOFFS—Semifinals: Pensacola defeated Fort Worth 3-1 and Lincoln defeated Wichita 3-2 in best-of-five series. **Finals:** Lincoln defeated Pensacola 3-2 in best-of-five series.

ATTENDANCE: St. Paul 267,398; El Paso 200,323; Fort Worth 177,807; Lincoln 172,445; Wichita 161,170; Grand Prairie 141,132; Sioux Falls 132,529; Shreveport-Bossier 86,635; Pensacola 71,797; Sioux City 70,978.

MANAGERS: El Paso—Butch Henry; Fort Worth—Chad Tredaway; Grand Prairie—Pete Incaviglia; Lincoln—Marty Scott; Pensacola—Talmadge Nunnari; St. Paul—George Tsamis; Shreveport—Rick Van Asselberg; Sioux City—Les Lancaster; Sioux Falls—Steve Shirley; Wichita—Kevin Hooper.

ALL-STAR TEAM: C—Joe Muich, Wichita; **1B**—John Allen, Fort Worth Cats; **2B**—Antoin Gray, Pensacola; **SS**—Josh Horn, Wichita; **3B**—Cesar Nicolas, Grand Prairie; **OF**—Brian Fryer, Fort Worth; Brent Krause, St. Paul; Greg Porter, Wichita; **DH**—Chase Burch, Pensacola.
LHP—Brad Davis, Wichita; **RHP**—Derek Blacksher, Wichita; **RP**—Chris Thompson, El Paso/Lincoln.
Player of the Year: Greg Porter, of, Wichita. **Manager of the Year:** Kevin Hooper, Wichita.

INDIVIDUAL BATTING LEADERS

BATTER, TEAM	AVG	G	AB	R	H	HR	RBI
Porter, Greg, Wichita	.372	95	376	67	140	21	86
Garcia, Christopher, Shreveport	.361	77	296	59	107	5	52
Torbert, Beau, Sioux Falls	.346	65	260	35	90	12	60
Burch, Chase, Pensacola	.341	90	334	60	114	9	65
Nicolas, Cesar, Grand Prairie	.335	96	358	83	120	14	103
Rodriguez, Andres, Shreveport	.327	95	379	51	124	6	67
Bibbs, Kennard, El Paso	.323	92	372	75	120	1	36

Rodriguez, Marcos, Pensacola	.319	92	385	47	123	0	60
Alvarez, Jorge, Shreveport	.319	96	408	71	130	9	76
Anthonsen, Joe, Sioux Falls	.318	91	365	67	116	0	34

INDIVIDUAL PITCHING LEADERS

PITCHER, CLUB	W-L		ERA	IP	H	BB	SO
Middleton, Kyle, Pensacola	5	2	1.75	87	79	21	83
Jung, Jae Hun, Fort Worth	7	3	2.59	125	106	16	48
Kintzler, Brandon, St. Paul	8	3	2.79	81	89	24	46
Savage, William, Wichita	5	7	2.94	125	119	48	49
Cowart, Adam, Wichita	8	5	3.05	100	97	19	39
Davis, Bradley, Wichita	8	7	3.35	105	112	29	57
Blacksher, Derek, Wichita	11	2	3.38	125	122	41	93
Mallett, Justin, El Paso	7	4	3.48	96	98	33	71
Kirsten, Joel, Fort Worth	9	5	3.61	127	126	31	76
Fox, Trevor, Sioux City	6	5	3.61	110	96	82	80

EL PASO DIABLOS

BATTERS		AVG	AB	R	H	2B	3B	HR	RBI	SB
1	Alvarez, Jorge, ss	.319	354	62	113	20	2	8	64	3
	Andrews, Bobby, ss	.182	33	5	6	0	0	0	1	1
*	Bernal, Hector, 1b	.239	339	32	81	15	6	1	38	4
*	Bibbs, Kennard, ss	.323	372	75	120	15	4	1	36	32
#	Camacho, Juan, 2b/c	.305	403	49	123	35	1	10	69	4
1*	Hale, Adam, ss	.281	135	19	38	11	1	3	19	3
	Imwalle, Matt, dh	.200	10	1	2	0	0	0	1	0
	Johnson, Tyler, ss	.249	201	33	50	10	3	5	22	20
	Maldonado, Edwin, 2b	.261	23	2	6	0	0	1	3	0
	Mejia, Roberto, 2b	.256	90	16	23	4	1	0	9	1
#	Ponce, Arnoldo, 3b	.276	399	69	110	24	3	6	59	6
	Provencher, Mike, ss	.280	239	31	67	16	3	2	35	2
2	Reynoso, Jonathan, ss	.244	41	8	10	4	0	0	7	7
	Rodriguez, Eddy, of	.264	295	36	78	17	0	8	42	0
*	Verastegui, Jerry, of	.278	194	26	54	8	0	0	27	0
*	Vincent, Jeff, ss	.312	202	31	63	12	7	4	35	21
	Washington, David, ss	.241	108	28	26	3	4	0	2	14

PITCHERS		W	L	ERA	G	SV	IP	H	BB	SO
	Bennett, Derek	0	1	9.82	3	0	3.2	5	3	2
	Cervera, Mike	2	1	4.86	29	9	33.1	38	15	33
	De La Rosa, Dane	1	4	8.07	15	1	35.2	51	20	37
	Dillard, Johnny	0	2	6.07	11	0	13.1	14	9	5
	Klein, Joseph	4	6	5.05	29	0	41	49	23	29
*	Luera, Chris	2	0	5.23	8	0	10.1	12	6	13
	Mallett, Justin	7	4	3.48	14	0	95.2	98	33	71
*	Martin, Nick	2	6	5.27	13	0	70	96	33	42
	Michael, Mark	1	2	4.71	4	0	21	22	7	17
	Montes, Albert	0	2	7.62	11	0	13	20	1	7
	Neitz, Josh	6	3	4.63	19	0	114.2	144	33	51
	Orosco Jr., Jesse	0	0	10.13	3	0	2.2	5	2	1
*	Piccola, Zachary	0	0	10.80	2	0	1.2	3	1	0
	Pluta, Tony	3	5	6.28	25	0	38.2	45	22	35
	Rivas, Ricardo	2	1	4.82	23	0	37.1	47	14	23
	Romero, Garvis	3	3	5.57	28	0	72.2	99	31	39
	Santana, Yury	2	0	5.67	24	1	27	29	16	25
	Short, Baron	0	1	5.23	7	0	10.1	17	1	5
2	Snipes, Clegg	1	2	4.47	8	0	48.1	61	16	22
1	Thompson, Chris	0	1	3.95	14	10	13.2	11	13	17
	Tucker, Cardoza	0	4	5.36	7	0	42	45	20	26
	Villalona, Bryan	1	6	8.93	9	0	43.1	71	15	20
	Whigham, David	3	0	3.88	9	0	53.1	62	21	37
	Wooley, Robert	2	0	8.40	10	0	15	22	14	5

FORT WORTH CATS

BATTERS		AVG	AB	R	H	2B	3B	HR	RBI	SB
	Allen, John, ss	.300	390	60	117	27	2	12	72	3
	Bell, Michael, 2b	.286	370	64	106	29	2	14	59	4
	Blair, Cameron, 3b	.278	363	61	101	15	2	2	42	12
	Carter, Charles, of	.215	130	12	28	4	0	0	8	1
	Combs, Matt, of	.136	59	5	8	4	0	0	4	0
	Davis, Aljay, ss	.242	91	22	22	2	0	1	9	10
	Dennis, Spenser, ss	.239	46	4	11	0	0	0	4	0
3	Fenwick, Ron, ss	.111	27	5	3	0	0	0	2	0

	AVG	AB	R	H	2B	3B	HR	RBI	SB
Fryer, Brian, ss	.307	424	60	130	21	1	1	48	38
Garcia, Isa, 1b	.292	336	48	98	22	0	5	40	6
Gulledge, Kelley, of	.268	299	47	80	24	0	7	46	0
O'Sullivan, Patrick, c	.309	372	53	115	14	1	14	65	9
Patterson, Ryan, ss	.284	391	61	111	27	1	12	66	11
Thompson, Kevin, ss	.238	42	5	10	1	0	1	4	2

PITCHERS	W	L	ERA	G	SV	IP	H	BB	SO
Cameron, Dustin	1	4	3.21	28	14	28	21	17	29
Casares, Kelly	0	1	3.18	6	0	5.2	8	4	6
Crow, Aaron	3	0	1.06	3	0	17	11	5	17
* Domangue, Eric	0	1	7.71	5	0	4.2	4	4	2
1* Garcia, Justin	1	1	5.40	8	0	8.1	10	7	5
Gibbs, Matt	2	3	5.45	18	0	67.2	79	38	23
Grybash, Dan	6	2	2.76	10	0	49	64	16	27
Gwaltney, Lee	5	2	3.54	10	0	56	53	14	28
2 Harris, Nat	3	4	4.10	10	0	52.2	57	18	16
Jung, Jae Hun	7	3	2.59	19	0	125	106	16	48
* Kirsten, Joel	9	5	3.61	20	0	127	126	31	76
Lee, Gary	0	3	3.12	28	6	34.2	39	8	21
1 Morales, Alex	1	2	6.56	26	2	23.1	25	19	23
* Parker, Taylor	2	1	6.05	29	0	41.2	40	31	23
Pearson, Tyler	3	1	5.08	29	1	33.2	44	17	34
* Riddle, Ryan	6	7	5.45	19	0	107.1	132	51	77
Trytten, Ryan	2	2	4.44	23	0	46.2	51	34	45
2 Vander Weg, Scott	2	1	1.61	20	5	22.1	17	7	25
Yates, Kyle	0	0	20.25	2	0	1.1	5	3	0

GRAND PRAIRIE AIRHOGS

BATTERS	AVG	AB	R	H	2B	3B	HR	RBI	SB
Berg, Daniel, 3b	.252	143	21	36	5	0	3	16	4
Brito, Javier, c	.316	212	40	67	22	0	12	62	0
* Carter, Brandon, 3b	.270	241	48	65	12	2	3	38	25
* Conroy, Mike, ss	.315	267	51	84	10	7	2	35	11
* Dziomba, Jonathan, 1b	.274	117	18	32	3	0	1	8	2
# Espinosa, David, 3b	.349	83	24	29	3	1	1	14	10
2 Fenwick, Ron, 1b	.257	70	14	18	3	0	0	10	1
Gabriel, Chad, ss	.316	307	48	97	19	2	9	60	7
Garza, Aaron, ss	.298	349	76	104	22	4	8	40	38
Holder, Drew, ss	.250	208	41	52	7	2	2	28	6
* Incaviglia, Thomas, ss	.214	28	4	6	2	0	0	4	0
Merrell, Cody, 1b	.162	37	4	6	2	1	0	3	0
* Munoz, Billy, c	.197	61	7	12	1	0	2	5	0
* Nicholson, Derek, ss	.225	240	33	54	12	2	1	34	5
Nicolas, Angel, ss	.208	24	2	5	1	0	0	2	0
Nicolas, Cesar, 2b	.335	358	83	120	30	0	14	103	6
Spiers, Joseph, 3b	.350	40	6	14	1	0	0	4	5
Trevino, Noel, ss	.176	85	9	15	2	0	0	9	3
Tucker, J.B., of	.257	369	48	95	25	1	5	45	4
Yaconetti, Jay, 2b	.260	104	11	27	7	1	0	14	2

PITCHERS	W	L	ERA	G	SV	IP	H	BB	SO
Camareno, Dimitri	4	3	4.42	11	0	55	57	30	36
Cordero, Jose	4	5	4.92	25	0	89.2	102	41	51
Crawford, Nathan	0	0	4.50	3	0	6	13	6	1
Crawford, Tristan	0	0	4.26	4	0	6.1	7	0	6
* Crowell, Cody	9	5	5.34	27	0	86	97	57	59
2* Garcia, Justin	1	1	6.75	15	0	25.1	31	14	19
Green, Matthew	7	6	5.49	25	0	101.2	115	52	100
Gronkiewicz, Lee	1	0	2.16	5	0	8.1	5	2	5
1 Harris, Nat	2	3	5.27	10	0	42.2	43	21	20
2 Jamnik, Jeff	0	0	6.32	7	0	15.2	30	6	6
* Jenkins, Aaron	0	0	4.86	11	0	16.2	12	16	15
Krause, Greg	2	2	6.20	22	1	20.1	26	11	18
MacFarland, Stephen	0	3	8.42	7	0	25.2	21	28	19
Macy, Thomas	0	0	15.43	3	0	7	14	3	4
1 Mahomes, Pat	1	6	6.44	13	1	57.1	74	27	38
1 Mattison, Kieran	4	3	5.72	14	0	72.1	83	44	52
1 Minor, Matthew	0	1	6.00	3	0	6	10	4	2
2 Morales, Alex	2	3	7.64	13	0	17.2	22	12	21
Morrison, James	4	3	4.06	49	20	57.2	47	27	49
Nelson, Ryne	0	0	1.93	4	0	4.2	2	1	3
Prihoda, Luke	3	1	1.89	21	3	38	29	6	27
Tata, Jordan	0	0	7.20	3	0	10	10	12	7
Wesley, John	0	2	6.35	5	0	5.2	9	4	5
2* Williamson, Logan	1	0	2.89	3	0	18.2	25	6	10

LINCOLN SALTDOGS

BATTERS	AVG	AB	R	H	2B	3B	HR	RBI	SB
Alexander, Steven, 3b	.236	296	36	70	12	0	11	49	3
2# Alvarez, Rafael, of	.369	111	23	41	10	1	4	19	4
Balet, Pichi, of	.313	201	22	63	10	0	1	31	2
Barbaro, Andrew, c	.263	19	2	5	0	0	0	0	0
* Burns, Deacon, of	.231	216	22	50	7	1	2	20	7
Burrus, Josh, of	.282	383	68	108	21	3	10	44	36
Dickey, Gavin, of	.336	113	13	38	10	1	1	17	3
Gonzalez, Ernesto, 2b	.225	71	10	16	4	1	0	6	1
* Hawke, Matthew, 1b	.311	360	59	112	20	1	12	61	1
1# Hutchins, Norm, dh	.313	16	3	5	0	0	1	3	0
* Jadlowski, Jake, ss	.240	25	7	6	0	0	0	5	4
2 Jones, Brandon, 3b	.267	225	29	60	10	0	6	37	2
# Machado, Albenis, ss	.277	346	64	96	9	0	2	34	20
Maloney, Matt, of	.215	121	13	26	1	1	5	13	0
McFeely, Shea, 2b	.279	344	43	96	20	0	5	41	4
McGill, Shawn, c	.270	311	49	84	18	1	7	48	22
Nunez, Argelis, of	.238	42	8	10	5	0	2	6	0
Povey, Tycen, c	.138	29	7	4	0	0	0	2	0
Rubin, Lee, c	.138	29	2	4	1	0	1	6	0

PITCHERS	W	L	ERA	G	SV	IP	H	BB	SO
Afify, Khalid	0	0	10.80	4	0	6.2	10	5	1
Arreola, Daryl	1	4	6.09	35	2	44.1	51	18	41
Brown, Tim	5	1	2.59	17	0	62.2	76	9	27
Campbell, Brian	3	5	5.66	15	0	76.1	84	51	30
* Chestnut, Nolan	0	1	5.95	13	0	19.2	20	14	13
* Cline, Zachary	6	5	4.36	23	0	95	103	29	50
* Cory, III, Forrest	1	1	5.85	25	0	20	25	10	12
* Daniels, Adam	7	4	2.98	46	0	54.1	47	22	54
* Davis, Vince	0	4	6.83	6	0	27.2	34	18	18
* Figueroa, Jonathan	3	4	3.45	13	0	60	56	40	59
Gardner, Jarrett	10	4	4.00	20	0	135	139	25	63
Giles, Joshua	1	1	10.38	9	0	13	17	15	14
Guevara, Carlos	0	1	4.22	11	6	10.2	16	5	11
Humen, David	0	0	3.86	4	0	4.2	4	3	0
Knoff, Justin	1	1	5.87	5	0	23	22	12	8
Martinez, Gregorio	1	0	4.35	4	0	10.1	13	1	10
Paduch, Jim	7	5	4.79	24	0	120.1	116	58	96
Petrusek, Matt	2	2	0.77	17	1	23.1	24	6	21
2 Reilly, Matthew	0	3	8.10	15	1	13.1	22	9	4
2 Thompson, Chris	1	1	1.61	28	20	28	18	16	34

PENSACOLA PELICANS

BATTERS	AVG	AB	R	H	2B	3B	HR	RBI	SB
1# Alvarez, Rafael, ss	.269	182	30	49	9	0	3	26	19
Bautista, Luis, 2b-C	.270	159	21	43	7	0	2	20	4
Burch, Chase, c	.341	334	60	114	20	1	9	65	1
Christison, Dallas, 3b	.273	267	44	73	10	0	1	26	15
Contreras, Lester, 2b	.261	92	13	24	4	0	1	14	0
* Darby, Adam, ss	.253	178	34	45	4	1	4	23	16
Deleo, Adam, c	.277	148	15	41	6	1	1	17	1
* Diaz, Jason, ss	.370	27	4	10	1	0	0	2	3
Gray, Antoin, 1b	.309	395	70	122	20	0	14	84	2
1 Guance, Luis, 3b	.266	248	36	66	12	0	1	34	22
Humphries, Kyle, ss	.221	113	13	25	6	0	4	16	1
LaMotta, Kyle, ss	.100	10	1	1	0	0	0	2	1
* Leandro, Francisco, ss	.310	345	70	107	23	1	1	34	28
McDougall, Marshall, 2b	.329	73	11	24	4	0	0	11	1
Mojica, Jimmy, 3b	.354	130	26	46	11	1	1	18	15
2 Palmisano, Lou, of	.223	148	19	33	7	2	2	21	1
Reynolds, Kevin, ss	.310	142	34	44	8	1	1	15	19
* Rodriguez, Marcos, ss	.319	385	47	123	16	1	6	60	11

PITCHERS	W	L	ERA	G	SV	IP	H	BB	SO
Bass, Corey	1	1	13.50	4	0	6	12	1	4
* Beam, Randall	10	7	4.54	20	0	119	121	39	93
* Brandenburg, Adam	2	2	7.12	8	0	36.2	47	36	25
Butto, Francisco	1	0	0.00	3	0	6.2	5	1	6
Cooper, Kevin	1	0	2.70	4	0	20	21	3	9
Davis, Hunter	3	1	1.79	35	22	40.1	26	21	40
DeValk, Dane	5	4	4.16	23	0	97.1	111	29	74
Hill, Ron	4	0	2.95	24	1	39.2	35	11	48
Jackson, Aaron	3	4	4.14	28	0	82.2	78	35	47

	W	L	ERA	G	SV	IP	H	BB	SO
2 Mattison, Kieran	2	0	0.82	2	0	11	7	1	5
Middleton, Kyle	5	2	1.75	13	0	87.1	79	21	83
* Navarro, Jason	1	2	8.33	6	0	31.1	51	6	21
Nelson, Bubba	3	5	5.65	15	0	57.1	62	25	52
Roque, Ulysses	4	5	4.09	34	0	50.2	47	29	31
* Smith, Dan	0	2	9.57	5	0	26.1	37	16	11
Snipes, Clegg	1	5	6.02	9	0	52.1	59	30	30
* Solich, Brent	1	1	3.00	16	0	27	26	8	19
Wedner, Joseph	0	0	7.33	12	0	23.1	27	12	21
* Wilson, Tyler	5	1	4.56	23	0	47.1	54	17	39

ST. PAUL SAINTS

BATTERS	AVG	AB	R	H	2B	3B	HR	RBI	SB
* Alley, Josh, ss	.322	171	25	55	10	0	2	26	7
Bennett, Andrew, 1b	.077	13	3	1	0	0	0	0	0
* Brazell, Craig, 2b	.581	31	9	18	4	0	4	12	0
Butler, Jacob, ss	.263	350	57	92	20	0	16	63	0
* Butler, Steve, 3b	.269	219	33	59	8	0	1	23	0
* Cooper, Jason, c	.288	208	43	60	14	3	11	44	2
* Derrick, Stephen, 2b	.083	12	1	1	0	0	0	1	0
DeSmidt, Jeff, of	.167	24	1	4	0	0	1	3	0
Eure, Jeffrey, 2b	.258	225	28	58	10	1	5	31	2
1 Fenwick, Ron, 1b	.173	110	11	19	2	0	0	9	0
Fonseca, Alex, 1b	.292	195	30	57	8	2	2	22	18
Herbert, Chris, of	.200	30	3	6	0	0	1	4	0
Johnson, Kyle, of	.214	14	1	3	1	0	0	1	0
Kaczrowski, Dan, 3b	.286	42	8	12	1	0	1	5	1
Knazek, Scott, of	.245	245	24	60	11	1	1	35	0
Krause, Brent, ss	.300	347	63	104	23	4	11	59	15
Kubal, Alex, ss	.167	12	1	2	1	0	0	1	0
Mansolino, Anthony, 1b	.226	190	25	43	5	1	0	13	1
Mays, Steve, 3b	.074	27	2	2	1	0	0	1	0
* Norman, Anthony, ss	.264	144	21	38	11	1	2	19	5
Roberts, Daron, ss	.282	124	14	35	11	1	2	22	8
* Schmiesing, Andrew, ss	.248	254	41	63	6	7	0	20	9
* Self, Todd, c	.319	144	33	46	12	0	4	27	2
Sheldon, Ole, dh	.340	106	22	36	7	0	6	19	0

PITCHERS	W	L	ERA	G	SV	IP	H	BB	SO
* Ariail, Ryan	1	0	1.72	27	4	31.1	25	19	21
Bille, Michael	2	6	2.40	36	4	56.1	44	23	58
Brower, Jim	0	0	3.77	11	3	14.1	16	6	9
Buske, Tom	5	5	4.07	14	0	79.2	84	26	35
* Cox, Adam	1	4	7.67	6	0	27	32	19	28
Dickert, Reed	4	6	5.51	27	0	94.2	102	51	74
Foster, Kyle	5	3	3.83	33	1	54	49	23	47
Kintzler, Brandon	8	3	2.79	14	0	80.2	89	24	46
Ligtenberg, Kerry	0	2	3.00	30	15	36	27	6	29
Mathison, Todd	3	1	3.38	6	0	34.2	28	13	18
Moriarty, Mark	2	5	6.27	17	0	60.1	68	41	47
Robinson, Lonnie	1	0	8.53	7	1	19	27	17	10
Ruud, Charlie	8	4	3.69	20	0	107.1	132	47	47
Scheppers, Tanner	1	1	3.32	4	0	19	17	11	20
1 Vander Weg, Scott	0	0	9.49	7	0	12.1	15	6	10
* Wagner, David	0	0	5.68	4	0	6.1	12	5	3
Wylie, Mitch	8	7	4.11	18	0	111.2	113	38	80

SHREVEPORT SPORTS

BATTERS	AVG	AB	R	H	2B	3B	HR	RBI	SB
2 Alvarez, Jorge, of	.315	54	9	17	2	0	1	12	1
Amyx, Brett, dh	.077	13	0	1	0	0	0	2	0
Bryant, Tommy, ss	.227	119	13	27	6	0	1	16	0
* Cone, Aaron, 1b	.129	31	2	4	2	0	0	3	0
# Fermin, Angelo, 2b	.220	82	10	18	3	0	1	5	9
* Garcia, Christopher, 1b	.361	296	59	107	17	0	5	52	0
* Gonzalez, Albert, 2b	.190	63	10	12	4	0	0	5	2
* Griffin, Kevin, ss	.264	220	32	58	9	3	2	33	6
2 Guance, Luis, 2b	.200	60	3	12	2	0	0	11	3
* Langaigne, Selwyn, 3b	.218	156	19	34	10	0	0	20	0
Medina, Rodney, 3b	.339	62	8	21	2	0	0	11	0
# Ozuna, Rafael, 2b	.250	100	11	25	6	0	0	13	2
Paz, Rich, of	.262	168	33	44	8	1	1	18	0
1 Reynoso, Jonathan, 3b	.285	291	44	83	14	1	2	33	8
Rodriguez, Andres, 1b	.327	379	51	124	30	4	6	67	4
Sabatella, Bryan, 3b	.303	175	35	53	6	0	0	13	16

	AVG	AB	R	H	2B	3B	HR	RBI	SB
Salazar, Jose, 2b	.211	19	3	4	0	0	0	1	1
Sanchez, Luany, ss	.194	93	6	18	3	0	0	7	1
Torres, Jose, 3b	.290	303	62	88	15	4	6	51	17
Urtuzuastegui, Joe, 1b	.250	76	10	19	3	0	0	7	0
* Wagner, Geoff, dh	.182	11	2	2	0	1	0	2	1
Wheeler, BJ, of	.244	82	18	20	3	1	1	11	0
* White, Dwayne, 3b	.261	349	44	91	15	2	1	43	5
Williams, Dan, 2b	.167	48	8	8	3	1	0	10	0

PITCHERS	W	L	ERA	G	SV	IP	H	BB	SO
Bone, Josh	0	0	6.75	8	0	16	23	9	9
* Coffey, Andrew	2	1	6.92	4	0	13	21	6	15
* Cunningham, Aaron	1	4	6.21	14	0	42	61	12	21
Cunningham, Jakob	4	1	2.91	34	5	43.1	34	15	39
1* Dowdy, Justin	0	3	2.37	37	13	38	29	13	47
Heard, Jimmy	7	1	1.76	11	0	66.1	58	21	50
Herman, Jason	0	0	0.00	4	0	8	3	5	3
Litchfield, B.J.	0	1	5.88	19	1	26	43	7	9
* Lowe, Ronald	7	11	5.70	19	0	102.2	130	46	60
* Lugo, Jorge	0	3	4.58	4	0	19.2	24	18	15
Markray, Thad	5	10	5.05	16	0	101.2	117	33	69
* Massetti, Luke	7	3	5.03	16	0	87.2	104	25	46
Miramontes, Derrick	0	1	3.95	19	0	41	54	9	25
Petty, Matt	5	1	3.71	47	1	51	50	28	37
Pierce, Tony	0	0	8.66	13	0	17.2	26	9	18
Romero, Robert	0	2	5.11	37	5	37	31	28	36
2* Salazar, Richard	2	1	2.41	3	0	18.2	19	3	19
1* Williamson, Logan	8	5	4.92	18	0	100.2	127	48	61

SIOUX CITY EXPLORERS

BATTERS	AVG	AB	R	H	2B	3B	HR	RBI	SB
* Arroyo, Carlos, ss	.321	28	5	9	2	0	0	1	2
* Berry, Boomer, ss	.286	91	20	26	4	2	2	15	5
# Boone, James, ss	.281	89	17	25	11	0	1	10	5
Camp, Landon, 2b	.244	82	12	20	1	1	1	11	2
* Colson, Jason, c	.280	168	21	47	10	0	6	33	2
Dean, Brent, of	.111	18	2	2	1	0	0	1	1
Figueroa, Luis, 2b	.216	51	3	11	0	0	0	5	0
* Franco, Andrew, of	.133	15	1	2	0	0	0	0	1
2* Hale, Adam, ss	.158	19	3	3	1	0	0	2	1
2# Hutchins, Norm, ss	.351	37	3	13	2	0	0	9	0
1 Jones, Brandon, 2b	.232	99	10	23	5	0	3	11	2
Jones, Dustin, ss	.264	337	57	89	13	3	3	24	32
Jordan, Daniel, of	.245	49	6	12	3	0	1	6	0
Lee, Matt, of	.200	10	2	2	0	0	0	0	0
* Llanos, Alex, 1b	.275	346	44	95	19	0	6	50	5
# McCoola, Nick, 3b	.262	351	54	92	12	1	0	39	10
* Meigs, Tyler, c	.278	36	2	10	3	0	0	4	0
* Mieras, Brett, of	.313	134	19	42	4	0	1	15	1
* Nelson, Justin, ss	.272	327	50	89	19	4	11	72	9
1 Palmisano, Lou, of	.257	74	10	19	2	0	0	6	2
Schermerhorn, Derek, 2b	.236	331	59	78	15	1	2	27	36
# Stevens, Greg, of	.233	150	20	35	10	0	2	22	2
Tellam, Justin, of-C	.167	12	0	2	1	0	0	0	0
Toole, Justin, 1b	.346	26	3	9	1	0	0	3	1
* Webster, Anthony, of	.297	155	28	46	9	2	1	23	7
Whitaker, Bo, 1b	.143	21	4	3	0	0	0	1	1
* Young, Walter, dh	.272	151	17	41	9	0	7	30	1

PITCHERS	W	L	ERA	G	SV	IP	H	BB	SO
1 Andrade, Steve	1	0	1.80	9	0	10	7	4	9
Bailey, Griffin	1	1	2.08	7	0	17.1	16	8	15
Benz, Charlie	1	0	5.40	6	0	11.2	15	3	1
* Campbell, Michael	1	1	8.71	8	0	20.2	26	17	12
* Chirino, Israel	2	2	14.46	11	0	9.1	16	15	5
* Fox, Trevor	6	5	3.61	20	0	109.2	96	82	80
Frets, Kyle	0	1	7.40	12	0	20.2	22	15	11
Harris, Ryan	2	2	5.32	7	0	44	52	22	23
1 Jamnik, Jeff	0	0	11.42	3	0	8.2	13	6	5
* Layden, Timothy	0	1	9.49	3	0	12.1	22	4	5
Marotz, Ty	6	9	4.20	29	0	120	137	55	82
Meigs, Tyler	1	8	4.78	36	0	79	86	32	60
* Pasma, Curtis	1	2	8.31	4	0	17.1	33	5	8
Phelps, Michael	2	2	2.95	12	0	36.2	26	25	18
Reid, Brett	1	3	3.77	40	17	43	36	18	44
Singleton, Nick	6	7	4.04	21	0	129.1	119	59	97

| | | 0 | 2 | 11.00 | 2 | 0 | 9 | 14 | 8 | 2 |
| Sottung, Nick |
| Spurgeon, Steven | | 5 | 5 | 5.24 | 17 | 0 | 79 | 82 | 29 | 52 |
| Trahan, David | | 6 | 5 | 2.75 | 35 | 0 | 59 | 52 | 26 | 72 |

SIOUX FALLS CANARIES

BATTERS	AVG	AB	R	H	2B	3B	HR	RBI	SB
* Anthonsen, Joe, 1b	.318	365	67	116	5	2	0	34	17
# Bardeguez, Alex, 1b	.087	23	2	2	1	0	0	1	0
Dempsey, Joe, of	.200	50	8	10	2	0	1	4	1
Eveland, Kyle, 2b	.266	79	14	21	4	0	0	9	2
Grant, Ryan, ss	.158	19	2	3	0	0	0	2	0
* Haerther, Cody, of	.294	160	27	47	5	0	2	20	0
Harris, Cory, ss	.307	352	43	108	17	0	10	61	5
1 Holmes, Fraser, of	.059	17	0	1	0	0	0	1	1
Hutting, Tim, 3b	.300	377	59	113	19	2	5	33	1
Lawhorn, Trevor, 2b	.279	373	45	104	29	1	7	49	0
* Lemieux, Jared, ss	.243	103	18	25	5	0	1	14	1
Lup, Ken, of	.215	219	19	47	7	1	0	14	0
* Reilly, Patrick, c	.248	355	46	88	19	2	8	42	13
Reininger, Jarrett, ss	.265	302	36	80	19	0	5	39	3
Smyth, Paul, of	.173	75	5	13	3	0	1	8	0
* Taylor, Reggie, ss	.330	91	12	30	1	0	5	18	2
Torbert, Beau, ss	.346	260	35	90	10	2	12	60	5
Van Iderstine, Ben, ss	.236	72	4	17	2	1	0	1	0

PITCHERS	W	L	ERA	G	SV	IP	H	BB	SO
Baca, Noel	3	7	5.42	20	0	94.2	102	44	38
Cotter, Aaron	4	1	3.22	21	9	22.1	18	3	18
* Ford, Ryan	3	10	5.20	20	0	119.1	158	51	57
* Gonzalez, Jino	4	7	4.29	18	0	100.2	105	41	54
Grant, Ryan	1	3	5.18	27	1	41.2	48	15	39
Kane, Travis	3	9	5.79	20	0	96.1	108	41	58
Lawler, Patrick	4	2	5.03	36	0	39.1	41	21	39
2 Mahomes, Pat	2	2	6.46	10	0	39	49	21	32
2 Minor, Matt	0	0	5.06	6	0	5.1	7	6	2
Moore, Benjamin	5	9	5.27	19	0	126.1	156	39	101
Morales, Angelo	2	4	5.91	18	0	35	40	7	29
Pluta, Andrew	4	0	3.12	24	0	26	26	7	9
* Regas, Kris	2	0	1.19	19	15	22.2	10	9	25
1 Reilly, Matthew	1	0	7.15	12	0	11.1	18	11	4
2 Stephens, Amad	1	0	3.63	15	0	17.1	15	12	9
* Weast, Chris	1	1	8.17	10	0	25.1	40	16	17

WICHITA WINGNUTS

BATTERS	AVG	AB	R	H	2B	3B	HR	RBI	SB
Blasi, Nicholas, ss	.263	358	55	94	15	4	5	34	16
Brooks, Patrick, ss	.252	155	25	39	6	0	2	11	0
Goldberg, Zach, of	.138	29	3	4	1	0	0	1	1
Herrera, Brenan, 1b	.280	328	47	92	20	2	4	37	6
Horn, Josh, 3b	.310	364	68	113	12	0	3	43	19
Hunt, Kelly, c	.259	382	55	99	21	1	21	66	1
Martin, John, of	.267	15	4	4	1	0	0	1	1
Mohr, Dustan, ss	.290	348	50	101	12	1	13	73	12
Muich, Joseph, of	.260	281	32	73	9	0	7	31	0
* Pearson, Steve, ss	.304	326	47	99	21	3	3	36	9
* Porter, Greg, ss	.372	376	67	140	25	2	21	86	4
Sharp, Mike, of	.325	40	6	13	2	0	0	5	1
Thompson, Michael, 2b	.268	355	49	95	32	1	7	45	3

PITCHERS	W	L	ERA	G	SV	IP	H	BB	SO
Blacksher, Derek	11	2	3.38	20	0	125	122	41	93
Cowart, Adam	8	5	3.05	17	0	100.1	97	19	39
D'Alessandro, Joe	2	1	4.56	23	8	23.2	24	16	30
* Davis, Bradley	8	7	3.35	18	0	104.2	112	29	57
2* Dowdy, Justin	0	1	1.50	6	4	6	3	3	5
Hurn, Doug	5	2	2.56	41	4	56.1	54	17	44
Medina, Gabriel	8	5	4.37	19	0	119.1	115	52	82
* Morales, Ronald	0	2	4.05	20	0	20	28	11	21
Rhoden, Robert	2	3	5.10	29	1	30	29	21	21
1* Salazar, Richard	3	0	3.44	29	3	49.2	49	16	33
Savage, William	5	7	2.94	19	0	125.1	119	48	49
Soto, Diego	1	0	1.06	10	0	17	8	7	12
1 Stephens, Amad	2	0	8.79	15	8	14.1	16	11	10
* Torres, Julio	0	0	6.14	8	0	7.1	9	4	6
Young, Justin	2	3	3.40	40	1	47.2	43	18	36

ATLANTIC LEAGUE

The Somerset Patriots are running out of Atlantic League records to break.

The Patriots became the first Atlantic League to defend their title, but even more impressively they won their fifth title in the 12-year history of the league by knocking off Southern Maryland in the Atlantic League championship series.

Stability is part of the key to Somerset's success. Sparky Lyle, who picked up his third manager of the year award, has been the team's manager since 1998. Third baseman Jeff Nettles, the championship series MVP, has been on the team for six years. He's set nearly every Somerset career record during that time, has won three titles, earned two championship series MVP awards and has made the all-star team in all six years.

Somerset may have won another title, but Southern Maryland's debut was nearly as impressive. The first-year expansion team had the second-best record in the league in addition to earning a sport in the championship series.

FIRST HALF

LIBERTY	W	L	PCT	GB
Southern Maryland	42	28	.609	—
Long Island	37	33	.520	5
Camden	33	37	.471	9
Bridgeport	33	37	.471	9

FREEDOM	W	L	PCT	GB
Somerset	43	27	.614	—
Newark	35	35	.500	8
Lancaster	33	37	.471	10
York	24	46	.343	19

SECOND HALF

LIBERTY	W	L	PCT	GB
Southern Maryland	37	33	.529	—
Long Island	37	33	.529	—
Bridgeport	32	38	.457	5
Camden	29	41	.414	8

FREEDOM	W	L	PCT	GB
Somerset	43	27	.614	—
Newark	39	31	.557	4
Lancaster	34	36	.486	9
York	29	41	.414	14

PLAYOFFS—Semifinals: Southern Maryland defeated Long Island 3-2 and Somerset defeated Newark 3-1 in best-of-five series. **Finals:** Somerset defeated Southern Maryland 3-1 in best-of-five series.
ATTENDANCE: Long Island 414,973; Somerset 355,429; Lancaster 314,228; York 276,446; Southern Maryland 239,541; Camden 234,519; Newark 163,736; Bridgeport 162,121.
MANAGERS: Bridgeport—Tommy John/Willie Upshaw; Camden—Joe Ferguson; Lancaster—Von Hayes/Tom Herr; Long Island—Gary Carter; Newark—Tim Raines; Somerset—Sparky Lyle; Southern Maryland—Butch Hobson. York—Chris Holies.
ALL-STAR TEAM: C—Salamon Manriquez, Newark; **1B**—Jesse Hoorelbeke, Bridgeport; **2B**—Matt Hagen, Somerset; **3B**—Jeff Nettles, Somerset; **SS**—Travis Garcia, So Maryland; Utility—Ray Navarrete, Long Island; **OF**—Charlton Jimerson, Newark; Brandon Sing, Bridgeport; James Shanks, So Maryland; Wayne Lydon, Camden; **DH**—Carl Everett, Newark.
RHP—Jim Magrane, Somerset; **LHP**—Troy Cate, Long Island; **RP**—Bill Simas, Long Island.
Player of the Year: Ray Navarrete, OF, Long Island. **Pitcher Of The Year:** Jim Magrane, Somerset. **Manager of the Year:** Sparky Lyle, Somerset.

INDIVIDUAL BATTING LEADERS

BATTER, CLUB	AVG	G	AB	R	H	HR	RBI
Jimerson, Charlton, Newark	.335	103	397	91	133	21	62
Ford, Lew, Long Island	.330	93	355	77	117	10	55
Hagen, Matt, Somerset	.317	120	451	88	143	10	75
Everett, Carl, Newark	.315	109	384	67	121	17	82
Pressley, Josh, Somerset	.314	109	369	61	116	15	72
Manriquez, Salomon, Newark	.311	106	354	52	110	7	51
Francia, Juan, Long Island	.310	125	452	88	140	4	43
Navarrete, Ray, Long Island	.309	139	531	106	164	25	96
Sing, Brandon, Bridgeport	.305	129	459	96	140	23	94
Rodriguez, Victor, Long Island	.301	97	392	34	118	4	56

INDIVIDUAL PITCHING LEADERS

PITCHER, CLUB	W	L	ERA	IP	H	BB	SO
Magrane, Jim, Somerset	15	4	2.70	183	162	50	134
Cate, Troy, Long Island	13	5	3.28	129	119	31	84
Yan, Esteban, Bridgeport	11	6	3.29	164	145	41	98
Reichert, Dan, Bridgeport	14	9	3.53	194	183	75	126
Brazelton, Dewon, Camden	6	8	3.69	127	130	38	84
Brey, Josh, Camden	9	8	3.90	132	122	45	58
Fritz, Ben, Lancaster	5	9	4.04	143	154	64	92
Parker, Zach, Lancaster	4	6	4.05	138	126	67	86
Harang, Daryl, York	10	12	4.08	154	182	54	85
Manon, Julio, Long Island	9	6	4.13	144	134	55	108

BRIDGEPORT BLUEFISH

BATTERS	AVG	AB	R	H	2B	3B	HR	RBI	SB
Asadoorian, Rick, dh	.273	11	2	3	0	0	0	2	0
# Batista, Wilson, 2b	.302	192	27	58	10	0	0	21	9
2 Bautista, Rayner, ss	.262	302	48	79	15	0	4	30	2
Caligiuri, Jay, 1b	.289	135	17	39	7	0	2	19	0
Czarniecki, Jordan, of	.179	39	4	7	2	0	1	1	2
2* Davenport, Ron, of	.111	27	1	3	1	0	0	3	0
Davison, Todd, 2b	.272	217	25	59	7	1	1	14	6
# Ezi, Travis, of	.118	34	5	4	1	0	0	1	1
* Greenberg, Adam, of	.248	508	89	126	19	8	3	42	53
Harris, Shea, c	.165	85	4	14	4	0	0	4	1
Hoorelbeke, Jesse, 1b	.293	437	74	128	27	1	23	88	0
Johnson, Timothy, ss	.309	55	9	17	3	0	0	6	2
Lisk, Charlie, c	.288	66	7	19	5	1	1	7	1
Lopez, Luis, 3b	.275	505	73	139	18	1	8	74	1
# Mateo, Henry, 2b	.416	101	25	42	4	1	0	13	7
# Pendergrass, Tyrone, of	.249	357	60	89	13	6	2	36	28
2 Polanco, Enohel, 2b	.274	168	18	46	7	3	2	20	5
Radmanovich, Ryan, of	.249	309	32	77	17	2	7	50	0
2* Roberson, Colin, of	.213	197	21	42	6	6	6	24	11
Rodriguez, Luis, c	.277	405	35	112	11	4	5	49	2
Rogers, Ed, ss	.299	127	9	38	7	0	1	12	5
Sing, Brandon, of	.305	459	96	140	34	1	23	94	4

PITCHERS	W	L	ERA	G	SV	IP	H	BB	SO
* Arroyo, Luis	0	2	3.75	2	0	12	15	1	7
Asadoorian, Rick	1	3	3.74	33	1	45.2	42	30	37
1 Carrasco, Hector	0	1	9.39	7	1	7.2	7	9	7
Cavazos, Andy	0	2	5.76	23	4	25	21	26	20
1* Dipietro, Ryan	0	1	3.45	6	0	15.2	13	5	6
Francisco, Alex	0	0	9.64	2	0	4.2	5	6	0
Hoorelbeke, Casey	3	3	4.66	43	1	56	61	29	37
Jackson, Kyle	11	11	5.37	28	0	157.2	164	63	101
Knotts, Gary	5	11	4.52	26	0	153.1	168	58	118
* Lee, Corey	4	7	5.38	25	0	90.1	102	53	63
Perez, Franklin	0	2	9.40	12	1	29.2	42	22	22
Pike, Matthew	7	10	3.80	33	1	109	113	46	79
Plefka, Jonathan	5	4	3.26	33	1	49.2	45	29	24
Reichert, Dan	14	9	3.53	28	0	193.2	183	75	126
Ryan, Patrick	1	1	0.73	21	4	24.2	19	6	25
Weimer, Andrew	3	0	2.14	41	5	59	55	15	35
Yan, Esteban	11	6	3.29	26	0	164.1	145	41	98
1* Youman, Shane	0	1	10.50	5	0	6	8	9	5

CAMDEN RIVERSHARKS

BATTERS	AVG	AB	R	H	2B	3B	HR	RBI	SB
Abernathy, Brent, 2b	.211	57	5	12	1	0	1	4	1
2 Barrows, Derek, dh	.250	4	0	1	0	0	0	0	0
* Bonvechio, Brett, 1b	.269	361	44	97	15	4	7	46	2
# Burgamy, Brian, 3b	.247	450	70	111	25	3	10	62	3
Chiaravalloti, Vito, 1b	.272	401	50	109	26	1	12	60	2
Dominguez, Carlos, c	.283	46	5	13	2	0	0	4	0
Fenwick, Ron, 2b	.216	37	1	8	2	0	0	3	0
Finegan, Brian, 2b	.232	228	32	53	11	0	3	24	3
* Guzman, Garrett, of	.298	151	27	45	9	1	4	29	2
* Haines, Kyle, ss	.253	79	5	20	1	1	0	7	2
2# Housel, David, of	.250	20	2	5	0	0	0	1	1
2# Infante, Jansy, ss	.077	26	4	2	0	0	0	1	0
Jacobs, Jason, c	.250	160	16	40	11	1	2	20	1
Knott, Jon, of	.328	265	39	87	24	2	8	43	5
2* Kotch, Kevin, of	.240	50	8	12	3	1	1	2	0

BATTERS	AVG	AB	R	H	2B	3B	HR	RBI	SB
Leon, Jose, 1b	.286	192	32	55	13	0	9	32	0
Lydon, Wayne, of	.273	542	99	148	12	13	5	54	72
* Majewski, Val, of	.310	100	16	31	3	0	4	12	6
# Nelson, Bryant, ss	.300	367	37	110	19	1	9	60	5
2 Purdom, John, c	.250	132	19	33	8	0	0	13	0
Spivey, Junior, 2b	.261	211	27	55	9	0	5	38	6
Torres, Frederick, c	.236	123	9	29	4	1	2	13	0
* Vincent, Jeff, of	.180	50	12	9	1	0	1	6	4
Walker, Chris, of	.254	520	83	132	12	9	5	58	61

PITCHERS	W	L	ERA	G	SV	IP	H	BB	SO
2 Barrows, Derek	0	0	9.53	4	0	5.2	7	1	4
2 Batson, Byron	0	0	5.79	3	0	4.2	8	2	1
2* Bittner, Tim	2	1	3.54	35	3	41	39	21	32
Brazelton, Dewon	6	8	3.69	22	0	126.2	130	38	84
* Brey, Josh	9	8	3.90	26	0	131.2	122	45	58
Bump, Nate	8	2	2.49	12	0	79.2	75	16	41
Capella, Anthony	1	1	5.11	11	0	12.1	14	7	2
Davey, Tom	8	2	2.33	15	0	85	75	20	72
2* DiPietro, Ryan	7	9	4.64	22	0	108.2	114	48	79
Drese, Ryan	1	4	3.34	9	0	32.1	33	16	7
Flannery, Mike	2	5	5.85	32	0	52.1	73	34	32
Gearhart, Kalen	1	4	6.83	18	0	54	70	22	23
Guerrero, Julio	1	5	4.80	63	1	81	103	14	47
Lawrence, Brian	4	3	3.44	8	0	49.2	45	13	26
Lewis, Jeremy	1	0	4.63	3	0	11.2	13	3	10
2 Mannix, Kevin	2	5	4.59	16	0	84.1	86	47	42
* Newman, Josh	1	3	10.02	13	0	21	33	13	22
* Parker, Shaun	0	1	33.75	3	0	1.1	1	5	0
2 Perez, Franklin	0	2	3.00	27	6	24	24	13	18
Ramos, Victor	0	1	0.00	1	0	0	2	2	0
Reith, Brian	1	1	7.31	24	0	32	41	16	32
Rodriguez, Felix	4	4	3.54	52	7	48.1	36	29	30
* Shaver, Christopher	3	4	3.83	46	7	47	46	14	35
1 Thorpe, Tracy	0	4	3.15	26	9	40	25	27	44
Vincent, Jeff	0	0	0.00	1	0	1	0	0	1

LANCASTER BARNSTORMERS

BATTERS	AVG	AB	R	H	2B	3B	HR	RBI	SB
* Ackerman, Eric, of	.000	1	0	0	0	0	0	0	0
* Biernbaum, L.J., of	.284	388	45	110	13	0	14	64	12
# Bravo, Danny, 2b	.255	208	39	53	16	0	1	20	2
* Campbell, Michael, of	.224	232	19	52	14	2	4	21	4
* Cooper, Jason, of	.145	62	9	9	2	0	3	9	0
* Foster, Quincy, of	.180	50	9	9	0	1	0	5	4
Gold, Nate, 1b	.213	47	4	10	2	1	0	7	0
Gutierrez, Vic, ss	.221	113	12	25	4	1	1	7	2
2 Haran, Gerard, c	.297	273	47	81	19	0	11	46	2
Herr, Aaron, 3b	.265	441	61	117	30	1	14	83	1
1# Housel, David, 2b-OF	.206	97	16	20	3	0	4	11	1
# Machado, Andy, ss	.193	171	18	33	7	3	3	17	9
* Medina, Rodney, of	.290	62	5	18	2	0	0	6	3
* Morris, Jed, c	.249	353	40	88	21	0	9	46	2
Mulhern, Ryan, 1b	.231	441	59	102	25	0	16	66	2
* Perry, Jason, of	.361	36	10	13	1	0	6	15	0
Sabatella, Bryan, 1b	.266	229	35	61	8	3	2	25	19
Shorsher, Adam, c	.224	58	6	13	3	0	2	7	0
Suarez, Cesar, 2b	.272	173	21	47	7	3	2	16	5
Turner, Lloyd, ss	.281	508	94	143	25	8	11	58	31
* Watson, Matt, of	.269	234	35	63	12	2	8	43	1
Williams, Dan, 2b	.100	10	1	1	0	0	0	1	1
Woods, Michael, of	.284	409	73	116	17	3	12	49	18
Zazueta, Amadeo, ss	.171	82	7	14	1	1	0	9	0

PITCHERS	W	L	ERA	G	SV	IP	H	BB	SO
Abel, Nick	2	4	3.09	29	1	35	33	10	31
* Ackerman, Eric	7	11	4.19	34	2	135.1	153	49	82
Alfonseca, Antonio	0	0	4.35	14	15	32.1	49	11	38
1 Barrows, Derek	0	0	13.50	2	0	2.2	5	4	1
Batson, Byron	0	0	54.00	1	0	0.1	1	1	0
* Camacho, Eddie	4	4	4.92	52	0	64	76	27	40
* Cochran, Tom	3	2	4.67	7	0	27	28	12	22
Cruz, Reymond	1	1	5.06	5	0	16	15	4	10
* Cullen, Ryan	4	3	2.08	22	7	26	26	8	24
D'Alessandro, Joe	1	1	4.43	18	0	22.1	22	12	15
Davis, Kane	0	0	9.00	7	0	5	7	2	1

	W	L	ERA	G	SV	IP	H	BB	SO
Fritz, Ben	5	9	4.04	25	0	142.2	154	64	92
Gomez, Ricardo	5	2	5.09	30	0	69	77	34	52
Hall, Josh	1	1	3.32	3	0	19	16	0	17
* Heuser, Jim	1	1	1.84	14	0	14.2	14	12	20
Hodges, Trey	5	5	4.31	21	0	108.2	98	48	62
Huber, Jon	1	0	3.63	18	2	22.1	24	8	25
Junge, Eric	4	1	2.25	6	0	32	27	9	41
Lundberg, Spike	0	0	13.50	3	0	1.1	3	2	0
Montero, Joanniel	1	1	3.45	17	1	28.2	28	5	32
* Musser, Neal	2	2	3.07	22	0	44	37	27	48
Ovalles, Juan	2	4	6.43	31	1	42	46	24	35
* Parker, Zach	4	6	4.05	25	0	137.2	126	67	86
* Peeples, Ross	2	2	5.92	49	2	51.2	64	20	35
Savage, William	1	0	3.24	2	0	8.1	6	2	5
Scobie, Jason	7	9	4.60	30	0	139	171	42	89

NEWARK BEARS

BATTERS	AVG	AB	R	H	2B	3B	HR	RBI	SB
* Anderson, Marlon, 1b	.240	25	2	6	0	0	0	1	0
* Buckman, Brandon, 1b	.254	122	13	31	4	0	3	11	1
* Cabreja, Rafael, of	.286	7	0	2	0	0	0	0	0
* Caruso, Mike, 2b	.111	18	2	2	0	0	0	0	0
2 Castillo, Alberto, c	.245	102	11	25	4	0	1	12	0
Castro, Ramon, ss	.333	9	2	3	0	0	0	1	0
Dellaero, Jason, ss	.313	48	12	15	3	0	1	11	0
# Everett, Carl	.315	384	67	121	18	0	17	82	2
* Gibbons, Jay, of	.233	163	16	38	13	0	4	19	0
1 Haran, Gerard, c	.208	24	2	5	0	0	1	2	0
Hernandez, Michael, of	.302	308	47	93	24	0	11	51	0
# Hill, Bobby, 2b	.265	83	17	22	6	0	0	9	4
1# Infante, Jansy, ss	.214	28	5	6	2	2	0	2	0
# Jimenez, D'Angelo, 2b	.326	144	26	47	10	0	2	20	3
Jimerson, Charlton, of	.335	397	91	133	27	1	21	62	38
* Jones, Jacque, of	.311	119	25	37	8	0	5	25	2
2* Jones, Kennard, of	.277	47	5	13	2	0	0	8	0
2* Loadenthal, Carl, of	.317	101	21	32	4	1	1	11	7
* Mackowiak, Rob, 3b	.323	288	59	93	18	2	14	52	3
Madera, Sandy, 1b	.375	256	50	96	14	0	12	62	1
Manriquez, Salomon, c	.311	354	52	110	20	3	7	51	2
1 Manuel, Anthony, 2b	.243	74	10	18	4	1	0	7	0
Martinez, Felix, ss	.266	192	24	51	7	0	5	24	3
Mercedes, Victor, ss	.289	201	29	58	16	4	1	36	3
Nieblas, Luis, c	.235	34	5	8	3	1	0	3	0
Nivar, Ramon, of	.331	127	19	42	6	0	3	15	8
# Nunez, Abraham, ss	.314	51	12	16	3	1	0	6	2
Otanez, Willis, 3b	.253	99	16	25	2	0	6	21	0
Perez, Andres, 2b	.306	229	44	70	15	4	17	54	2
1 Polanco, Enohel, 3b-SS	.364	11	3	4	1	0	0	0	1
Raines, Tim, of	.143	21	1	3	1	1	0	0	0
* Redman, Tike, of	.292	271	49	79	7	1	5	36	10
Sandoval, Michael, 3b	.291	175	27	51	13	0	3	23	0
Shubsda, Brian, c	.257	35	6	9	0	0	0	1	0
Smith, Dustin, of	.091	11	3	1	0	0	0	2	3
Tejeda, Juan, 1b	.306	62	9	19	1	1	3	8	0
Thompson, Kevin, of	.209	67	7	14	3	1	2	13	4
1* Tucker, Michael, of	.231	39	3	9	1	0	0	0	1
* Ward, Daryle, 1b	.222	27	2	6	2	0	0	2	0

PITCHERS	W	L	ERA	G	SV	IP	H	BB	SO
Almanzar, Carlos	2	0	2.87	12	0	15.2	14	7	15
Banks, Willie	1	0	6.43	17	0	28	36	26	21
1 Batson, Byron	1	1	5.27	7	0	13.2	14	5	7
Benitez, Armando	1	0	2.86	34	16	34.2	21	10	43
1* Bittner, Tim	0	0	2.45	11	0	11	11	10	12
Blacksher, Derek	0	1	2.45	3	1	11	9	2	11
Brownlie, Bobby	4	3	3.03	11	0	68.1	58	14	62
Bukvich, Ryan	2	6	7.93	17	0	53.1	52	66	37
Carrasco, Hector	1	1	6.00	2	0	9	8	6	5
Castillo, Francisco	1	1	8.44	2	0	5.1	5	4	0
Chacon, Shawn	3	3	4.29	7	0	42	41	16	29
Demko, Luke	2	0	5.46	14	0	31.1	27	21	25
Foulke, Keith	5	4	5.02	34	11	52	64	11	49
* Fultz, Aaron	1	1	9.92	6	0	16.1	24	10	10
Garcia, Jose	4	1	5.65	12	0	57.1	66	23	40
Gunter, Kevin	1	0	4.66	7	0	9.2	14	3	7

	W	L	ERA	G	SV	IP	H	BB	SO
2 Hrynio, Mike	4	2	5.92	14	0	51.2	55	25	32
* Kent, Steve	0	1	10.29	5	0	7	10	2	7
Kobernus, Kyle	3	5	5.86	15	0	71	77	41	39
Komine, Shane	8	7	4.50	20	1	90	94	35	60
1 Mannix, Kevin	0	0	7.94	3	0	5.2	5	6	5
Martinez, Edgar R.	1	3	6.09	12	0	54.2	57	30	20
* Melody, Matt	0	1	11.30	6	0	14.1	26	13	8
Mendoza, Ramiro	4	4	3.83	17	0	87	86	19	72
Nix, Michael	4	1	3.08	23	1	26.1	21	20	27
Nunez, Franklin	0	0	4.50	2	0	4	4	0	7
Perez, Franklin	0	1	7.59	2	0	11	18	6	8
Perez, Oneli	4	4	2.82	15	1	44.2	43	18	48
Ramos, Eddy	0	1	7.71	7	0	7	10	3	3
* Rice, Scott	2	1	9.00	9	0	13	19	8	9
Rleal, Sendy	3	2	3.65	26	0	37	29	20	22
Santiesteban, Danny	2	1	6.00	12	0	15	21	16	15
Santos, Victor	3	2	5.92	5	0	24.1	26	16	15
1 Shibilo, Andy	0	0	7.04	6	0	7.2	9	3	11
* Smith, Matt	3	3	7.52	14	0	46.2	60	37	28
Soler, Alay	0	1	9.69	7	0	13	19	6	10
Spurling, Chris	1	0	6.95	19	1	22	25	9	16
2 Thorpe, Tracy	0	1	2.31	12	4	11.2	12	2	15
Willey, Cory	3	2	4.75	50	1	55	58	24	52
Williamson, Scott	0	0	2.30	16	1	15.2	9	7	12

SOMERSET PATRIOTS

BATTERS	AVG	AB	R	H	2B	3B	HR	RBI	SB
Anderson, Travis, c	.306	265	52	81	15	1	8	58	5
Ayala, Elliott, of	.276	341	43	94	10	0	1	43	11
* Belcher, Jason, c	.283	343	47	97	18	3	5	53	2
* Burke, Joe, 1b	.279	373	47	104	17	1	3	41	13
# Granato, Anthony, ss	.248	391	77	97	21	0	7	46	42
Hagen, Matt, 2b	.317	451	88	143	36	3	10	75	25
Hall, Noah, of	.293	140	29	41	7	2	5	33	8
* Johnson, Brandon, 3b	.143	21	5	3	0	0	0	0	0
Nelson, Jon, of	.200	175	14	35	7	2	5	14	3
Nettles, Jeff, 3b	.295	502	75	148	29	1	15	93	1
Olivares, Teuris, 2b	.283	375	67	106	26	2	10	54	10
* Pressley, Josh, 1b	.314	369	61	116	21	0	15	72	1
* Rodriguez, Mike, of	.252	397	63	100	13	3	4	48	45
Smith, Sean, of	.262	500	93	131	21	3	8	56	52
Teilon, Nilson, 2b	.225	40	4	9	5	0	2	6	0

PITCHERS	W	L	ERA	G	SV	IP	H	BB	SO
* Adams, Brian	13	8	4.61	27	0	164	190	38	120
* Babula, Shaun	1	1	6.17	12	0	11.2	9	9	7
Basner, Ryan	3	2	2.88	54	6	50	51	23	40
Bouknight, Kip	6	8	5.17	25	0	101	112	40	68
Buglovsky, Chris	8	2	4.48	19	0	92.1	99	25	43
Bush, Paul	0	0	1.62	9	0	16.2	14	3	22
Cahill, Casey	6	3	3.33	51	2	51.1	50	31	27
Fairchild, Thomas	4	2	4.27	23	0	52.2	58	15	48
Gothreaux, Jared	7	8	4.77	38	0	100	127	20	71
* Henderson, Brian	4	1	2.32	45	2	54.1	52	11	29
Kirsten, Joel	0	1	1.29	1	0	7	8	0	2
# Lewis, Jeremy	2	0	5.63	12	0	16	17	7	12
Magrane, Jim	15	4	2.70	27	0	183.1	162	50	134
Miller, Josh	10	5	3.65	15	0	101	113	19	55
Minix, Travis	0	0	0.95	21	12	19	12	5	20
Nageotte, Clint	1	2	7.84	6	0	21	24	22	16
Prinz, Bret	1	2	2.04	40	21	39.2	27	17	51
Standridge, Jason	4	4	5.13	18	0	100	104	39	88
Van Es, Scott	1	1	4.41	20	0	32.2	40	16	26

SOUTHERN MARYLAND BLUE CRABS

BATTERS	AVG	AB	R	H	2B	3B	HR	RBI	SB
1 Acey, Jermy, 2b	.276	214	37	59	9	0	7	30	4
Bailey, Trae, 2b	.154	13	2	2	1	0	0	0	0
Burkhart, Lance, c	.242	322	40	78	14	1	13	48	1
* Conroy, Mike, of	.220	50	8	11	1	1	0	2	2
* Crozier, Eric, 1b	.314	175	30	55	13	2	8	24	4
Doetsch, Steve, of	.164	61	9	10	1	1	0	7	1
Garcia, Travis, ss	.353	326	49	115	19	1	16	63	5
# Giannotti, Rich, of	.293	290	34	85	18	3	5	39	6
Harvey, Ken, 1b	.381	126	26	48	8	0	4	16	0

	AVG	AB	R	H	2B	3B	HR	RBI	SB
Jeroloman, Charles, 3b	.190	306	44	58	9	0	11	38	1
Just, Mike, 2b	.274	354	55	97	14	0	2	32	9
Krause, Brent, of	.323	31	3	10	3	0	1	3	0
Martinez, Octavio, c	.262	275	31	72	11	2	4	48	1
Nicolas, Cesar, 1b	.289	38	5	11	2	0	4	9	0
Osborn, Pat, 3b	.268	477	63	128	29	1	14	69	1
Owens, Jeremy, of	.240	475	96	114	24	4	28	80	15
Perry, Anthony, 1b	.105	19	7	2	1	0	0	0	0
2 Polanco, Enohel, 2b	.400	10	1	4	0	0	0	1	0
Ramistella, John, of	.273	385	69	105	20	3	22	58	15
1* Rodriguez, Liu, ss	.280	143	23	40	4	0	3	14	2
Shanks, James, of	.293	536	87	157	22	7	17	93	12
# Spruill, Dustin, dh	.556	9	2	5	0	0	0	2	0
2* Tucker, Michael, 1b	.332	196	37	65	21	2	5	29	5

PITCHERS	W	L	ERA	G	SV	IP	H	BB	SO
3 Batson, Byron	1	3	11.32	8	0	10.1	17	4	5
Baugh, Kenny	6	3	4.52	13	0	69.2	85	29	44
Bicondoa, Ryan	11	6	4.66	29	0	164.1	200	58	89
Blanton, Jason	0	2	9.95	7	0	6.1	9	14	2
De La Rosa, Dane	1	1	1.11	18	3	24.1	16	7	32
* DeChristofaro, Vincent	0	1	7.71	10	0	4.2	6	9	1
Desalvo, Matt	0	1	5.40	1	0	5	5	2	4
* Ellison, Derrick	1	1	1.42	13	4	12.2	10	2	15
Estrada, Paul	4	1	3.54	37	2	41	46	18	39
Gannon, Joe	9	17	5.96	32	0	202.1	239	101	75
Grube, Jarrett	3	1	3.36	16	0	75	90	21	56
* Halama, John	8	1	1.96	10	0	69	64	13	39
Hensley, Matt	5	2	2.70	31	7	33.1	30	12	36
James, Mike	3	3	2.52	58	4	61	58	31	43
* Keisler, Randy	2	2	6.89	6	0	31.1	37	13	24
LaVorgna, Jason	0	1	3.86	10	0	11.2	19	5	7
Navarro, Jason	2	0	1.04	19	0	17.1	12	7	12
* O'Connor, Mike	2	0	3.13	4	0	23	24	4	21
* Ramsey, Keith	5	4	5.42	13	0	81.1	103	21	50
Rayborn, Kenny	8	5	3.06	17	0	103	100	36	52
Richardson, Jason	0	0	14.73	6	0	3.2	6	5	2
Righter, Matthew	1	3	2.66	14	0	23.2	19	13	13
Rodriguez, Edward	2	1	2.97	19	0	30.1	29	10	17
* Schweitzer, Matt	5	0	2.37	64	4	61	47	20	64
Serrano, Jim	0	2	6.09	30	0	34	41	24	27
Warden, Jim Ed	0	0	1.13	22	13	24	14	6	20

YORK REVOLUTION

BATTERS	AVG	AB	R	H	2B	3B	HR	RBI	SB
2 Acey, Jeremy, 2b	.158	76	16	12	0	0	0	4	1
Arhart, Josh, c	.170	47	6	8	2	0	3	11	0
* Aspito, Jason, of	.259	402	49	104	23	0	7	51	3
1 Bautista, Rayner, 3b	.091	11	0	1	1	0	0	0	0
Collaro, Tom, of	.274	507	62	139	27	5	15	75	4
# De Renne, Keoni, 2b	.289	470	70	136	24	2	5	34	18
* Eggleston, Aharon, of	.326	46	10	15	5	1	0	7	0
Esquivel, Matt, of	.259	421	72	109	19	3	21	68	21
Eure, Jeffrey, 3b	.234	124	7	29	3	0	1	8	2
Goleski, Ryan, of	.212	217	24	46	10	2	3	23	1
Hill, Jamar, of	.304	79	12	24	5	2	3	5	1
Johnson, Josh, c	.186	290	28	54	14	2	7	29	0
1* Jones, Kennard, of	.271	314	46	85	16	4	2	21	9
Ka'aihue, Kala, 1b	.217	23	4	5	3	0	1	4	0
1* Loadenthal, Carl, of	.200	75	8	15	1	1	0	3	5
2 Manuel, Anthony, ss	.158	38	1	6	0	0	0	3	1
* Padgett, Matt, 3b	.274	460	62	126	27	2	7	70	7
Pinckney, Brandon, ss	.315	54	5	17	1	2	0	5	0
1 Purdom, John, 1b	.216	51	3	11	3	0	0	5	0
1* Roberson, Colin, of	.118	34	4	4	0	0	0	4	1
2* Rodriguez, Liu, ss	.267	75	8	20	3	0	0	9	0
* Rogelstad, Matt, 1b	.280	325	36	91	22	3	7	39	5
2* Rose, P.J., 1b	.278	237	23	66	11	0	3	33	1
* Sandel, George, ss	.130	54	2	7	1	0	0	2	0
# Sandoval, Danny, ss	.191	110	6	21	3	0	3	4	
2 Taveras, Luis, c	.213	108	7	23	7	0	0	10	1

PITCHERS	W	L	ERA	G	SV	IP	H	BB	SO
Andrade, Steve	1	0	6.75	10	1	9.1	13	5	6
Baker, Jamie	1	1	3.24	7	0	8.1	5	5	5
Bauer, Rick	0	0	3.86	3	0	14	12	3	13

	W	L	ERA	G	SV	IP	H	BB	SO
Britton, Chris	2	5	4.91	39	3	40.1	44	10	19
Foli, Daniel	5	15	7.11	36	0	144.1	201	66	79
1* Franklin, Wayne	0	0	4.50	3	0	4	6	7	5
Freeman, Jesse	0	3	8.03	6	0	12.1	15	8	9
* Gassner, Dave	4	12	5.59	22	0	112.2	160	39	64
* Harang, Daryl	10	12	4.08	33	0	154.1	182	54	85
Harikkala, Tim	5	3	3.51	13	0	51.1	56	6	21
Hedrick, Shawn	1	2	4.43	4	0	22.1	26	5	9
* Holliday, Brian	3	3	4.81	35	0	76.2	83	29	47
Hughes, Travis	1	2	5.93	12	1	13.2	20	3	8
* Kershner, Jason	3	3	5.40	55	1	80	101	14	45
1 Olson, Jason	1	2	7.91	16	0	19.1	25	14	23
Padilla, Juan	0	0	0.00	10	3	11	4	4	7
Phelps, Travis	2	4	3.52	58	9	69	59	41	58
2 Richardson, Jason	0	0	4.50	3	0	4	4	0	5
Shafer, David	0	0	10.38	5	0	4.1	3	7	2
Sharpless, Josh	1	1	7.85	15	0	18.1	25	17	17
2 Shibilo, Andy	0	1	6.75	5	0	8	12	5	4
Smith, Mike	1	3	2.86	5	0	28.1	21	9	17
Sotolongo, Roberto	0	2	5.04	6	0	25	42	10	9
Thurman, Corey	4	3	3.28	16	0	85	87	28	57
Wade, Travis	0	0	3.12	6	0	8.2	9	6	7
Wilkerson, Wes	1	0	6.65	16	0	21.2	34	8	9
2* Youman, Shane	1	6	3.44	14	0	68	71	25	50
Zimmermann, Bob	6	4	4.43	38	8	89.1	91	60	61

CAN-AM LEAGUE

Eric Gagne's career will always be remembered for his dominating work as the Dodgers closer in the early years of the 2000s.

But in Quebec, the native son will be remembered fondly for his post-major league career as well.

The former all-star reinvented himself for a second career as an independent league starter in 2009. Gagne quickly became the face of the franchise in Quebec. While he wasn't dominating (he went 6-6, 4.65 during the regular season) he saved his best for his last start of the season, striking out eight in a complete-game win over Worcester in the Can-Am League finals. In the next game Karl Gelinas picked up the win as Quebec finished off the Tornadoes.

Gagne wasn't the only ex-big leaguer to star in the Can-Am League in 2009. Former Rays catcher Pierre-Luc LaForest returned to his Quebec home to win player of the year award.

FIRST HALF

	W	L	PCT	GB
New Jersey	28	19	.596	—
Brockton	26	20	.565	1½
Worcester	22	24	.478	5½
Quebec	22	25	.468	6
New Hampshire	21	26	.447	7
Sussex	21	26	.447	7

SECOND HALF

	W	L	PCT	GB
Quebec	31	16	.660	—
Brockton	30	17	.638	1
New Jersey	27	20	.574	4
Worcester	21	26	.447	10
Sussex	17	30	.362	14
New Hampshire	15	32	.319	16

PLAYOFFS—Semifinals: Worcester defeated New Jersey 3-0 and Quebec defeated Brockton 3-1 in best-of-five series. **Finals:** Quebec defeated Worcester 3-1 in best-of-five series.

ATTENDANCE: Quebec 164,009; Brockton 112,343; New Jersey 88,658; Worcester 78,174; Sussex 79,663; New Hampshire 40,361.

MANAGERS: Brockton—Chris Miyake; Nashua—Rick Miller; New Jersey—Joe Calfapietra; Quebec—Michel Laplante; Sussex—Hal Lanier; Worcester—Rich Gedman.

ALL-STARS: C—Pierre-Luc LaForest, Quebec; **1B**—Myron Leslie, New Jersey; **2B**—Melvin Falu, Brockton; **SS**—Mike DeJesus, New Jersey; **3B**—Chris Kelly, New Hampshire/Sussex; **OF**—Jerod Edmondson, New Hampshire/New Jersey; Maikel Jova, Sussex; Carlos Sosa, Worcester; **DH**—Palmer Karr, Brockton.

LHP—AJ Wideman, New Jersey; **RHP**—Wayne Lundgren, Brockton;

RP—Rusty Tucker, New Jersey.

Player of the Year: Pierre-Luc LaForest, Quebec. **Manager of the Year:** Joe Calfapietra, New Jersey.

INDIVIDUAL BATTING LEADERS

BATTER, CLUB	AVG	G	AB	R	H	HR	RBI
Edmondson, Jerod, New Jersey	.332	94	337	66	112	13	51
Falu, Melvin, Brockton	.328	91	326	46	107	7	63
Jova, Maikel, Sussex	.315	91	378	56	119	5	74
Salotti, Nick, Worcester	.315	88	324	43	102	4	42
Sosa, Carlos, Worcester	.314	83	312	55	98	15	69
Nunez, Alex, Quebec	.314	92	341	54	107	3	34
Valencia, Christopher, Brockton	.309	93	369	60	114	1	36
Tomlinson, Goef, Quebec	.302	81	334	58	101	5	55
Colabello, Chris, Worcester	.302	84	321	48	97	9	55
Scanzano, Mike, New Jersey	.301	83	276	36	83	0	28

INDIVIDUAL PITCHING LEADERS

PITCHER, CLUB	W	L	ERA	IP	H	BB	SO
Wideman, Aaron, New Jersey	10	1	2.51	115	90	18	81
Lundgren, Wayne, Brockton	9	5	2.75	128	120	31	78
Clements, Carter, Sussex	6	4	3.05	112	116	35	57
Knoff, Justin, Sussex	5	5	3.24	86	82	27	52
Zuercher, Zachary, Worcester	7	5	3.53	102	96	29	69
Long, Jeff, Brockton	6	4	3.55	84	84	15	42
Lobban, Ryan, Worcester	10	7	3.56	121	132	31	74
Anderson, Craig, Brockton	7	4	3.62	114	124	32	87
Pavlik, Isaac, New Jersey	6	6	3.66	111	103	17	75
Allen, Chris, Quebec	5	8	3.71	95	95	26	41

BROCKTON ROX

BATTERS	AVG	AB	R	H	2B	3B	HR	RBI	SB
Alcantara, Ervin, of	.320	25	3	8	2	0	0	3	0
* Brachold, Keith, of	.284	341	67	97	16	1	15	65	14
2 Brown, Morgan, 3b	.175	40	4	7	1	0	0	1	0
Calzado, Napoleon, of	.246	65	8	16	1	1	0	6	0
# Cuadrado, Phillip, 3b	.286	273	40	78	20	1	8	53	2
# Falu, Melvin, 2b	.328	326	46	107	25	2	7	63	9
Flores, Freddy, ss	.300	10	1	3	0	0	0	1	0
Gossard, Jon, c	.216	51	5	11	2	0	0	7	0
Grossman, Chris, c	.296	257	37	76	19	1	3	35	1
Karr, Palmer, of	.280	347	55	97	22	1	19	62	1
* Kinzler, Derek, 2b	.310	71	12	22	3	0	2	8	0
Ramos, Dominic, ss	.294	367	50	108	16	3	0	22	13
Stevens, Jeff, c	.278	18	1	5	1	0	0	1	0
Thigpen, Jud, of	.279	294	50	82	16	1	11	39	2
* Valencia, Christophe, of	.309	369	60	114	23	4	1	36	27
2* Williams, Clyde, 1b	.261	272	48	71	16	0	11	51	0

PITCHERS	W	L	ERA	G	SV	IP	H	BB	SO
* Anderson, Craig	7	4	3.62	19	0	114.1	124	32	87
Baker, Jamie	0	0	6.75	4	0	6.2	9	2	3
Delabar, Steven	3	3	3.76	12	0	26.1	22	12	23
Dunn, Gerald	0	1	3.44	36	24	36.2	38	12	34
Flores, Freddy	6	5	3.93	16	0	84.2	86	18	37
* Hertzler, Bradley	2	4	3.70	35	0	48.2	55	19	29
Kelly, John	2	3	6.23	8	0	30.1	38	11	22
Long, Jeff	6	4	3.55	14	0	83.2	84	15	42
Lundgren, Wayne	9	5	2.75	19	0	127.2	120	31	78
Lussier, Paul	3	0	4.02	11	0	40.1	38	15	24
* Morse, Bryan	1	0	3.45	4	0	15.2	13	9	6
Noe, Keith	5	2	3.83	31	0	40	30	20	48
2 Piechowski, Adam	2	0	3.72	7	0	9.2	8	6	8
* Robinson, Fraser	7	4	4.29	20	1	86	106	25	46
Tesseyman, John	0	0	2.70	5	1	10	11	1	5
Zachary, Matt	3	2	4.42	27	0	36.2	44	24	26

NEW HAMPSHIRE DEFENDERS

BATTERS	AVG	AB	R	H	2B	3B	HR	RBI	SB
Bergeron, Jabe, 1b	.276	261	34	72	9	2	9	44	0
* Berry, Boomer, 2b	.248	234	31	58	13	1	2	24	6
Bramasco, Jovanny, 3b	.219	32	3	7	2	0	0	6	0
Brown, Breland, of	.167	30	3	5	0	0	0	0	1
2 Brown, Morgan, 2b	.125	24	2	3	0	1	0	1	1
2* Cabreja, Rafael, of	.306	36	4	11	1	0	4	1	0
* Chavez, Zane, c	.269	212	21	57	6	0	5	30	3
1* Edmondson, Jerod, of	.315	276	54	87	17	0	13	42	13

2 Keel, Heath, of	.143	42	5	6	1	2	0	5	2
1 Kelly, Chris, 3b	.261	307	43	80	12	0	19	51	0
1* Lemon, Greg, ss	.282	287	38	81	12	3	0	17	4
Mojica, Albert, c	.250	16	3	4	2	0	0	4	0
Molina, Angel, of	.290	338	58	98	22	1	13	62	15
Nandin, Matt, ss	.244	160	10	39	3	1	0	11	2
2 O'Malley, Mike, 2b	.220	41	4	9	1	0	0	4	0
Ovalle, Edward, of	.279	305	36	85	20	1	4	35	8
* Pinto, Steve, of	.226	31	2	7	0	0	0	1	6
* Riley, Rob, of	.250	68	11	17	3	2	0	3	2
# Tavarez, Aregenis, c	.216	232	27	50	8	1	3	26	4
Weakley, Chris, ss	.095	21	3	2	0	0	1	4	0
1* Williams, Clyde, 1b	.195	82	15	16	2	0	5	13	0

PITCHERS	W	L	ERA	G	SV	IP	H	BB	SO
1 Asselin, Nick	9	6	3.96	16	0	100	112	26	38
* Bentz, Chad	0	1	9.82	2	0	3.2	3	6	0
Blanco, Nicolas	0	0	16.62	7	0	8.2	19	16	9
Brannan, Cooper	1	1	5.18	27	1	41.2	42	24	17
Burkett, Isaac	3	6	7.68	10	0	41	56	20	25
Cervantes, Francisco	1	5	6.69	8	0	35	42	32	23
Cuevas, Gabe	0	0	7.56	7	0	8.1	10	9	7
Driscoll, Pat	0	1	11.12	5	0	5.2	6	4	0
Flores, Miguel	6	5	5.21	19	0	103.2	124	53	61
Ford, Greg	0	0	6.43	2	0	7	9	1	4
Ledbetter, Lucas	2	2	4.21	31	3	66.1	70	36	40
McAllister, J.R.	0	1	22.24	4	0	5.2	17	7	3
Padilla, Juan	0	1	2.76	31	17	32.2	36	13	26
1 Palanski, Brett	1	3	15.00	7	0	15	32	7	4
1 Piechowski, Adam	3	2	3.22	27	2	36.1	41	12	32
2* Qualben, David	0	2	4.05	3	0	20	16	13	10
* Ramos, Luis	4	5	5.01	26	0	46.2	44	35	18
Renaud, Keith	0	0	8.31	14	0	17.1	27	13	11
* Riley, Rob	2	3	5.30	26	1	56	59	27	31
* Romanczuk, Mark	1	3	8.44	6	0	26.2	34	20	19
Valdez, Luis	0	6	5.72	12	0	39.1	50	23	33
Wasylak, David	1	0	3.60	10	1	15	18	8	16
Woodson, Alex	2	4	6.07	10	0	43	41	28	23

NEW JERSEY JACKALS

BATTERS	AVG	AB	R	H	2B	3B	HR	RBI	SB
1* Cabreja, Rafael, of	.308	13	4	4	0	0	0	2	0
Chiarappa, Christoph, c	.220	118	11	26	5	1	1	6	0
* Davis, Quentin, of	.344	122	25	42	8	3	1	16	11
* De Jesus, Michael, ss	.297	347	51	103	14	3	5	66	3
2* Edmondson, Jerod, of	.410	61	12	25	7	1	0	9	5
* Garcia, Chris, 1b	.318	22	3	7	1	0	0	1	0
Humphries, Justin, 1b	.333	15	2	5	2	0	0	3	0
* Kovatch, Billy, of	.247	227	22	56	8	2	0	23	8
Lauderdale, Matthew, c	.285	281	33	80	15	3	5	41	1
# Leslie, Myron, 1b	.272	316	71	86	10	3	18	75	8
* Perez, Timo, of	.338	80	13	27	5	1	0	17	5
* Rogowski, Ryan, of	.282	262	47	74	11	6	4	32	28
Sanders, Marcus, 2b	.296	365	74	108	16	5	1	36	23
Scanzano, Mike, 3b	.301	276	36	83	15	0	0	28	5
# Smithlin, Zach, of	.262	84	8	22	3	0	0	9	6
Stewart, Quinn, of	.259	266	41	69	16	4	9	44	11
Tejeda, Juan, 1b	.242	161	20	39	8	0	4	27	1

PITCHERS	W	L	ERA	G	SV	IP	H	BB	SO
2 Asselin, Nick	1	0	4.50	3	0	18	16	6	6
* Granitto, Giuseppe	2	4	5.28	20	0	73.1	79	33	51
Gunter, Kevin	8	1	4.29	34	0	50.1	46	28	41
Hicks, Romas	4	2	1.85	28	1	39	22	24	57
* Lorenston, Michael	0	0	5.40	7	0	10	12	2	2
Overbey, Seth	4	4	3.80	41	2	45	46	11	30
* Pavlik, Isaac	6	6	3.66	18	0	110.2	103	17	75
Pomerans, Stuart	5	6	6.50	16	0	73.1	90	31	48
1* Qualben, David	2	2	3.20	6	0	25.1	24	16	18
Serro, Ted	6	7	3.99	18	0	108.1	111	29	62
* Suchowiecki, Mark	0	1	5.24	32	0	44.2	51	19	43
* Thompson, Sean	1	2	7.33	6	0	23.1	30	12	13
* Tucker, Rusty	5	2	2.40	40	24	41.1	20	14	56
* Wideman, Aaron	10	1	2.51	18	0	114.2	90	18	81

QUEBEC CAPITALES

BATTERS	AVG	AB	R	H	2B	3B	HR	RBI	SB
* Boucher, Sebastien, of	.227	198	40	45	8	1	1	28	9
1 Brown, Morgan, ss	.385	13	1	5	2	0	0	5	0
Colafemina, Joshua, 2b	.245	314	55	77	2	1	0	27	33
D'Aoust, Patrick, c	.265	151	30	40	7	0	1	14	0
* Deschenes, Pat, 3b	.270	348	41	94	18	0	5	51	2
Gonzalez, Issael, of	.188	69	6	13	2	0	1	9	3
* LaForest, Pete, 1b-C	.277	336	69	93	22	1	24	82	5
Lantigua, Eddie, 1b	.261	295	39	77	9	0	11	49	1
* Lewis, Tony, of	.292	161	30	47	12	1	1	26	2
* Naccarata, Ivan, ss	.297	317	53	94	22	3	6	54	21
Nunez, Alex, of	.314	341	54	107	13	0	3	34	15
Scalabrini, Pat, 1b	.354	48	9	17	3	0	1	6	0
# Stevens, Greg, c	.230	100	14	23	2	0	4	16	0
* Tomlinson, Goef, of	.302	334	58	101	12	3	5	55	20
Toro, Douglas, of	.233	129	23	30	8	1	0	12	5

PITCHERS	W	L	ERA	G	SV	IP	H	BB	SO
Allen, Chris	5	8	3.71	16	0	94.2	95	26	41
* Barber, Rhett	1	2	6.75	5	0	24	26	7	12
Blanco, Juan	0	3	6.49	5	0	26.1	35	6	16
Castle, Cody	1	0	4.15	17	1	21.2	23	2	12
* Dumesnil, Brian	1	0	5.40	5	0	5	7	1	6
Freeman, Jesse	0	0	11.05	9	0	14.2	29	8	9
Gagne, Eric	6	6	4.65	17	0	102.2	108	34	64
Gelinas, Karl	4	2	4.43	13	0	61	71	19	51
Gregory, Sean	2	1	2.45	19	0	25.2	27	7	22
* Joyce, Mike	1	1	3.24	21	0	25	19	14	21
Klein, Joseph	1	0	10.13	1	0	5.1	5	5	0
* Matumoto, Jo	0	0	4.50	2	0	4	3	2	4
McDaid, Derek	4	0	1.51	34	6	41.2	28	8	33
2 Palanski, Brett	1	1	3.28	22	1	35.2	38	13	23
Purcell, Brad	0	1	6.14	1	0	7.1	11	1	2
Sausville, Dan	9	4	4.55	26	0	89	92	29	54
Schutt, Jason	4	5	3.43	37	10	39.1	46	12	28
Simard, Michel	9	6	4.16	20	0	125.1	136	25	81
Trias, Orlando	0	1	6.14	2	0	7.1	9	1	7

SUSSEX SKYHAWKS

BATTERS	AVG	AB	R	H	2B	3B	HR	RBI	SB
* Adamchick, David, c	.136	22	0	3	1	0	0	2	0
# Bardeguez, Alex, 3b	.250	20	4	5	1	0	0	2	0
Boelsen, Ryan, c	.224	49	2	11	1	0	0	3	0
Brown, Chris, 2b	.272	290	42	79	17	1	5	44	9
Crespi, Ryan, of	.250	348	63	87	15	6	4	30	23
Fuller, Jesse, ss	.222	18	4	4	1	0	0	2	0
Hunt, Jeremy, 3b	.267	311	49	83	17	0	10	40	0
Jova, Maikel, of	.315	378	56	119	26	1	5	74	2
2 Kelly, Chris, 3b	.275	40	3	11	3	0	0	4	0
Kmiecik, Kyle, ss	.215	172	13	37	5	0	0	11	3
Moreno, Jorge, of	.269	353	60	95	26	2	8	55	20
Pappas, Mark, ss	.232	233	30	54	15	1	2	28	0
* Perodin, Ron, of	.219	169	24	37	3	3	2	13	11
Serrano, Ray, c	.287	310	43	89	20	1	7	45	5
2# Soto, Luis, 1b	.230	113	11	26	5	0	3	13	4
* Urick, John, 1b	.273	297	39	81	18	0	8	43	3
* Weston, Matthew, 1b	.391	23	4	9	1	0	0	3	0

PITCHERS	W	L	ERA	G	SV	IP	H	BB	SO
* Campusano, Edward	1	1	5.33	21	0	27	34	20	32
Clements, Carter	6	4	3.05	18	1	112	116	35	57
* Douglas, James	1	2	6.53	18	0	30.1	42	15	21
Fox, Stephen	0	3	3.98	19	0	40.2	43	22	42
Knoff, Justin	5	5	3.24	14	0	86	82	27	52
Lane, Greg	1	2	3.48	21	2	33.2	40	11	22
* Lincoln, Roger	6	7	5.14	18	0	98	110	22	56
Nin, Sandy	3	7	2.61	34	10	48.1	44	13	56
Petrusek, Matt	0	5	7.79	16	3	17.1	33	8	13
Ruwe, Kyle	8	7	4.77	19	0	117	148	38	64
Schellinger, Mike	5	8	4.23	17	0	95.2	121	18	48
* Smith, Alex	0	1	4.40	22	1	45	54	21	28
Stanton, TJ	1	1	7.20	2	0	10	13	3	5
Stringer, Tim	1	3	3.50	7	0	36	35	19	30
Whalen, Stephen	0	0	12.71	2	0	5.2	9	4	4

WORCHESTER TORNADOES

BATTING	AVG	AB	R	H	2B	3B	HR	RBI	SB
Colabello, Chris, 3b	.302	321	48	97	22	0	9	55	3
Gilardo, Peter, c	.000	12	0	0	0	0	0	0	0
1 Keel, Heath, of	.243	185	22	45	7	1	3	18	6
LaHair, Jeff, 2b	.250	288	32	72	13	2	1	33	5
2* Lemon, Greg, ss	.282	39	8	11	2	1	0	0	0
Leonard, Michael, c	.242	124	7	30	5	0	1	12	1
MacMillan, Michael, 3b	.227	255	37	58	8	1	0	18	4
1 O'Malley, Mike, 3b	.233	30	3	7	2	0	0	1	0
Olson, Garrett, ss	.213	174	24	37	11	3	3	23	4
Pena, Alex, of	.297	101	13	30	6	1	5	21	0
Pena, Omar, ss	.304	115	15	35	6	0	1	14	3
* Pennell, Vinny, of	.249	293	43	73	14	7	3	29	11
Salotti, Nick, 1b	.315	324	43	102	24	0	4	42	1
Sosa, Carlos, of	.314	312	55	98	23	0	15	69	7
1# Soto, Luis, of	.190	21	1	4	2	0	0	0	0
Taylor, Lucas, of	.239	184	27	44	10	1	0	12	10
* Trezza, Alex, c	.298	248	35	74	14	1	8	33	1
Valera, Yohanny, c	.230	74	4	17	1	0	1	8	0

PITCHERS	W	L	ERA	G	SV	IP	H	BB	SO
* Anderson, Chris	2	2	6.40	35	0	45	54	29	32
Ayala, Albert	0	0	6.07	10	0	13.1	11	7	14
Cadoret, Steve	1	0	16.50	3	0	6	9	10	7
Conway, Nick	2	4	5.01	29	0	50.1	52	25	46
Farley, Chris	5	4	4.10	14	0	83.1	76	41	52
Frias, Jusef	4	2	4.60	24	0	94	90	50	65
* Lobban, Ryan	10	7	3.56	20	0	121.1	132	31	74
Mitchell, Ryan	1	0	4.71	5	0	21	26	5	15
Pellegrine, Dave	0	0	5.40	3	0	3.1	1	5	1
Pena, Alex	3	3	5.74	8	0	42.1	48	8	22
Pena, Eddie	2	4	3.47	30	0	46.2	50	16	22
Quinn, Ryan	0	3	5.03	5	0	19.2	21	21	15
Ramirez, Santiago	4	5	4.71	35	11	42	55	26	30
Short, Baron	1	1	4.50	6	0	30	25	7	27
Sullivan, Anthony	1	3	5.16	25	9	22.2	19	15	22
Thomas, Patrick	0	1	2.38	16	0	22.2	20	15	10
Weagle, Matt	1	4	6.82	7	0	31.2	44	12	16
* Zuercher, Zachary	7	5	3.53	18	0	102	96	29	69

CONTINENTAL LEAGUE

The Continental League's third season saw the league's most popular team win the title, but not without plenty of controversy.

The Alexandria Aces swept the Big Bend Cowboys at home in the best-of-three championship series to win the title in their first season in the league. How the league decided to play the championship series in Alexandria left another team unhappy.

The Aces were the only team in the six-team league to draw a significant number of fans—more than 45,000 of the roughly 63,000 fans who came to Continental League games came through the turnstiles in Alexandria. Because of that, the league decided to move the entire championship series to Alexandria for financial reasons, even though the top-seeded Bay Area Toros had won the other semifinal series. While Toros management agreed—they were guaranteed to lose money if they hosted the series—the players objected, so they were replaced by the Cowboys for the championship series, meaning that the Cowboys advanced to the championship by losing their semifinal series.

The playoff controversy wasn't the only problem the league faced in 2009. The league fielded two travel teams for the entire season. The South Louisiana Pipeliners were a typical travel team that struggled to a 15-41 record. But the Coastal Kingfish were one of the worst teams in the history of independent baseball. Coastal went 8-51 (.136) thanks in part to the league's decision that players could pay for a guaranteed spot on the roster. The team fielded a constantly rotating roster of 49 different position players and 45 different pitchers for its 59-game schedule.

FRONTIER LEAGUE

Expansion teams are supposed to take a couple of years to get their footing before reaching respectability. The Lake Erie Crushers accelerated that timetable dramatically.

In its debut season, Lake Erie had the second-best record during the regular season (only a half-game behind Kalamazoo) behind pitcher of

INDEPENDENT LEAGUES

the year Paul Fagan and followed it up by winning a pair of deciding Game Fives in the playoffs. In the first round against the Kings, Lake Erie scored four runs in the 10th inning of Game Five to advance. In the championship series, Lake Erie trailed by two in the deciding game before scoring seven runs in the fifth on their way to a 13-10 win.

Playoff MVP Andrew Davis (.324-1-6 in the playoffs), Eddie Tisdale (.389-1-8) and Tyler Johnson (.333-2-11) were the offensive stars in the playoffs for the Crushers, while Alberto Rolon (2-0, 1.32) led the way on the mound.

OVERALL STANDINGS

EAST	W	L	PCT	GB
Kalamazoo	58	38	.604	—
Lake Erie	57	38	.600	½
Florence	49	47	.510	9
Washington	43	53	.448	15
Traverse City	42	53	.442	15½
Midwest	42	54	.438	16

WEST	W	L	PCT	GB
River City	56	38	.596	—
Windy City	56	40	.583	1
Southern Illinois	56	40	.583	1
Rockford	44	50	.468	12
Gateway	40	54	.426	16
Evansville	28	66	.298	28

PLAYOFFS—Semifinals: River City defeated Windy City 3-0 and Lake Erie defeated Kalamazoo 3-2 in best-of-five series. **Finals:** Lake Erie defeated River City 3-2 in best-of-five series.

ATTENDANCE: Southern Illinois 209,477; Gateway 175,720; Traverse City 170,358; Lake Erie 153,654; Washington 133,881; Rockford 110,565; Evansville 104,829; Windy City 103,129; Florence 102,086; River City 89,776; Kalamazoo 70,499; Midwest 20,252.

MANAGERS: Evansville--Wayne Krenchicki; Florence--Toby Rumfield; Gateway--Phil Warren; Lake Erie--John Massarelli; Kalamazoo--Fran Riordan; Midwest--Eric Coleman; River City--Chad Parker; Rockford--Bob Koopman; Southern Illinois--Mike Pinto; Traverse City--Gregg Langbehn; Washington--Greg Jelks.

ALL-STAR TEAM: C—Charlie Lisk, Gateway; **1B**—Ernie Banks, Washington/River City; **2B**—Gilberto Mejia, Windy City; **SS**—Tony Roth, Southern Illinois; **3B**—Andrew Davis, Lake Erie **OFs**—Jason James, Rockford; Joey Metropoulos, Southern Illinois; Chad Maddox, River City; **DH**—Jacob Dempsey, Washington.

SP—Paul Fagan, Lake Erie. **RP**—Jason Lowey, River City.

Most Valuable Player: Joey Metropolous, Southern Illinois. **Pitcher of the Year:** Paul Fagan, Lake Erie. **Manager of the Year:** Chad Parker, River City.

INDIVIDUAL BATTING LEADERS

BATTER, TEAM	AVG	G	AB	R	H	HR	RBI
James, Jason, Rockford	.374	94	345	60	129	14	48
Short, Josh, Kalamazoo	.360	58	225	41	81	9	46
Banks, Ernie, River City	.353	77	289	65	102	24	75
Restko, J.T., Windy City	.334	92	344	51	115	18	76
Ramon, Amos, Kalamazoo	.327	85	278	49	91	8	59
Davis, Andrew, Lake Erie	.327	95	367	74	120	15	68
Mejia, Gilberto, Windy City	.324	95	377	83	122	9	55
Alonso, John, Traverse City	.319	73	270	43	86	15	52
Wehrle, Ryan, River City	.317	75	252	48	80	4	37
Metropolous, Joey, So. Illinois	.317	96	344	76	109	31	82

INDIVIDUAL PITCHING LEADERS

PITCHER, TEAM	W	L	ERA	IP	H	BB	SO
Wright, Kyle, Rockford	10	6	2.24	144	120	41	129
Jernstad, Matt, Windy City	7	4	2.31	78	55	23	97
Fagan, Paul, Lake Erie	14	3	2.70	140	114	33	83
Stout, Ross, Windy City	13	5	2.94	144	134	35	138
Lowey, Josh, River City	9	2	2.94	101	98	43	75
Brownell, John, Kalamazoo	11	5	3.48	134	118	46	106
Bird, Ryan, Southern Illinois	9	7	3.48	106	86	32	97
Augustine, Joe, Southern Illinois	7	5	3.50	111	110	43	84
Durand, Brett, Rockford	10	6	3.81	130	139	23	110
Bostelman, Brett, Traverse City	7	8	3.81	111	107	47	53

EVANSVILLE OTTERS

BATTERS	AVG	AB	R	H	2B	3B	HR	RBI	SB
Adamkiewicz, Felix, ss	.064	47	2	3	0	0	0	2	0
Alexander, Greg, of	.261	291	55	76	9	4	9	54	12
Blackwell, Eric, 3b	.250	164	24	41	8	0	5	21	2
Brown, Breland, of	.143	7	0	1	0	0	0	0	0
* Brown, Donald, of	.245	94	10	23	4	0	2	10	0
Brown, Javier, 2b	.296	243	35	72	14	0	2	19	6
Daleiden, Chad, ss	.108	37	4	4	2	0	0	1	0
Diamond, Tyler, 1b-C	.198	116	16	23	4	1	4	14	0
* Gilbert, Kenneth, of	.277	101	19	28	5	2	0	8	4
Gormon, Reece, c	.187	91	11	17	2	0	3	7	0
2 Hetherington, Luke, of	.241	137	25	33	9	0	4	20	4
* Howard, Josh, of	.254	248	30	63	4	3	1	23	4
Kampsen, Adam, 3b	.275	51	10	14	1	0	0	6	1
1* Koca, Dustin, of	.275	193	28	53	15	0	7	29	0
Liscinsky, Andre, ss	.251	231	21	58	5	2	2	30	3
* Mackey, Kevin, 1b	.245	155	18	38	6	2	2	18	1
# McCleary, Travis, 3b	.256	78	8	20	3	0	1	11	0
Meade, Francis, c	.296	280	52	83	14	0	16	58	1
* Pulley, Matthew, 3b	.254	138	18	35	5	2	0	16	1
1* Randall, Justin, 2b	.167	18	3	3	0	0	0	1	0
Rose, Marcus, 2b	.198	81	12	16	1	1	0	9	7
Satterwhite, Cameron, of	.315	111	10	35	7	3	0	15	0
* Schneider, Matt, ss	.234	94	9	22	1	0	1	13	0
Strack, Jeremy, of	.246	167	23	41	8	3	2	16	10

PITCHERS	W	L	ERA	G	SV	IP	H	BB	SO
Brock, Stephen	2	3	4.86	9	0	37	43	19	21
Cable, Jason	0	0	6.75	3	0	2.2	4	3	1
Cotto, Giovanni	0	0	10.38	3	0	4.1	9	3	4
Dahman, Kyle	1	4	8.15	10	0	38.2	51	20	36
Dill, Brandon	2	4	6.59	34	1	57.1	66	28	43
Ducey, John	3	11	5.48	18	0	110	130	39	73
Ford, Rashad	3	5	5.14	14	0	63	80	35	43
Kamppi, Kyle	0	0	5.19	6	0	8.2	9	5	1
* Mueller, Tom	0	0	7.20	7	0	5	8	4	4
Oates, Brian	0	4	11.78	5	0	18.1	27	19	14
Paxton, Ben	1	1	1.12	27	4	40.1	34	13	24
Phillips, Billy	0	2	12.27	2	0	7.1	16	2	6
Renfrow, Dustin	5	9	5.64	21	0	111.2	131	36	80
Smith, Justin	3	4	3.89	38	10	44	40	23	42
Sutton, Calen	0	2	8.10	11	0	23.1	40	8	8
1* Thompson, Sean	0	1	11.57	3	0	9.1	18	10	7
Tiegs, Jordan	0	2	8.00	5	0	18	23	8	11
* Tuomi, Kai	1	6	5.10	29	0	90	111	30	55
Utley, Nick	4	6	4.63	33	0	72	67	25	68
* Werner, Andrew	3	2	5.46	10	0	29.2	30	16	41
Ziegler, Beau	0	0	6.10	8	0	10.1	9	6	7

FLORENCE FREEDOM

BATTERS	AVG	AB	R	H	2B	3B	HR	RBI	SB
# Andrus, Erold, of	.302	348	56	105	20	3	9	48	15
* Baker, Jordan, 1b	.206	63	9	13	3	0	0	6	8
* Basham, Ryan, of	.313	377	61	118	25	0	16	64	5
Gil, Armando, 2b	.140	43	4	6	1	0	0	0	3
Goldberg, Zach, c	.189	74	3	14	2	0	0	1	0
* Grogan, Timothy, ss	.270	307	48	83	23	0	12	60	4
Hough, Brad, ss	.253	293	53	74	14	1	10	42	15
Johnson, Jay, of	.281	310	65	87	16	1	7	46	12
2* Koca, Dustin, of	.185	65	17	12	1	0	2	9	1
Magrass, Miguel, 1b	.150	20	1	3	2	0	0	1	0
* Miller, Jeff, 1b	.200	60	8	12	2	0	1	6	0
* Mottram, William, 2b	.281	370	73	104	15	4	23	79	30
Pickerell, Steven, c	.214	56	6	12	0	0	3	5	0
Pickett, Justin, c	.277	347	64	96	10	2	26	78	2
* Stiffler, Matt, of	.296	162	32	48	13	3	0	11	4
Underhill, Cory, of	.256	43	7	11	0	0	0	5	2
* Welch, John, 3b	.267	311	45	83	21	1	13	51	12
Williams, Dan, 3b	.500	2	3	1	0	0	0	0	0

PITCHERS	W	L	ERA	G	SV	IP	H	BB	SO
* Banks, Demetrius	7	4	3.53	44	0	63.2	41	41	77
Clark, Andy	3	4	5.20	27	0	90	111	25	62
Clark, David	0	1	11.05	5	0	7.1	10	9	6

	W	L	ERA	G	SV	IP	H	BB	SO
De La Rosa, Carlos *	1	0	5.56	14	0	22.2	29	10	13
Donato, Allan	0	2	4.91	5	0	18.1	20	13	13
Edwards, Jake 1	0	0	12.00	2	0	3	4	6	3
Hough, Brad	0	0	4.50	4	0	4	3	5	2
Hudnall, Jaeson	0	0	1.17	4	0	7.2	5	6	9
Melendez, Moises *	4	4	3.88	12	0	69.2	52	31	58
Miller, Jonathan	3	3	4.58	32	14	57	59	18	43
Neigebauer, Robert 2	0	1	9.64	2	0	4.2	9	5	4
Odquist, David *	0	0	6.55	7	0	11	13	8	7
Saul, Everett	12	7	5.23	23	0	130.2	138	49	105
Schlee, Billy	0	1	9.53	4	0	5.2	9	5	2
Schlenkerman, Todd	0	0	10.80	2	0	3.1	6	3	2
Shaffer, Nolan 1	1	1	5.18	18	0	41.2	42	24	35
Shivers, Ben 2	0	0	1.64	6	0	11	9	4	9
Short, Baron	1	2	9.20	5	0	14.2	13	9	13
Soriano, Julio	0	3	6.86	16	0	19.2	24	17	22
Stanley, Jimmy 1	0	1	3.50	18	3	18	15	10	15
Szkotak, Stephen	0	0	8.18	7	0	11	14	5	11
Tesseyman, John	1	0	2.61	28	0	31	25	10	18
Tiffany, Chuck *	5	2	4.23	8	0	38.1	32	21	32
Towns, Jordan	3	6	6.06	18	0	52	52	25	36
Vancil, Preston	6	4	3.26	11	0	66.1	42	44	61
Williams, Charles	2	1	8.00	23	0	27	35	16	14

GATEWAY GRIZZLIES

BATTERS	AVG	AB	R	H	2B	3B	HR	RBI	SB
Agreste, Joe, 1b *	.303	175	35	53	18	4	5	33	5
Cantu, Adrian, 2b *	.167	60	9	10	1	0	3	10	0
Douglas, Stephen, of 1*	.204	54	8	11	3	0	2	6	1
Draper, Breck, c	.253	150	25	38	9	1	7	27	5
Gordon, Casey, ss *	.000	11	0	0	0	0	0	0	0
Hale, Darrick, ss *	.154	26	0	4	1	0	0	2	0
Holdren, Stephen, of 1*	.318	233	61	74	19	1	17	42	2
Johnson, Brandon, ss	.281	210	50	59	10	0	14	46	17
Kerins, Alex, 2b	.269	208	24	56	12	1	6	26	1
Kotch, Kevin, c *	.077	52	8	4	0	0	1	3	1
Kubal, Alex, of	.083	12	2	1	0	0	0	2	1
Lape, Nathan, of	.217	60	13	13	5	0	4	11	0
Lisk, Charlie, c	.282	344	77	97	14	2	28	82	6
Matos, Wilson, 3b 2	.265	68	15	18	3	0	2	5	1
Maycock, Dan, dh #	.133	15	3	2	0	0	0	0	0
McClendon, Chris, 3b *	.190	21	4	4	1	0	0	2	0
Meade, Sonny, of	.067	15	1	1	0	0	0	0	0
Merrell, Cody, c	.056	18	4	1	1	0	0	2	1
Morrow, Danny, 3b	.241	108	14	26	9	0	2	19	2
Peters, Brandon, of #	.289	325	62	94	17	1	11	52	4
Quigley, Jon, c	.197	66	5	13	4	0	1	8	0
Rothford, Chad, 1b #	.255	220	32	56	10	0	14	41	1
Scaperotta, Joseph, of *	.291	333	63	97	15	1	22	62	5
Thoma, Brad, 2b	.236	72	9	17	4	2	2	8	0
Tountas, Peter, ss	.185	81	12	15	2	1	1	8	0
Ubbenga, Jon, ss	.125	16	1	2	1	0	0	0	0
West, Jareck, of	.254	276	60	70	18	4	7	40	21
White, Phillip, ss	.290	31	6	9	1	0	1	7	0

PITCHERS	W	L	ERA	G	SV	IP	H	BB	SO
Arneson, Jamie *	5	1	5.26	12	0	51.1	43	50	49
Boeschen, Joel *	2	6	5.68	30	10	69.2	70	40	84
Bowling, Adam	3	5	7.34	15	0	57.2	82	16	30
Brackman, Mark	6	10	4.93	20	0	127.2	148	38	112
Brennan, Collin	2	1	6.94	12	0	23.1	23	10	30
Castorri, Christian	3	2	7.01	8	0	43.2	59	17	30
Craft, Jordan 2	2	1	6.48	5	0	8.1	12	8	6
Draper, Breck	0	0	8.04	9	0	15.2	27	5	9
Dumont, Paige	5	5	5.75	13	0	81.1	111	24	51
Ellis, Shaun	1	0	11.37	8	0	6.1	4	11	12
Epperson, Chad	0	0	10.64	9	0	11	17	9	5
Gray, Zack	0	2	20.77	4	0	4.1	12	6	6
Hammon, Kevin	1	1	14.81	9	0	10.1	12	11	13
Kelly, Scott	1	1	6.85	30	0	47.1	57	29	65
Lilly, Justin 1	0	1	9.75	3	0	12	16	11	13
Maschino, John	2	2	6.87	12	1	18.1	25	8	21
Melek, Nathan	4	9	6.08	19	0	117	148	48	90
Revelette, Adam 1*	0	0	4.64	15	1	21.1	23	9	18
Ridener, Eric	1	2	8.28	23	2	29.1	35	25	39

	W	L	ERA	G	SV	IP	H	BB	SO
Seibert, Shaun	0	1	11.32	6	0	10.1	14	13	5
Shafer, Jake	0	0	14.73	3	0	3.2	6	4	4
Vesely, Tom	1	3	5.33	18	1	50.2	53	28	47
Wiman, Chris 2	1	1	3.55	8	3	12.2	14	5	15

KALMAZOO KINGS

BATTERS	AVG	AB	R	H	2B	3B	HR	RBI	SB
Anderson, Brandon, of #	.280	318	56	89	10	3	2	32	37
Billak, Scott, of 2	.134	67	14	9	1	0	1	6	4
Brown, Tim, 1b *	.249	293	50	73	17	0	12	55	1
Graves, Michael, c	.148	61	9	9	2	0	1	7	0
Grose, Jeff, of *	.294	109	20	32	4	0	1	16	5
Higgins, Kyle, ss	.235	349	55	82	16	2	8	36	20
Makonnen, Destan, 1b *	.272	158	28	43	9	1	12	37	0
Maloney, Matt, of	.333	48	5	16	3	2	1	11	0
Malvagna, Stephen, c	.091	11	2	1	0	0	0	3	1
Marquez, Bryan, 3b	.179	39	5	7	1	0	0	2	2
Moley, Randy, of	.077	13	0	1	0	0	0	1	2
Murphy, Brendan, of	.257	319	43	82	12	0	17	61	0
Ramon, Amos, 3b	.327	278	49	91	21	4	8	59	4
Ramos, Joseph, 2b	.315	365	76	115	19	1	12	62	31
Roblin, Brad, of	.250	4	0	1	0	0	0	0	0
Ruiz, Jett, c	.274	270	33	74	15	0	9	38	1
Short, Josh, of	.360	225	41	81	16	1	9	46	1
Stancil, Hans, 3b #	.160	50	5	8	4	0	0	4	5
Williams, Simon, of	.248	250	43	62	16	0	4	26	16

LAKE ERIE CRUSHERS

BATTERS	AVG	AB	R	H	2B	3B	HR	RBI	SB
Binkoski, Timothy, of *	.300	260	33	78	9	1	4	36	8
Bond, Wayne, of	.259	286	49	74	12	3	7	52	6
Cheshire, Levi, 2b-3B #	.190	21	5	4	0	0	0	0	0
Davis, Andrew, 3b #	.327	367	74	120	25	7	15	68	7
Gibson, Jesse, 2b	.169	65	16	11	1	0	0	2	8
Griffiths, Brad, c	.218	188	19	41	3	0	1	24	3
Gronkowski, Gordon, 1b	.305	311	62	95	19	2	19	79	4
Hash, Kylee, c #	.222	63	6	14	1	0	0	5	0
Hetherington, Luke, of 1	.281	185	44	52	6	1	8	26	8
Johnson, Tyler, of	.277	137	27	38	8	1	6	29	13
Maragas, Nick, c	.167	72	12	12	3	0	1	7	0
McIlvain, Scott, ss	.167	18	5	3	1	0	0	1	3
McWilliams, Arden, of	.257	288	51	74	7	3	12	52	10
Rivera, Jodam, ss #	.255	368	70	94	16	6	4	36	8
Saylor, Andrew, 2b	.302	381	70	115	26	2	10	62	3
Tisdale, Eddie, 1b *	.292	212	37	62	10	0	4	37	7

PITCHERS	W	L	ERA	G	SV	IP	H	BB	SO
Chambers, Brian	1	0	3.96	16	2	25	24	7	9
Charry, Jorge	0	5	6.62	9	0	35.1	35	20	28
Davidson, Brad *	1	1	5.84	12	0	24.2	23	6	19
DeFratus, Steven	0	0	11.12	4	0	5.2	10	1	3
DeLeon, Darwin	1	2	6.46	9	0	23.2	24	23	22
Fagan, Paul *	14	3	2.70	22	0	140	114	33	83
Faiola, Joshua	3	7	5.57	27	3	72.2	76	18	40
Gonell, Jacinto	3	4	4.63	36	11	44.2	42	32	44
Lysander, Brent	9	3	4.75	19	0	102.1	103	39	57
Mata, Cristobal	3	6	3.02	35	2	65.2	44	33	50
Morales, Ronnie *	2	0	2.43	23	1	29.2	21	12	30
Pacella, J.J.	3	2	2.63	29	9	41	26	32	54
Rigo, Chris	3	1	5.06	4	0	16	13	7	7
Rolon, Alberto	4	1	3.40	15	1	53	47	20	28
Skogley, Kevin *	3	2	4.63	10	0	58.1	59	20	44
Sprouse, Shannon	1	1	6.68	24	2	32.1	37	26	30
Tisone, Nick	2	0	5.63	4	0	8	10	5	3
Tucker, Cardoza	4	0	2.63	8	0	51.1	37	22	31
Vassella, Thomas *	0	0	7.71	2	0	7	9	7	4

MIDWEST SLIDERS

BATTERS	AVG	AB	R	H	2B	3B	HR	RBI	SB
Baker, Jimmy, 1b	.310	261	50	81	18	1	16	53	2
Barrone, Ben, c	.250	168	22	42	7	0	8	21	3
Bonner, Brian, ss	.263	266	36	70	16	2	2	33	2
Brodin, Joash, 1b #	.330	221	39	73	11	2	10	37	0
Castro, Jonathan, 2b-3B #	.300	10	2	3	0	0	0	1	1

INDEPENDENT LEAGUES

	AVG	AB	R	H	2B	3B	HR	RBI	SB
# De La Rosa, Maikel, 2b	.042	24	0	1	0	0	0	2	0
Deluca, Sam, 2b	.310	168	21	52	9	1	5	33	1
Flora, Stephen, c	.207	29	4	6	1	0	0	4	0
Gilliland, Eric, of	.000	17	0	0	0	0	0	0	0
Jones, Dennis, of	.150	20	3	3	0	0	0	0	1
# Jones, Jeremy, of	.245	143	18	35	13	0	0	20	5
# Kennedy, Ryan, 2b	.225	71	11	16	6	0	0	3	1
2 Knapp, Robbie, 3b	.287	282	39	81	13	0	9	56	1
Knoble, Jonnie, of	.220	259	37	57	11	5	3	36	22
Lombardi, Dominick, c	.343	35	5	12	4	1	0	4	0
Maines, Garrett, c	.185	54	4	10	2	1	0	2	0
* McCord, Clay, of	.299	187	33	56	9	1	0	24	9
Mena, Roberto, ss	.285	263	43	75	12	5	2	19	12
* Pace, Zack, of	.304	359	71	109	17	1	4	30	37
* Rosas, Ralph, 1b	.211	76	7	16	5	0	0	8	0
Rubin, Lee, c	.301	93	11	28	8	0	2	19	0
1 Zayas, Gil, 3b	.286	224	32	64	15	0	5	34	0

PITCHERS	W	L	ERA	G	SV	IP	H	BB	SO
Albury, James	6	2	2.40	11	0	63.2	48	31	51
Asjes, Arshwin	1	4	5.00	33	12	36	42	16	34
Brooks, Douglas	2	4	6.40	7	0	32.1	32	17	23
2 Dominick, Adam	3	0	6.29	9	0	24.1	29	7	26
Fischer, Jeffrey	5	5	4.46	17	0	72.2	81	42	56
* Gerard, Kevin	1	0	6.75	3	0	2.2	5	2	0
* Gilliland, Eric	0	1	5.60	28	1	35.1	30	20	38
Graham, Caleb	1	0	1.80	1	0	5	3	1	8
Haldis, Jonathan	3	3	4.14	17	0	37	31	15	28
2 Hayer, Kurt	0	0	2.45	3	0	3.2	4	3	1
* Horvath, Dan	0	0	9.38	11	0	24	31	15	15
Kafka, Nate	1	0	3.54	16	0	20.1	23	4	13
* Kearcher, Kyle	1	9	6.25	14	0	76.1	99	20	39
* Nyman, Chris	0	3	8.59	5	0	14.2	23	13	6
Oakes, Earl	3	1	5.52	37	7	45.2	46	26	56
Pannell, J.J.	0	0	7.13	14	0	17.2	21	18	13
Penn, Michael	7	5	4.57	16	0	100.1	104	26	76
Rollins, Christopher	0	1	11.81	5	0	10.2	18	9	8
2 Shaffer, Nolan	4	4	5.51	9	0	50.2	47	24	43
Van Es, Scott	1	1	4.68	5	0	25	23	13	22
Wink, Kyle	1	5	6.58	12	0	53.1	63	27	28
Zocchi, P.J.	2	4	4.95	22	1	56.1	63	20	41

RIVER CITY RASCALS

BATTERS	AVG	AB	R	H	2B	3B	HR	RBI	SB
Banda, Joshua, c	.303	33	6	10	1	0	2	5	0
2 Banks, Ernie, 1b	.376	85	13	32	6	0	5	20	0
Batten, Joseph, 2b	.305	318	60	97	21	2	4	43	11
Billick, Joseph, c	.316	95	12	30	6	0	2	14	0
1* Blackstock, Josh, 3b	.160	25	2	4	0	0	0	2	0
Chavarria, Joe, ss	.222	63	15	14	0	0	1	3	4
Colton, Chris, of	.249	334	67	83	8	0	18	69	34
1* Groth, Ryan, of	.270	100	16	27	4	1	3	14	6
Gutierrez, Jorge, ss	.266	308	36	82	17	0	7	42	9
Houin, Scott, of	.278	316	68	88	20	2	7	42	35
Howell, Cameron, c	.167	24	2	4	3	0	0	4	0
Maddox, Chadwick, of	.307	342	66	105	31	5	14	67	12
1* Paris, Pete, c	.359	39	4	14	3	0	0	9	1
1 Raniere, Chris, 2b	.400	15	2	6	1	0	0	2	1
Reilly, Andy, 3b	.240	96	13	23	3	1	1	11	4
Resnik, Bryan, 2b	.151	53	6	8	0	0	0	3	1
Reynolds, Kevin, of	.275	189	35	52	11	1	3	21	15
* Robinson, Scott, 1b	.309	278	55	86	17	1	13	57	10
Sawyer, Danny, c	.239	188	24	45	9	1	9	28	3
* Warters, Chris, 1b	.222	27	5	6	2	0	0	1	0
Washington, Johnny, 2b-SS	.118	17	1	2	1	0	0	3	1
Wehrle, Ryan, 3b	.317	252	48	80	16	0	4	37	12

PITCHERS	W	L	ERA	G	SV	IP	H	BB	SO
Alcorn, Michael	0	0	8.59	5	0	7.1	10	4	7
Ashner, Ryan	4	0	3.57	12	0	17.2	15	4	15
Cordell, Eric	1	1	6.75	11	0	10.2	15	0	6
Edwards, Jake	1	0	4.91	22	2	33	40	17	20
2 Flake, Stephen	5	2	5.22	8	0	39.2	37	25	39
* Graves, Brandon	1	0	1.29	3	0	7	4	2	8
Hart, Mike	1	1	5.68	24	0	31.2	27	21	28
Howard, Daniel	6	5	5.03	18	0	107.1	111	37	85

	W	L	ERA	G	SV	IP	H	BB	SO
1* Ingoglia, Chris	5	7	6.66	16	0	73	98	30	61
Kirbis, Anthony	0	0	13.50	4	0	5.1	11	3	1
* Laber, Jake	9	4	4.48	21	0	130.2	142	45	115
Lopez, Pablo	2	2	7.46	10	0	41	54	8	25
Lowey, Jason	3	2	3.43	41	24	42	38	19	56
Lowey, Josh	9	2	2.94	24	3	101	98	43	75
Marsala, Tony	2	4	3.83	40	2	49.1	53	14	44
* Monsma, Quinn	1	2	7.20	3	0	15	21	11	9
Musselwhite, Tyler	3	2	6.95	8	0	33.2	41	26	20
Rose, Josh	1	2	3.41	29	0	37	37	10	33
* Solich, Brent	1	1	1.25	19	1	21.2	18	7	18
Turmail, Scott	1	0	8.31	4	0	13	22	4	10

ROCKFORD RIVERHAWKS

BATTERS	AVG	AB	R	H	2B	3B	HR	RBI	SB
* Albano, Anthony, of	.222	27	4	6	3	0	1	4	0
# Bardeguez, Alex, 3b	.290	69	8	20	3	0	1	10	3
Blumenthal, Benjamin, c	.201	179	21	36	6	0	7	23	0
Brooks, Jonathan, ss	.221	276	45	61	14	3	7	27	30
* Brown, Javier, 2b	.143	21	4	3	0	0	0	0	1
* Cohen, Brandon, 1b	.310	155	20	48	11	1	7	30	0
* Cone, Aaron, 3b	.247	77	16	19	4	0	0	8	2
Dempsey, Joe, c	.111	18	2	2	1	0	0	1	0
Fields, Caleb, 3b	.299	231	46	69	16	2	7	37	17
* Goetz, Mike, of	.230	122	18	28	4	0	0	12	8
* James, Jason, of	.374	345	60	129	26	0	14	48	18
Kalina, Mike, of	.111	9	1	1	0	1	0	0	0
1 Knapp, Robbie, 3b	.267	75	12	20	8	0	4	9	0
* Martin, Todd, 1b	.343	108	26	37	9	1	5	27	0
* Mazurek, Matt, of	.243	235	38	57	5	0	5	27	19
McCoy, Ross, of	.283	286	42	81	18	0	5	44	8
Romans, Brandon, of	.206	34	8	7	4	0	0	2	0
* Sabates, Roberto, c	.264	273	30	72	13	1	5	47	1
Sanders, Doug, 2b	.289	315	47	91	17	1	4	49	12
* Simon, Scott, 1b	.194	31	5	6	1	0	0	4	0
Tansey, Mike, of	.250	28	4	7	1	0	0	3	0
Tejeda, Ferdin, dh	.000	2	0	0	0	0	0	0	0
Walker, Derrick, of	.297	148	28	44	8	1	5	25	8

PITCHERS	W	L	ERA	G	SV	IP	H	BB	SO
Cribby, Elliott	3	2	4.50	36	2	46	46	21	41
Durand, Brett	10	6	3.81	21	1	130	139	23	110
* Enderle, Matt	1	2	4.88	21	0	48	56	20	33
* Gomez, Fabian	4	4	5.77	17	0	43.2	47	20	34
Marcum, Kyffin	0	0	10.80	13	0	10	5	14	5
Mateo, Jose	1	1	6.25	17	0	31.2	36	15	22
* McKenzie, Marcus	0	2	6.30	26	0	30	34	24	25
Monti, Jason	7	7	4.25	19	0	101.2	111	38	81
Muller, John	2	3	2.60	23	12	27.2	21	13	30
1 Neigebauer, Robert	0	3	4.25	6	0	29.2	26	21	22
Pearson, Tyler	1	0	0.00	6	2	7.1	2	1	8
Rogers, Michael	1	5	8.05	9	0	34.2	44	26	27
Ryder, Mikael	0	1	4.50	1	0	8	7	1	7
* Sharp, Cody	0	0	9.95	9	0	6.1	11	6	3
Tejeda, Ferdin	1	3	9.69	10	1	13	19	10	11
Vasilyev, Viacheslav	0	1	6.06	14	1	16.1	16	7	21
Watson, Tanner	4	3	3.69	11	0	61	59	31	47
Wright, Kyle	10	6	2.24	20	0	144.1	120	41	129

SOUTHERN ILLINOIS MINERS

BATTERS	AVG	AB	R	H	2B	3B	HR	RBI	SB
Block, William, 2b	.254	134	26	34	6	0	1	17	3
Camp, Landon, 3b	.260	169	25	44	13	2	4	34	0
Crescenzi, Chris, c	.172	58	4	10	0	0	2	7	0
Goldsmith, Bradley, of	.237	38	5	9	1	2	0	8	1
* Hale, Adam, of	.243	148	32	36	9	1	10	33	4
* Higa, Mike, 2b	.182	66	10	12	0	1	0	12	2
2* Holdren, Stephen, of	.300	130	23	39	6	1	3	14	1
* Jackson, Travon, of	.222	144	22	32	4	2	0	13	8
* Koski, Kevin, of	.303	142	23	43	6	1	1	25	10
# Lopez, Pedro, ss	.225	71	9	16	2	1	0	6	3
Metropoulos, Joey, of	.317	344	76	109	22	0	31	82	1
Miller, Brad, 1b	.296	348	70	103	19	2	13	74	8
Milons, Jereme, of	.285	358	80	102	27	2	15	72	38
* Mochizuki, Gered, ss	.269	78	11	21	3	0	0	12	7

	AVG	AB	R	H	2B	3B	HR	RBI	SB
* Molina, Randy, 3b	.228	162	22	37	9	0	2	17	3
Netzel, Brad, ss	.286	42	5	12	2	1	0	7	1
2* Perry, Patrick, c	.132	38	5	5	1	0	0	3	0
2* Randall, Justin, of	.149	47	8	7	1	0	0	4	1
Roth, Tony, ss	.302	308	65	93	23	3	9	41	15
Stack-Babich, Tom, of	.222	45	5	10	1	0	3	7	0
# Sweet, Andrew, c	.247	271	41	67	10	0	2	33	4

PITCHERS	W	L	ERA	G	SV	IP	H	BB	SO
Augustine, Joe	7	5	3.50	19	0	110.2	110	43	84
Bird, Ryan	9	7	3.48	18	0	106	86	32	97
* Bradley, Anthony	3	2	8.06	8	0	25.2	36	16	13
Damchuk, Mike	5	4	2.63	29	6	41	38	17	39
Davis, Tyler	0	0	8.44	10	0	10.2	15	9	6
1* Dennehy, Timothy	0	1	7.71	3	0	4.2	6	6	2
Dooley, Kevin	0	0	6.75	15	1	13.1	21	7	11
Kussmaul, Ryan	4	1	2.57	9	0	35	24	10	41
* Lapinski, Cory	0	0	5.79	6	0	4.2	0	5	3
Maj, Jameson	0	0	4.91	6	0	7.1	11	4	8
McMurran, Jake	5	2	1.76	41	3	66.1	45	16	58
Miramontes, Derrick	0	0	6.43	7	0	7	6	3	4
Mitchell, Ryan	1	2	9.24	3	0	12.2	20	4	6
Moring, Justin	0	2	19.80	2	0	5	10	7	8
Phelps, Michael	2	1	4.76	19	5	22.2	23	14	20
2* Revelette, Adam	0	1	3.71	14	0	17	18	7	9
Rollin, Alex	1	1	9.67	15	0	22.1	31	12	23
Scarpetta, Brett	7	4	3.86	16	0	95.2	96	32	48
Spurgeon, Steve	1	1	4.22	7	0	21.1	22	9	17
Starnes, Nick	2	1	8.06	18	1	22.1	44	12	19
* Stewart, Chris	0	0	6.43	11	0	14	15	5	10
Stringer, David	0	0	5.40	7	0	6.2	9	7	6
1 Wiman, Chris	3	1	3.20	16	6	39.1	34	15	42
Zeffiro, Danny	6	4	4.69	20	0	109.1	120	30	57

TRAVERSE CITY BEACH BUMS

BATTERS	AVG	AB	R	H	2B	3B	HR	RBI	SB
Alcombrack, Robert, c	.246	183	24	45	10	1	10	27	1
Alonso, John, 1b	.319	270	43	86	18	2	15	52	3
Araiza, Jorge, 2b	.219	32	4	7	1	0	0	1	0
Barbaro, Andrew, c	.271	96	17	26	2	0	2	8	4
* Barbato, Al, 2b	.217	46	5	10	3	0	1	6	1
1 Billak, Scott, of	.222	81	8	18	4	1	0	9	4
* Campbell, Mike, of	.330	100	22	33	8	0	3	18	3
* D'Alfonso, Anthony, of	.223	94	6	21	4	0	1	12	0
2* Douglas, Stephen, of	.091	22	0	2	1	0	0	0	0
* Epping, Michael, of	.241	361	60	87	18	5	10	49	42
* Franco, Andrew, c	.347	121	19	42	5	0	4	22	1
* Frew, Bryan, 3b	.222	63	6	14	2	1	0	7	3
* Gerdes, Chase, of	.159	44	5	7	1	0	1	1	3
Guerrero, James, 2b	.265	102	23	27	6	0	0	3	10
Hoorelbeke, Sean, of	.202	84	7	17	3	1	0	8	3
Lapin, Brian, of	.288	271	32	78	11	4	3	35	2
Maunus, Kyle, 3b	.232	164	15	38	10	1	1	17	2
McArthur, Brandon, 3b	.190	79	12	15	2	0	2	8	1
Miller, Bradley, ss	.214	318	39	68	13	3	5	20	10
1* Perry, Patrick, c	.227	88	7	20	4	0	0	12	2
Stafford, Andrew, of	.217	157	8	34	7	0	0	9	3
2 Victor, Mike, 3b	.259	263	29	68	10	0	8	38	0
* Whiting, Corey, of	.196	92	20	18	4	0	0	7	11

PITCHERS	W	L	ERA	G	SV	IP	H	BB	SO
Bostelman, Brett	7	8	3.81	19	0	111	107	47	53
Dinelli, David	4	5	6.46	12	0	47.1	45	36	43
Ford, Greg	0	0	9.90	9	0	10	14	11	8
Hagen, B.J.	1	3	2.48	29	3	40	24	16	37
* Hurst, David	3	3	3.32	32	6	43.1	36	17	45
* Joy, Shawn	5	0	2.90	27	0	59	56	23	36
Kiley, Jason	6	10	5.26	20	0	114.2	134	32	57
Kruszka, Ryan	1	1	2.97	19	0	30.1	27	13	31
1 Kupillas, Christopher	0	1	3.86	9	0	14	13	9	15
* Locke, Jared	0	3	5.83	34	1	41.2	48	17	38
McEneaney, Peter	0	1	10.80	2	0	1.2	5	1	1
Nathanson, David	6	9	3.91	21	0	138	157	18	94
Pepper, Nick	0	0	2.08	11	0	13	12	3	9
Reese, Kevin	8	7	4.64	20	0	114.1	125	18	81
Roberts, Steve	1	1	3.38	3	0	16	18	4	11
Touchatt, Kyle	0	1	6.48	11	0	8.1	8	13	4
Williams, Jeff	0	0	0.78	23	13	23	14	6	23

WASHINGTON WILD THINGS

BATTERS	AVG	AB	R	H	2B	3B	HR	RBI	SB
Anderson, David, 1b	.400	5	1	2	0	0	1	1	0
1 Banks, Ernie, 1b	.343	204	52	70	9	2	19	55	1
2* Blackstock, Josh, 3b	.175	57	5	10	2	0	0	4	1
Busti, Shayne, ss	.077	13	1	1	0	0	0	0	0
* Davis, Matt, of	.091	11	0	1	0	0	0	2	0
# Demons, Chris, of	.180	50	10	9	2	0	4	10	6
# Dempsey, Jacob, of	.281	359	81	101	21	4	31	95	1
# Eachues, Josh, c	.100	10	1	1	0	0	0	0	0
Grandstrand, Brett, ss	.237	283	42	67	17	2	3	29	8
2* Groth, Ryan, of	.215	93	15	20	2	2	3	13	4
* Laurent, Phil, of	.335	179	37	60	17	3	8	40	1
Obal, Kyle, c	.182	11	1	2	0	0	0	1	0
Parker, Michael, 2b	.298	373	75	111	22	2	5	40	10
Psomas, Grant, 3b	.254	358	62	91	22	1	24	72	2
2 Raniere, Chris, 3b	.228	127	14	29	5	0	1	13	1
* Robbins, Alan, c	.236	242	25	57	7	3	4	25	3
Rochelle, Kris, c	.250	100	18	25	6	0	1	13	1
# Sidick, Chris, of	.240	338	61	81	9	7	9	38	24
Spiers, Joe, 2b	.276	29	2	8	3	0	0	3	2
* Sutton, Matt, of	.264	368	45	97	16	2	15	52	9

PITCHERS	W	L	ERA	G	SV	IP	H	BB	SO
Austin, Richard	1	1	6.00	5	0	9	6	6	7
Eachues, Josh	1	1	6.20	15	0	24.2	29	16	16
Edwards, Justin	4	5	5.40	43	3	60	58	23	70
* Evans, Eric	0	0	5.40	5	0	10	7	13	5
* Fuhrman, Aaron	1	2	7.66	11	0	22.1	29	16	13
Groh, Zach	6	5	4.17	19	0	110	101	40	95
Guinn, Aaron	0	0	4.91	9	0	11	10	8	7
Hedrick, Rob	0	0	5.59	12	0	19.1	25	12	18
1 Heimpel, Sean	1	5	9.25	10	0	36	45	22	19
2* Ingoglia, Chris	1	2	8.53	6	0	19	26	7	19
* Jenkins, A.J.	1	2	9.53	4	0	11.1	11	8	10
2 Kupillas, Christopher	1	0	5.50	12	1	18	18	13	16
Lucas, Michael	2	2	3.24	35	1	58.1	50	22	40
Maradeo, Matthew	1	0	8.22	12	0	15.1	13	12	12
* Martin, Kedrick	1	1	6.75	8	0	8	8	11	7
McCullough, Brian	6	5	5.03	15	0	77	81	40	42
Meyer, Keith	1	1	4.74	18	2	19	16	9	17
* Neitz, Jason	7	7	5.61	20	0	114	133	28	70
Peterson, Nicholas	1	4	5.31	35	10	39	36	29	57
Pitts, Zach	0	2	30.38	2	0	2.2	4	8	2
Schindling, Andy	4	3	4.80	11	0	60	60	36	29
* Snipp, Craig	3	4	5.45	15	0	76	79	30	57

WINDY CITY THUNDER BOLTS

BATTERS	AVG	AB	R	H	2B	3B	HR	RBI	SB
Aakhus, Zach, c	.286	105	13	30	8	1	2	14	6
Binick, Kraig, of	.323	99	16	32	2	0	0	14	17
Coe, Doug, c	.171	41	3	7	3	0	0	5	0
* Cook, Bryan, 1b	.295	302	45	89	19	0	16	53	8
Farrar, Tyler, of	.236	161	23	38	5	3	1	21	15
Gonzalez, Tony, of	.189	74	7	14	3	1	2	11	1
Hall, Nate, 3b	.291	223	28	65	16	0	2	31	5
Jordan, Dan, c	.226	168	23	38	10	0	9	25	2
* Lamont, Wade, 1b	.133	30	4	4	2	0	1	4	0
Martinez, Guillermo, ss	.304	293	59	89	16	3	3	31	28
1 Matos, Wilson, 3b	.203	128	22	26	5	0	6	11	1
# Mejia, Gilberto, 2b	.324	377	83	122	19	10	9	55	47
2* Paris, Pete, c	.286	105	16	30	6	0	2	24	0
* Perry, Robert, of	.397	209	47	83	14	4	6	38	20
Restko, J.T., 1b	.334	344	51	115	23	1	18	76	4
* Scarduzio, Vincent, of	.268	291	55	78	20	2	16	49	12
Spencer, Marcus, of	.063	16	4	1	0	0	1	2	4
* Sullivan, Mike, of	.360	50	11	18	7	0	2	16	2
Walcott, Damian, of	.178	129	23	23	2	3	2	30	5
2 Zayas, Gil, 3b	.246	65	5	16	3	0	1	6	2

PITCHERS	W	L	ERA	G	SV	IP	H	BB	SO
Axelrod, Dylan	3	1	2.21	22	6	61	51	14	60
2 Bryant, Carson	0	1	22.85	2	0	4.1	10	3	3
2* Dennehy, Timothy	0	0	5.94	16	0	16.2	17	10	14
1 Dominick, Adam	2	3	3.38	25	0	34.2	38	12	40

		W	L	ERA	G	SV	IP	H	BB	SO
1	Flake, Stephen	1	2	6.35	16	0	45.1	50	24	41
	Fry, Justin	0	1	11.12	4	0	5.2	11	3	5
	Garner, Brandon	3	4	8.63	30	1	48	56	39	38
	Hall, Nicholas	4	1	2.41	40	11	41	32	27	59
1	Hayer, Kurt	0	0	1.80	2	0	5	4	4	8
2	Heimpel, Sean	0	0	4.26	5	0	6.1	7	6	7
*	Jernstad, Matt	7	4	2.31	44	1	78	55	23	97
*	Kamine, Matt	0	0	4.15	8	0	13	15	9	11
*	Kelsey, Tyler	5	4	4.08	12	0	64	63	22	55
	Kloess, Brandon	0	1	4.82	3	0	9.1	6	6	10
*	Meinhold, Ricky	4	3	3.35	11	0	51	49	26	44
*	Pease, Dustin	12	7	3.85	30	0	133.1	127	38	106
	Petrick, Billy	1	0	2.13	11	3	12.2	13	3	15
*	Piccola, Zach	0	1	3.72	8	0	9.2	8	3	13
	Pryor, Ty	0	0	8.49	11	0	11.2	16	8	14
	Stout, Ross	13	5	2.94	21	0	143.2	134	35	138
	Thomsen, Mike	0	0	7.88	7	0	8	10	2	9
*	Zegarac, Shane	1	2	6.48	4	0	16.2	21	7	15

	AVG	G	AB	R	H	HR	RBI
Miller, Drew, Calgary	.364	75	275	71	100	11	56
Valentine, A.J., St. George	.359	82	312	72	112	17	82
Gailen, Blake, Chico	.355	74	279	43	99	5	38
Guerra, Nick, Orange County	.346	73	269	49	93	6	45
Gomes, Joey, Edmonton	.344	59	241	51	83	12	63

INDIVIDUAL PITCHING LEADERS

PITCHER, TEAM	W	L	ERA	IP	H	BB	SO
Ryder, Mikael, Chico	5	1	3.27	77	85	7	60
Gober, Dustin, Long Beach	5	0	3.38	61	63	18	49
Bello, Cibney, Tucson	5	2	3.39	66	61	35	38
Davis, Vince, Tucson	5	2	3.43	63	49	32	43
Honel, Kris, Long Beach	7	5	3.45	86	65	76	74
Diaz, Raymar, St. George	7	4	3.60	90	99	11	60
Fox, Ben, Long Beach	5	7	3.80	109	104	33	83
Durkin, Matt, Orange County	11	4	3.88	107	97	60	52
Sergent, Joe, Calgary	7	3	3.88	97	114	27	72
Lima, Jose, Edmonton	6	7	3.95	116	125	21	67

GOLDEN BASEBALL LEAGUE

FIRST HALF

NORTH	W	L	PCT	GB
Calgary Vipers	26	13	.667	—
Edmonton Capitals	23	18	.561	4
Chico Outlaws	19	19	.500	6½
Victoria Seals	17	24	.415	10

SOUTH	W	L	PCT	GB
St. George Roadrunners	25	15	.625	—
Long Beach Armada	20	18	.526	4
Orange County Flyers	17	20	.459	6½
Tucson Toros	17	21	.447	7
Yuma Scorpions	10	27	.270	13½

SECOND HALF

NORTH	W	L	PCT	GB
Calgary Vipers	23	14	.622	—
Edmonton Capitals	21	20	.512	4
Victoria Seals	15	26	.366	10
Chico Outlaws	14	25	.359	10

SOUTH	W	L	PCT	GB
Tucson Toros	21	14	.600	—
St. George Roadrunners	23	19	.548	1½
Long Beach Armada	20	18	.526	2½
Orange County Flyers	20	19	.513	3
Yuma Scorpions	19	20	.487	4

PLAYOFFS—Semifinals: Tucson defeated St. George 3-2 and Calgary defeated Edmonton 3-1 in best-of-five series. **Finals:** Calgary defeated Tucson 3-1 in best-of-five series.

MANAGERS: Calgary—Morgan Burkhart. Chico—Brent Bowers. Long Beach—Garry Templeton. Orange County—Phil Nevin. Tucson—Tim Johnson. St. George—Cory Snyder. Victoria—Darrell Evans. Yuma—Boris Villa.

ATTENDANCE: Tucson Toros 139,149; Victoria Seals 93,691; Chico Outlaws 89,276; Edmonton Capitals 84,813; Long Beach Armada 54,931; Calgary Vipers 54,910; St George Roadrunners 44,417; Yuma Scorpions 41,578; Orange County Flyers 28,344.

ALL-STAR TEAM: C—Jose Rodriguez, St. George; **1B**—A.J. Valentine, St. George; **2B**—Wilver Perez, Victoria; **3B**—Chad Ehrnsberger, Edmonton; **SS**—Nelson Castro, Calgary; **Util**—Damian Jackson, Orange County; **OFs**—Fehlandt Lentini, Calgary; Sergio Pedroza, Victoria; Colin Moro, Calgary; Drew Miller, Calgary; **DH**—Jim Rushford, Tucson. **SPs**—Matt Durkin, Orange County; Isaac Hess, Victoria; Lou Pote, Edmonton; Raymar Diaz, St. George; Kris Honel, Long Beach. **RPs**—Emiliano Fruto, Yuma; Reid Price, Tucson; Mac Suzuki, Calgary; Julio Castro, St. George; Justin Segal, Long Beach.

Most Valuable Player: Nelson Castro, Calgary. **Pitcher of the Year:** Matt Durkin, Orange County. **Manager of the Year:** Morgan Burkhart, Calgary.

INDIVIDUAL BATTING LEADERS

BATTER, TEAM	AVG	G	AB	R	H	HR	RBI
Castro, Nelson, Calgary	.410	69	300	80	123	11	81
Moro, Calvin, Calgary	.376	74	274	61	103	8	65
Lentini, Fehlandt, Calgary	.366	74	333	98	122	11	57
Yan, Ruddy, St. George	.364	54	217	46	79	1	33

CALGARY VIPERS

BATTERS	AVG	AB	R	H	2B	3B	HR	RBI	SB
Castro, Nelson	.410	300	80	123	18	10	11	81	33
Cosme, Caonabo	.387	124	28	48	6	1	7	28	0
Duncan, Carlos	.316	19	4	6	1	0	1	3	0
Gonzalez, Raul	.206	63	11	13	2	0	0	3	0
Guarno, Rick	.309	259	55	80	27	0	9	53	1
Jiannetti, Joe	.298	47	11	14	1	0	5	13	1
Johnston, Clint	.244	45	7	11	2	0	1	5	0
Lentini, Fehlandt	.366	333	98	122	33	3	11	57	33
Matsumoto, Yuki	.278	18	2	5	0	0	0	1	0
Mejia, Jorge	.341	299	64	102	17	3	6	57	24
Mermer, Terry	.256	39	4	10	5	0	1	8	0
Miller, Drew	.364	275	71	100	28	1	11	56	1
Morales, Buddy	.138	29	3	4	1	0	0	3	0
Moro, Colin	.376	274	61	103	17	2	8	65	5
Okano, Mark	.254	138	24	35	14	0	4	29	3
OKrane, Dillon	.275	138	17	38	9	1	2	16	0
Pedroza, Sergio	.367	49	11	18	4	0	5	19	1
Pellow, Kit	.319	69	8	22	3	0	1	18	0
Perez, Wilver	.526	19	5	10	3	0	1	8	0
Price, Kevin	.220	41	10	9	2	0	2	7	0
Recuenco, Rob	.167	36	8	6	3	0	0	5	2
Reyes, Ivan	.252	139	27	35	6	0	2	12	2

PITCHERS	W	L	ERA	G	SV	IP	H	BB	SO
Cillo, Cody	1	0	10.13	7	0	8.0	12	6	5
Demott, Andrew	3	2	7.98	30	1	44.0	74	21	17
Dessau, Erik	9	5	6.78	18	0	85.0	121	34	51
Greusel, Evan	6	3	6.81	15	0	76.2	122	12	60
Hess, Isaac	0	0	9.88	3	0	13.2	21	8	9
Hughes, Travis	3	0	4.50	15	0	22.0	27	17	20
Huizinga, Jon	1	1	5.59	21	5	19.1	34	7	20
James, Frank	0	1	4.50	10	0	8.0	8	10	6
Mahan, Dallas	3	4	4.17	22	0	60.1	78	26	55
Moser, Todd	2	0	4.64	20	0	21.1	28	10	16
Nagasaka, Hideki	3	0	7.44	13	0	52.0	73	21	21
Oliver, Brian	1	0	4.32	18	0	25.0	27	10	15
Rivard, Reggie	3	3	5.62	13	0	49.2	66	32	38
Sergent, Joe	7	3	3.88	17	0	97.1	114	27	72
Sikaras, Pete	2	1	5.79	10	0	9.1	15	3	10
Suzuki, Mac	4	3	2.01	35	12	49.1	34	13	76
Webb, Alan	0	1	6.88	17	0	17.0	20	16	18

CHICO OUTLAWS

BATTERS	AVG	AB	R	H	2B	3B	HR	RBI	SB
Alvarado, Andre	.148	27	3	4	0	0	0	3	2
Ash, Jonny	.313	256	38	80	11	0	4	35	6
Brown, Ryan	.239	184	24	44	6	0	3	16	1
Cronin, Shane	.287	164	15	47	5	0	5	23	0
Crosland, Jason	.231	208	27	48	13	0	6	30	7
DeJesus, Matt	.143	14	1	2	1	0	0	2	0
Farina, Pete	.281	32	8	9	0	0	1	5	0
Gailen, Blake	.355	279	43	99	15	3	5	38	18
Hale, Derrick	.233	60	9	14	2	1	2	6	2
Hutchins, Norm	.238	80	14	19	3	2	3	6	4

	AVG	AB	R	H	2B	3B	HR	RBI	SB
Janeway, Rich	.294	272	44	80	21	1	9	59	10
Luyben, Dan	.305	154	28	47	7	1	2	21	7
Mehl, Truan	.315	292	41	92	15	1	4	43	10
Reyes, Ivan	.342	38	4	13	1	0	0	3	1
Riley, Gabriel	.253	83	15	21	2	2	3	14	3
Silverman, Bryan	.237	177	33	42	7	1	4	24	3
Swinford, Dale	.285	246	52	70	5	1	0	22	27
Underkofler, BJ	.220	91	17	20	1	0	0	11	0

PITCHERS	W	L	ERA	G	SV	IP	H	BB	SO
Altman, Kevin	1	4	7.57	6	0	35.2	49	13	23
Alvarado, Andrew	0	4	7.05	21	0	46.0	63	13	43
Brandt, Donald	4	1	3.64	12	0	42.0	41	16	41
Cull, Blake	1	1	9.00	17	0	16.0	20	14	9
Dibernardo, Mark	1	2	3.51	11	0	33.1	39	9	22
Franklin, Wayne	3	4	4.33	11	0	62.1	66	32	38
Martin, Michael	2	5	6.06	10	0	55.0	84	25	28
Matumoto, Jo	4	8	5.09	17	0	99.0	119	31	88
Oster, Jesse	4	0	2.20	30	3	41.0	39	9	19
Redwine, Austin	0	0	0.00	7	1	12.2	5	4	7
Ryder, Mikael	5	1	3.27	20	2	77.0	85	7	60
Shockey, Ben	3	4	6.57	30	8	37.0	59	20	17
Tacker, Ryne	1	2	8.78	10	1	13.1	16	12	9
White, Evan	4	9	5.31	16	0	105.0	136	33	55

EDMONTON OUTLAWS

BATTERS	AVG	AB	R	H	2B	3B	HR	RBI	SB
Brinkley, Darryl	.297	344	68	102	23	0	13	82	26
Ceriani, Matt	.312	202	33	63	12	0	4	37	0
Cortes, Jorge	.316	282	70	89	21	4	10	51	23
Duncan, Carlos	.288	73	15	21	3	0	6	18	1
Ehrnsberger, Chad	.332	289	59	96	30	0	7	49	4
Gomes, Joey	.344	241	51	83	20	0	12	63	3
Graham, Mitch	.244	90	12	22	6	0	1	13	0
Harris, Gary	.222	72	11	16	0	1	3	9	3
Hornostaj, Aaron	.280	243	43	68	15	3	5	43	7
House, Kevin	.316	136	42	43	6	1	3	18	10
Hutchins, Norm	.324	185	24	60	13	1	3	23	4
Jiannetti, Joe	.285	130	24	37	11	0	6	21	4
Morban, Jose	.375	24	8	9	1	2	2	4	1
Nettles, Marcus	.276	185	35	51	9	4	0	16	23
Okano, Mark	.301	73	16	22	7	0	2	13	4
Pasieka, John	.176	85	7	15	3	0	0	2	0
Poulin, Max	.262	130	15	34	6	1	0	16	1
Young, Walter	.316	98	10	31	4	0	4	10	1

PITCHERS	W	L	ERA	G	SV	IP	H	BB	SO
Bevis, PJ	1	0	5.84	11	0	24.2	32	6	14
Caughey, Trevor	3	6	5.49	15	0	83.2	118	20	49
DePriest, Derrick	3	2	3.52	33	3	48.2	53	11	47
Dumont, Paige	3	1	6.05	8	0	22.1	32	7	15
Easton, Aaron	3	2	5.49	23	1	41.0	46	27	29
Honel, Kris	4	4	4.24	11	0	51.0	38	53	47
Johnson, Mike	2	4	8.34	9	0	45.1	71	17	24
Jordan, Justin	2	1	4.93	8	0	38.1	57	12	19
Ledbetter, Grant	0	1	6.75	5	0	8.0	13	4	5
Lima, Jose	1	2	6.48	5	0	33.1	41	11	16
Little, Chris	7	3	5.06	17	0	96.0	122	27	31
Moraga, David	1	2	8.38	6	0	19.1	35	6	6
Pearson, Jason	1	4	2.98	34	14	39.1	43	13	36
Pote, Lou	9	3	3.98	18	0	108.2	119	51	87
Privett, Todd	4	2	3.33	32	1	51.1	50	20	52

LONG BEACH ARMADA

BATTERS	AVG	AB	R	H	2B	3B	HR	RBI	SB
Bouchie, Andy	.290	214	33	62	15	3	7	42	1
Bramasco, Omar	.319	301	51	96	26	4	5	52	2
Calzado, Napoleon	.285	151	17	43	8	1	0	17	5
Edgecombe, Matt	.303	261	30	79	13	1	2	39	2
Garrison, Casey	.258	155	16	40	7	1	3	24	0
Hirsh, Matt	.125	24	3	3	0	0	1	1	0
Howard, Brandon	.290	162	26	47	7	1	1	18	10
Jones, Daryl	.238	244	39	58	14	2	4	23	3
Kaplan, Jonny	.282	209	32	59	13	4	4	29	12
Luyben, Dan	.197	76	10	15	3	0	0	5	2

	AVG	AB	R	H	2B	3B	HR	RBI	SB
Miller, Chad	.259	108	14	28	6	0	4	20	0
Moss, Steve	.304	112	22	34	5	0	2	13	4
Ramirez, David	.265	68	11	18	6	0	0	11	1
Shah, Asif	.345	58	7	20	3	0	1	7	1
Sherrill, J.J.	.373	102	21	38	10	0	1	18	5
Womack, Josh	.277	267	47	74	12	5	3	29	24
Young, Steve	.254	142	23	36	4	1	0	14	7

PITCHERS	W	L	ERA	G	SV	IP	H	BB	SO
Arneson, Jamie	0	1	8.03	3	0	12.1	13	15	14
Baran, Chase	0	0	9.64	6	0	9.1	18	4	8
Beal, Zach	1	1	6.75	4	0	17.1	24	9	10
Birosik, Dustin	0	0	5.63	8	0	8.0	11	4	4
Buller, Sean	0	1	2.84	16	3	19.0	15	5	18
Fox, Ben	5	7	3.80	17	1	109.0	104	33	83
Gober, Dustin	5	0	3.38	14	0	61.1	63	18	49
Honel, Kris	3	1	2.31	6	0	35.0	27	23	27
Irabu, Hideki	5	3	3.58	10	0	65.1	62	19	66
Jimenez, Juan	1	1	7.36	7	0	7.1	11	3	4
Jones, Rusty	2	3	3.46	26	4	39.0	31	10	38
Lima, Jose	5	5	2.93	11	0	83.0	84	10	51
Lonergan, Scott	5	6	5.95	15	0	72.2	99	22	47
Misawa, Koichi	2	3	4.36	27	10	31.0	33	5	36
Ramsey, Keith	2	3	6.08	5	0	23.2	42	6	11
Segal, Justin	2	1	1.23	31	2	44.0	32	7	27
Tacker, Ryne	0	0	3.31	19	5	16.1	9	20	18
Watson, Scott	2	0	3.22	15	0	22.1	28	8	12

ORANGE COUNTY FLYERS

BATTERS	AVG	AB	R	H	2B	3B	HR	RBI	SB
Bacani, David	.319	94	15	30	10	0	0	8	5
Becktel, Travis	.307	261	43	80	15	3	2	28	22
Benavidez, Julian	.310	281	45	87	15	1	9	38	1
Boggs, Scott	.285	200	39	57	6	1	0	25	11
Buschini, Shane	.209	43	8	9	2	0	2	4	4
Fick, Robert	.299	231	27	69	16	1	5	48	1
Goethals, Jim	.176	91	10	16	2	0	3	11	1
Guerra, Nick	.346	269	49	93	15	1	6	45	5
Jackson, Damian	.339	271	65	92	26	0	4	37	17
Johnson, Ben	.239	46	7	11	4	2	1	6	0
Keene, Willie	.111	27	1	3	0	0	1	3	0
LoNigro, Frank	.221	86	6	19	4	0	1	10	0
Morrow, Danny	.260	50	7	13	2	0	1	5	1
Pacheco, Fernando	.216	88	8	19	6	0	1	7	1
Perren, Derrek	.348	69	13	24	4	0	1	9	0
Rohan, Jimmy	.324	210	37	68	12	0	1	29	2
Senreiso, Juan	.284	134	24	38	7	0	3	23	11
Spiezio, Scott	.217	69	9	15	1	0	3	10	0

PITCHERS	W	L	ERA	G	SV	IP	H	BB	SO
Altman, Kevin	2	4	3.68	13	0	51.1	53	31	25
Ayala, Manny	2	5	6.16	10	0	49.2	61	35	30
Carrasco, Armando	1	1	6.82	25	1	30.1	41	27	29
Cosgrove, Mike	1	2	8.74	3	0	11.1	22	7	8
Cross, David	1	3	7.39	10	0	31.2	47	16	18
Durkin, Matt	11	4	3.88	18	0	106.2	97	60	52
Grady, Josh	0	0	11.57	2	0	7.0	11	8	3
Harris, Bryan	1	3	4.97	30	12	29.0	30	10	28
Johnson, Adam	2	5	8.21	15	0	49.1	68	24	26
Koons, Mike	2	2	3.03	29	0	38.2	27	15	35
Lawrence, Brian	1	0	0.00	1	0	7.0	1	1	7
Lorraine, Andrew	0	1	4.50	4	0	24.0	35	10	10
Rouwenhorst, Jonathan	0	1	3.17	34	0	34.0	34	12	28
Simpson, Andre	1	3	3.08	35	3	38.0	33	19	50
Smith, Jesse	10	5	4.44	17	0	99.1	109	38	74
Tucker, Cordosa	0	1	5.27	3	0	13.2	14	12	13

ST. GEORGE ROADRUNNERS

BATTERS	AVG	AB	R	H	2B	3B	HR	RBI	SB
Almario, Yosvany	.311	293	64	91	23	1	8	58	15
Calderon, Henry	.317	278	41	88	14	0	4	41	3
Dixon, DJ	.273	99	12	27	8	0	0	5	2
Gomez, Alexis	.340	53	15	18	1	0	6	20	8
Harris, Gary	.282	131	20	37	7	2	2	14	2
Leavitt, Chase	.310	87	13	27	4	1	1	17	2

INDEPENDENT LEAGUES

	AVG	AB	R	H	2B	3B	HR	RBI	SB
Netzel, Brad	.180	61	4	11	1	1	0	6	1
Nowlin, Cody	.302	202	33	61	12	2	5	31	3
Pringle, Eric	.193	150	27	29	7	0	1	15	6
Rodriguez, Jose	.333	249	49	83	25	2	9	65	1
Rodriguez, Liu	.185	27	7	5	0	0	0	2	0
Sanchez, Angel	.277	213	51	59	16	0	11	39	3
Serrano, Juan	.290	107	18	31	8	0	2	16	2
Stevenson, Ryan	.311	299	71	93	20	4	2	34	7
Valentine, AJ	.359	312	72	112	22	2	17	82	7
Yan, Ruddy	.364	217	46	79	10	0	1	33	25

PITCHERS	W	L	ERA	G	SV	IP	H	BB	SO
Abbott, Justin	2	5	6.40	18	0	57.2	88	25	35
Brito, Eude	4	1	3.74	25	0	53.0	61	16	31
Castro, Julio	2	0	1.45	32	9	37.1	20	11	41
Darensbourg, Vic	3	2	4.45	22	0	28.1	33	5	17
Diaz, Raymar	7	4	3.60	20	1	90.0	99	11	60
Fortunato, Bartolome	2	1	2.63	24	12	24.0	18	6	33
Gonzalez, Luis	6	5	4.86	13	0	76.0	100	21	50
Mansfield, Monte	1	2	11.42	16	0	34.2	60	20	27
Martin, Michael	2	1	2.74	6	0	23.0	22	9	6
Nelson, Mac	4	1	8.39	10	0	53.2	78	20	39
Seccombe, David	7	6	5.08	16	0	95.2	121	29	49
Van Slyke, Eric	7	6	5.42	15	0	98.0	132	38	76
Webb, Alan	0	0	8.56	9	0	13.2	17	13	12

TUCSON TOROS

BATTERS	AVG	AB	R	H	2B	3B	HR	RBI	SB
Adams, Skip	.305	302	72	92	19	5	10	50	12
Apodaca, Luis	.290	183	28	53	8	2	0	23	0
Garcia, Lino	.314	264	50	83	23	0	5	49	22
Gonzalez, Franklin	.196	51	11	10	2	1	0	4	2
Marshall, Andre	.308	273	54	84	17	5	9	42	8
Miaso, Curt	.247	215	29	53	11	3	1	24	3
Parzyk, Dylan	.268	112	16	30	6	0	3	9	0
Poole, Lyndon	.362	69	15	25	3	0	6	11	0
Priddy, Ryan	.321	212	40	68	16	3	3	27	4
Rushford, Jim	.333	291	35	97	18	0	5	66	2
Santana, Mayobanex	.284	250	27	71	11	0	1	30	2
Spivey, Junior	.366	112	28	41	8	1	3	22	5
Yount, Dustin	.310	287	56	89	19	0	11	58	1

PITCHERS	W	L	ERA	G	SV	IP	H	BB	SO
Barcelo, Lorenzo	8	5	4.20	16	0	109.1	122	7	96
Bello, Cibney	5	2	3.39	18	0	66.1	61	35	38
Daly, Brian	1	3	7.16	21	2	27.2	40	16	9
Davis, Vince	5	2	3.43	11	0	63.0	49	32	43
Garcia, Rene	0	2	4.40	8	1	14.1	14	6	16
Greenwalt, Danny	1	1	4.63	11	0	23.1	35	16	18
Hanna, Jason	1	1	7.38	22	0	22.0	28	8	14
Hartmann, Pete	2	2	4.80	5	0	30.0	38	5	14
Jacome, Jason	5	3	4.72	13	0	68.2	83	18	39
Knox, Dan	3	2	6.61	15	0	62.2	88	16	47
Luera, Chris	0	2	7.02	12	0	16.2	21	7	14
McCune, Matt	0	0	4.09	5	0	11.0	11	7	6
Muir, Jordan	1	4	4.95	22	1	36.1	36	9	30
Nordman, Toby	2	1	3.64	17	0	34.2	41	11	17
Price, Reid	4	1	1.51	29	11	35.2	21	10	29
Rosen, Mark	0	2	5.06	6	0	5.1	4	4	2
Wilhelmson, Tom	0	0	6.17	11	2	11.2	15	4	13

VICTORIA SEALS

BATTERS	AVG	AB	R	H	2B	3B	HR	RBI	SB
Arhart, Joshua	.325	246	45	80	22	0	11	52	0
Davidson, Trevor	.217	46	8	10	3	0	0	2	0
Duncan, Carlos	.289	142	33	41	6	3	6	17	0
Flowers, Brett	.302	291	41	88	19	0	6	49	5
Hill, Jamar	.289	284	64	82	15	1	19	64	8
Kavanaugh, Matt	.239	184	27	44	10	1	1	15	2
Krause, Billy	.169	65	11	11	3	0	0	8	4
LeVier, Bret	.230	261	37	60	15	0	4	33	3
Mermer, Terry	.244	90	9	22	3	0	6	19	2
Miyoshi, Takashi	.100	20	0	2	0	0	0	0	0
Montero, Pedro	.182	99	10	18	4	0	0	2	1
Nichols, Kyle	.224	58	4	13	0	0	1	5	0
Pedroza, Sergio	.325	255	51	83	17	1	15	62	11

	AVG	AB	R	H	2B	3B	HR	RBI	SB
Perez, Wilver	.318	296	74	94	25	2	9	39	24
Riley, Gabriel	.262	103	20	27	7	2	2	16	3
Rios, Brian	.319	248	37	79	19	0	6	37	1
VanRossum, Chris	.277	177	24	49	12	1	0	17	4

PITCHERS	W	L	ERA	G	SV	IP	H	BB	SO
Baeza, Eduardo	5	9	6.48	22	0	93.0	116	35	46
Bibens-Dirkx, Austin	2	2	3.70	8	0	48.2	50	13	54
Bodishbaugh, Chris	4	1	5.91	24	2	77.2	102	38	60
Campbell, Graham	1	1	7.36	31	0	47.2	63	21	42
Garcia, James	3	5	8.25	9	0	52.1	73	37	29
Garcia, Javier	3	6	4.63	25	9	35.0	30	17	35
Hess, Isaac	9	2	3.86	16	0	98.0	84	38	90
Karp, Josh	0	1	19.29	2	0	7.0	20	2	5
Katz, Ethan	1	3	6.75	27	0	41.1	51	21	43
Pluta, Anthony	0	3	7.59	8	0	10.2	15	17	10
Reeves, Mike	0	3	10.66	9	1	12.2	16	12	9
Ruvalcaba, Eziequiel	0	1	10.36	16	0	24.1	40	27	20
Sobkow, Phil	0	0	5.24	13	0	22.1	27	11	16
Sotolongo, Roberto	2	1	2.68	10	0	43.2	39	15	28
Trolia, Aaron	1	5	6.05	7	0	41.2	52	20	41
Wade, Travis	1	6	5.83	14	0	46.1	68	19	28

YUMA SCORPIONS

BATTERS	AVG	AB	R	H	2B	3B	HR	RBI	SB
Arroyo, Carlos	.316	231	32	73	12	0	4	27	8
Avila, Diover	.279	269	37	75	11	2	4	21	10
Balcazar, Carlos	.264	121	10	32	5	0	1	16	0
Castro, Ismael	.317	278	37	88	20	0	6	38	10
Del Rio, Cesar	.213	47	6	10	1	0	2	8	0
Gomez, Adolfo	.281	285	33	80	10	0	0	26	3
Hernandez, William	.192	125	12	24	4	1	1	13	1
Lozada, Jonathan	.253	182	24	46	8	1	0	16	2
Mosquera, Jose	.224	67	11	15	1	1	0	3	0
Pupo, Carlos	.210	162	22	34	10	0	5	19	1
Rivadeneira, Deivis	.273	227	46	62	6	0	2	15	5
Rodriguez, Reynaldo	.335	284	44	95	13	6	6	48	18
Villalobos, Carlos	.327	248	46	81	21	0	9	38	2

PITCHERS	W	L	ERA	G	SV	IP	H	BB	SO
Castro, Dorian	4	3	4.04	36	1	49.0	52	21	44
Correal, Reynaldo	1	6	8.64	18	0	66.2	89	52	40
Fruto, Emiliano	0	4	3.35	35	21	37.2	29	20	54
Ladeuth, Carlos	4	4	4.88	13	0	59.0	66	26	48
Mendoza, Cristian	3	4	5.45	31	1	36.1	38	15	34
Noel, Wilton	0	1	8.02	14	0	33.2	52	31	21
Ortiz, Javier	7	3	4.32	14	0	89.2	93	35	56
Ramirez, Ronald	2	7	5.80	17	0	71.1	97	40	42
Rodriguez, Jorge	0	0	6.86	11	0	19.2	25	16	13
Rojano, Rafael	1	2	11.12	18	0	34.0	42	29	19
Salazar, Yesid	6	5	6.11	17	0	73.2	89	30	63
Santiago, Julio	1	7	7.58	11	0	46.1	64	24	37
Sheridan, Eric	0	1	6.53	8	0	20.2	31	10	12

NORTHERN LEAGUE

	W	L	PCT	GB
Gary	57	39	.594	—
Winnipeg	55	41	.573	2
Fargo-Moorhead	53	42	.558	3½
Kansas City	46	50	.479	11
Schaumburg	43	53	.448	14
Joliet	33	62	.347	23½

PLAYOFFS—Semifinals: Fargo-Moorhead defeated Winnipeg 3-2 and Gary defeated Kansas City 3-2 in best-of-five series. **Finals:** Fargo-Moorhead defeated Gary 3-1 in best-of-5 series.

ATTENDANCE: Winnipeg 278,099; Kansas City 245,625; Schaumburg 202,112; Fargo-Moorhead 181,872; Gary 166,334; Joliet 146,258.

MANAGERS: Fargo-Moorhead—Doug Simunic; Gary Southshore—Greg Tagert; Joliet—Wally Backman; Kansas City—Andy McCauley; Schaumburg—Michael Busch; Winnipeg—Rick Forney.

ALL-STAR TEAM: C—Alan Rick, Fargo-Moorhead; **1B**—Freddie Thon, Joliet; **2B**—Josh Asanovich, Winnipeg; **3B**—Jeremiah Piepkorn, Fargo-Moorhead; **SS**—Zach Penprase, Fargo-Moorhead; **OF**—Nic Jackson, Fargo-Moorhead; Mike Coles, Fargo-Moorhead; Aharon Eggleston, Kansas

Fargo-Moorhead; Mike Coles, Fargo-Moorhead; Aharon Eggleston, Kansas City; **DH**—Juan Diaz, Winnipeg.
RHP—Ace Walker, Winnipeg; **LHP**—Tony Cogan, Gary SouthShore.
Player of the Year: Nic Jackson, OF, Fargo-Moorhead. **Pitcher of the Year:** Ace Walker, Winnipeg. **Manager of the Year:** Greg Tagert, Gary.

INDIVIDUAL BATTING LEADERS

BATTER, CLUB	AVG	G	AB	R	H	HR	RBI
Piepkorn, Jeremiah, F-M	.339	92	363	74	123	19	73
Coles, Mike, Fargo-Moorhead	.328	88	369	77	121	4	41
Brown, Dee, Winnipeg	.322	94	360	49	116	12	53
Harrison, Vince, Winnipeg	.322	91	339	54	109	11	45
Eggleston, Aharon, Kansas City	.318	90	387	74	123	4	44
Diaz, Juan, Winnipeg	.317	95	356	60	113	29	90
Brown, Neb, Kansas City	.313	67	227	48	71	9	37
Jackson, Nic, Fargo-Moorhead	.310	95	384	76	119	17	97
Jose, Felix, Schaumburg	.306	83	281	33	86	7	39
Thon, Freddy, Joliet	.302	95	384	40	116	11	63

INDIVIDUAL PITCHING LEADERS

PITCHER, CLUB	W	L	ERA	IP	H	BB	SO
Villarreal, Luis, Kansas City	5	3	3.07	97	87	40	87
Walker, Andrew, Winnipeg	12	6	3.32	149	156	29	77
Bay, Bear, Winnipeg	8	3	3.54	130	129	24	79
Cogan, Tony, Gary	8	7	3.60	150	134	37	105
Fogelson, Scott, Fargo-Moorhead	3	2	3.66	79	77	42	61
Jones, Christopher, Gary	6	3	3.75	84	80	25	53
McAllister, Cody, Kansas City	8	4	4.43	87	82	42	77
Knippschild, Ryan, Kansas City	4	8	4.44	126	130	41	103
Cruse, Andrew, Winnipeg	5	5	4.58	114	119	46	74
Fellman, Nick, Fargo-Moorhead	6	5	4.58	98	105	34	51

FARGO-MOORHEAD REDHAWKS

	BATTERS	AVG	AB	R	H	2B	3B	HR	RBI	SB
2	Coles, Mike, of	.330	367	77	121	28	2	4	41	27
	Cota, Carlo, 2b	.257	342	59	88	22	1	10	57	7
	DeCaster, Yurendell, 3b	.344	157	36	54	14	0	13	43	9
	Jackson, Nic, of	.310	384	76	119	26	0	17	97	26
	Johnson, Kyle, c	.241	29	3	7	1	0	0	1	0
*	Justice, Justin, of	.277	296	52	82	18	8	13	51	11
*	Koerber, Scott, 1b	.200	15	2	3	0	0	0	0	0
#	McDonald, Donzell, of	.327	55	12	18	2	0	0	8	7
	Penprase, Zach, ss	.300	373	100	112	24	4	6	46	45
	Piepkorn, Jeremiah, 3b	.339	363	74	123	20	2	19	73	8
*	Rick, Alan, c	.262	298	50	78	18	1	18	65	2
	Salazar, Ruben, 1b	.299	144	21	43	8	0	0	24	0
*	Simon, Randall, 1b	.281	303	42	85	11	1	13	51	4
	Stevens, Jeff, c	.202	84	5	17	5	0	0	14	1
	Zimmerman, Kole, c	.223	94	8	21	6	0	0	8	5

	PITCHERS	W	L	ERA	G	SV	IP	H	BB	SO
	Bakker, Garry	7	7	6.26	19	0	106.1	119	57	73
*	Coffman, Broc	9	6	5.16	17	0	90.2	104	45	42
	Fellman, Nick	6	5	4.58	24	0	98.1	105	34	51
	Finocchi, Mike	0	2	3.29	20	0	27.1	24	18	15
*	Fogelson, Scott	3	2	3.66	15	0	78.2	77	42	61
1	Giles, Joshua	1	0	5.02	9	0	14.1	10	13	16
*	Hauer, Jeremy	1	2	1.64	14	0	22	12	10	19
*	Ibanez, Yosandy	4	3	3.42	25	3	52.2	51	14	49
*	Icenogle, Jeffrey	3	2	5.23	7	0	43	40	22	38
*	Koerber, Scott	2	1	5.12	22	3	19.1	24	12	24
	Lavigne, Tim	1	1	1.13	7	3	8	9	3	7
1	Moore, Michael	0	0	6.48	5	0	8.1	7	7	2
	Mossey, Matt	4	3	5.40	32	1	86.2	94	40	48
	Quezada, Elvys	4	2	3.79	25	2	35.2	37	15	28
*	Rowe, Adam	1	0	5.54	20	1	13	11	8	4
	Stanton, T.J.	4	0	2.25	32	9	44	37	20	42
*	Tollefson, Adam	1	0	5.19	15	0	17.1	17	7	10
	Weber, Zachary	0	0	12.00	5	0	6	7	3	1
	Weitzman, Billy	2	3	5.55	13	0	48.2	46	29	29

GARY SOUTHSHORE RAILCATS

BATTERS	AVG	AB	R	H	2B	3B	HR	RBI	SB
Bartolucci, Paul, 2b	.294	17	3	5	1	0	0	0	0
Beachum, Jeffrey, 1b	.309	223	36	69	14	0	2	31	4
Carrara, Christopher, 3b	.327	98	13	32	3	3	0	15	9

	BATTERS	AVG	AB	R	H	2B	3B	HR	RBI	SB
	Czarniecki, Jordan, of	.223	323	44	72	23	3	6	46	6
	Esquer, Anthony, c	.275	171	25	47	5	0	1	17	1
	Guerrero, Cristian, of	.227	220	33	50	9	0	11	49	1
*	Haake, Steve, 1b	.262	351	54	92	23	5	10	67	21
	Marconi, Rob, of	.271	317	59	86	15	6	6	35	12
*	Massaro, Michael, of	.302	358	69	108	28	4	3	53	10
	McNamee, Eric, 2b	.266	327	48	87	16	0	0	36	6
1*	Omura, Isaac, 1b	.152	46	1	7	2	0	0	1	1
#	Pecci, Jay, ss	.292	325	50	95	17	1	2	48	2
*	Rohde, Mike, 3b	.274	325	49	89	12	6	2	32	14
	Wallace, Brett, c	.285	186	19	53	6	2	2	31	2

	PITCHERS	W	L	ERA	G	SV	IP	H	BB	SO
*	Cogan, Tony	8	7	3.60	22	0	150	134	37	105
	Cook, Aaron	2	3	3.23	24	2	30.2	36	14	20
	De la Cruz, Eddy	5	1	3.06	41	1	53	43	33	34
*	Facer, Tristan	0	3	3.74	20	0	21.2	20	16	23
	Fischer, Jeffrey	0	2	6.10	9	0	20.2	20	12	15
*	Goocher, Clint	1	0	8.44	4	0	5.1	8	3	5
	Heyne, Kyle	3	0	2.98	33	1	48.1	50	22	36
	Holleran, Garret	5	2	3.46	14	1	67.2	64	23	35
2	Johnson, Grant	4	4	6.89	22	2	49.2	65	22	43
	Jones, Christopher	6	3	3.75	15	0	84	80	25	53
*	Masaoka, Onan	1	5	6.02	12	0	55.1	61	26	51
	McCall, Derell	6	0	2.54	8	0	49.2	47	18	25
	Pfalzgraf, Christopher	0	0	6.75	1	0	4	4	3	3
1*	Quijano, Alain	0	0	7.71	5	0	4.2	8	1	3
	Rollin, Alex	1	0	7.96	16	0	26	34	8	22
2	Shipman, Andrew	4	3	1.85	36	13	39	29	11	34
*	Thornton, Tom	8	6	5.91	23	0	115.2	156	35	64
*	Walker, Edwin	3	0	3.26	16	3	19.1	14	10	29

JOLIET JACKHAMMERS

	BATTERS	AVG	AB	R	H	2B	3B	HR	RBI	SB
	Alberts, Tim, of	.305	200	22	61	14	0	1	21	5
	Arcadia, Ryan, 2b	.188	32	2	6	1	0	0	3	3
	Avlas, Phil, c	.266	218	36	58	15	0	5	15	8
*	Backman, Wally, of	.244	246	24	60	12	1	3	24	7
2	Correll, Brad, of	.286	147	29	42	14	0	7	38	2
*	Cox, Danny, 2b	.160	50	4	8	1	0	0	6	1
	Dahlberg, Rob, 2b	.253	99	8	25	3	0	0	14	3
	Davenport, James, 2b	.208	24	0	5	1	0	0	4	0
	Gaetti, Joe, of	.303	89	19	27	7	0	9	25	2
	Garcia, Michael, of	.283	53	5	15	4	0	1	8	0
	Gillingham, Tug, c	.228	57	7	13	0	0	0	3	1
	Gomes, Joey, of	.250	68	4	17	2	1	1	6	2
*	Harris, Gary, 2b	.225	80	6	18	2	1	0	7	3
2	Harrison, Vince, 3b	.282	71	10	20	2	0	0	5	1
	Herbert, Chris, c	.111	18	1	2	0	0	0	0	0
*	Herren, Karl, of	.180	89	7	16	3	0	2	7	1
*	Klein, Adam, of	.258	360	55	93	20	1	0	26	32
*	Lawrence, Horace, of	.063	16	2	1	1	0	0	0	0
	Lopez, Christian, c	.235	68	6	16	2	0	1	5	0
#	McGraw, James, of	.133	30	3	4	1	0	1	3	0
	Meadows, Tydus, of	.235	81	13	19	4	0	3	9	0
	Nichols, Kyle, dh	.231	65	7	15	3	0	2	12	0
2*	Omura, Isaac, 2b	.233	43	5	10	5	0	0	4	0
#	Pinckney, Andrew, 3b	.268	224	33	60	12	2	12	32	3
	Rios, Kevin, ss	.297	377	55	112	15	3	5	39	4
2	Scriven, Eric, of	.030	33	5	1	0	0	1	1	2
*	Thon, Freddy, 1b	.302	384	40	116	23	0	11	63	2
	Washington, Johnny, 2b	.286	14	3	4	2	0	0	0	0

	PITCHERS	W	L	ERA	G	SV	IP	H	BB	SO
*	Anderson, Devin	1	5	4.70	31	1	76.2	92	45	59
	Barrows, Derek	2	4	8.52	15	1	56	76	29	29
	Blackwell, Chad	3	4	4.61	52	4	80	95	24	64
1*	Gehring, Ryan	3	8	5.12	15	0	84.1	111	16	34
1	Johnson, Grant	1	3	6.19	4	0	16	20	8	13
	Lee, Trenton	0	0	9.00	6	0	7	15	5	4
*	Mumma, Brad	4	2	3.07	7	0	44	45	14	32
	Novak, Jason	2	7	7.65	21	0	62.1	71	44	27
	O'Loughlin, Luke	1	2	10.88	13	0	22.1	34	14	18
*	Paul, Ryan	3	3	2.70	39	0	46.2	34	30	50
1	Richardson, Jason	2	8	5.91	19	4	56.1	62	26	55
	Sevier, Nate	3	3	2.54	10	0	60.1	48	22	57

	W	L	ERA	G	SV	IP	H	BB	SO
Shortell, Rory	3	7	5.25	22	0	123.1	153	31	82
Trolia, Aaron	1	4	6.11	6	0	28	40	14	24

KANSAS CITY T-BONES

BATTERS

	AVG	AB	R	H	2B	3B	HR	RBI	SB
Blackwood, Jacob, 3b	.288	240	32	69	19	1	4	38	4
* Brown, Neb, 2b	.313	227	48	71	10	1	9	37	5
1 Correll, Brad, 3b	.262	130	18	34	10	2	6	21	4
Eggleston, Aharon, of	.318	387	74	123	18	2	4	44	13
* Fasano, James, 1b	.266	349	54	93	24	1	12	68	0
Fox, Ryan, of	.242	343	61	83	17	3	24	65	5
Harvey, Ken, 1b	.351	37	6	13	3	0	1	5	2
* Helps, Jeff, ss	.253	198	28	50	4	1	0	12	2
Hurba, Craig, c	.268	343	50	92	16	0	15	69	0
Jacobs, Greg, of	.300	313	56	94	23	2	11	65	3
1 Minicozzi, Mark, ss	.242	211	28	51	12	0	9	37	1
Rolls, Damian, 1b	.294	360	81	106	16	1	14	46	12
1 Scriven, Eric, of	.183	60	8	11	2	1	0	4	1
Terrero, Luis, of	.324	37	14	12	2	0	2	9	1
* Urick, John, of	.196	46	5	9	0	0	1	4	0

PITCHERS

	W	L	ERA	G	SV	IP	H	BB	SO
Bolton, Dustin	7	5	4.84	20	0	113.1	122	35	46
Cotton, Nate	0	4	4.84	23	12	22.1	21	10	14
* Curles, Weston	0	0	6.89	27	1	32.2	38	23	22
* Davis, Brett	2	0	5.19	4	0	26	33	5	22
Duclos, Derek	2	3	5.40	6	0	28.1	17	26	10
James, Justin	4	6	5.73	34	0	88	98	27	74
Johnson, Blair	1	1	3.68	5	0	7.1	12	2	4
* Knippschild, Ryan	4	8	4.44	20	0	125.2	130	41	103
Martinez, Brady	0	1	7.36	3	0	3.2	5	2	3
McAllister, Cody	8	4	4.43	31	2	87.1	82	42	77
* Moser, Todd	1	2	6.23	14	1	13	21	3	12
Rhoads, Chris	6	4	5.97	27	0	98	111	52	61
Sattler, Daniel	3	3	1.66	36	0	43.1	22	21	51
1 Shipman, Andrew	0	1	15.19	5	1	5.1	14	2	6
Trahan, David	2	1	15.75	5	1	4	9	2	5
* Tweddale, Payton	1	4	3.16	39	0	37	38	15	41
* Villarreal, Luis	5	3	3.07	16	0	96.2	87	40	87

SCHAUMBURG FLYERS

BATTERS

	AVG	AB	R	H	2B	3B	HR	RBI	SB
Brown, Travis, ss	.229	323	38	74	8	2	0	29	22
* Colson, Jason, 1b	.239	134	20	32	3	1	4	23	2
Dunbar, Jeffrey, of	.286	297	37	85	19	1	6	44	1
# Ezi, Travis, of	.185	119	16	22	3	1	2	7	8
Ferrante, Victor, of	.284	356	51	101	21	9	18	68	4
1 Harrison, Vince, 3b	.338	219	36	74	13	1	5	27	8
# Jose, Felix, dh	.306	281	33	86	12	0	7	39	2
* Maddox, Craig, 1b	.291	134	11	39	8	0	3	20	0
Mansolino, Anthony, 3b	.234	154	13	36	5	0	1	15	3
Mercado, Richard, c	.259	321	47	83	19	1	7	33	9
Pauley, Joe, 2b	.282	39	5	11	1	0	1	4	3
Poole, Lyndon, of	.296	115	17	34	6	2	3	10	12
# Richardson, Antoan, of	.287	94	20	27	3	4	0	6	20
Thames, Julius, of	.181	105	5	19	2	0	0	8	6
Toussas, John, of	.186	43	4	8	1	0	0	1	0
* Valdez, Jose, 2b	.288	226	36	65	13	4	4	26	8
Williams, Peanut, of	.200	20	3	4	0	0	1	3	0
* Wilson, TJ, of	.180	172	19	31	1	2	0	13	16
# Yoo, Stephen, 2b	.176	51	3	9	0	0	0	5	2

PITCHERS

	W	L	ERA	G	SV	IP	H	BB	SO
Almonte, Ed	6	10	4.89	19	0	114	117	44	68
Campbell, Joseph	0	0	7.78	10	0	19.2	32	14	11
Dunbar, Jeffrey	1	1	6.04	13	0	25.1	40	12	12
2* Gehring, Ryan	2	1	3.48	6	0	33.2	35	8	15
2 Giles, Joshua	2	1	5.70	16	0	23.2	24	19	25
Glant, Dustin	8	8	4.76	22	0	138	134	49	60
Howard, Adam	2	2	5.71	4	0	17.1	21	6	15
Howard, Cephas	3	1	1.71	31	6	42	33	16	47
2 Huizinga, Jon	0	0	7.94	4	0	5.2	6	5	8
James, Craig	2	1	2.25	14	7	16	9	10	17
Jiggitts, Kristopher	1	2	5.87	34	0	53.2	69	26	65
Lyons, Tom	2	6	6.00	21	0	51	62	21	41

	W	L	ERA	G	SV	IP	H	BB	SO
Patterson, Lonnie	0	0	1.59	4	0	5.2	5	5	3
* Pignatiello, Carmen	6	9	5.87	20	0	107.1	128	38	64
Popp, Jim	3	1	2.96	30	2	45.2	32	23	36
2* Quijano, Alain	5	6	5.36	19	0	87.1	96	35	59
2 Richardson, Jason	0	2	4.66	11	7	19.1	20	5	25
* Rieck, Garrett	0	1	9.77	20	0	15.2	26	12	17
Shippey, Steve	0	1	7.45	4	0	19.1	23	10	20

WINNIPEG GOLDEYES

BATTERS

	AVG	AB	R	H	2B	3B	HR	RBI	SB
Asanovich, Josh, 2b	.285	298	56	85	22	3	9	32	8
Brown, Dee, of	.322	360	49	116	22	0	12	53	2
Crowell, Kurt, of	.210	124	16	26	1	1	2	12	1
DeSmidt, Jeff, c	.286	77	7	22	6	0	1	13	0
Diaz, Juan, dh	.317	356	60	113	13	0	29	90	1
* Ehlers, Cody, 1b	.245	302	42	74	18	0	6	41	1
Frost, Adam, ss	.280	289	48	81	11	3	5	19	30
3 Harrison, Vince, 3b	.306	49	8	15	3	0	6	13	0
Long, Wesley, ss	.343	166	30	57	15	0	3	22	15
* Metheny, Brent, 3b	.256	305	49	78	20	2	12	49	13
2 Minicozzi, Mark, 2b	.205	44	3	9	3	0	0	7	0
Patton, Cory, of	.239	322	67	77	17	1	13	52	3
Richardson, Dustin, of	.229	223	38	51	18	0	3	20	5
West, Kevin, of	.285	369	58	105	22	0	19	66	13

PITCHERS

	W	L	ERA	G	SV	IP	H	BB	SO
* Baldwin, Zachary	4	4	3.71	35	0	63	70	19	34
Bay, Bear	8	3	3.54	22	0	129.2	129	24	79
Cruse, Andrew	5	5	4.58	25	0	114	119	46	74
Davis, Matt	5	7	5.12	38	13	45.2	54	16	32
Feldkamp, Derek	1	0	5.85	25	0	40	46	12	28
* Haigwood, Daniel	3	0	4.58	7	0	35.1	35	19	35
Homer, Chris	2	3	4.83	29	8	31.2	29	17	27
Michael, Mark	3	6	5.97	16	0	63.1	76	41	49
* Odom, Aaron	3	1	3.98	18	1	20.1	17	11	20
Pfinsgraff, Ben	2	2	6.75	4	0	21.1	37	4	15
* Pulsipher, Bill	4	2	3.35	6	0	40.1	30	13	35
Stewart, Jordan	3	1	2.91	41	2	55.2	45	10	38
* Thomas, Ian	0	1	2.81	11	0	16	16	9	16
Walker, Andrew	12	6	3.32	22	0	149	156	29	77

UNITED LEAGUE

The biggest success of the 2009 United League season was that it occurred at all.

The league declared bankruptcy after the 2008 season, which left its future plans up in the air. But thanks to a sale of the league, it reorganized in time to return to the field with largely the same slate of teams as it had in 2008.

On the field, Bryan Frichter led San Angelo to the best record during the regular season, but in the playoffs the Amarillo Dillas bounced back to win their second consecutive title.

The league did have its rocky points during the 2009 season as well. There are no final statistics for the league because the league had a billing dispute with the league's official statistician, Howe Sportsdata.

	W	L	PCT	GB
San Angelo Colts	48	32	.600	—
Edinburg Roadrunners	46	34	.575	2
Amarillo Dillas	44	35	.557	3½
Coastal Bend Thunder	39	40	.494	8½
Rio Grande Valley WhiteWings	39	41	.488	9½
Laredo Broncos	23	57	.288	25

PLAYOFFS—Semifinals: San Angelo defeated Coastal Bend 2-0 and Amarillo defeated Edinburg 2-1 in best-of-three series. **Finals:** Amarillo defeated San Angelo 3-2 in best-of-five series.

INTERNATIONAL

Japan, U.S. claim top international events

BY JOHN MANUEL

While 2009 was not an Olympic year, it was a watershed year for international baseball, on the field and off.

Baseball, which had been dropped from the Olympic roster for the 2012 London Games, sought a return when the International Olympic Committee added two sports to the docket for the 2016 Games. Rugby and golf will become Olympic sports, but baseball was denied and will not be in the Olympics for the foreseeable future, jeopardizing funding for national governing bodies around the world.

Yet 2009 also had two of the biggest international tournaments ever. In March, Major League Baseball (and the International Baseball Federation) staged the second World Baseball Classic, which saw Japan defend the championship it won in 2006 in the inaugural event. Team USA reached the semifinals, a significant accomplishment and an improvement over its second-round exit in 2006, but still fell short of its goal and failed to capture the interest of the many North American baseball fans.

The WBC now moves to a four-year interval between events, with the next scheduled for 2013. In the interim, the largest international baseball tournament becomes the World Cup, held every two years. IBAF staged the most ambitious World Cup ever in September, playing in seven countries throughout Europe, including baseball neophytes Croatia, Sweden and the Czech Republic. Only Germany saw robust attendance, as Europeans in general ignored the 22-team event, the largest field in World Cup history.

While fewer people paid much attention to the World Cup, USA Baseball fielded one of its strongest teams ever, a group of prospects that included eight players who had been drafted in the first round. With Rangers farmhand Justin Smoak winning MVP honors, Team USA won 14 consecutive games in Europe and defeated Cuba, 10-5, to win the gold medal.

On the Olympic front, the IOC had a solidly unfriendly summer toward baseball. First, the IOC met in Berlin in August to decide which sports to put into the 2016 Games, filling the spots created when baseball and softball were booted in 2005. Baseball and softball filed separately for reinstate-

Ichiro Suzuki had the game-winning hit for Japan in the WBC finale against Korea

LARRY GOREN

ment, but both were left out as golf and seven-man rugby won the day. That means baseball won't be in the Olympics until 2020 at the earliest, and outgoing IBAF president Harvey Schiller recommended in a letter to his constituents not to waste time trying to get back in the Olympics anytime soon.

"It makes much more sense to spend all our time, money and effort in continued development of the game around the world," he wrote, "as opposed to making futile attempts to work with a group that has no interest in partnering with baseball."

Baseball entered the Olympics in 1984, when it was a demonstration sport, then became a medal sport in 1992. Cuba won gold medals in 1992, 1996 and 2004. The United States took the gold in 2000, while South Korea won what may prove to be the last Olympic baseball tournament in 2008.

Ichiro, As In Hero

The end of Olympic baseball leaves the World Baseball Classic as the sport's top international event, and Japan is now batting 1.000 when it comes to the Classic.

Japan wound up playing South Korea four times

in the 2009 tournament, losing two of the first three but winning when it counted, in Dodger Stadium in the March 24 championship game. In front of a Classic-record crowd of 54,846, Japan's biggest star, Mariners outfielder Ichiro Suzuki, had the big hit, with a two-out, two-strike, two-run single in the 10th inning that provided the winning margin in the 5-3 game.

"It's an image that will be forever imprinted in my mind," Japan manager Tatsunori Hara said of Ichiro's game-winner. "I believe I will never forget it."

Red Sox righthander Daisuke Matsuzaka earned MVP honors for the second straight Classic, as he went 3-0, 2.45 overall in the event. Unlike 2006, though, Matsuzaka didn't pitch the title game, as Hara had plenty of pitching depth. He was able to use 22-year-old fireballer Yu Darvish out of the bullpen, closing out the U.S. in the semifinal, and he used him again in the championship game because he had Hisashi Iwakuma on hand to start it.

Iwakuma left with a lead after allowing just two runs and four hits over 7⅔ innings, but Korea rallied against Darvish to tie the game in the ninth inning on an RBI single by Bum Ho Lee. Darvish earned the victory after Ichiro's big hit and struck out five in two innings.

For Korea, it was another tough loss in WBC play, but the nation has proved it deserves a place in the discussion of top baseball nations, with its repeated strong showings in youth events as well as the '08 Olympic gold and strong performances in both WBCs.

Teams from the Western Hemisphere, meanwhile, fared poorly in the Classic. The United States was the best of the group, advancing to the semifinals for the first time. Cuba's club may have been stronger, but Cuba couldn't get out of its second-round pool in Mexico City, with a pair of shutout losses to Japan. The Americans had an easier road but still needed late heroics to beat Puerto Rico and advance to the final four.

Team USA, managed by Davey Johnson, lost 9-4 to Japan in the semifinal, and the American pitching wasn't good enough to win the event. Team USA also had four key players injured in the second round as Red Sox first baseman Kevin Youkilis sprained his left ankle, Red Sox second baseman Dustin Pedroia strained a muscle in his left side, Braves third baseman Chipper Jones strained a muscle in his right side and Marlins reliever Matt Lindstrom strained his right shoulder.

The U.S. team came up with its most dramatic WBC moment in the second-round victory against Puerto Rico, a 6-5 walk-off victory in Miami. While just 13,224 watched it, David Wright's soft

TEAM USA WORLD CUP STATISTICS									
BATTERS	AVG	AB	R	H	2B	3B	HR	RBI	SB
Jon Weber, lf	.412	51	10	21	4	1	3	13	0
Terry Tiffee, dh	.357	56	12	20	4	0	4	20	0
Lucas May, c	.355	31	7	11	3	0	3	8	1
Ike Davis, 1b/rf	.333	30	10	10	2	1	3	5	0
Buck Coats, cf	.321	56	13	18	3	1	4	12	5
Justin Smoak, 1b	.291	55	16	16	2	0	9	22	0
Josh Kroeger, rf	.268	56	13	15	4	0	1	6	1
Trevor Plouffe, ss	.262	61	13	16	2	0	3	7	2
Pedro Alvarez, 3b	.259	54	8	14	2	0	5	12	0
Tug Hulett, util	.258	31	11	8	2	3	2	5	2
Daniel Descalso, 2b	.238	21	4	5	1	0	1	2	1
Jason Castro, c	.130	23	1	3	0	0	0	2	0
PITCHERS	W	L	ERA	G	SV	IP	H	BB	SO
Lucas Harrell	3	0	0.00	3	0	10	2	2	7
Ehren Wasserman	1	0	0.00	6	1	9	3	3	6
Trevor Reckling	2	0	0.69	3	0	13	5	5	14
Todd Redmond	3	0	1.21	3	0	22	11	1	17
Cory Luebke	1	0	1.50	3	0	18	12	2	22
Kasey Kiker	1	0	2.08	3	0	13	5	14	17
Brad Lincoln	3	0	2.70	4	0	23	23	6	12
Nate Field	0	1	3.00	6	1	6	5	3	7
Geno Espineli	0	0	4.91	6	1	4	3	1	2
Cedrick Bowers	0	0	5.40	6	0	3	3	2	4
B.J. Rosenberg	0	0	6.35	5	0	6	5	3	11
Jason Childers	0	0	7.94	6	1	6	3	4	8

line-drive single that drove in two runs prompted a wild celebration as the Americans advanced.

"You're talking about representing the United States of America," Wright said. "You have that across the front of your chest. You're representing a nation, and to come up and be able to get that hit, that's got to be right up there at the top of the list."

Other teams from the Americas that had been expected to contend didn't fare as well. Canada played host to a first-round pool in Toronto's Rogers Centre but failed to advance. After a loud, well-played 6-5 loss to the U.S. in the opener, Canada was stunned 6-2 by Italy, sealing its first-round fate. More embarrassing, the Dominican Republic also failed to make it out of the first round, losing twice to the Netherlands in a pair of one-run games. The Dutch won despite getting just eight hits in 20-plus innings of play thanks to sloppy pitching and fielding by the Dominicans.

Americans Dominate In Europe

American teams fared much better in the World Cup in November, though, feasting on weaker European teams and thriving as Japan, South Korea and Taiwan each sent younger teams with amateurs mixed in with minor leaguers. Venezuela's roster was filled with former minor leaguers tuning up for winter ball, and yet Venezuela advanced to the event's third round.

Venezuela dealt the U.S. a defeat in the first game of the Cup, as the Americans blew a 7-2 lead and lost 13-9 in 11 innings. Team USA, which won the 2007 World Cup with a different cast of characters, rallied and didn't lose again in the tournament. Playing games in Regensburg, Germany, and at various sites in Italy, Team USA won 14 straight games, including a pair of victories against Cuba, which sent its top-level national team.

The Americans beat Cuba 10-5 in the championship game, rallying to break a 4-4 tie with a six-run seventh inning. The Americans scored all six runs after Cuban veteran Norge Vera retired the first two batters, getting a walk, a double and an error to break the tie, followed by five straight hits to break the game open. Reliever Brad Lincoln (Pirates) got the victory in relief.

Team USA was led by manager Eddie Rodriguez, who was born in Cuba and came to the U.S. in 1965 when he was 6 years old. Rodriguez, who was the third-base coach for the 2000 Olympic gold medalists, pushed all the right buttons for a team that came together quickly.

"Our guys really persevered through a lot of difficulties, with the bus rides, the travel, the late-night meals, and just grinded it out," Rodriguez said. "The guys never complained. They just came together and played their best, and everyone played their role. That's how this can happen."

While competition wavered from excellent to inept, the bigger story was the poor attendance. While more than 38,000 fans came out for six games in Germany, crowds for the second and third rounds in the Netherlands and Italy were sparse. According to European baseball Website misterbaseball.com, games in the Netherlands averaged 507 fans when the Dutch weren't involved, and all the games in Italy for the second round averaged just 635 fans. It was worse for the third and final round—an average of just 482 a game. The overall World Cup total of 126,799 for 106 games breaks down to a 1,196 average, but taking away the German games, the average dips to 888.

Maybe that makes it easier to see why European nations, which dominate the IOC, were quick to get baseball out of the Olympics.

WORLD BASEBALL CLASSIC

STANDINGS AND RESULTS

NATION	W	L	RF	RA
*Japan	7	2	50	16
*Venezuela	6	2	45	36
*South Korea	6	3	53	30
Cuba	4	2	36	24
Puerto Rico	4	2	31	10
*United States	4	4	50	54
Mexico	2	4	47	52
Netherlands	2	4	10	23

Justin Smoak earned MVP honors in the World Cup thanks to nine home runs

Dominican Republic	1	2	12	5
Italy	1	2	7	19
China	1	2	4	19
Australia	1	2	22	28
Canada	0	2	7	12
Panama	0	2	0	16
South Africa	0	2	4	22
Taiwan	0	2	1	13

*Advanced to championship round

Semifinals
South Korea 10, Venezuela 2; Japan 9, United States 4

Championship
Japan 5, South Korea 3 (10)

ALL-TOURNAMENT TEAM
C: Ivan Rodriguez, Puerto Rico. **1B:** Tae Kyun Kim, South Korea. **2B:** Jose Lopez, Venezuela. **3B:** Bum Ho Lee, South Korea. **SS:** Jimmy Rollins, United States. **OF:** Norichika Aoki, Japan; Frederich Cepeda, Cuba; Yoennis Cespedes, Cuba. **DH:** Hyun Soo Kim, South Korea. **P:** Jung Keun Bong, South Korea; Hisashi Iwakuma, Japan; *Daisuke Matsuzaka, Japan.
*MVP

INDIVIDUAL PITCHING LEADERS
(Minimum 6 IP)

PITCHER, NATION	W	L	ERA	G	SV	IP	H	BB	SO
Felix Hernandez, Ven	2	0	0.00	2	0	9	5	6	11
Pedro Martinez, D.R.	0	0	0.00	2	0	6	1	0	6
Toshiya Sugiuchi, Japan	0	0	0.00	5	1	6	0	2	6
Enrique Gonzalez, Ven	1	0	0.00	3	0	10	3	4	6
Nelson Figueroa, PR	0	0	0.00	4	0	7	2	3	6
Rob Cordemans, Ned	0	0	0.00	3	0	7	2	4	3
Jungkeun Bong, SK	2	0	0.51	4	0	18	14	6	4
Javier Vazquez, PR	2	0	0.96	2	0	9	8	1	5
Suk-Min Yoon, SK	2	0	1.13	4	0	16	13	1	13
Yuneski Maya, Cuba	0	1	1.23	3	0	7	5	2	4
Elmer Dessens, Mex	1	0	1.35	2	0	7	5	0	3
Hisashi Iwakuma, Japan	1	1	1.35	4	0	20	12	6	15

INDIVIDUAL BATTING LEADERS
(Minimum 10 Plate Appearances)

PLAYER, NATION	AB	R	H	2B	3B	HR	RBI	SB	AVG
Joey Votto, Can	9	2	5	2	0	1	2	0	.556
Frederich Cepeda, Cuba	24	5	12	2	0	3	10	0	.500
Trent Oeltjen, Aus	12	1	6	0	0	0	1	2	.500
Ivan Rodriguez, PR	20	6	10	3	0	2	6	0	.500
Yoennis Cespedes, Cuba	24	5	11	1	3	2	5	0	.458
Ray Chang, China	11	1	5	1	0	1	2	0	.455
Justin Morneau, Can	9	1	4	2	0	0	1	0	.444
Carlos Delgado, PR	16	4	7	2	0	2	5	0	.438
Carlos Beltran, PR	19	3	8	1	0	1	3	2	.421
Karim Garcia, Mex	19	5	8	0	0	3	5	0	.421
Jose Lopez, Ven	24	8	10	6	0	2	4	0	.417
Jimmy Rollins, USA	24	4	10	1	2	1	4	4	.417

Saltillo wins second Mexican League title

Saltillo won its second Mexican League championship (and first since 1980), beating Quintana Roo, 14-1, in the sixth and clinching game of the best-of-seven championship series behind four hits by midseason acquisition Hernando Arredondo.

Arredondo, who spent parts of three seasons in the Rays organization from 1996-98, spent the first half of the season with Tabasco. A career .286 hitter in 11 Mexican League seasons, he was batting just .268 in 60 games for the Olmecas before being acquired by Saltillo. While the Saraperos were just 28-26 in the second half, Arredondo caught fire, batting .385 with eight home runs in just 40 games with Saltillo. He also moved from second base to third base as a replacement for Kit Pellow, the 2008 Mexican triple-crown winner. Pellow left Saltillo for a contract with Calgary of the Golden League.

Arredondo then led the league with 21 postseason RBIs while batting .345 as Saltillo beat Quintana Roo, whose 71 regular-season victories led the league. Saltillo went 12-4 in the playoffs, batting .297 as a team with 29 home runs in 16 games. Former Diamondbacks farmhand Jesus Cota hit .377 with a team-best six homers, while 38-year-old righthander Rafael Diaz served as the postseason ace, giong 3-1, 3.34 in five starts. Diaz won the playoff clincher, tossing a complete-game eight-hitter.

As usual, Mexico was a hitter's paradise, with the league ERA being 4.96. The lack of power arms was evident as hitters struck out 8,379 times in 14,715.2 innings pitched, a ratio of 5.12 per nine innings. For comparison, the Pacific Coast League, an excellent league for hitters, had an ERA of 4.50 and 15,313 strikeouts in 20,224 innings, a 6.81 strikeouts per nine innings ratio.

Former Athletics farmhand Dionys Cesar won the league batting title and MVP award. Cesar, a second baseman playing for Laguna, also lead the league with 40 stolen bases, 36 doubles and 156 hits. Laguna eliminated the defending champion Mexico Red Devils in a seven-game quarterfinals playoff series.

OVERALL STANDINGS

NORTH	W	L	PCT	GB
*† Mexico	70	35	.667	—
Reynosa	58	47	.552	12
Saltillo	59	58	.551	12
Monclova	57	50	.533	14
Laguna	55	51	.519	15½
Monterrey	51	56	.477	20
Chihuahua	40	67	.374	31
Nuevo Laredo	35	71	.330	35½

SOUTH	W	L	PCT	GB
* Quintana Roo	71	36	.664	—
† Yucatan	68	38	.642	2½
Puebla	62	43	.590	8
Campeche	56	51	.523	15
Veracruz	51	56	.477	20
Oaxaca	42	63	.400	28
Tabasco	39	63	.382	29½
Minatitlan	34	73	.318	37

*First-half division winner. †Second-half division winner.

PLAYOFFS—Division Series: Puebla defeated Yucatan 4-1, Saltillo defeated Reynosa 4-2, Laguna defeated Mexico 4-3 and Quintana Roo defeated Campeche 4-3 in best-of-seven series. **Semifinals:** Saltillo defeated Laguna 4-0 and Quintana Roo defeated Puebla 4-1 in best-of-seven series. **Finals:** Saltillo defeated Quintana Roo 4-2 in best-of-seven series.

ATTENDANCE—Monclova, 430,059; Reynosa, 334,369; Laguna, 300,722; Saltillo, 279,410; Monterrey, 204,698; Yucatan, 203,680; Oaxaca, 200,822; Mexico City, 181,966; Veracruz, 162,264; Puebla, 155,540; Quintana Roo, 132,549; Nuevo Laredo, 112,984; Campeche, 109,300; Chihuahua, 104,949; Minatitlan, 91,746; Tabasco, 60,312.

INDIVIDUAL BATTING LEADERS

	AVG	AB	R	H	2B	3B	HR	RBI	BB	SO	SB
Cesar, Dionys, Lag	.380	411	92	156	36	4	5	58	58	36	40
Quintero, Edgar, Mty	.378	394	81	149	36	2	21	77	54	82	2
Soto, Saul, Mva	.370	395	79	146	23	0	28	93	59	64	1
Cruz, Jacob, Chi	.359	301	73	108	19	0	24	84	66	47	4
Rodriguez, Serafin, Pue	.358	416	87	149	26	3	5	42	16	39	7
Rivera, Carlos, Oax	.358	355	66	127	24	1	20	79	45	40	3
Alejos, Fernando, Yuc	.355	318	60	113	27	4	6	65	63	58	9
McDonald, Donzell, Mva	.355	372	91	132	25	9	10	56	66	67	17
Reyes, Rene, Pue	.355	392	85	139	33	4	12	87	56	53	12
Valdes, Pedro, Tab	.354	333	60	118	21	0	17	81	92	33	0
Arredondo, Eduardo, Mex	.354	435	97	154	23	13	6	64	32	26	11
Teilon, Nelson, Sal	.353	399	88	141	27	4	18	82	26	73	10
Robles, Oscar, Mex	.351	396	74	139	25	1	6	74	57	24	2
Matos, Luis, Yuc	.349	272	60	95	20	2	7	64	54	29	17
Otanez, Willis, Pue	.349	370	58	129	29	0	19	91	64	46	0

INDIVIDUAL PITCHING LEADERS

	W	L	ERA	G	GS	SV	IP	H	R	ER	BB	SO
Campos, Francisco, Cam	11	6	2.31	25	23	0	144	128	53	37	32	89
Oramas, Juan, Mex	9	1	2.31	25	14	0	90	72	24	23	44	89
Quintanilla, Enrique, Lar	6	7	2.48	21	20	0	138	110	41	38	20	71
Meza, Andres, Pue	15	2	2.72	20	20	0	126	112	39	38	34	46
Cruz, Rafael, Ver	12	7	2.81	22	22	0	144	128	50	45	23	67
Rodriguez, Nerio, Mva	11	5	2.85	22	21	1	136	131	48	43	35	11
Martinez, Javier, Yuc	11	4	2.95	21	21	0	128	144	52	42	30	59
Giron, Roberto, Ver	7	4	3.01	17	16	0	90	87	34	30	23	79
Ortega, Pablo, Tig	13	5	3.19	21	21	0	135	141	58	48	30	55
Rivera, Oscar, Mex	6	3	3.26	15	14	0	88	80	35	32	35	63
Ramirez, Roberto, Mex	13	4	3.45	22	22	0	123	139	52	47	31	72
Francisco, Alexander, Min	6	8	3.89	18	18	0	111	126	60	48	33	66
Tequida, Mauricio, Mex	7	3	3.90	33	10	0	97	120	44	42	24	44
Gonzalez, Leonardo, Tab	8	8	4.02	21	21	0	119	119	57	53	44	76
Verdugo, Oswaldo, Yuc	9	0	4.14	21	20	0	117	122	58	54	37	84

Yomiuri wins 21st Japan Series

BY WAYNE GRACZYK

The Yomiuri Giants won their first Japanese championship since 2002, defeating the Nippon Ham Fighters four games to two in the best-of-seven Japan Series. The powerhouse Giants, boasting a roster of superstar players similar to the New York Yankees, won their 21st Japan Series since the two-league system was inaugurated in Japan in 1950.

The Giants made it to the finals by beating the second-place Chunichi Dragons in Stage 2 of the Central League Climax Series playoffs. The Dragons had defeated the third-place Tokyo Yakult Swallows in Stage 1 of the Central League playoffs. Nippon Ham, based in Hokkaido, knocked off the second-place Tohoku Rakuten Golden Eagles in Stage 2 of the Pacific League Climax Series, after the Eagles eliminated the third-place Fukuoka SoftBank Hawks in Stage 1.

A total of 68 foreigners played in Japan in 2009, including players from the United States, Canada, Korea, Taiwan, Puerto Rico, Venezuela, Panama and the Dominican Republic. Among the non-Japanese standouts were Venezuelan outfielder Alex Ramirez and pitcher Dicky Gonzalez of the Giants and first baseman Tony Blanco of the Dragons.

Ramirez, a former major leaguer with the Indians and Pirates who was playing his ninth season in Japan, won the Central League batting title with a .322 average.

Gonzalez, who played for the Mets and Rays and is a six-year Japan veteran, chalked up a 15-2 record—remarkable because he began the season on the Yomiuri farm team and was not promoted until May 2. Blanco, in his first Japan season after playing part of 2005 with the Nationals, led the Central League with 39 homers and 110 RBIs.

Top foreign performers in the Pacific League included a trio of former major leaguers: first baseman/outfielder Terrmel Sledge of the Fighters and pitchers D.J. Houlton and Brian Falkenborg of the Hawks.

Sledge, playing his second season in Japan, hit 27 home runs and had 88 RBIs and was MVP of the playoff series against Rakuten. His performance included a dramatic come-from-behind, walkoff, grand slam to win Game One.

Houlton went 11-8, 2.89. Falkenborg was one of the top setup relievers, posting a 6-0, 1.74 record and 23 holds in 46 games. Saitama Seibu Lions third baseman Takeya Nakamura won the

Pacific League home run race for the second consecutive season, hitting 48. He also led the league with 122 RBIs. Outfielder Teppei Tsuchiya of Rakuten won the Pacific League batting title with a .327 average.

Pitchers Kazuki Yoshimi of the Dragons and Shohei Tateyama of the Swallows tied for the most victories in the Central League with 16, and Hideaki Wakui of Seibu posted 16 wins to lead the Pacific. Wakui, 16-6, 2.30, also won the Sawamura Award as Japan's top hurler. Dragons lefthander Chen Wei Yin had the best ERA in the Central League (1.54), and is considered a major league prospect. Nippon Ham phenom Yu Darvish, the Japanese-Iranian righthander, posted a 1.73 ERA to pace the Pacific League.

CENTRAL LEAGUE

	W	L	T	Pct.	GB
Yomiuri Giants	89	46	9	.659	—
Chunichi Dragons	81	62	1	.566	12
Tokyo Yakult Swallows	71	72	1	.497	22
Hanshin Tigers	67	73	4	.479	24½
Hiroshima Carp	65	75	4	.464	26½
Yokohama BayStars	51	93	0	.354	42½

CLIMAX SERIES PLAYOFFS—Stage One: Chunichi defeated Yakult 2-1 in best-of-three series. **Stage Two:** Yomiuri defeated Chunichi 4-1 in best-of-seven series.

INDIVIDUAL BATTING LEADERS
(MINIMUM 446 PLATE APPEARANCES)

	AVG.	AB	R	H	2B	3B	HR	RBI	SB
Ramirez, Alex, Giants	.322	577	66	186	35	0	31	103	4
Uchikawa, Seiichi, BayStars	.318	503	65	160	32	2	17	66	1
Ogasawara, Michihiro, Giants	.309	514	78	159	25	1	31	107	2
Sakamoto, Hayato, Giants	.306	581	87	178	33	3	18	62	5
Ibata, Hirozaku, Dragons	.306	569	80	174	24	2	5	39	13
Aoki, Norichika, Swallows	.303	531	87	161	23	2	16	66	18
Wada, Kazuhiro, Dragons	.302	517	73	156	24	4	29	87	5
Miyamoto, Shinya, Swallows	.294	469	43	138	26	4	5	46	3
Higashide, Akihiro, Carp	.294	558	71	164	16	8	0	26	14
Abe, Shinnosuke, Giants	.293	409	63	120	20	2	32	76	1
Kamei, Yoshiyuki, Giants	.290	490	79	142	25	4	25	71	12
Morino, Masahiko, Dragons	.289	546	83	158	42	3	23	109	4
Toritani, Takashi, Tigers	.288	538	84	155	31	2	20	75	7
Blanco, Tony, Dragons	.275	549	87	151	25	0	39	110	1
Sekimoto, Kentaro, Tigers	.271	377	45	102	18	2	3	44	3
Fukuchi, Kazuki, Swallows	.270	504	75	136	13	5	5	34	42
Hirano, Keiichi, Tigers	.270	404	56	109	15	5	0	18	3
Araki, Masahiro, Dragons	.270	582	80	157	21	1	2	38	37
Guiel, Aaron, Swallows	.267	409	62	109	26	1	27	80	2
Kanemoto, Tomoaki, Tigers	.261	518	66	135	37	0	21	91	8
Arai, Takahiro, Tigers	.260	558	68	145	32	1	15	82	4
Tanaka, Hiroyasu, Swallows	.258	434	48	112	24	2	4	35	6
Kurihara, Kenta, Carp	.257	521	68	134	21	0	23	79	1
Kawashima, Keizo, Swallows	.255	427	49	109	13	2	12	43	8
Yoshimura, Yuuki, BayStars	.248	528	62	131	26	2	16	54	13
Aikawa, Ryoji, Swallows	.247	413	26	102	21	1	5	43	2
McClain, Scott, Carp	.244	401	43	98	18	1	18	52	1
Ishikawa, Takehiro, BayStars	.242	463	38	112	15	3	2	24	19
Akamatsu, Masato, Carp	.232	423	58	98	15	3	6	43	14

	AVG.	AB	R	H	2B	3B	HR	RBI	SB
Brazell, Craig, Tigers	.291	285	29	83	14	0	16	49	0
D'Antona, Jamie, Swallows	.276	391	39	108	19	0	21	83	0
Phillips, Andy, Carp	.265	264	35	70	15	1	15	50	0
De La Rosa, Tomas, Dragons	.236	55	3	13	2	0	0	3	0
Johnson, Dan, BayStars	.215	325	43	70	6	1	24	57	0
Seabol, Scott, Giants	.213	127	9	27	3	1	4	11	1
Mench, Kevin, Tigers	.148	54	1	8	3	0	0	2	1
Alfonso, Edgardo, Giants	.146	41	3	6	0	0	2	4	0
Baldiris, Aarom, Tigers	.103	29	1	3	0	0	1	1	0

INDIVIDUAL PITCHING LEADERS
(MINIMUM 144 INNINGS)

	W	L	ERA	G	SV	IP	H	BB	SO
Chen, Wei Yin, Dragons	8	4	1.54	24	0	164	113	40	146
Yoshimi, Kazuki, Dragons	16	7	2.00	27	0	189	166	33	147
Gonzalez, Dicky, Giants	15	2	2.11	23	0	162	134	25	113
Nomi, Atsushi, Tigers	13	9	2.62	28	0	165	142	44	154
Otake, Kan, Carp	10	8	2.81	29	0	186	177	60	127
Takahashi, Hisanori, Giants	10	6	2.94	25	0	144	147	36	126
Utsumi, Tetsuya, Giants	9	11	2.96	27	0	180	161	36	115
Lewis, Colby, Carp	11	9	2.96	29	0	176	156	19	186
Tono, Shun, Giants	8	8	3.17	27	0	153	133	57	133
Miura, Daisuke, BayStars	11	11	3.32	28	0	195	175	37	138
Maeda, Kenta, Carp	8	14	3.36	29	0	193	194	29	147
Tateyama, Shohei, Swallows	16	6	3.39	27	0	188	195	45	126
Greisinger, Seth, Giants	13	6	3.47	25	0	161	173	26	91
Ishikawa, Masanori, Swallows	13	7	3.54	29	0	198	203	28	84
Kubo, Yasutomo, Tigers	9	8	3.75	26	0	151	140	50	113
Ando, Yuya, Tigers	8	12	3.90	28	0	164	180	51	97
Asakura, Kenta, Dragons	10	8	4.04	24	0	151	159	45	83

REMAINING U.S., AUSTRALIAN AND LATIN PLAYERS

	W	L	ERA	G	SV	IP	H	BB	SO
Kroon, Marc, Giants	1	3	1.26	46	27	50	36	19	57
Atchison, Scott, Tigers	5	3	1.70	75	0	90	60	20	81
Randolph, Stephen, BayStars	5	2	1.96	8	0	55	33	34	59
Payano, Nelson, Dragons	2	1	2.08	34	0	30	17	17	39
Schultz, Mike, Carp	5	3	2.28	73	1	75	57	22	72
Obispo, Wirfin, Giants	6	1	2.45	14	0	59	44	11	48
Williams, Jeff, Tigers	1	1	3.58	31	0	28	19	20	35
Nelson, Maximo, Dragons	1	3	3.58	26	1	50	48	16	49
Walrond, Les, BayStars	5	10	4.80	21	0	111	128	50	85
Glynn, Ryan, BayStars	3	15	5.11	23	0	118	135	35	69
Mastny, Tom, BayStars	1	5	5.69	15	0	62	79	25	43
Barrett, Ricky, Swallows	0	1	7.15	7	0	11	16	10	5
Dohmann, Scott, Carp	0	0	17.28	9	0	8	14	7	4
Kozlowski, Ben, Carp	0	0	54.00	1	0	1/3	3	0	0

PACIFIC LEAGUE

	W	L	T	Pct.	GB
Hokkaido Nippon Ham Fighters	82	60	2	.577	—
Tohoku Rakuten Golden Eagles	77	66	1	.538	5½
Fukuoka SoftBank Hawks	74	65	5	.532	6½
Saitama Seibu Lions	70	70	4	.500	11
Chiba Lotte Marines	62	77	5	.446	18½
Orix Buffaloes	56	86	2	.394	26

CLIMAX SERIES PLAYOFFS—**Stage One:** Rakuten defeated SoftBank 2-0 in best-of-three series. **Stage Two:** Nippon Ham defeated Rakuten 4-1 in best-of-seven series.

INDIVIDUAL BATTING LEADERS
(MINIMUM 446 PLATE APPEARANCES)

	AVG.	AB	R	H	2B	3B	HR	RBI	SB
Tsuchiya, Teppei, Eagles	.327	496	84	162	26	13	12	76	13
Sakaguchi, Tomotaka, Buffaloes	.317	526	82	167	23	7	5	50	16
Omura, Saburo, Marines	.314	427	71	134	24	2	22	68	4
Hasegawa, Yuya, Hawks	.312	509	69	159	31	3	7	44	10
Takahashi, Shinji, Fighters	.309	508	66	157	22	1	8	75	7
Nakajima, Hiroyuki, Lions	.309	560	100	173	31	3	22	92	20
Itoi, Yoshio, Fighters	.306	425	74	130	40	3	15	58	24
Kusano, Daisuke, Eagles	.305	462	55	141	28	0	7	54	3
Inaba, Atsunori, Fighters	.300	500	78	150	37	4	17	85	5

	AVG.	AB	R	H	2B	3B	HR	RBI	SB
Koyano, Eiichi, Fighters	.296	530	65	157	33	4	11	82	7
Omura, Naoyuki, Buffaloes	.291	419	32	122	21	0	0	30	5
Sato, G.G., Lions	.291	502	69	146	34	0	25	83	1
Nakamura, Takeya, Lions	.285	501	91	143	37	1	48	122	3
Tanaka, Kensuke, Fighters	.283	575	93	163	34	4	3	49	31
Ortiz, Jose, Hawks	.282	411	54	116	24	2	20	74	2
Iguchi, Tadahito, Marines	.281	448	71	126	24	3	19	65	4
Matsunaka, Nobuhiko, Hawks	.279	448	62	125	21	0	23	80	2
Watanabe, Naoto, Eagles	.276	463	79	128	24	2	1	28	26
Fukuura, Kazuya, Marines	.273	396	47	108	18	0	6	39	1
Omatsu, Shoitsu, Marines	.269	494	67	133	28	1	19	79	0
Kuriyama, Takumi, Lions	.267	569	78	152	24	6	12	57	18
Kokubo, Hiroki, Hawks	.266	533	64	142	27	0	18	81	2
Sledge, Terrmel, Fighters	.266	418	53	111	27	1	27	88	1
Honda, Yuichi, Hawks	.262	554	72	145	32	4	1	41	43
Fernandez, Jose, Buffaloes	.261	410	43	107	21	0	15	47	4
Kataoka, Yasuyuki, Lions	.260	588	92	153	32	4	13	58	51
Nishioka, Tsuyoshi, Marines	.260	501	84	125	14	5	14	41	26
Kawasaki, Munenori, Hawks	.259	540	73	140	26	8	4	34	44
Tanoue, Hidenori, Hawks	.251	463	47	116	16	1	26	80	0
Yamasaki, Takeshi, Eagles	.246	536	73	132	27	0	39	107	3
Satozaki, Tomoya, Marines	.234	414	39	97	22	1	10	49	0

REMAINING U.S. AND LATIN PLAYERS

	AVG.	AB	R	H	2B	3B	HR	RBI	SB
Cabrera, Alex, Buffaloes	.314	239	37	75	10	0	13	39	0
Rhodes, Tuffy, Buffaloes	.308	295	41	91	15	0	22	62	0
Linden, Todd, Eagles	.292	284	47	83	22	0	12	37	2
LaRocca, Greg, Buffaloes	.287	261	28	75	16	0	12	43	0
Agbayani, Benny, Marines	.265	272	23	72	14	1	7	31	0
Short, Rick, Eagles	.255	184	13	47	7	0	3	13	4
Seguignol, Fernando, Eagles	.253	316	37	80	18	0	14	54	1
Botts, Jason, Fighters	.238	21	4	5	3	0	1	6	0
Jiminez, Luis, Fighters	.231	121	13	28	5	0	5	14	0
Burnham Jr., Gary, Marines	.218	147	14	32	7	1	4	22	1
Bocachica, Hiram, Lions	.215	195	29	42	8	1	13	32	2
Lambin, Chase, Marines	.192	120	18	23	8	0	4	12	0
Aguila, Chris, Hawks	.095	42	0	4	0	0	0	0	0

INDIVIDUAL PITCHING LEADERS
(MINIMUM 144 INNINGS)

	W	L	ERA	G	SV	IP	H	BB	SO
Darvish, Yu, Fighters	15	5	1.73	23	0	182	118	45	167
Wakui, Hideaki, Lions	16	6	2.30	27	0	212	162	76	199
Tanaka, Masahiro, Eagles	15	6	2.33	25	1	190	170	43	171
Sugiuchi, Toshiya, Hawks	15	5	2.36	26	0	191	145	63	204
Kaneko, Chihiro, Buffaloes	11	8	2.57	32	0	172	149	34	165
Houlton, D.J., Hawks	11	8	2.89	25	0	171	137	43	138
Iwakuma, Hisashi, Eagles	13	6	3.25	24	0	169	179	43	121
Kishi, Takayuki, Lions	13	5	3.26	26	0	180	168	53	138
Naruse, Yoshihisa, Marines	11	5	3.28	23	0	154	146	28	156
Nagai, Satoshi, Eagles	13	7	3.42	26	0	171	153	50	144
Takeda, Masaru, Fighters	10	9	3.55	24	0	144	150	20	99
Hoashi, Kazuyuki, Lions	9	6	3.59	25	0	163	175	40	126
Ono, Shingo, Marines	8	7	3.81	23	0	144	158	37	77
Watanabe, Shunsuke, Marines	3	13	4.05	25	0	144	144	46	74
Yamamoto, Shogo, Buffaloes	9	7	4.23	27	0	160	176	47	110
Shimizu, Naoyuki, Marines	6	7	4.42	23	0	145	177	42	88
Kondo, Kazuki, Buffaloes	9	12	4.78	24	0	153	155	80	91

REMAINING U.S. AND LATIN PLAYERS

	W	L	ERA	G	SV	IP	H	BB	SO
Falkenborg, Brian, Hawks	6	0	1.74	46	1	52	39	9	62
Sikorski, Brian, Marines	8	5	2.19	55	15	66	41	19	73
Bayliss, Jonah, Lions	0	0	3.21	19	1	14	18	8	6
Gwyn, Marcus, Eagles	3	4	3.56	47	4	48	37	29	44
Germano, Justin, Hawks	5	4	4.38	14	0	76	92	10	42
Vogelsong, Ryan, Buffaloes	1	4	4.54	30	0	42	39	16	56
Leicester, Jon, Buffaloes	0	1	5.04	20	0	25	22	11	20
Wasdin, John, Lions	2	3	5.31	14	0	58	79	21	24
Sweeney, Brian, Fighters	5	8	5.32	21	0	118	144	52	58
Graman, Alex, Lions	0	2	5.40	6	3	5	6	2	1
Rasner, Darrell, Eagles	4	7	6.09	15	0	81	94	23	52
Loe, Kameron, Hawks	0	4	6.33	5	0	27	36	12	18
Childers, Matt, Eagles	0	0	10.38	3	0	4	8	2	2

INTERNATIONAL BASEBALL

Kia Walks Off With Title

Na Ji-wan hit two home runs in the seventh and deciding game, including a walk-off series ender, to give the Kia Tigers won their 10th Korean Baseball Organization championship but their first since becoming sponsored by Kia. The Tigers won 6-5 in Game Seven and beat the two-time defending champion SK Wyverns in seven games for the Korean Series crown.

The Tigers, an original KBO franchise, won the second-ever league championship in 1983 and won nine times in the first 16 seasons, most in KBO history. However, this was the franchise's first championship since 1997. Na's home run was the second winning walk-off in Korean Series history; the Samsung Lions won in similar fashion in 2002.

The Tigers and Wyverns were the league's top two clubs in the regular season, with Kia having a slightly better winning percentage. Kia also claimed the league MVP in third baseman Kim Sang-hyun, acquired in midseasaon from the LG Twins in a trade. Kim belted 36 home runs, 15 of them in August alone, and added 127 RBIs.

STANDINGS

	W	L	PCT	GB
Kia Tigers	81	48	.609	—
SK Wyverns	80	47	.602	—
Doosan Bears	71	60	.534	11
Lotte Giants	66	67	.496	17
Samsung Lions	64	69	.481	19
(Seoul) Heroes	60	72	.451	22 ½
LG Twins	54	75	.406	27
Hanwha Eagles	46	84	.346	35 ½

INDIVIDUAL BATTING LEADERS

	AVG	AB	R	H	2B	3B	HR	RBI	BB	SO	SB
Park Yong-taek, LG	.372	452	91	168	31	5	18	74	42	63	22
Hong Sung-hoon, Lotte	.371	426	71	158	33	0	12	64	54	55	9
Kim Hyun-su, Doosan	.357	482	97	172	31	6	23	104	84	59	6
Kim Dong-ju, Doosan	.353	354	63	125	28	0	19	86	69	55	3
Jung Keun-woo, SK	.350	480	98	168	29	4	9	59	78	55	53
Petagine, Roberto, LG	.332	388	62	129	16	0	26	100	104	70	2
Kim Sang-hyun, KIA	.315	448	77	141	30	2	36	127	47	103	7
Oh Taek-keun, Heroes	.311	456	84	142	26	0	15	66	77	59	43
Kim Joo-chan, Lotte	.310	435	77	135	30	5	7	51	34	56	34
Kang Bong-kyu, Samsung	.310	449	89	139	24	2	20	78	73	61	20

INDIVIDUAL PITCHING LEADERS

	W	L	ERA	G	SV	IP	H	R	ER	SO
Kim Kwang-hyun, SK	12	2	2.80	21	0	138	121	46	43	112
Jung Byung-do, SK	8	4	3.11	49	8	133	114	50	46	136
Aquilino Lopez, Kia	14	5	3.12	29	0	190	200	83	66	129
Song Eun-beom, SK	12	3	3.13	31	0	149	155	59	52	103
Yang Hyeon-jeong, Kia	12	5	3.15	29	0	148	133	55	52	139
Rick Guttormson, Kia	13	4	3.24	26	0	161	149	61	58	95
Bong Jung-keun, LG	11	12	3.29	26	0	172	160	70	63	127
Ryu Hyun-jin, Hanwha	13	12	3.57	28	0	189	180	80	75	188
Joh Jung-hoon, Lotte	14	9	4.05	27	0	182	189	97	82	175
Jang Won-joon, Lotte	13	8	4.15	28	0	162	175	83	75	108

Gambling Scandal Hits—Again

The biggest news in the Chinese Professional Baseball League came from off the field, not on it. Gambling and game-fixing scandals already had whittled the CPBL down to four franchises, and an error-filled championship series in 2009 resulted in another gambling probe that had eight players in the finals, accused of game fixing by November. Four Brother Elephants—pitchers Li Hao-jen, and Wu Bao-hsien and outfielder Chu Hung-shen—turned themselves in within a week of the end of their championship Series loss to the Uni-President Lions. Up to 12 Elephants players were implicated in the scandal, including former Rockies righthander Tsao Chin-Hui, who was the first Taiwanese pitcher to reach the major leagues.

It's the fifth game-fixing scandal to rock the CPBL in the last dozen years and threatens the future of the league. It spread beyond the top teams, as La New Bears ace Chang Chih-chia—a stalwart on Taiwan's international rosters—was linked in media reports as being involved in the scandal.

Only the champion Lions, who won their third-straight title, have escaped being linked to the gambling mess. The eight-game title series included a record-setting 17-inning game that was ruled a 3-3 tie. The Lions won the clincher 5-2.

STANDINGS

	W	L	T	PCT	GB
Uni-President Lions	63	54	3	.538	—
La New Bears	61	58	1	.513	3
Sinon Bulls	57	60	3	.487	6
Brother Elephants	54	63	3	.462	9

INDIVIDUAL BATTING LEADERS

	AVG	AB	R	H	2B	3B	HR	RBI	SB
Pan Wu-hsiung, Lions	.367	324	61	119	34	3	8	66	11
Peng Cheng-min, Elephants	.366	361	85	132	19	0	17	71	25
Wilton Veras, Bulls	.360	489	71	176	37	1	9	73	3
Cheng Da-hung, Bulls	.355	304	48	108	19	4	6	46	13
Lin Yi-chuan, Bulls	.348	486	92	169	33	4	18	113	6
Lin Zhi-sheng, Bears	.332	431	87	143	29	4	31	111	11
Zhang Jian-ming, Bulls	.328	451	75	148	25	7	5	59	9
Chen Chin-feng, Bears	.320	412	80	132	17	1	27	99	7
Zhou Zhi-chi, Elephants	.311	354	67	110	25	1	5	49	3

INDIVIDUAL PITCHING LEADERS

Player, Team	W	L	ERA	G	SV	IP	H	R	ER	BB	SO
Pan Wei-lung, Lions	10	8	3.30	22	0	134	62	49	23	81
Liao Yu-cheng, Elephants	11	6	3.31	22	0	131	60	48	83	64
Shen Yu-Jie, Bulls	7	5	3.42	65	5	100	40	38	27	77
Aaron Rakers, Bears	13	6	3.45	26	0	159	82	61	45	110
Tsao Chin-hui, Elephants	8	8	3.94	19	0	94	52	41	27	64
Lin Ke-chian, Bulls	10	7	4.02	28	0	146	77	65	52	67
Chang Chih-chia, Bears	10	9	4.31	26	0	136	70	65	54	94
Yu Wen-bin, Bulls	6	4	4.33	40	1	104	52	50	35	50
Lin Ying-chie, Bulls	6	6	4.44	27	1	116	60	57	32	93
Zheng Tian-su, Bulls	14	6	4.44	27	0	158	87	78	35	115

Foreign Talent Lifts Bologna

BY HARVEY SAHKER

Bologna defeated defending champion San Marino in five games to win its third Italy Series in the last seven years. What began as a tightly contested series ended as a romp. In the first three games, Bologna won twice by one run and lost once by two runs. It emphatically wrapped up the title with 17-7 and 16-2 blowout victories in San Marino.

Former Mariners farmhand Claudio Liverziani batted .571 for Bologna and was voted Italy Series MVP. Dominican Eddy Garabito, a Rockies and Orioles alumnus who won the regular-season batting title, hit three homers for Bologna in the series. Longtime American independent leaguer Richard Austin hit .471 in the series with a pair of homers and seven runs batted in.

The Italian Baseball League triple round-robin semifinal competition ended with San Marino on top, one game ahead of Bologna and Rimini. Bologna earned second place—and a berth in the Italy Series—by winning two of its three games against Rimini in the semis. Austin and Garabito hit four homers each in the semifinals and Austin amassed a staggering eighteen RBIs.

A pair of former Dutch Major League players from Curacao helped their respective Italian clubs qualify for the postseason. Ivanon Coffie played for Rimini and tied for the IBL lead in home runs with 10. The 32-year old former Oriole has now played in the American major leagues as well as leagues in Taiwan, the Netherlands and Italy. Johnny Balentina, a 38-year old former catcher for the Dutch national team, led Parma in stolen bases.

Reggio Emilia was relegated after a dismal campaign that included 10 shutout defeats. Paterno was promoted to the IBL at the end of the 2009 season after defeating Anzio in an exciting Serie A2 best-of-five final series that went the distance, including a final-day doubleheader and an 11-10 Paterno victory in 12 innings in the clincher.

Nettuno won the 2009 European Cup. The club claimed the continental club championship by defeating Bologna 1-0 in an all-Italian final. The winning pitcher in the game was former big leaguer Jeff Farnsworth, who logged 14 strikeouts in eight innings.

STANDINGS

	W	L	PCT	GB
Rimini	30	12	.714	—
Bologna	30	12	.714	—
San Marino	26	16	.619	4
Parma	24	18	.571	6
Nettuno	23	19	.548	7
Grosseto	17	25	.405	13
Godo	10	32	.238	20
Reggio Emilia	8	34	.190	22

PLAYOFFS—Semifinals: San Marino (6-3) and Bolonga (5-4) advance out of nine-game round robin among top three teams. Finals: Bologna defeated San Marina 4-1 in best-of-seven series.

INDIVIDUAL BATTING LEADERS

	AVG	AB	R	H	2B	3B	HR	RBI
Garabito, Eddie, Bol	.383	167	43	64	13	3	5	32
Carvajal, Jhonny, Par	.361	169	29	61	5	2	4	30
Connell, Lino, Godo	.354	158	17	56	10	0	5	24
Navarro, Dewis, Net	.339	127	23	43	12	0	2	26
Camilo, Juan, Net	.338	160	41	54	15	1	7	21
Dall'ospedale, Davide, Par	.331	148	29	49	8	0	2	17
Duran, Carlos, SM	.330	185	36	61	11	4	6	22
Crociati, Filippo, Rim	.329	149	21	49	6	2	0	23
Infante, Juan Carlos, Bol	.321	137	36	44	8	1	2	15
Imperiali, Francesco, SM	.319	135	20	43	12	0	0	16

INDIVIDUAL PITCHING LEADERS

	W	L	ERA	G	SV	IP	H	R	ER	BB	SO
Da Silva, Tiago, SM	9	1	1.10	14	0	90	57	16	11	13	107
Garcia, Rafael, Rim	10	1	1.16	14	0	93	58	15	12	24	96
Ramirez, Luis, SM	2	1	1.56	14	0	35	13	6	6	10	60
Figueroa, Juan, Gro	4	7	1.83	14	0	88	75	25	18	20	87
Estrada, Horacio, SM	9	2	1.96	14	0	92	67	25	20	21	79
Patrone, Sandy, Rim	8	1	2.02	13	0	76	65	19	17	22	72
Leal, Remigio, Net	3	2	2.12	15	4	47	39	15	11	15	47
Matos, Jesus, Bol	9	4	2.26	14	0	96	82	29	24	20	118
Grifantini, Marco, Par	5	3	2.45	14	0	73	51	24	20	36	74
Quattrini, Michele, Rim	2	1	2.68	14	4	37	24	11	11	16	30

CHINA

League Flags After Olympics

In the aftermath of the 2008 Olympics, baseball continues to struggle to find a foothold in China.

The Olympic baseball tournament—including a victory for China over Taiwan—was supposed to jumpstart the sport in China, but the professional league still generates little interest in the country.

While the China Baseball League did expand to seven teams in 2009—adding the Henan Elephants—the schedule got shorter, with teams playing just nine regular season games.

The league played a three-month season in previous years (though usually just a few games a week), but the loss of several Japanese corporate sponsors forced the CBL to play its entire season (including playoffs) in less than a month. The championship was also shortened to a one-game playoff, with the Beijing Tigers beating the Guangdong Leopards to take the CBL title.

Beijing emerged from the West/North Division, overcoming the Sichuan Dragon and Tianjin Lions, the defending league champion. Guangdong won the East/South Division, which included the Jiangsu Hopestars and Shanghai Golden Eagles in addition to Henan.

Major League Baseball continues to invest in the country, however, hoping to increase interest in the sport as well as looking for a source of potential talent. Major League Baseball International opened a baseball development center on Sept. 23, the first baseball training facility in China that provides professional baseball training for middle school and high school-aged

students within an academic school environment. The MLB Development Center is in Wuxi, in the eastern part of China on the Yangtze River. The center has an international team of baseball instructors. In addition to receiving academic education, the students will receive baseball training and lessons in English.

"One of the chief goals of Major League Baseball in China is increasing the popularity and participation of the game of baseball among young athletes," MLB president Bob DuPuy said. "The establishment of the MLB Development Center demonstrates Major League Baseball's commitment to expand the sport in China and to aid elite players in reaching their full competitive potential."

NETHERLANDS

Neptunus Wins Title

BY HARVEY SAHKER

Neptunus, the best team during the regular season, defeated Hoofddorp three games to one in the best-of-five Holland Series to claim its first Dutch Major League championship since 2005. The Rotterdam-based club tied the league record of 12 titles, held by the defunct Haarlem Nicols.

Belgium's Benjamin Dille was named Holland Series MVP. The Neptunus second baseman hit .467 in the series and led all players with seven hits and six runs. The series pitted the two stingiest pitching staffs in the league. Hoofddorp hurlers had a combined 2.57 ERA in the regular season. That impressive figure was mediocre compared to Neptunus, who had a puny 1.96 team ERA. Neptunus' dominance showed during a 15-game winning streak during the season.

Ryan Murphy of Hoofddorp won the pitching triple crown after leading the league in ERA (0.89), strikeouts (104) and tying for the league lead with 10 wins. The Canadian righthander played first base for the Pioniers when he wasn't on the mound, hitting .312 and finishing among the league leaders in RBIs and doubles. But he had a forgettable Holland Series, batting just .133 and giving up seven earned runs in his lone start.

Murphy was not the only DML player to excel both on the mound and as a position player in the regular season. Amsterdam Pirates first baseman Kenny Berkenbosch won the league batting crown and had a 3-0, 2.96 mark as a relief pitcher. The 24-year old Amsterdam native was a pitcher in the Marlins farm system in 2004 and 2005.

Fausto Alvarez, 48, had a fine season for the Pirates. The Cuban hit a league-best .500 with run-

ners in scoring position. He was among the league leaders in home runs, RBIs and batting average.

RCH, which had a 15-game losing streak at one point, dropped into the First Division at the end of the season after losing a best-of-five promotion/relegation playoff series to Almere '90, which will compete in the DML in 2010.

STANDINGS

	W	L	T	GB
Neptunus	32	9	1	—
Amsterdam	29	12	1	3
Hoofddorp	27	13	2	4½
Kinheim	26	16	0	6½
Sparta/Feyenoord	24	17	1	8
HCAW	11	30	1	21
ADO	10	31	1	22
RCH	5	36	1	27

PLAYOFFS—Semifinals: Neptunus defeated Kenheim 3-1, Hoofddorp defeated Amsterdam 3-1 in best-of-five series. **Finals:** Neptunus defeated Hoofddorp 3-1 in best-of-five series.

INDIVIDUAL BATTING LEADERS

	AVG	AB	R	H	HR	RBI	BB	SO	SB
Berkenbosch, Ken, Amst	.402	107	23	4	4	24	8	12	1
Rombley, Danny, Kin	.396	144	33	57	5	24	22	18	7
de Jong, Bas, Amst	.377	106	21	40	2	29	8	13	0
Kingsale, Eugene, Nep	.364	151	37	55	3	24	31	16	9
Legito, Raily, Nep	.363	160	29	58	2	32	22	18	18
Connor, Wesley, Amst	.353	173	31	61	1	24	6	12	10
Arends, Jeffrey, Nep	.353	156	26	55	2	48	19	18	3
Alvarez Rizo, Fausto, Amst	.350	137	24	48	4	43	23	22	2
Koeiman, Zair, Amst	.341	129	24	44	3	13	9	23	1
de Jong, Sidney, Amst	.333	147	31	49	1	21	30	12	2

INDIVIDUAL PITCHING LEADERS

	W	L	ERA	G	SV	IP	H	R	HR	BB	SO
Murphy, Ryan, Hoof	10	2	0.89	16	0	111	69	16	1	15	104
Cordemans, Rob, Spa	6	2	0.91	13	0	99	77	18	0	26	103
Ruzic, Dushan, Nep	7	2	1.05	20	6	60	33	7	1	9	55
Markwell, Diegomar, Nep	10	2	1.82	15	0	99	72	29	2	35	83
Bergman, David, Nep	8	6	2.02	15	0	107	80	34	4	18	88
Blackley, Adam, Amst	7	3	2.06	14	0	96	62	26	3	36	93
Heijstek, Kevin, Nep	10	3	2.13	15	0	93	72	28	2	18	53
Gaarman, Herman, Spa	5	2	2.22	22	4	49	40	13	0	40	24
Walsma, Pim, Amst	3	2	2.23	10	27	36	35	13	0	10	34
Gustina, Greg, Spa	6	6	2.36	14	0	92	94	33	0	20	46

INTERNATIONAL BASEBALL

Home Run Tide, Defections Rise

BY PETER BJARKMAN

Cuba's 48th National Series included some notable changes in league structure as well as a few surprises both on and off the field of play. A new regular season format debuted with two eight-team leagues replacing the four-division structure introduced back in 1992-93.

The season itself was split down the middle, just as it was in 2006 for the first World Baseball Classic. In order to accommodate national team participation in the event, Cuban domestic action was shut down from early February through late March. And the island also crowned a first-time-ever league champion when Habana Province rolled over Villa Clara in a five-game post-season finale. It was only the second time the Habana Province Cowboys had reached the championship finals during a quarter-century of Cuban League postseason play.

Aided in part by Japanese-made balls that have proved livelier than their Cuban-made counterparts, Cuban Leaguers provided a number of eye-opening individual performances during a campaign that witnessed a second-straight year of increased home run production. Alfredo Despaigne quickly erased Alexei Bell's one-year-old single-season home run standard, hitting his 32nd in the season's final weekend and earning MVP honors. While Bell disappeared from the headlines and national teams after being struck in the eye by a fastball during the season's opener, Despaigne followed up his performance with a World Cup-record 11 home runs in September as Cuba took home the silver medal.

Michel Enríquez won a second league batting crown, repeating the title he also captured during the earlier WBC-interrupted Cuban season of 2006. Six-time league batting champion Osmani Urrutia (Las Tunas) finally called it quits after 16 league campaigns and numerous national team appearances, retiring as the league's third-best hitter ever (.366). By year's end Enríquez himself had tied Omar Linares for the highest career batting mark with a lofty .368 14-season average.

Cuba continued to lose a noteworthy of number second-level stars as several former national team role players were part of more than 50 ballplayers departing the country. Outfielder Yasser Gómez and pitcher Yadir Martí abandoned the island on eve of the season and usual powerhouse Havana Industriales never seemed to recover from

its significant lineup losses, falling out of the playoff picture for the first time in 13 seasons. Significant losses included national team starters Yunieski Maya (National Series ERA runner-up) and Aroldis Chapman (last season's strikeout leader).

STANDINGS

WEST	W	L	PCT	GB
Habana Province Cowboys	57	33	.633	—
Pinar del Río Foresters	54	36	.600	3
Sancti Spíritus Roosters	48	42	.533	9
Isla de la Juventud Pine Cutters	43	47	.478	14
Matanzas Crocodiles	39	51	.433	18
Industriales Blue Lions	37	53	.411	20
Cienfuegos Elephants	34	56	.378	23
Metropolitanos Warriors	33	57	.367	24

EAST	W	L	PCT	GB
Ciego de Avila Tigers	64	26	.711	—
Santiago de Cuba Wasps	57	33	.633	7
Villa Clara Orangemen	53	37	.589	11
Holguín Dogs	47	43	.522	17
Guantánamo Indians	43	47	.478	21
Camagüey Potters	41	49	.456	23
Las Tunas Woodcutters	36	54	.400	28
Granma Stallions	34	56	.378	30

PLAYOFFS— Quarterfinals: Pinar del Río defeated Sancti Spíritus 4-1, Habana Province defeated Isla de la Juventud 4-1, Ciego de Avila defeated Holguín 4-0, Villa Clara defeated Santiago de Cuba 4-3 in best-of-seven series. **Semifinals:** Habana Province defeated Pinar del Río 4-2 and Villa Clara defeated Ciego de Avila 4-1 in best-of-seven series. **Finals:** Habana Province defeated Villa Clara 4-1 in best-of-seven series.

INDIVIDUAL BATTING LEADERS

PLAYER, TEAM	AVG	AB	H	R	HR	RBI	BB	SO
Michel Enríquez, Isla	.401	299	120	68	12	66	89	15
Yulieski Gourriel, SSP	.399	328	131	77	22	90	48	23
Yorelvis Charles, Ciego	.387	297	115	60	14	69	31	24
Giorvis Duvergel, Gtm	.386	319	123	79	16	73	82	18
Leslie Anderson , Cam	.381	299	114	45	13	66	56	36
Yoilan Cerce, Gtm	.375	363	136	85	14	50	27	43
Alfredo Despaigne, Granma	.375	328	123	73	32	97	61	45
Yariel Duque, Matanzas	.365	323	118	46	13	81	33	30
Henry Urrutia, Las Tunas	.365	271	99	49	6	46	41	29
Yunier Mendoza, SSP	.364	321	117	64	2	38	43	25
Yoandy Garlobo, Matanzas	.364	250	91	58	11	53	71	27
Yordanis Pérez, Ciego	.358	352	126	73	12	57	16	39
Yadil Mujica, Matanzas	.358	257	92	43	3	39	34	29
Reutilio Hurtado, Santiago	.357	294	105	58	10	70	58	61
Yusniel Ibañes, Cienf	.356	281	100	42	6	39	25	44

INDIVIDUAL PITCHING LEADERS

PITCHER, TEAM	ERA	W	L	PCT	G	IP	SO	BB
Yadier Pedroso, Habana	1.91	9	3	.750	16	113	114	33
Yunieski Maya, Pinar	2.22	13	4	.765	21	146	119	40
Alfredo Unzué, Ciego	2.54	8	3	.727	17	92	44	49
Maikel Folch, Ciego	2.69	11	4	.733	18	117	75	52
Wilber Pérez, Isla	2.74	12	4	.750	20	121	89	81
Pedro Luis Lazo, Pinar	2.79	9	2	.818	14	97	70	20
Miguel A. González, Habana	2.86	8	4	.667	18	126	101	30
Yulieski González, Habana	3.04	9	4	.692	17	118	99	35
Norge Luis Vera, Santiago	3.08	11	5	.688	16	111	67	15
Freddy A. Alvarez, Villa Clara	3.40	7	2	.778	17	95	54	32
Yaumier Sánchez , Santiago	3.47	10	3	.769	18	122	92	51
Oscar Jacomino, Isla	3.51	3	2	.600	25	90	38	26
Vicyohandri Odelín, Cam	3.58	7	4	.636	18	121	52	57
Yosvani Fonseca, Matanzas	3.59	7	7	.500	19	120	50	43
Alberto Bicet, Santiago	3.83	9	2	.818	36	99	38	35

INTERNATIONAL BASEBALL

Bullpen lifts Venezuela to 7th Caribbean title

Venezuela clinched the 2009 Caribbean Series championship early, as a 5-3 victory against Mexico left the host nation two games back of undefeated Venezuela with two games to play. Venezuela, represented by the Tigres de Aragua, wound up 5-1, earning Aragua its first-ever Caribbean Series title and the seventh in Venezuela history.

"We won . . . is that good?" excited Venezuelan manager Buddy Bailey (Red Sox) said to the media in the postgame press conference. He then credited the victory to the heart of the players and the superb performances by his bullpen.

One of those relievers was Francisco Butto, who wound up pitching in the Phillies system in 2009. Butto set a Caribbean Series record with four saves in Venezuela's first five games. His six career Caribbean Series saves also is a record, and he was named tournament MVP.

Bailey's strategy was to utilize his deep bullpen liberally throughout the series, usually limiting his pitchers to 30-35 pitches each. He said after the clinching victory that he didn't want Mexico's Gonzalez brothers, first baseman Adrian and second baseman Edgar, to see the same pitcher twice in the final game. In the ninth, he was able to avoid Adrian Gonzalez as Butto retired Christian Quintero on a flyout to center field to end the game with Gonzalez on deck. That nailed down the first Caribbean Series title for Aragua, which earned the right to represent Venezuela by defeating Caracas in a seven-game series for the Venezuelan League title.

Two other key pieces for Aragua were first baseman Hector Gimenez and Twins farmhands Wilson Ramos and Yohan Pino, who was traded during the 2009 season to the Indians in the Carl Pavano trade. Gimenez, a former Astros farmhand, hit the team's lone home run, a solo walk-off homer to push Venezuela to a 1-0 victory in its fourth game, also against Mexico's representative, the Mazatlan Deer. Ramos hit .385 and drew four walks in Venezuela's first five victories, after batting .317/.331/.475 in the Venezuelan League season. Pino posted a 3.38 ERA in relief during the Venezuelan League season and worked in middle relief in Bailey's deep bullpen.

Giants farmhand Pablo Sandoval was named

KEVIN PATAKY

Twins farmhand Wilson Ramos was one of Venezuela's top hitters in 2009

Baseball America's Winter Player of the Year. Setting the stage for his 2009 season, Sandoval kept hitting in his native Venezuela, batting .396/.449/.677 with 12 home runs. He had a 13-game hitting streak as well and set himself up for his huge first full season in the big leagues, when he batted .330/.387/.556 with 25 home runs, 44 doubles and 90s RBIs.

DOMINICAN LEAGUE

TEAM	W	L	PCT	GB
Gigantes	30	20	.600	—
Azucareros	28	22	.560	2
Licey	26	24	.520	4
Aguilas	26	24	.520	4
Escogido	25	25	.500	5
Estrellas	16	34	.320	14
ROUND ROBIN				
Licey	12	6	.667	—
Gigantes	12	7	.632	½
Azucareros	11	8	.579	1 ½
Aguilas	2	16	.111	10

FINALS: Licey defeated Gigantes 5-0.

INTERNATIONAL BASEBALL

INDIVIDUAL BATTING LEADERS

BATTER, CLUB	AVG	AB	R	H	2B	3B	HR	RBI	SB
Ozuna, Pablo, Est	.390	118	18	46	12	0	3	21	2
Hernandez, Anderson, Lic	.365	211	41	77	20	6	1	29	6
Francisco, Juan, Gig	.360	161	36	58	9	2	12	37	0
Fox, Jake, Lic	.353	116	21	41	13	0	3	31	0
Aybar, Erick, Lic	.348	164	32	57	6	1	5	30	3
German, Esteban, Azu	.344	157	32	54	5	4	2	23	19
Pena, Brayan, Gig	.341	164	38	56	9	2	8	38	4
Tatis, Fernando, Est	.338	148	22	50	15	1	2	18	4
Hernandez, Diory, Esc	.329	155	32	51	8	0	7	27	5
Polonia, Luis, Agu	.328	192	35	63	14	1	0	23	4

INDIVIDUAL PITCHING LEADERS

PITCHER, CLUB	W	L	ERA	G	SV	IP	H	BB	SO
Sosa, Jorge, Lic	6	2	2.53	11	0	57	51	16	24
Hughes, Dusty, Esc	3	1	2.56	11	0	39	30	27	31
Bastardo, Antonio, Gig	2	0	2.63	8	0	38	28	17	25
Lopez, Aquilino, Gig	3	1	2.84	9	0	44	39	7	36
Figueroa, Nelson, Agu	3	2	3.13	5	0	32	33	6	24
Perez, Beltran, Gig	3	0	3.38	16	0	32	30	18	27
Nippert, Dustin, Lic	2	2	3.48	7	0	34	30	18	33
Mateo, Julio, Esc	1	4	3.70	10	0	41	47	5	22
Valdez, Edward, Esc	0	3	4.08	15	0	40	49	10	23
Beltre, Omar, Azu	2	2	4.35	11	0	50	51	11	36

MEXICAN PACIFIC LEAGUE

TEAM	W	L	PCT	GB
Mazatlan	41	27	.603	—
Los Mochis	36	29	.554	3 ½
Guasave	37	31	.544	4
Hermosillo	36	32	.529	5
Mexicali	33	33	.500	7
Navojoa	31	37	.456	10
Obregon	29	38	.433	11 ½
Culiacan	26	42	.382	15

FINALS: Mazatlan defeated Los Mochis 4-0.

INDIVIDUAL BATTING LEADERS

PLAYER, TEAM	AVG	AB	R	H	2B	3B	HR	RBI	SB
Quintero, Christian, Maz	.357	185	36	66	15	0	4	20	5
Vazquez, Jorge, Cul	.348	198	37	69	12	0	15	46	0
Murillo, Agustin, Obr	.345	252	41	87	30	0	11	47	12
Roberson, Chris, Her	.323	260	46	84	15	3	2	25	16
Rodriguez, Jose, GSV	.314	258	40	81	13	1	9	40	5
Robles, Oscar, Mxc	.309	246	39	76	16	1	9	48	2
Pellow, Kit, Cul	.302	189	33	57	6	0	11	37	0
Cervantes, Refugio, Cul	.298	198	26	59	11	0	10	45	0
Gastelum, Carlos, Her	.298	205	34	61	6	0	3	18	3
Cesar, Dionys, GSV	.288	243	42	70	11	2	7	25	12

INDIVIDUAL PITCHING LEADERS

PITCHER, TEAM	W	L	ERA	G	SV	IP	H	BB	SO
Castillo, Ismael, Moc	5	5	2.86	13	0	72	60	25	34
Lara, Orlando, Nav	5	3	3.15	14	0	71	56	34	55
Silva, Walter, Maz	5	4	3.23	13	0	70	62	20	61
Armenta, Alejandro, Nav	2	4	3.25	15	1	72	57	30	61
Ramirez, Miguel, Her	5	4	3.80	15	0	69	61	22	30
Espinoza, Omar, Cul	7	4	3.82	14	0	73	65	30	44
Ortega, Pablo, Maz	5	6	3.84	14	0	80	86	19	39
Montemayor, Humberto, Mxc	3	6	4.17	14	0	73	70	27	57
Campos, Francisco, Her	2	4	4.29	14	0	84	86	23	63
Rodriguez, Jesus, Obr	3	6	5.38	15	0	72	85	31	53

PUERTO RICAN LEAGUE

TEAM	W	L	PCT	GB
Ponce	27	15	.643	—
Arecibo	22	18	.550	4
Mayaguez	20	23	.465	7 ½
Santurce	19	22	.463	7 ½
Caguas	19	24	.442	8 ½
Carolina	17	24	.415	9 ½

INDIVIDUAL BATTING LEADERS

PLAYER, TEAM	AVG	AB	R	H	2B	3B	HR	RBI	BB	SO	SB
Gonzalez, Andy, Ponce	.387	137	34	53	7	1	2	22	38	22	9
Valentin, Geraldo, Sant	.362	116	18	42	6	1	0	13	10	6	6
Matos, Luis, Cag	.362	163	28	59	12	1	6	21	20	25	10
Feliciano, Jesus, Are	.338	154	40	52	10	2	2	12	24	14	7
Martinez-Esteve, Eddy, Car	.331	127	20	42	11	0	4	23	14	18	2
Aviles, Mike, Sant	.321	112	13	36	9	5	0	13	10	15	5
Rivera, Carlos, Ponce	.321	131	16	42	9	1	2	31	8	13	1
Padilla, Jorge, Are	.317	139	30	44	7	2	10	44	22	26	1
Santos, Omir, Cag	.313	112	14	35	6	0	1	8	6	15	0
De Jesus Jr., Ivan, Car	.309	149	32	46	7	3	5	16	9	25	5

INDIVIDUAL PITCHING LEADERS

PITCHER, TEAM	W	L	ERA	G	SV	IP	H	BB	SO
Kennedy, Ian, May	2	2	1.56	6	0	35	19	12	31
Simas, Bill, May	2	1	1.93	21	0	33	27	6	15
Gee, Dillon, Ponce	4	0	2.22	10	0	49	43	13	43
Youman, Shane, Sant	4	1	2.28	11	1	51	53	8	22
Perkins, Vince, Cag	4	2	2.74	10	0	49	48	22	31
Matos, Josue, Car	5	2	2.89	12	0	53	48	15	32
Roman, Orlando, Cag	1	4	3.05	11	0	59	52	23	44
Santos, Jarrett, Cag	2	3	3.26	12	0	61	49	18	30
Villarreal, Luis, Sant	4	1	3.30	10	0	46	41	15	35
Antonini, Michael, Ponce	2	0	3.45	9	0	47	42	13	29

VENEZUELAN LEAGUE

TEAM	W	L	PCT	GB
Caracas	42	21	.667	—
Aragua	36	27	.571	6
Lara	33	30	.524	9
La Guaira	31	32	.492	11
Zulia	31	32	.492	11
Caribes	28	35	.444	14
Magallanes	28	35	.444	14
Margarita	23	40	.365	19

ROUND ROBIN

	W	L	PCT	GB
Caracas	10	7	.588	—
Aragua	10	8	.556	½
La Guaira	9	8	.529	1
Lara	7	9	.438	2½

FINALS: Aragua defeated Caracas 4-3.

INDIVIDUAL BATTING LEADERS

PLAYER, TEAM	AVG	AB	R	H	2B	3B	HR	RBI	SB
Sandoval, Pablo, Mag	.396	192	35	76	12	3	12	33	0
Salazar, Oscar, Lag	.352	179	38	63	15	2	6	26	3
Medina, Rodney, Zul	.351	171	32	60	11	1	2	20	0
Gonzalez, Luis, Ori	.350	217	36	76	9	1	6	30	2
Guzman, Jesus, Car	.349	232	48	81	15	4	13	67	4
Blanco, Gregor, Lag	.349	172	39	60	14	4	2	22	6
Gimenez, Hector, Ara	.335	203	43	68	16	0	7	44	0
Reyes, Rene, Mar	.332	196	23	65	11	0	5	30	4
Parra, Gerardo, Zul	.329	246	39	81	20	1	7	44	15
Jimenez, Luis Antonio, Lar	.329	146	29	48	7	0	6	31	2

INDIVIDUAL PITCHING LEADERS

PITCHER, TEAM	W	L	ERA	G	SV	IP	H	BB	SO
Austen, David, Zul	8	2	1.98	11	0	64	55	8	38
Gutierrez, Juan, Car	5	2	2.63	13	0	65	54	20	56
Morales, Franklin, Car	4	3	2.72	10	0	53	52	13	37
Bonilla, Henry, Lag	3	2	3.21	13	0	67	64	26	34
Estrada, Horacio, Ara	5	3	3.56	15	0	68	71	15	38
Zambrano, Victor, Mag	1	4	3.86	13	0	56	50	32	42
Randolph, Stephen, Lag	5	5	3.98	13	0	61	50	37	51
Totten, Heath, Zul	4	4	4.23	14	0	66	68	13	47
Gonzalez, Enrique, Lag	5	2	4.55	13	0	59	64	18	41
Granado, Jan, Zul	4	5	4.70	16	0	54	62	26	40

COLLEGE

CHRIS MACHLAN

LSU, the most dominant team of the 1990s, returned to the top of the college baseball world

Louisiana State wins sixth national title

BY AARON FITT

OMAHA

Louisiana State athletic director Joe Alleva waded through the throng around the Rosenblatt Stadium pitcher's mound and spotted a grinning Louis Coleman. With a hug and a handshake, Alleva said into Coleman's ear, "Thanks for coming back."

Moments earlier, Coleman had set off a wild celebration on that mound by striking out three straight Texas Longhorns to secure an 11-4 victory and the sixth national championship for LSU—the first since 2000. After getting Connor Rowe to swing through an 0-and-2 pitch, Coleman chucked his glove into the air and was speared to the ground by catcher Micah Gibbs. Within seconds, Coleman was enveloped by a writhing sea of yellow jerseys.

"There's no one better to close out that game than Louis," said LSU sophomore righthander Anthony Ranaudo, who started Game Three of the College World Series Finals and picked up his 12th victory of the season with 5⅓ innings of work. "What he did to sacrifice a year of professional ball to come back—he said he wanted to come back to win a national championship. I know everyone is happy he got to close it out for us and be the one at the bottom of the dogpile."

Ranaudo played his own key part in the clinching victory, though he didn't have his best stuff or sharpest control, as evidenced by his five walks. The Tigers staked him to an early 4-0 lead, and though Texas battled back to tie the score in the fifth inning, Ranaudo kept the Tigers in the game until LSU's patient, explosive offense could break it open with a five-run sixth.

"It's just the story of our year: When the pitcher might not have his best stuff, the hitters pick him up, and vice versa," Ranaudo said.

"I knew he was going to give us a chance," said LSU junior first baseman Sean Ochinko, who stepped into the cleanup spot and delivered four hits and three RBIs. "I put my head on the pillow last night knowing Anthony Ranaudo would give us a chance to win. And he did, he kept us right in there. We had a big five-run inning, and that was it."

Knowing their ace was on the mound, the Tigers came out loose and confident, and CWS Most Outstanding Player Jared Mitchell put them on top with a three-run homer down the right-field line in the first inning. After Texas tied the game at 4-4 with two runs in the bottom of the fifth, Mitchell sparked the big sixth-inning rally by working an eight-pitch walk to lead off the frame. He scored a batter later on freshman Mikie Mahtook's RBI double, and LSU never trailed again.

"I thought we were a little flat in those middle

COACHING CAROUSEL

SCHOOL	NEW COACH (PREVIOUS SCHOOL/JOB)	FORMER COACH (REASON FOR DEPARTURE)
Alabama	Mitch Gaspard (Alabama assistant)	Jim Wells (retired)
Alcorn State	Barret Rey (Grambling State head coach)	Willie McGowan (retired)
Grambling State	James Cooper (Grambling State assistant)	Barret Rey (Alcorn State head coach)
Indiana State	Rick Heller (Northern Iowa head coach)	Lindsay Meggs (Washington head coach)
Marist	Chris Tracz (Army pitching coach)	Dennis Healy (Wake Forest assistant)
Maryland	Erik Bakich (Vanderbilt assistant)	Terry Rupp (fired)
New Orleans	Bruce Peddie (New Orleans assistant)	Tom Walter (Wake Forest head coach)
UNC Asheville	Tom Smith (UNC Asheville assistant)	Willie Stewart (resigned)
Southern Mississippi	Scott Berry (Southern Mississippi assistant)	Corky Palmer (retired)
Wake Forest	Tom Walter (New Orleans head coach)	Rick Rembielak (fired)
Washington	Lindsay Meggs (Indiana State head coach)	Ken Knutson (fired)
Western Illinois	Mike Villano (Central Michigan assistant)	Stan Hyman (deceased)

innings," Ochinko said. "I knew when Jared came up there and fought really hard for that walk that that was going to start something."

Texas righthander Brandon Workman, who came in to start the third after starter Cole Green allowed four runs in the first two innings, had retired nine straight Tigers heading into the sixth, but Longhorns coach Augie Garrido pulled him after Mahtook's double, and relievers Austin Dicharry and Austin Wood could not provide any answers. LSU capitalized on two walks, two hit batsmen and a throwing error by Dicharry to score five times in the inning despite managing just two hits.

Ochinko, who moved into the cleanup spot because coach Paul Mainieri liked his chances against a lefthanded pitcher like Wood in a tight spot, faced the Longhorns senior and capped the rally with a two-run single through the left side of the infield.

Texas never threatened again, mustering just one hit of its own over the last four innings.

"Answering right back, it really was devastating," Texas second baseman Travis Tucker said of LSU's sixth. "They got the momentum back; we had it our way, they chipped it back to theirs. They're a great ballclub."

Garrido echoed Tucker's praise for the Tigers, who opened the season ranked second in the nation and finished it on top of the college baseball world. In between, LSU won the Southeastern Conference's regular-season and tournament titles, dropping just two weekend series all year.

"We've won several championships this year, but if we hadn't won this one, it probably would have left a little bit of an empty feeling," Mainieri said. "But we won't have to know that, because we did it."

Mainieri shook things up to improve his defense in April, inserting freshman Austin Nola at shortstop and sliding preseason All-America shortstop D.J. LeMahieu to second, and preseason All-America second baseman Ryan Schimpf to left

field. The Tigers went 28-5 from that point on, and any lingering doubt that they were the nation's best team in 2009 was erased with that 11-4 win against Texas in Game Three of the Finals.

"I don't think we lost this tournament; I think that they won it," Garrido said. "It was a great effort that combined all the things that baseball is about. They overcame adversity, came from behind, did things that couldn't be done, got good pitching when they needed it, got tremendous defensive plays. So a well-deserved championship for LSU."

The Tigers' sixth national title will require an addition to the new Alex Box Stadium. At the old stadium, which was replaced at the start of this year, a giant billboard—known as the Intimidator—stood behind the right-field wall, displaying the years of all five LSU national titles alongside a fearsome photo of a Tiger.

Toward the end of LSU's postgame press conference, Mainieri called out to Alleva standing at the back of the Hall of Fame room, "Joe, are we getting a new Intimidator with a new number on it?"

"Yeah, no doubt," Alleva called back.

For players like Mitchell, who grew up in Louisiana watching the Tigers dominate college baseball, putting a new number on that board is what it's all about.

"It's an unbelievable feeling to be put in position where basically you'll be remembered forever in Baton Rouge now," said Mitchell, who along with reliever Chad Jones also was part of LSU's 2007 Bowl Championship Series football title. "To be a part of that company with guys who've done it before is unbelievable. To put LSU baseball back on top where it belongs, for years to come—to be a part of that is something special."

Texas Looks To 2010

Augie Garrido finished second at the 1992 College World Series with a Cal State Fullerton team led by future big leaguer Phil Nevin.

"I know this: That 1992 team with Nevin and those guys that finished second, more of them have gone on to different professions—real estate, banking, dentistry," Garrido said. "They have a higher level of success rate in life than teams that won. I honestly believe it's because they never want to finish second in anything again. I have that experience—I know that to be true."

Garrido's 2004 Texas team also finished as the national runner-up—famously and notoriously failing to show up at home plate for the second-place trophy presentation. The Longhorns returned to Omaha in 2005 and won the CWS but did not even win a regional the next three years before getting back to Omaha and pushing Louisiana State to the third game of the CWS Finals in 2009. Even though the Longhorns fell short of a national title, there is reason to believe they could follow the example of the '05 team next year.

Texas will lose just two drafted players—closer Austin Wood and first baseman Brandon Belt—off this year's club. The Longhorns' rotation of rising juniors Chance Ruffin, Cole Green and Brandon Workman and rising sophomore Tyler Jungmann—who was the best pitcher in the CWS, as evidenced by his complete-game win over Louisiana State in the CWS Finals' second game—should be the best in the nation.

Texas also should get its biggest bats back in juniors Kevin Keyes, an outfielder; Cameron Rupp, a catcher/outfielder; and DH Russell Moldenhauer, who hit four homers in Omaha after going homerless during an injury-plagued season.

"I honestly believe this is the beginning of a new era for Texas baseball in Omaha," Garrido said. "There's a lot of very disappointed people, but the first team I ever brought to Omaha was Cal State Fullerton (in 1975)—the first time at the World Series, two and out. The first team I brought from Texas to Omaha (in 2000)—two and out. We didn't have a player with College World Series experience on this team, and we finished second in Omaha—pretty cool. (It was) the best team I've ever brought to Omaha without any experience, and the best finish, ever."

Despite its youth and inexperience, Texas put together a remarkable season that will be remembered fondly in Austin, even without a championship at the end of the road. The Longhorns won the Big 12's regular-season and tournament titles, losing just two weekend series all season. They survived the longest game in NCAA history—25 epic innings—in regionals against Boston College, then overcame a four-run ninth-inning deficit to beat Army on a walk-off grand slam in the regional clincher.

COLLEGE WORLD SERIES

STANDINGS

BRACKET ONE	W	L
Louisiana State	3	0
Arkansas	2	2
Virginia	1	2
Cal State Fullerton	0	2
BRACKET TWO	**W**	**L**
Texas	3	0
Arizona State	2	2
North Carolina	1	2
Southern Mississippi	0	2

CWS FINALS (BEST-OF-THREE)

June 22: Louisiana State 7, Texas 6
June 23: Texas 5, Louisiana State 1
June 24: Louisiana State 11, Texas 4
C: Cameron Rupp, Texas. **1B:** Dustin Ackley, North Carolina. **2B:** D.J. LeMahieu, Louisiana State. **3B:** Kyle Seager, North Carolina. **SS:** Tyler Cannon, Virginia. **OF:** Kole Calhoun, Arizona State; *Jared Mitchell, Louisiana State; Ryan Schimpf, Louisiana State. **DH:** Russell Moldenhauer, Texas. **P:** Taylor Jungmann, Texas; Anthony Ranaudo, Louisiana State.
*Named Most Outstanding Player.

BATTING
(MINIMUM 10 PA)

PLAYER	AVG	AB	R	H	2B	3B	HR	RBI	SB
Keith Werman, UVa.	.600	10	3	6	2	0	0	3	0
Tyler Cannon, UVa.	.600	10	3	6	0	1	0	1	0
Kole Calhoun, ASU	.563	16	5	9	2	0	3	11	0
Kyle Seager, UNC	.538	13	2	7	2	0	1	3	0
Dustin Ackley, UNC	.500	16	2	8	1	0	0	3	0
Mike Cavasinni, UNC	.462	13	1	6	0	0	0	1	0
Ben Tschepikow, Arkansas	.455	11	4	5	2	0	0	0	1
D.J. LeMahieu, LSU	.444	27	9	12	1	1	1	4	2
Travis Tucker, Texas	.400	25	6	10	1	0	1	3	0
Johnny Ruettiger, ASU	.385	13	3	5	1	0	0	0	0
Ben Bunting, UNC	.385	13	4	5	0	0	0	2	0

PITCHING
(MINIMUM 6 IP)

PITCHER	W-L	ERA	G	SV	IP	H	BB	SO
Taylor Jungmann, Texas	3-0	0.59	4	0	15	8	5	15
Alex White, UNC	0-0	1.00	1	0	9	7	3	12
Andrew Carraway, UVa.	1-1	1.50	2	0	6	7	2	4
Josh Spence, ASU	1-0	2.57	2	0	14	15	5	16
Dallas Keuchel, Arkansas	2-0	2.70	2	0	10	8	4	7
Danny Hultzen, UVa.	0-0	2.89	2	0	9	12	1	12
Anthony Ranaudo, LSU	2-0	3.68	3	0	15	17	9	12
Mike Bolsinger, Arkansas	0-0	4.00	3	1	9	8	2	11
Louis Coleman, LSU	1-0	4.20	4	0	15	16	4	18
Adam Warren, UNC	1-0	4.50	1	0	6	3	5	6

Then Texas won a tough three-game super regional against Texas Christian, and the 'Horns reached the CWS Finals with three dramatic wins—on a walk-off walk against Southern Mississippi, a comeback from a 6-0 deficit against Arizona State (and ace Mike Leake), and a walk-off homer against ASU.

"It's been amazing," fifth-year senior Preston

Clark said. "Every guy's pulled for each other. It's been the best team we've been apart of. Everybody pulls for one another. It was a great run.

"(LSU) played unbelievable ball today; they punched us in the mouth. Coach Garrido told us that would happen. We punched back, but they punched back harder and we couldn't get another rally going."

COLLEGE WORLD SERIES CHAMPIONS: 1947—2009   *Undefeated

YEAR	CHAMPION	COACH	RECORD	RUNNER-UP	MVP
1947	California*	Clint Evans	31-10	Yale	None selected
1948	Southern California	Sam Barry	40-12	Yale	None selected
1949	Texas*	Bibb Falk	23-7	Wake Forest	Charles Teague, 2b, Wake Forest
1950	Texas	Bibb Falk	27-6	Washington State	Ray VanCleef, of, Rutgers
1951	Oklahoma*	Jack Baer	19-9	Tennessee	Sid Hatfield, 1b-p, Tennessee
1952	Holy Cross	Jack Barry	21-3	Missouri	Jim O'Neill, p, Holy Cross
1953	Michigan	Ray Fisher	21-9	Texas	J.L. Smith, p, Texas
1954	Missouri	Hi Simmons	22-4	Rollins	Tom Yewcic, c, Michigan State
1955	Wake Forest	Taylor Sanford	29-7	Western Michigan	Tom Borland, p, Oklahoma State
1956	Minnesota	Dick Siebert	33-9	Arizona	Jerry Thomas, p, Minnesota
1957	California*	George Wolfman	35-10	Penn State	Cal Emery, 1b-p, Penn State
1958	Southern California	Rod Dedeaux	35-7	Missouri	Bill Thom, p, Southern California
1959	Oklahoma State	Toby Greene	27-5	Arizona	Jim Dobson, 3b, Oklahoma State
1960	Minnesota	Dick Siebert	34-7	Southern California	John Erickson, 2b, Minnesota
1961	Southern California*	Rod Dedeaux	43-9	Oklahoma State	Littleton Fowler, p, Oklahoma State
1962	Michigan	Don Lund	31-13	Santa Clara	Bob Garibaldi, p, Santa Clara
1963	Southern California	Rod Dedeaux	37-16	Arizona	Bud Hollowell, c, Southern California
1964	Minnesota	Dick Siebert	31-12	Missouri	Joe Ferris, p, Maine
1965	Arizona State	Bobby Winkles	54-8	Ohio State	Sal Bando, 3b, Arizona State
1966	Ohio State	Marty Karow	27-6	Oklahoma State	Steve Arlin, p, Ohio State
1967	Arizona State	Bobby Winkles	53-12	Houston	Ron Davini, c, Arizona State
1968	Southern California*	Rod Dedeaux	45-14	Southern Illinois	Bill Seinsoth, 1b, Southern California
1969	Arizona State	Bobby Winkles	56-11	Tulsa	John Dolinsek, of, Arizona State
1970	Southern California	Rod Dedeaux	51-13	Florida State	Gene Ammann, p, Florida State
1971	Southern California	Rod Dedeaux	53-13	Southern Illinois	Jerry Tabb, 1b, Tulsa
1972	Southern California	Rod Dedeaux	50-13	Arizona State	Russ McQueen, p, Southern California
1973	Southern California*	Rod Dedeaux	51-11	Arizona State	Dave Winfield, of-p, Minnesota
1974	Southern California	Rod Dedeaux	50-20	Miami	George Milke, p, Southern California
1975	Texas	Cliff Gustafson	56-6	South Carolina	Mickey Reichenbach, 1b, Texas
1976	Arizona	Jerry Kindall	56-17	Eastern Michigan	Steve Powers, dh-p, Arizona
1977	Arizona State	Jim Brock	57-12	South Carolina	Bob Horner, 3b, Arizona State
1978	Southern California*	Rod Dedeaux	54-9	Arizona State	Rod Boxberger, p, Southern California
1979	Cal State Fullerton	Augie Garrido	60-14	Arkansas	Tony Hudson, p, Cal State Fullerton
1980	Arizona	Jerry Kindall	45-21	Hawaii	Terry Francona, of, Arizona
1981	Arizona State	Jim Brock	55-13	Oklahoma State	Stan Holmes, of, Arizona State
1982	Miami	Ron Fraser	57-18	Wichita State	Dan Smith, p, Miami
1983	Texas	Cliff Gustafson	66-14	Alabama	Calvin Schiraldi, p, Texas
1984	Cal State Fullerton	Augie Garrido	66-20	Texas	John Fishel, of, Cal State Fullerton
1985	Miami*	Ron Fraser	64-16	Texas	Greg Ellena, dh, Miami
1986	Arizona	Jerry Kindall	49-19	Florida State	Mike Senne, of, Arizona
1987	Stanford	Mark Marquess	53-17	Oklahoma State	Paul Carey, of, Stanford
1988	Stanford	Mark Marquess	46-23	Arizona State	Lee Plemel, p, Stanford
1989	Wichita State	Gene Stephenson	68-16	Texas	Greg Brummett, p, Wichita State
1990	Georgia	Steve Webber	52-19	Oklahoma State	Mike Rebhan, p, Georgia
1991	Louisiana State*	Skip Bertman	55-18	Wichita State	Gary Hymel, c, Louisiana State
1992	Pepperdine*	Andy Lopez	48-11	Cal State Fullerton	Phil Nevin, 3b, Cal State Fullerton
1993	Louisiana State	Skip Bertman	53-17	Wichita State	Todd Walker, 2b, Louisiana State
1994	Oklahoma*	Larry Cochell	50-17	Georgia Tech	Chip Glass, of, Oklahoma
1995	Cal State Fullerton*	Augie Garrido	57-9	Southern California	Mark Kotsay, of-p, Cal State Fullerton
1996	Louisiana State*	Skip Bertman	52-15	Miami	Pat Burrell, 3b, Miami
1997	Louisiana State*	Skip Bertman	57-13	Alabama	Brandon Larson, ss, Louisiana State
1998	Southern California	Mike Gillespie	49-17	Arizona State	Wes Rachels, 2b, Southern California
1999	Miami*	Jim Morris	50-13	Florida State	Marshall McDougall, 2b, Florida State
2000	Louisiana State*	Skip Bertman	52-17	Stanford	Trey Hodges, rhp, Louisiana State
2001	Miami*	Jim Morris	53-12	Stanford	Charlton Jimerson, of, Miami
2002	Texas*	Augie Garrido	57-15	South Carolina	Huston Street, rhp, Texas
2003	Rice	Wayne Graham	58-12	Stanford	John Hudgins, rhp, Stanford
2004	Cal State Fullerton	George Horton	47-22	Texas	Jason Windsor, rhp, Cal State Fullerton
2005	Texas*	Augie Garrido	56-16	Florida	David Maroul, 3b, Texas
2006	Oregon State	Pat Casey	50-16	North Carolina	Jonah Nickerson, rhp, Oregon State
2007	Oregon State*	Pat Casey	49-18	North Carolina	Jorge Reyes, rhp, Oregon State
2008	Fresno State	Mike Batesole	47-31	Georgia	Tommy Mendonca, 3b, Fresno State
2009	Louisiana State	Paul Mainieri	56-17	Texas	Jared Mitchell, of, Louisiana State

Garrido, 70, did confess some regret over the way his pitching moves played out in the fateful sixth inning, when LSU broke a 4-4 tie with five runs. Workman, working in relief of Green, had retired nine straight heading into the inning, but Jared Mitchell walked to start the sixth and Mikie Mahtook doubled him home. Rather than give Workman a chance to get out of the inning, Garrido went to relievers Austin Dicharry and Austin Wood, and the move backfired as both struggled with their control.

"That was the decision we made; in hindsight it doesn't look so good," Garrido said. "We made the same kind of decision the other night (in the ninth inning of Game One of the Finals) and it didn't work out. When those decisions don't work out, they can be scrutinized, they can be questioned of course. That's why I don't like to take the credit for anything the players do, and I'm not going to take the blame.

"We played our cards, we thought they were the right ones, it didn't work out. To me it's credit to the opponent. They are the best team we played by far."

Wood, in fact, struggled throughout the postseason after his heroic appearance against Boston College. The nation's leader with 41 appearances, he threw 11 innings the rest of the way and gave up 16 hits and 10 runs (eight earned), posting a 6.55 ERA in that stretch. Prior to the CWS Finals, Garrido lauded Wood's grit and guts, then joked that if Wood—a fifth-round pick in this year's draft—comes down with a sore arm anytime in the next 10 years, he knows he'll be blamed.

More pertinent to 2009, the senior lefty wasn't able to be his best when the Longhorns needed him in Omaha, but they would never have gotten there without his Herculean effort against the Eagles. In 2010, Texas will have to get there without him.

CWS NOTES

■ Though attendance was down for the winner-take-all Game Three of the CWS Finals (19,986, the fourth-lowest attendance of the 15 CWS games in 2009), the overall attendance of 336,076 set a CWS record. Of course, last year's overall attendance set a record also, but that was because the NCAA changed the way attendance was measured. On average, attendance was down last year, as just 20,631 fans per game showed up. That number rebounded to 22,405 in 2009, thanks in part to the deep runs by two of the sport's top fan bases, LSU and Texas. The record for average attendance is 23,952, set in 2005.

■ LSU has reached the championship round of the CWS six times in its history and has won the national title all six times. The Tigers finished this season with 56 wins—the most by a national champion since Texas in 2005. They posted a .991 field-

RPI RANKINGS

The Ratings Percentage Index is an important tool used by the NCAA in selecting at-large teams for the 64-team Division I regional tournament. The NCAA now releases its RPI rankings during the season. These were the top 100 finishers for 2009. A team's rank in the final Baseball America Top 25 is indicated in parentheses, and College World Series teams are in bold.

1. Cal State Fullerton (4)	47-16	51. San Diego	29-25
2. Texas (2)	50-16	52. Notre Dame	36-23
3. Virginia (5)	49-15	53. Jacksonville	37-22
4. Louisiana State (1)	56-17	54. SE Louisiana	37-22
5. North Carolina (6)	48-18	55. Rhode Island	37-20
6. Arizona State (3)	51-14	56. Cal Poly	37-21
7. Arkansas (7)	41-24	57. Western Carolina	35-22
8. Texas Christian (14)	40-18	58. Tennessee	26-29
9. Georgia Tech (20)	38-19	59. Xavier	39-21
10. Florida (12)	42-22	60. Brigham Young	30-24
Rice (8)	43-18	61. Arizona	30-25
12. Clemson (16)	44-22	62. Coll. of Charleston	35-22
13. Miami	38-22	63. Eastern Illinois	36-14
14. Mississippi (13)	44-20	64. UNC Wilmington	31-23
15. Florida State (9)	45-18	65. Illinois	34-20
16. UC Irvine (10)	45-15	66. Tulane	34-25
17. Louisville (15)	47-18	67. Missouri State	34-20
18. Texas A&M	37-24	68. Hawaii	32-26
19. Oklahoma (18)	43-20	69. Troy	33-23
20. Georgia	38-24	70. Sam Houston State	36-24
21. South Carolina (25)	40-23	71. UCLA	27-29
22. Kansas State (19)	43-18	72. Connecticut	36-24
23. East Carolina (17)	46-20	73. South Florida	34-25
24. Elon (24)	41-18	74. Southern California	28-28
25. Minnesota (21)	40-19	75. Duke	35-24
26. Oklahoma State	34-24	76. Stanford	30-25
27. Vanderbilt	37-27	77. UC Riverside	33-20
28. Coastal Carolina	47-16	78. Kent State	43-17
29. Boston College	34-26	79. The Citadel	37-22
30. Baylor	30-26	80. San Jose State	41-20
31. Southern Miss (11)	40-26	81. Utah	28-31
32. Oral Roberts	33-15	82. Fla. International	34-23
33. Auburn	31-25	83. Appalachian State	33-21
34. Texas State	41-17	84. Texas-San Antonio	32-24
35. Missouri	35-27	85. UC Santa Barbara	29-23
36. Ohio State	42-19	86. Florida Atlantic	30-26
37. Georgia Southern	42-17	87. Maryland	27-27
38. Middle Tenn. State	44-18	88. New Mexico	35-22
39. Alabama	37-21	89. Mississippi State	25-29
40. Dallas Baptist	38-17	90. Indiana State	33-21
41. W. Kentucky (23)	42-20	91. Kennesaw State	30-22
42. Oregon State	37-19	92. Texas Tech	25-32
43. Florida Gulf Coast	36-18	93. Louisiana-Lafayette	27-30
44. Kansas	39-24	94. Loyola Marymount	30-29
45. San Diego State	41-23	95. Louisiana-Monroe	32-27
46. Kentucky	28-26	96. Wichita State	30-27
47. Gonzaga (22)	36-18	97. Georgia State	39-22
48. Washington State	32-25	98. James Madison	30-24
49. George Mason	42-14	99. N.C. State	25-31
50. Virginia Tech	32-21	100. San Francisco	28-28

ing percentage in Omaha, the second-highest ever for a national champion behind only the .993 mark they posted in 1991.

■ Texas hit just 39 home runs in 61 games during the regular season, but the Longhorns exploded for 14 homers in six games in Omaha, the third-most homers by any team at the CWS ever. LSU and Texas combined to hit 27 homers in Omaha, a record for the two teams playing for the championship. The 12 combined homers in the Finals is also a record, breaking last year's record of nine.

FIRST TEAM

POS.	NAME	YEAR	AVG	OBP	SLG	AB	R	H	HR	RBI	BB	SO	SB
C	Tony Sanchez, Boston College	Jr.	.346	.443	.614	228	63	79	14	51	30	40	1
1B	Dustin Ackley, North Carolina	Jr.	.412	.513	.776	250	73	103	22	70	50	32	13
2B	Derek McCallum, Minnesota	Jr.	.409	.484	.741	232	57	95	18	86	30	34	6
3B	Chris Dominguez, Louisville	Jr.	.345	.441	.698	258	80	89	25	82	32	55	19
SS	Stephen Cardullo, Florida State	Jr.	.376	.479	.612	237	76	89	10	51	45	46	20
OF	Jason Kipnis, Arizona State	Jr.	.385	.496	.729	221	71	85	16	71	48	30	26
OF	Marc Krauss, Ohio	Jr.	.402	.521	.852	209	73	84	27	70	46	29	6
OF	Kent Matthes, Alabama	Sr.	.358	.461	.858	204	67	73	28	81	32	46	13
DH	Rich Poythress, Georgia	Jr.	.376	.468	.764	25	86	89	25	86	42	39	4
UT	Bryce Brentz, Middle Tennessee State	So.	.465	.535	.930	230	79	107	28	73	31	32	7

POS.	NAME	YEAR	W	L	ERA	G	CG	SV	IP	H	BB	SO	AVG
SP	Louis Coleman, Louisiana State	Sr.	13	2	2.76	21	2	0	114	92	19	124	.217
SP	Mike Leake, Arizona State	Jr.	16	1	1.36	17	7	0	133	79	21	150	.175
SP	A.J. Morris, Kansas State	Jr.	14	1	2.09	16	5	0	116	98	30	100	.222
SP	Stephen Strasburg, San Diego State	Jr.	13	1	1.32	15	2	0	109	65	19	195	.172
RP	Kyle Bellamy, Miami	Jr.	3	1	0.97	30	0	16	46	23	20	63	.147
UT	Bryce Brentz, Middle Tennessee State	So.	5	3	4.57	15	2	0	89	90	31	63	.265

SECOND TEAM

POS.	NAME	YEAR	AVG	OBP	SLG	AB	R	H	HR	RBI	BB	SO	SB
C	J.T. Wise, Oklahoma	Sr.	.359	.414	.665	209	50	75	17	62	23	42	2
1B	Troy Channing, St. Mary's	Fr.	.379	.463	.723	206	45	78	20	75	26	44	2
2B	Chris Sedon, Pittsburgh	Jr.	.398	.449	.796	201	65	80	22	62	13	41	19
3B	Anthony Rendon, Rice	Fr.	.388	.461	.702	242	60	94	20	72	31	23	9
SS	Christian Colon, Cal State Fullerton	So.	.351	.438	.519	239	74	84	7	35	23	22	14
OF	Tyler Holt, Florida State	So.	.401	.520	.578	237	87	95	5	28	54	47	34
OF	Jarrett Parker, Virginia	So.	.364	.454	.684	253	75	92	16	65	35	71	19
OF	Tim Wheeler, Sacramento State	Jr.	.385	.494	.765	200	59	77	18	72	29	28	15
DH	Wade Gaynor, Western Kentucky	Jr.	.371	.457	.781	251	83	93	25	78	35	41	21
UT	Mike McGee, Florida State	So.	.379	.494	.768	19	78	75	19	78	40	47	13

POS.	NAME	YEAR	W	L	ERA	G	CG	SV	IP	H	BB	SO	AVG
SP	Eric Arnett, Indiana	Jr.	12	2	2.50	14	6	0	108	82	39	109	.212
SP	Daniel Bibona, UC Irvine	Jr.	12	1	2.63	15	1	0	106	78	26	108	.209
SP	Kyle Gibson, Missouri	Jr.	11	3	3.21	16	5	0	107	95	19	131	.236
SP	Deck McGuire, Georgia Tech	So.	11	2	3.50	16	0	0	101	86	41	118	.232
RP	Addison Reed, San Diego State	So.	0	0	0.65	25	0	20	28	20	7	38	.200
UT	Mike McGee, Florida State	So.	6	2	4.03	15	0	0	69	64	42	70	.248

THIRD TEAM

POS.	NAME	YEAR	AVG	OBP	SLG	AB	R	H	HR	RBI	BB	SO	SB
C	Josh Phegley, Indiana	Jr.	.344	.456	.633	221	58	76	16	66	45	34	2
1B	Paul Goldschmidt, Texas State	Jr.	.352	.470	.685	219	69	77	18	88	54	29	5
2B	Ryan Wood, East Carolina	Sr.	.379	.486	.628	264	87	100	14	57	50	41	14
3B	Tom Mendonca, Fresno State	Jr.	.339	.447	.721	233	54	79	27	78	33	64	2
SS	Ryan Goins, Dallas Baptist	Jr.	.371	.478	.765	221	76	82	22	70	46	36	11
OF	Jeremy Hazelbaker, Ball State	Jr.	.429	.550	.724	203	77	87	9	38	48	35	29
OF	A.J. Pollock, Notre Dame	Jr.	.365	.443	.610	241	69	88	10	52	30	24	21
OF	Tyler Townsend, Florida International	Jr.	.434	.512	.858	212	58	92	24	77	26	31	3
DH	Luke Murton, Georgia Tech	Sr.	.354	.496	.714	206	64	73	20	63	43	35	4
UT	Danny Hultzen, Virginia	Fr.	.333	.419	.430	186	40	62	3	33	28	32	8

POS.	NAME	YEAR	W	L	ERA	G	CG	SV	IP	H	BB	SO	AVG
SP	Justin Marks, Louisville	Jr.	11	3	3.77	18	1	1	105	86	35	129	.227
SP	Daniel Renken, Cal State Fullerton	So.	10	2	2.56	15	2	0	109	84	31	88	.210
SP	Josh Spence, Arizona State	Jr.	9	1	2.33	16	2	1	83	78	25	109	.234
SP	Alex Wimmers, Ohio State	So.	9	1	2.68	15	4	0	101	72	48	131	.199
RP	Brian Moran, North Carolina	Jr.	7	1	1.95	34	0	4	65	42	8	88	.184
UT	Danny Hultzen, Virginia	Fr.	9	1	2.09	15	0	0	86	76	27	95	.242

■ LSU has reached the championship round of the CWS six times in its history and has won the national title all six times. The Tigers finished this season with 56 wins—the most by a national champion since Texas in 2005. Texas, meanwhile, finished second for the sixth time, the most runner-up finishes of any program. The Tigers also were the first top-eight national seed to win the national championship since Rice in 2003. They posted a .991 fielding percentage in Omaha, the second-highest ever for a national champion behind only the .993 mark they posted in 1991.

■ Only one save was recorded in the entire CWS, the lowest save total since 1993, when there were no saves. Arkansas' Mike

Bolsinger got the save in the Razorbacks' 10-6 victory against Cal State Fullerton in the first game of the CWS.

■ From the individual achievement files, Texas junior DH Russell Moldenhauer tied a Series mark with four home runs. Moldenhauer, a third-round pick out of high school in 2006, missed much of this season while recovering from offseason knee surgery and didn't homer in the regular season. He wasn't drafted this year but became the 10th player in Series history to hit four home runs.

■ North Carolina's Dustin Ackley went 5-for-6 in the Tar Heels' only victory, an 11-4 win against Southern Mississippi. While he fell one hit short of tying the single-game CWS record for hits, he did set the career record. His 28 hits in three career CWS appearances (2007-2009) broke the mark of 24 set by Stanford's Sam Fuld from 2001-2003.

JOHN WILLIAMSON

Austin Wood's 13-inning outing was epic

OTHER TOP STORIES FROM 2009

■ Just when college baseball fans thought they had seen it all from San Diego State phenom Stephen Strasburg in 2008, when he struck out 23 in one game, the junior righthander managed to outdo himself in 2009, going 13-1, 1.32 with 195 strikeouts in 109 innings pitched. Strasburg's banner moment of the year came on May 8 against Air Force in his final start at Tony Gwynn Stadium, when he fanned 17 Cadets as part of a 117-pitch no-hitter.

■ In what is sure to remembered as one of the greatest postseason college baseball games ever, Texas' 3-2 victory over Boston College in the third game of the Austin Regional lasted 25 innings, making it the longest baseball game in NCAA history. The contest began at 7:02 p.m. EDT Saturday and concluded 7 hours, 3 minutes later at 2:05 a.m. Sunday. Longhorns senior lefthander Austin Wood turned in the greatest individual performance, striking out 14 over 13 innings of scoreless relief, the first 12^1/$_3$ of them hitless.

■ Set to retire at season's end, Southern Mississippi head coach Corky Palmer rallied the troops one last time. The Golden Eagles, who appeared in regionals each of the last seven years under Palmer, played in their first College World Series in school history after overcoming a five-run deficit against Florida in the second game of the Gainesville Super Regional.

■ The record books were never the same again after the final game of the Tallahassee Regional. The Seminoles jumped out to an unassailable 32-0 lead after 4^1/$_2$ innings, setting NCAA tournament records for hits (38), total bases (66) and runs scored in the process. FSU also tallied 15 doubles, which is an NCAA record for any game, postseason or otherwise.

■ Just one year after announcing a mandatory start date for the college baseball season that resulted in a compacted 13-week schedule, the NCAA reversed course and approved a proposal to add a week to the front of the regular season, effective 2010. The decision means teams will no longer have to grind through five-game weeks and student-athletes will have more time to focus on academics during the season.

■ College baseball took a blow from the economy in the first week of the season when both Vermont and Northern Iowa announced that they were cutting their baseball programs. Both schools cited budget deficits in their athletic departments as the chief motivator for the dissolutions.

■ Following an impressive run to the ACC tournament title—with wins against Clemson, North Carolina and Florida State—Virginia handed Strasburg his first loss of the year in its regional opener, and then defeated host UC Irvine (ranked No. 1 in the nation at the time) on consecutive days to win the Irvine Regional. Then Virginia took two of three from Mississippi in the Oxford Super Regional to find itself in Omaha for the first time school history. Virginia coach Brian O'Connor faced an emotional showdown against his former mentor, LSU coach Paul Mainieri, in UVa.'s CWS opener. The master bested the pupil 9-3.

■ In a landmark decision on Feb. 12, Oklahoma State lefthander Andrew Oliver won his lawsuit against the NCAA, invalidating the "no agent" rule. Oliver had originally been ruled ineligible on the eve of the 2008 Stillwater Regional when it came to light that his advisors had made contact with the Twins on his behalf after the organization drafted him out of high school in 2006. An Ohio judge restored Oliver's eligibility in time for the 2009 season, barring the NCAA from enforcing the "no agent" rule in the process. But Oliver and the NCAA reached a $750,000 settlement just before the damages phase of the trial was scheduled to begin in October, and the injunction against the "no agent" rule was dismissed in the process. The settlement therefore marked a return to the status quo.

■ The Pacific-10 Conference was certainly not up to scratch compared to previous years, as just three teams made it to the NCAA tournament in 2009 (with only one team, Arizona State, advancing past regionals). But the conference can hang its hat on the return of Oregon baseball, which played its first season in 27 years under former Cal State Fullerton coach George Horton. The Ducks struggled mightily in their first season, going 14-42 overall and 4-23 in Pac-10 play.

■ North Carolina State pitchers struck out 31 Akron hitters in a 5-4 win against the Zips that lasted 18 innings on March 4, setting a new single-game NCAA Division I record. The previous mark was held by Austin Peay State, whose pitchers fanned 26 against Murray State in a 15-inning game in 1987, before 11 different Wolfpack hurlers helped topple the 22-year-old record.

REGIONALS

MAY 29-JUNE 1
64 teams, 16 four-team, double-elimination tournaments. Winners advance to super regionals.

AUSTIN
Host: Texas (No. 1 national seed).
Participants: No. 1 Texas (41-13-1), No. 2 Texas State (41-15), No. 3 Boston College (33-24), No. 4 Army (34-19).
Champion: Texas (3-0).
Runner-Up: Army (2-2).
Outstanding Player: Austin Wood, lhp, Texas.

FORT WORTH
Host: Texas Christian
Participants: No. 1 Texas Christian (36-16), No. 2 Texas A&M (36-22), No. 3 Oregon State (35-17), No. 4 Wright State (22-28).
Champion: TCU (3-0).
Runner-Up: Oregon State (2-2).
Outstanding Player: Jason Coats, of, TCU.

ATLANTA
Host: Georgia Tech
No. 1 Georgia Tech (35-17-1), No. 2 Elon (40-16), No. 3 Southern Mississippi (35-23), No. 4 Georgia State (39-20).
Champion: Southern Miss (3-1).
Runner-Up: Georgia Tech (3-2).
Outstanding Player: B.A. Vollmuth, ss, Southern Miss.

GAINESVILLE, FLA.
Host: Florida (No. 8 national seed).
Participants: No. 1 Florida (39-20), No. 2 Miami (36-20), No. 3 Jacksonville (36-20), No. 4 Bethune-Cookman (32-26).
Champion: Florida (3-0).
Runner-Up: Miami (2-2).
Outstanding Player: Preston Tucker, 1b, Florida.

TEMPE, ARIZ.
Host: Arizona State (No. 5 national seed).
Participants: No. 1 Arizona State (44-12), No. 2 Oral Roberts (31-13), No. 3 Cal Poly (37-19), No. 4 Kent State (42-15).
Champion: Arizona State (3-0).
Runner-Up: Oral Roberts (2-2).
Outstanding Player: Mike Leake, rhp, Arizona State.

CLEMSON, S.C.
Host: Clemson.
Participants: No. 1 Clemson (40-19), No. 2 Alabama (37-19), No. 3 Oklahoma State (32-22), No. 4 Tennessee Tech (30-22-1).
Champion: Clemson (4-1).
Runner-Up: Oklahoma State (2-2).
Outstanding Player: Chris Epps, dh, Clemson.

GREENVILLE, N.C.
Host: East Carolina.
Participants: No. 1 East Carolina (42-17), No. 2 South Carolina (38-21) 25th appearance, at-large, fifth place in Southeastern Conference, No. 3 George Mason (42-12), No. 4 Binghamton (29-20).
Champion: East Carolina (4-1).

B.A. Vollmouth

Runner-Up: South Carolina (2-2).
Outstanding Player: Trent Whitehead, of, East Carolina.

CHAPEL HILL, N.C.
Host: North Carolina (No. 4 national seed).
Participants: No. 1 North Carolina (42-16), No. 2 Coastal Carolina (46-14), No. 3 Kansas (37-22), No. 4 Dartmouth (27-16).
Champion: North Carolina (3-0).
Runner-Up: Kansas (2-2).
Outstanding Player: Dustin Ackley, 1b, North Carolina.

FULLERTON, CALIF.
Host: Cal State Fullerton (No. 2 national seed).
Participants: No. 1 Cal State Fullerton (42-14), No. 2 Georgia Southern (42-15), No. 3 Gonzaga (35-16), No. 4 Utah (26-29).
Champion: Cal State Fullerton (3-0).
Runner-Up: Utah (2-2).
Outstanding Player: Dustin Garneau, c, Cal State Fullerton.

LOUISVILLE
Host: Louisville.
Participants: No. 1 Louisville (44-15), No. 2 Middle Tennessee State (43-16), No. 3 Vanderbilt (34-25), No. 4 Indiana (32-25).
Champion: Louisville (3-1).
Runner-Up: Vanderbilt (3-2).
Outstanding Player: Justin Marks, lhp, Louisville.

TALLAHASSEE, FLA.
Host: Florida State.
Participants: No. 1 Florida State (42-16), No. 2 Georgia (37-22), No. 3 Ohio State (40-17), No. 4 Marist (31-26).
Champion: Florida State (3-0).
Runner-Up: Ohio State (2-2).
Outstanding Player: Jason Stidham, 2b, Florida State.

NORMAN, OKLA.
Host: Oklahoma (No. 7 national seed).
Participants: No. 1 Oklahoma (44-18), No. 2 Arkansas (34-22), No. 3 Washington State (31-23), No. 4 Wichita State (30-25).
Champion: Arkansas (3-0).
Runner-Up: Oklahoma (2-2).
Outstanding Player: Andy Wilkins, 1b, Arkansas.

IRVINE, CALIF.
Host: UC Irvine (No. 6 national seed).
Participants: No. 1 UC Irvine (43-13), No. 2 Virginia (43-12-1), No. 3 San Diego State

(40-21), No. 4 Fresno State (32-28).
Champion: Virginia (3-0).
Runner-Up: UC Irvine (2-2).
Outstanding Player: Franco Valdes, c, Virginia.

OXFORD, MISS.
Host: Mississippi.
Participants: No. 1 Mississippi (40-17), No. 2 Missouri (34-25), No. 3 Western Kentucky (39-18), No. 4 Monmouth (32-23).
Champion: Mississippi (3-1).
Runner-Up: Western Kentucky (3-2).
Outstanding Player: Drew Pomeranz, lhp, Mississippi.

HOUSTON
Host: Rice.
Participants: No. 1 Rice (39-15), No. 2 Kansas State (41-16-1), No. 3 Xavier (38-19), No. 4 Sam Houston State (36-22).
Champion: Rice (4-1).
Runner-Up: Kansas State (2-2).
Outstanding Player: Taylor Wall, lhp, Rice.

BATON ROUGE
Host: Louisiana State (No. 3 national seed).
Participants: No. 1 Louisiana State (46-16), No. 2 Minnesota (38-17), No. 3 Baylor (29-24), No. 4 Southern (30-15).
Champion: LSU (3-0).
Runner-Up: Minnesota (2-2).
Outstanding Player: Anthony Ranaudo, rhp, LSU.

SUPER REGIONALS

JUNE 5-8
16 teams, eight best-of-three series. Winners advance to College World Series.

TEXAS CHRISTIAN AT TEXAS
Site: Austin.
Texas wins 2-1, advances to CWS.

SOUTHERN MISSISSIPPI AT FLORIDA
Site: Gainesville, Fla.
Southern Miss wins 2-0, advances to CWS.

CLEMSON AT ARIZONA STATE
Site: Tempe, Ariz.
Arizona State wins 2-0, advances to CWS.

EAST CAROLINA AT NORTH CAROLINA
Site: Chapel Hill, N.C.
North Carolina wins 2-0, advances to CWS.

LOUISVILLE AT CAL STATE FULLERTON
Site: Fullerton, Calif.
Fullerton wins 2-0, advances to CWS.

ARKANSAS AT FLORIDA STATE
Site: Tallahassee, Fla.
Arkansas wins 2-0, advances to CWS.

VIRGINIA AT MISSISSIPPI
Site: Oxford, Miss.
Virginia wins 2-1, advances to CWS.

RICE AT LOUISIANA STATE
Site: Baton Rouge.
LSU wins 2-0, advances to CWS.

Strasburg lives up to gigantic hype

As time passes, Stephen Strasburg might be remembered as the greatest pitcher in college baseball history, and his 2009 junior campaign as the most dominant season ever. San Diego State's 6-foot-4, 220-pound righthander went 13-1, 1.32 with 195 strikeouts and 19 walks in 109 innings to lead the Aztecs to regionals for the first time since 1991. His 16.1 strikeouts per nine innings ranks third on the NCAA's single-season list.

With an overpowering fastball that can reach triple digits, a devastating hard breaking ball and excellent feel for a changeup, Strasburg was a no-brainer choice for the No. 1 overall pick in the draft. He was also an easy selection for Baseball America's College Player of the Year, even though North Carolina's Dustin Ackley and Arizona State's Mike Leake put together seasons that would be enough to earn the award in almost any other year.

Stephen Strasburg

JESSE SOLL

We asked those who have coached Strasburg and coached against him, as well as Strasburg himself, to try to put his historic season into perspective.

San Diego State coach Tony Gwynn: "We were spoiled rotten, really. As the year went on and he got more and more attention, you would expect somewhere in there for him to have one where he wasn't effective. But he did what he needed to do. There were nights where he needed to punch a bunch of guys out, and he did that. There were nights he needed to pitch to contact, and he did that. I try to downplay everything because I know the expectations are through the roof with

him. But he did what he needed to do—I think that's the best description. Hey, if I put a bat in his hand, it wouldn't have surprised me if he'd gotten a knock—he was that good this year."

Texas Christian coach Jim Schlossnagle: "The thing that goes so underrated with him in my mind is his pitchability. The thing with Stephen is he throws like he's an 87-89 sinker-slider guy. He pitches at the knees with movement with the fastball. He's 1.1 (seconds) to the plate so you can't run on him even if you get on. And he fields his position well. He is obviously physically gifted, but he's the most complete package I've ever seen at the amateur level."

San Diego coach Rich Hill: "To do what he did from the mental side, to me, is the story. Every team schemed and planned on him this year, tried to bunt on him, tried to run on him, tried to get him rattled. Every single game, he's facing an offense that's had all week to prepare, it's going to make their season if they beat him. And still there was nothing you could do. You couldn't rattle him, you couldn't short game him, you couldn't do anything. We have a different perspective in San Diego because we've seen Stephen grow up and transform into this beast that he's become. It's remarkable."

Stephen Strasburg: "I think it's just something my parents have instilled in me at an early age. It's about hard work and dedication. If you want something bad enough, you can't let anything get in your way. I wanted to be the best, I still want to be the best, and I'm going to work as hard as I can to get there."

PREVIOUS WINNERS

1981: Mike Sodders, 3b, Arizona State	**1991:** David McCarthy, 1b, Stanford	**2001:** Mark Prior, rhp, Southern California
1982: Jeff Ledbetter, of/lhp, Florida State	**1992:** Phil Nevin, 3b, Cal State Fullerton	**2002:** Khalil Greene, ss, Clemson
1983: Dave Magadan, 1b, Alabama	**1993:** Brooks Kieschnick, dh/rhp, Texas	**2003:** Rickie Weeks, 2b, Southern
1984: Oddibe McDowell, of, Arizona State	**1994:** Jason Varitek, c, Georgia Tech	**2004:** Jered Weaver, rhp, Long Beach State
1985: Pete Incaviglia, of, Oklahoma State	**1995:** Todd Helton, 1b/lhp, Tennessee	**2005:** Alex Gordon, 3b, Nebraska
1986: Casey Close, of, Michigan	**1996:** Kris Benson, rhp, Clemson	**2006:** Andrew Miller, lhp, North Carolina
1987: Robin Ventura, 3b, Oklahoma State	**1997:** J.D. Drew, of, Florida State	**2007:** David Price, lhp, Vanderbilt
1988: John Olerund, 1b/lhp, Washington St.	**1998:** Jeff Austin, rhp, Stanford	**2008:** Buster Posey, c/rhp, Florida State
1989: Ben McDonald, rhp, Louisiana State	**1999:** Jason Jennings, rhp, Baylor	
1990: Mike Kelly, of, Arizona State	**2000:** Mark Teixeira, 3b, Georgia Tech	

Mainieri guides LSU back to top

BY AARON FITT

Paul Mainieri never wanted to be Mickey Mantle or Joe Morgan or Bob Gibson.

"Most kids grow up wanting to be major league baseball players, but I wanted to be a college baseball coach," Mainieri said. "Growing up talking about Bobby Winkles, and Rod Dedeaux, and Augie Garrido—those are my heroes."

And Demie Mainieri, of course. Demie, Paul's father, was the legendary coach at Miami Dade CC-North, where he became the first junior college coach to win 1,000 games in 1990.

Paul followed in his father's huge footsteps, getting into coaching after one season as a second baseman in pro ball. After three years as an assistant at Miami's Christopher Columbus High, and six as the head coach at Biscayne (Fla.) College (now called St. Thomas), and six more as the head coach at Air Force, and 12 at the helm at Notre Dame,

Paul Mainieri

Mainieri took over as the head coach at Louisiana State in 2006. In three seasons, he has led the Tigers out of a rough patch and back to the pinnacle of college baseball, culminating in the school's sixth national title in 2009. For restoring that proud program to its former glory—and doing it the right way at every step—Mainieri is Baseball America's Coach of the Year.

"I don't think anybody could have done it any faster or classier," Skip Bertman said of the turnaround from missing regionals in 2006 and '07 to reaching Omaha in '08 and '09. That praise means something coming from Bertman, the legendary former coach who led LSU to five national titles from 1991-2000. Bertman served as LSU's athletics director after retiring from coaching and hired Mainieri to replace Smoke Laval.

Junior outfielder/infielder Ryan Schimpf said Mainieri forms such a strong bond with his players that they feel like his own kids. But DH Blake Dean added that Mainieri strikes a pefrect balance between approachability and discipline.

But it's not just Mainieri's interpersonal skills that make him the Coach of the Year. Mainieri teaches the fundamentals of baseball extremely well and doesn't use "gadgets", as he puts it. And he has a great feel for when to make moves, both in games and when it comes to filling out his lineup card.

Case in point: The Tigers took off in 2009 after Mainieri shook up his lineup to improve his defense, which wasn't turning enough double plays. He moved preseason All-America shortstop D.J. LeMahieu to second base, shifted preseason All-America second baseman Schimpf to left field, and installed freshmen Austin Nola at shortstop and Mikie Mahtook in center field. LSU went 28-5 after Nola took over at short on April 21.

"Naturally he's very modest and always gives credit to the kids, as you should," Bertman said. "But in watching college baseball for 45 years as I have, I can tell you, he has great—I call it mojo. M-O-J-O. It's a magic, a mixture. Who knows exactly, really what it is, but he's got it."

PREVIOUS WINNERS

1981: Ron Fraser, Miami	**1990:** Steve Webber, Georgia	**2000:** Ray Tanner, South Carolina
1982: Gene Stephenson, Wichita State	**1991:** Jim Hendry, Creighton	**2001:** Dave Van Horn, Nebraska
1983: Barry Shollenberger, Alabama	**1992:** Andy Lopez, Pepperdine	**2002:** Augie Garrido, Texas
1984: Augie Garrido, Cal State Fullerton	**1993:** Gene Stephenson, Wichita State	**2003:** George Horton, Cal State Fullerton
1985: Ron Polk, Mississippi State	**1994:** Jim Morris, Miami	**2004:** David Perno, Georgia
1986: Skip Bertman, Louisiana State	**1995:** Pat Murphy, Arizona State	**2005:** Rick Jones, Tulane
Dave Snow, Loyola Marymount	**1996:** Skip Bertman, Louisiana State	**2006:** Pat Casey, Oregon State
1987: Mark Marquess, Stanford	**1997:** Jim Wells, Alabama	**2007:** Dave Serrano, UC Irvine
1988: Jim Brock, Arizona State	**1998:** Pat Murphy, Arizona State	**2008:** Mike Fox, North Carolina
1989: Dave Snow, Long Beach State	**1999:** Wayne Graham, Rice	

Rendon gives Rice elite power threat

BY MATT FORMAN

After watching the team play four fall scrimmages, Rice's boosters expressed their main concern to head coach Wayne Graham: Is there any player on the Owls' roster who can hit 10 home runs?

Graham gave them a simple response: Yes, Anthony Rendon. Graham predicted Rendon could even hit 15 home runs and be a power threat in the middle of Rice's lineup.

"It surprised them when I said Anthony because he hadn't hit any in the fall," Graham said. "But we watched batting practice every day and we watched the ball disappear every day."

Eight months later, Rendon proved any doubters wrong and one-upped Graham's prediction. The Houston native belted a freshman-best 20 home runs. Rendon also hit team-leading .388/.461/.702 with 72 RBIs.

ANDREW WOOLLEY

Anthony Rendon

FRESHMAN OF THE YEAR

After becoming the first player to garner Conference USA player of the year and freshman of the year honors in the same season, Rendon has new hardware for the trophy case. To go along with being a second-team All-America selection, Rendon is Baseball America's Freshman of the Year.

"He had the best freshman year we've ever had," Graham said. "Anthony's year offensively is pretty much transcendental."

Rendon is the second Rice player to win Freshman of the Year honors, joining Joe Savery in 2005. Both Rendon and Savery attended Lamar High, just two miles away from Rice's campus. But the Rendon-Savery comparisons stop there. Savery earned the award as much on the rubber as in the box, while Rendon powered his way to it.

"A lot of people go up there and think about what they're going to do—I just hit," Rendon said. "I relax and don't think about anything. I just want to hit the ball as hard and as far as I can."

PREVIOUS WINNERS

1982: Cory Snyder, 3b, Brigham Young
1983: Rafael Palmeiro, of, Mississippi State
1984: Greg Swindell, lhp, Texas
1985: Jack McDowell, rhp, Stanford
1986: Robin Ventura, 3b, Oklahoma State
1987: Paul Carey, of, Stanford
1988: Kirk Dressendorfer, rhp, Texas
1989: Alex Fernandez, rhp, Miami
1990: Jeffrey Hammonds, of, Stanford
1991: Brooks Kieschnick, rhp-dh, Texas
1992: Todd Walker, 2b, Louisiana State
1993: Brett Laxton, rhp, Louisiana State
1994: R.A. Dickey, rhp, Tennessee
1995: Kyle Peterson, rhp, Stanford
1996: Pat Burrell, 3b, Miami
1997: Brian Roberts, ss, North Carolina
1998: Xavier Nady, 2b, California
1999: James Jurries, 2b, Tulane
2000: Kevin Howard, 3b, Miami
2001: Michael Aubrey, of/lhp, Texas
2002: Stephen Drew, ss, Florida State
2003: Ryan Braun, ss, Miami
2004: Wade LeBlanc, lhp, Alabama
2005: Joe Savery, lhp, Rice
2006: Pedro Alvarez, 3b, Vanderbilt
2007: Dustin Ackley, 1b, North Carolina
2008: Chris Hernandez, lhp, Miami

FRESHMAN ALL-AMERICA TEAMS

FIRST TEAM

POS.	PLAYER, SCHOOL	AVG	OBP	SLG	AB	R	H	HR	RBI	SB-ATT
C	Jeremy Schaffer, Tulane	.311	.370	.566	212	40	66	14	56	1-4
1B	Preston Tucker, Florida	.364	.419	.628	242	48	88	15	85	5-7
2B	Matt Jensen, Cal Poly	.375	.493	.650	160	42	60	9	53	2-4
3B	Anthony Rendon, Rice	.388	.461	.702	242	60	94	20	72	9-11
SS	A.J. Pettersen, Minnesota	.353	.445	.438	224	65	79	2	45	8-13
OF	Kolton Wong, Hawaii	.341	.418	.597	226	46	77	11	52	11-15
OF	Jackie Bradley, South Carolina	.349	.431	.537	255	69	89	11	46	8-10
OF	George Springer, Connecticut	.358	.454	.679	212	75	76	16	57	12-15
DH	Troy Channing, St. Mary's	.379	.463	.723	206	45	78	20	75	2-3
UT	Danny Hultzen, Virginia	.327	.410	.422	199	40	65	3	37	9-9

POS.	PLAYER, SCHOOL	W	L	ERA	G	SV	IP	H	BB	SO
SP	Sean Gilmartin, Florida State	12	3	3.49	18	1	98	81	37	83
SP	Taylor Jungmann, Texas	10	3	2.10	23	0	86	60	32	92
SP	Trevor Bauer, UCLA	9	3	2.99	20	2	105	85	27	92
SP	Noe Ramirez, Cal State Fullerton	9	2	3.33	20	0	111	90	24	100
RP	Matty Ott, Louisiana State	3	2	2.85	36	16	47	46	5	66
UT	Danny Hultzen, Virginia	9	1	2.17	17	0	95	88	28	107

SECOND TEAM

C—C.J. Cron, Utah (.337-11-58). **1B**—Todd Brazeal, S. Fla. (.348-5-50). **2B**—Ross Heffley, W. Caro. (.391-4-51). **3B**—Matt Skole, Ga. Tech (.302-17-58). **SS**—Sam Mende, S. Fla. (.319-5-37). **OF**—Kam Brunty, S. Miss. (.336-7-53); Dusty Robinson, Fresno State (.319-15-45); Tyler Sibley, Texas State (.367-10-38, 14 SB). **DH**—Alex Dickerson, Ind. (.370-14-57). **UT**—Nick Ramirez, CS Fullerton (.287-10-31; 3-1, 2.61, 7 SV). **SP**—Jordan Cooper, Wichita State (8-6, 2.78, 97 IP/91 SO); Sam Gaviglio, Ore. State (10-1, 2.73, 63 IP/55 SO); Anthony Meo, Coastal Caro. (9-2, 2.93, 77 IP/68 SO); Tyler Pill, CS Fullerton (11-3, 4.06, 102 IP/74 SO). **RP**—Mitchell Lambson, Ariz. State (9-5, 3.01, 5 SV, 84 IP/99 SO).

Minimum 120 plate appearances, 3.0 plate appearances per team game

BATTING

BATTING AVERAGE

RANK NAME, TEAM	YEAR	G	AB	H	AVG
1. Bryce Brentz, Middle Tennessee State	So.	62	230	107	.465
2. Joey Bergman, College of Charleston	Jr.	56	221	100	.452
3. Jayson Langfels, Eastern Kentucky	So.	43	170	75	.441
4. Dan Dibartolomeo, West Virginia	So.	55	205	90	.439
5. Ryan Hamme, Campbell	Sr.	44	162	71	.438
6. Dillon Baird, Arizona	Jr.	49	194	84	.433
7. Justin Kline, North Dakota State	Fr.	35	125	54	.432
8. Matt Otteman, Texas-Arlington	Sr.	56	220	95	.432
9. Dan Paolini, Siena	Fr.	50	200	86	.430
10. Gary Helmick, Towson	Sr.	53	228	98	.430
11. Jeremy Hazelbaker, Ball State	Jr.	50	203	87	.429
12. Lance Durham, Cincinnati	Jr.	58	232	99	.427
13. Tyler Townsend, Florida International	Jr.	55	216	92	.426
14. Jared Jeffries, Florida A&M	Jr.	46	167	71	.425
15. Jeff Hanson, Sacred Heart	Sr.	49	186	79	.425
16. Matt Perry, Holy Cross	Jr.	49	182	77	.423
17. Mike Sodders, New Mexico State	Jr.	50	187	79	.422
18. Isaac Harrow, Appalachian State	Sr.	54	218	92	.422
19. Adam Buschini, Cal Poly	Jr.	49	185	78	.422
Brandon Haveman, Purdue	Sr.	43	185	78	.422
21. Jedd Gyorko, West Virginia	So.	55	228	96	.421
22. Scott Gladstone, Tennessee-Martin	Sr.	51	200	84	.420
23. Brent Greer, Western Carolina	Jr.	57	243	102	.420
24. Sean Rockey, George Washington	Jr.	55	193	81	.420
25. Nick Zaleski, Sam Houston State	Sr.	60	236	99	.419
26. Matt Davis, Eastern Kentucky	Sr.	49	196	82	.418
27. Vince Belnome, West Virginia	Jr.	55	213	89	.418
28. Dustin Ackley, North Carolina	Jr.	66	266	111	.417
29. Richie Derbak, Eastern Illinois	Jr.	50	187	78	.417
30. Andrew Kainer, Texas-Arlington	Sr.	53	204	85	.417
31. Tim Morris, St. John's	Jr.	52	217	90	.415
32. Rafael Neda, New Mexico	So.	55	205	85	.415
33. Bryan Marquez, New Mexico State	Sr.	60	215	89	.414
34. Mike Brownstein, New Mexico	Sr.	57	244	101	.414
35. Ross Babineaux, Delaware State	Sr.	44	145	60	.414
36. Griffin Benedict, Georgia Southern	Sr.	58	220	91	.414
37. Brayden Drake, Missouri State	Sr.	47	191	79	.414
38. Drew Lee, Morehead State	Jr.	52	208	86	.413
39. Michael Choice, Texas-Arlington	So.	56	225	93	.413
40. Jake McAloose, Old Dominion	Jr.	48	184	76	.413
41. Chris Henderson, George Mason	Jr.	56	235	97	.413
42. Wes Cunningham, Murray State	Jr.	51	192	79	.411
43. Derek McCallum, Minnesota	Jr.	59	232	95	.409
44. Eduardo Gonzalez, Alcorn State	Fr.	48	172	70	.407
45. Alex Gregory, Radford	Sr.	50	177	72	.407
46. Spenser Dennis, Texas State	Sr.	53	192	78	.406
47. Ryan Honeycutt, New Mexico	So.	56	197	80	.406
48. Tyler Elkins, Bowling Green	Sr.	42	165	67	.406
49. Tommy Nurre, Miami (Ohio)	Sr.	52	202	82	.406
50. Matt Lenski, Valparaiso	Sr.	45	170	69	.406
51. Steve Domecus, Virginia Tech	Jr.	40	143	58	.406
52. Ellis Lowe, Campbell	So.	51	223	90	.404
53. Brian Billigen, Cornell	Fr.	31	114	46	.404
54. Dewey Oriente, St. Joseph's	Jr.	39	144	58	.403
55. Brandon Kendricks, Prairie View A&M	Sr.	43	154	62	.403
56. David Arredondo, Texas Southern	Sr.	53	159	64	.403
57. Pat Irvine, Elon	Sr.	55	194	78	.402
58. Marc Krauss, Ohio	Jr.	53	209	84	.402
59. Rob Lyerly, Charlotte	Jr.	43	167	67	.401
Jimmy Roesinger, Dayton	So.	52	167	67	.401
61. Effrey Valdez, New York Tech	Jr.	49	192	77	.401
62. Nick Ciolli, Indiana State	Jr.	54	222	89	.401
63. Tyler Holt, Florida State	So.	63	237	95	.401
64. Billy Alvino, High Point	Sr.	53	210	84	.400

Bryce Brentz led the nation in batting

Kevin Atkinson, New Mexico	Sr.	57	230	92	.400
Jeremy Gillan, Jacksonville	Sr.	57	215	86	.400
Justin Lloyd, Gardner-Webb	Sr.	49	195	78	.400
Alfie Wheeler, High Point	Sr.	52	205	82	.400
69. Matt Rice, Western Kentucky	So.	61	253	101	.399
70. Jeremy Cruz, Stetson	Sr.	56	228	91	.399
71. Jacob Bruns, San Jose State	Sr.	51	178	71	.399
72. Rawley Bishop, Middle Tennessee State	Sr.	62	241	6	.398
73. Sean Meyers, Stephen F. Austin State	Sr.	55	206	82	.398
74. Chris Sedon, Pittsburgh	Jr.	48	201	80	.398
75. Marc Mimeault, Georgia State	Sr.	56	196	78	.398
76. C. J. Lauriello, Bethune-Cookman	Jr.	52	181	72	.398
77. Leo Aguirre, New Mexico State	Jr.	49	166	66	.398
78. Blake Crosby, Sacramento State	Sr.	54	209	83	.397
79. Sonny Meade, Citadel	Sr.	59	262	104	.397
80. Miles Hartsfield, Tennessee-Martin	Sr.	51	194	77	.397
Austin Wates, Virginia Tech	So.	47	194	77	.397
82. Dylan Craig, Belmont	Fr.	58	232	92	.397
Tyler Rehmel, Eastern Kentucky	Sr.	49	174	69	.397
84. Josh Fellhauer, Cal State Fullerton	Jr.	60	227	90	.396
85. Kevin Nieto, Manhattan	Jr.	46	187	74	.396
86. Clint Moore, Army	So.	53	185	73	.395
87. Michael Rockett, Texas-San Antonio	Sr.	56	251	99	.394
88. Zach Borenstein, Eastern Illinois	Fr.	40	137	54	.394
89. Jim Klocke, Southeast Missouri State	Jr.	51	188	74	.394
Jordan Kreke, Eastern Illinois	Sr.	48	188	74	.394
91. Jared Gruccio, Wagner	So.	48	155	61	.394
92. Hayden Johnston, Ohio	Sr.	53	234	92	.393
93. Kyle Seager, North Carolina	Jr.	66	262	103	.393
94. Dan Rhault, Rhode Island	Sr.	53	201	79	.393
95. Kyle Bluestein, Jacksonville State	Fr.	44	163	64	.393
96. Eddie Tisdale, Winthrop	Sr.	60	242	95	.393
97. Ruben Perez, Manhattan	Sr.	53	214	84	.393
98. Kipp Schutz, Indiana	So.	51	181	71	.392
99. Mark Stuckless, Hofstra	Sr.	43	176	69	.392
100. Kevin Nolan, Winthrop	Jr.	57	222	87	.392

ON-BASE PERCENTAGE

RANK	NAME, TEAM	OBP
1.	Joey Bergman, College of Charleston	.551
2.	Jeremy Hazelbaker, Ball State	.550
3.	Chris Bangi, Campbell	.538
4.	Bryce Brentz, Middle Tenn. State	.535
5.	Bryan Marquez, New Mexico State	.534
6.	Pat Irvine, Elon	.533
7.	Griffin Benedict, Georgia Southern	.528
8.	Ryan Hamme, Campbell	.527
9.	Danny Muno, Fresno State	.525
10.	Marc Krauss, Ohio	.521
11.	Tyler Holt, Florida State	.520
12.	Chris McGuiness, Citadel	.520
13.	Vince Belnome, West Virginia	.519
14.	Alex Gregory, Radford	.518
15.	Dan Black, Purdue	.518
16.	Dustin Ackley, North Carolina	.512
17.	Nick Zaleski, Sam Houston State	.509
18.	Tyler Stampone, William & Mary	.509
19.	Brady Shoemaker, Indiana State	.508
20.	Zach Borenstein, Eastern Illinois	.506
21.	Richard Stout, New Mexico State	.506
22.	Jeff Hanson, Sacred Heart	.505
23.	Mike Sodders, New Mexico State	.505
24.	Dillon Baird, Arizona	.504
25.	Sean Rockey, George Washington	.504
26.	Rafael Neda, New Mexico	.504
27.	Tyler Townsend, Fla. International	.504
28.	Clay McCord, College of Charleston	.504
29.	Justin Kline, North Dakota State	.503
30.	Jake McAloose, Old Dominion	.502
31.	Gary Helmick, Towson	.502
32.	Lance Durham, Cincinnati	.502
33.	Rawley Bishop, Middle Tenn. State	.502
34.	Isaac Harrow, Appalachian State	.500
	Jared Jeffries, Florida A&M	.500
	D.J. Johnson, Campbell	.500
	Ben Soignier, Louisiana-Monroe	.500
38.	Tommy Nurre, Miami (Ohio)	.498
39.	Jason Kipnis, Arizona State	.497
40.	Luke Murton, Georgia Tech	.496
41.	Earnest Rhone, Texas Southern	.496
42.	Mike McGee, Florida State	.494
43.	Clint Moore, Army	.494
44.	Matt Duffy, Vermont	.493
45.	Rob Lyerly, Charlotte	.493
46.	Michael Choice, Texas-Arlington	.492
47.	Tim Morris, St. John's	.492
48.	Matt Perry, Holy Cross	.491
49.	Erik Castro, San Diego State	.490
50.	Tim Wheeler, Sacramento State	.490

SLUGGING PERCENTAGE

RANK	NAME, TEAM	SLG
1.	Bryce Brentz, Middle Tenn. State	.930
2.	Devon Dageford, Louisiana Tech	.862
3.	Kent Matthes, Alabama	.858
4.	Marc Krauss, Ohio	.852
5.	Tyler Townsend, Fla. International	.843
6.	Jayson Langfels, Eastern Kentucky	.800
7.	Chris Sedon, Pittsburgh	.796
8.	Bryan Marquez, New Mexico State	.795
9.	Pat Irvine, Elon	.789
10.	Gary Helmick, Towson	.785
11.	Wade Gaynor, Western Kentucky	.781
12.	Chris Kersten, Louisiana Tech	.780
13.	Joey Bergman, College of Charleston	.778
14.	Cody Hawn, Tennessee	.773
15.	Mike McGee, Florida State	.768
16.	Ryan Goins, Dallas Baptist	.765
17.	Drew Lee, Morehead State	.764
18.	Rich Poythress, Georgia	.764
19.	Dustin Ackley, North Carolina	.763

20.	Tim Wheeler, Sacramento State	.760
21.	Tommy Nurre, Miami (Ohio)	.757
22.	Scott Krieger, George Mason	.757
23.	Kevin Nieto, Manhattan	.754
	Mike Sodders, New Mexico State	.754
25.	Tony Thompson, Kansas	.753
26.	Charles Derkoski, Texas Southern	.752
27.	Isaac Harrow, Appalachian State	.748
28.	Kevin Mahoney, Canisius	.746
29.	Derek McCallum, Minnesota	.741
30.	Paul Hoilman, East Tennessee State	.740
31.	Jose Hernandez, Texas-San Antonio	.739
32.	Brian Cavazos-Galvez, New Mexico	.737
33.	Joseph Sanders, Auburn	.737
34.	Jason Krizan, Dallas Baptist	.736
	Kolbrin Vitek, Ball State	.736
36.	David Anderson, Coastal Carolina	.732
37.	Matt Townsend, James Madison	.732
38.	Jeff Hanson, Sacred Heart	.731
39.	Adam Buschini, Cal Poly	.730
40.	Jake Smith, Alabama	.728
41.	Rob Lyerly, Charlotte	.725
42.	Clint Moore, Army	.724
43.	Jeremy Hazelbaker, Ball State	.724
44.	Troy Channing, St. Mary's	.723
45.	Mike Melillo, Elon	.722
46.	Tom Mendonca, Fresno State	.721
47.	Jeremy Cruz, Stetson	.719
48.	Ryan Hutson, Texas-San Antonio	.719
49.	Jordan Kreke, Eastern Illinois	.718
50.	Shane Eyler, Mount St. Mary's	.717

HOME RUNS

RANK	NAME, TEAM	HR
1.	Bryce Brentz, Middle Tennessee State	28
	Kent Matthes, Alabama	28
3.	Marc Krauss, Ohio	27
	Tom Mendonca, Fresno State	27
5.	Chris Dominguez, Louisville	25
	Wade Gaynor, Western Kentucky	25
	Rich Poythress, Georgia	25
8.	Tyler Townsend, Florida International	24
9.	Chase Austin, Elon	23
	Devon Dageford, Louisiana Tech	23
	Nick Ebert, South Carolina	23
	Mike Spina, Cincinnati	23
13.	Dustin Ackley, North Carolina	22
	Ryan Goins, Dallas Baptist	22
	Cody Hawn, Tennessee	22
	Kevin Mahoney, Canisius	22
	Bryan Marquez, New Mexico State	22
	Ryan Schimpf, Louisiana State	22
	Chris Sedon, Pittsburgh	22
20.	David Anderson, Coastal Carolina	21
	Cody Decker, UCLA	21
	Gaunlett Eldemire, Ohio	21
	Tony Thompson, Kansas	21
24.	Troy Channing, St. Mary's	20
	Nate Freiman, Duke	20
	A.J. Kirby-Jones, Tennessee Tech	20
	Scott Krieger, George Mason	20
	Luke Murton, Georgia Tech	20
	Anthony Rendon, Rice	20
	Kevin Sandberg, Northern Colorado	20
31.	Kyle Conley, Washington	19
	Chad Cregar, Western Kentucky	19
	Joey Lewis, Georgia	19
	Matt Mansilla, College of Charleston	19
	Bryce Massanari, Georgia	19
	Mike McGee, Florida State	19
	Connor Powers, Mississippi State	19
	Carlos Ramirez, Arizona State	19
	Joseph Sanders, Auburn	19
	Jesse Sawyer, South Dakota State	19

	Andy Wilkins, Arkansas	19
42.	Jeremy Cruz, Stetson	18
	Bennett Davis, Elon	18
	Paul Goldschmidt, Texas State	18
	Victor Gomez, Marshall	18
	Chris Kersten, Louisiana Tech	18
	Andrew Marshall, Eastern Michigan	18
	Derek McCallum, Minnesota	18
	Mike Melillo, Elon	18
	Ryan Rivers, Charlotte	18
	Jake Smith, Alabama	18
	Tim Wheeler, Sacramento State	18
	Phil Wunderlich, Louisville	18

RUNS BATTED IN

RANK	NAME, TEAM	RBI
1.	Paul Goldschmidt, Texas State	87
2.	Derek McCallum, Minnesota	86
	Rich Poythress, Georgia	86
4.	Bryan Marquez, New Mexico State	85
	Preston Tucker, Florida	85
6.	Vince Belnome, West Virginia	84
7.	David Anderson, Coastal Carolina	82
	Jared Clark, Cal State Fullerton	82
	Chris Dominguez, Louisville	82
	Tony Thompson, Kansas	82
11.	Chase Austin, Elon	81
	Cody Hawn, Tennessee	81
	Kent Matthes, Alabama	81
14.	Jeremy Cruz, Stetson	80
	Scott Krieger, George Mason	80
16.	Wade Gaynor, Western Kentucky	78
	Mike McGee, Florida State	78
	Tom Mendonca, Fresno State	78
	Phil Wunderlich, Louisville	78
20.	Tyler Townsend, Florida International	77
21.	Jeffrey Farnham, New Mexico State	76
	Jason Stidham, Florida State	76
23.	Troy Channing, St. Mary's	75
	Isaac Harrow, Appalachian State	75
	Joey Henshaw, Army	75
	Carlos Ramirez, Arizona State	75
	Kyle Roller, East Carolina	75
28.	Jason Krizan, Dallas Baptist	74
	Jeff Mercer, Wright State	74
	Brandon Sizemore, Col. of Charleston	74
31.	Dustin Ackley, North Carolina	73
	Bryce Brentz, Middle Tenn. State	73
	Nathan Hines, Middle Tenn. State	73
	Tony Plagman, Georgia Tech	73
35.	Nick Ebert, South Carolina	72
	Jayson Langfels, Eastern Kentucky	72
	Anthony Rendon, Rice	72
	Matt Rice, Western Kentucky	72
	Tim Wheeler, Sacramento State	72
40.	Blake Dean, Louisiana State	71
	Jason Kipnis, Arizona State	71
	Ben Soignier, Louisiana-Monroe	71
43.	Greg Folgia, Missouri	70
	Ryan Goins, Dallas Baptist	70
	Sam Honeck, Tulane	70
	Marc Krauss, Ohio	70
	Ryan Schimpf, Louisiana State	70
48.	Jeremy Barnes, Notre Dame	69
	Daniel Hill, Murray State	69
	Richard Jones, Citadel	69
	Brandon May, Alabama	69
	Matt Otteman, Texas-Arlington	69
	Mike Spina, Cincinnati	69

DOUBLES

RANK	NAME, TEAM	2B
1.	Zach Johnson, Campbell	29
2.	Jedd Gyorko, West Virginia	28

3. Nathan Hines, Middle Tenn. State 27
Tony Thompson, Kansas 27
Tyson Van Winkle, Gonzaga 27
6. Ryan Hamme, Campbell 26
Jeff Mercer, Wright State 26
Josh Powers, Sacramento State 26
Kyle Seager, North Carolina 26
10. C.J. Beatty, North Carolina A&T 25
Joey Bergman, College of Charleston 25
Khris Davis, Cal State Fullerton 25
Jose Hernandez, Texas-San Antonio 25
Hayden Johnston, Ohio 25
Danny Muno, Fresno State 25
Kolbrin Vitek, Ball State 25
17. Drew Robertson, Middle Tenn. State 24
Jason Stidham, Florida State 24
Trent Whitehead, East Carolina 24
Kurt Wideman, Pacific 24
21. Bryan Altman, Citadel 23
Mike Brownstein, New Mexico 23
Matt Carpenter, Texas Christian 23
Matt Collins, Towson 23
Andrew Crisp, South Carolina 23
Kevin David, Oklahoma State 23
Isaac Harrow, Appalachian State 23
Wes Hobson, Appalachian State 23
Tyler Holt, Florida State 23
Andrew Kainer, Texas-Arlington 23
Tyler Santos, Sacred Heart 23
Ty Summerlin, Southeastern La. 23
33. Jamie Abercrombie, Temple 22
Robert Anston, Boston College 22
Anthony Armenio, Manhattan 22
Matt Bowman, Nevada 22
Brent Greer, Western Carolina 22
Chris Henderson, George Mason 22
Jon Karcich, Santa Clara 22
Zach Kayne, Davidson 22
Ben Klafczynski, Kent State 22
Andy Leonard, Illinois-Chicago 22
Steven Liddle, Vanderbilt 22
Nick Liles, Western Carolina 22
Casey McGrew, Wright State 22
Sonny Meade, Citadel 22
Mike Nemeth, Connecticut 22
Steven Proscia, Virginia 22
Ben Soignier, Louisiana-Monroe 22
Jeff Taliaferro, Northern Iowa 22
Ryan Wood, East Carolina 22
Nick Zaleski, Sam Houston State 22

Tyler Holt scored 87 runs as a sparkplug atop FSU's lineup

TRIPLES

RANK NAME, TEAM	3B
1. Mike Brownstein, New Mexico	11
2. Dylan Craig, Belmont	9
Todd Cunningham, Jacksonville State	9
Gary Helmick, Towson	9
Nick Kuroczko, Utah	9
6. Aaron Conway, Missouri State	8
Jeremy Hazelbaker, Ball State	8
Drew Heid, Gonzaga	8
Matt Otteman, Texas-Arlington	8
10. Gary Brown, Cal State Fullerton	7
Brian Cavazos-Galvez, New Mexico	7
Bobby Coyle, Arizona	7
Dane Hamilton, New Mexico	7
Jonathan Johnson, Loyola Marymount	7
Branson Joseph, Canisius	7
Brandon Kendricks, Prairie View	7
John Lynch, Norfolk State	7
Austin Markel, West Virginia	7
Tj Mittelstaedt, Long Beach State	7
Chris Murrill, Nicholls State	7
Jarrett Parker, Virginia	7

Chad Watson, Troy	7
23. Kevin Atkinson, New Mexico	6
Avery Barnes, Florida	6
Aaron Barrows, Eastern Kentucky	6
Lance Brown, Texas-San Antonio	6
Matt Carpenter, Texas Christian	6
Joe Cotter, Villanova	6
Micheal Dabbs, Oklahoma State	6
Marshal Davis, Texas-San Antonio	6
Aaron Dunsmore, Dayton	6
Adam Eaton, Miami (Ohio)	6
Ryan Eden, New Orleans	6
Brian Ferguson, Stephen F. Austin	6
Cass Hargis, Southeastern La.	6
Isaac Harrow, Appalachian State	6
Nathan Hines, Middle Tennessee State	6
Zach Hurley, Ohio State	6
Brett Jackson, California	6
Alex Johnson, Cleveland State	6
Charlie Karstedt, Buffalo	6
Jayson Langfels, Eastern Kentucky	6
Danny Leach, Fordham	6
Matt Long, Santa Clara	6
Nick Longmire, Pacific	6
Kevin Nieto, Manhattan	6
Corey Overholtzer, UNC Greensboro	6
Martin Parra, Texas A&M-Corpus Christi	6
Jake Rife, Washington	6
Matt Sanford, Southern Utah	6
Joe Sclafani, Dartmouth	6
J.J. Sferra, UNLV	6
Matt Smedberg, Seton Hall	6
Cody Stanley, UNC Wilmington	6
Steven Sultzbaugh, Rice	6

STOLEN BASES

RANK NAME, TEAM	SB	CS
1. Rico Noel, Coastal Carolina	48	3
Josh Prince, Tulane	48	7
3. Brint Hardy, Ala.-Birmingham	46	3
4. Zach Kim, San Francisco	42	7
John McCambridge, Xavier	42	7
6. Jeff Squier, Miss. Valley State	41	4
7. Jordan Henry, Mississippi	38	6
Danny Menendez, Maine	38	8
9. Damian Csakai, Wagner	37	7
Brock Miller, Gardner-Webb	37	10
11. Jared Mitchell, Louisiana State	36	9

12. Tyler Holt, Florida State	34	5
13. Dexter Kelley, Savannah State	33	8
14. Darryl Evans, Florida A&M	32	5
Nate Fields, Ball State	32	3
Kyle Rhoad, Eastern Michigan	32	3
17. Justyn Carter, St. Peter's	31	7
Adam McConnell, Richmond	31	8
Tristan Smith, Savannah State	31	1
20. Trevor Collias, Western Carolina	30	5
Matt Maher, Fairleigh Dickinson	30	7
Kyle Wilson, North Carolina State	30	5
Scott Woodward, Coastal Carolina	30	3
24. Jeremy Hazelbaker, Ball State	29	6
Grant Hogue, Mississippi State	29	5
Danny Leach, Fordham	29	5
27. Deshaun Dilworth, Texas Southern	28	5
Adam Eaton, Miami (Ohio)	28	1
Clay McCord, Col. of Charleston	28	4
Mark Micowski, Vermont	28	8
Phil Vaughn, Md.-Eastern Shore	28	5
32. Evan Crawford, Indiana	27	5
Jason Kipnis, Arizona State	27	6
Ryan Lee, Cal Poly	27	3
James Lyons, Western Carolina	27	4
Chris Murrill, Nicholls State	27	5
37. Jesse Bosnik, St. Bonaventure	26	5
Daniel Cooke, Gardner-Webb	26	4
James Hayes, Rider	26	3
Chris Herron, Miss. Valley State	26	5
Matt Nohelty, Minnesota	26	5
Jim Viscomi, Evansville	26	10
David Washington, Savannah State	26	6
Adam Yeager, Marshall	26	8
45. Matt Davis, Eastern Kentucky	25	3
Andrew Diminio, VCU	25	5
Matt Hightower, Western Ky.	25	7
Scott Kimble, Longwood	25	4
Kevin Nieto, Manhattan	25	3
Brooks Raley, Texas A&M	25	4
Brendan Rowland, Albany	25	4
Tyler Wilson, Lipscomb	25	7

RUNS

RANK NAME, TEAM	R
1. Joey Bergman, College of Charleston	88
2. Tyler Holt, Florida State	87
Ryan Wood, East Carolina	87
4. Adam Duvall, Louisville	83

Wade Gaynor, Western Kentucky	83
Bryan Marquez, New Mexico State	83
7. Andrew Clark, Louisville	82
Christian Colon, Cal State Fullerton	82
9. Chris Dominguez, Louisville	80
10. Bryce Brentz, Middle Tennessee State	79
Cory Harrilchak, Elon	79
12. Rawley Bishop, Middle Tenn. State	78
Trent Whitehead, East Carolina	78
14. Jeremy Hazelbaker, Ball State	77
Tyler Sibley, Texas State	77
16. Avery Barnes, Florida	76
Stephen Cardullo, Florida State	76
Ryan Goins, Dallas Baptist	76
Jamie Johnson, Oklahoma	76
Jason Kipnis, Arizona State	76
Jarrett Parker, Virginia	76
Justin Parks, West Virginia	76
23. Dustin Ackley, North Carolina	75
Austin Markel, West Virginia	75
Clay McCord, College of Charleston	75
Rico Noel, Coastal Carolina	75
George Springer, Connecticut	75
28. Chase Austin, Elon	74
Jedd Gyorko, West Virginia	74
Danny Muno, Fresno State	74
31. Marc Krauss, Ohio	73
Tyler Link, Lamar	73
Ryan Schimpf, Louisiana State	73
Richard Stout, New Mexico State	73
Ty Wright, Georgia Southern	73
36. Mike Brownstein, New Mexico	72
Paul Goldschmidt, Texas State	72
Gary Helmick, Towson	72
Kevin Nieto, Manhattan	72
40. Stephen Batts, East Carolina	71
Boomer Blanchard, Louisiana-Monroe	71
Matt Davis, Eastern Kentucky	71
Ryan Enos, Dallas Baptist	71
Nate Shaver, New Mexico State	71
45. Jeffrey Farnham, New Mexico State	70
Chris Henderson, George Mason	70
Jordan Henry, Mississippi	70
Jon Prevost, Louisiana-Monroe	70
Ryan Shay, Bowling Green	70
50. Jackie Bradley, South Carolina	69
Ellis Lowe, Campbell	69
Tim Morris, St. John's	69
Matt Nohelty, Minnesota	69
Nick Orvin, Citadel	69
A.J. Pollock, Notre Dame	69
Rich Poythress, Georgia	69
Kyle Rhoad, Eastern Michigan	69

HITS

RANK NAME, TEAM	H
1. Dustin Ackley, North Carolina	111
Braeden Riley, Sam Houston State	111
3. Bryce Brentz, Middle Tennessee State	107
4. Trent Whitehead, East Carolina	105
5. Sonny Meade, Citadel	104
6. Kyle Seager, North Carolina	103
7. Brent Greer, Western Carolina	102
8. Mike Brownstein, New Mexico	101
Matt Rice, Western Kentucky	101
10. Joey Bergman, College of Charleston	100
Ryan Wood, East Carolina	100
12. Lance Durham, Cincinnati	99
Michael Rockett, Texas-San Antonio	99
Nick Zaleski, Sam Houston State	99
15. Gary Helmick, Towson	98
16. Chris Henderson, George Mason	97
17. Stephen Batts, East Carolina	96
Rawley Bishop, Middle Tenn. State	96

Dustin Ackley was a hitting machine for three years at UNC

CARL KLINE

Jedd Gyorko, West Virginia	96
D.J. Lemahieu, Louisiana State	96
Tony Thompson, Kansas	96
22. Bryan Altman, Citadel	95
Nathan Hines, Middle Tennessee State	95
Tyler Holt, Florida State	95
Richard Jones, Citadel	95
Nick Liles, Western Carolina	95
Derek McCallum, Minnesota	95
Matt Otteman, Texas-Arlington	95
Ben Paulsen, Clemson	95
Eddie Tisdale, Winthrop	95
31. Jarrett Parker, Virginia	94
Anthony Rendon, Rice	94
33. Kyle Bellows, San Jose State	93
Michael Choice, Texas-Arlington	93
Wade Gaynor, Western Kentucky	93
36. Kevin Atkinson, New Mexico	92
Chase Austin, Elon	92
Ben Bunting, North Carolina	92
Dylan Craig, Belmont	92
Isaac Harrow, Appalachian State	92
Ross Heffley, Western Carolina	92
Hayden Johnston, Ohio	92
DeAngelo Mack, South Carolina	92
Nick Orvin, Citadel	92
Tyler Townsend, Florida International	92
46. Griffin Benedict, Georgia Southern	91
Christian Colon, Cal State Fullerton	91
Jeremy Cruz, Stetson	91
Jason Kipnis, Arizona State	91
Jeff Mercer, Wright State	91
Whit Merrifield, South Carolina	91
Ben Orloff, UC Irvine	91

TOTAL BASES

RANK NAME, TEAM	TB
1. Bryce Brentz, Middle Tenn. State	214
2. Dustin Ackley, North Carolina	203
3. Wade Gaynor, Western Kentucky	196
4. Tony Thompson, Kansas	186
5. Tyler Townsend, Fla. International	182
6. Rich Poythress, Georgia	181
7. Chris Dominguez, Louisville	180
8. Gary Helmick, Towson	179
9. Chase Austin, Elon	178
Marc Krauss, Ohio	178

11. Jarrett Parker, Virginia	176
12. Kent Matthes, Alabama	175
Ryan Schimpf, Louisiana State	175
14. Joey Bergman, College of Charleston	172
Derek McCallum, Minnesota	172
16. Bryan Marquez, New Mexico State	171
17. Anthony Rendon, Rice	170
18. Ryan Goins, Dallas Baptist	169
Richard Jones, Citadel	169
20. Devon Dagefrod, Louisiana Tech	168
Jason Kipnis, Arizona State	168
Tom Mendonca, Fresno State	168
23. Nathan Hines, Middle Tenn. State	167
Michael Rockett, Texas-San Antonio	167
25. Ryan Wood, East Carolina	166
26. Chris Henderson, George Mason	165
Scott Krieger, George Mason	165
28. Jeremy Cruz, Stetson	164
Hayden Johnston, Ohio	164
Phil Wunderlich, Louisville	164
31. Isaac Harrow, Appalachian State	163
32. David Anderson, Coastal Carolina	161
Stephen Batts, East Carolina	161
Ryan Enos, Dallas Baptist	161
35. Brian Cavazos-Galvez, New Mexico	160
Ben Paulsen, Clemson	160
Chris Sedon, Pittsburgh	160
38. Drew Lee, Morehead State	159
39. Cory Harrilchak, Elon	158
40. Rawley Bishop, Middle Tenn. State	157
Tony Plagman, Georgia Tech	157
42. Jose Hernandez, Texas-San Antonio	156
Jamie Johnson, Oklahoma	156
Kevin Mahoney, Canisius	156
45. DeAngelo Mack, South Carolina	155
Kyle Seager, North Carolina	155
47. Bennett Davis, Elon	154
Blake Dean, Louisiana State	154
Nate Freiman, Duke	154
Paul Goldschmidt, Texas State	154
Mike Spina, Cincinnati	154
Trent Whitehead, East Carolina	154

WALKS

RANK NAME, TEAM	BB
1. Chris McGuiness, Citadel	65
2. Danny Muno, Fresno State	64

3. Dan Black, Purdue	62
4. Richard Stout, New Mexico State	59
5. Jared Mitchell, Louisiana State	57
6. Jordan Henry, Mississippi	56
7. Andrew Clark, Louisville	55
Paul Goldschmidt, Texas State	55
9. Tyler Holt, Florida State	54
Sam Honeck, Tulane	54
11. Nick Ebert, South Carolina	53
Clay McCord, College of Charleston	53
Brad Miller, Clemson	53
14. Seth Henry, Tulane	52
15. Matt Carpenter, Texas Christian	51
Jason Kipnis, Arizona State	51
Luke Stewart, Alabama-Birmingham	51
Colin Walsh, Stanford	51
19. Dustin Ackley, North Carolina	50
Blake Dean, Louisiana State	50
Cody McMurry, Alabama-Birmingham	50
Ryan Wood, East Carolina	50
23. Ben Braaten, Saint Louis	49
Chase Leavitt, Arkansas	49
Bryan Marquez, New Mexico State	49
26. Alan Ahmady, Fresno State	48
Jeremy Hazelbaker, Ball State	48
Alan Parks, Charlotte	48
Andy Wilkins, Arkansas	48
30. Tyler Link, Lamar	47
31. Bo Davis, Southern Mississippi	46
Ryan Goins, Dallas Baptist	46
Marc Krauss, Ohio	46
Logan Power, Mississippi	46
Carlos Ramirez, Arizona State	46
Aaron Senne, Missouri	46
Ben Soignier, Louisiana-Monroe	46
38. David Anderson, Coastal Carolina	45
Stephen Cardullo, Florida State	45
Chad Cregar, Western Kentucky	45
Pat Irvine, Elon	45
Mike Melillo, Elon	45
Josh Phegley, Indiana	45
Josh Prince, Tulane	45
Michael Reed, Texas Tech	45
Kyle Seager, North Carolina	45
47. LaDerek Camper, Jackson State	44
Erik Castro, San Diego State	44
Andy Mees, Northern Colorado	44
Max Most, Old Dominion	44
Jeremiah Sammy, Lamar	44
Ryan Schimpf, Louisiana State	44
Diego Seastrunk, Rice	44
Jason Stidham, Florida State	44
Stuart Tapley, Florida State	44
Murray Watts, Arkansas State	44
Derek Wiley, Belmont	44

TOUGHEST TO STRIKE OUT

RANK NAME, TEAM	AB/SO
1. Billy Alvino, High Point	52.5
2. Brandon Wikoff, Illinois	32.6
3. Carmen Del Mastro, Temple	31.8
4. Andy Leonard, Illinois-Chicago	24.2
5. Ryan Goetz, UC Riverside	23.9
6. Danny Stienstra, San Jose State	23.4
7. Corey Valine, San Jose State	23.3
8. Nick Overmyer, Purdue	21.4
9. Curran Redal, Liberty	21.3
10. Kyle Obal, Temple	21.1
11. Chris Mentrasti, Hofstra	19.6
12. Taylor Traub, Oakland	19.4
13. Kevin Winn, Louisiana Tech	19.4
14. Richie Derbak, Eastern Illinois	18.7
15. Tony Jusino, Temple	18.3
16. Ryan Dew, Ohio State	18.3

Texas freshman Brandon Loy led the nation in sacrifice bunts

JOHN WILLIAMSON

17. Jason Martin, San Jose State	17.6
18. Adam Tempesta, Massachusetts	17.6
19. Kyle Klee, Binghamton	17.4
20. Chris Collazo, Monmouth	16.7
21. Kevin Bowles, Georgia Southern	16.6
22. Wes Dorrell, Cal Poly	16.3
23. Eddie Tisdale, Winthrop	16.1
24. Chad Marshall, Stony Brook	16.0
25. Ben Orloff, UC Irvine	15.9

HIT BY PITCH

RANK NAME, TEAM	HBP
1. Chris Bangi, Campbell	30
2. Adam Eaton, Miami (Ohio)	26
3. Jason Martin, San Jose State	25
4. Griffin Benedict, Georgia Southern	24
Kyle Roller, East Carolina	24
6. Jordin Hood, Northern Illinois	23
Tim Jallen, North Dakota State	23
8. Ben Carlson, Missouri State	22
Cody Cotter, Saint Louis	22
Josh Cryer, Southeastern Louisiana	22
Casey Stevenson, UC Irvine	22
12. Brian Harris, Vanderbilt	21
Mark Onorati, Manhattan	21
Jacob Spaeth, Dayton	21
Kiko Vazquez, Central Florida	21
Evan Wells, Gonzaga	21
17. Brad Buell, Cleveland State	20
Marvin McWhorter, Jackson State	20
Dane Yelovich, Kansas State	20
20. Nate Brown, Arkansas-Little Rock	19
Justyn Carter, St. Peter's	19
Kevin Hoef, Iowa	19
Bryant Kraus, Portland	19
Jerry Mancuso, Saint Louis	19
Jeff Newman, Cal State Fullerton	19
Pablo Rosario, High Point	19

SACRIFICE BUNTS

RANK NAME, TEAM	SH
1. Brandon Loy, Texas	25
Joe Scott, Cal State Fullerton	25
3. Danny Menendez, Maine	20
4. Austin McDowell, Chicago State	16
Zak Presley, Houston	16
Chris Wade, Kentucky	16
7. Bret Atwood, Texas State	15
Joey Kenworthy, Texas Tech	15
Jeff Newman, Cal State Fullerton	15

Joe Rosati, Villanova	15
Tobias Streich, West Virginia	15
Max Willett, New Mexico	15
Jared Wolf, Western Illinois	15
Joey Wong, Oregon State	15
15. Dan Dibartolomeo, West Virginia	14
Andrew Gehr, Evansville	14
Tyrone Hambly, Oklahoma State	14
Matt Harughty, Oklahoma	14
Robby Price, Kansas	14
Riley Reynolds, Vanderbilt	14
Alfie Wheeler, High Point	14
22. Junior Arrojo, Florida International	13
Kevin Atkinson, New Mexico	13
Gavin Hedstrom, Fresno State	13
Chad Marshall, Stony Brook	13
Taylor Motter, Coastal Carolina	13
Rico Noel, Coastal Carolina	13
Brooks Raley, Texas A&M	13

SACRIFICE FLIES

RANK NAME, TEAM	SF
1. D.J. Gentile, Cal Poly	11
2. Blake Dean, Louisiana State	10
Aaron Dudley, Toledo	10
Grayson Evans, UNC Wilmington	10
Greg Folgia, Missouri	10
Paul Goldschmidt, Texas State	10
Jonathan Roof, Michigan State	10
Jason Stidham, Florida State	10
9. Dan Burkhart, Ohio State	9
Jared Clark, Cal State Fullerton	9
Mick Doyle, Notre Dame	9
Miles Hartsfield, Tennessee-Martin	9
Jeremy Schaffer, Tulane	9
14. Buck Afenir, Kansas	8
Kyle Bellows, San Jose State	8
Phil Cerreto, Longwood	8
Joe Charron, Binghamton	8
Nick Ciolli, Indiana State	8
Dylan Craig, Belmont	8
Jonathan Koscso, South Florida	8
Ryan LaMarre, Michigan	8
Clint Moore, Army	8
John Murrian, Winthrop	8
Wes Patterson, Tennessee-Martin	8
Josh Phegley, Indiana	8
Derek Poppert, San Francisco	8
Anthony Sosnoskie, Virginia Tech	8

Mike Leake was named Pacific-10 Conference Pitcher of the Year for the second straight season

BILL MITCHELL

PITCHING

Minimum 50 IP, 1 IP per team game

EARNED RUN AVERAGE

RANK NAME, TEAM, YEAR	G	IP	R	ER	ERA
1. Stephen Strasburg, San Diego State, Jr.	15	109	17	16	1.32
2. Mike Leake, Arizona State, Jr.	19	142	31	27	1.71
3. Michael Schum, Wright State, Fr.	34	74	24	16	1.95
4. Justin Robichaux, Louisiana-Lafayette, Jr.	17	59	25	13	1.98
5. Taylor Jungmann, Texas, Fr.	25	95	27	21	2.00
6. A.J. Morris, Kansas State, Jr.	16	116	35	27	2.09
7. Nick McCully, Coastal Carolina, Jr.	28	73	20	17	2.10
8. Mike Ojala, Rice, Jr.	13	66	21	16	2.17
9. Danny Hultzen, Virginia, Fr.	17	95	33	23	2.17
10. Brian Moran, North Carolina, Jr.	36	66	19	17	2.31
11. Daniel Calhoun, Murray State, Jr.	16	97	41	25	2.32
12. Josh Spence, Arizona State, Jr.	18	103	34	27	2.37
13. Pat Lehman, George Washington, Sr.	13	105	40	28	2.40
14. Ryan Berry, Rice, Jr.	14	82	28	22	2.42
15. Matt Way, Washington State, Sr.	16	107	44	29	2.43
16. Marc Oslund, Brigham Young, Fr.	22	65	33	18	2.49
17. Eric Arnett, Indiana, Jr.	14	108	39	30	2.50
18. Mark Serrano, Oral Roberts, Sr.	20	86	34	24	2.50
19. Austin Wood, Texas, Sr.	41	86	28	25	2.61
20. Daniel Bibona, UC Irvine, Jr.	15	106	37	31	2.63
21. Alex Kaminsky, Wright State, Jr.	13	85	31	25	2.66
22. Zach Varce, Portland, So.	23	60	25	18	2.69
23. Daniel Renken, Cal State Fullerton, So.	17	124	40	37	2.69
24. Sam Gaviglio, Oregon State, Fr.	18	63	20	19	2.73
25. Dan Perkins, Delaware State, Sr.	15	85	34	26	2.75
26. Andrew Wolcott, Duke, Sr.	14	94	36	29	2.77
27. Adam Wilk, Long Beach State, Jr.	15	94	33	29	2.78
28. Jordan Cooper, Wichita State, Jr.	15	97	35	30	2.78
29. Tim Kelley, Wichita State, So.	14	94	40	30	2.86
30. Robert Stock, Southern California, Jr.	20	78	32	25	2.90
31. Jeremy Johnson, Washington State, Jr.	28	59	27	19	2.90
32. Louis Coleman, Louisiana State, Sr.	25	129	48	42	2.93
33. Anthony Meo, Coastal Carolina, Fr.	17	77	32	25	2.93
34. Justin Moring, Arkansas-Pine Bluff, Sr.	12	73	35	24	2.95
35. Charlie Lowell, Wichita State, Fr.	12	64	25	21	2.95
36. Tyler Wilson, Virginia, So.	31	67	23	22	2.97
37. Andre Lamontagne, Oral Roberts, Sr.	16	76	39	25	2.97
38. Mike Bolsinger, Arkansas, So.	30	69	28	23	2.99
39. Trevor Bauer, UCLA, Fr.	20	105	39	35	2.99
40. Eric Harrington, Lamar, Fr.	15	84	40	28	3.01
Mitchell Lambson, Arizona State, Fr.	32	84	31	28	3.01
Joe Yermal, Charlotte, So.	14	84	42	28	3.01
43. Mike Recchia, Eastern Illinois, So.	13	66	26	22	3.01
44. Jeff Tardiff, Le Moyne, So.	13	95	41	32	3.02
45. Kelly McLain, Charlotte, Jr.	30	62	25	21	3.03
46. Kenneth Roberts, Middle Tenn. State, Jr.	16	104	45	35	3.04
47. Anthony Ranaudo, Louisiana State, So.	19	124	49	42	3.04
48. Erik Stavert, Oregon, Jr.	14	95	40	32	3.04
49. Tyler Lavigne, San Diego State, Jr.	15	94	35	32	3.05
Jarryd Summers, West Virginia, So.	14	94	41	32	3.05
51. David Palms, Princeton, So.	10	50	25	17	3.06
52. Cody Martin, Gonzaga, So.	23	59	25	20	3.07
53. Randy Fontanez, South Florida, So.	14	99	42	34	3.09
54. Matteo D'Angelo, Winthrop, So.	17	84	34	29	3.10
55. Jerry Sullivan, Oral Roberts, Jr.	15	98	47	34	3.12
56. Murphy Smith, Binghamton, Jr.	14	89	44	31	3.12
57. Kyle Blair, San Diego, So.	10	55	33	19	3.13
58. Andrew Dunn, Southern Illinois, Sr.	18	71	42	25	3.16
59. Brad Mincey, East Carolina, So.	25	83	43	29	3.16
60. Brad Boxberger, Southern California, Jr.	14	94	42	33	3.16
61. Chris Boggs, Old Dominion, Jr.	16	51	33	18	3.20
62. David Berner, San Jose State, Sr.	13	96	43	34	3.20
63. Kyle Gibson, Missouri, Jr.	16	107	39	38	3.21
64. Ali Simpson, Bethune-Cookman, Fr.	16	75	38	27	3.23
65. Buddy Baumann, Missouri State, Jr.	13	86	35	31	3.23
66. Rex Brothers, Lipscomb, Jr.	14	94	46	34	3.26
Chris Fetter, Michigan, Sr.	13	94	42	34	3.26
68. Jimmy Cornell, Southern Illinois, Jr.	15	66	28	24	3.26
69. Alex Wimmers, Ohio State, So.	16	105	43	38	3.27
70. Kane Holbrooks, Texas State, Sr.	16	101	46	37	3.29
71. Pat Dean, Boston College, So.	18	95	44	35	3.31
72. Adam Warren, North Carolina, Sr.	17	98	39	36	3.31
73. Chance Ruffin, Texas, So.	25	125	57	46	3.32
74. Robert Morey, Virginia, So.	18	68	27	25	3.32
75. A.J. Griffin, San Diego, Jr.	17	81	35	30	3.33
Noe Ramirez, Cal State Fullerton, Fr.	20	111	46	41	3.33
77. Cole Green, Texas, So.	21	110	45	41	3.35
78. Aaron Meade, Missouri State, So.	15	90	43	34	3.39
79. Seth Blair, Arizona State, So.	17	77	42	29	3.39
80. Joe Bircher, Bradley, Fr.	14	64	30	24	3.39
81. Drew Pomeranz, Mississippi, So.	16	95	47	36	3.40
82. Joe Gardner, UC Santa Barbara, Jr.	13	85	48	32	3.40
83. Matt Talley, Citadel, Sr.	18	71	36	27	3.42
84. Matt Hiserman, San Francisco, So.	19	89	43	34	3.43
85. Rob Gariano, Fairfield, Jr.	12	84	42	32	3.43
86. Lee Henry, Tennessee Tech, Jr.	21	79	38	30	3.43
Cameron Hobson, Dayton, Fr.	18	79	40	30	3.43
88. Zach Osborne, Louisiana-Lafayette, Jr.	16	84	40	32	3.44
89. John Hesketh, New Mexico, Sr.	15	89	39	34	3.45
90. Sean Weatherford, Sam Houston State, Fr.	22	81	47	31	3.46
91. Jayson Kramer, Hawaii, Sr.	15	93	46	36	3.47
92. Matt Fields, Gonzaga, Sr.	14	91	39	35	3.47
93. Adam Worthington, Illinois-Chicago, Sr.	15	96	43	37	3.48
94. Brandon Workman, Texas, So.	20	75	38	29	3.48
95. Keith Cantwell, Seton Hall, Sr.	13	93	45	36	3.48
96. Sean Gilmartin, Florida State, Fr.	18	98	48	38	3.49
97. John Straka, North Dakota State, Fr.	10	59	26	23	3.49
98. Gerrit Cole, UCLA, Fr.	15	85	46	33	3.49
99. Deck McGuire, Georgia Tech, So.	16	100	51	39	3.50
100. Jarrett Maloy, Southern, Jr.	12	72	40	28	3.50

WINS

RANK NAME, TEAM	W	L
1. Mike Leake, Arizona State	16	1
2. A.J. Morris, Kansas State	14	1
Louis Coleman, Louisiana State	14	2
4. Stephen Strasburg, San Diego State	13	1
5. Daniel Bibona, UC Irvine	12	1
Eric Arnett, Indiana	12	2
Drew Rucinski, Ohio State	12	2
Sean Gilmartin, Florida State	12	3
Anthony Ranaudo, Louisiana State	12	3
10. Buddy Baumann, Missouri State	11	1
Chris Mederos, Georgia Southern	11	1
Kenneth Roberts, Middle Tenn. State	11	1
Deck McGuire, Georgia Tech	11	2
Mike Modica, George Mason	11	2
Dean Wolosiansky, Ohio State	11	2
Daniel Calhoun, Murray State	11	3
Kyle Gibson, Missouri	11	3
Taylor Jungmann, Texas	11	3
Justin Marks, Louisville	11	3
Tyler Pill, Cal State Fullerton	11	3
Daniel Renken, Cal State Fullerton	11	3
22. Sam Gaviglio, Oregon State	10	1
Kane Holbrooks, Texas State	10	1
Josh Spence, Arizona State	10	1
Cody Wheeler, Coastal Carolina	10	1
Paul Applebee, UC Riverside	10	2
Chance Ruffin, Texas	10	2
Adam Warren, North Carolina	10	2
Chris Craycraft, Murray State	10	3
Brad Mincey, East Carolina	10	5
31. Doug Murray, San Francisco	9	0
Danny Hultzen, Virginia	9	1
Mark Serrano, Oral Roberts	9	1
Daniel Simon, New Mexico State	9	1
Jacob Wiley, Marist	9	1
Kevin Brandt, East Carolina	9	2
Andrew Carraway, Virginia	9	2
Jesse Darrah, Sacramento State	9	2
Shane Davis, Canisius	9	2
Aaron Meade, Missouri State	9	2
Anthony Meo, Coastal Carolina	9	2
Justin Moring, Arkansas-Pine Bluff	9	2
Noe Ramirez, Cal State Fullerton	9	2
Ali Simpson, Bethune-Cookman	9	2
Shawn Teufel, Liberty	9	2
Matt Watson, Wagner	9	2
Alex Wimmers, Ohio State	9	2
Trevor Bauer, UCLA	9	3
Christian Bergman, UC Irvine	9	3
Brett Bukvich, Mississippi	9	3
Tony Gonzales, Alcorn State	9	3
Lee Henry, Tennessee Tech	9	3
Dallas Keuchel, Arkansas	9	3
Seth Maness, East Carolina	9	3
Tyler Wilson, Virginia	9	3
Wes Wrenn, Citadel	9	3
Tom Buske, Minnesota	9	4
Blake Cooper, South Carolina	9	4
Sam Dyson, South Carolina	9	4
Billy Gross, West Virginia	9	4
Todd McInnis, Southern Mississippi	9	4
Garrett Richards, Oklahoma	9	4
Jesse Simpson, College of Charleston	9	4
Mitchell Lambson, Arizona State	9	5

SAVES

RANK NAME, TEAM	SV
1. Addison Reed, San Diego State	20
2. Jake Hale, Ohio State	18
3. Jarad Miller, Valparaiso	17
Thomas Girdwood, Elon	17
Eric Pettis, UC Irvine	17
6. Ryan Duke, Oklahoma	16

Kyle Bellamy, Miami	16
Matty Ott, Louisiana State	16
9. Scott Matyas, Minnesota	15
Coty Woods, Middle Tennessee State	15
Austin Wood, Texas	15
12. Tyler Mizenko, Winthrop	14
13. Jordan Conley, Xavier	13
Andrew Huebner, Wagner	13
Collin Cargill, Southern Mississippi	13
Michael Schum, Wright State	13
17. Joseph Kelly, UC Riverside	12
Chris Franklin, Southeastern Louisiana	12
Austin Hubbard, Auburn	12
David Erickson, Connecticut	12
Richard Folmer, Stephen F. Austin	12
22. Jordan Muir, Brigham Young	11
Luke Demko, Rhode Island	11
Ryan Smith, Dartmouth	11
Charlie Ruiz, Long Beach State	11
Kevin Arico, Virginia	11
Donnie Joseph, Houston	11
Zach Quate, Appalachian State	11
Billy Bullock, Florida	11
Jason Stoffel, Arizona	11
31. Matthew Kimball, Brown	10
Chad Sheppard, Northwestern State	10
Jeremy Johnson, Washington State	10
Jimmy Marshall, Florida State	10
Randy McCurry, Oklahoma State	10
Dean Weaver, Georgia	10
37. Matt Zahel, Toledo	9
Bill Henke, Jacksonville State	9
Shuhei Fujiya, Northern Iowa	9
Nick Pepitone, Tulane	9
Nick Gaudi, Pepperdine	9
Jason Patten, Radford	9
Kevin Rhoderick, Oregon State	9
Zach Varce, Portland	9
Eric Marshall, Texas Christian	9
Kevin Munson, James Madison	9
Michael Belfiore, Boston College	9
Anthony Vega, San Jose State	9
Jake Morgan, Mississippi	9
Paul Smyth, Kansas	9
David Burch, New Orleans	9
Adam Boydston, Texas-Arlington	9
Jake Geglein, Cincinnati	9
Brian Slover, Cal State Northridge	9
Daniel Tenholder, Austin Peay State	9
Stephen Richards, Arkansas	9
Seth Simmons, East Carolina	9

STRIKEOUTS

RANK NAME, TEAM	SO
1. Stephen Strasburg, San Diego State	195
2. Mike Leake, Arizona State	162
3. Anthony Ranaudo, Louisiana State	159
4. Louis Coleman, Louisiana State	142
5. Alex Wimmers, Ohio State	136
6. Rex Brothers, Lipscomb	132
Mark Serrano, Oral Roberts	132
8. Kyle Gibson, Missouri	131
9. Justin Marks, Louisville	129
10. Josh Spence, Arizona State	125
11. Drew Pomeranz, Mississippi	124
Matt Way, Washington State	124
13. Alex White, North Carolina	121
14. Alex Wilson, Texas A&M	120
15. Deck McGuire, Georgia Tech	118
16. Jerry Sullivan, Oral Roberts	116
17. James Paxton, Kentucky	115
Chance Ruffin, Texas	115
19. Mike Minor, Vanderbilt	114
20. Chris Mederos, Georgia Southern	113
21. Eric Arnett, Indiana	109

22. Matt Bashore, Indiana	108
Daniel Bibona, UC Irvine	108
Chris Rusin, Kentucky	108
25. Danny Hultzen, Virginia	107
26. Gerrit Cole, UCLA	104
Nathan Long, Texas-Arlington	104
28. Chris Fetter, Michigan	103
Daniel Renken, Cal State Fullerton	103
Adam Warren, North Carolina	103
31. Tim Kelley, Wichita State	102
32. Buddy Baumann, Missouri State	101
Taylor Jungmann, Texas	101
Jimmy Reyes, Elon	101
Josh Smith, Lipscomb	101
36. A.J. Morris, Kansas State	100
Noe Ramirez, Cal State Fullerton	100
Caleb Thielbar, South Dakota State	100
39. Victor Black, Dallas Baptist	99
Brad Boxberger, Southern California	99
Mitchell Lambson, Arizona State	99
Chris Masters, Western Carolina	99
Jarryd Summers, West Virginia	99
44. Cody Wheeler, Coastal Carolina	98
45. Tyler Blandford, Oklahoma State	97
Andrew Oliver, Oklahoma State	97
47. Nate Garcia, Santa Clara	96
B.J. Martin, Marist	96
49. Chris Dwyer, Clemson	95
Brooks Raley, Texas A&M	95
Brian Rorick, Delaware	95

STRIKEOUTS PER NINE INNINGS

RANK NAME, TEAM	SO/9
1. Stephen Strasburg, San Diego State	16.10
2. Mark Serrano, Oral Roberts	13.77
3. James Paxton, Kentucky	13.22
4. Rex Brothers, Lipscomb	12.64
5. Brian Moran, North Carolina	12.22
6. Alex Meyer, Kentucky	12.06
7. Alex Wilson, Texas A&M	12.04
8. Brad Gemberling, Princeton	11.88
9. Drew Pomeranz, Mississippi	11.71
10. Alex Wimmers, Ohio State	11.69
11. Anthony Ranaudo, Louisiana State	11.51
12. Tyler Blandford, Oklahoma State	11.19
13. Robert Morey, Virginia	11.17
14. Justin Marks, Louisville	11.06
15. Tyler Kehrer, Eastern Illinois	11.05

FEWEST HITS PER NINE INNINGS

RANK NAME, TEAM	H/9
1. Stephen Strasburg, San Diego State	5.37
2. Mike Leake, Arizona State	6.02
3. Gerrit Cole, UCLA	6.04
4. Brett Mooneyham, Stanford	6.15
5. Ryan Berry, Rice	6.17
6. Taylor Jungmann, Texas	6.18
7. Cole Cook, Pepperdine	6.18
8. Mitchell Lambson, Arizona State	6.24
9. Brian Moran, North Carolina	6.38
10. Nick McCully, Coastal Carolina	6.41

FEWEST WALKS PER NINE INNINGS

RANK NAME, TEAM	BB/9
1. Daniel Calhoun, Murray State	0.56
2. Jeff Thomson, Northeastern	0.65
3. Conrad Flynn, Tulane	0.72
4. John Walker, Longwood	0.87
5. Alex Kaminsky, Wright State	0.96
6. Shaeffer Hall, Kansas	0.97
7. Paul Bargas, UC Riverside	1.08
8. Brian Moran, North Carolina	1.09
9. Alex Gillingham, Loyola Marymount	1.10
10. Tyler Pill, Cal State Fullerton	1.15

BATTING

SCORING

RANK	TEAM	G	R	R/G
1.	New Mexico State	61	668	11.0
2.	Elon	59	604	10.2
3.	Campbell	51	516	10.1
4.	College of Charleston	57	554	9.7
5.	Georgia Southern	59	565	9.6
6.	West Virginia	55	525	9.5
7.	Dallas Baptist	55	515	9.4
8.	New Mexico	57	528	9.3
9.	Eastern Illinois	50	459	9.2
10.	Eastern Kentucky	51	468	9.2
11.	St. John's	52	473	9.1
12.	Manhattan	53	480	9.1
13.	Kent State	60	542	9.0
14.	Oral Roberts	48	425	8.9
15.	Jackson State	57	504	8.8
16.	Bowling Green	50	442	8.8
17.	Middle Tennessee State	62	545	8.8
18.	Alabama	58	509	8.8
19.	Florida State	63	550	8.7
20.	Western Kentucky	62	538	8.7
21.	Georgia Tech	58	501	8.6
22.	Louisiana Tech	51	438	8.6
23.	East Carolina	66	565	8.6
24.	Texas State	58	496	8.6
25.	Charlotte	55	470	8.5

BATTING AVERAGE

RANK	TEAM	AVG
1.	New Mexico	.363
2.	Eastern Illinois	.362
3.	West Virginia	.360
4.	New Mexico State	.353
5.	Manhattan	.349
6.	St. John's	.349
7.	Campbell	.346
8.	Bowling Green	.345
9.	College of Charleston	.345
10.	Eastern Kentucky	.345

HOME RUNS

RANK	TEAM	HR
1.	Elon	138
2.	New Mexico State	119
3.	Georgia Tech	111
4.	College of Charleston	110
5.	South Carolina	109
	Georgia	109
7.	East Carolina	108
8.	Alabama	107
	Louisiana State	107
10.	Auburn	103

DOUBLES

RANK	TEAM	2B
1.	Middle Tennessee State	164
2.	Florida State	163
3.	West Virginia	161
4.	New Mexico	158
5.	College of Charleston	156
6.	East Carolina	154
7.	New Mexico State	151
	Boston College	151
9.	St. John's	149
10.	Coastal Carolina	147

TRIPLES

RANK	TEAM	3B
1.	New Mexico	47
2.	Nevada-Las Vegas	35
3.	Arizona	33
4.	Arizona State	30
5.	Eastern Kentucky	29
6.	Virginia	28
	North Carolina	28

8.	Jackson State	26
	Ohio State	26
	Nicholls State	26

SLUGGING PERCENTAGE

RANK	TEAM	SLG
1.	New Mexico State	.599
2.	Elon	.596
3.	Eastern Illinois	.590
4.	College of Charleston	.590
5.	Dallas Baptist	.582
6.	Middle Tennessee State	.567
7.	Alabama	.566
8.	West Virginia	.564
9.	Towson	.556
10.	New Mexico	.554

STOLEN BASES

RANK	TEAM	SB	CS
1.	Savannah State	169	38
2.	Jackson State	149	25
	Kansas State	149	45
4.	Florida A&M	132	40
5.	Western Carolina	126	33
6.	Cal State Fullerton	125	49
7.	Eastern Kentucky	123	34
8.	Mississippi Valley State	122	40
9.	Coastal Carolina	121	34
10.	College of Charleston	120	27

WALKS

RANK	TEAM	BB
1.	New Mexico State	416
2.	Florida State	386
3.	Arizona State	380
4.	Louisiana State	350
5.	Fresno State	332
6.	Elon	326
7.	Tulane	318
8.	North Carolina	315
9.	Clemson	312
10.	Oregon State	304

PITCHING

EARNED RUN AVERAGE

RANK	TEAM	ERA
1.	Arizona State	2.90
2.	Texas	2.95
3.	Virginia	3.23
4.	Cal State Fullerton	3.53
5.	Clemson	3.68
6.	North Carolina	3.73
7.	Oral Roberts	3.78
8.	Oregon State	3.93
9.	Louisiana State	4.01
10.	Coastal Carolina	4.04
11.	San Diego State	4.04
12.	Mississippi	4.04
13.	Creighton	4.05
14.	Southern California	4.06
15.	Jackson State	4.19
16.	Rice	4.21
17.	UC Riverside	4.22
18.	Texas Christian	4.22
19.	Wichita State	4.26
20.	Florida	4.27
21.	UCLA	4.28
22.	Louisville	4.32
23.	Washington State	4.34
24.	Seton Hall	4.35
25.	Texas-Arlington	4.38

STRIKEOUTS PER NINE INNINGS

RANK	TEAM	IP	SO	SO/9
1.	Oral Roberts	424	498	10.6
2.	North Carolina	596	661	10.0
3.	Kentucky	475	523	9.9
4.	Mississippi	568	623	9.9

5.	Vanderbilt	556	604	9.8
6.	Louisiana State	644	679	9.5
7.	Texas A&M	540	568	9.5
8.	Arizona State	581	608	9.4
9.	UCLA	494	509	9.3
10.	Tennessee	485	494	9.2

FEWEST HITS PER NINE INNINGS

RANK	TEAM	IP	H	H/9
1.	Texas	613	512	7.52
2.	Pepperdine	472	410	7.82
3.	Virginia	583	516	7.97
4.	Arizona State	581	520	8.05
5.	Cal State Fullerton	569	517	8.18
6.	Oregon State	499	455	8.20
7.	North Carolina	596	547	8.26
8.	Oral Roberts	424	392	8.33
9.	Jackson State	432	401	8.35
10.	Rice	543	513	8.51

FEWEST WALKS PER NINE INNINGS

RANK	TEAM	IP	BB	BB/9
1.	Dartmouth	373	96	2.32
2.	UC Riverside	480	127	2.38
3.	Arizona State	581	157	2.43
4.	Murray State	457	124	2.44
5.	Cal State Fullerton	569	161	2.55
6.	San Diego State	573	165	2.59
7.	Louisiana State	644	186	2.60
8.	Tulane	512	149	2.62
9.	UC Irvine	538	160	2.68
10.	Illinois-Chicago	454	136	2.70

FIELDING

FIELDING PERCENTAGE

RANK	TEAM	PCT
1.	Creighton	.984
2.	Pepperdine	.982
3.	Western Kentucky	.979
4.	Duke	.979
5.	San Jose State	.978
6.	Stanford	.977
7.	Oregon State	.977
8.	Texas	.976
9.	UC Irvine	.976
10.	Oklahoma State	.976
11.	Indiana State	.976
12.	Cal State Fullerton	.976
13.	New Mexico	.976
14.	Hawaii	.975
15.	Liberty	.974
16.	Louisiana State	.974
17.	South Carolina	.974
18.	La Salle	.974
19.	San Diego State	.974
20.	Georgia Southern	.973
21.	Oklahoma	.973
22.	Tennessee	.972
23.	Pittsburgh	.972
24.	Kansas State	.972
25.	Vanderbilt	.972

DOUBLE PLAYS PER GAME

RANK	TEAM	G	DP	DP/G
1	Morehead State	52	70	1.35
2	Penn State	51	66	1.29
3	Nevada-Las Vegas	58	75	1.29
4	Maine	55	71	1.29
5	Nevada	56	71	1.27
6	Southern Miss.	66	83	1.26
7	Southern Utah	51	63	1.24
8	Creighton	56	69	1.23
9	Rice	61	73	1.20
10	Texas A&M-Corpus Christi	56	65	1.16

Batters: 10 or more at-bats. **Pitchers:** 5 or more innings.

1. LOUISIANA STATE

Coach: Paul Mainieri. **Record:** 56-17.

Player, Pos., Year	AVG	AB	R	H	2B	3B	HR	RBI	SB
D.J. LeMahieu, 2b, So.	.350	274	57	96	13	4	5	43	12
Chad Jones, of, So.	.343	35	8	12	2	0	1	6	1
Ryan Schimpf, of, Jr.	.336	262	73	88	19	1	22	70	18
Sean Ochinko, 1b, Jr.	.333	234	46	78	15	0	9	57	2
Blake Dean, dh, Jr.	.328	259	67	85	18	0	17	71	4
Jared Mitchell, of, Jr.	.327	226	64	74	14	5	11	50	36
Tyler Hanover, 3b, Fr.	.321	209	40	67	9	2	5	47	6
Mikie Mahtook, of, Fr.	.316	196	41	62	8	3	7	38	9
Buzzy Haydel, if, Sr.	.313	32	5	10	4	0	0	8	2
Leon Landry, of, So.	.300	170	38	51	10	0	12	41	9
Micah Gibbs, c, So.	.294	238	58	70	16	2	6	42	2
Chris McGhee, if, Sr.	.286	42	12	12	6	0	0	4	7
Nicholas Pontiff, of, Sr.	.279	43	9	12	1	0	2	6	0
Grant Dozar, if, Fr.	.265	34	9	9	0	0	2	6	0
Derek Helenihi, 3b, Sr.	.255	106	20	27	2	1	4	23	3
Austin Nola, ss, Fr.	.240	121	27	29	4	1	3	18	3

Player, Pos., Year	W	L	ERA	G	SV	IP	H	BB	SO
Matty Ott, rhp, Fr.	4	2	2.68	37	16	50	46	6	69
Chad Jones, lhp, So.	0	0	2.70	9	0	7	4	3	7
Louis Coleman, rhp, Sr.	14	2	2.93	25	0	129	108	23	142
Anthony Ranaudo, rhp, So.	12	3	3.04	19	0	124	93	50	159
Daniel Bradshaw, rhp, So.	4	0	3.04	25	1	50	45	11	33
Paul Bertuccini, rhp, Jr.	2	0	3.86	28	3	26	22	15	31
Nolan Cain, rhp, Sr.	5	0	4.01	19	0	34	36	10	38
Chris Matulis, lhp, Fr.	6	2	4.82	13	0	47	54	15	39
Austin Ross, rhp, So.	6	8	5.18	19	0	83	101	22	76
Buzzy Haydel, rhp, Sr.	0	0	5.40	9	0	8	9	2	6
Ryan Byrd, lhp, Sr.	1	0	5.81	13	0	26	31	8	24
Ben Alsup, rhp, So.	1	0	6.14	15	0	29	34	10	24
Shane Riedie, rhp, Fr.	0	0	8.10	4	1	7	5	4	9
Spencer Mathews, rhp, Fr.	0	0	9.45	5	1	7	13	2	4
Jordan Nicholson, rhp, So.	1	0	9.64	12	0	14	27	3	14

2. TEXAS

Coach: Augie Garrido. **Record:** 50-16-1.

Player, Pos., Year	AVG	AB	R	H	2B	3B	HR	RBI	SB
Brandon Belt, 1b, Jr.	.323	235	47	76	17	3	8	43	15
Kevin Lusson, if, Fr.	.310	42	13	13	4	0	0	11	1
Kevin Keyes, of, So.	.305	213	46	65	17	1	9	46	9
Michael Torres, 3b, Sr.	.298	245	36	73	11	2	5	33	12
Travis Tucker, 2b, Sr.	.297	266	52	79	12	2	3	30	13
Cameron Rupp, c, So.	.292	216	46	63	13	0	11	46	0
Brandon Loy, ss, Fr.	.288	233	34	67	8	1	0	30	9
Preston Clark, of, Sr.	.280	161	24	45	13	0	3	27	0
Connor Rowe, of, So.	.277	195	33	54	7	2	8	40	3
David Hernandez, if, Jr.	.273	99	10	27	0	0	0	12	3
Jordan Etier, if, Fr.	.267	15	6	4	0	0	0	2	0
Russell Moldenhauer, dh, Jr.	.262	84	10	22	5	0	4	14	0
Tant Shepherd, of, So.	.260	150	27	39	13	2	2	21	4
Tim Maitland, of, Jr.	.194	31	11	6	0	0	0	4	2
Kyle Lusson, of, Jr.	.170	47	7	8	2	0	0	3	3

Player, Pos., Year	W	L	ERA	G	SV	IP	H	BB	SO
Taylor Jungmann, rhp, Fr.	11	3	2.00	25	0	95	65	35	101
Stayton Thomas, rhp, So.	4	0	2.11	12	0	21	23	6	13
Austin Dicharry, rhp, Fr.	8	2	2.28	26	1	59	40	28	59
Keith Shinaberry, lhp, Sr.	1	0	2.53	13	0	11	15	2	2
Austin Wood, lhp, Sr.	6	1	2.61	41	15	86	68	18	74
Chance Ruffin, rhp, So.	10	2	3.32	25	2	125	109	25	115
Cole Green, rhp, So.	5	3	3.34	21	0	110	98	34	85
Brandon Workman, rhp, So.	3	5	3.48	20	0	75	58	28	82
Kendal Carrillo, rhp, Jr.	1	0	3.52	10	0	15	17	0	12
Andrew McKirahan, lhp, Fr.	1	0	5.68	11	0	13	17	7	12

3. ARIZONA STATE

Coach: Pat Murphy. **Record:** 51-14.

Player, Pos., Year	AVG	AB	R	H	2B	3B	HR	RBI	SB
Austin Barnes, c, Fr.	.412	17	4	7	0	1	0	2	1
Jason Kipnis, of, Jr.	.384	237	76	91	21	4	16	71	27
Johnny Ruettiger, of, Fr.	.360	100	28	36	6	2	1	13	12
Abe Ruiz, if, Fr.	.345	55	10	19	4	2	1	19	2
Carlos Ramirez, c, Jr.	.338	234	63	79	13	2	19	75	3
Kole Calhoun, of, Jr.	.313	211	54	66	117	2	12	53	10
Drew Maggi, ss, Fr.	.309	181	63	56	5	5	0	24	21
Matt Newman, of, So.	.305	236	42	72	15	1	7	54	6
Mike Leake, if, Jr.	.303	33	10	10	4	1	0	4	0
Andy Workman, of, So.	.292	48	11	14	4	0	0	7	2
Riccio Torrez, if, Fr.	.280	150	25	42	8	2	6	37	4
Zach Wilson, if, Fr.	.275	80	7	22	3	2	0	9	0
Zack MacPhee, 2b, Fr.	.270	204	48	55	8	1	4	39	8
Raoul Torrez, if, Jr.	.250	180	40	45	7	1	1	26	15
Jared McDonald, if, Jr.	.246	130	25	32	6	4	5	22	5
Mike Murphy, if, Jr.	.222	18	1	4	1	0	0	0	0
Jordan Swagerty, c, Fr.	.147	34	7	5	1	0	3	10	0
Brandon Magee, of, Fr.	.000	12	3	0	0	0	0	0	0

Player, Pos., Year	W	L	ERA	G	SV	IP	H	BB	SO
Mike Leake, rhp, Jr.	16	1	1.71	19	0	142	95	24	162
Jake Borup, rhp, Fr.	0	0	2.25	8	0	8	4	3	6
Jason Franzblau, rhp, Sr.	3	2	2.32	20	0	50	52	15	44
Josh Spence, lhp, Jr.	10	1	2.37	18	1	103	93	30	125
Kyle Brule, rhp, So.	0	0	2.79	10	1	10	11	1	7
Mitchell Lambson, lhp, Fr.	9	5	3.01	32	5	84	58	25	99
Seth Blair, rhp, So.	7	2	3.39	17	1	77	70	30	78
Jeeter Ishida, rhp, Fr.	0	0	3.52	7	0	8	10	7	7
Jordan Swagerty, rhp, Fr.	4	1	4.50	25	4	58	68	14	51
Matt Newman, lhp, So.	2	1	4.59	11	0	33	47	5	22
Kole Calhoun, lhp, Fr.	0	1	11.57	11	0	7	11	2	6

4. CAL STATE FULLERTON

Coach: Dave Serrano. **Record:** 47-16.

Player, Pos., Year	AVG	AB	R	H	2B	3B	HR	RBI	SB
Josh Fellhauer, of, Jr.	.396	227	49	90	12	0	6	55	18
Joey Siddons, 3b, Jr.	.371	124	24	46	5	0	0	33	9
Jared Clark, 1b, Sr.	.363	234	57	85	17	0	12	82	14
Christian Colon, ss, So.	.357	255	82	91	16	2	8	40	15
Gary Brown, of, So.	.340	259	64	88	17	7	3	40	23
Khris Davis, of, Jr.	.328	232	53	76	25	0	16	58	17
Joe Scott, 2b, Sr.	.313	166	34	52	6	4	1	39	9
Jeff Newman, of, Sr.	.296	152	38	45	2	0	0	10	11
Billy Marcoe, c, Jr.	.294	68	9	20	2	0	0	10	1
Nick Ramirez, dh, Fr.	.287	157	25	45	11	0	10	31	0
Dustin Garneau, c, Sr.	.284	155	34	44	7	1	5	28	6
Tyler Pill, of, Fr.	.269	26	2	7	2	0	0	6	0
Shevis Shima, if, Sr.	.268	41	12	11	1	0	0	2	0
Tony Harkey, if, So.	.237	38	4	9	3	0	0	11	1
Matthew Fahey, of, Sr.	.125	32	3	4	0	0	0	3	1

Player, Pos., Year	W	L	ERA	G	SV	IP	H	BB	SO
Colin O'Connell, rhp, Fr.	1	0	1.74	8	0	10	7	3	4
Brock Floro, rhp, So.	1	0	1.80	4	0	5	2	0	3
Kyle Mertins, rhp, Jr.	1	0	2.30	25	0	27	23	11	19
Nick Ramirez, lhp, Fr.	3	1	2.61	23	7	41	39	10	30
Daniel Renken, rhp, So.	11	3	2.69	17	0	124	93	35	103
Michael Morrison, rhp, Jr.	1	2	3.10	21	4	20	15	13	26
Noe Ramirez, rhp, Fr.	9	2	3.33	20	0	111	90	24	100
Ryan Ackland, rhp, Jr.	2	1	3.41	26	1	29	39	11	16
Tyler Pill, rhp, Fr.	11	3	4.06	17	0	102	97	13	74
Kevin Rath, lhp, So.	3	1	5.02	15	0	38	38	23	27
Travis Kelly, rhp, Jr.	0	0	5.25	10	0	12	13	3	6
Kyle Witten, rhp, Jr.	4	3	6.14	16	0	44	56	12	40

5. VIRGINIA

Coach: Brian O'Connor. **Record:** 49-15-1.

Player, Pos., Year	AVG	AB	R	H	2B	3B	HR	RBI	SB
John Bivens, of, Jr.	.438	16	7	7	0	0	0	2	2
Keith Werman, 2b, Fr.	.400	70	14	28	2	1	0	10	3
Dan Grovatt, of, So.	.356	247	53	88	8	4	8	51	14
Jarrett Parker, of, So.	.355	265	76	94	20	7	16	65	20
Tyler Cannon, ss, Jr.	.351	231	53	81	19	5	1	38	17
Steven Proscia, 3b, Jr.	.333	258	53	86	22	2	10	58	13
Danny Hultzen, 1b, Fr.	.327	199	40	65	8	1	3	37	9
Corey Hunt, if, So.	.317	60	10	19	2	0	0	12	2
Phil Gosselin, 2b, So.	.310	255	54	79	18	3	6	64	24
Tyler Biddix, if/of, So.	.308	13	5	4	0	0	0	2	1
John Hicks, c/of, Fr.	.307	254	51	78	13	3	8	39	6
David Coleman, of, So.	.307	75	10	23	4	1	1	10	1
John Barr, of, So.	.298	124	29	37	3	0	0	15	5
Franco Valdes, c, Jr.	.292	171	30	50	14	1	6	43	0
Jared King, if, Fr.	.250	64	13	16	2	0	0	15	1
Scott Silverstein, 1b, Fr.	.143	21	1	3	1	0	0	5	0

Player, Pos., Year	W	L	ERA	G	SV	IP	H	BB	SO
Justin Thompson, rhp, Fr.	0	0	0.00	7	0	8	3	3	5
Sean Lucas, lhp, Fr.	0	0	0.75	11	0	12	11	8	11
Shane Halley, rhp, Fr.	3	0	1.86	10	0	19	10	3	23
Danny Hultzen, lhp, Fr.	9	1	2.17	17	0	95	88	28	107
Robert Poutier, rhp, Sr.	3	0	2.21	13	0	37	31	15	50
Kevin Arico, rhp, So.	2	3	2.70	31	11	37	29	6	47
Tyler Wilson, rhp, So.	9	3	2.97	31	1	67	57	21	63
Roberty Morey, rhp, So.	3	0	3.33	18	2	68	52	28	84
Andrew Carraway, rhp, Sr.	9	2	3.96	18	0	91	84	22	75
Matt Packer, lhp, Jr.	3	5	4.13	32	3	61	59	25	59
Will Roberts, rhp, Fr.	4	0	4.14	11	0	37	36	12	38
Neal Davis, lhp, Jr.	2	0	4.63	16	1	23	25	5	16
Jeff Lorick, lhp, Jr.	2	1	5.61	8	0	26	27	13	15

6. NORTH CAROLINA

Coach: Mike Fox. **Record:** 48-18.

Player, Pos., Year	AVG	AB	R	H	2B	3B	HR	RBI	SB
Dustin Ackley, 1b, Jr.	.417	266	75	111	18	4	22	73	13
Kyle Seager, 3b, Jr.	.393	262	59	103	26	4	6	62	13
Ben Bunting, of, So.	.336	274	63	92	12	4	2	37	5
Garrett Gore, of, Sr.	.311	270	52	84	6	3	6	44	5
Mark Fleury, c, Jr.	.309	243	59	75	19	3	12	60	1
Levi Michael, 2b, Fr.	.290	262	54	76	15	4	13	57	5
Ryan Graepel, ss, Jr.	.283	247	36	70	17	1	2	42	2
Mike Cavasinni, of, Sr.	.272	217	43	59	5	4	0	24	9
Jacob Stallings, c, Fr.	.246	57	8	14	1	0	0	9	0
Brett Thomas, 1b, Sr.	.238	42	4	10	2	0	1	8	0
Seth Baldwin, of, Fr.	.229	48	9	11	1	0	3	14	1
Greg Holt, dh, So.	.190	42	2	8	0	0	1	5	1
Tarron Robinson, of/1b, Fr.	.174	46	5	8	1	1	1	7	0
Ryan Norton, of, Jr.	.156	32	9	5	1	0	0	2	2
Matt Harrison, if, Fr.	.130	23	2	3	1	0	0	0	0

Player, Pos., Year	W	L	ERA	G	SV	IP	H	BB	SO
Greg Holt, rhp, So.	0	0	1.69	7	1	11	9	5	10
Brian Moran, lhp, Jr.	7	1	2.31	36	4	66	47	8	90
Logan Munson, lhp, So.	1	1	2.61	19	2	21	25	11	22
Colin Bates, rhp, Jr.	4	4	3.15	34	6	60	53	19	59
Adam Warren, rhp, Sr.	10	2	3.31	17	0	98	83	39	103
Patrick Johnson, rhp, So.	2	2	3.49	23	1	57	46	37	77
Alex White, rhp, Jr.	8	4	3.87	16	0	107	93	44	121
Bryant Gaines, rhp, So.	4	0	4.08	10	1	35	37	14	38
Nate Striz, rhp, So.	2	0	4.12	26	1	24	37	14	38
Garrett Davis, rhp, Fr.	0	1	4.50	9	0	8	7	9	6
Matt Harvey, rhp, So.	7	2	5.40	21	1	75	88	42	81
Ryan Leach, rhp, So.	0	1	5.40	8	0	8	9	8	6
Jimmy Messer, rhp, Fr.	2	0	6.08	10	0	24	29	15	19

7. ARKANSAS

Coach: Dave Van Horn. **Record:** 41-24.

Player, Pos., Year	AVG	AB	R	H	2B	3B	HR	RBI	SB
Andy Wilkins, 1b, So.	.319	235	53	75	18	0	19	58	8
Ben Tschepikow, 2b/ss, Sr.	.317	240	54	76	12	4	9	47	17

Player, Pos., Year	AVG	AB	R	H	2B	3B	HR	RBI	SB
Tom Hauskey, c, Jr.	.308	26	3	8	0	0	0	3	0
Chase Leavitt, of, Sr.	.305	220	40	67	12	2	2	33	12
Scott Lyons, ss, Sr.	.295	241	37	71	11	1	8	46	2
Jacob House, of, So.	.282	110	13	31	5	0	2	15	0
Bo Bigham, 2b, Fr.	.280	75	16	21	2	1	1	6	4
Zack Cox, 3b, So.	.266	199	41	53	15	2	13	39	1
Travis Sample, of, So.	.263	76	11	20	7	0	2	16	1
Collin Kuhn, of, Fr.	.256	172	39	44	7	2	3	19	11
Andrew Darr, of, Sr.	.252	103	19	26	6	0	4	18	0
James McCann, c, Fr.	.242	128	18	31	6	0	1	11	0
Brett Eibner, of, So.	.231	147	34	34	3	1	12	34	3
Tim Carver, if, Fr.	.229	83	9	19	2	0	0	10	1
Jarrod McKinney, of, Fr.	.197	61	12	12	1	0	0	5	7
Ryan Cisterna, c, Sr.	.165	91	13	15	3	0	4	13	0

Player, Pos., Year	W	L	ERA	G	SV	IP	H	BB	SO
Stephen Richards, lhp, Jr.	6	2	2.19	31	9	37	30	20	52
Mike Bolsinger, rhp, Jr.	6	4	2.99	30	2	69	53	28	79
Christian Kowalchuk, lhp, Jr.	0	0	3.57	16	0	18	17	10	14
Dallas Keuchel, lhp, Jr.	9	3	3.92	18	0	108	114	32	69
Justin Wells, rhp, Sr.	2	1	4.38	26	3	49	62	16	34
Drew Smyly, lhp, Fr.	3	1	4.66	16	0	58	57	25	60
Kendall Wehrle, rhp, Fr.	0	0	4.70	9	0	15	12	7	15
Zack Cox, rhp, So.	5	1	4.82	14	1	19	24	3	15
Brett Eibner, rhp, So.	5	5	5.00	17	0	72	65	35	67
T.J. Forrest, rhp, Jr.	2	6	5.99	17	0	68	70	27	48
Sam Murphy, rhp, So.	3	1	6.15	21	0	41	47	20	40
Scott Limbocker, lhp, So.	0	0	9.00	8	0	7	9	9	5
Jeremy Heatley, rhp, Jr.	0	0	9.31	7	0	10	17	8	7
Bryan Bingham, rhp, Jr.	0	0	12.79	4	0	6	8	4	5

8. RICE

Coach: Wayne Graham. **Record:** 43-18.

Player, Pos., Year	AVG	AB	R	H	2B	3B	HR	RBI	SB
Anthony Rendon, 3b, Fr.	.388	242	60	94	14	1	20	72	9
Daniel Gonzales-Luna, of/if, Fr.	.360	50	12	18	3	0	1	7	3
Michael Fuda, of, So.	.359	181	43	65	14	2	3	21	8
Brock Holt, 2b, Jr.	.348	250	67	87	13	2	12	43	11
Steven Sutlzbaugh, of, Jr.	.324	222	47	72	6	6	8	31	7
Chad Mozingo, of, So.	.319	216	47	69	16	3	8	50	10
Rick Hague, ss, So.	.319	254	47	81	17	0	9	57	11
Craig Manuel, c, Fr.	.292	130	12	38	3	0	0	23	0
Ryan Lewis, of, Fr.	.289	45	5	13	3	1	0	9	1
Diego Seastrunk, c, Jr.	.288	226	46	65	15	1	7	45	1
Jimmy Comerota, 1b, Jr.	.285	214	51	61	5	4	1	26	11
Jess Buenger, if, Sr.	.250	40	6	10	0	1	0	11	0
Jeremy Rathjen, of, Fr.	.242	95	11	23	8	0	1	13	3
Dave Peterson, c/if, Jr.	.100	10	1	1	1	0	0	4	0

Player, Pos., Year	W	L	ERA	G	SV	IP	H	BB	SO
Mike Ojala, rhp, Jr.	5	0	2.17	13	1	66	61	26	74
Ryan Berry, rhp, Jr.	7	2	2.42	14	1	82	56	19	68
Travis Wright, rhp, So.	2	0	2.45	7	0	15	11	6	12
Taylor Wall, lhp, Fr.	7	8	3.72	18	1	94	83	37	77
Jordan Rogers, rhp, Sr.	8	3	4.33	30	7	54	39	29	53
Mark Haynes, rhp, Jr.	2	0	4.35	25	1	50	58	17	22
Abel Gonzales, lhp, So.	1	0	4.58	17	0	20	22	9	7
Andrew Benak, rhp, Fr.	1	1	5.70	15	0	24	30	10	12
Matthew Reckling, rhp, So.	2	2	5.84	20	2	37	34	30	34
Jared Rogers, rhp, Jr.	4	1	6.15	19	0	45	52	16	27
Matt Evers, lhp, So.	4	3	6.89	32	3	47	56	34	37

9. FLORIDA STATE

Coach: Mike Martin. **Record:** 45-18.

Player, Pos., Year	AVG	AB	R	H	2B	3B	HR	RBI	SB
Sean Gilmartin, of, Fr.	.600	10	4	6	2	0	0	4	0
Sherman Johnson, if, Fr.	.476	21	6	10	2	1	1	10	0
Tyler Holt, of, So.	.401	237	87	95	23	2	5	28	34
Mike McGee, of, So.	.379	198	66	75	18	1	19	78	13
Stephen Cardullo, ss, Jr.	.376	237	76	89	20	3	10	51	20
Jason Stidham, 2b, Jr.	.363	223	55	81	24	2	12	76	5
Mike Meschke, 1b, Jr.	.322	87	22	28	10	0	3	23	0
Stuart Tapley, 3b, So.	.316	215	46	68	18	0	13	60	8
D'Vontrey Richardson, of, So.	.304	79	23	24	6	1	0	10	2
James Ramsey, of/if, Fr.	.294	68	19	20	3	0	2	14	0

Player, Pos., Year	AVG	AB	R	H	2B	3B	HR	RBI	SB
Rafael Lopez, c, So.	.287	150	33	43	4	0	4	29	1
Ohmed Danesh, of, Jr.	.262	168	34	44	13	1	6	34	9
Tommy Oravetz, if, Sr.	.257	191	37	49	11	3	8	33	2
Parker Brunelle, c, So.	.239	71	12	17	2	2	0	22	0
Ruairi O'Connor, of, Sr.	.209	43	8	9	2	0	1	5	0
Jack Posey, 1b, So.	.203	138	18	28	5	0	5	28	0

Player, Pos., Year	W	L	ERA	G	SV	IP	H	BB	SO
Sean Gilmartin, lhp, Fr.	12	3	3.49	18	1	98	81	37	83
Brian Busch, lhp, Fr.	6	2	3.97	19	0	91	81	35	70
Mike McGee, rhp, So.	6	2	4.04	15	0	69	64	42	72
Jack Posey, rhp, So.	0	1	4.08	15	0	18	21	9	16
Tyler Everett, rhp, So.	0	0	4.62	21	1	37	38	18	30
Hunter Scantling, rhp, Fr.	3	1	4.63	19	0	35	33	14	20
Geoff Parker, rhp, Sr.	6	2	4.82	31	1	65	54	41	65
Jimmy Marshall, rhp, Sr.	3	2	4.85	28	10	26	24	24	39
John Gast, lhp, So.	5	3	5.12	28	0	39	43	21	24
Austin Wood, rhp, Fr.	0	0	6.35	9	0	23	24	25	13
Mark Peterson, rhp, Fr.	1	0	6.75	17	0	19	23	15	15
Bo O'Dell, rhp, Sr.	3	2	6.84	11	0	25	35	11	17

10. UC IRVINE

Coach: Mike Gillespie. **Record:** 45-15.

Player, Pos., Year	AVG	AB	R	H	2B	3B	HR	RBI	SB
Ronnie Shaeffer, c, Fr.	.388	165	34	64	12	0	4	36	4
Ben Orloff, ss, Sr.	.358	254	62	91	11	1	0	28	18
Eric Deragisch, if, Sr.	.355	203	49	72	11	3	3	39	7
Tommy Reyes, if, Fr.	.348	92	23	32	7	1	0	15	1
Casey Stevenson, 2b, Jr.	.346	191	44	66	19	1	3	41	8
Ryan Fisher, of/if, So.	.320	125	31	40	7	3	4	28	2
Maverick Olivares, of, So.	.316	19	2	6	3	0	0	4	0
Cory Olson, of, Jr.	.315	111	17	35	6	1	4	18	3
Jordan Leyland, if, Fr.	.310	42	5	13	0	0	1	7	0
Francis Larson, c, Jr.	.309	220	34	68	14	4	9	43	5
Jeff Cusick, 1b, Jr.	.293	215	41	63	13	0	6	40	2
Jordan Fox, if, Fr.	.289	38	9	11	1	1	0	8	1
Dillon Bell, of, Jr.	.274	84	21	23	5	0	2	11	1
D.J. Crumlich, of, Fr.	.261	161	29	42	7	0	1	30	4
Tony Asaro, of, Sr.	.230	61	15	14	3	1	0	10	2
Sean Madigan, of, Jr.	.227	22	2	5	2	0	0	3	0
Brock Bardeen, dh, So.	.226	31	9	7	0	0	6	16	0
Sammy Donabedian, c, Sr.	.148	27	3	4	1	0	0	5	0

Player, Pos., Year	W	L	ERA	G	SV	IP	H	BB	SO
Daniel Bibona, lhp, Jr.	12	1	2.63	15	0	106	78	26	108
Christian Bergman, rhp, Jr.	9	3	3.50	15	0	98	111	16	66
Eric Pettis, rhp, Jr.	5	2	3.68	29	17	42	47	7	37
Noel Avison, lhp, Sr.	3	1	3.86	28	0	37	34	10	25
Kyle Necke, rhp, Jr.	1	4	4.50	18	1	34	33	7	29
Crosby Slaught, rhp, So.	8	0	4.62	16	0	76	87	23	52
Brock Bardeen, rhp, So.	5	0	4.63	23	1	47	55	18	28
Matt Dufour, rhp, Sr.	2	0	5.85	24	1	40	54	12	27
Matt Summers, rhp, Fr.	0	0	7.71	6	0	7	10	5	6
Cory Hamilton, rhp, So.	0	2	7.96	20	0	37	45	29	33
Nick Hoover, rhp, So.	0	2	12.27	7	0	11	17	6	11

11. SOUTHERN MISSISSIPPI

Coach: Corky Palmer. **Record:** 40-26.

Player, Pos., Year	AVG	AB	R	H	2B	3B	HR	RBI	SB
Brian Dozier, ss, Sr.	.391	138	44	54	13	1	4	39	6
Bo Davis, of, Sr.	.359	209	67	75	6	4	14	53	10
Kameron Brunty, of, Fr.	.336	229	62	77	9	4	7	53	7
Adam Doleac, if, So.	.333	39	6	13	3	0	0	7	1
Corey Stevens, of, Sr.	.320	231	50	74	15	1	8	60	2
James Ewing, 2b, Sr.	.308	201	43	62	10	0	4	43	3
Joey Archer, 1b, Jr.	.306	229	42	70	14	0	10	62	2
Taylor Walker, 3b, Jr.	.305	243	64	74	11	1	3	29	7
Kyle Maxie, if, Jr.	.281	96	21	27	2	0	4	16	1
Tyler Koelling, of, So.	.269	167	25	45	6	1	2	27	4
Travis Graves, c, Jr.	.254	122	20	31	4	1	2	12	0
Michael Ewing, of, Sr.	.237	97	24	23	3	0	5	20	1
B.A. Vollmuth, ss, Fr.	.237	97	16	23	3	0	8	28	1
Josh Fields, if, Sr.	.237	114	18	27	10	0	2	14	0

Player, Pos., Year	W	L	ERA	G	SV	IP	H	BB	SO
Todd McInnis, rhp, So.	9	4	3.73	19	0	101	96	34	90
Collin Cargill, rhp, So.	4	3	3.55	28	13	38	31	22	32
Jeff Stanley, lhp, Jr.	4	2	4.23	16	0	45	48	21	24
Josh Fields, rhp, Sr.	2	1	4.38	8	1	12	9	5	14
J.R. Ballinger, rhp, Jr.	6	4	4.40	18	0	86	95	39	59
Jonathan Johnston, rhp, Sr.	1	0	4.42	30	1	39	38	9	29
Cody Schlagel, rhp, Jr.	5	1	5.37	26	0	52	54	28	45
Wade Weathers, lhp, Sr.	2	0	5.64	24	1	30	39	18	24
Kyle Lindsey, rhp, Jr.	3	3	6.28	16	0	53	70	25	54
Scott Copeland, rhp, Jr.	2	5	6.41	16	1	39	55	17	22
Seth Hester, rhp, So.	2	2	7.12	13	0	37	50	13	18
Moses Munoz, lhp, Jr.	0	1	8.51	11	0	24	33	17	21
Matt Warren, rhp, Fr.	0	0	8.79	9	0	14	20	2	6

12. FLORIDA

Coach: Kevin O'Sullivan. **Record:** 42-22.

Player, Pos., Year	AVG	AB	R	H	2B	3B	HR	RBI	SB
Avery Barnes, of, Sr.	.364	247	76	90	9	6	8	42	18
Preston Tucker, 1b, Fr.	.364	242	48	88	13	3	15	85	5
Jonathan Pigott, of, Jr.	.357	126	31	45	6	1	6	32	6
Josh Adams, if, So.	.342	240	58	82	11	1	8	52	5
Brandon McArthur, 3b, Sr.	.338	207	25	70	14	1	3	41	0
Teddy Foster, c, Sr.	.321	84	19	27	2	0	7	25	3
Mike Mooney, of, Sr.	.306	157	45	48	6	0	2	24	2
Daniel Pigott, of, Fr.	.301	133	28	40	6	0	3	21	4
Matt den Dekker, of, Jr.	.296	226	63	67	9	1	5	37	17
Buddy Munroe, c, Jr.	.270	159	23	43	7	0	5	26	3
Riley Cooper, of, So.	.247	89	16	22	5	2	2	8	3
Tyler Thompson, of, Fr.	.235	68	12	16	1	1	1	10	0
Clayton Pisani, if, Jr.	.226	93	17	21	5	1	2	16	2
Hampton Tignor, c, Jr.	.213	47	6	10	1	0	0	2	1
Jerico Weitzel, if, Fr.	.208	77	13	16	2	0	0	6	3
Ben McMahan, c, Fr.	.100	30	5	3	0	0	1	2	0

Player, Pos., Year	W	L	ERA	G	SV	IP	H	BB	SO
Tony Davis, lhp, Jr.	5	0	2.25	32	0	44	29	18	37
Billy Bullock, rhp, Jr.	3	3	2.64	34	11	48	40	22	50
Stephen Locke, lhp, Sr.	5	2	4.32	12	0	67	85	18	48
Alex Panteliodis, lhp, Fr.	6	5	4.38	22	1	64	82	16	43
Nick Maronde, rhp, Fr.	3	1	4.40	21	0	61	62	18	59
Jeff Barfield, rhp, Jr.	2	1	4.50	16	1	46	47	15	40
Anthony DeScalfani, rhp, Fr.	6	3	4.98	21	0	65	63	16	47
Patrick Keating, rhp, Sr.	4	4	5.12	22	0	58	80	13	41
Justin Poovey, rhp, Fr.	2	1	5.73	15	0	33	46	13	18
Kevin Chapman, lhp, So.	1	0	2.38	11	0	11	16	6	5
Clint Franklin, rhp, Jr.	2	0	3.00	9	0	15	10	5	5
Greg Larson, rhp, Fr.	3	2	3.45	29	0	31	33	18	16
Will Jolin, rhp, Fr.	0	0	5.54	11	0	13	13	6	14
Chas Spottswood, rhp, Jr.	0	0	12.00	5	0	6	11	2	2

13. MISSISSIPPI

Coach: Mike Bianco. **Record:** 44-20.

Player, Pos., Year	AVG	AB	R	H	2B	3B	HR	RBI	SB
Taylor Hightower, c, Fr.	.476	21	5	10	1	0	0	2	0
Tim Ferguson, if, So.	.358	123	28	44	6	4	2	21	18
Jordan Henry, of, Jr.	.343	230	70	79	12	1	0	31	38
Zach Miller, if, Jr.	.341	211	48	72	15	2	5	38	8
Kyle Henson, c, Sr.	.338	151	37	51	12	0	8	34	1
Matt Smith, 1b, Sr.	.336	232	52	78	15	2	8	59	4
Evan Button, if, Jr.	.325	117	20	38	5	2	2	19	2
Logan Power, of, Sr.	.311	238	58	74	20	1	7	58	8
Matt Snyder, if, Fr.	.298	141	25	42	3	0	8	31	0
Michael Hubbard, of, Sr.	.295	78	23	23	5	0	2	13	2
David Phillips, of, So.	.290	100	14	29	6	0	2	20	1
Brett Basham, c, Jr.	.287	101	14	29	7	0	3	18	2
Kevin Mort, ss, Jr.	.286	217	32	62	5	1	0	33	4
Jeremy Travis, of, Sr.	.279	122	21	34	8	1	7	30	2
Taylor Hashman, of, Jr.	.210	62	18	13	0	0	2	8	2
Mike Snyder, if, Fr.	.200	25	2	5	2	0	0	5	0
Cullan Kight, 1b, Sr.	.118	17	2	2	1	0	0	2	0
Logan Williams, if, So.	.045	22	1	1	0	0	0	1	0

Player, Pos., Year	W	L	ERA	G	SV	IP	H	BB	SO
Matt Tracy, lhp, So.	0	0	0.00	4	0	5	6	1	8
Wade Broyles, rhp, Jr.	0	1	1.80	7	0	10	3	2	13
Scott Bittle, rhp, Sr.	5	2	2.17	14	3	46	28	22	68
David Goforth, rhp, Fr.	1	1	2.80	25	3	35	25	11	20
Drew Pomeranz, lhp, So.	8	4	3.40	16	0	95	85	37	124
Jake Morgan, rhp, So.	4	1	3.46	27	9	42	40	7	55
Nathan Baker, lhp, Jr.	4	3	3.63	20	1	67	74	16	69
Phillip Irwin, rhp, Jr.	8	3	3.84	15	0	87	106	20	73
Brett Bukvich, lhp, Sr.	9	3	4.42	17	0	71	77	16	72
Rory McKean, rhp, Jr.	5	1	4.53	22	1	46	65	14	42
Kyle Barbeck, lhp, Fr.	0	0	5.89	11	0	18	26	13	15
Michael Park, rhp, Jr.	0	0	7.71	5	0	7	8	4	8
Aaron Barrett, rhp, Jr.	0	1	8.70	14	0	30	44	13	33
Chris Corrigan, rhp, Jr.	0	0	11.42	4	0	9	15	4	7

14. TEXAS CHRISTIAN

Coach: Jim Schlossnagle. **Record:** 40-18.

Player, Pos., Year	AVG	AB	R	H	2B	3B	HR	RBI	SB
Matt Vern, 1b, Sr.	.360	200	61	72	13	2	17	54	16
Matt Carpenter, 3b, Jr.	.333	207	58	69	23	6	11	47	13
Chris Ellington, of, Sr.	.331	236	40	78	21	2	6	52	2
Taylor Featherston, ss/2b, Fr.	.322	230	54	74	13	2	5	28	8
Jason Coats, of, Fr.	.316	193	36	61	17	2	6	32	2
Matt Curry, dh, Jr.	.315	162	30	51	10	1	3	31	2
Bryan Holaday, c, Jr.	.300	203	39	61	0	1	10	48	2
Corey Steglich, of/if, Sr.	.296	203	32	60	7	3	2	31	7
Ben Carruthers, 2b/ss, Jr.	.275	138	27	38	6	0	2	19	3
Jimmie Pharr, c, So.	.255	51	7	13	6	0	1	8	0
Aaron Schultz, of, Fr.	.254	71	11	18	1	0	2	9	2
Brance Rivera, if, Fr.	.250	32	9	8	0	0	0	6	2
Zac Jordan, of, Fr.	.250	16	3	4	3	0	0	2	0
Hunt Woodruff, c, Sr.	.217	46	5	10	1	1	2	6	0
Brett Medlin, of, So.	.200	20	3	4	1	1	0	2	0

Player, Pos., Year	W	L	ERA	G	SV	IP	H	BB	SO
Paul Gerrish, rhp, Jr.	7	2	3.84	17	1	61	61	16	59
Kyle Winkler, rhp, Fr.	7	1	4.15	17	0	74	70	35	48
Tyler Lockwood, rhp, Jr.	4	2	4.71	17	0	71	75	18	44
Eric Marshall, rhp, Jr.	2	2	1.48	24	9	30	22	5	20
Taylor Cragin, rhp, Jr.	5	0	2.50	17	0	58	41	17	37
Trent Appleby, rhp, So.	4	1	3.61	24	1	57	57	20	47
Greg Holle, rhp, So.	5	2	3.89	12	0	42	43	15	26
Erik Miller, rhp, Jr.	0	2	4.50	22	3	26	29	8	25
Kaleb Merck, rhp, Fr.	0	0	5.94	17	1	17	24	10	22
Steven Maxwell, rhp, So.	3	2	6.10	12	0	38	49	10	27
Derek VerHagen, lhp, Jr.	0	0	6.48	7	0	8	12	4	9
Sean Hoelscher, rhp, Jr.	2	2	7.03	9	0	24	23	20	22
Walker Kelly, rhp, Fr.	1	2	7.71	11	0	12	7	8	18

15. LOUISVILLE

Coach: Dan McDonnell. **Record:** 47-18.

Player, Pos., Year	AVG	AB	R	H	2B	3B	HR	RBI	SB
Phil Wunderlich, of, So.	.367	245	56	90	18	1	18	78	4
Andrew Clark, 1b, Jr.	.350	254	82	89	21	2	9	55	1
Chris Dominguez, 3b, Jr.	.345	258	80	89	12	2	25	82	19
Ryan Wright, of/if, Fr.	.335	257	43	86	16	2	5	66	12
Adam Duvall, 2b, Jr.	.328	268	83	88	21	2	11	51	12
Josh Richmond, of, So.	.307	238	54	73	14	4	7	31	5
Alec Lowrey, of, Sr.	.297	128	17	38	5	3	3	25	1
Jeff Arnold, c, Jr.	.246	187	37	46	6	1	3	32	13
John Dao, ss, Sr.	.245	200	17	49	8	2	0	22	3
Nate Holland, of, So.	.209	67	17	14	0	0	4	14	3
Drew Haynes, of, So.	.208	144	26	30	1	0	0	13	17
Kyle Cheesebrough, c, Sr.	.179	39	6	7	1	0	0	0	0
Tony Zych, if, Fr.	.172	29	4	5	1	0	0	1	0

Player, Pos., Year	W	L	ERA	G	SV	IP	H	BB	SO
Tony Zych, rhp, Fr.	6	2	3.25	21	2	44	38	10	31
Joe Stilphen, lhp, Fr.	0	0	3.38	7	0	5	7	1	4
Thomas Royse, rhp, So.	3	2	3.48	12	2	41	35	10	48
Mike Nastold, rhp, So.	2	0	3.52	8	1	38	34	12	28
Gabriel Shaw, rhp, Jr.	3	1	3.73	29	3	51	46	12	47
Justin Marks, lhp, Jr.	11	3	3.77	18	1	105	86	35	129
Neil Holland, rhp, So.	0	0	3.80	16	1	24	27	11	27

Player, Pos., Year	W	L	ERA	G	SV	IP	H	BB	SO
Keith Landers, lhp, Fr.	1	0	3.86	3	0	9	12	3	10
Derek Self, rhp, Fr.	7	0	3.88	22	1	46	47	14	34
Gavin Logsdon, lhp, Sr.	2	0	4.00	29	1	36	39	11	30
Bob Revesz, lhp, So.	4	2	4.40	23	1	61	74	12	28
Dean Kiekhefer, lhp, So.	6	5	5.00	18	0	77	96	21	63
Tyler Mathis, rhp, So.	1	3	6.00	14	0	30	26	13	28
Matt Lea, lhp, So.	1	0	9.26	11	0	23	21	14	27

16. CLEMSON

Coach: Jack Leggett. **Record:** 44-22.

Player, Pos., Year	AVG	AB	R	H	2B	3B	HR	RBI	SB
Ben Paulsen, 1b, Jr.	.367	259	56	95	18	4	13	61	3
Wilson Boyd, of, Jr.	.341	182	35	62	15	3	3	46	5
Mike Freeman, 2b, Jr.	.328	268	60	88	16	5	4	44	11
Jeff Schaus, of, So.	.320	247	60	79	14	1	13	50	9
Jason Stolz, 3b, Fr.	.315	143	29	45	7	0	1	21	7
John Nester, c/1b, So.	.304	168	25	51	11	0	5	33	1
Chris Epps, of, So.	.297	128	32	38	6	2	4	27	9
Matt Sanders, 3b, Sr.	.295	122	14	36	5	0	3	20	1
Brad Miller, ss, Fr.	.273	238	49	65	6	1	3	36	16
Will Lamb, of, Fr.	.268	56	8	15	3	0	0	6	4
Kyle Parker, of, So.	.255	231	48	59	7	0	12	52	6
Richard Mounce, 1b, Fr.	.238	42	1	10	4	0	1	8	0
Addison Johnson, of, So.	.217	138	25	30	6	0	2	14	9
Phil Pohl, c, Jr.	.194	67	9	13	4	0	1	3	0

Player, Pos., Year	W	L	ERA	G	SV	IP	H	BB	SO
Scott Weismann, rhp, Fr.	3	1	1.23	17	1	37	26	15	28
Kevin Brady, rhp, Fr.	0	0	1.69	4	0	11	9	5	8
Will Lamb, lhp, Fr.	0	0	2.45	15	1	22	22	8	15
Craig Gullickson, lhp, So.	1	0	2.45	9	0	11	4	9	10
Kyle Deese, rhp, Fr.	0	0	2.70	7	0	7	3	9	7
Matt Vaughn, rhp, Sr.	4	1	2.80	22	4	35	37	11	24
Tomas Cruz, rhp, Jr.	2	3	3.33	24	4	46	32	16	39
Trey Delk, rhp, Sr.	4	1	3.44	11	0	50	53	22	41
Graham Stoneburner, rhp, So.	7	4	3.52	20	1	64	70	19	71
Alex Frederick, rhp, So.	1	0	3.72	6	0	10	11	4	8
Ryan Hinson, lhp, Sr.	2	1	3.76	28	0	38	33	18	47
Casey Harman, lhp, Sr.	7	3	3.95	22	1	87	98	16	89
Clinton McKinney, rhp, Sr.	4	0	4.30	13	0	23	23	8	22
David Haselden, rhp, Fr.	1	0	4.58	7	0	18	21	1	16
Chris Dwyer, lhp, Fr.	5	6	4.92	17	0	86	76	33	95
Justin Sarratt, rhp, Jr.	3	2	5.10	16	1	42	41	9	26
Richard Mounce, rhp, Fr.	0	0	7.94	5	0	6	8	0	1

17. EAST CAROLINA

Coach: Billy Godwin. **Record:** 46-20.

Player, Pos., Year	AVG	AB	R	H	2B	3B	HR	RBI	SB
Corey Thompson, 3b, Jr.	.467	15	6	7	2	0	1	3	0
Ryan Wood, 2b, Sr.	.379	264	87	100	22	1	14	57	14
Trent Whitehead, of, So.	.376	279	78	105	24	2	7	47	10
Austin Homan, of, So.	.354	79	24	28	5	0	0	19	2
Stephen Batts, of, So.	.352	273	71	96	21	1	14	63	19
Devin Harris, of, So.	.344	212	44	73	8	0	14	48	13
Kyle Roller, 1b, Sr.	.336	256	63	86	12	1	16	75	4
Brandon Henderson, 1b, Sr.	.330	212	34	70	12	0	13	57	5
Jared Avchen, c, Jr.	.330	176	27	58	8	1	2	29	0
Dustin Harrington, ss, Jr.	.318	261	53	83	15	0	14	49	4
Drew Schieber, 3b, Sr.	.311	257	42	80	16	2	8	52	4
Jonathan Ratledge, of, Jr.	.300	10	3	3	0	0	0	1	0
Zach Wright, c, So.	.295	44	12	13	5	1	3	8	0
Cameron Freeman, 2b, So.	.261	23	11	6	2	0	1	3	1
Broc Sutton, 3b, Jr.	.200	15	4	3	1	0	1	6	0
Trent Ashcraft, of, Sr.	.053	19	5	1	0	0	0	3	1

Player, Pos., Year	W	L	ERA	G	SV	IP	H	BB	SO
Brad Mincey, rhp, So.	10	5	3.16	25	0	83	89	22	71
Britton Cole, rhp, So.	0	0	3.18	8	0	11	12	5	9
Kevin Brandt, lhp, Fr.	9	2	3.64	28	0	82	73	24	72
Seth Simmons, rhp, So.	3	1	3.69	33	9	39	36	20	50
Chris Heston, rhp, Jr.	7	0	4.17	17	0	91	90	32	88
Shawn Armstrong, rhp, Fr.	1	0	4.26	9	0	6	5	2	0
Bailey Daniels, rhp, Sr.	2	2	4.35	2	2	41	38	20	35
Seth Maness, rhp, So.	9	3	4.71	18	2	107	123	18	83
Patrick Somers, lhp, Fr.	2	2	5.64	24	0	30	31	20	25

Deck McGuire was ACC Pitcher of the Year

DAVID STONER

Mike Anderson, rhp, So.	1	1	5.86	9	0	28	32	14	22
Mike Wright, rhp, Fr.	1	2	7.66	15	0	22	28	9	23
Sthil Sowers, rhp, So.	1	2	8.65	14	0	26	44	14	24
Joe O'Malley, rhp, So.	0	0	10.12	6	0	5	7	2	4

18. OKLAHOMA

Coach: Sunny Galloway. **Record:** 43-20.

Player, Pos., Year	AVG	AB	R	H	2B	3B	HR	RBI	SB
J.T. Wise, c, Sr.	.359	209	50	75	13	0	17	62	2
Garrett Buechele, 3b, Jr.	.353	232	41	82	14	1	4	40	1
Jamie Johnson, of, Jr.	.353	255	76	90	17	5	13	44	18
Bryant Hernandez, ss, Jr.	.351	251	65	88	12	4	12	62	10
Kaleb Herren, of, Jr.	.319	91	14	29	8	1	0	15	1
Chris Ellison, of, Fr.	.316	117	27	37	5	1	3	22	4
Casey Johnson, of, So.	.307	205	44	63	10	4	7	44	9
Cameron Seitzer, if, Fr.	.307	75	22	23	6	0	4	21	0
Tyler Ogle, c, Fr.	.302	96	18	29	6	0	1	17	1
Aaron Baker, 1b, Jr.	.284	225	55	64	16	1	15	56	6
Matt Haraghty, 2b, Jr.	.273	227	59	62	10	2	8	43	12
Bryan Groth, c, Jr.	.273	11	4	3	1	0	1	1	0
Ross Hubbard, c/if, Jr.	.265	68	10	18	3	1	2	19	0
Elliott Blair, of, So.	.250	28	13	7	4	0	2	7	1
Trey Sperring, if, So	.250	24	3	6	1	0	2	7	1
Tyson Seng, if, So.	.231	13	4	3	0	0	0	2	0
Caleb Busyhead, if, Fr.	.083	12	4	1	0	0	0	1	0

Player, Pos., Year	W	L	ERA	G	SV	IP	H	BB	SO
Ryan Duke, rhp, So.	3	1	3.22	26	16	36	28	12	43
Jarrett Semler, rhp, Jr.	0	0	3.46	13	0	13	16	3	15
Jeremy Erben, rhp, Jr.	0	1	3.62	14	0	27	24	7	24
Andrew Doyle, rhp, Jr.	8	4	4.21	15	0	92	90	23	65
Michael Rocha, rhp, So.	5	3	4.84	20	0	58	58	22	41
Antwonie Hubbard, rhp, So.	2	3	4.84	13	0	25	34	19	39
C.J. Blue, lhp, Sr.	2	1	4.88	11	0	28	39	1	9
Kaleb Herren, rhp, Jr.	2	0	4.91	9	0	15	14	6	10
Chase Anderson, rhp, Jr.	3	1	4.97	26	0	51	44	19	60
Tyson Seng, rhp. So.	4	0	5.40	17	0	35	41	12	24
Stephen Porlier, rhp, Jr.	1	1	5.82	9	0	22	29	6	21
Garrett Richards, rhp, Jr.	9	4	6.00	17	0	75	78	38	85
J.R. Robinson, lhp, Jr.	3	1	6.49	23	0	53	68	17	49
Jason Chowning, rhp, Jr.	1	0	12.00	6	0	6	11	6	5

19. KANSAS STATE

Coach: Brad Hill. **Record:** 43-18.

Player, Pos., Year	AVG	AB	R	H	2B	3B	HR	RBI	SB
Matt Giller, if, Fr.	.400	15	5	6	0	0	1	6	0
Justin Bloxom, 1b, Jr.	.361	244	50	88	16	4	12	63	7
Carter Jurica, 2b, So.	.353	238	61	84	15	3	4	46	23
Nick Martini, of, Fr.	.336	232	54	78	17	2	4	50	19
Drew Biery, ss, Sr.	.329	207	53	68	17	1	9	44	6
Jordan Cruz, of, Sr.	.324	210	45	68	10	3	11	52	17
Daniel Dellasega, c, Jr.	.321	56	10	18	2	1	2	15	3
Jason King, 3b, So.	.316	247	49	78	16	5	7	61	14
Adam Muenster, of, Jr.	.292	202	44	59	11	2	2	18	24
Rob Vaughn, c, Sr.	.281	167	28	47	7	0	5	25	5
Dane Yelovich, of, Sr.	.275	222	42	61	8	0	1	27	24

Mike Kindel, of, Fr.	.250	28	4	7	2	0	0	3	1
David Masters, c, Jr.	.250	20	5	5	0	1	0	3	4
Dan Rumsey, of, Jr.	.250	12	1	3	0	0	0	3	1
Jake Brown, if, Fr.	.174	23	3	4	1	0	0	4	1

Player, Pos., Year	W	L	ERA	G	SV	IP	H	BB	SO
A.J. Morris, rhp, Jr.	14	1	2.09	16	0	116	98	30	100
Mark Joukoff, rhp, Jr.	0	0	3.86	4	0	7	6	3	5
Thomas Rooke, lhp, So.	5	2	4.33	32	4	54	47	14	58
Ryan Daniel, rhp, Jr.	4	1	4.44	17	0	51	70	15	40
Lance Hoge, lhp, Sr.	6	4	4.54	16	0	71	82	22	46
Kayvon Bahramzadeh, rhp, Fr.	2	1	4.58	11	0	35	37	8	35
Josh Crockett, rhp, Jr.	0	0	4.86	14	0	17	20	8	10
Matt Applegate, rhp, Fr.	2	2	4.88	24	1	28	33	14	19
Todd Vogel, rhp, Jr.	4	2	5.13	15	0	54	60	12	29
James Allen, rhp, Fr.	2	1	5.5	24	5	36	42	12	41
Evan Marshall, rhp, Fr.	2	2	6.39	28	0	31	41	9	19
Duston Hobbs, rhp, Fr.	1	0	7.36	12	0	15	18	8	22
Kyle Hunter, lhp, Fr.	1	2	8.35	17	1	32	46	14	29

20. GEORGIA TECH

Coach: Danny Hall. **Record:** 38-19.

Player, Pos., Year	AVG	AB	R	H	2B	3B	HR	RBI	SB
Luke Murton, of, Sr.	.354	206	64	73	12	1	20	63	4
Tony Plagman, 1b, Jr.	.354	246	59	87	18	2	16	73	4
Chase Burnette, of, So.	.351	97	26	34	7	1	8	29	1
Jeff Rowland, of, Sr.	.340	247	66	84	13	4	8	39	21
Derek Dietrich, ss, So.	.311	225	61	70	7	4	10	54	5
Jason Haniger, c, Sr.	.311	222	51	69	12	0	8	50	2
Evan Martin, of/if, Jr.	.311	45	8	14	0	1	1	11	3
Cole Leonida, c, So.	.306	72	16	22	3	0	5	14	0
Matt Skole, 3b, Fr.	.302	215	41	65	13	0	17	58	2
Chris House, of, Sr.	.293	140	29	41	5	1	3	24	1
Thomas Nichols, if, So.	.290	100	17	29	6	0	2	15	0
Jason Garofalo, 2b, Jr.	.286	98	19	28	6	2	3	19	0
Jay Dantzler, of, Jr.	.281	57	14	16	2	0	5	12	5
Jake Davies, 1b, Fr.	.250	12	2	3	0	0	1	2	0
Brandon Miller, c, Fr.	.222	18	5	4	1	0	2	3	0
Jarrett Didrick, of, Fr.	.214	14	3	3	2	0	0	0	0
Connor Winn, 2b, Fr.	.207	29	6	6	0	0	1	4	2
Patrick Long, if, Jr.	.163	43	11	7	4	0	0	4	2

Player, Pos., Year	W	L	ERA	G	SV	IP	H	BB	SO
Patrick Long, rhp, Jr.	0	1	3.24	17	0	17	18	5	21
Andrew Robinson, rhp, Jr.	1	0	3.35	27	1	46	56	20	34
Deck McGuire, rhp, So.	11	2	3.50	16	0	100	86	41	118
Jake Davies, lhp, Fr.	3	0	3.54	27	0	28	24	16	25
Zach Brewster, lhp, So.	1	3	3.73	32	1	31	24	16	35
Kevin Jacob, rhp, So.	5	3	4.69	22	0	56	58	29	54
Brandon Cumpton, rhp, So.	4	3	4.76	13	0	64	77	22	63
Jacob Esch, rhp, Fr.	0	0	4.82	14	1	19	21	6	19
Taylor Wood, lhp, So.	0	0	5.40	8	0	8	6	5	11
Zach Von Tersch, rhp, Jr.	6	2	5.79	14	0	61	62	35	52
Mark Pope, rhp, Fr.	5	1	6.00	25	8	27	32	16	27
Jed Bradley, lhp, Fr.	2	3	6.65	12	0	45	54	17	49
Thomas Nichols, rhp, So.	0	1	7.71	11	1	12	11	5	13

21. MINNESOTA

Coach: John Anderson. **Record:** 40-19.

Player, Pos., Year	AVG	AB	R	H	2B	3B	HR	RBI	SB
Derek McCallum, ss, Jr.	.409	232	57	95	17	3	18	86	6
A.J. Pettersen, 2b, Fr.	.353	224	65	79	7	3	2	45	8
Michael Kvasnicka, c/of, So.	.341	249	48	85	18	2	10	65	5
Justin Gominsky, of, Fr.	.338	157	35	53	11	1	3	25	11
Matt Nohelty, of, Jr.	.337	246	69	83	5	3	0	31	26
Eric Decker, of, Jr.	.319	213	43	68	13	3	4	25	11
Kyle Knudson, c, Jr.	.296	223	31	66	14	1	4	48	2
Sam Ryan, if, Fr.	.296	27	5	8	4	0	0	2	1
Nick O'Shea, c/1b, Fr.	.287	254	31	73	13	0	11	44	0
Kyle Geason, if, Fr.	.229	188	43	43	10	1	1	19	7
Brooks Albrecht, of, So.	.158	19	3	3	1	0	0	2	1
Jon Hummel, of, Sr.	.153	59	4	9	0	0	2	8	0
Trip Schultz, of, Fr.	.095	21	4	2	0	0	0	2	0

Player, Pos., Year	W	L	ERA	G	SV	IP	H	BB	SO
Scott Matyas, rhp, So.	0	1	2.22	23	15	28	21	7	45
Tom Buske, rhp, Sr.	9	4	3.57	15	0	96	78	26	75
Luke Rasmussen, lhp, So.	4	0	3.99	22	0	29	31	11	22
Tim Ryan, rhp, So.	1	2	4.09	16	0	22	25	6	9
Seth Rosin, rhp, So.	7	1	4.21	15	0	77	82	16	65
Chauncy Handran, rhp, Sr.	8	3	4.69	15	0	96	109	34	57
Austin Lubinsky, rhp, Fr.	3	1	4.78	15	2	38	41	14	23
Cullen Sexton, rhp, So.	4	0	5.16	21	1	30	34	17	23
Scott Fern, rhp, So.	3	1	5.18	15	0	33	43	16	24
Dustin Klabunde, rhp, So.	1	2	8.34	9	0	23	27	16	8
Tyler Oakes, rhp, Sr.	0	2	8.55	14	0	20	27	8	15
Phil Isaksson, lhp, So.	0	1	8.68	7	0	9	15	8	13
Allen Bechstein, rhp, Jr.	0	1	9.27	12	0	22	43	13	13

22. GONZAGA

Coach: Mark Machtolf. **Record:** 36-18.

Player, Pos., Year	AVG	AB	R	H	2B	3B	HR	RBI	SB
Tyson Van Winkle, c, Jr.	.362	232	45	84	27	0	5	61	0
Drew Heid, of, Jr.	.355	234	45	83	7	8	2	41	10
Anthony Synegal, c/of, Sr.	.333	175	30	58	9	1	8	36	3
Chris Sturdivant, of, Fr.	.333	45	9	15	3	0	0	5	1
Evan Wells, 2b, Sr.	.324	204	59	66	9	4	0	28	12
Ryan Weigand, 1b, Sr.	.318	223	44	71	21	0	7	65	1
Mark Castellitto, of, Jr.	.278	212	40	59	9	1	9	42	3
Ernesto Ortiz, ss, Fr.	.257	187	39	48	15	1	3	23	1
Jason Chatwood, if, Sr.	.242	198	43	48	4	0	4	24	5
Grant Kveder, of, Sr.	.233	103	15	24	2	0	0	9	5
Royce Bolinger, of, Fr.	.192	78	9	15	3	1	1	18	0
Brian Yardley, if, Jr.	.091	11	0	1	0	0	0	1	0

Player, Pos., Year	W	L	ERA	G	SV	IP	H	BB	SO
Cody Martin, rhp, So.	5	4	3.07	23	6	59	54	30	68
Matt Fields, rhp, Jr.	8	1	3.47	14	0	91	98	31	74
A.J. Proszek, rhp, Jr.	2	1	3.67	13	3	49	55	15	25
Steven Ames, rhp, Jr.	8	2	3.91	15	0	97	106	21	70
Andy Hunter, rhp, Fr.	1	0	4.82	11	0	19	20	6	20
Jacob Hiatt, rhp, Jr.	1	1	4.91	12	1	15	18	10	17
Tyler Olson, lhp, Fr.	1	1	5.09	11	0	18	20	8	19
Ryan Carpenter, lhp, Fr.	6	4	5.26	15	0	65	73	29	68
Reedy Berg, lhp, So.	0	0	5.40	17	0	47	51	11	49
Jeremy Stumetz, rhp, Jr.	0	0	10.80	5	0	5	10	5	2
C.J. McClure, rhp, Sr.	0	0	13.50	10	1	10	22	9	7

23. WESTERN KENTUCKY

Coach: Chris Finwood. **Record:** 42-20.

Player, Pos., Year	AVG	AB	R	H	2B	3B	HR	RBI	SB
C.J. Wamsley, c, Sr.	.462	13	3	6	1	0	1	7	0
Ryan Hook, of, Jr.	.400	5	3	2	0	0	0	2	0
Matt Rice, c, So.	.399	253	50	101	18	1	10	72	2
Kes Carter, of, Fr.	.383	94	26	36	6	1	1	20	4
Wade Gaynor, 3b, Jr.	.371	251	83	93	20	4	25	78	21
Drew Morgan, if, So.	.364	11	4	4	2	0	0	1	0
J.B. Paxson, c, Sr.	.345	84	21	29	6	0	5	24	2
Terrence Dayleg, ss, Sr.	.327	220	43	72	18	2	3	39	3
Chad Cregar, of, Sr.	.325	234	67	76	13	2	19	63	19
Jake Wells, 1b, Jr.	.314	229	49	72	15	0	5	36	0
Matt Payton, ss, Jr.	.307	202	49	62	12	5	3	34	7
Matt Hightower, of, Sr.	.300	223	56	67	6	3	11	53	25
Jared Andreoll, of, Fr.	.298	181	43	54	5	1	2	32	4
Casey Dykes, c, Fr.	.257	35	6	9	0	0	2	6	0
Jeremy Coleman, if, Sr.	.255	102	17	26	1	2	0	10	9
Logan Robbins, if, Fr.	.250	44	12	11	1	0	1	11	4
Matt Bracken, of, So.	.222	9	6	2	0	0	0	2	0

Player, Pos., Year	W	L	ERA	G	SV	IP	H	BB	SO
Matt Hightower, lhp, Sr.	4.01	7		3	15	0	85	92	33	55
Matt Ridings, rhp, Jr.	4.84	8		2	19	2	102	107	29	93
Shane Cameron, rhp, Jr.	5.03	5		2	15	0	77	80	30	59
Evan Teague, lhp, Sr.	3.32	5		3	35	3	41	37	17	38
Ross Hammonds, rhp, Fr.	4.09	0		0	7	1	11	13	2	6
Tyler Gilliand, rhp, So.	4.38	1		0	8	0	12	12	7	6
Bryce Jenney, rhp, So.	4.60	1		1	12	3	16	13	5	16
Bart Carter, lhp, Fr.	6.00	6		1	25	4	51	57	22	54
Ben Paxton, rhp, Sr.	6.06	1		1	28	0	33	34	15	10

Player, Pos., Year	W	L	ERA	G	SV	IP	H	BB	SO
Aaron Mayfield, rhp, Fr.	6.19	2	0	16	0	16	24	4	10
J.B. Paxson, rhp, Sr.	6.82	3	1	26	3	33	40	18	41
Chad Adcock, rhp, Sr.	7.26	1	3	29	1	31	39	13	27
Craig Stem, rhp, Fr.	9.00	0	1	4	0	7	6	11	10
Garrie Krueger, lhp, So.	9.49	1	1	24	2	12	17	4	16

24. ELON

Coach: Mike Kennedy. **Record:** 42-20.

Player, Pos., Year	AVG	AB	R	H	2B	3B	HR	RBI	SB
Pat Irvine, of/c, Jr.	.402	194	68	78	14	5	17	57	19
Chase Austin, 3b, Jr.	.359	256	74	92	11	3	23	82	19
Mike Melillo, c, Jr.	.344	209	67	72	19	3	18	59	7
Bennett Davis, 2b, Sr.	.343	233	63	80	16	2	18	64	11
Cory Harrilchak, of, Sr.	.336	256	79	86	18	3	16	61	10
Dallas Tarleton, c, Sr.	.293	191	44	56	8	2	13	47	5
Justin Hilt, of, Jr.	.289	228	68	66	12	3	16	55	15
Neal Pritchard, ss, So.	.276	174	41	48	15	0	10	42	1
Matt Kirchner, of/3b, Fr.	.375	16	6	6	1	0	0	3	0
Harry Austin, ss, Jr.	.351	94	23	33	3	1	0	14	18
Ryan Adams, 1b, Jr.	.333	90	18	30	9	0	2	27	2
Zeth Stone, if, Jr.	.309	94	22	29	3	2	0	15	7
Matt Hinson, of, Jr.	.308	13	2	4	0	0	2	7	0
Mike Lobacz, 1b, Sr.	.246	57	7	14	7	0	1	10	0
Matt Brown, c, Jr.	.200	10	1	2	0	0	0	0	0
Greg Annarummo, of, So.	.188	32	6	6	1	0	1	6	1
Alex Maruri, 3b/1b, Fr.	.087	23	5	2	0	0	0	1	0

Player, Pos., Year	W	L	ERA	G	SV	IP	H	BB	SO
Jimmy Reyes, lhp, So.	8	0	4.78	16	0	85	98	19	101
Ken Ferrer, rhp, So.	8	1	5.30	20	2	73	93	37	52
Thomas Girdwood, rhp, So.	0	3	5.33	29	17	25	29	14	38
Jordan Darnell, rhp, Fr.	3	0	5.60	25	1	27	22	18	22
Daniel Britt, rhp, Jr.	8	1	5.86	17	2	63	79	22	39
Cory Harrilchak, lhp, Sr.	3	1	6.04	11	0	48	56	17	37
Ryan Adams, rhp, Jr.	2	0	6.35	19	1	28	33	17	16
Jared Kernodle, rhp, So.	2	4	6.59	22	1	29	27	19	22
Tom Porter, rhp, So.	2	4	6.60	15	0	45	58	13	35
J.D. Reichenbach, lhp, Jr.	3	1	7.50	23	0	42	49	25	35
John Brebbia, rhp, Fr.	1	0	7.62	24	0	28	35	9	14
Bobby Kennedy, lhp, Jr.	1	3	8.89	14	0	27	31	25	23
Greg Amorosso, rhp, So.	0	0	12.46	9	0	9	13	7	8

25. SOUTH CAROLINA

Coach: Ray Tanner. **Record:** 40-23.

Player, Pos., Year	AVG	AB	R	H	2B	3B	HR	RBI	SB
DeAngelo Mack, of, Jr.	.361	255	57	92	14	3	14	60	7
Jackie Bradley, Jr., of, Fr.	.349	255	69	89	11	2	11	46	8
Whit Merrifield, of, Jr.	.340	268	67	91	16	3	11	49	15
Parker Bangs, dh, So.	.328	119	19	39	12	0	5	36	0
Justin Dalles, c, Jr.	.324	185	39	60	7	0	15	47	0
Nick Ebert, 3b, Jr.	.321	209	60	67	13	0	23	72	3
Andrew Crisp, 3b, So.	.313	262	39	82	23	0	10	53	4
Bobby Haney, ss, Jr.	.291	227	45	66	14	1	4	30	1
Adam Matthews , of, Jr.	.290	69	19	20	3	1	5	11	4
Kyle Enders, c, Jr.	.261	69	12	18	5	0	3	9	0
Jeffery Jones, if, Jr.	.228	79	9	18	7	0	1	12	0
Scott Wingo, 2b, So.	.196	153	27	30	5	1	5	17	3
Brady Thomas, c, Jr.	.174	23	4	4	1	0	1	3	0
Michael Roth, 1b, Fr.	.154	13	1	2	1	0	0	2	0

Player, Pos., Year	W	L	ERA	G	SV	IP	H	BB	SO
Steven Neff, rhp, So.	0	0	0.00	4	0	5	3	4	4
Jay Brown, rhp, Sr.	3	0	3.35	12	0	48	48	23	35
Matt Price, rhp, Fr.	1	1	4.05	7	0	20	16	10	15
Michael Roth, lhp, Fr.	1	1	4.22	16	0	32	31	13	28
Adam Westmoreland, lhp, Fr.	4	2	4.24	13	0	47	40	32	46
Blake Cooper, rhp, Jr.	9	4	4.50	17	0	86	100	29	65
Brandon Miller, lhp, Fr.	0	0	4.91	6	0	7	9	6	7
Alex Farotto, lhp, Sr.	4	2	4.96	20	7	33	25	25	37
Sam Dyson, rhp, So.	9	4	5.21	16	0	102	92	37	94
Nolan Belcher, lhp, Fr.	4	5	5.33	16	0	83	81	41	76
Curtis Johnson, rhp, So.	2	1	5.68	20	0	32	28	12	29
Parker Bangs, rhp, So.	3	2	5.88	15	0	34	37	20	39
Will Casey, lhp, So.	0	1	6.75	6	0	9	8	5	4
Jordan Propst, rhp, Jr.	0	0	10.12	5	0	5	7	6	8
Grimes Medlin, lhp, Jr.	0	0	12.15	10	1	7	13	4	6
Justin Hopper, rhp, So.	0	0	13.5	6	0	5	10	1	7

CONFERENCE STANDINGS & LEADERS

*Won automatic bid
Boldface: NCAA regional participant/conference department leader
#Conference department leader who is a non-qualifier

AMERICA EAST CONFERENCE

	Conference		Overall	
	W	L	W	L
*Binghamton	13	7	30	22
Albany	15	9	26	31
Stony Brook	14	10	29	23
Vermont	14	10	23	33
Maine	13	11	32	23
Hartford	7	15	15	32
Maryland-Baltimore County	4	18	9	36

ALL-CONFERENCE TEAM: C—Ryan Gugel, Sr., Albany. **1B**—Rob Dyer, Jr., Stony Brook. **2B**—Brad Brainer, Sr., UMBC. **3B**—Kyle Klee, Sr., Binghamton. **SS**—Matt Duffy, So., Vermont.**OF**—Corey Taylor, So., Binghamton; Kevin McAvoy, Sr., Maine; Brian Witkowski, Sr., Stony Brook. **DH**—Nick Thode, So., Stony Brook. **SP**—Murphy Smith, Jr., Binghamton; Mike Errigo, Sr., Stony Brook; Keith Rakus, Sr., Vermont; Justin Albert, Sr., Vermont. **RP**—Sean Gregory, Sr., Albany.
Player of the Year: Matt Duffy, Vermont. **Pitcher of the Year:** Murphy Smith, Binghamton. **Rookie of the Year:** David Ciocchi, Binghamton. **Coach of the Year:** Tim Sinicki, Binghamton.

INDIVIDUAL BATTING LEADERS
(Minimum 125 At-Bats)

	AVG	AB	R	H	2B	3B	HR	RBI	SB
Duffy, Matt, Vermont	.388	178	57	69	17	1	13	57	0
Retz, Shawn, UMBC	.383	162	29	62	13	0	10	32	1
Ciocchi, Dave, Binghamton	.381	147	33	56	12	0	5	41	3
McAvoy, Kevin, Maine	.379	174	41	66	15	1	10	39	3
Micowski, Mark, Vermont	.365	219	55	80	16	4	4	30	28
Thode, Nick, Stony Brook	.364	173	38	63	15	1	6	32	0
Drexel, Andy, Hartford	.362	160	33	58	13	4	7	49	5
Amendola, Mike, Hartford	.362	163	31	59	11	3	3	27	8
Calderone, Jim, Binghamton	.358	201	53	72	8	5	5	32	14
Leisenheimer, Ian, Maine	.356	160	28	57	4	2	5	41	2
Marshall, Chad, Stony Brook	.354	192	42	68	13	0	2	24	1
Mazzurco, Steve, Stony Brook	.348	178	37	62	12	0	1	20	5
Cather, Billy, Maine	.344	212	52	73	11	1	6	39	16
Brainer, Brad, UMBC	.343	166	37	57	14	0	3	15	11
Tansey, Michael, Stony Brook	.343	175	50	60	18	0	13	40	4
Witowski, Brian, Stony Brook	.341	176	43	60	15	2	12	36	10
Taylor, Corey, Binghamton	.340	191	50	65	13	2	16	56	11
Pitcheralle, Gary, Albany	.335	197	50	66	14	2	7	29	15
Lugbauer, Myckie, Maine	.321	168	29	54	9	0	4	32	3
Lukas, Jarrett, Maine	.320	175	30	56	12	2	5	35	3
Klee, Kyle, Binghamton	.319	191	40	61	5	3	5	36	9
Patane, Tony, Maine	.315	181	39	57	16	0	5	31	0
Sobocinski, Ben, Hartford	.315	162	27	51	7	1	0	29	17
Menendez, Danny, Maine	.312	189	44	59	9	1	2	29	38
Moylan, Corey, Vermont	.312	157	36	49	14	2	4	34	12
West, Dave, Albany	.306	206	31	63	8	0	4	39	6
Himmelstein, Max, UMBC	.304	135	18	41	8	0	3	26	0
Kelly, Tom, Vermont	.303	152	23	46	7	2	0	30	5
Gugel, Ryan, Albany	.303	195	44	59	11	2	9	49	16
Paquette, Ethan, Vermont	.296	199	33	59	12	1	8	46	1

INDIVIDUAL PITCHING LEADERS
(Minimum 50 Innings)

	W	L	ERA	G	SV	IP	H	BB	SO
Smith, Murphy, Binghamton	7	3	3.12	14	0	89	79	14	84
Scanlan, Kevin, Maine	6	3	3.96	14	2	61	59	23	44
Bazdanes, A.J., Maine	3	1	4.30	13	2	67	62	25	54
Jebb, Matt, Maine	7	3	4.33	13	0	79	91	16	37
Dennis, Jeff, Binghamton	6	5	4.37	13	0	68	77	29	49
Bilodeau, Keith, Maine	1	7	4.38	17	1	64	73	25	38
Albert, Justin, Vermont	5	5	4.55	14	0	89	106	32	65
Errigo, Mike, Stony Brook	4	4	4.78	12	0	75	81	22	58
#Lane, Greg, Binghamton	5	2	4.80	21	7	30	24	16	25
Giulietti, James, Binghamton	4	1	5.03	13	0	59	74	12	35
Gregory, Sean, Albany	6	2	5.05	33	6	66	86	20	49
Tropeano, Nick, Stony Brook	5	1	5.12	14	0	58	69	16	50
Clark, Kevin, UMBC	3	4	5.30	12	0	54	67	22	35
Johnson, Tyler, Stony Brook	5	3	5.32	13	0	64	67	21	58
Rakus, Keith, Vermont	7	3	5.40	14	0	68	79	33	49
Augliera, Mike, Binghamton	5	3	5.60	13	0	55	52	10	36
Kubiak, David, Albany	4	9	5.90	13	0	72	88	23	55
Bach, Ed, UMBC	1	10	6.02	13	0	64	102	20	33
Serafin, Joe, Vermont	4	7	6.16	14	0	83	108	26	62
Sobocinski, Steve, Hartford	3	4	7.15	15	0	57	67	36	25
Drewyer, Austin, UMBC	2	5	7.30	12	0	65	92	14	39

ATLANTIC COAST CONFERENCE

	Conference		Overall	
ATLANTIC	W	L	W	L
Florida State	19	9	45	18
Clemson	19	11	44	22
Boston College	13	15	34	26
Maryland	10	20	27	27
North Carolina State	10	20	25	31
Wake Forest	6	24	22	30
COASTAL	W	L	W	L
North Carolina	19	10	48	18
Georgia Tech	17	10	38	19
Miami	18	12	38	22
*Virginia	16	11	49	15
Duke	15	15	35	24
Virginia Tech	12	17	32	21

ALL-CONFERENCE TEAM: C—Tony Sanchez, Jr., Boston College. **1B**—Dustin Ackley, Jr. North Carolina. **2B**—Phil Gosselin, So., Virginia. **3B**—Kyle Seager, Jr., North Carolina. **SS**—Tyler Cannon, Jr., Virginia. **OF**—Dan Grovatt, So., Virginia; Tyler Holt, So., Florida State; Luke Murton, Sr., Georgia Tech; Jarrett Parker, So., Virgnia; Jeff Rowland, So., Georgia Tech; Jeff Schaus, So., Clemson. **UTIL**—Danny Hultzen, Fr., Virginia. **SP**—Sean Gilmartin, Fr., Florida State; Deck McGuire, So., Georgia Tech; Alex White, Jr., North Carolina. **RP**—Kyle Bellamy, Jr., Miami.
Player of the Year: Dustin Ackley, North Carolina. **Pitcher of the Year:** Deck McGuire, Georgia Tech. **Freshman of the Year:** Danny Hultzen, Virginia. **Coach of the Year:** Mike Martin, Florida State.

INDIVIDUAL BATTING LEADERS
(Minimum 125 At-Bats)

	AVG	AB	R	H	2B	3B	HR	RBI	SB
Ackley, Dustin, North Carolina	.417	266	75	111	18	4	22	73	13
Domecus, Steve, Virginia Tech	.406	143	37	58	11	1	4	42	6
Holt, Tyler, Florida State	.401	237	87	95	23	2	5	28	34
Wates, Austin, Virginia Tech	.397	194	50	77	20	3	5	42	16
Seager, Kyle, North Carolina	.393	262	59	103	26	4	5	62	13
McGee, Mike, Florida State	.379	198	66	75	18	1	19	78	13
Cardullo, Stephen, Florida State	.376	237	76	89	20	3	10	51	20
Paulsen, Ben, Clemson	.367	259	56	95	18	4	13	61	3
Stidham, Jason, Florida State	.363	223	55	81	24	2	12	76	5
Reed, Klint, Virginia Tech	.358	165	51	59	12	0	1	15	2
Grovatt, Dan, Virginia	.356	247	53	88	8	4	8	51	14
Parker, Jarrett, Virginia	.355	265	76	94	20	7	16	65	20
Murton, Luke, Georgia Tech	.354	206	64	73	12	1	20	63	4
Plagman, Tony, Georgia Tech	.354	246	59	87	18	2	16	73	4
Freiman, Nate, Duke	.352	219	47	77	15	1	20	62	3
Cannon, Tyler, Virginia	.351	231	53	81	19	5	1	38	17
Sanchez, Tony, Boston College	.346	228	63	79	19	0	14	51	1
Williams, Matt, Duke	.345	223	35	77	13	1	5	47	1
Anston, Robbie, Boston College	.344	247	55	85	22	3	1	30	15
Hassan, Alex, Duke	.342	219	56	75	17	4	3	3	3
Herrmann, Chris, Miami	.341	214	59	73	13	0	9	44	7
Boyd, Wilson, Clemson	.341	182	35	62	15	3	3	46	5
Gould, Jeremy, Duke	.340	241	43	82	20	0	7	37	6
Rowland, Jeff, Georgia Tech	.340	247	66	84	13	4	8	39	21
Kaminski, Mike, Virginia Tech	.340	159	41	54	11	2	6	38	4
Bunting, Ben, North Carolina	.336	274	63	92	12	4	2	37	5
Proscia, Steven, Virginia	.333	258	53	86	22	2	10	58	13

	AVG	AB	R	H	2B	3B	HR	RBI	SB
Lawson, Scott, Miami	.333	225	50	75	21	1	4	34	10
Freeman, Mike, Clemson	.328	268	60	88	16	5	4	44	11
Woodall, Weldon, Wake Forest	.328	186	41	61	15	0	9	39	7

INDIVIDUAL PITCHING LEADERS
(Minimum 50 Innings)

	W	L	ERA	G	SV	IP	H	BB	SO
#Bellamy, Kyle, Miami	3	1	0.97	30	16	46	23	20	63
Hultzen, Danny, Virginia	9	1	2.17	17	0	95	88	28	107
Moran, Brian, North Carolina	7	1	2.31	36	0	66	47	8	90
Wolcott, Andrew, Duke	8	3	2.77	14	0	94	90	21	71
Wilson, Tyler, Virginia	9	3	2.97	31	1	67	57	21	63
Dean, Pat, Boston College	6	4	3.30	18	0	95	109	16	90
Warren, Adam, North Carolina	10	2	3.31	17	0	98	83	39	103
Morey, Robert, Virginia	3	0	3.33	18	2	68	52	28	84
Gilmartin, Sean, Florida State	12	3	3.49	18	1	98	81	37	83
McGuire, Deck, Georgia Tech	11	2	3.49	16	0	100	86	41	118
Gillheeney, Jimmy, N.C. State	6	5	3.86	13	0	82	81	34	75
White, Alex, North Carolina	8	4	3.87	16	0	107	93	44	121
Harman, Casey, Clemson	7	3	3.95	22	1	87	98	16	89
Wright, Justin, Virginia Tech	7	2	3.95	12	0	66	70	17	59
Carraway, Andrew, Virginia	9	2	3.96	18	0	91	84	22	75
Busch, Brian, Florida State	6	2	3.97	19	0	91	81	35	70
McGee, Mike, Florida State	6	2	4.04	15	0	69	4	42	72
Ballard, Rhett, Virginia Tech	7	4	4.05	17	0	80	81	38	77
Stadler, Austin, Wake Forest	4	5	4.13	13	2	52	59	19	41
Gutierrez, David, Miami	4	6	4.38	16	0	72	73	31	55
Cumpton, Brandon, Georgia Tech	4	3	4.76	13	0	64	77	22	63

ATLANTIC SUN CONFERENCE

	Conference		Overall	
	W	L	W	L
Florida Gulf Coast	23	7	36	18
Kennesaw State	20	9	30	22
*Jacksonville	19	11	37	22
Lipscomb	17	13	24	32
Stetson	16	14	27	30
Belmont	15	15	29	29
North Florida	15	15	23	31
Mercer	12	15	23	23
East Tennessee State	10	20	25	28
Campbell	7	19	27	24
South Carolina-Upstate	7	23	17	37

ALL-CONFERENCE TEAM: C—Jeremy Gillan, Sr., Jacksonville. **1B**—Paul Hoilman, East Tennessee State. **2B**—Chuck Opachich, Jr., Jacksonville. **3B**—Tim Roberson, So., Florida Gulf Coast. **SS**—Casey Frawley, Jr., Stetson. **OF**—Ryan Hamme, Sr., Campbell; Josh Upchurch, Sr., Florida Gulf Coast; Jeremy Cruz, Sr., Stetson. **DH**—Zach Maxfield, So., Florida Gulf Coast. **SP**—Chris Sale, So., Florida Gulf Coast; Chad Jenkins, Jr., Kennesaw State; Rex Brothers, Jr., Lipscomb. **RP**—Kenny Faulk, Jr., Kennesaw State.

Player of the Year: Chad Jenkins, Kennesaw State. **Pitcher of the Year:** Jeremy Cruz, Stetson. **Freshman of the Year:** Dylan Craig, Belmont. **Coach of the Year:** Dave Tollet, Florida Gulf Coast.

INDIVIDUAL BATTING LEADERS
(Minimum 125 At-Bats)

	AVG	AB	R	H	2B	3B	HR	RBI	SB
Hamme, Ryan, Campbell	.438	162	61	71	26	0	4	51	15
Nelson, Kevin, Campbell	.409	110	26	45	5	1	1	16	11
Lowe, Ellis, Campbell	.404	223	69	90	14	3	5	62	16
Gillan, Jeremy, Jacksonville	.400	215	45	86	21	2	11	62	1
Cruz, Jeremy, Stetson	.399	228	62	91	19	0	18	80	2
Craig, Dylan, Belmont	.397	232	48	92	14	9	2	34	9
Maxfield, Zach, Fla. Gulf Coast	.383	214	59	82	16	0	20	66	4
Hoilman, Paul, ETSU	.380	200	55	76	19	1	17	66	2
Johnson, Zach, Campbell	.380	200	55	76	29	0	12	61	10
Opachich, Chuck, Jacksonville	.377	239	52	90	9	3	2	42	19
Karwatt, Steven, Mercer	.374	131	30	49	9	0	10	43	2
Sanders, Justin, Lipscomb	.373	220	48	82	15	5	12	53	8
Hale, Preston, North Florida	.371	221	46	82	17	1	10	43	1
Jones, Mark, Stetson	.363	226	45	82	12	1	7	44	6
Langley, Michael, Mercer	.358	179	39	64	13	1	7	27	4

	AVG	AB	R	H	2B	3B	HR	RBI	SB
Wickens, Steven, Fla. Gulf Coast	.356	225	44	80	9	1	1	36	7
Tanner, Jimmy, S.C.-Upstate	.354	226	41	80	15	0	2	34	0
Alvarez, Mikel, Fla. Gulf Coast	.352	210	51	74	7	0	1	44	3
Wilkins, Ryan, S.C.-Upstate	.352	108	26	38	5	3	1	17	6
Emory, Sean, Stetson	.350	160	43	56	6	1	1	29	3
Bishop, Ric, Kennesaw State	.350	206	43	72	16	1	6	51	1
Roberson, Tim, Fla. Gulf Coast	.349	252	56	88	12	1	19	65	0
Mendez, Troy, ETSU	.349	215	54	75	16	2	9	49	3
McCall, Brandon, Belmont	.344	212	51	73	15	0	8	48	9
Upchurch, Josh, Fla. Gulf Coast	.342	240	59	82	7	6	5	39	11
DiMauro, Nick, Mercer	.340	191	43	65	15	1	4	33	6
Tanis, Jacob, Mercer	.340	159	38	54	13	1	11	35	2
Crittenden, Aaron, Stetson	.339	224	46	76	9	0	13	66	2
Reeder, Bo, ETSU	.339	224	50	76	21	3	15	53	4
McCarty, Tyler, Mercer	.335	179	28	60	14	0	6	32	3
#Wilson, Tyler, Lipscomb	.315	203	39	64	4	1	0	25	25

INDIVIDUAL PITCHING LEADERS
(Minimum 50 Innings)

	W	L	ERA	G	SV	IP	H	BB	SO
Jenkins, Chad, Kennesaw State	8	1	2.54	13	0	92	80	15	98
#Kaminski, Chris, Jacksonville	5	1	2.70	25	8	33	38	5	33
Sale, Chris, Florida Gulf Coast	7	4	2.72	14	1	89	83	27	104
Frawley, John, North Florida	7	2	3.20	15	0	82	92	8	64
Brothers, Rex, Lipscomb	5	5	3.26	14	0	94	74	43	132
Heckathorn, Kyle, Kennesaw State	4	1	3.44	13	0	86	85	27	98
Smith, Josh, Lipscomb	7	4	3.86	15	0	89	70	48	101
#Odom, J.T., Mercer	5	5	3.88	32	3	49	37	21	61
Mauldin, Andry, Stetson	4	5	4.04	14	0	69	76	25	52
#Thompson, Ian, Stetson	1	1	4.13	35	0	28	27	14	29
Loosen, Matt, Jacksonville	4	4	4.16	18	2	80	71	31	91
Woodworth, Pete, Fla. Gulf Coast	5	2	4.25	11	0	66	68	25	60
Branham, Matt, S.C.-Upstate	2	5	4.39	15	0	82	87	27	82
Caldwell, Darren, ETSU	4	3	4.43	32	4	63	70	28	41
Crumbly, Craig, Florida Gulf Coast	7	3	4.61	22	2	68	87	15	47
#Stanley, Jimmy, Belmont	4	4	4.66	26	8	39	47	12	27
Andrew, Carson, Jacksonville	6	4	4.70	15	1	61	67	21	61
Rorbaugh, Phil, North Florida	2	4	5.07	16	0	71	71	21	51
McLurg, Brandon, Lipscomb	5	4	5.09	15	0	74	82	32	52
Donovan, Robby, Stetson	5	3	5.19	13	0	76	87	34	68
Rydman, Jeff, Campbell	5	1	5.43	14	0	65	97	29	45
Byrne, Chas, ETSU	6	4	5.53	16	0	83	107	33	67
Guyer, Lath, Mercer	2	4	5.55	15	0	71	76	33	76

ATLANTIC-10 CONFERENCE

	Conference		Overall	
	W	L	W	L
Dayton	21	6	38	19
Rhode Island	19	6	37	20
*Xavier	18	9	39	21
Charlotte	16	11	33	22
Massachusetts	16	11	27	26
Fordham	16	11	22	32
St. Louis	12	13	30	25
George Washington	11	15	22	33
Temple	11	15	17	33
Richmond	11	16	22	25
St. Bonaventure	9	17	24	25
St. Joseph's	9	17	16	30
LaSalle	8	18	19	30
Duquesne	7	19	14	41

ALL-CONFERENCE TEAM: C—Scott Dunwoody, Dayton. **1B**—Rob Lyerly, Jr., Charlotte. **2B**—Sean Rockey, Jr., George Washington. **3B**—Jimmy Roesinger, So., Dayton. **SS**—Dan Rhault, Sr., Rhode Island. **OF**—Sean Barksdale, Sr., Temple; Mike Donato, Jr., Massachusetts; Jacob Spaeth, Sr., Dayton. **DH**—Jim Macdonald, Sr., Massachusetts. **SP**—Pat Lehman, Sr., George Washington; Eric Smith, Jr. Rhode Island. **RP**—Jordan Conley, Sr., Xavier.

Player of the Year: Dan Rhault, Rhode Island. **Pitcher of the Year:** Pat Lehman, George Washington. **Rookie of the Year:** Cameron Hobson, Dayton. **Coach of the Year:** Tony Vittorio, Dayton.

INDIVIDUAL BATTING LEADERS
(Minimum 125 At-Bats)

	AVG	AB	R	H	2B	3B	HR	RBI	SB
Rockey, Sean, GW	.420	193	35	81	18	1	10	60	11
Oriente, Dewey, Saint Joseph's	.403	144	27	58	7	2	6	39	3
Roesinger, Jimmy, Duquesne	.401	167	39	67	14	3	3	38	11
Lyerly, Rob, Charlotte	.401	167	42	67	18	0	12	49	0
Rhault, Dan, Rhode Island	.393	201	48	79	15	1	12	60	11
Barksdale, Sean, Temple	.371	210	53	78	11	0	15	56	12
Valesente, David, Saint Joseph's	.369	176	39	65	15	2	5	35	1
Bennett, Ryan, St. Louis	.368	209	49	77	16	0	2	43	19
Spaeth, Jacob, Duquesne	.367	196	58	72	10	3	3	32	8
Wilson, Justin, Charlotte	.364	187	53	68	8	3	3	38	19
Jusino, Tony, Temple	.363	201	33	73	19	3	3	39	1
Bomann, Grant, Charlotte	.362	196	43	71	10	1	3	36	8
Del Mastro, Grant, Charlotte	.361	191	47	69	7	3	1	21	17
Navalinski, Max, Duquesne	.358	187	47	67	16	1	8	35	12
McConnell, Adam, Richmond	.355	197	48	70	9	1	1	25	31
Brown, Shane, Charlotte	.355	141	38	50	8	1	1	25	10
Jacob, Zach, Duquesne	.354	223	56	79	13	2	11	50	8
Zebroski, Tom, GW	.347	216	52	75	13	1	8	30	17
Macdonald, Jim, Massachusetts	.343	207	40	71	12	2	9	53	3
Palmer, Oliver, Rhode Island	.342	228	53	78	21	3	11	44	9
Tempesta, Adam, Massachusetts	.341	211	34	72	19	1	5	35	4
Brown, Cameron, Richmond	.340	197	50	67	13	1	11	39	3
Gorby, Kyle, St. Bonaventure	.340	150	24	51	13	1	6	39	3
Bray, Aaron, Charlotte	.339	189	43	64	10	1	1	36	11
Thomas, Ben, Xavier	.338	195	42	66	16	0	16	66	0
Brock, Danny, St. Louis	.336	211	37	71	15	1	2	38	4
Donato, Mike, Massachusetts	.336	217	36	73	13	2	5	40	3
Braaten, Ben, St. Louis	.335	170	42	57	11	0	8	41	1
Freking, Bobby, Xavier	.335	173	30	58	10	2	4	35	0
Cammans, Jeff, Rhode Island	.335	206	39	69	11	1	4	35	17
Abercrombie, Jamie, Temple	.320	202	44	49	22	0	3	40	11
Leach, Danny, Fordham	.332	223	52	74	9	6	0	29	29
Dunsmore, Aaron, Duquesne	.323	235	46	76	16	6	11	55	6
Rivers, Ryan, Charlotte	.313	208	53	65	11	1	18	65	2
#McCambridge, John, Xavier	.287	209	45	60	4	1	3	39	42

INDIVIDUAL PITCHING LEADERS
(Minimum 50 Innings)

	W	L	ERA	G	SV	IP	H	BB	SO
#Conley, Jordan, Xavier	1	1	2.20	25	13	29	23	8	48
Lehman, Pat, GW	7	4	2.40	13	0	105	93	23	89
Yermal, Joe, Charlotte	8	3	3.01	14	0	84	82	22	37
McLain, Kelly, Charlotte	6	2	3.03	30	5	62	54	15	71
Hobson, Cameron, Duquesne	7	1	3.43	18	2	79	79	16	83
Sever, Dave, Saint Louis	6	4	3.60	17	2	65	65	25	70
Greenwood, Nick, Rhode Island	7	3	3.61	16	1	92	88	16	74
Smith, Eric, Rhode Island	5	3	4.08	11	0	71	62	29	56
Clegg, Mitchell, Massachusetts	7	1	4.15	13	0	91	87	35	81
Kennedy, Ryan, LaSalle	4	1	4.29	12	0	57	69	20	27
Turmail, Scott, St. Louis	5	4	4.32	13	0	90	114	14	42
#Greenwell, Brett, Xavier	2	1	4.37	31	0	60	68	18	43
Bellitto, Sebastian, St. Bonaventure	3	3	4.41	10	0	49	56	26	34
Cantrell, Eric, George Washington	5	2	4.46	11	0	73	68	26	60
Fuqua, Kevin, LaSalle	4	5	4.52	14	0	88	95	34	50
Cotton, Bryant, St. Louis	5	4	4.64	14	0	76	101	11	52
LaPointe, Ryan, GW	4	3	4.69	22	2	56	69	25	46
Britton, Jim, St. Bonaventure	6	5	4.70	15	1	75	89	23	64
Johnson, Cael, St. Bonaventure	4	5	4.72	13	0	90	90	36	55
Sherba, Dennis, St. Bonaventure	8	2	4.74	17	0	74	75	44	55
Mower, Randy, St. Joseph's	5	5	4.80	12	0	81	108	20	44
Mack, J.P., Fordham	5	5	5.01	17	0	97	103	42	48
#Haselhorst, Quinn, Duquesne	8	5	5.93	17	0	91	133	25	45

BIG EAST CONFERENCE

	Conference		Overall	
	W	L	W	L
*Louisville	19	7	47	18
South Florida	18	9	34	25
West Virginia	17	10	37	18
St. John's	16	11	30	22
Notre Dame	15	12	36	23
Connecticut	14	13	36	24
Pittsburgh	13	13	28	21
Seton Hall	13	14	25	24
Cincinnati	13	14	29	29
Georgetown	8	18	17	34
Rutgers	8	19	22	31
Villanova	6	20	22	28

ALL-CONFERENCE TEAM: C—Tobias Streich, So., West Virginia. **1B**—Tim Morris, Jr., St. John's. **2B**—Chris Sedon, Jr., Pittsburgh. **3B**—Chris Dominguez, Jr., Louisville. **SS**—Jedd Gyorko, So., West Virginia. **OF**—Justin Parks, Sr., West Virginia; A.J. Pollock, Jr., Notre Dame; George Springer, Fr., Connecticut. **DH**—Chris Affinito, Sr., Seton Hall. **P**—Keith Cantwell, Sr., Seton Hall; Randy Fontanez, So., South Florida; Justin Marks, Jr., Louisville; Jarrod Summers, So., West Virginia.

Players of the Year: Chris Dominguez, Louisville. **Pitcher of the Year:** Justin Marks, Louisville. **Rookie of the Year:** George Springer, Connecticut. **Coach of the Year:** Lelo Prado, South Florida.

INDIVIDUAL BATTING LEADERS
(Minimum 125 At-Bats)

	AVG	AB	R	H	2B	3B	HR	RBI	SB
DiBartolomeo, Dan, West Virginia	.439	205	55	90	18	0	8	59	5
Durham, Lance, Cincinnati	.427	232	45	99	18	1	9	53	1
Gyorko, Jedd, West Virginia	.421	228	74	96	28	1	8	58	1
Belnome, Vince, West Virginia	.418	213	66	89	20	1	9	84	2
Morris, Tim, St. John's	.415	217	69	90	17	2	12	62	7
Sedon, Chris, Pittsburgh	.398	201	65	80	10	2	22	62	19
Carlin, Junior, South Florida	.384	164	31	63	4	2	0	27	3
Smedberg, Matt, Seton Hall	.382	186	41	71	12	6	2	26	7
Kemp, Brian, St. John's	.379	219	68	83	13	3	3	35	16
Parks, Justin, West Virginia	.374	230	76	86	14	1	12	41	4
Wunderlich, Phil, Louisville	.367	245	56	90	18	1	18	78	4
Pollock, A.J., Notre Dame	.365	241	69	88	19	5	10	52	21
Parque, Jimmy, St. John's	.360	228	53	82	17	1	5	61	2
Springer, George, Connecticut	.358	212	75	76	14	3	16	57	12
Markel, Austin, West Virginia	.357	207	75	74	11	7	15	56	4
Kosco, Jonathan, South Florida	.355	234	60	83	14	2	3	36	8
Clark, Andrew, Louisville	.350	254	82	89	21	2	9	55	1
Del Rosario, Carlos, St. John's	.350	163	35	57	17	1	1	35	8
Barnes, Jeremy, Notre Dame	.349	232	53	81	15	5	15	69	4
Fernandez, Erick, Georgetown	.349	169	28	59	16	1	5	28	2
Hopkins, Greg, St. John's	.349	169	41	59	11	1	7	45	2
Brazeal, Todd, South Florida	.348	204	48	71	15	0	5	50	1
Wessinger, Matt, St. John's	.347	150	37	52	15	0	2	31	6
Nemeth, Mike, Connecticut	.346	231	35	80	22	2	6	47	0
Szczur, Matt, Villanova	.346	188	45	65	10	2	1	24	18
Dominguez, Chris, Louisville	.345	258	80	89	12	2	25	82	19
Lang, Michael, Rutgers	.343	207	58	71	17	2	8	38	10
Spina, Mike, Cincinnati	.342	228	52	78	7	0	23	69	2
Koczirka, David, Villanova	.340	162	25	55	13	3	1	39	4
LePage, Pierre, Connecticut	.339	236	47	80	16	0	1	38	3
Duvall, Adam, Louisville	.328	268	83	88	21	2	11	51	12
#Tommy, Lee, Georgetown	.308	169	32	52	10	1	1	16	23

INDIVIDUAL PITCHING LEADERS
(Minimum 50 Innings)

	W	L	ERA	G	SV	IP	H	BB	SO
Summers, Jarryd, West Virginia	7	3	3.05	14	0	94	85	35	99
Fontanez, Randy, South Florida	7	3	3.09	14	0	99	90	24	57
#Erickson, David, Connecticut	0	2	3.21	27	12	28	23	11	33
Cantwell, Keith, Seton Hall	6	3	3.48	13	0	93	94	23	74
Marks, Justin, Louisville	11	3	3.77	18	1	105	86	35	129
Folino, John, Connecticut	6	3	3.92	10	0	64	81	18	58
Black, Sean, Seton Hall	4	6	3.99	13	0	86	87	37	70
Gross, Billy, West Virginia	9	4	4.23	13	0	87	105	26	58
Altemus, Andy, West Virginia	1	1	4.28	18	4	61	78	21	34

	W	L	ERA	G	SV	IP	H	BB	SO
Dirocco, Joe, Seton Hall	4	3	4.46	14	0	75	86	28	33
Stultz, Derrick, South Florida	5	4	4.48	13	0	76	70	27	63
Johnson, Cole, Notre Dame	7	3	4.56	15	0	95	88	36	64
Sanford, Shawn, South Florida	5	4	4.68	17	3	75	79	22	64
Glynn, Elliot, Connecticut	5	4	4.76	13	0	74	84	26	58
Maust, Eric, Notre Dame	6	3	4.94	14	0	86	104	28	26
Kiekehefer, Dean, Louisville	6	5	5.00	18	0	77	96	21	63
Cenatiempo, Nick, St. John's	5	3	5.17	17	0	54	65	27	28
Streilein, Brian, Villanova	5	8	5.46	14	0	84	103	29	54
Helisek, Kyle, Villanova	4	1	5.55	14	1	58	71	17	31
Gaynor, Casey, Rutgers	2	9	5.68	13	0	76	105	25	59
Kaye, David, Pittsburgh	3	4	5.82	16	0	73	93	28	42

BIG SOUTH CONFERENCE

	Conference		Overall	
	W	L	W	L
*Coastal Carolina	21	5	47	16
Winthrop	18	9	35	25
Liberty	17	9	33	21
Radford	16	9	26	24
Gardner-Webb	13	14	25	25
High Point	11	12	21	32
Virginia Military Institute	10	15	18	35
Charleston Southern	10	15	16	37
Presbyterian	7	19	13	38
UNC Asheville	5	21	9	42

ALL-CONFERENCE TEAM: C—Billy Alvino, Sr., High Point. **1B**—David Anderson, Sr., Coastal Carolina. **2B**—A.J. Yoder, Sr., VMI. **3B**—Justin Loyd, Sr., Gardner-Webb. **SS**—Alfie Wheeler, Sr., High Point. **DH**—Eddie Rohan, So., Winthrop. **OF**—Tommy Baldridge, Sr., Coastal Carolina; P.K. Keller, Sr., Liberty; David Sappelt, Jr., Coastal Carolina. **SP**— Anthony Meo, Fr., Coastal Carolina; Shawn Teufel, Jr., Liberty; Cody Wheeler, So., Coastal Carolina. **RP**—Nick McCully, Jr., Coastal Carolina.
Player of the Year: David Anderson, Coastal Carolina. **Pitcher of the Year:** Cody Wheeler, Coastal Carolina. **Freshman of the Year:** Jeff Kemp, Radford. **Coach of the Year:** Gary Gilmore, Coastal Carolina.

INDIVIDUAL BATTING LEADERS
(Minimum 125 At-Bats)

	AVG	AB	R	H	2B	3B	HR	RBI	SB
Gregory, Alex, Radford	**.407**	177	45	72	12	1	10	42	4
Alvino, Billy, High Point	.400	210	29	84	18	1	3	47	2
Wheeler, Alfie, High Point	.400	205	57	82	17	0	2	29	6
Loyd, Justin, Gardner-Webb	.400	195	51	78	20	0	9	56	7
Tisdale, Eddie, Winthrop	.393	**242**	61	**95**	11	1	10	53	11
Nolan, Kevin, Winthrop	.392	222	57	87	17	0	2	38	11
Redal, Curran, Liberty	.380	213	50	81	13	4	6	42	6
Anderson, David, Coastal Carolina	.377	220	53	83	11	2	21	82	0
Miller, Brock, Gardner-Webb	.373	193	61	72	8	3	2	16	37
Fulginiti, Kurt, Gardner-Webb	.370	162	34	60	9	2	8	39	0
Rice, Adam, Coastal Carolina	.368	242	54	89	20	1	7	59	5
Ballard, Jordan, VMI	.366	202	43	74	17	0	11	48	2
Bortnick, Tyler, Coastal Carolina	.363	226	65	82	13	0	11	44	10
Bream, Doug, Liberty	.355	166	31	59	13	0	6	33	1
Manion, Bill, High Point	.355	220	44	78	12	1	4	48	5
Cooke, Daniel, Gardner-Webb	.353	201	56	71	13	2	7	47	26
Yoder, A.J., VMI	.349	229	42	80	13	2	3	27	11
Rohan, Eddie, Winthrop	.348	227	41	79	18	0	14	53	6
Thielepape, Matt, Winthrop	.339	171	36	58	10	0	8	30	5
Chinners, Nick, Charleston Southern	.339	186	35	63	13	1	6	28	1
Bream, Tyler, Liberty	.337	187	35	63	16	2	8	57	0
Kemp, Jeff, Radford	.337	196	33	66	9	2	5	36	13
Roberts, Sam, VMI	.335	200	53	67	10	0	6	34	7
Bowman, Dan, Coastal Carolina	.333	222	53	74	14	2	13	54	5
Combs, Jared, Presbyterian	.332	211	34	70	16	0	8	51	2
Lyda, Cory, Presbyterian	.330	200	35	66	8	5	10	38	9
Sullivan, Sean, Winthrop	.327	217	41	71	11	0	3	44	13
Mahoney, Kyle, High Point	.327	217	38	71	16	0	3	38	2
Hollinger, Errol, Liberty	.327	208	36	68	19	1	8	35	0
Murrian, John, Winthrop	.327	205	42	67	19	1	6	42	3
#Noel, Rico, Coastal Carolina	.315	232	**75**	73	17	1	8	45	**48**
#Grammer, Gabe, Presbyterian	.304	171	29	52	3	**6**	5	29	7
#Henderson, Bryn, Winthrop	.298	235	51	70	**21**	1	6	37	10

INDIVIDUAL PITCHING LEADERS
(Minimum 50 Innings)

	W	L	ERA	G	SV	IP	H	BB	SO
McCully, Nick, Coastal Carolina	8	1	**2.10**	28	8	73	52	26	64
Meo, Anthony, Coastal Carolina	9	2	2.93	17	0	77	67	32	68
D'Angelo, Matteo, Winthrop	8	3	3.09	17	0	84	83	22	60
Wilson, Andrew, Liberty	5	3	3.52	24	5	64	61	21	70
Fleet, Austin, Coastal Carolina	7	2	3.53	15	0	64	63	17	28
#Mizenko, Tyler, Winthrop	2	4	3.77	**30**	**14**	45	44	19	42
Wheeler, Cody, Coastal Carolina	**10**	1	3.83	15	0	**92**	76	34	**98**
Evans, Steven, Liberty	7	2	3.96	16	1	73	82	26	45
Stackhouse, Brett, Gardner-Webb	5	6	4.27	17	0	65	65	37	44
Smink, Travis, VMI	8	4	4.33	18	0	87	100	32	72
Teufel, Shawn, Liberty	9	2	4.33	14	0	73	80	30	72
Montieth, Ken, Winthrop	3	5	4.34	16	0	66	84	16	34
Henderson, Chris, VMI	3	7	4.67	19	0	91	102	17	76
Taylor, Aerik, Radford	5	4	4.90	14	0	72	82	28	41
Odom, Mitchell, Presbyterian	5	3	4.94	21	0	75	86	27	37
Harmon, Jesse, Presbyterian	4	5	5.04	14	0	75	83	28	54
Gagg, Bobby, Coastal Carolina	4	4	5.35	18	5	66	75	12	40
Newman, Wade, Winthrop	4	4	5.42	15	0	76	87	30	55
Campbell, Devin, Gardner-Webb	3	4	5.51	14	0	64	74	30	42
Edwards, Matt, VMI	3	6	5.72	23	3	57	63	16	44
Pysh, Shane, Radford	3	4	5.94	13	0	67	73	34	52

BIG TEN CONFERENCE

	Conference		Overall	
	W	L	W	L
Ohio State	18	6	42	19
Minnesota	17	6	40	19
*Indiana	16	7	32	27
Illinois	16	8	34	20
Michigan State	13	11	23	31
Purdue	11	12	25	26
Michigan	9	15	30	25
Penn State	8	16	25	26
Northwestern	5	17	14	35
Iowa	4	19	16	35

ALL-CONFERENCE TEAM: C—Dan Burkhart, So., Ohio State; Josh Phegley, Jr., Indiana. **1B**—Mike Dufek, Jr., Michigan. **2B**—Derek McCallum, Jr., Minnesota. **3B**—Dominic Altobelli, Sr., Illinois. **SS**—Brandon Wikoff, Jr., Illinois. **OF**— Ryan Durant, Jr., Iowa; Kyle Hudson, Jr., Illinois; Kipp Schutz, So., Indiana; Brandon Haveman, Sr., Purdue. **DH**—Ryan Dew, Jr., Ohio State. **SP**—Eric Arnett, Jr., Indiana; Chris Fetter, Sr., Michigan; Alex Wimmers, So., Ohio State. **RP**—Jake Hale, Sr., Ohio State.
Player of the Year: Dan Burkhart, Ohio State. **Pitchers of the Year:** Eric Arnett, Indiana; Alex Wimmers, Ohio State. **Freshman of the Year:** Alex Dickerson, Indiana. **Coach of the Year:** Bob Todd, Ohio State.

INDIVIDUAL BATTING LEADERS
(Minimum 125 At-Bats)

	AVG	AB	R	H	2B	3B	HR	RBI	SB
Haveman, Brandon, Purdue	**.422**	185	39	78	**20**	2	4	26	7
McCallum, Derek, Minnesota	.409	232	57	**95**	17	3	**18**	**86**	6
Schutz, Kipp, Indiana	.392	181	36	71	10	0	5	34	2
Dew, Ryan, Ohio State	.388	219	53	85	15	1	7	42	6
Cappetta, Pete, Illinois	.384	151	37	58	10	4	2	30	7
Wikoff, Brandon, Illinois	.373	228	56	85	17	5	4	41	10
Durant, Ryan, Iowa	.370	181	27	67	12	1	2	29	8
Dickerson, Alex, Indiana	.370	238	45	88	15	1	14	57	2
Charles, Eric, Purdue	.369	160	45	59	9	3	2	21	7
Steranka, Jordan, Penn State	.365	192	39	70	9	3	6	42	3
Altobelli, Dominic, Illinois	.361	219	54	79	15	3	8	53	7
Argo, Willie, Illinois	.355	172	46	61	11	2	12	47	10
Burkhart, Dan, Ohio State	.354	209	48	74	13	3	10	62	2
Patterson, A.J., Minnesota	.353	224	65	79	7	3	2	46	8
Lynd, Blake, Penn State	.350	163	39	57	1	0	0	16	22
Hurley, Zach, Ohio State	.346	**257**	58	89	12	**6**	**6**	53	14
Toole, Hustin, Iowa	.346	156	31	54	13	1	2	25	15
Stephens, Michael, Ohio State	.346	237	61	82	10	5	14	63	10
Roof, Eric, Michigan State	.345	200	46	69	14	2	6	41	3
Phegley, Josh, Indiana	.344	221	58	76	11	1	17	66	2
LaMarra, Ryan, Michigan	.344	192	55	66	11	1	12	62	13

	AVG	AB	R	H	2B	3B	HR	RBI	SB
Sabourin, Jerrud, Indiana	.343	248	48	85	15	3	6	36	4
Kvasnicka, Michael, Minnesota	.341	249	48	85	18	2	10	65	5
Fellows, Kenny, Michigan	.340	203	40	69	14	1	0	28	21
Kovanda, Cory, Ohio State	.339	221	55	75	11	3	1	38	7
Gominsky, Justin, Minnesota	.338	157	35	53	11	1	3	25	11
Nohelty, Matt, Minnesota	.337	246	69	83	5	3	0	31	26
Parr, Josh, Illinois	.337	184	31	62	10	2	0	30	13
Johnson, Aaron, Illinois	.333	195	39	65	8	0	10	52	5
Jaffe, Alex, Purdue	.333	153	35	51	5	0	5	26	5
#Crawford, Evan, Indiana	.323	167	46	54	13	0	2	29	27

INDIVIDUAL PITCHING LEADERS
(Minimum 50 Innings)

	W	L	ERA	G	SV	IP	H	BB	SO
#Hale, Jake, Ohio State	0	1	1.31	40	18	55	39	15	67
Arnett, Eric, Indiana	12	2	2.50	14	0	108	82	39	109
Fetter, Chris, Michigan	7	3	3.26	13	0	94	93	17	103
Wimmers, Alex, Ohio State	9	2	3.27	16	0	105	80	55	136
Katzman, Eric, Michigan	7	4	3.53	17	1	74	65	41	64
Bucciferro, Tony, Michigan State	5	2	3.55	14	0	71	92	12	61
Buske, Tom, Minnesota	9	4	3.57	15	0	96	78	26	75
Achter, A.J., Michigan State	3	6	3.76	14	0	81	76	56	57
Strack, Will, Illinois	6	1	3.84	15	2	68	77	18	18
Bashore, Matt, Indiana	7	5	4.07	16	0	95	98	30	108
Rosin, Seth, Minnesota	7	1	4.21	15	0	77	82	16	65
Cianciolo, Paul, Penn State	4	1	4.34	17	0	58	76	15	31
Moody, Nolan, Minnesota	6	5	4.53	14	0	93	97	41	57
Chauncy, Handran, Minnesota	8	3	4.59	15	0	96	109	33	57
Morgan, Matt, Purdue	6	5	4.64	13	0	78	93	22	61
Monar, Blake, Indiana	5	3	4.64	14	0	78	75	39	59
Hippen, Jarred, Iowa	3	4	4.87	16	0	68	73	29	50
Haig, Phil, Illinois	7	3	4.92	16	0	82	99	24	44
Macy, T.J., Penn State	3	4	4.95	13	0	76	75	40	91
Muraski, Joe, Northwestern	3	5	5.20	13	0	81	86	32	65
Jokisch, Eric, Northwestern	4	7	5.48	14	0	89	105	32	57
Rucinski, Drew, Ohio State	12	2	5.54	36	2	75	85	32	62

BIG 12 CONFERENCE

	Conference		Overall	
	W	L	W	L
*Texas	17	9	50	16
Oklahoma	17	10	43	20
Missouri	16	11	35	27
Kansas State	14	11	43	18
Kansas	15	12	39	24
Texas A&M	14	13	37	24
Texas Tech	12	15	25	32
Baylor	10	16	30	26
Oklahoma State	9	16	34	24
Nebraska	8	19	25	28

ALL-CONFERENCE TEAM: C—J.T. Wise, Sr., Oklahoma. **1B**—Chris Richburg, Sr., Texas Tech. **2B**—Brodie Greene, Jr., Texas A&M. **3B**—Tony Thompson, So., Kansas. **SS**—Shaver Hansen, Jr., Baylor; Bryant Hernandez, Jr., Oklahoma. **OF**—Michael Dabbs, Sr., Oklahoma State; Greg Folgia, Jr., Missouri; Jamie Johnson, Jr., Oklahoma. **DH**—Dustin Dickerson, Jr., Baylor. **UTIL**—Brooks Raley, So., Texas A&M. **SP**—Kyle Gibson, Jr., Missouri; A.J. Morris, Jr., Kansas State; Chance Ruffin, So., Texas. **RP**—Austin Wood, Sr., Texas.
Player of the Year: J.T. Wise, Oklahoma. **Pitcher of the Year:** A.J. Morris, Kansas State. **Newcomer of the Year:** David Narodowski, Kansas. **Freshman of the Year:** Garrett Buechele, Oklahoma. **Coach of the Year:** Brad Hill, Kansas State.

INDIVIDUAL BATTING LEADERS
(Minimum 125 At-Bats)

	AVG	AB	R	H	2B	3B	HR	RBI	SB
Thompson, Tony, Kansas	.389	247	58	96	27	0	21	82	1
Dickerson, Dustin, Baylor	.377	228	50	86	16	0	10	41	4
Heere, Brian, Kansas	.362	210	55	76	12	4	5	40	7
Bloxom, Justin, Kansas State	.361	244	50	88	16	4	12	63	7
Wise, J.T., Oklahoma	.359	209	50	75	13	0	17	62	2
Narodowski, David, Kansas	.354	240	64	85	19	1	8	43	6
Buechele, Garrett, Oklahoma	.353	232	41	82	14	1	4	40	1
Johnson, Jamie, Oklahoma	.353	255	76	90	17	5	13	44	18
Jurica, Carter, Kansas State	.353	238	61	84	15	3	4	46	23
Hernandez, Bryant, Oklahoma	.351	251	65	88	12	4	12	62	10
Shofner, Caleb, Texas A&M	.348	198	49	69	12	3	7	42	4
Belza, Tom, Oklahoma State	.346	228	43	79	12	5	6	52	1
Greene, Brodie, Texas A&M	.344	221	50	76	12	2	11	35	11
Richburg, Chris, Texas Tech	.341	208	53	71	12	2	14	60	3
Dabbs, Michael, Oklahoma State	.337	196	46	66	14	6	13	38	11
Hambly, Tyrone, Oklahoma State	.336	217	42	73	11	1	10	41	2
Kenworthy, Joey, Texas Tech	.336	229	45	77	9	2	2	32	5
Martini, Nick, Kansas State	.336	232	54	78	17	2	4	50	19
Mach, Kyle, Missouri	.335	224	37	75	15	2	4	40	0
Afenir, Buck, Kansas	.333	219	54	73	12	1	10	63	0
Farst, Tyler, Nebraska	.333	189	36	63	15	0	3	36	2
Medchill, Neil, Oklahoma State	.332	223	63	74	17	2	14	57	2
Hansen, Shaver, Baylor	.330	218	52	72	15	0	17	59	5
Ashby, Taylor, Texas Tech	.330	224	27	74	17	0	1	46	12
Biery, Drew, Kansas State	.329	207	53	68	17	1	9	44	6
LeJeune, Scott, Texas Tech	.327	196	28	64	14	2	2	37	1
Booker, Ben, Baylor	.326	132	28	43	7	0	1	17	9
Folgia, Greg, Missouri	.326	224	58	73	16	3	12	70	0
Bailey, Adam, Nebraska	.325	194	35	63	15	1	12	50	2
Cruz, Jordan, Kansas State	.324	210	45	68	10	3	11	52	17
#Raley, Brooks, Texas A&M	.304	217	45	66	19	2	1	26	25

INDIVIDUAL PITCHING LEADERS
(Minimum 50 Innings)

	W	L	ERA	G	SV	IP	H	BB	SO
Jungmann, Taylor, Texas	11	3	2.00	25	0	95	65	35	101
Morris, A.J., Kansas State	14	1	2.09	16	0	116	98	30	100
Wood, Austin, Texas	6	1	2.61	41	15	86	68	18	74
Gibson, Kyle, Missouri	11	3	3.21	16	0	107	95	19	131
#Duke, Ryan, Oklahoma	3	1	3.22	26	16	36	28	12	43
Ruffin, Chance, Texas	10	2	3.32	25	2	125	109	25	115
Green, Cole, Texas	5	3	3.34	21	0	110	98	33	85
Workman, Brandon, Texas	3	5	3.48	20	0	75	58	28	82
Betis, Chad, Texas Tech	6	1	3.59	23	7	73	76	30	58
Raley, Brooks, Texas A&M	7	3	3.76	15	0	93	80	26	95
Lyons, Tyler, Oklahoma State	7	6	4.07	16	0	97	114	25	77
Hales, Ross, Texas A&M	6	2	4.11	19	0	77	79	22	76
Hall, Shaeffer, Kansas	5	6	4.18	15	0	93	104	10	65
Doyle, Andrew, Oklahoma	8	4	4.21	15	0	92	90	23	65
Wilson, Alex, Texas A&M	6	6	4.22	24	2	90	80	25	120
Volz, Kendal, Baylor	3	7	4.50	15	2	86	91	38	78
Hoge, Lance, Kansas State	6	4	4.54	16	0	71	83	22	46
Ridenhour, Lee, Kansas	6	3	4.65	17	1	79	86	23	49
Walz, T.J., Kansas	8	3	4.92	15	0	82	84	34	88
Nesseth, Mike, Nebraska	5	4	5.01	20	2	65	62	35	73
Bird, Erik, Nebraska	3	2	5.10	20	0	65	76	20	42

BIG WEST CONFERENCE

	Conference		Overall	
	W	L	W	L
*UC Irvine	22	2	45	15
Cal State Fullerton	17	7	47	16
Cal Poly	14	10	37	21
UC Riverside	12	12	33	20
UC Santa Barbara	11	13	29	23
Long Beach State	11	13	25	29
Pacific	9	15	21	32
Cal State Northridge	7	17	24	32
UC Davis	5	19	13	42

ALL-CONFERENCE TEAM: C—Francis Larson, Jr., UC Irvine. **1B**—Jared Clark, Sr., Cal State Fullerton. **2B**—Matt Jensen, Fr., Cal Poly. **3B**—Ryan Goetz, Jr., UC Riverside. **SS**—Ben Orloff, Sr., UC Irvine. **OF**—Khris Davis, Jr., Cal State Fullerton; Eric Deragisch, Sr., UC Irvine; Josh Fellhauer, Jr., Cal State Fullerton; Nick Longmire, So., Pacific. **DH**—Michael Hur, Jr., UC Riverside. **UTIL**—Adam Buschini, Jr., Cal Poly. **SP**—Daniel Bibona, So., UC Irvine; Joe Gardner, Jr., UC Santa Barbara; Daniel Renken, So., Cal State Fullerton. **RP**—Nick Ramirez, Fr., Cal State Fullerton. **CP**—Eric Pettis, Jr., UC Irvine.
Player of the Year: Ben Orloff, UC Irvine. **Pitcher of the Year:** Daniel Bibona, UC Irvine. **Freshman Player of the Year:** Matt Jensen, Cal Poly.

Freshman Pitchers of the Year: Tyler Pill, Cal State Fullerton; Noe Ramirez, Cal State Fullerton. **Coach of the Year:** Mike Gillespie, UC Irvine.

INDIVIDUAL BATTING LEADERS
(Minimum 125 At-Bats)

	AVG	AB	R	H	2B	3B	HR	RBI	SB
Buschini, Adam, Cal Poly	.422	185	50	78	18	3	11	61	13
Fellhauer, Josh, CS Fullerton	.396	227	49	90	12	0	6	55	18
Shaeffer, Ronnie, UC Irvine	.388	165	34	64	12	0	4	36	4
Longmire, Nick, Pacific	.385	218	60	84	16	6	6	37	8
Brown, J.B., Pacific	.378	222	45	84	17	0	7	58	3
Jensen, Matt, Cal Poly	.375	160	42	60	15	1	9	53	2
Cates, Richard, CS Northridge	.374	222	44	83	12	0	2	28	7
Hur, Michael, UC Riverside	.372	199	46	74	17	2	7	52	1
Clark, Jared, CS Fullerton	.363	234	57	85	17	0	12	82	14
Orloff, Ben, UC Irvine	.358	254	62	91	11	1	0	28	18
Colon, Christian, CS Fullerton	.357	255	82	91	16	2	8	40	15
Deragisch, Eric, UC Irvine	.355	203	49	72	11	3	3	39	7
Wideman, Kurt, Pacific	.351	194	41	68	24	2	5	41	6
Centanni, Joey, Pacific	.347	176	36	61	14	2	2	28	7
Stevenson, Casey, UC Irvine	.346	191	44	66	19	1	3	41	8
Walker, Mike, Pacific	.345	197	41	68	12	0	6	34	3
Tinoco, Steve, Long Beach State	.343	140	27	48	9	2	5	30	5
Valaika, Matt, UC Santa Barbara	.343	178	40	61	16	1	6	45	1
Cavan, Ryan, UC Santa Barbara	.341	173	50	59	11	3	4	36	3
Brown, Gary, CS Fullerton	.340	259	64	88	17	7	3	40	23
Goetz, Ryan, UC Riverside	.340	215	35	73	16	2	5	45	5
Schafer, Justin, UC Davis	.338	148	31	50	8	0	2	11	7
Martin, Brian, Pacific	.333	153	30	51	10	2	3	31	0
Smith, Kyle, Cal Poly	.332	214	50	71	16	2	5	41	13
Uhl, Carl, UC Riverside	.329	228	53	75	20	3	5	36	17
Lee, Ryan, Cal Poly	.328	265	65	87	11	2	3	30	27
Davis, Khris, CS Fullerton	.328	232	53	76	25	0	16	58	17
Oliver, Eric, UC Santa Barbara	.325	203	40	66	19	1	6	48	1
Crocker, Bobby, Cal Poly	.323	127	31	41	6	0	5	24	10
Fisher, Ryan, UC Irvine	.320	125	31	40	7	3	4	28	2

INDIVIDUAL PITCHING LEADERS
(Minimum 50 Innings)

	W	L	ERA	G	SV	IP	H	BB	SO
Bibona, Daniel, UC Irvine	12	1	2.63	15	0	106	78	26	108
Renken, Daniel, CS Fullerton	11	3	2.69	17	0	124	94	23	56
Ramirez, Noe, CS Fullerton	9	2	3.33	20	0	111	90	24	100
Gardner, Joe, UC Santa Barbara	7	1	3.40	13	0	85	79	31	69
Bergman, Christian, UC Irvine	9	3	3.50	15	0	98	111	16	66
Applebee, Paul, UC Riverside	10	2	3.74	14	0	89	84	20	63
#Pettis, Eric, UC Irvine	5	2	3.86	29	17	42	47	7	37
Pill, Tyler, CS Fullerton	11	3	4.06	17	0	102	97	13	74
Platt, Ryan, UC Riverside	4	0	4.15	13	0	65	61	22	67
DeVincenzi, Mark, Cal Poly	6	1	4.26	31	1	57	65	22	67
Bargas, Paul, UC Riverside	5	3	4.44	12	0	75	94	9	46
Slaught, Crosby, UC Irvine	8	0	4.62	16	0	76	87	23	52
Hollands, Mario, UC Santa Barbara	6	6	4.74	14	0	89	90	37	49
Mauldin, D.J., Cal Poly	5	5	4.75	16	1	108	135	31	65
Centanni, Joey, Pacific	5	6	4.82	15	0	99	122	20	44
Juarez, Ryan, CS Northridge	7	5	4.89	14	0	85	95	30	37
Eskew, Jared, Cal Poly	6	2	5.01	23	1	74	104	22	57
McCamey, Ryan, CS Northridge	1	4	5.26	18	0	50	56	24	41
Radeke, Mason, Cal Poly	6	2	5.31	14	1	76	102	20	754
Quist, Dayne, UC Davis	2	6	5.48	17	0	67	75	29	32
Briner, Tom, UC Davis	2	5	5.53	16	0	55	80	18	37
Thompson, Jake, Long Beach State	4	7	5.61	14	0	85	103	13	42

COLONIAL ATHLETIC ASSOCIATION

	Conference		Overall	
	W	L	W	L
George Mason	19	5	42	14
*Georgia State	12	9	39	22
UNC Wilmington	10	8	31	23
Northeastern	13	11	28	25
Old Dominion	13	11	22	27
Delaware	11	10	28	20
James Madison	12	11	30	24
Towson	12	12	28	25
William & Mary	9	14	24	25
Virginia Commonwealth	8	16	20	26
Hofstra	6	18	11	32

ALL-CONFERENCE TEAM: C—Chris Henderson, Jr., George Mason. **1B**—Justin Bour, Jr., George Mason. **2B**—Mike Fabiaschi, Jr., James Madison. **3B**—Jake McAloose, Jr., Old Dominion. **SS**—Gary Helmick, Sr., Towson. **OF**—Scott Krieger, Sr., George Mason; Mark Stuckless, Sr., Hofstra; Matt Townsend, Jr., James Madison. **DH**—Derek Simmons, Sr., Georgia State. **UTIL**—Trevor Knight, So., James Madison. **SP**— Kevin Crum, Jr., George Mason; Mike Modica, Sr., George Mason. **RP**—Kevin Munson, So., James Madison.

Players of the Year: Chris Henderson, George Mason; Scott Krieger, George Mason. **Defensive Player of the Year:** Chris Henderson, George Mason. **Rookie of the Year:** Brett Harris, Old Dominion. **Coach of the Year:** Bill Brown, George Mason.

INDIVIDUAL BATTING LEADERS
(Minimum 125 At-Bats)

	AVG	AB	R	H	2B	3B	HR	RBI	SB
Helmick, Gary, Towson	.430	228	72	98	12	9	17	51	15
McAloose, Jake, Old Dominion	.413	184	48	76	14	2	6	44	7
Henderson, Chris, George Mason	.413	235	70	97	22	2	14	58	1
Mimeault, Marc, Georgia State	.398	196	45	78	7	1	14	58	1
Stuckless, Mark, Hofstra	.392	176	43	69	11	4	5	25	14
Townsend, Matt, James Madison	.390	205	60	80	17	1	17	59	17
Stampone, Mark, Hofstra	.382	173	50	66	20	1	4	37	8
Alonso, Carlos, Delaware	.380	205	59	78	20	1	4	37	12
Knight, Trevor, James Madison	.377	223	60	84	13	2	14	55	15
Browning, Matt, James Madison	.376	218	49	82	19	0	9	59	14
Krieger, Scott, George Mason	.372	218	68	81	14	5	20	80	6
Merkler, Bill, Delaware	.371	194	48	72	9	0	17	54	2
Herbek, David, James Madison	.370	211	55	78	20	3	10	54	18
Collins, Matt, Towson	.367	221	46	81	23	0	8	52	3
Dameron, Pat, Delaware	.362	163	38	59	17	0	5	35	0
Van Horn, Matt, Georgia State	.360	197	44	71	13	2	6	39	12
Foltz, Alex, James Madison	.351	168	46	59	13	2	3	23	14
Nickle, Rob, William & Mary	.351	174	49	61	14	2	14	60	7
Tamsin, Mike, Northeastern	.347	213	42	74	10	3	5	45	4
Van Meter, Joe, VCU	.347	170	31	59	13	1	3	36	9
Jones, Jeff, William & Mary	.345	197	46	68	13	3	4	31	23
Prokopowicz, Matt, Hofstra	.344	151	18	52	9	1	3	30	4
Leskiw, Matt, VCU	.343	134	28	46	5	0	0	15	13
Otto, Doug, VCU	.343	169	38	58	12	0	2	25	8
Compagnone, Frank, Northeastern	.343	140	17	48	9	0	1	19	0
Rooney, Mike, UNC Wilmington	.341	182	42	62	10	4	2	41	5
Bour, Justin, George Mason	.339	221	48	75	14	0	17	66	0
Reed, Ryan, Delaware	.337	181	39	61	10	0	9	37	1
Most, Max, Old Dominion	.337	184	42	62	18	1	2	19	16
Collins, Kevin, Towson	.335	221	61	74	17	3	14	56	11
#Diminio, Andrew, VCU	.323	164	40	53	9	1	1	20	25

INDIVIDUAL PITCHING LEADERS
(Minimum 50 Innings)

	W	L	ERA	G	SV	IP	H	BB	SO
#Munson, Kevin, James Madison	3	3	2.85	24	9	47	38	23	67
Boggs, Chris, Old Dominion	5	2	3.20	16	1	51	67	13	39
#Booth, Bryan, UNC Wilmington	2	1	3.31	37	6	33	23	20	32
Tomchick, Ben, Old Dominion	5	3	3.51	14	0	82	72	28	60
Ross, J.T., Northeastern	5	1	3.90	13	0	62	60	22	52
Smith, Trevor, Northeastern	5	2	3.92	14	0	67	64	27	54
Williams, Tom, Northeastern	1	3	3.96	14	1	61	72	31	56
Francis, Aiden, Georgia State	5	1	4.15	21	3	56	49	18	58
Thomas, Ian, VCU	4	4	4.27	11	0	72	78	25	28
O'Donald, Rich, Delaware	5	4	4.32	11	0	77	69	29	47
Modica, Mike, George Mason	11	4	4.34	14	0	87	81	35	75
Moore, Ryan, Georgia State	7	2	4.41	16	0	86	86	29	64
Crum, Kevin, George Mason	8	4	4.64	14	0	83	85	22	56
Davenport, Matt, William & Mary	6	2	4.71	24	0	63	72	33	30
Landry, Kevin, William & Mary	4	6	4.72	20	0	76	71	30	91
Rodrick, Brian, Delaware	4	3	4.95	13	0	91	96	44	95
Harris, Brian, Old Dominion	6	4	4.95	11	0	80	100	19	49
Davis, Steven, UNC Wilmington	5	2	5.01	29	3	50	44	22	53
Neustifter, Jeremy, William & Mary	4	2	5.08	16	0	62	69	37	60
Phelps, Turner, James Madison	8	2	5.33	13	0	83	90	41	90
Cropper, Daniel, Georgia State	5	2	5.46	15	0	59	76	15	53

CONFERENCE USA

	Conference		Overall	
	W	L	W	L
East Carolina	17	7	46	20
*Rice	16	8	43	18
Tulane	13	11	34	25
Houston	13	11	27	31
Southern Mississippi	12	12	40	26
Alabama-Birmingham	11	12	31	26
Marshall	9	15	22	32
Central Florida	9	15	22	35
Memphis	7	16	21	32

ALL-CONFERENCE TEAM: C—Jeremy Schaffer, Fr., Tulane. **IF**—Victor Gomez, So., Marshall; Sam Honeck, Sr., Tulane; Anthony Rendon, Fr., Rice; Ryan Wood, Sr., East Carolina. **OF**—Stephen Batts, Sr., East Carolina; Bo Davis, Sr., Southern Miss; Brint Hardy, Sr., UAB. **DH**—Kyle Roller, Jr., East Carolina. **SP**—Ryan Berry, Jr., Rice; Chris Heston, Jr., East Carolina; Seth Maness, So., East Carolina; Todd McInnis, So., Southern Miss. **RP**—Donnie Joseph, Jr., Houston.

Player of the Year: Anthony Rendon, Rice. **Pitcher of the Year:** Todd McInnis, Southern Miss. **Freshman of the Year:** Anthony Rendon, Rice. **Newcomer of the Year:** Chris Heston, East Carolina. **Coach of the Year:** Billy Godwin, East Carolina.

INDIVIDUAL BATTING LEADERS
(Minimum 2.5 At-Bats Per Team Game)

	AVG	AB	R	H	2B	3B	HR	RBI	SB
Rendon, Anthony, Rice	.388	242	60	94	14	1	20	72	9
Wood, Ryan, East Carolina	.379	264	87	100	21	1	14	57	14
Whitehead, Trent, East Carolina	.376	279	78	105	24	2	7	47	10
Fuda, Michael, Rice	.359	181	43	65	14	2	3	21	8
Davis, Bo, Southern Miss	.359	209	67	75	6	4	14	53	10
Prince, Jared, Tulane	.353	218	54	77	15	4	6	31	48
Towe, Digger, UAB	.353	190	38	67	15	0	9	61	0
Batts, Stephen, East Carolina	.352	273	71	96	21	1	14	63	19
Holt, Brock, Rice	.348	250	67	87	13	2	12	43	11
Harris, Devin, East Carolina	.344	212	44	73	8	0	14	48	13
Brown, Shane, UCF	.341	214	39	73	20	0	6	44	2
McMurry, Cody, UAB	.339	192	58	65	18	1	11	51	3
Arnold, Colin, UCF	.337	184	41	62	9	3	5	20	7
Valle, Josh, Marshall	.337	199	46	67	14	2	4	35	0
Brunty, Kameron, Southern Miss	.336	229	62	77	9	4	7	53	7
Roller, Kyle, East Carolina	.336	256	63	86	12	1	16	75	4
Kelso, Blake, Houston	.335	254	45	85	16	3	2	23	12
Romans, Brandon, UCF	.333	195	39	65	9	0	14	49	3
Ramsey, Caleb, Houston	.332	238	41	79	11	2	4	46	16
Gomez, Victor, Marshall	.332	217	40	72	13	2	18	62	0
Henderson, Brandon, East Carolina	.330	212	34	70	12	0	13	57	5
Avchen, Jared, East Carolina	.330	176	27	58	8	1	2	29	0
Hardy, Brint, UAB	.326	218	65	71	12	1	5	50	46
Sultzbaugh, Steven, Rice	.324	222	47	72	6	6	8	31	7
Stevens, Corey, Southern Miss	.320	231	50	74	15	1	8	60	2
Mozingo, Chad, Rice	.319	216	47	69	16	3	8	50	10
Hague, Rick, Rice	.319	254	47	81	17	0	9	57	11
Manning, Andrew, UAB	.318	179	44	57	11	1	10	44	4
Harrington, Dustin, East Carolina	.318	261	53	83	15	0	14	49	4
Merritt, Jonathan, UAB	.317	230	48	73	18	5	2	30	20

INDIVIDUAL PITCHING LEADERS
(Minimum 1 Inning Per Team Game)

	W	L	ERA	G	SV	IP	H	BB	SO
Ojala, Mike, Rice	5	0	2.17	13	1	66	61	26	74
Berry, Ryan, Rice	7	2	2.42	14	1	82	56	19	68
Mincey, Brad, East Carolina	10	5	3.16	25	0	83	89	22	71
#Cargill, Collin, Southern Miss	4	3	3.55	28	13	38	31	22	32
Brandt, Kevin, East Carolina	9	2	3.64	28	0	82	73	24	72
#Simmons, Seth, East Carolina	3	1	3.69	33	9	39	36	20	50
Wall, Taylor, Rice	7	6	3.72	18	1	94	83	37	77
McInnis, Todd, Southern Miss	9	4	3.73	19	0	101	96	34	90
Farrell, Shane, Marshall	1	7	3.88	14	0	60	52	30	57
Flynn, Conrad, Tulane	8	3	3.93	14	0	87	91	7	58
Zeid, Josh, Tulane	6	0	4.01	14	0	76	68	28	45
Heston, Chris, East Carolina	7	0	4.17	17	0	91	90	32	88
Straily, Dan, Marshall	4	3	4.27	13	0	72	80	34	58

Ballinger, J.R., Southern Miss	6	4	4.40	18	0	86	95	39	59
Goodnight, Michael, Houston	5	5	4.43	15	0	65	68	31	58
Sweat, Kyle, UCF	3	4	4.60	18	1	74	86	20	50
Martin, Brennon, Memphis	6	4	4.66	13	0	83	95	18	59
Maness, Seth, East Carolina	9	3	4.71	18	2	107	123	18	83
Petiton, Matt, Tulane	5	3	5.13	15	0	67	71	23	45
Crawford, Shay, UAB	5	2	5.14	17	0	77	83	36	71
Ray, Jared, Houston	4	4	5.34	18	0	62	69	26	52
Roberson, Kyle, UAB	6	8	5.69	16	0	81	93	52	67

HORIZON LEAGUE

	Conference		Overall	
	W	L	W	L
Illinois-Chicago	17	6	29	23
Wisconsin-Milwaukee	14	9	28	27
*Wright State	14	12	33	30
Valparaiso	12	11	28	24
Cleveland State	12	13	21	31
Youngstown State	10	14	16	35
Butler	6	20	13	41

ALL-CONFERENCE TEAM: C—Matt Lenski, Sr., Vaparaiso. **1B**—Jeff Mercer, Sr., Wright State. **2B**—Andy Gerhartz, Sr., Wisconsin-Milwaukee. **3B**—Quentin Cate, Jr., Wright State. **SS**—Jacke Healey, Jr., Youngstown State. **OF**—Doug Dekoning, So., Wisconsin-Milwaukee; Casey McGrew, Jr., Wright State; Tim Patzman, Jr., Wisconsin-Milwaukee. **DH**—Josh Hungerman, Jr., Cleveland State. **UT**—Shawn Wozniak, Sr., Wisconsin-Milwaukee.

Player of the Year: Jeff Mercer, Wright State. **Pitcher of the Year:** Adam Worthington, Illinois-Chicago. **Rookie of the Year:** Quentin Cate, Wright State. **Coach of the Year:** Scott Doffek, Wisconsin-Milwaukee.

INDIVIDUAL BATTING LEADERS
(Minimum 125 At-Bats)

	AVG	AB	R	H	2B	3B	HR	RBI	SB
Lenski, Matt, Valparaiso	.406	170	33	69	16	0	5	43	2
Patzman, Tim, UWM	.389	193	39	75	18	2	11	44	3
Koehnlein, John, Youngstown State	.385	169	34	65	5	4	1	18	11
Groves, Josh, Cleveland State	.375	184	35	69	11	0	1	33	3
Mercer, Jeff, Wright State	.357	255	55	91	26	2	8	74	2
Cate, Quentin, Wright State	.352	250	47	88	17	1	12	57	4
Gundolff, R.J. Wright State	.347	222	52	77	7	5	2	24	9
Hungerman, Josh, Cleveland State	.345	194	41	67	11	2	11	50	4
McGrew, Casey, Wright State	.340	244	61	83	22	5	7	52	9
Dekonig, Doug, UWM	.338	198	44	68	13	1	5	28	6
Ganek, Jason, UIC	.333	189	35	67	13	1	5	7	5
Kraft, Cole, UWM	.333	186	37	68	6	2	1	32	6
Ashe, Ryan, Wright State	.330	206	37	68	6	2	1	32	2
Twede, Kory, Wright State	.329	216	33	71	17	1	8	45	9
Carr, Jake, UIC	.327	162	28	53	13	0	6	37	1
Schaefer, Brett, UIC	.323	158	31	51	12	0	4	33	1
Wozniak, Shawn, UWM	.320	200	39	64	16	0	8	39	4
Harwell, Brandon, UIC	.318	154	35	49	12	0	6	26	9
Fields, Aaron, Wright State	.314	226	36	71	12	0	2	25	7
Duncan, Luke, Butler	.308	156	25	48	3	4	0	22	3
Johnson, Alex, Cleveland State	.307	205	33	63	13	6	4	32	11
Scoby, Steven, Valparaiso	.307	176	34	54	7	1	1	22	6
Federico, Josh, Cleveland State	.304	138	19	42	6	0	0	10	8
Wynn, Tyler, Cleveland State	.303	155	28	47	5	0	11	35	3
Carter, Tom, Cleveland State	.302	172	30	52	6	0	4	22	6
Fillipitch, Grant, Butler	.302	202	32	61	17	0	7	30	1
Debruin, Dan, Valparaiso	.299	187	38	56	10	1	1	27	12
Leonard, Andy, UIC	.294	218	35	64	22	0	2	32	3
Healey, Jacke, Youngstown State	.293	188	37	55	17	1	8	36	7
#Gerhartz, Andy, UWM	.260	208	39	54	9	2	1	24	23

INDIVIDUAL PITCHING LEADERS
(Minimum 50 Innings)

	W	L	ERA	G	SV	IP	H	BB	SO
Schum, Michael, Wright State	5	7	1.95	34	13	74	62	10	57
#Miller, Jarad, Valparaiso	0	2	2.16	23	17	25	16	14	27
Kaminsky, Alex, Wright State	6	2	2.66	13	0	85	100	9	54
Worthington, Adam, UIC	4	5	3.48	15	0	96	93	21	73
Shafer, Bryce, Valparaiso	7	3	3.59	14	0	85	79	38	79

	W	L	ERA	G	SV	IP	H	BB	SO
Kovacevich, Chris, UIC	7	4	3.69	17	0	90	104	15	53
Heesch, Michael, UIC	5	0	4.02	21	0	54	54	17	32
Ostrosky, Rylan, Wright State	5	6	4.54	14	0	71	77	27	45
Hungerman, Josh, Cleveland State	5	6	4.60	13	0	88	75	37	91
Klein, Phil, Youngstown State	5	2	4.62	17	1	76	71	33	80
Lusti, Brad, UWM	5	4	4.94	14	0	93	110	18	68
Dearth, Cody, Youngstown State	2	5	4.96	13	0	53	67	22	25
Berry, Alex, Valparaiso	3	5	5.00	13	0	77	84	16	54
Schmidt, Kyle, UWM	3	4	5.13	13	0	60	68	19	43
Gulbransen, Jon, Valparaiso	5	7	5.33	13	0	79	91	15	57
Wagoner, Jared, Butler	0	5	5.59	17	0	58	71	22	46
Woytek, Michael, Wright State	4	3	5.89	3	0	66	91	24	46
Hetebrueg, Andy, UWM	3	4	5.93	13	0	71	79	27	50
Sinkiewicz, Jeff, Butler	1	6	6.05	16	1	58	79	13	40
Swenson, Aaron, Youngstown State	3	6	6.10	15	0	90	120	26	70
Kool, Mike, UIC	5	7	6.15	15	0	75	103	23	37

IVY LEAGUE

GEHRIG	Conference		Overall	
	W	L	W	L
Princeton	10	10	18	19
Cornell	10	10	17	23
Columbia	7	13	11	32
Penn	5	15	17	24

ROLFE	Conference		Overall	
*Dartmouth	16	4	27	18
Brown	15	5	24	19
Harvard	10	10	13	28
Yale	7	13	13	24

ALL-CONFERENCE TEAM: C—Jack Murphy, Jr., Princeton. **1B**—Trygg Larsson-Danforth, Jr., Yale. **2B**—Matt Nuzzo, Sr., Brown. **3B**—Nathan Ford, Sr., Cornell. **SS**—Joe Sclafani, Fr., Dartmouth. **OF**— Steve Daniels, Sr., Brown; Nick Santomauro, Jr., Dartmouth; Jim Wren, Jr., Dartmouth. **DH**—Ray Allen, Sr., Dartmouth. **UT**—Robert Papenhause, Sr., Brown. **Player of the Year:** Nick Santomauro, Dartmouth. **Pitcher of the Year:** Brandon Josselyn, Yale. **Rookie of the Year:** Joe Sclafani, Dartmouth. **Coach of the Year:** Bob Whalen, Dartmouth.

INDIVIDUAL BATTING LEADERS
(Minimum 100 At-Bats)

	AVG	AB	R	H	2B	3B	HR	RBI	SB
Brian Billigen, Cornell	.404	114	25	46	6	3	1	16	9
Papenhause, Robert, Brown	.377	151	40	57	11	2	6	33	2
Santomauro, Nick, Dartmouth	.372	164	41	61	13	0	8	40	1
Ford, Nathan, Cornell	.370	146	32	54	9	1	9	36	2
Grandieri, Tom, Pennsylvania	.357	157	42	56	19	0	5	32	0
Maas, Jeremy, Pennsylvania	.356	132	28	47	14	2	4	27	1
DeGeorge, Dan, Princeton	.349	152	26	53	12	2	2	21	2
Larsson-Danforth, Trygg, Yale	.344	131	27	45	7	1	7	37	5
Shapiro, Dan, Brown	.343	134	31	46	7	0	4	22	6
Douglas, Harry, Harvard	.342	152	29	52	13	2	3	27	8
Pagliarulo, Mike, Dartmouth	.340	150	36	51	12	1	6	40	0
Greskoff, Pete, Brown	.339	112	26	38	3	1	11	36	0
Sclafani, Joe, Dartmouth	.339	174	50	59	6	6	2	35	3
Williams, Dan, Pennsylvania	.337	166	38	56	10	1	4	42	4
Vigoa, Derek, Pennsylvania	.336	152	31	51	18	0	4	27	2
Allen, Ray, Dartmouth	.335	158	37	53	8	2	10	44	0
Meehan, Taylor, Harvard	.331	154	29	51	10	0	2	19	7
Eisen, Jon, Columbia	.331	145	25	48	7	1	0	20	11
Megee, Andy, Yale	.329	143	25	47	11	4	1	16	9
Gordon, Will, Pennsylvania	.327	153	27	50	12	2	10	48	0
Wren, Jim, Dartmouth	.325	154	25	50	11	1	5	44	0
Rogers, Matt, Harvard	.324	145	23	47	10	2	9	33	6
Schropp, Stefan, Yale	.324	139	24	45	8	1	3	28	6
Nuzzo, Matt, Brown	.324	173	34	56	14	2	11	45	1
O'Neill, Dillon, Harvard	.322	152	32	49	9	2	1	20	8
Santopadre, Johnathon, Dartmouth	.322	146	35	47	10	2	5	29	4
Tobolowsky, Zach, Yale	.320	100	13	32	6	1	5	18	1
Langseth, Matt, Cornell	.316	117	18	37	6	0	1	11	5
Daniels, Steve, Brown	.314	172	45	54	7	3	8	33	23
Gardner, Brett, Dartmouth	.314	102	24	32	5	1	4	22	6

INDIVIDUAL PITCHING LEADERS
(Minimum 40 Innings)

	W	L	ERA	G	SV	IP	H	BB	SO
Palms, David, Princeton	5	2	3.06	10	0	50	49	12	28
Schmeltzer, Jadd, Cornell	2	3	4.01	9	0	43	40	23	42
Josselyn, Brandon, Yale	5	3	4.29	11	0	57	57	15	51
Hale, David, Princeton	2	3	4.43	8	0	41	41	24	47
Gormley, Mark, Brown	6	2	4.55	12	0	61	56	13	50
Young, Robert, Dartmouth	5	4	4.63	12	0	68	81	22	42
Wilcox, Rob, Brown	4	2	4.76	14	0	59	76	9	31
Hendricks, Kyle, Dartmouth	6	3	4.84	12	0	67	84	15	50
Murray, Ben, Dartmouth	6	1	5.27	12	0	56	74	11	33
Pappel, Corey, Cornell	2	3	5.36	9	0	40	35	24	43
Scarlata, Joe, Columbia	4	5	5.52	10	0	60	71	12	30
Suter, Brent, Harvard	3	4	5.77	9	0	53	66	13	53
#Smith, Ryan, Dartmouth	2	3	5.88	25	11	34	42	4	28
Hulse, Conner, Harvard	1	5	6.11	12	0	56	79	18	33
Stuber, Langford, Princeton	3	4	6.12	8	0	43	52	21	35
Bracey, Dan, Columbia	2	6	6.23	9	0	48	64	11	24
McNulty, Chris, Pennsylvania	2	2	6.36	14	1	47	56	18	28
Aquino, Roger, Columbia	1	3	6.64	12	0	42	49	10	19
Cusick, Paul, Pennsylvania	4	3	6.64	10	0	42	48	26	43
Matt Hill, Cornell	2	6	6.66	11	0	53	62	20	41
#Gemberling, Brad, Princeton	5	3	6.67	10	0	55	67	17	73

METRO ATLANTIC ATHLETIC CONFERENCE

	Conference		Overall	
	W	L	W	L
Manhattan	18	6	35	18
Canisius	16	8	36	22
*Marist	15	9	31	28
Rider	14	10	26	23
Niagara	14	10	20	35
Fairfield	10	14	20	27
Siena	9	15	15	35
St. Peter's	7	17	17	37
Iona	5	19	6	40

ALL-CONFERENCE TEAM: C—Sean Olson, Sr., Rider. **1B**—Kevin Quaranto, So., Siena. **2B**—Kevin Mailloux, Sr., Canisius **3B**—Kevin Mahoney, Sr., Canisius. **SS**—Conor Mullee, Jr., St. Peter's. **OF**—Ian Choy, Jr., Canisius; Mike McCann, So., Manhattan; Kevin Nieto, Jr., Manhattan. **DH**—Anthony Armenio, Jr., Manhattan. **UTIL**—Anthony Giansanti, Jr., Siena. **SP**—Rob Gariano, Jr., Fairfield; Mike Gazzola, Jr., Manhattan; Michael Kellar, Sr., Niagara. **RP**—Jacob Wiley, Sr., Marist. **Player of the Year:** Kevin Mahoney, Canisius. **Pitcher of the Year:** Mike Gazzola, Manhattan. **Freshman of the Year:** Dan Paolini, Siena. **Coach of the Year:** Kevin Leighton, Manhattan.

INDIVIDUAL BATTING LEADERS
(Minimum 125 At-Bats)

	AVG	AB	R	H	2B	3B	HR	RBI	SB
Paolini, Dan, Siena	.430	200	42	86	12	3	11	53	7
Nieto, Kevin, Manhattan	.396	187	72	74	16	6	13	54	25
Perez, Ruben, Manhattan	.393	214	44	84	20	0	4	48	4
McCann, Mike, Manhattan	.388	219	65	85	17	1	13	59	10
Mailloux, Kevin, Canisius	.381	226	59	86	14	2	16	56	12
Salem, Chad, Manhattan	.380	205	51	78	13	1	8	45	3
Nathans, Tucker, Fairfield	.377	183	33	69	14	4	3	41	9
Choy, Ian, Canisius	.359	167	35	60	10	0	9	36	1
Deering, Brian, Niagara	.356	163	29	58	13	3	6	39	1
Giansanti, Anthony, Siena	.355	214	52	76	15	3	14	37	20
Onorati, Mark, Manhattan	.351	222	64	78	16	1	5	54	14
Olson, Sean, Rider	.351	185	50	65	10	0	12	58	2
Sheffield, Austin, Manhattan	.349	209	47	73	13	2	7	47	1
Quaranto, Kevin, Siena	.341	176	41	60	16	0	7	47	0
Willson, Shayne, Canisius	.340	194	46	66	14	2	9	37	8
Rafferty, Bill, Fairfield	.338	154	30	52	7	1	1	12	13
DeVito, Carmine, Fairfield	.336	128	24	43	9	3	1	18	5
Pacione, Ricky, Marist	.335	233	39	78	14	5	8	51	5
Albee, A.J., Rider	.333	183	44	61	15	3	5	32	3
Mahoney, Kevin, Canisius	.330	209	67	69	19	1	22	62	19
Hayes, James, Rider	.330	188	55	62	13	0	2	28	26
Fitzgerald, Jamie, Manhattan	.323	164	28	53	6	0	2	28	1

	AVG	AB	R	H	2B	3B	HR	RBI	SB
Nugent, Bryce, Marist	.318	179	28	57	9	0	8	42	1
Carter, Justyn, St. Peter's	.316	190	43	60	10	3	3	20	31
Williams, Maurice, Rider	.315	146	30	46	10	1	2	22	4
McQuail, Steve, Canisius	.314	188	42	59	14	0	10	45	3
Meyer, Kyle, Marist	.312	170	42	53	8	2	4	34	9
Koster, Brian, St. Peter's	.311	190	26	59	10	0	1	34	2
McDonough, Brian, Marist	.308	214	38	66	13	2	1	40	6
Armenio, Anthony, Manhattan	.308	198	49	61	22	0	9	61	0
#Joseph, Branson, Canisius	.305	220	42	67	13	7	7	57	16

INDIVIDUAL PITCHING LEADERS
(Minimum 50 Innings)

	W	L	ERA	G	SV	IP	H	BB	SO
#Wiley, Jacob, Marist	9	1	2.82	30	6	38	41	15	35
Gariano, Rob, Fairfield	5	4	3.43	12	0	84	77	19	88
Putnam, Kyle, Marist	4	4	4.08	15	1	75	89	20	46
Gazzola, Mike, Manhattan	7	1	4.15	14	0	93	91	45	54
Hasett, Will, Siena	3	3	4.30	15	0	75	75	30	56
Martin, B.J., Marist	5	6	4.36	15	0	87	84	39	96
Giordano, Mike, Manhattan	6	4	4.43	16	0	61	71	19	36
#Hayes, James, Rider	2	2	4.50	17	7	22	23	16	32
Robertson, Sam, Fairfield	2	2	4.67	11	0	54	51	28	45
Goemans, Mike, Canisius	7	6	4.68	15	0	90	104	32	48
Kellar, Michael, Niagara	6	4	4.88	13	0	76	84	42	50
Spaulding, Marcus, Niagara	4	5	5.06	12	0	75	87	32	60
Costigan, Tom, Manhattan	7	2	5.40	19	0	80	94	27	73
Callahan, Brian, Iona	3	5	5.46	11	0	58	70	22	21
Jackson, Ethan, St. Peter's	3	9	5.54	13	0	67	86	22	41
Jordan, Matt, Manhattan	4	5	5.56	15	1	55	67	35	47
Fico, Kevin, Fairfield	4	5	5.57	10	0	52	68	12	35
Rickards, Josh, Marist	5	3	5.60	16	0	80	84	50	53
Hughes, Craig, St. Peter's	4	5	5.88	19	1	64	75	29	54
Candelmo, Joe, Niagara	3	6	6.15	14	1	60	77	24	39
MacKenzie, Alex, Canisius	4	3	6.15	14	1	87	107	23	63
Sumple, Kyle, Siena	2	6	6.51	17	1	55	70	16	48
#Davis, Shane, Canisius	9	2	6.84	13	0	79	115	21	55

MID-AMERICAN CONFERENCE

	Conference		Overall	
EAST	W	L	W	L
Bowling Green State	18	8	28	22
Ohio	18	9	29	24
*Kent State	17	9	43	17
Miami (Ohio)	15	12	30	25
Akron	12	15	19	33
Buffalo	6	20	20	35
WEST	W	L	W	L
Ball State	14	10	26	25
Toledo	14	12	24	30
Eastern Michigan	13	14	25	35
Central Michigan	12	15	28	30
Northern Illinois	10	16	19	34
Western Michigan	8	18	14	35

ALL-CONFERENCE TEAM: C—Zach Dygert, Jr., Ball State. **1B**—Tom Nurre, Sr., Miami (Ohio). **2B**—Logan Meisler, Jr., Bowling Green. **3B**—Marc Krauss, Jr., Ohio. **SS**—Ryan Shay, Sr., Bowling Green State. **OF**—Adam Eaton, So., Miami (Ohio); Gauntlett Eldemire, So., Ohio; Jeremy Hazelbaker, Jr., Ball State. **DH**—Matt Skirving, So., Eastern Michigan. **UT**—Kolbrin Vitek, So., Ball State. **SP**—Matt Erwood, Sr., Miami (Ohio); Matt Malewitz, So., Bowling Green State; Chris Rigo, Sr., Ohio; Brennan Smith, So., Bowling Green State. **RP**—Andrew Chafin, Fr., Kent State.

Player of the Year: Marc Krauss, Ohio. **Pitcher of the Year:** Brennan Smith, Bowling Green State. **Freshman of the Year:** Andrew Chafin, Kent State. **Coach of the Year:** Danny Schmitz, Bowling Green State.

INDIVIDUAL BATTING LEADERS
(Minimum 125 At-Bats)

	AVG	AB	R	H	2B	3B	HR	RBI	SB
Hazelbaker, Jeremy, Ball State	.429	203	77	87	17	8	9	38	29
Elkins, Tyler, Bowling Green	.406	165	35	67	16	1	1	31	2
Nurre, Tommy, Miami (Ohio)	.406	202	53	82	18	1	17	54	16
Krauss, Marc, Ohio	.402	209	73	84	13	0	27	70	6
Johnson, Hayden, Ohio	.393	234	61	92	25	4	13	47	3

	AVG	AB	R	H	2B	3B	HR	RBI	SB
Vitek, Kolbrin, Ball State	.389	208	57	81	25	4	13	67	17
Shay, Ryan, Bowling Green	.387	212	70	82	17	3	13	52	18
Dudics, Chris, Toledo	.386	153	30	59	8	1	1	17	2
Spencer, Derek, Bowling Green	.385	192	50	74	9	2	15	59	2
Hood, Jordin, Northern Illinois	.382	199	57	76	15	2	10	46	14
Cielsa, Chris, Buffalo	.372	226	49	84	18	3	4	44	7
Berti, Jon, Bowling Green	.368	136	38	50	6	5	5	34	9
Petraitis, Jordan, Miami (Ohio)	.364	217	57	79	14	3	8	54	8
Meisler, Logan, Bowling Green	.361	194	36	70	8	1	4	45	1
Reynolds, Dave, Northern Illinois	.361	194	42	70	12	1	8	44	3
Dager, Pedro, Western Michigan	.360	161	29	58	13	1	3	19	3
Plata, Jake, Akron	.357	168	37	60	13	0	3	28	0
Nadeau, Chris, Miami (Ohio)	.356	233	42	83	19	2	5	50	3
Rider, Jimmy, Kent State	.353	218	62	77	11	2	5	46	5
Nielsen, Ian, Ball State	.352	216	34	76	15	2	9	53	2
Eaton, Adam, Miami (Ohio)	.350	214	67	75	12	6	11	48	28
Dygert, Zach, Ball State	.350	197	42	69	19	0	9	53	5
Rhoad, Kyle, Eastern Michigan	.349	232	69	81	13	2	12	34	32
Rohan, Greg, Kent State	.349	238	58	83	15	1	15	63	1
Skriving, Matt Eastern Michigan	.348	201	43	70	12	0	16	64	1
Tremblay, Chris, Kent State	.349	242	66	84	12	4	2	33	6
Kordal, Brian, Akron	.346	188	41	65	12	4	5	44	2
Roberts, Matt, Akron	.343	210	54	72	12	2	10	41	6
Yakubik, Jerod, Ohio	.342	190	39	65	12	1	5	37	3
Blanton, T.J., Bowling Green	.341	176	44	60	11	4	8	29	11
#Fields, Nate, Ball State	.308	208	56	64	16	1	1	30	32

INDIVIDUAL PITCHING LEADERS
(Minimum 50 Innings)

	W	L	ERA	G	SV	IP	H	BB	SO
Zelasko, Tom, Northern Illinois	2	4	3.26	32	4	47	45	24	53
#Dawes, Samuel, Miami (Ohio)	1	0	4.02	34	1	31	36	22	20
Kuna, Matt, Toledo	5	2	4.23	12	0	62	71	18	44
Smith, Brennan, Bowling Green	8	4	4.41	15	0	82	76	31	80
Erwood, Matt, Miami (Ohio)	7	3	4.46	14	0	79	95	11	53
Taylor, Dan, Central Michigan	4	7	4.53	14	0	87	106	22	80
Hallock, Kyle, Kent State	4	3	4.57	14	1	65	77	27	42
Howard, Trent, Central Michigan	5	2	4.71	13	0	65	71	16	52
Butt, Bryce, Ohio	6	6	4.80	24	5	60	77	19	52
Henderson, Bobby, Eastern Michigan	2	2	4.96	21	1	51	58	12	26
#Zahel, Matt, Toledo	2	0	5.14	19	9	21	25	12	12
Piatt, Brad, Ball State	5	2	5.34	14	0	62	80	23	36
Melling, Tyler, Miami (Ohio)	6	3	5.35	13	0	71	73	26	49
Malewitz, Matt, Bowling Green	5	3	5.62	14	0	80	80	35	53
Lukanen, Chuck, Northern Illinois	7	6	5.65	13	0	80	103	36	61
Vitek, Kolbrin, Ball State	4	3	5.65	12	0	57	62	9	56
Teno, Steve, Central Michigan	4	8	5.68	15	0	84	107	25	79
Stines, Brenden, Ball State	4	4	5.77	17	0	64	89	32	43
Lewis, Kendall, Eastern Michigan	4	5	5.80	16	0	50	67	29	30
Danziger, Benjamin, Akron	3	4	5.81	15	0	74	95	16	58
Glover, Jordan, Eastern Michigan	3	5	6.31	16	0	56	71	27	49
Heckaman, Eric, Western Michigan	3	3	6.41	12	0	59	66	27	35

MID-EASTERN ATHLETIC CONFERENCE

	Conference		Overall	
	W	L	W	L
*Bethune-Cookman	16	2	32	28
Florida A&M	10	8	24	30
Delaware State	10	8	19	25
Norfolk State	9	9	22	23
North Carolina A&T	9	9	22	23
Maryland-Eastern Shore	9	9	14	42
Coppin State	1	18	0	29

ALL-CONFERENCE TEAM: C—Peter O'Brien, Fr., Bethune-Cookman. **IF**—Ross Babineaux, Sr., Delaware State; Anselmo Cantu, Sr., Norfolk State; Jared Jeffries, Jr., Florida A&M; Tim Schalch, Jr., Florida A&M. **OF**—C.J. Beatty, Jr., North Carolina A&T; C.J. Lauriello, Jr., Bethune-Cookman; Xavier Macklin, Fr., North Carolina A&T. **DH**—Derrick Shaw, Fr., Florida A&M. **SP**—Dan Perkins, Sr., Delaware State; Ali Simpson, Fr., Bethune-Cookman. **RP**—Brandon Penick, Jr., Delaware State.

Player of the Year: Ross Babineaux, Delaware State. **Pitcher of the Year:** Dan Perkins, Delaware State. **Freshman of the Year:** Ali Simpson, Bethune-Cookman. **Coach of the Year:** Mervyl Melendez, Bethune-Cookman.

INDIVIDUAL BATTING LEADERS
(Minimum 125 At-Bats)

	AVG	AB	R	H	2B	3B	HR	RBI	SB
Jeffries, Jared, Florida A&M	.425	167	52	71	16	4	0	27	20
Babineaux, Ross, Delaware State	.414	145	30	60	8	1	1	33	11
Lauriello, C.J., B-CU	.398	181	45	72	19	2	4	36	12
Martin, Stavone, Florida A&M	.377	138	31	52	10	1	2	33	10
Eubank, Abe, Delaware State	.375	128	25	48	5	0	10	32	0
Macklin, Xavier, N.C. A&T	.371	205	53	76	20	5	10	48	14
Schalch, Timothy, Florida A&M	.370	181	38	67	3	1	0	25	7
Beatty, C.J., N.C. A&T	.368	185	50	68	25	2	8	42	9
Shaw, Derrick, Florida A&M	.366	172	34	63	9	2	3	42	3
Cantu, Anselmo, N.C. A&T	.350	157	34	55	9	2	7	31	7
Hairston, Brandon, Norfolk State	.348	155	38	54	11	1	1	23	5
Castro, Emmanuel, B-CU	.343	175	36	60	14	2	4	36	1
Evans, Darryl, Florida A&M	.342	228	57	78	19	5	6	46	32
Riley, Marquis, N.C. A&T	.338	142	32	48	12	0	3	21	6
Lynch, John, Norfolk State	.332	187	48	62	5	7	3	27	17
Jimenez, Alejandro, B-CU	.331	178	43	59	9	2	9	32	21
Rogers, Nick, N.C. A&T	.330	209	7	69	19	1	11	47	5
Farley, Jerrod, Norfolk State	.325	154	39	50	9	2	7	43	20
Suttmiller, Andrew, Norfolk State	.314	153	25	48	8	3	0	25	2
Vaughn, Phil, UMES	.310	184	34	57	6	4	1	30	28
Brown, Chris, B-CU	.310	168	35	52	16	2	8	29	4
Durrence, Ryan, B-CU	.307	153	36	47	14	1	11	48	2
Bittner, Justin, Delaware State	.307	153	36	47	11	0	7	42	6
Rizzuto, Mike, Delaware State	.305	128	36	39	7	1	1	17	1
Joyce, Chris, Norfolk State	.298	171	35	51	12	1	3	35	2
Adeyemi, Tobi, Florida A&M	.295	183	41	54	6	4	1	29	16
Brooks, Mark, B-CU	.291	151	34	44	4	1	2	24	16
Sanchez, Jose, Delaware State	.291	158	34	46	8	0	0	28	5
Hercinger, Pat, UMES	.285	186	29	53	6	2	1	23	4
Alston, Elliott, UMES	.284	169	28	48	9	1	2	15	12
Hines, George, N.C. A&T	.272	180	37	49	11	3	7	27	17
Griffin, TiQuan, Norfolk State	.270	126	25	34	3	0	1	20	14

INDIVIDUAL PITCHING LEADERS
(Minimum 50 Innings)

	W	L	ERA	G	SV	IP	H	BB	SO
#Penick, Brandon, Delaware State	0	2	2.16	22	5	25	22	7	22
Perkins, Dan, Delaware State	5	5	2.75	15	0	85	62	28	86
Simpson, Ali, B-CU	9	2	3.23	16	0	75	68	32	79
Burgos, Hiram, B-CU	6	3	3.74	14	0	79	73	24	94
Paulino, Esterlin, N.C. A&T	5	5	4.09	17	1	73	73	29	58
Davenport, Chase, Norfolk State	6	5	4.33	15	0	62	70	35	42
Parga, Miguel, Florida A&M	4	4	4.48	11	0	62	64	32	41
Barker, Jason, Norfolk State	6	3	4.78	16	1	85	106	34	47
Quinn Bright, Norfolk State	5	5	4.86	17	1	76	111	20	71
Thomas, Eric, B-CU	7	6	5.09	18	0	81	81	43	83
Munoz, Joseph, B-CU	3	6	5.14	20	2	56	7	22	35
Schalch, Timothy, Florida A&M	4	3	5.89	12	1	66	90	21	41
McCraw, Blaine, N.C. A&T	1	8	6.43	16	0	56	68	32	34
White, Matt, UMES	3	4	6.45	18	0	67	96	40	49
Schmidt, Josh, Delaware State	4	8	6.45	17	1	84	115	31	77
Smith, Jonathan, N.C. A&T	1	1	6.62	23	2	50	72	24	44
Espin, Anthony, Florida A&M	6	9	7.70	18	0	104	142	89	83
Watson, Chris, N.C. A&T	4	4	7.74	15	0	62	88	38	31
Deutschmann, Russel, UMES	2	8	8.04	14	0	59	104	16	19
Deschamps, John, UMES	3	5	8.25	23	1	80	127	29	47
#Garrett Braun, N.C. A&T	0	2	8.38	24	3	39	59	24	22
Zimmerman, Cameron, UMES	2	8	8.48	21	0	74	107	46	45

MISSOURI VALLEY CONFERENCE

	Conference		Overall	
	W	L	W	L
Missouri State	17	5	34	20
Indiana State	15	7	33	21
*Wichita State	11	7	30	27
Creighton	14	9	31	25
Southern Illinois	11	9	24	28
Illinois State	11	11	25	23
Northern Iowa	7	15	23	26
Evansville	7	17	25	30
Bradley	4	17	17	31

ALL-CONFERENCE TEAM: C—Dallas Hord, Jr., Missouri State. **1B**—Clint McKeever, Jr., Wichita State. **2B**—Kevin Medrano, Fr., Missouri State. **3B**—Brayden Drake, Sr., Missouri State. **SS**—Elliot Soto, So., Creighton. **OF**—Ben Carlson, Jr., Missouri State; Nick Ciolli, Jr., Indiana State; Brady Shoemaker, Sr., Indiana State. **DH**—Tyler Bullock, Jr., Southern Illinois. **UT**—Ryan Strausborger, Jr., Indiana State. **SP**—Buddy Baumann, Jr., Missouri State; Aaron Meade, So., Missouri State; Joe Rodriguez, Jr., Indiana State. **RP**—Bryant George, Jr., Southern Illinois; Jack Van Leur, So., Creighton.

Player of the Year: Brayden Drake, Missouri State. **Pitcher of the Year:** Buddy Baumann, Missouri State. **Newcomer of the Year:** Travis Bennett, Northern Iowa. **Freshman of the Year:** Kevin Medrano, Missouri State. **Coach of the Year:** Lindsay Meggs, Indiana State.

INDIVIDUAL BATTING LEADERS
(Minimum 125 At-Bats)

	AVG	AB	R	H	2B	3B	HR	RBI	SB
Drake, Brayden, Missouri State	.414	191	43	79	19	0	10	54	8
Ciolli, Nick, Indiana State	.401	222	51	89	18	3	5	50	11
Shoemaker, Brady, Indiana State	.389	203	65	79	19	1	14	50	11
Fieser, Luke, Indiana State	.351	191	48	67	9	1	2	31	2
Hord, Dallas, Missouri State	.347	196	41	68	11	3	8	37	11
Knight, Robbie, Creighton	.344	224	48	77	18	4	2	42	7
Strausborger, Ryan, Indiana State	.340	238	57	81	5	4	6	26	21
Bennett, Travis, Northern Iowa	.338	198	34	67	15	3	3	43	6
Brown, Taylor, Wichita State	.338	154	18	52	8	0	0	13	3
Mitidiero, Nick, Bradley	.337	175	30	59	10	0	4	27	12
Lafrenz, Bronco, Indiana State	.335	173	36	58	14	0	13	56	0
Kelly, Mark, Southern Illinois	.333	219	26	73	15	0	4	39	0
McKeever, Clinton, Wichita State	.333	216	34	72	18	1	6	43	6
Pascoe, Andy, Evansville	.331	175	20	58	9	0	1	21	2
Medrano, Kevin, Missouri State	.329	231	53	76	13	2	3	40	0
Stalowy, Mike, Illinois State	.328	183	41	60	15	4	3	38	12
Serritella, Chris, Southern Illinois	.325	160	32	52	8	2	4	24	0
Fitzgerald, Tommy, Bradley	.324	173	37	56	13	2	4	31	4
Douglas, Brett, Northern Iowa	.324	173	33	56	10	0	4	28	4
Court, Ryan, Illinois State	.323	164	40	53	8	2	5	41	3
Soto, Elliot, Creighton	.322	239	43	77	7	1	0	26	13
Becker, Nick, Creighton	.318	179	30	57	9	1	4	29	3
Taliaferro, Jeff, Northern Iowa	.316	193	27	61	22	0	1	35	0
Ruffolo, Anthony, Illinois State	.315	168	30	53	9	1	4	29	3
Cafaro, Vicente, Creighton	.313	198	36	62	16	2	5	35	4
Jim Viscomi, Evansville	.311	196	41	61	16	0	6	28	26
Kohli, Evan, Illinois State	.308	159	32	49	13	0	3	32	5
Salzenstein, Collin, Illinois State	.308	185	33	57	12	3	0	23	10
Fick, Cody, Evansville	.307	228	44	70	19	2	9	46	7
Playter, Chris, Missouri State	.307	215	43	66	14	3	2	46	15
#Carlson, Ben, Missouri State	.301	186	49	56	14	1	16	51	9
#Conway, Aaron, Missouri State	.291	220	58	64	10	8	4	29	18

INDIVIDUAL PITCHING LEADERS
(Minimum 50 Innings)

	W	L	ERA	G	SV	IP	H	BB	SO
Cooper, Jordan, Wichita State	8	6	2.78	15	0	97	87	20	91
Kelley, Tim, Wichita State	5	4	2.86	14	0	94	83	22	102
Lowell, Charlie, Wichita State	6	2	2.95	12	0	64	55	33	63
Carbonell, J.R., Evansville	3	1	3.14	28	2	52	43	24	53
Dunn, Andrew, Southern Illinois	8	4	3.15	18	0	71	84	10	29
Baumann, Buddy, Missouri State	11	1	3.23	14	0	86	71	32	101
Cornell, Jimmy, Southern Illinois	2	2	3.26	15	0	66	50	40	66
Meade, Aaron, Missouri State	9	2	3.39	15	1	90	79	31	89
Bircher, Joe, Bradley	4	2	3.39	14	0	64	67	17	50
Kirk, Nick, Northern Iowa	6	5	3.51	13	0	90	82	31	89
Copeland, Tom, Illinois State	4	5	3.63	14	1	92	84	15	69
#Fujiya, Shuhei, Northern Iowa	1	4	3.97	21	9	23	20	15	29
Foley, John, Evansville	6	3	3.77	18	1	86	97	18	58
Hauer, Jeremy, Creighton	2	6	3.78	20	0	81	81	24	63
Scahill, Rob, Bradley	3	3	4.05	10	0	60	55	30	59
Maines, Corey, Illinois State	6	5	4.26	14	0	87	86	29	69
Dufek, Jonas, Creighton	4	7	4.33	16	0	79	90	18	52
#VanLeur, Jack, Creighton	3	4	4.44	36	6	49	49	15	31
Curyinski, Adam, Southern Illinois	5	4	4.52	14	0	82	85	29	39
Camp, Ryan, Illinois State	6	3	4.73	13	0	78	72	44	50
Hellhake, Greg, Creighton	5	3	4.73	15	0	70	69	28	39
Petricka, Jacob, Indiana State	7	3	4.76	13	0	74	87	34	49

MOUNTAIN WEST CONFERENCE

	Conference		Overall	
	W	L	W	L
Texas Christian	15	5	40	18
New Mexico	15	8	37	20
San Diego State	15	9	41	23
Brigham Young	14	8	30	24
Nevada-Las Vegas	9	15	26	32
*Utah	8	16	9	28
Air Force	3	18	14	37

ALL-CONFERENCE TEAM: C—Rafael Neda, So., New Mexico. **1B**—Kevin Atkinson, Sr., New Mexico; Matt Vern, Sr., TCU. **2B**—Mike Brownstein, Sr., New Mexico. **3B**—Steve Parker, Jr., BYU. **SS**—Anthony Morel, Sr., UNLV. **OF**—Brian Cavazos-Galvez, Sr., New Mexico; J.J. Sferra, Sr., UNLV; Cory Vaughn, So., San Diego State. **DH/UTIL**—Kent Walton, Sr., BYU. **SP**—Trent Appleby, So., TCU; John Hesketh, Sr., New Mexico; Stephen Strasburg, Jr., San Diego State. **RP**—Addison Reed, So., San Diego State. **Player of the Year:** Mike Brownstein, New Mexico. **Pitcher of the Year:** Stephen Strasburg, San Diego State. **Freshman of the Year:** C.J. Cron, Utah. **Coach of the Year:** Jim Schlossnagle, TCU.

INDIVIDUAL BATTING LEADERS
(Minimum 125 At-Bats)

	AVG	AB	R	H	2B	3B	HR	RBI	SB
Neda, Rafael, New Mexico	.415	205	57	85	19	2	7	49	0
Brownstein, Mike, New Mexico	.414	244	72	101	23	11	1	49	20
Honeycutt, Ryan, New Mexico	.406	197	42	80	14	1	6	53	0
Atkinson, Kevin, New Mexico	.400	230	59	92	15	6	4	61	3
Cavazos-Galvez, Brian, New Mexico	.392	217	64	85	16	7	15	3	17
Alexander, Matt, Air Force	.383	214	53	82	19	3	15	65	4
Castro, Erik, San Diego State	.382	217	49	83	20	0	11	56	3
Walton, Kent, BYU	.377	199	50	75	10	2	9	41	16
Hamilton, Dane, New Mexico	.372	180	45	67	19	7	4	46	1
Sferra, J.J., UNLV	.364	236	47	86	9	6	0	22	5
Vern, Matt, TCU	.363	193	59	70	13	1	16	52	16
Parker, Steve, BYU	.361	205	52	74	13	4	9	34	6
Bowen, Michael, BYU	.355	200	38	71	15	1	6	53	13
Willett, Max, New Mexico	.355	220	50	78	15	2	4	46	12
Banks, Stetson, BYU	.354	178	33	63	9	1	3	18	23
Kuroczko, Nick, Utah	.353	224	47	79	10	9	6	44	4
Gentry, Addison, Air Force	.347	193	45	67	13	2	9	40	1
Walker, Daniel, Air Force	.346	156	24	54	5	2	2	26	9
Wright, Jesse, UNLV	.345	197	61	68	13	3	10	37	5
Shimada, Corey, Utah	.342	240	64	82	9	2	7	38	16
Yagi, Tyler, Utah	.341	182	32	62	12	1	0	33	1
Ellington, Chris, TCU	.341	229	40	78	21	2	6	52	2
Frierson, Jarred, UNLV	.340	191	35	65	7	4	4	35	4
Carpenter, Matt, TCU	.338	201	57	68	23	6	10	46	13
Cron, C.J., Utah	.337	246	39	83	19	1	11	57	1
Berke, Scott, UNLV	.329	170	32	56	12	1	2	40	10
Coats, Jason, TCU	.328	235	54	77	14	4	10	51	2
Thornton, Ryan, UNLV	.327	226	58	74	15	3	10	42	15
Resnick, Brian, UNLV	.327	202	46	66	9	3	7	35	13
Morel, Anthony, UNLV	.324	219	37	71	12	4	3	44	8

INDIVIDUAL PITCHING LEADERS
(Minimum 50 Innings)

	W	L	ERA	G	SV	IP	H	BB	SO
#Reed, Addison, San Diego State	0	0	0.64	25	20	28	20	7	38
Strasburg, Stephen, San Diego State	13	1	1.32	15	0	109	65	19	195
Oslund, Marc, BYU	7	1	2.49	22	1	65	57	24	59
Lavigne, Tyler, San Diego State	8	2	3.05	15	1	94	71	28	87
Hesketh, John, New Mexico	6	4	3.45	15	0	89	88	24	70
Appleby, Trent, TCU	4	1	3.61	24	1	57	57	20	47
Gerrish, Paul, TCU	6	2	4.00	16	1	54	56	16	53
Miller, Adam, BYU	3	3	4.04	12	0	56	63	35	33
Winkler, Kyle, TCU	7	1	4.15	17	0	74	70	35	48
Whatcott, Jordan, Utah	5	3	4.19	17	1	88	86	46	61
Lockwood, Tyler, TCU	4	1	4.41	16	0	67	71	17	43
Peters, Tanner, UNLV	5	7	4.90	15	0	79	86	19	59
#Krause, Greg, Utah	3	4	4.93	32	4	46	58	17	47
Card, Bryn, Utah	6	2	5.61	17	0	67	82	25	55
Torgerson, Blake, BYU	6	3	5.66	14	0	83	115	15	39
Budrow, Brian, Utah	5	5	5.75	17	1	99	129	30	79

Toole, Jeremy, BYU	5	5	5.77	15	0	83	85	52	68
Berger, Jon, San Diego State	4	5	5.83	15	0	88	111	12	71
Wilding, Andrew, Utah	2	5	6.29	14	0	79	107	13	49
Beresford, Andrew, UNLV	3	4	6.32	18	0	84	99	32	54
Bunch, Nathan, BYU	3	4	6.59	17	0	55	69	31	33

NORTHEAST CONFERENCE

	Conference		Overall	
	W	L	W	L
Wagner	17	9	31	21
Sacred Heart	16	10	29	27
Central Connecticut State	16	11	26	22
*Monmouth	15	11	32	25
Mount St. Mary's	15	11	23	25
Quinnipiac	11	17	8	13
Fairleigh Dickinson	11	17	16	34
Long Island	6	21	10	40

ALL-CONFERENCE TEAM: C—Jeff Heppner, Sr., Sacred Heart. **1B**—Jeff Hanson, Sr., Sacred Heart. **2B**—Chris Collazo, Sr., Monmouth. **3B**—Tyler Santos, Sr., Sacred Heart. **SS**—Anthony Scialdone, Jr., Central Connecticut State. **OF**—Damian Csakai, Jr., Wagner; Shane Eyler, So., Mount St. Mary's; Nick Pulsonetti, So., Monmouth. **DH**—Pat Epps, So., Central Connecticut State. **UTIL**—James Jones, Jr., Long Island. **P**— Ryan Buch, Jr., Monmouth; Matt Watson, Jr., Wagner. **Player of the Year:** Shane Eyler, Mount St. Mary's. **Pitcher of the Year:** Matt Watson, Wagner. **Rookie of the Year:** Matt Holsman, Fairleigh Dickinson. **Coach of the Year:** Joe Litterio, Wagner.

INDIVIDUAL BATTING LEADERS
(Minimum 125 At-Bats)

	AVG	AB	R	H	2B	3B	HR	RBI	SB
Hanson, Jeff, Sacred Heart	.425	186	48	79	19	1	12	54	1
Gruccio, Jared, Wagner	.394	155	30	61	10	0	0	32	11
Collazo, Chris, Monmouth	.385	226	57	87	13	1	2	46	6
Eyler, Shane, Mount St. Mary's	.380	166	39	63	11	0	15	46	5
Sand, Zachary, Fairleigh Dickinson	.379	145	40	55	14	3	5	38	7
Martutartus, Brian, Wagner	.366	172	28	63	14	4	2	35	18
Jones, James, Long Island	.364	173	47	63	11	3	9	32	20
Tantillo, Phil, Sacred Heart	.363	201	44	73	10	3	5	43	5
Parker, Sean, Central Conn. State	.361	144	21	52	14	2	6	46	1
Pulsonetti, Nick, Monmouth	.358	193	51	69	15	1	11	53	12
Santos, Tyler, Sacred Heart	.354	229	51	81	23	1	6	45	0
Dillon, Brian, Fairleigh Dickinson	.352	182	36	64	8	3	5	37	5
Heppner, Jeff, Sacred Heart	.351	221	40	74	17	2	13	63	0
Scialdone, Anthony, C. Conn. State	.351	174	40	61	8	3	5	37	4
Drowne, Mike, Sacred Heart	.348	178	51	62	10	4	7	29	18
Tri, Richie, Central Conn. State	.348	164	32	57	16	1	6	46	6
Holland, Brett, Monmouth	.347	193	47	67	11	2	3	26	19
Epps, Pat, Central Conn. State	.346	182	41	63	13	1	3	51	3
Dimasi, Frank, Long Island	.345	171	34	59	10	1	3	37	15
Guerino, Gabe, Quinnipiac	.343	134	22	46	5	0	3	27	0
Maher, Matt, Fairleigh Dickinson	.339	174	45	59	8	1	2	27	30
Winter, Josh, Mount St. Mary's	.333	132	20	44	8	3	4	33	3
Csakai, Damian, Wagner	.332	199	51	66	6	3	2	30	37
Terry, Ryan, Monmouth	.332	152	36	50	10	1	5	39	16
Dombrowski, Bobby, Monmouth	.329	152	36	50	10	1	5	33	3
Allaire, Sean, Central Conn. State	.329	213	53	70	12	3	1	23	5
Tedesco, Steve, Central Conn. State	.326	176	43	56	8	0	0	17	16
Holsman, Matt, Fairleigh Dickinson	.323	192	28	62	6	0	2	19	3
Kane, Kyle, Mount St. Mary's	.321	162	39	52	4	1	7	38	6
Schillaci, Jay, Central Conn. State	.320	175	35	56	17	4	7	38	3
#Bottigliero, Paul, Monmouth	.296	196	35	58	16	1	17	58	4
#Boyd, Josh, Monmouth	.281	160	40	45	5	5	1	30	19

INDIVIDUAL PITCHING LEADERS
(Minimum 50 Innings)

	W	L	ERA	G	SV	IP	H	BB	SO
#Huebner, Andrew, Wagner	1	2	3.16	26	13	31	33	12	29
Watson, Matt, Wagner	9	2	3.64	12	1	64	69	34	31
Buch, Ryan, Monmouth	7	4	4.11	13	0	72	78	31	87
Morrison, Kyle, Wagner	8	2	4.16	12	0	67	75	22	55
Vallillo, Nick, Monmouth	3	2	4.31	12	0	54	55	25	32
Balbach, Jared, Sacred Heart	8	2	4.32	14	0	83	104	24	55
Brach, Brett, Monmouth	7	2	4.61	14	1	68	65	12	69

	W	L	ERA	G	SV	IP	H	BB	SO
Gloor, Chris, Quinnipiac	7	4	4.63	13	0	82	81	35	81
Melchiorre, Nicholas, Fair. Dickinson	2	8	4.73	12	0	65	78	33	48
Kerski, Ken, Central Conn. State	6	5	4.79	14	0	73	108	25	48
Corcoran, Corey, Sacred Heart	2	1	4.97	15	0	54	55	23	15
Markoya, Dan, Central Conn. State	1	4	4.99	14	2	52	70	21	37
Kapothanasis, Costa, Mount St. Mary's	4	3	5.06	12	0	59	50	28	41
Duffy, Joe, Quinnipiac	2	10	5.36	18	1	84	104	23	64
Barthel, Chris, Sacred Heart	5	3	5.50	15	0	88	122	16	66
Oskandy, Michael, Quinnipiac	3	7	6.14	16	2	63	75	24	37
Meadus, John, Fairleigh Dickinson	2	6	6.30	12	0	60	67	34	47
Fitton, Matt, Sacred Heart	5	3	6.47	16	0	65	81	21	27
Mayer, Andy, Quinnipiac	5	3	6.59	12	0	68	89	19	52
Feigl, Brady, Mount St. Mary's	3	3	6.64	16	1	62	89	23	69
Breese, Kyle, Monmouth	5	3	7.28	13	0	59	74	23	42

OHIO VALLEY CONFERENCE

	Conference		Overall	
	W	L	W	L
Eastern Illinois	14	4	36	14
Murray State	13	8	34	21
Morehead State	12	10	20	32
Southeast Missouri State	12	11	26	25
*Tennessee Tech	10	11	31	24
Jacksonville State	10	13	31	26
Eastern Kentucky	10	13	27	24
Austin Peay State	7	12	22	30
Tennessee-Martin	9	15	20	31

ALL-CONFERENCE TEAM: C—Jim Klocke, Jr., Southeast Missouri State. **1B**—Wes Cunningham, Jr., Murray State. **2B**—Jordan Tokarz, Sr., Eastern Illinois. **3B**—Jayson Langfels, So., Eastern Kentucky. **SS**—Jordan Kreke, Sr., Eastern Illinois; Drew Lee, Jr., Morehead State. **OF**—Tyrell Cummings, Sr., Southeast Missouri State; Matt Davis, Sr., Eastern Kentucky; Daniel Hill, Jr., Murray State. **DH**—Jason Laws, Jr., Murray State. **UTIL**—Richie Derbak, Jr., Eastern Illinois. **SP**—Daniel Calhoun, Jr., Murray State; Mike Recchia, So., Eastern Illinois. **RP**—Bill Henke, So., Jacksonville State. **Players of the Year:** Jordan Kreke, Eastern Illinois. **Pitcher of the Year:** Daniel Calhoun, Murray State. **Rookie of the Year:** Kyle Bluestein, Jacksonville State. **Coach of the Year:** Rob McDonald, Murray State.

INDIVIDUAL BATTING LEADERS
(Minimum 150 At-Bats)

	AVG	AB	R	H	2B	3B	HR	RBI	SB
Langfels, Jayson, Eastern Ky.	.441	170	45	75	13	6	12	72	16
Gladstone, Scott, Tenn.-Martin	.420	200	46	84	9	0	7	30	2
Davis, Matt, Eastern Kentucky	.418	196	71	82	20	3	7	43	25
Derbak, Richie, Eastern Illinois	.417	187	34	78	12	0	5	41	0
Lee, Drew, Morehead State	.413	208	62	86	18	2	17	67	4
Cunningham, Wes, Murray State	.411	192	51	79	12	5	11	52	6
Hartsfield, Miles, Tenn.-Martin	.397	194	39	77	14	3	9	52	4
Rehmel, Tyler, Eastern Kentucky	.397	174	50	69	15	3	2	47	15
Borenstein, Zach, Eastern Illinois	.394	137	43	54	6	0	5	28	2
Klocke, Jim, Southeast Missouri	.394	188	56	74	20	1	9	46	0
Kreke, Jordan, Eastern Illinois	.394	188	50	74	16	3	13	59	5
Bluestein, Kyle, Jackson State	.393	163	48	64	21	0	9	46	0
Cummings, Tyrell, Southeast Mo.	.386	202	49	78	14	2	9	3	3
Lucas, Trey, Austin Peay State	.382	165	27	63	20	0	4	35	5
Lindquist, Ryan, Eastern Illinois	.375	144	38	54	12	2	6	27	2
Hartsfield, Mark, Tenn.-Martin	.373	212	56	79	10	3	12	42	9
Laws, Jason, Murray State	.373	153	32	57	10	3	3	39	0
Ashbrook, J.D., Morehead State	.371	202	65	75	16	3	14	36	9
Deeds, Andrew, Morehead State	.366	164	38	60	7	3	6	37	13
Daniel, Jacob, Eastern Kentucky	.361	147	40	53	5	5	3	30	10
Oberaker, Chad, Tennessee Tech	.354	195	51	69	8	4	4	27	11
Bottoms, Michael, Morehead State	.350	214	43	75	15	1	8	61	2
Tokarz, Jordan, Eastern Illinois	.350	200	55	70	10	3	13	52	5
Nelson, Ty, Tennessee-Martin	.345	165	34	57	11	0	6	27	3
Hill, Daniel, Murray State	.344	183	49	63	12	0	16	69	0
Frey, Elliot, Murray State	.344	189	57	65	9	3	4	36	6
Leach, Steven, Jacksonville State	.343	216	40	74	19	1	2	35	1
Bachman, Greg, Austin Peay State	.342	193	54	66	18	1	10	44	11
Ottrando, Anthony, Eastern Ky.	.340	188	41	64	9	1	8	50	11
Skidmore, Zach, Eastern Illinois	.340	159	46	54	11	1	11	49	2
Cunningham, Todd, Jacksonville State	.339	236	66	80	14	9	10	47	9
#Kirby-Jones, A.J., Tennessee Tech	.325	197	49	64	15	0	20	68	1

INDIVIDUAL PITCHING LEADERS
(Minimum 50 Innings)

	W	L	ERA	G	SV	IP	H	BB	SO
#Henke, Bill, Jacksonville State	2	3	2.10	20	9	26	26	9	21
Calhoun, Daniel, Murray State	11	3	2.32	16	1	97	90	6	85
#Tenholder, Daniel, Austin Peay State	3	2	2.93	30	9	46	41	21	41
Recchia, Mike, Eastern Illinois	8	2	3.02	13	0	66	54	24	62
Henry, Lee, Tennessee Tech	9	3	3.43	21	1	79	72	40	80
Dennick, Ryan, Tennessee Tech	4	2	3.88	21	2	72	67	33	58
Lucas, Austin, Jackson State	7	3	3.93	14	0	71	70	24	52
Freshour, Tanner, Jackson State	3	3	3.93	23	0	69	75	28	33
Craycraft, Chris, Murray State	10	3	4.05	14	0	100	110	22	80
Harper, Ryne, Austin Peay State	4	3	4.12	14	0	59	56	25	54
Bottoms, Michael, Morehead State	3	5	4.15	20	5	52	51	28	35
Kehrer, Tyler, Eastern Illinois	5	3	4.42	14	0	73	59	41	90
Marshall, Ricky, Austin Peay State	4	3	4.60	24	1	59	75	37	52
Harmon, Marc, Murray State	4	2	4.64	16	0	83	86	23	36
Mueller, Josh, Eastern Illinois	8	1	4.85	13	0	78	82	38	64
Bess, Tyler, Morehead State	5	7	4.86	18	0	87	107	13	61
Leigh, James, Southeast Missouri	7	3	4.89	16	0	85	95	35	87
Morrell, Brian, Eastern Illinois	3	2	4.89	25	2	53	59	24	45
Green, Coty, Tennessee-Martin	5	8	4.98	16	1	94	120	17	70
Watts, Daniel, Jacksonville State	5	5	5.16	20	0	59	60	29	53
Duncan, Paul, Eastern Kentucky	7	6	6.01	17	0	76	100	26	51
Morgan, Quentin, Morehead State	3	4	6.31	16	0	71	93	28	38

PACIFIC-10 CONFERENCE

	Conference		Overall	
	W	L	W	L
*Arizona State	21	6	51	14
Washington State	19	8	32	25
Oregon State	15	12	37	19
UCLA	15	12	27	29
Arizona	13	14	30	25
Stanford	13	14	30	25
Southern California	13	14	28	28
Washington	13	14	25	30
California	9	18	24	29
Oregon	4	23	14	42

ALL-CONFERENCE TEAM: C—Dwight Childs, Jr., Arizona; Ryan Ortiz, Jr., Oregon State; Carlos Ramirez, Jr., Arizona State. **IF**—Dillon Baird, Jr., Arizona; Mark Canha, So., California; Cody Decker, Sr., UCLA; Jeff Kobernus, Jr., California; Bryce Ortega, So., Arizona; Grant Green, Jr., USC. **OF**—Kyle Conley, Jr., Washington; Brett Jackson, Jr., California; Kellen Kiilsgaard, So., Stanford; Jason Kipnis, Jr., Arizona State; Jared Prince, Sr., Washington State. **DH**—Blake Smith, Jr., California. **UTIL**—Matt Newman, So., Arizona State. **P**—Trevor Bauer, Fr., UCLA; Brad Boxberger, Jr., USC; Gerrit Cole, Fr., UCLA; Jeremy Johnson, Jr., Washington State; Mitchell Lambson, Fr., Arizona State; Mike Leake, Jr., Arizona State; Josh Spence, Jr., Arizona State; Drew Storen, So., Stanford; Matt Way, Sr., Washington State. **Player of the Year:** Jason Kipnis, Arizona State. **Pitcher of the Year:** Mike Leake, Arizona State. **Defensive Player of the Year:** Jake Schlander, Stanford. **Freshman of the Year:** Trevor Bauer, UCLA. **Coach of the Year:** Pat Murphy, Arizona State.

INDIVIDUAL BATTING LEADERS
(Minimum 125 At-Bats)

	AVG	AB	R	H	2B	3B	HR	RBI	SB
Baird, Dillon, Arizona	.433	194	53	84	21	5	8	55	5
Kipnis, Jason, Arizona State	.384	237	76	91	21	4	16	71	27
Green, Grant, USC	.374	211	46	79	19	5	4	32	16
Pace, Hunter, Arizona	.372	148	41	55	7	5	2	29	15
Canha, Mark, California	.366	205	44	75	17	1	12	43	5
Ortiz, Ryan, Oregon State	.352	216	55	76	17	1	5	45	2
Prince, Jared, Washington State	.343	172	39	59	12	2	7	38	0
Kobernus, Jeff, California	.341	217	43	74	14	3	8	40	20
Ramirez, Carlos, Arizona State	.338	234	63	79	13	2	19	75	3
Lagreid, Greg, Washington State	.332	205	37	68	13	0	5	42	0
Rife, James, Washington	.328	192	41	63	5	6	9	39	3
Ortega, Bryce, Arizona	.324	210	57	68	9	3	3	33	16
Decker, Cody, UCLA	.322	199	55	64	9	0	21	53	2
Jackson, Brett, California	.321	218	42	70	17	6	8	41	11

	AVG	AB	R	H	2B	3B	HR	RBI	SB
Santos, Adalberto, Oregon State	.320	175	40	56	6	2	4	43	15
Walsh, Colin, Stanford	.320	194	44	62	11	0	0	25	4
O'Neill, Mike, USC	.319	191	40	61	6	4	3	17	7
Smith, Blake, California	.319	210	43	67	14	0	10	38	5
Uribe, Justin, UCLA	.318	151	27	48	11	0	3	23	3
Selsky, Steve, Arizona	.318	148	36	47	8	2	7	21	2
Coyle, Bobby, Arizona	.316	209	40	66	12	7	3	37	6
Guinn, Brian, California	.315	200	37	63	10	3	2	35	10
Oropesa, Ricky, USC	.314	185	35	58	8	1	13	48	3
Kiilsgaard, Kellen, Stanford	.313	201	37	63	14	1	9	46	1
Calhoun, Kole, Arizona State	.313	211	54	66	17	2	12	53	10
Maggi, Drew, Arizona State	.309	181	63	56	5	5	0	24	21
Vasquez, Anthony, USC	.307	202	36	62	13	2	6	42	6
Milleville, Brent, Stanford	.306	183	32	56	6	0	14	52	7
Haerther, Casey, UCLA	.305	203	31	62	7	0	9	42	4
Newman, Matt, Arizona State	.305	236	42	72	15	1	7	54	6
#Bandy, Jett, Arizona	.299	164	24	49	21	0	4	39	1

INDIVIDUAL PITCHING LEADERS
(Minimum 50 Innings)

	W	L	ERA	G	SV	IP	H	BB	SO
Leake, Mike, Arizona State	16	1	1.71	19	0	142	95	24	162
Spence, Josh, Arizona State	10	1	2.37	18	1	103	93	30	125
Way, Matt, Washington State	8	4	2.43	16	0	107	85	33	124
Gaviglio, Sam, Oregon State	10	1	2.73	18	1	63	45	9	55
Stock, Robert, USC	5	4	2.90	20	4	78	61	39	86
Johnson, Jeremy, Washington State	6	2	2.90	28	10	59	52	11	61
Bauer, Trevor, UCLA	9	3	2.99	20	2	105	85	27	92
Lambson, Mitchell, Arizona State	9	5	3.01	32	5	84	58	25	99
Stavert, Erik, Oregon State	5	6	3.04	14	0	95	78	36	82
Boxberger, Brad, USC	6	3	3.16	14	0	94	69	50	99
Blair, Seth, Arizona State	7	2	3.39	17	1	77	70	30	78
Cole, Gerrit, UCLA	4	8	3.49	15	0	85	57	38	104
Guilmet, Preston, Arizona	6	5	3.74	15	0	91	100	34	93
#Burns, Cory, Arizona	2	0	3.80	40	1	47	44	21	54
Triggs, Andrew, USC	5	3	3.96	15	0	75	79	20	50
Mooneyham, Brett, Stanford	6	3	4.14	13	0	67	46	54	72
Waldron, Tyler, Oregon State	6	4	4.15	16	0	93	96	31	70
Reyes, Jorge, Oregon State	6	2	4.20	15	0	81	84	29	75
Kittredge, Andrew, Washington	4	5	4.27	29	3	72	71	17	64
Vasquez, Anthony, USC	4	6	4.33	16	1	71	75	21	53
Erickson, Jason, Washington	5	4	4.34	14	0	75	81	18	55
#Stoffel, Jason, Arizona	2	1	4.67	39	11	54	44	25	55

PATRIOT LEAGUE

	Conference		Overall	
	W	L	W	L
*Army	13	7	36	21
Bucknell	13	7	22	25
Holy Cross	11	7	22	27
Lafayette	9	11	24	29
Navy	8	12	20	26
Lehigh	4	14	11	36

ALL-CONFERENCE TEAM: C—B.J. LaRosa, Jr., Bucknell. 1B—Kevin McKague, So., Army. 2B—Zach Price, Fr., Army. 3B—Matt Perry, Jr., Holy Cross. SS—Dan Bierce, Sr., Lafayette. OF—Andrew Brouse, Jr., Bucknell; Ben Koenigsfeld, Sr., Army; Andy Russell, So., Lehigh. DH—Joey Henshaw, So., Army. SP—Ben Koenigsfeld, Sr., Army; Chris Yamaguchi, Sr., Bucknell. RP—Tyler Anderegg, Sr., Army; Luke Roberts, So., Navy.

Player of the Year: Matt Perry, Holy Cross. Pitcher of the Year: Ben Koenigsfeld, Army. Rookie of the Year: Zach Price, Army. Coach of the Year: Gene Depew, Bucknell.

INDIVIDUAL BATTING LEADERS
(Minimum 100 At-Bats)

	AVG	AB	R	H	2B	3B	HR	RBI	SB
Matt, Perry, Holy Cross	.423	182	42	77	10	0	7	37	2
Moore, Clint, Army	.395	185	58	73	18	5	11	63	10
McKague, Kevin, Army	.389	203	45	79	8	1	6	44	7
Henshaw, Joey, Army	.383	209	47	80	12	2	13	75	5
Guadagnini, Mike, Navy	.374	195	42	73	6	4	3	24	9
Froio, Rob, Lafayette	.367	196	45	72	9	3	0	34	20
Allen, Ben, Bucknell	.366	186	47	68	14	1	2	22	7

	AVG	AB	R	H	2B	3B	HR	RBI	SB
Shribman, Doug, Bucknell	.360	164	33	59	15	1	6	42	2
Bierce, Daniel, Lafayette	.360	203	43	73	18	2	5	45	21
Price, Zach, Army	.355	197	59	70	10	2	0	25	14
Russell, Andrew, Lehigh	.348	164	35	57	13	4	7	38	10
Koenigsfeld, Ben, Army	.342	184	39	63	10	2	7	38	11
Campbell, Geoff, Lehigh	.342	149	21	51	8	3	3	17	4
Goldman, Billy, Lehigh	.333	162	22	54	8	0	0	16	7
Brouse, Andrew, Bucknell	.330	176	41	58	12	5	10	57	10
Bolt, Kendall, Navy	.328	183	33	60	10	2	3	48	9
Yoder, Ben, Bucknell	.323	161	38	52	3	1	7	35	4
LaRosa, B.J., Bucknell	.320	122	25	39	13	1	0	23	3
Ernesto, Andy, Army	.318	198	44	63	18	1	3	38	9
Mihalik, Kevin, Lehigh	.313	147	17	46	7	1	4	26	2

INDIVIDUAL PITCHING LEADERS
(Minimum 40 Innings)

	W	L	ERA	G	SV	IP	H	BB	SO
#Anderegg, Tyler, Army	8	2	4.04	27	1	49	45	17	43
Porter, Kirk, Army	6	3	4.18	12	0	60	63	25	40
Frahler, Trey, Bucknell	6	4	4.34	11	0	66	78	29	43
Yamaguchi, Chris, Bucknell	7	2	4.45	14	1	63	75	9	26
#McKague, Kevin, Army	0	0	4.57	23	7	21	17	17	17
Fouch, Matt, Army	7	5	4.70	16	0	90	93	44	65
Shea, Corey, Lafayette	4	3	4.81	14	0	67	80	22	33
Atkins, Jeremy, Lafayette	4	3	4.82	14	1	65	73	21	47
Koenigsfeld, Ben, Army	8	4	4.89	13	0	85	85	33	63
Berger, Andrew, Lehigh	2	6	5.31	11	0	58	75	13	44
Seip, Dan, Holy Cross	3	4	5.37	10	0	60	68	31	37
Fritz, Zach, Lafayette	2	6	5.50	13	0	74	80	29	62
Hanna, Ryan, Lafayette	6	3	5.68	19	0	71	98	12	41
Olson, Wes, Navy	3	5	5.69	10	0	55	68	24	39
Kerins, T.J., Navy	2	3	5.73	14	2	55	69	13	41
Shapiro, Matt, Holy Cross	3	4	6.40	10	0	58	75	16	41
Lebo, Mike, Lehigh	0	9	6.79	12	0	54	76	11	31
Seeley, Dylan, Bucknell	4	5	6.83	11	0	54	80	22	16
Sipe, Zach, Navy	3	4	7.22	11	0	57	74	27	53
Holmes, Bobby, Holy Cross	3	7	7.41	13	0	55	60	24	39
Jarrett, Eric, Bucknell	1	4	7.47	11	0	47	54	42	39

SOUTHEASTERN CONFERENCE

	Conference		Overall	
EAST	W	L	W	L
Florida	19	11	42	22
South Carolina	17	13	40	23
Georgia	15	15	38	24
Vanderbilt	12	17	37	27
Kentucky	12	18	28	26
Tennessee	11	19	26	29
WEST	W	L	W	L
*Louisiana State	20	10	56	17
Mississippi	20	10	44	20
Alabama	18	11	37	21
Arkansas	14	15	41	24
Auburn	11	19	31	25
Mississippi State	9	20	25	29

ALL-CONFERENCE TEAM: C—Blake Forsythe, So., Tennessee. 1B—Rich Poythress, Jr., Georgia. 2B—Josh Adams, So., Florida; Ross Wilson, So., Alabama. 3B—Jake Smith, Jr., Alabama. SS—Brian Harris, Jr., Vanderbilt; Josh Rutledge, So., Alabama. OF—Avery Barnes, Sr., Florida; Jordan Henry, Jr., Mississippi; Kent Matthes, Sr., Alabama. DH—Blake Dean, Jr., LSU. SP—Louis Coleman, Sr., LSU; Austin Hyatt, Sr., Alabama. RP—Matty Ott, Fr., LSU.

Player of the Year: Kent Matthes, Alabama. Pitcher of the Year: Louis Coleman, LSU. Freshmen of the Year: Matty Ott, LSU; Preston Tucker, Florida. Coach of the Year: Paul Mainieri, LSU.

INDIVIDUAL BATTING LEADERS
(Minimum 125 At-Bats)

	AVG	AB	R	H	2B	3B	HR	RBI	SB
Westlake, Aaron, Vanderbilt	.377	239	53	90	15	0	10	57	5
Poythress, Rich, Georgia	.376	237	69	89	17	0	25	86	4
Barnes, Avery, Florida	.364	247	76	90	9	6	8	42	18
Tucker, Preston, Florida	.364	242	48	88	13	3	15	85	5
Hawn, Cody, Tennessee	.364	198	46	72	15	0	22	81	0

	AVG	AB	R	H	2B	3B	HR	RBI	SB
Mack, DeAngelo, South Carolina	.361	255	57	92	15	3	14	60	7
Bisson, Chris, Kentucky	.360	222	49	80	9	3	2	52	13
Smith, Jake, Alabama	.359	195	42	70	14	2	18	54	2
Matthes, Kent, Alabama	.358	204	67	73	14	2	28	81	13
Wilson, Ross, Alabama	.353	215	59	76	15	2	9	47	8
DeLoach, Scott, Mississippi	.353	133	28	47	7	1	1	21	3
Dugas, Taylor, Alabama	.352	236	61	83	20	2	2	27	13
LeMahieu, D.J., LSU	.350	274	57	96	13	4	5	43	12
Bradley, Jackie, South Carolina	.349	255	69	89	11	2	11	46	8
Liddle, Steven, Vanderbilt	.348	250	62	87	22	2	10	51	1
Forsythe, Blake, Tennessee	.347	196	51	68	13	2	15	46	5
May, Brandon, Alabama	.347	222	53	77	18	2	12	69	1
Henry, Jordan, Mississippi	.343	230	70	79	12	1	0	31	38
Wright, Chad, Kentucky	.343	181	40	62	8	1	4	23	10
Adams, Josh, Florida	.342	240	58	82	11	1	8	52	5
Miller, Zach, Mississippi	.341	211	48	72	15	2	5	38	8
Merrifield, Whit, South Carolina	.340	268	67	91	16	3	11	49	15
May, Colby, Georgia	.339	224	58	76	14	1	11	42	3
McArthur, Brandon, Florida	.338	207	25	70	14	1	3	41	0
Smith, Matt, Mississippi	.336	232	52	78	15	2	8	59	4
Casali, Curt, Vanderbilt	.336	235	62	79	16	0	10	59	2
Schimpf, Ryan, LSU	.336	262	73	88	19	1	22	70	19
Butler, Jet, Mississippi State	.335	176	30	59	12	0	4	37	6
Ochinko, Sean, LSU	.333	234	46	78	15	0	9	57	2
#Crisp, Andrew, South Carolina	.313	262	39	82	23	0	10	53	4

INDIVIDUAL PITCHING LEADERS
(Minimum 50 Innings)

	W	L	ERA	G	SV	IP	H	BB	SO
#Ott, Matty, LSU	4	2	2.68	37	16	50	46	6	69
Coleman, Louis, LSU	14	2	2.93	25	0	129	108	23	142
Bolsinger, Mike, Arkansas	6	4	2.99	30	2	69	53	28	79
Ranaudo, Anthony, LSU	12	3	3.04	19	0	124	93	50	159
Pomeranz, Drew, Mississippi	8	4	3.40	16	0	95	85	37	124
#Harvill, Will, Georgia	4	3	3.54	37	0	48	49	26	41
Baker, Nathan, Mississippi	4	3	3.63	20	1	67	74	16	69
Hyatt, Austin, Alabama	8	3	3.76	15	0	103	89	15	88
Irwin, Phillip, Mississippi	8	3	3.84	15	0	87	106	20	73
Minor, Mike, Vanderbilt	6	6	3.90	17	1	111	109	37	114
Keuchel, Dallas, Arkansas	9	3	3.92	18	0	108	114	32	69
Cotham, Caleb, Vanderbilt	7	5	4.10	17	0	79	67	27	84
Routt, Nick, Mississippi State	5	3	4.15	13	0	87	87	28	87
Grimm, Justin, Georgia	4	4	4.15	15	0	78	82	26	72
Morgan, Adam, Alabama	4	2	4.17	13	0	58	64	20	44
Rusin, Chris, Kentucky	7	4	4.20	13	0	94	95	27	108
Locke, Stephen, Florida	5	2	4.32	12	0	67	85	18	48
Bukvich, Brett, Mississippi	9	3	4.42	17	0	71	77	16	72
Holder, Trevor, Georgia	7	5	4.48	15	0	92	94	30	72
Cooper, Blake, South Carolina	9	4	4.50	17	0	86	100	29	65
DeSclafani, Anthony, Florida	6	3	4.98	21	0	65	63	16	47
Eibner, Brett, Arkansas	5	5	5.00	17	0	72	65	35	67

SOUTHERN CONFERENCE

	Conference		Overall	
	W	L	W	L
Elon	23	4	41	18
*Georgia Southern	20	8	42	17
The Citadel	20	10	37	22
Western Carolina	19	10	35	22
College of Charleston	17	13	35	22
Appalachian State	15	13	33	21
Davidson	11	16	18	31
Furman	10	20	24	31
Samford	9	21	17	35
UNC Greensboro	7	21	20	29
Wofford	7	22	17	32

ALL-CONFERENCE TEAM: C—Richard Jones, Jr., Citadel. 1B—Chris McGuiness, Jr., Citadel. 2B—Brandon Sizemore, Sr., College of Charleston. 3B—Joey Bergman, Jr., College of Charleston. SS—Brent Greer, Jr., Western Carolina. OF—Cory Harrilchak, Sr., Elon; Pat Irvine, Sr., Elon; Sonny Meade, Sr., Citadel. DH—Ryan Daniels, Jr., College of Charleston. SP—Chris Mederos, Jr., Georgia Southern; Wes Wrenn, Sr., Citadel. RP—Thomas Girdwood, So., Elon; Zach Quate, Sr., Appalachian State.

Players of the Year: Chase Austin, Elon; Joey Bergman, College of Charleston. **Pitcher of the Year:** Wes Wrenn, Citadel. **Freshman of the Year:** Ross Heffley, Western Carolina. **Coach of the Year:** Mike Kennedy, Elon.

INDIVIDUAL BATTING LEADERS
(Minimum 125 At-Bats)

	AVG	AB	R	H	2B	3B	HR	RBI	SB
Bergman, Joey, Col. of Charleston	.452	221	88	100	25	1	15	57	24
Harrow, Isaac, Appalachian State	.422	218	57	92	23	6	12	75	13
Greer, Brent, Western Carolina	.420	243	49	102	22	2	8	52	2
Benedict, Griffin, Ga. Southern	.414	220	67	91	17	0	14	66	8
Irvine, Pat, Elon	.402	194	68	78	14	5	17	57	19
Meade, Sonny, Citadel	.397	262	59	104	22	0	5	67	3
Hatley, Mitchell, Western Carolina	.394	127	34	50	8	2	1	29	9
Heffley, Ross, Western Carolina	.391	235	48	92	18	2	4	51	7
McCord, Clay, Col. of Charleston	.382	225	75	86	14	2	5	31	28
Hobson, Wes, Appalachian State	.380	234	67	89	23	4	9	60	9
Jones, Richard, Citadel	.378	251	54	95	19	2	17	69	2
Greene, David, Citadel	.376	226	35	85	12	2	4	36	1
Altman, Bryan, Citadel	.368	258	63	95	23	3	7	47	11
McGuiness, Chris, Citadel	.367	207	55	76	15	1	15	59	1
Liles, Nick, Appalachian State	.367	259	66	95	22	2	9	49	24
Smith, Rand, Appalachian State	.365	241	68	88	17	3	10	42	10
Daniels, Ryan, Col. of Charleston	.363	193	44	70	13	0	10	64	0
Porter, Phillip, Georgia Southern	.362	243	68	88	9	2	11	51	11
Brodin, Joash, Col. of Charleston	.362	221	60	80	12	3	12	64	15
Pierce, Brian, Georgia Southern	.362	224	39	81	14	2	3	43	1
Austin, Chase, Elon	.359	256	74	92	11	3	23	81	19
Orvin, Nick, Citadel	.355	259	69	92	14	3	2	33	18
Ballard, Stephen, Samford	.350	200	42	70	15	2	2	21	3
Melillo, Mike, Elon	.344	209	67	72	19	3	18	60	7
Behrendt, Kyle, Wofford	.344	195	37	67	16	0	6	39	11
Davis, Bennett, Elon	.343	233	63	80	16	2	18	64	11
Kayne, Zach, Davidson	.340	209	41	71	22	1	10	37	10
Miller, Wayne, Samford	.339	218	48	74	11	2	3	28	24
Wright, Ty, Georgia Southern	.339	248	73	84	14	1	13	63	15
Harrilchak, Cory, Elon	.336	256	79	86	18	3	16	61	10
#Collias, Trevor, Western Carolina	.293	208	57	61	10	2	8	36	30

INDIVIDUAL PITCHING LEADERS
(Minimum 50 Innings)

	W	L	ERA	G	SV	IP	H	BB	SO
Talley, Matt, Citadel	8	1	3.42	18	0	71	72	33	52
Mahaffey, Drew, Citadel	2	3	3.60	30	7	50	38	14	71
Wrenn, Wes, Citadel	9	3	3.62	14	0	102	107	25	82
Slack, Warren, UNC Greensboro	4	0	3.77	23	1	62	61	21	50
Mederos, Chris, Georgia Southern	11	1	3.83	16	0	94	97	29	113
Crim, Matt, Citadel	8	4	4.10	14	0	83	98	33	62
Wojciechowski, Asher, Citadel	3	3	4.39	12	0	70	61	34	75
#Frongello, Mike, Davidson	3	2	4.47	34	1	44	52	11	29
Brown, Jake, Georgia Southern	6	3	4.50	17	0	88	106	22	64
Parish, Matt, UNC Greensboro	3	1	4.70	19	0	52	53	21	43
Murray, Matt, Georgia Southern	6	3	4.76	15	1	74	81	27	60
Reyes, Jimmy, Elon	8	0	4.78	16	0	85	98	19	101
Parry, Ian, Furman	3	5	4.87	15	0	78	91	27	86
Edens, Aubrey, Appalachian State	6	3	4.97	14	0	76	81	25	62
Dowdy, Josh, Appalachian State	6	3	5.07	20	0	76	89	19	68
Ferrer, Ken, Elon	8	1	5.30	20	2	73	93	37	52
#Girdwood, Thomas, Elon	0	3	5.33	29	17	25	29	14	38
Ozar, Garrett, Western Carolina	4	5	5.38	29	2	72	85	26	73
Tavernier, Mike, Western Carolina	7	6	5.49	20	0	82	105	33	67
Simpson, Jesse, Col. of Charleston	9	4	5.52	15	0	90	112	25	84
Knapp, David, Samford	3	5	5.54	13	0	67	93	39	50
Martin, Corey, Western Carolina	7	4	5.56	16	0	68	75	29	55

SOUTHLAND CONFERENCE

	Conference		Overall	
	W	L	W	L
Texas State	24	7	41	17
Southeastern Louisiana	21	12	37	22
Texas-San Antonio	20	12	32	24
Lamar	20	13	38	22
Texas-Arlington	19	13	30	26

Northwestern State	18	13	26	26
*Sam Houston State	18	14	36	24
Stephen F. Austin State	14	18	23	32
Central Arkansas	10	21	22	30
McNeese State	10	22	21	30
Nicholls State	9	23	19	32
Texas A&M-Corpus Christi	9	24	18	38

ALL-CONFERENCE TEAM: C—Taylor Freeman, Jr., McNeese State. **1B**—Paul Goldschmidt, Jr., Texas State. **2B**—Braeden Riley, So., Sam Houston State. **3B**—Lance Brown, Jr., UTSA. **SS**—Shon Landry, Sr., McNeese State. **OF**—Michael Choice, So., Texas-Arlington; Matt Otteman, Jr., Texas-Arlington; Michael Rockett, Sr., UTSA. **DH**—Andrew Kainer, Sr., Texas-Arlington. **P**—Eric Harrington, Fr., Lamar; Kane Holbrooks, Sr., Texas State; Nathan Long, Sr., Texas-Arlington.

Player of the Year: Paul Goldschmidt, Texas State. **Hitter of the Year:** Paul Goldschmidt, Texas State. **Pitcher of the Year:** Kane Holbrooks, Texas State. **Freshman of the Year:** Eric Harrington, Lamar. **Newcomer of the Year:** Keith Prestridge, Texas State. **Coach of the Year:** Ty Harrington, Texas State.

INDIVIDUAL BATTING LEADERS
(Minimum 125 At-Bats)

	AVG	AB	R	H	2B	3B	HR	RBI	SB
Otteman, Matt, Texas-Arlington	.432	220	52	95	15	8	9	69	4
Zaleski, Nick, Sam Houston	.419	236	57	99	22	0	9	56	7
Kainer, Andrew, Texas-Arlington	.417	204	35	85	23	0	5	46	14
Choice, Michael, Texas-Arlington	.413	225	64	93	13	3	11	52	5
Dennis, Spenser, Texas State	.406	192	49	78	11	1	6	51	16
Meyers, Sean, SFA	.398	206	41	82	17	2	7	49	4
Rockett, Michael, UTSA	.394	251	63	99	17	3	15	58	14
Riley, Braeden, Sam Houston	.387	287	56	111	13	3	2	39	12
Prestridge, Keith, Texas State	.376	170	35	64	10	2	7	51	2
Throneberry, Tye, Central Arkansas	.374	195	41	73	14	1	4	34	6
O'Neal, Justin, NW State	.373	201	45	75	15	0	11	52	3
Brown, Lance, UTSA	.372	226	50	84	17	6	4	40	9
Taylor, Brian, Lamar	.371	237	44	88	16	1	7	59	6
Urtuzuastegui, Joe, NW State	.371	151	42	56	1	21	8	45	4
Link, Tyler, Lamar	.369	233	73	86	14	3	7	40	15
Atwood, Bret, Texas State	.366	235	59	86	10	5	1	30	14
Smith, Dillon, Central Arkansas	.365	211	40	77	12	2	11	55	2
Lyles, Chase, NW State	.362	199	55	72	17	2	14	47	17
Hernandez, Jose, UTSA	.360	211	60	76	25	2	17	61	8
Sibley, Tyler, Texas State	.359	234	77	84	13	4	10	38	14
Goldschmidt, Paul, Texas State	.354	223	72	79	21	0	18	87	5
Hines, Tanner, SFA	.353	221	42	78	8	2	0	19	17
Knight, Tyler, Sam Houston	.350	217	45	76	12	2	7	57	10
Landry, Shon, McNeese State	.349	166	36	58	5	1	5	33	1
Moseley, Scott, Nicholls State	.346	179	34	62	12	4	2	37	16
Murrill, Chris, Nicholls State	.344	189	48	65	10	7	1	16	27
Fontenot, Matt, McNeese State	.343	166	37	57	7	0	3	25	2
Hutson, Ryan, UTSA	.343	178	46	61	12	2	17	43	4
Street, Brandon, Southeastern La.	.341	226	48	77	18	0	7	61	2
Riche', Andy, McNeese State	.340	159	29	54	8	1	3	23	9

INDIVIDUAL PITCHING LEADERS
(Minimum 50 Innings)

	W	L	ERA	G	SV	IP	H	BB	SO
#Franklin, Chris, Southeastern La.	5	2	2.60	24	12	35	27	20	33
Harrington, Eric, Lamar	8	1	3.01	14	0	84	94	26	63
Holbrooks, Kane, Texas State	10	1	3.29	16	0	102	111	20	57
Weatherford, Sean, Sam Houston	8	6	3.46	22	4	81	81	31	77
Smith, Matison, Lamar	6	6	3.52	15	0	77	75	33	53
Borski, Brian, Texas State	7	3	3.71	15	0	85	100	36	49
Long, Nathan, Texas-Arlington	6	4	3.76	14	0	93	107	29	104
Dunnam, Jarret, Nicholls State	3	8	3.80	13	0	71	84	34	45
#Brundridge, Tyler, Texas State	4	1	3.81	34	3	54	50	13	44
Robinson, Ryan, Texas-Arlington	6	2	3.89	13	0	79	94	12	45
Varner, Rett, Texas-Arlington	2	3	3.95	16	0	57	65	24	44
Testa, Ricky, Lamar	8	3	4.13	19	1	76	79	23	84
Lehmann, Erich, SFA	7	4	4.23	14	0	77	83	12	57
Needham, Brian, Lamar	4	3	4.26	31	2	61	64	16	58
Minto, Tyler, Nicholls State	3	3	4.26	12	0	74	85	17	49
Cross, Reece, Central Arkansas	4	4	4.48	17	0	66	55	33	54
Janway, Josh, Southeastern La.	4	2	4.50	15	1	60	64	23	33
Sauter, Andy, Texas-Arlington	4	2	4.55	11	1	57	55	16	44
Mitchell, Jason, Texas-Arlington	4	5	4.63	18	2	58	68	24	42

Tritz, Zach, Texas State	8	2	4.75	13	0	78	97	23	56
Powers, Brent, Sam Houston	3	2	4.77	15	0	72	83	26	61
Pritchett, Bobby, Central Arkansas	4	5	4.85	18	5	59	60	25	55
#Cloud, Jeremy, Central Arkansas	4	6	5.92	14	0	103	123	26	69

SOUTHWESTERN ATHLETIC CONFERENCE

	Conference		Overall	
EAST	**W**	**L**	**W**	**L**
Mississippi Valley State	15	5	20	30
Jackson State	15	9	36	21
Alcorn State	12	9	5	29
Alabama A&M	10	12	14	31
Alabama State	3	20	5	15
WEST	**W**	**L**	**W**	**L**
*Southern	17	6	30	17
Arkansas-Pine Bluff	13	11	5	21
Grambling State	10	13	17	37
Texas Southern	10	14	5	24
Prairie View A&M	9	15	5	21

ALL-CONFERENCE TEAM: C—Brandon Whitby, Sr., Prairie View A&M. **1B**—Frazier Hall, So., Southern. **2B**—LaDerek Camper, Jr., Jackson State. **3B**—David Arrendondo, Sr., Texas Southern. **SS**—Jeff Squier, Jr., Mississippi Valley State. **OF**—Victor Franklin, Sr., Southern; Jerome McCollum, Jr., Arkansas-Pine Bluff; Marvin McWhorter, Jr., Jackson State. **DH**—Adam Sellers, Sr., Texas Southern. **P**—Jarrett Maloy, Jr., Southern; Justin Moring, Sr., Arkansas-Pine Bluff; Scott Reid, Sr., Mississippi Valley State.

Player of the Year: David Arrendondo, Texas Southern. **Pitcher of the Year:** Justin Moring, Sr., Arkansas-Pine Bluff. **Hitter of the Year:** Victor Franklin, Southern. **Freshman of the Year:** Eduardo Gonzalez, Alcorn State. **Newcomer of the Year:** Marvin McWhorter, Jackson State.

INDIVIDUAL BATTING LEADERS
(Minimum 100 At-Bats)

	AVG	AB	R	H	2B	3B	HR	RBI	SB
Gonzalez, Eduardo, Alcorn State	.407	172	36	70	11	3	3	41	4
Kendricks, Brandon, Prairie View	.403	154	43	62	16	7	3	38	9
Arrendondo, David, Texas Southern	.403	159	32	64	5	0	1	53	0
Whitby, Brandon, Prairie View	.373	153	28	57	12	1	4	38	7
Solis, Frank, Jackson State	.372	148	30	55	5	1	0	39	11
Graham Jabar, Alcorn State	.370	146	49	54	11	0	6	52	8
Rhone, Earnest, Texas Southern	.367	177	55	65	15	3	5	56	7
Sellers, Adam, Texas Southern	.366	161	36	59	10	1	4	40	8
Camper, LaDerek, Jackson State	.366	172	55	63	7	2	2	36	15
McDavid, Brad, Southern	.359	131	32	47	12	1	8	52	1
Reed, Oscar, Prairie View	.356	146	20	52	15	2	3	33	1
Warren, Rodney, Alcorn State	.356	163	38	58	11	1	4	50	1
McCollum, Jerome, Ark.-Pine Bluff	.355	172	29	61	10	3	5	36	16
Squier, Jeff, Mississippi Valley	.354	164	38	58	7	5	8	26	41
Villapondo, John, Prairie View	.353	150	26	53	6	3	2	31	11
Wesley, Willie, Jackson State	.353	150	48	53	9	4	1	29	12
Bowens, Adrian, Alcorn State	.352	176	56	62	11	3	2	42	10
McWhorter, Marvin, Jackson State	.348	161	51	56	9	4	8	49	16
Armstrong, James, Southern	.345	142	39	49	11	2	8	40	3
Burchett, Lloyd, Ark.-Pine Bluff	.341	123	31	42	6	1	2	33	3
Griggs, Alexandria, Alabama State	.340	159	33	54	8	1	2	44	10
Brumfield, Josh, Alcorn State	.338	142	45	48	10	2	2	17	9
Hall, Frazier, Southern	.338	154	40	52	14	0	2	30	1
Ellison, Alton, Alabama A&M	.336	134	23	45	16	1	2	30	2
Reed, David, Alcorn State	.333	135	26	45	8	0	2	27	2
Franklin, Victor, Southern	.331	154	46	51	10	1	11	47	10
Kletke, Steve, Grambling State	.331	151	28	50	10	0	4	32	0
Rowan, Kenneth, Alcorn State	.328	137	30	45	14	0	2	36	4
Tyes, Jerome, Jackson State	.328	192	58	63	13	2	6	57	17
Del Grande, Joel, Alcorn State	.327	150	36	49	11	0	8	42	0
#Whitfield, Gregory, Southern	.291	158	30	46	11	1	12	36	3
#Mazierski, Arthur, Grambling State	.271	192	38	52	4	0	3	32	1

INDIVIDUAL PITCHING LEADERS
(Minimum 40 Innings)

	W	L	ERA	G	SV	IP	H	BB	SO
Moring, Justin, Ark.-Pine Bluff	9	2	2.95	12	0	73	63	37	71
Maloy, Jarrett, Southern	8	2	3.50	12	0	72	84	16	50
Huggins, Chris, Jackson State	6	3	3.66	12	0	59	49	29	44
Davis, Ajammi, Jackson State	8	2	3.70	20	1	80	85	30	56
Zachary, Marquise, Jackson State	8	4	3.94	16	0	89	79	45	72
Spear, James, Southern	5	2	4.20	12	0	60	73	18	35
Richard, Chase, Southern	6	4	4.26	14	0	76	100	18	40
Gonzales, Tony, Alcorn State	9	3	4.40	18	3	92	107	19	57
Bautista, Justin, Mississippi Valley	2	3	4.44	33	1	51	65	19	42
Hinton, Baron, Grambling State	3	5	4.59	19	0	69	73	61	41
Gathright, Daniel, Ark.-Pine Bluff	1	6	4.84	13	0	58	68	11	37
Mills, Chris, Mississippi Valley	4	5	5.23	15	0	76	97	29	51
Reid, Scott, Mississippi Valley	3	10	5.62	15	0	75	94	14	76
Arrendondo, David, Texas Southern	5	6	5.87	16	1	87	106	31	79
Blackburn, Ben, Prairie View	4	2	5.88	17	4	60	76	16	49
Breaux, Jeremy, Mississippi Valley	4	5	5.90	15	0	61	69	28	45
Aarmold, Collin, Alcorn	6	6	5.94	22	2	86	121	18	49
Moreno, Ehren, Texas Southern	7	4	6.33	14	0	85	103	31	56
McKinney, Bernard, Alabama A&M	3	6	6.34	13	0	55	65	30	33
Kendricks, Brandon, Prairie View	4	5	6.57	10	0	51	51	34	31

SUMMIT LEAGUE

	Conference		Overall	
	W	L	W	L
*Oral Roberts	16	2	33	15
Southern Utah	15	7	27	24
South Dakota State	17	10	26	30
Centenary	16	10	33	19
North Dakota State	10	14	16	28
Oakland	10	18	22	34
Western Illinois	8	16	13	33
IPFW	6	21	13	38

ALL-CONFERENCE TEAM: C—Seth Furmanek, Jr., Oral Roberts. **1B**—Stephen Turner, Sr., South Dakota State. **2B**—Keli'I Zablan, Sr., Southern Utah. **3B**—Jesse Sawyer, So., South Dakota State. **SS**—Juan Martinez, Jr., Oral Roberts. **OF**—Nick Freitas, Sr., Southern Utah; P.K. Sequeira, Jr., Oral Roberts; Justin Wilson, Sr., Oakland. **DH**—Johnny Roberts, Sr., Oral Roberts. **UTIL**—Tony Martin, Sr., South Dakota State. **SP**—Andre Lamontagne, Sr., Oral Roberts; Mark Serrano, Sr., Oral Roberts; Jerry Sullivan, Jr., Oral Roberts. **RP**—Chris LaLonde, Sr., Centenary. **Player of the Year:** Mark Serrano, Oral Roberts. **Pitcher of the Year:** Mark Serrano, Oral Roberts. **Newcomer of the Year:** Seth Furmanek, Oral Roberts. **Coach of the Year:** Rob Walton, Oral Roberts.

INDIVIDUAL BATTING LEADERS
(Minimum 125 At-Bats)

	AVG	AB	R	H	2B	3B	HR	RBI	SB
Kline, Justin, North Dakota State	.432	125	29	54	8	2	2	20	6
Cuthbertson, Bo, Southern Utah	.393	135	35	53	11	3	0	15	2
Leverson, Travis, Centenary	.386	184	56	71	15	1	4	40	18
Stafford, Andrew, Oakland	.381	215	45	82	13	1	8	46	8
Martinez, Juan, Oral Roberts	.377	199	55	75	12	1	16	66	6
Martin, Tony, South Dakota State	.374	214	39	80	15	5	4	36	4
Sanford, Matt, Southern Utah	.366	131	32	48	3	6	5	23	8
Laidig, Drew, Western Illinois	.360	172	42	62	12	0	6	41	0
Wilson, Chester, Southern Utah	.355	169	36	60	13	0	3	26	3
Wright, Ray, Southern Utah	.354	209	51	74	11	4	4	33	10
Ryan, Dan, Oakland	.354	198	39	70	12	2	4	32	4
Gottschall, Chris, IPFW	.354	198	38	70	21	1	7	47	6
Turner, Stephen, South Dakota State	.351	202	34	71	9	4	8	57	0
Blake, Joel, South Dakota State	.351	228	51	80	21	0	13	38	0
Ross, Tell, Centenary	.350	163	37	57	10	1	7	49	3
Wentz, Zach, North Dakota State	.349	169	28	59	11	1	3	25	4
Tompkins, Michael, Centenary	.348	181	44	63	13	0	8	45	2
Freitas, Nick, Southern Utah	.347	190	48	66	13	1	14	60	14
Sawyer, Jesse, South Dakota State	.346	211	61	73	18	0	19	58	2
Shepard, Cliff, Centenary	.345	177	33	61	13	3	7	40	3
Price, Colby, Oral Roberts	.340	141	28	48	10	1	6	37	0
Wilson, Justin, Oakland	.340	209	55	71	19	0	12	43	16
Stewart, Cooper, Western Illinois	.337	166	44	56	12	1	1	14	2

Furmanek, Seth, Oral Roberts	.333	183	51	61	14	2	17	63	0
Traub, Taylor, Oakland	.330	194	40	64	16	1	3	33	6
Sequeira, P.J., Oral Roberts	.330	188	50	62	14	2	9	38	5
Garewal, Tyler, Oral Roberts	.330	176	63	58	13	0	5	33	13
Ford, Colby, Southern Utah	.328	131	28	43	10	0	2	23	6
Jablonski, Tommy, Oakland	.328	177	35	58	8	2	2	29	9
Imperiali, Ricky, Centenary	.318	198	47	63	18	1	2	36	5

INDIVIDUAL PITCHING LEADERS
(Minimum 50 Innings)

	W	L	ERA	G	SV	IP	H	BB	SO
Serrano, Mark, Oral Roberts	9	1	2.50	20	0	86	62	25	132
Lamontagne, Andre, Oral Roberts	6	2	2.97	16	0	76	71	36	72
Sullivan, Jerry, Oral Roberts	8	3	3.12	15	0	98	93	27	116
Straka, John, North Dakota State	4	3	3.49	10	0	59	64	10	54
Kraft, Justin, Centenary	6	4	4.08	16	2	81	87	24	77
Whiting, Boone, Centenary	6	2	4.16	13	0	80	85	23	86
Walker, Samuel, IPFW	0	5	4.17	14	0	54	56	27	45
Tromblee, Stephen, Centenary	5	3	4.46	17	4	69	73	35	58
Johnson, Steve, Southern Utah	8	4	5.00	15	0	85	122	24	37
Somsen, Layne, South Dakota State	4	7	5.32	14	0	66	82	44	36
Thielbar, Caleb, South Dakota State	5	8	5.44	22	1	88	102	31	100
LaMothe, Matt, Oakland	4	4	5.45	17	1	68	80	34	42
Melling, Kyle, Southern Utah	7	3	5.58	15	1	81	99	31	55
Ries, Mark, North Dakota State	3	5	5.79	13	1	56	71	20	21
Reichle, Alec, Southern Utah	2	7	6.30	18	0	86	113	52	32
Welke, Greg, Oakland	4	6	6.48	16	0	67	85	26	31
Eden, Eric, Western Illinois	3	4	6.90	15	2	60	76	27	49
Robinson, Mike, South Dakota State	5	4	7.20	19	0	70	106	30	47
Wick, Aaron, Oakland	4	4	7.26	16	0	54	72	30	38
Pieczynski, Sam, South Dakota State	5	3	7.57	21	0	61	86	28	44
Johnson, Isaac, South Dakota State	4	3	7.87	15	0	59	65	41	30
Herrold, Stacy, IPFW	3	7	8.19	14	0	70	96	29	40
#Noyes, Jacob, Southern Utah	0	0	8.22	13	6	15	15	18	17
Baatz, Tyler, IPFW	1	6	8.23	20	0	63	85	40	43
Teague, Kyle, Oakland	2	4	9.21	14	0	58	89	25	40
#Emge, Andrew, IPFW	2	3	9.86	25	3	40	76	9	16

SUN BELT CONFERENCE

	Conference		Overall	
	W	L	W	L
*Middle Tennessee State	21	8	44	18
Western Kentucky	21	8	42	20
Troy	18	10	33	23
Florida International	18	12	34	23
Louisiana-Lafayette	14	15	27	30
South Alabama	13	16	25	30
Louisiana-Monroe	12	17	32	27
Florida Atlantic	12	17	30	26
Arkansas State	12	18	23	30
New Orleans	12	18	22	33
Arkansas-Little Rock	7	21	16	34

ALL-CONFERENCE TEAM: C—David Doss, Sr., South Alabama. **1B**—Mike Martinez, Fr., Florida International. **2B**—Ryan Mollica, Sr., Florida International. **3B**—Wade Gaynor, Jr., Western Kentucky. **SS**—Ben Soignier, Sr., Louisiana-Monroe. **OF**—Bryce Brentz, So., Middle Tennessee; Chad Cregar, Sr., Western Kentucky; Tyler Townsend, Jr., Florida International. **DH**—Tim Jobe, Jr., Florida International. **UT**—Michael Precise, Sr., Troy. **SP**—Matt Hightower, Sr., Western Kentucky; Kenneth Roberts, Jr., Middle Tennessee. **RP**—Coty Woods, Jr., Middle Tennessee. **Player of the Year:** Bryce Brentz, Middle Tennessee. **Pitcher of the Year:** Matt Hightower, Western Kentucky. **Freshman of the Year:** Tyler Ray, Troy. **Newcomer of the Year:** Boomer Blanchard, Louisiana-Monroe. **Coach of the Year:** Chris Finwood, Western Kentucky.

INDIVIDUAL BATTING LEADERS
(Minimum 125 At-Bats)

	AVG	AB	R	H	2B	3B	HR	RBI	SB
Brentz, Bryce, Middle Tennessee	.465	230	79	107	19	2	28	73	7
Townsend, Tyler, Fla. International	.426	216	58	92	16	1	24	77	3
Rice, Matt, Western Kentucky	.399	253	50	101	18	1	10	72	2
Bishop, Rawley, Middle Tennessee	.398	241	78	96	17	1	14	51	7
Heisler, Adam, South Alabama	.390	213	37	83	14	1	3	45	16
Doss, Davis, South Alabama	.378	230	53	87	20	1	12	59	5
Soignier, Ben, Louisiana-Monroe	.376	226	58	85	22	1	11	71	8
Gaynor, Wade, Western Kentucky	.371	251	83	93	20	4	25	78	21
Poche, Jordy, Louisiana-Monroe	.365	178	34	65	8	2	3	36	4
Smith, Perry, Louisiana-Monroe	.365	159	38	58	13	1	5	34	4
Jobe, Tim, Florida International	.364	206	45	75	15	1	10	48	0
Morris, Jay, New Orleans	.362	196	44	71	10	0	2	36	8
O'Reilly, Derek, South Alabama	.354	192	38	68	7	1	0	35	16
Mollica, Ryan, Fla. International	.354	178	35	63	13	0	8	50	3
Hines, Nathan, Middle Tennessee	.352	270	60	95	27	6	11	73	7
Blanchard, Boomer, La.-Monroe	.351	248	71	87	10	2	12	38	11
Hoyle, Miles, Troy	.350	180	36	63	13	1	9	35	2
Harris, Alan, New Orleans	.344	157	28	54	11	0	9	44	1
Burnett, Tyler, Middle Tennessee	.344	221	45	76	12	1	7	37	9
Wade, Nick, Louisiana-Monroe	.342	190	53	65	12	1	9	36	4
McDade, Blake, Middle Tennessee	.340	212	39	72	19	1	6	51	4
Wilson, David, Florida Atlantic	.338	216	51	73	10	2	7	32	11
Block, William, Florida Atlantic	.337	199	48	67	16	4	9	52	4
Overstreet, Jake, South Alabama	.336	220	45	74	18	1	4	39	8
Martinez, Mike, Fla. International	.335	182	41	61	7	2	6	37	3
Schwaner, Nick, New Orleans	.332	214	46	71	20	3	12	53	7
Prevost, Jon, Louisiana-Monroe	.332	229	70	76	13	1	15	52	20
Bohanan, Ryan, South Alabama	.330	203	32	67	13	0	3	29	1
Fontenot, Greg, La.-Lafayette	.329	213	38	70	10	1	2	31	9
Whipple, Travis, La.-Lafayette	.329	161	39	53	13	2	8	30	5
Reynolds, Clint, South Alabama	.328	201	43	66	5	3	1	38	18
Dayleg, Terrence, Western Kentucky	.327	220	43	72	18	2	3	39	3
Ditthardt, Ryan, Troy	.327	223	36	73	13	1	7	54	4
#Hightower, Matt, Western Ky.	.300	223	56	67	6	3	11	53	25

INDIVIDUAL PITCHING LEADERS
(Minimum 50 Innings)

	W	L	ERA	G	SV	IP	H	BB	SO
#Woods, Coty, Middle Tennessee	4	3	1.62	32	15	44	33	28	50
Robichaux, Justin, La.-Lafayette	3	3	1.98	17	0	59	60	13	16
Roberts, Kenneth, Middle Tennessee	11	1	3.04	16	0	104	87	35	28
#Teague, Kevin, Western Kentucky	5	3	3.32	35	3	41	37	17	38
Osborne, Zach, Louisiana-Lafayette	5	3	3.44	16	1	84	85	32	14
Baxter, Lance, South Alabama	3	3	3.74	21	0	67	81	28	28
Bullington, Joe, Arkansas State	2	3	3.95	29	0	57	57	25	30
Hightower, Matt, Western Kentucky	7	3	4.01	15	0	85	92	38	33
Ware, Chase, Arkansas State	5	3	4.22	13	1	85	86	40	30
Ebert, Tom, Florida International	6	5	4.39	15	6	28	4	54	39
Brentz, Bryce, Middle Tennessee	5	3	4.57	15	0	89	90	45	31
Ray, Tyler, Troy	7	3	4.60	14	0	88	104	45	20
Sage, Brandon, South Alabama	3	6	4.64	15	1	64	67	25	44
Rembisz, Scott, Fla. International	6	3	4.69	15	0	94	98	22	90
Walls, Jason, Troy	4	4	4.73	15	0	65	65	40	49
Ridings, Matt, Western Kentucky	8	2	4.84	19	2	102	107	29	93
Graham, Drew, Louisiana-Monroe	3	2	4.85	22	2	52	43	30	54
Christensen, Keith, Louisiana-Monroe	5	3	4.98	15	0	73	96	34	44
Cameron, Shane, Western Kentucky	5	2	5.03	15	0	77	80	30	59
Haagen, Blake, Louisiana-Monroe	2	5	5.19	29	4	50	51	25	37
Jackson, Matt, South Alabama	5	4	5.33	13	0	74	81	27	64
Rooks, Barry, Florida Atlantic	3	2	5.46	14	0	58	69	29	38

WEST COAST CONFERENCE

	Conference		Overall	
	W	L	W	L
*Gonzaga	14	7	36	18
Loyola Marymount	13	8	30	29
Pepperdine	12	9	31	23
San Francisco	12	9	28	28
San Diego	11	10	29	25
St. Mary's	9	12	28	27
Portland	7	14	25	26
Santa Clara	6	15	19	34

ALL-CONFERENCE TEAM: C—Geoff Klein, Jr., Santa Clara; Tyson Van Winkle, Jr., Gonzaga. **1B**—Kyle Jensen, Jr., St. Mary's; Ryan Wheeler, Jr., Loyola Marymount; Ryan Wiegand, Sr., Gonzaga. **2B**—Jonathan Johnson, So., Loyola Marymount. **3B**— Dane Braunecker, Sr., San Francisco; Troy Channing, Fr., St. Mary's; Zach Walters, So., San Diego. **SS**—Jon Karcich, Jr., Santa Clara; Sean Nicol, Sr., San Diego; Derek Poppert, Jr., San Francisco. **OF**—Drew Johnson, Sr., San Francisco; Zach Kim, Sr., San Francisco; James Meador, Jr., San Diego; Nate Simon, Sr., Pepperdine; Anthony Synegal, Sr., Gonzaga. **P**—Matt Bywater, So., Pepperdine; Matt Fields, Sr., Gonzaga; Nate Garcia, Jr., Santa Clara; Nick Gaudi, Sr., Pepperdine; A.J. Griffin, Jr., San Diego; Brian Justice, Sr., St. Mary's; Doug Murray, Jr., San Francisco; Lee Roberts. Sr., Loyola Marymount.

Player of the Year: James Meador, San Diego. **Pitcher of the Year:** Matt Fields, Gonzaga. **Defensive Player of the Year:** Denny Duron, Pepperdine. **Freshman of the Year:** Troy Channing, St. Mary's. **Coach of the Year:** Mark Machtolf, Gonzaga.

INDIVIDUAL BATTING LEADERS
(Minimum 125 At-Bats)

	AVG	AB	R	H	2B	3B	HR	RBI	SB
Channing, Troy, St. Mary's	.379	206	45	78	11	0	20	75	2
Klein, Geoff, Santa Clara	.379	214	32	81	21	0	5	56	1
Walters, Zach, San Diego	.377	191	35	72	13	4	1	26	4
Meador, James, San Diego	.376	213	42	80	17	2	6	45	7
Van Winkle, Tyson, Gonzaga	.362	232	45	84	27	0	5	61	0
Songco, Angelo, LMU	.360	214	65	77	17	3	15	63	5
Nicol, Sean, San Diego	.359	220	59	79	19	2	8	39	19
Engell, Chris, San Diego	.358	215	35	77	16	1	3	37	3
Heid, Drew, Gonzaga	.355	234	45	83	7	8	2	41	10
Karcich, Jon, Santa Clara	.354	192	37	68	22	0	2	22	7
Kim, Zach, San Francisco	.353	224	52	79	17	3	2	30	42
Poppert, Derek, San Francisco	.352	219	41	77	15	3	1	52	16
Henricks, Riley, Portland	.344	183	27	63	11	1	4	31	6
Kauppila, Kris, Portland	.336	214	46	72	20	0	4	21	8
Mulligan, Ryan, St. Mary's	.335	158	37	53	11	1	0	16	5
Aliotti, Anthony, St. Mary's	.333	171	35	57	9	0	6	39	6
Synegal, Anthony, Gonzaga	.331	175	30	58	9	1	8	36	3
Rooney, Collin, Pepperdine	.327	165	29	54	9	1	6	31	0
Carpenter, Cort, Portland	.327	147	19	48	6	0	8	37	0
Wells, Ryan, Gonzaga	.324	204	59	66	9	4	0	28	12
Enos, Ollie, LMU	.320	153	29	49	13	0	1	31	1
Wheeler, Ryan, LMU	.319	232	61	74	20	3	9	48	5
Kraus, Bryant, Pepperdine	.318	179	40	57	16	2	9	41	3
Wiegand, Ryan, Gonzaga	.318	223	44	71	21	0	7	65	1
Simon, Nate, Pepperdine	.317	186	30	59	9	2	9	51	7
Ethel, Bobby, San Francisco	.316	155	39	49	6	1	3	26	11
Smith, Craig, Portland	.315	162	30	51	10	0	5	21	9
Strazzara, Tony, San Diego	.313	134	26	42	9	0	0	17	0
Johnson, Drew, San Francisco	.312	208	40	65	11	0	6	35	18
Hawthorne, Ryan, LMU	.307	228	39	70	12	0	1	29	2
Johnson, Jonathan, LMU	.305	226	41	69	10	7	1	24	6
Madden, Kevin, Santa Clara	.305	128	21	39	11	1	0	10	4
Braunecker, Dane, San Francisco	.305	174	41	53	5	2	3	23	1
Humphries, Brian, Pepperdine	.305	220	34	67	13	1	2	38	8

INDIVIDUAL PITCHING LEADERS
(Minimum 50 Innings)

	W	L	ERA	G	SV	IP	H	BB	SO
Varce, Zach, Portland	3	5	**2.69**	23	**9**	60	55	23	62
Martin, Cody, Gonzaga	5	4	3.07	23	6	59	54	30	68
Blair, Kyle, San Diego	3	2	3.13	10	2	55	47	18	62
Griffin, A.J., San Diego	8	3	3.33	17	3	81	74	32	85
Anderson, Mark, St. Mary's	1	0	3.38	15	0	37	40	7	23
Hiserman, Matt, San Francisco	4	6	3.43	19	2	89	82	29	88
Fields, Matt, Gonzaga	8	1	3.47	14	0	91	98	31	74
Bywater, Matt, Pepperdine	6	1	3.57	12	0	63	50	24	66
#Gaudi, Nick, Pepperdine	5	3	3.52	23	**9**	36	29	12	47
Roberts, Lee, LMU	7	2	3.58	16	1	103	104	27	91
Cook, Cole, Pepperdine	7	3	3.69	16	1	83	57	20	79
Murray, Doug, San Francisco	**9**	0	3.77	13	0	88	95	18	95
Love, Cameron, San Francisco	4	1	3.83	24	0	51	52	21	27
Ames, Steven, Gonzaga	8	2	3.91	15	0	97	106	21	70
Kraus, Kyle, Portland	4	6	4.00	15	0	83	106	14	31
#Brynteson, Keeler, Portland	2	0	4.00	**28**	1	40	42	18	32
Alexander, Scott, Pepperdine	4	5	4.11	16	0	66	52	38	60
Justice, Brian, St. Mary's	6	3	4.31	13	0	77	87	16	59
Garcia, Nate, Santa Clara	7	5	4.33	13	0	96	95	30	**96**
Schneider, Scott, St. Mary's	6	4	4.54	13	0	75	94	21	67
Burris, Scott, Portland	5	4	4.70	13	0	69	68	28	31
Barraclough, Kyle, St. Mary's	4	5	4.70	15	0	54	59	25	51
Gonzalez, Nathan, St. Mary's	3	3	4.78	11	0	58	65	16	25

WESTERN ATHLETIC CONFERENCE

	Conference		Overall	
	W	L	W	L
San Jose State	15	7	41	20
Louisiana Tech	13	11	29	22
New Mexico State	12	12	44	17
*Fresno State	12	12	32	30
Hawaii	11	12	32	26
Nevada	10	13	25	31
Sacramento State	8	14	27	27

ALL-CONFERENCE TEAM: C—Travis Simas, Sr., Nevada. **1B**—Kevin Macdonald, Jr., Hawaii. **2B**—Danny Muno, So., Fresno State. **3B**—Tom Mendonca, Jr., Fresno State. **SS**—Kyle Bellows, Jr., San Jose State; Bryan Marquez, Sr., New Mexico State. **OF**—Devon Dageford, Jr., Louisiana Tech; Dusty Robinson, Fr., Fresno State; Tim Wheeler, Jr., Sacramento State; Kolten Wong, Fr., Hawaii. **DH**—Nick Melino, Fr., Nevada. **UTIL**—Matt Bowman, Sr., Nevada. **SP**—David Berner, Sr., San Jose State; Jayson, Kramer, Sr., Hawaii; Ryan Shopshire, Sr., San Jose State. **RP**—Holden Sprague, Sr., Fresno State.

Player of the Year: Tom Mendonca, Fresno State. **Pitcher of the Year:** Ryan Shopshire, San Jose State. **Freshman of the Year:** Kolten Wong, Hawaii. **Coach of the Year:** Sam Piraro, San Jose State.

INDIVIDUAL BATTING LEADERS
(Minimum 125 At-Bats)

	AVG	AB	R	H	2B	3B	HR	RBI	SB
Sodders, Mike, New Mexico State	**.422**	187	55	79	19	2	13	68	1
Marquez, Bryan, New Mexico State	.414	215	**83**	89	14	1	22	**85**	5
Bruns, Jacob, San Jose State	.399	178	47	71	16	1	7	42	5
Aguirre, Leo, New Mexico State	.398	166	43	66	11	3	8	47	0
Crosby, Blake, Sacramento State	.397	209	36	83	9	1	4	47	4
Bellows, Kyle, San Jose State	.389	**239**	62	**93**	16	**4**	10	57	10
Valine, Corey, San Jose State	.387	186	30	72	11	0	7	46	4
Dageford, Devon, Louisiana Tech	.385	195	59	75	18	3	23	68	9
Winn, Kevin, Louisiana Tech	.380	213	51	81	19	1	9	63	2
Wheeler, Tim, Sacramento State	.380	200	59	76	16	3	18	72	15
Muno, Danny, Fresno State	.379	224	74	85	25	1	3	41	13
Martin, Jason, San Jose State	.376	229	68	86	11	2	5	45	2
Thomas, Patrick, Louisiana Tech	.372	207	58	77	12	1	7	47	7
Kersten, Chris, Louisiana Tech	.372	191	49	71	20	2	18	58	3
Farnham, Jeffrey, New Mexico State	.371	237	70	88	16	1	13	76	18
Reynoso, Wade, New Mexico State	.370	230	56	85	16	2	11	68	0
Martinez, Hunter, Sacramento State	.364	239	67	87	11	2	5	32	14
Powers, Josh, Sacramento State	.358	212	41	76	**26**	0	3	44	11
Melino, Nick, Nevada	.352	165	28	58	15	2	4	39	3
Catricala, Vinnie, Hawaii	.349	218	51	76	13	1	13	44	3

Stout, Richard, New Mexico State	.346	188	73	65	11	3	2	42	**23**
Shaver, Nate, New Mexico State	.344	227	71	78	16	2	9	57	6
Wong, Kolten, Hawaii	.341	226	46	77	21	2	11	52	11
Mendonca, Tom, Fresno State	.339	233	54	79	8	0	**27**	78	2
Stienstra, Danny, San Jose State	.337	187	39	63	12	0	0	27	3
Shaffer, John, San Jose State	.335	161	31	54	8	0	4	26	3
Kort, Shaun, Nevada	.329	213	41	70	16	1	4	62	4
Ahmady, Alan, Fresno State	.326	175	47	57	6	2	8	53	1
Robinson, Dusty, Fresno State	.319	207	52	66	12	1	15	45	7
Grunenwald, Nick, Louisiana Tech	.315	184	49	58	7	1	3	31	19
Roth, Jeff, Sacramento State	.312	154	30	48	9	0	11	40	2

INDIVIDUAL PITCHING LEADERS
(Minimum 50 Innings)

	W	L	ERA	G	SV	IP	H	BB	SO
Berner, David, San Jose State	7	2	**3.20**	13	0	96	84	15	**84**
Kramer, Jayson, Hawaii	5	4	3.47	15	1	93	98	22	45
Shopshire, Ryan, San Jose State	6	1	4.04	14	2	62	59	30	69
Sprague, Holden, Fresno State	7	4	4.20	23	**4**	**99**	104	19	67
Sisto, Matthew, Hawaii	5	4	4.37	14	0	82	104	14	50
Peterson, Max, San Jose State	7	1	4.55	15	0	65	61	37	62
Simon, Daniel, New Mexico State	**9**	1	4.55	15	0	87	97	38	71
Achelpohl, Derek, Nevada	4	6	4.58	15	0	75	103	16	58
Morse, Matt, Fresno State	4	3	4.72	19	1	80	97	26	50
4Benny, Derek, Fresno State	4	4	5.09	16	1	87	101	22	59
Klein, Nathaniel, Hawaii	3	4	5.10	11	0	60	69	13	47
Sandoval, Brandon, Sac. State	5	4	5.49	14	0	77	86	36	56
#Vega, Anthony, San Jose State	0	4	5.59	26	**9**	39	48	13	41
Darrah, Jesse, Sacramento State	**9**	2	5.64	14	0	83	104	31	59
Jordan, Jared, New Mexico State	7	3	5.71	15	0	70	85	30	53
Garcia, Chris, Nevada	4	6	6.02	14	0	81	81	52	57
Jefferson, Mike, Louisiana Tech	3	3	6.10	**25**	1	51	53	38	39
Moseley, Dylan, Louisiana Tech	5	4	6.33	13	0	75	104	26	42
Vendette, Sebastien, NM State	8	2	6.37	15	0	89	109	39	67
Stefan, Jeb, Louisiana Tech	4	5	6.39	14	0	75	82	36	66
Stassi, Brock, Nevada	6	5	6.63	15	0	73	86	34	54
Sturdevant, Tyler, NM State	7	6	6.75	16	0	88	105	44	69
Elrod, Tommy, Sacramento State	4	4	6.93	16	0	62	82	29	45

INDEPENDENTS

	Overall	
	W	L
Dallas Baptist	38	17
Bryant	32	22
Longwood	26	22
Le Moyne	24	23
Savannah State	25	26
New York Tech	19	29
Northern Colorado	18	35
Utah Valley	18	35
North Dakota	14	29
Southern Illinois-Edwardsville	15	39
Cal State Bakersfield	13	37
Texas-Pan American	14	41
Houston Baptist	11	40
North Carolina Central	6	35
New Jersey Tech	4	33
Chicago State	3	38

ALL-INDEPENDENTS TEAM: C—Jeff Vigurs, Jr., Bryant. **1B**—Jake Magner, So., North Dakota. **2B**—Josh Street, Sr., SIU-Edwardsville. **3B**—Jace Brinkerhoff, Jr., Utah Valley. **SS**—Ryan Goins, Jr., Dallas Baptist. **OF**—Billy Burgess, Fr., Utah Valley; Ryan Enos, Jr., Dallas Baptist; Erik Hegstad, Sr., Northern Colorado. **DH/UTIL**—Jason Krizan, So., Dallas Baptist. **SP**—Eric Polvani, Jr., Bryant; Justin Smith, Jr., Utah Valley. **RP**—Mark Andrews, So., Bryant.

Player of the Year: Ryan Goins, Dallas Baptist. **Pitcher of the Year:** Eric Polvani, Bryant. **Newcomer of the Year:** Billy Burgess, Utah Valley. **Coach of the Year:** Dan Heffner, Dallas Baptist.

INDIVIDUAL BATTING LEADERS
(Minimum 125 At-Bats)

	AVG	AB	R	H	2B	3B	HR	RBI	SB
Brinkerhoff, Jace, Utah Valley	.433	217	46	94	19	0	5	39	2
Valdez, Effrey, New York Tech	.401	192	35	77	10	2	11	40	0
Magner, Jake, North Dakota	.393	168	30	66	13	2	10	51	4
Havers, Casey, Longwood	.391	169	42	66	14	0	5	38	5
Krizan, Jason, Dallas Baptist	.389	208	57	81	20	2	16	74	2
Vigurs, Jeff, Bryant	.389	203	37	79	23	1	9	70	7
Jones, Brant, Longwood	.387	191	60	74	17	4	7	44	7
Street, Josh, SIU-Edwardsville	.387	212	53	82	12	2	15	59	3
Burgess, Billy, Utah Valley	.381	139	37	53	8	3	8	42	2
Ross, Johnathan, Savannah State	.380	158	38	60	12	1	4	26	13
Enos, Ryan, Dallas Baptist	.376	229	71	86	20	2	17	56	13
Campbell, Nick, Bryant	.375	224	50	84	11	1	3	42	5
Goins, Ryan, Dallas Baptist	.371	221	76	82	17	2	22	70	11
Quigley, Jonathan, Longwood	.371	178	41	66	13	1	9	47	3
Budde, Seth, Northern Colorado	.370	127	31	47	12	2	2	31	0
Garcia, Abraham, UTPA	.368	182	38	67	15	1	6	33	13
Smiy Jr., David, Longwood	.367	180	30	66	18	3	2	27	4
Cerreto, Phil, Longwood	.367	180	45	66	13	0	8	52	12
Botsford, Brett, Le Moyne	.363	182	35	66	13	2	4	21	10
Smith, Brian, New York Tech	.361	208	47	75	10	2	7	30	10
Hegstad, Erik, Northern Colo.	.353	204	41	72	16	2	11	41	1
Sandberg, Kevin, Northern Colo.	.351	211	54	74	13	0	20	64	0
Dienna, Christian, New York Tech	.348	158	23	55	11	0	1	34	0
2Mendoza, Jose, UTPA	.348	204	44	71	9	2	1	28	7
Thompson, Ryan, Dallas Baptist	.346	191	51	66	13	4	8	48	9
McKenna, Pat, Bryant	.338	216	62	73	14	3	12	43	4
Mees, Andy, Northern Colorado	.338	198	58	67	16	3	10	57	2
Meiners, Travis, Dallas Baptist	.337	169	47	57	8	0	8	38	6
Benson, Chris, Utah Valley	.336	214	44	72	14	2	3	38	5
Mendez, Andrew, Savannah State	.335	164	42	55	15	0	1	37	10
#Rickenbach, Jake, Utah Valley	.322	211	44	68	13	5	7	43	5
#Kelley, Dexter, Savannah State	.318	173	46	55	5	1	9	45	33

INDIVIDUAL PITCHING LEADERS
(Minimum 50 Innings)

	W	L	ERA	G	SV	IP	H	BB	SO
Polvani, Eric, Bryant	8	2	2.04	12	1	79	82	15	58
Tardiff, Jeff, Le Moyne	6	2	3.02	13	0	95	94	27	68
Cobb, Kevin, Bryant	7	0	3.35	11	0	81	81	16	62
Roth, Mike, New York Tech	3	1	3.65	23	2	37	42	11	19
Nelson, Cory, Le Moyne	5	5	4.06	14	0	62	60	42	49
Black, Victor, Dallas Baptist	6	4	4.16	15	0	89	92	40	99
Guarrasi, Andrew, New York Tech	6	5	4.36	13	0	87	91	35	79
#Andrews, Mark, Bryant	2	4	4.38	21	10	25	29	11	20
Brunson, Keith, Houston Baptist	3	3	4.45	20	2	59	78	21	38
Ramsdale, Robert, Savannah State	4	5	4.66	13	1	66	76	30	38
Smith, Justin, Utah Valley	8	4	4.73	17	0	91	93	37	91
Quattrocchi, Dustin, SIU-Edwardsville	3	5	4.75	17	1	61	77	12	40
Smith, Michael, Dallas Baptist	6	0	5.15	21	0	51	61	19	40
Millard, Ryan, Dallas Baptist	7	2	5.20	11	0	64	76	14	47
Walker II, John, Longwood	5	4	5.23	13	0	72	102	7	39
Patton, Spencer, SIU-Edwardsville	4	6	5.24	16	0	69	83	29	77
Wingo, Scott, UTPA	4	6	5.56	14	0	89	93	43	68
Montgomery, Mark, Longwood	3	5	5.57	20	0	63	69	24	64
Allegretti, Michael, Savannah State	7	7	5.65	16	0	72	72	21	52
Jannis, Mickey, CS Bakersfield	2	8	5.76	13	0	75	91	31	61
Messmore, Spenser, CS Bakersfield	2	4	7.14	23	0	58	83	14	32
#Scott, Forbes, Northern Colorado	2	1	7.96	23	0	37	56	20	20
#Haney, Chris, Dallas Baptist	4	4	4.64	23	7	43	45	21	44

NCAA DIVISION II

Lynn (Fla.) won its first Division II College World Series after defeating Emporia State (Kan.) 2-1 in a classic pitchers' duel at the USA Baseball National Training Complex in Cary, N.C.

Lynn ace Dan Wright, a junior who transferred from Palm Beach (Fla.) CC, protected the 2-1 lead his team built in the third inning. Wright fired seven innings and allowed only one run on six hits. He fanned four batters and walked three.

Wright, who posted a 2.35 ERA and struck out 115 batters in 115 innings on the season, cruised after a shaky first inning, when Emporia plated its only run. He then worked six shutout innings, retiring eight straight batters at one point.

Emporia State's sidewinding righthander Ben Graham put together a valiant performance of his own by striking out 10 over eight innings. Lynn scrapped together a run each in the second and third innings before Graham retired 10 straight batters.

First baseman Chris Chavez drove in Lynn's first run with a line-drive single down the right-field line in the second inning. Senior shortstop Chad Crowe tacked on what proved to be the game-winner in the third with a sacrifice fly to left field.

Righthander Tommy Kahnle, who had made 13 starts and six relief appearances to go along with four saves for the Fighting Knights, entered the game in the eighth inning and shut the door with a perfect two-inning save. Kahnle recorded 12 shutout innings during the College World Series and was named the tournament's most outstanding player.

DIVISION II WORLD SERIES

Site: Cary, N.C.
Participants: Mesa State, Colo. (43-13); Belmont Abbey, N.C. (38-24); Grand Valley State, Mich. (45-14-1); Emporia State, Kan. (46-13); UC San Diego (39-13); Dowling, N.Y. (34-16); West Chester, Pa. (46-10); Lynn, Fla. (42-16).
Champion: Lynn.
Runner-Up: Emporia State.
Outstanding Player: Tommy Kahnle, Lynn.
PRELIMINARIES
Mesa State 7, Belmont Abbey 2
Emporia State 3, Grand Valley State 0
Dowling 3, UC San Diego 1
Lynn 7, West Chester 3
Belmont Abbey 5, Grand Valley State 4 (Grand Valley State eliminated)
UC San Diego 8, West Chester 6 (West Chester eliminated)
Emporia State 5, Mesa State 2
Lynn 6, Dowling 5
Belmont Abbey 9, Mesa State 2 (Mesa State eliminated)
UC San Diego 13, Dowling 1 (Dowling eliminated)
SEMIFINALS
Emporia State 5, UC San Diego 3 (UC San Diego eliminated)
Lynn 7, Belmont Abbey 5 (Belmont Abbey eliminated)
CHAMPIONSHIP
Lynn 2, Emporia State 1 (Emporia State eliminated)

NCAA DIVISION III

St. Thomas (Minn.) took two games from Wooster (Ohio) on the tournament's final day to come away with its second national championship.

St. Thomas took the opening game of the finals 6-4, and then pulled out a thrilling 3-2 win in a 12-inning marathon—the second-longest championship game in D-III history.

In the bottom of the 12th inning, St. Thomas outfielder and tournament most outstanding player Matt Olsen singled to left and was sacrificed into scoring position. Dan Leslie then singled through the left gap to walk off the field with the trophy.

"We consider ourselves very fortunate and lucky as (Wooster) was very good also," St. Thomas coach Dennis Denning said. "You want to play in big games. We finished at the end of the year playing in the biggest game(s) of the year and won two."

Wooster's Mark Miller pitched the entire second game, allowing three runs over 11⅓ innings.

"For three years (Miller) has done a phenomenal job and had a great effort," coach Tim Pettorini said. "Unfortunately we could not score a few more runs for him."

But it was St. Thomas' Brandon Stone who picked up the win, pitching seven shutout innings of relief in his first outing since the conference tournament. Stone surrendered just three hits.

St. Thomas forced the second game for the first time since 2003. The Tommies used some late-game magic in the opener as well, scoring two runs in the top of the ninth inning for the winning margin.

DIVISION III WORLD SERIES

Site: Grand Chute, Wis.
Participants: Carthage, Wis. (36-7); Wooster, Ohio (39-9); Kean, N.J. (38-9); Trinity, Conn. (33-5); Shenandoah, Va. (37-8); Farmingdale State, N.Y. (30-15); Chapman, Calif. (30-15); St. Thomas, Minn. (36-12).
Champion: St. Thomas.
Runner-Up: Wooster.
Outstanding Player: Matt Olson, St. Thomas.
PRELIMINARIES
Wooster 8, Carthage 1
Kean 8, Trinity 5
Shenandoah 12, Farmingdale State 2
St. Thomas 9, Chapman 1
Carthage 10, Trinity 1 (Trinity eliminated)
Chapman 4, Farmingdale State 2 (Farmingdale State eliminated)
Wooster 14, Kean 1
St. Thomas 16, Shenandoah 5
Carthage 9, Shenandoah 8 (Shenandoah eliminated)
Chapman 7, Kean 5 (Kean eliminated)
Wooster 3, St. Thomas 0
SEMIFINALS
Wooster 11, Chapman 7 (Chapman eliminated)
St. Thomas 3, Charthage 1 (11 innings; Carthage eliminated)
CHAMPIONSHIP
St. Thomas 6, Wooster 4
St. Thomas 3, Wooster 2 (12 innings; Wooster eliminated)

NAIA

Lubbock Christian (Texas) captured its second NAIA title, beating Point Loma Nazarene (Calif.) 11-8 in the finals. Lubbock won two straight against Point Loma after falling 2-1 earlier in the tournament. Lubbock's Will Stramp put Lubbock up for good in the third inning with a three-run homer to make the score 8-5. Stramp went 2-for-5 in the finale with his 27th homer and RBIs 97, 98 and 99—and collected tournament MVP honors.

NAIA WORLD SERIES

Site: Lewiston, Idaho
Participants: Campbellsville, Ky. (40-10); Lee, Tenn. (50-12); Berry, Ga. (45-14); Southern Poly State, Ga. (51-8); Embry-Riddle, Fla. (44-12); Point Loma Nazarene, Calif. (41-11); Lewis-Clark State, Idaho (39-13); Fresno Pacific, Calif. (39-19); Lubbock Christian, Texas (47-7); Oklahoma City (51-7).
Champion: Lubbock Christian.
Runner-Up: Point Loma Nazarene.
Outstanding Player: Will Stramp, Lubbock Christian.
PRELIMINARIES
Lee 5, Campbellsville 2
Berry 10, Southern Poly State 5
Point Loma Nazarene 10, Embry-Riddle 0 (8 innings)
Lewis-Clark State 5, Fresno Pacific 0
Southern Poly State 6, Campbellsville 5 (Campbellsville eliminated)
Fresno Pacific 8, Embry Riddle 6 (Embry-Riddle eliminated)
Lubbock Christian 11, Lee 0
Oklahoma City 10, Lewis-Clark State 8
Southern Poly State 9, Lewis-Clark State 6 (Lewis-Clark State eliminated)
Lee 5, Fresno Pacific 4 (Fresno Pacific eliminated)
Lubbock Christian 11, Berry 5
Point Loma Nazarene 8, Oklahoma City 3
Lee 5, Berry 3 (Berry eliminated)
Oklahoma City 8, Southern Poly State 4 (Southern Poly State eliminated)
SEMIFINALS
Point Loma Nazarene 2, Lubbock Christian 1
Lubbock Christian 14, Oklahoma City 4 (Oklahoma City eliminated)
Point Loma Nazarene 8, Lee 6 (Lee eliminated)
CHAMPIONSHIP
Lubbock Christian 5, Point Loma Nazarene 1
Lubbock Christian 11, Point Loma Nazarene 8 (Point Loma Nazarene eliminated)

JUNIOR COLLEGES

NJCAA DIVISION I

Howard (Texas) capped a 63-win season by defeating Santa Fe (Fla.) 7-4 in 10 innings to win the national title. Howard racked up a 57-game winning streak through an undefeated regular season before losing its only game of the season in regional play. Howard and Santa Fe were tied until the Hawks loaded the bases in the 10th, and Santa Fe walked in a run. Andrew Collazo followed with a two-out, two-run single.

Site: Grand Junction, Colo.
Participants: Cowley County, Kan. (47-13); Howard, Texas (58-1); Iowa Western (39-21); Middle Georgia (43-18); San Jacinto, Texas (41-9); Santa Fe, Fla. (32-20); Seminole State, Okla. (47-13); Shelton State, Ala. (43-16); Spartanburg Methodist, S.C. (54-8); Western Nevada (45-12).
Champion: Howard.
Runner-Up: Santa Fe.
Outstanding Player: Anthony Collazo, Howard.

NJCAA DIVISION II

Parkland (Ill.) breezed through the competition en route to an 11-3 win in the title game against Scottsdale (Ariz.). Parkland won its first five tournament games by a combined score of 51-20, and broke the NJCAA record for team batting average by hitting .408.

Site: Enid, Okla.
Participants: Allegany, Md. (49-13); Des Moines Area, Iowa (54-9); Kankakee, Ill. (48-12-1); Kellogg, Mich. (30-19); Louisiana State-Eunice (48-10); Lurleen B. Wallace, Ala. (47-9); Monroe, N.Y. (27-17); Parkland, Ill. (44-9); Scottsdale, Ariz. (36-20); Western Oklahoma State (49-13).
Champion: Parkland.
Runner-Up: Scottsdale.
Outstanding Player: Kevin Kiermaier, Parkland.

NJCAA DIVISION III

Richland (Texas) won its fourth national title, beating Montgomery-Germantown, 7-5 in the championship game. Richland's Kirk Pritchett was named tournament MVP after pitching a complete game, striking out 11 while giving up five earned runs.

Site: Tyler, Texas.
Participants: Brookdale, N.J. (39-8); Joliet, Ill. (39-14); Manchester, Conn. (26-17); Montgomery-Germantown, Md. (28-17); Richland, Texas (43-13); Riversland, Minn. (37-8); Suffolk County-Grant, N.Y. (32-13).
Champion: Richland.
Runner-Up: Montgomery-Germantown.
Outstanding Player: Kirk Pritchett, Richland.

CALIFORNIA COMMUNITY COLLEGE ATHLETIC ASSOCIATION

Orange Coast won the California JC title, beating San Joaquin Delta 10-7 in Fresno. Orange Coast capped a season when one redshirting player died, another was hospitalized with injuries from a flesh-eating virus, and coach John Altobelli was suspended for the last six weeks of the season following an April 14 ejection against Irvine Valley.

Site: Fresno.
Participants: Diablo Valley (35-15); Orange Coast (34-13); San Joaquin Delta (32-17); Santa Ana (37-17).
Champion: Orange Coast.
Runner-Up: San Joaquin Delta.
Outstanding Player: D.J. Arellano, Orange Coast.

NORTHWEST ATHLETIC ASSOCIATION OF COMMUNITY COLLEGES

Bellevue (Wash.) entered the NWAACC championship game with a 28-20 record but stunned Columbia Basin (Wash.) twice to win the title. It was Bellevue's second title in three seasons and the fourth in school history.

Site: Longview, Wash.
Participants: Clackamas (24-21); Columbia Basin (44-7); Bellevue (24-19); Green River (28-14); Lower Columbia (35-6); Mt. Hood (33-6); Treasure Valley (26-25); Skagit Valley (31-7).
Champion: Bellevue.
Runner-Up: Columbia Basin.
Outstanding Player: Ian Parmley, Bellevue.

The summer was a mixed bag for USA Baseball's collegiate national team, which fared very well against perhaps its weakest schedule in years but fell just short in its most meaningful test in the annual Japan Series.

In the final game of the summer, lefthander Drew Pomeranz (Mississippi) carried a no-hitter into the seventh inning to lead Team USA to an 8-1 win against Germany in the championship game of the Enbridge Nothern Gateway Pipeline World Baseball Challenge in Prince George, British Columbia. The Americans finished their summer campaign with a 19-5 record, including a 6-1 mark in the Challenge in Canada.

"That was a tough event," said Eric Campbell, USA Baseball's general manager of national teams. "In the annals of USA Baseball, was it the most challenging event we ever went to? No. But it was still a tough event. This group was on the cusp of some very, very historical things. It didn't happen, but they were still able to have a good summer."

The Americans also came within an out of winning the Japan Series on Japanese soil for the first time since 1974, but Japan rallied to overcome a three-run deficit in the ninth and went on to win the decisive game of the series in extra innings.

"It was a successful summer and it was good to finish on a positive note, but there's no question that not getting that final out in Japan was the only negative," Team USA coach Rick Jones said.

"We played so well over there. We took a 7-4 lead into the ninth and just couldn't hold it. It was just a disappointing thing."

Against Germany, Pomeranz allowed a run in the first inning on a hit batsman, a walk, a sacrifice bunt and an RBI groundout, but Germany couldn't touch him after that, and the Americans supported him with eight runs, three of them on solo homers. Pomeranz finished with 12 strikeouts over seven innings, allowing just one hit and two walks.

"Pomeranz had some command issues early, and he did the same thing against Canada in the first game, but once he settled in, it was really good," Jones said. "He was throwing his fastball to both sides of the plate, had a good breaking ball—just special."

Not to be outdone, righthander Gerrit Cole (UCLA) finished the summer at 4-0, 1.06 with 46 strikeouts and 10 walks in 34 innings. Cole carried USA to the title game with a complete-game, two-hit, seven-strikeout masterpiece in a 1-0 win against Canada two days earlier. He struck out the side in the ninth inning and finished with 100 pitches.

"I don't know if I've seen a more dominant pitching performance than what I saw out of Gerrit Cole," Jones said. "I know he touched 99 a couple times, and he had a great slider."

As they did almost all summer, setup man Nick Pepitone (Tulane) and closer Chad Bettis (Texas Tech) slammed the door against Germany in the

COLLEGIATE NATIONAL TEAM STATS

Year indicates 2009-2010 class standing

PLAYER, POS.	YEAR	SCHOOL	AVG	OBP	SLG	G	AB	R	H	2B	3B	HR	RBI	BB	SO	SB
Rick Hague, 3b	Jr.	Rice	.371	.406	.551	22	89	15	33	7	0	3	16	6	19	7
Tyler Holt, of	Jr.	Florida State	.371	.513	.427	23	89	28	33	5	0	0	14	24	12	19
Bryce Brentz, of	Jr.	Middle Tennessee State	.366	.416	.563	23	71	15	26	6	1	2	18	6	17	5
Christian Colon, ss	Jr.	Cal State Fullerton	.362	.459	.617	23	94	31	34	3	3	5	37	11	6	24
Michael Choice, of	Jr.	Texas-Arlington	.350	.453	.550	23	60	13	21	3	0	3	13	8	13	3
Casey McGrew, of	Sr.	Wright State	.341	.348	.386	19	44	8	15	2	0	0	11	1	7	7
Matt Newman, of	Jr.	Arizona State	.315	.403	.407	19	54	14	17	2	0	1	13	8	19	4
Blake Forsythe, c	Jr.	Tennessee	.293	.500	.466	21	58	22	17	4	0	2	9	21	16	3
Brad Miller, 2b	So.	Clemson	.255	.417	.255	23	55	13	14	0	0	0	8	16	12	8
Andy Wilkins, 1b	Jr.	Arkansas	.232	.365	.406	24	69	13	16	2	2	2	16	14	11	2
Kolten Wong, 2b/of	So.	Hawaii	.215	.316	.277	21	65	15	14	4	0	0	8	11	10	11
Yasmani Grandal, c	Jr.	Miami	.182	.291	.318	19	66	14	12	0	0	3	7	10	20	0

PITCHER, POS.	YEAR	SCHOOL	W	L	ERA	G	GS	CG	SV	IP	H	R	ER	BB	SO	AVG
Nick Pepitone, rhp	Jr.	Tulane	0	0	0.00	8	0	0	1	15	2	0	0	5	10	.045
Matt Newman, lhp	Jr.	Arizona State	0	0	0.00	1	0	0	0	1	0	0	0	0	2	.000
Sonny Gray, rhp	So.	Vanderbilt	3	1	0.75	8	2	0	0	24	11	4	2	8	27	.139
Gerrit Cole, rhp	So.	UCLA	4	0	1.06	6	5	1	0	34	11	4	4	10	46	.104
Drew Pomeranz, lhp	Jr.	Mississippi	4	1	1.75	5	5	0	0	26	14	11	5	9	48	.161
Asher Wojciechowski, rhp	Jr.	The Citadel	2	1	2.18	5	3	0	0	21	11	8	5	4	29	.153
Cody Wheeler, lhp	Jr.	Coastal Carolina	3	0	2.42	5	4	0	0	22	11	9	6	13	31	.151
T.J. Walz, rhp	Jr.	Kansas	2	0	2.89	5	2	0	0	19	18	6	6	6	22	.261
Tony Zych, rhp	So.	Louisville	0	1	2.93	6	0	0	0	15	13	8	5	5	17	.224
Chad Bettis, rhp	Jr.	Texas Tech	0	0	3.00	9	0	0	3	9	3	3	3	3	11	.100
Trevor Bauer, rhp	So.	UCLA	1	1	4.67	5	3	1	0	17	13	10	9	7	24	.213
Bryce Brentz, rhp	Jr.	Middle Tennessee State	0	0	5.40	5	0	0	0	10	11	6	6	8	15	.282

finale, each working a perfect inning of relief. Pepitone allowed just two hits and posted a 0.00 ERA in 15 innings on the summer, while Bettis used a mid-to-high-90s fastball to earn three saves and 11 strikeouts in nine innings.

Third baseman Rick Hague (Rice) received the tournament's best hitter award, batting .474 with two home runs. He went 2-for-4 with an RBI in the championship game and finished the summer tied with outfielder Tyler Holt (Florida State) for the team lead in batting (.371).

But scouts were largely disappointed with the team's overall talent level. After Cole, Team USA lacked sure-fire star power. Most of the other high-upside talents came with significant caveats, and the safest bets offered lower ceilings.

Bourne Wins 1st Cape Title

Kyle Roller

KEN BABBITT

A year after Harwich captured its first Cape Cod League title in the franchise's 21st year, the Bourne Braves followed suit. The Braves, which were formed in 1988, swept Cotuit in the championship series to win their first Cape League title. In the clincher, Bourne took the lead with a three-run third inning and never looked back, as starter Eric Cantrell (George Washington) limited Cotuit to one run over five-plus innings while striking out six.

Slugger Kyle Roller (East Carolina), who won the regular-season MVP award after finishing second in the league in batting and first in home runs and RBIs, also captured postseason MVP honors, batting .500 and accounting for eight of Bourne's 31 RBIs in four playoff games.

The Cape League remains college baseball's premier summer circuit, but talent evaluators weren't overwhelmed by the prospect crop in 2009.

"The talent level is the worst it's been since I've been coaching up here," said Mike Roberts, who has managed Cotuit for six seasons and had two previous one-year stints with Wareham. "Major League Baseball has signed more guys out of high school, and you can see where it's making a major dent on college baseball."

The Cape League wasn't bereft of talent and did serve as a coming-out party for several players. Yarmouth-Dennis' Chris Sale didn't draw a lot of

attention at Florida Gulf Coast, but his strong summer put him in position to be the first lefthander drafted in 2010. After working just eight innings as a freshman at Vanderbilt, Wareham righthander Jack Armstrong hit 96 mph during the league's all-star game at Fenway Park—where Arkansas third baseman Zack Cox earned MVP honors.

Righthander Jesse Hahn, who won four games in two seasons at Virginia Tech, reached 98 mph for Chatham. Falmouth outfielder Todd Cunningham won the batting title at .378, 39 points better than he hit with metal bats at Jacksonville State.

SUMMER LEAGUE ROUNDUP

■ The El Dorado Broncos posted the best record in the five-team Jayhawk League season, going 22-9, then led a strong Jayhawk showing in the National Baseball Congress World Series by winning the event. El Dorado got a strong start from tournament MVP Jake Sabol (seven innings, one run) in the championship game against the Anchorage Glacier-Pilots, and the Broncos won on David Allbritton's sacrifice fly in the bottom of the 11th inning. The Liberal Beejays (third place) and Hays Larks (tied for fourth) also performed well for the Jayhawk League in Wichita.

■ Budget constraints continued to take a toll on the tradition-rich Alaska League. The Mat-Su Miners finished the season with the best record at 28-17 and were awarded the Alaska League title. The Anchorage Bucs were the runner-up with a 26-19 record after getting four wins (and one tie) over their final 10 games. The third-place Glacier Pilots represented the Alaska League in the NBC World Series, as both the Miners and the Bucs declined to attend because of the travel expenses required.

■ Rochester won its fifth championship in the Northwoods League's 16 seasons, beating La Crosse 7-4 in the third game of the championship series. Iowa's Zach Robertson pitched six innings on three days' rest for the Honkers, who hit three home runs in the title clincher.

■ Forest City, which finished 51-9 overall, won the Petitt Cup championship after dominating the Coastal Plain League season. The Owls swept Peninsula in the championship series, sweeping all five playoff games after setting the league record with 46 regular-season victories. Forest City's 51 wins led all teams in all summer leagues.

■ The Newport Gulls became the first team to win four New England Collegiate League championships, defeating the Vermont Mountaineers two games to one in the best-of-three championship series. Righthander Andrew Kittredge (Washington) struck out 12 in Newport's Game One victory, and Troy Scott (Washington) drove in five—including a three-run homer that gave the Gulls the lead for good—in the title-clinching win in Game Three.

■ Luray won the Lineweaver Cup by sweeping Covington in the Valley League championship series. The Wranglers outscored the Lumberjacks 17-4 in three games. It was Luray's third consecutive appearance in the championship and its second title since joining the Valley in 2001.

Colon provides leadership on, off field

BY AARON FITT

Whenever coaches and scouts talk about Christian Colon, they invariably start and finish with praise for his baseball IQ, instincts, leadership skills and confidence. Colon is just a darn good baseball player, they'll say, a born winner who simply finds a way to get the job done.

Amidst the kudos for Colon's intangibles and makeup, it's easy to overlook his talent, and his production. A second-team All-American as Cal State Fullerton's sophomore shortstop this spring, Colon ratcheted his game to another level this summer, hitting .362/.459/.617 and leading Team USA in slugging, home runs (five), RBIs (37), runs (31) and stolen bases (24 in 26 attempts). He also drew 11 walks and struck out a team-low six times despite registering a team-high 94 at-bats.

BRIAN FLEMING PHOTOGRAPHY

Christian Colon

For his impressive offensive production—and, yes, for his valuable leadership—Colon is Baseball America's Summer Player of the Year.

"He's a special, special person and a special, special player," said Eric Campbell, USA Baseball's general manager of national teams. "He really believes in this uniform, and he wants to make history in this uniform."

Few players have ever contributed as much to USA Baseball as Colon, who first donned the stars and stripes for the 16-and-under national team in 2005 and has played for three other national teams since.

Colon was the lone returnee from the undefeated 2008 collegiate team. That wealth of experience, along with the respect Colon commanded in the USA dugout, prompted coach Rick Jones to name Colon the team's captain this summer.

"Four different times he's worn this uniform, and he's such a great leader that I felt like we needed to have him in that captain role," Jones said. "And he did a great job with it."

But Colon's summer was cut short in Team USA's penultimate game against Canada. Colon was covering second base on a bunt to third, and he received the throw in plenty of time to get the out and fire a relay to first. But the runner slid hard and late, colliding with Colon's shin. Colon suffered breaks in his fibia and tibia, forcing him to miss the title game of the World Baseball Challenge two days later.

Both breaks were clean, and Colon was already walking around 15 days after the surgery, albeit with a limp. During his downtime after the injury, Colon was largely confined to the couch. Leave it to Colon to find the silver lining in that fate.

"Now that I'm just sitting here waiting for this bone to heal, I'm just watching baseball all day," he said. "I look at their at-bats, their pitches, the way they throw to home, whether they use a slidestep or not—just trying to pick up some stuff. It's just love for the game."

PREVIOUS WINNERS

1984: Will Clark, 1b, Team USA; Rafael Palmeiro, of, Hutchinson (Jayhawk)
1985: Jeff King, 3b, Team USA; Bob Zupcic, of, Liberal (Jayhawk)
1986: Jack Armstrong, rhp, Wareham (Cape Cod); Mike Harkey, rhp, Fairbanks (Alaska)
1987: Cris Carpenter, rhp, Team USA
1988: Robin Ventura, 3b, Team USA; Ty Griffin, 2b, Team USA
1989: John Olerud, 1b-lhp, Palouse (Alaska)

1990: Calvin Murray, of, Anchorage Bucs (Alaska)
1991: Chris Roberts, of, Team USA
1992: Jeffrey Hammonds, of, Team USA
1993: Geoff Jenkins, of, Team USA
1994: Steve Carver, 1b, Anchorage Glacier Pilots (Alaska)
1995: Travis Lee, 1b, Team USA
1996: Seth Greisinger, rhp, Team USA
1997: Pat Burrell, 3b, Team USA
1998: Bobby Kielty, of, Bourne (Cape Cod)
1999: Xavier Nady, 3b, Team USA

2000: Mark Teixeira, 3b, Team USA
2001: Bobby Brownlie, rhp, Team USA
2002: Brad Sullivan, rhp, Team USA
2003: Jered Weaver, rhp, Team USA
2004: Daniel Carte, of, Falmouth (Cape Cod)
2005: Andrew Miller, lhp, Chatham (Cape Cod)
2006: David Price, lhp, Team USA
2007: Luke Greinke, of/rhp, Winchester (Valley)
2008: Mike Minor, lhp, Team USA

For players who played for two teams:
1: Stats with first team 2: Stats with second team T: combined stats

CAPE COD LEAGUE

EAST

	W	L	T	PCT	PTS
Yarmouth-Dennis	28	15	1	.651	57
Orleans	25	17	2	.595	52
Chatham	21	23	0	.477	42
Brewster	17	22	5	.436	39
Harwich	18	25	1	.419	37

WEST

	W	L	T	PCT	PTS
Bourne	25	17	2	.595	52
Cotuit	20	18	6	.526	46
Wareham	19	19	6	.500	44
Falmouth	17	24	2	.415	36
Hyannis	16	26	1	.381	33

PLAYOFFS—Semifinals: Bourne defeated Orleans 2-0 and Cotuit defeated Yarmouth-Dennis 2-1 in best-of-three series. **Finals:** Bourne defeated Cotuit 2-0 in best-of-three series.

TOP 30 PROSPECTS: 1. Chris Sale, lhp, Yarmouth-Dennis (Jr., Florida Gulf Coast). 2. Zack Cox, 3b, Cotuit (So., Arkansas). 3. Alex Wimmers, rhp, Bourne (Jr., Ohio State). 4. Jedd Gyorko, 3b/2b, Brewster (Jr., West Virginia). 5. Bryan Morgado, lhp, Bourne (Jr., Tennessee). 6. Jack Armstrong Jr., rhp, Wareham (So., Vanderbilt). 7. Brandon Workman, rhp, Wareham (Jr., Texas). 8. Jesse Hahn, rhp, Chatham (Jr. Virginia Tech). 9. Todd Cunningham, of, Falmouth (Jr., Jacksonville State). 10. Jorge Reyes, rhp, Orleans (SIGNED: Padres). 11. Brett Eibner, 1b/of/rhp, Wareham (Jr., Arkansas). 12. Zach Cone, of, Cotuit (So., Georgia). 13. Kyle Blair, rhp, Brewster (Jr., San Diego). 14. Leon Landry, of, Harwich (Jr., Louisiana State). 15. Austin Wates, of, Yarmouth-Dennis (Jr., Virginia Tech). 16. Rob Rasmussen, lhp, Orleans (Jr., UCLA). 17. Gary Brown, of, Orleans (Jr., Cal State Fullerton). 18. Justin Grimm, rhp, Cotuit (Jr., Georgia). 19. Jackie Bradley, of, Hyannis (So., South Carolina). 20. B.A. Vollmuth, ss, Falmouth (So., Southern Mississippi). 21. Mickey Wiswall, 1b, Yarmouth-Dennis (Jr., Boston College). 22. Logan Verrett, rhp, Chatham (So., Baylor). 23. Cameron Rupp, c, Cotuit (Jr., Texas). 24. Hunter Morris, 1b, Falmouth (Jr., Auburn). 25. Jarrett Parker, of, Brewster (Jr., Virginia). 26. Chad Bell, lhp, Cotuit (SIGNED: Rangers). 27. George Springer, of, Wareham (So., Connecticut). 28. Daniel Tillman, rhp, Cotuit (Jr., Florida Southern). 29. Nick Tepesch, rhp, Falmouth (Jr., Missouri). 30. Dallas Gallant, rhp, Hyannis (Jr., Sam Houston State).

INDIVIDUAL BATTING LEADERS
(MINIMUM 118 PLATE APPEARANCES)

	AVG	G	AB	R	H	HR	RBI
Cunningham, Todd, Falmouth	.378	43	156	31	59	3	22
Roller, Kyle, Bourne	.342	42	149	33	51	10	33
Gyorko, Jedd, Brewster	.323	34	127	18	41	5	18
Wates, Austin, Yarmouth-Dennis	.312	40	138	17	43	0	21
Brown, Gary, Orleans	.310	33	126	25	39	2	14
LePage, Pierre, Bourne	.308	43	159	26	49	0	14
Crawford, Nick, Hyannis	.304	34	125	23	38	0	4
Segedin, Robert, Bourne	.304	29	102	11	31	0	16
Wiswall, Mickey, Yarmouth-Dennis	.302	43	159	19	48	5	30
Casas, Jordan, Yarmouth-Dennis	.301	37	113	28	34	1	5

INDIVIDUAL PITCHING LEADERS
(MINIMUM 35 INNINGS)

	W	L	ERA	IP	H	BB	SO
Buchanan, Jake, Cotuit	3	1	0.84	43	33	6	38
Blair, Kyle, Brewster	3	1	1.42	44	25	30	51
Sale, Chris, Yarmouth-Dennis	4	2	1.47	55	37	9	57
Wilson, Tyler, Hyannis	3	1	1.60	39	27	5	28
Gaynor, Casey, Orleans	2	1	1.74	41	26	12	32
Lyons, Tyler, Chatham	2	4	1.77	46	35	8	44
Bell, Chad, Cotuit	3	1	1.77	46	27	15	46
Rasmussen, Rob, Orleans	4	0	1.80	35	24	11	42
Meade, Aaron, Harwich	3	1	1.91	42	33	18	47
Glynn, Elliot, Orleans	3	2	2.03	40	36	11	33

BOURNE

BATTING

	AVG	AB	R	H	2B	3B	HR	RBI	SB
Alonso, Carlos	.077	13	1	1	1	0	0	2	0
Band, Josh	.333	3	0	1	0	0	0	0	0
Bolt, Kendall	.143	7	1	1	0	0	0	1	0
Campbell, Raynor	.265	113	18	30	6	1	1	14	7
Freeman, Cody	.238	21	2	5	0	0	1	3	0
Hightower, Taylor	.074	27	2	2	0	0	0	1	3
Karmas, Paul	.186	43	2	8	3	0	0	2	2
Klafczynski, Ben	.212	85	13	18	6	0	0	7	1
LaRosa, Brandon	.227	22	1	5	0	0	0	4	0
Lee, Kurt	.500	2	0	1	0	0	0	0	1
LePage, Pierre	.308	159	26	49	8	2	0	14	17
MacPhee, Zack	.146	89	10	13	4	1	0	4	4
Rice, Adam	.145	62	8	9	1	0	1	6	4
Richmond, Josh	.167	6	0	1	0	0	0	0	0
Roller, Kyle	.342	149	33	51	13	1	10	33	1
Romero, Stefan	.234	124	20	29	5	1	5	23	1
1 Schwaner, Nick	.228	101	5	23	4	0	1	15	4
Segedin, Robert	.304	102	11	31	6	2	0	16	0
Wallace, Chris	.168	95	9	16	3	0	2	11	2
Whitmer, Jace	.333	6	0	2	1	0	0	0	0
Woodward, Scott	.246	118	20	29	2	1	1	4	28
Zebroski, Tom	.156	32	3	5	0	0	1	1	0

PITCHING

	W	L	ERA	G	SV	IP	H	BB	SO
Aizenstadt, Andrew	0	0	3.00	1	0	3	3	0	2
Billbrough, Logan	4	1	1.30	15	1	28	14	10	38
Bowen, Ricky	0	0	0.00	1	0	1	1	0	0
Cantrell, Eric	2	2	3.08	8	0	38	34	15	39
Dimock, Michael	2	0	3.42	9	0	24	19	5	25
Ferrer, Ken	0	1	5.40	4	0	5	3	9	7
Harrold, Stephen	0	1	1.23	15	6	15	7	5	14
Knight, Trevor	2	0	2.89	7	1	9	5	3	12
Maness, Seth	2	1	3.44	8	0	34	30	5	41
Matyas, Scott	0	1	10.80	2	0	2	2	2	1
Morey, Robert	3	1	4.44	6	0	26	27	12	21
Morgado, Bryan	2	1	3.06	8	0	32	17	15	47
Munson, Kevin	0	1	1.80	16	3	15	11	13	24
Oberg, Scott	0	0	1.80	3	0	5	5	0	1
Phelps, Turner	3	3	4.62	8	0	37	43	11	35
Poovey, Justin	0	0	3.00	16	1	21	14	8	22
Porlier, Stephen	0	0	1.50	1	0	6	2	0	4
Robles, Tanner	0	2	4.97	5	0	13	12	9	12
Rocha, Michael	0	0	1.69	3	0	5	6	1	3
Roth, Cameron	3	2	3.45	13	0	31	33	12	22
Wimmers, Alex	2	0	1.23	6	0	22	12	13	37

BREWSTER

BATTING

	AVG	AB	R	H	2B	3B	HR	RBI	SB
Allen, Lyle	.171	117	11	20	4	0	2	13	2
Barr, John	.288	118	14	34	5	1	0	8	12
1 Butler, Daniel	.250	44	9	11	2	0	1	4	1
Canha, Mark	.257	74	9	19	2	1	3	11	2
Coyle, Bobby	.186	43	5	8	0	1	1	4	2
Ferguson, Tim	.238	80	14	19	5	0	1	11	6
Gallego, Niko	.229	83	8	19	0	0	0	6	8
Gyorko, Jedd	.323	127	18	41	6	0	5	18	7
Holaday, Bryan	.050	20	0	1	0	0	0	1	0
Jones, Zach	.127	71	5	9	1	1	0	4	2
Klocke, James	.196	51	3	10	1	0	0	3	0
Martinez, Harold	.236	127	11	30	3	1	4	15	1
McCarthy, Michael	.000	10	0	0	0	0	0	0	0
Parker, Jarrett	.188	96	15	18	5	2	1	13	10
Shepherd, Tant	.247	73	9	18	4	0	3	13	2
Thornburg, Tyler	.000	2	1	0	0	0	0	0	0
Walsh, Colin	.255	102	13	26	4	0	0	5	6
Wright, Davy	.096	73	3	7	2	0	0	3	0
Yarrow, Stephen	.125	40	3	5	2	0	0	3	0
Zrenda, Ryan	.000	9	0	0	0	0	0	0	0

PITCHING	W	L	ERA	G	SV	IP	H	BB	SO
Alexander, Scott	1	0	4.55	5	0	30	24	13	27
Allen, Lyle	0	0	40.50	2	0	1	7	2	0
Baker, Nathan	0	1	3.00	3	0	9	8	4	7
Bard, Jared	0	0	7.27	4	0	9	10	7	3
Bierman, Sean	2	4	5.90	11	0	40	57	11	30
Blair, Kyle	3	1	1.42	8	0	44	25	30	51
Cotham, Caleb	1	0	0.00	4	0	13	7	1	15
Goeddel, Erik	0	0	5.40	1	0	2	2	2	2
Goforth, David	0	1	5.27	9	3	14	14	8	19
1 Gormley, Mark	1	1	5.00	3	0	9	6	5	10
Hoelscher, Sean	1	1	1.64	4	0	22	9	9	20
Klocke, James	0	1	4.50	1	0	2	3	2	2
Lujan, Matt	1	4	2.64	9	0	48	37	25	36
Maxwell, Steven	3	2	2.12	9	0	30	26	7	28
Panozzo, Michael	1	0	0.00	1	0	1	0	1	1
Regnault, Kyle	0	1	12.27	6	0	4	6	4	2
Ross, J.T.	0	0	27.00	1	0	0	0	1	0
Sandbrink, Danny	1	1	2.82	12	0	22	24	11	11
Schmidt, Casey	0	3	6.67	8	0	30	31	14	21
Thomas, Stayton	2	0	4.03	11	0	22	26	9	19
Thornburg, Tyler	0	0	2.60	15	8	17	15	10	18
Volz, Kendal	0	1	2.00	5	0	9	9	1	9

CHATHAM

BATTING	AVG	AB	R	H	2B	3B	HR	RBI	SB
Bangs, Parker	.193	57	2	11	1	0	0	2	0
Belza, Tom	.183	115	16	21	1	0	1	11	3
Brooks, Steven	.273	88	10	24	7	0	2	9	5
Carroll, George	.143	7	1	1	0	0	0	0	0
Duffy, Matt	.187	91	10	17	6	0	1	8	2
Green, Dean	.275	120	18	33	6	0	3	22	1
Harris, Brian	.206	102	13	21	1	0	1	11	1
Johnson, Addison	.155	71	4	11	0	0	0	2	6
Merrifield, Whit	.266	143	23	38	7	1	1	12	16
Murray, Mike	.347	72	8	25	2	0	1	5	0
Oropesa, Rick	.171	41	2	7	2	1	0	4	0
Perry, Matthew	.222	108	8	24	2	1	0	7	3
Pohl, Phillip	.179	56	4	10	0	0	0	0	0
Rahmatulla, Tyler	.101	69	8	7	2	0	0	6	4
Schaus, Jeff	.239	71	8	17	1	0	0	5	1
2 Schwaner, Nick	.267	30	4	8	2	0	0	3	0
T Schwaner, Nick	.237	131	15	31	6	0	1	18	4
Stallings, Jacob	.206	34	3	7	1	0	1	1	1
Terdoslavich, Joey	.234	111	6	26	7	0	0	14	1

PITCHING	W	L	ERA	G	SV	IP	H	BB	SO
Bangs, Parker	2	0	2.70	12	0	17	9	14	15
Brewer, Russell	2	1	1.90	21	10	24	23	9	33
Dennhardt, Mike	2	3	2.76	8	0	46	38	14	22
Fleck, Kaleb	0	2	4.50	8	0	18	21	8	17
Hahn, Jesse	1	1	5.28	9	1	15	8	6	17
Harvey, Matt	0	2	6.00	7	0	18	21	11	16
Hill, Taylor	2	1	1.44	18	2	31	25	10	35
Johnson, Patrick	2	1	2.76	7	0	29	20	10	24
Keeling, Thomas	1	1	8.76	10	1	12	46	13	15
Kennelly, Pete	0	0	0.00	4	1	11	3	7	11
Leach, Ryan	0	1	6.10	8	0	10	8	7	3
Lyons, Tyler	2	4	1.77	7	0	46	35	8	44
Scanlan, Kevin	1	1	3.86	16	0	26	26	8	18
Thompson, Jake	1	2	7.71	4	0	14	20	8	12
Tolleson, Shawn	3	3	5.45	8	0	40	41	14	39
Verrett, Logan	2	0	3.09	5	0	23	18	16	32

COTUIT

BATTING	AVG	AB	R	H	2B	3B	HR	RBI	SB
Bingham, Paul	.000	3	1	0	0	0	0	0	0
Bisson, Chris	.269	134	19	36	5	0	0	15	36
Cone, Zach	.243	136	16	33	3	0	3	20	10
Cooper, Riley	.000	5	0	0	0	0	0	0	1
Cox, Zack	.344	93	8	32	8	0	0	11	1
Guinn, Brian	.194	62	8	12	0	1	0	6	6
Harris, Devin	.067	15	1	1	0	0	0	1	1
Harrision, Brian	.000	14	2	0	0	0	0	0	0

	AVG	AB	R	H	2B	3B	HR	RBI	SB
Hillman, Drew	.000	12	1	0	0	0	0	0	1
Kelliher, Brandon	.400	5	0	2	1	0	0	1	0
Keyes, Kevin	.185	81	8	15	1	1	2	7	5
Maggard, Zach	.291	55	8	16	2	0	2	6	2
May, Brandon	.155	58	4	9	0	0	1	7	0
Noel, Rico	.233	116	25	27	2	0	2	8	26
Patterson, Kevin	.244	90	8	22	2	0	4	11	1
Plagman, Tony	.188	117	8	22	7	0	1	16	3
Rowland, Jeff	.240	129	11	31	3	2	0	8	7
Rupp, Cameron	.317	60	7	19	3	0	4	12	1
Stanley, Cody	.299	97	18	29	9	1	1	11	5
Vaughn, Cory	.242	99	12	24	3	0	3	9	3

PITCHING	W	L	ERA	G	SV	IP	H	BB	SO
Bell, Chad	3	1	1.77	11	0	46	27	15	46
Blair, Seth	3	2	2.75	7	0	39	37	16	30
2 Bowen, Ricky	1	1	8.03	4	0	12	9	15	10
T Bowen, Ricky	1	1	7.62	5	0	13	10	15	10
Buchanan, Jake	3	1	0.84	7	0	43	33	6	38
Caceres, Andres	0	0	4.91	6	0	11	11	10	13
Cumpton, Brandon	1	0	1.59	3	0	17	16	3	7
Dwyer, Chris	1	0	0.00	1	0	5	3	3	9
Fritsch, Craig	0	1	3.30	9	1	30	30	16	24
Gagnier, Drew	2	0	0.00	3	1	4	1	0	6
Grace, Matt	0	1	7.50	12	0	18	31	9	9
Grimm, Justin	1	4	2.84	8	0	44	49	14	47
Moore, Navery	1	1	7.88	8	0	8	3	15	4
Nesseth, Mike	0	3	6.26	11	0	23	26	14	17
Rowen, Ben	4	2	2.21	20	1	37	28	12	31
Russell, Max	0	1	9.64	2	0	5	5	3	4
Tillman, Daniel	0	0	0.00	16	5	22	13	7	31
Walters, Jeff	0	0	3.86	5	1	14	12	12	17

FALMOUTH

BATTING	AVG	AB	R	H	2B	3B	HR	RBI	SB
Adams, Josh	.215	93	7	20	0	0	0	10	0
Baumgartner, Todd	.143	7	2	1	0	0	0	0	1
Brodsky, Mickey	.250	4	0	0	0	0	0	0	0
Conley, Tom	.000	2	0	0	0	0	0	0	0
Cunningham, Todd	.378	156	31	59	8	1	3	22	11
Esposito, Jason	.198	111	11	22	2	0	0	8	6
Fletcher, Brian	.291	117	11	34	11	0	2	19	0
Grasso, Matt	.300	10	1	3	0	0	0	2	0
Jones, Ryan	.198	106	13	21	6	0	1	9	8
Lapensee, Ryan	.333	9	1	3	0	0	0	1	1
Lawson, Scott	.230	126	22	29	5	0	0	9	16
Mach, Conner	.179	84	7	15	1	0	3	10	1
Morris, Hunter	.239	109	16	26	2	0	8	19	3
Mortimer, Kevin	.333	3	0	1	0	0	0	0	0
Nester, John	.257	74	11	19	5	0	1	2	1
O'Brien, Chris	.230	100	12	23	5	0	0	15	1
Polk, P.J.	.000	2	0	0	0	0	0	0	0
Robertson, Drew	.000	5	0	0	0	0	0	0	0
Skole, Matt	.181	94	9	17	4	0	1	6	1
Stolz, Jason	.158	19	1	3	0	0	0	2	2
Vollmuth, B.A.	.230	100	14	23	3	3	5	18	0
Watts, Murray	.267	30	5	8	1	1	2	6	0

PITCHING	W	L	ERA	G	SV	IP	H	BB	SO
Collier, Tommy	3	2	3.23	6	0	31	22	8	35
Cooper, Jordan	1	2	2.09	7	0	39	33	16	29
Cooper, Patrick	2	1	0.66	17	1	27	15	10	39
Danielli, Evan	0	0	1.80	4	0	5	4	5	8
Farrell, Shane	0	1	6.35	8	0	16	17	5	7
Garvin, Grayson	0	0	3.86	8	0	16	17	5	22
Hill, Dennis	1	0	3.60	1	0	5	6	2	7
Koneski, Nate	0	0	0.00	3	0	5	4	2	4
Lowell, Charlie	0	1	6.52	6	0	10	9	9	10
Morman, Mitch	1	2	7.78	10	0	20	16	16	14
Pope, Mark	2	2	2.10	12	1	34	27	7	32
Sheppard, Chad	0	3	3.60	17	2	25	20	22	27
Tanner, Cecil	0	2	3.28	17	3	25	18	19	28
Tepesch, Nick	2	3	5.44	8	0	41	47	11	41
Wall, Taylor	3	3	2.62	7	0	34	32	14	26
Winkler, Kyle	2	2	3.62	7	0	32	29	12	31
Zylstra, Jason	0	0	5.40	7	0	8	12	9	5

HARWICH

BATTING	AVG	AB	R	H	2B	3B	HR	RBI	SB
Cardullo, Stephen	.000	12	0	0	0	0	0	0	0
Foltz, Alex	.059	17	1	1	0	0	0	1	0
Gedman, Matt	.000	1	0	0	0	0	0	0	0
Goebbert, Jacob	.091	11	0	1	0	0	0	1	0
Gosselin, Phil	.262	126	16	33	3	1	0	7	5
Grovatt, Daniel	.288	125	14	36	7	1	1	12	5
Hall, Dain	.250	8	2	2	0	0	0	0	1
Herbek, David	.141	71	11	10	1	1	1	8	0
Landry, Leon	.364	99	5	36	4	0	2	12	6
Lockwood, Ryan	.176	17	0	3	0	0	0	4	0
Loftus, Joe	.162	68	9	11	3	0	0	4	3
Michael, Levi	.247	93	11	23	1	0	1	6	7
Mummey, Trent	.250	140	22	35	6	3	3	14	22
Nidiffer, Marcus	.173	81	7	14	4	0	1	9	1
Powers, Connor	.205	127	13	26	4	1	2	17	1
Sosnoskie, Anthony	.213	61	7	13	2	0	2	10	0
Tapley, Stuart	.189	122	10	23	8	0	0	9	2
Vigurs, Jeff	.218	55	5	12	2	0	0	4	1
Wade, Chris	.260	50	6	13	1	1	0	3	3
Wiley, Keenan	.196	97	7	19	2	0	0	2	2

PITCHING	W	L	ERA	G	SV	IP	H	BB	SO
Bradshaw, Daniel	0	0	3.44	7	0	18	23	2	19
Bruening, Brett	0	3	2.55	6	0	25	20	20	22
Davis, Garrett	0	0	5.19	9	0	9	10	8	4
Dupra, Brian	2	1	5.48	13	2	23	20	7	25
Gariano, Rob	1	1	4.15	9	0	26	30	6	31
Gast, John	1	4	4.37	10	0	35	40	14	30
Gipson, Mike	2	4	3.89	8	0	39	37	11	50
Jokisch, Eric	1	2	1.36	8	0	33	22	9	26
Meade, Aaron	3	1	1.91	8	0	42	33	18	47
Parker, Geoff	0	1	2.70	5	0	17	13	4	17
Price, Mathew	2	2	2.97	12	1	36	28	13	34
Reid, Chase	2	2	3.74	10	0	22	24	9	28
Troyanowski, Glenn	0	2	2.51	13	4	14	10	6	22
Williams, Les	1	0	2.93	10	1	15	20	3	14
Wright, Justin	3	2	4.26	11	0	25	23	10	19

HYANNIS

BATTING	AVG	AB	R	H	2B	3B	HR	RBI	SB
Austin, Jamal	.125	16	1	2	0	0	0	0	2
Bradley Jr., Jackie	.275	153	16	42	6	4	0	14	10
Brown, Jay	.000	1	0	0	0	0	0	0	0
Burkhart, Dan	.295	78	11	23	2	1	0	6	0
Crawford, Nick	.304	125	23	38	3	1	0	4	8
Cuneo, Ryan	.270	159	17	43	10	0	5	29	1
Dunning, Jake	.000	1	0	0	0	0	0	0	0
Graepel, Ryan	.129	62	9	8	0	0	0	3	1
Haney, Chris	.000	1	0	0	0	0	0	0	0
Harrington, Dustin	.265	136	18	36	7	0	0	9	6
Hawn, Cody	.375	48	8	18	4	0	4	14	0
Johnson, Casey	.189	53	0	10	2	0	0	1	1
Kroker, Shane	.200	10	1	2	0	0	0	1	0
Manning, Andrew	.273	11	1	3	1	0	0	2	1
Norton, Tim	.200	15	0	3	1	0	0	0	0
Rohan, Eddie	.202	109	7	22	4	0	0	13	1
Ruettiger, Johnny	.255	98	16	25	4	1	0	6	14
Soto, Elliot	.194	124	9	24	3	0	0	10	6
Swab, Kenny	.146	82	8	12	3	0	0	3	4
Taylor, Patrick	.500	2	0	1	0	0	0	0	0
Whitehead, Trent	.264	129	10	34	7	2	0	16	12

PITCHING	W	L	ERA	G	SV	IP	H	BB	SO
Brandt, Kevin	1	2	3.92	11	0	39	35	21	32
Brown, Jay	1	5	4.74	9	0	44	45	9	35
Chowning, Jason	0	0	0.00	1	0	0	1	0	0
Dunning, Jake	0	0	3.38	3	0	3	6	0	5
Gallant, Dallas	2	1	1.95	14	2	28	17	13	43
Girdwood, Thomas	0	0	9.00	3	1	2	1	5	0
2 Gormley, Mark	0	4	3.67	16	1	27	24	6	32
T Gormley, Mark	1	5	4.00	19	1	36	30	11	42
Haney, Chris	0	1	4.15	11	2	17	14	8	12
Hudson, Austin	3	2	3.26	7	0	39	37	10	28

	W	L	ERA	G	SV	IP	H	BB	SO
Johnson, Cole	1	2	3.93	8	0	37	34	13	44
Maust, Eric	2	2	2.29	10	0	20	16	6	17
Messer, Jimmy	1	1	8.27	10	0	16	19	12	12
Moran, Kevin	0	2	1.93	12	1	19	16	7	20
Rosin, Seth	2	1	1.87	7	0	34	33	10	38
Ruettiger, Johnny	0	1	10.80	1	0	2	2	4	0
Torres, Raul	0	1	3.48	4	0	10	10	10	4
Weidig, Will	0	0	10.13	3	1	3	5	0	6
Wilson, Tyler	3	1	1.60	7	0	39	27	5	28

ORLEANS

BATTING	AVG	AB	R	H	2B	3B	HR	RBI	SB
Brown, Gary	.310	126	25	39	3	1	2	14	10
Gardner, Andersen	.231	13	2	3	0	0	0	1	1
Glynn, Elliot	.000	0	1	0	0	0	0	0	0
Gould, Jeremy	.211	123	14	26	3	1	3	17	5
Hassan, Alex	.289	114	19	33	5	2	1	20	4
Heffley, Ross	.198	101	13	20	1	0	0	8	2
Koch, Matt	.191	34	9	18	3	0	1	11	2
Lang, Michael	.188	16	0	3	0	0	0	0	3
Lohman, Devin	.219	128	15	28	3	1	2	11	3
Matthews, Jaren	.211	128	16	27	4	1	2	18	11
Moss, Westley	.273	11	1	3	1	0	0	0	1
Muno, Danny	.222	135	12	30	4	0	0	13	7
Muno, Kevin	.257	144	22	37	10	0	1	16	16
Olt, Michael	.218	124	18	27	3	1	3	14	2
1 Selsky, Steven	.243	70	10	17	2	0	2	5	4
Tignor, Hampton	.192	52	4	10	0	0	0	3	0
Torrez, Riccio	.346	52	7	18	4	1	2	11	2

PITCHING	W	L	ERA	G	SV	IP	H	BB	SO
Catapano, Rob	0	0	0.00	3	0	2	2	2	0
Cook, Cole	1	2	4.72	8	0	34	37	9	25
Esquivel, Xavier	0	1	24.30	4	0	3	10	2	5
Gaynor, Casey	2	1	1.74	8	0	41	26	12	32
Glynn, Elliot	3	2	2.03	8	0	40	36	11	33
Hassan, Alex	0	0	1.13	7	4	8	5	6	8
Hiserman, Matt	2	1	3.27	13	1	33	26	7	27
Kahnle, Tommy	2	2	2.41	15	1	19	9	13	23
Ness, Mike	0	1	3.12	8	0	9	8	6	5
Ottone, Daniel	2	1	3.86	14	3	16	20	6	15
Packer, Matt	2	0	1.90	11	0	24	16	10	29
Rasmussen, Rob	4	0	1.80	6	0	35	24	11	42
Reyes, Jimmy	3	2	3.40	8	0	48	47	7	38
Reyes, Jorge	1	2	1.06	6	0	34	19	10	40
Stassi, Brock	1	1	3.72	14	0	19	14	14	15
Weibley, Brett	2	1	1.23	16	0	22	17	5	26

WAREHAM

BATTING	AVG	AB	R	H	2B	3B	HR	RBI	SB
Albright, Tyler	.091	33	1	3	0	0	0	1	0
Armstrong, Jack	.000	0	0	0	0	0	0	0	0
Dickerson, Alex	.224	107	14	24	0	3	3	15	2
Dietrich, Derek	.211	152	26	32	7	1	3	10	4
Doleac, Adam	.000	3	1	0	0	0	0	0	0
Eibner, Brett	.240	50	7	12	3	1	3	7	1
Hannick, Chris	.170	53	2	9	2	0	1	7	0
Kral, Robert	.417	12	2	5	2	0	0	3	2
LaMarre, Ryan	.236	140	13	33	6	2	0	14	15
Lemmerman, Jake	.172	122	11	21	2	0	1	10	4
Leonida, Cole	.259	54	10	14	4	0	1	5	0
O'Hara, Sean	.000	1	0	0	0	0	0	0	0
Pfisterer, Eric	.111	9	0	1	0	0	0	1	0
Pineda, Ryan	.170	112	12	19	5	0	0	8	2
Rowe, Connor	.153	59	6	9	3	1	2	4	0
Springer, George	.261	134	19	35	3	1	3	25	12
Swagerty, Jordan	.286	56	10	16	1	1	1	2	1
Vucinich, Shea	.179	151	17	27	7	0	3	12	6
Wilson, Zach	.247	97	11	24	5	0	2	10	2

PITCHING	W	L	ERA	G	SV	IP	H	BB	SO
Armstrong, Jack	4	1	2.57	8	0	35	27	18	31
Barnes, Matt	1	3	4.78	9	0	26	23	10	33
Bilodeau, Keith	0	1	1.93	12	1	19	14	11	19
Brewster, Zach	0	0	5.40	6	0	7	9	3	7

	W	L	ERA	G	SV	IP	H	BB	SO
Eibner, Brett	1	0	2.19	3	0	12	7	7	14
Fischer, David	0	2	5.06	12	0	16	21	10	18
Green, Cole	1	1	3.12	4	0	26	20	8	33
Kern, Bruce	1	1	3.28	12	0	25	21	12	27
Kiekhefer, Dean	1	1	3.44	12	2	18	14	7	23
Monar, Blake	2	3	3.02	8	0	48	39	16	37
Mueller, Josh	2	0	3.34	6	0	32	28	18	31
Pepitone, Nick	0	0	5.40	1	1	2	2	1	0
Pfisterer, Eric	3	1	3.32	7	0	38	27	16	40
Rembisz, Scott	0	2	3.86	14	0	23	22	10	27
Slaats, Josh	2	1	0.95	13	1	19	14	11	24
Swagerty, Jordan	0	1	2.16	6	1	8	10	4	13
Workman, Brandon	1	1	5.06	5	1	21	22	11	24

YARMOUTH-DENNIS

BATTING	AVG	AB	R	H	2B	3B	HR	RBI	SB
2 Butler, Daniel	.240	25	3	6	1	0	0	0	0
T Butler, Daniel	.246	69	12	17	3	0	1	4	1
Casas, Jordan	.301	113	28	34	3	0	1	5	10
Chatwood, Steve	.215	130	13	28	6	0	1	19	3
Davidson, Chase	.222	18	0	4	0	0	0	0	0
Dunlap, Blair	.000	6	0	0	0	0	0	0	0
Gibbs, Micah	.212	52	6	11	1	0	3	9	0
Hanover, Tyler	.300	90	14	27	4	0	2	16	10
Hernandez, Brian	.244	131	10	32	7	0	3	16	0
Ingui, Derek	.125	8	1	1	0	0	0	0	0
Jones, Jonathan	.273	128	20	35	7	0	0	12	6
Kelso, Blake	.260	150	24	39	3	2	0	13	18
Lyman, Scott	.500	4	1	2	1	0	0	0	0
McMahan, Ben	.241	79	13	19	4	0	3	8	1
Ramsey, Caleb	.353	17	4	6	0	1	0	3	1
Rutledge, Josh	.250	112	17	28	2	0	0	11	7
Schlander, Jake	.175	63	5	11	1	0	0	5	1
2 Selsky, Steven	.067	15	1	1	0	0	0	0	0
T Selsky, Steven	.212	85	11	18	3	0	2	5	4
Wates, Austin	.312	138	17	43	8	2	0	21	12
Wiswall, Mickey	.302	159	19	48	8	0	5	30	1

PITCHING	W	L	ERA	G	SV	IP	H	BB	SO
Burgoon, Tyler	1	1	1.69	17	12	21	12	6	34
Campbell, Darrin	1	1	1.76	5	0	15	15	9	5
Coan, Austin	0	0	54.00	2	0	0	4	0	0
Dempsay, Chase	0	0	0.00	8	1	12	2	6	15
Goodnight, Michael	2	0	2.52	7	0	36	23	22	31
Hayes, Drew	3	0	1.25	10	1	22	12	9	19
Hollands, Mario	4	1	2.12	5	0	30	22	8	18
Holle, Greg	0	1	0.00	1	0	3	3	3	0
Leonard, John	2	1	2.57	10	1	35	33	10	26
Little, Matt	1	2	4.56	12	0	24	14	24	24
Lyman, Scott	0	0	2.93	9	0	15	12	14	16
Peavey, Greg	3	2	2.75	10	0	36	34	7	35
Ray, Jared	1	1	3.93	4	0	18	9	7	18
Rhoderick, Kevin	2	0	4.19	17	1	19	14	6	30
Ross, Austin	1	1	1.93	6	0	23	20	9	24
Sale, Chris	4	2	1.47	9	0	55	37	9	57
Serino, Nick	0	0	16.88	1	0	3	4	3	2
Simmons, Seth	2	1	5.79	13	0	14	12	10	18
Tone, Matt	1	1	3.60	2	0	5	5	3	5

ALASKA LEAGUE

FINAL STANDINGS	W	L	PCT	GB
Mat-Su Miners	28	17	.622	—
Anchorage Bucs	26	19	.578	2
Anchorage Glacier Pilots	25	20	.556	3
Alaska Goldpanners of Fairbanks	19	25	.431	9
Fairbanks AIA Fire	18	26	.409	9½
Kenai Peninsula Oilers	18	27	.400	10

TOP 10 PROSPECTS: 1. Kevin Jacob, rhp, Anchorage Bucs (Jr., Georgia Tech). 2. Ryan Carpenter, lhp, Anchorage Glacier Pilots (So., Gonzaga). 3. Jason Martinson, 3b, Anchorage Bucs (Jr., Texas State). 4. Scott Snodgrass, lhp, Peninsula (So., Stanford). 5. Ryan Woolley, rhp, Athletes In Action Fire (Jr., Alabama-Birmingham). 6. Logan Darnell, lhp, Anchorage Glacier Pilots (Jr., Kentucky). 7. Kellen Kiilsgaard, of, Anchorage Bucs (Jr.,

Stanford). 8. Jason Coats, of, Anchorage Glacier Pilots (Jr. Texas Christian). 9. James Ramsey, of, Mat Su (So., Florida State). 10. Drew Heid, of, Anchorage Glacier Pilots (Sr., Gonzaga).

INDIVIDUAL BATTING LEADERS
(MINIMUM 3 PLATE APPEARANCES PER TEAM GAME)

	AVG	AB	R	H	2B	3B	HR	RBI	SB
Heid, Drew, Glacier Pilots	.427	171	41	73	18	1	4	31	11
Torrez, Raoul, Goldpanners	.323	130	15	42	8	0	0	6	3
Ramsey, James, Mat-Su	.321	134	24	43	14	1	1	25	4
Hur, Michael, Bucs	.318	129	13	41	6	1	0	19	2
Enos, Ryan, Fairbanks AIA	.309	149	25	46	8	0	2	23	9
Kuykendall, Gary, Kenai	.305	128	14	39	2	5	0	13	14
Wimmer, Trey, Fairbanks AIA	.301	163	17	49	8	0	2	23	0
Johnson, Jonathan, Mat-Su	.295	132	28	39	3	2	0	7	7
Gebhart, Ryan, Fairbanks AIA	.294	153	24	45	2	1	1	14	12
Martinson, Jason, Bucs	.293	167	29	49	6	1	2	19	13

INDIVIDUAL PITCHING LEADERS
(MINIMUM .9 INNINGS PER TEAM GAME)

	W	L	ERA	G	SV	IP	BB	SO
Carpenter, Ryan, Glacier Pilots	2	2	0.67	10	0	40	12	54
Kraft, Justin, Mat-Su	3	2	1.44	12	0	50	7	33
Barracloug, Kyle, Kenai Peninsula	2	3	1.65	8	0	49	15	39
Darnell, Logan, Glacier Pilots	5	1	1.66	13	0	48	18	37
Stilley, David, Mat-Su	4	1	1.95	9	0	51	10	43
Carruth, Garret, Bucs	5	0	2.03	13	0	44	12	29
Millard, Ryan, Fairbanks AIA	4	0	2.86	9	0	50	30	38
Bergman, Christian, Bucs	2	2	3.06	12	0	47	6	39
Colvin, David, Goldpanners	0	5	3.07	8	0	41	11	27
Snodgress, Scott, Kenai Peninsula	2	3	3.07	9	0	41	25	51

ATLANTIC COLLEGIATE LEAGUE

WOLFF	W	L	PCT	GB
Jersey Pilots	26	11	.703	—
Kutztown Rockies	22	16	.579	4½
Lehigh Valley Catz	19	18	.514	7
Quakertown Blazers	17	19	.472	8½
Peekskill Robins	11	19	.367	11½
N. New Jersey Eagles	12	24	.333	13½

KAISER	W	L	PCT	GB
North Fork Ospreys	25	15	.625	—
Southampton Breakers	24	16	.600	1
Westhampton Aviators	24	16	.600	1
Riverhead Tomcats	22	18	.550	3
Sag Harbor Whalers	18	22	.450	7
Long Island Mustangs	7	33	.175	18

PLAYOFFS—Westhampton defeated Jersey in a one-game championship.

TOP 10 PROSPECTS: 1. Nick Tropeano, rhp, Riverhead (So., Stony Brook). 2. Brian Dudzinski, rhp, Lehigh Valley (Jr., Furman). 3. Nick Ahmed, ss/rhp, Westhampton (So., Connecticut). 4. Pete Greskoff, of/1b, Riverhead (Jr., Brown). 5. Nate Reed, lhp, Kutztown (Sr., Pittsburgh). 6. Andrew Leenhouts, lhp, Peekskill (So., Northeastern). 7. Alex Pracher, rhp, Westhampton (Jr., Stanford). 8. Justin Bradley, rhp, Westhampton (Jr., UNC Wilmington). 9. Grant Kernaghan, rhp, Lehigh Valley (Sr., Bloomsburg, Pa.). 10. Gardner Leaver, rhp, Sag Harbor (Jr., Rhode Island).

INDIVIDUAL BATTING LEADERS
(MINIMUM 74 PLATE APPEARANCES)

	AVG	AB	R	H	2B	3B	HR	RBI	SB
Gregory, Ken, Jersey	.405	111	30	45	9	1	4	34	2
Greskoff, Peter, Riverhead	.397	121	28	48	14	0	10	37	2
Rice, Bill, Jersey	.382	76	16	29	7	4	0	10	4
Oriente, Dewey, Kutztown	.368	106	18	39	6	4	1	17	5
Houck, Shane, Kutztown	.365	104	12	38	10	0	2	22	1
Cockman, Cameron, Quakertown	.363	124	16	45	7	0	0	20	9
Meade, Tom, Peekskill	.359	92	14	33	9	1	3	18	3
Flax, Jeffrey, Quakertown	.352	125	21	44	7	0	2	14	10
Haas, Jeremey, Quakertown	.352	91	14	32	3	3	1	5	4
Greig, T.J., Long Island	.350	100	13	35	7	0	1	13	9

INDIVIDUAL PITCHING LEADERS
(MINIMUM 35 INNINGS)

	W	L	ERA	G	SV	IP	H	BB	SO
Tropeano, Nick, Riverhead	7	3	1.61	10	0	50	36	14	77
McNamara, James, Sag Harbor	1	3	1.98	9	0	41	45	14	19
Zaccherio, Chris, Southampton	3	2	2.29	9	1	39	39	10	37
Saveri, C.J., Lehigh Valley	4	2	2.31	9	1	39	36	7	42
Lawrence, Casey, Kutztown	6	1	2.40	8	0	45	40	6	52
Dudzinski, Brian, Lehigh Valley	4	1	2.45	7	0	40	31	22	28
Sanchez, Joel, Jersey	3	1	2.50	9	1	40	36	11	38
Etienne, Daniel, North Fork	5	2	2.75	9	0	59	39	15	46
Marotta, Matt, N. New Jersey	4	1	2.77	10	0	39	31	23	34
Gussaroff, Scott, North Fork	5	2	3.06	8	0	53	66	3	26

CAL RIPKEN SR. LEAGUE

FINAL STANDINGS

	W	L	PCT	GB
Bethesda Big Train	31	10	.756	—
Youse's Orioles	29	12	.707	2
Maryland Redbirds	24	18	.571	7½
Herndon Braves	19	22	.463	12
Silver Spring-Takoma Thunderbolts	18	24	.429	13½
Alexandria Aces	17	25	.405	14½
College Park Bombers	17	25	.405	14½
Rockville Express	11	30	.268	20

PLAYOFFS—Bethesda defeated Maryland in the championship of a six-team, double-elimination tournament.
TOP 10 PROSPECTS: 1. Kevin Brady, rhp, Youse's Orioles, (So., Clemson). 2. Blake Hassebrock, rhp, Youse's Orioles (Jr., UNC Greensboro). 3. Joe Leonard, 3b, Youse's Orioles (Jr., Pittsburgh). 4. Beau Taylor, c, Herndon (So., Central Florida). 5. Scott Swinson, rhp, Youse's Orioles (Sr., Maryland). 6. Jed Bradley, lhp, Youse's Orioles, (So., Georgia Tech.). 7. Nolan Rudman, rhp, Bethesda (Jr., Lee, Tenn.). 8. Jarrod Parks, ss/3b, Bethesda, (Sr., Mississippi State). 9. Curtis Wilson, ss, Silver Spring (Jr., Southern). 10. Jim Moran, rhp, Youse's Orioles (Jr., South Florida).

INDIVIDUAL BATTING LEADERS
(MINIMUM 90 PLATE APPEARANCES)

	AVG	AB	R	H	2B	3B	HR	RBI	SB
Adkins, Luke, Bethesda	.380	137	22	52	13	4	0	37	7
Boike, Eli, Bethesda	.371	151	44	56	12	2	2	34	18
Parks, Jarrod, Bethesda	.366	123	41	45	8	1	6	27	0
Stienstra, Danny, Bethesda	.350	157	29	55	8	0	1	40	2
Taylor, Corey, Herndon	.348	138	30	48	9	3	6	22	7
Leonard, Joseph, Youse's	.346	130	17	45	7	1	0	25	4
Schafferman, Dan, Youse's	.333	129	29	43	7	1	4	16	5
Bernatz, Connor, Bethesda	.318	170	45	54	16	1	2	18	17
Kish, Colin, Youse's	.309	94	15	29	6	2	0	15	4
Blair, Patrick, Youse's	.306	108	18	33	6	1	0	15	4

INDIVIDUAL PITCHING LEADERS
(MINIMUM 30 INNINGS)

	W	L	ERA	G	SV	IP	H	BB	SO
Beck, Sander, Youse's	6	1	1.56	10	0	40	28	15	28
Abramson, Jonathan, Alexandria	3	2	1.59	10	1	45	34	18	42
Beistline, Jordan, Bethesda	5	2	1.95	9	0	51	40	15	35
Worthington, Kent, Alexandria	2	2	2.05	7	0	44	34	14	37
Love, Cameron, Bethesda	6	1	2.59	9	0	49	52	12	36
White, Ben, Maryland	2	3	2.76	8	0	46	28	19	30
Lapointe, Ryan, Silver Spring	4	0	2.88	7	0	34	33	10	23
Judson, Kyle, College Park	2	1	3.03	9	0	36	24	17	20
Stinsman, Daniel, College Park	3	1	3.13	8	0	37	34	18	20
Mazur, Justin, Alexandria	4	1	3.18	7	0	34	42	13	23

CALIFORNIA COLLEGIATE LEAGUE

FINAL STANDINGS

	W	L	PCT	GB
Santa Barbara Foresters	18	6	.750	—
Conejo Oaks	13	11	.542	5
San Luis Obispo Rattlers	11	13	.458	7
Santa Maria Packers	10	14	.417	8
MLB Academy Barons	8	16	.333	10

TOP 10 PROSPECTS: 1. Kevin Gelinas, lhp, Conejo (Jr., UC Santa Barbara). 2. Tyler Blandford, rhp, Santa Barbara (SIGNED: Mariners). 3. Sam Stafford, lhp, Santa Barbara (So., Texas). 4. Jeremy Rathjen, of, Santa Barbara (So., Rice). 5. Brandon Loy, ss, Santa Barbara (So., Texas). 6. Jack Marder, 2b, Conejo (Fr., Oregon). 7. A.J. Griffin, rhp, Santa Barbara (Sr., San Diego). 8. Matt Leonard, lhp, Santa Barbara (Jr., Cal Poly). 9. Matt Evers, lhp, Santa Barbara (Jr., Rice). 10. Shuehei Fujiya, rhp, MLB Academy (Sr., Southern California).

INDIVIDUAL BATTING LEADERS
(MINIMUM 62 AT-BATS)

	AVG	AB	R	H	2B	3B	HR	RBI	SB
Marder, Jack, Conejo	.375	120	20	45	8	2	0	27	3
Loy, Brandon, Santa Barbara	.370	81	17	30	6	1	0	17	10
Weik, Joe, San Luis Obispo	.347	173	32	60	17	1	2	30	4
Rathjen, Jeremy, Santa Barbara	.323	96	17	31	7	2	4	20	8
Fowble, Arin, Santa Maria	.322	152	29	49	10	1	5	26	0
Cutspec, Brice, Santa Maria	.322	90	16	30	8	0	0	20	4
McIntyre, Sean, Conejo	.321	109	10	35	6	0	1	13	0
Ornelas, Ben, Santa Maria	.319	69	13	22	5	1	0	9	6
Goetz, Ryan, Santa Barbara	.312	141	19	44	7	0	2	23	9
Jones, Kyle, Conejo	.308	198	51	61	10	9	1	33	17
Terry, Josef, Academy	.308	65	13	20	2	0	0	11	2

INDIVIDUAL PITCHING LEADERS
(MINIMUM 25 INNINGS PITCHED)

	W	L	ERA	G	SV	IP	BB	SO
Leonard, Matt, Santa Barbara	6	0	0.47	0	38	20	12	44
Selden, Robbie, Conejo	3	1	1.05	0	60	37	16	57
Kelley, Tim, Santa Barbara	6	1	1.24	0	51	31	16	56
Van Dam, Brandon, San Luis Obispo	0	2	1.26	0	29	17	8	27
Hutchison, Matt, Santa Barbara	4	3	1.31	6	34	22	7	26
Evers, Matt, Santa Barbara	2	1	1.44	0	31	25	12	34
Griffin, A.J., Santa Barbara	6	1	1.59	0	51	34	6	55
Cesar, Trevor, Santa Maria	4	3	1.72	0	52	34	19	38
Gelinas, Kevin, Conejo	2	2	1.96	3	37	23	20	54
Mirowski, Richie, San Luis Obispo	6	4	2.03	0	58	52	17	61

CLARK GRIFFITH LEAGUE

	W	L	PCT	GB
Vienna Senators	30	9	.769	—
Carney Pirates	29	10	.774	1
Southern Maryland Cardinals	19	19	.500	10½
Fairfax Nationals	17	21	.447	12½
D.C. Grays	16	22	.421	13½

PLAYOFFS—Southern Maryland defeated Carney in the championship of a five-team, double-elimination tournament.
TOP 10 PROSPECTS: 1. K.C. Hobson, 1b/of, Southern Maryland (SIGNED: Blue Jays). 2. Chad Morgan, c, Carney (Fr., Virginia Tech). 3. Ryan Camp, rhp, Vienna (Jr., Illinois State). 4. Matt Crouse, lhp, Carney (So., Mississippi). 5. Matt Snyder, 1b, Carney (So., Mississippi). 6. Jamie Bruno, 1b, Vienna (So., Tulane). 7. Johnny Bladel, of, Fairfax (Fr., James Madison). 8. Connor Mielock, rhp, Carney (So., Oakland). 9. Ryan Doiron, rhp, Vienna, (So., Tulane). 10. Pat Somers, lhp, Carney (So., East Carolina).

INDIVIDUAL BATTING LEADERS
(MINIMUM 90 AT-BATS)

	AVG	AB	R	H	2B	3B	HR	RBI	SB
Bladel, Johnny, Fairfax	.356	101	16	36	8	2	0	21	12
Mitchell, Tony, Vienna	.354	99	26	35	4	0	3	19	6
Wager, Kevin, D.C.	.333	129	19	43	5	1	1	18	3
Simons, Sam, D.C.	.327	104	20	34	9	1	2	20	0
Kuroczko, Nick, Vienna	.317	104	27	33	5	0	3	27	8
Booker, Austin, Vienna	.315	130	36	41	4	1	0	13	25
Dunigan, Foster, D.C.	.313	134	25	42	6	1	0	13	6
August, Mike, S. Maryland	.313	115	24	36	7	2	0	11	11
Bruno, Jamie, Vienna	.311	135	24	42	8	0	9	42	0
Swenson, Alex, Fairfax	.299	107	10	32	9	0	0	19	1

INDIVIDUAL PITCHING LEADERS
(MINIMUM 30 INNINGS PITCHED)

	W	L	ERA	G	SV	IP	H	BB	SO
Crouse, Matt, Carney	6	0	0.82	8	0	44	21	17	34
Hald, Kyle, Vienna	7	0	1.08	15	2	58	40	7	53
Mielock, Connor, Carney	4	2	2.08	9	0	48	45	11	28
Poretz, Austin, S. Maryland	7	0	2.09	11	0	56	50	24	42
Camp, Ryan, Vienna	5	0	2.74	13	0	43	33	22	44
Hoyt, Adam, Southern Maryland	3	3	3.24	9	0	50	44	22	53
Coker, Logan, S. Maryland	1	4	3.96	7	0	39	42	11	23
Paeplow, Kyle, Fairfax	2	2	4.06	10	0	44	50	24	32
Choate, Chason, Fairfax	4	4	4.30	10	0	52	50	15	37
Carpenter, Wyatt, D.C.	3	2	6.06	12	0	36	59	17	10

COASTAL PLAIN LEAGUE

NORTH	W	L	PCT	GB
Peninsula Pilots	35	21	.625	—
Outer Banks DareDevils	32	23	.582	2½
Edenton Steamers	29	27	.518	6
Petersburg Generals	19	37	.339	16

SOUTH	W	L	PCT	GB
Wilson Tobs	35	21	.625	—
Fayetteville SwampDogs	30	23	.566	3½
Florence RedWolves	30	25	.545	4½
Columbia Blowfish	19	36	.345	15½
Wilmington Sharks	19	36	.345	15½

WEST	W	L	PCT	GB
Forest City Owls	46	9	.836	—
Thomasville Hi-Toms	26	28	.481	19½
Gastonia Grizzlies	25	31	.446	21½
Martinsville Mustangs	22	34	.393	24½
Asheboro Copperheads	19	35	.352	26½

PLAYOFFS— Forest City defeated Peninsula in the championship game of an eight-team tournament.
TOP 10 PROSPECTS: 1. Will Lamb, lhp/of, Peninsula (So., Clemson). 2. Graham Stoneburner, rhp, Petersburg (SIGNED: Yankees). 3. Pratt Maynard, 3b/c, Forest City (So., North Carolina State). 4. Chris Epps, of, Thomasville (Jr., Clemson). 5. Russell Wilson, 2b, Gastonia (Jr., North Carolina State). 6. Gerard Hall, 2b/of, Edenton (SIGNED: Royals). 7. Daniel Cropper, rhp, Wilmington (Jr., UNC Wilmington). 8. Stewart Ijames, of, Thomasville (So., Louisville). 9. Trent Rothlin, rhp, Martinsville (Jr., Mississippi). 10. Spencer Patton, rhp, Forest City (Sr., Southern Illinois-Edwardsville).

INDIVIDUAL BATTING LEADERS
(MINIMUM 120 PLATE APPEARANCES)

	AVG	AB	R	H	2B	3B	HR
RBI					SB		
Diamaduros, Konstantine, FC	.376	178	37	67	11	5	4	45	0
Petrich, Dylan, Outer Banks	.374	163	37	61	12	1	2	26	2
Cerreto, Phil, Martinsville	.351	205	33	72	16	4	8	40	12
Epps, Chris, Thomasville	.344	122	40	42	10	5	6	22	12
Hamlet, Matthew, Gastonia	.342	158	26	54	4	0	0	23	6
Shaban, Ronnie, Petersburg	.333	183	30	61	16	0	7	38	5
Holton, Dylan, Martinsville	.328	134	26	44	3	1	0	12	16
LaPensee, Ryan, Martinsville	.328	131	20	43	5	1	0	19	16
Maynard, Pratt, Forest City	.318	176	42	56	16	0	4	38	6
Whitaker, Josh, Outer Banks	.318	195	30	62	3	3	6	47	21

INDIVIDUAL PITCHING LEADERS
(MINIMUM 44 INNINGS)

	W	L	ERA	G	SV	IP	H	BB	SO
Howard, Trent, Wilson	6	1	1.01	10	0	53	40	15	64
Patton, Spencer, Forest City	9	0	1.46	11	0	74	50	22	110
Taylor, John, Florence	4	4	1.58	14	2	63	38	15	54
Christman, Tyler, Columbia	2	5	1.77	10	0	61	38	19	58
Markham, Anthony, Edenton	7	1	1.83	10	0	59	46	20	66
Arrowood, Ryan, Forest City	10	0	1.88	10	0	72	52	17	64
McCray, Stephen, Florence	5	2	1.92	10	0	66	38	21	68
McSwain, Tyler, Peninsula	5	1	1.98	10	1	59	45	17	39
Cropper, Daniel, Wilmington	2	4	2.05	11	0	70	45	16	68
Brown, Jeff, Wilson	2	0	2.13	15	1	51	46	15	32

FLORIDA COLLEGIATE SUMMER LEAGUE

FINAL STANDINGS	W	L	PCT	GB
DeLand Suns	25	13	.658	—
Sanford River Rats	23	17	.575	3
Leesburg Lightning	21	18	.538	4½
Clermont Mavericks	19	24	.442	8½
Winter Park Diamond Dawgs	10	26	.278	14

PLAYOFFS— Leesburg defeated Clermont in the championship of a five-team playoff.
TOP 10 PROSPECTS: 1. Jabari Blash, of, DeLand (So., Miami-Dade CC). 2. Jimmy Nelson, rhp, DeLand (Jr., Alabama). 3. Taylor Wrenn, ss/2b, DeLand (So., Southern California). 4. Mike Dufek, 1b/rhp, Leesburg (Sr., Michigan). 5. Derek Luciano, ss/2b, DeLand (Jr., Central Florida). 6. Tyler White, rhp, DeLand (So., Alabama). 7. Nick DelGuidice, ss/2b, Leesburg (Jr., Florida Atlantic). 8. Robert Lake, rhp, Leesburg (Jr., Winthrop). 9. Josh Smith, rhp, Sanford (Sr., Lipscomb). 10. Delgis Soto, rhp, Sanford (Jr., Brewton-Parker, Ga.).

INDIVIDUAL BATTING LEADERS
(MINIMUM 2.0 AT-BATS PER TEAM GAME)

	AVG	AB	R	H	2B	3B	HR	RBI	SB
Figliolia, Anthony, Winter Park	.398	88	19	35	2	2	0	10	8
Taylor, Evan, Leesburg	.333	90	16	30	4	0	3	13	5
Schulze, David, Sanford	.319	138	31	44	11	0	3	27	18
Okey, Chase, Clermont	.318	132	22	42	6	0	0	26	1
Wethers, Tyrone, Clermont	.299	137	24	41	5	1	0	14	23
Luciano, Derek, DeLand	.299	134	23	40	7	3	3	30	8
Dye, Tim, Clermont	.296	152	23	45	10	3	4	26	7
Semeniuk, Ryan, Clermont	.293	116	20	34	10	0	1	14	8
Gore, Trae, Leesburg	.287	101	15	29	2	1	3	11	16
Venegas, Trace, Leesburg	.287	122	14	35	6	0	3	19	4

INDIVIDUAL PITCHING LEADERS
(MINIMUM 0.7 INNINGS PER TEAM GAME)

	W	L	ERA	G	SV	IP	H	BB	SO
Wilson, Nick, Sanford	3	1	1.20	14	0	30	20	10	15
Goodyear, Matt, Clermont	2	2	1.23	13	0	37	23	15	43
Strawn, Josh, DeLand	3	0	1.59	6	0	28	21	7	27
Caughel, Lindsey, DeLand	2	0	1.70	8	0	37	29	5	37
Brown, Bryan, Sanford	5	1	2.21	10	0	53	48	20	52
Ferrano, Trey, Sanford	5	2	2.23	9	0	48	45	13	40
Wahl, Kyle, DeLand	4	3	2.68	10	0	47	37	16	51
Nelson, Jimmy, DeLand	4	4	2.76	11	0	59	41	23	75
Prano, Charles, Clermont	5	2	2.91	12	0	46	44	22	25
Kalgstein, Rick, Leesburg	1	3	2.93	9	0	43	44	8	37

GREAT LAKES LEAGUE

FINAL STANDINGS	W	L	PCT	GB
Lima Locos	28	8	.778	—
Grand Lake Mariners	25	10	.714	2½
Cincinnati	23	12	.657	4½
Licking County Settlers	22	13	.629	5½
Southern Ohio Copperheads	18	16	.529	9
Xenia Athletes in Action	16	19	.457	11½
Hamilton	12	23	.343	15½
Lake Erie	12	24	.333	16
Stark County	11	23	.324	16
Anderson Servants	8	27	.229	19½

PLAYOFFS—Cincinnati defeated Southern Ohio in the championship of a six-team, double-elimination tournament.
TOP 10 PROSPECTS: 1. Kolbrin Vitek, 2b/rhp, Lake Erie (Jr., Ball State). 2. Perci Garner, rhp, Stark County (So., Ball State). 3. Mike Jefferson, lhp, Cincinnati (So., Louisiana Tech). 4. Kolby Wood, rhp, Lima (Jr., Michigan). 5. Ryan Strausborger, of, Cincinnati (Sr., Indiana State). 6. Jeff Shields, rhp, Lima (Kennesaw State). 7. Jared Hoying, ss, Grand Lake (Jr., Toledo). 8. Ian Kadish, rhp, Cincinnati (Sr., Marshall). 9. Andrew Meyer, rhp, Lima (Sr., Ashland, Ohio). 10. Tristan Moore, if/of, Lima (So., Wright State).

INDIVIDUAL BATTING LEADERS
(MINIMUM 70 PLATE APPEARANCES)

	AVG	AB	R	H	2B	3B	HR	RBI	SB
Vitek, Kolbrin, Lake Erie	.400	135	27	54	16	6	6	38	10
Strausborger, Ryan, Cincinnati	.384	138	41	53	14	5	4	21	22
Moore, Tristan, Lima	.375	104	29	39	4	1	0	17	10
Hoying, Jared, Grand Lake	.375	96	24	36	8	8	4	29	7
Jones, Terrell, Lima	.374	115	12	43	7	2	0	17	4
Thompkins, Aaron, Stark County	.364	99	17	36	3	3	0	10	6
Jones, Daniel, Lima	.355	76	10	27	2	2	0	16	1
Roberts, Aaron, Licking County	.336	110	20	37	4	0	0	16	5
Gillespie, Kevin, Lake Erie	.331	133	24	44	5	2	1	19	12
Spiteals, Reed, Anderson	.330	109	19	36	13	0	1	22	6

INDIVIDUAL PITCHING LEADERS
(MINIMUM 30 INNINGS)

	W	L	ERA	G	SV	IP	H	BB	SO
Jensen, Dave, Southern Ohio	2	0	0.30	7	0	30	15	10	24
Newhart, Tyler, Lima	3	0	1.09	7	0	33	23	5	29
Klein, Phil, Licking County	2	1	1.70	7	0	37	27	11	24
Bucciferro, Tony, Grand Lake	4	2	1.74	8	0	41	32	11	34
Starn, David, Southern Ohio	1	2	1.80	7	0	30	26	10	36
Kadish, Ian, Cincinnati	4	1	1.94	8	0	42	21	15	49
Meyer, Andrew, Lima	6	0	1.96	8	0	41	40	4	34
Hobson, Cameron, Southern Ohio	1	3	2.15	7	0	38	27	14	36
McNeil, Brent, Grand Lake	3	0	2.27	8	0	32	40	12	25
Kitchen, Bill, Hamilton	2	5	2.45	8	0	48	40	18	33

JAYHAWK LEAGUE

FINAL STANDINGS

	W	L	PCT	GB
El Dorado Broncos	22	9	.710	—
Hays Larks	17	13	.567	4½
Liberal Bee Jays	18	14	.563	4½
Derby Twins	16	16	.500	6½
Dodge City A's	5	25	.167	16½

TOP 10 PROSPECTS: 1. Wes Cunningham, 1b, El Dorado (Sr., Murray State). 2. Bobby Doran, rhp, Liberal (Jr., Texas Tech). 3. Andrew Heck, rhp/ss, Hays (Jr., Duquesne). 4. Justin Lindsey, rhp, El Dorado (So., Kansas State). 5. Jake Sabol, rhp, El Dorado (Jr., Central Michigan). 6. Matt Hauser, rhp, Liberal (Sr., San Diego). 7. Mitch Caster, rhp/of, Liberal (Jr., Wichita State). 8. Eric Sim, c, Derby (Jr., South Florida). 9. Chris Craycraft, rhp, El Dorado (Jr., Murray State). 10. Brandon Eckerle, of, Hays (Jr., Michigan State).

INDIVIDUAL BATTING LEADERS
(MINIMUM 80 PLATE APPEARANCES)

	AVG	AB	H	2B	3B	HR	RBI
Cunningham, Wes, El Dorado	.402	107	43	12	2	4	26
Eckerle, Brandon, Hays	.287	119	46	4	0	0	8
Sigala, Oscar, Dodge City	.359	103	37	9	0	3	18
Whipple, Travis, El Dorado	.356	104	37	13	0	7	29
Gordey, Justin, Liberal	.353	85	30	4	0	2	16
Gregorich, Brandon, Derby	.330	91	30	7	0	9	32
Rindels, Tanner, Liberal	.327	113	37	8	1	5	28
Haddow, Mark, Derby	.335	83	27	5	0	3	12
Waddell, Cole, Derby	.318	107	34	4	1	3	20
Williams, Dorrain, El Dorado	.314	86	27	1	1	0	9

INDIVIDUAL PITCHING LEADERS
(MINIMUM 20 INNINGS)

	W	L	ERA	IP	H	SO
Kelly, Mike, Derby	3	0	1.25	23	10	23
Craycraft, Chris, El Dorado	5	1	1.59	45	41	37
Heck, Andrew, Hays	2	0	2.05	54	53	39
Davis, Brett, Liberal	3	0	2.23	40	32	29
Sabol, Jake, El Dorado	4	0	2.27	33	25	20
Lacourse, Michael, Dodge City	2	1	2.35	23	15	26
St. John, Kirby, Derby	0	1	2.52	25	19	28
Hauser, Matt, Liberal	3	2	2.71	53	44	52
Trevino, Steve, El Dorado	3	0	2.78	32	35	12
Lisi, Don, Liberal	4	3	2.85	60	62	40

MINK LEAGUE

NORTH	W	L
Chillicothe Mudcats	21	13
Beatrice Bruins	20	13
St. Joe Mustangs	19	13
Topeka Golden Giants	18	15
Clarinda A's	14	14

SOUTH	W	L
Sedalia Bombers	21	12
Nevada Griffons	20	12
Joplin Outlaws	14	21
Mac-N-Seitz	13	22
Ozark Generals	6	28

PLAYOFFS—Chillicothe defeated Sedalia 2-0 in best-of-three championship series.

TOP 10 PROSPECTS: 1. Mike Morin, rhp, Mac-N-Seitz (Fr., North Carolina). 2. Adam Smith, ss/rhp, Beatrice (So., Texas A&M). 3. Nick Martini, of, Topeka (So., Kansas State). 4. Michael Fuda, of, Clarinda (Jr., Rice). 5. Johnny Coy, 3b/1b, St. Joseph (So., Wichita State). 6. Dominic D'Anna, 1b, Sedalia (Jr., Cal State Northridge). 7. Randall Thorpe, of, Beatrice (So., San Jacinto, Texas, JC). 8. Shane Minks, rhp, Beatrice (Sr., Texas A&M). 9. Mike Mariot, rhp, Beatrice (Jr., Nebraska). 10. Darian Sandford, cf/2b, Chillicothe (Sr., Park, Mo.).

NEW ENGLAND COLLEGIATE LEAGUE

EASTERN	W	L	PCT	GB
Newport Gulls	31	10	.756	—
Sanford Mainers	23	16	.590	7
North Shore Navigators	20	21	.488	11
New Bedford Bay Sox	17	24	.415	14
Manchester Silkworms	13	26	.333	17
Lowell All-Americans	13	28	.317	18

WESTERN	W	L	PCT	GB
Keene Swamp Bats	27	13	.675	—
North Adams SteepleCats	25	16	.610	2½
Vermont Mountaineers	20	19	.513	6½
Holyoke Blue Sox	20	21	.488	7½
Danbury Westerners	19	22	.463	8½
Pittsfield American Defenders	13	25	.342	13

PLAYOFFS— Quarterfinals: Newport defeated New Bedford 2-0, Sanford defeated North Shore 2-1, Keene defeated Holyoke 2-1, Vermont defeated North Adams 2-0. **Semifinals:** Newport defeated Sanford 2-1, Vermont defeated Holyoke 2-0. **Finals:** Newport defeated Vermont 2-1 in best-of-three championship series.

TOP 10 PROSPECTS: 1. Devin Jones, rhp, Danbury (So., Mississippi State). 2. Peter Verdin, of/c, Keene (So., Georgia). 3. Tyler Mizenko, rhp, Sanford (So., Winthrop). 4. Troy Scott, 1b, Newport (Jr., Washington). 5. Joey Bergman, 3b, Newport (Sr., College of Charleston). 6. Taylor Featherston, ss, New Bedford (So., Texas Christian). 7. Adam Conley, lhp, Keene (So., Washington State). 8. Chad Arnold, rhp, Newport (Jr., Washington State). 9. Andrew Benak, rhp, Vermont (So., Rice). 10. Andrew Kittredge, rhp, Newport (So., Washington).

INDIVIDUAL BATTING LEADERS
(MINIMUM 80 PLATE APPEARANCES)

	AVG	AB	R	H	2B	3B	HR	RBI	SB
Lytle, Casey, Pittsfield	.386	114	20	44	6	2	1	16	2
Wood, Jim, Holyoke	.353	133	21	47	9	0	3	25	3
Dunn, Henry, Vermont	.351	134	27	47	11	1	0	17	17
Bergman, Joey, Newport	.351	97	18	34	6	0	1	14	3
Pratt, Dylan, Sanford	.341	123	25	42	14	0	2	25	3
Jones, Clay, Vermont	.336	119	16	40	4	0	2	21	2
Thompson, Corey, Sanford	.330	91	8	30	7	0	0	13	2
Schultz, John, North Adams	.329	143	23	47	8	1	1	30	19
Micowski, Mark, Sanford	.328	137	34	45	3	7	1	10	10
Chester, Josh, Keene	.328	131	23	43	11	3	1	13	1

INDIVIDUAL PITCHING LEADERS
(MINIMUM 20 INNINGS)

	W	L	ERA	G	SV	IP	H	BB	SO
Conley, Adam, Keene	2	0	0.00	8	1	34	14	11	37
Murray, Doug, New Bedford	2	1	0.55	11	2	33	18	7	22
Peterson, Stephen, Newport	2	1	0.71	12	5	25	24	9	31
Branham, Matt, Newport	1	0	0.78	16	6	23	11	10	26
Murray, Matt, Sanford	2	1	0.80	6	0	34	17	9	27
Meo, Anthony, New Bedford	1	1	0.87	5	0	21	12	15	20
Holland, Neil, Sanford	3	3	0.90	17	1	20	16	8	23
Roberts, Will, Newport	3	0	1.00	5	0	27	21	3	24
Brown, Geoff, Newport	3	0	1.31	12	1	21	14	7	20
Kumbatovic, Rob, Vermont	5	1	1.35	7	0	47	32	9	21

NEW YORK COLLEGIATE LEAGUE

WEST	W	L	PCT	GB
Hornell Dodgers	30	12	.714	—
Brockport Riverbats	22	19	.527	7½
Alfred Oilers	22	20	.524	8
Geneva Red Wings	21	20	.512	8½
Webster Yankees	21	21	.500	9
Elmira Pioneers	20	22	.476	10
Allegany County Nitros	18	21	.462	10½
Niagara Power	11	29	.275	18

EAST	W	L	PCT	GB
Amsterdam Mohawks	30	12	.714	—
Glen Falls Golden Eagles	29	12	.707	1/2
Saratoga Phillies	19	22	.463	10½
Mohawk Valley DiamondDogs	17	24	.415	12½
Watertown Wizards	15	24	.385	13½
Albany Dutchmen	11	27	.289	17

PLAYOFFS—Quarterfinals: Amsterdam defeated Mohawk Valley 2-0, Hornell defeated Geneva 2-0, Glens Falls defeated Saratoga 2-1, Alfred defeated Geneva 2-0. **Semifinals:** Amsterdam defeated Glens Falls 2-0, Hornell defeated Alfred 2-0. **Championship:** Amsterdam defeated Hornell 2-0 in best-of-three championship series.

TOP 10 PROSPECTS: 1. Braden Kapteyn, rhp/1b, Amsterdam (So., Kentucky). 2. Tillman Pugh, of, Amsterdam (Jr., Sonoma State, Calif.). 3. Rodarrick Jones, of, Glens Falls (So., New Orleans). 4. Greg Holle, rhp, Saratoga (Jr., Texas Christian). 5. Mel Rojas Jr., of, Amsterdam (Fr., Wabash Valley CC, Ill.). 6. Corey Pappel, rhp, Elmira (Jr., Cornell). 7. Justin Fradejas, of, Amsterdam (Jr., Auburn). 8. Tony Dischler, rhp, Glens Falls (So., Louisiana-Monroe). 9. Nate Koontz, of, Webster (So., Ball State). 10. Chase Boruff, rhp, Hornell (Sr., Carson-Newman, Tenn.).

INDIVIDUAL BATTING LEADERS
(MINIMUM 100 PLATE APPEARANCES)

	AVG	AB	R	H	2B	3B	HR	RBI	SB
Hattori, Kosuke, Watertown	.377	151	36	57	5	1	0	13	22
Bennett, Trey, Hornell	.347	144	35	50	10	2	7	38	8
Johnson, Neiko, Watertown	.343	140	28	48	6	1	2	24	21
Jones, Brant, Watertown	.338	151	30	51	9	0	2	32	11
Edwards, J.J., Elmira	.338	157	24	53	6	2	0	18	6
Choy, Ian, Amsterdam	.336	110	22	37	7	0	3	17	6
Giansanti, Anthony, Glen Falls	.331	148	31	49	7	3	4	23	13
Keppler, Jonathan, Hornell	.327	107	35	35	4	0	0	19	7
Bailey, Shawn, Webster	.325	160	20	52	3	0	0	13	14
Muoio, Steve, Webster	.324	139	19	45	14	0	1	17	1

INDIVIDUAL PITCHING LEADERS
(MINIMUM 25 INNINGS PITCHED)

	W	L	ERA	G	SV	IP	H	BB	SO
Green, Chase, Amsterdam	3	0	0.71	16	0	25	11	14	25
Backes, Jordan, Hornell	6	1	1.34	9	0	47	24	30	52
Craig, Michael, Webster	5	1	1.50	9	0	42	26	15	19
Forer, Nathan, Glen Falls	5	2	1.52	8	0	47	37	13	34
Pappel, Corey, Elmira	4	3	1.55	11	1	52	28	35	59
Lambe, Erik, Hornell	4	3	1.70	12	0	48	30	14	32
Johnson, Kevin, Brockport	3	2	1.88	11	1	38	23	10	35
Bouthilette, Sean, Amsterdam	4	3	2.02	9	0	49	37	14	42
Shepard, Jon, Albany	0	3	2.03	19	3	27	29	5	22
Beard, Willie, Glen Falls	4	0	2.06	8	0	35	32	10	34

NORTHWOODS LEAGUE

NORTH	W	L	PCT	GB
Rochester Honkers	42	26	.618	—
Mankato MoonDogs	39	29	.574	3
Alexandria Beetles	38	30	.559	4
Brainerd Lakes Area Lunkers	34	34	.500	8
St. Cloud River Bats	32	36	.471	10
Thunder Bay Border Cats	27	41	.397	15
Duluth Huskies	25	43	.368	17

SOUTH	W	L	PCT	GB
La Crosse Loggers	41	27	.603	—
Madison Mallards	38	29	.567	2½
Battle Creek Bombers	37	30	.552	3½
Eau Claire Express	36	32	.529	5
Wisconsin Woodchucks	30	37	.448	10½
Green Bay Bullfrogs	30	37	.448	10½
Waterloo Bucks	25	43	.368	16

PLAYOFFS—Semifinals: Rochester defeated Mankato 2-0, La Crosse defeated Eau Claire 2-0. **Championship:** Rochester defeated La Crosse 2-1 in best-of-three championship series.

TOP 10 PROSPECTS: 1. Rob Brantly, c, La Crosse (So., UC Riverside). 2. Dixon Anderson, rhp, Green Bay (So., California). 3. Michael Kvasnicka, of/c, Brainerd Lakes Area (Jr., Minnesota). 4. Tony Thompson, 3b, Rochester (Jr., Kansas). 5. Matt Miller, rhp, Alexandria (So., Michigan). 6. Erik Johnson, rhp, Alexandria (So., California). 7. Brooks Pinckard, rhp/of, Eau Claire (Jr., Baylor). 8. Harold Riggings, 1b, Madison (So., North Carolina State). 9. Zach Varce, rhp, Green Bay (Jr., Portland). 10. Corey Jones, 2b/ss, Rochester (Jr., Cal State Fullerton).

INDIVIDUAL BATTING LEADERS
(MINIMUM 2.7 PLATE APPEARANCES PER TEAM GAME)

	AVG	AB	R	H	2B	3B	HR	RBI	SB
Brantly, Robert, La Crosse	.346	188	29	65	14	0	6	34	2
Lewis, Chris, Battle Creek	.344	253	49	87	11	5	4	43	10
Muller, Kurtis, Madison	.335	197	40	66	8	2	3	24	19
Giller, Michael, Waterloo	.335	263	36	88	12	0	4	40	14
Roof, Jonathon, St. Cloud	.332	241	43	80	11	1	0	24	25
Durant, Ryan, Mankato	.324	244	32	79	10	1	1	22	9
Fadness, Nolan, Eau Claire	.317	230	50	73	6	0	0	24	28
Jones, Corey, Rochester	.315	241	45	76	10	1	13	43	14
Serna, KC, Mankato	.314	175	30	55	7	2	0	16	25
Kvasnicka, Mike, Brainerd	.314	188	19	59	8	0	2	26	0

INDIVIDUAL PITCHING LEADERS
(MINIMUM 0.8 INNINGS PITCHED PER TEAM GAME)

	W	L	ERA	G	SV	IP	H	BB	SO
Butt, Bryce, Wisconsin	7	0	1.07	11	1	67	42	12	36
Demmin, Ryan, Mankato	5	4	1.36	12	0	80	56	16	72
Handley, Mitch, Alexandria	6	1	1.47	12	0	86	54	28	48
O Grady, Dennis, Brainerd Lakes	6	1	1.58	12	0	74	49	16	64
Griffin, Tim, Mankato	4	2	1.60	11	0	67	44	23	70
Anderson, Dixon, Green Bay	3	2	1.61	23	7	56	40	24	56
Deminsky, David, St. Cloud	6	3	1.64	11	0	71	56	15	38
Talley, Matt, Battle Creek	6	4	1.72	12	0	79	78	27	42
Varce, Zach, Green Bay	3	5	1.93	18	1	75	50	21	105
Whitmore, Bennett, Mankato	3	2	2.07	9	0	57	51	15	28

PROSPECT LEAGUE

EAST	W	L	PCT	GB
Chillicothe Paints	31	25	.554	—
North Coast Knights	28	24	.538	1
Butler Blue Sox	28	26	.519	2
Richmond River Rats	26	28	.481	4
Slippery Rock Sliders	22	31	.415	7½

WEST	W	L	PCT	GB
Quincy Gems	36	20	.643	—
Danville Dans	32	21	.604	2½
Dupage Dragons	26	28	.481	9
Dubois County Bombers	25	28	.472	9½
Springfield Sliders	22	32	.407	13
Hannibal Caveman	20	33	.377	14½

PLAYOFFS— Quincy defeated Chillicothe 2-0 in best-of-three championship series.

TOP 10 PROSPECTS: 1. Mikie Mahtook, of, Danville (So., Louisiana State). 2. Kyle Gaedele, of, Hannibal (So., Valparaiso). 3. Brett Huber, rhp, Danville (R-Fr., Mississippi). 4. Brian Billigen, of, Butler (So., Cornell). 5. Jason Nappi, 3b/of, Danville (Jr., Harding, Ark.). 6. Brad Goldberg, rhp, North Coast (So., Coastal Carolina). 7. Ashley Graeter, ss/rhp, Hannibal (So., Pearl River, Miss., CC). 8. Austin Nola, ss, Danville (So., Louisiana State). 9. Rusty Shellhorn, lhp, North Coast (So., Washington State). 10.Tyler Bullock, c/dh, Richmond (Sr., Southern Illinois).

INDIVIDUAL BATTING LEADERS
(MINIMUM 2.7 PLATE APPEARANCES PER TEAM GAME)

	AVG	AB	R	H	2B	3B	HR	RBI	SB
Villegas, Joseph, Richmond	.363	171	25	62	7	3	0	17	11
Youchak, Brian, Butler	.350	163	24	57	10	0	0	23	6
Nappi, Jason, Danville	.336	140	30	47	11	2	2	29	5
Melendez, Evan, N. Coast	.328	174	26	57	9	2	1	16	12
Allen, Ben, Chillicothe	.313	192	26	60	4	2	1	22	8
Billigen, Brian, Butler	.313	182	36	57	7	4	4	22	16
Bullock, Tyler, Richmond	.312	173	29	54	16	0	14	47	0
Brouse, Andy, Chillicothe	.311	190	33	59	14	2	4	17	6
Banks, Eian, Chillicothe	.308	185	25	57	13	2	5	27	6
Green, Austin, Danville	.305	164	30	50	11	2	3	26	0

INDIVIDUAL PITCHING LEADERS
(MINIMUM 0.8 INNINGS PITCHED PER TEAM GAME)

	W	L	ERA	G	SV	IP	H	BB	SO
Derbak, Richie, Quincy	4	0	1.10	11	1	49	29	10	63
Schreiber, Phil, Springfield	6	0	1.30	8	0	48	36	17	51
Oropeza, Joe, North Coast	5	1	1.42	12	0	57	42	18	49
Shellhorn, Rusty, North Coast	8	3	1.45	18	0	68	45	26	89
Schulz, Clayton, Chillicothe	6	2	1.48	10	0	61	35	31	48
Bertucci, Tony, Chillicothe	4	2	1.51	8	0	48	44	8	29
Webber, Casey, Dupage	2	2	1.57	15	1	52	36	21	67
Painter, Adam, Richmond	4	2	2.06	20	1	48	32	22	32
Wurdack, Drew, Springfield	2	3	2.15	9	0	59	55	16	51
Lambrix, Aaron, Danville	6	2	2.19	15	2	49	44	14	50

TEXAS COLLEGIATE LEAGUE

FINAL STANDINGS

	W	L	PCT	GB
Victoria Generals	30	14	.682	—
East Texas Pump Jacks	26	19	.578	4½
Coppell Copperheads	21	26	.447	10½
Brazos Valley Bombers	19	27	.413	12
McKinney Marshals	18	28	.391	13

PLAYOFFS—Semifinals: Coppell defeated East Texas 2-0, Victoria defeated Brazos Valley 2-0. **Championship:** Coppell defeated Victoria 2-0 in best-of-three championship series.

TOP 10 PROSPECTS: 1. Nathan Karns, rhp, Coppell (SIGNED: Nationals). 2. Riley Cooper, of, McKinney (SIGNED: Rangers). 3. David Rollins, lhp, East Texas (So., San Jacinto JC, Texas). 4. Rett Varner, rhp, Coppell (Jr., Texas-Arlington). 5. Mark Hudson, of, Victoria (Jr., Sam Houston State). 6. Carter Jurica, ss, McKinney (Jr., Kansas State). 7. Matt Juengel, 3b, East Texas (So., Texas A&M). 8. Zach Nuding, rhp, Victoria (So., Weatherford JC, Texas). 9. Mike Bolsinger, rhp, McKinney (Sr., Arkansas). 10. Brett Nicholas, c, East Texas (Jr., Missouri).

INDIVIDUAL BATTING LEADERS
(MINIMUM 50 PLATE APPEARANCES)

	AVG	AB	R	H	2B	3B	HR	RBI	SB
Hudson, Mark, Victoria	.386	127	29	49	15	4	1	27	6
Brown, J.B. McKinney	.356	149	19	53	9	1	1	17	2
Hale, John, B.V.	.333	51	11	17	5	0	0	6	1
Juengel, Matt, East Texas	.322	146	27	47	8	0	4	26	5
Foster, James, Coppell	.317	145	29	46	4	0	0	11	17
Biggins, Marcellous, Coppell	.317	82	14	26	3	2	2	13	5
Gonzales, Abel, East Texas	.314	70	8	22	3	0	0	11	3
Hoke, Creighton, Victoria	.299	67	13	20	1	0	0	12	1
Ogle, Tyler, McKinney	.295	112	23	33	7	0	2	11	3
Hinojosa, Joaquin, B.V.	.295	61	11	18	1	0	4	8	1

INDIVIDUAL PITCHING LEADERS
(MINIMUM 25 INNINGS)

	W	L	ERA	G	SV	IP	H	BB	SO
Varner, Rett, Coppell	4	2	1.17	7	0	46	26	7	57
Karns, Nathan, Coppell	4	0	1.20	6	0	30	13	17	47
Massey, Taylor, McKinney	1	3	1.22	18	2	37	26	16	23
Oros, Michael Victoria	3	0	1.53	10	0	29	20	11	26
Schwalenberg, Ian, East Texas	3	0	1.88	17	3	29	21	6	36
Steward, Garrett, Victoria	2	0	1.91	14	0	28	25	18	35
Rooke, Thomas, McKinney	3	0	2.31	8	0	47	39	22	44
Stafford, Jared, Coppell	2	3	2.41	7	0	37	36	11	34
Payne, Blake, Victoria	6	0	2.44	8	0	44	46	10	27
Rollins, David, East Texas	5	2	2.45	9	0	51	37	26	63

VALLEY LEAGUE

NORTH

	W	L	PCT	GB
Front Royal Cardinals	30	17	.638	—
Haymarket Senators	29	23	.558	3½
Winchester Royals	25	23	.521	5½
Fauquier Gators	21	23	.477	7½

CENTRAL

	W	L	PCT	GB
Luray Wranglers	27	20	.574	—
Woodstock River Bandits	24	22	.522	2½
New Market Rebels	24	25	.490	4
Harrisonburg Turks	20	24	.455	5½

SOUTH

	W	L	PCT	GB
Staunton Braves	27	17	.614	—
Covington Lumberjacks	26	27	.491	5½
Waynesboro Generals	18	26	.409	9
Rockbridge	9	33	.214	17

PLAYOFFS—Quarterfinals: Haymarket defeated Staunton 2-0, New Market defeated Luray 2-1, Covington defeated Front Royal 2-1, Winchester defeated Woodstock 2-1. **Semifinals:** Haymarket defeated New Market 2-0, Covington defeated Winchester 2-0. **Championship:** Haymarket defeated Covington 3-1 in best-of-five championship series.

TOP 10 PROSPECTS: 1. Daniel Bowman, of, Luray (So., Coastal Carolina). 2. Johnny Dishon, of, Staunton (So., Louisiana State). 3. Drew Rucinski, rhp, Luray (Jr., Ohio State). 4. Michael Lang, of, Haymarket (Jr., Rutgers). 5. Stephen McQuail, 3b, Front Royal (Jr., Canisius). 6. Todd Brazeal, 1b, Staunton (So., South Florida). 7. Greg Hopkins, 3b, Haymarket (Jr., St. John's). 8. Pablo Bermudez, of, Luray (So., Florida International). 9. Bobby Rauh, of, Winchester (SIGNED: Braves). 10. Chris Sorce, rhp, Harrisonburg (SIGNED: Mariners).

INDIVIDUAL BATTING LEADERS
(MINIMUM 125 PLATE APPEARANCES)

	AVG	AB	R	H	2B	3B	HR	RBI	SB
Mickens, Kenny, New Market	.365	126	25	46	15	1	1	22	1
Wirnsberger, A.J., Luray	.361	158	29	57	16	2	3	35	4
Lang, Michael, Haymarket	.357	140	40	50	8	1	7	21	7
Burford, Kent, Staunton	.348	135	38	47	3	0	0	10	14
Hopkins, Greg, Haymarket	.345	200	34	69	14	2	4	33	13
Brown, Bobby, Harrisonburg	.341	126	28	43	11	1	3	12	4
Dudley, Aaron, Staunton	.338	142	32	48	12	0	2	23	2
Oberacker, Chad, Fauquier	.337	163	24	55	12	1	2	21	17
Gonzalez, Richard, New Market	.331	169	22	56	10	1	0	31	7
Blackburn, Kyle, Staunton	.325	120	21	39	8	1	3	18	3

INDIVIDUAL PITCHING LEADERS
(MINIMUM 50 INNINGS)

	W	L	ERA	G	SV	IP	H	BB	SO
Sasser, Grant, Haymarket	6	1	1.77	12	2	61	43	16	58
Putnam, Kyle, Fauquier	4	2	1.91	9	0	57	48	15	43
Swenson, Aaron, Staunton	5	2	2.20	9	0	65	48	15	63
Hatfield, Heith, Woodstock	2	4	2.35	7	0	46	35	13	45
Baker, Garrett, New Market	3	3	2.53	10	0	64	65	16	55
Granier, Drew, Harrisonburg	5	1	2.64	8	0	44	42	13	49
VanSickler, Greg, Front Royal	5	1	2.68	9	0	57	50	10	54
Alessio, Eric, New Market	5	0	2.96	10	0	52	52	19	32
DeSimone, Danny, Covington	4	2	3.19	9	0	59	74	17	52
Patton, Michael, Fauquier	3	2	3.19	8	0	48	56	16	41

WEST COAST LEAGUE

EAST	W	L	PCT	GB
Wenatchee AppleSox	34	14	.708	—
Kelowna Falcons	24	24	.500	10
Spokane RiverHawks	19	29	.396	15
Moses Lake Pirates	10	38	.208	24

WEST	W	L	PCT	GB
Corvallis Knights	38	10	.792	—
Bend Elks	25	23	.521	13
Bellingham Bells	22	26	.458	16
Kitsap BlueJackets	20	28	.417	18

PLAYOFFS—Semifinals: Wenatchee defeated Kelowna 2-0, Corvallis defeated Bend 2-1. **Championship:** Wenatchee defeated Corvallis 2-0 in best-of-three championship series.
TOP 10 PROSPECTS: 1. Andrew Susac, c, Corvallis (Fr., Oregon State). 2. Matt Andriese, rhp, Corvallis, (So., UC Riverside). 3. Taylor Ard, 1b, Corvallis (So., Oregon State). 4. Bobby Crocker, of, Bend (So., Cal Poly). 5. Jordan Leyland, 1b, Bend (So., UC Irvine). 6. Chris Amezquita, 3b, Bellingham (So., Pepperdine). 7. Seth Harvey, rhp, Bellingham (Sr., Washington State). 8. Evan DeLuca, lhp, Wenatchee (SIGNED: Yankees). 9. Chris Casazza, 3b, Moses Lake (Jr., Tarleton State, Texas). 10. Kyle Johnson, of, Wenatchee (So., Washington State).

INDIVIDUAL BATTING LEADERS
(MINIMUM 1.8 AT-BATS PER TEAM GAME)

	AVG	AB	R	H	2B	3B	HR	RBI	SB
Ard, Taylor, Corvallis	.387	111	22	43	11	0	4	30	0
Jimenez, Richie, Corvallis	.354	161	33	57	7	2	0	20	6
Johnson, Kyle, Wenatchee	.340	162	31	55	9	2	0	25	1
Richter, Sam, Bellingham	.338	151	32	51	10	0	0	19	5
Valine, Corey, Bend	.336	131	16	44	6	0	0	14	2
Jenkins, Ryan, Kelowna	.333	129	19	43	9	0	1	21	3
Johnson, Phil, Spokane	.327	150	17	49	8	0	1	24	0
Leyland, Jordan, Bend	.327	147	17	48	11	1	2	25	1
Takayoshi, Josh, Wenatchee	.318	148	34	47	8	1	0	18	5
Johnson, D.J., Corvallis	.316	95	10	30	5	0	0	11	0

INDIVIDUAL PITCHING LEADERS
(MINIMUM 0.8 INNINGS PER TEAM GAME)

	W	L	ERA	G	SV	IP	H	BB	SO
Andriese, Matt, Corvallis	5	0	0.78	7	0	46	31	6	40
Kalush, Steve, Corvallis	3	1	1.49	12	3	42	41	6	32
O'Niel, Chris, Kelowna	3	3	1.58	6	0	40	41	9	18
Wagner, Chad, Wenatchee	3	0	1.61	11	1	56	43	14	34
Hamman, Kyle, Kitsap	4	3	1.87	13	0	6	60	17	33
Berg, Reedy, Wenatchee	3	2	1.88	11	0	43	43	9	34
Watt, Trey, Kitsap	6	4	2.01	12	0	67	60	21	46
Poggemeyer, Tyrell, Bellingham	4	1	2.17	9	0	66	56	23	43
Macey, David, Kitsap	1	2	2.23	18	3	44	37	13	29
Kraus, Kyle, Corvallis	6	1	2.24	11	0	60	53	14	38

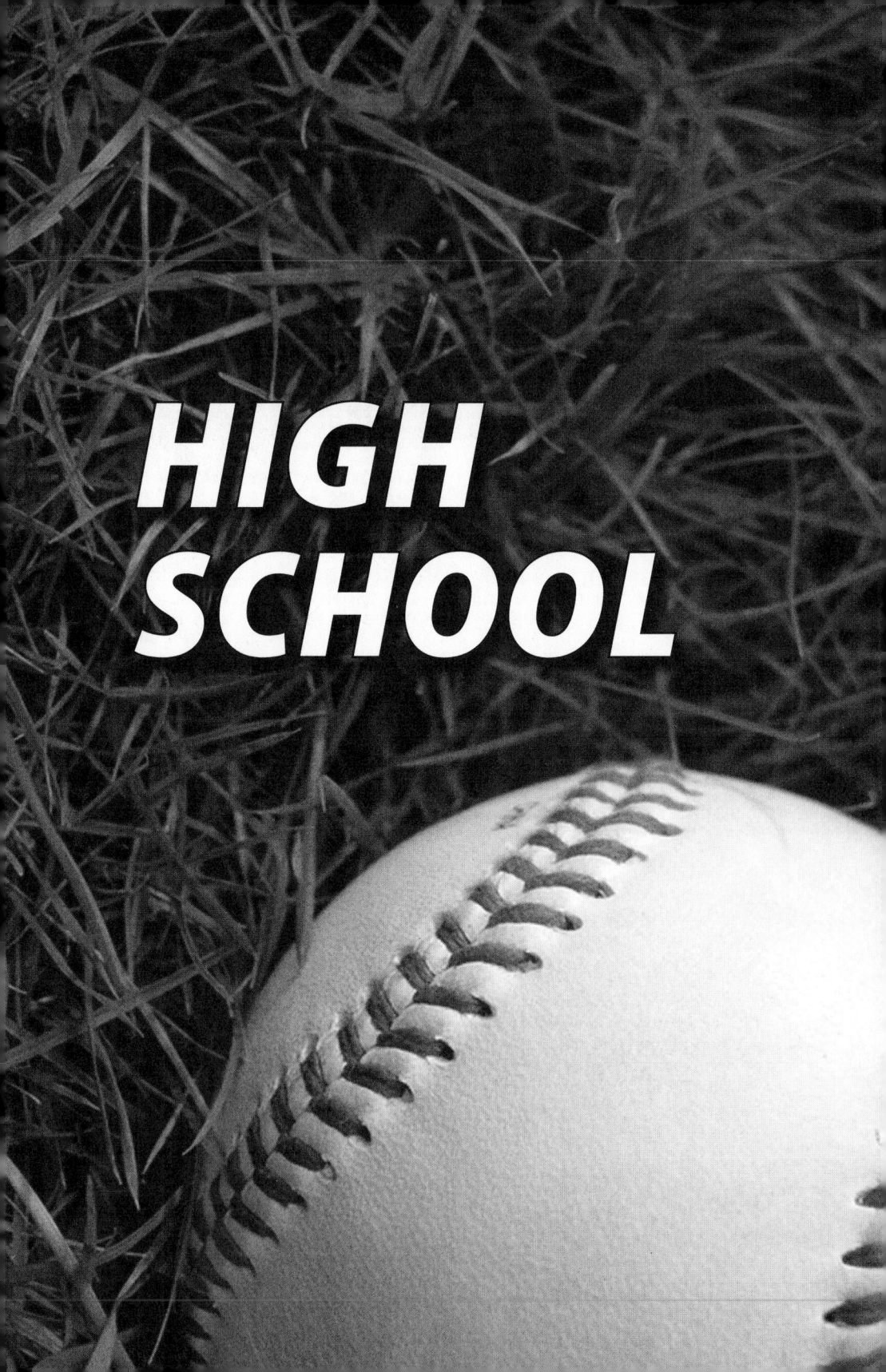

HIGH
SCHOOL

Bishop Gorman starts, finishes atop rankings

BY NATHAN RODE

After completing the spring season, Bishop Gorman High (Las Vegas) head coach Chris Sheff had his summer squad in Hawaii to play eight games in eight days. Despite the packed schedule and obvious distractions the islands of paradise can bring, Sheff and the Gaels were plenty in tune with what was happening back on the mainland.

Moody High of Corpus Christi, Texas, was heading into the state finals against Texarkana's Texas High and

Bishop Gorman's fourth state title also netted a national one

eyeing its second 4-A title in three years as well as a national crown. But Texas had different ideas, scoring late and holding on for the win. That spoiled Moody's shot at the titles and helped propel Bishop Gorman into elite company.

The Gaels won 39 of their final 40 games en route to winning their fourth-straight state title and claiming Baseball America's Team of the Year honors. And it comes as no surprise to Sheff and his team.

"Absolutely we were watching," he said. "I've got a father who was a sportswriter and loves stats and writes a blog for our program. He's very involved in activities that go on around the nation. It's hard not to follow it. Then you get to it and you start rooting for teams to lose. Down the stretch after we were done we were definitely paying attention."

With five seniors committed to Division I programs, three straight state titles and a 2008 finish at No. 2 in the country, Bishop Gorman was the pick for the preseason No. 1 spot. But the Gaels didn't come out of the gate like a No. 1 team. They traveled to Scottsdale, Ariz., to play in Horizon High's Big League Dugout National Tournament. Already 0-1 after an Opening Day loss, Bishop Gorman went 1-2 over the first three days of the event.

"Obviously we got off to a slow start," Sheff said. "Almost every poll had us No. 1 in the nation and we get off to a slow start, 1-3, and people are trying to figure out what's going on. We lost a couple close

ball games and weren't able to get it going. Our last game of the Horizon tournament probably was our turnaround game. We were down 7-0 and looking at going 1-4 and our offense gets rolling. We end up coming back and winning that game."

That game was against Canyon del Oro High (Oro Valley, Ariz.). Down 7-0 after three innings, Bishop Gorman put 12 runs on the board in the next three innings and held on for a thrilling victory. The Gaels returned to Nevada with a 2-3 record, but were ready to keep winning.

And win they did. They rode a 35-game win streak into the playoffs in convincing fashion. In those 35 games, Bishop Gorman outscored opponents 513-76. While 24 of those games were decided by 10 runs or more, their streak was not all about offense—it included 12 shutouts and opponents scored more than five runs just four times.

Las Vegas rival Cimarron Memorial interrupted that streak, taking Bishop Gorman down in the region championship. But there was still a way to win.

"I think the game we lost in the regional championship was as big a part of anything," Sheff said. "At that point we were in the hunt for a national championship but we knew you can't win a national without winning a state. That was a little deflating for our club. We still have a chance to win the tournament. We knew we had a play-in game the next day. My talk to the guys was we're going to win this

Bishop Gorman High (Las Vegas) finished the season at 40-4 and won a fourth straight state title. The staff of Baseball America and the National High School Baseball Coaches Association unanimously voted American Heritage as the final No. 1 team in the 2008 rankings. Records do not include ties.

Rank	Team	Record	Season conclusion
1	Bishop Gorman HS, Las Vegas	40-4	State 4-A Champion
2	Menchville HS, Newport News, Va.	25-2	State 3-A Champion
3	Owasso (Okla.) HS	34-4	State 6-A Champion
4	Northshore HS, Slidell, La.	34-2	State 5-A Champion
5	Naples (Fla.) HS	32-1	State 4-A Champion
6	Notre Dame Prep, Scottsdale, Ariz.	30-2	State 4-A II Runner-Up
7	Sumrall (Miss.) HS	36-0	State 3-A Champion
8	Farragut HS, Knoxville	38-5	State 3-A Champion
9	Moody HS, Corpus Christi, Texas	37-4	State 4-A Runner-Up
10	Pope HS, Marietta, Ga.	31-8	State 5-A Champion
11	Alonso HS, Tampa	30-3	State 6-A Champion
12	La Cueva HS, Albuquerque	29-2	State 5-A Runner-Up
13	Charlotte Christian School	30-3	State Private School Champion
14	Calallen HS, Corpus Christi, Texas	35-5	State 4-A Region Finalist
15	Cartersville (Ga.) HS	33-4	State 3-A Champion
16	Bellaire (Texas) HS	33-4	State 4-A Regional Finalist
17	Capistrano Valley HS, Mission Viejo, Calif.	26-6	CIF Southern Section Champion
18	Chatsworth (Calif.) HS	30-4	CIF City Section Champion
19	Columbus (Ga.) HS	33-4	State 3-A Runner-Up
20	Greenbrier Christian Academy, Chesapeake, Va.	28-2	State Private School D-II Champion
21	Severna Park (Md.) HS	22-2	State 4-A Champion
22	Hartselle (Ala.) HS	50-9	State 5-A Champion
23	Northgate HS, Newnan, Ga.	32-5	State 4-A Champion
24	Soccoro HS, El Paso, Texas	35-4	State 5-A Champion
25	Texas HS, Texarkana, Texas	31-7	State 4-A Champion
26	Bolles School, Jacksonville	31-4	State 3-A Champion
27	Lawrence (Kan.) HS	21-4	State 6-A Champion
28	South Fork HS, Stuart, Fla.	29-3	State 5-A Champion
29	Andrean HS, Merrillville, Ind.	33-2	State 3-A Champion
30	Calvert Hall HS, Towson, Md.	26-4	MIAA Champion
31	Hunterdon Central HS, Fleminton, N.J.	30-1	Group IV State Champion
32	Westide HS, Omaha	34-4	Class A State Champion
33	Yuba City (Calif.) HS	28-3	Sac-Joaquin Section Champion
34	Desert Ridge HS, Mesa, Ariz.	29-5	State 5-A II Champion
35	Kell HS, Charlotte	28-8	State 4-A Champion
36	Thomas HS, New York	24-0	PSAL Champion
37	De La Salle HS, Warren, Mich.	36-5	State D-I Champion
38	Moeller HS, Cincinnati	25-5	State D-I Champion
39	Richland (Wash.) HS	24-2	State 4-A Champion
40	Fort Zumwalt HS, O'Fallon, Mo.	28-6	State 4-A Champion
41	Walsh Jesuit HS, Cuyahoga Falls, Ohio	29-4	State D-II Runner-Up
42	Sylvan Hills HS, Sherwood, Ark.	32-4	State 5-A Semi-finalist
43	American Heritage HS, Plantation, Fla.	29-4	State 3-A Runner-Up
44	Rocky Mountain HS, Fort Collins, Colo.	22-4	State 5-A Runner-Up
45	St. Rita HS, Chicago	33-6	State 4-A Runner-Up
46	Snider HS, Fort Wayne, Ind.	25-3	State 4-A Champion
47	Orland Park (Ill.) HS	30-2	State 4-A Quarterfinalist
48	Central HS, Madison, Miss.	27-5	State 5-A Champion
49	Penn Charter HS, Philadelphia	19-4	State Independent Schools First Round
50	Mamaroneck (N.Y.) HS	23-4	State 2-A Champion

thing. At the end no one is going to remember who wins the regional championship. Everyone is going to remember who wins the state championship."

The next day, the Gaels beat Las Vegas High and advanced to the state tournament the following week. There they took down Henderson's Green Valley High and Minden's Douglas High to set up a rematch with Cimarron. Lefthander Joey Rickard pitched 5 1/3 innings, allowing just one run on three hits before giving way to Jeff Malm, who earned the save and prompted their fourth-straight dog pile.

"It's almost unreal," said Malm, who along the way matched the national record for career hits. "It's pretty incredible the run we've been able to put together. All of our hard work the past four years finally paid off. For me and our seniors, this year stands out. It's our last year and we're going out on top. Not just because it's recent but because of the struggles we had to go through early in the year. We never really had to go through those the other three years."

Sheff echoed what it meant for the senior class.

"Joey and Jeff have been the centerpiece of our program for four years," he said. "Joey got the base hit to win the first state championship as a freshman and pitches us to the state championship as a senior. Our infielders, (R.J.) Santigate and (Tyler) Wagner, they played big parts. They played every day and pitched for us in big games and the playoffs. Other than Malm, (Stephen) Manthei was our guy that we relied on in big games. So the the one-two punch of Malm and Manthei is really what got us there on the bump."

Only next year will reveal whether the book has closed on the Bishop Gorman dynasty. One thing is for sure: When Malm entered as a freshman and predicted they would win four-straight titles he not only proved he could possibly be a prophet, but he helped start a tradition of winning that usually sticks with a program for years to come. But for now, Bishop Gorman will bask in the glory of immortality.

"It's been a great group of seniors and they're going to be sorely missed," Sheff said. "It's been a talented group of kids, a group that knows how to win, doesn't let pressure get to them. For these seniors that have been here four years, its the perfect way to end a career by winning a national championship."

Four For Four

The goal of any high school baseball player is to ultimately win a state championship. A small percentage of participants get the chance to play in one and even fewer get that sweet taste of victory. The luckiest get to experience it more than once.

What Zack Von Rosenberg has experienced in his varsity career is simply unimaginable.

Not only did he just claim his fourth state championship ring, but he was the starting, and winning, pitcher in all four title clinchers. Read that again: He started and won a state championship game as a freshman, sophomore, junior and senior.

"It's a dream come true," Von Rosenberg said. "It's unbelievable to just win one. To win four you're like, 'Is that even possible?' It's like living in a dream world. You couldn't ask for a better high school career."

The ace righthander for Zachary (La.) High, just north of Baton Rouge, Von Rosenberg has an ideal pitcher's frame at 6-foot-5, 200 pounds, with a little room to fill out. He doesn't blow hitters away with overpowering heat, but the results rival many of the top pitching prospects. This season he went 11-1, 0.60 with two saves in 93 innings pitched. He allowed only 56 hits while striking out 141 and walking 18.

While his fastball sits 89-92 mph and can touch

Taillon, Wolters shine at Aflac

BY DAVE PERKIN

SAN DIEGO—For the first time in the series' history, the Aflac All-America Game resulted in a tie between the East and West teams. Neither team could scratch across a winning run and the game was called after 10 innings.

The West got on the board early when middle infielder Tony Wolters and outfielder Josh Sale reached base and eventually scored on a wild pitch. The East cut the lead to 2-1 in the fourth and then took the lead in the eighth after shortstop Jacoby Jones' RBI single and outfielder Michael Arencibia scampered home on a wild pitch.

Wolters, the game's MVP, tied the game 3-3 with a two-out RBI triple. In extra innings, each team started with the bases loaded and one out. Both scratched across one run in the 10th before the game was called.

This year's event was dominated by two distinctly-different elite high school baseball prospects: righthander Jameson Taillon and Wolters.

Taillon is a near-perfect pitching prospect while Wolters is noticeably unimpressive in build and tools, but inevitably impressive in results. He also received the award for top defensive player at the opening banquet.

After registering one strikeout in a quick first inning, Taillon (The Woodlands, Texas, HS) breezed through the second frame, striking out the side while barely breaking a sweat.

Wolters (Rancho Buena Vista HS, Vista, Calif.) is an electric player that makes things happen and has subtle strengths. A lefthanded-hitting middle infielder who profiles as a second baseman in pro ball, Wolters is an intelligent hitter with an advanced approach. He ripped an outside 92 mph fastball to left field for a hit early in the game. In the ninth, Wolters smartly dropped the bat head down to catch up to a low inside pitch, driving it down the right-field line for a triple which tied the score.

"It's almost for the best that we tied," Wolters said. "All of these guys are great players. We're all winners."

Preps pile on runs at Wrigley

BY NATHAN RODE

CHICAGO—In its second year at Wrigley Field, the Under Armour All-America Game yet again put on a major league event that saw the nation's top high school players put their tools to the test.

The Baseball Factory team prevailed once again, defeating Team One 11-6. Rain clouds parted the morning of the game as players prepared to play at Wrigley. ESPNU televised the game for the second-straight year and ESPN analyst Steve Phillips roamed the batting practice session, meeting with all of the players. Hall of Famer Ernie Banks made his rounds as well, talking baseball and throwing out the first pitch.

Once the game began, it didn't take long to realize the talent that would be on display.

In the bottom of the first inning, righthander Jameson Taillon (The Woodlands, Texas, HS) struck out the side with an electric 94-95 mph fastball and filthy mid-80s breaking ball. He threw 16 pitches, 10 of which were strikes.

Team One was first on the board after a laser home run by outfielder Austin Wilson (Harvard-Westlake HS, Los Angeles). Up against righthander Karsten Whitson (Chipley, Fla. HS), whose fastball was sitting 92-93 mph, Wilson was looking for a fastball in a 3-2 count and got exactly that. He deposited the 93 mph heater into the bleachers in left-center field to give Team One a 1-0 lead.

Nick Castellanos (Archbishop McCarthy HS, Southwest Ranches, Fla.) was the unquestionable MVP for Baseball Factory as he went 4-for-4 with four doubles, a walk, three runs scored and three RBIs.

Infielder Yordy Cabrera (Lakeland, Fla., HS) added a home run of his own for Baseball Factory in the sixth. Reggie Golden, an outfielder from Wetumpka (Ala.) High, had the most impressive home run, an absolute bomb to left-center that came just a few feet short of landing on the famous Waveland Avenue.

While this event was held in the middle of the Area Code Games, the talent on hand was undeniably good as Taillon (Team One) and Castellanos (Baseball Factory) were named MVPs of their respective teams.

94, Von Rosenberg shows exceptional command, polish and a feel for pitching. Von Rosenberg's prospect status hasn't been long standing despite his distinguished career, commitment to Louisiana State and the expectation of being drafted in the second or third round.

The German Assassin, as his coaches and teammates call him, actually started his career at the perennial Louisiana power of Barbe High in Lake Charles, less than 40 miles from Louisiana-Texas border. Barbe has produced baseball names like lefthander Wade LeBlanc, who was drafted in the second round in 2006 out Alabama by the Padres, as well as Carmen Angelini, a prep shortstop selected in 2007 by the Yankees. Angelini and Von Rosenberg were teammates on the 2006 squad that won the 5-A state title and finished with a 37-7 record.

Von Rosenberg was a runt then. He stood only 5-foot-7 and threw just a 78-79 mph fastball, which sometimes touched 80. Nonetheless he surrendered only one unearned run in a 2-1 win that netted his first state title. It looked like the start of another special talent for Barbe's program, but things changed quickly.

After the 2006 season, Von Rosenberg's parents were offered better jobs across the state in the school district that included Zachary High. So the family packed up and moved away from Lake Charles and Barbe. They weren't alone, however, as Jesse Cassard, an assistant under Glenn Cecchini at Barbe took over as head coach at Zachary.

Going into the new school year, the odds were against Cassard and his squad. A new regime was in town, as well as new players, and the returning athletes weren't in the physical shape that Cassard knew was needed to win.

"Our offseason workouts were gruesome," Cassard said. "They were so out of shape. From the first day of school up until the first game we had three-hour workouts every day. They were ridiculous. Some kids made it and some kids didn't. And fortunately the kids that were talented wanted to go through it."

Each player did what any strong program needs them to do. They bought into the philosophy of the coaching staff. Egos and differences were put aside and the team focused on winning.

Zachary won the next two state title games 7-0, with Von Rosenberg on the hill. During his sophomore year he was only throwing 83-84 while standing six feet tall. His junior year he was up to 6-foot-3, and 86-87 with his fastball.

In his senior year, Von Rosenberg had jumped to 6-foot-5 and was registering in the low 90s on radar guns while leading his team back to the state tournament and setting up the chance at a third-straight title and immortality. It wasn't as easy as the previous two though. Von Rosenberg gave up his first earned run in a state title game as Sam Houston High (Lake Charles, La.) jumped out to a 2-0 lead in the first inning. Zachary battled back and the game was tied 2-2 until the fourth when the Broncos made it 3-2. A couple of insurance runs in the sixth gave Zachary a 5-2 lead that held until the final out. It was then that Von Rosenberg was speared by his teammates and sent to the bottom of a dog pile for the fourth time in four years.

"Every time you lose your breath," he said. "You feel like you're choking because you can't breathe. But it's all worth it. You go a whole year without doing it and its worth it. I'll have those few seconds where I can't breathe to celebrate with my teammates. It's all part of the championship, it's just tradition. It's a great feeling."

Von Rosenberg and his family took a vacation after celebrating his latest achievement. Even though the high from winning another title was present, a big decision remained looming in the distance. Von Rosenberg was selected by the Pirates in the sixth round of the draft. Before the selection, he was showing no sign of preference.

"I guess you could say when I get drafted that'll be my favorite team," Von Rosenberg said in June. "I'm just thinking whatever happens, happens. If I feel I need to forgo LSU, I'll do it. It's going to be a decision where I weigh the options of LSU and pro ball. I can't make a bad decision with either. It's a decision I'd like to make rather than not have it."

Von Rosenberg opted to sign with the Pirates and received a bonus of $1.2 million. So what did the Pirates get in selecting him? Von Rosenberg has a competitive edge and mentality rarely seen in the everyday high schooler. His pitchability is advanced for his age, which stemmed from his habit of simply listening.

"When I was at Barbe and he was 12 years old he would ride with us on the bus trips," Cassard said. "He wouldn't say a word. It was hard to even get one word out of him. He'd sit there and listen to the coaches talk and take everything in. He'd figure out the game that way. He's a good learner. Every situation that comes up he's already got an answer for it. But he's still coachable. That's the biggest thing. He's been so focused on being good."

Not only did he listen intently to coaches at a young age, but Von Rosenberg wasn't shy about poking older athletes for info. Growing up next door to LeBlanc, he had a good one to pry for advice.

"When he was in high school I talked to him a lot about what to do," Von Rosenberg said. "I

asked him how do you pitch like that. He just said 'I throw strikes.' That was it. That was all he told me. And I said you know what, I'm going to throw strikes. That's what people say about me. I'm a strike-thrower. I don't walk people."

And the pro scouts have noticed.

"He throws a fastball, curveball and changeup," one scout said. "He commands all three and all three are major league average pitches. He's very polished right now. That's why he's been so successful. He's competitive and has great pitchability."

In the end the Pirates should be grateful for acquiring such a polished righthander. They should also be thankful for his physical health: It's a miracle Von Rosenberg survived four dog piles.

AROUND THE NATION

■ The 2009 season was one for the record books as two prospects made headlines with individual achievements. Malm, who signed with the Rays as a fifth-round pick, tied the national record for career hits (277) when he singled in his first at-bat of the state championship game. Patrick Schuster, a lefthander from Mitchell High (New Port Richey, Fla.), actually received air time from ESPN thanks to his run of no-hitters. Schuster threw four no-hitters in a row in April and his attempt at a fifth aired on ESPNews. A double in the third inning brought an end to the run. Schuster ended up being a 13th-round pick and opted to sign with the Diamondbacks for $450,000 instead of heading to Florida for college.

■ In 2007, two Corpus Christi, Texas baseball powers squared off in a region championship series. Moody and Calallen High played a three-game set at Whataburger Field, home of the Double-A Corpus Christi Hooks. The series gained national attention, not only because both teams were ranked and gunning for a state title, but also because of the number of people that witnessed the event. More than 18,000 people walked through the turnstiles and saw Moody win an epic battle and advance to the 4-A state tournament, which it eventually won.

The stars realigned in 2009 as a rematch was set between Moody and Calallen. Moody marched on with another region crown, but this was witnessed by even more. Again at Whataburger Field, the the three-game series drew more than 25,000 fans, who got to see another great series.

■ The 2009 draft was uncharacteristically heavy with high school pitchers. After the 2008 draft saw three prep arms drafted in the first round—and only two signed—the 2009 installment featured seven. Only one of them, Matt Purke of Klein (Texas) High, didn't sign. The six that signed netted $18,897,000 in signing bonuses.

Righthanders Matt Hobgood (fifth overall) and Shelby Miller (19th overall) were the only ones to see regular season action. Hobgood went 1-2, 4.72 in 27 innings with Rookie-level Bluefield of the Appalachian League. Miller had a cameo with low Class A Quad Cities. He made two appearances and pitched three innings, allowing two earned runs on five hits while walking two and striking out two.

Harper gains national stardom

BY NATHAN RODE

In a game that doesn't come easy to most, Bryce Harper makes it look effortless. Nevertheless, he has his own challenges to deal with.

Harper was well known to every opponent he faced this season, even though he was just a high school sophomore. So they were going to do everything they could to avoid getting beat by him.

But there is no avoiding Harper, and that was particularly true on high school diamonds this spring. His desire to win drove Harper to work harder and find a way to be successful, and the results make him Baseball America's High School Player of the Year. No junior had ever won the award, much less a sophomore, so Harper continues to go where no player has gone before.

Harper's sophomore season at Las Vegas High was effectively his senior year because he has enrolled at the CC of Southern Nevada and will pursue his GED diploma this fall. He certainly doesn't have anything left to prove at the high school level, with a line of .626/.723/1.339 in 115 at-bats with 14 home runs and 55 RBIs during his sophomore campaign. A spectacular line for any other high school player, Harper expected those numbers and says he wasn't at his best early on.

"I was getting walked a lot and getting frustrated," he said. "My coach and dad sat down with me. We were just talking about me being a little more patient. Seeing more pitches and working to the opposite field. I only hit 14 home runs."

Only 14 home runs? That's pretty good in most people's eyes.

"It's pretty all right," Harper said. "I pulled one ball for a home run. That was my key this year, to sit back on everything and work opposite field a lot."

Always Hitting

The conversations between Ron Harper and Las Vegas head coach Sam Thomas did the trick, as Harper racked up 72 hits in 39 games and ended the season on a 23-game hitting streak. His work in the batting cage, on top of his tremendous natural talent, helped Harper get his hits. He spends most of his cage time working on hitting to the opposite field and timing offspeed pitches. He takes hacks for 45 minutes, working from up the middle to the left

side. It's only in his last 20 cuts that he unleashes fury to all fields.

"That's what I've been working on my whole life, is working oppo," Harper said. "If I get a pitch inside, I'm going to crush it."

Not only did the effort show up in his numbers, but it was also evident in results only seen by those watching the games. Like his 13 home runs that cleared the fence to the left side of second base, or the ground balls that were hit so hard they rolled to the wall for extra bases.

"He hit a ball that the shortstop bailed out of the way and it rolled to the wall for a triple," Thomas recalled. "That's how hard it was hit. And it was opposite field. It could have been a good play by the shortstop, but it was hit so hard that he elected to move, which in my opinion, that was probably his best choice."

All of Harper's strength is put into his swing, but that's not all that he puts maximum effort into. It continues as he hustles down the line and takes extra bases on balls in the gap, overthrows and passed balls. Harper is the poster boy for a theory Thomas preaches at Las Vegas High: Every hit is a double. The defense has to hold you to a single.

Harper will now look to take the philosophy to new levels as he plays for Southern Nevada in the spring as one of the top draft prospects of all time.

PLAYER OF THE YEAR

PREVIOUS WINNERS

1992: Preston Wilson, of/rhp, Bamberg-Ehrhardt (S.C.) HS
1993: Trot Nixon, of/lhp, New Hanover HS, Wilmington, N.C.
1994: Doug Million, lhp, Sarasota (Fla.) HS
1995: Ben Davis, c, Malvern (Pa.) Prep
1996: Matt White, rhp, Waynesboro Area (Pa.) HS
1997: Darnell McDonald, of, Cherry Creek HS, Englewood, Colo.
1998: Drew Henson, 3b/rhp, Brighton (Mich.) HS
1999: Josh Hamilton, of/lhp, Athens Drive HS, Raleigh, N.C.
2000: Matt Harrington, rhp, Palmdale (Calif.) HS
2001: Joe Mauer, c, Cretin-Derham Hall HS, St. Paul, Minn.
2002: Scott Kazmir, lhp, Cypress Falls HS, Houston
2003: Jeff Allison, rhp, Veterans Memorial HS, Peabody, Mass.
2004: Homer Bailey, rhp, LaGrange (Texas) HS
2005: Justin Upton, ss, Great Bridge HS, Chesapeake, Va.
2006: Adrian Cardenas, ss/2b, Mons. Pace HS, Opa Locka, Fla.
2007: Mike Moustakas, ss, Chatsworth (Calif.) HS
2008: Ethan Martin, rhp/3b, Stephens County HS, Toccoa, Ga.

Bryce Harper

ALYSON BOYER

Jacob Turner

MIKE JANES

FIRST TEAM

Pos.	Player, School	Class	B/T	HT	WT	AVG	AB	R	H	2B	3B	HR	RBI	SB	Drafted
C	Bryce Harper, Las Vegas HS	So.	L/R	6-3	200	.626	115	76	72	22	9	14	55	36	Not Eligible
IF	Matt Davidson, Yucaipa (Calif.) HS	Sr.	R/R	6-3	210	.553	85	49	47	18	0	11	45	2	D'backs (1s)
IF	Kenny Diekroger, Menlo HS, Atherton, Calif.	Sr.	R/R	6-2	185	.586	58	31	34	10	3	4	20	15	Rays (2)
IF	Nick Franklin, Lake Brantley HS, Altamonte Springs, Fla.	Sr.	B/R	6-1	170	.538	78	49	42	12	3	10	30	15	Mariners (1)
IF	Jeff Malm, Bishop Gorman HS, Las Vegas	Sr.	L/L	6-3	215	.564	133	68	75	14	1	17	69	16	Rays (5)
OF	Randal Grichuk, Lamar Cons. HS, Rosenberg, Texas	Sr.	R/R	6-0	190	.597	72	45	43	9	1	19	43	7	Angels (1)
OF	Mike Trout, Millville (N.J.) HS	Sr.	R/R	6-1	190	.531	81	50	43	5	1	18	45	20	Angels (1)
OF	Max Walla, Albuquerque (N.M.) Academy	Sr.	L/L	5-11	195	.556	72	49	40	10	2	12	40	6	Brewers (2)
DH	Austin Maddox, Eagle's View Acad., Jacksonville, Fla.	Sr.	R/R	6-3	220	.554	79	23	43	11	0	9	33	5	Rays (37)
UT	Matt Hobgood, Norco (Calif.) HS	Sr.	R/R	6-4	245	.475	101	47	48	9	0	21	55	0	Orioles (1)

Pos.	Player, School	Class	B/T	HT	WT	W	L	ERA	G	SV	IP	H	BB	SO	Drafted
LHP	David Holmberg, Port Charlotte (Fla.) HS	Sr.	R/L	6-4	205	7	0	0.22	10	0	65	27	23	132	White Sox (2)
RHP	Keyvius Sampson, Ocala HS, Forest, Fla.	Sr.	R/R	6-1	180	9	2	0.84	12	1	75	24	21	134	Padres (4)
LHP	Patrick Schuster, Mitchell HS, New Port Richey, Fla.	Sr.	R/L	6-2	175	8	1	0.93	10	0	60	12	29	115	D'backs (13)
RHP	Jacob Turner, Westminster Academy, St. Louis	Sr.	R/R	6-1	205	7	2	0.60	9	0	58	21	13	118	Tigers (1)
RHP	Zack Wheeler, East Paulding HS, Dallas, Ga.	Sr.	B/R	6-4	185	9	0	0.46	13	0	76	31	18	149	Giants (1)
UT	Matt Hobgood, Norco (Calif.) HS	Sr.	R/R	6-4	245	11	1	0.92	13	0	68	39	26	101	Orioles (1)

SECOND TEAM

Pos.	Player, School	Class	B/T	HT	WT	AVG	AB	R	H	2B	3B	HR	RBI	SB	Drafted
C	J.R. Murphy, Pendleton School, Bradenton, Fla.	Sr.	R/R	6-0	190	.627	102	56	64	17	6	11	66	13	Yankees (2)
IF	Bobby Borchering, Bishop Verot HS, Fort Myers, Fla.	Sr.	B/R	6-4	195	.494	77	33	38	9	0	13	37	4	D'backs (1)
IF	Daniel Fields, University of Detroit Jesuit HS, Detroit	Sr.	L/R	6-2	200	.596	57	50	34	5	1	13	43	30	Tigers (6)
IF	Miles Head, Whitewater HS, Fayetteville, Ga.	Sr.	R/R	6-0	215	.528	72	30	38	8	1	14	48	0	Red Sox (26)
IF	Michael Ratteree, Memorial HS, Houston	Sr.	R/R	6-0	180	.517	89	45	46	10	1	12	41	11	Nationals (45)
OF	Daniel Aldrich, Wando HS, Mt. Pleasant, S.C.	Sr.	L/R	6-2	200	.461	89	35	41	6	1	13	43	9	Undrafted
OF	Jake Stewart, Rocky Mountain HS, Fort Collins, Colo.	Sr.	R/R	6-2	195	.544	90	46	49	8	2	12	56	8	Phillies (14)
OF	Donavan Tate, Cartersville (Ga.) HS	Sr.	R/R	6-3	200	.474	97	51	46	12	1	9	42	17	Padres (1)
DH	Wil Myers, Wesleyan Christian Acad., High Point, N.C.	Sr.	R/R	6-3	190	.532	62	29	33	7	0	14	41	13	Royals (3)
UT	Zack Von Rosenberg, Zachary (La.) HS	Sr.	R/R	6-5	205	.472	120	34	57	19	0	10	43	28	Pirates (6)

Pos.	Player, School	Class	B/T	HT	WT	W	L	ERA	G	SV	IP	H	BB	SO	Drafted
RHP	Tanner Bushue, South Central HS, Farina, Ill.	Sr.	R/R	6-4	180	8	3	0.62	13	1	68	31	22	140	Astros (2)
RHP	Dylan Floro, Buhach Colony HS, Atwater, Calif.	Sr.	L/R	6-2	170	7	1	0.46	14	2	61	25	11	109	Rays (20)
RHP	Shelby Miller, Brownwood (Texas) HS	Sr.	R/R	6-3	195	10	2	1.90	13	0	77	40	38	154	Cardinals (1)
LHP	Miguel Pena, La Joya (Texas) HS	Sr.	L/L	6-2	160	7	1	0.12	13	4	56	20	14	98	Nationals (5)
LHP	Josh Turley, Texas HS, Texarkana, Texas	Sr.	L/L	5-10	185	10	2	1.15	16	2	85	42	26	138	Brewers (36)
UT	Zack Von Rosenberg, Zachary (La.) HS	Sr.	R/R	6-5	205	11	1	0.60	14	2	93	56	18	141	Pirates (6)

Team USA earns youth trifecta

Baseball may be out of the Olympics, but USA Baseball is going to keep going for gold medals in other world championships. Team USA was 3-for-3 this summer, claiming gold medals with the 18U, 16U and 14U National teams.

Heading into the gold-medal game versus Cuba, the 18U team had outscored its opponents 93-13, rolling to a perfect 7-0 record in the COPABE Pan Am "AAA" 18U championships being played in Barquisimeto, Venezuela.

The championship game remained scoreless through the first six innings, but the Americans plated six runs in the top of the seventh inning, ultimately winning the final game, 6-1. All seven of Team USA's hits were singles, but five of them came in the seventh when the team batted around and also took advantage of two walks, two hit batters, a wild

pitch and a sac fly. The win gives the Team USA 18U team its first gold medal in the Pan Ams.

Righthander Jameson Taillon dominated the event going 2-0, 0.00 in 13 2/3 innings. He struck out 28 while walking just three and allowing seven hits.

The 16U team beat Cuba with a ninth-inning rally to at the 2009 IBAF World Youth Championships in Taichun, Taiwan.

Austin Cousino (Dublin, Ohio), who is scheduled to graduate high school in 2011, was named the tournament's MVP after hitting .581/.632/1.161 with two home runs, eight doubles, two triples and 18 RBIs in eight games. He was also 4-for-5 in stolen bases and scored 18 runs.

The 14U team defeated Puerto Rico 4-3 to win a gold medal in Ecuador.

AMATEUR/YOUTH CHAMPIONS 2009

TEAM USA

18-AND-UNDER

Event	Site	Champion	Runner-up
Tournament of Stars	Cary, N.C.	Babe Ruth	American Legion
COPABE Pan Am 'AAA' Championships	Barquisimeto, Venezuela	United States	Cuba

16-AND-UNDER

Event	Site	Champion	Runner-up
USA Junior Olympics—East	Palm Beach County, Fla.	All American Prospects Red	Triple Threat Baseball Academy
USA Junior Olympics—West	Peoria & Surprise, Ariz.	Team Anderson 2011	Conejo Oaks

ALL-AMERICAN AMATEUR BASEBALL ASSOCIATION (AAABA): HEADQUARTERS: ZANESVILLE, OHIO

Event	Site	Champion	Runner-up
World Series (21-and-Under)	Johnstown, Penn.	New Orleans Boosters	New Brunswick Matrix

AMATEUR ATHLETIC UNION (AAU): HEADQUARTERS: LAKE BUENA VISTA, FLA.

Event	Site	Champion	Runner-up
10-and-Under (65-foot)	Lake Buena Vista, Fla.	North Texas Bulldogs	East Cobb Bulldogs
11-and-Under (70-foot)	Lake Buena Vista, Fla.	Chet Lemon's Juice	Tampa Red Rage
12-and-Under (70-foot)	Richmond, Va.	Bullets Gold	Home Plate Chili Dogs
13-and-Under (90-foot)	Virginia Beach, Va.	Florida Flash	Gulf Coast Greyhounds
14-and-Under (90-foot)	Sarasota, Fla.	Tidewater Drillers	Unavailable
15-and-Under	Viera, Fla.	Team Connecticut Blue Jays	Royals Baseball
Junior Olympics/16 & U	Viera, Fla.	Unavailable	Unavailable
18/19-and-Under	Ft. Myers, Fla.	Florida Raiders/Akadema	Winegrass Cardinals

AMERICAN AMATEUR BASEBALL CONGRESS (AABC): HEADQUARTERS: FARMINGTON, N.M.

Event	Site	Champion	Runner-up
Gil Hodges	Brooklyn, N.Y.	Connecticut Bombers	Brooklyn Bonnie Seals
Pee Wee Reese (12 & U)	Toa Baja, Puerto Rico	Puerto Rico Vaqueros	Southwest Shamrocks
Sandy Koufax (13 & U)	Battle Creek, Mich.	Connecticut Naturals	Rockford Tri-Part
Sandy Koufax (14 & U)	Surprise, Ariz.	The All-Star Baseball Academy	Puerto Rico Warriors
Mickey Mantle (15 & U)	Owasso, Okla.	DBAT Mustangs Phillips	DBAT Mustangs McCabe
Mickey Mantle (16 & U)	McKinney, Texas	East Cobb Titans	Dallas Patriots
Connie Mack (18 & U)	Farmington, N.M.	Midland Redskins	DBAT Mustangs
Stan Musial (open)	Huntsville, Texas	Bayamon Vaqueros	Long Island Storm

AMERICAN LEGION BASEBALL: HEADQUARTERS: INDIANAPOLIS

Event	Site	Champion	Runner-up
World Series (19 & U)	Fargo, N.D.	Midland, Mich.	Medford, Ore.

BABE RUTH BASEBALL: HEADQUARTERS: TRENTON, N.J.

Event	Site	Champion	Runner-up
Cal Ripken (10&U)	Lamar, Colo.	West Raleigh, N.C.	Danbury, Conn.
Cal Ripken 12-year-old (60 feet)	Winchester, Mass.	West Lewis County, Wash.	Coosa, Ala.
13-year-old	Murray, Utah	Tallahassee-Leon, Fla.	Tri-Valley, Calif.
14-year-old	Appleton, Wisc..	Hamilton, Ariz.	Appleton, Wisc.
13-15-year-olds	Longview, Wash.	Tallahassee-Leon, Fla.	Torrence, Calif.
16-18-year-olds	Moses Lake, Wash.	Puget Sound, Wash.	Hammond, Ind.

CONTINENTAL AMATEUR BASEBALL ASSOCIATION (CABA): HEADQUARTERS: WESTERVILLE, OHIO

Event	Site	Champion	Runner-up
9-and-Under	Woodstock, Ill.	New Lenox (Illinois)	Cincinnati Flames
10-and-Under	Westfield, Ind.	Cincinnati Flames	Cincinnati Stix
11-and-Under	McHenry/Johnsburg, Ill.	IL Gravel	Cincinnati Flames
12-and-Under	Cincinnati, Ohio	Pennsylvania Revolution	Ohio Force
13-and-Under	Westfield/Carmel, Ind.	Summit City Sluggers (Indiana)	Louisville Panthers
14-and-Under (60x90)	Lebanon, Tenn.	South Oakland A's	Seattle Select (Washington)
15-and-Under	Northern Illinois	East Cobb Astros	Schaumburg Seminoles (Illinois)
16-and-Under	Marietta, Ga.	East Cobb Astros	6-4-3 DP Cougars
High school age	Euclid, Ohio	Top Tier	Team Florida Red
18-and-Under (wood)	Charleston, S.C.	S.C. Diamond Devils 17	S.C. Diamond Devils 18
18-and-Under (aluminum)	Youngstown, Ohio	Ohio Diamond Premier	Ohio Warhawks

LITTLE LEAGUE BASEBALL: HEADQUARTERS: WILLIAMSPORT, PA.

Event	Site	Champion	Runner-up
Little League (11-12)	Williamsport, Pa.	Chula Vista, Calif.	Chinese Taipei
Junior League (13-14)	Taylor, Mich.	Mountain View, Ariz.	Aruba
Senior League (15-16	Bangor, Maine	Houston	Fremont, Calif.
Big League (17-18)	Easley, S.C.	Dominican Republic (Latin America)	California (West)

NATIONAL AMATEUR BASEBALL FEDERATION (NABF): HEADQUARTERS: BOWIE, MD.

Event	Site	Champion	Runner-up
Sophomore (14 & U)	Lynchburg, Va.	Up-to-Bat Titans	Forest Cavaliers
Junior (16 & U)	Northville, Mich.	Long Island Titans	Dayton Dirtbags
High School (17 & U)	Lynchburg, Va.	Virginia Barnstormers	Maryland Orioles
Senior (18 & U)	Jackson, Miss.	Maryland Monarchs	Jackson 96ers Blue
College (22 & U)	Toledo, Ohio	Crystal Lake Cardinals	Dix Hills Dodgers
Major (open)	Louisville, Ky.	Detroit Jet Box	Beecher Muskies

PERFECT GAME/BCS FINALS: HEADQUARTERS: CEDAR RAPIDS, IOWA

Event	Site	Champion	Runner-up
14-and-Under	Fort Myers, Fla.	Dulins Dodgers	BigStix Gamers
15-and-Under	Fort Myers, Fla.	South Florida Elite	East Cobb Astros
16-and-Under	Fort Myers, Fla.	Dallas Yankees	Marucci Elite
17-and-Under	Fort Myers, Fla.	East Cobb Astros	All American Prospects Blue
18-and-Under	Fort Myers, Fla.	St. Louis Pirates	Syracuse Sports Zone Chiefs

PERFECT GAME/WWBA SUMMER CHAMPIONSHIPS: HEADQUARTERS: CEDAR RAPIDS, IOWA

Event	Site	Champion	Runner-up
14-and-Under	Marietta, Ga.	Dulins Dodgers	East Cobb Astros
15-and-Under	Marietta, Ga.	Houston Banditos Black	Washington RIPS Brewers
16-and-Under	Marietta, Ga.	Canes North	Florida Mustangs
17-and-Under	Marietta, Ga.	ABD Bulldogs Red	East Cobb Astros
18-and-Under	Marietta, Ga.	East Cobb Braves	Florida Bombers

PONY BASEBALL: HEADQUARTERS: WASHINGTON, PA.

Event	Site	Champion	Runner-up
Mustang (9-10)	Irving, Texas	Caguas (Villa Nueva), PR	Chino Hills, Calif.
Bronco (11-12)	Monterey, Calif.	Simi Valley, Calif.	Brooklyn, New York
Pony (13)	Chino Hills, Calif.	Houston (Kyle Chapman), Tx.	Mililani, Hi.
Pony (13-14)	Washington, Pa.	Chinese Taipei	Riverside, Calif.
Colt (15-16)	Lafayette, Ind.	Santa Clara, Calif.	Tampa, Fla.
Palomino (17-18)	San Jose, Calif.	Houston (Kyle Chapman), Tx.	Taoyuan County, Taiwan

REVIVING BASEBALL IN INNER CITIES (RBI): HEADQUARTERS: NEW YORK

Event	Site	Champion	Runner-up
Junior (13-15)	Miami	Urban Youth Academy	Santo Domingo
Senior (16-18)	Miami	Los Angeles	Detroit

U.S. SPECIALTY SPORTS ASSOCIATION (USSSA): HEADQUARTERS: PETERSBURG, VA.

Event	Site	Champion	Runner-up
10-and-Under/Majors Elite	Lake Buena Vista, Fla.	San Diego Stars	Banditos Black
11-and-Under/Majors Elite	Lake Buena Vista, Fla.	Tomateros de California	Strike Force
12-and-Under/Majors Elite	Lake Buena Vista, Fla.	Norwalk Stringrays	Arizona Desert Blaze
13-and-Under/Majors Elite	Lake Buena Vista, Fla.	East Cobb Astros	Terror Baseball
14-and-Under/Majors Elite	Lake Buena Vista, Fla.	East Cobb Astros	Team Orlando 14's

DRAFT

Strasburg fulfills expectations to earn No. 1 spot, top contract

The 2009 draft will be long remembered as the Season of Strasburg. The San Diego State righthander burst on the scene as a closer in 2007, his freshman year, and ranked as the No. 1 prospect in the New England Collegiate League that summer. The next year, Stephen Strasburg went national, setting a Division I record with 23 strikeouts against Utah, and later earning a spot on the U.S. Olympic team. While he took a loss against Cuba, Strasburg's profile was already higher than any college player in recent memory, and he got into Mark Prior/Jered Weaver/Mark Teixeira territory in 2009.

Strasburg dominated college baseball, going 13-1, 1.32 and leading the nation in ERA and strikeouts (195, an absurd 16.1 K's per nine innings) while reaching 100 mph regularly on radar guns. After he capped his regular season in late May with a no-hitter with 17 strikeouts against Air Force, the only question was whether the Nationals, drafting No. 1 overall, would be able to afford Strasburg. Put another way, could they afford not to draft him?

A Scott Boras Corp. client, Strasburg was rumored to have a price tag approaching the $50 million that free agent righty Daisuke Matsuzaka got from the Red Sox after the 2006 season. But Strasburg wasn't a free agent, and Nationals' interim general manager Mike Rizzo had plenty of experience dealing with Boras from his days as the Diamondbacks' scouting director.

When the night of the draft came, Rizzo and the Nats took Strasburg first overall then agreed to terms with him just before the Aug. 17 deadline on a major league contract with a record $7.5 million bonus and record $15.1 million guarantee.

With all the hype Strasburg's received, it could be difficult to live up to all the expectations—fair or not—placed on the shoulders of a 21-year-old.

"The bottom line is, all year I've never been worrying about the hype," Strasburg said in a press conference the morning after he was drafted. "I just want to go out there and help my team win a ballgame."

Plenty Of Prep Pitchers

Strasburg was the dominant storyline of the draft, and his record-setting contract helped a record-setting draft. The Nationals had two picks in the top 10, a first in draft history thanks to having a compensation pick at No. 10 overall for

Righthander Stephen Strasburg shattered the bonus record as 2009's No. 1 pick

failing to sign 2008 first-rounder Aaron Crow. While Stanford closer Drew Storen signed a below-slot deal, it was still a second seven-figure bonus to go with Strasburg's record. The Nats wound up spending $11,194,500 just on players in the first 10 rounds and two six-figure signings after the 10th round. That surpassed the Royals' 2008 record total of $11,148,000.

Aside from Strasburg, the other thing that stood out about this year's class was the strong crop of high school pitching. Seven high school arms were selected within the top 20 picks, the first time that's happened since Josh Beckett and six others were picked within the top 20 in 1999.

Norco (Calif.) High righthander Matt Hobgood was the first off the board, with the fifth-overall pick to the Orioles. It was somewhat of a surprise pick, but Hobgood is a physical 6-foot-4, 245 pounds and features a 90-94 mph fastball with late life and good movement. He also throws a sharp curveball, and occasionally mixes in a changeup and a slider. With the very next pick, the Giants selected righthander Zack Wheeler from East Paulding High in Dallas, Ga. Wheeler doesn't have Hobgood's thick frame, but still showed a mid-90s fastball and a slurvy breaking ball with late bite and depth.

The top righthander heading into the draft was Jacob Turner from Westminster Christian Academy in St. Louis. Turner showed a pro-ready, 6-foot-5, 205-pound frame and the stuff to match. He was sitting 92-94 mph and topping out at 98 with his fastball. He also has a hard curveball up to 83 mph and flashes a changeup. Turner benefitted from the tutelage of former big leaguers Andy Benes, Mike Matheny and Todd Worrell, who all had sons on his team. His price tag allowed the Tigers to pick him ninth overall and he signed on deadline day to a major league contract with a $4.7 million bonus, setting a new record for a high school pitcher.

The top lefthander heading into draft day was Tyler Matzek from Capistrano Valley High in Mission Viejo, Calif. But Matzek's price tag also scared some teams away and the Rockies were able to snag him 11th overall. Matzek's fastball peaked at 94 mph in the spring and he also throws a sharp-breaking curveball. He signed for $3.9 million.

Already sitting 92-95 with room to grow in his 6-foot-3, 180-pound frame, Klein (Texas) High lefthander Matt Purke rivaled Matzek as the class' top lefthander for much of the spring. He also throws a hard slider and occasionally works in a changeup. Purke was selected by the Rangers, 14th overall, but did not sign and will instead head to Texas Christian.

Lefthander Chad James was the Marlins' first-rounder out of Yukon (Okla.) High and right-hander Shelby Miller was the Cardinals' first-rounder, a pick later. James was clocked as high as 95 with his fastball during the spring and Miller was up to 97, though he normally sat at 92-93.

Unsigned Picks

It was the longest first round in draft history, as for the first time two teams had compensation picks in the first round added after they failed to sign their picks in 2008. The Nats had the 10th pick, and the Yankees picked 29th overall after failing to sign Gerrit Cole. That led to 32 first-round picks, and the same will happen in 2010 after the Rays failed to sign Florida high school outfielder LeVon Washington and the Rangers couldn't agree to terms with Purke.

Washington was not a consensus first-rounder, though he is a burner with top-of-the-scale speed and excellent hitting tools. He wound up going

DRAFT EXPENDITURES BY CLUB

Though MLB slashed its bonus recommendations by 10 percent in 2009, teams still set a new record for draft spending. The 30 clubs spent a total of $189,482,700 on bonuses, up slightly from the standard of $188,297,598 established in 2008. The Nationals led the way with $11,511,500 in bonuses, breaking the club record of $11,148,000 that the Royals set last year.

TEAM	SIGNED	1ST	SUPP.	'09 TOTAL	'08 TOTAL
Nationals	29	2	0	$11,511,500	$4,761,500
Mariners	35	2	1	$10,945,600	$4,295,000
Tigers	25	1	0	$9,395,100	$3,742,000
Diamondbacks	37	2	3	$9,328,200	$4,493,500
Padres	37	1	0	$9,136,500	$5,449,000
Pirates	23	1	1	$8,918,900	$9,780,500
Orioles	29	1	0	$8,730,200	$6,916,500
Rockies	40	2	1	$7,924,300	$4,157,000
Yankees	27	1	0	$7,564,500	$5,122,000
Red Sox	26	1	0	$7,095,400	$10,515,000
Angels	33	2	3	$6,792,900	$2,728,500
Brewers	32	1	2	$6,759,500	$8,395,800
Royals	32	1	0	$6,657,000	$11,148,000
Athletics	29	1	0	$6,439,400	$6,522,000
Giants	35	1	0	$6,289,000	$9,080,000
Reds	34	1	1	$5,855,400	$4,801,000
Cardinals	43	1	0	$5,388,500	$5,542,000
Indians	28	1	0	$4,943,000	$6,984,500
Blue Jays	34	1	0	$4,895,200	$4,359,500
Twins	24	1	1	$4,694,100	$7,330,498
Rangers*	25	1	1	$4,684,200	$7,388,300
Braves	24	1	0	$4,400,500	$5,091,500
Astros	36	1	0	$4,212,800	$6,544,500
White Sox	39	1	1	$4,178,600	$4,663,500
Marlins	35	1	0	$4,142,800	$5,377,000
Cubs	29	1	0	$4,044,200	$5,545,000
Dodgers	31	0	1	$4,037,100	$4,442,500
Rays*	32	1	0	$4,004,500	$9,921,000
Phillies	34	0	0	$3,229,500	$6,740,500
Mets	35	0	0	$3,134,300	$6,460,000
Total	**952**	**32**	**17**	**$189,332,700**	**$188,297,598**

*Didn't sign first-round pick. First = First-round picks. Supp. = Supplemental first-round picks.

30th overall, but the Boras Corp. client and the Rays didn't come particularly close to a deal. The Rays also failed to sign their second-rounder, athletic shortstop Kenny Diekroger, who chose to attend Stanford.

Though Purke has great stuff and had an impressive summer and spring, rumors about his price tag scared some teams off.

The Rangers had bigger problems, though, as owner Tom Hicks' financial problems began to hamstring the organization. Major League Baseball had significant input on Rangers decisions in 2009 as it helped keep the club functioning through Hicks' troubles and the search for a new owner. As a result, Texas' $4 million offer to Purke the night of the deadline wound up being too little, too late, and he chose to attend college and go into the 2011 draft as an eligible sophomore.

The Rangers made up for losing Purke a bit by signing supplemental first-rounder Tanner Scheppers in September, just before the Royals signed their first-rounder, Aaron Crow. With no college eligibility remaining, Scheppers and Crow were not bound by the deadline. Crow was a first-rounder for a second consecutive season and wound up getting a $1.5 million bonus as part of a major league contract.

Scheppers figured to be a top 10 pick in 2008 before he came down with a shoulder injury in May while pitching for Fresno State. He missed the Bulldogs' amazing College World Series championship run and fell to the second round, where the Pirates drafted him. He didn't sign with Pittsburgh and re-entered the draft, prepping with a four-start stint with the St. Paul Saints of the independent American Association. Scheppers wound up signing for a $1.25 million bonus.

The Blue Jays did sign their first-round pick, righthander Chad Jenkins out of Kennesaw State, but failed to sign their supplemental first-rounder, lefthander James Paxton out of Kentucky (and a native of British Columbia); second-round lefthander Jake Eliopoulos from Sacred Heart Catholic High in Newmarket, Ontario; and third-round righthander Jake Barrett from Desert Ridge High in Mesa, Ariz.

Toronto scouting director Jon Lalonde, who was reassigned as a pro scout in the fall, said the Blue Jays changed philosophies this year and decided to be more aggressive when selecting players that could be tougher to sign.

HIGHEST BONUSES EVER

Only one player ever had received a bonus of more than $6 million before the 2007 draft, but the last three drafts have seen eight bonuses of $6 million or more, including three of the top 10 players drafted in 2009. Nationals first overall pick, righthander Stephen Strasburg, led the way with his record-breaking $7.5 million bonus. For players who signed major league contracts, only the bonus is included.

PLAYER, POS.	CLUB, YEAR (ROUND)	BONUS
*Stephen Strasburg, rhp	Nationals '09 (1)	$7,500,000
*Dustin Ackley, cf	Mariners '09 (1)	$6,000,000
Donavan Tate, cf	Padres '09 (1)	$6,250,000
Buster Posey, c	Giants '08 (1)	$6,200,000
Tim Beckham, ss	Rays '08 (1)	$6,150,000
Justin Upton, ss	Diamondbacks '05 (1)	$6,100,000
*Pedro Alvarez, 3b	Pirates '08 (1)	$6,000,000
Eric Hosmer, 1b	Royals '08 (1)	$6,000,000
Matt Wieters, c	Orioles '07 (1)	$6,000,000
*David Price, lhp	Devil Rays '07 (1)	$5,600,000
Joe Borchard, of	White Sox '00 (1)	$5,300,000
Joe Mauer, c	Twins '01 (1)	$5,150,000
B.J. Upton, ss	Devil Rays '02 (1)	$4,600,000

*Received major league contract.

"I think if you look at the recent track record of the Blue Jays and our history of drafting pitchers and getting them to the big leagues, we thought that might have some sway," Lalonde said. "Obviously we took all three with the hope of getting them signed and we did everything we could to try and make that happen. They get lumped together because we didn't sign all of them, but they are three different players and three unique situations."

The Blue Jays will receive compensation picks for their failure to sign those players. Paxton will return to Kentucky, Eliopoulos will pitch for Chipola (Fla.) JC, so he will be eligible again in 2010 and Barrett will honor his commitment to Arizona State. Eliopoulos was one of seven Canadian players selected by Toronto, but the team didn't sign any of them.

The Rest Of The Story

■ For the first time, the draft was stretched into a three-day event. The first day started at 6 p.m. EDT and covered the first three rounds in about four hours. The first round was broadcast live on the MLB Network and Baseball America executive editor Jim Callis was in studio along with MLB Network host Greg Amsinger, MLB Network analysts Harold Reynolds and John Hart, MLB.com senior writer Jonathan Mayo and Major League

LARGEST BIG LEAGUE CONTRACTS

After the draft started in 1965, no player received a multiyear major league contract until the Royals gave fourth-round pick Bo Jackson a $1.066 million deal in 1986, luring the Heisman Trophy winner away from the NFL. A total of 43 players have received multiyear big league contracts, including a record-tying four in 2009: Stephen Strasburg ($7.5 million bonus, $15,107,104 guaranteed value), Dustin Ackley ($6 million bonus, $7.5 million guarantee), Jacob Turner ($4.7 million bonus, $5.5 million guarantee) and Aaron Crow ($1.5 million bonus, $3 million guarantee). Teams also gave our four major league contracts in 2000, 2004 and 2007.

Strasburg's deal was the largest guaranteed contract in draft history. Below are the 15 biggest such deals:

PLAYER, POS.	CLUB	YEAR (PICK)	BONUS	GUARANTEE
Stephen Strasburg, rhp	Nationals	2009 (No. 1)	$7,500,000	$15,107,104
Mark Prior, rhp	Cubs	2001 (No. 2)	$4,000,000	$10,500,000
Mark Teixeira, 3b	Rangers	2001 (No. 5)	$4,500,000	$9,500,000
David Price, lhp	Devil Rays	2007 (No. 1)	$5,600,000	$8,500,000
Pat Burrell, 1b/of	Phillies	1998 (No. 1)	$3,150,000	$8,000,000
Dustin Ackley, of	Mariners	2009 (No. 2)	$6,000,000	$7,500,000
J.D. Drew, of	Cardinals	1998 (No. 5)	$3,000,000	$7,000,000
Josh Beckett, rhp	Marlins	1999 (No. 2)	$3,625,000	$7,000,000
Rick Porcello, rhp	Tigers	2007 (No. 27)	$3,580,000	$7,000,000
Eric Munson, c	Tigers	1999 (No. 3)	$3,500,000	$6,750,000
Delmon Young, of	Devil Rays	2003 (No. 1)	$3,700,000	$5,800,000
Stephen Drew, ss	Diamondbacks	2004 (No. 15)	$4,000,000	$5,500,000
Jacob Turner, rhp	Tigers	2009 (No. 9)	$4,700,000	$5,500,000
Andrew Miller, lhp	Tigers	2006 (No. 6)	$3,550,000	$5,450,000
Mike Pelfrey, rhp	Mets	2005 (No. 9)	$3,550,000	$5,250,000
Luke Hochevar, rhp	Royals	2006 (No. 1)	$3,500,000	$5,250,000

Scouting Bureau director Frank Marcos providing coverage and analysis as the draft unfolded. The only player on hand for the televised portion of the draft was Millville (N.J.) High outfielder Mike Trout, whom the Angels selected 25th overall. The remaining 47 rounds of the draft stretched over the next two days and the conference call was streamed live on mlb.com.

■ For the first time ever, all 30 teams signed at least one player over MLB's slot recommendations. In 2008, the only time in the decade the commissioner's office gave clubs the go-ahead to value ability over signability, the Blue Jays, Cardinals, Mets and Tigers still toed the line.

■ Strasburg set new standards for the biggest bonus ($7.5 million) and largest guarantee ($15.1 million) in draft history. The bonus marks for a high school draftee (Donavan Tate, Padres, $6.25 million) and a high school pitcher (Jacob Turner, Tigers, $4.7 million bonus in major league deal) also were erased.

■ One of the themes for most of the spring was that Strasburg was far and away the top talent in the draft and there wasn't a clear No. 2 guy behind him. But North Carolina first baseman Dustin Ackley separated himself from the pack to become the second-best player in the class after he hit

ALYSON BOYER

Lefthander Tyler Matzek's bonus demands allowed Colorado to pick him 11th overall

.417/.512/.763. While he played primarily first base for the Tar Heels, he's a good athlete and was drafted as a center fielder by the Mariners.

■ The Pirates got some criticism for their selection of catcher Tony Sanchez with the fourth overall pick, as he was not seen as the fourth-best talent. However, their strategy was to pick a more signable player in that spot and use a "spread the wealth" strategy with the rest of their picks. Including Sanchez, who signed for $2.5 million, the Pirates signed 14 players for at least $100,000 and paid more than $200,000 to eight of them: right-hander Victor Black (supplemental first round), righthander Brooks Pounders (second round), outfielder Evan Chambers (third round), lefthander

DRAFT ORDER 2010

By virtue of finishing with a 59-103 record, the Nationals will have the No. 1 overall pick in the 2010 draft. They become just the second club to own the top choice in consecutive years, joining the 2007-08 Rays.

Below is the raw order for the first round of the 2010 draft, though it's subject to change with free agent compensation. If a team picking in the second half of the first round signs a Type A free agent (ranked in the top 20 percent at his position by a statistical formula) whose former club offered him arbitration, then it must surrender its first-round pick in return. However, the Rays wouldn't have to give up their No. 31 choice, because it's a compensation pick for their failure to sign 2009 first-rounder LeVon Washington.

1. Nationals (59-103)
2. Pirates (62-99)
3. Orioles (64-98)
4. Royals (65-97)
5. Indians (65-97)
6. Diamondbacks (70-92)
7. Mets (70-92)
8. Astros (74-88)
9. Padres (75-87)
10. Athletics (75-87)
11. Blue Jays (75-87)
12. Reds (78-84)
13. White Sox (79-83)
14. Brewers (80-82)
15. Rangers
   (for failure to sign Matt
   Purke)
16. Cubs (83-78)
17. Rays (84-78)
18. Mariners (85-77)
19. Tigers (86-77)
20. Braves (86-76)
21. Twins (87-76)
22. Rangers (87-75)
23. Marlins (87-75)
24. Giants (88-74)
25. Cardinals (91-71)
26. Rockies (92-70)
27. Phillies (93-69)
28. Dodgers (95-67)
29. Red Sox (95-67)
30. Angels (97-65)
31. Rays
   (for failure to sign LeVon
   Washington)
32. Yankees (103-59)

FIRST-ROUND TRENDS

Year	College	HS	Hitters	Pitchers	Average Bonus	Change
2000	12	18	13	17	$1,872,586	+3.5%
2001	18	12	10	*20	$2,154,280	+15.0%
2002	14	16	14	16	$2,106,793	-2.2%
2003	18	12	*20	10	$1,765,667	*-16.2%
2004	17	13	11	19	$1,958,448	+10.9%
2005	19	10	17	13	$2,018,000	+3.0%
2006	16	13	12	18	$1,933,333	-4.2%
2007	17	13	13	17	$2,098,083	+8.5%
2008	*21	9	11	19	*$2,458,714	+17.2%
2009	15	16	16	16	$2,434,800	-1.0%

ROUND	PLAYER, POS, TEAM	YEAR	BONUS
1st	Stephen Strasburg, rhp Nationals	2009	$7,500,000
Supp. 1st	Michael Garciaparra, ss, Mariners	2001	$2,000,000
2nd	Jason Young, rhp, Rockies	2000	$2,750,000
3rd	Matt Tuiasosopo, ss, Mariners	2004	$2,290,000
4th	Max Stassi, c, Athletics	2009	$1,500,000
5th	Ryan Westmoreland, of, Red Sox	2008	$2,000,000
6th	Jack McGeary, lhp, Nationals	2007	$1,800,000
7th	Brett Hunter, rhp, Athletics	2007	$1,100,000
8th	Colton Cain, lhp, Pirates	2009	$1,125,000
9th	Jason Middlebrook, rhp, Padres	1996	$750,000
10th	Luis Cota, rhp, Royals*	2003	$1,050,000
11th	Chris Huseby, rhp, Cubs	2006	$1,300,000
12th	Mike Rozier, lhp, Red Sox	2004	$1,575,000
13th	Jimmy Barthmaier, rhp, Astros	2003	$750,000
14th	Dexter Fowler, of, Rockies	2004	$925,000
15th	J.P. Ramirez, of, Nationals	2008	$1,000,000
Post-15th	Sean Henn, lhp, Yankees*	2000	$1,701,000

*Signed next year as draft-and-follow.

Rick Monday, the No. 1 overall pick in baseball's first-ever draft in 1965, signed with the Athletics for $100,000—a bonus record that lasted for a decade. The mark has been broken several times since and two 2009 draftees broke the record for the highest bonus ever, which had been the $6.2 million the Giants gave first No. 5 overall pick Buster Posey the year before. The Padres upped the mark to $6.25 million when they signed No. 3 overall choice Donavan Tate on Aug. 17, and the Nationals shattered it when they gave No. 1 overall selection Stephen Strasburg $7.5 million shortly before the midnight deadline. The figures below represent cash bonuses and don't include guaranteed money from major league contracts, college scholarship plans or incentives. They also don't factor in discount rates for bonuses spread over multiple years for two-sport athletes, such as Justin Upton. The list considers only players who signed with the clubs that drafted them and does not include the four loophole free agents from 1996. Among that group is former Devil Rays righthander Matt White, who established a bonus standard that still stands when he signed for $10.2 million.

YEAR	PLAYER, POS., CLUB (ROUND)	BONUS
1965	Rick Monday, of, Athletics (1)	$100,000
1975	Danny Goodwin, c, Angels (1)	$125,000
1978	Kirk Gibson, of, Tigers (1)	$150,000
	*Bob Horner, 3b, Braves (1)	$162,000
1979	Bill Bordley, lhp, Giants (1#)	$200,000
	Todd Demeter, 1b, Yankees (2)	$208,000
1988	Andy Benes, rhp, Padres (1)	$235,000
1989	Tyler Houston, c, Braves (1)	$241,500
	*Ben McDonald, rhp, Orioles (1)	$350,000
	*John Olerud, 1b, Blue Jays (3)	$575,000
1991	Mike Kelly, of, Braves (1)	$575,000
	Brien Taylor, lhp, Yankees (1)	$1,550,000
1994	Paul Wilson, rhp, Mets (1)	$1,550,000
	Josh Booty, 3b, Marlins (1)	$1,600,000
1996	Kris Benson, rhp, Pirates (1)	$2,000,000
1997	Rick Ankiel, lhp, Cardinals (2)	$2,500,000
	Matt Anderson, rhp, Tigers (1)	$2,505,000
1998	*J.D. Drew, of, Cardinals (1)	$3,000,000
	*Pat Burrell, 3b, Phillies (1)	$3,150,000
	Mark Mulder, lhp, Athletics (1)	$3,200,000
	Corey Patterson, of, Cubs (1)	$3,700,000
1999	Josh Hamilton, of, Devil Rays (1)	$3,960,000
2000	Joe Borchard, of, White Sox (1)	$5,300,000
2005	Justin Upton, ss, Diamondbacks (1)	$6,100,000
2008	Tim Beckham, ss, Rays (1)	$6,150,000
	Buster Posey, c, Giants (1)	$6,200,000
2009	Donavan Tate, cf, Padres (1)	$6,250,000
	*Stephen Strasburg, rhp, Nationals (1)	$7,500,000

*Major legue contract.

Zack Dodson (fourth round), righthander Zack Von Rosenberg (sixth round), righthander Trent Stevenson (seventh round), lefthander Colton Cain (eighth round) and righthander Jeff Inman (12th round).

■ Kennesaw State (Chad Jenkins) and Sacramento State (Tim Wheeler) produced their school's first-ever first-round picks in 2009.

■ Teams were also aggressive about drafting players with pre-determined injuries and signing them to above-slot deals because of what they showed before requiring surgery. The Rays selected Troup County High catcher Luke Bailey in the fourth round and signed him for $750,000. Bailey was considered one of the top high school catchers in the class before having Tommy John surgery in April. The Orioles liked Houston Christian High's Cameron Coffey enough to give him $990,000 as a 22nd-round pick. Before having Tommy John surgery in March, the lefthander showed a fastball that touched 94 mph.

■ As is always the case, many players drafted have relatives who played sports professionally. Outfielder Donavan Tate's (Padres, 1) father, Lars, was an NFL running back; outfielder Reymond Fuentes (Red Sox, 1) is a cousin of Carlos Beltran, righthander Brett Wallach's (Dodgers, 3) father, Tim, is a former all-star third baseman who manages the Dodgers' Triple-A Albuquerque affiliate and his brother Matt is a catcher in the system. Former Orioles all-star Al Bumbry is the father of Steve Bumbry, who the Orioles selected in the 12th round, and the Blue Jays signed a few players with baseball bloodlines. First baseman K.C. Hobson, their sixth-round pick, is the son of ex-Red Sox infielder and manager Butch; first baseman Lance Durham (14) is the son of former Cubs all-star Leon "Bull" Durham; and shortstop Jonathan Fernandez (34) is the son of former Jays all-star Tony Fernandez. The father of White Sox second rounder, outfielder Trayce Thompson, is former NBA No. 1 overall draft pick and ex-Lakers center Mychal Thompson. Lefthander Brian Moran (Mariners, 7) is the nephew of 1985's No. 1 MLB pick, B.J. Surhoff and the Rangers selected outfielder Ruben Sierra Jr. in the sixth round, to name a few. Another interesting connection is with Phillies' second-rounder, Kelly Dugan. His father, Dennis, has directed many Adam Sandler movies, including "Happy Gilmore" and "Big Daddy."

DRAFT

TONY FARLOW

Four years after he was the first-overall pick, Justin Upton hit .300/.366/.532.

YEAR	NO. 1 PICK	SCHOOL	HOMETOWN	BONUS	HIGHEST LEVEL	LARGEST BONUS (PICK NUMBER)	AMOUNT
1965	Rick Monday, of, Athletics	Arizona State	Santa Monica, Calif.	$100,000	Majors	same	$80,000
1966	Steve Chilcott, c, Mets	Antelope Valley HS	Lancaster, Calif.	75,000	Triple-A	Reggie Jackson, of, Athletics (2)	75,000
1967	Ron Blomberg, 1b, Yankees	Druid Hills HS	Atlanta	65,000	Majors	#Mike Adamson, rhp, Orioles	75,000
1968	Tim Foli, ss, Mets	Notre Dame HS	Sherman Oaks, Calif.	74,000	Majors	Lloyd Allen, rhp, Angels (12)	75,000
1969	Jeff Burroughs, of, Senators	Wilson HS	Long Beach, Calif.	88,000	Majors	same	
1970	Mike Ivie, c, Padres	Walker HS	Decatur, Ga.	75,000	Majors	#Dave Kingman, 1b, Giants	80,000
1971	Danny Goodwin, c, White Sox	Central HS	Peoria, Ill.	DNS	Majors	Ed Kurpiel, 1b, Cardinals (8)	83,750
1972	Dave Roberts, 3b, Padres	Oregon	Corvallis, Ore.	70,000	Majors	Jamie Quirk, ss, Royals (18)	78,000
1973	*David Clyde, lhp, Rangers	Westchester HS	Houston	65,000	Majors	^Alan Bannister, ss, Phillies	85,000
1974	*Bill Almon, ss, Padres	Brown	Warwick, R.I.	90,000	Majors	Willie Wilson, of, Royals (18)	90,000
1975	*Danny Goodwin, c, Angels	Southern	Peoria, Ill.	125,000	Majors	same	
1976	Floyd Bannister, lhp, Astros	Arizona State	Seattle	100,000	Majors	same	
1977	Harold Baines, of, White Sox	St. Michaels HS	St. Michaels, Md.	32,000	Majors	Paul Molitor, ss, Twins (3)	77,500
1978	*Bob Horner, 3b, Braves	Arizona State	Glendale, Ariz.	162,000	Majors	same	
1979	Al Chambers, 1b, Mariners	Harris HS	Harrisburg, Pa.	60,000	Majors	Todd Demeter, 1b, Yankees (51)	208,000
1980	Darryl Strawberry, of, Mets	Crenshaw HS	Los Angeles	152,500	Majors	same	
1981	Mike Moore, rhp, Mariners	Oral Roberts	Eakly, Okla.	100,000	Majors	Terry Blocker, of, Mets (4)	127,500
1982	Shawon Dunston, ss, Cubs	Jefferson HS	New York	135,000	Majors	Kenny Williams, of, White Sox (78)	160,000
1983	Tim Belcher, rhp, Twins	Mt. Vernon Nazarene	Sparta, Ohio	DNS	Majors	Kurt Stillwell, ss, Reds (2)	135,000
1984	Shawn Abner, of, Mets	Mechanicsburg HS	Mechanicsburg, Pa.	150,500	Majors	same	
1985	B.J. Surhoff, c, Brewers	North Carolina	Rye, N.Y.	150,000	Majors	Bobby Witt, rhp, Rangers (3)	179,000
1986	Jeff King, 3b, Pirates	Arkansas	Colorado Springs	180,000	Majors	Mark Merchant, of, Pirates (2)	165,000
1987	Ken Griffey Jr., of, Mariners	Moeller HS	Cincinnati	160,000	Majors	Jack McDowell, rhp, White Sox (5)	165,000
1988	Andy Benes, rhp, Padres	Evansville	Evansville, Ind.	235,000	Majors	same	
1989	*Ben McDonald, rhp, Orioles	Louisiana State	Denham Springs, La.	350,000	Majors	HJohn Olerud, 1b, Blue Jays (79)	575,000
1990	Chipper Jones, ss, Braves	The Bolles School	Jacksonville	275,000	Majors	*Todd Van Poppel, rhp, A's (14)	500,000
						Tony Clark, 1b, Tigers (2)	500,000
1991	Brien Taylor, lhp, Yankees	East Carteret HS	Beaufort, N.C.	1,550,000	Double-A	same	
1992	Phil Nevin, 3b, Astros	Cal State Fullerton	Placentia, Calif.	700,000	Majors	Jeffrey Hammonds, of, Orioles (4)	975,000
1993	*Alex Rodriguez, ss, Mariners	Westminster Christian HS	Miami	1,000,000	Majors	Darren Dreifort, rhp, Dodgers (2)	1,300,000
1994	Paul Wilson, rhp, Mets	Florida State	Orlando, Fla.	1,550,000	Majors	Josh Booty, ss, Marlins (5)	1,600,000
1995	Darin Erstad, of, Angels	Nebraska	Jamestown, N.D.	1,575,000	Majors	same	
1996	@Kris Benson, rhp, Pirates	Clemson	Kennesaw, Ga.	2,000,000	Majors	Matt White, rhp, Giants (7)	10,200,000
1997	Matt Anderson, rhp, Tigers	Rice	Louisville	2,505,000	Majors	same	
1998	*Pat Burrell, 3b, Phillies	Miami	Boulder Creek, Calif.	3,150,000	Majors	Corey Patterson, of, Cubs (3)	3,700,000
1999	Josh Hamilton, of, Devil Rays	Athens Drive HS	Raleigh, N.C.	3,960,000	Majors	same	
2000	Adrian Gonzalez, 1b, Marlins	Eastside HS	Chula Vista, Calif.	3,000,000	Majors	Joe Borchard, of, White Sox (12)	5,300,000
2001	Joe Mauer, c, Twins	Creten-Derham Hall	St. Paul, Minn.	5,150,000	Majors	same	
2002	Bryan Bullington, rhp, Pirates	Ball State	Fishers, Ind.	4,000,000	Majors	B.J. Upton, ss, Devil Rays (2)	4,600,000
2003	*Delmon Young, of, Devil Rays	Camarillo HS	Camarillo, Calif.	3,700,000	Majors	same	
2004	Matt Bush, ss, Padres	Mission Bay HS	El Cajon, Calif.	3,150,000	Class A	Jered Weaver, rhp, Angels	4,000,000
						Stephen Drew, ss, D-backs	4,000,000
2005	Justin Upton, ss, D'backs	Great Bridge HS	Chesapeake, Va.	6,100,000	Majors	same	
2006	*Luke Hochevar, rhp, Royals	No School	Fowler, Colo.	3,500,000	Majors	Andrew Miller, lhp, Tigers	3,550,000
2007	*David Price, lhp, Devil Rays	Vanderbilt	Murfreesboro, Tenn.	5,600,000	Majors	Matt Wieters, c, Orioles	6,000,000
2008	Tim Beckham, ss, Rays	Griffin HS	Griffin, Ga.	6,150,000	Short-season	Buster Posey, c, Giants	6,200,000
2009	Stephen Strasburg, rhp, Nationals	San Diego State	San Diego	$7,500,000	Did not play	same	

* Signed major league contract; cash bonus only reported. # Selected in January draft. @ Includes four loophole free agents; White signed with Devil Rays. ^ Selected in June secondary phase.

TOP 100 PICKS

ALYSON BOYER

North Carolina's Dustin Ackley emerged as the best hitter in the 2009 class

	TEAM	PLAYER	POS.	SCHOOL	BONUS
1.	Nationals	Stephen Strasburg	RHP	San Diego State	$7,500,000
2.	Mariners	Dustin Ackley	OF	North Carolina	$6,000,000
3.	Padres	Donavan Tate	OF	HS—Cartersville, Ga.	$6,250,000
4.	Pirates	Tony Sanchez	C	Boston College	$2,500,000
5.	Orioles	Matt Hobgood	RHP	HS—Norco, Calif.	$2,422,000
6.	Giants	Zack Wheeler	RHP	HS—Dallas, Ga.	$3,300,000
7.	Braves	Mike Minor	LHP	Vanderbilt	$2,420,000
8.	Reds	Mike Leake	RHP	Arizona State	$2,270,000
9.	Tigers	Jacob Turner	RHP	HS—St. Louis	$4,700,000
10.	Nationals	Drew Storen	RHP	Stanford	$1,600,000
11.	Rockies	Tyler Matzek	LHP	HS—Mission Viejo, Calif.	$3,900,000
12.	Royals	Aaron Crow	RHP	Fort Worth Cats	$1,500,000
13.	Athletics	Grant Green	SS	Southern California	$2,750,000
14.	Rangers	Matt Purke	LHP	HS—Klein, Texas	Did not sign
15.	Indians	Alex White	RHP	North Carolina	$2,250,000
16.	D'backs	Bobby Borchering	3B	HS—Fort Myers, Fla.	$1,800,000
17.	D'backs	A.J. Pollock	OF	Notre Dame	$1,400,000
18.	Marlins	Chad James	LHP	HS—Yukon, Okla.	$1,700,000
19.	Cardinals	Shelby Miller	RHP	HS—Brownwood, Texas	$2,875,000
20.	Blue Jays	Chad Jenkins	RHP	Kennesaw State	$1,359,000
21.	Astros	Jiovanni Mier	SS	HS—La Verne, Calif.	$1,358,000
22.	Twins	Kyle Gibson	RHP	Missouri	$1,850,000
23.	White Sox	Jared Mitchell	OF	Louisiana State	$1,200,000
24.	Angels	Randal Grichuk	OF	HS—Rosenberg, Texas	$1,242,000
25.	Angels	Mike Trout	OF	HS—Millville, N.J.	$1,215,000
26.	Brewers	Eric Arnett	RHP	Indiana	$1,197,000
27.	Mariners	Nick Franklin	SS	HS—Altamonte Springs, Fla.	$1,280,000
28.	Red Sox	Reymond Fuentes	OF	HS—Manati, P.R.	$1,134,000
29.	Yankees	Slade Heathcott	OF	HS—Texarkana, Texas	$2,200,000
30.	Rays	LeVon Washington	2B	HS—Gainesville, Fla.	Did not sign
31.	Cubs	Brett Jackson	OF	California	$972,000
32.	Rockies	Tim Wheeler	OF	Sacramento State	$900,000
33.	Mariners	Steve Baron	C	HS—Miami	$980,000
34.	Rockies	Rex Brothers	LHP	Lipscomb	$969,000
35.	D'backs	Matt Davidson	3B	HS—Yucaipa, Calif.	$900,000
36.	Dodgers	Aaron Miller	LHP	Baylor	$889,200
37.	Blue Jays	James Paxton	LHP	Kentucky	Did not sign
38.	White Sox	Josh Phegley	C	Indiana	$858,600
39.	Brewers	Kentrail Davis	OF	Tennessee	$1,200,000
40.	Angels	Tyler Skaggs	LHP	HS—Santa Monica, Calif.	$1,000,000
41.	D'backs	Chris Owings	SS	HS—Gilbert, S.C.	$950,000
42.	Angels	Garrett Richards	RHP	Oklahoma	$802,800
43.	Reds	Brad Boxberger	RHP	Southern California	$857,000
44.	Rangers	Tanner Scheppers	RHP	St. Paul Saints	$1,250,000
45.	D'backs	Mike Belfiore	LHP	Boston College	$725,000
46.	Twins	Matt Bashore	LHP	Indiana	$751,500
47.	Brewers	Kyle Heckathorn	RHP	Kennesaw State	$776,000
48.	Angels	Tyler Kehrer	LHP	Eastern Illinois	$728,100
49.	Pirates	Victor Black	RHP	Dallas Baptist	$717,000
50.	Nationals	Jeff Kobernus	2B	California	$705,500
51.	Mariners	Rich Poythress	1B	Georgia	$694,800
52.	Padres	Everett Williams	OF	HS—Austin	$775,000
53.	Pirates	Brooks Pounders	RHP	HS—Temecula, Calif.	$670,000
54.	Orioles	Mychal Givens	SS	HS—Tampa	$800,000
55.	Giants	Tommy Joseph	C	HS—Scottsdale, Ariz.	$712,500
56.	Dodgers	Blake Smith	OF	California	$643,500
57.	Reds	Billy Hamilton	SS	HS—Taylorsville, Miss.	$623,600
58.	Tigers	Andy Oliver	LHP	Oklahoma State	$1,495,000
59.	Rockies	Nolan Arenado	3B	HS—Lake Forest, Calif.	$625,000
60.	D'backs	Eric Smith	RHP	Rhode Island	$605,700
61.	White Sox	Trayce Thompson	OF	HS–Rancho Santa Margarita, Calif.	$625,000
62.	Rangers	Tommy Mendonca	3B	Fresno State	$587,700
63.	Indians	Jason Kipnis	OF	Arizona State	$575,000
64.	D'backs	Marc Krauss	OF	Ohio	$550,000
65.	Dodgers	Garrett Gould	RHP	HS—Maize, Kan.	$900,000
66.	Marlins	Bryan Berglund	RHP	HS—Simi Valley, Calif.	$572,500
67.	Cardinals	Robert Stock	C	Southern California	$525,000
68.	Blue Jays	Jake Eliopoulos	LHP	HS—Newmarket, Ont.	Did not sign
69.	Astros	Tanner Bushue	RHP	HS—Farina, Ill.	$530,000
70.	Twins	Billy Bullock	RHP	Florida	$522,000
71.	White Sox	David Holmberg	LHP	HS—Port Charlotte, Fla.	$514,000
72.	Mets	Steve Matz	LHP	HS—East Setauket, N.Y.	$895,000
73.	Brewers	Max Walla	OF	HS—Albuquerque	$499,000
74.	Brewers	Cameron Garfield	C	HS—Murrieta, Calif.	$492,200
75.	Phillies	Kelly Dugan	OF	HS—Sherman Oaks, Calif.	$485,000
76.	Yankees	J.R. Murphy	C	HS—Bradenton, Fla.	$1,250,000
77.	Red Sox	Alex Wilson	RHP	Texas A&M	$470,700
78.	Rays	Kenny Diekroeger	SS	HS—Atherton, Calif.	Did not sign
79.	Cubs	D.J. Lemahieu	2B	Louisiana State	$508,000
80.	Angels	Pat Corbin	LHP	Chipola (Fla.) JC	$450,000
81.	Nationals	Trevor Holder	RHP	Georgia	$200,000
82.	Mariners	Kyle Seager	2B	North Carolina	$436,500
83.	Padres	Jerry Sullivan	RHP	Oral Roberts	$430,200
84.	Pirates	Evan Chambers	OF	Hillsborough (Fla.) CC	$423,900
85.	Orioles	Tyler Townsend	1B	Florida International	$417,600
86.	Giants	Chris Dominguez	3B	Louisville	$411,300
87.	Braves	David Hale	RHP	Princeton	$405,000
88.	Reds	Donnie Joseph	LHP	Houston	$398,000
89.	Tigers	Wade Gaynor	3B	Western Kentucky	$392,400
90.	Rockies	Ben Paulsen	1B	Clemson	$391,000
91.	Royals	Wil Myers	C/3B	HS—High Point, N.C.	$2,000,000
92.	Athletics	Justin Marks	LHP	Louisville	$375,300
93.	Rangers	Robbie Erlin	LHP	Scotts Valley (Calif.) HS	$425,000
94.	Indians	Joe Gardner	RHP	UC Santa Barbara	$363,000
95.	D'backs	Keon Broxton	OF	Santa Fe (Fla.) CC	$358,000
96.	Dodgers	Brett Wallach	RHP	Orange Coast (Calif.) CC	$351,900
97.	Marlins	Marquise Cooper	OF	HS—Huntington Beach, Calif.	$345,000
98.	Cardinals	Joe Kelly	RHP	UC Riverside	$341,000
99.	Blue Jays	Jake Barrett	RHP	HS—Mesa, Ariz.	Did not sign
100.	Astros	Telvin Nash	OF	HS—Griffin, Ga.	$330,300

2009 CLUB-BY-CLUB SELECTIONS

ORDER OF SELECTION IN PARENTHESES   PLAYERS SIGNED IN BOLD

ARIZONA DIAMONDBACKS (15)

1. **Bobby Borchering, 3b, Bishop Verot HS, Fort Myers, Fla.**
1. **A.J. Pollock, of, Notre Dame** (Pick from Dodgers as compensation for Type A free agent Orlando Hudson)
1. **Matt Davidson, 3b, Yucaipa (Calif.) HS** (Supplemental pick—35th—for loss of Hudson)
1. **Chris Owings, ss, Gilbert (S.C.) HS** (Supplemental pick—41st—for loss of Type A free agent Juan Cruz)
1. **Mike Belfiore, lhp, Boston College** (Supplemental pick—45th—for loss of Type B free agent Brandon Lyon)
2. **Eric Smith, rhp, Rhode Island** (Pick from Royals for Cruz)
2. **Marc Krauss, of, Ohio**
3. **Keon Broxton, of, Santa Fe (Fla.) CC**
4. **David Nick, ss, Cypress (Calif.) HS**
5. **Ryan Wheeler, 1b, Loyola Marymount**
6. **Bradin Hagens, rhp, Merced (Calif.) JC**
7. **Matt Helm, 3b, Hamilton HS, Chandler, Ariz.**
8. **Paul Goldschmidt, 1b, Texas State**
9. **Chase Anderson, rhp, Oklahoma**
10. **Tyson Van Winkle, c, Gonzaga**
11. **Scottie Allen, rhp, Lyman HS, Longwood, Fla.**
12. **Charles Brewer, rhp, UCLA**
13. **Patrick Schuster, lhp, Mitchell HS, New Port Richey, Fla.**
14. **Brent Greer, ss, Western Carolina**
15. **David Narodowski, ss, Kansas**
16. **Ryan Robowski, lhp, Ohio Dominican**
17. **Andrew Wolcott, rhp, Duke**
18. **Roidany Aguila, c, Providencia HS, Rio Piedras, P.R.**
19. **Randy Hamrick, rhp, Brewton-Parker (Ga.)**
20. **Adam Worthington, rhp, Illinois-Chicago**
21. **Dan Taylor, lhp, Central Michigan**
22. **Evan Button, ss, Mississippi**
23. **Chris Odegaard, rhp, Minnesota State-Mankato**
24. **Brad Gemberling, rhp, Princeton**
25. Taylor Wrenn, ss, Manatee (Fla.) CC
26. **Dan Kaczrowski, ss, Hamline (Minn.)**
27. **Jake Hale, rhp, Ohio State**
28. **Brian Budrow, rhp, Utah**
29. Jake Williams, 1b, Brophy Prep, Phoenix
30. Jack Marder, ss, Newbury Park (Calif.) HS
31. **Keith Cantwell, rhp, Seton Hall**
32. **Will Harvil, rhp, Georgia**
33. **Brad Wilson, rhp, Cal Poly Pomona**
34. Patrick Cooper, rhp, Des Moines Area CC
35. Zach Morgan, rhp, Shasta (Calif.) JC
36. Mike Freeman, ss, Clemson
37. Chris Jacobs, of, Westchester HS, Los Angeles
38. Trevon Prince, lhp, Oakland, Calif.
39. Ryan Jones, of, Wichita State
40. **Tim Sherlock, of, Duke**
41. Cade Kreuter, 3b, Hart HS, Newhall, Calif.
42. Zach Hendrix, 2b, Emerald Ridge HS, Puyallup, Wash.
43. Brooklyn Foster, c, Walnut Grove SS, Langley, B.C
44. **Zach Varnell, c, Arkansas-Pine Bluff**
45. Beau Amaral, of, Huntington Beach (Calif.) HS
46. Matt Ozanne, of, Notre Dame Prep, Scottsdale, Ariz.
47. Mario Gallardo, lhp, West Los Angeles JC
48. Juan Avila, of, Narbonne HS, Harbor City, Calif.
49. Jordan Luvisi, of, Notre Dame Prep, Scottsdale, Ariz.
50. Frank Abbl, rhp, Mesa (Ariz.) CC

ATLANTA BRAVES (7)

1. **Mike Minor, lhp, Vanderbilt**
2. (Pick to Dodgers as compensation for Type A free agent Derek Lowe)
3. **David Hale, rhp, Princeton**
4. **Mycal Jones, ss, Miami Dade CC**
5. **Thomas Berryhill, rhp, Newberry (S.C.)**
6. Ryan Woolley, rhp, Alabama-Birmingham
7. **Robby Hefflinger, of, Georgia Perimeter JC**
8. **Kyle Rose, of, Northwest Shoals (Ala.) CC**

9. **Matt Weaver, ss, Burlington (N.J.) CC**
10. **Aaron Northcraft, rhp, Mater Dei HS, Santa Ana, Calif.**
11. **Chris Masters, lhp, Western Carolina**
12. **Chris Lovett, ss, Columbia State (Tenn.) CC**
13. **Jordan Kreke, 3b, Eastern Illinois**
14. **Cory Harrilchak, of, Elon**
15. Bennett Pickar, c, Eaton (Colo.) HS
16. **Riaan Spanjer-Furstenburg, 1b, Nova Southeastern (Fla.)**
17. **Jace Whitmer, c, Kennesaw State**
18. **Jakob Dalfonso, 3b, Middle Georgia JC**
19. **Ty'Relle Harris, rhp, Tennessee**
20. **Jeff Lorick, lhp, Virginia**
21. **Matt Crim, lhp, The Citadel**
22. **Ryan Weber, rhp, St. Petersburg (Fla.) JC**
23. **Lucas LaPoint, rhp, Knight HS, Palmdale, Calif.**
24. Casey Upperman, rhp, Notre Dame Prep, Scottsdale, Ariz.
25. Ethan Icard, rhp, Wilkes (N.C.) CC
26. Will Scott, rhp, Walters State (Tenn.) CC
27. Joey Leftridge, of, Howard (Texas) JC
28. Eric Swegman, rhp, Young Harris (Ga.) JC
29. **Bobby Rauh, of, Daytona Beach (Fla.) CC**
30. Vince Howard, of, Sikeston (Mo.) HS
31. **Derek Wiley, 1b, Belmont**
32. Jake Montgomery, rhp, Pope HS, Marietta, Ga.
33. Tyler Stubblefield, ss, Kennesaw State
34. Arby Fields, of, Los Osos HS, Rancho Cucamonga, Calif.
35. Matt Hartunian, c, Montclair Prep, Van Nuys, Calif.
36. **Andrew Wilson, rhp, Liberty**
37. Matt Moynihan, of, Cathedral Catholic HS, San Diego
38. Tripp Faulk, of, North Myrtle Beach HS, Little River, S.C.
39. Joey Bourgeois, rhp, Louisiana State-Eunice JC
40. Antonio Carrillo, of, San Ysidro HS, San Diego
41. Kyle Petter, lhp, El Camino (Calif.) JC
42. Josh Conway, of, Smithburg (Md.) HS
43. Alan Walden, rhp, Red Bank HS, Chattanooga
44. Corey Newsom, rhp, Bay HS, Panama City, Fla.
45. Nathan Dorris, lhp, Marion (Ill.) HS
46. Buck Farmer, rhp, Rockdale County HS, Conyers, Ga.
47. Colby Holmes, rhp, Conway (S.C.) HS
48. **Jamie Hayes, rhp, Rider**
49. Gabe Gutierrez, rhp, Apollo HS, Glendale, Ariz.
50. Josh Edgin, lhp, Francis Marion (Pa.)

BALTIMORE ORIOLES (5)

1. **Matt Hobgood, rhp, Norco (Calif.) HS**
2. **Mychal Givens, ss, Plant HS, Tampa**
3. **Tyler Townsend, 1b, Florida International**
4. **Randy Henry, rhp, South Mountain (Ariz.) CC**
5. **Ashur Tolliver, lhp, Oklahoma City**
6. **Justin Dalles, c, South Carolina**
7. **Aaron Wirsch, lhp, El Toro HS, Lake Forest, Calif.**
8. Devin Harris, of, East Carolina
9. **Ryan Berry, rhp, Rice**
10. **Jacob Cowan, rhp, San Jacinto (Texas) JC**
11. **Michael Ohlman, c, Lakewood Ranch HS, Bradenton, Fla.**
12. **Steve Bumbry, of, Virginia Tech**
13. **Ty Kelly, 2b, UC Davis**
14. **David Baker, rhp, Hemet (Calif.) HS**
15. Garrett Bush, rhp, Stanton College Prep HS, Jacksonville
16. **Ryan Palsha, rhp, Diablo Valley (Calif.) JC**
17. Jeff Walters, rhp, Georgia
18. **Jarret Martin, lhp, Bakersfield (Calif.) JC**
19. **Kipp Schutz, of, Indiana**
20. **James Brandhorst, rhp, Lamar**
21. **Kevin Landry, rhp, William & Mary**
22. **Cameron Coffey, lhp, Houston Christian HS**
23. **Mike Mooney, ss, Florida**
24. **Justin Anderson, lhp, Louisiana-Monroe**
25. Jay Johnson, lhp, Lethbridge (Alberta) JC
26. **Blake Mechaw, lhp, Shelton State (Ala.) CC**
27. **Mike Planeta, of, Glendale (Ariz.) CC**

28. Kyle Hoppy, of, Orchard Park (N.Y.) HS
29. Brandon Alexander, of, Oakville HS, St. Louis
30. **Brenden Webb, of, Palomar (Calif.) JC**
31. **Mike Flacco, 3b, Catonsville (Md.) CC**
32. Matt Nadolski, lhp, Casa Grande HS, Petaluma, Calif.
33. Tyler Naquin, of, Klein Collins HS, Spring, Texas
34. Malcolm Clapsaddle, rhp, Oviedo (Fla.) HS
35. Jeremy Lucas, c, West Vigo HS, Terre Haute, Ind.
36. Scott Firth, rhp, Stevenson HS, Lincolnshire, Ill.
37. Taylor Rogers, lhp, Chatfield HS, Littleton, Colo.
38. **Josh Dowdy, rhp, Appalachian State**
39. Kevin Alexander, rhp, Taravella HS, Coral Springs, Fla.
40. Bobby Shore, rhp, Palomar (Calif.) JC
41. Mason Magleby, rhp, Del Oro HS, Loomis, Calif.
42. Joe Valleggia, c, Old Dominion
43. Brad Decater, of, Cuesta (Calif.) JC
44. Kyle Westwood, rhp, Palm Harbor (Fla.) University HS
45. **David Rivera, of, Francisco Oller HS, Catano, P.R.**
46. Scott Swinson, rhp, Maryland
47. Nolan Martz, rhp, McKendree (Ill.)
48. Ryan Burnaman, 3b, San Jacinto (Texas) JC
49. Ashley Bulluck, rhp, South Broward HS, Hollywood, Fla.
50. **Tim Berry, lhp, San Marcos (Calif.) HS**

BOSTON RED SOX (27)

1. **Reymond Fuentes, of, Fernando Callejo HS, Manati, P.R.**
2. **Alex Wilson, rhp, Texas A&M**
3. **David Renfroe, ss, South Panola HS, Batesville, Miss.**
4. **Jeremy Hazelbaker, of, Ball State**
5. **Seth Schwindenhammer, of, Limestone HS, Bartonville, Ill.**
6. Branden Kline, rhp, Johnson HS, Frederick, Md.
7. **Madison Younginer IV, rhp, Maudlin (S.C.) HS**
8. **Shannon Wilkerson, of, Augusta State (Ga.)**
9. **Kendal Volz, rhp, Baylor**
10. **Brandon Jacobs, of, Parkview HS, Lilburn, Ga.**
11. **Jason Thompson, ss, Germantown (Tenn.) HS**
12. **Michael Thomas, c, Southern**
13. **Chris McGuiness, 1b, The Citadel**
14. **Willie Holmes, of, Chaffey (Calif.) JC**
15. **Michael Bugary, lhp, California**
16. Luke Bard, rhp, Charlotte Christian HS
17. Kraig Sitton, lhp, Oregon State
18. **Renny Parthemore, rhp, Cedar Cliff HS, Camp Hill, Pa.**
19. **Tom Ebert, rhp, Florida International**
20. **Alex Hassan, of/rhp, Duke**
21. Randall Fant, lhp, Texas HS, Texarkana, Texas
22. **Jordan Flasher, rhp, George Mason**
23. **Christopher Court, rhp, Stephen F. Austin State**
24. Dan Kemp, ss, Tantasqua Regional HS, Fiskdale, Mass.
25. Austin House, rhp, La Cueva HS, Albuquerque
26. **Miles Head, 3b, Whitewater HS, Fayetteville, Ga.**
27. Reed Gragnani, ss, Godwin HS, Richmond
28. **Eric Curtis, rhp, Miami Dade CC**
29. Cody Stubbs, 1b, Tuscola HS, Waynesville, N.C.
30. **Jeremiah Bayer, rhp, Trinity (Conn.)**
31. **Tim Webb, lhp, Palm Beach (Fla.) CC**
32. Mike Clark, lhp, American Heritage HS, Plantation, Fla.
33. Blaze Tart, rhp, Pendleton School, Bradenton, Fla.
34. Jimmy Patterson, lhp, Central Arizona JC
35. Matt Milroy, rhp, Marmion Academy, Aurora, Ill.
36. Mike Yastrzemski, of, St. John's Prep, Danvers, Mass.
37. Matt Koch, rhp, Washington HS, Cherokee, Iowa
38. Zeke DeVoss, of, Astronaut HS, Titusville, Fla.
39. Gavin McCourt, of, Harvard-Westlake HS, Los Angeles
40. Jimmy Dykstra, rhp, Rancho Bernardo HS, San Diego
41. **Kyle Rutter, rhp, North Carolina State**
42. Gera Sanchez, rhp, New Mexico JC
43. Luke Maile, c, Covington Catholic HS, Park Hills, Ky.
44. Derrick Thomas, of, Roswell (Ga.) HS
45. Kyle Arnsberg, c, Lamar HS, Arlington, Texas
46. John Pivach, rhp, New Orleans
47. **Jordan Sallis, 2b, Arkansas-Fort Smith JC**
48. Brian Heere, of, Kansas
49. Chris Constantino, 3b, Bishop Hendricken HS, Warwick, R.I.

50. Drew Hedman, 1b, Pomona-Pitzer (Calif.)

CHICAGO CUBS (29)

1. **Brett Jackson, of, California**
2. **D.J. Lemahieu, 2b, Louisiana State**
3. **Austin Kirk, lhp, Owasso (Okla.) HS**
4. **Chris Rusin, lhp, Kentucky**
5. **Wes Darvill, ss, Brookswood SS, Langley, B.C.**
6. **Brooks Raley, lhp, Texas A&M**
7. **Blair Springfield, ss, MacArthur HS, Decatur, Ill.**
8. **Robert Whitenack, rhp, SUNY Old Westbury**
9. **Richard Jones, c, The Citadel**
10. **Charles Thomas, 3b, Edward Waters (Fla.)**
11. **John Mincone, lhp, Suffolk County (N.Y.) CC-Grant**
12. **Runey Davis, of, Howard (Texas) JC**
13. Chad Taylor, ss, Jefferson HS, Tampa
14. **Danny Keefe, rhp, Tampa**
15. **Cody Shields, of, Auburn-Montgomery**
16. Keenyn Walker, of, Judge Memorial HS, Salt Lake City
17. B.J. Dail, rhp, Mount Olive (N.C.) (Contract voided)
18. **Matt Williams, c, Duke**
19. **Sergio Burruel, c, Browne HS, Phoenix**
20. Eric Erickson, lhp, Miami
21. **Greg Rohan, 1b, Kent State**
22. **D.J. Fitzgerald, 2b, Dyersburg State (Tenn.) CC**
23. Jeff Pruitt, of, Cal State Northridge (Contract voided)
24. Gerardo Esquivel, rhp, De La Salle Institute, Chicago
25. **Justin Bour, 1b, George Mason**
26. **Steve Grife, rhp, Mercyhurst (Pa.)**
27. **Corey Martin, rhp, Western Carolina**
28. **Jordan Petraitis, 3b, Miami (Ohio)**
29. **Tim Clubb, rhp, Missouri State**
30. Danny Sheppard, c, Downers Grove (Ill.) North HS
31. Andrew Clark, 1b, Louisville
32. **Trey McNutt, rhp, Shelton State (Ala.) CC**
33. John Lambert, lhp, North Carolina State
34. Rett Varner, rhp, Texas-Arlington
35. Kevin David, c, Oklahoma State
36. **Brandon May, 2b, Alabama**
37. Peter Mooney, ss, Palm Beach (Fla.) CC
38. **Bobby Wagner, 3b, Panola (Texas) JC**
39. **Nick Struck, rhp, Mount Hood (Ore.) CC**
40. Eric Whaley, rhp, Cardinal Gibbons HS, Fort Lauderdale
41. **Jake Schmidt, rhp, Concordia (Minn.)**
42. Trey Ford, ss, Chaparral HS, Scottsdale, Ariz.
43. Colin Kaepernick, rhp, Nevada
44. Frank DeJiulio, rhp, Daytona Beach (Fla.) CC
45. Addison Dunn, rhp, Warren (Pa.) Area HS
46. **Glenn Cook, of, Miami**
47. Joe Jocketty, 3b, Watkins HS, St. Louis
48. John Nasshan, rhp, Niles West HS, Skokie, Ill.
49. Christian Segar, of, McQuaid Jesuit HS, Rochester, N.Y.
50. Zach Cleveland, rhp, Central Arizona JC

CHICAGO WHITE SOX (22)

1. **Jared Mitchell, of, Louisiana State**
1. **Josh Phegley, c, Indiana** (Supplemental pick—38th—for loss of Type A free agent Orlando Cabrera)
2. **Trayce Thompson, of, Santa Margarita Catholic HS, Rancho Santa Margarita, Calif.** (Comp. pick from Athletics for Cabrera)
2. **David Holmberg, lhp, Port Charlotte (Fla.) HS**
3. Bryan Morgado, lhp, Tennessee
4. **Matt Heidenreich, rhp, T Canyon HS, Lake Elsinore, Calif.**
5. **Kyle Bellamy, rhp, Miami**
6. **Justin Collop, rhp, Toledo**
7. Justin Jones, lhp, Oakdale (Calif.) HS
8. **Ryan Buch, rhp, Monmouth**
9. **Matt Hopps, rhp, Cal State Dominguez Hills**
10. **Nick Ciolli, of, Indiana State**
11. **J.R. Ballinger, rhp, Southern Mississippi**
12. **Kyle Colligan, of, Texas A&M**
13. **Cameron Bayne, rhp, Concordia (Calif.)**
14. **Dan Black, 1b, Purdue**
15. Dane Williams, rhp, Archbishop McCarthy HS, Fort Lauderdale

16. **Daniel Wagner, 2b, Belmont**
17. Brian Goodwin, of, Rocky Mount (N.C.) HS
18. **Phil Negus, rhp, Wake Forest**
19. **Brady Shoemaker, of, Indiana State**
20. Nate Reed, lhp, Pittsburgh
21. **Jared McDonald, ss, Arizona State**
22. **Zach Kayne, ss, Davidson**
23. **Goldy Simmons, rhp, San Diego State**
24. **Jeff Tezak, 2b, Nebraska**
25. Mike Strong, lhp, Iowa Western CC
26. **Matt Harughty, 2b, Oklahoma**
27. **Kyle Davis, 2b, Delaware**
28. **Robby Cummings, 3b, UC Santa Barbara**
29. **Trey Delk, rhp, Clemson**
30. **Rob Vaughn, c, Kansas State**
31. **Ryan Hamme, of, Campbell**
32. **Jake Wilson, rhp, New Mexico State**
33. **Chase Cooney, rhp, Volunteer State (Tenn.) CC**
34. **Alex Farotto, lhp, South Carolina**
35. **Danny Wiltz, rhp, Tennessee**
36. Ryan Crowley, lhp, Morton West HS, Berwyn, Ill.
37. **Joe Serafin, lhp, Vermont**
38. **A.J. Casario, of, Maryland**
39. **Paul Burnside, rhp, Auburn**
40. **Leighton Pangilinan, 1b, Escalon (Calif.) HS**
41. **Ryan Lee, of, Cal Poly**
42. **Chris Zagyi, rhp, Middlesex (N.J.) CC**
43. Tyler Williams, 3b, Chaparral HS, Scottsdale, Ariz.
44. **Taylor Thompson, rhp, Auburn**
45. **Harold Baines Jr., of, McDaniel (Md.)**
46. Grant Monroe, rhp, Northwest Florida State JC
47. Jordan Yallen, of, Golden Valley HS, Santa Clarita, Calif.
48. Matthew Little, lhp, Bryan (Texas) HS
49. Theron Geith, lhp, Scottsdale (Ariz.) CC
50. Kevin Chapman, lhp, Florida

CINCINNATI REDS (8)

1. **Mike Leake, rhp, Arizona State**
1. **Brad Boxberger, rhp, Southern California** (Supplemental pick—43rd—for loss of Type B free agent Jeremy Affeldt)
2. **Billy Hamilton, ss, Taylorsville (Miss.) HS**
3. **Donnie Joseph, lhp, Houston**
4. **Mark Fleury, c, North Carolina**
5. **Daniel Tuttle, rhp, Randleman (N.C.) HS**
6. **Mark Serrano, rhp, Oral Roberts**
7. **Josh Fellhauer, of, Cal State Fullerton**
8. **Juan Silva, of, Puerto Rico Baseball Academy, Gurabo, P.R.**
9. **Brian Pearl, rhp, Washington**
10. **Tucker Barnhart, c, Brownsburg (Ind.) HS**
11. **Jacob Johnson, rhp, Trinity Christian HS, Lake Worth, Fla.**
12. **Josh Garton, of, Volunteer State (Tenn.) CC**
13. **Nick Christiani, rhp, Vanderbilt**
14. **Tim Crabbe, rhp, Westmont (Calif.)**
15. **Jamie Walczak, rhp, Mercyhurst (Pa.)**
16. Chase Fowler, c, South Forsythe HS, Cumming, Ga.
17. Deven Marrero, ss, American Heritage HS, Plantation, Fla.
18. Steven Perez, ss, Gulliver Prep HS, Miami
19. **Mitchell Clarke, lhp, Forest Heights HS, Kitchener, Ont.**
20. Matt Valaika, 2b, UC Santa Barbara
21. Jon Reed, rhp, Memorial HS, Tulsa
22. **Dave Stewart, 1b, Grayson County (Texas) CC**
23. **Chris Richburg, 1b, Texas Tech**
24. **Derrick Lowery, 1b, Young Harris (Ga.) JC**
25. Mike Monster, rhp, Rutland SS, Kelowna, B.C
26. **Trey Manz, c, South Florida**
27. Stefan Del Pino, lhp, Dorman HS, Roebuck, S.C.
28. Derek Poppert, ss, San Francisco
29. **Jason Braun, rhp, Corban (Ore.)**
30. **Yovan Gonzalez, c, Wabash Valley (Ill.) CC**
31. **Adian Kummet, rhp, St. Scholastica (Minn.)**
32. **Shane Carlson, ss, UC Santa Barbara**
33. **Will Stramp, 3b, Lubbock Christian (Texas)**
34. **Forest Cannon, rhp, UC Santa Barbara**
35. Oliver Santos, 3b, South Carolina-Salkehatchie JC

36. **Chris Burleson, ss, Southern Maine**
37. **Dayne Read, of, Chipola (Fla.) JC**
38. **Tommy Nurre, 1b, Miami (Ohio)**
39. Paul Barton, rhp, Kwalikum SS, Qualicum Beach, B.C
40. Michael Robertson, of, Bellevue (Wash.) CC
41. **Jake Wiley, rhp, Marist**
42. **Blair Carson, rhp, Anderson (S.C.)**
43. **Ricky Bowen, rhp, Mississippi State**
44. Jaron Shepherd, of, Navarro (Texas) JC
45. Brian Adams, of, South Forysth HS, Cumming, Ga.
46. Tim Dunn, rhp, Trevecca Nazarene (Tenn.)
47. Jason Hampton, rhp, Rocklin (Calif.) HS
48. Kenny Swab, c, Young Harris (Ga.) JC
49. Darion Hamilton, of, Taylorsville (Miss.) HS
50. Chris Page, 1b, Genesee (N.Y.) CC

CLEVELAND INDIANS (14)

1. **Alex White, rhp, North Carolina**
2. **Jason Kipnis, of, Arizona State**
3. **Joe Gardner, rhp, UC Santa Barbara**
4. **Kyle Bellows, 3b, San Jose State**
5. **Austin Adams, rhp, Faulkner (Ala.)**
6. **Ben Carlson, 1b, Missouri State**
7. **Jordan Henry, of, Mississippi**
8. **Cory Burns, rhp, Arizona**
9. **Preston Guilmet, rhp, Arizona**
10. **Brett Brach, rhp, Monmouth**
11. **Kirk Wetmore, lhp, Bellevue (Wash.) CC**
12. **Joseph Colon, rhp, Caguas, P.R.**
13. **Jeremy Johnson, rhp, Washington State**
14. **Kyle Smith, ss, Cal Poly**
15. **Mike Rayl, lhp, Palm Beach (Fla.) CC**
16. **Dale Dickerson, rhp, Nicholls State**
17. **Casey Frawley, of, Stetson**
18. **Dwight Childs, c, Arizona**
19. **Nick Kirk, lhp, Northern Iowa**
20. **Kyle C. Smith, rhp, Kent State**
21. Jeff Rowland, of, Georgia Tech
22. Merrill Kelly, rhp, Yavapai (Ariz.) JC
23. **Danny Jimenez, rhp, John A. Logan (Ill.) CC**
24. Michael Hamann, rhp, Danbury HS, Lakeside, Ohio
25. Blake Hauser, rhp, Manchester HS, Midlothian, Va.
26. **Antwonie Hubbard, rhp, Oklahoma**
27. **Tyler Sturdevant, rhp, New Mexico State**
28. **Nick Sarianides, rhp, Chattahoochee Valley (Ala.) JC**
29. Xorge Carrillo, c, Central Arizona JC
30. Bryson Smith, 3b, Young Harris (Ga.) JC
31. Raynor Campbell, 3b, Baylor
32. **Matt Packer, lhp, Virginia**
33. **Chris Kersten, 3b, Louisiana Tech**
34. Westley Moss, of, Nevada
35. Chris Beck, rhp, Jefferson (Ga.) HS
36. Austin Evans, rhp, Alabama
37. Steve Ewing, lhp, University HS, Orlando
38. Robert Sabo, rhp, Kent State
39. Brian Hernandez, 3b, UC Irvine
40. **Greg Folgia, ss, Missouri**
41. Max Muncy, of, Keller (Texas) HS
42. Jonathan Kountis, rhp, Ohio Dominican
43. D.J. Gentile, dh, Cal Poly
44. Jose Madrid, c, Memorial HS, Victoria, Texas
45. James Jones, rhp, John A. Logan (Ill.) CC
46. Scott Sommerfeld, of, Parkway South HS, Ballwin, Mo.
47. Christian Powell, rhp, Greenwood (S.C.) HS
48. **Vidal Nuno, lhp, Baker (Kan.)**
49. Burch Smith, rhp, Howard (Texas) JC
50. Tyler Joyner, lhp, Northern Nash HS, Rocky Mount, N.C.

COLORADO ROCKIES (10)

1. **Tyler Matzek, lhp, Capistrano Valley HS, Mission Viejo, Calif.**
1. **Tim Wheeler, of, Sacramento State** (Pick from Angels as compensation for Type A free agent Brian Fuentes)
1. **Rex Brothers, lhp, Lipscomb** (Supplemental pick—34th—for loss of Fuentes)

2. Nolan Arenado, 3b, El Toro HS, Lake Forest, Calif.
3. Ben Paulsen, 1b, Clemson
4. Kent Matthes, of, Alabama
5. Joseph Sanders, 3b, Auburn
6. Chris Balcom-Miller, rhp, West Valley (Calif.) JC
7. Erik Stavert, rhp, Oregon
8. Rob Scahill, rhp, Bradley
9. Wes Musick, lhp, Houston
10. Charlie Ruiz, rhp, Long Beach State
11. Avery Barnes, of, Florida
12. Jared Clark, 1b, Cal State Fullerton
13. Paul Bargas, lhp, UC Riverside
14. Jeff Squier, ss, Mississippi Valley State
15. Tyler Gagnon, rhp, Diablo Valley (Calif.) JC
16. Dom Altobelli, 3b, Illinois
17. Josh Hungerman, lhp, Cleveland State
18. Ricky Testa, rhp, Lamar
19. Dustin Garneau, c, Cal State Fullerton
20. Dallas Tarleton, c, Elon
21. Chandler Laurent, of, Delgado (La.) JC
22. David Born, lhp, Long Beach State
23. Jose Rivera, 2b, Universidad Interamericana (P.R.)
24. Joey Wong, ss, Oregon State
25. Trevor Gibson, rhp, San Jose State
26. Rhett Ballard, rhp, Virginia Tech
27. Dan Perkins, rhp, Delaware State
28. David DiNatale, of, Miami
29. Corey Dickerson, of, Meridian (Miss.) CC
30. Bryce Massanari, c, Georgia
31. Clint Tilford, rhp, Kentucky
32. Steve Junker, lhp, Bellevue (Neb.)
33. Coty Woods, rhp, Middle Tennessee State
34. Brandon Whitby, c, Prairie View A&M
35. Tym Pearson, of, Thurston HS, Springfield, Ore.
36. Jarrett Higgins, of, Bellaire (Texas) HS
37. Brandon Thomas, of, Pace Academy, Atlanta
38. Brett Hambright, c, Riverside (Calif.) CC
39. Eric Federico, rhp, Cal State Stanislaus
40. Jason Bagoly, c, Fitch HS, Austintown, Ohio
41. Matt Sanders, 3b, Clemson
42. Joe Scott, 2b, Cal State Fullerton
43. Franco Broyles, of, Fayetteville (Ark.) HS
44. Micah Green, of, Cherokee Trail HS, Aurora, Colo.
45. Heath Holliday, c, Bixby (Okla.) HS
46. Tyler Wallace, 3b, Eaton (Calif.) HS
47. Sterling Monfort, 1b, Eaton (Colo.) HS
48. Clint McKinney, rhp, Clemson
49. Mark Tracy, c, Duquesne
50. Nathan Hines, of, Middle Tennessee State

DETROIT TIGERS (9)

1. Jacob Turner, rhp, Westminster Christian Academy, St. Louis
2. Andy Oliver, lhp, Oklahoma State
3. Wade Gaynor, 3b, Western Kentucky
4. Edwin Gomez, ss, P.R. Baseball Academy, Gurabo, P.R.
5. Austin Wood, lhp, Texas
6. Daniel Fields, ss, University of Detroit Jesuit HS
7. Jamie Johnson, of, Oklahoma
8. Craig Fritsch, rhp, Baylor
9. John Murrian, c, Winthrop
10. Chris Sedon, 2b, Pittsburgh
11. Adam Wilk, lhp, Long Beach State
12. Matt Thompson, rhp, San Diego
13. Michael Rockett, of, Texas-San Antonio
14. Kevan Hess, rhp, Western Michigan
15. Mark Appel, rhp, Monte Vista HS, Danville, Calif.
16. Kenny Faulk, lhp, Kennesaw State
17. Nate Newman, rhp, Pepperdine
18. Eric Roof, c, Michigan State
19. Rawley Bishop, 3b, Middle Tennessee State
20. Jimmy Gulliver, ss, Eastern Michigan
21. Giovanni Soto, lhp, Carolina, P.R.
22. Matt Mansilla, of, Charleston
23. Cory Hamilton, rhp, UC Irvine

24. Wade Kapteyn, rhp, Evansville
25. Victor Roache, of, Lincoln HS, Ypsilanti, Mich.
26. Edgar Corcino, 3b, Adolfina Irizarry De Puig HS, Toa Baja, P.R.
27. Pat McKenna, ss, Bryant (R.I.)
28. Tobin Mateychick, rhp, Enid (Okla.) HS
29. Michael Morrison, rhp, Cal State Fullerton
30. James Robbins, 1b, Shorecrest HS, Shoreline, Wash.
31. Andrew Walter, rhp, Cactus HS, Glendale, Ariz.
32. Parker Markel, rhp, Mountain Ridge HS, Glendale, Ariz.
33. Cody Keefer, of, Davis (Calif.) HS
34. Derek Kline, rhp, Millersville (Pa.)
35. Patrick Biondi, of, Divine Child HS, Dearborn, Mich.
36. Chuck Crumpton, ss, Lakeside HS, Hot Springs, Ark.
37. Danny Canela, c, Florida Christian HS, Miami
38. Tarran Senay, of, South Park (Pa.) HS
39. Chad Duling, ss, Bishop Carroll HS, Wichita
40. Ben Bechtol, c, Neshannock HS, New Castle, Pa.
41. Larry Balkwill, c, Ursuline College Chatham SS, Chatham-Kent, Ont.
42. Nick Avila, rhp, Central Florida CC
43. Andrew Allen, 3b, Central Arizona JC
44. Charlie Markson, of, Whitefish Bay (Wis.) HS
45. Jimmy Brennan, of, Suffern (N.Y.) HS
46. Nate Goro, 3b, Lafayette HS, Wildwood, Mo.
47. Kevin Chambers, lhp, Capistrano Valley HS, Mission Viejo, Calif.
48. Jake Porcello, rhp, Seton Hall Prep, West Orange, N.J.
49. Cameron Giannini, rhp, Hargrave Military Academy, Chatham, Va.
50. Nico Rosthenhausler, of, South Mountain (Ariz.) CC

FLORIDA MARLINS (17)

1. Chad James, lhp, Yukon (Okla.) HS
2. Bryan Berglund, rhp, Royal HS, Simi Valley, Calif.
3. Marquise Cooper, of, Edison HS, Huntington Beach, Calif.
4. Dan Mahoney, rhp, Connecticut
5. Chase Austin, ss, Elon
6. Dustin Dickerson, 1b, Baylor (Contract voided)
7. Josh Hodges, rhp, Ingomar HS, New Albany, Miss.
8. Stephen Richards, lhp, Arkansas
9. Jobduan Morales, c, Jose S. Alegria HS, Dorado, P.R.
10. Matt Montgomery, rhp, UC Riverside
11. Chris Wade, ss, Kentucky
12. Kyle Jensen, of, St. Mary's
13. Tyler Curtis, rhp, JC of Southern Idaho
14. Sequoyah Stonecipher, of, Grossmont (Calif.) JC
15. Chad Cregar, of, Western Kentucky
16. David Peters, c, Lakewood (Calif.) HS
17. Brent Keys, of, Simi Valley (Calif.) HS
18. Brett Bukvich, lhp, Mississippi
19. Erick Carrillo, rhp, Cal State San Bernardino
20. Rand Smith, of, Appalachian State
21. A.J. Ramos, rhp, Texas Tech
22. Terrence Dayleg, ss, Western Kentucky
23. Tommy Peale, rhp, Lewis-Clark State (Idaho)
24. Mike Brady, ss, California
25. Sean Teague, rhp, Southern Polytechnic State (Ga.)
26. Brent Weaver, 3b, Oklahoma City
27. Nate Simon, 2b, Pepperdine
28. Holden Sprague, rhp, Fresno State
29. Jared Eskew, lhp, Cal Poly
30. Harold Brantley, of, Connecticut
31. Joey O'Gara, rhp, Indiana
32. Dallas Hord, c, Missouri State
33. Tom Buske, rhp, Minnesota
34. Isaac Morales, lhp, Cal State Los Angeles
35. Tyler Topp, rhp, Long Beach State
36. Kaleth Fradera, rhp, Puerto Rico Baseball Academy, Gurabo, P.R.
37. Alex Glenn, of, Henry County HS, McDonough, Ga.
38. Kevin Johnson, lhp, Cincinnati
39. Noah Perio, ss, De La Salle HS, Concord, Calif.
40. Mitch Patito, rhp, Patriot HS, Riverside, Calif.
41. Darnell Sweeney, ss, American Heritage HS, Plantation, Fla.
42. Jordan Poyer, of, Astoria (Ore.) HS
43. Donovan Gonzales, rhp, Twentynine Palms (Calif.) HS
44. Kenny Giles, rhp, Rio Grande HS, Albuquerque
45. Zach Hurley, of, Ohio State

DRAFT

46. Nick Ammirati, c, Seton Hall Prep, West Orange, N.J.
47. Cody Miller, c, River Valley HS, Yuba City, Calif.
48. Ryan Gibson, lhp, Yukon (Okla.) HS
49. Alan Williams, lhp, Meridian (Miss.) CC
50. **Adam Kam, 1b, Douglas HS, Parkland, Fla.**

HOUSTON ASTROS (20)

1. **Jiovanni Mier, ss, Bonita HS, La Verne, Calif.**
2. **Tanner Bushue, rhp, South Central HS, Farina, Ill.**
3. **Telvin Nash, of, Griffin (Ga.) HS**
3. **Jonathan Meyer, 3b, Simi Valley (Calif.)** HS (Supplemental pick—111th—for failure to sign '08 third-rounder Chase Davidson)
4. **B.J. Hyatt, rhp, South Carolina-Sumter JC**
5. **Brandon Wikoff, ss, Illinois**
6. **Enrique Hernandez, ss, Am. Military Academy, Toa Baja, P.R.**
7. **Dallas Keuchel, lhp, Arkansas**
8. **Brandt Walker, rhp, Stanford**
9. **Ben Orloff, ss, UC Irvine**
10. **Erik Castro, 3b, San Diego State**
11. **Bubby Williams, c, Crowder (Mo.) JC**
12. Geoff Thomas, rhp, Stephenson HS, Stone Mountain, Ga.
13. **Jake Goebbert, of, Northwestern**
14. **David Berner, lhp, San Jose State**
15. **Ryan Humphrey, of, St. Louis CC-Meramec**
16. **Ronald Sanchez, 1b, Manuela Toro Morice HS, Caguas, P.R.**
17. **Justin Harper, rhp, Oklahoma City**
18. **J.B. MacDonald, rhp, Boston College**
19. **Brian Kemp, of, St. John's**
20. **J.D. Martinez, of, Nova Southeastern (Fla.)**
21. **Barry Butera, 2b, Boston College**
22. **Mark Jones, rhp, Manheim Township HS, Lititz, Pa.**
23. **Robby Donovan, rhp, Stetson**
24. **Mike Modica, lhp, George Mason**
25. **Nick Stanley, 1b, Florida Southern**
26. Matt Watson, 1b, Pompano Beach (Fla.) HS
27. **Aaron Bray, 3b, Charlotte**
28. Eric Anderson, rhp, Mountain Vista HS, Highlands Ranch, Colo.
29. **Garen Wright, of, Putnam City HS, Oklahoma City**
30. Brandon Petite, rhp, Vauxhall Academy, Edmonton
31. **Travis Smink, lhp, Virginia Military Institute**
32. Greg Peavey, rhp, Oregon State
33. **Brenden Stines, rhp, Ball State**
34. **Scott Migl, rhp, Texas A&M**
35. **Grant Hogue, of, Mississippi State**
36. Tyler Saladino, ss, Palomar (Calif.) JC
37. **Raul Rivera, rhp, Paul HS, Santurce, P.R.**
38. **Sean Barksdale, of, Temple**
39. Rory Young, rhp, Mountain SS, Langley, B.C
40. **Dan Sarisky, rhp, Oglethorpe (Ga.)**
41. Carlos Escobar, c, Chatsworth (Calif.) HS
42. Ivory Thomas, of, Downey (Calif.) HS
43. Anthony Tzamtzis, rhp, La Salle HS, Miami
44. **Mike Schurz, rhp, Iowa**
45. Adrian Morales, 2b, Miami Dade CC
46. Justin Gonzalez, ss, Columbus HS, Miami
47. Matt Branham, rhp, South Carolina-Upstate
48. Paco Rodriguez, lhp, Gulliver Prep, Miami
49. Matt Smith, 1b, Mississippi
50. **Spencer Hylander, lhp, Oklahoma Baptist**

KANSAS CITY ROYALS (11)

1. **Aaron Crow, rhp, Fort Worth (American Association)**
2. (Pick to D'backs as compensation for Type A free agent Juan Cruz)
3. **Wil Myers, c/3b, Wesleyan Christian HS, High Point, N.C.**
4. **Chris Dwyer, lhp, Clemson**
5. **Louis Coleman, rhp, Louisiana State**
6. **Cole White, rhp, New Mexico**
7. **Buddy Baumann, lhp, Missouri State**
8. **Dusty Odenbach, rhp, Connecticut**
9. **Ben Theriot, c, Texas State**
10. **Geoff Baldwin, 1b, Grand Junction (Colo.) HS**
11. **Ryan Wood, rhp, East Carolina**
12. **Nick Wooley, rhp, William Woods (Mo.)**
13. Lane Adams, of, Red Oak (Okla.) HS

14. **Crawford Simmons, lhp, Statesboro (Ga.) HS**
15. **Scott Lyons, ss, Arkansas**
16. **Eric Diaz, lhp, New Mexico JC**
17. **Ben Tschepikow, 2b, Arkansas**
18. **Brendan Lafferty, lhp, UCLA**
19. **Ryan Stovall, 3b, Thomas (Ga.)**
20. **Patrick Keating, rhp, Florida**
21. **Chanse Cooper, of, Belhaven (Miss.)**
22. **Ryan Dennick, lhp, Tennessee Tech**
23. **Scott Kelley, rhp, Penn State**
24. Zach Jones, rhp, Santa Teresa HS, San Jose
25. **Richard Folmer, rhp, Stephen F. Austin State**
26. Matt Frazer, 1b, Nitro (W.Va.) HS
27. **Gabe MacDougall, of, Lynn (Fla.)**
28. Eric Peterson, inf, Liberty HS, Spangle, Wash.
29. Nick Zaharion, of, South Fork HS, Stuart, Fla.
30. **Josh Worrell, rhp, Indiana Wesleyan**
31. **Brian Peacock, lhp, Santa Ana (Calif.) JC**
32. Luke Voit, c, Lafayette HS, Wildwood, Mo.
33. **Claudio Bavera, lhp, Cochise (Ariz.) JC**
34. **Justin Trapp, ss, Fairfield Central HS, Winnsboro, S.C.**
35. Levi Cartas, of, Marysville-Pilchuck HS, Marysville, Wash.
36. Fabian Roman, rhp, Marist HS, Bayonne, N.J.
37. Tanner Poppe, rhp, Girard (Kan.) HS
38. Arthur Owens, ss, Sandy Creek HS, Tyrone, Ga.
39. Art Charles, 1b, Bakersfield (Calif.) JC
40. Mike Morin, rhp, Shawnee Mission South HS, Overland Park, Kan.
41. **Joey Lewis, c, Georgia**
42. **Jonathon Keck, lhp, Bethel (Tenn.)**
43. Jeff Soptic, rhp, Shawnee Mission East HS, Prairie Village, Kan.
44. Derrick Hudgins, ss, Middleton HS, Tampa
45. Derek Spencer, 3b, Bowling Green State
46. Hudson Randall, rhp, Dunwoody (Ga.) HS
47. **Anthony Howard, of, Quince Orchard HS, Gaithersburg, Md.**
48. Kevin Kuntz, ss, Union HS, Tulsa
49. Zac Fisher, c, Miller HS, Fontana, Calif.
50. **Anthony Scirrotto, ss, Penn State**

LOS ANGELES ANGELS (30)

1. **Randal Grichuk, of, Lamar Consolidated HS, Rosenberg, Texas** (Comp. pick from Mets for Type A free agent Francisco Rodriguez)
1. **Mike Trout, of, Millville (N.J.) HS** (Pick from Yankees as compensation for Type A free agent Mark Teixeira)
1. (Pick to Rockies as compensation for Type A free agent Brian Fuentes)
1. **Tyler Skaggs, lhp, Santa Monica (Calif.) HS** (Supplemental pick—40th—for loss of Teixeira)
1. **Garrett Richards, rhp, Oklahoma** (Supplemental pick—42nd—for loss of Rodriguez)
1. **Tyler Kehrer, lhp, Eastern Illinois** (Supplemental pick—48th—for loss of Type B free agent Jon Garland)
2. **Pat Corbin, lhp, Chipola (Fla.) JC**
3. **Josh Spence, lhp, Arizona State**
4. **Wes Hatton, 2b, Norco (Calif.) HS**
5. **Casey Haerther, 1b, UCLA**
6. **Danny Reynolds, rhp, Durango HS, Las Vegas**
7. **Jon Karcich, ss, Santa Clara**
8. **Carlos Ramirez, c, Arizona State**
9. **David Carpenter, rhp, Paris (Texas) JC**
10. **Jake Locker, of, Washington**
11. **Dillon Baird, 3b, Arizona**
12. **Travis Witherspoon, of, Spartanburg Methodist (S.C.) JC**
13. **Jeremy Cruz, of, Stetson**
14. **Sam Selman, lhp, St. Andrew's Episcopal HS, Austin**
15. **Mike Nesseth, rhp, Nebraska**
16. Andrew Del Colle, rhp, Newark Academy, Livingston, N.J.
17. **Jeremy Gillan, c, Jacksonville**
18. **Jamie Mallard, 1b, Hillsborough (Fla.) CC**
19. Adam Hornung, of, Baylor
20. **Dan Eichelberger, of, East Central (Miss.) CC**
21. **Rich Cates, of, Cal State Northridge**
22. **Stephen Locke, lhp, Florida**
23. **Jordan Drake, of, Elsinore HS, Wildomar, Calif.**
24. **Taylor Kinzer, rhp, Taylor (Ind.)**
25. **Michael Demperio, 2b, Georgia**

DRAFT

26. Garrett Cannizaro, 2b, Mandeville (La.) HS
27. Devon Zenn, of, Benicia (Calif.) HS
28. **Carson Andrew, rhp, Jacksonville**
29. **Heath Nichols, rhp, JC of Southern Idaho**
30. **Matt Long, of, Santa Clara**
31. Jordan Whatcott, rhp, Utah
32. Raoul Torrez, 2b, Arizona State
33. Ben Dew, rhp, Seminole (Fla.) CC
34. **Ryan Cisterna, rhp, Arkansas**
35. Robbie Harris, ss, Cardinal Gibbons HS, Baltimore
36. **Eric Oliver, 1b, UC Santa Barbara**
37. Erik Gregersen, rhp, Stephen F. Austin State
38. Justin Bellez, rhp, Mira Mesa (Calif.) HS
39. Ryan Hege, c, Cowley County (Kan.) CC
40. Asaad Ali, c, Niles (Mich.) HS
41. Joey Rapp, of, Chipola (Fla.) JC
42. Sam Wolff, rhp, Stevens HS, Rapid City, S.D.
43. Seth Harvey, rhp, Washington State
44. R.J. Santigate, 3b, Bishop Gorman HS, Las Vegas
45. **Phil Bando, 2b, JC of the Canyons (Calif.)**
46. Jonathan Paquet, rhp, Cardinal Roy SS, Ancienne-Lorette, Quebec
47. Jose Jimenez, 1b, Tampa
48. Jake Rife, of, Washington
49. Chunner Nyberg, rhp, Dixie HS, St. George, Utah
50. **Alibay Barkley, 1b, Washington HS, New York**

LOS ANGELES DODGERS (16)

1. (Pick to Diamondbacks as compensation for Type A free agent Orlando Hudson)
1. **Aaron Miller, lhp, Baylor** (Supplemental pick—36th—for loss of Type A free agent Derek Lowe)
2. **Blake Smith, of, California** (Comp. pick from Braves for Lowe)
2. **Garrett Gould, rhp, Maize (Kan.) HS**
3. **Brett Wallach, rhp, Orange Coast (Calif.) CC**
4. **Angelo Songco, of, Loyola Marymount**
5. **J.T. Wise, c, Oklahoma**
6. **Jan Vazquez, c, Puerto Rico Baseball Academy, Gurabo, P.R.**
7. **Brandon Martinez, rhp, Fowler (Calif.) HS**
8. **Jonathan Garcia, of, Luis Munoz Marin HS, Yauco, P.R.**
9. **Bryant Hernandez, ss, Oklahoma**
10. **Andy Suiter, lhp, UC Davis**
11. Connor Powers, 1b, Mississippi State
12. **Brian Cavazos-Galvez, of, New Mexico**
13. **J.B. Paxson, rhp, Western Kentucky**
14. **Casio Grider, ss, Newberry (S.C.)**
15. **Jeff Hunt, 3b, St. Benedict Catholic SS, Cambridge, Ont.**
16. **Mike Pericht, c, St. Joseph's (Ind.)**
17. **Steven Ames, rhp, Gonzaga**
18. **Greg Wilborn, lhp, Louisiana-Lafayette**
19. **Nick Akins, of, Vanguard (Calif.)**
20. Daniel Palo, rhp, Houston HS, Germantown, Tenn.
21. **Chris Henderson, 3b, George Mason**
22. **Stetson Banks, of, Brigham Young**
23. **Jimmy Marshall, rhp, Florida State**
24. Chad Kettler, ss, Coppell (Texas) HS
25. Richie Shaffer, 3b, Providence HS, Charlotte
26. Alex McRee, lhp, Georgia
27. Brian Johnson, lhp, Cocoa Beach (Fla.) HS
28. **Bobby Hernandez, rhp, Barry (Fla.)**
29. Reshawn Payne, 2b, Middle Georgia JC
30. **Nick Gaudi, rhp, Pepperdine**
31. **Austin King, of, Jackson State (Tenn.) CC**
32. **Graham Miller, lhp, Master's (Calif.)**
33. **Steve Cilladi, c, Kansas Wesleyan**
34. **Justin Dignelli, rhp, George Washington**
35. **David Iden, 2b, California Lutheran**
36. **K.J. Childs, rhp, Culver-Stockton (Mo.)**
37. Joel Effertz, rhp, Ladysmith (Wis.) HS
38. Kirby Pellant, 2b, Corona Del Sol HS, Tempe, Ariz.
39. Ryan Hander, rhp, Lincoln HS, Sioux Falls, S.D.
40. Ryan Christenson, lhp, South Mountain (Ariz.) CC
41. **Chris Handke, rhp, Cornell**
42. Tony Renda, ss, Serra HS, San Mateo, Calif.
43. Chad Gough-Fortenberry, c, Northshore HS, Slidell, La.

44. R.C. Orlan, lhp, Deep Run HS, Glen Allen, Va.
45. Stephen Piscotty, ss, Amador Valley HS, Pleasanton, Calif.
46. James Smith, 2b, Second Baptist HS, Houston
47. Cole Pembroke, of, Desert Vista HS, Phoenix
48. Travis Burnside, of, Laurens (S.C.) District HS
49. Christian Walker, 3b, Kennedy-Kenrick Catholic HS, Limerick, Pa.
50. David Garcia, ss, Kennedy HS, Granada Hills, Calif.

MILWAUKEE BREWERS (25)

1. **Eric Arnett, rhp, Indiana**
1. **Kentrail Davis, of, Tennessee** (Supplemental pick—39th—for loss of Type A free agent C.C. Sabathia)
1. **Kyle Heckathorn, rhp, Kennesaw State** (Supplemental pick—47th—for loss ot Type B free agent Brian Shouse)
2. **Max Walla, of, Albuquerque Academy** (Pick from Yankees as compensation for Sabathia)
2. **Cameron Garfield, c, Murrieta (Calif.) Valley HS**
3. **Josh Prince, ss, Tulane**
4. **Brooks Hall, rhp, Hanna HS, Anderson, S.C.**
5. **D'Vontrey Richardson, of, Florida State**
6. **Hiram Burgos, rhp, Bethune-Cookman**
7. **Khris Davis, of, Cal State Fullerton**
8. **Chad Stang, of, Midland (Texas) CC**
9. **Jon Pokorny, lhp, Kent State**
10. **Tyler Roberts, c, Jones County HS, Gray, Ga.**
11. **Andre Lamontagne, rhp, Oral Roberts**
12. **Rob Currie, rhp, Tusculum (Tenn.)**
13. **Sean Halton, 1b, Lewis-Clark State (Idaho)**
14. **Mike Brownstein, 2b, New Mexico**
15. **Del Howell, lhp, Alabama**
16. **Scooter Gennett, ss, Sarasota (Fla.) HS**
17. **Tyler Cravy, rhp, Napa Valley (Calif.) CC**
18. **Caleb Thielbar, lhp, South Dakota State**
19. **Scott Krieger, of, George Mason**
20. **Franklin Romero, of, Cerro Coso (Calif.) CC**
21. Brian Vigo-Suarez, ss, Fossil Ridge HS, Keller, Texas
22. **Michael Fiers, rhp, Nova Southeastern (Fla.)**
23. Austin Pressley, rhp, Franklin Monroe HS, Arcanum, Ohio
24. **Peter Fatse, 2b, Connecticut**
25. **Demetrius McKelvie, of, E. Columbus HS, Lk. Waccamaw, N.C.**
26. Lex Rutledge, lhp, Tupelo (Miss.) HS
27. **Ryan Platt, rhp, UC Riverside**
28. Geno Escalante, c, Rodriguez HS, Fairfield, Calif.
29. Chandler McLaren, of, Guelph (Ont.) Collegiate Vocational Institute
30. **Brandon Sizemore, 2b, Charleston**
31. **Jose Oviedo, rhp, Miami Dade CC**
32. **Chris Ellington, of, Texas Christian**
33. Jacobbi McDaniel, 3b, Madison (Fla.) County HS
34. Mike Ojala, rhp, Rice
35. **Matt Costello, lhp, Valdosta State (Ga.)**
36. Josh Turley, lhp, Texas HS, Texarkana, Texas
37. Cullen Sexton, rhp, Minnesota
38. Casey Stevenson, 2b, UC Irvine
39. Brady Rodgers, rhp, Lamar Consolidated HS, Rosenberg, Texas
40. Kyle Hansen, rhp, St. Dominic HS, Oyster Bay, N.Y.
41. Steven Sultzbaugh, of, Rice
42. Brad Schreiber, rhp, Kimberly (Wis.) HS
43. **Kyle Dhanani, 3b, Thompson Rivers (B.C.)**
44. Andrew Morris, rhp, Gulf Coast (Fla.) CC
45. Richard Stock, c, Agoura HS, Agoura Hills, Calif.
46. Jordan Wong, rhp, Vauxhall Academy, Edmonton
47. Trevor Kirk, of, CC of Southern Nevada
48. Rey Cotilla, rhp, Miami Dade CC
49. J.J. Altobelli, ss, Woodbridge HS, Irvine, Calif.
50. Darren Farmer, c, West Lauderdale HS, Collinsville, Miss.

MINNESOTA TWINS (21)

1. **Kyle Gibson, rhp, Missouri**
1. **Matt Bashore, lhp, Indiana** (Supplemental pick—46th—for loss of Type B free agent Dennys Reyes)
2. **Billy Bullock, rhp, Florida**
3. **Ben Tootle, rhp, Jacksonville State**
4. **Derek McCallum, 2b, Minnesota**
5. **Tobias Streich, c, West Virginia**

DRAFT

6. **Chris Herrmann, c, Miami**
7. **Brad Stillings, rhp, Kent State**
8. **Brian Dozier, ss, Southern Mississippi**
9. **Nick Lockwood, ss, Jesuit HS, Tampa**
10. Blake Dean, of, Louisiana State
11. Ronnie Richardson, of, Lake Region HS, Eagle Lake, Fla.
12. **Tony Davis, lhp, Florida**
13. Clarence Davis, ss, Campbell HS, Smyrna, Ga.
14. **Matt Tone, lhp, SUNY Cortland**
15. **Steven Liddle, of, Vanderbilt**
16. **Dakota Watts, rhp, Cal State Stanislaus**
17. **Nick Tindall, c, O'Fallon (Ill.) HS**
18. Beau Stoker, ss, Bishop Ward HS, Kansas City, Kan.
19. John Stilson, rhp, Texarkana (Texas) CC
20. Tommy Mackoul, lhp, UC Riverside
21. **Kane Holbrooks, rhp, Texas State**
22. **Buddy Munroe, c, Florida**
23. Eduardo Encinosa, rhp, Coral Park HS, Miami
24. Mario Hollands, lhp, UC Santa Barbara
25. Tony Bryant, rhp, Kennewick (Wash.) HS
26. Mike Giovenco, rhp, North Park (Ill.)
27. Eric Decker, of, Minnesota
28. Pat Light, rhp, Christian Brothers Academy, Lincroft, N.J.
29. Beau Wright, lhp, Los Alamitos (Calif.) HS
30. **Trayvone Johnson, c, Los Angeles, Calif.**
31. Cody Martin, 3b, Stephens County HS, Toccoa, Ga.
32. Aaron Senne, of, Missouri
33. **Nick Freitas, of, Southern Utah**
34. Ricky Claudio, rhp, American HS, Hialeah, Fla.
35. David Hurlbut, lhp, Diablo Valley (Calif.) JC
36. Jason Zylstra, rhp, Jacksonville State
37. David Gutierrez, rhp, Miami
38. **Peter Kennelly, rhp, Fordham**
39. Ryan Sadler, rhp, Naples (Fla.) HS
40. Ryan Abrahamson, of, Tartan HS, Oakdale, Minn.
41. Pat Butler, rhp, Chatham (N.J.) HS
42. Marc Bourgeois, of, Chipola (Fla.) JC
43. Jon Hedges, 1b, Olney Central (Ill.) CC
44. **Tyler Herr, rhp, Katy (Texas) HS**
45. **Eddie Ahorrio, rhp, Jesus Silverio Delgado HS, Arecibo, P.R.**
46. Jake Kretzer, of, Benton HS, St. Joseph, Mo.
47. **Richard Calcano, rhp, Dr. Jose M. Lazaro HS, Carolina, P.R.**
48. Cody Dordan, rhp, Newport (Ore.) HS
49. **Paul-Michael Klingsberg, 1b, Cal State Dominguez Hills**
50. Alberto Cardenas, rhp, Palmetto Ridge HS, Naples, Fla.

NEW YORK METS (23)

1. (Pick to Angels as compensation for Type A free agent Francisco Rodriguez)
2. **Steve Matz, lhp, Melville HS, East Setauket, N.Y.**
3. **Robbie Shields, ss, Florida Southern**
4. **Darrell Ceciliani, of, Columbia Basin (Wash.) CC**
5. Damien Magnifico, rhp, North Mesquite HS, Mesquite, Texas
6. David Buchanan, rhp, Chipola (Fla.) JC
7. **Darin Gorski, lhp, Kutztown (Pa.)**
8. **Taylor Freeman, c, McNeese State**
9. **Jeff Glenn, c, Winter Haven (Fla.) HS**
10. **Nick Santomauro, of, Dartmouth**
11. **Sam Honeck, 1b, Tulane**
12. **James Ewing, 2b, Southern Mississippi**
13. **Zach Dotson, lhp, Effingham County HS, Springfield, Ga.**
14. **R.J. Harris, of, Northwood (Texas)**
15. Casey Schmidt, rhp, San Diego
16. **Chase Greene, of, West Boca Raton (Fla.) Community HS**
17. **Alex Gregory, of, Radford**
18. **Cody Holliday, of, Wilmington (Del.)**
19. **Nelfi Zapata, c, English HS, Jamaica Plain, Mass.**
20. **Joey August, of, Stanford**
21. **Joe Bonfe, 3b, Sierra (Calif.) JC**
22. **Zach Von Tersch, rhp, Georgia Tech**
23. **John Church, rhp, West Florida**
24. **Michael Johnson, rhp, Concordia (Texas)**
25. **Josh Dunn, 3b, Sickles HS, Tampa**
26. **John Semel, of, Chapman (Calif.)**

27. **Kurt Steinhauer, of, Point Loma Nazarene (Calif.)**
28. **Brian Needham, rhp, Lamar**
29. **ZeErika Hall, of, East Central (Miss.) CC**
30. Jordan Harrison, lhp, New Caney (Texas) HS
31. Mitch Haniger, of, Archbishop Mitty HS, San Jose
32. **T.J. Chism, lhp, La Salle**
33. **James Schroeder, 3b, Southern Arkansas**
34. **Cam Maron, c, Hicksville (N.Y.) HS**
35. **Wes Wrenn, rhp, The Citadel**
36. **Lance Hoge, lhp, Kansas State**
37. **Brandon Sage, lhp, South Alabama**
38. **Will Cherry, of, Florida Southern**
39. **Taylor Whitenton, rhp, Darton (Ga.) JC**
40. Jerome Pena, 2b, Western Nevada CC
41. **Travis Ozga, 1b, Florida Atlantic**
42. Ryan Gunhouse, c, Clear Creek HS, League City, Texas
43. Bobby Rinard, rhp, Yavapai (Ariz.) JC
44. James Wooster, lhp, Alvin (Texas) CC
45. Jake Johansen, rhp, Allen (Texas) HS
46. Trey Pilkington, rhp, Oxford (Ala.) HS
47. **Ryan Mollica, 2b, Florida International**
48. Joe Mantiply, lhp, Tunstall HS, Dry Fork, Va.
49. Josh Easley, rhp, Weatherford (Texas) HS
50. Zack Godley, rhp, Bamberg-Ehrhardt HS, Bamberg, S.C.

NEW YORK YANKEES (24)

1. (Pick to Angels as compensation for Type A free agent Mark Teixeira)
1. **Slade Heathcott, of, Texas HS, Texarkana, Texas** (Supplemental pick—29th—for failure to sign 2008 first-rounder Gerrit Cole)
2. (Pick to Brewers as compensation for Type A free agent C.C. Sabathia)
2. **J.R. Murphy, c, Pendleton School, Bradenton, Fla.** (Supplemental pick—76th—for failure to sign 2008 second-rounder Scott Bittle)
3. (Pick to Blue Jays as compensation for Type A free agent A.J. Burnett)
4. **Adam Warren, rhp, North Carolina**
5. **Caleb Cotham, rhp, Vanderbilt**
6. **Rob Lyerly, 3b, Charlotte**
7. **Sean Black, rhp, Seton Hall**
8. **Sam Elam, lhp, Notre Dame**
9. **Gavin Brooks, lhp, UCLA**
10. Tyler Lyons, lhp, Oklahoma State
11. **Neil Medchill, of, Oklahoma State**
12. **Brett Gerritse, rhp, Pacifica HS, Garden Grove, Calif.**
13. **DeAngelo Mack, of, South Carolina**
14. **Graham Stoneburner, rhp, Clemson**
15. **Shane Greene, rhp, Daytona Beach (Fla.) CC**
16. **Bryan Mitchell, rhp, Rockingham County HS, Hamlet, N.C.**
17. Chad Thompson, rhp, El Toro HS, Lake Forest, Calif.
18. **Hector Rabago, c, Southern California**
19. **Luke Murton, 1b, Georgia Tech**
20. Thomas Keeling, lhp, Oklahoma State
21. **Joe Talerico, of, Brookdale (N.J.) CC**
22. Ben Soignier, ss, Louisiana-Monroe
23. **Kevin Mahoney, 3b, Canisius**
24. **Isaac Harrow, 2b, Appalachian State**
25. **Shaeffer Hall, lhp, Kansas**
26. Steve Bruno, ss, Gloucester Catholic HS, Gloucester City, N.J.
27. **Jeff Farnham, c, New Mexico State**
28. Aaron Meade, lhp, Missouri State
29. Scott Matyas, rhp, Minnesota
30. Kyle McKenzie, rhp, Thayer Academy, Braintree, Mass.
31. **Judd Golsan, of, Mountain Brook (Ala.) HS**
32. Nick Ebert, 1b, South Carolina
33. Andrew Aplin, of, Vanden HS, Fairfield, Calif.
34. Jake Petricka, rhp, Indiana State
35. Brett Bruening, rhp, Grayson County (Texas) CC
36. Kyle Ottoson, lhp, South Mountain (Ariz.) CC
37. **Justin Milo, of, Vermont**
38. Adam Bailey, of, Nebraska
39. Cody Stiles, rhp, Taravella HS, Coral Springs, Fla.
40. **Ben Watkins, rhp, Pittsburgh-Johnstown (Pa.)**
41. **Mariel Checo, rhp, Thomas HS, New York**
42. Danny Black, ss, Feather River (Calif.) CC
43. **Isaiah Brown, of, Paradise Valley (Ariz.) CC**
44. **Evan DeLuca, lhp, Immaculata HS, Somerville, N.J.**

45. Jeremy Baltz, of, Vestal (N.Y.) HS
46. Tony Plagman, 1b, Georgia Tech
47. Shane Brown, c, Central Florida
48. Patrick White, of, West Virginia
49. Xavier Esquivel, rhp, Loyola Marymount
50. Stephen Kaupang, 1b, Cypress (Calif.) JC

OAKLAND ATHLETICS (12)

1. **Grant Green, ss, Southern California**
2. (Pick to White Sox as comp. for Type A free agent Orlando Cabrera)
3. **Justin Marks, lhp, Louisville**
4. **Max Stassi, c, Yuba City (Calif.) HS**
5. **Steve Parker, 3b, Brigham Young**
6. **Ryan Ortiz, c, Oregon State**
7. **Ian Krol, lhp, Neuqua Valley HS, Naperville, Ill.**
8. **Rob Gilliam, rhp, UNC Greensboro**
9. **Myrio Richard, of, Prairie View A&M**
10. Sam Dyson, rhp, South Carolina
11. **Mike Spina, 3b, Cincinnati**
12. **Connor Hoehn, rhp, St. Petersburg (Fla.) JC**
13. **Murphy Smith, rhp, SUNY Binghamton**
14. Drew Gagnier, rhp, Oregon
15. **Anthony Aliotti, 1b, St. Mary's**
16. **Josh Leyland, c, Sam Dimas (Calif.) HS**
17. Pat Stover, of, Rocklin (Calif.) HS
18. **Max Peterson, lhp, San Jose State**
19. **Daniel Tenholder, rhp, Austin Peay**
20. Tyler Bernard, ss, Valley Center (Calif.) HS
21. Mike Faulkner, of, Germantown (Tenn.) HS
22. **Ryan Quigley, lhp, Northeastern**
23. **Kent Walton, of, Brigham Young**
24. **Dan Straily, rhp, Marshall**
25. **Chris Mederos, rhp, Georgia Southern**
26. **Nathan Long, rhp, Texas-Arlington**
27. **Michael Gilmartin, 2b, Wofford**
28. **Conner Crumbliss, 2b, Emporia State (Kan.)**
29. Michael Zunino, c, Mariner HS, Cape Coral, Fla.
30. **Royce Consigli, of, Notre Dame HS, Welland, Ont.**
31. Ian Texidor, 3b, C.E.D.E.A. HS, Rio Piedras, P.R.
32. Garett Claypool, rhp, UCLA
33. Mike Bolsinger, rhp, Arkansas
34. Dylan Brown, of, Oklahoma State
35. **Paul Smyth, rhp, Kansas**
36. **Jeremy Wells, 2b, Patten (Calif.)**
37. Colin Bates, rhp, North Carolina
38. Tristan Archer, rhp, Sullivan South HS, Blountville, Tenn.
39. Ryan Lockwood, of, South Florida
40. Chris O'Dowd, c, Regis Jesuit HS, Aurora, Colo.
41. Justin Hilt, of, Elon
42. **Blake Crosby, 1b, Sacramento State**
43. Ryan Lipkin, c, San Francisco
44. **A.J. Huttenlocker, lhp, Missouri Western State**
45. **Anthione Shaw, of, St. Augustine's (N.C.)**
46. **Joel Eusebio, 3b, Northeastern Oklahoma A&M JC**
47. Kyle Roller, 1b, East Carolina
48. Addison Johnson, of, Clemson
49. Anthony Giansanti, of, Siena
50. Tanner Biagini, 3b, Virginia Military Institute

PHILADELPHIA PHILLIES (26)

1. (Pick to Mariners as compensation for Type A free agent Raul Ibanez)
2. **Kelly Dugan, of, Notre Dame HS, Sherman Oaks, Calif.**
3. **Kyrell Hudson, of, Evergreen HS, Vancouver, Wash.**
4. **Adam Buschini, 2b, Cal Poly**
5. **Matt Way, lhp, Washington State**
6. **Steven Inch, rhp, Vauxhall Academy, Edmonton**
7. **Brody Colvin, rhp, St. Thomas More HS, Lafayette, La.**
8. **Jonathan Singleton, 1b, Millikan HS, Long Beach**
9. **Aaron Altherr, of, Agua Fria HS, Avondale, Ariz.**
10. **Josh Zeid, rhp, Tulane**
11. **Jeremy Barnes, ss, Notre Dame**
12. **Nick Hernandez, lhp, Tennessee**
13. **Ryan Sasaki, lhp, Connally HS, Austin**
14. Jake Stewart, of, Rocky Mountain HS, Fort Collins, Colo.

15. **Austin Hyatt, rhp, Alabama**
16. Andrew Susac, c, Jesuit HS, Carmichael, Calif.
17. **Mike Dabbs, of, Oklahoma State**
18. **Carl Uhl, of, UC Riverside**
19. **Stephen Batts, 1b, East Carolina**
20. **Darin Ruf, 1b, Creighton**
21. **Chase Johnson, rhp, South Mountain (Ariz.) CC**
22. **Bronco Lafrenz, c, Indiana State**
23. **Evan Porter, ss, Nebraska-Omaha**
24. **Justin Long, rhp, Bellevue (Neb.)**
25. **Eric Massingham, rhp, Cal Poly**
26. **Brian Gump, of, UC Santa Barbara**
27. **Marlon Mitchell, c, Hillsborough HS, Tampa**
28. **Justin Beal, rhp, Missouri Southern State**
29. **Mark Doll, rhp, Southern Polytechnic State (Ga.)**
30. Stephen Kohlscheen, rhp, Cowley County (Kan.) CC
31. **David Doss, c, South Alabama**
32. **Kevin Angelle, lhp, San Jacinto (Texas) JC**
33. **Colin Kleven, rhp, Mountain SS, Langley, B.C**
34. A.J. Griffin, rhp, San Diego
35. **Phil Aviola, c, Wilmington (Del.)**
36. **Matt McConnell, 2b, Metro State (Colo.)**
37. Brodie Greene, 2b, Texas A&M
38. **Cory Wine, 1b, Penn State**
39. Sam Kidd, rhp, Ohio County HS, Hartford, Ky.
40. Rob Amaro, 3b, Penn Charter HS, Philadelphia
41. Jeff Gelalich, of, Bonita HS, La Verne, Calif.
42. Matt Laney, lhp, Miami Dade CC
43. Francois Lafreniere, rhp, Ahuntsic (Quebec) JC
44. Brian Feekin, lhp, Iowa Western CC
45. Richard Bain, of, Trinity Christian Academy, Jacksonville
46. Jeff Ames, rhp, Skyview HS, Vancouver, Wash.
47. **Ryan Bollinger, 1b, Magic City HS, Minot, N.D.**
48. Wander Nunez, of, Frankford HS, Philadelphia
49. Chris Gosik, 3b, Malvern (Pa.) Prep HS
50. **David Hissey, of, Emory**

PITTSBURGH PIRATES (4)

1. **Tony Sanchez, c, Boston College**
1. **Victor Black, rhp, Dallas Baptist** (Supplemental pick—49th—for failure to sign 2008 second-rounder Tanner Scheppers)
2. **Brooks Pounders, rhp, Temecula (Calif.) Valley HS**
3. **Evan Chambers, of, Hillsborough (Fla.) CC**
4. **Zack Dodson, lhp, Medina Valley HS, Castroville, Texas**
5. **Nate Baker, lhp, Mississippi**
6. **Zach Von Rosenberg, rhp, Zachary (La.) HS**
7. **Trent Stevenson, rhp, Brophy Prep, Phoenix**
8. **Colton Cain, lhp, Waxahachie (Texas) HS**
9. **Brock Holt, 2b, Rice**
10. **Joey Schoenfeld, c, Santiago HS, Garden Grove, Calif.**
11. **Aaron Baker, 1b, Oklahoma**
12. **Jeff Inman, rhp, Stanford**
13. **Walker Gourley, 3b, Eastern Wayne HS, Goldsboro, N.C.**
14. Marcos Reyna, rhp, Bakersfield (Calif.) JC
15. Peter Bako, rhp, Connors State (Okla.) JC
16. Matt den Dekker, of, Florida
17. Jordan Cooper, rhp, Central HS, Shelbyville, Tenn.
18. **Ryan Beckman, rhp, Grayson County (Texas) CC**
19. Josh Urban, rhp, Dripping Springs (Texas) HS
20. Sam Spangler, rhp, Hawaii
21. **Phillip Irwin, rhp, Mississippi**
22. Carmine Giardina, lhp, Tampa
23. **Jose Hernandez, inf, Texas-San Antonio**
24. **Jason Erickson, rhp, Washington**
25. Aaron LaFountaine, of, North HS, Riverside, Calif.
26. Matt Dermody, lhp, Norwalk (Iowa) HS
27. Wes Luquette, c, Newman HS, New Orleans
28. Kyle Hooper, rhp, Saugus (Calif.) HS
29. Michael Heller, rhp, Cardinal Mooney HS, Bradenton, Fla.
30. **Ty Summerlin, ss, Southeastern Louisiana**
31. Zach Taylor, of, Statesboro (Ga.) HS
32. Niko Spezial, lhp, Don Bosco Prep, Ramsey, N.J.
33. **Pat Irvine, of, Elon**
34. **Zac Fuesser, lhp, Walters State (Tenn.) CC**

35. Chris McKenzie, rhp, San Jacinto (Texas) JC
36. Bobby Doran, rhp, Seward County (Kan.) CC
37. Zach Nuding, rhp, Weatherford (Texas) JC
38. Jake Lamb, 3b, Bishop Blancet HS, Seattle
39. Keifer Nuncio, rhp, Katy (Texas) HS
40. Brett Lee, lhp, West Florida HS, Pensacola, Fla.
41. Tyler Cannon, ss, Virginia
42. **Marc Baca, rhp, Nevada-Las Vegas**
43. **Teddy Fallon, rhp, South Carolina-Upstate**
44. Dexter Bobo, lhp, Georgia Southern
45. Kevin Gelinas, lhp, Central Arizona JC
46. Parker Bangs, rhp, South Carolina
47. Justin Earls, lhp, Georgia
48. Blake Brown, of, Normal (Ill.) West HS
49. Yasser Clor, rhp, California
50. Matt Taylor, lhp, Columbus (Ga.) HS

ST. LOUIS CARDINALS (18)

1. **Shelby Miller, rhp, Brownwood (Texas) HS**
2. **Robert Stock, c, Southern California**
3. **Joe Kelly, rhp, UC Riverside**
4. **Scott Bittle, rhp, Mississippi**
5. **Ryan Jackson, ss, Miami**
6. **Virgil Hill, of, Mission (Calif.) JC**
7. **Kyle Conley, of, Washington**
8. **Jason Stidham, ss, Florida State**
9. **Nick McCully, rhp, Coastal Carolina**
10. **Hector Hernandez, lhp, P.R. Baseball Academy, Gurabo, P.R.**
11. **Alan Ahmady, 1b, Fresno State**
12. **Pat Daugherty, lhp, Pearl River (Miss.) CC**
13. **Matt Carpenter, 3b, Texas Christian**
14. **Ross Smith, of, Middle Georgia JC**
15. **David Washington, 1b, University City HS, San Diego**
16. Daniel Bibona, lhp, UC Irvine
17. **Jonathan Rodriguez, 1b, Manatee (Fla.) CC**
18. **Anthony Garcia, c, San Juan Educational HS, San Juan, P.R.**
19. **Travis Tartamella, c, Cal State Los Angeles**
20. **Scott Schneider, rhp, St. Mary's**
21. **Trevor Rosenthal, rhp, Cowley County (Kan.) CC**
22. Joey Bergman, 2b, Charleston
23. **Matt Adams, c, Slippery Rock (Pa.)**
24. **Keith Butler, rhp, Wabash Valley (Ill.) CC**
25. **Josh Squatrito, rhp, Towson**
26. **C.J. Beatty, of, North Carolina A&T**
27. John Folino, rhp, Connecticut (Contract voided)
28. **Justin Edwards, lhp, Kennesaw State**
29. **Daniel Calhoun, lhp, Murray State**
30. **Chris Corrigan, rhp, Mississippi**
31. **Tyler Bighames, ss, Estero (Fla.) HS**
32. **Travis Lawler, rhp, Midland (Texas) JC**
33. **Devin Goodwin, ss, Delta State (Miss.)**
34. **David Kington, rhp, Southern Illinois**
35. **Andy Moss, rhp, Lincoln (Mo.)**
36. **Justin Smith, rhp, Utah Valley**
37. **Rich Racobaldo, 3b, Mount Olive (N.C.)**
38. **John Durham, lhp, Warner (Fla.)**
39. Taylor Terrasas, ss, Santa Fe (Texas) HS
40. **Jesse Simpson, rhp, Charleston**
41. **Cale Johnson, rhp, McKendree (Ill.)**
42. **Aaron Terry, rhp, Southern Arkansas**
43. **Manuel De La Cruz, lhp, Imperial Valley (Calif.) JC**
44. **Kyle Heim, lhp, Iowa**
45. Adam Heisler, of, South Alabama
46. Jim Klocke, c, Southeast Missouri State
47. **Michael Thompson, rhp, Bellarmine (Ky.)**
48. **Jason Novak, rhp, UCLA**
49. Andy Hillis, rhp, Brentwood (Tenn.) HS
50. **Tyler Lavigne, rhp, San Diego State**

SAN DIEGO PADRES (3)

1. **Donavan Tate, of, Cartersville (Ga.) HS**
2. **Everett Williams, of, McCallum HS, Austin**
3. **Jerry Sullivan, rhp, Oral Roberts**
4. **Keyvius Sampson, rhp, Forest HS, Ocala, Fla.**

5. **Jason Hagerty, c, Miami**
6. **James Needy, rhp, Santana HS, Santee, Calif.**
7. **Miles Mikolas, rhp, Nova Southeastern (Fla.)**
8. **Nate Freiman, 1b, Duke**
9. **Chris Fetter, rhp, Michigan**
10. **Ryan Hinson, lhp, Clemson**
11. Drew Madrigal, rhp, Mount San Jacinto (Calif.) JC
12. **Brayden Drake, 3b, Missouri State**
13. **Matt Vern, 1b, Texas Christian**
14. **Nick Greenwood, lhp, Rhode Island**
15. **Matt Lollis, rhp, Riverside (Calif.) CC**
16. **Griffin Benedict, c, Georgia Southern**
17. **Jorge Reyes, rhp, Oregon State**
18. Shuhei Fujiya, rhp, Northern Iowa
19. **Chris Tremblay, ss, Kent State**
20. John Wooten, 3b, Eastern Wayne HS, Goldsboro, N.C.
21. Kendall Korbal, rhp, Blinn (Texas) JC (Contract voided)
22. **Cody Decker, 1b, UCLA**
23. **Jeff Ibarra, lhp, Lee (Tenn.)**
24. **Bo Davis, of, Southern Mississippi**
25. **Ty Wright, of, Georgia Southern**
26. **Kevin Winn, rhp, Louisiana Tech**
27. **Cameron Monger, of, New Mexico**
28. **Vince Belnome, 2b, West Virginia**
29. **Robert Poutier, rhp, Virginia**
30. **Wande Olabisi, of, Stanford**
31. **Matt Jackson, rhp, South Alabama**
32. **David Erickson, rhp, Connecticut**
33. **Jon Berger, rhp, San Diego State**
34. Josh Cephas, rhp, Southern Nazarene (Okla.)
35. Adalberto Santos, of, Oregon State
36. **Dylan Tonneson, c, California**
37. Gaspar Santiago, lhp, Ranger (Texas) JC
38. **Kyle Loretelli, of, Cal State Stanislaus**
39. **Chris Ahearn, ss, Catawba (N.C.)**
40. **Tom Porter, rhp, Elon**
41. Dane Hamilton, 2b, New Mexico
42. Rey Delphey, rhp, Alonso HS, Tampa
43. **Chadd Hartman, of, Central Florida**
44. **Ryan Skube, 2b, Mountain Ridge HS, Glendale, Ariz.**
45. Derek Landis, rhp, Iowa Western CC
46. Mykal Stokes, of, Orange Coast (Calif.) CC
47. Zach Thomas, lhp, Cypress-Fairbanks HS, Cypress, Texas
48. Andrew Ruck, of, Sinclair SS, Whitby, Ont.
49. **Brett Holland, rhp, Texas-Tyler**
50. **Brett Basham, c, Mississippi**

SAN FRANCISCO GIANTS (6)

1. **Zack Wheeler, rhp, East Paulding HS, Dallas, Ga.**
2. **Tommy Joseph, c, Horizon HS, Scottsdale, Ariz.**
3. **Chris Dominguez, 3b, Louisville**
4. **Jason Stoffel, rhp, Arizona**
5. **Brandon Belt, 1b, Texas**
6. **Matt Graham, rhp, Oak Ridge HS, Spring, Texas**
7. **Nick Liles, 2b, Western Carolina**
8. **Gus Benusa, of, Riverview HS, Oakmont, Pa.**
9. **Evan Crawford, of, Indiana**
10. **Jeremy Toole, rhp, Brigham Young**
11. **John Eshleman, ss, Mount San Jacinto (Calif.) JC**
12. **Chris Heston, rhp, East Carolina**
13. **Shawn Sanford, rhp, South Florida**
14. **B.J. Salsbury, rhp, Mount San Jacinto (Calif.) JC**
15. **Kyle Vazquez, rhp, Franklin Pierce (N.H.)**
16. **Ryan Cavan, ss, UC Santa Barbara**
17. **Chris Gloor, lhp, Quinnipiac**
18. Jonathan Walsh, c, Coppell (Texas) HS
19. **Jason Walls, rhp, Troy**
20. Mitch Mormann, rhp, Des Moines Area CC
21. Zach Wasserman, 1b, Lake Shore HS, St. Clair Shores, Mich.
22. **Drew Biery, 3b, Kansas State**
23. Adam Champion, lhp, Arkansas-Little Rock
24. **Alex Burg, c, Washington State**
25. **Taylor Rogers, rhp, Tulane**
26. **Luis Munoz, of, Puerto Rico Baseball Academy, Gurabo, P.R.**

27. Kyle Mach, 3b, Missouri
28. Jamaine Cotton, rhp, Western Oklahoma State JC
29. Luke Demko, rhp, Rhode Island (Contract voided)
30. **Craig Westcott, rhp, Bellhaven (Miss.)**
31. Diego Seastrunk, c, Rice
32. **Luke Anders, 1b, Texas A&M**
33. **Jake Dunning, ss, Indiana**
34. Brandon Kirby, of, Lake Wales (Fla.) HS
35. **Brandon Graves, lhp, Valdosta State (Ga.)**
36. **Ryan Scoma, of, UC Davis**
37. **Ryan Lollis, of, Missouri**
38. **A.J. Proszek, rhp, Gonzaga**
39. **Kyle Henson, c, Mississippi**
40. **Jonathan White, of, Vanderbilt**
41. **Gary Moran, rhp, Sonoma State (Calif.)**
42. Nick Schwaner, 3b, New Orleans
43. Matt Jansen, lhp, Purdue
44. Joe Lewis, 1b, Pittsburg (Calif.) HS
45. Kyle Kramp, rhp, Westfield (Ind.) HS
46. **Juan Martinez, ss, Oral Roberts**
47. Michael Ness, rhp, Duke
48. Randolph Oduber, of, Western Oklahoma State JC
49. Austin Goolsby, c, Embry-Riddle (Fla.)
50. **Kaohi Downing, rhp, Point Loma Nazarene (Calif.)**

SEATTLE MARINERS (2)

1. **Dustin Ackley, of, North Carolina**
1. **Nick Franklin, ss, Lake Brantley HS, Altamonte Springs, Fla.**
   (Pick from Phillies for Type A free agent Raul Ibanez)
1. **Steve Baron, c, Ferguson HS, Miami** (Supplemental pick—33rd—for loss of Ibanez)
2. **Rich Poythress, 1b, Georgia**
3. **Kyle Seager, 2b, North Carolina**
4. **James Jones, of, Long Island**
5. **Tyler Blandford, rhp, Oklahoma State**
6. **Shaver Hansen, 3b, Baylor**
7. **Brian Moran, lhp, North Carolina**
8. **Jimmy Gillheeney, lhp, North Carolina State**
9. **Trevor Coleman, c, Missouri**
10. **Vinnie Catricala, 3b, Hawaii**
11. **Tim Morris, 1b, St. John's**
12. **Andrew Carraway, rhp, Virginia**
13. **Matt Cerione, of, Georgia**
14. Adam Nelubowich, 3b, Vauxhall Academy, Edmonton
15. Blake Keitzman, lhp, Western Oregon
16. Tillman Pugh, of, Gateway (Ariz.) CC
17. Joe Terry, 2b, Cerritos (Calif.) CC
18. **Anthony Vasquez, lhp, Southern California**
19. **Eric Thomas, rhp, Bethune-Cookman**
20. **John Hesketh, lhp, New Mexico**
21. **Daniel Cooper, rhp, Southern California**
22. Drew Hayes, rhp, Vanderbilt
23. David Rollins, lhp, San Jacinto (Texas) JC
24. **Carlton Tanabe, c, Pearl City (Hawaii) HS**
25. **Brandon Josselyn, rhp, Yale**
26. **Chris Sorce, rhp, Troy**
27. **Austin Hudson, rhp, Central Florida**
28. Regan Flaherty, 1b, Deering HS, Portland, Maine
29. **Brandon Haveman, of, Purdue**
30. **Brandon Bantz, c, Dallas Baptist**
31. Clint Dempster, lhp, Mississippi Gulf Coast JC
32. **Bennett Whitmore, rhp, Oregon**
33. **Hawkins Gebbers, 2b, Biola (Calif.)**
34. Scott Griggs, rhp, San Ramon Valley HS, Danville, Calif.
35. **Eric Valdez, rhp, Indiana State**
36. **John Housey, rhp, Miami**
37. **Chris Kessinger, rhp, Nebraska-Omaha**
38. Matt Nohelty, of, Minnesota
39. **Greg Waddell, of, Florida International**
40. **Jorden Merry, rhp, Washington**
41. **Kyle Witten, rhp, Cal State Fullerton**
42. Steve Hagen, 3b, Eastern Oklahoma State JC
43. Cameron Perkins, of, Southport HS, Indianapolis
44. **Mark Angelo, of, East Stroudsburg (Pa.)**

45. **Kevin Mailloux, 2b, Canisius**
46. Clay Cederquist, 1b, Fowler HS, Fresno
47. David Holman, rhp, Hutchinson (Kan.) CC
48. Sean Nolin, lhp, San Jacinto (Texas) JC
49. Dane Phillips, c, Central Heights HS, Nacogdoches, Texas
50. **Evan Sharpley, 3b, Notre Dame**

TAMPA BAY RAYS (28)

1. LeVon Washington, 2b, Buchholz HS, Gainesville, Fla.
2. Kenny Diekroeger, ss, Menlo HS, Atherton, Calif.
3. **Todd Glaesmann, of, Midway HS, Waco, Texas**
4. **Luke Bailey, c, Troup County HS, LaGrange, Ga.**
5. **Jeff Malm, 1b, Bishop Gorman HS, Las Vegas**
6. **Devin Fuller, rhp, Chandler-Gilbert (Ariz.) CC**
7. **Cody Rogers, of, Panola (Texas) JC**
8. **Brett Nommensen, of, Eastern Illinois**
9. **Kevin James, lhp, Whitefish Bay HS, Milwaukee**
10. Derek Dennis, ss, Forest Hills Central HS, Grand Rapids, Mich.
11. **Alex Koronis, rhp, Tampa**
12. **Andrew Bellatti, rhp, Steele Canyon HS, Spring Valley, Calif.**
13. **Hunter Hill, rhp, Howard (Texas) JC**
14. **Zach Quate, rhp, Appalachian State**
15. Pierce Johnson, rhp, Faith Christian Academy, Arvada, Colo.
16. **Tyler Bortnick, 2b, Coastal Carolina**
17. **Alex Diaz, of, Puerto Rico Baseball Academy, Gurabo, P.R.**
18. **Jacob Partridge, lhp, Rogers HS, Puyallup, Wash.**
19. **Scott Shuman, rhp, Auburn**
20. Dylan Floro, rhp, Buhach Colony HS, Atwater, Calif.
21. **Matt Swilley, rhp, El Camino HS, Oceanside, Calif.**
22. **Jake Sullivan, lhp, Arkansas-Little Rock**
23. Trevor Petersen, rhp, Hallsville (Texas) HS
24. Andrew Heaney, lhp, Putnam City HS, Oklahoma City
25. **Ryan Wiegand, 1b, Gonzaga**
26. **Dan Rhault, ss, Rhode Island**
27. Brady Wager, rhp, Globe (Ariz.) HS
28. **Zach Rosscup, lhp, Chemeketa (Ore.) CC**
29. **Gabe Cohen, of, UCLA**
30. **Marcus Proctor, rhp, Pinnacle HS, Phoenix**
31. **Aaron Dott, lhp, Wisconsin-Whitewater**
32. Alex Besaw, rhp, Skagit Valley (Wash.) CC
33. Ryan McCarney, rhp, Cal State Northridge
34. **Kyle Spraker, ss, Loyola Marymount**
35. **Chris Murrill, of, Nicholls State**
36. **Jeff Cinadr, rhp, Toledo**
37. Austin Maddox, c, Eagle's View HS, Jacksonville
38. Drew Hillman, 3b, Orange Coast (Calif.) CC
39. **Dan April, lhp, Mercer**
40. James Jones, lhp, Highland HS, Gilbert, Ariz.
41. **Matt Stabelfeld, lhp, Lewis-Clark State (Idaho)**
42. **Bennett Davis, 3b, Elon**
43. **Geno Glynn, 3b, Minnesota State-Mankato**
44. Kalani Brackenridge, ss, Kapolei (Hawaii) HS
45. Cole Nelson, lhp, Des Moines Area CC
46. Aaron Oates, 3b, Skyline HS, Oakland
47. **Jason Patton, of, Kent State**
48. Nate Roberts, of, Parkland (Ill.) JC
49. Vince Spilker, rhp, Raytown (Mo.) HS
50. **David Wendt, c, Dowling (N.Y.)**

TEXAS RANGERS (13)

1. Matt Purke, lhp, Klein (Texas) HS
1. **Tanner Scheppers, rhp, St. Paul** (American Association) (Supp. pick—44th—for loss of Type B free agent Milton Bradley)
2. **Tommy Mendonca, 3b, Fresno State**
3. **Robbie Erlin, lhp, Scotts Valley (Calif.) HS**
4. **Andrew Doyle, rhp, Oklahoma**
5. **Nick McBride, rhp, Ragsdale HS, Jamestown, N.C.**
6. **Ruben Sierra Jr., of, San Juan Educational HS, San Juan, P.R.**
7. **Braxton Lane, of, Sandy Creek HS, Tyrone, Ga.**
8. **Braden Tullis, rhp, Skagit Valley (Wash.) CC**
9. Jabari Blash, of, Miami Dade CC
10. Thomas Lemke, rhp, Northwest Christian HS, Phoenix
11. **Johnny Gunter, rhp, Chattahoochee Valley (Ala.) CC**
12. Vin DiFazio, c, Alabama

13. Justin Jamison, rhp, Strongsville (Ohio) HS
14. Chad Bell, lhp, Walters State (Tenn.) CC
15. Keith Campbell, rhp, Everett (Wash.) CC
16. Mike Revell, 3b, Florida HS, Tallahassee, Fla.
17. Paul Strong, lhp, Marina HS, Huntington Beach, Calif.
18. Mike Schaaf, rhp, Hill HS, Saginaw, Mich.
19. David Boyd, 3b, Tate HS, Cantonment, Fla.
20. Jerome Werniuk, rhp, Neil McNeil HS, Toronto
21. Chris Matlock, rhp, Central Missouri State
22. Sam Brown, rhp, North Carolina State
23. Daniel Lima, ss, Barry (Fla.)
24. Shawn Blackwell, rhp, Clear Creek HS, League City, Texas
25. Riley Cooper, of, Florida
26. Kevin Castner, rhp, Cal Poly
27. Aaron Barrett, rhp, Mississippi
28. Derek Law, rhp, Seton LaSalle Catholic HS, Pittsburgh
29. C.C. Watson, lhp, Cleburne County HS, Heflin, Ala.
30. Bryan Fogle, of, Erskine (S.C.)
31. Shon Landry, ss, McNeese State (Contract voided)
32. Reggie Williams Jr., of, Brooks-DeBartolo Collegiate HS, Tampa
33. Kyle Rhoad, of, Eastern Michigan
34. Jared Prince, of, Washington State
35. Tim Butler, rhp, Greenbrier Christian Academy, Chesapeake, Va.
36. Matt Carasiti, rhp, Berlin (Conn.) HS
37. Chad Nading, rhp, Nevada-Las Vegas
38. Anthony Hutting, of, Tesoro HS, Rancho San Margarita, Calif.
39. Jabari Henry, of, Olympia HS, Orlando
40. Taylor Vail, 3b, Cabrillo (Calif.) JC
41. Forrest Garrett, lhp, Norcross (Ga.) HS
42. Shane Zegarac, lhp, St. Joseph's (Ind.)
43. Joe Bonadonna, of, Illinois
44. Tyler Christman, rhp, South Carolina-Sumter JC
45. Dale Anderson, c, JC of Southern Idaho
46. Jerad Grundy, lhp, Johnsburg (Ill.) HS
47. Tyler Higgins, rhp, Mount Pleasant (Mich.) HS
48. Cole Frenzel, 3b, Dickinson (N.D.) HS
49. Cat Kendrick, rhp, Northgate HS, Newnan, Ga.
50. Ronald Melendez, of, Cowley County (Kan.) CC

TORONTO BLUE JAYS (19)

1. Chad Jenkins, rhp, Kennesaw State
1. James Paxton, lhp, Kentucky (Supplemental pick—37th—for loss of Type A free agent A.J. Burnett)
2. Jake Eliopoulos, lhp, Sacred Heart Catholic HS, Newmarket, Ont
3. Jake Barrett, rhp, Desert Ridge HS, Mesa, Ariz.
3. Jake Marisnick, of, Poly HS, Riverside, Calif. (Pick from Yankees as compensation for Burnett)
4. Ryan Goins, ss, Dallas Baptist
5. Ryan Schimpf, 2b, Louisiana State
6. K.C. Hobson, of, Stockdale HS, Bakersfield, Calif.
7. Egan Smith, lhp, CC of Southern Nevada
8. Brian Slover, rhp, Cal State Northridge
9. Aaron Loup, lhp, Tulane
10. Yan Gomes, c, Barry (Fla.)
11. Sean Ochinko, c, Louisiana State
12. Bryson Namba, 3b, Pearl City (Hawaii) HS
13. Matt Morgal, rhp, Southern Nazarene (Okla.)
14. Lance Durham, 1b, Cincinnati
15. Drew Hutchison, rhp, Lakeland (Fla.) HS
16. Dave Sever, rhp, Saint Louis
17. Steve Turnbull, rhp, Iowa
18. Daniel Webb, lhp, Northwest Florida State JC
19. Ryan Tepera, rhp, Sam Houston State
20. Kevin Nolan, ss, Winthrop
21. Kurt Giller, rhp, Manhattan (Kan.) HS
22. Matt Fields, rhp, Gonzaga
23. Brad Glenn, of, Arizona
24. Matt Nuzzo, ss, Brown
25. Sam Strickland, lhp, Texas A&M-Kingsville
26. Lance Loftin, rhp, Texas State
27. Brian Justice, rhp, St. Mary's
28. Zach Outman, rhp, Saint Louis
29. Zach Anderson, rhp, Buffalo
30. Tim McDonald, of, Edison HS, Fresno

31. Jack Murphy, c, Princeton
32. Ryan Shopshire, rhp, San Jose State
33. Robert Benincasa, rhp, Armwood HS, Seffner, Fla.
34. Jonathan Fernandez, ss, Guilford Tech (N.C.) CC
35. Evan Teague, lhp, Western Kentucky
36. Alex Pepe, lhp, Florida Atlantic
37. Shawn Griffith, rhp, George Mason
38. Yudelmis Hernandez, 1b, Barry (Fla.)
39. Josh Lucas, rhp, Lakeland (Fla.) HS
40. Jonathan Gilbert, of, Ahuntsic (Quebec) JC
41. Zach Kirksey, of, Louisiana State-Eunice JC
42. Michael Reeves, c, St. Peter's SS, Peterborough, Ont.
43. Maxx Tissenbaum, ss, York Mills Collegiate Institute, Toronto
44. Nick Wagner, of, Santa Margarita HS, Rancho Santa Margarita, Calif.
45. Brandon Kaye, rhp, Douglas (B.C.)
46. Carlos Castro, 3b, Lon Morris (Texas) JC
47. John Rigg, of, St. Petersburg (Fla.) JC
48. Jeff Gibbs, rhp, Birchmount Park Collegiate Institute, Toronto
49. Tommy Collier, rhp, San Jacinto (Texas) JC
50. Burke Seifrit, rhp, Semiahmoo SS, Surrey, B.C

WASHINGTON NATIONALS (1)

1. Stephen Strasburg, rhp, San Diego State
1. Drew Storen, rhp, Stanford (Supplemental pick—10th—for failure to sign 2008 first-rounder Aaron Crow)
2. Jeff Kobernus, 2b, California
3. Trevor Holder, rhp, Georgia
4. A.J. Morris, rhp, Kansas State
5. Miguel Pena, lhp, La Joya HS, Mission, Texas
6. Michael Taylor, ss, Westminster Academy, Fort Lauderdale
7. Dean Weaver, rhp, Georgia
8. Roberto Perez, ss, Dorado Academy, Dorado, P.R.
9. Taylor Jordan, rhp, Brevard (Fla.) CC
10. Paul Applebee, lhp, UC Riverside
11. Justin Bloxom, of, Kansas State
12. Nathan Karns, rhp, Texas Tech
13. Pat Lehman, rhp, George Washington
14. Naoya Washiya, of, JC of the Desert (Calif.)
15. Corey Davis, 1b, Coffee HS, Douglas, Ga.
16. Sean Nicol, ss, San Diego
17. Chad Jenkins, lhp, Cecil (Md.) CC
18. Marcus Stroman, ss, Patchogue-Medford HS, Medford, N.Y.
19. Frank Corolla, rhp, Houston (Contract voided)
20. Jack Walker, 3b, Concordia (Ill.)
21. Mitchell Clegg, lhp, Massachusetts
22. Danny Rosenbaum, lhp, Xavier
23. Kyle Breault, ss, Northville (Mich.) HS
24. Dustin Crane, rhp, Snead State (Ala.) CC
25. Matt Ridings, rhp, Western Kentucky
26. Gianison Boekhoudt, ss, Carroll HS, Southlake, Texas
27. Brandon King, rhp, Martinsburg (W.Va.) HS
28. Matt Swynenberg, rhp, Black Hawk (Iowa) JC
29. Evan Bronson, lhp, Trinity (Texas)
30. Rob Wort, rhp, Jefferson (Mo.) JC
31. J.J. Sferra, of, Nevada-Las Vegas
32. Kyle Morrison, rhp, Wagner
33. Nick DeSantiago, c, Hays HS, Kyle, Texas
34. Shane McCatty, rhp, Oakland
35. Jacob Morris, of, Coppell (Texas) HS
36. Josh Miller, lhp, O'Connor HS, Helotes, Texas
37. Josh Elander, c, Round Rock (Texas) HS
38. Chris Manno, lhp, Duke
39. Kyle Martin, rhp, St. Michael's Academy, Austin
40. Joseph Hughes, rhp, McMichael HS, Mayodan, N.C.
41. Dane Opel, of, Edwardsville (Ill.) HS
42. Daniel Cropper, rhp, UNC Wilmington
43. Cohl Walla, rhp, Lake Travis HS, Austin
44. Hoby Milner, lhp, Paschal HS, Fort Worth
45. Michael Ratterree, ss, Memorial HS, Houston
46. Seth Greene, rhp, Deep Run HS, Glen Allen, Va.
47. Darius Rudoph, 2b, Snead State (Ala.) CC
48. Zach Dygert, c, Ball State
49. Jose Sermo, of, Ileana de Gracia HS, Vega Alta, P.R.
50. Alvin Hines, of, Pelham (Ala.) HS

APPENDIX

■ **Nick Adenhart**, a righthander who was the top prospect in the Angels organization at the time of his passing, died April 9 in Orange, Calif., in an automobile accident. He was 22.

Adenhart, the Angels' 14th-round pick out of Williamsport (Md.) High in 2004, had developed into the team's top prospect and had earned a job in the starting rotation with a fine spring training performance. Adenhart was Baseball America's 2003 Youth Player of the Year after he led his summer league team to a All-American Amateur Baseball Association World Series title. The Angels decided to promote him in the summer of 2008 for three starts in the big leagues, although he struggled in his first taste of the majors. He had just thrown six scoreless innings against the Athletics on the night of his accident.

■ **Del Bates**, a catcher who appeared in 22 games for the 1970 Phillies, died Sept. 24 in Spokane, Wash. He was 69.

■ **Robert "Buddy" Blattner**, a second baseman who played five seasons in the majors in the 1940s, died Sept. 4 in Chesterfield, Mo. He was 89.

The 1946 season was Blattner's only one as a regular in the majors, as he hit .255 with 11 home runs for the Giants over 420 at-bats.

■ **Paul Busby**, an outfielder who played parts of two seasons in the majors with the Phillies, died Dec. 5, 2003, in Meridian, Miss. He was 85.

■ **Jackie Collum**, a lefthander who pitched nine seasons in the major leagues, died Aug. 28 in Grinnell, Iowa. He was 82.

Collum reached the big leagues in 1951, making three appearances for the Cardinals at the tail end of the season. Collum was traded to the Reds in May 1953, where he worked out of the bullpen for most of his time in Cincinnati, although he did make 17 starts for the Reds in 1955, when he went 9-8, 3.63. The Reds traded Collum back to the Cardinals after the '55 season, and he would go on to pitch for the Cubs, Dodgers, Indians and Twin before retiring in 1962.

■ **Jake Crawford**, an outfielder who made seven big league appearances with the St. Louis Browns in 1952, died Oct. 21, 2008, in Fort Worth. He was 80.

■ **Todd Cruz**, a shortstop who played six seasons in the majors, died Sept. 2, 2008, in Bullhead City, Ariz. He was 52.

Cruz was something of a journeyman throughout his big league career, though he was the everyday third baseman for the Orioles club that won the 1983 World Series, having moved to the hot

corner after being acquired during the season.

■ **Frank Dasso**, a righthander who spent parts of two seasons in the majors with the Reds, died June 8 in Seattle. He was 91.

Dasso spent most of his pro career pitching in the Pacific Coast League, debuting there with the San Francisco Seals in 1940 The Reds picked him up for the 1945 season and he appeared in 16 games, going 4-5, 3.66 in 96 innings. Dasso opened the 1946 season in Cincinnati, but returned to the PCL that June.

■ **Mike Derrick**, a first baseman who played one season in the major leagues as part of an 11 year pro career, died Jan. 14 in Lexington, S.C. He was 65.

The Red Sox claimed Derrick in the 1969 Rule 5 draft from the Tigers. He appeared in 24 games for the Red Sox during the 1970 season and hit .212 with five RBIs. Derrick was sent back to the minors the next year and played another two seasons,

■ **Dom DiMaggio**, an outfielder who played 11 seasons with the Red Sox and was a seven-time all-star, died May 8 in Marion, Mass. He was 92.

The younger brother of Yankees Hall of Famer Joe DiMaggio, Dom enjoyed great success as a rookie in 1940, hitting .301 with eight home runs and 46 RBIs in 418 at-bats. He made his first all-star team the next year, when he hit .283 with another eight home runs. DiMaggio hit a career-high 14 home runs in 1942 and made another all-star team, however he left baseball to enter the Navy after the season and did not return until being discharged in 1946.

DiMaggio never hit for a great deal of power, spending most of his career as a Boston's leadoff hitter and center fielder. He was always noted for his strong defensive play along with his hitting. DiMaggio returned to the Red Sox in 1946 and hit .316 while helping the Red Sox reach the World Series, where they lost in seven games to the Cardinals. DiMaggio hit .259 with three RBIs in the series. He never hit lower than .280 in any of his 11 big league seasons and made another four all-star games in consecutive years from 1949-52.

■ **Dock Ellis**, a righthander who pitched 12 seasons in the majors primarily for the Pirates, died Dec. 19, 2008, in Los Angeles. He was 63.

Ellis made the majors in 1968 after four seasons in the minors and wasted no time establishing himself as a member of the Pirates' staff, going 6-5, 2.51 in 104 innings as a rookie. He spent the next seven seasons as a member of Pirates' rotation and posted double-digit win totals in six of them. He threw a no-hitter in June 1970, though he later claimed to have been under the influence of LSD during the game, and had his finest season in the Pirates' championship year of 1971, going 19-9, 3.05.

■ **Mark Fidrych**, a righthander who was the 1976 AL Rookie of the Year, died April 13 in Northborough, Mass, after an apparent accident at his farm. He was 54.

Fidrych burst onto the scene in May 1976, having spent only one full season in the minors before making the Tigers' big league roster out of spring training at the age of 21. Fidrych made the AL all-star team and went on to finish the year 19-9, 2.34, while winning the rookie of the year award Fidrych also gained fame for his vibrant personality as much as his pitching exploits.

Unfortunately, Fidrych's peak was short lived. He was limited to only 11 starts in 1977 after tearing knee cartilage in spring training, although he was still able to go 6-4, 2.89 and made the all-star team again. However, the rest of his career would be plagued by arm troubles.

■ **Preston Gomez**, a shortstop who played briefly in the majors and later had a long executive career with the Angels, died Jan. 13 in Fullerton, Calif. He was 85.

Gomez had a brief stint in the majors with the Washington Senators in 1944. He appeared in eight games and went 2-for-7 with a double and two RBIs. After his playing career, Gomez embarked on a long managerial career, including stops in Mexico, Cuba and the big leagues. Gomez joined the Angels coaching staff in 1981 and later joined the club's front office. Gomez spent most of the rest of his life working for the Angels, primarily as an assistant to the general manager.

■ **Randy Gumpert**, a righthander who pitched 10 seasons in the majors with five different teams, died Nov. 25, 2008, in Wyomissing, Pa. He was 90.

Gumpert was signed by the Philadelphia Athletics out of the amateur ranks before the 1936 season and sent straight to the major leagues, where he worked primarily out of the bullpen en route to going 1-2, 4.79 in 62 innings as an 18-year-old and the second youngest player in the AL. He made another 10 appearances for the A's in 1937. Gumpert made it back to the majors with the Yankees in 1946, when he went 11-3, 2.30 in 133 innings, his best season as a big leaguer. Gumpert made his only all-star appearance in 1951 while going 9-8, 4.31 for the White Sox. He later played for the Red Sox and Washington Senators.

■ **Don Gutteridge**, a third baseman who played 12 seasons in the major leagues, died Sept. 7, 2008, in Pittsburg Kan. He was 96.

Gutteridge made his big league debut in September 1936 with the Cardinals. He quickly made a splash, hitting .319 and driving in 16 runs in 23 appearances with St. Louis. Gutteridge would spend the next three seasons as the Cardinals' everyday third baseman.

Gutteridge left the Cardinals after the 1940 season to play for Sacramento (Pacific Coast), before returning to the Gateway City in 1942. However, this time he would be suiting up for the St. Louis Browns. Gutteridge shifted over to second base for the Browns and spent four seasons as an everyday player there. Gutteridge didn't put up gaudy numbers, but he was a solid contributor.

■ **Ray Hamrick**, a shortstop who spent two seasons in the majors with the Phillies, died June 9 in Nashville. He was 88.

Hamrick reached the majors in 1943 after only two seasons in the minors. He made 44 appearances for the Phillies that season and hit .200 in 160 at-bats. He remained in Philadelphia for the 1944 season and made 74 appearances, but hit only .205 with one home run and 23 RBIs.

■ **Woodie Held**, a shortstop who played 12 seasons in the major leagues with seven teams, died June 10 in DuBois, Wyo. He was 77.

Held reached the majors full time in 1957, when he was called up again by the Yankees but subsequently traded to the Kansas City Athletics. Held went on to hit 20 home runs in 92 games for the A's, showing the kind of dependable power he would be well known for during his career, in which he hit 15 home runs or more eight times.

■ **Sidney Hudson**, a righthander who played 12 seasons in the major leauges, died on Oct. 10, 2008 in Waco, Texas. He was 93.

Hudson made his major league debut on April 13, 1940 with the Washington Senators and played with the team for the entire season. The then 25-year-old went 17-16, 4.57 over 252 innings.

In 1941, Hudson continued to pitch well, going 13-14, 3.46 over 250 innings and earning a spot on the American League All-Star team. He also earned a spot on the 1942 All-Star team and finished the 1942 season with a record of 10-17 and a 4.37 ERA over 239 innings. The only winning team Hudson played for was the 1953 Red Sox. That year, Hudson went 6-9, 3.52 over 156 innings. He finished his career in 1954.

■ **Larry Jansen**, a righthander who pitched nine seasons in the major leagues and was a two-time all-star, died Oct. 10 in Verboort, Ore. He was 89.

The New York Giants signed Jansen after the 1946 season and he won 21 games in his first big league season, going 21-5, 3.16. Jansen was known for his control, and he finished in the top 10 in the National League in walks per nine innings in each of his first five big league seasons. He earned his first trip to the all-star game in 1950 while going 19-13, 3.01 and leading the league with five shutouts. He won 23 games and returned to the all-star game again in 1951. Most famously, Jansen was the winning pitcher in the "Shot Heard Around The World" game against the Brooklyn Dodgers.

■ **Tommy Jones**, a former minor league player and major league executive, died Jan. 15 in Phoenix. He was 54.

Jones spent 12 seasons managing all around the country, ranging from places like Fort Myers (Florida State) in 1984 to San Bernardino (California) in 1991 with multiple stops in between. Jones eventually moved to the front office ranks and served seven seasons as the Diamondbacks' farm director from 1998 through 2004. Most recently, Jones was the director of baseball operations for the Arizona Fall League in 2008.

■ **Bill Kelso**, a righthander who pitched four seasons in the major leagues during the 1960s, died May 11 in North Kansas City, Mo. He was 69.

In what would be his only full season in the majors, Kelso was a mainstay of the Angels' bullpen in 1967, appearing in 69 games while compiling a 2.97 ERA over 112 innings.

■ **Barry Lersch**, a righthander who pitched five seasons with the Phillies, died Oct. 4 in Englewood, Colo. He was 65.

Lersch reached the big leagues for the first time in 1969 after four seasons in the minors, but went 0-3, 7.00 in 10 appearances for Philadelphia. He made it back to the big leagues in 1970 and pitched the next four seasons. He worked primarily as a reliever in his first full big league season, going 6-3, 3.26, but he transitioned to the Phillies' rotation in 1971 and put up a 3.79 ERA over 214 innings, though his record was just 5-14. The team moved him back to the bullpen for the 1972 season and he continued to flourish, putting up a career-best 3.03 ERA over 101 innings covering 36 appearances. Lersch remained in the bullpen in

1973, going 3-6, 4.41, though the Phillies traded him after the season.

■ **Carroll "Whitey" Lockman**, an outfielder who played 15 seasons in the majors primarily with the New York Giants, died March 17 in Scottsdale, Ariz. He was 82.

Lockman broke into the majors with the Giants in 1945, making 32 appearances and hitting .341 in 129 at-bats. However, he missed the 1946 season due to military service and wasn't able to rejoin the Giants full-time until the 1948 season. Lockman's career took off from there. He posted six consecutive seasons of batting .280 or better, the best of which came in 1949 when he hit .301 with 11 home runs and 65 RBIs in a career-high 617 at-bats. Lockman slugged a career high 16 home runs for the Giants in 1954, then followed that up with a 15 home run campaign in 1955, but his production fell off from there.

■ **Jack Lohrke**, a third baseman who played seven seasons in the major leagues, died April 29 in San Jose. He was 85.

Lohrke made his big league debut with the New York Giants in 1947, hitting .240 with 11 home runs in 329 at-bats. He spent another four seasons with the Giants, but was used mostly as a part-time player. He appeared in 97 games for the Giants in 1948 and hit .250 with five home runs, but he never approached playing that many games in a big league season again.

■ **Les McCrabb**, a righthander who pitched for parts of five seasons in the majors for the Philadelphia Athletics, died Oct. 8, 2008, in Lancaster, Pa. He was 93.

McCrabb made five appearances for the A's in the final weeks of the 1939 season, going 1-2, 4.00 in 36 innings. The 1941 season would be McCrabb's only full season in the majors. He made 23 starts for the A's that year and went 9-13, 5.50 with 11 complete games.

■ **Ron Moeller**, a lefthander who pitched in parts of four big league seasons, died Nov. 2 in Cincinnati. He was 70.

The Orioles signed Moeller at the age of 18 in 1956 and promoted him to the big leagues that September. Moeller made four appearances, including one start, for the Orioles over the season's final few weeks, going 0-1, 4.15 over nine innings. The Angels selected Moeller from Baltimore in the 1960 expansion draft and he saw his most extensive big league time in the new franchise's inaugural season. He made 33 appearances, 18 of them starts, for the Angels, going 4-8,

5.81 with one complete game in 113 innings.

■ **Dan Ozark**, a first baseman whose career spanned more than 40 years as a player and manager, died May 7 in Vero Beach, Fla. He was 85.

Ozark reached the big leagues as a manager when he took over the Phillies in 1973 and spent seven seasons with the club. Ozark's teams won three consecutive division titles from 1976-78, but lost in the NLCS each time. Including a brief stint managing the Giants in 1984, Ozark compiled a 594-510 record as a big league manager.

■ **Jack Phillips**, a first baseman who played in nine major league seasons, died Aug. 30 in Chelsea, Mich. He was 87.

Phillips originally came up through the Yankees system and made his big league debut in August 1947 after four years in the minors. Phillips opened 1949 with New York and was hitting .308 through 45 games before the Yankees sold him to the Pirates. Phillips played a part-time role for Pittsburgh over the next two seasons, seeing time both at third base and first. Phillips put up his best offensive season in the majors for Detroit in 1955, batting .316 over 117 at-bats with 20 RBIs.

■ **Brian Powell**, a righthander who pitched six seasons in the majors, died Oct. 5 in Tallahassee, Fla. He was 35.

Powell reached the big leagues for the first time in 1998, making 16 starts for the Tigers and going 3-8, 6.35 over 84 innings. The Tigers traded Powell to the Astros after the '98 season as part of a seven-player deal, and he would go on to make 10 appearances for Houston over the next three seasons Powell's final meaningful big league time came with the Phillies in 2004, when he worked primarily out of the bullpen while putting up a 5.03 ERA over 39 innings.

■ **Luis Quintana**, a lefthander who pitched in parts of two seasons for the California Angels in the 1970s, died July 27 in Lake Park, Fla. He was 57.

■ **Dave Roberts**, a lefthander who pitched 13 seasons in the major leagues primarily with the Padres and Astros, died Jan. 9 in Short Gap, W.Va. He was 64.

Roberts originally came up through the Pirates minor league system, but the Padres selected him in the 1968 expansion draft and he reached the majors for the first time the following year. Roberts had his breakout season two years later, when he went 14-17, 2.10 for the Padres in 1971. After the '71 season, Roberts was traded to the Astros, where he formed part of strong starting rotation with

Larry Dierker, J.R. Richard and Ken Forsch.

Roberts spent four seasons with the Astros, his best coming in 1973 when he went 17-11, 2.85 in 249 innings. Houston traded him to the Tigers after the 1975 season and he won 16 games for Detroit in 1976, but he struggled to maintain his numbers over the remainder of his career, pitching for six teams over his final five seasons.

■ **Eduardo Rodriguez**, a righthander who pitched seven seasons in the major leagues, died March 6 in Barceloneta, Puerto Rico. He was 57.

Rodriguez went 38-35, 3.78 in 660 innings in six seasons with the Brewers. His best season came in 1975 when he went 7-0, 3.49 in 88 innings, with most of his work coming in relief. In 1979, Rodriguez was purchased from the Brewers by the Royals, where he went 4-1, 4.84 over 74 innings in what was his last season in the majors.

■ **Freddie Rodriguez**, a righthander who pitched two seasons in the major leagues as part of an 18-year pro career, died June 11 in Miami. He was 86.

After 13 seasons spent bouncing around the minors, Rodriguez made it to the big leagues for the first time in 1958, appearing in seven games for the Cubs. Rodriguez made it back to the big leagues with the Phillies in 1959, but made only a single appearance.

■ **Preacher Roe**, a lefthander who was a five-time all-star in the 1940s and '50s, died Nov. 9, 2008, in West Plains, Mo. He was 92.

One of the aces of the "Boys of Summer"-era Dodgers of the '40s and 50s, Roe made the most of his first opportunity to pitch regularly in the big leagues, going 13-11, 3.11 for the Pirates in 1944. He earned his first trip to the All-Star Game the following season, when he put up a 14-13, 2.87 season while leading the league in strikeouts with 148.

The Pirates traded him to Brooklyn in December 1947, and the change immediately paid dividends for Roe. He went 12-8, 2.63 in his first season in Brooklyn, and in 1949, he began a streak of four straight all-star seasons, beginning with when he went 15-6, 2.79 in 1949 while helping the Dodgers reach the World Series. Roe's best season came in 1951, when he went 22-3, 3.04. Roe earned his last all-star selection in 1952 while the Dodgers returned to the World Series. Roe compiled a career record of 127-84.

■ **Johnny Schaive**, a second baseman who spent five seasons with the Washington Senators, died May 11 in Springfield, Ill. He was 75.

Schaive's only full campaign at the big league level came in 1962. He made 82 appearances for the Senators, hitting .253 with six home runs in 225 at-bats.

■ **Herb Score**, a lefthander who was the 1955 AL rookie of the year, died Nov. 11, 2008, in Rocky River, Ohio. He was 75.

Score burst onto the scene as a 22-year-old in 1955, going 16-10, 2.85 for the Indians and setting a rookie strikeout record of 245, a record which stood for 29 years. Score won 20 games at the age of 23 in 1956, when he went 20-9, 2.53. He led the league in strikeouts for the second straight year and was named to his second All-Star Game in as many years.

Score looked poised to become one of the game's elite pitchers, but his pitching career was changed forever on May 7, 1957, when he was struck in the head by a line drive. Score's injuries were severe, and he was never the same pitcher after the incident.

■ **Dave Smith**, a righthander who pitched 13 seasons in the majors and was a two-time all-star, died Dec. 17, 2008, in San Diego of an apparent heart attack. He was 53.

Smith worked exclusively as a reliever throughout his big league career, which he spent almost entirely with the Astros. Smith broke into the majors with Houston in 1980 and made 57 appearances, going 7-5, 1.92 with 10 saves. He worked in middle relief for the Astros for most of the next four seasons before becoming their closer in 1985. Smith racked up 27 saves that season while posting a 2.27 ERA in 79 innings. He finished third in the NL with a career-high 33 saves in 1986. He made the all-star game that season and helped the Astros win the NL West. Smith continued to shine for the Astros over the next four seasons, recording at least 23 saves in each of them and making the all-star team again in 1990. Smith retired as the Astros' all-time leader in appearances (563) and saves (199), although his saves mark has since been eclipsed by Billy Wagner.

■ **Billy Sorrell**, an outfielder who played parts of three seasons in the major leagues in the 1960s, died July 22, 2008, in Rancho Bernardo, Calif. He was 67.

■ **Craig Stimac**, an infielder who played parts of two seasons for the Padres, died Jan. 16 in San Marino, San Marino. He was 54.

■ **Tom Sturdivant**, a righthander who pitched 10 seasons in the major leagues, died Feb. 28 in Oklahoma City. He was 78.

Sturdivant started his pro career as a third baseman in 1948, but converted to pitching in 1952 after getting back from missing a season to serve in the military. He made it to the big leagues three years later, breaking in the with the Yankees in 1955. Sturdivant joined the Yankee rotation in 1956 and went 16-8, 3.30 in 158 innings. He followed that campaign up with what would be his career year in 1957. Sturdivant made 28 starts for the Yankees and went 16-6, 2.54 in 202 innings.

■ **Tom Tresh**, an infielder and outfielder who played 12 professional seasons, mostly with the Yankees, died Oct. 14, 2008 in Venice, Fla. He was 71.

As a 24-year-old, Tresh enjoyed an incredible rookie year for the Yankees in 1962. He hit .286/.359/.441 over 622 at-bats with 26 doubles, five triples and 20 home runs, helping the Yankees go 96-66 and win the World Series. He improved upon those numbers in 1963, putting up what would become his most impressive season at the plate, hitting .269/.371/487 over 520 at-bats with 28 doubles, five triples and 25 home runs. He made his second (and final) all-star appearance that year and finished 11th in the MVP voting.

■ **Ted Uhlaender**, an outfielder who played eight seasons in the major leagues, died Feb. 12 in Atwood, Kan. He was 69.

Uhlaender appeared in 13 games for the Twins in September 1965, hitting .182 with one RBI in his first taste of the majors. He took over as the Twins' everyday center fielder in 1966, although he hit only .226 with two home runs in 367 at-bats as the Twins finished second in the American League pennant race. Uhlaender upped his average to .258 in 1967, his first full season in the majors, then up to .283 with seven home runs, 21 doubles and 52 RBIs in 1968. Uhlaender was the Twins' primary leadoff hitter for much of the 1969 season, and he helped Minnesota reach the postseason with a .273 average in 554 at-bats.

The Twins traded Uhlaender to the Indians after the '69 season, and he hit a career high 11 home runs in his first season in Cleveland. Uhlaender then posted a career-high .288 average in 1971, but the Indians traded him to the Reds after the season. The 1972 season was Uhlaender's last in the majors, as he hit .159 in 113 at-bats for the Reds.

■ **Mickey Vernon**, a first baseman who was a seven-time major league all-star, died Sept. 24, 2008, in Media, Pa. He was 90.

The Washington Senators made Vernon their

everyday first baseman in 1941 and he settled into the role by hitting .299 with nine home runs and finished second on the team with 93 RBIs. Vernon was traded to the Indians after the 1948 season, but was tradede back to Washington after one season. Vernon spent another five seasons with Washington, where he was one of the few bright spots on teams that never finished higher than fifth in the AL standings. Vernon won his second AL batting title and was named to his third all-star team in 1953, when he hit .337 with 15 home runs and 115 RBIs.

The 1953 season began a streak of four consecutive all-star seasons for Vernon. He hit a career-high 20 home runs in 1954 and followed that season with consecutive campaigns of hitting over .300 once again. He batted .301 in 1955, his last season in Washington, then .310 for the Red Sox in 1956.

■ **Bill Werber**, a third baseman who played 10 seasons in the majors and was the oldest living former major leaguer at the time of his passing, died Jan. 22 in Charlotte. He was 100.

Werber attended Duke University and began his major league career in 1930 with the Yankees. He spent only a brief four game stint with the Yankees, going 4-for-14 at the plate, before being sent to Albany (Eastern), where he hit .339 in 316 at-bats. Werber made it back to the major leagues in 1933 with the Yankees, but his contract was purchased by the Red Sox that May. Werber hit his peak years with the Red Sox. He led the American League in stolen bases in three of the next four seasons, including back-to-back stolen base titles in 1934 and '35. He also hit .321 with 11 home runs in '34, although he never came close to equaling that mark again. Werber was traded to the Philadelphia Athletics for Pinky Higgins after the 1936 season and he enjoyed two strong seasons there. His contract was purchased by the Reds for the 1939 season and he would hit .277 with 12 home runs in 1940 and was a key part of Cincinnati's world championship team. He hit a healthy .370 (10-for-27) in the Reds' seven game triumph over the Tigers. However, his production tailed off in following seasons.

■ **Lee Wheat**, a righthander who made 11 major league appearances for the Athletics in 1954 and '55, died July 29, 2008, in Fort Lauderdale. He was 78.

■ **Davey Williams**, a second baseman who played six seasons for the New York Giants and was an all-star in 1953, died Aug. 17 in Farmer's Branch, Texas. He was 81.

Williams made his big league debut for the Giants as a 21-year-old in September 1949. He returned the minors for the next two seasons before making it to the big leagues full-time in 1952. Williams earned his only trip to the all-star game in 1953 thanks to a campaign that saw him hit .297 with three home runs and 34 RBIs. He helped the Giants win the World Series in 1954, though his offensive numbers dropped off and he hit just .222 with nine home runs.

■ **Frank Williams**, a righthander who pitched for parts of six seasons in the majors, died Jan. 9 in Victoria, B.C. He was 50.

The Giants picked Williams in the 11th round of the June 1979 draft and he reached the big leagues in 1984. A starter early in his career, Williams converted to relief while in Double-A in 1983 and worked exclusively as a reliever throughout his big league career. He made 61 appearances and threw 106 innings for the Giants as a rookie in 1984, going 9-4, 3.55. He spent another two seasons in San Francisco before being traded to the Reds after the 1986 season. He had his best big league season there in 1987, going 4-0, 2.30 over 85 appearances.

■ **George Williams**, a second baseman who played in parts of three big league seasons in the 1960s, died May 14 in Detroit. He was 69.

■ **Darrin Winston**, a lefthander who pitched two seasons for the Phillies, died of leukemia Aug. 15, 2008, in Freehold, N.J. He was 42.

■ **Hal Woodeschick**, a lefthander who pitched 11 seasons in the majors and was an all-star in 1963, died June 14 in Houston. He was 76.

Woodeschick enjoyed his greatest big league success in Houston. Woodeschick worked as a starter in his first season there and went only 5-16, 4.40 before converting back to the bullpen in 1963. He was the Colt .45's best reliever in '63, going 11-9, 1.97 in 55 appearances and earning his only all-star appearance. The following year, Woodeschick led the NL with 23 saves for a team that finished ninth in the standings.

■ **Sal Yvars**, a catcher who played eight seasons in the majors, died Dec. 10, 2008, in Valhalla, N.Y. He was 84.

Yvars made the New York Giants as a backup catcher in 1951. Yvars made a career-high 66 appearances for the Giants in 1952 and hit .245 with four home runs in 151 at-bats, but he was sold to the Cardinals in 1953 lasted only one more season in the majors.

APPENDIX

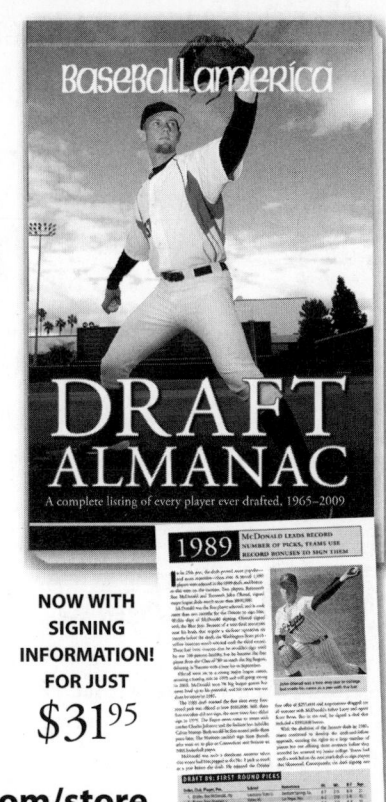

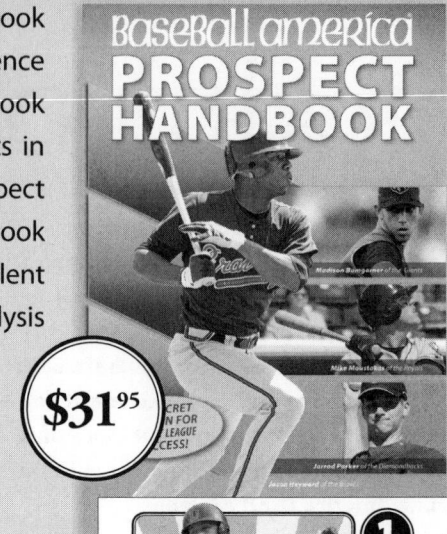